Fodor
Europe

(handwritten) 914.04 Fod 2008

PRAISE FOR FODOR'S GUIDES

*"Fodor's guides . . . are an admirable blend of the
cultural and the practical."*
—The Washington Post

*"Researched by people chosen because they lived or
have lived in the country, well-written, and with good
historical sections . . . Obligatory reading for millions
of tourists."*
—The Independent, *London*

*"Usable, sophisticated restaurant coverage, with an
emphasis on good value."*
—Andy Birsh, Gourmet restaurant columnist,
quoted by Gannett News Service

"Packed with dependable information."
—Atlanta Journal Constitution

*"Fodor's always delivers high quality . . . thoughtfully
presented . . . thorough."*
—Houston Post

"Valuable because of their comprehensiveness."
—Minneapolis Star-Tribune

Fodor's Travel Publications, Inc.
New York • Toronto • London • Sydney • Auckland

ISBN 0–679–02714–9

Fodor's Europe

Editor: Nancy van Itallie
Contributors: Robert Andrews, Barbara Angelillo, Mark Baker, Christopher Billy, Robert Blake, Toula Bogdanos, Rodney Bolt, Hannah Borgeson, Jules Brown, Robert Cohen, Brian Coleman, Roderick Conway-Morris, Samantha Cook, Nancy Coons, Fionn Davenport, Chris Drake, William Echikson, Mario Falzon, Nigel Fisher, Echo Garrett, Caroline Haberfeld, George Hamilton, Elva Harding, Emma Harris, Simon Hewitt, Alannah Hopkin, Rumyana Krasteva, Corinne LaBalme, David Lakein, Baty Landis, Graham Lees, David Low, Deborah Luhrman, Virginia Marsh, Bevin McLaughlin, Ian McMahon, Anne Merewood, Anne Midgette, Conrad Little Paulus, Kristen Perrault, Larry Peterson, Karina Porcelli, Mark Potok, Linda K. Schmidt, John Schoolcraft, Mary Ellen Schultz, Kate Sekules, Craig Seligman, George Semler, Alexandra Siegel, Eric Sjogren, Bjorn Sletto, Gilbert Summers, Enrique Tessieri, Robert Tilley, Julie Tomasz, Meltem Türköz, Anna Yates.
Creative Director: Fabrizio La Rocca
Cartographer: David Lindroth
Illustrator: Karl Tanner
Cover Photograph: Jean-Marie Truchet/TSW

Design: Vignelli Associates

Special Sales

Contents

Foreword *vii*

Highlights '95 *xi*

Fodor's Choice *xix*

Map of Europe *xxiv–xxv*

Map of World Time Zones *xxvi–xxvii*

1 Essential Information *1*

Before You Go *2*

Government Information Offices *2*
Tours and Packages *5*
Climate *10*
What to Pack *10*
Taking Money Abroad *11*
Getting Money from Home *12*
Long-Distance Calling *13*
Passports and Visas *13*
Customs and Duties *14*
Traveling with Cameras, Camcorders, and Laptops *15*
Staying Healthy *16*
Insurance *17*
Renting and Leasing Cars *18*
Rail Passes *20*
Home Exchange and Villa Rentals *21*
Student and Youth Travel *22*
Traveling with Children *23*
Hints for Travelers with Disabilities *24*
Hints for Older Travelers *25*
Hints for Gay and Lesbian Travelers *26*

Arriving and Departing *26*

From North America by Plane *26*
From North America by Ship *29*
From the United Kingdom by Plane *30*
From the United Kingdom by Car *32*
From the United Kingdom by Ferry/Ship *34*
From the United Kingdom by Train *35*
From the United Kingdom by Bus *36*

Getting Around Europe *37*

By Car *37*
By Train *39*
By Plane *41*
By Bus *42*
By Ferry/Ship *43*
By Bicycle *44*

Maps

2 Andorra 46   Andorra 48

3 Austria 55   Austria 57   Salzburg 84
Vienna 66–67   Innsbruck 90
The Danube Valley
80

4 Belgium 94   Belgium 96   Antwerp 119
Brussels 106–107   Brugge 124

5 Bulgaria 128   Bulgaria 130   Inland Bulgaria
Sofia 138   150
The Black Sea
Golden Coast 145

6 Cyprus 154   Cyprus 156

7 The Czech   The Czech   Prague 178–179
Republic 167   Republic 169   Bohemia 184

8 Denmark 187   Denmark 189   Fyn and the
Copenhagen   Central Islands
198–199   211
   Jylland 216

9 Finland 221   Finland 223   The Lakelands 241
Helsinki 232–233   Finnish Lapland 248

10 France 254   France 256–257   Burgundy 307
Paris Metro   The Loire Valley
268–269   314
Paris 272–273   The Riviera 319
Ile de France 293   Nice 323
Normandy 300   Monaco 324
Rouen 301

11 Germany   Germany   West Berlin
329   332–333   406–407
Munich 348–349   East Berlin 411
Frankfurt 364–365   Saxony and
Hamburg 374–375   Thuringia 422
The Rhine 381
The Black Forest
392

12 Great Britain   Great Britain   Stratford-upon-Avon
434   436–437   487
   London   Bath 490
   Underground 449   Cambridge 495
   London 456–457   York 501
   Windsor to   York Environs 503
   Bath 482   Edinburgh 508
   Oxford 485

Contents

Maps

13 Greece 513   Greece 516–517   Mainland Greece
Athens 526–527   547
The Peloponnese   The Greek Islands
540   553

14 Holland 558   Holland 560   The Hague, Delft,
Amsterdam   and Rotterdam
570–571   591
Historic Holland
584

15 Hungary 599   Hungary 601   The Danube Bend
Budapest 610–611   621
Lake Balaton 624

16 Iceland 627   Iceland 629
Reykjavík 635

17 Ireland 645   Ireland 648–649   Cork to Galway
Dublin 658–659   678
Dublin to Cork 673   Northwest Ireland 683

18 Italy 687   Italy 690–691   Milano (Milan) 747
Roma (Rome)   Venezia (Venice)
702–703   756–757
Firenze (Florence)   Campania 767
724–725
Toscana (Tuscany)
736

19 Luxembourg 776   Luxembourg 778
Luxembourg City
783

20 Malta 791   Malta 793

21 Norway 802   Norway 804   Through Telemark
Oslo 814–815   to Bergen 827
The Coast Road to
Stavanger 822

22 Poland 835   Poland 837   Gdańsk and the
Warsaw 844–845   North 855
Kraków 851

23 Portugal 858   Portugal 860   The Portuguese
Lisbon 870   Riviera 880
Belém 873   The Algarve 885

24 Romania 893   Romania 895   The Black Sea
Bucharest 906–907   Coast 911

25 Slovakia 915   Slovakia 917   The Tatras and
Bratislava 923   Eastern Slovakia 926

Maps

26 Spain *930*   *Spain 932–933*   *Seville 985*
Madrid 946–947 *Córdoba 988*
Madrid   *Granada 991*
Environs 959   *Costa del Sol 998*
Barcelona 972–973 *Gibraltar 1002*
Moorish Spain 983

27 Sweden *1012* *Sweden 1014*   *Uppsala and the*
Stockholm   *Folklore District*
1026–1027   *1037*
Stockholm   *The West Coast*
Environs 1028 *and the Glass*
Country 1041

28 Switzerland *1045* *Switzerland 1047* *Luzern 1077*
Zürich 1057   *Lugano 1084*
Geneva 1070–1071 *Bern 1089*

29 Turkey *1099* *Turkey 1101*   *The Mediter-*
Istanbul 1112–1113 *ranean Coast 1128*
The Aegean Coast *Central Anatolia*
1122   *and Cappadocia*
1133

Index   *1136*

Foreword

While every care has been taken to assure the accuracy of the information in this guide, the passage of time will always bring change, and consequently, the publisher cannot accept responsibility for errors that may occur.

All prices and opening times quoted here are based on information supplied to us at press time. Hours and admission fees may change, however, and the prudent traveler will avoid inconvenience by calling ahead.

Fodor's wants to hear about your travel experiences, both pleasant and unpleasant. When a hotel or restaurant fails to live up to its billing, let us know and we will investigate the complaint and revise our entries where the facts warrant it.

Send your letters to the editor of Fodor's Travel Publications, 201 East 50th Street, New York, NY 10022.

Highlights'95 and Fodor's Choice

Highlights '95

As a result of the Maastricht Treaty, the landmark general agreement on economic unity that went into effect November 1, 1993, the European Community changed its name to the European Union (EU) and removed all trade barriers between the 12 member states, turning much of Europe into one huge tariff-free market, the largest economic grouping in the world. Austria, Finland, Norway, and Sweden have applied to join the organization, and presumably a star for each will soon appear in the circle of stars on the blue field of the EU flag. Turkey, Cyprus, and Malta, all of which have applied (and were initially turned down for membership), should join the EU by the year 2000. Several Eastern European countries have or are negotiating association agreements with the Union.

Starting in 1993, citizens of EU-member countries no longer needed to show a passport when crossing borders, except into Britain. For travelers from non-EU countries entering EU countries, however, it is business as usual, with passport checks required at each border.

The collapse of communism in Eastern Europe has had the most tragic consequences in the former Yugoslavia. Heralded as the most open and "western" communist country under President Josip Broz Tito, this Balkan state has descended into a brutal war that has left tens of thousands of people dead and forced millions to flee their homes. At press time, U.S. State Department advisories were in effect for all republics except Slovenia. For the forseeable future travel is likely to be extremely hazardous in this once-beautiful region.

Austria This year's **music** and **opera** features in Salzburg include new productions of Richard Strauss' *Der Rosenkavalier* and Alban Berg's *Lulu* and *Wozzek*. Graz will mount a new production of Richard Wagner's *Tannhauser*. At the popular lakeside festivals, Bregenz will offer Beethoven's *Fidelio* on the lake stage, while the Mörbish festival south of Vienna has scheduled Karl Millöcker's *Der Bettelstudent* (*The Beggar Student*) on the lake. The Konzerthaus in Vienna will host the Vienna Festival Weeks (mid-May–mid-June) this year, with international orchestras and artists.

Of the major exhibits, one of the most interesting promises to be *The Esterhazy Princes: Tycoons, Diplomats, Patrons*, to be held from May through October in the Burgenland capital Eisenstadt, where the Esterhazy palace still stands. Focus will be on the painter Max Weiler's 85th birthday at a major show in Vienna's Belvedere Palace during the spring, and on the composer Paul Hindemith's relationship to Vienna at the Art History museum from mid-September to mid-November, after which medieval armaments from the 400-year-old collection of Duke Ferdinand go on display until March 1996.

Watch the colorful **folk festival** of the cows being herded back down from the alpine pastures in Pertisau, Tirol, on September 15. For **sports** enthusiasts, the year starts on January 4 with international ski jumping at the olympic jump in Innsbruck. Nearby Igls is the site of the second World Cup skibob race (dates yet to be set). Car collectors will gather at the Salzburg Ring, just outside the city, for an Oldtimer Grand Prix in mid-September.

Belgium The **Battle of Waterloo,** which took place in 1815, will be **reenacted** on June 17 and 18, 1995, by 3,000 local citizens, dressed as French, English, and Prussian soldiers, who stage realistic mock battles and cavalry charges, firing muskets and field guns. Unlike the real battle, which ended in over 40,000 deaths in a single day, this one ends with a grand parade by all participants. The Battle of Waterloo will not be staged again until the year 2000.

In medieval Brugge, the **Holy Blood Procession** on Ascension Day (May 25, 1995) is a magnificent pageant. Preceded by groups enacting scenes from the Old and New Testaments, the relic is carried through the streets of the city. It is enclosed in a golden reliquary, whose embellishments include a crown given by Mary of Burgundy and the black diamond donated by Mary Queen of Scots. Also in Brugge, the **Canal Festival** takes place August 17, 18, 21, 23, 25, and 26. Events of the ancient city's dramatic history are staged at various canalside sites, and spectators wander freely from one to the other.

The Czech Republic Like all of Eastern Europe, the Czech Republic is changing rapidly as the country pursues economic and cultural revitalization, aiming for membership in the EU by the year 2000. Old hotels, such as the Bohemia, an Art Nouveau jewel in the center of Prague, are being reopened; the influx of westerners has brought with it new restaurants offering Cajun, Mexican, vegetarian, and other exotic fare alongside the traditional ones serving pork and dumplings. New theater groups sprout everywhere, and the annual mid-May–early June **Prague Spring Music Festival** is attracting record numbers of music lovers. At press time, officials were planning to close Prague's art nouveau Obecni Dom in 1995 for long-needed repairs.

Finland Finland's decision to seek EU membership is considered by some leading Finnish academicians to be the most important move this country has made since it declared independence from Russia on December 6, 1917. As a result of the revaluation of the Finnmark in May 1993, Finland was transformed from one of the most expensive European countries to a veritable bargain-basement for tourists.

France The opening of the **Channel Tunnel** to vehicles in May 1994 and the start of high-speed passenger train service through it in July 1994 has put the French into closer touch with their neighbors across *La Manche* (the Channel).

Don't be surprised to find people at work in the **Jardin des Tuileries in Paris:** A project for restoring these elegant gardens to their original glory was adopted in 1992 and may continue into 1995.

The remodeling of the **Louvre** continues, with large new exhibition spaces making possible the display of art treasures long immured in the museum's basement, and cafés and escalators offering respite to tired feet. The **Très Grand Bibliothèque** (Very Large Library), scheduled for completion in 1995, is intended to anchor previously undeveloped eastern Paris, which will be linked to central Paris by a new metro line in 1996.

Outside Paris, **Eurodisney** is retrenching, offering lower rates for admissions, lodging, and dining. Elsewhere, too, the recession has kept prices down as the trend toward budget bistros continues.

Germany At press time it appeared that October 1994 **general elections** might bring a new government to power in Germany, possibly accompanied by higher taxes, which in turn could mean higher hotel rates and transport fares. Inflation is nevertheless expected to remain at a relatively low 5%, despite the lingering economic problems caused by reunification. Local and state elections in 1994 showed a leveling or even waning of support for far-right parties, and anti-foreigner sentiment appeared to be weakening, too.

The **Bamberg Symphony Orchestra** in northern Franconia has a new home, the Synfonie an der Regnitz, a grand concert and congress hall.

Two new east German castle hotels have joined the **Gast im Schloss** organization: Hotel Schloss Eckberg, a romantic, 19th-century neo-Gothic pile, complete with crenellated turrets, stands on the outskirts of Dresden; Hotel Schloss Blucher, a magnificent white-towered mansion built in 1847, sits amid the lakes and forests of the Mecklenburg plain about 100 miles north of Berlin. A new Rhineland hotel group is expanding into eastern Germany, starting with the **Balance Hotel Leipzig,** which opens in spring 1995. Generally, although new hotels are mushrooming everywhere in the east, moderately priced accommodations are still in short supply.

Motorists and passengers can cool off in Germany's first **autobahn swimming pool,** which opens in summer 1995. The heated open-air pool is at the junction of the A-4, A-5, and A-7 autobahns near Bad Hersfeld.

The privatization of the German **railway system** began in 1994 and is expected to take six years; routes, timetables, and fares may be changing in 1995. The electrification and renovation of the ancient tracks in the east has made big strides, allowing the extension there of the high-speed InterCity Express service, which previously linked only the cities of the west. The antiquated **telephone service** of the east has been brought completely up to date, but **roads** there are still under reconstruction.

Great Britain The often-delayed **Channel Tunnel** opened for cars, trucks, buses, and motorcycles in May 1994, ending Britain's age-old isolation from the Continent. Passenger train service began in July 1994 between London and Paris and London and Brussels. For more details, *see* Getting Around in Chapter 1, Essential Information.

As the **British telephone system** is modernized, **area codes throughout the country will add a 1 after the initial 0 in April 1995;** London's codes will thus become 0171 and 0181. There are a few exceptions to this system, so check before you make a call.

The new state-of-the-art Jewel House in the **Tower of London** opened in March 1994, allowing many more visitors to view the precious collection each day. **Glyndebourne's new opera house,** opened in May 1994, also accommodates much larger audiences, as well as more ambitious productions.

The **National Trust** celebrates its **centenary** in 1995 with events at many of the Trust's properties on the 570,000 acres of downs, moorlands, fens, farmland, woods, islands, nature reserves, inland waterways, and seacoast that it controls throughout the country.

Greece Despite the ongoing crisis in former Yugoslavia, Greek tourism officials remain optimistic, especially since tourism increased in 1994. To encourage and accommodate the influx, a number of schemes are in the works. The National Tourist Organization of Greece has plans for a new sea park, as well as three new golf courses in Halkidiki, Crete, and Kaifos in the Peloponnese. Olympic Airlines reinstated its inter-island flights from Thessaloniki to the eastern Aegean islands of Chios and Lesbos. The government has given the go-ahead for several projects to boost the country's modernization, including highways linking the western port of Igoumentisa across Corfu with the Turkish border in the east and Patras with the frontier post of Evzoni, bordering the former Yugoslav Republic of Macedonia. New catamarans are scheduled to make the Patras–Italy trip in half the usual time. There are also plans to introduce catamaran trips from Glyfada (near Athens) to Italy. A bridge over the strait between Antirio in mainland Greece and Rio on the north coast of the Peloponnese, which will cut travel time, is planned, as well as an underground railway in Thessaloniki. Work on the new Spata international airport in Athens continues, and in the city center, construction is underway to extend the metro, scheduled for completion in 1997. Despite Greece's high inflation, the strong dollar means Greece remains one of Europe's most affordable countries.

Holland Amsterdam celebrates its canals in 1995 with exhibitions and events relating to waterways. Also in 1995, the National Museum H. W. Mesdag in The Hague reopens after an extensive renovation program.

Hungary Delta and Malev, the Hungarian national airline, joined forces in May 1994 to merge their respective direct services between Budapest and the United States. The duo now offers **daily nonstop flights** between New York City's JFK and Budapest's Ferihegy airport.

Major chain hotels are expanding, and state-controlled hotels are going private and sprucing up. After finishing a $13-million overhaul, the **Budapest Marriott** revealed its impressive new face in June 1994. Outside the capital, a new chain of **castle hotels,** some attached to thermal spas, is preparing to open.

Travelers will find Hungary a bargain compared to western Europe, but rock-bottom prices are a thing of the past. At press time inflation was holding steady at 25%.

Iceland Although there has been investment in new hotels and expansion of existing ones over the past decade, the real growth area in Icelandic tourism has been at the less expensive end of the market: farmhouses, guesthouses, and camping holidays. Iceland has been going through a severe economic recession since the beginning of the 1990s, and this has led to efforts to keep prices down and attract more visitors from abroad. The cost of living is high in Iceland, and the country remains an expensive destination, but visitors now have a larger range of options in terms of accommodations and services.

Icelanders are realizing that it's not enough to be on an island in the middle of the ocean—atmospheric and marine pollution can still occur. The increase in tourism and the fact that visitors tend to travel in the highlands, where the environment is very sensitive, have led to serious discussion about limiting access to the most vulnerable areas.

Ireland Ireland used to rely on its unspoiled countryside and friendly, hospitable people to attract visitors. In the last five years, encouraged by the government, over IR £500 million has been invested in tourism, and the number of visitors is projected to double from 2 million to 4 million by 1996. Travelers can expect upgraded accommodations at all levels (most hotels and many bed-and-breakfasts now offer rooms with private bath, TV, and direct-dial phone), a wider choice of restaurants, better-organized cultural tourism, and greatly improved sporting facilities. Twenty-five new golf courses have been built, and as many again are in the making. Water sports, walking routes, fishing, cycling, and equestrian holidays have also been successfully developed.

Italy About 30 major national museums throughout Italy have extended their hours and are now open from 9 AM to 7 PM; in smaller museums, hours and closing days are being tailored for the public's convenience. Museum shops and bookstores, cafés and cafeterias are part of a plan to attract visitors to Italy's museums. In Rome, Florence, and Milan museumgoers can save on admission fees by purchasing Museum Cards. The three-year restoration of Michelangelo's *Last Judgment* in the Sistine Chapel in Vatican City has been completed. In Padua the Scrovegni Chapel will remain closed until late 1995 while Giotto's frescoes are restored; when it reopens access will probably be limited.

Luxembourg Luxembourg has been designated the **Cultural Capital of Europe for 1995** and has chosen *dialogue* as its theme. The choice has been inspired by the fact that all the "new" countries of Europe have sizable minorities—but none so large as in Luxembourg, where 30% of the population were born abroad. To learn the art of living together, dialogue is essential. Throughout 1995, each month will be devoted to a different aspect of culture as dialogue, with a different country invited to participate in the demonstrations, concerts, and performances. They will take place in a wide range of venues, including on ramparts and in fortresses, in theaters, and at the new Luxembourg City Historical Museum, which opens its doors in 1995. To accommodate events drawing really big crowds, a huge circus tent is being erected in the city.

Malta New hotels are popping up across the island, and Malta is also fast establishing itself as one of the top cruise destinations in the Mediterranean.

Norway Norway is expecting an unprecedented number of visitors in the wake of last year's Winter Olympics. The government has made tourism one of its highest priorities, particularly in the depressed northern part of the country, and prices are likely to fall as a result of the heightened competition.

The debate on future membership in the European Union (EU) is expected to come to a head in 1995, as Norway's closest neighbors, Sweden and Finland, are slated to join the EU this year. Polls show that Norwegians still are split, but favorable to EU membership should Finland and Sweden join. Already, Norway is a member of the European Economic Area, which has begun to exert a downward pressure on prices, including hotels and restaurants. A referendum may be held in 1995 on full EU membership, which will continue to make travel to Norway easier and less costly. Some Norwegian quirks, such as the ban on sales of alcohol in food stores, will disappear in the event of EU membership.

Poland The recently opened Warsaw air terminal has greatly improved the speed and comfort of arrival at Poland's capital. Getting about within Poland is also becoming easier. New car-rental firms are popping up, and gasoline is now readily available.

The range of accommodations continues to broaden. At the top end of the scale, older fine hotels are being renovated in Warsaw; there are also many new small private hotels and pensions countrywide.

Portugal Oddly perhaps (or not, if you're familiar with the tardiness of Portuguese officialdom), visitors can expect to reap the full benefit of Lisbon being **1994 European City of Culture** in 1995. After a face-lift, some of the country's best-loved monuments—including the **Torre de Belem** in Lisbon—should be looking as good as new; work goes on in the capital on improving the roads and transportation system.

In the Algarve, several new luxury hotels have come on line recently—the **Sheraton Algarve** is typical of these, while its associated golf course helps maintain the Algarve as one of Europe's top golfing destinations.

In the meantime, the upgrading of the **telephone system** continues to cause havoc for tourists and locals alike. Numbers throughout the country are changing in a rolling program, and though in many areas this is now complete, official publications are slow to catch up; always double check.

Romania Having established a democratic system, Romania is now trying to build a market economy. Peasants are being given back their land, and small private enterprises are being encouraged, leading to increasing variety in the shops and markets.

Spain The 1993 recession in Spain led to a weakening of the peseta, which, in turn, led to a record year for tourism in 1994. Visitors to Spain in 1995 will likely have to put up with climbing hotel and restaurant **prices** brought on by that boom. The biggest price hikes, however, will be at coastal resorts and in the Balearic and Canary Islands. Prices in Madrid and Barcelona should remain relatively stable, with especially good deals for tourists who schedule their city visits on weekends.

Rural Spain is an increasingly popular budget option. Farmhouses are being converted into charming **bed & breakfasts** throughout the country, and besides providing a low-cost way to travel they make it easier to mix in with the local culture. Provincial tourism offices can provide a brochure detailing rural tourism accommodations in their zone.

Also new to Spain in 1995 is the **Tibigardens** theme park, to be opened April 7 in Salou on the Costa Dorada. Owned in part by U.S. brewery Anhueser Busch, the park will have five theme areas: Polynesia, China, Mexico, the Wild West, and Catalonia.

Ski fans might also consider scheduling a visit to Spain in 1995. The Sierra Nevada resort near Granada will host the **World Ski Championships** in the early part of the year.

Sweden Construction of the 18-kilometer bridge over the Öresund, the sound separating Sweden and Denmark, was to have begun in 1993. At press time (spring 1994), the Swedish government had yet to give final approval to the project, awaiting the results of an environmental assessment. If approved, this rail-and-road bridge will create the first physical link between Sweden and the Continent.

Visitors will find that Sweden, due to a weak krona and a unified effort by the travel industry to bring hotel, restaurant, and travel costs in line with Continental Europe, is currently a bargain. American travelers can expect to find the country 40% less expensive than it was two years ago.

Switzerland As the member states of the **European Union** (EU) pool their resources and adjust to the brave new world of tariff-free borders, Switzerland—once aloof in its affluence—looks on from the sidelines and rejects (not without bitterness) the apparently unthinkable option of joining up.

Though other parts of the collection have been removed to Spain, Lugano's newly renovated **Villa Favorita** now displays to better advantage Baron von Thyssen-Bornemisza's 19th- and 20th-century paintings and water colors by European and American artists such as Thomas Hart Benton, Giorgio de Chirico, Lucien Freud, Franz Marc, and Edward Hopper.

For museum lovers with time for an all-day excursion (by car, train, or steamer from Geneva) to Lausanne, there are two new state-of-the-art options: the spectacular lakefront **Musée Olympique,** devoted entirely to the tradition of Olympic games, and the **Musée Romain,** also on the lakeshore, which traces the history of Roman settlement in the region.

A new sports trend is taking hold in the Swiss mountains: **snowshoe hiking,** newly refined with lightweight plastic raquettes that allow walkers to leave the trail and take off over the surface of snowbound forests and fields.

Turkey Visitors to Ankara may now see the prized **Lydian treasures** at the Museum of Anatolian Civilizations. The 363-piece gold and silver collection dating from the 6th century BC was reclaimed by Turkey from New York City's Metropolitan Museum of Art in late 1993, stirring speculation about the outcome of other such claims.

A new link in the **Hyatt Regency** chain opened near Istanbul's Taksim Square in 1994. Its modern architecture and decor reminiscent of Ottoman splendor mark it as yet another luxury hotel, but it nevertheless blends in with the city's surviving historical silhouette.

A tanker-freighter collision in the Bosporus in March 1994 sent hundreds of tons of crude oil gushing into the waters of the Bosporus and the Black Sea. At press time it was still unclear what the long-term effects of the **oil spill** will be, although initial predictions spell months of contamination for the western Black Sea coast and the Bosporus.

Fodor's Choice

No two people will agree on what makes a perfect vacation, but it's fun and can be helpful to know what others think. In compiling this list, we've included choices from each of the countries covered in the book, and we hope that you'll have a chance to experience some of them yourself. For more detailed information about each entry, refer to the appropriate chapters within this guidebook.

Sights to Remember

Belgium	The Burg and canals of Brugge at dusk
Bulgaria	The panorama from the ramparts of Veliko Târnovo
Denmark	Kronborg Castle overlooking the Baltic
Finland	Olavinlinna Castle, Savonlinna
France	Mont St-Michel at high tide
Germany	Neuschwanstein Castle, Bavaria
Great Britain	Tower Bridge and the Tower of London in floodlights
Greece	Sunset over the Caldera on the island of Santorini
Holland	Amsterdam canals by night
Hungary	Parliament building at night, Budapest
Iceland	Ice floes drifting on the Jökulsárlon lagoon (Skaftafell)
Ireland	Dusk over the lakes of Killarney
Italy	The Grand Canal in Venice at dawn
Malta	The Grand Harbor in Valletta
Norway	The midnight sun at the North Cape
Romania	The view from the clock tower in Sighisoara
Spain	The perched white villages of Andalusia
Switzerland	The Matterhorn from Gornergrat, Zermatt
Turkey	Istanbul skyline at sunset from Camliça Hill

Hotels

Austria	Imperial, Vienna (*Very Expensive*)
Belgium	SAS Royal Hotel, Brussels (*Very Expensive*)
Finland	Hotel Strand Inter-Continental, Helsinki (*Very Expensive*)
France	The Ritz, Paris (*Very Expensive*)

Any Logis et Auberges (Country Hotels and Inns) de France hotel (*Inexpensive*)

Germany The Grand, Berlin (*Very Expensive*)

Great Britain The Halkin, London (*Very Expensive*)

Greece Any of the "paradosiakoi oikismoi" (traditional homes)

Holland Amstel Inter-Continental, Amsterdam (*Very Expensive*)

Hungary Gellért, Budapest (*Expensive*)

Ireland Park, Kenmare (*Very Expensive*)

Italy Hassler-Villa Medici, Rome (*Very Expensive*)

Portugal Buçaco Hotel, Buçaco (*Expensive*)

Spain Parador of Siguenza (*Expensive*)

Switzerland Monte Rosa, Zermatt (*Expensive*)

Turkey Çirağan Palace, Istanbul (*Very Expensive*)

Restaurants

Austria Landhaus Bacher, Mautern (*Very Expensive*)

Belgium Comme Chez Soi, Brussels (*Very Expensive*)

Denmark Ida Davidsen, Copenhagen (*Moderate*)

Finland Palace Gourmet, Helsinki (*Very Expensive*)

France La Régalade, Paris (*Inexpensive–Moderate*)

Great Britain Bibendum, London (*Very Expensive*)

Greece Bajazzo, Athens (*Very Expensive*)

Holland Excelsior, Amsterdam (*Very Expensive*)

Hungary Gundel, Budapest (*Very Expensive*)

Iceland Perlan, Reykjavík (*Expensive*)

Ireland Arbutus Lodge, Cork (*Expensive*)

Italy El Toulà, Rome (*Very Expensive*)

Luxembourg La Bergerie, Echternach (*Very Expensive*)

Norway Theatercafeen, Oslo (*Expensive*)

Portugal Aviz, Lisbon (*Very Expensive*)

Spain Eldorado Petit, Barcelona (*Very Expensive*)

Sweden Den Gyldene Freden, Stockholm (*Expensive*)

Switzerland Bierhalle Kropf, Zürich (*Inexpensive*)

Monuments

The Czech Republic Starý Židovsky Hřbitov (Old Jewish Cemetery), Prague

Finland	The Sibelius Monument, Helsinki
Great Britain	Scott Monument, Edinburgh
Ireland	The Rock of Cashel
Luxembourg	The Devil's Altar, Diekirch
Poland	The Solidarity Monument, Gdańsk
Portugal	Monumento dos Descobrimentos (Monument to the Discoveries), Lisbon
Romania	Palace of the People, Bucharest

Museums and Galleries

Austria	Kunsthistorisches Museum, Vienna
Belgium	Groeninge Museum, Brugge
Bulgaria	National History Museum, Sofia
Finland	The Finnish National Gallery, Helsinki
France	Fondation Maeght, St-Paul-de-Vence
Great Britain	The British Museum, London
Greece	The N.J. Goulandris Museum of Cycladic Art, Athens
Holland	Rijksmuseum, Amsterdam
Hungary	Szépművészeti Múzeum (Museum of Fine Arts), Budapest
Portugal	Fundação Calouste Gulbenkian, Lisbon
Romania	Museum of the Peasant, Bucharest
Spain	Prado Museum, Madrid
Sweden	Vasa Museum, Stockholm
Switzerland	Musée International de la Croix-Rouge, Geneva
Turkey	Topkapi Palace and Harem, Istanbul

Festivals

Cyprus	Kataclysmos Festival
Denmark	The Copenhagen Jazz Festival
Finland	Kuhmo Chamber Music Festival, Kuhmo
Germany	Oktoberfest, Munich
Great Britain	Edinburgh International Festival
Holland	Queen's Day, Amsterdam
Hungary	Spring Festival, Budapest
Iceland	Reykjavík Arts Festival
Ireland	St. Patrick's Day Parade, Dublin
Italy	Venice Carnival

Norway	Bergen International Music Festival
Portugal	Santos Populares (Popular Saints) Festival, Lisbon
Sweden	Stockholm Water Festival

Churches, Temples, and Mosques

Austria	Karlskirche, Vienna
The Czech Republic	St. Vitus Cathedral, Prague
Finland	The Cathedral (Senate Square), Helsinki
France	Chartres Cathedral
Germany	Asamkirche, Munich
Great Britain	St. Paul's Cathedral, London
Hungary	Mátyás Templom (Matthias Church), Budapest
Malta	St. John's Co-Cathedral, Valletta
Portugal	Jerónimos Monastery, Belém, Lisbon
Spain	The 10th-century Mezquita (Mosque), Córdoba

Classical Sights

Bulgaria	Roman amphitheater, Plovdiv
Cyprus	Curium
Great Britain	The Roman baths, Bath
Greece	Delphi
Italy	Herculaneum and the temples of Paestum
Spain	Roman amphitheater, Merida
Turkey	Ruins of Ephesus

Parks and Gardens

Austria	Hellbrunn, Salzburg
Finland	Talvipuutarha, Helsinki
France	Monet's "Water Lily" garden, Giverny
Great Britain	Holyrood Park and Arthur's Seat, Edinburgh
Holland	Palace Het Loo, Apeldoorn
Ireland	Japanese Gardens, Tully, County Kildare
Poland	Łazienki Park, Warsaw
Sweden	Linné Gardens, Uppsala

For Children

Denmark	Legoland, Billund
Finland	Santa Claus's Workshop, Arctic Circle, near Rovaniemi
France	Le Jardin d'Acclimatation, Paris
	Ride to the top of the Eiffel Tower, Paris
Germany	Tierpark Hellabrun Zoo, Munich
Great Britain	The Planetarium, London
Holland	Musical Clock Museum, Utrecht
Italy	Exploring Castel Sant'Angelo, Rome
Norway	Cardamom Town, Kristiansand
Portugal	The beaches of the Algarve
Spain	Snowflake, the albino gorilla, Barcelona zoo

Shopping

Austria	Glass from the manufacturers at Neunagelberg
Belgium	Handmade Nihoul or Wittamer chocolates from Brussels
Finland	Iittala glass and Marimekko clothes
Great Britain	Cashmere sweaters from Edinburgh
Greece	Natural sponges from Athens
Holland	Tulip bulbs, Schiphol Airport, Amsterdam
Iceland	Handmade woolen goods from Reykjavík
Ireland	Hand knits from Dublin, Cork, and Galway
Luxembourg	Villeroy & Boch porcelain
Portugal	Hand-embroidered carpets from Arraiolos
Romania	Art and craftwork from Transylvania
Spain	Pottery from Seville and Talavera de la Reina, outside Madrid
Turkey	Hand-woven carpets from Bodrum

Europe

World Time Zones

World Time Zones

International Date Line

MONDAY
SUNDAY

+12 +13 -9 -7 -4 -3 0

-10 -5 -4 25

-11 -10 -7 -3:30

+11 -8 -6

+12 -4

-5 -4 -3

-5

-3

-3

| +11 | +12 | -11 | -10 | -9 | -8 | -7 | -6 | -5 | -4 | -3 | -2 |

Numbers below vertical bands relate each zone to Greenwich Mean Time (0 hrs.).
Local times frequently differ from these general indications,
as indicated by light-face numbers on map.

Algiers, **29**
Anchorage, **3**
Athens, **41**
Auckland, **1**
Baghdad, **46**
Bangkok, **50**
Beijing, **54**

Berlin, **34**
Bogotá, **19**
Budapest, **37**
Buenos Aires, **24**
Caracas, **22**
Chicago, **9**
Copenhagen, **33**
Dallas, **10**

Delhi, **48**
Denver, **8**
Djakarta, **53**
Dublin, **26**
Edmonton, **7**
Hong Kong, **56**
Honolulu, **2**

Istanbul, **40**
Jerusalem, **42**
Johannesburg, **44**
Lima, **20**
Lisbon, **28**
London (Greenwich), **27**
Los Angeles, **6**
Madrid, **38**
Manila, **57**

Mecca, **47**	Ottawa, **14**	San Francisco, **5**	Toronto, **13**
Mexico City, **12**	Paris, **30**	Santiago, **21**	Vancouver, **4**
Miami, **18**	Perth, **58**	Seoul, **59**	Vienna, **35**
Montréal, **15**	Reykjavík, **25**	Shanghai, **55**	Warsaw, **36**
Moscow, **45**	Rio de Janeiro, **23**	Singapore, **52**	Washington, D.C., **17**
Nairobi, **43**	Rome, **39**	Stockholm, **32**	Yangon, **49**
New Orleans, **11**	Saigon (Ho Chi Minh	Sydney, **61**	Zürich, **31**
New York City, **16**	City), **51**	Tokyo, **60**	

1 Essential Information

Before You Go

Government Information Offices

Austria **Austrian National Tourist Office. In the United States:** 500 Fifth Ave., Suite 2022, New York, NY 10110, tel. 212/944–6880, fax 212/730–4568; 500 N. Michigan Ave., Suite 1950, Chicago, IL 60611, tel. 312/644–8029, fax 312/644–6526; 11601 Wilshire Blvd., Suite 2480, Los Angeles, CA 90025, tel. 310/477–3332, fax 310/477–5141; 1300 Post Oak Blvd., Suite 1700, Houston, TX 77056, tel. 713/850–9999, fax 713/850–7857.
In Canada: 1010 Sherbrooke St. W, Suite 1410, Montreal, Quebec H3A 2R7, tel. 514/849–3709, fax 514/849–9577; 200 Granville St., Suite 1380, Vancouver, British Columbia V6C 1S4, tel. 604/683–5808, fax 604/662–8528; 2 Bloor St. E, Suite 3330, Toronto, Ontario M4W 1A8, tel. 416/967–3381, fax 416/967–4101.
In the United Kingdom: 30 St. George St., London W1R 0AL, tel. 071/629–0461.

Belgium **Belgian National Tourist Office. In North America:** 780 Third Ave., New York, NY 10017, tel. 212/758–8130, fax 212/355–7675.
In The United Kingdom: 29 Princes St., London W1R 7RG, tel. 071/629–0230, fax 071/629–0454.

Bulgaria **Bulgarian National Tourist Office. In North America:** Balkan Holidays (authorized agent), 41 E. 42nd St., Suite 508, New York, NY 10017, tel. 212/573–5530, fax 212/573–5538.
In the United Kingdom: 18 Princes St., London W1R 7RE, tel. 071/499–6988.

Cyprus **Cyprus Tourist Office. In North America:** 13 E. 40th St., New York, NY 10016, tel. 212/683–5280, fax 212/683–5282.
In the United Kingdom: 213 Regent St., London W1R 8DA, tel. 071/734–9822; **North Cyprus Tourist Office,** 28 Cockspur St., London SW1Y 5BN, tel. 071/930–5069.

The Czech Republic and Slovakia **Czech and Slovak Travel Bureau and Tourist Office (Čedok). In North America:** 10 E. 40th St., New York, NY 10016, tel. 212/689–9720.
In the United Kingdom: 17–18 Old Bond St., London W1X 3DA, tel. 071/629–6058.

Denmark **Danish Tourist Board. In the United States:** 655 Third Ave., New York, NY 10017, tel. 212/949–2333, fax 212/983–5260.
In Canada: c/o Helen Bergstrom, Box 636, Streetsville, Mississauga, Ontario, L5M 2C2, tel. 519/576–6213, fax 519/576–7115.
In the United Kingdom: Sceptre House, 169–173 Regent St., London W1R 8PY, tel. 071/734–2637.

Finland **Finnish Tourist Board. In the United States:** 655 Third Ave., New York, NY 10017, tel. 212/949–2333, fax 212/983–5260; 1900 Ave. of the Stars, Suite 1070, Los Angeles, CA 90067, tel. 310/277–5226.
In the United Kingdom: 66–68 Haymarket, London, SW1Y 4RF, tel. 071/839–4048.

France **French Government Tourist Office. In the United States:** Nationwide, tel. 900/990–0040 (costs 50¢ per minute); 610 Fifth Ave., New York, NY 10020, tel. 212/315–0888 or 212/757–1125, fax 212/247–6468; 645 N. Michigan Ave., Chicago, IL 60611, tel. 312/337–6301, fax 312/337–6339; 2305 Cedar Springs Rd., Dallas, TX 75201, tel. 214/720–4010, fax 214/720–0250; 9454 Wilshire Blvd., Beverly Hills, CA 90212, tel. 310/271–2358, fax 310/276–2835.

In Canada: 1981 McGill College Ave., Suite 490, Mor... H3A 2W9, tel. 514/288–4264, fax 514/845–4868; 30 S... Suite 700, Toronto, Ontario M5T 3A3, tel. 416/593–... 979–7587.

In the United Kingdom: 178 Piccadilly, London W1V OAL, tel. 071/491–7622.

Germany **German National Tourist Office. In the United States:** 122 E. 42nd St., New York, NY 10168, tel. 212/661–7200, fax 212/661–7174; 11766 Wilshire Blvd., Suite 750, Los Angeles, CA 90025, tel. 310/575–9799, fax 310/575–1565.

In Canada: 175 Bloor St. E, Suite 604, Toronto, Ontario M4W 3R8, tel. 416/968–1570.

In the United Kingdom: Nightingale House, 65 Curzon St., London W1Y 7PE, tel. 071/495–3990.

Gibraltar **Gibraltar Government Tourist Office. In North America:** 1155 15th St., NW, Room 710, Washington, DC 20005, tel. 202/452–1108, fax 202/872–8543.

In the United Kingdom: Arundel Great Court, 179 The Strand, London WC2R 1EH, tel. 071/836–0777.

Great Britain **British Tourist Authority. In the United States:** 551 5th Ave., Suite 701, New York, NY 10176, tel. 212/986–2200, fax 212/986–1188; 625 N. Michigan Ave., Suite 1510, Chicago, IL 60611, tel. 312/787–0490, fax 312/787–7746; World Trade Center, 350 S. Figueroa St., Suite 450, Los Angeles, CA 90071, tel. 213/628–3525, fax 213/687–6621; 2850 Cumberland Pkwy., Suite 470, Atlanta, GA 30339, tel. 404/432–9635, fax 404/432–9641.

In Canada: 111 Avenue Rd., Suite 450, Toronto, Ontario M5R 3J8, tel. 416/925–6326.

In the United Kingdom: British Travel Centre, 12 Regent St., London SW1Y 4PQ (no information by phone).

Greece **Greek National Tourist Organization. In the United States:** 645 Fifth Ave., New York, NY 10022, tel. 212/421–5777, fax 212/826–6940; 611 W. 6th St., Suite 2198, Los Angeles, CA 90017, tel. 213/626–6696, fax 213/489–9744; 168 N. Michigan Ave., Chicago, IL 60601, tel. 312/782–1084, fax 312/782–1091.

In Canada: 1233 Rue de la Montagne, Montreal, Quebec H3G 1Z2, tel. 514/871–1535, fax 514/871–1498; 1300 Bay St., Toronto, Ontario M5R 3K8, tel. 416/968–2220, fax 416/968–6533.

In the United Kingdom: 4 Conduit St., London W1R 0DJ, tel. 071/734–5997.

√ **Holland** **Netherlands Board of Tourism. In the United States:** 355 Lexington Ave., New York, NY 10017, tel. 212/370–0280, fax 212/370–9507; 225 N. Michigan Ave., Suite 326, Chicago, IL 60601, tel. 312/819–0300, fax 312/819–1740; 9841 Airport Blvd., Los Angeles, CA 90045, tel. 310/348–9333, fax 310/348–9344.

In Canada: 25 Adelaide St. E, Suite 710, Toronto, Ontario M5C 1Y2, tel. 416/363–1577, fax 416/363–1470.

In the United Kingdom: 25–28 Buckingham Gate, London SW1E 6LD, tel. 071/828–7900.

Hungary **Hungarian Travel Bureau (IBUSZ). In North America:** 1 Parker Plaza, Suite 1104, Fort Lee, NJ 07024, tel. 201/592–8585, fax 201/592–8736.

In the United Kingdom: Danube Travel Ltd. (authorized agent), 6 Conduit St., London W0R 9TG, tel. 071/493–0263.

Iceland **Iceland Tourist Board. In North America:** 655 Third Ave., New York, NY 10017, tel. 212/949–2333, fax 212/983–5260.

In the United Kingdom: 172 Tottenham Court Rd., 3rd floor, London W1P 9LG, tel. 071/388–5346.

Ireland **Irish Tourist Board. In the United States:** 345 Park Ave., New York, NY 10022, tel. 212/418–0800 or 800/223–6470, fax 212/371–9052.
In Canada: 160 Bloor St. E, Suite 1150, Toronto, Ontario M4W 1B9, tel. 416/929–2777, fax 416/929–6783.
In the United Kingdom: Ireland House, 150 New Bond St., London W1Y 0AQ, tel. 071/493–3201.

Italy **Italian Government Travel Office (ENIT). In the United States:** 630 Fifth Ave., Suite 1565, New York, NY 10111, tel. 212/245–4822, fax 212/586–9249; 12400 Wilshire Blvd., Suite 550, Los Angeles, CA 90025, tel. 310/820–0098, fax 310/820–6357.
In Canada: 1 Place Ville Marie, Suite 1914, Montreal, Quebec H3B 3M9, tel. 514/866–7667.
In the United Kingdom: 1 Princes St., London W1R 8AY, tel. 071/408–1254.

Luxembourg **Luxembourg Tourist Information Office. In North America:** 17 Beekman Pl., New York, NY 10022, tel. 212/935–8888, fax 212/935–5896.
In the United Kingdom: 122 Regent St., London W1R 5FE, tel. 071/434–2800.

Malta **Malta National Tourist Office. In North America:** Maltese Consulate, 249 E. 35th St., New York, NY 10016, tel. 212/213–6686, fax 212/213–6689.
In the United Kingdom: Mappin House, Suite 300, 4 Winsley St., London W1N 7AR, tel. 071/323–0506.

Monaco **Monaco Government Tourist and Convention Bureau. In North America:** 845 Third Ave., New York, NY 10022, tel. 212/759–5227, fax 212/754–9320.
In the United Kingdom: 3–18 Chelsea Garden Market, Chelsea Harbour, London SW10 0XE, tel. 071/352–2103.

Norway **Norwegian Tourist Board. In North America:** 655 Third Ave., New York, NY 10017, tel. 212/949–2333, fax 212/983–5260.
In the United Kingdom: Charles House, 5–11 Lower Regent St., London SW1Y 4LR, tel. 071/839–6255.

Poland **Polish National Tourist Office. In North America:** 275 Madison Ave., Suite 1711, New York, NY 10016, tel. 212/338–9412, fax 212/338–9283.
In the United Kingdom: 82 Mortimer St., London W1N 7DE, tel. 071/580–8028.

Portugal **Portuguese National Tourist Office. In the United States:** 590 Fifth Ave., 4th Floor, New York, NY 10036, tel. 212/354–4403, fax 212/764–6137.
In Canada: 60 Bloor St., Suite 1005, Toronto, Ontario M4W 3B8, tel. 416/921–7376, fax 416/921–1353.
In the United Kingdom: 22–25A Sackville St., London W1X 1DE, tel. 071/494–1441.

Romania **Romanian National Tourist Office. In North America:** 342 Madison Ave., Suite 210, New York, NY 10173, tel. 212/697–6971, fax 212/697–6972.
In the United Kingdom: 17 Nottingham Pl., London W1M 3RD, tel. 071/224–3692.

Slovakia *See* The Czech Republic and Slovakia, *above.*

Spain   **Spanish National Tourist Office. In the United States:** 665 Fifth Ave., New York, NY 10022, tel. 212/759–8822, fax 212/980–1053; 845 N. Michigan Ave., Chicago, IL 60611, tel. 312/642–1992, fax 312/642–9817; San Vicente Plaza Bldg., 8383 Wilshire Blvd., Suite 960, Beverly Hills, CA 90211, tel. 213/658–7188, fax 213/658–1061; 1221 Brickell Ave., Suite 1850, Miami, FL 33131, tel. 305/358–1992, fax 305/358–8223.
In Canada: 102 Bloor St. W, Suite 1400, Toronto, Ontario M5S 1M8, tel. 416/961–3131.
In the United Kingdom: 57–58 St. James's St., London SW1A 1LD, tel. 071/499–0901.

Sweden   **Swedish Travel and Tourism Council. In North America:** 655 Third Ave., 18th Floor, New York, NY 10017, tel. 212/949–2333, fax 212/983–5260.
In the United Kingdom: 73 Welbeck St., London W1M 8AN, tel. 071/487–3135, fax 071/935–5853.

Switzerland   **Swiss National Tourist Office. In the United States:** 608 Fifth Ave., New York, NY 10020, tel. 212/757–5944, fax 212/262–6116; 222 N. Sepulveda Blvd., Suite 1570, El Segundo, CA 90245, tel. 310/335–5980, fax 310/335–5982; 150 N. Michigan Ave., Suite 2930, Chicago, IL 60601, tel. 312/630–5840, fax 312/630–5848.
In Canada: 154 University Ave., Suite 610, Toronto, Ontario M5H 3Y9, tel. 416/971–9734.
In the United Kingdom: Swiss Centre, 1 New Coventry St., London W1V 8EE, tel. 071/734–1921.

Turkey   **Turkish Tourist Office. In North America:** 821 UN Plaza, New York, NY 10017, tel. 212/687–2194, fax 212/599–7568; 1717 Massachusetts Ave. NW, Suite 306, Washington, DC 20036, tel. 202/429–9844, fax 202/429–5649.
In Canada: c/o Turkish Embassy, 197 Wurtemburg St., Ottawa, Ontario K1N 8L9, tel. 613/789–4044.
In the United Kingdom: 170–173 Piccadilly, 1st floor, London W1V 9DD, tel. 071/734–8681.

U.S. Government Travel Briefings   The U.S. Department of State's **Overseas Citizens Emergency Center** (Room 4811, Washington, DC 20520; enclose S.A.S.E.) issues Consular Information Sheets, which cover crime, security, political climate, and health risks as well as embassy locations, entry requirements, currency regulations, and other routine matters. (Travel Warnings, which counsel travelers to avoid a country entirely, are issued in extreme cases.) For the latest information, stop in at any passport office, consulate, or embassy; call the interactive hotline (tel. 202/647–5225, fax 202/647–3000); or, with your PC's modem, tap into the Bureau of Consular Affairs' computer bulletin board (tel. 202/647–9225).

Tours and Packages

Should you buy your travel arrangements to Europe packaged or do it yourself? There are advantages either way. Buying packaged arrangements saves you money, particularly if you can find a program that includes exactly the features you want. You also get a pretty good idea of what your trip will cost from the outset. You have two options: fully escorted tours and independent packages.

Escorted tours mean having limited free time and traveling with strangers but they provide an overview of many places rather than an in-depth experience in just one. Escorted tours are most often via motorcoach, with a tour director in charge. Your baggage is handled, your time rigorously scheduled, and most meals planned. Escorted tours are therefore the most hassle-free way to see Europe, as well as generally the least expensive. Independent packages allow plenty of flexibility. They generally include airline travel and hotels, with certain options available, such as sightseeing, car rental, and excursions. Or they can be complex programs that include, in addition, travel by rail or cruise ship, special events, and entertainment. Independent packages are usually more expensive than escorted tours, but your time is your own.

While you can book directly through tour operators, you will pay no more to go through a travel agent, who will be able to tell you about tours and packages from a number of operators. Whatever program you ultimately choose, be sure to find out exactly what is included: taxes, tips, transfers, meals, baggage handling, ground transportation, entertainment, excursions, sports, or recreation (and rental equipment if necessary). Ask about the level of hotel used, its location, the size of its rooms, the kind of beds, and its amenities, such as pool, room service, or programs for children, if they're important to you. Find out the operator's cancellation penalties. Nearly everyone charges them, and the only way to avoid them is to buy trip-cancellation insurance (*see* Trip Insurance, *below*). Also ask about the single supplement, a surcharge assessed to solo travelers. Some operators do not make you pay it if you agree to be matched up with a roommate of the same gender, even if one is not found by departure time. Remember that a program that has features you won't use may not be the most cost-wise choice. In some countries, and particularly on budget programs, don't assume you will have a private bathroom. Ask!

Fully Escorted Tours Escorted tours are usually sold in three categories: deluxe, first-class, and tourist or budget class. The most important differences are the price and the level of accommodations. Some operators specialize in one category, while others offer a range. Among the larger companies who have been in business for some time, consider **Abercrombie & Kent** (1520 Kensington Rd., Oak Brook, IL 60521, tel. 800/323–7308), **Maupintour** (Box 807, Lawrence, KS 66044, tel. 800/255–4266), and **Tauck Tours** (11 Wilton Rd., Westport, CT 06881, tel. 800/468–2825) in the deluxe category; **Brendan Tours** (15137 Califa St., Van Nuys, CA 91411, tel. 818/785–9696 or 800/421–8446, fax 818/902–9876), **Caravan** (401 N. Michigan Ave., Suite 3325, Chicago, IL 60611, tel. 800/227–2826), **Certified Vacations** (Box 1525, Ft. Lauderdale, FL 33302, tel. 305/522–1414 or 800/233–7260), **CIT Tours** (342 Madison Ave., Suite 207, New York, NY 10173, tel. 212/697–2100 or 800/248–8687, fax 212/697–1394), **Collette Tours** (162 Middle St., Pawtucket, RI 02860, tel. 401/728–3805 or 800/832–4656), **Globus** (5301 S. Federal Circle, Littleton, CO 80123, tel. 303/797–2800 or 800/221–0090), **Grand European Tours** (4000 Kruse Way Pl., 2–245, Lake Oswego, OR 97035, tel. 503/635–9627 or 800/552–5545), **Olson-Travelworld** (Box 10066, Manhattan Beach, CA 90226, tel. 800/421–5785, or from CA, 800/421–2255), and **Trafalgar Tours** (21 E. 26th St., New York, NY 10010, tel. 800/854–0103) in the first-class category; and, in the budget category, **Cosmos Tourama,** a sister company of Globus at the same address, and the "Cost Savers" from **Trafalgar Tours.**

Most itineraries are jam-packed with sightseeing, so you see a lot in a short amount of time (usually one place per day). To judge just how fast-paced the tour is, review the itinerary carefully. If you are in a different hotel each night, you will be getting up early each day to head out, travel to your next destination, do some sightseeing, have dinner, and go to bed—then you'll start all over again. If you want some free time, make sure it's mentioned in the tour brochure; if you want to be escorted to every meal, confirm that any tour you consider does that. Also, when comparing programs, be sure to find out if the motorcoach is air-conditioned and has a rest room on board. Make your selection based on price and stops on the itinerary.

Independent Packages

Just about every airline that flies to Europe offers packages including round-trip airfare and hotels (plus breakfast in many cases). Contact **American Airlines Fly AAway Vacations** (tel. 800/321–2121), **Continental Airlines' Grand Destinations** (tel. 800/634–5555), **Delta Dream Vacations** (tel. 800/872–7786), **United Airlines' Vacation Planning Center** (tel. 800/328–6877). Others offering independent programs include **Abercrombie & Kent** (*see above*), **Euro-Connection** (1819 207th Place SW, Lynnwood, WA 98036, tel. 206/670–1140 or 800/645–3870), **Idyll, Ltd.** (Box 405, Media, PA 19063, tel. 215/565–5242), and **V E Tours** (1150 N.W. 72nd Ave., Suite 450, Miami, FL 33126, tel. 800/222–8383). **CIE Tours** (108 Ridgedale Ave., Box 2355, Morristown, NJ 07962-2355, tel. 800/243–8687) offers fly/drive packages to Great Britain and Ireland only. **Vantage Travel Wholesalers** (1324 E. North St., Greenville, SC 29607, tel. 803/233–7703 or 800/826–8268) includes "Castles & Villas" in France and Italy among its packages. **DER Tours** (11933 Wilshire Blvd., Los Angeles, CA 90025, tel. 800/782–2424) has an innovative voucher program; you travel either via rental car or rail, and select your travel dates and hotels as you go, paying with vouchers. While most vouchers are for tourist-class hotels, some first-class properties are available as well.

Special-Interest Travel

Special-interest programs may be fully escorted or independent. Some require a certain amount of expertise, but most are for the average traveler with an interest and are usually hosted by experts in the subject matter. When the program is escorted, it enjoys the advantages and disadvantages of all escorted programs; because your fellow travelers are apt to be passionate or knowledgeable about the subject, they can prove as enjoyable a part of your travel experience as the destination itself. The price range is wide, but the cost is usually higher—sometimes a lot higher—than for ordinary escorted tours and packages because of the expert guiding and special activities.

Adventure

If trekking through the Pyrenees in Spain, France, and Andorra or a breathtaking (in more ways than one) Alpine pass in Switzerland is your idea of fun, investigate **Mountain Travel/Sobek** (1089 Angels Camp, CA 95222, tel. 209/736–4524) and **Wilderness Travel** (801 Allston Way, Berkeley, CA 94710, tel. 510/548–0420 or 800/368–2794, fax 510/548–0347). Various cycling, skiing, backpacking, hiking, and walking tours are also available.

In the United Kingdom, **Top Deck Travel** (131–135 Earl's Court Rd., London SW5 9RH, tel. 071/244–8641) offers tours to Europe, with activities including flotilla sailing, a variety of water sports, and rafting.

Art and Architecture

Esplanade Tours (581 Boylston St., Boston, MA 02116, tel. 800/426–5492) are accompanied by expert guides; the Rhine River cruises emphasize art and architecture as well. **Archeological Tours** (271 Madison Ave., New York, NY 10016, tel. 212/986–3054, fax 212/370–1561) visits monuments and ancient cities in Italy, Greece, Spain, and Turkey, and the **Smithsonian Institution's** *Study Tours and Seminars* (1100 Jefferson Dr. SW, Room 3045, Washington, DC 20560, tel. 202/357–4700) offer a myriad of tours, ranging from

Christmas in Canterbury to exploring the remains of the Ottoman empire in western Anatolia.

In the United Kingdom, contact **Prospect Music & Art Tours Ltd.** (454–458 Chiswick High Rd., London W4 5TT, tel. 081/995–2151) and **Swan Hellenic Art Treasures Tours** (77 New Oxford St., London WC1A 1PP, tel. 071/831–1616).

Ballooning **Buddy Bombard Balloon Adventures** (6727 Curran St., McLean, VA 22101 tel. 800/862-8537) cover Austria, the Czech Republic, France, Italy, Switzerland, and Turkey, with days aloft and fine food and accommodations on the ground. **Abercrombie & Kent** (*see above*) also offers ballooning tours.

In the United Kingdom, **Air 2 Air** (Vauxhall House, Coronation Rd., Bristol BS3 1RN, tel. 0272/633333), a clearinghouse for balloon activities in Britain, has information about what's happening on the Continent.

Barges/Cruises **Avalon Tours** (1909 Alden Landing, Portsmouth, RI 02871, tel. 401/683–1782 or 800/662–2628) offers barge and yacht excursions along the rivers and waterways of France, Germany, and Holland. **Eurocruises** (303 W. 13th St., New York, NY 10014, tel. 212/691–2099 or 800/688–3876) has more than 60 ships; destinations range from the Canary Islands to Sweden, from Portugal to Russia. Other contacts are **Abercrombie & Kent** (*see above*) and **Lindblad's Special Expeditions** (720 Fifth Avenue, New York, NY 10019, tel. 212/765–7740 or 800/762–0003).

Biking The nonprofit **Bicycle Adventure Club** (3904 Groton St., San Diego, CA 92110, tel. 800/775-2453) keeps costs low on the 30 tours it runs each year by using inexpensive hotels and volunteer leaders. Destinations include England, France, Spain, and Russia. Among other contacts are **Backroads** (1516 5th St., Suite L101, Berkeley, CA 94710, tel. 510/527–1555 or 800/462–2848), **Butterfield & Robinson** (70 Bond St., Toronto, Ontario, Canada M5B 1X3, tel. 416/864–1354 or 800/387–1147), and **Classic Adventures** (Box 153-P, Hamlin, NY 14464, tel. 716/964–8488 or 800/777–8090).

Health and Fitness **DER Tours** (11933 Wilshire Blvd., Los Angeles, CA 90025, tel. 213/479–4411 or 800/937–1234) offers a menu of Europe's most acclaimed spa resorts. Some maintain sophisticated medical facilities; others are simply beautiful and healthy places to relax. **Health Tours** (25 W. 43rd St., Suite 805, New York, NY 10036, tel. 212/997–8510 or 800/443–0365) has excursions to take the waters in Czechoslovakia, Hungary, and Switzerland.

In the United Kingdom, **Moswin Tours Ltd.** (21 Church St., Oadby, Leicester LE2 5DB, tel. 0533/714982), has among its programs visits to health farms in Germany.

Music **Dailey-Thorp Travel** (330 W. 58th St., New York, NY 10019, tel. 212/307–1555; book through travel agents), specializing in classical music and opera programs throughout Europe, provides expert tour guides and tickets to events to which the general public would not have easy access. **Mozart's Europe** (Deer La., Pawlet, VT, tel. and fax 802/325–3656) offers tours featuring music festivals in Austria, Czechoslovakia, Germany, Italy, Hungary, and Switzerland. **Smolka Tours/All Around Travel** (Box 1108, Ridgefield, CT 06877, tel. 800/722–0057 or 203/431–9612 from CT) includes other performing arts as well as opera and music, and custom designs tours for art and history buffs.

In the United Kingdom, **Travel for the Arts** (117 Regent's Park Rd., London NW1 8UR, tel. 071/483–2290) takes groups to visit the musical highlights of regions throughout Europe. **Prospect Music & Art Tours** (*see* Art/Architecture Tours, *above*) has tours to many of the famous annual festivals, Savonlinna, Prague, Bregenz, and Munich among them.

Natural History
Questers Worldwide Nature Tours (257 Park Ave. S, New York, NY 10010, tel. 800/468–8668) explores the wild side of Europe in the company of expert guides. **Ryder-Walker Alpine Tours** (Box 947, Telluride, CO 81435, tel. 303/728–6481) takes group and individual hikes through Switzerland and Great Britain. **Earthwatch** (680 Mount Auburn St., Watertown, MA 02272, tel. 617/926–8000) recruits volunteers to serve in its EarthCorps as short-term assistants to scientists on research expeditions. **Esplanade Tours'** (*see* Art and Architecture, *above*) unusual itineraries explore the world's cultural traditions and wildlife.

In the United Kingdom, **Ramblers Holidays Ltd.** (Box 43, Welwyn Garden City, Herts. AL8 6PQ, tel. 0707/331133) arranges walking tours within Europe with walk leaders to point out natural features of interest.

Rail
Abercrombie & Kent (*see above*) has the market on Europe's luxury trains, including the transcontinental Venice–Simplon Orient Express and the Andalusian Express, the luxury train of Spain. Both trains are made up of vintage rail carriages from the 1920s. A&K's less costly "Great Rail Journeys of Great Britain and Europe" offers travel by regularly scheduled trains with stays in first-class and deluxe hotels, accompanied by a traveling bellboy so you don't have to lug your bags from train to hotel every morning and night.

Singles and Young Adults
Club Europa (802 W. Oregon St., Urbana, IL 61801, tel. 217/344–5863 or 800/331–1882) and **Contiki Holidays** (300 Plaza Alicante No. 900, Garden Grove, CA 93640, tel. 714/740–0808 or 800/266–8454) specialize in tours for people 18–35. **Trafalgar Tours** (*see above*) has a "Club 21" program of escorted bus tours through Europe and Great Britain for those ages 21 to 35.

Sports
Golf International (275 Madison Ave., New York, NY 10016, tel. 212/986–9176 or 800/833–1389) has golf packages to the United Kingdom, Ireland, and France. **Keith Prowse & Co.** (234 W. 44th St., Suite 100, New York, NY 10036, tel. 800/669–7469) specializes in sporting events on the Continent and in Britain, concerts, and events such as the Chelsea Flower Show. **Lindenmeyer Travel Ltd.** (19 E. 37th St., Suite 4R, New York, NY 10016, tel.800/248–2807) specializes in ski packages to the Alps; summer programs are also available. **Travel Concepts** (62 Commonwealth Ave., Suite 3, Boston, MA 02116, tel. 617/266–8450) packages prestigious sporting events but can also enroll you in polo school in England or a tennis clinic in Stockholm.

In the United Kingdom, **Owners Abroad** (Groundstar House, London Rd., Crawley RH10 2TB, tel. 071/221–6298) arranges visits to greens in Portugal, Spain, and Majorca. Companies offering alpine skiing packages include **Top Deck Ski** (131 Earls Court Rd., SW5 9RH, tel. 071/244–8641) and **Crystal Holidays** (Arlington Rd., Surbiton KT6 6BW, tel. 081/399–5144), both with a wide range of resorts at keen prices.

Wine and Food
Annemarie Victory Organization (136 E. 64th St., New York, NY 10021, tel. 212/486–0353, fax 212/751–3149) features deluxe gourmet tours in Belgium, Luxembourg, France, and Italy. **Endless Be-**

ginnings (9825 Dowdy Dr., Suite 105, San Diego, CA 92126, tel. 619/ 566–4166 or 800/822–7855) has sybaritic excursions to France and Italy, in addition to cooking school vacations in Italy, France, and England. **Travel Concepts** (*see above*) also specializes in gourmet food and wine tours, with departures to England, France, Germany, Ireland, Italy, Scandinavia, and Switzerland, and deluxe or first-class accommodations.

In the United Kingdom, **Alternative Travel Group Ltd.,** (69–71 Banbury Rd., Oxford OX2 6PE, tel. 0865/310344) has wine-tasting tours of Germany, along the Rhine, and France in the region of Alsace, as well as of other countries. They also stage orchid, truffle, and mushroom hunts to Italy, France, and Portugal.

Climate

For the average daily maximum and minimum temperatures of the major European cities, *see* When to Go in each country chapter. For current weather conditions and forecasts for cities abroad, plus the local time and helpful travel tips, call the **Weather Channel Connection** (tel. 900/932–8437; 95¢ per minute) from a touch-tone phone.

What to Pack

Clothing What you pack depends more on the season than on any particular dress code. In general, northern and central Europe have cold, snowy winters, and the Mediterranean countries have mild winters, though parts of southern Europe can be bitterly cold, too. In the Mediterranean resorts you may need a warm jacket for mornings and evenings, even in summer. The mountains usually are warm on summer days, but the weather, especially in the Alps, is unpredictable, and the nights are generally cool. The Pyrenees don't have much snow except in the higher elevations, but they have extremely damp, foggy weather and rain year-round.

For European cities, pack as you would for an American city; formal outfits for first-class restaurants and nightclubs, casual clothes elsewhere. Jeans are as popular in Europe as they are in the rest of the world and are perfectly acceptable for sightseeing and informal dining. Sturdy walking shoes are appropriate for the cobblestone streets and gravel paths that fill many of the parks and surround some of the historic buildings. For visits to churches and cathedrals, especially in southern Europe, avoid shorts and immodest outfits. Italians are especially strict, insisting that women cover their shoulders and arms (a shawl will do). Women, however, no longer have to cover their heads in Roman Catholic churches.

To discourage purse snatchers and pickpockets, take a handbag with long straps that you can sling across your body, bandolier-style, and with a zippered compartment for money and other valuables.

Miscellaneous If you stay in budget hotels, take your own soap: Many do not provide soap, and those that do often give guests only one tiny bar per room. Bring an extra pair of eyeglasses or contact lenses in your carry-on luggage. If you have a health problem that requires a prescription drug, pack enough to last the duration of the trip or have your doctor write a prescription using the drug's generic name, because brand names vary from country to country (you'll need a prescription from a doctor in the country you're visiting in order to get the medication from a pharmacy there). Always carry prescription drugs in their original packaging to avoid problems with customs officials. Don't pack them in luggage that you plan to check in case your bags go astray. Pack a list of the offices that supply refunds for lost or stolen traveler's checks.

Electricity The electrical current in most of Europe is 220 volts, 50 cycles alternating current (AC); the United States runs on 110-volt, 60-cycle AC. Unlike wall outlets in the United States, which accept plugs with two flat prongs, outlets in Europe take plugs of varying styles, often with two or three round prongs.

Adapters, To use U.S.-made electric appliances abroad, you'll need an adapter
Converters, plug. Unless the appliance is dual-voltage and made for travel, you'll
Transformers also need a converter. Hotels sometimes have 110-volt outlets for low-wattage appliances marked "For Shavers Only" near the sink; don't use them for a high-wattage appliance like a blow dryer. If you're traveling with an older laptop computer, carry a transformer. New laptop computers are auto-sensing, operating equally well on 110 and 220 volts (so you need only the appropriate adapter plug). When in doubt, consult your appliance's owner's manual or the manufacturer. Or get a copy of the free brochure "Foreign Electricity is No Deep Dark Secret," published by adapter-converter manufacturer Franzus Company (Customer Service, Dept. B50, Murtha Industrial Park, Box 142, Beacon Falls, CT 06403, tel. 203/723–6664).

Luggage Free airline baggage allowances depend on the airline, the route,
Regulations and the class of your ticket; ask in advance. In general, on domestic flights and on international flights between the United States and foreign destinations, you are entitled to check two bags—neither exceeding 62 inches, or 158 centimeters (length + width + height), or weighing more than 70 pounds (32 kilograms). A third piece may be brought aboard; its total dimensions are generally limited to less than 45 inches (114 centimeters), so it will fit easily under the seat in front of you or in the overhead compartment. In the United States the Federal Aviation Administration gives airlines broad latitude to limit carry-on allowances and tailor them to different aircraft and operational conditions. Charges for excess, oversize, or overweight pieces vary.

If you are flying between two foreign destinations, note that baggage allowances may be determined not by the piece method but by the weight method, which generally allows 88 pounds (40 kilograms) of luggage in first class, 66 pounds (30 kilograms) in business class, and 44 pounds (20 kilograms) in economy. If your flight between two cities abroad *connects* with your transatlantic or transpacific flight, the piece method still applies.

Safeguarding Before leaving home, itemize your bags' contents and their worth in
Your Luggage case they go astray. To minimize that risk, tag them inside and out with your name, address, and phone number. (If you use your home address, cover it so that potential thieves can't see it.) Put a copy of your itinerary inside each bag, so that you can easily be tracked. At check-in, make sure that the tag attached by baggage handlers bears the correct three-letter code for your destination. If your bags do not arrive with you, or if you detect damage, immediately file a written report with the airline before you leave the airport.

Taking Money Abroad

Traveler's Traveler's checks are preferable in metropolitan centers, although
Checks you'll need cash in rural areas and small towns. The most widely recognized are **American Express, Citicorp, Diners Club, Thomas Cook,** and **Visa,** which are sold by major commercial banks. Both American

Express and Thomas Cook issue checks that can be counter-signed and used by you or your traveling companion. Typically the issuing company or the bank at which you make your purchase charges 1% to 3% of the checks' face value as a fee. Some foreign banks charge as much as 20% of the face value as the fee for cashing traveler's checks in a foreign currency. Buy a few checks in small denominations to cash toward the end of your trip, so you won't be left with excess foreign currency. Record the numbers of the checks, cross them off as you spend them, and keep this list separate from the checks.

Travelers to western Europe can buy checks in the currency of the country they are visiting; banks will cash them with no fee, and they can be used as readily as cash in many hotels, restaurants, and shops.

Currency Exchange Banks offer the most favorable exchange rates. If you use currency exchange booths at airports, rail and bus stations, hotels, stores, and privately run exchange firms, you'll typically get less favorable rates, but you may find the hours more convenient.

You can avoid long lines at airport currency-exchange booths by getting a *small* amount of currency at **Thomas Cook Currency Services** (630 5th Ave., New York, NY 10111, tel. 212/757–6915 or 800/223–7373 for locations in major metropolitan areas throughout the United States) or **Ruesch International** (tel. 800/424–2923 for locations) before you depart. Check with your travel agent to be sure that the currency of the country you will be visiting can be imported.

Getting Money from Home

Cash Machines Many automated-teller machines (ATMs) are tied to international networks such as **Cirrus** and **Plus.** You can use your bank card at ATMs to withdraw money from an account and get cash advances on a credit-card account if your card has been programmed with a personal identification number, or PIN. Check in advance on limits on withdrawals and cash advances within specified periods. Ask whether your bank-card or credit-card PIN will need to be reprogrammed for use in the area you'll be visiting. Four digits are commonly used overseas. Note that Discover is accepted only in the United States. On cash advances you are charged interest from the day you receive the money from ATMs as well as from tellers. Although transaction fees for ATM withdrawals abroad may be higher than fees for withdrawals at home, Cirrus and Plus exchange rates are excellent because they are based on wholesale rates only offered by major banks. They also may be referred to abroad as "a withdrawal from a credit account."

Plan ahead: Obtain ATM locations and the names of affiliated cash-machine networks before departure. For specific foreign Cirrus locations, call 800/424–7787; for foreign Plus locations, consult the Plus directory at your local bank.

Wiring Money You don't have to be a cardholder to send or receive a **MoneyGram from American Express** for up to $10,000. Go to a MoneyGram agent in retail and convenience stores and American Express travel offices, pay up to $1,000 with a credit card and anything over that in cash. You are allowed a free long-distance call to give the transaction code to your intended recipient, who needs only present identification and the reference number to the nearest MoneyGram agent to pick up the cash. MoneyGram agents are in more than 70 countries (call 800/926–9400 for locations). Fees range from 3% to 10%, depending on the amount and how you pay.

You can also use **Western Union.** To wire money, take either cash or a cashier's check to the nearest agent or call and use MasterCard or Visa. Money sent from the United States or Canada will be available for pickup at agent locations in 100 countries within minutes. Once the money is in the system it can be picked up at 25,000 locations (call 800/325–6000 for the one nearest you; 800/321–2923 in Canada). Fees range from 4% to 10%, depending on the amount you send.

Long-Distance Calling

AT&T, MCI, and Sprint have international services that make calling home relatively affordable and convenient and let you avoid hotel surcharges. Before you go, call the company of your choice to learn the number you must dial in your destination country to reach its network: **AT&T** USA Direct (tel. 800/874–4000), **MCI** WorldPhone (tel. 800/444–4444), or **Sprint** Express (tel. 800/793–1153). All three companies offer message services to international travelers and have added debit cards so you don't have to fiddle with change.

Passports and Visas

If your passport is lost or stolen, report the loss immediately to the embassy, consulate, police. If you can provide the consular officer with the information contained in the passport, they will usually issue you a new passport promptly. For this reason, keep a photocopy of the data page of your passport separate from your money and traveler's checks. Also leave a photocopy at home.

U.S. Citizens All U.S. citizens, even infants, need a valid passport to enter the countries covered in this guide. You can pick up new and renewal application forms at any of the 13 U.S. Passport Agency offices and at some post offices and courthouses. Although passports are usually mailed within four weeks of your application's receipt, allow five weeks or more from April through summer. Call the Department of State Office of Passport Services' information line (tel. 202/647–0518) for fees, documentation requirements, and other details.

Canadian Citizens Canadian citizens need a valid passport to enter the countries covered in this guide. Application forms are available at 23 regional passport offices as well as post offices and travel agencies. Whether for a first or subsequent passport, you must apply in person. Children under 16 may be included on a parent's passport but must have their own to travel alone. Passports are valid for five years and are usually mailed within two weeks of an application's receipt. For fees, documentation requirements, and other information in English or French, call the passport office (tel. 819/994–3500 or 800/567–6868).

U.K. Citizens Citizens of the United Kingdom usually need a valid passport for travel within Europe. Applications for new and renewal passports are available from main post offices as well as at the six passport offices, located in Belfast, Glasgow, Liverpool, London, Newport, and Peterborough. You may apply in person at all passport offices, or by mail to all except the London office. Children under 16 may travel on an accompanying parent's passport. All passports are valid for 10 years. Allow a month for processing.

A British Visitor's Passport is valid for holidays and some business trips of up to three months to Andorra, Austria, Belgium, Denmark, Finland, France, Germany, Gibraltar, Greece, Iceland, Italy,

Liechtenstein, Luxembourg, Malta, Monaco, Netherlands, Norway, Portugal, Spain, Sweden, Switzerland, and Turkey. It can include both partners of a married couple. Valid for one year, it will be issued on the same day that you apply. You must apply in person at a main post office.

Customs and Duties

On Arrival Arrival formalities vary from country to country and are detailed in each chapter. In addition to specific duty-free allowances, most countries allow travelers also to bring in cameras and a reasonable amount of film and electronic equipment; most do not allow fresh meats, plants, weapons, and narcotics.

Returning Home If you are traveling with a foreign-made camera or other equipment, carry the original receipt or register it with U.S. Customs before leaving home (Form 4457) to avoid paying duty on your return.

U.S. Customs If you've been out of the country for at least 48 hours and haven't already used the exemption, or any part of it, in the past 30 days, you may bring home $400 worth of foreign goods duty-free. So can each member of your family, regardless of age; and your exemptions may be pooled, so one of you can bring in more if another brings in less. A flat 10% duty applies to the next $1,000 of goods; above $1,400, the rate varies with the merchandise. (If the 48-hour or 30-day limits apply, your duty-free allowance drops to $25, which may not be pooled.) Please note that these are the *general* rules, applicable to most countries.

Travelers 21 or older may bring back 1 liter of alcohol duty-free, provided the beverage laws of the state through which they reenter the United States allow it. In addition, 100 non-Cuban cigars and 200 cigarettes are allowed, regardless of your age. Antiques and works of art more than 100 years old are duty-free.

Gifts valued at less than $50 may be mailed to the United States duty-free, with a limit of one package per day per addressee, and do not count as part of your exemption (do not send alcohol or tobacco products or perfume valued at more than $5); mark the package "Unsolicited Gift" and write the nature of the gift and its retail value on the outside. Most reputable stores will handle the mailing for you.

For a copy of "Know Before You Go," a free brochure detailing what you may and may not bring back to the United States, rates of duty, and other pointers, contact the **U.S. Customs Service** (Box 7407, Washington, DC 20044, tel. 202/927–6724).

Canadian Customs Once per calendar year, when you've been out of Canada for at least seven days, you may bring in C$300 worth of goods duty-free. If you've been away less than seven days but more than 48 hours, the duty-free exemption drops to C$100 but can be claimed any number of times (as can a C$20 duty-free exemption for absences of 24 hours or more). You cannot combine the yearly and 48-hour exemptions, use the C$300 exemption only partially (to save the balance for a later trip), or pool exemptions with family members. Goods claimed under the C$300 exemption may follow you by mail; those claimed under the lesser exemptions must accompany you on your return.

Alcohol and tobacco products may be included in the yearly and 48-hour exemptions but not in the 24-hour exemption. If you meet the age requirements of the province through which you reenter Canada, you may bring in, duty-free, 1.14 liters (40 imperial ounces) of wine or liquor *or* two dozen 12-ounce cans or bottles of beer or ale. If you are 16 or older, you may bring in, duty-free, 200 cigarettes, 50 cigars or cigarillos, and 400 tobacco sticks or 400 grams of manufactured tobacco. Alcohol and tobacco must accompany you on your return.

An unlimited number of gifts valued up to C$60 each may be mailed to Canada duty-free. These do not count as part of your exemption. Label the package "Unsolicited Gift—Value under $60." Alcohol and tobacco are excluded.

For more information, including details of duties on items that exceed your duty-free limit, ask the Revenue Canada Customs, Excise and Taxation (2265 St. Laurent Blvd. S, Ottawa, Ontario, K1G 4K3, tel. 613/957–0275) for a copy of the free brochure "I Declare/Je Déclare."

U.K. Customs   If your journey was wholly within EU countries, you no longer need to pass through customs when you return to the United Kingdom. According to EU guidelines, you may bring in 800 cigarettes, 400 cigarillos, 200 cigars, and 1 kilogram of smoking tobacco, plus 10 liters of spirits, 20 liters of fortified wine, 90 liters of wine, and 110 liters of beer. If you exceed these limits, you may be required to prove that the goods are for your personal use or are gifts.

From countries outside the EU, you may import duty-free 200 cigarettes, 100 cigarillos, 50 cigars, or 250 grams of tobacco; 1 liter of spirits or 2 liters of fortified or sparkling wine; 2 liters of still table wine; 60 milliliters of perfume; 250 milliliters of toilet water; plus £136 worth of other goods, including gifts and souvenirs.

For further information or a copy of "A Guide for Travellers," which details standard customs procedures as well as what you may bring into the United Kingdom from abroad, contact HM Customs and Excise (Dorset House, Stamford St., London SE1 9PY, tel. 071/928–3344).

Traveling with Cameras, Camcorders, and Laptops

Cameras and Film   If your camera is new or if you haven't used it for a while, shoot and develop a few test rolls before you leave. Store film in a cool, dry place—never in the car's glove compartment or on the shelf under the rear window.

Airport security X-rays generally aren't harmful to film with ISO below 400. To protect your film, carry it with you in a clear plastic bag and ask for a hand inspection. Such requests are honored at U.S. airports, but left up to the inspector abroad. Don't depend on a lead-lined bag to protect film in checked luggage—the airline may increase the radiation to see what's inside. Call the Kodak Information Center (tel. 800/242–2424) for details.

Camcorders and Videotape   Before your trip, put camcorders through their paces, invest in a skylight filter to protect the lens, and check all the batteries. Most newer camcorders are equipped with batteries that can be recharged with a universal or worldwide AC adapter charger (or multivoltage converter) usable whether the voltage is 110 or 220. All that's needed is the appropriate plug.

Videotape is not damaged by X-rays, but it may be harmed by the magnetic field of a walk-through metal detector, so ask for a hand-check. Airport security personnel may ask you to turn on the camcorder to prove that it's what it appears to be, so make sure the battery is charged. Note that rather than the National Television

System Committee (NTSC) video standard used in the United States and Canada, some countries in Europe use PAL/SECAM technology. You will not be able to view your tapes through the local TV set or view movies bought there in your home VCR. Blank tapes bought in Europe can be used for NTSC camcorder taping, but they are pricey.

Laptops Security X-rays do not harm hard-disk or floppy-disk storage, but you may request a hand-check, at which point you may be asked to turn on the computer to prove that it is what it appears to be. (Check your battery before departure.) Most airlines allow you to use your laptop aloft except during takeoff and landing (so as not to interfere with navigation equipment). For international travel, register your foreign-made laptop with U.S. Customs as you leave the country. If your laptop is U.S.-made, call the consulate of the country you'll be visiting to find out whether or not it should be registered with customs upon arrival. Before departure, find out about repair facilities at your destination, and don't forget any transformer or adapter plug you may need (*see* Electricity, *above*).

Staying Healthy

There are no serious health risks associated with travel in Europe, and no inoculations are required. However, the Centers for Disease Control (CDC) in Atlanta advises that international travelers swim only in chlorinated swimming pools if there is any question about contamination of local beaches and freshwater lakes. The CDC also cautions that most of southern Europe is in the "intermediate" range for risk of contracting traveler's diarrhea. Part of this may be due to an increased consumption of olive oil and wine, which can have a laxative effect on stomachs used to a different diet. The American Medical Association recommends Pepto-Bismol for minor cases of traveler's diarrhea.

Finding a Doctor The **International Association for Medical Assistance to Travellers** (IAMAT, 417 Center St., Lewiston, NY 14092, tel. 716/754–4883; 40 Regal Rd., Guelph, Ontario N1K 1B5; 57 Voirets, 1212 Grand-Lancy, Geneva, Switzerland) publishes a worldwide directory of English-speaking physicians whose qualifications meet IAMAT standards and who have agreed to treat members for a set fee. Membership is free.

Assistance Companies Pretrip medical referrals, emergency evacuation or repatriation, 24-hour telephone hot lines for medical consultation, dispatch of medical personnel, relay of medical records, cash for emergencies, and other personal and legal assistance are among the services provided by several membership organizations specializing in medical assistance to travelers. Among them are **International SOS Assistance** (Box 11568, Philadelphia, PA 19116, tel. 215/244–1500 or 800/523–8930; Box 466, Pl. Bonaventure, Montréal, Qué. H5A 1C1, tel. 514/874–7674 or 800/363–0263), **Medex Assistance Corporation** (Box 10623, Baltimore, MD 21285, tel. 410/296–2530 or 800/874–9125), **Near Services** (450 Prairie Ave., Suite 101, Calumet City, IL 60409, tel. 708/868–6700 or 800/654–6700), and **Travel Assistance International** (1133 15th St. NW, Suite 400, Washington, DC 20005, tel. 202/331–1609 or 800/821–2828). Because these companies will also sell you death-and-dismemberment, trip-cancellation, and other insurance coverage, there is some overlap with the travel-insurance policies discussed under Insurance, *below*.

Publications *The Safe Travel Book* by Peter Savage ($12.95, Lexington Books, 866 3rd Ave., New York, NY 10022, tel. 212/702–4771 or 800/257–

5755, fax 800/562–1272) is packed with handy lists and phone numbers to make your trip smooth. *Traveler's Medical Resource* by William W. Forgey ($19.95, ICS Books, Inc., 1 Tower Plaza, 107 E. 89th Ave., Merrillville, IN 45410, tel. 800/541–7323) is also a good, authoritative guide to care overseas.

Insurance

U.S. Residents Most tour operators, travel agents, and insurance agents sell specialized health-and-accident, flight, trip-cancellation, and luggage insurance as well as comprehensive policies with some or all of these features. Before you make any purchase, review your existing health and homeowner policies to find out whether they cover expenses incurred while traveling.

Health-and-Accident Insurance Specific policy provisions of supplemental health-and-accident insurance for travelers include reimbursement for $1,000 to $150,000 worth of medical and/or dental expenses caused by an accident or illness during a trip. The personal-accident, or death-and-dismemberment, provision pays a lump sum to your beneficiaries if you die or to you if you lose one or both limbs or your eyesight; the lump sum awarded can range from $15,000 to $500,000. The medical-assistance provision may reimburse you for the cost of referrals, evacuation, or repatriation and other services, or it may automatically enroll you as a member of a particular medical-assistance company (*see* Assistance Companies, *above*).

Flight Insurance Often bought as a last-minute impulse at the airport, flight insurance pays a lump sum when a plane crashes either to a beneficiary if the insured dies or sometimes to a surviving passenger who loses eyesight or a limb. Like most impulse buys, flight insurance is expensive and basically unnecessary. It supplements the airlines' coverage described in the limits-of-liability paragraphs on your ticket. Charging an airline ticket to a major credit card often automatically entitles you to coverage and may also embrace travel by bus, train, and ship.

Baggage Insurance In the event of loss, damage, or theft on international flights, airlines' liability is $20 per kilogram for checked baggage (roughly about $640 per 70-pound bag) and $400 per passenger for unchecked baggage. On domestic flights, the ceiling is $1,250 per passenger. Excess-valuation insurance can be bought directly from the airline at check-in for about $10 per $1,000 worth of coverage. However, you cannot buy it at any price for the rather extensive list of excluded items shown on your airline ticket.

Trip Insurance **Trip-cancellation-and-interruption insurance** protects you in the event you are unable to undertake or finish your trip, especially if your airline ticket, cruise, or package tour does not allow changes or cancellations. The amount of coverage you purchase should equal the cost of your trip should you, a traveling companion, or a family member fall ill, forcing you to stay home, plus the nondiscounted one-way airline ticket you would need to buy if you had to return home early. Read the fine print carefully, especially sections defining "family member" and "preexisting medical conditions." **Default** or **bankruptcy insurance** protects you against a supplier's failure to deliver. Such policies often do not cover default by a travel agency, tour operator, airline, or cruise line if you bought your tour and the coverage directly from the firm in question. Tours packaged by one of the 33 members of the United States Tour Operators Association (USTOA, 211 E. 51st St., Suite 12B, New York, NY 10022, tel. 212/750–7371), which requires members to maintain $1 million each in an account to reimburse clients in case of default, are likely to present the fewest difficulties. Even better, pay for travel arrangements with a major credit card, so that you can refuse to pay the bill if services have not been rendered—and let the card company fight your battles.

Comprehensive Policies Companies supplying comprehensive policies with some or all of the above features include **Access America, Inc.** (Box 90315, Richmond, VA 23230, tel. 800/284–8300); **Carefree Travel Insurance** (Box 310, 120 Mineola Blvd., Mineola, NY 11501, tel. 516/294–0220 or 800/323–3149); **Tele-Trip** (Mutual of Omaha Plaza, Box 31762, Omaha, NE 68131, tel. 800/228–9792); **The Travelers Companies** (1 Tower Sq., Hartford, CT 06183, tel. 203/277–0111 or 800/243–3174); **Travel Guard International** (1145 Clark St., Stevens Point, WI 54481, tel. 715/345–0505 or 800/826–1300); and **Wallach and Company, Inc.** (107 W. Federal St., Box 480, Middleburg, VA 22117, tel. 703/687–3166 or 800/237–6615).

U.K. Residents Most tour operators, travel agents, and insurance agents sell specialized policies covering accident, medical expenses, personal liability, trip cancellation, and loss or theft of personal property. You can also buy an annual travel-insurance policy valid for every trip (usually of less than 90 days) you make during the year in which it's purchased. Make sure you will be covered if you have a preexisting medical condition or are pregnant.

For advice by phone or a free booklet, "Holiday Insurance," on what to expect from a holiday-insurance policy, with price guidelines, contact the **Association of British Insurers** (51 Gresham St., London EC2V 7HQ, tel. 071/600–3333; 30 Gordon St., Glasgow G1 3PU, tel. 041/226–3905; Scottish Providence Bldg., Donegall Sq. W, Belfast BT1 6JE, tel. 0232/249176; call for other locations).

Renting and Leasing Cars

Renting If you're traveling to more than one country, make sure your rental contract permits you to take the car across borders and that the insurance policy covers you in every country you visit.

Rental rates vary widely and depend on size and model and the number of days you use the car, and usually include unlimited free mileage and standard liability protection. Most major car-rental companies are represented in Europe, including **Alamo** (800/327–9633), **Avis** (tel. 800/331–1212, 800/879–2847 in Canada, 081/848–8765 in the United Kingdom); **Budget** (tel. 800/527–0700); **Hertz** (tel. 800/654–3131, 800/263-0600 in Canada, 081/679–1799 in the United Kingdom); **National** (tel. 800/227–7368, and 081/950–4080 in the United Kingdom). Unlimited-mileage rates vary, depending on where you rent the car and for how long, and usually do not include European value-added taxes (VAT), which also vary from country to country, ranging from zero in Switzerland to 18.6% in France.

Requirements Driver's licenses issued in the United States, Canada, and the United Kingdom are acceptable in Europe. Non-EC nationals must have Green Card insurance (*see* By Car in Getting Around Europe, *below*). An International Driver's Permit, available from the American or Canadian Automobile Association, is a good idea.

Extra Charges Picking up the car in one city and leaving it in another may entail substantial drop-off charges or one-way service fees. The cost of a collision or loss-damage waiver (*see below*) can be high, also. Some rental agencies will charge you extra if you return the car *before* the time specified on your contract. Ask before making unscheduled drop-offs. Be sure the rental agent agrees *in writing* to any changes in drop-off location or other items of your rental contract. Fill the tank just before you turn in the vehicle to avoid being charged for refueling at what you'll swear is the most expensive pump in town. In Europe, manual transmissions are standard and air-conditioning is a rarity and often unnecessary. Asking for an automatic transmission or air-conditioning can significantly increase the cost of your rental. Find out what the standard rentals are in the country you'll be visiting and weigh that factor when making your reservation.

Cutting Costs   Major international companies have programs that discount their standard rates by 15%–30% if you make the reservation before departure (anywhere from 24 hours to 14 days), rent for a minimum number of days (typically three or four), and prepay the rental. More economical rentals may come as part of fly/drive or other packages, even bare-bones deals that only combine the rental and an airline ticket (*see* Tours and Packages, *above*).

Several companies operate as wholesalers. They do not own their own fleets but rent in bulk from those that do and offer advantageous rates to their customers. Rentals through such companies must be arranged and paid for before you leave the United States. Among them are **Auto Europe** (Box 7006, Portland, ME 04112, tel. 207/828–2525 or 800/223–5555; 800/458–9503 in Canada); **Europe by Car** (mailing address, 1 Rockefeller Plaza, New York, NY 10020; walk-in address, 14 W. 49th St., New York, NY 10020, tel. 212/581–3040, 212/245–1713, or 800/223–1516; 9000 Sunset Blvd., Los Angeles, CA 90069, tel. 800/252–9401 or 213/272–0424 in CA); **Foremost Euro-Car** (5658 Sepulveda Blvd., Suite 201, Van Nuys, CA 91411, tel. 818/786–1960 or 800/272–3299); and the **Kemwel Group** (106 Calvert St., Harrison, NY 10528, tel. 914/835–5555 or 800/678–0678). You won't see these wholesalers' deals advertised; they're even better in summer, when business travel is down. Always ask whether the prices are guaranteed in U.S. dollars or foreign currency and if unlimited mileage is available. Find out about any required deposits, cancellation penalties, and drop-off charges, and confirm the cost of any required insurance coverage.

Insurance and Collision Damage Waiver   Until recently, standard rental contracts included liability coverage (for damage to public property, injury to pedestrians, and so on) and coverage for the car against fire, theft, and collision damage with a deductible. Due to law changes in some states and rising liability costs, several car rental agencies have reduced the type of coverage they offer. Before you rent a car, find out exactly what coverage, if any, is provided by your personal auto insurer. Don't assume that you are covered. If you do want insurance from the rental company, secondary coverage may be the only type offered. You may already have secondary coverage if you charge the rental to a credit card. Only Diner's Club (tel. 800/234–6377) provides primary coverage in the United States and worldwide.

In general, if you have an accident, you are responsible for the automobile. Car rental companies may offer a collision damage waiver (CDW), which ranges in cost from $4 to $14 a day. You should decline the CDW only if you are certain you are covered through your personal insurer or credit card company.

In Spain and Greece, make sure you carry insurance that provides bail bond in case of an accident. When driving a rental car in Greece, beware of damaging the underside of the vehicle on Greek roads, which are among the worst in Europe. Normal collision-damage waivers, even from one of the major international chains, may not cover such damage, and you could face a crippling fine.

Leasing For trips of 21 days or more, you may save money by leasing a car. With the leasing arrangement, you are technically buying a car and then selling it back to the manufacturer after you've used it. You receive a factory-new car, tax-free, with international registration and extensive insurance coverage. Rates vary with the make and model of car and length of time used. Car-leasing programs are offered by Renault, Citroën, and Peugeot in France and by Volkswagen, Ford, Audi, and Opel, among others, in Belgium. Delivery can be arranged outside France or Belgium for an additional fee. Before you go, compare long-term rental rates with leasing rates. Remember to add taxes and insurance costs to the car rentals, something you don't have to worry about with leasing. Companies that offer leasing arrangements include Kemwel and Europe by Car (*see* Renting, *above*).

Rail Passes

An excellent value if you plan to rack up the miles, **EurailPasses** provide unlimited first-class rail travel during their period of validity in Austria, Belgium, Denmark, Finland, France, Germany, Greece, Hungary, the Irish Republic, Italy, Luxembourg, the Netherlands, Norway, Portugal, Spain, Sweden, and Switzerland (but not England, Scotland, Northern Ireland, and Wales). Standard passes are available for 15 days ($498), 21 days ($648), one month ($728), two months ($1,098), and three months ($1,398). **Eurail Saverpasses** valid for 15 days cost $430 per person, for 21 days $550, for one month $678 per person; you must do all your traveling with at least one companion (two companions from April through September). **Eurail Youthpasses,** which cover second-class travel, cost $578 for one month, $768 for two months; you must be under 26 on the first day you travel. **Eurail Flexipasses** allow you to travel first class for 5 ($348), 10 ($560), or 15 ($740) days within any two-month period. **Eurail Youth Flexipasses,** available to those under 26 on their first travel day, allow you to travel second class for 5 ($255), 10 ($398), or 15 ($540) days within any two-month period. Another option is the **Europass,** featuring a minimum of 5 and a maximum of 15 days (within a two-month period) of unlimited rail travel in your choice of three to all five of the participating countries (France, Germany, Italy, Spain, and Switzerland); cost for five days is $280 first class, $198 second class (3 countries); for 8 days, $394 first class, $284 second class (4 countries), and for 11 days, $508 first class, $366 second class (all five countries). Each extra rail day costs $38 for first class and $28 for second class. Apply through your travel agent or **Rail Europe** (226–230 Westchester Ave., White Plains, NY 10604, tel. 800/438–7245 or 800/848–7245; or 2087 Dundas East, Suite 105, Mississauga, Ontario L4X 1M2, tel. 416/602–4195), **DER Tours** (Box 1606, Des Plaines, IL 60017, tel. 800/782–2424, fax 800/282–7474), or **CIT Tours Corp.** (342 Madison Ave., Suite 207, New York, NY 10173, tel. 212/697–2100 or 800/248–8687; 310/670–4269 or 800/248–7245 in western U.S.).

Eurail also sells single-country passes for Austria, Czechoslovakia, Finland, France, Germany, Greece, Hungary, Poland, Portugal, Russia, Spain, and Switzerland, as well as multi-country passes that cover Britain and France jointly, all of Scandinavia, and the Benelux nations. Typically these are flexipasses, valid for a 5, 10, and 15, or other specified number of days, within a longer time period; rail-and-drive schemes are also available.

Don't make the mistake of assuming that your rail pass guarantees you seats on the trains you want to ride. Seat reservations are required on some trains, particularly high-speed trains, and are a good idea on trains that may be crowded. You will also need reservations for overnight sleeping accommodations. Rail Europe can help you determine if you need reservations and can make them for you (about $10 each, less if you purchase them in Europe at the time of travel).

Home Exchange and Villa Rentals

Home Exchange You can find a house, apartment, or other vacation property to exchange for your own by becoming a member of a home-exchange organization, which then sends you its annual directories listing available exchanges and includes your own listing in at least one of them. Arrangements for the actual exchange are made by the two parties to it, not by the organization. For more information about the process contact the **International Home Exchange Association** (IHEA, 41 Sutter St., Suite 1090, San Francisco, CA 94104, tel. 415/673–0347 or 800/788–2489). Among the principal clearinghouses are: **Homelink International** (Box 650, Key West, FL 33041, tel. 800/638–3841), with thousands of foreign and domestic listings, which has four annual directories plus updates ($50 membership includes your listing in one book); **Intervac International** (Box 590504, San Francisco, CA 94159, tel. 415/435–3497), which has three annual directories ($62 membership or $72 to receive directories but remain unlisted); **Loan-a-Home** (2 Park La., Apt. 6E, Mount Vernon, NY 10552, tel. 914/664–7640) which specializes in long-term exchanges (no charge to list your home, but directories cost $35 or $45 depending on the number you receive); and **Villa Leisure** (Box 30188, Palm Beach, FL 33420, tel. 407/624–9000 or 800/526–4244), which facilitates swaps.

Apartment and Villa Rentals If you want a home base that's roomy enough for a family and comes with cooking facilities, a furnished rental may be the solution. It's generally cost-wise, too, although not always—some rentals are luxury properties (economical only when your party is large). Home-exchange directories do list rentals—often second homes owned by prospective house swappers— and some services search for a house or apartment for you (even a castle if that's your fancy) and handle the paperwork. Some send an illustrated catalogue and others send photographs of specific properties, sometimes at a charge; up-front registration fees may apply.

Among the companies are **At Home Abroad** (405 E. 56th St., Suite 6H, New York, NY 10022, tel. 212/421–9165); **Europa-Let** (92 N. Main St., Ashland, Oregon 97520, tel. 503/482–5806 or 800/462–4486); **Interhome Inc.** (124 Little Falls Rd., Fairfield, NJ 07004, tel. 201/882–6864); **Overseas Connection** (31 North Harbor Dr., Sag Harbor, NY 11963, tel. 516/725–9308 or 800/542–4007); **Property Rentals International** (1 Park West Circle, Suite 108, Midlothian, VA 23113, tel. 804/378–6054 or 800/220–3332); **Rent a Home International** (7200 34th Ave. NW, Seattle, WA 98117, tel. 206/789–9377 or 800/488–7368); **The Invented City** (*see* IHEA, *above*); **Vacation Home Rentals Worldwide** (235 Kensington Ave., Norwood, NJ 07648, tel. 201/767–9393 or 800/633–3284); **Villas and Apartments Abroad** (420 Madison Ave., Suite 1105, New York, NY 10017, tel. 212/759–1025 or 800/433–3020); and **Villas International** (605 Market St., Suite 510, San Francisco, CA 94105, tel. 415/281–0910 or 800/221–2260). **Hideaways International** (15 Goldsmith St., Box 1270, Littleton, MA 01460, tel. 508/486–8955 or 800/843–4433) functions as a travel club.

Membership ($99 yearly per person or family at the same address) includes two annual guides plus quarterly newsletters; rentals are arranged directly between members, not by the club staff.

Student and Youth Travel

Travel Agencies   **Council Travel Services (CTS),** a subsidiary of the nonprofit Council on International Educational Exchange, specializes in low-cost travel arrangements abroad for students and is the exclusive U.S. agent for several discount cards. Also newly available from CTS are domestic air passes for bargain travel within the United States. CIEE's twice-yearly *Student Travels* magazine is available at the CTS office at CIEE headquarters (205 E. 42nd St., 16th Floor, New York, NY 10017, tel. 212/661–1450) and in Boston (tel. 617/266–1926), Miami (tel. 305/670–9261), Los Angeles (tel. 310/208–3551), and at 43 branches in college towns nationwide (free in person, $1 by mail). **Campus Connections** (1100 East Marlton Pike, Cherry Hill, NJ 08034, tel. 800/428–3235) specializes in discounted accommodations and airline fares for students. The **Educational Travel Centre** (438 N. Frances St., Madison, WI 53703, tel. 608/256–5551) offers low-cost domestic and international airline tickets, mostly for flights departing from Chicago, and rail passes. Other travel agencies catering to students include **TMI Student Travel** (1146 Pleasant St., Watertown, MA 02172, tel. 617/661–8187 or 800/245–3672), and **Travel Cuts** (187 College St., Toronto, Ont. M5T 1P7, tel. 416/979–2406).

Discount Cards   For discounts on transportation and on museum and attractions admissions, buy the **International Student Identity Card** (ISIC) if you're a bona fide student, or the **International Youth Card** (IYC) if you're under 26. In the United States the ISIC and IYC cards cost $16 each and include basic travel accident and illness coverage and a toll-free travel assistance hot line. Apply to **CIEE** (*see* address *above,* tel. 212/661–1414; the application is in *Student Travels*). In Canada the cards are available for C$15 each from **Travel Cuts** (*see above*). In the United Kingdom they cost £5 and £4 respectively at student unions and student travel companies, including Council Travel's London office (28A Poland St., London W1V 3DB, tel. 071/437–7767).

Hostelling   A **Hostelling International** (HI) membership card is the key to more than 5,000 hostels in 70 countries; the sex-segregated, dormitory-style sleeping quarters, including some for families, go for $7 to $20 a night per person. Membership is available in the United States through **Hostelling International-American Youth Hostels** (HI-AYH, 733 15th St. NW, Suite 840, Washington, DC 20005, tel. 202/783–6161), the U.S. link in the worldwide chain, and costs $25 for adults 18 to 54, $10 for those under 18, $15 for those 55 and over, and $35 for families. Volume 1 of the *AYH Guide to Budget Accommodation* lists hostels in Europe and the Mediterranean ($13.95, including postage). HI membership is available in Canada through **Hostelling International-Canada** (205 Catherine St., Suite 400, Ottawa, Ontario K2P 1C3, tel. 613/748–5638) for $26.75, and in the United Kingdom through the **Youth Hostel Association of England and Wales** (Trevelyan House, 8 St. Stephen's Hill, St. Albans, Hertsfordshire. AL1 2DY, tel. 0727/855215) for £9.

Tour Operators   **AESU Travel** (2 Hamill Rd., Suite 248, Baltimore, MD 21210, tel. 410/323–4416 or 800/638–7640) and **Contiki** (300 Plaza Alicante #900, Garden Grove, CA 92640, tel. 714/740–0808 or 800/266–8454) specialize in package tours for travelers 18 to 35.

Traveling with Children

Publications *Family Travel Times*, published 10 times a year by **Travel With Your**
Newsletter **Children** (TWYCH, 45 W. 18th St., New York, NY 10011, tel. 212/
206–0688; annual subscription $55), covers destinations, types of va-
cations, and modes of travel.

Books *Traveling with Children—And Enjoying It*, by Arlene K. Butler
($11.95 plus $3 shipping per book; Globe Pequot Press, Box 833, 6
Business Park Rd., Old Saybrook, CT 06475, tel. 800/243–0495, or
800/962–0973 in CT), helps plan your trip with children, from tod-
dlers to teens. *Innocents Abroad: Traveling with Kids in Europe*,
by Valerie Wolf Deutsch and Laura Sutherland ($15.95 or $4.95
paperback, Penguin USA, 120 Woodbine St., Bergenfield, NJ
07621, tel. 800/253–6476), covers child- and teen-friendly activities,
food, and transportation. TWYCH (*see above*) also publishes *Cruising with Children* ($22) and *Skiing with Children* ($29).

Tour **Grandtravel** (6900 Wisconsin Ave., Suite 706, Chevy Chase, MD
Operators 20815, tel. 301/986–0790 or 800/247–7651) offers tours for people
traveling with their grandchildren. The catalogue, as charmingly
written and illustrated as a children's book, positively invites arm-
chair traveling with lap-sitters aboard. **Families Welcome!** (21 West
Colony Place, Suite 140, Durham, NC 27705, tel. 919/489–2555 or
800/326–0724; fax 919/490–5587) packages and sells family tours.
Rascals in Paradise (650 5th St., Suite 505, San Francisco, CA 94107,
tel. 415/978–9800, or 800/872–7225) specializes in adventurous, exotic, and fun-filled vacations for families to carefully screened resorts and hotels around the world.

Getting There On international flights, the fare for infants under age 2 not occupy-
Airfares ing a seat is generally either free or 10% of the accompanying adult's
fare; children ages 2 to 11 usually pay half to two-thirds of the adult
fare. On domestic flights, children under 2 not occupying a seat travel free, and older children currently travel on the "lowest applicable" adult fare.

Baggage In general, infants paying 10% of the adult fare are allowed one carry-on bag, not to exceed 70 pounds or 45 inches (length + width +
height) and a collapsible stroller; check with the airline before departure, because you may be allowed less if the flight is full. The
adult baggage allowance applies for children paying half or more of
the adult fare.

Safety Seats The FAA recommends the use of safety seats aloft and details approved models in the free leaflet **"Child/Infant Safety Seats Recommended for Use in Aircraft"** (available from the Federal Aviation
Administration, APA–200, 800 Independence Ave. SW, Washington, DC 20591, tel. 202/267–3479); Information Hotline, tel. 800/
322–7873). Airline policy varies. U.S. carriers allow FAA-approved
models bearing a sticker declaring their FAA approval. Because
these seats are strapped into regular passenger seats, airlines may
require that a ticket be bought for an infant who would otherwise
ride free. Foreign carriers may not allow infant seats, may charge
the child's rather than the infant's fare for their use, or may require
you to hold your baby during takeoff and landing, thus defeating the
seat's purpose.

Facilities Aloft Some airlines provide other services for children, such as children's
meals and freestanding bassinets (only to those with seats at the
bulkhead, where there's enough legroom). Make your request when
reserving. Biannually the February issue of *Family Travel Times*
details children's services on three dozen airlines ($12, *see above*).

"Kids and Teens in Flight" (free from the U.S. Department of Transportation's Office of Consumer Affairs (R-25, Washington, DC 20590, tel. 202/366–2220) offers tips for children flying alone.

Lodging **Novotel** hotels (tel. 800/221–4542) permit up to two children to stay free in their parents' room. Many Novotel properties have playgrounds. **Sofitel** hotels (tel. 800/221–4542) offer a free second room for children during July and August and over the Christmas holiday. **Happy Family Swiss Hotels,** 22 properties in Switzerland, offer outstanding programs for children at reduced prices; contact the Swiss National Tourist Office (608 Fifth Ave., New York, NY 10019, tel. 212/757–5944) for a brochure. Many of **Germany's castle hotels** (represented by Europa Hotels and Tours, tel. 206/486–9394 or 800/ 523–9570, and by DER Tours, tel. 310/479–4411 or 800/937–1234) are on parklike grounds and are enchanting for children, as are **Spain's Paradors** (Marketing Ahead, 433 Fifth Ave., New York, NY 10016, tel. 212/686–9213) in castles. The **Sol and Melia chains** (tel. 800/336–3542), also in Spain, permit children 12 and under to stay free with their parents. **Italy's CIGA hotels** (reservations, tel. 800/ 221–2340) welcome families as well.

Club Med (40 W. 57th St., New York, NY 10019, tel. 800/258–2633) has "Baby Clubs" (from age four months), "Mini Clubs" (for ages four to six or eight, depending on the resort), and "Kids Clubs" (for ages eight and up during school holidays) at many of its resort villages in France, Italy, Switzerland, and Spain.

Baby-Sitting For child-care agencies with English-speaking personnel, ask your **Services** hotel concierge, or call the American embassy or consulate. Some local tourist offices also maintain updated lists of local baby-sitters.

Hints for Travelers with Disabilities

Organizations Several organizations provide travel information for people with disabilities, usually for a membership fee, and some publish newsletters and bulletins. Among them are the **Information Center for Individuals with Disabilities** (Fort Point Pl., 27–43 Wormwood St., Boston, MA 02210, tel. 617/727–5540 or 800/462–5015 in MA between 11 AM and 4 PM, or leave message; TTY 617/345–9743); **Mobility International USA** (Box 10767, Eugene, OR 97440, tel. and TTY 503/ 343–1284; fax 503/343–6812), the U.S. branch of an international organization based in Britain (*see below*) that has affiliates in 30 countries; **MossRehab Hospital Travel Information Service** (tel. 215/ 456–9603, TTY 215/456–9602); the **Travel Industry and Disabled Exchange** (TIDE, 5435 Donna Ave., Tarzana, CA 91356, tel. 818/344– 3640, fax 818/344–0078); and **Travelin' Talk** (Box 3534, Clarksville, TN 37043, tel. 615/552–6670, fax 615/552–1182).

In the United Important information sources include the **Royal Association for** *Kingdom* **Disability and Rehabilitation** (RADAR, 12 City Forum, 250 City Rd., London EC1V 8AF, tel. 071/250–3222), which publishes travel information for people with disabilities in Britain, and **Mobility International** (228 Borough High St., London SE1 1JX, tel. 071/403– 5688), an international clearinghouse of travel information for people with disabilities.

Travel Agency **Flying Wheels Travel** (143 W. Bridge St., Box 382, Owatonna, MN **and Tour** 55060, tel. 507/451–5005 or 800/535–6790) is a travel agency specia- **Operator** lizing in domestic and worldwide cruises, tours, and independent travel itineraries for people with mobility problems. Adventurers should contact **Wilderness Inquiry** (1313 Fifth St. S.E., Minneapolis, MN 55414, tel. and TTY 612/379–3858 or 800/728–0719), which orchestrates action-packed trips such as white-water rafting, sea kayaking, and dog sledding to bring together people who have disabilities with those who don't.

Publications Several free publications are available from the U.S. Consumer Information Center (Pueblo, CO 81009): "New Horizons for the Air Traveler with a Disability" (include Dept. 608Y in the address), a U.S. Department of Transportation booklet describing changes resulting from the 1986 Air Carrier Access Act and from the 1990 Americans with Disabilities Act, and the Airport Operators Council's *Access Travel: Airports* (Dept. 5804), which describes facilities and services for people with disabilities at more than 500 airports worldwide.

Travelin' Talk Directory (*see* Organizations, *above*) was published in 1993. This 500-page resource book ($35 check or money order with a money-back guarantee) lists names and addresses of people and organizations who offer help for travelers with disabilities. **Twin Peaks Press** (Box 129, Vancouver, WA 98666, tel. 206/694–2462 or 800/637–2256) publishes the *Directory of Travel Agencies for the Disabled* ($19.95), listing more than 370 agencies worldwide. Add $2 for shipping.

Hints for Older Travelers

Organizations The **American Association of Retired Persons** (AARP, 601 E St. NW, Washington, DC 20049, tel. 202/434–2277) provides independent travelers who are members of the AARP (open to those age 50 or older; $8 per person or couple annually) with the Purchase Privilege Program, which offers discounts on lodging, car rentals, and sightseeing, and arranges group tours, cruises, and apartment living through AARP Travel Experience from American Express (400 Pinnacle Way, Suite 450, Norcross, GA 30071, tel. 800/927–0111 or 800/745–4567).

Two other organizations offer discounts on lodgings, car rentals, and other travel products, along with such nontravel perks as magazines and newsletters: the **National Council of Senior Citizens** (1331 F St. NW, Washington, DC 20004, tel. 202/347–8800; membership $12 annually) and **Mature Outlook** (6001 N. Clark St., Chicago, IL 60660, tel. 800/336–6330; $9.95 annually).

Note: Mention your senior-citizen identification card when booking hotel reservations for reduced rates, not when checking out. At restaurants, show your card before you're seated; discounts may be limited to certain menus, days, or hours. If you are renting a car, ask about promotional rates that might improve on your senior-citizen discount.

Educational Travel The nonprofit **Elderhostel** (75 Federal St., 3rd floor, Boston, MA 02110, tel. 617/426–7788) has offered inexpensive study programs for people 60 and older since 1975. Held at more than 1,800 educational and cultural institutions, courses cover everything from marine science to Greek myths and cowboy poetry. Participants generally attend lectures in the morning and spend the afternoon sightseeing or on field trips; they live in dormitory-type lodgings. Fees for two- to three-week international trips—including room, board, and transportation from the United States—range from $1,800 to $4,500.

Interhostel (University of New Hampshire, 6 Garrison Ave., Durham, NH 03824, tel. 603/862–1147 or 800/733–9753) caters to a slightly younger clientele—50 and over—and runs programs in some 25 countries. The idea is similar: Lectures and field trips mix with sightseeing, and participants stay in dormitories at cooperating educational institutions or in modest hotels. Programs usually last two weeks and cost $1,500–$2,100, excluding airfare.

Tour Operators The following tour operators specialize in older travelers: **Evergreen Travel Service** (4114 198th St. SW, Suite 3, Lynnwood, WA 98036, tel. 206/776–1184 or 800/435–2288), has introduced the "Lazy Bones" tours for those who like a slower pace. If you want to take your grandchildren, look into **Grandtravel** (*see* Traveling with Children, *above*); **Saga International Holidays** (222 Berkeley St., Boston, MA 02116, tel. 800/343–0273), caters to those over age 60 who like to travel in groups.

Publications *The 50+ Traveler's Guidebook: Where to Go, Where to Stay, What to Do* by Anita Williams and Merrimac Dillon ($12.95, St. Martin's Press, 175 5th Ave., New York, NY 10010) is available in bookstores and offers many useful tips. "The Mature Traveler" (Box 50820, Reno, NV 89513, tel. 702/786–7419; $29.95), a monthly newsletter, contains many travel deals.

Hints for Gay and Lesbian Travelers

Organizations The **International Gay Travel Association** (Box 4974, Key West, FL 33041, tel. 800/448–8550), which has 700 members, will provide you with names of travel agents and tour operators who specialize in gay travel. The **Gay & Lesbian Visitors Center of New York, Inc.** (135 W. 20th St., 3rd Floor, New York, NY 10011, tel. 212/463–9030 or 800/395–2315; $100 annually) mails a monthly newsletter, valuable coupons, and more to its members.

Tour Operators and Travel Agencies The dominant travel agency in the market is **Above and Beyond** (3568 Sacramento St., San Francisco, CA 94118, tel. 415/922–2683 or 800/397–2681). Tour operator **Olympus Vacations** (8424 Santa Monica Blvd., No. 721, West Hollywood, CA 90069; tel. 310/657–2220 or 800/965–9678) offers all-gay and lesbian resort holidays. **Skylink Women's Travel** (746 Ashland Ave., Santa Monica, CA 90405, tel. 310/452–0506 or 800/225–5759) handles individual travel for lesbians all over the world and conducts two international and five domestic group trips annually.

Publications The premiere international travel magazine for gays and lesbians is *Our World* (1104 N. Nova Rd., Suite 251, Daytona Beach, FL 32117, tel. 904/441–5367; $35 for 10 issues). "Out & About" (tel. 203/789–8518 or 800/929–2268; $49 for 10 issues, full refund if you aren't satisfied) is a 16-page monthly newsletter with extensive information on resorts, hotels, and airlines that are gay-friendly.

Arriving and Departing

Because the air routes between North America and Europe are among the world's most heavily traveled, the passenger can choose from many airlines and fares. But fares change with stunning rapidity, so consult your travel agent on which bargains are currently available.

From North America by Plane

Flights are either nonstop, direct, or connecting. A **nonstop** flight requires no change of plane and makes no stops. A **direct** flight stops at least once and can involve a change of plane, although the flight number remains the same; if the first leg is late, the second waits. This is not the case with a **connecting** flight, which involves a different plane and a different flight number.

Airlines The U.S. airlines that serve the major cities in Europe are **American Airlines** (tel. 800/433–7300); **Continental** (tel. 800/231–0856); **Delta** (tel. 800/241–4141); **Northwest** (tel. 800/447–4747); **TWA** (tel. 800/892–4141); and **United** (tel. 800/538–2929).

Many European national airlines fly directly from the United States to their home countries. The biggest advantage in arriving on a home airline is that the landing privileges are often better, as are the facilities provided at main airports. Here are the U.S. telephone numbers of those airlines that have representation in the United States; most of the numbers are toll-free.

Austria: Austrian Airlines (tel. 800/843–0002)
Belgium: Sabena Belgian World Airlines (tel. 800/955–2000)
Cyprus: Cyprus Airways (tel. 212/714–2190)
The Czech Republic and Slovakia: Czechoslovak Airlines (CSA, tel. 212/682–5833)
Denmark: Scandinavian Airlines (SAS, tel. 800/221–2350)
Finland: Finnair (tel. 800/950–5000)
France: Air France (tel. 800/237–2747)
Germany: Lufthansa (tel. 800/645–3880)
Great Britain: British Airways (tel. 800/247–9297); Virgin Atlantic (tel. 800/862–8621)
Greece: Olympic Airways (tel. 212/838–3600 or 800/223–1226 outside NY)
Holland: KLM Royal Dutch Airlines (tel. 800/777–5553)
Hungary: Malév Hungarian Airlines (tel. 212/757–6446)
Iceland: Icelandair (tel. 800/223–5500)
Ireland: Aer Lingus (800/223–6537)
Italy: Alitalia (tel. 800/223–5730)
Malta: Air Malta (tel. 415/362–2929)
Norway: Scandinavian Airlines (SAS, tel. 800/221–2350)
Poland: LOT Polish Airlines (tel. 212/869–1074)
Portugal: TAP Air Portugal (tel. 800/221–7370)
Romania: Tarom Romanian Airlines (tel. 212/687–6013)
Spain: Iberia Airlines (tel. 800/772–4642)
Sweden: Scandinavian Airlines (SAS, tel. 800/221–2350)
Switzerland: Swissair (tel. 800/221–4750)
Turkey: THY Turkish Airlines (tel. 212/986–5050)

Cutting Costs The Sunday travel section of most newspapers is a good source of deals. When booking, particularly through an unfamiliar company, call the Better Business Bureau and your local or state Consumer Protection Bureau to find out whether any complaints have been registered against the company, pay with a credit card if you can, and consider trip-cancellation and default insurance (*see* Insurance, *above*).

Promotional Less expensive fares, called promotional or discount fares, are
Airfares round-trip and involve restrictions, which vary according to the route and season. You must usually buy the ticket—commonly called an APEX (advance purchase excursion) when it's for international travel—in advance (7, 14, or 21 days are usual), although some of the major airlines have added no-frills, cheap flights to compete with new bargain airlines on certain routes.

With the major airlines the cheaper fares generally require minimum and maximum stays (for instance, over a Saturday night or at least 7 and no more than 30 days). Airlines generally allow some return date changes for a $25 to $50 fee, but most low-fare tickets are nonrefundable. Only a death in the family would prompt the airline to return any of your money if you cancel a nonrefundable ticket. However, you can apply an unused nonrefundable ticket toward a new ticket, again with a small fee. The lowest fare is subject to availability, and only a small percentage of the plane's total seats will be sold at that price. Contact the U.S. Department of Transportation's Office of Consumer Affairs (I–25, Washington, DC 20590, tel. 202/366–2220) for a copy of "Fly-Rights: A Guide to Air Travel in the U.S."

Consolidators Consolidators or bulk-fare operators—"bucket shops"—buy blocks of seats on scheduled flights that airlines anticipate they won't be able to sell. They pay wholesale prices, add a markup, and resell the seats to travel agents or directly to the public at prices that still undercut the airline's promotional or discount fares (higher than a charter ticket but lower than an APEX ticket and usually without the advance-purchase restriction). Moreover, some consolidators sometimes give you your money back. Carefully read the fine print detailing penalties for changes and cancellations. If you doubt the reliability of a company, call the airline once you've made your booking and confirm that you do, indeed, have a reservation on the flight.

The biggest U.S. consolidator, C.L. Thomson Express, sells only to travel agents. Well-established consolidators selling to the public include **UniTravel** (Box 12485, St. Louis, MO 63132, tel. 314/569–0900 or 800/325–2222); **Council Charter** (205 E. 42nd St., New York, NY 10017, tel. 212/661–0311 or 800/800–8222); and **Travac** (989 6th Ave., New York, NY 10018, tel. 212/563–3303 or 800/872–8800).

Charter Flights Charters usually have the lowest fares and the most restrictions. Departures are limited and seldom on time, and you can lose all or most of your money if you cancel. (The closer to departure you cancel, the more you lose, although sometimes you will be charged only a small fee if you supply a substitute passenger.) The charterer, on the other hand, may legally cancel the flight for any reason up to 10 days before departure; within 10 days of departure, the flight may be canceled only if it becomes physically impossible to operate it. The charterer may also revise the itinerary or increase the price after you have bought the ticket, but if the new arrangement constitutes a "major change," you have the right to a refund. Before buying a charter ticket, read the fine print for the company's refund policy and details on major changes. Money for charter flights is usually paid into a bank escrow account, the name of which should be on the contract. If you don't pay by credit card, make your check payable to the escrow account (unless you're dealing with a travel agent, in which case, his or her check should be payable to the escrow account). The U.S. Department of Transportation's Office of Consumer Affairs (I–25, Washington, DC 20590, tel. 202/366–2220) can answer questions on charters and send you its "Plane Talk: Public Charter Flights" information sheet.

Discount Travel Clubs Travel clubs offer members unsold space on airplanes, cruise ships, and package tours at as much as 50% below regular prices. Membership may include a regular bulletin or access to a toll-free hot line giving details of available trips departing from three or four days to several months in the future. Most also offer 50% discounts off hotel rack rates, but double check with the hotel to make sure it isn't offering a better promotional rate independent of the club. Clubs include **Discount Travel International** (114 Forrest Ave., Suite 203, Narberth, PA 19072, tel. 215/668–7184; $45 annually, single or family), **Entertainment Travel Editions** (Box 1014, Trumbull, CT 06611, tel. 800/445–4137; price ranges $28–$48), **Great American Traveler** (Box 27965, Salt Lake City, UT 84127, tel. 800/548–2812; $29.95 annually), **Moment's Notice Discount Travel Club** (425 Madison Ave., New York, NY 10017, tel. 212/486–0503; $45 annually, single or family), **Privilege Card** (3391 Peachtree Rd. NE, Suite 110, Atlanta GA 30326, tel. 404/262–0222 or 800/236–9732; domestic annual membership $49.95, international, $74.95), **Travelers Advantage** (CUC Travel Service, 49 Music Sq. W, Nashville, TN 37203, tel. 800/548–1116; $49 annually, single or family), and **Worldwide Discount Travel Club** (1674 Meridian Ave., Miami Beach, FL 33139, tel. 305/534–2082; $50 annually for family, $40 single).

Publications The monthly newsletters "Consumer Reports Travel Letter" (Consumers Union, 101 Truman Ave., Yonkers, NY 10703, tel. 800/234–1970) and "Travel Smart" (40 Beechdale Rd., Dobbs Ferry, NY 10522, tel. 800/327–3633; $44 a year) have a wealth of travel deals and indispensable consumer tips. Another helpful resource is *Airfare Secrets Exposed*, by Sharon Tyler and Matthew Wonder (Universal Information Publishing, $16.95), available in bookstores. *The Official Frequent Flyer Guidebook* by Randy Petersen (4715-C Town Center Dr., Colorado Springs, CO 80916, tel. 719/597–8899 or 800/487–8893; $14.99, plus $3 shipping and handling) yields valuable hints on getting the most for your air travel dollars. Also new and helpful is *202 Tips Even the Best Business Travelers May Not Know* by Christopher McGinnis, president of the Travel Skills Group (Box 52927, Atlanta, GA 30355, tel. 404/659–2855; $10 in bookstores.)

Enjoying the Fly at night if you're able to sleep on a plane. Because the air aloft is
Flight dry, drink plenty of fluids while on board. Drinking alcohol contributes to jet lag, as do heavy meals. Bulkhead seats, in the front row of each cabin—usually reserved for people who have disabilities, are elderly, or are traveling with babies—offer more legroom, but trays attach awkwardly to seat armrests, and all possessions must be stowed overhead.

Smoking Since February 1990, smoking has been banned on all domestic United States flights of less than six hours' duration; the ban also applies to domestic segments of international flights aboard U.S. and foreign carriers. On U.S. carriers flying to Europe and other destinations abroad, a seat in a no-smoking section must be provided for every passenger who requests one, and the section must be enlarged to accommodate such passengers if necessary as long as they have complied with the airline's deadline for check-in and seat assignment. If smoking bothers you, request a seat far from the smoking section.

Foreign airlines are exempt from these rules but do provide no-smoking sections, and some nations, including Canada as of July 1, 1993, have gone as far as to ban smoking on all domestic flights; other countries may ban smoking on flights of less than a specified duration. British Airways has banned smoking. The International Civil Aviation Organization has set July 1, 1996, as the date to ban smoking aboard airlines worldwide, but the body has no power to enforce its decisions.

From North America by Ship

Cunard Line (555 5th Ave., New York, NY 10017, tel. 800/221–4770 or 212/880–7545) operates four ships that make transatlantic crossings: The *Queen Elizabeth 2* is the only ocean liner that makes regular transatlantic crossings; the others—the *Sea Goddesses I* and *II* and the *Vistafjord*—make repositioning crossings twice a year, as one cruise season ends in Europe and another begins in North America. The *QE2* sails from April through December between Baltimore, New York City and Southampton, England. The *Sea Goddesses I* and *II* sail between Genoa, Italy, and St. Thomas in the U.S. Virgin Islands, for their repositioning crossings. The *Vistafjord* sails between Malaga, Spain, and Fort Lauderdale, Florida, on its repositioning crossings. Cunard Line offers fly-cruise packages and pre- and post-land packages.

Royal Viking Line (750 Battery St., San Francisco, CA 94111, tel. 800/634–8000) has three ships that cruise out of European ports. Two of the ships make repositioning crossings between Fort Lauderdale and Monte Carlo. Fly/cruise packages are available. The repositioning destinations vary from year to year, so be sure to check with shipping lines for current schedules.

American Star Lines (660 Madison Ave., New York, NY 10021, tel. 800/356–7677 and, in New York, 212/644–7900) makes transatlantic crossings in spring and fall between Greece and Barbados (in the British West Indies). The crossings are regular cruises, with ports of call in Portugal, Italy, Turkey, and the Greek islands. Summer cruises are from Piraeus (Athens), to the Greek islands, and Turkey. Fly/cruise packages are available.

Check the travel pages of your Sunday newspaper for other cruise ships that sail to Europe.

From the United Kingdom by Plane

Air travel from Britain to continental Europe has undergone a quiet revolution during the past few years. Thanks in part to the ever-growing demand for inexpensive charter flights, in part to the British government's determination to break down the cozy system of intergovernmental fare setting, and above all to a stronger sense of a shared European identity, more and more Britons regard flying as an everyday means of transportation rather than as an occasional luxury. The result, as expected, is more flights, greater choice, and lower fares.

But it isn't all good news. For one thing, not all European governments share Britain's enthusiasm for more competitive fares. Of long-term concern is the evident incapacity of European air networks to cope with an explosion in passenger numbers. And, at least at peak periods, more people traveling means more congestion and more delays.

It's not just those in the cheaper seats who suffer, either. Scheduled flights are just as likely to be delayed as charter flights, though they are, it's true, mostly spared the major delays that can afflict the summertime charter flights. Nonetheless, Europe's more militant air-traffic controllers have never been slow to grasp that the most effective way to draw attention to increased work loads and, in many cases, antiquated air-traffic control systems is to go on strike when maximum disruption is guaranteed—in other words, at the busiest times. Shots of beleaguered tourists gamely bedding down for another night at the airport have become commonplace on Britain's TV screens. France, Spain, and Greece currently head the list of countries with the most strike-happy air controllers.

None of which is intended to suggest that flying from Britain to the Continent is something that can be recommended only to those who don't mind not sleeping for three days. And not least, of course, because everyone agrees that Europe's prosperity depends more than ever on good communications, with air travel well up there in the forefront.

A unified European air-traffic control system in place of the current nationally operated systems may still be only a gleam in the eye of Utopian-minded Europhiles, but a new generation of air-traffic control systems is, at last, being installed in many countries. Once in place, they should improve dramatically the capacity of today's overworked machines. Likewise, in the certain knowledge that routine delays will eventually kill the goose that lays the golden egg, airlines, tour operators, and charter companies have exerted increasing pressure on governments to ensure that strikes become the exception, not the rule.

Scheduled Airlines If flying from a convenient airport, avoiding night flights at awkward hours, and relative reliability are more important to you than just finding the cheapest flight, scheduled flights are a better option than charters. London, with its two main airports—Heathrow and Gatwick—and three subsidiary airports—Luton, Stansted, and London City—is Europe's biggest air hub. Frequent scheduled services connect it with virtually every major European city and resort. British Airways (BA) is the largest single operator, but all other leading international European airlines have flights to and from their own countries. There is never less than one flight a day to all the European capitals; in most cases, many more.

The constantly changing airline hierarchy has meant that the smaller British airports have, if anything, become busier. Competition from up-and-coming airlines determined to grab customers from BA has increased the options available to travelers. These smaller airlines have pioneered routes to European capitals from regional British airports. Manchester, for instance, has become a busy northern hub for several carriers, with shuttle flights to London and several flights a day to Amsterdam and other European points. Other major European airlines also have flights from several regional British airports. Air France, for example, has daily flights from Edinburgh to Paris. (Both Glasgow and Edinburgh are linked to London by frequent shuttle flights.)

Most airlines' weekday schedules cater principally to business flyers, who want to fly at clearly defined peak times (generally weekdays, first thing in the morning and late afternoon/early evening). As a result, lower fares are available outside these peak times. Look for better fares on midday flights, and check into weekend fares. Some are less than half the regular economy fares, though note that nearly all require that you spend at least one Saturday night at your destination. As a basic rule of thumb, remember that the cheaper a fare is, the more likely it is to carry restrictions. Always make sure you find out what these are before you buy your ticket.

The busiest routes also tend to be the cheapest. There are evermore competitive fares between London and Paris and London and Frankfurt. Likewise, fares between London and Brussels are also lower than the European average, mile for mile. Fares between London and Amsterdam can be a bargain, the cheapest in Europe. What's more, there are excellent onward connections from Amsterdam to other European cities.

Finally, remember, too, that few European flights are longer than four hours; the majority, in fact, rarely top two hours. Such short journeys make flying business-class or first-class, where it exists, an unnecessary luxury for most travelers. It's also worth bearing in mind that on most European airlines business class is open to anyone with a full-fare economy (coach class) ticket.

Charter Airlines Charter airlines offer much cheaper fares to Europe than do the scheduled carriers, but the rules that bind them are more restrictive. While the British government turns a blind eye to sales of seat-only charter tickets, some European governments still require proof that you have bought an inclusive package vacation rather than just a flight. Most of the seat-only agencies will therefore give you a voucher stating that you have accommodations at a certain hotel. This is to comply with the rules—it won't necessarily get you a bed, even if you can find the hotel in question!

Greece specifically has expressed its determination to stamp out seat-only traffic by threatening passengers using such tickets with fines or deportation under international rules on charter sales. Its implementation of this rule has, though, been patchy so far.

Charter flights are by far the cheapest form of air transportation to main vacation destinations—particularly in the Mediterranean—and some of the charter fares available to last-minute buyers compare favorably even with bus or rail fares. Moreover, to destinations such as Spain, Greece, Turkey, and Italy, charter flights can give significant savings over scheduled fares. These are countries whose governments have vigorously resisted the introduction of cheaper scheduled fares and that remain zealously protective of their national airlines.

The main drawback of traveling by charter is rigid timetabling. Your return flight will be 7, 14, or 21 days from your departure date. The cheapest flights leave at inconvenient times—mainly in the early hours of the morning—and, in London, from airports a long way from the city center, such as Luton. The other major disadvantage is that charter flights are much more prone to delay than are scheduled flights. Delays of up to two days have been known, though these are admittedly exceptional. But on most flights it nonetheless makes sense to expect some delay, even if it's only an hour or so.

Arrival airports are often resorts rather than capital or major cities. In Spain, most charters fly to the Mediterranean coast rather than to Madrid or Seville; in Portugal, most flights arrive in the Algarve resort area rather than Lisbon. In Greece, this system can be an advantage rather than a drawback—many flights go to the islands rather than to Athens, so if your destination is, for example, Mykonos or Crete, you can fly there direct by charter without having to transfer to a domestic flight or ferry at Athens.

Charters bought at the last minute can be extremely cheap—check in travel agents' windows or in the classified sections of the London *Evening Standard* for cheap late-booking deals. Some of these may be so inexpensive that you may consider discarding the round-trip half of the ticket and traveling onward in Europe from your arrival point, rather than coming back to London.

From the United Kingdom by Car

Ferries Nearly all ferries from Britain to the Continent take cars, as does the long-awaited Channel Tunnel. Which route you take will be determined by your eventual destination and how much driving you want to do. The shortest routes are the fastest and the most popular: from Dover, Ramsgate, or Folkestone to Calais, Boulogne, and Ostend. These are the most convenient routes for much of France and Belgium, as well as central and southern Germany, Austria, Switzerland, Italy, and southeast Europe. If you're heading to western France or to Spain and Portugal, then Dieppe, Le Havre, Caen, Cherbourg, and St. Malo are better routes. Similarly, though the cost is much higher (though equally, the driving is greatly reduced) you should consider putting your car on the train in France or taking the ferry to Santander in northern Spain. The best routes to Holland and north Germany are from Dover and Felixstowe to Zeebrugge; from Sheerness to Vlissingen; and from Harwich to the Hook of Holland and Hamburg. If you're heading for Scandinavia, there are sailings from Harwich and Newcastle to Esbjerg in Denmark, Gothenburg in Sweden, and Stavangar and Bergen in Norway. There are regular sailings to Dublin from Holyhead and to Rosslare from Fishguard and Pembroke in Wales.

Unless you're traveling in the dead of winter, and sometimes even then, it's essential to book well in advance (*see* By Ferry/Ship, *below*, for addresses). Rates vary according to the length of your vehicle, the time of day and season you make the crossing. Morning and evening crossings in the summer months are most expensive, and national holidays should be avoided where possible.

Service Organizations   Both the **Automobile Association** (Fanum House, Box 31, Basingstoke, Hants. RG21 2BH; tel. 0256/492998) and the **Royal Automobile Club** (RAC House, Box 100, South Croydon CR2 6XW, tel. 0800/550–550) operate on-the-spot breakdown and repair services across Europe. Replacement cars can be provided in case of accidents. Both companies will also transport cars and passengers back to Britain in case of serious breakdowns. The AA's **5-Star Cover** costs £21.50 for 1 day, plus £1.50 per extra day, up to 25 days; after 25 days, add £7.50 per week. Cars over 10 years old incur a £25 surcharge, and non-AA members pay a £3 registration fee (tel. 0800/800–555 for credit card sales). The RAC's **Eurocover** costs £29.95 for 4 days, £37.95 for 9 days, £49.95 for 16 days, £52.95 for 23 days, or £55.95 for 31 days. Nonmembers pay a £3 surcharge; the surcharge for a car over 10 years old is £32.95. (tel. 0800/550–055 for credit card sales.)

For advice on whether to bring your own car or to buy or rent one on your trip, *see* Renting and Leasing Cars in Before You Go, *above*.

The Channel Tunnel   The **Channel Tunnel** opened officially in May 1994, providing the fastest route across the Channel—35 minutes from Folkestone to Calais, or 60 minutes from motorway to motorway. It consists of two large 50-kilometer (31-mile) long tunnels for trains, one in each direction, linked by a smaller service tunnel running between them. Scheduled to begin later in 1994, **Le Shuttle** (tel. 0345/353535 in the U.K., 800/388–3876 in the U.S.), a special car, bus, and truck train, is to operate a continuous loop, with services every 15 minutes at peak times and at least once an hour through the night. No reservations are necessary, although tickets may be purchased in advance from travel agents. Most passengers stay in their own car throughout the "crossing;" progress updates are provided on display screens and radio. Motorcyclists park their bikes in a separate section with its own passenger compartment, while foot passengers must book passage by coach (*see* By Train, *below*).

The Tunnel is reached from exit 11a of the M20/A20. Drivers purchase tickets from toll booths, then pass through frontier control before loading onto the next available train. Unloading at Calais takes eight minutes. Ticket prices start at £130 for a low-season five-day round trip in a small car and are based on season, time of day, length of stay, and car size regardless of the number of passengers. Peak season fares are not always competitive with ferry prices.

From the United Kingdom by Ferry/Ship

Ferry routes for passengers and vehicles link the North Sea, English Channel, and Irish Sea ports with almost all of Britain's maritime neighbors.

To France and Belgium By far the fastest and, for most visitors, the most convenient routes are those across the English Channel to France and Belgium. The principal routes are Dover–Calais (operated by **P&O European Ferries, Sealink,** and **Hoverspeed**); Dover–Boulogne (operated by P&O European Ferries and Hoverspeed); Ramsgate–Ostend (operated by **Sally Line**); Folkestone–Boulogne (operated by Sealink); and Ramsgate–Dunkirk (operated by Sally Line). Crossing times vary from 75 minutes for the Dover–Calais sailings to four hours for the Ramsgate–Ostend sailings, depending on sea conditions. Make reservations well in advance for peak periods (Easter, July, and August).

The passengers-only Ramsgate–Ostend Jetfoil (book through Sally Line) is a good bet if you're traveling by train. It makes the crossing in only 100 minutes. But note that it is both more expensive than the regular ferries and much more subject to cancellation in bad weather.

There is a wide choice of other sailings to France: Newhaven–Dieppe (operated by Sealink); Portsmouth–Le Havre or Cherbourg (operated by P&O European Ferries); Southampton–Cherbourg (operated by Sealink); Portsmouth–Caen (operated by **Brittany Ferries**); Portsmouth–St. Malo (operated by Brittany Ferries); Poole–Cherbourg (operated by Brittany Ferries, summer only); and Plymouth–Roscoff (operated by Brittany Ferries). Journey times are longer (ranging from four hours for the Newhaven–Dieppe route to nine hours for the Portsmouth–St. Malo route) and fares higher, but you can avoid a great deal of unnecessary driving across northern France. Again, make reservations well in advance for peak periods.

To Spain and Portugal Brittany Ferries, which runs the St. Malo service, also sails from Plymouth or Portsmouth to Santander in northern Spain. The crossings take 24 and 28 hours respectively, and the line's cruise ferries offer economy and luxury cabins, as well as entertainment facilities that include a cinema and restaurants. P&O European Ferries offers similar twice-weekly service between Portsmouth and Bilbao. If you are traveling by car and plan to tour Spain, this route offers you the option of looping back through France and returning to Britain without retracing your tracks. Onward travel into Spain without a car, however, will be time-consuming and is really an option only for those with plenty of time to spare.

To Holland, North Germany, and Scandinavia There are excellent ferry routes linking British east coast ports with Europe's North Sea coast. Crossings are longer than English Channel routes, and most North Sea ferry lines have adopted the ferry-cruise concept, with cabins with various degrees of comfort and on-board facilities that can include duty-free shopping, bars, restaurants, discos, and casinos.

For Holland and north central Germany, the best routes are Sheerness–Vlissingen (operated by **Olau Line**) and Harwich–Hook of Holland (operated by Sealink). If you're based farther north in England, the Hull–Rotterdam route (operated by **North Sea Ferries**) is also good. North Germany is best served by the Harwich–Hamburg route (operated by **Scandinavian Seaways**), the only direct ferry link with Germany. Services to Scandinavia include Harwich–Esbjerg, Denmark, and Newcastle–Esbjerg (both operated by

Scandinavian Seaways); Harwich–Gothenburg, Sweden, and Newcastle–Gothenburg (also operated by Scandinavian Seaways); Newcastle–Stavanger and Bergen, Norway (operated by **Color Line**).

To Ireland The principal ferry routes to Ireland are Holyhead–Dublin (operated by **B&I**); Holyhead–Dun Laoghaire (operated by Sealink); and Fishguard/Pembroke–Rosslare (operated by Sealink); and Pembroke–Rosslare (operated by B&I). There's a service between Swansea and Cork (operated by **Swansea Cork Ferries**) that runs from March through September. For Northern Ireland, take the Stranraer–Belfast ferry (operated by P&O European Ferries).

Useful Addresses For information on the services mentioned above, contact:

B&I Line UK Ltd. (150 New Bond St., London W1Y 0AQ, tel. 071/491–8682).

Brittany Ferries (Millbay Docks, Plymouth PL1 3EW, tel. 0752/221321).

Color Line (Tyne Commission Quay, Albert Edward Dock, North Shields NE29 6EA, tel. 091/296–1313).

Hoverspeed (Maybrook House, Queens Gardens, Dover, Kent CT17 9UQ, tel. 0304/240202).

North Sea Ferries (King George Dock, Hedon Rd., Hull HU9 5QA, tel. 0482/795141).

Olau Line (Ferry Terminal, Sheerness, Kent ME12 1SN, tel. 0795/666666).

P&O European Ferries (Channel House, Channel View Rd., Dover, Kent CT17 9TJ, tel. 0303/223000).

Sally Line (Argyle Centre, York St., Ramsgate CT11 9PL, tel. 0843/595522).

Scandinavian Seaways (Scandinavia House, Parkeston Quay, Harwich, Essex CO12 4QG, tel. 0255/240240).

Sealink (Charter House, Park St., Ashford, Kent TN24 8EX, tel. 0233/646801).

Swansea Cork Ferries (Kings Dock, Swansea SA1 8RU, tel. 0792/456116).

From the United Kingdom by Train

Air travel may offer the fastest point-to-point service, car travel the greatest freedom, and bus transportation the lowest fares, but there is still an unparalleled air of romance about setting off for Europe by train from one of the historic London stations.

Boat trains timed to meet ferries at Channel ports leave London from Victoria, Waterloo, Paddington, and Charing Cross stations and connect with onward trains at the main French and Belgian ports. Calais and Boulogne have the best quick connections for Paris (total journey time about six to seven hours using the cross-Channel Hovercraft); the Ramsgate–Ostend Jetfoil service is the fastest rail connection to Brussels (about 5½ hours, station to station), with good rail connections to Germany and points east.

Boat trains connecting with ferries from Harwich to the Dutch and Danish North Sea ports leave from London/Liverpool Street; there are good rail connections from the Dutch ports to Amsterdam and onward to Germany and Belgium and south to France.

For the Republic of Ireland, trains connecting with the ferry services across the Irish Sea leave from London/Paddington.

One-way and round-trip city-to-city tickets, including rail and ferry fares, can be booked in the United States through **BritRail**, either directly or through your travel agent. If you are traveling on one of the European rail passes bookable in the United States or in Britain, you may be entitled to free or discounted ferry crossings (*see* Rail Passes, *above*).

If all international rail journeys have a certain glamour, none has the cachet of the *Venice Simplon–Orient Express.* It's a reconditioned vintage train that, twice weekly from February through November, makes the 32-hour run between London/Victoria and Venice. Style and class abound. Prices are high. A peak-season one-way fare is £880; round-trip, £1,275. You can make reservations in Britain from **VSOE** (Sea Containers House, 20 Upper Ground, London SE1 9PF, tel. 071/620–0003). **Crystal Holidays** (Crystal House, Arlington Rd., Surbiton, Surrey KT6 6BW, tel. 081/390–8513) does short trips in Britain on the Orient Express from £145 (to Leeds Castle), including two lavish meals. In the United States, contact **Orient Express** (Suite 2841, One World Trade Center, New York, NY 10048, tel. 800/223–1588).

The Channel Tunnel **Eurostar** (for information tel. 071/922–4486 in the U.K., 800/942–4866 in the U.S.) high-speed train service was scheduled to begin in July 1994, with passenger-only trains whisking riders between new stations in Paris (Gare du Nord) and London (Waterloo) in 3 hours and between London and Brussels (Midi) in 3¼ hours. The service of five trains daily each way was scheduled to increase in January 1995 to 15 trains daily in each direction. At press time (spring 1994), ticket prices had not been set. Tickets are available in the United Kingdom through **InterCity Europe,** the international wing of BritRail (London/Victoria Station, tel. 071/834–2345 or 071/828–8092 for credit-card bookings), and in the United States through **Rail Europe** (tel. 800/942–4866) and **BritRail Travel** (1500 Broadway, New York, NY 10036, tel. 800/677–8585).

From the United Kingdom by Bus

Freeways (motorways) in the United Kingdom link London with the English Channel ferry ports and make bus travel—connecting with fast ferry, Jetfoil, or Hovercraft crossings—only a little slower than rail travel on the shorter routes into Europe.

Bus travel to cities such as Paris, Brussels, Amsterdam, Rotterdam, and Bruges is by fast and comfortable modern buses with reclining seats, air-conditioning, video entertainment, and airplane-style refreshment carts. There are frequent departures from central London pickup points. Fares by bus are a good deal less than the equivalent rail fare.

Euroways/Eurolines—an international consortium of bus operators—offers a range of day and night services linking London with Amsterdam, Paris, Antwerp, Brussels, and other points en route. Night services to Paris take about 10¼ hours; overnight journey time to Amsterdam is a little more than 13 hours.

Faster **Citysprint** daytime crossings use the Ramsgate–Ostend Jetfoil service en route to Amsterdam, reducing journey time to a little more than eight hours. The fast Hoverspeed crossing to France cuts the day trip time to Paris to just under seven hours. There are also one-day round-trips to Antwerp and Brussels and "Eurobreakaway" holiday packages with accommodations for two or three nights in Paris, Amsterdam, and Brussels.

National Express uses Sealink ferries to the Republic of Ireland. A connecting bus service in Ireland is operated by **Bus Eireann.** Sailings are from Fishguard to Rosslare—a 3½-hour crossing. The onward service goes via Waterford and Cork to Killarney and Tralee.

There are summer buses to the Spanish vacation resorts, aimed mainly at British families on a tight vacation budget. Winter coaches that run to Europe's less pricey ski destinations, notably Andorra and some Italian resorts, can also be inexpensive.

The situation in the former Yugoslavia at press time means that the road route to Greece through those countries is not an option.

Both Euroways/Eurolines and Hoverspeed City Sprint services can be booked in person at **National Express** offices at Victoria Coach Station (52 Grosvenor Gardens, London SW1W OAU, opposite Victoria Rail Station, tel. 071/730–0202), at any National Express agent throughout Britain, and at **Eurolines** (23 Crawley Rd., Luton LU1 1HX, tel. 0582/404–404511).

Getting Around Europe

By Car

Touring Europe by car has tremendous advantages over other ways of seeing the Continent. You can go where you want, when you want, traveling at your own pace, free of the petty restrictions of timetables. But there are pitfalls, too. For the American driver, used to a uniform system of signs and traffic rules from coast to coast, and accustomed to being able to ask directions in English, Europe can be a bewildering experience. On the excellent freeways of northern and central Europe, it's possible to drive through three or four countries in less time than it would take to cross one of the larger of the U.S. states—which means that in one day you may have to cope with perhaps four different languages and four sets of traffic rules!

Road Conditions In general, the richer European countries—France, Germany, Holland, Denmark, the Benelux countries, the United Kingdom, and Italy—all have excellent national highway systems. In Spain, freeway building is proceeding rapidly, and roads are much better than they were even 10 years ago.

By contrast, Greece has just two stretches of freeway-type road—the Odos Ethnikos, or National Road, between Athens and Thessaloníki, and the main road between Athens and Patras.

The Irish Republic's nearest equivalent to freeways are its National Primary Routes, but the low speed limit of 55 mph (88 kph) reflects the fact that their general size and standard falls below the usual European freeway network. Of the Western European countries, Portugal still lags furthest behind in freeway building, but the factor that holds it back—it is the poorest country in Western Europe—also means that far fewer people own cars, so its relatively poor roads are also less crowded.

In Scandinavia, the roads vary according to how far north they are. The harsh winters crack road surfaces in the far north of Norway, Sweden, and Finland. Minor roads have bumps and dips. Otherwise Scandinavia's main roads are well surfaced and refreshingly traffic-free.

Traffic Conditions On the freeway, U.S. drivers may find the pace of European traffic alarming. Speed limits in most countries are set much higher than those in the United States. Even on British motorways, where the upper limit is a very conservative 112 kph (70 mph), it is not uncommon to be passed by vehicles traveling 24–32 kph (15–20 mph) faster than that. On German *autobahns*, French *autoroutes*, or Italian *autostrade*, cars in the fast lane are often moving at 167 kph (100 mph). Much of the time traffic is heavier than is common on U.S. freeways outside major city rush hours.

Consequently, most tourists will find it more rewarding to avoid the freeways and use the alternative main routes. On these roads, where traffic moves more slowly, driving at a more leisurely pace is possible, and stopping en route is easier. This can also save money; many European freeways (such as those of France, Spain, Italy, and Greece) are toll roads, and a day's drive on them can be expensive. If you break down on any of the European highways, you can expect to pay a hefty fee for towing unless you have prudently joined one of the motorist plans offered by one of the many national associations such as the AA or RAC in Britain (*see* From the United Kingdom by Car in Getting to Europe, *above*).

As in many states in the United States, traffic officers in most European countries (with a few exceptions, such as the United Kingdom) are empowered to fine you on the spot for traffic violations. The language barrier will not make your case any easier. In Eastern Europe, police and frontier officials will pay much closer attention to your papers than they do in the West, but roads are emptier and foreign drivers are still a novelty. The language barrier may be greater, but the novelty value has been known to lead to foreigners being let off with a warning when local drivers might be fined for minor offenses.

Road Signs In some European countries—Bulgaria and Greece, for example—the language barrier is compounded by an alphabet barrier. Main road signs in Greece, for example, are written in the Greek alphabet. The only solution is to carry a good map.

Rules of the Road In the United Kingdom, the Republic of Ireland, Cyprus, and Gibraltar, cars drive on the left. In other European countries, traffic is on the right. Beware the transition when coming off ferries from Britain or Ireland to the Continent (and vice versa)!

Rush Hours During peak vacation periods, main routes can be jammed with holiday traffic. In the United Kingdom, try to avoid driving during any of the long bank-holiday (public holiday) weekends, when motorways, particularly in the south, can be totally clogged with traffic. In France and Italy, where huge numbers of people still take a fixed one-month vacation in August, avoid driving during *le départ*, the first weekend in August, when vast numbers of drivers head south; or *le retour*, when they head back.

Frontiers You may be surprised at the relatively casual approach many European countries have toward border controls for drivers. At many frontiers, you may simply be waved through; it is quite possible, for example, to drive from Amsterdam to Germany, via Belgium and France, without once being stopped for customs or immigration formalities. There are, however, spot checks at all borders, and at some—particularly those checkpoints used by heavy commercial truck traffic—there can be long delays at peak times. Ask tourist offices or motoring associations for latest advice on ways to avoid these tie-ups. If you are driving a rented car, the rental company will have provided you with all the necessary papers; if the vehicle is your own, you will need proof of ownership, certificate of roadworthiness (known in the United Kingdom as a Ministry of Transport, or MOT, road vehicle certificate), up-to-date vehicle tax, and a Green Card proof of insurance, available from your insurance company (fees vary depending on destination and length of stay).

By Train

European railway systems vary from the sublime to the ridiculous in terms of comfort and convenience. France, Germany, and the United Kingdom lead the field in developing high-speed trains, although the latter has fallen behind the other two. The **French National Railroads'** (SNCF's) Train à Grande Vitesse (TGV), for example, takes just 4½ hours to cover the 871 km (540 miles) from Paris to Marseille on the Mediterranean.

Rail Europe (230 Westchester Ave., White Plains, NY 10604, tel. 800/848–7245); has a catalog that outlines train, rental-car, and hotel programs in 23 European countries.

BritRail operates high-speed InterCity trains—with a top speed of 202 kph (125 mph)—on its main intercity routes in England and Scotland. Normal fares apply on the BritRail high-speed services, but there is a supplementary fare for travel on French TGV services.

The German rail system, **Deutsche Bundesbahn** (DB, known in the United States as GermanRail), last year wrested the world rail speed record from the French, and its high-speed InterCity trains make rail travel the best public transportation option within Germany.

Swiss trains are not the fastest in Europe, but they are the most punctual and reliable, making onward travel connections remarkably stress-free.

International trains link most European capital cities, including those of Eastern Europe; service is offered several times daily. Generally, customs and immigration formalities are completed on the train by officials who board when it crosses the frontier.

Most European systems operate a two-tier class system. First class costs substantially more; its only outstanding advantage is that it is likely to be less crowded on busier routes. Train journeys in Europe tend to be shorter than in the United States—trains are much faster and distances much shorter—so first-class rail travel is usually a luxury rather than a necessity. Some of the poorer European countries retain a third class, but avoid it unless you are on a rock-bottom budget.

A number of European airlines and railways operate fast train connections to their hub airports, and these can sometimes be booked through the airline's computer reservation service. The Zürich airport, for example, includes a train station where you can continue your journey to anywhere in Switzerland, Austria, France, or Germany.

Trains in Sweden and Norway offer supreme comfort, but greater distances and the more rugged terrain make for longer journey times; if you are on a tight schedule, you may prefer to take internal flights.

In Italy, there are some excellent rail services between major cities—but be sure that the train you book is a main intercity service, not one that stops at every minor station. Off the major lines, Italian rail services are slower and less frequent.

Trains are generally to be avoided in Spain and Portugal as point-to-point transportation—although a new high-speed train linking Madrid and Seville is one of the most modern and comfortable in Europe. In Greece and Turkey anyone but the most fanatical rail traveler will find the more modern, more comfortable buses, with their more frequent service, preferable to the slow, unreliable, crowded, and dirty trains.

Rail travel is vital in Eastern European countries, and services within and between them are better and more comfortable than you might expect. Though usually much slower than the more modern Western European trains, service is frequent and reliable.

Scenic Routes While the high-speed expresses are an ideal and comfortable way of getting from one place to another, travelers who delight in train travel for its own sake will find plenty to please them in Europe's smaller rail lines.

In Norway and Sweden, almost any train journey offers a superb view of some of Europe's most grandiose scenery. The trains of Switzerland, Austria, the Czech Republic, and Slovakia are also a comfortable way to view impressive mountain vistas.

In Switzerland, the *Glacier Express* running between the Alpine resorts of Zermatt, St. Moritz, and Davos is a regular train that has been taken over almost entirely by tourists attracted by the dramatic scenic route. It makes one round-trip a day in winter, and three in summer; reservations are essential.

In Portugal, there are some charming journeys to be made on small local trains. For instance, the rail line north from Oporto to Viana do Castelo and the Spanish border passes through picturesque small towns and crosses over two remarkable river bridges built by Gustav Eiffel, designer of Paris's famed landmark. Branch lines from the same route run through some of Europe's prettiest and least-developed rural countryside.

In many countries, there are special tourist trains, a number of them using historic rolling stock or original steam engines. The *Venice Simplon-Orient Express* uses the original sleeping and dining cars and coaches of Europe's most romantic train (*see* From the United Kingdom by Train in Arriving and Departing, *above*). In Scotland, the *Royal Scot* travels the spectacular glens of the Highlands with antique cars from the heyday of rail travel.

In Spain, a tourist special runs in summer through the pretty north coast country of Cantabria and Asturias, leaving from Santander. From Seville, the luxurious *Andalus Express* uses four vintage cars built in the 1920s and operates five-day rail cruises via Cordoba and Granada to Málaga. The train has its own bar, live music and dancing, restaurant cars, and a video and game room.

Almost all European countries offer discount rail passes. Many are available in the country (*see* country chapters). Others, for single countries and continent-wide, are available before you leave (*see* Rail Passes, *above*). In addition, travelers under 26 who have resided in Europe for at least six months qualify for the **Inter Rail Card**, an unbeatable value at £180. It gives unlimited rail travel in 24 countries, plus half-price travel within the United Kingdom and discounts of up to 50% on some ferry services to and from the United Kingdom. There are 15-day and one-month cards that allow for unlimited travel in 24 countries for £180, and £260, respectively. All cards are available from rail stations.

Useful Addresses Additional information on rail services and special fares is available from the addresses below or from national tourist offices.

In the United States and Canada **Belgian National Railways** (780 3rd Ave., Suite 1501, New York, NY 10017, tel. 212/758–8130).

BritRail Travel International Inc. (1500 Broadway, 10th Floor, New York, NY 10036, tel. 212/575–2667; 94 Cumberland St., Toronto, Ontario M5R 1A3, tel. 416/482–1777).

French National Railroads (Rail Europe, 226–230 Westchester Ave., White Plains, NY 10604, tel. 914/681–3203; Reservation Center, 2100 Central Ave., Suite 200, Boulder, CO 80301, tel. 303/443–5100 or 800/848–7245 reservations; 303/786–8200 sales; Reservation Centre, 2087 Dundas East, Mississauga, Ontario L4X 1M2, tel. 905/602–4195 or 800/361–7245).

German Rail (DER European Rail Services, 9501 W. Devon Ave., Suite 400, Rosemont, IL 60018, tel. 708/692–6300; rail passes 800/782–2424; DER Tours/German Rail, 904 The East Mall, Etobicoke, Ontario M9B 6K2, tel. 416/695–1211).

Italian State Railways (342 Madison Ave., New York, NY 10017, tel. 212/697–1482).

In the United Kingdom **Austrian Federal Railways** (30 St. George St., London W1R 0AL, tel. 071/629–0461).

Belgian National Railways (29 Princes St., London W1R 7RG, tel. 071/629–0230).

French Railways (French Railways House, 179 Piccadilly, London, W1V 0BA, tel. 071/493–9731).

German Federal Railways (DER Travel Services Limited, 18 Conduit St., London W1R 9TD, tel. 071/290–1111).

Italian State Railways (Italia, Marco Polo House, 3–5 Lansdowne Rd., Croydon, Surrey CR9 1LL, tel. 081/686–0677).

Netherlands Railways (25–28 Buckingham Gate, London SW1E 6LD, tel. 071/630–1735).

Norwegian State Railways Travel Bureau (21–24 Cockspur St., London SW1Y 5DA, tel. 071/930–6666).

Swiss Federal Railways (Swiss Centre, Swiss Court, London W1V 8EE, tel. 071/734–4577).

For information about rail networks in other European countries, contact their tourist boards in London.

By Plane

Air travel within the EU countries was decontrolled in 1993, spurring competition and prompting a slew of special deals. Airlines that once specialized in charter flights now offer scheduled services, and national carriers have moved into the lucrative markets of neighboring countries. The result has been somewhat chaotic for Europeans used to national monopolies, but prices have dropped considerably for those who can shop around. The best deals require a round-trip purchase and Saturday night stay-over. For one-way or mid-week travel the smaller airlines generally offer better prices; even if you buy a round-trip ticket and just use half of it, you'll usually come out ahead. For air travel within a single country, check with your transatlantic carrier. Many, Iberia for example, offer an air travel pass at a reasonable price that is good for numerous domestic flights.

Hub Airports As in the United States, airlines are developing hub and spoke-style services within Europe. The idea is that you take a transatlantic flight to an airline's hub, then continue on its intra-European services to other European cities. Thus, **SAS** is actively developing Copenhagen as a Scandinavian hub; the Dutch airline **KLM** is doing the same at Amsterdam's Schiphol; **British Airways** at London's Heathrow and Gatwick; and **Lufthansa** at Frankfurt. If you plan to fly to other European cities, one of these hubs is your obvious choice.

Domestic Services Most Western European countries have good internal services linking the capital city with major business and industrial centers and with more remote communities. In Germany, France, and Spain, regional flights tend to connect major business cities rather than areas of touristic interest—though in Spain there is a considerable overlap between the two.

In such countries as Sweden, Norway, Greece, and to some extent the United Kingdom, however, air services are a vital link between remote island and mountain communities and are often subsidized by the central government. In Greece, for example, you can fly very inexpensively between Athens and the islands—though not *between* islands.

Before booking an internal flight, consider the alternatives. Flights from London to Edinburgh take about one hour—airport to airport—while the competing BritRail InterCity train takes just over 4 hours. But if you add in the hour needed to get from central London to the airport, the need to check in as much as one hour before departure, the inevitable flight delays, the time spent waiting for luggage on arrival, and the transfer time back into town from Edinburgh Airport—you'll find you may not have saved any more than half an hour in travel time for a considerably higher fare. When looking into air travel as an option, remember that distances between European cities can be deceptively short to an eye accustomed to U.S. routings.

Formalities For scheduled flights, you will be asked to check in at least one hour before departure; for charter flights, generally two hours. These are guidelines; if you are traveling with just hand luggage, it is possible to check in as late as 30 minutes before takeoff.

You may be pleasantly surprised by the Green Channel/Red Channel customs systems in operation at most western European airports and at other international frontier posts. Basically, this is an honor system: If you have nothing to declare, you walk through the Green Channel, where there are only random spot luggage checks. If in doubt, go through the Red Channel.

Eastern Europe Eastern European countries need hard Western currency so badly that they try not to set airfares intolerably high. Most routes are served by Western as well as local carriers, and anyone with an eye to comfort and safety will prefer the former.

By Bus

If you have opted for land rather than air travel, the choice between rail and bus is a major decision. In countries such as Britain, France, Germany, and Holland, bus travel was, until recently, something of a poor man's option—slow, uncomfortable, but cheap. Today, though, fast modern buses travel on excellent highways and offer standards of service and comfort comparable to those on trains—but still at generally lower fares. Between major cities and over long distances, trains are almost always faster; buses will take you to places that trains often do not reach.

In several southern European countries—including Portugal, Greece, much of Spain, and Turkey—the bus has supplanted the train as the main means of public transportation, and is often quicker and more comfortable, with more frequent service, than the antiquated national rolling stock. In these countries choose the bus over the rail unless there is a particular scenic rail route or a special tourist train you want to use—but be prepared to discover that the bus is more expensive. Competition among lines is keen, so compare services, such as air-conditioning or reclining seats, before you buy.

Information Information on bus transportation in most countries is available from national or regional tourist offices. For reservations on major bus lines, contact your travel agent at home. For smaller bus companies on regional routes, you may have to go to a local travel agency or to the bus line office.

Note that travel agencies may be affiliated with a certain line and won't always tell you about alternative services—you may have to do some legwork to be sure of getting the best service.

By Ferry/Ship

Bounded by the sea on three sides and crossed by a number of major rivers, Europe offers an abundance of choices for anyone who loves water travel. Contact the appropriate national tourist office for more information.

The Baltic In the north, ferries ply daily between most of the major Baltic ports in Western Europe, as well as between Finnish ports and those of Russia. Baltic crossings are not for those in a hurry—several of them last overnight—and shipping lines operate luxury cruise-ferry vessels with all kinds of entertainment facilities and duty-free shopping.

Major lines include **Silja,** which operates between Finland and Sweden/Germany (book through Scandinavian Seaways); **Viking Line,** which operates between Finland and Sweden (book through Scantours); **Color Line,** which operates between Sweden and Norway; **Stena Line,** which operates between Norway and Sweden (book through Sealink); and **TT-Line,** which operates between Sweden and Germany (book through Olau Lines).

Local ferries ply the Norwegian fjords and are an excellent way of seeing the country, whether you are traveling by car or on public transportation; a fjord trip in midsummer, the time of the Midnight Sun in northern Norway, should not be missed.

Main international Baltic ports are Copenhagen, Gothenburg, Malmö, Stockholm, Helsinki, Kristiansand, and Oslo—also Travemunde in Germany.

Useful **Viking Line** (Scantours, 8 Spring Gardens, Trafalgar Sq., London
Addresses SW1A 2BG, tel. 071/839–2927).

For other Baltic ferry lines mentioned here, *see* From the United Kingdom by Ferry/Ship, *above.*

Scotland Ferry services are important, too, in the Scottish Western Isles, where the **Caledonian Macbrayne Ltd.** (Head Office, The Ferry Terminal, Gourock, Renfrewshire PA19 1QP, Scotland; tel. 0475/33755) has enjoyed a virtual monopoly for many years on its services linking the islands to west coast mainland ports. The northern Scottish islands of the Orkney and Shetland groups are served by **P&O Scottish Ferries** (Box 5, Jamieson's Quay, Aberdeen, AB9 8DL, tel. 0224/572615, fax 0224/574411) from Aberdeen and from Scrabster on the north coast of mainland Scotland—near John O'Groats.

Greece Many island communities have formed cooperative companies to operate services linking their island with others and with Piraeus, the port of Athens. While all Baltic ferries offer high standards of comfort, even luxury, Mediterranean ferry lines observe widely different standards. On Greek ships, for example, you can travel in a first- or second-class cabin or, for a much lower fare, rough it in deck class. The same is true for the international ferries plying between the Italian ports of Bari and Brindisi and the Greek ports of Corfu, Igoumenitsa, and Patras. The age of Greek ferry boats varies widely, too. Some are of pre–World War II vintage, while others—like the *Naxos*, which sails between Piraeus and Crete—are modern vessels.

Flying Dolphin Lines operates fast hydrofoil service from Piraeus to points popular with Athenian vacationers, including the Saronic Gulf islands and resorts on the eastern Peloponnese.

River Travel Major river systems crisscross Europe. Among the many attractive river trips available are a number of luxury cruises on the Rhine and Danube rivers. Contact national tourist offices for details.

The Danube passes through European countries in Western and Eastern Europe, and international cruises are possible. There is also an international hydrofoil service that operates several times a day on the Danube between Budapest in Hungary and Bratislava in Slovakia. For details of Rhine trips, contact **KD German Rhine Line** (170 Hamilton Ave., White Plains, NY 10601, tel. 914/948–3600; 28 South St., Epsom, Surrey KT18 7PF, tel. 0372/742033).

Though a great deal less spectacular than either the Rhine or the Danube, the smaller rivers of Belgium, Holland, France, and other Western European countries can also provide a relaxed and fascinating vacation.

By Bicycle

Bicycling in Europe can be sheer pleasure or unadulterated torment—depending on when you go, where you go, and what you try to do.

If you're planning a European bike trip, you are probably experienced enough not to need advice on equipment and clothing. But it needs to be said that some European countries are far more user-friendly than others toward bicyclists. In countries like Holland, Denmark, Germany, and Belgium, bikes are very much part of the landscape—mainly because the landscape tends to be uniformly flat. City streets and many main roads in these countries have special bike lanes set aside, and car drivers are used to coping with large numbers of bicycle riders.

Cycling is a major sport in Italy, Spain, and Portugal, as well as in France, and there are regular "Tour" road races. Cyclists also get a good deal in the Eastern Bloc countries, where for economic reasons, the bicycle is still an everyday form of transportation.

Northern Scandinavia and Iceland, plus the Alpine countries Austria and Switzerland, with their steep terrain, are destinations only for the serious cyclist. The Scandinavian countries have plenty of excellent-value campsites. Ireland has emptier roads and a gentler landscape than Sweden or Norway and is a pleasant country to bicycle in, though the temptation to sample just one more Guinness at each wayside pub can be a hazard in itself.

Of the wealthier European countries, Britain has the most shameful record when it comes to providing facilities for bicyclists or considering their interests. Riding in London traffic is a stomach-churning experience requiring nerves of steel. Except in remoter areas—such as the north of Scotland—main roads are overcrowded and often dangerous to cyclists.

Bicycle Transport Transporting your bicycle from the United Kingdom to Europe holds no big problems—some ferry lines transport bicycles free, others charge a nominal fee. Shop around. Surprisingly, you can transport your bicycle by air as checked baggage—you won't have to pay extra as long as you are within the 44-pound total baggage allowance.

Most European rail lines will transport bicycles free of charge or for a nominal fee, though you may have to book ahead. Check with the main booking office. One of the joys of biking in Europe is being able to bike one way and return by train or to board a train with your bike when you need to cover long distances or simply when you need to take a rest. SNCF (French Railways) has converted wagons on four of its Motorail services from Boulogne to carry bicycles. Transporting your bike by bus is also possible.

Renting Bicycles Bicycles can be rented by the day or week in most European capitals and are most readily available in cities like Amsterdam and Copenhagen, where cycling is part of the way of life. Local tourist boards are the best source of information on reliable rental agencies with safe bicycles to rent; remember to check on local traffic rules and make sure your insurance covers you in case of an accident. German **Rail (DB)**, French Rail (SNCF), and the Netherlands Railways (NS) rent bicycles at most stations at very reasonable prices.

2 Andorra

The 191-square-mile mountain paradise-turned-supermarket known as the coprincipality of Andorra drafted its constitution— somewhat grandly entitled the Carta Magna—and held elections in 1993, converting Europe's last bastion of feudalism into a democratic state. The bishop of Urgell and the president of France assumed even more symbolic roles as the co-princes of this unique Pyrenean country, which originally fell through the cracks between France and Spain when Charlemagne founded Andorra as an independent entity during his 8th-century battles with the Moors. His heir, Carles el Calb (Charles the Bald), made the bishop of Urgell overlord of Andorra in the 9th century, an overlordship contested by the French counts of Foix until a treaty providing joint suzerainty was agreed upon in 1278. The French monarchy inherited these rights and passed them on to the modern-day French presidents, while the bishop of Urgell's claim has remained rock-solid for the past thousand years. This dual protection has allowed Andorra to thrive as a low-tax, duty-free haven. Europe's new semiborderless unity, however, is in the process of eliminating this special status; the new Andorra aspires to an improved tourist industry and a more dignified economy than the smuggling and tax-evasion expertise for which it has acquired fame.

Winter sports, mountain climbing and hiking, and the cultural resources provided by a plethora of Romanesque chapels, bridges, and medieval farm and town houses are Andorra's once and future stock in trade, although numbered bank accounts will surely not be disappearing any time soon.

Essential Information

Before You Go

When to Go   Winter months bring a huge influx of ski buffs, though any time of year has always attracted consumers with an eye on Andorra's now less advantageous tax- and duty-free shopping status. Andorra is a paradise for lovers of the outdoors. In winter there is reliable snowfall from December to early April, and efficient ski resorts at Soldeu, Arinsal, Pas de la Casa, and La Massana. In summer, hikers will find magnificent trails on the Grande Randonnée (GR) network and a score of shorter but still demanding routes. Botanists and bird-watchers should arrive by early April, in time for the bird migrations up from Africa and the first flush of spring flowers on the slopes and in the valleys. Be warned that even in summer the nighttime temperatures can drop to freezing.

Climate   The following are the average daily maximum and minimum temperatures for Andorra.

Jan.	43F	6C	May	62F	17C	Sept.	71F	22C
	30	- 1		43	6		49	10
Feb.	45F	7C	June	73F	23C	Oct.	60F	16C
	30	- 1		39	4		42	6
Mar.	54F	12C	July	79F	26C	Nov.	51F	10C
	35	2		54	12		35	2
Apr.	58F	14C	Aug.	76F	24C	Dec.	42F	6C
	39	4		53	12		31	- 1

Currency   The Spanish peseta is the major Andorran currency, but French francs are equally acceptable, and all prices are quoted in both cur-

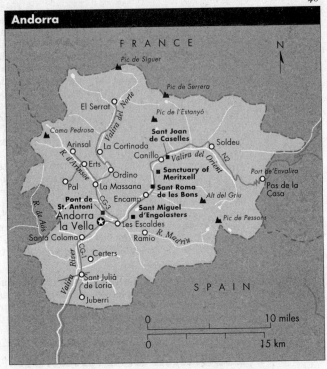

Andorra

rencies in Andorra. For exchange rates and coinage information, *see* Currency in Chapter 10, France, and Chapter 26, Spain.

What It Will Cost
Sample Prices

Andorra's prices are refreshingly easy on the wallet. At press time, some sample costs were as follows: Coca-Cola, 90 ptas.; cup of coffee, 60 ptas.; ham sandwich, 250 ptas.; glass of beer, 100 ptas.; one-mile taxi ride, 150 ptas.

Customs

Andorra has traditionally been famous for its liberality in the matter of customs, duties, visas, and the like. Non-Europeans need a passport to cross the border; Europeans enter with only an identity card. But now that the French-Spanish border is virtually a wave-by and usually not even that, Andorra's is less than a formality.

Language

Andorran nationalism is in the process of being invented, despite the fact that 82% of the country's population of 61,599, mainly Spanish and Portuguese nationals, do not speak Catalan, the coprincipality's official language. Spanish, French, and English are also commonly spoken by merchants and service personnel. Catalonia's "linguistic normalization," the establishment of Catalan as the area's first language, will certainly become a fact in the Andorran school system as well, and Andorra will join the estimated 6 million Catalan-speakers on both sides of the Pyrenees from the Delta del Ebro south of Barcelona to Perpignan in the French Rousillon.

Getting Around

By Car

The maintenance of Andorran roads varies. The one main artery from France into Spain via Andorra la Vella is excellent and copes with the heaviest traffic, as does the spur north toward the ski resorts at La Massana and Ordino. Elsewhere, roads are narrow, winding, and best suited to four-wheel-drive vehicles or, higher up, mules. During the winter, snow tires or chains are essential, especially on the eastern approach through the Puymorens pass to Pas de la Casa.

By Bus   Minibuses connect the towns and villages, and fares are low; 100 ptas. will take you 5 kilometers (3 miles). Details on fares and services are available at hotels and from tourist offices (*Sindicat d'Iniciativa*).

On Foot   Mountainous Andorra is a mecca for hikers, hill-walkers, and backpackers. The mountains are high and the terrain is wild, so a degree of care and experience is advisable. There are two long-distance trails: the GR7, which runs from Portello Blanca on the French frontier to Escaldes on the road to Spain, and the GR75, also called the Ordino Route, a magnificent, high-mountain trail that stretches across the central range. Get details on local treks and walks from tourist offices.

Staying in Andorra

Telephones   For the operator or local directory assistance, dial 11. It is not necessary to use Andorra's local area code, 628, when placing a call inside the country. To call Andorra from Spain the area code is 9738. Andorra's international country code is the same as France's: 33; the area code is 628.

Mail   You can buy Andorran stamps with French francs or Spanish pesetas, though the postal service within the country is free. The Spanish post office in Andorra la Vella is at Carrer Joan Maragall 10; the French post office is at 1 rue Père d'Urg.

Opening and Closing Times   **Banks** are open weekdays 9–1 and 3–5, and Saturday 9–noon. They are closed Sunday.

Churches. Andorra is predominantly Catholic. Most chapels and churches are kept locked around the clock, with the key being left at the closest house. Check with the tourist office for additional details.

Shops open daily 9–8, though some are closed between 1 and 3.

National Holidays   January 1; April 17 (Easter Monday); May 1; June 5 (Pentecost Monday); June 23 (St. John); September 8 (La Verge de Meritxell); November 1 (All Saints' Day); December 25.

Local Holidays   At Canillo: third Saturday in July and following Sunday and Monday; at Les Escaldes: July 25–27; at Sant Julià de Lòria: last Sunday in July and following Monday and Tuesday; at Andorra la Vella: first Saturday, Sunday, Monday in August; at Encamp and La Massana: August 15–17; at Ordino: September 16, 17.

Dining   Andorra is not known as a gastronomic paradise, but there are good restaurants serving French, Spanish, or Catalan cuisine and plenty of restaurants where the visitor will eat hearty Pyrenean fare at no great cost. Local dishes worth trying include *truite de carreroles* (a type of omelet with wild mushrooms); *trinyat*, a typical country specialty of potatoes and cabbage; and such local delicacies as *estofado de isard* (stewed mountain goat); local cheeses, such as *formatge de tupí;* and *rostes amb mel* (ham baked with honey). Although most restaurants offer fixed-price menus, a number of more expensive establishments offer only à la carte.

Mealtimes   True to the co-principality's predominantly Spanish flavor, Andorrans eat late: Dinners don't usually get underway until 8:30 or 9, and lunch is a substantial meal served between 2 and 4.

Dress   Casual dress is acceptable in all restaurants in Andorra, regardless of price category.

Ratings   The following ratings are for a three-course meal for one person, excluding wine. Best bets are indicated by a star ★.

Category	Cost
Very Expensive	over 5,000 ptas
Expensive	2,500–5,000 ptas
Moderate	1,000–2,500 ptas
Inexpensive	under 1,000 ptas

Lodging   The number of Andorran hotels continues to increase, and standards are improving. The architecture is usually functional, but the service is friendly and the facilities are excellent.

Most hotels are open year-round. Reservations are necessary during July and August. Hotel rates often include at least two meals.

Ratings   As a general guide, the following price ratings apply for two people in a double room. Best bets are indicated by a star ★.

Category	Cost
Very Expensive	over 9,000 ptas
Expensive	6,000–9,000 ptas
Moderate	4,000–6,000 ptas
Inexpensive	2,500–4,000 ptas

Tipping   Restaurants and cafés almost always tack on a 10%–15% service charge; if they don't, it's customary to leave a similar amount.

Arriving and Departing

By Plane   The nearest international airports are at Barcelona (200 kilometers, 125 miles), Perpignan (136 kilometers, 85 miles), and Toulouse-Blagnac (180 kilometers, 112 miles).

By Train   From Barcelona, take the train to Puigcerdà, then the bus to La Seu d'Urgell and Andorra la Vella; from Madrid, take the train to Lleida and then a bus to La Seu d'Urgell and Andorra la Vella; from Toulouse, take the train to Ax-les-Thermes and La Tour de Carol, then the bus to La Seu d'Urgell and Andorra la Vella. Alternatively, take the train from Toulouse to L'Hospitalet (the bus to Pas de la Casa and Andorra la Vella meets the morning train from Toulouse).

By Bus   A bus service runs twice daily from Barcelona (Ronda Universidad 4). During the summer there are direct buses from Perpignan and Toulouse to Andorra. The ride from Barcelona, Perpignan, or Toulouse to Andorra la Vella takes about 3 hours.

By Car   The fastest and most direct course from Barcelona to Andorra la Vella, the route with the fewest curves and the most tolls (around 3,000 ptas in all) runs through the Tunel del Cadí and the Cerdanya

Valley via Bellver and La Seu d'Urgell. The roads from Toulouse and Perpignan are beautiful but tortuous, approaching Andorra through its eastern Pas de la Casa entrance at its border with France.

Important Addresses and Numbers

Tourist Information
Andorra La Vella. Sindicat d'Iniciativa (National Tourist Office, C/. Dr. Vilanova, tel. 628/20214. Open Mon.–Sat. 10–1 and 3–7, Sun. and holidays 10–1).
Barcelona (C/. Marià Cubí, 159, tel. 93/200–0655, 93/200–0787).
Canillo (Unió Pro-Turisme, Caseta Pro-Turisme, tel. 628/51002).
Encamp (Unió Pro-Foment i Turisme, Plaça Consell General, tel. 628/31405).
Escaldes-Engordany (Unío Pro-Turisme, Plaça dels Co-Prínceps, tel. 628/20963).
La Massana (Unió Pro-Turisme, Plaça del Quart, tel. 628/35693).
Ordino (Oficina de Turisme, Cruïlla d'Ordino, tel. 628/36963).
Pas de la Casa (Unió Pro-Turisme, C./ Bernat III, tel. 628/55292).
St. Julià (Unió Pro Turisme, tel. 628/41352).

Consulates
U.S. (Pg. Reina Elisenda 23, Barcelona, tel. 93/280–2227). **Canadian** (Nuñez de Balboa 35, Madrid, tel. 91/225–9119). **U.K.** (Apartado de Correos 12111, Barcelona, tel. 93/322–2151).

Emergencies
Doctor (tel. 628/21905). **Police** (tel. 628/21222). **Ambulance and Fire** (tel. 628/20020).

Travel Agency
American Express: in the Relax travel agency (Roc dels Escolls 12, Andorra la Vella, tel. 628/22044).

Guided Tours
Tours of the capital and the surrounding countryside are offered by several firms; check with the tourist office for details or call **Excursion Nadal** (tel. 628/21138) or **Solineu Excursion** (tel. 628/23653).

Exploring Andorra

Exploring Andorra takes time. The roads are narrow and steep, the views compel frequent stops, and every village is worth examining. If possible, do as much sightseeing on foot as time permits.

Overlooking Andorra la Vella's main square is the stone bulk of the **Casa de la Vall** (House of the Valley), a medieval-looking building constructed in 1580 and the seat of the Andorran government. A charmingly rustic spot, the Casa contains many religious frescoes of note, some of which were carefully transported here from village churches high up in the Pyrenees. The kitchen is particularly interesting, with a splendid array of ancient copper pots and other culinary implements. *Carrer de la Vall s/n. Guided tours weekdays 10–1 and 3–7, Sat. 3–7.*

The spa town of **Les Escaldes** is about a 15-minute walk from Andorra la Vella. The Romanesque church of **Sant Miquel d'Engolasters** lies on a ridge northeast of the capital and can be reached on foot— allow half a day for the round-trip—or by taxi up a mountain road. The views are well worth the climb. Just beyond Encamp, 6 kilometers (4 miles) northeast, is the 12th-century church of **Sant Romà de les Bons,** situated in a particularly picturesque convergence of medieval buildings and mountain scenery.

Midway between Encamp and Canillo on the CG-2 is the **Sanctuary of Meritxell,** the focal point of the country's religious fervor. The Blessed Virgin of Meritxell is the principality's patron saint, though, oddly enough for such a religious country, this patronage wasn't declared until the late 19th century. The original sanctuary was destroyed by fire in 1972; the new gray stone building looks remarkably like a factory, but the mountain setting is superb. *Admission free. Open weekdays 9–1 and 3–7, Sat. 10–1.*

Another 3 kilometers (2 miles) farther, just before reaching the town of Canillo, you will see a Gothic seven-armed stone cross (actually six-armed, as one has broken off). A mile or so beyond is the Romanesque church of **Sant Joan de Caselles,** whose ancient walls have turned a lovely dappled brown hue over the centuries. The bell tower is stunning, three stories of weathered stone punctuated by rows of arched windows. Inside the main building is a good example of a reredos (a wall or screen positioned behind an altar). It dates from 1525 and depicts the life of St. John the Evangelist.

Retrace your way back to Andorra la Vella, and this time take the CG-3 due north out of the capital. After just 3 kilometers (2 miles) you'll come to a Romanesque stone bridge, the **Pont de Sant Antoni,** which spans a narrow river. Three kilometers (2 miles) farther is the picturesque mountain town of **La Massana;** take some time to stroll along its quaintly rustic streets. Another 5 kilometers (3 miles) farther is the tiny village of **Ordino.** Its medieval church is exceptionally pretty; to see it properly, go at night between 7 and 8, when mass is celebrated.

In **La Cortinada,** a mile or so farther, is the **Can Pal,** another fine example of medieval Andorran architecture. This time the building is a privately owned manor house (strictly no admittance), with a pretty dovecote attached. Note the turret perched high up on the far side.

Backtrack once more to Andorra la Vella, then take the CG-1 south. In 2½ miles you'll come to the pre-Romanesque church of **Santa Coloma,** in the village bearing the same name; parts of the church date from the 9th and 10th centuries, and there are splendid Romanesque frescoes on the interior walls.

Shopping

Visitors to Andorra have traditionally listed shopping as one of the main attractions, but not all the goods displayed are actually at bargain prices. Moreover, Andorra's appeal to bargain-seekers may be coming to an end. The French and Spanish come here to buy cigarettes, liquor, household items, and foodstuffs, but find electrical goods and cameras no cheaper than they are at home. Good buys are consumable items: perfume, cigarettes, whiskey, and gin. For cameras, tape recorders, and other imported items, compare prices and models carefully. The main shopping center is Andorra la Vella, but there are shops in all the new developments and in the towns close to the frontiers, at Pas de la Casa and Sant Julià de Lòria.

Dining and Lodging

For details and price-category definitions, *see* Dining and Lodging in Staying in Andorra, *above.*

Andorra la Vella
Dining

Chez Jaques. The varied menu features both classical and nouvelle French dishes, though other international cuisines are handled with flair. With good food and a cozy ambience, it's very popular with the locals. *Av. Tarragona, Edificio Terra Vella, tel. 628/20325. Reser-*

vations accepted. *AE, DC, MC, V. Closed July and Aug. Expensive.*

Moli dels Fanals. This quiet restaurant, built into an antique *borda*, or typical Andorran mountain hideaway, that has been recently and elegantly restored, offers international cuisine based on the high quality of its natural ingredients. Try the chateaubriand with foie-gras sauce. *Dr. Vilanova (Borda Casadet), tel. 628/21381. Reservations advised. Closed Sun. June–Aug. AE, DC, MC, V. Expensive.*

Borda Estevet. Another borda with a very Pyrenean feel, this simple spot offers a selection of Spanish and Andorran dishes, beef cooked and served on hot slabs of slate (*a la llosa*), four private dining rooms, and a terrace for outside dining in summer. *ctra. Comella 2, tel. 628/64026. AE, DC, MC, V. Moderate.*

★ **Versailles.** A tiny and authentic French bistro with only a handful of tables, Versailles is always packed. Leave room for pastries after the magret of duck! *Cap del Carrer 1, tel. 628/21331. Reservations advised. AE, DC, MC, V. Moderate.*

Lodging
★ **Andorra Palace.** The large and modern Palace is widely considered one of the capital's best hotels. The rooms are spacious and the furnishing smartly contemporary. The outdoor terrace is a pleasant spot in which to relax and watch the bustle below. *Carrer de la Roda s/n, tel. 628/21072, fax 628/28195. 140 rooms with bath. Facilities: restaurant, parking, bar, sauna, fitness center, pool. AE, DC, MC, V. Very Expensive.*

Andorra Park. The Park ranks with the Palace as one of Andorra la Vella's two top hotels. It's a grand building away from the city's congestion of traffic and pedestrians. The American Bar is a popular watering hole for local society. There's a pretty garden, as well as a terrace and the deluxe guest rooms have private balconies. *Carrer Les Canals 24, tel. 628/20979, fax 628/20983. 40 rooms with bath. Facilities: restaurant, tennis courts, croquet, parking, bar, pool. AE, DC, MC, V. Very Expensive.*

Hotel Eden Roc. This small hotel has all the amenities of larger hotels and offers an exceptional dining room and attentive personal service. *Av. Dr. Mitjavila 1, tel. 628/21000, fax 628/60319. 56 rooms with bath. Facilities: restaurant, bar, terrace. AE, V. Very Expensive.*

President. This modern hotel is clean and tidy and offers good value rather than charm. The restaurant commands a particularly dramatic mountain view. *44 av. Santa Coloma, tel. 628/22922, fax 628/61414. 88 rooms with bath. Facilities: bar, restaurant, sauna, pool. AE, DC, MC, V. Very Expensive.*

Florida. This cheerful hotel offers good value at relatively inexpensive rates. There's no restaurant, but there are several nearby. *Carrer La Llacuna 15, tel. 628/20105, fax 628/61925. 52 rooms with bath. Facilities: bar, lounge. AE, DC, MC, V. Moderate.*

Hotel La Mola. This friendly spot, midway between the ski slope and the brightish lights of Andorra la Vella, is a comfortable choice with all the basic facilities at a fraction of the price of some of the better-known Andorra hotels. *Av. Co-Princep Episcopal 62, tel. 628/31181. 48 rooms with bath. Facilities: restaurant, pool, tennis courts. AE, DC, MC, V. Inexpensive.*

Les Escaldes
Dining
★ **1900.** The 1900 is a small, beautifully decorated restaurant that serves the best food in the principality, with a mixture of French, Spanish, and Andorran cuisines. It's expensive for Andorra, but Chef Alain Despretz's inventive cuisine is often worth it. *11 Carrer de la Unio, tel. 628/26716. Reservations advised. AE, DC, MC, V. Closed Mon. and July. Expensive.*

Lodging
★

Roc Blanc. Sleek, modern, and luxurious trappings—and a wealth of facilities to pamper the body, from mud baths to acupuncture—are what the Roc Blanc is all about. The rooms are large, and the hotel's restaurant, El Pi, is consistently good. *Plaça Co-Princeps 5, tel. 628/21486, fax 628/60244. 250 rooms with bath. Facilities: restaurant, piano bar, 2 pools, sauna, tennis courts, health club, thermal baths, hairdresser, terrace. AE, DC, MC, V. Very Expensive.*

Ordino
Lodging

Hotel Coma. Surrounded by woods and meadows, this Swiss chalet–style hideaway just outside the village of Ordino offers scenery, silence, and simple Andorran fare at affordable prices. *Carretera General s/n, tel. 628/35116, fax 628/37909. 48 rooms with bath. Facilities: bar, restaurant, terrace, pool. AE, DC, MC, V. Moderate.*

Pas de la Casa
Dining

Le Grizzly. This is a popular French restaurant for lunch or dinner, especially during the ski season. The food is simple but well prepared, and it offers good value, with a choice of four fixed-price menus, from 800 ptas. to 1,300 ptas. Try the *entrecôte roquefort* (steak) and the thick Provençal soups. *Av. d'Encamp s/n, tel. 628/55227. Reservations advised. AE, DC, MC, V. Inexpensive–Moderate.*

Sant Julià de Lòria
Lodging
★

Pol. Gracefully modern surroundings and friendly staff are just two reasons why this hotel is so popular. Its disco is a popular nightspot. *Av. Verge de Canólich 52, tel. 628/41122, fax 628/41852. 80 rooms with bath. Facilities: restaurant, bar, garden, terrace. AE, MC, V. Moderate–Expensive.*

Santa Coloma
Dining

El Bon Racó. This is exactly what it says it is: a good corner, nook, or retreat. A traditional borda in design, it turns out good local cuisine at encouraging prices. Try to be there early; the *racó* is popular and fills quickly on weekends especially. *Carrer de l'Obach, tel. 628/22085. Reservations advised. AE, DC, MC, V. Inexpensive.*

3 Austria

What Austria lacks in size, it more than makes up for in diversity. Its Alps and mountain lakes in the central and southern provinces rival those of neighboring Switzerland; the vast Vienna Woods remind some of the Black Forest; the steppes of the province of Burgenland blend with those across the border in Hungary; and the vineyards along the Danube rival those of the Rhine and Mosel river valleys. In addition, nowhere else is there a Vienna or a Salzburg—or such pastry shops!

Austria has become considerably more expensive in recent years. But there are still bargains to be found, and discovering them can be one of the diversions of a vacation in Austria.

The country is highly accessible. There are virtually no outposts that are not served by public transport of one form or another. The rail network is well maintained, and trains are fast, comfortable, and punctual. Highways are superb and well marked. Public transportation in the cities, although not cheap, is safe, clean, and convenient. In short, the visitor to Austria spends more time having fun than coping with the logistics of getting from A to B.

The Austrians are for the most part friendly and welcoming. They are an outdoor people, given to heading off to the ski slopes, the mountains, the lakes, and the woods at a moment's notice. At the same time, they can be as melancholy as some of the songs of their wine taverns would suggest. Communication is seldom a problem, since most Austrians speak another language besides their native German, and English is the usual choice.

What you'll discover in conversation with Austrians is that they are more for evolution than revolution, so change is gradual, and old values tend to be maintained. Graceful dancers do execute the tricky "left waltz" on balmy summer evenings in Vienna, and at any time you may find an entire town celebrating some event, complete with brass band in lederhosen.

Essential Information

Before You Go

When to Go Austria has two main tourist seasons. The summer season starts at Easter and runs to about mid-October. The most pleasant months weather-wise are May, June, September, and October. June through August are the peak tourist months, and aside from a few overly humid days when you may wish for the wider use of air-conditioning, even Vienna is pleasant; the city literally moves outdoors in summer. The winter cultural season starts in October and runs into June; the winter sports season gets under way in December and lasts until the end of April, although you can ski in selected areas well into June and on some of the highest glaciers year-round. Some events—the Salzburg Festival is a prime example—make a substantial difference in hotel and other costs. Nevertheless, bargains are available in the (almost nonexistent) off-season.

Climate Summer can be warm; winter, bitterly cold. The southern region is usually several degrees warmer in summer, several degrees colder in winter. Winters north of the Alps can be overcast and dreary, whereas the south basks in winter sunshine.

The following are the average daily maximum and minimum temperatures for Vienna.

Jan.	34F	1C	May	67F	19C	Sept.	68F	20C
	25	– 4		50	10		53	11
Feb.	38F	3C	June	73F	23C	Oct.	56F	14C
	28	– 3		56	14		44	7
Mar.	47F	8C	July	76F	25C	Nov.	45F	7C
	30	– 1		60	15		37	3
Apr.	58F	15C	Aug.	75F	24C	Dec.	37F	3C
	43	6		59	15		30	– 1

Currency   The unit of currency is the Austrian schilling (AS), divided into 100 groschen. There are AS 20, 50, 100, 500, 1,000, and 5,000 bills; AS 1, 5, 10, and 20 coins; and 1-, 2-, 10-, and 50- groschen coins. The 1-, 2-, and 5-groschen coins are rare, and the AS20 coins are unpopular— though useful for some cigarette machines. The 500- and 100-schilling notes look perilously similar; confusing the two can be an expensive mistake.

At press time (spring 1994), there were about AS12 to the dollar and about AS18 to the pound sterling.

Credit cards are widely used throughout Austria, although not all establishments take all cards. American Express has money machines in Vienna at Parkring 10 (actually in Liebenberggasse, off Parkring) and at the airport. Many of the Bankomat money dispensers will also accept Visa cards if you have an international PIN number encoded.

Cash traveler's checks at a bank, post office, or American Express office to get the best rate. All charge a small commission; some smaller banks or "change" offices may give a poorer rate *and* charge a higher fee. All change offices at airports and the main train stations in major cities cash traveler's checks. Bank-operated change offices in Vienna with extended hours are located on Stephansplatz and in the Opernpassage. The Bank Austria machines on Stephansplatz and on Kärntnerstrasse 51 (to the right of the opera) and at the Raiffeisenbank on Kohlmarkt (at Michaelerplatz) change bills in other currencies into schillings, but rates are poor and a hefty commission is automatically deducted.

You may bring in any amount of foreign currency or schillings and take out any amount with you.

What It Will Cost   Austria is not inexpensive, but since inflation is relatively low, costs remain fairly stable. Vienna and Salzburg are the most expensive cities, along with such fashionable resorts as Kitzbühel, Seefeld, Badgastein, Bad Hofgastein, Velden, Zell am See, Pörtschach, Lech, and Zürs. Many smaller towns offer virtually identical facilities at half the price.

Drinks in bars and clubs are considerably higher than in cafés or restaurants. Austrian prices include service and tax.

Sample Prices   Cup of coffee, AS25; half-liter of draft beer, AS27–AS40; glass of wine, AS35; Coca-Cola, AS25; open sandwich, AS25; theater ticket, AS200; concert ticket, AS250; opera ticket, AS600 and up; 1-mile taxi ride, AS35.

Customs on Arrival   Austria's duty-free allowances are as follows: 200 cigarettes or 100 cigars or 250 grams of tobacco, 2 liters of wine and 1 liter of spirits, 1 bottle of toilet water (about 300-milliliter size), 50 milliliters of perfume for those aged 18 and over arriving from other European countries. These limits are being liberalized or eliminated under the terms of the European Economic Area agreement. Visitors arriving from the United States, Canada, or other non-European points may bring in twice the above amounts.

Language   German is the official national language. In larger cities and most resort areas, you will have no problem finding those who speak English; hotel and restaurant staff, in particular, speak English reasonably well. Most younger Austrians speak at least passable English, and fluency is increasing.

Getting Around

By Car   The highway system is excellent, and all roads are well maintained
Road and well marked. Secondary mountain roads may be narrow and
Conditions winding, but traffic is generally light. Check the condition of mountain roads in winter before starting out (tel. 0222/711–99–7). Many mountain passes are closed, though tunnels are kept open.

Rules of the Drive on the right. Seat belts are compulsory in front. Children un-
Road der 12 must sit in the back, and smaller children must have a restraining seat. Speed limits are as posted; otherwise, 130 kph (80 mph) on expressways, 100 kph (62 mph) on other main roads, 50 kph (31 mph) in built-up areas. Some city center areas have speed limits of 30 kph (19 mph). The right-of-way is for those coming from the right (especially in traffic circles) unless otherwise marked. A warning triangle—standard equipment in rental cars—must be set up in case of breakdown.

Parking Observe signs; tow-away in cities is expensive. Overnight parking in winter is forbidden on city streets with streetcar lines.

Gasoline Prices—AS9–AS10 per liter—are fairly consistent throughout the country. Only unleaded (*bleifrei*)—regular and premium—is sold in Austria.

Breakdowns Emergency road service is available from **ARBÖ** (tel. 123 nationwide) or **ÖAMTC** (tel. 120). Special phones are located along autobahns and major highways.

By Train   Trains in Austria are fast and efficient, and most lines have now been electrified. Hourly express trains run on the key Vienna–Salzburg route. All principal trains have first- and second-class cars, as well as smoking and nonsmoking areas. Overnight trains have sleeping compartments, and most trains have dining cars. If you're traveling at peak times, a reserved seat—available for a small additional fee—is always a good idea.

Fares If you're visiting other European countries, a **Eurail Pass** (*see* Getting Around Europe, in Chapter 1, for details), valid throughout most of Europe, is the best deal. Austria has only two discount tickets, but half-price fares are available to families, with children up to 15 years traveling free. Adults need a passport photo to get the family pass at rail stations. A **Bundesnetzkarte** offers unlimited travel for a month and costs AS5,400 for first class and AS3,600 for second class. The alternative is an **Österreich Puzzle** ticket including one or more of the four zones that cover the country. The ticket is good for unlimited travel on any four days within a 10-day period. For a single zone, a first-class Puzzle ticket costs AS1,485, second-class AS990. If you're 26 or under, the Puzzle Junior ticket costs AS900 first-class, AS600 second-class. Full details are available from travel agents or from the Austrian National Tourist Office.

By Plane   Domestic service is expensive. **Austrian Airlines** flies between Vienna and Linz, Salzburg, Graz, and Klagenfurt. **Tyrolean Airlines** has service from Vienna to Innsbruck. **Rheintalflug** flies between Vienna and Altenhausen, just over the border in Switzerland, with bus connections to Feldkirch, Bregenz, and Bludenz in Vorarlberg.

By Bus Service is available to virtually every community accessible by highway. Winter buses have ski racks. Vienna's central bus terminal (Wien-Mitte/Landstrasse Hauptstrasse, opposite the Hilton) is the arrival/departure point for international bus routes; in most other cities the bus station is adjacent to the train station.

By Boat Boats ply the Danube from Passau in Germany all the way to Vienna and from Vienna to Bratislava (Slovakia), Budapest (Hungary), and the Black Sea. Only East European boats run beyond Budapest. Overnight boats have cabins; all have dining. The most scenic stretches in Austria are from Passau to Linz and through the Wachau Valley (Melk, Krems). From Vienna, there are day trips you can take upstream to the Wachau and downstream to Bratislava and Budapest. There are also special moonlight dancing and jazz excursions. Make reservations from **DDSG** (the Danube Steamship Company, tel. 0222/727–50–0) in Vienna or travel agents.

By Bicycle Bicycles can be rented at many train stations and returned to any of them. Most trains and some postal buses will take bikes as baggage. Bikes can be taken on the Vienna subway (year-round, Sun. all day; Oct.–Apr., Sat. after 2 PM; May–Sept., weekdays 9–3 and after 6:30, Sat. after 9 AM). Marked cycling routes parallel most of the Danube.

Staying in Austria

Telephones Pay telephones take AS 1, 5, 10, and 20 coins. A three-minute local
Local Calls call costs AS1. Emergency calls are free. Instructions are in English in most booths. Add AS1 when time is up to continue the connection. If you will be phoning frequently, get a phone "credit card" at a post office. This works in all *Wertkartentelefon* phones; the cost of the call will be deducted from the card automatically. Cards cost AS190 for AS200 worth of phoning, AS95 for AS100 in calls, AS48 for calls totaling AS50.

Phone numbers throughout Austria are being changed. A sharp tone indicates no connection or that the number has been changed. Calls to Vienna from *outside* Austria use the city prefix 01 or 1; from *inside* Austria, 0222.

International The country code for Austria is 43. It costs more to telephone *from*
Calls Austria than it does to telephone *to* Austria. Calls from post offices are least expensive. Hotels time all calls and charge a "per unit" fee according to their own tariff, which can add AS100 or more to your bill. To avoid this charge, call overseas and ask to be called back or use an international credit card, available from ATT, Sprint, MCI, and others. To make a collect call—you can't do this from pay phones—dial the operator and ask for an *R* (pronounced "err")-*Gespräch*.

International Dial 08, 1611, or 1614. Most operators speak English; if yours
Information doesn't, you'll be passed to one who does.

Mail Airmail letters to the United States and Canada cost AS11.50 mini-
Postal Rates mum; postcards cost AS8.50. Letters to the United Kingdom cost AS7, postcards cost AS6, and both automatically go by air. An aerogram costs AS12.

Receiving Mail American Express offices in Vienna, Linz, Salzburg, and Innsbruck will hold mail at no charge for those carrying an American Express credit card or American Express traveler's checks.

VAT Refunds Value-added tax (VAT) at 20% is charged on all sales and is automatically included in prices. If you purchase goods worth AS1,000 or more, you can claim the tax back as you leave or once you've reached home. Ask shops where you buy the goods to fill out and give you the necessary papers. Get them stamped at the airport or border by customs officials (who may ask to see the goods). You can get an immediate refund of the VAT at the airport or at main border points, less a service charge, or you can return the papers by mail to the shop(s), which will then deal with the details. The VAT refund can be credited to your credit-card account or paid by check.

Opening and Closing Times **Banks** are open weekdays 8–noon or 12:30 and 1:30–3 or 4. Hours vary from one city to another. Principal offices in cities stay open during lunch.

Museums. Opening days and times vary considerably from one city to another and depend on the season, the size of the museum, budgetary constraints, and assorted other factors. Your hotel or the local tourist office will have current details.

Shops are open weekdays from 8 or 9 until 6 and Saturday until noon or 1 only, except the first Saturday of every month, when they stay open until 5. Some shops in larger cities are open on Thursday evening until 8 PM. Many smaller shops close for one or two hours at midday.

National Holidays January 1; January 6 (Epiphany); April 16, 17 (Easter); May 1 (May Day); May 25 (Ascension); June 4, 5 (Pentecost); June 15 (Corpus Christi); August 15 (Assumption); October 26 (National Day); November 1 (All Saints' Day); December 8 (Immaculate Conception); December 25, 26 (Christmas).

Dining Take your choice of sidewalk *Wurstl* (frankfurter) stands, *Imbissstube* (quick-lunch stops), cafés, Heuriger wine restaurants, self-service restaurants, modest *Gasthäuser* neighborhood establishments with local specialties, and full-fledged restaurants in every price category. Most establishments post their menus outside. Shops that sell coffee beans (such as Eduscho) also offer coffee by the cup at prices that are considerably lower than those in a café. Many Anker bakery shops also offer tasty *Schmankerl* (snacks) and coffee. Butcher shops (*Fleischer* or *Fleischhauer*) may also offer soup and a main course at noon. A growing number of shops and snack bars offer pizza by the slice.

Mealtimes Austrians often eat up to five meals a day: a very early Continental breakfast of rolls and coffee; a slightly more substantial breakfast *(Gabelfrühstück)* with eggs or cold meat, possibly even a small goulash, at mid-morning (understood to be 9, sharp); a main meal at noon; afternoon coffee *(Jause)* with cake at teatime; and, unless dining out, a light supper to end the day.

Dress A jacket and tie are generally advised for restaurants in the top price categories. Otherwise casual dress is acceptable, although in Vienna formal dress (jacket and tie) is preferred in some moderate restaurants at dinner. When in doubt, it's best to dress up.

Ratings Prices are per person and include soup and a main course, usually with salad, and a small beer or glass of wine. Meals in the top-price categories will include a dessert or cheese and coffee. Prices include taxes and service (but leaving an additional 4%–5% is customary). Best bets are indicated by a star ★.

Category	Major City	Other Areas
Very Expensive	over AS800	over AS600
Expensive	AS500–AS800	AS400–AS600
Moderate	AS200–AS500	AS170–AS400
Inexpensive	under AS200	under AS170

Lodging Austrian hotels and pensions are officially classified using from one to five stars. These grades broadly coincide with our own four-way rating system. No matter what the category, standards for service and cleanliness are high. All hotels in the upper three categories have either a bath or shower in the room; even the most inexpensive accommodations provide hot and cold water. Accommodations include castles and palaces, conventional hotels, country inns (*Gasthof*), motels (considerably less frequent), and the more modest pensions.

Ratings All prices quoted here are for two people in a double room. Though exact figures vary, a single room generally costs more than 50% of the price of a comparable double room. Breakfast—which can be anything from a simple roll and coffee to a full and sumptuous buffet—is usually included in the room rate. In the top five-star hotels, however, it is extra (and expensive). Best bets are indicated by a star ★.

Category	Major City	Other Areas
Very Expensive	over AS2,300	over AS1,800
Expensive	AS1,250–AS2,300	AS1,000–AS1,800
Moderate	AS850–AS1,250	AS700–AS1,000
Inexpensive	under AS850	under AS700

Tipping Railroad porters get AS10 per bag. Hotel porters or bellhops get AS5–AS10 per bag. Doormen get AS10 for hailing a cab and assisting. Room service gets AS10 for snacks and AS20 for full meals. Maids get no tip unless your stay is a week or more, or special service is rendered. In restaurants, 10% service is included. Add anything from AS5 to AS50, depending on the restaurant and the size of the bill.

Vienna

Arriving and Departing

By Plane All flights use Schwechat Airport (tel. 0222/71110–2231), about 16 kilometers (10 miles) southwest of Vienna.

Between the Airport and Downtown Buses leave from the airport for the city air terminal (tel. 0222/5800–35404) by the Hilton on Wien-Mitte-Landstrasse Hauptstrasse every half hour from 5 to 8:30 AM and every 20 minutes from 8:50 AM to 11:30 PM; the last bus is at midnight. Trains shuttle every half-hour between the rail terminal in the airport and Wien-Mitte/Landstrasse Hauptstrasse; check schedules and fares, as the new rail service may mean a change in bus service. Buses also run every hour (every half-hour on weekends) from the airport to the Westbahnhof (west train station) and the Südbahnhof (south train station). Be sure you get on the right bus! The one-way fare for all buses is AS60. A taxi from the airport to downtown Vienna costs about AS330–AS350; agree on the price in advance. Cabs (legally) do not meter the drive, as fares are more or less fixed (legally again) at about double the meter fare. A seat in a limousine costs less; book at the airport. **Mazur** (tel. 0222/711–10–6422 or 711–10–6491) offers cheaper pickup and delivery service by arrangement. If you are driving from the airport, follow signs to "Zentrum."

By Train Vienna has four train stations. The principal station, Westbahnhof, is for trains to and from Linz, Salzburg, and Innsbruck. Trains from Germany and France arrive here, too. The Südbahnhof is for trains to and from Graz, Klagenfurt, Villach, and Italy. Franz-Josefs-Bahnhof is for trains to and from Prague, Berlin, and Warsaw. Go to Wien-Mitte (Landstrasse) for local trains to and from the north of the city. Budapest trains use the Westbahnhof and Südbahnhof, and Bratislava trains use Wien-Mitte and Südbahnhof, so check.

By Bus If you arrive by bus, it will probably be at the central bus terminal, Wien-Mitte, opposite the city air terminal (and the Hilton).

By Boat All Danube riverboats dock at the DDSG terminal on Mexikoplatz. There's an awkward connection with the U-1 subway from here. Some boats also make a stop slightly upstream at Heiligenstadt, Nussdorf, from which there is an easier connection to the U-4 subway line.

By Car Main access routes are the expressways to the west and south (Westautobahn, Südautobahn). Routes to the downtown area are marked "Zentrum."

Getting Around

Vienna is fairly easy to explore on foot; as a matter of fact, much of the heart of the city—the area within the Ring—is largely a pedestrian zone. The Ring itself was once the city ramparts, torn down just over a century ago to create today's broad, tree-lined boulevard.

Public transportation is comfortable, convenient, and frequent, though not cheap. Tickets for bus, subway, and streetcar are available in most stations. Tickets in multiples of five are sold at cigarette shops, known as Tabak-Trafik, or at the window marked "Vorverkauf" at central stations such as Karlsplatz or Stephansplatz. A block of five tickets costs AS85, a single ticket AS20. If you plan to use public transportation frequently, get a **24-hour ticket** (AS50), a **three-day tourist ticket** (AS130), or an **eight-day ticket** (AS265). Maps and information are available at Stephansplatz, Karlsplatz, and Praterstern U-Bahn stations.

By Bus or Inner-city buses are numbered 1A through 3A and operate week-
Streetcar days to about 7:40 PM, Saturday until 2 PM. Reduced fares (buy a **Kurzstreckenkarte;** it gives four trips for AS34) are available for these routes as well as designated shorter stretches (roughly two to four stops) on all other bus or streetcar lines. Streetcars and buses are numbered or lettered according to route, and they run until about midnight. Night buses marked N follow special routes every hour on Saturdays and nights before holidays; the fare is AS25. The central terminal point is Schwedenplatz. The Nos. 1 and 2 streetcar lines run the circular route around the Ring, clockwise and counterclockwise, respectively.

By Subway Subway lines (U-Bahn; stations are marked with a huge blue "U") are designated U-1, U-2, U-3, U-4, and U-6 and are clearly marked and color-coded. Additional services are provided by a fast suburban train, the S-Bahn, indicated by a stylized blue "S" symbol. Both are tied into the general city fare system.

By Taxi Cabs can be flagged on the street if the "Frei" (free) sign is illuminated. Alternatively, dial 1718, 60160, 31300, or 40100 to call for one. All rides are metered. The basic fare is AS24 days, AS25 nights, but expect to pay AS60 for an average city ride. There are additional charges for luggage and a night and Sunday surcharge of AS10. Tip the driver AS3–AS5 by rounding up the fare.

Important Addresses and Numbers

Tourist Information City Tourist Office (Kärntnerstr. 38, behind the opera, tel. 0222/513–8892). Open daily 9–7.

Embassies U.S. (Gartenbaupromenade [Marriott Bldg., Parking 12a], tel. 0222/31339). Canadian (Fleischmarkt 19, tel. 0222/533–3691). U.K. (Jauresg. 12, tel. 0222/713–1575).

Emergencies Police (tel. 133), Ambulance (tel. 144), Doctor: ask your hotel, or in an emergency, phone your embassy or consulate (*see above*). Pharmacies: open weekdays 8–6, Saturday 8–noon.

English-Language Bookstores Big Ben Bookshop (Porzellang. 24, tel. 0222/319–6412), British Bookshop (Weihburgg. 24–26, tel. 0222/512–1945), Shakespeare & Co. (Sterng. 2, tel. 0222/535–5053).

Travel Agencies American Express (Kärntnerstr. 21–23, tel. 0222/51540), Austrian Travel Agency (Opernring 3–5, tel. 0222/588628), Wagons-Lits (Kärntner Ring 2, tel. 0222/501600).

Guided Tours

Orientation Tours Vienna Sightseeing Tours (tel. 0222/712–4683) offers a short highlights tour or a lengthier one to the Vienna Woods, Mayerling, and other areas surrounding Vienna. Tours start in front of or beside the opera house. Cityrama (tel. 0222/534130) provides city tours with hotel pickup; tours assemble opposite the InterContinental Hotel. Citytouring Vienna (tel. 0222/894–1417), with hotel pickup, starts from the City Air Terminal behind the Hilton hotel. Prices are similar, but find out which admissions are included or excluded, particularly to Schönbrunn and Belvedere palaces.

Special-Interest Tours Tours are available to the Spanish Riding School, the Vienna Boys Choir, operettas and concerts, the wine suburb of Grinzing, nightclubs, and Vienna by night. Check with the city tourist office or your hotel for details.

Walking Tours *Vienna from A to Z* (in English) is available at most bookstores; it explains the numbered plaques attached to all major buildings in Vienna. *Vienna: Downtown Walking Tours* by Henriette Mandl (may be out of print; check for a new edition) outlines suggested routes and provides information on sights.

Excursions Day bus trips are organized to the Danube Valley, the Hungarian border, the Alps south of Vienna, Salzburg, and Budapest; get information from the city tourist office.

Exploring Vienna

Vienna has been described as an "old dowager of a town," not a bad description for this onetime center of empire. It's not just the aristocratic and courtly atmosphere, with monumental doorways and stately facades of former palaces at every turn. Nor is it just that Vienna has a higher proportion of middle-aged and older citizens than any other city in Europe, with a concomitant sense of stability, quiet, and respectability. Rather, it's these factors, combined with a love of music; a discreet weakness for rich food (especially cakes); an adherence to old-fashioned and formal forms of address; a high, if unadventurous, regard for the arts; and a gentle mourning for lost glories, that produce a stiff but elegant, slightly other-worldly sense of dignity.

The Heart of Vienna Most main sights are in the inner zone, the oldest part of the city, encircled by the **Ring**, once the city walls and today a broad boulevard. Carry a ready supply of AS10 coins; many places of interest have coin-operated tape machines that provide English commentaries. As you wander around, train yourself to look upward; some of the most memorable architectural treasures are on upper stories and roof lines.

Numbers in the margin correspond to points of interest on the Vienna map.

Vienna's role as imperial city is preserved in the complex of buildings that make up the former royal palace. Start your tour at Albertinaplatz, behind the opera house. Head down Augustinerstrasse. To the right is the "Memorial to Victims of Fascism," disputed in part because the sculptor was once an admitted Communist. On your left is the **Albertina**, home to the world's largest collection of drawings, sketches, engravings, and etchings. There are works here by Dürer—these are perhaps the highlight of the collection—Rembrandt, Michelangelo, Corregio, and many others. The holdings are so vast that only a limited number can be shown at one time. Some original works are so delicate that they can be shown only in facsimile. *Augustinerstr. 1, tel. 0222/534830. Closed for renovations, but check to see whether parts of the collection are being shown elsewhere.*

Beethoven was a regular visitor at the Palais Lobkowitz across the street on Lobkowitzplatz. The renovated palace now houses the **Theater Museum**. Exhibits cover the history of theater in Vienna and the rest of Austria. A children's museum in the basement—alas, open only by appointment—is reached by a slide! *Lobkowitzpl. 2, tel. 0222/512–8800. Admission: AS40 adults, AS20 children. Open Tues.–Sun. 10–5.*

Go back to Augustinerstrasse to the 14th-century **Augustinerkirche**, a favorite on Sundays, when the 11 AM mass is sung in Latin. The Habsburg rulers' hearts are preserved in a chamber here. Nearby is the **Nationalbibliothek** (the National Library), with its stunning Baroque great hall. Don't overlook the fascinating collection of globes on the third floor. *Josefsplatz 1, tel. 0222/534–10–397. Admission: AS20 adults, children free. Open May–Oct., Mon. and Wed.–Sat. 10–4, Tues. 10–6, Sun. and holidays 10–1; Nov.–Apr., Mon.–Sat. 11–noon. Globe museum: tel. 534–10–297. Admission: AS10. Open Mon.–Wed., Fri. 11–noon, Thurs. 2–3.*

Josefsplatz is where much of *The Third Man* was filmed, specifically in and around the Palais Pallavicini across the street. The usual entrance to the **Spanische Reitschule,** the Spanish Riding School, is

Albertina, **1**
Augustinerkirche, **3**
Donner Brunnen, **18**
Hofburg, **6**
Hofburgkapelle, **9**
Hoher Markt, **28**
Imperial
Apartments, **7**
Jewish Museum, **19**
Kapuzinerkirche, **17**
Karlskirche, **14**
Kirche am Hof, **25**
Kunsthistorisches
Museum, **12**
Maria am Gestade, **27**
Mozart
Erinnerungsräume, **23**
Nationalbibliothek, **4**
Naturhistorisches
Museum, **11**
Neue Hofburg
Museums, **10**
Pestsäule, **20**
Peterskirche, **21**
Ruprechtskirche, **29**
Sacher Hotel, **16**
Schatzkammer, **8**
Schloss Belvedere, **31**
Schönbrunn
Palace, **30**
Schottenkirche, **24**
Spanische
Reitschule, **5**
Staatsoper, **15**
Stephansdom, **22**
Tabak Museum, **13**
Theater Museum, **2**
20th Century
Museum, **32**
Uhrenmuseum, **26**

Vienna

N

Votivkirche

Währinger Str.
Hörlg.
Koling.
Maria Theresien Str.
Börseg.

Roosevelt-
pl.
Alserstrasse
Universitätsstrasse
Schottenring
Wipplingerstr.
Börsepl.

Universität

Landesgerichtsstrasse
Grillparzerstr.
Oppolzerg. Mölker
Schottengasse Helferstorferstr.
Schottenbastei Hohenstaufeng.
Steig
Teinfaltstr.
Rosenstr.
Herrengasse
Freyung
Tiefer Graben
Renng.
Renng.

24

Am
Hof

Friedrich
Schmidt-Platz

Neues
Rathaus

Schenkeng.
Bankg.
Löwelstr.
Nagierg.
Wallnerstr.
Bognerg.

Stadiong.

Burgtheater

Minoritenkirche

Kohlmarkt

Auerspergstr.

Parliament

Dr. K. Renner Ring
Dr. Karl Lueger Ring

Volksgarten
Ballhaus-
pl.
Schauflerg.
Michaeler-
pl.
Stallburg.

Lerchen-
felderstr.

Museumstrasse

Bellariastr.

Burgring

Heldenpl.

6
7
9 8
5
4 3
10
1
2

Josefs-
pl.
Augustinerstr.
Hanuschg.

11

Maria
Theresien-
Platz

12

Burggasse

Messeplatz

Babenbergstr.
Eschenbachg.
Getreidemarkt

Opernring

Elizabethstr.
Schillerpl.
Nibelungeng.

Opernring

Siebensterng.

13

Burggarten

Goethg.

A

B

Mariahilferstrasse

Gumpendorferstr.
Gumpendorferstr.
Linke Wienzeile
Rechte Wienzeile
Wiedner Hauptstr.

KEY
AE American Express Office
i Tourist Information

30

here, too, though the famed white horses are actually stabled on the other side of the square. During renovations, the entrance to the school has been relocated in the main courtyard next to the Swiss Gate, beyond the Michaelertor rotunda dome. For tickets, write the Spanische Reitschule (Hofburg, A-1010 Vienna) or Austrian Tourist Office (Friedrichstr. 7, A-1010 Vienna) *at least* three months in advance. There are performances on Sunday at 10:45 AM from March through June, and from September through October. Evening performances are occasionally given on Wednesdays at 7 PM. Tickets for the few short performances on Saturday mornings at 9 AM are available only from ticket offices and travel agencies. You can watch the 10 AM–noon training sessions Tuesday to Saturday during much of the performance season; tickets are available only at the door (Josefspl., Gate 2; admission AS80 adults, AS20 children).

6 From here you're only a few steps from Michaelerplatz, the circular square that marks the entrance to the **Hofburg,** the royal palace. On one side of the square, opposite the entrance, on the corner of Herrengasse and Kohlmarkt, is the **Loos building** (1911), designed by Adolf Loos. Step inside to see the remarkable restoration of the foyer. Outside, it's no more than a simple brick-and-glass structure, but architectural historians point to it as one of the earliest "modern" buildings in Europe—a building where function determines style. In striking contrast is the Baroque **Michaelertor,** opposite, the principal gateway to the Hofburg.

Time Out Some insist that no visit to Vienna is complete without a visit to **Demel,** on the left just down the Kohlmarkt. The pastries and lunch are expensive even by Viennese standards, but new management has sought to bring back quality and service to match the elegant tradition. *Tel: 0222/533–5516. Reservations advised at lunchtime. AE, D, MC, V. Closes 6 PM.*

7 Head under the domed entrance of the Michaelertor to visit the **imperial apartments** of Emperor Franz Josef and Empress Elisabeth. Among the exhibits is the exercise equipment used by the beautiful empress. Here, too, is the dress she was wearing when she was stabbed to death by a demented Italian anarchist on the shores of Lake Geneva in 1898; the dagger marks are visible. *Michaelerplatz 1, tel. 0222/587–5554–515. Admission: AS40 adults, AS20 children. Open Mon.–Sat. 8:30–noon, 12:30–4; Sun. and holidays 8:30–12:30.*

8 Be sure to see the **Schatzkammer,** the imperial treasury, home of the magnificent crown jewels. *Hofburg, Schweizerhof, tel. 0222/533–7931. Admission: AS60 adults, AS30 children. Open Wed.–Mon. 10–6, Thurs. 10–9.*

9 The **Hofburgkapelle,** the court chapel, is where the Vienna Boys Choir sings mass at 9:15 AM on Sunday mid-September through June. You'll need tickets to attend; they are available at the chapel from 5 PM Friday (queue up by 4:30 and expect long lines) or by writing to Hofmusikkapelle, Hofburg, Schweizerhof, A-1010 Vienna. The city tourist office can sometimes help with ticket applications.

10 Head south to Heldenplatz, the vast open square punctuated with oversized equestrain statues of Prince Eugene and Archduke Karl, in front of the **Neue Hofburg Museums.** The ponderously ornate 19th-century edifice—Hitler announced the annexation of Austria from the balcony in 1938—now houses a series of museums. Highlights are the Waffensammlung (the weapons collection), the collections of musical instruments including a piano once owned by Beethoven, the ethnographic museum with Montezuma's feathered headdress, and the exciting Ephesus museum, with finds from the excavations at that ancient site. *Neue Hofburg, Heldenplatz 1, tel. 0222/521770. Admission: AS45 adults, AS20 children. Open Wed.–Mon. 10–6.*

Walk west again under the unmonumental Hero's Monument archway and across the Ring, the broad boulevard encircling the inner city, to the museum complex. The **Naturhistorisches Museum** (Natural History Museum) is on your right, the **Kunsthistorisches Museum** (Art History Museum) is on your left. The latter is one of the great art museums of the world; this is not a place to miss. The collections focus on old-master painting, notably Brueghel, Cranach, Titian, Canaletto, Rubens, and Velazquez. But there are important Egyptian, Greek, Etruscan, and Roman exhibits, too. *Burgring 5, tel. 0222/521770. Admission: AS60 adults, AS30 children. Open Tues.–Sun. 10–6, limited galleries also Tues. and Fri. 10–9.*

Time Out   Across the Messeplatz stretches Messepalast, the former court stables that now serve as a fair and exhibit space. Inside is one of Vienna's better-kept secrets, the **Glacis-Beisl** restaurant. Wine and the local specialties in the garden under the vine-clad arbors have to be experienced. *Tel. 0222/526–6795. Reservations advised. No credit cards. Closed Jan.–Feb., Sun., and holidays.*

At the Mariahilferstrasse end of the Messepalast complex is the small and fascinating **Tabak Museum,** the Tobacco Museum. *Mariahilferstr. 2, tel. 0222/526–1716. Admission: AS20 adults, AS10 children. Open Tues.–Fri. 10–5, weekends 10–2.*

Head east down the Getreidemarkt, with the Kunsthistorisches Museum on your left. Looming up ahead with the gilt cauliflower dome is the Sezession and beyond it a huge yellow and blue container. Both are art museums with changing exhibits. Beyond them, over Karlsplatz, is the heroic facade and dome, flanked by vast twin columns, of the **Karlskirche.** It was built around 1715 by Fischer von Erlach. The oval interior is surprisingly small, given the monumental facade: One expects something more on the scale of St. Peter's in Rome. The ceiling has airy frescoes, and stiff shafts of gilt radiate like sunbeams from the altar.

Take the pedestrian underpass back under the Ring to Opernplatz. This is the site of the **Staatsoper,** one of the best opera houses in the world and a focus of Viennese social life. Tickets are expensive and rare, so you may have to settle for a backstage tour. The tour schedule for the day is usually posted alongside the door under the right front arcade on the Kärntnerstrasse side and will depend on the activities going on inside.

Head up Kärntnerstrasse, Vienna's main thoroughfare, now a busy pedestrian mall. On your left is the creamy facade of the **Sacher Hotel.** Take a look inside at the plush red-and-gilt decor, a fin de siècle masterpiece. The hotel is also the home of the original Sachertorte—the ultimate chocolate cake. Back on Kärntnerstrasse, around the corner from the Sacher, is the city tourist office. Leading off Kärntnerstrasse, to the left, is the little street of Marco d'Aviano-Gasse. Follow it to **Kapuzinerkirche,** in whose crypt, called the **Kaisergruft** or the imperial vault, the serried ranks of long-dead Habsburgs lie. The oldest tomb is that of Ferdinand II; it dates from 1633. The most recent tomb is that of Empress Zita, widow of Austria's last kaiser, dating from 1989. *Neuer Markt 1, tel. 0222/512–*

6853–12. Admission: AS30 adults, AS20 children. Open daily 9:30–4.

⑱ In the center of the square is the ornate 18th-century **Donner Brunnen,** the Providence Fountain. The figures represent main rivers that flow into the Danube; Empress Maria Teresa thought the figures were obscene and wanted them removed or properly clothed.

Time Out	Coffee or tea and what are said, even by the French and Belgians, to be the best pastries in the world are available at the **Konditorei Oberlaa.** *Neuer Markt 16. Open weekdays 9–7, Sat. 9–6, Sun. and holidays 10–6.*

Turn down Plankengasse to Dorotheergasse. On your right, in the **⑲** former Eskeles palace, is the **Jewish Museum.** Permanent and changing exhibits try but, alas, fail to portray the rich Jewish culture and heritage of Vienna and Austria. Don't consider it a priority if you're pressed for time. *Dorotheergasse 11, tel. 0222/513–7907. Admission: AS50 adults, AS25 children. Open Sun.–Wed., and Fri. 10–6, Thurs. 10–9.*

Continue north through Dorotheergasse to reach pedestrians-only **⑳** Graben. The **Pestsäule,** or Plague Column, shoots up from the middle of the street, looking like a geyser of whipped cream touched with gold. It commemorates the Black Death of 1697. A small turning to the right, just past the column, leads to the Baroque **㉑** **Peterskirche.** The little church, the work of Johann Lukas von Hildebrandt, finished in about 1730, has what is probably the most theatrical interior in the city. The pulpit is especially fine, with a highly ornate canopy, but florid and swirling decoration is everywhere. Many of the decorative elements are based on a tent form, a motif suggested by the Turkish forces that camped outside the city walls during the great siege of Vienna at the end of the 17th century.

Walk down Goldschmiedgasse to Stephansplatz, site of the **㉒** **Stephansdom** (St. Stephen's Cathedral). Its towering Gothic spires and gaudy 19th-century tile roof are still the dominant feature of the Vienna skyline. The oldest part of the building is the 13th-century entrance, the soaring **Riesentor,** or Giant Doorway. Inside, the church is mysteriously dark, filled with an array of monuments, tombs, sculptures, paintings, and pulpits. Despite extensive wartime damage—and numerous Baroque additions—the building radiates an authentically medieval atmosphere. Climb up the 345 steps of **Alte Steffl,** Old Steven, the south tower, for a stupendous view over the city. An elevator goes up the north tower to **Die Pummerin,** the Boomer, a 22-ton bell first cast in 1711 from cannons captured from the Turks. Take a 30-minute tour of the crypt to see the copper jars in which the entrails of the Habsburgs are carefully preserved.

On a narrow street east of the cathedral is the house where Mozart **㉓** lived from 1784 to 1787. Today it's the **Mozart Erinnerungsräume,** the Mozart Museum. It was here that the composer wrote *The Marriage of Figaro* (thus the nickname Figaro House) and here, some say, that he spent the happiest years of his life. *Domgasse 5, tel. 0222/513–6294. Admission: AS15 adults, AS5 children. Open Tues.–Sun. 9–12:15 and 1–4:30.*

Other Corners of Vienna	Walk back down the Graben and the narrow Naglergasse and turn left into the Freyung. On your left is the **Palais Ferstl,** now a stylish shopping arcade. At the back is the skillfully restored **Café Central,** once headquarters for Vienna's leading literary figures. Cross the

24 Freyung to the dominant **Schottenkirche.** The monks who were brought to found it were actually Irish, not Scottish. Turn back through the Freyung to **Am Hof,** a remarkable square with the city's Baroque central fire station, possibly the world's most ornate. Cross
25 the square to the **Kirche am Hof.** The interior is curiously reminiscent of many Dutch churches.

Time Out For a typical meal or just a beer or coffee, stop at **Gustlbauer.** The restaurant is a regular stop for the Fiaker coachmen, who leave their livery and passengers briefly for a quick Schnapps. The waiter will help you decipher the handwritten menu. *Am Hof, Drahtgasse 2, tel. 0222/533–5889. Open Sun.–Fri. 10 AM–midnight, Sat. 10 AM–3.*

Continue to Judenplatz and turn right into Parisergasse to the
26 **Uhrenmuseum** (Clock Museum), located in a lovely Renaissance house. *Schulhof 2, tel. 0222/533–2265. Admission: AS30 adults, AS10 children. Open Tues.–Sun. 9–4:30.*

Turn down the Kurrentgasse and, via Fütterergasse, cross the Wipplingerstrasse into Stoss im Himmel (literally, a "thrust to
27 heaven"). To your left down Salvatorgasse is **Maria am Gestade,** originally a church for fishermen on the nearby canal. Note the ornate "folded hands" spire. Return along Wipplingerstrasse, across
28 Marc Aurel-Strasse, to **Hoher Markt,** with a central monument celebrating the betrothal of Mary and Joseph. Underground are **Roman ruins,** remains of the second-century Roman encampment. *Hoher Markt 3, tel. 0222/535–5606. Admission: AS15 adults, AS5 children; free on Fri. morning. Open Tues.–Sun. 9–12:15 and 1–4:30.*

On the north side of Hoher Markt is the amusing **Anker-Uhr,** a clock that tells time by figures moving across a scale. The figures are identified on a plaque at the lower left of the clock; it's well worth passing by at noon to catch the show. Go through Judengasse to
29 **Ruprechtskirche** (St. Rupert's). The oldest church in Vienna, dating from the 11th century, is small, damp, dark, and, unfortunately, usually closed, though you can peek through a window.

Vienna It's a 15-minute ride from the city center on subway line U-4 (stop
Environs either at Schönbrunn or Hietzing) to **Schönbrunn Palace,** the mag-
30 nificent Baroque residence built between 1696 and 1713 for the Habsburgs. Here Kaiser Franz Josef I was born and died. His "office" (kept as he left it in 1916) is a touching reminder of his spartan life; other rooms, however, reflect the elegance of the monarchy. The ornate public rooms are still used for state receptions. A guided tour covers 45 of the palace's 1,441 rooms; among the curiosities are the Chinese room and the gym fitted out for Empress Elisabeth, where she exercised daily to keep her figure. Ask about rooms open independent of a tour, but don't pass up the tour. *Schönbrunner Schlosstr., tel. 0222/81113–238. Admission: AS95 adults, AS40 children. Guided tours only. Open Nov.–Mar., daily 9–4:30; Apr.–June and Oct., daily 8:30–5, July–Sept., daily 8:30–5:30.*

Once on the grounds, don't overlook the **Tiergarten** (Zoo). It's Europe's oldest menagerie and, when established in 1752, was intended to amuse and educate the court. It contains an extensive assortment of animals, some of them in their original Baroque enclosures. *Tel. 0222/877–9294. Admission: AS80 adults, AS60 children. Open Nov.–Jan., daily 9–4:30; Feb., Oct., daily 9–5; Mar., daily 9–5:30; Apr., daily 9–6; May–Sept., daily 9–6:30.*

Follow the pathways up to the **Gloriette,** that Baroque ornament on the rise behind Schönbrunn, and enjoy superb views of the city. Originally this was to have been the site of the palace, but projected construction costs were considered too high. The restored edifice again incorporates a café, as the original did. *Admission: AS20 adults, AS10 children. Open May–Sept., daily 8–6; Oct., daily 8–5.*

The **Wagenburg** (Carriage Museum), near the entrance to the palace grounds, holds some splendid examples of early transportation, from children's sleighs to funeral carriages of the emperors. *Tel. 0222/877–3244. Admission: AS30 adults, AS15 children. Open Nov.–Mar., Tues.–Sun. 10–4; Apr.–Oct., Tues.–Sun. 10–6.*

③ Take the D streetcar toward the Südbahnhof to reach **Schloss Belvedere** (Belvedere Palace), a Baroque complex often compared to Versailles. It was commissioned by Prince Eugene of Savoy and built by Johann Lukas von Hildebrandt in 1721–22. The palace is made up of two separate buildings, one at the foot and the other at the top of a hill. The lower tract was first built as residential quarters; the upper buildings were reserved for entertaining. The gardens in between are among the best examples of natural Baroque ornamentation found anywhere. The buildings have contemporary significance: The State Treaty that gave Austria its independence in 1955 was signed in the great upper hall. The composer Anton Bruckner lived in an apartment to the north of the upper building until his death in 1896. Both sections now house outstanding art museums: the gallery of 19th- and 20th-century art in the Upper Belvedere (Klimt, Kokoschka, Schiele, Waldmüller, Markart) and the Baroque museum (including medieval Austrian art) in the Lower Belvedere. *Prinz-Eugen-Str. 27, tel. 0222/784158. Admission: AS60 adults, AS30 children. Open Tues.–Sun. 10–5.*

③ Continue across the Gürtel from the Upper Belvedere southward to the **20th Century Museum,** containing a small but extremely tasteful modern art collection. *Schweizer Garten, tel. 0222/782550. Admission: AS45 adults, AS25 children. Open Tues.–Sun. 10–6.*

You can reach a small corner of the **Vienna Woods** by streetcar and bus: Take a streetcar or the subway U-2 to Schottentor/University and, from there, the No. 38 streetcar (Grinzing) to the end of the line. Grinzing itself is out of a picture book; alas, much of the wine offered in the taverns is less enchanting. (For better wine and ambience, try the area around Pfarrplatz and Probusgasse in Hohe Warte—streetcar 37, bus 39A—or the suburb of Nussdorf—streetcar D.) To get into the woods, change in Grinzing to the No. 38A bus. This will take you to Kahlenberg, which provides a superb view over the Danube and the city. You can take the bus or hike to Leopoldsberg, the promontory over the Danube from which Turkish invading forces were repulsed during the 16th and 17th centuries.

Off the Beaten Track

Vienna's **Bermuda Triangle** (around Judengasse/Seitenstettengasse) is jammed with everything from good bistros to jazz clubs. Also check the tourist office's museum list carefully: There's something for everyone, ranging from Sigmund Freud's apartment to the Funeral and Burial Museum. The **Hundertwasserhaus** (Kegelgasse/Löwengasse; streetcar N), an astonishing apartment complex designed by artist Friedenreich Hundertwasser, with turrets, towers, odd windows, and uneven floors, will be of interest to those who do not think that architectural form has to follow function. The nearby **KunstHaus Wien** art museum offers Hundertwasser plus changing exhibits of modern works.

Children and adults alike will enjoy the charming **Doll and Toy Museum,** next door to the Clock Museum (*see* Exploring Vienna, *above*). It's filled with trains, dollhouses, and troops of teddy bears. *Schulhof 4, tel. 0222/535-6860. Admission: AS60 adults, AS30 children. Open Tues.–Sun. 10–6.*

Shopping

Antiques   The best (and most expensive) shops are in the inner city, many in and around **Dorotheergasse,** but there are good finds in some of the outer districts, particularly among the back streets in the **Josefstadt** (eighth) district.

Boutiques   Name brands are found along the **Kohlmarkt** and **Graben** and their respective side streets, and the side streets off the **Kärntnerstrasse.**

Folk   A good selection at reasonable prices is offered by the **NÖ**
Costumes   **Heimatwerk** (Herrengasse 6); also try **Trachten Tostmann** (Schottengasse 3a) or **Loden-Plankl** (Michaelerplatz 6).

Shopping   Tourists gravitate to the **Kärntnerstrasse,** but the Viennese do most
Districts   of their shopping on the **Mariahilferstrasse.**

Food and   The **Naschmarkt** (between Rechte and Linke Wienzeile; weekdays
Flea Markets   6 AM–mid-afternoon, Sat. 6–1) is a sensational open-food market, offering specialties from around the world. The **Flohmarkt** (flea market) operates year-round beyond the Naschmarkt (subway U-4 to Kettenbrückengasse) and is equally fascinating (Sat. 8–4). An **Arts & Crafts Market** with better offerings operates on Saturday (2–6) and Sunday (10–6) alongside the Danube Canal near the Salztorbrücke. Look for the seasonal markets in the Freyung square opposite Palais Ferstal.

Dining

In contrast to many cities, the leading Viennese hotels are in competition for the country's best cooks and therefore offer some of the city's best dining. Even the chain hotels have joined in the effort to see which can win over the leading chefs. The results are rewarding; you may not even have to leave your hotel to enjoy outstanding food and service. For details and price-category definitions, *see* Dining in Staying in Austria, *above.*

Very   **Korso.** You'll find outstanding food and atmosphere at this gourmet
Expensive   temple of "New Vienna Cuisine." Chef Reinhard Gerer produces ex-
★   quisite variations on Austrian standards such as pork and beef by borrowing accents from Asian cuisine. *Mahlerstr. 2, tel. 0222/ 51516–546. Reservations advised. AE, DC, MC, V. Closed Sat. lunch.*
Palais Schwarzenberg. The glassed-in restaurant with a view into the palace gardens is a perfect setting for the excellent fillet of beef, lamb in herb crust, or souffléd turbot. Wine prices are high, although special offers can be outstanding and reasonable. The house wines are good. *Schwarzenbergpl. 9, tel. 0222/798–4515. Reservations recommended. AE, DC, MC, V.*
Steirereck. Acclaimed as Austria's best restaurant, the Steirereck successfully espouses the lighter New Vienna Cuisine in an elegant atmosphere, with service that cannot be faulted. Try Styrian venison, turbot crêpes with asparagus, or even a schnitzel. The noontime fixed-price lunch offers choices and is an outstanding value.

Rasumofskygasse 2, tel. 0222/713–3168. Reservations required. AE, V. Closed weekends and holidays.

Zu den Drei Husaren. This is one of Vienna's enduring monuments to tradition, complete with candlelight and live piano music (except on Sunday). Casual visitors (as opposed to the "regulars") may have to settle for more atmosphere than service, however, but the food— mainly Viennese standards such as variations on rump steak—is of exceptional quality. The hors d'oeuvre trolleys are intentionally enticing and can easily double the lunch or dinner bill. *Weihburggasse 4, tel. 0222/512–1092. Reservations required. AE, DC, MC, V. Closed mid-July–mid-Aug.*

Expensive **Plachutta.** The feature here is superb *Tafelspitz* (boiled beef), served in its own delicious soup, for which you can order the day's "supplement"—*Frittaten* (thin pancake strips), perhaps, or *Leberknödel* (liver dumplings). You choose the cut or type of beef you prefer (all are outstanding) or select a steak or grilled fish, and finish with a rhubarb strudel. The house wines are fine; service is less so. *Wollzeile 38, tel. 0222/512–1577. Reservations required evenings, recommended at lunch. No credit cards.*

★ **Vier Jahreszeiten.** This restaurant effortlessly manages to achieve that delicate balance between food and atmosphere. The service is attentive without being overbearing. The lunch buffet offers both excellent food and value. Evening dining includes grill specialties and live piano music. *Hotel Intercontinental, Johannesgasse 28, tel. 0222/71122–143. Reservations advised. AE, DC, MC, V. Closed Sat. lunch and Sun. dinner.*

Zum Kuckuck. Wood paneling and the patina of years mark this intimate restaurant, candle-lit at night. Specials change daily but tend toward regional variations on pork, venison, or lamb. The fig cake with rum sauce is a house classic. *Himmelpfortgasse 15, tel. 0222/512–8470, fax 0222/523–3818. Reservations required. Jacket and tie advised. AE, DC, MC, V. Closed weekends.*

Moderate **Bastei-Beisl.** A comfortable, wood-paneled restaurant offering good traditional Viennese fare. Outdoor tables are particularly pleasant on summer evenings. *Stubenbastei 10, tel. 0222/512–4319. Reservations usually not necessary. AE, DC, MC. Closed Sun.*

Bei Max. The decor is somewhat bland, but the tasty Carinthian specialties—*Kasnudeln* and *Fleischnudeln* (a kind of cheese- and meat-filled ravioli) in particular—keep this friendly restaurant packed. *Landhausgasse 2/Herrengasse, tel. 0222/533–7359. Reservations advised. No credit cards. Closed Sat., Sun., last week July, first 3 weeks Aug.*

★ **Gigerl.** It's hard to believe you're right in the middle of the city at this imaginative and charming wine restaurant that serves hot and cold buffets. The rooms are small and cozy but may get smoky and noisy when the place is full—which it usually is. The food is typical of wine gardens on the fringes of the city: roast meats, casserole dishes, cold cuts, salads. The wines are excellent. The surrounding narrow alleys and ancient buildings add to the charm of the outdoor tables in summer. *Rauhensteingasse 3, tel. 0222/513–4431. Reservations advised. AE, DC, MC, V. Closed Sun. lunch.*

Kaiserwalzer. The rooms in this once-private house radiate the elegance of the old empire. Austrian specialties are prominent: the beet soup, roast chicken, and paprika sauces are all splendid. *Esterházygasse 9, tel. 0222/587–0494. Reservations advised. AE, DC, MC, V. Dinner only; closed Sun.*

Melker Stiftskeller. This is one of the city's half-dozen genuine wine taverns, or kellers; the food selection is limited but good, featuring pig's knuckle. House wines from the Wachau are excellent.

Schottengasse 3, tel. 0222/533–5530. Reservations usually not necessary. MC. Evenings only; closed Sun.

★ **Ofenloch.** This place is always packed, which speaks well not only of the excellent specialties from some Viennese grandmother's cookbook but also of the atmosphere. Waitresses are dressed in appropriate period costumes, and the furnishings add to the color. At times the rooms may be too smoky and noisy for some tastes. If you like garlic, try *Vanillerostbraten,* a rump steak with as much garlic as you request. *Kurrentgasse 8, tel. 0222/533–8844. Reservations required. AE, DC, MC, V.*

Stadtbeisl. Good standard Austrian fare is served at this popular eatery, which is comfortable without being pretentious. The service gets uneven as the place fills up, but if you are seated outside in summer, you probably won't mind. *Naglergasse 21, tel. 0222/533–3507. Reservations advised. No credit cards.*

Zu den drei Hacken. This is one of the few genuine Viennese *Gasthäuser* in the city center; like the place itself, the fare is solid if not elegant. Legend has it that Schubert dined here; the ambience probably hasn't changed much since then. There are tables outside in summer, although the extra seating capacity strains both the kitchen and the service. *Singerstr. 28, tel. 0222/512–5895. No reservations. AE, DC, V. Closed Sat. dinner and Sun.*

★ **Zu ebener Erde und erster Stock.** Ask for a table upstairs in this exquisite, tiny, utterly original Biedermeier house, which serves excellent Austrian fare; the downstairs space is really more for snacks. *Burggasse 13, tel. 0222/523–6254. Reservations advised. AE. Closed Sat. lunch, Sun., Mon., and late July–late Aug.*

Inexpensive **Figlmüller.** Known for its schnitzel, Figlmüller is always packed.
★ Guests share the benches, the long tables, and the experience. Food choices are limited, but nobody seems to mind. Only wine is offered to drink, but it is good. The small "garden" is now enclosed and is just as popular as the tables inside. *Wollzeile 5 (passageway), tel. 0222/512–6177. No reservations. No credit cards. Closed Sat. dinner and Sun.*

Ilona-Stüberl. Head to Ilona-Stüberl for a cozy Hungarian atmosphere—without the gypsy music. Be prepared to douse the fire if you ask for a dish with hot peppers! The tables outside in summer are pleasant but somewhat public. *Bräunerstr. 2, tel. 0222/533–9029. Reservations advised. AE, DC, MC, V. Closed Sun.*

Lodging

Vienna's inner city is the best base for visitors because it's so close to most of the major sights, restaurants, and shops. This accessibility translates, of course, into higher prices. For details and price-category definitions, *see* Lodging in Staying in Austria, *above.* Try bargaining for discounts at the larger international chain hotels during the off season.

Very **Bristol.** Opposite the opera house, the Bristol is classic Viennese,
Expensive preferred by many for the service as well as the location. The bar is
★ comfortable, though not overly private; the restaurants associated with the hotel are outstanding, especially Korso. Back and upper guest rooms are quieter. *Kärntner Ring 1, tel. 0222/515160, fax 0222/515–16550. 146 rooms with bath. Facilities: restaurants, bar. AE, DC, MC, V.*

★ **Imperial.** This former palace represents elegant old Vienna at its best, with such features as heated towel racks in some rooms. The location could hardly be better, although being on the Ring sometimes makes the front and lower rooms a bit noisy. The bar is intimate and pleasant. Lunch in the café is both reasonable and good; the hotel restaurant, Majestät, has a new chef but has yet to regain its erstwhile top-quality reputation. *Kärntner Ring 16, tel. 0222/ 501100, fax 0222/501–10410. 145 rooms with bath or shower. Facilities: beauty parlor, conference rooms. AE, DC, MC, V.*

★ **InterContinental.** Vienna's modern InterContinental has the reputation of being one of the chain's very best. The rooms are a cut above standard; the main restaurant, exceptional. But whereas the hotel succeeds in acquiring some Viennese charm, the bar fails hopelessly, as does the less formal Brasserie. Rooms in front overlooking the park are quieter, particularly in winter when the ice-skating rink at the back is in operation. *Johannesgasse 28, tel. 0222/711220, fax 0222/713–4489. 500 rooms with bath. Facilities: sauna, health club, laundry, dry cleaning service, barber, hair stylist, complimentary limousine, parking. AE, DC, MC, V.*

Marriott. The only Viennese aspect here is the service; all else is global modern. The atrium lobby, while pleasant, is anything but intimate. The restaurants are satisfactory if not quite up to the level of other top hotels, although Sunday brunch at the Marriott has become immensely popular (book at least a week in advance). *Parkring 12A, tel. 0222/515180, fax 0222/515–186722. 304 rooms with bath. Facilities: sauna, health club, pool, shops, garage. AE, DC, MC, V.*

Palais Schwarzenberg. The rooms are furnished with antiques and appropriately incorporated into a quiet wing of a Baroque palace, a 10-minute walk from the opera. The restaurant enjoys a good reputation; the view out over the formal gardens is glorious. *Schwarzenbergplatz 9, tel. 0222/784515, fax 0222/784714. 38 rooms with bath. Facilities: bar. AE, DC, MC, V.*

Sacher. The hotel's reputation has varied considerably during recent years, but it remains one of the legendary addresses in Europe, with its opulent decor highlighted by original oil paintings, sculptures, and objets d'art. The Blue and Red bars are intimate and favored by nonguests as well, as is the café, particularly in summer when tables are set up outside. Guest rooms are spacious and elegantly appointed. *Philharmonikerstr. 4, tel. 0222/514560, fax 0222/ 514–57810. 117 rooms with bath or shower. Facilities: coffee shop, bars. AE, DC, MC, V.*

Expensive **Altstadt.** You're one streetcar stop or a short walk from the main museums in this newly renovated old-Vienna residential building. Each of the spacious rooms is decorated individually, though the predominant scheme involves fine wood period furniture set against light and blue-gray walls. The upper rooms have views out over the city roofline. *Kirchengasse 41, tel. 0222/526–33990, fax 0222/423–4901. 25 rooms with bath or shower. Facilities: bar. AE, DC, MC, V.*

★ **Astoria.** Though the Astoria is one of Vienna's traditional old hotels, the rooms have been modernized considerably. The paneled lobby, however, has been preserved and retains an unmistakable Old World patina. The location is central, but because of the street musicians and the late-night crowds in the pedestrian zone, rooms overlooking the Kärntnerstrasse tend to be noisy in summer. *Fürichgasse 1, tel. 0222/515770, fax 0222/515–7782. 108 rooms with bath or shower. Facilities: restaurant. AE, DC, MC, V.*

Capricorno. This establishment overlooks the Danube Canal in a fairly central location. Although its facade is modern and somewhat short on charm, the hotel nonetheless represents good value. *Schwedenplatz 3–4, tel. 0222/533–3104, fax 0222/533–76714. 46 rooms with bath or shower. Facilities: garage. AE, DC, MC, V.*

Europa. The location—midway between the opera house and the cathedral—is ideal, but the rooms on the Kärntnerstrasse side are noisy in summer; ask for a room overlooking Neuer Markt. The building is postwar modern and lacks the charm of older hotels, but the staff is friendly and helpful. The café is popular, particularly in summer when tables are put outdoors. *Neuer Markt 3, tel. 0222/ 515940, fax 0222/513–8138. 102 rooms with bath. Facilities: restaurant, coffee shop, bar. AE, DC, MC, V.*

König von Ungarn. This utterly charming, centrally located hotel is tucked away in the shadow of the cathedral. The historic facade belies the modern efficiency of the interior, from the atrium lobby to the guest rooms themselves. Insist on written confirmation of bookings. *Schulerstr. 10, tel. 0222/515840, fax 0222/515848. 32 rooms with bath or shower. Facilities: restaurant, bar. DC, MC, V.*

Mailberger Hof. This is a favorite of opera stars, conductors, and those who want a central but quiet location. Some rooms have limited kitchenette facilities. The arcaded courtyard is very pretty. *Annagasse 7, tel. 0222/512–0641, fax 0222/512–064110. 40 rooms with bath or shower. AE, MC, V.*

Moderate **Austria.** This older hotel is on a quiet side street in a historic area. It
★ is popular with tourists. *Wolfengasse 3/Fleischmarkt, tel. 0222/ 51523, fax 0222/515–23506. 46 rooms, 42 with bath or shower. Facilities: bar. AE, DC, MC, V.*

★ **Kärntnerhof.** Though tucked away in a tiny, quiet side street, Kärntnerhof is nevertheless centrally located. It's known for its particularly friendly staff. The rooms are functionally decorated but clean and serviceable. *Grashofgasse 4, tel. 0222/512–1923, fax 0222/ 513–222833. 43 rooms, 41 with bath or shower. AE, DC, MC, V.*

Pension Christina. This quiet pension, just steps from Schwedenplatz and the Danube Canal, offers mainly smallish modern rooms, warmly decorated with attractive dark-wood furniture set off against beige walls. Room 524 is particularly spacious and inviting. *Hafnersteig 7, tel. 0222/533–2961, fax 0222/533–296111. 32 rooms with bath or shower. MC, V.*

★ **Pension Zipser.** This 1904 house, with an ornate facade and gilttrimmed coat of arms, has become a favorite with regular visitors to Vienna. It is slightly less central than some others on our list, but very comfortable. *Lange Gasse 49, tel. 0222/404–5400, fax 0222/ 408–526613. 46 rooms with bath or shower. Facilities: bar. AE, DC, MC, V.*

★ **Post.** Taking its name from the city's main post office, opposite, this is an older but updated hotel that offers a fine location, a friendly staff, and a good café. *Fleischmarkt 24, tel. 0222/515830, fax 0222/ 515–83808. 107 rooms, 77 with bath or shower. AE, DC, MC, V.*

Schweizerhof. This is more of a pension than a hotel, but the location is excellent and the smallish rooms are certainly adequate. *Bauernmarkt 22, tel. 0222/533–1931, fax 0222/533–0214. 55 rooms with bath or shower. AE, DC, MC, V.*

Wandl. The house is old and some of the rooms are small, but the Wandl's location and reasonable prices compensate for most of its deficiencies. *Petersplatz 9, tel. 0222/534550, fax 0222/534–5577. 134 rooms with bath or shower. No credit cards.*

The Arts

Theater and Check the monthly program published by the city; posters also show
Opera opera and theater schedules. The **Staatsoper,** one of world's great opera houses, features major stars in its almost-nightly performances in the original languages. The **Volksoper** offers lighter opera, operetta, and musicals, all in German. Performances at the **Burgtheater** and **Akadamietheater** are in German. Tickets for the

Staatsoper, Volksoper, and the Burg and Akademie theaters are available at the central ticket office to the left rear of the Staatsoper (**Bundestheaterkassen,** Hanuschgasse 3, tel. 0222/514–442959, fax 0222/514–442969; open weekdays 8–6, Sat. 9–2, Sun. and holidays 9–noon). Tickets go on advance sale a week before performances. Unsold tickets can be obtained at the evening box office. Plan to be there at least one hour before the performance; students can buy remaining tickets at lower prices, so they are usually out in force. Tickets can be ordered three weeks or more in advance in writing (or by fax) or six days in advance from anywhere in the world by phone (tel. 0222/513–1513; AE, DC, MC, V). Theater is offered in English at **Vienna English Theater** (Josefsgasse 12, tel. 0222/402–1260) and **International Theater** (Porzellangasse 8, tel. 0222/319–6272).

Music Most classical concerts are in either the **Konzerthaus** (Lothringerstr. 20, tel. 0222/712–1211, fax 0222/712–2872) or **Musikverein** (Dumbastr. 3, tel. 0222/505–8190, fax 0222/505–9409). Tickets can be bought at the box offices or ordered by phone (AE, DC, MC, V). Pop concerts are scheduled from time to time at the **Austria Center** (Am Hubertusdamm 6, tel. 0222/236–9150; U-1 subway to Vienna International Center stop). Tickets to various musical events are available via **Vienna Ticket Service** (tel. 0222/587–9843, fax 0222/587–9844), or at the "Salettl" gazebo ticket office on the Kärntnerstrasse next to the opera (tel. 0222/588–85–81).

Film Films are shown in English at **Burg Kino** (Opernring 19, tel. 0222/587–8406), **de France** (Schottenring 5, tel. 0222/345236), **Top Kino** (Rahlgasse 1, tel. 0222/587–5557), **Votiv Kino** (Währinger Str. 12, tel. 0222/343571), and **Film Museum** (Augustinerstr. 1, tel. 0222/533–7054). To find English-language movies, look for "OF" (Originalfassung) or "OmU" (original with subtitles) in the newspaper listings.

Nightlife

Cabarets Most cabarets are expensive and unmemorable. Two of the best are **Casanova** (Dorotheergasse 6, tel. 0222/512–9845), which emphasizes striptease, and **Moulin Rouge** (Walfischgasse 11, tel. 0222/512–2130).

Discos **Atrium** (Schwarzenbergpl. 10, tel. 0222/505–3594) is open Thursday through Sunday and draws a lively younger crowd. **Queen Anne** (Johannesgasse 12, tel. 0222/512–0203) is central, popular, and always packed. The **U-4** (Schönbrunnerstr. 222, tel. 0222/858307) ranks high among the young set. Live bands, dancing, and snacks are offered at **Chattanooga** (Graben 29, tel. 0222/533–5000).

Nightclubs A casual '50s atmosphere pervades the popular **Café Volksgarten** (Burgring 1, tel. 0222/533–0518), situated in the city park of the same name; tables are set outdoors in summer. The more formal **Eden Bar** (Liliengasse 2, tel. 0222/512–7450) is considered one of Vienna's classiest night spots; don't expect to be let in unless you're dressed to kill.

Wine Taverns For a traditional Viennese night out, head to one of the city's atmospheric wine taverns, some of which date as far back as the 12th century. You can often have full meals at these taverns, but the emphasis is mainly on drinking. **Melker Stiftskeller** (*see* Dining, *above*) is one of the friendliest and most typical. Other well-known ones: **Antiquitäten-Keller** (Magdalenenstr. 32, tel. 0222/566–9533; closed Aug.), which has a backdrop of classical music; **Augustinerkeller** (Augustinerstr. 1, tel. 0222/533–1026), open at lunchtime as well as during the evenings, in the same building as the Albertina collection; **Esterhazykeller** (Haarhof 1, tel. 0222/533–3482), a particularly mazelike network of rooms, with excellent wines; and **Zwölf-Apostelkeller** (Sonnenfelsgasse 3, tel. 0222/512–6777), near St. Stephen's Cathedral.

The Danube Valley

The Danube Valley stretches about 88 kilometers (55 miles) west of Vienna, and many visitors enjoy it as part of an excursion from the country's capital. What this region offers is magnificent countryside, some of Austria's best food and wines, and comfortable—in some cases elegant—accommodations. Above the river are the ruins of ancient castles. The abbeys at Melk and Göttweig, with their magnificent libraries, dominate their settings. Vineyards sweep down to the river, which is lined with fruit trees that burst into blossom every spring. People here live close to the land, and at certain times of year vintners open their homes to sell their own wines and produce. Roadside stands offer flowers, fruits, vegetables, and wines. And this is an area of legend: The Danube shares with the Rhine the story of the mythical Nibelungen, defenders of Siegfried, hero of German myth.

Getting Around

By Car If you're pressed for time, take the Autobahn to St. Pölten, turn north onto Route S-33, and follow the signs to Melk. For a more scenic route, leave Vienna along the south shore of the Danube via Klosterneuburg and Greifenstein, taking Routes 14, 19, 43, and 33. Cross the Danube at Melk, then return to Vienna along the north bank of the river (Route 3).

By Train Depart from the Westbahnhof for Melk, then take the bus along the north bank of the Danube to Dürnstein and Krems. Side bus trips can be made from Krems to Göttweig.

By Boat Travel upstream, with stops at Krems, Dürnstein, Melk, and points between. Return to Vienna by boat or by train from Melk (combination tickets available).

Guided Tours

Vienna travel agencies offer tours of the Wachau, as the Danube Valley is known. These range from one-day outings to longer excursions. For details, contact the **Lower Austria Tourist Office** (Heidenschuss 2, tel. 0222/533–3114, fax 0222/535–0319).

Tourist Information

Dürnstein (Parkplatz Ost, tel. 02711/219 or 02711/200).
Klosterneuburg (Niedermarkt, Postfach 6, tel. 02243/2038, fax 02243/86773).
Krems (Undstr. 6, tel. 02732/82676, fax 02732/70011—also covers **Stein an der Donau**).
Melk (Linzerstr. 3–5, tel. 02752/2307–32, fax 02752/2307–37).
Tulln (Albrechtsg. 32, tel. 02272/5836).

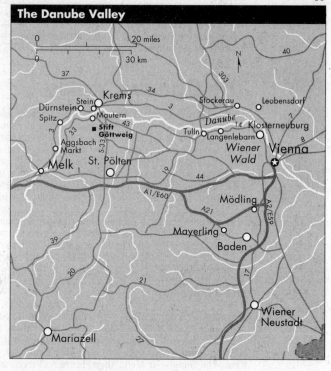

The Danube Valley

Exploring the Danube Valley

North of Vienna lies **Klosterneuburg,** whose huge **abbey** dominates the market town. The abbey's extensive vineyards offer excellent wines; the abbey itself is a major agricultural landowner in the region. *Guided tours every half hour (winter schedule may vary) Mon.–Sat. 9–11 and 1:30–5, Sun. 11 and 1:30–5.*

If you are driving, you have the choice of either following the riverbank or heading up over the village of St. Andrae and down to the river plain again. At **Tulln,** the **town hall** dominates the town square.

You will see **Stift Göttweig** long before you reach it. This impressive, 11th-century Benedictine abbey affords sensational views of the Danube Valley; walk around the grounds and view the impressive chapel. *Rte. 303, on the south bank of the Danube, opposite Krems.*

Time Out | Have lunch at the **Stiftskeller.** If the weather is clear, sit out on the open terrace and enjoy the magnificent views of the Danube in the distance. The local wines are excellent. *Open Apr.–Oct., daily.*

Farther along the valley is the abbey of **Melk,** holding a commanding position over the Danube. The library is rich in art as well as books; the ceiling frescoes are particularly memorable. *Tel. 02752/2312. Admission: AS45 adults, AS20 children. Admission (with guided tour): AS55 adults, AS30 children. Open April–Sept., daily 9–5; Oct., daily 9–4; Nov.–Mar., daily 11 and 2 (by tour only).*

Cross to the north of the river and head back downstream. The beautiful medieval town of **Dürnstein** is known for having kept Richard the Lionhearted imprisoned in its now-ruined castle for 13 months. The town is also known for its fine hotels, restaurants, and wines. Virtually next door is **Stein,** with its former **Imperial Toll House** and the 14th-century **Minoritenkirche,** a church that now serves as an exhibition showcase. Stein and Krems sit at the center of Austria's foremost wine-growing region.

The road back to Vienna now wanders away from the Danube, crossing through some attractive woodlands. When you reach Leobensdorf, you'll spot **Burg Kreuzenstein,** perched to the left upon a nearby hilltop. The castle includes a small museum of armor. *Tours daily 9–4, according to demand.*

Dining and Lodging

For details and price-category definitions, *see* Dining and Lodging in Staying in Austria, *above.*

Dürnstein
Lodging
★ **Schlosshotel.** This early Baroque castle has been luxuriously converted. Try for a room overlooking the Danube. Eat in the celebrated restaurant, and don't miss out on the house wines. *Dürnstein 2, tel. 02711/212, fax 02711/351. 37 rooms with bath or shower. Facilities: sauna, pool. Closed Nov.–Mar. AE, DC, MC, V. Very Expensive.*

Krems
Lodging
Alte Post. A 16th-century house with an arcaded courtyard, the Alte Post is conveniently positioned right in the center of town. In good weather the courtyard is used for dining. *Obere Landstr. 32, tel. 02732/82276, fax 02732/84396. 20 rooms, most with bath. No credit cards. Closed Jan. and Feb. Inexpensive.*

Langenlebarn
Dining
★ **Zum Roten Wolf.** This outstanding, elegant country restaurant serves traditional local foods and superb wines. *Bahnstr. 58, tel. 02272/2567. Reservations advised. Closed Mon. and Tues. AE, DC, MC, V. Expensive.*

Mautern
Dining
★ **Landhaus Bacher.** The Landhaus Bacher is one of Austria's best restaurants, elegant but entirely lacking in pretension. Dining in the garden during the summer adds to the experience. *Südtirolerplatz 208, tel. 02732/829–370, fax 02732/74337. Reservations required. Jacket and tie advised. Closed Nov.–Apr., Mon., Tues.; May–Oct. and late Jan.–late Feb., Mon. and Tues. lunch. DC, V. Very Expensive.*

Salzburg

Arriving and Departing

By Plane For information, phone Salzburg airport, tel. 0662/852091.

Between the Airport and Downtown Buses leave for the Salzburg train station at Südtirolerplatz every 15 minutes during the day, every half hour at night. Journey time is 18 minutes. Taxi fare runs about AS150–AS170.

By Train Salzburg's main train station is at Südtirolerplatz. Train information, tel. 0662/1717; telephone ticket orders and seat reservations, tel. 0662/1700.

By Bus The central bus terminal (post office bus information: tel. 0662/167; railroad bus information: tel. 0662/872150) is in front of the train station, although during construction of the underground garage in front of the rail station bus stops may be moved to various points around the square.

By Car Salzburg has several autobahn exits; study the map and decide which one is best for you. Parking is available in the cavernous garages under the Mönchsberg, and in other garages around the city; look for the large blue "P" signs.

Getting Around

By Bus and Trolleybus Service is frequent and reliable; route maps are available from the tourist office or your hotel. Save money by buying a Salzburg-1 (24-hour) or Salzburg-3 (72-hour) ticket that is good on all trolley and bus lines, on the funicular up to the fortress, on the Mönchsberg lift, and on the rail line north to Bergheim; half-price tickets for children 6–15. Local transportation information, tel. 0662/6205–5131.

By Taxi At festival time, taxis are too scarce to hail on the street, so order through your hotel porter or phone 0662/8111 or 0662/1716.

By Fiaker Fiakers, or horsedrawn cabs, are available at the railroad station and at Residenzplatz (tel. 0662/844772).

By Car Don't even think of it! The old part of the city is a pedestrian zone. Cars are totally forbidden in the entire Old City on weekends. Many other parts of the city have restricted parking (indicated by a blue pavement stripe), either reserved for residents with permits, or for a restricted period. Get parking tickets from coin-operated dispensers on street corners; instructions are also in English.

Guided Tours

Guided bus tours of the city and its environs are given by **Salzburg Sightseeing Tours** (Mirabellplatz 2, tel. 0662/881615) and **Salzburg Panorama Tours** (Mirabellplatz/St. Andrä Church, tel. 0662/ 874029). Both can organize chauffeur-driven tours for up to eight people. Your hotel will have details.

Tourist Information

Salzburg's official tourist office, **Stadtverkehrsbüro,** has an **information center** at Mozartplatz 5, tel. 0662/847568, and at the main train station, tel. 0662/871712. The main office is at Auerspergstrasse 7, tel. 0662/889870.

Exploring Salzburg

Numbers in the margin correspond to points of interest on the Salzburg map.

Salzburg is best known as the birthplace of Wolfgang Amadeus Mozart and receives its greatest number of visitors during the annual Music Festival in July and August. Dominated by a fortress on one side and a minimountain (Kapuzinerberg) on the other, this Baroque city is best explored on foot. Many areas are pedestrian precincts. Some of the most interesting boutiques and shops are found in the dozens of alleys and passageways that link streets and squares. And take an umbrella: Salzburg is noted for sudden, brief downpours that start as abruptly as they stop.

The Salzach River separates the old and new towns; for the best perspective on the old, climb the **Kapuziner** hill (pathways from the Linzerstrasse or Steingasse). Once back down at river level, walk up

① through Markartplatz to the **Landestheater,** where operas and operettas are staged during the winter months; the larger houses used during the festival are closed most of the year. Wander through the Baroque **Mirabell** gardens in back of the theater and enjoy a dramatic view of the Old City, with the castle in the background. If you are
② pressed for time, you can pass up the **Baroque Museum.** *Admission: AS40 adults, AS20 children. Open Tues.–Sat. 9–noon and 2–5, Sun. 9–noon.*

③ However, be sure to look inside **Schloss Mirabell.** It houses public offices, including that of the city's registrar; many couples come here for the experience of being married in such a sumptuous setting. The foyer and staircase, decorated with cherubs, are good examples of Baroque excess. *Mirabellplatz, tel. 0662/8072–2258. Open Mon.– Thurs. 8–4, Fri. 8–1.*

Head left down Schwarzstrasse, back toward the center of the city.
④ On your left is the famed **Mozarteum,** a music academy (Schwarzstr. 26, tel. 0662/889400) whose courtyard encloses the summerhouse in which Mozart wrote his opera *The Magic Flute.* Cross over the Markartsteg footbridge to the Old City side of the Salzach river.
⑤ Turn right and walk a short distance up the Kai to the **Carolino Augusteum Museum.** This is the city museum, whose collections include art, archaeology, and musical instruments. *Museumsplatz 1, tel. 0662/843145. Admission: AS40 adults, AS15 children; combined ticket with toy museum in Bürgerspital (see below), cathedral excavations, and Folklore Museum: AS60 adults, AS20 children. Open Tues.–Thurs. and weekends 9–5, Fri. 9–8.*

Time Out From the Carolinum, as the museum is called, turn the corner into Gstättengasse. On your right is the Mönchsberg elevator, which will take you to the top of the promontory. Once here, follow the signs and path south to **Burgerwehr-Einkehr** (Am Mönchsberg 19c, tel. 0662/841729); it offers superb views of the city, with the fortress in the background. It's a delightful hike over the ridge to the fortress from here (making the trip in reverse, however, will save you an uphill climb). *No credit cards. Closed mid-Oct.–May.*

---

⑥ Returning to city level, follow the Gstättengasse to the **Bürgerspital,** which houses a toy and musical instruments museum within its Renaissance arcades. *Bürgerspitalplatz 2, tel. 0662/847560. Admission: AS30 adults, AS10 children; combined ticket with Carolino Augusteum. Open Tues.–Sun. 9–5.*

Ahead is Herbert-von-Karajan-Platz, whose central **Pferde-schwemme** (Horse Fountain) is its most notable feature. Built into
⑦ the side of the mountain itself is the **Festspielhaus,** a huge complex where Salzburg's annual festival, the Festspiel, is held. *Hofstallgasse 1, tel. 0662/80450.*

From the Festspielhaus, turn left into the Wiener-Philharmoniker-
⑧ Strasse. The **Kollegienkirche** (Collegiate Church) on the left is the work of Fischer von Erlach and is one of the best examples of Baroque architecture anywhere; be sure to look inside. Cut under the covered passageway and turn right into Sigmund-Haffner Gasse. At
⑨ the corner on the left stands the 13th-century **Franziskanerkirche** (Franciscan Church), an eclectic mix of architectural styles, with Romanesque and Gothic accents. Nearby, at Domplatz, is the Salz-
⑩ burg **Dom** (cathedral), a magnificently proportioned building; note the great bronze doors as you enter.

Alter Markt, **14**
Baroque Museum, **2**
Bürgerspital, **6**
Carolino Augusteum
Museum, **5**
Dom, **10**
Festspielhaus, **7**
Festung
Hohensalzburg, **11**
Franziskanerkirche, **9**
Kollegienkirche, **8**
Landestheater, **1**
Mozarteum, **4**
Mozart's
Birthplace, **15**
Residenz, **13**
Schloss Hellbrunn, **16**
Schloss Mirabell, **3**
Stiftskirche
St. Peter, **12**

Salzburg

KEY

AE American Express Office

i Tourist Information

To reach the fortress on the hill above, walk under the arcade to the right side of the church and up the narrow Festungsgasse at the back end of Kapitalplatz. From here, you can either follow the footpath up the hill or take a five-minute ride on the Festungsbahn, the inclined railway cable car. On a sunny day, a far more pleasurable— and strenuous!—route is to hike up the Festungsgasse, turning frequently to enjoy the changing panorama of the city below.

Time Out **Stieglkeller** offers a wide choice of good Austrian fare, served outdoors in summer. The local beer is superb. Try the *Salzburger Nockerln,* a heavenly meringue dessert. Stop here during the day; evenings feature a *Sound of Music* dinner theater. *Festungsgasse 10, tel. 0662/842681. Closed Oct.–Apr.*

⓫ Once you've reached the **Festung Hohensalzburg** itself, you can wander around on your own (admission: AS30 adults, AS15 children) or take a tour (AS30 adults, AS15 children in addition to admission). The views from the 12th-century fortress are magnificent in all directions. A main attraction is **St. George's Chapel,** built in 1501. A year later, in 1502, the Festung acquired the 200-pipe barrel organ, which plays daily in summer at 7 AM, 11 AM, and 6 PM. *Mönchsberg, tel. 0662/8042–2133. Open June–Sept., daily 8–7; Oct.–May, daily 8–6. Guided tour schedule varies.*

⓬ Back down in the city, follow the wall to **Stiftskirche St. Peter** (St. Peter's Abbey). The cemetery lends an added air of mystery to the monk's caves cut into the cliff. The catacombs attached to the church can be visited by guided tour. *Just off Kapitalplatz, tel. 0662/844–5780. Admission: AS12 adults, AS8 children. Tours each hour May–Sept., daily 10–5; Oct.–Apr., daily 11–noon and 1:30–3:30.*

⓭ Head around the cathedral to the spacious Residenzplatz, a vast and elegant square. The **Residenz** itself includes prince-archbishop's living quarters and representative rooms. *Residenzpl. 1, tel. 0662/8042–2690. Admission: AS40 adults, children free. Tours Sept.–June, weekdays at 10–noon, 2, and 3; July–Aug., daily every 20 mins. from 10 to 4:40.*

The **Residenzgalerie,** in the same building complex, has an outstanding collection of 16th- to 19th-century European art. *Residenzplatz 1, tel. 0662/8042–2270. Admission: AS40 adults, children free. Combined ticket with state rooms: AS60. Open daily 10–5. Closed on Wed. Oct.–Jan.; closed Feb.–late Mar.*

⓮ From the lower end of Residenzplatz, cut across into the **Alter Markt,** which still serves as an open market. Salzburg's narrowest house is squeezed into the north side of the square. Turn left into Getreidegasse, a tiny street packed with boutiques and fascinating
⓯ shops. At the head of the tiny Rathausplatz is **Mozart's birthplace,** now a museum. *Getreidegasse 9, tel. 0662/844313. Admission: AS60 adults, AS15 children. Open daily 9–6; during festival, daily 9–7.*

Wander along Getreidegasse, with its ornate wrought-iron shop signs and the Mönchsberg standing sentinel at the far end. Don't neglect the warren of interconnecting side alleys: These include a number of fine shops and often open onto impressive inner courtyards that, in summer, are guaranteed to be filled with flowers.

⓰ One popular excursion from Salzburg is to **Schloss Hellbrunn,** about 5 kilometers (3 miles) outside the city. Take bus line 55. The castle was built during the 17th century, and its rooms have some fine trompe l'oeil decorations. The castle's full name is Lustschloss Hellbrunn—Hellbrunn Pleasure Castle. It was designed for the relaxation of Salzburg's prince-bishops and includes the **Wasserspiele,** or fountains, conceived by someone with an impish sense of humor. Expect to get sprinkled as water shoots up from unlikely spots, such as the center of the table at which you're seated. The Baroque fountains are also fascinating. Both the castle and the fountain gardens can be included on a tour. *Tel. 0662/820372. Admission: AS48 adults, AS24 children. Tours Apr. and Oct., daily 9–4:30; May–Sept., daily 9–5. Evening tours July–Aug. on the hour 6–10.*

The Hellbrunn complex houses the **Tiergarten** (zoo), which is outstanding because of the way in which the animals have been housed in natural surroundings. *Tel. 0662/820176. Admission: AS50 adults, AS25 children. Open Oct.–Mar., daily 8:30–4; Apr.–Sept., daily 8:30–6.* You can also visit the small **folklore museum.** *Admission: AS20 adults, AS10 children. Open Easter–Oct., daily 9–5.*

Dining

Some of the city's best restaurants are in the leading hotels. This is a tourist town, and popular restaurants are always crowded, so make reservations well ahead, particularly during festival time. For details and price-category definitions, *see* Dining in Staying in Austria, *above.*

Expensive **Goldener Hirsch.** The return to more traditional Austrian and international cuisine suits the preferences of the musical and theater celebrities who regularly dine in these chic rooms. But don't overlook such specialties as fillet of catfish in anchovy sauce or game in season. The same kitchen serves the cheaper **s'Herzl** next door. *Getreidegasse 37, tel. 0662/848511. Reservations required. AE, DC, MC, V.*

Mirabell. Although it's housed in a chain hotel (the Sheraton), the Mirabell is among the city's top restaurants. The menu mixes international dishes with adventurous versions of such local specialties as Wiener schnitzel and *Wild-schwein* (wild boar). *Auerspergstr. 4, tel. 0662/889995. Reservations advised. AE, DC, MC, V.*

★ **Zum Eulenspiegel.** The intimate rooms of an Old City house contribute to the charm of this city restaurant. *Hagenauerplatz 2, tel. 0662/843180. Reservations advised. MC, V. Closed Sun. except during festival, and early Jan.–mid-Mar.*

Moderate **Zipfer Bierhaus.** Such standards as tasty roast pork with bread dumplings seem appropriate in this informal setting of arched ceilings and brick floors, one of the oldest *Gasthäuser* in town. *Sigmund-Haffner-Gasse 12/Universitätsplatz 19, tel. 0662/840745. Reservations advised. No credit cards. Closed Sun.*

★ **Zum Mohren.** Arched ceilings in the lower rooms add atmosphere to this historic house. Duck and venison are specialties. *Judengasse 9, tel. 0662/842387. Reservations advised. No credit cards. Closed Sun. and holidays.*

Inexpensive **Mundenhammer.** Local favorites such as roast pork taste particularly good in this stylized rustic setting. The goulash soup is splendid, as are the steak sandwiches and vegetarian specialties. *Rainerstr. 2, tel. 0662/875693. Reservations advised. AE, DC, MC, V. Closed Sun. and holidays.*

Sternbräu. If you're not looking for anything too fancy, try the hearty sausages and roasted meats at this vast complex, which has a pleasant garden in summer. *Griesgasse 23, tel. 0662/842140. No credit cards.*

★ **Wilder Mann.** The atmosphere may be too smoky for some (choose the outside courtyard in summer), but the beamed ceiling and antlers are genuine, as are the food and value. Try the *Tellerfleisch* (boiled beef) or game in season. *Getreidegasse 20/Griesgasse 17 (passageway), tel. 0662/841787. Reservations advised. No credit cards. Closed Sun.*

Lodging

Reservations are always advisable and are essential at festival time (both Easter and summer). For details and price-category definitions, *see* Lodging in Staying in Austria, *above.*

Very Expensive

Bristol. The attractive Belle Epoque facade of the Bristol will prepare you for the comfortable rooms and period furnishings inside. It is one of Austria's classic hotels. *Markartplatz 3, tel. 0662/873557, fax 0662/873557–6. 65 rooms with bath or shower. Facilities: restaurant, bar, garage. AE, DC, MC, V. Closed Jan.–Mar.*

★ **Goldener Hirsch.** This old-timer—800 years old and an inn since 1564—is conveniently set right in the heart of the Old City. Arched corridors, vaulted stairs, rustic furniture, and antiques provide a medieval atmosphere; the essential modern appliances stay ingeniously hidden. The restaurant (*see* Dining, *above*) is excellent. *Getreidegasse 35–37, tel. 0662/848511, fax 0662/843349. 75 rooms with bath. Facilities: restaurant, garage. AE, DC, MC, V.*

Österreichischer Hof. Salzburg's grande dame occupies a lovely riverside location, and the favored rooms give views of the fortress and the Old City. The house restaurants are disappointing. *Schwarzstr. 5–7, tel. 0662/88977, fax 0662/88977–14. 120 rooms, 118 with bath or shower. Facilities: 4 restaurants, garage. AE, DC, MC, V.*

Schloss Mönchstein. With its sensational location overlooking the city, this is a top, if expensive, hotel. The restaurant is one of the best in the city. *Mönchsberg 26, tel. 0662/848555, fax 0662/848559. 17 rooms with bath. Facilities: restaurant, garage, tennis. AE, DC, MC, V.*

Sheraton. A Sheraton is a Sheraton, but this one has one of Salzburg's best restaurants. The location, beside the Mirabell Gardens, is a plus. *Auerspergstr. 4, tel. 0662/889990, fax 0662/881776. 165 rooms with bath. Facilities: restaurant, garage, indoor pools, laundry, health spa adjacent. AE, DC, MC, V.*

Expensive

Bayrischer Hof. Not as close to the downtown area as visitors may want, but only two blocks from the train station. The modern rooms are very comfortable—which may explain why they're almost always full. *Kaiserschützenstr. 1, tel. 0662/469700, fax 0662/46970–75. 60 rooms with bath or shower. Facilities: 3 restaurants, garage. AE, DC, MC, V.*

★ **Elefant.** This charming old inn in the heart of the Old City has been totally modernized without losing the carpets, country furniture, or resultant atmosphere. *Sigmund-Haffner-Gasse 4, tel. 0662/843397, fax 0662/840109–28. 36 rooms with bath or shower. Facilities: restaurant, garage. AE, DC, MC, V.*

Gablerbräu. A country inn transported to town, the Gablerbräu is convenient and an obvious favorite with repeat visitors. *Linzergasse 9, tel. 0662/88965, fax 0662/88965–55. 51 rooms with bath or shower. Facilities: restaurant. AE, DC, MC, V.*

Moderate

Markus Sittikus. This hotel is reasonably priced and more than reasonably comfortable. The train station is within walking distance unless you're loaded with luggage. *Markus-Sittikus-Str. 20, tel. 0662/871–1210, fax 0662/871121–58. 41 rooms with bath or shower. AE, DC, MC, V.*

★ **Wolf.** The family touch reins in this intimate, well-located hotel with spotless rooms in country decor. Book well ahead. *Kaigasse 7, tel. 0662/843453, fax 0662/842423–4. 12 rooms with bath. AE.*

The Arts

Festivals   Tickets for the festival performances are almost impossible to get once you are in Salzburg. Write or fax ahead to **Salzburger Festspiele,** Postfach 140, A-5010 Salzburg, fax 0662/846682.

Opera, Music,   Theater and opera are presented in the **Festspielhaus** (*see* Explor-
and Art   ing, *above*), opera and operetta at the **Landestheater** (Schwarzstr. 22, tel. 0662/871–5120), and concerts at the **Mozarteum** (Schwarzstr. 26, tel. 0662/873154). Chamber music—in costume—is performed in **Schloss Mirabell.** Special art exhibits in the **Carolino Augusteum** (*see* Exploring, *above*) are often outstanding.

Innsbruck

Arriving and Departing

By Plane   The airport is 4 kilometers (2 miles) to the west of the city. For flight information, phone 0512/22220.

Between the   Buses (Line F) to the city center (Maria-Theresien-Str.) run every
Airport and   20 minutes and take about 20 minutes. Get your ticket from the bus
Downtown   driver; it costs AS18. Taxis should take no more than 10–15 minutes into town, and the fare is about AS120–AS150.

By Train   All trains stop at the city's main station at Südtiroler-Platz. Train connections are available to Munich, Vienna, Rome, and Zurich. For train information, phone 0512/1717. Ticket reservations, tel. 0512/1700.

By Bus   The terminal is to the right of the main train station.

By Car   Exit from the east–west autobahn or from the Brenner autobahn running south to Italy. Much of the downtown area is pedestrian zone or paid-parking only; get parking vouchers at tobacco shops, coin-operated dispensers, or the city tourist office at Burggraben 3.

Getting Around

By Bus and   Most bus and streetcar routes begin or end at Südtiroler-Platz, site
Streetcar   of the main train station. The bus is the most convenient way to reach the six major ski areas outside the city. Many hotels offer free transportation with direct hotel pickup; for those staying in the Old City, the buses leave from in front of the Landestheater.

By Taxi   Taxis are not much faster than walking, particularly along the one-way streets and in the Old City. To order a radio cab, phone 0512/5311 or 0512/45500.

Guided Tours

Sightseeing   Bus tours lasting 2 hours cover the city's highlights and leave from
Tours   the hotel information office at the railroad station (Südtiroler-Platz) daily at noon and at 12:10 from the Hypobank, across from the Tiroler Landesreisebüro on Bozner-Platz. During the summer, additional buses are scheduled at 10 and 2, and there are shorter tours Monday through Saturday at 10:15, noon, 2, and 3:15. Your hotel or one of the tourist offices will have tickets and details.

Tourist Information

The city's two main tourist offices are at Burggraben 3 (tel. 0512/
5356, fax 0512/535643, daily 8–7—Innsbruck) and Wilhelm-Greil-
Strasse 17 (tel. 0512/532–0170, fax 0512/532–0175 weekdays 8:30–8,
Sat. 9–noon—Tirol).

American Express (Brixnerstr. 3, tel. 0512/582491, fax 0512/
573385).
Wagon-Lits Travel (Brixnerstr. 2, tel. 0512/520790, fax 0512/520–
7985).

Exploring Innsbruck

*Numbers in the margin correspond to points of interest on the Inns-
bruck map.*

Squeezed by the mountains and sharing the valley with the Inn River, Innsbruck is compact and very easy to explore on foot. The medieval city—it received its municipal charter in 1239—no doubt owes
much of its fame and charm to its unique situation. To the north, the
steep, sheer sides of the Alps rise like a shimmering blue-and-white
wall from the edge of the city, an awe-inspiring backdrop to the mellow green domes and red roofs of the picturesque Baroque town.

Modern-day Innsbruck retains close associations with three historical figures: Emperor Maximilian I and Empress Maria Theresa,
both of whom are responsible for much of the city's architecture, and
Andreas Hofer, a Tirolean patriot. You will find repeated references
to these personalities as you tour the city. A good starting point is
① the **Goldenes Dachl** (the Golden Roof), which made the ancient mansion whose balcony it covers famous. (It's actually made of copper
tiles guilded with 14 kg [31 lbs.] of gold.) The building now houses an
Olympic Museum, which features videotapes of the Innsbruck winter Olympics. *Herzog Friedrich-Str. 15, tel. 0512/536–0575. Admission: AS22 adults, AS11 children. Open daily 9:30–5:30. Closed on
Mon. Nov.–Feb.*

② A walk up the Hofgasse brings you to the **Hofburg,** the Rococo imperial palace, with its ornate reception hall decorated with portraits
of Maria Theresa's ancestors. *Rennweg 1, tel. 0512/587186. Admission: AS50 adults, AS10 children. Open mid-May–mid-Oct., daily
9–5; mid-Oct.–mid-May, Mon.–Sat. 9–5.*

③ Close by is the **Hofkirche,** the Imperial Church, built as a mausoleum for Maximilian. The emperor is surrounded by 24 marble reliefs
portraying his accomplishments, as well as 28 oversize statues of his
ancestors, including the legendary King Arthur. Andreas Hofer is
also buried here. Don't miss the silver chapel with its ornate altar.
The **Tiroler Volkskunstmuseum** (Tirolean Folk Art Museum) is
housed in the Hofkirche, too, and shows costumes, rustic furniture,
and farmhouse rooms decorated in styles ranging from Gothic to Rococo. *Universitätsstr. 2, tel. 0512/584302. Admission: AS20 adults,
children free (Hofkirche), AS40 adults, AS15 children (Volkskunstmuseum); combined ticket: AS50 adults. Hofkirche open Sept.–
June, daily 9–5; July–Aug. daily 9–5:30. Volkskunstmuseum open
Sept.–June, Mon.–Sat. 9–5, Sun. 9–noon; July–Aug., Mon.–Sat.
9–5:30, Sun. 9–noon.*

④ Follow Museumstrasse to the **Ferdinandeum,** which houses
Austria's largest collection of Gothic art, as well as paintings from
the 19th and 20th centuries. *Museumstr. 15, tel. 0512/594–8971. Admission: AS50 adults, AS20 children. Open May–Sept., daily 10–5,*

Innsbruck

Major Attractions
Annasäule, **6**
Ferdinandeum, **4**
Goldenes Dachl, **1**
Hofburg, **2**
Hofkirche, **3**
Triumphpforte, **5**

Other Attractions
Dom zu St. Jakob, **9**
Helblinghaus, **8**
Stadtturm, **7**
Tiroler Volkskunst-
museum, **10**

Thurs. eve. 7–9; Oct.–Apr., Tues.–Sat. 10–noon and 2–5, Sun. and holidays 10–1.

Time Out Relax over coffee, excellent pastries, and a newspaper in just about any language you want under the crystal chandeliers at **Café Central,** in the Hotel Central, just off Wilhelm Greil-Str. *Gilmstr. 5, tel. 0512/5920. AE, DC, MC, V. Closed Nov.*

➎ Cut back down Wilhelm Greil-Strasse to the **Triumphpforte** (Triumphal Arch), built in 1765, and walk up Maria Theresien-Strasse past
➏ the **Annasäule** (Anna Column) for a classic "postcard" view of Innsbruck with the Alps in the background.

Off the Beaten Track

Just 3 kilometers (2 miles) southeast of the city and easily reached by either bus or streetcar is **Schloss Ambras,** one of Austria's finest and best-preserved castles. Originally dating from the 11th century, it was later rebuilt as a residence for the archduke Ferdinand of Tirol (from 1564 to 1582), so most of what you now see is in German Renaissance style. The collection includes numerous pictures (including the only known portrait of Count Dracula), weapons, armor, objets d'art, and furniture. *In the village of Ambras (streetcar line 3 or bus K), tel. 0512/48446. Admission: AS60 adults, AS30 children. Open Apr.–Oct., Wed.–Mon. 10–5; Jan.–Mar. 2–3 only, by tour, for an additional AS20. Verify opening dates and times.*

In the mountains high above the city is the unique **Alpine Zoo,** with alpine animals and birds in their native environment and even an aquarium. And, of course, there's a restaurant at the top. You can either hike up or take the Hungerberg funicular, then the cable car. A combination funicular-cable entry card is available at the Hungerberg ticket office. *Weiherburggasse 37, tel. 0512/292323. Admission: AS56 adults, AS28 children. Open summer, daily 9–6; winter, daily 9–dusk.*

A visit to the 400-year-old operating **Grassmayr Bell Foundry** shows how bells are cast and tuned. Take Bus J, K, or S south to Grassmayrstrasse. *Leopoldstr. 53, tel. 0512/59418. Admission: AS20 adults, AS10 children. Open weekdays 9–6, Sat. 9–noon.*

Dining

For details and price-category definitions, *see* Dining in Staying in Austria, *above.*

Expensive **Europa-Stüberl.** Regional specialties and the resplendent setting are two reasons why the Hotel Europa's (*see* Lodging, *below*) restaurant is highly regarded by locals and visitors. *Brixnerstr. 6, tel. 0512/593–1648. Reservations advised. AE, DC, MC, V.*
Schwarzer Adler. This place drips with atmosphere, its massive-beamed rooms a perfect backdrop for typical Austrian dishes like *Knödeln* (dumplings) and *Tafelspitz* (boiled beef). *Kaiserjägerstr. 2, tel. 0512/587109. Reservations advised. AE, DC, MC, V. Closed Sun. and mid-Jan.*
★ **Tiroler Stuben.** The rustic pine setting in the Alpotel is just right for garlic soup and house specialties such as *Bauernschöpsenes,* a delicious lamb plate. *Innrain 13, tel. 0512/577931. Reservations required. AE, DC, MC, V. Closed Sat. lunch, Sun., and holidays.*

Moderate **Goethestube.** The wine tavern of the city's oldest inn, the Goldener Adler (*see* Lodging, *below*), is one of Innsbruck's best. It was here that Goethe (who lent his name to the tavern) sipped quantities of red South Tirolean wine during his stays in 1786 and 1790. *Herzog Friedrich-Str. 6, tel. 0512/586334. Reservations not necessary. AE, DC, MC, V. No lunch.*

★ **Hirschenstuben.** Old-fashioned hospitality and dark-wood trimmings are found in force at this charming local favorite. Game is particularly good here. *Kiebachgasse 5, tel. 0512/582979. Reservations advised. AE, DC, MC, V. Closed Sun.*

★ **Ottoburg.** A rabbit warren of rooms, in a 13th-century building, the Ottoburg is exactly right for an intimate, cozy lunch or dinner. It's packed with Austriana and is 100% genuine. Go for the trout if it's available. *Herzog Friedrich-Str. 1, tel. 0512/574652. Reservations advised. AE, DC, MC, V.*

Stieglbräu. Lovers of good beer will be delighted to find this popular rustic spot, which, in addition to its thirst-quenching brews, provides good, solid Austrian fare. Portions are huge, the garden exceptionally pleasant. *Wilhelm-Greil-Str. 25, 0512/584338. No credit cards.*

Inexpensive **Gasthaus Steden.** The substantial portions and unassuming (if occasionally smoky) atmosphere attract visiting business people as well as many local regulars to this thoroughly genuine *Gasthaus*. The roast pork is particularly tasty and the daily specials are a bargain. *Anichstr. 15, tel. 0512/580890. No reservations. No credit cards. Closed Sun.*

Weinhaus Happ. Some of the smaller rooms upstairs in this historic house may be a bit smoky, and service falters if groups arrive, but local specialties such as game in season are excellent. *Herzog Friedrich-Str. 14, tel. 0512/582980. Reservations advised. AE, DC, MC, V. Closed Sun.*

Lodging

For details and price-category definitions, *see* Lodging in Staying in Austria, *above.*

Very Expensive **Europa.** The Europa is a postwar building blessed with a considerable amount of charm. Some rooms have period furnishings; others are 20th-century modern. *Südtiroler Platz 2, tel. 0512/5931, fax 0512/587800. 132 rooms with bath. Facilities: restaurant, bar, beauty salon, sauna, solarium, garage. AE, DC, MC, V.*

★ **Goldener Adler.** The Golden Eagle has been an inn since 1390, and over the centuries it has welcomed nearly every king, emperor, duke, or poet who passed through the city. The facade looks suitably medieval, and inside, passages and stairs twist romantically and rooms crop up when least expected. The several restaurants offer well-prepared seasonal and local dishes. *Herzog Friedrich-Str. 6, tel. 0512/586334, fax 0512/584409. 40 rooms with bath or shower. Facilities: restaurants, bar, coffee shop. AE, DC, MC, V.*

Scandic Crown. Innsbruck's newest major hotel belongs to the leading Scandinavian chain. The rooms are modern plush; the facilities, including sauna, are extensive. The buffet lunch is good value and abundant. The train station is nearby. *Salurnerstr. 15, tel. 0512/59350, fax 0512/593-5220. 176 rooms with bath. Facilities: restaurants, bar, health club, pool, sauna, garage. AE, DC, MC, V.*

Schwarzer Adler. Rooms are individual, warm, and inviting in this traditional Romantik Hotel. It's an easy stroll to the Old City. *Kaiserjägerstr. 2, tel. 0512/587109, fax 0512/561697. 27 rooms. Facilities: 2 restaurants, bar, garage. AE, DC, MC, V.*

Expensive **Alpotel.** Abundant space, comfort, and modern style are the keys in this new hotel on the edge of the Old City. The staff is particularly helpful. Many rooms have balconies with splendid views. The Tiroler Stuben restaurant (*see* Dining, *above*) is very good. *Innrain 13 (Ursulinenpassage), tel. 0512/577931, fax 0512/577931–15. 75 rooms with bath. Facilities: restaurant, sauna, solarium, bar, café, garage, transportation to ski areas. AE, DC, MC, V.*

Moderate **Goldene Krone.** The smallish rooms in this older hotel are clean and
★ adequate, and the location on the main square is splendid, if not directly in the old city. You can easily walk the two longish blocks from the railroad station. Rooms on the Maximilianstrasse side are less quiet but look across to the attractive Art Deco building opposite. *Maria Theresien-Str. 48, tel. 0512/586160, fax 0512/580189–6. 35 rooms. Facilities: café. AE, DC, MC, V.*

Tautermann. A former villa north of the river but within walking distance of the city center is now a friendly, family-run hotel. Rooms are done in natural woods and white, and some upper rooms have bay windows with gorgeous views of the nearby mountains. Bus A from the main rail station to Höttinger Kirchenplatz will get you close to the door. *Stamser Feld 5/Höttingergasse, tel. 0512/281572, fax 0512/281572–10. 28 rooms. Facilities: breakfast room, parking. AE, DC, MC, V.*

★ **Weisses Kreuz.** Occupying an honored position just steps away from the famous Goldenes Dachl (*see* Exploring, *above*), Weisses Kreuz is itself a lovely old historic building. *Herzog Friedrich-Str. 31, tel. 0512/594790, fax 0512/59479–90. 39 rooms, 28 with bath or shower. Facilities: restaurant. AE, V.*

Inexpensive **Binder.** A short streetcar trip (Line 3) from the center of town shouldn't be too high a price to pay for less costly comfort at this small, friendly hotel. *Dr.-Glatz-Str. 20, tel. 0512/42236, fax 0512/42236–99. 32 rooms, most with bath or shower. AE, DC, MC, V.*

Riese Haymon. You're across the river in this quaint older but comfortable house and still just minutes from the Old City on foot. *Haymongasse 4, tel. 0512/589837, fax 0512/586190, 30 rooms with bath or shower. Facilities: parking. No credit cards.*

The Arts

Most hotels have a monthly calendar of events (in English). Tickets to most events are available at the main tourist office (Burggraben 3, tel. 0512/5356, fax 0512/535643). Opera, operetta, musicals, and concerts take place at the **Tiroler Landestheater** (Rennweg 2, tel. 0512/520744) and **Kongresshaus** (Rennweg 3, tel. 0512/5936–0).

4 Belgium

Belgium covers a strip of land just under 320 kilometers (200 miles) long and 160 kilometers (100 miles) wide bordering the North Sea between France and Holland. With more than 10 million people, Belgium is the second most densely populated country in the world. Both Parisians and Amsterdammers tend to think of Belgium as a substandard version of "pure" French or Dutch culture. However, Belgium has a distinctive culture, or rather, two: Flemish and Walloon. The Flemish, who speak Dutch (Flemish), inhabit the northern half of the country and account for 56% of the population. The French-speaking Walloons live in the other half. The capital, Brussels, is officially designated a dual-language area.

Belgium is the world's most heavily industrialized country, with only 5% of the working population engaged in agriculture (though they still manage to produce 165 different cheeses and any number of fine sausages). Besides being natural entrepreneurs, the Belgians also work very hard—partly to make up for what has so long been denied them. In the course of history, the Belgians have been ruled by the Romans, French, Spanish, Austrians, Dutch, English, and Germans. Many of Europe's greatest battles have been fought on Belgian soil—from the Hundred Years' War to Waterloo to the long-slogging encounters of World War I. During World War II, this territory witnessed both the initial blitzkrieg of Nazi Panzer units and Hitler's final desperate counterattack against the advancing Allies in the Ardennes—an offensive that has gone down in history as the Battle of the Bulge.

The south of the country is a wild wooded area, with mountains rising to more than 620 meters (2,000 feet). In the Dutch-speaking north, on the other hand, the land is flat and heavily cultivated, much as it is in neighboring Holland. Here stand the medieval Flemish cities of Ghent and Brugge, with their celebrated carillons and canals—not to mention the 68 kilometers (42 miles) of sandy beaches that make up the country's northern coastline. Due north of Brussels lies Antwerp, the country's dynamic seaport. This city, where the painter Rubens lived, is now the world's leading diamond-cutting center.

Brussels stands in the very center of the country. A booming, expanding, and often expensive city, it is now the capital of Europe. Here the European Union (EU) has its headquarters. The city boasts more ambassadors than any other in the world—approximately 160. Partly as a result of this concentration of power and partly because of the Belgians' celebrated love of good food, Brussels has become one of the most renowned gastronomic cities in the world.

As befits a bourgeois culture, the Belgians are great believers in the quality of life. In practice, this means that meals, parks, cars, and houses are large. Homes are highly individualistic and comfortable; trendy designer bars are cozy as well as chic. Except on the road, Belgians are generous and have time for old-fashioned courtesy.

But Belgians are not just creatures of the senses. A robust culture is celebrated in paintings by Bruegel and Rubens, Magritte, and Delvaux and by exciting Gothic, Renaissance, and Art Nouveau architecture. Belgium is no self-publicist, but quietly and confidently waits to be discovered.

Essential Information

Before You Go

When to Go The tourist season runs from early May to late September and peaks in July and August, when the weather is best. In recent years, however, off-season travel has become increasingly popular. In the coastal resorts, some hotels and restaurants remain open all year.

Climate Temperatures range from around 65 F in May to an average 73 F in July and August. In winter, temperatures drop to an average of about 40 to 45 F. Snow is unusual except in the mountains of the Ardennes, where cross-country and Alpine skiing are popular when weather permits.

The following are the average daily maximum and minimum temperatures for Brussels.

Jan.	40F	4C	May	65F	18C	Sept.	69F	21C
	30	– 1		46	8		51	11
Feb.	44F	7C	June	72F	22C	Oct.	60F	15C
	32	0		52	11		45	7
Mar.	51F	11C	July	73F	23C	Nov.	48F	9C
	36	2		54	12		38	3
Apr.	58F	14C	Aug.	72F	22C	Dec.	42F	6C
	41	5		54	12		32	0

Currency The unit of currency in Belgium is the franc. There are bills of 100, 500, 1,000, 2,000, and 10,000 francs in addition to coins of 1, 5, 20, and 50 francs. At press time (spring 1994), the exchange rate was about BF36 to the dollar and BF54 to the pound sterling.

Traveler's checks and credit cards are the safest and simplest ways to carry money. American Express, Bank of America, Barclays, Eurocheques, and Thomas Cook traveler's checks are all honored in Belgium. All major credit cards are widely accepted, too.

What It Will Cost Brussels is a considerably less expensive city than Paris, Zürich, or Frankfurt and on par with London and New York. Deluxe hotels are very expensive but offer substantially discounted weekend and summer rates. There is also a wide selection of reasonably priced establishments, and hotels away from the capital are generally less pricey. Top restaurants are in the $100 range, but you can eat very well in this land of gourmets for a third of that sum. Note that all taxes and service charges are included in hotel and restaurant bills. Gasoline prices conform to the high European average, but the excellent highways are toll free.

Sample Prices A cup of coffee in a café will cost BF45–BF60; a glass of beer, BF35–BF85; and a glass of wine, about BF100. Train travel averages BF6 per mile, the average bus/metro/tram ride costs BF45, theater tickets cost about BF500, and movie tickets about BF250.

Customs on Arrival Since the European Union's 1992 agreement on a unified European market, the limits of what visitors from EU countries may bring in have become generous to the point of being meaningless. For example, travelers from EU nations may now bring in 120 bottles of wine, 10 liters of alcohol, and 800 cigarettes. Duty-free amounts, however, remain unchanged: 300 cigarettes, 5 liters of wine, and 1½ liters of spirits. Visitors from non-EU countries can bring in 200 cigarettes or 50 cigars or 250 grams of tobacco, 2 liters of still wine and 1 liter of spirits or 2 liters of aperitif wine, and 50 grams of perfume. Other goods from non-EU countries may not exceed BF2,000 in value. There are no restrictions on the import or export of currency.

Language Language is a sensitive subject that has led to the collapse of at least two governments. There are three national languages in Belgium: French, spoken primarily in the south of the country (Wallonia); Flemish, spoken in the north; and German, spoken in a small area in the east. Brussels is bilingual, with both French and Flemish officially recognized, though French predominates. Many people speak English in Brussels and in the north (Flanders). If your French is good but your Flemish nonexistent, it is politic to speak English to Flemings. In Wallonia you may have to muster whatever French you possess, but in tourist centers you will be able to find people with at least basic English.

Getting Around

By Car Belgium has an excellent system of expressways, and the main roads
Road are generally very good. Road numbers for main roads have the pre-
Conditions fix N; expressways, the prefix A or E.

Rules of the Drive on the right and pass on the left (passing on the right is forbid-
Road den). Seat belts are compulsory in both front and rear seats. Each car must have a warning triangle to be used in the event of a breakdown or accident. At intersections, particularly in cities, traffic on the right has priority. Adhere strictly to this rule because there are few stop or yield signs. In Brussels, the system of tunnels and ring roads is generally effective. Cars within a traffic circle have priority over cars entering it, but not all drivers agree, so keep a wary eye on traffic from the right. Buses and streetcars have priority over cars. Maximum speed limits are 120 kph (70 mph) on highways, 90 kph (55 mph) on major roads, and 50 kph (30 mph) in cities.

Road Signs Road signs are written in the language of the region, so you need to know that Antwerpen (Flemish) is Anvers (French) and Antwerp to us; likewise, Brugge and Brussel (Flemish) are Bruges and Bruxelles (French); Gent (Flemish) is Gand (French) and Ghent (English). Even more confusing, Liège and Luik are the same place, as are Louvain and Leuven and Namur and Namen. Even more difficult is Mons (French) and its Flemish equivalent, Bergen, or Tournai (French), which becomes Doornik in Flemish!

Parking Most cities have metered on-street parking (parking meters take 5- or 20-franc coins) and parking lots.

By Train Fast and frequent trains connect all main towns and cities. If you intend to travel frequently, buy a **Benelux Tourrail Ticket,** which allows unlimited travel throughout Belgium, Luxembourg, and the Netherlands for any five days during a one-month period. If you are over 26, the cost of the five-day pass is BF5,670 first-class and BF3,780 second-class. For those under 26, the pass costs BF2,950 first-class and BF1,980 second-class. The **Belgian Tourrail Ticket** allows unlimited travel for five days in a 17-day period at a cost of BF2,700 first-class and BF1,800 second-class; for those under 26, BF2,030 first-class and BF1,350 second-class. Young people from 12 to 26 can purchase a **Go Pass** for BF990, valid for eight one-way trips in a six-month period on the Belgian rail network. All of the above are available at any Belgian train station.

Special weekend round-trip tickets are valid from Friday noon to Monday noon: A 40% reduction is available on the first traveler's ticket and a 60% reduction on companions' tickets. During the tourist season there are similar weekday fares to the seaside and the Ardennes.

By Bus Intercity bus service is almost nonexistent. Details of services are available at train stations and tourist offices.

By Bicycle You can rent a bicycle from Belgian railways at 48 stations throughout the country; train travelers get reduced rates. Bicycling is especially popular in the flat northern and coastal areas. Bicycle lanes are provided in many Flemish cities, but bicycling in Brussels is madness.

Staying in Belgium

Telephones Pay phones work mostly with Telecards, available in a number of de-
Local Calls nominations starting from BF200; some phones are coin-operated and take 5- and 20-franc coins. The Telecards can be purchased at any post office and at many newsstands. Most phone booths that accept Telecards have a list indicating where these cards are sold. An average local call costs BF10 or BF20.

International The least expensive method is to buy a high-denomination Telecard
Calls and make a direct call from a phone booth. A five-minute phone call to the United States at a peak time will cost about BF750 by this method. International calls can also be made at most hotels, but nearly all have a service charge that may double the cost. Operator-assisted international calls can also be made at most post offices.

Mail Airmail letters and postcards to the United States cost BF38 for the
Postal Rates first 10 grams and BF4 more for each additional 10 grams. Airmail letters to the United Kingdom are BF16 for the first 20 grams.

Receiving Mail You can have mail forwarded directly to your hotel. If you're uncertain where you'll be staying, have mail sent in care of **American Express** (1 pl. Louise, B-1000 Brussels). Cardholders are spared the $2-per-letter charge.

Shopping When you buy goods for export, you can ask most shops to fill out
Sales-Tax special forms covering VAT or sales tax. An itemized invoice show-
Refunds ing the amount of VAT will also do. When you leave Belgium, you must declare the goods at customs and have the customs officers stamp the documents. Once you're back home, you simply send the stamped forms back to the shop and your sales tax will be refunded. This facility is available in most boutiques and large stores and covers most purchases of more than BF2,000. There's another option as well: In shops displaying a "Europe Tax-Free" sign you will be given a check for slightly *less* than the amount of TVA you have paid; this check can then be redeemed at the airport. It's up to you to decide whether the convenience is worth the slight charge.

Opening and **Banks** are open weekdays from 9 to 4; some close for an hour at
Closing Times lunch. Exchange facilities are usually open on weekends, but you'll get a better rate during the week.

Museums are generally open from 10 to 5 six days a week. Closing day is Monday in Brussels and Antwerp, Tuesday in Brugge. Check individual listings.

Shops are open weekdays and Saturdays from 10 to 6 and generally stay open later on Friday. Some shops close for lunch. Bakeries and some groceries are open Sunday and closed Monday.

National January 1; April 17 (Easter Monday); May 1 (May Day); May 25 (As-
Holidays cension); June 5 (Pentecost Monday); July 21 (National Holiday);

August 15 (Assumption); November 1 (All Saints' Day); November 11 (Armistice); December 25.

Dining Nearly all Belgians take eating seriously and are discerning about fresh produce and innovative recipes. They are prepared to spend a considerable amount on a celebratory meal, and you will almost always find families sharing a meal even in the most expensive restaurants. At the top end of the scale, the *menus de dégustation* offer a chance to sample a large selection of the chef's finest dishes. Fixed-price menus are available in virtually all restaurants and often represent very considerable savings. Menus and prices are always posted outside. Belgian specialties include *lapin à la bière* (rabbit in beer), *faisan à la brabançonne* (pheasant with chicory), *waterzooi* (a rich chicken or fish hotpot), and *carbonnades* (chunky stews). Belgians love their *frites* (french fries) so much that they think they invented them. *Steack et frites* can be found everywhere, from the simplest to the fanciest eating place. For the best cut of beef, ask for *filet pur*.

Local specialties include truly marvelous asparagus from Mechelen, at their best in May; *salade Liègoise*, a hot salad with beans and bacon (Liège); wild strawberries and freshwater fish from the Meuse River (Namur); different permutations of sprouts, chicory, and pheasant (Brussels); and shrimps, oysters, and mussels (Flanders).

Belgian snacks are equally appetizing. The waffle *(gaufre/wafel)* has achieved world fame, but *couques* (sweet buns), *speculoos* (spicy gingerbread biscuits), and *pain d'amandes* (nutty after-dinner biscuits) are less well known. For lunch, cold cuts, rich pâtés, and *jambon d'Ardenne* (Ardenne ham) are popular, often accompanied by goat's cheese and rye or wholemeal bread.

Mealtimes Most hotels serve breakfast until 10. Belgians usually eat lunch between 1 and 3, some making it quite a long, lavish meal. However, the main meal of the day is dinner, which most Belgians eat between 7 and 10; peak dining time used to be about 8, but is now creeping closer to 9.

Dress Belgians tend to be fairly formal and dress conservatively when dining out in the evenings. Generally speaking, the more prestigious the restaurant, the more formal the dress. Younger Belgians favor stylish, casual dress in most restaurants.

Ratings Prices are per person and include a first course, main course, dessert, tip, and sales tax, but no wine. Best bets are indicated by a star ★.

Category	All Areas
Very Expensive	over BF3,500
Expensive	BF2,500–BF3,500
Moderate	BF1,500–BF2,500
Inexpensive	under BF1,500

Lodging You can trust Belgian hotels, almost without exception, to be clean and of a high standard. The more modern hotels in city centers can be very expensive, but there are smaller, well-appointed hotels, offering lodging at excellent rates. The family-run establishments in out-of-the-way spots, such as the Ardennes, can be surprisingly inexpensive, especially if you are visiting them out of season.

Pensions Pensions offer a double room with bath or shower and full board from BF2,500 to BF3,500 in Brussels and from BF2,000 to BF3,000 elsewhere. These terms are often available for a minimum stay of three days.

Youth Hostels For information about youth hostels, contact **Fédération Belge des Auberges de la Jeunesse** (tel. 02/215–31–00). In the United States: **American Youth Hostels, Inc.,** Box 37613, Washington, DC 20013. In the United Kingdom: **Camping and Caravan Club Ltd.,** 11 Lower Grosvenor Pl., London SW1, or **Youth Hostels Association International Travel Bureau,** 14 Southampton St., London WC2.

Camping Belgium is well supplied with camping and caravan sites. For details, contact the **Royal Camping and Caravaning Club of Belgium** (rue Madeleine 31, B-1000 Brussels, tel. 02/513–12–87).

Ratings Hotel prices are inclusive and are usually listed in each room. All prices are for two people in a double room. Best bets are indicated by a star ★.

Category	All Areas
Very Expensive	BF9,000–BF12,000
Expensive	BF6,500–BF9,000
Moderate	BF3,500–BF6,500
Inexpensive	under BF3,500

Tipping Tipping has been losing its hold in Belgium over the past few years because a service charge is almost always figured into the bill. For example, a tip of 16% is included in all restaurant and café bills. The tip is also included in taxi fares. If you want to give more, round the amount up to the nearest BF50 or BF100. Porters in railway stations ask a fixed per-suitcase price, BF30 in the day and BF35 at night. For moderately priced hotels, BF50 should be an adequate tip for bellhops and doormen; in the very expensive hotels, though, BF100 is usually more appropriate. At the movies, tip the usher BF20, whether or not he or she shows you to your seat. In theaters, tip about BF50 for programs. In restaurants, cafés, movie theaters, theaters, train stations, and other public places, you should tip the washroom attendant BF10.

Brussels

Arriving and Departing

By Plane All international flights arrive at Brussels's Zaventem Airport, about a 30-minute drive or a 16-minute train trip from the city center. **Sabena, American, Delta, TWA,** and **United** all fly into Brussels from the United States. **Sabena, British Airways,** and **British Midland** dominate the short-haul London (Heathrow)–Brussels route. **Air UK** flies to Brussels from London (Stansted), and **British Airways** from London (Gatwick). Several regional centers in the United Kingdom also have direct flights to Brussels.

Between the Airport and Downtown There is regular train service from the airport to the Gare du Nord (North Station) and the Gare Centrale (Central Station), which leaves every 20 minutes. The trip takes 16 minutes and costs BF220 (first-class round-trip) and BF140 (second-class round-trip); you can buy a ticket on the train for a BF30 surcharge. The first train from the airport runs at 6:00 AM and the last one leaves at 11:46 PM. A taxi to the city center takes about half an hour and costs about BF1,000. You can save up to 25% on Autolux airport taxi fares by buying a voucher for the return trip at the same time. Beware free-lance taxi drivers who offer their services in the arrival hall.

Via the Chunnel Using "Le Shuttle" under the English Channel cuts total driving time from Dover to Brussels to about three hours, but the 35-minute ride through the tunnel costs £110 to £140 one-way. "Eurostar" train service between London and Brussels via the tunnel, scheduled to start before the end of 1994, will cut travel time to 3 hours 8 minutes, and to 2 hours 35 minutes by 1996. There will be 15 trains a day. Fares (not announced at press time) will be competitive with air fares. Trains stop in Brussels at Gare du Midi, currently being rebuilt.

By Train and Boat/Jetfoil From London, the train service connects with the Ramsgate–Oostende ferry or jetfoil services. From Oostende, the train takes you to Brussels. The whole journey by jetfoil takes just under five hours, but is longer by boat. For reservations and times, contact **British Rail International** in London (tel. 071/834–2345). A one-way London–Brussels ticket costs £44, excluding the £6–£9 (depending on the season) jetfoil supplement.

By Bus and Hovercraft/ Ferry From London, the Hoverspeed City Sprint bus connects with the Dover–Calais Hovercraft, and the bus then takes you on to Brussels. The journey takes 6½ hours; a one-way ticket costs £30. For reservations and times, contact **Hoverspeed** (tel. 034/240–241).

Getting Around

By Métro, Tram, and Bus The métro, trams (streetcars), and buses run as part of the same system. All three are clean and efficient, and a single ticket costs BF50. The best buy is a 10-trip ticket, which costs BF290, or a 24-hour card costing BF220. You need to stamp your ticket in the appropriate machine on the bus or tram; in the métro, your card is stamped as you pass through the automatic barrier. You can purchase these tickets in any métro station or at newsstands. Single tickets can be purchased on the bus.

Detailed maps of the Brussels public transportation network are available in most métro stations and at the Brussels tourist office in the Grand' Place (tel. 02/513–89–40). You get a map free with the new **Tourist Passport** (also available at the tourist office), which for BF220 allows you a 24-hour transport card and BF500 worth of museum admissions.

By Taxi Taxis are expensive, but tips are included in the fare. To call a cab, phone (or have the restaurant or hotel call) **Taxis Verts** (tel. 02/349–49–49) or **Taxis Oranges** (tel. 02/513–62–00) or catch one at a cabstand. The price per kilometer is BF38, but airport taxis charge higher rates.

Important Addresses and Numbers

Tourist Information The main tourist office for **Brussels** is in the Hôtel de Ville on the Grand' Place (tel. 02/513–89–40), open daily 9–6 during the main tourist season (Sun. off-season 10–2; Dec.–Feb., closed Sun.) The main tourist office for the rest of **Belgium** is near the Grand' Place (rue Marché-aux-Herbes 61, tel. 02/504–03–90) and has the same opening hours. There is a tourist office at **Waterloo** (chaussée de

Bruxelles 149, tel. 02/354–99–10); it is open April–November 15, daily 9:30–6:30 and November 16–March, daily 10:30–5.

Embassies **U.S.** (blvd. du Régent 27, B–1000 Brussels, tel. 02/513–38–30). **Canadian** (av. de Tervuren 2, B–1000 Brussels, tel. 02/735–60–40). **U.K.** (rue d'Arlon 85, B–1040 Brussels, tel. 02/287–62–11).

Emergencies **Police** (tel. 101); **Accident** (tel. 100); **Ambulance** (tel. 02/649–11–22); **Doctor** (tel. 02/648–80–00 and 02/479–18–18); **Dentist** (tel. 02/426–10–26); **Pharmacy:** To find out which one is open on a particular night or on weekends, call 02/479–18–18.

English-Language Bookstores **House of Paperbacks** (chaussée de Waterloo 813, Uccle, tel. 02/343–11–22) is open Tuesday–Saturday 10–6. **W. H. Smith** (blvd. Adolphe Max 71–75, tel. 02/219–27–08) is open Monday–Saturday 9–6. **Librairie de Rome** (av. Louise 50b, tel. 02/511–79–37) is open Monday–Saturday 8 AM–10 PM, Sunday 9–6; the bookshop sells U.S. and U.K. newspapers, periodicals, and paperbacks.

Travel Agencies **American Express** (pl. Louise 2, B–1000 Brussels, tel. 02/512–17–40). **Wagons-Lits** (rue Ravenstein 22, tel. 02/512–98–78, and other locations).

Guided Tours

Orientation Tours **De Boeck Sightseeing** (tel. 02/513–77–44) operates city tours (BF700) with multilingual cassette commentary. Passengers are picked up at major hotels and at the tourist office in the town hall. More original are the tours run by **Chatterbus**, rue des Thuyas 12. For reservations, call 02/673–18–35 weekdays after 7 PM and weekends. Tours include a minibus tour of the main sites (BF600) and a walking tour that includes a visit to a bistro (BF250). Tours are operated early June–September.

Special-Interest Bus Tours **ARAU** organizes thematic city bus tours (in English), including "Brussels 1900: Art Nouveau," "Alternative Brussels," and "Brussels 1930: Art Déco." Tours begin in front of No. 2, rue du Midi (next to the Bourse); call 02/513–47–61 for times and bookings. The cost is BF500 for a half-day tour.

Regional Tours **De Boeck Sightseeing Tours** (rue de la Colline 8, Grand' Place, tel. 02/513–77–44) visits Antwerp, the Ardennes, Brugge, Ghent, Ieper, and Waterloo.

Exploring Brussels

Brussels is a city of individualists. Walk along almost any street, and you will be surprised at how different each house is from its neighbor, often embellished in Art Nouveau style, in contrast with impersonal office blocks. Stop in the Grand' Place during a son et lumière show and your mood softens, or watch from a cozy bar, its tables stacked high with pancakes or covered with bottles of Duvel beer. Brussels is an odd mixture of the provincial and the international. Underneath the bureaucratic surface, the city is a subtle meeting of the Walloon and Flemish cultures. As the heart of the ancient Duchy of Brabant, Brussels retains its old sense of identity and civic pride. A stone's throw from the steel-and-glass towers, there are cobbled streets and forgotten spots where the city's eventful and romantic past is plainly visible through its 20th-century veneer.

Numbers in the margin correspond to points of interest on the Brussels map.

The Grand'
Place
①

Begin in the **Grand' Place,** one of the most ornate market squares in Europe. There is a daily flower market and a colorful Sunday-morning bird market. On summer nights, the entire square is flooded with music and colored light. The Grand' Place also comes alive during local pageants, such as the *Mayboom;* the *Ommegang,* a splendid historical pageant (early July); and the biennial *Tapis de Fleurs,* when the entire square is covered by a carpet of flowers (mid-August, 1996).

② The bombardment of the city by Louis XIV's troops left only the **Hôtel de Ville** (town hall) intact. Civic-minded citizens started rebuilding the Grand' Place immediately, but the highlight of the square remains the Gothic town hall. The central tower, combining boldness and light, is topped by a statue of St-Michel, the patron saint of Brussels. Among the magnificent rooms are the Salle Gothique, with its beautiful paneling; the Salle Maximilienne, with its superb tapestries; and the Council Chamber, with a ceiling fresco of the *Assembly of the Gods* painted by Victor Janssens in the early 15th century. *Admission: BF75. English-speaking tours start Tues. at 11:30 and 3:45, Wed. at 3:45; no individual visits.*

③ Opposite the town hall is the **Maison du Roi** (King's House)—though no king ever lived there—a 16th-century palace housing the **City Museum.** The collection includes important ceramics and silverware—Brussels is famous for both—church sculpture, and statues removed from the facade of the town hall, as well as an extravagant collection of costumes for Manneken Pis (*see below*). *Grand' Place, tel. 02/511-27-42. Admission: BF80. Open Mon.–Thurs. 10–12:30 and 1:30–5 (Oct.–Mar. until 4), weekends 10–1.*

Time Out **La Rose Blanche** (Grand' Place 11, tel. 02/511-2754) is in a renovated three-story town house beside the town hall. Inside, brightly painted ceilings have been restored, but the minstrel's gallery, the creaking stairs, and the Chimay beer are original enough. Try a *fondue au parmesan* (cheese in batter) with a strong Chimay or a light *bière blanche.* A sweeter combination is coffee and a *dame blanche* (vanilla ice cream coated with hot chocolate sauce) or a *mousse au chocolat* (chocolate mousse). This is also the spot from which to view a son et lumière display on a summer's evening.

④ Southwest of the town hall, on the corner of the rue de l'Etuve and rue du Chêne, stands the famous **Manneken Pis,** a fountain with a small bronze statue of a chubby little boy urinating. Made by Jerome Duquesnoy in 1619, the statue is known as "Brussels's Oldest Citizen" and is often dressed in costumes that are kept in the City Museum. The present Manneken is a copy; the original was kidnapped by 18th-century French and English invaders (soldiers, not tourists!).

Leaving the Manneken, cross the Grand' Place in the direction of the Marché-aux-Herbes. Opposite the tourist office (rue Marché-aux-Herbes 61), take the Petite rue des Bouchers, the main restaurant street in the heart of the tourist maelstrom. In Brussels fashion, each restaurant advertises its wares by means of large signs and carts packed with a selection of game and seafood. As a general rule, however, remember that the more lavish the display, the poorer the

⑤ cuisine. From here, explore the network of galleries called **Galeries St-Hubert,** which includes the Galerie de la Reine, Galerie du Roi, and Galerie des Princes, all built in 1847. Written on the central galleries is the motto "Omnibus Omnia" (Everything for Everyone), which is not altogether appropriate, given the designer prices.

6 7 Head south along the rue Marché-aux-Herbes and the rue Madeleine until you come to the **equestrian statue of King Albert.** To the left of the statue is the Central Station and to the right, the **Bibliothèque Nationale** (National Library). Walk through the formal gardens next to the National Library and look back at the ornate clock, with moving figures, over the lower archway. Try to hear—and see—it at noon, when it strikes the hour.

Place Royale If you continue walking through the gardens, you will arrive at the **place Royale,** the site of the Coudenberg palace, where the sovereigns once lived. Here you have a superb view over the lower town.

8 On the northwest corner of the square is the **Musée d'Art Moderne** (Museum of Modern Art), housed in an exciting feat of modern architecture. On entry, a vertiginous descent into the depths reveals a sudden well of natural light. The paintings are displayed with the light and space they deserve. Although there are a few paintings by Matisse, Gauguin, Degas, and Dali, the surprise lies in the quality of Belgian modern art. See Magritte's luminous fantasies, James Ensor's masks and still lifes, and Spilliaert's coastal scenes. Do not miss Permeke's deeply brooding *Fiancés* or Delvaux's Surrealist works. *Pl. Royale 1, tel. 02/508–32–11. Admission free. Open Tues.–Sun. 10–1 and 2–5.*

9 Next door is the **Musée Royale d'Art Ancien** (Royal Museum of Ancient Art). Here the collection is of Flemish and Dutch paintings, ranging from magnificent 15th- and 16th-century works—Cranach, Matsys, and Bruegel the Elder, among them—to Rubens (several fine canvases), Van Dyck, and David. Do not miss Bruegel's dramatic *La Chute d'Icare (The Fall of Icarus)* or Hieronymous Bosch's *Le Dernier Jugement (The Last Judgment),* a malevolent portrait of humanity. *Rue de la Régence 10, tel. 02/508–32–11. Admission free. Open Tues.–Sun. 10–1 and 2–5.*

If you decide to divide your exploration of Brussels into two walks, this is a good place to break. You can pick up again at the same spot on the neoclassical place Royale. The Rue de la Régence runs from this square toward the Palais de Justice. The Sablon lies along this

10 street, on the right. The **Grand Sablon,** the city's most sophisticated square, is alive with cafés, restaurants, and antiques shops. Here, also, is the tempting Wittamer, the city's finest pastry shop. Toward the end of the square is the **church of Notre Dame du Sablon,** built in flamboyant Gothic style. Although much of the original workmanship was lost in restoration, it remains one of the city's best-loved churches. At night, the brilliant church windows illuminate the Grand Sablon and the Petit Sablon behind.

11 A small garden square, the **Petit Sablon** is surrounded by 48 statues representing Brussels's medieval guilds. Each craftsman carries an object that reveals his trade: The furniture maker holds a chair, for instance; the wine merchant, a goblet.

On the Petit Sablon is the **Musée Instrumental** (Museum of Musical Instruments). A huge collection of over 1,000 musical instruments is on display. Half of them are unique, and a few go back to the Bronze Age. The guide can often be persuaded to play one of the pianos. *Petit Sablon 17, tel. 02/511–35–95. Admission free. Open Tues., Thurs., and Sat. 2:30–4:30, Wed. 4–6, Sun. 10:30–12:30.*

Immediately behind the Petit Sablon is the **Palais d'Egmont,** at different times the residence of Christina of Sweden, Louis XV, and Voltaire. It is now used by the Belgian Ministry of Foreign Affairs for official meetings. If security allows, you can enter the Jardin d'Egmont, another small park, on this side. Come out of the en-

Bibliothèque
Nationale, **7**

Bourse, **19**

Cathédrale
St-Michel, **17**

Cinquantenaire, **23**

Equestrian Statue of
King Albert, **6**

European Community
Headquarters, **22**

Galeries St-Hubert, **5**

Grand' Place, **1**

Grand Sablon, **10**

Hôtel de Ville, **2**

Maison du Roi, **3**

Manneken Pis, **4**

Musée d'Art
Moderne, **8**

Musée Royale d'Art
Ancien, **9**

Notre Dame de la
Chapelle, **13**

Palais de Justice, **12**

Palais de la Nation, **16**

Palais Royal, **15**

Petit Sablon, **11**

Place des Martyrs, **18**

Place du Jeu
de Balle, **14**

Rue Antoine
Dansaert, **21**

Tour Noir, **20**

Brussels

trance on rue du Grand Cerf and turn left toward the boulevard de Waterloo, a wide street full of bars and designer shops.

Time Out Among the bars on your right, **Le Nemrod** is the most typical. In summer, there is a sidewalk café. The interior is decorated like a Belgian hunting lodge, with lifelike deer and other stuffed animal heads on the walls. At the first chill, the Nemrod's fireplace is surrounded by drinkers of Gueuze and Kriek beers.

Palais de Justice to the Black Tower At the end of the rue de la Régence is the **Palais de Justice,** constructed during the reign of the empire-builder, Leopold II. Often described as the ugliest building in Europe, the palais is designed to impress upon you the majesty of justice. It's on the site of the former Gallows Hill.

⑫

Down a rather steep hill from the Palais de Justice is the working-class **Marolles** district, where the artist Pieter Bruegel died in 1569.
⑬ His imposing marble tomb is in **Notre Dame de la Chapelle,** his local church on rue Haute, which has just been splendidly restored. From the church, head back to the Sablon via the cobbled rue Rollebeek. If you would rather see more of the authentic Marolles district, ignore the cluster of chic restaurants and designer shops on rue Rollebeek. Instead, from place de la Chapelle, take rue Blaes to the flea market
⑭ in **place du Jeu de Balle** (*see* Shopping, *below*). On the way, you will pass a number of rough Belgian bars and North African food shops. Until this century, bourgeois Belgians considered this labyrinth of small alleys a haven for thieves and political refugees. Although the Marolles continues to welcome immigrants and outsiders, it has lost its danger but kept its slightly raffish character.

Return via the Sablon to the place Royale. Directly ahead of you is
⑮ the **Parc de Bruxelles** (Brussels Park) with the **Palais Royal** (Royal Palace) at the end closer to you (open for visits from July 22 to early
⑯ September). You can walk through the park to the **Palais de la Nation** (Palace of the Nation) at the opposite end, where the two houses of the Belgian Parliament meet. When Parliament is not sitting, you can visit the building. *Guided tours weekdays 10–noon and 2–5 (Sat. until 4).*

Surrounding the park are elegant turn-of-the-century houses. The prime minister's office is next to the Parliament building. A walk downhill (rue des Colonies) toward the downtown area and a short
⑰ right-hand detour bring you to the **Cathédrale St-Michel.** The cathedral's chief treasure is the beautiful stained-glass windows designed by Bernard van Orley, an early 16th-century painter at the royal court. In summer the great west window is floodlit from inside to reveal its glories. In the crypt, you can see the remnants of the original 12th-century church.

⑱ Continue downhill to the **place des Martyrs,** a dignified square over a mass grave for local patriots who died in the 1830 battle to expel the Dutch. Renovation is now in progress of this nobly proportioned square. Cross the rue Neuve and continue on to the boulevard Adolphe-Max. Turn left and then right, in front of the imposing
⑲ **Bourse** (stock exchange), to place Ste-Catherine.

⑳ The 12th-century **Tour Noir** (Black Tower) here is part of the city's first fortifications. Archaeological excavations have begun under this shamefully neglected monument. Under the square runs the river Senne, channeled underground in the last century when the pollution of the canal basins and the stench from the open sewers became too great. As a result of its watery past, place Ste-Catherine and the old fish market (quai aux Briques) that extends north from it still have the city's best seafood restaurants. Return to the Bourse ❷① via the **Rue Antoine Dansaert,** which has lately become a trendy shopping street with boutiques and galleries.

Time Out **Le Pain Quotidien** (16, rue Dansaert) is open all day and serves superior sandwiches of crusty bread, salads, and cakes at a communal table. This is a highly popular place among young local people.

Parc du Cinquantenaire and Bois de la Cambre ❷② To see the **European Commission** headquarters at the Rond Point Schuman, take the metro (Line 1) from the center. The vast 13-story cruciform building is now undergoing restoration to remove asbestos ceilings and partitions. The Council offices are nearby. The new European Parliament building is a couple of blocks away on Rue Wiertz. Near it is the **Musée des Sciences Naturelles** (Museum of Natural Sciences), recently spruced up, which features a great collection of iguanodon dinosaurs and many imaginative displays. *Rue Vautier 29, tel. 02/627–42–11. Admission: BF120. Open Tues.–Sat. 9:30–4:45, Sun. 9:30–6.*

❷③ The **Cinquantenaire** is a huge, decorative archway, built in 1905 in a pleasant park. The buildings on either side of the archway house the **Royal Museums of Art and History.** Displays include Greek, Roman, and Egyptian artifacts and toys. *Parc du Cinquantenaire 10, tel. 02/ 741–72–11. Admission free. Open weekdays 9:30–12:30 and 1:30– 4:45, weekends 10–4:45.*

The new **Autoworld Museum,** also in the Cinquantenaire, has one of the world's handsomest collections of vintage cars. *Parc du Cinquantenaire 11, tel. 02/736–41–65. Admission: BF150. Open daily 10–6 (Nov.–Mar. until 5).*

Waterloo No history buff can visit Brussels without making the pilgrimage to the site of the **Battle of Waterloo,** where Napoleon was finally defeated on June 18, 1815. It is easily reached from the city and lies 19 kilometers (12 miles) to the south of the Forêt de Soignes; take a bus from place Rouppe or a train from Gare Centrale to Waterloo station.

Wellington's headquarters, now a museum, presents the complex battle through illuminated 3-D maps, scale models, and military memorabilia, including the general's personal belongings. *Chaussée de Bruxelles 149, tel. 02/345–78–06. Admission: BF60. Open Apr.– mid-Nov., daily 9:30–6:30; mid-Nov.–Mar., daily 10:30–5.*

Just south of town is the actual battlefield. Start at the **Visitors' Centre,** which has an audiovisual presentation that shows scenes of the battle. You can also book expert guides to take you around the battlefield. *Route du Lion 252–254, tel. 02/385–19–12. Admission: BF300. Open Apr.–Oct. 9:30–6:30; Nov.–Mar. 10:30–4. Guides 1815: Route du Lion 250, tel. 02/385–06–25. One hour BF1,400; 3 hours BF2,200.*

Overlooking the battlefield is the **Butte de Lion,** a pyramid-shape monument erected by the Dutch. After climbing 226 steps, you will be rewarded with a great view of the battlescene.

Time Out For a lunch of authentic Belgian cuisine, try the **Bivouac de l'Empereur,** an attractive 1720s farmhouse close to the Lion Monument. *Route de Lion 315, tel. 02/384–67–40. AE, DC, MC, V. Moderate.*

Off the Beaten Track

The **Atomium** is the trademark of Brussels, visible from all over the city. Erected in the hopeful 1950s as a symbol of science, it is an iron crystal molecule magnified 160 billion times, and from the highest sphere you have a panoramic view of Brussels. The structure also houses a future-oriented medical exhibition, **Biogenium**. *Blvd. du Centenaire, tel. 02/477–09–77. Metro Heysel. Admission: BF160. Open daily 10–6 (July and Aug. until 9:30).*

In the same area are the **Brussels Trade Mart, Heysel Stadium,** and **Bruparck,** including Mini-Europe (scale models of famous landmarks) and Kinepolis, a multi-cinema complex.

The Maison d'Erasme is a beautifully restored 15th-century house where Erasmus, the great humanist, lived in 1521. Every detail of this atmospheric house is authentic, with period furniture, paintings by Holbein, Dürer, and Hieronymous Bosch and early editions of Erasmus's works, including *In Praise of Folly*. *Rue du Chapitre 31, tel. 02/521–13–83. Metro Saint-Guidon. Admission: BF20. Open Wed.–Thurs. and Sat.–Mon., 10–noon and 2–5.*

The new **Musée de la Bande Dessinée** celebrates the comic strip, emphasizing such famous Belgian graphic artists as Hergé, Tintin's creator. Hergé pioneered the *ligne claire*, a simple, bold style of drawing. The display is housed in Victor Horta's splendid Art Nouveau building, once a department store. Horta's juggling of steel, glass, and light has created an exciting backdrop. *Rue des Sables 20, tel. 02/219–19–80. Tram Nos. 92, 93, 101. Admission: BF150. Open Tues.–Sun. 10–6.*

The **Musée Horta** (Horta Museum) was once the home of the Belgian master of Art Nouveau, Victor Horta. From the attic to the cellar, every detail of the house displays the exuberant curves of Art Nouveau style. Horta, who designed the house for himself, wanted to put nature back into daily life. Here his floral motifs, organic style, and refined curves of iron and stone succeed magnificently. *Rue Américain 25, tel. 02/537–16–92. Admission: BF150. Open Tues.–Sun. 2–5:30. Tram No. 92 or bus No. 60.*

Shopping

Gift Ideas

Crystal The Val-St-Lambert mark is the only guarantee of hand-blown, hand-carved lead crystal tableware. You can buy it in many stores, including **Art and Selection** (Marché-aux-Herbes 83) and **Buss,** across the street at No. 84, near the Grand' Place.

Chocolate For "everyday" chocolate, try the Côte d'Or variety, available in any chocolate shop or larger store. For the delicious pralines—rich chocolates filled with every fruit, liqueur, or nut imaginable—try the brands made by Godiva, Neuhaus, or Leonidas, available at shops scattered throughout the city. Godiva is the best known, Neuhaus the best-tasting, and Leonidas the best value for money. Exclusive handmade pralines can be bought at **Wittamer** (Grand Sablon 16) and **Nihoul** (Ave. Louise 300).

Lace To avoid disappointment, ask the store assistant outright whether the lace is handmade Belgian or made in the Far East. As preparation, visit the **Lace Museum** (rue de la Violette 6, near the Grand' Place). **La Maison F. Rubbrecht,** on the Grand' Place, sells authentic, handmade Belgian lace. For a large choice of old and modern lace, try **Manufacture Belge de Dentelles** (Galerie de la Reine 6–8).

Shopping Districts For boutiques and stores, the main districts are in the **ville basse** (low town), the **Galeries St-Hubert** (luxury goods or gift items), **rue Neuve** (inexpensive clothes), and **City 2** and the **Anspach Center** (large shopping malls). In City 2, **FNAC** is a cherished French institution: As well as being an outlet for books, records, cameras, and stereo equipment at the best prices in town, it is also a trendy cultural and exhibition center.

You'll find designer names and department stores (such as **Sarmalux**) in the **ville haute** (high town). **Avenue Louise** is its center, complete with the arcades **Galerie Louise** and **Espace Louise,** while the **Galerie de la Toison d'Or** branches off from the appropriately named street of the Golden Fleece! To offset prices, many of these stores operate sales-tax refunds (*see* Shopping in Staying in Belgium, *above*). The **place du Grand Sablon** is an equally expensive but more charming shopping district. This is the center for antiques, small art galleries, and designer shops. Around the Sablon and its neighboring streets, **rue des Minimes** and **rue Lebeau**, it is possible to buy anything from Persian carpets and African primitives to 18th-century paintings and Art Nouveau.

Markets On Saturdays (9–5) and Sundays (9–1), the Sablon square is transformed into an **antiques market.** The **flower market** on the Grand' Place (Tues.–Sun. 8–4) is a colorful diversion, as is the Sunday-morning **bird market** in the same square. **Midi Market** is far more exotic (by Gare du Midi train station). On Sunday morning (5 AM–1 PM) the whole area becomes a colorful *souk* (bazaar) as the city's large North African community gathers to buy and sell exotic foods and household goods. The **Vieux Marché** (Old Market) in place du Jeu de Balle is a rough flea market worth visiting for the authentic atmosphere of the working-class Marolles district. The market is open daily 7–2. To make real finds, get there as early in the morning as you can.

Dining

Apart from hearty Belgian cuisine, Brussels is proud of its foreign restaurants: Chefs from at least 50 countries work in the city, and many Asian restaurants provide a tasty and inexpensive alternative to European fare. The local cuisine is, in the more expensive restaurants, an imaginative variant of French cuisine. The ambience tends to be formal, dignified, and old-fashioned in the more exclusive restaurants and cozy or jovial in the simpler brasseries or bistros. Servings are plentiful everywhere. Most places offer fixed-price menus, which, especially at lunch, can reduce the bill by half. Less expensive restaurants also feature a *plat du jour* (daily special) at a reasonable price.

For details and price-category definitions, *see* Dining in Staying in Belgium, *above*.

Very Expensive ★ **Comme Chez Soi.** Pierre Wynants, the perfectionist owner-chef, has decorated the restaurant in Art Nouveau style. Every detail is authentic, from the stained-glass panels to the carved mahogany woodwork and the artistic menus. The inventive French cuisine, excellent wine list, and attentive service complement the warm decor. The specialties include fillets of sole with a white wine mousseline and shrimps, saddle of young rabbit with lemon and basil, venison, partridge, and pheasant. Many dishes are served for a minimum of two persons. Tables for two are so close together that you're likely to hear as much of your neighbors' conversation as your own. You need to make reservations at least a couple of months ahead. *Pl. Rouppe,*

tel. 02/512–29–21, fax 02/511–80–52. Reservations required. AE, DC, MC, V. Closed Sun., Mon., July, and Christmas to New Year's.
Les Délices de la Mer. Michel Beyls, one of the most talented chefs of his generation, has moved around a lot throughout his career. Brussels gourmets hope he will stay for a while at this address, a splendid villa in suburban Uccle. Beyls is the kind of magician who can turn a poached egg on a mousse of wild mushrooms into a memorable culinary experience. Seafood has pride of place on the menu. Try the quickly sautéed sea scallops in a light curry sauce, or turbot baked in a salt crust. *Chaussée de Waterloo 1020, tel. 02/375–54–67. Reservations required. AE, DC, MC, V. Closed Sat. lunch and Sun.*
Maison du Cygne. With decor to match its classical cuisine, this restaurant is set in a grand 17th-century guild hall on the Grand' Place. The formal dining room upstairs features paneled walls hung with old masters, and a small room on the mezzanine floor contains two priceless Bruegels. Service is flawless in the grand manner of old. Typical French-Belgian dishes include *lotte aux blancs de poireaux*, a monkfish-and-leeks specialty. *Rue Charles Buyls 2, tel. 02/511–82–44. Reservations required. AE, DC, MC, V. Closed Sat. lunch, Sun.*

Expensive   **L'Ecailler du Palais Royal.** This fish restaurant just off the Grand Sablon seems more like a comfortable club, and many of the clients seem to have known each other and the staff for years. Risotto of prawns *au Champagne*, baked lobster custard, and the best turbot you're likely to taste for a long time are among specialties on offer. A little care is required not to stray over the line into Very Expensive. *Rue Bodenbroek 18, tel. 02/512–87–51. Reservations required. AE, DC, MC, V. Closed Mon., Easter week, and Aug.*

★   **Les Brigittines,** on the edge of the Marolles, faces the recently cleaned facade of the church where Bruegel is buried. The *Belle Epoque* interior is remarkably attractive, with numerous paintings and flower arrangements. One room is dominated by a splendid old bar and the other by a huge open fireplace. The young chef serves up delicacies such as browned escalopes of goose liver with caramelized apple, sea scallops with braised chicory, and grilled John Dory with lobster bearnaise. *Pl. de la Chapelle 5, tel. 02/512–68–91. Reservations advised. AE, DC, MC, V. Closed Sat. lunch, Sun., and Aug.*
Ogenblik. This is a true bistro, with green-shaded lamps over marble-topped tables, sawdust on the floor, ample servings, and a great ambience. The long and imaginative menu changes frequently, but generally includes such specialties as *mille-feuille* of lobster and salmon and saddle or leg of lamb with fresh, young vegetables. *Galerie des Princes 1, tel. 02/511–61–51. No reservations after 8 PM. AE, DC, MC, V. Closed Sun.*

Moderate   **Aux Armes de Bruxelles.** This restaurant is one of the few to escape the "tourist trap" label in this hectic little street. Inside, a lively atmosphere fills three rooms: The most popular section overlooks the street theater outside, but locals prefer the cozy rotunda. Service is fast and friendly, and portions are large. Specialties include *waterzooi de volaille* (a rich chicken stew) and *moules au vin blanc* (mussels in white wine). Order the crêpe suzette if you want to see your table engulfed by brandy flames! *Rue des Bouchers 13, tel. 02/511–55–98. Reservations advised. AE, DC, MC, V. Closed Mon. and June.*
Brasserie Georges. This hugely successful restaurant, open every day until past midnight, was the first of its kind in Brussels and still the best. The *brasserie* formula calls for a splendid display of shellfish at the entrance, an Art Deco interior with tile floor and potted plants, fast and friendly service by waitresses in black and white,

and traditional fare such as *choucroute* (sauerkraut), poached cod, and *confit de canard* (potted duck). The *crème brûlée* is an outstanding dessert. Unusually, 25 different wines are sold by the glass. *Av. Winston Churchill 259, tel. 02/347–21–00. Reservations advised. AE, DC, MC, V.*

★ **La Quincaillerie.** The name means "the hardware store"—and the character has been retained, with tables perched on the balcony and a zinc oyster bar downstairs. The three-course *menu du patron* is a bargain. Excellent game dishes are nicely presented by a staff who, like the clientele, is young and pleasant. *Rue du Page 45, tel. 02/538–25–53. Reservations advised. AE, DC, MC, V.*

Inexpensive **Chez Leon.** This 100-year-old restaurant continues to do land-office business and has over the years expanded into a row of eight old houses. Heaping plates of mussels and other Belgian specialties, like eels in a green sauce, are served nonstop from noon to midnight all year round. *Rue des Bouchers 18, tel. 02/511–14–15. No reservations. AE, DC, MC, V.*

★ **Falstaff.** Some things never change, and Falstaff is one of them. This huge tavern, with an interior that is pure Art Nouveau, fills up for lunch and keeps going until 5 AM, with an ever-changing crowd from students to pensioners. Cheerful waitresses punch in your orders for onion soup, filet mignon, salads, and other straightforward dishes on electronic order pads. Falstaff II at No. 25 has the same food but not the ambience. *Rue Henri Maus 19, tel. 02/511–87–89. Reservations advised. AE, DC, MC, V.*

L'Armagnac. As the name implies, this restaurant specializes in dishes of Southwest France. The premises may be a wee bit run-down, but the faithful, mostly middle-aged clientele appreciates the reliability of the $25 fixed-price menu, which provides a choice among half a dozen dishes for each of the three courses. Scampi in lobster sauce, lamb's tongues, and fillet steak with wild mushrooms and braised pheasant are among the favorites. *Chaussée de Waterloo 591, tel. 02/345–92–79. Reservations advised. AE, DC, MC, V. Closed Sun., Mon. eve., and July 20–Aug. 20.*

Lodging

The *Hotel Guide,* published every year by Tourist Information Brussels (TIB), provides the most reliable and up-to-date information on prices and services. In general, finding accommodations is not difficult. There has been a boom in hotel construction lately, adding several more hotels in all price categories. Substantial weekend and summer rebates are available in many hotels; be sure to check when you book. The main hotel districts are in the Grand' Place area and around the avenue Louise shopping district. Avoid the cheap hotel districts near Gare du Midi and Gare du Nord train stations. Hotels can be booked at the tourist office on the Grand' Place (tel. 02/513–89–40), and a deposit is required (deductible from the final hotel bill).

For details and price-category definitions, *see* Lodging in Staying in Belgium, *above.*

Very **Conrad.** President Bill Clinton slept here. The Conrad, which
Expensive opened in 1993, seeks to combine the European grand hotel tradition with American taste and amenities and does quite a good job of it. The classical facade of the Maison Godefroy from 1865 has been retained. As a result rooms come in many different shapes but are uniformly spacious, with three telephones, bathrobes, and in-room checkout. The Maison de Maître restaurant is getting good notices in

the gourmet press, and the large bar is pleasantly clublike. Business travelers can arrange to have PCs and fax machines brought to their rooms. *av. Louise 71, tel. 02/542–42–42, fax 02/542–43–42. 268 rooms. Facilities: 2 restaurants, bar, conference facilities, parking. AE, DC, MC, V.*

Hilton International. The 27-story Hilton was one of the first high rises in Brussels back in the '60s and remains a distinctive landmark. It is continuously being refurbished floor by floor. Corner rooms are the most desirable. The top-floor restaurant, Plein Ciel (lunch only), has a terrific view over the city. The second-floor Maison du Boeuf is an outstanding restaurant and the ground-floor Cafe d'Egmont highly popular. Centrally located, it is next to the main luxury shopping area and overlooks the quiet Parc d'Egmont. *Blvd. de Waterloo 38, tel. 02/504–11–11, fax 02/504–21–11. 450 rooms with bath. Facilities: health club, sauna, 2 restaurants, coffee shop, bar, solarium. AE, DC, MC, V.*

★ **SAS Royal Hotel.** This 1990 hotel, a few minutes' walk through the Galerie de la Reine from Grand' Place, was built for business travelers. The rooms are decorated in different styles: Scandinavian, Oriental, Italian, and Art Deco. A portion of the city wall from 1134, discovered during construction, forms part of the Atrium. A business service center and fully equipped conference rooms cater to businesspeople's needs. The Sea Grill has become one of the city's top seafood restaurants. Rooms for nonsmokers and for guests with diabilities are available. Travelers aged 65 or older qualify for special weekend and summer rates. *Rue du Fossé-aux-Loups 47, tel. 02/ 219–28–28, fax 02/219–62–62. 281 rooms with bath. Facilities: 2 restaurants, valet parking, fitness center, in-room checkout, airline check-in, Atrium coffee shop, bar. AE, DC, MC, V.*

Expensive **Amigo.** This world-famous, family-owned hotel, off the Grand'
★ Place, was built in the 1950s, but it has the charm of an older age. No one would guess that it was built on the site of the city prison. Each room is individually decorated, often in silk, velvet, and brocades. A recent refurbishing has smartened up bedrooms and public rooms. The bar is very pleasant, though the restaurant is not memorable. Room rates vary considerably, with the less expensive options being on lower floors. *Rue d'Amigo 1, tel. 02/547–47–47, fax 02/513–52– 77. 183 rooms with bath. Facilities: restaurant, bar, parking. AE, DC, MC, V.*

Metropole. A major restoration has returned the Metropole to its Art Nouveau glory. The lobby sets the tone, with its high coffered ceiling, chandeliers, marble, and Oriental carpets. The theme extends seamlessly to the bar with its potted palms and deep leather sofas, to the gourmet restaurant and to the café, which opens onto a heated terrace on the Place Brouckère. Most of the guest rooms have been discreetly done over in pastel shades and Art Deco style, but the very high ceilings can be disconcerting. *Place de Brouckère 31, tel. 02/217–23–00, fax 02/218–02–20. 410 rooms. Facilities: restaurant, bar, café, conference rooms, fitness room, airport courtesy bus. AE, DC, MC, V.*

Sofitel. Opened in 1989, the six-floor Sofitel has a great location in the heart of the chic shopping center. There's even a boutique-lined arcade on the ground floor, and you reach the lobby on an escalator. Public rooms and bedrooms are decorated in warm brown and beige tones. There's no extra charge for double occupancy. Bathroom telephones and bathrobes are standard. *Av. de la Toison d'Or 40, tel. 02/ 514–22–00, fax 02/514–57–44. 171 rooms. Facilities: restaurant, bar. AE, DC, MC, V.*

Moderate **Cadettt.** This 1991 addition to the Swiss Mövenpick chain does spell its name with three *t*'s. The large, bright rooms have blond wood furniture, modem phone jacks, and Lay-Z-Boy chairs. The atrium bar and restaurant serves copious Swiss breakfasts and a limited selection of Mövenpick specialties. The Caveau wine bar offers wine tasting and light snacks. *Rue Paul Spaak 15, tel. 02/645–61–11, fax 02/646–63–11. 128 rooms with bath. Facilities: restaurant, bars, café, sauna, fitness room, nonsmoking rooms, parking. AE, DC, MC, V.*

Le Dixseptième. Pronounced "disset-yehm," this hotel occupies the 18th-century residence of the Spanish ambassador. Stylishly restored, it opened in 1993. Rooms, named for Belgian artists, surround a pleasant interior court. All feature white-washed walls, plain floorboards, exposed beams, suede-upholstered sofas, and colorful draperies. Rooms also have kitchenettes and bathrobes, while suites have working fireplaces and fax machines. *Rue de la Madeleine 25, tel. 02/502-57-44, fax 02/502-64-24. 12 rooms, 13 suites. Facilities: breakfast room, bar. AE, DC, MC, V.*

★ **Manos Stéphanie.** The Louis XV furniture, marble lobby, and plentiful antiques set a standard of elegance rarely encountered in a hotel in this price category. Even the corridors are decorated with paintings and mirrors. This 1992 hotel occupies a converted town house, and most rooms have good-sized sitting areas. Avenue Louise is just a few minutes' walk away. *Chaussée de Charleroi 28, tel. 02/539–02–50, fax 02/537–57–29. 55 rooms. Facilities: restaurant, bar, parking. AE, DC, MC, V.*

Inexpensive **Mozart.** The entrance to the Mozart, which opened in 1993, is between two Greek pita joints; the reception is up a flight of stairs. The lack of an elevator is a drawback, but the oak-beamed, spacious rooms, in shades of salmon, are attractive; each has a refrigerator and a shower. Complimentary breakfast is served in a cozy nook. The multilingual Moroccan owner, Ben, and his Swedish wife also own the remarkably inexpensive restaurant Boccaccio across the street. *Rue Marché aux Fromages 15A, tel. 02/502–66–61, fax 02/502–77–58. 23 rooms. Facilities: breakfast room. AE, DC, MC, V.*

Orion. This residential hotel opened in 1990 in the old fish market, which has become a lively restaurant district. The reception area is always staffed, but you make your own bed. Linen is changed weekly. Rooms are decorated in a cheerful, crisp red-and-white modern scheme. There are fully equipped kitchenettes in the studio rooms and two-room apartments and a quiet interior courtyard. *Quai au Bois-à-Brûler 51, tel. 02/221–14–11, fax 02/221–15–99. 169 rooms with bath. Facilities: parking. AE, DC, MC, V.*

★ **Welcome/Truite d'Argent.** Among the charms of the smallest hotel in Brussels are the young owners, Michel and Sophie Smeesters. The six rooms, with king- or queen-size beds, are as comfortable as those in much more expensive establishments. This little hotel is much in demand, so book early. There's a downstairs breakfast room cum dining room for hotel guests, while the rather expensive "Silver Trout" around the corner on the Fish Market serves excellent seafood. *Rue du Peuplier 5, tel. 02/219–95–46, fax 02/217–18–87. 6 rooms. Facilities: 2 restaurants, garage, seminar rooms. AE, DC, MC, V.*

The Arts

The best way to find out what's going on is to buy a copy of the English-language weekly magazine *The Bulletin*. It's published every Thursday and sold at newsstands for BF80.

Music   Major classical music concerts are generally held at the **Palais des Beaux-Arts** (rue Ravenstein 23, tel. 02/507–82–00). Alternatively, there are many free Sunday morning concerts at various churches, including the Cathédrale St-Michel and the Petite Église des Minimes (rue des Minimes 62). Major rock and pop concerts are given at Forest National (av. du Globe 36, tel. 02/347–03–55).

Opera and   The national opera company, Compagnie Royale Belge de l'Opera, is
Dance   based at the **Théâtre Royal de la Monnaie** (pl. de la Monnaie, tel. 02/218–12–02). The Monnaie is an attractive opera house, and its productions are of international quality. Tickets cost from BF500 to BF2,000 and are very hard to come by. Touring dance and opera companies often play at the **Cirque Royal** (rue de l'Enseignement 81, tel. 02/218–20–15).

Theater   At Brussels's 30 theaters, actors perform in French, Flemish, and occasionally in English. The loveliest theater is the **Théâtre Royal du Parc** (in Parc de Bruxelles at Rue de la Loi 3, tel. 02/512–23–39), which plays Molière and other French classics. Avant-garde theater is performed at the enterprising **Théâtre Varia** (rue du Sceptre 78, tel. 02/640–82–58) and **Théâtre de Poche** (in Bois de la Cambre at Chemin du Gymnase, tel. 02/649–17–27). Puppet theater is a Belgian experience not to be missed. In Brussels, visit the intimate **Théâtre Toone VII** (impasse Schuddeveld, Petite rue des Bouchers 21, tel. 02/511–71–37). In this atmospheric medieval house, satirical plays are performed in a Bruxellois dialect.

Film   Movies are mainly shown in their original language, so many are in English. **The Acropole** (Galeries de la Toison d'Or, tel. 02/511–43–28), the new **UCG** complex (pl. de Brouckère, tel. 02/218–06–07), and the multiscreen **Kinepolis** (av. du Centenaire 1, tel. 02/478–04–50) feature comfortable armchairs and first-run movies. For unusual movies or screen classics, visit the **Musée du Cinéma** (Cinema Museum; rue Baron Horta 9, tel. 02/513–41–55). Five movies are shown daily, at only BF50 each.

Nightlife

Nightclubs   These are mostly sad, seedy, and exploitative. The best of an undistinguished lot is **Show Point** (pl. Stéphanie 14, tel. 02/511–53–64).

Disco   **Griffin's** (rue Duquesnoy 5, tel. 02/511–42–15) at the Royal Windsor Hotel appeals to young adults and business travelers. **Le Mirano** (Chaussée de Louvain 38, tel. 02/218–57–72) attracts a self-styled jet set (Sat. only), while **Le Garage** (rue Duquesnoy 16, tel. 02/512–66–22) draws a younger crowd. The current favorite among the BCBG *(bon chic, bon genre)* is the **Jeux d'Hiver** in the Bois de la Cambre (Thurs. and Sat.), which is a members-only club; you'll be admitted if you look the part. In all of the above, the action does not start much before midnight.

Bars   The diversity is greater here than in many other European capitals. These are just a few of the best: **La Fleur en Papier Doré** (rue des Aléxiens 53, tel. 02/511–16–59) is a quiet bar that attracts an artistic audience to drink local beer and look at the ancient walls covered with surreal paintings and old etchings. **Cirio** (rue de la Bourse 18, tel. 02/512–13–95) is a pleasantly quiet bar with nice decor. **Rick's Café** (av. Louise 344, tel. 02/647–75–30) is as popular with homesick Americans as it is with the British expatriate community. It serves fairly expensive American and Tex/Mex food. **De Ultieme Hallucinatie** (rue Royale 316, tel. 02/217–06–14) is another popular Art Nouveau bar and restaurant that serves imaginative cocktails, a full range of beers, and a short but appealing menu. **Henry J. Bean's** (rue du Montagne-aux-Herbes-Potagères 40, tel. 02/219–28–28) is a 1950s style bar and grill much frequented by the younger set.

Jazz Among the best venues are **Travers** (rue Traversière 11, tel. 02/218–40–86), **Preservation Hall** (Place de Londres 4, tel. 02/502–15–97), and **Sounds** (Rue de la Tulipe 28, tel. 02/512–92–50).

Antwerp

Arriving and Departing

By Plane Antwerp International Airport lies just 3 kilometers (2 miles) southeast of the city. For flight information, call 03/218–12–11. Antwerp is served by a small number of flights from neighboring countries. Most passengers arrive via Brussels National Airport, which is linked with Antwerp by hourly bus service (50 minutes one way).

Between the Airport and Downtown Buses bound for Antwerp's central station leave about every 20 minutes; travel time is around 15 minutes. Taxis are readily available as well.

By Train Express trains run between Antwerp and Brussels; the trip takes 35 minutes. Antwerp Central Station is at Koningin Astridplein 27 (tel. 03/233–39–15). Four trains leave every hour from Antwerp's central station.

By Car Several major highways converge on Antwerp's inner-city ring expressway. It's a 10-lane racetrack, so be sure you maneuver into the correct lane well before you exit. Antwerp is an easy 45-kilometer (28-mile) drive from Brussels on E19.

Getting Around

By Streetcar In the downtown area, the streetcar (or tram) is the best, and most common, means of transportation. Some lines have been rebuilt underground (look for signs marked "M"); the most useful line runs between the central station (metro stop Diamant) and the Groenplaats (for the cathedral). For detailed maps of the transportation system, stop at the tourist office.

Guided Tours

Orientation tours by minibus (50 minutes) depart from the Grote Markt daily at 2, 3, and 4 (mid-Nov. to mid-Mar., weekends only). Tickets (BF330 adults, BF200 children) are sold on the bus. The tourist office operates a **Guide's Exchange** and, with a week's notice, is able to meet most requirements for city guides. Guides charge BF600 an hour, with a minimum of two hours.

Tourist Information

The tourist office is near the cathedral (Grote Markt 15, tel. 03/232–01–03). It is open Monday–Saturday 9–6, Sunday 9–5. Ask for their booklet on walks, which includes the famous "Rubens Walk." Various other popular walks are signposted throughout the city.

Exploring Antwerp

Antwerp, lying on the Scheldt River 50 kilometers (31 miles) north of Brussels, is the world's fifth-largest port and the main city of

Belgium's Flemish region. Its name, according to legend, is derived from *handwerpen*, or "hand throwing." It seems a Roman soldier once cut off the hand of a malevolent giant and flung it into the river; his feat is commemorated by a statue on the Grote Markt. In the 16th century, Emperor Charles V made Antwerp the world's most important trading center, and during the 17th century Rubens and other painters made their city an equally important center of the arts. Enterprising craftsmen began practicing diamond-cutting at about this time, and the city is still a world leader in the diamond trade. Much of the glory that was Antwerp has been preserved, and Antwerp's year as Cultural Capital of Europe 1993 resulted in a much-improved cultural infrastructure.

Numbers in the margin correspond to points of interest on the Antwerp map.

❶ Antwerp's **Centraalstation** is a good place to start exploring the city. This elegant neo-Classical building, restored to its former glory, was built early in this century as a virtual "railway cathedral." To
❷ the east of the station is **Antwerp Zoo,** a huge, well-designed complex that includes a winter garden, a planetarium, a good restaurant, and a natural-history museum. *Koningin Astridplein 26, tel. 03/231–16–40. Admission: BF390 adults, BF240 children. Open July–Aug., daily 8:30–6:30; Sept.–Feb., daily 9–5; Mar.–June, daily 8:30–6.*

Near the central station, along the Pelikaanstraat and the streets running off it, lies the **Diamond Quarter.** You can visit the spectacu-
❸ lar showrooms of **Diamondland** to see both rough and polished diamonds, slide shows and films illustrating the history of the industry, and diamond cutters at work. Stones purchased here are accompanied by a Diamond High Council guarantee. *Appelmansstraat 33A, tel. 03/234–36–12. Admission free. Open Mon.–Sat. 9:30–5:30.*

The broad De Keyserlei leads west from the central station to the main shopping area, the **Meir.** South of the Meir, on Wapper, is
❹ **Rubenshuis** (Rubens House). The artist lived here from 1610 until his death in 1640. It is a patrician's home, enriched with paintings by Rubens and his contemporaries. *Wapper 9. Admission: BF75. Open Tues.–Sun. 10–5.*

Turn left at the **Torengebouw,** which Antwerpers claim to be Europe's first skyscraper, and you find yourself in a shopping district where the tone is set by the Antwerp Six, pioneers of "grunge"
❺ fashion. A few blocks south is the **Museum Mayer van den Bergh,** whose masterpiece is Bruegel's "Mad Meg," a powerful anti-war allegory that may be his greatest work. *Lange Gasthuisstraat 19, tel. 03/232–42–37. Admission: BF75. Open Tues.–Sun. 10–5.*

Turn back, and let yourself be guided by its white, 400-foot spire to
❻ the **Onze-Lieve-Vrouwekathedraal** (Cathedral of Our Lady), the largest church in the Low Countries. Just thoroughly renovated, it is an inspiring Gothic monument. Three Rubens altarpieces are among its art treasures. *Admission: BF60. Open weekdays 10–5, Sat. 10–3, Sun. 1–4.*

The **Grote Markt,** flanked by the 16th-century city hall and surrounded by old guild houses, is just a few steps north of the cathedral. The area north of the square, with its narrow streets, churches, and old merchants' houses, is the heart of old Antwerp.

Returning to the cathedral, walk the short distance west along the
❼ Suikerrui to the river. To your right is the fortresslike **Steen,** the oldest building in Antwerp. From the terraces around the Steen,

Antwerp

Antwerp Zoo, **2**
Centraalstation, **1**
Diamondland, **3**
Koninklijk Museum voor Schone Kunsten, **10**
Museum Mayer van den Bergh, **5**
Onze-Lieve-Vrouwekathedraal, **6**

Plantin-Moretus Museum, **9**
Rubenshuis, **4**
St. Annatunnel, **8**
Steen, **7**
Vogelmarkt, **11**

you can see the main port installations. For a close look, a 2½-hour **boat excursion** (from Easter to late Sept.) around the port leaves from Quay 13 on weekdays and from Steen Landing stage on Sunday. *Cost: BF375 adults, BF240 children. Information from n.v. Flandria, Steenplein 1, tel. 03/231–31–00.*

Walking along the river south of the Steen, you come to a foot tunnel, **❽** the **St. Annatunnel,** leading to the left bank of the river. Turn east, **❾** and walk two blocks to the **Plantin-Moretus Museum,** a famous printing works founded in the 16th century. The building is a fine example of Renaissance architecture and is magnificently furnished. Among its treasures are many first editions, engravings, and a copy of Gutenberg's Bible. Plantin was printer to Emperor Charles V, and thousands of liturgical books were printed here. Two of the typefaces designed here, Plantin and Garamond, are still in use. The presses are still in working order, and you can purchase a copy of Plantin's *Ode to Happiness. Vrijdagmarkt 22. Admission: BF75. Open Tues.–Sun. 10–5.*

From the Plantin, walk through the Vrijdagmarkt and up the Oude Koornmarkt to the Groenplaats and catch tram no. 8 to the **❿** **Koninklijk Museum voor Schone Kunsten** (Royal Museum of Fine Arts). It lies in the southern part of the old city and contains more than 1,500 paintings by old masters, including a magnificent array of works by Rubens, Van Dyck, Hals, and Bruegel. The second floor houses one of the best collections of paintings by Flemish Primitives of the 15th and 16th centuries. The first floor is given over to more modern paintings. *Leopold de Waelplaats 1–9. Admission free. Open Tues.–Sun. 10–5.*

⓫ On Sunday morning you can see the famous **vogelmarkt,** or bird market, a few blocks south of Rubenshuis on the Oude Vaartplaats. You'll find everything from birds and domestic pets to plants, clothes, and food.

Time Out More than 350 kinds of Belgian beer and 150 foreign brews are available in **Café Kulminator**—including the lethal EKU-28, claimed by Kulminator to be "the strongest beer on Earth." The beers are best accompanied by the excellent cheeses. *Vleminckveld 32, tel. 03/232–45–38. No credit cards. Closed Sun. Inexpensive.*

Dining

Local specialties include herring and eel dishes and *witloof* (endives) cooked in a variety of ways. As for drink, there are 20 local beers; a city gin called *jenever;* and a strong liqueur, *Elixir d'Anvers.*

For details and price-category definitions, *see* Dining in Staying in Belgium, *above.*

Very Expensive **La Pérouse.** When the good ship *La Pérouse,* which carries tourists on pleasure trips in summer, ties up at the Steen for the winter season, it is converted into an outstanding restaurant. The emphasis is naturally on seafood, such as bass cooked in salt crust and served with saffron butter, but meat dishes are also excellent. This floating dining room is small, so early reservations are a must. *Steenplein, tel. 03/231–31–51. Reservations required. AE, DC, MC, V. Closed Sun., Mon., and May–mid-Sept.*

Expensive **De Matelote.** At a tiny restaurant in a small house down a narrow **★** street, the gifted chef concocts inventive dishes such as grilled asparagus with fresh morels and a poached egg, or langoustines in a light curry sauce. Local gourmets consider this the best fish restaurant in town. For dessert, try the outstanding *crème brûlée*. *Haarstraat 9, tel. 03/231–32–07. Reservations advised. AE, DC, MC, V. Closed Mon. and Sat. lunch, Sun., 3 weeks in July.*

Petrus. This small restaurant is opposite the marvelous early 19th-century Bourla Theater, and the fixed-price theater menu is an especially good buy. One specialty is a terrine of duck's liver interleaved with *filet d'Anvers* (lightly smoked beef). The sliced, sautéed sea scallops on a galette of potatoes with olive oil and white truffles are a dream. Serious wine lovers should visit the extensive cellar. *Kelderstraat 1, tel. 03/225–27–34. Reservations advised. AE, DC, MC, V. Closed weekend lunch, Mon., and 2 weeks in July.*

Moderate **Neuze Neuze.** Five tiny houses have been cobbled together to create
★ this handsome, split-level restaurant with white-washed walls, dark brown beams, and a blazing fireplace. Salmon smoked *à la minute* and served with endives in a white beer sauce, scallops with rhubarb preserve, and monkfish rolls with caviar are some of the dishes, conceived and executed with the flair of pricier establishments. *Wijngaardstraat 19, tel. 03/232–57–83. Reservations advised. AE, DC, MC, V. Closed Sun. and 3 weeks in July/Aug.*

Sir Anthony Van Dijck. The owner/chef has abandoned his two-star rating, cut prices in half, increased the number of tables, and introduced simpler, brasserie-type dishes based on less expensive products. The antiques-filled interior is still the same, and so is the setting in the charming Vlaaykensgang alley. *Oude Koornmarkt 16, tel. 03/231–61–70. AE, DC, MC, V. Closed Sun. and most of Aug.*

Inexpensive **Panaché.** At this Antwerp institution, you can savor the best sandwiches in town or, in the back room, simple but satisfying fare. *Statiestraat 17, tel. 03/232–69–05. AE, DC, MC, V.*

Zuiderterras. A stark glass-and-black-metal construction, this riverside café and restaurant was designed by avant-garde architect bOb (his spelling) Van Reeth. Here you can have a light meal for about $15 and enjoy seeing the river traffic on one side and, on the other, a view of the Cathedral and the old town. *Ernest Van Dijckkaai, tel. 03/234–12–75. AE, DC, MC, V.*

Lodging

The tourist office (Grote Markt 15) can reserve rooms for you at reduced prices. Write for a form and return it, specifying your needs. For details and price-category definitions, *see* Lodging in Staying in Belgium, *above.*

Very **De Rosier.** A 17th-century mansion provides discreet luxury for the
Expensive privileged few. Cloistered behind double doors on a narrow street,
★ its presence announced only by a small brass plaque, it focuses on the aristocratic garden court and lavishly furnished interiors. Rooms vary from skylighted, modernized garrets to the beamed and leaded-glass Renaissance suite. *Rosier 21–23, tel. 03/225–01–40, fax 03/231–41–11. 12 rooms. Facilities: breakfast room, garden terrace, indoor pool. AE, DC, MC, V.*

Hilton. The newest contender among luxury hotels in Antwerp opened in mid 1993, and with just five floors, it is architecturally well integrated in Groenplaats, next to the cathedral. Afternoon tea is served in the marble-floor lobby; buffet breakfast, lunch, and dinner in the "Isabella and Helena" restaurant, named for Rubens's two wives. Rooms are equipped with mahogany doors, three telephones, safes, and executive desks. *Groenplaats, tel. 03/204–12–12, fax 03/204–12–13. 211 rooms. Facilities: 2 restaurants, bar, sauna, fitness*

center, conference rooms, ballroom, nonsmoking floors, garage.
AE, DC, MC, V.

Expensive **Alfa De Keyser.** This well-maintained deluxe hotel is handily situated only 100 meters from the central station and near the diamond center. It has a restaurant that prides itself on its adaptation of local ingredients to nouvelle cuisine. *De Keyserlei 66, tel. 03/234–01–35, fax 03/232–39–70. 117 rooms with bath. Facilities: airport express bus that stops opposite the hotel, restaurant, café, bar, nightclub, parking, videos available. AE, DC, MC, V.*

Moderate **Firean.** An Art Deco gem, built in 1929 and restored in 1986, it offers
★ the personal service of a family-owned and operated hotel. Rooms are decorated in peaceful pastels, offset by rich fabrics. Bathrooms come with robes and a private line of toiletries. There's a tiny bar cum breakfast room, where eggs are brought to the table in floral-print cosies. The location is not central, but there's a tram outside the door to the Old Town. *Karel Oomsstraat 6, tel. 03/237–02–60, fax 03/238–11–68. 11 rooms plus 6 in annex. Facilities: breakfast room, bar. AE, DC, MC, V. Closed first half of Aug. and Christmas Eve–weekend after Epiphany (Jan. 6).*

Prinse. Opened in 1990, this hotel occupies a 400-year-old building surrounding an interior courtyard. Rooms are a neutral modern; those on the top floor, with exposed beams, have more character. The Prinse offers peace and quiet, close to both sightseeing and shopping districts. *Keizerstraat 63, tel. 03/226–40–50, fax 03/225–11–48. 30 rooms. Facilities: breakfast room, 3 conference rooms, parking. AE, DC, MC, V.*

Inexpensive **Pension Cammerpoorte** (formerly Antwerpja). Private chauffeurs sleep here when their employers stay at De Rosier. There's no elevator, and rooms (some with a view of the Cathedral) are full of bright pastels and sad-clown art. Buffet breakfast, included in the price, is served in the tidy brick-and-lace café downstairs. *Steenhouwersvest 55, tel. 03/231–28–36, fax 03/226–29–68. 9 rooms with toilet and shower. Facilities: breakfast room. AE, DC, MC, V.*

Waldorf. This pleasant, modern hotel is near the diamond center. The smallish rooms are attractively decorated in gray and brown. *Belgielei 36, tel. 03/230–99–50, fax 03/230–78–70. 100 rooms with bath. Facilities: restaurant, bar. AE, DC, MC, V.*

Brugge

Arriving and Departing

By Train Trains run hourly at 28 and 59 minutes past the hour from Brussels (Gare du Midi) to Brugge. The London–Brussels service stops here as well. The train station is south of the canal that surrounds the downtown area; for information, tel. 050/38–23–82. Travel time from Brussels is 53 minutes.

By Car Brugge lies 97 kilometers (61 miles) northwest of Brussels. The most direct route between the two cities is the A10/E40.

Getting Around

By An expensive means of seeing the sights is provided by the horse-
Horse-Drawn drawn cabs that congregate in the Burg square, March–November,
Cab daily 10–6. A 35-minute trip will cost BF800, and the cabs take up to four people.

Guided Tours

Boat Trips Boat trips along the city canals are run by several companies and depart from five separate landings. Boats ply the waters March–November, 10–6. There is no definite departure schedule; boats leave when enough people have gathered, but you'll never have to wait more than 15 minutes or so. During the summer months, special evening cruises can be arranged.

Orientation Tours Fifty-minute minibus trips of the city center leave every hour on the hour from the Market Square in front of the post office. Tours are given in seven languages (individual headphones). Cost: BF330 (BF200 children). For further information and a full list of companies, check with the tourist office.

Tourist Information

The **Brugge Tourist Office** (Burg 11, tel. 050/44–86–86).

Exploring Brugge

Brugge (also known by its French name, Bruges) is an exquisitely preserved medieval town. It was Brugge's good fortune to be linked with the sea by a navigable waterway, and the city became a leading member of the Hanseatic League in the 13th century. Europe's first stock exchange was established here. Brugge was ignored for centuries after the Zwin River silted up in the 15th century, and the port became a romantic Flemish backwater. This past misfortune is its present glory. Little has changed in this city of interlaced canals, overhung with humpbacked bridges and weeping willows. The **Burg,** an intimate medieval square, is the inspiring setting for summer classical concerts.

Numbers in the margin correspond to points of interest on the Brugge map.

1 The best place to start a walking tour is the **Markt** (Market Square).
2 From the top of the **Belfort** (Belfry) there's a panoramic view of the town. The belfry has a carillon notable even in Belgium, where they are a matter of civic pride. On summer evenings, the Markt is brightly lit. *The Belfort. Admission: BF100. Open Apr.–Sept., daily 9:30–5. Oct.–Mar., 9:30–12:30 and 1:30–5. Carillon concerts Oct.–mid-June, Sun., Wed., and Sat. 2:15–3; mid-June–Sept., Mon., Wed., and Sat. 9–10 PM, Sun. 2:15–3.*

3 On the eastern side of the Markt stands the **Provinciaal Hof,** the neo-Gothic provincial government building. Walk east from the Markt along Breidelstraat, to the Burg, a square at the center of ancient
4 Brugge. On the left is the **Landshuis** (Provost's House), built in 1665. Across the square is a row of magnificent buildings—the
5 **Stadhuis** (town hall), dating from the 14th century, its wonderfully
6 ornate facade covered with statues; **Oude Griffie,** the former Recorder's House dating from the 1530s, and also ornamented with impressive windows; and the **Heilig-Bloed Basiliek** (the Basilica of the
7 Holy Blood), a double chapel consisting of a Romanesque 12th-century crypt and an upper chapel, rebuilt in Gothic style in the 15th century and decorated with 19th-century murals. Here the relic of the Holy Blood is worshipped every Friday. Here, too, is a **Heilig-Bloed Museum** (Museum of the Holy Blood), with many treasures associated with the cult. The Procession of the Holy Blood on Ascension Day (May 25 in 1995) is a major pageant that combines religious and historical elements. *Stadhuis—Admission: BF60. Open Apr.–*

Brugge

Begijnhof, **14**

Belfort, **2**

Dijver, **8**

Groeninge
Museum, **9**

Gruuthuse
Museum, **10**

Heilig–Bloed
Basiliek, **7**

Landshuis, **4**

Markt, **1**

Memling Museum, **11**

Minnewater, **13**

Onze-Lieve-
Vrouwekerk, **12**

Oude Griffie, **6**

Provinciaal Hof, **3**

Stadhuis, **5**

Sept., daily 9:30–5; Oct.–Mar., daily 9:30–12:30 and 2–5. Heilig-Bloed Basiliek—Admission: BF40. Open Apr.–Sept., daily 9:30–noon and 2–6; Oct.–Mar., daily 10–noon and 2–4.

⑧ Walk through a passage between the town hall and the Oude Griffie and you'll come to the **Dijver,** the city canal. Canal boat trips leave from here. *Boats leave on demand. Average trip 30 minutes. Cost: BF150.*

⑨ Walking south along the Dijver, you'll soon reach a group of museums. The **Groeninge Museum,** on the Dijver Canal, has a very rich, wide-ranging collection of Flemish masterpieces, with works by Van Eyck, Memling, Bosch, and Bruegel, among many others, plus some contemporary works. *Dijver 12. Admission: BF130. Open Apr.–Sept., daily 9:30–5; Oct.–Mar., Wed.–Mon. 9:30–12:30 and 2–5.*

⑩ The **Gruuthuse Museum,** in the 15th century a palace of the aristocratic Gruuthuse family, contains archaeological exhibitions and a display of lace from all over Belgium. *Dijver 17. Admission: BF130; combined ticket for BF350 covers the Groeninge, Gruuthuse, and Memling museums* (see below). *Open Apr.–Sept., daily 9:30–5; Oct.–Mar., Wed.–Mon. 9:30–12:30 and 2–5.*

⑪ Here, too, is the **Memling Museum,** dedicated to the work of one of Brugge's most famous sons, the painter Hans Memling (?1440–94), perhaps the most spiritual of all the Flemish Primitives, housed in the former Sint Jans Hospital (Hospital of St. John), where the artist was nursed back to health after being wounded in France. *Mariastraat 38. Admission: BF130. Open Apr.–Sept., daily 9:30–5; Oct.–Mar., Thur.–Tues. 9:30–12:30 and 2–5.*

⑫ Next to the Memling Museum is the **Onze-Lieve-Vrouwekerk** (Church of Our Lady), with, at 116 meters (375 feet), the highest tower in Belgium, a notable collection of paintings and carvings— especially a small *Madonna* by Michelangelo—and some splendidly colorful tombs. *Mausoleums—Admission: BF30. Open Apr.–Sept., weekdays 10–11:30 and 2:30–5, Sun. 2:30–5; Oct.–Mar., weekdays 10–11:30 and 2:30–4:30, Sun. 2:30–4:30. No visits during services.*

Time Out Walk south on Katelijnestraat, turn right on the narrow Stoofstraat, and find yourself on Walplein, one of Brugge's many charming squares. Treat yourself to a **Straffe Hendrik** (Strong Henry) beer: crystal clear, natural, and indeed quite strong, at the eponymous brewery pub, or a snack at **Nieuw 't Walnutje** across the street.

⑬ Continue south to the enchanting **Minnewater** (Lake of Love) Park. From the Minnewater visit the adjoining 16th-century lockkeeper's house, usually surrounded by contented white swans, the symbol of the city.

⑭ Beside Minnewater, a picturesque bridge leads to the **Begijnhof,** the former almshouses and the most serene spot in Brugge. Founded in 1245 by the countess of Constantinople, the Begijnhof was originally a home for widows of fallen Crusaders. These women took partial vows and lived a devout life while serving the community. Although the last Béguines left in 1930, a Benedictine community has replaced them. The Begijnhof has kept its cloistered charm. Notice the harmonious pattern made by the gabled white houses, the expanse of green lawn, and the crooked trees that stretch diagonally across your view.

Dining

For details and price-category definitions, *see* Dining in Staying in Belgium, *above.*

Very Expensive ★ **De Karmeliet.** One of Belgium's top culinary landmarks is in a lovely 18th-century house with a graceful English garden. The highly talented young chef serves up escalopes of goose liver with truffled potatoes, turbot with bacon, crisp potato nests with langoustines (Dublin Bay prawns), and fabulous desserts. *Langestraat 19, tel. 050/33–82–59. Reservations required. AE, DC, MC, V. Closed Sun. dinner (and Sun. lunch in July and Aug.), Mon., and 2 weeks in Aug./Sept.*

Expensive ★ **'t Boergoensche Cruyce.** Claiming one of the most romantic canalside settings in Brugge it has salmon-and-copper decor that is reflected in the water. The cuisine is equally romantic: lamb lightly flavored with fennel and cinnamon, delicate smoked halibut, saddle of hare. *Wollestraat 41, tel. 050/33–79–26. Reservations advised. AE, MC, V. Closed Tues., Wed. lunch, Feb., and mid-Nov.–mid-Dec.*

Moderate **De Castillion.** The restaurant and hotel bears the name of Jean-Baptiste de Castillion, whose residence it was during the 18th century. Predinner drinks and postprandial coffee are served in a handsome Art Deco salon, decorated in shades of blue and green. Filet mignon of venison in a Pomerol stock, duck's liver and a fricassée of tourbot and wild salmon are among the offerings. The hotel side comprises 18 rooms and 2 suites. *Hetlige Geeststraat 1, tel. 050/34–30–01, fax 050/33–94–75. Reservations advised. AE, DC, MC, V. Closed Tues. and first half of Jan.*

Inexpensive **Taverna Curiosa.** You have to descend a short but steep staircase to arrive at the cross-vaulted crypt. Snacks include very good omelettes, sandwiches, and a smoked fish plate. *Vlamingstraat 22, tel. 050/34–23–34. AE, MC, V. Closed Mon.*

Lodging

In proportion to its size, Brugge has a large number of hotels; in fact, many more than Antwerp. Prices are relatively high, but so are the standards. For details and price-category definitions, *see* Lodging in Staying in Belgium, *above.*

Expensive ★ **De Tuilerieen.** This stately mansion with its Venetian glass windows was converted into a patrician hotel in 1988 and furnished with discreet antique reproductions, weathered marble, and warm mixed-print fabrics. The bar is furnished with tartan wing-backs, and the breakfast room has a coffered ceiling. Canalside rooms have great views; courtyard rooms are quieter. *Dijver 7, tel. 050/34–36–91, fax 050/34–04–00. 26 rooms. Facilities: breakfast room, bar, parking, indoor pool, whirlpool, sauna, solarium. AE, DC, MC, V.*

Holiday Inn Crowne Plaza. This superbly located hotel has been successfully integrated into the heart of the city. The rooms are modern and agreeable. In the basement, next to the conference area, you can see remnants of the old ramparts, and a small museum contains objects found during construction. *Burg 10, tel. 050/34–58–34, fax 050/34–56–15. 96 rooms and suites with bath. Facilities: restaurant, bar, fitness center, sauna, solarium, swimming pool. AE, DC, MC, V.*

Moderate **Egmond.** This manorlike inn on the Minnewater park offers garden views from every room as well as parquet floors and the odd fireplace or dormer ceiling. The hotel is a pleasant retreat from the tourist bustle of the center, 10 minutes away. *Minnewater 15, tel. 050/34–14–45, fax 050/34–29–40. 9 rooms. Facilities: breakfast room. AE, DC, MC, V.*

Inexpensive   **De Pauw.** At this spotless, family-run hotel, the warmly furnished rooms have names rather than numbers, and breakfast comes with six different kinds of bread and a soft-boiled egg. The two rooms with shower are a super value. *St. Gilliskerkhof 8, tel. 050/33–71–18, fax 050/34–51–40. 8 rooms, 6 with bath. AE, DC, MC, V.*

Fevery. In this friendly, comfortable hotel you are made to feel a personal guest. There's even a baby monitor to enable parents to relax downstairs. Rooms have been upgraded with new carpets and fresh chenille; all have bathrooms. *Collaert Mansionstraat 3, tel. 050/33–12–69, fax 050/33–17–91. Facilities: bar. AE, DC, MC, V.*

5 Bulgaria

Bulgaria, a land of mountains and seascapes, of austerity and rustic beauty, lies in the eastern half of the Balkan peninsula. From the end of World War II until recently, it was the closest ally of the former Soviet Union and presented a rather mysterious image to the Western world. This era ended in 1989 with the overthrow of Communist party head Todor Zhivkov. Since then, Bulgaria has gradually opened itself to the West as it struggles along the path toward democracy and a free-market economy.

Endowed with long Black Sea beaches, the rugged Balkan range in its interior, and fertile Danube plains, Bulgaria has much to offer the tourist year-round. Its tourist industry is quite well developed and is being restructured to shield visitors better from shortages of goods and services and the other legacies of rigid central planning.

The Black Sea coast along the country's eastern border is particularly attractive, with secluded coves and old fishing villages, as well as wide stretches of shallow beaches that have been developed into self-contained resorts. The interior landscape offers great scenic beauty, and the traveler who enters it will find a tranquil world of forested ridges, spectacular valleys, and rural communities where folklore is a colorful part of village life.

Founded in 681, Bulgaria was a crossroads of civilization even before that date. Archaeological finds in Varna, on the Black Sea coast, give proof of civilization from as early as 4600 BC. Bulgaria was part of the Byzantine Empire from AD 1018 to 1185 and was occupied by the Turks from 1396 until 1878. The combined influences are reflected in Bulgarian architecture, which has a truly Eastern feel. Five hundred years of Muslim occupation and nearly half a century of Communist rule did not wipe out Christianity, and there are many lovely, icon-filled churches to see. The 120 monasteries, with their icons and many frescoes, provide a chronicle of the development of Bulgarian cultural and national identity, and several merit special stops on any tourist's itinerary.

The capital, Sofia, is picturesquely situated in a valley near Mount Vitosha. There is much of cultural interest here, and the city has good hotels and restaurants serving traditional and international cuisine. Other main towns are Veliko Târnovo, the capital from the 12th to the 14th centuries and well worth a visit for the old, characteristic architecture; Plovdiv, southeast of Sofia, which has a particularly interesting old quarter; and Varna, the site of one of Europe's first cultural settlements and the most important port in Bulgaria.

Essential Information

Before You Go

When to Go The ski season lasts from mid-December through March, while the Black Sea coast season runs from May to October, reaching its crowded peak in July and August. Fruit trees blossom in April and May; in May and early June the blossoms are gathered in the Valley of Roses (you have to be up early to watch the harvest); the fruit is picked in September, and in October the fall colors are at their best.

Climate Summers are warm, winters are crisp and cold. The coastal areas enjoy considerable sunshine, though March and April are the wettest months inland. Even when the temperature climbs, the Black Sea breezes and the cooler mountain air prevent the heat from being overpowering.

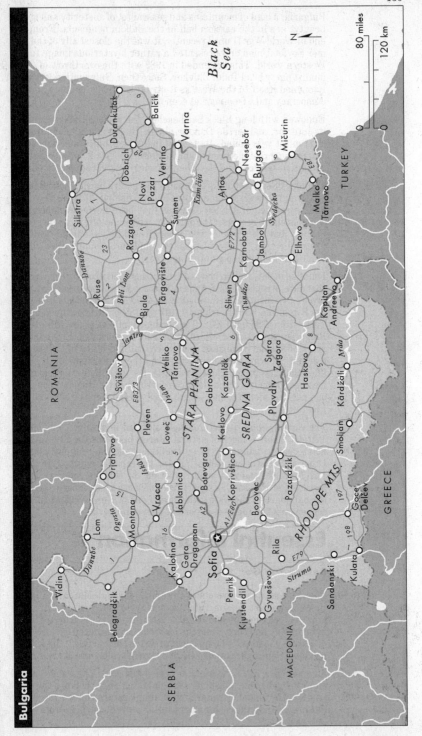

Bulgaria

The following are the average daily maximum and minimum temperatures for Sofia.

Jan.	35F	2C	May	69F	21C	Sept.	70F	22C
	25	– 4		50	10		52	11
Feb.	39F	4C	June	76F	24C	Oct.	63F	17C
	27	– 3		56	14		46	8
Mar.	50F	10C	July	81F	27C	Nov.	48F	9C
	33	1		60	16		37	3
Apr.	60F	16C	Aug.	79F	26C	Dec.	38F	4C
	42	5		59	15		28	– 2

Currency The unit of currency in Bulgaria is the lev (plural leva), divided into 100 stotinki. There are bills of 1, 2, 5, 10, 20, 50, 100, and 200 leva; coins of 1, 2, and 5 leva; and coins of 1, 2, 5, 10, 20, and 50 stotinki. At press time (spring 1994), as part of efforts at economic reform, hard-currency payments for goods and services are no longer permitted. The only legal tender for commercial transactions and tourist services in Bulgaria is the lev. These services include air, train, and long-distance bus travel; all accommodations, from camping to hotels; and car rentals and Balkantourist package tours. You may import any amount of foreign currency, including traveler's checks, and exchange it at branches of the Bulgarian State Bank, commercial banks, Balkantourist hotels, airports, border posts, and other exchange offices, which quote their daily selling and buying rates. The rate quoted by the Bulgarian State Bank at press time is 57 leva to the U.S. dollar, 85.5 leva to the pound sterling.

It is forbidden either to import or to export Bulgarian currency. Unspent leva must be exchanged at frontier posts on departure before you go through passport control. You will need to present your official exchange slips to prove that the currency was legally purchased.

The major international credit cards are accepted in the larger stores, hotels, and restaurants.

What It Will Cost Prices in Bulgaria have been low for years, but this is changing as the government tries to revive the economy and open it up to the West. If you choose the more moderate hotels, accommodations won't be very expensive. It is possible to cut costs even more by staying in a private hotel or private room in a Bulgarian house or apartment—also arranged by Balkantourist or other tourism companies—or by camping. The favorable cash exchange rate, linked to foreign-currency fluctuations, makes such expenses as taxi and public transport fares, museum and theater admission, and meals in most restaurants seem comparatively low by international standards. A little hard currency, exchanged at this rate, goes a long way. Shopping for imported and domestic wares in the duty-free shops also helps to keep travel expenses down. The following price list, correct as of spring 1994, can therefore be used only as a rough guide.

Sample Prices Trip on a tram, trolley, or bus, 3 leva; theater ticket, 20–40 leva; coffee in a moderate restaurant, 5 leva–20 leva; bottle of wine in a moderate restaurant, 40 leva–100 leva.

Museums Museum admission is very inexpensive, ranging from 10 leva to 30 leva (less than 40¢).

Visas All visitors need a valid passport. Those traveling in groups of six or more do not require visas, and many package tours are exempt from the visa requirement. Americans do not need visas when traveling as tourists. Other tourists, traveling independently, should inquire about visa requirements at a Bulgarian embassy or consulate before entering the country, since fees may be higher for visas obtained at the border.

Customs on Arrival
You may import duty-free into Bulgaria 250 grams of tobacco products, plus 1 liter of hard liquor and 2 liters of wine. Items intended for personal use during your stay are also duty-free. Travelers are advised to declare items of greater value—cameras, tape recorders, etc.—so there will be no problems with Bulgarian customs officials on departure.

Language
The official language, Bulgarian, is written in Cyrillic and is very close to Old Church Slavonic, the root of all Slavic languages. English is spoken in major hotels and restaurants, but is unlikely to be heard elsewhere. It is essential to remember that in Bulgaria, a nod of the head means "no" and a shake of the head means "yes."

Getting Around

By Car
Road Conditions
Main roads are generally well engineered, although some routes are poor and narrow for the volume of traffic they have to carry. A large-scale expressway construction program has begun to link the main towns. Completed stretches run from Kalotina—on the Serbian border—to Sofia and from Sofia to Plovdiv. Highway tolls of some $20 total are paid at the border; be prepared for delays during the summer season at border points (open 24 hours) while documents are checked and stamped.

Rules of the Road
Drive on the right, as in the United States. The speed limits are 50 or 60 kph (31 or 36 mph) in built-up areas, 80 kph (50 mph) elsewhere, except on highways, where it is 120 kph (70 mph). The limits for a car towing a trailer are 50 kph (31 mph), 70 kph (44 mph), and 100 kph (62 mph), respectively. You must obtain a Green Card or Blue Card from your car insurance company, as recognized international proof that your car is covered by International Civil Liability (third-party) Insurance. You may be required to show one of these cards at the border. Balkantourist recommends that you also take out collision, or Casco, insurance. You are required to carry a first-aid kit, fire extinguisher, and breakdown triangle in the vehicle, and you must not sound the horn in towns. Front seat belts must be worn. The drinking-driving laws are extremely strict—you are expressly forbidden to drive after consuming any alcohol at all.

Parking
Park only in clearly marked parking places. If you are in doubt, check with the hotel or restaurant.

Gasoline
Stations are regularly spaced on main roads but may be few and far between off the beaten track. All are marked on Balkantourist's free motoring map. As of press time, service stations sell unlimited quantities of fuel, supplies permitting, for leva (in spring 1994, 38¢ per liter, or $1.52 per gallon, for regular leaded). For motorist information contact the automobile club **Shipka,** located at 6 Sveta Sofia Street, Sofia (tel. 2/87–88–01 or 2/88–38–56).

Breakdowns
In case of breakdown, telephone 146. The **S.B.A.** (Bulgarian Automobile Touring Association) trucks carry essential spares, but it's wise to carry your own spare-parts kit. Fiat, Ford, Volkswagen, Peugeot, and Mercedes all have car-service operations in Bulgaria offering prompt repairs by skilled technicians.

Car Rental
The **Balkan Holidays/Hertz Rent-a-Car** organization has offices in most of the major hotels and at Sofia Airport (tel. 2/72–01–57). Its main headquarters in Sofia are at 41 Vitosha Boulevard (tel. 2/83–

34–87 or 2/88–52–05). Rental cars and fly/drive arrangements can be prebooked through Balkantourist agents abroad. These agents can also provide you with a driver for a small extra charge. **Avis** (tel. 2/79–14–77) and **Europe Car** (tel. 2/72–01–57) also have offices in Sofia.

By Train Buy tickets in advance at a ticket office—there is one in each of the major centers—and avoid long lines at the station. Trains are very busy; seat reservations are obligatory on expresses. All medium- and long-distance trains have first- and second-class carriages and limited buffet services; overnight trains between Sofia and Black Sea resorts have first- and second-class sleeping cars and second-class couchettes. From Sofia there are six main routes—to Varna and Burgas on the Black Sea coast, to Plovdiv and on to the Turkish border, to Dragoman and the Serbian border, to Kulata and the Greek border, and to Ruse on the Romanian border. The main line is powered by electricity. Plans to electrify the rest are under way.

By Plane **Balkanair** (Balkan Bulgarian Airlines) has regular services to Varna and Burgas, the biggest ports of the Black Sea. Book through Balkantourist offices; this can take time, however, and overbooking is not unusual. Group travel and air-taxi services are available through privately run Hemus Air and Air Via. Business flights to other destinations in the country are also arranged by Hemus Air.

By Bus The routes of the crowded buses are mainly planned to link towns and districts not connected by rail. Within the cities a regular system of trams and trolley buses operates for a single fare of 3 leva. Ticket booths, at most tram stops, sell single or season tickets; you can also pay the driver. The tourist information offices have full details of routes and times.

By Boat Modern luxury vessels cruise the Danube from Passau in Austria to Ruse. Hydrofoils link main communities along the Bulgarian stretches of the Danube and the Black Sea, and there are coastal excursions from some Black Sea resorts. A ferry from Vidin to Calafat links Bulgaria with Romania.

Staying in Bulgaria

Telephones Calls can be made from hotels or from public telephones in the post office in each major town or resort. Elsewhere, there is a new system of international telephones—modern, direct-dial phones with no coin slots—that operate only with special cards paid for in leva. Directions for buying the cards are given, often in English, on the phones.

Mail Letters and postcards to the United States cost 10 leva, 7 leva to the United Kingdom.

Opening and Closing Times **Banks** are open weekdays 9–3. **Museums** are usually open 8–6:30 but are often closed on Monday or Tuesday. **Shops** are open Monday–Saturday 9–7. Many shops are open on Sunday, and most grocery stores are open round-the-clock.

National Holidays January 1 (New Year's); March 3 (Independence Day); April 23 and 24 (Easter Sunday and Monday; the date is determined by the Eastern Orthodox Church every year); May 1 (Labor Day); May 24 (Bulgarian Culture Day); December 24, 25, 26 (Christmas).

Dining There is a choice of hotel restaurants with their international menus, Balkantourist restaurants, or the inexpensive restaurants and cafeterias run privately and by cooperatives. The best bets are the small folk-style restaurants that serve national dishes and local specialties. The word *picnic* in a restaurant name means that the tables are outdoors. Standards have improved, but food is still rarely served piping hot, and visitors should be prepared for loud background music.

Specialties Balkan cooking revolves around lamb and pork, sheep cheese, potatoes, peppers, eggplant, tomatoes, onions, carrots, and spices. Fresh fruit, vegetables, and salads are particularly good in season, and so are the soups. Bulgaria invented yogurt (*kiselo mleko*), with its promise of good health and longevity, and there are excellent cold yogurt soups (*tarator*) during the summer. Rich cream cakes and syrupy *baklava* are served to round out a meal.

Bulgarian wines are good, usually full-bodied, dry, and inexpensive. The national drink is *rakia*—plum or grape brandy *slivova* or *grosdova*—but vodka is popular, too. Coffee is strong and is often drunk along with a cold beverage, such as cola or a lemon drink. Tea is taken with lemon instead of milk.

Dress In Sofia, formal dress (jacket and tie) is customary at Expensive and Very Expensive restaurants. Casual dress is appropriate elsewhere.

Ratings Prices are per person and include a first course, main course, dessert, and tip, but no alcohol. Best bets are indicated by a star ★.

Category	All Areas
Very Expensive	over 180 leva
Expensive	100 leva–180 leva
Moderate	40 leva–100 leva
Inexpensive	20 leva–40 leva

Credit Cards Increasingly, even restaurants in the Moderate category are accepting credit cards, although the list of cards accepted may not always be correctly posted. Before you place an order, check to see whether you can pay with your card.

Lodging There is a wide choice of accommodations, ranging from hotels—most of them dating from the '60s and '70s—to apartment rentals, rooms in private homes, hostels, and campsites. Although hotels are improving, they still tend to suffer from temperamental wiring and erratic plumbing, and it is a good idea to pack a universal drain plug, as plugs are often missing in hotel bathrooms. In moderate and inexpensive hotels, bathrooms often look unusual. Don't be surprised if strangely placed plumbing turns the entire bathroom into a shower. Due to power cuts in the winter, flashlights and other battery-powered utilities are strongly recommended.

Hotels Until recently, most hotels used by Western visitors were owned by Balkantourist and Interhotels. At press time (spring 1993), many of the government-owned or -operated hotels listed below were on the verge of privatization. The conversion is expected to take up to five years. Hotels may be closed for renovation for extended periods or may be permanently shut down. Visitors are strongly urged to call ahead to hotels to get the latest information. Some hotels were always privately run or run by municipal authorities or organizations catering to specific groups (Sipka for motorists, Orbita for young people, Pirin for hikers). Most have restaurants and bars; the large, modern ones have swimming pools, shops, and other facilities. Some coastal resorts have complexes where different categories of hotels are grouped, each with its own facilities.

Rented Accommodations Rented accommodations are a growth industry, with planned, modern complexes as well as picturesque cottages. Cooking facilities tend to be meager, and meal vouchers are included in the deal. An English-speaking manager is generally on hand.

Private Accommodations Staying in private homes, arranged by Balkantourist, is becoming a popular alternative to hotels as a means not only of cutting costs but of offering increased contact with Bulgarians. There are one-, two-, and three-star private accommodations. Some offer a bed or bed and breakfast only; some provide full board. Three-star rooms are equipped with kitchenettes. Booking offices are located in most main tourist areas. In Sofia, contact **Balkantourist** at 27 Stambolijski Boulevard (tel. 2/88–52–56), or go to the private accommodations office at 37 Dondukov Boulevard.

Hostels Hostels are basic, but clean and cheap. Contact **Orbita** (45a Stambolijski Boulevard, Sofia, tel. 2/80–15–03 and 48 Hristo Botev Blvd., Sofia, tel. 2/80–01–02).

Campsites There are more than 100 campsites, many near the Black Sea coast. They are graded one, two, or three stars, and the best of them offer hot and cold water, grocery stores, and restaurants. Balkantourist provides a location map.

Ratings Prices are for two people in a double room with half-board (breakfast and a main meal). Best bets are indicated by a star ★. You can pay in either Western or local currency, but if you pay in leva, you must show your exchange slips to prove that the money was legally changed.

Category	Sofia	Other Areas
Very Expensive	over 5000 leva	over 2000 leva
Expensive	2000–5000 leva	1500–2000 leva
Moderate	1000–2000 leva	800–1500 leva
Inexpensive	500–1000 leva	200–800 leva

Tipping To tip, round out your restaurant bill 3%–5%.

Sofia

Arriving and Departing

By Plane All international flights arrive at Sofia airport. For information on international flights, tel. 2/79–80–35 or 2/72–06–72; domestic flights, tel. 2/72–24–14 or 2/88–13–94.

Between the Airport and Downtown Bus No. 84 (nonstop) serves the airport. Fares for taxis taken from the airport taxi stand run about 50 leva–120 leva for the 9-kilometer (6-mile) ride into Sofia. Avoid the taxi touts; they tend to overcharge or to insist on payment in hard currency.

By Train The central station is at the northern edge of the city. For information, tel. 2/3–11–11 or 2/59–71–97. The ticket offices in Sofia are in the underpass of the National Palace of Culture (1 Bulgaria Sq., tel. 2/59–71–97) or at the Rila International Travel Agency (5 Gurko St., tel. 2/87–07–77 or 2/87–59–35). There is a taxi stand at the station.

By Car Heading to or from Serbia, the main routes are E80, going through the border checkpoint at Kalotina on the Niš-Sofia road, or E871 going through the checkpoint at Gyueshevo. Traveling from Greece, take E79, passing through the checkpoint at Kulata; from Turkey, take E80, passing through checkpoint Kapitan-Andreevo. Border crossings to Romania are at Vidin on E79 and at Ruse on E70 and E85.

Getting Around

By Bus Buses, trolleys, and trams run fairly often. Buy a ticket from the ticket stand near the streetcar stop and punch it into the machine as you board. (Watch how the person in front of you does it.) For information, tel. 2/3–12–41 or 2/88–13–53.

By Taxi Since private taxi drivers were given permission to operate in 1990, it has become easier to find cabs in Sofia. Hail them in the street or at a stand—or ask the hotel to call one. Daytime taxi rates (at press time) run 5–7 leva per kilometer, 7.50–9 leva per kilometer after 10 PM. There is a 10-leva surcharge for taxis ordered by phone. To order by phone, call 142 or 68–01–01, 2/12–82, or 2/12–88. To tip, round out the fare 5%–10%.

By Rented Car You can rent a car, with or without driver, through Balkantourist, at the airport, and at hotel reception desks.

On Foot The main sites are centrally located, so the best way to see the city is on foot.

Important Addresses and Numbers

Since late 1990, a national commission has been working to rename cities, streets, and monuments throughout the country. Names given in the following sections were correct as of spring 1993 but are subject to change.

Tourist Information **Balkantourist Head Office** (tel. 2/4–33–31) is at 1 Vitosha Boulevard; the tourist and accommodations office (tel. 2/88–44–30 or 2/88–03–62; 2/88–06–55; 2/80–07–37) is at 37 Dondukov Boulevard. It also has offices or desks in all the main hotels. **Balkantour** is at 27 Stambolijski Blvd., tel. 2/88–52–56 **Pirin** is at 30 Stambolijski Blvd., tel. 2/88–41–22.

Embassies **U.S.** (1 Stambolijski Blvd., tel. 2/88–48–01). **U.K.** (65 Levski Blvd., tel. 2/88–53–61).

Emergencies **Police:** Sofia City Constabulary (tel. 166), **ambulance** (tel. 150), **Fire** (tel. 160), **Doctor:** Clinic for Foreign Citizens (Mladost 1, 1 Eugeni Pavlovski St., tel. 2/7–43–91), **"Pirogov"** Emergency Hospital (tel. 2/5–15–31), **pharmacies** (tel. 178 for information about all-night pharmacies).

Guided Tours

Orientation Tours Guided tours of Sofia and environs are arranged by Balkantourist from either of the main Sofia offices or from Balkantourist desks at the major hotels. Among the possibilities are three- to four-hour tours of the principal city sights by car or minibus or a longer four- to five-hour tour that goes as far as Mount Vitosha.

Excursions Balkantourist offers 23 types of special-interest tours of various lengths, using Sofia as the point of departure. There are trips to the most beautiful monasteries, such as the Rila Monastery, 118 kilometers (74 miles) south of Sofia; to museum towns, such as Nesebâr and Koprivshtitsa; to sports areas and spas; to the Valley of Roses; and to other places of exceptional scenic or cultural interest.

Evening Tours Balkantourist has a number of evening tours, from a night out eating local food and watching folk dances to an evening at the National Opera.

Exploring Sofia

Sofia is set on the high Sofia Plain, ringed by mountain ranges: the Balkan range to the north; the Lyulin Mountains to the west; part of the Sredna Gora Mountains to the southeast; and, to the southwest, Mount Vitosha, the city's playground, which rises to 2,325 meters (7,500 feet). The area has been inhabited for about 7,000 years, but the visitor's first impression is of a modern city with broad streets, light traffic, spacious parks, and open-air cafés. As recently as the 1870s it was part of the Turkish Empire, and one mosque still remains. Most of the city, however, was planned after 1880. There are enough intriguing museums and high-quality musical performances to merit a lengthy stay, but if time is short, you need only two days to see the main sights and another day, at least, for Mount Vitosha.

Numbers in the margin correspond to points of interest on the Sofia map.

❶ **Ploshtad Sveta Nedelya** (St. Nedelya Square) is a good starting point for an exploration of the main sights. The south side of the square is **❷** dominated by the 19th-century **Tzarkva Sveta Nedelya** (St. Nedelya Church). Go behind it to find Vitosha Boulevard, a lively pedestrian street with plenty of stores, cafés, and dairy bars.

The first building along this boulevard, on the west side of the **❸** street, is the former Courts of Justice, now the **Natzionalen Istoricheski Musei** (National History Museum). Its vast collections, vividly illustrating the art history of Bulgaria, include priceless Thracian treasures, Roman mosaics, enameled jewelry from the First Bulgarian Kingdom, and glowing religious art that survived the years of Ottoman oppression. The courts are due to return to this location as soon as a new home is found for the National History Museum collection. *2 Vitosha Blvd., tel. 2/88–41–60. Open Tues.–Fri. and weekends 10:30–6:15.*

Return to the northeast side of St. Nedelya Square, and in the courtyard of the Sheraton Sofia Balkan Hotel you will see the **❹** **Rotonda Sveti Georgi** (Rotunda of St. George). Built in the 4th century as a Roman temple, it has served as a mosque and church, and recent restoration has revealed medieval frescoes. It is not open to the public. Head east to the vast and traffic-free Alexander **❺** Batenberg Square, which is dominated by the **Partiyniyat Dom** (the former headquarters of the Bulgarian Communist party).

Facing the square, but entered via Alexander Stambolijski Boulevard, is the former Great Mosque, which now houses the **❻** **Natzionalen Archeologicheski Musei** (National Archaeological Museum). The 15th-century building itself is as fascinating as its contents, which illustrate the culture of the different peoples who inhabited Bulgaria up to the 19th century. *Tel. 2/88–24–06. Open Tues.–Sun. 10–noon and 2–6.*

❼ On the next block to the east is the former **Mavsolei Georgi Dimitrov** (Georgi Dimitrov Mausoleum), which until 1990 contained the embalmed body of the first general secretary of the Bulgarian Commu-

Sofia

Banya Bashi
Djamiya, **16**
Borisova Gradina, **13**
Hram-pametnik
Alexander Nevski, **11**
Mavsolei Georgi
Dimitrov, **7**
Nacionalen Dvoretz na
Kulturata **14**

Natzionalen
Archeologicheski
Musei, **6**
Natzionalen
Etnografski Musei, **8**
Natzionalen
Istoricheski Musei, **3**
Natzionalna
Hudozhestvena
Galeria, **9**
Partiyniyat Dom, **5**
Ploshtad Sveta
Nedelya, **1**

Rotonda Sveti
Georgi, **4**
Tsentralen
Universalen
Magazin, **15**
Tsentralni Hali, **17**
Tzarkva Sveta
Nedelya, **2**
Tzarkva Sveta
Sofia, **12**
Tzarkva Sveti
Nikolai, **10**

nist party, who died in Moscow in 1949 and was known as the "Father of the Nation." His remains have been moved to the Central Cemetery, and there is talk of converting the mausoleum into a museum, or destroying it.

8 Across from the mausoleum is the former palace of the Bulgarian Czar, which currently houses the **Natzionalen Etnografski Musei** (National Ethnographical Museum), with displays of costumes, handicrafts, and tools that illustrate the agricultural way of life of the country people until the 19th century. *Alexander Batenberg Sq., tel. 2/88–42–09. Open Wed.–Sun. 10–noon and 1:30–5:30.*

9 In the west wing of the same building is the **Natzionalna Hudozhestvena Galeria** (National Art Gallery). It houses a collection of the best works of Bulgarian artists, as well as a foreign art section that contains some graphics of famous artists. *1 Knyaz Al. Batemberg, tel. 2/88–35–59. Open Tues.–Sun. 10:30–6.*

10 Nearby stands the ornate Russian **Tzarkva Sveti Nikolai** (Church of St. Nicholas), erected 1912–14.

From here you'll enter Tzar Osvoboditel Boulevard, with its monument to the Russians, topped by the equestrian statue of Russian Czar Alexander II. It stands in front of the National Assembly. Behind the National Assembly, just beyond Shipka Street, you'll be confronted by the neo-Byzantine structure with glittering onion domes whose image you may recognize from almost every piece of tourist literature, and which really does dominate the city. This is **11** the **Hram-pametnik Alexander Nevski** (Alexander Nevski Memorial Church), built by the Bulgarian people at the beginning of this century as a mark of gratitude to their Russian liberators. Inside are alabaster and onyx, Italian marble and Venetian mosaics, magnificent frescoes, and space for a congregation of 5,000. Attend a service to hear the superb choir, and, above all, don't miss the fine collection of icons in the **Crypt Museum.** *Ploshtad Alexander Nevski, tel. 2/87–76–97. Admission: 20 leva. Open Wed.–Mon. 10:30–6:30.*

12 Cross the square to the west to pay your respects to the much older **Tzarkva Sveta Sofia** (Church of St. Sofia), which dates to the 6th century, though remains of even older churches have been found during excavations. Its age and simplicity are in stark contrast to its more glamorous neighbor.

13 Return to Tzar Osvoboditel Boulevard and continue east to the **Borisova Gradina** (Boris's Garden), with its lake and fountains, woods and lawns, huge sports stadium, and open-air theater. From the park take Dragan Tsankov west (back toward St. Nedelya Square) briefly, before going left on Patriarh Evtimij, toward Južen Park. The formal gardens and extensive woodlands here are to be extended as far as Mount Vitosha.

14 At the entrance to the park stands a large modern building, the **Natzionalen Dvoretz na Kulturata** (National Palace of Culture), with its complex of halls for conventions and cultural activities. Its underpass, on several levels, is equipped with a tourist information office, shops, restaurants, discos, and a bowling alley. *1 Bulgaria Sq., tel. 2/5–15–01. Admission: 5 leva. Open 10:30–6:30. Closed Tues.*

15 Back at St. Nedelya Square, follow Knyaginya Maria-Luiza Boulevard to the train station. The large building on the right is the recently refurbished **Tsentralen Universalen Magazin** (Central Department Store). *2 Knyaginya Maria-Luiza Blvd. Open Mon.–Sat. 8–8.*

16 Just beyond is a distinctive building, a legacy of Turkish domination, the **Banya Bashi Djamiya** (Banja Basi Mosque); it is closed to visitors. Nearby you will see the Public Mineral Baths. Across the boul-

17 evard is the busy **Tsentralni Hali** (Central Market Hall), which is closed for renovations until the end of 1994.

Time Out Anyone doing the full tour is going to need at least one refreshment stop. There are several places to eat on the northern length of Vitosha Boulevard; three of the best cafés are **Magura, Medovina,** and **One Dollar.** A café huddles near the 14th-century church of **Sveta Petka Samardzijska** (St. Petka of the Saddles) in the underpass leading to the Central Department Store. Or take a break in a café in the underpass at the National Palace of Culture or on St. Nedelya Square itself at the Complex Roubin.

Off the Beaten Track

The little medieval church of **Boyana,** about 10 kilometers (6 miles) south of the city center, is well worth a visit as is the small, elegant restaurant of the same name, next door. The church itself is closed for restoration, but a replica, complete with copies of the exquisite 13th-century frescoes, is open to visitors.

The **Dragalevci Monastery** stands in beechwoods above the nearby village of Dragalevci. The complex is currently a convent, but you can visit the 14th-century church with its outdoor frescoes. Shepherds can often be seen tending their flocks in the surrounding woods. From here take the chair lift to the delightful resort complex of **Aleko,** and another nearby chair lift to the top of Malak Rezen. There are well-marked walking and ski trails in the area. Both Boyana and Dragalevci can be reached by taking the No. 64 bus.

Shopping

Gifts and There are good selections of arts and crafts at the shop of the **Union**
Souvenirs **of Bulgarian Artists** (6 Tzar Osvoboditel Blvd.) and at the **Bulgarian Folk Art Shop** (14 Vitosha Blvd.). You will find a range of souvenirs at **Sredec** (7 Lege St.), **Souvenir Store** (7 Stambolijski Blvd.), and **Prizma Store** (2 Tzar Osvoboditel Blvd). If you are interested in furs or leather, try **4 Slavjanska St., 7 Car Kalojan St.,** or **2 Tzar Osvoboditel Blvd.** For recordings of Bulgarian music, go to the **National Palace of Culture** (*see* Exploring Sofia, above).

Shopping The latest shopping center is in the underpass below the modern **Na-**
Districts **tional Palace of Culture,** where stores sell fashions, leather goods, and all forms of handicrafts. The pedestrians-only area along **Vitosha Boulevard** features many new, privately owned shops. The colorful small shops along **Graf Ignatiev Street** also merit a visit.

Department Sophia's biggest department store is the newly renovated **Central**
Stores **Department Store** (2 Knyaginya Maria-Luiza Boulevard).

Dining

Eating in Sofia can be enjoyable and even entertaining if the restaurant has a nightclub or folklore program. Be prepared to be patient and make an evening of it, as service can be slow at times. Or try a *mehana,* or tavern, where the atmosphere is informal and the service sometimes a bit quicker. For details and price-category definitions, *see* Dining in Staying in Bulgaria.

Very Expensive

Club Restaurant of the Hunting and Fishing Union. Here you can choose from an excellent menu of game, fish, and fowl. *31–33 Vitosha Blvd., tel. 2/87–94–65. Reservations essential. AE, DC, MC, V.*

Coop-35 Vitosha. Continental cuisine is served in a friendly, homey atmosphere that makes it a good choice for both business dinners and more intimate dining. *Dragalevci District, 1 Narcis St., tel. 2/67–11–84. No credit cards.*

Dionyssos Vip. This club and restaurant above the Central Department Store (Zum), opposite the Sheraton Hotel, provides a rich selection of international and Bulgarian cuisine spiced with a three-hour floor show. *2 Knyaginya Maria-Luiza Blvd., tel. 2/81–37–26. Reservations advised. DC, MC, V.*

Krim. This Russian restaurant serves the best beef Stroganoff in town. *17 Slavydnska, tel. 2/87–01–31. Reservations advised. AE.*

Expensive

Berlin. German food is the specialty in this sophisticated restaurant in the Serdika Hotel. *2 Yanko Sakazov Blvd., tel. 2/44–12–58. Reservations accepted. AE, DC, MC, V.*

★ **Budapest.** This place enjoys a reputation as one of the best restaurants in Sofia for good food, wine, and live music. As the name suggests, Hungarian food takes center stage. *145 G.S. Rakovski St., tel. 2/87–37–50. Reservations accepted. AE, DC, MC, V.*

Havana. Cuban food is featured in this popular restaurant near the center of town. *27 Vitosha Blvd., tel. 2/80–05–44. Reservations accepted. No credit cards.*

Moderate

Boyansko Hanche. Local and national specialties are the main features in this restaurant and folklore center, 6 miles from downtown (take bus No. 63, 64, or 107). *Near Bojanska church, tel. 2/56–30–16. AE, DC, MC, V.*

Phenyan. This place is known for its Far Eastern ambience and chinese specialties. *24 Assen Zlatarov St., tel. 2/44–34–36. DC, MC, V.*

Ropotamo. With its central location and reasonable prices, Ropotamo is a good bet for visitors on a budget. *63 Trakia Blvd., tel. 2/72–25–16. AE, DC, MC, V.*

Rubin. This eating complex in the center of Sofia has a snack bar and an elegant restaurant that serves Bulgarian and international food. A full meal can sometimes push the cost into the Expensive bracket. *4 St. Nedelya Sq., tel. 2/87–47–04. AE, DC, MC, V.*

Vodeničarski Mehani. The English translation is "Miller's Tavern," which is appropriate, since it's made up of three old mills linked together. It is at the foot of Mount Vitosha and features a folklore show and a menu of Bulgarian specialties. *Dragalevci District (bus No. 64), tel. 2/67–10–21. AE, DC, MC, V.*

Inexpensive

Party Club. This restaurant features international and Chinese cuisine. *3 Vasil Levski Blvd., tel. 2/81–05–44 or 2/81–43–43. Reservations accepted. AE, DC, MC, V.*

Zheravna. Candlelight, stone walls, and wood tables set the scene for Zherzavna's country cuisine. *26 Levski Blvd., tel. 2/87–21–86. No credit cards.*

Zlatnite Mostove. This restaurant on Mount Vitosha has live music in the evenings. *Vitosha District, 19 km (12 mi) from the city center. No credit cards.*

Lodging

The following hotels maintain a high standard of cleanliness and are open year-round unless otherwise stated. If you arrive in Sofia without reservations, go to Interhotels Central Office (4 Sveta Sofia St.),

Balkantourist (37 Dondukov Blvd.), Bureau of Tourist Information and Reservations (35 Eksarh Josif St.), the National Palace of Culture (1 Bulgaria Sq.), or the central rail station. For details and price-category definitions, *see* Lodging in Staying in Bulgaria.

Very **Novotel Europa.** This member of the French Novotel chain is near
Expensive the train station and not far from the center of the city. *131 Knyaginya Maria-Luiza Blvd., tel. 2/3–12–61. 600 rooms with bath. Facilities: 2 restaurants, cocktail bar, coffee shop, shops. AE, DC, MC, V.*

★ **Sheraton Sofia Hotel Balkan.** The former Grand Hotel Balkan has recently been done up to Sheraton standards. It is now a first-class hotel with a central location that is hard to match. It also has excellent restaurants. *1 St. Nedelya Sq., tel. 2/87–65–41. 188 rooms with bath. Facilities: 3 restaurants, fitness center, whirlpool, nightclub, bars. AE, DC, MC, V.*

★ **Vitosha.** There is a distinct Oriental flavor to this towering, trim Interhotel, which is not surprising, since it was designed by the Japanese. It is hard to match the range of services and activities available here. The Vitosha also has a superb Japanese restaurant. *100 James Boucher Blvd., tel. 2/6–25–11. 454 rooms with bath. Facilities: 5 restaurants, 6 bars, shopping and business center, tennis courts, sauna, fitness center, pool, nightclub, casino. AE, DC, MC, V.*

Expensive **Grand Hotel Sofia.** This five-story, centrally located Interhotel conveys an atmosphere of relative intimacy, compared with some of its larger rivals in the capital. *4 Narodno Sobranie Sq., tel. 2/87–88–21. 204 rooms with bath. Facilities: 3 restaurants, coffee shop, folk tavern, nightclub, cocktail bar, and shops. AE, DC, MC, V.*

Park Hotel Moskva. The pleasant park setting makes up for the fact that this hotel is not as centrally located as some other comparable hotels. The excellent Panorama restaurant is hidden away on the rooftop. *25 Nezabravka St., tel. 2/7–12–61 or 2/83–32–15. 390 rooms with bath. Facilities: 4 restaurants, coffee shop, cocktail bar, nightclub, shops. AE, DC, MC, V.*

Rodina. Sofia's highest building is not far from the city center and boasts the latest in modern facilities. *8 Tzar Bovis III Blvd., tel. 2/5–16–31. 536 rooms with bath. Facilities: 3 restaurants, coffee shop, cocktail bar, shops, summer and winter gardens, pool, gym, nightclub. AE, DC, MC, V.*

Moderate **Bulgaria.** Despite its central location, this small hotel is quiet and a bit old-fashioned. *4 Tzar Osvoboditel Blvd., tel. 2/88–22–11 or 2/87–01–91. 85 rooms, some with bath or shower. Facilities: restaurant, tavern, coffee shop, cocktail bar. AE, DC, MC, V.*

Deva-Spartak. This small new hotel is located behind the National Palace of Culture. It offers excellent sports facilities. *Valdo Georgiev St., tel. 2/66–12–61. 16 rooms with bath. Facilities: restaurant, indoor and outdoor swimming pools, Spartak sports complex, shop. No credit cards.*

Hemus. This is a smaller place near the Vitosha Hotel. Guests can take advantage of the facilities of its larger neighbor while saving money for the casino or nightclub. *31 Cherni Vrah Blvd., tel. 2/6–39–51 or 2/66–13–19. 240 rooms, most with bath or shower. Facilities: restaurant, folk tavern, nightclub, shops. AE, DC, MC, V.*

Pliska-Cosmos. Part of the Balkan Airlines hotel chain, the Pliska-Cosmos, located at the entrance to Sofia, has been recently renovated. *87 Tzarigradsko Shose Blvd., tel. 2/71–281. 200 rooms with shower. Facilities: restaurant, cocktail bar, shops, casino. DC, MC, V.*

Rila. A convenient, central downtown location makes it a low-cost alternative to the Sheraton. *6 Kaloyan St., tel. 2/88–18–61. 120 rooms with bath or shower. Facilities: restaurant, coffee shop, folk tavern, art gallery, fitness center. AE, DC, MC, V.*

Inexpensive **Serdika.** The centrally located Serdika has an old Berlin-style restaurant that serves German specialties. *2 Yanko Sakazov Blvd., tel. 2/44–34–11. 140 rooms, most with shower. DC, MC, V.*

The Arts

The standard of music in Bulgaria is high, whether it takes the form of opera, symphonic, or folk music, which has just broken into the international scene with its close harmonies and colorful stage displays. Contact Balkantourist or the **Concert Office** (2 Tzar Osvoboditel Blvd., tel. 2/87–15–88) for general information.

You don't need to understand Bulgarian to enjoy a performance at the **Central Puppet Theater** (14 Gourko St., tel. 2/88–54–16) or at the **National Folk Ensemble** (check with the tourist office for details).

There are a number of fine art galleries: The art gallery of the **Sts. Cyril and Methodius International Foundation** has a collection of Indian, African, Japanese, and Western European paintings and sculptures (Alexander Nevski Sq., tel. 2/88–49–22; open Wed.– Mon. 10:30–6). The art gallery of the **Union of Bulgarian Artists** has exhibitions of contemporary Bulgarian art (6 Shipka St., tel. 2/44–61–15; open daily 10:30–6). The **City Art Gallery** has both permanent exhibits 19th-century and modern Bulgarian paintings as well as changing exhibits by contemporary artists (1 Gen. Gurko, tel. 2/87–21–81).

The **Odeon, Serdika,** and **Vitosha cinemas** show recent foreign films in their original languages with Bulgarian subtitles.

Nightlife

Nightclubs The following hotel bars have floor shows and a lively atmosphere: **Bar Sofia** (Grand Hotel Sofia, 1 Narodno Sobranie Sq., tel. 2/87–88–21); **Bar Variety Ambassador** (Vitosha Hotel, 100 James Boucher Blvd., tel. 2/6–24–51); **Bar Variety** (Park Hotel Moskva, 25 Nezabravka St., tel. 2/7–25–11); **Bar Fantasy** (Sheraton Sofia Hotel Balkan, 1 St. Nedelya Sq., tel. 2/87–65–41).

Discos There is a disco, nightclub, and bowling alley at the **National Palace of Culture** (1 Bulgaria Sq.). Other choices are **Orbylux,** known as the classiest disco in town (76 James Boucher Blvd., tel. 2/66–89–97); **Angel** (centrally located at Narodno Sobranie Sq.); and **Sky Club,** a big, two-tier disco (63 Hristo Botev Blvd., tel. 2/54–81–40).

Casino Gamblers can try their luck at the casino in the **Vitosha Hotel,** (100 James Boucher Blvd., tel. 2/62–41–51) at the **Sheraton Sofia Hotel** (1 St. Nedelya Sq., tel. 2/82–65–43), or at **Pliska Cosmos** (87 Tzari-gradsko Shose, tel. 2/71–281).

The Black Sea Golden Coast

Bulgaria's most popular resort area attracts visitors from all over Europe. Its sunny, sandy beaches are backed by the easternmost slopes of the Balkan range and by the Strandja Mountains. Although the tourist centers tend to be huge state-built complexes with a somewhat lean feel, they have modern amenities. Sunny Beach, the largest of the resorts, with more than 100 hotels, has plenty of children's amusements and play areas; baby-sitters are also available.

The historic port of Varna is a good center for exploration. It is a focal point of land and sea transportation and has museums, a variety of restaurants, and some nightlife. The fishing villages of Nesebâr and Sozopol are more attractive. Lodgings tend to be scarce in these villages, so private accommodations, arranged on the spot or by Balkantourist, are a good option. Whatever resort you choose, all offer facilities for water sports and some have instructors. Tennis and horseback riding are also available.

Getting Around

Buses make frequent runs up and down the coast and are inexpensive. Buy your ticket in advance from the kiosks near the bus stops. **Cars** and **bicycles** can be rented; bikes are particularly useful for getting around such sprawling resorts as Sunny Beach. A **hydrofoil** service links Varna, Nesebâr, Burgas, and Sozopol. A regular **boat** service travels the Varna–Sveti Konstantin (St. Konstantin)–Golden Sands–Albena–Balčik route.

Guided Tours

A wide range of excursions are arranged from all resorts. There are bus excursions to Sofia from Golden Sands, Sveti Konstantin, Albena, and Sunny Beach; a one-day bus and boat trip along the Danube from Golden Sands, Sveti Konstantin, and Albena; and a three-day bus tour of Bulgaria, including the Valley of Roses, departing from Golden Sands, Sveti Konstantin, and Albena. All tours are run by Balkantourist (*see* Tourist Information, *below*, or check with your hotel information desk).

Tourist Information

There is a Balkantourist office in most towns and resorts.

Albena (tel. 057/21–52 or 057/23–12).
Burgas (1 Gani-Ganev St., tel. 056/4–81–11).
Golden Sands (tel. 052/85–54–07).
Nesebâr (18 Yana Luskova St., tel. 0554/–28–55).
Sunny Beach (tel. 0554/69–01 or 69–10 or 0554/23–12 or 23–15).
Sveti Konstantin (tel. 052/82–10–45).
Varna (main office, 3 Moussala St., tel. 052/22–55–24 or 052/22–22–72 private accommodations office, 3 Kniaz Boris I Blvd.).

Exploring the Black Sea Golden Coast

Varna **Varna**, Bulgaria's third-largest city, is easily reached by rail (about 7½ hours by express) or road from Sofia. If you plan to drive, allow

The Black Sea Golden Coast

N

Durankulak

Dobrich

Balčik

Shabla

Novi Pazar

Albena

Kavarna

Vetrino

A2

Zlatni Pjasâci
(Golden Sands)

Sveti Konstantin

Varna

Goljama

Staro Orjahovo

Kamčija

Bjala

Kamčija

Obzor

Orizare

Black Sea

Slånčev Brjag
(Sunny Beach)

Ajtos

Nesebâr

Pomorie

Burgas

Sredecka

Sozopol

Djuni

Primorsko

Mičurin

Ahtopol

TURKEY

| 0 | | 40 miles |
| 0 | | 60 km |

---

time to see the Stone Forest (Pobiti Kammani) just off the Sofia-Varna road between Devnya and Varna. The unexpected groups of monumental sandstone tree trunks are thought to have been formed when the area was the bed of the Lutsian Sea. There is plenty to see in the port city of Varna. The ancient city, named Odessos by the Greeks, became a major Roman trading center and is now an important shipbuilding and industrial city. The main sights can be linked by a planned walk.

Begin with the **Archeologicheski Musei,** one of the great—if lesser known—museums of Europe. The splendid collection includes the world's oldest gold treasures from the Varna necropolis of the 4th millennium BC, as well as Thracian, Greek, and Roman treasures and richly painted icons. *41 Osmi Primorski Polk Blvd., tel. 052/23-70-57. Open Tues.–Sun. 10-6.*

Near the northeastern end of Osmi Primorski Polk Boulevard are numerous shops and cafés; the western end leads to Mitropolit Simeon Square and the monumental **cathedral** (1880–86), whose lavish murals are worth a look. Running north from the cathedral is Vladislav Varnenchik Street, with shops, movie theaters, and eateries. Opposite the cathedral, in the City Gardens, is the **Old Clock Tower,** built in 1880 by the Varna Guild Association. On the south side of the City Gardens, on Nezavisimost Square, stands the magnificent Baroque **Stoyan Bucharov National Theater.**

Leave the square to the east and walk past the Moussala Hotel. The **tourist information office** is at 3 Moussala Street (tel. 052/22-55-24). Nearby, on the corner of Kniaz Boris I Boulevard and Shipka Street, are the remains of the **Roman fortress wall** of Odessos. Kniaz

Boris I Boulevard is another of Varna's shopping streets. At No. 44 you can buy handcrafted souvenirs from one of the outlets of the Union of Bulgarian Artists.

Walk south along Odessos Street to Han Krum Street. Here you'll find the Holy Virgin Church of 1602 and the substantial remains of the **Roman Thermae**—the public baths, dating from the 2nd to the 3rd century AD. Buy the excellent English guidebook here to get the most out of your visit.

Not far from the baths, moving west, is old Drǎzki Street, recently restored and comfortingly lined with restaurants, taverns, and coffeehouses.

Head toward the sea and November 8 Street. Continue to Primorski Boulevard and follow it, with the sea on your right, to No. 2 for the **Naval Museum** (tel. 052/24–06; open daily 8–6:30), with its displays of the early days of navigation on the Black Sea and the Danube. The museum is at the edge of the extensive and luxuriant **Marine Gardens,** which command a wide view over the bay. In the gardens there are restaurants, an open-air theater, and the fascinating **Copernicus Astronomy Complex** (tel. 02/82–94; open weekdays 8–noon and 2–5) near the main entrance.

Sveti Konstantin Eight kilometers (5 miles) north along the coast from Varna is **Sveti Konstantin,** Bulgaria's oldest Black Sea resort. Small and intimate, it spreads through a wooded park near a series of sandy coves. Warm mineral springs were discovered here in 1947, and the five-star **Grand Hotel Varna,** the most luxurious on the coast, offers all kinds of hydrotherapy under medical supervision (*see* Lodging, *below*).

In contrast to the sedate atmosphere of Sveti Konstantin is lively **Zlatni Pjasâci** (Golden Sands), a mere 8 kilometers (5 miles) to the north, with its extensive leisure amenities, mineral-spring medical centers, and sports and entertainment facilities. Just over 4 kilometers (2 miles) inland from Golden Sands is **Aladja Rock Monastery,** one of Bulgaria's oldest, cut out of the cliff face and made accessible to visitors by sturdy iron stairways.

From Sveti Konstantin, if time permits, take a trip 16 kilometers (10 miles) north to **Balčik.** Part of Romania until just before World War II, it is now a relaxed haven for Bulgaria's writers, artists, and scientists. On its white cliffs are crescent-shaped tiers populated with houses, and by the Balčik Palace, the beautiful **Botanical Gardens** are dotted with curious buildings, including a small Byzantine-style church.

Albena, the newest Black Sea resort, is located between Balčik and Golden Sands. It is well known for its long, wide beach and clean sea. The most luxurious among its 35 hotels is the **Dobrudja,** with extensive hydrotherapy facilities.

Slânčev Brjag Another popular resort, this time 36 kilometers (22.5 miles) south of Varna, is **Slânčev Brjag** (Sunny Beach). It is enormous and especially suited to families because of its safe beaches, gentle tides, and facilities for children. During the summer there are kindergartens for young vacationers, children's concerts, and even a children's discotheque. Sunny Beach has a variety of beachside restaurants, kiosks, and playgrounds.

Nesebâr is 5 kilometers (3 miles) south of Sunny Beach and accessible by regular excursion buses. It would be hard to find a town that exudes a greater sense of age than this ancient settlement, founded by the Greeks 25 centuries ago on a rocky peninsula reached by a narrow causeway. Among its vine-covered houses are richly decorated medieval churches. Don't miss the frescoes and the dozens of small, private, cozy pubs all over Nesebâr.

Continue traveling south along the coast. The next place of any size is **Burgas,** Bulgaria's second main port on the Black Sea. Burgas is rather industrial, with several oil refineries, though it does have a pleasant **Maritime Park** with an extensive beach below.

For a more appealing stopover, continue for another 32 kilometers (20 miles) south to **Sozopol,** a fishing port with narrow cobbled streets leading down to the harbor. This was Apollonia, the oldest of the Greek colonies in Bulgaria. It is now a popular haunt for Bulgarian and, increasingly, foreign writers and artists who find private accommodations in the rustic Black Sea–style houses, so picturesque with their rough stone foundations and unpainted wood slats on the upper stories. It is also famous for the Apollonia Arts Festival, held each September.

Ten kilometers (6 miles) farther south is the vast, modern resort village of **Djuni,** where visitors can stay in up-to-date cottages, in the modern Monastery Compound, or in the Seaside Settlement. The wide range of amenities—cafés, folk restaurants, a sports center, shopping center, yacht club, and marina—make it another attractive vacation spot for families.

Dining and Lodging

For details and price-category definitions, *see* Dining and Lodging in Staying in Bulgaria. Gradually, even restaurants in the moderate category are beginning to accept credit cards. Check with a restaurant before ordering.

Albena
Dining

Bambuka (Bamboo Tree). This open-air restaurant serves international and Bulgarian cuisine and seafood. *Albena Resort, tel. 5772/24–04. Moderate. No credit cards.*

Lodging

Dobrudja Hotel. This is a big, comfortable hotel with a mineral-water health spa. *Albena Resort, tel. 5722/20–20. 272 rooms with bath. Facilities: restaurants, nightclub, coffee shops, cocktail bars, shops, indoor and outdoor swimming pools, fitness center, hydrotherapy. DC, MC, V. Moderate.*

Burgas
Dining

Starata Gemia. The name of this restaurant translates as "old boat," appropriate for a beachfront restaurant featuring fish specialties. *39 Aleksandrovska St., tel. 056/45708. Moderate. No credit cards.*

Lodging

Bulgaria. The Bulgaria is a high-rise Interhotel in the center of town. It features its own nightclub with floor show and a restaurant set in a winter garden. *21 Aleksandrovska St., tel. 056/4–28–20. 200 rooms, most with bath or shower. DC, MC, V. Moderate.*

Slânčev Brjag
Dining

Hanska Šatra. Situated in the coastal hills behind the sea, this combination restaurant and nightclub has been built to resemble the tents of the Bulgarian khans of old. It has entertainment well into the night. *4.8 km (3 mi) west of Slânčev Brjag, tel. 0554/2811. No credit cards. Moderate.*
Ribarska Hiza. This lively beachside restaurant specializes in fish and has music until 1 AM. *Northern end of Slânčev Brjag Resort, tel. 0554/2437. No credit cards. Inexpensive.*

Lodging

Burgas. Large and comfortable, this hotel lies at the southern end of the resort. *Slânčev Brjag Resort, tel. 0554/23–58. 250 rooms with* *bath or shower. Facilities: restaurant, 2 pools, sports hall, coffee shop, cocktail bar. AE, DC, MC, V. Moderate.*

★ **Globus.** Considered by many to be the best in the resort, this hotel combines a central location with modern facilities. *Slânčev Brjag Resort, tel. 0554/22–45. 100 rooms with bath or shower. Facilities: indoor pool, restaurant, sports hall, coffee shop, cocktail bar. AE, DC, MC, V. Moderate.*

Kuban. Near the center of the resort, this large establishment is just a short stroll from the beach. *Slânčev Brjag Resort, tel. 0554/23–09. 216 rooms, most with bath or shower. Facilities: restaurants, coffee shops. AE, DC, MC, V. Moderate.*

Čajka. This hotel offers the best location at a low cost. *Slânčev Brjag Resort, tel. 0554/23–08. 36 rooms, some with bath or shower. No credit cards. Inexpensive.*

Sveti Konstantin
Dining

Bulgarska Svatba. This folk-style restaurant with dancing is on the outskirts of the resort; charcoal-grilled meats are especially recommended. *Sveti Konstantin Resort, tel. 052/861283. No credit cards. Moderate.*

Manastirska Izba. Centrally located, this eatery is a modest but pleasant restaurant with a sunny terrace. *Sveti Konstantin Resort, tel. 0566–11–77. No credit cards. Moderate.*

Lodging
★

Grand Hotel Varna. This Swedish-built hotel has a reputation for being the best hotel on the coast. It is set just 139 meters (150 yards) from the beach and offers a wide range of hydrotherapeutic treatments featuring the natural warm mineral springs. *Sveti Konstantin Resort, tel. 052/86–14–91. 325 rooms with bath. Facilities: 3 restaurants, nightclub, 2 swimming pools, sports hall, tennis courts, bowling alley, coffee shops, cocktail bars, shops. AE, DC, MC, V. Expensive.*

Čajka. Čajka means "sea gull" in Bulgarian, and this hotel has a bird's-eye view of the entire resort from its perch above the northern end of the beach. *Sveti Konstantin Resort, tel. 052/861332. 130 rooms, most with bath or shower. No restaurant. No credit cards. Moderate.*

Varna
Dining

Orbita. Don't come here for the ambience (it's a dark room with tables) but to experience the the typical East European food in vast quantities. This cheap hole-in-the-wall is extremely popular with the locals, who come here for the lentil soup, grilled kebabs with potatoes, or Bulgarian sausage in a pot. *Czar Osvoboditel 25, in Hotel Orbita, off Knjaz Boris I, tel. 052/22–52–75. No credit cards. Moderate.*

Horizont. This restaurant in Seaside Garden near the Delphinerium has a good selection of seafood as well as a view of the Black Sea from its outside tables. It's not too busy during the day, but at night the live music draws a crowd. *Morskaya Gradina, tel. 052/88–60–26. No credit cards. Inexpensive.*

Lodging
★

Černo More. One of the best things about this modern Interhotel is the panoramic view from the 22nd floor; another is the modern facilities. *33 Slivnitza Blvd., tel. 052/23–21–15. 230 rooms with bath or shower. Facilities: 3 restaurants, ground-floor café with terraces, nightclub, cocktail bar. AE, DC, MC, V. Expensive.*

Inland Bulgaria

Inland Bulgaria is not as well known to tourists as the capital and the coast, but an adventurous traveler, willing to put up with limited hotel facilities and unreliable transportation, will find plenty to photograph, paint, or simply savor. Wooded and mountainous, the interior is dotted with attractive "museum" villages (entire settlements listed for preservation because of their historic cultural value) and ancient towns; the folk culture is a strong survivor from the past, not a tourist-inspired re-creation of it. The foothills of the Balkan Range, marked Stara Planina ("old mountains") on most maps, lie parallel with the lower Sredna Gora Mountains, with the verdant Valley of Roses between them. In the Balkan range is the ancient capital of Veliko Târnovo; south of the Sredna Gora stretches the fertile Thracian plain and Bulgaria's second-largest city, Plovdiv. Between Sofia and Plovdiv is the enchanting old town of Koprivshtitsa. To the south, in the Rila Mountains, is Borovec, first of the mountain resorts. A round-trip covering all these towns, with a side excursion to Rila Monastery, could be made in four or five days, although more time is recommended.

Getting Around

Rail and bus services cover all parts of inland Bulgaria, but the timetables are not easy to follow and there are frequent delays. The best bet is to rent a car. You may also prefer to hire a driver; Balkantourist can arrange this.

Guided Tours

Organized tours set out from Sofia, each covering different points of interest. Check with your Sofia hotel information desk or with Balkantourist for specific information.

Tourist Information

Plovdiv (34 Bulgaria Blvd., tel. 032/5–38–48 or 032/22–25–60 and 032/55–28–07).
Veliko Târnovo (1 Vasil Levski St., tel. 062/2–02–36).

Exploring Inland Bulgaria

Koprivshtitsa **Koprivshtitsa,** one of Bulgaria's showpiece villages, is set in mountain pastures and pine forests, about 930 meters (3,000 feet) up in the Sredna Gora range. It is 105 kilometers (65 miles) from Sofia, reached by a minor road south from the Sofia–Kazanlak expressway. Founded during the 14th century, it became a prosperous trading center with close ties to Venice during the National Revival period 400 years later. The architecture of this period, also called the Bulgarian Renaissance, features carved woodwork on broad verandas and overhanging eaves, brilliant colors, and courtyards with studded wooden gates. Throughout the centuries, artists, poets, and wealthy merchants have made their homes here, and many of the historic houses can be visited. The town has been well preserved and revered by the Bulgarians as a symbol of freedom since April 1876, when the rebellion that led, two years later, to the end of Turkish occupation ignited.

Return to the main road and turn right. After 15 kilometers (9 miles) you'll reach **Klisura** and the beginning of the **Rozova Dolina** (Valley of

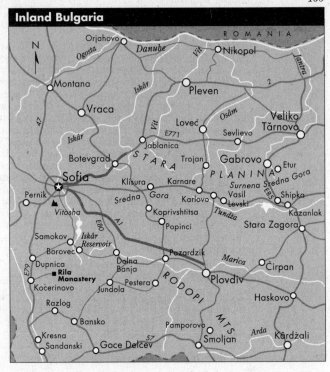

Inland Bulgaria

Roses). Here the famous Bulgarian rose water and attar, or essence, are produced. Each May and June, the whole valley is awash in fragrance and color. After another 17 kilometers (11 miles), turn at the village of Karnare; take the winding scenic road north over the Balkan range to the town of Trojan; and, a few miles away, you'll see the **Trojan Monastery,** built during the 1600s in the heart of the mountains. Trojan Monastery Church was painstakingly remodeled during the 19th century, and its icons, wood carvings, and frescoes are classic examples of National Revival art. Back at Trojan, continue north on the mountain road until it meets highway E771, where you turn right for Veliko Târnovo, 82 kilometers (50 miles) away.

Veliko
Târnovo

Veliko Târnovo, a town of panoramic vistas, rises up against steep mountain slopes through which the river Jantra runs its jagged course. During the 13th and 14th centuries, this was the capital of the Second Bulgarian Kingdom. Damaged by repeated Ottoman attack, and again by an earthquake in 1913, it has been reconstructed and is now a museum city of marvelous relics. The town warrants two or three days of exploration, but even in a short visit some sights should not be missed. Ideally, you should begin at a vantage point above the town in order to get an overview of its design and character. Next, seek out **Tszarevec** to the west (Carevec on some maps), protected by a river loop. This is where medieval czars and patriarchs had their palaces. The area is under restoration, and steep paths and stairways now provide opportunities to view the extensive ruins of the Patriarchite and the royal palace. In summer, there is a spectacular sound-and-light show, presented at night, which can be seen from the surrounding pubs.

The prominent feature to the south is **Baldwin's Tower,** the 13th-century prison of Baldwin of Flanders, onetime Latin emperor of Constantinople. Nearby are three important churches: the 13th-century **church of the Forty Martyrs,** with its Târnovo school frescoes and two inscribed columns, one dating to the 9th century; the **church of Saints Peter and Paul,** with vigorous murals both inside and out; and, across the river, reached by a bridge near the Forty Martyrs, the restored **church of Saint Dimitrius,** built on the spot where the Second Bulgarian Kingdom was launched in 1185.

Back toward the center of town, near the Yantra Hotel, is Samovodene Street, lined with restored crafts workshops—a fascinating place to linger in and a good place to find souvenirs, Turkish candy, or a charming café. On nearby Rakovski Street are a group of buildings of the National Revival period. One of the finest is **Hadji Nikoli,** a museum that was once an inn. *17 Georgi Sava Rakovski, tel. 62/2–17–10 for opening times.*

Moving east from Veliko Târnovo toward Varna on E771, you can go back farther in time by visiting the ruins of the two capitals of the First Bulgarian Kingdom in the vicinity of Šumen (spelled Shoumen in some English translations). The first ruins are the fortifications at **Pliska,** 23 kilometers (14 miles) southeast of Šumen, and date from 681. At **Veliki Preslav,** 21 kilometers (13 miles) southwest of Šumen, there are ruins from the second capital that date from 893 to 927. The 8th- to 9th-century **Madara Horseman,** a bas-relief of a rider slaying a lion, appears 18 kilometers (11 miles) east of town on a sheer cliff face.

If you leave Veliko Târnovo by E85 and head south toward **Plovdiv,** you can make three interesting stops en route. The first, near the industrial center of Gabrovo—interesting in itself for its House of Humor Museum—is the museum village of **Etur,** 8 kilometers (5 miles) to the southeast. Its mill is still powered by a stream, and local craftsmen continue to be trained in traditional skills. The second is the **Shipka Pass,** with its mighty monument on the peak to the 200,000 Russian soldiers and Bulgarian volunteers who died here in 1877, during the Russian-Turkish Wars. The third is **Kazanlak,** at the eastern end of the Valley of Roses, where you can trace the history of rose production, Bulgaria's oldest industry. Here, in early June, young rose pickers dress in traditional costumes for rose parades and other carnival processions. There is also a highly decorated replica of a Thracian tomb of the 3rd or 4th century BC, set near the original, which remains closed for its preservation.

Plovdiv From Kazanlak, take the road west through the **Valley of Roses** to either Vasil Levski or Karlovo, another Rose Festival town. Then turn south for **Plovdiv,** Bulgaria's second-largest city, one of the oldest cities in Europe and a major industrial center. The old town, on the hillier southern side of the Marica River, is worth a visit.

Begin at the **National Ethnographical Museum** in the House of Arghir Koyumdjioglu, an elegant example of National Revival style that made its first impact in Plovdiv. The museum is filled with artifacts from that important period. *2 Čomakov St. Open Tues.–Sun. 9–noon and 1:30–5.*

Below the medieval gateway of Hissar Kapiya are the attractive **Georgiadi House,** on Starina Street, and the steep, narrow **Strumna Street,** lined with workshops and boutiques, some reached through little courtyards. Follow Saborna Street westward to its junction with the pedestrians-only Kniaz Alexander I Street; here you'll find the remains of a **Roman stadium.** Nearby, the **Kapana District** has many restored and traditional shops and restaurants. Turn east off Kniaz Alexander I Street and walk to the fine hilltop **Roman Amphitheater,** sensitively renovated and frequently used for dramatic and musical performances. On the other side of the old town, toward the river, is the **National Archaeological Museum,** which holds a replica of the 4th-century BC Panagjuriste Gold Treasure, the original of which is in Sofia. *1 Suedinie Sq., Open Tues.–Sun. 9–12:30 and 2–5:30.*

Travel west along the E80 Sofia Road. At Dolna Banja, turn off to **Borovec,** about 1,333 meters (4,300 feet) up the northern slopes of the Rila Mountains. This is an excellent walking center and winter sports resort, well equipped with hotels, folk taverns, and ski schools. The winding mountain road leads back to Sofia, 70 kilometers (44 miles) from here, past Lake Iskar, the largest in the country.

On the way back to Sofia, you should consider a visit to the **Rila Monastery,** founded by Ivan of Rila during the 10th century. Cut across to E79, travel south to Kočerinovo, and then turn east to follow the steep forested valley past the village of Rila. The monastery has suffered so frequently from fire that most of it is now a grand National Revival reconstruction, although a rugged 14th-century tower has survived. The atmosphere in this mountain retreat, populated by many storks, is still heavy with a sense of the past—although part of the complex has been turned into a museum and some of the monks' cells are now guest rooms. The visitor can see 14 small chapels with frescoes from the 15th and 17th centuries, a lavishly carved altarpiece in the new Assumption church, the sarcophagus of Ivan of Rila, icons, and ancient manuscripts—a reminder that this was a stronghold of art and learning during the centuries of Ottoman rule. It is well worth the detour of 120 kilometers (75 miles)—or a special trip from Sofia.

Dining and Lodging

For details and price-category definitions, *see* Dining and Lodging in Staying in Bulgaria. In the moderate hotels and restaurants, check to see whether your credit card will be accepted.

Koprivshtitsa
Dining

Djedo Liben Inn. This attractive folk restaurant with cocktail bar and nightclub is built in the traditional style of the area—with half-timbered, high stone walls. The menu reflects similar attention to traditional detail. *Tel. 997184/21–09. No credit cards. Moderate.*
Barikadite. This small hotel is located on a hill 15 kilometers (9 miles) from Koprivshtitsa. *Tel. 997184/20–91. 20 rooms with shower. Facilities: restaurant, nightclub, cocktail bar. No credit cards. Inexpensive.*

Lodging

Koprivshtitsa. This good-value hotel is popular with Bulgarians themselves and is just over the river from the center of town. *Tel. 997184/21–18. 30 rooms. No credit cards. Inexpensive.*

Plovdiv
Dining

Pldin. This is an attractive folk restaurant in the center of town. A video presentation in the lobby highlights the city's past. *3 Knyaz Tseretelev St., tel. 032/23–17–20. AE, DC, MC, V. Expensive.*
Alafrangite. This charming folk-style restaurant is located in a restored 19th-century house with wood-carved ceilings and a vine-covered courtyard. *17 Nektariev St., tel. 032/22–98–09 or 032/26–95–95. No credit cards. Moderate.*
Filipopoli. This is an elegant folk-style restaurant with a menu combining traditional Bulgarian, Greek, and international cuisine (in-

cluding seafood), served by candlelight with the accompaniment of a jazz piano. Try the rich salads and *chushka byurek*. *56 Stamat Matanov St., tel. 032/22-52-96. Reservations accepted. No credit cards. Moderate.*

Rhetora. This coffee bar is in a beautifully restored old house near the Roman amphitheater in the old part of the city. *8A G. Samodoumov St., tel. 032/22-20-93. No credit cards. Moderate.*

Lodging **Novotel Plovdiv.** The large, modern, and well-equipped Novotel is across the river from the main town, near the fairgrounds. *2 Zlatju Boyadjiev St., tel. 032/55-51-71 or 032/5-58-92. 322 rooms with bath. Facilities: restaurant, folk tavern, nightclub, cocktail bar, sports hall, swimming pools, shop. AE, DC, MC, V. Expensive.*

Trimontium. This centrally located Interhotel built in the 1950s is comfortable and ideal for exploring the old town. *2 Kapitan Raico St., tel. 032/2-34-91. 163 rooms with bath or shower. Facilities: restaurant, cocktail bar, folk tavern, shop. AE, DC, MC, V. Expensive.*

Marica. This is a large, modern hotel that offers a less expensive alternative to its neighbor, the Novotel. *5 Vazrazhdane St., tel. 032/55-27-35. 171 rooms with bath or shower. Facilities: restaurant, bar. AE, DC, MC, V. Inexpensive.*

Veliko **Boljarska Izba.** In the center of the busy district just north of the **Târnovo** river, this place is a folk tavern. *Dimiter Blagoev St., no telephone.* *Dining* *No credit cards. Moderate.*

Lodging **Veliko Târnovo.** Located right in the middle of the most historic part of the town, this modern Interhotel boasts some of the best facilities for this class of hotel. *2 Emile Popov St., tel. 062/3-05-71. 195 rooms with bath or shower. Facilities: 2 restaurants, cocktail bar, coffee shop, disco, sports hall, indoor pool, shops. AE, DC, MC, V. Expensive.*

Yantra. The Yantra has some of the best views in town, looking across the river to Tsaravec. *1 Velchova Zavera Sq., tel. 062/2-03-91. 60 rooms, most with shower. Facilities: restaurant, coffee shop, bar. DC, MC, V. Moderate.*

Etur. This moderate-size hotel, with an address near the more expensive Veliko Târnovo, makes it a good base for sightseeing within town. *I. Ivailo St., tel. 062/2-68-51. 80 rooms, most with shower. Facilities: restaurant, coffee shop, bar. AE, DC, MC, V. Inexpensive.*

6 Cyprus

The Mediterranean island of Cyprus was at one time a center for the cult of Aphrodite, the Greek goddess who is said to have risen naked and perfect from the sea near what is now the beach resort of Paphos. Wooded and mountainous, with a 751-kilometer-long (466-mile-long) coastline, Cyprus lies just off the southern coast of Turkey. Oranges, olives, lemons, grapes, and cherries grow here, and fish are plentiful. The summers are hot and dry, the spring gentle. Snow covers the Troodos Mountains in winter, making it possible to ski in the morning and sunbathe on a beach in the afternoon.

Cyprus's strategic position in the eastern Mediterranean has made it subject to regular invasions by powerful countries. Greeks, Phoenicians, Assyrians, Egyptians, Persians, Romans, and Byzantines—all have ruled here. In the Middle Ages, the English King Richard I took Cyprus from the Byzantine Empire by force and gave it to Guy of Lusignan. Guy's descendants ruled the island until the late 15th century, when it was annexed by the Venetians. From the 16th century to the 19th century it was ruled by the Turks. It became a British colony in 1914.

The influence of diverse cultures especially adds to the island's appeal to tourists. Many fortifications built by the Crusaders and the Venetians still stand. The tomb of the Prophet Mohammed's aunt (Tekke of Hala Sultan), located on the shores of the great salt lake near Larnaca, is one of Islam's most important shrines. A piece of the true cross is said to exist in the Monastery of Stavrouni, and Paphos has the remains of a pillar where St. Paul was allegedly tied and beaten for preaching Christianity.

The upheavals are not over. Following independence in 1960 the island became the focus of Greek-Turkish contention. Currently nearly 80% of the population are Greek Cypriots and 18% are Turkish Cypriots. Since 1974 Cyprus has been divided by a thin buffer zone occupied by United Nations forces between the Turkish Cypriot north and the Greek Cypriot south. The zone cuts right through the capital city of Nicosia. Talks aimed at uniting the communities into one bizonal federal state have been going on for years, lately under the auspices of the United Nations secretary-general. Both communities offer comfortable tourist facilities.

Essential Information

Before You Go

When to Go   The tourist season runs throughout the year, though prices tend to be lower from November through March. Spring and fall are best, usually warm enough for swimming but not uncomfortably hot.

Climate   The rainy season is in January and February, and it often snows in the highest parts of the Troodos Mountains from January through March. January and February can be cold and wet; July and August are always very hot and dry.

The following are the average daily maximum and minimum temperatures for Nicosia.

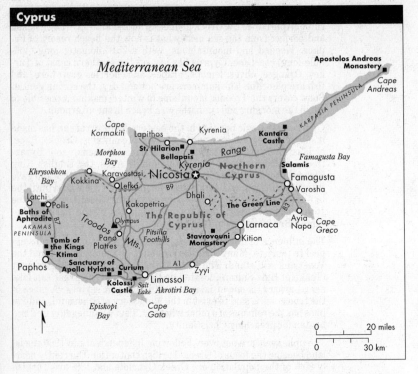

Jan.	59F	15C	May	85F	29C	Sept.	92F	33C
	42	5		58	14		65	18
Feb.	61F	16C	June	92F	33C	Oct.	83F	28C
	42	5		65	18		58	14
Mar.	66F	19C	July	98F	37C	Nov.	72F	22C
	44	7		70	21		51	10
Apr.	75F	24C	Aug.	98F	37C	Dec.	63F	17C
	50	10		69	21		45	7

Visas No visas are necessary for holders of valid passports from the United States, Canada, the United Kingdom, and other European countries.

Customs on Arrival Duty-free allowances are: 250 grams of tobacco, 1 liter of spirits, 750 ml of wine, 300 ml of perfume, and up to C£50 in other goods.

The export of antiques and historical artifacts, whether gathered on land or during undersea explorations, is strictly forbidden unless a license is obtained from the Ministry of Tourism in Nicosia.

Language Greek is the main language, but English is widely spoken in hotels, tavernas, and other tourist haunts. Off the beaten track, sign language may have to do.

Credit Cards Major credit cards are widely accepted, especially in shops and hotels. Banks usually allow you to draw cash upon your credit card account, so payment is rarely a problem.

The Republic of Cyprus

Currency

The monetary unit in the Republic of Cyprus is the Cyprus pound (C£), which is divided into 100 cents. There are notes of C£20, C£10, C£5, C£1, and 50 Cyprus cents and coins of 50, 20, 10, 5, 2, and 1 Cyprus cents. At press time (spring 1994) there were C£0.52 to the U.S. dollar and C£0.75 to the pound sterling.

What It Will Cost

A cup of coffee or tea costs Cyprus 50¢–80¢; a glass of beer 75¢–C£1; a kebab around C£1–C£1.50; a bottle of local wine 90¢–C£2. Admission to museums and galleries costs 50¢–C£1.

Arriving and Departing

By Plane There are no direct flights from the United States. **Cyprus Airways** and **British Airways** fly direct from London, Birmingham, and Manchester to Larnaca and Paphos. **Cyprus Airways** also operates from Athens, Amsterdam, Brussels, Frankfurt, Munich, Paris, Vienna, and Zurich. **Alitalia** flies from Rome. **United Airlines** and **Swiss Air** have good connections.

By Boat Passenger ships connect Cyprus with various Greek, Egyptian, Italian, and Middle Eastern ports.

Getting Around

By Car An international or national license is acceptable for driving in Cyprus. Drive on the left. Main roads between large towns are good. Minor roads can be unsurfaced, narrow, and winding. Gas costs 36.7¢ per liter and is available around the clock in larger towns. Cars may be rented from C£18 per day. Lower rates are available off season.

By Bus This is the cheapest form of transportation in urban areas; the fare is 25¢–40¢. Buses operate every half-hour and cover an extensive network. In Nicosia, buses run until 7:30 PM (winter 6:30 PM). In tourist areas during the summer, services extend until midnight.

Intercity bus fares range between C£2 and C£3. For information on the Nicosia–Limassol–Paphos route, tel. 02/464636; or on the Limassol–Larnaca–Ayia Napa route, tel. 05/351031.

By Service Taxi Shared taxis accommodate four to seven passengers and are a cheap, fast, and comfortable way of traveling between towns. Taxis operate between the main towns—Nicosia, Limassol, Larnaca, and Paphos. Tariffs are from C£2 to C£3.50. Seats must be booked by phone, and passengers may embark/debark anywhere within the town boundaries. The taxis run every half-hour (Mon.–Sat. 5:45 AM–6:30 PM). Sunday service is less frequent and rides must be booked one day ahead. Contact the **Kypros Taxi Office** (tel. 02/464811), **Karydas** (tel. 02/463126), or **Kyriakos** (tel. 02/444141).

By Private Taxi Private taxis operate 24 hours throughout the island. They are generally very cheap within towns but far more expensive than service taxis between towns. Telephone from your hotel or hail one in the street. Urban taxis have an initial charge of 55¢ and charge 21¢ per mile in the daytime, more at night. Drivers are bound by law to use and display a meter. Ask the driver what it will cost before you depart, and don't be afraid to barter. In-town journeys range from C£1.50 to about C£3.

Staying in the Republic of Cyprus

Telephones Pay phones take 2¢, 10¢, and 20¢ coins. Some newer pay phones also take 5¢ coins, and others take telecards of C£2, C£5, and C£10, which can be purchased at post offices, souvenir shops, and kiosks. Local, national, and international calls can be made from these phones; cheaper rates apply from 10 PM to 8 AM and all day Sunday. Hotels will add a service charge for placing a call for you. For telephone inquiries service, dial 192 in all towns. Cyprus's country code is 357.

Mail At press time (spring 1994), a 20-gram letter to the United States costs 36¢, a postcard, 26¢. To Europe, a 20-gram letter costs 31¢, and a postcard 21¢. Post offices are open Mon.–Fri. 7:30 AM–2:30 PM. Stamps are also sold at hotels, newsstands, and kiosks.

Opening and Closing Times **Banks** are open Monday–Friday 8:15AM–12:30 PM. Some have afternoon tourist services and will cash traveler's checks weekdays 3–6 in winter, 4–7 in summer, and Saturday 8:30–noon.

Museum hours vary greatly. It pays to check ahead. Generally, museums are closed for lunch and on Sunday. Most ancient monuments are open from dawn to dusk.

Shops are open Monday–Saturday 8–1 and 4–7 PM (summer); 2–5:30 PM (winter). Shops are closed Wednesday and Saturday afternoons and on Sundays. In tourist areas shops generally maintain longer hours.

National Holidays January 1; January 6 (Epiphany); April 21–24 (Greek Easter); May 1 (May Day); June 12 (Pentecost Monday); August 15 (Assumption); October 1 (Cyprus Independence Day); October 28 (Greek National Day); December 25, 26.

Tipping A service charge of 10%, a 3% charge by the Cyprus Tourist organization, and an 8% VAT are usually added to all bills. If service has been especially good, add 5%.

Important Addresses and Numbers The main **tourist information office** is in Nicosia (19 Limassol Ave., tel. 02/315715). This is the head office; for personal and telephone inquiries, call the other Nicosia office at Laiki Yitonia (tel. 02/444264). There are local offices at all major resorts.

Embassies or High Commissions **U.S. Embassy** (Metochiou Ploutarchou, Box 4536, Engomi, Nicosia, tel. 02/476100, fax 02/465944). **British High Commission** (Alexander Pallis St., Nicosia, tel. 02/473131–7, fax 02/367198).

Emergencies **Ambulance, Fire Brigade,** and **Police** (tel. 199). **Doctor: Nicosia General Hospital** (tel. 02/451111); **Limassol Hospital** (tel. 05/330333); **Paphos Hospital** (tel. 06/240111). **Pharmacies** (tel. 192 for information about opening times in English). A list with additional opening details appears in the English-language *Cyprus Mail* and *Cyprus Weekly*.

Guided Tours Guided tours are often the best way to see Cyprus and learn about its rich history. Try **National Sightseeing Tours** (c/o Louis Tourist Agency, 54–58 Evagoras Ave., Nicosia, tel. 02/442114) for half-day and full-day trips—expect to pay C£7–C£12. Night tours are quite popular, and typically include dinner at a local taverna, folk dancing, and bouzouki music. In Limassol, **Laikon Shipping** (124 Ayias Paraskevis St., tel. 05/326108) arranges coastal cruises on the *Lady Thetis* that usually include lunch on board or at a seaside restaurant.

Exploring the Republic of Cyprus

Nicosia

Nicosia, the capital, is twice divided. The picturesque Old City is contained within 16th-century Venetian fortifications that separate it from the wide, tree-lined streets, large hotels, and high rises of the modern section. The second division is political and more noticeable. The so-called Green Line (set up by the United Nations) divides the island between the Republic of Cyprus and Turkish-occupied Northern Cyprus. It is possible, at press time (spring 1994), to arrange a day trip from the Greek to the Turkish sector through the official checkpoint in Nicosia (Ledra Palace), though it is essential to return by 5 PM. Visits in the other direction are not permitted.

In the Greek sector a good starting point is **Laiki Yitonia** at the southern edge of the Old City, an area of winding alleys and traditional architecture. Tavernas, cafés, and crafts workshops line the shaded, cobbled streets. Here you will encounter everyday Cypriot life. Just to the west lies Ledra Street, where modern shops alternate with yet more crafts shops. Head north of the tourist information center (19 Limassol Ave., tel. 02/444264) in Laiki Yitonia to visit the tiny **Tripiotis Church.** This Greek Orthodox church, with its ornately carved golden iconostasis and silver-covered icons, dates from 1690.

The **Leventis Museum,** also in Laiki Yitonia, traces the history of Nicosia from 2,000 BC to the present with exhibits on crafts and daily life. *17 Hippocratous St., tel. 02/451475. Admission free. Open Tues.–Sun. 10–4:30.*

Within the walls to the east of the Old City is a cluster of museums. Housed in a wing of the Archbishopric, built in 1960 in neobyzantine style, the new **Archbishop Makarios III Cultural Foundation** consists of the **Byzantine Art Museum,** with fine displays of icons spanning 1,000 years, and the **Greek War of Independence Gallery,** with a collection of maps, paintings, and mementoes of 1821. *Archbishop Kyprianou Sq., tel. 02/456781. Admission: C£1. Open weekdays 9–1 and 2–5 (winter 2–5:30), Sat. 9–1.*

Next door, the **Museum of the National Struggle** has dramatic displays of the Cypriot campaigns against the British during the preindependence years 1955–59; exhibits include letters, newspapers, photos, and even torn uniforms, together with other memorabilia. *Archbishop Kyprianou Sq., tel. 02/302465. Admission: 25¢. Open weekdays 7:30–1:30 (winter 7:30–2) and 3–5, Sat. 7:30–1:30.*

Close by is the **Cyprus Folk Art Museum** (housed in the old part of the Bishopric, dating from the 14th century), which offers demonstrations of ancient weaving techniques and displays of ceramics, olive and wine presses, and Cypriot costumes and embroideries. *Archbishop Kyprianou Sq., tel. 02/463205. Admission: 50¢. Open weekdays 8:30–4, Sat. 8:30–1.*

Don't miss **St. John's Cathedral** (Ayios Ioannis), built in 1662 within the courtyard of the Archbishopric. Look for the 18th-century wall paintings, which illustrate Cypriot moments of religious significance, including a depiction of the tomb of St. Barnabas. **Famagusta Gate** is just a short walk to the east. It was the strongest and most elaborate of three gateways into the old city. Now a cultural center, it houses exhibitions, a lecture hall, and a theater. *Athina St., tel. 02/430877. Open weekdays 10–1 and 4–7, Sat. 10–1.*

To the west of the city stands the **Cyprus Museum.** Located outside the city walls near the Paphos Gate, it has extensive archaeological displays ranging from Neolithic to Roman times. Exhibits are well arranged and labeled in English. This stop is essential to understanding the island's ancient sites. *Museum St., tel. 02/302189. Admission: C£1. Open Mon.–Sat. 9–5, Sun. 10–1.*

Across the street from the museum lie the neoclassical style **Municipal Theatre** (1960) and the lush **Municipal Gardens.**

Larnaca Many visitors choose to stay in the seaside resorts. Both Larnaca and Paphos, each of which has its own airport, make excellent centers. **Larnaca,** 51 kilometers (32 miles) southeast of Nicosia, is famous as the burial place of Lazarus and for its flamboyant Whitsuntide celebration, *Cataklysmos.* It has fine beaches, palm trees, and a modern harbor and marina, the starting point for boat trips. The tourist office at Democratias Square (tel. 04/654322; open weekdays, hours vary), is right at the marina district, and just a short walk from **Larnaca Museum,** with its displays of treasures including outstanding sculptures and Bronze-Age seals from the island's archaeological sites. *Kimon and Kilkis Sts., tel. 046/630169. Admission: 50¢. Open weekdays 7:30–2:30, Thurs. 4–7 (winter 3–6).*

A short walk north from the museum, along Kyman Street, will bring you to the site of **Kition** (the old Larnaca of biblical times and one of the most important ancient city-kingdoms), where you can observe the excavations from specially constructed walkways. Architectural remains of ancient temples date from the 13th century BC. *Admission: 50¢. Open weekdays 7:30–2:30 and 3–5.*

Southward from the marina is the 17th-century **Turkish fort,** built in the 9th century by Emperor Leo VI, open the same hours as the museum. The fort contains finds from Hala Sultan Tekke (*see below*) and Kition. The view from the top is impressive. On the way to the ancient fort is the **Pierides Collection,** a private collection of over 3,000 pieces distinguished by amusing Bronze-Age terra-cotta figures and fine carvings from gravestones. *Paul Zenon Kitieus St. near Lord Byron St., tel. 04/622345. Admission: 50¢. Open Mon.–Sat. 9–1.*

Walk inland from the fort to the town center and to one of the island's more important churches, **Ayios Lazarus,** resplendent with icons. It has a fascinating crypt containing Lazarus's sarcophagus.

South of Larnaca on the airport road is the 2½-square-mile **Salt Lake.** Water fills the lake in spring, but by July you can watch local villagers collecting its salt. In winter it's a refuge for migrating birds. On the lake's edge, a mosque stands in an oasis of palm trees guarding the **Hala Sultan Tekke**—burial place of the prophet Mohammed's aunt. This is Islam's third most important shrine.

Nearby, the **Panayia Angeloktistos Church,** in Kiti, is famous for its outstanding Byzantine wall mosaics, which date from the 6th and 7th centuries.

Ayia Napa A decade ago, **Ayia Napa,** which is 30 kilometers (20 miles) from Larnaca, was a small coastal fishing village, anchored by a **16th-century monastery** and renowned for its white, sandy beaches and views of the brilliant sea. Today's emergence of tavernas, bars, restaurants, and fine hotels reflects the town's transformation into Cyprus's premier vacationland: Water-sports fanatics and bons vivants now flock here from points north and west. The town maintains the flavor of its historic past, however, and from the monastery's 14th-century sycamore tree, you can still enjoy the panoramic view of the Mediterranean.

Paphos **Paphos,** 142 kilometers (89 miles) southwest of Nicosia, in the west of the island, combines superb sea-swimming with archaeological sites and a rich history. Paphos, the birthplace of Aphrodite—the Greek goddess of love and beauty—is a modern town center with numerous ancient sights, including a picturesque harbor and a 13th-century fort. Begin at the tourist office on Gladstone Street (tel. 06/232841; open weekdays, hours vary) in Upper Paphos.

The **Paphos District Museum** is famous for its pottery, jewelry, and statuettes from the Roman villas. *Grivas Dighenis Ave., Ktima, tel. 06/240215. Admission: 50¢. Open weekdays 7:30–2:30 and 4–6 (winter 7:30–2 and 3–5), weekends 10–1.*

Nearby are the charming **Ethnographical Museum** (1 Exo Vrysi, tel. 06/232010) and notable icons in the **Byzantine Museum** (Andreas Ioannou St., tel. 06/232092) in the Archbishopric.

Don't miss the elaborate mosaics in the **Roman Villa of Theseus,** in the **House of Dionysos,** and in the recently excavated **House of Aion,** all in New Paphos. The mosaics are considered by many to be among the finest in the Eastern Mediterranean and have been expertly preserved and restored. The town bus stops nearby. Also worth seeing are the **Tombs of the Kings,** an early necropolis dating from 300 BC. Natural caves have been extended and linked by passages, and though the coffin niches are empty, a powerful sense of mystery remains. *Admission: C£1 (mosaics) and 50¢ (Tombs of the Kings). Open daily 7:30–sunset (winter 7:30–5:30).*

Limassol **Limassol,** a commercial port and wine-making center on the south coast, 75 kilometers (47 miles) from Nicosia, is a bustling, cosmopolitan town popular with tourists. Luxury hotels, apartments, and guest houses stretch along 12 kilometers (7 miles) of sea-frontage. The nightlife is the liveliest on the island. In Central Limassol, the elegant modern shops of Makarios Avenue contrast with those of the old part of town, where you'll discover local handicrafts.

The tourist information office (Spyros Araouzos St., tel. 05/362756) is open Monday through Saturday; hours vary. A short walk takes you to **Limassol Fort,** near the old port. This 14th-century castle was built on the site of an earlier Byzantine fortification. According to tradition, Richard the Lionhearted married his future queen of England here in 1191. The **Cyprus Medieval Museum** is housed here and displays a variety of medieval armor and relics. *Tel. 05/330132. Admission: 50¢. Open weekdays 7:30–5, Sat. 9:30–5, Sun. 10–1.*

For a glimpse of Cypriot folklore, visit the **Folk Art Museum** on St. Andrews Street. The collection includes national costumes and fine examples of the island's crafts and woven materials. *Tel. 05/362303. Admission: 30¢. Open Mon. and Wed.–Fri. 8:30–1:30 and 4–7 (winter 3–5:30); Tues. 8:30–1:30.*

For a nice side trip, try the **KEO Winery,** just west of the town, which welcomes visitors daily. *Roosevelt Ave., toward new port, tel. 05/362053. Admission free. Tours are given weekdays 10–6.*

Troodos The **Troodos Mountains,** north of Limassol, are popular in summer
Mountains for the shade of their cedar and pine forests and the coolness of their lakes and mineral spas. Small, painted churches in the Troodos and **Pitsilia foothills** are rich examples of a rare indigenous art form. **Asinou Church** and **St. Nicholas of the Roof,** south of Kakopetria, are especially noteworthy. Nearby is the **Tall Trees Trout Farm,** a shady oasis serving delicious fresh fish meals. In winter, skiers take over. **Platres,** in the foothills of Mount Olympus, is the principal resort. Be sure to visit the **Kykko Monastery,** whose prized icon of the Virgin is

reputed to have been painted by St. Luke. Founded in the 12th century, the monastery now operates in buildings and a lavish church added in the 19th century.

Off the Beaten Track

Stavrovouni Monastery stands on a mountain west of Larnaca. It was founded by St. Helena (mother of the Emperor Constantine) in AD 326, though the present buildings date from the 19th century. Ideally, it should be visited in a spirit of pilgrimage rather than sightseeing, out of respect for the monks, though the views of the island are splendid. Male visitors are allowed inside the monastery daily from sunrise to sunset, except between noon and 3 (noon and 1 in winter). The monks have decreed that female visitors will be admitted only on Sunday mornings.

Curium (Kourion), west of Limassol, has numerous Greek and Roman ruins. There is an **amphitheater,** where actors occasionally present classical and Shakespearean drama. Next to the theater is the **Villa of Eustolios,** a summer house that belonged to a wealthy Christian; its mosaic floors are still in good condition. A nearby **Roman stadium** has been partially rebuilt. Two miles farther along the main Paphos road is the **Sanctuary of Apollo Hylates** (of the woodlands), an impressive archaeological site. *Admission: C£1. Open daily 7:30–sunset (winter 7:30–5:30).*

Other places to visit include **Kolossi Castle,** a Crusader castle of the Knights of St. John, a 15-minute drive outside Limassol; and the fishing harbor of **Latchi** on the west coast, 32 kilometers (20 miles) north of Paphos. Nearby are the **Baths of Aphrodite,** where the goddess of love is said to have seduced swains. The wild and undeveloped Akamas Peninsula is perfect for a hike through fields of wildflowers or a swim off isolated beaches.

Dining

Most hotels have restaurants, but these tend to serve bland international-style food garnished with french fries. Visitors with a sense of adventure may want to dine in local restaurants or in one of the informal, family-run tavernas featuring live music. Meals start with a variety of *mezes* (snacks)—many of Middle Eastern origin. Kebabs are popular, as are *dolmades*—stuffed grape leaves or cabbage leaves—stews, fresh fish, and various lamb dishes. End with fruit or honey pastries and Greek coffee. Moderate establishments display a menu; in inexpensive ones it is the custom to go into the kitchen and choose your meal. Food is cheap in Cyprus, and the quality is good.

Prices are for a three-course meal for one person, not including drinks or tip.

Category	All Areas
Expensive	over C£12
Moderate	C£6–C£11
Inexpensive	under C£5

Larnaca **Miliges.** This sea-view restaurant is popular with tourists and locals. Near the old fort, Miliges has a village ambience. *Kleftico* (lamb and goat meat wrapped in bay leaves) cooked in traditional clay ovens and *sheftalia* (minced-meat-and-herb rissole) are specialties. *42 Bia-Pasha, tel. 04/655867. No credit cards. Moderate.*

Monte Carlo. On the road to the airport, this spot has outdoor seating on a balcony extending over the sea. Service is efficient, and the dining area is clean. Particularly worthy Cypriot dishes are the meat meze and casseroles. *28 Piale Pashia, tel. 04/653815. AE, DC, MC, V. Moderate.*

Limassol   Ladas. This pleasant seafood restaurant is in Old Harbor. All the fish here is fresh; try the tender and sweet fried calamari and grilled *soupies* (ink fish). *1 Sadi St., tel. 05/365760. Closed Sunday. AE, DC, MC, V. Moderate.*

Porta. This quaint restored warehouse is home to a varied menu of international and Cypriot dishes, such as *foukoudha barbecue* (grilled strips of steak) and trout baked in prawn and mushroom sauce. On many nights, you'll be entertained by folk dancers and guitarists. *17 Yenethliou Mitella, Old Castle, tel. 05/360339. MC, V. Moderate.*

Nicosia   Archondiko. A lively meeting place for business or pleasure, it has tables on the walking path of the restored Laiki Yitonia area, indoors in cooler weather. Cypriot cuisine includes savory *lountza* (smoked fillet of pork) and grilled *haloumi* (a salty local cheese). *27 Aristokyprou St., Laiki Yitonia, tel. 02/450080. AE, DC, MC, V. Moderate.*

Cellari. This romantic, candlelit inn is lent a festive touch by a pair of guitarists strumming mellow Greek and Cypriot favorites. The highlight of this traditional cuisine is *chiromeri* (smoked pork). *22 Korai St., tel. 02/448338. No credit cards. Moderate.*

Paphos   Naftikos Omilos (Nautical Club). This huge seaside eatery seats more than 180. Fresh fish and kleftiko are your best bets. *St. Paul's Ave., Old Harbor, tel. 062/33745. DC, MC, V. Moderate.*

Panicos Corallo Restaurant. Sheltered from the main road by grapevines, this traditional family-run restaurant is just outside Paphos on the northern coastal road toward Coral Bay. The veal is recommended, as is the swordfish, a house specialty. Meals are served with fresh vegetables, many of which are home-grown. *Peyia, tel. 06/621052. No credit cards. Moderate.*

Lodging

All hotels listed below have private bath or shower, but check when making reservations. Most have at least partial air-conditioning. In resort areas, hotel/apartments are a convenient choice for groups or families—many have kitchens.

Prices are for two people sharing a double room and include breakfast.

Category	All Areas
Expensive	over C£60
Moderate	C£40–C£60
Inexpensive	under C£40

Ayia Napa   Nissi Beach. This modern, fully air-conditioned, family-style hotel is set in magnificent gardens overlooking a sandy beach. Its rooms and bungalows were recently refurbished. *Box 10, Ayia Napa, tel. 03/*

721021, fax 03/721623. 270 rooms. Facilities: pool, disco, restaurant. AE, MC, DC, V. Expensive.

Pernera Beach Sun Hotel. Even on a budget, you can enjoy this hotel with a view of the beach. All rooms are air-conditioned. *Pernera Beach, Box 38, tel. 03/831011, fax 03/831020. 92 rooms. AE, DC, MC, V. Moderate.*

Larnaca **Golden Bay.** Comfort is high on the list at this beach hotel to the east of the town center. All rooms have balconies and views of the sea. The extensive range of sports facilities makes it ideal for summer or winter vacations. *Larnaca-Dhekelia Rd., Box 741, tel. 046/23444, fax 046/23451. 194 rooms. Facilities: 2 restaurants, pool, minigolf, tennis. AE, DC, MC, V. Expensive.*

Pasithea. This apartment/hotel near Salt Lake is a short stroll from the sandy beach. The management is friendly, the apartments spacious. *4 Michael Angelou, Box 309, Larnaca, tel. 046/25740, fax 046/25848. AE, DC, MC, V. Moderate.*

Cactus Hotel. This recent addition to Larnaca's hotels is 20 minutes from the seafront, with all its tavernas. The hotel offers bed-and-breakfast only. *6–8 Shakespeare St., Box 188, tel. 046/27400, fax 046/26966. 56 rooms. Facilities: pool. AE, MC, V. Inexpensive.*

Limassol **Le Meridien.** This spacious, luxurious hotel has a striking lobby—pink marble and glass. You'll find all the amenities expected in a first-class hotel—health and beauty club, gym, steam baths—as well as the island's largest swimming pool. *Old Limassol/Nicosia Rd., Box 6560, tel. 05/327000, fax 05/329222. 191 rooms and 57 villas. Facilities: 3 restaurants, pool, water sports. AE, DC, MC, V. Expensive.*

Azur Beach. This fine apartment/hotel has two restaurants, a sandy beach, and helpful management. *Potamios Yermasoyias, Box 1318, tel. 05/322667, fax 05/321897. 24 apartments. DC, MC, V. Moderate.*

Continental. This family hotel is close to the castle and has a great sea view. *137 Spyros Araouzos Ave., Box 398, tel. 05/362530, fax 05/373030. 27 rooms. AE, DC, MC, V. Inexpensive.*

Nicosia **Cyprus Hilton.** This is among the island's best hotels, with standards you'd expect from a Hilton. It has its own pool, sports facilities, dancing, and more. *Archbishop Makarios Ave., Box 2023, tel. 02/377777, fax 02/377788. 230 rooms. Facilities: pool, tennis, nightclub. AE, DC, MC, V. Expensive.*

Cleopatra Hotel. Visitors enjoy its convenient location, cordial service, and well-prepared food served at poolside. *8 Florina St., Box 1397, tel. 02/445254, fax 02/452618. 55 rooms. Facilities: restaurant, pool. AE, DC, MC, V. Moderate.*

Kennedy Holiday Inn. Centrally located in the old city, the Kennedy has smallish rooms decorated in Greek Cypriot style with balconies overlooking city streets. Rooms in the new wing are larger. *70 Regina St., Box 1212, tel. 02/475131, fax 02/473337. 140 rooms. Facilities: 3 restaurants, bar, rooftop pool and garden, indoor pool, Roman bath. AE, DC, MC, V. Moderate.*

Paphos **Paphos Beach.** There are many facilities at this recently renovated hotel surrounded by attractive gardens. Accommodations are either in the main hotel or in spacious bungalows on the grounds. *Posidonos St., Box 136, tel. 06/233091, fax 06/242818. 190 rooms. Facilities: pool, tennis. AE, DC, MC, V. Expensive.*

Amalthea Hotel. On the beach amid banana groves, the hotel has a friendly, personal atmosphere fostered by the resident owner/managers. The impressive, open lobby furnished with gray leather couches and large plants overlooks the water, and the rooms have balconies with sea views. *Kissonerga Rd., Box 323, tel. 06/247777,* *fax 06/245963. 168 rooms. Facilities: restaurant, bar, indoor and outdoor pools, gym, sauna, tennis and squash courts. AE, DC, MC, V. Moderate.*

Ficardos Hotel Apartments. Clean, spacious apartments are located in Lower Paphos, a five-minute walk from the old port. *Contact Iris Travel, 10 Gladstone Ave., Upper Paphos, tel. 062/237585, fax 062/233960. 8 apartments. DC, MC, V. Moderate.*

Northern Cyprus

Currency

The monetary unit in Northern Cyprus is the Turkish lira (TL). There are bills for 500,000, 250,000, 100,000, 50,000, 20,000, 10,000, 5,000, 1,000, 500, 100, 50, 20, and 10 TL, and coins for lesser sums. The Turkish lira is subject to considerable inflation, so most of the prices in this section are quoted in dollars.

What It Will Cost

Prices for food and accommodations tend to be lower than those in the Republic of Cyprus. Wine and spirits, on the other hand, are imported from Turkey, and drinks will be slightly more expensive.

Sample Prices A cup of coffee should cost less than a dollar, a glass of beer about $1.00. Wine is good and cheap at around $3.00 per bottle. Taxis are also a bargain—an 80-kilometer (50-mile) ride costs about $12. Admission to museums costs less than $1.

Arriving and Departing

Turkish Airlines, Cyprus Turkish Airlines, and **Noble Air** run all flights via mainland Turkey, usually with a change of plane at Istanbul. There are also direct flights from Izmir and Ankara to Ercan Airport near Nicosia. Ferries run from Mersin and Tasucu in Turkey to Famagusta and Kyrenia, respectively. *It is not possible to enter Northern Cyprus from the Republic except for a day trip from Nicosia.*

Getting Around

By Car *See* Getting Around by Car in the Republic of Cyprus, *above.*

By Bus Buses and the shared taxi *(dolmuş)* are the cheapest forms of transportation. Service is frequent on main routes.

Fares A bus from Nicosia to Kyrenia costs about U.S. 40¢, and to Famagusta about 70¢. A seat in a dolmus for the same trips would cost about 90¢ and $3.00, respectively.

Exploring Northern Cyprus

The main tourist information office is at the Public Information Office on Mehmet Akif Avenue in Lefkoşa (Nicosia) (tel. 905/20/84133). (The postal address is Lefkoşa-KKTC, Mersin–10, Turkey.)

There are two important things to bear in mind in Northern Cyprus. One is to obey the "no photographs" signs wherever they appear. The other is to note that as Turkish is the language used here, Turkish names designate the cities and towns: **Nicosia** is known as **Lefkoşa, Kyrenia** as **Girne,** and **Famagusta** as **Gazimagusa.** A useful map showing these and other Turkish names is available free from tourist offices.

Lefkosa (Nicosia) The Turkish half of **Nicosia** is the capital of Northern Cyprus. In addition to the Venetian walls already mentioned (*see* Exploring the Republic of Cyprus, *above*), it contains the **Selimiye Mosque** (Selimiye St.), formerly the 13th-century Cathedral of St. Sophia and a fine example of Gothic architecture, to which a pair of minarets has been added. Near the Girne Gate is the **Mevlevi Tekke ve Etnografy Müzesi** (Mevlevi Sacred Place and Ethnographic Museum), the former home of the Mevlevi Dervishes, a Sufi order popularly known as Whirling Dervishes. The building now houses a museum of Turkish history and culture. *Girne St. Open Mon.–Fri. 8–1 and 2–5, Sat. 8–1, Sun. 10–1.*

A walk around the **Old City,** within the encircling walls, is rich with glimpses from the Byzantine, Lusignan, and Venetian past. There is a great deal of restoration and reconstruction work going on, especially in the parts of the city beyond the walls.

Girne (Kyrenia) Of the coastal resorts, **Girne** (Kyrenia), with its yacht-filled harbor, is the most appealing. There are excellent beaches to the east and west of the town. **Girne Castle,** overlooking the harbor, is Venetian, though on the site of a much older Byzantine defensive structure. It now houses the **Batık Gemi Müzesi** (Shipwreck Museum), whose prize possession is the remains of a ship that sank around 300 BC. *Open Mon.–Fri. 8–1 and 2–5, Sat. 8–1, Sun. 10–1.*

Gazimagusa (Famagusta) **Gazimagusa** (Famagusta), the chief port of Northern Cyprus, has massive and well-preserved Venetian walls and the late-13th-century Gothic Cathedral of St. Nicholas, now **Lala Mustafa Pasha Mosque.** The **Old Town,** within the walls, is the most intriguing part to explore.

Off the Beaten Track

It is well worth making two short excursions from Girne—to **St. Hilarion** and to **Bellapais.** The fantastic ruins of the **Castle of St. Hilarion** stand on a hilltop 11 kilometers (7 miles) to the southwest. It's a strenuous walk, so take a taxi; the views are breathtaking. The ruins of the former **Abbey of Bellapais,** built in the 12th century by the Lusignans, are just as impressive. They lie on a mountainside 6 kilometers (4 miles) to the southeast. The showpiece is the refectory, but there are also dormitories, storerooms, and a church with frescoes.

Salamis, north of Gazimagusa, is an ancient ruined city, perhaps the most dramatic archaeological site on the island. St. Barnabas and St. Paul arrived in Salamis and set up a church near here. The present ruins date largely from the 12th-century Lusignan rulers of Cyprus, who came from France and used this as their major port before Gazimagusa was developed by the mid–16th-century Turks. Salamis does contain relics of earlier civilizations, including Greek and Roman settlements. The city was frequently devastated by earthquakes, but the setting is beautiful, and some of the ruins are sufficiently overgrown to give the visitor a satisfying sense of discovery.

7 The Czech Republic

Just three years after the dramatic but peaceful revolution that overthrew a Communist regime that had been in power for 40 years, Czechoslovakia again made world headlines in 1993 when its two constituent republics, Czech and Slovak, officially parted ways to form independent countries.

To observers from abroad, the rush to split the republics following federal elections in 1992 came as something of a surprise. Formed from the ruins of the Austro-Hungarian empire at the end of World War I, *Czecho-Slovakia* had portrayed itself to the world as a modern-day success story: a union of two peoples that had managed to overcome divisive nationalism in the higher interest of stabilizing a potentially volatile region.

Popular perceptions were reinforced by a long list of achievements. During the difficult 1930s, the Czechoslovak republic was the model democracy in Central Europe. The 1968 Prague Spring, an intense period of cultural renewal when Communists spoke openly of creating a more humane socialism, was centered largely on Czech territory, but was led by a courageous Slovak, Alexander Dubček. In 1989 the Communists were brought down by students in both Prague and Bratislava who shared a similar faith in the power of democracy and freedom.

The forces for separation, however, proved in the end to be too powerful. For all its successes, Czechoslovakia was ultimately an artificial creation, masking important and longstanding cultural differences between two outwardly similar peoples. The Czech Republic, linking the old Austrian crown lands of Bohemia and Moravia, can look to a rich cultural history going back some 600 to 700 years when the Bohemian Kingdom was at the center of the Holy Roman Empire. Bohemia and Moravia played pivotal roles in the great religious and social conflicts of European history.

Slovakia, by contrast, languished for nearly a millennium as the agrarian half of the Hungarian empire. Although great strides were made in the years following World War II to bring Slovakia's schools and industries to the level of their cousins to the west, many Slovaks are still stung by the label of cultural inferiority. Given the state of the national ego, independence was probably inevitable.

Although officially separate as of January 1993, the two republics still present themselves to the visitor in many respects as one country. Combining a visit to Prague with an excursion to Slovakia's breathtaking High Tatras is as easy at it ever was (*see* Chapter 25, Slovakia).

Most visitors to the Czech Republic head straight for the Gothic, Baroque, and Art Nouveau splendors of Prague. But don't pass up a chance to visit the famous spas of western Bohemia or the lovely towns and castles of southern Bohemia. The crumbling Renaissance river town of Český Krumlov stands out as a "must-see."

It should be noted that the country still bears the scars of 40 years of Communism, in the form of Kafkaesque bureaucracies and, outside Prague, dilapidation and pollution. Unlike much of the West, however, most cities have remained much as they were, and streets are safe and have a refreshing lack of commercial hype. Tourist amenities certainly lack polish, and service can be frustratingly bad, but the beauty of the towns and the countryside and the rich heritage of art and architecture go a long way to compensate for these discomforts.

The Czech Republic

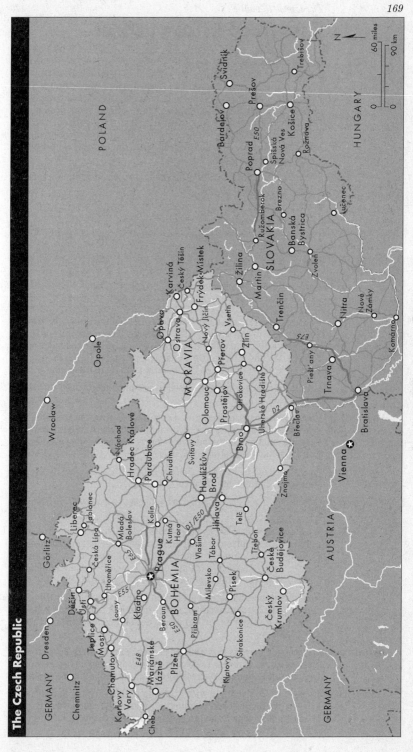

Essential Information

Before You Go

When to Go Organized sightseeing tours run from April or May through October. Some monuments, especially castles, either close entirely or open for shorter hours during the winter. Hotel rates drop during the off-season except during festivals. May, the month of fruit blossoms, is the time of the Prague Spring Music Festival. During the fall, when the forests are glorious, Brno, the cultural center of Moravia, hold its own music festival.

Climate The following are the average daily maximum and minimum temperatures for Prague.

Jan.	36F	2C	May	66F	19C	Sept.	68F	20C
	25	- 4		46	8		50	10
Feb.	37F	3C	June	72F	22C	Oct.	55F	13C
	27	- 3		52	11		41	5
Mar.	46F	8C	July	75F	24C	Nov.	46F	8C
	32	0		55	13		36	2
Apr.	58F	14C	Aug.	73F	23C	Dec.	37F	3C
	39	4		55	13		28	- 2

Currency The unit of currency in the Czech Republic is the crown, or koruna, written as Kč, and divided into 100 haléř. There are bills of 20, 50, 100, 500, 1,000, and 5,000 Kč and coins of 10, 20, and 50 haléř and 1, 2, 5, 10, 20, and 50 Kč. At press time (spring 1994), the koruna was trading at around 30 Kč to the dollar and 42 Kč to the pound.

Credit cards are widely accepted in establishments used by foreign tourists.

What It Will Cost Costs are highest in Prague and only slightly lower in the Bohemian resorts and main spas, though even in these places you can now find very reasonable accommodations in private rooms. The least expensive area is southern Bohemia.

Sample Prices Cup of coffee, 10 Kč; beer (½ liter), 15 Kč; Coca-Cola, 15 Kč; ham sandwich, 30 Kč; 1-mile taxi ride, 100 Kč.

Museums Admission to museums, galleries, and castles ranges from 5 Kč to 50 Kč.

Visas U.S. and British citizens do not need visas to enter the Czech Republic. Visa requirements have been temporarily reintroduced for Canadian citizens; check whether this is still the case with the consulate. Apply to the Consulate of the Czech Federal Republic, 50 Rideau Terrace, Ottawa, Ontario K1M 2A1, tel. 613/749–4442.

Customs *On Arrival* Valuable items should be entered on your customs declaration. You can bring in 250 cigarettes (or their equivalent in tobacco), 2 liters of wine, 1 liter of spirits, ½ liter of eau de cologne, and gifts to the value of 1,000 Kč.

On Departure Crystal not purchased with hard currency may be subject to a tax of 100% of its retail price. To be on the safe side, hang on to all receipts. Only antiques bought at specially appointed shops may be exported.

Language English is spoken fairly widely among both the young and those associated with the tourist industry. You will come across English speakers elsewhere, though not frequently. German is widely understood throughout the country.

Getting Around

By Car
Road Conditions Main roads are usually good, if sometimes narrow, and traffic is light, especially away from main centers. An expressway links Prague, Brno, and Bratislava. Other highways are single-lane only.

Rules of the Road Drive on the right. Speed limits are 60 kph (37 mph) in built-up areas, 90 kph (55 mph) on open roads, and 110 kph (68 mph) on expressways. Seat belts are compulsory outside built-up areas; drinking and driving is strictly prohibited.

Parking Except for those belonging to hotel guests, all cars are banned in the center of Prague. In some areas of the capital you can pay to park for a limited period. If you're staying in a private room near Wenceslas Square, a good option is to look for a spot on one of the streets behind the National Museum, where parking is free and unrestricted. Whatever you do, don't park in a no-parking area; your car is likely to be towed away. Elsewhere in the country there's little problem.

Gasoline At about $3 a gallon, gasoline is expensive. Service stations are usually located along main roads on the outskirts of towns and cities. Finding a station in Prague is notoriously difficult. Fill up on the freeway as you approach the city to avoid frustration. Lead-free gasoline, known as "Natural," is still only available at select stations, so tank up when you see it.

Breakdowns The "Yellow Angels" (tel. 02/773455) operate a patrol service on main highways. The emergency telephone number for motorists is 154; for ambulances, 155; for police (traffic accidents), 02/2366464.

By Train There is an extensive rail network throughout the country. As elsewhere in Eastern Europe, fares are relatively low and trains can be crowded. Also, you have to pay a supplement on all express trains. Most long-distance trains have dining cars; overnight trains between main centers have sleeping cars.

By Plane Remarkably good internal air service links Prague with several other towns, including Brno, Bratislava, Poprad (for the High Tatras), Karlovy Vary, and Piešt'any. Prices are reasonable.

Make reservations at Čedok offices or directly at ČSA, Czechoslovak Airlines (tel. 02/2146).

By Bus A wide-ranging bus network provides quicker service than trains at somewhat higher prices (though they are still very low by Western standards). Buses are always full, and, on long-distance routes especially, reservations are advisable.

Staying in the Czech Republic

Telephones
Local Calls To use a public phone, buy a Phone Card at a newsstand or tobacconist. Cards cost 100 Kč for 50 units or 190 Kč for 100 units. Local calls cost one unit, international rates vary according to destination. To place a call, lift the receiver, insert the card, and dial.

International Calls You'll pay through the nose if you make calls from your hotel. There's automatic dialing to many countries, including North America and the United Kingdom. Special international pay booths in central Prague will take 5 Kč coins, but your best bet is to go to the main post office (Jindřišská 24, near Wenceslas Square). For international inquiries, dial 0132 for the United States, Canada, or the United Kingdom. ATT's USADirect number for the Czech Republic is 004200010.

Mail
Postal Rates

Airmail letters to the United States and Canada cost 11 Kč up to 10 grams, postcards 6 Kč. Airmail letters to the United Kingdom cost 8 Kč up to 20 grams, postcards 5 Kč.

Receiving Mail

Mail can be sent to Poste Restante at the main post office in Prague (Jindřišská 24, window 28) or to any other main post office. There's no charge. The American Express office on Wenceslas Square in Prague will hold letters addressed to cardholders or holders of American Express traveler's checks for up to one month free of charge.

Opening and Closing Times

Banks are open weekdays 8–3. **Museums** are usually open Tues.–Sun. 10–5. **Shops** are generally open weekdays 9–6 (9–8 on Thurs.); some close between noon and 2. Many are also open Sat. 9–noon (department stores, 9–4).

National Holidays

January 1; April 17 (Easter Monday); May 1 (Labor Day); May 9 (Liberation Day); July 5 (SS Cyril and Methodius); July 6 (Jan Hus); December 25, 26.

Dining

Dining options include restaurants, wine cellars *(vinárna)*, the more down-to-earth beer taverns *(pivnice)*, cafeterias, and a growing number of coffee shops and snack bars. Eating out is popular, and in summer you must reserve in advance. Most restaurants are remarkably reasonable, but privatization is beginning to push up prices in a few places.

Prague ham makes a favorite first course, as does soup, which is less expensive. The most typical main dish is roast pork (or duck or goose) with sauerkraut. Dumplings in various forms, generally with a rich gravy, accompany many dishes.

Mealtimes

Lunch is usually from 11:30 to 2 or 3; dinner from 6 to 9:30 or 10. Some places are open all day, and you might find it easier to find a table in off-hours.

Dress

A jacket and tie are recommended for Very Expensive and Expensive restaurants. Informal dress is appropriate elsewhere.

Ratings

Prices are reasonable by American standards, even in the more expensive restaurants. Czechs don't normally go in for three-course meals, and the following prices apply only if you're having a first course, main course, and dessert (excluding wine and tip). Best bets are indicated by a star ★.

Category	Prague	Other Areas
Very Expensive	over 800 Kč	over 400 Kč
Expensive	350 Kč–800 Kč	250 Kč–400 Kč
Moderate	200 Kč–350 Kč	100 Kč–250 Kč
Inexpensive	under 200 Kč	under 100 Kč

Lodging

There's a choice of hotels, motels, private accommodations, and campsites. Many older properties are gradually being renovated, and the best have great character and style. There is still an acute shortage of hotel rooms during the peak season, so make reservations well in advance. Many private room agencies are now in operation, and as long as you arrive before 9 PM, you should be able to get a room. The standards of facilities and services hardly match those in the West, so don't be surprised by faulty plumbing or indifferent reception clerks.

Hotels These are officially graded with from one to five stars. Many hotels used by foreign visitors—Interhotels—belong to Čedok and are mainly in the three- to five-star categories. These will have all or some rooms with bath or shower. Čedok can also handle reservations for some non-Čedok hotels, such as those run by Balnea (the spa treatment organization); CKM (the Youth Travel Bureau); and municipal organizations, some of which are excellent.

Hotel bills can be paid in crowns, though some hotels still try to insist on hard currency.

Private Prague is full of travel agencies offering accommodation in private
Accommodations homes. These are invariably cheaper and often more comfortable than hotels, though you may have to sacrifice something in privacy. The best room-finding service is probably **AVE** in the main train station (open 7 AM–10:30 PM). Insist on a room in the center, however, or you may find yourself in a dreary, far-flung suburb. Another helpful agency is **Hello Ltd.** (Senovážné nám. 3, Prague 1, tel. 02/224283). Elsewhere, look for signs declaring "Room Free" or, more frequently, in German, "Zimmer Frei" or "Privatzimmer" along main roads. Čedok offices can also frequently help in locating private accommodation.

Camping Campsites are run by a number of organizations. A free map and list are available from Čedok.

Ratings Prices are for double rooms, generally not including breakfast. Prices at the lower end of the scale apply to low season. At certain periods, such as Easter or during festivals, there may be an increase of 15%–25%. Best bets are indicated by a star ★.

Category	Prague	Other Areas
Very Expensive	over $200	over $100
Expensive	$100–$200	$50–$100
Moderate	$50–$100	$15–$50
Inexpensive	under $50	under $15

Tipping Reward good service in restaurants with a few crowns, given directly to the waiter on paying your bill. As a rule of thumb, round up to the nearest multiple of 10 (i.e., if the bill comes to 83 Kč, give the waiter 90 Kč). Give 10% on big or group tabs. For taxis, add 10 Kč. In the better hotels, doormen should get 5 Kč for each bag they carry to the check-in desk; bellhops get up to 10 Kč for taking them up to your rooms. In Moderate or Inexpensive hotels, you'll have to lug them yourself.

Prague

Arriving and Departing

By Plane All international flights arrive at Prague's Ruzyně Airport, about 20 kilometers (12 miles) from downtown. For arrival and departure times, tel. 02/367814 or 02/367760.

Between the Czechoslovak Air Lines (ČSA) provides bus services linking the air-
Airport and port with Town Terminal Vltava (Revoluční 25) and major hotels.
Downtown Buses depart every 20 minutes during the day, every half hour evenings and on weekends. The trip into Prague costs 15 Kč and takes

about 30 minutes. A special shuttle service serves main hotels and costs 50 Kč; buy the ticket before boarding. The cheapest way to get into Prague is by regular bus No. 119; the cost is 6 Kč, but you'll need to change to the subway at the Dejvická station for the last leg of the trip. By taxi, expect to pay 300 Kč.

By Train The main station for international and domestic routes is Hlavni nádraží (tel. 02/24217654), Wilsonova, not far from Wenceslas Square. Some international trains arrive at and depart from Nádraží Holešovice, on the same metro line (C) as the main station.

By Bus The main bus station is Florenc (at Na Florenci, tel. 02/24211060), not far from the train station. Take metro line C to Florenc station.

Getting Around

Public transportation is a bargain. Jizdenky (tickets) cost 6 Kč and can be bought at hotels, newsstands, and from dispensing machines in the metro stations. For the metro, punch the ticket in the station before getting on the escalators; for buses and trams, punch the ticket inside the vehicle. You can also buy one-day passes allowing unlimited use of the system for 50 Kč, two-day for 85 Kč, three-day for 110 Kč, and five-day for 170 Kč. The passes can be purchased at the main metro stations and at some newsstands.

By Subway Prague's three modern subway lines are easy to use and spotlessly clean. They provide the simplest and fastest means of transportation, and most new maps of Prague mark the routes.

By Tram/Bus You need to buy a new ticket every time you change vehicles. Express buses (marked with green badges) serve the suburbs and cost 6 Kč.

By Taxi Taxi scams are common. Avoid taxi stands in heavily touristed areas. Instead, hail cabs from the street or order them in advance by telephone. Reputable firms include **AAA** (tel. 02/322444) and **Taxi** (tel. 02/24911560). The basic charge is 10 Kč, increased by 12 Kč per kilometer. Be warned: Many drivers don't put on the meter. Either agree on a price beforehand (no more than 100 Kč within the city) or ask them to put on the meter. Some larger hotels have their own fleets, which are a little more expensive.

Important Addresses and Numbers

Tourist Information The main **Čedok** office (Na příkopě 18, tel. 02/24197111) is close to Wenceslas Square.

Embassies U.S. (Tržiště 15, Malá Strana, tel. 02/24510847). **Canadian** (Mickiewiczova 6, Hradčany, tel. 02/24311108). **U.K.** (Thunovská 14, Malá Strana, tel. 02/24510439).

Emergencies **Police** (tel. 158); **Ambulance** (tel. 155); **Diplomatic Health Center for Foreigners** (Na homolce 724, Prague 5, weekdays tel. 02/5292–2146, evenings and weekends tel. 02/5292–2191); **24-Hour Pharmacy** (Na příkopě 7, near Wenceslas Sq., tel. 02/24210229). Prague now has a **Lost Credit Card Hotline** (02/2366688).

English-Language Bookstores The **Globe Bookstore and Coffeehouse** (Janovského 14, Prague 7; Metro: Vltavska) has the city's best selection of English books. **Bohemian Ventures** (nám. Jana Palacha 2) at the Philosophical Faculty of Charles University near the Staroměstská metro station) stocks a large selection of paperbacks and modern fiction. For hiking maps and atlases, try **Melantrich** (Na příkopě 3, Prague 1, tel. 02/267166).

Guided Tours

Čedok arranges a variety of tours in and around Prague; they can either be arranged before you leave or booked in Prague.

Orientation Tours Čedok offers a daily three-hour tour of the city, starting at 10 AM from the Čedok office at Bílkova 6 (tel. 02/2318255), opposite the Hotel Intercontinental. Contact any Čedok office for the current schedule and itinerary. From May to September, the organization also operates an afternoon tour, starting at 1:30. Both tours cost about 350 Kč.

Martin-Tour (tel. 02/527456) offers a similar but cheaper tour departing from náměstí Republiky daily at 9:30, 11:30, 1:30, and 3:30 (cost: about 270 Kč).

Special-Interest Tours The "U Fleku" brewery and beer-tasting tour departs on Friday mornings from Wenceslas Square 24 and lasts 1½ hours. For cultural tours, call Čedok *(see above)*. These include performances of folklore, Laterna Magika *(see* The Arts, *below)*, opera, and concerts. You can save money by buying tickets—if any are available—at box offices, but this will take time.

Excursions Čedok's one-day tours out of Prague cover principal historic and scenic sights and include lunch. The "Treasures of Bohemian Gothic" tour includes an excursion to the lovely medieval town of Kutná Hora; "Romantic Bohemian Paradise" features the bizarre sandstone and rock formations of northern Bohemia. Other tours include visits to famous spa towns and castles.

Personal Guides Contact Čedok *(see above)* to arrange a personal walking tour of the city. Times, prices, and itinerary are negotiable. Prices start at around 400 Kč per hour.

Exploring Prague

Prague is one of the most enchanting cities in Europe. Like Rome, Prague is built on seven hills, sprawling within the confines of a broad loop of the Vltava River. The riverside location, enhanced by a series of graceful bridges, makes a great setting for two of the city's most notable features: its extravagant, fairy-tale architecture and its memorable music. Mozart claimed that no one understood him better than the citizens of Prague, and he was only one of several great masters who lived or lingered here.

It was under Charles IV (Karel IV) during the 14th century that Prague briefly became the seat of the Holy Roman Empire—virtually the capital of Western Europe—and acquired its distinctive Gothic imprint. At times you'll need to look quite hard for this medieval inheritance; it's still here, though, under the overlays of graceful Renaissance and exuberant Baroque.

Prague escaped serious wartime damage, but it didn't escape neglect. Because of the long-term restoration program now under way, some part of the city is always under scaffolding. But what's completed—which is nearly all that's described in the following itineraries—is hard to find fault with as an example of sensitive and painstaking restoration.

Numbers in the margin correspond to points of interest on the Prague map.

The Nové Město and Staré Město

❶ ❷ ❸ **Václavské náměstí** (Wenceslas Square) is the Times Square of Prague. Confusingly, it's not actually a square at all but a broad boulevard sloping down from the **Národní muzeum** (National Museum) and the equestrian **statue of St. Wenceslas.** The lower end is where all the action is. Na příkopě, once part of the moat surrounding the Old Town, is now an elegant pedestrian mall. Čedok's main **❹** office is here, on your way to the **Prašná brána** (Powder Tower), a 19th-century neo-Gothic replacement of the medieval original.

❺ Turn into Celetná and you're on the old **Royal Route,** once followed by coronation processions, past the foreboding Gothic spires of the **❻** Týn Church through **Staroměstské náměstí** (Old Town Square), **❼** down **Karlova,** across **Karlův most** (Charles Bridge), and up to the castle. Along this route, you can study every variety or combination of Romanesque, Gothic, Renaissance, and Baroque architecture. Two good examples are the town buildings at 12 Celetná and 8 Karlova. On Staroměstské náměstí, the crowds regularly gather below the famous **Clock Tower,** where, on the hour, the complex 16th-century mechanism activates a procession that includes the Twelve Apostles. Note the skeleton figure of Death that tolls the bell.

❽ **Franz Kafka's birthplace** is just north of Staroměstské náměstí on U radnice. Following the 1989 revolution, Kafka's popularity has soared, and the works of this German Jewish writer are now widely available in Czech. A fascinating little museum has been set up in the house. *U radnice 5. Admission: 10 Kč. Open daily 10–6.*

❾ In the **Starý židovský hřbitov** (Old Jewish Cemetery) in **Josefov** (Joseph's Town, the old Jewish quarter), ancient tombstones lean and jostle each other; below them, in a dozen layers, are 12,000 graves. As you stand by the tomb of the scholar Rabbi Low, who died in 1609, you may see, stuffed into the cracks, scraps of paper bearing prayers and requests. Be sure to visit the tiny Gothic **Staronová synagóga** (Old-New Synagogue), which, along with the **❿** cemetery, forms part of the **Státní židovské múzeum** (State Jewish Museum). *Červená 101. Admission: 20 Kč. Open Sun.–Fri. 9–4:30 (9–5 in summer); closed Sat. and religious holidays.*

When you stand on Charles Bridge, you'll see views of Prague that would still be familiar to the 14th-century architect Peter Parler and to the sculptors who added the 30 Baroque statues in the early 18th century (a few have been replaced). They're worth a closer look, especially the 12th on the left (starting from the Old Town side of the bridge) (St. Luitgarde, by Matthias Braun, circa 1710), and the 14th on the left (in which a Turk guards suffering saints, by F. M. Brokoff, circa 1714).

⓫ The **museum** devoted to Prague composer **Bedřich Smetana,** located nearby at Novotného lávka, is small, and its exhibits mainly documentary. But it's a lovely quiet oasis in which to listen to tapes of Smetana's music—and admire the views across the Vltava and up to the castle. *Novotného lávka. Admission: 20 Kč. Open Wed.–Mon. 10–5.*

⓬ The **Betlémska kaple** (Bethlehem Chapel) has been completely reconstructed since Jan Hus thundered his humanitarian teachings from its pulpit in the early 15th century to congregations that could number 3,000. But the little door through which he came to the pulpit is original, as are some of the inscriptions on the wall. *Betlémské náměstí. Open daily 9–6.*

Malá Strana and Hradčany (Lesser Quarter and Castle)

⓭ Cross Charles Bridge and follow Mostecká up to Malostranské náměstí. After the turbulence of the Counter-Reformation at the start of the 17th century, Prague witnessed a great flowering of what became known as Bohemian Baroque. The architects (Dientzenhofer, father and son) of the **Chram svatého Mikuláše** (Church of St. Nicholas) were among its most skilled exponents. If you're in Prague when a concert is being given in this church, fight for a ticket. The lavish sculptures and frescoes of the interior make for a memorable setting. *Malostranské náměstí. Open daily 10–4 (9–6 in summer).*

⓮ The monumental complex of **Hradčany** (Prague Castle) has witnessed the changing fortunes of the city for more than 1,000 years. The scaffolding has only recently been removed from the latest restoration of the castle's **Chram svatého Víta** (St. Vitus Cathedral). It took from 1344 to 1929 to build, so you can trace the whole gamut of styles from Romanesque to Art Nouveau. This is the final resting place for numerous Bohemian kings. Charles IV lies in the crypt. Good King Wenceslas has his own chapel in the south transept, studded with semiprecious stones. Knightly tournaments often accompanied coronation ceremonies in the **Královský palác** (Royal Palace), next to the cathedral, hence the broad Riders' Staircase leading up to the grandiose **Vladislavský sál** (Vladislav Hall) of the Third Courtyard. Oldest of all the buildings, though much restored, is the Romanesque complex of **Bazilika svatého Jiří** (St. George's Church and Monastery). Behind a Baroque facade, it houses a superb collection of Bohemian art from medieval religious sculptures to decadent Baroque paintings. *Hradčanské náměstí. Admission to each museum building in the castle: 10 Kč. All are open Tues.–Sun. 10–5.*

⓯ The Baroque church and shrine of **Loreto** is named for the Italian town to which the Virgin Mary's House in Nazareth was supposedly transported by angels to save it from the infidel. The crowning glory of its fabulous treasury is the glittering monstrance of the *Sun of Prague,* set with 6,222 diamonds. Arrive on the hour to hear the 27-bell carillon. *Loreta 12. Admission: 10 Kč. Open Tues.–Sun. 9–noon and 1–4:30.*

Off the Beaten Track

Cross the Vltava at the Hotel InterContinental (via the Čechův bridge) and climb the steps to the **Letenské sady** (Gardens on the Ramparts) for sweeping views of Prague.

Almost as old as the oldest parts of Prague Castle, the ruins of **Vyšehrad Castle** crown a rock bluff rising out of the Vltava, about 2 miles downstream from the Old Town. The quiet cemetery adjoining the **Church of Sts. Peter and Paul** is a place to pay homage to some of the nation's cultural giants, among them Bedřich Smetana and the writer Karel Čapek.

Across the river, in Prague 5 district, Mozart stayed in the peaceful **Bertramka Villa,** and here completed his opera *Don Giovanni.* With luck, your trip will coincide with a concert here. If not, taped music will accompany your walk through the villa, restored to what it was in his day.

Although it's no longer possible to stroll around the grounds, you can still glimpse **Franz Kafka's grave** through the gates of the **Židovské hřbitovy** (New Jewish Cemetery) in Vinohrady, a rather depressing part of Prague. Take metro line A to Želivského, turn

Prague

HRADČANY

14

15

Pod Bruskou

Kosárkovo nábř.

Dvořákovo nábř.

Mánesův most

nám. Jana Palacha

Valdštejnská

Letenská

Thunovska

Nerudova

Vojanovy Gardens

Veleslavinova

Malostranské nám.

13

Tržiště

Mostecká

Karlův most

7

Křižovnická

K

Jánský vršek

Karmelitská

Maltézské nám.

Na Kampě

11

Liliova

Křižovnické nám.

Velkopřevorské nám.

N

Hellichova

Vltava

Betlémská

Konviktská

MALÁ STRANA

Všehrdova

Malostranské nábř.

Střelecký ostrov

Smetanovo nábř.

B

Újezd

Petřín Gardens

Vítězná

most Legii

Ostrovni

Pštrossova

0   1/4 mile

0   1/4 km

Plaská

Zborovská

Janáčkovo nábř.

Masarykovo nábřeží

Petřínská

KEY

AE American Express Office

i Tourist Information

Holečkova

Malátova

Dětský ostrov

Slovanský ostrov

K

Betlémská kaple, **12**
Chram svatého
Mikuláše, **13**
Hradčany (Prague
Castle), **14**
Kafka's Birthplace, **8**
Karlův most, **7**
Loreto, **15**
Národní muzeum, **2**

Starý židovský
hřbitov, **9**
Prašná brána, **4**
Royal Route, **5**
Smetana Museum, **11**
Staroměstské
náměstí, **6**
Státni židovské
muzeum, **10**
Statue of
St.Wenceslas, **3**
Václavské náměstí, **1**

Na Františku

nábř. Ludvíka Svobody

U Milosrdných

Klimentská

Bílkova

Soukenická

Haštalská

17. listopadu

Pařížská

Široká

Dlouhá

Zlatnická

Havlíčkova

9

10

STARÉ MĚSTO

Rybná

Masná

Truhlářská

Na poříčí

Na Florenci

Maiselova

Jakubská

Kaprová

8

Staroměstské nám.

nám. Republiky

Platnéřská

6

5 Celetná **4**

Hybernská

Malé nám.

Železná

Havelská

Havířská

Na příkopě

Karlova

Melantrichova

i

nám. M. Gorkého

Liliová

Jilská

Nekázanka

Panská

Train Station (Hlavní Nádraží)

12

Betlémské nám.

Martinská

Růžová

Václavské náměstí

Jindřišská

Politických vězňů

Bartolomějská

Na Perštýně

třída

Jungmannovo nám.

Opletalova

Wilsonova

Národní

1

(Wenceslas Square)

Washingtonova

Spálená

Vladislavova

Jungmannova

Vodičkova

AE

Španělská

Italská

Lazarská

3

Mánesova

NOVÉ MĚSTO

Štěpánská

Ve Smečkách

Královská

2

Křemencova

Školská

Vinohradská

Černá

Myslíkova

Žitná

right at the main cemetery gate, and follow the wall for about 100 yards. Kafka's thin, white tombstone lies at the front of section 21.

Shopping

Specialty Shops Look for the name **Dilo** for objets d'art and prints; **ULUV** or **UVA** for folk art. **Moser** (Na příkopě 12) is the most famous for glass and porcelain. Shops specializing in Bohemian crystal, porcelain, ceramics, and antiques abound.

Shopping Districts Many of the main shops are in and around Wenceslas Square and Na příkopě, as well as along Celetná and Pařížská.

Department Stores Four central stores are **Bílá Labut'** (Na poříčí 23), **Krone** (Václavské nám. 21), **Kotva** (nám. Republiky 8), and Kmart (Narodní 26).

Dining

Eating out in Prague is a very popular pastime, so it's advisable to make reservations whenever possible, especially for dinner. For details and price-category definitions, *see* Dining in Staying in the Czech Republic, *above.*

Very Expensive **U Malířů.** This recently privatized old restaurant now serves exclusively French food and wines at the highest prices you'll see in the entire country. The specialty of the house is lobster, but the chef prepares a couple of elaborate set menus daily. *Maltézké náměstí 11, Malá Strana, tel. 02/24510269. Reservations advised. AE, DC, MC, V. Closed Sun.*

★ **U Zlaté Hrušky.** Careful restoration has returned this restaurant to its original 18th-century style. It specializes in Moravian wines, which go down well with fillet steaks and goose liver. *Nový Svět 3, Castle area, tel. 02/531133. Reservations required. No credit cards. Dinner only.*

Vzátiší. White walls and casual grace accentuate the subtle flavors of smoked salmon, roast beef, and other non-Czech specialties. It's a favorite spot with the expatriate crowd and visiting businesspeople on expense accounts. *Liliova 1, Staré Město, tel. 02/24228977. Reservations advised. AE, DC, MC, V.*

Expensive **Opera Grill.** Though called a grill, this is one of the most stylish small
★ restaurants in town, complete with antique Meissen candelabra and Czech specialties. *K. Světlé 35, Staré Město, tel. 02/265508. Reservations required. AE, DC, MC, V. Dinner only.*

U Labutí. Located in tastefully remodeled stables in the castle area, "At the Swans" has a stylish—if slightly rich and heavy—menu (haunch of venison, goose liver with ham and almonds), which includes some Expensive dishes. The place is rich in atmosphere, too. *Hradčanské náměstí 11, tel. 02/536962. Reservations required. AE, DC, MC, V. Dinner only.*

★ **U Mecenáše.** This wine restaurant manages to be both medieval and elegant despite the presence of an ancient gallows! Try to get a table in the back room. The chef specializes in thick, juicy steak, served with a variety of sauces. *Malostranské náměstí 10, Malá Strana, tel. 02/533881. Reservations required. AE, DC, MC, V. Dinner only.*

Moderate **Myslivna.** They took the antlers off the walls of this rustic restaurant a year or so after the Velvet Revolution, but the cooks still know their way around pheasant, boar, and quail. Try leg of venison in wine sauce with walnuts or wild boar, all prepared to please the eye and palette. *Jagellonská 21, Vinohrady, tel. 02/6270209. Reservations advised. AE, DC, MC, V.*

Penguin's. A trendy crowd comes here for some of the best Czech cooking and freshest vegetables in town (and because they know they're getting excellent value for their money). The muted mauve and matte-black walls make a casually elegant setting. *Zborovská 5, tel. 02/545660. Reservations advised. No credit cards.*

Pezinok. You'll get good, hearty fare served in a relaxed, no-frills atmosphere at this restaurant located behind Národní Třída in the New Town. The homemade sausage, accompanied by hearty Slovak wine, is excellent. The large *palačinky* (crêpes) for dessert are some of the best in Prague. *Purkyňova 4, tel. 02/291996. Reservations advised. AE.*

U Lorety. Sightseers will find this an agreeable spot—peaceful except for the welcoming carillon from neighboring Loreto Church. The service here is discreet but attentive, the tables are private, and the food is consistently good. Venison and steak are specialties. *Loretánské námestí 8, near the Castle, tel. 02/24510109. Reservations advised. AE, DC, MC, V. Closed Mon. (and Tues. in winter).*

Inexpensive **Na Zvonařce.** This bright beer hall serves very good traditional fare at unbeatable prices. Sit on the terrace during the summer to escape the noisy crowd. Noteworthy dishes include fried chicken and English roast beef. Fruit dumplings for dessert are a rare treat. Service is slow. *Šafaříkova 1, tel. 02/6911311. Reservations advised. No credit cards.*

U Koleje. The friendly staff at this popular, laid-back pub suitable for the whole family serves good traditional pork and beef dishes and excellent beer. You may have to share a table. *Slavíkova 24, tel. 02/6274163. Reservations advised. No credit cards.*

U Zlatého Tygra. This impossibly crowded hangout is the last of a breed of authentic Czech *pivnice* (pubs). The smoke and stares preclude a long stay, but it's still worth dropping in for typical pub staples like ham and cheese plates or roast pork. The service is surly, but the beer is good. *Husova 17. No phone. No reservations. No credit cards. Evenings only. Closed Sun.*

V Krakovské. This clean pub noted for its excellent traditional fare is the place to try Bohemian duck: it's cooked just right and offered at an excellent price. Wash it down with good dark beer from Domažlice in western Bohemia. *Krakovská 20, tel. 02/261537. Reservations advised. No credit cards.*

Lodging

Many of Prague's older hotels—some of which have great style—have recently been or are due to be renovated. For details and price-category definitions, *see* Lodging in Staying in the Czech Republic, *above*.

Very Expensive ★ **Diplomat.** Completed in 1990 as part of a joint venture with an Austrian company, the Diplomat succeeds in fusing elegance with "Western" efficiency. The effect is marred only by an unfortunate location, four subway stops from Staré Město (about a 15-minute ride). *Evropská 15, tel. 02/24394111, fax 02/341731. 387 rooms with bath. Facilities: sauna, nightclub. AE, DC, MC, V.*

★ **Palace Praha** (Interhotel). Beautifully renovated in art nouveau style, the newly reopened Palace is Prague's most elegant and luxurious hotel. Its central location just off Wenceslas Square makes this an excellent choice. *Panská 12, tel. 02/24093111, fax 02/24221240. 125 rooms with bath. Facilities: saunas, health club, nightclub. AE, DC, MC, V.*

U Páva. Recently remodeled suites in this svelte, neoclassical inn on a cobblestone street in Malá Strana afford unforgettable views of the Castle. The Old World staff is courteous, and the reception and public areas are elegant and discreet. *U lužického semináře 106, Prague 1, tel. 02/24510922, fax 02/533379. 11 rooms with bath. AE, DC, MC, V.*

Expensive **Forum** (Interhotel). This modern 28-story high rise is near ancient Vyšehrad Castle, two subway stops south of the city center. Prices include half-board. *Kongresová ul., tel. 02/61191111, fax 02/420684. 531 rooms with bath. Facilities: saunas, pool, bowling alleys, miniature golf, gym, nightclub, roulette. AE, DC, MC, V.*

Jalta (Interhotel). The Jalta has a plum location on Wenceslas Square. Recently remodeled, it deserves at least four of the five stars awarded by Čedok. *Václavské náměstí 45, tel. 02/24229133, fax 02/24229066. 90 rooms with bath. Facilities: 2 nightclubs. AE, DC, MC, V.*

Paříž. Despite its overpriced rooms, this Art Nouveau gem near the center of the Old Town continues to be in high demand. Request a room away from the street. *U Obecního domu 1, Prague 1, tel. 02/24222151, fax 02/24225475. 86 rooms with bath. AE, DC, MC, V.*

Moderate **Atlantic.** Something of the 1970s hangs in the air of this well-run establishment, situated a stone's throw from the Powder Tower in central Prague. Dark, carpeted interiors and overstuffed leather chairs set the subdued mood. The slickly appointed rooms, all with television sets and clean, modern bathrooms, date from a 1989 renovation. *Na poříčí 9, tel. 02/24811084, fax 02/24812378. 60 rooms with bath. Facilities: restaurant, bar. AE, DC, MC, V.*

Kampa. An early Baroque armory-turned-hotel, the Kampa is tucked away in a shady corner just south of Malá Strana. The rooms are clean, if spare, but the bucolic setting compensates for any discomforts. *Všehrdova 16, Prague 1, tel. 02/24510409, fax 02/24510377. 85 rooms with bath. Facilities: restaurant, café. AE, DC, MC, V.*

Meteor Plaza. Costly renovation and incorporation into the Best Western chain recently pushed this hotel from Inexpensive to the top end of Moderate. It may be worth a splurge, though: This elegant Baroque building is in a lovely setting just five minutes on foot from downtown. *Hybernská 6, tel. 02/24192111, fax 02/24213005. 86 rooms with bath. Facilities: restaurant, business center, terrace. AE, DC, MC, V.*

The Arts

Prague's cultural life is one of its top attractions and its citizens like to dress up for it, but performances are usually booked far ahead. You can get a monthly program of events from the Prague Information Service, Čedok, or many hotels. The two English-language newspapers, *The Prague Post* and *Prognosis*, carry detailed entertainment listings. The main ticket agencies are **Bohemia Ticket International** (Salvátorská 6, tel. 02/261889) and **Tiketpro** (Štěpánská 61, Lucerna passage, tel. 02/3118780). It's much cheaper, however, to buy tickets at the box office.

Concerts Performances are held in the **National Gallery** in Prague Castle; the **National Museum;** the **Gardens** below the castle (where music comes with a view); the **churches of St. Nicholas** in both the Old Town Square and in Malá Strana; and **St. James's Church** on Malá Stupartská (Staré Město), where the organ plays amid a flourish of Baroque statuary.

Year-round concert halls include the newly renovated **Rudolfinum** (home of the Czech Philharmonic Orchestra, Alšovo nábř. 12, Prague, tel. 02/24893352), and **Smetana Hall** (Obecní dum, nám. Republiky 5, tel. 02/2322501).

Opera and Ballet Opera is of an especially high standard in the Czech Republic. The main venues in the grand style of the 19th century are the beautifully restored **National Theater** (Národní třida 2, tel. 02/24912673) and the **State Opera of Prague** (Wilsonova 4, tel. 02/24227693; formerly the Smetana Theater). The even older **Theater of Estates** (Ovocný trh 1, tel. 02/24215001; formerly the Týl Theater) is occasionally used for opera performances.

Theater You won't need to know the language at **Divadlo na Zábradlí** (Theater on the Balustrade, Anenské nám. 3, tel. 02/24221933), home of the famous Black Theater mime group when it is (rather rarely) in Prague. **Laterna Magika** (Magic Lantern, Národní třída 4, tel. 02/24914129) is a popular extravaganza combining live actors, mime, and sophisticated film techniques.

Puppet Shows These are brought to a high art form at the **Špejbl and Hurvínek Theater** (Římská 45).

Nightlife

Cabaret The **Alhambra** (Václavské náměstí 5, tel. 02/220467) has a three-part floor show. More moderately priced is **Variété Praha** (Vodičkova 30, tel. 02/2350861). You'll find plenty of fellow foreigners at both.

Discos and Clubs Discos catering to a young crowd (mostly 14- to 18-year-olds) line Wenceslas Square. The best bet is to stroll down the square and listen for the liveliest music. Excellent jazz can be heard nightly in Prague at several venues. Try **Reduta** (Národní třída 20, tel. 02/24912246) or **Agharta** (Krakovská 5, tel. 02/24212914). For live rock, check out the **Rock Cafe** (Národní třída 20, tel. 02/206656) or **Malostranská Beseda** (Malostranské nám. 21, tel. 02/539024).

Bohemian Spas and Castles

The Bohemian countryside is a restful world of gentle hills and thick woods. It is especially beautiful during fall foliage or in May, when the fruit trees that line the roads are in blossom. In such settings lie the two most famous of the Czech Republic's scores of spas: Karlovy Vary and Mariánské Lázně. During the 19th and early 20th centuries, the royalty and aristocrats of Europe who came to ease their overindulged bodies (or indulge them even more!) knew these spas as Karlsbad and Marienbad.

To the south, the higher wooded hills of Šumava, bordering Germany, have their own folklore and give rise to the headwaters of the Vltava. You'll follow its tortuous course as you enter South Bohemia, which has probably spawned more castles than any other region of comparable size. The medieval towns of South Bohemia are exquisite, though be prepared to find them in various stages of repair or decay. In such towns was the Hussite reformist movement born during the early 15th century, sparking off a series of religious conflicts that eventually embroiled all of Europe.

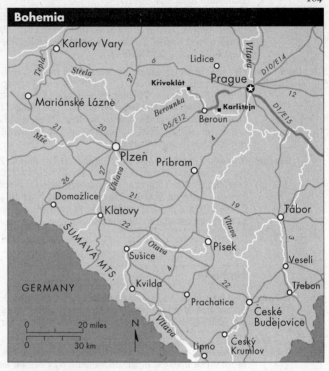

Bohemia

Getting Around

There are bus or train connections to every corner of this region. The service is cheap, frequent, and reliable, though you may be frustrated by incomprehensible small print when trying to decipher timetables. The most convenient way to follow this entire itinerary is by car.

Guided Tours

Many of the attractions on this itinerary, and some additional ones in Moravia, are covered by Čedok's escorted seven-day "Short Tour of the Czech Republic" out of Prague. Most of them can also be visited during a series of day trips from the capital.

Tourist Information
České Budějovice (Hronznova 21, tel. 038/32381).
Český Krumlov (Svornosti náměstí, tel. 0337/2062).
Karlovy Vary (Tržiště 23, tel. 017/27798).
Mariánské Lázně (Odborářů 48, tel. 0165/2500).
Tábor (Tř. 9 května 1282, tel. 0361/144585).

Exploring Bohemian Spas and Castles

If you're traveling by car, the best—though not fastest—route is to head south from Prague on Highway 4, then west along minor roads up the Berounka Valley, taking in the castles of **Karlštejn** and **Křivoklát**. The first is an admirable restoration of the 14th-century castle built by Charles IV, but it isn't worth the uphill slog unless the stunning Chapel of the Holy Rood is reopened, its walls covered with 128 Gothic paintings and encrusted with 2,000 gems. Křivoklát's main attractions are its glorious woodlands, a favorite royal hunting ground in times past. *Both castles open May–Oct., Tues.–Sun. 9–6; closed the day after public holidays.*

Karlovy Vary, or Karlsbad, was named after Charles IV, who, while out hunting, was supposedly led to the main thermal spring of Vřídlo by a fleeing deer. In due course, the spa drew not only many of the crowned heads and much of the blue blood of Europe but also leading musicians and writers. The same parks, promenades, and colonnades still border the little river Teplá, beneath wooded hills. For all its later buildings and proletarian patients, Karlovy Vary still has a great deal of elegance. The waters from the spa's 12 springs are uniformly foul-tasting. The thing to do is sip them while nibbling rich Karlovy Vary wafers (*oplatky*), then resort to the "13th spring," Karlovy Vary's tangy herbal liqueur called *Becherovka.*

Karlovy Vary and **Mariánské Lázně** have the Czech Republic's two best golf courses. As a spa, Mariánské Lázně is younger and smaller, yet its more open setting gives it an air of greater spaciousness. It was much favored by Britain's Edward VII, though from all accounts, he didn't waste too much time on strict diets and rigorous treatments.

The spas of west Bohemia have long catered to foreign travelers. As you head south to the higher Šumava Mountains bordering Germany, you'll be following much less frequented trails. **Domažlice** is the heart of the region of the Chods, for centuries guardians of Bohemia's frontiers, a function that earned them a number of privileges. Their special folk culture is still very much alive, not least in their pottery and their contagious dances accompanied by local bagpipes (main festival in mid-August). It is a bustling if neglected little town with a lovely arcaded square, old fortifications, and a castle that houses the **Chod Museum** of local folk culture. *Open May–Oct., Tues.–Sun. 8–noon and 1–4:30.*

From Domažlice runs a tortuous but extremely pretty route, mainly along minor roads, through Sušice along the upper Otava River and over the hills to Prachatice and back to **Kvilda,** where the road joins the young Vltava River. Downstream, the Vltava has been trapped to form the great reservoir and recreational area of **Lipno.** You skirt part of it before turning northeast to Český Krumlov.

This entire part of South Bohemia has strong associations with such feudal families as the Rožmberks, who peppered the countryside with their castles and created lake-size "ponds" in which to breed highly prized carp, still the main feature of a Czech Christmas dinner. Once the main seat of the Rožmberks, **Ceský Krumlov** is a magical town dominated by a forbidding Renaissance castle, complete with romantic elevated walkways and delicate towers. The Vltava River snakes through the town, which is steeply stacked on either bank, with flights of steps linking various levels and twisting narrow lanes that converge on **Svornosti náměstí,** the main square of the Old Town. There are arcades, courtyards, and landscaped castle gardens with an 18th-century theater.

České Budějovice is on a much larger scale, and here your main stop should be the massive but handsome **Přemysla Ottokara II Square.** Previously named for the Hussite leader Žižka, the square's name was changed in 1991 to reflect historical reality—the town was firmly on the side of the Catholics. This is the home of the Czech version of Budweiser beer, known in Czech as Budvar, and well worth trying.

Farther north along Highway 3 is **Tábor,** the very cradle of the Hussite movement. Its twisting streets were designed to confuse the enemy. A labyrinth of tunnels and cellars below the town were used both as living quarters and as links with the outer defenses. Their story is told in the **Hussite Museum** just off Žižka Square. *Open Tues.–Sun. 9–5.*

Dining and Lodging

For details and price-category definitions, *see* Dining and Lodging in Staying in the Czech Republic, *above.*

Český Krumlov   **Růže.** This former Renaissance monastery was lovingly restored in 1992, and now holds its own with other impressive sights in this enchanting town. Guest rooms are spacious and well-appointed; some are furnished in period style. *Horní ul. 153, tel. 0337/2245, fax 0337/3881. 110 rooms with bath. AE, DC, MC, V. Expensive.*

Krumlov. This 19th-century town house is a charming and very comfortable hotel, renovated in 1988. It's in the center of the old town. *Svornosti náměstí 14, tel. 0337/2255–8. 36 rooms, 13 with bath. AE, DC, MC, V. Moderate.*

Karlovy Vary   **Dvořak.** Opened in 1991, this Austrian-built hotel offers imaginative decor, friendly efficiency, and a superb array of facilities. *Nova louka 11, tel. 017/24145, fax 017/22819. 79 rooms with bath. Facilities: pool, fitness room, spa center. AE, DC, MC, V. Very Expensive.*

★   **Grand Hotel Pupp.** Founded in 1701, the Pupp still features a fine 18th-century hall, Slavností sál. It's one of the oldest surviving hotels in Europe, with a glittering list of guests, both past and present. *Mírové náměstí 2, tel. 017/22121–5. 358 rooms with bath. Facilities: saunas, tennis courts, golf, riding, 2 nightclubs, several restaurants and taverns. AE, DC, MC, V. Very Expensive.*

Atlantic. This hotel is right in the middle of town and is run by the nearby Hotel Central. The turn-of-the-century building was renovated recently, but it still bears its characteristic grotesque porcelain statues on the roof. *Divadelní náměstí, tel. 017/24715. 38 rooms, some with bath. AE, DC, MC, V. Moderate.*

Mariánské Lázně   **Golf.** Built in 1924 and renovated in 1982, this hotel is located a bit out of town by the golf course. The decor is traditional and the restaurant serves good regional dishes, such as dumplings. *Zádub 55, tel. 0165/2651, fax 0165/2655. 26 rooms with bath. Facilities: pool, tennis, golf, riding. AE, DC, MC, V. Very Expensive.*

Palace Praha. Built in 1875 during the spa's heyday, this elegant building is conveniently situated just within the resort center. French foods are the specialty at one of the hotel's two restaurants. *Třída Odborářů 67, tel. 0165/2222. 35 rooms, 23 with bath. Facilities: nightclub. AE, DC, MC, V. Expensive.*

8 Denmark

Ebullience and a sense of humor have earned the Danes a reputation as "the Italians of Scandinavia." While one might expect a country comprising more than 400 islands to develop an island mentality, the Danes are famous for their friendliness and have a word— *hyggelig*—for the feeling of well-being that comes from their own brand of cozy hospitality.

The stereotype of melancholic Scandinavia doesn't hold here: not in the café-studded streets of the larger cities, where musicians and fruit vendors hawk their wares to passersby; not in the tiny coastal towns, where the fishing boats are as brightly painted as fire trucks; not in the jam sessions that erupt in the Copenhagen jazz clubs, nor in the equally joyous "jam" sessions involved in the production of *smørrebrød* (the famous open-face Danish sandwich). Even the country's indoor/outdoor museums, where history is reconstructed through full-scale dwellings out in the open, indicate that Danes don't wish to keep life behind glass.

They even joke about their undeniably flat landscape. One of the country's highest hills—dwarfed by any self-respecting peak abroad—stands in Jutland, at 139.5 meters (450 feet). The Danes have dubbed it Himmelbjerget, or Sky Mountain. This is a land of well-groomed agriculture, where every acre is rich in orchard and field. Nowhere are you far from water, as you drive on and off the ferries and bridges linking the three regions of Jutland, Fyn, and Zealand.

It is the sea surrounding the land that has helped shape Denmark's history. The Vikings were magnificent seafarers and had seen much of the world by the 8th century. Today the Danes remain expert navigators, using the 4,480 kilometers (2,800 miles) of coastline for sport—there are regattas around Zealand and Funen—as well as for fishing and trading.

Long one of the world's most liberal countries, Denmark has a highly developed social welfare system. The hefty taxes are the subject of grumbles and jokes, but Danes remain proud of their state-funded medical and educational systems. Evidence of the strong sense of community spirit is the uniquely Danish institution of the People's High School, or Folkehøjskole, where pupils live in and where the shared experience is deemed as important as the courses taken. In the summer, adults and even entire families attend these "schools for life," studying anything from weaving to the philosophy of Wittgenstein.

The country that gave the world Isak Dinesen, Hans Christian Andersen, and Søren Kierkegaard has a long-standing commitment to culture and the arts. In what other nation does the royal couple translate the writings of Simone de Beauvoir or the queen design costumes for the ballet? The Danish Ballet is world-renowned, while the provinces boast numerous theater groups and opera houses.

Perhaps Denmark's greatest charm is its manageable size—about half that of Maine. The ferry journey from Esbjerg, on the western coast of Jutland, to Copenhagen, on the eastern coast of Zealand, takes around five hours. From here you can make comfortable, unhurried expeditions by boat, car, bus, or train to cover what is one of the world's most civilized countries.

Denmark

North
Sea

Skagerrak

TO
GREENLAND
TO
FAROE ISLANDS

SWEDEN

Skagen
Hirtshals
Hjørring
Frederikshavn
Sæby
Brønderslev
Læsø

Hanstholm
Limfjord
Limfjord
Aalborg
Thisted
Nykøbing
Hadsund
Aalborg
Bugt
Kattegat

Lemvig
Skive
Viborg
Randers
Grenå
Anholt

Struer
Holstebro
Jylland

Ringkøbing
Herning
Silkeborg
Århus
Ebeltoft

Grindsted
Skanderborg
Horsens
Samsø

Skjern
Billund
Vejle
Nykøbing
Tisvildeleje
Hornbæk

Esbjerg
Holsted
Fredericia
Kalundborg
Holbæk
Helsingør
Frederikssund
Hillerød

Fanø
Kolding
Middelfart
Jyderup
Roskilde
Copenhagen

Ribe
Vojens
Odense
Kerteminde
Storebælt
Slagelse
Sjælland
Amager

Rømø
Haderslev
Assens
Fyn
Nyborg
Køge
Bugt

Skærbæk
Åbenrå
Fåborg
Ringsted
Køge
St.
Heddinge

Tønder
Als
Svendborg
Langeland
Næstved
Karrebæksminde

Sønderborg
Troense
Tranekær
Vordingborg
Stege
Møn

Ærøskøbing
Rudkøbing
Nakskov
Nykøbing
Falster

Ærø
Marstal
Maribo
Rødby
Nysted
Lolland
TO
BORNHOLM

Ostsee

GERMANY

SWEDEN
Baltic
Sea

Bornholm

Rønne

0   50 miles
0   75 km

Essential Information

Before You Go

When to Go Most travelers visit Denmark during the warmest months, July and August, but there are advantages to going in May, June, or September, when sights are less crowded and many establishments offer off-season discounts. However, few places in Denmark are ever unpleasantly crowded, and when the Danes make their annual exodus to the beaches, the cities have even more breathing space. Visitors may want to avoid the winter months, when the days are short and dark and when important attractions, Tivoli included, close for the season.

Climate The following are the average daily maximum and minimum temperatures for Copenhagen.

Jan.	36F	2C	May	61F	16C	Sept.	64F	18C
	28	-2		46	8		51	11
Feb.	36F	2C	June	67F	19C	Oct.	54F	12C
	28	-2		52	11		44	7
Mar.	41F	5C	July	71F	22C	Nov.	45F	7C
	31	-1		57	14		38	3
Apr.	51F	11C	Aug.	70F	21C	Dec.	40F	4C
	38	3		56	14		34	1

Currency The monetary unit in Denmark is the krone (kr. or DKK), which is divided into 100 øre. At press time (winter 1994), the krone stood at 6.62 kr. to the dollar and 9.91 kr. to the pound sterling. Most well-known credit cards are accepted in Denmark, though the American Express card is accepted less frequently than others. Traveler's checks can be changed in banks and in many hotels, restaurants, and shops.

What It Will Cost Denmark's economy is stable, and inflation remains reasonably low, without wild fluctuations in exchange rates. While Denmark is slightly cheaper than Norway and Sweden, the standard and the cost of living are nonetheless high, especially for such luxuries as alcohol. Prices are highest in Copenhagen, while the least expensive areas are Fyn and Jutland.

Sample Prices Cup of coffee, 14–20 kr.; bottle of beer, 15–25 kr.; soda, 10–15 kr.; ham sandwich, 30–35 kr.; 1-mile taxi ride, 30 kr.

Customs on Arrival If you purchase goods in a country that is a member of the European Union (EU) and pay that country's value-added tax (VAT) on those goods, you may import duty-free 1½ liters of liquor; 300 cigarettes or 150 cigarillos or 75 cigars or 400 grams of tobacco.

If you are entering Denmark from a non-EU country or if you have purchased your goods on a ferryboat or in an airport not taxed in the EU, you must pay Danish taxes on any amount of alcoholic beverages greater than 1 liter of liquor or 2 liters of strong wine, plus 2 liters of other wine. For tobacco, the limit is 200 cigarettes or 100 cigarillos or 50 cigars or 250 grams of tobacco. Other articles (including beer) are allowed up to a maximum of 350 kr.; you are also allowed 50 grams of perfume.

Language A wit once said that Danish was not so much a language as "a disease of the throat." It is a difficult tongue for foreigners, except those from Norway and Sweden, to understand, let alone speak. Danes are good linguists, however, and almost everyone, except elderly people in rural areas, speaks English well.

Getting Around

By Car Roads here are good and largely traffic-free (except around Copenhagen); you can reach many islands by toll-free bridges.

Rules of the Road The driver needs a valid driver's license, and, if you're using your own car, it must have a certificate of registration and national plates. A triangular hazard-warning sign is compulsory in every car and is provided with a rented car. No matter where they are seated, all passengers traveling in cars must wear seat belts, and cars must have low-beam lights on at all times. Motorcyclists must always wear helmets and use low-beam headlights. All drivers must pay attention to cyclists, who drive on the outer right lane and have the right-of-way.

Drive on the right and give way to traffic from the left. A red-and-white triangular Yield sign, or a line of white triangles across the road, means you must yield to traffic on the road you are entering. Do not turn right on a red light. Speed limits are 50 kph (30 mph) in built-up areas; on highways, 100 kph (60 mph); and on other roads, 80 kph (50 mph). If you are towing a trailer, you must not exceed 70 kph (40 mph). Speeding and, especially, drinking and driving, are punished severely.

Parking "Parkering/Standsning Forbudt" means no parking and no stopping, though you are allowed a three-minute grace period to load and unload. In towns, automatic parking-ticket machines are used. Drop in coins, push the silver button, and a ticket will drop down with the expiration time. Display the ticket clearly on the dash. Parking for an hour is 6 kr.–15 kr. in Copenhagen, 7 kr. elsewhere.

Gasoline Gas costs around 5.90 kr. a liter.

Breakdowns Members of organizations affiliated with Alliance International de Tourisme (AIT) can get technical and legal assistance from the **Danish Motoring Organization** (FDM), (Firskovej 32, DK 2800 Lyngby, tel. 45/93–08–00). All highways have emergency phones, and you can even phone the car-rental company for help. If you cannot drive your car to a garage for repairs, the rescue corps, **Falck** (tel. 33/14–22–22), can help anywhere, night or day.

By Train and Bus Traveling by train or bus is easy because Danish State Railways (DSB) (tel. 33/14–17–01) and a few private companies cover the country with a dense network of train services, supplemented in remote areas by buses. Hourly intercity trains connect the main towns in Jutland and Fyn with Copenhagen and Zealand, using high-speed diesels, called IC-3s, on the most important stretches. All these trains make the one-hour ferry crossing of the Store Bælt (Great Belt), the waterway separating Funen and Zealand. You can reserve seats on intercity trains and Lyntog, and you *must* have a reservation if you plan to cross the Great Belt. Buy tickets at stations for trains, buses, and connecting ferry crossings. You can usually buy tickets on the bus itself. For most cross-country trips, children between 4 and 11 accompanied by an adult travel free, though they must have a seat reservation (30 kr.). Ask about discounts for senior citizens and groups.

Fares The **Scanrail pass** is a good buy for 21 days of unlimited travel by rail and on some sea routes in Denmark, Norway, Sweden, and Finland.

The price for an adult traveling second-class is 1,930 kr., 1,450 kr. for young adults (12–25), and 965 kr. for children (4–11).

By Boat There is frequent service to Germany, Poland, Sweden, Norway, and the Faroe Islands (in the Atlantic Ocean, north of Scotland), as well as to Britain. Domestic ferries provide services between the three areas of Jutland, Funen, and Zealand and to the smaller islands, 100 of which are inhabited. Danish State Railways and several private shipping companies publish timetables in English, and you should reserve on domestic as well as overseas routes. Ask about off-season discounts.

By Bicycle Some say the Danes have the greatest number of bikes per capita in the world. Indeed, with its flat landscape and uncrowded roads, Denmark is a cycler's paradise. You can rent bikes at some train stations and many tourist offices, as well as from private firms. Contact the **Danish Cyclists' Association** (Dansk Cyklist Forbund) (Rømersgade 7, DK 1362 Copenhagen, tel. 33/32–31–21) for additional information. Danish tourist offices publish the pamphlet "Cycling Holiday in Denmark."

Staying in Denmark

Telephones Pay phones take 1-, 5-, and 10-kr. coins. You must use the area codes
Local Calls even when dialing a local number. Calling cards, which are sold at DSB stations, post offices, and some kiosks, cost 25, 50, or 100 kr., and are used at certain phones.

International Dial 009, then the country code, the area code, and the number. Ho-
Calls tels add a hefty service charge, so use a pay phone or, in the larger cities, the telephone "butik" in the post office.

Operators and To speak to an operator, most of whom speak English, dial 118; for
Information an international operator, dial 113.

Mail Surface and airmail letters, as well as aerograms, to the United
Postal Rates States cost 5 kr. for 20 grams; postcards also cost 5 kr. Letters and postcards to the United Kingdom and other EU countries cost 3.75 kr. Stamps are sold at post offices and some shops.

Receiving Mail If you do not know where you will be staying, have mail sent Poste Restante to any post office. American Express holds mail free of charge, but only for card- and/or traveler's check–holders. If no post office is specified, letters will be sent to the main post office in Copenhagen (Tietgensgade 37, DK 1704).

Shopping Visitors from a non-EU country can save about 20% by obtaining a
VAT Refunds refund of the value-added tax (VAT) at the more than 1,500 shops displaying Tax Free signs. If the shop sends your purchase directly to your home address, you pay only the sales price, exclusive of VAT. If you want to take the goods home yourself, pay the full price in the shop and get a VAT refund at the Danish duty-free shopping center at the Copenhagen airport. Get a copy of the *Tax-Free Shopping Guide* from the tourist office.

Opening and **Banks** in Copenhagen are open weekdays 9:30–4 and Thursdays un-
Closing Times til 6. Several *bureaux de change*, including the ones at Copenhagen's central station and airport, stay open until 10 PM. Outside Copenhagen, banking hours vary.

Museums are generally open 10–3 or 11–4 and closed Mondays. In winter, opening hours are shorter, and some museums close for the season. Check the local papers or ask at tourist offices.

Shops are generally open weekdays 10–5:30; most stay open on Fridays until 7 or 8 and close on Saturdays at 1 or 2.

National Holidays January 1; April 14–16 (Easter); May 12 (Common Prayer); May 25 (Ascension); June 4 (Pentecost); June 5 (Constitution Day; shops close at noon); and December 24–26.

Dining Danes take their food seriously, and Danish food, however simple, is excellent, with an emphasis on fresh ingredients and careful presentation. Fish and meat are both of top quality in this farming and fishing country, and both are staple ingredients of the famous smørrebrød. Some smørrebrød are huge meals in themselves: Innocent snackers can find themselves faced with a dauntingly large (but nonetheless delicious) mound of fish or meat, slathered with pickle relish, all atop *rugbrød* (rye bread) and *franskbrød* (French bread). Another specialty is *wienerbrød* (a Danish pastry), an original far superior to anything billing itself "Danish pastry" elsewhere.

All Scandinavian countries have versions of the cold table, but Danes claim that theirs, *det store kolde bord*, is the original and the best. It's a celebration meal; the setting of the long table is a work of art—often with paper sculpture and silver platters—and the food itself is a minor miracle of design and decoration.

In hotels and restaurants the cold table is served at lunch only, though you will find a more limited version at hotel breakfasts—a good bet for budget travelers because you can eat as much as you like.

Liquid refreshment is top-notch. Denmark boasts more than 50 varieties of beer made by as many breweries; the best-known come from Carlsberg and Tuborg. Those who like harder stuff should try *snaps*, the famous aquavit traditionally drunk with cold food. Do as the locals do, and knock it back after eating some herring. The Danes have a saying about the herring-snaps combo: "The fish should be swimming."

Mealtimes The Danes start work early, which means they generally eat lunch at noon. Evening meals are also eaten early, but visitors can be certain of being able to eat and drink until 10.

Dress The Danes are a fairly casual lot, and few restaurants require a jacket and tie. Even in the most chic establishments, the tone is elegantly casual.

Ratings Meal prices vary little between town and country. While approximate gradings are given below, remember that careful ordering can get you a Moderate meal at a Very Expensive restaurant. Prices are per person and include a first course, main course, and dessert, plus taxes and tip, but not wine. Best bets are indicated by a star ★.

Category	All Areas
Very Expensive	over 400 kr.
Expensive	200 kr.–400 kr.
Moderate	120 kr.–200 kr.
Inexpensive	under 120 kr.

Lodging Accommodations in Denmark range from the spare and comfortable to the resplendent. Even inexpensive hotels offer simple designs in good materials and good, firm beds. Many Danes prefer a shower to a bath, so if you particularly want a tub, ask for it, but be prepared to pay more. Except in the case of rentals, breakfast and taxes are usually included in prices, but check when making a reservation.

Hotels Luxury hotels in the city or countryside offer rooms of a high standard, and in a manor-house hotel you may find yourself sleeping in a four-poster bed. Less expensive accommodations, however, are uniformly clean and comfortable.

Inns A cheaper and charming alternative to hotels are the old stagecoach kro inns scattered throughout Denmark. You can save money by contacting **Kro Ferie** (Vejlevej 16, 8700 Horsens, tel. 75/64–87–00) to invest in a book of Inn Checks, valid at 80 inns. Each check costs 375 kr. per person or 535 kr. per couple and includes one overnight stay in a double room with bath, breakfast included. Family checks, for three (595 kr.) and four (685 kr.) are also available.

Farm Vacations These are perhaps the best way to see how the Danes live and work. You stay on a farm and share meals with the family; you can even get out and help with the chores. There's a minimum stay of three nights; bed-and-breakfast is 160 kr., while half board runs 230. (Full board can be arranged.) Children under 4 get 75% off; 4–11 get 50%. Contact the **Horsens Tourist Office** (Søndergade 26, DK 8700 Horsens, Jutland, tel. 75/62–38–22, fax 75/62–61–51) for details.

Youth Hostels The 100 youth hostels in Denmark are open to everyone regardless of age. If you have an International Youth Hostels Association card (obtainable before you leave home), the average rate is 60 kr. Without the card, there's a surcharge of 22 kr. For more information, contact **Danmarks Vandrehjem** (Vesterbrogade 39, DK–1620 V, tel. 31/31–36–12).

Rentals Many Danes rent out their summer homes, and a stay in one of these is another good way to see the countryside on your own terms. A simple house with room for four will cost from 1,000 kr. per week. Contact the Danish Tourist Board for details.

Camping Denmark has over 500 approved campsites, with a rating system of one, two, or three stars. You need an International Camping Carnet or Danish Camping Pass (available at any campsite and valid for one year). For more details on camping and discounts for groups and families, contact **Campingrådet** (Hesseløgade 10, tel. 39/27–88–44).

Ratings Prices are for two people in a double room and include service and taxes and usually breakfast. Best bets are indicated by a star ★.

Category	Copenhagen	Other Areas
Very Expensive	over 1,100 kr.	over 850 kr.
Expensive	800 kr.–1,100 kr.	650 kr.–850 kr.
Moderate	670 kr.–800 kr.	450 kr.–650 kr.
Inexpensive	under 670 kr.	under 450 kr.

Tipping The egalitarian Danes do not expect to be tipped. The exception is hotel porters, who get around 5 kr. per bag; you should also leave 1 or 2 kr. for the use of a public toilet, if there is an attendant.

Copenhagen

Arriving and Departing

By Plane The main airport for both international and domestic flights is Copenhagen Airport, 10 kilometers (6 miles) outside of town.

Between the Airport and Downtown There is frequent bus service to the city; the airport bus to the central station leaves every 15 minutes, and the trip takes about 25 minutes. You pay the 27 kr. fare on the bus. Public buses cost 18 kr. and run as often but take twice as long. Bus No. 32 or No. 32H takes you to Rådhus Pladsen, the city-hall square. A taxi ride takes 15 minutes and costs about 120 kr.

By Train Copenhagen's recently renovated central station is the hub of the train networks. Express trains leave hourly, on the hour, from 6 AM to 10 PM for principal towns in Fyn and Jutland. Find out more from **DSB Information** (tel. 33/14–17–01) at the central station. You can make reservations at the central station (tel. 33/14–88–00) and most other stations and through travel agents. In Copenhagen, public shower facilities at the main train station are open 5:30 AM–midnight and cost 15 kr.

Getting Around

By Bus and Suburban Train The best bet for visitors is the **Copenhagen Card,** affording unlimited travel on buses and suburban trains (S-trains), admission to some 60 museums and sights around Zealand, and a reduction on the ferry crossing to Sweden. Buy the card, which costs about 140 kr. (one day), 230 kr. (two days), or 295 kr. (three days)—half price for children 5–11—at tourist offices, hotels, or from travel agents.

Buses and suburban trains operate on the same ticket system and divide Copenhagen and environs into three zones. Tickets are validated on the time system: On the basic ticket, which costs 9.50 kr. for an hour, you can travel anywhere in the zone in which you started. You can buy a packet of 10 basic tickets for 70 kr. Get zone information from the 24-hour information service: tel. 36/45–45–45 for buses, 33/14–17–01 for S-trains. Buses and S-trains run from 5 AM (6 AM on Sundays) to 12:30 AM.

By Car Copenhagen is a city for walkers, not drivers. The charm of its pedestrian streets is paid for by a complicated one-way road system and difficult parking. Leave your car in the garage: Attractions are relatively close together, and public transportation is excellent.

By Taxi Taxis are not cheap, but all are metered. The base charge is 12 kr., plus 8–10 kr. per kilometer. A cab is available when it displays the sign Fri (Free); it can be hailed or picked up at a taxi stand, or tel. 31/35–35–35.

By Bicycle More than half the 5 million Danes are said to ride bikes, which are popular with visitors as well. Bike rental costs 30–50 kr. a day, with a deposit of 100–200 kr. Contact **Danwheel-Rent-a-Bike** (Colbjørnsensgade 3, tel. 31/21–22–27) or **Urania Cykler** (Gammel Kongevej 1, tel. 31/21–80–88).

Important Addresses and Numbers

Tourist Information The main tourist information office is **Danmarks Turistråd** (Danish Tourist Board) (Bernstoffsgade 1, DK–1577 V, Copenhagen, tel. 33/11–13–25). Located on the Tivoli grounds, it is open May, weekdays

9–6, Sat. 9–2, Sun. 9–1; June–Sept., daily 9–6; Oct.–Apr., week-days 9–5, Sat. 9–noon, closed Sun. There are also offices at Elsinore, Hillerød, Køge, Roskilde, Gilleleje, Hundersted, and Tisvildeleje. Youth information in Copenhagen is available at **Huset** (Rådhusstraede 13, tel. 33/15–65–18).

Embassies **U.S.** (Dag Hammarskjöldsallé 24, tel. 31/42–31–44). **Canada** (Kristen Benikowsgade 1, tel. 33/12–22–99). **U.K.** (Kastelsvej 40, tel. 35/26–46–00).

Emergencies **Police, Fire, Ambulance** (tel. 112). **Doctor** (after 4 PM, tel. 33/12–00–41. Fees payable in cash only; night fees around 400–500 kr.). **Dentist: Dental Emergency Service,** Tandlægevagten, 14, Oslo Plads, near Østerport station (no telephone; emergencies only; cash only). **Pharmacies:** The following are open 24 hours in central Copenhagen: **Steno Apotek** (Vesterbrogade 6C, tel. 33/14–82–66); **Sønderbro Apotek** (Amagerbrogade 158 [Amager area], tel. 31/58–01–40); **Glostrup Apotek** (Hovedvegen 101 [Glostrup area], tel. 43/96–00–20).

English-Language Bookstores English-language publications can be found at the central-station newsstand and in most bookstores around town. **Boghallen** (Rådhus Pladsen 37) has a particularly good selection.

Travel Agencies **American Express** (Amagertorv 18, tel. 33/12–23–01). **Spies** (Nyropsgade 41, tel. 33/32–15–00) arranges charter flights and ac-commodations all over Europe.

Guided Tours

Orientation Tours Tours are a good way to get acquainted with Copenhagen. The "Har-bor and Canal Tour" (by boat; May–mid-Sept., daily every ½-hour 10–5) leaves from Gammel Strand and the east side of Kongens Nytorv, while the following bus tours, conducted by **Copenhagen Excursion** (tel. 31/54–06–06), leave from the Lur Blower Column in the Rådhus Pladsen: "City Tour" (mid-May–mid-Oct., daily at 10; June 15–Aug., daily at 10, 12, 4); "Grand Tour of Copenhagen" (Nov.–Mar., Sun.–Fri. and Sat. at 11, 1:30; Apr.–Oct., daily at 11, 1:30, 3); "Royal Tour of Copenhagen" (June–mid-Sept., Tues., Thurs., and Sat. at 10); "City and Harbor Tour" (combined bus and boat; May–mid-Sept., daily at 9:30, 1, 3). Tickets are available aboard the bus and boat or from travel agencies.

Special-Interest Tours The "Carlsberg Brewery Tour," which includes a look into the draft-horse stalls, meets at the Elephant Gate (Ny Carlsbervej 140) on weekdays at 11 and 2 or by arrangement for groups (tel. 33/27–13–14). Tuborg Breweries also provides tours (Strandvejen 54, bus No. 6 or the Svanemøllen train station) weekdays at 10, 12:30, and 2:30 or by arrangement for groups (tel. 33/27–22–12). The "Royal Co-penhagen Porcelain" tour (Smallegade 45, tel. 31/86–48–48) is given on weekdays at 9, 10, and 11.

Walking Tours The tourist board supplies maps and brochures and can recommend a walking tour. **Golden Ring** (tel. 31/51–25–90) offers scheduled walking tours in the summer and by special arrangement.

Regional Tours The Danish Tourist Board has full details of excursions outside the city, including visits to castles (such as Hamlet's castle), the Viking Ship Museum, and Sweden.

Personal Guides The tourist information center can recommend multilingual guides for individual needs, while travel agents have details on hiring a lim-ousine and guide.

Discover The Europe Called Denmark.

Visit Denmark, Europe's oldest kingdom, a royal land where the Golden Age lives on through art, architecture, ballet, opera and design.

Start your vacation on Scandinavian Airlines, America's favorite airline to Denmark. SAS offers the greatest variety of vacation packages.

Stroll Copenhagen's narrow, winding streets. Roam its medieval castles and stately museums – and a mile-long shopping street for pedestrians only. Browse Royal Copenhagen's shops, brimming with the finest crystal, porcelain and silverware. Everywhere you turn, the Royal Denmark experience awaits; and everywhere the English-speaking Danes will give you a warm welcome.

For a Danish Travel Planner, call 1-800-835-2335 or your travel agent.

ROYAL DENMARK

Fortunately, when you travel on Rail Europe, there are some sights you'll miss.

No goofy hats. No big sunglasses. No plaid shirts with striped shorts. Instead, on Rail Europe, you'll experience Europe the way Europeans do. You'll enjoy scenic countryside no one else can show you. And meet unique and interesting people. In short, you'll explore Europe the way it was meant to be explored. When it comes to visiting 33 European countries, get real. Go Rail Europe. Because traveling any other way could end up showing you some pretty dreadful sights. To learn more, call your travel agent or 1-800-4-EURAIL. (1-800-438-7245)

Rail Europe

Europe. To the trained eye.

Exploring Copenhagen

When Denmark ruled Norway and Sweden in the 15th century, Copenhagen was the capital of all three countries. Today it is still the liveliest Scandinavian capital, with about 1 million inhabitants. It's a city meant for walking, the first in Europe to recognize the value of pedestrian streets in fostering community spirit. As you stroll through the cobble streets and squares, you'll find that Copenhagen combines the excitement and variety of big-city life with a small-town atmosphere. If there's such a thing as a cozy metropolis, you'll find it here.

Nor are you ever far from water, be it sea or canal. The city itself is built upon two main islands, Slotsholmen and Christianshavn, connected by drawbridges. Walk down Nyhavn Canal, an area formerly haunted by a fairly salty crew of sailors. Now it's gentrified, and the 18th-century houses lining it are filled with chic restaurants. You should linger, too, in the five main pedestrian streets known collectively as "Strøget," with shops, restaurants, cafés, and street musicians and vendors. In summer Copenhagen moves outside, and the best views of city life are from the sidewalk cafés in the sunny squares.

Numbers in the margin correspond to points of interest on the Copenhagen map.

Rådhus Pladsen and Slotsholmen

❶ The best place to start a stroll is the Rådhus Pladsen (City Hall Square), the hub of Copenhagen's commercial district. The mock-Renaissance building dominating it is the **Københavns Rådhus** (city hall), completed in 1905. A statue of Copenhagen's 12th-century founder, Bishop Absalon, sits atop the main entrance. Inside you can see the first World Clock, an astrological timepiece invented and built by Jens Olsen and put in motion in 1955. If you're feeling energetic, take a guided tour up the 350-foot tower for a panoramic view. *Rådhus Pladsen, tel. 33/66–25–82. Open weekdays 10–3. Tours in English: weekdays at 3, Sat. at 10. Tower tours: Mon.–Sat. at noon; additional tours June–Sept. at 10, noon, 2. Admission: tour 20 kr., tower 10 kr.*

❷ On the east side of Rådhus Pladsen is **Lurblæserne** (Lur Blower's Column), topped by two Vikings blowing an ancient trumpet called a *lur*. The artist took a good deal of artistic license—the lur dates from the Bronze Age, 1500 BC, while the Vikings lived a mere 1,000 years ago. The monument is a starting point for sightseeing tours of the city.

If you continue to the square's northeast corner and turn right, you will be in Frederiksberggade, the first of the five pedestrian streets **❸** that make up the **Strøget**, Copenhagen's shopping district. Walk past the cafés and trendy boutiques to the double square of **Gammel and Nytorv**, where, farther along, the street has been hand inlaid with mosaic tiles.

Turn down Rådhusstræde toward Frederiksholms Kanal, and continue to Nye Vestergade. Here you'll find the entrance to the **❹** **Nationalmuseet** (National Museum), with extensive collections that chronicle Danish cultural history to modern times and display Egyptian, Greek, and Roman antiquities. Viking enthusiasts will want to see the Runic stones in the Danish cultural history section. *Nye Vestergade 10, tel. 33/13–44–11. Admission: 30 kr. adults, 20 kr. students and senior citizens, free for children under 16. Open Tues.–Sun. 10–5.*

Amalienborg, **16**

Amaliehavn, **15**

Børsen, **10**

Botanisk Have, **28**

Christiansborg Slot, **5**

Den Hirschsprungske Samling, **30**

Den Lille Havfrue, **22**

Det Kongelige Bibliotek, **7**

Frihedsmuseet, **20**

Helligånds Kirken, **12**

Kastellet, **21**

Københavns Rådhus, **1**

Københavns Synagoge, **25**

Københavns Universitet, **24**

Kongelige Teater, **14**

Kunstindus-trimuseet, **19**

Lurblæserne, **2**

Marmorkirken, **17**

Nationalmuseet, **4**

Nikolaj Kirke, **13**

Ny Carlsberg Glyptotek, **32**

Rosenborg Slot, **27**

Rundetårn, **26**

Russiske Ortodoks Kirke, **18**

Statens Museum for Kunst, **29**

Strøget, **3**

Teaterhistorisk Museet, **8**

Thorvaldsens Museum, **6**

Tivoli, **31**

Tøjhusmuseet, **9**

Tycho Brahe Planetarium, **33**

Vor Frelsers Kirke, **11**

Vor Frue Kirke, **23**

Copenhagen

KEY

American Express Office

Tourist Information

Rail Lines

Cross Frederiksholms Kanal to Castle Island, dominated by the
⑤ massive gray **Christiansborg Slot** (Christiansborg Castle). The complex, which contains the Folketinget (Parliament House) and the
Royal Reception Chambers, is situated on the site of the city's first
fortress, built by Bishop Absalon in 1167. While the castle that
stands was being built at the turn of the century, the National Museum excavated the ruins beneath the site. *Christiansborg ruins, tel.
33/92–64–92. Admission: 12 kr. adults, 5 kr. children. Open May–
Oct., daily 9:30–3:30; closed Nov.–Apr., Mon. and Sat. Folketinget,
tel. 33/37–55–00. Admission free. Tours every hour (except noon)
on Sun., 10–4. Reception Rooms. Admission: 27 kr. adults, 10 kr.
children. Open May–Oct., Tues.–Sun., English tours at 10, noon,
and 2; Sept.–Apr., Tues.–Thurs., and Sun., English tours at 11
and 3.*

⑥ Just north of the castle is **Thorvaldsens Museum.** The 19th-century
Danish sculptor Bertel Thorvaldsen, buried at the center of the museum, was greatly influenced by the statues and reliefs of classical
antiquity. In addition to his own works, there is a collection of paintings and drawings by other artists illustrating the influence of Italy
on Denmark's Golden Age artists. *Porthusgade 2, tel. 33/32–15–32.
Admission free. Open Tues.–Sun. 10–5.*

⑦ Nearby, **Det Kongelige Bibliotek** (Royal Library) houses the country's largest collection of books, newspapers, and manuscripts.
Look for early records of the Viking journeys to America and Greenland and the statue of the philosopher Søren Kierkegaard in the garden. *Christians Brygge 8, tel. 33/93–01–11. Admission free. Open
weekdays 9–7, Sat. 10–7.*

⑧ Close to the library is the **Teaterhistorisk Museet** (Theater History
Museum), in the Royal Court Theater of 1767. You can see extensive
exhibits on theater and ballet history, then wander around the
boxes, stage, and dressing rooms to see where it all happened.
*Christianborg Ridebane 18, tel. 33/11–51–76. Admission: 20 kr.
adults, 10 kr. senior citizens and students, 5 kr. children. Open
Wed. 2–4, Sun. noon–4.*

⑨ Across the street that bears its name is **Tøjhusmuseet** (Royal Armory), with impressive displays of uniforms, weapons, and armor in
an arched hall 200 yards long. *Tøjhusgade 3, tel. 33/11–60–37. Admission: 20 kr. adults, 5 kr. children 6–17. Open Tues.–Sun. 10–4.*

⑩ A few steps from Tøjhuset is the old stock exchange, **Børsen,** believed to be the oldest still in use—although it functions only on special occasions. It was built by the 16th-century monarch King
Christian IV, a scholar and warrior, and architect of much of the
city. The king is said to have had a hand at twisting the tails of the
four dragons that form the structure's distinctive green copper
spire. With its steep roofs, tiny windows, and gables, the recently
renovated building is one of Copenhagen's treasures.

From Børsen, look east across the drawbridge (Knippelsbro) that
connects Slotsholmen with Christianshavn, one of the oldest parts
⑪ of Copenhagen, to the green-and-gold spire of **Vor Frelsers Kirke**
(Our Savior's Church). The Gothic structure was built in 1696. Local
legend has it that the staircase encircling it was built curling the
wrong way around, and that when its architect reached the top and
saw what he had done, he jumped. Unfortunately, the delicate steeple is under repair (and scaffolding) until 1996. *Skt. Annægade 9,
tel. 31/57–27–98. Admission free. Open Mar. 15–May, Mon.–Sat.
9–4:30, Sun. noon–3:30; June–Aug., Mon.–Sat. 9–4:30, Sun.*

*noon–4:30; Sept.–Oct., Mon.–Sat. 9–3:30, Sun. noon–3:30. Nov.–
Mar. 14, Mon.–Sat. 10–1:30, Sun. noon–1:30. Tower closed.*

Head back to Strøget, turning left along the Amagertov section. Toward the end and to the right (5 Niels Hemmingsens Gad) is the
⑫ 18th-century **Helligånds Kirken** (Church of the Holy Ghost). The
choir contains a marble font by the sculptor Thorvaldsen.

In Østergade, the easternmost of the streets that make up Strøget,
⑬ you cannot miss the green spire of **Nikolaj Kirke** (Nikolaj Church).
The building that currently stands was built in the 20th century; the
previous structure, which dated from the 13th century, was destroyed by fire in 1728. Today the church's role is secular—it's an art
gallery and an exhibition center.

Time Out **Café Nikolaj,** inside the old Nikolaj Kirke, is a good place to stop for a
Danish pastry or a light meal. *Open Mon.–Sat. noon–3 for lunch,
until 5 for drinks and cakes. Inexpensive.*

While Strøget is famous as a shopping area, and elegant stores
abound, it's also where Copenhagen comes to stroll. Outside the
posh displays of the fur and porcelain shops, the sidewalks have the
festive aura of a street fair.

Royal Palace **Kongens Nytorv** (the King's New Market) is the square marking the
Area end of Strøget. The **Kongelige Teater** (Danish Royal Theater), home
⑭ of Danish opera and ballet as well as theater, sits on the south side.
The Danish Royal Ballet remains one of the world's great companies, with a repertoire ranging from classical to modern. On the
western side of the square you'll see the stately facade of the hotel
D'Angleterre, the grande dame of Copenhagen hotels.

The street leading southeast from Kongens Nytorv is **Nyhavn.** The
recently gentrified canal was a longtime haunt of sailors. Now restaurants and boutiques outnumber the tattoo shops, but on hot summer nights the area still gets rowdy, with Scandinavians reveling
amid a fleet of old-time sailing ships and well-preserved 18th-century buildings. Hans Christian Andersen lived at both nos. 18 and 20.
Nearer the harbor are old shipping warehouses, including two—
Nyhavn 71 and the Admiral—that have been converted into comfortable hotels.

Turn left at the end of Nyhavn to see the harbor front and then make
an immediate left onto Sankt Annæ Plads. Take the third right onto
⑮ Amaliegade. Continue straight ahead for **Amalienborg,** the principal royal residence since 1784. When the royal family is in residence
during the fall and winter, the Royal Guard and band march through
the city at noon to change the palace guard. Since spring of 1994 the
second division of the Royal Collection (the first is at Rosenborg) has
been open to the public at Amalienborg. Among the museum's highlights are the study of King Christian IX (1818–1906) and the drawing room of his wife, Queen Louise. They were called the Father- and
Mother-in-law of Europe, as their offspring ascended to, and married into several European monarchies. The rooms are packed with
family gifts and regal baubles, ranging from a tacky polar-bear-and-
pink-umbrella doohickey to Fabergé treasures. The collection also
includes Rococo banquet silver, highlighted by a bombastic Viking
ship centerpiece, and a small costume collection. *Amalienborg Museum, tel. 31/12–21–86. Admission 35 kr. adults, 5 kr. children.
Open Mar.–Oct., daily 11–4; late-Oct.–Feb., Tues.–Sun. 11–4.*

Rest a moment on the palace's harbor side, amid the trees and foun
⑯ tains of **Amaliehavn.** Across the square, it's just a step to Bredgade

⑰ and the **Marmorkirken** (Marble Church), a 19th-century Baroque church with a dome that looks several sizes too large for the building beneath it.

⑱ Bredgade is also home to the exotic onion domes of the **Russiske Ortodoks Kirke** (Russian Orthodox Church). Farther on is the
⑲ **Kunstindustrimuseet** (Museum of Decorative Art), with a large selection of European and Oriental handicrafts, as well as ceramics, silver, and tapestries. *Bredgade 68, tel. 33/14–94–52. Admission: 30 kr. adults, 20 kr. students and senior citizens, children under 16 free. Permanent exhibition open Tues.–Sun. 1–4; special exhibitions open Tues.–Sat. 10–4, Sun. 1–4.*

A little farther, turn right onto Esplanaden and you'll come to
⑳ **Frihedsmuseet** (Liberty Museum), situated in Churchill Parken. It gives an evocative picture of the heroic Danish Resistance movement during World War II, which managed to save 7,000 Jews from the Nazis by hiding them in homes and hospitals, then smuggling them across to Sweden. *Esplanaden, tel. 33/13–77–14. Admission free. Open Sept. 16–April, Tues.–Sat. 11–3, Sun. 11–4; May–Sept. 15, Tues.–Sat. 10–4, Sun. 10–5.*

At the park's entrance stands the English church, St. Alban's, and,
㉑ in the center, the **Kastellet** (Citadel), with two rings of moats. This was the city's main fortress in the 18th century, but, in a grim reversal during World War II, the Germans used it as the headquarters of their occupation of Denmark. *Admission free. Open 6 AM to sunset.*

Continue on to the Langelinie, which on Sunday is thronged with
㉒ promenading Danes, and at last to **Den Lille Havfrue** (The Little Mermaid), the 1913 statue commemorating Hans Christian Andersen's lovelorn creation, and the subject of hundreds of travel posters.

Around From Langelinie, take the train or bus from Østerport station back
Strøget to the center. Walk north from the Strøget on Nørregade until you
㉓ reach **Vor Frue Kirke** (The Church of Our Lady), Copenhagen's cathedral since 1924. The site itself has been a place of worship since the 13th century, when Bishop Absalon built a chapel here. The spare neoclassical facade is a 19th-century revamp, that repaired the damage incurred during Nelson's famous bombing of the city in 1801. Ordinarily you can see Thorvaldsen's marble sculptures of Christ and the Apostles, but a new organ is being installed through 1995, so opening times are irregular. *Nørregade, Frue Plads, tel. 33/15–10–78.*

㉔ Head north up Fjolstraede until you come to the main **Københavns Universitet** (Cophenhagen University), built in the 19th century on the site of the medieval bishops' palace. Past the university, turn
㉕ right onto Krystalgade. On the left is the **Københavns Synagoge** (Copenhagen Synagogue), designed by the famous contemporary architect Gustav Friedrich Hetsch. Hetsch drew on the Doric and Egyptian styles to create the arklike structure.

㉖ Just across Købmagergade is the **Rundetårn**, a round tower built as an observatory in 1642 by Christian IV. It is said that Peter the Great of Russia drove a horse and carriage up the 600 feet of the inner staircase. You'll have to walk, but the view is worth it. *Købmagergade, tel. 33/93–66–60. Admission: 12 kr. adults, 5 kr. children. Open Dec.–May and Sept.–Oct., Mon.–Sat. 10–5, Sun. noon–4; June–Aug., Mon.–Sat. 10–8, Sun. noon–8. Observatory and telescope open, with astronomer on hand to answer questions, mid-Oct.–mid-Mar., Tues.–Wed. 7–10.*

Turn right at Rundetårn onto Landemærket, then left onto Åbenrå.
If your appetite for museums is not yet sated, turn right out of
Åbenrå until you reach Gothersgade, where another right, onto
㉗ Øster Voldgade, will bring you to **Rosenborg Slot.** This Renaissance
castle—built by Renaissance man Christian IV—houses the Crown
Jewels, as well as a collection of costumes and royal memorabilia.
Don't miss Christian IV's pearl-studded saddle. *Øster Voldgade 4A,
tel. 33/15–32–86. Admission: 35 kr. adults, 5 kr. children. Open
Apr.–May, daily 11–3; June–Aug., daily 10–4; Sept.–Oct., daily
11–3; Nov.–Mar., Tues., Fri., and Sun. 11–2.*

The palace is surrounded by gardens, and just across Øster
㉘ Voldgade is **Botanisk Have,** Copenhagen's 25 acres of botanical gardens, with a rather spectacular Palm House containing tropical and
subtropical plants. There's also an observatory and a geological museum. *Admission free. Open May–Aug., daily 8:30–6; Sept.–Apr.,
daily 8:30–4. Palm House open daily 10–3.*

㉙ Leave the gardens through the north exit to get to the **Statens Museum for Kunst** (National Art Gallery), where the collection ranges
from modern Danish art to works by Rubens, Dürer, and the Impressionists. Particularly fine are the museum's 20 Matisses.
*Sølvgade 48–50, tel. 33/91–21–26. Admission: 20 kr. adults (30 kr.
for special exhibits), children under 16 free. Open Tues.–Sun. 10–
4:30, Wed. until 9 PM.*

Time Out The subterranean **cafeteria** in the museum makes an excellent place
to stop for lunch or coffee. Art posters deck the walls, and a cheerful
staff serves hearty lunches. *Inexpensive.*

㉚ A nearby building houses **Den Hirschsprungske Samling** (the
Hirschsprung Collection) of 19th-century Danish art. The cozy museum features works from the Golden Age, in particular those by a
group of late-19th-century painters called the Skagen school.
*Stockholmsgade 20, tel. 31/42–03–36. Admission: 20 kr. adults, 10
kr. students and senior citizens, children under 16 free. Open Wed.–
Sat. 1–4, Sun. 11–4.*

From Stockholmsgade, turn right onto Sølvgade and then left onto
Øster Søgade, just before the bridge. Continue along the canal (the
street name will change from Øster Søgade to Nørre Søgade to
Vester Søgade) until you reach the head of the harbor. Walk straight
ahead and turn left onto Vesterbrogade.

㉛ On the right lies Copenhagen's best-known attraction, **Tivoli.** In the
1840s, the Danish architect Georg Carstensen persuaded King
Christian VIII that an amusement park was the perfect opiate of the
masses, preaching that "when people amuse themselves, they forget
politics." In the comparatively short season, from May to September, about 4 million people come through the gates. Tivoli is more
sophisticated than a mere funfair: It boasts a pantomime theater
and open-air stage; elegant restaurants; and numerous classical,
jazz, and rock concerts. On weekends there are elaborate fireworks
displays and maneuvers by the Tivoli Guard, a youth version of the
Queen's Royal Guard. Try to see Tivoli at least once by night, when
the trees are illuminated along with the Chinese Pagoda and the
main fountain. *Tel. 33/15–10–01. Admission: 38 kr. adults, 20 kr.
children. Open mid-Apr.–mid-Sept., daily 10 AM–midnight.*

At the southern end of the gardens, on Hans Christian Andersens
㉜ Boulevard, is the **Ny Carlsberg Glyptotek** (New Carlsberg Picture
Hall). This elaborate neoclassical building houses a collection of

works by Gauguin and Degas and other Impressionists, as well as Egyptian, Greek, Roman, and French sculpture. *Dantes Plads 7, tel. 33/41–81–41. Admission: 15 kr. adults, children free; adults free on Wed. and Sun. Open Sept.–Apr., Tues.–Sat. noon–3, Sun. 10–4; May–Aug., Tues.–Sun. 10–4.*

㉝ Tucked between St. Jorgens Lake and the main arteries of Vesterbrogade and Gammel Kongevej is the new **Tycho Brahe Planetarium**. The modern cylindrical building is filled with astronomy exhibitions and an Omnimax Theater, which takes visitors on a visual journey up through space and down under the seas. Changing Omnimax films range in topics from the Rolling Stones to the Kuwait fires of the Gulf War. *Gammel Kongevej 10, tel. 33/12–12–24. Admission: 65 kr. for exhibition and theater, 6–10 PM; exhibition only, 15 kr. Reservations advised for theater. (Children under 7 are not permitted in the Omnimax theater.) Open daily 10:30–9.*

Excursions from Copenhagen

Helsingør-Kronborg Castle Shakespeare immortalized the town and castle when he chose **Kronborg Castle** as the setting for *Hamlet*. Completed in 1585, the gabled and turreted structure is about 600 years younger than the fortress we imagine from the setting of Shakespeare's tragedy. Well worth seeing is the 200-foot-long dining hall, the luxurious chapel, and the royal chambers. The ramparts and 12-foot walls are a reminder of the castle's role as coastal bulwark—Sweden is only a few miles away. The town of **Helsingør**—about 29 miles north of Copenhagen—has a number of picturesque streets with 16th-century houses. There is frequent train service to Helsingør station, and then it's a 20-minute walk around the harbor to the castle. *Helsingør, tel. 49/21–30–78. Admission: 25 kr. adults, 10 kr. children. Open Easter and May–Sept., daily 10:30–5; Oct. and Apr., Tues.–Sat. 11–4; Nov.–Mar., Tues.–Sun. 11–3.*

Louisiana A world-class modern art collection is housed in a spectacular building on the "Danish Riviera," the North Zealand coast. Even those who can't tell a Rauschenberg from a Rembrandt should make the 35-kilometer (22-mile) trip to see the setting: It's an elegant, rambling structure set in a large park with views of the sound, and, on a clear day, Sweden.

Louisiana is well worth the half-hour train ride from Copenhagen to Humlebæk. The museum is a 10-minute walk from the station. It's also accessible by the E4 highway and the more scenic coastal road, Strandvejen. *Gammel Strandvej 13, Humlebæk, tel. 42/19–07–19. Admission: 60 kr. adults, children free. Open Mon., Tues., and Thurs., 10–5, Wed. and Fri. 10–10, weekends 10–6. A combined train and admission ticket for 89 kr. (from Copenhagen) is available from DSB.*

Roskilde History buffs should head 30 kilometers (19 miles) west of Copenhagen to the bustling market town of **Roskilde.** A key administrative center during Viking times, it remained one of the largest towns in northern Europe through the Middle Ages. Its population has dwindled, but the legacy of its 1,000-year history lives on in the spectacular cathedral. Built on the site of Denmark's first church, the **Domkirke** (cathedral) has been the burial place of Danish royalty since the 15th century. *Domkirkeplasden, Roskilde. Admission: 5 kr. adults, 2 kr. children. Open Apr.–Sept., weekdays 9–4:45, Oct.–Mar., weekdays 10–2:45; May–Aug., Sun. 12:30–4:45; Sept.–Apr., Sun. 12:30–3:45. For varying Sat. hrs, tel. 42/35–27–00.*

A 10-minute walk south and through the park takes you to the water and to the **Viking Ship Museum.** Inside are five Viking ships, discovered at the bottom of the Roskilde Fjord in 1962. Detailed placards in English chronicle Viking history. There are also English-language films on the excavation and reconstruction. *Strandengen, Roskilde, tel. 42/35–65–55. Admission: 30 kr. adults, 20 kr. children. Open Apr.–Oct., daily 9–5; Nov.–Mar., daily 10–4.*

Rungstedlund About halfway between Copenhagen and Helsingør is **Rungstedlund,** the former manor of Karen Blixen. The author of *Out of Africa* and several accounts of aristocratic Danish life, Blixen wrote under the pen name Isak Dinesen. The manor, where she lived as a child and to which she returned in 1931, opened as a museum in 1991, and includes manuscripts, as well as photographs and memorabilia documenting her years in Africa and Denmark. A half-hour train ride from Copenhagen, the estate is a 10-minute walk from Rungsted station. *Rungsted Strandvej 111, Rungsted Kyst, tel. 42/57–10–57. Admission: 30 kr. adults, children free. Open May–Sept., daily 10–5; Oct.–Apr., Wed.–Fri. 1–4, Sat.–Sun. 11–4.*

Shopping

Gift Ideas Copenhagen is a mecca for shoppers in search of impeccable designs and top-notch quality, with prices for most Danish-made items less than they would be at home. Several ideas for inexpensive gifts include simple table decorations—a porcelain candle holder or ashtray or the long-lasting candles, often handmade, for which Scandinavia is famous. Denmark also produces tasteful reproductions of Viking ornaments and jewelry, in bronze as well as silver and gold.

Specialty Shops Synonymous with shopping are Strøget's pedestrian streets. For glass, try **Holmegaard** at Østergade. Just off the street is Pistolstræde, a typical old courtyard that's been lovingly restored and filled with intriguing boutiques. **Illum** and **Magasin** offer department-store variety, and **Illums Bolighus** offers home furnishings in near-gallery surroundings. There are such specialists as **Royal Copenhagen Porcelain,** which has a small museum attached, as does **Georg Jensen,** one of Denmark's most famous silversmiths.

Off the eastern end of Strøget on Ny Østergade, the **Pewter Center** has a large pewterware collection, and on Fridjof Nansens Plads there's another pewter designer, **Royal Selangor,** founded in 1885. Back along Strøget, **Birger Christensen** will offer you a glass of sherry while you look at the furs, unless you decide to take your patronage to their competition, **A. C. Bang. FONA** is the place to buy Bang and Olufsen stereo systems, so renowned that they are in the permanent design collection of New York's Museum of Modern Art.

Dining

Food remains one of the great pleasures of a stay in Copenhagen, a city with over 2,000 restaurants. Traditional Danish fare spans all the price categories: You can order a light lunch of the traditional smørrebrød, snack from a *store kolde bord* (cold buffet), or dine out on lobster and Limfjord oysters. Those who are strapped for cash can enjoy fast food Danish style, in the form of *pølser* (hot dogs) sold from trucks on the street. Team any of this with some pastry from a bakery (look for them under the sign of the upside-down gold pretzel), and you've got yourself a meal on the go.

For details and price-category definitions, *see* Dining in Staying in Denmark, *above.*

Very   **Kong Hans Kaelder.** Chef Daniel Letz's French-inspired cooking is
Expensive   superb, while the setting is subterranean and mysterious, with
★   whitewashed arching ceilings, candles, and wooden carvings. *Vingårdstræde 6, tel. 33/11–68–68. Reservations advised. AE, DC, MC, V. Dinner only. Closed mid-July–mid-Aug., Dec. 24 and 25, and Sun.*

Pakhuskælderen. Surrounded by thick white walls and raw timbers, Nyhavn 71 hotel's intimate restaurant attracts a mix of business and holiday guests and is known for its fresh, classically prepared seafood. Look for store kolde bord at lunchtime. *Nyhavn 71, tel. 33/11–85–85. Reservations required. AE, DC, MC, V.*

★   **Skt. Gertrude's Kloster.** The history of this monastery goes back 700 years. In its vaulted stone dining room, predominantly French food is served in the mysterious light of 2,000 candles, among vaulted spiral stairways and ecclesiastical antiques. *Hauser Plads 32, tel. 33/14–66–30. Reservations required. AE, DC, MC, V. Dinner only.*

Expensive   **Els.** When it opened in 1853, the intimate Els was the place to be
★   seen before the theater, and the painted muses on the walls still watch diners rush to make an 8 o'clock curtain. Antique wooden columns and Royal Copenhagen tile tables complement a nouvelle Danish/French menu. The menu changes daily and incorporates game, fish, and market-fresh produce. *Store Strandstæde 3, tel. 33/14–13–41. Reservations advised. AE, DC, MC, V. Closed Dec. 24–25 and 31, Jan. 1.*

La Brasserie. This is the place where Copenhagen's see-and-be-seen set goes to eat. Diners enjoy French-inspired food in charming bistro surroundings, under a giant illuminated clock suspended from the ceiling. *Hotel D'Angleterre, Kongens Nytorv 34, tel. 33/32–01–22. Reservations advised. AE, DC, MC, V. Closed Sun.*

L'Alsace. Set in a cobbled courtyard, this peaceful and quiet restaurant is hung with paintings by Danish surrealist Wilhelm Freddie. The hand-drawn menu includes a hearty choucrôute of cabbage, sausage, and pork, as well as superb fruit tarts and cakes. Ask for a seat with a view of the old courtyard on Pistolstraede. *Ny Østergade 9, tel. 33/14–57–43. Reservations advised. AE, DC, MC, V. Closed Sun. and holidays.*

Moderate   **Copenhagen Corner.** Diners get a great view of the Rådhus Pladsen
★   here, and terrific smørrebrød besides. Plants hang from the ceiling; waiters hustle platters of herring, steak, and other Danish/French dishes; and businesspeople clink glasses. In summer you can eat outside. *Rådhus Pladsen, tel. 33/91–45–45. Reservations advised. AE, DC, MC, V. Closed Dec. 24.*

El Meson. Ceiling-hung pottery, knowledgeable waiters, and a topnotch menu make this Copenhagen's best Spanish restaurant. Choose carefully for a moderately priced meal, which might include beef spiced with spearmint, lamb with a honey sauce, or paella valenciano for two. *Hauser Plads 12 (behind library), tel. 33/11–91–31. Reservations advised. AE, DC, MC, V. Dinner only; closed Sun.*

Havfruen. A life-size wooden mermaid swings langorously from the ceiling in this snug fish restaurant in Nyhavn. Copenhagen natives love the maritime-bistro ambience and the French-inspired fish specialties. *Nyhavn 39, tel. 33/11–11–38. Reservations advised. DC, MC, V. Closed Sun.*

★   **Ida Davidsen.** Five generations old, this world-renowned lunch place has become synonymous with smørrebrød. Choose from creative open-face sandwiches, piled high with such ingredients as pâté, bacon, and steak tartare, as well as smoked duck, served with a beet salad and potatoes. *Skt. Kongensgade 70, tel. 33/91–36–55. Reservations required. DC, MC, V. Lunch only. Closed weekends and July.*

Peder Oxe. In a 17th-century square this lively bistro is countrified, with rustic tables and 15th-century Portuguese tiles. Their mainly grilled fish and beef menu also includes an excellent all-you-can-eat salad bar. *Gråbrødertorv 11, tel. 33/11–00–77. Reservations accepted. DC, MC, V.*

Inexpensive **Flyvefisken.** Silvery stenciled fish swim along blue-and-yellow stenciled walls in this funky Thai eatery. Among the city's more experimental (and spicy) restaurants, it offers chicken with cashew nuts, spicy shrimp soup with lemongrass, and herring shark in basil sauce. There is also a less expensive vegetarian café in the basement. *Larsbjørnsstræde 18, tel. 33/14–95–15. No reservations. AE, DC, MC, V. Closed Sun., Dec. 24–26 and 31.*

Quattro Fontane. Just west of the lakes, one of Copenhagen's best Italian restaurants is a busy, noisy affair, complete with chatty waiters. Homemade fare includes a dozen pasta dishes and pizza, as well as excellent ice cream, which you can also pick up from their carry-out in Frederiksberg (Falkoner Allé 42, tel. 31/39–49–82). *Guldbergsgade 3, tel. 31/39–39–31. Reservations advised. No credit cards. Closed Dec. 24 and 25.*

Riz Raz. Located on a corner off Strøget, this Middle Eastern restaurant hops with young locals who pack it on weekends. The very inexpensive all-you-can-eat buffet is heaped with healthy dishes, including lentils, falafel, bean salads, and occasionally pizza. *Kompagnistræde 20, tel. 33/15–05–75. Reservations advised (required on weekends). DC, MC, V. Closed Dec. 24 and 25 and Jan. 1.*

Victor. This French-style corner café offers great people-watching and bistro fare. It's best during weekend lunches, when young and old gather for specialties like rib roast, homemade pâté, smoked salmon, and cheese platters—and the menu changes—and becomes pricier—after 6. *Ny Østergade 8, tel. 33/13–36–13. Reservations advised. AE, DC, MC, V.*

Lodging

Copenhagen is well served by a wide range of hotels, and you can expect your accommodations to be clean, comfortable, and well run. Most Danish hotels include a substantial breakfast in the room rate, but this isn't always the case. In summer reservations are always recommended, but if you should arrive without one, try the hotel booking service in the tourist office. They can also give you a "same-day, last-minute price," which is about 200–250 kr. for a single hotel room. This service will also locate rooms in private homes, with rates starting at about 140 kr. for a single. Young travelers should head for "Use It" (Huset) at Rådhusstræde 13 (tel. 33/15–65–18); in summer after hours, they can check the bulletin board outside for suggestions.

For details and price-category definitions, *see* Lodging in Staying in Denmark, *above.*

Very **D'Angleterre.** Just when the "grande dame" of Copenhagen hotels
Expensive was fraying around the edges, a new group of owners took over and
★ made the painfully needed repairs and changes. While these include a swimming pool and a night club, the hotel still retains its Old World, old-money aura. The rooms are done in pinks and blues, with

overstuffed chairs and antique escritoires and armoires. There's a liberal use of brass, mahogany, and marble in the bathrooms. *Kongens Nytorv 34, tel. 33/12–00–95, fax 33/12–11–18. 130 rooms with bath. Facilities: 2 restaurants, bar, barber, beauty salon, swimming pool, nightclub. AE, DC, MC, V.*

Nyhavn 71. This cozy hotel started life in 1804 as a humble harbor warehouse, though its subsequent metamorphosis has won several design awards. Ask for a room overlooking the harbor—the quaint, porthole-style windows add to the charm. *Nyhavn 71, tel. 33/11–85–85, fax 33/93–15–85. 82 rooms with bath. Facilities: restaurant, bar. AE, DC, MC, V.*

SAS Scandinavia. Near the airport, this is one of northern Europe's largest hotels and Copenhagen's token skyscraper. The immense lobby is streamlined and modern, as are the rooms, which means this is a good choice if you prefer convenience to character. *Amager Blvd. 70, tel. 33/11–23–24, fax 31/57–01–93. 542 rooms with bath. Facilities: casino, sauna, pool, 4 restaurants, bar, coffee shop. AE, DC, MC, V.*

Expensive **Kong Frederik.** West of Rådhus Pladsen, near Strøget, this intimate hotel is a cozy version of its grand sister, D'Angleterre. The sunny Queen's Garden restaurant serves a hearty all-you-can-eat breakfast buffet; the rooms are elegant with Oriental vases, mauve carpets, and plain blue spreads. *Vester Voldgade 25, tel. 33/12–59–02, fax 33/93–59–01. 110 rooms, 17 suites. Facilities: restaurant, bar, room service, meeting rooms, parking. Breakfast not included. AE, DC, MC, V.*

Neptun. Renovated and expanded, the centrally situated Neptun has been in business for nearly 150 years and shows no signs of flagging. Guest rooms are decorated with blond wood and are usually reserved ahead by American visitors. *Skt. Annæ Plads 18, tel. 33/13–89–00, fax 33/14–12–50. 137 rooms, 10 apartments, all with bath. Facilities: restaurant, café, conference rooms. AE, DC, MC, V. Closed Dec. 24–Jan. 2.*

The Phoenix. This luxury hotel welcomes guests with automatic glass doors, crystal chandeliers, and gilt everywhere. The staff shuffles between languages while they register business as well as cruise guests. The suites and executive-class rooms have Biedermeier furniture and 18-karat-gold bathroom fixtures, while the standard rooms are very small, at barely 9′×15′. While it's convenient to central-city attractions, light sleepers should ask for a room above the second floor to avoid street noise. *Bredgade 37, 1260 Kbh K, tel. 33/95–95–00, fax 33/33–98–33. 212 rooms, 7 suites. Facilities: restaurant, 1 pub (closed Sun.), meeting and banquet room. AE, DC, MC, V.*

Moderate **Ascot.** A charming old building in the city's downtown area, the Ascot features a classically columned entrance and an excellent breakfast buffet. The rooms have colorful geometric-pattern bedspreads and cozy bathrooms. Many have been recently remodeled; a few have kitchenettes. *Studiestræde 61, tel. 33/12–60–00, fax 33/14–60–40. 143 rooms, 30 apartments, all with bath. Facilities: conference rooms, fitness room, solarium, restaurant (breakfast only), bar. AE, DC, MC, V.*

Copenhagen Admiral. A five-minute stroll from Nyhavn, this one-time granary is now a no-nonsense hotel. With massive stone walls broken by rows of tiny windows, it's one of the less expensive top hotels, cutting frills and prices. *Toldbodgade 24–28, tel. 33/11–82–82, fax 33/32–55–42. 365 rooms with bath. Facilities: restaurant, bar, café, nightclub, shop, sauna. AE, DC, MC, V.*

Triton. Streamlined and modern, the Triton has a cosmopolitan clientele and a central location. The large rooms, in blond wood and warm tones, are equipped with every modern convenience, and many of the bathrooms have been recently updated. The buffet breakfast is exceptionally generous. *Helgolandsgade 7–11, tel. 31/ 31–32–66, fax 31/31–69–70. 123 rooms with bath. Facilities: restaurant (breakfast only), bar. AE, DC, MC, V.*

Inexpensive **Cab-Inn Scandinavia.** Copenhagen's answer to Japanese-style hotel minirooms is more cozy than futuristic, with shiplike "berths" brightly decorated. All offer standard hotel furnishings, including private shower and small wall-hung desks with chairs. *Vodroffsvej 55, tel. 35/36–11–11, fax 35/36–11–14. 201 rooms with shower. Facilities: café, gym. (Also an 86-room location at Danasvej 32, tel. 31/21–04–00, fax 31/21–74–09.) AE, DC, MC, V.*
Viking. A comfortable, century-old former mansion close to Amalienborg Castle, Nyhavn, and the Little Mermaid, the Viking is convenient to most sights and public transportation. The rooms are surprisingly spacious. *Bredgade 65, tel. 33/12–45–50, fax 33/12–46– 18. 89 rooms, 19 with bath. Facilities: restaurant (breakfast only). AE, DC, MC, V.*

The Arts

Copenhagen This Week has good information on musical and theatrical events, as well as on special events and exhibitions. Concert and festival information is available from the **Dansk Musik Information Center (DMIC,** Gråbrødretorv 16, tel. 33/11–20–66). Copenhagen's main theater and concert season runs from September through May, and tickets can be obtained either directly from theaters and concert halls or from ticket agencies; ask your hotel concierge for advice.

Music **Tivoli Concert Hall** (Vesterbrogade 3, tel. 33/15–10–12), offers more than 150 concerts each summer, featuring a host of Danish and foreign soloists, conductors, and orchestras.

Theater, The **Royal Theater** (Kongens Nytorv, tel. 33/14–10–02) regularly
Opera, and holds theater, ballet, and opera performances. For English-lan-
Ballet guage theater, call either the professional **London Toast Theatre** (tel. 33/33–80–25) or the amateur **Copenhagen Theatre Circle** (tel. 31/62–86–20).

Film Copenhagen natives are avid movie buffs, and since the Danes rarely dub films or television imports, you can often see original American and British movies and TV shows.

Nightlife

Many of the city's restaurants, cafés, bars, and clubs stay open after midnight, some as late as 5 AM. Copenhagen is famous for jazz, but you'll find night spots catering to musical tastes ranging from bop to ballroom music. Younger tourists should make for the **Minefield,** the district around the Nikolaj Kirke, which has scores of trendy discos and dance spots, with admission only the price of a beer. **Privé** (Ny Østergade 14) and **U-Matic** (Vestergade 10) are particularly popular with the young set.

A few streets behind the railway station is Copenhagen's red-light district, where sex shops share space with grocers. While the area is fairly well lighted and lively, women may feel uncomfortable going there alone at night.

Nightclubs Some of the most exclusive nightclubs are in the biggest hotels: **Fellini's** in the SAS Royal (Hammerichsgade 1, tel. 33/93–32–39).

Jazz Copenhagen has a worldwide reputation for sophisticated jazz clubs though, sadly, many have closed in the past couple of years. These are a few of the best: **Jazzhus Slukefter** (Tivoli); **La Fontaine** (Kompagnistræde 11); and **Kridhuset** (Nørregade 1).

Fyn and the Central Islands

It was Hans Christian Andersen, the region's most famous native, who dubbed Fyn (Funen) "The Garden of Denmark." Part orchard, part farmland, Fyn is sandwiched between Zealand and Jylland, and with its tidy, rolling landscape, seaside towns, manor houses, and castles, it is one of Denmark's loveliest islands. Its capital is 1,000-year-old Odense in the north, one of Denmark's best-known cities and the birthplace of Hans Christian Andersen. It has two museums detailing his life and works. In a country crowded with castles, Fyn has two of the best-preserved ones: the 12th-century castle Nyborg Slot, in the east, and the famed 16th-century Egeskov Slot, near Svendborg, in the south. From Svendborg it's easy to hop on a ferry and visit some of the smaller islands, such as Tåsinge, Langeland, and Ærø, whose main town, Ærøskøbing, with its twisting streets and half-timbered houses, seems caught in a time warp. The local people speak with a slightly singsong accent, and claim it is the tongue spoken by angels on Sundays!

Getting Around

The best starting point is Nyborg on Fyn's east coast, just across the Store Bælt (Great Belt) from Korsør on Zealand. From Nyborg, the easiest way to travel is by car, though public transportation is good. (Get details of car rentals from local tourist offices.) Distances on Fyn and its islands are short, but there is much to see and you can easily spend two or three days here. The choice is to circle the islands from Nyborg or to base yourself in Odense or Svendborg and make excursions. Whichever you choose, you can use the itinerary given below.

Guided Tours

There are few organized tours of any area of Denmark outside Copenhagen. The Fyn town of Odense has a two-hour tour that operates Monday through Saturday during July and August. Expect to see anything and everything to do with native son Hans Christian Andersen.

There's also a day trip to Odense from Copenhagen every Sunday from mid-May to mid-September. Lasting about 11 hours, the trip includes stops at several picturesque villages and a lightning visit to Egeskov Slot. Departure is at 8:45 AM from Copenhagen's city-hall square.

Tourist Information

Nyborg (Torvet 9, tel. 65/31–02–80).
Odense (Rådhuset, tel. 66/12–75–20).
Svendborg (Centrumpladsen, tel. 62/21–09–80).

Fyn and the Central Islands

KEY
— Rail Lines
⛴ Ferry

Exploring Fyn and the Central Islands

The 13th-century town of **Nyborg** was Denmark's capital during the
Middle Ages, as well as an important stop on a major trading route
between Zealand and Jutland. From 1200 to 1413, Nyborg housed
the Danehof, the early Danish parliament. Nyborg's major landmark is its 12th-century castle, the **Nyborg Slot.** It was here that
Erik Glipping granted the first Danish constitution, the Great
Charter, in 1282. *Slotspladsen, tel. 65/31–02–07. Admission: 20 kr.
adults, 10 kr. children under 16. Open Mar.–June, Tues.–Sun.
10–3; July–Aug., daily 10–5; Sept.–Oct., Tues.–Sun. 10–3.*

Take Route 165 20 kilometers (12½ miles) along the coast to
Kerteminde, Funen's most important fishing village, as well as a picturesque summer resort. It's worth strolling down the Langegade
to see its half-timbered houses.

Viking enthusiasts will want to head a few kilometers south to the
village of **Ladby.** Stop here to see the **Ladbyskibet,** the 1,100-year-
old underground remains of a Viking chieftain's burial, complete
with his 72-foot-long ship. The warrior was equipped for his trip to
Valhalla (the afterlife) with his weapons, 4 hunting dogs, and 11
horses. *Vikingsvej 123, tel. 65/32–16–67. Admission: 15 kr. adults,
10 kr. students and senior citizens, children under 16 free. Open
May–Sept., Tues.–Sun. 10–6; Oct.–Apr., Tues.–Sun. 10–3.*

Twenty kilometers (12½ miles) southwest on Route 165 lies **Odense,**
Denmark's third-largest city. Plan on spending at least one night
here; in addition to its museums and pleasant pedestrian streets,
Odense gives a good feel for a provincial capital.

If you can't take quaintness, don't go to the **H. C. Andersens Hus** (Hans Christian Andersen Museum). The surrounding area has been carefully preserved, with cobbled pedestrian streets and low houses with lace curtains. Inside, exhibits use photos, diaries, drawings, and letters to convey a sense of the man and the time in which he lived. Attached to the museum is an extensive library with Andersen's works in more than 100 languages, where you can listen to fairy tales on tape. *Hans Jensenstræde 37–45, tel. 66/13–13–72. Admission: 20 kr. adults, 10 kr. children under 14. Open Sept.– May, daily 10–4; June–Aug., daily 9–6.*

Nearby is the **Carl Nielsen Museum,** a modern structure with multimedia exhibits on Denmark's most famous composer (1865–1931) and his wife, the sculptress Anne Marie Carl-Nielsen. *Claus BergsGade 11, tel. 66/13–13–72, ext. 4671. Admission: 15 kr. adults, 5 kr. children. Open daily 10–4.*

Montegården, Odense's museum of cultural and urban history fills four houses built from the Renaissance to the 18th century, all grouped around a shady cobble courtyard. The innovative exhibits inside feature dioramas, an extensive coin collection, clothed dummies, toys, and tableaux. *Overgade 48–50. Admission: 15 kr. adults, 5 kr. children. Open daily 10–4.*

Brandt's Passage, off Vestergade, is a heavily boutiqued walking street. At the end of it, in what was once a textile factory, is a four-story art gallery, the Brandts Klædefabrik, incorporating the **Museum for Photographic Art,** the **Graphic Museum,** and other spaces, with temporary exhibits for video art. It's well worth the short walk to see Funen's version of a Soho loft. *37–43 Brandts Passage, tel. 66/13–78–97. Admission: photography museum, 20 kr. adults, 10 kr. children; graphics museum, 15 kr. adults, 10 kr. children; combined admission, 40 kr. adults, 10 kr. children. Open Tues.–Fri. 10–5, weekends 11–5.*

Don't neglect **Den Fynske Landsby** (Funen Village), 3 kilometers (2 miles) south; an enjoyable way of getting there is to travel down the Odense River by boat. The open-air museum-village is made up of 20 farm buildings, including workshops, a vicarage, a water mill, and a windmill. There's a theater, too, which in summer stages adaptations of Andersen's tales. *Sejerskovvej 20, tel. 66/13–13–72, ext. 4642. Admission: 20 kr. adults, 10 kr. children. Open Apr.–May and Sept.–mid-Oct., daily 10–4; June–Aug., daily 10–7:30; mid-Oct.–Mar., Sun. and holidays only, 10–4.*

Head 30 kilometers (18 miles) south on Route 43 to **Fåborg,** a lovely little town dating from the 12th century. Four times a day, it echoes with the dulcet chiming of the Klokketårnet's (Belfry's) carillon, the largest in Fyn. Dating from 1725, **Den Gamla Gård** (the Old Merchant's House) chronicles the cultural history of Funen. *Holkegade 1, tel. 62/61–33–38. Admission: 20 kr. adults, 3 kr. children under 14. Open May 15–Sept. 15, daily 10:30–4:30.*

Visit the **Fåborg Museum for Fynsk Malerkunst** (Art Gallery for Funen Artists), which has a good collection of paintings and sculpture—dating mainly from 1880 to 1920—by the Fyn Painters, whose works are full of the dusky light that so often illuminates Scandinavian painting. *Grønnegade 75, tel. 62/61–06–45. Admission: 20 kr. adults, children under 15 free. Open Apr.–May and Sept.–Oct., daily 10–4; June–Aug., daily 10–5; Nov.–Mar., daily 11–3.*

From Fåborg, take the car ferry to Søby at the northern tip of Ærø Island, the "Jewel of the Archipelago," where roads wend through fertile fields and past thatched farmhouses. South from Søby on Route 16, 13 kilometers (8 miles), is the charming town of Ærøskøbing on the island's north coast. When you've spent an hour walking through its cobbled 17th- and 18th-century streets, you'll understand its great appeal.

From Ærøskøbing, the ferry takes just over an hour to reach Svendborg, Funen's southernmost town. It's also the gateway to the country's southern islands, so leave it for the moment and cross over the bridge onto the tiny island of **Tåsinge**.

Dating from around 1640, **Valdemars Slot,** now a sumptuously furnished home, is one of Denmark's oldest privately owned castles. Upstairs, the rooms are furnished to the smallest detail. Downstairs is the castle church, illuminated only by candlelight. There's a restaurant (*see* Dining and Lodging, *below*) situated beneath the church. The Tea Pavilion is now a café overlooking Lunkebugten Bay, with one of south Fyn's best stretches of beach. *Slotsalleen 100, Troense, tel. 62/22–61–06. Admission: 45 kr. adults, 15 kr. children. Open May–Oct., daily 10–5; Apr. and Oct., weekends 10–5.*

Pretty **Troense** is one of Denmark's best-preserved villages. Once the home port for many sailing ships, both commercial and Viking, today the harbor is stuffed with pleasure yachts.

Tåsinge is connected with the island of **Langeland** by a causeway-bridge. The largest island in the southern archipelago, Langeland is rich in relics of the past, and the beaches are worth scouting out.

Head back now, passing through Tåsinge, to Fyn's **Svendborg.** Just north of town is **Egeskov Slot,** one of the best-preserved island castles in Europe. Egeskov means "Oak Forest," and an entire one was felled around 1540 to form the piles on which the rose-stone structure stands. The park contains noteworthy Renaissance, Baroque, English, and peasant gardens and an antique-car museum. Unfortunately, little of the castle is open to the public. *Egeskovgade 18, Kvaerndrup, tel. 62/27–10–16. Admission (to castle and museum): 95 kr. adults, 47.50 kr. children under 12. Castle open May 1–Sept. 30, daily 10–5. Museum open June 1–Aug. 31, daily 9–6.*

Dining and Lodging

Fyn boasts a wide range of hotels and inns, many of which offer off-season (October through May) rates, as well as special weekend deals. The islands are also endowed with numerous campsites and youth hostels, all clean and attractively located. Some, like Odense's youth hostel, are set in old manor houses. For information, contact the local tourist office. For details and price-category definitions, *see* Dining and Lodging in Staying in Denmark, *above.*

Ærøskøbing
Lodging

Ærøhus. A half-timbered building with a steep red roof, the Ærøhus looks more like a rustic cottage than a hotel. Inside you'll find cozy simplicity in the modest wooden furniture and cheerful curtains and duvets. The garden's eight cottages have small terraces. *Vestergade 38 (Ærø), tel. 62/52–10–03, fax 62/52–21–23. 35 rooms, 14 with bath; 8 cottages. Facilities: restaurant, garden, terrace. Closed Dec. 24–Jan. 20. Moderate.*

Fåborg
Dining and Lodging

Falsled Kro. Once a smuggler's hideaway, the 500-year-old Falsled Kro is among Denmark's most elegant inns. The rooms are furnished in a mixture of antiques and contemporary Danish designs; most have a sitting area and a stone fireplace. The superb restaurant specializes in game and seafood. Try the fresh mussels from the local bed, and order some wine from the exceptional selection. *Assensvej 513, Falsled, 13 km (8 mi) northwest of Fåborg on the Millinge–Assens highway, tel. 62/68–11–11, fax 62/68–11–62. 14 rooms with bath, 3 apartments. AE, DC, MC. Closed Jan.–Feb. Very Expensive.*

Steensgård Herregårdspension. A long avenue of beeches leads to this 700-year-old moated manor that is tucked 7 kilometers (4½ miles) northwest of Fåborg. The interior elegantly blends wood paneling, parquet floors, antiques, and porcelain stoves. The candle-lit restaurant is top-notch. Try the game if it's on the menu. *Steensgård 4 (Funen), in Millinge, tel. 62/61–94–90, fax 62/61–78–61. 15 rooms, 13 with bath. Facilities: tennis, horseback riding, restaurant. AE, DC, MC, V. Closed Jan. Expensive.*

Nyborg
Lodging

Nyborg Strand. A seaside location adds to the charm of this typical Danish hotel that welcomes guests with a sculpture of a polar bear. It's clean, bright, and popular, with a friendly staff. *Østerøvej 2, tel. 65/31–31–31, fax 65/31–37–01. 240 rooms with bath. Facilities: pool, sauna, game room, restaurant, bar, garden. AE, DC, MC, V. Moderate.*

Odense
Dining

Restaurant Provence. A few minutes from the pedestrian mall, this cozy, blue-and-white dining room puts a Danish twist on Provençal cuisine. Specialties include venison with blackberry sauce, and duck breast cooked in sherry. *Pogstræde 31, tel. 66/12–12–96. Reservations advised. DC, MC, V. Moderate.*

Rudolf Mathis. You'll enjoy delectable seafood specialties and a splendid view of Kerteminde Harbor at this traditional Danish restaurant. *Dosseringen 13, Kerteminde, 13 km (8 mi) northeast of Odense on Rte. 165, tel. 65/32–32–33. Reservations accepted. No credit cards. Closed Mon. Moderate.*

Målet. A spirited local clientele frequents this sports club and restaurant filled with soccer memorabilia. Schnitzels are the specialty, prepared with mushrooms, paprika, or even Italian and Madagascar style. *Jernbanegade 17, tel. 66/17–82–41. No reservations. No credit cards. Inexpensive.*

Lodging

Grand Hotel. They don't make spacious, gracious places like this anymore. Dating from 1897, the Grand offers spruced-up fin-de-siècle elegance. The decor is cool and green, and there are lovely marble bathrooms in the rooms, as well as a sweeping staircase and a spectacular Pompeiian red dining room. *Jernbanegade 18, tel. 66/11–71–71, fax 66/14–11–71. 137 rooms with bath. Facilities: sauna, solarium, restaurant, bar, parking. AE, DC, MC, V. Closed Christmas–New Year's Day. Very Expensive.*

Hotel Ydes. This bright, colorful hotel is a good bet for students and budget-conscious travelers tired of barrack-type accommodations. The plain, white hospital-style rooms are clean and comfortable. *Hans Tausensgade 11, tel. 66/12–11–31. 30 rooms, 24 with shower. Facilities: café. MC, V. Inexpensive.*

Svendborg
Dining

Sandig. At this austere white eatery, just near the harbor, the food is owner-chef-waiter-dishwasher Volkert Sandig's priority. His daily French-Danish menu includes inventive fish and beef specialties, such as cod served with mussel and garlic sauce. *Kullinggade 1b, tel. 62/22–92–11. Reservations advised. DC, MC, V. Closed Sun. and Dec. 24–Jan. 4. Moderate.*

Troense
Dining

Valdemars Slot. Situated in the ancient vaults beneath the church of Valdemar Castle, this restaurant provides a cool retreat and an excellent meal. Arched ceilings, tiled floors, and candlelight set the elegant tone. *Slotsalleen 100, Tåsinge, tel. 62/22–59–00. Reservations advised. MC. Closed Mon. Expensive.*

Jylland and the Lakes

The peninsula of Jylland (Jutland) is the only part of Denmark that is attached to the mainland of Europe; its southern boundary is the frontier with Germany. It's a region of carefully groomed pastures punctuated by stretches of rugged beauty. The windswept landscapes of *Babette's Feast,* the film version of Isak Dinesen's novel, are in northwest Jylland. One-tenth of the peninsula consists of moors and sand dunes; the remaining land is devoted to agriculture and forestry. To the east of the peninsula, facing Fyn, lie the well-wooded fjords, which run inland for miles. The region of rustic towns and stark countryside also boasts gracious castles, parklands, and the famed Legoland. Ribe, Denmark's oldest town, lies to the south, while to the east is Århus, Denmark's second-largest city, with its superb museums and new concert hall.

Getting Around

If you're following this itinerary directly after the tour around Fyn, head northwest from Odense through Middlefart and then on to Vejle. By train, either from Odense or Copenhagen, the starting point is Kolding, to the south of Vejle. While there are good train and bus services between all the main cities, this tour is best done by car. Delightful though they are, the offshore islands are suitable only for those with a lot of time, since many involve an overnight stay.

Guided Tours

Guided tours are scarce in these parts. However, you can stop by any tourist office for maps and suggestions for a walking tour. Århus also offers a "Round and About the City" tour, which leaves from the tourist office daily from mid-June to mid-Aug. at 10 AM.

Tourist Information

Aalborg (Østerå 8, tel. 98/12–60–22).
Århus (Rådhuset, tel. 86/12–16–00).
Billund (c/o Legoland A/S, tel. 75/33–19–26).
Herning (Bredgade 2, tel. 97/12–44–22).
Kolding (Axeltorv 8, tel. 75/53–21–00).
Randers (Erik Menveds Plads 1, tel. 86/42–44–77).
Ribe (Torvet 3–5, tel. 75/42–15–00).
Silkeborg (Godthåbsvej 4, tel. 86/82–19–11).
Vejle (Søndergade 14, tel. 75/82–19–55).
Viborg (Nytorv 9, tel. 86/61–16–66).

Exploring Jylland and the Lakes

If **Kolding** is your starting point, don't miss the well-preserved 13th-century **Koldinghus** castle, a royal residence during the Middle Ages. *Tel. 75/50–15–00. Admission: 30 kr. adults, children free. Open April–Sept., daily 10–5; Oct.–Mar., Mon.–Fri. noon–3, weekends 10–3.*

Jylland

The Den Geografiske Have (Geographical Garden) has a rose garden with more than 120 varieties, as well as some 2,000 plants from all parts of the world, arranged geographically. *Admission: 30 kr. adults, children free. Open June and Aug., daily 9–7; July, daily 9–8; Sept.–May, daily 10–6.*

Vejle, about 20 kilometers (12 miles) to the north of Kolding, is beautifully positioned on the fjord; amid forest-clad hills, the town looks out toward the Kattegat, the strait that divides Jylland and Fyn. You can hear the time of day chiming on an old Dominican monastery clock; the clock remains, but the monastery has long since given way to the town's imposing 19th-century city hall.

Leaving Vejle, take the road 10 kilometers (6 miles) north through the Grejs Valley to **Jelling.** In Jelling you'll find two 10th-century burial mounds marking the seat of King Gorm the Old and his wife, Thyra. Between the mounds are the Jelling runic stones, one of which is known as "Denmark's Certificate of Baptism" because it shows the oldest known figure of Christ in Scandinavia. The inscription explains that the stone was erected by Gorm's son, King Harald Bluetooth, who brought Christianity to the Danes in AD 960.

Head north toward **Silkeborg,** set on the banks of the river Gudena in Jylland's lake district. The region stretches from Silkeborg in the west to Skanderborg in the east and contains some of Denmark's loveliest scenery, as well as one of the country's meager "mountains." The best way to explore the area is by water because the Gudena winds its way some 160 kilometers (100 miles) through lakes and wooded hillsides down to the sea. You can take one of the excursion boats or, better still, the world's last coal-paddle steamer, *Hjejlen*, which runs in the summer and is based at Silkeborg. Since 1861, it has paddled its way through narrow stretches of fjord, where the treetops meet overhead, to the foot of the Himmelbjerget at Lake Julso. From that point you can clamber up the narrow paths through the heather and trees to the top, where an 80-foot tower stands sentinel, placed there on Constitution Day in 1875 in memory of King Frederik VII.

Silkeborg's other attraction is housed in the **Silkeborg Kulturhistoriske Museum** (Museum of Culture and History): the 2,200-year-old Tollund Man, one of the so-called bog people, whose corpse was preserved by natural ingredients in the soil and water. *Hovedgaardsvej 7, tel. 86/82–14–99. Admission: 20 kr. adults, 5 kr. children. Open Apr. 15–Oct. 23, daily 10–5; Oct. 24–Apr. 14, Wed. and weekends noon–4.*

On the coast, lying directly east of Silkeborg, is **Århus,** Denmark's second-largest city. The town is at its liveliest during the 10-day Århus Festival in September, which brings together everything from classical concerts to jazz and folk music, clowning, theater, exhibitions, beer tents, and sports. The town's cathedral, the 15th-century **Domkirke,** is Denmark's longest church; it contains a beautifully executed three-panel altarpiece. Look up at the whimsical sketches around the drains on the ceiling.

Nearby is the **Vor Frue Kirke,** formerly a Dominican abbey. Underneath the 13th-century structure is the eerie but interesting crypt church, rediscovered in 1955 and, dating from 1060, one of the oldest preserved stone churches in Scandinavia. The vaulted room houses a replica of an old Roman crucifix.

Not to be missed is the town's open-air museum, known as **Den Gamle By** (The Old Town). A sophisticated version of Disneyland, it features 65 half-timbered houses, a mill, and a millstream. The meticulously re-created period interiors range from the 15th to the early 20th century. *Viborgvej, tel. 86/12–31–88. Admission: 40 kr. adults, children under 16 free. Open Jan.–Mar. and Nov., daily 11–3; Apr. and Oct., daily 10–4; May and Sept., daily 10–5; June–Aug., daily 9–6; Dec., Mon.–Sat. 10–3, Sun. 10–4. Grounds always open.*

Set in a 250-acre forest in a park south of Århus is the indoor/outdoor **Moesgård Prehistoric Museum,** with exhibits on ethnography and archaeology, including the famed Grauballe Man, an eerie, well-preserved corpse from 2,000 years ago. Take the "Prehistoric Trail" through the forest, which leads past Stone and Bronze Age displays to some reconstructed houses from Viking times. *Ny Moesgård Allé 20, Højbjerg, tel. 86/27–24–33. Admission: 25 kr. adults, children under 15 free. Open Jan.–Apr. and Sept. 16–Dec., Tues.–Sun. 10–4; May–mid-Sept., daily 10–5.*

Heading north 21 kilometers (15 miles), you'll come to the medieval town of **Randers,** where, in 1340, the Danish patriot Niels Ebbesen killed the German oppressor, Count Gert the Bald of Holstein, whose army was then occupying most of Jutland. To the east of Randers is the Djursland Peninsula, a popular vacation area, with fine manor houses open to the public. If time is of the essence, choose **Gammel Estrup,** a grand 17th-century manor in the tiny village of **Auning;** it's full of rich period furnishings, including an alchemist's cellar. *Tel. 86/48–30–01. Admission: 20 kr. adults, 5 kr. children. Manor and farm open May–Oct., daily 10–5; Nov.–Apr., (manor) Tues.–Sun. 11–3, (farm) daily 10–5.*

Aalborg, 71 kilometers (44 miles) north of Randers, is set at the narrowest point of the Limfjord, the great waterway of northern Jutland and the gateway between north and south. You'll find charming combinations of new and old; twisting lanes filled with medieval houses; and, nearby, broad modern boulevards. Jomfru Ane Gade is a tiny cobble street in the center of Aalborg, with a number of restaurants, inns, and sidewalk cafés. Major sights include the magnificent **Jens Bangs Stenhus** (Jens Bang's Stone House). A five-story building dating from 1642, it has an atmospheric restaurant and an excellent wine cellar. You'll also want to take in the Baroque cathedral, the **Budolfi Kirke,** dedicated to the English saint Butolph, and the 15th-century **Helligåndsklosteret** (Monastery of the Holy Ghost). One of Denmark's best-preserved monasteries, it is now a home for the elderly.

If you have some time to spare, head north up to the tip of Jylland, to **Skagen,** where the picturesque streets and the luminous light have inspired painters and writers alike. The 19th-century Danish artist Holger Drachmann (1846–1908) and his friends founded the Skagen school of painting; you can see their efforts on display in the local **Skagens Museum.** *4 Brøndumsvej, tel. 98/44–64–44. Admission: 25 kr. adults, children free. Open Apr. and Oct., Tues.–Sun. 11–4; May and Sept., daily 10–5; June–Aug., daily 10–6; Nov.–Mar., Wed.–Fri. 1–4, Sat. 11–4, Sun. 11–3.*

Heading south once more, you next come to **Viborg,** a town whose history goes back to the 8th century, when it was a trading post and a place of pagan sacrifice. Later it became a center of Christianity, with monasteries and an episcopal residence. The 1,000-year-old **Haervejen,** the old military road that starts near here, was once Denmark's most important connection with the outside world. Legend has it that in the 11th century, King Canute set out from Viborg to conquer England; he succeeded and ruled from 1016 to 1035.

Built in 1130, Viborg's **Domkirke,** the cathedral, was once the largest granite church in the world. Today the crypt is all that remains of the original building, restored and reopened in 1876. The early 20th-century biblical frescoes are by Danish painter Joakim Skovgaard.

There's terrific walking country 8 kilometers (5 miles) south of Viborg, beside **Hald Sø** (Hald Lake) and on the heatherclad **Dollerup Bakker** (Dollerup Hills). Next head southwest 45 kilometers (28 miles) to **Herning,** an old moorland town. There you'll find a remarkable circular house, with a 400-foot outer frieze by Carl-Henning Pedersen; it houses the **Carl-Henning Pedersen and Else Afelt's Museum,** set within a sculpture park. *Uldjydevej 1, tel. 97/22–10–79. Admission: 30 kr. adults, children free. Open May–Oct., Tues.–Fri. noon–5, weekends 10–5; Nov.–Apr., Tues.–Sun. noon–5.*

About 100 kilometers (60 miles) to the south, but well worth the extra driving time, is **Ribe,** Denmark's oldest town, where the medieval town center is preserved by the Danish National Trust. From May to mid-September, a night watchman goes around the town telling of its ancient history and singing traditional songs. Visitors can accompany him nightly by gathering in the main square at 10 PM.

Before heading back to Vejle, stop off at **Billund** to see the country's most famous tourist attraction. **Legoland** is a park filled with scaled-down versions of cities, towns, and villages, as well as working harbors and airports, a Statue of Liberty, a statue of Sitting Bull, Mount Rushmore, a safari park, even a Wild West saloon—all constructed of millions of Lego bricks. There are also exhibits of toys from pre-Lego days, including Legoland's high point, Titania's Palace, a sumptuous dollhouse built in 1907 by Sir Neville Wilkinson for his daughter. *Billund, tel. 75/33–13–33. Admission: 95 kr. adults, 80 kr. children under 14. Open May–Sept. 15, daily 10–7.*

Dining and Lodging

For details and price-category definitions, *see* Dining and Lodging in Staying in Denmark, *above.*

Aalborg
Dining
★

Duus Vinkælder. Occupying part of Jens Bang's house, and with 300 years of tradition behind it, Duus Vinkælder is one of Aalborg's best-known restaurants. The wine cellar is phenomenal. *9 Østerå, tel. 98/12–50–56. Reservations required. No credit cards. Closed Sun. Moderate.*

Spisehuset Kniv og Gaffel. In a 400-year-old building near Jomfru Ane gade, this busy restaurant is crammed with boisterous diners, oak tables, crazy slanting floors, and young waitresses negotiating the mayhem to deliver inch-thick steaks—the house specialty. *Maren Turisgade 10, tel. 98/16–69–72. Reservations advised. Dress: casual but neat. DC, MC, V. Closed Sun. Moderate.*

Dining and Lodging

Helnan Phønix. A centrally located hotel in a historic building, Helnan Phønix is discreet, traditional, and exceptionally popular. The rooms are comfortable and spacious, the staff pleasant and helpful. One of the Phønix's restaurants, the Halling, serves excellent French and Danish cuisines. *Vesterbro 77, tel. 98/12–00–11, fax 98/16–31–66. 179 rooms with bath. Facilities: sauna, solarium, game room, 2 restaurants, bar, café. AE, DC, MC, V. Very Expensive.*

Århus
Dining
★

Restaurant Mahler. Located on a busy street lined with ethnic eateries, this elegant French restaurant is trimmed with swag curtains, sprays of dried spices, and gem-colored flasks of oil. Every two weeks, the menu features the fare of another region of France, using the freshest Danish ingredients. *Vestergade 39, tel. 86/19–06–96. Reservations advised. Dress: casual but neat. AE, DC, MC, V. Closed Mon., Sat lunch, holidays, and Dec. 24–Jan. 2. Expensive.*
Kashmir. In his popular, casual eatery, owner Mirza Zaman serves spicy Pakistani and Indian specialties made from his grandmother's recipes. *Vesterbrogade 36, tel. 86/13–16–37. Reservations advised. MC. Dinner only. Inexpensive.*

Lodging

Royal Hotel. Open since 1838, Århus's grand hotel has recently been restored and rebuilt, with its period elegance left intact. Cool pastels abound, as does cheerful chintz. The bathrooms are marble; the service is excellent. *Store Torv 4, tel. 86/12–00–11, fax 86/76–04–04. 106 rooms with bath. Facilities: 5 cinemas, restaurant, nightclub, casino, sauna, solarium. AE, DC, MC, V. Very Expensive.*
Youth Hostel Pavilionen. As in all Danish youth and family hostels, the rooms here are clean, bright, and functional, while the secluded, wooded setting near the fjord is downright beautiful. Unfortunately, it can get a little noisy, with guests ranging from carousing business parties to budget-conscious backpackers. *Marienlundsvej 10, tel. 86/16–72–98, fax 86/10–55–60. 30 rooms, 11 with private shower; 4 communal showers and toilets. Facilities: cafeteria (breakfast only), kitchen, parking. AE, MC, V. Closed mid-Dec.–mid-Jan. Inexpensive.*

Ribe
Dining and
Lodging

Hotel Dagmar. Occupying a building dating from 1581, the Dagmar is a cozy place, encapsulating all the charm of the 16th century, with stained-glass windows, frescoes, sloping floors, and carved chairs. The restaurant has a delightful central fireplace, and the food is first-class. Try the fillet of veal à la Dagmar. *Torvet 1, tel. 75/42–00–33, fax 75/42–36–52. 50 rooms with bath. Facilities: restaurant (reservations advised). AE, DC, MC, V. Expensive.*

Skagen
Dining and
Lodging

Brøndums Hotel. With an attractive beachside location, the Brøndums is a friendly hotel, decorated throughout with paintings by 19th-century artists of the Skagen school. The restaurant has lots of fish specialties and outside dining in the summer. *Anchersvej 3, tel. 98/44–15–55, fax 98/45–15–20. 46 rooms with bath. Facilities: restaurant (reservations advised). AE, MC, V. Expensive.*

Vejle
Dining and
Lodging

Munkebjerg. A remote location and marvelous views characterize this establishment, which dates from 1880. The original building has long since gone, but the nearby beech woods and fjord remain. Guest rooms are modern and light, with fresh colors and stripped-pine decor. The Munkebjerg has two fine restaurants specializing in French cuisine. *Munkebjergvej 125, tel. 75/72–35–00, fax 75/72–08–86. 148 rooms with bath. Facilities: 2 restaurants, casino, café, fitness room, pool, sauna, solarium, game room, tennis, heliport, horseback riding, golf course, and biking, jogging, and walking trails. AE, DC, MC, V. Very Expensive.*

9 Finland

If you like majestic open spaces, fine architecture, and civilized living—and can afford the prices—Finland is for you. It is a land of lakes, 187,888 at the last count, and forests. It is a land where nature is so prized that even the design of city buildings reflects the soaring spaces of the countryside.

The music of Sibelius, Finland's most famous son, tells you what to expect from this Nordic landscape. Both can swing from the somber nocturne of midwinter darkness to the tremolo of sunlight slanting through pine and bone-white birch or from the crescendo of a sunset before it fades into the next day's dawn. Similarly, the Finnish people reflect the changing moods of their land and climate. They can get annoyed when described as "children of nature," but the description is apt. Their affinity with nature has produced some of the world's greatest designers and architects. Many American cities have buildings designed by Alvar Aalto and the Saarinens, Eliel and son Eero. In fact, Eliel and his family moved to the United States in 1923 and became American citizens—but it was to a lonely Finnish seashore that Saarinen had his ashes returned.

Until 1917, Finland (the Finns call it *Suomi)* was under the domination of its nearest neighbors, Sweden and Russia, who fought over it for centuries. After more than 600 years under Swedish rule and 100 under the czars, the country inevitably bears many traces of these two cultures, including a small (6%) but influential Swedish-speaking population and a scattering of Russian Orthodox churches.

But the Finns themselves are neither Scandinavian nor Slavic. All that is known of their origins is that they are descended from wandering groups of people who probably came from west of the Ural Mountains before the Christian era and settled on the swampy shores of the Gulf of Finland.

There is a tough, resilient quality in the Finns. No other people fought the Soviets to a standstill as the Finns did in the Winter War of 1939–40. This resilience, in part, stems from the turbulence of the country's past, but also comes from the people's strength and determination to work the land and survive the long winters. No wonder there is a poet-philosopher lurking in most Finns, one who sometimes drowns his melancholic, darker side in the bottle. For the Finn is in a state of constant confrontation—with the weather, the land, and most recently a huge eastern neighbor that is engulfed in political and economic turmoil. The Finn is stubborn, patriotic, and self-sufficient, yet not aggressively nationalistic. On the contrary, rather than being proud of past battles, the Finn is proud of finding ways to live in peace. His country's neutrality and his own personal freedom are what he tenaciously holds on to and will never easily relinquish.

The average Finn doesn't volunteer much information, but that's due to reserve, not indifference. Make the first approach and you may have a friend for life. Finns like their silent spaces, though, and won't appreciate back-slapping familiarity—least of all in the sauna, still regarded by many as a spiritual, as well as a cleansing, experience.

Finland

NORWAY

Utsjoki

Karigasniemi

Inarijärvi

Kilpisjärvi

Inari
Ivalo

Enontekiö

Porttipahdan tekojärvi

COMMONWEALTH OF
INDEPENDENT STATES
(RUSSIA)

Muonio

Lokan tekojärvi

Kittilä

Sodankylä

SWEDEN

LAPLAND

Kemijärvi
Joutsijärvi

Arctic Circle

Arctic Circle

Rovaniemi

Perä-Posio
Posio
Kuusamo

Tornio

Kemi

20

5

Pudasjärvi

Hailuoto

Puolanka

Suomussalmi

Raahe

Oulu

E63

22

8

4

Kalajoki

Pulkkila

Oulujärvi
Kajaani

Nivala

85

Otanmäki

Kuhmo

Kokkola

Kärsämäki

E63

of

Haapajärvi

Iisalmi

Nurmes

Bothnia

E75

Pielinen

Vaasa

Kyyjärvi

5

Kuopio

16

17

Joensuu

Kallavesi

Seinäjoki

Äänekoski

Orivesi

8

9

12

Jyväskylä

23

Varkaus

Savonlinna

23

E63

14

23

Parkano

9

Mikkeli

Kokonselkä

Punkaharju

Pori

Näsijärvi

Päijänne

Saimaa

11

Tampere

Heinola

Rauma

Imatra

*Lake
Ladoga*

8

Hämeenlinna

12

Lahti

6

Lappeenranta

3

Kouvola

M5

1

*Åland
(Ahvenanmaa)*

2

Turku

Kotka

RUSSIA

1

Salo

Helsinki

Porvoo

E18

Mariehamn
(Maarianhamina)

Ekenäs

Gulf of Finland

Baltic Sea

Hanko
(Hangö)

0   50 miles

0   50 km

N

Essential Information

Before You Go

When to Go The tourist summer season runs from mid-June until mid-August, a magnificently sunny and generally dry time marked by unusually warm temperatures in recent years. Outside this period, many amenities and attractions either close or operate on much reduced schedules. But there are advantages to visiting Finland off-season, not the least being that you avoid the mosquitoes, which can be fearsome, especially in the north. Also, hotel rates, especially in vacation villages, may drop by up to 50%, (between 25% and 30% in Helsinki during the summer) and the fall colors (from early September in the far north, October in the south) are spectacular. January through March (through April in the north) is the main cross-country skiing season. Spring is brief but magical, as the snows melt, the ice breaks up, and nature explodes into life almost overnight.

Climate Generally speaking, the spring and summer seasons begin a month earlier in the south of Finland than they do in the far north. You can expect warm (not hot) days in Helsinki from mid-May; in Lapland from mid-June. The midnight sun can be seen from May to July, depending on the region. In midwinter there is a corresponding period when the sun does not rise at all, but it is possible to see magnificent displays of the Northern Lights. Even in Helsinki, summer nights are brief and never really dark, whereas in midwinter daylight lasts only a few hours.

The following are average daily maximum and minimum temperatures for Helsinki.

Jan.	30F	– 1C	May	64F	18C	Sept.	53F	11C
	26	– 3		48	9		39	4
Feb.	34F	1C	June	60F	16C	Oct.	46F	8C
	24	– 4		48	9		36	2
Mar.	36F	2C	July	68F	20C	Nov.	32F	0C
	26	– 3		55	13		26	– 3
Apr.	46F	8C	Aug.	64F	18C	Dec.	32F	0C
	32	0		53	12		24	– 4

Currency The unit of currency in Finland is the Finnmark (FIM), divided into 100 penniä. There are bills of FIM 20, 50, 100, 500, and 1,000. Coins are 10 and 50 penniä, and FIM 1, FIM 5, and FIM 10. At press time (spring 1994), the exchange rate was about FIM 5.60 to the dollar and FIM 8.45 to the pound sterling. Credit cards are widely accepted even in many taxicabs. Traveler's checks can be changed only in banks.

What It Will Cost Prices are highest in Helsinki; otherwise they vary little throughout the country. Taxes are already included in hotel and restaurant charges, and there is no airport departure tax. However, the price of many goods includes an 18% sales tax, less on food (*see* Shopping in Staying in Finland, *below*).

Sample Prices Cup of coffee, FIM 7; glass of beer, FIM 10–FIM 20; Coca-Cola, FIM 10; ham sandwich, FIM 15–FIM 20; 1-mile taxi ride, FIM 25.

Customs on Arrival Europeans age 16 and over entering Finland may bring in 200 cigarettes or 250 grams of other tobacco; visitors from outside Europe may bring in twice as much. All visitors aged 20 or over may also bring in 2 liters of beer, 1 liter of alcohol under 22% volume, and 1 liter over 22% volume; or 2 liters of beer and 2 liters of alcohol under 22%. Visitors aged 18 or over may import 2 liters of beer and 2 liters of alcohol under 22% volume. Goods up to a value of FIM 1,500 may be imported.

Language The official languages of Finland are Finnish and Swedish, though only a small minority (about 6%) speak Swedish. English is widely spoken among people in the travel industry and by many younger Finns, though they're often shy about using it. Nearly all tourist sites and attractions provide texts in English. In the north the Lapp people, called *Same*, have their own language.

Getting Around

By Car Finland has no superhighways, but there is an expanding network of
Road efficient major roads, some of which are multilane. In some areas,
Conditions however, especially in the north, you can expect long stretches of dirt road. These roads are usually adequate to good, although during the spring thaw they become difficult to negotiate. Away from the larger towns, traffic is light, but take moose and reindeer warning signs seriously.

Rules of the Drive on the right. At intersections, cars coming from the right have
Road priority. Speed limits (usually marked) are 50 kph (30 mph) in built-up areas and between 80 kph and 100 kph (50 mph and 62 mph) in the country and on main roads. Low-beam headlights must be used at all times outside city areas, seat belts are compulsory (on rear as well as front seats), and you must carry a warning triangle in case of breakdown.

Parking Parking is a problem only in some city centers. Major cities offer multistory garages; most towns have on-street meters. Illegally parked cars may be towed away.

Breakdowns The **Automobile and Touring Club of Finland** (Autoliitto ry,
and Accidents Hämeentie 105 A, PL 35, 00550 Helsinki, tel. 90/774761) operates a 24-hour road patrol service (tel. 90/774–76400), and a weekend road-patrol service (tel. 9700/8080) on the main roads from 6 PM Friday to 10 PM Sunday. If you're involved in an accident, report it without delay to the **Finnish Motor Insurers' Bureau** (Liikennevakutuskeskus, Bulevardi 28, Helsinki, tel. 90/680401) as well as to the police.

By Train Finland's extensive rail system reaches all main centers of the country and offers high standards of comfort and cleanliness. A special **Finnrail Pass** entitles you to unlimited travel for three, five, or 10 days within a month; second-class prices are FIM 480 (three days), FIM 650 (five days), and FIM 900 (10 days); first-class tickets are FIM 20 (three days), FIM 975 (five days), and FIM 1,350 (10 days). Children pay half fare. These tickets can be purchased both inside and outside the country. In Finland, the Finnrail Pass is available from the Finnish State Railways (VR) (tel. 90/010–0127). In the United States and Canada they can be purchased by calling **Rail Europe** (tel. 800/438–7245) in the United Kingdom, from **Finlandia Travel** (tel. 071/409–7334).

By Plane **Finnair** (tel. 90/818800) operates an elaborate network of flights linking 22 towns in Finland. For $300, a **Holiday Ticket** guarantees you unlimited travel for 15 days; visitors aged 17–24 can get a **Youth Holiday Ticket** for $250. These tickets are available in most countries, and in Finland they can be purchased at major travel agencies.

By Bus Bus travel plays a leading role in Finland, and the country's bus system provides the most extensive travel network of all; it can take you virtually anywhere. A **Coach Holiday Ticket,** available from bus stations and travel agencies, entitles you to 1,000 kilometers (625 miles) of bus travel for FIM 340 for two weeks.

By Boat Helsinki and Turku have regular sea links with the Åland Islands in the Baltic Sea. From mid-June to mid-August you can cruise the labyrinthine lakes of the Finnish interior. Complete timetables are available from the Finnish Tourist Board.

By Bicycle Planned bicycle routes are provided in many areas. The main advantages for the cyclist are the lack of steep hills and the absence of heavy traffic. Bikes can be rented in some youth hostels. The Finnish **Youth Hostel Association** (Yrjönkatu 38B, Helsinki, tel. 90/694–0377) offers accommodation packages of seven or 14 days to tie in with visitors' cycling tours.

Staying in Finland

Telephones Hotels charge a substantial fee for all calls. You can avoid this fee by
Local Calls using the pay phones provided in most lobbies. Have some FIM 1 and FIM 5 coins ready. Note that the Finnish letters å, ä, and ö come at the end of the alphabet; this may be useful when looking up names in the telephone book.

International You can dial directly to Britain and the United States from any-
Calls where in Finland. Calls to other countries can be made from a telegraph office; these are marked "Lennätin" or "Tele" and usually adjoin the post office. An operator will assign you a private booth and collect payment at the end of the call.

Operators and For information about telephone charges, dial 92020; for number in-
Information quiries, dial 118.

Mail At press time (spring 1994), airmail rates to North America were
Postal Rates FIM 3.40 for a letter of up to 20 grams. Letters to the United Kingdom cost FIM 2.90.

Receiving Mail If you're uncertain about where you'll be staying, be sure that mail sent to you is marked "Poste Restante" and addressed to the Main Post Office, Mannerheimintie 11, 00100 Helsinki, or to major post offices in other towns. American Express offers a free clients' mail service and will hold mail for up to one month (*see* Important Addresses and Numbers in Helsinki, *below*). The Finland Travel Bureau also provides a free mail service for foreigners: Mail should be addressed to its Mail Department, Box 319, 00101 Helsinki, and collected from the office at Kaivokatu 10A.

Shopping If you purchase goods worth more than FIM 100 in any of the many
Sales Tax shops marked "tax-free for tourists," you can get a 10%–16% refund
Refunds when you leave Finland. Show your passport and the store will give you a check for the appropriate amount that you can cash at most departure points.

Opening and **Banks** are open weekdays 9:15–4:15. **Museums.** Opening hours vary
Closing Times considerably, so check individual listings. Most close one day a week, usually Monday. Many museums in the countryside are open only during the summer months. **Shops** are generally open weekdays 9–6, Saturday 9–2. Department stores and supermarkets stay open until 8 from Monday through Friday. **Sightseeing.** Schedules for most attractions vary widely outside the main tourist season. Check local tourist offices for opening days and hours.

National January 1; January 6 (Epiphany Day); April 14–17 (Easter); May 1
Holidays (May Day); May 12 (Ascension); May 22 (Pentecost); June 24 (Mid-

summer's Eve); June 25 (Midsummer's Day); November 1 (All Saints' Day); December 6 (Independence Day); December 25–26.

Dining You can choose among restaurants, taverns, coffeehouses, and snack bars. As in other parts of Scandinavia, the *voileipäpöytä* (cold table) is often a work of art as well as a feast. Special Finnish dishes include *poronkäristys* (reindeer casserole; superb in Lapland); salmon, herring, and various freshwater fish; and *lihapullia* (meatballs) with a tasty sauce. Crayfish parties are popular between the end of July and early September. For a delicious dessert, try cloudberries (related to blackberries) and other forest fruits.

Mealtimes The Finns eat early; lunch runs from 11 or noon to 1 or 2, dinner from 4 to 7 (a bit later in Helsinki).

Dress Except for the most elegant restaurants, where a jacket and tie are preferred, casual attire is acceptable for restaurants in all price categories; however, jeans are not allowed in some of the Expensive and Very Expensive establishments.

Ratings Prices are per person and include first course, main course, dessert, and service charge—but not wine. All restaurant checks include a service charge (*sisältää palvelupalkkion*). If you want to leave an additional tip—though it really isn't necessary—it's enough to round the figure off to the nearest FIM 5 or FIM 10. Best bets are indicated by a star ★ .

Category	Helsinki	Other Areas
Very Expensive	over FIM 200	over FIM 170
Expensive	FIM 150–FIM 200	FIM 140–FIM 170
Moderate	FIM 80–FIM 150	FIM 80–FIM 140
Inexpensive	under FIM 80	under FIM 80

If you select the fixed-price menu, which usually covers two courses and coffee and is served at certain hours in many establishments, the cost of the meal can be as little as half these prices.

Lodging The range of accommodations available in Finland includes hotels, motels, boarding houses, private homes, rented chalets and cottages, farmhouses, youth hostels, and campsites. There is no official system of classification, but standards are generally high. If you haven't reserved a room in advance, you can make reservations at the **Hotel Booking Center** at the Railway Station (Rautatieasema, 00100 Helsinki, tel. 90/171133) or through a travel agency; the booking fee is FIM 10.

Hotels Nearly all hotels in Finland are modern or will have been recently renovated; a few occupy fine old manor houses. Most have rooms with bath or shower. Prices generally include breakfast and often a morning sauna and swim. The **Finncheque** voucher system, operating in many hotels from June through August, offers good discounts. Only the first night can be reserved, but subsequent reservations can be made free from any Finncheque hotel. For additional information, inquire at the Hotel Booking Center or the Finnish Tourist Board (Eteläesplanadi 4, 00130 Helsinki, tel. 90/403011).

Summer Hotels University students' accommodations are turned into "summer hotels" from June through August; they offer modern facilities at slightly lower-than-average prices.

Boarding Houses, Private Homes, and Rentals	These provide the least expensive accommodations and are found only outside Helsinki. Local tourist offices have lists. The choice of rentals is huge, and the chalets and cottages are nearly always in delightful lakeside or seashore settings. For comfortable (not luxurious) accommodations, count on paying FIM 1,000–FIM 3,000 for a four-person weekly rental. A central reservations agency is **Lomarengas** (Malminkaari 23C, 00700 Helsinki, tel. 90/3516–1321, or Eteläesplanadi 4, 00130 Helsinki, tel. 90/170611).
Farmhouses	These are located in attractive settings, usually near water. A central reservations agency is **Suomen 4H-liitto** (Abrahaminkatu 7, 00180 Helsinki, tel. 90/642233).
Youth Hostels	These range from empty schools to small manor houses. There are no age restrictions, and prices range from FIM 50 to FIM 150 per bed. The Finnish Tourist Board can provide a list of hostels.
Camping	There are about 350 Finnish campsites, all classified into one of three grades. All offer showers and cooking facilities, and many include cottages for rent. A list is available from the Finnish Tourist Board.
Ratings	Prices are for two people in a double room and include breakfast and service charge. Best bets are indicated by a star ★ .

Category	Helsinki	Other Areas
Very Expensive	over FIM 750	over FIM 650
Expensive	FIM 550–FIM 750	FIM 500–FIM 650
Moderate	FIM 350–FIM 550	FIM 350–FIM 500
Inexpensive	under FIM 350	under FIM 350

Tipping	The Finns are less tip-conscious than other Europeans. (For restaurant tips, *see* Dining, *above*.) You can give taxi drivers a few small coins, but it's not essential. Train and airport porters have a fixed charge. It's not necessary to tip hotel doormen for carrying bags to the check-in counter, but give bellhops FIM 5–FIM 10 for carrying bags to your room. The obligatory checkroom fee of FIM 3–FIM 4 is usually clearly indicated; if not, give FIM 3–FIM 10, depending on the number in your party. FIM 5 is a standard tip for all minor services.

Helsinki

Arriving and Departing

By Plane	All international flights arrive at Helsinki's Vantaa Airport, 20 kilometers (12 miles) north of the city. For arrival and departure information, call 9700–8100.
Between the Airport and Downtown	Finnair buses leave two to three times an hour for the city terminals, located at the Inter-Continental hotel (Töölönkatu 21, tel. 90/818–7670) and the main Railway Station. The trip takes about 30 minutes and costs FIM 20. A local bus service (No. 615), which takes about 40 minutes, goes to the train station and costs FIM 15. Expect to pay between FIM 100 and FIM 120 for a taxi into the city center. If you are driving, the way is well marked to Highway 137 (Tuusulantie) and Keskusta (downtown Helsinki).

By Train Helsinki's Railway Station is in the heart of the city. For train information, call 90/010–0121.

By Bus The terminal for many local buses is the Railway Station square, Rautatientori. The main long-distance bus station is located off Mannerheimintie between Salomonkatu and Simonkatu. For information, phone 9600–4000.

By Sea The Silja Line terminal for ships arriving from Stockholm is at Olympialaituri, on the west side of the South Harbor. The Finnjet-Silja Line and Viking Lines terminal for ships arriving from Travemünde and Stockholm is at Katajanokka, on the east side of the South Harbor.

Getting Around

The center of Helsinki is compact and best explored on foot. If you want to use public transportation, your best buy is the **Helsinki Card,** which gives unlimited travel on city public transportation, as well as free entry to many museums, a free sightseeing tour, and a variety of other discounts. It's available for one, two, or three days (FIM 85, FIM 110, and FIM 130; about half-price for children). You can buy it at some hotels, travel agencies, Stockmann's, and at the Helsinki City Tourist Office.

By Subway Helsinki's only subway line runs from the western suburb of Ruoholahti to Mellunmäki, in the eastern suburbs. It runs from around 5:45 AM to 11:20 PM, and each ride costs FIM 9; you can transfer for free if you do so within an hour from the start of travel. Each trip costs FIM 7.50 if you buy a 10-trip ticket. Tickets are available from some kiosks and vending machines.

By Streetcar These run from 6 AM to 1:30 AM, depending on the line. They can be very handy, but be sure to get route advice because route maps are practically nonexistent. The fare is the same as for the subway. The 3T streetcar follows a figure-eight circuit around the city center and, during summer, provides commentary on an electric screenboard in several languages.

By Taxi Taxis are all marked "taksi." The meters start at FIM 16, with the fare rising on a kilometer basis. There is a surcharge after 6 PM and 10 PM, and on weekends. Car services have a minimum charge and should be ordered well in advance. A listing of all taxi companies appears in the white pages under "Taksi"—try to choose one that is located nearby, because they charge from point of dispatch. Many accept credit cards.

By Boat In summer there are regular boat services from the South Harbor market square to the islands of Suomenlinna and Korkeasaari.

Important Addresses and Numbers

Tourist Information The **Helsinki City Tourist Office** is near the South Harbor (Pohjoisesplanadi 19, tel. 90/169–3757); open May 2–Sept., weekdays 8:30–6, weekends 10–3; Oct. 1–Apr. 28, 8:30–4, closed weekends. The **Finnish Tourist Board's Tourist Information Office** (covering all Finland) is nearby at Eteläesplanadi 4, tel. 90/4030–1211 or 90/4030–1300; open June–Aug., weekdays 8:30–5, weekends 10–2; Sept.–May, weekdays 8:30–4.

Embassies U.S. (Itäinen Puistotie 14, tel. 90/171931). **Canadian** (Pohjois-esplanadi 25B, tel. 90/171141). U.K. (Itäinen Puistotie 17, tel. 90/661293).

Emergencies **General** (tel. 112); **Police** (tel. 112); **Ambulance** (tel. 112); **Doctor** (tel. 10023); **Dentist** (tel. 90/736166); **Pharmacy: Yliopiston Apteekki,** Mannerheimintie 96, open 24 hours (tel. 90/415778).

English-Language Bookstores You'll find a good selection of books and newspapers in English at **Akateeminen Kirjakauppa** (Keskuskatu 1) and **Suomalainen Kirjakauppa** (Aleksanterinkatu 23).

Travel Agencies **American Express** (Area Travel Agency, Pohjoisesplanadi 2, 00170 Helsinki, tel. 90/628788. **Thomas Cook** (Finland Travel Bureau, Kaivokatu 10A, Box 319, tel. 90/18261).

Guided Tours

Orientation Tours **Suomen Turistiauto** (tel. 90/588–5166) runs a "City Tour" (1½ hours; Jan.–Apr., Sun. 11 AM; May, daily 9 AM (South Harbor), and 11 AM (Asema aukio); June–Aug., daily 10:30, 12:30, 2:30 (South Harbor), and daily 11:30 and 1 (Asema aukio); Sept. daily 9 (South Harbor), and daily 11 (Asema aukio); 11 AM; Oct.–Dec., Sun. 11 AM) that covers the main city-center sights. The tour starts from Asema aukio, across from the main post office, and you can buy tickets on the bus 15 minutes before departure. **Ageba Travel Agency** (tel. 90/669193) offers a similar tour (2 to 2½ hours), starting from the Olympic Terminal (Apr.–Oct., daily 9:30 AM and 11 AM; Nov.–Mar., Sat. and Sun. 11 AM). **Royal Line Rautakorpi** (tel. 90/351–1885) operates "Helsinki by Sea" boat tours (1½ hours; May 13–Sept. 10, daily 11 AM, 1 PM, and 3 PM; June 10–Aug. 20, daily 10, noon, 2, and 4; evening cruises June 29–Aug. 20 Wed. and Sat. 8:15 PM) from the South Harbor market square in the summer. The same agency runs "Porvoo Old Town Cruises" (7 hours; June 18–Aug. 6, Tues., Thurs., Sat., and Sun. 10:30 AM; Aug. 13, 20, and 28 Sun. 10:30 AM).

Excursions **Helsingin Matkailuyhdistys** (Lönnrotinkatu 7B, Helsinki, tel. 90/645225) offers four-hour tours of historic homes of Finnish artists. No-visa trips by sea to St. Petersburg, Russia, and Tallinn, Estonia, are offered by **Finnsov Tours** (tel. 90/694–2011). **Atlas Cruising Center** offers visa-free cruises to Tallinn (one-day), and St. Petersburg (three-days) (tel. 9800/22584 or 90/651011).

Exploring Helsinki

Helsinki is a city of the sea. It was built on peninsulas that stab into the Baltic, and streets and avenues curve around bays, bridges arch over to nearby islands, and ferries reach out to islands farther offshore. Sweet-tasting salt air hovers over the city, and the sounds from the vessels steaming into port resonate off the city's buildings.

Like other European capitals, Helsinki has expanded its boundaries and now absorbs about one-sixth of the Finnish population, and the suburbs sprawl from one peninsula to another. Helsinki residents must know the peninsulas in order to know their city. However, most of the city's sights, hotels, and restaurants cluster on one peninsula, thus forming a compact hub that is of special interest to the traveler.

Unlike most other European capitals, Helsinki is "new." About 400 years ago, King Gustav Vasa of Sweden decided to woo trade from the Estonian city of Tallinn and thus challenge the monopoly of the Hanseatic League. To do this, he commanded the people of four Finnish towns to pack up their belongings and relocate at the rapids on the river Vantaa. This new town became Helsinki.

For three centuries, Helsinki had its ups and downs as a trading town. Turku, to the west of Helsinki, remained the capital and the center of the country's intellectual pursuits. Ironically, not until Finland was thrust under the dominance of Russia did Helsinki's fortunes improve. Czar Alexander I wanted Finland's political center closer to Russia and, in 1812, selected Helsinki as the new capital. Shortly after the capital was moved from Turku to Helsinki, Turku suffered a monstrous fire. So great was the inferno that the university was also moved to Helsinki. From then on Helsinki's future was secure.

Fire was indeed fortuitous for the future of Helsinki. Just before the czar's proclamation, a fire had swept through the town, permitting the construction of new buildings suitable for a nation's capital. The German-born architect Carl Ludvig Engel was commissioned to rebuild the city, and, as a result, Helsinki has some of the purest neoclassical architecture in the world. Add to this foundation the stunning outlines of the Jügend period (early 20th century) and the modern buildings designed by talented Finnish architects, and you have a European capital city that is as architecturally eye-catching as it is different from its Scandinavian neighbors or the rest of Europe.

Numbers in the margin correspond to points of interest on the Helsinki map.

❶ Across from the city tourist office and beside the South Harbor is the **Kauppatori** (Market Square). Sometimes it seems that half the city is here seeking the best buys for the day or simply catching up on the gossip. All around are stalls selling everything from colorful, freshly cut flowers to ripe fruit, from vegetables trucked in from the hinterland to handicrafts made in small villages. Look at the fruit stalls—mountains of strawberries; raspberries; blueberries; and, if you're lucky, *lakka* (cloudberries), which grow largely above the Arctic Circle in the midnight sun. Closer to the dock are fresh fish, caught that morning in the Baltic Sea and still flopping. You can't miss the **statue of Havis Amanda** standing in the square. This beautiful lady is loved by all Finns, and every May Day eve she is embraced by students who wade through the protective moat to crown her with their white caps.

The market ends at 2 PM, and, in the summer, the fruit and vegetable stalls are replaced with arts-and-crafts stalls. This happens at 3:30 PM and lasts until about 8 PM.

❷ Another heartbeat of Helsinki is across the street, on the other side of **Pohjoisesplanadi** (North Esplanade). The uniformed guards will prevent you from entering, but the building is the **Presidentinlinna** (President's Palace), and next to it are the city hall and various administrative offices. Across from the palace is the waterfront, where ferries and sightseeing boats set out into the bay. On a summer's day it is a sailor's vision: sails hoisted and taut to the wind, yacht clubs beckoning, and island waters to explore. The redbrick edifice ❸ perched above the east side of the market is the Orthodox **Uspenskin Katedraali** (Uspenski Cathedral).

Just behind the cathedral is the district of **Katajanokka.** Here the 19th-century brick warehouses are slowly being renovated to form a complex of boutiques, arts-and-crafts studios, and restaurants. You'll find innovative designs at these shops, and the restaurants tend to offer lighter fare, which can make this a tempting area to stop for lunch. While in Katajanokka, you might enjoy a visit to

Finlandiatalo, **15**
Kauppatori, **1**
Market Hall, **6**
Parliament House, **14**
Pohjoismainen
Taidekeskus, **8**
Presidentinlinna, **2**
Railway Station, **11**
Senaatintori, **4**
Statue of Marshal
Mannerheim, **13**
Stockmann's, **10**
Suomen
Kansallismuseo, **17**
Suomen
Kansallisoopera, **16**
Suomenlinna, **7**
Svenska Teatern, **9**
Temppeliaukion
Kirkko, **18**
Tuomiokirkko, **5**
Uspenskin
Katedraali, **3**
Valtion Taidemuseo
Ateneum, **12**

Helsinki

N

Eläintarhantie

Suonionk.
Siltasaarenk.
Porthanink.
Hämeentie

Sörnäistenrantatie

Kaisaniemenlahti

Siltavuoren-
satama

Sörnäistensatama

Unioninkatu
Siltavuorenranta

Kluuvi
Gloet

Mauink.

Liisank.

Maneesik

Meritullink.

Vironk.

Rauhank.

Kirkkok.

Mariank.

Pohjoisranta

Pohjoissatama
(North Harbor)

Snellmaninkatu

Fabianink.

Kaisaniemenk.

Unioninkatu

**Railway
Station**

11

13 Kaivok.

Mannerheimintie

Keskusk.

12

Mikonk.

5

Hallitusk.

4

Aleksanterink.

2

3

Laivastok.

Luotsik.

10

Kauppiaank.

Kruunuvuorenk.

Kanavak.

Katajanokanlaituri

i

Pohjoisesplanadi

9

Yrjönk.

Eteläesplanadi

Eteläranta

1

Annank.

Uudenmaank.

Pohj Makasiink.

7 **8**

Etel Makasiink.

6

Pieni
Roobertink.

Kasarmink.

Bernhardink.

Laivasillank.

**Eteläsatama
(South Harbor)**

Roobertink.

Punavuorenk.

Valkosaari

Merimiehenk.

Jääkärink.

Tähtitornink.

Luoto

Pursimiehenk.

Vuorimiehenk.

Ryssänsaari

Sepänk.

Ehrenströmintie

Pikkuluoto

Tehtaankatu

Neitsytpolku

Puistok.

Rehbinderintie

Pietarink.

Skepparegatan

Laivanvarustajank.

Puistotie

Kaivopuisto

Ehrensvärd Tie

Merisatamaranta

Ehrenströmintie

Merikatu

Merisatama

0   1/4 mile

0   1/4 km

Wanha Satama, a small complex of cafés and food stores attached to an art gallery.

4 A one-minute stroll north of city hall will take you into **Senaatintori** (Senate Square), the heart of neoclassical Helsinki and one of the most graceful squares in Europe, dominated by the domed **5** **Tuomiokirkko** (Lutheran Cathedral). The square is the work of Carl Ludvig Engel. The harmony created with the Tuomiokirkko, the university, and the state council building places you amid one of the purest styles of European architecture. Senaatintori has a dignified, stately air, enlivened in summer by sun worshipers who gather on the wide steps leading up to Tuomiokirkko and throughout the year by the bustle around the **Kiseleff Bazaar** on the square's south side.

Back on the market, head southward along the western shore of the South Harbor on Eteläranta Street. You'll soon come to the old brick **6** **Market Hall**—it's worth taking a look at the voluminous displays of meat, fish, and other gastronomic goodies (open weekdays 8–5, Saturday 8–2). A little farther on is the **Olympia Terminal,** where the huge ferries from Sweden, Estonia, and Poland berth. Beyond this is **Kaivopuisto,** the elegant parkland district much favored by Russian high society during the 19th century. It is now popular as a strolling ground for Helsinki's citizens and as a residential area for diplomats.

Time Out Perched on the shore is the **Ursula café.** However welcome the refreshments may be, the view of the harbor with its waterborne traffic is all the reason you need to stop here.

You can avoid the long walk back by cutting across Kaivopuisto to Tehtaankatu and catching streetcar No. 3T to the marketplace. **7** From here, there's a frequent ferry service to **Suomenlinna.** *Suomenlinna* means "Finland's Castle," and for good reason. In 1748 the Finnish army helped build this fortress, which grew so over the years that today Suomenlinna is a series of interlinked islands. For a long time the impregnable fortress was referred to as the "Gibraltar of the North." While it has never been taken by assault, its occupants did surrender twice without a fight—once to the Russians in the war of 1808–19 and then to the British, who bombarded the fortress, causing fires.

Although still a fortress, Suomenlinna is today a collection of museums, parks, and gardens. In early summer it is engulfed in mauve and purple mists of lilacs, the trees introduced from Versailles by the Finnish architect Augustin Ehrensvärd. One of the museums **8** you may care to visit is the **Pohjoismainen Taidekeskus** (Nordic Arts Center), which exhibits and promotes Scandinavian art. *Admission free. Open Tues.–Sun. 11–6.*

Back on the mainland, head west from the marketplace up Pohjoisesplanadi. To your left are the Esplanade gardens. On your right are the showrooms and boutiques of some of Finland's top fashion de- **9** signers (*see* Shopping, *below*). The circular **Svenska Teatern** (Swedish Theater) marks the junction of the Esplanade and Helsinki's main artery, Mannerheimintie.

10 If you take a right up Keskuskatu, you'll come to **Stockmann's,** Helsinki's most famous store, well worth a shopping stop. Next **11** you'll come to the **railway station** and its square, the bustling commuting hub of the city. The station's huge red-granite figures are by Emil Wikström, but the solid building they adorn was designed by

⑫ Eliel Saarinen, one of the founders of the early 20th-century National Romantic style. The **Valtion Taidemuseo Ateneum** (Finnish National Gallery) is on the south side of the square facing the **National Theater.** *Admission: FIM 10 adults, children free. Open year-round Tues. and Fri. 9–5, Wed. and Thurs. 9–9, weekends 11–5.*

Time Out **Café Socis,** in the Seurahuone Hotel opposite the Railway Station, provides a restful turn-of-the-century atmosphere for a fixed-price lunch or afternoon tea. **Ekberg's café** has gained a good reputation for its traditional confectionery line. Located at Bulevardi 9, it is a favorite of literary people and the various publishing companies in the vicinity.

⑬ In front of the main post office west of the station is the **statue of Marshal Mannerheim** gazing down Mannerheimintie, the major thoroughfare named in his honor. Perhaps no man in Finnish history is so revered as Marshal Baron Carl Gustaf Mannerheim, the military and political leader who guided Finland through much of the turbulent 20th century. When he died in Switzerland on January 28, 1951, his body was flown back to his native land to lie in state in the cathedral. For three days, young war widows, children, and soldiers filed past his bier by the thousands.

⑭⑮⑯ About half a mile along, past the colonnaded red-granite **Parliament House,** stands **Finlandiatalo** (Finlandia Hall), one of the last creations of Alvar Aalto, and, a bit farther up Mannerheimintie, the new **Suomen Kansallisoppera** (Finnish National Opera), a striking example of Scandinavian architecture. If you can't make it to a concert there, take a guided tour. Finlandia Hall will be shut for interior renovations from 1994 to February 1995. Behind the hall and the Opera House lies the inland bay of Töölönlahti, and almost opposite the ⑰ hall stands the **Suomen Kansallismuseo** (National Museum), another example of National Romantic exotica in which Eliel Saarinen played a part. *Admission: FIM 10 adults, FIM 5 children. Free on Tues. Open June–Aug., Wed.–Sun. 11–5, Tues. 11–8; Sept.–May, Wed.–Sun. 11–4, Tues. 11–8.*

⑱ Tucked away in a labyrinth of streets to the west is the strikingly modern **Temppeliaukion Kirkko** (Temple Square Church). Carved out of solid rock and topped with a copper dome, this landmark is a center for religious activities, church services, and concerts. From here it's only a short distance back to Mannerheimintie, where you can pick up any streetcar for the downtown area. *Lutherinkatu 3. Open weekdays 10–8, Sat. 10–6, Sun. hours vary.*

Off the Beaten Track

Located in Espoo, Helsinki's next-door neighbor, is the garden city of **Tapiola,** one of Finland's architectural highlights. Designed by Alvar Aalto, the urban landscape of alternating high and low residential buildings, fountains, gardens, and swimming pools blends into the natural surroundings. What began as an experiment in communal, affordable housing has now lost its radical appeal, but Tapiola still holds interest for anyone interested in urban planning. Sightseeing tours are available from the Espoo City Tourist Office, tel. 90/460311.

Akseli Gallen Kallela (1865–1931) was one of Finland's greatest artists. His studio-home can be seen at Gallen-Kallelan tie 27, Tarvaspää. To get there, take tram No. 4 to Munkkiniemi, then it's a 1 ½-mile walk through the woods. *Admission: FIM 35 adults, FIM*

15 children. Open mid-May–Aug., Mon.–Thurs. 10–8, Fri.–Sun.
10–5; Sept.–mid-May, Tues.–Sat. 10–4, Sun. 10–5.

Shopping

Shopping Districts and Specialty Shops You should find everything you need on **Pohjoisesplanadi** (North Esplanade) and **Aleksanterinkatu**, in the **Forum Shopping Mall** at Mannerheimintie 20, or on the pedestrian mall **Iso Roobertinkatu.** You can make purchases until 10 PM, seven days a week, in the shops along the Tunneli underpass leading from the Railway Station.

Some of the shops in **Kiseleff Bazaar** and along Eteläesplanadi and Pohjoisesplanadi are open on Sundays from noon to 4 in summer. Along the latter you'll find some of Finland's top design houses: **Hackman Arabia** (Iittala and Nuutajärvi) ceramics and glass at No. 25; **Pentik** leather at No. 27C; **Aarikka** accessories, and wooden toys at No. 25–27 and Eteläesplanadi 8; **Marimekko** fashions at No. 31 and Eteläesplanadi 14; and **Artek** furniture and ceramics at Eteläesplanadi 18. Helsinki's three top jewelry boutiques are almost adjacent: **Galerie Björn Weckström**, Unioninkatu 30; **Kalevala Koru,** Unioninkatu 25; and **Kaunis Koru,** Kiseleff Bazaar.

Department Stores **Stockmann's,** a huge store that fills an entire block between Aleksanterinkatu, Mannerheimintie, and Keskuskatu, is your best bet if you want to find everything under one roof.

Markets The **Kauppatori market** beside the South Harbor (*see* Exploring Helsinki, *above*) is an absolute must. Also try to find time for the variety of goods at the **Hietalahti flea market,** located at the west end of Bulevardi on Hietalahti. (Open Mon.–Sat. 8 AM–2 PM; mid-May–Aug., also open weekdays 3:30 PM–8 PM and Sat. 10 AM–4 PM.)

Dining

For details and price-category definitions, *see* Dining in Staying in Finland, *above*. Best bets are indicated by a star ★.

Very Expensive **Alexander Nevski.** Helsinki has gained a reputation for having the best Russian-cuisine restaurants in Scandinavia. Situated right
★ across from the Havis Amanda statue is Finland's most celebrated Russian restaurant, Alexander Nevski. The decor of the restaurant is dominated by hues of green and palm trees, in the Russian-French style of 19th-century St. Petersburg restaurants. Be sure to try the blinis and yellow grouse baked in a clay pot. *Pohjoisesplanadi 17, tel. 90/639610. Reservations advised. AE, DC, MC, V. No dinner Sun, closed Christmas, and June 24–25.*

★ **Amadeus.** Situated in an old town house near the South Harbor, Amadeus specializes in game dishes, such as baked ptarmigan, smoked duck, and reindeer fillets. *Sofiankatu 4, tel. 90/626676. Reservations advised. AE, DC, MC, V. Closed Sun., Christmas, June 24–25, and bank holidays.*

Galateia. Located on top of the Hotel Inter-Continental with a magnificent view of Töölö bay and the city is Helsinki's best seafood restaurant. Try the sautéed jumbo shrimps with prosciutto, nuts, and basil vinaigrette for starters, followed by broiled salmon with sweetbread mousse and pork sauce. *Mannerheimintie 46, tel. 90/405-5900 or 90/40551. Reservations advised. AE, DC, MC, V. Open weekday evenings only. Closed weekends, and bank holidays.*

★ **Palace Gourmet.** One of Helsinki's top restaurants, Palace Gourmet offers elegant surroundings with a splendid view of South Harbor. Chef Markus Maulavirta has been with the restaurant for two years and specializes in French and Finnish fare. For an appetizer try the tartar steak with aspic and caviar, and follow it with glow-fried perch. *Eteläranta 10, tel. 90/134561. Reservations advised. AE, DC, MC, V. Closed weekends, bank holidays, and July.*

Savoy. With its airy dining room overlooking the Esplanade park, the Savoy is a favorite for business lunches. The interior was designed by the architect Alvar Aalto in the functionalist style. The restaurant was Finnish statesman Marshal Baron Carl Gustaf Mannerheim's favorite, and he is rumored to have introduced the *Vorschmack* (minced lamb and anchovies) recipe to the restaurant. *Eteläesplanadi 14, tel. 90/176571. Reservations advised. AE, DC, MC, V. Closed weekends, Easter, June 24–25, and bank holidays.*

Expensive **Bellevue.** Established in 1917, Bellevue is one of Helsinki's oldest
★ restaurants. Despite its French name, the restaurant is Russian, both in decor and cuisine. Fillet à la Novgorod and chicken à la Kiev are the authentic articles here. *Rahapajankatu 3, tel. 90/179560. Reservations advised. AE, DC, MC, V. No lunch weekends. Closed Christmas, Easter, June 25 and 26.*

Kosmos. Located only a short walking distance from Stockmann's is Kosmos, which serves good food at reasonable prices for Helsinki. The restaurant is a favorite among artists, writers, and journalists during the evenings, and it's popular among business people during lunchtime. One of Kosmos's specialties is sweetbread. *Kalevankatu 3, tel. 90/607603. Reservations advised. AE, DC, MC, V. Closed weekends and national holidays.*

Sipuli. Sipuli, at the foot of the Russian Orthodox Uspenski Cathedral, gets its name from the golden onion-shape cupolas that adorn the cathedral. In a brick warehouse building dating from the late 19th century, Sipuli specializes in game and fish dishes. The skylight offers a spectacular view of the cathedral. *Kanavaranta 3, tel. 90/179900. Reservations advised. AE, DC, MC, V. No lunch. Closed weekends, Christmas, and June 24–July 1.*

Svenska Klubben. The restaurant resembles an English stately home. You can enjoy an aperitif before having lunch or dinner at the lobby bar, which has a fireplace and big, comfortable armchairs. Svenska Klubben specializes in local fish, roe, game, and fowl dishes. *Maurinkatu 6, tel. 90/135–4706. Reservations advised. AE, DC, MC, V. Closed weekends, Christmas, June 20–Aug. 15, and bank holidays.*

Troikka. The Troikka takes you back to czarist times in decor, paintings, and music, and offers exceptionally good food and friendly service. Try the Siberian *pelmens* (small meat pasties). *Caloniuksenkatu 3, tel. 90/445229. Reservations advised. AE, DC, MC, V. Closed July 1–15, Sun., and national holidays.*

Moderate **Café Raffaello.** This spot has gained a good reputation for its reasonable prices and tasty pasta, salad, and meat dishes. Raffaello's Italian decor in strong browns adds a pleasant touch of warmth. *Aleksanterinkatu 46, tel. 90/653930. Reservations advised. AE, DC, MC, V. Closed Christmas.*

Omenapuu. This cozy family restaurant, set in the midst of a busy shopping district, features special dishes for weight watchers. *Keskuskatu 6, second floor, tel. 90/630205. Reservations advised for lunch. AE, DC, MC, V. Closed Christmas.*

Inexpensive **China.** Located in the heart of Helsinki, China specializes in Cantonese fare. The Peking Duck is recommended. *Annankatu 25, tel. 90/640258. Reservations advised. AE, DC, MC, V. Closed Christmas, June 24–25.*

Perho Mechelin. This is the restaurant connected with Helsinki's catering school. During summer the emphasis is on Finnish food, particularly salmon. *Mechelininkatu 7, tel. 90/493481. Reservations advised. AE, DC, MC, V. Closed Christmas, Easter, and June 24–25.*

Pizzeria Dennis. This pleasant spot serves the best pasta and pizza in town. *Fredrikinkatu 36, tel. 90/694–5271. Reservations advised. DC, MC, V. Closed Christmas, June 24–25.*

Lodging

For details and price-category definitions, *see* Lodging in Staying in Finland, *above*. Best bets are indicated by a star ★.

Very Expensive

Hesperia. Enlarged and redecorated in 1986, the Hesperia is modern in the best Finnish tradition and just a short stroll from the center of the city. *Mannerheimintie 50, 00260, tel. 90/43101, fax 90/431–0995. 360 rooms, 287 with bath and 73 with shower. Facilities: sauna, pool, golf simulator, nightclub, helipad. AE, DC, MC, V. Closed Christmas.*

★ **Inter-Continental.** This is the most popular hotel in the city—with American visitors, at least. It's modern and close to Finlandia Hall, although its rooms are on the small side. Restaurant noise may disturb guests staying on the top floor. *Mannerheimintie 46–48, 00260, tel. 90/40551, fax 90/405–5255. 555 rooms with bath. Facilities: sauna, pool, 2 restaurants, coffee shop, bar, barber shop. AE, DC, MC, V.*

Palace. The Palace has a splendid location overlooking the South Harbor—but make sure you ask for a room with a view; these rooms are on the ninth floor. *Eteläranta 10, 00130, tel. 90/134561, fax 90/654786. 50 rooms with bath or shower. Facilities: 2 restaurants, sauna. AE, DC, MC, V. Sometimes closed during Christmas.*

Ramada Presidentti. Located in the heart of Helsinki is the Ramada Presidentti, one of the city's top luxury hotels. Apart from its spacious rooms, the hotel also offers a wide range of facilities. In 1991, Finland's first international casino was inaugurated at the hotel. The hotel's main restaurant, Four Seasons, serves tasty buffet meals. *Eteläinen Rautatiekatu 4, 00100, tel. 90/6911, fax 90/694–7886. 495 rooms with bath. Facilities: sauna, pool, nightclub, casino, 2 restaurants, 2 coffee shops. AE, DC, MC, V.*

Rivoli Jardin. Rivoli Jardin is a central town house, with all rooms overlooking a quiet courtyard. The rooms are rather small but well equipped and attractively designed. Breakfast is served in the winter garden, but there's no restaurant. *Kasarmikatu 40, 00130, tel. 90/177880, fax 90/656988. 53 rooms with shower. Facilities: sauna. AE, DC, MC, V. Closed Christmas.*

SAS Royal Hotel. This luxury hotel is centrally located and a 10-minute walk from the Railway Station. The rooms are elegant and decorated in one of three styles: Scandinavian (light woods), Oriental (lots of bamboo), and Italian (strong colors). If you want more space and privacy, try the business class rooms (art deco style) located on the hotel's top floors. The Johan Ludvig restaurant specializes in tasty dishes like prime rib of beef. The hotel's other restaurant, Ströget, is cheaper and serves pasta, salads, hamburgers, and Danish sandwiches. *Runeberginkatu 2, 00100, tel. 90/69580, fax 90/6958–7100. 260 rooms with bath. Facilities: 2 restaurants, sauna, bar, summer terrace. AE, DC, MC, V.*

★ **Strand Inter-Continental.** Centrally located, the hotel is adjacent to the Old City on the waterfront. The hotel's distinctive use of stone, granite, and marble in the central lobby is accentuated by a soaring atrium and softened by a cozy fireplace. There is a choice of restaurants—from Pamir's elegant gourmet dishes of seafood, steak, and game to the Atrium Plaza's buffet restaurant for light meals. *John Stenbergin ranta 4, 00530, tel. 90/39351, fax 90/761362. 200 rooms with bath. Facilities: 2 restaurants, sauna, indoor pool, lounge-bar. AE, DC, MC, V.*

Expensive **Hotel Grand Marina.** Housed in an early 19th-century customs warehouse in the plush Katajanokka Island neighborhood, the Hotel Grand Marina is one of the best congress centers in Finland. The hotel's good location, friendly service, and ample modern facilities have made it a favorite among tourists. *Katajanokkalaituri 7, 00160 Helsinki, tel. 90/16661, fax 90/664764. 462 rooms with shower or bath. Facilities: 5 restaurants, congress center, bar, pub, sauna. AE, DC, MC, V. Moderate (weekends)–Expensive (weekdays).*

Lordhotel. In a handsome stone castle built in 1903, each room offers contemporary-style furnishing in peaceful blue and gray tones. *Lönnrotinkatu 29, 00180, tel. 90/680–1680, fax 90/680–1315. 49 rooms with shower or bath (17 rooms with Jacuzzi). Facilities: restaurant, bar, saunas, banquet hall, conference rooms, free parking. AE, DC, MC, V.*

Rantasipi Airport Hotel. Just 3.2 kilometers (2 miles) from the airport, the Rantasipi was built in 1981 and expanded in 1986. The rooms are rather small, but airport shuttle service is provided. *Robert Huberintie 4, 01510 Vantaa, tel. 90/87051, fax 90/822846. 300 rooms with shower. Facilities: restaurant, sauna, pool, piano bar. AE, DC, MC, V.*

★ **Seurahuone.** This is a traditional town house from 1914, renovated in 1982, facing the Railway Station. The room decor ranges from sleek modern to crystal chandeliers and brass bedsteads. Streetside rooms get some traffic noise. *Kaivokatu 12, 00100, tel. 90/170441, fax 90/664170. 118 rooms; 95 with bath, 23 with shower. Facilities: sauna, café, pub. AE, DC, MC, V.*

Moderate **Arthur.** A property of the Helsinki YMCA, Arthur is located on a quiet, central street and is unpretentious but comfortable. *Vuorikatu 17B, 00100, tel. 90/173441, fax 90/626880. 144 rooms with bath or shower. Facilities: sauna, restaurant. AE, DC, MC, V. Closed Christmas.*

Aurora. About a mile from the city center, the Aurora is just opposite the Linnanmäki amusement park. Reasonable prices, cozy rooms, and good facilities have made this hotel a favorite with families. *Helsinginkatu 50, 00530, tel. 90/717400, fax 90/714240. 70 rooms with shower, 6 with bath. Facilities: restaurant, sauna, pool, squash courts, health spa. AE, DC, MC, V. Closed Dec. 23–Jan. 3.*

Marttahotelli. The rooms here are small but pleasantly decorated. The hotel is only a 10-minute walk from the Railway Station. *Uudenmankatu 24, 00120, tel. 90/646211, fax 90/680–1266. 45 rooms with shower or bath. Facilities: sauna. AE, DC, MC, V. Closed Christmas, Easter, and June 24–25.*

Merihotelli. Located on the seafront, the Merihotelli is a 10-minute walk from the center of town. The rooms are somewhat small but modern; those with a sea view get some traffic noise. *John Stenbergin ranta 6, 00530, tel. 90/708711, fax 90/760271. 87 rooms with shower. Facilities: sauna, 2 restaurants, coffee shop. AE, DC, MC, V.*

Inexpensive **Academica.** Fully renovated in 1992, the Academica is a town house with simple but adequate rooms, 10 minutes' walk from the town center. *Hietaniemenkatu 14, 00100, tel. 90/402–0206, fax 90/441201. 115 rooms with shower and kitchenette. Facilities: sauna, pool, indoor tennis, disco (weekends), self-service laundry, solarium. AE, DC, MC, V. Closed Sept.–May.*

Skatta. Located in the elegant neighborhood of Katajanokka Island, and 3 kilometers (2 miles) from the Railway Station, is modest Skatta. Each room has a kitchenette. *Linnankatu 3, 00160, tel. 90/ 659233 or 90/669984, fax 90/631352. 24 rooms with shower. Facilities: sauna, gym, solarium. AE, DC, MC, V. Sometimes closed during Christmas.*

The Arts

For a list of events, pick up the free publication *Helsinki This Week*, available in hotels and tourist offices. For recorded program information in English, dial 0700–9–2010. A central reservations office for all events is **Lippupalvelu,** Mannerheimintie 5, tel. 9700–4700 or 90/664466 when calling from abroad. Call **Tiketti,** Yrjönkatu 29C, tel. 90/693–2255, when making reservations for small concerts.

Theater   Although all performances are in Finnish or Swedish, summertime productions in such bucolic settings as **Suomenlinna Island, Kekuspuisto Park, Mustikkamaa Island,** the **Rowing Stadium** (operettas), **Indoor Ice Rink** (rock concerts), and the **Savoy Theater** (ballet and music performances) make enjoyable entertainment. The splendid Kansallisooppera (Finnish National Opera) opened in 1993 in a waterside park by **Töölönlahti** just a few hundred feet from Finlandia Hall.

Concerts   The two main locations for musical events are **Finlandia Hall** (tel. 90/ 40241) and **Temppeliaukio Church** (*see* Exploring, *above*).

Festivals   Finland holds many festivals throughout the country, especially during the summer months. The **Helsinki Festival** is said to be the biggest in Scandinavia. For more than two weeks during August to September, the city is turned over to the arts. Scores of musical happenings and art exhibitions are organized throughout Helsinki. Each Helsinki Festival has a theme. Composer Esa Pekka Salonen was named festival director for 1995. Contact Helsinki Festival, Unioninkatu 28, tel. 90/659688. For more information on festivals, call Finland Festivals, Mannerheimintie 40, B49, tel. 90/445763 or 90/445686.

Nightlife

Nightclubs   The most popular nightclub in town is the **Hesperia** (Hesperia, Kivelänkatu 2, tel. 90/43101). **Fizz** (Arctia Hotel Marski, Mannerheimintie 10, tel. 90/68061), **Fennia** (Mikonkatu 17, tel. 90/666355), **Page** (Keskuskatu 3, tel. 90/175655), and **Kaivohuone** (Kaivohuone Kaivopuisto, tel. 90/177881) are also popular.

Discos   The liveliest and most popular are **Old Baker's** (Mannerheimintie 10, tel. 90/641579) and **Fanny & Alexander** (Pitkänsillanranta 3, tel. 90/ 701–4424). The most popular among young people is **KY Exit** (Pohjoinen Rautatiekatu 21, tel. 90/407238).

The Lakelands

This is a region of lakes, forests, and islands in southeastern and central Finland. The light in these northern latitudes has a magical softness, and the vistas are constantly changing. For centuries the lakeland region was a buffer between the warring empires of Sweden and Russia. After visiting the people of the lakelands, you should have a basic understanding of the Finnish word *sisu* (guts), a

The Lakelands

quality that has kept Finns independent, fiercely guarding their neutrality.

Getting Around

Savonlinna is the best-placed town in the Lakelands and can make a convenient base from which to begin exploring. You can fly to the Savonlinna area from Helsinki in 40 minutes; a connecting bus takes you the remaining 16 kilometers (10 miles) into town. By train, the journey takes 5½ hours; by bus, 6 hours.

If you travel by car, you can do the lake trips as separate excursions. The alternative is to take advantage of the excellent network of air, rail, bus, and boat transportation. Take the boat from Savonlinna to Kuopio in 12 hours (**Roll Cruises,** tel. 971/262–6744). From Kuopio, take the 320-kilometer (200-mile) cross-country bus ride via Jyväskylä to Tampere. Continue by boat to Hämeenlinna for a little over eight hours (**Finnish Silverline,** tel. 931/124803). The final leg by bus or train back to Helsinki takes about 1¼ hours.

Guided Tours

A program of **Friendly Finland Tours,** available through a number of travel agencies, offers escorted lakeland packages from two to 11 days, starting from Helsinki. Brochures are available from the **Finnish Tourist Board** (Eteläesplanadi 4, tel. 90/403011) and its overseas offices (*see* Government Tourist Offices in Chapter 1).

Tourist Information

Hämeenlinna (Sibeliuksenkatu 5A, 13100 Hämeenlinna, tel. 917/
621–2388). Open June and July, weekdays 9–5, Sat. 9–2; Aug.–
May, weekdays 9–5.

Kuopio (Haapaniemenkatu 17, 70110 Kuopio, tel. 971/182584). Open
weekdays 9–5; June–Aug., weekdays 9–6, Sat. 10–2.

Savonlinna (Puistokatu 1, 57100 Savonlinna, tel. 957/273492). Open
June and Aug., daily 8–6; July, daily 8 AM–10 PM; Sept.–May, weekdays 9 AM–4 PM.

Tampere (Verkatehtaankatu 2, 33211 Tampere, tel. 931/212–6652).
Open June–Aug., weekdays 8:30 AM–8 PM, Sat. 8:30–6, Sun. 11:30–6;
Sept.–May, weekdays 8:30–5.

Exploring the Lakelands

Savonlinna   The center of **Savonlinna** is a series of islands linked by bridges.
First, stop at the tourist office for information; then cross the bridge
east to the **open-air market** that flourishes alongside the main passenger quay. It's from here that you can catch the boat to Kuopio. In
days when waterborne traffic was the major form of transportation,
Savonlinna was the central hub of the passenger fleet serving
Saimaa, the largest lake system in Europe. Now the lake traffic is
dominated by cruise and sightseeing boats.

A 10-minute stroll from the quay to the southeast brings you to
Savonlinna's most famous sight, the castle of **Olavinlinna.** First built
in 1475 to protect Finland's eastern border, the castle retains its
medieval character and is one of Scandinavia's best-preserved historic monuments. Still surrounded by water that once formed part
of its defensive strength, the fortress rises majestically out of the
lake. The Savonlinna Opera Festival is held in the courtyard each
July. The combination of music and setting is spellbinding. You will
need to make reservations well in advance (tel. 957/514700 or 957/
273492), both for tickets and for hotel rooms. *Castle admission:
FIM 14 adults, FIM 7 children; includes a guided tour. Open June–
Aug., daily 10–5; Sept.–May, daily 10–3.*

Close to the castle are the 19th-century steam schooners, *Mikko,
Salama,* and *Savonlinna.* The *Salama* houses an excellent museum
on the history of lake traffic, including the fascinating floating tim-
ber trains that are still a common sight on Saimaa today. *Admission:
FIM 12 adults, FIM 6 children. Open July, daily 10–8; Aug.–June,
Tues.–Sun. 11–5.*

The most popular excursion from Savonlinna is to **Taidekeskus
Retretti** (Retretti Art Center). You can take either a two-hour boat
ride or a 30-minute, 29-kilometer (18-mile) bus trip. The journey by
bus takes you along the 8-kilometer (5-mile) ridge of **Punkaharju.**
This amazing ridge of pine-covered rocks, which rises out of the water and separates the lakes on either side, predates the Ice Age. At
times it narrows to only 25 feet, yet it still manages to accommodate
a road and train tracks. *Admission: FIM 60 adults, FIM 55 senior
citizens and students, FIM 25 children. Open July, daily 10–7; May
21–June and Aug., daily 10–6.*

Near Retretti is the **Punkaharju National Hotel.** The building
started as a gamekeeper's lodge for Czar Nicholas I in 1845, but has
been subsequently enlarged and restored; it is now a restful spot for
a meal or an overnight visit.

Kuopio The 12-hour boat trip from Savonlinna to **Kuopio** is probably the best opportunity you'll get to feel the soul of the Finnish lakeland. Meals are available on board. The boat arrives at Kuopio passenger harbor, where you'll find a small evening market in action daily from 3 to 10. If you go by car, the best route is by Highways 14, 464, and 5, via Rantasalmi and Varkaus.

The Kuopio Tourist Office is located close to the **Tori** (marketplace). The Tori should be one of the places you visit first, for it is one of the most colorful outdoor markets in Finland. *Open May–Aug., Mon.–Sat. 7–3; Sept.–Apr., Mon.–Sat., 7–2.*

Only a 15-minute walk from the heart of Kuopio is another picturesque market square by the Kuopio passenger harbor. *Open May 15–Aug. 31, daily noon–10.*

The **Orthodox Church Museum** has one of the most interesting and unusual collections of its kind in the world. When Karelia was ceded to the Soviet Union after World War II, the religious art was taken out of the monasteries and brought to Kuopio. The collection is eclectic and, of its type, one of the rarest in the world. *Karjalankatu 1, Kuopio, tel. 971/261-8818. Open May–Aug., Tues.–Sun. 10–3; Sept.–Apr., weekdays noon–3, weekends noon–5.*

Visitors who are fascinated by the treasures in the museum will want to visit the Orthodox convent of Lintula and the **Monastery of Valamo.** The monastery is a center for Russian Orthodox religious and cultural life in Finland. The precious 18th-century icons and sacred objects are housed in the main church and in the icon conservation center. The Orthodox library is the most extensive in Finland and is open to visitors. Church services are held daily. There is a café-restaurant, and hotel and hostel accommodations are available at the monastery. It can be reached by car and bus routes from Kuopio, Joensuu, and Varkaus. *Uusi Valamo, tel. 972/561911 (972/561959 for hotel reservations). Admission free. Guided tours: FIM 20 adults, FIM 5 children. Open daily 10–6.*

The **convent of Lintula** can be reached by boat from Valamo, or you can visit both the convent and the monastery by boat on scenic day excursions from Kuopio that run from June 16 through August 14. Tickets, available from the tourist office, cost FIM 210 for adults and FIM 90 for children.

Puijo Tower is best visited at sunset, when the lakes shimmer with reflected light. The slender tower is located 3 kilometers (2 miles) northwest of Kuopio. It has two observation decks and a revolving restaurant on top where you can enjoy the marvelous views. *Open June 1–Aug., daily 10 AM–10 PM; Sept.–May, daily 10–8.*

Tampere The 320-kilometer (200-mile) journey from Kuopio to **Tampere** will take four to five hours, whether you travel by car or bus. The train ride from Helsinki to Tampere takes about two hours. Almost every guide will inform you that Tampere, the country's third-largest city, is Finland's Pittsburgh. However, the resemblance begins and ends with the concentrated presence here of industry—the settings themselves have little in common.

From about the year 1000, this part of Finland was a base from which traders and hunters set out on their expeditions to northern Finland and even to Lapland. But it was not until 1779 that a Swedish king, Gustav III, actually founded the town of Tampere. One hundred and three years later, a Scotsman by the name of James Finlayson came to the infant city and established a factory for spinning cotton. This was perhaps the beginning of "big business" in

Finland. The firm of Finlayson exists today and is still one of the country's large industrial enterprises.

An isthmus, little more than half a mile wide at its narrowest point, separates the lakes Näsijärvi and Pyhäjärvi, and at one spot the **Tammerkoski Rapids** provide an outlet for the waters of one to cascade through to the other. Called the "Mother of Tampere," these rapids provide a small part of the power on which the town's livelihood depends. Their natural beauty has been preserved in spite of the factories on either bank, and the well-designed public buildings of the city grouped around them enhance their general effect. Also in the heart of town is **Hämeensilta Bridge,** with its four statues by the well-known Finnish sculptor Wäinö Aaltonen.

Close to the Hämeensilta bridge, near the high-rise Hotel Ilves, are some old factory buildings that have been restored as shops and boutiques. Nearby, at Verkatehtaankatu 2, is the city tourist office, where you can buy a 24-hour **Tourist Ticket** (FIM 25 adults, FIM 20 children) that allows unlimited travel on local city transportation.

Parts of the ridge of **Pyynikki** separating the two lakes form a natural park, including the Särkänniemi peninsula, about a 20-minute walk northwest of the city center. On the way there, visit one of Tampere's best small museums, **The Amuri Museum of Workers' Housing.** It consists of a block of old timber houses, with descriptions and illustrations of how the original tenants lived; it is so well done that you half expect them to return at any minute. *Makasiininkatu 12. Admission: FIM 15 adults, FIM 5 children. Open May 11–Sept. 19, Tues.–Sat. 9–5, Sun. 11–5.*

At Särkänniemi, a 15-minute walk from downtown Tampere, is Finland's tallest structure, the 168-meter (550-foot) **Näsinneula Observation Tower.** There is an observatory on top, as well as a revolving restaurant. The views are magnificent, commanding the lake, forest, and town. The contrast between the industrial maze of Tampere at your feet and the serenity of the lakes stretching out to meet the horizon is unforgettable. *Open May–Aug., daily 10–10; Sept.–Apr., weekdays 9–3, weekends 11–6.*

The same building complex houses the first **planetarium** in Scandinavia and a well-planned **aquarium,** which includes a separate dolphinarium. Near this complex is another striking example of Finnish architecture, the **Sarah Hildén Art Museum,** where modern Finnish and international artists (including Miró, Leger, Picasso, and Chagall) are on display. *Joint admission: FIM 60 adults, FIM 30 children; Hildén Museum only: FIM 15 adults, FIM 5 children. Open June–Aug., daily 11–6; Sept.–May, Tues.–Sun. 11–6.*

On the east side of the town is the modern **Kaleva Church.** What may appear from the outside to be a grain elevator is, in fact, as seen from the interior, a soaring monument to space and light. *Open May–Aug., daily 10–6; Sept.–Apr., daily 11–3.*

Most buildings in Tampere, including the cathedral, are comparatively modern. However, though the cathedral was built only in 1907, it is worth a visit to see some of the best-known masterpieces of Finnish art, including Magnus Encknell's frescoes, *The Resurrection,* and a few works by Hugo Simberg, such as *Wounded Angel* and *Garden of Death.*

It was in Tampere that Lenin and Stalin first met, and this fateful occasion is commemorated with displays of photos and mementoes in the **Lenin Museum.** *Hämeenpuisto 28. Admission: FIM 10 adults, FIM 3 children. Open weekdays 9–5, weekends 11–4.*

One of the most popular excursions from Tampere is the **Poet's Way** boat tour along Lake Näsijärvi. The boat passes through the agricultural parish of Ruovesi, where J. L. Runeberg, Finland's national poet, used to live. Shortly before the boat docks at Virrat, you'll pass through the straights of Visuvesi, where many artists and writers spend their summers. *Finnish Silverline and Poet's Way, PL 87, Verkatehtaankatu 2, 33221 Tampere, tel. 931/212-4804. Round-trip fare: FIM 220.*

Hämeenlinna   The Finnish Silverline's white motor ships leave Tampere for **Hämeenlinna** from the Laukontori terminal. If you're traveling by car, take Highway 3 and stop en route at the famous **Iittala Glassworks,** which offers guided museum tours and has a shop. The magnificent glass is produced by top designers, and the "seconds" are bargains you won't find elsewhere. *Museum open May–Aug., daily 10–8; Sept.–Apr., daily 10–4; shop open May–Aug., daily 9–8.*

Hämeenlinna's secondary school has educated many famous Finns, among them composer Jean Sibelius (1865–1957). The only surviving timber house in the town center is the **birthplace of Sibelius,** a modest dwelling built in 1834. Here you can listen to tapes of his music and see the harmonium he played when he was a child. *Hallituskatu 11. Admission: FIM 10 adults, FIM 5 children; admission includes a free guided tour. Open May–Aug., daily 10–4; Sept.–Apr., daily noon–4.*

The much-altered medieval **Häme Castle,** Finland's oldest castle, on the lakeshore half a mile north of the town center, doesn't compare with Savonlinna's, but it has seen a lot of action in its time and has been used as a granary and a prison. *Admission: FIM 14 adults, FIM 7 children. Open May–Aug., daily 10–6; Sept.–Apr., daily 10–4.*

Hattula Church, 6 kilometers (3½ miles) to the north, is the most famous of Finland's medieval churches. The interior is a fresco gallery of biblical scenes whose vicious little devils and soulful saints are as clear and fresh as when they were first painted around 1510. The admission fee includes entry to **Hämeenlinna Art Museum** (Viipurintie 2, tel. 917/621–2669) and to the **Hämeenlinna History Museum** (Lukionkatu 6, tel. 917/621–2560), which offers exhibitions on 19th-century life in the city. *Admission: FIM 20 adults, FIM 10 children. Open May 15–Aug. 15, daily 11–5.*

Rail and bus departures to Helsinki are frequent. If you're traveling by car, take the new Highway 12. As you pass by **Riihimäki,** you'll see signs to the **Finnish Glass Museum.** Follow them! It's an outstanding display of the history of glass from early Egyptian times to the present, beautifully arranged in an old glass factory. *Admission: FIM 15 adults, FIM 10 children. Open Apr.–Sept., daily 10–6; Oct.–Dec., Feb., Mar., Tues.–Sun. 10–6.*

Dining and Lodging

For details and price-category definitions, *see* Dining and Lodging in Staying in Finland, *above.* Best bets are indicated by a star ★.

Hämeenlinna   **Huviretki.** Located in the heart of the city at the Cumulus Hotel,
Dining   Huviretki offers friendly service and a wide range of standard international fare, such as pepper steak and honey chicken. *Raatihuonentie 16–18, tel. 917/64881. Reservations advised. AE, DC, MC, V. Moderate.*
Piiparkakkutalo. Located in a renovated old timber building,

Piiparkakkutalo offers fine Finnish fare. *Kirkkorinne 2, tel. 917/ 612–1606. Reservations advised. AE, DC, MC, V. Moderate.*

Lodging ★ **Rantasipi Aulanko.** One of Finland's top hotels sits on the lakeshore in a beautifully landscaped park 6.4 kilometers (4 miles) from town. *13210 Hämeenlinna, tel. 917/658801, fax 917/21922. 245 rooms with bath. Facilities: saunas, pool, tennis, golf, riding, boating, night-club, tax-free shop. AE, DC, MC, V. Expensive.*

Kuopio
Dining **Mustalammas.** Located near the passenger harbor, Mustalammas has been attractively adapted from a beer cellar and features steaks and basic fish dishes. *Satamakatu 4, tel. 971/262–3494. Reservations advised. AE, DC, MC, V. Closed lunch. Expensive.*

Sampo. Situated in the town center, Sampo specializes in *muikku* (vendace), a kind of whitefish. Try the smoked variety. The atmosphere is unpretentious and lively. *Kauppakatu 13, tel. 971/261– 4677. AE, DC, MC, V. Moderate.*

Lodging **Arctia.** Completed in 1987, the Arctia is the most modern and best equipped of local hotels. It has all the advantages of a lakefront location and is close to the center of town. *Satamakatu 1, 70100 Kuopio, tel. 971/195111, fax 971/195170. 141 rooms with bath or shower. Facilities: sauna, swimming pool, Jacuzzi, solarium, boat rental. AE, DC, MC, V. Expensive.*

Hotelli Iso-Valkeinen. Located by the lakeshore and only 5 kilometers (2.5 miles) from the town center, this hotel has large, quiet rooms. *Päiväranta, 70420 Kuopio, tel. 971/364–1444, fax 971/364– 1344. 100 rooms with shower. Facilities: 2 restaurants, nightclub, 2 saunas, swimming pool, mini-golf, tennis, swimming beach, fishing, boat rental. AE, DC, MC, V. Moderate.*

Rauhalahti. About 4.8 kilometers (3 miles) from the town center, Rauhalahti is set near the lakeshore and has a number of amenities catering to sportsmen and families. The hotel has three restaurants, including the tavern-style Vanha Apteekkari—a local favorite. *Katiskaniementie 8, 70700 Kuopio, tel. 971/361–1700, fax 971/361– 1843. 106 rooms with bath or shower, 15 apartments, and 5 inexpensive youth hotel rooms. Facilities: 3 restaurants, saunas, Jacuzzi, solarium, gymnasium, children's playroom, nightclub, tennis, horseback riding, squash, spa, boat rental. AE, DC, MC, V. Inexpensive–Moderate.*

Savonlinna
Dining **Rauhalinna.** This romantic turn-of-the-century timber villa was built by a general in the Imperial Russian Army. From town it's 16 kilometers (10 miles) by road, 40 minutes by boat. Both the food and atmosphere are old Russian, but some Finnish specialties are also available. *Lehtiniemi, tel. 957/523119. Reservations required during festival season. AE, DC, MC, V. Closed mid-Aug.–May. Expensive.*

Majakka. Centrally located, Majakka goes in for home cooking and a family atmosphere. *Satamakatu 11, tel. 957/21456. Reservations required during festival season. AE, DC, V. Moderate.*

Paviljonki. Paviljonki is connected with the Savonlinna restaurant school. Located 1 kilometer (½ mile) west of the city center, the restaurant serves homemade Finnish dishes. *Rajalahdenkatu 4, tel. 957/520960. MC, V. Moderate.*

Snellman. This small 1920s-style mansion is in the center of town. Meals are served against a quiet background of classical music. One of the specialties of the house is cold-salted salmon and steak with morel sauce. *Olavinkatu 31, tel. 957/273104. Reservations advised. AE, DC, MC, V. Moderate.*

Lodging **Casino Spa.** Built in the 1960s and renovated in 1986, the Casino Spa has a restful lakeside location on an island linked by a pedestrian bridge to the center of town. *Kylpylaitoksentie, Kasinosaari, 57130 Savonlinna, tel. 957/57500, fax 957/272524. 80 rooms with shower. Facilities: restaurant, saunas, pool, marina, spa treatment. AE, DC, MC, V. Expensive.*

Savonlinnan Seurahuone. This old town house is located near the market and passenger harbor. A new extension opened in 1989. Some older rooms are small. *Kauppatori 4–6, 57130 Savonlinna, tel. 957/5731, fax 957/273918. 84 rooms with shower. Facilities: 6 restaurants, lobby bar, saunas, disco, nightclub. AE, DC, MC, V. Expensive.*

Vuorilinna Summer Hotel. Guests at this modern hotel use the facilities, including the restaurant, of the nearby Casino Spa Hotel. *Kasinonsaari, 57130 Savonlinna, tel. 957/57500, fax 957/272524. 220 rooms, with shower for every 2 rooms. AE, DC, MC, V. Closed Sept.–May. Inexpensive.*

Tampere **Tiiliholvi.** Tiiliholvi is a romantic cellar restaurant that specializes in
Dining fish, meat, and game dishes. *Kauppakatu 10, tel. 931/212–1220. Reservations advised. AE, DC, MC, V. Expensive.*

Astor. The Astor has gained a good reputation for its tasty reindeer and snow grouse dishes. The romantic decor is dominated by dark red tones and wood paneling. In the evenings, candlelight and live piano music set the ambience. *Aleksis Kivenkatu 26, tel. 931/213–3522. Reservations advised. AE, DC, MC, V. Moderate.*

Bodega Salud. Bodega Salud has a well-earned reputation for Spanish specialties, though it also features such unconventional dishes as grilled alligator, rattlesnake soup, and stewed kangaroo. *Otavalankatu 10, tel. 931/223–5996. Reservations advised. AE, DC, MC, V. Moderate.*

Silakka. Although its atmosphere is casual and unpretentious, Silakka (Baltic herring) has earned a great reputation for its Finnish fish specialties. *Hatanpään valtatie 1, Koskikeskus, tel. 931/149740. DC, MC, V. Moderate.*

Lodging **Cumulus Koskikatu.** Overlooking the tamed rapids of Tammerkoski, Cumulus Koskikatu is central and modern. The Finnair terminal is in the same building. *Koskikatu 5, 33100 Tampere, tel. 931/242–4111, fax 931/242–4399. 230 rooms with shower. Facilities: restaurant, wine bar, nightclub, saunas, pool. AE, DC, MC, V. Moderate.*

Ilves. This hotel soars above a newly gentrified area of old warehouses near the city center. It is favored by Americans. *Hatanpään valtatie 1, 33100 Tampere, tel. 931/212–1212, fax 931/213–2565. 336 rooms with bath or shower, special floor for nonsmokers. Facilities: 3 restaurants, nightclub, gymnasium, saunas, pool, Jacuzzi. AE, DC, MC, V. Moderate.*

Domus Summer Hotel. About 3 kilometers (2 miles) from the center of town in the Kaleva district, this hotel is a good value. *Pellervonkatu 9, 33540 Tampere, tel. 931/550000, fax 931/222–5409. 197 rooms, 85 with shower. Facilities: saunas, pool. MC, V. Closed Sept.–May. Inexpensive.*

Finnish Lapland

Lapland is often called Europe's last wilderness, a region of endless forests, fells, and great silences. So often the arrival of settlers has obliterated all that came before, but here people have walked gently and left the virgin solitude of this country almost unspoiled. Now easily accessible by plane, train, or bus, this Arctic outpost offers

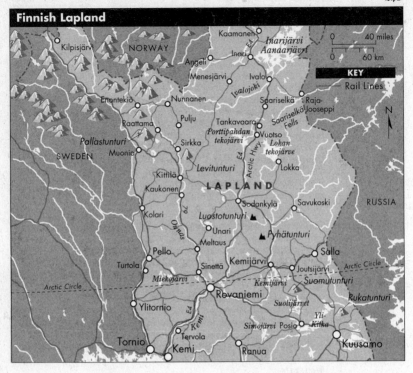

Finnish Lapland

comfortable hotels and modern amenities, yet you won't have to go very far to find yourself in an almost primordial solitude.

The oldest traces of human habitation in Finland have been found in Lapland, and hoards of Danish, English, and even Arabian coins indicate the existence of trade activities many centuries ago. The origins of the Lapps themselves are lost in the mists of history. There are only about 4,500 pure Lapps still living here; the remainder of the province's population of 220,000 are Finns. Until the 1930s, Lapland was still largely unexploited, still a region where any trip was an expedition. Then the Canadian-owned Petsamo Nickel Company completed the great road that connects Rovaniemi with the Arctic Sea. Building activities increased along this route (later to be known as the Arctic Highway), the land was turned and sown, and a few hotels were built to cater to increasing numbers of visitors.

Summer has the blessing of daylight up to 24 hours long and often beautiful weather to go with it. In early fall the colors are so fabulous that the Finns have a special word for it: *ruskaa*. If you can take the intense but dry cold, winter is also a fascinating time in Lapland, not only for the Northern Lights but for such experiences as the reindeer roundups.

In December and January, reindeer owners round up their herds from all over Lapland province and corral them by the thousands. Sometimes dressed in colorful costumes, the Lapps (and also many Finns) lasso the reindeer in true Wild West fashion, recognizing their own animals by brand marks on the ears. The roundups are attended by many buyers, for reindeer meat is considered a delicacy and is exported to the south and abroad.

To get to some of the remoter roundups, you may have to travel by taxi plane, though other corrals are near the road, especially around Ivalo, Inari, and Enontekiö. Most Lapps and northern Finns get there on the motorized sledges that have almost entirely replaced the much more attractive (and silent) reindeer-drawn *pulkka* (a kind of boat-shaped sleigh on one runner). In southern Lapland especially, an increasing number of roundups occur in the fall. Finding out exactly when and where a roundup is taking place isn't easy, for much depends on the whims of the weather and the reindeer, so you must check locally. The information offices in Rovaniemi, however, will be able to give some guidance.

A few words should be said about the Lapps—a proud, sensitive, and intelligent people who prefer their own name for themselves, *Same* (pronounced Sah-me)—some of whom resent visitors who regard them as a tourist attraction put there for their benefit. Modern influences (and intermarriage) have regrettably changed many aspects of their traditional way of life; for example, the attractive costumes are less frequently seen, except on festive occasions. The young, especially, have been affected by the changes, and many of them are far more interested in becoming teachers, lawyers, or engineers than in breeding reindeer or hunting from their remote homesteads. Yet others have found profit from selling souvenirs to the tourists. But most prefer to go about their daily lives, minding their own business. The Lady Day Church Festival in Enontekiö in March is a particularly colorful event, attended by many Lapps in their most brilliant costumes and usually featuring reindeer racing or lassoing competitions.

The experienced traveler who would like to roam through the wilds for days on end without meeting a fellow human being can still do so without any problem at all. Be warned, however, that climatic conditions change rapidly and often unpredictably, especially on those lonely Arctic fells. Always seek local advice and let your hotel and friends know where you're heading and how long you intend to be away. An attractive alternative is provided by organized canoeing or hiking trips with nights in huts or tents in the wilderness.

Getting Around

Rovaniemi is the best base for traveling around the Arctic area. It connects with Helsinki and the south by road, rail, and air links; there is even a car-train from Helsinki. Within the area, driving is the best way to get around, although a regular bus service connects most centers. There are also daily flights from Rovaniemi to Ivalo.

Guided Tours

Friendly Finland Tours (tel. 90/182–6333) features an escorted five-day "North Cape Tour" in summer or a five-day "Polar Safari Adventure Tour" in winter out of Helsinki. You can get details from the Finnish Tourist Board's overseas offices (*see* Government Tourist Offices in Chapter 1) or at Eteläesplanadi 4, 00130 Helsinki, tel. 90/403–01211.

Tourist Information

Inari (99870 Inari, tel. 9697/12521.

Rovaniemi (Ainonkatu 1, 96200, tel. 960/346270). Open June–Aug., weekdays 8–6, weekends 11:30–4; Sept.–May, weekdays 8–4. For further information on the region, contact **Lapland Travel** (Maakuntakatu 10, tel. 960/346052).

Saariselkä (Tuntturihotelli, PL 22, 99831 Saariselkä, tel. 9697/668122).

Sodankylä (Sodänkylän Matkailu Oy) (Jäämerentie 9, 99600, tel. 9693/13474).

Exploring Lapland

Rovaniemi Your best launching point is the town of **Rovaniemi,** where the Ounas and Kemi rivers meet almost on the Arctic Circle. Rovaniemi is the so-called Gateway to Lapland and the administrative hub and communications center of the province.

If you're expecting an Arctic shanty town, you're in for a surprise. Rovaniemi was nearly razed by the retreating German army in 1944, so what you'll see today is a modern city strongly influenced by Alvar Aalto's architecture. The old way of life is preserved in museums. During the process of rebuilding, the population rose from 8,000 to around 34,000, so be prepared for a contemporary city on the edge of the wilderness, with various amenities and some incredible architecture—notably **Lappia Hall,** the concert and congress center that also houses the world's northernmost professional theater, designed by Aalto. Rovaniemi also has the best shops in the region.

After collecting information from the tourist office, find a window table in the restaurant of the nearby **Pohjanhovi Hotel,** and plan your itinerary while gazing out at the fast-flowing Kemi River.

You can get a good instant introduction to the region and its natural history at the **Museum of the Province of Lapland** at the **Arktikum** (Arctic Research Center), located 1 kilometer (½ mile) north of Lappia House. The collection also includes exhibits of Same culture. *Pohjoisranta 4, Rovaniemi, tel. 960/317840. Admission: FIM 40 adults, FIM 10 children. Open June 15–Aug., daily 10–8; Sept.– June 14, Tues.–Sun. 10–6.*

But you'll get more of a feel for the living past from the **Pöykköla Museum,** located in 18th-century farm buildings 3 kilometers (2 miles) from the town center. *Admission: FIM 5 adults, FIM 2 children. Open June–Aug., Tues.–Sun. 1–4. Bus service available.*

Arctic The Arctic Highway (Highway 4) is the main artery of central and
Highway northern Lapland; you'll follow it north for most of this tour. Eight kilometers (5 miles) north of Rovaniemi, right on the Arctic Circle, is **Santa Claus's Workshop,** where gifts can be bought in midsummer for shipping any time of year, with a special Santa Claus Land stamp. For most visitors, however, the main attractions are Santa Claus and to mail postcards home from the special Arctic Circle post office. There's also a very good souvenir shopping complex and the impressive sight of the mountains of mail that pour in from children all over the world. Yes, all of it gets answered. *Admission free. Open June–Aug., daily 8–8; Sept.–Nov., weekdays 9–5; Dec., daily 9–7; Jan.–May, daily 9–5.*

After driving north for a couple of hours, you may want to take a short detour to the modern tourist center at **Luostotunturi** in the fell district of southern Lapland—you'll turn right onto a secondary road 16 kilometers (10 miles) south of Sodankylä and follow it 22 kilometers (14 miles) to the center.

Continue north, through the village of Vuotso, to **Tankavaara,** the most accessible and the best developed of several gold-panning areas. The **Gold Museum** tells the century-old story of Lapland's hardy fortune seekers. For a small fee (FIM 45 per hour), authentic prospectors will show you how to sift gold dust and tiny nuggets from the dirt of an ice-cold stream. You can keep what you find, but don't expect to be able to retire early. *Admission: June–Sept., FIM 30 adults, FIM 10 children; Oct.–May, FIM 20 adults, FIM 5 children. Open June 1–Aug. 16, daily 9–6; Aug. 17–Sept., daily 9–5; Oct.–May, hours vary, so check locally.*

Thirty kilometers (19 miles) north of Tankavaara is the holiday center of **Saariselkä,** which has a variety of accommodations and makes a sensible base from which to set off on a trip (alone or in a group) into the true wilderness; during the snowy months, there is some of the best cross-country and downhill skiing in Finland. There are marked trails through forests and over fells where nothing much has changed since the last Ice Age and where you can experience the timeless silence of the Arctic landscape. More than 2,500 square kilometers (965 square miles) of this magnificent area has been named the **Urho Kekkonen National Park.**

Northern   Just south of the village of Ivalo, the highway passes the **Ivalo River**
Lapland   (Ivalojoki). Canoeing trips are organized on its fast waters down to Lake Inari, returning by bus. The village of **Ivalo** is the main center for northern Lapland. However, except for a first-class hotel, an airport, and many of the amenities of a modern community, it has little to offer the tourist in search of a wilderness experience.

The huge island-studded expanses of **Lake Inari** (Inarinjärvi), north of Ivalo, offer endless possibilities for wilderness exploration. It is a beautiful 40-kilometer (25-mile) drive northwest from Ivalo, along the lakeshore, to **Inari.** This is a good base for summer boat excursions. The **Sami Museum,** on the village outskirts, covers all facets of Lapp culture. *Admission: FIM 12 adults, FIM 5 children. Open June 1–Aug. 10, daily 8–10; Aug. 11–30, daily 8–8; Sept. 1–20, daily 9–3:30.*

In recent years, a growing number of small holiday villages have blossomed near Inari and to the north of it, usually with a small restaurant and shop attached. Amenities are simple, but the locations are often magnificent and bring you very close to the true pulse of Lapland. Usually there will be a boat at your disposal, fishing possibilities, and the experience of preparing your own sauna. From Kaamanen, north of Inari, a side road leads to **Sevettijärvi,** home of the Skolt Lapps, and eventually into Norway.

It is an attractive drive back south from Inari to **Menesjärvi** along a relatively new, secondary road that passes through a wilderness of forest and swamp. Take every opportunity to leave your car and do some walking; it's the only way to experience the vastness of these Arctic spaces. The hills get gentler and the ride less dramatic as you continue south to Levitunturi, the last of the gently sloping fells before you reach the banks of the Ounas River and return to Rovaniemi via Highway 79.

Dining and Lodging

For details and price-category definitions, *see* Dining and Lodging in Staying in Finland, *above.*

Inari   **Kultahovi.** This recently renovated old inn is located on the wooded
Lodging   banks of a swiftly flowing river. *99870 Inari, tel. 9697/51221, fax*

9697/51250. 29 rooms with shower. Facilities: restaurant, saunas. DC, MC, V. Moderate.

Ivalo
Lodging

Hotel Ivalo. Right on the riverside about a kilometer (½ mile) from the village center, Ivalo is modern and well equipped. One of its two restaurants serves Lapland specialties, including *poronkäristys*, a reindeer casserole. *Ivalontie 34, 99800 Ivalo, tel. 9697/661911, fax 9697/661905. 94 rooms with bath or shower. Facilities: 2 restaurants, saunas, pool, boating. AE, DC, MC, V. Inexpensive–Moderate.*

Kultahippu. Located in the heart of Ivalo, next to the Ivalo River, Kultahippu claims to have the northernmost nightclub in Finland. The guest rooms are cozy. *Petsamontie 1, 99800 Ivalo, tel. 9697/661825, fax 9697/662510. 30 rooms (7 with saunas). Facilities: restaurant, nightclub, sauna, Jacuzzi, swimming beach. AE, DC, MC, V. Inexpensive.*

Levitunturi
Lodging

Levitunturi. Built in traditional log style at the foot of the fells, Levitunturi is a particularly well-equipped and modern tourist complex. *99130 Sirkka, tel. 9694/641301, fax 9694/641434. 121 rooms with shower. Special floor for nonsmokers. Facilities: saunas, pool, Jacuzzi, squash, gymnasium, tennis, boating, cross-country skiing, spa amenities. AE, DC, MC, V. Moderate–Expensive.*

Luostotunturi
Lodging

Arctia Hotel Luosto. Situated amid the fells southeast of Sodankylä, this small-scale hotel is modern and comfortable. It is built in traditional timber style. *99600 Luostotunturi, tel. 9693/624400, fax 9693/624410. 54 cabins. Facilities: saunas, boating, cross-country skiing. AE, DC, MC, V. Moderate.*

Rovaniemi
Dining

Fransmanni. Located at the Vakunna Hotel in the heart of Rovaniemi, Fransmanni specializes in international, Finnish, and Lapp specialties. *Koskikatu 4, tel. 960/332211. Reservations advised. AE, DC, MC, V. Moderate.*

Ounasvaaran Pirtit. Ounasvaara is one of Rovaniemi's favorite restaurants, specializing in traditional Finnish and Lapp food. Try the fried salmon with cream. *Antinmukka 4, tel. 960/369056. Reservations advised. AE, DC, MC, V. Moderate.*

Lodging

Hotel Lapponia. Opened in 1992, Hotel Lapponia is one of the newest luxury hotels in Lapland. *Koskikatu 23, 96200 Rovaniemi, tel. 960/33661, fax 960/313770. 151 rooms with shower, 8 with sauna, and 8 with Jacuzzi. Facilities: 4 restaurants, pub, nightclub, lobby bar, saunas. AE, DC, MC, V. Expensive.*

Gasthof. Built in 1986, the Gasthof is a comfortable small hotel with a restaurant featuring Finnish specialties. *Koskikatu 41, 96100 Rovaniemi, tel. 960/23222, fax 960/23226. 44 rooms with shower. Special floor for nonsmokers. Facilities: restaurant, saunas, pool. AE, DC, MC, V. Moderate.*

Hotelli Pohjanhovi. With its pleasant location overlooking the Kemi River, this hotel is an old favorite with travelers to the north. It has been extended and modernized over the years. *Pohjanpuistikko 2, 96200 Rovaniemi, tel. 960/33711, fax 960/313997. 216 rooms with bath or shower. Special floor for nonsmokers. Some rooms in neighboring building. Facilities: saunas, pool, boating, disco. AE, DC, MC, V. Moderate.*

Sky Hotel Ounasvaara. Located on a hilltop 3 kilometers (2 miles) from the center of town, Sky Hotel is the top choice for views and a tranquil atmosphere, but it's best if you have a car. *Hiihtokeskus, 96400 Rovaniemi, tel. 960/346001, fax 960/318789. 69 rooms (47 with saunas). Facilities: restaurant, saunas, cross-country skiing. AE, DC, MC, V. Moderate.*

Vaakuna. Opened in January 1992, the Vaakuna is a recent addition to the high-class hotel scene in Rovaniemi. *Koskikatu 4, 96200 Rovaniemi, tel. 960/332211, fax 960/332–2199. 159 rooms (all doubles) with shower. Facilities: 4 restaurants, saunas, nightclub, pub, gymnasium. AE, DC, MC, V. Moderate.*

Oppipoika. This hotel belongs to the Hotel School of Rovaniemi. The rooms are spacious and comfortable, but the real reason to come here is the food: Chef Tapio Sointu has created the "Lappi à la Carte" program, featuring a variety of Lapland specialties. *Korkalonkatu 33, 96200 Rovaniemi, tel. 960/388–8111, fax 960/ 346969. 40 rooms with bath or shower. Facilities: restaurant, saunas, pool. AE, DC, MC, V. Inexpensive.*

Saariselkä
Lodging

Riekonlinna. The latest and best-equipped addition to this developing tourist complex on the fringes of the wilderness fells, Riekonlinna makes good use of its location. *99830 Saariselkä, tel. 9697/ 668601, fax 9697/668602. 124 rooms with shower. Facilities: saunas, tennis, boating, squash, cross-country skiing. AE, DC, MC, V. Very Expensive.*

Tankavaara
Dining

Wanhan Waskoolimiehen Kahvila. Lapp specialties are featured in this attractive café and restaurant; try the gold prospector's reindeer beefsteak with mashed potatoes. Accommodations are limited in the vicinity. *Tankavaara Gold Village, tel. 9693/626158. No reservations. AE, DC, MC, V. Moderate.*

10 France

The French are a Mediterranean people—temperamental and spontaneous, closer to the Spanish and Italians than to northern Europeans. At the same time, they are heirs to the Cartesian tradition of logic ("I think, therefore I am"), as well as being inveterate theorizers. Their reluctance to take a shortcut to an obvious solution often frustrates English-speaking pragmatists.

The essence of French *savoir-vivre* is simplicity. Everyday things count: eating, drinking, talking, dressing, shopping. Get in the mood: Daily rituals are meant to be enjoyed. Food is the best example. The French don't like rushing their meals. They plan them in advance, painstakingly prepare them, look forward to them over an *apéritif*, admire the loving presentation of each dish, savor each mouthful. The pace is unhurried and the wine flows steadily.

French towns and villages are quietly attractive and historic. Chances are that the ornate *mairie* (town hall) has been there since the Revolution, and the church or cathedral since the Middle Ages. The main streets tend to be lined with sturdy trees planted before living memory. The 20th century is kept firmly at bay. Modern buildings—such as supermarkets—are banished to the outskirts or obliged to fit architecturally.

There is a bewildering variety of man-made marvels in France: Southern France is rich in Roman remains. Western France is dotted with Romanesque churches from the 10th and 11th centuries, with some of the best examples in Poitiers. Gothic architecture was born in the Ile de France around Paris: Such huge cathedrals as Notre-Dame rank among the world's finest. The Renaissance yielded the sumptuous Loire châteaux and the Palace of Fontainebleau, paving the way for the haughty Baroque of Versailles.

France boasts as much natural as man-made variety. You'll find ski slopes and towering peaks in the Alps and Pyrenees; beaches and cliffs in Brittany or along the Mediterranean; limitless horizons beyond the golden grain fields of the Beauce or the misty plains of the north; haunting evergreen forests stretching from the Ardennes down to the Midi (south); marsh and canals in the Marais Poitevin, the "Green Venice" of the west; lush, softly lit valleys along the Seine and Loire; steep-climbing terraces above the Rhône; and wherever you go, the swirl and sway of ripening vines.

Whatever you've heard, France is a welcoming country. Don't be misled by superficial coldness: They are a formal people who don't go out of their way to speak to strangers (except in anger). Above all, don't suppose that all Frenchmen are like Parisians—most are more approachable and friendly.

France considers itself to be, above all, a European power. It borders seven countries (Belgium, Luxembourg, Germany, Switzerland, Italy, Spain, Andorra) and looks across the Channel at an eighth (Great Britain). France played a crucial role in the creation of the European Union (EU).

Still, deep down, most of the French are chauvinists who are proud of *La douce France*, worship Napoleon, and feel that the Liberty-Equality-Fraternity motto of the French Revolution confers moral superiority upon their country—as they showed during the patriotic celebrations in 1989 that marked the bicentennial of the Revolution.

France

ENGLAND

La Manche
(English Channel)

Boulogne
Le Touquet

Cherbourg
Dieppe

Le Havre
Deauville
Caen
Rouen

Seine

Roscoff
St-Malo
Brest
N12
Morlaix
St-Brieuc
Mont St-Michel

Quimper
N165
N24
Rennes
Laval
Chartres
A11
Le Mans
Orléans
A10

Lorient
Vannes
N137
Angers
Blois
Nantes
Saumur
Loire
Tours

ATLANTIC
OCEAN

Les Sables
d' Olonne
Poitiers
A10
Niort
La Rochelle
Saintes
Limoges
Royan
Cognac
Angoulême

Bay of Biscay

Périgueux

Bordeaux
Garonne
Brive-la-
Gaillarde
Arcachon
Dordogne
Langon
Cahors
Agen
A62
Montauban
Albi

Bayonne
N10
N117
Pau
Tarbes
Toulouse
Biarritz
Lourdes
A61

SPAIN
Carcassonne

ANDORRA

Calais

BELGIUM

A26

Lille

Arras
Amiens

Cambrai
St. Quentin

A1

Beauvais

Laon

Reims

A4

Paris

Fontainebleau

Sens

Troyes

Châlons-sur-
Marne

Metz

Nancy
Strasbourg

A31

Colmar

Mulhouse

LUXEMBOURG

GERMANY

Corsica

Calvi

Bastia

Corte

Ajaccio

N198

Bonifacio

Auxerre

A6

Bourges

Nevers

Beaune

Autun

Montluçon

A71

Mâcon

Dijon

A36

Belfort

Besançon

SWITZERLAND

Saône

Bourg-en-
Bresse

Clermont-
Ferrand

A72

Lyon

Rhône

A43

Chambéry

ITALY

Aurillac

Le Puy

Grenoble

Rhône

Rodez

Millau

Montélimar

Gap

Nîmes

Avignon

Montpellier

A9

Aix-en-Provence

A8

Monte Carlo
Nice

Cannes

Narbonne

A19

Marseille

Toulon

Perpignan

0   50 mi

0   75 km

Mediterranean Sea

Corsica

Essential Information

Before You Go

When to Go   June and September, free of the mid-summer crowds, are the best months to be in France. June offers the advantage of long daylight hours, while slightly cheaper prices and frequent Indian summers (often lasting well into October) make September attractive. The second half of July and all of August are spoiled by inflated prices and huge crowds on the beaches. And July and August heat can be stifling in southern France. Paris, though pleasantly deserted, can be stuffy in August, too.

The ski season in the Alps and Pyrenees lasts from Christmas through Easter—steer clear of February (school vacation time) if you can. Anytime between March and November offers a good chance to soak up the sun on the Riviera. The weather in Paris and the Loire is unappealing before Easter. If you're dreaming of Paris in the springtime, May (not April) is your best bet.

Climate   France's climate changes regionally. North of the Loire (including Paris), France has a northern European climate—cold winters, pleasant if unpredictable summers, and frequent rain. Southern France has a Mediterranean climate: mild winters, long, hot summers, and sunshine throughout the year. The more continental climate of eastern and central France is a mixture of these two extremes: Winters can be very cold and summers very hot. France's Atlantic coast has a temperate climate even south of the Loire, with the exception of the much warmer Biarritz.

The following are the average daily maximum and minimum temperatures for Paris and Marseille.

Paris										
	Jan.	43F	6C	May	68F	20C	Sept.	70F	21C
		34	1		49	10		53	12
	Feb.	45F	7C	June	73F	23C	Oct.	60F	16C
		34	1		55	13		46	8
	Mar.	54F	12C	July	76F	25C	Nov.	50F	10C
		39	4		58	15		40	5
	Apr.	60F	16C	Aug.	75F	24C	Dec.	44F	7C
		43	6		58	15		36	2

Marseille										
	Jan.	50F	10C	May	71F	22C	Sept.	77F	25C
		35	2		52	11		58	15
	Feb.	53F	12C	June	79F	26C	Oct.	68F	20C
		36	2		58	14		51	10
	Mar.	59F	15C	July	84F	29C	Nov.	58F	14C
		41	5		63	17		41	5
	Apr.	64F	18C	Aug.	83F	28C	Dec.	52F	11C
		46	8		63	17		37	3

Currency   The unit of French currency is the franc, subdivided into 100 centimes. Bills are issued in denominations of 20, 50, 100, and 500 francs (frs); coins are 5, 10, 20, and 50 centimes and 1, 2, 5, 10, and 20 francs. In 1992, the Banque de France began to issue bright blue 50-franc notes depicting characters from Antoine de St-Exupery's children's story *Le Petit Prince*. The small, copper-color 5-, 10-, and 20-centime coins have considerable nuisance value, but can be used for tips in bars and cafés.

International credit cards and traveler's checks are widely accepted throughout France, except in rural areas. At press time (spring 1994), the dollar was worth 5.5 frs, the Canadian dollar was worth 4.70 frs, and the pound sterling was worth 8 frs.

What It Will Cost Hotel and restaurant prices compensate for travel expenses. Prices are highest in Paris, on the Riviera, and in the Alps during the ski season. But even in these areas, you can find pleasant accommodations and excellent food for surprisingly reasonable prices.

All taxes must be included in posted prices in France. The initials TTC *(toutes taxes comprises*—taxes included) are sometimes included on price lists but, strictly speaking, they are superfluous. Restaurant and hotel prices must *by law* include taxes and service charges: If they are tacked onto your bill as additional items, you should complain.

Sample Prices Prices vary greatly depending on the region, proximity to tourist sites, and—believe it or not—whether you're sitting down or standing up in a café! Here are a few samples: cup of coffee, 5–9 frs; glass of beer, 10–13 frs; soft drink, 10–15 frs; ham sandwich, 12–15 frs; 1-mile taxi ride, 35 frs.

Visas Citizens of the United States, Canada, and Britain do not require a visa to visit France.

Customs on Arrival There are two levels of duty-free allowance for travelers entering France: one for goods obtained (tax paid) within another European Union (EU) country and the other for goods obtained anywhere outside the EU or for goods purchased in a duty-free shop within the EU.

In the first category, you may import duty-free: 300 cigarettes or 150 cigarillos or 75 cigars or 400 grams of tobacco; 5 liters of table wine and (1) 1½ liters of alcohol over 22% volume (most spirits), (2) 3 liters of alcohol under 22% by volume (fortified or sparkling wine), or (3) 3 more liters of table wine; 90 milliliters of perfume; 375 milliliters of toilet water; and other goods to the value of 2,400 francs (620 frs for those under 15).

In the second category, you may import duty-free: 200 cigarettes or 100 cigarillos or 50 cigars or 250 grams of tobacco (these allowances are doubled if you live outside Europe); 2 liters of wine and (1) 1 liter of alcohol over 22% volume, (2) 2 liters of alcohol under 22% volume, or (3) 2 more liters of table wine; 60 milliliters of perfume; 250 milliliters of toilet water; and other goods to the value of 300 francs (150 frs for those under 15).

Language The French study English for a minimum of four years at school, but few are fluent. English is widely understood in major tourist areas, and in most tourist hotels there should be at least one person who can converse with you. Be courteous, patient, and speak slowly: France has visitors from many countries and is not heavily dependent for income on English-speaking visitors. Even if your own French is rusty, try to master a few words: The French are more cooperative when they think you are at least making an effort to speak their language.

Getting Around

By Car France's roads are classified into five types, numbered and prefixed
Road A, N, D, C, or V. Roads marked A *(Autoroutes)* are expressways.
Conditions There are excellent links between Paris and most French cities, but poor ones between the provinces (the principal exceptions being A62

between Bordeaux and Toulouse and A9/A8 the length of the Mediterranean coast). It is often difficult to avoid Paris when crossing France—this need not cause too many problems if you steer clear of the rush hours (7–9:30 AM and 4:30–7:30 PM). A *péage* (toll) must be paid on most expressways: The rate varies but can be steep. The N *(Route Nationale)* roads—which are sometimes divided highways—and D *(Route Départementale)* roads are usually wide and fast, and driving along them can be a real pleasure. Don't be daunted by smaller (C and V) roads, either. The yellow regional Michelin maps—on sale throughout France—are invaluable.

Rules of the Road You may use your own driver's license in France but must be able to prove you have third-party insurance. Drive on the right. Be aware of the French tradition of yielding to drivers coming from the right. Seat belts are obligatory for all passengers, and children under 12 may not travel in the front seat. Speed limits are 130 kph (80 mph) on expressways, 110 kph (70 mph) on divided highways, 90 kph (55 mph) on other roads, 50 kph (30 mph) in towns. French drivers break these limits and police dish out hefty on-the-spot fines with equal abandon.

Parking Parking is a nightmare in Paris and often difficult in other large towns. Meters and ticket machines (pay and display) are common: Make sure you have a supply of 1-fr coins. Parking is free during August in most of Paris, but be sure to check the signs. In smaller towns, parking may be permitted on one side of the street only—alternating every two weeks—so pay attention to signs.

Gasoline Fuel is more expensive on expressways and in rural areas. Don't let your tank get too low—you can go for many kilometers in the country without passing a gas station—and keep an eye on pump prices as you go. These vary enormously; anything from 5 to 6 frs per liter.

Breakdowns If your car breaks down on an expressway, go to the nearest roadside emergency telephone and call the breakdown service. If you have a breakdown anywhere else, find the nearest garage or contact the police (dial 17).

By Train SNCF, the French national railroad, is generally recognized as Europe's best national train service: fast, punctual, comfortable, and comprehensive. The high-speed TGVs, with a top speed of 190 mph, are the best domestic trains, heading south–east from Paris to Lyon, the Riviera, and Switzerland; west to Nantes; southwest to Bordeaux; and north to Lille. Most TGV trains require passengers to pay a supplement—usually 20–40 frs, but a bit more during peak periods. Also, you need a seat reservation—easily obtained at the ticket window or from an automatic machine. Seat reservations are reassuring but seldom necessary on other French trains, except at holiday times.

You need to punch your train ticket in one of the orange machines you'll encounter alongside platforms. Slide your ticket in faceup and wait for a "clink" sound. (The small yellow tickets and automatic ticket barriers used for most suburban Paris trains are similar to those in the métro/RER.) The ticket collectors will present you with an on-the-spot fine of 100 frs if your ticket hasn't been validated before boarding.

If you take an overnight train, you have a choice between *wagons-lits* (private sleeping cars), which are expensive, and *couchettes* (bunks), which sleep six to a compartment in second class and four to a compartment in first class (sheet and pillow provided) and are more affordable (around 89 frs). Ordinary compartment seats do not pull together to enable you to lie down. There are special summer night trains from Paris to Spain and the Riviera geared for a younger market, with discos and bars.

Fares Various reduced-fare passes are available from major train stations in France and from SNCF travel agents. If you are planning a lot of train travel, buy a special **France Vacances** card (around 1,400 frs for nine days). Families and couples are also eligible for big discounts. So are senior citizens (over 60) and young people (under 26), who qualify for different discount schemes (**Carte Vermeil** and **Carrissimo**). You can get 50% discounts in blue periods (most of the time) and 20% most of the rest of the time (white periods: noon Friday to noon Saturday; 3 PM Sunday to noon Monday). On major holidays (red periods) there are no reductions. Calendars are available at stations. The **Carte Kiwi** (395 frs) enables children and up to four accompanying adults to travel half-price.

By Plane Domestic flights from Paris, which are on **Air Inter,** leave from Orly. Contact your travel agent or Air Inter (tel. 45–46–90–00). Train service may be faster when you consider time spent to and from the airport.

By Bus Because of excellent train service, the rare long-distance buses are found mainly where train service is inadequate. Bus tours are organized by the **SNCF** and other tourist organizations, such as **Horizons Européens:** Ask for their brochures at any major travel agent, or contact France-Tourisme at 3 rue d'Alger, 75001 Paris, tel. 42–61–85–50.

By Boat France has Europe's busiest inland waterway system. Canal and river vacations are popular: Visitors can either take an organized cruise or rent a boat and plan their own leisurely route. Contact a travel agent for details or ask for a "Tourisme Fluvial" brochure in any French tourist office. Some of the most picturesque stretches are in Brittany, Burgundy, and the Midi. The Canal du Midi between Toulouse and Sète, constructed in the 17th century, is a historic marvel. Contact the French national tourist offices or **Bourgogne Voies Navigables** (1 quai de la République, 89000 Auxerre, tel. 86–52–18–99).

By Bicycle There is no shortage of wide empty roads and flat or rolling countryside in France suitable for biking. The French are great cycling enthusiasts—witness the Tour de France. For around 40 frs a day bikes can be rented from 260 train stations; you need to show your passport and leave a deposit of about 500 frs (unless you have a Visa or MasterCard). Bikes may be sent as accompanied luggage from any station in France; some trains in rural areas don't even charge for this. Tourist offices supply details on the more than 200 local shops that rent bikes, or obtain the SNCF brochure "Guide du Train et du Vélo."

Staying in France

Telephones The French telephone system is modern and efficient. Phone booths
Local Calls are plentiful; they are nearly always available at post offices and cafés. A local call in France costs 73 centimes plus 12 centimes per minute; half-price rates apply between 9:30 PM and 8 AM and between 1:30 PM Saturday and 8 AM Monday.

Some French pay phones take 1-, 2-, and 5-fr coins (1 fr minimum), but most phones are now operated by *télécartes* (phone cards), sold in post offices, Metro stations, and cafés sporting a red "Tabac" sign outside (cost: 40 frs for 50 units; 96 frs for 120).

French phone numbers have eight digits; a code is required only when calling the Paris region from the provinces (dial 16–1, then the number) and for calling the provinces from Paris (dial 16, then the number).

International Calls Dial 19 and wait for the tone, then dial the country code, area code, and number. Calls from your hotel room are very expensive. To reach an **AT&T** long distance operator, dial 19–0011, for **MCI,** dial 19–0019, and for **Sprint,** 19–0087. Dial 12 for local operators. France's country code is 33.

Mail
Postal Rates Airmail letters to the United States and Canada cost 4.30 frs for 20 grams. Letters to the United Kingdom cost 2.80 frs for up to 20 grams, as do letters within France. Postcards cost 2.40 frs within France and if sent to EU countries (2.40 frs for surface or 3.80 frs for airmail to North America). Stamps can be bought in post offices and tabacs.

Receiving Mail If you're uncertain where you'll be staying, have mail sent to American Express (if you're a cardmember), Thomas Cook, or Poste Restante at most French post offices.

Shopping
VAT Refunds A number of shops, particularly large stores in cities and holiday resorts, offer value-added tax (VAT) refunds to foreign shoppers. You are entitled to an export discount of 13% or 23%, depending on the item purchased, though this often applies only if your purchases in the same store reach a minimum 2,800 frs (for residents of EU countries) or 1,200 frs (all others).

Bargaining Shop prices are clearly marked and bargaining is not a way of life. Still, at outdoor markets, flea markets, and in antiques stores, you can try your luck. If you're thinking of buying several items in these places, you have nothing to lose in cheerfully suggesting to the proprietor, *"Vous me faites un prix?"* ("How about a discount?").

Hours **Banks** are open weekdays 9:30–4:30, but times vary. Most close for an hour to an hour and a half for lunch.

Museums are closed one day a week (usually Tuesday) and on national holidays. Usual times are from 9:30 to 5 or 6. Many museums close for lunch (noon–2); on Sunday many are open afternoons only.

Shops in big towns are open from 9 or 9:30 to 7 or 8 without a lunch break and have recently begun to open on Sunday. Smaller shops often open earlier and close later, but take a lengthy lunch break (1–4). This siesta-type schedule is more typical in the south of France. Corner grocery stores frequently stay open until around 10 PM.

National Holidays January 1; April 17 (Easter Monday); May 1 (Labor Day); May 8 (VE Day); May 25 (Ascension); June 5 (Pentecost Monday); July 14 (Bastille Day); August 15 (Assumption); November 1 (All Saints' Day); November 11 (Armistice); December 25.

Dining Eating in France is serious business, at least for two of the three meals each day. For a light meal, try a *brasserie* (steak and french fries remain the classic), a picnic (a *baguette* loaf with ham, cheese, or pâté makes a perfect combination), or one of the fast-food places that have sprung up in urban areas over recent years.

French breakfasts are relatively modest—strong coffee, fruit juice if you insist, and croissants. International chain hotels are likely to offer American or English breakfasts, but in cafés you will probably be out of luck if this is what you want.

Mealtimes Dinner is the main meal and usually begins at 8. Lunch begins at 12:30 or 1.

Dress Jacket and tie are recommended for Very Expensive and Expensive restaurants, and at some of the more stylish Moderate restaurants as well. When in doubt, it's best to dress up. Otherwise casual dress is appropriate.

Precautions Tap water is perfectly safe, though not always very palatable (least of all in Paris). Mineral water is a good alternative; there is a vast choice of *eaux plates* (plain) as well as *eaux gazeuses* (fizzy).

Ratings Prices are per person and include a first course, main course, and dessert plus taxes and service (which are always included in displayed prices), but not wine. Best bets are indicated by a star ★.

Category	Cost*: Major City	Cost*: Other Areas
Very Expensive	over 550 francs	over 500 francs
Expensive	300–550 francs	250–500 francs
Moderate	175–300 francs	125–250 francs
Inexpensive	under 175 francs	under 125 francs

*per person for a three-course meal, including tax (18.6%) and tip but not wine

Lodging France has a wide range of accommodations, from rambling old village inns to stylishly converted châteaus. Prices must, by law, be posted at the hotel entrance and should include taxes and service. Prices are always by room, not per person. Breakfast is not always included, but you are usually expected to have it and often are charged for it whether you have it or not. In smaller rural hotels, you may be expected to have your evening meal at the hotel, too.

The quality of rooms, particularly in older properties, is uneven; if you don't like the room you're given, ask to see another. If you want a private bathroom, state your preference for *douche* (shower) or *baignoire* (bath)—the latter always costing more. Tourist offices in major train stations can reserve hotels for you, and so can tourist offices in most towns.

Hotels Hotels are officially classified from one-star to four-star-deluxe. France has—but is not dominated by—big hotel chains: Examples in the upper price bracket include Frantel, Holiday Inn, Novotel, and Sofitel. The Ibis and Climat de France chains are more moderately priced. Chain hotels, as a rule, lack atmosphere, with the following exceptions:

Logis de France. This is a group of small, inexpensive hotels that can be relied on for comfort, character, and regional cuisine. Look for its distinctive yellow and green sign. The Logis de France paperback guide is widely available in bookshops (cost: around 68 frs) or from Logis de France (83 av. d'Italie, 75013 Paris, tel. 45–84–83–84).
France-Accueil is another chain of friendly low-cost hotels. You can get a free booklet from France-Accueil (163 av. d'Italie, 75013 Paris, tel. 45–83–04–22).
Relais et Châteaux. You can stay in style at any of the 150 members of this prestigious chain of converted châteaus and manor houses. Each hotel is distinctively furnished, provides top cuisine, and often stands in spacious grounds. A booklet listing members is available in bookshops or from Relais et Châteaux (15 rue Galvani, 75017 Paris, tel. 45–72–90–00, fax 45–72–90–30).

Rentals *Gîtes Ruraux* offers families or small groups the opportunity for an economical stay in a furnished cottage, chalet, or apartment. These can be rented by the week or month. Contact either the **Fédération Nationale des Gîtes de France,** 35 rue Godot-de-Mauroy, 75009 Paris, tel. 49–70–75–75 (indicate the region that interests you), or the French Government Tourist Office in New York or London (*see* Before You Go in Chapter 1, Essential Information).

Bed-and-Breakfasts Known as *chambres d'hôte,* these are increasingly popular in rural areas and can be a great bargain. Check local tourist offices for details.

Youth Hostels With inexpensive hotel accommodations in France so easy to find, you may want to think twice before staying in a youth hostel—especially as standards of French hostels don't quite approximate those in neighboring countries. Contact **Fédération Unie des Auberges de Jeunesse** (4 blvd. Jules Ferry, 75011 Paris, tel. 43–57–02–60, fax 40–21–79–92).

Villas The French Government Tourist Offices in London and New York publish extensive lists of agencies specializing in villa rentals. You can also write to **Rent-a-Villa Ltd.** (3 W. 51st St., New York, NY 10019) or, in France, **Interhome** (15 av. Jean-Aicard, 75011 Paris).

Camping French campsites have a good reputation for organization and amenities but are crowded in July and August. Many campsites welcome advance reservations, and in summer, it makes sense to book in advance. A guide to France's campsites is published by the **Fédération Française de Camping et de Caravaning,** 78 rue de Rivoli, 75004 Paris, tel. 42–72–84–08. They'll send it to you directly for 70 frs, plus shipping.

Ratings Prices are for double rooms and include all taxes. Best bets are indicated by a star ★.

Category	Cost*: Major City	Cost*: Other Areas
Very Expensive	over 1,200 francs	over 800 francs
Expensive	750–1,200 francs	400–800 francs
Moderate	450–750 francs	200–400 francs
Inexpensive	under 450 francs	under 200 francs

*All prices are for a standard double room for two, including tax (18.6%) and service charge.

Tipping The check in a bar or restaurant will include service, but it is customary to leave some small change unless you're dissatisfied. The amount varies, from 30 centimes for a beer to a few francs after a meal. Tip taxi drivers and hairdressers about 10%. Give ushers in theaters 1–2 frs. Cloakroom attendants will expect nothing if there is a sign saying *Pourboire interdit*—no tip; otherwise give them 5 frs. Washroom attendants usually get 5 frs—a sum that is often posted. Bellhops should get 10 frs per item.

If you stay in a moderately priced hotel for more than two or three days, it is customary to leave something for the chambermaid—perhaps 10 frs per day. Expect to tip 10 frs for room service—but nothing is expected if breakfast is routinely served in your room.

Service station attendants get nothing for giving you gas or oil, and 5 or 10 frs for checking tires. Train and airport porters get a fixed sum (6–10 frs) per bag. Museum guides should get 5–10 frs after a guided tour. It is standard practice to tip guides (and bus drivers) after an excursion.

Paris

Arriving and Departing

By Plane International flights arrive at either Charles de Gaulle Airport (Roissy), 24 kilometers (15 miles) northeast of Paris, or at Orly Airport, 16 kilometers (10 miles) south of the city.

Between the **From Charles de Gaulle:** Buses operated by **Air France** leave every
Airport and 20 minutes from 5:40 AM to 11 PM. The fare is 48 frs and the trip takes
Downtown 40 minutes (up to 1½ hours during rush hour). You arrive at the Arc de Triomphe or Porte Maillol, on the Right Bank by the Hotel Concorde-Lafayette. Alternatively, the **Roissybus,** operated by RATP, runs directly to and from rue Scribe at Paris Opera every 15 minutes and costs 30 frs.

From Orly: Buses operated by **Air France** leave every 12 minutes from 6 AM to 11 PM and arrive at the Air France terminal near Les Invalides on the Left Bank. The fare is 32 frs, and the trip takes between 30 and 60 minutes, depending on traffic. RATP also runs the **Orlybus** to and from Denfert-Rochereau and Orly every 15 minutes for 23 frs.

Both airports provide free bus shuttles to the nearest train stations, where you can take the RER service to Paris. The advantages of this are speed, price (33 frs to Paris from Charles de Gaulle in Roissy, 45 frs from Orly on the shuttle-train **Orlyval**), and the fact that the RER trains link up directly with the métro system. The disadvantage is having to lug your bags around. Taxi fares from airports to Paris range from 150 to 200 frs, with a 5 fr surcharge per bag.

By Train Paris has five international stations: Gare du Nord (for northern France, northern Europe, and England via Calais or Boulogne); Gare de l'Est (for Strasbourg, Luxembourg, Basle, and central Europe); Gare de Lyon (for Lyon, Marseille, the Riviera, Geneva, Italy); Gare d'Austerlitz (for the Loire Valley, southwest France, Spain); Gare St-Lazare (for Normandy, England via Dieppe). The Gare Montparnasse serves western France (mainly Nantes and Brittany) and is the terminus for the new TGV Atlantic service from Paris to Bordeaux. For train information, tel. 45–82–50–50. You can reserve tickets at any Paris station regardless of the destination. Go to the Grandes Lignes counter for travel within France or to the Billets Internationaux (international tickets) desk if you're heading out of France.

By Bus Long-distance bus journeys within France are uncommon, which may be why Paris has no central bus depot. The leading Paris-based bus company is **Eurolines Nord** (3 av. de la Porte de la Villette, 19e, tel. 40–38–93–93).

By Car The highway system fans out from Paris. You arrive from the north (England/Belgium) via A1; from Normandy via A13; from the east via A4; from Spain and the southwest via A10; from the Alps, the Riviera, and Italy via A7. Each of these expressways connects with the *Périphérique* (beltway). Note that exits here are named by "Porte" and are not numbered. The "Périphe" can be extremely fast—but it gets very busy and is best avoided between 8 and 10 AM and between 5 and 7:30 PM.

Getting Around

Paris is relatively small as capital cities go, and most of its prize monuments and museums are within walking distance of one another. A river cruise is a pleasant way to get an introductory overview. The most convenient form of public transportation is the métro; buses are a slower alternative, though they do allow you to see more of the city. Taxis are not expensive but not always easy to hail, either. Car travel within Paris is best avoided because parking is chronically difficult.

By Métro   There are 13 métro lines crisscrossing Paris and the nearby suburbs, and you are seldom more than a five-minute walk from the nearest station. It is essential to know the name of the last station on the line you take, since this name appears on all signs within the system. A connection (you can make as many as you please on one ticket) is called a *correspondance*. At junction stations, illuminated orange signs, bearing the names of each line terminus, appear over the corridors leading to the various correspondances.

The métro runs from 5:30 AM to 1:15 AM. Some lines and stations in the seedier parts of Paris are a bit risky at night—in particular Line 2 (Porte-Dauphine–Nation) and the northern section of Line 13 from St-Lazare to St-Denis/Asnières. The long, bleak corridors at Jaurès and Stalingrad are a haven for pickpockets and purse snatchers. But the Paris métro is relatively safe, as long as you don't walk around with your wallet hanging out of your back pocket or travel alone (especially women) late at night.

The métro network connects at several points in Paris with RER trains that race across Paris from suburb to suburb: RER trains are a sort of supersonic métro and can be a great time-saver. All métro tickets and passes are valid for RER and bus travel within Paris. Métro tickets cost 6.50 frs each, though a *carnet* (10 tickets for 39 frs) is a far better value. If you're staying for a week or more, the best deal is the *coupon jaune* (weekly) or *carte orange* (monthly) ticket, sold according to zone. Zones 1 and 2 cover the entire métro network (cost: 59 frs per week or 208 frs per month). If you plan to take a suburban train to visit monuments in the Ile de France, you should consider a four-zone ticket (Versailles, St-Germain-en-Laye; 109 frs per week) or a six-zone ticket (Rambouillet, Fontainebleau; 142 frs per week). For these weekly or monthly tickets, you need to obtain a pass (available from train and major métro stations) and provide a passport-size photograph.

Alternatively there are one-, three-, and five-day unlimited travel tickets for the metro, bus, and RER (*Formule 1* and *Paris Visite*). The advantage is that unlike the *coupon jaune*, which is good from Monday morning to Sunday evening, the latter are valid starting any day of the week and give you discounts on a limited number of museums and tourist attractions. The price is 36, 90, and 145 francs for Paris only; 85, 200, and 275 francs for suburbs including Versailles, St-Germain-en-Laye, and Euro Disney.

Access to métro and RER platforms is through an automatic ticket barrier. Slide your ticket in flat and pick it up as it pops up farther along. Keep your ticket; you'll need it again to leave the RER system.

By Bus   Most buses run from around 6 AM to 8:30 PM; some continue until midnight. Night buses (called *Noctambus*) operate from 1 AM to 6 AM between Châtelet and nearby suburbs. They can be stopped by hailing them at any point on their route. You can use your metro tickets on the buses, or you can buy a one-ride ticket on board. You need to show weekly/monthly/special tickets to the driver as you get on; if you have individual tickets, you should state your destination and be prepared to punch one or more tickets in the red and gray machines on board the bus.

By Taxi There is no standard vehicle or color for Paris taxis, but all offer good value. Daytime rates (7 AM to 7 PM) within Paris are about 2.80 frs per kilometer, and nighttime rates are around 4.50 frs, plus a basic charge of 11 frs. Rates outside the city limits are about 40% higher. It is best to ask your hotel or restaurant to call for a taxi, since cruising cabs can be hard to find. There are numerous taxi stands, but you have to know where to look. Note that taxis seldom take more than three people at a time.

Important Addresses and Numbers

Tourist Information Paris Tourist Office (127 av. des Champs-Elysées, tel. 49–52–53–54). Open daily 9 AM–8 PM. (Closed Dec. 25, Jan 1.) Offices in major train stations are open daily 8–8.

Embassies U.S. (2 av. Gabriel, 75008 Paris, tel. 42–96–12–02). **Canada** (35 av. Montaigne, 75008 Paris, tel. 44–43–32–00). **U.K.** (35 rue du Faubourg St-Honoré, 75008 Paris, tel. 42–66–91–42).

Emergencies Police: dial 17 for emergencies. Automatic phone booths can be found at various main crossroads for use in police emergencies *(Police-Secours)* or medical help *(Services Médicaux)*; **Ambulance** (tel. 15 or 43–78–26–26); **Doctor** (tel. 47–07–77–77); **Hospitals: American Hospital** (63 blvd. Victor-Hugo, Neuilly, tel. 46–41–25–25); **British Hospital** (3 rue Barbes, Levallois-Perret, tel. 47–58–13–12); **Dentist** (tel. 43–37–51–00; open 24 hours). **Pharmacies: Dhéry** (Galerie des Champs, 84 av. des Champs-Elysées, tel. 45–62–02–41; open 24 hours); **Drugstore** (corner of blvd. St-Germain and rue de Rennes, 6e; open until 2 AM); **Pharmacie des Arts** (106 blvd. Montparnasse, 6e; open until midnight).

English-Language Bookstores W. H. Smith (248 rue de Rivoli); **Galignani** (224 rue de Rivoli); **Brentano's** (37 av. de l'Opéra); **Shakespeare & Co.** (rue de la Bûcherie).

Most newsstands in central Paris sell *Time, Newsweek,* and the *International Herald Tribune,* as well as the English dailies.

Travel Agencies American Express (11 rue Scribe 75009 Paris, tel. 47–77–70–00). **Wagons-Lits** (8 rue Auber, 75009 Paris, tel. 42–66–57–33).

Guided Tours

Orientation Tours Bus tours of Paris offer a good introduction to the city. The two largest operators are **Cityrama** (tel. 44–55–61–00) and **Paris Vision** (tel. 42–60–31–25). Tours start from their respective offices, 4 pl. des Pyramides and 214 rue de Rivoli. Both are in the first *arrondissement* (ward), opposite the Tuileries Gardens (toward the Louvre end). Tours are generally given in double-decker buses with either a live guide or a tape-recorded commentary. They last two to three hours and cost about 150 frs. The same operators also offer a variety of other tours with a theme (Historic Paris, Modern Paris, Paris by Night) lasting from 2½ hours to all day and costing between 120 and 300 frs. For a more intimate tour of the city, Cityrama also runs minibus excursions that pick up and drop off at your hotel. Costs run between 210 and 350 frs per person; reservations are necessary.

Paris Métro

Boat Trips Boat trips along the Seine are a must for first-time Paris visitors. The two most famous services are the **Bâteaux Mouches,** which leaves from the Pont de l'Alma, at the end of the avenue George V, and the **Vedettes du Pont-Neuf,** which sets off from the square du Vert Galant, on the western edge of the Ile de la Cité. Price per trip is around 35 frs. Boats depart in season every half-hour from 10:30 AM to 5 PM (slightly less frequently in winter). Evening cruises are available most of the year and, thanks to the boats' powerful floodlights, offer unexpected views of Paris's riverbanks.

Canauxrama (tel. 42–39–15–00) organizes canal tours in flat-bottom barges along the picturesque but relatively unknown St-Martin and Ourcq Canals in East Paris. Departures from 5 bis quai de la Loire, 19e (métro Jaurès), or the Bassin de l'Arsenal, opposite 50 blvd. de la Bastille, 12e (métro Bastille). Times vary, so phone to check hours. Tours cost from 70 frs, depending on the time of day and length of trip.

Walking Tours There are numerous special-interest tours concentrating on historical or architectural topics. Most are in French, however. Charges vary between 30 and 50 frs, depending on fees that may be needed to visit certain buildings. Tours last about two hours and are generally held in the afternoon. Details are published in the weekly magazines *Pariscope* and *L'Officiel des Spectacles* under the heading "Conférences."

Bike Tours **Paris by Cycle** organizes daily bike tours around Paris and the environs (Versailles, Chantilly, and Fontainebleau) for about 220 frs, 120 frs for bike rental (99 rue de la Jonquiere, 17e, tel. 42–63–36–63).

Excursions The **RATP** (Paris Transport Authority) organizes many guided excursions in and around Paris. Ask at its tourist service on the place de la Madeleine (north of place de la Concorde), or at the RATP office at St-Michel (53 quai des Grands-Augustins). **Cityrama** and **Paris Vision** *(see* Orientation Tours, *above)* organize half- and full-day trips to Chartres, Versailles, Fontainebleau, the Loire Valley, and Mont St-Michel at a cost of between 150 and 750 frs.

Personal Guides **International Limousines** (182 blvd. Pereire, 17e, tel. 45–74–77–12) and **Executive Car** (5 rue d'Astorg, 8e, tel. 42–65–54–20) have limousines and minibuses that take up to seven passengers around Paris or to surrounding areas for a minimum of three hours. The cost starts from about 200 frs per hour. Phone for details and reservations.

Exploring Paris

Paris is a compact city. With the possible exception of the Bois de Boulogne and Montmartre, you can easily walk from one sight to the next. Paris is divided in two by the River Seine, with two islands (Ile de la Cité and Ile St-Louis) in the middle. The south—or Left—Bank has a more intimate, bohemian flavor than the haughtier Right Bank. The east–west axis from Châtelet to the Arc de Triomphe, via the rue de Rivoli and the Champs-Elysées, is the principal thoroughfare for sightseeing and shopping on the Right Bank.

A special **Carte Musées et Monuments** pass, allowing access to most Paris museums and monuments, can be obtained from museums or métro stations (price: one-day pass, 60 frs; three days, 120 frs; five days, 170 frs).

Though attractions are grouped into four logical touring areas, there are several "musts." If time is a problem, explore Notre-Dame and the Latin Quarter; head to place de la Concorde and enjoy the vista from the Champs-Elysées to the Louvre; then take a boat along the Seine for a waterside rendezvous with the Eiffel Tower. You could finish off with dinner in Montmartre and consider it a day well spent.

Numbers in the margin correspond to points of interest on the Paris map.

Notre-Dame and the Left Bank

❶ The most enduring symbol of Paris, and its historic and geographic heart, is **Notre-Dame Cathedral,** around the corner from Cité métro station. This is the logical place from which to start any tour of the city—especially as the tour starts on the Ile de la Cité, one of the two islands in the middle of the Seine, where Paris's first inhabitants settled around 250 BC. Notre-Dame has been a place of worship for more than 2,000 years; the present building is the fourth on this site. It was begun in 1163, making it one of the earliest Gothic cathedrals, although it was not finished until 1345. The facade seems perfectly proportioned until you notice that the north (left) tower is wider than the south. The interior is at its lightest and least cluttered in the early morning. Bay-by-bay cleaning is gradually revealing the original honey color of the stone. Window space is limited and filled with shimmering stained glass; the circular rose windows in the transept are particularly delicate. The 387-step climb up the towers is worth the effort for a perfect view of the famous gargoyles and the heart of Paris. *Cathedral admission free. Towers admission 30 frs adults, 16 frs children. Open daily 10–5. Treasury (religious and vestmental relics) open Mon.–Sat. 10–6, Sun. 2–6. Admission: 15 frs adults, 10 frs students, 5 frs children.*

The pretty garden to the right of the cathedral leads to a bridge that crosses to the city's second and smaller island, the **Ile St- Louis,** barely 600 meters (1,868 feet) long and an oasis of inner-city repose.

❷ The rue des Deux Ponts bisects the island. Head left over the Pont de la Tournelle. To your left is the **Tour d'Argent,** one of the city's most famous restaurants (*see* Dining, *below*).

❸ Continue along quai de la Tournelle past Notre-Dame, then turn left at rue St-Jacques. A hundred yards ahead, on the right, is the back end of the **Eglise St-Séverin,** an elegant and unusually wide 16th-century church. Note the spiraling column among the forest of pillars behind the altar.

❹ Turn left out of the church, cross the bustling boulevard St-Germain, and take rue de Cluny to the left. This leads to the **Hôtel de Cluny,** which houses the **Musée National du Moyen-Age,** a museum devoted to the late Middle Ages and Renaissance. Look for the *Lady with the Unicorn* tapestries and the beautifully displayed medieval statues. *6 pl. Paul-Painlevé. Admission: 26 frs adults, 17 frs students and children; 17 frs for all on Sun. Open Wed.–Mon. 9:30–5:15.*

❺ Head up rue de la Sorbonne to the **Sorbonne,** Paris's ancient university. Students here used to listen to lectures in Latin, which explains why the surrounding area is known as the Quartier Latin (Latin Quarter). The Sorbonne is the oldest university in Paris—indeed, one of the oldest in Europe—and has for centuries been one of France's principal institutions of higher learning.

❻ Walking up rue Victor-Cousin and turning left into rue Cujas, you come to the **Panthéon.** Its huge dome and elegant colonnade are reminiscent of St. Paul's in London but date from a century later (1758–89). The Panthéon was intended to be a church, but during the Revo-

Paris

0 ⎯⎯⎯⎯⎯⎯⎯ 1 mile
0 ⎯⎯⎯⎯⎯⎯⎯ 1 km

Arc de Triomphe, **20**
Arènes de Lutèce, **7**
Beaubourg, **39**
Bois de Boulogne, **19**
Eglise de la
Madeleine, **28**
Eglise St-Séverin, **3**
Eiffel Tower, **17**

Fauchon's, **29**
Grand Palais, **21**
Hédiard's, **30**
Hôtel de Cluny, **4**
Hôtel de Ville, **44**
Jardin des Plantes, **8**
Jardin des
Tuileries, **23**
Les Grands
Magasins, **34**
Les Halles, **38**

L'Hôtel des
Invalides, **15**
Louvre, **24**
Louvre des
Antiquaires, **36**
Moulin Rouge, **27**
Musée d'Orsay, **13**
Musée Marmottan, **18**
Musée Picasso, **40**

Musée Rodin, **16**
Notre-Dame
Cathedral, **1**
Opéra, **33**
Palais Bourbon, **14**
Palais de Justice, **46**
Palais du
Luxembourg, **10**
Palais-Royal, **35**
Panthéon, **6**
Petit Palais, **22**

Place de la Bastille, **42**
Place des Vosges, **41**
Place du Tertre, **26**
Place Vendôme, **31**
Ritz, **32**
Sacré-Coeur, **25**
St-Eustache, **37**
St-Germain-
des-Prés, **12**
Saint-Paul-Saint-
Louis, **43**

St-Sulpice, **11**
Sorbonne, **5**
Square du Vert
Galant, **47**
Tour d'Argent, **2**
Tour St-Jacques, **45**
Val de Grâce, **9**

lution it was swiftly earmarked as a secular hall of fame. Its crypt contains the remains of such national heroes as Voltaire, Rousseau, and Zola. The interior is empty and austere, with principal interest centering on Puvis de Chavanne's late 19th-century frescoes, relating the life of Geneviève, patron saint of Paris. *Admission: 26 frs adults, 17 frs senior citizens, 6 frs children. Open daily 10–5:30.*

Behind the Panthéon is **St-Etienne du Mont,** a church with two claims to fame: its ornate facade and its curly Renaissance rood-screen (1521–35) separating nave and chancel—the only one of its kind in Paris. Don't forget to check out the fine 17th-century glass in the cloister at the back of the church.

Take the adjoining rue Clovis, turn right into rue Descartes, then left at the lively place de la Contrescarpe down rue Rollin. Cross rue Monge to rue de Navarre. On the left is the **Arènes de Lutèce** (always open during daylight hours, admission free), a Gallo-Roman arena rediscovered only in 1869; it has since been landscaped and excavated to reveal parts of the original amphitheater, and counts as one of the least-known points of interest in Paris.

Rue de Navarre and rue Lacépède lead to the **Jardin des Plantes** (Botanical Gardens), which have been on this site since the 17th century. The gardens have what is reputedly the oldest tree in Paris, a robinia planted in 1636 (allée Becquerel), plus a zoo, alpine garden, hothouses, aquarium, and maze. Natural science enthusiasts will be in their element at the various museums, devoted to insects (Musée Entomologique), fossils and prehistoric animals (Musée Paléontologique), and minerals (Musée Minéralogique). *Admission: 12–25 frs. Museums open Wed.–Mon. 9–11:45, 1–4:45.*

Head back up Rue Lacépède from the Jardin des Plantes. Turn left into rue Gracieuse, then right into rue Ortolan, which soon crosses the rue Mouffetard—site of a colorful market and many restaurants. Continue along rue du Pot-de-Fer and rue Rataud. At rue Claude-Bernard, turn right; then make your first left up rue St-Jacques.

Set slightly back from the street is the **Val de Grâce,** a domed church designed by the great architect Jules Hardouin-Mansart and erected in 1645–67 (after the Sorbonne church but before the Invalides). Its two-tiered facade, with capitals and triangular pedestals, is directly inspired by the Counter-Reformation Jesuit architectural style found more often in Rome than in Paris. The Baroque style of the interior is epitomized by the huge twisted columns of the baldachin (ornamental canopy) over the altar.

From the crossroads by the Closerie des Lilas, there is an enticing view down the tree-lined avenue de l'Observatoire toward the **Palais du Luxembourg.** The palace was built by Queen Maria de' Medici at the beginning of the 17th century in answer to Florence's Pitti Palace. It now houses the French Senate and is not open to the public. In the surrounding gardens, mothers push their baby carriages along tree-lined paths among the majestic fountains and statues.

Head through the gardens to the left of the palace into rue de Vaugirard. Turn left, then right into rue Madame, which leads down to the enormous 17th-century church of **St-Sulpice.** Stand back and admire the impressive, though unfinished, 18th-century facade, with its unequal towers. The interior is overwhelmingly impersonal, but the wall paintings by Delacroix, in the first chapel on the right, are worth a visit.

Rue Bonaparte descends to boulevard St-Germain. You can hardly
⑫ miss the sturdy pointed tower of **St-Germain-des-Prés,** the oldest
church in Paris (begun around 1160, though the towers date to the
11th century). Note the colorful nave frescoes by the 19th-century
artist Hippolyte Flandrin, a pupil of Ingres.

Time Out The spirit of writers Jean-Paul Sartre and Simone de Beauvoir still
haunts the **Café de Flore** opposite the church, though this, and the
neighboring **Les Deux Magots,** have more tourists than literary luminaries these days. Still, you can linger over a drink while watching what seems to be all of Paris walking by. *Blvd. St-Germain. No
credit cards.*

Rue de l'Abbaye runs along behind St-Germain-des-Prés to place
Fürstemberg, a charming little square where fiery Romantic artist
Eugène Delacroix (1798–1863) had his studio. If you go there on a
summer evening, you'll sometimes find young Frenchmen singing
love songs to guitar accompaniment. Turn left into rue Jacob and
continue along rue de l'Université. You are now in the heart of the
Carré Rive Gauche, the Left Bank's district of art dealers and galleries.

About a quarter of a mile along rue de l'Université, turn down rue de
⑬ Poitiers. Ahead is the sandstone bulk of the **Musée d'Orsay.** Follow it
around to the left to reach the main entrance. The new Musée
d'Orsay—opened in late 1986—is already one of Paris's star tourist
attractions, thanks to its imaginatively housed collections of the arts
(mainly French) spanning the period 1848–1914. Exhibits take up
three floors, but the visitor's immediate impression is one of a single, vast hall. This is not surprising: The museum was originally
built in 1900 as a train station. The combination of hall and glass roof
with narrow, clanky passages and intimate lighting lends Orsay a
human, pleasantly chaotic feel.

The chief artistic attraction, of course, is the Impressionist collection, transferred from the inadequate Jeu de Paume museum
across the river. Other highlights include Art Nouveau furniture, a
faithfully restored Belle Epoque restaurant (formerly part of the
station hotel), and a model of the Opéra quarter beneath a glass
floor. *1 rue Bellechasse, tel. 40–49–48–14. Admission: 31 frs, 16 frs
students, senior citizens, children, and Sun. Open Tues., Wed.,
Fri., Sat. 10–5:30; Thurs. 10–9:30; Sun. 9–5:30.*

⑭ Farther along on rue de l'Université is the 18th-century **Palais Bourbon,** home of the French National Legislature (Assemblée
Nationale). The colonnaded facade commissioned by Napoleon is a
sparkling sight after a recent cleaning program (jeopardized at one
stage by political squabbles as to whether cleaning should begin
from the left or the right). There is a fine view across to place de la
Concorde and the Madeleine.

Follow the Seine down to the exuberant **Pont Alexandre III.** The
Grand and Petit Palais are to your right, across the river. To the left,
⑮ the silhouette of **L'Hôtel des Invalides** soars above expansive if hardly manicured lawns. The Invalides was founded by Louis XIV in
1674 to house wounded (or "invalid") war veterans. Although only a
few old soldiers live here today, the military link remains in the form
of the **Musée de l'Armée**—a vast, albeit musty, collection of arms,
armor, uniforms, banners, and pictures. The **Musée des Plans-Reliefs** contains a fascinating collection of scale models of French towns
made by the military architect Vauban in the 17th century.

The museums are far from being the only reason for visiting the Invalides. It is an outstanding Baroque ensemble, designed by Bruand and Mansart, and its church possesses the city's most elegant dome as well as the tomb of Napoleon, whose remains are housed in a series of no less than six coffins within a tomb of red porphyry. *Admission to museums and church: 32 frs adults, 22 frs children and senior citizens. Open daily 10–6 (10–5 in winter).*

16 Alongside is the **Musée Rodin.** Together with the Picasso Museum in the Marais, this is the most charming of Paris's individual museums, consisting of an old house (built 1728) with a pretty garden, both filled with the vigorous sculptures of Auguste Rodin (1840–1917). The garden also has hundreds of rosebushes, with dozens of different varieties. *77 rue de Varenne. Admission: 26 frs, 17 frs Sun. Open Tues.–Sun. 10–5.*

Take avenue de Tourville to avenue de La Motte-Picquet. Turn left,
17 and in a few minutes you will come face-to-face with the **Eiffel Tower.** It was built by Gustave Eiffel for the World Exhibition of 1889. Recent restorations haven't made the elevators any faster—long lines are inevitable—but decent shops and two good restaurants have been added. Consider coming in the evening, when every girder is lit in glorious detail. Such was Eiffel's engineering precision that even in the fiercest winds the tower never sways more than 11½ centimeters (4½ inches). Today, of course, it is the best-known Parisian landmark. Standing beneath it, you may have trouble believing that it nearly became 7,000 tons of scrap-iron when its concession expired in 1909. Only its potential use as a radio antenna saved the day; it now bristles with a forest of radio and television transmitters. The view from 1,000 feet up will enable you to appreciate the city's layout and proportions. *Admission: on foot, 8 frs; elevator, 18–52 frs, depending on the level. Open July–Aug., daily 9 AM–midnight; Sept.–June, Sun.–Thurs. 9:30 AM–11 PM, Fri., Sat. 10 AM–midnight.*

West Paris Our second itinerary starts at the **Musée Marmottan.** To get there,
and take the métro to La Muette, then head down chaussée de la Muette,
the Louvre through the small Ranelagh park to the corner of rue Boilly and ave-
18 nue Raphaël. The museum is a sumptuous early 19th-century mansion, replete with many period furnishings, and probably is the most underestimated museum in Paris. It houses a magnificent collection of paintings by Claude Monet, along with other Impressionist works and some delicately illustrated medieval manuscripts. *2 rue Louis-Boilly. Admission: 35 frs adults, 15 frs children and senior citizens. Open Tues.–Sun. 10–5:30.*

Continue along rue Boilly and turn left on boulevard Suchet. The
19 next right takes you into the **Bois de Boulogne.** Class and style have been associated with "Le Bois" (The Woods) ever since it was landscaped into an upper-class playground by Haussmann in the 1850s. The attractions of this sprawling 891-hectare (2,200-acre) wood include cafés, restaurants, gardens, waterfalls, and lakes. Pass Auteuil racetrack on the left and then walk to the right of the two lakes. An inexpensive ferry crosses frequently to an idyllic island. Rowboats can be rented at the far end of the lake. Just past the boathouse, turn right on the route de Suresnes and follow it to Porte Dauphine, a large traffic circle.

Cross over to avenue Foch, with the unmistakable silhouette of the Arc de Triomphe in the distance. Notice the original Art Nouveau iron-and-glass entrance to Porte Dauphine métro station, on the left. Continue along avenue Foch, the widest and grandest
20 boulevard in Paris, to the **Arc de Triomphe.** This 51-meter (164-foot)

arch was planned by Napoleon to celebrate his military successes. Yet when Empress Marie-Louise entered Paris in 1810, it was barely off the ground and an arch of painted canvas had to be strung up to save appearances. Napoleon had been dead for more than 20 years when the Arc de Triomphe was finally finished in 1836.

Place Charles de Gaulle, referred to by Parisians as **L'Etoile** (The Star), is one of Europe's most chaotic traffic circles. Short of a death-defying dash, your only way to get over to the Arc de Triomphe is to take the pedestrian underpass from either the Champs-Elysées (to your right as you arrive from avenue Foch) or avenue de la Grande Armée (to the left). France's Unknown Soldier is buried beneath the archway; the flame is rekindled every evening at 6:30.

From the top of the Arc you can see the "star" effect of Etoile's 12 radiating avenues and admire two special vistas: one, down the Champs-Elysées toward place de la Concorde and the Louvre, and the other, down avenue de la Grande Armée toward La Tête Défense, a severe modern arch surrounded by imposing glass and concrete towers. Halfway up the Arc there is a small museum devoted to its history. *Museum and platform. Admission: 31 frs adults, 20 frs senior citizens, 6 frs children. Open daily 10–5:30; 10–5 in winter.*

The Champs-Elysées is the site of colorful national ceremonies on July 14 and November 11; its trees are often decked out with French tricolors and foreign flags to mark visits from heads of state. It is also where the cosmopolitan pulse of Paris beats strongest. The gracefully sloping 2-kilometer (1¼-mile) boulevard was originally laid out in the 1660s by André Le Nôtre as a garden sweeping away from the Tuileries. There is not much sign of that as you stroll past the cafés, restaurants, airline offices, car showrooms, movie theaters, and chic arcades that occupy its upper half. Farther down, on ② the right, is the **Grand Palais,** which plays host to Paris's major art exhibitions. Its glass roof makes its interior remarkably bright. *Admission varies. Usually open 10:30–6:30.*

The Grand Palais also houses the **Palais de la Découverte,** with scientific and mechanical exhibits and a planetarium. Entrance is in the avenue Franklin-Roosevelt. *Admission: 22 frs adults, 11 frs students; additional 15 frs (10 frs students) for planetarium. Open Tues.–Sat. 9:30–6, Sun. 10–7.*

② Directly opposite the main entrance to the Grand Palais is the **Petit Palais,** built at the same time (1900) and now home to an attractively presented collection of French paintings and furniture from the 18th and 19th centuries. *Admission: 26 frs adults, 14 frs students. Open Tues.–Sun. 10–5:40.*

Continue down to place de la Concorde, built around 1775 and scene of more than a thousand deaths at the guillotine, including those of Louis XVI and Marie-Antoinette. The obelisk, a gift from the viceroy of Egypt, was erected in 1833.

② To the east of the place de la Concorde is the **Jardin des Tuileries:** formal gardens with trees, ponds, and statues, currently undergoing renovations as part of the **Grand Louvre Project.** Standing guard on either side are the **Jeu de Paume** and the **Orangerie,** identical buildings erected in the mid-19th century. The Jeu de Paume, home of an Impressionist collection before its move to the Musee d' Orsay, has been completely transformed. Its spacious, austere, white-walled rooms now house temporary exhibits of contemporary art, usually at its most brazen. The Orangerie contains fine early 20th-century

French works by Monet (including his *Water Lilies*), Renoir, Marie Laurencin, and others. *Admission to Jeu de Paume: 30 frs adults, 20 frs students. Open Tues. noon–9:30, Wed.–Fri. noon–7, weekends 10–7. Admission to Orangerie: 26 frs, 14 frs Sun. Open Wed.–Mon. 9:45–5:45.*

Pass through the Tuileries to the Arc du Carrousel, a rather small triumphal arch erected more quickly (1806–08) than its big brother at the far end of the Champs-Elysées. Towering before you is the ❷❹ **Louvre,** with its glass pyramids. The Louvre, originally a royal palace, is today the world's largest and most famous museum. I. M. Pei's pyramids are the highlight of a major modernization program begun in 1984 and scheduled for completion in 1996. The plans include the extension of the museum collections into the Richelieu wing and cleaning of the facades, restoration of the gardens between the Louvre and the Tuileries, and the construction of an underground garage and shopping arcade, the **Carrousel du Louvre,** centered around an inverted glass pyramid. In the course of construction, the medieval foundations of the palace were unearthed and are maintained and displayed as an integral part of the museum's collection.

The Louvre was begun as a fortress in 1200 (the earliest parts still standing date from the 1540s) and completed under Napoleon III in the 1860s. The Louvre used to be even larger; a wing facing the Tuileries Gardens was razed by rampaging revolutionaries during the bloody Paris Commune of 1871.

Whatever the aesthetic merits of Pei's new-look Louvre, the museum has emerged less cramped and more rationally organized. Yet its sheer variety can seem intimidating. The main tourist attraction is Leonardo da Vinci's *Mona Lisa* (known in French as *La Joconde)*, painted in 1503. The latest research, based on Leonardo's supposed homosexuality, would have us believe that the subject was actually a man! The *Mona Lisa* may disappoint you; it's smaller than most imagine, it's kept behind glass, and it's invariably encircled by a mob of tourists.

Turn your attention instead to some of the less-crowded rooms and galleries nearby, where Leonardo's fellow Italians are strongly represented: Fra Angelico, Giotto, Mantegna, Raphael, Titian, and Veronese. El Greco, Murillo, and Velázquez lead the Spanish; Van Eyck, Rembrandt, Frans Hals, Brueghel, Holbein, and Rubens underline the achievements of northern European art. English paintings are highlighted by works of Lawrence, Reynolds, Gainsborough, and Turner. Highlights of French painting include works by Poussin, Fragonard, Chardin, Boucher, and Watteau—together with David's *Coronation of Napoleon*, Géricault's *Raft of the Medusa*, and Delacroix's *Liberty Guiding the People*.

Famous statues include the soaring *Victory of Samothrace*, the celebrated *Venus de Milo*, and the realistic Egyptian *Seated Scribe*. Be sure to inspect the Gobelins tapestries, the Crown Jewels (including the 186-carat Regent diamond), and the 9th-century bronze statuette of Emperor Charlemagne. *Admission 32 frs adults, 20 frs students and Sun., children under 18 free. Open Wed.–Mon. 9–6 (9–9:45 PM Mon. and Wed.).*

Montmartre If you start at the Anvers métro station and head up rue de Steinkerque, with its budget clothing shops, you will be greeted by the most familiar and spectacular view of the Sacré Coeur basilica ❷❺ atop the Butte Montmartre. The **Sacré-Coeur** was built in a bizarre, mock-Byzantine style between 1876 and 1910. It is no favorite with aesthetes, yet it has become a major Paris landmark. It was built as an act of national penitence after the disastrous Franco-Prussian War of 1870—a Catholic show of strength at a time when conflict between Church and State was at its most bitter.

26 Around the corner is the **place du Tertre,** full of would-be painters and trendy, overpriced restaurants. The painters have been setting up their easels on the square for years; avoid being talked into having your portrait done.

Despite its eternal tourist appeal and ever-growing commercialization, Montmartre has not lost all its traditional bohemian color. Walk down rue Norvins and descend the bustling rue Lepic to place Blanche and one of the favorite haunts of Toulouse-Lautrec and oth-
27 er luminaries of the Belle Epoque—the legendary **Moulin Rouge** cabaret.

Montmartre is some distance from the rest of the city's major attractions, so go left up boulevard de Clichy as far as **place Pigalle,** then take the métro to Madeleine.

Central Paris The **Eglise de la Madeleine,** with its array of uncompromising col-
28 umns, looks like a Greek temple. The only natural light inside comes from three shallow domes; the walls are richly but harmoniously decorated, with plenty of gold glinting through the dim interior. The church was designed in 1814 but not consecrated until 1842, after efforts to turn the site into a train station were defeated. The portico's majestic Corinthian colonnade supports a huge pediment with a sculptured frieze of the *Last Judgment.* From the top of the steps you can admire the vista down rue Royale across the Seine. Another vista leads up boulevard Malesherbes to the dome of **St-Augustin,** a mid-19th-century church notable for its innovative use of iron girders as structural support.

Place de la Madeleine is in the heart of Paris's prime shopping dis-
29 **30** trict: Jewelers line rue Royale; **Fauchon's** and **Hédiard's,** behind the Madeleine, are high-class delicatessens. Alongside the Madeleine is a **ticket kiosk** selling tickets for same-day theater performances at greatly reduced prices (open Tues.–Sat. 12:30–8).

Continue down boulevard de la Madeleine and turn right into rue des Capucines. This nondescript street leads to rue de la Paix. Im-
31 mediately to the right is **place Vendôme.** This is one of the world's most opulent squares, a rhythmically proportioned example of 17th-century urban architecture that shines in all its golden-stoned splendor since being sandblasted several years ago. Other things shine here, too, in the windows of jewelry shops that are even more upscale (and discreet) than those in rue Royale—fitting neighbors
32 for the top-ranking **Ritz** hotel. The square's central column, topped by a statue of Napoleon, is made from the melted bronze of 1,200 cannons captured at the Battle of Austerlitz in 1805.

Time Out Rue de la Paix leads, logically enough, to the **Café de la Paix** on the corner of the place de l'Opéra. There are few grander cafés in Paris, and fewer places where you can perch with as good a tableau before you.

33 Dominating the northern side of the square is the imposing **Opéra,** the first great work of the architect Charles Garnier, who in 1860 won the contract to build the opera house. He used elements of neoclassical architecture—bas reliefs on facades and columns—in an exaggerated combination that borders on parody. The lavishly upholstered auditorium, with its delightful ceiling painted by Marc

Chagall in 1964, seems small—but this is because the stage is the largest in the world, accommodating up to 450 players. It was the Opéra Garnier that inspired Gaston Leroux's penny dreadful, **The Phantom of the Opera,** as it was rumored that a diabolical genius who lived in the cellar lured the opera singers down to his murky chambers. *Admission: 30 frs adults, 15 frs students and children. Open daily 10–4:30.*

㉞ Behind the Opéra are **les grands magasins,** Paris's most venerable department stores. The nearer of the two, the **Galeries Lafayette,** is the more outstanding because of its elegant turn-of-the-century glass dome. But **Printemps,** farther along boulevard Haussmann to the left, is better organized and has an excellent view from its rooftop cafeteria.

㉟ Take the métro at Chaussée d'Antin, near the Galeries Lafayette, and travel three stops (direction Villejuif) as far as **Palais-Royal.** This former royal palace, built in the 1630s, has a charming garden, bordered by arcades and boutiques, that many visitors overlook.

㊱ On the square in front of the Palais-Royal is the **Louvre des Antiquaires,** a chic shopping mall full of antiques dealers. It deserves a browse whether you intend to buy or not. Afterward, head east along rue St-Honoré and left into rue du Louvre. Skirt the circular **Bourse du Commerce** (Commercial Exchange) and head toward the **㊲** imposing church of **St-Eustache,** (1532–1637), an invaluable testimony to the stylistic transition between Gothic and Classical architec-**㊳** ture. It is also the "cathedral" of **Les Halles**—the site of the central market of Paris until the much-loved glass-and-iron sheds were torn down in the late '60s. The area has since been transformed into a trendy—and already slightly seedy—shopping complex, Le Forum.

Head across the topiary garden and left down rue Berger. Pass the square des Innocents, with its Renaissance fountain, to boulevard de Sébastopol. Straight ahead lies the futuristic, funnel-topped **㊴** **Beaubourg** (Pompidou Center)—a must for lovers of modern art. The Beaubourg, also known as the Pompidou Centre, was built in the mid-1970s and named in honor of former French president Georges Pompidou (1911–74). This "cultural Disneyland" is always crowded, housing a **Museum of Modern Art,** a huge library, experimental music and industrial design sections, a children's museum, and a variety of activities and exhibitions. Musicians, magicians, fire-eaters, and other street performers fill the large forecourt near the entrance. *Admission free. Art museum: 30 frs; 20–50 frs for special exhibitions; 50 frs for daily pass covering all sectors of the center. Open Mon., Wed.–Fri. noon–10; weekends 10–10. Guided tours in English 3:30 PM weekdays and 11 AM weekends during summer and Christmas season.*

Note on the right side of Beaubourg as you face it the large digital clock, dubbed the **Genitron,** which counts down the seconds to the year 2000 at what seems like an apocalyptic pace. Peek into the café-lined **square Stravinsky** just to the right; kids will delight in the lively fountain animated by the colorful and imaginative sculptures and aquatic mechanisms by French artists Niki de Saint Phalle and Jean Tinguely. Continue east to the **Marais,** one of the most historic quarters of Paris. The spacious affluence of its 17th-century mansions, many restored to former glory, contrasts with narrow winding streets full of shops and restaurants. Rue de Rambuteau leads from the Centre Pompidou into rue des Francs-Bourgeois. Turn left on rue Elzivir to rue Thorigny, where you will find the Hôtel Salé and **㊵** its **Musée Picasso.** This is a convincing experiment in modern museum layout, whether you like Picasso or not. Few of his major works are here, but many fine, little-known paintings, drawings, and engravings are on display. *5 rue Thorigny. Admission: 26 frs., free under 18 yrs. Open Wed.–Mon. 9:30–6.*

41 Double back down rue Elzivir and turn left along rue des Francs-Bourgeois until you reach the **place des Vosges.** Built in 1605, this is the oldest square in Paris. The square's harmonious proportions, soft pink brick, and cloisterlike arcades give it an aura of calm. In the far corner is the **Maison de Victor Hugo,** containing souvenirs of the great poet's life and many of his surprisingly able paintings and ink drawings. *6 pl. des Vosges. Admission: 12 frs., 6.50 frs students and children. Open Tues.–Sun. 10–5:40.*

42 Rue Birague leads from the middle of the place des Vosges down to rue St-Antoine. About 250 yards along to the left is the **place de la Bastille.** Unfortunately, there are no historic vestiges here; not even the soaring column, topped by the figure of Liberty, commemorates the famous storming of the Bastille in 1789 (the column stands in memory of Parisians killed in the uprisings of 1830 and 1848). Only the new **Opéra de la Bastille,** which opened in 1989, can be said to mark the bicentennial.

43 Retrace your steps down rue St-Antoine as far as the large Baroque
44 church of **Saint-Paul-Saint-Louis** (1627–41). Then continue down the rue de Rivoli to the **Hôtel de Ville.** This magnificent city hall was rebuilt in its original Renaissance style after being burned down in 1871, during the violent days of the Paris Commune. The vast square in front of its many-statued facade is laid out with fountains and bronze lamps.

45 Avenue de Victoria leads to place du Châtelet. On the right is the **Tour St-Jacques.** This richly worked 52-meter (170-foot) stump is all that remains of a 16th-century church destroyed in 1802.

46 From Châtelet take the pont-au-Change over the Seine to the Ile de la Cité and the **Palais de Justice** (law courts). Visit the turreted **Conciergerie,** a former prison with a superb vaulted 14th-century hall (Salles des Gens d'Armes) that often hosts temporary exhibitions. The **Tour de l'Horloge** (clock tower) near the entrance on the quai de l'Horloge has a clock that has been ticking off time since 1370. Around the corner in the boulevard du Palais, through the imposing law court gates, is the **Sainte-Chapelle,** built by St-Louis (Louis IX) in the 1240s to house the Crown of Thorns he had just bought from Emperor Baldwin of Constantinople. The building's lead-covered wood spire, rebuilt in 1854, rises 75 meters (246 feet). The somewhat garish lower chapel is less impressive than the upper one, whose walls consist of little else but dazzling 13th-century stained glass. *Conciergerie and Sainte-Chapelle. Admission: joint ticket 40 frs; single ticket 26 frs, 17 frs students. Open daily 9:30–6:30; winter 10–5.*

47 From boulevard du Palais turn right on quai des Orfèvres. This will take you past the quaint place Dauphine to the **square du Vert Galant** at the westernmost tip of the Ile de la Cité. Here, above a peaceful garden, you will find a statue of the Vert Galant: gallant adventurer Henry IV, king from 1589 to 1610.

Off the Beaten Track

Few tourists venture into east Paris, but there are several points of interest tucked away here. The largest is the **Bois de Vincennes,** a less touristy version of the Bois de Boulogne, with several cafés and lakes. Rowboats can be taken to the two islands in Lac Daumesnil or to the three in Lac des Minimes. There is also a zoo, cinder racetrack *(hippodrome)*, and an extensive flower garden (Parc Floral, route de la Pyramide). The **Château de Vincennes** (av. de Paris) is an imposing, high-walled castle surrounded by a dry moat and dominated by a 53-meter (170-foot) keep. It contains a replica of the Sainte-Chapelle on Ile de la Cité and two elegant classical wings added in the mid-17th century. *Best métro access to the woods is at Porte Dorée; to the flower garden and castle (admission: 25 frs, 14 frs students and senior citizens, 6 frs under 7; open summer 10–6, winter 10–4), at Château de Vincennes.*

Cemeteries aren't every tourist's idea of the ultimate attraction, but **Père Lachaise** is the largest, most interesting, and most prestigious in Paris. It forms a veritable necropolis with cobbled avenues and tombs competing in pomposity and originality. Steep slopes and lush vegetation contribute to a powerful atmosphere; some people even bring a picnic lunch. Leading incumbents include Chopin, Molière, Proust, Oscar Wilde, Sarah Bernhardt, Jim Morrison, Yves Montand, and Edith Piaf. Get a map at the entrance and track them down. *Av. du Père-Lachaise, 20e; métro Gambetta. Open daily 8–6, winter 8–5 .*

The **Canal St-Martin** starts life just south of the Place de la Bastille but really comes into its own during the 1.5-kilometer (1-mile) stretch north across the 10th arrondissement. It has an unexpected flavor of Amsterdam, thanks to its quiet banks, locks, and footbridges. *Closest métro stations: Jaurès to the north and Jacques-Bonsergent to the south.*

Hidden away in a grid of narrow streets not far from the Opéra is Paris's central auction house, the **Hôtel Drouot.** It is open six days a week (except at Christmas, Easter, and midsummer), and its 16 salesrooms make a fascinating place to browse, with absolutely no obligation to bid—though you may wish to do so! Everything from stamps and toy soldiers to Renoirs and 18th-century commodes is available. The mixture of fur-coated ladies with money to burn, penniless art lovers desperate to unearth an unidentified masterpiece, and scruffy dealers trying to look anonymous makes up Drouot's unusually rich social fabric. *Viewing takes place 11–noon and 2–6, with auctions starting at 2. Entrance at the corner of rue Rossini and rue Drouot, métro Richelieu-Drouot.*

Some of Paris's less-frequented arrondissements afford great walks. The **Bercy** section of the 12e arrondissement (métro: Bercy) is the focus of a massive renovation project scheduled for completion in 1996. Once filled with warehouses for the storing of wine from the provinces, the neighborhood has seen a total transformation, which was kicked off in the mid-80s with the creation of the **Palais Omnisports,** the grassy-walled, pyramid-shaped sports complex and the installation in 1989 of the **French Finance Ministry** in their quaiside glass and steel offices. These buildings serve as cornerstones for the **Parc de Bercy,** which is also bordered by a large food and wine business complex and the new American Center, a venue for American art and cultural events designed by architect Frank Gehry.

Enjoy an afternoon stroll along the tree-lined streets of Paris's so-called **Beaux Quartiers,** concentrated in the 16e arrondissement (métro: Eglise d'Auteil, Ranelagh, La Muette), which are punctuated with some superb examples of 20th-century architecture. Of greatest interest are the art nouveau buildings built by **Hector**

Guimard (particularly 34 rue Boileau; 8 av. de la Villa-de-la-Reunion; and 14, 17, and 19 rue de la Fontaine); and **Le Corbusier's** first private houses, featuring Villa La Roche (1923), on a small cul-de-sac off rue du Docteur Blanche.

Finally, for those weary of monument gazing, Paris's **Chinatown**—concentrated between the high rises of rue Tolbiac, av. de Choisy and bd Massena (métro: Tolbiac) in the 13e—though not as ornamental as that of New York or San Francisco, boasts a delightful array of Chinese restaurants, supermarkets, and clothing stores.

Shopping

Gift Ideas Paris is the home of fashion and perfume. Old prints are sold in *bouquinistes* (stalls) along the Left Bank of the Seine. For state-of-the-art home decorations, the shop in the **Musée des Arts Décoratifs** in the Louvre (107 rue de Rivoli) is well worth visiting. Regional specialty foods, herbs, and pâtés can be found at **Fauchon** and **Hédiard,** two upscale grocers at 26 and 21 place de la Madeleine, 8e.

Antiques Antiques dealers proliferate in the **Carré Rive Gauche** between St-Germain-des-Prés and the Musée d'Orsay. There are also several dealers around the Drouot auction house near Opéra (corner of rue Rossini and rue Drouot; métro: Richelieu-Drouot). The **Louvre des Antiquaires,** near the Palais-Royal (*see* Exploring, *above*), and the **Village Suisse,** near the Champ de Mars (78 av. de Suffren), are stylish shopping malls dominated by antiques.

Boutiques Only Milan can compete with Paris for the title of Capital of European Chic. The top shops are along both sides of the Champs-Elysées, along the avenue Montaigne and the rue du Faubourg St-Honoré, and at Place des Victoires. St-Germain-des-Prés, rue de Grenelle, and rue de Rennes on the left bank are centers for small specialty shops and boutiques. If you're on a tight budget, search for bargains along the shoddy streets around the foot of Montmartre (*see* Exploring, *above*), or in the designer discount shops (Cacharel, Rykiel, Dorotennis) along rue d'Alésia in Montparnasse. The streets to the north of the Marais, close to Arts-et-Métiers métro, are historically linked to the cloth trade, and some shops offer garments at wholesale prices.

Department Stores The most famous department stores in Paris are **Galeries Lafayette** and **Printemps,** on boulevard Haussmann. Others include **Au Bon Marché** on the Left Bank (métro Sèvres–Babylone) and the **Samaritaine,** overlooking the Seine east of the Louvre (métro Pont-Neuf).

Food and Flea Markets The sprawling **Marché aux Puces de St-Ouen,** just north of Paris, is one of Europe's largest flea markets. Best bargains are to be had early in the morning (open Sat.–Mon.; métro Porte de Clignancourt). There are smaller flea markets at the Porte de Vanves and Porte de Montreuil (weekends only).

Dining

Eating out in Paris should be a pleasure, and there is no reason why choosing a less expensive restaurant should spoil the fun. After all, Parisians themselves eat out frequently and cannot afford five-star dining every night, either. For details and price-category definitions, *see* Dining in Staying in France, *above*.

Left Bank
Very Expensive **Jules Verne.** Distinctive all-black decor, stylish service, and a top chef—not to mention its location on the 400-foot second level of the

Eiffel Tower—have made the Jules Verne one of the hardest dinner reservations to get in Paris. The colorful, flavorful cuisine (including soufflé of giant crab, and lobster tournedos in a veal and butter sauce) is most accessible at lunch, when a table is easier to snag and there is a good fixed-price menu. *Eiffel Tower, 7e, tel. 45–55–61–44. Reservations required at least 3 weeks in advance. Jacket and tie required. AE, DC, MC, V.*

★ **La Tour d'Argent.** Dining at this temple to haute cuisine is a theatrical and unique event—from apéritifs in the ground-floor bar to dinner in the top-floor dining room, with its breathtaking view of Notre Dame. Come for the setting; the food does not reach the same standard. In recent years owner Claude Terrail has hired a series of young chefs, and today's menu is a mix of Tour classics and contemporary creations, including *caneton* Tour d'Argent (pressed duck), and scallop salad with truffles. The wine list is one of the greatest in the world. *15 quai de la Tournelle, 5e, tel. 43–54–23–31. Reservations required at least 1 week in advance. Jacket and tie required at dinner, advised at lunch. AE, DC, MC, V. Closed Mon.*

Moderate– **La Timonerie.** Only a few steps along the quai from La Tour
Expensive d'Argent, this small, elegant restaurant avoids all theatrics and
★ sticks to fine cooking. Philippe de Givenchy works with a small staff, but his proposals are consistently interesting and well executed. In his hands, simple products such as rosemary and lemon mackerel are turned into high-class eating experiences. *35 quai de la Tournelle, 5e, tel. 43–25–44–42. Reservations advised. Jacket and tie advised. MC, V. Closed Sun. and Mon.*

Moderate **Campagne et Provence.** This small establishment, on the quai across from Notre Dame, specializes in country cooking. Fresh, colorful Provençal-inspired cuisine includes vegetables stuffed with *brandade* (creamed salt cod), ratatouille, and beer *daube* (stew) with olives. The list of reasonably priced regional wines helps keep the cost down. *25 quai de la Tournelle, 5e, tel. 43–54–05–17. Reservations advised. Dress: casual. MC, V. Closed Mon. and Sat. lunch, Sun.*

Lipp. Politicians, entertainers, rubber-necking tourists, and everyone else vie for tables here, especially in the ground-floor dining room of this classic Left Bank brasserie. Food is classic brasserie-style, too: herring in cream, *choucroute garni* (sausages and cured pork served with sauerkraut), and *mille-feuille* (puffed pastry). Attractive 1920s decor includes historic ceramics. *151 blvd. St-Germain, 6e, tel. 45–48–53–91. No reservations; expect lines. Jacket required. AE, DC, MC, V. Closed mid-July–mid-Aug.*

La Rotisserie d'En Face. A long rotisserie is part of the attractive country-elegant decor at this bistro created by renowned chef Jacques Cagna. The cuisine includes roast chicken with mashed potatoes and grilled salmon with spinach. The menu is fixed-price only, and it's cheaper at lunch. *2 rue Christine, 6e, tel. 43–26–40–98. MC, V. Closed Sat. dinner.*

Inexpensive **La Régalade.** This is one of the most talked about new restaurants in
★ Paris. The address, right next to the highway, is nothing to write home about, but Yves Camdeborde's cooking is stunning. Although a veteran of the Crillon, he has kept his prices remarkably low—$30 for a three-course feast. Tables are booked as much as a month in advance, but service does continue until midnight, and often you can sneak in later in the evening. *49 av Jean-Moulin, 14e, tel. 45–45–68–58. Reserve 1 month in advance. Dress: casual. MC, V. Closed Sat. lunch, Sun., Mon., Aug.*

West Paris
Very Expensive
★

Jamin/Robuchon. Surely it's the most difficult reservation to obtain in France. Chef-owner Joël Robuchon, though under 50, has already attained cult status, and his influence on cooks around the globe is great. Under his inspired vision, everything from cream of cauliflower with caviar to John Dory with ginger, saddle of lamb in a salt crust to pig's head becomes a visual and gustatory revelation. The big news here is that Robuchon has moved out of his old, cramped quarters into a brighter, airier space in a sparkling new hôtel particulier. *59 av Raymond-Poincaré, 16e, tel. 47–27–12–27. Reservations required. Jacket and tie required. MC, V. Closed weekends and July.*

Taillevent. Many say it's the best restaurant in Paris. Within the wood-paneled main dining rooms of this mid-19th-century mansion you will find exceptional, subtle service, a world-renowned wine list, and the neoclassic cuisine of young chef Philippe Legendre. Specials here include lobster boudin and lamb with cabbage. Book three to four weeks ahead. *15 rue Lamennais, 8e, tel. 45–63–39–94. Reservations required. Jacket and tie required. AE, MC, V. Closed weekends and Aug.*

Moderate

La Fermette Marbeuf. It's a favorite haunt of French TV and movie stars, who like the spectacular Belle Epoque mosaics, tiles, and stained glass (discovered by accident when the restaurant was being redecorated), and the solid, updated classic cuisine. Try *gâteau* of chicken livers and sweetbreads, lamb *navarin* (stew), and bitter chocolate fondant. La Fermette becomes animated late, around 9. Prices here are surprisingly reasonable, considering the quality, surroundings, and neighborhood. *5 rue Marbeuf, 8e, tel. 47–20–63–53. Reservations advised. Dress: casual but elegant. AE, DC, MC, V.*

Inexpensive

La Ferme St. Hubert. Reserve ahead for lunch, as this unpretentious spot serving primarily cheese dishes is mobbed then. The owner has a cheese shop next door—one of the best in the city—and from its shelves come the main ingredients for fondue, raclette, and the best *croque St-Hubert* (toasted cheese sandwich) in Paris. The house wines are decent, and the location is convenient to the fancy food shop, Fauchon, on the place de la Madeleine. *21 rue Vignon, 8e, tel. 47–42–79–20. Reservations essential at lunch, advised at dinner. Dress: casual. AE, MC, V. Closed Sun.*

Right Bank
Very Expensive

Le Grand Véfour. This sumptuously decorated restaurant is perhaps the most beautiful in Paris, and its 18th-century origins make it one of the oldest. Chef Guy Martin impresses with his unique blend of sophisticated yet rustic dishes, including rabbit with carrot and curry and cabbage ravioli with truffle cream. Luminaries from Napoléon to Colette to Jean Cocteau have frequented this intimate address under the arcades of the Palais Royal; you can request to be seated at their preferred table. *17 rue Beaujolais, 1er, tel. 42–96–56–27. Reservations advised 1 week in advance. Jacket and tie required. AE, DC, MC, V. Closed Sat., Sun., and Aug.*

Expensive

Miravile. This latest Miravile—the third for successful young owners Gilles and Muriel Epié—has vaguely California decor and a Provençal-inspired menu. Mr. Epié's celery *remoulade* with foie gras, and chocolate mille-feuille exemplify his full-flavored style. The restaurant is popular with staff members from the adjacent Hôtel de Ville (city hall). *72 quai de l'Hôtel de Ville, 4e, tel. 42–74–72–22. Reservations advised. Dress: casual. MC, V. Closed Sat. lunch, Sun.*

Moderate **Coconnas.** On a soft summer evening, there is no prettier place in Paris than a table at the terrace of this restaurant on the Place des Vosges. The owner is Claude Terrail, owner of the celebrated Tour d'Argent, and as at the Tour d'Argent, the emphasis here is more on the setting than the food. Certainly you won't eat poorly, but you'll enjoy watching the world go by more than concentrating on your plate. *2 Pl. des Vosges, 4e, tel. 42–78–58–16. Reservations advised. Dress casual. Closed Mon., Tues., and Jan. 10–Feb. 10. AE, DC, MC, V.*

Inexpensive **Chez Jenny.** Order the filling choucroute Jenny and a carafe of Alsation wine, then sit back and watch the bustle at this large, Alsatian brasserie. Waitresses in regional costume wend their way through many salons on two levels, serving hearty fare. Decor includes museum-quality marquetry and woodwork. Although the clientele is not the chic crowd found in other brasseries, everyone's having just as much fun. *39 blvd. du Temple, 3e, tel. 42–74–75–75. Reservations advised. Dress: casual. AE, DC, MC, V.*

Montmartre and East Paris *Very Expensive* **A. Beauvilliers.** Pickwickian owner Edouard Carlier is a born party-giver, and his flower-filled restaurant is one of the most festive in Paris. The three dining rooms are filled with his personal collection of paintings and valuable bibelots, and a tiny, vine-covered terrace makes for delightful summer dining. Chefs here come and go, but Mr. Carlier maintains quality, serving both original creations and reinterpreted classics. Recommended are the red mullet *en escabèche*, foie gras, lobster, sweetbread *tourte*, and *rognonnade* of veal. The mouth-puckering lemon tart is not to be missed. One drawback: Service can be distant if you are not known. *52 rue Lamarck, 18e, tel. 42–54–54–42. Reservations required. Jacket and tie required. AE, MC, V. Closed Sun. and Mon. lunch.*

Expensive ★ **La Table d'Anvers.** One of the best restaurants near Montmartre, La Table d'Anvers serves an interesting menu, with Italian and Provençal touches in dishes like gnocchi of langoustines and *girolles* (wild mushrooms), saddle of rabbit with polenta, and *croustillant* of asparagus with scampi. Desserts are among the best in Paris; serious sweet tooths can indulge in an all-dessert menu, which includes a fish dish. *2 pl. d'Anvers, 9e, tel. 48–78–35–21. Reservations advised. Dress: casual but elegant. AE, MC, V. Closed Sat. lunch, Sun., and mid-Aug.*

Moderate **Chez Philippe/Pyrénées-Cévennes.** Old-timers refer to this comfortable bistro by its original name—Pyrénées-Cévennes—while others know it as Chez Philippe. The eclectic menu combines the cooking of Burgundy, central France—even Spain—in such dishes as snails in garlic butter, coq au vin, cassoulet, and paella. An attentive staff bustles amid cozy surroundings that include a beamed ceiling and polished copper. *106 rue de la Folie-Méricourt, 11e, tel. 43–57–33–78. Reservations advised. Dress: casual. MC, V. Closed weekends and Aug.*

Lodging

Paris is popular throughout the year, so make reservations early. For details and price-category definitions, *see* Lodging in Staying in France, *above*.

Left Bank and Ile St-Louis *Very Expensive* **L'Hotel.** Rock idols and movie stars adore this expensive but eccentric Left Bank hotel filled with flowers and antiques. Oscar Wilde died in room 16. "I am dying beyond my means," he wrote. One small double is covered entirely in leopardskin; another handsome suite features the mirrored art deco boudoir furniture that belonged to the nightclub star Mistinguett. Warning: Many rooms are extremely small. The hotel has a fine restaurant, Le Belier, whose decor includes a fountain with a live tree. The bar, open until 1 AM, is popular with a well-heeled international crowd. *13 rue des Beaux-Arts, 75006, 6e, tel. 43–25–27–22, fax 43–25–64–81. 16 rooms with bath, 8 with shower, 3 suites. Facilities: restaurant, bar, room service, English spoken. AE, DC, MC, V.*

Expensive **Deux-Iles.** This cleverly converted 17th-century mansion on the residential Ile St-Louis has long won plaudits for charm and comfort. Flowers and plants are scattered around the stunning hall. The fabric-hung rooms, though small, have exposed beams and are fresh and airy. Ask for a room overlooking the little garden courtyard. The lounge is dominated by a fine chimneypiece. *59 rue St-Louis-en-l'Ile, 75004, 4e, tel. 43–26–13–35, fax 43–29–60–25. 17 rooms, 8 with bath, 9 with shower. English spoken. No credit cards.*

★ **Fleurie.** Entirely air-conditioned, this spiffy family-run hotel established in 1988 offers a good location (a quiet sidestreet near the place de l'Odéon), prettily furnished pastel rooms, and many luxury amenities: built-in hairdryers, mini-bars, private safe deposit boxes, marble-clad bathrooms, heated towel racks, and color TV with CNN. *32–34 rue Grégoire-de-Tours, 75006, 6e, tel. 43–29–59–81, fax 43–29–68–44. 29 rooms with bath. Facilities: bar/salon. English spoken. AE, DC, MC, V.*

Moderate **Grandes Ecoles.** Recently upgraded from no stars to two, this delightful hotel in three small old buildings is set far off the street in a beautiful garden. There are parquet floors, antiques, and a piano in the breakfast area. Most rooms have beige carpets and flowery wallpaper. You won't find a quieter, more charming hotel for the price. There's a faithful American clientele, including some back-packers. The rooms with bathroom facilities on the well-lit landings are inexpensive. *75 rue du Cardinal Lemoine, 75005, 5e, tel. 43–26–79–23, fax 43–25–28–15. 29 rooms with bath, 20 with shower, 9 with shared bath. English spoken. V.*

★ **Jardin des Plantes.** Across the street from the lovely Jardin des Plantes botanical gardens on the edge of the Latin Quarter, this pleasant two-star hotel offers botanical-theme decor and very reasonable prices. There's a fifth-floor terrace where you can breakfast or sunbathe in summer, and a sauna and ironing room in the cellar. *5 rue Linné, 75005, 5e, tel. 47–07–06–20, fax 47–07–62–74. 29 rooms with bath, 4 with shower. Facilities: sauna, bar-tearoom, terrace. English spoken. AE, DC, MC, V.*

West Paris **Le Bristol.** Luxury and discretion are the Bristol's trump cards. The
Very Expensive understated facade on rue du Faubourg St-Honoré might mislead
★ the unknowing, but the Bristol ranks among Paris's top four hotels. Some of the air-conditioned and spaciously elegant rooms have authentic Louis XV and Louis XVI furniture, and the management has filled public areas with old-master paintings, sculptures, sumptuous carpets, and tapestries. The marble bathrooms are simply magnificent. Nonguests can take tea in the vast garden or dine in the tented summer restaurant or the wood-paneled winter restaurant; later, you can listen to the pianist in the bar, open till 1 AM. There's an enclosed pool on the roof, complete with solarium and sauna for guests only. The service throughout is impeccable. *112 rue du Faubourg St-Honoré, 75008, 8e, tel. 42–66–91–45, fax 42–66–68–68. 155 rooms with bath, 45 suites. Facilities: restaurant, bar, pool, sauna, fitness machines, solarium, parking. English spoken. AE, DC, MC, V.*

★ **Crillon.** The Crillon is the crème de la crème of the Paris "palace hotels," set as it is in two 18th-century town houses on the place de la Concorde, site of the French Revolution's infamous guillotine. Marie-Antoinette, who met her end there, took singing lessons at the Hôtel de Crillon, where one of the original *grands appartements*, now sumptuous salons protected by the French National Historic Landmark Commission, has been named for the queen. Guests must pay dearly for a balcony overlooking the great square, with seemingly all of Paris at their feet; only the suites have them. Lesser mortals still get magnificent digs, individually decorated with Rococo and Directoire antiques, crystal and gilt wall sconces, and gold fittings. Most double rooms have separate sitting rooms, and the bathrooms, stocked with wonderful Annick Goutal toiletries, are clad in marble. The sheer quantity of the marble downstairs—in the lobby, the adjacent lounge, and especially the grand, top-rated Les Ambassadeurs restaurant—is staggering. The staff anticipates your every need. *10 pl. de la Concorde, 75008, 8e, tel. 44–71–15–00, fax 44–71–15–02. 120 rooms and 43 suites, all with bath. Facilities: 2 restaurants, 2 bars, shop. English spoken. AE, DC, MC, V.*

George V. Some say the George V lacks the this-could-only-be-Paris atmosphere of other super-deluxe Parisian hotels; its style is more international. But there's no lack of authentic period furniture, or, indeed, of excellent, highly trained staff. Most rooms are impeccably decorated and imposing, although the penthouse suites are the only ones to enjoy a commanding view over the city. There are two restaurants; the better is Les Princes, where, in summer, you can eat on the leafy patio. *31 av. George V, 75008, 8e, tel. 47–23–54–00, fax 47–20–40–00. 298 rooms with bath, 53 suites. Facilities: 2 restaurants, bar, tea salon, hairdresser. English spoken. AE, DC, MC, V.*

Moderate **Etoile-Pereire.** Pianist Ferrucio Pardi, owner and manager of the
★ Etoile-Pereire, has created a unique small hotel, set behind a quiet, leafy courtyard in a chic residential district. All rooms and duplexes are decorated in soothing pastels—pinks, grays, and apricots— with Laura Ashley curtains and chair covers, and prints on the walls. There's no house restaurant, but room service can be arranged. A copious breakfast is available—with 40 different jams and jellies. The bar is always busy in the evening. For a lively, personally run hotel, few places beat this likeable spot. *146 blvd. Pereire, 75017, 17e, tel. 42–67–60–00, fax 42–67–02–90. 18 rooms with bath, 3 with shower, 4 duplexes, 1 suite. Facilities: bar. English spoken. AE, DC, MC, V.*

Keppler. Ideally located on the edge of the 8th and 16th Arrondissements near the Champs-Elysées, this small two-star hotel in a 19th-century building bursts with amenities (room service, small bar) at extremely reasonable prices. The spacious and airy rooms are simply decorated with modern furnishings. Some rooms with shower are inexpensive. *12 rue Keppler, 75116, 16e, tel. 47–20–65–05, fax 47–23–02–29. 31 rooms with bath, 18 with shower. Facilities: bar. English spoken. AE, MC, V.*

Inexpensive **Argenson.** This friendly, family-run hotel provides what may well be
★ the best value in the swanky 8th Arrondissement. Top sights are just a 10-minute walk away. Old furniture, molded ceilings, and skillfull flower arrangements add to the charm. Room-by-room renovation means new bathrooms in many. The best rooms have full bath, but they are moderately priced; reserve well in advance for one of these. The small rooms with shared baths are very inexpensive. *15 rue d'Argenson, 75008, 8e, tel. 42–65–16–87, fax 47–42–02–06. 5 rooms with bath, 19 with shower, 3 with shared bath. Some English spoken. MC, V.*

Montmartre and Central Paris

Very Expensive

Grand Hotel Inter-Continental. Paris's biggest luxury hotel has endless hallways and a facade that seems as long as the Louvre. After a thorough restoration completed mid-1991, this 1862 gem sparkles like new. The grand salon and the painted ceilings of the Opéra and Café de la Paix restaurants are registered landmarks. The latter is one of the city's great rendezvous and people-watching spots. *2 rue Scribe, 75009, 9e, tel. 40–07–32–32, fax 42–66–12–51. 470 rooms with bath, 23 suites. Facilities: 3 restaurants, 2 bars, health club, shops, parking. English spoken. AE, DC, MC, V.*

Pavillon de la Reine. The best hotel in the Marais, it's set around two flower-filled courtyards behind the historic Queen's Pavilion on the 17th-century place des Vosges. Although this cozy mansion looks old, it was actually reconstructed from scratch in 1986 following original plans and using period timbers, rough-hewn paving stones, Louis XIII fireplaces, and antiques. Ask for a duplex with French windows over the first courtyard (there are no rooms overlooking the place des Vosges). Breakfast is served in a vaulted cellar. *28 pl. des Vosges, 75003, 3e, tel. 42–77–96–40, fax 42–77–63–06. 31 rooms with bath, 24 suites. Facilities: parking. English spoken. AE, DC, MC, V.*

★ **Ritz.** The Paris Ritz, on the stunning place Vendôme, is one of the world's most renowned hotels, located on the most famous and elegant square in the city. Millions of dollars have been lavished on the hotel by Egyptian-born owner Mohammed al-Fayed (who also owns Harrods in London). The building is a sumptuous 18th-century town house, a delightful combination of elegance and comfort. The vast, marble-clad bathrooms, some with turn-of-the-century fixtures, are renowned. The centerpiece of the health club here is a huge, delightful pool. The luxurious suites are named after just some of the guests who have stayed here—Coco Chanel, Marcel Proust, and Edward VII among them. L'Espadon is one of the finest hotel restaurants in the city, and the Vendôme Bar is notably chic. *15 pl. Vendôme, 75001, 1er, tel. 42–60–38–30, fax 42–86–00–91. 142 rooms and 45 suites, all with bath. Facilities: 2 restaurants, bar, health and sports complex with indoor pool. AE, DC, MC, V.*

Moderate

★ **Gaillon-Opéra.** The oak beams, stone walls, and marble tiles of the Gaillon-Opéra single it out as one of the most charming hotels in the Opéra neighborhood. The plants throughout and a flower-filled patio also delight. *9 rue Gaillon, 75002, 2e, tel. 47–42–47–74, fax 47–42–01–23. 26 rooms with bath, 1 suite. English spoken. AE, DC, MC, V.*

Inexpensive

Castex. This family-run, two-star hotel in a 19th-century building is a real find. The decor is strictly functional, but the extremely friendly owners and rock-bottom prices mean the Castex is often fully booked months ahead. There's a large American clientele. The eight least expensive rooms, two per floor, share toilets on the immaculate, well-lit landings. There's no elevator, and the only TV is in the lobby. *5 rue Castex, 75004, 4e, tel. 42–72–31–52, fax 42–72–57–91. 4 rooms with bath, 23 with shower. English spoken. MC, V.*

★ **Place des Vosges.** A loyal American clientele swears by the small, historic Place des Vosges, which is located on a charming street just off the exquisite square of the same name. Oak-beamed ceilings and rough-hewn stone in public areas and some of the guest rooms add to the atmosphere. Ask for the top-floor room, the hotel's largest, with a view of Marais rooftops. Some rooms, the size of walk-in closets, are inexpensive. There's a welcoming breakfast room. *12 rue de Birague, 75004, 4e, tel. 42–72–60–46, fax 42–72–02–64. 11 rooms with bath, 5 with shower. English spoken. AE, DC, MC, V.*

Regyn's Montmartre. Despite small rooms (all recently renovated), this small, owner-run hotel on Montmartre's place des Abbesses is rapidly gaining an enviable reputation for simple, comfortable accommodations. A predominantly young clientele and a correspondingly relaxed atmosphere have made this an attractive choice for some. Try for one of the rooms on the upper floors, with great views over the city. *18 pl. des Abbesses, 75018, 18e, tel. 42–54–45–21, fax 42–23–76–69. 14 rooms with bath, 8 with shower. English spoken. MC, V.*

The Arts

The monthly magazine *Paris Boulevard* (in English) and the weekly magazines *Pariscope, L'Officiel des Spectacles,* and *7 à Paris* give detailed entertainment listings. The Paris Tourist Office has set up a **24-hour hot line in English** with information about weekly events (tel. 49–52–53–56). Buy tickets at the place of performance; otherwise, try hotels, travel agencies (try **Paris-Vision** at 214 rue de Rivoli), and special ticket counters (in the **FNAC** stores at 26 av. de Wagram, near the Arc de Triomphe and the Forum des Halles). Half-price tickets for same-day theater performances are available at the ticket stand at the west side of the Madeleine church.

Theater There is no Parisian equivalent to Broadway or the West End, although a number of theaters line the grand boulevards between Opéra and République. Shows are mostly in French; classical drama is at the distinguished **Comédie Française** (by Palais-Royal). A completely different charm·is to be found in the tiny **Théâtre de la Huchette,** near St-Michel, where Ionesco's short modern plays make a deliberately ridiculous mess of the French language.

Concerts The principal venues for classical music are the **Salle Pleyel** (252 rue du Faubourg St-Honoré), near the Arc de Triomphe, the new **Opéra Bastille,** and the **Chatelet** theater (pl. Chatelet). You can also attend one of the many inexpensive organ or chamber music concerts in churches throughout the city.

Opera The **Opéra** itself, or **Opéra Garnier** (pl. de l'Opéra, 9e), has, alas, conceded its role as Paris's main opera house to the **Opéra Bastille** (pl. de la Bastille, tel. 44–73–13–00), which stages both traditional opera and symphony concerts. Getting a ticket for an opera or ballet performance is not easy, though, and requires either luck, much preplanning, or a well-connected hotel receptionist. The **Opéra Comique** (the French term for opera with spoken dialogue), close by in the rue Favart, is more accessible.

Dance The highlights of the Paris dance year usually take place at the **Opéra Garnier,** which, in addition to being the sumptuous home of the well-reputed Paris Ballet, also bills dozens of major foreign troupes ranging from classical to modern. Other major venues include the **Théatre de la Ville** (tel. 42–74–22–77) at Châtelet and the **Palais des Congrès** (tel. 40–68–22–22) at Porte Maillot.

Film There are hundreds of movie theaters in Paris and some of them, especially in principal tourist areas such as the Champs-Elysées and the boulevard des Italiens near the Opéra, run English films marked "V.O." *(version originale*—i.e., not dubbed). Admission is around 35–45 frs, with reduced rates on Wednesday. Movie fanatics should check out the **Centre Pompidou** and **Musée du Cinéma** at Trocadéro, where old and rare films are often screened.

Nightlife

Cabaret This is what Paris is supposed to be all about. Its nightclubs are household names—more so abroad than in France, it would seem, judging by the hefty percentage of foreigners present at most shows. Prices range from 200 frs (basic admission plus one drink) up to 650 frs (dinner included). For 350–450 frs, you can get a good seat plus half a bottle of champagne.

The **Crazy Horse** (12 av. George-V, tel. 47–23–32–32) is one of the field leaders in pretty women and dance routines: It features lots of humor and a lot less clothes. The **Moulin Rouge** (place Blanche, tel. 46–06–00–19) is an old favorite at the foot of Montmartre. Nearby is the **Folies-Bergère**, (32 rue Richer, tel. 42–46–77–11), which re-opened at the end of 1993 with an all-new show reminiscent of its music-hall origins. The **Lido** (116 bis av. des Champs-Elysées, tel. 40–76–56–10) is all razzle-dazzle.

Bars and Nightclubs Upscale nightclubs are usually private, so unless you have a friend who is a member, forget it. Give the wildly popular **Niel's** (27 av. Ternes, 17e) or **Sheherazade** (93 rue de Liege, 9e) a try on weeknights only, or you run the risk of spending the evening waiting in line on the sidewalk.

The Pigalle area in Montmartre is becoming the place to be nowadays, despite its reputation as a seedy red-light district. Among hot places here are **Moloko** (26, rue Fontaine, 9e), a smoky late-night bar; **Le Dépanneur** (next door at 27 rue Fontaine), which caters to more of a gin-drinking yuppie crowd; and **Lili la Tigresse** (98 rue Blanche, 9e), a sexy bar with a trendy crowd; and—not to be missed—the brasserie **Pigalle** (22 blvd. de Clichy, 18e), whose '50s frescoes and ceramics have been classified as a national treasure.

The nightlife is still hopping in and around the Bastille: the **China Club** (50 rue de Charenton, 12e) is a trendy bar with an Orient Express theme; **Le Casbah** (18 rue de la Forge Royale, 11e), a bar and dance club with a touch of Casablanca; and **Le Pistou Pelican** (15 rue de Bagnolet, 20e) a favorite among Beaux-Arts students with a laid-back ambience and occasional live music.

For a more leisurely experience in an atmosphere that is part bar and part gentlemen's club, try an old haunt of Hemingway, Fitzgerald, and Gertrude Stein: **Harry's Bar** (5 rue Danou), a cozy wood-paneled spot for Americans, journalists, and sportsmen.

Gay and Lesbian Gay and lesbian bars and clubs are mostly concentrated in the Marais and include some of the most happening addresses in the city. The very trendy **Banana Café** (13 rue de la Ferronnerie, 1e) attracts an energetic and scantily-clad mixed crowd; dancing on the tables is the norm. For men, **Le Quetzal** (10 rue de la Verrerie, 4e), which features a chrome-and-blue-light atmosphere, gets very crowded and smoky on weekends; **The Trap** (10 rue Jacob, 6e) contains a ground floor video bar with a staircase leading to a darker, more social area. For a more relaxed atmosphere try **Subway** (35 rue Saint-Croix-de-la-Bretonnerie, 4e), a popular hangout with pinball and pool.

For women, **La Champsmelé** (4 rue Chabanais, 2e) is the hub of lesbian nightlife with a back room reserved for women only; **Le Memorie's** (2 pl. de Pte. Maillol, 16e), though situated in a staid neighborhood, is Paris's most renowned lesbian dance club.

Jazz Clubs The Latin Quarter is a good place to track down Paris jazz, and the doyen of clubs is the **Caveau de la Huchette** (5 rue de la Huchette), where you can hear Dixieland in a hectic, smoke-filled atmosphere. **Le Slow Club** (130 rue de Rivoli), another favorite, tries to resurrect the style of early Bourbon street, and nearly succeeds.

Rock Clubs **Le Sunset** (60 rue des Lombards) is a small, whitewashed cellar with first-rate live music and a clientele that's there to listen. **New Morning** (7 rue des Petites Ecuries) is a top spot for visiting American musicians and good French bands.

Discos **Club Zed** (2 rue des Anglais off blvd. St.-Germain), is the best place for rock and roll. The long-established **Balajo** (9 rue de Lappe, 11e) is crowded and lots of fun, with plenty of nostalgic '60s sounds on some nights. **Memphis** (3 impasse Bonne-Nouvelle) boasts some impressive lighting and video gadgetry.

Ile de France

The area surrounding Paris is called the Ile (island) de France, reflecting the role it has played over the centuries as the economic, political, and religious center of the country. For many visitors to Paris, it is the first taste of French provincial life, with its slower pace and fierce devotion to the soil. Although parts of the area are fighting a losing battle to resist the encroaching capital, you can still see the countryside that was the inspiration for the Impressionists and other 19th-century painters and is home to a wealth of architecture dating to the Middle Ages. The most famous buildings are Chartres—one of the most beautiful of French cathedrals—and Versailles, the monumental château of Louis XIV, the Sun King. Before the completion of Versailles, king and court resided in the delightful château of St-Germain-en-Laye, west of Paris. This is within easy day-trip range of Paris, as are the châteaux of Vaux-le-Vicomte, Rambouillet, and Fontainebleau, and the newest Disney venture, Euro Disney.

Getting Around

The region is reached easily from Paris by car and by regular suburban train services. But you might find it convenient to group some sights together: Versailles, Rambouillet, and Chartres are all on the Paris–Chartres train line; Fontainebleau, Barbizon, and Vaux-le-Vicomte are all within a few miles of each other.

By Train Three lines connect Paris with Versailles; on each, the trip takes about 30 minutes. Best for the château is RER C5 (Express métro line) to Versailles Rive Gauche station. Trains from Gare St-Lazare go to Versailles Rive Droite. Trains from Gare Montparnasse go to Versailles Chantiers and then on to Rambouillet and Chartres. Fontainebleau is served by 20 trains a day from Gare de Lyon; buses for Barbizon leave from in front of the main post office in Fontainebleau. The RER-A4 line will take you to Euro Disneyland.

By Car Expressway A13, from the Porte d'Auteuil, followed by A12, will take you from Paris to Versailles. Alternatively, you can get to Chartres on A10 or N10 south from Porte d'Orleans. For Fontainebleau, take A6 from Porte d'Orleans or, for a more attractive route through the forest of Sénart and the northern part of the forest of Fontainebleau, take N6 from Porte de Charenton via Melun. Vaux-le-Vicomte is 6 kilometers (4 miles) northeast of Melun via N36 and D215. The 32-kilometer (20-mile) drive along the A4 expressway from Paris to Euro Disneyland takes about 30 minutes, longer in heavy traf-

Ile de France

fic. Euro Disneyland is 4 kilometers (2½ miles) off the A4; follow the signs for the park.

Guided Tours

Two private companies, **Cityrama** and **Paris Vision,** organize regular half-day and full-day tours from Paris with English-speaking guides. Times and prices are identical. Tours are subject to cancellation, and reservations are suggested. Cityrama tours depart from 4 place des Pyramides, 1er (tel. 44–55–61–00). Paris Vision leaves from 214 rue de Rivoli, 1er (tel. 42–60–31–25).

Versailles and Les Trianons. Daily excursions starting at 9:30 include a complete tour of Paris in the morning followed by an afternoon at Versailles. Half-day excursions of Versailles leave mornings and afternoons daily (9:30 and 2:30, 285 frs) and include a guided tour of the château, Hall of Mirrors, and Queen's Suite. On Thursday only, a daylong excursion (420 frs) extends the tour to include an afternoon visit (starting 1:30) to the Trianons. Separate afternoon visits to the Trianons, again on Thursday, start at 1:30 (200 frs).

Chartres. Both companies organize half-day tours to Chartres on Tuesday, Thursday, and Saturday afternoons (departure at 1:30 PM, 250 frs), but if you're short of time or cash, you'd be better off taking the **Versailles–Chartres** day trips on Tuesday and Saturday (departure at 9:30, 435 frs).

Fontainebleau and Barbizon. Half-day trips (departure at 1:30, 295 frs) on Wednesday, Friday, and Sunday run to Fontainebleau and nearby Barbizon (which is otherwise difficult to reach), but can be linked to a Versailles tour leaving at 9:30 on the same days.

Tourist Information

Barbizon (41 rue Grande, tel. 60–66–41–87).
Chartres (Pl. de la Cathédrale, tel. 37–21–50–00).
Euro Disney (Euro Disney S.C.A., Central Reservations Office, Box 105 F77777, Marne-la-Vallée, Cedex 4 France, tel. 49–41–49–10).
Fontainebleau (31 pl. Napoléon-Bonaparte, tel. 64–22–25–68).
Rambouillet (8 pl. de la Libération, tel. 34–83–21–21).
Versailles (7 rue des Réservoirs, tel. 39–50–36–22).

Exploring the Ile de France

Versailles **Versailles** is the location of one of the world's grandest palaces and one of France's most popular attractions. Wide, tree-lined avenues, broader than the Champs-Elysées and bordered with massive 17th-century mansions, lead directly to the Sun King's château. From the imposing place d'Armes in front of the château, you enter the Cour des Ministres, a sprawling cobbled forecourt. Right in the middle, the statue of Louis XIV stands triumphant, surveying the town that he built from scratch to house those of the 20,000 noblemen, servants, and hangers-on who weren't lucky enough to get one of the 3,000 beds in the château.

The building of the château in its entirety took 50 years. Hills were flattened, marshes drained, forests transplanted, and water for the magnificent fountains was channeled from the Seine several miles away. Visit the **Grands Appartements,** the six salons that made up the royal living quarters, and the famous **Galerie des Glaces** (Hall of Mirrors). Both can be visited without a guide, but you can get a cassette in English. There are also guided tours of the **petits appartements,** where the royal family and friends lived in relative intimacy, and the miniature opera house—one of the first oval rooms in France, built on the *aile nord* (north wing) for Louis XV in 1770. *Grands Appartements and Galerie des Glaces. Admission: 40 frs adults, 20 frs students and senior citizens. Open Tues.–Sun. 9–6:30, 9–5:30 in winter.*

The château's vast grounds are masterpieces of formal landscaping. At one end of the Petit Canal, which crosses the Grand Canal at right angles, is the **Grand Trianon,** a scaled-down pleasure palace built in the 1680s. The **Petit Trianon,** nearby, is a sumptuously furnished 18th-century mansion, commissioned by Louis XVI for Marie-Antoinette, who would flee here to avoid the stuffy atmosphere of the court. Nearby, she built the village, complete with dairy and mill, where she and her companions would dress as shepherdesses and lead a make-believe bucolic life. *Château grounds. Admission: 20 frs adults June–Sept. only. Open 8:30–dusk. Grand Trianon. Admission: 20 frs adults, 13 frs children and senior citizens. Open June–Sept., daily 10–6:30, Oct.–May, daily 10–12:30 and 2–5:30. Petit Trianon. Admission: 12 frs adults, 8 frs children and senior citizens. Open June–Sept., daily 10–6:30; Oct.–May, daily 2–5:30.*

Rambouillet Just a little more than 20 kilometers (12 miles) southwest of Versailles is the small town of **Rambouillet,** home of a château, adjoining park, and 13,770 hectares (34,000 acres) of forest. Since 1897, the château has been a summer residence of the French president; today, it is also used as a site for international summits. You can visit the château only when the president is not in residence—fortunately, he's not there often.

French kings have lived in the château since it was built in 1375. Highlights include the **Appartements d'Assemblée,** decorated with finely detailed wood paneling, and Napoleon's bathroom, with its Pompeii-inspired frescoes. The park stretches way behind the château. Beyond the **Jardin d'Eau** (Water Garden) lies the English-style garden and the **Laiterie de la Reine** (Marie-Antoinette's Dairy). This was another of her attempts to "get back to nature." *Château, tel. 34–83–00–25. Admission: 26 frs adults, 17 frs children and senior citizens. Open Apr.–Sept., Wed.–Mon. 10–11:30 and 2–5:30; Oct.–Mar. 10–11:30 and 2–4:30. Park. Admission free. Open sunrise-sunset. Marie-Antoinette's Dairy: Admission 13 frs. Open same hours as Château; closes at 4 in winter.*

Chartres From Rambouillet, N10 will take you straight to **Chartres.** Long before you arrive you will see its famous cathedral towering over the plain of the Beauce, France's granary. The attractive old town, steeped in religious history and dating to before the Roman conquest, is still laced with winding medieval streets.

Today's Gothic cathedral, **Notre-Dame de Chartres,** is the sixth Christian church to have been built on the site; despite a series of fires, it has remained virtually the same since the 12th century. The **Royal Portal** on the main facade, presenting "the life and triumph of the Savior," is one of the finest examples of Romanesque sculpture in the country. Inside, the 12th- and 13th-century rose windows come alive even in dull weather, thanks to the deep Chartres blue of the stained glass: Its formula remains a mystery to this day. *Cathedral tours available: Ask at the Maison des Clercs, 18 rue du Cloître Notre-Dame. Tours in English daily noon and 2:45.*

Since the rest of the tour is on another side of Paris, it is probably easier to return to the capital to continue (*see* Getting Around in Ile de France, *above*).

Fontainebleau In the early 16th century, the flamboyant Francis I transformed the medieval hunting lodge of **Fontainebleau** into a magnificent Renaissance palace. His successor, Henry II, covered the palace with his initials, woven into the *D* for his mistress, Diane de Poitiers. When he died, his queen, Catherine de' Medici, carried out further alterations, later extended under Louis XIV. Napoleon preferred the relative intimacy of Fontainebleau to the grandeur of Versailles. Before he was exiled to Elba, he bade farewell to his Old Guard in the courtyard now known as the **Cour des Adieux** (Farewell Court). The emperor also harangued his troops from the **Horseshoe Staircase.** Ask the curator to let you see the **Cour Ovale** (Oval Court), the oldest and perhaps most interesting courtyard. It stands on the site of the original 12th-century fortified building, but only the keep remains today.

The **Grands Appartements** (royal suites and ballroom) are the main attractions of any visit to the château. The **Galerie de François I** is really a covered bridge (built 1528–30) looking out over the Cour de la Fontaine. The overall effect inside the Galerie—and throughout Fontainebleau—is one of classical harmony and proportion, combining to create a sense of Renaissance lightness and order. Francis I appreciated the Italian Renaissance, and the ballroom is decorated with frescoes by Primaticcio (1504–70) and his pupil, Niccolò dell'Abbate. If you're there on a weekday, you will also be able to join a guided tour of the Petits Appartements, used by Napoleon and Josephine. *Pl. du Gal-de-Gaulle, tel. 64–22–27–40. Admission: 30 frs, 19 frs under 25 and Sun., free under 18. Open 9:30–12:30 and 2–5. Closed Tues. and holidays.*

Barbizon The **Rochers des Demoiselles,** just south of the town, are good for an afternoon stroll. The **Gorges d'Apremont,** which offer the best views of the rocks, are near **Barbizon,** on the edge of the forest, 10 kilometers (6 miles) northwest of Fontainebleau. This delightful little village is scarcely more than a main street lined with restaurants and boutiques, but a group of landscape painters put it on the map in the mid-19th century. Théodore Rousseau and Jean-François Millet both had their studios here. Sculptor Henri Chapu's bronze medallion, sealed to one of the famous sandstone rocks in the forest nearby, pays homage to the two leaders of what became known as the Barbizon group.

Drop in at the **Ancienne Auberge du Père Ganne** (Père Ganne's Inn), where most of the landscape artists ate and drank, while in Barbizon. They painted on every available surface, and even now you can see some originals on the walls and in the buffet. Closed for restoration in 1994, the Auberge is scheduled to reopen in mid-1995. *Rue Grande.*

Next to the church, in a barn that Rousseau used as a studio, you'll find the **Musée de l'Ecole de Barbizon** (Barbizon School Museum), containing documents of the village as it was in the 19th century as well as a few original works. *55 rue Grande, tel. 60–66–22–38. Admission: 15 frs adults, children free. Open Apr.–Sept., Wed.–Sun. 10:30–12:30 and 2–6; Oct–Mar., Wed.–Sun. 10:30–12:30 and 2–5.*

From Barbizon, D64 offers a pleasant shortcut to Melun and then on to the château of **Vaux-le-Vicomte,** one of the greatest monuments of 17th-century French architecture. It was to have been Nicolas Fouquet's pride and joy, but turned out to be his downfall. This superintendent of France's finances under Louis XIV tended to use state resources for his own benefit—the château itself is damning evidence—and the Sun King eventually had him imprisoned for life. From the visitor's point of view, though, Fouquet's *folie de grandeur* is a treat. He had excellent taste (and a large budget) and chose the best-qualified team to build Vaux-le-Vicomte. Louis liked the results enough to reemploy them all when he built Versailles. Visit the kitchens, which have been preserved just as they were in the 17th century. The gardens (admission: 22 frs) are open all day. *Guided tours of château. Admission: 43 frs. Open Apr.–Oct., daily 10–6; Nov–Mar., daily 11–5. Candlelit visits. Admission: 50 frs. Open May–Sept., Sat. 8:30–11:30.*

Euro Disney The resort is on A4 (Exit 14—"Parc Euro Disneyland"). The express metro (RER line A4) from Paris runs directly to Marne-la-Vallée, a short walk from the theme park entrance (travel time 40 minutes, 35 frs one way); as of June 1994 a new TGV line will connect Euro Disney with Gare Montparnasse.

Now you can get a dose of American pop culture in between visits to the Louvre and the Left Bank. In April 1992 the **Euro Disney** complex opened in Marne-la-Vallée, just 32 kilometers (20 miles) east of Paris, much to the consternation of French cultural partisans. The complex is divided into several areas, including **Euro Disneyland,** the pay-as-you-enter theme park that is the main reason for coming here. Occupying 136 acres, the park is less than half a mile across and ringed by a railroad with whistling steam engines. Although smaller than its U.S. counterparts, Euro Disneyland was built with great attention paid to the tiniest detail. Smack in the middle of the park is the soaring Sleeping Beauty Castle, which is surrounded by a plaza from which you can enter the four "lands" of Disney: **Frontierland, Adventureland, Fantasyland,** and **Discoveryland.** In addition, Main Street U.S.A. connects the castle to Euro Disneyland's entrance, under the pointed pink domes of the Disneyland Hotel. In October 1993 Euro Disney inaugurated its newest attraction, **"Indiana Jones et le Temple de Peril"** ("Indiana Jones and the Temple of Doom"), a thrilling roller-coaster adventure ride. *Admission to Euro Disneyland (prices vary according to season): 250–175 frs adults, 175–125 frs children under 12; 2-day Passport 475–335 frs adults, 335–240 frs children; 3-day Passport 630–440 frs adults, 440–315 frs children. Open mid-June–mid-Sept., daily 9 AM–10 PM; mid-Sept.–Nov. and Jan.–mid-June, daily 10–6; Dec. and spring school holidays, daily 10–9.*

There are six hotels in the 4,800-acre Euro Disney complex, all part of a section called the **Euro Disney Resort,** just outside the theme park. The resort also comprises parking lots, a train station, and the Festival Disney entertainment center, with restaurants, a theater, dance clubs, shops, a post office, and a tourist office. Cheaper accommodations—log cabins and campsites—are available at Camp Davy Crockett, but it is located farther away from the theme park.

Dining and Lodging

For details and price-category definitions, *see* Dining and Lodging in Staying in France, *above.*

Barbizon
Dining

Le Relais. The delicious specialties—particularly the beef and the game (in season)—are served in large portions and there is a good choice of fixed-price menus. The Relais is spacious, its walls covered with paintings and hunting trophies, and there is a big open fire. The owner is proud of the large terrace where you can eat in the shade of lime and chestnut trees. *2 av. Charles de Gaulle, tel. 60-66-40-28. Weekend reservations required. MC, V. Closed Tues. eve., Wed. Inexpensive–Moderate.*

Dining and
Lodging

Auberge des Alouettes. This delightful 19th-century inn is set on 8,000 square meters (2 acres) of grounds. The interior has been redecorated in '30s style, but many rooms still have their original oak beams. The restaurant, with a large open terrace, features nouvelle cuisine in sizable portions. *4 rue Antoine Barye, tel. 60-66-41-98. 22 rooms with bath or shower. Facilities: restaurant, tennis, parking, TV. Weekend-dinner reservations required. AE, DC, MC, V. Moderate.*

Chartres
Dining

Vieille Maison. Located in a recently refitted 14th-century building only a stone's throw from the cathedral, Vieille Maison offers excellent nouvelle cuisine as well as more traditional dishes. Try the regional *menu beauceron* for the homemade foie gras and duck dishes or the mouth-watering *menu gourmand*, if the wallet allows. *5 rue au Lait, tel. 37-34-10-67. Reservations advised. AE, MC, V. Closed Sun. evening, Mon. Expensive.*

Buisson Ardent. Set in an attractive old oak-beamed building within sight of the cathedral's south portal, Buisson Ardent is a popular restaurant providing inexpensive fixed-price menus (especially good on weekdays) and a choice of imaginative à la carte dishes with delicious sauces. The wine list is comprehensive. *10 rue au Lait, tel. 37-34-04-66. Reservations advised. AE, DC, MC, V. Closed Sun. evenings. Moderate.*

Lodging

Grand Monarque. The most popular rooms in this 18th-century coaching inn are in a separate turn-of-the-century building overlooking a garden. Rooms have the level of comfort and consistency you would expect from a Best Western. The hotel also has an excellent reasonably priced restaurant. *22 pl. des Epars, tel. 37-21-00-*

72. 54 rooms with bath or shower. Facilities: restaurant. AE, DC, MC, V. Expensive.

Euro Disney
Dining and
Lodging

Euro Disneyland is peppered with places to eat, ranging from snack bars and fast-food joints to full-service restaurants—all with a distinguishing theme. In addition, all Disney hotels have restaurants that are open to the public. As these are outside the theme park, you may not want to waste time traveling to them for lunch. Disney now offers wine and beer in some locations within the park. Eateries serve nonstop as long as the park is open. The resort has six hotels and 5,000 rooms all a short distance from the park, ranging from the luxurious Euro Disney Hotel to the not-so-rustic Camp Davy Crockett. *Euro Disney S.C.A., Central Reservations Office, Box 105 F77777, Marne-la-Vallée, Cedex 4 France, tel. 49–41–49–10, fax 49–41–49–49; for hotel-restaurant reservations, tel. 60–45–65–40. Reservations advised for sit-down restaurants. AE, DC, MC, V accepted at sit-down restaurants; no credit cards at others. Counter-service restaurants: Inexpensive; sit-down restaurants: Moderate; hotels: Expensive–Very Expensive.*

Fontainebleau
Dining

Le Dauphin. Prices are reasonable in this homey, rustic restaurant located near the town hall and just five minutes from the château. Specialties include snails, confit of duck, and a variety of homemade desserts. *24 rue Grande, tel. 64–22–27–04. Reservations advised. MC, V. Closed Tues. evening, Wed., Feb., and Sept. 1–8. Inexpensive.*

Lodging

Londres. The balconies of this tranquil, family-style hotel look out over the palace and the Cour des Adieux; the 19th-century facade is preserved by government order. Inside, the decor evokes a Louis XV–style ambience. *1 pl. Général de Gaulle, tel. 64–22–20–21. 22 rooms with bath or shower. Facilities: restaurant, tea room, bar, parking. AE, DC, MC, V. Closed Dec. 20–Jan. 5. Moderate.*

Rambouillet
Dining

La Poste. Traditional, unpretentious cooking is the attraction of this former coaching inn, close to the château. The restaurant's two dining rooms are often packed with a lively group. The service is good, as is the selection of inexpensive fixed-price menus, even on Sunday. *101 rue du Général-de-Gaulle, tel. 34–83–03–01. Reservations advised. AE, MC, V. Closed Sun. eve. and Mon. Inexpensive.*

Versailles
Dining

Trois Marches. This, the best-known restaurant in town, is also recognized as one of the best in France for its nouvelle cuisine. Don't miss Gerard Vié's bisque of lobster, salmon with fennel, or turbot *galette*. Vié's 1992 move here to the sumptuous Trianon Palace Hotel, overlooking the château park—and the restaurant's huge, spanking-new kitchens—seem to have inspired him. *1 blvd. de la Reine, tel. 39–50–13–21. Reservations required. AE, DC, MC, V. Closed Sun., Mon., and Aug. Very Expensive.*

La Grande Sirène. An appealing lunch menu served every day but Sunday makes this pretty spot near the château a popular noontime choice. Zesty simmered snails and well-prepared fish are good choices here. *25 rue du Maréchal-Foch, tel. 39–53–08–08. Reservations advised. Dress: casual. AE, MC, V. Closed Mon. Moderate.*

Quai N° l. Fish enthusiasts don't have to spend a fortune in Versailles, as a visit to this atmospheric restaurant—awash in wood and brass and decked out in seafaring paraphernalia—will underline. Smoked salmon is the house specialty, and *crème brûlée* the pick of the desserts. *1 av. de St-Cloud, tel. 39–50–42–26. Reservations advised. MC, V. Closed Sun. evening and Mon. Moderate.*

Normandy

Jutting out into the Channel, Normandy has had more connections with the English-speaking world than any other part of France. The association continues today. Visitors flock here not only to see historic monuments but to relax in the rich countryside amid apple orchards, lush meadows, and sandy beaches.

The historic cities of Rouen and Caen, capitals of Upper and Lower Normandy, respectively, are full of churches, well-preserved buildings, and museums. The Seine Valley is lined with abbeys and castles from all periods: St-Wandrille, for example, dates to the 7th century. Richard the Lionhearted's 12th-century Château Gaillard, at Les Andelys, is still imposing. Normandy also has one of France's most enduring tourist attractions: Mont St-Michel, a remarkable Gothic abbey perched on a rocky mount off the Cotentin peninsula.

Etretat and Fécamp on the Alabaster Coast and Deauville, Trouville, and Honfleur on the Côte Fleurie (Flowered Coast) are among Normandy's many seaside resorts. Hotels, restaurants, and beaches cater to the simpler pleasures of life, while casinos make the rich poor—and sometimes the other way around, too. Normandy is also recognized as one of France's finest gastronomic regions; try some of the excellent cheeses with local cider, Calvados (the apple brandy), or the wide range of seafood dishes.

Getting Around

Normandy is best visited by car, although there are regular daily trains from Paris to Rouen, Caen, and Bayeux. Limited train connections make cross-country traveling difficult. Visiting many historic monuments and some towns—such as Honfleur, which has no train station—means using buses whose connections are not always convenient.

Guided Tours

Paris Vision (214 rue de Rivoli, 75001 Paris, 1er, tel. 42–60–31–25) and **Cityrama** (4 pl. des Pyramides, Paris, 1er, tel. 44–55–61–00) organize identical one-day excursions to Mont St-Michel from Paris, leaving at 7:15 Saturday morning and taking you by bus to Mont St-Michel in time for lunch at the Terrasse Poulard restaurant (*see* Dining and Lodging, *below*). There is a guided tour of the mount and the abbey, and you return by first-class train from Laval to Gare Montparnasse. *Cost: 900 frs.*

Tourist Information

Regional Centers
Caen (Lower Normandy) (Pl. du Canada, tel. 31–86–53–30).
Rouen (Upper Normandy) (2 bis rue du Petit-Salut, tel. 35–88–61–32).

Local Offices
Les Andelys (Rue Philippe Auguste, tel. 32–54–41–93).
Bayeux (2 rue des Cuisiniers, tel. 31–92–16–26).
Caen (12 pl. St-Pierre, tel. 31–86–27–65).
Deauville (Pl. de la Mairie, tel. 31–88–21–43).
Etretat (Pl. de la Mairie, tel. 35–27–05–21).
Fécamp (Pl. Bellet, tel. 35–28–20–51).
Honfleur (9 rue de la Ville, tel. 31–89–23–30).
Mont St-Michel (Corps de Garde des Bourgeois, tel. 33–60–14–30).
Rouen (25 pl. de la Cathédrale, tel. 35–71–41–77).

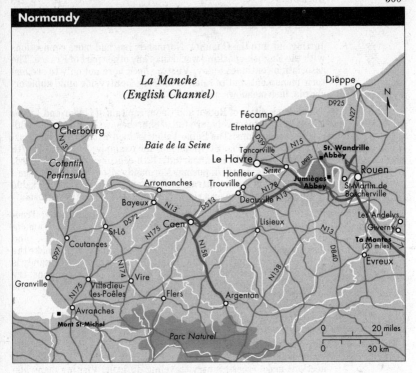

La Manche
(English Channel)

Dieppe

Fécamp
Etretat

St. Wandrille Abbey

Baie de la Seine
Cherbourg
Tancarville
Le Havre
Rouen
Cotentin
Peninsula
Honfleur
Seine
Jumièges Abbey
St-Martin de Boscherville
Arromanches
Trouville
Deauville
Bayeux
Caen
Lisieux
Les Andelys
Giverny
St-Lô
To Mantes (20 miles)
Coutances
Evreux
Granville
Vire
Villedieu-les-Poêles
Flers
Argentan
Avranches
Mont St-Michel
Parc Naturel

0   20 miles
0   30 km

Exploring Normandy

Take Expressway A13 from Paris (Porte d'Auteuil) as far as Meulan or Mantes and cross the Seine to the right bank. Then follow D913 or make a short stop in the village of **Giverny,** where you can visit the house and gardens in which Claude Monet lived and worked. *Admission: 30 frs. Open Tues.–Sun. 10–6.*

D313 goes to **Les Andelys,** a small town on the banks of the Seine, dominated by the imposing **Château Gaillard,** the fortress built in 1196 by Richard the Lionhearted, King of England, and duke of Normandy. *Admission: 15 frs. Open mid-Mar.–mid-Nov., Thurs.–Mon. 10–12:30 and 2–5, Wed. 2–5.*

Numbers in the margin correspond to points of interest on the Rouen map.

Rouen
①
②

③

④ ⑤
⑥

Rouen, the capital of Upper Normandy, has a remarkable number of historic churches, from the city's **Cathédrale Notre-Dame,** dating from the 12th century, to the modern, fish-shaped **Eglise Jeanne d'Arc** on the old market square, where Joan of Arc was burned at the stake in 1431. The tourist office organizes a guided tour leaving from the place de la Cathédrale and visiting the city's main churches, the **Palais de Justice,** and the lively old quarter around the rue du Gros-Horloge, where you can see the giant Renaissance clock that was built in 1527. The most noteworthy churches are located on the right bank, around the old quarter, and can be visited on foot. Try to visit **Eglise St-Maclou,** with its five-gabled facade; **Abbaye St-Ouen,** a beautifully proportioned 14th-century abbey; and the **Eglise St-Godard,** with well-preserved stained-glass windows.

Rouen

Abbaye
St-Ouen, **5**

Cathédrale
Notre-Dame, **1**

Eglise Jeanne
d'Arc, **2**

Eglise St-
Godard, **6**

Eglise St-
Maclou, **4**

Musée de la
Céramique, **9**

Musée des
Beaux-Arts, **7**

Musée du Gros-
Horloge, **10**

Musée Le Secq
des Tournelles, **8**

Palais de
Justice, **3**

One ticket will get you into several of Rouen's best museums,
7 notably the **Musée des Beaux Arts** (Fine Arts Museum), near Eglise
St-Godard (on Square Vedral). This specializes in 17th- and 19th-
century French paintings, with a particular emphasis on artists who
lived and worked locally. There is an outstanding collection of macabre paintings by Romantic painter Géricault. Nearby museums in-
8 clude the **Musée Le Secq des Tournelles** (rue Jacques Villon, in the
Eglise St-Laurent), which has an unusual collection of wrought iron;
9 the **Musée de la Céramique** (rue Faucon), which now houses Rouen's
10 porcelain collections; and the **Musée du Gros-Horloge** (rue du Gros-
Horloge), where you can study the mechanism of the Renaissance
clock that gives its name to the museum. *Museums. Admission: 15
frs. Open Thurs.–Mon. 10–noon and 2–6, Wed. 2–6.*

Follow D982 across the Forest of Roumare and along the Seine via
St-Martin de Boscherville, with its mighty 12th-century Romanesque abbey church of St-Georges, to **Jumièges Abbey,** once a powerful Benedictine center, founded in the 7th century. The abbey was
dismantled during the Revolution, but you can still wander through
the remains of the chapter house and several of the chapels. *Admission: 24 frs adults, 15 frs senior citizens, 10 frs children. Open Apr.–
Sept. daily 10–noon and 2–6; Oct.–Mar., weekdays 10–noon and
2–4, weekends 2–5.*

The nearby **St-Wandrille Abbey,** off D982, founded in 649, still has a
Benedictine community. Arrive early in the morning to hear the
Gregorian chants at Mass. *Morning Mass Mon.–Sat. at 9:30; Sun.
and holidays at 10. Guided tours weekdays 3 and 4 PM; cost, 18 frs
adults.*

Fécamp **Fécamp,** at the foot of the highest cliffs in Normandy, was the region's first place of pilgrimage. Legend has it that in the first century, an abandoned boat washed ashore here with a bottle containing Christ's blood. The 11th-century **Eglise de la Trinité** was built to accommodate all the pilgrims. *Guided tours May–Oct., Sun. at 11, 3, and 5.*

Fécamp is also home of the famous Bénédictine liqueur. The museum devoted to its production—rebuilt in 1892 after a fire—is one of the most popular attractions in Normandy. *Musée de la Bénédictine. 110 rue Alexandre-le-Grand. Admission: 30 frs. Open Easter–Oct., daily 9:30–11:30 and 2–5:30; Nov.–Mar., daily 10–1:30 and 3:30–4:30.*

Follow the pretty coast road about 12 kilometers (7 miles) to **Etretat,** where the sea has cut into the cliff to create two immense archways that lead to the neighboring beaches at low tide. For a view over the bay and the **Aiguille,** which is an enormous rock towering in the middle, take the little path up the Falaise d'Aval cliff.

To avoid doubling back to Fécamp, take D39 to the Tancarville Bridge, which links Upper and Lower Normandy. Have some small change ready for the toll. Turn right on N178 and drive south for 14 kilometers (9 miles) to a major crossroads. Turn right and drive the same distance to Honfleur.

Honfleur Once an important port for maritime expeditions, **Honfleur** became a favorite spot for painters, including the Impressionists. Today, Honfleur's lively cobbled streets, inland harbors full of colorful yachts, and the Eglise Ste-Catherine, a little 15th-century wooden church, make it the most picturesque town on the north coast. In the summer or on weekends, be prepared for lines at restaurants and cafés.

The popular resorts of **Trouville** and **Deauville** are 16 kilometers (10 miles) along the Côte de Grâce, on D513. Deauville is the swankier of the two, with its palaces, casino, horse racing, and film festival. Its more modest neighbor, Trouville, with its active fishing fleet, is a better place to get a feel for traditional Normandy.

Caen, slightly inland from these resorts, is the capital of Lower Normandy. It was badly bombed in 1944 but has been rebuilt with care and imagination. William the Conqueror was responsible for Caen's large **fortress** perched on a hill behind the town: Its ramparts now encircle the public garden. William and his queen, Mathilde, also built Caen's "his and hers" abbeys—**Abbaye aux Hommes** and **Abbaye aux Femmes.** The city hall is alongside the Abbaye aux Hommes, which has hourly guided tours (admission: 10 frs); Abbaye aux Femmes is now a hospital, and only the church is open to visitors.

Bayeux **Bayeux,** a few miles inland from the D-Day beach via N13, was the first French town freed by the Allies in June 1944. But it is known primarily as the home of **La Tapisserie de la Reine Mathilde** (the Bayeux Tapestry), which tells the epic story of William's conquest of England in 1066. It is on show at the **Centre Culturel Guillaume le Conquérant** (William the Conqueror Cultural Center). *Rue St-Exupère. Admission: 28 frs adults, 15 frs students. Open June–Sept., daily 9–7; Oct.–May, daily 9:30–12:30 and 2–7. Closed Dec. 25, Jan. 1.*

Head up rue de Nesmond to rue Larchet, turning left into lovely place des Tribuneaux, where you'll find the **Musée Baron Gérard** with a fine collection of Bayeux porcelain and lace, ceramics from

Rouen, a marvelous array of apothecary jars of the 17th and 18th centuries, and furniture and paintings from the 16th to 19th centuries. *1 rue la Chaine, tel. 31–92–14–21. Admission: 16 frs adults, 10 frs senior citizens. Open June–Aug., daily 9–7; Sept.–mid-Oct. and Mar.–May, 9:30–12:30 and 2–6:30; mid-Oct.–Mar., 10–12:30 and 2–6.*

Behind the museum, with an entrance on rue de Bienvenu, sits Bayeux's most important historic building, the **Cathédrale Notre-Dame,** a harmonious mixture of Norman and Gothic architecture. Note the portal on the south side of the transept, which depicts the assassination of English Archbishop Thomas à Becket in Canterbury Cathedral in 1170.

The **Musée de la Bataille de Normandie** (Museum of the Battle of Normandy) traces the history of the Allied advance against the Germans in 1944. It overlooks the British Military Cemetery. *Blvd. Général-Fabian-Ware. Admission: 22 frs adults, 10 frs students. Open June–Aug., daily 9–7; Sept.–mid-Oct. and mid-Mar.–May, daily 9:30–12:30 and 2:30–6:30; mid-Oct.–mid-Mar., daily 10–12:30 and 2–6.*

Bayeux is a good base for excursions up the Cotentin coast, to Mont-St-Michel, and the D-Day beaches. In **Arromanches** harbor, you can see the remains of **Mulberry B,** an artificial port built for the British D-Day landings. Mulberry A, where American troops landed farther up the coast on what is now known as **Omaha Beach,** was destroyed by a storm a few months after the landings. The **Musée du Débarquement** (Landings Museum) on Arromanches seafront shows the landing plan and a film (in English) on the operation. *Admission: 16 frs. Open June–mid-Sept., daily 9–6:30; mid-Sept.–mid-Apr., daily 9–11:30 and 2–5:30. Closed Dec. 25, Jan. 1–18.*

Mont-St-Michel Drive through the fertile heartland of Normandy, among the rolling hills and orchards that produce Calvados and cider. Take D972 to **St-Lô** and then D999 to **Villedieu-les-Poeles,** a town famous for its kitchen copperware. Now join N175 and continue to **Avranches,** where you will have your first view of **Mont-St-Michel,** the Gothic abbey and village rising up from the sea. The mount's fame comes not just from its location—until the causeway was built, it was cut off from the mainland at high tide—but from the dramatic nature of its construction in the 8th century, when tons of granite were brought from the nearby Chausey Islands and Brittany and hauled up the 265-foot peak. It has been a pilgrimage center ever since.

For most of the year, Mont-St-Michel is surrounded by sandy beach. The best time to see it is during the high tides of spring and fall, when the sea comes pounding in—dangerously fast—and encircles the mount. **La Merveille** (the Wonder) is the name given to the collection of Gothic buildings on top. What looks like a fortress is in fact a series of architectural layers that trace the evolution of French architecture from Romanesque to late-Gothic. You can join a guided tour (in English). *Admission: 32 frs adults, 15 frs students and senior citizens, 7 frs children. Open mid-May–Sept., daily 9–11:30 and 1:30–6; Oct.–mid-May, Wed.–Mon. 9:30–11:45 and 1:45–4:15.*

Dining and Lodging

For details and price-category definitions, *see* Dining and Lodging in Staying in France, *above.*

Bayeux **L'Amaryllis.** This small, simply decorated restaurant with fewer
Dining than 15 tables produces good Norman fare at very reasonable prices.

For 98 frs you'll get a three-course dinner that might include a half dozen oysters, sole with a cider-based sauce, and pastries for dessert. *32 rue St-Patrice, tel. 31–22–47–94. AE, DC, MC, V. Closed Mon. and Dec. 20–Jan. 15. Inexpensive.*

Dining and Lodging **Grand Hotel du Luxembourg.** Les Quatre Saisons, the restaurant at this fairly run-of-the-mill hotel, has the best kitchen in town. Chef Daniel Rivième's classical repertoire from Normandy includes a *galette* of salmon, chicken roasted with cider, and veal in a sauce strongly scented with calvados. The hotel's guest rooms are adequate. All but two face the courtyard garden and away from any street noise. *25 rue des Boucchers, 14403, tel. 31–92–54–26, fax 31–92–54–26. 19 rooms with bath, 3 suites. Facilities: restaurant, elevator, bar, nearby disco, free parking. AE, DC, MC, V. Moderate.*

Lodging **Hôtel d'Argouges.** This popular 18th-century hotel in the city center has quiet, simple rooms furnished with the ubiquitous candlewick bedspreads and heavy-duty carpeting of two-star hotels. Only continental breakfast is served, but the owners will happily make restaurant reservations. *21 rue St-Patrice, 14400 Bayeux, tel. 31–92–88–86, fax 31–92–69–16. 25 rooms, 20 with bath, 5 with shower; 2 suites. Facilities: garden, free parking. AE, DC, MC, V. Moderate.*

Caen **Bourride.** Michel Bruneau, owner and chef of this famous restaurant *Dining* set in one of the town's oldest streets, bases his inventive recipes almost exclusively on local and regional produce. Specialties include skate caramelized in honey and cider and meat pastry cooked in cider vinegar. *15 rue du Vaugueux, tel. 31–93–50–76. Reservations advised. AE, DC, MC, V. Closed Sun., Mon., Jan. 1–24, and Aug. 15–31. Expensive.*

Lodging **Le Dauphin.** Although small, the rooms in this old priory are clean and renovated. Many of them overlook the quiet hotel courtyard. Le Dauphin also has an excellent restaurant serving Norman dishes topped by unusually light sauces, with an emphasis on seafood. *29 rue Gémare, 14000, tel. 31–86–22–26, fax 31–86–35–14. 21 rooms with bath or shower. Facilities: restaurant, parking. AE, DC, MC, V. Closed part of Feb. and mid-July–mid-Aug.; restaurant closed Sat. Moderate.*

Deauville **Spinnaker.** Here is a handy—and affordable—restaurant in the cen- *Dining* ter of this chic resort. The atmosphere is informal and the food is local, with special emphasis on seafood. Try the delicious fresh pasta and crab salad. *52 rue Mirabeau, tel. 31–88–24–40. Reservations advised. MC, V. Closed Wed. out of season, Thurs., and Jan. 15–Feb. 15. Moderate.*

Etretat **Roches Blanches.** Situated back from the sandy beach, this family- *Dining* owned restaurant is a concrete post–World War II eyesore on the outside. Inside, it's another matter: There's a view of the sea and the cliffs, and the seafood is superbly fresh. Besides other dishes, such as veal escalope with mushrooms and flambéed in Calvados, be sure to try the mussels. *Rue Abbé Cochet, tel. 35–27–07–34. Reservations required. MC, V. Closed Wed. in summer, Tues.–Thurs. in winter, and Oct. and Jan. Moderate.*

Dining and Lodging **Le Donjon.** This charming little château, in a park overlooking the resort, offers lovely bay views. The individually furnished guest rooms are spacious, comfortable, and quiet. Reliable French cuisine is served with flair in a cozy, romantic restaurant. *Chemin de St-Clair, 76790, tel. 35–27–08–23, fax 35–29–92–24. 8 rooms, 6 with bath. Facilities: pool, parking. AE, DC, MC, V. Moderate.*

Fécamp
Dining and
Lodging

Auberge de la Rouge. The quaint inn is in a little hamlet a mile or so south of Fécamp. Its menu features a good mix of classic and modern dishes and includes many local specialties—try the *coquilles St-Jacques* (scallops in a sherry cream sauce, with a scent of herbs in the shell) or the pressed duck. *Commune de St-Léonard, 76400, tel. 35–28–07–59, fax 35–28–70–55. Reservations advised. 8 rooms with bath. Facilities: restaurant. AE, DC, MC, V. Closed Sun. dinner and Mon. Moderate.*

Honfleur
Dining

Absinthe. The magnificent 17th-century dining room dominates the ground floor, where you will also find the pub-style bar, the Ivanhoe. But in warm weather, the place to be is on the sunny terrace on the quayside. The menu features both nouvelle and traditional cuisines, with the accent on seafood. *10 quai de la Quarantaine, tel. 31–89–39–00. Reservations advised. AE, DC, MC, V. Closed Mon. evening and Tues., except in midsummer; and Nov. 11–Dec. 20. Expensive.*

L'Assiette Gourmande. Next door to the Cheval Blanc (*see below*) is Honfleur's unsung top restaurant. If Chef Gérard Bonnefoy should stir out of his kitchen into the dining room, you'll find he's a master at deciding what you would enjoy most after a few minutes of culinary conversation. The season influences the menu, but you may be lucky enough in the fall to have a superb coquilles St-Jacques grilled with sautéed asparagus in a raspberry vinaigrette and reduced orange sauce or the noix de St-Jacques (huge succulent scallops) with a risotto of hazelnuts. Or you may enjoy lobster salad, tartare of smoked salmon in a caviar-based cream, roast turbot marinated in a basil mussel sauce, or roast lamb from the salt marshes. *2 quai des Passagers, tel. 31–89–24–88. Dress: casual but neat. Reservations advised. Closed Mon. dinner and Tues. Moderate–Expensive.*

Ancrage. Vast seafood platters are the specialty in this charming old restaurant overlooking the Vieux Bassin (old harbor), but meat dishes are good, too, particularly the calf sweetbreads braised in cider. *16 rue Montpensier, tel. 31–89–00–70. Reservations advised in summer. MC, V. Closed Tues. evening, Wed.; Jan. 2–Feb. 2. Moderate.*

Lodging

Le Cheval Blanc. In a renovated, 15th-century building on the harborfront, owners Alain Petit and his wife run this friendly inn. All the guest rooms have recently been redecorated and offer fine views of the port across the main road. Room 34 (slightly more expensive than the others) has gabled ceilings supported by triangle and cross beams pegged together and a small sitting area, as well as a whirlpool bath. *2 quai des Passagers, 14600, tel. 31–81–65–00, fax 31–89–52–80. 35 rooms, 14 with bath. Facilities: breakfast room, parking in nearby lot. MC, V. Closed Jan. Moderate.*

Mont-St-
Michel
Lodging

Terrasses Poulard. This collection of town houses, while still overpriced, is the less expensive sister hotel to the exorbitant Mère Poulard; each room takes the name of a famous local Norman personality and is decorated accordingly. Several rooms have breathtaking views of the bay, while others look out onto a little garden. The restaurant, crowded with American, British, and Canadian tourists, has its best views upstairs. *Grande Rue, 50116, tel. 33–60–14–09, fax 33–60–37–31. 29 rooms with bath. Facilities: restaurant. AE, DC, MC, V. Expensive.*

Le Manoir de la Roche Turin. An appealing alternative to the high-priced hotels in Mont-St-Michel is this small ivy-clad manor house 9 kilometers (6 miles) away. Rooms are pleasantly old-fashioned, but the bathrooms are modern and the owners run a delightful dining room. The *agneau pré-salé* (lamb from the salt marshes) is superb, but lobster and fresh fish are also available on the 150-fr and 200-fr menus. *50220 Courtils, tel. 33-70-96-55, fax 33-48-35-20. 11 rooms, 1 suite. Facilities: restaurant (closed Mon.), free parking. MC, V. Closed mid-Nov.–mid-Mar. Moderate.*

Rouen **La Couronne.** Built in 1345, La Couronne claims to be the oldest inn
Dining in France. The oak beams, leather upholstery, and woodwork provide an attractive setting for a collection of sculptures. The traditional cuisine features homemade foie gras, duck *à l'orange,* and turbot in flaky pastry. Keep to the "menu Normand," for 180 frs, or expect a hefty bill if you order à la carte. *31 pl. du Vieux-Marché, tel. 35-71-40-90. Reservations required. AE, DC, MC, V. Expensive.*

Dining and **Hotel de Dieppe.** A newly renovated 19th-century hotel opposite the
Lodging train station, Hotel de Dieppe offers two types of rooms: modern and period-style. The buffet-style breakfast is substantial—unlike most in France—and the popular restaurant serves a range of grilled meats, as well as duckling Rouennaise à la presse, a traditional Norman recipe prepared at your table. *Pl. Bernard-Tissot, 76000, tel. 35-71-96-00, fax 35-89-65-21. 40 rooms with bath or shower. Facilities: restaurant. AE, DC, MC, V. Moderate.*

Burgundy and Lyon

For a region whose powerful medieval dukes held sway over large tracts of Western Europe and whose current image is closely allied to its expensive wine, Burgundy is a place of surprisingly rustic, quiet charm.

Despite the mighty Gothic cathedrals of Sens and Auxerre, Burgundy's leading religious monument is the Romanesque basilica at Vézelay. Once one of Christianity's most important pilgrimage centers, Vézelay is today a tiny village hidden in the folds of rolling, verdant hills. In its time, the abbey of Cluny farther south was equally important, but few of its buildings remain.

The heart of Burgundy consists of the dark, brooding Morvan Forest. Dijon is the region's only city and retains something of its medieval opulence. Its present reputation is essentially gastronomic, however; top-class restaurants abound, and local industries involve the production of mustard, *cassis* (black-currant liqueur), snails, and—of course—wine. The vineyards extending down toward the ancient town of Beaune are among the world's most distinguished and picturesque.

The vines continue to flourish as you head south along the Saône Valley, through the Mâconnais and Beaujolais, toward Lyon, one of France's most appealing cities. The combination of frenzied modernity and unhurried *joie de vivre* give Lyon a sense of balance. The only danger is a temptation to overindulge in its rich and robust cuisine.

Burgundy's winters are cold, its summers hot. The ideal times to come are late May, when the countryside is in flower, and September or October, for the wine harvest.

Getting Around

Burgundy is a region best visited by car. Its meandering country roads invite leisurely exploration. There are few big towns, and traveling around by train is unrewarding, especially as the infre-

Burgundy

quent cross-country trains steam along at the speed of a legendary Burgundy snail.

Guided Tours

The Dijon branch of the regional tourism office organizes a series of tours using Dijon as a base. These include wine tastings and historic tours of the famous religious centers. Write to Comité Régional de Tourisme (21 blvd. Brosses, 21000 Dijon).

Tourist Information

Auxerre (1 quai de la République, tel. 86–52–06–19).
Beaune (Rue de l'Hôtel-Dieu, tel. 80–22–24–51).
Dijon (29 pl. Darcy, tel. 80–43–42–12).
Lyon (Pl. Bellecour, tel. 78–42–25–75).
Sens (Pl. Jean-Jaurès, tel. 86–65–19–49).

Exploring Burgundy and Lyon

It makes sense for **Sens** to be your first stop on the way down to Burgundy, as it lies just 120 kilometers (75 miles) from Paris on N6—a fast, pretty road that hugs the Yonne Valley south of Fontainebleau. Sens is home to France's senior archbishop and is dominated by the 12th-century **Cathédrale St-Etienne.** This is one of the oldest cathedrals in France and has a foursquare facade topped by towers and an incongruous little Renaissance campanile. The vast, harmonious interior contains outstanding stained glass of various periods.

The 13th-century **Palais Synodal** alongside, now a local museum, provides a first encounter with Burgundy's multicolored tiled roofs; from its courtyard, there is a fine view of the cathedral's south transept, constructed in the fluid Flamboyant Gothic style of the 16th century. *Rue des Déportés de la Résistance. Admission: 13 frs. Open Mar.–mid-Dec. daily 10–noon and 2–5; mid-Dec.–Feb., Thurs.–Tues. 2–4:30.*

Auxerre   N6 continues to **Auxerre**, a small, peaceful town with its own **Cathédrale St-Etienne**, perched on a steepish hill overlooking the Yonne. The muscular cathedral, built between the 13th and 16th centuries, has a powerful north tower similar to that at Clamecy. The former **abbey of St-Germain** nearby contains an underground church dating from the 9th century. *Rue Cochois. Guided tour of crypt. Admission: 10 frs. Open Wed.–Mon. 10–noon and 2–5.*

Chablis, famous for its dry white wine, makes an attractive excursion 16 kilometers (10 miles) to the east of Auxerre, along N65 and D965. Beware of village tourist shops selling local wines at unpalatable prices. The surrounding vineyards are dramatic: Their towering, steeply banked hills stand in marked contrast to the region's characteristic gentle slopes.

Clamecy   From Auxerre, take N151 43 kilometers (27 miles) south along the Yonne to **Clamecy**. This sleepy town is not on many tourist itineraries, but its tumbling alleyways and untouched, ancient houses epitomize *la France profonde*. The many-shaped roofs of Clamecy, dominated by the majestic square tower of the **church of St-Martin**, are best viewed from the banks of the Yonne. The river played a crucial role in Clamecy's development: Trees from the nearby Morvan Forest were cut down and floated in huge convoys to Paris. The history of this curious form of transport *(flottage)*, now extinct, is detailed in the town **museum**. *Rue Bourgeoise. Admission: 10 frs. Open July–Sept., Wed.–Mon. 10–noon and 2–5; rest of the year by appointment.*

Vézelay lies 24 kilometers (15 miles) east of Clamecy, along D957. The **Basilica** is perched on a rocky crag, with commanding views of the surrounding countryside. It rose to fame in the 11th century as the resting place of the relics of St. Mary Magdalene and became a departure point for the great pilgrimages to Santiago de Compostela in northwest Spain. The church was rescued from decay by the 19th-century Gothic Revival architect Eugène-Emmanuel Viollet-le-Duc and counts as one of the foremost Romanesque buildings in existence. Its interior is long and airy, with superbly carved column capitals; the facade boasts an equally majestic tympanum.

Avallon is 13 kilometers (8 miles) farther along from Vézelay, via D957. Its site, on a promontory, is spectacular, and its old streets and ramparts make agreeable places to stroll. The imagination of medieval stone carvers ran riot at the portals of the venerable church of **St-Lazarus**.

The expressway passes close by Avallon and can whisk you along to Dijon, 96 kilometers (60 miles) away, in less than an hour. If you're in no rush, take the time to explore part of the huge **Morvan Regional Park**; the road twists and turns through lakes, hills, and forests. Take D10 south to **Quarré-les-Tombes**—so called because of the empty prehistoric stone tombs discovered locally and eerily arrayed in a ring around the church—before continuing southeast toward Saulieu. The **Rocher de la Pérouse**, 8 kilometers (5 miles) from Quarré-les-Tombes, is a mighty outcrop worth climbing for the view of the Cousin Valley. Continue to **Saulieu** via the N6, D264, and D977.

Saulieu's reputation belies its size (just 3,000 inhabitants). It is renowned for good food (Rabelais, that 16th-century authority, extolled its hospitality) and Christmas trees (a million are harvested each year). The **Basilica of St-Andoche** is almost as old as Vézelay's, though less imposing and much restored. The adjoining town **museum** (admission: 20 frs; open Wed.–Mon., 10–noon and 2–5) contains a room devoted to the sculptor of art deco animals, François Pompon.

Dijon N6 and then D977 link Saulieu to the Dijon-bound A38 expressway to the east. **Dijon** is capital of both Burgundy and gastronomy. Visit its restaurants and the **Palais des Ducs** (Ducal Palace), testimony to bygone splendor and the setting for one of France's leading art museums (Admission: 12 frs. Open Wed.–Mon. 10–6). The tombs of Philip the Bold and John the Fearless head a rich collection of medieval objects and Renaissance furniture. Outstanding features of the city's old churches include the stained glass of **Notre-Dame,** the austere interior of the **cathedral of St-Bénigne,** and the chunky Renaissance facade of **St-Michel.** Don't miss the exuberant 15th-century gateway at the **Chartreuse de Champmol**—all that remains of a former charterhouse—or the adjoining **Puits de Moïse,** a "well" with six large, realistic medieval statues on a hexagonal base.

Beaune A31 connects Dijon to **Beaune,** 40 kilometers (25 miles) to the south, but you may prefer a leisurely trip through the vineyards. Take D122, then N74 at Chambolle-Musigny; just to the south is the Renaissance **Château du Clos de Vougeot,** famous as the seat of Burgundy's elite company of wine tasters, the Confrérie des Chevaliers du Tastevin, who gather here in November at the start of the three-day festival Les Trois Glorieuses—which includes a wine auction at the Hospices de Beaune. *Château du Clos de Vougeot. Admission: 22 frs. Guided tours daily 9–11:30 and 2–5:30. Closed Dec. 24–Jan. 3.*

The **Hospices** (or Hôtel-Dieu) **de Beaune** owns some of the finest vineyards in the region yet was founded in 1443 as a hospital. Its medical history is retraced in a **museum** that also features Roger van der Weyden's medieval Flemish masterpiece *The Last Judgment,* plus a collection of tapestries, though a better series (late 15th century, relating the *Life of the Virgin*) hangs in Beaune's main church, the **Collégiale Notre-Dame,** which dates from 1120. *Hospices de Beaune. Admission: 27 frs adults, 14 frs children. Open Apr.–Nov., daily 9–6:30; Dec.–Mar., daily 9–11:30 and 2–5:30.*

The history of local wines can be explored at the **Musée du Vin de Bourgogne,** housed in a mansion built in the 15th and 16th centuries (Admission: 10 frs. Open Apr.–Oct., daily 9–noon and 1:30–6; Nov.–Mar., daily 10–noon and 2–5:30). The place to drink the stuff is in the candlelit cellars of the **Marché aux Vins** (wine market), on rue Nicolas Rolin, where you can taste as much as you please for 40 frs.

Autun **Autun** is 48 kilometers (30 miles) west of Beaune along D973 but is worth a detour, if only for the Renaissance **château of Sully** on the way. (Admission: 12 frs. Visits to grounds only, daily in summer, 10–noon and 2–5.) The town's importance dates back to Roman times, as you can detect at the **Porte St-André,** a well-preserved archway, and the **Théâtre Romain,** once the largest arena in Gaul. The leading monument in Autun is the church of **St-Lazarus,** a curious Gothic cathedral redone in the Classical style by 18th-century clerics trying to follow fashion. The building actually dates back to the first half of the 12th century. Note the majestic picture by Ingres, the *Martyrdom of St-Symphorien,* in one of the side chapels. Across from the cathedral is the **Musée Rolin** (admission: 15 frs; open Wed.–Mon. 10–noon and 2–5; Sun. 2–5), with several fine paintings from the Middle Ages.

Cluny From Autun, head southeast along N80 and D980, via industrial Montceau-les-Mines, to **Cluny,** 80 kilometers (50 miles) away. The **Abbey** of Cluny, founded in the 10th century, was the largest church in Europe until St. Peter's was built in Rome in the 16th century. The ruins give an idea of its original grandeur. Note the **Clocher de l'Eau-Bénite,** a majestic bell tower, and the 13th-century **Farinier** (flour mill) with its fine chestnut roof and collection of statues. *Guided tours of ruins. Admission: 28 frs adults, 9 frs children. Open Easter–Oct., daily 9–noon and 2–5; Nov.–Easter, daily, late morning–early afternoon.*

A model of the original abbey can be seen in the **Musée Ochier,** the 15th-century abbot's palace. *Rue Conant. Admission: 8 frs. Open Wed.–Mon. 10–noon and 2–5. Closed Jan. 1–15.*

Cluny is a mere 28 kilometers (16 miles) northwest of **Mâcon,** a bustling town best known for its wine fair in May and for its stone bridge across the Saône; the low arches are a headache for large river barges. At Mâcon take N6 or A6 due south to Lyon, where the river Rhône runs parallel to the Saône before the two converge south of the city center.

Lyon In recent years, **Lyon** has solidified its role as one of Europe's leading commercial centers, thanks to France's policy of decentralization and the TGV train that puts Paris at virtual commuter distance (two hours). Much of the city has an appropriate air of untroubled prosperity, and you will have plenty of choices when it comes to good eating.

The clifftop silhouette of **Notre-Dame de Fourvière** is the city's most striking symbol: The 19th-century basilica is an exotic mish-mash of styles with an interior that's pure decorative overkill. Climb the Fourvière heights for the view instead and then go to the nearby Roman remains. *Théâtres Romains. Admission free. Open Mar.–Oct., 8–noon and 2–5, Sat. 9–noon and 3–6, Sun. 3–6; Nov.–Feb., weekdays 8–noon and 2–5.*

The pick of Lyon's museums is the **Musée des Beaux-Arts** (open Wed.–Mon. 11–6). It houses sculpture, classical relics, and an extensive collection of Old Masters and Impressionists. Don't miss local artist Louis Janmot's 19th-century mystical cycle *The Poem of the Soul,* 18 canvases that took nearly 50 years to complete. *20 pl. des Terreaux, tel. 78–28–81–11. Admission: 20 frs adults, 10 frs students, children under 18 free. Open Wed.–Sun. 10:30–6.*

Dining and Lodging

For details and price-category definitions, *see* Dining and Lodging in Staying in France, *above.*

Auxerre **Jardin Gourmand.** As its name implies, the Jardin Gourmand has a
Dining pretty garden where you can eat *en terrasse* during the summer. The interior, accented by light-colored oak, is equally congenial. The cuisine is innovative—try the ravioli and foie gras or the duck with black currants—and the service is discreet. *56 blvd. Vauban, tel. 86–51–53–52. Reservations advised. MC, V. Closed Mon. and Tues. lunch. Moderate.*

Lodging **Normandie.** This picturesque creeper-covered construction is right in the town center, with its own garden but no restaurant. The rooms are well equipped and unpretentious. *41 blvd. Vauban, tel. 86–52–57–80, fax 86–51–54–33. 47 rooms, some with bath or shower. AE, DC, MC, V. Inexpensive.*

Avallon **Moulin des Ruats.** The hotel is housed in an old flour mill just south-
Lodging west of Avallon along D427. The rooms, many with their own balcony, are rustic. Most look onto the sparkling river Cousin, and in the summer you can eat on the riverbank. The traditional dishes that make up the large menu are served in the wood-panelled restaurant at other times. Try the *coq au vin* (chicken cooked in local Burgundy wine). This hotel is popular, so make sure to have a reservation if you come in July or August. *Vallée du Cousin, tel. 86–34–07–14. 27 rooms, some with shower or bath. Facilities: restaurant. AE, DC, MC, V. Closed winter. Moderate.*

Beaune **L'Ecusson.** Despite its unprepossessing exterior, L'Ecusson is a
Dining comfortable, friendly, thick-carpeted restaurant, with four fixed-price menus offering outstanding value. For around 200 frs, you can have rabbit terrine with tarragon followed by leg of duck in oxtail sauce, then cheese, and dessert. *2 rue du Lieutenant-Dupuis, tel. 80–24–03–82. Reservations advised. AE, DC, MC, V. Closed Sun., mid-Feb.–mid-Mar. Moderate.*

La Grilladine. At this small, warm restaurant chef Pierre Lenko's fare, while not elaborate, is good and hearty Burgundy cooking with such items as boeuf bourgignon and *oeufs en meurette*. One of the two cheerful dining rooms has rose-pink table cloths, exposed stone walls, and a mammoth ancient wood beam supporting the ceiling's center. The other is lighter, more open, and less rustic. *17 rue Maufoux, tel. 80–22–22–36. Reservations advised. MC, V. Closed Mon. Inexpensive–Moderate.*

Lodging **Le Cep.** Within the ramparts and only a five-minute walk from the main square, Beaune's top hotel offers spacious, tastefully decorated rooms furnished with antiques and large tile bathrooms. Rooms facing the courtyard are quieter. The hotel is a combination of several ancient town houses—the oldest is circa 1547—and their courtyards have been made into a small garden. On the ground floor, especially in the lounge where a log fire burns during the chillier months, the large beams are exposed. Service can become a little harried when tour groups, albeit of fairly small size, check in and out. *27 rue Maufoux, 21200, tel. 80–22–35–48, fax 80–22–76–80. 52 rooms. Facilities: restaurant (closed Mon., Tues. lunch), garage. AE, DC, MC, V. Expensive.*

Chablis **Hostellerie des Clos.** Guest rooms at this inn are quite simple and or-
Dining and dinary, given color by the cheerful floral curtains and quilts on the
Lodging beds. The attraction is Michel Vignaud's superb culinary art. His *sandre* (perchlike freshwater fish) is served with a chicken-based sauce that stands in tasty juxtaposition to the fish. The casserole of hare (available only in the autumn) is wonderfully robust. Most exciting is the appetizer of *huîtres d'Isigny* (small oysters) in a dill-and-chablis sauce. Desserts are equally splendid; perhaps try the *feuilles de chocolat* with red fruits. *Rue Jules-Rathier, 89800, tel. 86–42–10–63, fax 86–42–17–11. 26 rooms with bath. Facilities: restaurant. AE, DC, MC, V. Moderate–Expensive.*

Cluny **Bourgogne.** It is hard to find a better place to get into the medieval
Dining and mood of Cluny than this old-fashioned hotel, right next door to the
Lodging ruins of the famous abbey. There is a small garden and an atmos-
★ pheric restaurant with sober pink decor and refined cuisine: foie

gras, snails, and fish with ginger are specialties. *Pl. de l'Abbaye, tel. 85–59–00–58, fax 85–59–03–73. 14 rooms with bath or shower. Facilities: restaurant. AE, DC, MC, V. Closed Wed. lunch, Mon., and mid-Nov.–mid-Feb. Moderate–Expensive.*

Dijon **Jean-Pierre Billoux.** M. Billoux's restaurant is reputedly the best of
Dining all in this most gastronomic of French cities. It is magnificently situated in a spacious, restored town house with garden, bar, and stone-vaulted restaurant. Service is charming. Specialties include steamed frogs' legs served with cress pancakes and guinea fowl with foie gras. *14 pl. Darcy, tel. 80–30–11–00. Reservations required. MC, V. Closed Sun. evening, Mon., part of Feb., and first half Aug. Expensive.*

Lodging **Chapeau Rouge.** This is a good choice if you want to be sure of getting a quiet, tasteful room in the center of town—it's close to Dijon cathedral. The Chapeau is even a better choice for its restaurant, renowned as a haven of regional cuisine. Snails, pigeon, and veal in mustard top the list of specialties. *5 rue Michelet, tel. 80–30–28–10, fax 80–30–33–89. 29 rooms with bath or shower. Facilities: restaurant. Reservations required. AE, DC, MC, V. Moderate–Expensive.*

Lyon **Léon de Lyon.** A mixture of regional tradition (dumplings, hot sau-
Dining sages) and eye-opening innovation keep Léon de Lyon at the fore-
★ front of Lyon's restaurant scene. It consists of two floors in an old house full of alcoves and wood panelling. The blue-aproned waiters melt into the old-fashioned decor, and such dishes as fillet of veal with celery or leg of lamb with fava beans will linger in your memory. *1 rue Pléney, tel. 78–28–11–33. Reservations required. MC, V. Closed Sun. dinner, Mon. lunch, and Aug. Expensive.*
A Ma Vigne. Here is a restaurant that's popular with tourists; it provides straightforward meals as a break from too much gourmet Lyonnais dining. French fries, *moules* (mussels), roast ham, and tripe lead the menu. Locals appreciate this, too, so get there early, especially at lunchtime. *23 rue Jean-Larrivé, tel. 78–60–46–31. Reservations not necessary. MC, V. Closed Sun., Aug. Moderate.*

Lodging **Royal.** The Royal is on the spacious and elegant place Bellecour in the very heart of Lyon. Beware of the huge range in room prices (590–890 frs); many rooms have been stylishly renovated and some of the most expensive (with their own Jacuzzi) are positively luxurious. *20 pl. Bellecour, tel. 78–37–57–31, fax 78–37–01–36. 80 rooms, most with bath or shower. Facilities: parking, restaurant. AE, DC, MC, V. Expensive.*

Sens **Paris et Poste.** This hotel makes a pleasant stopping point on the way
Lodging to Burgundy from Paris. The helpful service and sumptuous breakfasts (rare in France) confirm a sense of well-being created by the robust evening meal (with fixed-price menus including duck, snails, and steak) served in the large, solemn restaurant, whose decor can be described as rustic Burgundian. *97 rue de la République, tel. 86–65–17–43, fax 86–64–48–45. 25 rooms with bath or shower. Facilities: Restaurant. AE, DC, MC, V. Moderate.*

Vézelay **L'Espérance.** In the small neighboring village of St-Père-sous-
Dining and Vézelay, L'Espérance is one of France's premier restaurants. Chef
Lodging Marc Meneau is renowned for the subtlety and originality of his cui-
★ sine. Parisian gourmets think nothing of driving down to Burgundy to eat here: A second restaurant, **Le Pré des Marguerites,** offers more traditional fare, much simpler, and less expensive. L'Espérance also has 40 luxurious rooms. Thirteen are pretty, but rather small rooms in the main house; the others, slightly larger, are in

nearby buildings. *St-Père-sous-Vézelay, tel. 86–33–20–45, fax 86–33–26–15. Reservations required. Jacket and tie required. AE, DC, MC, V. Closed Tues., Wed. lunch, and Jan. 1–Feb. 15. Very Expensive.*

Loire Valley

The Loire is the longest river in France, rising near Le Puy in the east of the Massif Central and pursuing a broad northwest curve on its 1,000-kilometer (620-mile) course to the Atlantic Ocean near Nantes. The region traditionally referred to as the Loire Valley—château country—is the 225-kilometer (140-mile) stretch between Orléans, 113 kilometers (70 miles) south of Paris and Angers, 96 kilometers (60 miles) from the Atlantic coast. Thanks to its mild climate, soft light, and lush meadowland, this area is known as the Garden of France. Its leading actor—the wide, meandering Loire—offers two distinct faces: fast-flowing and spectacular in spring, sluggish and sandy in summer.

To the north lies the vast grain plain of the Beauce; to the southeast the marshy, forest-covered Sologne, renowned for mushrooms, asparagus, and game. The star attractions along the rocky banks of the Loire and its tributaries—the Rivers Cher, Indre, Vienne, and Loir—are the famous châteaux: stately houses, castles, or fairy-tale palaces. Renaissance elegance is often combined with fortresslike medieval mass. The Loire Valley was fought over by France and England during the Middle Ages. It took the example of Joan of Arc, the "Maid of Orléans" (scene of her most rousing military successes), for the French finally to expel the English.

The Loire Valley's golden age came under Francis I (1515–47), France's flamboyant contemporary of England's Henry VIII. He hired Renaissance craftsmen from Italy and hobnobbed with the aging Leonardo da Vinci, his guest at Amboise. His salamander emblem is to be seen in many châteaus, including Chambord, the mightiest of them, begun in 1519.

The best months to visit are June through October, though the weather can sometimes be hot and sticky in midsummer. Nature in the region is at its best in late spring and early fall, when there are fewer crowds. In peak season (especially August), it is essential to have your accommodations reserved.

Getting Around

The easiest way to visit the Loire châteaus is by car; N152 hugs the riverbank and offers excellent sightseeing possibilities. Trains run along the Loire Valley every two hours, supplemented by local bus services. A peaceful way to explore the region is to rent a bicycle at one of the SNCF train stations (some trains even transport bikes for free).

Guided Tours

Bus tours for the main châteaus leave daily in summer from Tours, Blois, Angers, Orléans, and Saumur. Ask at the relevant tourist office for latest times and prices. Most châteaus insist that visitors follow one of their own tours anyway, but try to get a booklet in English before joining the tour, as most are in French only.

The Loire Valley

Tourist Information

Angers (Pl. du Président Kennedy, tel. 41–87–72–50).
Blois (3 av. du Docteur Jean-Laigret, tel. 54–74–06–49).
Orléans (Pl. Albert-Ier, tel. 38–53–05–95).
Tours (rue B. Palissy, tel. 47–05–58–08).

Exploring the Loire Valley

Châteaudun Orléans, little more than an hour away by expressway (A10) or train, is the most obvious gateway to the Loire Valley if you're coming from Paris. Apart from its art museum and majestic Ste-Croix cathedral, however, Orléans has little going for it. Instead take the expressway from Paris to Chartres, then N10 to **Châteaudun,** whose colossal château, standing resplendent on a steep promontory contains graceful furniture and lavish tapestries. In its chapel are 15 statues produced locally in the 15th century. *Admission: 32 frs. Open mid-Mar.–Sept. 9:30–11:45 and 2–6; Oct.–mid-Mar. 10–11:45 and 2–6.*

Continue along N10 to **Vendôme,** 40 kilometers (25 miles) to the southwest, where the Loir river (not to be confused with the larger and more famous *Loire* to the south) splits into many arms, lending the town a canal-like charm that harmonizes with its old streets and bridges. The large but little-known main church, **Eglise de la Trinité,** an encyclopedia of different styles, with brilliantly carved choir stalls and an exuberant west front, is the work of Jean de Beauce, best known for his spire at Chartres Cathedral. Vendôme also has a ruined **castle** with ramparts and pleasant, uncrowded gardens. *Admission to castle: 12 frs. Open Mar.–June, Wed.–Mon. 10–noon and 2–6; July and Aug., daily 10–noon and 2–6.*

Blois **Blois** lies 32 kilometers (20 miles) southeast of Vendôme along D957. It is the most attractive of the major Loire towns, with its tumbling alleyways and its château. The **château** is a mixture of four different styles: Feudal (13th century); Gothic-Renaissance transition (circa 1500); Renaissance (circa 1520); and Classical (circa 1635). *Admission: 30 frs. Open May–Aug., daily 9–6:30; Sept.–Apr., daily 9–noon and 2–5.*

Blois makes an ideal launching pad for a visit to the châteaux of Chambord and Cheverny. **Chambord** (begun 1519) is 20 kilometers (11 miles) east of Blois along D33, near Bracieux. It stands in splendid isolation in a vast forest and game park. There's another forest on the roof: 365 chimneys and turrets, representing architectural self-indulgence at its least squeamish. Grandeur or a mere 440-room folly? Judge for yourself, and don't miss the superb spiral staircase or the chance to saunter over the rooftop terrace. *Admission: 31 frs adults, 7 frs children. Open July–Aug., daily 9:30–6:30; Sept.–June, daily 9:30–11:45 and 2–sunset.*

About 20 kilometers (12 miles) south of Blois, along D751, stands the sturdy château of **Chaumont,** built between 1465 and 1510—well before Benjamin Franklin became a regular visitor. There is a magnificent Loire panorama from the terrace, and the stables—where purebreds dined like royalty—show the importance attached to fine horses, for hunting or just prestige. *Admission: 25 frs adults, 13 frs students and senior citizens. Open Apr.–Sept., daily 9–12:30 and 2–4:30; Oct.–Mar., daily 9:30–12:30 and 2–3:30.*

Amboise Downstream (westward) another 16 kilometers (10 miles) lies the bustling town of **Amboise,** whose **château,** with charming grounds, a rich interior, and fine views over the river from the battlements, dates from 1500. It wasn't always so peaceful: In 1560, more than 1,000 Protestant "conspirators" were hanged from these battlements during the Wars of Religion. *Admission: 30 frs adults, 20 frs students, 10 frs children. Open July–Aug., daily 9–6:30; Sept.–June, daily 9–noon and 2–5.*

The nearby **Clos-Lucé,** a 15th-century brick manor house, was the last home of Leonardo da Vinci, who was invited to stay here by Francis I. Da Vinci died here in 1519, and his engineering genius is illustrated by models based on his plans and sketches. *Admission: 31 frs adults, 25 frs students and senior citizens. Same hours as château, but open till 6:30 in winter.*

The early 16th-century château of **Chenonceau,** 16 kilometers (10 miles) south of Amboise along D81 and then D40, straddles the tranquil river Cher like a bridge. It is surrounded by elegant gardens and a splendid avenue of plane trees. Inside, note the fine paintings, colossal fireplaces, and richly worked ceilings. A waxworks museum lurks in an outbuilding. *Admission: 35 frs adults, 25 frs children. Open mid-Feb.–mid-Mar., daily 9–sunset; mid-Nov.–mid-Feb., daily 9–4:30.*

Tours **Tours,** 25 kilometers (15 miles) farther on, is the unofficial capital of the Loire. It retains a certain charm despite its sprawling size (250,000 inhabitants) and extensive postwar reconstruction. Its attractive old quarter, Vieux Tours, around place Plumereau, has been tastefully restored, while the **Cathedral of St-Gatien** (1239–1484) numbers among France's most impressive churches. The influence of local Renaissance sculptors and craftsmen is much in evidence on the ornate facade. The stained glass in the choir is particularly delicate; some of it dates from 1320.

The château of **Villandry**, 16 kilometers (10 miles) southwest of Tours along the river Cher, is known for its painstakingly relaid 16th-century gardens, with their long avenues of 1,500 manicured lime trees. The château interior, restored like the gardens in the mid-19th century, is equally beguiling. Note the painted and gilded ceiling from Toledo and the collection of Spanish pictures. *Admission: château and gardens, 37 frs; garden only, 24 frs. Open daily 9–6; gardens open 9–dusk.*

Langeais **Langeais** is just 14 kilometers (9 miles) west of Villandry: Keep on D7 to Lignières before turning right onto D57 and crossing the Loire. A massive **castle** built in the 1460s and never altered dominates this small town. Its apartments contain a superb collection of tapestries, chests, and beds. *Admission: 35 frs adults, 25 frs senior citizens, 17 frs students and children. Open Easter–Oct., daily 9–6:30; Nov.–Easter, Tues.–Sun. 9–noon and 2–5. Closed Mon.*

Azay-le-Rideau (1518–29), one of the prettiest of the Loire châteaux, lies on the river Indre 10 kilometers (6 miles) south of Langeais along D57. It has harmonious proportions and exquisite grounds, with a domesticated moat that is really a lake. This graceful ensemble compensates for the château's spartan interior, as does the charm of the surrounding village. *Admission: 26 frs adults, 17 frs senior citizens, 6 frs children. Open Apr.–Sept., daily 9:30–noon and 2–6; Oct.–Mar., daily 9:30–noon and 2–4:15.*

A short ride down the Indre Valley (on D17 and then D7) from Azay will help you judge whether **Ussé** really is, as the brochures claim, the fairy-tale setting that inspired *Sleeping Beauty*. Its bristling roofs and turrets, flowered terraces, and forest backcloth have undeniable romance. Don't forget the **chapel** in the park, built 1520–38 in purest Renaissance proportions. *Admission: 49 frs adults, 20 frs students. Open mid-Mar.–Nov., daily 9–noon and 2–6.*

Chinon **Chinon**, 13 kilometers (8 miles) from Ussé via D7 and D16, is an ancient town nestled by the river Vienne, with a rock-of-ages **castle** patrolling the horizon. This 12th-century fortress, with walls 370 meters (400 yards) long, is mainly in ruins, though small museums are installed in the Royal Chambers and sturdy Tour de l'Horloge (clock tower). There are excellent views from the ramparts over Chinon and the Vienne Valley. *Admission: 23 frs adults, 18 frs senior citizens, 16 frs children under 19. Open Nov.–mid-Mar., Thurs.–Tues. 9–noon and 2–5, closed Wed.; mid-Mar.–June and Sept., daily 9–6; July and Aug., daily 9–7; Oct., daily 9–5.*

From just south of Chinon, D751 heads off up the Vienne Valley toward **Fontevraud**, 21 kilometers (13 miles) away. This quiet village is dominated by its medieval **abbey**, where English kings Henry II and Richard the Lionhearted are buried. The church, cloisters, Renaissance chapter house, long-vaulted refectory, and octagonal kitchen are all still standing. The guided tours are in French, but you can get a brochure in English to keep track of where you are. *Admission: 25 frs. adults, 15 frs senior citizens, 7 frs children. Open June–mid-Sept., daily 9–noon and 2–6:30; Sept.–Apr., daily 9:30–12:30 and 2–5:30.*

Saumur, 16 kilometers (10 miles) west along the Loire from Fontevraud via D947, is a prosperous town famous for its riding school, wines, and château—a white 14th-century castle that towers above the river. The château contains two outstanding museums:

the **Musée des Arts Décoratifs** (Decorative Arts Museum), featuring porcelain and enamels, and the **Musée du Cheval** (Equine Museum), with saddles, stirrups, skeletons, and Stubbs engravings. *Admission: 32 frs adults, 22 frs students and senior citizens. Open July–Sept., daily 9–6:30; Nov.–Mar., Wed.–Mon. 10–5.*

Angers   **Angers** is a large, historic town on the river Maine just to the north of the Loire. D952 runs along the Loire Valley from Saumur, 45 kilometers (28 miles) away. The feudal **château** was built by St-Louis (1228–38) and has a dry moat, drawbridge, and 17 round towers along its half-mile-long walls. A modern, well-integrated gallery houses an exquisite tapestry collection, notable for the enormous *Tapestry of the Apocalypse,* woven in Paris around 1380. *Admission: 31 frs adults, 15 frs students and senior citizens, 6 frs children. Open July–Aug., daily 10–7; Sept.–June, daily 9:30–noon and 2–5:30.*

Dining and Lodging

For details and price-category definitions, *see* Dining and Lodging in Staying in France, *above.*

Angers   **La Treille.** For traditional, simple fare, try this small two-story
Dining   mom-and-pop restaurant just off the Place Ste-Croix (next to the cathedral). The prix-fixe menu may start with a salade au chevre chaud (warm goat cheese salad), followed by confit of duck and an apple tart. A bottle of local wine completes the meal. Madame runs the small bar while the husband serves the food with a warm welcoming smile. The upstairs dining room has a party atmosphere; downstairs is better for quiet conversation. *12 rue Montault, tel. 41–88–45–51. Reservations not required. Dress: casual. Closed Sun. MC, V. Inexpensive.*

Dining and   **Pavillon Paul Le Quéré.** In 1992, Paul Le Quéré created a luxurious
Lodging   boutique hotel to complement his restaurant in a renovated mansion set back from the main avenue. The rooms, decorated by his wife, Martine, in classic modern style, have flashy marble bathrooms. The chef happily juggles tradition with modern innovations, be it roast lobster tails, fillet of sole sautéed in the juice of oysters, or diced beef with mussels. One opulent dining room is in a glass rotunda, splendid for lunch, while the formal dining room with a Charles X fireplace sets a classic tone for dinner. *3 blvd. Foch, 49100, tel. 41–20–00–20, fax 41–20–06–20. 6 rooms, 4 suites. Facilities: restaurant, parking. AE, DC, MC, V. Expensive.*

Hôtel d'Anjou. An old friend of a hotel, this has spacious, well-modernized rooms and is handily situated by the Jardin du Mail, a pleasant park. Its restaurant, La Salamandre, prides itself on its classic cuisine (menus at 110 frs and 220 frs) served in a Renaissance-style dining room. *1 blvd. du Mal-Foch, 49100, tel. 41–88–24–82, fax 41–87–22–21. 53 rooms with bath or shower. Facilities: restaurant, parking. AE, DC, MC, V. Restaurant closed Sun. Moderate.*

Blois   **Au Rendez-vous des Pêcheurs.** Located on the right bank of the Loire
Dining   below the castle, this extremely modest restaurant has simple decor but offers excellent value in its creative cooking. Chef Eric Reithler has brought inventiveness to his fish-based specialties. *27 rue du Foix, tel. 54–74–67–48. Reservations accepted. MC, V. Closed Sun., Mon. dinner. Moderate.*

Chambord   **Hôtel St-Michel.** Considering its location right across from the châ-
Lodging   teau, the St-Michel offers good value. Some of its rooms afford
★   splendid views of the château, its lawns, and the forest backdrop, as

does the conveniently situated terrace, an ideal place for summer morning coffee before the tourist hordes arrive. *41250 Chambord, tel. 54–20–31–31. 38 rooms, some with bath or shower. Facilities: restaurant, tennis court, parking. MC, V. Closed Nov. 12–Dec. 19. Moderate.*

Chinon
Dining and Lodging

Château de Marcay. In a smartly renovated château whose early beginnings were a medieval fortress, a professional and efficient staff serve the fashion-conscious guests who come to stay and dine. Chef Pascal Bodin prepares an excellent carpaccio de canard for a starter and follows with, perhaps, tournedos of salmon bathed in a Chinon wine sauce and served with a confit of aubergine. Rooms in the château are furnished with valuable antiques; space is generous, beams and gables add warmth, and bathrooms are marbled and vast. Ground-floor rooms in the west wing have private patios. Rooms in the newly constructed Pavilion 50 yards from the château, though pleasantly furnished, have less charm. *Marcay (6 km/4 mi south of Chinon by D49 and D116), 37500 Chinon, tel. 47–93–03–47, fax 47–93–45–33. 35 rooms (27 in château). Facilities: restaurant, gardens, pool, tennis, parking. AE, DC, MC, V. Closed 2nd week of Jan.–mid-Mar. Expensive.*

Saumur
Lodging

Anne d'Anjou. Close to the center of town, this hotel facing the river offers views of the château (floodlit at night) perched above. Inside the 18th-century building the staircase has wrought iron banisters that circle up to the top floor. Rooms are simple, with either old furniture or contemporary decor. Room 102, the pride and joy of the hotel's owners, Yves and Anne-Marie Touzé, has wood panel paintings and Empire furnishings. The restaurant, Les Menestreles, offers traditional fare. *32–33 quai Mayaud, 49400 Saumur, tel. 41–67–30–30, fax 41–67–51–00. 50 rooms. Facilities: restaurant, street parking. AE, DC, MC, V. Moderate.*

Tours
Dining and Lodging

Domaine de la Tortinière. Ten kilometers (6 miles) due south of Tours along N10, this turreted building dates from the mid-19th century. It stands proudly on a hill amid vast fields and woodland. The bedrooms are individually decorated in styles ranging from conventionally old-fashioned to brash ultramodern. The airy restaurant looks out over the gardens. Salmon, pigeon, and rabbit with truffles are menu highlights. *10 rte de Ballan, 37250 Veigné, tel. 47–26–00–19, fax 47–65–25–70. 14 rooms with bath. Facilities: restaurant. MC, V. Closed mid-Dec.–Feb. Restaurant closed Wed. lunch and Tues. in Nov., Dec., and Mar. Expensive.*

Hotel de l'Univers. A complete renovation completed in 1993 has made the most of the building's old charm. The rooms vary slightly, but common to all is a clever use of space to form desk and sitting areas separate from the beds. The use of wood panels and soft colorings adds warmth. Bathrooms are spacious. Most rooms look onto a garden. The lobby is decorated with murals depicting some of the famous people who have stayed here, such as Winston Churchill, Rudyard Kipling, and Maurice Chevalier. *5 blvd. Heurteloup, 37000, tel. 47–02–37–12, fax 47–61–51–80. 89 rooms, 10 suites. Facilities: restaurant, bar, parking. AE, DC, MC, V. Expensive.*

The Riviera

Few places in the world have the same pull on the imagination as France's fabled Riviera, the Mediterranean coastline stretching from St-Tropez in the west to Menton on the Italian border. Cooled by the Mediterranean in the summer and warmed by it in winter, the climate is almost always pleasant. Avoid the area in July and Au-

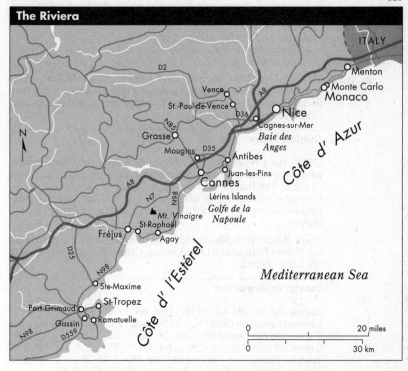

The Riviera

gust, however—unless you love crowds. To see the Riviera at its best, plan your trip in the spring or fall, particularly in May or September.

The Riviera is a land of contrasts. While the coastal resorts seem to live exclusively for the tourist trade and have often been ruined by high-rise blocks, the hinterlands remain relatively untarnished. The little villages perched high on the hills behind medieval ramparts seem to belong to another century. One of them, St-Paul-de-Vence, is the home of the Maeght Foundation, one of the world's leading museums of modern art.

Artists, attracted by the light, have played a considerable role in popular conceptions of the Riviera, and their presence is reflected in the number of modern art museums: the Musée Picasso at Antibes, the Musée Renoir and the Musée d'Art Moderne Mediterranée at Cagnes-sur-Mer, and the Musée Jean Cocteau near the harbor at Menton. Wining and dining are special treats on the Riviera, especially if you are fond of garlic and olive oil. *Bouillabaisse*, a spicy fish stew, is the most popular regional specialty.

The tiny principality of Monaco, which lies between Nice and Menton, is included in this section despite the fact that it is a sovereign state. Although Monaco has its own army and police force, its language, food, and way of life are French. Its famous casino, the highly visible royal Grimaldi family, and the wealth of jetsetters, chic fashions, and opulent yachts all ensure that it maintains its reputation as a "golden ghetto."

Getting Around

By Car Expressway A8 is the only way to get around the Riviera quickly, but for the drama of mountains and sea, take one of the famous Corniche roads.

By Train The train line follows the coast from Marseille to the Italian border, providing excellent access to the seaside resorts, but you will have to take local buses (marked *Gare Routière*) or guided tours to visit Grasse and the perched villages.

Guided Tours

SNCF, the French national railroad company, runs the greatest number of organized tours. For information, contact the Nice Tourist Office (*see* Tourist Information, *below*). Tours are most valuable to areas otherwise impossible to reach by public transportation: St-Paul-de-Vence, Upper Provence, and the spectacular Verdon Gorges.

Boats operate from Nice to Marseille; from St-Tropez to the charming Hyères Islands; and from Antibes, Cannes, and Juan-les-Pins to the Lérins Islands.

Tourist Information

Cagnes-sur-Mer (6 blvd. du Mal-Juin, tel. 93–20–61–64).
Cannes (Palais des Congrès, La Croisette, tel. 93–39–24–53).
Fréjus (325 rue Jean-Jaurès, tel. 94–17–19–19).
Grasse (22 cours Honoré-Cresp, tel. 93–36–03–56).
Juan-les-Pins (51 bd. Guillaumont, tel. 93–61–04–98).
Menton (Palais de l'Europe, Av. Boyer, tel. 93–57–57–00).
Monaco (2a blvd. des Moulins, tel. 92–16–61–16).
Nice (Av. Thiers, tel. 93–87–07–07; 5 av. Gustave-V, tel. 93–87–60–60).
St-Paul-de-Vence (Maison Tour, rue Grande, tel. 93–32–86–95).
St-Tropez (Quai Jean-Jaurès, tel. 94–97–45–21).
Vence (Pl. du Grand-Jardin, tel. 93–58–06–38).

Exploring the Riviera

St-Tropez **St-Tropez** was just another pretty fishing village until it was "discovered" in the 1950s by the "beautiful people," a fast set of film stars, starlets, and others who scorned bourgeois values while enjoying bourgeois bank balances. Today, its summer population swells from 6,000 to 60,000. In season, its top hotels, restaurants, nightclubs, and chic little shops are jammed. In the winter, it's hard to find a restaurant open. The best times to visit, therefore, are early summer or fall. May and June are perhaps the best months, when the town lets its hair down during two local festivals.

The **old port** is the liveliest part of town. You can kill time here at a café terrace, watching the rich and famous on their gleaming yachts. Between the old and new ports is the **Musée de l'Annonciade,** set in a cleverly converted chapel, which houses paintings by artists drawn to St-Tropez between 1890 and 1940—including Paul Signac, Matisse, Derain, and Van Dongen. *Quai de l'Épi, tel. 94–97–04–01. Admission: 22 frs adults, 11 frs children. Open June–Sept., Wed.–Mon. 10–noon and 3–7; Oct.–May, Wed.–Mon. 10–noon and 2–6.*

Across the place de l'Hôtel de Ville lies the old town, where twisting, narrow streets, designed to break the impact of the terrible mistral (the cold, dry northerly wind common to this region), open onto tiny squares and fountains. A long climb up to the **citadel** is rewarded by a splendid view over the old town and across the gulf to **Ste-Maxime,** a quieter, more working-class family resort with a decent beach and reasonably priced hotels. St-Tropez is also a good base for visiting **Port Grimaud,** a pastiche of an Italian fishing village (take D558) and the nearby hilltop villages: the old Provençal town of **Ramatuelle** and the fortified village of **Gassin.**

The **Corniche des Issambres** (N98) runs along the coast from Ste-Maxime to **Fréjus,** a Roman town built by Caesar in 49 BC, standing on a rocky plateau between the Maures and Esterel hills. Two main roads link Fréjus and Cannes. Tortuous N7, originally a Roman road, skirts the northern flank of the rugged Esterel hills. Look for an intersection called the "carrefour du Testannier" and follow the signs to **Forêt Domaniale de l'Esterel** and **Mont Vinaigre** for a magnificent view over the hills.

Cannes   In 1834, a chance event was to change the town of **Cannes** forever. Lord Brougham, Britain's lord chancellor, was en route to Nice when an outbreak of cholera forced the authorities to freeze all travel to prevent the disease from spreading. Trapped in Cannes, he fell in love with the place and built himself a house there to use as an annual refuge from the British winter. The English aristocracy, czars, kings, and princes soon caught on, and Cannes became a community for the international elite. Grand palace hotels were built to cater to them, and Cannes came to symbolize dignified luxury. Today, Cannes is also synonymous with the **International Film Festival.**

Cannes is for relaxing—strolling along the seafront on the **Croisette** and getting tanned on the beaches. Almost all the beaches are private, but that doesn't mean you can't use them, only that you must pay for the privilege. The Croisette offers splendid views of the **Napoule Bay.** Only a few steps inland is the old town, known as the **Suquet,** with its steep, cobbled streets and its 12th-century watchtower.

Grasse is perched in the hills behind Cannes. Take N85 or just follow your nose to the town that claims to be the perfume capital of the world. A good proportion of its 40,000 inhabitants work at distilling and extracting scent from the tons of roses, lavender, and jasmine produced here every year. The various perfumers are only too happy to guide visitors around their fragrant establishments. Fragonard is the best known (20 blvd. Fragonard, tel. 93–36–44–65). The old town is attractive, with its narrow alleys and massive, somber **cathedral.** Three of the paintings inside the cathedral are by Rubens and one is by Fragonard, who lived here for many years.

Take N85 back down to the coast, but fork left at **Mougins,** an attractive fortified hilltop town, famous for one of France's best restaurants, Le Moulin de Mougins. D35 takes you to **Antibes** and **Juan-les-Pins,** originally two villages that now form one town on the west side of the **Baie des Anges** (Angels' Bay).

Antibes   **Antibes,** the older village, dates back to the 4th century BC, when it was a Greek trading port. Today, it is renowned throughout Europe for its industrial flower and plant production. Every morning, except Monday, the market on the Cours Masséna comes alive with the colors of roses, carnations, anemones, and tulips. The Grimaldis, the family that rules Monaco, built **Château Grimaldi** here in the 12th century on the remains of a Roman camp. Today, the château's main attraction is the **Musée Picasso**—a bounty of paintings, ceramics, and lithographs inspired by the sea and Greek mythology. *Pl. du Château, tel. 92–90–54–20. Admission: 26 frs adults, 13 frs students and senior citizens. Open Dec.–Oct., Wed.–Mon. 10–noon and 2–6.*

Nice The 20-kilometer (13-mile) stretch of flat coast between Antibes and Nice lacks charm, but the hinterland makes up for it. With its population of 400,000, its own university, new congress hall, and nearby science park, Nice is the undisputed capital of the Riviera. Founded by the Greeks as Nikaia, it has lived through several civilizations and was attached to France only in 1860. It consequently boasts a profusion of Greek, Italian, British, and French styles. Tourism may not be the main business of Nice, but it is a deservedly popular center with much to offer. The double blessing of climate and geography puts its beaches within an hour-and-a-half's drive of the nearest ski resorts. There is an eclectic mixture of old and new architecture, an opera house, museums, flourishing markets, and regular concerts and festivals, including the Mardi Gras festival and the Battle of Flowers.

Numbers in the margin correspond to points of interest on the Nice map.

① The **place Masséna** is the logical starting point for an exploration of Nice. This fine square was built in 1815 to celebrate a local hero: one **②** of Napoleon's most successful generals. The **Promenade des Anglais,** built by the English community here in 1824, is only a short stroll **③** past the fountains and the **Jardin Albert Ier.** It now carries heavy traffic but still forms a splendid strand between town and sea. The narrow streets in the old town are the prettiest part of Nice: Take **④** the rue de l'Opéra to see **St-François-de-Paule** church (1750) and the **⑤** **opera house.** At the northern extremity of the old town lies the vast **⑥** **place Garibaldi** —all yellow-ocher buildings and formal fountains.

⑦ The **Musée Chagall** is just off the boulevard de Cimiez, near the Roman ruins. The museum was built in 1972 to house the Chagall collection, including the 17 huge canvases of *The Message of the Bible,* which took 13 years to complete. *Av. du Dr-Ménard, tel. 93–81–75– 75. Admission: 27 frs adults, 18 frs students and senior citizens. Open July–Sept., Wed.–Mon. 10–7; Oct.–June, Wed.–Mon. 10– 12:30 and 2–5:30.*

Numbers in the margin correspond to points of interest on the Monaco map.

Monaco Sixteen kilometers (10 miles) along the coast from Nice is **Monaco.** For more than a century Monaco's livelihood was centered in its **①** splendid copper-roof **casino.** The oldest section dates from 1878 and was conceived by Charles Garnier, architect of the Paris opera house. It's as elaborately ornate as anyone could wish, bristling with turrets and gold filigree, and masses of interior frescoes and bas-reliefs. There are lovely sea views from the terrace, and the gardens out front are meticulously tended. The main activity is in the American Room, where beneath the gilt-edged ceiling busloads of tourists feed the one-armed bandits. *Pl. du Casino, tel. 92–16–21– 21. Persons under 21 not admitted. Admission for American Room free. Open daily noon–4 AM. Closed May 1.*

② The **Musée National des Automates et Poupées d' Autrefois** (Museum of Antique Dolls and Automatons) has a compelling collection of 18th- and 19th-century dolls and mechanical figures, the latter shamelessly showing off their complex inner workings. It's magically set in a 19th-century seaside villa (designed by Garnier). *17 av.*

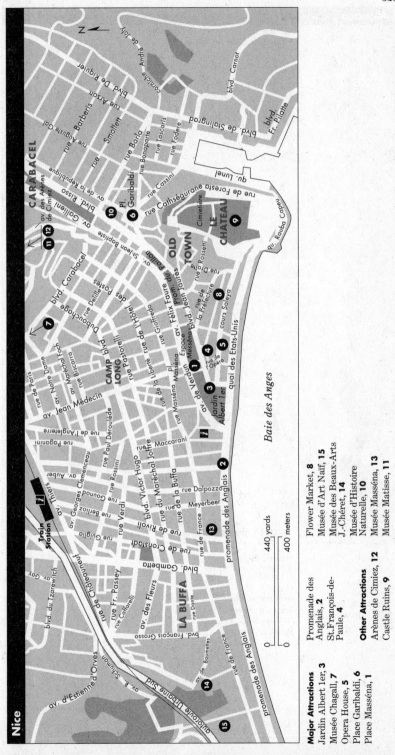

Nice

Baie des Anges

Major Attractions
Jardin Albert 1er, **3**
Musée Chagall, **7**
Opera House, **5**
Place Garibaldi, **6**
Place Masséna, **1**

Promenade des
Anglais, **2**
St.François-de-
Paule, **4**

Other Attractions
Arènes de Cimiez, **12**
Castle Ruins, **9**

Flower Market, **8**
Musée d'Art Naïf, **15**
Musée des Beaux-Arts
J.-Chéret, **14**
Musée d'Histoire
Naturelle, **10**
Musée Masséna, **13**
Musée Matisse, **11**

Monaco

MONTE CARLO

LA CONDAMINE

Train Station

FONTVIEILLE

0   220 yards
0   200 meters

Casino, **1**
Cathedral, **4**
Fort Antoine
Theater, **7**
Jardin Exotique, **8**
Musée Historial des
Princes de Monaco, **5**

Musée National des
Automates et Poupées
d'Autrefois, **2**
Musée
Océanographique, **6**
Museum of Prehistoric
Anthropology, **9**
Palais du Prince, **3**

*Princesse-Grace, tel. 93–30–91–26. Admission: 26 frs adults, 15 frs
children. Open daily 10–12:15 and 2:30–6:30.*

Monaco Town, the principality's old quarter, has many vaulted passageways and exudes an almost tangible medieval feel. The magnificent **Palais du Prince** (Prince's Palace), a grandiose Italianate
structure with a Moorish tower, was largely rebuilt in the last century. Here, since 1297, the Grimaldi dynasty has lived and ruled.
The spectacle of the **Changing of the Guard** occurs each morning at
11:55; inside, guided tours take visitors through the state apartments and a wing containing the **Palace Archives** and **Musée Napoléon** (Napoleonic Museum). *Pl. du Palais, tel. 93–25–18–31. Palace
open June–Oct., daily 9:30–12:30 and 2–6:30. Admission: 40 frs
adults, 20 frs children. Musée Napoléon and Palace Archives open
year-round, Tues.–Sun. Admission: 20 frs adults, 10 frs children.*

Monaco's **cathedral** (4 rue Colonel Bellando de Castro) is a late 19th-
century neo-Romanesque confection in which Philadelphia-born
Princess Grace lies in splendor along with past members of the Gri-
maldi dynasty. Nearby is the **Musée Historial des Princes de Monaco**
(Waxworks Museum), a Monégasque Madame Tussauds, with none-
too-realistic wax figures stiffly portraying various episodes in the
Grimaldi history. The waxworks may not convince, but the rue
Basse is wonderfully atmospheric. *27 rue Basse, tel. 93–30–39–05.
Admission: 24 frs. Open May–Sept., daily 9–8; Oct.–Dec., daily
10:30–6; Jan.–Apr., daily 9–6:30.*

Next to the **St-Martin Gardens**—which contain an evocative bronze
monument in memory of Prince Albert I (Prince Rainier's great-
grandfather, the one in the sou'wester and flying oil skins, benignly
guiding a ship's wheel)—is the **Musée Océanographique** (Oceanog-
raphy Museum and Aquarium). This museum is also an internationally renowned research institute founded by the very Prince Albert
who is remembered outside as an an eminent marine biologist in his
day; the well-known underwater explorer Jacques Cousteau is the
present director. The aquarium is the undisputed highlight, however, where a collection of the world's fish and crustacea live out their
lives in public, some colorful, some drab, some the stuff nightmares
are made of. *Av. St-Martin, tel. 93–15–36–00. Admission: 60 frs
adults, 30 frs children. Open Sept.–Oct. and May–June, daily
9:30–7; Nov.–Apr., daily 9:30–6; July and Aug., daily 9–8.*

Before heading back inland, take a stroll to the eastern tip of the
rock, to the **Fort Antoine Theater** (av. de la Quarantaine, tel. 93–30–
19–21), a converted 18th-century fortress that certainly looks a lot
prettier now than it would have in more warlike times, covered as it
is in ivy and flowering myrtle and thyme. In the summer, this is an
open-air theater seating 350.

The Moneghetti area is the setting for the **Jardin Exotique** (Garden
of Exotic Plants), where 600 varieties of cacti and succulents cling to
the rock face, their improbable shapes and sometimes violent color-
ing a further testimony to the fact that Mother Nature will try anything once. Your ticket also allows you to explore the **caves**, next to
the gardens, and to visit the **Museum of Prehistoric Anthropology**,
adjacent. *Blvd. du Jardin Exotique, tel. 93–15–80–06. Admission:
39 frs adults, 26 frs senior citizens, 15 frs children. Open Oct.–May,
daily 9–5:30; June–Sept., daily 9–7.*

Menton   **Menton** also once belonged to the Grimaldis and, like Nice, was attached to France only in 1860. Because of its popularity among British visitors, the western side of the town was developed at the turn
of the century to cater to the influx of the rich and famous, with spa-

cious avenues, first-class hotels, and the inevitable casino. The eastern side of town long remained the domain of the local fishermen but has been developed to cater to the needs of tourists. A large marina was built and the **Sablettes,** once a tiny beach, has been artificially extended.

Down by the harbor stands a small 17th-century fort, where Jean Cocteau, the artist, writer, and filmmaker, once worked. It now houses the **Musée Jean Cocteau,** with a collection of his work. *111 quai Napoléon, tel. 93–57–72–30. Admission free. Open mid-June–mid-Sept., Wed.–Sun. 10–noon and 3–6; mid-Sept.–mid-June, 10–noon and 2–6.*

Dining and Lodging

For details and price-category definitions, *see* Dining and Lodging in Staying in France, *above.*

Antibes
Lodging

Auberge Provençale. The rooms and service are sunny, partly a reflection of the manageable size of the hotel. Its popular restaurant serves lobster and shellfish as well as *boudin de rascasse,* a minced fish shaped into a sausage. *61 pl. Nationale, tel. 93–34–13–24, fax 93–34–89–88. 6 rooms with bath. Restaurant reservations required. AE, DC, MC, V. Facilities: restaurant. Closed mid-Nov.–mid-Dec. Restaurant closed Mon., Tues. lunch. Moderate.*

Cagnes
Lodging

Cagnard. This hotel is in an attractive 15th-century building in the old village. The restaurant—once the Grimaldi Château Guards Room—dates back to the early 14th century. The hotel has several suites in two houses in the garden and a third up the road. The view from them all—over the Cap d'Antibes—is memorable. *54 rue Sous-Bari, tel. 93–20–73–22, fax 93–22–06–39. 19 rooms and suites with bath. Facilities: restaurant. AE, DC, MC, V. Restaurant closed Thurs. lunch and Nov.–mid-Dec. Expensive.*

Cannes
Dining

Mirabelle. For many, this is a favorite restaurant in the Suquet. The cuisine is inventive, the sauces light, and the desserts special. *24 rue St-Antoine, tel. 93–38–72–75. Reservations advised. MC, V. Closed Tues., Jan. 15–Feb. 15, and Nov. 15–30. Expensive.*

Lodging

Majestic. Unlike most luxury hotels lining the Croisette on the seafront, the Majestic has a discreet atmosphere. The rooms are spacious and traditional but refreshingly decorated in pastels. The restaurant also offers a reasonably priced evening meal in winter. *14 La Croisette, tel. 92–98–77–00. 283 rooms with bath. Facilities: private beach, swimming pool, air-conditioning, parking lot, tennis, golf, horseback riding. AE, DC, MC, V. Closed Nov. 11–Dec. 20. Very Expensive.*

Beverly. Despite extensive renovations and a 1993 name change, the Beverly (formerly the Bristol) continues to offer an intimate, wallet-friendly contrast to the big names nearby on La Croisette. Prices start at around 180 frs, but be prepared to go a bit higher if you fancy one of the 10 (quieter) rooms with a balcony at the back of the building. The beach, train station, and Palais des Festivals are all within a three-minute walk. *14 rue Hoche, tel. 93–39–10–66, fax 92–98–65–63. 19 rooms, 15 with bath or shower. AE, MC, V. Closed Dec.–mid-Jan. Inexpensive–Moderate.*

Grasse
Lodging

Panorama. The excellent views of the Massif d'Estérel and right across to Cannes are the vindication of this hotel's name. It is modern and well run and has ample parking. Most rooms have good views, but there is no restaurant. *2 pl. du Cours, tel. 93–36–80–80,* *fax 93–36–92–04. 36 rooms with bath. Facilities: parking. MC, V. Moderate.*

Menton
Dining and
Lodging

Chez Mireille-l'Ermitage. Best known for its restaurant, this elegant yet cozy hotel stands on the promenade du Soleil, overlooking the beach. Each room has its own style and all are different, although many have good views. The restaurant is a favorite for local specialties: *bourride* (fish soup) and bouillabaisse, salmon, and bass fillets. *30 av. Carnot, tel. 93–41–62–85. 21 rooms with bath or shower. AE, DC, MC, V. Facilities: restaurant. Hotel closed first half Dec., part of Jan.; restaurant closed Mon. evening, Tues., mid-Nov–mid-Apr. Moderate.*

Monaco
Dining
★

Louis XV. A strong contender for the best-in-Monaco award, Louis XV's opulent decor and chef Alain Ducasse's beautifully conceived dishes, such as ravioli with foie gras and truffles, contribute to the formal atmosphere. The wine cellar is exceptional. *Hôtel de Paris, pl. du Casino, tel. 92–16–30–01. Reservations required. AE, DC, MC, V. Very Expensive.*

Port. Harbor views from the terrace and top-notch Italian food make the Port a good choice. A large, varied menu includes shrimp, pastas, lasagna, fettuccine, fish risotto, and veal with ham and cheese. *Quai Albert Ier, tel. 93–50–77–21. Reservations advised. Dress: casual. AE, DC, MC, V. Closed Mon. and Nov. Moderate–Expensive.*

Polpetta. This popular trattoria is close enough to the Italian border to pass for authentic. It's excellent value for the money, with delicious home cooking to boot. *2 rue Paradis, tel. 93–50–67–84. Reservations required in high season. MC, V. Closed Sat. lunch, Tues., Feb. 15–Mar. 15, Oct. 15–30. Moderate.*

Lodging
★

Hôtel de Paris. An exceptional establishment, where elegance, luxury, dignity, and Old World charm are the watchwords. Built in 1864, it still exudes the gold-plated splendor of an era when kings and grand dukes stayed here. *Pl. du Casino, tel. 92–16–30–00, fax 93–15–90–03. 245 rooms with bath. Facilities: 2 restaurants, bar, pool, health club, shops, tennis court. AE, DC, MC, V. Very Expensive.*

Balmoral. Despite the name, there's nothing even vaguely Scottish about this somewhat old-fashioned hotel overlooking the harbor. Rooms are a reasonable size, if bland; many have balconies. *12 av. de la Costa, tel. 93–50–62–37, fax 93–15–08–69. 75 rooms with bath or shower, half with air-conditioning. Facilities: restaurant. AE, DC, MC, V. Restaurant closed Nov. Moderate.*

France. The modest hotel France, near the train station, can't begin to compete with the opulence of some of the others listed here, but it's one of the cheapest around and worth a look if you are on a tight budget. *6 rue de La Turbie, tel. 93–30–24–64, fax 92–16–13–34. 26 rooms, 18 with bath or shower. DC, MC, V. Inexpensive.*

Mougins
Dining and
Lodging

Le Moulin de Mougins. Roger Vergé has created one of France's finest restaurants in a converted mill about 1½ miles from the village along D3. The cuisine ranges from apparently simple salads to rich, complicated sauces for lobster, salmon, or turbot. Considering that it is a gourmet favorite, the restaurant has a surprisingly informal atmosphere. There are five elegantly rustic guest rooms as well. *Quartier Notre-Dame-de-Vie, 424 Chemin du Moulin, tel. 93–75–78–24, fax 93–90–18–55. Reservations required. AE, DC, MC, V. Closed Thurs. lunch and Mon., Feb.–Mar. Very Expensive.*

Nice
Dining

Ane-Rouge. Famous for generations as *the* place for Nice's best fish and seafood, this tiny, family-run restaurant is popular with locals, not least for the Vidalots, the pleasant couple who run it. *7 quai des*

Deux-Emmanuel, tel. 93–89–49–63. Reservations advised. MC, V. Closed weekends, mid-July–end of Aug. Expensive.

Dining and **Negresco.** Opened in 1912, the Negresco is officially listed as a his-
Lodging toric monument and is a byword for Old World elegance. The public
★ rooms have antique coffered ceilings and magnificent fireplaces. No
two bedrooms are alike, but they all have antique furniture and
paintings. Its main restaurant, Le Chantecler, is without doubt the
best in Nice. *37 promenade des Anglais, tel. 93–88–00–58, fax 93–
88–35–68. 130 rooms with bath. Facilities: 2 restaurants (reservations required). AE, DC, MC, V. Restaurants closed mid-Nov.–
mid-Dec. Very Expensive.*

St-Tropez **Byblos.** This hotel is unique. Its luxury rooms and suites are built
Dining and around tiled courtyards, fragrant with magnolia and orange trees,
Lodging like a miniature Provençal village. Each room is different, with
amusing touches and subtle lighting. Les Caves du Roy, one of its
two nightclubs, and Le Chabichou, an independent restaurant within the complex, are considered among the best in town. Specialties
include foie gras and lobster. Les Arcades, the hotel's other restaurant, offers slightly more moderately priced meals. *Av. Paul Signac, tel. 94–97–00–04, fax 94–97–40–52. 59 rooms and 48 suites
with bath. Facilities: 2 restaurants, 2 nightclubs, sauna, pool, hairdresser. AE, DC, MC, V. Closed winter. Very Expensive. Le
Chabichou, tel. 94–54–80–00. Reservations required. AE, DC, MC,
V. Closed Oct. 10–May 1. Very Expensive.*

11 Germany

A reunited Germany offers the traveler a unique experience. Today one country exists where previously there were two, and although the 40-year division was an artificial one, differences that developed during this period will take some years to even out. Travelers crossing from "west" to "east" Germany will soon notice the big gap in wealth between the two halves. In western Germany, a stable economy has resulted in cared-for cities, towns, and villages and in a manicured countryside. In eastern Germany, many cities and rural areas are scarred by a 19th-century approach to industrialization that had little or no concern for the environment. Still, the former Communist authorities did attempt to preserve and renovate some historic buildings.

Former West Germany was a founding member of the European Common Market, now the European Union (EU), and its government has always championed efforts to expand the "club." Apart from security checks, Germany abandoned bureaucratic border formalities with its EU neighbors (France, Holland, Belgium, Luxembourg, and Denmark) when all trade barriers within the EC were lifted at the beginning of 1993.

In many ways, Germany is already one country: the same language, the same currency, the same federal political structure. But some of the differences can be quirky. The united Germany is still a young country; the two sides came together again only on October 3, 1990.

Rapid reunification—critics said it was too hasty—has had a damaging effect on the German economy, which had previously been unaffected by the recession in other parts of the western world. The bid to quickly rejuvenate former East Germany and provide its 17 million inhabitants with better standards of living has so far proved elusive, while costing western German taxpayers thousands of millions of Deutschemarks. By the end of 1992, the effects of reunification had virtually stopped the great German economic locomotive, resulting in higher prices and the threat of higher taxes—and causing much grumbling in the west. The determined effort of the powerful German federal bank, the Bundesbank, to curb inflation at all costs, has been blamed by neighboring west European governments for slowing up their efforts to recover from the recession.

The problems of reunification, and the attendant social unrest in the east, also coincided with the massive influx of several hundred thousand "political" refugees as word spread far and wide that Germany had the most liberal asylum laws in the world, one of the central planks of a deliberately liberal post-Nazi constitution. The refugees—many of whom are believed to be economic rather than political—have added to the strains on the economy.

In the eastern part of the country Germans still earn less than their fellow countrymen in the west. But many basic costs of living are lower. Apartment rents, for example, are often considerably less than what Germans in the west pay, although rents and utility costs are rising. Eastern German shops are less numerous and elegant, but they are already filled with the sort of material goods that were unobtainable under the Communist regime. During the first six months after the fall of the Berlin Wall, the number of car owners in eastern Germany rose by 600,000.

Germans tend to rise very early; they may be found hammering away at a building site by 7 AM or seated at an office desk by 8 AM, but they take their leisure time just as seriously. Annual vacations of up to six weeks are the norm, and secular and religious festivals occupy another 12 days. Every town and village, and many city neighborhoods, manage at least one "Fest" a year, when the beer barrels are rolled out and sausages are thrown on the grill. The seasons have their own festivities: Carnivals (Fasching) herald the end of winter, countless beer gardens open up with the first warm rays of sunshine, fall is celebrated with the Munich Oktoberfest, and Advent brings Christkindlmarkt, colorful pre-Christmas markets held in town and city squares.

Eastern Germany's emergence from communism has not so much inspired a new sense of nationhood there as it has revived regional traditions and identities. The villages south of Leipzig and Dresden have more in common with their neighbors in northern Bavaria, from whom they were cut off for four decades, than with Berlin bureaucrats. Five old states—with their capitals in Dresden, Erfurt, Magdeburg, Potsdam, and Schwerin—have been re-created, making a total of 16 for all of reunited Germany. Each new state, with its own regional parliament, is certain to develop a cultural identity.

The great outdoors have always been an important escape hatch for the Germans, and *Lebensraum* (living space) is even more highly prized in the era of high technology and pressurized urban life. Germany does its best to meet the needs of its hardworking inhabitants. A Bavarian mountain inn, the glow of its lights reflected on the blanket of snow outside, may be only a short drive from Munich. The busy industrial city of Stuttgart lies at the gateway to the Black Forest (Schwarzwald), the popular region of spas, hiking trails, and its tempting cake. Berlin is surrounded by its own lakes and green parklands. The Green Party is a political expression of this appreciation for the outdoors and nature.

The transportation system that links these various regions is a godsend to the visitor. German trains are fast, clean, and punctual, and a drive on a speed limit–free autobahn will give you an idea of just how fast all those BMW and Mercedes sports cars are meant to go.

Essential Information

Before You Go

When to Go The main tourist season in Germany runs from May to late October, when the weather is naturally at its best. In addition to many tourist events, this period has hundreds of folk festivals. The winter sports season in the Bavarian Alps runs from Christmas to mid-March. Prices everywhere are generally higher during the summer, so you may find considerable advantages in visiting out of season. Most resorts offer out-of-season (*Zwischensaison*) and "edge-of-season" (*Nebensaison*) rates, and tourist offices can provide lists of hotels offering special low-price inclusive weekly packages (*Pauschalangebote*). Similarly, many winter resorts offer lower rates for the periods immediately before and after the Christmas and New Year high season (*Weisse Wochen*, or "white weeks"). The other advantage of out-of-season travel is that there aren't as many crowds. The disadvantages of visiting out of season, especially in winter, are that the weather is often cold and gloomy and many tourist attractions, especially in rural areas, are closed. Ski resorts are an exception.

The major cities, especially Munich and Berlin, are active year-round. Avoid Leipzig around the first weeks in March and September, when the trade fair commandeers all accommodations and prices soar.

Germany

Climate Germany's climate is generally temperate. Winters vary from mild and damp to very cold and bright. Particularly chilly regions include the Baltic coast, the Alps, the Harz Mountains, and the Black and Bavarian forests. Summers are usually sunny and warm, though be prepared for a few cloudy and wet days. In Alpine regions, spring often comes late, with snow flurries well into April. Fall is sometimes spectacular in the south: warm and soothing. The only real exception to the above is the strikingly variable weather in southern Bavaria (Bayern) caused by the *Föhn*, a warm Alpine wind that brings sudden barometric changes and gives rise to clear but oppressive conditions in summer and, in winter, can cause snow to disappear overnight.

The following are the average daily maximum and minimum temperatures for Munich.

Jan.	35F	1C	May	64F	18C	Sept.	67F	20C
	23	− 5		45	7		48	9
Feb.	38F	3C	June	70F	21C	Oct.	56F	13C
	23	− 5		51	11		40	4
Mar.	48F	9C	July	74F	23C	Nov.	44F	7C
	30	− 1		55	13		33	0
Apr.	56F	14C	Aug.	73F	23C	Dec.	36F	2C
	38	3		54	12		26	− 3

Currency The unit of currency in Germany is the Deutschemark, written as DM and generally referred to as the mark. It is divided into 100 pfennig. There are bills of 5 (rare), 10, 20, 50, 100, 200, 500, and 1,000 marks and coins of 1, 2, 5, 10, and 50 pf and 1, 2, and 5 marks. At press time (spring 1994), the mark stood at DM 1.68 to the dollar and DM 2.50 to the pound sterling.

The Deutschemark is legal tender throughout reunited Germany. The cost of living is still much lower in the former GDR (German Democratic Republic), where most people earn considerably less than their western colleagues doing the same jobs, and some of these lower costs benefit tourists—for example, on public transportation, in cafés and beer restaurants, and in simple accommodations such as country inns and private guest houses. But a growing number of places that cater specifically to visitors are now charging western rates.

Major credit cards are widely accepted in Germany, though not universally so. You can buy a seat on a Lufthansa flight with a credit card but not on a German train, for example. Most hotels, a significant number of restaurants, and all leading car-rental companies accept credit cards, however. A growing number of shops also honor them, but don't be surprised if you are offered a discount for cash.

What It Will Cost The early 1990s has seen inflation creeping up (at press time, the annual rate of inflation was around 4%), primarily because of the cost of financing the rejuvenation and integration of former Communist East Germany. For example, a "reunification" tax has been levied on basic commodities such as gas, and telephone charges have risen. There were further modest increases in fares for most forms of public transportation.

The most expensive areas to visit are the major cities, notably Frankfurt, Hamburg, and Munich. Out-of-the-way rural regions, such as north and east Bavaria, the Saarland on the French border, and many parts of eastern Germany, offer the lowest prices.

Sample Prices Cup of coffee in a café, DM 3.50, in a stand-up snack bar DM 1.80; mug of beer in a beer hall, DM 4.50, a bottle of beer from a supermarket, DM 1.50; soft drink, DM 2; ham sandwich, DM 4; 2-mile taxi ride, DM 12.

Visas To enter the new Germany, only passports are required of visitors from the United States, Canada, and the United Kingdom, although U.S. citizens must obtain a visa if they plan to stay longer than three months. A passport is valid for travel throughout the country, and, of course, there are no limitations on movement in Berlin.

Customs The establishment in 1993 of a single, unrestricted market within the European Union (EU) means that there no longer are any restrictions on importing items duty-free for citizens of the 12 member countries traveling among EU countries.

If you are entering Germany as a citizen of a country that does not belong to the EU, you may import duty-free: (1) 200 cigarettes or 50 cigars or 250 grams of tobacco; plus (2) 1 liter of spirits more than 22% proof or 2 liters of spirits less than 22% proof, and 2 liters of still wine; plus (3) 50 grams of perfume and ¼ liter of toilet water; plus (4) other goods to the value of DM 115.

Tobacco and alcohol allowances are for visitors aged 17 and over. Other items intended for personal use may be imported and exported freely. There are no restrictions on the import and export of German currency.

Language English has long been taught in high schools in the western part of Germany. Consequently, many people under age 40 speak some English, although the level of understanding varies considerably. Older people in rural areas are less familiar with the English language, but a substantial number have retained some basic words of communication from the immediate post-war years when American and British forces occupied the country. English is not as widely understood in eastern parts of the country, where before the collapse of communism Russian was the first foreign language taught in many schools. Still, young people exposed to American and British pop music are becoming increasingly familiar with basic English.

Germans who speak some English will take every opportunity to practice what they know, and they are delighted when someone makes an effort—no matter how elementary—to speak their language. For a visitor attempting to practice his or her German, the country's many dialects pose the biggest problem. Probably the most difficult to comprehend is Bavaria's, which is like another language—even books are written in "Bayerisch." Nonetheless, except for older people in remote, rural districts, virtually everyone can also speak Hoch Deutsch, the German equivalent of Oxford English. Hoch Deutsch is always used on TV and radio.

Getting Around

By Car
Road
Conditions The autobahn system in western Germany is of the highest standard. These roads are marked either A (on blue signs), meaning inter-German highways, or E (on green signs), meaning they form part of the Europe-wide *Europastrasse* network. All autobahns are toll-free. Local roads are called *Bundesstrassen* and are marked by their number on a yellow sign. All local roads are single lane and slower than autobahns.

The condition of the road system in eastern Germany has improved enormously. Many major roads have been repaired, and new autobahns are being added, most notably those linking Berlin with both western and eastern destinations.

Rules of the Road Rules of the road are now the same in both parts of reunited Germany, with no difference in the speed limits. Officially, there's no speed limit on autobahns, although you'll find signs recommending that motorists stay below 130 kph (80 mph). You'll also find blue signs on autobahns stating the recommended minimum speed on that stretch. Germans are fast drivers and autobahn speeds of over 160 kph (100 mph) are common. Unless you're driving at that speed, keep to the right-hand lane on autobahns, using the faster-paced left-hand lanes only for passing. There are speed limits on other roads—100 kph (60 mph) on main roads (Bundesstrassen), 80 kph (50 mph) on country roads, between 30 kph (18 mph) and 60 kph (36 mph) in built-up urban areas. Fines for exceeding the speed limit can be heavy and penalties for driving under the influence of alcohol are even more severe, so make sure to keep within the legal limit— equivalent to the consumption of two small beers or a glass of wine. Alcohol-free beer is sold at all autobahn restaurants and refreshment stops and even at gas stations.

Parking Daytime parking in cities is very difficult. If you can find one, use a parking lot or you'll risk having your car towed. Parking restrictions are not always clearly marked and can be hard to understand when they are. At night, parking-meter spaces are free.

Gasoline Both leaded and unleaded gas and diesel are generally available all over Germany. At press time (spring 1994), the price of a liter of gas ranged from DM 1.05 to DM 1.55, depending on the grade. (To encourage the use of the more environmentally friendly unleaded gas, the government has made it cheaper.)

Breakdowns The **ADAC,** the major German automobile organization, gives free help and advice to tourists, though you have to pay for any spare parts and labor you need. All autobahns have regularly spaced telephones with which you can call for help. The contact address for the ADAC is Am Westpark 8, 8000 Munich 70 (tel. 089/76760).

By Train The German railway system is in the process of being privatized, so routes, timetables, and fares could change by 1995. The privatization began in 1994 and is expected to take at least six years to complete. The special tickets and fares we list below applied in 1994, and a spokesperson for **Deutsche Bundesbahn** (German Railways) predicted no sweeping changes for 1995. The two separate rail networks of the former East and West Germany merged in 1994, bringing Berlin and the cities of the old German Democratic Republic much closer to the main railheads of the west. The electrification and renovation of the ancient tracks in the formerly Communist-run East also made big strides forward, allowing the extension there of the high-speed InterCity Express service that previously linked only the cities of the west. InterCity and EuroCity services were improved and expanded, and the regional InterRegio network was extended nationwide. Train travel times were reduced so dramatically that journeys between many cities—Munich–Frankfurt, for example—can be completed faster by rail than by plane. All overnight InterCity services and the slower D-class trains have sleepers, with a first-class service that includes breakfast in bed. All InterCity and InterCity Express trains have restaurant cars and the Hamburg–Berchtesgaden service has introduced an on-board MacDonald's as an experiment. A DM 6 surcharge is added to the ticket price on all InterCity journeys irrespective of distance (DM 12 round-trip), while InterCity Express fares are about 20% more expensive than normal ones.

Seat reservations are free of charge. Bikes cannot be transported on InterCity and InterCity Express services, but InterRegio trains have special storage facilities aboard and compartments where cyclists can travel next to their bikes.

Fares European union is bringing a greater degree of cooperation between the railroad authorities of individual countries, and new deals allowing more freedom and flexibility were being worked out in 1994. One deal that will be in effect by 1995 is a new and more comprehensive version of the popular InterRail ticket. It's complicated, but big savings can be made by young travelers (you must be 26 years old or younger) touring just one area of Europe. The system divides Europe into seven zones, with different InterRail tariffs within each one. Germany belongs to Zone C, along with Switzerland, Austria, and Denmark. A one-month InterRail ticket for travel within this zone costs DM 580, and a two-week ticket DM 420. Young travelers intending to tour only Germany can get an even better deal with a Tramper ticket, allowing one month's rail travel on all German trains (including the high-speed InterCity Express) for DM 465. No age limit is linked to other special deals, such as the "Saver" and "Super Saver" which offer big savings on return journeys made on off-peak days. One tip: There is very little difference in comfort between first- and second-class compartments in the sleek new InterCity Express trains but there's a big difference in fares.

The Rail Pass is also valid on all buses operated by the Deutsche Bundesbahn (DB; German Railway), as well as on tour routes along the Romantic and Castle roads served by **Deutsche Touring Gesellschaft** (Am Römerhof 17, D-60486 Frankfurt/Main, tel. 069/ 79030). It includes free rides on the Rhine and Mosel rivers, with cruises operated by the Köln-Düsseldorfer (KD) Line between Mainz and Cologne (Köln) and Koblenz and Cochem, as well as free admission to the Transportation Museum in Nürnberg (Lessingstrasse 6).

By Bus Long-distance bus services in Germany are part of the Europe-wide Europabus network. Services are neither as frequent nor as comprehensive as those on the rail system, so make reservations. Be careful in selecting the service you travel on: All Europabus services have a bilingual hostess and offer small luxuries that you won't find on the more basic, though still comfortable, regular services. For details and reservations, contact DTG (*see* By Train, *above*). Reservations can also be made at any of the Deutsche Touring offices in Cologne, Hanover, Hamburg, Munich, Nuremberg (Nürnberg), and Wuppertal and at travel agents.

Rural bus services are operated by local municipalities and some private firms, as well as by DB and the post office. Services are variable, however, even when there is no other means to reach your destination by public transportation.

By Plane Germany's national airline, **Lufthansa,** serves all major cities. **LTU International Airways** (in the United States, tel. 800/888–0200; in Germany, tel. 0211/410941) has connections between Düsseldorf and Munich and between Frankfurt and Munich (summer only). Regular fares are high, but you can save up to 40% with Flieg und Spar ("fly and save") specials; several restrictions apply, such as a DM 100 penalty for changing flights. Contact Lufthansa at Frankfurt International Airport (D-60549 Frankfurt, tel. 069/6961; in the United States at 750 Lexington Ave., New York, NY 10022, tel. 718/895–1277 or 800/645–3880; in Great Britain at 23–26 Piccadilly, London W1V 0EJ, tel. 071/355–4994 or 071/408–0442). A British Airways subsidiary, **Deutsche BA,** competes with Lufthansa on many domestic routes, including those between Berlin and Munich, Frankfurt, and Düsseldorf. The airline, Germany's newest, planned to set up its headquarters at Munich Airport in April 1994.

By Boat For a country with such a small coastline, Germany is a surprisingly nautical nation: You can cruise rivers and lakes throughout the country. The biggest fleet, and most of the biggest boats, too, belongs to the Cologne-based KD line, the Köln-Düsseldorf Rheinschiffahrt. It operates services on the Rivers Rhine, Moselle, and Main, ranging from luxurious five-day trips from Amsterdam or Rotterdam in Holland all the way down the Rhine to Basel in Switzerland, to short "riverboat shuffles" with jazz bands and freely flowing wine. For details, write **KD River Cruises of Europe** (Rhine Cruise Agency), 170 Hamilton Ave., White Plains, NY 10601) or **KD German Rhine Line** (Frankenwerft 15, D-50667 Köln).

Services on the 160-kilometer (100-mile) stretch of the Danube (Donau) between the spectacular Kelheim gorge and Passau on the Austrian border are operated by **Donauschiffahrt Wurm & Köck** (Höllgasse 26, D-94032 Passau). The company has daily summer cruises on the Rivers Danube, Inn, and Ilz, which meet at Passau; some two-day cruises into Austria are also offered. Bodensee (Lake Constance), the largest lake in Germany, located at the meeting point of Germany, Austria, and Switzerland, has up to 40 ships crisscrossing it in summer. Write **Deutsche Bundesbahn,** Bodensee-Schiffsbetriebe, Hafenstrasse 6, D-78462 Konstanz. Bavaria's five largest lakes—Ammersee, Chiemsee, Königsee, Tegernsee, and Starnbergersee—have regular summer cruises and excursions. Details are available from local tourist offices.

KD has two new luxury cruise ships now plying the Elbe. Several different itineraries are being offered, ranging from five to eight days. All cruises stop at Dresden, and some include free bus transfers to Hamburg, Berlin, and Prague.

By Bicycle Bicycles can be rented at nearly 400 train stations throughout Germany from Apr. 1–Oct. 31. The basic cost is DM 6 per day with a valid train ticket; otherwise it's DM 10. Two marks extra per day gets you a bike with gears. You can pick up a bike at one station and return it to another, provided the station is on the list of those renting bikes. Mountain bikes can be rented for DM 20 a day at Garmisch-Partenkirchen Station and three other Alpine Stations (Immenstadt, Oberstdorf, and Sonthoten). There is a small charge for taking a bike on the train; Intercity and Intercity Express (ICE) trains do not carry bikes. Most cities also have bike-rental companies, usually priced about DM 15 per day or DM 80–DM 90 a week.

Staying in Germany

Telephones Telephone lines between western and eastern Germany are now much improved after an initial period of difficulty following reunification. All but the more remote eastern regions can be reached by direct dialing.

Since reunification, all phones in the east and west use the same coins: 10 pf, DM 1, and DM 5 for long-distance calls. A local call costs 30 pf and lasts six minutes. Card phones are rapidly replacing coin-operated phones: Cards cost DM 12 or DM 50 and can be purchased at the post office.

You'll also find public booths at the post office; if you have no change or need to make a lengthy overseas call, the counter clerk gets you a line, and you pay him or her afterward. If possible, avoid making international phone calls from your hotel room because the rates are double or more.

Mail   Airmail letters to the United States and Canada cost DM 3; postcards cost DM 2. Airmail letters to the United Kingdom cost DM 1; postcards cost 80 pf.

You can arrange to have mail sent to you in care of any German post office; have the envelope marked "Postlagernd." This service is free. Alternatively, have mail sent to any American Express office in Germany. There's no charge to cardholders, holders of American Express traveler's checks, or anyone who has booked a vacation with American Express. Otherwise, you pay DM 2 per collection (not per item).

Shopping   German goods carry a 15% value-added tax (VAT). You can claim this
VAT Refunds   back either as you leave the country or once you've returned home. When you make a purchase, ask the shopkeeper for a form known as an "Ausfuhr-Abnehmerbescheinigung"; he or she will help you fill it out. As you leave the country, give the form, plus the goods and receipts, to German customs, which will give you an official export certificate or stamp. In the unlikely event that there's a branch of the Deutsche Bank on the spot, you can take the stamped form to it, where you will receive the refund on the spot. Otherwise, send the form back to the shop, and it will send the refund.

Opening and   **Banks.** Times vary from state to state and city to city, but banks are
Closing Times   generally open weekdays from 8:30 or 9 to 3 or 4 (5 or 6 on Thursday). Most banks close from 12:30 to 1:30. Branches at airports and main train stations open as early as 6:30 AM and close as late as 10:30 PM. Many banks in eastern Germany have shorter hours but are slowly conforming to western times.

Museums are generally open Tuesday to Sunday 9–5. Some close for an hour or more at lunch, and some are open on Monday. Many stay open until 9 on Thursdays.

Shops are generally open weekdays from 8:30 or 9 until 6:30 PM and Saturdays until 1 or 2 PM. On the first Saturday of each month, many larger shops and department stores in Germany are open until 6. Some stores stay open until 8:30 PM on Thursdays.

National   January 1; January 6 (Epiphany); April 14 (Good Friday); April 17
Holidays   (Easter Monday); May 1; May 25 (Ascension); June 5 (Pentecost Monday); June 15 (Corpus Christi, south Germany only); August 15 (Assumption Day); October 3 (German Unity Day); October 31 (Reformation Day, only in northern Germany); November 1 (All Saints' Day); November 22 (Day of Prayer and Repentance), December 24–26.

Dining   It's hard to generalize about German food beyond saying that standards are high and portions are large. In fact, the range of dining experiences is vast: everything from highly priced nouvelle cuisine to hamburgers. As a visitor, you should search out local restaurants if atmosphere and regional specialties are your priority. Beer restaurants in Bavaria, *Apfelwein* taverns in Frankfurt, and *Kneipen*—the pub on the corner cum local café—in Berlin nearly always offer best value and atmosphere. But throughout the country you'll find *Gaststätten* and/or *Gasthöfe*—local inns—where atmosphere and regional specialties are always available. Likewise, just about every town will have a *Ratskeller*, a cellar restaurant in the town hall, where exposed beams, huge fireplaces, sturdy tables, and immense portions are the rule.

In larger towns and cities throughout the country, Germans like to nibble at roadside or market snack stalls, called *Imbisse*. Hot sausages, spicy meatballs (*Fleischpflanzerl*), meatloaf topped with a fried egg (*Leberkäs*), in the south, and sauerkraut are the traditional favorites. But foods eaten on the hoof are creeping in, too: french fries, pizzas, gyros, and hamburgers. In eastern Germany, the old state-run self-service worker cafeterias may still be operating in some towns, but these are rapidly being replaced by commercial enterprises.

The most famous German specialty is sausage. Everyone has heard of frankfurters, but if you're in Munich, try *Weisswurst*, a delicate white sausage traditionally eaten only between midnight and noon. Nürnberg's sausage favorite is the *Nürnberger Bratwurst;* its fame is such that you'll find restaurants all over Germany serving it. Look for the "Bratwurststube" sign. Dumplings (*Knödeln*) can also be found throughout the country, though their natural home is probably Bavaria; farther north, potatoes often take their place.

The natural accompaniment to German food is either beer or wine. Munich is the beer capital of Germany, though there's no part of the country where you won't find the amber nectar. Say "Helles" or Export if you want light beer; "Dunkles" if you want dark beer. In Bavaria, try the sour but refreshing beer brewed from wheat, called *Weissbier*. Germany is a major wine-producing country, also, and much of it is of superlative quality. You will probably be happy with the house wine in most restaurants or with one of those earthenware pitchers of cold Moselle wine. If you want something more expensive, remember that all wines are graded in one of three basic categories: *Tafelwein* (table wine); *Qualitätswein* (fine wines); and *Qualitätswein mit Prädikat* (top-quality wines).

Mealtimes Lunch is served from around 11:30 (especially in rural areas) to around 2; dinner is generally from 6 until 9:30 PM, or earlier in some quiet country areas. Big city hotels and popular restaurants serve later. Lunch tends to be the main meal, a fact reflected in the almost universal appearance of a lunchtime *Tageskarte*, or suggested menu; try it if you want maximum nourishment for minimum outlay. This doesn't mean that dinner is a rushed or skimpy affair, however; the Germans have too high a regard for food for any meal to be underrated. Breakfast, served anytime from 6:30 to 10, is often a substantial meal, with cold meats, cheeses, rolls, and fruit. Many city hotels offer Sunday "brunch," and the custom is rapidly catching on.

Dress Jacket and tie are recommended for restaurants in the Very Expensive and Expensive categories. Casual dress is appropriate elsewhere.

Ratings Prices are per person and include a first course, main course, dessert, and tip and tax. Best bets are indicated by a star ★.

The following chart gives price ranges for restaurants in the western part of Germany. Food prices in the territory of former East Germany are still somewhat unstable, although in the bigger cities many of the better quality restaurants are already starting to mimic "western" rates. Generally speaking, the prevailing price structure in the eastern part of the country, except for restaurants in the priciest hotels, falls into the Inexpensive to Expensive categories listed below. Bills in simple restaurants in country areas of the eastern region will, however, still come well below DM 35.

Category	Major Cities and Resorts	Other Areas
Very Expensive	over DM 100	over DM 90
Expensive	DM 75–DM 100	DM 55–DM 90
Moderate	DM 50–DM 75	DM 35–DM 55
Inexpensive	DM 25–DM 50	under DM 35

Lodging The standard of German hotels, from top-notch luxury spots (of which the country has more than its fair share) to the humblest pension, is generally excellent. Prices can be high, but not disproportionately so in comparison to other northern European countries. You can expect courteous service; clean and comfortable rooms; and, in rural areas especially, considerable old-German atmosphere.

In addition to hotels proper, the country also has numerous *Gasthöfe* or *Gasthäuser* (country inns); pensions or *Fremdenheime* (guest houses); and, at the lowest end of the scale, *Zimmer*, meaning, quite simply, rooms, normally in private houses. Look for the sign "Zimmer frei" or "zu vermieten," meaning "for rent." A red sign reading "besetzt" means there are no vacancies.

Lists of hotels are available from the German National Tourist Office (Beethovenstr. 69, D-60325 Frankfurt/Main 1, tel. 069/75720), and from all regional and local tourist offices. Tourist offices will also make reservations for you—they usually charge a nominal fee—but may have difficulty doing so after 4 PM in peak season and on weekends. A reservations service is also operated by the German National Tourist Office (Allgemeine Deutsche Zimmer-reservierung, Cornelius-str. 34, D-60325 Frankfurt/Main, tel. 069/740–767). The service is free of charge.

Most hotels have restaurants, but those describing themselves as *Garni* will provide breakfast only.

Tourist accommodations in eastern Germany are beginning to blossom under free enterprise after the straitjacket of state monopoly, although the choice and facilities are still far behind the western half of the country. The former state-owned Interhotel chain (34 hotels with several thousand rooms) has been dismantled, its components sold individually. Other hotel groups are keen to build new properties in the region or to convert old buildings with the potential for atmospheric lodgings. But for now, accommodations remain tight at the top- and middle-quality levels. It cannot be too greatly stressed: If you want to stay in good hotels in eastern Germany, book well in advance. Hotel rooms in the cities are under pressure year-round because of the comings and goings of businesspeople involved in rebuilding the east's economy. Traditional inn accommodations have run down during the past 40 years, and those that survive are rather antiquated—still, you may well come across the odd gem.

The real boom in lodgings has been at the inexpensive end of the market, where thousands of beds are now available for the adventurous traveler. For relatively few marks every village can now provide somewhere for the tourist to put his or her head and perhaps offer a simple but wholesome evening meal. Many guest houses have sprung up under the enterprising stewardship of housewives eager to supplement the family income. For a list of approved addresses, consult the local tourist office.

Romantik Hotels Among the most delightful places to stay and eat in Germany are the aptly named Romantik Hotels and Restaurants. All are in historic buildings—this is a precondition of membership—and are personally run by the owners. The emphasis generally is on solid comfort, good food, and style. A detailed listing of all Romantik Hotels is available in the United States from **Harm Meyer Romantik Hotels** (14178 Woodinville-Duval Road, Box 1278, Woodinville, WA 98072, tel. 206/486–9394; for reservations only, tel. 800/826–0015).

Castle Hotels **Gast im Schloss** is a similar hotel association, though some of the simpler establishments lack a little in the way of comfort, and furnishings can be basic. But most can be delightful, with antiques, imposing interiors, and out-of-the-way locations setting the tone. Prices are mostly moderate. Ask the German National Tourist Office or your travel agent for the "Castle Hotels in Germany" brochure. It details a series of good-value packages, most for stays of four to six nights.

Ringhotels This association groups 130 individually owned and managed hotels in the medium price range. Many are situated in the countryside or in pretty villages. Package deals of 2–3 days are available. Contact **Ringhotels** (Belfortstrasse 8, D-81667 Munich, tel. 089/482720).

Rentals Apartments and hotel homes, most accommodating from two to eight guests, can be rented throughout Germany. Rates are low, with reductions for longer stays. Charges for gas and electricity, and sometimes water, are usually added to the bill. Local and regional tourist offices have lists of apartments in their areas; otherwise contact the **German National Tourist Office** (*see* Lodging in Staying in Germany, *above*).

Farm Vacations Taking an *Urlaub auf dem Bauernhof*, as the Germans put it, has increased dramatically in popularity over the past four or five years. Almost every regional tourist office has listings of farms by area offering bed and breakfast, apartments, or whole farmhouses to rent. Alternatively, write the **German Agricultural Association** (DLG), Zimmerweg 16, D-60325 Frankfurt/Main. It produces an annual listing of more than 1,500 farms, all of them inspected and graded, that offer accommodations. The brochure costs DM 7.50.

Camping There are 2,600 campsites in Germany, about 1,600 of which are listed by the **German Camping Club** (DCC), Mandlstrasse 28, D-80802, Munich. For details of camping facilities in eastern Germany, where facilities are neither common nor modern, contact **Camping und Caravanverband,** Postfach 105, 1080 Berlin. The German National Tourist Office also publishes a listing of sites. Most are open from May through October, with about 400 staying open year-round. They tend to become crowded during the summer, so it's always worthwhile to make reservations a day or two ahead. Prices range from DM 15 to DM 20 per night for two adults, a car, and trailer (less for tents).

Youth Hostels Germany's youth hostels—*Jugendherberge*—are probably the most efficient and up-to-date in Europe. There are 600 in all, many located in castles, adding a touch of romance to otherwise utilitarian accommodations. There's an age limit of 27 in Bavaria; elsewhere, there are no restrictions, though those under 20 take preference if space is limited. You'll need an International Youth Hostel card to stay in a German youth hostel; write **American Youth Hostels Association** (Box 37613, Washington, DC 20013) or **Canadian Hostelling Association** (333 River Rd., Ottawa, Ontario K1L 8H9). In Great Britain, contact the **Youth Hostels Association** (22 Southampton St.,

London WC2). The International Youth Hostel card can also be obtained from the **Deutsches Jugendherbergswerk** (Bismarckstr. 8, D-32756 Detmold, tel. 05231/74010), which provides a complete list of the 650 German hostels for DM 6.50.

Hostels must be reserved well in advance for midsummer, especially in eastern Germany. Bookings for hostels in the new German states (former East Germany) of Saxony, Thuringia, Saxony-Anhalt, Brandenburg, and Mecklenburg can be made directly through **Jugendtourist** (Alexanderplatz 5, D-10178 Berlin; or Münzstr. 14, tel. 030/281–7449).

Ratings   Service charges and taxes are included in all quoted room rates. Similarly, breakfast is usually, but not always, included, so check before you book in. Rates are often surprisingly flexible in German hotels, varying considerably according to demand. Major hotels in cities often have lower rates on weekends or other periods when business is quiet. If you're lucky, you can find reductions of up to 60%. Likewise, rooms reserved after 10 PM will often carry a discount, on the basis that an occupied room at a reduced rate is better than an empty one. Although it's worthwhile to ask if your hotel will give you a reduction, don't count on finding rooms at lower rates late at night, especially in the summer. Prices are for two people in a double room. Best bets are indicated by a star ★.

The following chart is for hotels throughout Germany. Rooms in many of the bigger hotels of eastern Germany were priced similar to those in western Germany, even before reunification, and most of these hotels are now being bought by private chains. But smaller hotels in the east are often much cheaper—and shorter on facilities.

Category	Major Cities or Resorts	Other Areas
Very Expensive	over DM 300	over DM 200
Expensive	DM 200–DM 300	DM 160–DM 200
Moderate	DM 140–DM 200	DM 100–DM 160
Inexpensive	under DM 140	under DM 100

Tipping   The Germans are as punctilious about tipping as they are about most facets of life in their well-regulated country. Overtipping is as frowned upon as not tipping at all, though the kind of abuse you risk in some countries for undertipping is virtually unknown here. Nonetheless, tips are expected, if not exactly demanded. Follow these simple rules and you won't go wrong.

In restaurants, service is usually included (under the heading *Bedienung*, at the bottom of the check), and it is customary to round out the check to the next mark or two, a practice also commonplace in cafés, beer halls, and bars. For taxi drivers, also round out to the next mark or two: for DM 11.20, make it DM 12; for DM 11.80, make it DM 13. Railway and airport porters (if you can find any) have their own scale of charges, but round out the requested amount to the next mark. Hotel porters get DM 1 per bag. Doormen are tipped the same amount for small services, such as calling a cab. Room service should be rewarded with at least DM 2 every time you use it. Maids should get about DM 1 per day. Double all these figures at luxury hotels. Service-station attendants get 50 pf or DM 1 for checking oil and tires or cleaning windshields.

Munich

Arriving and Departing

By Plane Munich's Franz Josef Strauss (FJS) Airport, named after a former state premier, opened in May 1992. It is 28 kilometers (17½ miles) northeast of the city center.

Between the The S8 suburban train line links FJS Airport with the city's main
Airport and train station (Hauptbahnhof). Trains depart in both directions ev-
Downtown ery 20 minutes from 3:55 AM to 12:55 AM daily. Intermediate stops are made at Ostbahnhof (good for hotels located east of the River Isar) and city center stations such as Marienplatz. The 38-minute trip costs DM 9.30 if you purchase a multi-use strip ticket (*see* Getting Around, *below*) and use 8 strips; otherwise an ordinary one-way ticket is DM 12 per person. A tip for families: Up to five people (maximum of two adults) can travel to or from the airport for only DM 20 by buying a Tageskarte (*see* Getting Around, *below*). This is particularly advantageous if you are arriving in Munich, because you can continue to use the Tageskarte in the city for the rest of the day. The only restriction is that you cannot use this special day ticket before 9 AM weekdays.

The suburban train (S-Bahn) service has proved so popular that the airport bus service has been discontinued. A taxi will cost between DM 80 and DM 100. If you are driving from the airport into the city, follow the Munich autobahn signs to A92 and A9.

By Train All long-distance services arrive at and depart from the main train station, the Hauptbahnhof. Trains to and from destinations in the Bavarian Alps usually use the adjoining Starnbergerbahnhof. For information on train times, tel. 089/19419; English is spoken by most information office staff. For tickets and information, go to the station or to the ABR travel agency right by the station on Bahnhofplatz.

By Bus Munich has no central bus station. Long-distance buses arrive at and depart from the north side of the train station on Arnulfstrasse. A taxi stand is 20 yards away.

By Car From the north (Nürnberg, Frankfurt), leave the autobahn at the Schwabing exit and follow the "Stadtmitte" signs. The autobahn from Stuttgart and the west ends at Obermenzing; again, follow the "Stadtmitte" signs. The autobahns from Salzburg and the east, from Garmisch and the south, and from Lindau and the southwest all join up with the city beltway, the Mittlerer Ring. The city center is well posted.

Getting Around

Downtown Munich is only about one mile square, so it can easily be explored on foot. Other areas—Schwabing, Nymphenburg, the Olympic Park—are best reached on the efficient and comprehensive public transportation network. It incorporates buses, streetcars, subways (U-Bahn), and suburban trains (S-Bahn). Tickets are good for the entire network, and you can break your trip as many times as you like using just one ticket, provided you travel in one direction only and within a given time limit. If you plan to make only a few trips, buy strip tickets (Streifenkarten)—blue for adults, red for children. Fares were due to rise 5.8% in 1994, but at press time, an adult ticket of 12 strips cost DM 14; children got the same number for DM 8. For adults, short rides that span up to 4 stations cost 1 strip; trips spanning more than 4 stations cost 2 strips. Children pay 1 strip per ride. All tickets must be validated by time-punching them in the automatic machines at station entrances and on all buses and streetcars. The best buy is the Tageskarte: Up to two adults and three children can use this excellent-value ticket for unlimited journeys between 9 AM and the end of the day's service (about 2 AM). It costs DM 10 for the inner zone, which covers central Munich. A Tageskarte for the entire system, extending to the Starnbergersee and Ammersee lakes, costs DM 20. Holders of a Eurail Pass, a Youth Pass, an Inter-Rail Card, or a DB Tourist Card travel free on all S-Bahn trains.

By Taxi Munich's cream-colored taxis are numerous. Hail them in the street or call 089/21610 (there's an extra charge for the drive to the pickup point). Rates start at DM 3.90 and rise by DM 2.20 per kilometer (about DM 4 per mile). There are additional charges of DM 1 for each piece of luggage. Figure on paying around DM 12 for a short trip within the city.

Important Addresses and Numbers

Tourist Information The address to write to for information in advance of your visit is **Fremdenverkehrsamt München**, Postfach, München. This address also deals with lodging questions and bookings. Two other offices provide on-the-spot advice: at the Hauptbahnhof (tel. 089/239–1256), daily between 8 AM and 11 PM, and at the corner of Rindermarkt and Pettenbeckstrasse, behind Marienplatz (tel. 089/239–1272), open weekdays between 9:30 AM and 6 PM.

Consulates **U.S. Consulate General** (Königinstrasse 5, tel. 089/28880). **British Consulate General** (Bürkleinstr. 10, tel. 089/211090). **Canadian Consulate** (Tal 29, tel. 089/222–661).

Emergencies **Police** (tel. 110). **Ambulance** and **emergency medical attention** (tel. 089/558661). **Dentist** (tel. 089/723–3093). **Pharmacies: Internationale Ludwigs-Apotheke**, Neuhauserstrasse 8, tel. 089/260–3021; **Europa-Apotheke**, Schützenstrasse 12 (near the Hauptbahnhof), tel. 089/595423. Open weekdays 8–5:30, Saturday 8–1. Outside these hours, call 089/594475.

English-Language Bookstores The **Anglia English Bookshop** (Schellingstrasse 3, tel. 089/283642) has the largest selection of English-language books in Munich. Also try the **Hugendubel** bookshops at Marienplatz and Karlsplatz. A library of English-language books is kept in **Amerika Haus** (Karolinenplatz 3, tel. 089/595369).

Travel Agencies **American Express** (Promenadeplatz 6, tel. 089/21990). **ABR,** the official Bavarian travel agency, has outlets all over Munich; tel. 089/12040 for information.

Guided Tours

Orientation Tours City bus tours are operated by **Panorama Tours** (Arnulfstr. 8, tel. 089/120–4248). Tours run daily and take in the city center, the Olympic Park, and Nymphenburg. Departures are at 10 AM and 2:30 PM (and 11:30 AM in midsummer) from outside the Hertie department store across from the train station, and the cost is between DM 15 and DM 27 per person, depending on the duration of the tour.

Walking and Cycling Tours Under the auspices of the city council, students conduct walking tours of the historic center on Monday, Tuesday, and Thursday at 10 AM. The walks start from the Fischbrunnen (Fish Fountain) at

Marienplatz and cost DM 6. Bike tours of the city, including bike rentals, are offered through **City Hopper Touren** (tel. 089/272-1131). Charges run from DM 40 per person in a group of two to DM 20 for larger groups. Tours on foot, by bicycle, and by streetcar are organized by **Radius Touristik** (Arnulfstr 3, north side of Hauptbahnhof, tel. 089/596113).

Excursions **Panorama Tours** (Arnulfstr. 8, tel. 089/591504) organizes bus trips to most leading tourist attractions outside the city, including the "Royal Castles Tour" (Schlösserfahrt) of "Mad" King Ludwig's dream palaces. This tour, which takes in Neuschwanstein, costs DM 65 per person. Reservations for these tours can also be made through all major hotels. All tours leave from outside the Hertie department store in front of the Hauptbahnhof.

Exploring Munich

Germans in other parts of the country sometimes refer to Munich as the nation's "secret capital." This sly compliment may reflect the importance of Munich—it's the number-one tourist destination in Germany, as well as the most attractive major German city—but there's nothing "secret" about the way Münchners make this brave claim. Indeed, the noise with which the people of Munich trumpet the attractions of their city could be dismissed as so much Bavarian bombast were it not for the fact that it is so enthusiastically endorsed by others. Flamboyant, easygoing Munich, city of beer and Baroque, is starkly different from the sometimes stiff Prussian influences to be found in Berlin, the gritty industrial drive of Hamburg, or the hardheaded commercial instincts of high-rise Frankfurt. This is a city to visit for its good-natured and relaxed charm—*Gemütlichkeit*, they call it here—and for its beer halls, its museums, its malls, its parks, and its palaces.

Munich is a crazy mix of high culture (witness its world-class opera house and art galleries) and wild abandon (witness the vulgar frivolity of the Oktoberfest). Its citizenry seems determined to perpetuate the lifestyle of 19th-century king Ludwig I, the Bavarian ruler who brought so much international prestige to his home city after declaring: "I want to make out of Munich a town which does such credit to Germany that nobody knows Germany unless he has seen Munich." He kept his promise with an architectural and artistic renaissance—before abdicating because of a wild romance with a half-caste Irish-born dancing girl, Lola Montez (who died in exile in New York).

The Historic *Numbers in the margin correspond to points of interest on the Mu-*
Heart *nich map.*

❶ Begin your tour of Munich at the **Hauptbahnhof,** the main train station and an important orientation point. The city tourist office is here, too, ready with information and maps. Cross the street and you're at the start of a kilometer (½ mile) of pedestrian shopping malls, the first being Schützenstrasse. Facing you are **Hertie,**
❷ Munich's leading department store, and **Karlsplatz** square, known locally as *Stachus*. The huge, domed building on your left is the late-19th-century **Justizpalast** (Palace of Justice). It's one of Germany's finest examples of *Gründerzeit*, the 19th-century versions of Medieval and Renaissance architectural styles.

Head down into the pedestrian underpass—it's another extensive shopping area—to reach the other side and one of the original city
❸ gates, **Karlstor.** The city's two principal shopping streets—

Neuhauserstrasse and **Kaufingerstrasse**—stretch away from it on the other side. Two of the city's major churches are here, too: the **4 5** **Bürgersaal** and the **Michaelskirche.** The latter is one of the most magnificent Renaissance churches in Germany, a spacious and handsome structure decorated throughout in plain white stucco. It was built for the Jesuits in the late 16th century and is closely modeled on their church of the Gesù in Rome. The intention was to provide a large preaching space, hence the somewhat barnlike atmosphere. Ludwig II is buried here; his tomb is in the crypt. The large neoclassical tomb in the north transept is the resting place of Eugène de Beauharnais, Napoleon's stepson. The highly decorated Rococo interior of the Bürgersaal makes a startling contrast with the simplicity of the Michaelskirche. Guided tours of the church are given every Wed. at 2 PM and cost DM 5.

6 A block past the Michaelskirche to your left is Munich's late-15th-century cathedral, the **Frauenkirche,** or Church of Our Lady. Towering above it are two onion-shaped domes, symbols of the city (perhaps because they resemble brimming beer mugs, cynics claim). They were added in 1525 after the body of the church had been completed. Step inside and you'll be amazed at the stark simplicity of the church. This is partly the result of the construction that followed the severe bombing in World War II. The crypt houses the tombs of numerous Wittelsbachs, the family that ruled Bavaria for seven centuries until forced to abdicate in 1918. The cathedral—after a two-year, $17 million renovation—reopened in 1994, just in time for the 500th anniversary of the cathedral's consecration.

7 From the Frauenkirche, walk to the **Marienplatz** square, the heart of the city, surrounded by shops, restaurants, and cafés. It takes its name from the 300-year-old gilded statue of the Virgin in the center. When it was taken down to be cleaned in 1960, workmen found a small casket containing a splinter of wood said to have come from the **8** cross of Christ. The square is dominated by the 19th-century **Neues Rathaus,** the new town hall, built in the fussy, turreted style so **9** loved by Ludwig II. The **Altes Rathaus,** or old town hall, a medieval building of great charm, sits, as if forgotten, in a corner of the square. At 11 AM and noon daily (also June–Oct. at 5 PM and 9 PM), the **Glockenspiel,** or chiming clock, in the central tower of the town hall, swings into action. Two tiers of dancing and jousting figures perform their ritual display. It can be worthwhile scheduling your day to catch the clock. Immediately after the war, an American soldier donated some paint to help restore the battered figures and was rewarded with a ride on one of the knight's horses, high above the cheering crowds. April through October, a lift whisks visitors to an observation point near the top of one of the towers. On a clear day the view is spectacular. But beware, there are 86 steps to climb before reaching the lift. The lift is in operation 10–5; the fare is DM 4, DM 2 children.

Time Out You can get a fine view of the Glockenspiel from the sixth-floor **Hoch-Cafe,** opposite the City Hall. Claim a window-side table early, however, particularly on rainy days, when all Munich seems to have the same idea. The café is open until 10 PM daily and serves medium-priced light meals, as well as morning coffee and afternoon tea.

10 Heading south down Rosenstrasse to Sendlingerstrasse, you come to the **Asamkirche** on your right. Some consider the Asamkirche a preposterously overdecorated jewel box; others consider it one of Europe's finest late-Baroque churches. One thing is certain: If you have any interest in church architecture, this is a place you shouldn't

Alte Pinakothek, **20**
Altes Rathaus, **9**
Asamkirche, **10**
Bürgersaal, **4**
Englischer Garten, **18**
Feldherrnhalle, **16**
Frauenkirche, **6**
Hauptbahnhof, **1**
Haus der Kunst, **19**
Hofgarten, **14**
Karlsplatz, **2**
Karlstor, **3**
Marienplatz, **7**
Michaelskirche, **5**
Nationaltheater, **13**
Neue Pinakothek, **21**
Neues Rathaus, **8**
Residenz, **12**
Siegestor, **17**
Theatinerkirche, **15**
Viktualienmarkt, **11**

TO SCHWABING

17

Schackstr.

Blütenstr.

Türkenstr.

Adalbertstr.

University

Prof.-Huberpl.

Veterinärstr.

Schellingstr.

Amalienstr.

Ludwigstr.

Kaulbachstr.

Königinstr.

Englischer Garten

18

Oettingenstr.

Türkenstr.

Theresienstr.

Schönfeldstr.

Oskar-von-Miller-Ring

Von-der-Tann Str.

Prinzregentenstr.

19

Lerchenfeldstr.

Oettingenstr.

Reitmorstr.

Galeriestr.

Odeons-pl.

Hofgarten

14

Salvator-pl.

Kard.-Faulhaber-Str.

Theatinerstr.

Residenzstr.

Hofgartenstr.

K.-Scharnagl-Ring

Unsoldstr.

St.-Anna-Pfarrstr.

St. Anna Pl.

Liebigstr.

Sternstr.

Widenmayerstr.

15

16

AE

12

Christophstr.

Max-Joseph-Pl.

13

Marstallstr.

Bürkleinstr.

Maffeistr.

Dienerstr.

Am Kosttor

Platzl

Maximilianstr.

Maximiliansbr.

6

Frauen-pl.

Weinstr.

Pfisterstr.

8

Marien-pl.

7 **9**

Tal

Th.-Wimmer-Ring

Knöbelstr.

Isar

Rosental

11

Isar Tor-Pl.

Kanalstr.

Steinsdorfstr.

Frauenstr.

Innere Wiener Str.

Blumenstr.

Corneliusstr.

Rumfordstr.

Klenzestr.

Zweibrückenstr.

Kellerstr.

Gärtner-pl.

Ludwigsbr.

Rosenheimerstr.

Klenzestr.

Reichenbachstr.

Baaderstr.

Erhardtstr.

Deutsches Museum

HAIDHAUSEN

Fraunhofer

N

miss. It was built around 1730 by the Asam brothers—Cosmas Damian and Egid Quirin—next door to their home, the Asamhaus. They dedicated it to St. John Nepomuk, a 14th-century Bohemian monk who was drowned in the Danube. Pause before you go in to see the charming statue of angels carrying him to heaven from the rocky riverbank. Inside, there is a riot of decoration: frescoes, statuary, rich rosy marbles, billowing clouds of stucco, and gilding everywhere. The decorative elements and the architecture merge to create a sense of seamless movement and color.

⑪ Go back to Marienplatz and turn right for the **Viktualienmarkt,** the food market. Open-air stalls sell cheese, wine, sausages, fruit, and flowers. Fortified with Bavarian sausage and sauerkraut, plunge ⑫ into local history with a visit to the **Residenz,** home of the Wittelsbachs from the 16th century to their enforced abdication at the end of World War I. From Max-Joseph-Platz you'll enter the great palace, with its glittering Schatzkammer, or treasury, and glorious Rococo theater, designed by court architect François Cuvilliès. Also facing the square is the stern neoclassical portico of ⑬ the **Nationaltheater,** built at the beginning of the 19th century and twice destroyed. *Residenz and Schatzkammer, Max-Joseph-Platz 3. Admission to each: DM 4 adults, DM 2.50 children. Open Tues.– Sun. 10–4:30 PM. Cuvilliès Theater admission: DM 2.50 adults, DM 1.50 children. Open Mon.–Sat. 2–5, Sun. 10–5.*

⑭ To the north of the Residenz is the **Hofgarten,** the palace gardens. Two sides of the gardens are bordered by sturdy arcades designed by Leo von Klenze, whose work for the Wittelsbachs in the 19th century helped transform the face of the city. Dominating the east side of the Hofgarten is the Bavarian state chancellery, an eclectic and controversial mixture of styles that incorporates the dome of Bavaria's former Army Museum, destroyed in World War II.

Time Out   Munich's oldest café, the **Annast,** is located on Odeonsplatz, right by the west entrance to the Hofgarten. Sit at one of the tables under the Hofgarten trees at the back of the café. The Hofgarten was a favorite haunt of Hitler, before and after he came to power—he and his cronies used to frequent the garden tables of another café farther down the street.

Odeonsplatz itself is dominated by two striking buildings. One is the ⑮ **Theatinerkirche,** built for the Theatine monks in the mid-17th century, though its handsome facade, with twin eye-catching domes, was added only in the following century. Despite its Italian influences, the interior, like that of the Michaelskirche, is austerely white. The ⑯ other notable building here is the **Feldherrnhalle,** built by Ludwig I and modeled on the Loggia dei Lanzi in Florence, and later used by the Nazis as a speakers' rostrum. For years it was a key Nazi shrine, for in the neighboring street, Residenz-Strasse, Hitler's unsuccessful 1923 putsch came to its bloody end.

The Feldherrnhalle looks north along one of the most imposing boulevards in Europe, the **Ludwigstrasse,** which in turn becomes the **Leopoldstrasse.** Von Klenze was responsible for much of it, replacing the jumble of old buildings that originally stood here with the clean, high-windowed lines of his restrained Italianate buildings. The state library and the university are located along it, while, halfway ⑰ up it, is the **Siegestor,** or Arch of Victory, modeled on the Arch of Constantine in Rome. Beyond it is **Schwabing,** once a student and artist quarter but now much glossier, with a mix of bars, discos (*see* Nightlife, *below*), trendy cafés, and boutiques. Nightlife centers around Wedekindplatz, near the Münchener Freiheit subway station.

Back on Leopoldstrasse, wander down to the university, turn on to Professor-Huber-Platz (he was a Munich academic executed by the Nazis for his support of an anti-Hitler movement), and take Veterinärstrasse. It leads you to Munich's largest park, the magnificent **Englischer Garten.** You can rent a bike (tel. 089/282-500) at the entrance to the park on summer weekends (May-Oct.). The cost is DM 5 per hour and DM 25 for the day.

The Englischer Garten, 4½ kilometers (3 miles) long and over a ½ kilometer (¼ mile) wide, was laid out by Count Rumford, a refugee from the American War of Independence. He was born in England, but it wasn't his English ancestry that determined the park's name as much as its open, informal nature, a style favored by 18th-century English aristocrats. You can rent boats, visit beer gardens—the most famous is at the foot of a Chinese Pagoda—ride your bike (or ski in winter), or simply stroll around. Ludwig II used to love to wander incognito along the serpentine paths. What would he say today, now that so much of the park has been taken over by Munich's nudists? This is no misprint. Late-20th-century Germans have embraced nature worship with almost pagan fervor. A large section of the park right behind the **Haus der Kunst,** Munich's leading modern art gallery and a surviving example of Third Reich architecture — has been designated a nudist area. The building underwent major renovations in 1992. One wing also houses one of the city's most exclusive discos, the PI. *Haus der Kunst, Prinzregentenstr. 1. Admission: DM 3.50 adults, 50 pf children; Sun. and holidays free. Open Tues.-Sun. 9-4:30, also Thurs. 7 PM-9 PM.*

Munich's two leading picture galleries, the Alte (meaning "old") and the Neue (meaning "new") Pinakothek, are located on Barerstrasse, just to the west of the university. The **Alte Pinakothek** is usually the repository of some of the world's most celebrated Old Master paintings; it is also an architectural treasure in its own right, though much scarred from wartime bomb damage. It was built by von Klenze at the beginning of the 19th century to house Ludwig I's collections. In 1994, the museum closed for renovations scheduled to take at least three years. Its most famous paintings (including most of the Dürers, Rembrandts, Rubenses, and two celebrated Murillos) are now on display at the Neue Pinakothek (*see below*) until the renovations are completed.

The **Neue Pinakothek** was another of Ludwig I's projects, built to house his "modern" collections, meaning, of course, 19th-century works. The building was destroyed during World War II, and today's museum opened in 1981. The low, brick structure—some have compared it with a Florentine palazzo—is an unparalleled environment in which to see one of the finest collections of 19th-century European paintings and sculpture in the world. *Barerstr. 29. Admission: DM 6 adults, DM 1 children; free Sun. and holidays. Open Tues.-Sun. 9-4:30; also Tues. 7 PM-9 PM. Take the No. 18 streetcar or the U2 subway to Königsplatz from Karlsplatz.*

Suburban Attractions There are two trips you can take to attractions just out of the city center. One is to the **Olympic Park,** a 10-minute U-Bahn ride (U3); the other is to Nymphenburg, 6 kilometers (4 miles) northwest and reached by the U1 subway to Rotkreuzplatz, then the No. 12 streetcar.

Perhaps the most controversial buildings in Munich are the circus tent–shaped roofs of the **Olympic Park.** Built for the 1972 Olympics, the park, with its undulating, transparent tile roofs and modern housing blocks, represented a revolutionary marriage of technology and visual daring when first unveiled. Sports fans might like to join the crowds in the Olympic stadium when the local soccer team, Bayern Munich, has a home game. Call 089/699310 for information and tickets. There's an amazing view of the stadium, the Olympic Park, and the city from the Olympic tower. An elevator speeds you to the top in seconds. *Admission: DM 5 adults; DM 2.50 children; combined tower and park tour (until 5 PM) DM 7 adults, DM 4 children. Admission to stadium alone: DM 1 adults, 50 pf children. Tower open daily 9 AM–midnight. Olympic stadium open daily 9–4:30.*

Schloss Nymphenburg was the summer palace of the Wittelsbachs. The oldest parts date from 1664, but construction continued for more than 100 years, the bulk of the work being undertaken in the reign of Max Emmanuel between 1680 and 1730. The gardens, a mixture of formal French *parterres* (trim, ankle-high hedges and gravel walks) and English parkland, were landscaped over the same period. The interiors are exceptional, especially the Banqueting Hall, a Rococo masterpiece in green and gold. Make a point of seeing the Schönheits Galerie, the **Gallery of Beauties.** It contains more than 100 portraits of women who had caught the eye of Ludwig I; duchesses rub shoulders with butchers' daughters. Among them is Lola Montez. Seek out the **Amalienburg,** or Hunting Lodge, on the grounds. It was built by Cuvilliès, architect of the Residenz Theater in Munich. That the lodge was designed for hunting of the indoor variety can easily be guessed by the sumptuous silver and blue stucco and the atmosphere of courtly high life. The palace also contains the **Marstallmuseum** (the Museum of Royal Carriages), containing a sleigh that belonged to Ludwig II, among the opulently decorated vehicles, and, on the floor above, the **Nymphenburger Porzellan,** with examples of the porcelain produced here between 1747 and the 1920s. *Schloss Nymphenburg. Admission: Combined ticket to all Nymphenburg attractions: DM 6. Combined ticket to Schloss, Gallery of Beauties, Amalienburg, and Marstallmuseum: DM 4.50. Botanic gardens: DM 1.50. Children under 15 free. Open Apr.– Sept., Tues.–Sun. 9–12:30 and 1:30–5; Oct.–Mar., Tues.–Sun. 10– 12:30 and 1:30–4. Gardens open daily.*

Off the Beaten Track

Even though the Olympic Tower is higher, romantics say the best view of Munich and the Alps is from the top of the **Alte Peter** church tower (DM 2.50 adults, DM 1.50 children); it's just off Marienplatz. Check that a white disk is hanging on the wall outside the entrance: It means that visibility is good. There are 302 steps to climb to the top. For the most inexpensive sightseeing tour of the center, take a No. 19 streetcar from outside the train station at Bahnhofplatz and ride it to **Wienerplatz,** itself located in Haidhausen, one of Munich's most interesting areas. On a fine day, join the chess players at their open-air boards in Schwabing's **Münchener Freiheit** square. On a rainy day, pack your swimsuit and splash around in the Art Nouveau setting of the **Müllersches Volksbad** pool; it's located on the corner of the Ludwigsbrücke, one of the bridges over the Isar.

Shopping

Gift Ideas   Munich is a city of beer, and beer mugs and coasters make an obvious gift to take home. There are many specialist shops in downtown Munich, but **Ludwig Mory,** located in the town hall on Marienplatz, is about the best. Munich is also the home of the famous Nymphenburg porcelain factory; its major outlet is on Odeonsplatz. You can also buy direct from the factory located on the half-moon–shaped road—Schlossrondell—in front of Nymphenburg Palace. *Nördliche Schlossrondell 8, tel. 089/1791–9710. Salesroom open weekdays 8:30–noon and 12:30–5.*

Shopping Districts From Odeonsplatz you are poised to plunge into the heart of the huge pedestrian mall that runs through the center of town. The first street you come to, **Theatinerstrasse,** is also one of the most expensive. In fact, it has only one serious rival in the money-no-object stakes: **Maximilianstrasse,** the first street to your left as you head down Theatinerstrasse. Both are lined with elegant shops selling desirable German fashions and other high-priced goods from around the world. Leading off to the right of Theatinerstrasse is **Maffeistrasse,** where **Loden-Frey** has Bavaria's most complete collection of traditional wear, from green "loden" coats to Lederhosen. Maffeistrasse runs parallel to Munich's principal shopping streets: **Kaufingerstrasse** and **Neuhauserstrasse,** the one an extension of the other.

Department Stores All the city's major department stores—other than **Hertie** (*see* Exploring, *above*)—are along Maffeistrasse, Kaufingerstrasse, and Neuhauserstrasse. **Kaufhof** and the newly expanded **Karstadt-Oberpollinger** are probably the best. Both have large departments stocking Bavarian arts and crafts, as well as clothing, household goods, jewelry, and other accessories.

Antiques Antique hunters should visit **Blumenstrasse, Ottostrasse, Türkenstrasse,** and **Westenriederstrasse.** Also try the open-air Auer Dult fairs held on Mariahilplatz at the end of April, July, and October (streetcar No. 25), or the Saturday markets at the old Riem airport (take the S-6 to Riem).

Dining

Münchners love to eat just as much as they love their beer, and the range of food is as varied and rich as the local breweries' output. Some of Europe's best chefs are to be found here, purveyors of French nouvelle cuisine in some of the most noted—and pricey—restaurants in Germany. But these restaurants are mainly for the gourmet. For those in search of the local cuisine, the path leads to Munich's tried-and-true wood-paneled, flagstone beer restaurants and halls where the food is as sturdy as the large measure of beer that comes to your table almost automatically. Provided your pockets are deep enough, the choice is limitless—from a mountainous roast pork knuckle with dumplings to delicate slivers of salmon and truffle salad. The high-brow restaurants offer a low-key, library-quiet atmosphere, while many of the lower-brow establishments provide ear-splitting conviviality. Try the *Weisswurst* (white veal sausages with herbs), brought to your table in a tureen of boiling water to keep them fresh and hot. They are served with a sweet mustard and pretzels and are a breakfast or midmorning favorite. Equally good is *Leberkäs*, wedges of piping-hot meat loaf with a fried egg on top and pan-fried potatoes.

For details and price-category definitions, *see* Dining in Staying in Germany, *above.*

Very Expensive ★ **Aubergine.** German gourmets swear by the upscale nouvelle cuisine of Eckart Witzigmann, chef and owner of this sophisticated restaurant. The decor is a bit loud, incorporating aubergine, white, and silver into the color scheme. If you want a gastronomic experience on the grand scale, try the turbot in champagne or the breast of pigeon with artichoke and truffle salad. The equally exotic wine list includes an 1832 Lafite Rothschild. *Maximilianplatz 5, tel. 089/598171. Reservations required. DC, MC, V. Closed Sun., Mon. lunch, all public holidays, and first 3 weeks of Aug.*

Königshof. Located on the second floor of the postwar Königshof Hotel and overlooking the Karlstor at the northern entrance to the pedestrian-only center, the Königshof is without doubt Munich's most opulent restaurant. The neo-baroque style includes ceiling frescoes, subdued chandelier lighting, and heavy drapery. The kitchen offers nouvelle cuisine dishes—breast of goose with truffles, or veal in basil cream and mushroom sauce, for example. *Karlsplatz 25, tel. 089/551360. Reservations advised. AE, DC, MC, V.*

Sabitzer's. Further evidence of upscale Munich's love affair with nouvelle cuisine, though with Bavarian influences, is provided by the fabulous fare at Sabitzer's. Within its elegant gold-and-white 19th-century interior, you'll dine on such specialties as wolffish in sea urchin sauce or salmon lasagne. *Reitmorstr. 21, tel. 089/298584. Reservations required. AE, DC, MC, V. Closed Sun. and Aug.*

Expensive **Hunsingers Bouillabaisse.** Werner Hunsinger has moved his restaurant into the city center from the southern suburbs, bringing with him his talent and reputation for excellent cuisine. The sleek and elegant decor of his new restaurant, just off fashionable Maximilianstrasse, is a change in style from the solid traditional look of his previous location, but the cuisine is the same. The predominantly French menu is full of light and imaginative dishes created from the simplest of ingredients—calves' tongue, for instance, with avocado vinaigrette, or black noodles with mussels. *Falkenturmstr. 10, tel. 089/297909. Reservations advised. AE, DC, MC, V. Closed Sun. and last 3 weeks of Aug.*

Käferschanke. Fresh fish, including lobster, crab, salmon, trout, and halibut, is imported daily. Try the grilled prawns in a sweet-sour sauce. The rustic decor, complemented by some fine antique pieces, is a delight. The restaurant is located in the classy Bogenhausen suburb, a 10-minute taxi ride from downtown. *Käfer-Schänke Prinzregentenstr. 73, tel. 089/416–8247. Reservations advised. AE, DC, MC. Closed Sun. and holidays.*

★ **Le Gourmet.** Imaginative combinations of French and Bavarian specialties have won this small bistro substantial praise from local critics. Try chef Otto Koch's soufflé of sole in lemongrass sauce, or filled marrowbones with *Röstli* (Swiss-style pan-fried potatoes). *Hartmannstr. 8, tel. 089/212–0958. Reservations advised. AE, DC, MC. Closed Sun., Mon., and first 10 days of Jan.*

★ **Preysing Keller.** Devotees of all that's best in modern German food— food that's light and sophisticated but with recognizably Teutonic touches—will love the Preysing Keller, a hotel/restaurant. It's in a 16th-century cellar, though this has been so overrestored that there's practically no sense of its age or original character. Never mind; it's the food, the extensive wine list, and the perfect service that make this place special. *Innere-Wiener-Str. 6, tel. 089/481015. Reservations required. No credit cards. Closed Sun., Christmas, and New Year's Day.*

Moderate **Altdeutsche Weinstube.** Piano music is served nightly at this unabashedly old-fashioned wine restaurant in the heart of Munich's up-market central Lehel quarter. There's usually a singer among the diners, ready to join in an impromptu version of a selection or two from a favorite operetta. The menu offers traditional German dishes, with prices that swing wildly from expensive, in the evening, to an unmatchable lunch-time bargain of three courses for less than DM 20. *Tattenbachstr. 6, tel. 089/225268. Reservations advised. MC.*

Augustiner Keller. This 19th-century establishment, renovated from top to bottom in 1992, is the flagship beer restaurant of one of Munich's oldest breweries, Augustiner. The decor emphasizes wood—from the refurbished parquet floors to the wood barrels from which the beer is drawn. This is more the place to meet locals in a communal atmosphere of two baronial hall-like rooms, rather than a venue for a quiet meal for two. The menu changes daily and offers a full range of Bavarian specialties, but try to order *Tellerfleisch*—cold roast beef with lashings of horse radish, served on a big wood board. Follow that with *Dampfnudeln* (suet pudding served with custard) and you won't feel hungry again for 24 hours. *Arnulfstr. 52, tel. 089/594393. Reservations not necessary. No credit cards.*

Grüne Gans. This small, chummy restaurant near Viktualienmarkt is popular with local entertainers, whose photographs clutter the walls. International fare with regional German influences dominates the menu, although there are a few Chinese dishes. Try the chervil cream soup, followed by calves' kidneys in tarragon sauce. *Am Einlass 5, tel. 089/266228. Reservations required. MC. Closed lunch and Sat.*

James Cafe. Chef-owner James is an immigrant from Kenya, but you'll find no African specialties on his small but very fine menu. Instead, James cooks Italian, and so well that his cozy café is considered by aficionados as one of *the* Italian eating places in town. One of Munich's leading restaurant critics said the city's Italian cooks should turn "green, white, and red (the Italian national colors) with shame." James changes his menu every day, and if Italian-style pheasant is on it, then that's the dish to order. *Hochbrückenstr. 14, tel. 089/298940. Reservations not required. MC. Closed Sun. lunch.*

Weinhaus Neuner. Originally a seminary, this early 18th-century building houses Munich's oldest surviving wine hostelry, in the Neuner family since 1852. There is a timeless atmosphere in the high-ceilinged dining rooms lined with dark oak paneling. Look for the herb-filled pork fillets with noodles, and veal with Morchela mushroom sauce. *Herzogspitalstr. 8, tel. 089/260–3954. Reservations required. AE, DC, MC, V. Closed Sat. lunch, Sun., and holidays.*

Inexpensive
★

Altes Hackerhaus. This upscale beer restaurant on one of Munich's ritziest shopping streets is full of bric-a-brac and mementos that harken back to its origins as a medieval brewery and one-time home of the Hacker family, for whom one of the city's largest breweries is named. Beer has been brewed or served here since 1570. On a cold day, duck into one of the cozy little rooms and choose from the selection of hearty soups, then try a plate of *Käsespätzle* (egg noodles with melted cheese). In the heat of summer, try for a table in the tiny cool inner courtyard, probably the smallest beer garden in Munich. *Sendlingerstr. 75, tel. 089/260–5026. Reservations not necessary. No credit cards.*

Brauhaus zur Brez'n. A hostelry bedecked in the blue-and-white checked colors of the Bavarian flag. The eating and drinking are spread over three floors and cater to a broad clientele—from local business lunchers to hungry night owls emerging from Schwabing's bars looking for a bite at 2 AM. Brez'n offers a big all-day menu of traditional roasts, to be washed down with a choice of three draft beers. *Leopoldstrasse 72, tel. 089/390092. Reservations not necessary. No credit cards.*

Dürnbräu. A fountain plays outside this picturesque old Bavarian inn. Inside, the mood is crowded and noisy. Expect to share a table; your fellow diners will range from businessmen to students. The food is resolutely traditional. Try the cream of spinach soup and the boiled beef. *Dürnbräugasse 2, tel. 089/222195. Reservations not necessary. AE, DC, MC, V.*

Franziskaner. Vaulted archways, cavernous rooms interspersed with intimate dining areas, bold blue frescoes on the walls, and long wooden tables create a spick-and-span medieval atmosphere. Aside from the late-morning Weisswurst, look out for *Ochsenfleisch* (boiled ox meat) and dumplings. *Perusastr. 5, tel. 089/231–8120. No reservations. No credit cards.*

Haxnbauer. You can still order meat dishes here—*Bratwurstl* (roast sausages), *Schweinshaxe* (roast pork knuckle)—that have been cooked over an open charcoal fire. And, surprisingly for a Munich beer restaurant, the beer is from a north German brewery! The decor in the series of interlocking rooms is plain, with chunky, dark wood furniture. *Münzstr. 2, tel. 089/221922. Reservations advised. MC, V.*

Hofbräuhaus. The heavy stone vaults of the Hofbräuhaus contain the most famous of the city's beer restaurants. Crowds of singing, shouting, swaying beer drinkers fill the cavernous, smoky hall. Picking their way past the tables are hefty waitresses in traditional garb bearing frothing steins. The menu is strictly solid Bavarian. If you're not here solely to drink, try the more subdued upstairs restaurant, where the service is not so brusque and less beer gets spilled. It's located between Marienplatz and Maximillianstrasse. *Platzl 9, tel. 089/221676. No reservations. No credit cards.*

Hundskugel. This is Munich's oldest tavern, with a history stretching back to 1440. If *Spanferkel*—roast suckling pig—is on the menu, make a point of ordering it. This is simple Bavarian fare at its best. *Hotterstr. 18, tel. 089/264272. Reservations advised. No credit cards. Closed Sun.*

★ **Pfälzer Weinprobierstube.** A warren of stone-vaulted rooms of various sizes, wooden tables, glittering candles, dirndl-clad waitresses, and a vast range of wines add up to an experience as close to your picture of timeless Germany as you're likely to get. The food is reliable rather than spectacular. Local specialties predominate. *Residenzstr. 1, tel. 089/225628. No reservations. No credit cards.*

Lodging

Make reservations well in advance and be prepared for higher-than-average rates. Though Munich has a vast number of hotels in all price ranges, most are full year-round. If you plan to visit during the "fashion weeks" (Mode Wochen) in March and September or during the Oktoberfest at the end of September, make reservations at least several months in advance. Munich's tourist offices will handle only written or personal requests for reservations assistance. Write to: Fremdenverkehrsamt, Sendlinger Str. 1, D-80331 Munich, fax 089/2391313. Your best bet for finding a room if you haven't reserved is the tourist office at the Hauptbahnhof, by the Bayerstrasse entrance. The staff will charge a small fee.

Consider staying in a suburban hotel—where rates are often, but not always, lower—and taking the U-Bahn or S-Bahn into town. A 15-minute train ride is no obstacle to serious sightseeing. Check out the city tourist office "Key to Munich" packages. These include reduced-rate hotel reservations, sightseeing tours, theater visits, and low-cost travel on the U- and S-Bahn. Write to the tourist office (*see* Important Addresses and Numbers in Munich, *above*).

For details and price-category definitions, *see* Lodging in Staying in Germany, *above*.

Very Expensive

Bayerischer Hof. This is one of Munich's most traditional luxury hotels. Public rooms are decorated with antiques, fine paintings, marble, and painted wood. Old-fashioned comfort and class abound in the older rooms; some of the newer rooms are rather functional. *Promenadeplatz 2–6, tel. 089/21200, fax 089/212–0906. 383 rooms with bath and 45 apartments. Facilities: 3 restaurants, nightclub, rooftop pool, garage, sauna, masseur, hairdresser. AE, DC, MC, V.*

Rafael. A character-laden lodging in the heart of the old town (close to the Hofbräuhaus), the Rafael, which opened in 1989, retains many of the architectural features of its late-19th-century origins, including a sweeping staircase and stuccoed ceilings. Rooms are individually furnished and extravagantly decorated. The hotel restaurant, Mark's, is rapidly making a name for itself with its "new German" cuisine. *Neuturmstr. 1, tel. 089/290980, fax 089/222539. 67 rooms and 7 suites with bath. Facilities: restaurant, bar, indoor pool, sauna. AE, DC, MC, V.*

★ **Vier Jahreszeiten.** The Vier Jahreszeiten—it means the Four Seasons—has been playing host to the world's wealthy and titled for more than a century. It has an unbeatable location on Munich's premier shopping street and is only a few minutes' walk from the heart of the city. Elegance and luxury set the tone throughout; many rooms have handsome antique pieces. *Maximilianstr. 17, tel. 089/230390, fax 089/2303–9693. (Reservations in the U.S. from Kempinski International, tel. 800/426–3135). 277 rooms with bath, 45 apartments, presidential suite. Facilities: 3 restaurants, nightclub, rooftop pool, sauna, garage, car rental, Lufthansa check-in desk. AE, DC, MC, V.*

Expensive

Eden Hotel Wolff. Chandeliers and dark wood paneling in the public rooms underline the old-fashioned elegance of this downtown favorite. It's directly across the street from the train station and the airport bus terminal. The rooms are comfortable, and most are spacious. Dine on excellent Bavarian specialties in the intimate Zirbelstube restaurant. *Arnulfstr. 4, tel. 089/551150, fax 089/5511–5555. 210 rooms with bath. Facilities: restaurant, parking. AE, DC, MC, V.*

Hotel Erzgiesserei Europe. Its location—a dull little street in an uninteresting section of town—is the only drawback to this attractive new addition to Munich's hotel scene. The nearby subway whisks you in five minutes to central Karlsplatz, convenient for the pedestrian shopping area and the main railway station. Rooms are particularly bright, and are decorated in soft pastel tones with good-quality art reproductions on the walls. The cobblestone garden café is a peaceful haven in summer. *Erzgiessereistr. 15, tel. 089/126–820, fax 089/123–6198. 106 rooms with bath. Facilities: restaurant, bar, garden café, parking. AE, DC, MC, V.*

★ **Pannonia Hotel Königin Elisabeth.** Housed in a 19th-century neoclassical building, which was completely restored and opened for the first time as a hotel in 1989, the Elisabeth is modern and bright, with an emphasis on pink decor. The restaurant offers Hungarian specialties. The Elisabeth is a 15-minute streetcar ride northwest of the city center en route to Nymphenburg. *Leonrodstr. 79, tel. 089/126860, fax 089/126–86459. 80 rooms with bath. Facilities: bar, beer garden, sauna, solarium, and keep-fit equipment. AE, DC, MC, V.*

Platzl. This is a Bavarian-rustic–style but modern hotel in a building dating to 1573 and located in the heart of Munich's historic quarter—opposite the famous Hofbräuhaus beer hall. In fact, the Platzl is owned by an out-of-town brewery, Ayingerbräu. The rooms are smallish but comfortable. *Sparkassenstr. 10, tel. 089/237030, fax 089/2370–3800 (toll-free booking in the U.S., tel. 800/448–8355). 167 rooms with bath. Facilities: equipped for physically disabled guests, sauna, solarium, fitness rooms, rooftop terrace, restaurant, bar, underground garage. AE, DC, MC, V.*

Torbräu. This atmospheric lodging, tucked away next to the city's 14th-century eastern gate, the *Isartor* (Tor means gate), is just a few minutes' walk from Marienplatz. Rooms were recently renovated and offer a high level of comfort. There's an Italian restaurant and a coffee shop that bakes its own cakes. *Tal 41, tel. 089/225–016, fax 089/225–019. 82 rooms with bath, 4 suites. Facilities: restaurant, coffee shop, bowling alley. AE, MC, V.*

Moderate   **Arosa.** This plain, well-worn but friendly lodging in the old town is just a 5-minute walk to Marienplatz. If you're driving, make sure you reserve a spot in the hotel garage; parking in the area is difficult. Munich's oldest pub, the Hundskugel, is right down the street. *Hotterstr. 2, tel. 089/267087, fax 089/263–104. 77 rooms, some with bath. Facilities: restaurant, bar, garage. AE, DC, MC, V.*

Bauer. If the rustic Bavarian style of pinewood, blue-and-white check, and red geraniums appeals to you, you'll feel at home at the Bauer, a 20-minute ride east on the S-6 suburban train, or just a few miles by car along the A94 autobahn. The Bauer gives excellent value and facilities for the price. *Münchnerstr. 6, tel. 089/90980, fax 089/909–8414. 103 rooms with bath. Facilities: restaurant, terrace café, sauna, indoor pool. AE, DC, MC, V.*

Gästehaus am Englischer Garten. Despite the slightly basic rooms, you need to reserve well in advance to be sure of getting one in this converted, 200-year-old watermill. The hotel, complete with ivy-clad walls and shutter-framed windows, stands right on the edge of the Englischer Garten, no more than a five-minute walk from the bars and shops of Schwabing. Be sure to ask for a room in the main building; the modern annex down the road is cheaper but charmless. There's no restaurant, but in summer, breakfast is served on the terrace. *Liebergesellstr. 8, tel. 089/392034, fax 089/391–233. 34 rooms, some with bath. No credit cards.*

Hotel Amba. Families get an especially good deal at the Amba, which is part of a hotel group that prides itself on being child-friendly. A modern, brightly furnished double room comes for as low as DM 110, and additional beds cost DM 35. The hotel is right across the street from the main railway station and has its own porter service. A bus operated by the hotel picks up guests from the airport. *Arnulfstr. 20, tel. 089/592–921, fax 089/554–160. 85 rooms, most with bath. Facilities: restaurant, coffee bar, parking. AE, DC, MC, V.*

Hotel Carlton. This is a diplomats' favorite—a small, elegant, discreet hotel on a quiet side street in the best area of downtown Munich. The American and British consulates are nearby, as are some of the liveliest Schwabing bars and restaurants. Art galleries, museums, and cinemas are also in the neighborhood. Rooms are on the small side, but there are also several apartments with cooking facilities. *Fürstenstr. 12, tel. 089/282–061, fax 089/284–391. 40 rooms with bath. AE, DC, MC, V.*

Tele-Hotel. This modern, well-appointed hotel on the outskirts of Munich is close to the television studios at Unterföhring (hence the name), and is conveniently located along the airport S-Bahn line 8, only a 15-minute ride from downtown. TV types escape their studio cafeteria's drab fare by popping into the hotel's Bavarian Hackerbräu restaurant, where a lunchtime menu for less than DM 30 is a hot favorite. *Bahnhofstr. 15, Unterföhring, tel. 089/950–146, fax 089/950–6652. 60 rooms with bath, 1 apartment. Facilities: restaurant, bar, roof terrace, bowling alley, parking. AE, DC, MC, V.*

Inexpensive **Am Markt.** Although tucked away in a corner of the colorful Viktualienmarkt in the heart of the old town, this old-fashioned hotel has long ceased to be a secret. Its central location and slightly seedy charm make up for the lack of luxury. It's very popular, so book well in advance. Parking in the area is a problem. *Heiliggeistr. 6, tel. 089/225014, fax 089/224–017. 28 rooms, some with bath. No credit cards.*

Hotel-Pension Beck. American and British guests receive a particularly warm welcome from the anglophile owner of the rambling, friendly Beck. Rooms may be furnished in a somewhat haphazard and even garish style, but this pension has a prime location in the heart of fashionable Lehel—handy for museums and the English Garden. *Thierschstr. 36, tel. 089/220–708 or 089/225–768, fax 089/ 220–925. 44 rooms, 4 with shower. No credit cards.*

Mariandl. Large families are catered to at this rambling, friendly pension with huge rooms furnished in a variety of homey styles. Only four of the rooms have their own showers, however, so be specific when booking. The ground floor is taken up by a Viennese-style restaurant, with Biedermeier furnishings and a menu featuring every variety of Wiener schnitzel. The large grand piano isn't in here just for decoration—evening soirees in the style of those once enjoyed by Franz Schubert and his friends in Vienna are held here Monday through Friday (portraits of the composer adorn the walls). If you like your schnitzel with Lieder, then you'll love this place. *Goethestr. 51, tel. 089/534–108 or 089/535–158. 30 rooms, 4 with shower. AE, V.*

The Arts

Details of concerts and theater performances are available from the *Vorschau* or *Monatsprogramm* booklets obtainable at most hotel reception desks. Some hotels will make ticket reservations; otherwise use one of the ticket agencies in the city center: **Hieber Max** (Liebfrauenstr. 1, tel. 089/226571) or the **Residenz Bücherstube** (Residenzstr. 1, concert tickets only, tel. 089/220868). You can also book tickets at the two kiosks on the concourse below Marienplatz.

Concerts Munich's Philharmonic Orchestra entertains in Germany's biggest concert hall, the **Gasteig Cultural Center.** Tickets can be bought directly at the box office (the Gasteig center is on Rosenheimerstrasse, on a hill above the Ludwigsbrücke Bridge (tel. 089/4809–8614). The Bavarian Radio Orchestra performs Sunday concerts here. In summer, concerts are held at two Munich palaces, **Nymphenburg** and **Schleissheim,** and in the open-air interior courtyard of the **Residenz.**

Opera Munich's **Bavarian State Opera** company is world-famous, and tickets for major productions in its permanent home, the State Opera House, are difficult to obtain. Book far in advance for the annual opera festival held in July and August; contact the tourist office for the schedule of performances and ticket prices. The opera house box office (Maximilianstr. 11, tel. 089/221316) takes reservations one week in advance only. It's open weekdays 10:30–1 and 3:30–5:30, Saturday 10–12:30.

Dance The ballet company of the Bavarian State Opera performs at the **State Opera House**. Ballet productions are also staged at the attractive late-19th-century **Gärtnerplatz Theater** (tel. 089/201–6767).

Film Munich hosts an annual film festival each June. English-language films are shown regularly at several downtown cinemas: **Ricks and Hollywood** (Schwantalerstr. 2–6), **Cinema** (Nymphenburgerstr. 31), the **Film Museum** (St. Jakobs Platz), and the **Museum Lichtspiele** (Ludwigsbrücke).

Theater There are two state theater companies, one of which concentrates on the classics. More than 20 other theater companies (some of them performing in basements) are to be found throughout the city. Regular English-language productions, featuring an American cast and director, are staged at **America House** (tel. 089/595–367).

Nightlife

Bars, Cabaret, Nightclubs Although it lacks the racy reputation of Hamburg, Munich has something for just about all tastes. For spicy striptease, explore the train station district (Schillerstrasse, for example) or the Hofbräuhaus neighborhood, perhaps along Maderbräu-strasse.

Jazz The best jazz can be heard at the **Scala Music Bar** (Oscar-von-Miller Ring 3), the **Unterfahrt** (Kirchenstr. 96), and the **Podium** (Wagnerstr. 1). Or try **Jenny's Place in the Blue Note** (Moosacherstr. 24, tel. 089/351–0520), named for an English singer who settled in Munich.

Discos Disco bars abound in the side streets off Freilitzschstrasse surrounding Münchener Freiheit in Schwabing. **babalu** (Leopoldstr. 19) is among the best and a real old-timer on Munich's changing disco scene. More upscale are **Nachtcafe** (Maximiliansplatz 5), open all night on weekends, and **P1** (in the Haus der Kunst, Prinzregentenstr. 1). **Nachtwerk** (Landsbergerstr. 185) has everything from punk to avant garde, plus live bands.

For Singles Every Munich bar is singles territory. Three you might like to try are **Schumann's** (Maximilianstr. 36) anytime after the curtain comes down at the nearby opera house; **Alter Simpl** (Türkenstr. 57) but not before midnight; and **O'Reilly's**, an atmospheric Irish bar incongruously located on fashionable Maximilianstrasse (Maximilianstr. 29). For the student, beards, and pipe scene, try **Bunte Vogel** in Schwabing (Herzogstr. 44), which also features an unusual collection of table lamps.

Frankfurt

Arriving and Departing

By Plane Frankfurt airport, the busiest in mainland Europe, is about 10 kilometers (6 miles) southwest of the city.

Between the Airport and Downtown There are several ways to get into town. Two suburban (S-Bahn) lines connect the airport and the center. The S-14 runs between the Hauptwache station and the center. The S-15 from the main train station, the Hauptbahnhof. The S-14 runs every 20 minutes and takes 15 minutes; the S-15 leaves every 10 minutes and takes 11 minutes. The trip costs DM 4.20 (DM 5.60 in rush hour, 6:30–8:30 AM and 4–6:30 PM. InterCity and InterCityExpress (ICE) trains also stop at Frankfurt airport train station on hourly direct runs to Cologne, Dortmund, Hamburg, and Munich. A No. 61 bus runs from the airport to the Südbahnhof station in Sachsenhausen, where there is access to the U-Bahn (subway) lines U-1 and U-3; the fare is DM 4.20 (DM 5.60 during rush hours). Taxi fare from the airport to downtown is about DM 40. By rented car, follow the signs to Frankfurt ("Stadtmitte") via the B-43 main road.

By Train Frankfurt's main train station, the Hauptbahnhof, and the airport station are directly linked with all parts of the country by fast Euro-City and InterCity services and by the high-speed InterCityExpress (ICE) trains. For train information, tel. 069/19419. For tickets and general information, go directly to the station or to the DER travel office at the Hauptbahnhof.

By Bus Long-distance buses connect Frankfurt with more than 200 European cities. Buses leave from the south side of the Hauptbahnhof. Tickets and information are available from **Deutsche Touring GmbH** (Am Römerhof 17, tel. 069/79030).

By Car From the north, leave autobahn A5 at the Nordwestkreuz, join A66 and follow it to its end, in the Nordend district. From the east, A66 brings you into Enkheim, from where you follow the signs to the downtown area, the "Stadtmitte." From the west, leave autobahn A3 at the Frankfurt-south ("Frankfurt-Süd") exit and enter the city on B43/44. From the south, leave the autobahn at the Offenbach exit (the "Anschluss-stelle Offenbach") and enter the city on B459.

Getting Around

By Public Transportation A combination of subway and suburban train, streetcar, and bus services provides speedy transportation. Tickets cover travel on the complete network, which is divided into tariff zones. A single ticket for travel within the city costs DM 2.20 (DM 2.80 during rush hour). A day ticket (for use during one calendar day) offers unlimited journeys in the inner zone for DM 6. Buy all tickets at newspaper kiosks or from blue automatic dispensing machines. If you're caught without a ticket, you'll have to pay a fine of DM 60 to the plain-clothes "controllers" who patrol the trains. For further information or assistance, call 069/269463.

By Taxi Taxi meters start at DM 3.80, and the fare is DM 2.15 per kilometer (about DM 3 per mile), or DM 2.35 on weekends. Count on paying DM 10 to DM 12 for a short city ride. Taxi drivers charge 50 pf for each piece of luggage carried. To order a taxi, call 069/250001 or 069/545011.

Important Addresses and Numbers

Tourist Information There are three city information offices. One is at the Hauptbahnhof, across from platform 23 (tel. 069/212–8849). It's open Monday–Saturday 8 AM–10 PM (November–March until 9 PM), Sunday and holidays 9:30 AM–8 PM. The other is in the town hall in the old town at Römerberg 27 (tel. 069/21238708). It's open weekdays 9 AM–6 PM, weekends and holidays 9:30AM–6PM. Both offices will help you find accommodations. A third information office (tel. 069/690–6211) is in the airport Arrival Hall B, daily 8 AM–9 PM. The DER Deutsches Reisebüro, Arrival Hall B6 (tel. 069/693071), can also help you find rooms. Open daily 8 AM–9 PM (tel. 069/693071). For information in advance of your trip, contact the **Verkehrsamt Frankfurt/Main** (Kaiserstrasse 52, 6000 Frankfurt, tel. 069/212–38800).

Consulates U.S. (Seismayerstrasse 21, tel. 069/75350). U.K. (Bockenheimer Landstrasse 42, tel. 069/170–0020).

Emergencies **Police** (tel. 110). **Doctor or Ambulance** (tel. 069/112). **Dentist** (tel. 069/660–7271). **Pharmacy Information** (tel. 069/11500).

English- The **British Bookshop** (Börsenstrasse 17, tel. 069/280492) and the
Language **American Book Center** (Jahnstrasse 36, tel. 069/552816) carry En-
Bookstores glish-language titles.

Travel **American Express** (Kaiserstr. 8, tel. 069/210548). **DER Deutsches**
Agencies **Reisebüro** (Emil-von-Behring Strasse 6, tel. 069/958–8360).

Guided Tours

Orientation Daily bus tours of the city, including visits to Goethe's House and
Tours the Europa Tower for a view over Frankfurt depart at 10:15 AM and
2:15 PM from outside the tourist information office at the main train
station, and at 10 AM and 2 PM from the Römer tourist office. The tour
lasts about two and a half hours and costs DM 36 (children up to 16, half
price). **Gray Line** (tel. 069/230492) offers city tours four times a day;
they cost DM 50 (DM 40 children). On weekend afternoons, a gaily
painted old streetcar, "The Ebbelwei Express," trundles around
the city and Sachsenhausen, on the south side of the Main. The 40-
minute ride—starting and ending at the Ostbahnhof train station,
at Danzigerplatz in Frankfurt's Ostend district—includes a glass of
apple cider (*Ebbelwei*) and a pretzel in the DM 3 fare. Further information and tickets can be obtained from the tourist offices (*see* Important Addresses and Numbers, *above*). Visitors who like to go at
their own pace can buy a cassette in English for DM 12 from the tourist office at the Römer. The tape describes a one-hour walking tour.
You can also rent a portable cassette player there.

Excursions Bus tours of the surrounding countryside, as far as the Rhine, are
offered by **Noblesse Limousine Service** (tel. 06101/12055) in Bad
Vilbel, the **Deutsche Touring GmbH** (Am Römerhof 17, tel. 069/
7903268), and **Gray Line** (*see above*). One-day excursions are also offered by German Railways, the Deutsche Bundesbahn. These are
described in a brochure, *"Der Schöne Tag,"* obtainable from the
main train station and the DER tourist office. A "Casino-Express"
bus service runs daily from Frankfurt (departing from the south
side of the train station) to the casino at Bad Homburg in the Taunus
Mountains. The DM 9.50 fare includes the entrance charge to the casino. The bus departs hourly, from 2 to 11 PM. Pleasure boats of the
Primus Line cruise the Main and Rhine rivers from Frankfurt, sailing as far as the Lorelei and back in a day. For schedules and reservations, contact **Frankfurter Personenschiffahrt** (Mainkai 36, tel.
069/281884).

Exploring Frankfurt

*Numbers in the margin correspond to points of interest on the
Frankfurt map.*

At first glance, Frankfurt-am-Main doesn't seem to have much to offer the tourist. Virtually flattened by bombs during the war, it now
bristles with skyscrapers, the visible sign of the city's role as
Germany's financial capital. Yet the inquisitive and discerning visitor will find many remnants of Frankfurt's illustrious past (besides
being well placed for excursions to other historic cities, such as Heidelberg and Würzburg, and within easy reach of the Rhine).

Originally a Roman settlement, Frankfurt was later one of
Charlemagne's two capitals (the other being Aachen). Still later, it
was for centuries the site of the election and coronation of the em-

perors of that unwieldy entity, the Holy Roman Empire, which was
the forerunner of a united Germany. It was also the birthplace of the
poet and dramatist Goethe (1749–1832). The house in which he was
born is one of many restored and reconstructed old buildings that
inject a flavor of bygone days into the center of this busy modern
city.

Although the true center of Frankfurt is its ancient **Römerberg
Square,** where the election of Holy Roman emperors was traditionally proclaimed and celebrated, this tour of the city begins slightly to
❶ the north, at the **Hauptwache,** an 18th-century guardhouse that today serves a more peaceful purpose as a café. The lower ground floor
houses Interpress, an information office that assists young visitors,
including finding moderately priced accommodations. *Open weekdays 10–6, Sat. 10–1.*

❷ Head south along Kornmarkt, passing on the left the **Katerinenkirche** (Church of St. Catherine), the historic center of Frankfurt Protestantism, in whose 17th-century font Goethe was con-
firmed. After crossing Berlinerstrasse, and still heading south,
❸ you'll pass the **Paulskirche** (Church of St. Paul). It was here that the
first all-German parliament convened in 1848, and the church is
therefore an important symbol of German unity and democracy.
Continue down Buchgasse and within a few minutes you're on the
north bank of the river **Main.** Turn left toward the iron footbridge
known as the **Eiserner Steg** and at the **Rententurm,** one of the city's
medieval gates, bear left again and you'll arrive at the spacious
❹ **Römerberg,** center of Frankfurt civic life over the centuries. In the
center of the square stands the 16th-century **Fountain of Justitia**
(Justice): At the coronation of Emperor Matthias in 1612, wine instead of water spouted from the stonework. The crush of people was
so great, however, that the Germans have not repeated the trick
since.

❺ Compared with many city halls, Frankfurt's **Römer** is a modest affair, with a gabled Gothic facade. It occupies most of one side of the
square and is actually three patrician houses (the Alt-Limpurg, the
Römer—from which it takes its name—and the Löwenstein). The
mercantile-minded Frankfurt burghers used the complex not only
for political and ceremonial purposes, but for trade fairs and commerce. The most important events to take place in the Römer, however, were the elections of the Holy Roman emperors. The
Kaisersaal (Imperial Hall) was last used in 1792 to celebrate the election of Emperor Francis II, who was later forced to abdicate by
arch-egomaniac Napoleon Bonaparte. (A 16-year-old Goethe smug-
gled himself into the banquet celebrating the coronation of Emperor
Joseph II in 1765 by posing as a waiter.) Today, visitors can see the
impressive full-length 19th-century portraits of the 52 emperors of
the Holy Roman Empire that line the walls of the reconstructed banquet hall. *Admission: DM 3 adults, DM 1 children. Open Tues.–
Sun. 11–3. Closed Mon. and during official functions.*

Charlemagne's son, Ludwig the Pious, established a church on the
present site of the Römerberg in AD 850. His church was replaced by
a much grander Gothic structure, one used for imperial coronations;
❻ it became known as the **Kaiserdom,** the Imperial Cathedral. The cathedral suffered only superficial damage during World War II, and it
still contains many of its original treasures, including a fine 15th-
century altar.

On the south side of the square stands the 13th-century
❼ **Nikolaikirche** (St. Nicholas's Church). It's worth trying to time your

Frankfurt

KEY

AE American Express Office

i Tourist Information

Alte Brücke, **14**

Alte Oper, **11**

Börse, **12**

Goethehaus und
Goethemuseum, **10**

Hauptwache, **1**

Jewish Museum, **17**

Kaiserdom, **6**

Karmeliterkirche, **9**

Katerinenkirche, **2**

Kuhhirtenturm, **15**

Leonhardskirche, **8**

Museum of Modern
Art, **13**

Nikolaikirche, **7**

Paulskirche, **3**

Römer, **5**

Römerberg, **4**

Städelsches
Kunstinstitut und
Städtische Galerie, **16**

visit to the square to coincide with the chimes of the glockenspiel carillon, which ring out three times a day. *Carillon chimes daily at 9, noon, and 5. Nikolaikirche open Mon–Sat. 10–5.*

From the Römerberg, stroll south toward the river, but turn right this time, past the riverside **Leonhardskirche** (St. Leonhard's Church), which is filled with wonderful things including a fine 13th-century porch and a beautifully carved circa 1500 Bavarian altar, then into the narrow Karmelitergasse to the **Karmeliterkloster** (Carmelite Church and Monastery). The secularized and renovated church houses the **Museum of Prehistory and Early History;** next door, the main cloister contains the largest religious fresco north of the Alps, a 16th-century representation of the birth and death of Christ. *Admission to museum: DM 5 adults, DM 2.50 children; open Tues.–Sun. 10–5. Admission to cloister: DM 3 adults, DM 1.50 children; open Tues.–Sun. 11–6.*

From here, it's only a short way to the **Goethehaus und Goethemuseum** (Goethe's House and Museum). It was here that the poet was born in 1749, and though the house was destroyed by Allied bombing, it has been carefully restored and is furnished with pieces from Goethe's time, some belonging to his family. The adjoining museum is closed for renovations. *Grosser Hirschgraben 23–25, tel. 069/282824. Admission: DM 4 adults, DM 3 children. Open Apr.–Sept., Mon.–Sat. 9–6, Sun. 10–1; Oct.–Mar., Mon.–Sat. 9–4, Sun. 10–1.*

From the Goethehaus, retrace your steps to the Hauptwache via Rossmarkt. From there, take a window-shopping stroll past the elegant boutiques of Goethestrasse, which ends at Opernplatz and Frankfurt's reconstructed opera house, the **Alte Oper.** Wealthy Frankfurt businessmen gave generously for the construction of the opera house during the 1870s (provided they were given priority for the best seats), and Kaiser Wilhelm I traveled from Berlin for the gala opening in 1880. Bombed in 1944, the opera house remained in ruins for many years while controversy raged over its reconstruction. The new building, in the classical proportions and style of the original, was finally opened in 1981.

Looking out from the Alte Oper, you'll see the skyscrapers that have earned Frankfurt its nickname of Mainhattan; some of these house the headquarters of West Germany's biggest and richest banks. Cross Opernplatz and bear left down Grosse Bockenheimer Strasse (known locally as Fressgasse—literally "Food Street"—because of its abundance of gourmet shops and restaurants), turn left into Börsenstrasse, and you'll hit the center of the financial district. Just around the corner from Fressgasse is the Frankfurt **Börse,** Germany's leading stock exchange and financial powerhouse. It was founded by Frankfurt merchants in 1558 to establish some order in their often chaotic dealings. Today's dealings can also be quite hectic; see for yourself by slipping into the visitors' gallery. *Admission free. Gallery open weekdays 10:30–1:30.*

From the Börse, turn right into Schillerstrasse, and within two minutes you're back at the Hauptwache. Here begins Frankfurt's main shopping street, the **Zeil,** which claims the highest turnover per square yard of stores in all Germany. Resist if you can the temptations that shriek from the shop windows on both sides of this crowded pedestrian zone and head eastward to the nearby point where it is crossed by Hasengasse. Turn right into Hasengasse and you'll see the striking wedge form of Frankfurt's newest museum rising straight ahead of you. The **Museum of Modern Art** opened in

June 1991 and contains an important collection of works by such artists as Siah Armajani, Joseph Beuys, Walter de Maria, and Andy Warhol. *Domstr. 10, tel. 069/21238819. Admission DM 7 adults, DM 3.50 children. Open Tues.–Sun. 10–5, Wed. 10–8.*

Across the Main lies the district of **Sachsenhausen.** It's said that Charlemagne arrived here with a group of Saxon families during the 8th century and formed a settlement on the banks of the Main. It was an important bridgehead for the crusader Knights of the Teutonic Order and, in 1318, officially became part of Frankfurt. Cross to Sachsenhausen over the **Alte Brücke.** Along the bank to your left you'll see the 15th-century **Kuhhirtenturm,** the only remaining part of Sachsenhausen's original fortifications. The composer Paul Hindemith lived and worked in the tower from 1923 to 1927.

The district still has a medieval air, with narrow back alleys and quiet squares that have escaped the destructive tread of the city developer. Here you'll find Frankfurt's famous *Ebbelwei* taverns. Look for a green pine wreath over the entrance to tell passersby that a freshly pressed—and alcoholic—apple wine or cider is on tap. You can eat well in these little inns, too.

Time Out The main street in Sachsenhausen, **Neuer Wall,** is lined with atmospheric old taverns offering home-brewed apple wine and solid local fare. A favorite is Dauth-Schneider (Neuer Wall 7, closed Mon. in winter).

No fewer than eight top-ranking museums line the Sachsenhausen side of the Main, on **Schaumainkai** (locally known as the **Museumsufer** or Museum Bank). These range from exhibitions of art and architecture to the German Film Museum. The **Städelsches Kunstinstitut und Städtische Galerie** (Städel Art Institute and Municipal Gallery) has one of the most significant art collections in Germany, with fine examples of Flemish, German, and Italian Old Masters, plus a sprinkling of French Impressionists. *Schaumainkai 63. Admission: DM 8 adults, DM 4 children; free on Wed. Open Tues.–Sun. 10–5, Wed. until 8.*

Across the river from this impressive lineup of museums is Frankfurt's **Jewish Museum** (cross the Untermain Bridge to reach it). The fine city mansion houses a permanent exhibit tracing the history of Frankfurt's Jewish community; its library is Germany's main registry for Jewish history. *Untermainkai 14–15, tel. 069/212–35000. Admission DM 5 adults, DM 2.50 children. Open Tues. and Thurs.–Sun. 10–5, Wed. 10–8.*

Dining

Several Frankfurt restaurants close for the school summer vacation break, a six-week period that falls between mid-June and mid-September. Always check to avoid disappointment.

For details and price-category definitions, *see* Dining in Staying in Germany, *above.*

Expensive **Avocado.** This classy restaurant is as ideal for a romantic dinner as for a business lunch. Excellent service and huge arrangements of fresh flowers help create a fitting ambience for the fine French bistro food. *Hochstr. 27, tel. 069/292–867. Reservations advised. AE, MC. Closed Sun.*

★ **Bistrot 77.** Mainly Alsatian specialties are served at this bright, light, and cheerful French restaurant in Sachsenhausen. *Ziegelhüt-*

tenweg 1–3, tel. 069/614040. Reservations accepted. AE, DC, MC, V. Closed Sat. lunch, Sun., and mid-June–mid-July.

Erno's Bistro. Small, chic, and popular with visiting power brokers, Erno's has become something of a Frankfurt institution. The menu features classy nouvelle specialties, with fish—flown in daily, often from France—predominating. All the waiters speak English and are both able and happy to choose your meal for you. *Liebigstr. 15, tel. 069/721–997. Reservations required. AE, DC, MC, V. Closed weekends and mid-June–mid-July.*

Weinhaus Brückenkeller. *Keller* is German for "cellar," and that's where the Brückenkeller is situated. The ancient vaulted interior (the restaurant has been in business since 1652) is set off by carefully selected antiques. The wine-list choice of 180 different labels is supported by an extraordinary stock of 85,000 bottles. But more than anything, it's the fine cuisine that has earned this restaurant its two Michelin stars. *Schützenstr. 6, tel. 069/284238. Reservations advised. AE, DC, MC, V. Dinner only. Closed Sun.*

Moderate **Altes Zollhaus.** In this beautiful, 200-year-old half-timbered house, you can sample very good versions of traditional German specialties. Try some of the game dishes. In summer, you can eat in the beautiful garden. *Friedberger Landstr. 531, tel. 069/472707. Reservations advised. AE, DC, MC, V. Closed Mon.*

Börsenkeller. Solid Germanic food, with just a hint of French style, is served here to fortify the business community from the nearby stock exchange (*Börse* means "money market"). Steaks are a specialty. *Schillerstr. 11, tel. 069/281115. Reservations accepted. AE, DC, MC, V. Closed Sat. dinner and Sun.*

Casa Nova. The inviting exterior is fully matched by the cozy interior of this superior Italian restaurant, in an attractive Sachsenhausen house. Fish is prepared with imagination and skill, and if the pasta proves too plentiful, half-portions are willingly served. *Stresemannallee 59, tel. 069/632473. Reservations advised. AE, DC, MC, V. Closed Sat. and 2 weeks in Aug.*

Zur Müllerin. The *müllerin* (miller's wife) is Lieselotte Müller, who has been running this restaurant since the 1950s. Her regulars are artists and actors from the nearby theaters; you'll find expressions of appreciation for the cooking skills of their beloved müllerin decorating the restaurant walls. *Weissfrauenstr. 18, tel. 069/285182. Reservations advised. AE, DC, MC, V. Closed for lunch on Sat. and Sun.*

Inexpensive **Café GegenwART.** The accent really is on art at this friendly, bustling café-restaurant. Art can be found both on the walls and in the cooking; exhibitions change as regularly as the menu. In summer, the tables spill out onto the sidewalk. Do try the freshly caught angler fish or tomato fondue if they are available. *Berger Str. 6, tel. 069/4970544. Reservations not necessary. MC.*

Lux. This stylish and reasonably priced bar/restaurant at the center of town pulls in a twenty-something crowd who come for the salads, afternoon snacks, or simply coffee as much as for hearty evening meals. *Kornmarkt 11, tel. 069/281–529. Reservations not necessary. No credit cards.*

★ **Zum Gemalten Haus.** This is the real thing, a traditional wine tavern in the heart of Sachsenhausen. Its name means "At the Painted House," a reference to the frescoes that cover the place inside and out. In the summer and on fine spring and autumn days, the courtyard is the place to be (the inner rooms can get a bit crowded). But if you can't at first find a place at one of the bench-lined long tables, order an apple wine and hang around until someone leaves: It's worth the wait. *Schweizerstr. 67, tel. 069/614559. Reservations not necessary. No credit cards. Closed Mon. and Tues.*

Lodging

For details and price-category definitions, *see* Lodging in Staying in Germany, *above*.

Very Expensive ★ **Gravenbruch Kempinski.** This spacious, elegant hotel retains the atmosphere of the manor house that once stood on its parkland site in leafy Neu Isenburg (a 15-minute drive south of Frankfurt). Some of its luxuriously appointed rooms and suites are arranged as duplex penthouse apartments. Make sure you get a room overlooking the lake. *63243 Neu Isenburg, tel. 06102/5050, fax 06102/505445. 288 rooms with bath. Facilities: 3 restaurants, indoor and outdoor pools, tennis courts, health spa, hairdresser, Lufthansa check-in service, limo service to airport and city (both 15 minutes away). AE, DC, MC, V.*

Hessischer Hof. This former palace is still owned by a prince of Hesse, and fine antiques are deftly positioned in many guest rooms. A daily supply of fresh fruit delivered to all rooms is part of the outstanding service. One of the two bars, Jimmy's, numbers among Frankfurt's best, and the hotel restaurant is highly prized both for its gourmet cuisine and its refined ambience. *Friedrich-Ebert-Anlage 40, tel. 069/75400, fax 069/7540924. 117 rooms with bath. Facilities: restaurant, 2 bars, garage. AE, DC, MC, V.*

★ **Steigenberger Hotel Frankfurter Hof.** The Frankfurter Hof is one of the city's oldest established hotels, in the Victorian grand style. The German kaiser once slept here. *Am Kaiserplatz 17, tel. 069/21502, fax 069/215860. 347 rooms with bath. Facilities: 4 restaurants, café, 2 bars. AE, DC, MC, V.*

Expensive **An der Messe.** This place—the name means "at the fairgrounds"—is a small but stylish hotel with chicly appointed rooms. Comfort and attentive service push this venue into the quality class, despite the absence of a restaurant. *Westendstr. 104, tel. 069/747979, fax 069/748349. 46 rooms with bath. Facilities: garage. AE, DC, MC, V.*

Dorint Hotel. A palm-fringed, rooftop pool beckons after a day of touring downtown Frankfurt, which is a short walk across the river from this stylish member of the Dorint group. The hotel has all the comfort and facilities expected from this respected hotel chain. *Hahnstr. 9, tel. 069/663060, fax 069/66306600. 183 rooms with bath, 8 suites. Facilities: restaurant, 2 bars, indoor pool, sauna, parking. AE, DC, MC, V.*

Palmenhof. The city's west end houses this luxuriously modernized turn-of-the-century hotel. In the basement is a cozy restaurant, the Bastei, which has an expensive nouvelle menu. *Bockenheimer Landstr. 89–91, tel. 069/753–0060, fax 069/75300666. 47 rooms with bath, plus 35 apartments. Facilities: restaurant, garage. AE, DC, MC, V.*

Moderate **Arcade.** This modern hotel is situated on the north bank of the Main river, just five minutes' walk from the train station. The rooms are furnished basically, though all have TV, and two are specially equipped for disabled guests. *Speicherstr. 3–5, tel. 069/273030, fax 069/237024. 233 rooms with bath. Facilities: restaurant, bar, parking. AE, DC, MC, V.*

★ **Maingau.** This excellent-value hotel is in the city's Sachsenhausen district, within easy reach of the downtown area and just a stone's throw from the lively Altstadt quarter, with its cheery apple-cider taverns. The rooms are spartanly furnished, though clean and comfortable, and all have TV. *Schifferstr. 38–40, tel. 069/617001, fax 069/620790. 100 rooms with bath. Facilities: restaurant, garage. AE, MC.*

Neue Kräme. This small, friendly hotel is located on a quiet pedestrians-only street right in the downtown area. The rooms are basic, but all have TV and minibar. There's no restaurant, but drinks and snacks are available. *Neue Kräme 23, tel. 069/284046, fax 069/296288. 21 rooms with bath. AE, DC, MC, V.*

Inexpensive **Am Zoo.** This hotel provides modest but comfortable accommodations in Frankfurt's east end and, as the name suggests, is near the city's famous big zoo. *Alfred-Brehm-Platz 6, tel. 069/490771, fax 069/439868. 85 rooms with bath. Facilities: restaurant. AE, DC, MC, V. Closed Christmas.*

Hotel-Schiff *Peter Schlott*. Watch your step when returning to this unusual hotel after a night out in Frankfurt—it's a "hotel ship," moored on the River Main in the suburb of Höchst, a 15-minute train or tram ride from the city center. Guest cabins are predictably on the small side, but the marvelous river views more than compensate. *Mainberg, tel. 069/315480, fax 069/3004680. 19 rooms, about half with shower. Facilities: restaurant, parking. MC.*

Waldhotel "Hensel's Felsenkeller." Helmut Braun's traditional old hotel has the woods that ring Frankfurt as its backyard, yet the city center is just a 15-minute tram ride away (the nearest stop is a three-minute walk away from the hotel). Rooms are quite basic, but there are plans to modernize them to add more comfort. *Buchrainerstr. 95, tel. 069/652086, fax 069/658371. 14 rooms, 7 with bath. Facilities: restaurant, parking. MC.*

Hamburg

Arriving and Departing

By Plane Hamburg's international airport, Fuhlsbüttel, is 11 kilometers (7 miles) northwest of the city. Lufthansa flights connect Hamburg with all other major German cities and European capitals.

Between the Airport and Downtown A bus service between Hamburg's central bus station and the airport (stopping also at the hotels Atlantic and Plaza and the Schauspielhaus Theater) operates daily at 20-minute intervals between 5:40 AM and 9:30 PM. The first bus leaves the airport for the city at 6:30 AM. It takes about 25 minutes. One-way fare, including luggage, is DM 8. There is also an "Airport Express" bus, No. 110, which runs between the airport and the Ohlsdorf S-Bahn (suburban line) and U-Bahn (subway) station. The fare is DM 3.60. Taxi fare from the airport to the downtown area is about DM 25. By rented car, follow the signs to "Stadtmitte" (Downtown), which appear immediately outside the airport area.

By Train Hamburg is a terminus for mainline services to northern Germany; trains to Schleswig-Holstein and Scandinavia also stop here. There are two principal stations: the main train station (Hauptbahnhof) and Hamburg-Altona. EuroCity, InterCity, and high-speed InterCityExpress services connect Hamburg with all German cities and the European rail network. For train information, tel. 040/19419.

By Bus Hamburg's bus station, the Zentral-Omnibus-Bahnhof, is in Adenauerallee, behind the Hauptbahnhof. For tickets and information, contact the **Deutsche Touring Gesellschaft** (Am Römerhof 17, D–60486 Frankfurt/Main, tel. 069/79030).

By Car Hamburg has proportionately fewer cars than most other German cities and an urban road system that is the envy of many of them. Incoming autobahns end at one of Hamburg's three beltways, which then connect easily with the downtown area ("Stadtmitte").

Getting Around

By Public Transportation The comprehensive city and suburban transportation system includes a subway network (U-Bahn), which connects efficiently with S-Bahn (suburban) lines, and an exemplary bus service. Tickets cover travel by all three, as well as by harbor ferry. A ticket costs DM 2.30 (DM 3.60 for travel outside the inner city) and can be bought at the automatic machines found in all stations and most bus stops. A day's ticket permitting unlimited travel in the entire Hamburg urban area from 9 AM costs DM 6.90 for one adult and up to three children (DM 12.20 for a group of up to four adults and three children); a three-day ticket costs DM 19. The all-night buses (Nos. 600–640) tour the downtown area, leaving the Rathausmarkt and the Hauptbahnhof every hour. Information can be obtained from the **Hamburg Passenger Transport Board** (HHV); Steinstrasse 1, tel. 040/322911.

By Taxi Taxi meters start at DM 3.60, and the fare is DM 2.20 per kilometer (or about DM 3.16 per mile). To order a taxi, phone 040/441011, 040/686868, or 040/611061.

Important Addresses and Numbers

Tourist Information The principal Hamburg tourist office is at Bieberhaus, Hachmannplatz, next to the Hauptbahnhof (tel. 040/300–51244; open weekdays 7:30–6, Saturday 8–3). There's also a tourist information center inside the Hauptbahnhof itself (tel. 040/300–51230, open daily 7 AM–11 PM) and in the arrivals hall of Hamburg Airport (tel. 040/300–51240 open daily from 8 AM to 11 PM). Other tourist offices can be found in the Hanse-Viertel shopping arcade (tel. 040/300–51220; open weekdays 10–6:30, Sat. 10–3, Sun. 11–3) and at the Landungsbrücken (tel. 040/300–51200; open Mar.–Oct., daily 9–6; Nov.–Feb., daily 10–5). All centers will reserve hotel accommodations.

Consulates U.S. (Alsterufer 28, tel. 040/411710). U.K. (Harvestehuder Weg 8a, tel. 040/446071).

Emergencies **Police** (tel. 110). **Doctor** (tel. 040/228022). **Dentist** (tel. 11500). **Ambulance** (tel. 112). **Pharmacy Information** (tel. 040/228022).

Books in English Try **Frensche** (Spitalerstr. 26e, tel. 040/327585) for a selection of English-language books.

Travel Agencies **American Express** (Rathausmarkt 5, tel. 040/33114). **Thomas Cook** (Ballindamm 39, tel. 040/309–08120).

Guided Tours

Orientation Tours Bus tours of the city, with an English-speaking guide, leave from Kirchenallee (across from the Hotel Europäischer Hof and in front of the Hauptbahnhof) at regular intervals (six times daily during the summer). The two-hour tour costs DM 18 for adults, DM 9 for children. A 2½-hour tour, taking in more of the city, starts at 10 and 2 daily from the same place. The fare is DM 22 for adults, DM 11 for children. From late March to early November, a night tour of the city sets off from the Kirchenallee at 8 and returns shortly after midnight (Tues.–Sat.). The fare of DM 80 includes a drink at each stop.

Boat Tours Hamburg is a city dominated by water, and one of the best ways of getting a feel of the place is by taking one of the many boat trips offered. Tours of the harbor leave at regular intervals throughout the year from piers (Landungsbrucken) 1–7. The one-hour tour costs DM 12 (DM 6 for children). A special harbor tour with English-speaking guide leaves pier 1 at 11:15 daily from March 1 to October 30 (cost: DM 14 for adults, DM 7 for children). The Störtebeker line has a special party boat where you can wine, dine (a six-course banquet), and dance. The boat casts off at pier 6 every evening at 8. The all-inclusive cost of the cruise is DM 99, and reservations can be made by calling 040/2202552.

Cruises of the Binnenalster and Aussenalster leave from the Jungfernstieg every half hour between 10 and 6, April–October. The fare is DM 10 for adults, DM 5 for children. A tour including canals leaves three times daily (DM 17 and DM 8.50, respectively). For information, tel. 040/341141.

Excursions Bus tours of the surrounding countryside are offered by **Jasper-Reisebüro** (Colonnaden 72, tel. 040/343751).

Exploring Hamburg

The comparison that Germans like to draw between Hamburg and Venice is—like all such comparisons with the *Serenissima*—somewhat exaggerated. Nevertheless, Hamburg is, like Venice, a city on water: the great river Elbe, which flows into the North Sea; the small river Alster, which has been dammed to form two lakes, the Binnenalster and Aussenalster; and many canals. Once a leading member of the Hanseatic League of cities, which dominated trade on the North Sea and the Baltic during the Middle Ages, Hamburg is still a major port, with 33 individual docks and 500 berths for oceangoing vessels.

Apart from its aquatic aspects, the most striking thing about Hamburg is its contradictions. Within the remaining traces of its old city walls, Hamburg combines the seamiest, steamiest streets of dockland Europe with the sleekest avenues to be found anywhere between Biarritz and Stockholm. During World War II and afterward, Hamburg was wrecked from without and within—by fire, then by Allied bombing raids, and finally by philistine town planners, who tore down some of the remaining old buildings to make way for modernistic glass-and-steel boxes. The result is a city that is, in parts, ugly, but still a fascinating mixture of old and new.

It is also a city in which escaping the urban bustle is relatively easy, since it contains more than 800 kilometers (500 miles) of riverside and country paths within its boundaries. The following itinerary includes a few detours, some by boat, which will enhance your enjoyment of Hamburg.

Numbers in the margin correspond to points of interest on the Hamburg map.

❶ Hamburg's main train station, the **Hauptbahnhof,** is not only the start of the city tour but very much part of it. It's not often you are tempted to linger at a train station, but this is an exception. Originally built in 1906 and modernized since, it has a remarkable spaciousness and sweep, accentuated by a 148-meter-wide (160-yard-wide) glazed roof, the largest unsupported roof in Germany. Gather city travel guides and maps from the city tourist office here and ride one stop on the S-Bahn (suburban railroad) to the Dammtor station. Compare this Art Nouveau–style building with the one you've just left. You'll find splendid examples of Germany's version of Art Nouveau, the *Jugendstil*, throughout your tour of Hamburg.

The Dammtor station brings you out near Theodor-Heuss-Platz in **Wallringpark,** a stretch of parkland that runs for more than a kilometer alongside what was once the western defense wall of the city. The first two sections of the park—the **Alter Botanischer Garten** (Old Botanical Garden) and the **Planten un Blomen**—have lots to attract the attention of gardeners and flower lovers. In summer, the evening sky over the Planten un Blomen lake is lighted up by the colored waters of its fountain, dancing what the locals romantically call a "water ballet."

The section of the park known as **Grosse Wallanlagen**—to the southwest—is interrupted abruptly by the northern edge of the **St. Pauli** district and its most famous—or infamous—thoroughfare, the **Reeperbahn** (*see* Nightlife, *below*). Unlike other business sections of Hamburg, this industrious quarter works around the clock; although it may seem quiet as you stroll down its tawdry length in broad daylight, any tourist who stops at one of its bars will discover that many of the girls who work this strip are on a day shift.

If it's a Sunday morning, join the late revelers and the early joggers and dog-walkers for breakfast at the **Fischmarkt** (fish market), down at the Elbe riverside between the St. Pauli Landungsbrücken (the piers where the excursion boats tie up) and Grosse Elbstrasse. The citizens of Hamburg like to breakfast on pickled herring, but if that's not to your taste, there's much more than fish for sale, and the nearby bars are already open. *The fish market is held every Sun., 5 AM–10 AM, starting at 7 AM in winter.*

The nearby **Landungsbrücken** is the start of the many boat trips of the harbor that are offered throughout the year (*see* Guided Tours, *above*).

Along the north bank of the Elbe is one of the finest walks Hamburg has to offer. The walk is a long one, about 13 kilometers (8 miles) from the St. Pauli Landungsbrücken to the attractive waterside area of **Blankenese,** and that's only three-quarters of the route. But there are S-Bahn stations and bus stops along the way, to give you a speedy return to the downtown area. Do, however, try to reach Blankenese, even if you have to catch an S-Bahn train from downtown to Blankenese station and walk down to the riverbank from there.

Blankenese is another of Hamburg's surprises—a city suburb that has the character of a fishing village. If you've walked all the way from St. Pauli, you may not be able to face the 58 flights of stairs (nearly 5,000 individual steps) that crisscross through Blankenese between its heights and the river. But by all means attempt an exploratory prowl through some of the tiny lanes, lined with the retirement retreats of Hamburg's sea captains and the cottages of the fishermen who once toiled here.

A ferry connects Blankenese with Hamburg's St. Pauli, although the S-Bahn ride back to the city is much quicker. Back at St. Pauli, resume your tour at the riverside and head back toward the downtown area through Elb Park, crossing Helgolander Allee to the **Bismarckdenkmal** (Bismarck Memorial)—an imposing statue of the Prussian "Iron Chancellor," the guiding spirit of the 19th-century unification of Germany. Cross the square ahead of you and make for the **Museum für Hamburgische Geschichte** at Holstenwall 24. This fascinating display of Hamburg's history has a department (the His-

Hamburg

Alter Botanischer Garten, **2**

Bismarckdenkmal, **8**

Blankenese, **7**

Fischmarkt, **5**

Hauptbahnhof, **1**

Jungfernstieg, **13**

Kunsthalle, **14**

Landungsbrücken, **6**

Michaeliskirche, **10**

Museum für Hamburgische Geschichte, **9**

Planten un Blomen, **3**

Rathaus, **12**

Rathausmarkt, **11**

Reeperbahn, **4**

toric Emigration Office) of great interest to American descendants of German immigrants, who can arrange to have called up from the microfilm files information about any ancestors who set out for the New World from Hamburg. *Holstenwall 24, tel. 040/35042360. Admission: DM 6 adults, DM 1 children. Open Tues.–Sun. 10–5.*

Cross Holstenwall to Peterstrasse, where you'll find a group of finely restored, 18th-century half-timbered houses. Turn right down Neanderstrasse and cross Ost-West-Strasse to Hamburg's principal ⑩ Protestant church, the **Michaeliskirche** (St. Michael's Church), the finest Baroque church in northern Germany. Twice in its history, this well-loved 17th-century church has given the people of Hamburg protection—during the Thirty Years' War and again in World War II. From its 132-meter (440-foot) tower, there is a magnificent view of the city and the Elbe, and twice a day the watchman blows a trumpet solo from up there. *Cost for the elevator up to the tower: DM 3 adults, DM 1.50 children.*

From the Michaeliskirche, return to Ost-West-Strasse, turn right, then left down Brunnenstrasse to Wexstrasse. Follow Wexstrasse to Grosse Bleichen, cross the Bleichenbrücke and Adolphsbrücke (Bleichen and Adolph bridges), over two of Hamburg's canals (known as the Fleete), turn left into Alter-wall, and you'll come to ⑪ the **Rathausmarkt,** the town hall square. The designers of the square deliberately set out to create a northern version of the Piazza San Marco in Venice and, to a certain extent, succeeded. The 100- ⑫ year-old **Rathaus** is built on 4,000 wooden piles sunk into the marshy ground beneath. It is the home not only of the city council but of the Hamburg state government, for Hamburg is one of Germany's federal, semiautonomous states. The sheer opulence of its interior is hard to beat. It has 647 rooms, 6 more than Buckingham Palace. Although visitors can tour only the state rooms, the tapestries, huge staircases, glittering chandeliers, coffered ceilings, and gilt-framed portraits convey forcefully the wealth of the city in the last century. *Marktplatz. Admission: DM 1. Guided tours in English Mon.–Thurs. every hour 10:15–3:15, Fri.–Sun. hourly 10:15–1:15.*

If you've had enough sightseeing by this time, you've ended up at the right place, for an arcade at the western edge of the Rathausmarkt signals the start of Europe's largest undercover shopping area, nearly a kilometer of airy arcades, cool in summer and warm in winter, bursting with color and life. Three hundred shops, from cheap souvenir stores to expensive fashion boutiques, are crammed into this consumer-age labyrinth. There are expensive restaurants and cozy cafés, and one of the rare opportunities in Germany (or anywhere) to eat lobster and sip good wine at a fast-food outlet. It's easy to get lost here, but all the arcades lead at some point to the wide, ⑬ seasidelike promenade, the **Jungfernstieg,** which borders Hamburg's two artificial lakes, the **Binnenalster** and the **Aussenalster.** Although called lakes, they are really dammed-up sections of the Alster River, which rises only 56 kilometers (35 miles) away in Schleswig Holstein. The river was originally dammed up at the beginning of the 13th century to form a millrace before it spilled into the Elbe. The original muddy dam wall is today the elegant Jungfernstieg promenade. From the Jungfernstieg, you can take a boat tour of the two Alster lakes and the canals beyond (*see* Guided Tours, *above*), passing some of Hamburg's most ostentatious homes, with their extensive grounds rolling down to the water's edge (the locals call it "Millionaires' Coast").

Hamburg has its share of millionaires, enriched by the city's thriving commerce and industry. But they, in turn, can claim to have enriched the artistic life of Hamburg. For example, it was a group of wealthy merchants who, in 1817, founded the Kunstverein, from which grew Hamburg's famous Kunsthalle collection. The **⑭ Kunsthalle** is well placed at the end of our Hamburg tour, next to the Hauptbahnhof, and its collection of paintings is one of Germany's finest. You'll find works by practically all the great northern European masters from the 14th to the 20th century, as well as by such painters as Goya, Tiepolo, and Canaletto. For many visitors, the highlight of the entire collection is the *Grabow Altarpiece*, painted in 1379 by an artist known only as Master Bertram; the central scene is the Crucifixion, but numerous side panels depict the story of man from Genesis to the Nativity. *1 Glockengiesserwall, tel. 040/ 24862612. Admission: DM 6 adults, DM 1 children. Open Tues.– Sun. 10–6, Thurs. 10–9.*

Dining

For details and price-category definitions, *see* Dining in Staying in Germany, *above.*

Expensive **La Mer.** Located in the elegant Hotel Prem, on the southwest bank of the Aussenalster, La Mer offers a fine and varied menu. Try the marinated inoki mushrooms with imperial oysters and salmon roe or the spring venison with elderberry sauce. *An der Alster 9, tel. 040/ 245454. Reservations advised. AE, DC, MC, V. Closed Sat. and Sun. lunch.*

Landhaus Dill. Proprietor Volkmar Preis has moved his restaurant up the road into a fine fin de siècle building with views of the Elbe. The restaurant has the same air of cool elegance, with crisp linen and glistening tiled floors, and the high standard of cuisine hasn't changed, either. The lobster salad is still prepared at your table; the rack of lamb comes hot from the kitchen with an aromatic thyme sauce. If anything, the dessert section of the menu has improved— try the rhubarb compote with vanilla cream, a dream of a dish. *Elbchaussee 94, tel. 040/3905077. Reservations advised. Jacket and tie advised. AE, DC, MC, V.*

Landhaus Scherrer. A popular, country house-style restaurant located in the city's Altona district, Landhaus Scherrer specializes in fine regional cuisine and prides itself on its extensive wine list. It offers a separate bistro for lunches. *Elbchaussee 130, tel. 040/880– 1325. Reservations required. AE, DC, MC. Closed Sun.*

L'Auberge Française. Generally regarded as Hamburg's most authentic French restaurant, L'Auberge Française specializes in traditional seafood dishes and fine wines. *Rutschbahn 34, tel. 040/410– 2532. Reservations required. AE, DC, MC, V. Closed Sun.*

★ **Peter Lembcke.** This formal, traditional restaurant located just north of the train station offers the best of German cuisine. There's no better place to eat eel soup or the traditional Hamburg dish *Labskaus*. Steaks are another specialty. *Holzdamm 49, tel. 040/ 243290. Reservations advised. AE, DC, MC, V. Closed Sat. lunch, Sun., and public holidays.*

Moderate **Ahrberg.** Located on the river in Blankenese, the Ahrberg has a
★ pleasant terrace for summer dining, and, for a warm retreat on cooler days, a cozy, wood-paneled dining room. The menu features a range of traditional German dishes and seafood specialties—often served together. Try the shrimp and potato soup and fresh carp in season. *Strandweg 33, tel. 040/860438. Reservations advised. AE, DC, MC. Closed Sun.*

Fischerhaus. Hamburg's famous fish market is right outside the door of this traditional old restaurant, which accounts for the variety and quality of fish dishes on its menu. Meat-eaters are also catered to, and the soups are legendary (the fish soup is understandably the pride of the house). *St. Pauli Fischmarkt 14, tel. 040/314053. No reservations. AE, DC, MC, V.*

Noblesse. The Ramada Renaissance Hotel's stylish restaurant has won awards for the standard of its cuisine and service. The extensive menu is a combination of German traditional and nouvelle cuisine; the wine list embraces the best labels from Germany, France, and Italy. The buffet is a particularly good value. *Grosse Bleichen, tel. 040/349180. Reservations advised. Jacket and tie required. AE, DC, MC, V.*

Inexpensive **Atnali.** This is one of Hamburg's oldest and most popular Turkish restaurants. It is friendly and comfortable with a very reasonable and extensive menu. It stays open late—until 1 AM. *Rutschbahn 11, tel. 040/410–3810. Reservations advised. AE, DC, MC, V.*

Avocado. This popular, modern restaurant offers excellent value and an imaginative menu. Try the salmon in Chablis. *Kanalstr. 9, tel. 040/220–4599. Reservations required. No credit cards. Dinner only. Closed Sun., Mon.*

Lodging

For details and price-category definitions, *see* Lodging in Staying in Germany, *above.*

Very Expensive **Atlantic Hotel Kempinski Hamburg.** Since it first opened in 1909, the luxuriously appointed Atlantic, close by the Aussenalster and near the Hauptbahnhof, has been a focal point of the Hamburg social scene. The Atlantic Restaurant, stunning with its bird's-eye maple Empire-style decor and inlaid marble floor, serves haute cuisine, while the Atlantic Mühle serves traditional German fare in a rustic setting. *An der Alster 72, tel. 040/28880, fax 040/247129. 243 rooms and 13 suites. Facilities: 2 restaurants, bar, indoor pool, sauna, solarium, hairdresser, massage, Lufthansa check-in desk, garage. AE, DC, MC, V.*

Hamburg Marriott. The U.S. Marriott group chose downtown Hamburg as the site of its first hotel in Germany. It opened in 1988 amid the city's shopping arcades and smart restaurants. Among its many refinements are two floors reserved for nonsmokers. *ABC-Str. 52, Kleiner Gänsemarkt, tel. 040/35050, fax 040/35051777. 276 rooms with bath. Facilities: restaurant, pool, sauna, solarium, beauty salon, fitness center, sea grill, piano lounge, café. AE, DC, MC, V.*

★ **Vier Jahreszeiten.** This hotel, with its antique-style rooms, impeccable service, and excellent food, is rated among the world's best. It is continually being refurbished to maintain an impeccable standard, but you won't notice a blip in the hotel's smooth routine. Centrally located, it offers scenic views of the Binnenalster. *Neuer Jungfernstieg 9–14, tel. 040/34940, fax 040/3494602. 148 rooms and 23 apartments, all with bath. Facilities: 2 restaurants, 2 bars, nightclub, pâtisserie, beauty salon. AE, DC, MC, V.*

Expensive **Aussen Alster.** Only seven minutes from the train station and a few steps from the Alster Lake, the Aussen Alster is a small, tranquil hotel occupying a gracious 19th-century house. The cool, modern decor is given warmth by a log-fed fireplace and friendly bar. *Schmilinskystr. 11, tel. 040/241557, fax 040/2803231. 27 rooms with bath or shower. Facilities: restaurant, bar, sauna, solarium, bike rental. AE, DC, MC, V.*

Moderate– Expensive **Hotel Graf Moltke.** The sturdy old Graf Moltke, which rules majestically over central Steindamm street (a short walk from the main railway station), was completely renovated in 1991. Some rooms were enlarged and all were equipped with soundproofing. Special weekend deals are offered for families. *Steindamm 1, tel. 040/2801154, fax 040/2802562. 97 rooms with bath or shower. Facilities: restaurant, bar, boutiques. AE, DC, MC, V.*

Moderate **Baseler Hof.** Centrally located near the inner lake and the State Opera House, this hotel offers friendly and efficient service and neatly furnished rooms. There is no charge for children under 10 sharing a room with parents. *Esplanade 11, tel. 040/359060, fax 040/35906918. 140 rooms with bath. Facilities: restaurant, café. AE, DC, MC, V.*

Haus Emde. If you're touring northern Germany by car, this small, friendly hotel is ideally located as a base for exploring Hamburg; it's located just 5 minutes from the autobahn A–7 Bahrenfeld exit. By rail it can be reached from the S-I S-Bahn line Hamburg-Othmarschen stop. Although it's not central, the hotel offers suburban peace and quiet in a charming city mansion set in its own grounds. Rooms were recently renovated to a high level of comfort. *Lüdemannstr. 1, tel. 040/893626, fax 040/8100689. 10 rooms, 2 suites, with bath or shower. Facilities: parking. AE, DC, MC, V.*

Wedina. Fully renovated and refurbished in 1992, the Wedina now offers a very high standard of accommodation in two attractive city mansions on a quiet street running down to the Alster. It has a bar, an outdoor pool in the attractive garden, and a sauna. *Gurlittstr. 23, tel. 040/243011, fax 040/2803894. 23 rooms with bath or shower. Facilities: sauna, outdoor pool. AE, DC, MC, V. Closed Dec. 18–Jan. 1.*

Inexpensive **Alameda.** The Alameda offers guests good, basic accommodations. All rooms feature TV, radio, and minibar. *Colonnaden 45, tel. 040/344000, fax 040/343439. 15 rooms with shower. AE, DC, MC, V.*

Metro Merkur Minotel. Centrally located near Hamburg's main train station, the recently renovated Metro Merkur is a convenient, functional hotel. *Bremer Reihe 12–14, tel. 040/247266, fax 040/240284. 100 rooms, most with bath. AE, DC, MC, V.*

Nightlife

Few visitors can resist taking a look at the **Reeperbahn,** if only by day. At night, however, from 10 onward, the place really shakes itself into life, and *everything* is for sale. Among the Reeperbahn's even rougher side streets, the most notorious is the Grosse Freiheit, which means "Great Freedom." A stroll through this small alley, where the attractions are on display behind plate glass, will either tempt you to stay or send you straight back to your hotel. Three of the leading clubs on the Grosse Freiheit are the **Colibri** (No. 34, tel. 040/313233), the **Safari** (No. 24, tel. 040/315400), and the **Nightlife-Club** (No. 32, tel. 040/3174996).

The Reeperbahn area is not just a red-light district, however. Side streets are rapidly filling up with a mixture of yuppie bars, restaurants, and theaters that complement the seamen's bars and sex shops. The **Hans-Albers-Platz** is a center of this revival, where the stylish bar La Paloma provides contrast to the Hans-Albers-Ecke, an old sailors' bar. The **Theater Schmidt** (Spielbudenplatz 24, tel. 040/314804) offers variety shows most evenings to a packed house.

A few tips for visiting the Reeperbahn: Avoid going alone; demand a price list whenever you drink (legally, it has to be on display), and pay as soon as you're served; if you have trouble, threaten to call the cops. If that doesn't work—call the cops.

The Rhine

None of Europe's many rivers is so redolent of history and legend as the Rhine. For the Romans, who established forts and colonies along its western banks, the Rhine was the frontier between civilization and the barbaric German tribes. Roman artifacts can be seen in museums throughout the region. The Romans also introduced viticulture—a legacy that survives in the countless vineyards along the riverbanks—and later, Christianity. Throughout the Middle Ages, the river's importance as a trade artery made it the focus of sharp, often violent, conflict between princes, noblemen, and archbishops. Many of the picturesque castles that crown its banks were the homes of robber barons who held up passing ships and barges and exacted heavy tolls to finance even grander fortifications.

For poets and composers, the Rhine—or *"Vater* (Father) *Rhein,"* as the Germans call it—has been an endless source of inspiration. As legend has it, the Lorelei, a treacherous, craggy rock, was home to a beautiful and bewitching maiden who lured sailors to a watery grave. Wagner based four of his epic operas on the lives of the medieval Nibelungs, said to have inhabited the rocky banks. To travel the Rhine by boat, especially in autumn, when the rising mists enshroud the castles high above, is to understand the place the river occupies in the German imagination.

The Rhine does not belong to Germany alone, but it is in Germany—especially the stretch between Mainz and Köln (Cologne) known as the Middle Rhine—that the riverside scenery is most spectacular. This is the "typical" Rhine: a land of steep and thickly wooded hills, terraced vineyards, tiny villages hugging the banks, and a succession of brooding castles.

Getting Around

By Train One of the best ways to visit the Rhineland in very limited time is to take the scenic train journey from Mainz to Köln along the western banks of the river. The views are spectacular, and the entire trip takes less than two hours. Choose an InterCity train for its wide viewing windows. If you're traveling north toward Köln, make sure you get a window seat on the right-hand side. Better still, sit in the restaurant car where you can enjoy a meal or beverage while you watch the scenery unfold. Contact Deutsche Bundesbahn (German Railways) in Frankfurt, Reisedienst, Friedrich-Ebert-Anlage 43, tel. 069/19419, or get details at any big train station travel office.

By Boat Passenger ships traveling up and down the Rhine and its tributaries offer a pleasant and relaxing way to see the region. **KD River Cruises of Europe** (2500 Westchester Ave., Purchase, NY 10577, tel. 914/696–3600; 323 Geary, San Francisco, CA 94102, tel. 415/392–8817) operates a fleet of ships that travel daily between Düsseldorf and Frankfurt, from Easter to late October. They also offer cruises along the entire length of the Rhine. Passengers have a choice of buying an excursion ticket or a ticket to a single destination. This company also offers trips up the Mosel as far as Trier. From March through November, the **Hebel-Line** (tel. 06742/2420) in Boppard offers a scenic cruise of the Lorelei Valley; night cruises feature music and dancing. For information about Neckar River excursions, contact **Neckar Personen Schiffahrt** in Stuttgart, tel. 0711/541073 or 0711/541074.

The Rhine

TO KÖLN
Bonn
Bad Godesberg
Königswinter
Remagen
Siebengebirge
Sieg
255
257
9
Rhine
42
Lahn
Koblenz
Bad Ems
N
A48/E44
Boppard
Burg Maus
St. Goarshausen
St. Goar
Lorelei
Oberwesel
Kaub
Wiesbaden
Bacharach
42
327
50
Rüdesheim
Mainz
Moselle
41
A63
Bad
Kreuznach
Trier
A1
0   20 miles
0   30 km

By Car If you prefer to drive, the Rhineland offers a comprehensive high-way network that takes in some of the region's most spectacular scenery. Roads crisscross the entire province, from the historic vineyards of the Mosel Valley to the beautiful castle and wine-growing country of the Rhine's west bank. For information about routes available, contact the **German Automobile Club** (AVD; Lyonerstrasse 16, 60528 Frankfurt-am-Main, tel. 069/66060).

By Bicycle Tourist offices in all the larger towns will provide information and route maps. German Railways offers bikes for hire at numerous stations. For information, call 069/19419 or ask for the "Bikes for Rent" (*"Fahrrad am Bahnhof"*) brochure at any station.

Tourist Information

For general information on the region, contact the Fremdenverkehrsverband Rheinland-Pfalz, Löhrstrasse 103, tel. 0261/31079.

Bacharach (Fremdenverkehrsamt, Oberstrasse 1, tel. 06743/2968).
Boppard (Verkehrsamt, Karmeliterstrasse 2, tel. 06742/10319).
Koblenz (Fremdenverkehrsamt, Hauptbahnhof, tel. 0261/31304).
Köln (Verkehrsamt, Unter Fettenhennen 19, tel. 0221/221–3345).
Königswinter (Verkehrsamt, Drachenfelsstrasse 7, tel. 02223/889325).
Mainz (Verkehrsverein, Bahnhofstrasse 15, tel. 06131/286210).
Rüdesheim (Verkehrsamt, Rheinstrasse 16, tel. 06722/2962).

Guided Tours

In addition to a number of special-interest cruises, **KD River Cruises of Europe** operates a series of guided excursions covering the towns along its routes (*see* Getting Around, *above*). The British-run **European Yacht Cruises Ltd.** conducts a variety of Rhine cruises, some with optional shore excursions (tel. in London 081/462–8843). The tourist offices in Mainz, Köln, and Koblenz also offer tours (in English) of their respective cities.

Exploring the Rhine

Köln **Köln** (Cologne) is the largest city on the Rhine, marking the northernmost point of the river's scenic stretch before it becomes a truly industrial waterway through the Ruhr Valley. It's a very old city—first settled by the Romans in 38 BC—and today is a vibrant, zestful Rhineland center, with a very active cultural life and a business and commercial infrastructure that supports trade fairs year-round. It derives its name from the Latin Colonia Claudia Ara Agrippinensium, the title given to it by the Roman emperor Claudius in honor of his wife, Julia Agrippina, who was born there. The Franks and Merovingians followed the Romans before Charlemagne restored the city's fortunes in the 9th century, appointing its first archbishop and ensuring its ecclesiastical prominence for centuries.

By the Middle Ages, Köln was the largest city north of the Alps, and, as a member of the powerful Hanseatic League, it was more important commercially than either London or Paris. Ninety percent of the city was destroyed in World War II, and in the rush to rebuild it many mistakes were made. But although today's Köln lacks the aesthetic unity of many other rebuilt German cities, the heart of the Altstadt (Old Town), with its streets that follow the line of the medieval city walls, has great charm, and at night it throbs with life.

Towering over the old town is the extraordinary Gothic cathedral, the **Kölner Dom**, dedicated to Sts. Peter and Mary. It's comparable to the best French cathedrals; a visit to it may prove a highlight of your trip to Germany. What you'll see is one of the purest expressions of the Gothic spirit in Europe. Spend some time admiring the outside of the building (you can walk almost all the way around it). Notice that there are practically no major horizontal lines—all the accents of the building are vertical. It may come as a disappointment to learn that the cathedral, begun in 1248, was not completed until 1880. Console yourself with the knowledge that it was still built to original plans. At 157 meters (515 feet) high, the two west towers of the cathedral were by far the tallest structures in the world when they were finished (they are still the tallest in a church). The length of the building is 143 meters (470 feet); the width of the nave is 45 meters (147 feet); and the highest part of the interior is 42½ meters (140 feet).

The cathedral was built to house what were believed to be the relics of the Magi, the three kings or wise men who paid homage to the infant Jesus. Today the relics are kept just behind the altar, in the same enormous gold-and-silver **reliquary** in which they were originally displayed. The other great treasure of the cathedral is the **Gero Cross**, a monumental oak crucifixion dating from 971. Impressive for its simple grace, it's in the last chapel on the left as you face the altar.

Other highlights to admire are the stained-glass windows, some of which date from the 13th century; the 15th-century altar painting;

and the early 14th-century high altar with its surrounding arcades of glistening white figures and its intricate choir screens. The choir stalls, carved from oak around 1310, are the largest in Germany, seating 104 people. There are more treasures to be seen in the **Dom Schatzkammer,** the cathedral treasury, including the silver shrine of Archbishop Engelbert, who was stabbed to death in 1225. *Admission: DM 3 adults, DM 1.50 children. Open Mon.–Sat. 9–5, Sun. 1–5.*

Outside again, you have the choice of either more culture or commerce. Köln's **shopping district** begins at nearby **Wallrafplatz.** Grouped around the cathedral is a collection of superb museums. If your priority is painting, try the ultramodern **Wallraf-Richartz-Museum** and **Museum Ludwig** complex. Together, they form the largest art collection in the Rhineland. The Wallraf-Richartz-Museum contains pictures spanning the years 1300 to 1900, with Dutch and Flemish schools particularly well represented (Rubens, who spent his youth in Köln, has a place of honor). The Museum Ludwig is devoted exclusively to 20th-century art; its Picasso collection is outstanding. *Bischofsgartenstr. 1. Admission to both museums: DM 8 adults, DM 4 children. Open Tues.–Fri. 10–6, weekends 11–6.*

Opposite the cathedral is the **Römisch-Germanisches Museum,** built from 1970 to 1974 around the famous Dionysus mosaic that was uncovered at the site during the construction of an air-raid shelter in 1941. The huge mosaic, more than 91½ meters (100 yards) square, once covered the dining-room floor of a wealthy Roman trader's villa. Its millions of tiny earthenware and glass tiles depict some of the adventures of Dionysius, the Greek god of wine and, to the Romans, the object of a widespread and sinister religious cult. The pillared 1st-century tomb of Lucius Publicius, a prominent Roman officer, some stone Roman coffins, and a series of memorial tablets are among the museum's other exhibits. *Roncallipl. 4. Admission: DM 5 adults, DM 2.50 children. Open Tues.–Fri. 10–4, weekends 11–4.*

Now head south to the nearby **Alter Markt** and its **Altes Rathaus,** the oldest town hall in Germany (if you don't count the fact that the building was entirely rebuilt after the war). The square has a handsome assembly of buildings—the oldest dating from 1135—in a range of styles. There was a seat of local government here in Roman times, and directly below the current Rathaus are the remains of the Roman city governor's headquarters, the Praetorium. Go inside to see the 14th-century **Hansa Saal,** whose tall Gothic windows and barrel-vaulted wood ceiling are potent expressions of medieval civic pride. The figures of the prophets, standing on pedestals at one end, are all from the early 15th century. Ranging along the south wall are nine additional statues, the so-called *Nine Good Heroes,* carved in 1360. Charlemagne and King Arthur are among them.

Now head across Unter Käster toward the river and one of the most outstanding of Köln's 12 Romanesque churches, the **Gross St. Martin.** Its massive 13th-century tower, with distinctive corner turrets and an imposing central spire, is another landmark of Köln. Gross St. Martin is the parish church of Köln's colorful old city, the **Martinsviertel,** an attractive combination of reconstructed, high-gabled medieval buildings, winding alleys, and tastefully designed modern apartments and business quarters. Head here at night— the place comes to vibrant life at sunset.

To complete your daytime Köln tour, however, leave the Martinsviertel along Martinstrasse and turn right into Gürzenichstrasse, passing the crenellated Gothic-style Gürzenich civic reception/concert hall. Take a left turn into Hohestrasse and another right turn into Cäcilienstrasse. At No. 29, you'll find the 12th-century St. Cäcilien church, and within its cool, well-lit interior one of the world's finest museums of medieval Christian art, the **Schnütgen Museum.** The museum is named after the cathedral capitular Alexander Schnütgen, who bequeathed his collection of religious art to the city in 1906. Enlarged considerably over the years, the collection was moved to St. Cäcilien in 1956. Although the main emphasis of the museum falls on early and medieval sacred art, the collection also covers the Renaissance and Baroque periods. *Cäcilienstr. 29, tel. 0221/2212310. Admission: DM 5 adults, DM 2.50 children. Open Tues.–Fri. 10–6, weekends 11–6. Guided tours on Sun. at 11.*

Around the corner, on Leonhard-Tietz-Strasse, is **St. Peter's Church,** where the painter Peter Paul Rubens was christened. There's a fine Rubens painting in the altar recess, joined recently by a modern triptych by the British painter Francis Bacon.

A few steps away is the expansive **Neumarkt** square, at whose western end is one of Köln's finest Romanesque basilicas, **St. Aposteln.** The Neumarkt was an early trading center; the church was built in the 11th century amid the hustle and bustle of a daily market. Today, its weighty east front, surmounted by two graceful hexagonal towers and the more traditional four-sided west steeple, dominates a very different scene, a green city park lined with elegant shops and offices.

South of Köln lies Germany's former capital, **Bonn,** preparing now to hand most of its legislative and administrative functions over to Berlin. **Bad Godesberg,** just south of Bonn, is the leafy community where many diplomats live and work, and across the river is **Königswinter,** site of one of the most visited castles on the Rhine. The ruins of **Drachenfels** crown the highest hill in the **Siebengebirge** (Seven Hills) area commanding a spectacular view of the river. The castle was built during the 12th century by the archbishop of Köln. Its name commemorates a dragon said to have lived in a nearby cave. As legend has it, the dragon was slain by Siegfried, the Niebelunglied hero.

Continuing south along the west bank, you come to the ancient, half-timbered town of **Remagen.** Originally a Roman village built near the source of a mineral spring, where the Ahr River meets the Rhine, Remagen was an important bridgehead during World War II. Here, American forces were able to capture the bridge and speed their advance into Germany. The Ahr Valley, lined with picturesque, terraced vineyards, produces some of Germany's finest red wines.

Koblenz   In the heart of the Middle Rhine region, at the confluence of the Rhine and Moselle rivers, lies the city of **Koblenz,** the area's cultural and administrative center and the meeting place of the two great wine-producing districts. It is also one of the most important traffic points along the Rhine. Here you are ideally placed to sample and compare the light, fruity Moselle wines and the headier Rhine varieties. The city's **Weindorf** area, just south of the **Pfaffendorfer Bridge,** has a wide selection of taverns, where you can try the wines in traditional Römer glasses, with their symbolic amber and green bowls.

The city of Koblenz began as a Roman camp—Confluentes—more than 2,000 years ago. The vaults beneath **St. Florin Church** contain an interesting assortment of Roman remains. A good place to begin your tour of Koblenz is the **Deutches Eck,** or "Corner of Germany," the tip of the sharp peninsula separating the Rhine and Moselle rivers. In the 12th century, the Knights of the Teutonic Order established their center here. The towering equestrian statue of Kaiser Wilhelm that once stood here was destroyed by Allied bombs during World War II; last year's plan to install a replica was met with controversy, because opponents feel that the statue is more a celebration of Prussian military might than of German unity. On summer evenings, concerts are held in the nearby **Blumenhof Garden.** Most of the city's historic churches are also within walking distance of the Deutsches Eck. The **Liebfrauenkirche** (Church of Our Lady), completed in the 13th century, incorporates Romanesque, late Gothic, and Baroque elements. **St. Florin,** a Romanesque church built around 1100, was remodeled in the Gothic style in the 14th century. Gothic windows and a vaulted ceiling were added in the 17th century. The city's most important church, **St. Kastor,** also combines Romanesque and Gothic elements and features some unusual altar tombs and rare Gothic wall paintings.

Although the city lost 85% of its buildings during wartime air raids, some of the old buildings survived and others have been built in complementary styles. Much of the **Old Town** of Koblenz is now a pedestrian district, and an attractive area for a leisurely stroll. Many of the ancient cellars beneath the houses have been rediscovered and now serve as wine bars and jazz clubs.

Koblenz also offers an assortment of castles and palaces. The former residence of the archbishop of Trier now houses the city administrative offices. The original 18th-century building was demolished during the war; today only the interior staircase remains. Across the river, on the Rhine's east bank, towers the city's most spectacular castle, the **Ehrenbreitstein.** The fortifications of this vast structure date to the 1100s, although the bulk of it was built much later, in the 16th and 17th centuries. To reach the fortress, take the cable car (*Sesselbahn*) or, if you're in shape, try walking up. The view alone is worth the trip. The fortress contains an interesting museum, the **Landesmuseum,** with exhibits tracing the industrial development of the Rhine Valley, including a reconstructed 19thcentury tobacco factory and a pewter works. *Admission free. Open Mar.–Nov., Tues.–Sun. 9–12:30 and 1–5.*

Koblenz also has two noteworthy art galleries. The **Ludwig Museum**—opened in 1992—presents rotating exhibitions of contemporary art, much of it from the enormous collection of Koblenz-born tycoon Peter Ludwig, Germany's top collector (also responsible for the Museum Ludwig in Köln). The setting is spectacular—converted rooms of the historic Deutschherrenhaus on the Danziger Freiheit square. *Admission: DM 5 adults, children free. Open Tues.–Wed. and Fri.–Sat. 11–5; Thurs. 11–8; Sun. 11–6.*

The other gallery, the **Mittelrhein Museum,** features Rhenish art and artifacts from the Middle Ages to the present day. *15 Florinsmarkt. Admission: DM 5 adults, children free. Open Tues. and Thurs.–Sat. 11–5, Wed. 11–8, Sun. 11–6.*

Rhine Gorge Between the cities of Koblenz and Mainz, the Rhine flows through the 64-kilometer (40-mile) stretch known as the **Rhine Gorge.** It is here that the Rhine lives up to its legends and lore and where the river, in places, narrows to a width of 200 yards. Once it was full of treacherous whirlpools, sudden shallows, and stark rock outcroppings that menaced passing ships. Today, vineyards occupy every inch of available soil on the steep, terraced slopes. High above, ancient castles crown the rocky shelves.

South of Koblenz, at a wide, western bend in the river, lies the quiet old town of **Boppard,** once a bustling city of the Holy Roman Empire. Now the remains of its Roman fort and castle are used to house a museum of Roman artifacts and geological specimens. There are also several notable churches, including the **Carmelite Church,** with its fine Baroque altar, and the Romanesque Church of **St. Severus.** Boppard also offers a wonderful view across the Rhine to the ruined castles of **Liebenstein** and **Sterrenberg,** known as the "hostile brothers." As legend has it, the castles were built by two feuding brothers to protect their respective interests.

Continuing south from Boppard, you come to the little town of **St. Goar,** crowded against the steep gorge cliff and shadowed by the imposing ruin of **Rheinfels Castle.** A steep, narrow road takes you up to the castle—a fine spot for scenic river vistas. Rheinfels was built in the mid-13th century by Count Dieter von Katzenelnbogen (whose name means "cat's elbow"). The count's enormous success in collecting river tolls provoked the other river barons to join together and lay siege to his castle. What transpired is unclear, but through the years Rheinfels survived numerous sieges. It was finally destroyed by the French in 1797. During the 19th century, the ruins served as a source of inspiration for a host of Romantic poets and artists. It is now in the process of restoration, and a luxury hotel has been built on the site (*see* Dining and Lodging, *below*). *Admission: DM 4, children DM 2. Open Apr.–Oct., daily 9–5.*

On the east bank of the river, just across from the town of St. Goar, lies its sister village, **St. Goarshausen.** An hourly ferry service links the two. St. Goarshausen is dominated by **Burg Katz** (Cat Castle), a massive fortress built by a later Count von Katzenelnbogen. Tourists are not permitted inside, but the top of the cliff offers a lovely view of the famous Lorelei rock. About 3.2 kilometers (2 miles) north of St. Goarshausen is the **Burg Maus,** or Mouse Castle. Legend has it that an archbishop of Trier built the fortress to protect a strip of land he owned at the base of the cliff. The Count von Katzenelnbogen, annoyed at what he considered an intrusion into his territory, sent the archbishop a message explaining that his "Cat" (Burg Katz) was sufficient to protect the electoral "Mouse." Hence the nickname, Burg Maus.

Many tourists visit St. Goarshausen for its location—only a few kilometers from the legendary **Lorelei rock.** To get to Lorelei, follow the road marked with "Lorelei-Felsen" signs. Here the Rhine takes a sharp turn around a rocky, shrub-covered headland. This is the narrowest and shallowest part of the Middle Rhine, full of treacherous currents. According to legend, the beautiful maiden, Lore, sat on the rock here, combing her golden hair and singing a song so irresistible that passing sailors forgot the navigational hazards and were swept to their deaths.

Oberwesel, on the west bank, is a medieval wine town encircled by ancient walls and towers. Sixteen of the original 21 towers remain. Two churches deserve a visit: **St. Martin,** built in the 14th and 15th centuries, features a distinctive, brightly painted nave; the **Liebfrauen Kirche** (known as the "red church" because of its fiery facade) contains a magnificent choir screen, some fine sculpture, and an altarpiece depicting the magnanimous deeds of St. Nicholas.

One of the most photographed sites of the Middle Rhine region is the medieval village of **Kaub,** just south of Oberwesel on the east side of the river. Its unusual castles are well worth a visit. The **Pfalzgrafenstein,** situated on a tiny island in the middle of the Rhine, bristles with sharp-pointed towers and has the appearance of a small sailing ship. In the 14th century, the resident *Graf,* or count, was said to have strung chains across the Rhine in order to stop riverboats and collect his tolls. A special boat takes visitors to the island. *Ferry runs every ½-hour 9–1 and 2–5. Fare: DM 2.50 adults, DM 2 children; castle admission: DM 4 adults, DM 1.50 children.*

On a hillside above Kaub hovers another small castle: **Burg Gutenfels.** Built in the 13th century, Gutenfels was renovated completely at the end of the 18th century and is now an exquisite hotel (*see* Dining and Lodging, *below*).

The picturesque little village of **Bacharach,** encircled by 15th-century walls, is the best-preserved town of the Middle Rhine. It takes its name from the Roman "Baccaracum," or "altar of Bacchus"—a great stone that stood here until it was dynamited by river engineers during the last century. As its name implies, Bacharach is also a wine-trade center.

Farther south, on the Rhine's east bank and at the center of the Rheingau region, lies another famous wine town. According to legend, **Rüdesheim's** first vines were planted by Charlemagne. More recent vintages can be enjoyed in the many taverns lining **Drosselgasse,** a narrow, colorful street in the heart of town. Rüdesheim is a tourist magnet—about the most popular destination on the Rhine—so if you plan to stay overnight, be sure to reserve well in advance. Besides its half-timbered houses, hidden courtyards, and medieval castles, Rüdesheim offers an interesting museum, **Rheingau und Weinmuseum,** devoted to the history of wine making and local lore. *Rheinstr. 2. Admission: DM 3 adults, DM 2 children. Open mid-Mar.–Oct., daily 9–6.*

Mainz On the west side of the Rhine, at the mouth of the river Main, stands the city of **Mainz,** an old university town that's the capital of the Rhineland-Palatinate state. During Roman times, Mainz was a camp called Moguntiacum. Later it was the seat of the powerful archbishops of Mainz. But it is perhaps best known as the city in which, around 1450, printing pioneer Johannes Gutenberg established his first movable press. (He's such an important figure in Mainz that he has his own festival, Johannisnacht, celebrated in mid-June.) He is commemorated by a monument and square bearing his name and a museum containing his press and one of his Bibles. *Liebfrauenplatz 5. Admission free. Open Tues.–Sat. 10–6, Sun. and holidays 10–1. Closed Jan.*

Today, Mainz is a bustling, modern city of nearly 200,000 inhabitants. Although it was heavily bombed during World War II, many of the buildings have been faithfully reconstructed, and the city retains much of its historic charm. On **Gutenbergplatz** in the **Old Town** stand two fine Baroque churches, **Seminary Church** and **St. Ignatius.** The Gothic church of **St. Stephen** features six windows by the French artist Marc Chagall. The city's **Dom** (cathedral) is one of the finest Romanesque churches in Germany. The Old Town also boasts the country's oldest Renaissance fountain—the **Marktbrunnen**—and the **Dativius-Victor-Bogen Arch,** dating to Roman times. The **Römisch-Germanisches Museum,** in the **Kurfürstliches Schloss,** contains a notable collection of archaeological finds. *Rheinstr. Admission free. Open Tues.–Sun. 10–6.*

Dining and Lodging

When it comes to cuisine, the Rhineland offers a number of regional specialties. Be sure to sample the wide variety of sausages available, the goose and duck dishes from the Ahr Valley, and Rhineland *Sauerbraten*—accepted by many as the most succulent of pot roasts. Hotels in the Rhineland range from simple little inns to magnificent castle hotels. Many smaller towns have only small hotels and guest houses, some of which close during the winter months. During the peak summer season and in early autumn—wine festival time—accommodations are scarce, so it is advisable to reserve well in advance.

For details and price-category definitions, *see* Dining and Lodging in Staying in Germany, *above*.

Bacharach **Hotel-Restaurant Steeger Weinstube.** Hearty three-course meals for
Dining under DM 20 are offered at this friendly, family-run tavern/restaurant located just off the Rhine tourist route. The menu changes daily, but Rhineland-style sauerbraten, homemade potato dumplings, and in-season venison are often featured. *Blucherstr. 149, Bacharach-Steeg, tel. 06743/1240. Reservations not necessary. AE, MC. Closed Wed. Inexpensive.*

Lodging **Altkölnischer Hof.** This is a small but cozy rustic-style hotel. *Blücherstr. 2, tel. 06743/1339, fax 06743/2793. 18 rooms with bath. Facilities: restaurant, car park. AE, V. Closed Nov.–Easter. Moderate.*

Bonn **Halbedel's Gasthaus.** Rainer-Maria Halbedel's fine establishment in
Dining the Bad Godesberg diplomatic quarter is no ordinary German "Gasthof," but a restaurant of distinction. The decor is country-house style, with lead-paned windows and mahogany paneling and furniture. Herr Halbedel reigns supreme in the kitchen while his wife Irmgard runs the restaurant—a highly successful combination. *Rheinallee 47, tel. 0228/354253. Reservations advised. MC. Closed Mon. Expensive.*

Rhapsody. This restaurant in the Scandic Crown Hotel offers fish specialties in the Swedish style, courtesy of chef Joachim Lassner. *Berliner Freiheit 2, tel. 0228/72690. Reservations advised. AE, DC, MC, V. Closed Sun., holidays. Expensive.*

Lodging **Königshof.** The sleek, modern Königshof is a favorite hotel among
★ diplomatic visitors only partly for its convenient location near the Old Town and close to the Rhine. Patrons of the fine terrace restaurant enjoy an excellent river view. There is also a well-stocked wine cellar. *Adenauerallee 9, tel. 0228/26010, fax 0228/2601529. 137 rooms with bath. Facilities: restaurant, bar, childcare service. AE, DC, MC, V. Expensive.*

Rheinhotel Dreesen. The Rhine rolls by right outside this historic hotel, which recently underwent a complete renovation. Despite the modernization, a belle epoque atmosphere lingers in its stately public rooms, and on weekends an orchestra still strikes up for afternoon tea. *Rheinstr. 45–49, Bad Godesberg, tel. 0228/82020, fax 0228/8202153. 74 rooms, 4 apartments and suites. Facilities: restaurant, bar, café-terrace, parking. AE, DC, MC, V. Expensive.*

Sternhotel. For good value, solid comfort, and a central location in the old town, the family-run Stern is tops. Rooms can be small, but all are pleasantly furnished. There's no restaurant, but snacks are available at the bar. *Markt 8, tel. 0228/72670, fax 0228/726715. 81 rooms with bath. AE, DC, MC, V. Moderate.*

Boppard
Lodging

Bellevue Rheinhotel. This is one of the most majestic hotels of the Rhineland, an imposing turn-of-the-century building whose elegant white-and-yellow facade, under steep slate eaves, faces directly onto the river. *Rheinallee 41–42, tel. 06742/1020, fax 06742/102602. 95 rooms with bath. Facilities: restaurant, beer cellar, bar, indoor pool, sauna, Turkish bath, fitness center, tennis courts. AE, DC, MC, V. Expensive.*

Kaub
Lodging
★

Burg Gutenfels. The terrace of this luxurious castle hotel offers one of the finest views in the Rhine Valley. Guests can also enjoy wine from the hotel's own vineyard. Be sure to reserve well in advance. *Tel. 06774/220, fax 06774/1760. 10 rooms with bath. Facilities: restaurant, private chapel. AE, DC, MC. Very Expensive.*

Koblenz
Dining

Wacht am Rhein. The name of this attractive riverside restaurant, Watch on the Rhine, sums it up. In summer, take a table on the outside terrace and watch the river traffic roll by; in winter, choose a window table and dine with the Rhine outside and the atmospheric warmth of the fin de siècle fittings and furnishings inside. Fish is the basis of the extensive menu. *Adenauer-Ufer 6, tel. 0261/15313. Reservations not necessary. AE. Moderate.*

Weinhaus Hubertus. This restaurant, named for the patron saint of hunting, lives up to its sporting image. Its decor is 17th-century rustic, its specialty, fresh game in season. Guests enjoy generous portions and a congenial atmosphere. *Florinsmarkt 6, tel. 0261/31177. Reservations advised. No credit cards. Closed lunch and Tues. Moderate.*

Lodging

Hohenstaufen. Hohenstaufen is located near the train station in a postwar building that was renovated in 1985. Facilities include a Chinese restaurant and garage. *Emil-Schüller-Str. 41–43, tel. 0261/37081, fax 0261/32303. 50 rooms with bath or shower. AE, DC, MC, V. Expensive.*

Scandic Crown. This elegant, modern hotel stands directly on the Rhine river bank; most rooms have fine views of the river and Ehrenbreitstein fortress. A lovely garden and terrace also overlook the river. *Julius-Wegeler-Str. 6, tel. 0261/1360, fax 0261/1361199. 159 rooms with bath. Facilities: 2 restaurants, bar, sauna, whirlpool. AE, DC, MC, V. Expensive.*

Köln
Dining
★

Bado-La Poêle d'Or. At first glance, the heavy furnishings and hushed atmosphere of the Poêle d'Or make it seem like the last place you'd find light and sophisticated nouvelle cuisine in Germany. But for some years, those in the know have been claiming this as one of the finest dining establishments in Europe. Even such apparently simple dishes as onion soup have been winning plaudits. Order salmon with lemon-ginger sauce if you want to sample the full glory of the place. *Komödienstr. 50–52, tel. 0221/134100. Reservations required. AE, DC, MC, V. Closed Sun., Mon. for lunch. Expensive.*

Gaststätte Früh am Dom. For real down-home German food, there are few places to compare with this time-honored former brewery. Bold frescoes on the vaulted ceilings establish the mood. Such dishes as Hämchen provide an authentically Teutonic experience. The beer garden is delightful for summer dining, and a tavern room, the Glockenstube, has been added recently. *Am Hof 12–14, tel. 0221/2580394. Reservations advised. No credit cards. Moderate.*

★ **Weinhaus im Walfisch.** The black-and-white gabled facade of this 400-year-old restaurant signals that here, too, you'll come face-to-face with no-holds-barred traditional specialties in a time-honored atmosphere. Try *Himmel und Erde* (a mixture of potatoes, onions, and apples) and any of the wide range of wines. The restaurant is tucked away between the Heumarkt (Haymarket) and the river.

Salzgasse 13, tel. 0221/2580397. Reservations advised. AE, DC, MC, V. Closed weekends and holidays. Moderate.

Lodging **Dom-Hotel.** The Dom is in a class of its own. Old-fashioned, formal,
★ and gracious, with a stunning location right by the cathedral, it offers the sort of Old World elegance and discreetly efficient service few hotels aspire to these days. The antique-filled bedrooms are subdued in color, high-ceilinged, and spacious. The view of the cathedral is something to treasure; enjoy it from the glassed-in Atelier am Dom, where you can dine on anything from wild boar served with chanterelle ragout to tofu piccata with ratatouille and curried rice. *Domkloster 2A, tel. 0221/20240, fax 0221/2024444. 126 rooms with bath. Facilities: 2 restaurants, terrace café, bar, parking. AE, DC, MC, V. Very Expensive.*

★ **Excelsior Hotel Ernst.** The Empire-style lobby in sumptuous royal blue, bright yellow, and gold is striking, and a similar boldly conceived grandeur extends to all the public rooms in this hotel founded in 1863, just down the street from the main train station and across from the cathedral. Old Master paintings (including a Van Dyke) are everywhere; you'll be served breakfast in a room hung with Gobelins tapestries. Guest rooms are appropriately more intimate in scale, with spectacular marble bathrooms and ultramodern fixtures. Looking like anything but a *Stube*, the lacquered-wood-paneled restaurant serves classic French cuisine imaginatively prepared. The wine cellar is renowned for its French Burgundies and Bordeaux. *Domplatz, tel. 0221/2701, fax 0221/135150. 160 rooms with bath. Facilities: restaurant, piano bar, hair salon, masseuse, fitness room. AE, DC, MC, V. Very Expensive.*

Weisser Schwan. An ordinary little hotel in the city center was transformed in 1992 into a luxurious establishment that owner Kurt Bohlscheid boasts is a Rhineland showplace. Each room is individually decorated, with fabric-covered walls, brass bedsteads, and fine Victorian antiques. An Italian restaurant is on the ground floor. *Thieboldsgasse 133–135, tel. 0221/217697, fax 0221/238516. 15 rooms with bath. No credit cards. Expensive.*

★ **Alstadt.** Located close by the river in the old town, this is the place for charm and low rates. Each room is furnished differently, and the service is impeccable—both welcoming and efficient. There's no restaurant. *Salzgasse 7, tel. 0221/2577851, fax 0221/2577853. 28 rooms with bath. Facilities: sauna. AE, DC, MC, V. Closed Christmas. Moderate.*

Königswinter **Zum Alten Bräuhaus.** Located in a pleasant, shady garden in the
Dining center of town, Zum Alten Bräuhaus features hearty German fare, served with a selection of local wines and beers. *Hauptstr. 454, tel. 02223/22528. Reservations not necessary. No credit cards. Moderate.*

Lodging **Günnewig Rheinhotel.** A modern hotel situated right on the banks of the Rhine, Günnewig Rheinhotel offers pleasant river views. *Rheinallee 9, tel. 02223/24051, fax 0223/26694. 50 rooms with bath. Facilities: restaurant, bar, pool, sauna, solarium. AE, DC, MC, V. Expensive.*

Mainz **Drei Lilien.** This beautifully appointed restaurant has antique fur-
Dining nishings and excellent nouvelle cuisine. *Ballplatz 2, tel. 06131/*
★ *225068. Reservations advised. AE, DC, MC, V. Closed Sun. and Mon. Expensive.*

Rats-und Zunftstuben Heilig Geist. Although the decor is predominantly modern, this popular restaurant also incorporates some Roman remains and offers a traditional atmosphere. The cuisine is hearty German fare. *Rentengasse 2, tel. 06131/225757. Reservations required. AE, DC, MC, V. Closed Sun. Moderate.*

Lodging **Hotel-Restaurant Am Lerchenberg.** The location isn't ideal—some 4 miles from the city center—but there's a bus stop right outside the door and open countryside only short steps away. Family-run, the hotel is friendly, comfortable, and peaceful. *Hindemithstr. 5, tel. 06131/73001, fax 06131/73004. 53 rooms with bath. Facilities: restaurant, sauna, solarium, fitness room. AE, DC, MC, V. Moderate–Expensive.*

Rüdesheim **Krone.** The extensive restoration work carried out on the 450-year-
Dining old Krone Hotel included a complete renovation of its restaurant, which now ranks among the most outstanding in the region. Chef Herbert Pucher's terrines and pâtés draw regular customers from as far away as Frankfurt. His fish dishes are supreme, and the Rhine wines are the best. *Rheinuferstr. 10, Assmannshausen, tel. 06722/4030. Reservations advised. AE, DC, MC. Closed Jan. and Feb. Moderate–Expensive.*

Lodging **Central.** This friendly, family-run hotel recently became a member of the Ring group and now offers all the comfort and facilities expected from that chain. It has a fine restaurant. *Kirchstr. 6, tel. 06722/3036, fax 06722/2807. 53 rooms with bath. AE, DC, MC, V. Closed Jan. and Feb. Moderate.*

Rudesheimer Hof. For a taste of Rheingau hospitality, try this typical inn. There's a terrace for summer dining on excellent local specialties, which you can enjoy along with any of the many wines offered. *Geisenheimerstr. 1, tel. 06722/2011, fax 06722/48191. 42 rooms with bath. Facilities: restaurant, terrace, parking. AE, DC, MC, V. Closed mid-Nov.–mid-Feb. Moderate.*

Hotel und Weinhaus Felsenkeller. Located just around the corner from Drosselgasse, Hotel and Weinhaus Felsenkeller is a traditional 18th-century establishment offering modern comforts. *Oberstr. 39–41, tel. 06722/2094, fax 06722/47202. 60 rooms with shower. AE, MC, V. Inexpensive.*

St. Goar, St. **Roter Kopf.** This is a historic wine restaurant brimming with rustic
Goarshausen Rhineland atmosphere. *Burgstr. 5, St. Goarshausen, tel. 06771/
Dining 2698. Reservations advised. No credit cards. Moderate.*

Lodging **Schlosshotel-Burg Rheinfels.** Situated high above St. Goar, on a hill commanding spectacular river views, the Schlosshotel-Burg Rheinfels rises from the ruins of the adjacent castle (*see* Exploring, above). *Schlossberg 47, tel. 06741/8020, fax 06741/7652. 59 rooms with shower. Facilities: restaurant, pool, sauna. AE, DC, MC, V. Expensive.*

Rhein Hotel Adler. Perched right on the edge of the Rhine, this is a turn-of-the-century, family-run establishment. Facilities include an attractive garden and terrace. *St. Goarshausen, Bahnhofstr. 6, tel. 06771/2613, fax 06771/1447. 73 rooms with bath. Facilities: restaurant, pool, solarium. AE, DC, MC, V. Moderate.*

The Black Forest

Only a century ago, the Black Forest (Schwarzwald) was one of the wildest stretches of countryside in Europe. It had earned its somber name because of the impenetrable stretches of dark forest that clothed the mountains and shielded small communities from the outside world. Today, it's a friendly, hospitable region, still extensively forested but with large, open valleys and stretches of verdant farmland. Among the trailblazing tourists of the adventurous 19th centu-

The Black Forest

0 — 20 miles
0 — 30 km

FRANCE

Karlsruhe

A8

Pforzheim

294

Bad Liebenzell

Stuttgart

29

Baden-Baden

Calw

Talmühle

B463

Zavelstein

Kehl

Mummelsee

Nagold

N

Baiersbronn

Offenburg

Freudenstadt

Neckar

415

Zell

Alpirsbach

27

Lahr

B294

Wolfach

Gutachtal Valley

Schiltach

B294

Rottweil

Rhine

Kaiserstuhl

Triberg

Danube

Freiburg

Furtwangen

Himmelreich

Titisee

A81/E41

Tuttlingen

Staufen

Schluchsee

Zell

Radolfzell

Rheinfelden

34

Friedrichshafen

Bodensee

SWITZERLAND

ry was Mark Twain, who wrote enthusiastically about the natural beauty of the region. The deep hot springs first discovered by the Romans were rediscovered, and small forgotten villages became wealthy spas. Hikers treasured the lonely trails that cut through the forests and rolling uplands, skiers opened the world's first lift on the slopes of the region's highest mountain, and horseback riders cut bridle paths through the tangle of narrow river valleys.

The Black Forest is the southernmost German wine region and the custodian of some of the country's best traditional foods. (Black Forest smoked ham and Black Forest cake are world-famous.) It retains its vibrant clock-making tradition, and local wood-carvers haven't yet died out. Best of all, though, it's still possible to stay overnight in a Black Forest farmhouse and eat a breakfast hearty enough to last the day, all for the price of an indifferent meal at a restaurant in, say, Munich or Frankfurt.

Getting Around

Today the Black Forest is easily accessible from all parts of the country. The Rhine Valley autobahn, the A5, runs the entire length of the Black Forest and connects at Karlsruhe with the rest of the German expressway network. Well-paved, single-lane highways traverse the region. A main north-south train line follows the Rhine Valley, carrying EuroCity and InterCity trains that call at hourly intervals at Freiburg and Baden-Baden, connecting those two centers directly with Frankfurt and many other German cities. Local lines connect most Black Forest towns, and two local east-west services, the Black Forest Railway and the Höllental Railway, are spectacular scenic runs. The nearest airports are at Stuttgart; Strasbourg, in the neighboring French Alsace; and the Swiss border city of Basel, just 64 kilometers (40 miles) from Freiburg.

Tourist Information

Baden-Baden (Augustaplatz 8, tel. 07221/275200).
Freiburg (Rotteckring 14, tel. 0761/3689090).
Freudenstadt (Promenadenplatz 1, tel. 07741/86420).
Pforzheim (Marktplatz 1, tel. 07231/302314).

Guided Tours

Guided bus tours of the Black Forest begin in both Freiburg and Baden-Baden. A choice of 25 day tours from Freiburg includes the French Alsace region, the Swiss Alps, and various attractions in the Black Forest. Prices range from DM 20 to DM 42 and include English-speaking guides. In Baden-Baden, tours are offered by the **Deutsches Reisebüro** (Sophienstr. 1b, tel. 07221/21050) and concentrate on the Black Forest.

Exploring the Black Forest

The regional tourist authority has worked out a series of scenic routes covering virtually every attraction the visitor is likely to want to see (obtainable from the **Fremdenverkehrsverband,** Bertoldstr. 45, D-79098 Freiburg, tel. 0761/31317). Routes are basically intended for the motorist, but most points can be reached by train or bus. The following itinerary is accessible by all means of transportation and takes in parts of the Black Forest High Road, Low Road, Spa Road, Wine Road, and Clock Road.

The ancient Roman city of **Pforzheim** is the starting point here, accessible either from the Munich–Karlsruhe autobahn or by train from Karlsruhe, Frankfurt, or Stuttgart. Known even beyond Germany's borders as the Gold City because of its association with the jewelry trade, Pforzheim has the world's finest museum collection of jewelry in the **Reuchlinhaus,** spanning four centuries. (Jahnstr. 42, tel. 07231/392–126; admission charges were being set in 1994; Tues.–Sun. 10–5). Pforzheim was almost completely destroyed by wartime bombing and is a fine example of reconstruction work: Visit the centrally located parish church of **St. Michael** to see how faithfully the experts stuck to the original mixture of sturdy Romanesque and later, finer Gothic styles. For a contrast, take a look at Pforzheim's **St. Matthew's Church,** a tentlike construction erected in 1953 when the designers of the similarly styled Olympic stadium in Munich were still at the drawing board.

On the way out of Pforzheim, toward B463, the Nagold Valley road, gardeners should make a detour to the **Alpine Garden** on the Tiefenbronn road. More than 100,000 varieties of plants, including the rarest Alpine flowers, are found here, and many are for sale. *Open Mar.–Oct., daily 8–7.*

Bad Liebenzell, our first stop on B463, is one of the oldest spas of the Black Forest, with the remains of 15th-century installations. Visitors are welcome to take the waters at the **Paracelsus baths** on the Nagold riverbank. *Tel. 07052/408250. Admission: DM 11.50 adults, DM 5 children for 3 hours. Open Mon., Thurs. 8:30–5; Tues., Wed., Fri., Sat. 8:30–8; Sun. 8:30–7.*

Leave plenty of time to explore **Calw** (pronounced Calve), the next town on the road south. Its famous native son, the novelist and poet Hermann Hesse, called it the "most beautiful [town] of all I know." And Hesse, who died in Switzerland in 1962, had seen more than a few in his extensive travels. Pause on the town's 15th-century bridge over the rushing Nagold River—if you're lucky, you'll see a local tanner spreading hides over the river wall to dry, as his ancestors did for centuries past.

Back on the main road south, turn off at Talmühle for the **Neubulach silver mine.** Once the most productive workings of the Black Forest, the mine is now open to visitors. *Admission: DM 4 adults, DM 3 children (includes entry to mineral museum). Open Apr.–Oct., Mon.–Sat. 10–4, Sun. 9:30–5.*

Time Out In the town of **Nagold,** visit the 1697-built half-timbered **Alte Post** inn on Bahnhofstrasse 2. Kings and queens have taken refreshment here on journeys through the Black Forest. Enjoy the local beer and a plate of Black Forest smoked ham or a pot of strong coffee and a slice of delectable Black Forest cake.

From Nagold, the road travels on through lush farmland to **Freudenstadt,** another war-flattened German city that has been painstakingly restored. It was originally built during the early 17th century as a model city to house not only workers in nearby silver mines but refugees from religious persecution in what is now Austrian Carinthia. The streets are still laid out in the grid pattern decreed by the original planners, while the vast central square continues to wait for the palace that was intended to stand here. It was to have been built for the city's founder, Prince Frederick I of Württemberg, but he died before work could begin. Don't miss Freudenstadt's **Protestant parish church,** just off the square. It's L-shaped, a rare architectural liberty during the early 17th century, when this imposing church was built.

Quench your thirst at nearby **Alpirsbach,** where the unusually soft water gives the local beer an especially smooth quality. The brewery was once part of a monastic settlement whose pretty **Romanesque church** next to the brewhouse is well worth a visit. The brewery still produces a strong monastery beer *(Klosterbock)* and maintains the tradition of brewing a special Christmas beer.

South of Alpirsbach, stop at **Schiltach** to admire (and possibly giggle at) the frescoes on the 16th-century town hall that depict the history of this exceptionally pretty village. The devil figures prominently in the frescoes: He was blamed for burning Schiltach down on several occasions.

From here, take B294 to **Wolfach** to visit the last Black Forest factory where glass is blown by centuries-old techniques once common throughout the region. *Die Dorotheen-Glashütte, Glashüttenweg 4, tel. 07834/751. Admission: DM 4 adults, DM 3 children. Open weekdays 9–4:30, Sat. 9–2.*

The **Gutachtal Valley,** south of Wolfach, is famous for its traditional costumes, and if you're there at the right time (holidays and some Sundays), you'll see the married women sporting black pompoms on their hats to denote their matronly status (red pompoms are for the unmarried). At the head of the valley, at **Triberg,** are Germany's highest waterfalls, which reach a height of nearly 155 meters (500 feet). This is also cuckoo clock country. The **Clock Museum (Uhrenmuseum)** at Furtwangen is the largest in Germany. Its collection includes an astronomical timepiece weighing more than one ton. *Gerwigstr. 11, tel. 07723/656117. Admission: DM 4 adults, DM 2 children. Open Apr.–Oct., daily 9–5; Nov.–Mar., Mon.–Sat. 10–4.*

From Furtwangen, the road leads to the lakeland of the Black Forest. The two largest lakes, **Titisee** and **Schluchsee,** are beautifully set amid fir-clad mountains, but try to avoid them at the height of the summer holidays, when they are quite crowded. From here, it's a short run to Freiburg, capital of the Black Forest. The most direct route goes via the aptly named Höllental (Hell Valley). The first stop outside the narrow, gorgelike valley is called, appropriately enough, **Himmelreich,** meaning "Kingdom of Heaven." The village is said to have been given the name by railway engineers who were grateful finally to have run a line through Hell Valley. The Black Forest railway, more than 100 years old, still tackles the mountainous route, connecting Freiburg and the resort of Hinterzarten; details and tickets are available from the **Deutsche Bundesbahn** (German Railways) in Freiburg (tel. 0761/19419).

Perched on the western slopes of the Black Forest, **Freiburg** was founded as a free market town in the 12th century. It was badly bombed in World War II. Towering over the rebuilt, medieval streets of the city is its most famous landmark, the cathedral, or **Münster.** The cathedral took three centuries to build and has one of the finest spires in the world. April through October, English-language walking tours of the old town include an explanation of the Münster's numerous architectural styles. Tours are led daily, except Tuesdays, at 10 AM and last two hours. *Admission: DM 6 adults, DM 3 children. (Contact tourist office; see above.)*

Try to visit Freiburg on a Friday, which is market day. The square in front of the cathedral then becomes a mass of color and movement, while a fitting backdrop is provided by **Kaufhaus,** the 16th-century market house.

Time Out   Stroll up to the Oberlinden Square and stop in at **Zum Roten Bären** (The Red Bear), reputedly Germany's oldest inn; it has a documented history dating from 1091! Order a "Viertel" of the local wine and perhaps a plate of locally smoked ham—and if you like the atmosphere, why not stay the night?

Once you've braved Hell Valley to get to Freiburg, a visit to the nearby town where Dr. Faustus is reputed to have made his deal with the devil should hold no horrors. **Staufen,** which claims the inquisitive doctor as one of its early burgers, is some 19 kilometers (12 miles) south of Freiburg. Local records show there really was an alchemist named Faustus who blew himself up in his laboratory. According to legend, the devil dragged him off to hell from the **Gasthof zum Löwen** (Hauptstr. 47, tel. 07633/7078), an old inn in the village center. The inn has a tap room named for Faust, and there are comfortable guest rooms if you fancy staying the night.

From Staufen, turn northward to Baden-Baden along the **Wine Road,** skirting the French border to your left, through the southernmost vineyards of Germany, source of the prized Baden wine. Some of the best vineyards are situated on a volcanic outcrop known as the **Kaiserstuhl** (Emperor's Chair). Sample a glass of wine in the village of **Achkarren,** which has a fascinating **wine museum.** *Admission: DM 2 adults, DM 1 children. Open Apr.–Oct., weekdays 2–5, weekends 10:30–4.*

All the vineyards along the Wine Road offer tastings, so don't hesitate to drop in and try one or two. Leave the Wine Road at the town of Lahr and head inland, on B415, through the narrow Schuttertal valley to Zell, and from there to the Black Forest **High Road.** This is the land of fable and superstition, and if you're here during the mist-days of autumn, stop off at the mystery-shrouded **Mummelsee Lake,** immortalized by the poet Mörike in his ballad *The Spirits of the Mummelsee.* Legend has it that sprites and other spirits of the deep live in the cold waters of the small, round lake in its forest setting. It's true that no fish are found in the lake, but scientific sorts say this is a result of the high mineral content of the water.

From the Mummelsee, it's downhill all the way to fashionable **Baden-Baden,** idyllically set in a wooded valley of the northern Black Forest. The town sits on top of extensive underground hot springs that gave the city its name (*Bad,* German for "spa"). The Romans first exploited the springs, which were then rediscovered by wealthy 19th-century travelers. By the end of the 19th century, there was scarcely a crowned head of Europe who had not dipped into the healing waters of Baden-Baden. The town became the unofficial summer residence of numerous royal and titled families, and they left their imprint in the form of palatial houses that grace its tree-lined avenues.

One of the grand buildings of Baden-Baden's Belle Epoque is the pillared **Kurhaus,** home of Germany's first casino, which opened its doors to the world's gamblers in 1853. Entrance costs a modest DM 5, though visitors are required to sign a declaration that they enter with sufficient funds to settle subsequent debts! *Jacket and tie required. Passport necessary as proof of identity. Open Sun.–Fri. 2 PM–2 AM, Sat. 2 PM–3 AM. Daily tours (DM 3) from Apr.–Sept., daily 9:30–noon; Oct.–Mar., 10–noon.*

If jackets and ties are customary attire at the casino, no clothes at all are de rigueur at Baden-Baden's famous Roman baths, the **Friedrichsbad.** You "take the waters" here just as the Romans did nearly 2,000 years ago—nude. *Römerplatz 1, tel. 07221/275920. Admission: DM 28 for 3 hours (DM 38 with massage). Children under 16 not admitted. Open Mon.–Sat. 9 AM–10 PM.*

The remains of the Roman baths that lie beneath the Friedrichsbad can be visited from April through October. *Admission: DM 2.*

Time Out   Step into the warm elegance of the **Café König** in the nearby Lichtentalerstrasse pedestrian zone. Order a pot of coffee and a wedge of Black Forest cake and listen to the hum of contentment from the monied spa crowd who have made this quiet corner their haunt.

The attractions of the Friedrichsbad are rivaled by the neighboring **Caracalla baths,** renovated and enlarged in 1985. The huge, modern complex has five indoor pools, two outdoor ones, numerous whirlpools, a solarium, and what is described as a "sauna landscape"— you look out through windows at the countryside while steaming. *Römerplatz 11, tel. 07221/275940. Admission: DM 18 for 2 hours. Open daily 8 AM–10 PM.*

Dining and Lodging

For details and price-category definitions, *see* Dining and Lodging in Staying in Germany, *above.*

Baden-Baden
Dining and
Lodging

Pospisil's Merkurius. A log fire on cool days adds to the already warm atmosphere of this country-style restaurant and small hotel in the district of Varnhalt on the southern fringe of Baden-Baden. The menu offers classic and regional dishes with a light touch—goose-liver soufflé and imaginative preparations of wild hare and pheasant, for example. The wine list offers an extensive selection of very fine vintages. The restaurant borders on the expensive (menus range up to DM 125), but the four comfortable hotel rooms are very reasonably priced (DM 110–130). *Klosterbergstr. 2, tel. 07223/5474, fax 07223/60996. Reservations required. No credit cards. Closed Sat. lunch, Mon., and Tues. Expensive.*

Stahlbad. The Gallo-Germanic menu here is echoed by the restaurant's furnishings—19th-century French oils adorn the walls, while French and German china are reflected in the mahogany gleam of antique tables and sideboards. An abundance of green velvet catches the tone of the parklike grounds of the stately house that accommodates this elegant restaurant. *Augustaplatz 2, tel. 07221/24569. Reservations advised. AE, DC, MC, V. Closed Sun. dinner and Mon. Expensive.*

Gasthaus zur Traube. Regional specialties, such as smoked bacon and homemade noodles, take pride of place in this cozy inn, south of the city center in the Neuweier district. If you like the food, you can also spend the night in one of the 18 neatly furnished and moderately priced rooms. *Mauerbergstr. 107, tel. 07223/57216. Reservations not essential. AE, DC, MC, V. Closed Wed. Moderate.*

Lodging

Brenner's Park Hotel. This exceptional stately mansion is set in spacious private grounds. All rooms are luxuriously furnished and appointed—as they should be, since they cost up to DM 980 per day, with 20 apartments going for up to DM 2,000. *Schillerstr. 6, tel. 07221/9000, fax 07221/38772. 68 rooms with bath and balcony, 32 suites. Facilities: 2 restaurants, hairdresser, beauty salon, indoor pool, sauna, bridge room, bicycle hire. AE, DC, MC. Very Expensive.*

★ **Der Kleine Prinz.** Each room of this beautifully modernized 19th-century mansion is decorated in a different style, from romantic Art Nouveau to Manhattan modern (owner Norbert Rademacher was director of New York's Waldorf-Astoria for several years). Some rooms have whirlpool baths. The hotel's elegant restaurant offers "new German cuisine" with a French touch. *Lichtentalerstr. 36, tel. 07221/3464, fax 07221/38264. 39 rooms with bath. Facilities: restaurant. AE, DC, MC, V. Restaurant closed first 2 weeks of Jan. Expensive.*

Deutscher Kaiser-Etol. This centrally located old, established hotel, a few minutes' stroll from the Kurhaus, offers homey and individually styled rooms at comfortable prices in an otherwise expensive town. All the double rooms have balconies on a quiet street off one of the main thoroughfares. *Merkurstr. 9, tel. 07221/2700, fax 07221/270270. 44 rooms with bath. Facilities: restaurant (closed Sun. dinner), bar, wine and beer tavern, bicycle hire. AE, DC, MC, V. Moderate.*

Hotel am Markt. The Bogner family has run this historic, 250-year-old hotel for more than 30 years. It's friendly, popular, and right in the center of town. *Marktplatz 17–18, tel. 07221/22747. 28 rooms, 14 with bath or shower. Facilities: restaurant, terrace. AE, DC, MC, V. Inexpensive.*

Bad
Liebenzell
Lodging

Thermen-Hotel. This spacious spa hotel, on the edge of Bad Liebenzell's spa park, is one of the region's most distinctive buildings: a flower-smothered, half-timbered mansion (and its more modern annex) where the Black Forest creeps to the very edge of the garden. Rooms are spacious and comfortable and most have pergola-like balconies. *Am Kurpark, tel. 07052/408300, fax 07052/408305. 23 rooms with bath or shower. Facilities: restaurant, garden café, terrace, fitness center, sauna, parking. MC. Moderate.*

Baiersbronn
Dining and Lodging

Bareiss. The beautiful mountain resort of Baiersbronn is blessed with two of Germany's leading restaurants. The Bareiss (in the luxury hotel of the same name) has dark-wood furniture and tapestry-papered walls warmly lit by candles and traditional lamps. It attracts French guests from neighboring Alsace who value its light, classic cuisine and carefully selected wines (30 brands of champagne alone). The hotel itself is among the most luxurious and best-equipped in the Black Forest. Suites (DM 700 upwards) have their own sauna, solarium, and whirlpool baths. *Gärtenbühlweg 14, Mitteltal, tel. 07442/470, fax 07442/47320. 51 rooms with bath, 42 apartments, 7 suites. Facilities: 2 restaurants, bar, 3 swimming pools, fitness room, sauna, solarium, billiard room, bowling, bikes, tennis. AE, DC, MC, V. Very Expensive.*

Traube Tonbach. Baiersbronn's second world-class restaurant, the Schwarzwaldstube, is also part of a luxurious hotel, the Traube Tonbach. The hotel has two outstanding restaurants, and if the Schwarzwaldstube is full or too pricey for your budget (menus range from DM 150 to DM 200), then the Köhlerstube is a very acceptable alternative. In both, you dine beneath beamed ceilings at tables bright with fine silver and glassware. The hotel is a harmonious blend of old and new furnishings and decor, each room enjoying sweeping views of the Black Forest. Guests are virtually outnumbered by a small army of helpful and friendly staff. *Tonbachstr. 237, Tonbach, tel. 07442/4920, fax 07442/492–692. 134 rooms with bath, 38 apartments, 8 suites. Facilities: 2 restaurants, bars, cafeteria, terraces, gardens, 3 swimming pools, sauna, solarium, fitness room, bowling, bikes, tennis. AE, DC, MC, V. Very Expensive.*

Hotel Lamm. The half-timbered exterior of this 200-year-old hotel beckons the traveler and holiday-maker into a comfortable house of long tradition. In its beamed restaurant, you can order fish taken from the hotel's own trout pools. Rooms are furnished in traditional Black Forest style, with heavy oak fittings and some fine antiques. In winter, logs flicker in the open fireplace of the lounge. Skiers can board a lift right outside the front door. *Ellbacherstr. 4, tel. 07442/4980, fax 07442/49878. Facilities: restaurant, indoor pool, sauna, solarium, billiard room, table tennis. AE, DC, MC, V. Moderate.*

Calw
Dining and Lodging

Hotel Kloster Hirsau. This country-house hotel on the wooded outskirts of Calw stands on the site of a 900-year-old monastery, whose Gothic cloisters are still largely intact. A small Renaissance palace, a Romanesque chapel, and some fine medieval half-timbered buildings are just a short walk away. The hotel prides itself on its award-winning restaurant, where owner-chef Joachim Ulrich's menu changes daily. The emphasis is on regional dishes enhanced with a light French touch: featured are Swabian farmhouse noodles along with truffle vinaigrette. *Wildbaderstr. 2, tel. 07051/56213, fax 07051/51795. 43 rooms with bath. Facilities: restaurant, bar, indoor pool, garden terrace, parking. DC, MC, V. Expensive.*

Ratsstube. This historic house in the center of Calw was fully renovated in 1989, though most of its traditional features (centuries-old beams and brickwork) were kept intact. The restaurant offers sturdy German fare (marinated beef and noodles, thick soups, Black Forest sausage). Rooms aren't particularly spacious but they are brightly decorated and furnished, with pastel colors and floral patterns dominating. *Marktpl. 12, tel. 07051/1864, fax 07051/70826. 13* rooms with bath. Facilities: restaurant, parking. No credit cards. Moderate.

Freiburg
Dining

Enoteca. Three dining possibilities are now offered by the refurbished and recently reopened Enoteca. Lunch is served in the crowded, friendly bistro, while dinner is a more leisurely affair in the adjacent restaurant, where subdued lighting glistens on honey-colored paneling. Late-night diners can get light meals at the Enoteca bar, which is open until 1:30 AM. Proprietor Manfred Schmitz is a respected local wine connoisseur as well as an accomplished chef, and he can be relied on to recommend just the right vintage to accompany such specialties as veal roulade with gorgonzola. *Gerberau 21–23, tel. 0761/30751. Restaurant reservations advised. AE, MC, V. Closed Sun. Moderate–Expensive.*

Ratskeller. In the shadow of the cathedral, the popular Ratskeller has a typical Black Forest ambience (lots of wood paneling and beams), which is matched by a menu of mostly traditional dishes (roasts and rich sauces). *Münsterplatz 11, tel. 0761/37530. Reservations advised. AE, DC, MC, V. Closed Sun. dinner, Mon. Moderate.*

Dining and
Lodging

Colombi. Freiburg's most luxurious hotel also has the city's finest and most original restaurant and two reconstructed 18th-century Austrian farmhouse guest cottages, now luxuriously furnished and decorated with antiques (including a handsome cuckoo clock, of course). In the rustic section of the restaurant (named for Black Forest artist Hans Thoma) you can order hearty local dishes, such as lentil soup and venison, while its more elegant section's menu goes decidedly up-market, combining traditional meat and fish dishes with imaginatively innovative sauces. The hotel is centrally located and quiet. *Am Colombi Park, tel. 0761/21060, fax 0761/31410. 80 rooms with bath, 12 suites. Reservations required at restaurant (closed Sun.). AE, DC, MC, V. Expensive–Very Expensive.*

Zum Roten Bären. Germany's oldest inn (it dates back to 1311) is now the showpiece hotel of the Ring Group. It has retained its individual character, however, offering very comfortable lodging and excellent dining in a cozy warren of four restaurants and taverns. If it's a chilly evening, order a table next to the large tiled oven, which dominates the main, beamed restaurant. A tour of the two basement floors of cellars, dating from the original 12th-century foundation of the town of Freiburg and now well stocked with fine wines, is also recommended. *Oberlinden 12, tel. 0761/36913, fax 0761/36916. 19 rooms with bath, 3 apartments. Facilities: restaurant, wine tavern, sauna, parking. AE, DC, MC, V. Expensive.*

Markgräfler Hof. Even the French make a pilgrimage from Alsace to dine in Hans Leo Kempchen's restaurant in this traditional old hotel in Freiburg's quaint pedestrian zone. Kempchen rewards travelers with special gourmet menus and unbeatable two-day deals that include accommodations, a wine tasting, and a guided tour of the city. Call well in advance to reserve rooms—otherwise the French will have most likely beaten you to it. *Gerberau 22, tel. 0761/32540, fax 0761/37947. 18 rooms with bath or shower. Facilities: restaurant, parking. AE, DC, MC, V. Moderate.*

Lodging

Panorama Hotel Mercure. This modern hotel is situated high above Freiburg, although it's only a few minutes by car to the downtown area. It was recently taken over by the French Mercure group, who have maintained standards. All rooms have south-facing balconies, with fine views of the city and surrounding countryside. *Wintererstr. 89, tel. 0761/51030, fax 0761/5103300. 85 rooms with* *bath. Facilities: restaurant, indoor pool, sauna, solarium, tennis, ping-pong, bicycle hire. AE, DC, MC, V. Very Expensive.*

★ **Romantik Hotel Stollen.** You'll need a car to reach this luxuriously decorated half-timbered country house located 9½ kilometers (6 miles) outside the town in Gutach im Elztal. The hotel is best reached from the Karlsruhe-Basel autobahn by taking the Freiburg north exit and following the Waldkirch road. The restaurant has won awards for its excellent concoctions. *7809 Gutach im Elztal, tel. 07685/207, fax 07685/1550. 11 rooms with bath and balcony, 1 suite. AE, MC, V. Moderate–Expensive.*

Gasthaus und Pension Hirschen. This charming converted farmhouse has been in the possession of the Winterhalter family for four centuries, and today's Winterhalters take as much care in making their guests feel at home as did their ancestors. The pension is in the village of Wittnau, a 10-minute drive or 15-minute bus trip from Freiburg, but the disadvantages of its distance from the city are more than offset by its peaceful location amid open countryside, a walker's paradise. *Schönberg 11, 7801 Wittnau, tel. 0761/402137. 20 rooms, most with bath. Facilities: restaurant, bowling alley, parking. No credit cards. Moderate.*

Rappen Hotel. You'll sleep like a pampered farmhouse guest here, in brightly painted rustic beds, beneath soft feather quilts. It's as quiet as a country village, too: The Rappen is in the center of the traffic-free old city. In the countrified but comfortable restaurant, patrons have the choice of more than 200 regional wines. *Am Münsterplatz 13, tel. 0761/31353, fax 0751/382252. 25 rooms, 13 with bath. Facilities: bar-restaurant, terrace. AE, DC, MC, V. Moderate.*

Freudenstadt
Dining

Ratskeller. If it's cold outside, ask for a place near the Ratskeller's *Kachelofen*, a large, traditional, tiled heating stove. Swabian dishes and venison are prominent on the menu, but if the homemade trout roulade with crab sauce is featured, go for it. *Marktplatz 8, tel. 07441/2693. Reservations advised. MC, V. Closed Mon. Moderate.*

Dining and
Lodging

Bären. The sturdy old Gasthof Bären, in the same family since 1878, accents Black Forest tradition and service with a personal touch. Rooms are modern but with homey touches such as farmhouse-style bedsteads and cupboards. The beam-ceiling restaurant is a favorite with the locals; its menu combines heavy Black Forest dishes (roasts and hearty sauces) and lighter international fare. The trout is caught locally. *Lange Str. 33, tel. 07441/2779, fax 07441/2887. 23 rooms with bath. Facilities: restaurant, parking. MC. Moderate–Expensive.*

Warteck. The centrally located Warteck's Biedermeier-style restaurant is first a feast for the eye—flowers are everywhere: freshly picked posies adorn the linen-covered tables and the nooks and crannies between the handsome, lead-paned windows. The imaginative menu offers succulent lamb in meadow herbs, venison with Swabian noodles, or veal in mushroom sauce. When asparagus is in season it is prepared here in an aromatic hazelnut vinaigrette. The Biedermeier decor extends to the comfortable furnishings of the hotel's guest rooms as well. *Stuttgarter Str. 14, tel. 07441/7418, fax 07441/2957. 13 rooms with bath. Restaurant closed Tues.; restaurant and hotel closed first 3 weeks after Easter. DC, V. Moderate.*

Lodging

Lutz Posthotel. This is an old coaching inn in the heart of the town that has been managed by the same family since 1809. But there's nothing old-fashioned about the rooms, which are both modern and cozy. The restaurant offers Swabian delicacies. During the summer there's a coffee terrace. *Stuttgarterstr. 5, tel. 07441/2421, fax 07441/*

84533. 45 rooms with bath, some with balcony. Facilities: wine bar, library. AE, DC, MC, V. Moderate.

Hinterzarten
Lodging
★

Park Hotel Adler. This hotel has been in the possession of the Riesterer family for more than five centuries: Since 1446, when an early ancestor gave 17 schillings for the original property, it has been developing into one of Germany's finest hotels. The hotel complex stands in nearly 10 acres of grounds ringed by the Black Forest. Among the seven rooms devoted to eating and drinking are a French restaurant and a paneled 17th-century dining room. An orchestra accompanies dinner and later moves to the bar for dancing. *Adlerplatz 3, tel. 07652/1270, fax 07652/127717. 84 rooms with bath. Facilities: 2 restaurants, bar, pool, sauna, solarium, tennis (indoor and outdoor), horseback riding, bicycle hire, beauty salon, hairdresser, library, game rooms, child-care facilities. AE, DC, MC, V. Very Expensive.*

Nagold
Dining

Romantik Restaurant Alte Post. This centuries-old half-timbered inn has the kind of atmosphere lesser establishments believe can be built in with false beams. The menu ranges from Swabian traditional to pricey French, so stay with the local dishes (veal in a rich mushroom sauce or, in season, venison in the Baden-Baden style) and you won't be shocked by the bill. *Bahnhofstr. 2, tel. 07452/4221. Reservations required. AE, DC, MC, V. Closed Fri. lunch. Moderate.*

Lodging

Hotel Post Gästehaus. Run by the former proprietors of the adjacent Alte Post restaurant, this hotel is made up of an old coaching inn and modern additions. It offers a high degree of comfort—and homemade preserves for breakfast. *Bahnhofstr. 3, tel. 07452/4048, fax 07452/4040. 23 rooms with bath. Facilities: English-language cable TV. AE, DC, MC, V. Expensive.*

Pforzheim
Dining

Silberburg. This is a rustic restaurant offering classic and regional cooking at bargain prices. For best value, ask to see the *Tagesempfehlungen*—the chef's daily recommendations. *Dietlingerstr. 27, tel. 07231/41159. Reservations necessary. AE, DC, MC, V. Closed Mon., Tues. lunch, and 3 weeks in Aug. Inexpensive.*

Titisee
Lodging

Romantik Hotel Adler Post. This hotel is in the Neustadt district of Titisee, about 4½ kilometers (3 miles) from the lake. The solid old building has been in the possession of the Ketterer family for more than 140 years. The guest rooms are comfortably and traditionally furnished. The hotel's restaurant, the Rôtisserie zum Postillon, is noted for its regional cuisine. *Hauptstr. 16, tel. 07651/5066, fax 07651/3729. 24 rooms, 4 apartments, all with bath. Facilities: pool, sauna, solarium, game room, library. AE, DC, MC, V. Moderate.*

Triberg
Dining and Lodging

Römischer Kaiser. The "Roman Emperor" has been in the same Triberg family for more than 150 years, and the place exudes Black Forest tradition. Rooms are comfortably furnished in solid Black Forest style, with heavy wooden bedsteads and painted furniture. The restaurant serves German and international dishes, all with a perceptible French flair. Fresh mountain trout is almost always on the menu. *Sommeraustr. 35, Nussbach, tel. 07722/4418, fax 07722/4401. 26 rooms with bath. Facilities: restaurant, terrace, parking. AE, DC, MC, V. Moderate.*

Lodging

Hotel Central Garni. From the sunny rooftop terrace of this hotel you have a sweeping view of the surrounding Black Forest, with Triberg's bustling market square directly below. The hotel occupies the upper floors of a new office building: Rooms are bright and airy, with selected Black Forest antiques giving them a homely feel. There's no restaurant, but the hotel's central location means you'll find plenty within a few minutes' walk. *Am Marktpl., tel. 07722/ 4360. 14 rooms with shower. Facilities: terrace, parking. MC. Moderate.*

Berlin

Berlin is now a united metropolis—again the largest in continental Europe—and only two small sections of the Wall have been left in place to remind visitors and residents alike of the hideous barrier that divided the city for nearly 30 years. Old habits die hard, however, and it will be a long time before Germans and even Berliners themselves can get accustomed to regarding Berlin as one entity with one identity. You'll still hear Berliners in the western, more prosperous half talking about "those Ossies over there" when referring to people in the still down-at-the-heels eastern part. All restrictions on travel within and beyond the city have, of course, disappeared. But there's still a strong feeling of passing from one world into another when crossing the scar that marks the line where the Wall once stood. It's not just the very visible differences between the glitter of West Berlin and the relative shabbiness of the east. Somehow the historical heritage of a long-divided city permeates the place and penetrates the consciousness of every visitor. You'll almost certainly arrive in and depart from the western part of Berlin, but just as surely your steps will lead you into the east. On the way, ponder the miracle that made this easy access to a onetime fortress of communism possible.

Arriving and Departing

By Plane **Tegel** airport is centrally located, only 7 kilometers (4 miles) from downtown. Airlines flying to Tegel include American, Delta, TWA, Air France, British Airways, Deutsche BA, Lufthansa, and some charter specialists. Because of increased air traffic at Tegel following unification, the former military airfield at **Tempelhof** (even closer to downtown) is being used more and more. East Berlin's **Schönefeld** airport is about 24 kilometers (15 miles) outside the downtown area. For information on arrival and departure times at Tegel, call 030/41011; at Tempelhof, call 030/69510; for Schönefeld, call 030/60910.

Between the Airports and Downtown The No. 109 bus runs every ten minutes between Tegel airport and downtown. The journey takes 30 minutes and the fare is DM 3.50 for adults, DM 2.30 for children. A taxi fare will cost about DM 25. If you've rented a car at the airport, follow signs for the "Stadtautobahn" highway.

A shuttle bus leaves Schönefeld airport every 10–15 minutes for the nearby S-Bahn (metropolitan train) station. S-Bahn trains leave every 20 minutes for the Friedrichstrasse and Zoologischer Garten stations. The trip takes about 30 minutes, and you can get off at whatever stop is nearest your hotel. The fare by bus or subway is DM 3.50 and covers all public transportation throughout Berlin. Taxis are usually available at the stops from Hauptbahnhof onward. You can also take a taxi from the airport; the fare to your hotel will be about DM 30–DM 35, and the trip will take about 40 minutes. By car, follow the signs for "Stadtzentrum Berlin."

By Train There are six major rail routes to Berlin from the western half of the country (from Hamburg, Hannover, Köln, Frankfurt, Munich, and Nürnberg), and the network has expanded considerably, making the rest of eastern Germany more accessible. Service between Berlin and Eastern Europe has also significantly improved, resulting in shorter traveling times. For the latest information on routes call **Deutsche Bundesbahn** (tel. 030/19419) or inquire at the local main train station. Three people or more can often travel at discounted group rates.

Most trains now stop at and depart from all of Berlin's four main train stations, but generally west-originated trains arrive at Friedrichstrasse and Zoologischer Garten, east-originated trains at Hauptbahnhof and Lichtenberg. Train information: tel. 030/49541 for international trains, 030/49531 for domestic services.

By Bus Long-distance bus services link Berlin with numerous western German and other western European cities. For travel details, if you're in Berlin, call the main bus station (Messedam, tel. 030/301–8028), or if you're in western Germany, inquire at the local tourist office.

By Car The eight former "transit corridor" roads linking the western part of Germany with Berlin have now been incorporated into the country-wide autobahn network, but some are ill prepared for the vast increase of motor traffic between east and west that has followed unification. Be prepared for large traffic jams, particularly during weekends. At the time of writing, speed restrictions of 100 kph (60 mph) still apply on some autobahn sections, but on others they have now been raised to 120 kph (74 mph) or 130 kph (81 mph). You must carry your driver's license, car registration, and insurance documents. Seat belts must be worn at all times, even in the backseat.

Getting Around

By Public Transportation Berlin is surprisingly large, and only the center can comfortably be explored on foot. Fortunately, the city is blessed with an excellent public transportation system: A combination of U-Bahn (subway) and S-Bahn (metropolitan train) lines, buses, streetcars, and even a ferry across the Wannsee lake allows easy access to the whole city. The nine U-Bahn lines alone have 161 stations. Extensive all-night bus and streetcar service (they are marked by the letter N next to their number) are in operation all week, and the subway lines U9 and U12 run all night on weekends. For DM 3.50 (DM 2.30 children) you can buy a ticket that covers travel on the entire system for 2 hours. A multiple ticket, valid for four trips, costs DM 12 (DM 7.80 children). Or, you can pay DM 13 (DM 6.50 children) for a 24-hour ticket that allows unlimited use (except on the Wannsee Lake ferries). If you're staying for more than a few days, the week tourist pass for DM 32 is the best bargain. Information can be obtained at all ticket-selling booths or from the main office of the city transport authority, the Berliner Verkehrsbetriebe (BVG) at Hardenbergplatz, in front of the Bahnhof Zoo, or by calling 030/752–7020.

The fare structure now covers both parts of Berlin, although slightly cheaper tickets are still sold to East Berlin residents. These tickets are only valid with accompanying East Berlin identification, so don't be tempted to buy one if you're traveling in East Berlin. If you're caught without any ticket or one for East Berliners, the fine is DM 60.

By Taxi Taxi meters start at DM 3.60, and the fare is DM 1.79 (DM 1.99 after midnight). Taxi drivers charge 50 pf for each piece of heavy luggage carried. A drive along the Kurfürstendamm will cost about DM 15. Taxis can be ordered by telephone: Call 030/6902, 030/210–202, 030/8644, or 030/344–4059.

Important Addresses and Numbers

Tourist Information The main tourist office, **Verkehrsamt Berlin,** is at the Europa Center (Budapesterstr., tel. 030/262–6031). It's open Mon.–Sat. 8 AM–10:30 PM, Sun. 9–9. There are other offices at the main hall of **Tegel** airport (tel. 030/4101–3145, open daily 8 AM–11 PM); at **Zoologischer Garten,** (tel. 030/313–9063, open Mon.–Sat. 8 AM–11 PM); and at the **Hauptbahnhof** (tel. 030/279–5209; open daily 8–8) in East Berlin. Accommodations can be reserved at all offices, which also issue a free English-language information brochure, "Berlin Turns On." Pretravel information on Berlin can be obtained by writing to the Verkehrsamt Berlin (Martin-Luthar-Str. 105, 10825 Berlin).

Consulates U.S. (Neustädtische Kirchstr. 4–5, tel. 030/238–5174). **Canada** (International Trade Center, Friedrich Str. 95, tel. 030/261–1161). **Great Britain** (Unter den Linden 32–34, tel. 030/220–2431).

Emergencies **Police** (tel. 030/110). **Ambulance and emergency medical attention** (tel. 030/310–031). **Dentist** and **emergency pharmaceutical assistance** (tel. 030/1141).

English-Language Bookstores **Marga Schoeller** (Knesebeckstr. 33, tel. 030/881–1112) and **Buchhandlung Kiepert** (Hardenbergstr. 4–5, tel. 030/311–0090) sell English-language publications.

Guided Tours

By Bus English-language bus tours of West and East Berlin are offered by a number of operators, the chief of which are **Severin & Kühn** (Kurfürstendamm 216, Charlottenburg, tel. 030/883–1015); **Berliner Bären Stadtrundfahrt** (Rankestr. 35, corner of Kurfürstendamm, tel. 030/213–4077); **Reisebüro Berolina** (Kurfurstendamm 22, corner Meinekestr., tel. 030/882–2091); and **Bus Verkehr Berlin** (**BVB,** Kurfürstendamm 225, tel. 030/885–9880). These four companies offer more or less identical tours in English, covering all the major sights in West and East Berlin, as well as day tours to Potsdam and Dresden. The Berlin tours cost DM 30–DM 45, those to Potsdam and the Sanssouci Palace, the favorite residence of Frederick the Great, DM 60–DM 70. Inquire about tour operators that offer specialty (cultural, historical, walking) tours at the main city tourist office at the Europa-Center (Budapesterstr., tel. 030/262–6031).

By Boat Berlin is a city of waterways, and boat trips can be made on the Spree River, on the canals that connect the city's network of big lakes, and on the lakes themselves. For details, contact the main city tourist office.

Exploring Berlin

Visiting Berlin is a bittersweet experience, as so many of the triumphs and tragedies of the past are tied up with the bustling present. The result can be either dispiriting or exhilarating. And by European standards, Berlin isn't that old: Köln was more than 1,000 years old when Berlin was born from the fusion of two tiny settlements on islands in the Spree River. Although already a royal residence in the 15th century, Berlin really came into its own three centuries later, under the rule of King Friedrich II—Frederick the Great—whose liberal reforms and artistic patronage led the way as the city developed into a major cultural capital.

The events of the 20th century would have crushed the spirit of most other cities. Hitler destroyed the city's reputation for tolerance and plunged Berlin headlong into the war that led to the wholesale destruction of monuments and houses. And after World War II, Berlin was still to face the bitter division of the city and the construction of the infamous wall in 1961. But a storm of political events, beginning in 1989, brought the downfall of the Communist regime; the establishment of democracy in the east; and finally, in October 1990, the unification of Berlin and of all Germany. Now you can travel from one end of Berlin to the other and in and out of the long-isolated city as easily as you would in any other Western metropolis.

Numbers in the margin correspond to points of interest on the West Berlin map.

West Berlin The **Kurfürstendamm,** or Ku'damm as the Berliners call it, is one of Europe's busiest thoroughfares, throbbing with activity day and ❶ night. At its eastern end is the **Kaiser Wilhelm Gedächtniskirche** (Kaiser Wilhelm Memorial Church). This landmark has come to symbolize not only West Berlin, but the futile destructiveness of war. The shell of the tower is all that remains of the church that was built at the end of the 19th century and dedicated to the memory of Kaiser Wilhelm. Surrounding the tower are the new church and bell tower, referred to as the "powder box" and the "lipstick" by Berliners. Inside is a historical exhibition of the devastation of World War II. *At Breitscheidpl., tel. 030/218–5023. Admission free. Open Tues.–Sat. 10–4.*

❷ Cross Budapesterstrasse to enter the **Zoologischer Garten,** Berlin's zoo. It has the world's largest variety of individual types of fauna along with a fascinating aquarium. *Budapesterstr. 34, tel. 030/254–010. Admission to zoo only: DM 9 adults, DM 4.50 children. Combined ticket to zoo and aquarium: DM 13.50 adults, DM 6.50 children. Open daily from 9–6 PM or to dusk in winter.*

Double back across Breitscheidplatz and take Tauentzienstrasse to Wittenbergplatz to catch bus No. 142 to Kemperplatz. Among the ❸ buildings that comprise the **Kulturforum** (Cultural Forum) on the large square is the **Philharmonie** (Philharmonic Hall), home of the famous Berlin Philharmonic orchestra, whose musical director is Claudio Abbado. You'll recognize it by its roof, which resembles a great wave. The main hall, built in 1963, reopened in the spring of 1992 after an ambitious renovation. *Matthäikirchstr. 1, tel. 030/254–880. Ticket office open weekdays 3:30–6 and weekends 11–2.*

Opposite is the **Kunstgewerbemuseum** (Museum of Decorative Arts), which displays arts and crafts of Europe from the Middle Ages to the present day. Among its treasures is the Welfenschatz (Guelph Treasure), a collection of 16th-century gold and silver plate from Nürnberg. *Matthäikirchpl. 6, tel. 030/266–2902. Admission: DM 4 adults, DM 2 children. Combined day pass to 4 Tiergarten museums: DM 8 adults, DM 4 children. Free Sun. Open Tues.–Fri. 9–5, weekends 10–5.*

Leave the museum and walk south past the mid-19th-century church of St. Matthaeus to the **Neue Nationalgalerie** (New National Gallery), a modern glass-and-steel building designed by Mies van der Rohe and built in the mid-1960s. The gallery's collection consists of paintings, sculpture, and drawings from the 19th and 20th centuries, with an accent on works by the Impressionists. *Potsdamerstr. 50, tel. 030/266–2651. Admission: DM 4 adults, DM 2 children. Combined day pass to 4 Tiergarten museums: DM 8 adults, DM 4 children. Free Sun. Open Tues.–Fri. 9–5, weekends 10–5.*

West Berlin

Ägyptisches
Museum, **15**

Berliner Mauer, **9**

Brandenburger Tor, **6**

Gemäldegalerie, **16**

Grunewald, **17**

Haus am Checkpoint
Charlie, **11**

Kaiser Wilhelm
Gedächtniskirche, **1**

Kreuzberg, **12**

Kulturforum, **3**

Potsdamer Platz, **8**

Prinz-Albert-
Gelände, **10**

Rathaus
Schöneberg, **13**

Reichstag, **7**

Schloss
Charlottenburg, **14**

Siegessäule, **4**

Sowjetisches
Ehrenmal, **5**

Zoologischer Garten, **2**

Paulstr.

Lüneburgerstr.

Moltkestr.

Str. des 17 Juni

Entlastungsstr.

Tiergarten

Tiergarten Str.

7

5

6

Unter den Linden

Wilhelmstr.

Friedrichstr.

AE

Gendarmen-
markt

Marx
Engels
Pl.

Karl-Liebknecht-Str.

Alexander · Pl.

Rathausstr.

Stralauerstr.

Wallstr.

8

Potsdamer
Pl.

Leipzigerstr.

FORMER LOCATION
OF BERLIN WALL

11

9

10

Wilhelmstr.

Friedrichstr.

Lindenstr.

Oranienstr.

Ritterstr.

H. Heine-Str.

Prinzenstr.

3

Lützowstr.

Potsdamerstr.

-shöferstr.

Schönebergerstr.

Möckernstr.

Bülowstr.

Gitschinerstr.

Urban - str.

Potsdamerstr.

Yorckstr.

Yorckstr.

Möckernstr.

Monumentenstr.

Kreuzbergstr.

Mehringdamm

Gneisenaustr.

Baerwaldstr.

Bergmannstr.

Volkspark
Hasenheide

12
Victoria
Park

Dudenstr.

Columbiadamm

Kolonnenstr.

Ebertstr.

Westtangente

0   1/2 mile

0   3/4 km

N

The Kulturforum is adjacent to the 255-hectare (630-acre) **Tiergarten** (Animal Park), the Elector's former hunting grounds, which has at last recovered from the war, when it was not only ripped apart by bombs and artillery, but was stripped of its woods by desperate, freezing Berliners in the bitter cold winter of 1945–46. The column in the center of a large traffic circle in the park is the

❹ **Siegessäule** (Victory Column), erected in 1873 to commemorate four Prussian military campaigns against the French. The granite and sandstone monument originally stood in front of the Reichstag (parliament building), but was moved to its present site in 1938 as part of the Nazi's grand architectural designs for Berlin. Climb the 285 steps to its 65-meter (210-foot) summit and you'll be rewarded with a fine view of both West Berlin and East Berlin. *Am Grossen Stern, Admission: DM 1.50 adults, DM 1 children. Open Mon. 3–6, Tues.–Sun. 9–6.*

At the base of the Siegessäule, go east down the wide Strasse des 17 Juni (June 17th Street), named in memory of the day, in 1953, when 50,000 East Germans staged an uprising that was put down by Sovi-

❺ et tanks. On the left, you'll pass the **Sowjetisches Ehrenmal** (Soviet Honor Monument), a semicircular colonnade topped with a statue of a Russian soldier and flanked by what are said to be the first Soviet tanks to have fought their way into Berlin in 1945.

❻ Ahead of you is **Brandenburger Tor** (Brandenburg Gate), built in 1788 as a victory arch for triumphant Prussian armies. The horse-drawn chariot atop the arch was reerected after the war. The monumental gate was cut off from West Berlin by the Wall, and it became a focal point of celebrations marking the unification of Berlin and of all Germany. It was here that German politicians formally sealed unification.

❼ Just north of the Brandenburg Gate is the **Reichstag**, which served as Germany's parliament building from its completion in 1894 until 1933, when it was gutted by fire under suspicious circumstances. When the federal government relocates to Berlin (scheduled for 1998), the Bundestag, the lower house of parliament, will convene here. The Reichstag houses an excellent exhibition on German history entitled "Questions on German History." *Pl. der Republic, tel. 030/3977–3172. Admission free. Open Tues.–Sun. 10–5.*

❽ Walk south along where the Wall used to stand to **Potsdamer Platz** (Potsdam Square). It was one of Berlin's busiest pre-war squares, but then had the distinction to be the widest expanse of No-Man's Land separating East and West Berlin. Follow farther along the Wall's former location to see the real thing, one of three still-stand-

❾ ing segments of the famous **Berliner Mauer** (Berlin Wall), to find the

❿ **Prince-Albert-Gelände** (Prince-Albert-Grounds) along Niederkircherstrasse. Buildings that once stood here housed the headquarters of the Gestapo and other Nazi security organizations from 1933 until 1945. After the war, they were leveled and remained so until 1987, when what was left of the buildings was excavated and an exhibit documenting their history and Nazi atrocities was opened. *Exhibit: Topography of Terrors, Stresemannstr. 110, tel. 030/2548–6703. Admission free. Open Tues.–Sun. 10–6.*

The history of the hideous frontier fortification can be followed in the museum that arose at its most famous crossing point, at Friedrichstrasse, the second cross street heading east. Checkpoint Charlie, as it was known, disappeared along with the Wall, but the

⓫ **Haus am Checkpoint Charlie** (House at Checkpoint Charlie–The Wall Museum) is still there. Be sure to give yourself at least a few hours to see the many excellent exhibits and films. *Friedrichstr. 44, tel. 030/251–1031. Admission: DM 7.50 adults, DM 4.50 children. Open daily 9 AM–10 PM.*

Time Out Try to visualize the former Checkpoint Charlie crossing and the Wall from a window seat at **Café Adler** (Friedrichstr. 206, tel. 030/ 251–8965), which bumped right up against the Wall here. The soups and salads are all tasty and cheap.

Find the nearby Kochstrasse U-Bahn station and go two stops south on the U6 line to Mehringdamm. Head for Kreuzbergstrasse. Just ⑫ on the left is the 62-meter (200-foot) **Kreuzberg,** West Berlin's highest natural hill. (There are higher hills made of the rubble gathered from the bombed-out ruins of the city when reconstruction began in 1945.) The monument on the top of the hill was erected in 1821 to commemorate the 1813–15 Wars of Liberation.

Bordering Kreuzberg to the west is the Schöneberg district, where ⑬ you'll find **Rathaus Schöneberg** (Schöneberg City Hall), the former West Berlin city hall. (In 1991 the city administration moved back to the Rotes Rathaus in the Mitte district.) In the belfry of the Rathaus is a replica of the Liberty Bell, donated to Berliners in 1950 by the United States and rung every day at noon. It was in front of the Rathaus that President Kennedy made his famous "Ich bin ein Berliner" speech, in the spring of 1963.

Take the U-Bahn north one stop from Rathaus Schöneberg station and change to the U7 line for eight stops, to Richard-Wagner-Platz station. From the station, walk east along Otto-Suhr-Allee to the ⑭ handsome **Schloss Charlottenburg** (Charlottenburg Palace) and its beautiful, calming grounds, which have French and English gardens and a swan-filled pond. Built at the end of the 17th century by King Frederick I for his wife, Queen Sophie Charlotte, the palace was progressively enlarged for later royal residents. Frederick the Great's suite of rooms can be visited. *Luisenplatz, tel. 030/320–911. Admission: DM 4 adults, DM 2 children. Combined day pass to 4 Charlottenburg museums: DM 8 adults, DM 4 children. Free Sun. Open Tues.–Fri. 9–5, weekends 10–5.*

⑮ Opposite the palace is the **Ägyptisches Museum** (Egyptian Museum), home of perhaps the world's best-known portrait sculpture, the beautiful Nefertiti. The 3,300-year-old Egyptian queen is the centerpiece of a fascinating collection of Egyptology that includes one of the finest preserved mummies outside Cairo. *Schlosstr. 70, tel. 030/320–911. Admission: DM 4 adults, DM 2 children. Combined day pass to 4 Charlottenburg museums: DM 8 adults, DM 4 children. Free Sun. Open Mon.–Thurs. 9–5, weekends 10–5. Closed Fri.*

Take U-Bahn line U7 back toward Schöneberg until Fehrbelliner Platz, where you change to line U2 southwest for five stops to Dahlem-Dorf station. This is the stop for the magnificent **Dahlem museums,** chief of which is West Berlin's leading picture gallery, the ⑯ **Gemäldegalerie.** The collection includes many works by the great European masters, with 26 Rembrandts and 14 by Rubens. *Arnimallee 23/27, tel. 030/83011. Admission: DM 4 adults, DM 2 children. Combined day pass to 8 Dahlem museums: DM 8 adults, DM 4 children. Free Sun. Open Tues.–Fri. 9–5, weekends 10–5.*

No visit to West Berlin is complete without an outing to the city's ⑰ outdoor playground, the **Grunewald** (Green Forest). Bordering the Dahlem district to the west, the park is a vast green space, with meadows, woodlands, and lakes. There are a string of 60 lakes within Berlin's boundaries; some are kilometers long, others are no more than ponds. The total length of their shorelines—if stretched out in one long line—is 209½ kilometers (130 miles), longer than Germany's Baltic Coast. There are nudist beaches on the banks of the Wannsee lake, while in winter a downhill ski run and even a ski jump operate on the modest slopes of the Teufelsberg hill.

East Berlin The infamous Wall is now gone, but the spirit of division remains in a city that was physically split for 28 years. The stately buildings of the city's past are not as overwhelmed by new high-rise construction as in West Berlin, but East Berlin's postwar architectural blunders are just as monumental in their own way. These will be obvious—along with the sad shabbiness of years of neglect—as you explore the side streets together with the main thoroughfares.

Numbers in the margin correspond to points of interest on the East Berlin map.

⑱ For a sense of déjà vu, enter the eastern part of Berlin at **Checkpoint Charlie,** the most famous crossing point between the two Berlins during the Cold War; American and Soviet tanks faced each other here during the tense months of the Berlin Blockade in 1948. At this point both ends of Friedrichstrasse—north and south—are lined with attractive new shops and trendy restaurants. Turn right onto ⑲ Mohrenstrasse and you'll arrive at **Gendarmenmarkt,** with its beautifully reconstructed **Schauspielhaus**—built in 1818, and now one of the city's main concert halls—and the twin **Deutsche und Französische Dome** (German—south side, undergoing restoration—and French Cathedrals). In the latter, you'll find the ⑳ **Hugenottenmuseum** (Huguenot Museum), which has some interesting collections of the history and art of the French Protestant Huguenots who took refuge in Germany after being expelled from Catholic France in 1685. *Gendarmenmarkt, tel. 030/229–1760. Admission: DM 2 adults, DM 1 children. Open Tues.–Thurs., Sat. noon–5; Sun. 1–5.*

Time Out The **Arkade Café** (Französischer Str. 25) on the northwest corner of the plaza is perfect for a light snack; some excellent pastry; and a beer, coffee, or tea.

Continue east along the Französischer Strasse and turn left into Hedwigskirchgasse to reach Bebelplatz. The peculiar round shape ㉑ of **St. Hedwigs Kathedrale** (St. Hedwig's Cathedral) calls to mind Rome's Pantheon. The tiny street named Hinter der Katholischen Kirche (Behind the Catholic Church) is a reminder that though Berlin was very much a Protestant city, St. Hedwig's was built (about 1747) for Catholics.

Walk north across Bebelplatz to Unter den Linden, the elegant cen- ㉒ tral thoroughfare of Old Berlin. On your right is the **Deutsche Staatsoper** (German State Opera), the great opera house of Berlin, now with an entirely new interior. Just after Oberwallstrasse is the former crown prince's palace, the **Kronprinzenpalais,** now restored and used to house official government visitors.

Look back down the street to the western sector and you'll see the ㉓ monumental **Brandenburger Tor** (Brandenburg Gate), its chariot-and-horses sculpture now turned to face the east. Cross Unter den ㉔ Linden and look into the courtyard of **Humboldt Universität** (Humboldt University): It was built as a palace for the brother of Friedrich II of Prussia but became a university in 1810, and today is

East Berlin

KEY

AE American Express Office

Altes Museum, **26**
Berliner Dom, **30**
Bodemuseum, **29**
Brandenburger Tor, **23**
Checkpoint Charlie, **18**
Deutsche
Staatsoper, **22**
Deutsches Historisches
Museum, **25**
Fernsehturm, **34**
Gendarmenmarkt, **19**

Hugenotten-
museum, **20**
Humboldt
Universität, **24**
Marienkirche, **33**
Märkisches
Museum, **37**
Nationalgalerie, **27**
Nikolaikirche, **36**

Palast der
Republik, **31**
Pergamon Museum, **28**
Rotes Rathaus, **35**
St. Hedwigs
Kathedrale, **21**
Staatsrat, **32**
Synagogue, **38**

one of Germany's largest institutions of higher learning. Marx and Engels were its two most famous students. Beyond the war memorial, housed in a onetime arsenal (1695–1705) is the **Deutsches Historisches Museum** (German Historical Museum), which has a partial inventory of its exhibit tracing German History from 1789 to the present on display. *Unter den Linden 2, tel. 030/215–020. Admission: DM 4 adults, DM 2 children. Open Thurs.–Tues. 10–6.*

Turning left along the Spree canal (along Am Zeughaus and Am Kupfergraben) will bring you to East Berlin's museum complex, at the northern end of what is known as **Museumsinsel** (Museum Island). The first of the Big Four that you'll encounter is the **Altes Museum** (entrance on Lustgarten), an austere neoclassical building just to the north of Marx-Engels-Platz. The collections here include postwar art from some of Germany's most prominent artists and numerous etchings and drawings from the Old Masters. Next comes the **Nationalgalerie,** on Bodestrasse, which features 19th- and 20th-century painting and sculpture. The **Pergamon Museum,** on Am Kupfergraben, is one of Europe's greatest museums. Its name derives from the museum's principal exhibit and the city's number-one attraction, the Pergamon Altar, a monumental Greek altar dating from 180 BC that occupies an entire city block. Almost as impressive is the Babylonian Processional Way. The Pergamon Museum also houses vast Egyptian, early Christian, and Byzantine collections, plus a fine array of sculpture from the 12th to the 18th centuries. To the north is the **Bodemuseum** (also on Am Kupfergraben, but with its entrance on Monbijoubrücke), with an outstanding collection of early Christian, Byzantine, and Egyptian art, as well as exhibits of Italian Old Masters paintings. *For all of Museumsinsel: tel. 030/ 203–550. Admission to each museum: DM 4 adults, DM 2 children. Combined day pass to 4 Museumsinsel museums: DM 8 adults, DM 4 children. Free Sun. Museum complex open Wed.–Sun. 9–5; Pergamon's architectural halls only: Mon. and Tues. 9–5.*

From the museum complex, follow the Spree river south to Unter den Linden and the vast **Berliner Dom** (Berlin Cathedral). The cathedral's impressive main nape was reopened in June 1993 after a 20-year renovation. The hideous modern building in bronze mirrored glass opposite is the **Palast der Republik** (Palace of the Republic), a postwar monument to socialist progress that also housed restaurants, a theater, and a dance hall. Since 1991 the Palast has been closed while the politicians argue about whether it should be torn down or used for other purposes. It formerly housed the Volkskammer, East Germany's People's Chamber (Parliament). The building at the south end of Marx-Engels-Platz used to house East Germany's **Staatsrat** (Federal Senate). From the balcony of the preserved older entrance, on November 18, 1919, Karl Liebknecht declared the birth of the doomed German Socialist Republic.

Head east on Karl-Liebknecht-Strasse for a closer look at the 13th-century **Marienkirche** (Church of St. Mary), especially noting its late-Gothic *Dance of Death* fresco. You are now at the lower end of Alexanderplatz. Just ahead is the massive **Fernsehturm** (TV Tower), which stands 365 meters high (not accidentally 215 meters *higher* than West Berlin's broadcasting tower). It offers the best view of Berlin and the city's highest café. *Alexanderplatz, tel. 030/242– 3333. Admission: 5 DM adults, 2.50 DM children. Open daily 9– noon.*

The red building southwest of the tower is the **Rotes Rathaus** (Red City Hall). The building's redbrick design and the frieze depicting scenes from the city's history are impressive. In the fall of 1991 the city administration and seat of the governing mayor were transferred from Rathaus Schöneberg back to the Rotes Rathaus, renewing its prewar function. The area adjacent to the Rathaus, known as the **Nikolai Viertel** (Nikolai Quarter), has been handsomely rebuilt and is now filled with delightful shops, cafés, and restaurants. On the quarter's Probst Strasse, Berlin's oldest building, the **36** **Nikolaikirche** (Nikolai Church), can be found. The church, dating from 1230, was heavily damaged in the war, but has been beautifully restored and is now a museum. Wander back down Muhlendamm into the area around the Breitestrasse—there are some lovely old buildings here—and on over to the **Fischerinsel** area. The throbbing heart of Old Berlin of 750 years ago, Fischerinsel retains a tangible medieval flavor.

Time Out   The **Alt-Cöllner Schankstuben** (Friedrichsgracht 50), overlooking the Spree canal is as charming and friendly a restaurant as you'll find in East Berlin. On a sunny day, enjoy a glass of beer at an outdoor table.

37   Nearby is the **Märkisches Museum** (Mark Museum), which has different exhibits on Berlin's history, in addition to an amusing section devoted to automaphones—"self-playing" musical instruments. These are demonstrated Sundays 10–noon and Wednesdays 3–4. Live bears—the city's symbol—are in a pit next to the museum. *Am Köllnischen Park 5, tel. 030/270–0514. Admission: DM 3 adults, DM 1 children. Instrument demonstration: 2 DM. Open Tues.–Sun. 10–6.*

Take the U2 subway from Märkisches Museum station three stops to Stadtmitte, then change to the U6, traveling three stops to Oranienburger Tor. Walk a few blocks down Oranienburger Strasse **38**   to reach the city's largest **synagogue.** Completed in 1866, in oriental style, the synagogue was one of Germany's most beautiful until it was seriously damaged on November 9, 1938, the infamous *Kristallnacht* (crystal night) when synagogues and Jewish stores across Germany were vandalized, looted, and burned. Nearly destroyed by Allied bombing in 1943, it remained a ruin until renovation began under the East Germany regime only in the mid-80's.

Shopping

Berlin is a city of alluring stores and boutiques. Despite the new capital's cosmopolitan gloss, prices are generally lower than in cities like Munich and Hamburg. Most stores offer tax-free shopping for non-European Union citizens, so be sure to ask about it before making your purchase.

Fine porcelain is still produced at the former Royal Prussian Porcelain Factory, now called **Staaliche Porzellan Manufactur,** or KPM. This delicate, handmade, hand-painted china is sold at KPM's store at Kurfürstendamm 26A (tel. 030/881–1802), but it may be more fun to visit the factory salesroom at Wegelystrasse 1. It sells seconds at reduced prices. If you long to have the Egyptian Queen Nefertiti on your mantlepiece at home, try the **Gipsformerei der Staatlichen Museen Preussicher Kulturbesitz** (Sophie-Charlotte-Str. 17, tel. 030/321–7011, open weekdays 9–4). It sells plaster casts of this and other treasures from the city's museums.

Shopping   The liveliest and most famous shopping area in West Berlin is the
Districts   **Kurfürstendamm** and its side streets, especially between **Breitscheidplatz** and **Oliver Platz**. The **Europa Center** at

Breitscheidplatz encompasses more than 100 stores, cafés, and restaurants—this is not a place to bargain-hunt, though! Running east from Breitscheidplatz is **Tauenzientstrasse,** another shopping street. Elegant malls include the **Gloria Galerie** (opposite the Wertheim department store on Ku'damm) and the **Uhland-Passage** (connecting Uhlandstrasse and Fasanenstrasse). In both, you'll find leading name stores as well as cafés and restaurants.

For trendier clothes, try the boutiques along **Bleibtreustrasse.** One of the more avant-garde fashion boutiques is **Durchbruch** (Schlutterstr. 54), around the corner. The name means "breakthrough," and the store lives up to its name by selling six different designers' outrageous styles. Less trendy and much less expensive is the shopping strip along **Wilmersdorferstrasse** (U7 station of same name), where price-conscious Berliners do their shopping. It's packed on weekends.

East Berlin's chief shopping areas are along the **Friedrichstrasse, Unter den Linden,** and in the area around **Alexanderplatz.** The **Berliner Markthalle** (corner Karl-Liebknecht-Str. and Rosa-Luxemburg-Str.) is one of the East's newest and largest malls.

Department Stores The classiest department store in Berlin is **KaDeWe,** the Kaufhaus des Westens (Department Store of the West, as it's modestly known in English), at Wittenbergplatz. The biggest department store in Europe, the KaDeWe is a grand-scale emporium in modern guise. Be sure to check out the food department, which occupies the whole sixth floor. The other main department store downtown is **Wertheim** on the Ku'damm. Neither as big nor as attractive as the KaDeWe, Wertheim nonetheless offers a large selection of fine wares.

The main department store in East Berlin is **Kaufhof** (formerly Centrum), at the north end of Alexanderplatz. Under the old regime, you could find ridiculously cheap subsidized prices here. Now it is filled with mainly Western-made products, superior, of course, but the prices are higher.

Antiques On Saturdays and Sundays from 10 to 5, the colorful and lively antiques and handicrafts fair on Strasse des 17 Juni swings into action. Don't expect to pick up any bargains—or to have the place to yourself. Not far from Wittenbergplatz is **Keithstrasse,** a street given over to antiques stores. Eisenacherstrasse, Fuggerstrasse, Kalckreuthstrasse, Motzstrasse, and Nollendorfstrasse—all close to Nollendorfplatz—have many antiques stores of varying quality. Another good street for antiques is **Suarezstrasse,** between Kantstrasse and Bismarckstrasse.

In East Berlin, antiques are sold in the Nikolai quarter at the **Antikenmarkt** under the tracks at Friedrichstrasse and in the restored Husemannstrasse. Some private stores along the stretch of Friedichstrasse north of the Spree Bridge sell old books and prints.

Dining

Dining in Berlin can mean sophisticated nouvelle creations in upscale restaurants with linen tablecloths and hand-painted porcelain plates or hearty local specialties in atmospheric and inexpensive inns. The range is as vast as the city. Specialties include *Eisbein mit Sauerkraut,* knuckle of pork with pickled cabbage; *Rouladen,* rolled stuffed beef; *Spanferkel,* suckling pig; *Berliner Schüsselsülze,* potted meat in aspic; *Schlachtplatte,* mixed grill; *Hackepeter,* ground beef; and *Kartoffelpuffer,* fried potato cakes. *Bockwurst* is a chubby frankfurter that's served in a variety of ways and sold in restaurants and at Bockwurst stands all over the city. *Schlesisches Himmerlreich* is roast goose or pork served with potato dumplings in rich gravy. *Königsberger Klopse* consists of meatballs, herring, and capers—it tastes much better than it sounds.

East Berlin now has some of the city's most fashionable and expensive restaurants, ranging from French and New German Cuisine to even more exotic fare, such as Japanese, Thai, and Indonesian; most of the restaurants featuring the national cuisine of other one-time socialist states are now gone. Wines and spirits imported from other former East Bloc countries can still be found in many restaurants, however, and are quite good; try Hungarian, Yugoslav, and Bulgarian wines (the whites are lighter), and Polish and Russian vodkas.

For details and price-category definitions, *see* Dining in Staying in Germany, *above*.

West Berlin
Expensive
★

Bamberger Reiter. Considered by Berliners to be one of the city's best restaurants, Bamberger Reiter is the pride of its chef, Tirolean Franz Raneburger. He relies heavily on fresh market produce for his *neue deutsche Küche* (new German cuisine), so the menu changes from day to day. Fresh flowers, too, abound in his attractive, oakbeamed restaurant. *Regensburgerstr. 7, tel. 030/218–4282. Reservations required. AE, DC, V. Dinner only. Closed Sun., Mon., Jan. 1–15.*

Frühsammer's Restaurant an der Rehwiese. From your table you can watch chef Peter Frühsammer at work in his open kitchen. He's ready with advice on the daily menu: Salmon is always a treat here. The restaurant is located in the annex of a turn-of-the-century villa in the southern district of Zehlendorf (U-Bahn to Krumme Lanke and then bus No. 53 to Rehwiese). *Matterhornstr. 101, tel. 030/803–8032. Reservations strongly advised. No credit cards. Dinner only.*

Paris Bar. This top-class restaurant in Charlottenburg attracts a polyglot clientele of film stars, artists, entrepreneurs, and executives. The cuisine is high-powered, high-quality French. *Kantstr. 152, tel. 030/313–8052. Reservations advised. AE.*

Moderate

Alt-Nürnberg. Step into the tavernlike interior and you could be in Bavaria: The waitresses even wear dirndls. The Bavarian colors of blue and white are everywhere, and such Bavarian culinary delights as *Schweinshaxe* (knuckle of pork) are well represented on the menu. If you prefer to eat in the Prussian style, the calves' liver *Berliner Art* is recommended. *Europa Center, tel. 030/261–4397. Reservations advised. AE, DC, MC, V.*

★ **Blockhaus Nikolskoe.** Prussian King Wilhelm III built this Russianstyle wooden lodge for his daughter Charlotte, wife of Russia's Czar Nicholas I. It's located in the southwest of the city, on the eastern edge of Glienicke Park. In summer, you can eat on the open terrace overlooking the Havel River. In character with its history and appearance, the Blockhaus features game dishes. *Nikolskoer Weg, tel. 030/805–2914. Reservations advised. DC, MC, V.*

Gado Gado. This quaint restaurant just north of Savigny Platz serves some of the city's best Thai food. The soft lighting and tropical umbrellas lining the walls and the friendly service won't transport you to Thailand, but you'll almost feel like you're there once you sample some of the delicately prepared food. The coconut soup is the very embodiment of smoothness. *Goethestr. 6, tel. 030/316–067. Reservations advised. No credit cards. Dinner only.*

Hecker's Deele. You could find yourself seated in one of the antique church pews that complete the oak-beamed interior of this restaurant that features Westphalian dishes. The *Westfälische Schlachtplatte* (a variety of meats) will set you up for a whole day's sightseeing—the Ku'damm is right outside. *Grolmannstr. 35, tel. 030/88900. No reservations. AE, DC, MC, V.*

Mundart Restaurant. Too many cooks don't spoil the broth (and certainly not the excellent fish soup) at this popular restaurant in the Kreuzberg district. Two chefs are at work in the spacious kitchen. Fortunately, they agree on the day's specials, and you can follow their advice with impunity. *Muskauerstr. 33/34, tel. 030/612-2061. No reservations. No credit cards. Dinner only.*

Inexpensive **Eierschale.** This is one of the better breakfast cafés, located just off Ku'damm. In the evenings, it serves mostly Berlin fare and features jazz bands in the neighboring room. Sunday mornings are Frühschoppen time when live jazz accompanies the buffet brunch. *Rankestr. 1, tel. 030/882-5305. Reservations accepted. AE, MC.*

Thürnagel. Located in the Kreuzberg district, Thürnagel is a vegetarian restaurant where it's not only healthy to eat but fun. The seitan in sherry sauce or the tempeh curry are good enough to convert a seasoned carnivore. *Gneisenaustr. 57, tel. 030/691-4800. Reservations advised. No credit cards. Dinner only.*

East Berlin **Ermeler-Haus.** The wine restaurant in a series of upstairs rooms re-
Very Expensive flects the elegance of this restored patrician house, which dates from 1567 (it was moved to its present location in 1969, however). The atmosphere is subdued, the wines are imported, and the service matches the international specialties. There's dancing on Saturday evening. *Märkisches Ufer 12, tel. 030/279-4028. Reservations advised. AE, DC, MC, V. Closed Mon.*

Moderate **Borchardt.** This fashionable meeting place has columns, red plush benches, and an art nouveau mosaic, all of which helps create the impression of a 1920s salon. The restaurant serves entrées that have a French accent, it's also well known for its luscious seafood platter (DM 58). Sunday brunches are particularly popular, so plan a bit ahead for that. *Französischestr. 47, tel. 030/229-3144. Reservations advised. AE, MC, V.*

Französicher Hof. The ceilings in this classy restaurant are as high as the wine list is long. International fare, with an emphasis on French dishes, is served with impeccable service. The maître d' claims that guests can find here "an oasis of calm and relaxation," and he's right. In summer the terrace offers seats practically on Gendarmenmarkt. *Jägerstr. 56, tel. 030/229-3969. Reservations advised. AE, DC, MC, V.*

Reinhard's. This restaurant in the Nikolai quarter is one of Berlin's newer popular eating establishments. Berliners of all stripes meet here to enjoy the carefully prepared entrées and sample spirits from the amply stocked bar. It's all served to you by friendly, bright-tie-wearing waiters. The honey-glazed breast of duck "Adlon" is one of the house specialties. *Poststr. 28, tel. 030/242-5295. Reservations advised for lunch and dinner. AE, DC, MC, V.*

★ **Turmstuben.** Not for the infirm or those who are afraid of heights, the Turmstuben restaurant is tucked away below the cupola of the French Cathedral, which sits on the north side of the beautiful Gendarmenmarkt. The restaurant, which runs a circular course around the base of the cupola, is approached by a long, winding staircase. The reward at the top of the stairs is a table in one of Berlin's most original and attractive restaurants. It's worth the wait for a table in the upstairs dining hall. The menu is as short as the stairway is long, but there's an impressive wine list. *Gendarmenmarkt, tel. 030/229-9313. Reservations strongly advised on weekends (the frustration of being turned away after that climb could spoil anyone's day). No credit cards.*

Zur Rippe. This famous eating place in the Nikolai Quarter serves wholesome food in an intimate setting with oak paneling and ceramic tiles. Specialties include the herring casserole. *Poststr. 17, tel. 030/2431–3234. Reservations not necessary. No credit cards.*

Inexpensive **Alt-Cöllner Schankstuben.** A charming and genuine old Berlin house is the setting for this conglomerate of no fewer than three tiny restaurants, all of which provide exceptionally friendly service. *Friedrichsgracht 50, tel. 030/242–5972. Reservations accepted. AE, DC, MC, V.*

★ **Zur Letzten Instanz.** Established in 1621, Berlin's oldest restaurant combines the charming atmosphere of Old-World Berlin with a limited (but tasty) choice of dishes. Napoleon is said to have sat alongside the tiled stove in the front room and Mikhail Gorbachev enjoyed a beer here during a visit to Berlin in 1989. The emphasis here is on beer, both in the recipes and in the mug. Service can be erratic, though engagingly friendly. *Waisenstr. 14–16, tel. 030/242–5528. Reservations advised for both lunch and dinner. AE, DC, V.*

Lodging

Berlin lost all its grand old luxury hotels in the bombing during World War II; though some were rebuilt, many of the best hotels today are modern. Although they lack little in service and comfort, you may find some short on atmosphere. For first-class or luxury accommodations, East Berlin is easily as good as West, because the East German government, eager for hard currency, built several elegant hotels—the Grand, Palast, Dom (now the Hilton International), and Metropol—which are up to the very best international standards and place in the very top price category. If you're seeking something more moderate, the better choice may be West Berlin, where there are large numbers of good-value pensions and small hotels, many of them in older buildings with some character. In East Berlin, however, the hostels run by the Evangelical Lutheran church offer outstanding value for your money.

In West Berlin, business conventions year-round and the influx of summer tourists mean that you should make reservations well in advance. If you arrive without reservations, consult the board at Tegel Airport that shows hotels with vacancies or go to the tourist office.

For details and price-category definitions, *see* Lodging in Staying in Germany, *above.*

West Berlin **Bristol Hotel Kempinski.** Located in the heart of the city, this grand
Very Expensive hotel has the best of Berlin's shopping on its doorstep. English-style furnishings give the "Kempi" an added touch of class. All the rooms and suites are luxuriously decorated and equipped, with marble bathrooms, air-conditioning, and cable TV. Children under 12 stay for free if they share their parents' room. *Kurfürstendamm 27, tel. 030/884–340, fax 030/883–6075. 315 rooms with bath, 52 suites. Facilities: 3 restaurants, bar, garden room, winter garden, indoor pool, sauna, fitness room, solarium, masseur, hairdresser, boutiques, 24-hour room service, limousine service. AE, DC, MC, V.*

Grand Hotel Esplanade. Opened in 1988, the Grand Hotel Esplanade exudes luxury. Uncompromisingly modern architecture, chicly styled rooms, and works of art by some of Berlin's most acclaimed artists are some of its outstanding visual aspects. Then there are the superb facilities and impeccable service. *Lützowufer 15, tel. 030/261–011, fax 030/265–1171. 369 rooms with bath, 33 suites. Facilities: 2 restaurants, pub, bar, pool-side bar, pool, sauna, whirlpool, steam bath, solarium, fitness center, masseur, hairdresser, bou-*

tique, 24-hour room service, free bicycle rental, library. AE, DC, MC, V.

★ **Inter-Continental Berlin.** The "Diplomaten Suite" is expensive, but it is in a class of its own: It's as large as a suburban house and furnished in modern Italian style. The other rooms and suites are not as luxuriously furnished but still show exquisite taste. The lobby is a quarter the size of a football field, opulently furnished, and just the place for afternoon tea and pastries. *Budapesterstr. 2, tel. 030/26020, fax 030/2602–80760. 511 rooms with bath, 70 suites. Facilities: 3 restaurants (including a rooftop garden), 2 bars, indoor pool, sauna, non-smoking floor, 24-hour room service, boutiques. AE, DC, MC, V.*

Expensive **Berlin Excelsior Hotel.** This modern, well-run establishment is part of the Blue Band Hotels group in Berlin and is only five minutes from the Ku'damm. The comfortable rooms are furnished in dark teak, and the helpful front-office staff will arrange sightseeing tours and will try to obtain hard-to-get theater and concert tickets. *Hardenbergerstr. 14, tel. 030/31550, fax 030/3155–1002. 320 rooms with bath. Facilities: 2 restaurants, bar, garden terrace, winter garden, garage. AE, DC, MC, V.*

★ **Palace.** This ideally located hotel just completed an impressive renovation that has enhanced its luxurious looks, and the service has also been upgraded considerably. The rooms are comfortable and tastefully furnished. The ninth floor is an all-suite floor that offers maximum privacy. Ask for a room in the Spielbank wing, where the view is memorable. The Palace is part of Berlin's Europa Center, and guests have free use of the center's health club (including pool, fitness room, steam bath, sauna, and masseur). *Europa Center, tel. 030/25020, fax 030/262–6577. 322 rooms with bath, 18 suites. Facilities: 2 restaurants, bar, bistro, garage. AE, DC, MC, V.*

Schweizerhof Inter-Continental. There's a rustic, Swiss look about most of the rooms in this centrally located hotel, but they have a high standard of comfort and facilities. Ask to be placed in the west wing, where the rooms are larger. The indoor pool is the largest of any Berlin hotel, and the hotel is opposite Tiergarten Park. *Budapesterstr. 21–31, tel. 030/26960, fax 030/269–6900. 430 rooms with bath, 26 suites. Facilities: 2 restaurants, bar, indoor pool, pool-side bar, steam bath, masseur, sauna, solarium, fitness room, boutique, nonsmoking floor, garage. AE, DC, MC, V.*

Moderate **Hotel Casino.** The hotel is a former Prussian military barracks but bears little evidence of its former role: The rooms are large and comfortable and well equipped—the soldiers never had it so good. The hotel is located in the Charlottenburg district. *Königin-Élisabeth-Str. 47a, tel. 030/303090, fax 030/303–0945. 25 rooms with bath. Facilities: all-night snack bar. AE, DC, MC, V.*

★ **Ravenna.** This small, friendly hotel is located in the Steglitz district, close to the Botanical Garden and the Dahlen Museum. All the rooms are well equipped, but suite 111B is a bargain: It includes a large living room and kitchen for the rate of only DM 305. *Grunewaldstr. 8–9, tel. 030/792–8031, fax 030/794–412. 55 rooms with bath or shower, 4 suites. Facilities: bar. AE, DC, MC, V.*

Riehmers Hofgarten. Located in the interesting Kreuzberg district, this hotel, in a late-19th-century building, is a short walk from the Kreuzberg hill, is surrounded by bars and restaurants, and has fast connections to the center of town. The high-ceilinged rooms are elegantly furnished. *Yorckstr. 83, tel. 030/781–011, fax 030/786–6059. 21 rooms with bath or shower. AE, DC, MC, V.*

Inexpensive **Econtel.** Families are well cared for at this hotel that's situated within walking distance of Charlottenburg Palace. Lone travelers also appreciate the touches in the rooms, which come with free closet safes and cable. The breakfast buffet offers a dazzling array of choices and will fill you up for a day of sightseeing. *Sommeringstr. 24, tel. 030/346–810, fax 030/344–7034. 205 rooms with bath or shower. Facilities: bar. MC, V.*

East Berlin **Hilton International.** The city's newest hotel (opened in 1990) the
Very Expensive Hilton International is located on the beautiful Gendarmenmarkt in the center of East Berlin. The rooms feature heated tubs; house facilities are equally plush. *Gendarmenmarkt, tel. 030/23–820, fax 030/2382–4269. 355 rooms with bath, 24 suites. Facilities: 2 restaurants, cafeteria, winter garden, pub, wine cellar, bar, discotheque, pool, sauna, solarium, masseur, health club, bowling, squash, hairdresser, beauty salon, art gallery, shop, 24-hour room service, rooms for disabled guests, garage, car rental. AE, DC, MC, V.*

★ **Maritim Grand Hotel.** East Berlin's most expensive hotel lives up to its name—it's grand in every sense of the word. From the moment you step into the atrium lobby, you'll wonder how this grandiose bit of capitalist decadence ever fit into a socialist society. From the lobby on in, all is couched in luxury. *Friedrichstr. 158–164, corner Behrenstr., tel. 030/23–270, fax 030/2327–3362. 349 rooms with bath, 16 suites. Facilities: 4 restaurants, Bierstube, concert café, bar, pool, sauna, solarium, fitness room, shopping arcade, hairdresser, theater-ticket office, 24-hour room service, nonsmoking floor, garage. AE, DC, MC, V.*

★ **Metropol.** This hotel, recently acquired by the German Maritim hotel group, is the businessperson's choice, not least for its excellent location opposite the International Trade Center. The best rooms are those in front, with a view toward the north. The main specialty restaurant (left of the lobby) is now one of the city's best and is full at noon (reservations advised). *Friedrichstr. 150–153, tel. 030/23875, fax 030/238–74209. 341 rooms with bath, 31 suites. Facilities: 2 restaurants, bar, fitness room, sauna, health club, shops, garage, car rental. AE, DC, MC, V.*

Radisson Plaza. This is another of Berlin's mega-facility hotels. Ask for a room overlooking the Spree River; those on Alexanderplatz can be noisy if you like your windows open. The two new restaurants are both to be highly recommended, especially the Orangerie, with its view of the Spree. *Karl-Liebknecht-Str. 5, tel. 030/23–828, fax 030/2382–7590. 503 rooms with bath, 37 suites. Facilities: 2 restaurants, bar, pool, sauna, health club, massage, beauty salon, hairdresser, travel office, boutique, shopping arcade, garage, car rental. AE, DC, MC, V.*

Expensive **Berlin Hilton Krone.** The Krone is part of the Hilton Hotel complex, sharing the Hilton's excellent location on East Berlin's beautiful Gendarmenmarkt, but not its high prices. The rooms are not as lavish, but they are all comfortable and adequately furnished, and Krone guests can use all the Hilton facilities free of charge. *Mohrenstr. 30, tel. 030/23820, fax 030/238–24269. 148 rooms with bath. Facilities: 2 restaurants, cafeteria, pub, wine cellar, bar, discotheque, indoor pool, sauna, solarium, fitness room, squash, bowling, beauty salon, shop, art gallery, 24-hour room service, rooms for disabled guests, garage. AE, MC, V.*

Forum Hotel. With its 40 stories (it's the city's largest hotel), the Forum Hotel (owned by Inter-Continental), at the top end of Alexanderplatz, competes with the nearby TV tower for the title City Landmark. The roof dining room, Panorama 37, features not only good food and service but stunning views as well; reservations are essential. *Alexanderplatz, tel. 030/23–890, fax 030/2389–4305. 943 rooms with bath, 11 suites. Facilities: 3 restaurants, bar, sauna, fitness room, garage. AE, DC, MC, V.*

Moderate   **Charlottenhof.** This popular hotel-pension, ideally located on East Berlin's Gendarmenmarkt, was taken over by a large West German group in 1991. Luckily the room prices have remained moderate and the homey, friendly nature of the original establishment has come through intact. *Charlottenstr. 52, tel. 030/238–060, fax 030/2380–6100. 86 rooms with bath, 1 suite. AE, DC, MC, V.*

Gendarm Garni Hotel. This well-run hotel is also by the Gendarmenmarkt. All the rooms are neat and pleasantly furnished. Ask for the corner suite facing the square; the view and the large living room (for DM 225) is one of the better deals in town. *Charlottenstr. 60, tel. 030/200–4180, fax 030/208–2482. 25 rooms with bath, 4 suites. Facilities: lobby bar. AE, DC, MC, V.*

Inexpensive   **Albrechtshof.** For reasons of both price and convenience, this Lutheran hostel tends to be heavily booked months in advance. It appeals to families, so the public rooms are not always restful. *Albrechstr. 8, tel. 030/284–030, fax 030/2840–3100. 99 rooms, most with bath. Facilities: 3 restaurants, chapel, fitness room, sauna. AE, DC, MC, V.*

Märkischer Hof. This small hotel is conveniently located just off Friedrichstrasse with all of downtown Old Berlin within easy walking distance. Be sure to ask about the special weekend rates. *Linienstr. 133, tel. 030/282–7155, fax 030/282–4331. 20 rooms, most with bath. AE, MC, V.*

The Arts

West Berlin   Today's Berlin has a tough task in trying to live up to the reputation it gained from the film *Cabaret*, but if nightlife is a little toned down since the '20s, the arts still flourish. Apart from the many hotels that book seats, there are numerous ticket agencies, including **Europa-Center** (Tauentzienstrasse 9, tel. 030/261–7051); **Theaterkasse Centrum** (Meinekestrasse 25, tel. 030/882–7611); and the **Top Ticket** branches (in all major stores, such as Hertie, Wertheim, and KaDeWe).

The Berlin Philharmonic, one of the world's leading orchestras, performs in the **Philharmonie** (Matthaikirchstrasse 1, tel. 030/2548–8132). It plays a major role in the annual festival months of August, September, and October. The **Deutsche Oper** (Opera House, Bismarckstrasse 35), by the U-Bahn stop of the same name, is the home of opera and ballet companies.

East Berlin   The quality of opera and classical concerts in East Berlin is impressively high. Tickets are available at most ticket agencies and the theaters' own box offices, either in advance or an hour before the performance. Tickets are also sold at the ticket offices in the Radisson Plaza and Grand hotels, or from your hotel service desk. Check the monthly publication *Berlin Programm*.

Concerts   **Schauspielhaus** (Gendarmenmarkt, tel. 030/2090–2122).

Opera and   **Deutsche Staatsoper** (Unter den Linden 7, tel. 030/200–4762);
Ballet   **Komische Oper** (Behrenstrasse 55–57, tel. 030/229–2555); **Metropol Theater** (Friedrichstrasse 101, tel. 030/203–640).

Nightlife

West Berlin Nightlife in West Berlin is no halfhearted affair. It starts late (from 9 PM) and runs until breakfast. Almost 50 bars (*Kneipen*) have live music of one kind or another, and there are numerous small cabaret clubs and discos. The heart of this nocturnal scene is the Kurfürstendamm, but some of the best bars and discos are to be found around Nollendorfplatz (try **Metropol** for late-night dancing, Nollendorfplatz 5) in Charlottenburg, and along Oranienstrasse and Wienerstrasse in Kreuzberg (head straight for the secret back room at **Bierhimmel,** Oranienstr. 183).

West Berlin is still Germany's drag-show capital, as you'll see if you go to **Chez Nous** (Marburgerstrasse 14). It's essential to book ahead (tel. 030/213–1810). The women are for real next door (No. 15) at the **Scotch Club 13.**

Berlin is a major center for jazz in Europe. If you're visiting in the fall, call the tourist office for details of the annual international Jazz Fest. Throughout the year a variety of jazz groups appear at the **Eierschale** (Podbielskiallee 50), and **Quasimodo** (Kantstr. 12a).

East Berlin Nightlife in East Berlin offers just as much excitement and variety as that in the West, and new bars and clubs open almost weekly. Most of the action is in Mitte along Oranienburgerstrasse and points north. **Zosch** (Tucholskystr. 30) has a great basement bar and Prenzlauerberg along Knaackstrasse and around Kollwitzplatz. **Café Westfall** (Kollwitzstr. 64) is one of few places left over from Communist days. For clubs with music and atmosphere, try one of the following: **Checkpoint** (Leipziger Strasse 55); **Franz** (Schönhauser Allee 36–39); **Knaack** (Greifswalderstr. 224); **Sophienklubb** (Sophienstr. 6); **Tacheles** (Oranienburgerstr. 53–56).

Saxony and Thuringia

Saxony and Thuringia—the very sound of those names conjures up images of kingdoms and forest legends, of cultural riches and booming industrial enterprises. The reality after 40 years of communism is markedly less glamorous. Isolated from the West for decades, these two regions in eastern Germany are today struggling to make the transition from state-planned economies to a free-market system. Slowly, progress is being made, thanks to massive injections of cash from the federal government and the arrival of foreign and western German investors. But many people have been made jobless in the process. In January 1992, the opening up of the "Stasi" secret police files revealed the full horror and extent of former East Germany's monitoring of its citizens' lives. Closely tied politically and economically to the former Soviet Union for 45 years, many eastern Germans remain uncomfortable with their newly won freedoms and uncertain about the future. In Saxony, though, people seem happy enough with their new "Freistaat Sachsen" title, something they share in common with the Free State of Bavaria.

Dresden was once the capital of the kingdom of Saxony, and no city could be prouder of its history. The sculpture of August the Strong atop his horse was back in his original place many years before East Berlin, remembering its Prussian past, removed the statue of Frederick the Great from its hiding place and put it back on show again on the Unter den Linden in the late 1970s.

Since German reunification, Saxony has thrown open its doors to visitors. Tourists are proudly conducted around the world-famous porcelain factory in Meissen. In Colditz, a small town southeast of Leipzig, foreigners are courteously shown the town's forbidding castle, which during World War II housed captured Allied officers. Leipzig may be renowned for its East-West trade fairs, but its true fame lies in its music and literary tradition, proudly upheld by the internationally famous Gewandhaus Orchestra and by its annual book fair.

Thuringia's fame, it is sometimes said, begins and ends with its vast green forests, an unfair assessment given its many other historical facets and the fact that for centuries it was the home of dozens of kingdoms. Back in the 14th century, Thuringia was known as the Rynestig or Rennsteig (literally, fast trail), when it attracted traders from the dark forested depths of the Thuringer Wald (Woods) to the prospering towns of Erfurt (today the state capital), Eisenach, and Weimar, then already 600 years old. It was in Weimar that the privy councillor and poet, Johann Wolfgang von Goethe, was inspired by the pristine beauties of the 168 kilometers (104 miles) of the Rennsteig in 1777 to write that "tranquility crowns all its peaks." Goethe enjoyed his time in Weimar—he stayed 57 years—as did his friend and contemporary Friedrich von Schiller, professor and poet, who taught history in Jena but preferred Weimar's cultured atmosphere in which to live with his family. The Hungarian composer Franz Liszt regularly spent the summer in Weimar, where he conducted the royal court's orchestra and championed the works of his friend and son-in-law, Richard Wagner, who was born in Leipzig. But it is Goethe who reigns supreme in Weimar. His face graces many a monument, and his sayings adorn the town's libraries.

Although the railway systems of the two halves of long-divided Germany have now been fully fused together, services in the east—and particularly in country regions—still tend to be slower and less frequent than in the west. Long-neglected road works are still in progress and can result in big delays on the autobahns linking Leipzig, Dresden, and Berlin. The antiquated telephone service of the east has been brought completely up to date, however. Although new hotels are mushrooming everywhere, there is still a shortage of moderately priced accommodations. Tourist offices have lists of guesthouses and private quarters for visitors who shrink from paying the high room rates demanded by most of the new hotels. Remember that most hotels offer lower rates on weekends. If you plan to visit Leipzig when one of its fairs is being held—Dresden during a music festival or Weimar at any time—book well in advance. Changes are still occurring in this part of Germany at such a pace that we suggest that you contact the German National Tourist Office for the latest information, or phone ahead to confirm information locally.

Getting Around

By Car Some 1,600 kilometers (1,000 miles) of autobahn and 11,300 kilometers (7,000 miles) of secondary roads crisscross the five new federal states in the east. Resurfacing of some of the Communist-built highways has now resulted in the lifting of the previous strictly enforced 100 kph (62 mph) speed limits on autobahns.

Gasoline is available at Minol or Intertank filling stations, although increasingly you find the familiar signs of gasoline brands you know. Remember that diesel fuel may not be available at all stations, and unleaded fuel is often sold only on expressways and in main towns. On back roads, filling stations can be scarce, so be careful not to let fuel reserves get too low.

By Train The railway systems of East and West Germany have now been completely fused, although many stretches of line in Saxony and Thuringia are still being modernized and electrified. InterCity and EuroCity trains now connect Dresden and Leipzig with Berlin and other major German cities, with InterRegio services completing the older and slower D and E network in country areas. All InterCity and EuroCity trains have restaurant cars, the InterRegio ones have bistro-bars while on the longer D and E routes a trolley buffet is in service. It is advisable to make advance reservations at major stations or through travel agents, as trains are popular and they are often full.

Leipzig has an S-bahn city railway system. Tickets must be obtained in advance, at various prices according to the number of rides in a block. Get S-bahn tickets at the main railway station.

By Bus and Streetcar Within Saxony and Thuringia, most areas are accessible by bus, but service is infrequent and serves chiefly to connect with rail lines. Check schedules carefully. In Dresden, Leipzig, and Weimar, public transport in the form of buses and streetcars is cheap and efficient.

By Taxi Taxis in Dresden are inexpensive, but the city is small and walking is the best way to discover its hidden surprises. Leipzig has more cabs than any other eastern German city because of the number needed to cope with peak traffic at fair time. Weimar's chief attractions are within walking distance, but you may want to take a taxi from the main train station, which is somewhat removed from the city center.

By Boat The **Weisse Flotte** (White Fleet) of inland boats, including paddle side-wheelers, ply the river Elbe, with their starting point at Dresden or at the beautiful forested border town of Bad Schandau, and on into Czechoslovakia. The **KD River Cruises of Europe** (2500 Westchester Ave., Purchase, NY 10577, tel. 914/696–3600; 323 Geary, San Francisco, tel. 415/392–8817) operates luxury cruises in both directions from May to October on the Elbe.

Tourist Information

Dresden (Pragerstr. 10–11, tel. 0351/495–5025). A museum card good for one day and covering admission to all museums in the Staatlichen Kunstsammlungen, including the museums at the Albertinum and the Zwinger, is available at the participating institutions. The card costs DM 10 for adults, DM 5 for children.
Leipzig (Sachsenplatz 1, tel. 0341/79–590).
Weimar (Marktstr. 4, tel. 03643/2173 or 03643/65690).

Guided Tours

The tourist information office in **Leipzig** leads regularly scheduled bus and tram tours of the city. Although the guides ordinarily conduct the tours in German, they are happy to translate into English on request. Daily two-hour bus tours leave from near the tourist office at Am Brühl at 1:30 PM (additional tours in summer at 10 AM); reservations are advised (tel. 0341/79–590). The cost is DM 20 adults, DM 10 children. Walking tours start from the Thomaskirche at 4 and 7, and cost DM 10.

Seven tours daily of **Dresden** and the surrounding countryside (as far as Pillnitz Palace) are organized by the tourist office. Buses depart central Postplatz (near the main post office) and stop en route at the Augustusbrucke. Two-hour city tours (10:30, 12:30, and 2:30) cost DM 28 (DM 14 children), a Grand Tour (10:30) costs DM 58 (DM 30 children), while a city tour including a visit to Pillnitz Palace (12:30) costs DM 38 (DM 20 children). There are also afternoon tours to Pillnitz Palace for DM 38 (DM 20 children). Day tours to Prague (DM 89) and Meissen (DM 58) are also offered.

Walking tours of **Weimar** start from outside the tourist office, Weimar-Information, daily at 11 and 4. Cost is DM 5 adults and DM 2.50 children. The tourist office can also arrange individual tours of the city.

Exploring Dresden

Dresden, superbly located on the banks of the river Elbe, suffered appalling damage during World War II but has been lovingly rebuilt. Italianate influences are everywhere, most pronounced in the glorious Rococo and Baroque buildings in pastel shades of yellow and green. Although many of Dresden's architectural and cultural treasures were destroyed during a fateful night of British bombing in 1945, some gems still remain.

The **Semper Opera House,** at Theaterplatz in the center of Dresden, is a mecca for music lovers. Named after its architect, Gottfried Semper, the hall has premiered Wagner's *The Flying Dutchman* and *Tannhäuser* (conducted by the composer) and nine operas of Richard Strauss. Dating from 1871–78 (the first building by Semper burned down in 1869), the opera house fell victim to the 1945 bombings, but fortunately Semper's architectural drawings had been preserved, so it was rebuilt on the same lines and reopened with much pomp in 1985. At concert intermissions, guests often mingle on the high-up balconies, which have breathtaking views of the city. Tickets are in great demand at the Semper (tel. 0351/484–20); try booking through your travel agent before you go or ask at your hotel. As a last resort, line up at the Abendkasse (Evening Box Office) half an hour before the performance begins. Tours of the opera house are also offered (tel. 0351/4842496).

From Theaterplatz, stroll down the Sophienstrasse to the largely 18th-century **Zwinger** palace complex, which remains one of the city's cultural wonders in the heart of the Altstadt. Completely enclosing a central courtyard of lawns and pools, the complex consists of six linked pavilions decorated with a riot of garlands, nymphs, and other Baroque ornamentation and sculpture, all created under the direction of Matthäus Daniel Pöppelmann.

The Zwinger complex is the home of the world-renowned **Sempergalerie** (Gemäldegalerie Alte Meister) collection of Old Master paintings, among them works by Dürer, Holbein the Younger, Rembrandt, Vermeer, Raphael, Correggio, and Canaletto. The Zwinger's other treasures include the Porzellansammlung (Porcelain Collection)—famous for its Meissen pieces—Zoological Museum, and salon displaying marvelous old scientific instruments (Mathematisch-Physikalischer Salon), remain on view at the palace. *Tel. 0351/484–0120. Gemäldegalerie Alte Meister admission: DM 7 adults, DM 1.50 children. Open Tues.–Sun. 10–6. Porzellansammlung admission: DM 3 adults, DM 1.50 children. Open Fri.–Wed. 10–6. Mathematisch-Physikalischer Salon admission: DM 3 adults, DM 1.50 children. Open Fri.–Wed. 9:30–5. Zoological Museum admission: DM 3 adults, DM 1.50 children. Open Tues.–Sun. 9–4.*

After leaving the Zwinger, head eastward along Ernst-Thälmann-Strasse and turn into the **Neumarkt** (New Market), which is, despite its name, the historic heart of old Dresden. The ruined shell on the right is all that remains of the mighty Baroque **Frauenkirche,** once Germany's greatest Protestant church, after the bombing raids of February 1945. The ruined church is being painstakingly rebuilt. Work is scheduled to be completed in time for the 800th anniversary of the foundation of Dresden in 2006.

Behind the Frauenkirche looms Dresden's leading art museum, the **Albertinum.** This large, imperial-style building gets its name from Saxony's King Albert, who between 1884 and 1887 converted a royal arsenal into a convenient setting for the treasures he and his forebears had collected.

Permanent exhibits at the Albertinum include the **Gemäldegalerie Neue Meister** (New Masters Gallery), displaying outstanding 19th- and 20th-century European pictures that include French Impressionist and Post-Impressionist works and Caspar David Friedrich's haunting *Das Kreuz im Gebirge*.

Despite the rich array of paintings, it is the **Grünes Gewölbe** (Green Vault) that invariably attracts most attention. Named after a green room in the palace of August the Strong, this part of the Albertinum (entered from Georg-Treu-Platz) contains an exquisite collection of unique objects d'art fashioned from gold, silver, ivory, amber, and other precious and semiprecious materials. Among them is the world's biggest "green" diamond, 41 carats in weight, and a dazzling group of tiny, gem-studded figures, some of which can be admired only through a magnifying glass. Somewhat larger and less delicate is the drinking bowl of Ivan the Terrible, perhaps the most sensational of the treasures to be found in this extraordinary museum. Next door is the **Skulpturensammlung** (Sculpture Collection), which includes ancient Egyptian and classical objects and Italian Mannerist works. *Tel. 0351/495-3056. Gemaldegalerie Neue Meister, Grünes Gewölbe and Skulpturensammlung admission (combined ticket for all three galleries): DM 7 adults, DM 3.50 children. Open Fri.-Wed. 10-6.*

The southern exit of the Albertinum, at Augustus-Strasse, brings you back to the Neumarkt and leads you to another former royal building now serving as a museum, the 16th-century **Johanneum,** once the royal stables. Instead of horses, the Johanneum now houses the **Vekehrsmuseum** (Transport Museum), a collection of historical vehicles, including vintage automobiles and engines. *Am Neumarkt, tel. 0351/495-3002. Admission: DM 4 adults, DM 2 children. Admission half-price on Fri. Open Tues.-Sun. 10-5.*

On the outside wall of the Johanneum is a prime example of Meissen porcelain art: a 102-meter-long (335-foot-long) painting on Meissen tiles of a royal procession. More than 100 members of the royal Saxon house of Wettin, half of them on horseback, are depicted on the giant jigsaw made up of 25,000 porcelain tiles, painted from 1904 to 1907.

Follow this unusual procession to the end and you arrive at the former royal palace, the **Herzogschloss,** where major restoration work will continue until the mid-1990s behind the fine Renaissance facade. Rooms now in use host historical exhibitions. *Sophienstr., tel. 0351/495-3110. Admission: DM 3 adults, DM 1.50 children. Open Fri.-Wed. 10-6.*

Standing next to the Herzogschloss is the **Katholische Hofkirche,** also known as the Cathedral of St. Trinitas, Saxony's largest church. The son of August the Strong, Frederick Augustus II (ruled 1733–63) brought architects and builders from Italy to construct this Catholic church, consecrated in 1754, in a city that had been the first large center of Lutheranism. In the cathedral's crypt are the tombs of 49 Saxon rulers and a precious vessel containing the heart of August the Strong.

Moving away from the treasures near the river, along the St. Petersburger Strasse, make a left into Lingnerplatz. The **Deutsches Hygiene-Museum** (German Health Museum) reflects Dresden's important role in the history of medicine. The most famous object is a glass model of a human, which caused a sensation when it was first displayed in 1930. *Lingnerplatz 1, tel. 0351/48460. Admission: DM 4 adults, DM 1.50 children. Open Tues.-Sun. 9-5.*

Two fine examples of Baroque architecture, both designed by Pöppelmann, general designer of the Zwinger palace, are within easy reach from Dresden. Take bus No. 85 from Schillerplatz to the chinoiserie-bedecked **Schloss Pillnitz** (tel. 0351/39325), once the summer residence of the Saxon court and situated in a huge park on the Elbe that embodies both Baroque and English landscape styles. The complex consists of two major palaces—the Wasserpalais (admission: DM 3 adults, DM 1.50 children; open Easter–Oct., Wed.–Mon. 9:30–5:30) and the Bergpalais (DM 3 adults, DM 1.50 children; open Easter–Oct., Tues.–Sun. 9:30–5:30)—both housing arts and crafts collections. The palace park is open throughout the year. Schloss Moritzburg, an imposing 17th-century hunting lodge once used by the Saxon royal family, was renovated and enlarged by Pöppelmann in the Baroque style and is now called the Jägerhof (Hunter's Court). Today it is home to the **Folk Art Museum,** where a decorative arts collection, much of the building's original furniture, and a collection of hunting trophies is displayed. You can get there by taking the Grossenhein bus from the main train station in Dresden. *Köpckestr. 1, tel. 0351/570–817. Admission: DM 3 adults, DM 1.50 children. Open Tues.–Sun. 10–6.*

Exploring Leipzig

With a population of about 560,000, Leipzig is the second-largest city (after Berlin) in the eastern half of Germany. Since the Middle Ages it has been an important market town and a center for printing, book publishing, and the fur industry. Nowadays, its twice-yearly fairs, staged in March and September, maintain Leipzig's position as a commercial center. If commerce still plays a strong role, it is music and literature that most people associate with Leipzig. Johann Sebastian Bach (1685–1750) was organist and choir director at St. Thomas's church. The composer Richard Wagner was born in Leipzig in 1813. The Romantic writers Johann Wolfgang von Goethe (1749–1832) and Friedrich von Schiller (1759–1805) are also closely associated with the city and its immediate area. Trade and the arts are just two aspects of the city's fame. One of the greatest battles of the Napoleonic Wars—the Battle of the Nations—was fought here in 1813 and was instrumental in leading to the French general's defeat. Little remained of old Leipzig following the devastation of World War II, but reminders of its medieval and Renaissance character are still to be found in the city center.

Railroad buffs may want to start their tour of Leipzig at the **Hauptbahnhof,** the main train station. With its 26 platforms, majestic staircase, and great arched ceiling, it is Europe's biggest and is unique among German railway stations.

Cross the Platz der Republik to the pedestrian area, leading to Sachsenplatz and the **Markt,** the old market square. Here, in the rebuilt 12th-century marketplace, you will find the **Altes Rathaus,** the Renaissance town hall, now housing the municipal museum, where Leipzig's illustrious past is well documented. *Markt 1, tel. 0341–70921. Admission: DM 3 adults, DM 1.50 children. Open Tues–Fri. 10–6, weekends 10–4.*

On all sides of the Markt, small streets leading from the square attest to Leipzig's rich trading past. Tucked in among them are glass-roofed arcades of surprising beauty and elegance. At the **Apotheke** at Hainstrasse 9, you enter surroundings that haven't changed for 100 years or more, redolent of powders and perfumes, home cures and foreign spices. It's spectacularly Jugendstil, all stained glass and rich mahogany. Nearby, on Grimmaischestrasse, is Leipzig's finest arcade, the **Mädlerpassage.** Here, at No. 2, you'll find the **Auerbachs Keller** restaurant, built in 1530, and made famous in Goethe's tale of Faust (*see* Dining and Lodging, *below*).

Continuing west, Grimmaischestrasse becomes Thomasgasse, site of the **Thomaskirche,** where Johann Sebastian Bach worked for 27 years; he composed most of his cantatas for the church's boys' choir. Once the heart of a 13th-century monastery, rebuilt in the 15th century, the tall Gothic church now stands by itself, with only the names of adjacent streets recalling the cloisters that once surrounded it. The great composer's burial place, it is to this day the home of the Thomasknabenchor and a center of Bach tradition.

Time Out In the **Teehaus** café opposite the church you can take your choice of more than a dozen exotic kinds of tea. The café is quite exotic, too, another splendid example of Leipzig Jugendstil.

Another church of more than historic interest is the **Nikolaikirche,** behind Grimmaischestrasse on Nikolaistrasse, where tens of thousands of East Germans demanding reform gathered in the months before the collapse of the Communist regime. *"Wir sind das Volk"* (We are the people) was their chant as they defied the government's efforts to silence them. The church, more impressive inside than outside, has an ornate 16th-century pulpit and an unusual diamond-pattern ceiling supported by classical pillars that are crowned with palm-tree-like flourishes.

Looming above the Nikolaikirche in the city center is the 143-meter-high (470-foot-high) **Leipzig University tower,** dubbed the "Jagged Tooth" by students. Using the university skyscraper as a landmark, you come to **Augustus-Platz,** on which stands the modernistic **Opera House** and **Neues Gewandhaus** concert hall, both centers of Leipzig's musical life. By heading across the Ring and up the Grimmaisch Steinweg, you reach the **Grassimuseum** complex. It includes the newly renovated **Museum of Arts and Crafts** (tel. 0341/2142170; open Tues.–Fri. 10–6, Wed. 10–8, weekends 10–5), the **Geographical Museum** (open Tues. and Wed. 9:30–5:30, Thurs. and Fri. 9:30–1:45, Sun. 10–8), and the **Musical Instruments Museum** (enter from Taubchenweg 2; open Tues.–Fri. 9–5, Sat. 10–5, Sun. 10–1). *Johannesplatz 5–11. Admission to each museum: DM 3 adults, DM 1.50 children.*

Back on the Ring and heading clockwise (west), turn left into Harkorstrasse. You'll come to the city's most outstanding museum, the **Museum der Bildenden Kunste,** an art gallery of international stature that is especially strong in German and Dutch painting. *Georgi-Dimitroff-Platz 1, tel. 0341/216990. Admission: DM 5 adults, DM 2.50 children; free Sun. Open Tues. and Thurs.–Sun. 9–5, Wed. 10–4.*

Still further out, reached by streetcar nos. 15, 20, 21, or 25, is the **Exhibition Pavilion** at Pragerstrasse 210. Its main feature is a vast diorama portraying the Battle of the Nations of 1813 (admission: DM 2 adults, DM 1 children; open May–Sept., Tues.–Sun. 10–6; Oct.–Apr., Tues.–Sun. 9–4; admission: DM 3.50 adults, DM 2 children). Nearby on Pragerstrasse is the massive **Völkerschlacht-denkmal** (open May–Oct., daily 10–5; Nov.–Apr., daily 9–4) a 91-meter-high (300-foot-high) granite and concrete memorial in a formal park; it, too, commemorates the battle. You must climb 500 steps to take in the view from the platform near the top. The Prussians did make one concession to Napoleon in designing the monument: A stone marks the spot where he stood during the battle.

Exploring Weimar

Weimar, wedged between Erfurt and Jena and southwest of Leipzig, sits prettily on the Ilm River between the Ettersberg and Vogtland hills, and has a place in German political and cultural history out of all proportion to its size (population 63,000). Its civic history, not long by German standards, began as late as 1410, but by the early 19th century Weimar had become one of Europe's most important cultural centers, where Goethe and Schiller were neighbors, Carl Maria von Weber wrote some of his best music, and Liszt was director of music, presenting the first performance of Wagner's *Lo-*

hengrin. Walter Gropius founded his Staatliches Bauhaus design school in Weimar in 1919, and it was there in 1919–20 that the German National Assembly drew up the constitution of the Weimar Republic. After the collapse of the ill-fated Weimar government, a shadow was cast over the unsuspecting city when Hitler chose it as the site for the first national congress of his new Nazi Party, and later built—or forced prisoners to build for him—the notorious Buchenwald concentration camp on the outskirts of Weimar.

Weimar's greatness is bound up with the activity of the widowed Countess Anna Amalia, who in the late 18th century set about attracting cultural figures to enrich the glittering court her Saxon forebears had set up in the town. Goethe, who served the Countess as a councillor, advising on financial matters and town design, was one of them; Schiller was another. In front of the National Theater on **Theaterplatz** a statue of the famous pair, showing Goethe with a patronizing hand on the shoulder of the younger Schiller, commemorates them.

Adjacent to the National Theater is the Baroque **Wittumspalais,** once the home of Countess Anna Amalia. In the exquisite drawing room where her soirees were held, you find the original cherrywood table at which company sat. In the east wing is a small museum that is a fascinating memorial to her cultural gatherings. *Theaterpl. 9. Admission: DM 3 adults, DM 2 children. Open Mar.–Oct., Tues.– Sun. 9–noon and 1–5; Nov.–Feb., Tues.–Sun. 9–noon and 1–4.*

Goethe spent 57 years in Weimar, 47 years in the house that has since become a shrine for millions of visitors. **Goethehaus** is two blocks south of Theaterplatz on a street called Frauenplan. The museum it contains is testimony not only to the great man's literary might but also his interest in the sciences, particularly medicine, and his administrative skills (and frustrations) as Weimar's exchequer. Here you find the desk at which Goethe stood to write (he liked to work standing up), his own paintings (he was an accomplished watercolorist), and the modest bed on which he died. *Frauenplan 1, tel. 03643/ 62041. Admission: DM 5 adults, DM 3 children. Open Mar.–Oct., Tues.–Sun. 9–5; Nov.–Feb., Tues.–Sun. 9–4.*

On a tree-shaded square around the corner from Goethe's house is Schiller's green-shuttered home, **Schillerhaus,** in which he and his family spent a happy, all-too-brief three years (Schiller died there in 1805). The poet and playwright's study, dominated by the desk where he probably completed *William Tell,* is tucked up underneath the mansard roof. *Schiller Str. 17, tel. 03643/62041. Admission: DM 5 adults, DM 3 children. Open Mar.–Oct., Wed.–Mon. 9–5; Nov.– Feb., Wed.–Mon. 9–4.*

Another historic house worth visiting is found on the **Marktplatz,** the central town square. It was the home of the painter Lucas Cranach the Elder, who lived there during his last years, 1552–53. Its imposing facade, richly decorated, bears the coat of arms of the Cranach family. In its ground floor it now houses a private modern art gallery.

Around the corner and to the left is Weimar's 16th-century castle, the **Stadtschloss,** with its restored classical staircase, festival hall, and falcon gallery. The castle houses an impressive art collection, including several fine paintings by Cranach the Elder and many early 20th-century works by such artists as Böcklin, Liebermann, and Beckmann. *Burgplatz. Admission: DM 3 adults, DM 2 children. Open May–Sept., Tues.–Sun. 9–6; Oct.–Apr., Tues.–Sun. 9–5.*

In Weimar's old, reconstructed town center stands the Late Gothic **Herderkirche,** with its large winged altarpiece started by Lucas Cranach the Elder and finished by his son in 1555. Nearby in Jakobstrasse you'll spot the Baroque facade of the **Kirms-Krackow** house.

A short walk south, past Goethehaus and across Wieland Platz, brings you to the cemetery, **Historischer Friedhof** (Historic Cemetery), where Goethe and Schiller are buried. Their tombs are in the classical-style chapel. The Goethe-Schiller vault can be visited daily 9–1 and 2–5.

On the other side of the Ilm, amid meadowlike parkland, is Goethe's beloved **Gartenhaus** (Garden House), where he wrote much poetry and began his masterpiece *Iphigenie auf Tauris* (admission: DM 3 adults, DM 2 children; open daily 9–noon and 1–5; Nov.–Feb., 9–noon and 1–4). Goethe is said to have felt very close to nature here, and you can soak up the same rural atmosphere today on footpaths along the peaceful little river, where time seems to have stood still. Just across the river from the Gartenhaus is a generous German tribute to another literary giant, William Shakespeare, a 1904 statue that depicts him jauntily at ease on a marble plinth, looking remarkably at home in his foreign surroundings.

Just south of the city (take the No. 1 bus from Goetheplatz) is the lovely 18th-century **Schloss Belvedere,** now housing a museum of Baroque art and an exhibition of coaches and other old vehicles but once was a hunting and pleasure castle. The formal gardens were in part laid out according to Goethe's concepts. *Tel. 0621/661831. Admission: DM 4 adults, DM 2 children. Open Apr.–Oct., Wed.–Sun. 10–6. Closed Nov.–Mar.*

North of Weimar, in the Ettersberg Hills, is a blighted patch of land that contrasts cruelly with the verdant countryside that so inspired Goethe: **Buchenwald,** where, from 1937 to 1945, 65,000 men, women, and children from 35 countries met their deaths through disease, starvation, and gruesome medical experiments. Each is commemorated today by a small stone placed on the outlines of the former barracks (no longer existing), and by a massive memorial tower. Buses depart hourly for the camp from the main railway station between 9 and 3:30, or you can take the more frequent bus no. 6 to Ettersburg. *Contact Weimar Tourist Information, tel. 03643/2173 or 03643/65690. Campsite admission free. Open Tues.–Sun. 8:45–4:30.*

Dining and Lodging

Many of the best restaurants in Saxony and Thuringia are to be found in the larger hotels. You can expect hearty food in both regions. Roast beef, venison, and wild boar are often on Saxon menus, and in the Vogtland you'll find *Kaninchentopf* (rabbit stew). In Thuringia, regional specialties include *Thüringer Rehbraten* (roast venison); roast mutton served in a delicate cream sauce; tasty grilled Thuringian sausages; *Thüringer Sauerbraten mit Klössen* (marinated beef with dumplings); *Börenschinken* (cured ham); and roast mutton shepherd-style, with beans and vegetables. The light Meissner Wein, wine from the Meissen region, is splendid.

Dining out in Saxony and Thuringia can still be relatively inexpensive, but hotel prices are high because of the ongoing shortage of accommodations. Although hotels are being built at a brisk pace, building costs are so high that they are directly reflected in room rates. Cheaper hotels tend to be the unimproved and sometimes substandard hold-overs from the old German Democratic Republic; it's often better to seek cheap but clean accommodation from the lists of private bed-and-breakfast houses available at most tourist offices.

For details and price-category definitions, *see* Dining and Lodging in Staying in Germany.

Dresden **Kügelnhaus.** A combination grill/coffee shop/restaurant/beer cellar,
Dining Kügelnhaus is extremely popular, so either get there early or reserve your table in advance. You'll find the usual hefty local dishes, but prepared with a deft touch. *Str. der Befreiung 13, tel. 0351/ 52791. Reservations advised. No credit cards. Moderate.*

Haus Altmarkt. The choice of cuisine in this busy corner of the colonnaded Altmark is enormous—from the McDonald's which has insinuated itself into the landscape to the up-market Amadeus restaurant on the first floor. In between are a jolly bistrolike café and, downstairs, a vaulted restaurant, Zum Humpen, with a secluded bar. The restaurant offers good value, with midday menus under DM 20. In warm weather you can eat outside on a terrace and watch the marketplace's bustle. *Am Altmarkt 1, tel. 0351/4951212. No reservations. No credit cards. Inexpensive–Moderate.*

Lodging **Hotel Bellevue.** This modern hotel across the river from the Zwinger palace incorporates an old town house, now restored. The hotel views of the historic center are terrific, the rooms luxurious, and the service good. Its Cafe Pöppelmann is especially recommended for its atmosphere and hearty dishes. *Meissnerstr., tel. 0351/56–620. 328 rooms with bath. Facilities: 5 restaurants, wine cellar, café, beer pub, bar, nightclub, shops, sauna, solarium, jogging course. AE, DC, MC, V. Very Expensive.*

Leipzig **Auerbachs Keller.** This historic restaurant (built in 1530) in the base-
Dining ment of a stylish city shopping arcade is immortalized in Goethe's
★ *Faust.* The menu features regional dishes from Saxony, often with Faustian names. There is a good wine list. Both a visit and a reservation are musts. *Grimmaischestr. 2–4, tel. 0341/2161040. Reservations required. Jacket and tie required. AE, DC, MC, V. Expensive.*

★ **Altes Kloster.** Game is featured in this fascinating restaurant, once part of a cloister. The Old World ambience enhances the excellent food. *Klostergasse 5, tel. 0341/282–252. Reservations advised. No credit cards. Moderate.*

★ **Paulaner.** This intimate restaurant is recommended for its quiet atmosphere and good regional cooking. *Klostergasse 3, tel. 0341/211– 3115. Reservations advised. No credit cards. Moderate.*

Ratskeller. This large restaurant, which also has a *Jagdzimmer* (Hunting Room), prides itself on its good *Bürgliche* cooking. Specialties include the popular *Ratskeller Topf*, a savory stew with vegetables; homemade pasta; and *Schweineschnitzel* (pork cutlet). *Lotterstr. 1, tel. 0341/123–6202. Reservations advised. No credit cards. Closed Sun. dinner. Moderate.*

Zill's Tunnel. The tunnel refers to the barrel-ceilinged ground-floor restaurant, where foaming glasses of excellent local beer are cheerily served by the friendly staff who can help decipher the Old Saxon descriptions of the menu's traditional dishes. Upstairs there's a larger wine restaurant, with a welcoming open fireplace. Despite the distinction between floors, you can drink just what you choose on either floor. Wine buffs will single out the rare Saxon wine from a Saale valley vineyard. Goose in a variety of forms is a staple here and among the soups is a potent mixture of vegetables, beer and gin. *Barfussgässchen 9, tel. 0341/200–446. Reservations advised. Dress: casual. No credit cards. Moderate.*

Thüringer Hof. This fine old tavern-restaurant has been in business for centuries and its dark-paneled walls have history carved deep within the wood. The roast wild boar is served just as Leipzigers would have ordered it in ages past, and the traditional Thüringian dishes couldn't be more authentic—marinated beef, Thüringian dumplings, and red cabbage sweetened with apple, to name just one. *Burgstr. 19–23, tel. 0341/209–884. Reservations not necessary. No credit cards. Closed Fri. and Sat. dinner. Inexpensive.*

Lodging **Astoria.** This older, well-worn hotel is still preferred by many for its genteel ambience and central location next to the main rail station. Traffic in the area is considerable; ask for a room at the rear. *Platz der Republik 2, tel. 0341/72220, fax 0341/722–4747. 309 rooms with bath. Facilities: 2 restaurants, bar, café, nightclub, sauna, parking. AE, DC, MC, V. Very Expensive.*

Hotel Inter-Continental Leipzig. The city's most luxurious accommodation, now part of the Inter-Continental chain, is imposing for its high-rise profile as well as its Japanese restaurant and garden. It's close to the main rail station and is fully air-conditioned. *Gerberstr. 15, tel. 0341/7990, fax 0341/799–1229. 429 rooms with bath, 18 suites. Facilities: 4 restaurants, 2 bars, coffee bar, nightclub, indoor pool, sauna, solarium, bowling, jogging course, fitness club, casino, shops, garage. AE, DC, MC, V. Very Expensive.*

Corum. In 1993 the former, and slightly seedy, Hotel Zum Löwen was dazzlingly transformed into a smart and very comfortable hotel. Unchanged is the excellent location, across the street from Leipzig's main railway station. Rooms still tend to be small but lack nothing in terms of comfort and facilities. The bar and lounge are a lively evening meeting spot. *Rudolf-Breitscheid-Str. 3, tel. 0341/125100, fax 0341/12510100. 108 rooms, 14 suites. Facilities: restaurant, bar, parking. AE, DC, MC, V. Expensive.*

Hotel Stadt Leipzig. Considering its central location, this hotel is surprisingly quiet. Public rooms are attractive; dark wooden paneling in the Vignette restaurant sets the tone for a quiet meal. *Richard-Wagner-Str. 1–5, tel. 0341/21450, fax 0341/2145600. 352 rooms with a bath. Facilities: 3 restaurants, cafe, bar, nightclub, sauna, shops, car rental, parking. AE, DC, MC, V. Expensive.*

Zum Goldenen Adler. This traditional old Leipzig inn got a complete face-lift in 1992 and now offers up-to-date comfort and facilities within its handsome framework. Rooms are bright and modern, with dark woods and red upholstery dominating the decor. The bistro-bar Day & Night is a popular nightspot in town and though conveniently part of the hotel it's well sound-proofed. *Portitzerstr. 10, tel. 0341/688–0976, fax 0341/66326. 20 rooms with bath. Facilities: bistro-bar, parking. AE, MC, V. Expensive.*

Balance. This third hotel of a newly formed Rhineland-based group is scheduled to open in spring 1995. It is being planned along the same lines as its sister hotels in Neuss-Düsseldorf and Neu-Isenburg, with about half the rooms in the form of self-service suites and apartments, complete with kitchenettes. Rooms are large and have luxury furnishings, yet rates are kept reasonable. *Wasserturmstr. (tel. and fax numbers have not yet been allotted, but rooms at all 3 Balance hotels can be booked in U.S. at 800/223–5652). 150 suites and apartments. Facilities: restaurant, bar, sauna. AE, DC, MC, V. Moderate–Expensive.*

Weimar **Weisser Schwan.** This historic restaurant in the center of town, right
Dining by Goethehaus, dates to 1500. It offers high-quality international cuisine and Thuringian specialties, particularly fish and grilled meats. *Frauenstorstr. 23, tel. 03643/61715. Reservations essential. Jacket and tie advised. AE, DC, MC, V. Closed Mon. Expensive.*

Gastmahl des Meeres. Centrally located, this restaurant offers a wide range of fish dishes, as well as meat. It has fast service and friendly waiters but tends to get crowded between 1 and 2 PM, so it's best to arrive early for lunch. *Herder Platz 16, tel. 03643/4521. No reservations. No credit cards. Inexpensive.*

Ratskeller. This is one of the region's most authentic city hall cellar restaurants, its whitewashed, barrel-vaulted ceiling attesting to centuries of tradition. Tucked away at the side is a cozy bar, where you can enjoy a drink beneath a spectacular art nouveau colored-glass skylight. There's one exotic touch to an otherwise traditionally Thuringian menu—Madagascar green pepper soup. If venison is in season, try it; also recommended are the wild duck or wild boar in red wine sauce. *Markt 10, tel. 03643/64142. Reservations advised. Closed Sun. dinner. AE, MC, V. Inexpensive.*

Scharfe Ecke. This is the place to try Thuringia's traditional *Knödel* (dumplings) at their best. But be patient; they are made to order and take at least 20 minutes to make the journey from kitchen to table (the wait is well worth it, however). The Knödel come with just about every dish, from roast port to venison stew. And the ideal accompaniment to any of the choices here is the locally brewed beer. *Eisfeld 2, tel. 03643/202430. No reservations. Closed Mon. and Sun. dinner. No credit cards. Inexpensive.*

Lodging

Weimar Hilton. Weimar's most modern hotel, the Belvedere, was taken over by Hilton in 1991, and now combines luxury with smooth-running service. The riverside Belvedere park—which Goethe helped to lay out—is just across the road, and the rococo Belvedere Palace, with its museum of ancient vehicles, is a short walk away. Weimar town center *is* quite a hike from here, but bus service is frequent. *Belvederer Allee 25, tel. 03643/7220, fax 03643/722–741. 300 rooms with bath. Facilities: 2 restaurants, café, beer tavern, 3 bars, indoor pool, sauna, solarium, fitness room, spa, parking. AE, DC, MC, V. Very Expensive.*

Elephant. This hotel, dating to 1696, is one of Germany's most famous; you'll follow the choice of Goethe, Schiller, Herder, Liszt—and Hitler—all of whom have been guests here. The rooms are comfortable and modern, thanks to recent renovations. A sense of the historic past is ever present. Book well in advance. *Am Markt 19, tel. 03643/61471, fax 03643/65310. 116 rooms with bath. Facilities: 4 restaurants, bar, nightclub, sauna, garage. AE, DC, MC, V. Expensive.*

Russischerhof. This charming hotel built in 1805 was modernized and expanded in 1989. The pleasing rooms are attractively furnished, each equipped with bath, shower, TV, and radio. *Goethe Platz 2, tel. 03643/7740, fax 03643/62337. 79 rooms with bath. Facilities: 2 restaurants, bar, beer cellar, garage. AE, DC, MC, V. Expensive.*

12 Great Britain

Great Britain is a small country with a long history spread out for all to see. Two factors have helped to ensure the preservation of so much of the nation's past. The first is the absence of fighting on British soil. Although for centuries Britain's armies crossed the Channel to take part in European wars and during the 18th and 19th centuries the nation won for itself an extensive worldwide empire, the physical fact of the English Channel has kept Britain's shores from invasion for more than 900 years, blocking the process of destruction and reconstruction seen in much of the rest of Europe. In addition, the nation's internal conflicts, though bloody, have generally been brief. The second factor is the innate sense of history (some would call it conservatism) of the British, who generally prefer the old to the new and are often reluctant to contemplate any kind of change, especially in their physical surroundings.

All this means that Great Britain is an ideal holiday destination for anyone with a feel for the past. Here you'll find soaring medieval cathedrals, tributes to the faith of the churchmen and masons who built them; grand country mansions of the aristocracy filled with treasures—paintings, furniture, tapestries—and set in elegantly landscaped grounds; and grim fortified castles, their gray stone walls set fast against all challengers.

But Britain is not merely a historical theme park, and the visitor who concentrates solely on such traditional sights misses the essence of the land and the people. Many of the pleasures of exploration away from the main tourist routes derive from the constantly changing variety of the countryside. A day's drive from York, for example, will take you through long stretches of wild, heather-covered moorland, ablaze with color in the fall, or past the steep, sheep-dotted mountainsides of the Dales, cut by deep valleys and scattered with isolated stone-built hamlets.

Wandering off the beaten track will also allow you to discover Britain's many distinctive small country towns and villages, which move at a notably slower pace than the metropolitan centers. A medieval parish church, a high street of 18th-century buildings interrupted by occasional survivors from earlier centuries, and a grandiose Victorian town hall, all still in use today, help to convey a sense of a living past.

This direct continuity of past into present can be experienced in such a celebrated and tourist-filled place as Stratford-upon-Avon, but even more in such communities as the little town of Chipping Campden, set in the rolling Cotswold Hills, and Bury St. Edmunds, in the gentle Suffolk countryside east of Cambridge. In such places, the visitor's understanding is often helped by small museums devoted to explaining local history, full of intriguing artifacts and information on trade, traditions, and social life. Such towns, too, are the places to look for specialty goods, such as knitwear, pottery, glass, and pictures, the product of a 1980s renaissance in craftsmanship.

In contrast is the hectic, at times aggressive, pace of life in London. This is a city that scarcely seems to sleep, with a vibrant artistic, cultural, and commerical life. Yet here, too, the links with the past are plain for all to see. For instance, despite all the recent rebuilding, the basic street pattern of the City (the financial quarter between St. Paul's Cathedral and the Tower of London) is the one that evolved in the Middle Ages, more than 600 years ago, and still standing is much of the work of Christopher Wren, the master architect chiefly responsible for reconstruction after the disastrous fire of

Great Britain

1666. Most notable of these works is St. Paul's itself. Here again, exploration off the beaten track will reward you with the discovery of a London relatively untouched by tourists.

Finally, it is important to remember that Great Britain consists of three nations—England, Scotland, and Wales—and that 640 kilometers (400 miles) north of London lies another capital city, Edinburgh, whose streets and monuments bear witness to the often turbulent and momentous history of the Scottish people. Cardiff, 272 kilometers (170 miles) west of London, is a busy port and the focal point of two of the famous Welsh passions—singing and rugby.

Essential Information

Before You Go

When to Go The main tourist season runs from mid-April to mid-October. In recent years, however, parts of the winter—especially December—have been almost as busy. Winter is also the height of London's theater, ballet, and opera season. Springtime reveals the countryside at its most verdant and beautiful, while fall offers soft vistas of muted, golden color. May, September, and October are the months to visit the northern moorlands and Scottish highlands, while June is best for Wales and the Lake District. Most British people take their vacations during July and August, when costs are high and accommodations at a premium.

Climate On the whole, Britain's winters are rarely bitter, except in northern Scotland. Recent summers have been scorchers all over the country. Wherever you are, and whatever the season, be prepared for sudden changes. What begins as a brilliant, sunny day often turns into a damp and dismal one by lunchtime. Take an umbrella and raincoat wherever you go, particularly in Scotland, where the temperatures are somewhat cooler.

The following are the average daily maximum and minimum temperatures for London.

Jan.	43F	6C	May	62F	17C	Sept.	65F	19C
	36	2		47	8		52	11
Feb.	44F	7C	June	69F	20C	Oct.	58F	14C
	36	2		53	12		46	8
Mar.	50F	10C	July	71F	22C	Nov.	50F	10C
	38	3		56	13		42	6
Apr.	56F	13C	Aug.	71F	22C	Dec.	45F	7C
	42	6		56	13		38	3

Currency The British unit of currency is the pound sterling, divided into 100 pence (p). Bills are issued in denominations of 5, 10, 20, and 50 pounds (£); new, smaller £10 and £5 notes are also in circulation. Coins are £1, 50p, 20p, 10p, 5p, 2p, and 1p; the 10p and 5p are new, smaller coins. Scottish banks issue Scottish currency, of which all coins and notes—with the exception of the £1 notes—are accepted in England. At press time (spring 1994), exchange rates were approximately U.S.\$1.53 and C\$2.14 to the pound.

Traveler's checks are widely accepted in Britain, and many banks, hotels, and shops offer currency-exchange facilities. You will probably lose from 1¢ to 4¢ on the dollar, however, depending on where you change them; banks offer the best rates. In London and other big cities, bureaux de change abound, but it definitely pays to shop around: They usually have a minimum charge of £1 and often a great deal more. Credit cards are universally accepted, too. The most commonly used are MasterCard and Visa.

What It Will Cost In general, transportation in Britain is expensive in comparison with other countries. You would be well advised to take advantage of the many reductions and special fares available on trains, buses, and subways. Always ask about these when buying your ticket. Gasoline prices are about the same as those on the Continent.

London now ranks with Tokyo as one of the world's most expensive hotel capitals. Finding budget accommodations—especially during July and August—can be difficult; you should try to book well ahead if you are visiting during these months. Many London hotels offer special off-season (October–March) rates, however. Dining out, even in moderate restaurants, can be prohibitively expensive, but a large number of pubs offer excellent food at reasonable prices, and fast-food facilities are widespread. Many ethnic restaurants also tend to be better value for your money.

Remember that the gulf between prices in the capital and outside is wide. Take advantage of one ubiquitous bargain: Nearly all state-owned museums are free to visitors. Be prepared to pay a value-added tax (VAT) of 17½% on almost everything you buy; in most cases it is included in the advertised price.

Sample Prices For London: cup of coffee, 80p; pint of beer, £1.40; glass of wine, £1.40; soda, 60p; 1-mile taxi ride, £2.50; ham sandwich, £1.75.

Customs on Arrival There are two levels of duty-free allowance for people entering the United Kingdom: one, for goods bought outside the European Union (EU) or for goods bought in a duty-free shop within the EU; two, for goods bought in an EU country.

In the first category, you may import duty-free 200 cigarettes or 100 cigarillos or 50 cigars or 250 grams of tobacco *(Note:* If you live outside Europe, these allowances are doubled), plus 1 liter of alcoholic drinks over 22% volume or 2 liters of alcoholic drinks not over 22% volume or fortified or sparkling wine, plus 2 liters of still table wine, plus 60 cc/ml of perfume, plus 250 cc/ml of toilet water, plus other goods to the value of £36.

In the second category, you may import duty-free a considerable amount of liquor and tobacco—800 cigarettes, 400 cigarillos, 200 cigars, 1 kilogram of pipe tobacco, 10 liters of spirits, 90 liters of wine, and 110 liters of beer.

In addition, no animals or pets of any kind may be brought into the United Kingdom without a six-month quarantine. Penalties for evading this regulation are severe and strictly enforced.

Getting Around

By Car Britain has superhighways (called motorways) running almost the
Road length of the country, with links connecting them in the South, Mid-
Conditions lands, and North. Motorways, given the prefix M on maps and road signs, have two or three lanes in each direction and are designed for high-speed rather than scenic travel.

The main north–south road between London and Leeds is the M1. Other principal routes are the M5, running from the Midlands to the Southwest, and the M6, from the Midlands north to Scotland. The M4 covers the route from London to Wales via Bristol. Encircling London is the M25, which provides access to the countryside and southeast coast. It is, however, heavily traveled and not capable of supporting the volume of traffic it sees. Be ready for lengthy traffic jams.

Divided A roads are usually shown on maps as thick, red lines and, except for occasional traffic lights, are similar to motorways. Most other major routes are the 19th-century coach and turnpike roads designed for horses and carriages. Although they—and the even narrower, winding village roads—will allow you to see much more of the real Britain, your journey could end up taking twice the time. In remote country areas, road travel can be slow, especially in an icy winter. Good planning maps are available from the **AA** (Automobile Association) and the **RAC** (Royal Automobile Club); for in-depth exploring, try the Ordnance Survey 1:50,000-series maps. These show every road, track, and footpath in the country. You might also consult the very useful Ordnance Survey *Motoring Atlas*.

Rules of the Road You can use either your driver's license or an International Driving Permit in Britain. Drive on the left-hand side of the road and pay close attention to the varying—and abruptly changing—speed limits. Seat belts are obligatory for front-seat passengers (and back-seat ones when the cars are fitted with them). In general, speed limits are 30 mph in the center of cities and built-up areas, 40 mph in suburban areas, 70 mph on motorways and divided highways, and 60 mph on all other roads.

Parking Parking in London and other large cities can be a nightmare. On-street meters are hard to find and can be very expensive. Cheaper pay-and-display lots (the driver inserts money into a machine to receive a sticker for the car with the amount of time allowed for parking) are common in smaller towns and suburban areas. But wherever you are, in town or city, beware of yellow or red lines. A single yellow line denotes no parking during the daytime. Double yellow lines or red lines indicate a more extensive prohibition on stopping. The exact times can always be ascertained from nearby signs, usually attached to lamp posts. Illegal parking can result in having your vehicle removed or wheelclamped, which can lead to a great deal of inconvenience as well as a hefty fine. Be sure to check street signs carefully before parking. In Central London, where there is good bus and underground service and taxis are plentiful, the use of a car is not recommended.

Gasoline In Britain gas (called petrol) comes in three grades, though the price difference among them is negligible. Strangely enough, though most gas stations advertise prices by the gallon, pumps actually measure in liters. A British Imperial gallon is larger than its American equivalent—four of the former equal five of the latter. At press time (spring 1994), the price of gasoline was about £2.60 per gallon, less for lead-free. A recent campaign to promote lead-free gas has been fairly successful, helped by the fact that it's slightly cheaper (£2.05 per gallon) than the leaded variety.

By Train Despite severe financial restrictions and frequent complaints from commuters, Britain offers one of the fastest, safest, and most comfortable rail services in the world. All trains are run by the state-owned **British Rail**, although there are plans afoot to privatize parts of the system.

The country's principal—and most efficient—service is the Inter-City network, linking London with every major city in the country. The most modern high-speed trains travel up to 200 kph (125 mph) and offer comfortable, fully air-conditioned cars, both first- and second-class, with restaurant or buffet facilities. Local train services are not quite as reliable, particularly around congested city centers such as London. In general, seat reservations are not necessary except during peak vacation periods and on popular medium- and long-distance routes. Reserving a standard-class seat costs £1.

Fares British Rail fares are high when compared with those in other countries. However, the network does offer a wide, and often bewildering, range of ticket reductions, and these can make a tremendous difference. The information office in each station is generally the most reliable source of information. Information and tickets can also be obtained from British Rail Travel Centers within the larger train stations and from selected travel agents displaying the double-arrow British Rail logo.

One of the best bargains available to overseas visitors is the **BritRail Pass** or the **BritRail Youth Pass,** the U.K. equivalent of the Eurail ticket. It provides unlimited standard and first class travel over the entire British Rail network (and associated ferry and bus routes) for periods of 8, 15, or 22 days, or one month. The cost of a **BritRail standard ticket** for 8 days is $219; for 15 days, $339; for 22 days, $425; and for a month, $495. The **Youth Pass,** for those aged 16 to 25, provides unlimited second-class travel and costs $179 for 8 days, $269 for 15 days, $339 for 22 days, and $395 for one month. The **Senior Citizen Standard Pass** entitles passengers over 60 to unlimited first-class travel. It costs $199 for 8 days, $305 for 15 days, $379 for 22 days, and $445 for one month. There is also a **Flexi Pass,** which allows 4, 8, or 15 days' travel in one month. These passes can be purchased only outside Britain, either in the United States, before you leave, or in one of 46 other countries. British Rail has its own information offices in New York, Los Angeles, Chicago, Dallas, Vancouver, and Toronto. The quoted prices are in U.S. dollars. Canadian tickets are slightly higher.

If you are planning to travel only short distances, be sure to buy inexpensive same-day return tickets ("cheap day returns"). These cost only slightly more than ordinary one-way, standard-class tickets but can be used *only* after 9:30 AM and on weekends. Other special offers are regional **Rover** tickets, giving unlimited travel within local areas, and **Saver** returns, allowing greatly reduced round-trip travel during off-peak periods. For information about routes and fares, contact the **British Travel Centre** (12 Regent Street, London SW1Y 4PQ, tel. 071/730–3400). Also inquire at main rail stations for details about reduced-price tickets to specific destinations.

By Plane For a comparatively small country, Britain offers an extensive network of internal air routes. These are run by about six different airlines. Hourly shuttle services operate every day between London and Glasgow, Edinburgh, Belfast, and Manchester. Seats are available on a no-reservations basis, and you can generally check in about half an hour before flight departure time. Keep in mind, however, that Britain's internal air services are not as competitive as those in the United States. And with modern, fast trains and relatively short distances, it is often much cheaper—and not much more time-consuming—to travel by train.

By Bus Buses provide the most economical form of public transportation in Britain. Prices are invariably half those of train tickets, and the network is just as extensive. In recent years, both short- and long-distance buses have improved immeasurably in speed, comfort, and frequency. There is one important semantic difference to keep in mind when discussing bus travel in Britain. Buses (either double- or single-decker) are generally part of the local transportation system in towns and cities and make frequent stops. Coaches, on the other hand, are comparable to American Greyhound buses and are used only for long-distance travel.

National Express offers the largest number of routes of any coach operator in Britain. It also offers a variety of discount tickets, including the **BritExpress Card** and the **Tourist Trail Pass** for overseas visitors. The BritExpress Card (£12) is a discount card providing a reduction on every journey made in any 30-day period. The Tourist Trail Pass costs £49 for 3 consecutive days' travel, £79 for 5 days' travel out of 10 consecutive days, £119 for 8 days out of 16, and £179 for 15 days out of 30. Passes can be bought from travel agents in the United States; in London, at the Victoria Coach Station (Buckingham Palace Road, SW1 9TP) or at main train stations in Edinburgh and Glasgow. Information about all services can be obtained from the National Express Information Office at Victoria Coach Station (tel. 071/730–0202) or from **SMT** (St. Andrew Sq., tel. 031/556–8464) in Edinburgh.

By Boat Britain offers more than 2,400 kilometers (1,500 miles) of navigable inland waterways—rivers, lakes, canals, locks, and loughs—for leisure travel. Particular regions, such as the Norfolk Broads in East Anglia, the Severn Valley in the West Country, and the sea lochs and canals of Scotland, are especially popular among the nautically minded. Although there are no regularly scheduled waterborne services, hundreds of yachts, canal boats, and motor cruises are available throughout the year. The **British Tourist Authority's** booklet "U.K. Waterway Holidays" is a good source of information. You can also contact the **Inland Waterways Association** (114 Regents Park Road, London NW1 8UQ, tel. 071/586–2510) or the **British Waterways Board** (Willow Grange, Church Rd., Watford WD1 3QA, tel. 0923/226422).

By Bicycle Cycling provides an excellent way to see the countryside, and most towns—including London—offer bike-rental facilities. Any bike shop or tourist information center should be able to direct you to the nearest rental firm. Rental fees generally run from £15 per day, plus a fairly large deposit, though this can often be put on your credit card. If you're planning a tour and would like information on rental shops and special holidays for cyclists, contact a British Tourist Authority office in the United States before you leave home. In Britain, contact the **Cyclists' Touring Club** (Cotterell House, 69 Meadrow, Godalming, Surrey GU7 3HS, tel. 0483/417217).

On Foot Many organizations conduct group walking holidays during the summer months. These are especially popular in the Welsh mountains, the Lake District, Dartmoor, and Exmoor. Details are available from the British Tourist Authority.

Staying in Great Britain

Telephones For years, both foreign visitors and the British themselves have cursed the country's inefficient and antiquated phone system. The privatization of British Telecom has brought little improvement, though the system is gradually being modernized. *NOTE:* On April 5, 1995, an extra digit will be added to area codes nationwide; in most areas a "1" will be added after the initial "0."

Local Calls Public telephones are plentiful in British cities, especially London, although you will ordinarily find a high proportion out of order. Other than on the street, the best place to find a bank of pay phones is in a hotel or large post office. As part of Telecom's modernization ef-

forts, the distinctive red phone booths are gradually being replaced by generic glass and steel cubicles, but the red boxes still remain in more remote areas of the country. The workings of coin-operated telephones vary, but there are usually intructions in each unit. The oldest kind takes only 10p coins; the new ones take 10p, 20p, 50p, and £1 coins. A Phonecard is also available; it comes in denominations of 10, 20, 40, and 100 units and can be bought in a number of retail outlets. Cardphones are clearly marked with a special green insignia, and they will not accept coins.

A local call during the peak period (9 AM–1 PM) costs 20p for three minutes. A peak period call to the United States will cost 65p a minute. Each large city or region in Britain has its own numerical prefix, which is used only when you are dialing from outside the city. In provincial areas, the dialing codes for nearby towns are often posted in the booth, and some even list international codes.

Telephone numbers are being changed in a haphazard fashion all over the country, as equipment is modernized. All numbers are expected to have an additional digit added in 1994.

International Calls The cheapest way to make an overseas call is to dial it yourself. But be sure to have plenty of coins or Phonecards close at hand. After you have inserted the coins or card, dial 010, the international code, then the country code—for the United States, it is 1—followed by the area code and local number. To make a collect or other operator-assisted call, dial 155. The United Kingdom's country code is 44.

Operators and Information For information anywhere in Britain, dial either 142 or 192. For the operator, dial 100. For assistance with international calls, dial 155.

Mail
Postal Rates Airmail letters to the United States and Canada cost 41p for 10 grams; postcards, 35p; aerograms, 36p. Letters and postcards to Europe weighing up to 20 grams cost 30p (25p to EU-member countries). Letters within the United Kingdom: first-class, 25p; second-class and postcards, 19p. These rates are likely to have risen by early 1995.

Receiving Mail If you're uncertain where you'll be staying, you can arrange to have your mail sent to American Express, 6 Haymarket, London SW1Y 4BS. The service is free to cardholders; all others pay a small fee. You can also collect letters at London's main post office. Ask to have them sent to Poste Restante, Main Post Office, London. The point of collection is King Edward Building (King Edward Street, London EU1A 1AA). Hours are Monday, Tuesday, Thursday, and Friday 8:30 AM–6:30 PM; Wednesday 9 AM–6:30 PM; closed weekends. You'll need your passport or other official form of identification.

Shopping
VAT Refunds Foreign visitors can avoid Britain's crippling 17½% value-added tax (VAT) by taking advantage of a variety of special refund and export schemes. The easiest and most common way of getting a refund is the Over-the-Counter method. To qualify for this, you must buy goods worth £75 or more (stores vary; if you are from the EU, it can be as much as £420). The shopkeeper will attach a special paper—Form VAT 407—to the invoice, and upon leaving the United Kingdom, you present the goods, form, and invoice to the customs officer. Allow plenty of time to do this at the airport; there are often long lines. The form is then returned to the store, and the refund forwarded to you, minus a small service charge. The Direct Export method is another option. With this method, you are also issued

Form VAT 407, but your purchases are sent home separately, and upon returning home, you must have the form certified by customs or a notary public. You then return the form to the store, and your money is refunded.

Opening and Closing Times **Banks.** Most banks are open weekdays 9:30–4:30. Some have extended hours on Thursday evenings, and a few are open on Saturday mornings.

Museums. Museum hours vary considerably from one part of the country to another. In large cities, most open Tuesday–Saturday 10–5; many are also open on Sunday afternoons. The majority close one day a week. Be sure to double-check the opening times of historic houses, especially if the visit involves a difficult trip.

Shops. Usual business hours are Monday–Saturday 9–5:30. Outside the main centers, most shops observe an early closing day once a week, often Wednesday or Thursday; they close at 1 PM and do not reopen until the following morning. In small villages, many also close for lunch. In large cities—especially London—department stores stay open for late-night shopping (usually until 7:30 or 8) one day midweek. Apart from some big supermarkets, DIY stores, newsstands, and small food stores, almost all shops are closed on Sunday.

National Holidays England and Wales: January 1; April 14 (Good Friday); April 17 (Easter Monday); May 1 (May Day); May 29 (Spring Bank Holiday); August 28 (Summer Bank Holiday); December 25, 26. Scotland: January 1–3; April 14; May 1, 29; August 7, December 25, 26.

Dining British food was once condemned the world over for its plainness and mediocrity. But nowadays the problem is not so much bad food as expensive food; you might want to check the menu outside the restaurant for prices before going in. The best of traditional British cooking is solid and straightforward and dependent on top-quality, fresh materials, such as succulent spring beef and seasonal vegetables. Nearly all restaurant menus also include some vegetarian dishes.

Mealtimes These vary somewhat, depending on the region of the country you are visiting. But in general, breakfast is served between 7:30 and 9 and lunch between noon and 2. Tea—an essential and respected part of British tradition and often a meal in itself—is generally served between 4:30 and 5:30. Dinner or supper is served between 7:30 and 9:30, sometimes earlier, but rarely later outside the metropolitan areas. High tea, at about 6, replaces dinner in some areas, and in large cities, after-theater suppers are often available.

Dress Jacket and tie are suggested for the more formal restaurants in the top-price categories, but, in general, casual chic or informal dress is acceptable in most establishments.

Ratings Prices quoted here are per person and include a first course, a main course, and dessert, but not wine or service. Best bets are indicated by a star ★.

Category	Cost
Very Expensive	over £45
Expensive	£35–£45

Moderate	£15–£35
Inexpensive	under £15

Lodging   Britain offers a wide variety of accommodations, ranging from enormous, top-quality, top-price hotels to simple, intimate farmhouses and guest houses.

Hotels   British hotels vary greatly, and there is no reliable official system of classification. Most have rooms with private bathrooms, although there are still many—usually older hotels—that offer some rooms with only wash basins; in this case, showers and bathtubs (and toilets) are usually just down the hall. Many also have "good" and "bad" wings. Be sure to check the room before you take it. Generally, British hotel prices include breakfast, but beware: Many offer only a Continental breakfast—often little more than tea and toast. A hotel that includes a traditional British breakfast in its rates is usually a good bet. Hotel prices in London can be significantly higher than in the rest of the country, and often the quality is not as good. Tourist information centers all over the country will reserve rooms for you, usually for a small fee. A great many hotels offer special weekend and off-season bargain packages. For extra thrills (or chills), the British Tourist Authority can recommend overnight accommodations in one of Britain's "haunted" hotels.

Bed-and-Breakfasts   These small, simple establishments are a special British tradition. They offer modest, inexpensive accommodations, usually in a family home. Few have private bathrooms, and most offer no meals other than breakfast. Guest houses are a slightly larger, somewhat more luxurious, version. Both provide the visitor with an excellent glimpse of everyday British life that's seldom seen in large city hotels.

Farmhouses   Such accommodations have become increasingly popular in recent years. Farmhouses rarely offer professional hotel standards, but they have a special appeal: the rustic, rural experience. Prices are generally very reasonable. Ask for the British Tourist Authority booklets "Farmhouse Vacations" and "Stay on a Farm." A car is vital for a successful farmhouse stay. The **Farm Holiday Bureau** (National Agricultural Centre, Stoneleigh, Kenilworth, Warwickshire CV8 2LZ, tel. 0203/696909), a network of farming and country people who offer B&B accommodation, is a good source for regional tourist board inspected and approved properties.

Holiday Cottages   Furnished apartments, houses, cottages, and trailers are available for weekly rental in all areas of the country. These vary from quaint, cleverly converted farmhouses to brand-new buildings set in scenic surroundings. For families and large groups, they offer the best value-for-money accommodations. Lists of rental properties are available free of charge from the British Tourist Authority. Discounts of up to 50% apply during the off-season (October to March). A useful publication on the subject is the *Good Holiday Cottage Guide* (Swallow Press).

Historic Buildings   Do you dream of spending your vacation in a gothic banqueting house, an old lighthouse, or maybe in a gate house that sheltered Mary, Queen of Scots in 1586? There are some half-dozen organizations in Great Britain that have specially adapted historic buildings to rent. Most of them have cooking facilities, so for a short while you can pretend to have lived there all your life. Two of the leading charities that have such buildings for rent are **The Landmark Trust** (Shottesbrooke, Maidenhead, Berkshire SL6 3SW, tel. 0628/

825925) and the **National Trust** (Box 101, Western Way, Melksham, Wiltshire SN12 8EA, tel. 0225/705676). All the buildings have been adapted and modernized, with due respect to their historic status, so you don't have to worry about medieval plumbing or Tudor kitchens. There are, however, no TVs in the Landmark Trust properties. Other organizations are **Portmeirion Cottages** (Portmeirion, Gwynedd, Wales LL48 6ER, tel. 0766/770228) and the rather upscale **Rural Retreats** (Retreat House, Station Rd., Blockley, Moreton-in-Marsh, Gloucestershire GL56 9DZ, tel. 0386/701177).

University Housing In larger cities and in some towns, certain universities offer their residence halls to paying vacationers. The facilities available are usually compact sleeping units, and they can be rented on a nightly basis. For information, contact the **British Universities Accommodation Consortium** (Box 880, University Park, Nottingham NG7 2RD, tel. 0602/504571).

Youth Hostels There are more than 350 youth hostels throughout England, Wales, and Scotland. They range from very basic to very good. Many are located in remote and beautiful areas; others can be found on the outskirts of large cities. Despite the name, there is no age restriction. The accommodations are inexpensive and generally reliable and usually include cooking facilities. For additional information, contact the **YHA Headquarters** (Trevelyan House, 8 St. Stephen's Hill, St. Albans, Hertfordshire AL1 2DY, tel. 0727/855215).

Camping Britain offers an abundance of campsites. Some are large and well equipped; others are merely small farmers' fields, offering primitive facilities. For information, contact the British Travel Authority in the United States or the **Camping and Caravan Club, Ltd.** (Greenfields House, Westwood Way, Coventry CV4 8JH, tel. 0203/694995).

Ratings Prices are for two people in a double room and include all taxes. Best bets are indicated by a star ★.

Category	London	Other Areas
Very Expensive	over £150	over £150
Expensive	£100–£150	£90–£150
Moderate	£55–£100	£50–£90
Inexpensive	under £55	under £50

Tipping Some restaurants and most hotels add a service charge of 10%–15% to the bill. Check if this has been done. In this case do not tip. If no service charge is indicated, add 10% to your total bill. Taxi drivers should also get 10%. You are not expected to tip theater or cinema ushers, elevator operators, or bartenders in pubs. Hairdressers and barbers should receive 10%–15%.

London

Arriving and Departing

By Plane International flights to London arrive at either Heathrow Airport, 19.4 kilometers (12 miles) west of London, or at Gatwick Airport, 40.3 kilometers (25 miles) south of the capital. Most—but not all—flights from the United States go to Heathrow, while Gatwick generally serves European destinations. American Airlines flights from Chicago, and AirTransit flights from Toronto and Vancouver, land at a third airport, Stansted.

Between the Airport and Downtown

The Piccadilly Line serves Heathrow (all terminals) with a direct Underground (subway) link. The 40-minute ride cost £3 at press time. Three special buses also serve Heathrow: A1 leaves every 30 minutes for Victoria Station; A2 goes to Euston Station every 30 minutes and takes 80 minutes. The one-way cost is £5. Bus 390 runs to Victoria eight times daily and costs £4 one-way.

From Gatwick, the quickest way to London is the nonstop rail Gatwick Express, costing (at press time) £8.60 one-way and taking 30 minutes to reach Victoria Station. Regular bus services are provided by Greenline Coaches, including the Flightline 777 to Victoria Station. This takes about 70 minutes and costs £6 one-way.

Cars and taxis drive into London on the M4; the trip can take more than an hour, depending on traffic. The taxi fare is about £25, plus tip. If you are driving from Gatwick, take the M23 and then A23 to central London. The taxi fare is at least £35, plus tip; traffic can be very heavy.

By Train

London is served by no fewer than 15 train stations, so be absolutely certain of the station for your departure or arrival. All have Underground stops either in the train station or within a few minutes' walk from it, and most are served by several bus routes. The principal routes that connect London to other major towns and cities are on an InterCity network.

Seats can be reserved by phone only with a credit card. You can, of course, apply in person to any British Rail Travel Centre or directly to the station from which you depart. Below is a list of the major London rail stations and the areas they serve.

Charing Cross (tel. 071/928–5100) serves southeast England, including Canterbury, Margate, Dover/Folkestone.
Euston/St. Pancras (tel. 071/387–7070) serves East Anglia, Essex, the Northeast, the Northwest, and North Wales, including Coventry, Stratford-upon-Avon, Birmingham, Manchester, Liverpool, Windermere, Glasgow, and Inverness.
King's Cross (tel. 071/278–2477) serves the east Midlands; the Northeast, including York, Leeds, and Newcastle; and north and east Scotland, including Edinburgh and Aberdeen.
Liverpool Street (tel. 071/928–5100) serves Essex and East Anglia.
Paddington (tel. 071/262–6767) serves the south Midlands, west and south Wales, and the west country, including Reading, Bath, Bristol, Oxford, Cardiff, Swansea, Exeter, Plymouth, and Penzance.
Victoria (tel. 071/928–5100) serves southern England, including Gatwick Airport, Brighton, Dover/Folkestone (from May), and the south coast.
Waterloo (tel. 071/928-5100) serves the southwestern United Kingdom, including Salisbury, Bournemouth, Portsmouth, Southampton, Isle of Wight, Jersey, and Guernsey.

Fares

The fare structures are slowly changing as the formerly nationalized British Rail is sold off to various independent operators. Generally speaking, though, it is less expensive to buy a return (round trip) ticket, especially for day trips not far from London, and you should always inquire at the information office to find out what discount fares are available for your route. You can hear a recorded summary of timetable and fare information to many destinations by dialing the appropriate "dial and listen" numbers listed under British Rail in the telephone book.

By Bus The **National Express** coach service has routes to over 1,000 major
towns and cities in the United Kingdom. It's considerably cheaper
than the train, although the trips usually take longer. National Express offers two types of service: an ordinary service, which makes
frequent stops for refreshment breaks, and a Rapide service, which
has hostess and refreshment facilities on board. Day returns are
available on both, but booking is advised on the Rapide service. National Express coaches leave Victoria Coach Station (Buckingham
Palace Rd.) at regular intervals, depending on the destination. For
travel information, dial 071/730–0202. For reservations with a credit card, dial 071/730–3499.

Getting Around

**By
Underground**
Known as "the tube," London's extensive Underground system is by
far the most widely used form of city transportation. Trains run
both beneath and above ground out into the suburbs, and all stations
are clearly marked with the London Underground circular symbol.
(A "subway" sign refers to an under-the-street crossing.) Trains are
all one class; smoking is *not* allowed on board or in the stations.

There are ten basic lines—all named—plus the East London line,
which runs from Shoreditch and Whitechapel across the Thames
south to New Cross, and the Docklands Light Railway, which runs
from Stratford in London's East End to Greenwich, with an extension to the Royal Docks to be completed. The Central, District,
Northern, Metropolitan, and Piccadilly lines all have branches, so
be sure to note which branch is needed for your particular destination. Electronic platform signs tell you the final stop and route of the
next train, and some signs also indicate how many minutes you'll
have to wait for the train to arrive.

From Monday to Saturday, trains begin running around 5:30 AM; the
last services leave central London between midnight and 12:30 AM. On
Sundays, trains start two hours later and finish about an hour earlier.
The frequency of trains depends on the route and the time of day, but
normally you should not have to wait more than 10 minutes in central
areas.

A pocket map of the entire tube network is available free from most
Underground ticket counters. There should also be a large map on the
wall of each platform, and the new computerized database, *Routes*, is
available at LT's 14 Travel Information Centres (*see below*).

Fares For both buses and tube fares, London is divided into six concentric
zones; the fare goes up the farther afield you travel. Ask at Underground ticket counters for the London Transport (LT) booklet
"Tickets," which gives details of all the various ticket options and
bargains for the tube; after some experimenting, you'll soon know
which ticket best serves your particular needs. Till then, here is a
brief summary of the major ticket categories, but note that these
prices are subject to increases.

Singles and Returns. For one trip between any two stations, you can
buy an ordinary single for travel anytime on the day of issue; if
you're coming back on the same route the same day, then an ordinary return costs twice the single fare. Singles vary in price from
90p in the central zone to £3 for a six-zone journey—not a good option for the sightseer who wants to make several journeys.

One-Day Off-Peak Travelcards. These allow unrestricted travel on
the tube, most buses, and British Rail trains in the Greater London
zones and are valid weekdays after 9:30 AM, weekends, and all public

London Underground

holidays. They cannot be used on airbuses, night buses, Route 128, for special services, or on tours and excursions. The price is £2.70–£3.70.

Visitor's Travelcard. These are the best bet for visitors, but they must be bought before leaving home and are available in both the United States and Canada. They are valid for periods of three, four, or seven days ($25, $32, $49 adults; $11, $13, $21 children) and can be used on the tube and virtually all buses and British Rail services in London. One-day Visitor's Travelcards can be bought in London for £3.70. All these cards also include a set of money-saving discounts to many of London's top attractions. Apply to travel agents or to BritRail Travel International.

For more information, there are **LT Travel Information Centres** at the following tube stations: Euston, *open Sat.–Thurs. 7:15–6, Fri. to 7:30;* King's Cross, *open Sat.–Thurs. 8:15–6, Fri. to 7:30;* Oxford Circus, *open Mon.–Sat. 8:15–6;* Piccadilly Circus, *open Mon.–Sun. 8:15–6;* Victoria, *open Mon.–Sun. 8:15–9:30;* and Heathrow, *open Mon.–Sun. (to 9 or 10 PM in Terminals 1 and 2).* For information on all London bus and tube times, fares, and so on dial 071/222–1234; the line is operated 24 hours a day.

By Bus London's bus system now consists of the bright red double- and single-deckers, plus other buses of various colors. Destinations are displayed on the front and back, with the bus number on the front, back, and side. By no means do all buses run the full length of their route at all times, so always check the termination point, preferably with the conductor or driver, before boarding. Some buses are still operated with a conductor whom you pay after finding a seat, but these days you will more often find one-man buses, in which you pay the driver upon boarding.

Buses stop only at clearly indicated stops. Main stops—at which the bus *should* stop automatically—have a plain white background with a red LT symbol on it. There are also request stops with red signs, a white symbol, and the word "Request" added; at these you must hail the bus to make it stop. Smoking is not allowed on any bus. Although you can see much of the town from a bus, *don't* take one if you want to get anywhere in a hurry; traffic often slows travel to a crawl, and during peak times you may find yourself waiting at least 20 minutes for a bus and not being able to get on it once it arrives. If you intend to go by bus, ask at a Travel Information Centre for a free Londonwide Bus Map.

Fares Single fares start at 50p for short distances (90p in the central zone). Travelcards are good for tube, bus, and British Rail trains in the Greater London Zones. There are also a number of bus passes available for daily, weekly, and monthly use, and prices vary according to zones. A photograph is required for weekly or monthly bus passes; this also applies to children and older children who may need a child-rate photocard to avoid paying the adult rate.

By Taxi London's black taxis are famous for their comfort and for the ability of their drivers to remember the mazelike pattern of the capital's streets. Hotels and main tourist areas have ranks (stands) where you wait your turn to take one of the taxis that drive up. You can also hail a taxi if the flag is up or the yellow "for hire" sign is lighted. Fares start at £1 and increase by units of 20p per 291 yards or 1 minute. A surcharge of 60p is added in the evenings until midnight, on Sundays, and on holidays.

By Car The best advice is to avoid driving in London because of the illogical street patterns and the chronic parking shortage. A constantly changing system of one-way streets adds to the confusion.

Things are a lot easier outside the rush hours (8 AM–10 AM and 4 PM–6 PM), and if you drive through central London in the early hours of the morning, you'll see that the traffic-choked arteries of daytime (such as the Strand and Oxford Street) are convenient ways to cross London.

Important Addresses and Numbers

Tourist Information The main **London Tourist Information Centre** at Victoria Station Forecourt provides details about London and the rest of Britain, including general information; tickets for tube and bus; theater, concert, and tour bookings; and accommodations. Open Apr.–Oct., daily 9–8:30; rest of the year, Mon.–Sat. 9–7, Sun. 9–5.

Other information centers are located in **Harrods** (Brompton Rd., SW1 7XL) and **Selfridges** (Oxford St., W1A 2LR) and are open store hours only; at **Tower of London** (West Gate, EC3W 4AB), open summer months only; and **Heathrow Airport** (Terminals 1, 2, and 3). **Visitorcall** is the London Tourist Board's phone service—a premium-rate (48p per minute; 36p off-peak) recorded information line, with different numbers for theater, events, museums, sports, getting around, and so on. To access the list of options, tel. 0839/123456, or see the display advertisement in the phone book. An events calendar via fax is also available, tel. 0839/401278.

Embassies and Consulates **American Embassy** (24 Grosvenor Sq., W1A, 1AE, tel. 071/499–9000). Located inside the embassy is the **American Aid Society,** a charity set up to help Americans in distress. Dial the embassy number and ask for extension 570 or 571.

Canadian High Commission (Canada House, Trafalgar Sq., London SW1 Y 5BJ, tel. 071/629–9492).

Emergencies For police, fire brigade, or ambulance, dial 999.

The following **hospitals** have 24-hour emergency rooms: **Charing Cross** (Fulham Palace Rd., W6, tel. 081/846–1234); **Guys** (St. Thomas St., SE1, tel. 071/955–5000); **Royal Free** (Pond St., Hampstead, NW3, tel. 071/794–0500); **St. Bartholomew's** (West Smithfield, EC1, tel. 071/601–8888); **St. Thomas's** (Lambeth Palace Rd., SE1, tel. 071/928–9292); **Westminster** (Dean Ryle St., Horseferry Rd., SW1, tel. 071/828–9811, adults only).

Pharmacies Chemists (drugstores) with late opening hours include **Bliss Chemist** (50–56 Willesden Lane, NW6, tel. 071/624–8000, open daily 9 AM–midnight, also the branch at 5 Marble Arch, W1, tel. 071/723–6116, open daily 9 AM–midnight) and **Boots** (44 Piccadilly Circus, W1, tel. 071/734–6126, open Mon.–Sat. 8:30–8, also the branch at 439 Oxford St., W1, tel. 071/409–2857, open Thurs. 8:30–7).

Travel Agencies **American Express** (6 Haymarket, SW1, tel. 071/930–4411, and at 89 Mount St., W1, tel. 071/499–4436). **Thomas Cook** (4 Henrietta St., WC2, tel. 071/240–4872; 1 Marble Arch, W1, tel. 071/706–4188; and branches).

Credit Cards Should your credit cards be lost or stolen, here are some numbers to dial for assistance: **Access (MasterCard)** (tel. 081/450–3122); **American Express** (tel. 071/222–9633, 24 hours, or 0800/521313 for traveler's checks); **Barclaycard (Visa)** (tel. 0604/230230); **Diners Club** (tel. 0252/516261).

Guided Tours

Orientation Tours

By Bus

London Transport's London Plus sightseeing tours (tel. 071/828–6449) offer passengers a good introduction to the city from double-decker buses (seating capacity 64–72). Tours run daily every half hour 10–5, from Marble Arch, Harrods, Trafalgar Square, Victoria, Piccadilly, and around 30 more places of interest. You may board and alight at any stop to view the sights, and then get back on the next bus. Tickets cost £12 and can be bought from the driver, any London Transport Travel Information Centre, or Tourist Information Centres. Other reputable agencies offering half- and full-day bus tours include **Evan Evans** (tel. 071/930–2377), **Frames Rickards** (tel. 071/837–3111), and **The Big Bus Company** (tel. 081/944–7810). These tours have a smaller seating capacity of approximately 50 passengers and include stops at places such as St. Paul's Cathedral and Westminster Abbey. Prices and pick-up points vary according to the sights visited, but many pick-up points are at major hotels.

By River

From April to October, boats cruise up and down the Thames, offering a different view of the London skyline. Most leave from Westminster Pier (tel. 071/930–4097), Charing Cross Pier (Victoria Embankment, tel. 071/839–3312), and Tower Pier (tel. 071/488–0344). Downstream routes go to the Tower of London, Greenwich, and Thames Barrier; upstream destinations include Kew, Richmond, and Hampton Court. Most of the launches seat between 100 and 250 passengers, have a public-address system, and provide a running commentary on passing points of interest. Depending upon the destination, river trips may last from one to four hours. For more information, call **Catamaran Cruisers** (tel. 071/839–3572), or **Tidal Cruises** (tel. 071/928–9009).

By Canal

During summer, narrow boats and barges cruise London's two canals, the Grand Union and Regent's Canal; most vessels (seating about 60) operate on the latter, which runs between Little Venice in the west (the nearest tube is Warwick Ave. on the Bakerloo Line) and Camden Lock (about 200 yards north of Camden Town tube station). **Jason's Trip** (tel. 071/286–3428) operates one-way and round-trip narrow boat cruises on this route. During April, May, and September, there are two cruises per day; from June to August there are four. Trips last 1½ hours. **Canal Cruises** (tel. 071/485–4433) also offers cruises from March to October on the *Jenny Wren* and all year on the cruising restaurant *My Fair Lady*.

Walking Tours

One of the best ways to get to know London is on foot, and there are many guided walking tours from which to choose. **The Original London Walks** (tel. 071/624–3978), **City Walks** (tel. 071/700–6931), and **Citisights** (tel. 081/806–4325) are just a few of the better-known firms, but your best bet is to peruse a variety of leaflets at the London Tourist Information Centre at Victoria Station. The duration of the walks varies (usually 1–3 hours), and you can generally find one to suit even the most specific of interests—Shakespeare's London, say, or a Jack the Ripper tour. Prices are around £4 for adults.

If you'd rather explore on your own, then the City of London Corporation has laid out a **Heritage Walk** that leads through Bank, Leadenhall, and Monument; follow the trail by the directional stars set into the sidewalks. A map of this walk can be found in *A Visitor's Guide to the City of London*, available from the City Information Centre across from St. Paul's Cathedral. Another option is to follow the **Silver Jubilee Walkway,** created in 1977 in honor of the 25th anniversary of the reign of the present queen. The entire route covers 16 kilometers (10 miles) and is marked by a series of silver crowns set into the sidewalks; Parliament Square makes a good starting point. Several guides offering further London walks to follow are available in bookshops.

Excursions LT, Evan Evans, and Frames Rickards (*see* Orientation Tours, *above*) all offer day excursions (some combine bus and boat) to places of interest within easy reach of London, such as Windsor, Hampton Court, Oxford, Stratford, and Bath. Prices vary and may include lunch and admission prices or admission only.

Personal Guides With 30 years' experience of providing a customized sightseeing service, **British Tours** (tel. 071/629–5267) will pick you up from your hotel and take you anywhere in the United Kingdom. Tour prices include car and driver-guide expenses and range from £75 for two people in a medium-size car going on a three-hour tour of London to £255 for four people in a large car taking in Bath and Stonehenge (10 hours). A good choice of tours, for one to six people, is available all year. Details of similar private operators can be found at the London Tourist Information Centre in Victoria Station or at Heathrow.

Exploring London

Traditionally London has been divided between the City, to the east, where its banking and commercial interests lie, and Westminster to the west, the seat of the royal court and of government. Today the distinction between the two holds good, and even the briefest exploration will demonstrate that each enjoys a quite distinct atmosphere. It is also in these two areas that you will find most of the grand buildings that have played a central role in British history: the Tower of London and St. Paul's Cathedral, Westminster Abbey and the Houses of Parliament, Buckingham Palace, and the older royal palace of St. James's.

These sites are natural magnets for visitors to London, as the crowds of people and the ubiquitous tourist coaches demonstrate. But visitors who restrict their sightseeing to these well-known tourist areas miss much of the best the city has to offer. Within a few minutes' walk of Buckingham Palace, for instance, lie St. James's and Mayfair, two neighboring quarters of elegant town houses built for the nobility in the 17th and early 18th centuries and now notable for the shopping opportunities they house. The same lesson applies to the City, where, tucked away in quiet corners, stand many of the churches Christopher Wren built to replace those destroyed during the Great Fire of 1666.

Other parts of London worth exploring include Covent Garden, where a former fruit and flower market has been converted into a lively shopping and entertainment center with a bazaar where craftspeople sell their own wares. The atmosphere here is informal, and you can stroll for hours enjoying the friendly bustle of the streets. Hyde Park and Kensington Gardens, by contrast, offer a great swathe of green parkland across the city center, preserved by past kings and queens for their own hunting and relaxation. A walk across Hyde Park will bring you to the museum district of South Kensington, with three major national collections: the Natural History Museum, the Science Museum, and the Victoria and Albert Museum, which specializes in costume and the fine and applied arts.

The south side of the river Thames has its treats as well. A short stroll across Waterloo Bridge brings you to the South Bank Arts Complex, which includes the National Theatre, the Royal Festival Hall, the Hayward Gallery (with changing exhibitions of international art), the National Film Theatre, and the Museum of the Moving Image (MOMI)—a must for movie buffs. The views from here are stunning—to the west are the Houses of Parliament and Big Ben, to the east the dome of St. Paul's is just visible on London's changing skyline.

London, although not simple of layout, is a rewarding walking city, and this remains the best way to get to know its nooks and crannies. The infamous weather may not be on your side, but there's plenty of indoor entertainment to keep you amused if you forgot the umbrella. More than in most cities, though, London's centuries of history are revealed as much in the quotidian street life and residential districts as in the grand national monuments, so keep your eyes peeled, and discover it for yourself.

Numbers in the margin correspond to points of interest on the London map.

Westminster   **Westminster** is the royal backyard—the traditional center of the royal court and of government. Here, within a kilometer or so of each other, are virtually all London's most celebrated buildings (St. Paul's Cathedral and the Tower of London excepted), and there is a strong feeling of history all around you. Generations of kings and queens and their offspring have lived here since the end of the 11th century, in no less than four palaces, three of which (Buckingham, St. James's, and Westminster) still stand.

❶ Start at **Trafalgar Square,** which is on the site of the former Royal Mews. Both the square's name and its present appearance date from about 1830. A statue of Lord Nelson, victor over the French in 1805 at the Battle of Trafalgar, at which he lost his life, stands atop a column. Lions guard the base of the column, which is decorated with four bronze panels depicting naval battles against France and cast from French cannons captured by Nelson. The bronze equestrian statue on the south side of the square is of the unhappy Charles I; he is looking down Whitehall toward the spot where he was executed in 1649.

❷ In the **National Gallery,** which occupies the long neoclassical building on the north side of the square, is a comprehensive collection of paintings, with works from virtually every famous artist and school from the 14th to the 19th century. The gallery is especially strong on Flemish and Dutch masters, Rubens and Rembrandt among them, and on Italian Renaissance works. The Sainsbury Wing houses the early Renaissance collection. *Trafalgar Sq., tel. 071/839-3321; 071/839-3526 (recorded information). Admission free; charge for Sainsbury Wing exhibitions. Open Mon.–Sat. 10–6, Sun. 2–6; June–Aug., Wed. until 8.*

Around the corner, at the foot of Charing Cross Road, is a second ❸ major art collection, the recently renovated **National Portrait Gallery,** which contains portraits of well-known (and not so well-known) Britons, including monarchs, statesmen, and writers. *2 St. Martin's Pl., tel. 071/930-1552. Admission free. Open weekdays 10–5, Sat. 10–6, Sun. 2–6.*

The Gallery's entrance is opposite the distinctive neoclassical ❹ church of **St. Martin-in-the-Fields,** built in about 1730. Regular lunchtime music recitals are held here.

Time Out   Both **The Brasserie** in the Sainsbury Wing of the National Gallery and **Café in the Crypt** in St. Martin's serve ambitious hot meals at lunchtime, as well as sandwiches, salads, snacks, cakes, and coffee during opening hours.

⑤ Admiralty Arch guards the entrance to **The Mall**, the great ceremonial way that leads alongside **St. James's Park** to Buckingham Palace. The Mall takes its name from a game called "pell mell," a version of croquet that society people, including Charles II and his courtiers, used to play here in the late 1600s. The park, one of central London's smallest and most attractive, with superbly maintained flowerbeds, was developed by successive monarchs, most recently by George IV in the 1820s, having originally been used for hunting by Henry VIII. Join office workers relaxing with a lunchtime sandwich, or stroll here on a summer's evening when the illuminated fountains play and Westminster Abbey and the Houses of Parliament beyond the trees are floodlit.

On the other side of the Mall, you'll pass along the foot of the imposing **⑥ Carlton House Terrace,** built in 1827–32 by John Nash. A right turn up Marlborough Road brings you to the complex of royal and **⑦** government buildings known collectively as **St. James's Palace.** Although the earliest parts of this lovely brick building date from the 1530s, it had a relatively short career as the center of royal affairs, from the destruction of Whitehall Palace in 1698 until 1837, when Victoria became queen and moved the royal household down the road to Buckingham Palace. A number of royal functionaries have offices here, however, and various court functions are held in the state rooms. Foreign ambassadors are still accredited to the "Court of St. James's."

At the end of Marlborough Road, beyond the open-sided **Friary ⑧ Court,** turn left along **Cleveland Row,** and walk past **York House,** the London home of the duke and duchess of Kent. Another left turn **⑨** into **Stable Yard Road** takes you to **Lancaster House,** built for the duke of York by Nash in the 1820s and used today for government receptions and conferences. On the other side of Stable Yard is **⑩ Clarence House,** so called because it was designed and built by Nash in 1825 for the duke of Clarence, who later became King William IV. It was restored in 1949 and is now the home of the Queen Mother. Inside the palace is the **Chapel Royal,** said to have been designed for Henry VIII by the painter Holbein; it was heavily redecorated in the mid-19th century. The ceiling still has the initials H and A, intertwined, standing for Henry VIII and his second wife, Anne Boleyn, the mother of Elizabeth I and the first of his wives to lose her head. The public can attend Sunday morning services here between the first week of October and Good Friday.

⑪ Buckingham Palace, at the end of the Mall, is the London home of the queen and the administrative hub of the entire royal family. When the queen is in residence (on weekdays except in January, August, September, and part of June), the royal standard flies over the east front. Inside there are dozens of splendid state rooms used on such formal occasions as banquets for visiting heads of state. The private apartments of Queen Elizabeth and Prince Philip are in the north wing. Behind the palace lie some 40 acres of private gardens, a haven for wildlife in the midst of the capital.

The ceremony of the **Changing of the Guard** takes place in front of the palace at 11:30 daily, May through July, and on alternate days during the rest of the year. It's advisable to arrive early; the Queen Victoria Memorial in the middle of the traffic round-about provides a grandstand view.

London

Admiralty Arch, **5**

Albert Memorial, **29**

Bank of England, **45**

Banqueting House, **20**

Barbican, **42**

British Museum, **38**

Buckingham Palace, **11**

Cabinet War Rooms, **15**

Carlton House Terrace, **6**

Cenotaph, **19**

Clarence House, **10**

Covent Garden, **33**

Guildhall, **43**

Horse Guards Parade, **21**

Hyde Park Corner, **25**

Jewish Museum, **39**

Kensington Palace, **31**

Lancaster House, **9**

Leadenhall Market, **48**

Lloyd's of London, **49**

London Transport Museum, **35**

Mansion House, **47**

Museum of London, **41**

Museum of Mankind, **24**

National Gallery, **2**

National Portrait Gallery, **3**

Natural History Museum, **27**

Palace of Westminster, **17**

Parliament Square, **16**

Portobello Road, **32**

Queen's Gallery, **12**

Round Pond, **30**

Royal Academy, **23**

KEY

AE American Express Office

i Tourist Information

0   1 mile

0   1 km

Royal Exchange, **46**

Royal Mews, **13**

Royal Opera House, **37**

St. James's Church, **22**

St. James's Palace, **7**

St. Martin-in-the-Fields, **4**

St. Mary-le-Bow, **44**

St. Paul's Cathedral, **40**

St. Paul's Church, **34**

Science Museum, **26**

Theatre Museum, **36**

Tower of London, **50**

Trafalgar Square, **1**

Victoria and Albert Museum, **28**

Wellington Barracks, **14**

Westminster Abbey, **18**

York House, **8**

Parts of **Buckingham Palace** are open to the public during August and September, while the former chapel, bombed during World War II, rebuilt in 1961, and now the **Queen's Gallery,** shows paintings from the vast royal art collections from March through December. *Buckingham Palace Rd., tel. 071/799–2331. Admission: Buckingham Palace, £8 adults, £3.50 children, £5.50 senior citizens; Queen's Gallery £2.50 adults, £1.20 children, £1.80 senior citizens. Open Tues.–Sat. 10–5, Sun. 2–5; closed between exhibitions.*

Just along Buckingham Palace Road from the Queen's Gallery is the **Royal Mews,** where some of the queen's horses are stabled and the elaborately gilded state coaches are on view. *Tel. 071/799–2331. Admission: £2.50 adults, £1.20 children, £1.80 senior citizens. Combined ticket with Queen's Gallery: £4.50 adults, £1.90 children, £3.10 senior citizens. Open Oct.–Mar. Wed. noon–4; April–Sept. Tues.–Thurs. noon–4; closed March 25–30, Oct. 1–6, Dec. 23–Jan. 5.*

Birdcage Walk, so called because it was once the site of the royal aviaries, runs along the south side of St. James's Park, past the **Wellington Barracks.** These are the regimental headquarters of the Guards Division, the elite troops that traditionally guard the sovereign and mount the guard at Buckingham Palace. The **Guards Museum** relates the history of the Guards from the 1660s to the present; paintings of battle scenes, uniforms, and a cat o'nine tails are among the items on display. *Tel. 071/930–4466, ext. 3430. Admission: £2 adults, £1 children under 16 and senior citizens. Open Sat.–Thurs. 10–4.*

The **Cabinet War Rooms,** between the Foreign Office and the Home Office, are the underground offices used by the British High Command during World War II. Among the rooms on display are the Prime Minister's Room, from which Winston Churchill made many of his inspiring wartime broadcasts, and the Transatlantic Telephone Room, from which he spoke directly to President Roosevelt in the White House. *Clive Steps, King Charles St., tel. 071/930–6961. Admission: £3.80 adults, £1.90 children under 16, £2.80 senior citizens. Open daily 10–5:15.*

Parliament Square is flanked, on the river side, by the Palace of Westminster. Among the statues of statesmen long since dead are those of Churchill, Abraham Lincoln, and Oliver Cromwell, the Lord Protector of England during the country's sole, brief republican period (1648–60).

The **Palace of Westminster** was the monarch's main residence from the 11th century until 1512, when the court moved to the newly built Whitehall Palace. The only part of the original building to have survived, however, is **Westminster Hall,** which has a fine hammer-beam roof. The rest was destroyed in a disastrous fire in 1834 and was rebuilt in the newly popular mock-medieval Gothic style with ornate interior decorations. The architect, Augustus Pugin, provided many delightful touches, such as Gothic umbrella stands. In addition to Westminster Hall, which is used only on rare ceremonial occasions, the palace contains the debating chambers and committee rooms of the two Houses of Parliament—the Commons (whose members are elected) and the Lords (whose members are appointed or inherit their seats). There are no tours of the palace, but the public is admitted to the Public Gallery of each House; expect to wait in line for several hours (the line for the Lords is generally much shorter than that for the Commons).

The most famous features of the palace are its towers. At the south end is the 104-meter (336-foot) **Victoria Tower** (currently undergoing restoration). At the other end is **St. Stephen's Tower**, better known, but inaccurately so, as Big Ben. That name properly belongs to the 13-ton bell in the tower on which the hours are struck; Big Ben himself was Sir Benjamin Hall, commissioner of works when the bell was installed in the 1850s. A light shines from the top of the tower during a night sitting of Parliament.

18 **Westminster Abbey** is the most ancient of London's great churches and the most important, for it is here that Britain's monarchs are crowned. It is unusual for a church of this size and national importance not to be a cathedral. The abbey dates largely from the 13th and 14th centuries, although **Henry VII's Chapel,** an exquisite example of the heavily decorated late Gothic style, was not built until the early 1600s, and the twin towers over the west entrance are an 18th-century addition. There is much to see inside, including the memorial to Winston Churchill; the tomb of the Unknown Warrior, a nameless World War I soldier buried in earth brought with his corpse from France; and Poets' Corner, where some of the country's finest writers are commemorated. Behind the high altar are the royal tombs, including those of Queen Elizabeth I, Mary Queen of Scots, and Henry V. In the Chapel of Edward the Confessor stands the Coronation Chair. Among the royal weddings that have taken place here are those of the present queen and most recently, in 1986, the duke and duchess of York.

It is all too easy to forget, swamped by the crowds trying to see the abbey's sights, that this is a place of worship. Early morning is a good moment to catch something of the building's atmosphere. Better still, take time to attend a service. *Broad Sanctuary, tel. 071/ 222–5152. Admission to the nave is free, to Poets' Corner and Royal Chapels, £3 adults, £1 children, £1.50 students and senior citizens (Royal Chapels, free Wed. 6–7:45 PM). Open weekdays 9–4, Sat. 9–2 and 3:45–5; Sun. all day for services only; museum and cloisters open Sun.; closed weekdays to visitors during services; Royal Chapels closed Sun. No photography except Mon. evening.*

The Norman **Undercroft,** off the original monastic cloisters, houses a small museum with exhibits on the abbey's history. In the **Pyx Chamber** next door are fine examples of silver vessels and other treasures. The nearby **Chapter House** was where the English Parliament first met. *Tel. 071/222–5152. Joint admission: £2 adults, £1.60 students and senior citizens, £1 children. Open daily 10:30–1:45.*

19 From Parliament Square, walk up **Parliament Street** and **Whitehall** (this is a single street—its name changes), past government offices, toward Trafalgar Square. The **Cenotaph,** in the middle of the road, is the national memorial to the dead of both world wars. On the left is the entrance to **Downing Street,** an unassuming row of 18th-century houses. The prime minister's office is at No. 10 (he has a private apartment on the top floor). The chancellor of the exchequer, the finance minister, occupies No. 11.

20 On the right side of Whitehall is the **Banqueting House,** built by the architect Inigo Jones in 1625 for court entertainments. This is the only part of Whitehall Palace, the monarch's principal residence in the 16th and 17th centuries, that was not burned down in 1698. It has a magnificent ceiling by Rubens, and outside there is an inscription that marks the window through which King Charles I stepped to his execution. *Tel. 071/930–4179. Admission: £2.75 adults, £2.10* *students and senior citizens, £1.90 children. Open Tues.–Sat. 10–5, Sun. 2–5.*

㉑ Opposite is the entrance to **Horse Guards Parade,** the former tilt yard of Whitehall Palace. This is the site of the annual ceremony of Trooping the Colour, when the queen takes the salute in the great military parade that marks her official birthday on the second Saturday in June (her real one is on April 21). There is also a daily guard-changing ceremony outside the guard house, at 11 AM (10 on Sunday).

St. James's and Mayfair After such a concentrated dose of grand, historical buildings, it's time to explore two of London's elegant shopping areas. Start by walking west from Piccadilly Circus along **Piccadilly,** which contains a mixture of airline offices, shops (including **Hatchards,** the booksellers, and **Fortnum and Mason,** the queen's grocer), and academic societies.

㉒ **St. James's Church** was designed by the 17th-century architect Christopher Wren and contains beautiful wood carvings by Grinling Gibbons.

Time Out | **The Wren** at St. James's is a friendly café in the church precincts. Coffee, pastries, and light lunches are served.

Jermyn Street, south of Piccadilly, is famous for upscale shops selling costly shirts, ties, and sweaters. **Paxton & Whitfield** sells an extraordinary variety of cheeses. Shops along **Duke Street** and **Bury Street** specialize in paintings, the former in Old Masters, the latter in early English watercolors. Don't be put off by the exclusive appearance of these establishments—anyone is free to enter, and there is no obligation to buy. **King Street** is home to **Christie's,** the fine art auctioneer, and to **Spink and Son,** renowned for Oriental art.

㉓ On the north side of Piccadilly, **Burlington House** contains the offices of many learned societies and the headquarters of the **Royal Academy.** The RA, as it is generally known, stages major visiting art exhibitions. The best known is the Summer Exhibition (May–Aug.), featuring works by living British artists.

Burlington Arcade, beside the RA, is a covered walkway with tiny shops selling primarily jewelry and craft goods, such as woolens. Built in 1819, it was the first shopping precinct in the country, and it retains something of its original atmosphere. A uniformed beadle is on duty to ensure that no one runs, whistles, or sings here.

㉔ The **Museum of Mankind,** behind the RA, contains the British Museum's ethnographic collection, though this will shortly be transferred to the British Museum when the British Library moves to its new premises in St. Pancras. There are displays on the South Seas, the Arctic, and other regions of the world. *6 Burlington Gardens, tel. 071/323–8043. Admission free. Open Mon.–Sat. 10–5, Sun. 2:30–6.*

There are three special shopping streets in this section of Mayfair, each with its own specialties. **Savile Row** is the home of gentlemen's tailors. Nearby **Cork Street** has many dealers in modern and classical art. **Bond Street** (divided into two parts, Old and New, though both are some 300 years old) is the classiest shopping street in London, the home of haute couture, with such famous names as **Gucci, Hermès,** and **St. Laurent,** and costly jewelry from such shops as **Asprey, Tiffany,** and **Cartier.**

Some of the original 18th-century houses survive on the west side of **Berkeley Square.** Farther along is **Curzon Street,** which runs along the northern edge of **Shepherd Market,** a maze of narrow streets full of antiques shops, restaurants, and pubs that retain something of a village atmosphere.

Time Out   **L'Artiste Musclé** is a popular bistro serving French food with a few picturesque tables outside in summer. *1 Shepherd Market.*

Hyde Park and Beyond **㉕**   A great expanse of green parkland begins at **Hyde Park Corner** and cuts right across the center of London. **Hyde Park,** which covers about 137 hectares (340 acres), was originally a royal hunting ground, while **Kensington Gardens,** which adjoins it to the west, started life as part of the royal Kensington Palace. These two parks contain many fine trees and are a haven for wildlife. The sandy track that runs along the south edge of the parks has been a fashionable riding trail for centuries. Though it's called **Rotten Row,** there's nothing rotten about it. The name derives from *route du roi* ("the King's Way")—the route William III and Queen Mary took from their home at Kensington Palace to the court at St. James's. There is boating and swimming in the **Serpentine,** the S-shaped lake formed by damming a stream that used to flow here. Refreshments can be had at the Serpentine bars, buffet, and restaurant complex, and the **Serpentine Gallery** holds noteworthy exhibitions of modern art (tel. 071/402–6075).

㉖   Leave the park at **Exhibition Road** and visit three of London's major museums. The **Science Museum** is the leading national collection of science and technology, with extensive hands-on exhibits on outer space, astronomy, computers, transportation, and medicine. *Tel. 071/938–8000; 071/938–8123 (recorded information). Admission: £4 adults, £2.10 children under 15 and senior citizens. Open Mon.– Sat. 10–6, Sun. 11–6.*

㉗   The **Natural History Museum** is housed in an ornate late-Victorian building with striking modern additions. As in the Science Museum, its displays on topics such as human biology and evolution are designed to challenge visitors to think for themselves. *Cromwell Rd., tel. 071/938–9123; 042/692–7654 (recorded information). Admission: £4.50 adults, £2.20 children under 15 and senior citizens; free weekdays 4:30–5:50. Open Mon.–Sat. 10–6, Sun. 2:30–6.*

㉘   The **Victoria and Albert Museum** (or V & A) originated in the 19th century as a museum of decorative art and has extensive collections of costumes, paintings, jewelry, and crafts from every part of the globe. The collections from India, China, and the Islamic world are especially strong. *Cromwell Rd., tel. 071/938–8500; 071/938–8441 (recorded information). Suggested voluntary contribution: £3.50 adults, £1 children and senior citizens. Open Mon.–Sat. 10–5:50, Sun. 2:30–5:50.*

Time Out   The **V & A restaurant** is just the place to recuperate after visiting the museum. You can enjoy morning coffee, hot lunchtime dishes, or afternoon tea.

㉙   Back in Kensington Gardens, the **Albert Memorial** commemorates Queen Victoria's much-loved husband, Prince Albert, who died in 1861 at the age of 42. The monument, itself the epitome of high Victorian taste, commemorates the many socially uplifting projects of the prince, among them the Great Exhibition of 1851, whose catalog he is holding. The Memorial, which has been badly eroded by pollution, is currently being restored.

From the **Flower Walk,** behind the Albert Memorial, carefully planted so that flowers are in bloom virtually throughout the year, ㉚ strike out across Kensington Gardens to the **Round Pond,** a favorite place for children to sail toy boats.

㉛ **Kensington Palace,** across from the Round Pond, has been a royal home since the late 17th century—and is one still, for the prince and princess of Wales and Princess Margaret. From the outside it looks less like a palace than a country house, which it was until William III bought it in 1689. Inside, however, are state rooms on a grand scale, mostly created in the early 18th century. Such distinguished architects as Wren, Hawksmoor, Vanbrugh, and William Kent were all employed here. Queen Victoria lived at Kensington Palace as a child, and several rooms are furnished as they were during her time. The public part of the palace also contains an exhibition of court dress. *Tel. 071/937–9561. Admission: £3.90 adults, £2.95 students and senior citizens, £2.60 children. Open Mon.–Sat. 9–5, Sun. 1–5.*

North of Kensington Gardens is the lively **Notting Hill** district, full of restaurants and cafés where young people gather. The best-㉜ known attraction in this area is **Portobello Road,** where the lively antiques and bric-a-brac market is held each Saturday (arrive early in the morning for the best bargains). The street is also full of regular antiques shops that are open most weekdays.

Time Out **Geales** (2 Farmer St.) is a superior Notting Hill fish-and-chips restaurant, popular with locals and visitors alike.

Covent You could easily spend a half day exploring the block of streets north
Garden of the Strand known as **Covent Garden.** The heart of the area is a for-
㉝ mer wholesale fruit and vegetable market, established in 1656. The market moved to more modern and accessible premises only in 1974. **The Piazza,** the Victorian Market Building, is now a vibrant shopping center, with numerous boutiques, crafts shops, and cafés. On the south side of the market building is the lively and much less formal **Jubilee market,** with crafts and clothing stalls.

㉞ The atmosphere in Covent Garden is friendly and informal. Look for the open-air entertainers performing under the portico of **St. Paul's Church**—you can enjoy an excellent show for the price of a few coins thrown in the hat that's passed among the onlookers. The church, entered from Bedford Street, is known as the Actors' Church, and inside are numerous memorials to theater people. The **Royal Opera House** and the **Theatre Royal Drury Lane,** two of London's oldest theaters, are close by.

Time Out There's a good selection of eating places in and around the Market Building. **Crank's,** at No. 11, serves delicious quiches, salads, and cakes. The **Calabash,** in the basement of the Africa Center at 38 King Street, serves authentic African dishes at reasonable prices.

For interesting specialty shops, head north of the Market Building. Shops on **Long Acre** sell maps, art books, clothing, and glass; shops on **Neal Street** sell clothes, pottery, jewelry, and goods from the Far East.

㉟ The collection of vehicles at the **London Transport Museum** includes a steam locomotive, a tram, a subway car, and an Underground train simulator. Visitors are encouraged to operate many of the vehicles, and the exhibits and the space were recently upgraded. The shop sells T-shirts, books, souvenirs, and current and historic London Transport posters. *The Piazza (southeast corner), tel. 071/379–6344. Admission: £3.95 adults, £2.50 children 5–16 and senior citizens, children under 5 free. Open daily 10–5:15.*

㊱ The **Theatre Museum** contains a comprehensive collection of material on the history of the English theater—not merely the classic drama but also opera, music hall, pantomime, and musical comedy. Scripts, playbills, costumes, and props are displayed; there is even a re-creation of a dressing room filled with memorabilia of former stars. *Russell St., tel. 071/836–7891. Admission: £3 adults, £1.50 children under 14, students, and senior citizens. Open Tues.–Sun. 11–7.*

㊲ On **Bow Street** is the **Royal Opera House,** home of the Royal Ballet and the Royal Opera Company. The plush interior captures the richness of Victorian England.

Bloomsbury **Bloomsbury** is a semiresidential district to the north of Covent Garden that contains some spacious and elegant 17th- and 18th-century squares. It could claim to be the intellectual center of London, since both the British Museum and the University of London are found here. The area also gave its name to the Bloomsbury Group, a clique of writers and painters who thrived here in the early 20th century. The antiquarian and specialist bookshops, publishing houses, restaurants, and pubs frequented by the local literati add to the academic-cum-bohemian ambience of the area.

㊳ The **British Museum** houses a vast and priceless collection of treasures, including Egyptian, Greek, and Roman antiquities; Renaissance jewelry; pottery; coins; glass; and drawings from virtually every European school since the 15th century. It's best to pick out one section that particularly interests you—to try to see everything would be an overwhelming and exhausting task. Some of the highlights are the **Elgin Marbles,** sculptures that formerly decorated the Parthenon in Athens; the **Rosetta Stone,** which helped archaeologists to interpret Egyptian script; a copy of the **Magna Carta,** the charter signed by King John in 1215 to which is ascribed the origins of English liberty; and the **Mildenhall treasure,** a cache of Roman silver found in East Anglia in 1842. *Great Russell St., tel. 071/636–1555; 071/580–1788 (recorded information). Admission free; guided tours of museum's highlights, £6. Open Mon.–Sat. 10–5, Sun. 2:30–6.*

㊴ The **Jewish Museum** has a small but interesting collection of antiquities illustrating Judaism, Jewish life, and history. There are also audiovisual programs on Jewish festivals and ceremonies. *Woburn House, Upper Woburn Pl., tel. 071/388–4525. Admission: £1 adults, 50p students and children, under 15 free. Open Tues.–Thurs. (and Fri. in summer) 10–4, Sun. (and Fri. in winter) 10–12:45.*

The City The **City,** the traditional commercial center of London, is the most ancient part of the capital, having been the site of the great Roman city of Londinium. Since those days, the City has been built and rebuilt several times. The wooden buildings of the medieval City were destroyed in the Great Fire of 1666. There were further waves of reconstruction in the 19th century, and then again after World War II, to repair the devastation wrought by air attacks. The 1980s have seen the construction of many mammoth office developments, some undistinguished, others incorporating adventurous and exciting ideas.

Throughout all these changes, the City has retained its unique identity and character. The lord mayor and Corporation of London are still responsible for the government of the City, as they have been for many centuries. Commerce remains the lifeblood of the City, which is a world financial center rivaled only by New York, Tokyo, and Zurich. The biggest change has been in the City's population. Until the first half of the 19th century, many of the merchants and traders who worked in the City lived there, too. Today, despite its huge daytime population, scarcely 8,000 people live in the 274 hectares (677 acres) of the City. Try, therefore, to explore the City on a weekday morning or afternoon. On weekends its streets are deserted, and many of the shops and restaurants, even some of the churches, are closed.

40 Following the Great Fire, **St. Paul's Cathedral** was rebuilt by Sir Christopher Wren, the architect who was also responsible for designing 50 City parish churches to replace those lost in the Great Fire. St. Paul's is Wren's greatest work. Fittingly, he is buried in the crypt, under the simple epitaph composed by his son: "Reader, if you seek his monument, look around you." The cathedral has been the site of many famous state occasions, including the funeral of Winston Churchill in 1965 and the marriage of the prince and princess of Wales in 1981. There is much fine painting and craftsmanship—the choir stalls are by the great 17th-century wood carver Grinling Gibbons—but overall the atmosphere is somewhat austere and remote. The cathedral contains many monuments and tombs. Among those commemorated are George Washington; the essayist and lexicographer Samuel Johnson; and two military heroes—Nelson, victor over the French at Trafalgar in 1805, and Wellington, who defeated the French on land at Waterloo 10 years later. In the ambulatory (the area behind the high altar) is the American Chapel, a memorial to the 28,000 U.S. citizens stationed in Britain during World War II who lost their lives while on active service.

The greatest architectural glory of the cathedral is the dome. This consists of three distinct elements: an outer, timber-framed dome covered with lead; an interior dome built of brick and decorated with frescoes of the life of St. Paul by the 18th-century artist Sir James Thornhill; and, in between, a brick cone that supports and strengthens both. There is a good view of the church from the **Whispering Gallery,** high up in the inner dome. The gallery is so called because of its remarkable acoustics, whereby words whispered on one side can be clearly heard on the other, 35 meters (112 feet) away. Above this gallery are two others, both external, from which there are fine views over the City and beyond. *Tel. 071/248–2705. Admission to cathedral free; Ambulatory (American Chapel), Crypt, and Treasury: £2.50 adults, £2 senior citizens and students, £1.50 children; to galleries: £2.50 adults, £2 senior citizens and students, £1.50 children, combined ticket: £4.50 adults, £3.50 senior citizens and students, £2.50 children. Cathedral open Mon.–Sat. 7:30–6, Sun. 8–6; the Ambulatory, Crypt, and Galleries weekdays 10–4:15, Sat. 11–4:15. Tours weekdays 11, 11:30, 2, 2:30.*

A short walk north of the cathedral, to **London Wall,** so called because it follows the line of the wall that surrounded the Roman settlement, brings you to the **Museum of London.** Its displays enable you to get a real sense of what it was like to live in London at different periods of history, from Roman times to the present day. Among the highlights are the Lord Mayor's Ceremonial Coach, an imaginative reconstruction of the Great Fire, and the Cheapside Hoard, jewelry hidden during an outbreak of plague in the 17th century and never recovered by its owner. A gallery devoted to the 18th century was opened in 1989. The 20th-century exhibits include a Woolworth's counter and elevators from Selfridges; both stores were founded by Americans and had an immense impact on the life of Londoners. *London Wall, tel. 071/600–3699. Admission £3 adults, £1.50 under 18 and senior citizens. Open Tues.–Sat. 10–6, Sun. 2–6.*

42 The **Barbican** is a vast residential complex and arts center built by the City of London. It takes its name from the watchtower that stood here during the Middle Ages, just outside the City walls. The arts center contains a concert hall, where the London Symphony Orchestra is based, two theaters, an art gallery, a cinema, and several cafés and restaurants. The theaters are the London home of the Royal Shakespeare Company.

43 On the south side of London Wall stands **Guildhall,** the much reconstructed home of the Corporation of London; the lord mayor of London is elected here each year with ancient ceremony. *King St., tel. 071/606–3030. Admission free. Open weekdays 10–5.*

Now walk south to **Cheapside.** This was the chief marketplace of medieval London (the word *ceap* meant "market"), as the street names hereabouts indicate: Milk Street, Ironmonger Lane, etc. Despite rebuilding, many of the streets still run on the medieval pat-
44 tern. The church of **St. Mary-le-Bow** in Cheapside was rebuilt by Christopher Wren after the Great Fire; it was built again after being bombed during World War II. It is said that to be a true Cockney, you must be born within the sound of Bow bells.

Time Out | **The Place Below** (St Mary-le-Bow, Cheapside) serves a very high standard of meatless soup-quiche-salad lunches, then metamorphoses into a fancy restaurant two nights a week. *Closed weekends.*

A short walk east along Cheapside brings you to a seven-way inter-
45 section. The **Bank of England,** which regulates much of Britain's financial life, is the large windowless building on the left. At the northern side of the intersection, at right angles to the bank, is the
46 **Royal Exchange,** originally built in the 1560s as a trading hall for merchants. The present building, opened in 1844 and the third on the site, is now occupied by the **London International Financial Futures Exchange.** If you call ahead, you can watch the hectic trading from the Visitors' Gallery. *Tel. 071/623–0444. Admission free. Visitors' Gallery open by appointment to groups from relevant organizations.*

The third major building at this intersection, on its south side, is the
47 **Mansion House,** the official residence of the lord mayor of London.

Continue east along **Cornhill,** site of a Roman basilica and of a medieval grain market. Turn right into Gracechurch Street and then left
48 into **Leadenhall Market.** There has been a market here since the 14th century; the present building dates from 1881.

Just behind the market is one of the most striking pieces of contem-
49 porary City architecture: the headquarters of **Lloyd's of London,** built by the modernist architect Richard Rogers. Its main feature is a 62-meter-high (200-foot-high) barrel vault made of sparkling glass. The underwriters of Lloyd's provide insurance for everything imaginable, from oil rigs to a pianist's fingers, though they suffered a crash in 1993, with most of the so-called Names, whose millions formed the Lloyd's backbone, losing major money. An exhibit traces the history of Lloyd's from the 17th century. *1 Lime St., tel. 071/*

623–7100, ext. 6210 or 5786. Admission free. Open by appointment to groups from recognized organizations.

Time Out   Lloyd's started life in a coffeehouse, and so **Lloyd's Coffee House,** at the foot of the modern building, is an apt place for coffee and pastries, a full lunch, or afternoon tea.

㊿ From here it's a short walk east to the **Tower of London,** one of London's most famous sights and one of its most crowded, too. Come as early in the day as possible and head for the Crown Jewels so you can see them before the crowds arrive.

The tower served the monarchs of medieval England as both fortress and palace. Every British sovereign from William the Conqueror in the 11th century to Henry VIII in the 16th lived here, and it remains a royal palace, in name at least. The **History Gallery,** south of the White Tower, is a walk-through display designed to answer questions about the inhabitants of the tower and its evolution over the centuries.

The **White Tower** is the oldest and also the most conspicuous building in the entire complex. Inside, the **Chapel of St. John** is one of the few unaltered parts. A structure of great simplicity, it is almost entirely lacking in ornamentation. The **Royal Armories,** England's national collection of arms and armor, occupies the rest of the White Tower. Armor of the 16th and 17th centuries forms the centerpiece of the displays, including pieces belonging to Henry VIII and Charles I.

Among other buildings worth seeing is the **Bloody Tower.** This name has been traced back only to 1571; it was originally known as the Garden Tower. Sir Walter Raleigh was held prisoner here, in relatively comfortable circumstances, between 1603 and 1616, during which time he wrote his *History of the World;* his rooms are furnished much as they were during his imprisonment. The little princes in the tower—the boy king Edward V and his brother Richard, duke of York, supposedly murdered on the orders of Gloucester, later crowned Richard III—certainly lived in the Bloody Tower, and may well have died here, too. Another bloody death is alleged to have occurred in the **Wakefield Tower,** when Henry VI was murdered in 1471 during England's medieval civil war, the Wars of the Roses. It was a rare honor to be beheaded in private inside the tower; most people were executed outside, on **Tower Hill,** where the crowds could get a much better view. Important prisoners were held in the **Beauchamp Tower;** the walls are covered with graffiti and inscriptions carved by prisoners.

The **Crown Jewels** are a breathtakingly beautiful collection of regalia, precious stones, gold, and silver. The Royal Scepter contains the largest cut diamond in the world. The Imperial State Crown, made for the 1838 coronation of Queen Victoria, contains some 3,000 precious stones, largely diamonds and pearls. The Jewels moved to their new home in the Duke of Wellington's Barracks in spring 1993. Look for the ravens whose presence at the tower is traditional. It is said that if they leave, the tower will fall and England will lose her greatness. *Tower Hill, tel. 071/709–0765. Admission: £6.70 adults, £5.10 students and senior citizens, £4.40 children under 16, family ticket £19. Reduced admission charges apply during Feb. when the Jewel House is closed. Small additional admission charge to the Fusiliers Museum only. Open Mar.–Oct., Mon.–Sat. 9:30–6, Sun. 10–6; Nov.–Feb., Mon.–Sat. 9:30–4.*

Yeoman Warder guides conduct tours daily from the Middle Tower, no charge, but a tip is always appreciated. Subject to weather and availability of guides, tours are conducted about every 30 minutes until 3:30 in summer, 2:30 in winter.

Off the Beaten Track

Camden Lock Walk along the bank of the **Grand Union Canal** (Regent's Canal) from the northwest corner of Regent's Park eastward to **Camden Lock,** where there are lots of little shops selling gifts, secondhand clothes, crafts, and antiques. On weekends there's an outdoor market, and the area overflows with hordes of twentysomethings.

You can extend the excursion in two different directions from Camden Lock. Either walk east along the canal towpath through the elegant streets of Islington and then through increasingly less prosperous areas until you reach the Thames at Limehouse or turn north to **Hampstead** and **Hampstead Heath.**

Hampstead Hampstead is a village within the city, where many famous poets and writers have lived. Today it is a fashionable residential area, with a main shopping street and some rows of elegant 18th-century houses. The heath is one of London's largest and most attractive open spaces. In **Keats Grove,** on the southern edge of the heath, is the house where the Romantic poet John Keats (1795–1821) lived. *Wentworth Pl., tel. 071/435–2062. Admission free. Visitors are advised to call in advance for exact opening times.*

Standing alone in its own landscaped grounds on the north side of the heath is **Kenwood House,** built in the 17th century and remodeled by Robert Adam, the talented exponent of classical decoration, at the end of the 18th. The house contains a collection of superb paintings by such masters as Rembrandt, Vermeer, Turner, Reynolds, Van Dyck, and Gainsborough, which gain enormously by being displayed in the grand country-house setting for which they were originally intended. The lovely landscaped grounds, with lake, provide the setting for symphony concerts in summer. *Hampstead Lane, tel. 071/435–2062. Admission free. Open Apr.–Oct., weekdays 2–6, Sat. 10–1 and 2–5, Sun. 2–5; Nov.–Mar., weekdays 1–5, Sat. 10–1 and 2–5 , Sun. 2–5.*

Greenwich The historical and maritime attractions at **Greenwich,** on the Thames, some 8 kilometers (5 miles) east of central London, make it an ideal place for a day out. You can get to Greenwich by riverboat from Westminster and Tower Bridge piers, by ThamesLine's high-speed river buses, or by train from Charing Cross station. You can also take the Docklands Light Railway from Tower Gateway to Island Gardens and walk a short distance along a pedestrian tunnel under the river.

Visit the **National Maritime Museum,** a treasure house of paintings; maps; models; sextants; and, best of all, ships from all ages, including the ornate royal barges. *Romney Rd., tel. 081/858–4422. Joint admission with the Royal Observatory: £3.75 adults, £2.75 children and senior citizens. Open late Mar.–late Oct., Mon.–Sat. 10–6, Sun. 2–6; late Oct.–late Mar., Mon.–Sat. 10–5, Sun. 2–5.*

Two ships now in dry dock are the glorious 19th-century clipper ship ***Cutty Sark*** and the tiny ***Gipsy Moth IV,*** which Sir Francis Chichester sailed single-handed around the world in 1966. *Cutty Sark, King William Walk, tel. 081/858–3445. Admission: £3.25 adults, £2.25 children under 16 and senior citizens. Open late Mar.–Sept., Mon.–Sat. 10–5:30, Sun. noon–5:30; Oct.–Mar., Mon.–Sat.*

10–4:30, Sun. noon–4:30. Gipsy Moth IV, King William Walk, tel. 081/853–3589. Admission: 50p adults, 30p children and senior citizens. Open Apr.–Oct., Mon.–Sat. 10–5:30, Sun. noon–5:30.

The **Royal Naval College** was built in 1694 as a home, or hospital, for old sailors. You can see the magnificent **Painted Hall**, where Nelson's body lay in state following the Battle of Trafalgar, and the College Chapel. *Tel. 081/858–2154. Admission free. Open Fri.–Wed. 2:30–4:30.*

Behind the museum and the college is **Greenwich Park**, originally a royal hunting ground and today an attractive place in which to wander and relax. On top of the hill is the **Old Royal Observatory**, founded in 1675, where original telescopes and other astronomical instruments are on display. The prime meridian—zero degrees longitude—runs through the courtyard of the observatory. *Greenwich Park, tel. 081/858–4422. Joint admission with National Maritime Museum: £3.75 adults, £2.75 children and senior citizens; day passport to all Greenwich sights, plus one return visit £7.45 adults, £5.45 children and senior citizens. Open Apr.–Oct., Mon.–Sat. 10–6, Sun. 2–6; Nov.–Mar., Mon.–Sat. 10–5, Sun. 2–5.*

Shopping

Shopping is one of London's great pleasures. Different areas retain their traditional specialties, as described below, but there are also numerous pockets of local shops to explore, and it's fun to seek out the small crafts, antiques, and gift stores, designer clothing resale outlets, and high-street favorites.

Shopping Districts   **Chelsea** is a mecca for those in search of up-to-the-minute fashions, antiques, and classy home furnishings, especially around **Brompton Cross** in South Kensington. The **King's Road,** which was the center of youth culture for two decades, now tends to be touristy and tired.

Covent Garden is the home of crafts shops, trendy boutiques, and the daily Jubilee Market. Antiques are the main draw in **Kensington,** especially along **Kensington Church Street.** Representatives of the better high-street clothing chains line **Kensington High Street.**

The great Edwardian bulk of Harrods dominates **Knightsbridge,** but don't neglect the boutiques and art galleries on other shopping streets in the area, such as **Sloane Street, Beauchamp Place,** and **Walton Street.**

In **Mayfair,** the area between **Piccadilly** and **Oxford Street,** the emphasis is on traditional British clothing for men and women. Traffic-free **South Molton Street** is good for top women's labels—especially **Browns.** Go to **Bond Street** for designer-label fashions and world-famous jewelry. Both quality and prices are tops here.

Noisy, crowded **Oxford Street** is to be endured rather than enjoyed. **Selfridges, Marks and Spencer,** and **John Lewis** are all good department stores here, and little **St. Christopher's Place,** almost opposite Bond Street tube, adds a chic touch.

There are still a number of classy stores along **Piccadilly,** including **Simpsons** (clothes), **Hatchards** (books), and **Fortnum and Mason** (foodstuffs, fashions). Several elegant shopping arcades lead off Piccadilly, the best-known of which is the **Burlington Arcade.**

China, clothes, fabrics, and good department stores help to make **Regent Street** an appealing alternative to neighboring Oxford Street. Don't miss **Liberty**—the city's most appealing department store, still with its original emphasis on Oriental goods, and **Hamley's**—London's largest toy store.

Though his suits may be made in Savile Row, the English gentleman comes to **St. James's** for the rest of his outfit, which includes shoes, shirts, silk ties, hats, and all manner of accessories. The prices mirror the quality.

Markets   Street markets are one aspect of London life not to be missed. Here are some of the more interesting markets:

Bermondsey. Arrive as early as possible for the best treasure—or junk. *Tower Bridge Rd., SE1. Open Fri. 4:30 AM–noon. Take the tube to London Bridge and walk or take the No. 15 or 25 bus to Aldgate and then a No. 42 bus over Tower Bridge to Bermondsey Square.*

Camden Lock. This is just the place for an unusual and inexpensive gift; it's also a picturesque place to wander around. There's an openair antiques market on weekends, but it gets horribly crowded. *Chalk Farm Rd., NW1. Open Tues.–Sun. 9:30–5:30. Take the tube or the No. 24 or 29 bus to Camden Town.*

Camden Passage. The rows of little antiques shops are a good hunting ground for silverware and jewelry. Stalls open Wednesday and Saturday, a books and prints market opens Thursdays, and shops open the rest of the week. *Islington, N1. Open Wed.–Sat. 8:30–3. Take the tube or No. 19 or 38 bus to the Angel.*

Petticoat Lane. Look for budget-priced leather goods, dazzling knitwear, and fashions, plus cameras, videos, stereos, antiques, books, and bric-a-brac. *Middlesex St., E1. Open Sun. 9–2. Take the tube to Liverpool Street, Aldgate, or Aldgate East.*

Portobello Market. Saturday is the best day for antiques, though this neighborhood is London's melting pot and increases in vibrancy year after year. Find fabulous small shops, the city's trendiest restaurants, and a Friday and Saturday flea market at the far end. *Portobello Rd., W11. Open Fri. 5–3, Sat. 8–5. Take the tube or No. 52 bus to Notting Hill Gate or Ladbroke Grove or No. 15 bus to Kensington Park Road.*

Dining

For details and price-category definitions, *see* Dining in Staying in Great Britain, *above.*

Bloomsbury
Moderate

Chez Gerard. This purveyor of *steak-frites* and similarly simple gallic offerings is reliable, relaxed, and usefully located near Oxford Street. Some say these are London's best fries—of the shoestring variety. *8 Charlotte St., tel. 071/636–4975. Reservations advised. AE, DC, MC, V. Closed Christmas.*

Museum Street Café. The young owners of this tiny, spartan place near the British Museum offer a short menu featuring fresh ingredients intelligently and plainly cooked: for lunch, soup and stilton on walnut bread; for dinner, corn-fed chicken with pesto, and chocolate cake. Bring your own wine. *47 Museum St., tel. 071/405–3211. Reservations required for dinner. No credit cards. Closed weekends, public holidays.*

Inexpensive   **The North Sea Fish Restaurant.** Good old British fish 'n' chips—battered and deep-fried fish with thick fries—cooked to a turn and always fresh is served in this popular haunt. It's a bit tricky to find—three blocks south of St. Pancras station, down Judd Street. You can eat in or take out. *7–8 Leigh St., tel. 071/387–5892. Reservations advised. AE, DC, MC, V. Closed Sun., holidays, 10 days at Christmas.*

★ **Wagamama.** Japanese noodles here are fast and delicious, served in soup, topped with meat or fish, or supplemented by rice and vegetable dishes. Staff take your order on hand-held computers for fast, high-tech service. You will have to share a table, such is its popularity. *4 Streatham St., tel. 071/323–9223. No reservations. No credit cards. Closed Christmas.*

Chelsea
Very Expensive

La Tante Claire. This spot is justly famous for Pierre Koffmann's superb haute cuisine: hot foie gras on shredded potatoes with a sweet wine and shallot sauce or his famous signature dish of pig's trotter stuffed with sweetbreads and wild mushrooms. *68 Royal Hospital Rd., tel. 071/352–6045. Reservations 3–4 weeks in advance. AE, DC, MC, V. Closed weekends, 10 days at Easter and Christmas, 3 weeks in Aug.–Sept.*

Expensive

Chutney Mary. London's only Anglo-Indian restaurant provides a fantasy version of the British Raj, with colonial cocktails and authentic recreations of comforting, rich dishes like Country Captain (chicken with almonds, raisins, chilis, and spices) and Masala roast lamb. *535 King's Rd., tel. 071/351–3113. Reservations advised. AE, DC, MC, V. Closed Christmas dinner, Dec. 26.*

Moderate

Gavvers. This is the down-market branch of the Gavroche empire, located two blocks below Sloane Square. The set menus at about £15 for lunch and £25 for dinner offer simpler versions of the Roux brothers' classic French dishes. The place is rather cramped and noisy but full of character. *61–63 Lower Sloane St., tel. 071/730–4772. Reservations essential. AE, DC, MC, V. Closed Sat. lunch, Sun.*

Inexpensive

Henry J. Bean's. Hamburgers and Tex-Mex food are served to American oldies music. Order food at the bar, then wait—in the big patio garden if you're lucky—for your number to come up on the TV screen. *195–197 King's Rd., tel. 071/352–9255. No reservations. No credit cards. Closed Dec. 25, 26, 31.*

The City
Expensive

Bill Bentley's. Once a wine merchant's vault with bare walls and arched ceiling, this atmospheric institution has a menu dominated by seafood of many varieties and tables filled with lunching City workers. There are four other branches, including one at Beauchamp Place near Harrods. *Swedeland Ct., 202 Bishopsgate, tel. 071/283–1763. Reservations required. AE, DC, MC, V. Open weekdays for lunch only.*

Le Poulbot. Here you'll find one of the most popular and reliable fixed-price lunches in the City, at around £30 for three courses and aperitif. Onion tart, cold poached salmon with chervil, and summer pudding are typical of the frequently changing French menu, served smartly in a comfortably red-plush dining room. Try the moderately priced brasserie upstairs, too. *45 Cheapside, tel. 071/236–4379. Reservations required. AE, DC, MC, V. Open weekdays for lunch only.*

Moderate

Sweetings. City gents stand in line to lunch at this tiny, basic Victorian restaurant close to the remains of a Roman temple. The service is Old World courteous; the fish, cheese, and puddings are comforting and well prepared. *39 Queen Victoria St., tel. 071/248–3062. No reservations. No credit cards. Open weekdays for lunch only; closed Christmas, holidays.*

Covent
Garden
Very Expensive
★

The Savoy Grill. Continuing to attract more than its fair share of mostly male power-brokers, from newspaper editors to tycoons, this paneled French-English salon exudes comfort, from the avuncular, yet deferential, service to the glorious nursery food, which most choose over the more modern, more French side of the menu. The daily dish is the way to go—or something British, like jugged hare (a stew of hare, with blood), or the omelet Arnold Bennett (with cheese and smoked fish), invented here for that novelist. *Strand, tel. 071/836–4343. Reservations essential for lunch and for Thurs.–Sat. dinner. AE, DC, MC, V. Closed Sat. lunch, Sun., and Aug.*

Expensive ★ **The Ivy.** The epitome of style without pretension, this restaurant beguiles everybody, including media, literary, and theatrical movers and shakers, who table-hop. The menu's got it all: fish-and-chips, sausage-and-mash, Caesar salad, burgers, squid-ink risotto, bang-bang chicken, sticky toffee pudding, and all good. *1 West St., tel. 071/836–4751. Reservations required. AE, DC, MC, V. Closed Dec. 25–26.*

Rules. This city's oldest restaurant (it's been here since 1798) is traditional from soup to nuts, or rather, from venison and Dover sole to trifle and Stilton. Nowadays there's the odd nod to newer cuisines, but the clientele of expense-accounters and tourists in search of olde London Towne remains. *35 Maiden La., tel. 071/836–5314. Reservations at least 1 day in advance. AE, DC, MC, V. Closed Sun., Dec. 25.*

Moderate ★ **Bertorelli's.** Opposite the stage door of the Royal Opera House, Bertorelli's is a favorite with opera goers. Chic decor complements Maddalena Bonino's modern Italian food—try the poached cotechino sausage on lentils, followed by the monkfish, fennel, and tomato ragout. *44a Floral St., tel. 071/836–3969. Reservations advised. AE, DC, MC, V. Closed Sun., Dec. 25.*

★ **Joe Allen.** This basement restaurant behind the Strand Palace Hotel follows the style of its New York counterpart, is descended on by packs of theatrical types after curtain, and is forever noisy. The menu, too, is straight from Manhattan—there's a great Caesar, BBQ ribs with black-eye peas and wilted greens, brownies with ice cream—and it's open late. *13 Exeter St., tel. 071/836–0651. Reservations required. No credit cards. Closed Christmas.*

Inexpensive ★ **Food for Thought.** This is a simple downstairs vegetarian restaurant, with seats for only 50, so there's almost always a waiting line. The menu—stir fries, casseroles, salads, and dessert—changes daily, and each dish is freshly made. No alcohol is served here. *31 Neal St., tel. 071/836–0239. No reservations. No credit cards. Closed Sun., Sat. after 4:30 PM, weekdays after 8 PM, 2 weeks at Christmas, holidays.*

Kensington **Bibendum.** Upstairs in the renovated 1911 Michelin building, this
Very Expensive excellent restaurant has been the flavor of the month for some time
★ now with chef Simon Hopkinson continually showered with well-deserved accolades. From the scallops in a citrus sauce to the passion-fruit *bavarois*, all the dishes are unpretentious but perfectly done every time. *81 Fulham Rd., tel. 071/581–5817. Reservations required. MC, V. Closed Christmas and holidays.*

Moderate ★ **Bistrot 190.** Chef-restaurateur Antony Worral-Thompson seems to know exactly what the people want, which, in this case, is big plates of happy, hearty food from southern Europe (liver and wild mushroom terrine; grilled squid with red and green salsa; lemon tart). The decor incorporates hardwood floors and art-laden walls. Next door is **Downstairs at 190**—similar, but offering fish and seafood in all guises and all sizes. *190 Queensgate, tel. 071/581–5666. No reservations. AE, DC, MC, V. Closed Sat. lunch, Sun., Dec. 25–26, Jan. 1.*

★ **Wodka.** This modern Polish restaurant in a quiet backstreet serves stylish food to a fashionable group and often has the relaxed atmosphere of a dinner party. Try herring blinis, roast duck with figs and port, and the several flavored vodkas. *12 St. Albans Grove W8, tel. 071/937-6513. Reservations advised. AE, DC, MC, V. Closed weekend lunch, Dec. 25–26.*

Knightsbridge
Moderate

Grill St. Quentin. This is a popular French spot just five blocks west of Harrods. Choose from a selection of fresh meat or fish, which is then cooked on an open grill. The set lunch at £12.50 is excellent value for shoppers. *2 Yeoman's Row, tel. 071/583–8377. Reservations advised. AE, DC, MC, V. Closed Sun.*

Inexpensive

Stockpot. Speedy service is the mark of this large, jolly restaurant full of students and shoppers. The food is filling and wholesome; try the homemade soups, the Lancashire hot pot, and the apple crumble. Breakfast is also served Monday–Saturday. Other Stockpot branches can be found in Old Compton Street, Soho, and behind Leicester Square in Panton Street. *6 Basil St., tel. 071/589–8627. Reservations accepted. No credit cards. Closed Dec. 25, New Year's Day.*

Mayfair
Very Expensive
★

Le Gavroche. Long regarded as a top temple of *haute cuisine*, this dark and rich dining room dropped its third *Michelin* star when Albert Roux's son, Michel, took over the kitchen in '93, but no drop in quality seemed to ensue. Dining here is an unashamedly sybaritic and costly experience, punctuated with foie gras, oysters, and lobster, but one that becomes accessible with the three-course lunch for £36, inclusive of coffee, wine, and service. *43 Upper Brook St., tel. 071/408–0881. Reserve at least 1 week in advance. AE, DC, MC, V. Closed weekends, 10 days at Christmas, holidays.*

★

Nico at Ninety. Those with refined palates and very deep pockets should not miss Nico Ladenis's exquisite gastronomy. He is one of the world's great chefs, and is famous for knowing it. Nowhere is food taken more seriously; the menu is in French (untranslated); vegetarians and children are not welcome. *90 Park La., tel. 071/409–1290. Reservations required. AE, DC, MC, V. Closed weekends, public holidays, 3 weeks in Aug.*

Expensive

Langan's Brasserie. Langan's is as much a haunt of tourists as of celebrities these days. If you do manage to get in, you'll be impressed by the modern art on the walls, the vast menu, the frank service (the waiters sometimes advise against certain dishes), and the top-quality food. Try the spinach soufflé with anchovy sauce or the black pudding—a sausage made mostly from blood. *Stratton St., tel. 071/493–6437. Reservations required far in advance. AE, DC, MC, V. Closed Sat. lunch, Sun., holidays.*

★

Mulligans. Anyone with Irish blood (though it's not compulsory . . .) should not miss this friendly and relaxing slice of Dublin. The cooking is unpretentious and satisfying—London's finest black pudding served with calvados and spiced apples; steak, Guinness, and kidney pie; and, of course, a sublime Irish stew. There's a separate bar at street level. *13–14 Cork St., W1, tel. 071/409–1370. Reservations advised. AE, DC, MC, V. Closed Sat. lunch, Sun. dinner, Dec. 25–26, Jan. 1.*

Moderate

Criterion. This welcome point of light in the Piccadilly desert offers a fresh California-Italian menu (corn and asparagus risotto; roast salmon on cucumber noodles; rosemary mashed potatoes), substantial desserts, afternoon tea, and sanctuary. The setting is a palatial neo-Byzantine mirrored, marbled hall with a splendid gold mosaic ceiling; there's a bar at the back, behind the giant, blue-lit glass clock. *Piccadilly Circus, tel. 071/925–0909. Reservations advised. AE, DC, MC, V. Closed Christmas.*

Inexpensive **The Chicago Pizza Pie Factory.** Huge pizzas with salad and garlic bread are served at reasonable prices in this loud basement, the first of the ubiquitous Bob Payton's London restaurants (he co-owns the Criterion too). These pies are American-style with a thick chewy base and a somewhat limited choice of toppings; try the American sausage and mushroom. *17 Hanover Sq., tel. 071/629–2669. Reservations advised for lunch. No credit cards. Closed Dec. 25, 26.*

Notting Hill Gate
Expensive **Clarke's.** There's no choice of dishes at dinner (and only a limited choice at lunch); chef Sally Clarke plans the meal according to what is freshest and best in the market each day. Her style is natural and unfussy West Coast cuisine, accompanied by fabulous homemade breads. *124 Kensington Church St., tel. 071/221–9225. Reservations advised. MC, V. Closed weekends, 10 days at Christmas, Easter, 3 weeks in Aug.*

Kensington Place. Trendy and loud, this ever-popular place features enormous plate-glass windows through which to be seen, and plenty of fashionable food. Try foie gras with sweet-corn pancake, rack of lamb, and baked tamarillo with vanilla ice cream. *201 Kensington Church St., W8, tel. 071/727–3184. Reservations advised. MC, V. Closed Aug. bank holiday, Dec. 25–26.*

Moderate **L'Artiste Assoiffé.** An eccentric Victorian house stuffed with antiques, inhabited by a cage of macaws and a pair of labradors, it has a nonfoodie clientele (including actors and minor royals) that remains loyal to the bohemian ambience rather than the mediocre bistro food. Steak caramelized with Dijon mustard and spinach pancakes with nuts and cheese are typical dishes. *122 Kensington Park Rd., tel. 071/727–4714. Reservations required. AE, DC, MC, V. Closed Sun., holidays; no lunch weekdays.*

Inexpensive **Tootsies.** A useful burger joint characterized by loudish rock and vintage advertisements on the walls, Tootsies serves some of London's better burgers, as well as chili, chicken, BLTs, taco salad, apple pie, fudge cake, and ice cream. There are five other branches. *115 Notting Hill Gate, W11, tel. 071/727–6562. MC, V.*

St. James's
Very Expensive **The Ritz.** The British menu here hasn't always lived up to its setting, but since this Louis XVI marble, gilt, and *trompe l'oeil* treasure, with its view over Green Park, is known as London's most magnificent dining room, that's not such a crime. The latest chef, David Nicholls, retains the French accent and ingredients as rich as the decor (foie gras terrine with fig preserve; lobster thermidor). He also offers British specialties—Irish stew, braised oxtail, steak-and-kidney pie, and a daily roast—that are the most enticing part of the menu. A three-course lunch at £26 and four-course dinner at £39.50 make the check more bearable, but the wine list is pricey. *Picadilly, W1, tel. 071/493–8181. Jacket and tie required. Reservations required. AE, DC, MC, V.*

Expensive **Le Caprice.** The cool and elegant decor here matches the often well-known clientele exactly. The international menu should appeal to all tastes, with dishes from North Africa, France, and the Far East. Finish with a mousse of dark and white chocolate. It's owned by the Ivy people. *Arlington House, Arlington St., tel. 071/629–2239. Reservations required. AE, DC, MC, V. Closed 10 days at Christmas.*

Soho
Expensive **Alastair Little.** A favorite among table-hopping media types, here the eponymous Little—one of Britain's most innovative and exciting chefs—serves his much-imitated eclectic (with influences from Japan, via Sicily to Scandinavia), seafood-dominated fare. The set lunch is, at £18 for three courses, a more affordable way to enjoy the constantly changing menu. The decor is functional and space at a

premium. *49 Frith St., tel. 071/734–5183. Reservations required. AE, MC, V. Closed Sat. lunch, Sun., Christmas, Easter.*

Moderate **Chiang Mai.** The interior is modeled on a traditional Thai stilt house. The food is delicious and spicy, all easy to order from an English menu. Try a *Tom Yum* (hot-and-sour soup) or a *Pad Kra Prow* (beef, pork, or chicken with fresh Thai basil and chili). *48 Frith St., tel. 071/437–7444. Reservations advised. AE, MC, V. Closed Sun. and holidays.*

dell'Ugo. London's favorite 1992 opening was this three-storied Mediterranean café-restaurant from the Antony Worral-Thompson stable (*see* Bistrot 190, *above*). Both the street level café and the upstairs restaurant serve heartwarming country food—spaghetti with roasted peppers, anchovy, and chili; tuna tartare with spicy gazpacho; and bruschetta with pears, watercress, and gorgonzola. *56 Frith St., tel. 071/734–8300. Reservations required for restaurant, not accepted for café. AE, MC, V. Closed Sun., Christmas.*

Inexpensive **Crank's.** This restaurant belongs to a popular vegetarian chain that has weathered the storms of food fashion since the '60s, despite (or because of) a certain worthiness of menu—mixed salads and thick soups; dense, grainy breads; and sugarless cakes. It is self-service, and many branches, though not this one, close at 8 PM. *8 Marshall St., tel. 071/437–9431. Reservations advised for dinner. AE, DC, MC, V. Closed Sun., Dec. 25.*

Poon's. A popular Chinese restaurant (there are long lines in the evening), Poon's specializes in wind-dried meats. There are two other Poon's, but this one is the cheapest and most authentic. *4 Leicester St., tel. 071/437–1528. Reservations required. Closed Sun., Dec. 25, 26.*

Lodging

Although British hotels traditionally included breakfast in their nightly tariff, these days many of London's most expensive establishments charge extra for breakfast. For details and price-category definitions, *see* Lodging in Staying in Great Britain, *above.*

Bayswater **Whites.** This cream-faced Victorian "country mansion" has a
Very Expensive wrought-iron portico and a view of Kensington Gardens, especially
★ grand when floodlit at night. Thick carpets, gilt and mirrors, marble balustrades, swagged silk draperies, and Louis XV-style furniture all help to give a sense of deep luxury. Some of the bedrooms have balconies; all have seating areas and personal safes. Colors are muted: powder blue, old rose, and pale green. *90–92 Lancaster Gate, W2 3NR, tel. 071/262–2711, fax 071/262–2147. 54 rooms with bath. Facilities: restaurant, lounge, valet service, free in-house movies. AE, DC, MC, V.*

Expensive **Abbey Court.** A short walk from Kensington Gardens brings you to this luxury bed-and-breakfast establishment in a historic 1850 building. Each bedroom is individually designed with 19th-century French furniture, Venetian mirrors, and oil portraits; some have four-poster beds. *20 Pembridge Gardens, W2 4DU, tel. 071/221–7518, fax 071/792–0858. 22 rooms with bath. Facilities: Jacuzzis, conservatory, drawing room, garden. AE, DC, MC, V.*

Portobello. A faithful core of visitors returns again and again to this eccentric hotel in a Victorian terrace near the Portobello Road antiques market. Some rooms are tiny, but the suites have sitting rooms attached, and the atmosphere is relaxed and informal. *22 Stanley Gardens, W11 2NG, tel. 071/727–2777, fax 071/792–9641. 25* *rooms with bath or shower. Facilities: restaurant, 24-hour bar. AE, DC, MC, V. Closed 10 days at Christmas.*

Moderate ★ **Camelot.** This affordable hotel, recently refurbished and extended, has beautifully decorated rooms and a friendly staff. The few bathless single rooms are bargains. *45–47 Norfolk Sq., W2 1RX, tel. 071/723–9118, fax 071/402–3412. 43 rooms, 33 with bath or shower. Facilities: lounge, free in-house videos. MC, V.*

Bloomsbury– Regent's Park *Very Expensive* ★ **The Regent.** The onetime Great Central Hotel and former BritRail headquarters was resuscitated by a three-year injection of £75 million, and transformed into London's latest most elegant and understated luxury hotel. The palm-filled, six-story "Winter Garden" atrium is overlooked by guest rooms; even standard rooms here are among the largest in London. This Hong Kong-based hotel group is famous for glamorous bathrooms—these are marble and chrome, complete with robe and hair dryer. Unsurprisingly, the Regent is very near Regent's Park; it's also near Madame Tussauds. The West End is a 15-minute walk away. *222 Marylebone Rd., NW1 6JO, tel. 071/631–8000, fax 071/631–8080. 309 rooms with bath. Facilities: restaurant, 2 bars, health club with pool, cable TV, VCR and personal fax on request, business center. AE, DC, MC, V.*

Moderate **Academy.** Convenient to the British Museum and area shops, the Academy is in a Georgian building and has a bar, library/lounge, and patio garden. *17–21 Gower St., WC1E 6HG, tel. 071/631–4115, fax 071/636–3442. 32 rooms, 24 with bath. Facilities: restaurant, lounge, bar. AE, DC, MC, V.*

Morgan. This charming family-run hotel in an 18th-century terrace house has rooms that are small and comfortably furnished, but friendly and cheerful. The tiny paneled breakfast room is straight out of a doll's house. The back rooms overlook the British Museum. *24 Bloomsbury St., WC1B 3QJ, tel. 071/636–3735. 14 rooms with bath or shower. No credit cards.*

Inexpensive **Ridgemount.** The kindly owners, Mr. and Mrs. Rees, make you feel at home in this tiny hotel by the British Museum. There's a homey, cluttered feel in the public areas and some bedrooms overlook a leafy garden. *65 Gower St., WC1E 6HJ, tel. 071/636–1141. 15 rooms, none with bath. Facilities: lounge. No credit cards.*

Chelsea and Kensington *Very Expensive* ★ **Blakes.** Patronized by musicians and film stars, this hotel is one of the most exotic in town. Its Victorian exterior contrasts with the 1980s ultrachic interior, with an arty mix of Biedermeier, leather, and bamboo furniture; rich fabrics; four-poster beds; and Oriental enameled screens. The bedrooms have individual designs ranging from swaths of black moiré silk to an entirely pink suite. *33 Roland Gardens, SW7 3PF, tel. 071/370–6701. 52 rooms with bath. Facilities: restaurant, bar, satellite TV. AE, DC, MC, V.*

Expensive ★ **The Gore.** Every wall of every room in this very friendly and quiet hotel near the Albert Hall is smothered in prints and etchings, and antiques pepper the rooms. Some of these are spectacular follies—like Tudor-style room 101, with its minstrel gallery and four-poster, or room 211, with its ceramic Greek goddess mural. Despite all that, it manages to remain most elegant, and certainly unique. *189 Queen's Gate, SW7 5EX, tel. 071/584–6601, fax 071/589–8127. 54 rooms with bath. Facilities: lounge. AE, DC, MC, V.*

Inexpensive **Abbey House.** Standards are high and the rooms unusually spacious in this hotel in a fine residential block near Kensington Palace and Gardens. *11 Vicarage Gate, W8 4AG, tel. 071/727–2594. 15 rooms, none with bath. Facilities: orthopedic beds. No credit cards.*

Vicarage Hotel. This genteel establishment, run by the same husband-wife team for the past 40 years, has high standards of cleanliness throughout. Bedrooms are traditional and comfortable with solid English furniture. It attracts many repeat visitors from the United States and welcomes single travelers. *10 Vicarage Gate, W8 4AG, tel. 071/229–4030. 20 rooms, none with bath. Facilities: small TV lounge. No credit cards.*

Knightsbridge, Belgravia, and Victoria

Very Expensive

Berkeley. This is a luxurious, spacious, air-conditioned modern building into which a period country mansion has been decanted. One very special feature is the penthouse health club, with a pool whose roof opens in good weather. Bedrooms are elegant and sophisticated and there are some spectacular suites, including one with a sauna. *Wilton Pl., SW1X 7RL, tel. 071/235–6000. 160 rooms, all with bath. Facilities: 2 restaurants, bar, lounges, health club, hairdresser, florist, movie theater. AE, DC, MC, V.*

Goring. Around the corner from Buckingham Palace and often used by visiting VIPs, this hotel was built in 1910 and is now run by the third generation of Gorings. The atmosphere remains opulently Edwardian: marble fixtures in the bathrooms, with brass trim and the original fitted closets in some of the bedrooms. *17 Beeston Pl., Grosvenor Gardens, SW1W 0JW, tel. 071/834–8211. 90 rooms with bath. Facilities: restaurant, bar, lounge. AE, DC, MC, V.*

★ **Halkin.** This peaceful, ultra-modern haven for the design-conscious has many high-tech features in the bedrooms, like personal fax, video player, two phone lines and a key pad for operating lights and TV. Everything is cool and beautiful from the charcoal gray curved corridors to the Armani staff uniform. But it's surprisingly friendly. *Halkin St., SW1X 7DJ, tel. 071/333–1000. 41 rooms, all with bath. Facilities: restaurant, cable TV, video library, fax (on request), Reuters news service. AE, DC, MC, V.*

The Lanesborough. Brocades and Regency stripes, moiré silks and fleurs-de-lys, antiques, oils, and reproductions in gilded splendor—everything undulates with richness in this multimillion-pound conversion of the old St. George's Hospital at Hyde Park Corner. To register you just sign the book, then retire to your room to find a personal butler, business cards with your in-room fax and phone numbers, VCR and CD player, umbrella, robe, huge flacons of unguents for bathtime, and a drinks tray. Such a palace should be nearer the shops. *1 Lanesborough Pl., SW1X 7TA, tel. 071/259–5599, fax 071/259–5606. 95 rooms with bath. Facilities: 2 restaurants, bar, satellite TV, video and CD library. AE, DC, MC, V.*

Expensive

★ **Basil Street.** Women guests here are granted automatic membership in the ladies' organization called "Parrot Club." Family-run for some 75 years, this is a gracious Edwardian hotel on a quiet street. The rooms are filled with antiques. The Gallery is a writing area, with desks in the window alcoves, unusual paintings on glass, polished wooden floors, and fine Oriental carpets. *Basil St., SW3 1AH. tel. 071/581–3311. 96 rooms, 72 with bath. Facilities: 2 restaurants, wine bar, lounge, ladies' club. AE, DC, MC, V.*

Beaufort. "Hotel" would be a misnomer for this elegant pair of country house-style Victorian houses; there's a sitting room instead of a reception area, and guests have a front door key. The rates include drinks, breakfast, and anything from the 24-hour service menu, plus membership at a local health club. *33 Beaufort Gdns., SW3 1PP, tel. 071/584–5252, fax 071/589–2834. 29 rooms with bath. Facilities: sitting room with complimentary bar, video library, access to health club. AE, DC, MC, V.*

The Pelham. Eighteenth-century pine paneling in the drawing room, glazed chintz and antique lace, four-posters in some rooms, fireplaces in others—this is another hotel that feels more like an elegant home. It's opposite South Kensington tube, near the big museums, and there's a garden nearby with a heated pool for guests' use. *15 Cromwell Pl., SW7 2LA, tel. 071/589–8288, fax 071/584–8444. 37 rooms with bath. Facilities: restaurant, air-conditioning, access to garden with pool, valet. AE, MC, V.*

Moderate **Claverley.** Located on a quiet, tree-lined street, the Claverley offers friendly, attractive surroundings, some four-poster beds, and the wealthy world of Knightsbridge shopping, just around the corner. *13–14 Beaufort Gdns., SW3 1PS, tel. 071/589–8541, fax 071/584–3410. 31 rooms with bath. AE, V.*

Ebury Court. This small, old-fashioned, country house–style hotel is near Victoria Station. The rooms are small, with chintz and antique furniture to give them extra character. The reception area, lounge, and restaurant have all been recently renovated and some new guest rooms were added—ask the rate, since this varies considerably. *26 Ebury St., SW1W 0LU, tel. 071/730–8147. 45 rooms, 36 with bath. Facilities: restaurant, bar. MC, V.*

West End **Brown's.** Close to Bond Street, Brown's is like a country house in the
Very Expensive middle of town, with wood paneling, grandfather clocks, and large fireplaces. Both Roosevelts used to stay here and it has remained popular with Anglophile Americans ever since. *34 Albemarle St., W1A 4SW, tel. 071/493–6020, fax 071/493–9381. 133 rooms with bath. Facilities: restaurant, lounge, writing room, cocktail bar. AE, DC, MC, V.*

★ **Claridges.** This legendary hotel has one of the world's classiest guest lists. The liveried staff are friendly, not at all condescending, and the rooms are luxurious. The hotel was founded in 1812, but present decor is either 1930s Art Deco or country-house style. Have a drink in the foyer and hear the orchestra, or retreat to the peaceful reading room. The rooms are spacious, the sweeping staircase grand. *Brook St., W1A 2JQ, tel. 071/629–8860, fax 071/499–2210. 200 rooms with bath. Facilities: 2 restaurants, lounge (with orchestra), hairdresser, valet, AE, DC, MC, V.*

Duke's. This small Edwardian hotel is situated in a cul-de-sac in St. James's and enjoys a distinct Old World character, helped by the portraits of dukes adorning the walls. The top-floor bedrooms are the most spacious. *35 St. James's Pl., SW1A 1NY, tel. 071/491–4840, fax 071/493–1264. 62 rooms with bath. Facilities: restaurant, bar. AE, DC, MC, V.*

Four Seasons. Once one of Howard Hughes's hideaways, this opulent hotel, with its polished marble entrance hall has lost Bruno Loubet, the star chef from its eponymous restaurant, but gained a fitness center, with a conservatory overlooking the hotel's terrace. The strikingly decorated rooms have gigantic beds and plenty of extras, such as guest bathrobes and phone extensions in the bathrooms. *Hamilton Pl., Park Lane, W1A 1AZ, tel. 071/499–0888, fax 071/ 493–1895. 228 rooms with bath. Facilities: 2 restaurants, coffee shop, bar, lounge, fitness center, shopping arcade, free in-house movies, garden. AE, DC, MC, V.*

★ **Savoy.** This grand, historic late-Victorian hotel has been the byword for luxury for just over a century. Spacious bedrooms feature antiques and cream plasterwork, and the best ones overlook the Thames. More than a hint of 1920s style remains, not least in the bathrooms with their original splendid fittings. The Fitness Gallery is a new addition, situated on top of the freshly restored historic Savoy Theatre. *Strand, WC2R 0EU, tel. 071/836–4343, fax 071/ 240–6040. 202 rooms with bath. Facilities: 3 restaurants, 2 bars,* *grill room, health club, coffee shop, florist, theater-ticket desk, free in-house movies. AE, DC, MC, V.*

Expensive **Chesterfield.** This former town house of the earls of Chesterfield is very popular with U.S. visitors, who are often return guests. It is deep in the heart of Mayfair, with welcoming, paneled public rooms; a good restaurant; spacious bedrooms; and an outstandingly helpful staff. *35 Charles St., W1X 8LX, tel. 071/491–2622, fax 071/491–4793. 113 rooms, all with bath. Facilities: restaurant, in-house movies. AE, DC, MC, V.*

★ **Dorset Square.** The same husband (architect) and wife (interior designer) team who own the Pelham (above), created this stunning, comfortable small hotel in a fine pair of Regency townhouses north of Oxford Street almost a decade ago, but it remains fresh. Service is personal and charming; there's an "honesty bar" in the parlor, where you help yourself and own up later, and the owner's vintage Bentley will chauffeur you on request. *39–40 Dorset Sq., NW1 6QN, tel. 071/723–7874, fax 071/724–3328. 37 rooms, all with bath. Facilities: bar/restaurant, garden, 24-hr room service, air-conditioning. AE, MC, V.*

Hazlitt's. Still Soho's sole hotel, this, the last home of Hazlitt the essayist (1778–1830), is crammed with prints on every wall, Victorian claw-foot baths, assorted antiques, plants, and bits of art. There's no elevator, the sitting room is minuscule, floors can be creaky and bedrooms tiny, but Hazlitt's legion of devotees don't mind. And who needs room service when you live on Restaurant Row? The Gore (above) is under the same management. *6 Frith St., W1V 5TZ, tel. 071/434–1771, fax 071/439–1524. 23 rooms with bath. AE, DC, MC, V.*

Moderate **Bryanston Court.** Three 18th-century houses have been converted into a traditional English family-run hotel with open fires and comfortable armchairs; the bedrooms are more contemporary. *56–60 Great Cumberland Pl., W1H 7FD, tel. 071/262–3141, fax 071/262–7248. 56 rooms with bath or shower. Facilities: restaurant, bar, lounge, satellite TV. AE, DC, MC, V.*

Edward Lear. The former home of Edward Lear, the artist and writer of nonsense verse, this hotel has an imposing entrance leading to a black-and-white tiled lobby. The peacefulness of the rooms varies—ask for one of the quieter rooms to the rear—as does their size (No. 14 is the smallest). *28–30 Seymour St., W1H 5WD, tel. 071/402–5401, fax 071/706–3766. 32 rooms, 12 with bath or shower. V.*

The Arts

For a list of events in the London arts scene, visit a newsstand or bookstore to pick up the weekly magazine: *Time Out.* The city's evening paper, the *Evening Standard,* carries listings, as do the major Sunday papers; the daily *Independent* and *Guardian;* and, on Friday, *The Times.*

Theater London's theater life can broadly be divided into three categories: the government-subsidized national companies; the commercial, or "West End," theaters; and the fringe.

The main national companies are the **Royal National Theatre Company** (NT) and the **Royal Shakespeare Company** (RSC). Each has its own custom-designed facilities, in the South Bank arts complex and in the Barbican Arts Centre, respectively. Each presents a variety of plays by writers of all nationalities, ranging from the classics of Shakespeare and his contemporaries to specially commissioned modern works. Box office: NT, tel. 071/928–2252; RSC, tel. 071/638–8891.

The West End theaters largely stage musicals, comedies, whodunits, and revivals of lighter plays of the 19th and 20th centuries, often starring television celebrities. Occasionally there are more serious productions, including successful productions transferred from the subsidized theaters, such as RSC's *Les Liasons Dangereuses* and *Les Misérables*.

The two dozen or so established fringe theaters, scattered around central London and the immediate outskirts, frequently present some of London's most intriguing productions, if you're prepared to overlook occasional rough staging and uncomfortable seating.

Most theaters have an evening performance at 7:30 or 8 daily, except Sunday, and a matinee twice a week (Wednesday or Thursday and Saturday). Expect to pay from £7 to £10 for a seat in the upper balcony to at least £20 for a good seat in the stalls (orchestra) or dress circle (mezzanine)—more for musicals. Tickets may be booked in person at the theater box office; over the phone by credit card; or through ticket agents, such as **First Call** (tel. 071/497–9977). In addition, the ticket booth in Leicester Square sells half-price tickets on the day of performance for about 45 theaters; there is a small service charge. Beware of unscrupulous ticket agents who sell tickets at four or five times their box-office price (a small service charge is legitimate) and scalpers, who stand outside theaters offering tickets for the next performance; they've been known to charge £200 for a sought-after show.

Concerts Ticket prices for symphony orchestra concerts are still relatively moderate—between £5 and £15, although you can expect to pay more to hear big-name artists on tour. If you can't book in advance, arrive half an hour before the performance for a chance at returns.

The London Symphony Orchestra is in residence at the **Barbican Arts Centre** (tel. 071/638–8891), although other top symphony and chamber orchestras also perform here. The **South Bank arts complex** (tel. 071/928–8800), which includes the **Royal Festival Hall** and the **Queen Elizabeth Hall,** is another major venue for choral, symphony, and chamber concerts. For less expensive concert going, try the **Royal Albert Hall** (tel. 071/589–8212) during the summer Promenade season; special tickets for standing room are available at the hall on the night of performance. **The Wigmore Hall** (tel. 071/935–2141) is a small auditorium, ideal for recitals. Inexpensive lunchtime concerts take place all over the city in smaller halls and churches, often featuring string quartets, singers, jazz ensembles, and gospel choirs. **St. John's, Smith Square** (tel. 071/222–1061), a converted Queen Anne church, is one of the more popular venues. It has a handy crypt cafeteria.

Opera The **Royal Opera House** ranks alongside the New York Met. Prices range from £8.50 (in the upper balconies, from which only a tiny portion of the stage is visible) to £392 for a box in the Grand Tier. Bookings are best made at the box office (tel. 071/240–1066). The **Coliseum** (tel. 071/836–3161) is the home of the English National Opera Company; productions are staged in English and are often innovative and exciting. The prices, which range from £6.50 to £43, are much cheaper than those of the Royal Opera House.

Ballet The Royal Opera House also hosts the **Royal Ballet.** The prices are slightly more reasonable than for the opera, but be sure to book well ahead. The **English National Ballet** and visiting companies perform at the Coliseum from time to time, especially during the summer. **Sadler's Wells Theatre** (tel. 071/278–8916) hosts regional ballet and international modern dance troupes. Prices here are reasonable.

Film Most West End cinemas are in the area around Leicester Square and Piccadilly Circus. Tickets run from £5 to £8. Matinees and Monday evenings are cheaper. Cinema clubs screen a wide range of films: classics, Continental, underground, rare, or underestimated masterpieces. A temporary membership fee is usually about £1. One of the best-value clubs is the **National Film Theatre** (tel. 071/928–3232), part of the South Bank arts complex.

Nightlife

London's night spots are legion, and there is only space here to list a few of the best known. For up-to-the-minute listings, buy *Time Out*.

Jazz **Bass Clef** (85 Coronet St., tel. 071/729–2476), situated in an out-of-the-way warehouse on the northern edge of the City, (the nearest tube is Old Street), offers some of the best live jazz in town and a mainly vegetarian menu. **Ronnie Scott's** (47 Frith St., tel. 071/439–0747) is the legendary Soho jazz club where a host of international performers have played.

Nightclubs **Legends** (29 Old Burlington St., tel. 071/437–9933) has an impressive high-tech interior; a large choice of cocktails is served at the upstairs bar, while the downstairs area is graced with a large cool dance floor and central bar. Glitzy **Stringfellows** (16 Upper St. Martin's Lane, tel. 071/240–5534) has an Art Deco upstairs restaurant, mirrored walls, and a dazzling light show in the downstairs dance floor. **The Limelight** (136 Shaftesbury Ave., tel. 071/434–0572), in a converted church, is one of London's enduringly popular night spots, with lots of one-nighter shows and special events. Liveliest on the weekend.

Casinos By law, you must apply in person for membership in a gaming house; in many cases, clubs prefer an applicant's membership to be proposed by an existing member. Approval usually takes about two days.

Crockford's (30 Curzon St., tel. 071/493–7771) is a civilized and unflashy 150-year-old club with a large international clientele; American roulette, punto banco, and blackjack are played.
Sportsman Club (3 Tottenham Court Rd., tel. 071/637–5464) has a dice table as well as punto banco, American roulette, and blackjack.

Discos **Camden Palace** (1A Camden High St., tel. 071/387–0428) is perennially popular with both London and visiting youth. This multi-tier dance hall features different theme nights, three bars, and a colorful light show. American-style food is served. The **Hippodrome** (Cranbourn St., tel. 071/437–4311) is a hugely popular and lavish disco with an exciting sound-and-laser light system, live bands and dancing acts, video screen, bars, and restaurant.

Rock **The Forum** (9–17 Highgate Rd., Kentish Town, tel. 071/284–0303) is a premier venue for medium-to-big acts; a little out of the way, but worth it.
The Rock Garden (67 The Piazza, Covent Garden, tel. 071/240–3961) is famous for encouraging younger talent; Talking Heads, U2, and The Smiths are among those who played here while still virtually unknown. Music is in the standing-room-only basement.
The Marquee (105 Charing Cross Rd., tel. 071/437–6603), Soho's

original rock club, is now in new premises; at least two live bands perform every night.

Cabaret The best comedy in town can be found in the bigger, brighter, new-look **Comedy Store** (Haymarket House, Oxendon St., near Piccadilly Circus, tel. 0426/914433). There are two shows, at 8 and midnight on Friday and Saturday, at 8 only Tuesday to Thursday. **Madame Jo Jo's** (8 Brewer St., tel. 071/734–2473) is possibly the most fun of any London cabaret, with its outrageous, glittering drag shows. The place is luxurious, and civilized. There are two shows, at 12:15 and 1:15 AM, and the food and drinks are reasonably priced.

Windsor to Bath

The Thames, England's second-longest river, winds its way toward London through an accessible and gracious stretch of countryside. An excursion west from the capital, roughly following the river toward its source in the Cotswold Hills, allows you to explore historic townships, such as Windsor, where the castle is still regularly used by the royal family; Oxford, home of the nation's oldest university; and Shakespeare's birthplace at Stratford-upon-Avon. Traveling south, you come to Bath, whose 18th-century streets recall an age more elegant than our own.

Getting Around

By Train Suburban services run from London (Waterloo and Paddington stations) to Windsor. Regular fast trains run from Paddington to Oxford and Bath, and less frequent and slower services requiring at least one change, to Stratford. For information, call 071/262–6767. An alternative route to Stratford is from London's Euston Station to Coventry, from which Guide Friday operates bus connections (summer four times daily, winter three times daily); telephone 0789-294466 for details.

By Bus Regular long-distance services leave from Victoria Coach Station. For information, call 071/730–0202.

By Car The M4 and the M40 are the main highways out of London serving Oxford, the Cotswolds, and Bath. Once you're clear of London, take to the country roads and explore tiny villages and the countryside—your trip may take a bit longer, but you'll be rewarded by the best of the English countryside.

Tourist Information

Bath (The Colonnades, 11–13 Bath St., tel. 0225/462831).
Chipping Campden (Woolstaplers Hall Museum, High St., tel. 0386/840101).
Oxford (St. Aldate's, opposite the town hall, tel. 0865/726871).
Stratford (Bridgefoot, next to the canal bridge, tel. 0789/293127).
Warwick (The Court House, Jury St., tel. 0926/492212).
Windsor (Central Station, Thames St., tel. 0753/852010).

Guided Tours

National Holidays operates five-day trips in the Cotswolds, some in Bath. There are agents throughout the country. **Frames Rickards** (tel. 071/837–3111) runs full-day sightseeing tours to Windsor, Stratford-upon-Avon, and Bath. **Guide Friday** (Windsor: tel. 0753/

855755; Oxford: tel. 0865/790522; and Stratford: tel. 0789/294466) offers excellent tours of Windsor, Oxford, and Shakespeare country.

Exploring Windsor to Bath

Windsor Windsor, some 40 kilometers (25 miles) west of London, has been a royal citadel since the days of William the Conqueror in the 11th century. In the 14th century, Edward III revamped the old castle, building the Norman gateway, the great round tower, and new apartments. Almost every monarch since then has added new buildings or improved existing ones; over the centuries, the medieval fortification has been transformed into the lavish royal palace the visitor sees today.

The following are some of the highlights of the castle: **St. George's Chapel,** more than 71 meters (230 feet) long with two tiers of great windows and hundreds of gargoyles, buttresses, and pinnacles, is one of the noblest buildings in England. Inside, above the choir stalls, hang the banners, swords, and helmets of the Knights of the Order of the Garter, the most senior Order of Chivalry. The many monarchs buried in the chapel include Henry VIII and George VI, father of the present queen. The magnificent art collection at Windsor contains paintings by such masters as Rubens, Van Dyck, and Holbein; drawings by Leonardo da Vinci; and Gobelin tapestries, among many other treasures. There are splendid views across to Windsor Great Park, the remains of a former royal hunting forest. Make time to view **Queen Mary's Dolls' House,** a charming toy country house with every detail complete, including electricity, running water, and miniature books on the library shelves. It was designed in 1921 by the architect Sir Edwin Lutyens for the present queen's grandmother.

The terrible fire of November 1992, which started in the Queen's private chapel, completely destroyed some of the **State Apartments.** Miraculously, a swift rescue effort meant that hardly any works of art were lost. The repairs will take years to complete. It is not clear, at press time, how much of the castle will be open to the public in 1995, though St. George's Chapel, which was untouched by the fire, will be, as will the State Apartments that were spared and Queen Mary's Dolls' House. *Windsor Castle, tel. 0753/831118 (recorded message). Admission: Precincts—free; State Apartments—£4 adults, £1.50 children, £2.50 senior citizens; Dolls' House and Carriages, each—£1.60 adults, 80p children, £1.40 senior citizens. Opening times are extremely complicated and subject to change. We recommend that you check before visiting.*

After seeing the castle, stroll around the town and enjoy the shops; antiques are sold in cobbled Church Lane and Queen Charlotte Street.

Time Out The **Adam and Eve** pub (Thames St.) opposite the walls of Windsor Castle serves hot snacks and plowmen's lunches, while **The Courtyard** (8 King George V Pl.) is an inviting spot for lunch or a cream tea.

A short walk over the river brings you to **Eton,** Windsor Castle's equally historic neighbor and home of the famous public school. (In Britain, so-called public schools are private and charge fees.) Classes still take place in the distinctive redbrick Tudor-style buildings; the oldest are grouped around a quadrangle called School Yard. The **Museum of Eton Life** has displays on the school's history, and a guided tour is also available. *Brewhouse Yard, tel. 0753/ 863593. Admission: £2.20 adults, £1.50 children; with tour–£3 or £5 adults, £2.50 or £4.50 children (depending on length of tour). Open daily during term 2–4:30, 10:30–4:30 on school holidays. Guided tours Mar.–Oct., daily at 2:15 and 3:15.*

A relatively uncrowded route from Windsor to Oxford is along the river through Marlow and Henley on the A404, then the A4155 and A423. In **Marlow,** there are some stylish 18th-century houses on Peter and West streets, and several princes of Wales have lived in Marlow Place on Station Road, which dates from 1721. Mary Shelley wrote her celebrated horror story *Frankenstein* in the town.

Henley has been famous since 1839 for the rowing regatta it holds each year around the first Sunday in July. For the spectators, the social side of the regatta is as entertaining as the races themselves; elderly oarsmen wear brightly colored blazers and tiny caps, businessmen entertain wealthy clients, and everyone admires the ladies' fashions. The town is worth exploring for its small but good selection of specialty shops, such as Saffron on Bell Street (crafts items) and Thames Gallery on Thameside (Georgian and Victorian silver). The Red Lion Hotel near the 200-year-old bridge has been visited by kings, dukes, and writers; the duke of Marlborough stayed there while Blenheim Palace was being built. St. Mary's Church has a 16th-century "checkerboard" tower made of alternate squares of flint and stone, and the **Chantry House,** built in 1420 as a school for poor boys, is an unspoiled example of the rare overhanging timberframe design. *Hart St., tel. 0491/577340. Admission free. Open Thurs. and Sat. 10–noon.*

Numbers in the margin correspond to points of interest on the Oxford map.

Oxford Continue along A423 north to **Oxford.** The surest way to absorb Oxford's unique blend of history and scholarliness is to wander around the tiny alleys that link the honey-colored stone buildings topped by elegant "dreaming" spires, exploring the colleges where the undergraduates live and work. Oxford University, like Cambridge University, is not a single building but a collection of 35 independent colleges; many of their magnificent chapels and dining halls are open

❶ to visitors—times are displayed at the entrance lodges. **Magdalen College** (pronounced "maudlin") is one of the most impressive, with cloisters more than 500 years old and lawns leading down to a deer

❷ park and the river Cherwell. **St. Edmund Hall,** the next college up the High Street, has one of the smallest and most picturesque quad-

❸ rangles, with an old well in the center. **Christ Church,** on St. Aldate's, has the largest quadrangle, known as Tom Quad; hanging in the medieval dining hall are portraits of former pupils, including John Wesley, William Penn, and no fewer than 14 prime ministers.

❹ The doors between the inner and outer quadrangles of **Balliol College,** on Broad Street, still bear the scorch marks from the flames that burned Archbishop Cranmer and Bishops Latimer and Ridley at the stake in 1555 for their Protestant beliefs.

❺ The **Oxford Story** on Broad Street is a dramatic multimedia presentation of the university's 800-year history, in which visitors travel through depictions of college life. *Broad St., tel. 0865/790055. Admission: £4.25 adults, £2.95 children, £3.65 senior citizens, £13 family ticket. Open Apr.–June and Sept.–Oct., daily 9:30–5; Jul.–Aug., daily 9:30–7; Nov.–Mar., daily 10–4.*

❻ Also on Broad Street is the **Sheldonian Theatre,** which St. Paul's architect Christopher Wren designed to look like a semi-circular Roman amphitheater; it's one of his earliest works. Graduation ceremonies are held here. *Broad St., tel. 0865/277299. Admission: 50p adults, 25p children. Open Mon.–Sat. 10–12:45 and 2–4:45; closes at 3:45 Dec.–Feb.*

❼ The **Ashmolean Museum,** which you encounter by turning right out of Broad Street into Magdalen Street, then taking the first left, is Britain's oldest public museum, holding priceless collections of Egyptian, Greek, and Roman artifacts; Michelangelo drawings; and European silverware. *Beaumont St., tel. 0865/278000. Admission free. Open Tues.–Sat. 10–4, Sun. 2–4.*

For a relaxing walk, make for the banks of the river Cherwell, either through the University Parks area or through Magdalen College to Addison's Walk, and watch the undergraduates idly punting a summer's afternoon away. Or rent one of these narrow flat-bottom boats yourself. But be warned: Navigating is more difficult than it looks!

Time Out The **St. Aldate's Coffee House** (94 St. Aldate's) is run by the church next door and is a great place for lunch or coffee. The **Eagle and Child** is a historic pub on St. Giles. On the outskirts of the city are two excellent pubs, the **Perch** at Binsey and the **Trout** at Godstow. Connoisseurs go to the former at lunchtime to sit on the wide lawn, savor the exotic sandwiches, and listen to the cooing of white doves. In the evening, they visit the Trout for a meal or simply to enjoy a drink while watching the peacocks strutting by the tumbling weir.

Blenheim Palace, about 13 kilometers (8 miles) north of Oxford on the A44 (Woodstock Road), is a vast mansion in neoclassical style

Oxford

University Parks

Little Clarendon St.
Woodstock Rd.
Keble Rd.
Banbury Rd.
Museum Rd.
South Parks Rd.
St. Cross Rd.

0   220 yards
0   200 meters

N

St. Giles
Pusey St.
Pusey Ln.
St. John St.
Beaumont St.
Parks Rd.
Savile Rd.
Jowett Walk
Magdalen Grove
Magdalen St.
Holywell St.
St. Cross Rd.

Gloucester Green
George St.
Broad St.
Catte St.
Queen's Ln.
Longwall St.

Train Station
Ship St.
St. Michael's St.
Cornmarket St.
Turl St.
Market St.
Market
High St.

New Inn Hall St.
New Rd.
Queen St.
High St. (The High)
Magpie Ln.
High St.

Castle St.
St. Ebb's St.
St. Aldate's
Blue Boat St.
Bear St.
Oriel Sq.
Merton St.
Dead Man's Walk

Main Information Office
AE

Pembroke St.
Brewer St.
Rose Pl.
Clarks Row
Broad Walk

Norfolk St.
Thames St.
Speedwell St.

Abingdon Rd.
New Walk
Christ Church Meadow
Cherwell

KEY
AE American Express Office
i Tourist Information

Thames
Folly Bridge
Isis

Major Attractions

Ashmolean Museum, **7**
Balliol College, **4**
Christ Church, **3**
Magdalen College, **1**
Oxford Story, **5**
St. Edmund Hall, **2**
Sheldonian Theatre, **6**

Other Attractions

All Souls College, **13**
Bodleian Library, **16**
Exeter College, **17**
Jesus College, **19**
Keble College, **10**
Radcliffe Camera, **15**
St. Giles' Church, **9**
St. Mary Magdalen Church, **20**

Trinity College, **18**
University Church (St. Mary's), **14**
University Museum, **11**
Wadham College, **12**
Worcester College, **8**

built in the early 18th century by the architect Sir John Vanbrugh; it stands in 1,012 hectares (2,500 acres) of beautiful gardens landscaped later in the 18th century by "Capability" Brown, perhaps the most famous of all English landscape gardeners. The house was built by the soldier and statesman John Churchill, first duke of Marlborough, on land given to him by Queen Anne and with money voted him by Parliament on behalf of a "grateful nation" as a reward for his crushing defeat of the French at the Battle of Blenheim in 1704. The house is filled with fine paintings, tapestries, and furniture. Winston Churchill, a descendant of Marlborough, was born in the palace; some of his paintings are on display, and there is an exhibition devoted to his life. *Woodstock, tel. 0993/811325. Admission: £6.30 adults, £3.10 children under 15, £4.70 senior citizens. Open mid-Mar.–Oct., 10:30–4:45. Grounds open all year 9:30–dusk. Restaurant and cafeteria.*

Sir Winston Churchill (1874–1965) is buried in the nearby village of **Bladon.** His grave in the small tree-lined churchyard is all the more touching for its simplicity.

The Cotswolds The A34 runs northwest from Oxford and Blenheim across the Cotswold Hills to Stratford-upon-Avon. The **Cotswolds** are high, bare hills patterned by patches of ancient forest and stone walls that protect the sheep that have grazed here from the earliest times. In the Middle Ages, English wool commanded high prices, and the little towns and villages nestling in valleys and on hillsides grew in prosperity. Although the wool trade has now dwindled in importance, the legacy of those days remains in the solid, substantial churches, cottages, and manor houses built of the mellow, golden-gray local stone. Burford, Stow-on-the-Wold, Upper Slaughter, Bourton-on-the-Water, Broadway, and Moreton-in-Marsh are just a few of the picturesque towns connected by pleasant country roads.

Stratford- Even without its most famous son, **Stratford-upon-Avon** would be **upon-Avon** worth visiting. The town's timbered buildings bear witness to its prosperity in the 16th century, when it was a thriving craft and trading center, and attractive 18th-century buildings are also of note.

Numbers in the margin correspond to points of interest on the Stratford-upon-Avon map.

The main places of Shakespearean interest are run by the **Shakespeare Birthplace Trust.** They all have similar opening times (Mar.–Oct., weekdays 9:30–5:30, Sun. 10–5:30; Nov.–Mar., weekdays 9:30–4, Sun. 10:30 (or 1:30)–4) and you can get an inclusive ticket for them all—£7.50 adults, £3.25 children, £7 senior citizens—or pay separate entry fees if you want to visit only one or two. The ❶ ❷ **Shakespeare Centre** and **Shakespeare's Birthplace** contain the costumes used in the BBC's dramatization of the plays and an exhibition of the playwright's life and work. *Henley St., tel. 0789/204016. A Shakespeare Birthplace Trust property.*

Time Out **Mistress Quickly** (59–60 Henley Street) serves light refreshments and meals throughout the day; an unusual feature is the jigsaw tree sculpture on the stairs. The **Black Swan**—better known locally as the Dirty Duck—is a riverside pub beside the theater, serving good ales and bar meals.

Two very different attractions reveal something of the times in which Shakespeare lived. Originally a farmhouse, the girlhood home ❸ of Shakespeare's mother, **Mary Arden's House,** is now an extensive

Major Attractions

Anne
Hathaway's
Cottage, **9**

Hall's Croft, **4**

Holy Trinity
Church, **8**

Mary Arden's
House, **3**

The Other
Place, **7**

Royal
Shakespeare
Theatre, **5**

Shakespeare
Centre, **1**

Shakespeare's
Birthplace, **2**

Swan, **6**

Other Attractions

American
Fountain, **15**

Grammar School
and Guildhall, **11**

Guild Chapel, **12**

Harvard
House, **14**

Shakespeare
Institute, **10**

Town Hall, **13**

Stratford-upon-Avon

museum of farming and country life. It was built in the 16th century and many of the original outbuildings are intact, together with a 600-nesting-hole dovecote. There are falconry displays and a garden planted with trees mentioned in Shakespeare's plays. *Wilmcote (4.8 km [3 mi] northwest of Stratford, off A34 and A422), tel. 0789/ 204016. Also reachable by train in a few minutes from Stratford. A Shakespeare Birthplace Trust property.*

4 A complete contrast is **Hall's Croft,** a fine Tudor town house that was the home of Shakespeare's daughter Susanna and her doctor husband; it is furnished in the decor of the day, and the doctor's dispensary and consulting room can also be seen. *Old Town, tel. 0789/ 292107. A Shakespeare Birthplace Trust property.*

❺ The **Royal Shakespeare Theatre** occupies a perfect position on the banks of the Avon—try to see a performance if you can. The company (always referred to as the RSC) performs several Shakespeare plays each season, as well as plays by a wide variety of other playwrights, between March and January. Beside the main theater

❻ there is the smaller **Swan**, the gift of an anglophile American, Frederick Koch. Modeled on an Elizabethan theater, the Swan provides a very exciting auditorium for in-the-round staging. A new auditori-

❼ um for experimental productions, **The Other Place,** is located just down the street. It's best to book well in advance for RSC productions, but a very few tickets for the day of performance are always available, and it is also worth asking if there are any returns. *Programs are available starting in February from the Royal Shakespeare Theatre, Stratford-upon-Avon, Warwickshire CV37 6BB, tel. 0789/205301.*

❽ It is in **Holy Trinity Church,** close to the Royal Shakespeare Theatre, that Shakespeare and his wife are buried.

❾ **Anne Hathaway's Cottage,** in Shottery on the edge of the town, is the early home of the playwright's wife. *Tel. 0789/292100. A Shakespeare Birthplace Trust property.*

Warwick **Warwick,** some 13 kilometers (8 miles) north of Stratford along A46, is an unusual mixture of Georgian redbrick and Elizabethan half-timbered buildings, although some unattractive postwar developments have spoiled the town center. **Warwick Castle** is one of the finest medieval structures of its kind in England, towering on a precipice above the river Avon. Most of the present buildings date from the 14th century; look for the remarkable gate house, which consists of a pair of towers above the doorway passage, and two massive towers, Guy's and Caesar's, both about 40 meters (130 feet) tall, the latter with a system of double battlements. The interior contains magnificent collections of armor, paintings, and furniture and a waxworks display by Madame Tussaud's, while, outside, peacocks strut in the 24 hectares (60 acres) of landscaped riverside gardens. Some battlements are open to the public, and a restored Victorian boathouse features a flora-and-fauna exhibition and a nature walk. *Castle Hill, tel. 0926/495421. Admission: £6.75 adults, £4.25 children, £4.75 senior citizens, £18.50 and £20.50 family tickets. Open Mar.–Oct., daily 10–6; Nov.–Feb., daily 10–4:30.*

Time Out The paneled bar in the **Zetland Arms** (11 Church St.) serves good local beer and simple meals. There is also a quiet, attractive little garden.

Chipping From Stratford take an easy detour via A34 and B4632 to **Chipping**
Campden **Campden.** If you have time to visit only one Cotswold town, make it this one. The broad High Street is lined with houses in an attractive disarray of styles, many dating from the 17th century. Look for the group of almshouses built in 1624 and raised above street level and for the gabled **Market Hall** built three years later for the sale of local produce.

One of the town's earliest buildings, dating from the 14th century, is the **Woolstaplers Hall,** which contains a museum of local history; besides material on the wool trade, there is a 1920s cinema and collections of medical equipment. *High St., tel. 0386/840101. Admission: £2 adults, £1 children. Open Apr.–Oct., daily 10–5.*

Five kilometers (3 miles) outside Chipping Campden is **Hidcote Manor Garden,** a 20th-century garden created around a Cotswold manor house (not open to the public). The garden consists of a series of open-air rooms divided by walls and hedges, each in a different style. *Hidcote Bartrim, tel. 0386/438333. Admission: £4.40 adults, £1.20 children, £12.10 family ticket. Open Apr.–Oct., Sat.–Mon., Wed., Thurs. 11–7. Last admission 6 PM or 1 hour before sunset.*

The A46 runs along the western edge of the gently rolling Cotswold Hills, through Cheltenham, once the rival of Bath in its Georgian elegance. While it's now marred by modern developments, there are still some fine examples of the Regency style in its graceful secluded villas, lush gardens, and leafy crescents and squares.

Bath   Bath lies at the southern end of the Cotswolds (at the end of A46), some 112 kilometers (70 miles) from Stratford. A perfect 18th-century city, perhaps the best preserved in all Britain, it is a compact place, easy to explore on foot; the museums, elegant shops, and terraces of magnificent town houses are all close to one another.

Numbers in the margin correspond to points of interest on the Bath map.

It was the Romans who first took the waters at Bath, building a temple in honor of their goddess Minerva and a sophisticated series of baths to make full use of the curative hot springs. To this day, these springs gush from the earth at a constant temperature of 115.7°F

❶ (46.5°C). In the **Roman Baths Museum,** underneath the 18th-century Pump Room, you can see the excavated remains of almost the entire baths complex. *Abbey Churchyard, tel. 0225/461111. Admission: £4 adults, £2 children. Combined ticket for Roman Baths and Costume Museum: £5 adults, £2.50 children. Open Mar.–Oct., daily 9–6, Aug. also 8 PM–10 PM; Nov.–Feb., Mon.–Sat. 9–5, Sun. 10–5.*

❷ Next to the Pump Room is the **Abbey,** built in the 15th century. There are superb fan-vaulted ceilings in the nave.

In the 18th century, Bath became the fashionable center for taking the waters. The architect John Wood created a harmonious city from the mellow local stone, building beautifully executed terraces, crescents, and villas. The heart of Georgian Bath is the perfectly

❸ ❹ proportioned **Circus** and the Royal Crescent. On the corner, **No. 1 Royal Crescent** is furnished as it might have been when Beau Nash, the master of ceremonies and arbiter of 18th-century Bath society, lived in the city. *Tel. 0225/428126. Admission: £3 adults, £2 children, £2.50 senior citizens. Open Mar.–Oct., Tues.–Sun. 11–5; Nov.–Dec. 12, Tues.–Sun. 10:30–4.*

❺ Also near the Circus are the **Assembly Rooms,** frequently mentioned by Jane Austen in her novels of early 19th-century life. This neoclassical villa now houses a Museum of Costume, which was lavishly redesigned and opened in mid-1990. *Bennett St., tel. 0225/461111, ext. 2789. Admission: £2.40 adults, £1.40 children. Opening times are slightly later than at the Roman Baths Museum.*

Across the Avon, in an elegant 18th-century building, is the
❻ **Holburne Museum and Crafts Study Centre,** which houses a superb collection of 17th- and 18th-century fine art and decorative arts. There are also works by 20th-century craftsmen in the study center. *Great Pulteney St., tel. 0225/466669. Admission: £2.50 adults, £1 children, £2 senior citizens, family tickets £6. Open Easter–Oct., Mon.–Sat. 11–5, Sun. 2:30–6; Nov.–mid-Dec. and mid-Feb.–Easter, Tues.–Sat. 11–5, Sun. 2:30–6.*

Major Attractions

Abbey, **2**

Assembly Rooms, **5**

Circus, **3**

Holburne Museum and Crafts Study Center, **6**

No. 1 Royal Crescent, **4**

Roman Baths Museum, **1**

Other Attractions

Camden Works Museum, **7**

Carriage Museum, **8**

Octagon and National Center of Photography, **10**

Pulteney Bridge, **11**

Sally Lunn's, **12**

Theatre Royal, **9**

Bath

KEY

AE American Express Office

i Tourist Information

Time Out	Bath has a good selection of spots for coffee or lunch. Try the **Pump Room** (Abbey Churchyard) for morning coffee or afternoon tea in grand surroundings, perhaps listening to the music of a string quartet, or, in nearby North Parade Passage, **Sally Lunns**, where the famous Sally Lunn bun is still baked.

Dining and Lodging

For details and price-category definitions, *see* Dining and Lodging in Staying in Great Britain, *above*.

Bath Dining	**Popjoys Restaurant.** Beau Nash entertained the best of 18th-century society here, and Popjoys retains its air of elegance. *Sawclose, tel.*

0225/460494. Reservations advised. AE, MC, V. Closed Sun. and Mon. Moderate.

Number Five. This candlelit bistro off Pulteney Bridge has a relaxed ambience and offers simple pasta with olive oil and grilled eggplant or more elaborate dishes such as confit of duck or roast breast of chicken with sun-dried tomatoes. Wednesday is fish day. *5 Argyle St., tel. 0225/444499. MC, V. Closed Sun. and Mon. lunch. Inexpensive–Moderate.*

Rascals. Located in a mazelike cellar of interconnecting rooms just south of the abbey, Rascals is a cheerful bistro-style restaurant offering excellent food, fine wines at low prices, and a noisy, relaxed atmosphere. Chef and proprietor Nick Anderson provides an international range of dishes, such as breast of Barbary duck and goujons of brill, though the menu changes regularly. Vegetarian dishes are also available, and homemade ice cream features among the desserts. *8 Pierrepoint Pl., tel. 0225/330201. Reservations advised. Dress; casual. MC, V. Closed Sun. lunch. Inexpensive.*

Theatre Vaults. These busy stone cellars house a very handy restaurant that serves light meals at lunchtime and early evening or full-scale dinner menus later. *Sawclose, tel. 0225/442265. AE, DC, MC, V. Closed Sun. Inexpensive.*

Lodging **Royal Crescent.** The Royal Crescent is the ultimate in luxury living, in a gracious, lavishly converted building, situated on one of England's most famous terraces. Each bedroom has been individually designed to recapture the elegance of Bath's heyday. *16 Royal Crescent, BA1 2LS, tel. 0225/319090, fax 0225/339401. 42 rooms, including 13 suites, all with bath. Facilities: whirlpool bath, garden, croquet. AE, DC, MC, V. Very Expensive.*

Francis Hotel. Overlooking one of Bath's attractive Georgian squares, the Francis consists of six Georgian houses and a new wing. Bedrooms in the old building are decorated in period style. *Queen Sq., BA1 2HH, tel. 0225/424257, fax 0225/319715. 93 rooms with bath. AE, DC, MC, V. Expensive.*

Pratt's. Just a few minutes' walk from the center of town and the main sights, Pratt's is a fine Georgian house. Once the home of novelist Sir Walter Scott, it is now a comfortable hotel with an innovative restaurant. *South Parade, BA2 4AB, tel. 0225/460441, fax 0225/448807. 46 rooms with bath. Facilities: restaurant, bar, conference rooms, parking nearby. AE, DC, MC, V. Moderate.*

The Tasburgh Hotel. This refurbished Victorian house, surrounded by gardens with beautiful views over the Avon Valley, has tastefully furnished rooms complete with every modern comfort. It's situated a mile from city center. *Warminster Rd., Bathampton, BA2 6SH, tel. 0225/425096, fax 0225/463842. 14 rooms, 10 with bath. Facilities: extensive gardens, fishing and mooring rights. AE, DC, MC, V. Moderate.*

Oxford **Elizabeth's.** These small, elegant dining rooms in a 16th-century
Dining bishop's palace overlook Christ Church and have the best views of any restaurant in Oxford. Salmon quenelles and roast lamb are among the Spanish chef's specialties, and there are outstanding wines. *82 St. Aldates, tel. 0865/242230. Reservations advised. AE, DC, MC, V. Closed Mon. Moderate.*

Fifteen North Parade. Just outside the city center, this is an intimate, stylish restaurant with cane furniture and a bright, open feeling. The menu changes regularly and may feature steamed breast of chicken with morel mousse, served with truffle noodles, pot-roast pheasant, or pumpkin pie with nutmeg. Set menus are available. *15 North Parade, tel. 0865/513773. Reservations advised. MC. Closed weekday lunch and Sun. evening. Moderate.*

Gee's. This brasserie is found in a conservatory just north of the town center. The large menu features Italian food and is very popular with both town and gown. *61 Banbury Rd., tel. 0865/53540. Reservations required. MC, V. Moderate.*

Munchy Munchy. A daily changing menu of spicy Malaysian dishes and a good selection of fresh fruit and vegetables make this a refreshing and popular spot. The surroundings are unpretentious and the prices are reasonable. *6 Park End St., tel. 0865/245710. Reservations accepted. No credit cards. Closed Sun. and Mon. Inexpensive.*

Lodging **The Randolph.** Oxford's only large central hotel has undergone extensive restoration of its elaborate Victorian Gothic interior. It's across from the Ashmolean Museum. *Beaumont St., OX1 2LN, tel. 0865/247481, fax 0865/791678. 109 rooms with bath. AE, DC, MC, V. Expensive–Very Expensive.*

The Eastgate Hotel. This welcoming hotel has the traditional style of an inn. Its bar is a favorite with undergraduates and is a good place for getting an insight into university life. *The High, OX1 4BE, tel. 0865/248244, fax 0865/791681. 42 rooms with bath. AE, DC, MC, V. Expensive.*

The Old Parsonage. It's rare to find an attractive country house-hotel, with stone gables and mullioned windows, in the middle of a city, but that is just what awaits at the Old Parsonage. Just a few yards behind St. Giles church, close to Somerville and Keble colleges, the Old Parsonage was originally established in 1660 and was completely restored and refurbished in 1991. Open fires, fascinating pictures, comfortable rooms, and immaculate service make this a hotel to remember—and revisit. *1 Banbury Rd., OX2 6NN, tel. 0865/310210, fax 0865/311262. 30 rooms with bath. Facilities: restaurant, garden. AE, DC, MC, V. Expensive.*

Stratford **Box Tree Restaurant.** In the Royal Shakespeare Theatre, this ele-
Dining gant restaurant overlooks the river and is a favored spot for pre- and post-theater dining. Specialties include noisettes of lamb Box Tree and poached Scotch beef fillet. *Waterside, tel. 0789/293226. Reservations required. Jacket and tie required. AE, MC, V. Closed Sun. Expensive.*

The Opposition. Located near the Royal Shakespeare Theatre, the Opposition caters to the pre- and post-theater dining crowd (as do all sensible restaurants in Stratford). It is extremely popular with the locals, so book in advance. The American and Continental dishes change constantly—if you're lucky there'll be Cajun chicken or aubergine pie on the menu. *13 Sheep St., tel. 0789/269980. Reservations required. MC, V. Closed Sun. lunch. Moderate.*

The River Terrace. For less expensive fare at the theater, this spot provides informal meals and light refreshments. Hot dishes include lasagna and shepherd's pie, and there are also salads, cakes, and sandwiches. *Waterside, tel. 0789/293226. No reservations. No credit cards. Inexpensive.*

The Slug and Lettuce. Don't let the name put you off. This is a pine-paneled pub that serves excellent meals; the long-standing favorites are chicken breast baked in avocado and garlic, and salmon escalope. This place can get very busy, so arrive early. *38 Guild St., tel. 0789/299700. Reservations advised. MC, V. Inexpensive.*

Lodging **The Falcon Hotel.** Licensed as an alehouse since 1640, it still has a friendly-inn atmosphere. The heavily beamed rooms in the older part are small and quaint; those in the modern extension are in standard international style. *Chapel St., CV37 6HA, tel. 0789/205777,* fax *0789/414260. 73 rooms with bath. Facilities: restaurant, 2 bars, parking, garden. AE, DC, MC, V. Expensive.*

The Shakespeare Hotel. For a touch of typical Stratford, stay at this timbered Elizabethan town house in the heart of the town, close to the theater and to most of the attractions. It has been luxuriously modernized while still retaining its Elizabethan character. *Chapel St., CV37 6ER, tel. 0789/294771, fax 0789/415411. 63 rooms with bath. AE, DC, MC, V. Expensive.*

Arden Hotel. Next to the theater, these refurbished 18th-century town houses have been successfully converted into a comfortable Old World hotel with beamed bedrooms. *44 Waterside, CV37 6BA, tel. 0789/294949. 65 rooms with bath. Facilities: restaurant, garden. AE, DC, MC, V. Moderate.*

Windsor and Eton
Dining

The Cockpit. Cockfighting once took place in the courtyard of this smart 500-year-old inn with oak beams, located on Eton's quiet main street. Specialties include guinea fowl and a casserole of bacon in mushroom sauce. *47–49 High Street, Eton, tel. 0753/860944. Reservations advised. AE, DC, MC, V. Closed Mon. Moderate–Expensive.*

The Hideaway. This relaxed bistro, just outside the castle walls, is located down by the river. With its exposed brick walls and modern prints, it is an ideal spot for a casual lunch during a sightseeing trip. *12 Thames St., tel. 0753/842186. AE, MC, V. Moderate.*

Lodging

Oakley Court. This Victorian mansion is set in leafy grounds beside the river, just outside Windsor. Most of the bedrooms are in a bright modern annex. It has the excellent Oak Leaf Room restaurant. *Windsor Rd., Water Oakley, SL4 5UR, tel. 0628/74141, fax 0628/37011. 92 rooms with bath. Facilities: 2 restaurants, 9-hole golf course, conference suite. AE, DC, MC, V. Very Expensive.*

Sir Christopher Wren's House. As the name suggests, this house was built by the famous architect, though modern additions have been made to convert it into a hotel. The restaurant overlooks the river, and the cream teas served on the terrace are renowned. *Thames St., Windsor, SL4 1PX, tel. 0753/861354, fax 0753/860172. 39 rooms with bath. AE, DC, MC, V. Moderate–Expensive.*

Christopher Hotel. The owners have done a good job of converting this former coaching inn on Eton High Street; some of the rooms in the courtyard annexes have been redecorated as well. It is also a good spot for solid, home-cooked meals. *110 High St., Eton, SL4 6AN., tel. 0753/852359, fax 0753/830914. 34 rooms with bath. Facilities: restaurant, bar. AE, DC, MC, V. Moderate.*

Cambridge

Cambridge, home of England's second-oldest university, is an ideal place to explore. Students began studying here in the late 13th century, and virtually every generation since then has produced fine buildings, often by the most distinguished architects of their day. The result is a compact gallery of the best of English architecture. There is also good shopping in the city, as well as relaxing riverside walks.

A short excursion outside Cambridge will introduce you to some characteristic East Anglian landscapes. To the north, on the edge of the Fens, is **Ely,** which boasts an impressive medieval cathedral. To the east is **Bury St. Edmunds,** a bustling market town rich with 17th- and 18th-century buildings and surrounded by cornfields, gentle hills, and tiny villages, each with its medieval church.

Getting Around

By Train   Hourly trains from London's Liverpool Street Station (tel. 071/928–5100) and King's Cross Station (tel. 071/278–2477) run to Cambridge. Average journey time is 60 to 90 minutes, depending on the day of week or time of day. Regular local services connect Cambridge with both Ely and Bury St. Edmunds.

By Bus   There are twelve buses daily from Victoria Coach Station that take just under two hours. Tel. 071/730–0202.

By Car   The M11 is the main highway from London to Cambridge. This connects with the fast A45 road east to Bury St. Edmunds. Ely is reached along the A10 from Cambridge. The main car rental companies have offices in Cambridge.

Tourist Information

Bury St. Edmunds (6 Angel Hill, tel. 0284/764667).
Cambridge (Wheeler St., off King's Parade, tel. 0223/322640).
Ely (Oliver Cromwell's House, 29 St. Mary's St., tel. 0353/662062).

Guided Tours

The **Cambridge Tourist Information Center** offers two-hour guided walking tours of the city and the colleges daily. Tickets (£3.10) are available up to 24 hours in advance, and booking is essential as the tours are very popular. **Guide Friday** (tel. 0223/62444), in Cambridge, operates a city open-top bus tour every 30 minutes throughout the day (Oct.–May, hourly); tickets (£6 adults, £1.50 children) can be bought from the driver or the office at Cambridge train station.

Exploring Cambridge

The university is in the very heart of **Cambridge.** It consists of a number of colleges, each of which is a separate institution with its own distinct character and traditions. Undergraduates join an individual college and are taught by dons attached to the college, who are known as "fellows." Each college is built around a series of courts, or quadrangles; because students and fellows live in these courts, access is sometimes restricted, especially during examination weeks in early summer. Visitors are not normally allowed into college buildings other than chapels and halls. It is best to check first with the city tourist office to find out which colleges may be visited.

Numbers in the margin correspond to points of interest on the Cambridge map.

❶ **King's College,** off King's Parade, is possibly the best known of all the colleges. Its chapel, started by Henry VI in 1446, is a masterpiece of late Gothic architecture, with a great fan-vaulted roof supported only by a tracery of soaring side columns. Behind the altar hangs Rubens's painting *Adoration of the Magi.* Every Christmas Eve the college choir sings the Festival of Nine Lessons and Carols, which is broadcast all over the world.

King's runs down to the "Backs," the tree-shaded grounds on the banks of the river Cam, which is the background of many of the colleges. From King's make your way along the river and through the
❷ **❸** **❹** narrow lanes past **Clare College** and **Trinity Hall** to **Trinity.** This is

Cambridge

KEY

AE American Express Office

i Tourist Information

Clare College, **2**

Downing College, **13**

Emmanuel College, **14**

Fitzwilliam Museum, **12**

Kettle's Yard, **8**

King's College, **1**

Magdalene College, **7**

Merton Hall, **6**

Pembroke College, **10**

Peterhouse, **11**

Queen's College, **9**

St. John's, **5**

Silver Street Bridge, **15**

Trinity, **4**

Trinity Hall, **3**

the largest college, established by Henry VIII in 1546. It has a handsome 17th-century Great Court, around which are the chapel, hall, gates, and a library by Christopher Wren. In the massive gate house is Great Tom, a large clock that strikes each hour with high and low notes. Prince Charles was an undergraduate here during the late 1960s.

⑤ Beyond Trinity lies **St. John's,** the second-largest college. The white crenellations of the enormous mock-Gothic **New Building** of 1825 have earned it the nickname "the wedding cake." It is reached across a facsimile of the Bridge of Sighs in Venice. Among St. John's buildings is one of the oldest houses in Cambridge, **Merton Hall,** with its
⑥ origins in the 12th century (although the building itself largely dates from the 16th century).

Up Northampton and across **Magdalene** (pronounced "maudlin")
⑦ Street you come to **Magdalene College,** with its pretty redbrick courts. The **Pepys Library** contains the 17th-century diarist's own books and desk. *Admission free. Open Oct.–Mar., daily 2:30–3:30; Apr.–Sept., daily 11:30–12:30 and 2:30–3:30.*

⑧ Beyond Magdalene is **Kettle's Yard.** This was originally the home of Jim Ede, a connoisseur of 20th-century art. Here he displayed his collections to the public; a gallery extension now houses temporary exhibits. *Castle St., tel. 0223/352124. Admission free. House open Tues.–Sun. 2–4; gallery currently under renovation; check with the tourist office for new opening times.*

Returning the way you've just come, along the Backs from King's,
⑨ you'll see **Queen's College,** where Isaac Newton's **Mathematical Bridge** crosses the river. This arched wooden structure was originally held together by gravitational force; when it was taken apart to see how Newton did it, no one could reconstruct it without using nails.

⑩ Back from the river, on Trumpington Street, sits **Pembroke College,** which contains some 14th-century buildings and a chapel by Wren,
⑪ and **Peterhouse,** the oldest college, dating from 1281. Next to
⑫ Peterhouse is the **Fitzwilliam Museum,** which contains outstanding art collections (including paintings by Constable, Gainsborough, and the French Impressionists) and antiquities (especially from ancient Egypt). *Trumpington St., tel. 0223/332900. Admission free. Open Tues.–Sat. lower galleries 10–2, upper galleries 2–5; Sun. all galleries 2:15–5.*

⑬ Other colleges worth visiting include **Downing College,** which has a unique collection of neoclassical buildings dating from about 1800,
⑭ and **Emmanuel College,** whose chapel and colonnade are by Christopher Wren. Emmanuel's spacious gardens have a pretty duck pond with several unusual breeds. Among the portraits of famous Emmanuel men hanging in the hall is one of John Harvard, founder of Harvard University.

⑮ If you have time, hire a punt at **Silver Street Bridge** or at **Magdalene Bridge** and navigate down past St. John's or upstream to **Grantchester,** the pretty village made famous by the Edwardian poet Rupert Brooke. On a sunny day, there's no better way to absorb Cambridge's unique atmosphere—somehow you will seem to have all the time in the world.

Time Out The coffee shop in the **Fitzwilliam Museum** is an excellent choice for a pastry or a light lunch. So is **The Copper Kettle** (King's Parade), a traditional students' hangout. The **Fort St. George,** on Jesus Green, is a riverside pub overlooking the college boathouses, with plenty of outdoor space for summer drinking.

From Ely to Bury St. Edmunds Some 24 kilometers (15 miles) north of Cambridge, on A10, is the small, compact town of **Ely.** Dominating the town is the **Cathedral,** whose commanding position atop one of the few Fenland ridges makes it visible from kilometers away; not for nothing is it nicknamed "the ship of the Fens." Within the cathedral, which was begun by the Normans in 1083, is one of the marvels of medieval construction: a vast stained-glass skylight that replaced the central tower when it collapsed in 1322. The **Lady Chapel,** restored during the 1970s with financial help from the United States, contains delicate decorative carving and a superb fan-vaulted ceiling. There is also a **Stained-Glass Museum.** *Chapter Office, The College, tel. 0353/ 667735. Cathedral admission: £2.80 adults, £2 senior citizens; up to 2 children free; free Sun. Open Apr.–Oct., daily 7–7; Nov.–Mar., daily 7:30–5. Stained-Glass Museum admission: £1.50 adults, 70p children and senior citizens. Open Easter–Oct., Mon.–Sat. 10:30–4, Sun. noon–3:30.*

Around the cathedral are the well-preserved buildings of the cathedral courtyard, where many of the clergy live, and of the **King's School,** which provides the cathedral with its choristers. To the north is the little market square and shopping streets that lead down to the attractive riverside.

Time Out The **Steeplegate Café and Gallery** (Steeplegate St.), on a street that connects the cathedral grounds with High Street, is a convenient spot for lunch.

The route from Cambridge to Bury St. Edmunds, 47 kilometers (29 miles) along A45, passes by **Newmarket,** headquarters of British horse racing. The town is known both for its first-class racecourse and as a breeding and training center. The **National Horseracing Museum** traces the history of the sport and has a fine collection of paintings. *High St., tel. 0638/667333. Admission charges and opening hours currently under review; call for latest information.*

Tours can be made of the **National Stud,** one of Britain's principal racing stables, where you can see the horses being trained. *Tel. 0638/663464. Tours offered from the end of Apr. to Sept., weekdays 11:15 and 2:30 and sometimes Sat. in summer at 11:15 and Sun. at 2:30. Admission: £3.50 adults, £2.50 children, students, and senior citizens. Advance booking essential.*

Bury St. Edmunds is a quintessential English country town with a picturesque gate tower and the ruins of a great 11th-century Norman abbey, which are located on **Angel Hill.** Medieval buildings along one side of the street face elegant 18th-century houses on the other; there are also some striking public buildings along **Abbeygate Street.**

Farther along Angel Hill from the abbey and then to the left, down Honey Hill, is the **Manor House Museum.** Housed in a Georgian mansion facing the abbey grounds are excellent art and horological collections: clocks, watches, paintings, furniture, and ceramics from the 17th to the 20th centuries. *Honey Hill, tel. 0284/757072. Admission: £2 adults, £1 children. Open Mon.–Sat. 10–5, Sun. 2–5.*

Time Out The lounge of the **Angel Hotel** (Angel Hill) makes a restful spot for an old-fashioned English tea.

The **Theatre Royal,** built in 1819 and now owned by the National Trust, is a perfect example of a working Regency theater and a delightfully intimate place to watch a performance. If rehearsals are not taking place, you can look around during the day. *Westgate St., tel. 0284/755127. Admission free. Open Mon.–Sat. 10–8. Advance booking advised for tours.*

As if to remind visitors that Bury St. Edmunds remains a working town, not a museum piece, a livestock market is held every Wednesday and Saturday off **Risbygate.**

Dining and Lodging

For details and price-category definitions, *see* Dining and Lodging in Staying in Great Britain, *above.*

Dining
★
Midsummer House. A classy restaurant set beside the river Cam, Midsummer House is lovely in summer. There's a comfortable conservatory. Set menus for lunch and dinner parade a selection of gourmet haute cuisine—mussel and rockfish soup with saffron, and pesto-filled supreme of chicken on black olive sauce are current favorites. Desserts are a specialty—try the pear tart with honey ice cream. There's an excellent wine list. *Midsummer Common, tel. 0223/69299. Reservations essential. AE, DC, MC, V. Closed Mon., Sat. lunch, Sun. dinner. Moderate.*

Three Horseshoes. This is an early 19th-century thatched cottage, with a recently added conservatory. A pub restaurant serves beautifully prepared grilled fish, and the conservatory menu offers traditional English fare and seafood, also beautifully presented. *Madingley, tel. 0954/210221 (3 mi outside Cambridge). AE, DC, MC, V. Moderate.*

Twenty-Two. This intimate restaurant occupies a modest house a half-mile from the city center. New owners haven't changed a winning formula. There's an extremely good-value fixed price dinner, featuring modern British specialties such as baked salmon with herb crust. *22 Chesterton Rd., tel. 0223/351880. Reservations advised. MC, V. Closed lunch and Sun., Mon., and Dec. 25–26. Moderate.*

Brown's. This huge, airy French-American style brasserie-diner was converted from the outpatient department of the old Addenbrooke's Hospital, directly opposite the Fitzwilliam Museum. Large fans still keep things cool in the pale yellow dining room. The wide-ranging menu runs from toasted tuna sandwiches to steak and Guiness pie, hamburgers, spaghetti, and salads; check the daily specials, too—there's usually fresh fish. You may have to wait in line on weekends. *23 Trumpington St., tel. 0223/461655. No reservations. No credit cards. Closed Dec. 25–26. Inexpensive–Moderate.*

Hobbs Pavilion. Housed in an old cricket pavilion on the western edge of Parker's Piece, this is a cheery place for pancakes, both sweet and savory. The ice cream is also recommended, homemade from free-range eggs, double cream, and honey. Three-course fixed price menus are a special bargain. *Park Terrace, tel. 0223/67480. Reservations unnecessary. No credit cards. Closed Sun. and Mon. Inexpensive.*

Lodging
★
The Garden House. Set among the colleges, this fairly luxurious, modern hotel makes the most of its riverside location. Its gardens, lounge, cocktail bar, and conservatories all have river views, as do most of the guest rooms—if you want one, make it clear when you make your reservation, as some of the rooms at the rear of the L-shaped hotel have less desirable views. The brightly furnished

guest rooms are comfortable, with minibars, TVs, and fine bathrooms. *Granta Pl., Mill La., CB2 1RT, tel. 0223/63421, fax 0223/316605. 118 rooms with bath. Facilities: restaurant, bar, in-house movies, punt rentals, garden. AE, DC, MC, V. Expensive.*

University Arms Hotel. There has been continuing refurbishment of the public areas and bedrooms in this city-center De Vere hotel; most rooms have now been attractively upgraded without impairing the hotel's original 19th-century elegance. Space is at a premium in central Cambridge and it shows here: Guest rooms are comfortable and well-appointed without being large, though views of Parker's Piece from many rooms compensate. The central lounge provides a cozy and comfortable place for afternoon tea, where you can sit by the fire enjoying a pot of Darjeeling and smoked salmon sandwiches. *Regent St., CB2 1AD, tel. 0223/351241, fax 0223/315256. 117 rooms with bath. Facilities: restaurant, 3 bars, TV, 24-hr room service. AE, DC, MC, V. Expensive.*

Arundel House. This hotel occupies a converted terrace of Victorian houses overlooking the river. The bedrooms are comfortably furnished with locally made mahogany furniture. A videotape tour of the city can be viewed on the hotel's TV information channel. *53 Chesterton Rd., CB4 3AN, tel. 0223/67701, fax 0223/67721. 88 rooms, with bath or shower. Facilities: restaurant, bar, videos, garden. AE, DC, MC, V. Moderate.*

York and Environs

Once England's second city, the ancient town of York has survived the ravages of time, war, and industrialization to remain one of northern Europe's few preserved walled cities. It was King George VI, father of the present queen, who once remarked that the history of York is the history of England. Even in a brief visit to the city, you can see evidence of life from every era since the Romans, not only in museums but in the very streets and houses. On a more contemporary note, the city also boasts some upmarket shops.

York is surrounded by some of the grandest countryside England has to offer. A fertile plain dotted with ancient abbeys and grand aristocratic mansions leads westward to the hidden valleys and jagged, windswept tops of the Yorkshire Dales and northward to the brooding mass of the North York Moors. This is a land quite different from the south of England—it's friendlier, emptier, and less aggressively materialistic. No visitor to Britain should overlook it.

Getting Around

By Train Regular fast trains run from London's King's Cross Station to York. The trip takes two hours. For information, call 071/278-2477.

By Bus Regular *Rapide* buses leave from Victoria Coach Station daily. The trip takes 4½ hours. For information, call 071/730-0202.

By Car Take the A1, the historic main route from London to the north, which branches east onto the A64 near Tadcaster for the final 19½ kilometers (12 miles) to York. Alternatively, take the M1, then the M18, and finally the A1. The drive from London takes a minimum of four hours. The main car rental companies have offices in York.

The best way to explore the area around York is by car—although it's inadvisable to take a car into the crowded city center. Bus tours (*see* By Bus, *above*) visit most of the nearby attractions.

Tourist Information

There is a tourist information office at De Grey Rooms (Lendel Bridge, Exhibition Square, North Yorkshire Y01 2HB, tel. 0904/ 621756) and smaller ones at the York railway station (tel. 0904/ 643700) and in Rougier Street (tel. 0904/620557).

Guided Tours

Guide Friday (8 Tower St., tel. 0904/640896) runs frequent city tours that allow you to get on and off the bus as you please (£5.50 adults, £1.50 children, £3.50 senior citizens). They also conduct tours of the surrounding countryside, including Fountains Abbey and Castle Howard.

The **York Association of Voluntary Guides** (in De Grey Rooms, Exhibition Square, tel. 0904/640780) arranges short walking tours around the city (free, but a gratuity is appreciated) each morning at 10:15, with additional tours at 2:15PM from April through October, and one at 7 PM from July through August.

Exploring York

Numbers in the margin correspond to points of interest on the York map.

❶ York's greatest glory is the **Minster,** the largest Gothic church in England and one of the finest in Europe. Take time to gaze at the soaring columns and intricate tracery of the 14th-century nave, the choir screen portraying the kings of England, and the imposing tracery of the mighty rose window—one of 128 stained-glass windows in the minster—which commemorates the marriage of Henry VII and Elizabeth of York. Visit the exquisite 13th-century **Chapter House** and the Roman and Saxon remains in the **Undercroft Museum and Treasury.** Climb the 275 steps of the **Central Tower** for an unrivaled view of the city and the countryside beyond. The **Crypt** features some of the cathedral's oldest and most valuable treasures, among them the Romanesque 12th-century statue of a heavy-footed Virgin Mary. *York Minster Undercroft Museum and Treasury, Chapter House, Central Tower, and Crypt, tel. 0904/624426. Admission: Minster free (£1.50 donation appreciated); Undercroft £1.80 adults, 50p children and senior citizens; Chapter House 60p adults, 30p children and senior citizens; Central Tower £2 adults, £1 children and senior citizens; Crypt 60p adults, 30p children and senior citizens. Minster open summer daily 7–8:30; winter 7–5; Undercroft, Chapter House, Central Tower, and Crypt open Mon.–Sat. 10–6:30, Sun. 1–6:30.*

❷ At the **Jorvik Viking Centre,** south of the Minster through tiny medieval streets, you can take another journey into history—whisked back in little "time cars" to the sights, sounds, and even the smells of a Viking street, which archaeologists have re-created in astonishing detail. *Coppergate, tel. 0904/643211. Admission: £3.80 adults, £1.90 children, £2.85 senior citizens. Open Apr.–Oct., daily 9–7; Nov.–Mar., daily 9–5:30.*

❸ Walk south down Castlegate and onto Tower Street, where you'll find the **Castle Museum,** housed in an 18th-century prison. It has a series of realistic period displays that bring the past to life. Highlights include a Victorian street scene, an 18th-century dining room, and a moorland farmer's cottage. Don't miss the Coppergate Helmet, one of only three Anglo-Saxon helmets ever found. *Clifford St.,*

York

Train Station

Marygate
CITY WALLS
Bootham

Museum Gardens

Gillygate

Lord Mayor's Walk

St. Leonard's Pl.
CITY WALLS
Deanery Gardens

Duncombe Pl.

Museum St.
Lendal
Blake St.
Stonegate
Darygate
Davygate
COURSE OF ROMAN WALL

Minster
Deangate
College St.
Low Petergate
Swinegate
Church St.
St. Sampson's Sq.
The Shambles
St. Andrewgate
Goodramgate
Spen Ln.

Station Rd.
Rougier St.
Tanner Row
Hudson St.
North St.
Micklegate Bridge
Toft Green
Micklegate
Trinity Ln.
Priory St.
Bishophill Junr.
Fetter Ln.
Bishophill Senior

Queen St.
Blossom St.
Nunnery Ln.
Dale St.
Swann St.
Victor St.
Fairfax St.
Hampden St.
Victor St.
Kyme St.
Cromwell Rd.
Prices Ln.
Nunnery Ln.
CITY WALLS

Low Ousegate
High Ousegate
Coppergate
King St.
Clifford St.
Castlegate
Tower St.
Parliament St.
Piccadilly
Fossgate
The Stonebow
Peaseholme Green
St. Saviourgate

River Foss

Bishopgate St.
Ouse
Tower St.
St. Georges Field
Fishergate
Piccadilly
Paragon St.
George St.
Walmgate
Walmgate
Navigation Rd.
Foss Islands Rd.
Barbican Rd.

KEY

AE American Express Office
i Tourist Information

0   200 yards
0   200 meters

Major Attractions
Castle Museum, 3
Jorvik Viking
Centre, 2
Merchant
Adventurers' Hall, 6
Minster, 1
National Railway
Museum, 7
Shambles, 4
Stonegate, 5

Other Attractions
All Saints, 8
Assembly Rooms, 9
Cholera Burial
Ground, 13
St-Michael-le-
Belfry, 10
Theater Royal, 11
York Story (Heritage
Center), 12

tel. 0904/653612. Admission: £3.80 adults, £2.70 children and senior citizens, family ticket £10.50. Open Apr.–Oct., Mon.–Sat. 9:30–5:30, Sun. 10–5:30; Nov.–Mar., Mon.–Sat. 9:30–4, Sun. 10–4.

Even more than the wealth of museums, it is the streets and city walls that bring the city's past to life. A walk along the **walls,** most of which date from the 13th century, though with extensive restoration, provides delightful views across rooftops and gardens and the Minster itself. The narrow paved path winds between various fortified gates where the old roads ran out of the city.

Within the walls, the narrow streets still follow the complex medieval pattern. The **Shambles,** in the heart of this walled city, is a ④ well-preserved example; the half-timbered shops and houses have such large overhangs that you can practically reach from one second-⑤ floor window to another. **Stonegate** is a narrow pedestrian street of 18th-century (and earlier) shops and courts. Along a narrow passage off Stonegate, at 52A, you will find the remains of a 12th-century Norman stone house—one of the very few surviving in England.

⑥ The **Merchant Adventurers' Hall** is a superb medieval building (1357–68) built and owned by one of the richest medieval guilds; it contains the largest timber-framed hall in York. *Fossgate, tel. 0904/654818. Admission: £1.80 adults, 50p children under 15, £1.50 senior citizens. Open Mar.–Nov., daily 8:30–5; Dec.–Feb., Mon.–Sat. 8:30–3.*

⑦ One very different attraction is the **National Railway Museum,** just outside the city walls, by the train station. This houses Britain's national collection of railway locomotives, including such giants of the steam era as *Mallard,* holder of the world speed record for a steam engine (126 mph), early rolling stock, and pioneer diesel and electric locomotives. *Leeman Rd., tel. 0904/621261. Admission: £3.95 adults, £2 children under 16, £2.60 senior citizens, £11 family ticket. Open Mon.–Sat. 10–6, Sun. 11–6.*

Time Out York's eating places tend to specialize in wholesome, traditional English cooking. In St. Helens Square, **Betty's** has been a York institution since 1912, serving teas with mouth-watering cakes and desserts as well as light meals and a splendid selection of exotic coffees. The 15th-century **Black Swan** pub on Peaseholme Green makes genuine Yorkshire pudding, served, as it should be, with onion gravy.

Outside York Traveling west on the A59, once a Roman road, you soon reach the **Yorkshire Dales,** made world-famous by the writings of a local veterinarian, James Herriot, and inspiration for, among others, the poet William Wordsworth and the quintessentially English painter J. M. Turner. The fertile river valleys of the Dales are separated from one another by areas of wild, high moorland that offers many opportunities for exhilarating walks and drives. At **Bolton Abbey,** about 57 kilometers (36 miles) west of York, the ruins of a 13th-century priory lie on a grassy embankment contained within a great curve of the river Wharfe. (There's unrestricted access during daylight.) Explore the ruins and walk through some of the most romantic woodland scenery in England, past the legendary **Strid,** where the river plunges through a rocky chasm only a few yards wide.

Northwest from Bolton Abbey, off B6160, is **Grassington,** a village of stone houses with an ancient, cobbled marketplace—a convenient center from which to explore the wild landscapes of Upper

York Environs

Wharfedale. The **National Park Centre** has a wide choice of guide-books, maps, and bus schedules to help you enjoy a day in the Dales. Organized tours depart from the center with qualified guides who explain the botanical and geological features of the area. *Colvend, Hebdon Rd., tel. 0756/752748. Open Apr.–Oct., daily 9:30–5:30; Nov.–Mar., Sat. and Sun. 9:30–5:30.*

About 24 kilometers (15 miles) east from Grassington, along B6265, across the moors, is **Fountains Abbey and Studley Royal,** on the very edge of the hills. Here, the extensive ruins of a 12th-century monastery are set beside an 18th-century landscaped water garden and deer park, complete with lakes, half-moon ponds, statuary, and pseudo-Greek temples. *Tel. 0765/608888. Admission: £3.80 adults, £1.60 children, family ticket £9. Open Apr.–Sept., daily 10–7; Oct.–Mar., daily 10–5 or dusk. Guided tours daily Apr.–Oct. at 2:30.*

Nearby **Newby Hall**—5 kilometers (3 miles) due east of Fountains Abbey along pleasant country roads—has some restored interiors by the 18th-century master architect Robert Adam and some equally celebrated gardens with a collection of old breeds of roses and rare shrubs. There is a handy restaurant. *Skelton-on-Ure, tel. 0423/322583. Admission: £5.20 adults, £3 children, £4 senior citizens, family tickets £14.90 and £17.50; gardens only, £3.30 adults, £2.20 children, £2.60 senior citizens, family tickets £8.50 and £10.50. Open Apr.–Sept., Tues.–Sun., grounds 11–5:30, house noon–5.*

To the northeast, across the Vale of York, lie the **North York Moors,** dominated by a vast expanse of dense woodland and heather moorland that in late summer turns a rich blaze of crimson and purple.

Nestled in deep valleys are charming villages built of brownstone—a contrast with the gray stone of the Dales.

Helmsley is a pleasant market town on the southern edge of the Moors, a good starting point for a more detailed exploration. It is not far, by road (B1257 north) or footpath, from the ruins of **Rievaulx Abbey,** a medieval seat of monastic learning whose graceful arches occupy a dramatic riverside setting. The ruins are best seen from the **Rievaulx Terraces,** a long grassy walkway on the hillside above, terminating in the remains of several classical temples. *Rievaulx Abbey, tel. 04396/228. Admission: £2 adults, £1 children, £1.50 senior citizens. Open Apr.–Sept., daily 10–6; Oct.–Mar., daily 10–4. Rievaulx Terrace, tel. 04396/340. Admission: £2.10 adults, 90p children. Open Apr.–Oct., 10:30–6.*

Returning south to York, stop off at **Nunnington Hall** (off B1257), a largely late-17th-century manor house set on the river Rye containing a paneled hall with a carved chimneypiece, fine tapestries and china, and a superb collection of miniature rooms with intricate dollhouse furniture of different periods. *Nunnington, tel. 04395/283. Admission: £3.50 adults, £1.50 children; gardens only £2, children free. Open Apr.–June and Sept.–Oct., Tues.–Thurs. and Sat.–Sun. 2–6; July–Aug., Tues.–Fri. 2–6, Sat.–Sun. noon–6.*

Time Out Teas (and light lunches on summer weekends) can be enjoyed at Nunnington Hall's excellent **tearoom.**

In marked contrast to Nunnington is the palatial majesty of **Castle Howard** (south off B1257 at Slingsby), the setting for the TV series "Brideshead Revisited." The great central domed tower, flanked by two huge and richly decorated wings, took 60 years—from 1699 to 1759—to build. The central hall, with its painted ceiling, leads to a series of grand state rooms and galleries, filled with paintings, sculpture, furniture, and porcelain. On the grounds is a mock classical landscape, with bridges, obelisks, even pyramids. *Coneysthorpe, tel. 065384/333. Admission: £5.50 adults, £3 children, £5 senior citizens. Open mid-Mar.–late Oct., daily, grounds 10–4:30, house 11–4:30.*

Dining and Lodging

For details and price-category definitions, *see* Dining and Lodging in Staying in Great Britain, *above.*

York
Dining

19 Grape Lane. The narrow, slightly cramped restaurant is housed in a typically leaning timbered York building in the heart of town. Hugely popular, it serves modern English food from a blackboard of specials such as pan-fried salmon on a bed of pasta with a red-wine sauce. *19 Grape La., tel. 0904/636366. Reservations advised. Dress: casual. MC, V. Closed Sun. and Mon., 2 wks in Feb., 2 wks in Sept. Expensive.*

Melton's. Just 10 minutes from the Minster, this unfussy restaurant has local art on the walls and an open kitchen. The excellent seasonal menu, cooked up by chef Michael Hjort, an alumnus of the Roux empire, offers modern English, Continental, and fish dishes. Tuesday the menu focuses on fish, Wednesday on desserts, and Thursday on vegetarian dishes. *7 Scarcroft Rd., tel. 0904/634341. Reservations advised. Dress: casual. MC, V. Closed Sun. dinner, Mon. lunch, 3 wks at Christmas, and 1 wk in Sept. Moderate–Expensive.*

Partners. The restaurateur is Polish, so you'll find the occasional Eastern European dish among the modern English cuisine in this simple, elegant restaurant, tucked well off the road and arranged around a pretty paved courtyard. Mushrooms are also a specialty, served in a variety of delicious guises; try the Kulibiak Russian fish pie with oyster mushrooms in olive oil, spring onions, and olives. *13a High Ousegate, tel. 0904/627929. Reservations advised. Dress: casual. AE, MC, V. Closed Sun. Moderate–Expensive.*

Hudson's Below Stairs. Eat traditional roast beef and yorkshire pudding in this atmospheric Victorian hotel restaurant five minutes' walk from the Minster. Morning coffee, lunch, and afternoon teas are also served. *60 Bootham, tel. 0904/621267. Reservations advised. Dress: casual. AE, DC, MC, V. Moderate.*

Kites. Climb a steep, narrow staircase to find an innovative restaurant serving off-beat, health-conscious food, using herbs from the owner's garden. Try the goat cheese and hazelnut soufflé and the rose-petal ice cream. *13 Grape La., tel. 0904/640750. Reservations advised. Dress: casual. MC, V. Closed lunch Mon.–Sat. Moderate.*

Four Seasons. This cheery restaurant in the heart of York's medieval center serves homemade pies and traditional English meat dishes in a 16th-century beamed hall with a stone floor. *45 Goodramgate, tel. 0904/633787. Reservations advised. Dress: casual. AE, DC, MC, V. Inexpensive–Moderate.*

Dining and Lodging **Middlethorpe Hall.** This handsome, superbly restored 18th-century mansion is located on the edge of the city beside the racetrack. The rooms are filled with antiques, paintings, and fresh flowers, and the extensive grounds boast a lake, a 17th-century dovecote, and "ha-has"—drops in the garden level that create cunning views. The large kitchen garden grows fresh vegetables for the hotel's award-winning Anglo-French restaurant, where you can eat in the original dining room by candlelight. *Bishopthorpe Rd., YO2 1QB, tel. 0904/ 641241, fax 0904/620176. 30 rooms with bath. Facilities: restaurant (reservations essential; jacket and tie required), garden, croquet. AE, DC, MC, V. Expensive–Very Expensive.*

Mount Royale Hotel. Two elegant town houses, dating from the 1830s, have been furnished in a traditional English country-cottage style to make a comfortable hotel about 15 minutes from the town center. The open-plan "garden rooms" are decorated with tropical plants and open out onto the hotel's lovely grounds. The fine Anglo-French restaurant serves dishes based on local produce. *119 The Mount, Y02 2DA, tel. 0904/628856, fax 0904/611171. 23 rooms with bath. Facilities: restaurant, garden, health center, open air pool, satellite TV. AE, DC, MC, V. Closed Christmas Eve to New Year's Eve. Moderate–Expensive.*

Lodging **Dean Court.** Directly opposite the Minster, this family-run establishment in a Victorian house has comfortably furnished rooms with plump sofas, TVs, and great views overlooking the Minster. Parking is a few minutes from the hotel, but there is a valet parking service. The restaurant serves good English cuisine. *Duncombe Place, YO1 2EF, tel. 0904/625082, fax 0904/620305. 40 rooms with bath. Facilities: coffee shop, bar, lounge, in-house movies. AE, DC, MC, V. Expensive.*

Grasmead House. The large, comfortable bedrooms in this small family-run hotel all boast four-poster beds, as well as tea and coffee-making facilities, and the friendly owners are more than willing to share their local knowledge with you. It's an easy walk from the city center. *1 Scarcroft Hill, YO2 1DF, tel. 0904/629996. 6 rooms with bath or shower (3 nonsmoking rooms). Facilities: bar, lounge, parking. MC, V. Moderate.*

Savages. Despite its name, this small hotel on a leafy road near the town center is eminently refined, with a reputation for attentive service. Once a Victorian home, it has a stylish and comfortable interior, and there's a bar in which to relax. *15 St Peter's Grove, YO3 6AQ, tel. 0904/610818, fax 0904/627729. 18 rooms with bath. Facilities: restaurant, bar, garden, baby-listening service. AE, DC, MC, V. Moderate.*

Abbey Guest House. This quaint, pretty guest house is 10 minutes' walk from the train station and town center. It enjoys a peaceful garden right on the river. *14 Earlsborough Terr., Marygate, YO3 7BQ, tel. 0904/627782. 7 rooms with basins. Facilities: lounge, baby-sitting service, parking, picnic lunches and evening meal on request. AE, DC, MC, V. Inexpensive.*

Edinburgh

Scotland and England *are* different—and let no Englishman tell you otherwise. Although the two nations have been united in a single state since 1707, Scotland retains its own marked political and social character, with, for instance, legal and educational systems quite distinct from those of England. And by virtue of its commanding geographic position, on top of a long-dead volcano, and the survival of a large number of outstanding buildings carrying echoes of the nation's history, Edinburgh proudly ranks among the world's greatest capital cities.

Getting Around

By Train Regular fast trains run from London's King's Cross Station to Edinburgh Waverley; the fastest journey time is just over 4 hours. For information in London, call 071/278–2477; in Edinburgh, 031/556–2451 (recorded information lines: weekday service 031/557–3000; Saturday service 031/557–2737; Sunday service 031/557–1616).

By Plane **British Airways** operates a shuttle service from London's Heathrow Airport to Edinburgh; reservations are not necessary, and you are guaranteed a seat. Flying time from London is one hour, 15 minutes. For information, call 081/759–2525 or 0345/222111. **British Midland** also flies from Heathrow (call 081/745–7321 or 0345/554554). **Air UK** flies from Gatwick (0293/567977) and Stansted (0279/662816)—both airports are far less crowded than Heathrow, and are as easy to reach by rail. From Edinburgh, call 0345/666777 for Air UK flights to both Gatwick and Stansted. Transatlantic flights direct to Scotland use Glasgow Airport, from which there are regular rail connections to Glasgow city center and on to Edinburgh.

By Bus Regular services are operated by **National Express** between Victoria Coach Station, London, and St. Andrew Square bus station, Edinburgh, three times a day. The 405-mile journey takes approximately eight hours.

By Car London and Edinburgh are 640 kilometers (400 miles) apart; allow a comfortable nine hours for the drive. The two principal routes to the Scottish border are the A1 (mostly a small but divided road) or the eight-lane M1, then M6. From there, the choice is between the dual-carriageway A74, which can be unpleasantly busy, followed by the A701 or A702, and the slower but much more scenic A7 through Hawick. All the main car-rental agencies have offices in Edinburgh.

Tourist Information

The **Edinburgh and Scotland Information Centre** (3 Princes Street, tel. 031/557–1700) gives expert advice on what to see and do in Edinburgh and throughout Scotland. Services include information and literature, accommodation reservations, route planning, coach tour tickets, entertainment reservations, a Scottish bookshop, and currency exchange. Visitors can also buy National Trust, Historic Scotland, and Great Britain Heritage passes.

Guided Tours

Both **Lothian Region Transport** (deep-red-and-white buses) and **S.M.T.** (green buses) operate tours in and around the city. For information, call 031/220–4111 (Lothian) or 031/313–1515 (for S.M.T. bus times, call 031/556–8464). Tickets allowing unlimited travel on city buses for various periods are also available.

The Cadies and **Witchery Tours** (352 Castlehill, 3rd floor, tel. 031/225–6745) offer a highly popular murder and mystery tour, and historical, and other special-interest tours.

Exploring Edinburgh

The key to understanding Edinburgh is to make the distinction between the Old and New Towns. Until the 18th century, the city was confined to the rocky crag on which its castle stands, straggling between the fortress at one end and the royal residence, the Palace of Holyroodhouse, at the other. In the 18th century, during a civilizing time of expansion known as the "Scottish Enlightenment," the city fathers fostered the construction of another Edinburgh, one a little to the north. This is the New Town, whose elegant squares, classical facades, wide streets, and harmonious proportions remain largely intact and lived-in today.

Numbers in the margin correspond to points of interest on the Edinburgh map.

The Royal Mile ❶ **Edinburgh Castle,** the brooding symbol of Scotland's capital and the nation's martial past, dominates the city center. The castle's attractions include the city's oldest building—the 11th-century **St. Margaret's Chapel;** the **Crown Room,** where the Regalia of Scotland are displayed; **Old Parliament Hall;** and **Queen Mary's Apartments,** where Mary, Queen of Scots, gave birth to the future King James VI of Scotland (who later became James I of England). In addition, military features of interest include the **Scottish National War Memorial** and the **Scottish United Services Museum.** *Tel. 031/244–3101. Admission: £5 adults, £3 senior citizens, £1 children under 16. Open Apr.–Sept., daily 9:30–5:15; Oct.–Mar., daily 9:30–4:15.*

❷ The **Royal Mile,** the backbone of the Old Town, starts immediately below the **Castle Esplanade,** the wide parade ground that hosts the annual Edinburgh Military Tattoo—a grand military display staged during a citywide festival every summer (*see below*). The Royal Mile consists of a number of streets, running into each other—**Castlehill, Lawnmarket, High Street,** and **Canongate**—leading downhill to the Palace of Holyroodhouse, home to the Royal Family when they visit Edinburgh. Tackle this walk in leisurely style; the many original Old Town "closes," narrow alleyways enclosed by high tenement buildings, are rewarding to explore and give a real sense of the former life of the city.

508

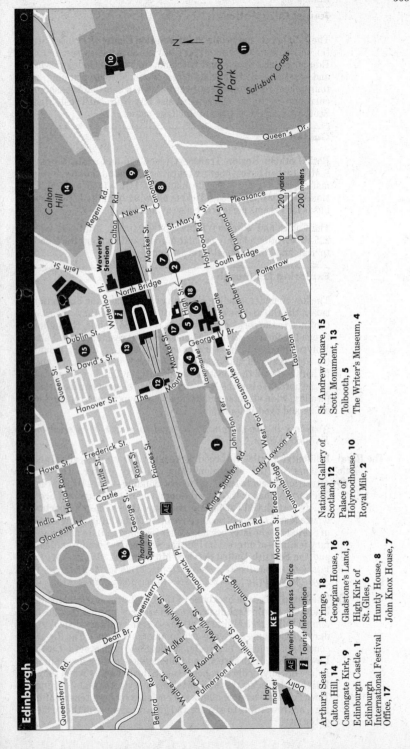

❸ In Lawnmarket, the six-story tenement known as **Gladstone's Land** dates from 1620. It has a typical arcaded front and first-floor entrance and is furnished in the style of a merchant's house of the time; there are magnificent painted ceilings. *747B Lawnmarket, tel. 031/ 226–5856. Admission: £2.50 adults, £1.30 children and senior citizens. Open Apr.–Oct., Mon.–Sat. 10–5, Sun. 2–5 (last admission 4:30).*

❹ Close by is **The Writers' Museum,** housed in Lady Stair's House, a town dwelling of 1622 that recalls Scotland's literary heritage with exhibits on Sir Walter Scott, Robert Louis Stevenson, and Robert Burns. *Lady Stair's Close, Lawnmarket, tel. 031/225–2424, ext. 4901. Admission free. Open June–Sept., Mon.–Sat. 10–6; Oct.– May, Mon.–Sat. 10–5, Sun. 2–5 during the festival.*

A heart shape set in the cobbles of the High Street marks the site of
❺ the **Tolbooth,** the center of city life until it was demolished in 1817.
❻ Nearby stands the **High Kirk of St. Giles,** Edinburgh's cathedral; parts of the church date from the 12th century, the choir from the 15th. *High St. Admission free. Open Mon.–Sat. 9–5 (7 in summer), Sun. 2–5 and for services.*

❼ Farther down High Street you'll see **John Knox House.** Its traditional connections with Scotland's celebrated religious reformer are tenuous, but it gives a flavor of life in the Old Town during Knox's time. *45 High St., tel. 031/556–2647. Admission: £1.25 adults, 75p children, £1 senior citizens. Open Mon.–Sat. 10–4:30.*

Next door is the **Netherbow Arts Centre,** with a theater, an art gallery, and a café *(tel. and opening hours as for John Knox House).*

Canongate was formerly an independent burgh, or trading commu-
❽ nity, outside the city walls of Edinburgh. **Huntly House,** built in 1570, is a museum featuring Edinburgh history and social life. *142 Canongate, tel. 031/225–2424, ext. 4143. Admission free. Open June–Sept., Mon.–Sat. 10–6; Oct.–May, Mon.–Sat. 10–5, Sun. 2–5 during the festival.*

❾ Some notable Scots are buried in the graveyard of the **Canongate Kirk** nearby, including the economist Adam Smith and the poet Robert Fergusson.

Time Out   Two places that serve a good cup of tea and a sticky cake (a notable Scottish indulgence) are **Clarinda's** in Canongate and the **Abbey Strand Tearoom,** near the palace gates. The **crypt of St. Giles** houses the popular **Lower Aisle Tearoom.**

❿ The **Palace of Holyroodhouse,** still the Royal Family's official residence in Scotland, was founded by King James IV at the end of the 15th century and was extensively remodeled by Charles II in 1671. The state apartments, with their collections of tapestries and paintings, can be visited. *Tel. 031/556–7371. Admission: £3.50 adults, £1.75 children, £3 senior citizens, £8.50 family ticket. Open Apr.– Oct., Mon.–Sat. 9:30–5:15, Sun. 10:30–4:30; end Oct.–Mar., Mon.– Sat. 9:30–3:45; closed during royal and state visits.*

The open grounds of **Holyrood Park** enclose Edinburgh's distinctive
⓫ originally volcanic minimountain, **Arthur's Seat,** with steep slopes and miniature crags.

In 1767, the competition to design the New Town was won by a young and unknown architect, James Craig. His plan was for a grid of three east–west streets, balanced at each end by a grand square. The plan survives today, despite all commercial pressures. Princes,

George, and Queen streets are the main thoroughfares, with St. Andrew Square at one end and Charlotte Square at the other.

⑫ The **National Gallery of Scotland,** on the Mound, the street that joins
the Old and New Towns, contains works by the Old Masters and the
French Impressionists and has a good selection of Scottish paintings. This is one of Britain's best national galleries, and is small
enough to be taken in easily on one visit. *Tel. 031/556–8921. Admission free; charge for special exhibitions. Open Mon.–Sat. 10–5,
Sun. 2–5. Print Room, weekdays 10–noon and 2–4 by arrangement.*

To the east along Princes Street is the unmistakable soaring Gothic
⑬ spire of the 62-meter- (200-foot-) high **Scott Monument,** built in the
1840s to commemorate the celebrated novelist of Scots history.
There is a statue of Sir Walter and his dog within. The views from
the top are well worth the 287-step climb. *Tel. 031/225–2424. Admission: £1. Open Apr.–Sept., Mon.–Sat. 9–6; Oct.–Mar. Mon.–Sat.
9–3.*

⑭ There are more splendid views from **Calton Hill:** north across the
Firth (or estuary) of Forth to the Lomond Hills of Fife and to the
Pentland Hills that enfold the city from the south. Among the various monuments on Calton Hill are a partial reproduction of the **Parthenon,** in Athens, begun in 1824 but left incomplete because the
money ran out; the **Nelson Monument;** and the **Royal Observatory.**

⑮ Make your way to **St. Andrew Square,** then along George Street,
where there is a wide choice of shops, and on to **Charlotte Square,**
whose north side was designed by the great Scottish classical archi-
⑯ tect Robert Adam. The rooms of the elegant **Georgian House** are
furnished to show the domestic arrangements of a prosperous
late-18th-century Edinburgh family. *7 Charlotte Sq., tel. 031/225–
2160. Admission: £3 adults, £1.50 children and senior citizens.
Open Apr.–Oct., Mon.–Sat. 10–5, Sun. 2–5 (last admission 4:30).*

Time Out Bianco's, in Hope Street, close to the Georgian House, is good for
coffee and croissants.

Finally, a word about the **Edinburgh International Festival,** the celebration of music, dance, and drama that the city stages each summer
(the 1995 dates are Aug. 13–Sept. 2), featuring international artists
of the highest caliber. The **Festival Fringe,** the unruly child of the
official festival, spills out of halls and theaters all over town, offering
visitors a cornucopia of theatrical and musical events of all kinds—
some so weird that they defy description. While the official festival
is the place to see top-flight performances by established artists, at
a Fringe event you may catch a new star, or a new art form, or a controversial new play in the making. Or then again, you may not; it's
very much up to luck. Advance information, programs, and ticket
⑰ sales for the festival are available from the **Edinburgh International**
⑱ **Festival Office** (21 Market St., tel. 031/226–4001), and for the **Fringe**
from its office (180 High St., tel. 031/226–5257/5259).

Dining and Lodging

For details and price-category definitions, *see* Dining and Lodging
in Staying in Great Britain, *above.*

Dining **The Pompadour.** The decor here is inspired by the France of Louis
XV, with ornate gilts and reds prevailing. A sophisticated French
menu in the evening is balanced by a Scots flavor at lunchtime. The

Caledonian has a second, less pricey restaurant, **Carriages,** that also offers a Scottish menu. *Caledonian Hotel, Princes St., tel. 031/225–2433. Reservations advised. Jacket and tie required. AE, DC, MC, V. Carriages: Moderate; Pompadour: Expensive–Very Expensive.*

Jackson's Restaurant. Intimate and candlelit in a historic Old Town close halfway down the Royal Mile, Jackson's offers good Scots fare. Aberdeen Angus steaks and Border lamb are excellent; there are vegetarian and seafood specialties, too. *2 Jackson Close, 209–213 High St., tel. 031/225–1793. Reservations advised. AE, MC, V. Closed for lunch Sat. and Sun. Moderate.*

Martin's. This very small spot is good for imaginative vegetarian dishes, game, and fresh seafood. Try the succulent halibut with leeks and carrot-and-basil coulis, or the breasts of mallard and pigeon with red cabbage and raisins. There's a good-value set lunch. *70 Rose St., North Lane (between Castle and Frederick Sts.), tel. 031/225–3106. Reservations essential. Jacket and tie advised. AE, DC, MC, V. Open lunch Tues.–Fri., dinner Tues.–Sat. Moderate–Expensive.*

L'Auberge. An established restaurant, L'Auberge is comfortably old-fashioned. The French-style cuisine uses the best Scottish ingredients. Try the brill with oysters or the tender venison. There are excellent three-course, fixed-price menus available. *56–58 St. Mary's St., tel. 031/556–5888. Reservations advised. AE, DC, MC, V. Moderate.*

Vintners Room. This atmospheric old wine warehouse lies outside the city center, in Leith, an old section of town. The fine, 17th-century, candle-blackened plasterwork gives the place a traditional feeling. The food is served in large portions: Try the rabbit terrine with lime pickle or the paupiettes of veal with hazlenuts and balsamic vinegar. *87 Giles St., Leith, tel. 031/554–6767. Reservations advised. AE, DC, MC, V. Closed Sun. and 2 weeks at Christmas. Moderate.*

Henderson's. This friendly place claims to be the city's original vegetarian restaurant, long before such places became fashionable. Try the vegetarian haggis! *94 Hanover St., tel. 031/225–2131. Reservations accepted. AE, MC, V. Inexpensive.*

Howie's. Howie's is a simple, neighborhood bistro, unlicensed, so you have to take your own bottle. The steaks are tender Aberdeen beef, the Loch Fyne herring are sweet-cured to Howie's own recipe, and the clientele's lively. *75 St. Leonard's St., tel. 031/668–2917 and 63 Dalry Rd., tel. 031/313–3334. Reservations advised. MC, V. Open lunch Tues.–Sun., dinner daily. Inexpensive.*

Pierre Victoire. There are four branches of this very popular bistro chain in Edinburgh. They are fairly chaotic, friendly, enjoyable eateries, serving healthy portions at low prices. The fish is fresh and especially good—try the baked oysters with bacon and hollandaise. *38 Grassmarket, tel. 031/226–2442; 10 Victoria St., tel. 031/225–1721 (closed Sun.); 8 Union St., tel. 031/557–8451 (closed Mon.); 5 Dock Place, Leith, tel. 031/556–6178 (closed Sun.) MC, V. Inexpensive.*

Lodging   **The Caledonian Hotel.** Popularly known as "the Caley," this hotel echoes the days of the traditional great railway hotel, though its neighbor station has long since closed. The imposing Victorian decor has been preserved in a total refurbishment. There are also two excellent restaurants (*see* Pompadour, *above*). *Princes St., EH1 2AB, tel. 031/225–2433, fax 031/225–6632. 239 rooms with bath. Facilities: 2 restaurants, in-house movies. AE, DC, MC, V. Very Expensive.*

George Hotel. This extensively refurbished city-center hotel has elegant 18th-century features in the public rooms and up-to-date bedrooms. Though busy, the staff takes time to be helpful. *19 George St., EH2 2PB, tel. 031/225–1251, fax 031/226–5644. 195 rooms with bath. Facilities: 2 restaurants, bar. AE, DC, MC, V. Very Expensive.*

Scandic Crown. One of the latest hotels to open in Edinburgh, the Scandic Crown has been designed to blend in with the surrounding ancient buildings. The bedrooms are roomy and follow the color scheme of each floor. If what you want is modern ambience but proximity to the sights, this is the place. *80 High St., The Royal Mile, EH1 1TH, tel. 031/557–9797, fax 031/557–9789. 238 rooms with bath. AE, DC, MC, V. Expensive–Very Expensive.*

Mount Royal Hotel. This modern hotel is ideally located for sightseeing and shopping. The front rooms have views of the castle. It has a friendly staff. *53 Princes St., EH2 2DG, tel. 031/225–7161, fax 031/220–4671. 160 rooms with bath. AE, DC, MC, V. Expensive.*

The Albany Hotel. Three fine 18th-century houses with many original features have been carefully converted into a comfortable city-center hotel. There's a good restaurant in the basement. *39 Albany St., EH1 3QY, tel. 031/556–0397, fax 031/557–6633. 20 rooms with bath. MC, V. Moderate.*

Brunswick Hotel. This bed-and-breakfast, close to the city center and near the Playhouse Theatre, is in a fine Georgian building that offers easy parking. All rooms have tea/coffee making facilities and TVs; two of them have four posters. *7 Brunswick St., EH7 5JB, tel. and fax 031/556–1238. 10 rooms with shower. AE, MC, V. Moderate.*

Dorstan Private Hotel. A Victorian villa in a quiet area, the Dorstan has fully modernized rooms decorated in bright, country-cottage colors. *7 Priestfield Rd., EH16 5HJ, tel. 031/667–6721, fax 031/668–4644. 14 rooms, 9 with bath or shower. MC, V. Moderate.*

13 Greece

You cannot travel far across the land in Greece without meeting the sea or far across the sea without meeting one of its roughly 2,000 islands. About the size of New York State, Greece has 15,019 kilometers (9,312 miles) of coastline, more than any other country of its size in the world. The sea is everywhere, not on three sides only but at every turn, reaching through the shoreline like a probing hand. The land itself is stunning, dotted with cypress groves, vineyards, and olive trees, carved into gentle bays or dramatic coves with startling white sand, rolling hills, and rugged mountain ranges that plunge straight into the sea. This natural beauty and the sharp, clear light of sun and sea, combined with plentiful archaeological treasures, make Greece one of the world's most inviting countries.

Poetry, music, architecture, politics, medicine, law—all had their Western birth here in Greece centuries ago, alongside the great heroes of mythology who still seem to haunt this sun-drenched land. Among the great mountains of mainland Greece are the cloud-capped peak of Mount Olympus, fabled home of the Greek gods, and Mount Parnassus, favorite haunt of the sun-god Apollo and the nine Muses, goddesses of poetry and science. The remains of the ancient past—the Acropolis and the Parthenon, the temples of Delphi, the Tombs of the Kings in Mycenae—and a later procession of Byzantine churches, Crusader castles and fortresses, and Turkish mosques are spread throughout the country.

Of the hundreds of islands and islets scattered across the Aegean Sea in the east and the Ionian Sea in the west, fewer than 250 are still inhabited. This world of the farmer and seafarer has largely been replaced by the world of the tourist. More than 8 million holiday makers visit Greece each year, almost as many as the entire native population; in fact, tourism has overtaken shipping as the most important element in the nation's economy. On some of the islands, the impact of the annual influx of visitors has meant the building of a new Greece, more or less in their image. But traditionalism survives: Now, pubs and bars stand next door to *ouzeri*, discos are as popular as *kafeneia*, and pizza and hamburger joints compete with *tavernes;* once-idyllic beaches have become overcrowded and noisy, and fishing harbors have become flotilla sailing centers. Prices rose steeply after Greece joined the European Community in 1981, and the simplicity and hardships of a peasant economy have largely disappeared from the islands' way of life.

Although mass tourism has taken over the main centers, it is still possible to strike out and find your own place among the smaller islands and the miles of beautiful mainland coastline. Except for some difficulty in finding accommodations (Greek families on vacation tend to fill the hotels in out-of-the-way places during high summer), this is the ideal way to see traditional Greece. Those who come only to worship the classical Greeks and gaze at their temples, seeing nothing but the glory that was, miss today's Greece. If you explore this fascinating country with open eyes, you'll enjoy it in all its forms: its slumbering cafés and buzzing tavernas; its elaborate religious rituals; its stark, bright beauty; and the generosity, curiosity, and kindness of its people.

Essential Information

Before You Go

When to Go Although the tourist season runs from May through October, the heat can be unpleasant in July and August, particularly in Athens. On the islands, a brisk northwesterly wind, the *meltemi*, can make life more comfortable. If you want to move about the country and avoid all the other tourists, the ideal months are May, June, and September. The winter months tend to be damp and cold virtually everywhere.

The following are the average daily maximum and minimum temperatures for Athens.

Jan.	55F	13C	May	77F	25C	Sept.	84F	29C
	44	6		61	16		67	19
Feb.	57F	14C	June	86F	30C	Oct.	75F	24C
	44	6		68	20		60	16
Mar.	60F	16C	July	92F	33C	Nov.	66F	19C
	46	8		73	23		53	12
Apr.	68F	20C	Aug.	92F	33C	Dec.	58F	15C
	52	11		73	23		47	8

Currency The Greek monetary unit is the drachma (dr.). Bank notes are in denominations of 50, 100, 500, 1,000, and 5,000 dr.; coins, 5, 10, 20, 50, and 100. At press time (spring 1994), there were approximately 225 dr. to the U.S. dollar and 355 dr. to the pound sterling. Daily exchange rates are prominently displayed in banks. You'll get a better exchange rate at banks than from hotels or stores.

What It Will Cost Inflation in Greece is rather high—just under 12% a year—and fluctuations in currency make it impossible to do accurate budgeting long in advance, so keep an eye on the exchange rates before your vacation. On the whole, Greece offers good value compared with many other European countries. The values are especially good for modest hotels and restaurants, transportation, and entertainment.

There are few regional price differences for hotels and restaurants. A modest hotel in a small town will charge only slightly lower rates than a modest hotel in Athens, with the same range of amenities. The same is true of restaurants. The spread of tourism has made Rhodes, Corfu, and Crete as affordable as many other islands. Car rentals are expensive in Greece, but taxis are inexpensive even for long-distance runs.

Sample Prices At a central-city café, you can expect to pay about 300 dr. to 500 dr. for a cup of coffee or a bottle of beer, 200 dr. to 300 dr. for a soft drink, and around 300 dr. for a toasted cheese sandwich. These prices can, of course, vary considerably from one place to another. A 1½-kilometer (1-mile) taxi ride costs about 300 dr.

Customs on Arrival You may take in one carton of cigarettes or cigars or ¼ pound of smoking tobacco; 1 liter of alcohol, or 2 liters of wine; and gifts up to a total value of $50. There's no duty on articles for personal use. Foreign bank notes amounting to more than $1,000 must be declared for re-export. There are no restrictions on traveler's checks. Foreign visitors may take in 40,000 dr. in Greek currency and export up to $1,760 in foreign currencies but no Greek money. Larger amounts may be exported, depending on your export declaration on arrival.

Greece

BULGARIA

MACEDONIA

ALBANIA

Stavroupoli
Sidirókastro
Séres
Philippi
Kilkis
Eleftheroúpoli
Kavala
Edessa
Gianitsa
Amfipoli
E86
Florina
Alexandria
Thessaloniki
E90
Kastoria
Ptolemaïda
Veria
Thérmi
Nea
Apolonia
Vatopedia
Kozani
Katerini
Polygyros
Ormylia
Ivirion
Siatista
Gulf of
Thermaikos
Dafni
Athos
Konitsa
Grevena
Mount
Olympus
Gulf of Kassandra
Delvinákio
Elassona
Kalithéa
Metsovo
Kalambaka
Tirnavos
Palioúri
Kerkira
Corfu
Igoumenítsa
Ioanina
Agia
Paramythia
Trikala
Larissa
SPORADES
Parga
Karditsa
Volos
Arta
Stavros
Farsala
Skiathos
Aliki
Almiros
Preveza
Lamia
Skopelos
Lefkas
Karpenissi
Skyros
Vassiliki
EVIA
Kymi
Kephalonia
Ithaki
Agrinio
Orhomenos
Delphi
Itea
Livadia
Halkida
Lixouri
Sami
Messolongi
Nefpaktos
Galaxidi
Thebes
Patras
Gulf of Corinth
Rafina
Karystos
Diakofto
Megara
Piraeus
Athens
Killini
Corinth
Glyfada
Loutra
Nemea
Voula
Lavrio
Kea
Zakynthos
Amalias
Egina
Pyrgos
Olympia
Argos
Poros
Sounio
Erm
Zakynthos
Kaiafas
Tripoli
Náflio
Toló
Andritsena
Ermioni
Ydra
Kythnos
S
Kyparissia
PELOPONNESE
Spetses
Serifos
Messini
Sparta
Leonidio
Gargaliani
Kalamata
Mystras
Geraki
Pilos
Kyparíssi
C
Methoni
Skala
Mirtoan
Sea
Koroni
Gythio
Monemvassia
Areopoli
Milos

Ionian Sea

Agía Pelagia
Kythira
Kythira

Mediterranean Sea

Hania

CRETE

0 —— 100 miles
0 —— 300 km

N

Language English is widely spoken in hotels and elsewhere, especially by young people, and even in out-of-the-way places someone is always happy to lend a helping hand.

In this guide, names are given in the Roman alphabet according to the Greek pronunciation except when there is a familiar English form, such as "Athens."

Getting Around

By Car Driving in Greek cities is not recommended unless you have iron
Road nerves. For the ratio of collisions to the number of cars on the road,
Conditions Greece has one of the worst accident rates in Europe. This is due, in part, to extremely varied road conditions. Motorways tend to be good; tolls are between 200 dr. and 700 dr. and are charged according to distance. Many country roads are narrow but free of traffic. If you do decide to drive in Greece, keep your wits about you and expect the unexpected. Red traffic lights are frequently ignored, and it is not unusual to see motorists passing on hills and while rounding corners.

Rules of the Unless you are a citizen of an EU (European Union) country, you
Road must have an International Driver's License. The **Automobile and Touring Club of Greece** (*see below*) issues them for 17,700 dr. Bring a photo and your driver's license. Driving is on the right, and although the vehicle on the right has the right-of-way, don't expect this or any other driving rule to be obeyed. The speed limit is 120 kph (74 mph) on the National Road, 80 kph (49 mph) outside built-up areas, and 50 kph (31 mph) in town. Seat belts are compulsory, as are helmets for motorcyclists.

Parking In Greece's half-dozen large cities, parking spaces are hard to find. In Athens or Thessaloniki, you can pay to use one of the many temporary parking areas set up in vacant lots, but you're better off leaving your car in the hotel garage and walking or taking a cab. Elsewhere, however, parking is easy. There is free or cheap parking at most archaeological sites outside Athens.

Gasoline At press time gas cost about 184 dr.–189 dr. a liter (about 786 dr.–808 dr. a gallon). Gas pumps and service stations are everywhere, and lead-free gas is widely available. Be aware that many stations close at 7 PM.

Breakdowns **The Automobile and Touring Club of Greece** (ELPA, Athens Tower, Messoghion 2–4, Athens, tel. 01/779–1615 or fax 01/778–6642; in an emergency, tel. 104) assists tourists with breakdowns free of charge for those who are ELPA members; otherwise, there is a charge, depending on the agreement made between ELPA and the driver's own automobile association.

By Bicycle Jeeps, dune buggies, pedal cycles, mopeds, and motorcycles can be rented on the islands. Use extreme caution. Crash helmets, although technically compulsory for motorcyclists, are not usually available, and injuries are common.

By Train Few tourists use the trains because they are slow and railway networks are limited. The main line runs north from Athens to the former Yugoslavia. It divides into three lines at Thessaloniki. The main line continues on to Belgrade, a second line goes east to the Turkish border and Istanbul, and a third line heads northeast to Bulgaria. The Peloponnese in the south is served by a narrow-gauge line dividing at Corinth into the Mycenae–Argos section and the Patras–Olympia–Kalamata section. For information, tel. 01/524–0601.

By Plane **Olympic Airways** (Syngrou 96, Athens, tel. 01/966–6666) has service between Athens and several cities and islands. Thessaloniki is also linked to the main islands, and there are several interisland connections. Reservations can be made by telephone daily from 7 AM to 10 PM. For information on arrivals and departures for Olympic Airways flights (West Terminal), call 01/936–3363; for other carriers (East Terminal), call 01/969–9466.

By Bus Travel by bus is inexpensive, usually comfortable, and relatively fast. The journey from Athens to Thessaloniki, for example, takes roughly the same amount of time as the slow train, though the express covers the distance 1¼ hours faster. In the Peloponnese, however, buses are much faster than trains. Bus information and timetables are available at tourist information offices throughout Greece. Make reservations at least one day before your planned trip, earlier for holiday weekends. Railway-operated buses leave from the Peloponnisos railway station in Athens. All other buses leave from one of two bus stations: Liossiou 260—for central and eastern Greece and Evia; Kifissou 100—for the Peloponnese and northwestern Greece.

By Boat There are frequent car ferries and hydrofoils from Piraeus, the port of Athens, to the central and southern Aegean islands and Crete. Nearby islands are also served by hydrofoils and ferries from Rafina, east of Athens. Ships to the Ionian islands sail from ports nearer to them, such as Patras. Connections from Athens/Piraeus to the main island groups are good, connections from main islands to smaller ones within a group less so, and services between islands of different groups or areas—such as Rhodes and Crete—are less frequent. Travel agents and shipping offices in Athens and Piraeus and in the main towns on the islands have details. Buy your tickets two or three days in advance, especially if you are traveling in summer or taking a car. Reserve your return journey or continuation soon after you arrive.

Timetables change very frequently, and boats may be delayed by weather conditions, so your itinerary should allow for some flexibility.

Staying in Greece

Telephones
Local Calls Most curbside kiosks have pay telephones for local calls only. You pay the kiosk owner 10 to 15 dr. per call after you've finished. It's easier, though, to buy a phone card from the Telecommunications Office (OTE); kiosks, or convenience shops and use it at the now ubiquitous card phones.

International
Calls Although you can buy phone cards with up to 5,000 dr. credit, if you plan to make and pay for several international phone calls, go to an OTE office, usually located in the center of towns and villages. There are several branches in Athens. Calls to the United States and Canada cost 355 dr. a minute; the price is reduced by 30% from 3 PM Saturday to 9 AM Monday. There is a three-minute minimum charge for operator-assisted station-to-station calls, a four-minute minimum for person-to-person connections. Hotels tend to add a hefty service charge for long-distance calls. You can call the United States collect or use your calling card by dialing the **AT&T** operator (tel. 00/800–1311), the **MCI** operator (tel. 00/800–1211), or the **Sprint** operator (tel. 00/800–1411).

Operators and There are English-speaking operators on the International Ex-
Information change. Ask your hotel reception desk or an employee at the OTE for
help in reaching one. It takes up to an hour for the operator to connect you, so using the AT&T, MCI, or Sprint numbers is much faster
for collect or prepaid calls.

Mail Airmail letters or postcards for delivery within Europe cost 90 dr.
Postal Rates for 20 grams and 180 dr. for 50 grams; outside Europe the cost is 120
dr. for 20 grams and 220 dr. for 50 grams. If you are mailing a package, you must bring it open with your wrapping materials to the
post office so it can be inspected.

Receiving Mail Except for the main office on **Syntagma Square** (open weekdays 8–8,
Sat. 7:30–2, Sun. 9–1), most post offices are open weekdays 8–2. You
can have your mail sent to Poste Restante, Aeolou 100, Athens 10200
(take your passport to pick up your mail), or to American Express,
Ermou 2, Athens, 10225. For holders of American Express cards or
traveler's checks, there is no charge for the service. Others pay 400
dr. for each pickup.

Shopping Prices quoted in shops include the VAT. There are no VAT refunds.
Prices in large stores are fixed. Bargaining may take place in small
owner-managed souvenir and handicrafts shops and in antiques
shops. In flea markets, bargaining is expected.

Export Permits Antiques and Byzantine icons require an export permit (not normally given if the piece is of any value), but beautiful replicas can be
bought fairly cheaply, although even these require a certificate stating they are copies.

Opening and Office and shopping hours vary considerably and may also change
Closing Times according to the season. Check with your hotel for up-to-the-minute
information on opening and closing times. Below is a rough guide:

Banks are open weekdays 8–2; closed weekends and public holidays.

Museums and Archaeological Sites are open 8:30–3, with longer
hours in summer. Generally, museums are closed on Monday. Admission is free on Sunday. EU students enjoy free admission, students from other EU countries pay half the fee, and seniors often
get a discount as well. Hours vary from one site to another and often
change without notice; always check with tourist offices or travel
agencies before visiting. *See* Exploring, *below*, for hours, which
were correct at press time (spring 1994) but may change by summer.

Shops are open Tuesday, Thursday, and Friday, 9–2 and 5:30–8;
Monday, Wednesday, and Saturday, 9–2.

National January 1; January 6 (Epiphany); March 6 (Clean Monday); March
Holidays 25 (Independence); April 21 (Good Friday); April 23 (Easter Sunday); April 24 (Easter Monday); May 1 (Labor Day); June 11 (Pentecost); August 15 (Assumption); October 28 (Ochi Day); December
25–26.

Dining Greek cuisine cannot be compared to that of France, and few visitors
would come to Greece for its food alone. You'll certainly be able to
find a delicious and inexpensive meal, but don't look in hotel restaurants, where the menus usually consist of bland, unimaginative international fare (although it's only here that you will find a
reasonably priced fixed menu). The principal elements of Greek cuisine are such vegetables as eggplants, tomatoes, and olives, fresh
and inventively combined with lots of olive oil and such seasonings as
lemon juice, garlic, and oregano. While meat dishes are limited
(veal, lamb, and chicken being the most common), fish is often the
better, though more expensive choice, particularly on the coast.

Your best bet is to look for tavernas and *estiatoria* (restaurants) and choose the one frequented by the most Greeks. The *estiatorio* serves oven-baked dishes called *magirefta*, precooked and left to stand, while tavernas offer similar fare plus grilled meats and fish. The decor of both types of establishment may range from simple to sophisticated, with prices to match.

Traditional fast-food in Greece consists of the *giro* (slices of grilled meat with tomato and onions in pita bread), *souvlaki* (shish kebab), and pastries filled with a variety of stuffings (spinach, cheese, or meat)—but hamburgers and pizzas can now be found even on the smaller islands.

Mealtimes Lunch in Greek restaurants is served from 12:30 until 3. Dinner begins at about 9 and is served until 1 in Athens and until midnight outside Athens.

Precautions Tap water is safe to drink everywhere, but it is often heavily chlorinated. Excellent bottled mineral water, such as *Loutraki*, is available.

Dress Throughout the Greek islands you can dress informally for dinner, even at Expensive restaurants; in Athens, you may want to wear a jacket at some of the top-price restaurants.

Ratings Prices are per person and include a first course, main course, dessert (generally fruit and cheese or a sticky pastry, such as baklava), and the 12%–15% service charge. They do not include drinks. Best bets are indicated by a star ★.

Category	Athens/ Thessaloniki	Other Areas
Very Expensive	over 10,000 dr.	over 7,000 dr.
Expensive	6,000 dr.– 10,000 dr.	5,000 dr.–7,000 dr.
Moderate	3,500 dr.–6,000 dr.	2,500 dr.–5,000 dr.
Inexpensive	under 3,500 dr.	under 2,500 dr.

Lodging Most accommodations are in standard hotels, sometimes called motels. There are a number of "village" complexes, especially at the beaches, and as part of some hotels. On islands and at beach resorts, large hotels are complemented by family-run pensions and guest houses—usually clean, bright, and recently built—and self-catering apartment and bungalow complexes. In a very few places, there are state-organized "traditional settlements"—houses with guest accommodations in buildings that are representative of the local architecture.

Greek hotels are classified as Deluxe, A, B, C, etc. Within each category, which is set by the government, quality varies greatly, but prices usually don't. Still, you may come across an A-class hotel that charges less than a B-class, depending on facilities. In this guide, hotels are classified according to price. All Very Expensive and Expensive hotels are assumed to have air-conditioning, so our listings in these categories mention it only when it is absent. If a Moderate or an Inexpensive hotel is air-conditioned, this is indicated. All have been built or completely renovated during the past 20 years, and all have private baths.

Prices quoted by hotels usually include service, local taxes, and VAT. At many hotels, breakfast is included. At certain times, though, you can negotiate the price, sometimes by eliminating breakfast. The official price should be posted on the back of the door or inside a closet. Seaside hotels, especially those in the Very Expensive and Expensive categories, frequently insist that guests take half-board (lunch or dinner included in the price).

Ratings Prices quoted are for a double room in high season, including taxes and service, but not breakfast unless noted. Rates are the same throughout the country for each category. Best bets are indicated by a star ★.

Category	All Areas
Very Expensive	over 39,000 dr.
Expensive	22,000 dr.–39,000 dr.
Moderate	13,000 dr.–22,000 dr.
Inexpensive	under 13,000 dr.

Tipping There are no absolute rules for tipping. In restaurants, cafés, and tavernas, you should leave a tip for the waiter of around 10%. This should be left on the table for your waiter and not on the plate, where it will be taken by the head waiter. In hotels, tip porters 50 dr. or 100 dr. per bag for carrying your luggage—more in a top hotel. For taxi drivers, Greeks usually round off the fare. Hairdressers usually get 10% or slightly more. In legitimate theaters, tip ushers 50 dr. if you are shown to your seat. In movie theaters, tip about the same if you receive a program from the usher. On cruises, cabin and dining-room stewards get about 400 dr. per day.

Athens

Arriving and Departing

By Plane Most visitors arrive by air at **Ellinikon** Airport, about 10 kilometers (6 mi) from the city center. All Olympic Airways flights, both international and domestic, use the Western terminal next to the ocean. All other flights arrive and depart from the Eastern terminal on the opposite side of the airport.

Between the Airport and Downtown A blue-and-yellow coach service connects the two air terminals, Syntagma Square, Omonia Square, and Piraeus. Between Athens and the terminals, the express bus runs every 30 minutes 5:30 AM–12:30 AM (160 dr). The night express buses (200 dr.) run at irregular intervals; ask for a schedule from a Greek National Tourist Organization (GNTO) office. From the terminals to Piraeus (5 AM–12:20 AM) and between the terminals (6 AM–1:20 AM), the express buses run about every 45 minutes and cost 160 dr. In most cases it's easier to take taxis: about 1,400 dr. to Piraeus; 800 dr. between terminals; 1,200–1,500 dr. to the center, depending on which terminal. The price goes up by about two-thirds between midnight and 5 AM.

By Train Athens has two railway stations, side by side, not far from Omonia Square. International trains from the north arrive at, and depart from, Stathmos Larissis, (tel. 01/524–0646, -7, -8). Take trolley No. 1 from the terminal to Omonia Square. Trains from the Peloponnese use the marvelously ornate and old-fashioned Stathmos Peloponnisos (tel. 01/513–1601) next door. To Omonia and Syntagma squares, take bus No. 57. Since the phones are almost always busy and agents often don't speak English, it's easier to get information and buy tickets at a railway office downtown (Sina 6, tel. 01/362–4402, -3, -4, -5, -6; Filellinon 17, tel. 01/323–6747; or Karolou 1, tel. 01/524–0646, -7, -8).

By Bus Greek buses arrive either at Terminal A (100 Kifissou, tel. 01/512–4910) or Terminal B (Liossion 260, tel. 01/831–7153). From Terminal A, take bus No. 51 to Omonia; from Terminal B, take bus No. 24 downtown. International buses drop their passengers off on the street, usually in the Omonia or Syntagma Square areas or at Stathmos Larissis.

By Car Whether you approach Athens from the Peloponnese or from the north, you enter by the National Road and then follow signs for the center. Leaving Athens, routes to the National Road are well marked; signs usually name Lamia for the north and Corinth or Patras for the southwest.

By Ship Except for cruise ships, few passenger ships from other countries call at Piraeus, the port of Athens, 10 kilometers (6 miles) from Athens' center. If you do dock at Piraeus, you can take the metro right into Omonia Square. The trip takes 20 minutes and costs 100 dr. Alternatively, you can take a taxi, which may well take longer due to traffic and will cost around 1,000 dr.

Getting Around

Many of the sights you'll want to see, and most of the hotels, cafés, and restaurants, are within a fairly small central area. It's easy to walk everywhere.

By Metro An electric (partially underground) railway runs from Piraeus to Omonia Square and then on to Kifissia. It is not useful for getting around the central area. The standard fare is 75 dr. or 100 dr., depending on the distance. There are no special fares or day tickets for visitors, and there is, as yet, no public transport map.

By Bus The fare on blue buses and the roomier yellow trolley buses is 75 dr. Tickets should be purchased beforehand at one of the yellow kiosks, or from booths at one of the terminals. Validate your ticket on the bus by stamping it in the orange machine, or you may be fined 1,500 dr. Buses run from the center to all suburbs and suburban beaches until about midnight. For suburbs beyond central Kifissia, you have to change at Kifissia. Attica has an efficient bus network. Most buses to the east Attica coast, including those for Sounion and Marathon, leave from the KTEL terminal, Platia Aigyptiou on Mavromateon, at the corner of Patission and Alexandras avenues.

By Taxi Taxis are plentiful except during rush hours and rainstorms. But drivers seem to lead a maverick life—those without occupants often refuse to pick up passengers, while those with occupants often stop to pick up more. Although you will eventually find an empty taxi, it's often more successful to shout your general destination to one carrying passengers; if the taxi is going in that direction, the driver will pick you up. Be sure to note the fare on the meter, so you can subtract your charge from the original amount. Most drivers speak basic English and are familiar with the city center, though not necessarily with the suburbs. The meter starts at 200 dr. There is a 300 dr. minimum and a basic charge of 48 dr. per kilometer; this increases to 94 dr. between midnight and 5 AM. There is an additional 200 dr. charge for trips to and from the airport, and 100 dr. for trips to and from the port, the train stations, and the bus terminals. There is also a 40 dr. charge per item for baggage over 10 kilograms. Some drivers overcharge foreigners, especially on trips from the airport or from Piraeus; insist that they turn on the meter as soon as you get in, and make sure they use the high tariff ("Tarifa 2") between only midnight and 5 AM. You can also call a radio taxi, which charges you an additional 300 dr. for the pickup. Some reliable companies are **Kosmos** (tel. 01/490–6914, 01/492–0505, 01/493–3811, or 01/493–1304) and **Hellas** (tel. 01/643–3400, 01/643–2240, or 01/643–7198).

Important Addresses and Numbers

Tourist Information There are **Greek National Tourist Organization** offices at Karageorgi Servias 2, in the bank, tel. 01/322–2545; at East Ellinikon Airport, tel. 01/961–2722; at Ermou 1, inside the General Bank building, tel. 01/323–4130; and at Piraeus, NTOG Building, Zea Marina, tel. 01/413–5716.

Embassies U.S. (Vasilissis Sofias 91, tel. 01/721–2951); **Canadian** (Gennadiou 4, tel. 01/725–4011); **U.K.** (Ploutarchou 1, tel. 01/723–6211).

Emergencies **Police:** Tourist Police (tel. 171); Traffic Police (tel. 01/523–0111); and City Police (tel. 100). **Fire** (tel. 199). **Ambulance** (tel. 166). **Doctors:** Top hotels usually have one on staff; any hotel will call one for you. You can also call your embassy. **Dentist:** Ask your hotel or embassy. **Pharmacies:** Many pharmacies in the central area have someone who speaks English and knows all the usual medical requirements. Try **Marinopoulos** (Kanari 23, tel. 01/361–3051). For information on late-night pharmacies, tel. 107, or check the *Athens News* in the Useful Information section.

English-Language Bookstores **Pantelides** (Amerikis 9–11, tel. 01/362–3673); **Eleftheroudakis** (Nikis 4, tel. 01/323–1051); **Compendium** (Nikis 28, upstairs, tel. 01/322–1248); **Reymondos** (Voukourestiou 18, tel. 01/354–8188).

Travel Agencies **American Express** (Ermou 2, tel. 01/324–4975); **CHAT Tours** (Stadiou 4, tel. 01/322–2886); **Condor Travel** (Stadiou 47, off Omonia Sq., tel. 01/321–2453); **Travel Plan** (Christou Lada 9, tel. 01/323–8801, -2, -3, -4).

Guided Tours

Orientation Tours All tour operators offer a four-hour morning bus tour of Athens, including a guided tour of the Acropolis, for around 6,950 dr. Make reservations at your hotel or at a travel agency; besides those agents already mentioned, there are hundreds of others, many situated around Filellinon and Nikis streets off Syntagma Square.

Special-Interest Tours For those interested in folk dancing, there is a four-hour evening tour (May–September) for around 6,650 dr. that begins with a son et lumière (sound-and-light-show) of the Acropolis from Pnyx Hill and then goes on to a performance of Greek folk dances in the open-air theater nearby. Another evening tour offers a dinner show at a taverna in the Plaka area, after the son et lumière, for around 9,600 dr. Any travel agency can arrange these tours—and the excursions below—for you, but go first to **CHAT Tours** (*see* Travel Agencies, *above*) for reliable and efficient service.

Excursions The choice is almost unlimited. A one-day tour to Delphi will cost up to 14,900 dr., with lunch included; a two-day tour to Corinth, Mycenae, Nafplion, and Epidaurus, around 25,750 dr., with meals and accommodations included. A full-day cruise from Piraeus, visiting three nearby islands—Aegina, Poros, and Ydra—costs around

13,800 dr. (including buffet lunch on the ship), and a three-day classical tour to Delphi and the breathtaking Meteora monasteries costs from 62,000 dr. (including half-board in standard-class hotels).

Personal Licensed Greek guides are some of the best in Europe, each having
Guides completed a two-year course at the national guide school. All the major tourist agencies can provide English-speaking guides for personally organized tours. Only hire one licensed by the GNTO.

Exploring Athens

Athens is essentially a village that outgrew itself, spreading out from the original settlement at the foot of the Acropolis. Back in 1834, when it became the capital of modern Greece, the city had a population of fewer than 10,000. Now it houses more than a third of the Greek population—around 4 million. A modern concrete city has engulfed the old village and now sprawls for 388 square kilometers (244 square miles), covering almost all the surrounding plain from the sea to the encircling mountains.

The city is very crowded, very dusty, and overwhelmingly hot during the summer. It also has an appalling air-pollution problem, caused mainly by traffic fumes; in an attempt to lessen the congestion, it is forbidden to drive private cars in central Athens on alternate workdays. Despite the smog, heat, and dust, Athens is an experience not to be missed. It has a tangible vibrancy that makes it one of the most exciting cities in Europe, and the sprawling cement has failed to overwhelm the few striking and astonishing reminders of ancient Athens.

The central area of modern Athens is small, stretching from the Acropolis to Mount Lycabettos, with its small white church on top. The layout is simple: Three parallel streets—Stadiou, Venizelou (a.k.a. Panepistimiou), and Akademias—link two main squares—Syntagma and Omonia. Try to wander off this beaten tourist track to catch some of the real flavor of living Athens. Seeing the Athenian butchers in the central market near Monastiraki sleeping on their cold, marble slabs during the heat of the afternoon siesta may give you more of a feel for the city than seeing hundreds of fallen pillars.

Keep in mind that most museums and archaeological sites are free on Sundays and holidays. It usually costs 1,000 dr. to bring in a video camera, 500 dr. if you want to use a flash.

Numbers in the margin correspond to points of interest on the Athens map.

The Historic At the center of modern Athens is **Syntagma (Constitution) Square.**
Heart It has several leading hotels, airline and travel offices, and numer-
❶ ❷ ous cafés. Along one side of the square stands the **Parliament Building,** completed in 1838 as the royal palace for the new monarchy. In front of the palace, you can watch the changing of the vividly costumed **Evzone guard** at the **Tomb of the Unknown Soldier.** Amalias Avenue, leading out of Syntagma, will take you to the **National Gardens,** a large oasis in the vast sprawl of this largely concrete city.

Time Out There are several breakfast/lunch spots around Syntagma Square.
Brazilian, at Voukourestiou 1B, two blocks from the square, is ideal for a quick coffee and snack. **Jimmy's,** at Valaoritou 7 in a pedestrian zone, is also a popular place for a snack, with outside tables.

❸ Across the street, at the far end of the National Gardens, you will see the columns of the once-huge **Temple of Olympian Zeus.** This fa-

Academy, **15**

Acropolis, **8**

Acropolis Museum, **10**

Agora, **11**

Byzantine Museum, **22**

Evzone Guards' barracks, **19**

Hadrian's Arch, **4**

Hephaisteion, **12**

Little Cathedral, **14**

Mount Lycabettos, **23**

Museum of Agora Excavations, **13**

Museum of Cycladic Art, **21**

National Archaeological Museum, **18**

National Library, **17**

Odeon of Herod Atticus, **7**

Panathenaic Stadium, **5**

Parliament Building, **2**

Parthenon, **9**

Presidential Palace, **20**

Senate House of the University, **16**

Syntagma (Constitution) Square, **1**

Temple of Olympian Zeus, **3**

Theater of Dionysos, **6**

Athens

mous temple was begun in the 6th century BC, and, when it was finally completed 700 years later, it exceeded in magnitude all other temples in Greece. It was destroyed during the invasion of the Goths in the 4th century, and today only a few towering sun-browned columns remain. *Vas. Olgas 1, tel. 01/922–6330. Admission: 400 dr. Open Tues.–Sun. 8:30–3.*

❹ Nearby stands **Hadrian's Arch,** built at the same time as the temple by the Roman emperor. It consists of a Roman archway, with a Greek superstructure of Corinthian pilasters. Visiting heads of state are officially welcomed here.

❺ About three-quarters of a kilometer (a half mile) east, down Vasilissis Olgas, you'll come to the marble **Panathenaic Stadium** built for the first modern Olympic Games in 1896; it is a blindingly white, marble reconstruction of the ancient Roman stadium of Athens and can seat 80,000 spectators.

❻ From Hadrian's Arch, take Dionysiou Areopagitou, a few blocks west to the **Theater of Dionysos,** built during the 6th century BC. Here the famous ancient dramas and comedies were originally performed in conjunction with bacchanalian feasts. *Tel. 01/322–4625. Admission: 400 dr. Open daily 8:30–2:30.*

❼ A little farther along, on the right, you'll see the massive back wall of the much better preserved **Odeon of Herodes Atticus,** built by the Romans during the 2nd century AD. Here, on pine-scented summer evenings, the **Athens Festival** takes place. It includes opera, ballet, drama, and concerts (*see* The Arts, *below*). *Tel. 01/321–0219. It is not otherwise open to the public.*

❽ Beyond the theater, a steep, zigzag path leads to the **Acropolis.** After a 30-year building moratorium at the time of the Persian wars, the Athenians built this complex during the 5th century BC to honor the goddess Athena, patron of the city. It is now undergoing conservation as part of an ambitious 20-year rescue plan launched with international support in 1983 by Greek architects. The first ruins you'll see are the **Propylaea,** the monumental gateway that led worshipers from the temporal world into the spiritual world of the sanctuary; now only the columns of Pentelic marble and a fragment of stone ceiling remain. Above, to the right, stands the graceful **Temple of Wingless Victory** (or Athena Nike), so called because the sculptor depicted the goddess of victory without her wings in order to prevent her from flying away. The elegant and architecturally complex **Erechtheion temple,** most sacred of the shrines of the Acropolis and later turned into a harem by the Turks, has now emerged from extensive repair work. Dull, heavy copies of the infinitely more beautiful Caryatids (draped maidens) now support the roof. The Acropolis Museum houses five of the six originals, their faces much damaged by acid rain; only four are on display, since one is being restored. The sixth is in the British Museum in London.

❾ The **Parthenon** dominates the Acropolis and indeed the Athens skyline. Designed by Ictinus, with Phidias as master sculptor, it is the most architecturally sophisticated temple of that period. Even with hordes of tourists wandering around the ruins, you can still feel a sense of wonder. It was completed in 438 BC. The architectural decorations were originally picked out in vivid red and blue paint, and the roof was of marble tiles, but time and neglect have given the marble pillars their golden-white shine, and the beauty of the building is all the more stark and striking. The British Museum houses the largest remaining part of the original 162-meter (523-foot) frieze (the Elgin Marbles). The building has 17 fluted columns along each side and 8 at the ends, and these lean slightly inward and bulge to cleverly counterbalance the natural optical distortion. The Parthenon has had a checkered history: It was made into a brothel by the Romans, a church by the Christians, and a mosque by the Turks. The Turks also stored gunpowder in the Propylaea, and when this was hit by a Venetian bombardment in 1687, a fire raged for two days and 28 columns were blown out, leaving the Parthenon in its present condition. *Tel. 01/321–0219. Admission: 1,500 dr., joint ticket to Acropolis and museum. Open weekdays 8–6:45 (8–4:45 in winter), weekends and holidays 8:30–2:45.*

⑩ The **Acropolis Museum,** just below the Parthenon, contains some superb sculptures from the Acropolis, including the Caryatids and a large collection of colored *kore* (statues of women dedicated by worshipers to the goddess Athena, patron of the ancient city). *Tel. 01/ 323–6665. Admission: 1,500 dr., joint ticket to the Acropolis. Open weekdays 8–6:30 (8–3:30 in winter), weekends and holidays 8–2:30.*

On **Areopagus,** the rocky outcrop facing the Acropolis, St. Paul preached to the Athenians; the road leading down between it and the hill of Pnyx is called Agiou Pavlou (St. Paul). To the right stands the
⑪ **Agora,** which means "marketplace," the civic center and focal point of community life in ancient Athens. The sprawling confusion of stones, slabs, and foundations is dominated by the best-preserved
⑫ temple in Greece, the **Hephestaion** (often wrongly referred to as the Theseion), built during the 5th century BC. Nearby, the impressive Stoa of Attalos II, reconstructed by the American School of Classical Studies in Athens with the help of the Rockefeller Foundation,
⑬ houses the **Museum of the Agora Excavations.** *Tel. 01/321–0185. Admission: 800 dr. Open Tues.–Sun. 8:30–2:45.*

Stretching east from the Agora is the **Plaka,** almost all that's left of 19th-century Athens. During the 1950s and '60s, the area became garish with neon as nightclubs moved in and residents moved out. Renovation in recent years has restored the Plaka, and it is again lined with attractive red-tile-roofed houses and the vine-shaded courtyards of open-air tavernas and bars.

Below the Plaka, in Cathedral Square, stands a charming 12th-cen-
⑭ tury Byzantine church known as the "Old" or **"Little Cathedral,"** nestled below the vast structure of the 19th-century **Cathedral of Athens.** From here, a short walk up Mitropoleos will take you back to Syntagma.

Time Out Visit the **De Profundis Tea Room** in an old mansion at Hatzimichali 1 for pastries and a large variety of teas. **Kostis,** on the main square in Plaka at Kidathineon 18, is good for a Greek lunch—wild greens, roast chicken, *imam* (a spicy eggplant dish). It's the perfect place to people-watch, and you won't be overcharged for this prime location. Or, go around the corner to the kafenion **Glikis** at Aggelou Geronta 2 for an inexpensive Greek coffee or ouzo and a *mikri pikilia* (a small plate of appetizers, including cheese, sausage, olives, and dips).

Downtown If you walk along Venizelou Avenue (Panepistimiou) from the
Athens square, you will pass, on the right, three imposing buildings in Clas-
⑮ ⑯ sical style: the **Academy,** the **Senate House of the University,** and the
⑰ **National Library.** When you reach **Omonia Square,** a bedlam of touts and tourists, you are in the heart of downtown Athens.

⑱ Try to spare time to see the **National Archaeological Museum.** Despite being somewhat off the tourist route, a good 10-minute walk north of Omonia Square, it is well worth the detour. This is by far the most important museum in Athens. It houses one of the most exciting collections of antiquity in the world, including sensational archaeological finds made by Heinrich Schliemann at Mycenae, 16th-century BC frescoes from the Akrotiri ruins on Santorini, and the 6½-foot-tall bronze sculpture *Poseidon*, an original work of circa 470 BC, possibly by the sculptor Kalamis, which was found in the sea off Cape Artemision in 1928. *Patission 44 (28 Oktovriou Ave.), tel. 01/821–7717. Admission: 1,500 dr. Open Mon. 11–5, Tues.–Fri. 8–7 (8–5 in winter), weekends and holidays 8:30–3.*

⑲ **⑳** Alternatively, from Syntagma you can take Vassilissis Sofias Avenue along the edge of the National Gardens to reach the **Evzone Guards' barracks.** From here you can turn right onto Herodes Atticus, which leads to the **Presidential Palace,** the former royal palace, now occupied by President Constantine Karamanlis.

㉑ Or, you can cross the street and turn up Neofytou Douka to the **Museum of Cycladic Art.** The collection spans 5,000 years, with nearly 100 exhibits of the Cycladic civilization (3,000–2,000 BC), including many of the slim marble figurines that so fascinated artists like Picasso and Modigliani. *Neofytou Douka 4, tel. 01/722–8321. Admission: 250 dr. Open Mon. and Wed.–Fri. 10–4, Sat. 10–3.*

㉒ A little farther along Vassilissis Sofias is the **Byzantine Museum,** housed in an 1848 mansion that was built by an eccentric French aristocrat. Since the museum is undergoing renovation, not all its pieces are on display, but it has a unique collection of icons and the very beautiful 14th-century Byzantine embroidery of the body of Christ in gold, silver, yellow, and green. Sculptural fragments provide an excellent introduction to Byzantine architecture. *Vassilissis Sofias 22, tel. 01/721–1027. Admission: 500 dr. Open Tues.–Sun. 8:30–3.*

㉓ **Kolonaki,** the chic shopping district and one of the most fashionable residential areas, occupies the lower slopes of **Mount Lycabettos** and is only a 10-minute walk northeast of Syntagma; it's worth a stroll around if you enjoy window-shopping and people-watching. Three times the height of the Acropolis, Lycabettos can be reached by funicular railway from the top of Ploutarchou Street (the No. 23 bus from Kolonaki Square will drop you at the station; fare: 400 dr. round-trip; open daily 8:45 AM–midnight (Thurs. 10:30 AM–midnight). The view from the top—pollution permitting—is the finest in Athens. You can see all Athens, Attica, the harbor, and the islands of Aegina and Poros laid out before you.

Time Out Take a cappuccino break at one of the many trendy but friendly cafés, such as **Peros** or **Da Capo** at the start of the pedestrian zone off Kolonaki Square, or sip an ouzo with your *mezedes* (appetizers) on Mount Lycabettos at **I Prasini Tenta** (the Green Awning), with its resplendent view of the city and the Acropolis. To get there, take the funicular to the top and walk back down the road about 10 minutes.

Off the Beaten Track

Outside central Athens, on the slopes of Mount Ymitos (ancient Mount Hymettus), is one of the city's most evocative Byzantine remains, the **Kaisariani monastery.** Take a taxi or the No. 224 bus from the terminal on Akademias (across from the Municipal Cultural Center) for 6 kilometers (4 miles) east of central Athens until you pass through the working-class suburb of Kaisariani. The monastery is an additional 30-minute walk along the paved road that climbs Mount Ymitos. The well-restored 11th-century church, built on the site of a sanctuary of Aphrodite, has some beautiful frescoes dating from the 17th century. A few minutes' walk beyond the monastery, there are plenty of shady places under the trees where you can sit and contemplate the view over Athens. If you feel particularly energetic, you can continue walking up Mount Ymitos—the roads wind through the forested slopes for 19 kilometers (12 miles)—and take your pick of the many picnic spots. *Tel. 01/723-6619. Admission 500 dr. Open Tues.–Sun. 8:30–3.*

Beyond the port of Piraeus, the little harbor of **Mikrolimano** is famed for its many seafood restaurants—22 at last count—but has lost favor with some Athenians because its pretty, crescent-shaped harbor suffers from pollution. The delightful atmosphere remains intact, however, and the harbor is crowded with the small yachts of its enthusiastic clientele. While it's not a particularly cheap place to eat, the freshness and quality of the fish and seafood at the Mikrolimano matches any elsewhere in Greece. If you don't like seafood, you'll still be enchanted by the terraces of lovely houses tucked up against the sloping hillsides, the elegant yachts, and the sturdy fishing craft. To get there from Athens, take the subway from Omonia Square to Neo Faliron or a bus from Filellinon Street to the Neo Faliron train station; it's only five minutes' walk from there. Alternatively, a relatively expensive (1,800 dr.) taxi ride will take you 16 kilometers (10 miles) along the coastal road toward **Glyfada,** where the fish restaurants give you wonderful views of the Saronic Gulf.

Shopping

Gift Ideas Better tourist shops sell copies of traditional Greek jewelry, silver filigree, enamel, Skyrian pottery, onyx ashtrays and dishes, woven bags, attractive rugs (including *flokates*—shaggy wool rugs, often brightly colored), good leather items, and furs. Furs made from scraps are inexpensive. Some museums sell replicas of small items that are in their collections. The best handicrafts are sold in the **National Welfare Organization shop** (Ypatias 6) near the cathedral. Other shops sell dried fruit, packaged pistachios, and canned olives. Natural sponges, which are cheaper than those to be found in the United States, also make good gifts.

Antiques Many shops, especially on **Pandrossou Street,** sell small antiques and icons. Keep in mind, however, that there are many fakes around, and that you must have permission from the government to export genuine objects from the Greek, Roman, or Byzantine periods.

Shopping Areas The central shopping area lies between Syntagma and Omonia. The **Syntagma** area has good jewelers, shoe shops, and handicrafts and souvenir shops, especially along **Voukourestiou. Stadiou Street** is the best bet for men's clothing. Try **Ermou Street** for shoes and the fascinating small streets that lead off it for fabrics and housewares. Go to **Mitropoleos** for rugs and souvenirs. This is also the main furrier street, and most of the moderately priced fur shops are here, including **Hydra** (Mitropoleos 3–5) and **Voula Mitsakou** (Mitropoleos 7). Ermou runs west to **Monastiraki,** a crowded market area popular with Athenians. Below the cathedral, **Pandrossou** has antiques, sandals (an especially good buy), and inexpensive souvenirs. **Kolonaki** has the most expensive shops. Here you'll find unique jewelry by the famous **Ilias Lalaounis** (Panepistimiou 6), with **La Chrysoteque Zolotas** just down the street (Panepistimiou 10), and designer boutiques, such as **Gianni Versace** (Anagnostopoulou 3) and **Gianfranco Ferre** (Anagnastopoulou 4), as well as Greek designers like **Sotris** (Leventi 3), who offers creative yet classic fashions. For a broader selection, try **Bettina** (Voukourestiou 4) for women's clothing and **Artisti Italiani** (Kanari 5) for men's.

Flea Market The flea market, based on **Pandrossou** and **Ifestou streets,** operates on Sunday mornings and sells almost anything: secondhand clothes, daggers, cooking pots and pans, old books, guitars, *bouzouki* (stringed instruments), old furniture and carpets, and backgammon sets. Pontians—Greeks who lived in the former Soviet Union—sell Russian caviar, vodka, and table linen. However little it costs, you should haggle. Ifestou Street, where the coppersmiths have their shops, is more interesting on a weekday—and you can pick up copper wine jugs, candlesticks, cooking ware, etc., for next to nothing.

Dining

Be adventurous and go looking for the places that have at least half a dozen tables occupied by Athenians—they're discerning customers. Alternatively, if you would like a change of cuisine and don't object to higher prices, pick up a copy of the weekly English-language magazine, *Athenscope*, available at most bookshops and central kiosks. It lists all kinds of ethnic restaurants—from French to Lebanese to Chinese—with relevant addresses and telephone numbers. For details and price-category definitions, *see* Dining in Staying in Greece, *above*.

Very Expensive ★ **Bajazzo.** This elegant wood-paneled restaurant, serving perhaps the best and most creative cooking in Athens, is housed in a converted neoclassical mansion in fashionable Kolonaki. The food is exquisitely presented, and specialties include duck with sour cherries, salmon roulade, various game dishes—including pheasant, partridge, and red deer—and fillet of sole with smoked salmon mousse, mascarpone cheese, and chive sauce. The luscious desserts include pear cake with chocolate mousse. *Ploutarchou 35, Kolonaki, tel. 01/ 729–1420. Reservations advised. AE, DC, MC, V. No Sun. dinner.*

Expensive **Aglamair.** The most civilized and expensive of the fish restaurants lining the picturesque Mikrolimano harbor, this is also one of the best in Athens. It's practically on the water's edge, so you can dine watching the lights shimmer across the bay. The decor is cheerful but sophisticated, with red tablecloths and green-and-black chairs. The menu includes lobster, shrimp, prawns, octopus, and squid, as well as house specialties like the *saganaki garides* appetizer (fried cheese with shrimp) and *ekmek*, a dessert made with shredded wheat and ice cream. *Akti Koumoundourou 54–56, Mikrolimano, tel. 01/411–5511, -2, -3, -4, -5. Reservations advised. AE, DC, MC, V.*

La Fenice. For those staying near the coast, this is the place to spend a romantic evening dining on beautifully presented, imaginative Italian food. You'll feel well taken care of the minute you enter this soothing, elegant restaurant, which also offers al fresco dining in the courtyard. Try the spaghetti with lobster, rigatoni with partridge ragout, crayfish wrapped in pastry, fresh sea bass with onions, or fillet of beef with balsamic vinegar. There is a rotating dessert menu of 20 choices; if it's available, don't miss the sorbet made from lotus fruit. *Zisimopoulou 10, Glyfada, tel. 01/894–9454. Reservations required. AE, DC, V. No lunch. Closed Sun.*

Rose. Though it may be slightly out of the way for tourists, this bar-restaurant has become a favorite with Greek yuppies (media stars), political consultants, and young entrepreneurs. Despite the occasionally indifferent service, the food is excellent—carpaccio with parmesan, sliced fresh sea bream with minced red peppers, salmon in pastry with champagne sauce, and fresh ravioli with spinach. For dessert, skip the rather watery crème brûlée and sample the white and dark chocolate mousse instead. *Kifissias 227 in Anavrita shopping center, Maroussi (take any bus leaving center for Kifissia and get off near KAT hospital), tel. 01/612–3051, -3. Reservations advised. DC. No lunch. Closed Sun.*

Symposio. After a show at the nearby Herodes Atticus, sit in the glass-enclosed dining room, which is open to the garden in summer, and enjoy some interesting culinary combinations—crepes with caviar and smoked salmon, pasta with metsovone cheese, fillets of St. Peter fish with oysters, and duck livers with sauce made from myrtle berries. Desserts include American cheesecake (hard to find in Greece) and *negraki*, a chocolate cake made with rum and raisins and served with hot chocolate sauce. The menu changes weekly. *Erecthiou 46, Makriyianni, tel. 01/922–5321. Reservations advised. AE, MC, V. No lunch. Closed Sun.*

Moderate **Apotsos.** A famous ouzerie, close to Syntagma Square but hidden away down an arcade, this is an echoing barn of a place—truly Athenian in atmosphere. Politicians, journalists, and artists gather here at lunchtime. As well as ouzo, wine and beer are served, along with dishes of mezedes—though three or four of these will add up to a substantial meal. The walls are decorated with old advertisements; the tabletops are of well-worn marble. *Panepistimiou 10 in the arcade, Syntagma, tel. 01/363–7046. Reservations not necessary. No credit cards. Lunch only Mon.–Sat. (11:30–5).*

Botsaris. Tucked away in a residential area, this bustling corner restaurant is a welcome alternative to the usual pricey seafood spots. Try grilled octopus, fish soup with large chunks of seafood and shrimp, or one of many fresh catches—red mullet, sea bream, grouper. Service is friendly and prompt. *Zisimopoulou 24, Paleo Faliron, tel. 01/941–3022. Reservations not necessary. AE, DC, V. No lunch Mon.–Sat. No dinner Sun.*

Ideal. This old Athenian restaurant, which opened in 1922, has been refurbished with an art deco interior after a disastrous fire and still attracts Athenians of all ages, as well as students from the nearby university. It has an extensive menu featuring Greek and Continental dishes such as mincemeat kebab and lamb fricassee. *Panepistimiou 46, Omonia, tel. 01/361–4604 or 01/363–1000. Reservations not necessary. AE, DC, MC, V. Closed Sun.*

Kostoyannis. If you're looking for authenticity, this is the place to go. One of the oldest and most popular tavernas in the area, located behind the Archaeological Museum, it has an impressively wide range of Greek dishes—including excellent shrimp salads, stuffed mussels, rabbit stifado, and sautéed brains. *Zaimi 37, Exarchia, tel. 01/821–2496. Reservations advised in summer. No credit cards. Dinner only. Closed Sun.*

★ **Vlassis.** Relying on traditional recipes from Thrace, Roumeli, Thessaly, and the islands, the cooks here whip up Greek home cooking in generous portions. The best way to sample as much as possible is to order several appetizers for a meal (there are more than 20, all reasonably priced). Musts are the *fava*, a dip made with chick peas, olive oil, and onion, and the octopus *stifado* (like a stew), tender and sweet with lots of onions. Also good are the kebabs, the *seftalies*, a tasty mix of lamb liver bits and onions wrapped in intestines, oven-baked pork, and *katsiki ladorigani* (goat with oil and oregano). Fresh fish is also available, and for dessert, the baked quince is delicious. *Armatolon and Klefton 20, Ambelokipi, tel. 01/642–5337. Reservations advised. No credit cards. No lunch. Closed Sun. and mid-July–Aug.*

Xynos. Step into the courtyard of this Plaka taverna, and you walk into a time warp: Athens in the '50s. According to loyal customers, nothing's changed much since then, including the excellent food. Start with the classic appetizer of stuffed grape leaves, then move on to the taverna's forte—cooked dishes like lamb *yiouvetsi*, made with tiny noodles called *kritharakia;* livers with sweetbreads in vinegar sauce and oregano; and *tsoutsoukakia*, meat patties made from spicy sausage and liberally laced with cinnamon. In summer, tables move outside, and all year roving musicians charm the crowd of regulars as they croon ballads of yesteryear. *Aggelou Geronta 4, Plaka (entrance down walkway next to kafenion Glikis), tel. 01/322–1065. Reservations advised. No credit cards. No lunch. Closed weekends and part of July.*

Inexpensive **Eden.** This vegetarian restaurant, in a neoclassical Plaka house, serves vegetable pies and such hearty dishes as vegetable lasagna; quiche with potatoes, corn, and cauliflower; vegetable kebabs; and spinach with cheese, rice, and carrots—a welcome experience for those who are tired of seeing lamb roasted on a spit at every corner. *Lyceou 12, Plaka, tel. 01/324–8858. Reservations not necessary. AE, DC. Closed Tues.*

Karavitis. A neighborhood favorite, this taverna near the Olympic Stadium has outdoor garden seating and a winter dining room decorated with huge wine casks. In summer, try to arrive early to get a seat in the courtyard rather than on the sidewalk, which can be noisy. The classic Greek cuisine is well prepared, including pungent *tzatziki* (yogurt-garlic dip), *bekri meze* (lamb chunks in a spicy red sauce), and *stamnaki* (beef baked in a clay pot). *Arktinou 35 and Pausaniou 4, Pangrati, tel. 01/721–5155. Reservations not necessary. No credit cards. No lunch.*

★ **O Platanos.** Set in a picturesque corner of the Plaka, this is one of the oldest tavernas in the area. It has a shady courtyard for outdoor dining. Don't miss the oven-baked potatoes, the roast lamb, and the exceptionally cheap but delicious barrel *retsina*. Although it's extremely friendly, not much English is spoken. *Diogenous 4, Plaka, tel. 01/322–0666. Reservations not necessary. No credit cards. Closed Sun.*

★ **Vasilenas.** Longtime residents and frequent visitors rejoice in this vestige of the good old days, a family-run taverna that is probably still as good a bargain now as it was 60 years ago. The decor is minimal, and in summer the operation moves to the upper terrace. Come here ravenously hungry with friends, so you can do justice to the set menu of 16 dishes, brought in a steady stream to your table. Zesty shrimp *yiouvetsi* and prawn croquettes are two standouts, as is the new dessert called *tiganites*, a sort of fried bread filled with walnuts. *Etolikou 72, Agia Sofia, Piraeus, tel. 01/461–2457. Reservations required for groups and on weekends. No credit cards. No lunch. Closed Sun. and 2 weeks in Aug.*

Lodging

Since Athens is the starting point for so many travelers, its hotels are very full, and it's always advisable to reserve a room in advance. Both traditional and modern hotels can be found in the center of town and out along the seacoast toward the airport. Modern hotels are more likely to be air-conditioned in the heat of summer, but in winter, look for double-glazed windows; the center of Athens can be so noisy that it's hard to get a good night's sleep. Except where noted, breakfast is not included in the rate, though it is often provided—sometimes in the form of a lavish buffet. For details and price-category definitions, *see* Lodging in Staying in Greece, *above.*

Very Expensive

Andromeda Athens Hotel. Athens's newest luxury hotel caters to business travelers with a mixture of deluxe rooms, studios, suites, and penthouses. The spacious rooms have a salmon color scheme, with quilted headboards, wall-to-wall carpeting, minibars, and TVs (computers are available on request). The hotel is on a quiet street near the U.S. Embassy, and the bedrooms have double-glazed windows. The White Elephant Polynesian restaurant is excellent. If you happen to be Greek, please note that while you may not get first dibs on the rooms, the price drops by half. *Timoleondos Vassou 22, Mavili Sq., 11521, tel. 01/643-7302, -3, -4, fax 01/646-6361. 30 rooms with bath. Facilities: 2 restaurants, 2 banquet halls, convention space. AE, DC, MC, V.*

★ **Astir Palace.** Operated by Conrad Hotels since 1994, this 80-acre complex of three hotels on a pine-covered promontory has its own beach, helicopter pad, and breathtaking views over Vouliagmeni Bay. This is Greece's most prestigious seaside hotel, 25 kilometers (16 miles) from Athens, and staying here in summer, among tycoons and celebrities at play, carries a certain cachet. The Nafsika, built into the hillside, has the loveliest location, but prices are the same for all hotels, and American breakfast is included. *Laimos Vouliagmeni, 16671, tel. 01/896-0211, fax 01/896-2582. Aphrodite: 165 rooms with bath. Facilities: restaurant, bar, 2 lounges, outdoor pool. Nafsika: 165 rooms with bath. Facilities: restaurant, bar, outdoor pool. Arion: 165 rooms with bath, 77 bungalows. Facilities: 2 restaurants, bar, gym, indoor pool, children's outdoor pool. Hotel also has 4 tennis courts and meeting rooms. AE, DC, MC, V.*

Athenaeum Inter-Continental. One of Athens's plushest hotels, the Inter-Continental has a marble atrium lobby that boasts a private art collection and spacious rooms with sitting areas and marble bathrooms; ask for one with an Acropolis view. All floors except the eighth and ninth were recently renovated, and the suites have pantries and dining nooks. In the morning a shuttle takes guests to the airport, and the rest of the day until 9:30 PM it travels hourly between the hotel and Syntagma Square, 15 minutes away. *89–93 Syngrou Ave., Neos Kosmos, 11745, tel. 01/902-3666, fax 01/924-3011. 551 rooms with bath, including 38 suites. Facilities: 4 restaurants, 2 bars, health club, outdoor pool, secretarial services, meeting rooms. AE, DC, MC, V.*

Athens Hilton. Set in a commanding position on a hill near the U.S. Embassy, the Hilton is about a 20-minute walk from Syntagma Square. All rooms and suites have balconies, double-glazed windows, and fine views of either the Acropolis or Mt. Hymettos. All rooms were renovated in late 1993. On summer evenings, there's a poolside barbecue, and the Byzantine, open virtually all the time, has Sunday brunch for those who crave this distinctly non-Greek institution. *Vasilissis Sofias 46, Hilton area, 11528, tel. 01/725-0201, fax 01/725-3110. 453 rooms with bath, including 3 deluxe suites with Jacuzzi. Facilities: 2 restaurants, lounge, piano bar, outdoor pool with food and beverage service, shops. AE, DC, MC, V.*

Grande Bretagne. The G.B., as it is known, is centrally located on Syntagma Square. An internationally famous landmark and the hub of Athenian social life, this distinguished hotel had a face-lift in 1992 in an effort to bring back its grandeur from the days when Churchill was a guest. Ask for an inside room overlooking the courtyard to escape the noise of the traffic, or try one of the coveted Syntagma rooms with large balconies and Acropolis views. The hotel houses the G.B. Corner restaurant, where you may catch a glimpse of prominent national politicians taking a break from Parliament. *Syntagma Square, 10563, tel. 01/323-0251, fax 01/322-8034. 364 rooms with bath. Facilities: restaurant, 2 bars, lounge, secretarial services, meeting rooms. AE, DC, MC, V.*

Ledra Marriott. Between Athens center and the sea near the Inter-Continental, this is a popular chain hotel known for comfort and service well above the standard. The rooms, renovated in 1993, have a pastel color scheme, vast closet space, and armchairs and sofas. There is also the Executive Level, which offers fax, secretarial services, a private dining area, and separate check-in and checkout. Its cafés and restaurants are fashionable meeting places, and it is renowned for its variety of dining options: You can sample Polynesian fare beside a cascading waterfall at Kona Kai, enjoy Japanese delights at Teppanyaki, or graze at Zephyros's filling Sunday brunch. The rooftop swimming pool is spectacular. Shuttles run to and from Syntagma Square for groups. *Syngrou 115, Kallithea, 11745, tel. 01/934-7711, fax 01/935-9153. 259 rooms with bath, including a presidential suite. Facilities: 4 restaurants, outdoor pool, shops, meeting rooms, secretarial services. AE, DC, MC, V.*

St. George Lycabettos. High on the wooded slopes of Mount Lycabettos in upscale Kolonaki, this hotel has a splendid view. Getting there, however, involves a steep short walk or a ride up (remember, taxis are inexpensive). In 1992 plush new rooms and suites were added. The hotel has, as its trump card, Le Grand Balcon, a two-tiered rooftop restaurant with good food, a terrace, and a wonderful view. It also has an attractive ground-floor bistro. Continental breakfast is included in the price. *Kleomenous 2, Kolonaki, 10675, tel. 01/729-0711, fax 01/724-7610. 162 rooms with bath. Facilities: 2 restaurants, bar, outdoor pool, roof garden. AE, DC, MC, V.*

Expensive **Elektra Palace.** At the edge of Plaka, this hotel offers cozy rooms done in warm hues—complete with TV, balconies, and minibar—for comparatively low prices. Keep in mind that rooms from the fifth floor up are smaller, but have bigger balconies. The staff is helpful, the American breakfast abundant (and included in the price), and best of all you can spend hours by the rooftop pool, sipping wine while gazing upon the Acropolis. *Nikodimou 18, Plaka, 10557, tel. 01/324-1401, -2, -3, -4, -5, -6, -7, fax 01/324-1875. 106 rooms with bath. Facilities: restaurant, bar, pool, roof garden. AE, DC, MC, V.*

Ilissia Hotel. This small hotel located near the Hilton, was taken over in 1992 by Best Western. Although the rooms are rather functional, it is within walking distance of many fine restaurants and night spots. Continental breakfast is included in the price. *Mihalakopoulou 25, Hilton area, 10439, tel. 01/724-4051, fax 01/724-1847. 90 rooms with bath. Facilities: air-conditioning. AE, MC, V.*

Novotel Athenes. Although not central, this hotel is just a 10-minute walk to the rail station and the national museum. One of the city's better values, it has an elegant lobby and soundproof rooms with sofas, minibars and TVs. The rooftop pool is beside an Italian restaurant where, in summer, you can watch the sun set behind the Acropolis. *M. Voda 4-8, Vathis Sq., 10439, tel. 01/825-0422, fax 01/883-7816. 195 rooms with bath. Facilities: 2 restaurants, boutique, bar, pool, air-conditioning. AE, DC, MC, V.*

Moderate **Acropolis View Hotel.** This hotel in a quiet neighborhood below the
★ Acropolis has agreeable rooms, most with Parthenon views. The staff members who man the homey lobby are efficient and friendly, and major sights lie a stone's throw away. American breakfast is in-

cluded in the price. *Webster 10, Acropolis, 11742, tel. 01/921–7303, -4, -5, fax 01/923–0705. 32 rooms with bath. Facilities: bar (summer), roof garden, air-conditioning. AE, MC.*

Astor. A no-frills hotel near Syntagma Square, the Astor offers convenience and the usual amenities—TV, air-conditioning, room service—of a more expensive place. If possible, request a room from the sixth floor and up for a memorable view of the Acropolis. Continental breakfast is included in the price. *Karageorgi Servias 16, Syntagma, 10562, tel. 01/325–5111, fax 01/325–5115. 130 rooms with bath. Facilities: restaurant, bar, air-conditioning. AE, DC, V.*

Austria. This small, unpretentious hotel on Filopappou Hill, opposite the Acropolis, is ideal as a base for wandering around the heart of ancient Athens. It has no restaurant, but it is at the bottom of the moderate price range and is well worth considering. Continental breakfast is included in the quoted rate but is not required (600 dr. per person). *Mouson 7, Filopappou, 11742, tel. 01/923–5151, fax 01/924–7350. 37 rooms with bath. Facilities: most rooms have air-conditioning. AE, DC, MC, V.*

Inexpensive **Aphrodite Hotel.** This is near Syntagma and perfectly comfortable. With all the facilities of other, more costly hotels, it offers excellent value for the money, and buffet breakfast is included in the price. Don't be put off by its cold-looking entrance. *Apollonos 21, Center, 10557, tel. 01/323–4357, -8, -9, fax 01/322–5244. 84 rooms with bath. Facilities: bar, air-conditioning. AE, DC, MC, V.*

★ **Art Gallery Pension.** On a quiet side street near the Acropolis, this friendly place, much prized by visiting students and single travelers, draws a congenial crowd. The handsome house has an old-fashioned look with family paintings on the muted white walls, comfortable beds, hardwood floors, and overhead fans to make up for the lack of air-conditioning. Most rooms have balconies with views of Filopappou or the Acropolis. *Erecthiou 5, Koukaki, 11742, tel. 01/923–8376, fax 01/923–3025. 21 rooms with bath. Facilities: bar. No credit cards. Closed Nov.–Feb.*

Attalos Hotel. The market area, where the Attalos is located, is full of life and color by day, but deserted at night. The hotel is pleasant and well run and has an exceptionally fine view of the Acropolis and Mount Lycabettos. Try to get a room on the 5th or 6th floor or in the rear, where the street noise is less. *Athinas 29, Psiri, 10554, tel. 01/321–2801, -2, -3, fax 01/324–3124. 80 rooms with bath. Facilities: bar, roof garden (summer only). No credit cards.*

President. Perhaps the most inexpensive A-class hotel in Athens, the President is a favorite with athletic teams and tourist groups. The staff is helpful, and the rooms, though unexceptional, are quiet, air-conditioned, and have city views (the Acropolis is visible from the sixth floor and up). Taxis stop often at the hotel, and there are trolley and bus stops nearby for the 20-minute journey to the center. Rather than order at the bar, which is particularly expensive, you can get bottled water and snacks at a handy kiosk outside. Continental breakfast is included in the price. *Kifissias 43, Ambelokipi, 11523, tel. 01/692–4600, fax 01/692–4968. 513 rooms with bath. Facilities: restaurant, taverna, bar, outdoor roof pool. AE, DC, MC, V.*

The Arts

The **Athens Festival** runs from late June through September and includes concerts, recitals, opera, ballet, folk dancing, and drama. Performances are in various locations, including the open-air theater of Herodes Atticus at the foot of the Acropolis, nearby

Filopappou Hill, and Mount Lycabettos. Tickets are available a few days before the performance from the festival box office in the arcade at Stadiou 4 (tel. 01/322–1459). Admission ranges from 1,500 dr. to 10,000 dr.

Though rather corny, the **son-et-lumière** shows showcase the Acropolis with dramatic lighting and a brief narrated history. Performances are given nightly from April through October, in English, at 9 PM (the time is subject to change), and admission is 1,000 dr. The entrance is on Dionysiou Areopagitou, opposite the Acropolis, and from your seat on the top of Filopappou Hill, you have a clear view of the monuments.

Cultural activity has improved enormously with the opening in 1991 of the **Megaron Athens Concert Hall** (tel. 01/728–2333), with two auditoriums equipped with state-of-the-art acoustics. Daily listings are published year-round in *The Athens News*, available in hotels and newsstands. Both it and the weekly magazine *Athenscope* list concerts, exhibitions, and showings of films in English.

Concerts Concerts are given September through June at the Megaron by Greek and world-class international orchestras. Information and tickets are available from the **Athens festival box office** (Stadiou 4, tel. 01/322–1459) or from the Megaron itself (Vasilissis Sofias and Kokkali, tel. 01/728–2333) next to the U.S. embassy. Prices range from 1,000 dr. to 20,000 dr, with lower rates for students and children ages 8 to 18. Tickets go on sale a few weeks in advance but are sold out within hours for popular events. The best way to be sure of getting a seat is to stand in line on the first day of sales (or ask a patient local friend); you must go yourself if you want to use a credit card.

Opera The **Lyriki Skini Opera Company** has a winter season (Oct.–May) and a small—not very good—ballet season at the Olympia Theater (Akademias 59, tel. 01/361–2461). In summer they perform at the Herodes Atticus theater. The best seats cost about 5,000 dr.

Films Almost all cinemas now show foreign films, usually managing to show the latest Hollywood offerings within a few months of their New York and London openings. *The Athens News*, *Athenscope*, and *Greek News* list them in English. Downtown cinemas are the most comfortable and best equipped. Near Syntagma try the **Astor** (Stadiou 28, tel. 01/323–1297) or the **Apollon** (Stadiou 19, tel. 01/323–6811) or near Omonia, the **Ideal** (Panepistimiou 46, tel. 01/362–6720), which has the best seats in Athens. Unless they have air-conditioning, most cinemas close June–September, giving way to wonderful outdoor movie theaters, such as the **Thission** (Pavlou 7, tel. 01/342–0864 or 01/347–0980), where you have a view of the Acropolis as a backdrop, and **Cine Paris** (Kidathineon 22, tel. 01/322–2071) in Plaka. At both, the films change every few days, and you can order drinks from the bar during the screening.

Nightlife

Athens has an active nightlife, with hundreds of places offering some sort of entertainment, much of it distinctly Greek. One way to get a taste is to take an "Athens by Night" guided tour, which can be arranged for you by any good travel agent (*see* Important Addresses and numbers, *above*). If you want to go on your own, try a *bouzoukia*, or a taverna with a floor show. Tavernas with floor shows are concentrated in the Plaka area.

Be forewarned that you will have to pay for an overpriced, second-rate meal at most places. At the bouzoukia, there is usually a per-person minimum or a prix-fixe menu; a bottle of whiskey costs about 25,000 dr. The name, style, and quality of tavernas and bouzoukias change frequently. Ask your hotel for recommendations.

Tavernas   **Palia Taverna Kritikou.** Here's a fun, although touristy, taverna where there's room for you to indulge in Greek dances to the amusement of the few Greek customers. *Mnisikleous 24, tel. 01/322–2809 or 01/325–0092. Reservations advised. AE, DC, V. Moderate.*

Stamatopoulou Palia Plakiotiki Taverna. Here in a converted 1822 Plaka house you'll find good food along with an acoustic band of three guitars, bouzouki, and accordion playing old Athenian songs. Greeks will often get up and dance, beckoning you to join them, so don't be shy. *Lyceou 26, tel. 01/322–8722. Reservations unnecessary. DC, V. Inexpensive.*

Rembetika   **Anifori.** Rembetika, the blues sung by Asia Minor refugees who
Clubs   came to Greece in the 1920s, still enthrall Greeks, even young people with whom the music has come back in fashion. At this small upstairs club, the band usually starts off slowly, but by 1 AM, they're wailing their *aman* to a packed dance floor. You don't need to order a complete dinner; a bottle of wine or drinks will do. *Vas. Georgiou 47, Pasalimani, Piraeus, tel. 01/411–5819. Reservations advised. No credit cards. Closed Mon.–Thurs. and July–Sept. Moderate.*

Bouzoukias   **Diogenes Palace.** Currently the "in" place with Athenians who want to hear Greece's most popular singers like Leftheris Pantazis, Iannis Parios, and Konstantina; it's also the most expensive. *Leoforos Syngrou 259, Nea Smyrni, tel. 01/942–4267. Reservations required. AE, DC, MC, V. Closed Mon. and usually July–Aug. Expensive.*

Posidonio. Decadence reigns as diners dance the seductive *tsifteteli* with enthusiasm and order flower vendors to shower gardenias on their favorite singers. *Posidonios 18, Elliniko, tel. 01/894–1033. Reservations advised. No credit cards. Closed Mon. and June–Sept. Expensive.*

The Peloponnese

Suspended from the mainland of Greece like a large leaf, with the isthmus of Corinth as its stem, the ancient land of Pelops offers beautiful scenery—rocky coasts, sandy beaches, and mountains—and a fascinating variety of ruins: temples, theaters, mosques, churches, palaces, and medieval castles built by crusaders.

Legend and history meet in Mycenae, where Agamemnon, Elektra, and Orestes played out their grim family tragedy. This city dominated the entire area from the 18th to the 12th century BC, and may even have conquered Minoan Crete. According to Greek mythology, Paris, son of the king of Troy, abducted the beautiful Helen, wife of Menelaus, the king of Sparta. Agamemnon, the king of Mycenae, was Menelaus's brother. This led to the Trojan War in which Troy was defeated. The story of the war is told in Homer's *Iliad.* Following Heinrich Schliemann's discoveries of gold-filled graves and a royal palace during excavations in 1874, Mycenae has become a world-class archaeological site and, of all the sites in the Peloponnese, is most worthy of a visit.

Sparta, once a powerful city-state, is today, unfortunately, devoid of charm or character. Like Corinth, once the largest, richest, and most pleasure-loving city of ancient Greece, Sparta now appears

The Peloponnese

sadly lifeless and unattractive. Neither of these modern townships seems to bear any relation to their original vibrancy; Corinth, in fact, was destroyed by earthquakes in 1858 and 1928, and each time experienced a more practical and banal reconstruction, the last of which left it 5 kilometers (3 miles) from its original site.

During the Middle Ages, the Peloponnese was conquered by leaders of the Fourth Crusade and ruled as a feudal state by French and Italian nobles. It formed the cornerstone of Latin (Christian) power in the eastern Mediterranean during the 13th and 14th centuries. In 1821, when the bishop of Patras raised the standard of revolt against Turkish domination, the Peloponnese played a key role in the Greek War of Independence. Nafplion was, for a short time during the 1800s, the capital of Greece. Among the region's many fine contributions to humanity are the Olympic Games, begun in 776 BC in Olympia.

Getting Around

The best way to see all the important sights of the Peloponnese at your own pace is by car. If you take the car ferry from Italy to Patras, capital of the Peloponnese, or if you rent a car in Patras, you can tour the area on the way to Athens. Otherwise, your tour will begin in Athens. Take the route suggested in the itinerary below. You could encounter a shortage of hotel rooms in summer, especially at Nafplio, so plan in advance.

Guided Tours

CHAT Tours (4 Stadiou, Athens, tel. 01/322–2886) and **Wagons-Lits Travel** (Stadiou 5, Athens, tel. 01/324–2281) both organize tours in the Peloponnese. A four-day tour of the Peloponnese and Delphi, including the sites, a qualified guide, and accommodations at first-class hotels, costs around 84,000 dr. A two-day tour, again including accommodations, to Corinth, Mycenae, and Epidauros, will cost around 25,000 dr. A six-day grand tour of the Peloponnese, taking in all the main sites and with accommodations at the best available hotels, costs around 120,000 dr., but it is not offered as often.

Tourist Information

In Patras, visit the **Greek National Tourist Office** (Iroon Polytechniou 110, Glyfada, tel. 061/653–358) or the **American Express** representative at **Albatros Travel** (Othonos 48, tel. 061/220–993). The **Tourist Police** are at Patreos 53 (tel. 061/220–902, -3). There are many tourist agencies along this street; Albatros can help you with all travel arrangements, including boat excursions to the Ionian islands, yacht hire, car hire, and rail bookings. The **Olympic Airlines** office is at Ayios Andreou 16 (tel. 061/222–901). The **Automobile and Touring Club of Greece** (ELPA) has a branch office at Patroon Athinon 18 in Patras (tel. 061/425–411). In Olympia you'll find the **Tourist Office** at Kondili 75 (tel. 0624/23–100). The **Tourist Police** are at Spiliopoulou 15 (tel. 0624/22–550).

Exploring the Peloponnese

Eleven kilometers (7 miles) northwest of Athens, after you have passed the last houses of the Athenian urban sprawl, you'll come to the 6th-century monastery of **Daphni.** It was sacked in 1205 by Frankish crusaders, who later installed Cistercian monks from Burgundy to rebuild it. The monastery has superb mosaics. *End of Iera Odos, tel. 01/581–1558. Admission: 500 dr. Open daily 8:30–3.*

Descending from Daphni to the sea, you face the narrow straits of Salamis, where the Persian fleet of Xerxes was defeated in 480 BC by Sparta. Shortly beyond are the ruins of **Eleusis,** site of antiquity's most important harvest celebrations, the Eleusinian Mysteries, where participants underwent rites commemorating the gift of corn cultivation given by Demeter, goddess of grain. Now the area is unattractive, surrounded by factories and their pollution, and there is almost nothing left of the ancient Eleusis but a few fallen pillars and overgrown pathways. Admission to the site includes entrance to a small museum. *Iera Odos 2, tel. 01/554–6019. Admission: 400 dr. Open Tues.–Sun. 8:30–3.*

When you cross the **Corinth Canal,** about 84 kilometers (52 miles) from Athens, you will have entered the **Peloponnese.** Modern **Corinth** lies by the sea; the ancient Greek city stood higher up. An important ruin is the **Doric Temple of Apollo,** built during the 6th century BC and one of the few buildings that still stood when Julius Caesar decided to restore Corinth. In AD 51, St. Paul fulminated against the sacred prostitutes who served Aphrodite on the **Acrocorinth,** the peak behind the ancient city. A museum beside the ruins contains finds from the excavations. *Tel. 0741/31–207. Admission: 1,000 dr. Open daily 8:45–7 (8:45–3 in winter).*

Drive from the square of ancient Corinth or hire a taxi to take you to the tourist pavilion below the **Fort of Acrocorinth,** then continue on foot for 200 meters to explore the imposing Franco-Turkish fortifications. *Tel. 0741/31–207. Admission: 400 dr. Open daily 8:30–7 (8:30–3 in winter).*

Mycenae, 44 kilometers (28 miles) from Corinth, was the fabulous stronghold of the Achaean kings of the 13th century BC. Destroyed in 468 BC, it was forgotten until 1874 when German archaeologist Heinrich Schliemann, who discovered the ruins of ancient Troy, uncovered the remains of this ancient fortress city. Mycenae was the seat of the doomed House of Atreus—of King Agamemnon and his wife, Clytemnestra, sister of Helen of Troy, and of their tragic children, Orestes and Elektra. When Schliemann uncovered six shaft graves (so named because the kings were buried standing up) of the royal circle, he was certain that one was the tomb of Agamemnon. The gold masks and diadems, daggers, jewelry, and other treasures found in the graves are now in the Athens Archaeological Museum; the new local museum is dedicated to archaeological studies. Along with the graves, you'll find the astounding beehive tombs built into the hillsides outside the reconstructed wall, the **Lion Gate,** dating to 1250 BC, and the castle ruins crowning the bleak hill, all remnants of the first great civilization in continental Europe. The tombs, the acropolis, the palace, and the museum can all be explored for the cost of admission. *Tel. 0751/76–585. Admission: 1,000 dr. Open weekdays 8–7 (8–5 in winter), weekends and holidays 8–3.*

Moving south, 11 kilometers (7 miles) from Mycenae, you'll pass **Argos,** prominent during the 8th century BC, and the Cyclopean ramparts (huge, irregular stones) of **Tiryns.** One version of the legend has Tiryns as the birthplace of Hercules, but the present remains, including the walls, date mostly from the 13th century BC when Tiryns was one of the most important Mycenaean cities.

Farther on is **Nafplion,** a picturesque town below the Venetian fortifications. Modern Greece's first king lived for a year or two within the walls of the higher fortress when Nafplion was capital of Greece. His courtiers had to climb 999 steps to reach him; you can still climb the long staircase or drive up to the **fortress.** *Tel. 0752/28–036. Admission: 400 dr. Open weekdays 8–7 (8:30–4:45 in winter), weekends and holidays 8:30–2:45.*

The **Venetian naval arsenal** on the town square houses a museum crowded with Mycenaean finds. *Tel. 0752/27–502. Admission: 400 dr. Open Tues.–Sun. 8:30–3.*

Epidauros, 24 kilometers (15 miles) east of Nafplion, was the sanctuary of Asklepios, the Greek god of healing. You can visit the foundations of the temples and ancient hospital. The most important site is the ancient open-air theater, which seats 14,000. In summer, during the **Epidauros Festival,** ancient Greek plays are staged here (*see* The Arts, *below*). The theater merits a visit anytime of year. The acoustics are so good that you can sit in the top row and hear a whisper onstage. *Tel. 0753/22–009. Admission: 1,000 dr. Museum and theater open weekdays (except Mon. when museum opens at 10) 7:30–7 (7:30–5 in winter), weekends and holidays 8:30–7 (8:30–3 in winter).*

From here you can return to Athens along the coast, a lovely drive, or continue on to **Olympia** by way of the rugged mountains of Arcadia. The site of ancient Olympia lies a few kilometers from the sea, northwest of **Megalopolis,** where a huge assembly hall was built to hold the Ten Thousand representatives of the Arcadian League. The first Olympic Games were held in Olympia in 776 BC and continued to be celebrated every four years until AD 393, when the Roman emperor Theodosius I, with his Christian sensibility, banned these "pagan rites." Women were excluded from the games under penalty of death, although no one was ever executed. They always held their own games a few weeks prior. Archaeologists are still uncovering statues and votive offerings among the pine trees surrounding **Olympic Stadium** and the imposing **ruins of the temples of Zeus and Hera** within the sacred precinct. *Stadium tel. 0624/22–517, museum tel. 0624/22–529. Admission: 1,000 dr. museum; 1,000 dr. stadium. Stadium open weekdays 7:30–7 (8–5 in winter), weekends 8:30–3. Museum open same hours except Mon. 11–7 (11–5 in winter).*

The **International Olympic Academy,** 6.4 kilometers (4 miles) east, houses the **Museum of the Olympic Games,** with its collection of commemorative postage stamps and mementos. *Tel. 0624/22–544. Admission: 500 dr. Open weekdays 8–3:30, weekends 9–4:30.*

North of Olympia, 122 kilometers (76 miles) away, is **Patras,** the third-largest city in Greece, its main western port, and the hub of the business world in the Peloponnese. Walk up to the **Byzantine kastro,** built on the site of the ancient acropolis, to take a look at the fine view along the coast. The **Cathedral of St. Andrew's,** reputedly the largest in Greece and built on the site of the crucifixion of St. Andrew, is also worth exploring. Its treasure is the saint's silver-mounted skull, returned to Patras in 1964 after 500 years in St. Peter's, Rome. The cathedral is on the far west side of the harbor at the end of Ag. Andreou. Apart from the kastro and the cathedral, there is little of particular interest here. The city's prettiest features are its arcaded streets and its squares, surrounded by neoclassical buildings.

The shortest route back to Athens follows the National Road along the southern shore of the Gulf of Corinth, an exceptionally beautiful drive. You could instead cross the entrance to the gulf and visit Delphi (*see* Exploring in Mainland Greece, *below*) on your way back to Athens.

Dining and Lodging

Many of the hotels in the Peloponnese have good dining rooms, so try these as well as the usual tavernas serving their traditional Greek cuisine and fresh seafood. For details and price-category definitions, *see* Dining and Lodging in Staying in Greece, *above.*

Nafplion
Dining

Savouras. Fresh seafood is served in this unpretentious taverna overlooking the bay; it is generally regarded as one of the best fish restaurants in the area. Specialties are red mullet, pandora, and dorado. *Bouboulinas 79, tel. 0752/27–704. Reservations not necessary. No credit cards. Moderate.*

Karamanlis. This simple taverna near the courthouse is crowded at lunch with civil servants who come for its tasty though limited number of *magirefta* (dishes cooked in advance). The light fish soup makes a good appetizer, followed by *yiouvelakia* (meat-rice balls) with egg-lemon sauce, baked potatoes, wild greens, and barrel wine. Fresh fish is also available at very good prices. *Staikopoulou 13, tel. 0752/27–668. Reservations not necessary. No credit cards. Inexpensive.*

Lodging
★

Amalia. The attractive hotel occupies a fine neoclassical building in large gardens 3 kilometers (2 miles) outside town, on the sea, near ancient Tiryns. The public rooms are spacious and comfortable, the service attentive, and the swimming pool very inviting. With a beach nearby, this makes the ideal base for a relaxing stay, and a buffet breakfast is included in the price. *National Road to Argos outside Nafplion, 21100, tel. 0752/24–401, fax 0752/24–400. 171 rooms with bath. Facilities: restaurant, cafeteria, bar, outdoor pool, gardens. AE, DC, MC, V. Expensive.*

Xenia Palace. Compulsory half-board boosts the price, but Xenia Palace has an unbeatable location. It's the only hotel built within the citadel of Akronafplio. Rooms are spacious, the bougainvillea-framed pool overlooks the harbor, and in the lounge you can sip a pot of hot chocolate or coffee for under 300 dr. (the best deal in town) while gazing upon the isle of Bourtzi. Check out the bizarre elevator to the hotel, tunneled out of the rock. *Akronafplio 21100, tel. 0752/ 28–981, -2, -3, -4, -5, fax 0752/28–987. 111 rooms with bath, including 3 suites and 57 bungalows. Facilities: restaurant, bar, pool. AE, MC, V. Expensive.*

Dioscouri. Located above the old town, with a fine view across the gulf of Nafplion, this family-run hotel is cool and quiet, and Continental breakfast is included in the price. *Zigomala 6, 21100, tel. 0752/28–550, fax 0752/21–202. 51 rooms with bath. No credit cards. Inexpensive.*

Olympia
Dining

Pete's Den. Owned by a Greek-German couple, this restaurant mixes traditional Greek and German cuisines, with sensational results. *Saganaki* (the name refers to the oval platter in which it is baked) is served hot and bubbling with cheese and brandy, and the toasted bread—complete with hot garlic butter—is a delightful change from the usual heavy white bread. *Main St., tel. 0624/22–066. Reservations not necessary. No credit cards. Closed Nov.–Feb. except Dec. weekends. Inexpensive.*

Thraka. This family-run taverna has a large variety of home-cooked Greek food including *lahanokeftedes* (fried vegetable balls), *arnaki giouvetsi* (lamb with bite-size noodles), *kokkinisto* (beef in red sauce), and *stifado* (beef stew with onions) made the old-fashioned way, with vinegar and garlic. Desserts are from the family's nearby pastry shop. Off-season, the cook (and family matriarch) will still prepare meals for you; just give her a call. *Main St., tel. 0624/22–575; off-season, 0624/22–475. Reservations not necessary. AE, DC, MC, V. Closed Nov.–Mar. Inexpensive.*

Lodging
★

Amalia. Pleasantly situated a little outside the village near the museum, the Amalia is comfortable and well run. Unfortunately, the Greek- and European-style fare in the restaurant is served with little panache, but the other facilities of the hotel make up for this drawback. *Pirgos-Olympia Rd., 27065, tel. 0624/22–190, -1, fax 0624/22–444. 160 rooms with bath. Facilities: restaurant, bar, jewelry shop, pool, roof garden. AE, DC, MC, V. Expensive.*

Altis. The Altis is reasonably priced and in a convenient location, opposite the old museum and near the archaeological site. The rooms have balconies and plenty of light, and the garden is ideal for enjoying the restaurant's hearty *spesiota* (perch baked with onion). Continental breakfast is included in the price. *Platia Dimarchiou (town hall sq.), 27065, tel. 0624/23–101, -2, fax 0624/22–525. 61 rooms with bath. Facilities: cafeteria-style restaurant, air-conditioning. AE, DC, MC, V. Closed Nov.–Mar. Moderate.*

Hotel Europa. Run by the friendly Spiliopoulos family, this Best Western hilltop hotel overlooks ancient Olympia, the Arcadian mountains, Alfios valley, and the sea in the distance. Rooms have large beds, flokati rugs, and marble bathrooms. Most face the pool, but try to book one of the six that look onto the archaeological site. Buffet breakfast is included in the price. *Off rd. to ancient Olympia, at Oikismou Drouba, 27065, tel. 0624/22–650 or 0624/22–700, fax 0624/23–166. 42 rooms with bath. Facilities: restaurant, bar,* taverna *(summer), tennis court, horseback riding, pool, air-condi-tioning. AE, DC, MC, V. Moderate.*

Patras
Dining

Kalypso. One of the newer and better restaurants, with garden seat-ing, Kalypso offers fresh grilled red mullet and dorado, its special-ty, *midia saganaki* (mussels with fried cheese), and a lemon-fish soup, in addition to grilled meats and the usual Greek *magirefta.* The wine list features several Patras vintages as well as barrel wine. Top it off with baked apple with whipped cream. *Iroon Politechniou 74, tel. 061/432–944. Reservations advised. AE, DC, MC, V. Moder-ate.*

Faros. During the day, the owner is out hauling in his catch, which he serves up to locals the same night. If it's atmosphere you want, forget it. This is a bare-bones, often noisy place, without a menu or even tablecloths, but it serves the freshest fish at the lowest prices. Nobody speaks English, but all you have to do is point (you pay by the kilo), round out your meal with a Greek salad, sit back and enjoy. *Othonos-Amalias 101, tel. 061/336–500. Reservations not neces-sary. No credit cards. No lunch. Inexpensive.*

Trikoyia. Down by the port, the Trikoyia family cooks delicious food in its traditional taverna, where a typical menu showcases *kalofaga* (beef baked with ham) and fresh grilled fish. Enjoy the ocean view as you complete your meal with a piece of baklava. *Amalias 46, tel. 061/279–421. Reservations not necessary. AE, DC, MC, V. Inex-pensive.*

Lodging

Astir. Recently renovated, this large hotel enjoys an excellent loca-tion on the waterfront near the center of town. Spacious and pleas-ant, it looks out on the busy harbor and to the mountains across the gulf. Continental breakfast is included in the price. *Ag. Andreou 16, 26223, tel. 061/277–502, fax 061/271–644. 120 rooms with bath (about 30 with TV). Facilities: restaurant, roof garden, bar, outdoor pool, conference rooms, sauna, air-conditioning. AE, DC, V. Ex-pensive.*

★ **Porto Rio.** There's a large and varied selection of rooms and cottages with a wide range of prices at this hotel complex on the sea at Rion, about 8 kilometers (5 miles) from Patras. Rooms over the front have outstanding views across the narrow entrance to the Gulf of Cor-inth. Continental breakfast is included in the price. *National Road, 26500, tel. 061/992–212, fax 061/992–115. 267 rooms and cottages with bath. Facilities: 2 restaurants, outdoor pool, 4 tennis courts, children's playground, air-conditioning. AE, DC, MC, V. Moder-ate–Expensive.*

The Arts

The **Festival of Ancient Drama** in the theater at Epidauros takes place from mid-July to mid-September, weekends only, at 9 PM. Tickets can be bought either at the theater itself before performances or in advance from the festival box office at Stadiou 4, Athens, tel. 01/322–1459. Patras also stages a lively summer arts festival. Check with the Greek National Tourist Office (061/653–358, -9) for details. You're in for a treat if you're in Patras for Carnival. In the several weeks be-fore Lent there are masquerade balls, fireworks, and on the last Sun-day the Grand Parade, with entrants competing for the best costume. Buy tickets for seats at the Grand Parade (3,000 dr.) at the Carnival office in the Municipal Cultural Center (Koryllon 1, tel. 061/226–063).

Mainland Greece

The dramatic rocky heights of mainland Greece provide an appropriate setting for man's attempt to approach divinity. The ancient Greeks placed their gods on snowcapped Mount Olympus and chose the precipitous slopes of Parnassus, "the navel of the universe," as the site for Delphi, their most important religious center. Many centuries later, pious Christians built a great monastery (Ossios Loukas) in a remote mountain valley. Others settled on the rocky mountain peninsula of Athos, the Holy Mountain. Later, devout men established themselves precariously on top of strange, towerlike rocks and, to be closer to God, built monasteries like those at Meteora. In fact, many of mainland Greece's most memorable and interesting sites are closely connected with religion—including the remarkable Byzantine churches of Thessaloniki.

In this land of lonely mountain villages, narrow defiles, and dark woods, bands of *klephts* (a cross between brigands and guerrillas) earned their place in folk history and song during the long centuries of Turkish rule. The women of Souli, one of the mountain strongholds of the klephts, threw themselves dancing and singing over a cliff rather than be captured by the Turks. From these same mountains during the German occupation of World War II, guerrilla bands descended to the valleys and plains to harry and attack the occupying army and drive it from their land.

Since Greece joined the European Union farmers have flourished, and few villages, even those tucked away in the hills, are still poor and isolated. But despite the arrival of video clubs and discos, the traditional way of life still survives. This is a beautiful area to explore. The mainland Greeks see fewer tourists and have more time for those they do see, hotels are unlikely to be full, and the sights— steep, wooded mountains, cypress trees like candles, narrow gorges, the soaring monasteries of Meteora—are beautiful.

Getting Around

This proposed itinerary begins in Athens. It can be done by public transportation, car, or guided tour. A one-day trip to Delphi is rushed; two days will give you more leisure time. Your best bet is a three-day trip that includes Delphi and Meteora. The five-day tour takes in more remote parts of western Greece, Epirus, and other main sights. A longer trip through the mainland should include Ossios Loukas. Thessaloniki is usually included only in lengthy guided tours of northern Greece. If you don't have a car, you can leave the Delphi–Meteora tour at Trikala, take the train to Thessaloniki, and return to Athens by plane or train. In September, during the Thessaloniki International Trade Fair, make hotel reservations well in advance.

Guided Tours

Travel agencies in Athens with tours of mainland Greece include **American Express** (Ermou 2 and in the Hilton Hotel), **CHAT Tours** (Stadiou 4), and **Key Tours** (Kallirois 4, in the Royal Olympic Hotel). American Express also has a representative in Thessaloniki at **Doucas Travel** (Eleftherios Venizelou 8, tel. 031/224–100 or 031/269–984, -5, -6, fax 061/286–610). A one-day tour to Delphi, with lunch, costs around 14,900 dr., without lunch 12,900 dr. A three-day trip to Delphi and Meteora with half-board (hotel, breakfast, and lunch or

Mainland Greece

dinner) ranges between 56,950 and 62,750 dr. A six-day Macedonia tour, including Delphi, Meteora, Thessaloniki, Philippi, Kavala, Pella, and Vergina costs around 147,000 dr. with half-board accommodations.

Tourist Information

In **Delphi,** visit the Delphi Tourist Office on Friderikis 44 for helpful service (tel. 0265/82–900); the Tourist Police is at Apollonos 46 (tel. 0265/82–220). At **Kalambaka,** the Tourist Police can be found at Hatzipetrou 10–11 (tel. 0432/22–813). In **Thessaloniki,** visit the Greek National Tourist Office (Mitropoleos 34 on Platia Aristotelous, tel. 031/222–935, or at the airport, tel. 031/421–170); here, the Tourist Police is at Egnatia 10 (tel. 031/251–662 or 031/251–835).

Exploring Mainland Greece

To get from Athens to Delphi, take the National Road toward Thessaloniki and turn off to **Thebes** (Thiva), the birthplace of the legendary Oedipus, who unwittingly fulfilled the prophesy of the Delphic Oracle by slaying his father and marrying his mother. Little now remains of the ancient city. At **Livadia,** 45 kilometers (28 miles) farther along the road, the ruins of a medieval fortress tower above the springs of Lethe (Oblivion) and Mnemosyne (Remembrance). Halfway between Livadia and Delphi is the crossroads where, according to mythology, Oedipus killed his father.

The road to the left leads to a serene upland valley and the **Monastery of Ossios Loukas,** a fine example of Byzantine architecture and decoration. Built during the 11th century to replace the earlier shrine of a local saint, it has some of the world's finest Byzantine mosaics. *Tel. 0267/22–797. Admission: 600 dr. Open daily 8–7 (8–5 in winter).*

Back on the road to Delphi, you'll climb a spur of Mount Parnassus to reach the village of **Arahova,** 32 kilometers (20 miles) from Livadia, known for handmade items in brightly colored wools, especially rugs. From Arahova, a short, spectacular drive down to Delphi will take you across the gorge of the Pleistos. You'll see a great cliff called the Phaedriades split by the **Castalian spring,** which gushes with cool, pure water. It was here that pilgrims to the Delphic Oracle came for purification.

The ancient Greeks believed that **Delphi** was the center of the universe because two eagles released by the gods at opposite ends of Earth met here. For hundreds of years, the worship of Apollo and the pronouncements of the Oracle here made Delphi the most important religious center of ancient Greece. As you walk up the Sacred Way to the **Temple of Apollo,** the **theater,** and the **stadium,** you'll see Mount Parnassus above; silver-green olive trees below; and, in the distance, the blue Gulf of Itea. This is one of the most rugged and lonely sites in Greece, and one of the most striking; if you can get to the site in the early morning or evening, avoiding the busloads of tourists, you will feel the power and beauty of the place. You may even see an eagle or two. First excavated in 1892, most of the ruins date from the 5th to the 3rd century BC. *Tel. 0265/82–313. Admission: 1,000 dr. Open Tues.–Fri. 8–7 (7:30–5:30 in winter), Mon. 11–7 (11–5:30 in winter), weekends and holidays 8–3.*

Don't miss the famous bronze charioteer (early 5th century BC) in the **Delphi Museum.** Other interesting and beautiful works of art here include a statue of Antinoüs, Emperor Hadrian's lover; pediments from the Temple of Apollo; the statues of Kleobis and Viton who, according to legend, pulled their mother 80 kilometers (50 miles) by chariot to the Temple of Hera so she could worship, then died from exhaustion; and the stone *omphalos*, representing the navel of the earth. Don't miss the delicate ivory statuettes and the bull made out of silver leaf; both are in an air-conditioned inner gallery. *Tel. 0265/82–313. Admission: 1,000 dr. Open Tues.–Fri. 8–7 (7:30–5:30 in winter), Mon. 11–7 (11–5:30 in winter), weekends and holidays 8–3.*

From Delphi, the road descends in sharp bends past groves of gnarled, ancient olive trees. Continue 17 kilometers (11 miles) to Amfissa and over the Pournaraki (Bralos) Pass to the town of **Lamia.** Follow the road to Karditsa and around the Thessalian plain to Trikala. You will then arrive at **Kalambaka** (139 kilometers, or 86 miles, from Lamia), the base for visits to the monasteries of **Meteora,** which sit atop gigantic rocks above the town. Monks and supplies once reached the top of the slopes by ladders or baskets. Today steps are cut into the boulders, and some of the monasteries can easily be reached by car. Not all of them are open to the public, however. Of the original 24 monasteries, only six can now be visited. Female visitors should wear skirts to the knee, not shorts, and men should wear long pants.

The fortresslike **Varlaam** monastery is easy to reach and has beautiful Byzantine frescoes. To get a better idea of what living in these monasteries was like 300 years ago, climb the steep rock steps to the

Megalo Meteoron, the largest of the monasteries. Make sure that you allow time for the trek up if it's nearing closing hours. The monasteries are all closed during midday. The hours vary from place to place, but they are generally open 9–1 and 3–6, although to complicate matters Varlaam is closed on Friday and Megalo Meteoron on Tuesday. *Tel. 6432/22–270 (Megalo Meteoron), 0432/22–277 (Varlaam). Admission: 400 dr. each.*

En route to Thessaloniki, the road east from Trikala crosses the plain of Thessaly (one of Europe's hottest places during the summer) and joins the National Road at Larissa. Eventually you will see Mount Olympus, Greece's highest mountain. The road runs for 154 kilometers (96 miles) through the valley of Tempe and then goes up the coast to **Thessaloniki**—Greece's second-largest city, its second port after Piraeus, and the capital of northern Greece. It is the cocapital of the country as a whole; as a shopping center it is possibly superior to Athens.

Although Thessaloniki still has some remains from the Roman period, it is best known for its fine Byzantine churches. The city is compact enough for you to see the main sights on foot. Start at the 15th-century grayish **White Tower,** landmark and symbol of Thessaloniki, previously named "Tower of Blood," referring to its use as a prison. Now it temporarily houses a museum, with an exhibition on the history and art of Byzantine Thessaloniki, including pottery, mosaics, and ecclesiastical objects. *Pavlou Mela and Nikis, tel. 031/267–832. Admission: 500 dr. Open Mon. 10:30–5, Tues.–Fri. 8–7 (8–5 in winter), weekends 8:30–3.*

Then walk up Pavlou Mela toward Tsimiski, the elegant tree-lined shopping street, and cut across to the green-domed basilica-style church of **Aghia Sophia,** which dates from the 8th century and has beautifully preserved mosaics.

Walk to Egnatia, which partially traces the original Roman road leading from the Adriatic to the Bosphorous. Continue north along the **Roman Agora** (town center) to **Agios Dimitrios,** the principal church. Though it is only a replica of the original 7th-century church that burned down in 1917, it is adorned with many 8th-century mosaics that were in the original building. Follow Aghiou Dimitriou east to **Agios Georgios,** a rotunda built by Roman emperor Galerius as his tomb during the 4th century AD. His successor, Constantine the Great, the first Christian emperor, turned it into a church. If the current restoration has been completed and it's open, have a look at the superb 4th-century mosaics of flowers, birds, and fish.

Return to Egnatia and the **Arch of the Emperor Galerius,** built shortly prior to the rotunda to commemorate the Roman victories of Galerius over forces in Persia, Armenia, and Mesopotamia. A short walk downhill to Tsimiski, where you turn left, will eventually bring you to the **Archaeological Museum.** Among its many beautiful objects are a huge bronze vase and a delicate, gold myrtle wreath from Derveni, as well as gold artifacts from recent excavations of the royal tombs of Vergina, including a 10-kilogram gold casket standing on lions' feet that contains bones thought to be those of Philip II, father of Alexander the Great. *Platia Hanth, tel. 031/830–538. Admission: 1,000 dr. Open Mon. 10:30–7 (10:30–5 in winter), Tues.–Fri. 8–7 (8–5 in winter), weekends and holidays 8:30–3.*

Dining and Lodging

For details and price-category definitions, *see* Dining and Lodging in Staying in Greece, *above*.

Delphi **Topiki Gefsi.** Traditional Greek cuisine, with many local specialties,
Dining is what this excellent *mezedopolion* (a place serving appetizers) offers. In winter, warm yourself at the fireplace while listening to
nightly piano music; in summer, dine on the veranda overlooking
Delphi. Especially good are the regional *kokkora krasato* (rooster
stewed in wine), pork with celery, *hortopites* (vegetable pies), lamb
on the spit, and lamb *kleftiko* (baked in a pastry shell with vegetables). Seafood is occasionally available, as is another house specialty, *mides saganaki* (mussels in fried cheese). *Vas. Pavlou and
Friderikis 19, tel. 0265/82–480. Reservations not necessary. AE,
DC, MC, V. Moderate.*

Dining and **Kastalia.** Designed to fit in with the other village houses, Fedriades'
Lodging sister hotel has simple rooms with paintings of the area and views
either over Mt. Parnassus or to the Corinthian gulf. The restaurant
is quite good, serving Greek food with a twist; lamb *fricassee*, for
example, has lettuce rather than the typical cabbage. Be sure to
sample the local sweet cheese, *formaella*. Continental breakfast is
included in the price. *Vas. Pavlou and Friderikis 13, 33054, tel.
0265/82–205, -6, -7, fax 0265/82–208. 26 rooms with bath. Facilities:
restaurant. AE, DC, MC, V. Closed weekdays Nov.–Mar. Moderate.*

Lodging **Hotel Vouzas.** The hotel sits on the edge of a gorge and has wonderful
★ views from every room. It was renovated in 1991, with air-conditioning added, and buffet breakfast is included in the price. There's a
cozy living room with a fireplace, which fills up on winter weekends
with Athenians who come to ski Mt. Parnassus. *Vas. Pavlou and
Friderikis 1, 33054, tel. 0265/82–232, fax 0265/82–033. 59 rooms
with bath. Facilities: restaurant. MC, V. Expensive.*

Apollo. This delightful hotel is owned and operated by a husband-
and-wife team—"She's the decorator; I do the public relations,"
says he. The *saloni* (living room) has traditional wall hangings and
old prints among its carefully selected furnishings. The light wood
furniture in the cheerful bedrooms is set off by blue quilts and
striped curtains. Many rooms have wood balconies with black-iron
railings, all have hair dryers (rare in country hotels), and a full
breakfast is included in the price. *Vas. Pavlou and Friderikis 59B,
33054, tel. 0265/82–580 or 0265/82–244, fax 0265/82–455. 21 rooms
with bath. Facilities: bar, breakfast room, air-conditioning. MC, V.
Closed weekdays Oct.–Mar. except Christmas and Carnival. Moderate.*

Fedriades. Named after Delphi's famous rocks, this 1992 hotel has a
neoclassical exterior, which gives way to a light, airy lobby and
rooms done in marble and wood with views of the Gulf of Itea. Buffet
breakfast is included in the price. *Vas. Pavlou and Friderikis 38,
33054, tel. 0265/82–919 or 0265/82–370, fax 0265/82–208. 24 rooms
with bath. Facilities: cafeteria, bar. AE, DC, MC, V. Closed weekdays Nov.–Mar. Moderate.*

Kalambaka **Gertzos.** A local favorite since 1925, this family restaurant relies on
Dining the cooking of matriarch Ketty Gertzos, who prepares such succu-
★ lent dishes as *tsoutsoukakia smirnaika* (spicy meat patties Smyrna
style), rabbit stew, and chicken in wine with green peppers and garlic. The wine list is heavily regional. *Ekonomou 4, on town hall sq.,
tel. 0432/22–316. Reservations not necessary. No credit cards.
Closed Nov.–Mar. Inexpensive.*

Lodging
★ **Motel Divani.** Below the Meteora is a hotel (in spite of its name) that is more comfortable than you might expect to find so far off the beaten path. Rooms are quiet and air-conditioned; those in the back have a view toward Meteora. American breakfast is included in the price. *Trikalon 1, 42200, tel. 0432/22-583, fax 0432/23-638. 165 rooms with bath. Facilities: restaurant, snack bar, outdoor pool with summer bar. AE, DC, MC, V. Expensive.*

Hotel Edelweiss. Bright and clean, this hotel shines like a new pin. Its comfortable rooms (with TVs) look out over the swimming pool to the daunting Meteora rocks towering beyond. The hotel bar is a lively and crowded local meeting spot. *E. Venizelou 3, 42200, tel. 0432/23-966, fax 0432/24-733. 50 rooms with bath. Facilities: restaurant, outdoor pool, snack bar, disco, air-conditioning. MC, V. Inexpensive.*

Thessaloniki
Dining

Vita-Vita. For a romantic evening made memorable by a flawless meal, try this trendy favorite, where there's a decidedly French influence. Don't miss the fresh mushrooms in parsley-and-fennel sauce before moving on to lamb with artichokes in an egg-lemon sauce, or the fresh salmon diablo, followed perhaps with Vita-Vita's famous profiteroles, made with a hard chocolate sauce. There's an extensive wine list—French, Greek, and California vintages—and nightly piano music sets the mood. *Tsimiski 46, tel. 031/287-443. Reservations advised. DC, MC. Open for dinner Mon.–Sat. Closed July–Aug. Expensive.*

Krikelas. A Thessaloniki landmark, this family-run taverna has been serving classic Greek dishes for more than half a century. Its eggplant dip has the faint smoky taste that's evident only in the homemade variety, and its gyros are heaped high with succulent lamb. You can even get *dandourma*—a special kind of homemade ice cream topped with cherry syrup—that's rarely found in Greek restaurants. In winter, Krikelas specializes in game like wild pig and venison; fresh fish is served year-round. *Ethnikis Antistasis 32, Kalamaria, tel. 031/451-690 or 031/451-289. Reservations advised. DC, V. Moderate.*

★ **O Kipos ton Pringipon (the Princes' Garden).** The Milos enclave, where this ouzeri is located, is an entertaining place to spend an evening. The former mill complex in the city's slaughterhouse area was renovated in the early 1990s into a nightlife center, with a café, bars playing everything from light jazz to heavy Greek music, and exhibition spaces for art shows and live performances. The ouzeri has traditional appetizers—*saganaki*, sausages, fried whitebait—as well as such specialties as their own *bekri meze*, diced beef in a mushroom and red-wine sauce topped with cheese. *Andrea Georgiou 56, Sfagia, tel. 031/251-838, 031/516-945, or 031/516-836. Reservations advised on weekends. No credit cards. Inexpensive–Moderate.*

Lodging
★ **Electra Palace.** This renovated hotel is built in a neo-Byzantine style to match the other buildings on the square. It's conveniently located in the center of town, and it has a nonsmoking floor, rare in Greece. Rooms have refrigerators and TV; American breakfast is included in the price. *Platia Aristotelous 5, 54624, tel. 031/232-221, -2, -3, -4, -5, -6, -7, -8, -9, -30, fax 031/235-947. 131 rooms with bath. Facilities: restaurant. AE, DC, MC, V. Expensive.*

Panorama. If you don't mind taking a taxi this is a delightful hotel tucked into the wealthy, foothill suburb of Panorama, about 10 kilometers (6 miles) from downtown. Rooms are modern and quiet, and those in front have a sweeping vista of the city below. The terrace is a good place to retreat on a sultry summer afternoon, where you can enjoy the city view unhurriedly with an iced coffee or frozen sherbet. *Analipseos 26, Panorama, 55236, tel. 031/341-123, 031/*

341–266, fax 031/341–229. 50 rooms with bath. Facilities: restaurant, bar. AE, DC, V. Expensive.

Capsis. Two blocks from the rail station, this hotel is popular with Greek business travelers for its convenient downtown location. Rooms are simply furnished; several have TVs. Buffet breakfast is included in the price. During the two weeks of the International Trade Fair, the room price increases considerably. *Monastiriou 18, 54629, tel. 031/321–421, -2, -3, -4, -5, -6, -7, -8, -9, fax 031/510–555. 428 rooms with bath. Facilities: restaurant, pool, roof garden. AE, DC, MC, V. Moderate.*

Queen Olga Hotel. Though it's starting to show its age, this hotel is slowly renovating piecemeal. Its location near the International Fairgrounds and its helpful staff make it appealing to the budget-minded traveler. Rooms have TV, air-conditioning, and minibars; those in the front have a sea view. *Vas. Olgas 44, 54641, tel. 031/824–621, -2, -3, -4, -5, -6, -7, -8, -9, -30, fax 031/830–550. 147 rooms with bath. Facilities: restaurant, bar, air-conditioning. AE, MC, V. Moderate.*

The Greek Islands

The islands of the Aegean have colorful legends of their own—the Minotaur in Crete; the lost continent of Atlantis, which some believe was Santorini; and the Colossus of Rhodes, to name a few. Each island has its own personality. Mykonos has windmills, dazzling whitewashed buildings, hundreds of tiny churches and chapels on golden hillsides, and small fishing harbors. Visitors to volcanic Santorini sail into what was once a vast volcanic crater and anchor near the island's forbidding cliffs. Crete, with its jagged mountain peaks, olive orchards, and vineyards, contains the remains of the Minoan civilization. In Rhodes, a bustling modern town surrounds a walled town with a medieval castle.

Getting Around

The simplest way to visit the Aegean Islands is by cruise ship. Visitors might consider a three-day cruise to the four most popular islands—Mykonos, Rhodes, Crete, and Santorini. Car and passenger ferries sail to these main destinations from Piraeus, the port of Athens; other ferries sail from Rafina, 20 miles north of Athens. (*See* Getting Around, By Boat, at the beginning of this chapter.) There is also frequent air service from Athens, and most flights are full, especially in summer. It's vital to book well in advance and to confirm and reconfirm in order to be sure of your seat.

Guided Tours

Aegean Cruises From April through October there are many cruises to the Greek Islands from Piraeus. Try any of the following: **Chandris Cruises** (tel. 01/429–0300), **Epirotiki** (tel. 01/429–1000), **Royal Cruise Lines** (tel. 01/428–2440 or 800/792–2992 in the U.S.), **Saronic Cruises** (tel. 01/323–4292), or **Sun Line** (tel. 01/452–3417 or 800/872–6400 in the U.S.). They all offer one- to seven-day cruises. In the United Kingdom, contact **Epirotiki Cruises** (Westmoreland House, 127/131 Regent St., London W1R, tel. 071/734–0805).

The Greek Islands

[Map showing: Athens, Piraeus, Voula, Cape Sounion, Kythnos, Ydra, Kea, Tinos, Andros (Andros), Syros, Mykonos, Mykonos, Delos, Serifos, Paros, Naxos, Milos, Oia, Thira, Santorini, Akrotiri, Anafi, Ios, Astypalea, Amorgos, CYCLADES, Aegean Sea, Samos, Samos, Ikaria, Agios Kirykos, Pythagorio, Pátmos, Leros, Kos, Kos, Bodrum (Halicarnassus), Ephesus, Nissyros, Symi, Rhodes, Kameiros, Tilos, Halki, Lindos, Rhodes, DODECANESE, Sea of Crete, Karpathos, Kassos, Hania, Iraklio, Mallia, Elounda, Siteia, Ayios Nikólaos, Knossos, Phaestos, Ierapetra, CRETE; scale 0–50 miles, 0–75 miles; N compass]

Tourist Information

There are **Greek National Tourist Organization** offices on **Crete,** at Kriari 40, Hania (tel. 0821/92–624), and at Xanthoulidou 1, Heraklion (tel. 081/228–203); on **Mykonos,** at the harbor, near the departure point for Delos (tel. 0289/22–482 or 0289/22–716); on **Rhodes,** at Archbishop Makarios and Papagou 5, Rhodes (tel. 0241/23–655).

Exploring the Greek Islands

The Cyclades   Cruise ships and car ferries to Mykonos leave from Piraeus or Rafina. If you sail from Piraeus, you will be able to see one of the great sights of Greece: the Temple of Poseidon looming on a hilltop at the edge of Cape Sounion, about two hours from Athens, at the tip of mainland Greece.

Mykonos   Mykonos is the name of the island and also of its chief village—a colorful maze of narrow, paved streets lined with whitewashed houses, many with bright blue doors and shutters. Every morning, women scrub the sidewalks and streets in front of their homes, undaunted by the many donkeys that pass by each day. During the 1960s, the bohemian jet set discovered Mykonos, and most of the old houses along the waterfront are now restaurants, nightclubs, bars, and discos—both gay and straight, all blaring loud music until the early morning; a quiet café or taverna is hard to find. Mykonos is still a favorite anchorage with the international yacht set, as well as being *the* holiday destination for the young, lively, and liberated—finding yourself alone on any of its beaches is unlikely.

Delos A half hour by boat from Mykonos and its 20th-century holiday pleasures is the ancient isle of Delos, the legendary sanctuary of Apollo. Its **Avenue of the Lions,** a remarkable group of five Naxian marble sculptures from the 7th century BC, is a must. Worth seeing, too, are some of the houses of the Roman period, with their fine floor mosaics. The best of these mosaics are in a museum, the **sanctuary of Dionysos.** *Tel. 0289/22-259. Admission (including entrance to the museum): 1,000 dr. Open Tues.-Sun. 8:30-3.*

Santorini The best way to approach Santorini is to sail into its harbor, once the vast crater of its volcano, and dock beneath its black and red cliffs. In some parts, the cliffs rise nearly 310 meters (1,000 feet) above the sea. The play of light across them can produce strange color effects. The white houses and churches of the main town, **Thira** (Fira), cling inside the rim in dazzling white contrast to the somber cliffs.

Most passenger ferries now use the new port, Athinios, where visitors are met by buses, taxis, and a gaggle of small-hotel owners hawking rooms. The bus ride into Thira takes about a half hour, and from there you can make connections to **Oia,** the serene town at the northern tip and to other towns on the island. Despite being packed with visitors in the summer, the tiny town is charming and has spectacular views. It has the usual souvenir and handicrafts shops and several reasonably priced jewelry shops. Be sure to try the local wines. The volcanic soil produces a unique range of flavors from light and dry to rich and aromatic.

The island's volcano erupted during the 15th century BC, destroying its Minoan civilization. At **Akrotiri,** on the south end of Santorini, the remains of a Minoan city buried by volcanic ash are being excavated. The site, believed by some to be part of the legendary Atlantis, is well worth visiting. *Tel. 0286/81-366. Admission: 1,000 dr. Open Tues.-Sun. 8:30-3, weekends and holidays 9:30-2:30.*

At **Ancient Thira,** a clifftop site on the east coast of the island, a well-preserved ancient town includes a theater and agora, houses, fortifications, and ancient tombs. *Tel. 0286/22-217. Admission free. Open Tues.-Sun. 8:30-3.*

For an enjoyable but slightly unnerving excursion, take the short boat trip to the island's still-active small offshore volcanoes called the **Kamenes** or Burnt Islands. You can descend into a small crater, hot and smelling of sulfur, and swim in the nearby water that has been warmed by the volcano.

The Dodecanese **Rhodes** The large island of Rhodes, 170 kilometers (106 miles) southeast of Mykonos and 11.2 kilometers (7 miles) off the coast of Turkey, is the chief island of the group of 12 called the Dodecanese. The northern end of the island is one of Greece's major vacation centers, and the Old Town of Rhodes is full of crooked cobbled streets, charming cityscapes, and echoes of antiquity. It is also full of the trappings of tourism, mainly evident in the pubs and bars that cater to the large Western European market. The island as a whole is not particularly beautiful—but it has fine beaches and an excellent climate. It is also a good base for visiting other islands of the Dodecanese, with their mixture of Aegean and Turkish architecture.

The town of Rhodes has an attractive harbor with fortifications; the gigantic bronze statue of the Colossus of Rhodes, once supposed to have straddled the entrance, was one of the wonders of the ancient world. The fascinating **old walled city,** near the harbor, was built by crusaders—the Knights of St. John—on the site of an ancient city. The Knights ruled the island from 1309 until they were defeated by the Turks in 1522. Within the fine medieval walls, on the Street of the Knights, stands the **Knights' Hospital,** now the Archaeological Museum, housing ancient pottery and sculpture, including the exquisite small marble of a crouching Aphrodite, shown washing her hair. *Tel. 0241/21–954. Admission: 600 dr. Open Tues.–Sun. 8:30–3.*

Another museum that deserves your attention is the restored and moated medieval **Palace of the Grand Master.** Destroyed in 1856 by a gunpowder explosion, the palace was renovated by the Italians as a summer retreat for Mussolini. Note its splendid Roman and early Christian floor mosaics. *Tel. 0241/21–954. Admission: 800 dr. Open Tues.–Sun. 8:30–3.*

To get the best overall view of the walled city, including the surviving Turkish buildings, go to one of the flower-filled parks that surround it. Try to see the son et lumière—performances in English are held on Sunday evening.

Many attractive souvenir and handicrafts shops in the old town and just outside the walls sell decorative Rhodian pottery, local embroidery, sea sponges, and relatively inexpensive jewelry.

From the town of Rhodes, drive about 60 kilometers (37 miles) down the east coast to the enchanting village of **Lindos.** Take a donkey from the village center and ride, or put on your comfortable shoes and walk up the steep hill to the ruins of the ancient **Acropolis of Lindos,** which is circled by a medieval castle. The sight of its beautiful colonnade with the sea far below is unforgettable. Look for little St. Paul's Harbor, beneath the cliffs of the acropolis; seen from above, it appears to be a lake, as the tiny entrance from the sea is obscured by the rocks. *Tel. 0241/21–954. Admission: 800 dr. Open Tues.–Sun. 8:30–3.*

Crete   Greece's largest island, situated in the south Aegean, was the center of Europe's earliest civilization, the Minoan, which flourished from about 2000 BC to 1200 BC. It was struck a mortal blow in about 1450 BC by some unknown cataclysm, now thought to be political.

The most important Minoan remains are to be seen in the **Archaeological Museum in Heraklion,** Crete's largest (and least attractive) city. The museum houses many Minoan treasures, including some highly sophisticated frescoes and elegant ceramics depicting Minoan life. *Plateia Eleftherias, tel. 081/226–092. Admission: 1,000 dr. Open Mon. 11–5, Tues.–Fri. 8–5, weekends and holidays 8:30–3.*

Not far from Heraklion is the partly reconstructed **Palace of Knossos,** which will also give you a feeling for the Minoan world. Note the simple throne room, which contains the oldest throne in Europe, and the bathrooms with their efficient plumbing. The palace was the setting for the legend of the Minotaur, a monstrous offspring of Queen Pasiphae and a bull, which King Minos confined to the Labyrinth under the palace. *Tel. 081/231–940. Admission: 1,000 dr. Open Tues.–Sun. 8:30–3.*

Crete belonged to Venice from 1210 until 1669, when it was conquered by the Turks. The island did not become part of Greece until early in this century. The **Venetian ramparts** that withstood a 24-year Turkish siege still surround Heraklion. In addition to archaeological treasures, Crete can boast beautiful mountain scenery and a large number of beach resorts along the north coast. One is **Mallia,** which contains the remains of another Minoan palace and has good sandy beaches. Two other beach resorts, **Ayios Nikolaos** and the nearby **Elounda,** are farther east. The south coast offers good, quieter beaches for those who want to get away from it all.

Dining and Lodging

For details and price-category definitions, *see* Dining and Lodging in Staying in Greece, *above.*

Crete Heraklion has many moderately priced open-air restaurants in the
Dining central area around Platia Venizelou and Platia Daedelou. In Hania, the Venetian harbor is surrounded by tavernas offering almost identical menus; in Ayios Nikolaos the seafront is the most popular place to eat. The island is known for its fine local wine, fresh seafood, and local produce, which is available year-round.

Kyriakos. This popular Heraklion taverna, with pink tablecloths and green chairs, offers a wide range of salads, fish dishes, and such Cretan specialties as snail stew and baked iris bulbs in olive oil. *Leoforos Dimokratias 53, tel. 081/224-649. AE, DC. Moderate.*

Lodging **Elounda Beach.** Located 4.8 kilometers (3 miles) north of Ayios Nikolaos, this is probably the best seaside resort complex on Crete. It is spacious, attractive, and spotlessly maintained. It's set in beautiful grounds—the pool is cleverly landscaped among carob trees—and has a private beach. *Tel. 0841/41-412/3. 301 rooms with bath. Facilities: restaurants, outdoor pool, miniature golf, tennis courts, nightclub, cinema. AE. Closed Nov.-Mar. Very Expensive.*

Casa Delfino. In the heart of Hania's old town, this small hotel was once part of a Venetian Renaissance Palace. Rooms decorated in cool pastel colors with modern furniture surround a courtyard paved in pebble mosaic. *Theofanous 9, Palio Limani, tel. 0821/42-613. 12 rooms with bath. Facilities: minibars, air-conditioning. DC, MC, V. Expensive.*

★ **Mediterranean.** This is another comfortable hotel in the center of Heraklion and 4.8 kilometers (3 miles) from the beach. It's priced at the top of its category. *Smyrnis 1, tel. 081/289-331. 55 rooms with bath. Facilities: restaurant, roof garden, partially air-conditioned. AE, MC, V. Moderate.*

Mykonos **Chez Cat'rine.** A favorite with Greeks as well as foreigners, this is
Dining where you can enjoy simple but superbly cooked French dishes, plus a selection of mouth-watering Greek fare, in an informal, brightly furnished dining room. *In town, opposite St. Gerasimos's church, tel. 0289/22-169. Reservations necessary. AE, MC, V. Dinner only. Expensive.*

Lodging **Cavo Tagoo.** Within walking distance of the center of town, this
★ small, charming hotel sits above a beach. Built to blend in with the Mykonian architecture, it has an attractively designed saltwater pool in the garden and is well worth the high rates. *Tagoo Beach, tel. 0289/23-692/4. 25 rooms with bath. Facilities: restaurant, outdoor pool. AE, MC, V. Closed Nov.-Mar. Expensive.*

Kouneni Hotel. This is a comfortable family-run hotel in the town center, and it's quieter than most. It is set in a cool green garden, a rarity on Mykonos. Rooms are fairly large; the slightly shabby, but cozy lounge has a tiled floor. *Tria Pigadia, tel. 0289/22-301. 20 rooms with bath. No credit cards. Moderate.*

Rhodes **Casa Castelana.** Set in a 15th-century Inn of the Knights, this res-
Dining taurant has a wonderful medieval atmosphere indoors; outdoors, there's an elegant but comfortable garden area for dining. The food is unusual and delicious, featuring a combination of non-Greek dishes and Rhodian specialties—including *trahanas,* an island vil-

lage soup, and *stifado*, a pot-au-feu-style lamb dish. *Aristotelous 35, tel. 0241/28–803. Reservations advised. AE, DC, V. Expensive.*

Plaka Taverna. This restaurant on the first floor, overlooking the fountain in the square, offers one of the prettiest settings in the town. The specialty here is fresh seafood, grilled or fried to order; the red mullet is particularly tasty. *Ippocratous Sq., tel. 0241/22–477. Reservations not necessary. AE, DC. Expensive.*

Reni. Nearly halfway to Lindos on the way from Rhodes is this quintessential beach restaurant, where you sit outdoors under straw sunshades and stuff yourself with all kinds of seafood. After lunch, if you can move, waddle across the beach and plunge right into the Aegean. *Afandou Beach, tel. 0241/51280. No reservations. No credit cards. Inexpensive–Moderate.*

Kavo d'Oro. You can't go wrong at this tiny restaurant, which is one of the best in the town of Rhodes and possibly on the entire island. *Sokratous 41, tel. 0241/36–181. Reservations not necessary. No credit cards. Inexpensive.*

Lodging **Grand Hotel Astir Palace.** This beachfront establishment, on the edge of the town of Rhodes, houses one of Greece's three casinos, as well as two restaurants and cocktail bars, an English-style pub, and the Isabella nightclub. Although the beach is ordinary, the setting is a great asset. Some rooms with verandas face the gardens, lawns, and pools; others, slightly more expensive, face the sea with views of the coast of Turkey. *Vass. Konstantinou St., tel. 0241/26–284/9. 378 rooms with bath. Facilities: restaurants, 1 indoor and 2 outdoor pools, private beach, tennis courts, casino. AE, DC, MC, V. Very Expensive.*

Steps of Lindos. This hotel, 4.8 kilometers (3 miles) out of the village of Lindos, is built on a sloping hillside above a long, good beach. The steps—and there are lots of them—link the whitewashed buildings to the pool and beach. The service is friendly and efficient, and the food is plentiful, although variable. *Vlyha Lindos, tel. 0244/42–262. 156 rooms with bath. Facilities: restaurant, outdoor pool, tennis courts, beach. AE. Closed Nov.–Mar. Expensive.*

Spartalis Hotel. Many rooms in this simple but lively hotel near the city's port have balconies overlooking the bay. *Plastira 2, tel. 0241/24–371/2. 79 rooms with bath. AE, V. Moderate.*

Santorini **Camille Stefani.** This is one of the island's best restaurants, where
Dining you can enjoy seafood, Greek and Continental cuisine, and the local wines. A taste of the mellow Santorini Lava red wine, a product of the volcanic ash, is a must! *Main St., Thira, tel. 0286/22–265. Reservations advised. AE, MC, V. Moderate.*

Lodging **Atlantis Hotel.** Located in the main village, this is the island's best hotel. It has a magnificent view. *Thira, tel. 0286/22–232. 26 rooms with bath. Facilities: bar. AE, DC, MC, V. Closed Nov.–Mar. Expensive.*

Perivolas. This group of traditional houses has been carefully restored by the Greek National Tourist Organization. Located in the beautiful village of Oia, they overlook the sea and the volcano and offer comfortable, self-catering accommodations in an authentic island setting. *Tel. 0286/71–308. 12 houses, each with 2 rooms and bath. Facilities: kitchen. AE, MC, V. Closed Nov.–Mar. Expensive.*

14 Holland

If you come to the Netherlands expecting to find its residents shod in wooden shoes, you're years too late; if you're looking for windmills at every turn, you're looking in the wrong place. The bucolic images that brought tourism here in the decades after World War II have little to do with the Netherlands of the '90s. Sure, tulips grow in abundance in the bulb district of Noord and Zuid Holland provinces, but today's Netherlands is no backwater operation: This tiny nation has an economic strength and cultural wealth that far surpass its size and population. Sophisticated, modern Netherlands has more art treasures per square mile than any other country on earth, as well as a large number of ingenious, energetic people with a remarkable commitment to quality, style, and innovation.

The 41,040 square kilometers (15,785 square miles) of the Netherlands are just about half the number in the state of Maine, and its population of 15 million is slightly less than that of the state of Texas. Size is no measure of international clout, however. The Netherlands is second only to Great Britain and Japan as an investor in the American economy. The Netherlands encourages internal accomplishments as well, particularly of a cultural nature. Within a 120-kilometer (75-mile) radius are ten major museums of art and several smaller ones that together contain the world's richest and most comprehensive collection of art masterpieces from the 15th to the 20th centuries, including the majority of paintings by Rembrandt and nearly every painting produced by Vincent van Gogh. In the same small area are a half dozen performance halls offering music, dance, and internationally known performing arts festivals.

The marriage of economic power and cultural wealth is nothing new to the Dutch; in the 17th century, for example, money raised through their colonial outposts overseas was used to buy or commission portraits and paintings by young artists such as Rembrandt, Hals, Vermeer, and van Ruisdael. But it was not only the arts that were encouraged: the Netherlands was home to the philosophers Descartes, Spinoza, and Comenius; the jurist Grotius; the naturalist van Leeuwenhoek, inventor of the microscope; and others like them who flourished in the country's enlightened tolerance. The Netherlands continues to subsidize its artists and performers, and it supports an educational system in which creativity in every field is respected, revered, and given room to express itself.

The Netherlands is the delta of Europe, located where the great Rhine and Maas rivers and their tributaries empty into the North Sea. Near the coast, it is a land of flat fields and interconnecting canals; in the center of the country it is surprisingly wooded, and in the far south are rolling hills. The country is too small for there to be vast natural areas, and it's too precariously close to sea level, even at its highest points, for there to be dramatic landscapes. Instead, the Netherlands is what the Dutch jokingly call a big green city. Amsterdam is the focal point of the nation; it also is the beginning and end point of a 50-kilometer (31-mile) circle of cities that includes The Hague (the Dutch seat of government and the world center of international justice), Rotterdam (the industrial center of the Netherlands and the world's largest port), and the historic cites of Haarlem, Leiden, Delft, and Utrecht. The northern and eastern provinces are rural and quiet; the southern provinces that hug the Belgian border are lightly industrialized and sophisticated. The great rivers that cut through the heart of the country provide both geographical and sociological borders. The area "above the great rivers," as the Dutch phrase it, is peopled by tough-minded and practical Calvinists; to the south are more ebullient Catholics. A tra-

560

Holland

North Sea

Wadden Islands

Schiermonnikoog

Ameland

Terschelling

Vlieland

Texel

Dokkum

Groningen

Delfzijl

Winschoten

Leeuwarden

Drachten

Assen

Emmen

Harlingen

Bolsward

Sneek

Den Helder

IJsselmeer

Enkhuizen

Hoogeveen

Meppel

Schagen

Alkmaar

Hoorn

Lelystad

Zwolle

Almelo

Hengelo

Enschede

Purmerend

Deventer

Zaanstad

Amsterdam

Apeldoorn

Haarlem

Bussum

Winterswijk

Hilversum

Amersfoort

Arnhem

Doetinchem

Leiden

Utrecht

Nijmegen

Rhine

GERMANY

Den Haag
(The Hague)

Tiel

Delft

Oss

Rotterdam

's Hertogenbosch

Dordrecht

Veghel

Haringvliet

Overflakkee

Grevelingen

Breda

Tilburg

Eindhoven

Schouwen/
Duiveland

Steenbergen

Weert

Roermond

Tholen

Oosterschelde

Bergen op Zoom

Goes

Walcheren

Beveland

Middelburg

Westerschelde

Breskens

Terneuzen

Antwerp

Sittard

Maastricht

Aachen

Vaals

BELGIUM

Liège

KEY

Ferry

Brussels

0   40 miles

0   60 km

dition of tolerance pervades this densely populated land; aware that they cannot survive alone, the Dutch are bound by common traits of ingenuity, personal honesty, and a bold sense of humor.

Essential Information

Before You Go

When to Go The prime tourist season in Holland runs from April through October and peaks during school vacation periods (Easter, July, and August), when hotels may impose a 20% surcharge. Dutch bulb fields bloom from late March to the end of May—not surprisingly, the hotels tend to fill up then, too. June is the ideal time to catch the warm weather and miss the crowds, but every region of the Netherlands has its season. Delft is luminous after a winter storm, and fall in the Utrecht countryside can be as dramatic as in New England.

Climate Summers are generally warm, but beware of sudden showers and blustery coastal winds. Winters are chilly and wet but are not without clear days. After a cloudburst, notice the watery quality of light that inspired Vermeer and other great Dutch painters.

The following are the average daily maximum and minimum temperatures for Amsterdam.

Jan.	40F	4C	May	61F	16C	Sept.	65F	18C
	34	1		50	10		56	13
Feb.	41F	5C	June	65F	18C	Oct.	56F	13C
	34	1		56	13		49	9
Mar.	47F	8C	July	70F	21C	Nov.	47F	8C
	38	3		59	15		41	5
Apr.	52F	11C	Aug.	68F	20C	Dec.	41F	5C
	43	6		59	15		36	2

Currency The unit of currency in Holland is the *guilder*, written as NLG (for Netherlands guilder), Fl., or simply F. (from the centuries-old term for the coinage, *florin*). Each guilder is divided into 100 cents. Bills are in denominations of 1,000, 250, 100, 50, 25, and 10 guilders. Denominations over Fl. 100 are rarely seen, and many shops refuse to change them. Coins are 5, 2.5, and 1 guilder and 25, 10, and 5 cents. Be careful not to confuse the 2.5- and 1-guilder coins and the 5-guilder and 5-cent coins. Bills have a code of raised dots that can be identified by touch; this is for people who are blind.

At press time (spring 1994), the exchange rate for the guilder was Fl. 1.90 to the U.S. dollar and Fl. 2.90 to the pound sterling.

Most major credit cards are accepted in hotels, larger restaurants, and shops, but check first.

What It Will Cost Holland is a prosperous country with a high standard of living, so overall costs are similar to those in other northern European countries. Prices for hotels and other services in major cities are 10%–20% above those in rural areas. Amsterdam and The Hague are the most expensive. Hotel and restaurant service charges and the 6% value-added tax (VAT) are usually included in the prices quoted.

The cost of eating varies widely in Holland, from a snack in a bar or a modest restaurant offering a *dagschotel* (day special), or "tourist menu" at around Fl. 25 to the considerable expense of gourmet cuisine. A traditional Dutch breakfast is occasionally included in the overnight hotel price.

One cost advantage Holland has over other European countries is that because it is so small, traveling around is inexpensive—especially if you use the many price-saving transportation deals available.

Sample Prices   Half-bottle of wine, Fl. 25; glass of beer, Fl. 3.50; cup of coffee, Fl. 2.75; ham and cheese sandwich, Fl. 5; 1-mile taxi ride, Fl. 10.

Museums   The **Museumkaart,** which can be purchased from some museums and all tourist offices, provides a year's free admission to about 350 museums. It costs Fl. 40, Fl. 25 if you're over 65, and Fl. 15 if you're under 18. A photo and passport are required for purchase. If your time is limited, you might want to check the list; not all museums participate.

Customs on Arrival   For travelers arriving from a country that is not a member of the European Union (EU) or those coming from an EU country who have bought goods in a duty-free shop, the allowances are (1) 200 cigarettes or 50 cigars or 100 cigarillos or 250 grams of tobacco, (2) 1 liter of alcohol more than 22% by volume or 2 liters of liqueur wine or 2 liters of sparkling wine, (3) 50 grams of perfume or 25 centiliters of toilet water, and (4) other goods to the value of Fl. 125.

Since Jan. 1, 1993, allowances for travelers within the EU member states have been effectively removed, provided that goods have been bought duty-paid (i.e., not in a duty-free shop) and are for personal use. You would have to have a pretty good excuse, such as a wedding reception, if you were found taking a few hundred liters of whisky over the border.

All personal items are considered duty-free, provided you take them with you when you leave Holland. Tobacco and alcohol allowances are for those 17 and older. There are no restrictions on the import and export of Dutch currency.

Language   Dutch is a difficult language for foreigners, but luckily the Dutch are fine linguists, so almost everyone speaks at least some English, especially in larger cities and tourist centers.

Getting Around

By Car   Holland has one of the best road systems in Europe, and even the
Road   longest trips between cities take only a few hours. Multilane ex-
Conditions   pressways (toll-free) link major cities, but the smaller roads and country lanes provide more varied views of Holland. In towns many of the streets are narrow, and you'll have to contend with complex one-way systems and cycle lanes. Information about weather and road conditions can be obtained by calling 06/9622.

Rules of the   The speed limit on expressways is 120 kph (75 mph); on city streets
Road   and in residential areas it is 50 kph (30 mph) or less, according to the signs. Driving is on the right.

Parking   Parking in the larger towns is difficult and expensive, with illegally parked cars quickly towed away or subject to a wheel clamp. Fines for recovery can reach Fl. 300. So consider parking on the outskirts of a town and using public transportation to get to the center.

Gasoline   Gas, *benzine* in Dutch, costs around Fl. 1.86 per liter for regular, Fl. 1.92 for super, and Fl. 2.03 for unleaded.

Breakdowns   Experienced, uniformed mechanics of the **Wegenwacht** patrol the highways in yellow cars 24 hours a day. Operated by ANWB (Royal Dutch Touring Club), they will help if you have car trouble. ANWB also maintains phone boxes along major roads on which to call for assistance. To use these services, you may be asked to take temporary membership in ANWB.

By Train Fast, frequent, and comfortable trains operate throughout the country. All trains have first- and second-class cars, and many intercity trains have buffet or dining-car services. Intercity trains run every 30 minutes and regular trains run to the smaller towns at least once an hour. Sometimes one train contains two separate sections that divide during the trip, so be sure you are in the correct section for your destination. Trains have specially designed entryways for people using wheelchairs.

Fares To get the best value out of rail travel it is advisable to purchase one of the three available rail passes before you leave. The **Benelux Tourrail** gives you unlimited travel throughout Holland, Belgium, and Luxembourg on any five days within one month ($205 first class, $137 second class). A **Euro Domino Holland** ticket allows unlimited travel throughout Holland for three, five, or ten days within any 30-day period (first class: 3-day, $81, 5-day $135, 10-day $243; second class: 3-day $63, 5-day $88, 10-day $159). A **Railrover** entitles you to unlimited travel within Holland for seven consecutive days (first class $127, second class $85). For an additional $14 the **Linkrover** offers free travel on public transport as well. The Netherlands Board of Tourism's (NBT) offices abroad have information on train services, as do overseas offices of Netherlands Railways (*see* Before You Go in Chapter 1, *above*). Your passport may be needed when you purchase these tickets. The Benelux Tourrail must be bought abroad, but the others are available in the Netherlands. **Dagtochtkaartjes** are special combined tickets covering train, boat, and bus trips. Ask about these fares at railway information bureaus or local tourist offices.

By Plane **KLM Royal Dutch Airlines,** under the banner of CityHopper, operates several domestic services connecting major cities. In this small country, however, you'd probably travel just as fast by car or train.

By Bus Holland has an excellent bus network between towns that are not connected by rail and also within towns. Bus excursions can be booked on the spot and at local VVV offices. In major cities, the best buy is a **strippenkaart** ticket (Fl. 11), which can be used for all bus, tram, and metro services. Each card has 15 strips, which are canceled either by the driver as you enter the buses or by the stamping machine at each door of the trams. More than one person can travel on a strippenkaart—it just gets used up more quickly. A strippenkaart with 45 strips is available for Fl. 32.25. You can buy it at train stations, post offices, and some VVV offices, or in Amsterdam at the GVB (national bus system) ticket office in the plaza in front of the central railway station and at many newsagents. **Dagkaart,** a travel-anywhere ticket, covers all urban bus/streetcar routes and costs Fl. 12 for one day, Fl. 16 for two days, and Fl. 19.75 for three days.

By Bicycle Holland is a "cyclist-friendly" country with specially designated cycle paths, signs, and picnic areas. Bikes can usually be rented at train stations in most cities and towns, and Dutch trains are "cycle-friendly," too, with extra spacious entryways designed to accommodate bicycles. You will need an extra ticket for the bike, however. There are some restrictions on carrying bicycles on trains, so it is worthwhile to check first. The flat rate single fare for a bike to anywhere in the country is Fl. 9, though on Mondays and Fridays in July and August this can rise to Fl. 15. Rental costs for bicycles are around Fl. 10 per day or from Fl. 40 per week, plus a deposit of Fl.

50–Fl. 200. Many larger railway stations hire bicycles to holders of valid train tickets at Fl. 6 per day and Fl. 24 per week. Advice on rentals and routes is available from offices of The Netherlands Board of Tourism in North America or in Holland, or from local VVV offices; cycling packages can be booked at the larger offices.

Staying in Holland

Telephones
Local Calls
The telephone system in Holland is excellent and reliable. All towns and cities have area codes that are to be used only when you are calling from outside the area. Most pay phones take 25¢ or Fl. 1 coins, though newer ones also accept other denominations. Increasingly, public phone booths are being converted to a phonecard system. Phonecards may be purchased from post offices, railway stations, and some newsagents for Fl. 5, Fl. 10, or Fl. 25. Queues at coin-operated boxes tend to be longer, so a phonecard is worth the investment, especially if you intend to make international calls.

International Calls
Direct-dial international calls can be made from any phone booth. Lower rates to the United States are charged from 7 PM to 10 AM weekdays, and from 7 PM Friday to 10 AM Monday. The average cost per minute to the U.S. is Fl. 1.95 (Fl. 1.70 nights and weekends). Think twice about making international calls from your hotel room because high service charges may double or triple the cost over and above the already doubled or tripled rates that are charged for calls from Europe to North America.

Operators
In Holland, dial 06/022911 to reach **ATT USA Direct;** tel. 06/0229122 to reach **MCI Call USA;** tel. 06/0229116 to reach **Bell Canada.** To telephone elsewhere internationally, call 06–0410 for an English-speaking operator; to call within Holland, dial the same number.

Mail
Postal Rates
The Dutch post office is as efficient as the telephone network. Airmail letters to the United States cost Fl. 1.60 for the first 20 grams; postcards cost 90¢; aerograms cost Fl. 1.20. Airmail letters to the United Kingdom cost 90¢ for the first 20 grams; postcards cost 70¢; aerograms cost Fl. 1.20.

Receiving Mail
If you're uncertain where you'll be staying, have mail sent to Poste Restante, GPO, in major cities along your route, or to American Express offices, where a small charge is made on collection to non–American Express customers.

Shopping
VAT Refunds
Purchases of goods in one single store in one single day amounting to Fl. 300 or more qualify for a value-added tax (VAT) refund of 17.5%, which can be claimed at the airport or main border crossing when you leave Holland, or by mail. Ask the salesperson for a VAT refund form when you buy anything that may qualify.

Bargaining
The prices in most shops are fixed, but you can try to bargain for items in any of the open-air markets.

Opening and Closing Times
Banks are open weekdays from 9 to 4. You can also change money at GWK Border Exchange Offices at major railway stations and Schiphol Airport, which are open Monday–Saturday 8–8 and Sunday 10–4. GWK offices in major cities or at border checkpoints are open 24 hours. Many VVV offices exchange funds, too.

Museums now close on Monday, but not all, so check with local VVV offices. In rural areas, some museums close or operate shorter hours during winter. Usual hours are 10–5.

Shops are open weekdays and Saturdays from 8:30 or 9 to 5:30 or 6, but outside the cities, some close for lunch. Department stores and most shops, especially in shopping plazas (in The Hague and Amsterdam) do not open on Monday until 1 PM, and a few close one afternoon a week on whichever day they choose. Late-night shopping usually can be done until 9 PM on Thursday or Friday. Few shops are open Sunday.

National Holidays January 1; April 16–17, (Easter); April 30 (Queen's Day; shops are open unless it falls on Sunday); May 5 (Liberation); May 25 (Ascension); June 4–5 (Pentecost); December 25–26.

Dining Of the many earthly pleasures the Dutch indulge, eating probably heads the list. There is a wide variety of cuisines from traditional Dutch to Indonesian—the influence of the former Dutch colony.

Breakfast is hearty and substantial—including several varieties of bread, butter, jam, ham, cheese, chocolate, boiled eggs, juice, and steaming coffee or tea. Dutch specialties for later meals include *erwtensoep*, a rich, thick pea soup with pieces of tangy sausage or pigs' knuckles, and *hutspot*, a meat, carrot, and potato stew; both are usually served only during winter. *Haring* (herring) is particularly popular, especially the "new herring" caught between May and September and served raw in brine, garnished with onions. If Dutch food begins to pall, try an Indonesian restaurant, where the chief dish is *rijsttafel*, a meal made up of 20 or more small dishes, many of which are hot and spicy.

The indigenous Dutch liquor is potent and warming *jenever* (gin), both "old" and "new." Dutch liqueurs and beers are also popular.

Eating places range from snack bars, fast-food outlets, and modest local cafés to gourmet restaurants of international repute. Of special note are the "brown cafés," traditional pubs of great character that normally offer snack-type meals.

Mealtimes The Dutch tend to eat dinner around 6 or 7 PM, especially in the country and smaller cities, so many restaurants close at about 10 PM and accept final orders at 9. In larger cities dining hours vary, and some restaurants stay open until midnight.

Dress Jacket and tie are suggested for restaurants in the Very Expensive and Expensive categories. The Dutch are tolerant, and almost any outfit is acceptable in most eateries.

Ratings Prices are per person including three courses (appetizer, main course, and dessert), service, and sales tax but not drinks. For budget travelers, many restaurants offer a tourist menu at an officially controlled price, currently Fl. 25. Best bets are indicated by a star ★.

Category	Amsterdam	Other Areas
Very Expensive	over Fl. 85	over Fl. 65
Expensive	Fl. 60–Fl. 85	Fl. 45–Fl. 65
Moderate	Fl. 35–Fl. 60	Fl. 30–Fl. 45
Inexpensive	under Fl. 35	under Fl. 30

Lodging Holland offers a wide range of accommodations, from the luxurious Dutch-owned international Golden Tulip hotel chain to traditional, small-town hotels and family-run guest houses. For young or adventurous travelers, the provinces abound with modest hostels, camping grounds, and rural bungalows. Travelers with modest budgets may prefer to stay in friendly bed-and-breakfast establishments;

these are in short supply and must be booked well ahead at local VVV offices.

Hotels Dutch hotels are generally clean, if not spotless, no matter how modest their facilities, and service is normally courteous and efficient. There are many moderate and inexpensive hotels, most of which are relatively small. In the provinces the range of accommodations is more limited, but there are pleasant, inexpensive family-run hotels that are usually centrally located and offer a friendly atmosphere. Some have good—if modest—dining facilities. English is spoken or understood almost everywhere. Hotels usually quote room prices for double occupancy, and rates usually include breakfast, service charges, and VAT.

To book hotels in advance, you can use the free **National Reservation Center** (Box 404, 2260 AK Leidschendam, tel. 070/3202500, fax 070/ 3202611). Alternatively, for a small fee, VVV offices can usually make reservations at short notice. Bookings must be made in person, however.

Ratings Prices are for two people sharing a double room. Best bets are indicated by a star ★.

Category	Amsterdam	Other Areas
Very Expensive	over Fl. 450	over Fl. 300
Expensive	Fl. 300–Fl. 450	Fl. 200–Fl. 300
Moderate	Fl. 200–Fl. 300	Fl. 150–Fl. 200
Inexpensive	under Fl. 200	under Fl. 150

Tipping Hotels and restaurants almost always include 10%–15% service and 6% VAT in their charges. Give a doorman from Fl. 3 for calling a cab. Bellhops in first-class hotels should be tipped Fl. 2 for each bag they carry. Hat-check attendants expect at least 25¢, and washroom attendants get 50¢. Taxis in almost every town have a tip included in the meter charge, but you are expected to make up the fare to the nearest guilder nevertheless.

Amsterdam

Arriving and Departing

By Plane Most international flights arrive at Amsterdam's Schiphol Airport, one of Europe's finest. Immigration and customs formalities on arrival are relaxed, with no forms to be completed.

Between the Airport and Downtown The best transportation between the airport and the city center is the direct rail link to the central station, where you can get a taxi or tram to your hotel. The train runs every 10 to 15 minutes throughout the day and takes about half an hour. Second-class fare is Fl. 5.50.

Taxis from the airport to central hotels cost about Fl. 50.

By Train The city has excellent rail connections with the rest of Europe. Fast services link it to Paris, Brussels, Luxembourg, and Cologne. Centraal Station is conveniently located in the center of town.

Getting Around

By Bus, Tram, and Metro A zonal fare system is used. Tickets (starting at Fl. 3) are bought from automatic dispensers on the metro or from the drivers on trams and buses; or buy a money-saving **strippenkaart** (*see* Getting Around, By Bus, *above*). Even simpler is the **dagkaart,** which covers all city routes for Fl. 12. These discount tickets can be obtained from the main GVB ticket office in front of Centraal Station and many newsstands along with route maps of the public transportation system. The **Canalbus,** which travels between the central station and the Rijksmuseum, is Fl. 15 for a hop-on, hop-off day card.

By Taxi Taxis are expensive: A short 3-mile ride costs around Fl. 20. Taxis are not usually hailed on the street but are picked up at stands near stations and other key points. Alternatively, you can dial 020/67777777. Water taxis (tel. 020/6222181) are even more expensive (standard size water taxis—for up to eight people—cost Fl. 60 for the first half hour plus Fl. 30 pickup charge and Fl. 2 per minute).

By Car Parking in Amsterdam has always been difficult. Frequent attempts to ban cars from the city center are scuppered by the opposition of local big business. The city's concentric ring of canals, one-way systems, and lack of parking facilities will continue to plague drivers. It's best to put your car in one of the parking lots on the edge of the old center and abandon it for the rest of your stay.

By Bicycle Rental bikes are readily available for around Fl. 10 per day with a Fl. 50–Fl. 200 deposit. Bikes are an excellent and inexpensive way to explore the city. Several rental companies are close to the central station, or ask at VVVs for details. Lock your bike up at all times, preferably to something immovable; thieves have been known to abscond with them in fewer than 30 seconds. Also, check with the rental company what your liability is under their insurance terms.

By Boat The **Museum Boat** (*see* Guided Tours, *below*), which makes seven stops near major museums, is Fl. 19 for adults, Fl. 15 for children.

On Foot Amsterdam is a small, congested city of narrow streets, which makes it ideal for exploring on foot. The VVV issues seven excellent guides that detail walking tours around the center. The best are "The Jordaan," a stroll through the lively canalside district, and "Jewish Amsterdam," a walk past the symbolic remains of Jewish housing and old synagogues.

Important Addresses and Numbers

Tourist Information There are three main VVV offices: one across from the central station in the Old Dutch Coffee House (open daily 9–5), another at Leidsestraat 106 (open fall–spring, daily 9–7; summer daily 9–9) and one on Stadion Square (open daily 9–5). The general number for telephone inquiries is 06/34034066 (not such a good idea, as you are charged 50¢ per minute and kept waiting in an electronic queue).

Consulates U.S. (Museumsplein 19, tel. 020/6790321). **Canadian** (7 Sophialaan, The Hague, tel. 070/3614111). **U.K.** (Koningslaan 44, tel. 020/6764343).

Emergencies The general number for emergencies is 06–11, but note direct numbers. **Police** (tel. 020/6222222); **Ambulance** (tel. 020/5555555); **Doctor Academisch Medisch Centrum** (Meibergdreef 9, tel. 020/5669111). **Central Medical Service** (tel. 020/612–3766) will give you names of pharmacists and dentists as well as doctors. **Dentist Practice AOC** (W.G. Plein 167, tel. 020/6161234) is also open on weekends.

English-Language Bookstores	**American Discount Book Center** (Kalverstraat 85, 020/6255537). **Athenaeum Boekhandel** (Spui 14, tel. 020/6233933). **English Bookshop** (Lauriergracht 71, tel. 020/6264230).

Travel Agencies	**American Express** (Damrak 66, tel. 020/5207777, Van Baerlestraat 38, tel. 020/6738550); **Holland International** (Rokin 54, tel. 020/5512812); **Key Tours** (Dam 19, tel. 020/6247310); **De Vries & Co.** (Damrak 90, tel. 020/5550888); **Thomas Cook** (Bureau de Change, 31a Leidseplein, tel. 020/6267000) and Van Baerlestraat 40, tel. 020/6766101.

Guided Tours

Boat Tours The most enjoyable way to get to know Amsterdam is by taking a boat trip along the canals. Several operators run trips, usually in glass-top boats. There are frequent departures from points opposite the central station, along the Damrak and along the Rokin and Stadhouderskade (near the Rijksmuseum). For a tour lasting about 1 hour, the cost is around Fl. 11, but the student guides expect a small tip for their multilingual commentary. On summer evenings, longer cruises include wine and cheese or a full buffet dinner. A few tours feature increasingly drunken stops for wine tastings in canalside bars. Costs range from Fl. 39.50 for wine and cheese tours upwards of Fl. 99 for a candlelight dinner. Trips can be booked through the VVV.

Alternatively, you may want to rent a pedal-boat and make your own canal tour. At **Canal-Bike,** prices begin at Fl. 19.50 per hour; for details, tel. 020/6239886.

The **Museum Boat** (Stationsplein 8, tel. 020/6222181) combines a scenic view of the city with seven stops near 20 museums. Tickets, good for the entire day, are Fl. 19; a combination ticket for Fl. 35 includes free entrance to three museums.

Bus Tours Guided bus tours around the city are also available and provide an excellent introduction to Amsterdam. A combined bus-and-boat tour includes the inevitable trip to a diamond factory. Costing Fl. 25–Fl. 35, the comprehensive three-hour tour can be booked through **Lindbergh** (Damrak 26–27, tel. 020/6222766) or **Key Tours** (Dam 19, tel. 020/6247310).

Exploring Amsterdam

Amsterdam is a gem of a city for the tourist. Small and densely packed with fine buildings, many dating from the 17th century or earlier, it is easily explored on foot or by bike. The old heart of the city consists of canals, with narrow streets radiating out like the spokes of a wheel. The hub of this wheel and the most convenient point to begin sightseeing is the central station. Across the street, in the same building as the Old Dutch Coffee House, is a VVV tourist information office that offers helpful tourist advice.

Amsterdam's key points of interest can be covered within two or three days, with each walking itinerary taking in one or two of the important museums and galleries. The following exploration of the city center can be broken up into several sessions.

Around the Dam *Numbers in the margin correspond to points of interest on the Amsterdam map.*

1 Start at the **Centraal Station** (Central Station). Designed by P. J.H. Cuijpers and built in 1884–89, it is a good example of Dutch architecture at its most flamboyant. The street directly in front of the station square is Prins Hendrikkade. To the left, a good vantage point

② for viewing the station, is **St. Nicolaaskerk** (Church of St. Nicholas), consecrated in 1888.

Around the corner from St. Nicolaaskerk, facing the harbor, is the

③ **Schrierstoren** (Weepers' Tower), where seafarers used to say goodbye to their women before setting off to sea. The tower was erected in 1480, and a tablet marks the point from which Henrik (aka Henry) Hudson set sail on the *Half Moon* on April 4, 1609, on a voyage that took him to what is now New York and the river that still bears his name. Today the Weeping Tower is used as a combined reception and exhibition center, which includes a maritime bookshop.

Three blocks to the southwest along the Oudezijds Voorburgwal is

④ the **Museum Amstelkring,** whose facade carries the inscription "Ons Lieve Heer Op Solder" ("Our Dear Lord in the Attic"). In 1578, Amsterdam embraced Protestantism and outlawed the church of Rome. So great was the tolerance of the municipal authorities, however, that secret Catholic chapels were allowed to exist; at one time there were 62 in Amsterdam alone. One such chapel was established in the attics of these three neighboring canalside houses, built around 1661. The lower floors were used as ordinary dwellings, while services were held in the attics regularly until 1888, the year St. Nicolaaskerk was consecrated for Catholic worship. Of interest are the baroque altar with its revolving tabernacle, the swinging pulpit that can be stowed out of sight, and the upstairs gallery. *Oudezijds Voorburgwal 40, tel. 020/6246604. Admission: Fl. 5. Open Mon.– Sat. 10–5, Sun. 1–5.*

⑤ Just beyond, you can see the **Oude Kerk,** the city's oldest church. Built during the 14th century but badly damaged by iconoclasts after the Reformation, the church still retains its original bell tower and a few remarkable stained-glass windows. From the tower, there is a typical view of old Amsterdam stretching from St. Nicolaaskerk to medieval gables and, if your eyesight is good, to glimpses of negotiations between a prostitute and a prospective client immediately below! *Oudekerksplein 23, tel. 020/624–9183. Admission: Fl. 3.50. Open Apr.–Oct., Mon.–Sat. 11–5, Sun. 1:30–5; Nov.–Mar., Fri.– Sun. 1–5.*

This area, bordered by Amsterdam's two oldest canals (Oudezijds Voorburgwal and Oudezijds Achterburgwal), is the heart of the *rosse buurt,* the red-light district. In the windows at canal level, women in sheer lingerie slouch, stare, or do their nails. Drawn red curtains above suggest a brisker trade. Although the area can be shocking, with its sex shops and porn shows, it is generally safe, but midnight walks down dark side streets are not advised. If you do decide to explore the area, take care; purse snatching is common.

⑥ Return to the Damrak and continue to the **Dam** (Dam Square), the broadest square in the old section of the town. It was here that the fishermen used to come to sell their catch. Today it is circled with shops and people, and bisected with traffic; it is also a popular center for outdoor performers. At one side of the square you will notice a simple monument to Dutch victims of World War II. Eleven urns contain soil from the 11 provinces of Holland, while a 12th contains soil from the former Dutch East Indies, now Indonesia.

⑦ In a corner of the square is the **Nieuwe Kerk** (New Church). A huge Gothic church, it was gradually expanded until 1540, when it reached its present size. Gutted by fire in 1645, it was reconstructed in an imposing Renaissance style, as interpreted by strict Calvin-

Amsterdam Historisch Museum, **12**

Anne Frankhuis, **10**

Begijnhof, **13**

Centraal Station, **1**

Concertgebouw, **27**

Dam, **6**

Dokwerker, **22**

Flower Market, **16**

Gouden Bocht, **17**

Het Koninklijk
Paleis, **8**

Joods Historisch
Museum, **23**

Jordaan, **28**

Leidseplein, **14**

Muntplein, **15**

Museum Amstelkring, **4**

Museum Het
Rembrandthuis, **19**

Muziektheater/
Stadhuis, **20**

Nederlands Theater
Instituut, **18**

Nieuwe Kerk, **7**

Noorderkerk, **11**

Oude Kerk, **5**

Portuguees Israelitische
Synagogue, **21**

Rijksmuseum, **24**

Rijksmuseum Vincent
van Gogh, **25**

St. Nicolaaskerk, **2**

Schreierstoren, **3**

Stedelijk Museum, **26**

Westermarkt, **9**

Amsterdam

Het IJ

Centraal
Station

**CENTRAAL
STATION**
Front

de Ruyterkade

Oosterdokskade

Oosterdokskade

Oosterdok

Hendrikkade

Binnen
Waals
kant
eilandsgracht
Oude waal
Bantam
Recht Boomssloot

Schans

Rapenburg

**NIEUW-
MARKT**

Oude

Nieuwe Uilenburgerstraat

Uilenburgergracht

Valkenburgerstraat

Rapenburgerstraat

Jodenbreestraat

**Mr.
Visser
plein**

WATERLOOPLEIN

Plantage Parklaan

Wertheim Park

Plantage
Middenlaan

Nieuwe

Keizersgracht

Amstel

Nieuwe

Nieuwe

Kerkstraat

Weesperstraat

Prinsengracht

Nieuwe Achter

Valckenierstraat

Sarphatistraat

WEESPERPLEIN

Mauritskade

Stadhouderskade

KEY	
AE	American Express Office
i	Tourist Information
M	Metro Stops
—	Metro Lines
···	Tram Lines
—	Railroad

0   220 yards

0   200 meters

ists. The superb oak pulpit, the 14th-century nave, the stained-glass windows, and the great organ (1645) are all shown to great effect on national holidays, when the church is bedecked with flowers. As befits Holland's national church, the Nieuwe Kerk is the site of all inaugurations (as the Dutch call their coronations), including that of Queen Beatrix in 1980. But in democratic Dutch spirit, the church is also used as a meeting place and is the home of a lively café, temporary exhibitions, and concerts. *Tel. 020/6268168. Open daily 11–5, but closed often for special occasions and exhibitions.*

Time Out   **De Drie Fleschjes** (The Three Bottles). In a bell-gabled house on a crooked, medieval street behind the Nieuwe Kerk, this is one of the most typical 17th-century *proeflokalen* (wine- and spirit-tasting houses). The tone is set by the burnished wood interior, the candlelit bar, and the profusion of kegs and taps. Brokers are big buyers here when the markets close. Although the main emphasis is on drink, light snacks are also available. *Gravenstraat 18. Open Mon.–Sat. noon–8.*

8   Dominating Dam Square is the **Het Koninklijk Paleis te Amsterdam** (Royal Palace at Amsterdam), or **Dam Palace**, a vast, well-proportioned structure on Dam Square that was completed in 1655. It is built on 13,659 pilings sunk into the marshy soil. The great pedimental sculptures are an allegorical representation of Amsterdam surrounded by Neptune and mythological sea creatures. *Open Wed. noon–4; daily noon–4 during Easter, summer, and fall holidays. Sometimes closed for state events.*

9   From behind the palace, Raadhuisstraat leads west across three canals to the **Westermarkt** and the **Westerkerk** (West Church), built in 1631. The church's 85-meter (275-foot) tower is the highest in the city. It also features an outstanding carillon (set of bells). Rembrandt and his son Titus are buried in the church. On summer afternoons, you can climb to the top of the tower for a fine view over the city.

10   Opposite, at Westermarkt 6, is the house where René Descartes, the great 17th-century French philosopher ("Cogito, ergo sum"—"I think, therefore I am") lived in 1634. Another more famous house lies farther down Prinsengracht. This is the **Anne Frankhuis** (Anne Frank House), immortalized by the poignant diary kept by the young Jewish girl from 1942 to 1944, when she and her family hid here from the German occupying forces. A small exhibition on the Holocaust can also be seen in the house. *Prinsengracht 263, tel. 020/5567100. Admission: Fl. 8. Open June–Aug., Mon.–Sat. 9–7, Sun. 10–7; Sept.–May, Mon.–Sat. 9–5, Sun. 10–5.*

11   Continuing across the Prinsengracht, you'll reach the **Noorderkerk,** built in 1623. In the square in front of the church, the Noorderplein, a bird market, is held every Saturday.

South of the Dam   Turn down Kalverstraat, a shopping street leading from the Royal Palace. You will notice a striking Renaissance gate (1581) that guards a series of tranquil inner courtyards. In medieval times, this area was an island devoted to piety. Today the bordering canals are filled in.

12   The medieval doorway just around the corner in St. Luciensteeg leads to the former Burgerweeshuis (City Orphanage), once a nunnery but now the **Amsterdam Historisch Museum** (Museum of History). The museum traces the city's history from its origins as a fishing village through the 17th-century Golden Age of material and artistic wealth to the decline of the trading empire during the 18th century. The engrossing story unfolds through a display of old maps, documents, and paintings, often aided by a commentary in English. *Kalverstraat 92, tel. 020/5231822. Admission: Fl. 6.50. Open weekdays 10–5, weekends 11–5.*

A small passageway and courtyard link the museum with the **®** **Begijnhof,** an enchanting, enclosed square of almshouses founded in 1346. The *beguines* were women who chose to lead a form of convent life, often taking the vow of chastity. The last beguine died in 1974 and her house, No. 26, has been preserved as she left it. No. 34, dating from the 15th century, is the oldest and the only one to keep its wooden Gothic facade. *Tel. 020/6233565. Open weekdays 11–4.*

In the center of the square is a church given to Amsterdam's English and Scottish Presbyterians more than 300 years ago. On the church wall and also in the chancel are tributes to the Pilgrim Fathers who sailed from Delftshaven to New York in 1620. Opposite the church is another of the city's secret Catholic chapels, built in 1671.

Continuing along Kalverstraat, you soon come to Spui, a lively square in the heart of the university area. It was a center for student rallies in revolutionary 1968. Now it is a center for bookstores and bars, including the cozy "brown cafés."

Beyond is the Singel Canal and, following the tram tracks, Leidsestraat, an important shopping street that terminates in the **®** **Leidseplein,** a lively square that is one of the nightlife centers of the city.

If you continue straight along Kalverstraat instead of turning at **®** Spui, you'll soon reach the **Muntplein,** with its **Munttoren** (Mint Tower, built in 1620), a graceful structure whose clock and bells still seem to mirror the Golden Age. Beginning at the Muntplein is the **®** floating **Flower Market** on the Singel Canal. *Open Mon.–Sat. 9:30–5.*

From the Singel, take Leidsestraat to the Herengracht, the city's most prestigious "Gentlemen's Canal." The stretch of canal from **®** here to Huidenstraat is named the **Gouden Bocht** (Golden Bend) for its sumptuous patrician houses with double staircases and grand entrances. Seventeenth-century merchants moved here from the Amstel River to escape the disadvantageous byproducts of their wealth: the noisy warehouses, the unpleasant smells from the breweries, and the risk of fire in the sugar refineries. These houses display the full range of Amsterdam facades: from neck, bell, and step gables to grander Louis XIV–style houses with elaborate cornices and frescoed ceilings. In particular, look at Nos. 364–370, as well as No. 380, with its sculpted angels and Louis XIV facade; Nos. 390 and 392 display neck-shaped gables surmounted by statues of a couple in matching 17th-century garb. These houses are best seen from the east side of the canal. For more gables, turn down Wolvenstraat into the Keizersgracht, the Emperor's Canal. Walk northward toward Westerkerk and the Anne Frank Huis (*see above*).

Time Out | On the corner of Keizersgracht and Reestraat is the wellrestored **Pulitzer Hotel** and restaurant complex. Inside, you can wander around quiet inner courtyards and a modern art gallery before sitting down in the **Café Pulitzer,** which overlooks the canal, for a well-deserved apple tart or pastry. *Keizersgracht 236. Open daily 11–4.*

® Along Herengracht, parallel to the Westerkerk, is the **Nederlands Theater Instituut.** This theater museum is a dynamic find on such a genteel canal. Two frescoed Louis XIV–style merchants' houses form the backdrop for a history of the circus, opera, musicals, and drama. Miniature theaters and videos of stage productions are just two entertaining features. During the summer, the large garden is open for buffet lunches. *Herengracht 168, tel. 020/6235104. Admission: Fl. 5. Open Tues.–Sun. 11–5.*

Jewish Take the Museumboat or the metro from the central station to
Amsterdam Waterlooplein and walk east to Jodenbreestraat. This is the heart of **Jodenbuurt,** the old Jewish district and an important area to all Amsterdammers. The original settlers here were wealthy Sephardic Jews from Spain and Portugal, later followed by poorer Ashkenazic refugees from Germany and Poland. At the turn of the century, this was a thriving community of Jewish diamond polishers, dyers, and merchants. During World War II, the corner of Jodenbreestraat marked the end of the *Joodse wijk* (Jewish neighborhood), by then an imposed ghetto. Although the character of the area was largely destroyed by highway construction in 1965, and more recently by construction of both the metro and the Town Hall–Muziektheater complex, neighboring Muiderstraat has retained much of the original atmosphere. Notice the gateways decorated with pelicans, symbolizing great love; according to legend, the pelican will feed her starving young with her own blood.

From 1639 to 1658, Rembrandt lived at Jodenbreestraat No. 4, now
⑲ the **Museum Het Rembrandthuis** (Rembrandt's House). For more than 20 years, the ground floor was used by the artist as living quarters; the sunny upper floor was his studio. It is fascinating to visit, both as a record of life in 17th-century Amsterdam and as a sketch of Holland's most illustrious artist. It contains a superb collection of his etchings and engravings. From St. Antonies Sluis bridge, just by the house, there is a canal view that has barely changed since Rembrandt's time. *Jodenbreestraat 4–6, tel. 020/6249486. Admission: Fl. 5. Open Mon.–Sat. 10–5, Sun. 1–5.*

After visiting Rembrandt's House, walk back to the canal and go left to pass the Waterlooplein flea market. Ahead of you is the Amster-
⑳ dam **Muziektheater/Stadhuis** (Music Theater/Town House) complex, which presents an intriguing combination of bureaucracy and art. Amsterdammers come to the Town Hall section of the building by day to obtain driving licenses, to pick up welfare payments, and to be married. They return by night to the rounded part of the building facing the river to see opera and ballet by Holland's well-known performing companies. Feel free to wander into Town Hall (there are some interesting sculptures and other displays to see). Opera and ballet fans can go on a tour of the Muziektheater, which takes you around the dressing rooms, dance studios, and even the wig department. *Amstel 3, tel. 020/5518054. Cost: Fl. 8.50. Guided tours every Wed. and Sat. at 4.*

㉑ Facing the Muziektheater is the 17th-century **Portuguees Israel-itische Synagogue** (Portuguese Israeli Synagogue). As one of Amsterdam's four neighboring synagogues, it was part of the largest Jewish religious complex in Europe. The austere interior is still intact, even if the building itself is marooned on a traffic island. *Tel. 020/6245351. Admission: Fl 5. Open May–Oct., Sun.–Fri. 10–4; Nov.–Apr., Mon.–Thurs. 10–4, Fri. 10–3. Closed daily 12:30–1.*

Jonas Daniel Meijerplein is a square behind the Portuguese Syna-
㉒ gogue. In the center is a statue of the **Dokwerker** (Dockworker), a profession that has played a significant part in the city's history. The statue commemorates the 1942 strike by which Amsterdam

dockworkers expressed their solidarity with persecuted Jews. A memorial march is held every year on February 25.

❷❸ On the other side of the square is the intriguing **Joods Historisch Museum** (Jewish History Museum), set in a complex of three ancient synagogues. These synagogues once served a population of 100,000 Jews, which shrank to less than 10,000 after 1945. The new museum, founded by American and Dutch Jews, displays religious treasures in a clear cultural and historical context. Since the synagogues lost most of their treasures in the war, their architecture and history are more compelling than the individual exhibits. *Jonas Daniël Meijerplein 2–4, tel. 020/6269945. Admission: Fl. 7. Open daily 11–5.*

Time Out **Cafeteria Kosher.** Situated within the oldest part of the museum, the cafeteria is built above the former kosher meat halls that later became ritual baths. It still looks like part of a clandestine Catholic church, the original model for the synagogue. Jewish delicacies include fish cakes, cheese tarts, bagels, and spicy cakes with gingerbread and almond cream filling. *Open daily 11–5.*

Instead of returning on foot, you can catch the Museum Boat from the Muziektheater to the central station or to a destination near your hotel. If you feel like a breath of fresh air, stroll along Nieuwe Herengracht, once known as the "Jewish Gentlemen's Canal." In Rembrandt's day, there were views of distant windjammers sailing into port, but today the canal is oddly deserted.

The Museum Quarter By crossing the bridge beyond the Leidseplein and walking a short distance to the left on Stadshouderskade, you'll find three of the most distinguished museums in Holland—the Rijksmuseum, the Stedelijk Museum, and the Rijksmuseum Vincent van Gogh. Of the **❷❹** three, the **Rijksmuseum,** easily recognized by its towers, is the most important, so be sure to allow adequate time to explore it. It was founded in 1808, but the current, rather lavish, building dates from 1885. The museum contains significant collections of furniture, textiles, ceramics, sculpture, and prints, as well as Italian, Flemish, and Spanish paintings, many of which are of the highest quality. But the museum's fame rests on its unrivaled collection of 16th- and 17th-century Dutch masters. Of Rembrandt's masterpieces, make a point of seeing *The Nightwatch*, concealed during World War II in caves in Maastricht. The painting was misnamed because of its dull layers of varnish; in reality it depicts the Civil Guard in daylight. Also worth searching out are Frans Hals's family portraits, Jan Steen's drunken scenes, Van Ruysdael's romantic but menacing landscapes, and Vermeer's glimpses of everyday life bathed in his usual pale light. *Stadhouderskade 42, tel. 020/6732121. Admission: Fl. 10. Open Tues.–Sat. 10–5, Sun. 1–5.*

❷❺ A few blocks beyond is the **Rijksmuseum Vincent van Gogh.** This museum contains the world's largest collection of the artist's works—200 paintings and nearly 500 drawings—as well as works by some 50 of his contemporaries. *Paulus Potterstraat 7, tel. 020/5705200. Admission: Fl. 10 adults, Fl. 5 children. Open daily 10–5.*

❷❻ Next door is the **Stedelijk Museum** (Municipal Museum), with its neo-Renaissance facade that complements the Rijksmuseum's neo-Gothic turrets. The museum has a stimulating collection of modern art and ever-changing displays of contemporary art. Before viewing the works of Cézanne, Chagall, Kandinsky, and Mondrian, check the list of temporary exhibitions in Room 1. Museum policy is to trace the development of the artist rather than merely to show a few masterpieces. Don't forget the museum's restaurant overlooking a garden filled with modern sculptures. *Paulus Potterstraat 13, tel. 020/ 5732911. Admission: Fl. 7.50. Open daily 11–5.*

㉗ Diagonally opposite the Stedelijk Museum, at the end of the broad Museumplein, is the **Concertgebouw,** home of the country's foremost orchestra, the world-renowned Concertgebouworkest. Many visiting orchestras also perform here. The building has two auditoriums, the smaller of which is used for chamber music and recitals. A block or two in the opposite direction is **Vondelpark,** an elongated rectangle of paths, lakes, and pleasant shady trees. A monument honors the 17th-century epic poet Joost van den Vondel, for whom the park is named. From Wednesday to Sunday during the summer, free concerts and plays are performed in the park.

The Jordaan One old part of Amsterdam that is certainly worth exploring is the ㉘ **Jordaan,** the area bordered by Prinsengracht, Lijnbaansgracht, Brouwersgracht, and Raadhuisstraat. The canals and side streets here are all named for flowers and plants. Indeed, at one time, when this was the French quarter of the city, the area was known as *le jardin* (the garden), a name that over the years has become Jordaan. The best time to explore this area is on a Sunday morning, when there are few cars and people about, or in the evening. This part of the town has attracted many artists and is something of a bohemian quarter, where rundown buildings are being renovated and converted into restaurants, antiques shops, boutiques, and galleries.

Time Out The Jordaan is the best part of Amsterdam for relaxing in a brown café, so named because of the rich wood furnishings and—some say—the centuries-old pipe-tobacco stains on the ceilings. You can while away a rainy afternoon chatting with friendly strangers over homemade meatballs or apple tarts. Spend an hour or three over a beer or coffee at either **'t Doktorje** (Rozenboomsteegweg 4) or **De Gijs** (Lindegracht 249).

Off the Beaten Track

Another "see-worthy" district is the burgeoning **Maritime Quarter.** To reach it, walk from the central station along the Prins Hendrikkade and the Eastern Harbor, the hub of shipping activity during Holland's Golden Age. A growing permanent collection of restored vessels is moored at the **National Maritime Museum** (Scheepvaart Museum), a former naval complex at Kattenburgerplein 1. A short stroll farther down the Kattenburgergracht-Wittenburgergracht to the footbridge over the canal leads to the **Kromhout Museum** (Hoogte Kadijk 147). Many early steamships were built at this wharf, where models and motors are on display.

About three blocks from the central station, at **Haarlemmerstraat 75,** a plaque commemorates the occasion, in 1623, when the directors of the Dutch West India Company planned the founding of Nieuw Amsterdam on the southernmost tip of the island of Manhattan. In 1664, this colony was seized by the English and renamed New York.

An otherwise unremarkable building at **Singel 460** (near Herengracht) has special significance for Americans. In this building John Adams raised the first foreign loan ($2 million) for the United States from the banking house of Van Staphorst in 1782. Additional loans from this and other banks soon followed, for a total of $30 million—a gesture of Dutch confidence in the future of America.

Beer lovers—or anyone with an interest in the production of a world-class product—will want to take time to visit the **Heine-kenontvangstgebouw,** formerly the Heineken Brewery. The guided weekday tours (year-round 9:30 and 11, additional summer tours at 1 and 2:30) take in a slide presentation, the old brewery stables, and, of course, include free beer at the end of the tour. *Van der Helstraat, tel. 020/5239436. Admission: Fl. 2. Children under 18 not admitted.*

Shopping

Amsterdam is a cornucopia of interesting markets, quirky specialist shops, antiques, art, and diamonds.

Gift Ideas **Diamonds.** Since the 17th century, "Amsterdam cut" has been synonymous with perfection in the quality of diamonds. You can see this craftsmanship at any of the diamond-cutting houses. The cutters explain how the diamond's value depends on the four *c*'s—carat, cut, clarity, and color—before encouraging you to buy. There is a cluster of diamond houses on the Rokin. Alternatively, try **Van Moppes Diamonds.** *Albert Cuypstraat 2–6, tel. 020/6761242. Open daily 9–5.*

Porcelain. The Dutch have been producing Delft, Makkum, and other fine porcelain for centuries. **Focke and Meltzer** stores have been selling it since 1823. The objects vary from affordable, newly painted tiles to expensive Delft blue-and-white pitchers. One store is near the Rijksmuseum (P.C. Hooftstraat 65–67, tel. 020/6642311).

Shopping Districts Amsterdam's chief shopping districts, which have largely been turned into pedestrianized areas, are the **Leidsestraat, Kalverstraat,** and **Nieuwendijk. Rokin,** hectic with traffic, houses a cluster of boutiques and renowned antiques shops selling 18th- and 19th-century furniture, antique jewelry, Art Deco lamps, and statuettes. By contrast, some of the **Nieuwe Spiegelstraat**'s old curiosity shops sell a more inexpensive range. Haute couture and other fine goods are at home on P.C. Hooftstraat, Van Baerlestraat, and Beethovenstraat. For trendy small boutiques and unusual crafts shops, locals browse through the Jordaan. For A-to-Z shopping in a huge variety of stores, visit the new **Magna Plaza** shopping center, built inside the glorious old post office behind the Royal Palace. When leaving Holland, remember that Schiphol Airport is Europe's best tax-free shopping center.

Department Stores **De Bijenkorf** (Dam Square), the city's number-one department store, is excellent for contemporary fashions and furnishings. Running a close second is **Vroom and Dreesman** (Kalverstraat 201), with well-stocked departments carrying all manner of goods. More sedate is **Maison de Bonneterie en Pander** (Rokin 140–142 and Beethovenstraat 32). The restaurants and cafés in these department stores are also worth trying.

Markets There is a lively open-air **flea market** on Waterlooplein around the Muziektheater (Mon.–Sat. 9:30–4). The **floating flower market** on the Singel is popular with locals and visitors alike (Open Mon.–Sat. 9:30–5). An unusual Saturday **bird market** is held in the Noordermarkt. Philatelists will not want to miss the **stamp market** at Nieuwezijds Voorburgwal (Wed. and Sat. 1–4). For antiques, especially silver and toys, visit the **Sunday Waterlooplein Market** during the summer. You can also try the **Antiekmarkt de Looier** (Elandsgracht 109. Open Sun.–Wed. 11–5, Thurs. 11–9). During the summer, art lovers can buy etchings, drawings, and watercolors at the Sunday **art markets** on Thorbeckeplein and the Spui.

Dining

Amsterdammers are less creatures of habit than are the Dutch in general. Even so, set menus and early dinners are preferred by these health-conscious citizens. For travelers on a diet or budget, the blue-and-white "Tourist Menu" sign guarantees an economical (Fl. 25) yet imaginative set menu created by the head chef. For traditionalists, the "Nederlands Dis" soup tureen sign is a promise of regional recipes and seasonal ingredients. "You can eat in any language" is the city's proud boast, so when Dutch restaurants are closed, Indonesian, Chinese, and Turkish restaurants are often open. Between meals, you can follow your nose to the nearest herring cart or drop into a cozy brown café for coffee and an apple tart. For details and price-category definitions, *see* Dining in Staying in Holland, *above*.

Very Expensive **★** **Amstel Inter-Continental.** This world-class restaurant in a recently renovated grand hotel is fit for royalty. There are three differently decorated rooms, two of which have canal views. The French cuisine, with an awe-inspiring "truffle menu" of dishes prepared with exotic (and expensive) ingredients, is nonpareil and can be tailored to meet your every whim. Epicureans seeking the ultimate should inquire about the "Chef's table": With a group of six you can sit in the heart of the kitchen and watch chefs describe each of your courses as it is prepared. *Professor Tulpplein 1, tel. 020/622–6060. Reservations advised. Jacket and tie required. AE, DC, MC, V.*

★ **Excelsior.** Hôtel de l'Europe's renowned restaurant offers a varied menu of French cuisine that is based on local ingredients. There is a splendid array of seafood dishes and an elaborate vegetarian menu. The service is discreet and impeccable. *Nieuwe Doelenstraat 2–4, tel. 020/6234836. Reservations required. Jacket and tie required. AE, DC, MC, V. Closed Sat. lunch.*

★ **'t Swarte Schaep.** The Black Sheep is named after a proverbial 17th-century sheep that once roamed the area. With its creaking boards and array of copper pots, the interior is reminiscent of a ship's cabin. The Dutch chef uses seasonal ingredients to create classical French dishes with regional flourishes. Dinner orders are accepted until 11 PM—unusually late even for Amsterdam. *Korte Leidsedwarsstraat 24, tel. 020/6223021. Reservations required. AE, DC, MC, V.*

Expensive **★** **De Silveren Spiegel.** In an alarmingly crooked 17th-century house, enjoying the personal attention of the owner at one of just a small cluster of tables, you can have one of the best meals in town. Local ingredients such as Texel lamb and wild rabbit are cooked with subtlety and flair. *Kattengat 4–6, tel. 020/6246589. Reservations advised. AE, MC, V.*

Le Tout Court. This small, meticulously appointed restaurant features seasonal specialties (spring lamb, summer fruits, game during autumn and winter) personally prepared by owner-chef John Fagel, a member of Holland's first family of food. *Runstraat 13, tel. 020/6258637. Reservations advised. AE, DC, MC, V.*

Yamazoto. Japanese ex-pats laud this as the top Japanese restaurant in town. An award-winning chef blends the freshest local ingredients with exotica flown in daily from the Land of the Rising Sun. The full seasonal set menu will cost you over Fl. 100, but there is a score of less pricey options. At a separate sushi bar fresh sushi is prepared before your eyes. The adjoining Sazanaka Restaurant specializes in Teppan Yaki (food grilled at the table). *Hotel Okura, Fer-*

dinand Bolstraat 333, tel. 020/6787111. Reservations advised. AE, DC, MC, V.

Moderate–Expensive **Eerst Klas.** Amsterdam's best-kept secret is in the most obvious of places: the former first-class waiting lounge of the central train station. The classic, dark-wood paneling and soft interior lighting create the perfect hideaway from the city's hustle and bustle. The convenient location is also perfect for business lunches. Diners munch their way through tasty salads, steaks, and fish dishes. *Stationsplein 15, Spoer 2B, tel. 020/6250131. AE, DC, MC, V. Reservations advised.*

★ **Pier 10.** Perched on the end of a pier behind the Centraal Station, this intimate restaurant was built in the '30s as a shipping office. Water laps gently just beneath the windows, and the harbor lights twinkle in the distance. Culinary adventures might include eel in herb sauce with pasta or goose with smoked mushrooms. *De Ruyterkade Steiger 10, tel. 020/6248276. Reservations required. AE, MC, V.*

Moderate **Haesje Claes.** Traditional Dutch food is served here in a traditional Dutch environment, with prices that are easy on the wallet; it sounds like a tourist's dream and, in ways, it is. There's a cozy feeling here and a relaxed simplicity. Menu choices can be as basic as traditional *stamppot* (mixed potatoes and sauerkraut) or as elaborate as filet of salmon with lobster sauce. There is a tourist menu. *Spuistraat 273–275, tel. 020/6249998. Reservations advised. AE, DC, MC, V. Closed Sun. lunch.*

Lucius. Outstanding fish and seafood are simply served in a plain setting. Not for the queasy, though—as you tuck into your fish, its live cousins eye you from a tank along the wall. *Spuistraat 247, tel. 020/6241831. Reservations advised. AE, DC, MC, V. Closed Sun.*

Oesterbar. As its name suggests, the Oyster Bar specializes in seafood, some of which eyes you from the tank. The upstairs dining room is more formal than the downstairs bistro, but prices don't vary. Salmon, seawolf, and halibut are favorite seafood entrées; oysters are a good, if pricey, appetizer. *Leidseplein 10, tel. 020/ 6232988. Reservations advised. AE, DC, MC.*

Rose's Cantina. This perennial favorite of the sparkling set offers spicy Tex-Mex food, lethal cocktails, and a high noise level. Pop in for a full meal or a sundowner. *Reguliersdwarsstraat 38, tel. 020/ 6259797. Reservations required weekends. AE, DC, MC, V.*

Speciaal. Although set in the Jordaan area, this Indonesian restaurant is slightly off the beaten track. From the outside, the Speciaal looks very mundane, but inside, the soothing Indonesian prints, raffia work, and bamboo curtains create an intimate atmosphere. Along with the usual rijsttafel, chicken, fish, and egg dishes provide tasty variants on a sweet-and-sour theme. *Nieuwe Leliestraat 142, tel. 020/6249706. Reservations accepted. AE, MC, V.*

★ **Toscanini.** This cavernous, noisy Italian restaurant has superb cuisine. Try the pasta with game sauce, the scrumptious selection of antipasti, the rabbit, or the fresh fish dishes. *Lindengracht 75, tel. 020/6232813. Reservation required. No credit cards. Closed lunch and Tues.*

Inexpensive **De Keuken van 1870.** "The Kitchen of 1870" was a soup-kitchen through the Great Depression and two world wars and now serves up hearty Dutch food at unbeatably low prices. Tourists, punks, and pensioners sit at plain wooden tables spread out on a traditional black-and-white tiled floor. Enormous white plates emanate from the steamy kitchen piled high with good, nutritious meat and vegetables doused in gravy. *Spuistraat 4, tel. 020/6248965. No reservations. No credit cards.*

Eettuin. An "eating garden" in the heart of the arty Jordaan area, there's something here for everyone—from vegetarian dishes to spare ribs and the house special, pork. Unusual for Europe is the salad bar. *Tweede Tuindwarsstraat 10, tel. 020/6237706. Reservations advised. No credit cards. No lunch.*

Pancake Bakery. Here is a chance to try a traditionally Dutch way of keeping eating costs down. The name of the game is pancakes—for every course including dessert, for which the topping can be ice cream, fruit, or liqueur. The Pancake Bakery is not far from Anne Frankhuis. *Prinsengracht 191, tel. 020/6251333. No reservations. No credit cards.*

Lodging

Accommodations are tight from Easter to summer, so early booking is advised if you wish to secure a popular hotel. The other snag is parking. Since few hotels have parking lots, cars are best abandoned in a multistory parking ramp for the duration of your stay. Many visitors like to stay inside the concentric ring of canals, an atmospheric area of historic gable-roofed merchants' houses. Others prefer the quieter museum quarter, convenient for the Rijksmuseum and near enough to the Vondelpark for light jogging. For details and price-category definitions, *see* Lodging in Staying in Holland, *above.*

Very Expensive ★ **Amstel Inter-Continental.** Amsterdam's grand dame opened in 1867 and was completely renovated in late 1992. The result is spectacular. It is frequented by many of the nation's top businesspeople and visited at times by the royal family. *Professor Tulpplein 1, tel. 020/6226060, fax 020/6225808. 79 rooms with bath. AE, DC, MC, V.*

Amsterdam Hilton. This hotel is the site of John Lennon and Yoko Ono's famous bedroom strike, when the couple stayed in bed protesting for world peace; you can still stay in the room, now the honeymoon suite. One of the first international chain hotels to open in Amsterdam, the Hilton is in a residential part of the city overlooking the attractive Noorder Amstelkanaal. All the rooms are luxuriously appointed. *Apollolaan 138, tel. 020/6780780, fax 020/6626688. 274 rooms with bath. Facilities: casino. AE, DC, MC, V.*

Golden Tulip Barbizon Palace. The newest Golden Tulip Hotel in Amsterdam combines past and present with fantasy and flair. Sneak a peak at the adjoining conference center, which was built recently in the ruins of a 15th-century chapel. *Prins Hendrikkade 59–72, tel. 020/5564564, fax 020/6243353. 268 rooms with bath; 5 suites. AE, DC, MC, V.*

Grand Amsterdam. Amsterdam's former city hall has recently been converted into a luxury hotel. Parts of the building date back to the 16th century, but most of it belongs to the early part of the 20th, when the country's best artists and architects were commissioned to create a building the city could be proud of. Many of the original fittings remain, including a valuable mural by the painter Karel Appel. The rooms are pamperingly luxurious and the kitchens are under the supervision of the incomparable Albert Roux. *Oudezijds Voorburgwal 197, tel. 020/5553111, fax 020/5553222. 166 rooms with bath. Facilities: spa, restaurant, garden. AE, DC, MC, V.*

★ **Hôtel de l'Europe.** Owned by the Heineken brewers, the hotel hides its modern facilities behind a Renaissance-style facade. It has larger-than-average rooms, often decorated with old prints and Empire furniture. Apart from its world-renowned Excelsior restaurant, de l'Europe houses a sophisticated leisure complex and hotel swimming pool in Roman style. *Nieuwe Doelenstraat 2–4, tel. 020/ 6234836, fax 020/6242962. 100 rooms with bath. Facilities: restaurant, pool, leisure complex. AE, DC, MC, V.*

Expensive **Ciga Pulitzer.** The Pulitzer succeeds in making living in the past a
★ positive pleasure. Recent renovations make this excellent hotel even better. This is one of Europe's most ambitious hotel restorations, using the shells of a row of 17th-century merchants' houses. Inside, the refined atmosphere is sustained by the modern art gallery, the lovingly restored brickwork, oak beams, and split-level rooms—no two are alike. The tranquil inner courtyards are equally adapted to contemplation and outdoor concerts. *Prinsengracht 315–331, tel. 020/5235235, fax 020/6262646. 236 rooms with bath. Facilities: restaurant, bar. AE, DC, MC, V.*

Grand Hotel Krasnapolsky. This is one of the fine, Old World hotels in Amsterdam, dominated by its Winter Gardens restaurant recently restored to its original 1818 luster. The cosmopolitan atmosphere carries through all the rooms, with decor ranging from Victorian to Art Deco. Each room is well equipped, and there is a choice of restaurants. *Dam 9, tel. 020/5549111, fax 020/6228607. 300 rooms with bath. Facilities: parking. AE, DC, MC, V.*

Moderate **Ambassade.** With its beautiful canalside location, its Louis XV–
★ style decoration, and its Oriental carpets, the Ambassade seems more like a stately home than a hotel. Service is attentive and room prices include breakfast. For other meals, the neighborhood has a good choice of restaurants for eating out. *Herengracht 341, tel. 020/ 6262333, fax 020/6245321. 49 rooms with bath. AE, MC, V.*

Atlas Hotel. Renowned for its friendly atmosphere, this small hotel has moderate-size rooms decorated in Art Nouveau style. It's also very handy for Museumsplein, whose major museums are within easy walking distance. *Van Eeghenstraat 64, tel. 020/6766336, fax 020/6717633. 22 rooms with bath. Facilities: bar, restaurant. AE, DC, MC, V.*

Het Canal House. The American owners of this canalside hotel also opt to put antiques rather than televisions in the rooms. Spacious rooms overlook the canal or the illuminated garden. A hearty Dutch breakfast comes with the room. *Keizergracht 148, tel. 020/6225182, fax 020/6241317. 26 rooms with bath or shower. AE, DC, MC, V.*

Hotel de Filosoof. In a quiet street near the Vondel Park, this hotel attracts artists, thinkers, and people looking for something a little different. Bone fide Amsterdam philosophers are regularly to be found in the comfy armchairs of the salon. Each room is decorated in a different cultural motif—there's an Aristotle room, and a Goethe room adorned with texts from Faust. *Anna van den Vondelstraat 6, tel. 020/6833013, fax 020/6853750. 23 rooms with bath, 4 without bath. Facilities: bar. AE, MC, V.*

Inexpensive– **Agora.** Near the Singel flower market, this small hotel reflects the
Moderate cheerful bustle. The rooms are light and spacious, some decorated
★ with vintage furniture; the best overlook the canal or the university. Recently refurbished, this 18th-century house has a considerate staff, and a relaxed neighborhood ensures the hotel's popularity. Book well in advance. *Singel 462, tel. 020/6272200, fax 020/6272202. 11 rooms with bath or shower, 4 without bath. AE, DC, MC, V.*

Inexpensive **Botel.** This floating hotel moored near the Centraal Station is an appropriate place to stay in watery Amsterdam. The rooms are small, but the windows are large, offering fine views across the water to the city. Make sure you don't get a room on the land side of the vessel, or you'll end up staring at an ugly postal sorting office.

*Oosterdokskade 224, tel. 020/6264247, fax 020/6391952. 176 rooms
with shower. Facilities: bar. AE, DC, MC, V.*

Hotel Seven Bridges. Named for the scene beyond its front steps, this
small canal-house hotel offers clean, simple rooms with private
bathrooms (also small but clean). The Rembrandtsplein is nearby.
For a stunning view of the city, request one of the two large double
rooms. *Reguliersgracht 31, tel. 020/6231329, no fax. 6 rooms with
bath. No credit cards.*

Quentin Hotel. A stone's throw from the hectic Leidseplein is this
small, family-run hotel. It is simply decorated with plain colors and
modern prints, and flooded with light through large windows. The
best rooms are the spacious corner ones that overlook a canal.
*Leidsekade 89, tel. 020/6262187, fax 020/6220121. 16 rooms without
bath. AE, MC, V.*

The Arts

The arts flourish in tolerant and cosmopolitan Amsterdam. The best
sources of information about performances are the monthly publications *Time Out Amsterdam* (in English) and *Uit Krant* (in Dutch)
and the biweekly *What's On in Amsterdam*, which can be obtained
from the VVV office, where you can secure tickets for the more popular events. Tickets must be booked in person from Monday to Saturday, 10 to 4. You also can book at the **Amsterdam Uit Buro,**
Stadsschouwburg, Leidseplein 26, tel. 020/6211211.

Classical Classical music is featured at the **Concertgebouw** (Concertgebouw-
Music plein 2–6), home of one of Europe's finest orchestras. A smaller auditorium in the same building is used for chamber music, recitals,
and even jam sessions. While ticket prices for international orchestras are fairly high, most concerts are good value and the Wednesday lunchtime concerts are free. The box office is open from 9:30 to 7;
you can make telephone bookings (020/6718345) from 10 to 5.

Opera and The Dutch national ballet and opera companies are housed in the
Ballet new **Muziektheater** (tel. 020/625–5455) on Waterlooplein. Guest
companies from foreign countries perform there during the three-
week Holland Festival in June.

Theater **Stalhouderij Theater** (1e Bloemdwarsstraat 4, tel. 020/6262282). An
international cast performs a wide range of English-language plays
in a former stable in the Jordaan. For experimental theater and colorful cabaret in Dutch, catch the shows at **Felix Meritis House**
(Keizersgracht 324, tel. 020/6231311).

Film The largest concentration of movie theaters is around Leidseplein
and near Muntplein. Most foreign films are subtitled rather than
dubbed, which makes Amsterdam a great place to catch up on movies you missed at home. The **City 1–7** theater near Leidseplein is the
biggest (seven screens), but the Art Deco–era **Tuschinski** on
Reguliersbreestraat is the most beautiful cinema house.

Nightlife

Amsterdam has a wide variety of discos, bars, and exotic shows. The
more respectable—and expensive—after-dark activities are in and
around Leidseplein, Rembrandtsplein, and Thorbeckeplein; fleshi-
er productions are on Oudezijds Achterburgwal. Names and locations change from year to year, but most bars and clubs are open
every night from 5 PM to 2 AM or 5 AM. On weeknights, very few clubs
charge admission, though the more lively ones sometimes ask for a
"club membership" fee of Fl. 20 or more. Drink prices are for the most

part not exorbitant. It is wise to steer clear of the area behind the central station at night.

Bars   **De Jaren** (Nieuwe Doelenstraat 20, tel. 020/6255771) is a spacious, high-ceilinged café with a canalside terrace. The smart young business set come in for a drink after work; arts and media people use it as a communal sitting-room; and the trendy pass through on their way out night-clubbing.

Jazz Clubs   Set in a converted warehouse, the **Bimhuis** is currently the most fashionable jazz club. Ticket holders can sit in the adjoining BIMcafé and enjoy a magical view across Oude Schans to the port (Oude Schans 73–77, tel. 020/6233373. Open Thurs.–Sat. from 9 PM). If you long for good Dixieland jazz, go to **Joseph Lam Jazz Club** (Van Diemenstraat 242, tel. 020/6228086); it's only open on Saturdays.

Rock Clubs   **Paradiso** (Weteringschans 6–8, tel. 020/6264521) is an Amsterdam institution; converted from a church, it has become a vibrant venue for rock, new age, and even contemporary classical music.

Discos   Mostly only hidden in cellars around the Leidseplein, the discos fill up after midnight. **Roxy** (Singel 465, tel. 020/6200354) is the Netherland's current hot spot. Also popular are **Escape** (Rembrandtsplein 11–15, tel. 020/6223542) and **It** (Amstelstraat 24, tel. 020/6250111), generally straight Thurs., Sun.; gay Fri.–Sat.). **Mazzo** (Rozengracht 114, tel. 020/6267500) uses dramatic lighting and slick videos to attract gay and straight student poseurs, would-be musicians, and artists.

Casinos   Blackjack, roulette, and slot machines have come lately—but not lightly—to the thrifty Dutch. Now everyone wants to play. The newest and most elegant venue, **Holland Casino** (Max Euweplein 62, tel. 020/6201006), just off Leidseplein, opened in 1991. You'll need your passport to get in; the minimum age is 18.

Gay and Lesbian Bars   Amsterdam has a vibrant gay and lesbian community, concentrated principally on Warmoestraat, Reguliersdwarsstraat, Amstelstraat, and Kerkstraat near Leidseplein. The **Gay & Lesbian Switchboard** (tel. 020/6236565) can provide information on the city's nightlife.

Historic Holland

This circular itinerary can be followed either clockwise or counterclockwise, but whichever way you decide to follow it, you'll be sure to see some of Holland's most characteristic sights. There are the historic towns of Leiden and Utrecht and the major museums in Haarlem; in between these towns, you'll see some of Holland's windmill-dotted landscape and pass through centers of tulip growing and cheese production.

Getting Around

The most convenient way to cover the following itinerary is by rented car out of Amsterdam. If you want someone else to do the navigating, then all the towns listed below can be reached by bus or train. From Amsterdam there are, for example, three direct trains per hour to Haarlem, Leiden, and Utrecht. Check with the VVV office in Amsterdam for help in planning your trip, or inquire at the central station.

Historic Holland

Guided Tours

Alternatively, these towns are covered, in various permutations, by organized bus tours out of Amsterdam. Brochures for tour operators are available from the **VVV** offices in Amsterdam: Stationplein 10, Leidsestraat 106, or on Stadionplein; the central telephone number is 06/34034066.

The VVV in Utrecht organizes several excursions, including a boat trip along the canals and a sightseeing flight over the city. There are also day trips to country estates and castles, often enclosed by Dutch baroque gardens.

Tourist Information

Amersfoort (Stationsplein 9–11, tel. 033/635151).
Apeldoorn (Stationsplein 6, tel. 055/788421).
Gouda (Markt 27, tel. 01820/13666).
Haarlem (Stationsplein 1, tel. 023/319059).
Leiden (Stationsplein 210, tel. 071/146846).
Lisse (Grachtweg 53a, tel. 02521/14262).
Utrecht (Vredenburg 90, tel. 06/34034085).
Zandvoort (Schoolplein 1, tel. 02507/17947).

Exploring Historic Holland

Amersfoort Traveling southeast from Amsterdam, 90 kilometers (56 miles) along highway A1, you will reach Apeldoorn, but if you have time, stop off at **Amersfoort** en route. Although today it is a major industrial town, Amersfoort still manages to retain much of its medieval character and charm. Starting at the **Koopelport,** the imposing water gate across the Eem, dating from 1400, walk down Kleine Spui. On the right is **St. Pieters-en-Bloklands Gasthuis,** a hospice founded in 1390. Close by is the **Museum Flehite,** with its unusual medieval collections that give a fascinating insight into the history of the town. *Westsingel 50, tel. 033/619987. Admission: Fl. 4. Open Tues.– Fri. 10–5, weekends 2–5.*

Continuing along Breestraat, you'll come to the graceful, 102-meter- (330-foot-) high **Onze Lieve Vrouwetorn** (Tower of Our Lady). The musical chimes of this Gothic church can be heard every Friday between 10 and 11 AM. Turning left down Langstraat, past the Gothic **St. Joriskerk,** you will come to the **Kamperbinnenpoort,** the turreted land gate dating from the 15th century. Making your way left down Muurhuizen, you'll come to a short canal, the **Hovik,** which was once the old harbor.

Apeldoorn The main attraction at **Apeldoorn** is the **Rijksmuseum Paleis Het Loo.** This former royal palace was built during the late 17th century for Willem III and has been beautifully restored to illustrate the domestic surroundings enjoyed by the House of Orange for more than three centuries. The museum, which is housed in the stables, has a fascinating collection of royal memorabilia, including cars and carriages, furniture and photographs, silver and ceramics. The formal gardens and the surrounding parkland offer attractive walks. *Tel. 055/212244. Admission Fl. 10. Open Tues.–Sun. 10–5.*

From Apeldoorn, it is well worth the 5-kilometer (3-mile) drive on N304 to the **Kröller-Muller Museum.** In the woods in the middle of a national park, it displays one of the finest collections of modern art in the world. It possesses 278 works by Vincent van Gogh, as well as paintings, drawings, and sculptures by such masters as Seurat, Redon, Braque, Picasso, and Mondrian. The building, too, is part of the experience; it seems to bring the museum's wooded setting right into the galleries with you. The major sculptures are shown in the garden; don't miss them. *National Park De Hoge Veluwe, tel. 08382/ 1041. Admission: Fl. 7.50. Open Tues.–Sat. 10–5, Sun. 10–5 (Nov.–Apr. 1–5). Sculpture garden closes ½ hour earlier.*

Arnhem If you have children in tow, consider a visit to the **Nederlands Openlucht Museum** (Open Air Museum) in **Arnhem,** 15 kilometers (9¼ miles) from Apeldoorn on A90. In a 44-acre park, the curators have brought together original buildings and furnishings from all over the Netherlands to establish both a comprehensive display of Dutch rural architectural styles as well as a depiction of traditional ways of living. There are farmhouses and barns, workshops, and windmills—animals, too. *Schelmseweg 89, tel. 085/576111. Admission: Fl. 12.50. Open Apr.–Oct., weekdays 9:30–5, weekends 10–5.*

Utrecht West of Apeldoorn, 72 kilometers (44 miles), is the city of **Utrecht.** The high gabled houses of the Nieuwegracht, the canals with their water gates, the 13th-century wharves and storage cellars of the Oudegracht, and the superb churches and museums are just some of the key attractions, most of which are situated around the main cathedral square. The **Domkerk** is a late-Gothic cathedral containing a series of fine stained-glass windows. The Domtoren (bell tower) opposite the building was connected to the cathedral until a hurricane hit in 1674. The bell tower is the tallest in the country, and it has 456 steep steps that lead to a magnificent view. A guide is essential in the labyrinth of steps and passageways. *Domplein, tel. 030/310403.*

Admission free to cathedral; Fl. 4 to Domtoren. Open May–Sept., Mon.–Sat. 10–5; Sun 2–4; Oct.–Apr., Mon.–Sat. 11–4, Sun. 2–4.

Not far from the cathedral is the merry **Rijksmuseum van Speelklok tot Pierement** (National Museum from Musical Clock to Street Organ), devoted solely to music machines—from music boxes to street organs and even musical chairs. During the guided tour, music students play some of the instruments. The museum is housed in Utrecht's oldest parish church. *Buurkerkhof 10, tel. 030/312789. Admission: Fl. 7.50. Open Tues.–Sat. 10–5, Sun. 1–5.*

Behind the museum is **Pieterskerk,** the country's oldest Romanesque church, built in 1048. The grandeur of the city's churches reflects the fact that Utrecht was Holland's religious center during the Middle Ages. Most churches are open during the summer and a church concert is held almost every day.

Walk south out of Domplein, down Lange Nieuwstraat. Halfway down is the **Rijksmuseum Het Catharijneconvent.** In addition to its collection of holy relics and vestments, this museum contains the country's largest display of religious art and history. *Nieuwegracht 63, tel. 030/317296. Admission: Fl. 5. Open Tues.–Fri. 10–5, weekends 11–5.*

There are more museums to be explored on Agnietenstraat, which crosses Lange Nieuwstraat. The **Centraal Museum** houses a rich collection of contemporary art and other city exhibits. Amid the clutter is an original Viking ship (discovered in 1930) and a 17th-century dollhouse complete with period furniture, porcelain, and miniature old masters. *Agnietenstraat 1, tel. 030/362362. Admission: Fl. 5. Open Tues.–Sat. 10–5, Sun. noon–5.*

An important part of the Central Museum's collection is a house that is located just a few blocks away; it is known as the **Rietveld Schröder House.** Designed in 1924 by the architect Gerrit Rietveld working with Truus Schröeder, this is considered to be the architectural pinnacle of the style known as De Stijl (The Style). The use of primary colors (red, yellow, blue) and black and white, and the definition of the interior space are unique and innovative even today. The experience of the house is, as one art historian phrased it, "like wandering into a Mondrian painting." The house was completely restored to its original condition in 1987. Allow 15 minutes to walk to the house; there is a guided tour through the rooms. *Prins Hendrikiaan 50, tel. 030/362310. Admission: Fl. 9. Open Wed.–Sat. 11–5. Call for appointment.*

Gouda West of Utrecht, 36 kilometers (22 miles) along the A12, you'll come to **Gouda,** famous for its cheese. Try to be there on a Thursday morning in July or August, when the cheese market, centered around the **Waag,** or Weigh House, is held. Brightly colored farm wagons are loaded high with orange cheeses. Take a good look at the **Stadhuis** (Town Hall); it's one of Holland's quaintest, with parts dating to 1449. (Admission: Fl. 1. Open weekdays 9–4, weekends 11–3; often closed for weddings.) After trying all five types of Gouda cheese, leave some space for syrup waffles, the city's other specialty.

By the side of the market square is **Sint Janskerk** (Church of St. John); what you see today was built during the 16th century. It has the longest nave in the country, and 70 glorious stained-glass windows, the oldest of which dates from 1555. Around the corner from the cathedral is the Catharina Gasthuis, now the **Stedelijk Museum Het Catharina Gasthuis,** the municipal museum that houses many unusual exhibits, including a fearsome medieval torture chamber and an equally horrific operating room. *Oosthaven 9, Achter de Kerk 14, tel. 01820/88440. Admission: Fl. 3.50. Open Mon.–Sat. 10–5, Sun. noon–5.*

Leiden   Heading north on N11, you'll come to the ancient city of **Leiden,** renowned for its spirit of religious and intellectual tolerance and known for its university and royal connections. Start at the **Lakenhal,** built in 1639 for the city's cloth merchants and now an art gallery, cloth, and antiques museum. Pride of place in the collection goes to the 16th- and 17th-century Dutch paintings, with works by Steen; Dou; Rembrandt; and, above all, Lucas van Leyden's *Last Judgment*—the first great Renaissance painting in what is now the Netherlands. Other rooms are devoted to furniture and to the history of Leiden's medieval guilds: the drapers, tailors, and brewers. *Oude Singel 32, tel. 071/165361. Admission: Fl. 5. Open Tues.–Fri. 10–5, weekends noon–5.*

Near the Lakenhal is the **Molenmuseum De Valk** (Windmill Museum), housed in an original windmill, built in 1747, which was worked by 10 generations of millers until 1964. The seven floors still contain the original workings, an old forge, washrooms, and living quarters. On summer Saturdays, the mill turns—but for pleasure, not business. *2e Binnenvestgracht 1a, tel. 071/165355. Admission: Fl. 3. Open Tues.–Sat. 10–5, Sun. 1–5.*

Crossing the canal and walking into bustling Breestraat and then down the narrow Pieterskerk-Choorsteeg, you'll come to the imposing **St. Pieterskerk,** with its memories of the Pilgrim Fathers who worshiped here and of their spiritual leader, John Robinson, who is buried here. A narrow street by the **Persijnhofje** almhouse, dating from 1683, takes you downhill to the gracious, tree-lined Rapenburg Canal, crossed by triple-arched bridges and bordered by stately 18th-century houses. To the right is the **Rijksmuseum van Oudheden** (National Museum of Antiquities), the country's leading archaeological museum. The prize exhibit is the entire 1st-century AD Temple of Taffeh, donated by the Egyptian government. There is also a floor devoted to finds in The Netherlands. *Rapenburg 28, tel. 071/163163. Admission: Fl. 5. Open Tues.–Sat. 10–5, Sun. noon–5.*

On the other side of the canal, a little farther down, you find the **Academie** (university) and the **Hortus Botanicus** gardens. The university was founded by William the Silent as a reward to Leiden for its victory against the Spanish in the 1573–74 siege. During the war, the dikes were opened and the countryside flooded so that the rescuing navy could sail right up to the city walls. Founded in 1587, the botanical gardens are among the oldest in the world. The highlights are a faithful reconstruction of a 16th-century garden, the herb garden, the colorful orangery, and the ancient trees. *Rapenburg 73. Admission: Fl. 3.50. Open Apr.–Oct., Mon.–Sat. 9–5, Sun. 10:30–5; Nov.–Mar., weekdays 9–4:30, Sun. 10:30–3.*

Follow Keiserstraat out of Rapenburg and turn left into Boisotkade. On your left is the **Pilgrim Fathers Documentatie Centrum.** This tiny museum contains photocopies of documents and maps related to the Pilgrims during their stay in Leiden, before they went to Delftshaven on the first stage of their arduous voyage to the New World. *Vliet 45, tel. 071/120191. Admission free. Open weekdays 9:30–4:30.*

Lisse/Aalsmeer   North from Leiden toward Haarlem, you can stop to visit (in spring only) the 70-acre **Keukenhof Gardens.** Set in a park intersected by canals and lakes, the world's largest flower show draws huge spring crowds to its regimental lines of tulips, hyacinths, and daffodils. (A lazier way of seeing the flowers is from the windows of the Leiden–Haarlem train.) *Admission: Fl. 15. Open late Mar.–late May, daily 8–7:30.*

During the rest of the year, or certainly as a complement to a spring visit to Keukenhof, you will want to see how flowers are marketed. Flowers are very big business to the Dutch, and the Netherlands is home to the world's largest complex of flower auction houses. The biggest of these auction facilities (it also is the single largest in the world) is the **Bloemenveiling** (Flower Auction) in the town of Aalsmeer near the national airport and not far from Amsterdam. In a building the size of three football fields, there are three separate auction rooms all functioning at the same time. Flowers, plants, greens, and even dried flowers are bought and sold in staggering quantities five days a week, year round. Get there early; it's all over by 10 AM. *Legmeerdijk 313, tel. 02977/34567. Open weekdays 7:30–11 AM. Closed weekends and holidays.*

Haarlem With its secret inner courtyards and pointed gables, **Haarlem** can resemble a 17th-century canvas, even one painted by Frans Hals, the city's greatest painter. The area around the **Grote Markt,** the market square, provides an architectural stroll through the 17th and 18th centuries. Some of the facades are adorned with such homilies as "The body's sickness is a cure for the soul." Haarlem's religious faith can also be sensed in any of its 20 almshouses. The **Stadhuis** (Town Hall) was once a hunting lodge. Nearby is the **Vleeshal,** or meat market, which has an especially fine gabled front. This dates from the early 1600s and is now used as an art gallery and a museum of local history. *Lepelstraat. Admission free. Open Mon.–Sat. 11–5, Sun. 1–5.*

Across from the Vleeshal is the **Grote Kerk,** dedicated to St. Bavo. The church, built between 1400 and 1550, houses one of Europe's most famous organs. This massive instrument has 5,000 pipes, and both Mozart and Handel played on it. It is still used for concerts, and an annual organ festival is held here in July. Make your way down Damstraat, behind the Grote Kerk, and turn left at the **Waag** (Weigh House). On the left is the **Teylers Museum,** which claims to be the oldest museum in the country. It was founded by a wealthy merchant in 1778 as a museum of science and the arts; it now houses a fine collection of The Hague school of painting as well as a collection of drawings and sketches by Michelangelo, Raphael, and other non-Dutch masters. Since the canvases in this building are lit by natural light, try to see the museum on a sunny day. *Spaarne 16, tel. 023/319010. Admission: Fl. 6.50. Open Tues.–Sat. 10–5, Sun. 1–5.*

Follow the Binnen Spaarn and turn right into Kampervest and then Gasthuisvest. On your right, in Groot Heiligland, you'll find the **Frans Hals Museum.** This museum, in what used to be a 17th-century hospice, contains a marvelous collection of the artist's work; his paintings of the guilds of Haarlem are particularly noteworthy. The museum also has works by Hals's contemporaries. *Groot Heiligland 62. Admission: Fl. 6.25. Open Mon.–Sat. 11–5, Sun. 1–5.*

Dining and Lodging

In towns such as Apeldoorn and Gouda, which have few good hotels, bed-and-breakfast accommodations, booked through the VVV office, make a more interesting choice. Rooms in Utrecht are often in short supply, so book in advance or immediately upon arrival. For details and price-category definitions, *see* Dining and Lodging in Staying in Holland, *above.*

Apeldoorn
Dining

De Echoput. Near to Het Loo, this delightful restaurant is a member of the Alliance Gastronomique Nederlandaise, a guarantee of an expensive meal of local and gourmet specialties. There is an attractive terrace, overlooking fountains and greenery, for summer dining. *Amersfoortseweg 86, tel. 057691248. Reservations required. AE, DC, MC, V. Closed Sat. lunch, Mon. Very Expensive.*

Lodging

Hotel de Keizerskroon. A perfect complement to the nearby royal palace is a stay at the Keizerskroon (the name means Emperor's Crown). In style and amenities it is a business hotel; in comfort and cordiality it is a traveler's hotel; in setting—at the edge of the city on a quiet street leading toward the woods—it is a weekend getaway inn. *Koningstraat 7, tel. 055/217744. 100 rooms with bath. AE, DC, MC, V. Expensive.*

Gouda
Dining

Goudsche Salon. Wooden floors, a big table of newspapers and magazines, and a friendly atmosphere combine with tasty cuisine to make this an ideal place for a lunch or dinner break. There are healthy salads and a good-value, seasonally changing set menu that might include such delights as rabbit cooked in mustard and tarragon. *Wijdstraat 13, tel. 01820/12330. Reservations accepted. AE, MC, V. Moderate.*

Haarlem
Dining

Café Restaurant Brinkman. This elegant, classic grand café overlooks the magnificent St Bavo's church. You can while away the afternoon over a single coffee or choose from a wide menu of salads, pastas, and local dishes. *Grote Markt 9–13, tel. 023/323111. Reservations accepted. AE, DC, MC, V. Moderate.*

Lodging

Golden Tulip Lion d'Or. Just five minutes from the old city center and conveniently near the railway station, this comfortable but unprepossessing hotel offers all the luxuries associated with a Golden Tulip hotel. Special weekend deals include reduced room prices, gourmet evening meals, and free cocktails. *Kruisweg 34–36, tel. 023/321750. 36 rooms with bath. Facilities: restaurant, conference rooms. AE, DC, MC, V. Expensive.*

Leiden
Dining

Jill's. A delightful, bright restaurant run by a cheerful staff and situated just a few minutes' walk from the De Valk windmill, this spot is ideal for a relaxing meal. A variety of set menus with Italian, Oriental, and Dutch influences allows you to find something to satisfy almost every palate. There is fresh fish daily. *Morsstraat 6, tel. 071/143722. AE, MC. Moderate.*

Annie's Verjaardag. A low-arched cellar full of cheery students and a water-level canalside terrace make Annie's popular in all weather. There is a modest but well-prepared selection of salads and baguettes and usually at least one daily special of something more substantial (such as mussels or pork medallions in a creamy casserole). *Hoogstraat 1a, tel. 071/125737. No credit cards. Inexpensive–Moderate.*

Dining and Lodging
★

Nieuw Minerva. This family-run hotel is a conversion of eight 15th-century buildings. While the original part of the hotel is decorated in Old Dutch style, the newer part is better equipped but has slightly less character. Many of the rooms overlook a quiet tributary of the Rhine. The restaurant caters to most tastes and pockets. The excellent three-course tourist menu offers separate fish, meat, and vegetarian menus. A monthly menu is served with four or six courses of one own's choice. Delicacies are also found on the à la carte menu. *Boommarkt 23, tel. 071/126358, fax 071/142674. 40 rooms, 30 with bath or shower. Facilities: restaurant. AE, DC, MC, V. Moderate.*

Lodging **Hotel De Doelen.** This small hotel is in a characteristic patrician house. The spartan decor is in keeping with the character of the 15th-century house, but the 16 rooms are comfortable and much sought after. *Rapenburg 2, tel. 071/120527, fax 071/128453. 4 rooms with bath, 12 with shower. AE, DC, MC, V. Moderate.*

Utrecht **Town Castle Oudaen/"Between Heaven and Earth."** In medieval
Dining times Utrecht's Oudegracht (Old Canal) was lined with many "town castles" such as this one, and some would say that along with the Dom Tower, this is one of the finest examples of medieval architecture in Utrecht. As a restaurant it is a curious place. You may be confused by the clublike atmosphere as you enter, but you'll find the dining room on the second floor (which may be why it is called "Between Heaven and Earth") and an excellent café at ground level. Another unique feature of the Oudaen is that they brew their own beer in the basement and, in addition to serving it on tap, use it as an ingredient in many of their dishes. *Oudegracht 99, tel. 030/311864. Reservations accepted. AE, DC, MC, V. Closed lunch (except café). Moderate.*

De Soepterrine. This snug restaurant offers steaming bowls of homemade soups. Some 10 different varieties are made daily, usually including Dutch specialties such as thick *erwtensoep* (pea soup). Each bowl comes with crusty bread and herb butter. Quiches and generous salads fill up those extra corners. *Zakkendragerssteeg 40, tel. 030/317005. AE, MC, V. Inexpensive.*

Lodging **Malie.** The Malie hotel is on a quiet leafy street, a 15-minute walk from the old center. This small, friendly hotel has an attractive breakfast room overlooking the garden and terrace. *Maliestraat 2–4, tel. 030/316424, fax 030/340661. 29 rooms with bath or shower. Facilities: bar, breakfast room. AE, DC, MC, V. Moderate.*

The Hague, Delft, and Rotterdam

Within this itinerary you can visit the Netherlands' most dignified and spacious city—the royal, diplomatic, and governmental seat of Den Haag (in English, better known as The Hague)—and its close neighbor, the leading North Sea beach resort of Scheveningen. Also nearby are Delft, a historic city with many canals and ancient buildings, and the energetic and thoroughly modern international port city of Rotterdam. It is known to the Dutch as "Manhattan on the Maas," both for its office towers and its cultural attractions.

Getting Around

The Hague and Delft are each about 60 kilometers (37½ miles) southwest of Amsterdam and can be reached within less than an hour by fast and frequent trains. The heart of both towns is compact enough to be explored on foot. Scheveningen is reached from The Hague's center by bus or tram. Travelers will find public transportation more convenient than driving because of severe parking problems at the resort. The RET Metro is an easy-to-use option for getting around Rotterdam. There are two main branches (north–south and east–west), and they cross in the heart of the business district at a major transfer center, which connects one branch to the other.

The Hague, Delft, and Rotterdam

0 ——— 5 miles
0 ——— 5 km

North Sea

Noordwijk-Binnen

Katwijk aan Zee

A44

Rijn

Leiden

Wassenaar

Scheveningen

N44

A4

The Hague
(Den Haag)

Voorberg

Zoetermeer

A12

Rijkswijk

E30

Monster

Poeldijk

N213

Delft

A13

N209

A20

A16

Hoek van
Holland

N20

Naaldwijk

Europoort

Nieuwe

A20

Rotterdam

Maassluis

Maas

A15

Guided Tours

Boat Trips   From The Hague, various boat companies run short day trips and longer candlelight dinner cruises. These can be booked at The Hague VVV or through **Rondvaartbedrijf RVH** (Spui 256, near the central station, tel. 070/3462473). Scheveningen offers fishing-boat tours around the Dutch coast. Contact **Sportsviscentrum Trip 3** (Scheveningen, tel. 070/3541122). In Delft, the VVV organizes boat tours along the unspoiled canal system.

Depending on the time available (or the time of year) and the extent of your interest, you can cruise the port of Rotterdam on a basic tour of 1¼ hours (year-round) or choose one that lasts as long as 9 hours (midsummer only). **Spido Havenrondvaarten** (Willemsplein, tel. 010/4135400), the main boat company, also operates summer evening music-and-dinner cruises of the inner harbor. The 1¼-hour tour costs Fl. 12. The pier can be reached by taking the Metro blue line toward Spijkenisse to the Leuvehaven station and walking to the end of the boulevard.

Orientation   City sightseeing tours of The Hague can be arranged by or through
Tours   the main VVV office next to the central station. The size and diversity of the city make a bus tour a logical choice. The "Royal Bus Tour" leaves from outside the VVV office at 1 PM every day between April and September. The 2½- to 3-hour trip includes background on the royal family and takes passengers past Queen Beatrix's residences. Book in advance at the VVV; cost: Fl. 19.

Scheveningen and Delft are best seen on foot. The Delft VVV office organizes tours, while the Scheveningen VVV will advise on coastal strolls.

In the long summer season (April through September), there are daily two-hour bus tours of Rotterdam conducted by the Rotterdam Tourist Office. The tours, which leave from the VVV at 1:30 PM, cost Fl. 25.

Tourist Information

Delft (Markt 85, tel. 015/126100).
The Hague (Babylon Center, Koningin Julianaplein 30, next to the central station, tel. 06/34035051).
Rotterdam (Coolsingel 67, in Centraal Station, tel. 06/34034065).
Scheveningen (Gevers Deynootweg 126, tel. 070/3546200).

If you're planning to spend a few days in The Hague or Rotterdam, ask for the VVV brochure on city events and entertainment. Tickets for concerts and other entertainment can be reserved in person at the VVV office.

Exploring the Hague, Delft, and Rotterdam

The Hague During the 17th century, when Dutch maritime power was at its zenith, **The Hague** was known as "The Whispering Gallery of Europe" because it was thought to be the secret manipulator of European politics. Although the Golden Age is over, The Hague remains a powerful world diplomatic capital, quietly boastful of its royal connections. It also is the seat of government for the Netherlands.

Its heart is the **Hofvijver** reflecting pool and the complex of gracious **Parliament Buildings** reflected in it. At the center of it all is the **Ridderzaal** (Knight's Hall). Inside are vast beams spanning a width of 18 meters (59 feet), flags, and stained-glass windows. A sense of history pervades the 13th-century great hall. It is now used mainly for ceremonies: Every year the queen's gilded coach brings her here to open Parliament. The two government chambers sit separately in buildings on either side of the Ridderzaal and can be visited by guided tour only when Parliament is not in session. Tours in English are conducted by Stichting Bezoekerscentrum Binnenhof (tel. 070/3646144), located just to the right of the Ridderzaal. Groups should book in advance. *Binnenhof 8a. Open Mon.–Sat. 10–4. Cost: Fl. 5.50.*

On the far side of the **Binnenhof,** the inner court of the Parliament complex, is a small, well-proportioned Dutch Renaissance building called the **Mauritshuis,** one of the finest small art museums in the world. This diminutive 17th-century palace contains a feast of art from the same period, including six Rembrandts; of these the most powerful is *The Anatomy Lesson of Dr. Tulp,* a theatrical work depicting a gruesome dissection of the lower arm. Also featured are Vermeer's celebrated *Girl Wearing a Turban* and his masterpiece, the glistening *View of Delft,* moodily emerging from a cloudburst. *Korte Vijverberg 8, tel. 070/3469244, Admission: Fl. 7.50. Open Tues.–Sat. 10–5, Sun. 11–5.*

Outside the Mauritshuis, follow the Korte Vijverberg past the reflecting pool, which is bordered by patrician houses with revamped 18th- and 19th-century facades, a sign of the area's continuing popularity with the local aristocracy. Only the presence of huge ducks ruffles the surface of this stately lake.

Turn right at Lange Vijverberg and walk a short way until you come to Lange Voorhout, a large L-shaped boulevard. During the last century, horse-drawn trams clattered along its cobbles and deposited dignitaries outside the various palaces. Apart from the trams, not much has changed. Diplomats still eat in the historic Hotel des Indes. For more than 100 years, Hotel des Indes has hosted ambassadors and kings, dancers and spies. Memories of famous guests remain in the form of Emperor Haile Selassie's gold chair and the ballerina Anna Pavlova's silver candlesticks. Pavlova and the spy Mata Hari both have suites named for them. No. 34 once belonged to William I, the first king of the Netherlands, but later it became the royal library; it is now the **Supreme Court.** With its clumsy skewed gable, the headquarters of the Dutch Red Cross at No. 6 seems out of place on this stately avenue. A few doors down, at the corner of Parkstraat, is The Hague's oldest church, the **Kloosterkerk,** built in 1400 and once used by the Black Friars. During the spring, the adjoining square is covered with yellow and purple crocuses; on Thursdays during the summer, it is the scene of a colorful antiques market.

North of Lange Voorhout is the **Panorama Mesdag,** a 122-meter (400-foot) painting-in-the-round that shows the nearby seaside town of Scheveningen as it looked in 1880. Housed in a specially designed building, the painting encircles you. Hendrik Mesdag was a late-19th-century marine painter, and his calming seascape is painted in the typically melancholic colors of The Hague School. Mesdag was assisted by his wife, who painted much of the fishing village, and by a friend, who painted the sky and dunes. *Zeestraat 65b, tel. 070/ 3642563. Admission: Fl. 4. Open Mon.–Sat. 10–5, Sun. noon–5.*

Just around the corner in Laan van Meerdervoort is the painter's home, now transformed into the **Rijksmuseum H.W. Mesdag.** Paintings by Mesdag and members of The Hague School are hung beside those of Corot, Courbet, and Rousseau. These delicate landscapes represent one of the finest collections of Barbizon School painting outside France. At press time (spring 1994) the museum was closed for renovation and was scheduled to re-open sometime in 1995. *Laan van Meerdervoort 7f.*

The **Vredespaleis** (Peace Palace), near Laan van Meerdervoort, is a monument to world peace through negotiation. Following the first peace conference at The Hague in 1899, the Scottish-American millionaire Andrew Carnegie donated $1.5 million for the construction of a building to house a proposed international court. The Dutch government donated the grounds, and other nations offered furnishings and decorations. Although it still looks like a dull multinational bank, the building has been improved by such gifts as Japanese wall hangings, a Danish fountain, and a grand staircase presented by The Hague. Today the **International Court of Justice,** consisting of 15 jurists, has its seat here. There are guided tours when the court is not in session. *Carnegieplein 2, tel. 070/3469680. Admission: Fl. 3. Open weekdays 10–noon and 2–4.*

The nearby **Haags Gemeentemuseum** (Municipal Art Museum) is the home of the largest collection of Mondrians in the world plus two vast collections of musical instruments—European and non-European. The building itself is also fascinating. It was built in 1935 and is an example of the International Movement in modern architecture. *Stadhouderslaan 41, tel. 070/3512873. Admission: Fl. 8. Open Tues.–Sun. 11–5.*

Behind the Gemeentemuseum, overlooking Zorgvliet (the western-most park of the Scheveningse Bosjes, a vast stretch of green that separates The Hague from Scheveningen), is the **Omniversum,** described as Europe's first space theater. It is housed in a cylindrical building with a 23-meter (75-foot) dome that acts as a screen for the projection of six–10 daily video presentations of outer space and oceanic voyages. *President Kennedylaan 5, tel. 070/3545454 for reservations and show times. Admission: Fl. 15. Open Tues.–Thurs. 11–4, Fri.–Sun. 11–9.*

Between The Hague and Scheveningen is **Madurodam,** a miniature Holland where the country's important buildings and facilities are duplicated at a scale of 1/52 of what its life-size counterpart would be. None of the details has been forgotten, from the harbor, with its lighthouse and quayside cranes, to the hand-carved furniture in the gabled houses. Son-et-lumière (sound-and-light) shows are planned for the summer months. *Haringkade 17, tel. 070/3520930. Admission: Fl. 14 adults, Fl. 8.50 children. Open late March–May, 9 AM–10:30 PM; June–Aug., 9 AM–11 PM; Sept., 9 AM–9:30 PM; Oct.–early Jan., 9–6.*

Scheveningen is adjacent to The Hague along the North Sea coast. A fishing village since the 14th century, it became popular as a beach resort during the last century, when the grand Kurhaus Hotel was built, which still is a focal point of this beach community.

The beach itself, protected from tidal erosion by stone jetties, slopes gently into the North Sea in front of a high promenade whose function is to protect the boulevard and everything behind it from winter storms. The surface of the beach is fine sand, and you can bicycle or walk for miles to the north.

At the turn of the century, the **Kurhaus Hotel** stood alone at the center of the beach as a fashionable and aristocratic resort. After being in decline for a long time, it was restored and reopened, having added a casino among its new attractions. There is a painted ceiling over the large central court and buffet restaurant.

Part of the new design around the Kurhaus area includes the Golfbad, a surf pool complete with artificial waves. **The Pier,** completed in 1962, stretches 372 meters (1,200 feet) into the sea. Its four circular end buildings provide a sun terrace and restaurant, a 43-meter- (141-foot-) high observation tower, an amusement center with children's play area, and an underwater panorama. At 11 on summer evenings, the Pier is the scene of dramatic fireworks displays.

Delft   Thirteen kilometers (8 miles) along the A13 from The Hague, you'll enter **Delft.** There is probably no town in the Netherlands that is more intimate, more attractive, or more traditional than this mini-metropolis, whose famous blue-and-white earthenware is popular throughout the world. Compact and easy to explore, despite its web of canals, Delft is best discovered on foot—although canal boat excursions are available April through October, as are horse-drawn trams that leave from the marketplace. Every street is lined with attractive medieval Gothic and Renaissance houses that bear such names as Wijnhaus (Wine House) and Boter Brug (Butter Bridge).

In the marketplace, the only lively spot in this tranquil town, is the **Nieuwe Kerk** (New Church), built during the 14th century, with its piercing Gothic spire 93 meters (300 feet) high, a magnificent carillon of 48 bells, and the tomb of William the Silent. Beneath this grotesque black marble sarcophagus is a crypt containing the remains of members of the Orange-Nassau line, including all members of the royal family since King William I ascended the throne during the mid-16th century. *Admission: Fl. 2.50. Tower: Fl. 3.50. Open Apr.–Oct., Mon.–Sat. 9–5; Nov.–Mar., Mon.–Sat. 11–4.*

Walk around the right side of the Nieuwe Kerk, then left at the back and along the Vrouwenregt canal for a few steps before taking another left turn into Voldergracht. To the left, the backs of the houses rise straight from the water as you stroll to the end of the street, which is marked by the sculptured animal heads and outdoor stairs of the old **Meat Market** on the right. Cross the Wijnhaven and turn left along its far side to the Koornmarkt, a stately canal spanned by a high, arching bridge that is one of the hallmarks of Delft.

Turn right at the Peperstraat to reach the **Oude Delft canal,** the city's oldest waterway. A few blocks farther along the canal is the **Prinsenhof,** formerly the Convent of St. Agatha, founded in 1400. The chapel inside dates from 1471; its interior is remarkable for the wooden statues under the vaulting ribs. Today the Prinsenhof is a museum that tells the story of the liberation of the Netherlands after 80 years of Spanish occupation (1568–1648). For Dutch royalists, the spot is significant for the assassination of Prince William of Orange in 1584; the bullet holes can still be seen in the wall. *St. Agathaplein 1. Admission: Fl. 3.50. Open Tues.–Sat. 10–5, Sun. 1–5.*

Across the Oude Delft canal is the **Oude Kerk** (Old Church), a vast Gothic monument of the 13th century. Its beautiful tower, surmounted by a brick spire, leans somewhat alarmingly. *Oudegracht. Admission: Fl. 2.50. Open Apr.–Oct., Mon.–Sat. 10–5.*

Beyond the Prinsenhof on the same side of the Oude Delft canal is the **Lambert van Meerten Museum,** a mansion whose timbered rooms are filled with the country's most complete collection of old Dutch tiles as well as Delft pottery. *Oude Delft 199. Admission: Fl. 3.50. Open Tues.–Sat. 10–5, Sun. 1–5.*

While in Delft, you will want to see the famous local specialty—Delftware. Decorated porcelain was brought to Holland from China on East India Company ships and was so much in demand that Dutch potters felt their livelihood was being threatened. They therefore set about creating pottery to rival Chinese porcelain. There are only two manufacturers that still make hand-painted Delftware: **De Delftse Pauw** and the more famous "Royal" **De Porceleyne Fles.** *De Delftse Pauw: Delftweg 133, tel. 015/124920. Admission free. Open Apr.–mid–Oct., daily 9–4:30; mid–Oct.–Mar., weekdays 9–4, weekends 11–1. De Porceleyne Fles: Rotterdamsweg 196, tel. 015/560234. Admission free. Open Apr.–Oct., Mon.–Sat. 9–5, Sun. 10–4; Nov.–Mar., weekdays 9–5, Sat. 10–4.*

Rotterdam Thirteen kilometers (8 miles) farther along A13 is **Rotterdam,** one of the few thoroughly modern cities in the Netherlands and the site of the world's largest and busiest port. Art lovers know Rotterdam for its extensive and outstanding collection of art; philosophers recall it as the city of Erasmus. It is a major stop on the rock 'n' roll concert circuit, and its soccer team is well known, but the city's main claim to fame is its extraordinary concentration of adventurous modern architecture. Oddest buildings of the lot are a series of cube-shaped apartments, turned to balance on one corner at the top of a tall stem. One of these precarious-looking houses, the **Kijk-Kubus,** just east of the center, is open to the public. *Overblaak 70, tel. 010/4142285. Admission: Fl. 2.50. Open Tues.–Fri. 10–5, weekends 11–5.*

The biggest surprise in Rotterdam is the remarkable 30-mile-long **Europoort,** which handles more than 250 million tons of cargo every year and more ships than any other port in the world. It is the delta for three of Europe's most important rivers (the Rhine, the Waal, and the Meuse/Maas) and a seemingly endless corridor of piers, warehouses, tank facilities, and efficiency. You can get to the piers at Willemsplein by tram or Metro (blue line to the Leuvehaven station) from the central station. The 1¼-hour harbor tour (*see* Boat Trips in Guided Tours, *above*) illuminates Rotterdam's vital role in world trade.

As an alternative to the boat tour, you also can survey the harbor from the vantage point of the **Euromast** observation tower. Get there via the Metro red line to Dijkszicht. *Parkhaven 20, tel. 010/ 4364811. Admission: Fl. 14.50. Open Apr.–June and Sept., daily 10–7; July and Aug., Sun. and Mon. 10–7, Tues.–Sat. 10 AM–10:30 PM; Oct.–Mar., daily 10–5.*

After the harbor tour, walk down the boulevard past the Metro station into Leuvehaven. On your right as you stroll along the inner harbor is **IMAX Rotterdam,** a gigantic theater in which films are projected onto a screen six stories high. There are earphones for English translation. *Leuvehaven 77, tel. 010/4048844. Admission: Fl. 14. Shows Tues.–Sun. 2, 3, 7:30, 10:30. Mon. also during holiday periods.*

Past the theater is a hodgepodge of cranes, barges, steamships, and old shipbuilding machines, even a steam-operated grain elevator. What looks at quick glance to be a sort of maritime junkyard is in fact a work in progress: Volunteers are working daily to restore these vessels and machines. The whole operation is an open-air museum of shipbuilding, shipping, and communications that is part of the **Prins Hendrick Maritime Museum,** housed in a large gray building at the head of the quay. Also moored in this inner harbor adjacent to the museum is the historic 19th-century Royal Dutch Navy warship *De Buffel.* Within the museum are exhibits devoted to the history and activity of the great port outside. *Leuvehaven 1, tel. 010/4132680. Admission: Fl. 6. Open Tues.–Sat. 10–5, Sun. 11–5.*

From the nearby Churchillplein Metro station, take the red line toward Marconiplein to the first stop at Eendrachtsplein, where you will walk along the canal toward the Museumpark. As a welcome contrast to the industrial might of the Europoort and Holland's maritime history, the **Boymans–van Beuningen Museum** is an impressive refresher course in Western European art history. The collection includes paintings by many famous master painters, Dutch and otherwise, from the 14th century to the present day. There is an Old Arts section that includes the work of Brueghel, Bosch, and Rembrandt and a renowned print gallery with works by artists as varied as Dürer and Cézanne. Dali and Magritte mix with the Impressionists in the Modern Arts collection. *Mathenesserlaan 18–20, tel. 010/4419400. Admission: Fl. 6. Open Tues.–Sat. 10–5, Sun. 11–5.*

Beside this long-established museum is the spanking-new **Nederlands Architectuurinstituut,** which houses changing exhibitions in the field of architecture and interior design. Across the park is the recently built **Kunsthal,** which plays host to all manner of major temporary exhibitions—from Andy Warhol retrospectives to rows of compact cars. *Nederlands Architectuurinstituut, Museumpark 25, tel. 010/4401200. Admission: Fl. 6. Open Tues.–Sat. 10–5, Sun.*

11–5. Kunsthal, Westzeedijk 341, tel. 010/4400300. Admission: Fl. 10. Open. Tues.–Sat. 10–5, Sun. 11–5.

Three stops farther west along the Metro line is Delfshaven, the last remaining nook of old Rotterdam. (From the Metro station double back along Schiedamseweg, then turn right down Aelbrechtskolk.) Rows of gabled buildings line the waterfront, and there is even a windmill. Nowadays Delfshaven is an up-and-coming area of trendy galleries, cafés, and restaurants.

Dining and Lodging

For details and price-category definitions, *see* Dining and Lodging in Staying in Holland.

Delft
Dining
Spijshuis De Dis. At this favorite neighborhood spot, a friendly staff serves typically Dutch delicacies. Even after a hearty meal of mussels in garlic sauce (a house specialty) or another of the myriad seafood dishes, save room for the chef's pièce de résistance: cinnamon parfait. *Beestenmarket 36, tel. 015/131782. Reservations advised. AE, MC, V. Moderate.*

Dining and
Lodging
Hotel Grand Cafe Central. This is the hot spot in central Delft for afternoon coffee or delicious hot chocolate, best enjoyed with one of the creamy cakes. Simple lunches and dinners are available. The hotel is clean, but rooms are modest in size. *Wijnhaven 6–8, tel. 015/123442, fax 015/125164. AE, DC, MC, V. Inexpensive.*

Lodging
Hotel De Ark. This bright, airy hotel in the center of old Delft comprises three canal houses joined so that nearly every room has a view of the canal or the large garden in back. Rooms are clean and modern. *Koornmarkt 59–65, tel. 015/157999, fax 015/144997. 16 rooms with bath, 8 apartments. Facilities: parking. AE, DC, MC, V. Expensive.*

Hotel Leeuwenbrug. This is a traditional Dutch family-style hotel on one of the prettiest canals in Delft. There are two buildings, one more traditional and simpler, with smaller, cheaper rooms; the annex is more contemporary and businesslike. Everyone enjoys breakfast overlooking the canal, however, and rooms on the top floor of the annex overlook the city. *Koornmarkt 16, tel. 015/147741, fax 015/147741. 38 rooms with bath. Facilities: parking. AE, MC, V. Moderate.*

The Hague
Dining
Djawa. Whether or not it is a result of the city's diplomatic heritage is unknown, but The Hague is said to have Holland's highest concentration of Indonesian restaurants. Among them is this cozy, family-run, neighborhood restaurant located not far from the center. *Mallemolen 12a, tel. 070/3635763. Reservations accepted. AE, DC, MC, V. Closed lunch. Moderate–Expensive.*

Le Haricot Vert. Built in 1638 as a staff house for the nearby palace, it is nowadays an intimate, candlelit restaurant in The Hague's city center. Dishes combine Dutch simplicity with French flair. Succulent meats swimming in sauce appear on large white plates with a colorful tangle of vegetables. Owner Herman van Overdam is to be seen chatting at diners' tables, or flitting back into the kitchen to create one of his sinfully laden dessert platters. Menus change frequently according to what is in season. *Molenstraat 9a–11, tel. 070/3652278. Reservations advised. AE, MC, V. Moderate–Expensive.*

Dining and
Lodging
Corona. Overlooking a charming square in the center of the city is this pride and joy of the Hague. The restaurant is one of the best in town, and the hotel is first-class, too. For less expensive meals, try

the brasserie. *Buitenhof 39–42, tel. 070/3637930, fax 070/3615785, AE, DC, MC, V. Expensive.*

Rotterdam **Millers.** This converted canalside warehouse in the attractive
Dining Delfshaven area dates from 1620. There is a spacious downstairs bistro for drinks and lighter meals and more intimate nooks under the rafters for candlelit dinners. The chef is influenced by Italian, French, and Japanese cuisines and comes up with imaginative dishes such as smoked breast of goose with beer and mustard. *Voorhaven 3, tel. 010/4775181. Reservations advised. AE, DC, MC, V. Moderate–Expensive.*

Inn the Picture. This trendy café offers a wide selection of typical Dutch fare. The salads are especially inviting. In summer, tables offer a view of passing crowds in the shopping district. *Karel Doormanstraat 294, tel. 010/4133204. AE, DC, MC, V. Moderate.*

Dining and **Intell.** Not the least of the attractions of the Hotel Intell are its views
Lodging of Rotterdam harbor—from the rooms, the restaurant, and even from the fully equipped rooftop health club that includes an 8-by-4-meter swimming pool. This is a busy, cheerful, modern hotel located adjacent to the IMAX super theater and near both the maritime museum and the Spido harbor tour pier. Named Le Papillon, the Intell's restaurant is a lively, intimate dining room with the best view in the house! The menu is French-influenced, offering such delicacies as cod in pink pepper sauce. Both the Metro and tram stop outside the door. *Leuvehaven 80, tel. 010/4134139, fax 010/4133222. 150 rooms with bath. Facilities: parking, bar, restaurant, health club, sauna, pool. AE, DC, MC, V. Expensive.*

15 Hungary

Hungary sits at the crossroads of Central Europe, having retained its own identity by absorbing countless invasions and foreign occupations. Its industrious, resilient people have a history of brave but unfortunate uprisings: against the Turks in the 17th century, the Habsburgs in 1848, and the Soviet Union in 1956. Each has resulted in a period of readjustment, a return to politics as the art of the possible.

The '60s and '70s saw matters improve politically and materially for the majority of Hungarians. Communist party leader János Kádár remained relatively popular at home and abroad, allowing Hungary to expand and improve trade and relations with the West. The bubble began to burst in the 1980s, however, when the economy stagnated and inflation escalated. The peaceful transition to democracy began when young reformers in the party shunted aside the aging Mr. Kádár in 1988 and began speaking openly about multiparty democracy, a market economy, and cutting ties with Moscow. Events quickly gathered pace, and by spring 1990, as the Iron Curtain fell, Hungarians went to the polls in the first free elections in 40 years. A center-right government led by the late Prime Minister József Antall took office, sweeping away the Communists and their renamed successor party, the Socialists, who finished fourth.

Two rivers cross the country. The famous Duna (Danube) flows from the west through Budapest on its way to the southern frontier, while the smaller Tisza flows from the northeast across the Nagyalföld (Great Plain). What Hungary lacks in size, it makes up for in beauty and charm. Western Hungary is dominated by the largest lake in Central Europe, Lake Balaton. Although some overdevelopment has blighted its splendor, its shores are still lined with Baroque villages, relaxing spas, magnificent vineyards, and shaded garden restaurants serving the catch of the day. In eastern Hungary, the Nagyalföld offers visitors a chance to explore the folklore and customs of the Magyars (the Hungarians' name for themselves and their language). It is an area of spicy food, strong wine, and the proud *csikós* (horsemen).

However, it is Budapest, a city of more than 2 million people, that draws travelers from all over the world. The hills of Buda rise from the brackish waters of the Danube, which bisects the city; on the flatlands of Pest are an imposing array of hotels, restaurants, and shopping areas. Throughout Hungary, comfortable accommodations can be found for comparatively modest prices, and there's an impressive network of inexpensive guest houses.

Hungarians are known for their hospitality and love talking to foreigners, although their strange language, which has no links to other European tongues, can be a problem. Today, however, everyone seems to be learning English, especially young people. Trying out a few words of German will delight the older generation. But what all Hungarians share is a deep love of music, and the calendar is star-studded with it, from Budapest's famous opera to its annual spring music festival and the serenades of gypsy violinists during evening meals.

Essential Information

Before You Go

When to Go Many of Hungary's major fairs and festivals take place in the spring and fall. During July and August, Budapest can be hot and the re-

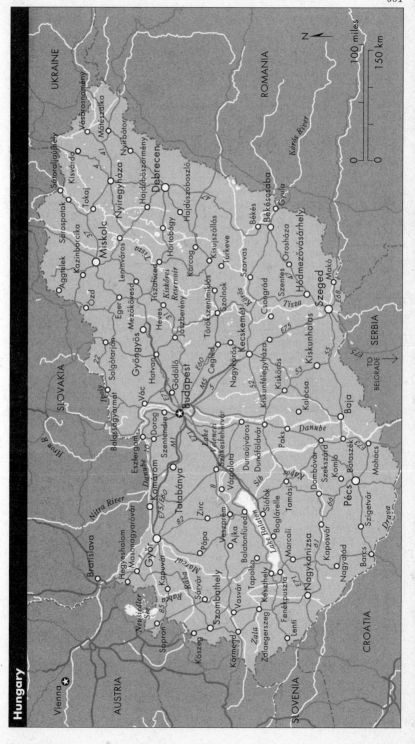

Hungary

sorts at Lake Balaton crowded, so spring (May) and the end of summer (September) are the ideal times to visit.

Climate The following are average daily maximum and minimum temperatures for Budapest.

Jan.	34F	1C	May	72F	22C	Sept.	73F	23C
	25	- 4		52	11		54	12
Feb.	39F	4C	June	79F	26C	Oct.	61F	16C
	28	- 2		59	15		45	7
Mar.	50F	10C	July	82F	28C	Nov.	46F	8C
	36	2		61	16		37	3
Apr.	63F	17C	Aug.	81F	27C	Dec.	39F	4C
	45	7		61	16		30	- 1

Currency The unit of currency is the forint (Ft.), divided into 100 fillérs (f.). There are bills of 50, 100, 500, 1,000, and 5,000 forints and coins of 1, 2, 5, 10, 20, and the new but less common 100 and 200 forints and 10, 20, and 50 fillérs. A newly designed series of the same coins was introduced into the system in late 1993, precipitating mild confusion and general frustration with pay phones and other coin-operated machines that still accept only the old coins. The tourist exchange rate was approximately 102 Ft. to the dollar and 151 Ft. to the pound sterling at press time (spring 1994). Note that official exchange rates are adjusted at frequent intervals.

Hungary does not require you to change a certain sum of money for each day of your stay. Exchange money as you need it at banks, hotels, or travel offices, but take care not to change too much, because although in theory you can change back 50% of the original sum when you leave (up to U.S. $100)—provided you've kept the exchange receipts—it may prove difficult in practice, at least until the forint becomes convertible.

Most credit cards are accepted, though don't rely on them in smaller towns or less expensive accommodations and restaurants. Eurocheque holders can cash personal checks in all banks and in most hotels. American Express, which now has a full-service office in Budapest (V Deák Ferenc utca 10, tel. 1/267–2024, 1/267–2022, or 1/266–80680; fax 1/267–2029), also dispenses cash to its cardholders.

There is still a black market in hard currency, but changing money on the street is illegal and the bank rate almost always comes close. Stick with official exchange offices.

What It Will Cost Although first-class hotel chains in Budapest charge standard international prices, quality hotels are still modest by Western standards. Even though the introduction of value-added tax (VAT) in 1988 has increased many of the prices in the service industry by up to 25%, and the annual inflation rate is 25%, enjoyable vacations with all the trimmings remain less expensive than in nearby Western cities like Vienna.

Sample Prices Cup of coffee, 60 Ft.; bottle of beer, 100 Ft.–120 Ft.; soft drinks, 20 Ft.–50 Ft.; ham sandwich, 100 Ft.; 1-mile taxi ride, 60 Ft.; museum admission, 30 Ft.–80 Ft.

Visas Only a valid passport is required of U.S., British, and Canadian citizens. For additional information, contact the Hungarian Embassy in the United States (3910 Shoemaker St., NW, Washington, DC 20008, tel. 202/362–6730) or Canada (7 Delaware Ave., Ottawa K2P OZ2, Ontario, tel. 613/234–8316), or the Hungarian Embassy in London (35b Eaton Pl., London SW1X 8BY, tel. 071/235–2664).

Customs
On Arrival Objects for personal use may be imported freely. If you are over 16, you may also bring in 250 cigarettes or 50 cigars or 250 grams of tobacco, plus 2 liters of wine, 1 liter of spirits, and .25 liter of perfume. A customs charge is made on gifts valued in Hungary at more than 8,000 Ft.

On Departure Take care when you leave Hungary that you have the right documentation for exporting goods. Keep receipts of any items bought from Konsumtourist, Intertourist, or Képcsarnok Vállalat. A special permit is needed for works of art, antiques, or objects of museum value. You are entitled to a VAT refund on new goods (i.e., not works of art, antiques, or objects of museum value) valued at more than 25,000 Ft.

For further information, inquire at the **National Customs and Revenue Office** (VIII Keleti train station arrivals area, tel. 1/114–0203 or 1/114–0280). If you have trouble communicating, ask **Tourinform** (tel. 1/117–9800) for help.

Language Hungarian (Magyar) tends to look and sound intimidating to everyone at first because it is a non-Indo-European language. However, there is a major trend, especially among young people, to learn English, and most people in the tourist trade, from bus drivers to waiters, speak some English or German.

Getting Around

By Car
Documentation To drive in Hungary, U.S. and Canadian visitors need an International Driver's License—although their domestic licenses are usually accepted anyway—and U.K. visitors may use their own domestic license.

Road
Conditions There are three classes of roads: highways (designated by the letter M and a single digit), secondary roads (designated by a two-digit number), and minor roads (designated by a three-digit number). Highways and secondary roads are generally excellent. The condition of minor roads varies considerably. There are no toll charges on highways.

Rules of the
Road Hungarians drive on the right and observe the usual Continental rules of the road. Unless otherwise noted, the speed limit in developed areas is 50 kph (30 mph), on main roads 90 kph (55 mph), and on highways 120 kph (75 mph). Seat belts are compulsory and drinking alcohol is strictly prohibited—the penalties are very severe.

Gasoline Gas stations are plentiful in and around major cities, and major chains are also opening modern all-service stations on highways in the provinces. A gallon of gasoline *(benzin)* costs about $3. Unleaded gasoline, only slightly more expensive, is usually available at all stations, as is diesel. Interag Shell and Áfor stations at busy traffic centers stay open all night; elsewhere, from 6 AM to 8 PM.

Breakdowns The **Hungarian Automobile Club** runs a 24-hour "Yellow Angels" breakdown service from Budapest XIV (Francia út 38/A, tel. 1/252–8000). There are repair stations in all the major towns and emergency telephones on the main highways.

By Train Travel by train from Budapest to other large cities or to Lake Balaton is cheap and efficient. Remember to take *gyorsvonat* (express trains) and not *személyvonat* (locals), which are extremely slow. A *helyjegy* (seat reservation), which costs about 40 Ft. (130 Ft. for Inter-City trains) and is sold up to 60 days in advance, is advisable for all express trains, especially for weekend travel in summer. It is also worth paying a little extra for first-class tickets.

Fares Only Hungarian citizens are entitled to student and senior citizen discounts. InterRail cards are available for those under 26, and the Rail Europe Senior Travel Pass entitles senior citizens to a 30% reduction on all trains. Snacks and drinks can be purchased on all express trains, but the supply often runs out quickly, especially in summer, so pack a lunch just in case. For more information about rail travel, contact the **MÁV Passenger Service** (Andrássy út 35, Budapest VI, tel. 1/122–8049 or 1/122–8275).

By Bus Long-distance buses link Budapest with many main cities in Eastern and Western Europe. Services to the eastern part of the country leave from Népstadion station (tel. 1/252–4496). Buses to the west and south leave from the main Volán bus station at Erzsébet tér in the Inner City (tel. 1/118–2122). Although inexpensive, they tend to be crowded, so reserve your seat.

By Boat Hungary is well equipped with nautical transport, and Budapest is situated on a major international waterway—the Danube. Vienna is five hours away by hydrofoil, and many Hungarian resorts are accessible by hydrofoil or boat. For information about excursions or pleasure cruises, contact **MAHART Tours** (Belgrád rakpart, Budapest V, tel. 1/118–1704, 1/118–1586, or 1/118–1743) or **IBUSZ** (Hungarian Travel Bureau; Károly körút 3/C, Budapest VII, tel. 1/121–1000 or 1/121–2932).

By Bicycle A land of rolling hills and flat plains, Hungary lends itself to bicycling. The larger train stations around Lake Balaton rent bicycles for about 200 Ft. a day. For information about renting in Budapest, contact **Tourinform** (Sütő utca 2, tel. 1/117–9800). **IBUSZ Riding and Hobbies** department provides a variety of guided bicycle tours (Ferenciek tere 10, Budapest V, tel. 1/118–2967).

Staying in Hungary

Telephones Pay phones use 5-Ft. coins—the cost of a three-minute local call—
Local Calls and also accept 10- and 20-Ft. coins. At press time (spring 1994), pay phones had still not been converted to accept Hungary's new coins. Most towns in Hungary can be dialed directly—dial 06 and wait for the buzzing tone, then dial the local number. It is unnecessary to use the city code, 1, when dialing within Budapest.

International Direct calls to foreign countries can be made from Budapest and all
Calls major provincial towns only by using the push-button telephones, or from hotels and post offices, and by dialing 00 and waiting for the international dialing tone. Gray card-operated telephones are on their way to outnumbering coin-operated phones in Budapest and throughout the Balaton region. The cards—available at post offices and most newsstands and kiosks—come in units of 50 (250 Ft.) and 200 (600 Ft.) calls and save you from having to continually feed coins into the slot while you're making your call.

Operators International calls can be made through the operator by dialing 09; for operator-assisted calls within Hungary, dial 01. Be patient: The telephone system is antiquated, especially in the countryside.

Information Dial 1/117–0170 for directory assistance. Some operators speak English and, depending on their mood, may assist you in English.

Mail The post offices near Budapest's Keleti (East) (VII. Baross tér 11c) and Nyugati (West) (VI. Teréz körút 105–107) train stations are open 24 hours.

Postal Rates An airmail postcard to the United States, the United Kingdom, and the rest of Western Europe costs 41 Ft., and an airmail letter costs from 56 Ft. Postcards to the United Kingdom and the rest of Western Europe cost 35 Ft., letters from 50 Ft.

Receiving Mail A poste restante service, for general delivery, is available in Budapest. The address is Magyar Posta, H-1052 Budapest, Petőfi Sándor utca 17–19. The roman numeral prefix listed in a Budapest address refers to one of the city's 22 districts.

Opening and Closing Times Banks are generally open weekdays 8–1; many close at noon on Fridays.

Museums are generally open daily from 10 to 6 and are closed on Mondays.

Department stores are open weekdays 10 to 5 or 6, Saturday until 1. Grocery stores are generally open weekdays 7 or 8 AM to 7 PM; "nonstops" or *éjjeli-nappali* are open 24 hours.

National Holidays January 1; March 15 (Anniversary of 1848 Revolution); April 16 and 17 (Easter and Easter Monday); May 1 (Labor Day); June 4 and 5 (Pentecost); August 20 (St. Stephen's and Constitution Day); October 23 (1956 Revolution Day); December 24–26.

Dining There are plenty of good, affordably priced restaurants offering a variety of Hungarian dishes. Meats, rich sauces, and creamy desserts predominate, but the health-conscious will also find salads, even out of season. There are self-service restaurants *(önkiszolgáló étterem)*, sit-down snack bars *(bistró* or *étel bár)*, snack counters *(büfé)*, cafés *(eszpresszó)*, and bars *(drink-bár)*. The pastry shops *(cukrászda)* are also worth a try.

In almost all restaurants, an inexpensive fixed-price lunch, called a *menü*, is available, usually for as little as 350 Ft. It includes soup or salad, an entrée, and a dessert.

Mealtimes Hungarians eat early—you risk off-hand service and cold food after 9 PM. Lunch, the main meal for many, is served from noon to 2.

Dress At most moderately priced and inexpensive restaurants, casual but neat dress is acceptable.

Ratings Prices are per person and include a first course, main course, and dessert, but no wine or tip. Prices in Budapest tend to be a good 30% higher than elsewhere in Hungary. Best bets are indicated by a star ★.

Category	All Areas
Very Expensive	over 2,000 Ft.
Expensive	1,400 Ft.–2,000 Ft.
Moderate	800 Ft.–1,400 Ft.
Inexpensive	under 800 Ft.

Lodging There are few expensive hotels outside Budapest, but the moderate-
Hotels ly priced hotels are generally comfortable and well-run, although single rooms with baths are scarce. Inexpensive establishments—more numerous every year as Hungarians convert unused rooms or second apartments into rental units for tourists—seldom have private baths, but plumbing is adequate almost everywhere.

Rentals Apartments in Budapest and cottages at Lake Balaton are available. Rates and reservations can be obtained from tourist offices in Hungary and abroad. A Budapest apartment might cost 15,000 Ft. a week, while a luxury cottage for two on Lake Balaton costs around 35,000 Ft. a week. Bookings can be made in Budapest at the **IBUSZ** on Petőfi tér 3 (tel. 1/118–5707 or 1/118–4842), which is open 24 hours a day, or through IBUSZ offices in the United States and Great Britain. (*See* Government Tourist Offices in Chapter 1.)

Guest Houses Also called pensions, these offer simple accommodations—well suited to people on a budget. Some offer simple breakfast facilities. Arrangements can be made through local tourist offices or travel agents abroad.

In the provinces it is safe to accept rooms that you are offered directly: They will almost always be clean and in a relatively good neighborhood, and the prospective landlord will probably not cheat you. *Szoba kiadó* (or the German *Zimmer frei*) means "Room to Rent." The rate per night for a double room in Budapest or at Lake Balaton is around 2,000 Ft., which includes the use of a bathroom but not breakfast. Reservations and referrals can also be made by any tourist office, and if you go that route, you have someone to complain to if things don't work out.

Camping Most of the 140 campsites in Hungary are open from May through September. As rates are no longer state-regulated, prices vary. An average rate is about 600 Ft. a day. There's usually a small charge for hot water and electricity plus an accommodations fee—around 100 Ft. per person per night. Children often get a 50% reduction. Camping is forbidden except in appointed areas. Information can be obtained through travel agencies or through the **Hungarian Camping and Caravanning Club** (Budapest VIII, Üllői út 6, tel. 1/133–6536), which publishes an informative brochure listing campsites and their facilities in English.

Ratings The following price categories are in forints for a double room with bath and breakfast during the peak season; rates are even lower off-season and in the countryside, sometimes under 1,500 forints for two. For single rooms with bath, count on about 80% of the double-room rate. Most large hotels require payment in hard currency. Best bets are indicated by a star ★.

Category	Budapest	Balaton
Very Expensive	over 20,000 Ft.	over 9,000 Ft.
Expensive	13,000–20,000 Ft.	7,000–9,000 Ft.
Moderate	6,000–13,000 Ft.	3,500–7,000 Ft.
Inexpensive	under 6,000 Ft.	under 3,500 Ft.

During the peak season (June through August), full board may be compulsory at the Lake Balaton hotels. During the off-season (in Budapest, September through March; at Lake Balaton, in May and September), rates can be considerably lower than those given above.

Tipping Four decades of socialism didn't alter the Hungarian habit of tipping generously. Cloakroom and gas-pump attendants, hairdressers, waiters, and taxi drivers all expect tips. At least 10% should be added to a restaurant bill or taxi fare. If a gypsy band plays exclusively for your table, you can leave 100 Ft. in the plate discreetly provided for that purpose.

Budapest

Arriving and Departing

By Plane Hungary's international airport, **Ferihegy,** is about 22 kilometers (14 miles) southeast of the city. All **Malév** and **Lufthansa** flights operate from the new Terminal 2 (tel. 1/157–8268); other airlines use Terminal 1. For same-day flight information, call the airport authority (tel. 1/157–7155). The staff takes its time to answer calls, and may not be cordial; be prepared.

Between the Airport and Downtown Minibuses to and from Erzsébet tér station (Platform 1) in downtown Budapest leave every half hour from 10 AM to 6 PM. The trip takes 30–40 minutes (longer in rush hours) and costs 200 Ft. The modern minivans of the fast, friendly, and reliable LRI Airport Shuttle service (tel. 1/157–8555) transport you to any destination in Budapest, door to door, for 600 Ft., even less than the least expensive taxi—and most employees speak English. At the airport, buy tickets at the LRI counter in the arrivals hall near baggage claim; for your return trip, just call ahead for a pick-up. A taxi ride to the center of Budapest should cost no more than 1,000 Ft., and take about the same time. Avoid drivers who offer their services before you are out of the arrivals lounge.

By Train There are three main train stations in Budapest: Keleti (East), Nyugati (West), and Déli (South). Trains from Vienna usually operate from the Keleti station, while those to the Balaton depart from the Déli.

By Bus Most buses to Budapest from the western region of Hungary, including those from Vienna, arrive at **Erzsébet tér** station.

By Car The main routes into Budapest are the M1 from Vienna (via Győr) and the M7 from the Balaton.

Getting Around

Budapest is best explored on foot. The maps provided by tourist offices are not very detailed, so arm yourself with one from any of the bookshops in Váci utca or from downtown stationery shops and newsstands.

By Public Transportation The public transportation system—a metro (subway), buses, streetcars, and trolleybuses—is cheap, efficient, and simple to use but closes down around midnight. However, certain trams and buses run on a limited schedule all night. A day ticket *(napijegy)* costs 200 Ft. (three-day, 400 Ft.) and allows unlimited travel on all services within the city limits. You can also buy tickets for single rides for 30 Ft. from metro stations or newsstands. You can travel on all trams, buses, and on the subway with this ticket, but you can't change lines.

Bus, streetcar, and trolleybus tickets must be canceled on board—watch how other passengers do it; metro tickets are canceled at station entrances. Don't get caught without a ticket: Spot checks are frequent, and you can be fined several hundred forints.

By Taxi Taxis are plentiful and a good value, but make sure that they have a meter that is working. The average initial charge is 30 Ft., plus 40 Ft. per kilometer plus 12 Ft. per minute of waiting time. There are too many taxis in Budapest, and some drivers try to charge outrageous prices. Avoid unmarked, "freelance" taxis; stick with those affiliated with an established company. The best rates are with **Főtaxi** (tel. 1/222–2222), **6 X 6** (tel. 1/266–6666), **Citytaxi** (tel. 1/153–3633 or 1/211–1111), **Volántaxi** (tel. 1/166–6666), and **Teletaxi** (tel. 1/155–5555).

By Boat In summer a regular boat service links the north and south of the city, stopping at points on both banks, including Margit-sziget (Margaret Island). From May through September boats leave from the quay at Vigadó tér on 1½-hour cruises between the Árpád and Petőfi bridges. The trip, organized by **MAHART,** runs twice a day and costs around 300 Ft. (tel. 1/118–1704).

Important Addresses and Numbers

Tourist Information **Tourinform** (Sütő utca 2 [Metro: Deák Tér], tel. 1/117–9800) is open daily 8–8. **IBUSZ Accommodation Office** (Petőfi tér 3, tel. 1/118–5707 or 1/118–4842) is open 24 hours. **Budapest Tourist** (Roosevelt tér 5, tel. 1/117–3555) is also helpful. *The Budapest Sun,* an English-language weekly newspaper that covers news, business and culture, carries general orientation tips for tourists and listings of concerts and foreign-language films.

Embassies **U.S.** Szabadság tér 12 (Budapest V, tel. 1/112–6450). **Canadian** Budakeszi út 32 (Budapest XII, tel. 1/176–7711). **U.K.** Harmincad utca 6 (Budapest V, tel. 1/266–2888). **Australian** Délibáb utca 30 (Budapest VI, tel. 1/153–4233 or 1/153–4577).

Emergencies **Police** (tel. 07). **Ambulance** (tel. 04). **Doctor:** Ask your hotel or embassy for recommendations. **I.M.S.** (International Medical Services) (XIII. Váci út 202, tel. 1/129–8423) is a private clinic staffed by English-speaking doctors offering 24-hour medical service. U.S. and Canadian visitors are advised to take out full medical insurance. U.K. visitors are covered for emergencies and essential treatment.

English-Language Bookstores **Foreign-Language Book Store** (V Váci utca 32), **Central Secondhand Bookshop** (V Múzeum körút 15), **Idegennyelvű Könyvesbolt** (Foreign-language Bookstore, V Petőfi Sándor utca 1), **Longman ELT** (VIII Köcsey utca 2), **Interbright** (XII Tartsay Vilmos út 11–13), **Bestsellers** (V Október 6. utca 11), and **Universum** (V Váci utca 31–33). Foreign publications—including those in English—can be bought at the reception desks of major hotels and at newsstands at major traffic centers.

Travel Agencies **American Express** (V Déak Ferenc utca 10, tel. 1/267–2024, 1/267–2022, or 1/266–8680, fax 1/267–2029). **Getz International** (V Falk Miksa utca 5, tel. 1/112–0645, fax 1/112–1014). **Vista** (VII Károly körút 21, tel. 1/269–6032, 1/142–9316, 1/142–1534, fax 1/269–6031).

Guided Tours

Orientation Tours **IBUSZ** (*see* Important Addresses and Numbers, *above*) sponsors three-hour bus tours of the city, which operate all year and cost about 2,000 Ft. Starting from Erzsébet tér, they take in parts of both Buda and Pest. **Gray Line Cityrama** (V Báthori utca 22, tel. 1/132–5344) also offers a three-hour city bus tour, as well as the three-hour "Budapest Potpourri" boat tour, which includes a stop to look inside the Parliament; both cost 2,200 Ft. per person.

Special-Interest Tours and Excursions **IBUSZ, Cityrama,** and **Budapest Tourist** organize a number of unusual tours, including trips to the Buda Hills and goulash parties as well as visits to the National Gallery and Parliament and other traditional sights. These tour companies will provide personal guides on request. Several enterprising tour operators now offer oddities such as day trips to former Soviet army bases and historical excursions focusing on Budapest's remaining Communist monuments. Also check at your hotel's Hostess Desk.

Excursions farther afield include day-long trips to the *Puszta* (the Great Plain), the Danube Bend, and Lake Balaton. IBUSZ's **Riding and Hobbies** department (*see* Getting Around in Essential Information, *above*) offers a variety of special-interest tours, including horseback riding, bicycling, and angling, as well as special stays in many of Hungary's historic castles and mansions.

Exploring Budapest

Budapest, situated on both banks of the Danube, unites the colorful hills of Buda and the wide boulevards of Pest. Though it was the site of a Roman outpost in the 1st century, the city was not actually created until 1873, when the towns of Óbuda, Pest, and Buda were joined. The cultural, political, intellectual, and commercial heart of the nation beats in Budapest; for the 20% of the nation's population who live in the capital, anywhere else is simply "the country."

Much of the charm of a visit to Budapest lies in unexpected glimpses into shadowy courtyards and in long vistas down sunlit cobbled streets. Although some 30,000 buildings were destroyed during World War II and in 1956, the past lingers on in the often crumbling architectural details of the antique structures that remain and in the memories and lifestyles of Budapest's citizens.

The principal sights of the city fall roughly into three areas, each of which can be comfortably covered on foot. The Budapest hills are best explored by public transportation. Note that street names are always being changed to purge all reminders of the Communist regime. If the street you're looking for seems to have disappeared, ask any local—though he or she may well be as bewildered as you are.

Numbers in the margin correspond to points of interest on the Budapest map.

① ② Take a taxi or bus (No. 16 from **Erzsébet tér**) to **Dísz tér,** at the top of **Várhegy** (Castle Hill), where the painstaking work of reconstruction has been in progress since World War II. Having made their final stand in the Royal Palace itself, the Nazis left behind them a blackened wasteland. Under the rubble, archaeologists discovered the medieval foundations of the palace of King Matthias Corvinus, who, in the 15th century, presided over one of the most splendid courts in Europe.

③ The **Királyi Palota** (Palace), now a vast museum complex and cultural center, can be reached on foot from Dísz tér—it is one block to the south—or by funicular railway *(Sikló)* from Clark Ádám tér. Until recently, the northern wing of the building was devoted to the **Legújabbkori Történeti Múzeum** (Museum of Contemporary History), but at press time (spring 1994) plans were underway to close it by 1995 and transfer the entire collection to the "most recent" end of the National Museum's epic Hungarian history exhibit. The **Ludwig Múzeum** (Ludwig Museum), with a collection of more than 200 pieces of Hungarian and contemporary world art, including works by Picasso and Lichtenstein, has shared the northern wing with the Museum of Contemporary History since 1991 and was bidding to spread eventually into the building's vacated areas. The central block houses the **Magyar Nemzeti Galéria** (Hungarian National Gallery), exhibiting a wide range of Hungarian fine art, from medieval paintings to modern sculpture. Names to look for are Munkácsy, a

Állami Operaház, **17**
Belvárosi plébánia templom, **12**
Dísz tér, **2**
Erzsébet tér, **1**
Hadtörténeti Múzeum, **8**
Halászbástya, **5**
Királyi Palota, **3**
Március 15 tér, **11**
Mátyás templom, **4**
Medieval synagogue, **7**
Mezőgazdasági Múzeum, **21**
Millenneumi Emlékmű, **18**
Műcsarnok, **20**
Néprajzi Múzeum, **15**
Parliament, **14**
Roosevelt tér, **9**
Szépművészeti Múzeum, **19**
Szt. István Bazilika, **16**
Váci utca, **13**
Vigadó tér, **10**
Zenetörténeti Múzeum, **6**

Budapest

19th-century Romantic painter, and Csontváry, an early Surrealist whom Picasso much admired. *Ludwig Museum: Buda Castle (Wing A), Dísz tr 17, tel. 1/175–7533. Admission: 80 Ft. Open Tues.–Sun. 10–6. Hungarian National Gallery: Buda Castle (Wing C), Dísz tér 17, tel. 1/175–7533. Admission: 40 Ft. adults, children free; free on Sat. Open mid-Mar.–mid-Nov., Tues.–Sun. 10–6; mid-Nov.–mid-Mar., Tues.–Sun. 10–4; closed Mon.*

The southern block contains the **Budapesti Történeti Múzeum** (Budapest History Museum). Down in the cellars are the original medieval vaults of the palace, portraits of King Matthias and his second wife, Beatrice of Aragon, and many late-14th-century statues that probably adorned the Renaissance palace. *Buda Castle (Wing E), Szt. György tér 2, tel. 1/175–7533. Admission: 40 Ft. Open Mar.–Oct., Wed.–Mon. 10–6; Nov.–Dec., Wed.–Mon. 10–5; Jan.–Feb., Wed.–Mon. 10–4.*

❹ The **Mátyás templom** (Matthias Church), northeast of Dísz tér, with its distinctive patterned roof, dates from the 13th century. Built as a mosque by the occupying Turks, it was destroyed and reconstructed in the 19th century, only to be bombed during World War II. Only the south porch is from the original structure. The Habsburg emperors were crowned kings of Hungary here, including Charles IV in 1916. High mass is celebrated every Sunday at 10 AM with an orchestra and choir, and organ concerts are often held in the summer on Friday at 8 PM. *Szentháromság tér 2, tel. 1/155–5657. Open daily 7 AM–8 PM. Admission free, except during concerts.*

❺ The *turn-of-the-century* **Halászbástya** (Fishermen's Bastion) is on your left as you leave the church. It was built as a lookout tower to protect what was once a thriving fishing settlement. Its neo-Romanesque columns and arches frame views over the city and river. Near the church, in Hess András tér, are remains of the oldest church on Castle Hill, built by Dominican friars in the 13th century. These have now been tastefully integrated into the modern Hilton hotel.

The town houses lining the streets of the Castle District are largely occupied by offices, restaurants, and diplomatic residences, but the ❻ house where Beethoven stayed in 1800 is now the **Zenetörténeti Múzeum** (Museum of Music History), which hosts intimate classical music recitals and displays rare manuscripts and antique instruments. *Táncsics Mihály utca 7, tel. 1/175–9011. Admission: 40 Ft. Open mid-Mar.–mid-Nov., Mon. 4–6 (until 9 during concerts), Wed.–Sun. 10–6; mid-Nov.–mid-Mar., Mon. 3–6 (until 9 during concerts), Wed.–Sun. 10–5.*

❼ The remains of a **medieval synagogue** are also in the neighborhood and open to the public. On display are a number of objects relating to the Jewish community, including religious inscriptions, frescoes, and tombstones dating from the 15th century. *Táncsics Mihály utca 26, tel. 1/155–8764. Admission: 40 Ft. adults, 20 Ft. children. Open May–Oct. 31, Tues.–Fri. 10–2, weekends 10–6. Group tours Oct.–May.*

❽ The **Hadtörténeti Múzeum** (Museum of Military History) is at the far end of Castle Hill. The collection includes uniforms and regalia, many belonging to the Hungarian generals who took part in the abortive uprising against Austrian rule in 1848. Other exhibits trace the military history of Hungary from the original Magyar conquest in the 9th century through the period of Ottoman rule and right to the middle of this century. *Tóth Árpád sétány 40, tel. 1/156–9522 or 1/156–9770. Admission: 20 Ft.; free Sat. Open Mar.–Oct., Tues.–Sat. 9–5, Sun. 10–6; Nov.–Feb., Tues.–Sat. 10–4, Sun. 10–6.*

Nearby stands a monument to Abdurrahman, the last pasha of Buda, commander of the Turkish troops in Hungary, who died, sword in hand, in 1686. For a good view of the Vérmező (Blood Meadow) and the surrounding Buda hills, stroll the length of Tóth Árpád sétány, along the rampart that defended Castle Hill to the west.

The Heart of the City **⑨** Cross the **Széchenyi lánchíd** (Chain Bridge) from Clark Adám tér to reach **Roosevelt tér** in Pest, with the 19th-century neo-classical Academy of Sciences on your left. Pest fans out from the **Belváros** (Inner City), which is bounded by the **Kiskörút** (Little Circular Road). The **Nagykörút** (Grand Circular Road) describes a wider semicircle from the Margaret Bridge to Petőfi Bridge. To your right, an elegant promenade, the **Korzó,** runs south along the river.

Time Out The **Bécsi Kávéház** (Vienna Coffeehouse) in the Forum Hotel serves the best coffee and cream pastries in town. *Apáczai Csere János utca 12–14.*

---

⑩ A square called **Vigadó tér** is dominated by the Danube view and Vigadó concert hall, built in a Romantic mix of Byzantine, Moorish, and Romanesque styles, with Hungarian motifs thrown in for good measure. Liszt, Brahms, and Bartók all performed here. Completely destroyed during World War II, it has been rebuilt in its original **⑪** style. Another square, **Március 15 tér,** commemorates the 1848 struggle for independence from the Habsburgs with a statue of the poet Petőfi Sándor, who died later in the uprising. Every March 15, the national holiday commemorating the revolution, the square is packed with patriotic Hungarians. Behind the square is the 12th-**⑫** century **Belvárosi plébánia templom** (Inner City Parish Church), the oldest in Pest. The church has been redone in a variety of western architectural styles; even Turkish influences, such as the Muslim prayer niche, remain. Liszt, who lived only a few yards away, often played the organ here.

⑬ Parallel to the Korzó, Pest's riverside promenade, lies Budapest's most upscale shopping street, **Váci utca. Vörösmarty tér,** a handsome square in the heart of the Inner City, is a good spot to sit and relax. Street musicians and sidewalk cafés make it one of the liveliest places in Budapest.

Time Out **Gerbeaud,** an elegant pastry shop founded in 1857, retains the old imperial style and has a terrace overlooking the square. A fashionable meeting place, it always seems crowded with tourists and locals devouring the rich chocolate cake known as *dobos torta,* their pleasure undiminished by the surliness of the waitresses. *Vörösmarty tér 7, tel. 1/118–1311.*

---

⑭ North of Roosevelt tér is the riverfront's most striking landmark, the imposing neo-Gothic **Parliament,** now minus the red star on top (open for tours only; call IBUSZ, tel. 1/118–5776, Budapest Tourist, tel. 1/117–3555, or Omnibusz Travel, tel. 1/117–2300). To its left sits an expressive statue of József Attila (1905–37), who, in spite of his early death, became known as one of Hungary's greatest poets.

⑮ Across from the Parliament is the **Néprajzi Múzeum** (Museum of Ethnography), with impressive exhibits—captioned in English—depicting folk traditions and such social customs as Hungarian costume and folklore. These are the authentic pieces you can't see at touristy folk shops. *Kossuth Lajos tér 12, tel. 1/112–4878 or 1/132–6340. Admission: 80 Ft. Open Tues.–Sun. 10–6.*

16 Dark and massive, the 19th-century **Szent István Bazilika** (St. Stephen's Basilica) is one of the chief landmarks of Pest. It was planned early in the 19th century as a neoclassical building, but was in the neo-Renaissance style by the time it was completed more than 50 years later. During World War II, the most precious documents from the Municipal Archives were placed in the cellar of the basilica—one of the few available bombproof sites. The mummified right hand of St. Stephen, Hungary's first king and patron saint, is preserved in the basilica as a relic. *V Szt. István tér, tel. 1/117–2859. Open Mon.–Sat. 7 AM–7 PM, Sun 1 PM–6 PM.*

17 Andrássy út runs 3.2 kilometers (2 miles) from the basilica to **Hősök tere** (Heroes' Square). On the left is the **Állami Operaház** (State Opera House), with its statues of the Muses in the second-floor corner niches. Completed in 1884, it was the crowning achievement of architect Miklós Ybl. It has been restored to its original ornate glory—particularly inside—and has been spared attempts at modernization. Foreign-language tours, held daily at 3 PM and 4 PM, meet in front of the Opera House. The cost is about 250 Ft. There are no performances in summer, except for the week-long BudaFest summer opera festival in mid-August.

Városliget Park In the center of Heroes' Square stands the 36.5-meter (118-foot) **Millenneumi Emlékmű** (Millennium Monument), begun in 1896 to **18** commemorate the 1,000th anniversary of the Magyar Conquest. Statues of Prince Árpád and six other founders of the Magyar nation occupy the base of the monument, while Hungary's greatest rulers and princes are between the columns on either side.

19 The **Szépművészeti Múzeum** (Fine Arts Museum) stands on one side of the square. Egyptian, Greek, and Roman artifacts dominate an entire section of the museum, and the collection of ceramics includes many rare pieces. The institution's largely unknown Spanish collection, which includes many works by El Greco and a magnificent painting by Velásquez, is considered the best of its kind outside Spain. *Dózsa György út 41, tel. 1/142–9759. Admission: 30 Ft.; free Sat. Open Tues.–Sun. 10–5:30; closed Jan.–Mar.*

Closed for exhaustive renovations since 1991, the striking 1895 **20** **Műcsarnok** (Art Gallery), on the other side of the square, was, at press time (spring 1994), due to reopen its doors to the public in spring or summer 1995, to once again bless Budapest with its magnificent visiting exhibitions of contemporary Hungarian and international art and its rich series of films, theater, and concerts *Tel. 1/142–4915.*

The **Városliget** (City Park) extends beyond the square; on the left as you enter it are the zoo, state circus, amusement park, and outdoor swimming pool of the Széchenyi mineral baths. On the right is the **Vajdahunyad Castle,** an art historian's Disneyland, created for the Millennial celebration in 1896 that blends elements from all of Hungary's historic architectural past. Housed in one building is the **21** surprisingly interesting **Mezőgazdasági Múzeum** (Agricultural Museum), with displays on subjects including animal husbandry, forestry, and horticulture. *XIV Városliget, Széchényi Island, tel. 1/142–0573. Admission: 50 Ft.; Tues. free. Open Mar.–Nov., Tues.–Fri. 10–5, weekends 10–6; Dec.–Feb., Tues.–Fri. 10–4, weekends 10–5.*

On the shores of the artificial lake stands the statue of George Washington, erected in 1906 from donations by Hungarians living in the United States. The **Olaf Palme sétány** (walk) is a pleasant route through the park.

Off the Beaten Track

A *libegő* (chair lift) will take you to the highest point in Budapest, **Jánoshegy** (János Hill), where you can climb a lookout tower for the best view of the city. *Take bus No. 158 from Moszkva tér to last stop, Zugligeti út, tel. 1/156–7975 or 1/176–3764. Admission: 60 Ft. one way, 100 Ft. round-trip. Open May 15–Sept. 15, daily 9–4; mid-Sept.–mid-May (depending on weather), daily 9:30–4. Closed alternate Mons.*

For another good view, make the strenuous climb up the staircase that ascends the high cliff overlooking the Danube at the Buda end of the Szabadság Bridge. This will lead you to **Gellért-hegy** (Gellert Hill), named for an 11th-century bishop who was hurled to his death here by some pagan Magyars. During the Middle Ages the hill was associated with witches; nowadays there is a towering memorial to the liberation of Budapest by the Red Army.

Shopping

You'll find plenty of folk art and souvenir shops, foreign-language bookshops, and classical record shops in or around **Váci utca,** but a visit to some of the smaller, more typically Hungarian shops on **Erzsébet** and **Teréz boulevards** and to the modern **Skála-Coop** department store near the Nyugati train station may prove more interesting.

The **central market hall** at IX Vámhaz körút 1–3 is closed for rebuilding, but the **Ecseri Piac** (flea market) some way out on Nagykőrösi utca 156 (take bus No. 54 from Boráros tér) stocks antiques, clothes, lamps, and such relics of the former Soviet empire as Red Army caps, Lenin statues, and Gorbachev dolls.

Dining

Private restaurateurs are breathing excitement into the Budapest dining scene. You can choose among Chinese, Mexican, Italian, French, and Czech cuisines—there is even a vegetarian restaurant. Or you can stick to solid, traditional Hungarian fare. Be sure to check out the less expensive spots favored by locals. For price-category definitions, *see* Dining in Staying in Hungary, *above.*

Very Expensive ★ **Gundel.** Kings, prime ministers, and Communist party bosses have dined in this turn-of-the-century palazzo since it was founded in 1894, but its elegance and grandeur dissipated under state control. Now relaunched by New York–based restaurateur George Lang, it showcases all that's best in Hungarian cuisine—here prepared with less fat and salt than is usual elsewhere. Waiters in black tie serve traditional favorites such as tender veal in a paprika-and-sour-cream sauce and carp Dorozsma (pan-fried, with mushrooms) to the accompaniment of Gypsy music led by one of Hungary's legendary Gypsy violinists. The cheese and the lively salads come from a special private farm, the strudel is hand-pulled, and the house specialty, Gundel palacsinta, is as rich as it sounds: a thin pancake filled with nuts and raisins and topped with a rum-spiked chocolate sauce. The tab for all this is high by Budapest standards, but the bistro menu served in the garden, open as weather permits, offers salads, smoked salmon sandwiches, and cold sliced breast of duck from the same accomplished kitchen at moderate prices. Linger here on balmy summer evenings and listen to the lions roar in the nearby zoo. *XIV Allatkerti út 2, tel. 1/121–3550, fax 1/142–2917. Reserva-*

tions required for main dining room but not for garden. Jacket and tie required. AE, DC, MC, V.

Kisbuda Gyöngye. This is the reincarnation of a venerable Budapest favorite that fell victim to foreign buyers. The long-time management, now at a new address in Obuda, has made their establishment better than ever with mixed antique furniture and walls creatively decorated with a patchwork of antique carved wooden cupboard doors. A violin-piano duo with a repertoire favoring Mozart set a romantic mood. Try the chicken Cumberland (grilled boneless breasts marinated in basil and spices) or the fresh trout smothered in a cream sauce nutted with mushrooms and capers. *III Kenyeres utca 34, tel. 1/168–6402 or 1/168–9246. Reservations advised 2 days ahead. AE. Closed Sun. dinner.*

Vadrózsa. The name means "wild rose," and there are always fresh ones on the table at this restaurant in an old villa in Buda's exclusive Rózsadomb district. It's elegant to the last detail—even the service is white glove—and the garden is delightful in summer. *II Pentelei Molnár utca 15, tel. 1/135–1118. Reservations advised. AE, DC, MC, V. No lunch. Closed Mon.*

Expensive **Kacsa.** Hungarian and international dishes with a focus on duck are done with a light touch and served by candlelight, with quiet chamber music in the background, in this small restaurant just a few steps from the river. Try the crisp wild duck stuffed with plums. *II Fő utca 75, tel. 1/201–9992. Reservations advised. AE, MC, V. Closed lunch.*

Légrádi. The debonair Légrádi brothers look after your every wish here. The scattering of antiques, the lovely Herend china, and the discreet guitar-violin duo complement the unhurried Old World service. The prices soar to expense-account levels. *V Magyar utca 23, tel. 1/118–6804. Reservations advised. AE. Closed lunch and weekends.*

Múzeum. Fans swear that this elegant, candlelit salon with mirrors, mosaics, and swift-moving waiters has the best dining in Budapest. The salads are generous, the Hungarian wines excellent, and the chef dares to be creative. *VIII Múzeum körút 12, tel. 1/138–4221. Reservations advised. AE.*

Moderate **Kispipa.** The street outside, a lane full of crumbling old buildings, ★ makes this restaurant's gleaming brass fixtures, stylish art deco chairs, and convivial crowd seem that much more polished. On the extensive menu, the game dishes stand out, and the venison stew with tarragon is outstanding. *VII Akácfa utca 38, tel. 1/142–2587. Reservations advised. No credit cards. Closed Sun. and holidays.*

Tabáni Kakas. Situated just below Castle Hill, this popular restaurant has a distinctly warm and friendly atmosphere. It specializes in large helpings of poultry dishes, particularly goose. Try the catfish paprikás or the roast duck with steamed cabbage. A pianist entertains every evening except Monday. *I Attila út 27, tel. 1/175–7165. Reservations advised. AE, MC.*

Inexpensive **Bohémtanya.** There's always a wait for a table at this rustic lively hangout, but it pays to be patient. The reward: heaping plates of stuffed cabbage, fried pork chops filled with goose liver, and other Hungarian specialties. The trilingual menu is extra budget-conscious: it's in price order. *VI Paulay Ede utca 6, tel. 1/122–1453. Reservations advised. No credit cards.*

Szerb. Down a sawdust-covered stairway, this lively cellar serves grilled meats on a skewer and other Serbian dishes for a song, along with giant pitchers of beer. *V Nagy Ignác utca 16, tel. 1/111–1858. Reservations advised. No credit cards. Closed Sun. dinner.*

Lodging

Some 30 million tourists come to Hungary every year, and the boom has encouraged hotel building; yet there is sometimes a shortage of rooms, especially in summer.

If you arrive in Budapest without a reservation, go to the IBUSZ travel office at Petőfi tér (tel. 1/118–5707 or 1/118–4842) or to one of the tourist offices at any of the train stations or at the airport. For details and price-category definitions, *see* Lodging in Staying in Hungary, *above.*

Very Expensive ★
Budapest Hilton. Built in 1977 around a 13th-century monastery, adjacent to the Matthias Church and overlooking the Danube from the choicest site on Castle Hill, this perfectly integrated architectural wonder is unique. Every ample Hilton-contemporary room has a remarkable view; Danube vistas cost more. Service and facilities are of the highest caliber. Note: breakfast is not included in room rates. *I Hess András tér 1–3, tel. 1/175–1000, fax 1/156–0285; in U.S. and Canada, tel. 800/445–8667. 323 rooms, 28 suites. Facilities: 3 restaurants, café, 2 bars, wine cellar, casino, hairdresser, cosmetic salon, conference rooms, ballroom, parking, gift shops, flower shop, boutiques, antiques shop, IBUSZ travel agency. AE, DC, MC, V.*

Fórum. This boxy modern riverside hotel consistently wins applause for its gracious appointments, friendly service, and gorgeous views across the Danube to Castle Hill. The central location makes it popular with businesspeople. *V Apáczai Csere János utca 12–14, tel. 1/117–8088, fax 1/117–9808. 392 rooms with bath, 16 suites. Facilities: 2 restaurants, 2 cafés, bar, fitness center, business center, airport transfer, drugstore, travel desk, car rental, doctor. AE, DC, MC, V.*

Expensive
Alba Hotel. Tucked behind an alleyway at the foot of Castle Hill, this spotless, modern gem of a hotel is a short walk, via the Chain Bridge, from lively business and shopping districts. Swiss management assures efficient service. *I Apor Péter utca 3, tel. 1/175–9244, fax 1/175–9899. 95 rooms with bath. Facilities: nonsmoking rooms, bar, conference room, underground parking. AE, DC, MC, V.*

★
Gellért. Nowadays this plump grand old lady of city hotels is shining. The turn-of-the-century architecture is regal, and the thermal bath are wonderfully ornate. (They're like regular swimming pools but more elegant; jets of water come shooting up through the floor at odd moments, and fountains dribble hot water onto the heads of bathers.) *XI Gellért tér 1, tel. 1/185–2200, fax 1/166–6631. 239 rooms with bath, 15 suites. Facilities: business center, baby-sitting service, parking, spa, thermal pools, terrace restaurant, coffee shop. AE, DC, MC, V.*

Grand Hotel Corvinus Kempinski. Opened in August 1992, the sleek Kempinski is the newest of Budapest's luxury hotels and has already become a focal point of elite goings-on, such as hosting Sotheby's debut art auction in Hungary. The location offers no Danube views but is about as city-central as you can get. The building's dramatic modern design alternates surfaces of glass and polished stone arrayed in stylish geometries. Room decor is understated, with an emphasis on functional touches such as three phones in every room. Note: breakfast is not included in the room rates. *V Erzsébet tér 7–8, tel. 1/226–1000, in the U.S. and Canada, tel. 800/426–3135; fax 1/226–2000. 340 rooms with bath, 28 suites. Facilities: 3 restaurants, 3 bars, business center, conference room, indoor swimming pool, sauna, fitness center, private parking, airport transfer, IBUSZ travel agency, boutiques. AE, DC, MC, V.*

Korona. Modern and functional, this Austrian-built hotel is on busy

Kálvin tér, near the river and close to the National Museum and other sights. *V Kecskeméti utca 14, tel. 1/117–4111, fax 1/118–3867. 433 rooms with bath. Facilities: pool, restaurant, bar, parking garage. AE, DC, MC, V.*

Radisson Béke. Traditional mixes with modern at this luxury hotel in the heart of the city. While the rooms are modern, the hotel's entrance is presided over by liveried doormen, and the lobby is full of mosaics and statuary. *VI Teréz körút 43, tel. 1/132–3300, fax 1/153–3380. 238 rooms with bath, 8 suites. Facilities: 2 restaurants, café, 2 bars, casino, business center, conference rooms, travel agency, parking, swimming pool, health club. AE, DC, MC, V.*

The Ramada Grand Hotel. This venerable 100-year-old hotel is completely modern, yet retains its period look, with high ceilings and Old World furnishings. It's in a tranquil park, surrounded by gardens on a car-free island in the Danube; the city is closer than it seems. *XIII Margit-sziget, tel. 1/1111–000, fax 1/1533–029; for reservations, tel. 1/131–7769; in U.S., tel. 800/228–9898. 162 rooms with bath, 10 suites. Facilities: restaurant, coffee shop, bar, thermal baths, fitness center, beauty shop. AE, DC, MC, V.*

Thermal Hotel Helia. A sleek Scandinavian design and quiet location away from downtown pollution make this spa hotel on the Danube a relaxing retreat. Special health packages—including anything from Turkish baths to electrotherapy and "Alfamassage"—are available. *XIII Kárpát utca 62–64, tel. 1/270–3277, fax 1/270–2262; in U.S. and Canada, tel. 800/223–5652. 254 rooms with bath; 8 suites, 4 with sauna. Facilities: 2 restaurants (1 with summer terrace), café, bar, spa, fitness center, tennis courts, business center. AE, DC, MC, V.*

Moderate **Astoria.** Revolutionaries and intellectuals once gathered in the marble-and-gilt Art Deco lobby here. Recent renovations have remained faithful to the Empire-style decor and furnishings and have not obscured the 81-year-old hotel's distinct charm; rather, they have meant the addition of other comforts—most notably soundproofing, essential since the Astoria is located at the city's busiest intersection. *V Kossuth Lajos utca 19–21, tel. 1/117–3411, fax 1/118–6798. 128 rooms with bath or shower. Facilities: nightclub, café, brasserie, conference room, parking. AE, DC, MC, V.*

Hotel Centrál. Relive history—stay in this hotel, well situated in a leafy diplomatic quarter just one block from Heroes' Square, as visiting Communist dignitaries once did. The architecture and furnishings are straight out of the 1950s, but rooms are comfortable and have unusually large bathrooms. Suites are classically elegant, with turn-of-the-century Hungarian eclectic furnishings; ask for Rudolf Nureyev's favorite. *VI Munkácsy Mihály utca 5–7, tel. 1/121–2000, fax 1/121–2008. 36 rooms with bath, 6 suites. Facilities: restaurant. AE, DC, MC, V.*

Nemzeti. The baby-blue Baroque facade stands out in this dingy neighborhood, which turns seedy after dark. The high-ceilinged lobby and public areas with pillars, arches, and wrought-iron railings are elegant, but rooms are small and unexceptional. For a quieter night, ask for a room facing the inner courtyard. The homey atmosphere is the real draw. *VIII József Körút 4, tel. 1/133–9160, fax 1/114–0019. 76 rooms with bath. Facilities: restaurant, brasserie, drugstore, garage. AE, DC, MC, V.*

Victoria. The dark, stately Parliament building and city lights twinkling over the river is the view from every room at this three-year-old establishment right on the Danube that mixes the charm of an inn in the country with ultramodern comforts. The absence of conventions is a plus. *II Bem rakpart 11, tel. 1/201–8644, fax 1/2015–816. 24 rooms with bath, 2 with balcony; 1 suite. Facilities: 24-hr.*

room service, bar, sauna, conference room, garage. *AE, DC, MC, V*.

Inexpensive **Ifjúság.** The concrete "Youth" hotel is a boxy remnant of Socialist architecture, but the location—a quiet, residential street at the top of a hill—is lovely and the rooms are modern and clean. Ask for a room with a view and a balcony, and you won't be sorry. *II Zivatar utca 3, tel. 1/135–3331, fax 1/1353–989. 100 rooms with bath. Facilities: restaurant. AE, DC, MC, V.*

Kulturinnov. One wing of what looks like a Gothic castle now houses basic budget accommodations. Rooms are clean, and the neighborhood—one of Budapest's most famous squares in the luxurious Castle District—is unbeatable. *I Szentháromság tér 6, tel. 1/155–0122 or 1/175–1651, fax 1/175–1886. 17 rooms, some with 3 or 4 beds, all with shower. Facilities: snack bar, reading room. AE.*

Medosz. One of Budapest's better small hotels, the Medosz provides a central location near Oktogon, a major transport hub, and lovely Andrássy út; the Opera House is a block away. Request a room facing the rear if you prefer quiet. *VI Jókai tér 9, tel. 1/153–1700 or 1/ 153–1434, fax 1/132–4316. 63 rooms, 7 suites. Facilities: restaurant (for groups only). No credit cards.*

The Arts

Budapest's English-language newspapers are the most up-to-date sources for arts information. *The Budapest Sun*'s Style section maps out the week's entertainment happenings, gallery exhibits, and all else going on culturally. *The Sun* is sold for about $1 at many newsstands and in well-trafficked areas. Hotels and tourist offices will provide you with a copy of the monthly publication *Programme*, which contains details of all cultural events in the city. Tickets can be bought at venue box offices, your hotel desk, many tourist offices, or any of several ticket agencies, the biggest of which are the **National Philharmonic Ticket Office** (V Vörösmarty tér 1, tel. 1/117–6222) and the **Central Theater Booking Office** (VI Andrássy ut 18, tel. 1/ 112–0000).

There are two opera houses, for which dress can be informal. Concerts are given all year at the **Academy of Music** on Liszt Ferenc tér, the **Pesti Vigadó** on Vigadó tér, and at the **Old Academy of Music** on Vörösmarty utca. Displays of Hungarian folk dancing are held at the **Cultural Center** on Corvin tér.

Arts festivals fill the calendar beginning in early spring. The season's first and biggest, the **Budapest Spring Festival** (beginning early to mid-Mar.), showcases Hungary's best opera, music, theater, and dance as well as visiting foreign artists. It's followed by the smaller annual **Jazz Festival** (Apr.), and after the opera season ends, by the **Summer Opera Festival** (July–Aug.) at the Opera House and occasionally at the open-air theater on Margitsziget. Information and tickets are available from the ticket sources, above.

Nightlife

Budapest is a lively city by night. Establishments stay open late and Western European–style *drink-bárs* have sprung up all over the city. For quiet conversation, there are such bars in most hotels, but beware of the inflated prices. Hotel nightclubs are convenient but pricey and not usually among the "in" places to be.

Bars and Clubs

High-Life advertises itself as Budapest's biggest disco. It's a vast complex of futuristic effects, strobe lights, and pounding techno-music. *III Kalap utca 15. Open Wed.–Sun. from 9 PM.*

Mad Block is a popular disco in the ornate Baroque theater that once housed the Moulin Rouge nightclub. Live bands play weekdays, disco on weekends. *VI Nagymező utca 17, tel. 1/112–4492. Open daily 9 PM–6 AM.*

Merlin, Budapest's most famous jazz club, features the biggest names in Hungarian jazz and frequent international guests. On weekdays, it's a good restaurant. *V Gerlóczy utca 4, tel. 1/117–5935. Jazz club Fri.–Sun. 10 PM–1 AM.*

Piaf is popular with arts sophisticates; it's classy and just a touch pretentious, with red velvet chairs and low, candlelit tables in cozy brick rooms. Open only from 10 PM, it often is still serving enthusiasts at 6 and 7 in the morning. *VI Nagymező utca 20, tel. 1/112–3823. Open daily 10 PM–5 AM (or when the last person leaves).*

Picasso Point, a very popular, spacious bar with a hip, coffeehouse feel and Pablo-themed decor, hosts local art exhibits and live jazz ensembles. *V Hajós utca 31, tel. 1/1132–4750. Open daily noon–4 AM.*

Pierrot is an elegant café and piano bar well suited for secret rendezvous. *I Fortuna utca 14, tel. 1/175–6971. Open 11 AM–1 AM. No credit cards.*

Casinos

Gresham Casino. In the Gresham Palace. *V Roosevelt tét 5, tel. 1/117–2407. Open daily 2 PM–4 AM.*

Las Vegas Casino. *V Roosevelt tér 2, tel. 1/117–6022. Open 24 hours a day.*

Várkert Casino. *I Miklós Ybl tér 9, tel. 1/202–4244. Open daily 2 PM–4 AM.*

The Danube Bend

About 40 kilometers (25 miles) north of Budapest, the Danube abandons its eastward course and turns abruptly south toward the capital, cutting through the Börzsöny and Visegrád hills. This area is called the Danube Bend and includes the Baroque town of Szentendre, the hilltop castle ruins and town of Visegrád, and the cathedral town of Esztergom. The attractive combination of hillside and river should dispel any notion that Hungary is one vast, boring plain.

Here, in the heartland, are the traces of the country's history—the remains of the Roman Empire's frontiers, the battlefields of the Middle Ages, and the relics of the Hungarian Renaissance. Although the area can be covered by car in a day—the round-trip from Budapest is only 124 kilometers (78 miles)—two days, with a night in Visegrád or Esztergom, would be a better way to savor its charms.

Getting Around

The most pleasant way to get around is by boat or hydrofoil on the Danube. The three main centers—Szentendre, Esztergom, and Visegrád—all have connections with each other and with Budapest. There is also regular bus service connecting all three with each other and with Budapest. Szentendre can also be reached by HÉV commuter rail, departing from the Batthyány tér metro; the fare is 60 Ft.

The Danube Bend

Guided Tours

IBUSZ organizes day trips from Budapest along the Danube from May through October (4,000 Ft. with lunch) and to Szentendre only on Sundays, May through October. Boat trips run on Wednesdays and Saturdays; buses go on Tuesdays, Fridays, and Saturdays. There is also a special bus trip to Szentendre departing on different days, depending on the season.

Tourist Information

Budapest (Dunatours, VI Bajcsy-Zsilinszky út 17, tel. 1/131–4533 or 1/111–5630, fax 1/111–6827).
Esztergom (IBUSZ Office, Lőrinc utca 1, tel. 33/312–552).
Szentendre (Dunatours, Bogdányi ut. 1, on the quay, tel. 26/311–311).

Exploring the Danube Bend

Heading north from Budapest toward Szentendre, 19 kilometers (12 miles) by car on Road 11, or by train, on your right look for the reconstructed remains of **Aquincum,** capital of the Roman province of Pannonia. Careful excavations have unearthed a varied selection of artifacts and mosaics, giving a tantalizing inkling of what life was like on the northern fringes of the Roman Empire.

Szentendre, nowadays a flourishing artists' colony with a lively Mediterranean atmosphere, was first settled by Serbs and Greeks fleeing the advancing Turks in the 14th and 17th centuries. There is a

Greek Orthodox church in the main square and a Serbian Orthodox cathedral on the hill. The narrow cobbled streets are lined with cheerfully painted houses. Part of the town's artistic reputation can be traced to the life and work of the ceramic artist Margit Kovács, whose work blended Hungarian folk art traditions with motifs from modern art. The **Margit Kovács Pottery Museum,** devoted to her work, is housed in a small 18th-century merchant's house with an attractive courtyard. *Vastag György utca 1, tel. 26/310–244. Admission: 60 Ft. Open Apr.–Oct., daily 10–6; Nov.–Mar., Tues.–Sun. 10–4.*

A short drive up Szabadság Forrás út, or a bus ride from the train station, will take you to the **Szabadtéri Néprajzi Múzeum** (Open-Air Ethnographical Museum), where a collection of buildings has been designed to show Hungarian peasant life and folk architecture in the 19th century. *Szabadság Forrás út, tel. 26/312–304. Admission: 60 Ft. Open Apr.–Oct., Tues.–Sun. 10–5.*

Visegrád, 23 kilometers (14 miles) from Szentendre, was the seat of the kings of Hungary in the 14th century. The ruins of the Palace of King Matthias in the main street have been excavated and reconstructed, and there are jousting tournaments here in June. A winding road leads up to a haunting late-medieval fortress, from which you have a fine view of the Danube Bend.

Esztergom, 21 kilometers (13 miles) farther upriver, stands on the site of a Roman fortress. St. Stephen, the first Christian king of Hungary, was crowned here in the year 1000. The kings are long gone, but Esztergom is still the home of the archbishop of Esztergom, the cardinal primate, head of the Catholic church in Hungary.

Thousands of pilgrims visit the imposing **cathedral,** the largest in Hungary, which stands on a hill overlooking the town. It was here, in the center of Hungarian Catholicism, that the famous anti-Communist cleric, Cardinal József Mindszenty, was finally reburied in 1991, ending an era of religious intolerance and prosecution and a sorrowful chapter in Hungarian history. The cathedral also houses a valuable collection of ecclesiastical art. Below it are the streets of Viziváros (Watertown), lined with Baroque buildings. The **Keresztény Múzeum** (Museum of Christian Art) is situated in the Primate's Palace. It is the finest art gallery in Hungary, with a large collection of early Hungarian and Italian paintings. The Italian collection of 14th- and 15th-century works is unusually large for a museum outside Italy. This collection, coupled with the extensive number of early Renaissance paintings from Flanders and the Lower Rhine, provides insights into the transition of European sensibilities from medieval Gothic to the humanistic Renaissance. *Berényi utca 2, tel. 33/313–880. Admission: 50 Ft. Open Tues.–Sun. 10–5:30.*

To the south of the cathedral, on **Szt. Tamás Hill,** is a small church dedicated to St. Thomas à Becket of Canterbury. From here you can look down on the town and see how the Danube temporarily divides, forming an island that locals use as a base for water skiing and swimming in spite of the pollution. This part of the Danube forms the frontier with Czechoslovakia.

Dining and Lodging

For details and price-category definitions, *see* Dining and Lodging in Staying in Hungary, *above.*

Esztergom
Dining

Primáspince. Arched ceilings and exposed brick walls make a charming setting for refined Hungarian fare at this restaurant just below the cathedral. Try the tournedos Budapest-style, tender beef with sautéed vegetables and paprika, or the thick stuffed pork chops Fiaker-style (stuffed with ham and melted cheese). *Szent István tér 4, tel. 33/13–495. Reservations advised. AE, DC, MC, V. Expensive.*

Fili Falatozó. The hearty German fare is heavy on meat and potatoes. The location on Esztergom's most pleasant old street, just a short stroll from the Danube. *Bajcsy-Zsilinszky utca 51 (no telephone). No reservations or credit cards accepted. Closed Jan.–Feb. Inexpensive.*

Lodging

Alabárdos Panzió. Conveniently located downhill from the basilica, this cozy, remodeled home provides an excellent view of Castle Hill. The rooms (doubles and quads) are large. If the caretaker isn't in, you might find him working at the adjoining restaurant. *Bajcsy-Zsilinsky utca 49, tel. 33/312–640. 13 rooms with bath. Facilities: restaurant. No credit cards. Moderate.*

Ria Panzió. In this small, friendly guest house near the cathedral, all rooms face a garden courtyard. *Batthyány utca 11, tel. 33/313–115. 4 rooms. No credit cards. Inexpensive.*

Szentendre
Dining

Angyal Borozó. This wine bar, also a restaurant, serves hefty portions of Hungarian food. *Alkotmány utca 4, tel. 26/310–160. No credit cards accepted. Moderate.*

Rab Ráby. Fish soup and fresh grilled trout are the specialties in this popular restaurant with wood beams and equestrian decorations. *Péter Pál utca 1, tel. 26/310–819. Reservations advised in summer. No credit cards. Moderate.*

Lodging

Bükkös Panzió. Impeccably clean, this stylishly modernized old house is on a small canal just a few minutes' walk from the town center. *Bükkös part 16, tel. 26/312–021 or 26/310–782. 16 rooms with bath. Facilities: restaurant. No credit cards. Moderate.*

Visegrád
Lodging

Silvanus. Located on a hill, Visegrád hegy, this hotel offers spectacular views. It's recommended for motorists and offers linking trails in the forest for the more active. *Fekete-hegy, tel. 26/398–311, fax 26/398–170. 74 rooms, most with bath; 4 suites. Facilities: restaurant, brasserie, terrace café. AE, DC, MC, V. Moderate.*

Haus Honti. This intimate, alpine-style pension, named after its owner, József Honti, is situated in a quiet residential area far from the main highway but close to the Danube ferry. A stream running close to the house creates a rustic ambience. *Fő utca 66, tel. 26/398–120. 5 rooms with bath. No credit cards. Inexpensive.*

Lake Balaton

Lake Balaton, the largest lake in Central Europe, stretches 80 kilometers (50 miles) across western Hungary. It is within easy reach of Budapest by any means of transportation. Sometimes known as the nation's playground, it goes some way toward making up for Hungary's much-lamented lack of coastline. On its hilly northern shore, ideal for growing grapes, is **Balatonfüred,** the country's oldest and most famous spa town.

The national park on the Tihany Peninsula is just to the south, and regular boat service links Tihany and Balatonfüred with Siófok on the southern shore. This shore is not as attractive as the northern one—being flatter and more crowded with resorts, cottages, and high-rise hotels once used as Communist trade-union retreats. Still,

Lake Balaton

it is worth visiting for its shallower, warmer waters, which make it a better choice for swimming than other locations.

A circular tour taking in Veszprém, Balatonfüred, and Tihany could be managed in a day, but two days, with a night in Tihany or Balatonfüred, would be more relaxed and allow for detours to Herend and its porcelain factory, or to the castle at Nagyvázsony.

The region is crowded in July and August, so visit at any other time if you can.

Getting Around

Trains from Budapest serve all the resorts on the northern shore; a separate line links the resorts of the southern shore. Road 71 runs along the northern shore; M7 covers the southern. Buses connect most resorts. Regular ferries link the major ones. On summer weekends, traffic can be heavy and driving slow around the lake. Book bus and train tickets in advance then. In winter, note that schedules are curtailed, so check before making plans.

Guided Tours

IBUSZ has several tours to Balaton from Budapest; inquire at the head office in Budapest (*see* Important Addresses and Numbers in Budapest, *above*). Other tours more easily organized from hotels in the Balaton area include boat trips to vineyards, folk music evenings, and overnight trips to local inns.

Tourist Information

Budapest (Balatontourist, VIII Üllői út 52/A, tel. 1/1336–982, fax 1/1339–929).
Balatonfüred (Balatontourist, Blaha L. utca 5, tel. 86/342–822).
Tihany (Balatontourist, Kossuth utca 20, tel. 86/348–519).
Veszprém (Balatontourist, Kossuth Lajos utca 10, tel. 88/426–874).

Exploring Lake Balaton

Hilly **Veszprém** is the center of cultural life in the Balaton region. **Várhegy** (Castle Hill) is the most attractive part of town, north of Szabadság tér. **Hősök Kapuja** (Heroes' Gate), at the entrance to the Castle, houses a small exhibit on Hungary's history. Just past the gate and down a little alley to the left, is the **Tűztorony** (Fire Tower); note that the lower level is medieval while the upper stories are Baroque. There is a good view of the town and surrounding area from the balcony. *Exhibit admission: 10 Ft. Open May–Oct., Tues.–Sun. 10–6.*

Vár utca, the only street in the castle area, leads to a small square in front of the **Bishop's Palace** and **Cathedral;** outdoor concerts are held here in the summer. Vár utca continues past the square up to a terrace erected on the north staircase of the castle. Stand beside the modern statues of St. Stephen and his queen, Gizella, for a far-reaching view of the old quarter of town.

If you are traveling by car, go 5 kilometers (3 miles) west to the village of **Nemesvámos,** where you can slake your thirst or conquer your hunger at **Vámosi Csárda** (Highwayman's Inn). This 18th-century Baroque building takes its name from Savanyu Jóska ("Sour Joe"), an infamous 19th-century highwayman who claimed it as one of his bases. Go down to the cellar to see the tables and seats made from tree trunks—a local architectural feature.

Herend, 16 kilometers (10 miles) northwest of Veszprém on Road 8, is the home of Hungary's renowned hand-painted porcelain. The factory, founded in 1839, displays many valuable pieces in its **museum.** *Tel. 88/361–144. Admission: 30 Ft. Open Sat., Sun., Mon. 10–6.*

From Veszprém, take Road 73 about 20 kilometers (12 miles) south to **Balatonfüred,** a spa and resort with good beaches. It is also one of the finest wine-growing areas of Hungary. Above the main square, where medicinal waters bubble up under a colonnaded pavilion, the hillsides are thick with vines.

A seven-minute boat trip takes you from Balatonfüred to the **Tihany Peninsula,** a national park rich in rare flora and fauna and an ideal place for strolling. From the ferry port, follow green markers to the springs (Oroszkút) or red ones to the top of **Csúcs-hegy,** a hill from which there is a good view of the lake.

The village of **Tihany,** with its famous **abbey,** is on the eastern shore. The abbey building houses a **museum** with exhibits related to the Balaton area. Also worth a look are the pink angels floating on the ceiling of the abbey church, and the abbey organ, on which recitals are given in summer. Consider a special detour to the Rege pastry shop at Batthyány út 38, not far from the abbey. *Első András tér 1, tel. 86/348–405. Admission: 20 Ft. Open Tues.–Sun., Oct.–Apr. 10–3, May–Sept. 10–5.*

The castle of **Nagyvázsony,** about 20 kilometers (12 miles) northwest of Balatonfüred, dates to the early 15th century. The 28-meter-high (92-foot-high) keep is the oldest part, and its upper rooms now house the **Castle Museum.** Try to get to the highest balcony in late afternoon for the best view. The surrounding buildings, preserved in their original style, date from the period when post horses were changed here. *Tel. 88/331–015. Museum admission: 30 Ft. Open Tues.–Sun. 10–6.*

Dining and Lodging

For details and price-category definitions, *see* Dining and Lodging in Staying in Hungary, *above.*

Balatonfüred
Dining

Vitorlás. This old villa has a pleasant lake-view terrace where you can watch the yachts and sailboats in the water as you eat good grilled trout and bean soup. *Tagore Sétány 1, tel. 86/43–407. Reservations advised. Dress: casual but neat. AE, DC, MC, V. Moderate.*

Lodging **Annabella.** The cool, spacious guest quarters in this large, Miami-style high rise are especially pleasant during summer heat. It is surrounded by gardens, away from other hotels but just around the corner from the main square in town. *Deák Ferenc utca 25, tel. 86/342–222, fax 86/343–084. 390 rooms; all double rooms have bath. Facilities: restaurant, indoor/outdoor pool, windsurfing. AE, DC, MC, V. Closed mid-Oct.–mid-Apr. Moderate.*

★ **Margaréta.** This attractive apartment-hotel stands across the street from the lakefront Hotel Marina. It is smaller and more intimate than most of its neighbors, and its restaurant is popular locally. Each room has a kitchen, a balcony, a phone, a TV, and a radio. *Szécsenyi ut 29, tel. and fax 86/343–824. 52 rooms with bath. Facilities: restaurant, bar, snack bar, parking. AE, DC, MC, V. Moderate.*

Tihany **Halásztanya.** The relaxed atmosphere and gypsy music in the eve-
Dining ning help contribute to the popularity of the Halásztánya, which specializes in fish. *Visszhang utca 11 (no phone). No reservations. Closed Nov.–Mar. Moderate.*

Pál Csárda. Two thatched cottages make up this simple restaurant, where cold fruit soup and fish stew are the specialties. Or you can eat in the garden, which is decorated with gourds and strands of peppers, from which paprika is made. *Visszhang utca 19, no phone. No reservations. Dress: casual. No credit cards. Closed Dec.–Mar. Moderate.*

Lodging **Park.** Lush landscaped gardens surround this stately mansion on
★ the water's edge. Inside, it's all understated elegance; rooms have balconies, views, and crisp sheets. *Fürdötelepi út 1, tel. 86/48–611. 26 rooms with bath. Facilities: restaurant, private beach. AE, DC, MC, V. Summer: Expensive; other seasons: Moderate.*

Kolostor. The cozy, wood-paneled rooms are built into an attic above a restaurant in the heart of Tihany village. *Kossuth út, tel. 86/348–408. 7 rooms with bath. Facilities: breakfast room. No credit cards. Moderate.*

Veszprém **Diana.** The Diana is just a little southwest of the town center, but
Dining worth the trip if you want to experience the old-fashioned charm of a
★ small provincial Hungarian restaurant. The decor could be called "cozy traditional," and the fish and game specialties are perennial favorites. There is also a 10-room pension on the premises. *József Attila utca 22, tel. 88/421–061. Reservations advised. No credit cards. Moderate.*

Tüztorony Sörklub. At this restaurant on the winding cobblestone street leading to the castle, you can order game specialties such as venison soup and veal stew. Try the cherry strudel for dessert. *Vár utca 1, tel. 88/326–220. No reservations. Dress: casual. No credit cards. Closed Sun. in winter. Inexpensive.*

Lodging **Veszprem.** This modern, comfortable hotel in the center of town now has a fresh paint job and pleasant new furniture. *Budapesti utca 6, tel. 88/324–677, fax 88/324–076. 72 rooms, 4 suites. Facilities: restaurant. No credit cards. Inexpensive.*

16 Iceland

Iceland is anything but icy. Though glaciers cover about 10% of the country, summers in Iceland are relatively warm, and the winter climate is milder than New York's. Coastal farms lie in green, pastoral lowlands, where cows, sheep, and horses graze alongside raging streams. Distant waterfalls plunge from heather-covered mountains with great spiked ridges and snowcapped peaks.

Iceland's name can be blamed on Hrafna-Flóki, a 9th-century Norse settler who failed to plant enough crops to see his livestock through their first winter. Leaving in a huff, he passed a northern fjord filled with pack ice and cursed the country with a name that's kept tourism in cold storage for 1,100 years.

The second-largest island in Europe, Iceland is in the middle of the North Atlantic, where the warm Gulf Stream from the south meets the cold currents from the north, providing a choice environment for the fish on which the nation depends for 80% of its export revenue. Beneath some of the country's glaciers are burning fires that become visible during volcanic eruptions—fires that heat the hot springs and geysers that are all over the country. The springs, in turn, provide heat to the country's homes, hospitals, and public swimming pools, keeping the nation's air smokeless and smogless. Except for fish and agricultural products, almost all consumer goods are imported, thus the cost of living is high by any standard.

The first permanent settlers arrived from Norway in 874, though some Irish monks had arrived a century earlier. The country came under foreign rule in 1262 and did not win complete independence until 1944. Today nearly three-fifths of the country's 260,000 people live in Reykjavík and its suburbs.

Essential Information

Before You Go

When to Go The best time to visit is from May through November. The months of June and July are highly recommended, because during that time there is perpetual daylight. In Reykjavík the sun disappears behind the mountains for only a couple of hours, and in the northern part of the island it barely sets at all. The weather is unpredictable: In June, July, and August, sunny days alternate with spells of rain showers and driving winds. Winter weather fluctuates bewilderingly, with temperatures as high as 50°F (10°C) or as low as –14°F (–10°C.). During December the sun shines for only three hours a day, but on a clear and cold evening you can see the Northern Lights dancing among the stars.

Climate Iceland enjoys a temperate ocean climate with cool summers and surprisingly mild winters. In the northern part of the country, the weather is more stable than in the south, which gets more wind and rain.

The following are the average daily maximum and minimum temperatures for Reykjavík.

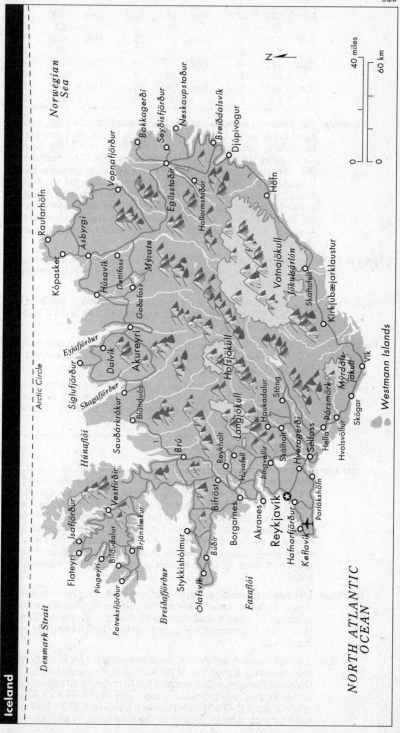

Iceland

Jan.	35F	2C	May	50F	10C	Sept.	52F	11C
	28	-2		39	4		43	6
Feb.	37F	3C	June	54F	12C	Oct.	45F	7C
	28	-2		34	7		38	3
Mar.	39F	4C	July	57F	14C	Nov.	39F	4C
	30	-1		48	9		32	0
Apr.	43F	6C	Aug.	56F	14C	Dec.	36F	2C
	33	1		47	8		29	-2

Currency The Icelandic monetary unit is the króna (plural krónur), which is equal to 100 aurar. Coins are the ISK 1, 5, 10, and 50. There are krónur bills in denominations of 100, 500, 1,000, and 5,000. At press time (spring 1994), the rate of exchange was ISK 73 to the dollar and ISK 109 to the pound sterling, but in the generally unstable economic climate, considerable fluctuation occurs. You are not permitted to import or export more than ISK 8,000, but you may bring any amount of foreign currency, which is easily exchanged for krónur at the Icelandic banks. Major credit cards, especially MasterCard and Visa, are widely accepted in the capital and by most businesses in the countryside.

What It Will Cost Iceland is expensive. Hotels and restaurants cost about 20% more in Reykjavík than elsewhere in the country. The airport departure tax is about ISK 1,300.

Sample Prices A cup of coffee or soft drink costs about ISK 150; a bottle of beer costs ISK 250; a sandwich or snack about ISK 300; and a 2-mile taxi ride, about ISK 500.

Customs on Arrival Tourists can bring in 6 liters of beer or 1 liter of wine containing up to 21% alcohol, 1 liter of liquor with up to 47% alcohol content, and 200 cigarettes.

Language The official language is Icelandic, brought to the country by early Norse settlers. It's a highly inflected North Germanic tongue that has changed little over the centuries. English is widely understood and spoken, particularly by the younger people.

Getting Around

By Car Most of the Ring Road, which encircles the island, is asphalt. But elsewhere, driving can be a very bumpy experience, often along lava track or dirt and gravel surfaces. But the superb scenery more than makes up for it. Although service stations and garages are few and far between, the main roads are patrolled, and fellow motorists are friendly and helpful. If you are traveling off the beaten path, you'll need a four-wheel-drive vehicle. An international driver's license is required—you can apply for one at the local police station if you are at least 20 years old and in possession of a valid driver's license from home.

By Plane Icelandair, Íslandsflug, Norlandair, and a few other airlines have domestic flights to some 50 towns and villages. Special discounts are available on certain combinations of domestic air routes. Some of these must be arranged when you book your Icelandair flight to Iceland.

By Bus A comprehensive network of buses compensates for the lack of any train network. A good buy, if you want to explore extensively, is the **Omnibus Passport,** which permits you to travel on all scheduled bus routes for one to four weeks. It costs ISK 14,300–ISK 28,500. Another choice is the **Full Circle Passport,** which costs ISK 12,900 and is valid for a trip around Iceland on the Ring Road. It will take you to some of the most popular attractions, but if you want to see more, there are scheduled bus tours for which you will have to pay extra. An **Air/Bus Rover Ticket** entitles the bearer to additional discounts on certain Central Highland tours, camping grounds, youth hostels, and ferries. For further information, contact **Reykjavík Central Bus Terminal**, BSÍ (Vatnsmýrarvegur 10, tel. 552–2300, fax 552–9973).

Staying in Iceland

Telephones
Local Calls Pay phones take ISK 10 and ISK 50 coins and are found in hotels, shops, bus stations, and post offices. There are not many outdoor telephone booths in the towns and villages. Phonecards cost ISK 500 and are sold at post offices, hotels, etc. Beginning in May 1995, all telephone numbers in Iceland will have seven digits; regional codes will no longer exist. Telephone numbers are given here in this new form. If you make calls in Iceland before May, use a regional code plus the last four, five, or six digits of the number listed in this book. Figure out the phone number as follows: If the number listed starts with 5 or 55, drop the five(s), and the regional code is (91). For example, the number 552–2322 is 91/22322 before May. If the first digits are 42, drop them and the regional code is (92). For 43, (93); 46, (96); 47, (97); and 48, (98). 45-numbers take the regional code (95), but be careful—numbers starting with 456 are just four digits and the regional code is (94).

International Calls You can dial direct to almost anywhere in Europe and the United States. Hotels in Iceland, as elsewhere, add hefty service charges to international calls, so ask about the charges before you place a call from your room.

Operators and Information For collect calls and assistance with overseas calls, dial 09; for local calls dial 02; for information dial 03; for direct international calls dial 00.

Mail
Postal Rates Airmail letters to the United States cost ISK 65; letters to Europe, ISK 35.

Receiving Mail You can have your mail sent to the post office in any town or village in Iceland. In Reykjavík, have mail sent to the downtown post office (R/O Pósthússtræti, 101 Reykjavík).

Opening and Closing Times **Banks** are open weekdays 9:15–4. Some branches are also open Thursday 5–6. The bank at Hotel Loftleiðir in Reykjavík is open weekends for foreign exchange only.

Museums are usually open 1–4:30, but some open as early as 10 and others stay open until 7.

Shops are open weekdays 9–6 and Saturdays 9–noon (shopping malls 9–4).

National Holidays January 1; April 13–17 (Easter); April 20 (first day of summer); May 1 (Labor Day); May 25 (Ascension Day); June 4–5 (Pentecost); June 17 (National Day); August 7 (public holiday); December 24–26.

Dining Seafood and lamb are the local specialties, and they are recommended. The restaurants are small and varied—East Asian, French, Italian classical, and trendy. A number of them are located in historic, though not always attractive, buildings. Street vendors sell tasty hot dogs with fried onions.

Mealtimes Dinner, served between 6 and 9, is the main meal; a light lunch is usually served between noon and 2. Most restaurants are open from mid-morning until midnight.

Dress   Casual dress is acceptable in all but the most formal restaurants, where a jacket and tie are recommended.

Ratings   The following ratings are for a three-course meal for one person. Prices include taxes and service charges but not wine or cocktails. Best bets are indicated by a star ★.

Category	Reykjavík	Other Areas
Expensive	over ISK 3,500	over ISK 3,000
Moderate	ISK 2,500–ISK 3,500	ISK 2,000–ISK 3,000
Inexpensive	under ISK 2,500	under ISK 2,000

Lodging   There is a wide range of accommodations designed to meet the demands of foreign visitors. The hotels are modern, without luxuries, but they are clean, quiet, and friendly. Reykjavík and most villages have guest houses and private accommodations. Hostels are few and only functional. Lodging in farmhouses is highly recommended: Over 100 participating farms are listed with **Icelandic Farm Holidays** (tel. 551–9200 or 562–3640, fax 562–3644), and many offer fishing, guided tours, and horseback riding. The **Iceland Tourist Board** (tel. 552–7488, fax 562–4749) offers additional information on where to stay.

Ratings   Prices are for two people sharing a double room. Best bets are indicated by a star ★.

Category	Reykjavík	Other Areas
Expensive	over ISK 11,000	over ISK 9,000
Moderate	ISK 8,000–ISK 11,000	ISK 6,000–ISK 9,000
Inexpensive	under ISK 8,000	under ISK 6,000

Tipping   Tipping is not customary in Iceland.

Reykjavík

Arriving and Departing

By Plane   Flights from the United States and Europe arrive at Keflavík Airport, 50 kilometers (30 miles) from Reykjavík. For information on arrivals and departures at Keflavík Airport, call 569–0100.

Between the Airport and Downtown   Buses connect with all flights to and from Keflavík. The drive takes 45 minutes and costs ISK 500. Taxis are also available, but they cost at least ISK 4,500.

By Boat   During the summer, the North Atlantic ferry *Norröna* sails from the Faroe Islands, Denmark, and Norway to Seyðisfjörður, one of the magnificent fjords on the east side of Iceland, 720 kilometers (450 miles) from Reykjavík. From Seyðisfjörður, Reykjavík is a 1-hour flight or a 10-hour drive. For information, contact **Smyril Line Passenger Department** (Box 370, 3800 Torshavn, Faroes, or Norræna ferðaskrifstofan, Laugavegur 3, Reykjavík, tel. 562–6362).

Getting Around

Most of the interesting sites are in the city center, within easy walking distance of one another. Sightseeing tours are also a good way to familiarize yourself with the city.

By Bus Buses run from 7 AM to midnight. The flat fare for Reykjavík and suburbs is ISK 100 for adults and ISK 25 for children under 13. Exact change is required. Strips of tickets are available from bus drivers and at bus stations.

By Taxi Rates start at about ISK 300. Because Reykjavík is small, most taxi rides do not exceed ISK 700. The best taxis to call are: **Hreyfill** (tel. 568–5522), **BSR** (tel. 561–1720), and **Bæjarleiðir** (tel. 553–3500).

Important Addresses and Numbers

Tourist Information The tourist information center, Bankastræti 2 (tel. 562–3045, fax 562–4749), is adjacent to the main shopping district. It's open summer, Mon.–Fri. 8:30–6, Sat. 8:30–2, Sun. 10–2; fall–spring, Mon.–Fri. 10–4, Sat. 10–2.

Embassies U.S. (Laufásvegur 21, tel. 552–1900). U.K. (Laufásvegur 49, tel. 551–5883). **Canadian Consulate** (Suðurlandsbraut 10, tel. 568–0820).

Emergencies Police (tel. 551–1166). **Ambulance** (tel. 551–1100). **Doctors and dentists** (weekdays 8 AM–5 PM, tel. 569–6600; weekdays 5 PM–8 AM and weekends, tel. 552–1230). **Pharmacies** operate on a rotating basis during nights and weekends. For information on which pharmacies are open evenings and weekends, call 551–8888.

Books in English Eymundsson-Penninn (Austurstræti, tel. 552–7077). **Mál og menning** (Laugavegur 18, tel. 552–4240).

Travel Agencies Iceland Tourist Bureau (Skógarhlíð 18, tel. 562–3300, fax 562–5895). Samvinn Travel (Austurstræti 12, tel. 552–7077). **Úrval–Útsýn Travel** (Álfabakki 16, tel. 569–9300).

Guided Tours

Tour operators use clean, comfortable buses that hold from 16 to 45 people. For information, call the tourist information center (tel. 562–3045).

Orientation Tours Reykjavík Excursions (tel. 562–1011 or 568–8922) offers "Reykjavík City Sightseeing," a daily tour that takes about 2½ hours and includes commercial centers, folk museums, and art centers.

Excursions Reykjavík Excursions (*see above*) has many different types of tours. Perhaps the most interesting are the daily "Gullfoss/Geysir" tours, an eight-hour visit to volcanic craters, geysers, and waterfalls; a half-day trip that includes a visit to the unique **Blue Lagoon**, where you can bathe in hot mineral-rich springs from the depths of the earth; and three-hour pony-trekking trips. For trout-fishing excursions, contact **Úrval–Útsýn Travel** (tel. 569–9300). For inexpensive, guided hikes lasting from an afternoon to several weeks, try the **Touring Club of Iceland** (Mörkin 6, tel. 568–2533) or **Outdoor Life Tours** (Grófin 1, tel. 551–4606).

Exploring Reykjavík

Numbers in the margin correspond to points of interest on the Reykjavík map.

❶ The heart of Reykjavík is **Austurvöllur,** a small square in the center of the city. The 19th-century **Alþingi** (Parliament building), one of the oldest stone buildings in Iceland, faces the square. In the center of the square is a statue of Jón Sigurðsson (1811–79), the national hero who led Iceland's fight for independence, which it achieved fully in 1944.

❷ Next to Alþingi is the **Dómkirkjan** (Lutheran Cathedral), a small, charming stone church. Behind it is **Tjörnin,** a natural pond by which the Reykjavík City Hall opened in 1992. One corner of the pond does not freeze; here thermal springs feed warm water, making it an attraction for birds year-round. Overlooking Tjörnin stands the **National Gallery,** which houses a collection of Icelandic art.

❸ Head back along Lækjargata, beyond Austurvöllur to **Lækjartorg** Square. On the right is the **Bernhöftstorfa** district, a small hill with colorful two-story wooden houses from the mid-19th century. No attempts have been made to modernize the area, and it keeps the spirit of the past. For a century and a half, the biggest building has housed the oldest educational institution in the country,

❹ **Menntaskólinn í Reykjavík,** a college whose graduates have from the early days dominated political and social life in Iceland. On the north side of Lækjartorg is one of the two city bus centers. During the summer this square is lively, with an outdoor market, shops, and cafés.

Time Out **Café Hressó** is one of the oldest coffee shops in Reykjavík. The sweets are delicious, though other places are better for meals. An attractive back garden is open in the summertime. *Austurstræti 20, tel. 551-4353. Moderate.*

Leading west out of the square is Austurstræti, a semipedestrian shopping street with the main post office on the right. From here you can take bus No. 10 or 110 from the bus station for a 20-minute
❺ ride to the **Arbæjarsafn** (Open-Air Museum), a "village" of 18th- and 19th-century houses. *Tel. 558-4094. Admission: ISK 300 adults, ISK 150 children 12–18 years, and free for children under 12. Open June–Aug., Tues.–Sat. 10–6; Sept., weekends 10–6; Oct.–May, by appointment.*

❻ You can also take bus No. 4 from the square to the **Ásmundur Sveinsson Gallery.** Sveinsson was a social-realist sculptor who started his career during the 1920s. Some of his originals are in the surrounding garden, which is accessible at all times free of charge. *v/Sigtún, tel. 553-2155. Admission: ISK 200. Open June–Sept., daily 10–4; Oct.–May, Tues., Thurs., and weekends 1–4.*

❼ Most downtown buses pass the **Náttúrufræðistofnun** (Museum of Natural History), located on Hlemmtorg Square along with the city's main bus station. The exhibits here vary from stuffed peacocks to giant sea turtles. *Tel. 552-9822. Admission free. Open Tues. and Thurs.–Sun. 1:30–4:30.*

Leading east out of Lækjartorg square is Bankastræti. On the left-hand side is an 18th-century white building, **Government House.**
❽ Originally built as a prison, it now houses the offices of Iceland's president and prime minister.

Walk left toward Arnarhóll Hill. On top of the hill is a statue of Viking **Ingólfur Arnarson,** the first settler in Iceland. He arrived in 874
❾ and lived in Reykjavík. Nearby is the modern Central Bank. The bank's basement car park takes on new life on weekends, when it houses the Kolaport Market. Across the hill is a 19th-century build-

Reykjavík

KEY

AE American Express Office

i Tourist Information

Arbæjarsafn (Open-Air Museum), **5**

Ásgrímur Jónsson Museum, **15**

Ásmundur Sveinsson Gallery, **6**

Austurvöllur, **1**

Dómkirkjan (Lutheran Cathedral), **2**

Einar Jónsson Museum, **14**

Government House, **8**

Hallgrímskirkja, **13**

High Court, **10**

Icelandic Opera, **12**

Ingólfur Arnarson statue, **9**

Kjarvalsstaðir, **16**

Lækjartorg, **3**

Menntaskólinn í Reykjavík, **4**

Náttúrufræðistofnun (Museum of Natural History), **7**

Norræna Húsið (Nordic House), **18**

Perlan, **17**

Þjóðleikhús (National Theater), **11**

Þjóðminjasafn (National Museum), **19**

⑩ ⑪ ing that is now the **High Court.** Behind it is the Þjóðleikhús (National Theater), built during the 1940s. Most of the other buildings in the area house government ministries.

⑫ Walk along Ingólfsstræti. To the right is the **Icelandic Opera** building, which was Iceland's first cinema and later its first opera house. A bit farther up, across Bankastræti, is the tourist information center. Turn left along Bankastræti. If you walk straight ahead, you'll be able to enjoy the various shops of what used to be the greatest shopping street in Iceland, Laugavegur.

Time Out **Café Solon Islandus.** The trendy place to see and be seen, this café serves light meals all day, is a popular bar in the evening, and offers such delights as art shows, live music, and intimate theater. *Bankastræti 7A, tel. 551–2666. Moderate.*

⑬ To continue the tour from Bankastræti, turn right onto Skólavörðustígur. At the end of that street towers **Hallgrímskirkja,** a church with a 65-meter (210-foot) gray stone tower that dominates the city's skyline. The church, which took more than 40 years to build and was completed in the '80s, is open to the public during the day. The **church tower** offers a panoramic view of the compact and colorful city center and its spacious suburbs. *Tel. 551–0745. Admission to tower: ISK 200 adults, ISK 100 children under 12. Open daily 10–6.*

⑭ Art lovers will want to visit the neighboring **Einar Jónsson Museum,** devoted to the works of Iceland's leading sculptor early in this century. His monumental sculptures have a strong symbolic and mystical content. *v/Skólavörðuholt. Admission: ISK 100. Open weekends, 1:30–4. Sculpture garden open daily, 11–4.*

⑮ Nearby is the **Ásgrímur Jónsson Museum,** which features the works of the popular post-Impressionist painter Ásgrímur Jónsson (1870–1968). *Bergstaðastræti 74. Admission free. Open weekdays 4–10, weekends 2–10.*

⑯ **Kjarvalsstaðir,** a municipal art gallery named in honor of Jóhannes Kjarval (1889–1972), the nation's best-loved painter, is a 10-minute walk away from Hallgrímskirkja. It is pleasantly situated in the **Miklatún,** one of two spacious parks in Reykjavík. Temporary exhibits show the work of Icelandic and visiting artists. *v/Flókagata, tel. 552–6131. Admission free, except for private exhibitions. Open daily 2–8.*

⑰ From the Municipal Art Gallery, cross Miklabraut and head south along any one of the short side streets to the reflective glass dome of the atrium, **Perlan,** perched high on a hill atop five huge hot-water reservoirs that heat the capital area. There's a fine restaurant here as well. *Öskjuhlíð, tel. 562–0200. Admission free. Open daily 11:30 AM–10 PM.*

⑱ Return to Miklabraut and walk west until you reach the city's other major park, Hljómskálagarður. On your left is **Norræna Húsið** (Nordic House), a cultural center with exhibitions, lectures, and concerts. *Call for information, tel. 551–7030. Open daily 2–7.*

⑲ Northwest of the Nordic House is the campus of the **University of Iceland** (founded 1911). On the campus grounds is the **Þjóðminjasafn** (National Museum), and a visit here is compulsory for anyone interested in Icelandic culture. On display are Viking artifacts, national costumes, weaving, wood carving, and silver works. *Suðurgata 41,*

*tel. 552–8888. Small admission fee. Open June–Sept., daily 1:30–4;
Oct.–May, Tues., Thurs., and weekends 1:30–4.*

From the National Museum, it is a 10-minute walk back to the pond
and the city center.

Shopping

The shops that sell the most attractive Icelandic woolen goods and
arts and crafts are on Aðalstræti, Hafnarstræti, and Vesturgata
streets. Stores to look for include **Icelandic Handcrafts Center** (Falcon House, Hafnarstræti 3, tel. 551–1784); the **Handknitting Association of Iceland,** (Skólavörðustígur 19, tel. 552–1890 or 552–1912);
and **Rammagerðin** (Hafnarstræti 19, tel. 551–7910 and Kringlan,
tel. 568–9960).

Dining

Most Reykjavík restaurants feature excellent seafood dishes,
cooked in a wide variety of ways. Many serve European cuisine as
well as local fish and lamb specialties. Reservations are vital on
weekends in the better restaurants. Jacket and tie are appreciated
but rarely required. Most are open from noon to midnight, and most
take major credit cards. Some offer discount lunch or tourist menus.
For details and price-category definitions, *see* Dining in Staying in
Iceland, *above.*

Expensive **Hótel Holt.** First-class service and fare are the trademarks of this
fine hotel dining room. The decor is chosen from the owner's unmatched private collection of Icelandic art. *Bergstaðastræti 37, tel.
552–5700. Reservations advised. AE, DC, MC, V.*

★ **Perlan.** In this rotating restaurant under the Perlan dome, you may
pay a bit more for the food, but the splendid view, especially at sunset, more than compensates for the price. *Öskjuhlíð, tel. 562–0200.
Reservations advised. No lunch. AE, DC, MC, V.*

★ **Vid Tjörnina.** This restaurant has a homey atmosphere. The chef is a
pioneer of Icelandic seafood cuisine—his marinated codcheeks are
not to be missed. *Templarasund 3, tel. 551–8555. Reservations advised. AE, MC, V.*

Moderate **Hornið.** The emphasis is on pizzas and pasta, but good meat and fish
dishes also are featured at this appealing bistro, which has a cosmopolitan flair. *Hafnarstræti 15, tel. 551–3340. Reservations advised.
AE, DC, MC, V.*

Oðinsvé. This hotel restaurant has a reputation for fine food at reasonable prices. *Oðinstorg, tel. 552–5090. Reservations advised.
AE, DC, MC, V.*

Potturinn og Pannan. This small restaurant on the edge of the downtown area has service that is brisk and efficient without being impersonal. Lamb and fish dishes and American-style salads are the
specialties. *Brautarholt 22, tel. 551–1690. Reservations advised.
AE, MC, V.*

Þrír Frakkav. This fine little restaurant offers an interesting range
of seafood dishes. *Balduvsgata 14, tel. 552–3939. Reservations advised. AE, DC, MC, V.*

Inexpensive **Café Hressó.** This is the place for a quick snack and some local color;
it's as close to a French café as you'll get in Iceland. *Austurstræti 20,
tel. 551–4353. Reservations not necessary. MC, V.*

Coffee Wagon. On the waterfront in West Reykjavík, this is the spot
where local fishermen typically enjoy their hearty lunches. Try the

filling and economical "fish of the day." *Grandagarði 10, tel. 551–5932. Reservations not necessary. No credit cards.*

Lodging

For details and price-category definitions, *see* Lodging in Staying in Iceland, *above*.

Expensive **Holt.** One of Reykjavík's finest hotels, the Holt is in a central resi-
★ dential district. Many of the rooms are furnished with Icelandic works of art. The restaurant (*see* Dining, *above*) is especially good. *Bergstaðastræti 37, tel. 552–5700, fax 562–3025. 40 rooms with bath or shower and 9 suites. Facilities: restaurant and lounge. AE, DC, MC, V.*

Ísland. Reykjavík's newest luxury hotel opened in 1991, in the eastern part of the city, with superb sea and mountain views. *Ármúli 9, tel. 568–8999, fax 568–9957. 119 rooms with bath, 3 suites. Facilities: restaurant, bar, nightclub. AE, DC, MC, V.*

Loftleiðir. The Loftleiðir accommodates both tourists and those attending meetings and conventions. Located near the domestic airport, it's 15 minutes from the center of town. *Reykjavík Airport, tel. 552–2322, fax 552–5320. 218 rooms with bath. Facilities: indoor pool, sauna, solarium, meeting rooms, restaurant, cafeteria, and several lounges. AE, DC, MC, V.*

★ **Saga.** In a class of its own, this hotel is very popular with American businesspeople. All rooms are above the fourth level and have spectacular views of the city and beyond. It's within walking distance of most museums, shops, and restaurants. *Hagatorg, tel. 552–9900, fax 562–3928. 162 rooms with bath. Facilities: meeting rooms, restaurant with live music and dancing, rooftop grill, 6 bars, sauna, in-room video. AE, DC, MC, V.*

Moderate **City Hotel.** A comfortable hotel, it's convenient to the center of town yet on a quiet street. *Ránargata 4A, tel. 551–8650, fax 552–9040. 31 rooms with bath or shower. Facilities: meeting rooms, restaurant. AE, DC, MC, V.*

Hotel Leifur Eiríksson. Adjacent to the hilltop church, Hallgrímskirkja, this hotel is an easy walk from all the city's main attractions. *Skólavörðustígur 45, tel. 562–0800, fax 562–0804. 29 rooms with shower. Restaurant serving breakfast and dinner. AE, DC, MC, V.*

Lind. Near the Hlemmur city bus station and a 10-minute walk from downtown, it offers few frills but plenty of clean rooms and easy access to the city's best shopping, museums, and galleries. *Rauðarárstígur 18, tel. 562–3350, fax 562–3150. 44 rooms with bath. Facilities: meeting rooms, restaurant, lounge. AE, DC, MC, V.*

Inexpensive **Garður.** This is a student residence, open as a hotel only during the summer, when the students are on vacation. It has basic but comfortable rooms, adequate for travelers on a tight budget. It's within easy reach of the National Museum and other attractions. *Hringbraut, tel. 551–5656. 44 rooms without bath. No credit cards. Closed in winter.*

Snorra Guest House. These accommodations are basic but clean, and the rooms have washbasins. The main bus station is close by. *Snorrabraut 52, tel. 551–6522. 18 rooms. No credit cards.*

The Icelandic Countryside

The real beauty of Iceland is in the countryside: the fjords of the east, the stark mountains of the north, the sands of the south, the rough coastline of the west, and the lava fields of the interior.

Getting Around

There are daily flights to most of the large towns. Although flights are expensive, special family fares and vacation tickets are available. There are car-rental agencies in Reykjavík, as well as in many towns around the country. The few scheduled ferries travel mainly to the Westmann Islands, from Þorlákshöfn on the south coast, and to Akranes, from Reykjavík. If you do not have your own car, your best bet is to buy one of the special bus tickets that cover scheduled routes throughout the country (*see* Getting Around in Staying in Iceland, *above*).

Guided Tours

Because of the remoteness of the countryside and the hassles of driving on roads that are often in poor condition, many people prefer a guided bus tour from Reykjavík; both day excursions and longer journeys are available. Such tours are an excellent way to relax and enjoy Iceland's spectacular scenery. Most longer tours operate between June and September and cost from ISK 25,000 to ISK 150,000 per person, including overnight accommodations and three meals a day. On some tours you'll stay in hotels; on others you'll camp out or sleep in tents. Tours typically last from 3 to 19 days and can be booked from abroad through **Icelandair** or travel agencies. For information on tour operators, contact the **Iceland Tourist Board** (Gimli, Lækjargata 3, Reykjavík, tel. 552–9488, fax 562–4749).

Local Tours One-day tours are available in all the major towns in Iceland and can be arranged through agencies in Reykjavík (*see* Important Addresses and Numbers, *above*).

From Akureyri there are several excursions: Tours to **Lake Mývatn** take about 10 hours and cost about ISK 3,500 per person. On the "Midnight Sun Tour," you'll drive along Eyjafjörður and watch the sun reach its lowest point and then rise again. This is a four-hour tour and costs about ISK 3,000 per person.

From Egilsstaðir there's a tour to Mjóifjörður across the rough mountain passes—a strenuous eight-hour tour costing about ISK 2,500 per person. From Höfn in Hornafjörður you can go by bus on a "Glacier Tour," which lasts 10 hours and costs about ISK 5,000 per person. Boat tours from Stykkishólmur in West Iceland, Ísafjörður in the west Fjords, and in the Westmann Islands are excellent and priced reasonably.

Tourist Information

Akureyri (Tourist Center, Hafnarstræti 82, tel. 462–4442).
Egilsstaðir (Kaupvangur 6, tel. 471–2000).
Höfn (Hótel Höfn, Hornafjörður, tel. 478–1240).
Ísafjörður (Tourist Bureau, Aðalstræti 11, tel. 456–3557).
Lake Mývatn (Hótel Reynihlíð, Mývatnssveit, tel. 464–4170).
Ólafsvík (Hótel Nes, Ólafsbraut 19, tel. 436–1300).
Seyðisfjörður (Austfar, Fjarðargata 8, tel. 472–1111).
Snæfellsnes (Hótel Búðir, tel. 435–6700).

Exploring the Iceland Countryside

See the Iceland map for the location of towns on this tour.

The South Iceland is not a crowded place. There can be up to 80 kilometers (50 miles) between tourist accommodations, so you must be prepared for some considerable traveling every day. Start your tour around Iceland from Reykjavík, heading east on the main ring road around the country (Road 1), which you will follow for most of your tour.

In **Hveragerði**, some 40 kilometers (25 miles) away, there are some interesting hot springs and botanic greenhouses where fruits and vegetables are grown. When you have passed **Selfoss**, 8 kilometers (5 miles) farther, you'll be in the heartland of Icelandic farming, and soon you'll cross the longest river in the country, Þjórsá. For an overnight stop in this area, the Edda hotels in **Skógar**, 120 kilometers (75 miles) east of Selfoss, and **Kirkjubæjarklaustur**, 80 kilometers (50 miles) farther east on road 205, are recommended (*see* Dining and Lodging, *below*).

The landscape around Kirkjubæjarklaustur is shaped by 200-year-old lava deposits. When the volcano Laki erupted in 1783, it produced the greatest amount of lava from a single eruption in recorded history.

Traveling the route along the south coast on a clear day, you'll see that the landscape is the area's major tourist attraction. Don't miss the **Skaftafell National Park**. There you can put down your tent for ISK 400 a night. The park is at the foot of the glacier Svínafellsjökull, and farther up is the highest peak in Iceland, Hvannadalshnjúkur, rising to 2,119 meters (6,300 feet). In the park you can walk for an hour or a day through a rare combination of green forest, clear waters, waterfalls, sands, mountains, and glaciers. About 32 kilometers (20 miles) east of the park is the adventure world of the **Jökulsárlón** glacial lagoon, with its eerie icefloes. Boat tours can be arranged on arrival for about ISK 1,000. Information is available at Skaftafell National Park.

One-day downhill skiing and snowmobiling tours to **Vatnajökull** are scheduled from June through September from **Höfn** in Hornafjörður, Road 99. These tours are a once-in-a-lifetime opportunity, as the trip takes you through some great nature spots. Details and general tourist information are available from Glacier Tours in Höfn (tel. 478–1240).

The East From Höfn the journey continues to Djúpivogur, Road 98, and the east coast, where one fjord lies beside another. From **Breiðdalsvík** there are two alternative routes. The coastal one runs through the fishing villages of **Stöðvarfjörður**, **Fáskrúðsfjörður**, and **Reyðarfjörður**, which can be reached via Roads 97, 96, and 92, respectively.

From Reyðarfjörður the ring road continues for 32 kilometers (20 miles) to **Egilsstaðir**. If you decide not to follow the coastline from Breiðdalsvík, you'll reach Egilsstaðir across Breiðdalsheiði, which, at approximately 775 meters (2,500 feet), is the highest mountain road in Iceland. The road is excitingly steep and, unfortunately, not the best example of Icelandic highland road engineering. In Egilsstaðir you are about 768 kilometers (480 miles) from Reykjavík, or halfway around the island, so you can either turn back the way you came or continue north. There is a tourist information center where you can get some traveling tips (Kaupvangur 6, tel. 471–1510).

Some 24 kilometers (15 miles) south of Egilsstaðir on Road 931 is **Hallormsstaðarskógur,** the largest forest in Iceland. There you can stop for the night at an Edda hotel, or pitch a tent by the Lögur lagoon. Perhaps you'll spot the Icelandic equivalent to the Loch Ness monster, which, according to myth, lives in the lagoon. This lovely, peaceful spot is strongly recommended.

From there you can travel around the **Hérað district** and to **Seyðisfjörður,** 48 kilometers (30 miles) from Egilsstaðir on Road 93. Check with the tourist office there for information on such activities as boat trips and pony trekking. Here the Faroese ferry *Norröna* docks weekly on its North Atlantic summer sailing route.

From Egilsstaðir the ring road continues for more than 160 kilometers (100 miles) across remote highlands to **Lake Mývatn.** On this day-long journey through a remote area, you will pass the highest inhabited farm in the country, Möðrudalur, approximately 418 meters (1,350 feet) above sea level. Lake Mývatn, with its incredibly rich variety of waterfowl, is a mecca for bird lovers and also offers fantastic geological formations. Few people live in the area, but there are two good hotels with restaurants (*see* Dining and Lodging, *below*). Information about bike rentals, fishing, and other activities is available at Hótel Reynihlíð (tel. 464–4170).

From Lake Mývatn there are two possible routes. One is to go directly along Road 1 to **Akureyri,** the capital of the north, a journey of 96 kilometers (60 miles). An astonishing attraction on this route is the graceful waterfall **Goðafoss.**

The other alternative is to go to **Húsavik** (Road 87) and **Tjörnes** (Road 85) for a day or so, a detour of more than 160 kilometers (100 miles). The major attractions in this area are the thundering waterfall **Dettifoss** (Road 864) and the great rocky haven of **Ásbyrgi,** which legend says is a giant hoofprint left by Sleipnir, the eight-legged horse of the ancient pagan god Odin.

The North and the West The natural surroundings in **Akureyri** are unequaled by any other Icelandic town. Late-19th-century wooden houses give the city center a sense of history, as well as architectural variety. The **Botanic Gardens** (admission free, open daily 8 AM–11 PM) have a fine collection of arctic flora. Akureyri also has the northernmost 18-hole golf course in the world, host of the **Midnight Sun Open Golf Tournament** each year around midsummer. For information, call the Iceland Tourist Board, tel. 562–3300, fax 562–5895.

From Akureyri you can go for an evening tour north along the coast of **Eyjafjörður** (Road 82) to see the midnight sun; June and July are the brightest months. Information for traveling in the north of the country is available at the Akureyri tourist center.

Driving from Akureyri to Reykjavík, a journey of 400 kilometers (250 miles) takes an entire day, so if there is time to spare, a stay in **Sauðárkrókur** (Roads 75 and 76), **Blönduós,** or **Borgarnes** can be both pleasant and peaceful. Holders of the Omnibus Passport (*see* Getting Around in Iceland, *above*) should not miss the 320-kilometer (200-mile) detour to the peninsula of **Snæfellsnes,** via Roads 54 and 57. A night in the presence of the glacier Snæfellsjökull, where Jules Verne's *Journey to the Center of the Earth* begins, is recommended.

From **Ólafsvík,** snowmobile tours to the top of the glacier can be arranged. The trip costs ISK 3,000 per person; information is available from the Hótel Nes (tel. 436–1300).

Another interesting detour, which can take up to a week, is to **Vestfirðir** (the West Fjords) (Roads 68, 69, and 61). From Ísafjörður, trips to the inhabitable parts of Strandasýsla may be of interest to those who are keen on walking and mountaineering. Information is available at the Vestfirðir Tourist Bureau (Aðalstræti 11, tel. 456–3457).

Dining and Lodging

If you tour Iceland on your own, whether by public transportation or by car, get a list of hotels and guesthouses in the regions from the **Tourist Information Center** (Bankastræti 2, tel. 562–3045, fax 562–4749). You can also contact **Icelandic Farm Holidays** (551–9200 or 562–3640) for a wide listing of participating farms. In addition, the **Icelandic Touring Club** operates a number of huts for mountaineers and hikers in the remote parts of the country. The huts are clean, warm, and comfortable, but are available during the summer months only. Club members have priority.

Most restaurants outside Reykjavík are in hotels, and the following list is largely a selection of hotel/restaurants. The cost of lodging in the countryside is less than in Reykjavík, but the meals cost about the same. Most hotels are moderately priced, around ISK 8,000 for a double room with breakfast. Youth hostels and farmhouse lodging are also available around the country, ranging from ISK 1,500 to ISK 3,000 per person. For details and price-category definitions, *see* Dining and Lodging in Staying in Iceland, *above*.

Akureyri ★ **Hótel KEA.** You'll receive first-class hotel service, and the price is a surprise—real value for the money. There is an excellent kitchen, and moderately priced food is available in the cafeteria. *Hafnarstræti 97, tel. 462–2200, fax 462–1009. 72 rooms with shower. AE, MC, V. Expensive.*

Hótel Norðurland. Renovated and well situated in the center of town, this hotel has a restaurant/bar. *Geislagata 7, tel. 462–2600, fax 462–7833. 28 rooms with bath. Facilities: satellite TV, minibars, phones. AE, DC, MC, V. Expensive.*

Hótel Edda. There is good service and a cafeteria here. *Menntaskólinn, tel. 462–4055. 77 rooms without bath. Facilities: swimming pool. AE, MC, V. Moderate.*

Lónsá Youth Hostel. It's lodging only, but there are kitchen facilities available. *Glæsibæjarhreppur, tel. 462–5037. 11 rooms without bath. AE, MC, V. Inexpensive.*

Blönduós **Hótel Blönduós.** This small hotel, located in the center of town, has a restaurant. *Aðalgata 6, tel. 452–4126, fax 452–4989. 18 rooms, 11 with shower. AE, MC, V. Inexpensive.*

Borgarnes **Hótel Borgarnes.** One of the biggest and most popular hotels on the west coast, this establishment offers both a cafeteria and an elegant restaurant. *Egilsgata 14–16, tel. 437–1119, fax 437–1443. 36 rooms with shower. AE, DC, MC, V. Expensive.*

Breiðdalsvík **Hótel Bláfell.** This is a newly built hotel, but it has no dining facilities. *Sólvellir 14, tel. 475–6770, fax 475–6668. 15 rooms without bath. AE, MC, V. Inexpensive.*

Búðir **Hótel Búðir.** Under the magical glacier Snæfellsjökull and close to a beach of black lava and golden sand, this rustic hotel has an excellent restaurant. *Snæfellsnes, tel. 435–6700. 10 rooms without bath. AE, DC, MC, V. Moderate. Closed out of season.*

Djúpivogur **Hótel Framtíð.** This small hotel by the harbor has a dining room where home-style food is served in a friendly atmosphere. *Tel. 478–8887, fax 478–8187. 10 rooms without bath. AE, MC, V. Moderate.*
Berunes Youth Hostel. This small summer hostel offers lodging for 15 people. *Beruneshr., tel. 478–8988. No credit cards. Closed winter. Inexpensive.*

Egilsstaðir **Hótel Valaskjálf.** This hotel is large and practical, with a restaurant and a cafeteria. There is dancing on the weekends. *v/Skógarströnd, tel. 471–1500, fax 471–1501. 66 rooms with shower. AE, MC, V. Moderate.*
Hótel Egilsstaðir. This is a charming farmhouse hotel. *Tel. 471–1114. 10 rooms without bath. No credit cards. Inexpensive.*
Húsey Youth Hostel. A distance from town, this hostel offers lodging only. *Hróarstunga, tel. 471–3010, fax 471–3009. No credit cards. Inexpensive.*

Hallormsstaður **Hótel Edda.** The hotel offers guests little to write home about, but the harmony of forest, lake, and quiet bays more than makes up for its shortcomings. It has a good restaurant. *Hallormsstað, tel. 471–1705. 17 rooms without bath. AE, DC, V. Closed Oct.–Apr. Moderate.*

Höfn **Hótel Höfn.** This clean and comfortable hotel has a restaurant with good food and service. Try the excellent almond trout. Fast food is also available at the grill, and there is dancing on the weekends. *Tel. 478–1240, fax 478–1996. 40 rooms, half with shower. AE, MC, V. Moderate.*

Húsavík **Hótel Húsavík.** Popular as a ski hotel during winter, this comfortable hotel has both a restaurant and a reasonably priced cafeteria. *Ketilsbraut 22, tel. 464–1220, fax 464–2161. 33 rooms with shower. AE, DC, MC, V. Expensive.*

Hveragerði **Hótel Örk.** Newly built with a health spa, the Örk has expensive rooms, but meals in the ground-floor restaurant are reasonable. Three- to seven-day "spa cure" retreat packages are available. *Breiðamörk 1, tel. 483–4700, fax 483–4775. 76 rooms with shower. AE, MC, V. Expensive.*
Ból Youth Hostel. This is a basic youth hostel with 2, 3, or 5 beds to a room. *Hveramörk 14, tel. 483–4198. No dining facilities. 24 beds. No credit cards. Inexpensive.*

Ísafjörður **Hótel Ísafjörður.** This is a good family hotel. The restaurant offers a great variety of tasty seafood. *Silfurtorg 2, tel. 456–4111, fax 456–4767. 20 rooms with shower. AE, MC, V. Moderate.*

Kirkjubæjarklaustur **Hótel Edda.** This is an ordinary hotel with a restaurant. *Tel. 487–4799. 55 rooms with shower. Facilities: swimming pool. AE, MC, V. Moderate.*

Mývatn **Hótel Reynihlíð.** This popular hotel offers a good tourist information service and a restaurant. *Mývatnssveit, tel. 464–4170, fax 464–4371. 44 rooms with shower. AE, DC, MC, V. Expensive.*
Hótel Reykjahlíð. This small hotel and restaurant have an exclusive location by the lake. *Mývatnssveit, tel. 464–4142. 7 rooms without bath. AE, MC, V. Closed Oct.–Apr. Moderate.*

Ólafsvík **Hótel Nes.** This functional hotel is close to the harbor. Its cafeteria offers good food at moderate prices. *Ólafsbraut 19, tel. 436–1300. 38 rooms without bath. No credit cards. Moderate.*

Sauðárkrókur **Hótel Mælifell.** This attractive hotel has a restaurant and dancing on the weekends. *Aðalgata 7, tel. 453–5265, fax 453–5640. 6 rooms with shower. AE, MC, V. Moderate.*

Seyðisfjörður **Hótel Snæfell.** This is a new hotel in an old wooden house. Its
★ glassed-in restaurant, by a picturesque pond, serves good food.
*Austurvegur 3, tel. 472–1460, fax 472–1570. 9 rooms with shower.
AE, MC, V. Moderate.*

Skaftafell **Hótel Freysnes.** This newly built guest house is adjacent to
Skaftafell National Park. *Skaftafell, 785 Fagurhólsmýri, tel. 478–
1945, fax 478–1946. MC, V. Moderate.*

Skógar **Hótel Edda.** Close to the waterfall Skógafoss, this summer hotel is
beautifully located and has views to the sea and to the mountains and
glaciers. It has a restaurant. *Skógar, tel. 487–8870. 36 rooms without bath. AE, MC, V. Closed Oct.–Apr. Moderate.*

17 Ireland

Ireland, one of the westernmost countries in Europe, is a small island on which you are never more than an hour's drive from the sea. It's actually two countries in one. The northeast corner of the island, Northern Ireland, remains a part of the United Kingdom, while the Republic, with a population of only 3½ million, has been independent since 1921.

The Republic of Ireland is virtually free from the "troubles" that dominate the news from Northern Ireland. Over the past few years, millions of pounds have been spent on upgrading tourist facilities, but the attractions of Ireland as a vacation destination remain the same as ever: those of a small, friendly country with a mild climate and a relaxed pace of life, where simple pleasures are to be found in its scenery, its historical heritage, its sporting opportunities, and the informal hospitality of its loquacious inhabitants.

Dublin, the capital, is a thriving modern city. It's a strikingly elegant city, too, a fact of which the Dubliners are well aware. Trinity College, Dublin Castle, and the magnificent public buildings and distinctive Georgian squares of the city have all been restored, allowing the elegance of 18th-century Dublin to emerge again after centuries of neglect.

The Irish way of life is unpretentious and informal. Pubs play an important part in it. The Irish will be found at their most convivial when seated in front of a pint of their famous black beer, Guinness, consumed here in vast quantities. Even if you do not usually frequent bars, a visit to an Irish pub or two will add greatly to the enjoyment of your visit.

The pace of life outside Dublin is even more relaxed. When a local was asked for the Irish-language equivalent of *mañana*, the reply came that there is no word in Irish to convey quite the same sense of urgency. An exaggeration, of course, but the farther you travel from the metropolis, the more you will be inclined to linger. Apart from such sporting attractions as championship golf, horse racing, deep-sea fishing, and angling, the thing to do in Ireland is to take it easy, and look around you.

The lakes of Killarney—a chain of deep-blue lakes—surrounded by romantic, boulder-strewn mountains are justifiably the country's most famous attractions. The Ring of Kerry provides the motorist with a day-long tour through lush coastal vegetation. By contrast, you will have to explore the eerie limestone desert called The Burren, in County Clare, on foot in order to find its rare Alpine and Mediterranean flowers. Likewise, if you want to stand on the summit of the Cliffs of Moher to watch the Atlantic breakers pounding on the rocks 217 meters (700 feet) below you, you'll have to walk a bit first. The blue hills of Connemara remain the inspiration for many paintings. The history buff will delight in the Shannon region, peppered with numerous castles, some of which have been meticulously restored. Throughout the country, there are prehistoric and early Christian remains to be discovered. You can also seek out the places made famous by James Joyce, William Butler Yeats, John Millington Synge, and other well-known writers and gain a new insight into the land and the people who inspired them.

Essential Information

Before You Go

When to Go   The main tourist season runs from June to mid-September. The attractions of Ireland are not as dependent on the weather as those in most other northern European countries, and the scenery is just as attractive in the off-peak times of fall and spring. Accommodations are more economical in winter, although some of the smaller attractions are closed from October through March. In all seasons the visitor can expect to encounter rain.

Climate   Winters are mild though wet; summers can be warm and sunny, but there's always the risk of a sudden shower. No one ever went to Ireland for a suntan.

The following are the average daily maximum and minimum temperatures for Dublin.

Jan.	46F	8C	May	60F	15C	Sept.	63F	17C
	34	1		43	6		48	9
Feb.	47F	8C	June	65F	18C	Oct.	57F	14C
	35	2		48	9		43	6
Mar.	51F	11C	July	67F	19C	Nov.	51F	11C
	37	3		52	11		39	4
Apr.	55F	13C	Aug.	67F	19C	Dec.	47F	8C
	39	4		51	11		37	3

Currency   The unit of currency in Ireland is the pound, or punt (pronounced "poont"), written as IR£ to avoid confusion with the pound sterling. The currency is divided into the same denominations as in Britain, with IR£1 divided into 100 pence (written *p*). There is likely to be some variance in the rates of exchange between Ireland and the United Kingdom (which includes Northern Ireland). Change U.K. pounds at a bank when you get to Ireland (pound coins not accepted); change Irish pounds before you leave.

U.S. dollars and British currency are accepted only in large hotels and shops licensed as bureaux de change. In general, visitors are expected to use Irish currency. Banks give the best rate of exchange. The rate of exchange at press time (spring 1994) was 63 pence to the U.S. dollar and 99 pence to the British pound sterling.

What It Will Cost   Dublin is one of Europe's most expensive cities—an unfortunate state of affairs that manifests itself most obviously in hotel and restaurant rates. You can generally keep costs lower if you visit Ireland on a package tour. Alternatively, consider staying in a guest house or one of the multitude of bed-and-breakfasts; they provide an economical and atmospheric option (*see* Lodging in Staying in Ireland, *below*). The rest of the country—with the exception of the better-known hotels and restaurants—is less expensive than Dublin. That the Irish themselves complain bitterly about the high cost of living is partly attributable to the high rate of value-added tax (VAT)—a stinging 21% on "luxury" goods and 10% on hotel accommodations. Some sample costs make the point. For instance, while a double room in a moderate Dublin hotel will cost about IR£90, with breakfast sometimes another IR£9 per person, the current rate for a country B&B is around IR£16 per person. A modest small-town hotel will charge around IR£25 per person.

Sample Prices Cup of coffee, 70p; pint of beer, IR£2; Coca-Cola, 95p; ham sandwich, IR£1.80; 1-mile taxi ride, IR£3.50.

Customs on Two categories of duty-free allowance exist for travelers entering
Arrival the Irish Republic: one for goods obtained outside the European
Community, on a ship or aircraft, or in a duty-free store within the
EC; and the other for goods bought in the EC, with duty and tax
paid.

In the first category, you may import duty-free: (1) 200 cigarettes or
100 cigarillos or 50 cigars or 250 grams of smoking tobacco; (2) 2 liters of wine, and either 1 liter of alcoholic drink over 22% volume or 2
liters of alcoholic drink under 22% volume (sparkling or fortified
wine included); (3) 50 grams of perfume and ¼ liter of toilet water;
and (4) other goods to a value of IR£34 per person (IR£17 per person
for travelers under 15 years of age); you may import 12 liters of beer
as part of this allowance.

Duty paid allowances increased substantially in 1993. Travelers are
now entitled to purchase (1) 800 cigarettes, (2) 10 liters of spirits, (3)
45 liters of wine, and (4) 55 liters of beer. The allowances apply only
to goods bought in shops in EC countries, including Britain and
Northern Ireland, which already have the duty paid.

Goods that cannot be freely imported include firearms, ammunition,
explosives, drugs (e.g., narcotics, amphetamines), indecent or obscene books and pictures, oral smokeless tobacco products, meat
and meat products, poultry and poultry products, plants and plant
products (including shrubs, vegetables, fruit, bulbs, and seeds), domestic cats and dogs from outside the United Kingdom, and live animals from outside Northern Ireland.

Language Officially, the Irish language is the first language of the Republic,
but the everyday language of the majority of Irish people is English.
Except for the northwest, where many signs are not translated,
most signs in the country are written in Irish with an English translation underneath. There is one important exception to this rule,
with which all visitors should familiarize themselves: *Fir* and *mná*
translate respectively into "men" and "women." The *Gaelteacht*—
areas in which Irish *is* the everyday language of most people—comprises only 6% of the land, and all its inhabitants are, in any case,
bilingual.

Getting Around

By Car Ireland is one country in which a car is more or less essential for suc-
Road cessful travel. Despite improvements in public transportation, both
Conditions the train and bus networks are limited, and many of the most intriguing areas are accessible only by car. Roads are reasonable,
though the absence of turnpikes means that trip times can be long;
on the other hand, you'll soon find that driving past an everchanging
and often dramatic series of unspoiled landscapes can be very much
part of the fun. There's a bonus in the fact that traffic is normally
light, though you can easily find yourself crawling down country
lanes behind an ancient tractor or a flock of sheep. This is not a country for those with a taste for life in the fast lane.

All principal roads are designated by the letter N, meaning National
Primary Road. Thus, the main highway north from Dublin is N1, the
main highway northwest is N2, and so on. Road signs are usually in
both Irish and English; in the northwest, most are in Irish only, so
make sure you have a good road map. Distances on the new green

signposts are in kilometers; the old white signposts give distances in miles.

Rules of the Road Driving is on the left. There is a general speed limit of 96 kph (60 mph) on most roads; in towns, the limit is 48 kph (30 mph). In some areas, the limit is 64 kph (40 mph); this is always clearly posted. At traffic circles, traffic from the right takes priority.

Seat belts must be worn by the driver and front-seat passengers. Children under 12 must ride in the back. Drunk-driving laws are strict.

Parking Despite the relative lack of traffic, parking in towns is a real problem. Signs with the letter P indicate parking lots, but if there's a stroke through the P, keep away or you'll collect a stiff fine, normally around IR£20. After 6 PM, restrictions are lifted. Give lot attendants about 20p when you leave.

Frontier Posts There are 20 approved routes for crossing the border between the Republic of Ireland and Northern Ireland. If you plan to drive into Northern Ireland in a rented car, be sure the rental company furnishes the necessary papers. Formalities of crossing the border are minimal, though you may find additional checks just north of the border. *Do not* drive on roads near the border marked "Unapproved Road."

By Train **Iarnód Eireann** (Irish Rail) and **Bus Eireann** (Irish Bus) are independent components of the state-owned public transportation company **Coras Iompair Eireann** (CIE). The rail network, although much cut back in the past 25 years, is still extensive, with main routes radiating from Dublin to Cork, Galway, Limerick, Tralee, Killarney, Westport, and Sligo; there is also a line for the north and Belfast. All trains are diesel; cars on principal expresses have air-conditioning. There are two classes on many trains—Super Standard (first class) and Standard (second class). Dining cars are carried on main expresses. There are no sleeping cars.

Speeds are slow in comparison with those of other European trains. Dublin, however, now has a modern commuter train—the DART—running south from the suburb of Howth through the city to Bray on the Wicklow coast, with various stops along the way.

Fares There is an eight-day **Rambler** ticket (rail and bus) for IR£78, valid for any 8 days in a 15-day period. One- and four-day round-trip train tickets are also available at discounted rates. The **Irish Rover** ticket includes travel in Northern Ireland via rail, bus, and Ulsterbus; it costs IR£70 for 5 days travel out of 15 consecutive days.

By Plane Distances are not great in Ireland, so air travel plays only a small role in internal travel. There are daily flights from Dublin to Shannon, Cork, Waterford, Kerry, Knock, and Galway; all flights take around 30 minutes. There is frequent service to the Aran Islands, off Galway Bay, from Connemara Airport, Galway. The flight takes 5 minutes.

By Bus For the strictly independent traveler, the 15-day **Rambler** ticket gives unlimited travel by bus and is an excellent value at IR£95. It can be purchased from any city bus terminal and is valid for travel on any 15 days in a 30-day period. The provincial bus system operated by Bus Eireann is widespread—more so than the train system—although service can be infrequent in remote areas. But the routes cover the entire country and are often linked to the train services (*see* By Train, *above*) for details of combined train and bus discount tickets.

By Boat   Exploring Ireland's lakes, rivers, and canals is a delightful offbeat way to get to know the country. Motor cruisers can be chartered on the Shannon, the longest river in the British Isles. The Irish Tourist Board has details of the wide choice of trips and operators available.

For drifting through the historic Midlands on the Grand Canal and river Barrow, contact **Celtic Canal Cruisers,** 24th Lock, Tullamore, County Offaly, tel. 0506/21861.

By Bicycle   Biking can be a great way to get around Ireland. Details of bicycle rentals are available from the Irish Tourist Board. Rates average IR£7.50 per day or IR£35 per week. You must pay a IR£30 deposit. Be sure to make reservations, especially in July and August. If you rent a bike in the Republic, you may *not* take it into Northern Ireland; nor may you take a bike rented in Northern Ireland into the Republic.

Staying in Ireland

Telephones   There are pay phones in all post offices and most hotels and bars, as
Local Calls   well as in street booths. Local calls cost 20p for three minutes, calls within Ireland cost about 50p for three minutes, and calls to Britain cost about IR£1.75 for three minutes. Rates go down by about a third after 6 PM and all day Saturday and Sunday.

International   For calls to the United States and Canada, dial 001 followed by the
Calls   area code. For calls to the United Kingdom, dial 0044 followed by the number, dropping the beginning zero. Don't make international calls from your hotel room unless absolutely necessary. Most hotels add a 200–300% surcharge to calls.

Mail   Airmail rates to the United States, Canada, and the Commonwealth
Postal Rates   are 52p for the first 10 grams, air letters 45p, and postcards 38p. Letters to Britain and continental Europe cost 32p, postcards 28p.

Receiving Mail   A general delivery service is operated free of charge from Dublin's General Post Office (O'Connell St., Dublin 1, tel. 01/872–8888).

Shopping   Visitors from outside Europe can take advantage of the "cash-back"
VAT Refunds   system on value-added tax (VAT) if their purchases total more than IR£50. A cash-back voucher must be filled out by the retailer at the point of sale. The visitor pays the total gross price, including VAT, and receives green and yellow copies of the invoice; both must be retained. These copies are presented to and stamped by customs, as you leave the country. Take the stamped form along to the cashier, and the VAT will be refunded.

Opening and   **Banks** are open weekdays 10–4, and until 5 on selected days. In
Closing Times   small towns they may close for lunch from 12:30–1:30.

Museums are usually open weekdays 10–5, Saturday 10–1, Sunday 2–5. Always make a point of checking, however, as hours can change unexpectedly.

Shops are open Monday–Saturday 9–5:30, closing earlier on Wednesday, Thursday, or Saturday, depending on the locality.

National   January 2; March 17 (St. Patrick's Day); April 14 (Good Friday);
Holidays   April 17 (Easter Monday); June 5 (Whit Monday); August 7 (August Monday); and December 25, 26. If you're planning a visit at Easter, remember that theaters and cinemas are closed for the last three days of the preceding week.

Dining   When it comes to food, Ireland has some of the best raw materials in the world: prime beef, locally raised lamb and pork, free-range poultry, game in season, abundant fresh seafood, and locally grown seasonal vegetables. Despite the near-legendary awfulness of much Irish cooking in the recent past, times are definitely changing, and a new generation of chefs is beginning to take greater advantage of this abundance of magnificent produce. In almost all corners of the country, you'll find a substantial choice of restaurants, many in hotels, serving fresh local food that is imaginatively prepared and served.

If your tastes run toward traditional Irish dishes, there are still a few old-fashioned restaurants serving substantial portions of excellent, if plain, home cooking. Look for boiled bacon and cabbage, Irish stew, and *colcannon* (cooked potatoes diced and fried in butter with onions and either cabbage or leeks and covered in thick cream just before serving). The best bet for daytime meals is "pub grub"—a choice of soup and soda bread, two or three hot dishes of the day, salad platters, or sandwiches. Most bars serve food, and a growing number offer coffee and tea as an alternative to alcohol. Guinness, a dark beer, or "stout," brewed with malt, is the Irish national drink. Even if you never go out for a drink at home, you should visit at least one or two pubs in Ireland. The pub is one of the pillars of Irish society, worth visiting as much for entertainment and conversation as for drinking.

Mealtimes Breakfast is served between 8 and 10—earlier by special request only—and is a substantial meal of cereal, bacon, eggs, sausage, and toast. Lunch is eaten between 12:30 and 2. The old tradition of "high tea" taken around 5, followed by a light snack before bed, is still encountered in many Irish homes, including many bed-and-breakfasts. Elsewhere, however, it is generally assumed that you'll be eating between 7 and 9:30 and that this will be your main meal of the day.

Dress A jacket and tie or upscale casual dress are suggested for expensive restaurants. Otherwise casual dress is acceptable.

Ratings Prices are per person and include a first course, a main course, and dessert, but no wine or tip. Sales tax at 10% is included in all Irish restaurant bills. Some places, usually the more expensive establishments, add a 12% or 15% service charge, in which case no tip is necessary; elsewhere a tip of 10% is adequate. Highly recommended restaurants are indicated by a star ★.

Category	Cost
Expensive	over IR£28
Moderate	IR£16–IR£28
Inexpensive	under IR£16

Lodging Accommodations in Ireland range all the way from deluxe castles and renovated stately homes to thatched cottages and farmhouses to humble B&Bs. Standards everywhere are high, and they continue to rise. Pressure on hotel space reaches a peak between June and September, but it's a good idea to make reservations in advance at any time of the year, particularly at the more expensive spots. Rooms can be reserved directly from the United States; ask your travel agent for details. The Irish Tourist Board's Central Reservations Service (14 Upper O'Connell St., Dublin 1, tel. 01/874–7733, fax 01/874–3660) can make reservations, as can local tourist board offices.

The Irish Tourist Board (ITB) has an official grading system and publishes a detailed price list of all approved accommodations, including hotels, guest houses, farmhouses, B&Bs, and hostels. No hotel may exceed this price without special authorization from the ITB; prices must also be displayed in every room. Don't hesitate to complain either to the manager or to the ITB, or both, if prices exceed this maximum.

In general, hotels charge per person. In most cases (but not all, especially in more expensive places), the price includes a full breakfast. VAT is included, but some hotels—again, usually the more expensive ones—add a 10–15% service charge. This should be mentioned in their price list. In moderate and inexpensive hotels, be sure to specify whether you want a private bath or shower; the latter is cheaper. Off-season (October–May) prices are reduced by as much as 25%.

Guest Houses Some smaller hotels are graded as guest houses. To qualify, they must have at least five bedrooms. A few may have restaurants; those that do not will often provide evening meals by arrangement. Few will have a bar. Otherwise these rooms can be as comfortable as those of a regular hotel, and in major cities they offer very good value for the money, compared with the inexpensive hotels.

Bed-and- Bed-and-breakfast means just that. The bed can vary from a four-
Breakfasts poster in the wing of a castle to a feather bed in a whitewashed farmhouse or the spare bedroom of a modern cottage. Rates are generally around IR£16 per person, though these can vary significantly. Although many larger B&Bs offer rooms with bath or shower, in some you'll have to use the bathroom in the hall and, in many cases, pay 50p–IR£1 extra for the privilege.

Camping There are a variety of beautifully sited campgrounds and trailer parks, but be prepared for wet weather! All are listed in *Guest Accommodation* (IR£4), available from the ITB.

Ratings Prices are for two people in a double room, based on high season (June–September) rates. Best bets are indicated by a star ★.

Category	Cost
Very Expensive	over IR£160
Expensive	IR£120–IR£160
Moderate	IR£80–IR£120
Inexpensive	under IR£80

Tipping Other than in upscale hotels and restaurants, the Irish are not really used to being tipped. Some hotels and restaurants will add a service charge of about 12% to your bill, so tipping isn't necessary unless you've received particularly good service.

Tip taxi drivers about 10% of the fare if the taxi has been using its meter. For longer journeys, where the fare is agreed in advance, a tip will not be expected unless some kind of commentary (solicited or not) has been provided. In luxury hotels, porters and bellhops will expect IR£1; elsewhere, 50p is adequate. Hairdressers normally expect a tip of about IR£1. You don't tip in pubs, but if there is waiter service in a bar or hotel lounge, leave about 20p.

Dublin

Arriving and Departing

By Plane All flights arrive at Dublin's Collinstown Airport, 10 kilometers (6 miles) north of town. For information on arrival and departure times, call individual airlines.

Between the Airport and Downtown Buses leave every 20 minutes from outside the Arrivals door for the central bus station in downtown Dublin. The ride takes about 30 minutes, depending on the traffic, and the fare is IR£2.50. A taxi ride into town will cost from IR£9 to IR£12, depending on the location of your hotel.

By Train There are three main stations. Heuston Station (at Kingsbridge) is the departure point for the south and southwest; Connolly Station (at Amiens Street), for Belfast, the east coast, and the west; Pearse Station (on Westland Row), for Bray and connections via Dun Laoghaire to the Liverpool/Holyhead ferries. Tel. 01/836–6222 for information.

By Bus The central bus station, Busaras, is at Store Street near the Custom House. Some buses terminate near Connolly Bridge. Tel. 01/873–4222 for information on city services (Dublin Bus); tel. 01/836–6111 for express buses and provincial services (Bus Eireann).

By Car The main access route from the north is N1; from the west, N4; from the south and southwest, N7; from the east coast, N11. On all routes there are clearly marked signs indicating the center of the city: "An Lar."

Getting Around

Dublin is small as capital cities go—the downtown area is positively compact—and the best way to see the city and soak in the full flavor is on foot.

By Train An electric train commuter service, DART (Dublin Area Rapid Transport), serves the suburbs out to Howth, on the north side of the city, and to Bray, County Wicklow, on the south side. Fares are about the same as for buses. Street-direction signs to DART stations read Staisiun/Station. The **Irish Rail** office is at 35 Lower Abbey Street; for rail inquiries, tel. 01/836–6222.

By Bus Most city buses originate in or pass through the area of O'Connell Street and O'Connell Bridge. If the destination board indicates "An Lar," that means that the bus is going to the city's central area. Timetables (IR£2) are available from the **Dublin Bus** office (59 Upper O'Connell St., tel. 01/873–4222) and give details of all routes, times of operation, and price codes. The minimum fare is 55p.

By Taxi Taxis do not cruise, but are located beside the central bus station, at train stations, at O'Connell Bridge, at St. Stephen's Green, and near major hotels. They are not of a uniform type or color. Make sure the meter is on. The initial charge is IR£2; the fare is displayed in the cab. A one-mile trip in city traffic costs about IR£3.50.

Important Addresses and Numbers

Tourist Information There is a tourist information office in the entrance hall of the **Irish Tourist Board** headquarters (Baggot Street Bridge, tel. 01/676–5871); open weekdays 9–5. More conveniently located is the office at

14 Upper O'Connell St. (tel. 01/874–7733); open weekdays 9–5:30, Saturday 9–1. There is also an office at the airport (tel. 01/844–5387). From mid-June to September, there is an office at the Ferryport, Dun Laoghaire (tel. 01/280–6984).

Embassies **U.S.** (42 Elgin Rd., Ballsbridge, tel. 01/688–8777), **Canadian** (65 St. Stephen's Green, tel. 01/478–1988), **U.K.** (33 Merrion Rd., tel. 01/269–5211).

Emergencies **Police** (tel. 999), **Ambulance** (tel. 999), **Doctor** (tel. 01/679–0700), **Dentist** (tel. 01/679–4311), **Pharmacy** (Hamilton Long, 5 Upper O'Connell St., tel. 01/874–8456).

Travel **American Express** (116 Grafton St., tel. 01/677–2874), **Thomas Cook**
Agencies (118 Grafton St., tel. 01/677–1721).

Guided Tours

Orientation Both **Bus Eireann** (tel. 01/836–6111) and **Gray Line Sightseeing** (tel.
Tours 01/661–9666) offer bus tours of Dublin and its surrounding areas. Both also offer three- and four-hour tours of the main sights in the city center. During the summer **Dublin Bus** (tel. 01/873–4222) has a daily three-hour city-center tour using open-top buses in fine weather (£7). From mid-April through September Dublin Bus runs a continuous guided open-top bus tour (IR£5) that allows you to hop on and off the bus as often as you wish and visit some 15 sights along its route.

Special- **Bus Eireann** has a "Traditional Irish Music Night" tour. **Elegant Ire-**
Interest **land** (tel. 01/475–1665) organizes tours for groups interested in ar-
Tours chitecture and the fine arts; these include visits with the owners of some of Ireland's stately homes and castles.

Walking Tours **Tour Guides Ireland** (tel. 01/679–4291) offers a selection of walking tours, including "Literary Dublin," "Georgian Dublin," and "Pub Tours." The **Irish Tourist Board** has a "Tourist Trail" walk, which takes in the main sites of central Dublin and can be completed in about three hours.

Excursions **Bus Eireann** (tel. 01/836–6111) and **Gray Line Sightseeing** (tel. 01/661–9666) offer day-long tours into the surrounding countryside and longer tours elsewhere; price includes accommodations, breakfast, and admission costs. **CIE Tours International** offers vacations lasting from one to 10 days that include touring by train or bus, accommodations, and main meals. Costs range from around IR£240 (IR£345, including round-trip airfare from London) to IR£370 (IR£410 from London) for an eight-day tour in July and August.

Exploring Dublin

Numbers in the margin correspond to points of interest on the Dublin map.

Dublin is a small city with a population of just over 1 million. For all that, it has a distinctly cosmopolitan air, one that complements happily the individuality of the city and the courtesy and friendliness of its inhabitants. Originally a Viking settlement, Dublin is situated on the banks of the river Liffey. The Liffey divides the city north and south, with the more lively and fashionable spots, such as the Grafton Street shopping area, to be found on the south side. Most of the city's historically interesting buildings date from the 18th century, and, although many of its finer Georgian buildings disappeared in the overenthusiastic redevelopment of the '70s, enough remain, mainly south of the river, to recall the elegant Dublin of the past. The slums romanticized by writers Sean O'Casey and Brendan Behan have virtually been eradicated, but literary Dublin can still be recaptured by those who want to follow the footsteps of Leopold Bloom's progress, as described in James Joyce's *Ulysses*. And Trinity College, alma mater of Oliver Goldsmith, Jonathan Swift, and Samuel Beckett, among others, still provides a haven of tranquillity.

Dubliners are a talkative, self-confident people, eager to have visitors enjoy the pleasures of their city. You can meet a lively cross section of people in the city's numerous bars, probably the best places to sample the famous wit of the only city to have produced three winners of the Nobel Prize for Literature: William Butler Yeats, George Bernard Shaw, and Samuel Beckett.

O'Connell Street
Begin your tour of Dublin at **O'Connell Bridge,** the city's most central landmark. Look closely and you will notice a strange feature: ❶ The bridge is wider than it is long. The north side of O'Connell Bridge is dominated by an elaborate memorial to Daniel O'Connell, "The Liberator," erected as a tribute to the great 19th-century orator's achievement in securing Catholic Emancipation in 1829. Today **O'Connell Street** is the city's main shopping area, though it seems decidedly parochial to anyone accustomed to Fifth Avenue or Rodeo Drive. Turn left just beyond the General Post Office and take a look at Henry Street. This pedestrians-only shopping area leads to the colorful **Moore Street Market,** where street vendors recall their most famous ancestor, Molly Malone, by singing their wares—mainly flowers—in the traditional Dublin style.

❷ The **General Post Office,** known as the GPO, occupies a special place in Irish history. It was from the portico of its handsome classical facade that Padraig Pearse read the Proclamation of the Republic on Easter Monday, 1916. You can still see the scars of bullets on its pillars from the fighting that ensued. The GPO remains the focal point for political rallies and demonstrations even today and is used as a viewing stand for VIPs during the annual St. Patrick's Day Parade.

❸ **The Gresham Hotel,** opposite the GPO, has played a part in Dublin's history since 1817, although, along with the entire O'Connell Street area, it is less fashionable now than it was during the last century. Just north of the Gresham is the Irish Tourist Board information office; drop in for a free street map, shopping guides, and information on all aspects of Dublin tourism. Opposite is the main office of Bus Eireann, which can supply bus timetables and information on excursions.

❹ At the top of O'Connell Street is the **Rotunda,** the first maternity hospital in Europe, opened in 1755. Not much remains of the once-elegant Rotunda Assembly Rooms, a famous haunt of fashionable Dubliners until the middle of the last century. The **Gate Theater,** housed in an extension of the Rotunda Assembly Rooms, however, continues to attract crowds to its fine repertoire of classic Irish and European drama. The theater was founded by the late Micheál MacLiammoir in 1928.

❺ Beyond the Rotunda, you will have a fine vista of **Parnell Square,** one of Dublin's earliest Georgian squares. You will notice immediately that the first-floor windows of these elegant brick-face buildings are much larger than the others and that it is easy to look in from street level. This is more than simply the result of the architect's desire to achieve perfect proportions on the facades: These rooms were designed as reception rooms, and fashionable hostesses liked passers-

Abbey Theatre, **9**

Archbishop Marsh's Library, **23**

Brown Thomas, **20**

Christ Church Cathedral, **25**

City Hall, **27**

Civic Museum, **22**

Custom House, **34**

Dublin Castle, **26**

Dublin Writers Museum, **7**

Four Courts, **33**

Genealogical Office, **18**

General Post Office, **2**

Gresham Hotel, **3**

Guinness Brewery, **29**

Halfpenny Bridge, **35**

Hugh Lane Municipal Gallery of Modern Art, **6**

Irish Whiskey Corner, **32**

Kilkenny Design Workshops, **12**

Leinster House, **15**

Merrion Square, **13**

National Gallery, **14**

National Library, **17**

National Museum, **16**

O'Connell Bridge, **1**

Parliament House, **10**

Parnell Square, **5**

Phoenix Park, **30**

Powerscourt Town House, **21**

Rotunda, **4**

Royal Hospital Kilmainham, **36**

Royal Irish Academy, **19**

St. Mary's Pro Cathedral, **8**

St. Michan's, **31**

St. Patrick's Cathedral, **24**

Temple Bar, **28**

Trinity College, **11**

Dublin

N

Annamoe Ter.

North Circular Rd.

Prussia St.

Aughrim St.

Manor St.

St. Brendan's Hospital

Grangegorman Upper

St. Lawrence Hospital

Phibsborough Rd.

Constitution Hill

Brunswick St. North

King St. North

Arbour Hill

Blackhall Pl.

32

Bow St.

Church St.

Me

Montpelier Hill

30

Parkgate

Benburb St.

31

Liffey

Ellis Quay

Arran Quay

33

Inns Quay

King's Br.

Heuston Station

Victoria Quay

Victoria Br.

Ushers

Queen's Br.

Quay

Whitworth Br.

Merchants Qua

Steven's Lane

Bridgefoot St.

Bridge St.

High St.

James's St.

29

Thomas St. West

Meath St.

36

The Coombe

Marrowbone Lane

Lane

Cork St.

Ardee St.

0 _____ 1/2 mile

0 _____ 3/4 km

KEY

AE American Express Office

by to be able to peer in and admire the distinguished guests at their luxurious, candle-lit receptions.

6 **Charlemont House,** whose impressive Palladian facade dominates the top of Parnell Square, now houses the **Hugh Lane Municipal Gallery of Modern Art.** Sir Hugh Lane, a nephew of Lady Gregory, who was Yeats's curious, high-minded aristocratic patron, was a keen collector of Impressionist paintings. The gallery also contains some interesting works by Irish artists, including Yeats's brother Jack. *Parnell Sq., tel. 01/6741903. Admission free. Open Tues.–Fri. 9:30–6, Sat. 9:30–5, Sun. 11–5.*

7 The Parnell Square area is rich in literary associations, which are explained and illustrated in the **Dublin Writers Museum,** which opened in 1991 in two carefully restored 18th-century buildings. Paintings, letters, manuscripts, and photographs relating to James Joyce, Sean O'Casey, George Bernard Shaw, W. B. Yeats, Brendan Behan, and others are on permanent display. There are also temporary exhibitions, lectures, and readings, as well as a bookshop. *18–19 Parnell Sq. N, tel. 01/872–2077. Admission: IR£2.25. Open Mon.–Sat. 10–5, Sun. 1–5.*

8 Return to O'Connell Street, where a sign on the left will lead you to **St. Mary's Pro Cathedral,** the main Catholic church of Dublin. Try to catch the famous Palestrina Choir on Sunday at 11 AM. John McCormack is one of many famous voices to have sung with this exquisite en-
9 semble. Turn right, down Marlborough Street, the **Abbey Theatre,** a brick building dating from 1966, was given a much-needed new facade in 1991. It has some noteworthy portraits and mementos in the foyer. Seats are usually available at about IR£12, and with luck you may just have a wonderful evening.

Time Out | On Westmoreland Street is **Bewley's Coffee House** (there's another one nearby on Grafton Street), an institution that has been supplying Dubliners with coffee and buns since 1842. The aroma of coffee is irresistible, and the dark interior, with marble-top tables, original wood fittings, and stained-glass windows, evokes a more leisurely Dublin of the past. *12 Westmoreland St. and 78 Grafton St. Open Mon.–Sat. 9–5:30.*

Trinity and Stephen's Green | It is only a short walk across O'Connell Bridge to **Parliament House.** Today this stately early 18th-century building is no more than a branch of the Bank of Ireland; originally, however, it housed the
10 Irish Parliament. The original House of Lords, with its fine coffered ceiling and 1,233-piece Waterford glass chandelier, is open to the public during banking hours (weekdays 10–12:30 and 1:30–3). It's also worth taking a look at the main banking hall, whose judicial character—it was previously the Court of Requests—has been sensitively maintained.

11 Across the road is the facade of **Trinity College,** whose memorably atmospheric campus is a must for every visitor. Trinity College, Dublin (familiarly known as TCD) was founded by Elizabeth I in 1591 and offered a free education to Catholics—provided that they accepted the Protestant faith. As a legacy of this condition, right up until 1966, Catholics who wished to study at Trinity had to obtain a dispensation from their bishop or face excommunication. Today more than 70% of Trinity's students are Catholics, a clear indication of how far away those days seem to today's generation.

The facade, built between 1755 and 1759, consists of a magnificent portico with Corinthian columns. The design is repeated on the interior, so the view from outside the gates and from the quadrangle inside is the same. On the sweeping lawn in front of the facade are statues of two of the university's illustrious alumni—statesman Edward Burke and poet Oliver Goldsmith. Other famous students include the philosopher George Berkeley, who gave his name to the San Francisco area campus of the University of California; Jonathan Swift; Thomas Moore; Oscar Wilde; John Millington Synge; Henry Grattan; Wolfe Tone; Robert Emmet; Bram Stoker; Edward Carson; Douglas Hyde; and Samuel Beckett.

The 18th-century building on the left, just inside the entrance, is the chapel. There's an identical building opposite, the Examination Hall. The oldest buildings are the library in the far right-hand corner and a row of redbrick buildings known as the Rubrics, which contain student apartments; both date from 1712.

Ireland's largest collection of books and manuscripts is housed in **Trinity College Library.** There are more than 2½ million volumes gathering dust here; about half a mile of new shelving has to be added every year to keep pace with acquisitions. The library is entered through the library shop. Its principal treasure is the **Book of Kells,** a beautifully illuminated manuscript of the Gospels dating from the 8th century. Because of the beauty and the fame of the Book of Kells, at peak hours you may have to wait in line to enter the library; it's less busy early in the day. Apart from the many treasures it contains, the aptly named Long Room is impressive in itself, stretching for 65 meters (209 feet). Originally it had a flat plaster ceiling, but the perennial need for more shelving resulted in a decision to raise the level of the roof and add the barrel-vaulted ceiling and the gallery bookcases. *Tel. 01/677–2941. Admission: IR£2.50. Open Mon.–Sat. 9:30–4:45, Sun. noon–5.*

In the Thomas Davis Theatre in the Arts Building, The **Dublin Experience** is an audiovisual presentation devoted to the history of the city over the last 1,000 years. *Tel. 01/677–2941. Admission: IR£2.75 (£5 with library). Open May–Oct., daily 10–5. Show runs every hour on the hour.*

Leave Trinity by the Nassau Street exit, a covered way beside the Arts Building. Shoppers will find a detour along Nassau Street in order here. As well as being well endowed with bookstores, it contains the **Kilkenny Design Workshops,** which, besides selling the best in contemporary Irish design for the home, also holds regular exhibits of exciting new work by Irish craftsmen. *Open Mon.–Sat. 9–5.*

Time Out The **Kilkenny Kitchen,** a self-service restaurant on the first floor of the Kilkenny Design Workshops, overlooking the playing fields of Trinity, is an excellent spot for a quick, inexpensive lunch in modern, design-conscious surroundings. The emphasis is on natural fresh foods and home baking. *Nassau St. Open Mon.–Sat. 9–5.*

Nassau Street will lead you into **Merrion Square,** past a distinctive corner house that was the home of Oscar Wilde's parents. Merrion Square is one of the most pleasant in Dublin. Its flower gardens are well worth a visit in the summer months. Note the brightly colored front doors and the intricate fanlights above them—a distinctive feature of Dublin's domestic architecture.

The **National Gallery** is the first in a series of important buildings on the west side of the square. It is one of Europe's most agreeable and compact galleries, with more than 2,000 works on view, including a major collection of Irish landscape painting, 17th-century French works, paintings from the Italian and Spanish schools, and a collection of Dutch masters. *Merrion Sq., tel. 01/661–5133. Admission free. Open Mon.–Wed., Fri. and Sat. 10–5:30, Thurs. 10–8:30, Sun. 2–5.*

⑮ Next door is **Leinster House,** seat of the Irish Parliament. This imposing 18th-century building has two facades: Its Merrion Square facade is designed in the style of a country house, while the other facade, in Kildare Street, is in the style of a town house. Visitors may be shown the house when the Dail (pronounced "Doyle"), the Irish Parliament, is not in session.

Time Out   A half-block detour to your left, between Merrion Square and Stephen's Green, will bring you to the door of **Doheny & Nesbitt's,** an old Victorian-style bar whose traditional "snugs"—individual wood-paneled booths—are popular any time. Usually noisy and smoky, but always friendly, it is one of the few authentic pubs left in the city.

Stephen's Green, as it is always called by Dubliners, suffered more from the planning blight of the philistine '60s than did its neighbor, Merrion Square. An exception is the magnificent **Shelbourne Hotel,** which dominates the north side of the green. It is still as fashionable—and as expensive—as ever.

Time Out   Budget-conscious visitors should put on their finery and try afternoon tea in the elegant splendor of the Shelbourne's **Lord Mayor's Room.** You can experience its old-fashioned luxury for around IR£9 (including sandwiches and cakes) per head.

⑯ ⑰ Around the corner on Kildare Street, the town-house facade of Leinster House is flanked by the **National Museum** and the **National Library,** each featuring a massive colonnaded rotunda entrance built in 1890. The museum (Admission: free. Open Tues.–Sat. 10–5, Sun. 2–5) houses a remarkable collection of Irish treasures from 6000 BC to the present, including the Tara Brooch, the Ardagh Chalice, and the Cross of Cong. Every major figure in modern Irish literature, from James Joyce onward, studied in the National Library at some point. In addition to a comprehensive collection of Irish authors, it contains extensive newspaper archives. *Kildare St., tel. 01/661–8811. Admission free. Open Mon. 10–9, Tues.–Wed. 2–9, Thurs.–Fri. 10–5, Sat. 10–1.*

⑱ The **Genealogical Office**—the starting point for ancestor-tracing—also incorporates the **Heraldic Museum,** which features displays of flags, coins, stamps, silver, and family crests that highlight the uses and development of heraldry in Ireland. *2 Kildare St., tel. 01/661–8811. Genealogical Office: open weekdays 10–5. Heraldic Museum: admission free. Guided tours Mar.–Oct., cost IR£1. Open weekdays 10–12:30 and 2:30–4.*

⑲ The **Royal Irish Academy,** on Dawson Street, is the country's leading learned society; it has many important manuscripts in its unmodernized 18th-century library (open Mon.–Fri. 9:30–5:15). Just below the academy is **Mansion House,** the official residence of the Lord Mayor of Dublin. Its Round Room was the location of the first assembly of the Dail Eireann—the Irish Parliament—in January 1919. It is now used mainly for exhibitions.

Grafton Street, which runs between Stephen's Green and Trinity **⑳** College, is a magnet for shoppers. Check out **Brown Thomas,**

Ireland's most elegant and old-fashioned department store; it has an extremely good selection of sporting goods and Waterford crystal—an odd combination. Many of the more stylish boutiques are just off the main pedestrians-only areas, so be sure to poke around likely corners. Don't miss the **Powerscourt Town House,** an imaginative shopping arcade installed in and around the covered courtyard of an impressive 18th-century building. Nearby is the **Civic Museum,** which contains drawings, models, maps of Dublin, and other civic memorabilia. *58 S. William St., tel. 01/679–4260. Admission free. Open Tues.–Sat. 10–6, Sun. 11–2.*

A short walk from Stephen's Green will bring you to one of the smaller and more unusual gems of old Dublin, **Archbishop Marsh's Library.** It was built in 1701, and access is through a tiny but charming cottage garden. Its interior has been unchanged for more than 300 years and still contains "cages" into which scholars who wanted to peruse rare books were locked. (The cages were to discourage students who, often impecunious, may have been tempted to make the books their own.) *St. Patrick's Close, tel. 01/454–8511. Open Mon., Wed., and Fri. 10–12:45 and 2–4, Sat. 10:30–12:45.*

Opposite, on Patrick Street, is **St. Patrick's Cathedral.** Legend has it that St. Patrick baptized many converts at a well on the site of the cathedral in the 5th century. The building dates from 1190 and is mainly early English in style. At 93 meters (300 feet), it is the longest church in the country. Its history has not always been happy. In the 17th century, Oliver Cromwell, dour ruler of England and no friend of the Irish, had his troops stable their horses in the cathedral. It wasn't until the 19th century that restoration work to repair the damage was put in hand. St. Patrick's is the national cathedral of the Protestant Church of Ireland and has had many illustrious deans. The most famous was Jonathan Swift, author of *Gulliver's Travels,* who held office from 1713 to 1745. Swift's tomb is in the south aisle, and Dean Swift's corner at the top of the north transept contains his pulpit, his writing table and chair, his portrait, and his death mask. Memorials to many other celebrated figures from Ireland's past line the walls of St. Patrick's. *Patrick St., tel. 01/475–4817. Admission: IR£1.*

St. Patrick's originally stood outside the walls of Dublin. Its close neighbor, **Christ Church Cathedral** (Christ Church Rd.), on the other hand, stood just within the walls and belonged to the See of Dublin. It is for this reason that the city has two cathedrals so close to each other. Christ Church was founded in 1172 by Strongbow, a Norman baron and conqueror of Dublin for the English crown, and it took 50 years to build. Strongbow himself is buried in the cathedral beneath an impressive effigy. The vast and sturdy **crypt** is Dublin's oldest surviving structure and should not be missed.

Signs in the Christ Church area will lead you to **Dublin Castle.** Guided tours of the lavishly furnished state apartments are offered every half hour and provide one of the most enjoyable sightseeing experiences in town. Only fragments of the original 13th-century building survive; the elegant castle you see today is essentially an 18th-century building. The state apartments were formerly the residence of the English viceroys and are now used by the president of Ireland to entertain visiting heads of state. The state apartments are closed when in official use, so phone first to check. *Off Lord Edward St., tel. 01/677–7129. Admission: IR£1.75. Open weekdays 10–12:15 and 2–5, weekends 2–5.*

㉗ Step into the **City Hall** on Dame Street to admire the combination of grand classical ornament and understated Georgian simplicity in its circular main hall. It also contains a good example of the kind of gently curving Georgian staircase that is a typical feature of most large town houses in Dublin.

Time Out A mosaic stag's head in the pavement of Dame Street marks the entrance to a narrow alley and a beautiful pub, **The Stag's Head** (1 Dame Court), dating from the early 19th century. Amid tall mirrors, stained-glass skylights, and mounted stags' heads, of course, you can enjoy a typical selection of lunchtime pub grub—smoked salmon sandwiches, hot meat dishes—and a pint of anything.

㉘ Between Dame Street and the river Liffey is a new semipedestrianized area known as **Temple Bar,** which should interest anyone who wants to discover "young Dublin." The area is chock-full of small, imaginative shops; innovative art galleries; and inexpensive restaurants.

㉙ The **Guinness Brewery,** founded by Arthur Guinness in 1759, dominates the area to the west of Christ Church, covering 60 acres. Guinness is proud of its brewery and invites visitors to attend a 30-minute film shown in a converted hops store next door to the brewery itself. After the film, you can sample the famous black beverage. *Guinness Hop Store, Crane St., tel. 01/453–6700. Admission: IR£2. Open weekdays 10–3.*

Phoenix Park and the Liffey Across the Liffey is **Phoenix Park,** 7,122 square kilometers (1,760 **㉚** acres) of green open space. Though the park is open to all, it has only two residents: the president of Ireland and the American ambassador. The park is dominated by a 64-meter-high (205-foot) obelisk, a tribute to the first duke of Wellington. Sunday is the best time to visit: Games of cricket, soccer, polo, baseball, hurling—a combination of lacrosse, baseball, and field hockey—or Irish football will be in progress.

㉛ Returning to the city's central area along the north bank of the Liffey, you pass through a fairly run-down section that's scheduled for major redevelopment. A diversion up Church Street to **St. Michan's** will be relished by those with a macabre turn of mind. Open coffins in the vaults beneath the church reveal mummified bodies, some more than 900 years old. The sexton, who can be found at the church gate on weekdays, will guide you around the church and crypt.

㉜ **Irish Whiskey Corner** is just behind St. Michan's. A 90-year-old warehouse has been converted into a museum to introduce visitors to the pleasures of Irish whiskey. There's an audiovisual show and free tasting. *Bow St., tel. 01/872–5566. Admission: IR£3. Tours weekdays at 3:30, or by appointment.*

㉝ The Liffey has two of Dublin's most famous landmarks, both of them the work of 18th-century architect James Gandon and both among the city's finest buildings. The first is the **Four Courts,** surmounted by a massive copper-covered dome, giving it a distinctive profile. It is the seat of the High Court of Justice of Ireland. The building was completed between 1786 and 1802, then gutted in the Civil War of the '20s; it has since been painstakingly restored. You will recognize **㉞** the same architect's hand in the **Custom House,** farther down the Liffey. Its graceful dome rises above a central portico, itself linked by arcades to the pavilions at either end. Behind this useful and elegant landmark is an altogether more workaday structure, the central bus station, known as Busaras.

Midway between Gandon's two masterpieces is the Metal Bridge, otherwise known as the **Halfpenny Bridge,** so called because, until early in this century, a toll of a half-penny was charged to cross it. The poet W. B. Yeats was one among many Dubliners who found this too high a price to pay—more a matter of principle than of finance—and so made the detour via O'Connell Bridge. Today no such high-minded concern need prevent you from marching out to the middle of the bridge to admire the view up and down the Liffey as it wends its way through the city.

The **Royal Hospital Kilmainham** is a short ride by taxi or bus from the center; it's well worth the trip. The hospital is considered the most important 17th-century building in Ireland and has recently been renovated. It was completed in 1684 as a hospice—the original meaning of the term "hospital"—for veteran soldiers. Note especially the chapel with its magnificent Baroque ceiling. It also houses the **Irish Museum of Modern Art,** which opened in 1991. Parts of the old building, used as a national cultural center, are occasionally closed to the public. *District of Kilmainham, tel. 01/671–8666. Guided tours: Sun. noon–5 and holidays 2–5; cost IR£2. Exhibitions: open Tues.–Sat. 10–5:30, Sun. noon–5:30.*

Devotees of James Joyce may wish to take the DART train south to **Sandycove,** about 8 kilometers (5 miles) out of the city center. It was here, in a Martello tower (a circular fortification built by the British as a defense against possible invasion by Napoleon at the beginning of the 19th century), that the maverick Irish genius lived for some months in 1904. It now houses the **Joyce Museum.** *Sandycove Coast. Admission: IR£1.50 adults, 60p children. Open Apr.–Oct., Mon.–Sat. 10–1 and 2–5, Sun. 2:30–6. Also by appointment, tel. 01/280–8571.*

Off the Beaten Track

It is all too easy for the visitor to forget how close Dublin is to the sea: Take advantage of fine weather and visit the fishing village of **Howth**—it's easily reached on the DART train—and watch the fishermen mending their nets on the pier. Or take the DART in the opposite direction to **Sandycove,** where intrepid all-weather swimmers brave the waves at the men-only **Forty Foot** bathing beach.

Everyone has heard of Waterford glass, but what about Dublin crystal? The **Dublin Crystal Glass Co.** is open year-round, and visitors are welcome to watch skilled crystal cutters at work and to purchase crystal—seconds are available, too—at a discount. Phone for an appointment. *Carysfort Ave., Blackrock, tel. 01/288–7932.*

The **Irish Jewish Museum** was opened in 1985 by Chaim Herzog, the president of Israel and an ex-Dubliner himself, and displays memorabilia of the Irish-Jewish community covering approximately 120 years of history. *3–4 Walworth Rd., tel. 01/283–2703.*

Shopping

Although the rest of the country is well supplied with crafts shops, Dublin is the place to seek out more specialized items—antiques, traditional sportswear, haute couture, designer ceramics, books and prints, silverware and jewelry, and designer handknits.

Shopping Districts The most sophisticated shopping area is around **Grafton Street:** The new **St. Stephen's Green Center** contains 70 stores, large and small, in a vast Moorish-style glass-roof building on the Grafton Street corner. **Molesworth** and **Dawson Streets** are the places to browse for antiques; **Nassau** and **Dawson Streets,** for books; the smaller cross side streets for jewelry, art galleries, and old prints. The pedestrianised **Temple Bar** area, with its young offbeat ambience, has a number of small art galleries, specialty shops (including music and books), and inexpensive and adventurous clothes shops. The area is further enlivened by buskers (street musicians) and street artists.

Department Stores

The shops north of the river tend to be less expensive and less design-conscious; chain stores and lackluster department stores make up the bulk of them. The **ILAC Shopping Center,** on Henry Street, is worth a look, however. **Switzers** and **Brown Thomas** are Grafton Street's main department stores; the latter is Dublin's most elegantly decorated department store, with many international fashion labels on sale. **Arnotts,** on Henry Street, is Dublin's largest department store and has a good range of cut crystal. Visit **Kilkenny Design Workshops** on Nassau Street for the best selection of Irish designs for the home.

Tweeds and Woolens

Ready-made tweeds for men can be found at **Kevin and Howlin,** on Nassau Street, and at **Cleo Ltd.,** on Kildare Street. The **Blarney Woollen Mills,** on Nassau Street, has a good selection of tweed, linen, and woolen sweaters in all price ranges. The **Woolen Mills,** at Halfpenny Bridge, has a good selection of handknits and other woolen sweaters at competitive prices.

Dining

The restaurant scene in Dublin has improved beyond recognition in recent years. Though no one is ever likely to confuse the place with, say, Paris, the days of chewy boiled meats and soggy, tasteless vegetables are long gone. Food still tends to be substantial rather than subtle, but more and more restaurants are at last taking advantage of the magnificent livestock and fish that Ireland has in such abundance. For details and price-category definitions, *see* Dining in Staying in Ireland, *above.*

Expensive

Celtic Mews. This long-established oasis of calm is in a Georgian mews off Baggot Street. A deep wine-colored interior is the backdrop for a collection of fine antiques, and tuxedo-clad waiters provide full silver service at polished or white-clothed tables. Despite the elegance of the setting, the atmosphere is cozy and informal. The chefs have successfully blended classical French and Irish cooking styles, with cuisine ranging from the very rich—Celtic filet mignon, cooked at the table and served in a whiskey and cream sauce—to upscale versions of traditional dishes such as Irish stew made with center loin chops. *109A Lower Baggot St., tel. 01/676-0796. Reservations advised. AE, DC, MC, V. No lunch Sat. Closed Sun. and holidays.*

The Commons Restaurant. In the basement of the Georgian showplace, Newman House, you will find this elegantly modern restaurant, where the cream and dark blue walls are hung with specially commissioned Irish art, and French windows open onto a patio used for al fresco lunches. The menu is international with French and Middle-Eastern influences; main courses lean towards fish, but other favorites include lamb cutlets roasted in garlic and thyme. *85-86 St. Stephen's Green, tel. 01/478-0530. Reservations required. AE, DC, MC, V. No lunch Sat. Closed Sun. and holidays.*

Ernie's. This luxurious place is built around a small floodlit courtyard shaded by an imposing mulberry tree. The rustic interior's granite walls and wood beams are adorned by 135 paintings of Kerry, where, for generations, the late Ernie Evans's family ran the famous Glenbeigh Hotel. The Evans family serves generous portions of the very best seafood—try scallops Mornay or prawns in garlic butter—and steaks. *Mulberry Gardens, Donnybrook, tel. 01/269–3300. Reservations advised. AE, DC, MC, V. Dinner only Sat. Closed Sun., Mon.*

★ **King Sitric.** This quayside restaurant in the fishing village-cum-suburb of Howth is a 20-minute ride north of Dublin by DART or cab. It's worth the journey to taste the succulent selection of locally caught seafood; try wild Irish salmon steaks with Hollandaise sauce, or *goujons* of turbot with saffron. You eat in the quietly elegant Georgian dining room of the former harbormaster's house under the supervision of owner-chef Aidan MacManus. *East Pier, Howth, tel. 01/8325235. Reservations advised. AE, DC, MC, V. Dinner only. Closed Sun., holidays, Dec. 24–Jan. 1, and the week preceding Easter.*

★ **Le Coq Hardi.** Award-winning owner-chef John Howard is noted for his wine cellar and for such specialties as Coq Hardi smokies—smoked haddock baked in tomato, cream, and cheese—and (in season) roast loin of venison with fresh cranberries and port wine. The seriousness of the cooking is complemented by the polished wood and brass and the gleaming mirrors of the sumptuous interior. *35 Pembroke Rd., Ballsbridge, tel. 01/268–9070. Reservations required. AE, DC, MC, V. Closed Sun. and holidays.*

Patrick Guilbaud. This is an authentic, rather formal French restaurant with a consistently good reputation, decked out in a refreshing combination of pink, white, and green with hanging plants. The emphasis is firmly on traditional bourgeois cuisine; the Gallic connection is reinforced by the all-French staff. *46 James Pl., tel. 01/676–4192. Reservations advised. AE, DC, MC, V. Closed Sun., Mon., and holidays.*

Moderate   **Elephant & Castle.** American visitors may be familiar with the New York cousin of this "Left Bank" restaurant. Traditional American food on an eclectic and flavorful menu incorporates everything from spicy nachos to ginger-laced stir fry. The diner-style decor is sparse, the noise level high, and the portions large—but this suits the typically voracious clientele. The central location attracts a young crowd. *18 Temple Bar, tel. 01/679–3121. No reservations. AE, DC, MC, V.*

La Pigalle. This is a charming and unpretentious French restaurant in an old and crooked building that forms part of the archway leading to the Ha'penny Bridge. It is in the heart of, and very much part of, the Temple Bar area scene. The decor is old-fashioned and well-worn, the atmosphere relaxed and the food authentically French, with a menu that changes daily. Typical dishes include fresh asparagus tart, sea trout fillet with sorrel and muscadet, duck breast with apples and calvados. *14 Temple Bar, tel. 01/671–9262. Reservations advised. MC, V. Lunch weekdays, dinner Mon.–Sat. Closed Sun.*

★ **Le Caprice.** This Italian restaurant with busy decor and white linen tablecloths is located right in the city center. The menu includes traditional Continental dishes such as prawn cocktail, deep-fried scampi, and roast duckling a l'orange, as well as an interesting selection of authentic Italian dishes including pasta and veal. This place can develop a real party atmosphere later in the evening if the pianist is in the right mood. *12 St. Andrew's St., tel. 01/679–4050. Reservations accepted. AE, DC, MC, V. Dinner only.*

Inexpensive   **Bad Ass Café.** Definitely one of Dublin's loudest restaurants, this barnlike place, situated in the trendy Temple Bar area, between the Central Bank and the Halfpenny Bridge, is always a fun place to eat.

American-style fast food—burgers, chili, and pizzas—and the pounding rock music attract a lively crowd, both the young and the young at heart. Look out for the old-fashioned cash shuttles whizzing around the ceiling! *9–11 Crown Alley, tel. 01/671–2596. Reservations for large parties recommended. AE, MC, V. Closed Good Friday, and Dec. 25–26.*

Corncucopia Wholefoods. This recently refurbished vegetarian restaurant above a health-food shop provides good value for the money in simple rustic surroundings. It's popular with student types from nearby Trinity College. The menu includes red lentil soup, avocado quiche, vegetarian spring roll, and vegetarian curry—all of them regular favorites. *19 Wicklow St., tel. 01/677–7583. No reservations. No credit cards. Closed Sun.*

Gallagher's Boxty House. Located behind the Central Bank in the lively Temple Bar area, this highly original Irish eatery has a country cottage ambience, with antique pine furniture complementing the dark green decor. Boxty is a traditional Irish potato bread or cake that is served here as a pancake thin enough to wrap around savory fillings such as bacon and cabbage, chicken with leeks, and smoked fish. Follow these with "brown bread and Bailey's" ice cream or the superb bread-and-butter pudding. *20 Temple Bar, tel. 01/ 677–2762. No reservations. V. Closed Christmas and Good Friday.*

Pizzeria Italia. This tiny, one-room pizza-bar and restaurant is decorated in the red, white, and green of the Italian flag and adorned by a nostalgia-provoking collection of Italian travel posters. It is all delightfully cheap and cheerful: Either take a place at the one large central table or perch on a bar stool at a wallside counter. The delicious herby aromas signal a good selection of freshly prepared pizzas and classic pasta dishes, but there is also a choice of light snacks, steaks, ribs, and chicken at very reasonable prices. *22 Temple Bar, tel. 01/677–8528. No reservations. No credit cards. Closed Sun., Mon., and holidays.*

Pub Food All the pubs listed here serve food at lunchtime; some also have food in the early evening. They form an important part of the dining scene in Dublin and make a pleasant and informal alternative to a restaurant meal. In general, a one-course meal should not cost much more than IR£4–IR£5, but a full meal will put you in the lower range of the Moderate category. In general, credit cards are not accepted.

Barry Fitzgerald's. Salads and a freshly cooked house special are available in the upstairs bar at lunch on weekdays. Pretheater dinners are served in the early evening. *90 Marlboro St., tel. 01/677– 4082.*

Davy Byrne's. James Joyce immortalized Davy Byrne's in his sprawling novel *Ulysses*. Nowadays it's more akin to a cocktail bar than a Dublin pub, but it's good for fresh and smoked salmon, salads, and a hot daily special. Food is available at lunchtime and in the early evening. *21 Duke St., tel. 01/671–1298.*

Kitty O'Shea's. Kitty O'Shea's cleverly, if a little artificially, recreates the atmosphere of old Dublin. *23–25 Grand Canal St., tel. 01/660–9965. Reservations accepted for lunch and Sun. brunch.*

Lord Edward Bar. With its Old World ambience, the Lord Edward Bar serves a wide range of salads and a hot dish of the day at lunchtime only. *23 Christ Church Pl., tel. 01/4542158.*

Old Stand. Located conveniently close to Grafton Street, the Old Stand offers grilled food, including steaks. *37 Exchequer St., tel. 01/ 677–0821.*

Lodging

Although only a few major hotels have opened in Dublin in the past few years, considerable investment in redevelopment, updating of facilities, and refurbishing of some of the older establishments is taking place. As in most major cities, there is a shortage of mid-range accommodations. For value-for-the-money, try one of the registered guest houses; in most respects they are indistinguishable from small hotels. Most economical of all is the bed-and-breakfast. Both guest houses and B&Bs tend to be located in suburban areas—generally a 10-minute bus ride from the center of the city. This is not in itself a great drawback, and savings can be significant.

The Irish Tourist Board (14 Upper O'Connell St.) can usually help if you find yourself without reservations.

There is a VAT of 10% on hotel charges, which should be included in the quoted price. A service charge of 12–15% is also included and listed separately in the bills of top-grade hotels; elsewhere, check to see if the service is included. If it's not, a tip of between 10% and 15% is customary—if you think the service is worth it. For details and price-category definitions, *see* Lodging in Staying in Ireland, *above*.

Very Expensive
Berkeley Court. The most quietly elegant of Dublin's large modern hotels, Berkeley Court is located in Ballsbridge—a leafy suburb about a 10-minute cab ride from the center of town. Its new conservatory gives freshness and spaciousness to the atmosphere of the public rooms; among the other new features are five luxury suites, each with its own Jacuzzi. *Lansdowne Rd., Ballsbridge, Dublin 4, tel. 01/660–1711, fax 01/661–7238. 207 rooms with bath. Facilities: 2 restaurants, parking. AE, DC, MC, V.*

Conrad. A subsidiary of Hilton Hotels, the Conrad is firmly aimed at the international business executive. The seven-story redbrick and smoked-glass building is well located just off Stephen's Green. The spacious rooms are decorated in pastel shades of green and brown, the bathrooms fitted in Spanish marble. Alfie Byrne's, the main bar, attempts to re-create the traditional Irish pub atmosphere in spite of its high-powered clientele. *Earlsfort Terrace, tel. 01/676–5555, fax 01/676–5076. 190 rooms with bath. Facilities: restaurant, 2 bars, coffee shop, sauna, gym, sporting facilities available by arrangement, parking. AE, DC, MC, V.*

★ **Shelbourne.** The Shelbourne is one of Europe's grand old hotels whose guestbook contains names ranging from the Dalai Lama and Princess Grace to Laurel and Hardy, Richard Burton, and Peter O'Toole. The blazing open fire in its bustling marble lobby, flanked by two huge rose brocade sofas, is proof that the Shelbourne has not lost the sense of grandeur of its past. Between 1986 and 1988, IR£7 million was lavished on major refurbishment, which included restoring many original Georgian features and emphasizing them with luxurious drapes and a prominently displayed collection of fine antiques and heirlooms. A supplement is charged for rooms overlooking the leafy but busy green; the back bedrooms without views are far quieter, however. *27 Stephen's Green, tel. 01/676–6471, fax 01/661–6006. 165 rooms with bath. Facilities: 2 bars, restaurant, sporting facilities available by arrangement. AE, DC, MC, V.*

Expensive
Burlington. Dublin's largest hotel is popular with American tour groups and Irish and European business travelers. It is about five minutes by car from the city's central area. At night the Burlington's disco and Irish cabaret turn it into a lively spot for overseas visitors. Bedrooms are the usual modern plush in neutral tones. *Upper Leeson St., tel. 01/660–5222, fax 01/660–8496. 477 rooms with*

bath. Facilities: restaurants, bars, disco, and cabaret. AE, DC, MC, V.

Hibernian. An early 20th-century Edwardian nurses' home was converted into this hotel in 1993. The distinct red-and-amber brick facade has been retained, and every room is a different shape, decorated in light pastel shades with deep pile carpets. The public rooms are slightly small, but are attractively done up in cheerful chintz and stripes. There is a library off the lobby and a small restaurant that provides intimate dinners and lunches. *Eastmoreland Place, off Upper Baggot St., Dublin 4, tel. 01/668-7666, fax 01/660-2655. 30 rooms. Facilities: restaurant, bar. AE, DC, MC, V.*

Jury's. This lively and fashionable spot has more atmosphere than most comparable modern hotels. It's a short cab ride from the center of town. Bedrooms are relatively spacious, standard modern plush, and each comes with a picture-window view of town. Exclusive facilities for businesspeople are provided in the 100-room Towers annex. *Ballsbridge, Dublin 4, tel. 01/660-5000, fax 01/660-5540. 390 rooms with bath. Facilities: indoor/outdoor pool, Jacuzzi, 2 bars, 3 restaurants, cabaret May-Oct. AE, DC, MC, V.*

Westbury. This comfortable, modern hotel has an excellent location, right off the fashionable shopping mecca of Grafton Street. The spacious main lobby on the mezzanine level is furnished with attractive antiques and large sofas where guests sit to take afternoon tea. Bedrooms are rather utilitarian with pastel color schemes, although the suites, which combine European decor with Japanese prints and screens, are more inviting. The flowery Russell Room serves formal lunches and dinners; the Sandbook, a ground floor seafood bar is less enticing. *Grafton St., Dublin 2, tel. 01/679-1122, fax 01/679-7078. 214 rooms. Facilities: 2 restaurants. AE, DC, MC, V.*

Moderate **Ariel Guest House.** This is Dublin's leading guest house, just a block
★ away from the elegant Berkeley Court and a 10-minute walk from Stephen's Green. The lobby lounge and restaurant of this Victorian villa are furnished with leather and mahogany heirlooms, as are most of their spacious bedrooms, 13 of which were added to the house in 1991. This is a good bet if you're in town for a leisurely, relaxing holiday. *52 Lansdowne Rd., tel. 01/668-5512, fax 01/668-5845. 27 rooms with bath. Facilities: refreshments, parking. MC, V. Closed Dec. 21-Jan. 31.*

Lansdowne. In the leafy suburb of Ballsbridge, convenient to the city center, this small establishment offers a very friendly ambience. The cozy, modest rooms are painted in pastel shades, and have all the basics. The basement bar is a popular hangout for local businesspeople and fans of the international rugby matches held at nearby Lansdowne Road; photos of sporting personalities hang on the walls. Parker's Restaurant is better than the average hotel spot and specializes in steaks and seafood. *27 Pembroke Rd., Dublin 4, tel. 01/688-4079, fax 01/688-5585. 28 rooms. Facilities: restaurant, bar. AE, DC, MC, V.*

Temple Bar. Previously a city center bank, these premises were converted into this well-appointed hotel in 1993. Although the decor is unexceptional, the triangular shape of the building on the corner of two streets makes the layout rather interesting. It is just around the corner from Trinity College and on the edge of the lively Temple Bar district. Busker's Pub is a popular street-level bar, and there is also a quieter lounge bar and a conservatory-style restaurant and coffee shop. *Fleet St., Temple Bar, Dublin 2, tel. 01/677-3333, fax 01/677-3088. 108 rooms with bath. Facilities: restaurant, 2 bars. AE, DC, MC, V.*

Inexpensive   **Dublin International Youth Hostel.** Housed in a converted convent, it offers dormitory accommodations (up to 25 people per room) and also family-size rooms that can take up to four people. This is a spartan, low-cost alternative to hotels. Non-members of the youth hostelling organization can stay for a small extra charge. The hostel is north of Parnell Square, near the Mater Hospital. *51 Mountjoy St., Dublin 1, tel. 01/830–1766, fax 01/830–1600. 500 beds. Facilities: restaurant. No credit cards.*

Isaac Tourist Hotel. This cheap cheerful alternative for budget travelers provides either bunk beds in small dormitories or private rooms from about IR£6 per person. At the top of the range here—about IR£17 per night—there are eight rooms en suite available for singles and doubles. *2 Frenchman's Lane, Dublin 1, tel. 01/836–3877, fax 01/874–1574. 21 private rooms, 16 dormitory rooms. Facilities: restaurant. No credit cards.*

Jury's Christchurch Inn. Jury's has now introduced functional budget hotels into its hitherto upmarket hotel chain. There are very few frills, but this hotel does offer good value for sharers with a fixed room rate for up to 3 adults or 2 adults and 2 children. The main advantage is the pleasant location, facing Christ Church Cathedral and within walking distance of most city center attractions. The rooms are decorated in pastel colors with utilitarian furniture. A bar offers a pub lunch, and the restaurant serves breakfast and dinner. *Christchurch Place, Dublin 8, tel. 01/475–0111, fax 01/475–0488. 183 rooms. Facilities: restaurant, bar, car park (fee). AE, DC, MC, V.*

Kilronan House. This guest house, a five-minute walk from St. Stephen's Green, is a favorite with vacationers. The large, late-19th-century terraced house is well converted, and the decor and furnishings are updated each year by the Murray family, who have run the place for the past 30 years. The bedrooms are pleasantly furnished with plush carpeting and pastel colored walls. *70 Adelaide Rd., Dublin 2, tel. 01/475–5266, fax 01/478–2841. 12 rooms with bath. Facilities: restaurant (wine license only). MC, V. Closed Dec. 21–Jan. 1.*

Mount Herbert Guest House. Located close to the swank luxury hotels in the tree-lined inner suburb of Ballsbridge, a 10-minute bus ride from Dublin's center of town, the Mount Herbert is popular with budget-minded American visitors in the high season. Bedrooms are small, but all have 10-channel TV and hair dryers. There is no bar on the premises, but there are plenty to choose from nearby. *7 Herbert Rd., Ballsbridge, tel. 01/668–4321, fax 01/660–7077. 135 rooms with bath. Facilities: restaurant (wine license only). AE, DC, MC, V.*

The Arts

The fortnightly magazine *In Dublin* contains comprehensive details of upcoming events, including ticket availability. In peak season, consult the free ITB leaflet "Events of the Week."

Theaters   Ireland has a rich theatrical tradition. The **Abbey Theatre,** Marlborough Street, is the home of Ireland's national theater company, its name forever associated with J. M. Synge, William Butler Yeats, and Sean O'Casey. The **Peacock Theatre** is the Abbey's more experimental small stage. The **Gate Theatre,** Parnell Square, is an intimate spot for modern drama and plays by Irish writers. The **Gaiety Theatre,** South King Street, features musical comedy, opera, drama, and revues. The **Olympia Theatre,** Dame Street, has seasons of comedy, vaudeville, and ballet. The **Project Arts Centre,** East Essex Street, is an established fringe theater. The new **National Concert Hall,** in Earlsfort Terrace, just off Stephen's Green, is the place to go for classical concerts.

Nightlife

Dublin does not have sophisticated nightclubs in the international sense. Instead, there is a choice of discos (often billed as nightclubs) and cabarets, catering mainly to visitors. There is also a very animated bar-pub scene—some places with live music and folksinging. No visit to this genial city will be complete without spending at least one evening exploring them.

Discos   **Annabels** (Mespil Rd., tel. 01/660–5222) is a popular late-evening spot; so is **The Pink Elephant** (S. Frederick St., tel. 01/677–5876).

Cabarets   The following all offer Irish cabaret, designed to give visitors a taste of Irish entertainment: **Burlington Hotel** (Upper Leeson St., tel. 01/660–5222, open May–Oct.); **Jury's Hotel** (Ballsbridge, tel. 01/660–5000, open May–mid-Oct.); **Abbey Tavern** (Howth, Co. Dublin, tel. 01/839–0307).

Pubs   Check advertisements in evening papers for "sessions" of folk, ballad, Irish traditional, or jazz music. The **Brazen Head** (20 Lower Bridge St., tel. 01/677–9549)—Dublin's oldest pub, dating from 1688—and **O'Donoghue's** (15 Merrion Row, tel. 01/661–4303) feature some form of musical entertainment on most nights. Several of Dublin's centrally located pubs are noted for their character and ambience; they're usually at their liveliest from 5 to 7 PM and again from 10. The **Bailey** (2 Duke St.) is mentioned in *Ulysses* (under its original name, Burton's) and retains something of its Edwardian character, while **William Ryan's** (28 Parkgate St.) is a beautifully preserved Victorian gem. **Henry Grattan** (47–48 Lower Baggot St.) is popular with the business and sporting crowd; **O'Neill's Lounge Bar** (37 Pearse St.) is always busy with students and faculty from nearby Trinity College; and the **Palace Bar** (21 Fleet St.) is a journalists' haunt. You can eavesdrop on Dublin's social elite and their hangers-on at the expensive **Horseshoe Bar** in the Shelbourne Hotel or bask in the theatrical atmosphere of **Neary's** (Chatham St.)

For details on pubs serving food, *see* Dining in Staying in Ireland, *above.*

Dublin to Cork

Ireland can be covered in three itineraries that, taken together, form a clockwise tour of the country, starting and ending in Dublin. Distances in Ireland seem short—the total mileage of the three itineraries combined is less than 960 kilometers (600 miles)—but roads are small and often twisty and hilly, and side attractions are numerous, so you should aim for a daily mileage of no more than 240 kilometers (150 miles). The consistently dazzling scenery, intriguing ruins, and beguiling villages will lead to many impromptu stops and explorations along the way. (We have tried to provide full addresses for hotels, restaurants, and sights, though many of Ireland's villages and towns are so tiny they barely have street names, much less numbers. If in any doubt, just ask for directions.)

The first tour takes you southwest from Dublin to hilly Cork, the Republic's second-largest city. On the way, you'll see the lush green fields of Ireland's famous stud farms and imposing Cashel, where

Dublin to Cork

Ireland built its reputation as the "Land of Saints and Scholars" while most of Europe was slipping into the Dark Ages.

Getting Around

By Train The terminus at Cork is Kent Station. There are direct services from Dublin and Tralee and a suburban line to Cobh (tel. 021/506766 for information).

By Bus The main bus terminus in Cork is at Parnell Place (tel. 021/508188).

By Car All the main car-rental firms have desks at Cork Airport. Be sure to get a map of Cork's complicated one-way system.

By Bicycle Bicycles can be rented from **Kilgrews Cycle Centre** (6 Kyle St., Cork, tel. 021/276255).

Guided Tours

CIE operates a number of trips from Parnell Place in Cork (tel. 021/506066).

Tourist Information

Tourist House (Grand Parade, Cork, tel. 021/273251, fax 021/273504).

Exploring Dublin to Cork

Leaving Dublin by N7 for **Naas** (pronounced "Nace"), you will pass through the area known as The Pale—that part of Ireland in which English law was formally acknowledged up to Elizabethan times. Beyond Naas, the road takes you to the center of the Irish racing world. **Goff's Kildare Paddocks** at Kill sells more than 50% of all Irish-bred horses. Naas has its own racecourse and lies just 4.8 kilometers (3 miles) from Punchestown, famous for its steeplechases. The **Curragh** begins just after Newbridge and is the biggest area of common land in Ireland, containing about 31 square kilometers (12 square miles). You will see the **Curragh Racecourse,** home of the Irish Derby, on your right-hand side; to the left is the training depot of the Irish army.

If you are interested in horses, **Kildare,** the traditional home of St. Brigid, is not to be missed. The main attraction is the **National Stud and Horse Museum** and its **Japanese Gardens.** *Tel. 045/21617. Admission: IR£1.50. Open Easter–Oct., Mon.–Sat. 10–5, Sun. 2–6. Guided tours on request.*

At Portlaoise (pronounced "Portleash")—the location of Ireland's top-security prison—follow N8 to **Cashel.** Your first glimpse of the famous **Rock of Cashel** should be an unforgettably majestic sight: It rises imposingly to a height of 62 meters (200 feet) above the plains and is crowned with a magnificent group of gray stone ruins. The kings of Munster held it as their seat for about seven centuries, and it is here that St. Patrick reputedly plucked a shamrock from the ground, using it as a symbol to explain the mystery of the Trinity, giving Ireland, in the process, its universally recognized symbol. The central building among the ruins is a 13th-century Gothic cathedral; next to it is the Romanesque Cormac's chapel. *Tel. 062/61437. Admission: IR£1.50 adults, 80p children and senior citizens. Open June–Sept., daily 9–7:30; mid-Mar.–May, daily 9:30–5:30; Oct.–mid-Mar., daily 9:30–4.*

Cashel and the next town, **Cahir** (pronounced "Care"), are both popular stopping places to break the Dublin–Cork journey. In the center of Cahir, you will discover a formidable **medieval fortress** with a working portcullis, the gruesome barred gate that was lowered to keep out attackers. An audiovisual display can be seen in the castle complex. *Tel. 052/41011. Admission: IR£1 adults, 40p children and senior citizens. Open June–Sept., daily 9–7:30; Oct.–May, Tues.–Sat. 10–6, Sun. 2–6.*

The road continues through Mitchelstown and Fermoy, both of them busy market towns serving Cork's dairy farmers. A short detour at Mitchelstown will allow you to visit President Reagan's ancestral home, **Ballyporeen,** a pretty little village with wide streets built to accommodate the open-air cattle markets held there until the '60s.

The road to **Cork City** passes through the beautiful wooded glen of Glanmire and along the banks of the river Lee. In the center of Cork, the Lee divides in two, giving the city a profusion of picturesque quays and bridges. The name Cork derives from the Irish *corcaigh,* meaning a marshy place. The city received its first charter in 1185 and grew rapidly in the 17th and 18th centuries with the expansion of its butter trade. It is the major metropolis of the south, and, with a population of about 135,000, the second-largest city in Ireland.

The main business and shopping center of Cork lies on the island created by the two diverging channels of the Lee, and most places of interest are within walking distance of the center. **Patrick Street** is the focal point of Cork. Here, you will find the city's most famous statue, that of **Father Theobald Mathew** (1790–1861), who led a nationwide temperance crusade, no small feat in a country as fond of a drink (or two) as this one. In the hilly area to the north of Patrick Street is the famous 120-foot **Shandon Steeple,** the bell tower of St. **Anne's Church.** It is shaped like a pepper pot and houses the bells immortalized in the song "The Bells of Shandon." Visitors can climb the tower; read the inscriptions on the bells; and, on request, have them rung over Cork. *Admission: IR£1, with bell tower IR£1.50. Open May–Oct., Mon.–Sat. 9:30–5; Nov.–Apr., Mon.–Sat. 10–3:30.*

Patrick Street is the main shopping area of Cork, and here you will find the city's two major department stores, **Roches** and **Cash's.** Cash's has a good selection of Waterford crystal. The liveliest place in town to shop is just off Patrick Street, to the west, near the city center parking lot, in the pedestrians-only **Paul Street** area. The **House of James** stocks the best in modern Irish design, including tableware, ceramics, knitwear, hand-woven tweeds, and high fashion. The **Donegal Shop** next door specializes in made-to-order tweed suits and rain wear. At the top of Paul Street is the **Crawford Art Gallery,** which has an excellent collection of 18th- and 19th-century views of Cork and mounts adventurous exhibitions by modern artists. *Emmet Place, tel. 021/273377. Admission free. Open weekdays 10–5, Sat. 9–1.*

One of Cork's most famous sons was William Penn (1644–1718), founder of the Pennsylvania colony. He is only one of thousands who sailed from Cork's port, the Cove of Cork on Great Island, 24 kilometers (15 miles) down the harbor. **Cobh,** as it is known nowadays, can be reached by train from Kent Station, and the trip provides excellent views of the magnificent harbor. Cobh is an attractive hilly town dominated by its 19th-century **cathedral.** It was the first and last European port of call for transatlantic liners, one of which was the ill-fated *Titanic.* Cobh has other associations with shipwrecks: It was from here that destroyers were sent out in May 1915 to search for survivors of the *Lusitania,* torpedoed by a German submarine with the loss of 1,198 lives. Cobh's maritime past and its links with emigration are documented in a new IR£2 million heritage center known as **The Queenstown Project,** which opened in the town's old railway station in 1993. *Tel. 021/893591. Admission: IR£3.50 adults, IR£2 children and senior citizens. Open Easter–Sept., weekdays 9:30–7:30, weekends 10–7; Oct.–Easter, daily 10–5.*

Fota Island, midway between Cork and Cobh, is a recent and very welcome addition to Cork's tourist attractions. The Royal Zoological Society has created a 238-square-kilometer (70-acre) wildlife park here. *Tel. 021/812678. Admission: IR£3.10 adults, IR£1.75 children and senior citizens. Car park: IR£1 per car. Open Easter–Oct., Mon.–Sat. 10–6, Sun. 11–6.*

Most visitors to Cork want to kiss the famous **Blarney Stone** in the hope of acquiring the "gift of gab." Blarney itself, 8 kilometers (5 miles) from Cork City, should not, however, be taken too seriously as an excursion. All that is left of **Blarney Castle** is its ruined central keep containing the celebrated stone. This is set in the battlements, and to kiss it, you must lie on the walk within the walls, lean your head back, and touch the stone with your lips. Nobody knows how the tradition originated, but Elizabeth I is credited with giving the word *blarney* to the language when, commenting on the unfulfilled promises of Cormac MacCarthy, Lord Blarney of the time, she remarked, "This is all Blarney; what he says, he never means." Adjoining the castle is a first-rate crafts shop, and the outing provides a good opportunity to shop around for traditional Irish goods at competitive prices. *Tel. 021/385252. Admission: IR£3 adults, IR£1.50 senior citizens, IR£1 children. Open Mon.–Sat. 9 to sundown, Sun. 9:30–5:30; winter, 9:30–sundown.*

Dining and Lodging

For details and price-category definitions, *see* Dining and Lodging in Staying in Ireland, *above.*

Cahir **Kilcoran Lodge Hotel.** Set in its own grounds on the main road,
Lodging Kilcoran Lodge Hotel is an ideal place to break the journey with coffee or a plainly cooked lunch. It occupies a bucolic country setting on the southern slope of the Galtees. *Co. Tipperary, just off N8, tel. 052/41288, fax 052/41994. 23 rooms with bath. Facilities: indoor pool, sauna. AE, DC, MC, V. Moderate.*

Cashel **Chez Hans.** Fresh local produce cooked with a French accent is
Dining served in this converted chapel at the foot of the famous rock. *Tel. 062/61177. MC, V. Dinner only. Closed Sun., Mon., first 3 weeks Jan. Expensive.*

Lodging **Cashel Palace.** This elegant Palladian mansion was once a bishop's palace. It has luxurious rooms and a beautiful garden. *Main St., Co. Tipperary, tel. 062/61411, fax 062/61521. 20 rooms with bath. AE, DC, MC, V. Closed Dec. 25–26. Very Expensive.*

Cork **Arbutus Lodge.** One of Ireland's most highly acclaimed restaurants,
Dining the Arbutus Lodge is run by the Ryan family and is famous for its
★ excellent wine list. There are 20 rooms as well. *Middle Glanmire Rd., Montenotte, tel. 021/501237. Reservations required. AE, DC, MC, V. Closed Sun. and 1 week at Christmas. Expensive.*

★ **Ballymaloe House.** This country-house hotel is half an hour's drive from the city, but it's well worth the effort because the restaurant—run by Myrtle Allen, a world expert on Irish cookery—is outstanding. *Shanagarry, near Ballycotton, tel. 021/652531. Reservations advised. AE, DC, MC, V. Expensive.*

Clifford's. Cork's most fashionable restaurant, just a short walk from Jury's hotel, serves seriously good food in a fun atmosphere. The ground floor of a Georgian house has been strikingly modernized and decorated in black and white. Choose from the owner/chef's small set menu (4 or 5 choices for each course), which includes items such as black sole and prawn in a pepper and lime sauce or medallions of beef in a light port and Chetwynd cheese sauce. *18 Dyke Parade, tel. 021/275333. Reservations advised. AE, DC, MC, V. Closed Sun., Mon., and Sat. lunch. Expensive.*

The Gallery Café. If you can't make it out to Ballymaloe, you can sample their distinctive cooking style at the Crawford Gallery Café—the best inexpensive food in the city, served amid statues and prints from the municipal art collection. *Crawford Gallery, Emmet Pl., tel. 021/274415. Open Mon., Tues., and Sat. 10:30–4:30; Wed.–Fri. 6:30–9:30. Inexpensive.*

Lodging **Jury's.** This modern two-story hotel has a lively bar and occupies a riverside location just five minutes' walk from the downtown area. *Western Rd., tel. 021/276622, fax 021/274477. 185 rooms with bath. Facilities: 2 restaurants, indoor and outdoor pools, health club, sauna, tennis. AE, DC, MC, V. Closed Dec. 25, 26. Expensive.*

Silver Springs. Situated on its own grounds overlooking the river Lee, five minutes' drive from the town center, this modern low-rise reopened in 1989 after major refurbishment. A popular choice for tour groups, it also has the most up-to-date leisure facilities in town. *Tivoli, tel. 021/507533, fax 021/507641. 110 rooms with bath. Facilities: indoor pool, sauna, gym, squash, tennis, 2 bars, 2 restaurants, bowling, 9-hole golf. AE, DC, MC, V. Expensive.*

★ **Arbutus Lodge.** This exceptionally comfortable hotel has an outstanding restaurant and panoramic views of the city and the river. *Middle Glanmire Rd., Montenotte, tel. 021/501237, fax 021/502893. 20 rooms with bath. AE, DC, MC, V. Closed 1 week at Christmas. Moderate.*

Moore's. Good for its central location on a quiet part of the riverbank, the hotel has a fine reputation for friendliness and personal attention. *Morrison's Island, tel. 021/271291, fax 021/272485. 36 rooms, most with bath. AE, DC, MC, V. Moderate.*

★ **Victoria Lodge.** Originally built in the early 20th century as a Capuchin monastery, this exceptionally well-appointed B&B is located a five-minute drive from the town center; it is also on several bus routes. The rooms are simple but comfortable, with views over the lodge's own grounds. Breakfast is served in the spacious old refectory. *Victoria Cross, tel. 021/542233, fax 021/542572. 22 rooms with bath. Facilities: restaurant (wine license only), TV lounge. MC, V. Inexpensive.*

Cork to Galway

The trip from Cork to Galway is about 300 kilometers (188 miles) and includes stops in Killarney and Limerick. Killarney and the mysterious regions of the Burren are two very different areas of outstanding natural beauty. The Shannon region around Limerick is littered with castles, both ruined and restored.

Getting Around

By Train   Trains run from Cork to Tralee, via Killarney, and from Cork to Limerick, changing at Limerick Junction.

By Bus   Buses offer a more flexible service than do trains; details are available from local tourist information offices.

By Car   All major rental companies have facilities at Shannon Airport. **Killarney Autos Ltd.** (Park Rd., tel. 064/31355) is the major firm in Killarney. Taxis do not operate on meters; agree on the fare beforehand.

By Bicycle   You can rent bicycles from **O'Callaghan Bros.** (College St., Killarney, tel. 064/31175), **D. O'Neill** (Plunkett St., Killarney, tel. 064/31970), and **Emerald Appliances** (1 Patrick St., Limerick, tel. 061/416983).

Guided Tours

Bus Eireann offers day tours by bus from Killarney and Tralee train stations; check with the tourist office or rail station for details. **Shannon Castle Tours** (tel. 061/61788) and **Destination Killarney** (tel. 064/32638) also operate tours.

Tourist Information

All tourist information offices are open weekdays 9–6, Sat. 9–1.

Killarney (Town Hall, tel. 064/31633, fax 064/34506).
Limerick (Arthur's Quay, tel. 061/317522, fax 061/317939).

Cork to Galway

Shannon Airport (tel. 061/471664).
Tralee (Ashe Memorial Hall, tel. 066/21288).

Exploring Cork to Galway

Beyond Macroom, the main Cork–Killarney road passes through the west-Cork **Gaelteacht**—a predominantly Irish-speaking region—and begins its climb into the Derrynasaggart Mountains. A detour to the left at Ballyvourney will take you to the lake of **Gougane Barra**, source of the river Lee and now a national park. The 6th-century monk St. Finbar, founder of Cork, had his cell on an island in the lake; this island can now be reached by causeway.

Killarney itself is an undistinguished market town, well developed to handle the tourist trade that flourishes here in the peak season. To find the famous scenery, you must head out of town toward the lakes that lie in a valley running south between the mountains. Part of Killarney's lake district is within **Killarney National Park.** At the heart of the park is the 40,470-square-kilometer (10,000-acre) **Muckross Estate** (open Easter–May and Sept.–Oct., daily 8–7; June–Aug., daily 9–5). Cars are not allowed in the estate, so if you don't want to walk, rent a bicycle in town or take a trip in a jaunting car—a small two-wheeled horse-drawn cart. At the center of the estate is **Muckross House**, a 19th-century manor that contains a folk museum and visitor center. *Tel. 064/31440. Admission: IR£2.50 adults, IR£1 children. Open Sept.–June, daily 9–5:30; July and Aug., daily 9–7.*

To get an idea of the splendor of the lakes and streams—of the massive glacial sandstone and limestone rocks and lush vegetation that characterize the Killarney district—take one of the day-long tours of the **Gap of Dunloe, the Upper Lake, Long Range, Middle** and **Lower lakes,** and **Ross Castle.** The central section, the Gap of Dunloe, is not suitable for cars, but horses and jaunting cars are available at **Kate Kearney's Cottage,** which marks the entrance to the gap.

The **Ring of Kerry** will add about 176 kilometers (110 miles) to your trip, but in good weather it provides a pleasant experience. Leave Killarney by the Kenmare road. **Kenmare** is a small market town 34 kilometers (21 miles) from Killarney at the head of Kenmare Bay. Across the water, as you drive out along the Iveragh Peninsula, will be views of the gray-blue mountain ranges of the Beara Peninsula. **Sneem,** on the estuary of the river Ardsheelaun, is one of the prettiest villages in Ireland. Beyond the next village, Caherdaniel, is **Derrynane House,** home of the 19th-century politician and patriot Daniel O'Connell, "The Liberator," and completed by him in 1825. It still contains much of its original furniture. *Tel. 066/75113. Admission: IR£1 adults, 40p children and senior citizens. Open mid-June–Sept., daily 10–1 and 2–7; Oct.–mid-June, Tues.–Sat. 10–1, Sun. 2–5. Park: admission free.*

The village of **Waterville** is famous as an angling center; it also has a fine sandy beach and a championship golf course. Offshore, protruding in conical shapes from the Atlantic, are the **Skellig Rocks,** which contain the cells of early Christian monks. To learn more about the history and bird life of these islands, visit **The Skellig Experience,** an interpretative center situated where the bridge joins Valentia Island. Landing is prohibited on the Skelligs without a special permit, but the one-and-a-half hour boat cruise offered (weather permitting) at the center is a good substitute. *Tel. 064/31633. Admission: IR£3 adults, IR£1.50 children; with cruise, IR£15 adults, IR£8 children. Open Apr.–June and Sept., daily 9:30–5; July–Aug., daily 9:30–7. Call to confirm cruise times.*

Beyond Cahirciveen, you are on the other side of the Ring, with views across Dingle Bay to the rugged peaks of the Dingle Peninsula. At the head of the bay is **Killorglin,** which has a three-day stint of unbridled merrymaking the first weekend in August, known as Puck Fair.

If time and the weather are on your side, turn off the main Killorglin–Tralee road and make a tour of the **Dingle Peninsula**— one of the wildest and least spoiled regions of Ireland—taking in the **Connor Pass, Mount Brandon, the Gallarus Oratory,** and stopping at **Dunquin** to hear some of Ireland's best traditional musicians. For an adventure off the beaten path, arrange for a boat ride to the **Blasket Islands** and spend a few blissful hours wandering along the cliffs. Dingle town is a handy touring base, with a surprisingly wide choice of good restaurants, open Easter–October.

Tralee is the commercial center of Kerry, but has little to recommend it unless you happen to be visiting in September, when the "Rose of Tralee" is selected from an international lineup of young women of Irish descent. Listowel is similarly transformed during its race week in October. From **Tarbert** (where a ferry provides a handy shortcut directly to County Clare and the Burren), the road skirts the estuary of the river Shannon. **Limerick** is the third-largest city in the Republic, with a population of 60,000; it's also arguably the least attractive city in Ireland. Its Newtown area, however, is dominated by attractive Georgian buildings.

Bunratty Castle is a famous landmark midway between Limerick and Shannon Airport. It is one of four castles in the area that offer nightly medieval banquets, which, though as fake as they come, at least offer some fairly uninhibited fun. The castle was the stronghold of the princes of Thomond and is the most complete and—despite its ye-olde-world banquets—authentic medieval castle in Ireland, restored in such a way as to give an idea of the 15th- and 16th-century way of life. The **Folk Park** on its grounds has farm buildings and crafts shops typical of the 19th century. *Tel. 061/ 361511. Admission: IR£4.00 adults, IR£3.75 students and senior citizens, IR£1.90 children. Open June–Aug., daily 9:30–7.*

Time Out Drop in to **Durty Nelly's,** beside Bunratty Castle—it's one of Ireland's most popular old-time bars.

There is an incredible number of castles—almost 900—in the Shannon area, ranging from such fully restored examples as **Knappogue** at Quin, 14 kilometers (9 miles) from Bunratty, to the multitude of crumbling ruins that loom up all over the area.

Beyond Shannon Airport is County Clare and its principal town, **Ennis,** the campaigning base of Eamon de Valera, the New York-born politician whose character and views dominated the Republic during its early years. Just beyond Ennis, a detour to **Corofin** will take you to the **Clare Heritage Center,** which explains the traumatic story of Ireland in the 19th century, a story of famines and untold misery that resulted in the mass emigrations of the Irish to England and the United States. *Tel. 065/27955. Admission: IR£1.75 adults, 75p children. Open Apr.–Oct., daily 10–6; Nov.–Mar. by appointment.*

Ennistymon or Lisdoonvarna, both quiet villages with an old-fashioned charm, make excellent bases for touring the Burren. **Lisdoonvarna** has developed something of a reputation over the years as a matchmaking center, with bachelor farmers and single women converging here each year around harvesttime in order to get to know each other better. This strange, rocky, limestone district is a superb nature reserve, with a profusion of unique wildflowers that are at their best in late May. Huge colonies of puffins, kittiwakes, shags, guillemots, and razorbills nest along its coast. The **Burren Display Center** at **Kilfenora** explains the extraordinary geology and wildlife of the area in a simple audiovisual display. *Tel. 065/88030. Admission: IR£2 adults, IR£1 children. Open mid-Mar.–Apr.and Sept.–Oct., daily 10–6; May–Aug., daily 10–6.*

The dramatic **Cliffs of Moher** are a must: They rise vertically out of the sea in a wall that stretches 8 kilometers (5 miles) and varies in height from 217 to 440 meters (700 feet), with **O'Brien's Tower** at their highest point. This contains a visitor center (open Mar.–Oct., 10–6). On a clear day, the **Aran Islands** are visible from the cliffs, and in the summer there are regular day trips to them from **Doolin,** a small village popular with young travelers and noted for its spontaneous traditional music sessions.

At **Ailwee Cave** near Ballyvaughan, you can take a guided tour into the underworld of the Burren, where 1,041 meters (1,120 yards) of cave, formed millions of years ago, can be explored. *Tel. 065/77036. Admission: IR£3.20 adults, IR£2 children. Open early Mar.–early Nov., daily 10–6 (last tour 5:30); July and Aug. daily 10–7 (last tour 6:30).*

The coast road continues into County Galway, through the pretty fishing village of Kinvara. Galway City itself is approached through **Clarinbridge,** the village that hosts Galway's annual Oyster Festival in September, featuring the superlative products of the village's oyster beds.

Dining and Lodging

For details and price-category definitions, *see* Dining and Lodging in Staying in Ireland, *above.*

Clarinbridge
Dining

Moran's of the Weir. This waterside traditional thatched cottage is one of Ireland's simplest yet most famous seafood eateries. The specialty here is oysters, but they also serve crab, prawns, mussels, and smoked salmon. *The Weir, Kilcolgan, Co. Galway, tel. 091/96113. AE, MC, V. Inexpensive.*

Dingle
Dining

Beginish. The best of several small but sophisticated restaurants in town, this relaxing place serves local meat and seafood in a generous version of nouvelle cuisine. *Green St., tel. 066/51588. AE, DC, MC, V. Closed Mon. and Nov. 1–Mar. Moderate.*

Doyle's Seafood Bar. This is Dingle's best-known seafood restaurant, specializing in simply prepared local fish and shellfish. There are also 8 comfortable bedrooms. *John St., tel. 066/51174, fax 066/51816. Reservations advised. AE, MC, V. Closed Sun. and mid-Nov.–early Mar. Moderate.*

Lodging

Benner's. This busy town-center hotel has been beautifully restored with country-pine antique furniture in all bedrooms. *Main St., tel. 066/51638, fax 066/51412. 25 rooms with bath. Facilities: 2 bars, restaurant. AE, DC, MC, V. Moderate.*

Ennis
Lodging
★

Old Ground. A gracious, creeper-clad old building, Old Ground has been carefully updated. *O'Connell St., tel. 065/28127, fax 065/28112. 60 rooms with bath. AE, DC, MC, V. Expensive.*

West County. This is a lively modern hotel with adequate rooms and Irish cabaret nightly in summer. *On N18 Limerick road, tel. 065/28421, fax 065/28801. 109 rooms with bath. AE, DC, MC, V. Moderate.*

Kenmare
Lodging
★

Park. A guest feels truly pampered at this antique-laden hotel, widely considered to be one of Ireland's best. The French restaurant is superb. *Tel. 064/41200, fax 064/41200. 48 rooms with bath. Facilities: tennis, parkland, garden. DC, MC, V. Very Expensive.*

Killarney
Dining
★

Foley's. This popular eatery specializes in seafood, steaks, and Kerry mountain lamb. *23 High St., tel. 064/31217. AE, DC, MC, V. Moderate.*

★

Gaby's. For simple and fresh seafood, Gaby's can't be beat. *17 High St., tel. 064/32519. AE, DC, MC, V. Closed Sun. (except for dinner in July and Aug.), Mon. lunch, and Dec.–mid-Mar. Moderate.*

Lodging

Aghadoe Heights. This luxury hotel overlooks the lakes and has the most romantic view of all the hotels in Killarney. The restaurant is outstanding. *Aghadoe Heights, tel. 064/31766, fax 064/31345. 57 rooms with bath. Facilities: restaurant, bar, indoor heated pool, sauna, Jacuzzi, tennis court, fishing. AE, DC, MC, V. Very Expensive.*

Great Southern. The Great Southern is housed in a vast 19th-century redbrick building set in large gardens. *Tel. 064/31262, fax 064/31642. 180 rooms with bath. Facilities: heated indoor pool. AE, DC, MC, V. Closed Jan.–mid-Mar. Expensive.*

Arbutus. Newly refurbished and centrally located, the Arbutus benefits from a lively bar and an Old World atmosphere. *College St., tel. 064/31037, fax 064/34033. 35 rooms with bath. AE, DC, MC, V. Moderate.*

Lahinch
Lodging

Aberdeen Arms. Golfers abound among the clientele of this comfortably refurbished Victorian seaside hotel. *Lahinch, Co. Clare, tel. 065/81100, fax 065/81228. 55 rooms with bath. Facilities: 2 restaurants, 2 bars, snooker, sauna, Jacuzzi, 10 tennis courts. AE, DC, MC, V. Moderate.*

Limerick
Dining

De La Fontaine. The French owner-chef uses only the best local produce to present imaginative "cuisine moderne" creations in this intimate hideaway. *12 Gerald Griffin St., tel. 061/414461. Reservations advised. AE, DC, MC, V. Closed Sun.; lunch served only on Fri. Moderate.*

Lodging

Greenhills. This suburban, modern low rise is convenient for Shannon Airport and also makes a good touring base. The friendly owner-manager welcomes families. *Ennis Rd., tel. 061/453033, fax 061/453307. 55 rooms with bath. Facilities: restaurant, bar, coffee shop, indoor heated pool, sauna, Jacuzzi, steam room, gym, tennis court. AE, DC, MC, V. Moderate.*

Jury's. This bright modern hotel is set in its own grounds overlooking the Shannon, about a three-minute walk from the town center. There is good French cuisine in the Copper Room restaurant and live music most nights in the bar. *Ennis Rd., tel. 061/55366, fax 061/326400. 96 rooms with bath. Facilities: restaurant, bar. AE, DC, MC, V. Moderate.*

Lisdoonvarna
Lodging

Ballinalacken Castle. It's not a castle, but a converted Victorian shooting lodge on the very edge of the Burren that commands a breathtaking view of the Atlantic. Rooms are modest but characterful. *Co. Clare, tel. 065/74025. 12 rooms with bath. Facilities: restaurant, bar. MC, V. Closed early Nov.–Easter. Inexpensive.*

Sheedy's Spa View. This is a friendly, family-run establishment with open turf fires and an excellent restaurant. *Sulphir Hill, tel. 065/74026, fax 065/74555. 11 rooms with bath. Facilities: restaurant, tennis. AE, DC, MC, V. Closed Oct.–Mar. Inexpensive.*

The Northwest

This route from Galway to Sligo and then back to Dublin, via Kells, takes you through the rugged landscape of Connemara to the fabled Yeats country in the northwest and then skirts the borders of Northern Ireland before returning to Dublin. The entire trip is about 400 kilometers (250 miles) and passes through some of the wildest and loneliest parts of Ireland.

Getting Around

By Train
Trains to Galway, Westport, and Sligo operate from Dublin's Heuston or Connolly (Sligo) stations. There is no train service north of Sligo.

By Bus
Travel within the area is more flexible by bus; details are available from local tourist information offices.

By Car
In Galway, cars can be rented from **Avis** (tel. 091/68886), **Budget** (tel. 091/66376), or **Murray's** (tel. 091/62222). Taxis do not operate on meters; agree on the fare beforehand.

By Bicycle
You can rent bikes from **Cycle Logical** (Galway City, tel. 091/68223), **John Mannion** (Railway View, Clifden, tel. 095/21160), or **Gary's Cycles** (Quay St., Sligo, tel. 071/45418).

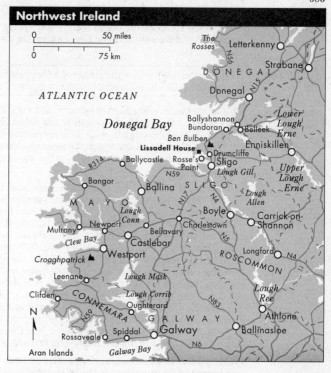

Northwest Ireland

ATLANTIC OCEAN

Donegal Bay

Guided Tours

CIE Tours International operates day tours of Connemara out of Galway City and bus tours into the Donegal highlands from Sligo train station; details are available from local tourist offices. **CIE** (tel. 01/302222 Bus Eireann) and **Gray Line** (tel. 01/661–9666) offer tours of the Boyne Valley and County Meath out of Dublin.

Tourist Information

All are open weekdays 9–6, Sat. 9–1.

Galway (off Eyre Sq., tel. 091/63081, fax 091/65201).
Sligo (Temple St., tel. 071/61201, fax 071/60360).
Westport (The Mall, tel. 098/25711, fax 098/26709).

Exploring the Northwest

Galway City is the gateway to the ancient province of Connacht, the most westerly seaboard in Europe. Galway City was well established even before the Normans arrived in the 13th century, rebuilding the city walls and turning the little town into a flourishing port. Later its waterfront was frequented by Spanish grandees and traders. The salmon fishing in the river Corrib, which flows through the lower part of the town, is unsurpassed. In early summer, you can stand on the **Weir Bridge** beside the town's cathedral and watch thousands of salmon as they leap and twist through the narrow access to the inner lakes. **Lynch's Castle** in Shop Street, now a bank, is a good example of a 16th-century fortified house—fortified because the neighboring Irish tribes persistently raided Galway City, whose commercial life excluded them. Nowadays the liveliest part of town is around the area between **Eyre Square** (the town's center) and **Spanish Arch.**

Time Out Drop in at **Noctan's** pub on the corner of Abbeygate Street for food at lunchtime and the latest news of what's on in town.

On the west bank of the Corrib estuary, just outside of the Galway town walls, is the **Claddagh,** said to be the oldest fishing village in Ireland. **Salthill Promenade,** with its lively seaside amenities, is the traditional place "to sit and watch the moon rise over Claddagh, and see the sun go down on Galway Bay"—in the words of the city's most famous song.

Connemara is a land of romantic, underpopulated landscapes, and rugged craggy coastlines, where the Irish language is still used by many people. **Rossaveale,** a port on the coast road beyond Spiddal, is the handiest port for a trip to the Aran Islands, 48 kilometers (30 miles) off the coast, where J. M. Synge drew the inspiration for his play *Riders to the Sea.* The islands are still 100% Irish speaking and retain an atmosphere distinct from that of the mainland, which will be appreciated by those in search of the peace and quiet of a past century. **Inishmaan,** the middle island, is considered the most unspoiled of the three and will delight botanists, ornithologists, and walkers. *Sailings daily from Rossaveale and less frequently from Galway; round-trip fare about IR£12. Details from Galway Tourist Information Office. Also accessible by air from Connemara Airport (tel. 091/93034): daily flights, round-trip fare about IR£25.*

Oughterard is an important angling center on Lough Corrib. Boats can be rented for excursions to the lake's many wooded islands. The road to Clifden runs between the Maamturk and the Cloosh Mountains beside a string of small lakes. **Clifden,** the principal town of Connemara, has an almost Alpine setting, nestling on the edge of the Atlantic with a spectacular mountain backdrop. Just beyond Clifden is the **Connemara National Park,** with its many nature trails offering views of sea, mountain, and lake. Its visitor center features an audiovisual presentation and has a collection of farm furniture. *Tel. 095/41054. Admission free. Open Apr.–Oct., daily 10–6.*

Westport is a quiet, mainly 18th-century town overlooking Clew Bay—a wide expanse of water studded with nearly 400 islands. The distinctive silhouette of **Croagpatrick,** a 775-meter mountain, dominates the town. Today some 25,000 pilgrims climb it on the last Sunday in July in honor of St. Patrick, who is believed to have spent 40 days fasting on its summit in AD 441. Whether he did or not, the climb is an exhilarating experience and can be completed in about three hours; it should be attempted only in good weather, however.

County Sligo is noted for its seaside resorts, the famous golf course at Rosse's Point (just outside Sligo Town), and its links with Ireland's most famous 20th-century poet, William Butler Yeats, who is buried just north of **Sligo Town** at Drumcliffe. An important collection of paintings by the poet's brother, Jack B. Yeats, can be seen in the **Sligo Museum** (Stephen St., tel. 071/42212), which also has displays on the folk life of the area. Take a boat from Sligo up to **Lough Gill** and see the **Lake Isle of Innisfree** and other places immortalized in the poetry of W. B. Yeats. His grave is found beneath the slopes of Ben Bulben, just north of the town. Nearby is **Lissadell House,** a substantial mansion dating from 1830 that features prominently in his writings. It was the home of Constance Gore-Booth, later Countess Markeviecz, who took part in the 1916 uprising. *Tel. 071/63150. Admission: IR£2 adults, 50p children. Open June–Sept., Mon.–Sat. 10:30–noon, 2–4:30.*

Bundoran, the southernmost town of Donegal, is one of Ireland's major seaside resorts, with excellent sandy beaches. From **Donegal Town,** you can set off to tour the ever-changing landscape of Donegal's rugged coastline and highlands, visiting the "tweed villages" on the coast at the Rosses, where the famous Donegal tweed is woven.

This route heads back to Dublin through **Belleek,** on the borders of Counties Donegal and Fermanagh, known for its fragile, lustrous china; a factory visit can be arranged (tel. 08/0365–65501). For the remaining towns on this tour, *see* the Ireland country map. Belleek is a frontier post on an approved road that skirts the shores of Lower Lough Erne in Northern Ireland, passing through Enniskillen and reemerging in Belturbet, County Cavan, on the main N3 Dublin road. (Tourists in private cars can cross the border here with a minimum of formality.) The N3 continues across a beautiful patchwork of lakes, the heart of the low-lying lakelands. In **Cavan** you may want to visit the **Crystal Factory,** which runs daily tours of the premises, showing visitors the techniques for blowing and cutting glass. *Dublin Rd., tel. 049/31800. Admission free. Open Mon.–Fri. 9–5; closed first two weeks in Aug.*

The N3 returns you to Dublin by way of **Kells,** in whose 8th-century abbey the Book of Kells was completed; a facsimile can be seen in **St. Columba's Church.** Among the remains of the abbey is a well-preserved round tower and a rare example of a stone-roof church dating from the 9th century. There are five richly sculptured stone crosses in Kells. Just south of **Navan** is the **Hill of Tara,** the religious and cultural capital of Ireland in ancient times. Its importance waned with the arrival of Christianity in the 5th century, and today its crest is, appropriately enough, crowned with a statue of the man who brought Christianity to Ireland—St. Patrick.

Dining and Lodging

For details and price-category definitions, *see* Dining and Lodging in Staying in Ireland, *above.*

Cashel Bay
Dining and Lodging

Cashel House. One of Ireland's outstanding country-house hotels, luxurious and secluded, Cashel House attracts an affluent outdoor-loving international clientele. *Cashel Bay, Connemara, Co. Galway, tel. 095/31001, fax 095/31077. 32 rooms with bath. Facilities: bar, restaurant, horseback riding, tennis, private beach, bicycles, fishing. AE, DC, MC, V. Expensive.*

Clifden
Lodging

Abbeyglen Castle. This comfortable hotel is quietly set a half-mile west of town, featuring panoramic views over the rolling green hillsides. The secluded garden is a haven for travelweary souls. *Sky Rd., tel. 095/21201, fax 095/21797. 46 rooms with bath. Facilities: heated pool, tennis. AE, DC, MC, V. Closed Jan. Moderate.*

Rock Glen Manor House. Dating from 1815, this converted hunting lodge is 1½ kilometers (1 mile) south of town in exceptionally peaceful surroundings. *Tel. 095/21035, fax 095/21737. 29 rooms with bath. AE, DC, MC, V. Closed Nov.–Feb. Moderate.*

Collooney
Dining and Lodging

Markree Castle. This magnificent 17th-century castle, which also houses the renowned Knockmuldowney Restaurant, is situated on a 1,000-acre estate. The host family offers bed and breakfast, delectable home-cooked French food at dinner, and a traditional Sunday lunch. *11 km (7 mi) south of Sligo Town on N4, Co. Sligo, tel. 071/ 67800, fax 071/67840. 14 rooms with bath. AE, DC, MC, V. Expensive.*

Cong
Lodging
★

Ashford Castle. This imposing castle is set in its own park on the edge of Lough Corrib and has a superb restaurant, the Connaught Room. President Reagan stayed here in 1984. *Tel. 092/46003, fax 092/46260. 82 rooms with bath. Facilities: 9-hole golf course, tennis, fishing, horseback riding, garden. AE, DC, MC, V. Very Expensive.*

Galway City
Dining

de Burgos. This Old World basement restaurant serves an extensive French-influenced menu focused around local seafood and char-grilled steaks. *15 Augustine St., tel. 091/62188. AE, DC, MC, V. Closed Sun. Moderate.*

Noctan's. This excellent, small French restaurant is situated above a popular pub. *17 Cross St., tel. 091/66172. MC, V. Dinner only. Closed Sun.–Mon. Moderate.*

Lodging

Great Southern. Recently refurbished, this old-style town hotel enjoys a conveniently central location. *Eyre Sq., tel. 091/64041, fax 091/66704. 120 rooms with bath. Facilities: roof-top heated pool, sauna, health complex. AE, DC, MC, V. Expensive.*

Ardilaun House. This hotel is set in pleasant grounds midway between Galway City and the seaside suburb of Salthill. *Taylors Hill, tel. 091/21433, fax 091/21546. 91 rooms with bath. AE, DC, MC, V. Moderate.*

Moycullen
Dining

Drimcong House. The chef-owner prepares his award-winning meals in a 300-year-old lakeside house, 13 kilometers (8 miles) from Galway City. *1½ km (1 mi) northwest on N59, tel. 091/85115. AE, DC, MC, V. Open Tues.–Sat., dinner only. Closed Christmas–mid-Mar. Moderate.*

Oughterard
Lodging

Connemara Gateway. This modern low rise makes a convenient touring base and has relatively spacious rooms with views of the Connemara hills. *Oughterard, Co. Galway, tel. 091/82328, fax 091/ 82332. 62 rooms with bath. Facilities: indoor pool, sauna, tennis court. DC, MC, V. Closed Dec. and Jan. Moderate.*

Sligo Town
Lodging

Ballincar House. Just outside of town, this converted country house with gardens serves excellent food. *Rosses Point Rd., tel. 071/45361, fax 071/44198. 25 rooms with bath. Facilities: squash, tennis, sauna, solarium. AE, DC, MC, V. Moderate.*

Silver Swan. In the town center overlooking the Garavogue river, this '60s-style hotel has recently been refurbished, with quite effective results. *Hyde Bridge, tel. 071/43231, fax 071/42232. 29 rooms with bath. AE, DC, MC, V. Moderate.*

Sligo Park. This is a modern two-story building, set in spacious grounds. *Pearse Rd., tel. 071/60291, fax 071/69556. 60 rooms with bath. AE, DC, MC, V. Moderate.*

Westport
Dining

Asgard. The Asgard is a pub with award-winning food in both its bar and second-floor restaurant. *The Quay, tel. 098/25319. AE, DC, MC, V. Moderate.*

Lodging

Hotel Westport. A modern low rise, this quiet hotel is five minutes' walk from the town center and overlooks the grounds of Westport House. *Newport Rd., tel. 098/25122, fax 098/26739. 49 rooms with bath. Moderate.*

Old Railway. A delightful Victorian hotel in the town center, the Old Railway has been fully refurbished with no loss of character. *The Mall, tel. 098/25166, fax 098/25090. 20 rooms with bath. Facilities: 2 restaurants, 2 bars, fishing. AE, DC, MC, V. Inexpensive.*

18 Italy

Where else in Europe can you find the blend of great art, delicious food and wine, and sheer verve that awaits you in Italy? This Mediterranean country has made a profound contribution to Western civilization, producing some of the world's greatest thinkers, writers, politicians, saints, and artists. Impressive traces of their lives and works can still be seen in the great buildings and lovely countryside.

The whole of Italy is one vast attraction, but the triangle of its most-visited cities—Rome (Roma), Florence (Firenze), and Venice (Venezia)—gives a good idea of the great variety to be found here. In Rome and Florence, especially, you can feel the uninterrupted flow of the ages, from the Classical era of the ancient Romans to the bustle and throb of contemporary life carried on in centuries-old settings. Venice, by contrast, seems suspended in time, the same today as it was when it held sway over the eastern Mediterranean and the Orient. Each of these cities presents a different aspect of the Italian character: the Baroque exuberance of Rome, Florence's serene stylishness, and the dreamy sensuality of Venice.

The uninhibited Italian lifestyle can be entertaining or irritating, depending on how you look at it. Rarely do things run like clockwork here; you are more likely to encounter unexplained delays and incomprehensible complications. Relax: There's usually something you can smile about even in the darkest circumstances.

Trying to soak in Italy's rich artistic heritage is a great challenge. The country's many museums and churches draw hordes of visitors, all wanting to see the same thing at the same time. From May through September, the Sistine Chapel, Michelangelo's *David*, St. Mark's Square, and other key sights are more often than not swamped by mobs of tourists. Try to see the highlights at off-peak times in the day. If they are open during lunch—and many are not— that is often a good time. Again, relax: Seeing some attractions— such as the scrubbed facades of Rome's glorious Baroque churches—entails no opening hours and no lines at all.

Along with hordes of tourists, large Italian cities are plagued by automobiles. Recent regulations barring some traffic from the centers of Rome and Florence have made them less noisy in spots, but air pollution remains a serious problem. Plans are now afoot to curtail the auto traffic that swirls around the Colosseum, sparing it some of the pollution and vibration it has suffered as perhaps the world's most extravagant *spartitraffico* (traffic circle).

Even in the major tourist cities, Italians generally take a friendly interest in their visitors. Only the most blasé waiters and salespeople will be less than courteous and helpful. However, the persistent attention Italian males pay to foreign females can be oppressive and annoying. If you're not interested, the best tactic is to ignore them. It's important to be attentive to matters of personal security in certain parts of the country; always be on guard against pickpockets and purse snatchers in the main tourist cities and in Naples. Especially in Rome and Florence, watch out for bands of gypsy children, expert at lifting wallets. Small cities and towns are usually safe.

Making the most of your time in Italy doesn't mean rushing through it. To gain a rich appreciation for Italy, don't try to see everything all at once. Do what you really want to do, and if that means skipping a museum to sit at a pretty café, enjoying the sunshine and a cappuccino, you're getting into the Italian spirit. Art—and life—are to be enjoyed, and the Italians can show you how.

Essential Information

Before You Go

When to Go The main tourist season in Italy runs from mid-April to the end of September. The best months for sightseeing are April, May, June, September, and October, when the weather is generally pleasant and not too hot. Foreign tourists crowd the major cities at Easter, when Italians flock to resorts and the countryside. Avoid traveling in August, when the heat can be oppressive and when vacationing Italians cram roads, trains, and planes, as well as beach and mountain resorts. Especially around the August 15 holiday, such cities as Rome and Milan are deserted, and many restaurants and shops close. Except for such year-round resorts as Taormina and a few on the Italian Riviera, coastal resorts close up tight from October or November to April. The best time for resorts is June and September, when the weather is usually fine and everything is open but not crowded.

The hottest months are July and August, when brief afternoon thunderstorms are common in inland areas. Winters are relatively mild in most places on the tourist circuit, but there are always some rainy spells.

Although low-season rates do not officially apply in Rome, Florence, and Milan you can usually bargain for discounted rates in Rome and Milan in summer (when business travelers are few) and in Florence in winter. Ask for *la tariffa scontata*. You can save on hotel accommodations in Venice and in such resorts as Sorrento and Capri during their low seasons—the winter, early spring, and late-autumn months.

Climate The following are average daily maximum and minimum temperatures for Rome.

Jan.	52F	11C	May	74F	23C	Sept.	79F	26C
	40	5		56	13		62	17
Feb.	55F	13C	June	82F	28C	Oct.	71F	22C
	42	6		63	17		55	13
Mar.	59F	15C	July	87F	30C	Nov.	61F	16C
	45	7		67	20		49	9
Apr.	66F	19C	Aug.	86F	30C	Dec.	55F	13C
	50	10		67	20		44	6

The following are average daily maximum and minimum temperatures for Milan.

Jan.	40F	5C	May	74F	23C	Sept.	75F	24C
	32	0		57	14		61	16
Feb.	46F	8C	June	80F	27C	Oct.	63F	17C
	35	2		63	17		52	11
Mar.	56F	13C	July	84F	29C	Nov.	51F	10C
	43	6		67	20		43	6
Apr.	65F	18C	Aug.	82F	28C	Dec.	43F	6C
	49	9		66	16		35	2

Currency The unit of currency in Italy is the lira (plural, lire). There are bills of 1,000, 2,000, 5,000, 10,000, 50,000, and 100,000 lire; coins are worth 10, 20, 50, 100, 200, and 500 lire. At press time (spring 1994), the exchange rate was about 1,600 lire to the dollar and 2,400 lire to

Italy

the pound sterling. Sooner or later the zeros will be lopped off the lire in order to simplify money dealings and life in general. The long-heralded move has not yet been made, but it seems imminent. If it does come to pass, 5,000 lire would become 5 lire, 50 lire would become 50 centesimi. When it does happen, both old and new values will be in effect until people become accustomed to the new system.

While the present system continues, especially when your purchases run into hundreds of thousands of lire, beware of being shortchanged, a dodge that is practiced at ticket windows and cashiers' desks, as well as in shops and even banks. *Always count your change before you leave the counter.*

Always carry some smaller-denomination bills for sundry purchases; you're less likely to be shortchanged, and you won't have to face the eye-rolling dismay of cashiers chronically short of change.

Credit cards are generally accepted in shops and hotels, but may not be welcome in restaurants, so always look for those little signs in the window or ask when you enter to avoid embarrassing situations. When you wish to leave a tip beyond the 15% service charge (*see* Staying in Italy, Tipping, *below*) that is usually included with your bill, leave it in cash rather than adding it to the credit card slip.

What It Will Cost Rome, Milan, and Venice are the more expensive Italian cities to visit. Taxes are usually included in hotel bills; a cover charge may appear as a separate item in restaurant checks, as does the service charge, usually about 15%, if added. There is a 19% tax on car rentals.

Sample Prices A cup of espresso consumed while standing at a bar costs from 1,000 lire to 1,400 lire, triple that for table service. A bottle of beer costs from 2,200 lire to 3,800 lire, a soft drink about 2,000 lire. A *tramezzino* (small sandwich) costs about 2,200 lire, a more substantial one about 3,500. You will pay about 10,000 lire for a short taxi ride in Rome and Florence, more in Milan. Admission to a major museum is about 10,000 lire; a three-hour sightseeing tour, about 38,000 lire.

Customs on Arrival Two still cameras and one movie camera can be brought in duty-free. Travelers arriving in Italy from an EU (European Union) country are allowed, duty-free, a total of 300 cigarettes (*or* 150 cigarillos *or* 75 cigars), 1½ liters of spirits plus 5 liters of still wine, and 75 milliliters of perfume if duty and taxes have been paid on them at the time of purchase. Visitors traveling directly from non-European countries are allowed 400 cigarettes and cigars or tobacco not exceeding 500 grams, 1 liter of spirits, and 2 liters of still wine. Not more than 20 million lire in Italian bank notes may be taken into or out of the country.

Language Italy is accustomed to English-speaking tourists, and in major cities you will find that many people speak at least a little English. In smaller hotels and restaurants, a smattering of Italian comes in handy.

Getting Around

By Car The extensive network of *autostrade* (toll superhighways) connecting all major towns is complemented by equally well-maintained but toll-free *superstrade* (express highways), *strade statali* (main roads), and *strade provinciali* (secondary roads).

Road Conditions

All are clearly signposted and numbered. The ticket issued on entering an autostrada must be returned on leaving, along with the toll. On some shorter autostrade, mainly connections, the toll is payable on entering. Have small bills and change handy for tolls; shortchanging is a risk, so always count your change before leaving the toll booth. If you will be using autostrade extensively, buy a Viacard, an automatic toll card, for 50,000 or 100,000 lire at autostrada locations.

The Autostrada del Sole (A1, A2, and A3) crosses the country from north to south, connecting Milan to Reggio Calabria. The A4 from west to east connects Turin to Trieste.

Rules of the Road Driving is on the right. The speed limit on an autostrada for a medium-size car is 130 kph (81 mph). On other roads it is 90 kph (56 mph). Other regulations are largely as in the United States except that the police have the power to levy on-the-spot fines—even as high as $500!

Parking Check with your hotel to determine the best place to park. Parking is greatly restricted in the center of most major Italian cities. Parking in a "Zona Disco" is for limited periods. City garages cost up to 30,000 lire per day.

Gasoline Gas costs the equivalent of more than $5 per U.S. gallon, or about 1,500 lire per liter. Except on the autostrade, most gas stations are closed Sunday; they also close from 12:30 PM to 3:30 PM and at 7 PM for the night. Self-service pumps can be found in most cities and towns.

Breakdowns Dial 116 for towing and repairs; breakdown service (emergency repairs and towing on autostrada) is free for tourists with foreign license plates or with cars rented in Italy, which have breakdown insurance. Dial 113 for ambulance and highway police.

By Train The fastest service on the FS (Ferrovie dello Stato), the state-owned railroad, are the *Pendolino*, or ETR 450, trains for which you pay a special supplement and for which seat reservations are required in both first and second class; service includes airline-type meals. Also fast are *Intercity* (IC) and *Eurocity* (EC) trains, for which you pay a supplement in both classes and for which reservations may be required. Trains designated *Interregionale* are slower, making more stops. *Regionale* trains are locals, serving a single region. You can buy tickets and make seat reservations at travel agencies displaying the FS symbol up to two months in advance, thereby avoiding long lines at station ticket windows. You pay a 20% penalty if you purchase your ticket on board the train. Tickets within a 100-km (62-mi) range can be purchased at any *tabacchi* (tobacconist's shop). They also must be stamped in the yellow machines before boarding. There is a refreshment service on all long-distance trains. Tap water on trains is not drinkable. Carry compact bags for easy overhead storage. Trains are very crowded at holiday times; always reserve.

By Plane **Alitalia** and domestic affiliate **ATI,** plus some privately owned companies such as **Meridiana,** provide service throughout Italy. Alitalia offers several discount fares; inquire at travel agencies or at Alitalia agencies in major cities.

By Bus Regional bus companies provide service over an extensive network of routes throughout Italy. Route information and timetables are usually available at tourist information offices and travel agencies, or at bus company ticket offices. Among the interregional companies providing long-distance service is **SITA** (Viale Cadorna 105, Florence, tel. 055/47821).

By Boat Ferries connect the mainland with all the major islands. Car ferries operate to Sicily, Sardinia, Elba, Ponza, Capri (though cars are not advised), and Ischia, among others. Lake ferries connect the towns on the shores of the Italian lakes: Como, Maggiore, and Garda.

Staying in Italy

Telephones Pay phones take either 100- or 200-lire coins, a *gettone* (token), or
Local Calls magnetic card. Tokens can be purchased from the token machine or from the cashier of the store, bar, or other facility where the phone is located. Local calls cost 200 lire for a minimum of 4 minutes. For *teleselezione* (long-distance direct dialing), place several coins in the slot; unused coins are returned when you push the large yellow knob. Buy magnetic cards at tobacconists.

International Since hotels tend to add exorbitant service charges for long-distance
Calls and international calls, it's best to go to the "Telefoni" telephone exchange, where the operator assigns you a booth, can help place your call, and will collect payment when you have finished. Telefoni exchanges (usually marked *SIP* or, in Rome, *ASST)* are found in all cities. The cheaper and easier option, however, will be to use your AT&T, MCI, or Sprint calling card. For AT&T dial access number 172–1011 and for MCI dial access number 172–1022. For Sprint, dial access number 172–1877. An English-speaking operator will then ask for your calling card number and proceed to connect you with the United States.

Operators and For Europe and the Mediterranean area, dial 15; for intercontinen-
Information tal service, dial 170.

Mail The Italian mail system is notoriously erratic and often excruciatingly slow. Allow up to 21 days for mail to and from the United States and Canada, almost as much to and from the United Kingdom, and much longer for postcards.

Postal Rates Airmail letters to the United States cost 1,200 lire for up to 20 grams; postcards with a short greeting and signature cost 1,000 lire, but cost letter rate if the message is lengthy. Airmail letters to the United Kingdom cost 750 lire, postcards 650 lire.

Receiving Mail You can have mail sent to American Express offices or to Italian post offices, marked "Fermo Posta" and addressed to you c/o Palazzo delle Poste, with the name of the city in which you will pick it up. In either case you must show your passport and pay a small fee.

Shopping Italy's IVA-refund system is complicated. Foreign tourists who
Sales-Tax have spent more than 300,000 lire (before tax) in one store can take
Refunds advantage of it, however. At the time of purchase, with passport or ID in hand, ask the store for an invoice describing the article or articles and price. If your destination when you leave Italy is a non-EU country, you must have the invoice stamped at Customs upon departure from Italy; if your destination is another EU country, you must obtain the customs stamp upon departure for that country. Once back home—and within 90 days of the date of purchase—you must send the stamped invoice back to the store, which should forward the IVA rebate directly to you. If the store participates in the Europe Tax-free Shopping System (those that do display a sign to the effect), things are simpler. The invoice provided is a Tax-free Cheque in the amount of the tax refund, which can be cashed at the Tax-Free Cash Refund window in the transit area of major airports and border crossings.

Bargaining Most shops now have *prezzi fissi* (fixed prices), but you may be able to get a discount on a large purchase. Always bargain with a street vendor or at a market (except for food).

Opening and Closing Times

Banks. Banks are open weekdays 8:30–1:30 and 2:45–3:45.

Churches. Churches are usually open from early morning to noon or 12:30, when they close for about two hours or more, opening again in the afternoon until about 7 PM.

Museums. National museums are usually open until 2 and are often closed on Monday, but there are many exceptions. Nonnational museums have entirely different hours, which may vary according to season. Archaeological sites are usually closed on Monday. At all museums and sites, ticket offices close an hour or so before official closing time. Always check with the local tourist office for current hours and holiday closings.

Shops. Shops are open, with individual variations, from 9 to 1 and from 3:30 or 4 to 7 or 7:30. They are open from Monday through Saturday, but close for a half-day during the week; for example, in Rome most shops (except food shops) are closed on Monday morning (Saturday afternoon in July and August). Some tourist-oriented shops are open all day, every day, as in downtown Rome, Florence, and Venice.

National Holidays

January 1; January 6 (Epiphany); April 4 (Easter Monday); April 25 (Liberation Day); May 1 (May Day); August 15 (the religious feast of the Assumption, known as Ferragosto, when cities are literally deserted and most restaurants and shops are closed); November 1 (All Saints Day); December 8 (Immaculate Conception); December 25 and 26.

Dining

Generally speaking, a *ristorante* pays more attention to decor, service, and menu than does a *trattoria*, which is simpler and often family-run. An *osteria* used to be a lowly tavern, though now the term may be used to designate a chic and expensive eatery. A *tavola calda* offers hot dishes and snacks, with seating. A *rosticceria* has the same, to take out.

The menu is always posted in the window or just inside the door of an eating establishment. Check to see what is offered, and note the charges for *coperto* (cover) and *servizio* (service), which will increase your check. A *menu turistico* includes taxes and service, but beverages are extra.

Mealtimes

Lunch hour in Rome lasts from 1 to 3, dinner from 8 to 10. Service begins and ends a half-hour earlier in Florence and Venice, later in the south. Practically all restaurants close one day a week; some close for winter or summer vacation.

Precautions

Tap water is safe in large cities and almost everywhere else unless noted *Non Potabile*. Bottled mineral water is available everywhere, *gassata* (with bubbles) or *non gassata* (without). If you prefer tap water, ask for *acqua semplice*.

Dress

Except for restaurants in the Very Expensive and occasionally in the Expensive categories, where jacket and tie are advisable, casual attire is acceptable.

Ratings

Prices are per person and include first course, main course, dessert or fruit, and house wine, where available. Best bets are indicated by a star ★.

Category	Rome, Milan*	Other Areas
Very Expensive	over 120,000 lire	over 80,000 lire
Expensive	65,000–120,000 lire	45,000–80,000 lire

| Moderate | 40,000–65,000 lire | 25,000–45,000 lire |
| Inexpensive | under 40,000 lire | under 25,000 lire |

Note that restaurant prices in Venice are slightly higher than those in Rome and Milan; in small cities prices are usually lower.

Lodging Italy, and especially the main tourist capitals of Rome, Florence, and Venice, offers a good choice of accommodations. Room rates are on a par with other European capitals, although porters, room service, and in-house cleaning and laundering are disappearing in all but the most elegant hotels. Taxes and service are included in the room rate. Breakfast also is usually included in the quoted room rate. Actually, breakfast is an extra charge, but you can decline to take breakfast in most hotels (though the desk may not be happy about it); make your preference clear when booking or checking in. Air-conditioning also may be an extra charge. In older hotels, room quality may be uneven; if you don't like the room you're given, ask for another. This applies to noise, too; some front rooms are bigger and have views but get street noise. Specify if you care about having either a bathtub or shower, as not all rooms have both. In Moderate and Inexpensive places, showers may be the drain-in-the-floor type guaranteed to flood the bathroom. Major cities have hotel reservation service booths in the rail stations.

Hotels Italian hotels are classified by regional tourist boards from five-star (deluxe) to one-star (modest hotels and small inns). The established price of the room appears on a rate card on the back of the door of your room or inside the closet door, though you may be able to get a lower rate by asking. Any variations above the posted rate should be cause for complaint and should be reported to the local tourist office. CIGA, Jolly, Space, Atahotels, Best Western, and Italhotels are among the reliable chains or groups operating in Italy, with CIGA among the most luxurious. Sheraton hotels are making an impact in Italy in a big way, though most, located in Rome, Florence, Bari, Padua, and Catania, tend to be geared toward convention and business travel. There are a few Relais et Châteaux member hotels that are noted for individual atmosphere, personal service, and luxury; they are also expensive. The AGIP chain is found mostly on main highways. The Family Hotels group, comprised mostly of small Moderate and Inexpensive family-run hotels, offers good value, reliability, and special attention to families.

Standards in one-star hotels are very uneven. At best, rooms are usually spotlessly clean but basic, with shower and toilets down the hall.

Rentals More and more people are discovering the attractions of renting a house, cottage, or apartment in the Italian countryside. These are ideal for families or for groups of up to eight people looking for a bargain—or just independence. Availability is subject to change, so it is best to ask your travel agent or the nearest branch of ENIT, the Italian tourist board, about rentals.

Camping Italy has a wide selection of campgrounds, and the Italians themselves are taking to camping by the thousands, which means that beach or mountain sites will be crammed in July and August. It's best to avoid these peak months. An international camping *carnet* (permit) is required; get one from your local association before leaving home. You can buy a campsite directory such as the detailed guide published by the Touring Club Italiano (available in bookstores) or obtain the free directory of campsites published by the Federazione Italiana del Campeggio (Casella Postale 23, 50041

Calenzano, Florence, fax 055/882–5918) in tourist information offices or by mail from the organization if you send three international reply coupons.

Ratings The following price categories are determined by the cost of two people in a double room. Best bets are indicated by a ★. As with restaurant prices, the cost of hotels in Venice is slightly more than those shown here.

Category	Rome, Milan	Other Areas
Very Expensive	over 450,000 lire	over 350,000 lire
Expensive	300,000–450,000 lire	200,000–350,000 lire
Moderate	160,000–280,000 lire	120,000–200,000 lire
Inexpensive	under 160,000 lire	under 120,000 lire

Tipping Tipping practices vary depending on where you are. Italians tip smaller amounts in small cities and towns, often not at all in cafés and taxis north of Rome. The following guidelines apply in major cities at a Moderate level.

In restaurants, a 15% service charge is usually added to the total, but it doesn't all go to the waiter. In large cities and resorts it is customary to give the waiter a 5% tip in addition to the service charge made on the check.

Charges for service are included in all hotel bills, but smaller tips to staff members are appreciated. In general, chambermaids should be given about 1,000 lire per day, 4,000 lire–5,000 lire per week; bellhops, 1,000 lire–2,000 lire; doormen, about 500 lire. Give the concierge about 15% of his bill for services. Tip a minimum of 1,000 lire for room service and valet service.

Taxi drivers are happy with 5%–10%. Porters at railroad stations and airports charge a fixed rate per suitcase; tip an additional 500 lire per person, more if the porter is very helpful. Service-station attendants are tipped 500 lire–1,000 lire if they are especially helpful. Tip guides about 2,000 lire per person for a half-day tour, more if they are very good.

Rome

Arriving and Departing

By Plane Rome's principal airport is at Fiumicino, 29 kilometers (18 miles) from the city. Though its official name is Leonardo da Vinci Airport, everybody calls it Fiumicino. For flight information, tel. 06/65951. The smaller airport of Ciampino is on the edge of Rome and is used as an alternative by international and domestic lines, especially for charter flights.

Between the Airport and Downtown To get to downtown Rome from Fiumicino airport you have a choice of two trains. Inquire at the airport (at EPT or train information counters) as to which takes you closest to your hotel. The non-stop Airport-Termini express takes you directly to Track 22 at Termini station, Rome's main train terminal, well served by taxis and the hub of Metro and bus lines. The ride to Termini takes 30 minutes;

departures are hourly, beginning at 7:50 AM from the airport, with the final departure at 10:55 PM. Tickets cost 12,000 lire. The other airport train has its terminal at Tiburtina train station, east of downtown Rome. It makes several stops, including Trastevere and Ostiense stations, on the southern fringes of downtown Rome. This train runs from 6 AM to 10 PM, with departures every 20 minutes. The ride to Tiburtina takes 40 minutes. Tickets cost 7,000 lire. For either train you buy your ticket at automatic vending machines (you need Italian currency). There are ticket counters at some stations (Termini Track 22, Trastevere, Tiburtina).

A taxi to or from the airport at Fiumicino costs about 60,000 lire, including supplements. At a booth inside the terminal you can hire a 4- or 5-passenger car with driver for a little more. If you decide to take a taxi, use only yellow or the newer white cabs, which must wait outside the terminal; make sure the meter is running. Gypsy cab drivers solicit your trade as you come out of customs; they're not reliable, and their rates may be rip-offs.

Ciampino is connected with the Anagnina station of the Metro Line A by bus (every half-hour). A taxi between Ciampino and downtown Rome costs about 35,000 lire.

By Train Termini station is Rome's main train terminal, while Tiburtina and Ostiense stations are used principally by commuters. For train information, try the English-speaking personnel at the Information Office in Termini, or at any travel agency. Tickets and seats can be reserved and purchased at travel agencies bearing the FS (Ferrovie dello Stato) emblem. Short-distance tickets are also sold by tobacconists and from ticket machines (instructions in English) in the stations.

By Bus There is no central bus station in Rome; long-distance and suburban buses terminate either near Termini station or near strategically located metro stops.

By Car The main access routes from the north are the Autostrada del Sole (A1) from Milan and Florence, and the Aurelia highway (SS 1) from Genoa. The principal route to or from points south, such as Naples, is the southern leg of the Autostrada del Sole (A2). All highways connect with the GRA (Grande Raccordo Anulare), a beltway that encircles Rome and funnels traffic into the city. Markings on the GRA are confusing; take time in advance to study which route into the center best suits you.

Getting Around

The best way to see Rome is to choose an area or a sight that you particularly want to see, reach it by bus or Metro (subway), then explore the area on foot, following one of our itineraries or improvising one to suit your mood and interests. Wear comfortable, sturdy shoes, preferably with thick rubber soles to cushion you against the cobblestones. Heed our advice on security, and try to avoid the noise and polluted air of heavily trafficked streets, taking parallel byways wherever possible.

You can buy transportation route maps at newsstands and at ATAC (bus company) information and ticket booths.

By Metro The subway, or Metro, provides the easiest and fastest way to get around. The Metro opens at 5:30 AM, and the last train leaves each terminal at 11:30 PM. Line A runs from the eastern part of the city to Termini station and past Piazza di Spagna and Piazzale Flaminio to

Ottaviano, near St. Peter's and the Vatican Museums. Line B serves Termini, the Colosseum, and the Tiburtina station (also terminal of the Fiumicino airport train). The fare is currently 1,000 lire. There are change booths and/or ticket machines on station mezzanines; it's best to buy single tickets or books of 5 or 10 ahead of time at newsstands and tobacco shops. A daily tourist ticket known as a **BIG** is good on buses as well, costs 4,000 lire, and is sold at Metro and ATAC ticket booths.

By Bus Orange ATAC (tel. 06/4695–4444) city buses (and two streetcar lines) run from about 6 AM to midnight, with skeleton *notturno* services on main lines throughout the night. The fare is 1,200 lire, and tickets are valid on all ATAC lines for 90 minutes; you must buy your ticket before boarding. They are sold singly or in books of 10 at tobacco shops and newsstands. Weekly tourist tickets cost 18,000 lire and are sold at ATAC booths. When entering a bus, remember to board at the rear and exit at the middle.

By Taxi Taxis wait at stands and, for a small extra charge, can also be called by telephone. The meter starts at 6,400 lire; there are supplements for service after 10 PM, on Sundays and holidays, and for each piece of baggage. Use yellow or the newer white cabs only, and be very sure to check the meter. To call a cab, tel. 06/3570, 06/3875, 06/4994, or 06/88177.

By Bicycle Bikes provide a pleasant means of getting around when traffic isn't heavy. There are bike-rental shops at Via di Porta Castello 43, near St. Peter's, and at Piazza Navona 69, next to Bar Navona. Rental concessions are at the Piazza di Spagna and Piazza del Popolo Metro stops, and at Largo San Silvestro and Largo Argentina. There are also some in Villa Borghese, at Sector III of the underground parking lot and at Viale della Pineta and Viale del Bambino on the Pincio.

By Moped You can rent a moped or scooter and mandatory helmet at **Scoot-a-Long** (Via Cavour 302, tel. 06/678–0206) or **St. Peter Moto** (Via di Porta Castello 43, tel. 06/687–5714).

Important Addresses and Numbers

Tourist Information The main **EPT** (Rome Provincial Tourist) office is at Via Parigi 5, 00185 (tel. 06/488–3748, open Mon.–Fri. 8:15–7:15, Sat. 8:15–1:15). There are also EPT booths at Termini station and Leonardo da Vinci Airport. A booth on the main floor of the **ENIT** (National Tourist Board) building at Via Marghera 2 (tel. 06/497–1293. Open Mon., Wed., Fri. 9–1 and 4–6; Tues., Thurs. 9–1) can provide information on destinations in Italy outside Rome.

Consulates U.S. (Via Veneto 121, tel. 06/46741). **Canadian** (Via Zara 30, tel. 06/440–3082). U.K. (Via Venti Settembre 80a, tel. 06/482–5441).

Emergencies **Police** (tel. 06/4686); **Carabinieri** (tel. 06/112); **Ambulance** (tel. 06/5100 Red Cross). **Doctor:** for a recommendation call your consulate, the private **Salvator Mundi Hospital** (tel. 06/589–4867), or the **Rome American Hospital** (tel. 06/22551), which has English-speaking staff members. **Pharmacies:** You will find American and British medicines (or their equivalents) and English-speaking personnel at **Farmacia Internazionale Capranica** (Piazza Capranica 96, tel. 06/679–4680), **Farmacia Internazionale Barberini** (Piazza Barberini 49, tel. 06/482–5456), and **Farmacia Doricchi** (Via Venti Settembre 47, tel. 06/487–3880), among others. They are open 8:30–1 and 4–8; some stay open all night.

English-
Language
Bookstores
You'll find English-language books and magazines at newsstands in the center of Rome, especially on Via Veneto. Also try the **Economy Book and Video Center** (Via Torino 136, tel. 06/474–6877), the **Anglo-American Bookstore** (Via della Vite 57, tel. 06/679–5222), or the **Lion Bookshop** (Via del Babuino 181, tel. 06/322–5837).

Travel
Agencies
American Express (Piazza di Spagna 38, tel. 06/67641). **CIT** (Piazza della Repubblica 64, tel. 06/47941). **Wagons-Lits Travel** (Via Boncompagni 25, tel. 06/481–7655). **Thomas Cook** representative: **World Vision** (Via Paolo Mercuri 6, tel. 06/686–8941).

Guided Tours

Orientation
Tours
American Express (tel. 06/67641), **CIT** (tel. 06/47941), and **Appian Line** (tel. 06/488–4151) offer three-hour tours in air-conditioned buses with English-speaking guides, covering Rome with four separate itineraries: "Ancient Rome" (including the Roman Forum and Colosseum), "Classic Rome" (including St. Peter's Basilica, Trevi Fountain, and the Janiculum Hill, with its panorama of the city), "Christian Rome" (some major churches and the Catacombs), and the "Vatican Museums and Sistine Chapel." Most tours cost about 36,000 lire, though the Vatican Museums tour is about 48,000 lire. American Express tours depart from Piazza di Spagna, CIT from Piazza della Repubblica, and Appian Line picks sightseers up at their hotels. The least expensive organized bus tour is run by **ATAC**, the municipal bus company, and lasts three hours. Book tours for about 10,000 lire at the ATAC information booth in front of Termini station. There is at least one tour daily, departing at 2:30 (3:30 in summer).

American Express can provide a car for up to three persons, limousine for up to seven, and minibus for up to nine, all with English-speaking driver. Guide service is extra. A minibus costs about 425,000 lire for three hours. Almost all operators offer "Rome by Night" tours, with or without dinner and entertainment. Reservations can be made through travel agents.

Special-
Interest Tours
You can make your own arrangements (at no cost) to attend a public papal audience in the Vatican or to be at the Sunday blessing at the Pope's summer residence at Castelgandolfo, or do it through **CIT** (tel. 06/47941), **Appian Line** (tel. 06/488–4151), or **Carrani** (tel. 06/488–0510).

Excursions
Most operators offer half-day excursions to Tivoli to see the Villa d'Este's fountains and gardens; Appian Line's and CIT's half-day tours to Tivoli also include Hadrian's Villa and its impressive ancient ruins. Most operators have all-day excursions to Assisi, to Pompeii and/or Capri, and to Florence.

Personal
Guides
Visitors can arrange for a personal guide through **American Express** (tel. 06/67641), **CIT** (47941), or the main **EPT** tourist office (tel. 06/488–99201).

Exploring Rome

Antiquity is taken for granted in Rome, where successive ages have piled the present on top of the past—building, layering, and overlapping their own particular segments of Rome's 2,500 years of history to form a remarkably varied urban complex. Most of the city's major sights are located in a fairly small area known as the *centro*. At its heart lies ancient Rome, where the Forum and Colosseum stand. It was around this core that the other sections of the city grew up through the ages: medieval Rome, which covered the horn of land that pushes the Tiber toward the Vatican and extended across the river into Trastevere; and Renaissance Rome, which was erected upon medieval foundations and extended as far as the Vatican, creating beautiful villas on what was then the outskirts of the city.

The layout of the centro is highly irregular, but several landmarks serve as orientation points to identify the areas that most visitors come to see: the Colosseum, the Pantheon and Piazza Navona, St. Peter's, the Spanish Steps, and Villa Borghese. You'll need a good map to find your way around; newsstands offer a wide choice. Energetic sightseers will walk a lot, a much more pleasant way to see the city now that some traffic has been barred from the centro during the day; others might choose to take taxis, buses, or the Metro. The important thing is to relax and enjoy Rome. Don't try to see everything, but do take time to savor its pleasures. If you are in Rome during a hot spell, do as the Romans do: Start out early in the morning, have a light lunch and a long siesta during the hottest hours, then resume sightseeing in the late afternoon and end your evening with a leisurely meal outdoors, refreshed by cold Frascati wine and the *ponentino*, the cool evening breeze.

Ancient Rome *Numbers in the margin correspond to points of interest on the Roma (Rome) map.*

❶ Start your first tour at the city's center, in **Piazza Venezia.** Behind the enormous marble monument honoring the first king of unified ❷ Italy, Victor Emmanuel II, stands the **Campidoglio** (Capitol Square) on the Capitoline Hill. The majestic ramp and beautifully proportioned piazza are Michelangelo's handiwork, as are the three palaces. **Palazzo Senatorio** at the center is still the ceremonial seat of Rome's city hall; it was built over the Tabularium, where ancient Rome's state archives were kept.

The palaces flanking the Palazzo Senatorio contain the **Capitoline** ❸ **Museums.** On the left, the **Museo Capitolino** holds some fine classical sculptures, including the gilded bronze equestrian statue of Marcus Aurelius that once stood on the pedestal in the piazza, as well as the *Dying Gaul,* the *Capitoline Venus,* and a fascinating series of portrait busts of ancient philosophers and emperors. In the courtyard ❹ of the **Palazzo dei Conservatori,** on the right of the piazza, you can use the mammoth fragments of a colossal statue of the emperor Constantine as amusing props for snapshots. Inside you will find splendidly frescoed salons, as well as sculptures and paintings. *Piazza del Campidoglio, tel. 06/671–02071. Admission: 10,000 lire. Open May–Sept., Tues. 9–1:30, 5–8; Wed.–Fri. 9–1:30; Sat. 9–1:30, 8–11; Sun. 9–1. Oct.–Apr., Tues. and Sat. 9–1:30, 5–8; Wed.–Fri. 9–1:30; Sun. 9–1.*

The Campidoglio is also the site of the very old church of the ❺ **Aracoeli,** which you can reach by way of the stairs on the far side of the Museo Capitolino. Stop in to see the medieval pavement; the Renaissance gilded ceiling that commemorates the victory of Lepanto; some Pinturicchio frescoes; and a much-revered wooden statue of the Holy Child. The Campidoglio gardens offer some good views of the heart of ancient Rome, the Imperial Fora, built when the original Roman Forum became too small for the city's burgeoning needs.

❻ In the valley below the Campidoglio, the **Foro Romano** (Roman Forum), once only a marshy hollow, became the political, commercial, and social center of Rome, studded with public meeting halls, shops, and temples. As Rome declined, these monuments lost their impor-

Aracoeli, **5**
Arch of Constantine, **8**
Baths of Caracalla, **9**
Campidoglio, **2**
Campo dei Fiori, **32**
Castel Sant'
Angelo, **21**
Church of Santa Maria
della Concezione, **19**
Church of the Gesù, **27**
Colosseum, **7**
Fabricio Bridge, **36**
Fontana di Trevi, **16**
Foro Romano
(Roman Forum), **6**
Galleria Borghese, **20**
Museo Capitolino, **3**
Palazzo Barberini, **18**
Palazzo dei
Conservatori, **4**
Palazzo Farnese, **34**
Pantheon, **29**
Piazza Barberini, **17**
Piazza del Popolo, **10**
Piazza Farnese, **33**
Piazza Navona, **31**
Piazza San Pietro, **22**
Piazza Venezia, **1**
San Luigi dei
Francesi, **30**
Santa Maria del
Popolo, **11**
Santa Maria Sopra
Minerva, **28**
Spanish Steps, **15**
St. Peter's Basilica, **24**
Tiberina Island, **35**
Trinità dei Monti, **14**
Vatican Gardens, **25**
Vatican Museums, **26**
Vatican Palace, **23**
Via Condotti, **13**
Via del Babuino, **12**

Roma (Rome)

tance and eventually were destroyed by fire or the invasions of barbarians. Rubble accumulated (though much of it was carted off later by medieval home-builders as construction material), and the site reverted to marshy pastureland; sporadic excavations began at the end of the 19th century.

You don't really have to try to make sense of the mass of marble fragments scattered over the area of the Roman Forum. Just consider that 2,000 years ago this was the center of the then-known world. Wander down the Via Sacra and climb the Palatine Hill, where the emperors had their palaces and where 16th-century cardinals strolled in elaborate Italian gardens. From the belvedere you have a good view of the Circus Maximus. *Entrances on Via dei Fori Imperiali, Piazza Santa Maria Nova and Via di San Gregorio, tel. 06/699–0110. Admission: 10,000 lire. Open Apr.–Sept., Mon., Wed.–Sat. 9–6, Tues., Sun. 9–1; Oct.–Mar., Mon., Wed.–Sat. 9–3, Tues., Sun. 9–1.*

⑦ Leave the Forum from the exit at Piazza Santa Maria Nova, near the Arch of Titus, and head for the **Colosseum,** inaugurated in AD 80 with a program of games and shows that lasted 100 days. On opening day alone 5,000 wild animals perished in the arena. The Colosseum could hold more than 50,000 spectators; it was faced with marble, decorated with stuccos, and had an ingenious system of awnings to provide shade. Try to see it both in daytime and at night, when yellow floodlights make it a magical sight, though parts may be shrouded during ongoing restoration. The Colosseum, by the way, takes its name from a colossal, 36-meter (115-foot) statue of Nero that stood nearby. You must pay a fee to explore the upper levels. *Piazza del Colosseo, tel. 06/700–4261. Admission: 6,000 lire to upper levels. Open Mon., Tues., and Thurs.–Sat. 9–one hour before sunset; Sun. and Wed. 9–1.*

Time Out   For delicious ice cream try **Ristoro della Salute,** one of Rome's best *gelaterie. Piazza del Colosseo 2a.*

⑧ Stroll past the **Arch of Constantine.** The reliefs depict Constantine's victory over Maxentius at the Milvian Bridge. Just before this battle in AD 312, Constantine had a vision of a cross in the heavens and heard the words, "In this sign thou shalt conquer." The victory led not only to the construction of this majestic marble arch but, more important, was a turning point in the history of Christianity: Soon afterward a grateful Constantine decreed that it was a lawful religion and should be tolerated throughout the empire.

⑨ A fairly long but pleasant walk takes you to the **Baths of Caracalla,** which numbered among ancient Rome's most beautiful and luxurious, inaugurated by Caracalla in 217 and used until the 6th century. An ancient version of a swanky athletic club, the baths were open to the public; citizens could bathe, socialize, and exercise in huge pools and richly decorated halls and libraries, now towering ruins. At press time it was uncertain that the famous open-air opera season would continue in this venue. *Via delle Terme di Caracalla. Admission: 6,000 lire. Open Apr.–Sept., Tues.–Sat. 9–6, Sun. and Mon. 9–1; Oct.–Mar., Tues.–Sat. 9–3, Sun.–Mon. 9–1.*

Piazzas and Fountains **⑩** **Piazza del Popolo** is one of Rome's most vast and airy squares, but for many years it was just an exceptionally beautiful parking lot with a 3,000-year-old obelisk in the middle. Now most traffic and parking has been barred, and the piazza is open to strollers. The **⑪** church of **Santa Maria del Popolo** over in the corner of the piazza near the arch stands out more, now that it has been cleaned, and is rich in art, including two stunning Caravaggios in the chapel to the left of the main altar.

Time Out | **Rosati** is a café that has never gone out of style, forever a rendezvous of literati, artists, and actors. Its sidewalk tables, tearoom, and upstairs dining room can revive you with an espresso, snack, lunch, or dinner—all with a hefty price tag. *Piazza del Popolo 4. Closed Tues.*

⑫ If you're interested in antiques, stroll along **Via del Babuino.** If trendy fashions and accessories suit your fancy, take Via del Corso **⑬** and turn into **Via Condotti,** Rome's most elegant and expensive shopping street. Here you can ogle fabulous jewelry, designer fashions, and accessories in the windows of Buccellati, Ferragamo, Valentino, Gucci, and Bulgari.

Time Out | The more-than-200-year-old **Antico Caffè Greco** is the haunt of writers, artists, and well-groomed ladies toting Gucci shopping bags. With its small marble-topped tables and velour settees, it's a nostalgic sort of place—Goethe, Byron, and Liszt were regulars here, and even Buffalo Bill stopped in when his road show came to town. Table service is expensive. *Via Condotti 86. Closed Sun.*

⑭ Via Condotti gives you a head-on view of the Spanish Steps in **Piazza di Spagna,** and of the church of **Trinità dei Monti.** In the center of the piazza is Bernini's **Fountain of the Barcaccia** (Old Boat), around which Romans and tourists cool themselves on hot summer nights. **⑮** The 200-year-old **Spanish Steps,** named for the Spanish Embassy to the Holy See, opposite the American Express office, is a popular rendezvous, especially for the young people who throng this area. On weekend afternoons, Via del Corso is packed with wall-to-wall teenagers, and McDonald's, tucked away in a corner of Piazza di Spagna beyond the American Express office, is a mob scene. In contrast, **Babington's Tea Room,** to the left of the Spanish Steps, is a stylish institution that caters to an upscale clientele.

To the right of the Spanish steps is the **Keats and Shelley Memorial House.** Once the home of these romantic poets, it's now a museum. *Piazza di Spagna 26, tel. 06/678-4235. Admission: 4,000 lire. Open June–Sept., weekdays 9–1 and 3–6; Oct.–May, weekdays 9–1 and 2:30–5:30.*

⑯ Head for Via del Tritone and cross this heavily trafficked shopping street into narrow Via della Stamperia, which leads to the **Fontana di Trevi** (Trevi Fountain), a spectacular fantasy of mythical sea creatures and cascades of splashing water. Legend has it that visitors must toss a coin into the fountain to ensure their return to Rome, but you'll have to force your way past crowds of tourists and aggressive souvenir vendors to do so. The fountain as you see it was completed in the mid-1700s, but there had been a drinking fountain on the site for centuries. Pope Urban VIII almost sparked a revolt when he slapped a tax on wine to cover the expenses of having the fountain repaired.

⑰ At the top of Via del Tritone, **Piazza Barberini** boasts two fountains by Bernini: the jaunty **Triton** in the middle of the square and the **Fountain of the Bees** at the corner of Via Veneto. Decorated with the heraldic Barberini bees, this shell-shaped fountain bears an inscription that was immediately regarded as an unlucky omen by the superstitious Romans, for it erroneously stated that the fountain had been erected in the 22nd year of the reign of Pope Urban VIII, who had commissioned it, while in fact the 21st anniversary of his election was still some weeks away. The wrong numeral was hurriedly erased, but to no avail: Urban died eight days before the beginning of his 22nd year as pontiff.

⓲ A few steps up Via delle Quattro Fontane is **Palazzo Barberini,** Rome's most splendid 17th-century palace, now surrounded by rather unkempt gardens and occupied in part by the **Galleria Nazionale di Arte Antica.** Visit the latter to see Raphael's *Fornarina,* many other good paintings, some lavishly frescoed ceilings, and a charming suite of rooms decorated in 1782 on the occasion of the marriage of a Barberini heiress. *Via delle Quattro Fontane 13, tel. 06/481–4591. Admission: 6,000 lire. Open Tues.–Sat. 9–2, Sun. 9–1.*

⓳ One of Rome's oddest sights is the **crypt** of the **Church of Santa Maria della Concezione** on Via Veneto, just above the Fountain of the Bees. In four chapels under the main church, the skeletons and scattered bones of some 4,000 dead Capuchin monks are arranged in decorative motifs, a macabre practice peculiar to the Baroque age. *Via Veneto 27, tel. 06/462850. Admission free, but a donation is encouraged. Open daily 9–noon and 3–6.*

The lower reaches of Via Veneto are quiet and sedate, but at the intersection with Via Bissolati, otherwise known as "Airline Row," the avenue comes to life. The big white palace on the right is the U.S. Embassy, and the even bigger white palace beyond it is the luxurious **Hotel Excelsior.** Together with Doney's next door and the Café de Paris across the street, the Excelsior was a landmark of La Dolce Vita, that effervescent period during the 1950s when movie stars, playboys, and exiled royalty played hide-and-seek with press agents and *paparazzi,* ducking in and out of nightclubs and hotel rooms along the Via Veneto. The atmosphere of Via Veneto is considerably more sober now, and its cafés cater more to tourists and expensive pickups than to barefoot cinema *contesse.*

Via Veneto ends at **Porta Pinciana,** a gate in the 12-mile stretch of defensive walls built by Emperor Aurelian in the 3rd century; 400 years later, when the Goths got too close for comfort, Belisarius reinforced the gate with two massive towers. Beyond is **Villa Borghese,** most famous of Rome's parks, studded with tall pines that are gradually dying off as pollution and age take their toll. Inside the **⓴** park, strike off to the right toward the **Galleria Borghese,** a pleasure palace created by Cardinal Scipione Borghese in 1613 as a showcase for his fabulous sculpture collection. In the throes of structural repairs for several years, the now-public gallery is, at press time, only partially open to visitors. It's still worth a visit to see the seductive reclining statue of Pauline Borghese by Canova, and some extraordinary works by Bernini, among them the unforgettable *Apollo and Daphne,* in which marble is transformed into flesh and foliage. With restorations dragging on, probably into 1995, a few of the best works, including Caravaggio's, have been moved from the upstairs picture gallery, which is closed, to the San Michele complex in Trastevere, where they are on view (Via di San Michele, tel. 06/581–6732; admission: 4,000 lire; open Tues.–Sat. 9–7, Sun.–Mon. 9–1). *During reconstruction the entrance to the Galleria Borghese is on Via Raimondi, reached from Via Pinciana. Via Pinciana (Piazzale Museo Borghese–Villa Borghese), tel. 06/858577. Admission: 4,000 lire. Open May–Sept., Tues.–Sat. 9–7, Sun. 9–1; Oct.–Apr., Tues.–Sat. 9–2, Sun. 9–1.*

Castel Sant'Angelo– St. Peter's– Vatican Museums

㉑

Ponte Sant'Angelo, an ancient bridge spanning the Tiber, is decorated with lovely Baroque angels designed by Bernini. From the bridge there are fine views of St. Peter's, in the distance, and of the nearby **Castel Sant'Angelo,** a formidable fortress that was originally built as the tomb of Emperor Hadrian in the 2nd century AD. In its early days, it looked much like the **Augusteo,** or Tomb of Augustus, which still stands more or less in its original form across the river. Hadrian's Tomb was incorporated into the town walls and served as a military stronghold during the barbarian invasions. According to legend it got its present name in the 6th century, when Pope Gregory the Great, passing by in a religious procession, saw an angel with a sword appear above the ramparts to signal the end of the plague that was raging. Enlarged and fortified, the castle became a refuge for the popes, who fled to it along the **Passetto,** an arcaded passageway that links it with the Vatican. Inside the castle you see ancient corridors, medieval cells and Renaissance salons, a museum of antique weapons, courtyards piled with stone cannonballs, and terraces with great views of the city. There's a pleasant bar with outdoor tables on one level. The highest terrace of all, under the newly restored bronze statue of the legendary angel, is the one from which Puccini's heroine, Tosca, threw herself. *Lungotevere Castello 50, tel. 06/687–5036. Admission: 8,000 lire. Open Mon. 2–6, Tues., Wed., Fri., Sat. 9–1, Thurs. 9–6, Sun. 9–noon.*

㉒

Via della Conciliazione, the broad avenue leading to St. Peter's Basilica, was created by Mussolini's architects by razing blocks of old houses. This opened up a vista of the basilica, giving the eye time to adjust to its mammoth dimensions, and thereby spoiling the effect Bernini sought when he enclosed his vast square (which is really oval) in the embrace of huge quadruple colonnades. In **Piazza San Pietro** (St. Peter's Square), which has held up to 400,000 people at one time, look for the stone disks in the pavement halfway between the fountains and the obelisk. From these points the colonnades seem to be formed of a single row of columns all the way around.

㉓

When you enter Piazza San Pietro (completed in 1667), you are entering Vatican territory. Since the Lateran Treaty of 1929, **Vatican City** has been an independent and sovereign state, which covers about 44 hectares (108 acres) and is surrounded by thick, high walls. Its gates are watched over by the Swiss Guards, who still wear the colorful dress uniforms designed by Michelangelo. Sovereign of this little state is John Paul II, 264th Pope of the Roman Catholic Church. At noon on Sunday, the Pope appears at his third-floor study window in the **Vatican Palace,** to the right of the basilica, to bless the crowd in the square. (Note: Entry to St. Peter's, the Vatican Museums, and all other sites within Vatican City [e.g., the Gardens] is barred to those wearing shorts, miniskirts, sleeveless T-shirts, and otherwise revealing clothing. Women should carry scarves to cover bare shoulders and upper arms or wear blouses that come to the elbow. Men should dress modestly, in slacks and shirts.) A free 90-minute tour of St. Peter's Basilica is offered in English daily (Mon.–Sat. 3 PM, Sun. 2:30 PM) by volunteer guides. They start at the information desk under the basilica portico.

㉔

St. Peter's Basilica is one of Rome's most impressive sights. It takes a while to absorb the sheer magnificence of it, however, and its rich decoration may not be to everyone's taste. Its size alone is overwhelming, and the basilica is best appreciated when providing the lustrous background for ecclesiastical ceremonies thronged with the faithful. The original basilica was built in the early 4th century AD by the emperor Constantine, over an earlier shrine that supposedly marked the burial place of St. Peter. After more than a thousand years, the old basilica was so decrepit it had to be torn down. The task of building a new, much larger one took almost 200 years and employed the architectural genius of Alberti, Bramante, Raphael, Peruzzi, Antonio Sangallo the Younger, and Michelangelo, who died before the dome he had planned could be completed. Finally, in 1626, St. Peter's Basilica was finished.

The basilica is full of extraordinary works of art. Among the most famous is Michelangelo's *Pietà* (1498), seen in the first chapel on the right just as you enter the basilica. Michelangelo has four *Pietàs* to his credit. The earliest and best known can be seen here. Two others are in Florence, and the fourth, the *Rondanini Pietà*, is in Milan.

At the end of the central aisle is the bronze statue of **St. Peter,** its foot worn by centuries of reverent kisses. The bronze throne above the altar in the apse was created by Bernini to contain a simple wood and ivory chair once believed to have belonged to St. Peter. Bernini's bronze *baldacchino* (canopy) over the papal altar was made with metal stripped from the portico of the Pantheon at the order of Pope Urban VIII, one of the powerful Roman Barberini family. His practice of plundering ancient monuments for material to implement his grandiose schemes inspired the famous quip, *"Quod non fecerunt barbari, fecerunt Barberini"* ("What the barbarians didn't do, the Barberini did").

As you stroll up and down the aisles and transepts, observe the fine mosaic copies of famous paintings above the altars, the monumental tombs and statues, and the fine stucco work. Stop at the **Treasury** (Historical Museum), which contains some priceless liturgical objects.

The entrance to the so-called **Vatican Grottoes,** or crypt, is in one of the huge piers at the crossing. It's best to leave this visit for last, as the crypt's only exit takes you outside the church. The crypt contains chapels and the tombs of many popes. It occupies the area of the original basilica, over the necropolis, the ancient burial ground where evidence of what may be St. Peter's burial place has been found. You can book special tours of the necropolis. To see the roof and dome of the basilica take the elevator or climb the stairs in the courtyard near the exit of the Vatican Grottoes. From the roof you can climb a short interior staircase to the base of the dome for an overhead view of the interior of the basilica. Only if you are in good shape should you attempt the very long, strenuous, and claustrophobic climb up the narrow, one-way stairs to the balcony of the lantern atop the dome, where the view embraces the Vatican Gardens as well as all of Rome. *St. Peter's Basilica, tel. 06/6988–4466. Open daily Apr.–Sept., 7–7, Oct.–Mar. 7–6. Treasury (Museo Storico-Artistico): entrance in Sacristy. Admission: 3,000 lire. Open Apr.–Sept., daily 9–6:30; Oct.–Mar., daily 9–5:30. Roof and Dome: entrance in the courtyard to the left as you leave the basilica. Admission: 6,000 lire, including use of elevator to roof, 5,000 lire if you climb the spiral ramp on foot. Open Apr.–Sept., daily 8–6; Oct.–Mar., daily 8–5. Vatican Grottoes (Tombs of the Popes): entrance alternates among the piers at the crossing. Admission: free. Open Apr.–Sept., daily 7–6; Oct.–Mar., daily 7–5. Necropolis: Apply a few days in advance to Ufficio Scavi, left beyond the Arco delle Campane entrance to the Vatican, or try in the morning for the same day, tel. 06/6988–5318. Admission: 10,000 lire for 2-hour guided visit, 6,000 lire with tape cassette. Ufficio Scavi office hours: Mon.–Sat. 9–5; closed Sun. and religious holidays.*

For many visitors, a **papal audience** is the highlight of a trip to Rome. Mass audiences take place on Wednesday morning in a modern audience hall (capacity 7,000) off the left-hand colonnade. Tickets are necessary, but you can also see the Pope when he appears at the window of the **Vatican Palace** to bless the crowd in the square below at noon on Sunday. He also blesses the public on summer Sundays when he's at the papal residence at **Castel Gandolfo.** *For audience tickets, write well in advance to the Prefettura della Casa Pontificia (00120 Vatican City), indicating the date you prefer, the language you speak, and the hotel in which you will be staying. You can pick up free tickets from 4–6 PM at the North American College, Via dell 'Umiltà 30 (tel. 06/678–9184), or apply to the Papal Prefecture (Prefettura), which you reach through the Bronze Door in the right-hand colonnade, tel. 06/6988–4466. Open Mon. and Tues. 9–1. Or arrange for tickets through a travel agent: Carrani Tours, Via V.E. Orlando 95, tel. 06/488–0510; Appian Line, Via Barberini 109, tel. 06/488–4151. Admission: about 36,000 lire (including transportation) if booked through an agent or hotel concierge.*

㉕ Guided tours through the **Vatican Gardens**—an hour by bus and an hour on foot—show you some attractive landscaping, a few historical monuments, fountains, and the lovely 16th-century house of Pius IV by Pirro Ligorio. These tours give you a different perspective on the basilica itself. *Tickets at information office, on the left side of St. Peter's Square, tel. 06/6988–4466. Open Mon.–Sat. 8:30–7. Garden tour cost: 16,000 lire. Available Mon., Tues., and Thurs.–Sat.*

From the St. Peter's Square information office you can take a shuttle bus (cost: 2,000 lire) direct to the Vatican Museums. This operates every morning, except Wednesday and Sunday, gives you a glimpse of the Vatican Gardens, and saves you the 15-minute walk that goes left from the square and continues along the Vatican walls.

㉖ The collections in the **Vatican Museums** cover nearly 8 kilometers (5 miles) of displays. If you have time, allow at least half a day for Castel Sant'Angelo and St. Peter's, and another half-day for the museums. Posters at the museum entrance plot out a choice of four color-coded itineraries; the shortest takes about 90 minutes, the longest more than four hours, depending on your rate of progress.

No matter which tour you take, it will include the famed **Sistine Chapel.** In 1508, Pope Julius II commissioned Michelangelo to fresco the more than 930 square meters (10,000 square feet) of the chapel's ceiling. For four years Michelangelo dedicated himself to painting over fresh plaster, and the result was his masterpiece. Recent cleaning operations, now completed, have removed centuries of soot and revealed its original and surprisingly brilliant colors.

You can try to avoid the tour groups by going early or late, allowing yourself enough time before the closing hour. In peak season, the crowds definitely detract from your appreciation of this outstanding artistic achievement. Buy an illustrated guide or rent a taped commentary in order to make sense of the figures on the ceiling. A pair of binoculars also helps.

The Vatican collections are so rich that unless you are an expert in art history, you will probably want only to skim the surface, concentrating on pieces that strike your fancy. If you really want to see the museums thoroughly, you will have to come back again and again. Some of the highlights that might be of interest on your first tour include the newly reorganized Egyptian collection and the *Laocoön*, the *Belvedere Torso*, and the *Apollo Belvedere*, which inspired Michelangelo. The Raphael Rooms are decorated with masterful frescoes, and there are more Raphaels in the Picture Gallery *(Pinacoteca)*. At the Quattro Cancelli, near the entrance to the Picture Gallery, a rather spartan cafeteria provides basic nonalcoholic refreshments. *Viale Vaticano, tel. 06/6988-3332. Admission: 13,000 lire, free on last Sun. of the month. Open Easter period and July–Sept., weekdays 8:45–5, Sat. 8:45–2; Oct.–June, Mon.–Sat. 8:45–2. Ticket office closes 1 hour before museums close. Closed Sun., except last Sun. of the month, and on religious holidays: Jan. 1, Jan. 6, Feb. 11, Mar. 19, Easter Sun. and Mon., May 1, Ascension Thurs., Corpus Christi, June 29, Aug. 15–16, Nov. 1, Dec. 8, Dec. 25–26.*

Time Out Near the Vatican are many good neighborhood trattorias better than the touristy eateries opposite the Vatican Museums entrance. At moderately priced **La Caravella** (Via degli Scipioni 32, corner of Via Vespasiano, off Piazza Risorgimento, closed Thurs.) you can lunch on pizza or try the homemade pasta and other specialties of Roman and Abruzzo cooking. **Hostaria Tonino** (Via Leone IV 60, near Largo Trionfale; closed Sun.) is a typical Roman tavern, of a type in danger of extinction, with paper-covered tables and a limited choice of inexpensive local fare. There are also several trattorias on and around Borgo Pio.

Old Rome Take Via del Plebiscito from Piazza Venezia to the huge **Church of**
㉗ **the Gesù.** This paragon of Baroque style is the tangible symbol of the power of the Jesuits, who were a major force in the Counter-Reformation in Europe. Encrusted with gold and precious marbles, the Gesù has a fantastically painted ceiling that flows down over the pillars, merging with painted stucco figures to complete the three-dimensional illusion.

㉘ On your way to the Pantheon you will pass **Santa Maria Sopra Minerva,** a Gothic church built over a Roman temple. Inside there are some beautiful frescoes by Filippo Lippi; outside there is a charming elephant by Bernini with an obelisk on its back.

Originally built in 27 BC by Augustus's general Agrippa and rebuilt
㉙ by Hadrian in the 2nd century AD, the **Pantheon** is one of Rome's most perfect, best-preserved, and perhaps least appreciated ancient monuments. Romans and tourists alike pay little attention to it, and on summer evenings it serves mainly as a backdrop for all the action in the square in front. It represents a fantastic feat of construction, however. The huge columns of the portico and the original bronze doors form the entrance to a majestic hall covered by the largest dome of its kind ever built, wider even than that of St. Peter's. In ancient times the entire interior was encrusted with rich decorations of gilt bronze and marble, plundered by later emperors and popes. *Piazza della Rotonda. Open Mon.–Sat. 9–2, Sun. 9–1.*

Time Out There are several sidewalk cafés on the square in front of the Pantheon, all of which are good places to nurse a cappuccino while you observe the scene. Serious coffee drinkers also like **Tazza d'Oro** (Via degli Orfani 84), just off Piazza della Rotonda. And for a huge variety of ice cream in natural flavors, **Giolitti** (Via Uffici del Vicario 40; closed Mon.) is generally considered by *gelato* addicts to be the best in Rome. It also has good snacks and a quick-lunch counter.

㉚ On Via della Dogana Vecchia, stop in at the church of **San Luigi dei Francesi** to see the three paintings by Caravaggio in the last chapel on the left; have a few hundred-lire coins handy for the light machine. The clergy of San Luigi considered the artist's roistering and unruly lifestyle scandalous enough, but his realistic treatment of sacred subjects was just too much for them. They rejected his first version of the altarpiece and weren't particularly happy with the other two works either. Thanks to the intercession of Caravaggio's patron, an influential cardinal, they were persuaded to keep them—a lucky thing, since they are now recognized to be among the artist's finest paintings. *Open Fri.–Wed. 7:30–12:30 and 3:30–7, Thurs. 7:30–12:30.*

③① Just beyond San Luigi is **Piazza Navona,** an elongated 17th-century piazza that traces the oval form of the underlying Circus of Diocletian. At the center, Bernini's lively **Fountain of the Four Rivers** is a showpiece. The four statues represent rivers in the four corners of the world: the Nile, with its face covered in allusion to its then unknown source; the Ganges; the Danube; and the River Plate, with its hand raised. And here we have to give the lie to the legend that this was Bernini's mischievous dig at Borromini's design of the facade of the church of **Sant'Agnese in Agone,** from which the statue seems to be shrinking in horror. The fountain was created in 1651; work on the church's facade began some time later. The piazza dozes in the morning, when little groups of pensioners sun themselves on the stone benches and children pedal tricycles around the big fountain. In the late afternoon the sidewalk cafés fill up for the aperitif hour, and in the evening, especially in good weather, the piazza comes to life with a throng of street artists, vendors, tourists, and Romans out for their evening *passeggiata* (promenade).

Time Out The sidewalk tables of the **Tre Scalini** café (Piazza Navona 30; closed Wed.) offer a grandstand view of this gorgeous piazza. Treat yourself to a *tartufo*, the chocolate ice-cream specialty that was invented here. The restaurant is a pleasant place for a moderately priced lunch. For a salad or light lunch, go to **Cul de Sac** (Piazza Pasquino 73, just off Piazza Navona) or to **Insalata Ricca** (Via del Paradiso, next to the church of Sant'Andrea della Valle). Both are informal and inexpensive.

③② Across Corso Vittorio is **Campo dei Fiori** (Field of Flowers), the site of a crowded and colorful daily morning market. The hooded bronze figure brooding over the piazza is philosopher Giordano Bruno, who **③③** was burned at the stake here for heresy. The adjacent **Piazza Farnese,** with fountains made of Egyptian granite basins from the Baths **③④** of Caracalla, is an airy setting for **Palazzo Farnese,** now the French Embassy, one of the most beautiful of Rome's many Renaissance palaces. There are several others in the immediate area: **Palazzo Spada,** a Wedgwood kind of palace encrusted with stuccos and statues; **Palazzo della Cancelleria,** a massive building that is now the Papal Chancellery, one of the many Vatican-owned buildings in Rome that enjoy extraterritorial privileges; and the fine old palaces along Via Giulia.

This is a section to wander through, getting the feel of daily life carried on in a centuries-old setting, and looking into the dozens of antiques shops. Stroll along Via Arenula into a rather gloomy part of Rome bounded by Piazza Campitelli and Lungotevere Cenci, the ancient Jewish ghetto. Among the most interesting sights here are the pretty **Fountain of the Tartarughe** (Turtles) on Piazza Mattei, the **Via Portico d'Ottavia,** with medieval inscriptions and friezes on the old buildings, and the **Teatro di Marcello,** a theater built by Julius Caesar to hold 20,000 spectators.

35 A pleasant place to end your walk is on **Tiberina Island.** To get there,
36 walk across the ancient **Fabricio Bridge,** built in 62 BC, the oldest
bridge in the city.

Off the Beaten Track

If the sky promises a gorgeous sunset, head for the **Terrazza del
Pincio** above Piazza del Popolo, a vantage point prized by Romans.

For a look at a real patrician palace, see the **Galleria Doria Pamphili,**
still the residence of a princely family. You can visit the gallery housing the family's art collection and part of the magnificently furnished private apartments, as well. *Piazza del Collegio Romano
1/a, near Piazza Venezia, tel. 06/679–4365. Admission: 5,000 lire;
additional 3,000 lire for guided visit of private rooms. Open Tues.,
Fri., weekends 10–1; closed Mon., Wed., and Thurs.*

Make an excursion to **Ostia Antica,** the well-preserved Roman port
city near the sea, as rewarding as an excursion to Pompeii and much
easier to get to from Rome. There's a regular train service from the
Ostiense station (Piramide Metro stop). *Via dei Romagnoli, Ostia
Antica, tel. 06/565–1405. Admission: 8,000 lire. Open daily 9–1
hour before sunset.*

Delve into the world of the Etruscans, who inhabited Italy even in
pre-Roman times and have left fascinating evidence of their relaxed,
sensual lifestyle. Visit the **Museo Nazionale di Villa Giulia,** in a gorgeous Renaissance mansion with a full-scale Etruscan temple (and a
small coffee bar) in the garden. You'll see a smile as enigmatic as that
of the Mona Lisa on deities and other figures in terracotta, bronze,
and gold. Ask especially to see the **Castellani collection of ancient
jewelry** (and copies) hidden away on the upper floor. *Piazza di Villa
Giulia 9, tel. 06/320–1951. Admission: 8,000 lire. Open Wed. 9–7:30,
Tues. and Thurs.–Sat. 9–2, Sun. 9–1.*

Shopping

Shopping is part of the fun of being in Rome, no matter what your
budget. The best buys are leather goods of all kinds, from gloves to
handbags and wallets to jackets; silk goods; and high-quality knitwear. Shops are closed on Sunday and on Monday morning; in July
and August, they close on Saturday afternoon as well.

Antiques A well-trained eye will spot some worthy old prints and minor antiques in the city's fascinating little shops. For prints, browse among
the stalls at **Piazza Fontanella Borghese** or stop in at **Casali** (Piazza
della Rotonda 81a), at the Pantheon, or at **Tanca** (Salita dei
Crescenzi 10), also near the Pantheon. For minor antiques, **Via dei
Coronari** and other streets in the **Piazza Navona** area are good. The
most prestigious antiques dealers are situated in **Via del Babuino**
and its environs.

Boutiques **Via Condotti,** directly across from the Spanish Steps, and the
streets running parallel to Via Condotti, as well as its cross streets,
form the most elegant and expensive shopping area in Rome. Lower-
price fashions may be found on display at shops on **Via Frattina** and
Via del Corso.

Shopping In addition to those mentioned, Romans themselves do much of their
Districts shopping along **Via Cola di Rienzo** and **Via Nazionale.** Among the
huge new shopping malls dotting Rome's outskirts, CinecittàDue is
easiest to reach; just take Metro A to the Subaugusta stop. It has
100 shops, as well as snack bars and cafés.

Religious Articles These abound in the shops around St. Peter's, on **Via di Porta Angelica** and **Via della Conciliazione,** and in the souvenir shops tucked away on the roof and at the crypt exit in St. Peter's itself.

Department Stores You'll find a fairly broad selection of women's, men's, and children's fashions and accessories at the **Rinascente** stores on Piazza Colonna and at Piazza Fiume and at the **Coin** department store on Piazzale Appio near San Giovanni Laterano. The **UPIM** and **Standa** chains have shops all over the city that offer medium-quality, low-price goods. The **Croff** chain features housewares.

Food and Flea Markets The open-air markets at **Campo dei Fiori** and in many neighborhoods throughout the city are colorful sights. The flea market held at **Porta Portese** on Sunday morning is stocked mainly with new or second-hand clothing. If you go, beware of pickpockets and purse snatchers.

Dining

There are plenty of fine restaurants in Rome serving various Italian regional cuisines and international specialties with a flourish of linen and silver, as well as a whopping *conto* (check) at the end. If you want family-style cooking and prices, try a *trattoria*, a usually smallish and unassuming, often family-run place. Fast-food places and Chinese restaurants are proliferating in Rome. Fixed-price tourist menus can be scanty and unimaginative. The lunch hour in Rome lasts from about 1 to 3 PM, dinner from 8 or 8:30 to about 10:30, though some restaurants stay open much later. During August many restaurants close for vacation. A few hotels (such as the Hassler, Hilton, and De la Ville) serve Sunday brunch.

For details and price-category definitions, *see* Dining in Staying in Italy, *above.*

Very Expensive
★ **El Toulà.** On a little byway off Piazza Nicosia in Old Rome, El Toulà has the warm, welcoming atmosphere of a 19th-century country house, with white walls, antique furniture in dark wood, heavy silver serving dishes, and spectacular arrangements of fruits and flowers. There's a cozy little bar off the entrance where you can sip a *prosecco*, the aperitif best suited to the chef's Venetian specialties, among them the classic *pasta e fagioli* (bean soup), risotto with radicchio, and *fegato alla veneziana* (liver with onions). *Via della Lupa 29/b, tel. 06/687–3750. Reservations required. AE, DC, MC, V. Closed Sat. lunch, Sun., Aug., and Dec. 24–26.*
Le Jardin. Housed in the posh Lord Byron Hotel in the Parioli residential district, Le Jardin is one of Rome's classiest restaurants. Mirrors, fresh flowers, frescoed walls, and soft lights set the mood for dining on selections from an imaginative seasonal menu that might include risotto with seafood or vegetable sauce and *maiale con miele e zenzero* (pork with honey and ginger); everything is beautifully presented, and the service is of a very high standard. *Hotel Lord Byron, Via Giuseppe De Notaris 5, tel. 06/322–0404. Reservations required. Jacket and tie advised. AE, DC, MC, V. Closed Sun.*

Expensive
★ **Andrea.** Ernest Hemingway and King Farouk used to eat here; FIAT supremo Gianni Agnelli and other Italian power brokers still do. A half-block off Via Veneto, Andrea offers classic Italian cooking in an intimate, clubby ambience in which snowy table linens gleam against a discreet background of dark green paneling. The menu features delicacies such as homemade *tagliolini* (thin noodles) with shrimp and spinach sauce, spaghetti with seafood, and mouth-watering *carciofi all'Andrea* (artichokes simmered in olive oil). *Via*

Sardegna 26, tel. 06/482-1891. Reservations advised. AE, DC, MC, V. Closed Sat. lunch, Sun., and most of Aug.

Coriolano. The only tourists who find their way to this classic restaurant near Porta Pia are likely to be gourmets looking for quintessential Italian food—that means light homemade pastas, choice olive oil, and market-fresh ingredients, especially seafood. Although seafood dishes vary, *tagliolini all'aragosta* (thin noodles with lobster sauce) is usually on the menu, as are *porcini* mushrooms (in season) cooked to a secret recipe. The wine list is predominantly Italian but includes some French and California wines. *Via Ancona 14, tel. 06/855-1122. Reservations advised. AE, DC, MC, V. Closed Sun. and Aug. 1-25.*

★ **Ranieri.** On a quiet street off fashionable Via Condotti near the Spanish Steps, this historic restaurant was founded by a former chef of Queen Victoria's. It remains a favorite with tourists for its traditional atmosphere and decor, with damask-covered walls, velvet banquettes, crystal chandeliers, and old paintings. Among the many specialties on the vast menu are *gnocchi alla parigina* (souffléed gnocchi with cheese sauce) and *mignonettes alla Regina Vittoria* (veal with pâté and an eight-cheese sauce). *Via Mario dei Fiori 26, tel. 06/678-6505. Reservations advised. AE, DC, MC, V. Closed Sun.*

Moderate **Colline Emiliane.** Located near Piazza Barberini, the Colline Emiliane is an unassuming trattoria offering exceptionally good food. Behind an opaque glass facade, there are a couple of plain little dining rooms where you are served light homemade pastas, a very special chicken broth, and meats ranging from pot roast to *giambonetto di vitella* (roast veal) and *cotoletta alla bolognese* (veal cutlet with cheese and tomato sauce). *Via degli Avignonesi 22, tel. 06/481-7538. Reservations advised. No credit cards. Closed Fri. and Aug.*

La Campana. An inconspicuous trattoria off Via della Scrofa, this is a place with a long tradition of hospitality; there has been an inn on this spot since the 15th century. The atmosphere is now that of a classic Roman eating place, with friendly but businesslike waiters and a menu that offers Roman specialties such as *vignarola* (sautéed fava beans, peas, and artichokes), rigatoni with prosciutto and tomato sauce, and *olivette di vitello* (tiny veal rolls, served with mashed potatoes). *Vicolo della Campana 18, tel. 06/686-7820. Dinner reservations advised. AE, MC, V. Closed Mon. and Aug.*

Le Maschere. This cellar restaurant hidden between Largo Argentina and Piazza Campo dei Fiori offers informal ambience and southern Italian (Calabrian) cuisine. Colored paper garlands and old utensils hang on dark, rustic walls, and you pour wine from pottery jugs. There is a large antipasto buffet and a glowing pizza oven; the menu also features pasta with tomato-and-eggplant sauce, grilled meats, and seafood. *Via Monte della Farina 29, tel. 06/687-9444. Reservations advised. AE, DC, MC, V. No lunch. Closed Mon. and mid-Aug.-mid-Sept.*

Orso 80. A bustling trattoria located in Old Rome, near Piazza Navona, it is known for a fabulous antipasto table. The egg pasta is freshly made, and the *bucatini all'amatriciana* (thick spaghetti with a tangy tomato and bacon sauce) is a classic Roman pasta. There's seafood on the menu, but it can be pricey. For dessert, try the ricotta cake, a Roman specialty. *Via dell'Orso 33, tel. 06/686-4904. Reservations advised. AE, DC, MC, V. Closed Mon. and Aug. 10-20.*

Paris. Off Piazza Santa Maria in Trastevere, Paris is reassuring and understated, with none of the flamboyant folklore of so many eateries in Trastevere, a characteristically colorful but clearly gentrified neighborhood. "Paris" is a traditional man's name in Rome, and this restaurant remains true to classic Roman cuisine, serving, among other things, homemade *fettuccine* and delicate *fritto misto* (morsels of vegetables fried in batter). Before or after your meal, take a stroll through the neighborhood (staying vigilant against purse snatchers). *Piazza San Callisto 7/a, tel. 06/581–5378. Dinner reservations advised. AE, DC, MC, V. Closed Sun. evening, Mon. and Aug.*

Pierluigi. Pierluigi, in the heart of Old Rome, is a longtime favorite. On busy evenings it's almost impossible to find a table, so make sure you reserve well in advance. Seafood predominates—if you fancy a splurge, try the lobster—but traditional Roman dishes are offered, too, such as *orecchiette con broccoli* (disk-shaped pasta with greens) and *abbacchio* (roast lamb). In warm weather ask for a table in the piazza. *Piazza dei Ricci 144, tel. 06/687–8717. Reservations advised. AE. Closed Mon. and 2 weeks in Aug.*

★ **Romolo.** Generations of Romans have enjoyed the romantic garden courtyard and historic dining room of this charming Trastevere haunt, reputedly once home of Raphael's ladylove, *La Fornarina*. In the evening, a guitarist serenades diners. The cuisine is appropriately Roman; specialties include *mozzarella alla fornarina* (deep-fried mozzarella with ham and anchovies) and *braciolette d'abbacchio scottadito* (grilled baby lamb chops). Alternatively, try one of the vegetarian pastas featuring carciofi or radicchio. *Via di Porta Settimiana 8, tel. 06/581–8284. Reservations advised. AE, DC, V. Closed Mon. and Aug. 2–23.*

Inexpensive
★ **Abruzzi.** This simple trattoria off Piazza Santi Apostoli near Piazza Venezia specializes in regional cooking of the Abruzzi, a mountainous region southeast of Rome. The straightforward menu and reasonable prices make it a lunchtime favorite for politicians, priests, and both students and professors from the nearby Gregorian papal university. Specialties include *tonnarelli Abruzzi* (square-cut pasta with mushrooms, peas, and ham) and *abbacchio* (roast lamb). *Via del Vaccaro 1, tel. 06/679–3897. Lunch reservations advised. V. Closed Sat and Aug.*

Armando. One of the best of the many trattorias in this neighborhood in the shadow of the Vatican, Armando's is a family-run favorite of regulars and tourists-in-the-know. The menu features Roman cooking, such as *fettuccine al ragù* (pasta with meat sauce) and *petto alla fornara* (roast veal breast) with potatoes. *Via degli Ombrellari 41 (at Borgo Vittorio), tel. 06/686–1602. Dinner reservations advised. AE, DC, MC, V. Closed Wed.*

Baffetto. Rome's best-known inexpensive pizza restaurant is plainly decorated and *very* popular; you'll probably have to wait in line outside on the *sampietrini*—the cobblestones. The interior is mostly given over to the ovens, the tiny cash desk, and the simple paper-covered tables. *Bruschetta* (toast) and *crostini* (mozzarella toast) are the only variations on the pizza theme. Expect to share a table. *Via del Governo Vecchio 114, tel. 06/686–1617. No reservations. No credit cards. Closed lunch, Sun., and Aug.*

Fratelli Menghi. A neighborhood trattoria that has been in the same family as long as anyone can remember, Fratelli Menghi consists of several modest dining rooms off the busy kitchen, which produces typical Roman fare for faithful customers, many of whom work nearby. There's usually a thick, hearty soup such as minestrone, *pasta e ceci* (with chick peas), and other Roman standbys including *involtini* (meat roulades). *Via Flaminia 57, tel. 06/320–0803. No reservations. No credit cards. Closed Sun.*

Hostaria Farnese. This is a tiny trattoria between Campo dei Fiori and Piazza Farnese, in the heart of Old Rome. Papa serves, Mamma cooks, and depending on what they've picked up at the Campo dei Fiori market, you may find rigatoni with tuna and basil, spaghetti with vegetable sauce, *spezzatino* (stew), and other homey specialties. *Via dei Baullari 109, tel. 06/654–1595. Reservations advised. AE, V. Closed Thurs.*

Pollarola. Located near Piazza Navona and Campo dei Fiori, this typical Roman trattoria has flowers (artificial) on the tables and an antique Roman column embedded in the rear wall, evidence of its historic site. You can eat outdoors in fair weather. Try a pasta specialty such as *fettuccine al gorgonzola* (noodles with creamy gorgonzola sauce) and a mixed plate from the temptingly fresh array of antipasti. The house wine, white or red, is good. *Piazza della Pollarola 24 (Campo dei Fiori), tel. 06/6880–1654. Reservations advised for groups. AE, V. Closed Sun.*

Lodging

The list below covers mostly those hotels that are within walking distance of at least some sights and that are handy to public transportation. Those in the Moderate and Inexpensive categories do not have restaurants but serve Continental breakfast. Rooms facing the street get traffic noise throughout the night, and few hotels in the lower categories have double glazing. Ask for a quiet room, or bring earplugs.

We strongly recommend that you always make reservations in advance, even if only a few days in advance, by phone or fax. Always inquire about special low rates, often available in both winter and summer and when occupancy is low. Should you find yourself in the city without reservations, however, contact one of the following EPT offices: at Leonardo da Vinci Airport (tel. 06/650–10255); Termini train station (tel. 06/487–1270); or the main information office at Via Parigi 5 (tel. 06/488–3748), which is near Piazza della Repubblica.

For details and price-category definitions, *see* Lodging in Staying in Italy, *above*.

Very Expensive **Cavalieri Hilton.** Though it is outside the main part of Rome and a taxi or courtesy shuttle-bus ride to wherever you are going, this is a large, elegant hotel set in its own park with two excellent restaurants. *Via Cadlolo 101, 00136, tel. 06/35091, fax, 06/315–12241. 378 rooms with bath. Facilities: 2 restaurants, pool, terrace. AE, DC, MC, V.*

★ **Hassler-Villa Medici.** Guests can expect a cordial atmosphere and magnificent service at this hotel, just at the top of the Spanish Steps. The public rooms are memorable, especially the first-floor bar (a chic city rendezvous), and the glass-roof lounge, with gold marble walls and hand-painted tile floor. The elegant bedrooms are decorated in a variety of classic styles; some feature frescoed walls. *Piazza Trinità dei Monti 6, 00187, tel. 06/678–2651, fax 06/678–9991. 100 rooms with bath. Facilities: garage, bar, garden restaurant, roof restaurant. AE, MC, V.*

Lord Byron. The most elegant hotel in Rome is the Lord Byron. Located in the diplomatic residential section of Rome away from its bustling center, the small villa has neat, fresh, and cheerful bedrooms. Renovations in 1991 included enlarging rooms and adding suites on top floors. The staff offers the best service of any Rome hotel, and its dining room has extremely creative Italian cooking. *Via*

Giuseppe De Notaris 5, 00197, tel. 06/322–0404, fax 06/322–0405. 28 rooms and 9 suites with bath. Facilities: bar, restaurant, garden. AE, DC, MC, V.

Majestic. In the 19th-century tradition of grand hotels, this prestigious establishment on Via Veneto has been entirely renovated and refurbished in turn-of-the-century style but with up-to-date comforts, including air-conditioning, CNN, and personal safes. Spacious rooms are sumptuously decorated with opulent flower prints, regal stripes, and extravagant drapes, and boast white Carrara marble bathrooms. *Via Veneto 50, 00187, tel. 06/48641, fax 06/488–0984. 105 rooms with bath. Facilities: restaurant, bar with terrace, garage. AE, DC, MC, V.*

Expensive **Farnese.** Located near both the Lepanto Metro station and St. Peter's, this 1906 mansion was renovated in 1991 in faithful Art Deco style. Sitting rooms on the main floor and high-ceilinged bedrooms are soberly elegant, with boiseries and rich fabrics. Bathrooms are dazzlingly modern. Guests highly rate service and atmosphere. Rates include a lavish buffet breakfast. *Via Alessandro Farnese 30, 00192, tel. 06/321–2553, fax 06/321–5129. 25 rooms with bath. Facilities: parking, bar, roof garden. AE, DC, MC, V.*

Forum. A centuries-old palace converted into a fine hotel, the Forum is on a quiet street within hailing distance of the Roman Forum and Piazza Venezia. The wood-paneled lobby and street-level bar are warm and welcoming, as are the smallish, pink-and-beige bedrooms. The view of the Colosseum from the roof-top restaurant is superb: Breakfast here—or a nightcap at the roof bar—can be memorable. *Via Tor dei Conti 25, 00184, tel. 06/679–2446, fax 06/678–6479. 76 rooms with bath. Facilities: bar, restaurant. AE, DC, MC, V.*

★ **Victoria.** Oriental rugs, oil paintings, welcoming armchairs, and fresh flowers add charm to the public rooms of this hotel, a favorite of American businesspeople who prize the personalized service and restful atmosphere. Some upper rooms and the roof terrace overlook the Villa Borghese. *Via Campania 41, 00187, tel. 06/473931, fax 06/487–1890. 110 rooms with bath. Facilities: bar, restaurant. AE, DC, MC, V.*

Moderate **Britannia.** A central but quiet location off Via Nazionale is only one ★ of the attractions of this small and special hotel, where guests are coddled with luxury touches such as English-language dailies and local weather reports delivered to their room each morning. The sybaritic bathrooms and well-furnished rooms, especially the clubby tartan-and-wood decor on the second floor, indicate that the management really cares about giving guests superior service and value. *Via Napoli 64, 00184, tel. 06/488–3153, fax 06/488–2343. 32 rooms with bath. Facilities: lounge, bar. AE, DC, MC, V.*

D'Este. Within hailing distance of Santa Maria Maggiore and close to Termini station, the hotel occupies a solidly renovated and roomy 19th-century building. The fresh, pleasing decor evokes turn-of-the-century comfort with brass bedsteads and lamps and walnut furniture. Rooms are quiet, light, and spacious; many can be adapted to suit family groups. The attentive owner-manager makes sure everything works, and he encourages inquiries about special rates, particularly during the slack summer months. *Via Carlo Alberto 4/b, 00185, tel. 06/446–5607, fax 06/446–5601. 37 rooms with bath. Facilities: bar, garden, terrace. AE, DC, MC, V.*

La Residenza. A converted town house near Via Veneto, this hotel offers good value and first-class comfort at reasonable rates. Public areas are spacious and furnished nicely and have a private-home atmosphere. Guest rooms are comfortable and have large closets, TV, fridge bar, and air-conditioning. The color scheme throughout the property is aquamarine and beige. The hotel's clientele is mainly American, and rates include a generous buffet breakfast. *Via Emilia 22, 00187, tel. 06/488–0797, fax 06/485721. 27 rooms with bath. Facilities: bar, roof terrace, parking. No credit cards.*

Inexpensive **Amalia.** Handy to the Vatican and the Cola di Rienzo shopping district, this small, former *pensione* is owned and operated by the Consoli family—Amalia and her brothers. On several floors of a 19th-century building, it has 21 newly renovated rooms with TV sets, direct-dial telephones, pictures of angels on the walls, and gleaming marble bathrooms (hair dryers included). Four more guest rooms will be redone in the future. The Ottaviano stop of Metro line A is a block away. *Via Germanico 66, 00192, tel. 06/397–23354, fax 06/397–23365. 25 rooms, 21 with bath or shower. Facilities: bar, breakfast room. AE, MC, V.*

★ **Margutta.** Centrally located near the Spanish Steps and Piazza del Popolo, this small hotel has an unassuming lobby but bright, attractive bedrooms with wrought-iron bedsteads and modern baths. *Via Laurina 34, 00187, tel. 06/322–3674. 21 rooms with bath. AE, DC, MC, V.*

Romae. Strategically located near Termini station, this midsize hotel has clean, spacious rooms with light-wood furniture and small but bright bathrooms. The cordial, helpful management offers special winter rates and welcomes families. TVs and hair dryers in the rooms plus low rates that include breakfast make this a good value. *Via Palestro 49, 00185, tel. 06/446–3554, fax 06/446–3914. 20 rooms with bath. AE, MC, V.*

The Arts

Pick up a copy of the *Carnet di Roma* at EPT tourist offices; issued monthly, it's free and has an exhaustive listing of scheduled events and shows. The bi-weekly booklet *Un Ospite a Roma*, free from concierges at some hotels, is another source of information, as is *Wanted in Rome*, available at newsstands. If you want to go to the opera, ballet, or to a concert, it's best to ask your concierge to get tickets for you. They are sold at box offices only, just a few days before performances.

Opera The **Teatro dell'Opera** is on Via del Viminale (tel. 06/6759–5725 for information in English; tel. 06/6759–5721 to book tickets in English); its summer season from May through August is famous for spectacular performances but at press time was in search of a venue after having been evicted from the Roman ruins of the Baths of Caracalla. Tickets are sold at the opera box office.

Concerts The main concert hall is the **Accademia di Santa Cecilia** (Via della Conciliazione 4, tel. 06/687–0743). The Santa Cecilia Symphony Orchestra has a summer season of concerts.

Film The only English-language movie theater in Rome is the **Pasquino** (Vicolo del Piede, just off Piazza Santa Maria in Trastevere, tel. 06/580–3622). The program is listed in Rome's daily newspapers.

Nightlife

Rome's "in" nightspots change like the flavor of the month, and many fade into oblivion after a brief moment of glory. The best source for an up-to-date list is the weekly entertainment guide, "Trovaroma," published each Thursday in the Italian daily *La Repubblica*.

Bars Jacket and tie are in order in the elegant **Blue Bar** of the Hostaria dell'Orso (Via dei Soldati 25, tel. 06/686–4250), and in **Le Bar** of Le Grand hotel (Via Vittorio Emanuele Orlando 3, tel. 06/4709). **Jeff Blynn's** (Via Zanardelli 12, tel. 06/686–1990), near Piazza Navona, is an upscale watering hole open from 7 PM to 2 AM, with a happy hour from 7 to 10. **Flann O'Brien** (Via Napoli 29, tel. 06/488–0418) has the look and atmosphere of a good Irish pub but also serves cappuccino.

Informal wine bars are popular with young Romans. Near the Pantheon is **Spiriti** (Via Sant'Eustachio 5, tel. 06/689–2499); both **Enoteca Roffi** (Via della Croce 76/a, tel. 06/679–0896) and **Trimani Wine Bar** (Via Cernaia 37/b, tel. 06/446–9630) offer light meals. **Birreria Marconi** (Via di Santa Prassede 9c, tel. 06/486636), near Santa Maria Maggiore, is a beer-hall pizzeria. Near the Pantheon, a hub of after-dark activity is **Antico Caffè della Pace** (Via della Pace 3, tel. 06/686–1216). Brazilian music is big in Rome; Trastevere especially draws carioca clubs. **Clarabella** (Piazza San Cosimato 39, tel. 0337/801772) has live music and is open from 10 PM to 4 AM. **Mambo** (Via dei Fienaroli 30/a, tel. 06/589–7196) lives up to its name with lively Latin music and dancing.

Discos and Nightclubs There's deafening disco music for an under-30s crowd at the **Frankie Go** (entrance at Via Luciani 52, tel. 06/322–1251). Special events such as beauty pageants and theme parties are a feature, and there's a restaurant on the premises. **Gilda Swing** (Via Mario dei Fiori 97, tel. 06/678–4838) is a combination supper club–disco–piano bar, often featuring theme parties and special events. **Spago** (Via di Monte Testaccio, tel. 06/574–4999) has a trendier atmosphere, with late-night dining, piano bar and dancing to disco music, funk, and soul; it's not easy to find, so take a taxi.

Singles Scene Locals and foreigners of all ages gather at Rome's cafés in **Piazza della Rotonda** in front of the Pantheon, at **Piazza Navona,** and **Piazza Santa Maria in Trastevere.** The cafés on **Via Veneto** and the bars of the big hotels draw tourists mainly and are good places to meet other travelers in the over-30 age group. In fair weather, under-30s will find crowds of contemporaries on the **Spanish Steps,** where it's easy to strike up a conversation.

Florence

Arriving and Departing

By Plane The nearest, medium-size airport is the Galileo Galilei Airport at Pisa (tel. 050/500707), connected with Florence by train direct from the airport to the Santa Maria Novella Station. Service is hourly throughout the day and takes about 60 minutes. When departing, you can buy train tickets for the airport and check in for all flights leaving from Pisa-Galilei Airport at the Florence Air Terminal at Track 5 of Santa Maria Novella train station (flight information tel. 055/216703). Some domestic and European flights use Florence's Vespucci Airport at Peretola (tel. 055/373498), connected by SITA bus to the downtown area. Passengers flying Alitalia to Rome's Leonardo da Vinci airport can take the twice-daily Airport Train from Rome directly to Florence (reserve rail connection when purchasing plane ticket). The trip takes about three hours.

By Train The main train station is Santa Maria Novella Station, abbreviated SMN on signs. There is an Azienda Transporti Autolinee Fiorentine (ATAF) city bus information booth across the street from the exit on the left side of the station (and also at Piazza del Duomo 57/r). Inside the station is an Informazioni Turistiche Alberghiere (ITA) hotel association booth, where you can get hotel information and bookings. The booking fee is from 3,000 to 10,000 lire, depending on the category.

By Bus The SITA bus terminal is on Via Santa Caterina da Siena, near Santa Maria Novella train station. The CAP bus terminal is at Via Nazionale 13, also near the station.

By Car The north–south access route to Florence is the Autostrada del Sole (A1) from Milan or Rome. The Florence–Mare autostrada (A11) links Florence with the Tyrrhenian coast, Pisa, and the A12 coastal autostrada.

Getting Around

On Foot You can see most of Florence's major sights on foot, as they are packed into a relatively small area in the city center. It's best not to plan to use a car in Florence; most of the center is off-limits and ATAF buses will take you where you want to go. Wear comfortable shoes and wander to your heart's content. It is easy to find your way around in Florence. There are so many landmarks that you cannot get lost for long. The system of street addresses is unusual, with commercial addresses (those with an "r" in them, meaning *rosso*, or red) and residential addresses numbered separately (32/r might be next to or a block away from plain 32).

By Bus ATAF city buses run from about 5:15 AM to 1 AM. Buy tickets before you board the bus; they are on sale singly or in books of eight at many tobacco shops and newsstands. The cost is 1,200 lire for a ticket good for 60 minutes on all lines, 1,500 lire for 120 minutes, and 9,000 lire for a book of eight 60-minute tickets, called a *multiplo*. An all-day ticket (*turistico*) costs 5,000 lire.

By Taxi Taxis wait at stands. Use only authorized cabs, which are white with a yellow stripe or rectangle on the door. The meter starts at 3,200 lire. To call a taxi, tel. 055/4798 or 055/4390.

By Bicycle You can rent a bicycle at **Alinari** (Via Guelfa 85/r, tel. 055/280500), which has several locations in Florence; **Motorent** (Via San Zanobi 9/r, tel. 055/490113); and at city concessions in several locations, including Piazza della Stazione, Piazza Pitti, and Fortezza da Basso.

By Moped For a moped, go to **Alinari** or **Motorent** (*see* By Bicycle, *above*), or to **Ciao e Basta** (Lungarno Pecori Girardi 1, tel. 055/234–2726).

Important Addresses and Numbers

Tourist Information The municipal tourist office is at Via Cavour 1/r (tel. 055/276–0382; open 8:30–7). Another municipal information office is next to the train station. The **Azienda Promozione Turistica (APT)** tourist board has its headquarters and an information office at Via Manzoni 16, 50121 (tel. 055/234–6284; open Mon.–Sat. 8:30–1:30). There is another information office near Piazza della Signoria, at Chiasso dei Baroncelli 17/r (tel. 055/230–2124).

Consulates U.S. (Lungarno Vespucci 38, tel. 055/239–8276). U.K. (Lungarno Corsini 2, tel. 055/284133).

Emergencies **Police** (tel. 113). **Ambulance** (tel. 118 or 055/212222). **Doctor:** Call your consulate for recommendations, or call the **Tourist Medical Service** (tel. 055/475411), associated with IAMAT, for English-speaking medical assistance 24 hours a day. **Pharmacies:** There are 24-hour pharmacies at Via Calzaiuoli 7/r (tel. 055/289490); Piazza

San Giovanni 20/r (tel. 055/284013); and at the train station (tel. 055/289435).

English-Language Bookstores You'll find English-language magazines and paperbacks on the newsstands in Piazza della Repubblica. **The Paperback Exchange** (Via Fiesolana 31/r, tel. 055/247–8154), in the Santa Croce area, has new and used paperbacks for sale. **The BM Bookshop** (Borgo Ognissanti 4/r, tel. 055/294575) has a good selection of English-language books.

Travel Agencies **American Express** (Via Guicciardini 49/r, tel. 055/288751). **CIT** (Via Cavour 54/r, tel. 055/294306). **Wagons-Lits** (Via del Giglio 27/r, tel. 055/218851).

Guided Tours

Orientation Tours **American Express** (tel. 055/288751), **CIT** (tel. 055/294306), and **SITA** (through hotels and travel agents) offer three-hour tours in air-conditioned buses. Two tours cover most of the important sights: The morning itinerary gives you a look at the outside of the cathedral, baptistry, and bell tower, takes you to the Accademia to see Michelangelo's *David*, to Piazzale Michelangelo for the view, and perhaps then to the Pitti Palace to visit the Palatine Gallery; the afternoon tour includes Piazza della Signoria, a visit to the Uffizi Gallery and to Santa Croce, and an excursion to Fiesole. The cost is about 45,000 lire for a three-hour tour, including entrance fees, and bookings can be made through travel agents.

Personal Guides **American Express** (tel. 055/288751) can arrange for limousine or minitours and personal guide services. **Europedrive** (Via Bisenzio 35, tel. 055/422–2839) will provide cars with English-speaking drivers.

Special-Interest Tours Inquire at travel agents or at **Agriturist Regionale** (Piazza San Firenze 3, tel. 055/287838) for visits to villa gardens around Florence from April through June, or for visits to farm estates during September and October.

Excursions Operators offer a half-day excursion to Pisa, usually in the afternoon, costing about 38,000 lire, and a full-day excursion to Siena and San Gimignano, costing about 58,000 lire. Pick up a timetable at ATAF information offices near the train station, at SITA (Via Santo Caterina da Siena 17, tel. 055/214721), or at the APT Tourist Office (*see* Tourist Information in Important Addresses and Numbers, *above*).

Both ATAF and tourist information offices may offer a free booklet containing information on interesting excursions in the vicinity of Florence, complete with timetables of local bus and train services.

Exploring Florence

Founded by Julius Caesar, Florence has the familiar grid pattern common to all Roman colonies. Except for the major monuments, which are appropriately imposing, the buildings are low and unpretentious. It is a small, compact city of ocher and gray stone and pale plaster; its narrow streets open unexpectedly into spacious squares populated by strollers and pigeons. At its best, it has a gracious and elegant air, though it can at times be a nightmare of mass tourism. Plan, if you can, to visit Florence in late fall, early spring, or even in winter, to avoid the crowds.

A visit to Florence is a visit to the living museum of the Italian Renaissance. The Renaissance began right here in Florence, and the city bears witness to the proud spirit and unparalleled genius of its artists and artisans. In fact, there is so much to see that it is best to savor a small part rather than attempt to absorb it all in a muddled vision.

For 10,000 lire you can purchase a special museum ticket valid for six months at seven city museums, including Palazzo Vecchio, the Museum of Firenze Com'Era (museum of Florentine history), and the Museum of Santa Maria Novella. Inquire at any city museum.

Numbers in the margin correspond to points of interest on the Firenze (Florence) map.

Piazza del Duomo and Piazza della Signoria

❶ The best place to begin a tour of Florence is **Piazza del Duomo,** where the cathedral, bell tower, and baptistry stand in the rather cramped square. The lofty **cathedral of Santa Maria del Fiore** is one of the longest in the world. Begun by master sculptor and architect Arnolfo di Cambio in 1296, its construction took 140 years to complete. Gothic architecture predominates; the facade was added in the 1870s but is based on Tuscan Gothic models. Inside, the church is cool and austere, a fine example of the architecture of the period. Among the sparse decorations, take a good look at the frescoes of equestrian monuments on the left wall; the one on the right is by Paolo Uccello, the one on the left by Andrea del Castagno. The dome frescoes by Vasari have been hidden by the scaffolding put up some years ago in order to study a plan for restoring the dome itself, Brunelleschi's greatest architectural and technical achievement. It was also the inspiration of such later domes as Michelangelo's dome for St. Peter's in Rome and even the Capitol in Washington. You can climb to the cupola gallery, 463 fatiguing steps up between the two skins of the double dome for a fine view of Florence and the surrounding hills. *Dome entrance is in the left aisle of cathedral. Admission: 5,000 lire. Open Mon.–Sat. 10–5. Cathedral open daily 10–5:30.*

❷ Next to the cathedral is Giotto's 14th-century **bell tower,** richly decorated with colored marble and fine sculptures (the originals are in the Museo dell'Opera del Duomo). The 414-step climb to the top is less strenuous than that to the cupola. *Piazza del Duomo. Admission: 5,000 lire. Open Mar.–Oct., daily 8:30–7; Nov.–Feb., daily 9–4:30.*

❸ In front of the cathedral is the **baptistry** (open Mon.–Sat. 1:30–6, Sun. 9–1), one of the city's oldest and most beloved edifices, where, since the 11th century, Florentines have baptized their children. The most famous of the bapistry's three portals are Ghiberti's east doors (facing the Duomo), dubbed the "gates of Paradise" by Michelangelo; a gleaming copy now replaces the originals, which have been **❹** removed to the **Museo dell'Opera del Duomo** (Cathedral Museum). The museum contains some superb sculptures by Donatello and Luca della Robbia—especially their *cantorie,* or choir decorations—as well as an unfinished *Pietà* by Michelangelo, which was intended for his own tomb. *Piazza del Duomo 9, tel. 055/230–2885. Admission: 5,000 lire. Open Mar.–Oct., Mon.–Sat. 9–7:30; Nov.–Feb., Mon.–Sat. 9–5:30.*

❺ Stroll down fashionable Via Calzaiuoli to the church of **Orsanmichele,** for centuries an odd combination of first-floor church and second-floor wheat granary. The statues in the niches on the exterior (many of which are now copies) constitute an anthology of the work of eminent Renaissance sculptors, including Donatello, Ghiberti, and Verrocchio, while the tabernacle inside is an extraordinary piece by Andrea Orcagna. Some of the original statues can be seen in the Bargello or Palazzo della Signoria.

Continuing another two blocks along Via Calzaiuoli you'll come upon **Piazza della Signoria,** the heart of Florence, and the city's largest square. During the long and controversial process of replacing the paving stones over the past few years, well-preserved remnants of Roman and medieval Florence came to light and were thoroughly examined and photographed before being buried again and covered with the new paving. In the center of the square a slab marks the spot where in 1497 Savonarola—the Ayatollah Khomeini of the Middle Ages—induced the Florentines to burn their pictures, books, musical instruments, and other worldly objects—and where a year later he was hanged and then burned at the stake as a heretic. The square, the **Neptune Fountain** by Ammanati, and the surrounding cafés are popular gathering places for Florentines and for tourists who come to admire the massive **Palazzo della Signoria** (better
❻ known as the **Palazzo Vecchio**), the copy of Michelangelo's *David* on its steps, and the frescoes and artworks in its impressive salons. *Piazza della Signoria, tel. 055/276–8465. Admission: 8,000 lire; Sun. free. Open weekdays 9–7, Sun. 8–1.*

Time Out Stop in at **Rivoire,** a Florentine institution, for some of its delectable ice cream and/or chocolate goodies. *Piazza della Signoria 5/r.*

If you'd like to do a little shopping, make a brief detour off Piazza
❼ della Signoria to the **Loggia del Mercato Nuovo** on Via Calimala. It's crammed with souvenirs and straw and leather goods at reasonable prices; bargaining is acceptable here. *Open Mon.–Sat. 8–7 (closed Mon. AM).*

❽ If time is limited, this is your chance to visit the **Uffizi Gallery,** which houses Italy's most important collection of paintings. (Try to see it at a leisurely pace, though—it's too good to rush through!) The Uffizi Palace was built to house the administrative offices of the Medicis, onetime rulers of the city. Later their fabulous art collection was arranged in the Uffizi Gallery on the top floor, which was opened to the public in the 17th century—making this the world's first public gallery of modern times. The emphasis is on Italian art of the Gothic and Renaissance periods. Make sure you see the works by Giotto, and look for the Botticellis in Rooms X–XIV, Michelangelo's *Holy Family* in Room XXV, and the works by Raphael next door. In addition to its art treasures, the gallery offers a magnificent close-up view of Palazzo Vecchio's tower from the little coffee bar at the end of the corridor. Authorities have done wonders in repairing the 1993 bomb damage, and most of the art works involved should again be on view before 1995. *Loggiato Uffizi 6, tel. 055/23885. Admission: 10,000 lire. Open Tues.–Sat. 9–7, Sun. 9–2.*

Accademia, San Marco, San Lorenzo, Santa Maria Novella
❾ Start at the **Accademia Gallery,** and try to be first in line at opening time so you can get the full impact of Michelangelo's *David* without having to fight your way through the crowds. Skip the works in the exhibition halls leading to the *David;* they are of minor importance and you'll gain a length on the tour groups. Michelangelo's statue is a tour de force of artistic conception and technical ability, for he was using a piece of stone that had already been worked on by a lesser sculptor. Take time to see the forceful *Slaves,* also by Michelangelo; the roughhewn, unfinished surfaces contrast dramatically with the highly polished, meticulously carved *David.* Michelangelo left the *Slaves* "unfinished" as a symbolic gesture, to accentuate the figures'

Accademia Gallery, **9**
Baptistry, **3**
Bell Tower, **2**
Boboli Gardens, **20**
Casa Guidi, **21**
Cathedral of Santa
Maria del Fiore
(Duomo), **1**
Church of San
Lorenzo, **13**
Loggia del Mercato
Nuovo, **7**
Medici Chapels, **14**
Museo
Archeologico, **10**
Museo dell'Opera del
Duomo, **4**
Museo di San
Marco, **11**
Museo Nazionale, **16**
Orsanmichele, **5**
Palazzo Medici
Riccardi, **12**
Palazzo Pitti, **19**
Palazzo Vecchio, **6**
Ponte Vecchio, **18**
Santa Croce, **17**
Santa Maria del
Carmine, **23**
Santa Maria
Novella, **15**
Santo Spirito, **22**
Uffizi Gallery, **8**

struggle to escape the bondage of stone. *Via Ricasoli 60, tel. 055/214375. Admission: 10,000 lire. Open Tues.–Sat. 9–2, Sun. 9–2.*

You can make a detour down Via Cesare Battisti to Piazza Santissima Annunziata to see the arcade of the **Ospedale degli Innocenti** (Hospital of the Innocents) by Brunelleschi, with charm-ing roundels by Andrea della Robbia, and the **Museo Archeologico** (Archaeological Museum) on Via della Colonna, under the arch. The latter has some fine Etruscan and Roman antiquities, and a pretty garden. *Via della Colonna 36, tel. 055/247–8641. Admission: 6,000 lire. Open Tues.–Sat. 9–2, Sun. 9–1.*

⑪ Retrace your steps to Piazza San Marco and the **Museo di San Marco,** housed in a 15th-century Dominican monastery. The unfortunate Savonarola meditated on the sins of the Florentines here, and Fra Angelico decorated many of the austere cells and corridors with his brilliantly colored frescoes of religious subjects. (Look for his mas-terpiece, *The Annunciation.*) Together with many of his paintings arranged on the ground floor, just off the little cloister, they form an interesting collection. *Piazza San Marco 1, tel. 055/238–8608. Admission: 6,000 lire. Open Tues.–Sat. 9–2, Sun. 9–2.*

⑫ Lined with shops, Via Cavour leads to **Palazzo Medici Riccardi,** a massive Renaissance mansion (*see* Off the Beaten Track, *below*).
⑬ Turn right here to the elegant **Church of San Lorenzo,** with its Old Sacristy designed by Brunelleschi, and two pulpits by Donatello. Rounding the church, you'll find yourself in the midst of the sprawl-ing **San Lorenzo Market,** dealing in everything and anything, includ-ing some interesting leather items. *Piazza San Lorenzo, Via dell'Ariento. Open Tues.–Sat. 8–7.*

Time Out On Via Sant'Antonino near the big covered food market, **Palla d'Oro** is a favorite with market workers for a quick sandwich or plate of pasta, which they usually eat standing at the counter. You can sit at the tables in the back for an extra charge. It's impossibly crowded between 1 and 1:30. *Via Sant'Antonino 45/r. Closed Sun.*

⑭ Enter the **Medici Chapels** from Piazza Madonna degli Aldobrandini, behind San Lorenzo. These remarkable chapels contain the tombs of practically every member of the Medici family, and there were a lot of them, for they guided Florence's destiny from the 15th century to 1737. Cosimo I, a Medici whose acumen made him the richest man in Europe, is buried in the crypt of the Chapel of the Princes, and Donatello's tomb is next to that of his patron. The chapel upstairs is decorated in an eye-dazzling array of colored marble. In Michelangelo's New Sacristy, his tombs of Giuliano and Lorenzo de' Medici bear the justly famed statues of *Dawn* and *Dusk*, and *Night* and *Day*. *Piazza Madonna degli Aldobrandini, tel. 055/238–8602. Admission: 9,000 lire. Open Tues.–Sat. 9–2, Sun. 9–2.*

Time Out **Baldini** is an unpretentious trattoria, low on atmosphere but offer-ing a good range of antipasti and delicious *fazzoletti*, pasta filled with ricotta and spinach. *Via Panzani 57. Closed Wed.*

⑮ You can take either Via Panzani or Via del Melarancio to the large square next to the massive church of **Santa Maria Novella,** a hand-some building in the Tuscan version of Gothic style. See it from the other end of Piazza Santa Maria Novella for the best view of its fa-cade. Inside are some famous paintings, especially Masaccio's *Trini-ty*, a Giotto crucifix in the sacristy, and Ghirlandaio's frescoes in the apse. *Piazza Santa Maria Novella, tel. 055/210113. Open daily 7–11:30 and 3:30–6.*

Next door to the church is the entrance to the **Museum of Santa Maria Novella,** worth a visit for its serene atmosphere and the restored Paolo Uccello frescoes in the Green Cloister. *Piazza Santa Maria Novella 19, tel. 055/282187. Admission: 4,000 lire. Open Mon.–Thurs., Sat. 9–2, Sun. 8–1.*

Only a few blocks behind Piazza della Signoria is the **Bargello,** a fortresslike palace that served as residence of Florence's chief magistrate in medieval times, and later as a prison. Don't be put off by its grim look, for it now houses Florence's **Museo Nazionale** (National Museum), a treasure house of Italian Renaissance sculpture. In a historically and visually interesting setting, it displays masterpieces by Donatello, Verrocchio, Michelangelo, and many other major sculptors. This museum is on a par with the Uffizi, so don't shortchange yourself on time. *Via del Proconsolo 4, tel. 055/238–8606. Admission: 6,000 lire. Open Tues.–Sat. 9–2, Sun. 9–1.*

Time Out From Piazza San Firenze follow Via degli Anguillara or Borgo dei Greci toward Piazza Santa Croce. Don't miss the chance to taste what's held by many to be the best ice cream in Florence, at **Vivoli,** on a little side street, the second left off Via degli Anguillara as you head toward Santa Croce. *Via Isole delle Stinche 7/r. Closed Mon.*

The mighty church of **Santa Croce** was begun in 1294; inside, Giotto's frescoes brighten two chapels and monumental tombs of Michelangelo, Galileo, Machiavelli, and other Renaissance luminaries line the walls. In the adjacent museum, you can see what remains of a Giotto crucifix, irreparably damaged by a flood in 1966, when water rose to 16 feet in parts of the church. The **Pazzi Chapel** in the cloister is an architectural gem by Brunelleschi. *Piazza Santa Croce, tel. 055/244619. Church open Apr.–Sept., Mon.–Sat. 8–6:30, Sun. 8–12:30 and 3–6:30; Oct.–Mar., Mon.–Sat. 8–12:30 and 3–6:30, Sun. 3–6. Opera di Santa Croce (Museum and Pazzi Chapel), tel. 055/244619. Admission: 4,000 lire. Open Mar.–Sept., Thurs.–Tues. 10–12:30 and 2:30–6:30; Oct.–Feb., Thurs.–Tues. 10–12:30 and 3–5.*

The monastery of Santa Croce harbors a leather-working school and showroom, with entrances at Via San Giuseppe 5/r and Piazza Santa Croce 16. The entire Santa Croce area is known for its leather factories and inconspicuous shops selling gold and silver jewelry at prices much lower than those of the elegant jewelers near Ponte Vecchio.

Time Out You have several eating options here. For ice cream, the **bar** on Piazza Santa Croce has a tempting selection. If it's a snack you're after, the **Fiaschetteria** (Via dei Neri 17/r) makes sandwiches to order and has a choice of antipasti and a hot dish or two. And if you're homesick for brownies and chocolate chip cookies, head for **Carlie's American Bakery** (Via delle Brache, aka Via dei Legnaioli, 12/r, a narrow street off Via dei Neri between Via dei Benci and Via dei Rustici; open 10–1:30 and 3:30–7:30)

Now head for the **Ponte Vecchio,** Florence's oldest bridge. It seems to be just another street lined with goldsmiths' shops until you get to the middle and catch a glimpse of the Arno flowing below. Spared during World War II by the retreating Germans (who blew up every other bridge in the city), it also survived the 1966 flood. It leads into the **Oltrarno district,** which has its own charm and still preserves much of the atmosphere of oldtime Florence, full of fascinating craft workshops.

⑲ But for the moment you should head straight down Via Guicciardini to **Palazzo Pitti,** a 15th-century extravaganza that the Medicis acquired from the Pitti family shortly after the latter had gone deeply into debt to build the central portion. The Medicis enlarged the building, extending its facade on the immense piazza. Solid and severe, it looks like a Roman aqueduct turned into a palace. The palace houses several museums: One displays the fabulous Medici collection of objects in silver and gold; another is the **Gallery of Modern Art.** The most famous museum, though, is the **Palatine Gallery,** with an extraordinary collection of paintings, many hung frame-to-frame in a clear case of artistic overkill. Some are high up in dark corners, so try to go on a bright day. *Piazza dei Pitti, tel. 055/210323. Gallery of Modern Art. Admission: 4,000 lire. Palatine Gallery. Admission: 8,000 lire. Monumental Royal Apartments. Admission 8,000 lire. Silver Museum. Admission: 6,000 lire (includes admission to the Historical Costume Gallery and to the Porcelain Museum at the top of the Boboli Gardens). All open Tues.–Sat. 9–2, Sun. 9–2.*

⑳ Take time for a refreshing stroll in the **Boboli Gardens** behind Palazzo Pitti, a typical Italian garden laid out in 1550 for Cosimo de' Medici's wife, Eleanor of Toledo. *Piazza dei Pitti, tel. 055/213440. Admission: 5,000 lire. Open Tues.–Sun. Apr., May, and Sept., 9–6:30; June–Aug., 9–7:30; Oct. and Mar.–Apr., 9–5:30; Nov.–Feb., 9–4:30.*

㉑ In the far corner of Piazza dei Pitti, poets Elizabeth Barrett and Robert Browning lived in the **Casa Guidi,** facing the smaller Piazza San Felice. *Piazza San Felice 8, tel. 055/284393. Admission free. Open by appointment.*

Time Out From Piazza San Felice it's not far to the **Caffè Notte,** a wine and sandwich shop featuring a different salad every day (corner of Via delle Caldaie and Via della Chiesa, closed Mon.). For more substantial sustenance, go to the **Cantinone del Gallo Nero,** an atmospheric wine cellar where Chianti is king and locals lunch on soups, pastas, and salads (Via Santo Spirito 6/r. Closed Mon.). A block from the church of Santo Spirito, **Casalinga** (Via dei Michelozzi 9, closed weekends) is a large, popular trattoria, fine for a hearty, inexpensive lunch.

㉒ The church of **Santo Spirito** is important as one of Brunelleschi's finest architectural creations, and it contains some superb paintings, including a Filippino Lippi *Madonna.* Santo Spirito is the hub of a colorful neighborhood of artisans and intellectuals. An **outdoor market** enlivens the square every morning except Sunday; in the afternoon, pigeons, pet owners, and pensioners take over. An arts and crafts fair is held in the square on the second Sunday of the month. The area is definitely on an upward trend, with new cafés, restaurants, and upscale shops opening every day.

㉓ Walk down Via Sant'Agostino and Via Santa Monaca to the church of **Santa Maria del Carmine,** of no architectural interest but of immense significance in the history of Renaissance art. It contains the celebrated frescoes painted by Masaccio in the **Brancacci Chapel,** unveiled not long ago after a lengthy and meticulous restoration. The chapel was a classroom for such artistic giants as Botticelli, Leonardo da Vinci, Michelangelo, and Raphael, since they all came to study Masaccio's realistic use of light and perspective and his creation of space and depth. *Piazza del Carmine, tel. 055/212331. Admission: 5,000 lire. Open Mon. and Wed.–Sat. 10–4:30, Sun. 1–4:30.*

Time Out The small trattoria on the square has a friendly atmosphere and is a delightful spot where you can eat outdoors and enjoy the view. *Piazza del Carmine 18/r. Closed Sat. evening and Sun.*

Off the Beaten Track

Few tourists get to see one of Florence's most precious works of art, Benozzo Gozzoli's glorious frescoes in the tiny chapel on the second floor of **Palazzo Medici Riccardi,** representing the Journey of the Magi as a spectacular cavalcade with Lorenzo the Magnificent on a charger. *Via Cavour 1, tel. 055/276–0340. Admission: 6,000 lire. Open Mon.–Tues., Thurs.–Sat. 9–1 and 3–6, Sun. 9–1.*

The **English Cemetery** is on a cypress-studded knoll in the middle of heavily trafficked Piazza Donatello, not far from the botanical garden. Here you can walk with the shades of Elizabeth Barrett Browning, Algernon Swinburne, and other poets. You will need to ask the custodian to let you into the cemetery. It is kept locked. *Piazza Donatello. Ring bell at entrance for admission.*

See some of Florence's smaller museums. **The Davanzati Museum** is a dusky and imposing medieval palazzo furnished with antiques from the 14th century on. *Via Porta Rossa 13, tel. 055/238–8610. Admission: 4,000 lire. Open Tues.–Sun. 9–2.*

Casa Buonarroti, which was Michelangelo's home from 1508 until his death in 1564 and subsequently belonged to his heirs, highlights the artist's early works and drawings in evocative surroundings. *Via Ghibellina 70, tel. 055/241752. Admission: 8,000 lire. Open Wed.–Mon. 9:30–1:30.*

The **Stibbert Museum,** a Victorian mansion full of objets d'art and armor, was donated to Florence by 19th-century collector Frederick Stibbert. This is the city's most eclectic and bizarre museum. *Via Stibbert 26, tel. 055/486049. Admission: 5,000 lire. Open Mon.–Wed., Fri., and Sat. 9–2, Sun. 9–12:30.*

Take the No. 12 or 13 bus from the train station or cathedral up to Piazzale Michelangelo, then walk along Viale dei Colli and climb to **San Miniato al Monte,** a charming green-and-white marble Romanesque church full of artistic riches.

Visit the **synagogue** on Via Farini and the **Jewish Museum** next door, which contains antique scrolls and ritual objects. *Via Farini 4; tel. 055/245252. Call in morning for opening hours.*

Shopping

Florence offers top quality for your money in leather goods, linens and upholstery fabrics, gold and silver jewelry, and cameos. Straw goods, gilded wooden trays and frames, hand-printed paper desk accessories, and ceramic objects make good inexpensive gifts. Many shops offer fine old prints.

Shopping The most fashionable streets in Florence are **Via Tornabuoni** and
Districts **Via della Vigna Nuova.** Goldsmiths and jewelry shops can be found on and around the **Ponte Vecchio** and in the **Santa Croce area,** where there is also a high concentration of leather shops.

Antiques Most of Florence's many antiques dealers are located in **Borgo San Jacopo** and **Borgo Ognissanti,** but you'll find plenty of small shops throughout the center of town.

Department **Principe,** in Piazza Strozzi, is a quality apparel store incorporating
Stores several designer boutiques. At the other end of the price range, **UPIM,** in Piazza della Repubblica and various other locations, has inexpensive goods of all types.

Markets The big food market at **Piazza del Mercato Centrale** is open in the morning (Mon.–Sat.) and is worth a visit. The **San Lorenzo market** on Piazza San Lorenzo and Via dell'Ariento is a fine place to browse for buys in leather goods and souvenirs (open Tues. and Sat. 8–7; also Sun. in summer). The **Mercato Nuovo,** Via Calimala, which is sometimes called the **Mercato del Porcellino** because of the famous bronze statue of a boar at one side, is packed with stalls selling souvenirs and straw goods (open Tues.–Sat. 8–7; closed Sun. and Mon. mornings in winter). There's a colorful neighborhood market at **Sant'Ambrogio,** Piazza Ghiberti (open Mon.–Sat. mornings), and a permanent flea market at **Piazza Ciompi** (open Mon.–Sat. 9–1 and 4–7, Sun. 9–1 in summer). A huge weekly market takes over Viale Lincoln in the Cascine park every Tuesday morning.

Dining

Mealtimes in Florence are 12:30 to 2 and 7:30 to 9 or later. Many Moderate and Inexpensive places are small, and you may have to share a table. Reservations are always advisable; to find a table at inexpensive places, get there early.

For details and price-category definitions, *see* Dining in Staying in Italy, *above.*

Very **Enoteca Pinchiorri.** In the beautiful Renaissance palace and its
Expensive charming garden courtyard that was home to Giovanni da Verrazza-
★ no (a 15th-century Florentine navigator), husband-and-wife team Giorgio Pinchiorri and Annie Feolde have created an exceptional restaurant that ranks as one of Italy's best. Guests can enjoy Annie's rediscoveries of traditional Tuscan dishes, or her own brand of imaginatively creative nouvelle cuisine, while Giorgio oversees the extraordinary wine cellar. At upward of 150,000 lire per person, meals here are for real connoisseurs; a fixed menu costs about 95,000 lire. *Via Ghibellina 87, tel. 055/242777. Reservations well in advance are advised at all times. AE, MC, V. Closed Sun., Mon. lunch, Aug. and Dec. 24–28.*

Expensive **Il Verrocchio.** In an elegant 18th-century villa, now a deluxe hotel, this restaurant is about 20 minutes from downtown Florence by car or taxi and well worth the ride. The indoor dining room has a huge fireplace, columns, and a high vaulted ceiling. Outdoors you dine on a terrace overlooking the Arno. The menu changes with the seasons but can be described as creative Tuscan, with such offerings as *agnello con salsa di albicocche* (lamb with apricot sauce) and delicate, fresh pasta dishes. *Villa La Massa, Via La Massa 6, Candeli, tel. 055/630051. Reservations advised. Jacket and tie required. AE, DC, MC, V. Closed Mon. and Tues. lunch Nov.–Mar.*

★ **Terrazza Brunelleschi.** The rooftop restaurant of the hotel Baglioni has the best view in town. The dining room, decorated in pale blue and creamy tones, has big picture windows; the summer-dining terrace is charming, with tables under arbors and turrets for guests to climb to get an even better view. The menu offers such traditional Tuscan dishes as *minestra di fagioli* (bean soup) and other more innovative choices, such as a pâté of peppers and tomato. *Hotel Baglioni, Piazza Unità Italiana 6, tel. 055/215642. Reservations advised, especially in summer. AE, DC, MC, V.*

Moderate **Alle Murate.** Between the Duomo and Santa Croce, this sophisticated but informal restaurant features creative versions of classic Tuscan food, along with specialties of other regions, such as the Calabrian *cavatelli con broccoli* (pasta with broccoli and cheese). In a smaller room called the *vineria*, the menu and service are simpler and prices lower. *Via Ghibellina 52/r, tel. 055/240618. Reservations advised. No credit cards. No lunch. Closed Mon.*

★ **Angiolino.** This bustling little trattoria has a real charcoal grill and an old wood-burning stove to keep its customers warm on nippy days. Glowing with authentic atmosphere, Angiolino offers such Tuscan specialties as *ribollita* (minestrone) and juicy *bistecca alla fiorentina* (T-bone steak basted in olive oil and black pepper). The bistecca will push the bill up, as you pay by weight (order one for two). *Via Santo Spirito 36/r, tel. 055/239–8976. Reservations advised in the evening. No credit cards. Closed Sun. dinner, Mon., and last 3 weeks in July.*

Buca Mario. Visitors can expect to share a table at this characteristically unadorned *buca* (downstairs trattoria), whose menu includes such hearty down-to-earth Tuscan food as homemade *pappardelle* (noodles) and *stracotto* (beef stew with beans). It's near Santa Maria Novella. *Piazza Ottaviani 16/r, tel. 055/214179. Reservations advised in evening. AE, DC, MC, V. Closed Thurs. lunch and Wed. and Aug.*

Cavallini. It makes sense that this restaurant, with its outdoor café, is touristy, particularly since it's situated right on Piazza della Signoria. But it is also consistently good, it's open on Sundays, and it's so handy for collapsing in after a hard day at the Uffizi. The cooking is pure Tuscan, with broad pappardelle noodles, bean soup, and grilled meat on the menu. *Via delle Farina 6/r, tel. 055/215818. Reservations advised, especially for outdoor tables. AE, DC, MC, V. Closed Tues eve., Wed., and Aug. 1–22.*

★ **Il Cibreo.** The young chefs of this upscale trattoria near the Sant'Ambrogio market prepare updated versions of traditional Florentine dishes and present them with flair, as in *passato di peperoni gialli* (yellow-pepper soup) and *anatra farcita* (boned duck with a meat, raisin, and pine-nut stuffing). Tables are set outdoors in June and July. It has a café annex across the street and an inexpensive tavern annex around the corner. *Via dei Macci 118/r, tel. 055/234–1100. Reservations advised for dinner. AE, DC, MC, V. Closed Sun. and Mon. July 25–Sept. 5 and Dec. 31–Jan. 7.*

Il Fagioli. This typical Florentine trattoria near Santa Croce has a simple decor and a menu in which such local dishes as *ribollita* (a sort of minestrone) and involtini predominate. The antipasti are always tempting here, but you're expected to have a two-course meal, besides. *Corso Tintori 47/r, tel. 055/244285. Reservations advised. Dress: informal. No credit cards. Closed Sun. (also Sat., in July and Aug.) and Christmas Day.*

La Giostra. A five-minute walk from the back of the cathedral or from Santa Croce, the Giostra has the typically unpretentious and rustic look of a Florentine trattoria, but with a difference: the gourmet touch of the courteous owner-chef. Try his ravioli or veal *agli agrumi* (with an unusual and delicate citrus sauce) or *spianata di carne* (a generous portion of thinly sliced beef redolent of herbs). Like the menu, the wine list offers good value. Service is informal. *Borgo Pinti 10/r, tel. 055/241341. Reservations advised in evening. AE, MC, V. Check locally for new closing day.*

Le Fonticine. This roomy restaurant near Santa Maria Novella has a warm, rustic atmosphere, with paintings and ceramics covering the walls. Owner Silvano Bruci and his staff are cordial, the homemade pasta is exquisite (try the *tortellini* or *tortelli*, with meat or cheese stuffing), and the menu offers a good choice of main courses. *Via Nazionale 79/r, tel. 055/282106. Reservations advised in evening. AE, DC, MC, V. Closed Sun., Mon., and July 25–Aug. 25.*

Mario da Ganino. Highly informal, rustic, and cheerful, this trattoria greets you with a taste of mortadella, and offers homemade pastas and *gnudoni* (ravioli without pasta), plus a heavenly cheesecake for dessert. There are plenty of other taste-tempters on the menu. It's tiny, seating only 35, double that in summer at outdoor tables. *Piazza dei Cimatori 4/r, tel. 055/214125. Reservations advised. AE, DC. Closed Sun. and Aug. 15–25.*

Inexpensive **La Maremmana.** A lavish display of produce at the entrance holds promise of what's in store at this typical Florentine trattoria near Santa Croce. The fixed-price menu includes generous servings of local favorites such as *ribollita* (vegetable soup) and *stracotto* (beef stew). There is an à la carte menu, too, and outdoor tables in the garden. *Via dei Macci 77/r, tel. 055/241226. MC, V. Closed Sun. Reservations advised.*

Za-Za. Near the San Lorenzo market, this is an informal but trendy trattoria with posters of movie stars on the walls and a lively Italian clientele. The food is classic Florentine: ribollita, fagioli served several ways, and good steaks, with everything fresh from the market. *Piazza Mercato Centrale 16/r, tel. 055/215411. Reservations advised. AE, DC, MC, V. Closed Sun. and Aug.*

Lodging

What with mass tourism and trade fairs, rooms are at a premium in Florence for most of the year. Make reservations well in advance. If you arrive without a reservation, the ITA office in the railway station (open 8:20 AM–9 PM) can help you, but there may be a long line. Now that much traffic is banned in the downtown area, many central hotel rooms are quieter. Local traffic and motorcycles can still be bothersome, however, so check the decibel level before you settle in. From November through March ask for special low winter rates.

For details and price-category definitions, *see* Lodging in Staying in Italy, *above*.

Very Expensive ★ **Grand.** A Florentine classic with Old World elegance and the luxurious amenities of the Ciga hotels. Smaller and more intimate than the Excelsior, its sister hotel across the square, the Grand has public areas and most rooms decorated in rich Renaissance style. Some rooms have balconies overlooking the Arno. *Piazza Ognissanti 1, 50123, tel. 055/288781, fax 055/217400. 107 rooms with bath. Facilities: restaurant, winter garden, bar, parking. AE, DC, MC, V.*

Regency. One of the Ottaviani family's small, select hotels, the Regency has the intimate and highly refined atmosphere of a private villa, luxuriously furnished with antiques and decorated with great style. Just outside the historic center of the city, it has a charming garden and the pleasant Le Jardin restaurant. *Piazza Massimo d'Azeglio 3, 50121, tel. 055/245247, fax 055/234–2937. 33 rooms with bath. Facilities: garage. AE, DC, MC, V.*

Villa Cora. Located in a residential area on a hill overlooking the Oltrarno section of Florence and across the Arno to the Duomo and bell tower, the Villa Cora is a converted private villa. Furnishings are exquisite and the atmosphere is quietly elegant. There are gardens in which to stroll, a pool in which to wallow, and a formal but charming restaurant in which to dine. There is a Mercedes shuttle service between the hotel and the center of Florence. *Viale Machiavelli 18, 50125, tel. 055/229–8451, fax 055/229086. 48 rooms with bath. AE, DC, MC, V.*

Expensive **Baglioni.** Spacious, elegant, and very grand, the Baglioni has well-
★ proportioned rooms tastefully decorated in antique Florentine style. The hotel also has a charming roof terrace, and the splendid Terrazza Brunelleschi restaurant (*see* Dining, *above*), which has the best view in all Florence. *Piazza Unità Italiana 6, 50123, tel. 055/23580, fax 055/235–8895. 197 rooms with bath. Facilities: garage. AE, DC, MC, V.*

★ **Brunelleschi.** This unique hotel in the heart of Florence encompasses a Byzantine tower, a medieval church, and an 18th-century palazzo. Sections of ancient stone walls and brick arches set off the tasteful contemporary decor in the public rooms. Bedrooms are decorated with textured, coordinated fabrics in soft colors, and the beige marble bathrooms are luxurious. *Piazza Sant'Elisabetta (Via dei Calzaiuoli), 50122, tel. 055/562068, fax 055/219653. 94 rooms with bath. Facilities: restaurant, bar. AE, DC, MC, V.*

★ **Monna Lisa.** Staying here is like living in an aristocratic palace in the heart of Florence. American visitors in particular are fond of its smallish but homey bedrooms and sumptuously comfortable sitting rooms. Ask for a room on the quiet 17th-century courtyard, especially the one with the delightful balcony. A lavish buffet breakfast is included in the price. Reserve well in advance. *Borgo Pinti 27, 50121, tel. 055/247–9751, fax 055/247–9755. 30 rooms with bath. Facilities: garden, bar, parking. AE, DC, MC, V.*

Moderate **Hermitage.** Comfort and charm are the attributes of this hotel occupying the top two floors of a *palazzo* next to the Ponte Vecchio and the Uffizi. In the inviting living room overlooking the Arno, the bright breakfast room, the flowered roof terrace, and the well-lighted bedrooms, decor and atmosphere are those of a well-kept Florentine home. Double glazing, air conditioning, and attentive maintenance sustain the relaxing ambience. (The hotel is served by an elevator located at the top of a short flight of stairs). *Vicolo Marzio 1 (Piazza del Pesce–Ponte Vecchio), 50122, tel. 055/287216, fax 055/212208. 30 rooms with bath. Facilities: roof terrace. AE, MC, V.*

★ **Loggiato dei Serviti.** You'll find the Loggiato dei Serviti tucked under an arcade in one of the city's quietest and most attractive squares. Vaulted ceilings and tasteful furnishings (some of them antiques) go far to make this hotel a real find for those who want to get the genuine Florentine feel and who will appreciate the 19th-century town house surroundings while enjoying modern creature comforts. There is no restaurant. *Piazza Santissima Annunziata 3, 50122, tel. 055/239–8280, fax 055/289595. 29 rooms with bath. AE, DC, MC, V.*

Morandi alla Crocetta. This charming and distinguished residence near Piazza Santissima Annunziata, was once a monastery, and access is up a flight of stairs. It is furnished in the classic style of a gracious Florentine home, and guests feel like privileged friends of the family. Small and exceptional, it is also a good value and must be booked well in advance. *Via Laura 50, 50121, tel. 055/234–4747, fax 055/248–0954. 9 rooms with bath. AE, DC, MC, V.*

Villa Azalee. In a residential area about five minutes from the train station, this century-old mansion is set in a large garden. It has a private-home atmosphere and comfortable living rooms. Bedrooms are decorated individually and are air-conditioned. *Viale Fratelli*

Rosselli 44, 50123, tel. 055/214242, fax 055/268264. 24 rooms with bath. AE, DC, MC, V.

Inexpensive **Apollo.** A hospitable Italian-Canadian couple owns and manages this conveniently located hotel near the station, offering good value in spacious rooms decorated in Florentine style, with gleaming new bathrooms that, though compact, have such amenities as hair dryers. The staff is helpful and attentive to guests' needs. *Via Faenza 77, 50123, tel. 055/284119, fax 055/210101. 15 rooms with bath. AE, DC, MC, V.*

★ **Bellettini.** Very centrally located, this small hotel occupies two floors of an old but well-kept building near the Church of San Lorenzo, in an area with plenty of inexpensive eating places. Rooms are ample, with Venetian or Tuscan decor, and bathrooms are modern. The management is friendly and helpful. *Via dei Conti 7, 50123, tel. 055/213561, fax 055/283551. 27 rooms, 23 with bath. Facilities: bar, lounge. AE, DC, MC, V.*

Nuova Italia. Near the train station, in a well-kept town house, this hotel is run by a cordial English-speaking family. It's bright with pictures and posters. The clean, ample rooms have a fresh look; many can accommodate extra beds. The low bargain rates include breakfast. *Via Faenza 26, 50123, tel. 055/268430, fax 055/210941. 20 rooms with bath. AE, DC, MC, V.*

The Arts

For a list of events, pick up a "Florence Concierge Information" booklet from your hotel desk, or the monthly information bulletin published by the **Comune Aperto** city information office (Via Cavour 1/r). This information is also available at information offices at the station, at Via Cavour 1/r, and at Chiasso dei Baroncelli.

Music and Most major musical events are staged at the **Teatro Comunale** (Corso
Ballet Italia 16, tel. 055/277–9236). The box office (closed Sun. and Mon.) is open from 9 to 1, and a half-hour before performances. It's best to order your tickets by mail, however, as they're difficult to come by at the last minute. You can also order concert and ballet tickets through **Universalturismo** (Via degli Speziali 7/r, tel. 055/217241). **Amici della Musica** (Friends of Music) puts on a series of concerts at the **Teatro della Pergola** (box office, Via della Pergola 10a/r, tel. 055/247–9651). For program information, contact the Amici della Musica directly at Via Sirtori 49 (tel. 055/608420).

Film English-language films are shown at the **Cinema Astro,** on Piazza San Simone near Santa Croce. There are two shows every evening, Tuesday through Sunday. It closes in July.

Nightlife

Bars Many of the top hotels have piano bars; that of the **Plaza Lucchesi** (Lungarno della Zecca Vecchia 38, tel. 055/264141) is particularly spacious and pleasant. The terrace of the hotel **Baglioni** (*see* Lodging, *above*) has no music but has one of the best views in Florence, candlelit tables, and a wonderful atmosphere. Music is on tape at the **Champagneria** (Via Lambruschini 15/r, tel. 055/490804, closed Sun.), a bistro-type meeting place for a fairly sophisticated mélange of young Florentines and an international crowd. **Caffè Voltaire** (Via della Scala 9/r, tel. 055/218255; closed Mon.) serves Brazilian food and drink and plays Latin music to a lively crowd.

Nightclubs **The River Club** (Lungarno Corsini 8, tel. 055/282465) has winter-garden decor and a large dance floor (closed Mon.). **Meccanò** (in the

Cascine park at Viale degli Olmi 1, tel. 055/331371, closed Mon.) offers a multimedia experience, with videos, art, and music, in a high-tech disco with a late-night restaurant, the Pomodoro d'Acciaio.

Discos **Jackie O** (Via dell'Erta Canina 24a, tel. 055/234–2442) is a glittering Art Deco disco with lots of mirrors and marble and a trendy clientele (closed Wed.). **Space Electronic** (Via Palazzuolo 37, tel. 055/239–3082) is exactly what its name implies: ultramodern and psychedelic (closed Mon., except from Mar. to Sept., when it's open every night). **Yab** (Via Sassetti 5/r, tel. 055/282018) is another futuristic-style disco popular with the young international set. It's closed Sunday and Monday.

Tuscany

Tuscany is a blend of rugged hills, fertile valleys, and long stretches of sandy beach that curve along the west coast of central Italy and fringe the pine-forested coastal plain of the Maremma. The gentle, cypress-studded green hills may seem familiar: Leonardo and Raphael often painted them in the backgrounds of their masterpieces. The cities and towns of Tuscany were the cradle of the Renaissance. Come to Tuscany to enjoy its unchanged and gracious atmosphere of good living, and, above all, its unparalleled artistic treasures, many still in their original settings in tiny old churches and patrician palaces.

Getting Around

By Train The main train network connects Florence with Arezzo and Prato. Another main line runs to Pisa, while a secondary line goes from Prato to the coast via Lucca. Trains also connect Siena with Pisa (via Empoli), a two-hour ride.

By Bus The entire region is crisscrossed by bus lines, good alternatives to trains, especially from Florence to Prato, a 30-minute trip, and from Florence to Siena, which can take from 75 minutes (by express bus) to 2 hours. Use local buses to tour the many pretty hill towns around Siena, such as San Gimignano, and then take a Tra-In or Lazzi bus from Siena to Arezzo, where you can get back onto the main Rome–Florence train line.

By Car The main autostrade run parallel to the train routes. Roads throughout Tuscany are in good condition, though often narrow.

Guided Tours

American Express (Via Guicciardini 49/r, tel. 055/288751) and **SITA** (Via Santa Caterina da Siena 17, tel. 055/214721) operates one-day excursions to Siena and San Gimignano out of Florence. American Express also can arrange for cars, drivers, and guides for special-interest tours in Tuscany. **CIT** (Via Cavour 54/r, tel. 055/294306) has a three-day Carosello bus tour from Rome to Florence, Siena, and San Gimignano, as well as a five-day tour that also takes in Venice.

Tourist Information

Arezzo (Piazza Risorgimento 116, tel. 0575/23952).
Cortona (Via Nazionale 72, tel. 0575/630557).
Lucca (Piazza Guidiccione 2, tel.. 0583/491205).
Pisa (Piazza della Stazione 11, tel. 050/42291; Piazza del Duomo 8, tel. 050/560464).

Toscana (Tuscany)

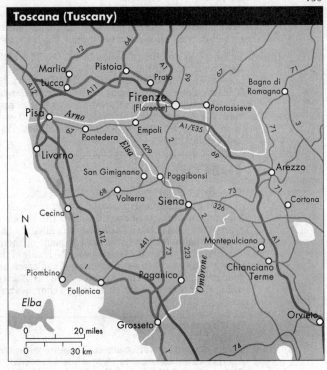

Pistoia (Piazza del Duomo 4, tel. 0573/21622).
Prato (Via Cairoli 48, tel. 0574/24112).
San Gimignano (Piazza del Duomo, tel. 0577/940008).
Siena (Via di Città 43, tel. 0577/42209; Piazza del Campo 56, tel. 0577/280551).

Exploring Tuscany

Starting from Florence, you can go west to Prato and Pistoia, work-aday cities with a core of fine medieval buildings, then to the historic cities of Lucca and Pisa. Lucca makes a good base for an excursion to Pisa, which is only about 30 minutes away by car, bus, or train. Heading south from Florence you can explore the Chianti district by car. You can make Siena your base for excursions by car or local bus to some picturesque hill towns: San Gimignano, Montepulciano, and Pienza.

Prato   Since the Middle Ages, **Prato,** 21 kilometers (13 miles) northwest of Florence, has been Italy's major wool-producing center, and it remains one of the world's largest manufacturers of cloth. Ignore the drab industrial outskirts and devote some time to the fine old buildings in the downtown area, crammed with artworks commissioned by Prato's wealthy merchants during the Renaissance. The **Duomo** (cathedral), erected during the Middle Ages, was decorated with paintings and sculptures by some of the most illustrious figures of Tuscan art, among them Fra Filippo Lippi, who took 12 years to complete the frescoes in the apse (perhaps because in the meantime he was being tried for fraud and was also wooing a nun with whom he then eloped). Look in particular for his passionate portrayals of

Herod's Feast and *Salome's Dance. Piazza del Duomo. Open daily 7–noon and 4–7.*

In the former bishop's palace, now the **Museo dell'Opera del Duomo,** you can see the original reliefs by Donatello for the Pulpit of the Holy Girdle (Mary's belt, supposedly given to Doubting Thomas as evidence of her assumption; the relic is kept in a chapel of the cathedral). *Piazza del Duomo 49, tel. 0574/29339. Admission: 5,000 lire (ticket valid for other Prato museums). Open Mon. and Wed.–Sat. 9:30–12:30 and 3–6:30, Sun. 9:30–12:30.*

Architects and architecture buffs rhapsodize over the church of **Santa Maria delle Carceri,** off Via Cairoli. Built by Giuliano Sangallo in the 1490s, it was a landmark of Renaissance architecture. Next to it, the formidable **castle** built for Frederick II of Hohenstaufen is another impressive sight, the only castle of its type to be seen outside southern Italy. *Piazza Santa Maria delle Carceri. Admission free. Open Tues.–Sat. 9–noon and 3–6, Sun. 9–noon.*

Pistoia **Pistoia** lies about 15 kilometers (9 miles) northwest of Prato. A floricultural capital of Europe, it's surrounded by greenhouses and plant nurseries. Flowers aside, Pistoia's main sights are all in the downtown area, so you can easily see them on the way to Lucca. The Romanesque **Duomo** (cathedral) is flanked by a 13th-century bell tower, while in a side chapel dedicated to San Jacopo (St. James) there's a massive **silver altar** that alone makes the stopover in Pistoia worthwhile. Two hundred years in the making, it's an incredible piece of workmanship, begun in 1287. *Piazza del Duomo. Illumination of altarpiece: 2,000 lire.*

Take a look at the unusual Gothic baptistry opposite the Duomo, then follow Via delle Pappe (to the left behind the Duomo) to admire the superb frieze by Giovanni della Robbia on the Ospedale del Ceppo. Continue on to the church of **Sant'Andrea** (Via Sant'Andrea) to see Pistoia's greatest art treasure, Giovanni Pisano's powerfully sculpted 13th-century **pulpit.** Heading back toward the train station and bus terminal, stop on the way to take in the green-and-white marble church of **San Giovanni Fuorcivitas** (Via Francesco Crispi, off Via Cavour). Highlights here include a *Visitation* by Luca della Robbia, a painting by Taddeo Gaddi, and a holy water font by Giovanni Pisano.

Lucca Your next destination is **Lucca,** Puccini's hometown and a city well-loved by sightseers who appreciate the careful upkeep of its medieval look. Though it hasn't the number of hotels and other tourist trappings that, say, Pisa does, for that very reason it's a pleasant alternative. You can easily make an excursion to Pisa from here—it's only 22 kilometers (14 miles) away. First enjoy the views of the city and countryside from the tree-planted 16th-century ramparts that encircle Lucca. Then explore the city's marvelously elaborate Romanesque churches, fronted with tiers and rows of columns, and looking suspiciously like oversize marble wedding cakes.

From vast **Piazza Napoleone,** a swing around the Old Town will take you past the 11th-century **Duomo** on Piazza San Martino, with its 15th-century tomb of Ilaria del Carretto by Jacopo della Quercia. Don't neglect a ramble through the **Piazza del Mercato,** which preserves the oval form of the Roman amphitheater over which it was built, or the three surrounding streets that are filled with atmosphere: **Via Battisti, Via Fillungo,** and **Via Guinigi.** In addition to the Duomo, Lucca has two other fine churches. **San Frediano** (Piazza San Frediano) is graced with an austere facade ornamented by 13th-century mosaic decoration. Inside, check out the exquisite reliefs by

Jacopo della Quercia in the last chapel on the left. **San Michele in Foro** (Piazza San Michele) is an exceptional example of the Pisan Romanesque style and decorative flair peculiar to Lucca: Note its facade, a marriage of arches and columns crowned by a statue of St. Michael.

The **Villa Reale** is 8 kilometers (5 miles) outside town, at Marlia. Gardening buffs, especially, will appreciate this handsome villa, surrounded by attractive parkland and gardens laid out in the 17th century. *Marlia, tel. 0583/30108. Admission: 5,000 lire. Guided visits on the hour, July–Sept., Tues.–Thurs. and Sun. 10, 11, 4, 5, and 6; Oct. and Mar.–June, Tues.–Sun. 10, 11, 3, 4, 5. Closed Nov.– Feb.*

Pisa   As you drive southwest, the next Tuscan town of note you'll come to is **Pisa,** a dull, overcommercialized place, though even skeptics have to admit that the **Torre Pendente** (Leaning Tower) really is one of the world's more amazing sights. Theories vary as to whether the now-famous list is due to shifting foundations or to an amazing architectural feat by Bonanno Pisano (the first of three architects to work on the tower). A 294-step staircase spirals its way up the tower, but since the tower was permanently closed to visitors in 1990 because the rate of its tilt was increasing too rapidly, you won't be able to get in. If you want a two-foot marble imitation of the Leaning Tower, perhaps even illuminated from within, this is your chance to grab one at a souvenir stand. *Campo dei Miracoli.*

Pisa has two other fine buildings, and, conveniently enough, they're next to the Leaning Tower. The **baptistry** was begun in 1153 but not completed until 1400, the Pisano family doing most of its decoration. Test out the excellent acoustics (occasionally the guard will slam the great doors shut and then sing a few notes—the resulting echo is very impressive, and costly, too, since he'll expect a tip). *Piazza del Duomo, in the Campo dei Miracoli. Open daily 9–sunset.*

Pisa's **Duomo** is elegantly simple, its facade decorated with geometric and animal shapes. The cavernous interior is supported by a series of 68 columns, while the pulpit is a fine example of Giovanni Pisano's work. Be sure to note the suspended lamp that hangs across from the pulpit; known as Galileo's Lamp, it's said to have inspired his theories on pendular motion. *Piazza del Duomo. Open daily 8– 12:45 and 3–sunset.*

Visitors may find it more convenient to take a train back to Florence and get a bus or train there for the 85-minute trip to Siena. For a more leisurely look at the Tuscan countryside, investigate the possibility of taking local trains from Pisa to Siena, changing trains at Empoli and then passing through **Certaldo,** a pretty hill town that's the birthplace of Giovanni Boccaccio, 14th-century author of the *Decameron.*

Siena   **Siena** is one of Italy's best-preserved medieval towns, rich both in works of art and in expensive antique shops. The famous **Palio** is held here, a breakneck, 90-second horse race that takes place twice each year in the Piazza del Campo, on July 2 and August 16. Built on three hills, Siena is not an easy town to explore, for everything you'll want to see is either up or down a steep hill or stairway. But it is worth every ounce of effort. Siena really gives you the chance of seeing and feeling what the Middle Ages must have been like: dark stone palaces that look like fortresses, Gothic church portals, and narrow streets opening out into airy squares.

Siena was a center of learning and art during the Middle Ages, and
almost all the public buildings and churches in the town have enough
artistic or historical merit to be worth visiting. Unlike most
churches, Siena's **Duomo** has a mixture of religious and civic symbols ornamenting both its interior and exterior. The cathedral museum in the unfinished transept contains some fine works of art,
notably a celebrated *Maestà* by Duccio di Buoninsegna. The animated frescoes of papal history in the Piccolomini Library (with an
entrance off the left aisle of the cathedral) are credited to
Pinturicchio and are worth seeking out. *Piazza del Duomo. Cathedral Museum. Admission: 5,000 lire. Open Mar. 14–Sept., daily 9–
7:30; Oct.–Nov. 3, daily 9–6:30; Nov. 4–Dec., daily 9–1:30; Jan. 2–
Mar. 13, daily 9–1. Library. Admission: 2,000 lire. Open mid-
Mar.–Sept., daily 9–7:30; Oct.–Nov. 3, 9–6:30; Nov. 4–Mar. 13,
daily 10–1 and 2:30–5.*

Nearby, the fan-shaped **Piazza del Campo** is Siena's main center of
activity, with 11 streets leading into it. Farsighted planning has
preserved it as a medieval showpiece, containing the 13th-century
Palazzo Pubblico (City Hall) and the **Torre del Mangia** (Bell Tower).
Try to visit both these buildings, the former for Lorenzetti's frescoes on the effects of good and bad government, the latter for the
wonderful view (you'll have to climb 503 steps to reach it, however).
*Piazza del Campo, tel. 0577/292111. Bell Tower. Admission: 4,000
lire. Open Mar. 15–Nov. 15, daily 10–1 hour before sunset; Nov. 15–
Mar. 14, daily 10–1:30. Palazzo Pubblico (Civic Museum). Admission: 5,500 lire. Open Mar. 15–Nov. 15, Mon.–Sat. 9:30–7:30, Sun.
9:30–1:30; Nov.–Mar., daily 9:30–1:30.*

Time Out   There are several *gelaterie* on Piazza del Campo, but if you need
something more substantial, walk east from Piazza del Campo to
Verrocchio (Logge del Papa 2; closed Wed.), a restaurant serving local fare.

From Siena, **San Gimignano** is only about a half hour away by car
and an hour by Tra-In bus (change buses in Poggibonsi). San
Gimignano is perhaps the most delightful of the Tuscan medieval hill
towns. There were once 79 tall towers here, symbols of power for the
wealthy families of the Middle Ages. Thirteen are still standing, giving the town its unique skyline. The bus stops just outside the town
gates, from which you can stroll down the main street to the picturesque Piazza della Cisterna.

Just around the corner is the church of the **Collegiata**. Its walls, and
those of its chapel dedicated to Santa Fina, are decorated with radi-
ant frescoes (have plenty of 100-lire coins at hand for the light machines; to get a closer look at the chapel frescoes, buy a ticket for the
Municipal Museum in Palazzo del Popolo, admission 5,000 lire).
From the steps of the church you can observe the town's countless
crows as they circle the tall towers. In the pretty courtyard on the
right as you descend the church stairs, there's a shop selling Tuscan
and Deruta ceramics, which you'll also find in other shops along the
Via San Giovanni. The excellent San Gimignano wine could be another souvenir of your visit; it's sold in gift cartons from just about
every shop in town.

If you have a car, you can drive northeast of Siena on Route 222,
through hilly Chianti country, or southeast of Siena to the Abbey of
Monte Oliveto Maggiore and the hill towns of Montepulciano and
Pienza, each worth seeing and much less crowded than San

Gimignano. You can also reach Montepulciano and Pienza by bus from Siena, though service is often haphazard.

Arezzo   A local bus takes you from Siena to **Arezzo,** about 48 kilometers (30 miles) east. The route meanders past thickly wooded hills, past vineyards and wheat fields, and past the broad ribbon of the Autostrada del Sole in the fertile Chiana valley, known for its pale beef cattle that provide the classic *bistecca alla fiorentina.* Arezzo is not a particularly beautiful town, though the old, upper town still has a good assortment of medieval and Renaissance buildings. What makes Arezzo worth a visit, however, is its fine array of Tuscan art treasures, including frescoes, stained glass, and ancient Etruscan pottery.

The **Museo Archeologico** (Archaeological Museum) is near the train station, next to what's left of an ancient **Roman amphitheater.** The museum has a rich collection of Etruscan art, artifacts, and pottery, which has been copied by Arezzo's contemporary artisans and is sold in the local ceramic shops. *Via Margaritone 10, tel. 0575/20882. Admission: 6,000 lire. Open Tues.–Sat. 9–2, Sun. 9–1.*

Via Guido Monaco, named after the 11th-century originator of the musical scale, leads to the church of **San Francesco,** in which sit some of the town's main attractions, among them the frescoes by Piero della Francesca. Due for restoration after intensive studies of suitable methods, these frescoes may be at least partially hidden for a few years. Though faded, they still rank among the outstanding examples of Italian painting, and art lovers are looking forward to seeing them in renewed splendor. *Push the button on the black box for light. Via Cavour.*

Now you enter the old part of Arezzo, where the poet Petrarch (1304–74), the artist Vasari (1511–74), and the satirical author Pietro Aretino (1492–1556) all lived. Climb Via Cesalpino uphill to the fine Gothic **cathedral** (Piazza del Duomo), then stroll past **Petrarch's House** to **Piazza Grande,** an attractive, sloping square where an extensive open-air fair of antiques and old bric-a-brac is held the first weekend of every month. The shops around the piazza also specialize in antiques, with prices lower than those you will encounter in Florence. The colonnaded apse and bell tower of the Romanesque church of **Santa Maria della Pieve** grace one end of this pleasant piazza.

Cortona   A full day may be enough for you to get the feel of Arezzo, but you may wish to stay overnight, especially during the antiques fair, or if you want to use the town as a base for an excursion to **Cortona,** about 30 kilometers (18 miles) south. This well preserved, unspoiled medieval hill town is known for its excellent small art gallery and a number of fine antiques shops, as well as for its colony of foreign residents. Cortona has the advantage of being on the main train line, though you will have to take a local bus from the station up into the town, passing the Renaissance church of **Santa Maria del Calcinaio** on the way.

The heart of Cortona is formed by **Piazza della Repubblica** and the adjacent **Piazza Signorelli.** Wander into the courtyard of the picturesque **Palazzo Pretorio,** and, if you want to see a representative collection of Etruscan bronzes, climb its centuries-old stone staircase to the **Museo dell'Accademia Etrusca** (Gallery of Etruscan Art). *Piazza Signorelli 9, tel. 0575/630415. Admission: 5,000 lire. Open Apr.–Sept., Tues.–Sun. 10–1 and 4–7; Oct.–Mar., Tues.–Sun. 9–1 and 3–5.*

So, you're getting away from it all.

Just make sure you can get back.

AT&T Access Numbers
Dial the number of the country you're in to reach AT&T.

Country	Number	Country	Number	Country	Number
*AUSTRIA†††	022-903-011	*GREECE	00-800-1311	NORWAY	800-190-11
*BELGIUM	078-11-0010	*HUNGARY	00◇-800-01111	POLAND†♦²	0◇010-480-0111
BULGARIA	00-1800-0010	*ICELAND	999-001	PORTUGAL†	05017-1-288
CANADA	1-800-575-2222	IRELAND	1-800-550-000	ROMANIA	01-800-4288
CROATIA¹♦	99-38-0011	ISRAEL	177-100-2727	*RUSSIA† (MOSCOW)	155-5042
*CYPRUS	080-90010	*ITALY	172-1011	SLOVAKIA	00-420-00101
CZECH REPUBLIC	00-420-00101	KENYA†	0800-10	S. AFRICA	0-800-99-0123
*DENMARK	8001-0010	*LIECHTENSTEIN	155-00-11	SPAIN•	900-99-00-11
*EGYPT¹ (CAIRO)	510-0200	LITHUANIA♦	8◇196	*SWEDEN	020-795-611
*FINLAND	9800-100-10	LUXEMBOURG	0-800-0111	*SWITZERLAND	155-00-11
FRANCE	19◇-0011	F.Y.R. MACEDONIA	99-800-4288	*TURKEY	00-800-12277
*GAMBIA	00111	*MALTA	0800-890-110	UKRAINE†	8◇100-11
GERMANY	0130-0010	*NETHERLANDS	06-022-9111	UK	0500-89-0011

Countries in bold face permit country-to-country calling in addition to calls to the U.S. **World Connect**℠ prices consist of **USADirect**® rates plus an additional charge based on the country you are calling. Collect calling available to the U.S. only. *Public phones require deposit of coin or phone card. ◇Await second dial tone. †May not be available from every phone. †††Public phones require local coin payment through the call duration. ♦Not available from public phones. • Calling available to most European countries. ¹Dial "02" first, outside Cairo. ²Dial 010-480-0111 from major Warsaw hotels. ©1994 AT&T.

Here's a travel tip that will make it easy to call back to the States. Dial the access number for the country you're visiting and connect right to AT&T. It's the quick way to get English-speaking AT&T operators and can minimize hotel telephone surcharges.

If all the countries you're visiting aren't listed above, call **1 800 241-5555** for a free wallet card with all AT&T access numbers. Easy international calling from AT&T. **TrueWorld Connections.**

AT&T

American Express offers Travelers Cheques built for two.

Cheques *for Two*℠ from American Express are the Travelers Cheques that allow either of you to use them because both of you have signed them. And only one of you needs to be present to purchase them.

Cheques *for Two* are accepted anywhere regular American Express Travelers Cheques are, which is just about everywhere. So stop by your bank, AAA* or any American Express Travel Service Office and ask for Cheques *for Two*.

AMERICAN EXPRESS **Travelers Cheques** ®

The nearby **Museo Diocesano** (Diocesan Museum) houses an impressive number of large and splendid paintings by native son Luca Signorelli, as well as a beautiful *Annunciation* by Fra Angelico, a delightful surprise to find in this small, eclectic town. *Piazza del Duomo 1, tel. 0575/62830. Admission: 5,000 lire. Open Apr.–Sept., Tues.–Sun. 9–1 and 3–6:30; Oct.–Mar., Tues.–Sun. 9–1 and 3–5.*

Dining and Lodging

For details and price-category definitions, *see* Dining and Lodging in Staying in Italy, *above*.

Arezzo
Dining
★

Buca di San Francesco. Travelers and passing celebrities come to this rustic and historic cellar restaurant for the 13th-century cantina atmosphere, but locals love it for the food, especially ribollita and *sformato di verdure* (vegetable pie). *Piazza San Francesco 1, tel. 0575/23271. Dinner reservations advised. AE, DC, MC, V. Closed Mon. dinner, Tues., and July. Moderate.*

Tastevin. Arezzo's purveyor of creative *nuova cucina* serves traditional Tuscan dishes as well, in two attractive rooms in warm Tuscan provincial style and one in more sophisticated Art Deco. At the cozy bar the talented owner plays and sings Sinatra songs in the evening. Specialties are *risotto Tastevin*, with cream of truffles, and *tagliata Tastevin*, sliced beef with olive oil and rosemary. *Via dei Cenci 9, tel. 0575/28304. Dinner reservations advised. AE, DC, MC, V. Closed Mon., (Sun. in summer), and Aug. Moderate.*

Spiedo d'Oro. Cheery red-and-white tablecloths add a colorful touch to this large, reliable trattoria near the Archaeological Museum. The menu offers such Tuscan home-style specialties as *zuppa di pane* (bread soup), *pappardelle oll'ocio* (noodles with duck sauce), and *ossobuco aretina* (sautéed veal shank). *Via Crispi 12, tel. 0575/22873. Reservations accepted. No credit cards. Closed Thurs. and first 2 weeks in July. Inexpensive.*

Lodging

Continental. The circa-1950 Continental has fairly spacious rooms decorated in white and bright yellow, gleaming bathrooms, and the advantage of a central location within walking distance of all major sights. *Piazza Guido Monaco 7, 51200, tel. 0575/20251, fax 0575/340485. 74 rooms with bath. Facilities: restaurant. AE, DC, MC, V. Inexpensive.*

Cortona
Dining
★

Tonino. The place to eat in Cortona, it's known for its delicious *antipastissimo* and for succulent steaks of Chiana valley beef. It's best on weekdays, when it's quieter. Both service and food have a touch of class. The dining rooms, on two floors, have large picture windows overlooking the valley. *Piazza Garibaldi, tel. 0575/630500. Weekends reservations advised. AE, DC, MC, V. Closed Mon. dinner and Tues. Moderate.*

Lucca
Dining
★

La Mora. You'll need a car or a taxi to take you to this charming old way station 10 kilometers (6 miles) outside Lucca, but its authentic local cooking is worth every effort. It is widely considered to be one of the best regional restaurants in Italy. *Via Sesto di Moriano 1748, Ponte a Moriano, tel. 0583/406402. Reservations advised. AE, DC, MC, V. Closed Wed. dinner, Thurs., June 25–July 8, Oct. 10–30. Moderate–Expensive.*

★ **Buca di Sant'Antonio.** A Lucca favorite, located near the church of San Michele, Buca di Sant'Antonio was around more than a century ago, and it still retains something of its rustic look. It specializes in traditional local dishes, some unfamiliar but well worth trying, among them *ravioli di ricotta alle zucchine* (cheese ravioli with zucchini) and kid or lamb roasted with herbs. *Via della Cervia 3, tel.*

*0583/55881. Dinner reservations advised. AE, DC, MC, V. Closed
Sun. dinner, Mon., and July 9–29. Moderate.*

Il Giglio. Off vast Piazza Napoleone, Il Giglio has a quiet, turn-of-
the-century charm and a dignified atmosphere. In the summer the
tables outdoors have a less formal air. The menu is classic: *crostini*
(savory Tuscan chicken liver, anchovy and caper paste on small
pieces of toast), *stracotto* (braised beef with mushrooms), and seafood, as well. *Piazza del Giglio 3, tel. 0583/494058. Dinner reservations advised. AE, DC, MC, V. Closed Tues. dinner and Wed.
Moderate.*

Lodging **Villa La Principessa.** This pretty 19th-century country mansion, 3½
★ kilometers (2 miles) outside Lucca, is an exclusive hotel whose
rooms feature original beamed ceilings. All rooms are individually
and tastefully decorated. Antique floors, furniture, and portraits
set the tone, and the restaurant is known for its fine Tuscan dishes.
*Massa Pisana, 55100, tel. 0583/370037, fax 0583/379019. 44 rooms
with bath. Facilities: park, pool, restaurant. AE, DC, MC, V.
Closed Nov. 1–Mar. 31. Expensive.*

La Luna. There's an aura of Old World charm in this family-run hotel
on one of Lucca's most central and historic streets. Recent, extensive renovations have endowed the establishment with gleaming
modern bathrooms, leaving the atmosphere intact. A plus for anyone touring by car is the hotel's own garage and parking area. *Corte
Compagni 12 (corner of Via Fillungo), 55100, tel. 0583/493634, fax
0583/490021. 30 rooms with bath. AE, DC, MC, V. Closed Dec. 24–
Jan. 6. Moderate.*

Ilaria. This small, family-run hotel sits in a pretty location on a minuscule canal within easy walking distance of the main sights. The
rooms are smallish but fresh and functional. *Via del Fosso 20, 55100,
tel. 0583/47558. 17 rooms, 12 with bath or shower. AE, DC, MC, V.
Inexpensive.*

Montepulciano **Cittino.** A few plants outside the door mark this plain, family-run
Dining trattoria off one of the town's main streets. *Pici* (homemade spa-
ghetti) with meat sauce and local *pecorino* (sheep's milk) cheese are
good choices. The house wine is local, too. *Vicolo Via Nuovo 2 (Via
Voltaia), tel. 0578/757335. No reservations. No credit cards. Closed
Wed. Inexpensive.*

Pievescola **La Suvera.** In this luxurious hotel in the Tuscan countryside, 27 ki-
(Casola lometers (17 miles) from Siena and 56 kilometers (35 miles) from
d'Elsa) Florence you can savor living on an aristocratic estate that was once
Dining and owned by Pope Julius II. Rooms and suites are magnificently fur-
Lodging nished with antiques and endowed with up-to-the-minute comforts.
With salons, a library, Italian garden, swimming pool, and
L'Oliviera restaurant (serving estate wines) to enjoy, guests find it
hard to tear themselves away. *Pievescola (Casola d'Elsa), off Rte.
541, 53030, tel. 0577/960300, fax 0577/960220. 25 rooms with bath, 10
suites. Facilities: restaurant, bar, park, heated swimming pool,
sauna, tennis, riding, heliport, conference rooms. AE, DC, MC, V.
Closed Nov. 16–Mar. 14. Expensive.*

Pisa **Bruno.** A country-inn look, with beamed ceilings and soft lights,
Dining makes Bruno a pleasant place to lunch on classic Tuscan dishes, from
zuppa alla pisana (vegetable soup) to *baccalà con porri* (cod with
leeks). It's just outside the old city walls and only a short walk from
the bell tower and cathedral. *Via Luigi Bianchi 12, tel. 050/560818.
Reservations advised. AE, DC, MC, V. Closed Mon. dinner, Tues.,
Aug. 1–20. Moderate.*

La Pergoletta. Located in a medieval tower on a street named for its
"Beautiful Towers," La Pergoletta is small and simple, with a shady

garden for outdoor dining. The owner presides over the kitchen, and she offers traditional Tuscan *minestra di farro* (wheat soup) and *grigliata* (grilled beef, veal, or lamb). *Via delle Belle Torri 36, tel. 050/542458. Reservations advised. MC, V. Closed Tues. and Aug. Moderate.*

Pistoia
Dining

La Casa degli Amici. The name means "the house of friends," and that's the atmosphere that the two industrious ladies who own it succeed in creating in this restaurant, located outside Pistoia's old walls, on the road toward the A11 autostrada exit. They offer homey specialties, such as ribollita, *pasta e fagioli* (pasta and bean soup), and *coniglio alla Vernaccia* (rabbit in white wine). There's a terrace for outdoor dining in the summer. *Via Bonellina 111, tel. 0573/380305. Reservations advised. AE, DC, MC, V. Closed Tues., Sun. eve, and Aug. Moderate.*

Il Duomo. This unpretentious trattoria is practically on Piazza del Duomo, and locals as well as tourists enjoy its typical Tuscan ribollita and *carne in umido* (stewed meats) at very reasonable prices. *Via Bracciolini 5, tel. 0573/31948. Reservations accepted. No credit cards. Closed Sun. Inexpensive.*

Prato
Dining

Stefano. At the lower end of the moderate price range, this trattoria is popular with the locals. A simple place, it serves regional dishes such as ribollita, fagioli laced with local olive oil, and grilled meat. *Via Pomeria 23, tel. 0574/34665. No reservations. No credit cards. Closed Sun. Moderate.*

San Gimignano
Dining

Bel Soggiorno. Bel Soggiorno is attached to a small hotel. It has fine views, refectory tables set with linen and candles, and leather-covered chairs. Specialties are *pappardelle alla lepre* (egg noodles with hare sauce) and herbed grilled meat. *Via San Giovanni 89, tel. 0577/940375. Reservations advised. AE, DC, MC, V. Closed Mon. and Jan. 7–Feb. 7. Moderate.*

Dining and Lodging

Pescille. This rambling stone farmhouse, about 3 kilometers (2 miles) outside San Gimignano, with a good view of the town, has been restored as a hotel and furnished in attractive rustic-chic style. The upscale Cinque Gigli restaurant serves Tuscan *zuppe* (soups), *arrosti* (roasted meats), and other local specialties. *Località Pescille, 53037, tel. 0577/940186, fax 0577/940186. 40 rooms with bath. Facilities: restaurant (closed Wed.), bar, garden, swimming pool, tennis. Closed Nov. 15–Feb. 28. AE, DC, MC, V. Moderate.*

Siena
Dining
★

Ai Marsili. Located in a medieval palace near the Duomo, Ai Marsili is a spacious, brick-vaulted wine cellar with refectory tables and excellent Tuscan cuisine; it's a place for a leisurely meal accompanied by classic Chianti wines. Specialties include *pici* (homemade spaghetti) with mushroom sauce, and *piccione* (squab). *Via del Castoro 3, tel. 0577/47154. Reservations advised. AE, DC, MC, V. Closed Mon. Moderate.*

Osteria Le Logge. Just off Piazza del Campo, this is a fine choice for an informal but memorable meal. Get there early to claim a table. Among the specialties are *pennette all'Osteria* (creamy pasta) and *tagliata alla rucola* (sliced steak with arugula). *Via del Porrione 33, tel. 0577/48013. Reservations advised. DC, MC, V. Closed Sun., June 10–23 and Nov. 6–24. Moderate.*

Tullio Tre Cristi. To find this historic trattoria, take Via dei Rossi from Via Banchi di Sopra. Even though it was discovered by tourists long ago, it remains true to typical Sienese cooking and atmosphere. Try *spaghetti alle briciole*, a poor-man's pasta with bread crumbs, tomato, and garlic. *Vicolo di Provenzano 1, tel. 0577/280608. Reser-*

vations advised. MC, V. Closed Sun. eve., Mon., and Jan. Moderate.

Le Tre Campane. Boasting a convenient location between Piazza del Campo and the Duomo, this small trattoria displays the colorful banners of Siena's 17 districts. Popular with the locals, it specializes in Tuscan fare and a *trittico* (trio) of pastas. *Piazzetta Bonelli 5, tel. 0577/286091. Reservations advised. No credit cards. Closed Tues. and Jan.–Feb. Inexpensive.*

Lodging **Certosa di Maggiano.** An easy and attractive walk (less than a mile) southeast of Siena takes you to this old Carthusian monastery, which has been converted into a sophisticated oasis furnished in impeccable style. The bedrooms have every comfort, and the atmosphere is that of an aristocratic family villa. *Strada di Certosa 82, 53100, tel. 0577/288180, fax 0577/288189. 18 rooms with bath. Facilities: pool, tennis. AE, DC, MC, V. Closed Dec.–Feb. Very Expensive.*

★ **Park Hotel.** Just outside the walls of the old city, this is a handsome 15th-century villa on its own grounds. Furnished in classic Tuscan style, with antiques and luxuriant plants in gleaming copper planters on highly polished terra-cotta floors, it has a simple but sophisticated ambience, in which you can pretend you're a house guest of the Medicis. There's a fine restaurant and garden terrace. *Via di Marciano 18, 53100, tel. 0577/44803, fax 0577/49020. 69 rooms with bath. Facilities: restaurant, garden terrace, pool, tennis. AE, DC, MC, V. Very Expensive.*

Chiusarelli. A handy location near a parking area and the long-distance bus terminal make this a good choice, and it is only a 10-minute walk from the main sights. In a well-kept neoclassic villa complete with caryatids, it has functional rooms that are airy and reasonably quiet. There is a small garden and a restaurant. *Viale Curtatone 9, 53100, tel. 0577/280562, fax 0577/271177. 50 rooms with bath. MC, V. Moderate.*

★ **Duomo.** Occupying the top floor of a 17th-century building in the center of Siena, near Piazza del Campo, the hotel is quiet and is furnished in a neat contemporary style, with traces of the past showing in the artfully exposed brickwork in the breakfast room. Many rooms have superb views of the city's towers and the hills beyond. Two rooms are endowed with balconies. *Via Stalloreggi 38, 53100, tel. 0577/289088, fax 0577/43043. 23 rooms with bath. AE, MC, V. Inexpensive–Moderate.*

Milan

Arriving and Departing

As Lombardy's capital and the most important financial and commercial center in northern Italy, Milan is well connected with Rome and Florence by fast and frequent rail and air service, though the latter is often delayed in winter by heavy fog.

By Plane Linate Airport, 11 kilometers (7 miles) outside Milan, handles mainly domestic and European flights (tel. 02/7485–2200). Malpensa, 50 kilometers (30 miles) from the city, handles intercontinental flights (tel. 02/7485–2200).

Between the Airport and Downtown Buses connect both airports with Milan, stopping at the central station and at the Porta Garibaldi station. Fare from Linate is 4,000 lire on the special airport bus or 1,200 lire on municipal bus no. 73 (to Piazza San Babila); from Malpensa 12,000 lire. A taxi from Linate to the center of Milan costs about 25,000 lire, from Malpensa about 110,000 lire.

By Train The main train terminal is the central station in Piazzale Duca d'Aosta (tel. 02/67500). Several smaller stations handle commuter trains. There are several fast Intercity trains daily between Rome and Milan, stopping in Florence. A nonstop Intercity leaves from Rome or Milan morning and evening, taking about four hours to go between the two cities.

By Car From Rome and Florence, take the A1 Autostrada. From Venice, take the A4. With bans on parking throughout the center of Milan, it's easier to park on the outskirts and use public transportation.

Getting Around

By Subway Milan's subway network, the Metropolitana, is modern, fast, and easy to use. "MM" signs mark Metropolitana stations. There are at present three lines. The ATM (city transport authority) has an information office on the mezzanine of the Duomo Metro station (tel. 02/875495). Tickets are sold at newsstands at every stop, and in ticket machines *for exact change only*. The fare is 1,200 lire, and the subway runs from 6:20 AM to midnight.

By Bus and Buy tickets at newsstands, tobacco shops, and bars. Fare is 1,200
Streetcar lire. One ticket is valid for 75 minutes on all surface lines, and one subway trip. Daily tickets valid for 24 hours on all public transportation lines are sold at the Duomo Metro station ATM information office, and at Stazione Centrale Metro station. Twenty-four-hour tickets cost 3,800 lire; 48-hour tickets cost 6,600 lire.

By Taxi Use yellow cabs only. They wait at stands or can be telephoned in advance (tel. 6767, 8585, or 8388).

Guided Tours

City Tours Three-hour morning or afternoon sightseeing tours depart Tues.– Sun. from Piazzetta Reale, next to the Duomo; the cost is about 50,000 lire and tickets can be purchased at some travel agencies or aboard the bus.

Excursions From April through September the **Autostradale** bus company (Via Pompeo Marchesi 55, tel. 02/4820–3177) and **Autostradale Viaggi** (Piazza Castello 1, tel. 02/801161) offer an all-day tour of Lake Maggiore, including a boat trip to the Borromean Islands and lunch. The cost is about 105,000 lire.

Museumcard The **Museumcard** is valid 6 months for admission to 20 Milan museums, including the Brera, Duomo Museum, Leonardo da Vinci Science Museum, and the Refectory of Santa Maria delle Grazie (*Last Supper*). It costs 37,000 lire and is available at Milan APT offices (*see below*), museum ticket offices, and major travel agencies.

Tourist Information

APT information offices (Via Marconi 1, 20121, tel. 02/809662; Central Station, tel. 02/669–0432). **Municipal Information Office** (Galleria Vittorio Emanuele at the corner of Piazza della Scala, tel. 02/6208–3101).

Exploring Milan

Numbers in the margin correspond to points of interest on the Milano (Milan) map.

① The center of Milan is the Piazza del Duomo. The massive **Duomo** is one of the largest churches in the world, a mountain of marble fretted with statues, spires, and flying buttresses. The interior is a more solemn Italian Gothic. Take the elevator or walk up 158 steps to the roof, from which—if it's a clear day—you can see over the city to the Lombard plain and the Alps beyond, all through an amazing array of spires and statues. The **Madonnina,** a gleaming gilt statue on the highest spire, is a Milan landmark. *Entrance to elevator and stairway outside the cathedral, to the right. Admission: stairs, 4,000 lire; elevator, 6,000 lire. Open Mar.–Oct., daily 9–5:45; Nov.– Feb. 9–4:15.*

② Outside the cathedral to the right is the elegant, glass-roofed **Galleria,** where the Milanese and visitors stroll, window-shop, and sip pricey cappuccinos at trendy cafés. At the other end of the **③** Galleria is **Piazza della Scala,** with Milan's city hall on one side and **④** **Teatro alla Scala,** the world-famous opera house, opposite.

Via Verdi, flanking the opera house, leads to Via Brera, where the **⑤** **Pinacoteca di Brera** houses one of Italy's great collections of paintings. Most are of a religious nature, confiscated in the 19th century when many religious orders were suppressed and their churches closed. *Via Brera 28, tel. 02/864–63501. Admission: 8,000 lire. Open Tues.–Sat. 9–5:30, Sun. 9–12:30.*

Time Out A pleasant café with tables outdoors in fair weather is open to Brera visitors, just inside the entrance to the gallery.

After an eyeful of artworks by Mantegna, Raphael, and many other Italian masters, explore the Brera neighborhood, dotted with art galleries, chic little restaurants, and such offbeat cafés as the **⑥** **Jamaica** (Via Brera 26), once a bohemian hangout. Take Via dei Fiori Chiari in front of the Brera and keep going in the same direc- **⑦** tion to the moated **Castello Sforzesco,** a somewhat sinister 19th-century reconstruction of the imposing 15th-century fortress built by the Sforzas, who succeeded the Viscontis as lords of Milan in the 15th century. It now houses wide-ranging collections of sculptures, antiques, and ceramics, including Michelangelo's *Rondanini Pietà,* his last work, left unfinished at his death. *Piazza Castello, tel. 02/ 6236 ext. 3947. Admission free. Open Tues.–Sun. 9:30–5:30.*

From the vast residence of the Sforzas it's not far to the church of **⑧** **Santa Maria delle Grazie.** Although portions of the church were designed by Bramante, it plays second fiddle to the **Refectory** next door, where, over a three-year period, Leonardo da Vinci painted his megafamous fresco, *The Last Supper.* The fresco has suffered more than its share of disaster, beginning with the experiments of the artist, who used untested pigments that soon began to deteriorate. *The Last Supper* is now a mere shadow of its former self, despite meticulous restoration that proceeds at a snail's pace. To save what is left, visitors are limited in time and number, and you may have to wait in line to get a glimpse of this world-famous work. *Piazza Santa Maria delle Grazie 2, tel. 02/498–7588. Admission: 6,000 lire. Open Tues.–Sun. 9–1:15. (Hours may vary; check locally.)*

If you are interested in medieval architecture, go to see the medieval **⑨** church of **Sant'Ambrogio** (Piazza Sant'Ambrogio). Consecrated by

Milano (Milan)

0 — 440 yards
400 meters

Pta. Nuova
Stazione Centrale
Vle. Crispi
Bast. di Pta. Nuova
V. S. Gregorio
Pza. d. Repubblica
Vle. Tunisia
Vle. Vittorio Veneto
V. Lazzaretto
V. Melzi d'Eril
V. Bramante
V. Montello
V. Volta
V. Solferino
C. Pta. Nuova
Bastioni di Pta. Venezia
V. Bertani
V. Niccolini
V. Legnano
C. Garibaldi
V. Statuto
V. San Marco
V. Moscova
V. Palermo
V. Montebello
V. Filippo Turati
V. Manin
Giardini Publici
Parco Sempione
V. Pontaccio
V. Fiori Chiari
V. Brera
Mercato
V. Fatebenefratelli
V. Borgonuovo
V. d. Giardini
V. d. Marchi
V. d. Senato
C. Venezia
V. Leopardi
Stazione Nord
Pza. Castello
Foro Buonaparte
Cusani dell'Orso
V. Broletto
Monte di Pietà
V. Manzoni
Monte N. S. Spirito
V. Andrea Spiga
V. Mozart
V. Monti
V. Boccaccio
V. Dante
V. Verdi
C. Matteotti
C. Mon forte
Pza. S. Maria delle Grazie
C. Magenta
V. G. Carducci
V. Meravigli
V. Orefici
Pza. del Duomo
C. V. Emanuele
V. di Modrone
V. Passione
V. San Vittore
Luini
V. S. M. Fulcorina
V. Bocchetto
V. Mazzini
V. Fil. Corridoni
V. Olona
V. S. Orsola
Cappuccio
V. Circo
V. Torino
C. Porta Romana
V. Velasca
V. Larga
V. Francesco Sforza
C. Porta Vittoria
V. Edmondo de Amicis
C. Pta. Ticinese
V. Mulino d'Armi
Corso Italia
V. S. Sofia
V. S. Barnaba
V. D. Commenda
V. Freguglia
V. Manara
V. Ariberto
V. M. d'Oggioni
D. Naviglio
S. Croce
V. G. Mercalli
V. Lamarmora
V. Orti
Vle. Caldara
Pta. Genova
Vle. G. d'Annunzio
V. Gorizia
Pta. Ticinese
Vle. Galeazzo
Vle. Col di Lana
V. S. Martino
V. Bianca di Savoia
V. Quadronno
V. Carlo Crivelli
Vle. Beatrice d'Este
Pta. Vigentina
Pta. Romana

Castello Sforzesco, **7**
Corso Buenos Aires, **16**
Duomo, **1**
Galleria, **2**
Jamaica, **6**

Piazza della Scala, **3**
Pinacoteca di Brera, **5**
San Lorenzo Maggiore, **10**
San Satiro, **11**
Santa Maria delle Grazie, **8**
Sant'Ambrogio, **9**

Teatro alla Scala, **4**
Via della Spiga, **14**
Via Manzoni, **13**
Via Monte Napoleone, **12**
Via Sant'Andrea, **15**

St. Ambrose in AD 387, it's the model for all Lombard Romanesque churches, and contains some ancient works of art, including a remarkable 9th-century altar in precious metals and enamels, and some 5th-century mosaics. On December 8, the day after the feast day of St. Ambrose, the streets around the church are the scene of a

⑩ lively flea market. Another noteworthy church is **San Lorenzo Maggiore** (Corso di Porta Ticinese), with 16 ancient Roman columns in front and some 4th-century mosaics in the Chapel of St. Aquilinus.

⑪ Closer to Piazza del Duomo on Via Torino, the church of **San Satiro** is another architectural gem in which Bramante's perfect command of proportion and perspective, a characteristic of the Renaissance, made a small interior seem extraordinarily spacious and airy.

Time Out   Stop in at the **Peck** shops a few steps from San Satiro. One is a gourmet delicatessen; another has a tempting array of snacks to eat on the premises. *Via Spadari 9; Via Cantù 3.*

⑫ Now head for Milan's most elegant shopping streets: **Via Monte**
⑬ ⑭ ⑮ **Napoleone, Via Manzoni, Via della Spiga,** and **Via Sant'Andrea.** The **Café Cova** (Via Monte Napoleone 8) is famous for its pastries; Hemingway loved them. And the **Sant'Ambroeus,** not far away, is the epitome of a genteel tearoom (Corso Matteotti 7). If the chic goods of
⑯ this area are a shock to your purse, make your way to **Corso Buenos Aires,** near the central station, which has hundreds more shops and accessible prices, too.

Dining

For details and price-category definitions, *see* Dining in Staying in Italy, *above.*

Expensive   **Biffi Scala.** The elegant Biffi Scala caters mainly to the after-opera crowd that pours in around midnight. Built in 1861, it features a high ceiling and polished wood walls. Specialties include *crespelle alle erbette* (pancakes stuffed with wild mushrooms and other vegetables) and *carpaccio alla Biffi Scala* (thin slices of cured raw beef with a tangy sauce). *Piazza della Scala, tel. 02/866651. Dinner reservations required, especially after the opera. AE, DC, MC, V. Closed Sun., Aug. 10–20, and Dec. 24–Jan. 6.*

★ **Boeucc.** Milan's oldest restaurant is situated not far from La Scala and is subtly lighted, with fluted columns, chandeliers, thick carpet, and a garden for warm-weather dining. In addition to the typical Milanese foods, it also serves such exotica as *penne al branzino e zucchine* (pasta with sea bass and zucchini sauce) and *gelato di castagne con zabaglione caldo* (chestnut ice cream with hot zabaglione). *Piazza Belgioioso 2, tel. 02/760–22880. Reservations required. AE. Closed Sat., Sun. lunch, Dec. 24–Jan. 2, and Aug.*

Don Lisander. This 17th-century chapel has been drastically redecorated, and now features designer lighting, abstract prints, and a modern terra-cotta tile floor, creating an uncompromisingly contemporary effect. Try the *scaloppe di fegato con menta* (calf's-liver scaloppine with fresh mint leaves) or else go for the *branzino al timo* (sea bass with thyme). *Via Manzoni 12A, tel. 02/760–20130. Reservations required. AE, DC, MC, V. Closed Sat. dinner, Sun., 2 weeks in mid-Aug., and 2 weeks at Christmas.*

Giannino. You'll find great character and style at this roomy, old-fashioned restaurant, with oak beams, stained-glass windows, and a huge lobster aquarium. If it's on the menu, be daring and try the *dadolata di capriolo* (venison in cream sauce) or *quaglie con risotto*

(quails with rice). *Via A. Sciesa 8, tel. 02/551–95585. Dinner reservations required. AE, DC, MC, V. Closed Sun., Aug.*

★ **Savini.** Red carpets and cut-glass chandeliers characterize the classy Savini, a typical, Old World Milanese restaurant whose dining rooms spread over three floors. There's also a "winter garden" from which patrons can people-watch shoppers in the Galleria. The *risotto al salto* (rice cooked as a pancake, tossed in the pan, a Milanese specialty) is excellent here, as is the *costoletta di vitello* (breaded veal cutlets). *Galleria Vittorio Emanuele, tel. 02/720–03433. Dinner reservations advised. AE, DC, MC, V. Closed Sun., 3 weeks in Aug., and 2 weeks at Christmas.*

Moderate **Antica Brasera Meneghina.** A huge fireplace, ornate mirrors, black-
★ and-white tiled floor, and bentwood chairs lend this restaurant a 17th-century air, while the long garden, shaded by a 450-year-old wisteria and containing fig trees, fountains, and frescoes, make it absolutely delightful in the summer. The menu features typical Milanese dishes such as *rustin negàa* (veal cooked in white wine with ham, bacon, sage, and rosemary) and *cassoeula* (casserole of pork, sausage, and cabbage). *Via Circo 10, tel. 02/808108. Winter reservations advised. AE, DC, MC, V. Closed Mon., Aug.*

Antica Trattoria della Pesa. Though the management has changed, the turn-of-the-century decor and atmosphere, dark wood paneling, and old-fashioned lamps still look much as they must have when it opened one hundred years ago. This is authentic Old Milan, and the menu is right in line, with risotto, minestrone, and *osso buco* (stewed veal shin). *Viale Pasubio 10, tel. 02/655–5741. Reservations advised evenings. AE, DC, MC, V. Closed Sun. and 2 weeks in Aug.*

Antica Trattoria Milanese. In the business district near the Castello Sforzesco, this small, family-run trattoria is crowded with white-collar workers at lunch and regulars at dinner, when lingering is allowed. With a name like this, the cuisine could be nothing but Milanese, with classic risotto and *costoletta alla milanese* at the head of the list. *Via Camperio 21, tel. 02/864–62333. No reservations. No credit cards. Closed Sun. and Aug.*

Inexpensive **Al Cantinone.** Operagoers still come to the Cantinone bar for a drink after the final curtain, just as they did a century ago. The decor is basic, the atmosphere lively, the service fast, and the food reliable. The proprietor stocks 240 different wines. Try the *costolette al Cantinone* (veal cutlets with mushrooms, olives, and a cream and tomato sauce). *Via Agnello 19, tel. 02/807666. Reservations advised. AE, MC, V. Closed Sat. lunch, Sun., Aug., Christmas, and Easter.*

Birreria-Bistro San Tomaso. A popular lunch spot for trendy Milanese, this place has the informal atmosphere of an old beer hall. At the self-service counter you can have a salad made to order, a cheese platter, or other light fare. It's usually quieter at night, and the kitchen stays open until 1 AM. *Via San Tomaso 5, tel. 02/874510. Reservations advised in evening. No credit cards. Closed Sun.*

La Bruschetta. A winning partnership of Tuscans and Neapolitans runs this tiny, busy, and first-class pizzeria near the Duomo. It features the obligatory wood-burning stove, so you can watch your pizza being cooked, though there are plenty of other dishes to choose from as well—try the *spaghetti alle cozze e vongole* (spaghetti with clams and mussels). *Piazza Beccaria 12, tel. 02/802494. Reservations advised, but service is so fast you don't have to wait long. No credit cards. Closed Mon., 3 weeks in Aug, a few days at Christmas and Easter.*

La Giara. At this tavern with bare wooden tables and benches, the menu offers a limited selection of southern Italian specialties, notably a varied vegetable antipasto. Meat is grilled on a range at the front of the restaurant and served with crusty bread and dense olive oil from the Puglia region. It is located in the vicinity of Piazzale Loreto. *Viale Monza 10, tel. 02/285–3835. Reservations not necessary; you may be asked to share a table. No credit cards. Closed Wed.*

La Piazzetta. A popular lunch spot in the Brera quarter, it's usually crowded with journalists, actors, and politicians. There's a salad bar, but you'll find hot dishes, too, such as the typically Milanese *ossobuco con risotto* (braised veal shanks with white wine and tomato. *Via Solferino 25, tel. 02/659–1076. No reservations. No credit cards. Closed Sun., Easter, and Aug.*

Lodging

Make reservations well in advance, particularly when trade fairs are on, which can be most of the year except for August (when many hotels close) and mid-December to mid-January. March and October are months with the highest concentration of fairs, and it's virtually impossible to find a room at this time. Should you arrive without reservations, there's a booking service at Via Palestro 24 (tel. 02/782072).

For details and price-category definitions, *see* Lodging in Staying in Italy, *above.*

Very Expensive ★
Duomo. Just 20 yards from the cathedral, this hotel's first-, second-, and third-floor rooms all look out onto the church's Gothic gargoyles and pinnacles. The rooms are spacious and snappily furnished in contemporary style. *Via San Raffaele 1, 20121, tel. 02/8833, fax 02/864–62027. 140 rooms with bath. Facilities: restaurant, bar. AE, DC, MC, V. Closed Aug.*

Four Seasons. The elegant restoration of a 14th-century monastery on an exclusive shopping street in the center of Milan has produced a gem, and a precious one, at the highest rates in the city. The hotel blends European class with American comfort. Individually furnished rooms have opulent marble bathrooms; most rooms face the quiet courtyard. Downstairs is the hotel's popular Il Teatro restaurant. *Via Gesù 8, tel. 02/77088, fax 02/770–85000. 78 rooms, all with bath. Facilities: restaurant (Expensive), bar, convention facilities, business center. AE, DC, MC, V.*

Galileo. In spite of its location on busy Corso Europa, this hotel is surprisingly quiet. The rooms have chic designer lighting, tartan carpets, and original modern prints on the walls. The bathrooms are particularly grand, with two basins each. *Corso Europa 9, 20122, tel. 02/7743, fax 02/760–20584. 76 rooms with bath. AE, DC, MC, V.*

Pierre. Luxury keynotes rooms individually furnished with elegant fabrics and an assortment of modern and antique furniture. Electronic gadgetry controls curtains and lights. The Pierre is located near the medieval church of Sant'Ambrogio. *Via De Amicis 32, 20123, tel. 02/720–00581, fax 02/805–2157. 47 rooms with bath. Facilities: restaurant, bar. AE, DC, MC, V.*

Principe di Savoia. The most fashionable and glitzy hotel in Milan, this is where fashion buyers and expense-account businesspeople stay. Dark wood paneling and period furniture, brass lamps, and a stucco lobby are all reminiscent of early 1900s Europe. *Piazza della Repubblica 17, 20124, tel. 02/6230, fax 02/659–5838. 287 rooms with bath. Facilities: restaurant, bar. AE, DC, MC, V.*

Expensive
Carlton-Senato. This hotel is in the heart of Milan's chic shopping district. The atmosphere is light and airy, and there are lots of little touches (such as complimentary chocolates and liqueurs in the

rooms) to make up for the rather functional furnishings. *Via Senato 5, 20121, tel. 02/760–15535. Fax 02/783–300. 79 rooms with bath. Facilities: restaurant, bar, garage. AE, MC, V. Closed Aug.*

Moderate **Canada.** This friendly, small hotel is close to Piazza del Duomo on the edge of a district full of shops and restaurants. Recently renovated, it offers good value; all rooms have TV, air-conditioning, and fridge bar. *Via Santa Sofia 16, 20122, tel. 02/583–04844, fax 02/583–00282. 35 rooms with bath. AE, DC, MC, V.*

Casa Svizzera. A faithful clientele considers this one of Milan's best small hotels in the moderate price category, so it's advisable to make early reservations. The location, adjacent to the Duomo and a few yards from the Galleria, is central and handy to Metro and bus lines. The hotel has been totally renovated and soundproofed. Rooms have air conditioning, TV and fridge-bar, and they are decorated in cheery floral-printed fabric. *Via San Raffaele 3, 20123, tel. 02/8692246, fax 02/72004690. 45 rooms with bath. Facilities: bar. AE, DC, MC, V. Closed Aug.*

Centro. The fragments of a Roman column and bust in the entrance lead you to expect something more old-fashioned and classier than is the case: The rooms are decorated in 1960s modern, with floral wallpaper and bare wood floors. Avoid rooms on the Via Broletto side—cars rumbling over cobblestones sound like thunder. *Via Broletto 46, 20121, tel. 02/869–2821, fax 02/875578. 54 rooms with bath. Facilities: bar. AE, DC, MC, V.*

Gritti. This bright, clean hotel has a cheerful atmosphere. Rooms are adequate, with picturesque views from the upper floors over the tiled roofs to the gilt Madonnina on top of the Duomo, only a few hundred yards away. *Piazza Santa Maria Beltrade (north end of Via Torino), 20123, tel. 02/801056, fax 02/890–10999. 48 rooms with bath. AE, DC, MC, V.*

Inexpensive **Città Studi.** Near the University and Piazzale Susa, this hotel is modern and functionally furnished, undistinguished but with a reputation as a reliable, reasonably comfortable place to stay. Most rooms have private showers. *Via Saldini 24, 20133, tel. 02/744666, fax 02/713122. 45 rooms, 38 with bath. AE, MC, V.*

London. Close to the Duomo, the London has clean, good-size, simply furnished rooms and an English-speaking staff. It also has an arrangement with the Opera Prima restaurant in the same building, where guests may take their meals if they wish. *Via Rovello 3, 20121, tel. 02/720–20166, fax 02/805–7037. 29 rooms with shower. MC, V. Closed Dec. 25–Jan. 3, Aug.*

San Francisco. In a residential area between the central station and the university, this medium-size pension is handy to subway and bus lines. It also has the advantages of a friendly management, rooms that are bright and clean, and a charming garden. *Viale Lombardia 55, 20131, tel. 02/236–1009, fax 02/266–80377. 31 rooms with bath or shower. AE, DC, MC, V.*

The Arts

The most famous spectacle in Milan is the one at **La Scala,** which presents some of the world's most impressive operatic productions. The house is invariably sold out in advance; ask at your hotel whether tickets can be found for you. You can book in advance by mail or fax (02/887–9297). You can also book tickets at CIT travel agencies elsewhere in Italy and in other countries, but no more than 10 days before the performance. The opera season begins December 7 (St. Ambrose Day) and ends in May. The concert season runs from May to the end of June and from September through November. There is a brief ballet season in September. Programs are available at principal travel agencies and tourist information offices in Italy and abroad. *Box Office, Teatro alla Scala, Piazza della Scala, tel. 02/ 809126. Open daily noon-7, noon-8:15 on performance days. Closed national holidays and July 28-Aug. 28.*

Venice

Arriving and Departing

By Plane Marco Polo International Airport is situated about 10 kilometers (6 miles) northeast of the city on the mainland. For flight information, tel. 041/661262.

Between the Blue ATVO buses make the 25-minute trip in to Piazzale Roma,
Airport and where the road to Venice terminates; the cost is around 5,000 lire.
Downtown From Piazzale Roma visitors will most likely have to take a *vaporetto* (water bus) to their hotel (*see* Getting Around, *below*). The Cooperative San Marco motor launch (fare 15,000 lire) can be a more convenient way to reach the city, depending on where your hotel is located. It runs from the airport, via the Lido, dropping passengers across the lagoon at Piazza San Marco. (It works on a limited schedule in winter.) Land taxis are available, running the same route as the buses; the cost is about 45,000 lire. Water taxis (slick high-power motorboats) are very expensive: Negotiate the fare in advance, usually upward of 100,000 lire (the official scale of tariffs is published in the "Guest in Venice" booklet; *see* The Arts, *below*).

By Train Make sure your train goes all the way to Santa Lucia train station in Venice's northwest corner; some trains leave passengers at the Mestre station on the mainland. All trains traveling to and from Santa Lucia stop at Mestre, so to get from Mestre to Santa Lucia, or vice versa, (a journey of about 10 minutes), take the first available train. The APT information booth (tel. 041/719078, open daily 8-8) and the baggage depot in the station are sometimes very busy. If you need a hotel room, go to the AVA hotel association desk (open Apr.-Oct., daily 8 AM-10 PM; Nov.-Mar., daily 8 AM-9:30 PM); there are others at the airport and at the city garage at Piazzale Roma. The deposit (15,000 lire-60,000 lire, depending on the hotel category) is discounted on your hotel bill. Vaporetto landing stages are directly outside the station. *Make sure you know how to get to your hotel before you arrive.* Don't take water taxis, since they are expensive and probably can't take you right to the door of your hotel. By water taxi or vaporetto you'll have to walk some distance anyway. For this reason, try to obtain a map of Venice before you arrive—and take a luggage cart; porters are not always available, and rates are quite high (15,000 lire for one bag and about 5,000 lire for each additional piece of luggage).

By Car If you bring a car to Venice, you will have to pay for a garage or parking space during your stay. Do not on any account allow yourself to be waylaid by illegal touts, often wearing fake uniforms, who will try to flag you down and offer to arrange parking and hotels; keep driving until you reach the automatic ticket machines. Parking at Piazzale Roma (run by the municipality) costs about 13,000 lire-23,000 lire per day, depending on the size of the car. Parking at the Tronchetto parking area (privately run) costs around 30,000 lire per day under cover, and 18,000 outside. (Do not leave valuables in your car. There is a left-luggage office next door to the Pullman Bar on the ground floor of the Municipal Garage in Piazzale Roma.) The Venetian Hoteliers Association (AVA) has arranged a discount of around 40% for hotel guests who use the official Tronchetto parking facility. Ask for a voucher on checking into your hotel. Present the voucher at Tronchetto when you pay the parking fee.

There is a vaporetto (currently number 82) from Tronchetto to Piazzale Roma and Piazza San Marco. (In thick fog or when tides are extreme, a bus runs instead to Piazzale Roma, where you can pick up a vaporetto.) Avoid taking private boats—they are a rip-off.

Getting Around

First-time visitors find that getting around Venice presents some unusual problems: the complexity of its layout (the city is made up of more than 100 islands, all linked by bridges); the bewildering unfamiliarity of waterborne transportation; the apparently illogical house numbering system and duplication of street names in its six districts; and the necessity of walking whether you enjoy it or not. It's essential to have a good map showing all street names and water bus routes; buy one at any newsstand.

By Vaporetto ACTV water buses run the length of the Grand Canal and circle the city. There are several lines, some of which connect Venice with the major and minor islands in the lagoon. **Line 1** is the Grand Canal local, calling at every stop, and continuing via San Marco to the Lido. (It takes about 45 minutes from the station to San Marco.) As the result of recent (extremely confusing and unpopular) rerouting, there are now two **Line 52** routes: one, running from the railway station to San Zaccaria, skirting the north of the city, via Fondamente Nove (where boats leave for the islands of the northern lagoon) and Murano, and continuing via the Arsenal; the other acting as a fast service via Zattere on the Giudecca Canal, south of the city, to San Marco and the Lido. There are also two **Line 82** routes from the Tronchetto: one going via Piazzale Roma, the railway station, and Rialto, and continuing, during the day, down the Grand Canal, with fewer stops than the Line 1, to San Marco and, in the summer, on to the Lido; the other taking the southern route through the Giudecca Canal, via Zaterre and also stopping on Giudecca, to San Marco, and again, in the summer, continuing to the Lido. The fare is 2,500 on most lines, but 3,500 on the 52 Zattere-Lido route and on the 82 Grand Canal route. A 24-hour tourist ticket costs 14,000 lire, while a 3-day tourist ticket costs 20,000; these are not valid on the 52 Zattere-Lido route or the 82 Grand Canal route, but can be especially worthwhile if you are planning to visit the islands. Timetables are posted at every landing stage, but there is not always a ticket booth operating. You may get on a boat without a ticket, but you will have to pay a higher fare on the boat. For this reason, it may be useful to buy a book of tickets (un blochetto) in advance. Landing stages are clearly marked with name and line number, but check before boarding, particularly with the 52, to make sure the boat is going in your direction.

By Water Taxi Known as *motoscafi*, or *taxi*, these are excessively expensive, and the fare system is as complex as Venice's layout. A minimum fare of about 40,000 lire gets you nowhere, and you'll pay three times as much to get from one end of the Grand Canal to the other. *Always agree on the fare before starting out.* It's probably worth considering taking a water taxi only if you are traveling in a small group.

By Traghetto Few tourists know about the two-man gondolas that ferry people across the Grand Canal at various fixed points. It's the cheapest and shortest gondola ride in Venice, and it can save a lot of walking. The fare is 500 lire, which you hand to one of the gondoliers when you get on. Look for "Traghetto" signs.

By Gondola   Don't leave Venice without treating yourself to a gondola ride, preferably in the quiet of the evening when the churning traffic on the canals has died down, the palace windows are illuminated, and the only sounds are the muted splashes of the gondolier's oar. Make sure he understands that you want to see the *rii*, or smaller canals, as well as the Grand Canal. There's supposed to be a fixed minimum rate of about 70,000 lire for 50 minutes. (Official tariffs are quoted in the "Guest in Venice" booklet; *see* The Arts, *below*.) Come to terms with your gondolier *before* stepping into his boat.

On Foot   This is the only way to reach many parts of Venice, so wear comfortable shoes. Invest in a good map that names all the streets, and count on getting lost more than once.

Important Addresses and Numbers

Tourist Information   The main Venice **APT Tourist Office** (tel. 041/522–6356) is at Calle dell'Ascensione 71C, just off Piazza San Marco, under the arcade in the far left corner opposite the basilica. Open every day except public holidays 8:30–6:30 (sometimes slightly later in summer). There are APT information booths at the Santa Lucia station (tel. 041/719078) and on the Lido (Gran Viale S.M. Elisabetta 6A, tel. 041/526–5721, fax 041/529–8720). Another office is due to open in the newly restored former coffeehouse pavilion in the corner of the Giardini Reali, on the waterfront near the San Marco vaporetto stop.

Consulates   U.K. (Campo Santa Maria della Carità 1051, Dorsoduro, tel. 041/522–7207). U.S. (The nearest U.S. Consulate is in Milan, at Largo Donegani 1, tel. 02/652841).

Emergencies   **Police** (tel. 113). **Ambulance** (tel. 041/523–0000). **Doctor:** Try the emergency room at Venice's hospital (tel. 041/529–4517), or call the British Consulate (*see above*) and ask for recommendations. **Pharmacies: Farmacia Italo-Inglese** (Calle della Mandola, tel. 041/522–4837); **Farmacia Internazionale** (Calle Larga XXII Marzo, tel. 041/522–2311). Pharmacies are open weekdays 9–12:30 and 4–7:45; Saturday 9–12:45; Sunday and night service by turns, with details posted outside every chemist, or available by dialing tel. 192.

Travel Agencies   **American Express** (San Moisè 1471, tel. 041/520–0844). **Wagons-Lits Travel** (Piazzetta dei Leoncini 289, tel. 041/522–3405).

Guided Tours

Orientation Tours   American Express and other operators offer two-hour walking tours of the San Marco area, taking in the basilica and the Doge's Palace. The cost is about 30,000 lire. American Express also has an afternoon walking tour from April through October that ends with a gondola ride. The cost is about 35,000 lire.

Special-Interest Tours   Some tour operators offer group gondola rides with serenade. The cost is about 35,000 lire. During the summer free guided tours of the Basilica di San Marco are offered by the Patriarchate of Venice; information is available at a desk in the atrium of the church (tel. 041/520–0333). There are several tours daily, except Sunday, and some tours are in English, including one at 11 AM.

Excursions   American Express can book you on a tour of the islands of Murano, Burano, and Torcello (daily at 9:30 and 2:30, San Marco; about 20,000 lire per person). However, it is best to avoid organized tours to the islands, particularly those operating from offices around Piazza San Marco. Tours tend to be annoyingly commercial and emphasize glass factory showrooms, pressuring you to buy, often at higher prices than normal. You can easily do these islands on your own. To get to Burano and Torcello, take the Line 52 Vaporetto to Fondamente Nuove and change to Line 12. For Murano, take the Line 52 all the way to Murano. (You can also pick up the Line 12 at Murano to continue to Burano and Torcello.) **American Express** offers a day trip by car to the Venetian Villas, Padua and Asolo, available all year round. The cost is about 120,000 lire per person, and bookings need to be made the day before.

Personal Guides **American Express** can provide guides for walking or gondola tours of Venice, or cars with driver and guide for excursions on the mainland. Pick up a list of licensed guides and their rates from the **APT** Information Office in Piazza San Marco (tel. 041/522–6356).

Exploring Venice

Venice—La Serenissima, the Most Serene—is disorienting in its complexity, an extraordinary labyrinth of narrow streets and waterways, opening now and again onto some airy square or broad canal. The majority of its magnificent palazzi are slowly crumbling; though this sounds like a recipe for a down-at-the-heels slum, somehow in Venice the shabby, derelict effect is magically transformed into one of supreme beauty and charm, rather than horrible urban decay. The place is romantic, especially at night when the lights from the vaporetti and the stars overhead pick out the gargoyles and arches of the centuries-old facades. For hundreds of years Venice was the unrivaled mistress of trade between Europe and the Orient, and the staunch bulwark of Christendom against the tide of Turkish expansion. Though the power and glory of its days as a wealthy city-republic are gone, the art and exotic aura remain.

To enjoy the city, you will have to come to terms with the crowds of day trippers, who take over the center around San Marco, from May through September. Hot and sultry in the summer, Venice is much more welcoming in early spring and late fall. Romantics like it in the winter when prices are much lower, the streets are often deserted, and the sea mists impart a haunting melancholy to the *campi* (squares) and canals. Piazza San Marco (St. Mark's Square) is the pulse of Venice, but after joining with the crowds to visit the Basilica di San Marco and the Doge's Palace, strike out on your own and just follow where your feet take you—you won't be disappointed.

Numbers in the margin correspond to points of interest on the Venezia (Venice) map.

Piazza San Marco and the Accademia Even the pigeons have to fight for space on **Piazza San Marco,** the most famous piazza in Venice, and pedestrian traffic jams clog the surrounding byways. Despite the crowds, San Marco is the logical
❶ starting place of each of our various itineraries. Pick up pamphlets at the **APT Information Office** in the far left corner of Piazza San Marco, opposite the basilica. The information office is in the Ala Napoleonica, a wing built by order of Napoleon to complete the much earlier palaces on either side of the square, enclosing it to form what he called "the most beautiful drawing room in all of Europe."
❷ Upstairs is the **Museo Correr,** with eclectic collections of historical objects and a picture gallery of fine 13th–17th-century paintings. *Piazza San Marco, Ala Napoleonica, tel. 041/522–5625. Admis-*

Venezia (Venice)

Basilica di San Marco, **3**

Ca' d'Oro, **18**

Ca' Foscari, **17**

Ca' Rezzonico, **16**

Campanile di San Marco, **5**

Fondaco dei Turchi, **20**

Frari, **10**

Galleria dell'Accademia, **8**

Museo Correr, **2**

Palazzo Ducale, **4**

Palazzo Vendramin Calergi, **19**

Peggy Guggenheim Museum, **15**

Piazza San Marco, **1**

Rialto Bridge, **14**

San Moisè, **6**

San Zanipolo, **13**

Santa Maria Formosa, **11**

Santa Maria dei Miracoli, **12**

Santa Maria del Giglio, **7**

Scuola di San Rocco, **9**

Canale delle Navi

Sacca della Misericordia

San Michele

0 ___ 440 yards
0 ___ 400 meters

C. Racchetta
Fondamente
Rio S. Caterina
R. d.
Gesuiti Nuove

Strada Nuova
18

Rio d. Santi Apostoli
C. d. Festa
C. della Panada
C. d. Squero
Cal. dei Mendicanti

Campo d. Pescheria

Campo Santi Giovanni e Paolo
12
13
R. Barbaria delle Tole

Rio d. S. Marina
Giustina
R. d. S.

Elberia
del Vin
14
Riga

R. d. S. Francesco
R. d. S.

Riva del Carbon
R. d. Fava
Sal. di S. Lio
11
R. d. S. Severo
R. d. S. Lorenzo
C. Lion
C. d. Furlani
Canale d. Galeazze

C. d. Bande
Giuffa
Campo Manin
Fabbri
Fond. Osmarin
R. d. Pietà
R. d. Greci
R. d. Scudi
R. d. Gorna
Darsena Grande
Rio d. Vergini
di S. Pietro

Trezzaria
2 1 3
5 4
R. d. Palazzo
Molo
Riva degli
Schiavoni
Rio d. S. Daniele
6
R. d. S. Moisè
Piazza San Marco
R. d. Arsenale
Rio della Tana
V. Garibaldi
Rio d. S. Anna
Can. di S.

Riva dei Sette Martiri
R. d. S. Giuseppe

Canale di S. Marco

Isola di S. Giorgio Maggiore

Viale Trieste
Rio dei Giardini

Fond. delle Zitelle

ci

Calle Michelangelo

KEY
___ Rail Lines
▲ Boat stop

sion: 5,000 lire. Open Apr.–Oct., Wed.–Mon. 9–7; Nov.–Mar., Wed.–Mon. 9–4.

❸ The **Basilica di San Marco** (St. Mark's Basilica) was begun in the 11th century to hold the relics of St. Mark the Evangelist, the city's patron saint, and its richly decorated facade is surmounted by copies of the four famous gilded bronze horses (the originals are in the basilica's upstairs museum). Inside, golden mosaics sheathe walls and domes, lending an extraordinarily exotic aura, half Christian church, half Middle Eastern mosque. Be sure to see the **Pala d'Oro,** an eye-filling 10th-century altarpiece in gold and silver, studded with precious gems and enamels. From the atrium, climb the steep stairway to the museum: The bronze horses alone are worth the effort. *The Basilica is open from early morning, but tourist visits are allowed Mon.–Sat. 9:30–5:30, Sun. 2:30–5:30. No admission to those wearing shorts or other revealing clothing. Pala d'Oro and Treasury. Admission: 2,000 lire. Open Mon.–Sat. 10–4, Sun. 1:45–4. Gallery and Museum. Admission: 2,000 lire. Open Apr.–Sept., daily 9:30–5:30; Oct.–Mar., daily 10–4.*

❹ Next to St. Mark's is the **Palazzo Ducale** (Doge's Palace), which, during Venice's prime, was the epicenter of the Serene Republic's great empire. More than just a palace, it was a combination White House, Senate, Supreme Court, torture chamber, and prison. The building's exterior is striking; the lower stories consist of two rows of fragile-seeming arches, while above rests a massive pink-and-white marble wall whose solidity is barely interrupted by its six great Gothic windows. The interior is a maze of vast halls, monumental staircases, secret corridors, state apartments, and the sinister prison cells and torture chamber. The palace is filled with frescoes, paintings, carvings, and a few examples of statuary by some of the Renaissance's greatest artists. Don't miss the famous view from the balcony, overlooking the piazza and St. Mark's Basin and the church of San Giorgio Maggiore across the lagoon. *Piazzetta San Marco, tel. 041/522–4951. Admission: 8,000 lire. Open Apr.–Oct., daily 9–7; Nov.–Mar., daily 9–4 (last entry one hour before closing time).*

For a pigeon's-eye view of Venice take the elevator up to the top of ❺ the **Campanile di San Marco** (St. Mark's bell tower) in Piazza San Marco, a reconstruction of the 1,000-year-old tower that collapsed one morning in 1912, practically without warning. Fifteenth-century clerics found guilty of immoral acts were suspended in wooden cages from the tower, sometimes to live on bread and water for as long as a year, sometimes to die of starvation and exposure. (Look for them in Carpaccio's paintings of the square that hang in the Accademia.) *Piazza San Marco, tel. 041/522–4064. Admission: 4,000 lire. Open Apr.–Oct., daily 10–8; Nov.–Mar. 10–4.*

Time Out **Caffè Florian** is a Venetian landmark located on the square. It's a great place to nurse a Campari or a cappuccino. The pleasure of relaxing amid so much history does not come cheap. A pot of hot chocolate indoors runs about $6—and there's an extra charge if you're served when the orchestra is playing. If you drink sitting at the bar, there is no service charge.

Armed with a street map, head west out of San Marco (with the facade of the basilica to your back), making your way past the Ameri-
❻ can Express office, across the bridge in front of **San Moisé**'s elaborate Baroque facade, and on to Calle Larga 22 Marzo. Continue
❼ on to the church of **Santa Maria del Giglio,** behind the **Gritti Palace**

hotel. Across the bridge behind the church, **Piazzesi** on Campiello Feltrina is famous for its handprinted paper and desk accessories.

Time Out You must cross another two bridges to get to Campo Santo Stefano, also known as Campo Morosini, where you can indulge yourself with some of the best ice cream you've ever eaten, at **Paolin,** a bar with tables outside in summer.

Join the stream of pedestrians crossing the Grand Canal on the wooden **Accademia Bridge,** and head straight on for the **Galleria dell'Accademia** (Accademia Gallery), Venice's most important picture gallery and a must for art lovers. Try to spend at least an hour viewing this remarkable collection of Venetian art, which is attractively displayed and well lighted. Works range from 14th-century Gothic to the Golden Age of the 15th and 16th centuries, including oils by Giovanni Bellini, Giorgione, Titian, and Tintoretto, and superb later works by Veronese and Tiepolo. *Campo della Carità, tel. 041/522-2247. Admission: 8,000 lire. Open daily, Apr.–Oct. 9–7, Nov.–Mar. 9–2.*

Once again consulting your map, make your way through Calle Contarini, Calle Toletta, and Campo San Barnaba to Rio Terra Canal, where **Mondonovo** ranks as one of the city's most interesting mask shops (Venetians, who originated Italy's most splendid carnival, love masks of all kinds, from gilded lions to painted sun faces and sinister death's heads). Just around the corner is Campo Santa Margherita, which has a homey feel.

Continue past Campo San Pantalon to Campo San Rocco, just beside the immense church of the Frari. In the 1500s, Tintoretto embellished the **Scuola di San Rocco** with more than 50 canvases; they are an impressive sight, dark paintings aglow with figures hurtling dramatically through space amid flashes of light and color. *The Crucifixion* in the Albergo (the room just off the great hall) is held to be his masterpiece. *Campo di San Rocco, tel. 041/523-4864. Admission: 7,000 lire. Open Apr.–Oct. weekdays 9–5:30; Nov.–Mar. 10–1; year-round Sat. and Sun. 10–4.*

The church of Santa Maria Gloriosa dei Frari (known simply as the **Frari)** is one of Venice's most important churches, a vast soaring Gothic building of brick. Since it is the principal church of the Franciscans, its design is suitably austere to reflect that order's vows of poverty, though paradoxically it contains a number of the most sumptuous pictures in any Venetian church. Chief among them are the magnificent Titian altarpiece, the immense *Assumption of the Virgin* over the main altar. Titian was buried here at the ripe old age of 88, the only one of 70,000 plague victims to be given a personal church burial. *Campo dei Frari. Admission: 1,000 lire. Open Apr.–Oct., Mon.–Sat. 9–noon and 2:30–6, Sun. 3–6; Nov.–Mar., Mon.–Sat. 9:30–noon and 3–5:30, Sun. 3–5:30.*

San Zanipolo and the Rialto Backtracking once again to Piazza San Marco, go to the arch under the Torre dell'Orologio (Clock Tower) and head northeast into the **Merceria,** one of Venice's busiest streets and, with the **Frezzeria** and **Calle dei Fabbri,** part of the shopping area that extends across the Grand Canal into the **Rialto district.** At Campo San Zulian, turn right into Calle della Guerra and Calle delle Bande to the graceful white marble church of **Santa Maria Formosa;** it's situated right on a lively square (of the same name) with a few sidewalk cafés and a small vegetable market on weekday mornings.

Use your map to follow Calle Borgoloco into Campo San Marina, where you turn right, cross the little canal, and take Calle Castelli to
⑫ **Santa Maria dei Miracoli** (Campo dei Miracoli). Perfectly proportioned and sheathed in marble, this late-15thcentury building embodies all the classical serenity of the early Renaissance. The interior is decorated with marble reliefs by the church's architect, Pietro Lombardo, and his son Tullio.

Retrace your steps along Calle Castelli and cross the bridge into Calle delle Erbe, following signs for "SS. Giovanni e Paolo." The
⑬ massive Dominican church of Santi Giovanni e Paolo—**San Zanipolo,** as it's known in the slurred Venetian dialect—is the twin (and rival) of the Franciscan Frari. The church is a kind of pantheon of the doges (25 are buried here), and contains a wealth of artworks. Outside in the campo stands Verrocchio's equestrian statue of Colleoni, who fought for the Venetian cause in the mid-1400s.

Cross the canal in front of the church, and continue along Calle Larga Giacinto Gallina, crossing a pair of bridges to Campiello Santa Maria Nova. Take Salizzada San Canciano to Salizzada San Giovanni Crisostomo to find yourself once again in the mainstream of pedes-
⑭ trians winding their way to the **Rialto Bridge.** Street stalls hung with scarves and gondolier's hats signal that you are entering the heart of Venice's shopping district. Cross over the bridge, and you'll find yourself on the edge of the famous market. Try to visit the Rialto market when it's in full swing (Tues.–Sat. mornings; Mondays are quiet because the fish market is closed), with fruit and vegetable vendors hawking their wares in a colorful and noisy jumble of sights and sounds. Not far beyond is the fish market, where you'll probably find sea creatures you've never seen before (and possibly won't want to see again). A left turn into Ruga San Giovanni and Ruga del Ravano will bring you face to face with scores of shops: At **La Scialuppa** (Calle Saoneri 2695) you'll find hand-carved wooden models of gondolas and their graceful oar locks known as *forcole.*

The Grand Just off Piazzetta di San Marco (the square in front of the Doge's Pal-
Canal ace) you can catch Vaporetto Line 1 at either the San Marco or San Zaccaria landing stages (on Riva degli Schiavoni), to set off on a boat tour along the **Grand Canal.** Serving as Venice's main thoroughfare, the canal winds in the shape of an "S" for more than 3½ kilometers (2 miles) through the heart of the city, past some 200 Gothic-Renaissance palaces. Although restrictions have been introduced to diminish the erosive effect of wash on buildings, this is still the route taken by vaporetti, gondolas, water taxis, mail boats, police boats, fire boats, ambulance boats, barges carrying provisions and building materials, bridal boats, and funeral boats. Your vaporetto tour will give you an idea of the opulent beauty of its palaces and a peek into the side streets and tiny canals where the Venetians go about their daily business. *Vaporetto Line 1. Cost: 2,500 lire.*

Here are some of the key buildings that this tour passes, departing from the San Marco landing: The **Accademia Gallery,** with its fine collection of 14th- to 18th-century Venetian paintings, that were vis-
⑮ ited earlier. The **Peggy Guggenheim Museum,** housed in the incomplete Palazzo Venier dei Leoni, has an exceptional modern art
⑯ collection (*see* Off the Beaten Track, *below*). The **Ca' Rezzonico** was built between the mid-17th and 18th centuries and is now a museum
⑰ of 18th-century Venetian paintings and furniture. **Ca' Foscari** is a 15th-century Gothic building that was once the home of Doge Foscari, who was unwillingly deposed and died the following day!
⑱ Today it's the headquarters of Venice's university. **Ca' d'Oro** is the most flowery palace on the canal; it now houses the Galleria

⑲ Franchetti. The **Palazzo Vendramin Calergi** is a Renaissance building where Wagner died in 1883. It's also the winter home of the mu-
⑳ nicipal casino. The **Fondaco dei Turchi** was an original Byzantine
"house-warehouse" of a rich Venetian merchant, but the building
suffered some fanciful remodeling during the 19th century. It is now
the Natural History Museum.

Off the Beaten Track

Explore the **Ghetto,** where Venice's Jewish community lived in
cramped quarters for many centuries, and visit the **Museo Ebraico**
(Jewish Museum, Campo del Ghetto Nuovo, tel. 041/715359; admission 4,000 lire, with tour 10,000 lire; open June–Sept., Sun.–Fri.
10–7, Oct.–May, Sun.–Fri. 10–4:30.) and the Ghetto's several synagogues. In the same area, go to view the Tintorettos in the Gothic
church of the **Madonna dell'Orto** (off Fondamenta Madonna dell'
Orto).

Visit late heiress Peggy Guggenheim's house and collection of modern art at the **Palazzo Venier dei Leoni** on the Grand Canal. *Entrance: Calle San Cristoforo, Dorsoduro, tel. 041/520–6288.
Admission: 10,000 lire. Open Sun.–Mon., Wed.–Sat. 11–6.*

Have an ice cream at one of the cafés on the Zattere and watch the
big ships steam slowly down the Giudecca Canal.

Explore the island of San Pietro di Castello, at the end of Via Garibaldi. The Renaissance church of **San Pietro** and its tipsy bell tower
stand on a grassy square surrounded by workaday canals and boat-
yards. San Pietro was Venice's cathedral for centuries (San Marco
was officially the Doges' private chapel).

Take Vaporetto Line 20 from Riva degli Schiavoni to visit the Armenian monastery on the island of San Lazzaro degli Armeni, near the
Lido. *Tel. 041/526–0104. Donation welcome. Open daily 3–5.*

Shopping

Glass Venetian glass is as famous as the city's gondolas, and almost every
shop window displays it. There's a lot of cheap glass for sale; if you
want something better, among the top showrooms are **Venini**
(Piazzetta dei Leoncini 314), **Pauly** (Calle dell' Ascensione 72, opposite the APT information office), **Salviati** (Piazza San Marco 78 and
110), **Cenedese** (Piazza San Marco 139), and **Isola** (Campo San Moisè
and Merceria San Zulian 723). On the island of Murano, where prices
are generally no lower than in Venice, **Domus** (Fondamenta dei
Vetrai) has a good selection.

Fabrics **Norelene** (Calle della Chiesa 727, in Dorsoduro, near the Guggenheim) has stunning hand-painted fabrics that make wonderful wall-
hangings or elegantly styled jackets and chic scarves, while **Venetia
Studuim** (Campo San Fantin 1997, opposite La Fenice opera house,
and also at Calle Larga XXII Marzo 2430), is a treasure-trove of
Fortuny-inspired lamps, furnishings, clothes, and accessories.

Shopping The main shopping area extends from Piazza San Marco through the
District Mercerie and Calle dei Fabbri toward the Rialto.

Department The **Coin** store (off Campo San Bartolomeo) specializes in fashion
Stores and accessories. **Standa** has stores on Campo San Luca and Strada
Nuova, where you can pick up medium-price goods of all kinds.

Dining

Venetians love seafood, which figures prominently on most restaurant menus, sometimes to the exclusion of any meat dishes. However, fish is generally expensive, and you should bear this in mind when ordering: The price given on menus for fish as a main course is often per 100 grams, not the total cost of what you are served, which could be two or three times that amount. This is not sharp practice, but a conventional way of pricing fish in Italy. Venice is not a particularly cheap place to eat, but there are good restaurants huddled along Venice's squares and seemingly endless canals. City specialties include *pasta e fagioli* (pasta-and-bean soup); risotto and all kinds of seafood; and the delicious *fegato alla veneziana*, thin strips of liver cooked with onions, served with grilled *polenta* (cornmeal cakes).

For details and price-category definitions, *see* Dining in Staying in Italy, *above*.

Very Expensive
★ **Da Fiore.** Long a favorite with Venetians, Da Fiore has been discovered by tourists, so reservations are imperative. It's known for its excellent seafood dinners, which might include such specialties as *pasticcio di pesce* (fish pie) and *seppioline* (little cuttlefish). Not easy to find, it's just off Campo San Polo. *Calle dello Scaleter 2202, San Polo, tel. 041/721308. Reservations required. AE, DC, MC, V. Closed Sun., Mon., Aug. 10–early Sept., and Dec. 25–Jan. 15.*

★ **Grand Canal.** The Hotel Monaco's restaurant is a favorite with Venetians, who enjoy eating on the lovely canal-side terrace on sunny days, looking across the mouth of the Grand Canal to the island of San Giorgio Maggiore, and in the cozy dining room in winter. All the pasta is made fresh daily on the premises, and the smoked and marinaded salmon are also produced in the restaurant's kitchen. The traditional Venetian dishes are very well prepared; the chef, Angelo Maiocco, also offers delicious meat and fish dishes, such as *scampi alla Ca'd'Oro* (scampi in cognac sauce, served with rice). *Calle Vallaresso 1325, San Marco, tel. 041/520–0211. Reseverations advised. Jacket advised at dinner. AE, DC, MC, V.*

La Caravella. La Caravella is decorated like the dining saloon of an old Venetian sailing ship, with lots of authentic touches. The menu is long and slightly intimidating, though the highly competent mâitre d' will advise you well. The *granseola* (crab) is marvelous in any of several versions. (The same kitchen also serves the slightly less expensive **Cortile** restaurant next door, which has a pretty garden court for summer and wood-paneled salons for winter.) *Calle Larga XXII Marzo 2397, San Marco, tel. 041/520–8901. Reservations required. AE, DC, MC, V. Closed Wed. Nov.–Apr.*

Expensive
Da Arturo. The tiny Da Arturo is a refreshing change from the numerous seafood restaurants of which Venetians are so fond. The cordial proprietor prefers, instead, to offer varied and delicious seasonal vegetable and salad dishes, tasty, tender and generous meat courses like *braciola alla veneziana* (pork chop schnitzel with vinegar), and an authentic, creamy home-made tiramisu for dessert. *Calle degli Assassini 3656, San Marco, tel. 041/528–6974. Reservations required. No credit cards. Closed Sun., 3 weeks in Aug., and Dec. 20–31.*

Fiaschetteria Toscana. This is one of the city's best restaurants, which is why you'll see so many Venetians in the pleasant upstairs dining room or under the arbor in the square out front. Courteous, cheerful waiters serve such specialties as *rombo* (turbot) with capers and an exceptionally good *pasta alla buranella* (pasta with shrimp, au gratin). *Campo San Giovanni Crisostomo 5719, Cannaregio, tel. 041/528–5281. Reservations advised. AE, DC, MC, V. Closed Tues. and first 2 weeks in July.*

Moderate **Al Mondo Novo.** This excellent fish restaurant is owned by a fish wholesaler in the Rialto market, so you can be sure that everything is absolutely fresh. Specialties prepared by Signora Trevisan, the owner's wife, include *cape sante* (pilgrim scallops) and *cape longhe* (razor clams), risottos and pasta dishes, and charcoal-grilled fish. Meat dishes are also available. The manager, Pino Calliandro, offers set menus on request to suit your taste and pocket, and service continues till midnight or later if there's a demand for it. *Salizzada San Lio 5409, Castello, tel. 041/520–0698. Reservations advised. AE, MC, V. Closed Wed. Feb.–Mar.*

Da Gigio. An attractive, friendly, family-run trattoria on the quayside of a canal just off the Strada Nuova. Da Gigio is popular with Venetians and visiting Italians, who appreciate the affable service and excellently cooked, homemade pasta, fish and meat dishes, and high-quality draft wine. Its barroom makes a pleasant, informal setting for simple lunches. *Fondamenta de la Chiesa 3628A, Cannaregio, tel. 041/528–5140. Reservations advised for dinner. AE, DC, MC, V. Closed Sun. dinner, Mon., 2 weeks in mid-Jan., and 2 weeks in Aug.*

Da Ignazio. A smiling waiter will welcome you to this attractive little trattoria in the San Polo district, where you'll find a tempting display of fruits and vegetables fresh from the Rialto market. Specialties include pasta e fagioli and *seppie* (cuttlefish). *Calle dei Saoneri, near San Polo, tel. 041/523–4852. Dinner reservations advised. AE, DC, MC, V. Closed Sat.*

Inexpensive **L'Incontro.** This trattoria has a faithful clientele of Venetians and visitors, attracted by generous meat dishes, friendly waiters, and reasonable prices. Menu choices include juicy steaks, wild duck, boar, and (with advance notice) roast suckling pig. L'Incontro is between San Barnaba and Campo Santa Margherita. *Rio Terra Canal 3062A, Dorsoduro, tel. 041/522–2404. Reservations advised. MC, V. Closed Mon.*

Metropole Buffet. Here at the Hotel Metropole's buffet, in a charming, comfortable room overlooking the waterfront by the Pietà Church, you can eat a substantial and tasty lunch or dinner, helping yourself from a varied selection of starters, soup, pastas, hot and cold fish and meat dishes, and desserts, all for around 45,000 lire. The price even includes a highly drinkable Bianco di Custoza (a light white wine from the Veneto region) on draft. *Riva degli Schiavoni 4149, Castello, tel. 041/520–5044. Reservations advised. AE, DC, MC, V.*

Vino Vino. This is an informal annex of the upscale Antico Martini around the corner, and it's one of the few places where you can eat lightly at almost any time of the day (it's open 10 AM–midnight). The place has a 1920s look: cream-colored walls covered with small prints and ceramic plates, marble tables, and café chairs. Venetians stop in for a glass of wine from an impressive assortment. *Calle delle Veste 2007/a (off Campo San Fantin), San Marco, tel. 041/523–7027. No reservations. AE, DC, MC, V. Closed Tues.*

Lodging

Venice is made up almost entirely of time-worn buildings, so it stands to reason that the majority of hotels are in renovated palaces. However, space is at a premium in this city, and even in the best hotels, rooms can be small and with little natural light. Preservation restrictions on buildings often preclude the installation of such amenities as elevators, air-conditioning systems, and satellite dishes (if any of these facilities is of paramount importance to you, check on their availability before booking). So don't come to Venice expecting to find the standard modern hotel room—you will almost certainly be disappointed. On the other hand, Venice's luxury hotels can offer rooms of fabulous opulence and elegance, and even in the more modest hotels you can find comfortable rooms of great charm and character, sometimes with stunning views.

Venice attracts visitors all year round, although the winter months are generally much quieter, and most hotels offer lower rates during this period. It is always worth booking in advance, but if you haven't, the AVA (Venetian Hoteliers Association) desk at the railway station (tel. 041/715016 and 041/715288; open Apr.–Oct., daily 8 AM–10 PM, Nov.–Mar., daily 8 AM–9:30 PM), at the airport (open Apr.–Oct., daily 10–9; Nov.–Mar., daily 10:30–6:30), and at the municipal parking garage at Piazzale Roma (open Apr.–Oct., daily 9 AM–10 PM; Nov.–Mar., daily 9–9) will help you find a room after your arrival in the city.

For details and price-category definitions, *see* Lodging in Staying in Italy, *above*.

Very Expensive

Cipriani. A sybaritic oasis of stunningly decorated rooms and suites with marble baths and Jacuzzis, the Cipriani is located across St. Mark's Basin on the island of Giudecca (pronounced Joo-DEK-ka), offering a panorama of romantic views of the entire lagoon. The hotel launch whisks guests back and forth to Piazza San Marco at any hour of the day or night. Cooking courses and fitness programs are offered as special programs to occupy the guests. Some rooms have pretty garden patios. The newly restored Palazzo Vendramin annex of the Cipriani (with 7 suites and 3 double rooms) is open all year. *Giudecca 10, tel. 041/520–7744, fax 041/520–3930. 104 rooms with bath. Facilities: restaurant, bar, pool, gardens, tennis, health club. AE, DC, MC, V. Closed Nov.–mid-Mar.*

Danieli. Parts of this rather large hotel are built around a 15th-century palazzo bathed in sumptuous Venetian colors, though the Danieli also has several modern annexes that some find bland and impersonal, and the lower-price rooms can be exceedingly drab. Still, it's a favorite with celebrities and English-speaking visitors, and the dining terrace does have a fantastic view of St. Mark's Basin. *Riva degli Schiavoni 4196, Castello, tel. 041/522–6480, fax 041/520–0208. 235 rooms with bath. AE, DC, MC, V.*

★ **Gritti Palace.** The atmosphere of an aristocratic private home is what the management is after here, and they succeed beautifully. Fresh flowers, fine antiques, sumptuous appointments, and Old World service make this a terrific choice for anyone who wants to be totally pampered. The dining terrace overlooking the Grand Canal is best in the evening when boat traffic dies down. *Campo Santa Maria del Giglio 2467, San Marco, tel. 041/794611, fax 041/520–0942. 88 rooms with bath. AE, DC, MC, V.*

Expensive

Londra Palace. You get the obligatory view of San Giorgio and St. Mark's Basin at this distinguished hotel whose rooms are decorated in dark paisley prints, with such sumptuous touches as canopied beds. French chefs preside over Les Deux Lions restaurant, now a haven of *cuisine française*, and the piano bar is open late. The hotel offers a complimentary Mercedes for one-day excursions and free entrance to the casino. *Riva degli Schiavoni 4171, Castello, tel. 041/520–0533, fax 041/522–5032. 69 rooms with bath. Facilities: terrace, solarium. AE, DC, MC, V.*

★ **Metropole.** Guests can step from their water taxi or gondola into the lobby of this small, very well-run hotel, rich in precious antiques, just five minutes from Piazza San Marco. Many rooms have a view of the lagoon, others overlook the garden at the back, but all are furnished with style. *Riva degli Schiavoni 4149, Castello, tel. 041/520–5044, fax 041/522–3679. 72 rooms with bath. Facilities: buffet restaurant (see* Dining, *above), bar. AE, DC, MC, V.*

Moderate **Accademia.** There's plenty of atmosphere and a touch of the romantic in this delightful hotel in a 17th-century villa. Many rooms overlook the gardens, where you can sit in warm weather. *Fondamenta Bollani 1058, Dorsoduro, tel. 041/523–7846, fax 041/523–9152. 27 rooms, most with bath. Facilities: gardens, bar. AE, DC, MC, V.*

Inexpensive **Alboretti.** This small hotel is simply but attractively furnished. Despite its size and central location, it has a little garden courtyard off the breakfast room and a lounge upstairs from the tiny lobby and bar area. There is no elevator. Together with its moderately priced restaurant, the Alboretti is a good value. *Rio Terra Sant'Agnese 882, Dorsoduro, tel. 041/523–0058, fax 041/521–0158. 19 rooms with bath. Facilities: restaurant. AE, MC, V.*

Bucintoro. This friendly, family-run hotel on the waterfront by the Arsenal, slightly off the tourist track, is the only hotel in Venice where every room has a view over the lagoon. The rooms are clean and simple, and the price unbeatable for such a spectacular position. *Riva San Biagio 2135, Castello, tel. 041/522–3240, fax 041/523–5224. 28 rooms, 18 with bath. No credit cards. Closed Jan.–mid-Feb.*

La Residenza. A Gothic palace makes a delightful setting for this charming hotel, conveniently close to both San Marco and the San Zaccaria landing stage. Breakfast is served in a real antique-furnished Venetian salon. Make reservations well in advance. *Campo Bandiera e Moro 3608, Castello, tel. 041/528–5315, fax 041/523–8859. 19 rooms, some with bath. AE, DC, MC, V. Closed 2nd week Jan.–mid-Feb., mid-Nov.–2nd week Dec.*

Locanda Fiorita. This welcoming, newly refurbished hotel is tucked away in a sunny little square (where breakfast is served in the summer), just off Campo Santo Stefano, near the Accademia Bridge, and is very central for sightseeing. The rooms have beamed ceilings and are simply furnished. *Campiello Novo 3457, San Marco, tel. 041/523–4754. 10 rooms, 7 with shower. AE, MC, V. Closed 2 weeks Nov.–Dec.*

Paganelli. This charming, small hotel, located on the waterfront near Piazza San Marco and with an annex on the quiet square of Campo San Zaccaria, is tastefully decorated in the Venetian style. Three rooms overlook the lagoon, and six have good views over the square. *Riva degli Schiavoni 4182, Castello, tel. 041/522–4324, fax 041/523–9267. 22 rooms, 19 with bath or shower. AE, DC, MC, V.*

Riva. This small hotel close to San Marco stands in a picturesque spot at the junction of three canals much used by all manner of Venetian watercraft—endlessly fascinating to watch but a little noisy early in the morning. It has recently been well refurbished by its enthusiastic new owner. *Ponte dell'Angelo 5310, Castello, tel. 041/522–7034. 12 rooms, 10 with bath. No credit cards. Closed mid-Nov.–Feb. 1, except for 2 weeks at Christmas.*

The Arts

For a program of events, pick up the free "Guest in Venice" booklet, available from the Assessorato al Turismo (Ca' Giustinian, 2nd floor, Calle del Ridotto), near Piazza San Marco, or at most hotel desks. Your hotel may also be able to get you tickets for some events.

Concerts There are regular concerts at the Pietà Church, with an emphasis on Vivaldi, and at San Stae—though prices tend to be high and the quality of performance uneven. Concerts, sometimes free, are also held by visiting choirs and musicians in other churches. For information on these often short-notice events, ask at the APT office, and look for posters on walls and in restaurants and shops. The **Kele e Teo Agency** (Piazza San Marco 4930, tel. 041/520–8722) supplies tickets for many of the city's musical events.

Opera The season at **Teatro La Fenice** (Campo San Fantin, tel. 041/521–0161, fax 041/522–1768) runs all year, except for August, with opera or concert performances most months. The box office is open September to July, Monday–Saturday 9:30–12:30 and 4–6, except when there's a performance on Sunday, in which case the box office is open Sunday and remains closed the following Monday.

Nightlife

The **Martini Scala Club** (Calle delle Veste, near Teatro La Fenice, tel. 041/522–4121) is an elegant piano bar with late-night restaurant. The bars of the top hotels stay open as long as their customers keep on drinking. Dedicated nighthawks should get a copy of *Notturno Veneziano (Venetian Nightlife)*, a guide to live music venues, discos, and late bars in and around Venice, published by the Assessorato alla Gioventù, the municipality's Youth Department (Corte Contarini 1529, 4th floor, near Piazza San Marco). It's available free at APT information offices, at present only in Italian, but with useful maps and easy-to-follow notes. Night spots popular with young people are **Ai Canottieri** (Fondamenta San Giobbe 690, Cannaregio, tel. 041/71548, live music Tues., closed Sun.) and **Paradiso Perduto** (Fondamenta Misericordia 2540, Cannaregio, tel. 041/720581, live music usually on weekends, closed Wed.).

Campania

Campania (the region of Naples, the Amalfi coast, and other sights) is where most people's preconceived ideas of Italy become a reality. You'll find lots of sun, good food that relies heavily on tomatoes and mozzarella, acres of classical ruins, and gorgeous scenery. The exuberance of the locals doesn't leave much room for efficient organization, however, and you may have to revise your concept of real time; here minutes dilate into hours at the drop of a hat.

Once a city that rivaled Paris as a brilliant and refined cultural capital, Napoli (Naples) is afflicted by acute urban decay and chronic delinquency. You need patience, stamina, and a healthy dose of caution to visit Naples on your own, but it's worth it for those who have a sense of adventure and the capacity to discern the enormous riches the city has accumulated in its 2,000-year existence.

On the other hand, if you want the fun without the hassle, head for Sorrento, Capri, and the Amalfi coast, legendary haunts of the sirens who tried to lure Odysseus off course. Sorrento is touristy but has some fine old hotels and beautiful views; it's a good base for a leisurely excursion to Pompeii. Capri is a pint-size paradise, though sometimes too crowded for comfort, while the Amalfi coast has some enchanting towns and spectacular scenery.

Campania

Volturno · A/E45 · Benevento · 264 · Capua · Caserta · 7 · Montesarchio · 7a · Aversa · A1 · A2 · A16 · Avellino · Pozzuoli · Napoli (Naples) · 268 · A3 · Vesuvio · 88 · 841 · Bácoli · Herculaneum · Pompeii · Ischia · Bay of Naples · A3 · Ischia · Ravello · Sorrento · 163 · Amalfi · Salerno · Grotta Azzurra · Positano · Anacapri · Capri · Capri · Tyrrhenian Sea

0 — 20 miles
0 — 30 km

N

Getting Around

By Plane   There are several daily flights between Rome and Naples's Capodichino Airport (tel. 081/709–2815), 8 kilometers (5 miles) north of the downtown area. During the summer months there's a direct helicopter service between Capodichino, Capri, and Ischia; for information, tel. 081/789–6273 or 081/584–1481.

By Train   A great number of trains run between Rome and Naples every day; Intercity trains make the journey in less than two hours. There are several stations in Naples, and a network of suburban trains connects the city with diverse points of interest in Campania. The central station is at Piazza Garibaldi. For train information, tel. 081/553–4188. Naples has a Metropolitana (subway); though it's old and trains are infrequent, it beats the traffic. The fare is 1,200 lire.

By Bus   For bus information, call **SITA** (tel. 081/552–2176) or the Naples Transport Board (tel. 081/553–4188).

By Car   The Naples–Pompeii–Salerno toll road has exits at Ercolano (Herculaneum) and Pompeii, and connects with the tortuous coastal road to Sorrento and the Amalfi coast at the Castellammare exit. Driving within Naples is not recommended: Window smashing and robbery are not uncommon.

By Boat   Most boats and hydrofoils for the islands, the Sorrento peninsula, and the Amalfi coast leave from the Molo Beverello, near Naples's Piazza Municipio. **Caremar** (tel. 081/551–3882), **Navigazione Libera del Golfo** (tel. 081/552–7209), and **Lauro** (tel. 081/551–3236) operate a frequent passenger and car ferry service, while hydrofoils of the Caremar, Navigazione Libera del Golfo, and **Alilauro** (tel. 081/761–

1004) lines leave from both Molo Beverello and the hydrofoil station at Mergellina pier, from which **SNAV** (tel. 081/761–2348) also operates.

Guided Tours

Aside from the one-, two-, or three-day guided tours of the area departing from Rome, offered by **American Express** (tel. 06/67641), **CIT** (tel. 06/47941), **Appian Line** (tel. 06/488–4151) and other operators, **CIT** in Naples (Piazza Municipio 72, tel. 081/552–5426) has a wide range of half-day and all-day tours on the mainland and to the islands. Similar tours are offered by **Tourcar** (Piazza Matteotti 1, tel. 081/552–0429).

Tourist Information

Capri (Marina Grande pier, tel. 081/837–0634; and Piazza Umberto I, Capri town, tel. 081/837–0686).
Naples. EPT Information Offices (Piazza dei Martiri 58, tel. 081/405311; central station, tel. 081/268779; hydrofoil station, Mergellina, summer only, tel. 081/761–4585; and Capodichino Airport, tel. 081/780–5761). AAST Information Office (Piazza del Gesù, tel. 081/552–3328).
Sorrento (Via De Maio 35, tel. 081/878–1115).

Exploring Campania

Naples   Founded by the Greeks, **Naples** became a playground of the Romans and was ruled thereafter by a succession of foreign dynasties, all of which left traces of their cultures in the city and its environs. The most splendid of these rulers were the Bourbons, who were responsible for much of what you will want to see in Naples, starting with the 17th-century **Palazzo Reale** (Royal Palace), still furnished in the lavish Baroque style that suited them so well. *Piazza del Plebiscito, tel. 081/413888. Admission: 6,000 lire. Open Apr.–Oct., daily 9–7:30; Nov.–Mar., Mon.–Sat. 9–2, Sun. 9–1.*

Across the way is the massive stone **Castel Nuovo,** which was built by the city's Aragon rulers in the 13th century; some rooms recently opened to the public contain sculptures and frescoes of the 14th and 15th centuries. *Admission: 5,000 lire. Open Mon.–Fri. 9–2, Sat. 9–1, closed Sun.*

Walk up Via Toledo, keeping an eye on the antics of the Neapolitans, whose daily lives are fraught with theatrical gestures and fiery speeches. They all seem to be actors in their own human comedy.

Time Out   Stop in at **Caflisch,** a historic café that has recently added a good fast-food counter, and try a *sfogliatella*, a delicious, clam-shaped Neapolitan pastry. *Via Toledo 253.*

Continue along Via Toledo, also known as Via Roma, and make a detour to the right to see the oddly faceted stone facade and elaborate Baroque interior of the church of the **Gesù** (Via Benedetto Croce) and, directly opposite, the church of **Santa Chiara,** built in the early 1300s in Provençal Gothic style. A favorite Neapolitan song celebrates the quiet beauty of its cloister, decorated in delicate floral tiles.

Time Out   For an authentic Neapolitan pizza in a genuine pizzeria, stop in at **Lombardi,** where you can have a classic pizza made in a wood-fired brick oven or a full meal in a tiny, crowded setting with no frills and lots of atmosphere. *Via Benedetto Croce 59.*

Another detour off Via Toledo, to the left this time, takes you from **Piazza Dante** to the Montesanto funicular, which ascends to the Vomero hill, where you can see the bastions of **Castel Sant'Elmo** and visit the museum in the **Certosa di San Martino,** a Carthusian monastery restored in the 17th century. It contains an eclectic collection of Neapolitan landscape paintings, royal carriages, and *presepi* (Christmas crèches). Check out the view from the balcony off room No. 25. *Certosa di San Martino, tel. 081/578–1769. Admission: 6,000 lire. Open Tues.–Sun. 9–2.*

Return to Piazza Dante and follow Via Pessina (an extension of Via Toledo) to the **Museo Archeologico Nazionale.** Dusty and unkempt, the museum undergoes perpetual renovations, but it holds one of the world's great collections of antiquities. Greek and Roman sculptures, vividly colored mosaics, countless objects from Pompeii and Herculaneum, and an equestrian statue of the Roman emperor Nerva are all worth seeing. *Piazza Museo, tel. 081/440166. Admission: 8,000 lire. Open May–Sept., Mon.–Sat. 9–7, Sun. 9–1; Oct.–Apr., Mon.–Sat. 9–2, Sun. 9–1.*

About a mile north on the same road (take a bus or a taxi), you'll come to the **Museo di Capodimonte,** housed in an 18th-century palace built by Bourbon king Charles III, and surrounded by a vast park that must have been lovely when it was better cared for. In the picture gallery are some fine Renaissance paintings; climb the stairs to the terrace for a magnificent view of Naples and the bay. Downstairs you can visit the State Apartments and see the extensive collection of porcelain, much of it produced in the Bourbons' own factory right here on the grounds. *Parco di Capodimonte, tel. 081/744–1307. Admission: 8,000 lire. Tues.–Sat. 9–2, Sun. 9–1.*

Herculaneum   **Herculaneum** (Ercolano) lies 14 kilometers (9 miles) southeast of Naples. Reputed to have been founded by the legendary Hercules, the elite Roman resort was devastated by the same volcanic eruption that buried Pompeii in AD 79. Recent excavations have revealed that many died on the shore in an attempt to escape, as a slow-moving mud slide embalmed the entire town by covering it with an 11-meter-deep (35-foot-deep) blanket of volcanic ash and ooze. While that may have been unfortunate for Herculaneum's residents, it has helped preserve the site in pristine detail for nearly two millenia. *Corso Ercolano, tel. 081/739–0963. Admission: 8,000 lire. Open daily 9–one hour before sunset (ticket office closes 2 hours before sunset).*

Pompeii   **Pompeii,** a larger community 8 kilometers (5 miles) farther to the east, lost even more residents. An estimated 2,000 of them perished on that fateful August day. The ancient city of Pompeii was much larger than Herculaneum, and excavations have progressed to a much greater extent (though the remains are not as well preserved, due to some 18th-century scavenging for museum-quality artworks, most of which you are able to see at Naples's Museo Archeologico Nazionale; *see above*). This prosperous Roman city had an extensive forum, lavish baths and temples, and patrician villas richly decorated with frescoes. It's worth buying a detailed guide of the site in order to give meaning and understanding to the ruins and their importance. Be sure to see the **Villa dei Misteri,** whose frescoes are in mint condition. Perhaps that is a slight exaggeration, but the paintings are so rich with detail and depth of color that one finds it difficult to believe that they are 1,900 years old. Have lots of small change handy to tip the guards at the more important houses so they will unlock the gates for you. *Pompeii Scavi, tel. 081/861–0744. Admission: 10,000 lire. Open daily 9–one hour before sunset (ticket office closes 2 hours before sunset).*

Sorrento   Another 28 kilometers (18 miles) southwest is **Sorrento,** in the not-too-distant past a small, genteel resort for a fashionable elite. Now the town has spread out along the crest of its fabled cliffs. Once this was an area full of secret haunts for the few tourists who came for the beauty of this coastline. Now, it has been "discovered" and the secret haunts are the playground for package tours. In Sorrento's case, however, the change is not as grim as it sounds, since nothing can dim the delights of the marvelous climate and view of the Bay of Naples. For the best views go to the **Villa Comunale,** near the old church of **San Francesco** (in itself worth a visit), or to the terrace behind the **Museo Correale.** The museum, an attractive 18th-century villa, houses an interesting collection of decorative arts (furniture, china, and so on) and paintings of the Neapolitan school. *Via Correale. Admission: 5,000 lire; gardens only, 3,000 lire. Open Apr.–Sept., Mon. and Wed.–Sat. 9–12:30 and 5–7, Sun. 9–12:30; Oct.–Mar., Mon. and Wed.–Sat. 9–12:30 and 3–5, Sun. 9–12:30.*

Capri   Sorrento makes a convenient jumping-off spot for a boat trip to **Capri.** No matter how many day-trippers crowd onto the island, no matter how touristy certain sections have become, Capri remains one of Italy's loveliest places. Incoming visitors disembark at Marina Grande, from where you can take some time out for an excursion to the **Grotta Azzurra** (Blue Grotto). Be warned that this must rank as one of the country's all-time great rip-offs: Motorboat, rowboat, and grotto admissions are charged separately, and if there's a line of boats waiting, you'll have little time to enjoy the grotto's marvelous colors. At Marina Grande you can also embark on a boat excursion around the island.

A cog railway or bus service takes you up to the town of Capri, where you can stroll through the **Piazzetta,** a choice place from which to watch the action, and window-shop expensive boutiques or browse in souvenir shops along Via Vittorio Emanuele on your way to the **Gardens of Augustus,** which have gorgeous views. The town of Capri is deliberately commercial and self-consciously picturesque. To get away from the crowds, hike to **Villa Jovis,** one of the many villas that Roman emperor Tiberius built on the island, at the end of a lane that climbs steeply uphill. The walk takes about 45 minutes, with pretty views all the way and a final spectacular vista of the entire Bay of Naples and part of the Gulf of Salerno. *Via Tiberio. Admission: 4,000 lire. Open daily 9–one hour before sunset.*

Or take the bus or a jaunty open taxi to **Anacapri** and look for the little church of **San Michele,** off Via Orlandi, where a magnificent handpainted majolica tile floor shows you an 18th-century vision of the Garden of Eden. *Admission: 2,000 lire. Open Easter–Oct., Mon.–Sat. 10–6, Sun. 10–2.*

From Piazza della Vittoria, picturesque Via Capodimonte leads to **Villa San Michele,** charming former home of Swedish scientist-author Axel Munthe. *Via Axel Munthe. Admission: 5,000 lire. Open May–Sept., daily 9–6; Oct.–Apr., daily 10:30–3:30.*

Amalfi and   From Sorrento, the coastal drive down to the resort town of Amalfi
Positano   provides some of the most dramatic and beautiful scenery you'll find in all of Italy. **Positano**'s jumble of pastel houses, topped by white-washed cupolas, clings to the mountainside above the sea. The town—the prettiest along this stretch of coast—attracts a sophisti-

cated group of visitors and summer residents who find that its relaxed and friendly atmosphere more than compensates for the sheer effort of moving about this exhaustingly vertical town, most of whose streets are stairways. This former fishing village has now opted for the more regular and lucrative rewards of tourism and commercialized fashion. Practically every other shop is a boutique displaying locally made casual wear. The beach is the town's main focal point, with a little promenade and a multitude of café-restaurants.

Amalfi itself is a charming maze of covered alleys and narrow byways straggling up the steep mountainside. The piazza just below the cathedral forms the town's heart—a colorful assortment of pottery stalls, cafés, and postcard shops grouped around a venerable old fountain. The cathedral's exterior is its most impressive feature, so there's no need to climb all those stairs unless you really want to.

Ravello   Do not miss **Ravello,** 8 kilometers (5 miles) north of Amalfi. Ravello is not actually on the coast, but on a high mountain bluff overlooking the sea. The road up to it is a series of switchbacks, and the village itself clings precariously on the mountain spur. The village flourished during the 13th century and then fell into a tranquillity that has remained unchanged for the past six centuries. The center of the town is **Piazza Duomo,** with its cathedral, founded in 1087 and recently restored. Note the fine bronze 12th-century doors and, inside, two pulpits richly decorated with mosaics: one depicting the story of Jonah and the whale; the other—more splendid—carved with fantastic beasts and resting on a pride of lions.

To the right of the cathedral is the entrance to the 11th-century **Villa Rufolo.** The composer Richard Wagner once stayed in Ravello, and there is a Wagner festival every summer on the villa's garden terrace. There is a moorish cloister with interlacing pointed arches, beautiful gardens, an 11th-century tower, and a belvedere with a fine view of the coast. *Admission: 3,000 lire. Open summer, daily 9:30–1 and 3–7:30; winter, daily 9:30–1, 2–4:30.*

Across the square from the cathedral is a lovely walk leading to the **Villa Cimbrone.** At the entrance to the villa complex is a small cloister that looks medieval but was actually built in 1917, with two bas-reliefs: one representing nine Norman warriors, the other illustrating the seven deadly sins. Then, the long avenue leads through peaceful gardens scattered with grottoes, small temples, and statues to a belvedere and terrace where, on a clear day, the view stretches out over the Mediterranean Sea. *Admission: 5,000 lire. Open daily 8:30–1 hour before sunset.*

Dining and Lodging

For details and price-category definitions, *see* Dining and Lodging in Staying in Italy, *above.*

Amalfi   **La Caravella.** Tucked away under some arches lining the coast road,
Dining   the Caravella has a nondescript entrance but a pleasant interior decorated in a medley of colors and paintings of old Amalfi. It's small and intimate, and proprietor Franco describes the cuisine as "*sfiziosa*" (taste-tempting). Specialties include *scialatielli* (homemade pasta with shellfish sauce) and *pesce al limone* (fresh fish with lemon sauce). *Via M. Camera 12, tel. 089/871029. Reservations advised. AE, MC, V. Closed Tues. and Nov. 10–30. Moderate.*

Lodging   **Santa Caterina.** A large mansion perched above terraced and flow-
★   ered hillsides on the coast road just outside Amalfi proper, the Santa

Caterina is one of the best hotels on the entire coast. The rooms are tastefully decorated, and most have small terraces or balconies with great views. There are lounges and terraces for relaxing, and an elevator whisks guests down to the seaside saltwater pool, bar, and swimming area. Amid lemon and orange groves, there are two romantic villa annexes. Some rooms and suites are in the Very Expensive category. *Strada Amalfitana 9, tel. 089/871012, fax 089/871351. 54 rooms with bath. Facilities: restaurant, bar, pool, beach bar, parking. AE, DC, MC, V. Expensive–Very Expensive.*

Capri **La Capannina.** Only a few steps away from Capri's social center, the
Dining Piazzetta, La Capannina has a delightful vine-hung courtyard for summer dining and a reputation as one of the island's best eating places. Antipasto features fried ravioli and eggplant stuffed with ricotta, and house specialties include chicken, scaloppine and a refreshing, homemade lemon liqueur. *Via Botteghe 14, tel. 081/837–0732. Reservations advised. AE. Closed Wed. (except during Aug.) and Nov.–mid-Mar. Moderate–Expensive.*

★ **Al Grottino.** This small family-run restaurant, with a handy location near the Piazzetta, sports autographed photographs of celebrity customers. House specialties are gnocchi with mozzarella and *linguine con gamberini* (pasta with shrimp sauce). *Via Longano 27, tel. 081/837–0584. Dinner reservations advised. AE, MC, V. Closed Tues. and Nov. 3–Mar. 20. Moderate.*

Da Gemma. One of Capri's favorite places for a homey atmosphere and a good meal, Da Gemma features *pappardelle all'aragosta* (egg noodles with lobster sauce) and fritto misto. If you're budgeting, don't order fish that you pay for by weight; it's always expensive. You can have pizza as a starter in the evening. *Via Madre Serafina 6, tel. 081/837–0461. Reservations advised. AE, DC, MC, V. Closed Mon. and Nov. Moderate.*

Lodging **Quisisana.** One of Italy's poshest hotels is sited right in the center of the town of Capri. The rooms are spacious, and many have arcaded balconies with views of the sea; the decor is traditional or contemporary, with some antique accents. From the small terrace at the entrance you can watch all Capri go by, but the enclosed garden and pool in the back are perfect for getting away from it all. The bar and restaurant are casual in a terribly elegant way. *Via Camerelle 2, tel. 081/837–0788, fax 081/837–6080. 150 rooms with bath. Facilities: restaurant, pool, tennis. AE, DC, MC, V. Closed Nov.–mid-Mar. Very Expensive.*

★ **Villa Brunella.** The glassed-in bar of this family-run hotel is on the lane leading to Punta Tragara and the Faraglioni. From that level you descend to the restaurant, with the rooms and the swimming pool all on lower levels. Furnishings are tastefully casual and comfortable, and the views from all levels are wonderful. Be prepared to climb stairs; there's no elevator. *Via Tragara 24, tel. 081/837–0122, fax 081/837–0430. 18 rooms with bath. Facilities: restaurant, bar, pool. AE, DC, MC, V. Closed Nov.–Mar. Expensive.*

Villa Sarah. Just a 10-minute walk from the Piazzetta, the Sarah is a whitewashed Mediterranean villa with bright, simply furnished rooms. There's a garden and small bar, but no restaurant. *Via Tiberio 3/A, tel. 081/837–0689, fax 081/837–7215. 20 rooms with bath. AE, MC, V. Closed Nov.–Mar. Moderate.*

Naples **La Sacrestia.** This lovely restaurant is in an elevated position, above
Dining Mergellina, with a fine view and a delightful summer terrace. The menu offers traditional Neapolitan cuisine; among the specialties are *linguine in salsa di scorfano* (pasta in scorpion-fish sauce) and *spigola* (sea bass), either steamed or baked. *Via Orazio 116, tel. 081/*

761–1051. Reservations advised. AE, DC, MC, V. Closed Mon. (Sept.–June), Sun. (in July), and Aug. Expensive.

★ **Ciro a Santa Brigida.** Centrally located off Via Toledo near the Castel Nuovo, this no-frills restaurant is a favorite with businesspeople, artists, and journalists. Tables are arranged on two levels, and the decor is classic trattoria. This is the place to try traditional Neapolitan *sartù di riso* (a rich rice dish with meat and peas) and *melanzane alla parmigiana* or *scaloppe alla Ciro*, eggplant or veal with prosciutto and mozzarella. There's pizza, too. *Via Santa Brigida 71, tel. 081/552–4072. Reservations advised. AE, DC, MC, V. Closed Sun. and Aug. Moderate.*

La Bersagliera. This restaurant has been making tourists happy for years, with a great location on the Santa Lucia waterfront, cheerful waiters, mandolin music, and good spaghetti *alla disgraziata* (with tomatoes, capers, and black olives) and *mozzarella in carrozza* (cheese fried in batter). *Borgo Marinaro 10, tel. 081/764–6016. Reservations advised. AE, DC, MC, V. Closed Tues. Moderate.*

Lodging **Excelsior.** Splendidly located on the shore drive, the Excelsior has views of the bay from its front rooms. The spacious bedrooms are well furnished in informal floral prints or more formal Empire style; all have a comfortable, traditional air. The salons are formal, with chandeliers and wall paintings, and the excellent Casanova restaurant is elegant. *Via Partenope 48, tel. 081/764–0111, fax 081/764–9743. 102 rooms with bath. Facilities: restaurant, bar, sauna, garage. AE, DC, MC, V. Very Expensive.*

★ **Jolly Ambassador.** This hotel occupies the top 14 floors of a downtown skyscraper, and its rooms and roof restaurant have wonderful views of Naples and the bay. It's furnished in dark brown, beige, and white in the functional, modern style typical of this reliable chain, which promises comfort and efficiency in a city where these are scarce commodities. *Via Medina 70, tel. 081/416000, fax 081/551–8010. 251 rooms with bath. Facilities: restaurant, bar. AE, DC, MC, V. Moderate–Expensive.*

Rex. This hotel occupies a fairly quiet location near the Santa Lucia waterfront. It is situated on the first two floors of an Art Nouveau building and lacks an elevator. The decor ranges from 1950s modern to fake period pieces and even some folk art, haphazardly combined. Although it has no restaurant, there are many in the area. *Via Palepoli 12, tel. 081/764–9389, fax 081/764–9227. 40 rooms, 37 with bath or shower. Facilities: bar, garage. AE, DC, MC, V. Moderate.*

Positano **Capurale.** Among all the popular restaurants on the beach prome-
Dining nade, Capurale (just around the corner) has the best food and lowest prices. Tables are set under vines on a breezy sidewalk in the summer, upstairs and indoors in winter. Spaghetti con melanzane and *crêpes al formaggio* (cheese-filled crepes) are good choices here. *Via Marina, tel. 089/875374. Reservations advised for outdoor tables. AE, DC, MC, V. Closed Tues. (Nov.–Mar). Moderate.*

Lodging **Le Sirenuse.** The most fashionable hotel in Positano is this converted 18th-century villa that has been in the same family for eight generations. The hotel is set into the hillside about 200 feet above Positano's harbor. Most of the bedrooms face the sea—these are the best. Because of the hotel's location, the dining room is like a long, closed-in terrace overlooking the village of Positano—a magnificent view. The cuisine varies from acceptable to excellent. *Via Cristoforo Colombo 30, tel. 089/875066, fax 081/811798. 60 rooms with bath. Facilities: restaurant, pool, sauna. AE, DC, MC, V. Very Expensive.*

San Pietro. Situated on the side of a cliff, this is quite possibly one of the world's most attractive hotels because of its magnificent views of the sea and the Amalfi coast. The decor of the hotel is eclectic, with unusual antiques and, everywhere, hanging bougainvillea. The furnishings are perfectly arranged to give a sense of openness and create a feeling of opulence. The guest rooms are decorated with an eye to detail, but their views steal the show. Verdant with plants, the light, open dining room offers fine Italian cuisine. An elevator takes guests to the hotel's small beach area. *Via Laurito 2, tel. 089/875455, fax 089/811449. 60 rooms with bath. Facilities: restaurant, beach, pool, tennis. AE, DC, MC, V. Closed Nov.–Mar. Very Expensive.*

Palazzo Murat. The location is perfect, in the heart of town, near the beachside promenade, but set within a walled garden. The old wing is a historic palazzo, with tall windows and wrought-iron balconies; the newer wing is a whitewashed Mediterranean building with arches and terraces. Guests can relax in antique-strewn lounges or on the charming vine-draped patio. *Via dei Mulini 23, tel. 089/875177, fax 089/811419. 28 rooms with bath. Facilities: bar, garden. AE, DC, MC, V. Closed Nov. 5–Mar. Expensive.*

Santa Caterina. There is more to this newly refurbished hotel than meets the eye, with rooms descending on three levels down the steep slope. The exquisite view over the town and seashore can be relished from each of the somewhat cramped rooms as well as the generous balconies and terraces. On street level (the top floor), there is also a good fish restaurant, well patronized by the locals. It's quite a hike down to the beach—a good 15 minutes down the steps—but that's nothing new in Positano. *Via Pasitea 113. tel. 089/811513. 12 rooms with bath or shower. Facilities: bar, restaurant. AE, DC, MC, V. Closed Nov.–Mar. Inexpensive.*

Ravello **Hotel Palumbo.** Of all the hotels on the Amalfi coast, the Hotel
Lodging Palumbo is the most genteel—a refined 12th-century retreat. Some of the bedrooms do tend to be small, but they are beautifully furnished and full of character. The rooms facing the sea are the choice ones—and the more expensive. The lounge area is filled with the owner's antiques and, with the greatest of ease, guests quickly come to view the Hotel Palumbo as their private palazzo. *Via Toro 28, tel. 089/857244, fax 089/857347. 12 rooms with bath. Facilities: restaurant, bar, garden. AE, DC, MC, V. Very Expensive.*

Sorrento **Antica Trattoria.** This is a homey, hospitable place with a garden for
Dining summer dining. The specialties of the house are a classic *pennette al profumo di bosco* (pasta with a creamy mushroom and ham sauce), fish (which can be expensive), and *melanzane alla parmigiana* (eggplant with mozzarella). *Via Giuliani 33, tel. 081/807–1082. Dinner reservations advised. No credit cards. Closed Mon., Jan. 10–Feb. 10. Moderate.*

Il Mulino. Occupying a 19th-century villa perched on the edge of the vine-covered gorge of the Mulini, this is an elegant veranda restaurant. Try the *scialatielli alla siciliana* (homemade pasta with mozzarella and eggplant). *Via Fuorimura 7, tel. 081/878–1216. Reservations advised. AE, DC, MC, V. Closed Tues. Moderate.*

★ **Parrucchiano.** One of the town's best and oldest, Parrucchiano features greenhouse-type dining rooms dripping with vines and dotted with plants. Among the antipasti, try the *panzarotti* (pastry crust filled with mozzarella and tomato), and for a main course, the *scaloppe alla sorrentina*, again with mozzarella and tomato. *Corso Italia 71, tel. 081/878–1321. Reservations advised weekends and Aug. MC, V. Closed Wed. Nov.–May. Moderate.*

Lodging **Cocumella.** In a lovely cliffside garden in a quiet residential area just outside Sorrento, this historic old villa (it features a 17th-century chapel) has been totally renovated for comfort. Furnishings are a tasteful blend of antique and modern; there are vaulted ceilings and archways, a dining veranda, and stunning tiled floors. Cocumella has an exclusive, elegant atmosphere without being stuffy. *Via Cocumella 7, tel. 081/878-2933, fax 081/878-3712. 60 rooms with bath. Facilities: restaurant, garden, parking, pool, tennis. AE, DC, MC, V. Very Expensive.*

Excelsior Vittoria. In the heart of Sorrento, but removed from the main square by an arbored walk, the Excelsior Vittoria is right on the cliff and has old-fashioned, Art Nouveau furnishings, some very grand, though faded. Tenor Enrico Caruso's bedroom is preserved as a relic; guest bedrooms are spacious and elegant in a turn-of-the-century way. It overlooks the bay and is recommended for those who like a lot of atmosphere with their views. *Piazza Tasso 34, tel. 081/807-1044, fax 081/877-1206. 106 rooms with bath. Facilities: restaurant, pool, garden, parking. AE, DC, MC, V. Expensive.*

Imperial Hotel Tramontano. Incorporating the birthplace of the poet Torquato Tasso—the first of an impressive list of literary credentials—this palatial villa lies within a semitropical garden in the center of Sorrento. The sumptuous furnishings and Belle-Epoque tone are set off by the spectacular views out to sea. *Via Veneto 1, tel. 081/878-2588, fax 081/807-2344. 120 rooms with bath or shower. Facilities: restaurant, bar, garden, private beach, parking, conference rooms. Closed Apr.-Nov. Expensive.*

Eden. Eden occupies a fairly quiet but central location, with a garden. The bedrooms are bright but undistinguished; the lounge and lobby have more character. It's an unpretentious but friendly hotel, although it can get crowded in high season. *Via Correale 25, tel. 081/878-1909, fax 081/807-2016. 60 rooms with bath. Facilities: restaurant, bar, parking, pool. AE, MC, V. Closed Nov.-Feb. Moderate.*

City. The central location and excellent value-for-money are the best reasons to stay in this modest establishment, close to the bus and train stations. Bedrooms are small and functional, but the atmosphere is relaxed and the management always ready with information and advice. *Corso Italia 221, tel. 081/877-2210. 12 rooms with bath. MC, V. Inexpensive.*

19 Luxembourg

Luxembourg, one of the smallest countries in the United Nations, measures only 2,587 square kilometers (999 square miles), less than the size of Rhode Island. It is dwarfed by its neighbors—Germany, Belgium, and France—yet from its history of invasion, occupation, and siege, you might think those square miles were built over solid gold. In fact, it was Luxembourg's very defenses against centuries of attack that rendered it all the more desirable: From AD 963, when Siegfried built a castle on the high promontory of the Bock, the once-grander duchy encased itself in layer upon layer of fortifications until by the mid-19th century its very invulnerability was considered a threat to those not commanding its thick stone walls. After successive invasions—by the Burgundians, the Spanish, the French, the Austrians, the French again, the Dutch, and the Prussians—Luxembourg was ultimately dismantled in the name of peace, its neutrality guaranteed by the 1867 Treaty of London, and its function reduced to that of a buffer zone. What remains of its walls, while impressive, is only a reminder of what was one of the strongholds of Europe—the "Gibraltar of the North."

Luxembourg is besieged again, this time by bankers and Eurocrats. Its Boulevard Royal bristles with international banks—enough to rival Switzerland—and just outside the old city, a new colony has been populated by *fonctionnaires* for the European Union, the heir to the Common Market. Fiercely protecting its share of the expanding bureaucracy from competitive co-capitals Strasbourg and Brussels, Luxembourg digs its heels in once again, vying not only for political autonomy but for its newfound prosperity and clout. Thus the national motto takes on new meaning: *Mir wëlle bleiwe wat mir sin,* or "We want to stay what we are"—nowadays, a viable Grand Duchy in the heart of modern Europe.

Visitors will find evidence of Luxembourg's military past scattered around the Grand Duchy's luxurious countryside: There are castles by the dozen, set in the densely wooded hills of La Petite Suisse (Little Switzerland) to the east, in the crests and valleys of the Ardennes to the north, and along the riverbanks of the Our and the Moselle, the latter renowned for its crisp white wines.

Essential Information

Before You Go

When to Go The main tourist season in Luxembourg is the same as in Belgium—early May to late September, with spring and fall the nicest times. But temperatures in Luxembourg tend to be cooler than those in Belgium, particularly in the hilly north, where there is frequently snow in winter.

Climate In general, temperatures in Luxembourg are moderate. It does drizzle frequently, however, so be sure to bring a raincoat.

The following are the average daily maximum and minimum temperatures for Luxembourg.

Luxembourg

Jan.	37F	3C	May	65F	18C	Sept.	66F	19C
	29	– 1		46	8		50	10
Feb.	40F	4C	June	70F	21C	Oct.	56F	13C
	31	– 1		52	11		43	6
Mar.	49F	10C	July	73F	23C	Nov.	44F	7C
	35	1		55	13		37	3
Apr.	57F	14C	Aug.	71F	22C	Dec.	39F	4C
	40	4		54	12		32	0

Currency In Luxembourg, as in Belgium, the unit of currency is the franc (abbreviated *Flux*). Luxembourg issues its own currency in bills of 100, 500, 1,000 and 5,000 francs and coins of 1, 5, 20, and 50 francs. Belgian currency can be used freely in Luxembourg, and the two currencies have exactly the same value. However, Luxembourg currency is not valid in Belgium. At press time (spring 1994), the exchange rate was Flux 36 to the U.S. dollar and Flux 54 to the pound sterling.

What It Will Cost Luxembourg is a developed and sophisticated country with a high standard and cost of living. Luxembourg City is an international banking center, and a number of European institutions are based there, a fact that tends to push prices slightly higher in the capital than in the countryside.

Sample Prices Cup of coffee, Flux 50; glass of beer, Flux 40–60; movie ticket, Flux 170–200; 3-mile taxi ride, Flux 600.

Customs on Arrival For information on customs regulations, *see* Customs on Arrival in Belgium.

Language Native Luxembourgers speak three languages fluently: Luxembourgish (best described as a dialect of German), German, and French. Many also speak English.

Staying in Luxembourg

Telephones You can find public phones both on the street and in city post offices. A local call costs Flux 5 per 3-minute period from a public phone (slightly more from restaurants and gas stations). The cheapest way to make an international call is to dial direct from a public phone; in a post office, you may be required to make a deposit before the call. Post offices also sell a *Telekaart* in units of 50 and 150, which can be used in nearly half the booths in the Grand Duchy. For operator-assisted calls, dial 0010.

Mail
Postal Rates Airmail postcards and letters weighing less than 20 grams cost Flux 22 to the United States. Letters and postcards to the United Kingdom cost Flux 14.

Receiving Mail If you are uncertain where you'll be staying, have your mail sent in care of American Express (34 av. de la Porte-Neuve, 2227 Luxembourg).

Shopping
Sales Tax
Refunds Purchases of goods for export may qualify for a sales tax (TVA) refund of 12%. Ask the shop to fill out a refund form. You must then have the form stamped by customs officers on leaving either Luxembourg, Belgium, or Holland.

Opening and
Closing Times Banks generally are open weekdays 8:30–noon and 1:30–4:30, though more and more remain open through the lunch hour.

Museums. Opening hours vary, so check individual listings. Many close on Monday, and most also close for lunch between noon and 2.

Shops. Large city department stores and shops are generally open weekdays, except Monday morning, and Saturday 9–noon and 2–6. A few small family businesses are open Sunday morning from 8 to noon.

National
Holidays January 1; February 27, 28 (Carnival); April 17 (Easter Monday); May 1 (May Day); May 25 (Ascension); June 5 (Pentecost Monday); June 23 (National Day); August 15 (Assumption); November 1 (All Saints' Day); November 2 (All Souls Day); December 25, 26.

Dining Restaurants in Luxembourg offer their best deals at lunch, when you can find a *plat du jour* (one-course special) or *menu* (two or three courses included in price) at bargain rates. Pizzerias offer an excellent and popular source of cheap food, with pasta, risotti, and wood-oven pizzas making a full meal. Light lunches—easy on the stomach if not always the wallet—can be found in chic pastry shops, where you point to the dishes in the display case (a slice of *pâté en croute*, an egg salad, a few small casseroles to be heated), then take your number upstairs to the *salon de consommation*, where your drink order will be taken and your meal served.

Mealtimes Most hotels serve breakfast until 10. Lunch hours are noon–2, sometimes extending until 3. Long accustomed to the Continental style of dining heavily at midday, business-conscious Luxembourgers now eat their main meal in the evening between 7 and 10.

Lodging
Hotels Most hotels in the capital are relatively modern and vary from the international style, mainly near the airport, to family-run establishments in town. Outside Luxembourg City, many hotels are housed in more picturesque buildings, often in beautiful countryside settings. Prices vary considerably between town and country, but as

Luxembourg City is an important business center, many of its hotels offer reduced rates on weekends, particularly out of season.

Youth Hostels Inexpensive youth hostels are plentiful in Luxembourg. They are often set in ancient fortresses and castles. For information, contact **Centrale des Auberges de Jeunesse** (18 pl. d'Armes, L-1136, Luxembourg, tel. 225588).

Camping The Grand Duchy is probably the best-organized country in Europe for camping. It offers some 120 sites, all with full amenities and most with scenic views. Listings are published annually by the National Tourist Office.

Tipping In Luxembourg hotels and restaurants, taxes and service charges are included in the overall bill and it is not necessary to leave more. If you wish to, round off the sum to the nearest Flux 50 or 100. Bellhops and doormen should receive between Flux 50 and 100, depending on the grade of the hotel. At the movies, tip the usher Flux 20 if you are seated personally. In theaters, tip about Flux 20 for checking your coat, and the same to the program seller. In public washrooms the attendant will usually expect between Flux 5 and 10. Taxi drivers expect a tip; add about 15% to the amount on the meter.

Luxembourg City

Arriving and Departing

By Plane All international flights arrive at Luxembourg's Findel Airport, 6 kilometers (4 miles) from the city.

Between the Bus No. 9 leaves the airport at regular intervals for Luxembourg's
Airport and main bus depot, located just beside the train station. From there,
Downtown Bus No. 4 (and, less directly, Nos. 11 and 12) goes to the city center. Individual tickets cost Flux 30. A taxi will cost you about Flux 600. If you are driving, follow the signs for the Centre Ville (city center).

Getting Around

One of the best transportation options in Luxembourg is the **Oeko-Carnet,** a block of five one-day tickets good for unlimited transportation on trains and buses throughout the country. Cards are on sale for Flux 540 at Gare Centrale (the main train station) in Luxembourg City, or at Aldringen Center, located underground in front of the central post office.

By Bus Luxembourg City has a highly efficient bus service. The blue-and-yellow buses outside the city train station will take you all around the city and also to some of the outlying areas. Get details about services at the information counter in the station arrivals hall. Fares are low, but the best bet is to buy a 10-ride ticket (Flux 270), available from banks or from the bus station in the Aldringen Center. Other buses, connecting Luxembourg City with towns throughout the country, leave from Gare Centrale.

By Train Luxembourg is served by frequent direct trains from Paris and Brussels. From Paris, travel time is about four hours; from Brussels, just under three hours. From Amsterdam, the journey is via Brussels and takes about six hours. There are connections from most German cities via Koblenz. Outside Luxembourg City, three major train routes extend north, south, and east into the Moselle Valley. For all train information, phone 492424. All service is from Gare Centrale in place de la Gare.

By Car A car is a liability in this small, walkable city. You can easily see the rest of the country in a day or two, and you might want to rent a car for this purpose. Major highways and smaller roads are excellent and fairly uncrowded. Speed limits are 120 kph (70 mph) on highways, 90 kph (55 mph) on major roads, and 50 kph (30 mph) in built-up areas.

Street parking in Luxembourg City is difficult. Make use of one of the underground parking lots, or park at the sizable Parking Glacis next to the Municipal Theater, five minutes' walk from the city center.

By Bicycle Bicycling is a popular sport in Luxembourg, and it is an excellent way to see the city and outlying regions. A new brochure, "Cycling Tracks," is available from the Luxembourg National Tourist Office, Box 1001, L-1010 Luxembourg. Bikes can be rented in Luxembourg City at **Luxembourg DELTA** (8 Bisserwee, tel. 4796–2383), from March 30 through October 31; in Reisdorf, Diekirch, and Echternach, rent bikes at the tourist office (**Syndicat d'Initiative**). Maps are available from the tourist office.

By Taxi There are taxi stands near Gare Centrale and the main post office; it is almost impossible to stop one in the streets. To call a taxi, phone 480058 or 482233.

Important Addresses and Numbers

Tourist Information The main **Office National du Tourisme (ONT)** in Luxembourg City (Aerogare [Air Terminal] bus depot, place de la Gare, tel. 481199) is open daily (except Sun. Nov.–Mar.) 9–noon and 2–6:30 (July–mid-Sept., 9–7:30). The Luxembourg City tourist office (place d'Armes, tel. 222809) is open mid-Sept.–mid-June, Mon.–Sat. 9–1 and 2–6; mid-June–mid-Sept., weekdays 9–7, Sat. 9–1 and 2–7, Sun. 10–noon and 2–6.

Embassies **U.S.** (22 blvd. Emmanuel Servais, tel. 460123). **U.K.** (14 blvd. F. D. Roosevelt, tel. 229864). **Canada:** The Brussels embassy (ave. de Tervuren 2, 1040 Brussels, tel. 00322/7356040) covers Luxembourg.

Emergencies **Police, Ambulance, Doctor, Dentist** (tel. 012). **Pharmacies** in Luxembourg stay open nights on a rotation system. Signs listing late-night facilities are posted outside each pharmacy.

Books in English For books and magazines in English, try **Magasin Anglais** (13 allée Scheffer, tel. 224925).

Travel Agencies **American Express** (34 av de la Porte-Neuve, tel. 228555). **C.I.T.** (pl. de la Gare, tel. 485102). **Keiser Tours** (34 rue Philippe II, tel. 472717). **Wagons Lits (Thomas Cook)** (99 Grand-rue, tel. 460315). **Emile Weitzel** (15 rue Notre-Dame, tel. 22931). **Sotour** (including youth travel) (15 pl. du Theatre, tel. 461514).

Guided Tours

Orientation Tours **Sales-Lentz** offers tours of the city every morning during the peak tourist season (Apr. 1–Oct. 31). The tours leave from the bus station, next to the railway station, platform 5, or from place de la Constitution, under the Gelle Fra, visiting the historic sights of the center, the new European area, and some of the villas on the city outskirts, together with the military cemeteries: General Patton is buried in the American one. Tours cost Flux 290. Another tour of the city and countryside takes visitors to the monuments of Luxembourg City, the cemeteries, and the restored castle of Bourglinster.

(Apr., May, and Oct., weekends 2:30–5:45; June–Sept., Tues., Thurs., Sat., and Sun. 2:30–5:45. Cost: Flux 320) Other more complete tours of the Grand Duchy are available to groups of 10 or more. For information and bookings, contact Sales-Lentz (26 rue du Curé, L-1368, tel. 461818). From April through October, minitrain tours of the Old Town and the Petrusse Valley start from the place de la Constitution (tel. 461617; Flux 220 adults, Flux 160 children under 17).

Walking Tours A self-guided city tour with headphones and cassette can be rented at the bus booth on the place de la Constitution for Flux 100–120, depending on length of tape. Information on weekend walking tours can be obtained from the tourist office or from the **Fédération Luxembourgeoise des Marches Populaires** (Boite Postale 794, L-2018 Luxembourg). Also consult the *Agenda Touristique,* published by the National Tourist Office.

Excursions Pick up the booklet "Circuits Auto-Pedestres," available at newsstands, bookstores, and the central tourist office (Flux 895), for information on combination driving-walking tours outside the city.

Exploring Luxembourg City

Numbers in the margin correspond to points of interest on the Luxembourg City map.

This walk takes you through Luxembourg City's maze of ancient military fortifications, now transformed into peaceful paths. Begin at Gare Centrale, in the southern section of the city. As you head right from the station toward the city center along avenue de la Gare, you will pass through a bustling shopping district.

❶ Take the **Passerelle Viaduct,** a 19th-century road bridge that links the station with the valley of the Petrusse. The Petrusse is more of a brook than a river and is now contained by concrete, but the valley has become a singularly beautiful park. From here you'll see the rocky ledges—partly natural, partly man-made—on which the city was founded.

At the cathedral end of the Passerelle, on the right, take the steps
❷ and curving sidewalk up to **Monument de la Solidarité Nationale** (National Monument to Luxembourg Unity), and admire its perpetual flame. It was erected in 1971 to commemorate Luxembourg's sacrifices and intact survival following World War II.

To the right of the monument, follow the road along the remains of
❸ the old city fortifications, known as the **Citadelle du St-Esprit** (Citadel of the Holy Spirit). This 17th-century citadel was built by Vauban, the French military engineer, in the typical style of thrusting wedges. From the end you can see the three spires of the cathedral, the curve of the Alzette, and the incongruous white tower of the European parliament.

Retrace your steps along the old city fortifications, cross boulevard
❹ F. D. Roosevelt, and continue on to the **place de la Constitution,** marked by the war memorial, a striking gilt *Gëlle Fra,* or Golden Woman. Here you'll find the entrance to the ancient **Petrusse casemates,** military tunnels carved into the bedrock. During the many phases of the fortress's construction, the rock itself was hollowed out to form a honeycomb of passages running for nearly 24 kilometers (15 miles) below the town. These were used both for storage and as a place of refuge when the city was under attack. Two sections of the passages are open to the public. These sections contain former

Luxembourg City

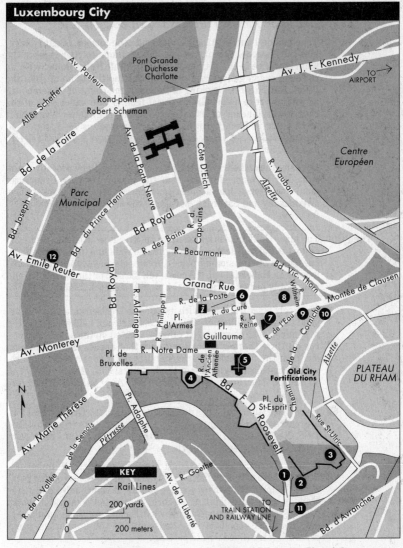

Bock, **10**

Cathédrale
Notre-Dame, **5**

Chapelle de
St-Quirin, **11**

Citadelle du
St-Esprit, **3**

Grand Ducal Palace, **7**

Maquette, **6**

Monument de la
Solidarité Nationale, **2**

Musée National, **8**

Passerelle, **1**

Place de la
Constitution, **4**

St-Michel, **9**

Villa Vauban, **12**

barracks, cavernous abattoirs, bakeries, and a deep well. *Admission: Flux 50 adults, Flux 30 children. Open July–Sept.*

Take rue de l'ancien Athénée alongside the former Jesuit college, now the National Library. In rue Notre-Dame to your right is the ❺ main entrance to the 17th-century **Cathédrale Notre-Dame,** with its Baroque organ gallery and crypt containing the tomb of John the Blind, the 14th-century king of Bohemia and count of Luxembourg as well as those of the Grand Ducal family. The valley side of the church was annexed in 1935; the roof of the main tower was rebuilt after a fire in 1985. *Open Easter–Oct., weekdays 10–5, Sat. 8–6, Sun. 10–6; Nov.–Easter, weekdays 10–11:30 and 2–5, Sat. 8–11:30 and 2–5, Sun. 10–5.*

Opposite the cathedral lies the place Guillaume, known locally as the Knuedler, a name derived from the girdle worn by Franciscan monks who once had a monastery on the site. On market days (Wednesday and Saturday mornings) the square is noisy and colorful.

Time Out The place Guillaume is an excellent spot to sit in an outdoor café and enjoy the passing scene. You might also walk one block north along rue Chimay to the smaller place d'Armes and have lunch at the fashionable **Le Rabelais** (4 pl. d'Armes, tel. 222202) or the traditional and reasonably priced **l'Académie** (11 pl. d'Armes, tel. 227131).

The lively place d'Armes, with its cafés and restaurants, lies just beyond the place Guillaume. Open-air concerts are held every evening in summer. The town tourist office is located on the square, and on ❻ rue du Curé there is a small museum that houses the **Maquette,** a model of the fortress at various stages of its construction: It provides a fascinating glimpse of the historical city. *Admission: Flux 40 adults, Flux 20 children. Open July–Aug. only, 10–12:30 and 2–6.*

❼ From place Guillaume, rue de la Reine leads to the **Grand Ducal Palace,** currently closed for renovations but expected to reopen by June 1995. Restoration of the facade of the oldest wing has been completed, and the result is superb.

Behind the palace is the oldest part of town, the Marché-aux-Poissons, site of the old fish market and originally the crossing point of two Roman roads. Now a quiet square, it comes alive on Easter Monday with the quaint, if obscure, Emais'chen Festival in which lovers exchange terra-cotta bird whistles and everyone indulges in *thüringer* (the standard local sausage) and the ubiquitous *gromperekichelcher* (fried potato patties).

❽ On the left is the **Musée National** (National Museum), set in an attractive row of 16th-century houses. The museum contains an eclectic collection of exhibits from the Stone Age to the Space Age, encompassing humble village crafts and fine arts. The Gallo-Roman collection features a fascinating assortment of small treasures— toga buckles, miniature deities—unearthed along the ancient routes that crisscrossed Luxembourg in the first centuries AD. Dramatic views over the ramparts compensate for the slightly confusing museum route. The museum now houses the spectacular Bentinck-Thyssen collection of 15th- to 19th-century art, including works by Breugel, Rembrandt, Canaletto, and other masters. *Admission free. Open Tues.–Fri. 10–4:45, Sat. 2–5:45, Sun. 10–11:45 and 2–5:45.*

Time Out In the rue Wiltheim, which runs alongside the Musée National, is the **Welle Man,** the quintessentially Luxembourgish museum bar. Sit on the tiny terrace and enjoy the magnificent view along the Alzette Valley or admire the massive carved furniture inside. Sip a glass of Elbling or Rivaner, local white wines, or try a kir, made from black-currant liqueur and white wine. Open until 7 PM. *rue Wiltheim 12. No credit cards. Closed Mon. Inexpensive.*

9 At the bottom of rue Wiltheim is the gate of **St.-Michel** and its Trois Tours (Three Towers), the oldest of which was built around 1050. During the French Revolution, the guillotine was set up in these towers. From here you can clearly see the source of Luxembourg's strength as a fortress.

10 Facing the valley, to your right is the **Bock** promontory, the site of the earliest castle (AD 963) and always the duchy's most fortified point. From the Bock, steep cliffs plunge downward to the Alzette Valley. The Bock also has a series of passages similar to the Petrusse Casemates. *Admission: Flux 50 adults, Flux 30 children. Open Mar.–Oct., daily 10–5.*

The scenic ramparts of the Bock's **Corniche** provide a view over the lower town, known as the Grund. Many of the houses on the right were refuges, used in times of danger by nobles and churchmen from the surrounding area. The massive towers on the far side of the valley date to the Wenceslas fortifications, which, in 1390, extended the protected area, and the blocklike *casernes* (barracks) were built in the 17th century by the French.

At the ruined fortifications of the Citadelle du St-Ésprit, take the elevator down to the Grund, and turn right on leaving the tunnel. As you follow the valley below the cliffs, you'll see two signs marking the high-water points of two devastating floods; that's why the rivers have been tamed with locks and concrete today. Turn right into **11** the green Petrusse Valley park. On the left, the little **chapelle de St-Quirin** (Chapel of St. Quirin) is built into the rock near the Passerelle Viaduct. The cave it surrounds is said to have been carved by the Celts; it is known to have housed a chapel since at least the 4th century. The relics of St-Quirin, transferred in 1050 from Avignon to Deutz-on-Rhine, spent a night in the chapel. At Pont Adolphe, walk back up to city level and you are suddenly face-to-face with the 20th century. The boulevard Royal, once the main moat of the fortress, is now Luxembourg's Wall Street, packed with the famous names of the international banking scene.

From here you can either take avenue de la Liberté, an important shopping street, toward the station or head back into town, perhaps to the Grand Rue shopping area. Or if you want to extend your tour, **12** take avenue Emile Reuter to the municipal park and **Villa Vauban,** the Duke's temporary lodging during palace renovations. Portions of its permanent collection of Dutch and Flemish paintings may be seen at the Musée National.

Off the Beaten Track

Walk up boulevard Royal to rond-point Robert Schuman, named for one of the founders of the European Common Market, and cross the Pont Grande Duchesse Charlotte (with stunning views of the valley) to **Plateau Kirchberg,** a moonscape of modern architecture housing the European Court of Justice and various branches of the European Union. The most prominent structure—at 23 stories, Luxembourg's only skyscraper—is home to the secretariat of the European Parliament. The Plateau is increasingly adorned with modern sculpture. Recent additions include a work by Henry Moore near the Court of Justice, a replica of Carl Fredrik Reutersward's *Non-Violence* in front of the Jean Monnet Building, and a sculpture by Frank Stella in rue Alphonse Weicker. Note also German architect Gottfried Boehm's Deutsche Bank building on boulevard Konrad Adenauer.

Shopping

Luxembourg City has two main shopping areas: the **Grand-Rue** and the **avenue de la Gare.** Jewelry and designer fashions are particularly well represented in the Grand-Rue. There are a few small department stores near the train station, but most of the stores in this area are specialty shops. Luxembourg chocolates, called *knippercher,* are popular purchases, available from the best pastry shops. A leading patisserie is Oberweis (19 Grand-Rue) Luxembourg's most famous product is Villeroy and Boch porcelain, available in most gift shops here. Feast your eyes at the glossy main shop, located at rue du Fossé 2, then buy at the excellent second-quality factory outlet (rue Rollingergrund 330).

Excursions from Luxembourg City

It would be a shame to leave Luxembourg without having explored some of the areas around the capital. To see the Ardennes, take Route N7 to **Diekirch,** where there is a church dating from the 7th century with Frankish tombs in the crypt. There are traces here of even older civilizations: the **Devil's Altar,** a Celtic dolmen, and some 4th-century Roman mosaics from nearby villas.

Another rewarding drive is northeast on Route E29 to **Echternach,** where St. Willibrord, a 7th-century English missionary, founded a Benedictine abbey. Many of the abbey buildings are now schools, but each year on the Tuesday after Pentecost, 15,000 pilgrims flock to the basilica, which is built on the site of the original chapel. In the crypt are frescoes dating to the 11th century and St. Willibrord's original sarcophagus. There's a charming, small hotel in Echternach, La Bergerie (47 route de Luxembourg, tel. 728504-1, fax 728508). A shuttle service links the hotel with the restaurant of the same name, set in the woods 7 kilometers (4 miles) away, a true gem. (1 Geyershof, tel. 79464).

Between Echternach and Luxembourg City, a detour via Gorge de Loup (direction Diekirch) and Mullerthal takes you through the **Petite Suisse** and Luxembourg's prettiest scenery.

To take in some of Luxembourg's best castles, allow a full day to take E27 northeast toward Junglinster, then cut north to **Bourglinster,** fully restored and complete with café; **Larochette,** its castle still inhabited, although the owners allow visitors to wander the older ruins out back; and **Beaufort,** a dramatic mix of ruins and restored chambers. Then follow the German border north to **Vianden,** perhaps the most spectacular of all, until recently in the possession of the grand-duke's family.

Dining

"French quality, German quantity"—that's an apt and common description of Luxembourg cuisine. Yet this tiny country has its own earthy specialties, fresh off the farm: *judd mat gardebounen* (salted pork with fava beans); *Eslecker ham* or *jambon d'Ardennes* (pearly-pink raw-smoked ham served cold with pickled onions); *choucroute* (sauerkraut); *treipen* (blood pudding); and batter-fried *merlan* (whiting). A few restaurants still feature them, though nowadays you're as likely to find Chinese, Thai, Japanese, Indian, and—leading the ethnic selection by several laps—Italian. And there are more star-studded *"gastronomique"* restaurants in Luxembourg per capita than in any other European country. Many restaurants—including some of these world-class venues—offer an accessibly priced menu at lunch. Crisp, fruity white wines from the banks of the Moselle range from the humble Elbling and Rivaner to fine Pinot Gris and Riesling.

Dress Stylish, casual dress is generally acceptable in most restaurants, but when in doubt, err on the formal side. In expensive French restaurants, formal dress is taken for granted.

Ratings Prices quoted here are per person and include a first course, main course, and dessert, but not wine. Best bets are indicated by a star ★.

Category	All Areas
Very Expensive	over Flux 3,000
Expensive	Flux 1,500–3,000
Moderate	Flux 750–1,500
Inexpensive	under Flux 750

Very Expensive **Clairefontaine.** Next to the foreign ministry, this lavish but dignified gastronomic dining spot attracts luminaries and heads of state (including François Mitterrand and the pope), who are pampered by chef Tony Tintinger. His inspirations include a showcase of foie gras specialties, innovative fish dishes (soufflé of langoustines perfumed with star anise), and game novelties (tournedos of doe larded with wild mushrooms). There's a business lunch, a three-course prix-fixe, and a thorough menu dégustation, all complemented by an extensive wine cellar. It's less expensive, if less romantic, than St-Michel (*see below*). *9 pl. de Clairefontaine, tel. 462211. Reservations required. AE, DC, MC, V. Closed Sat. dinner, Sun., 3 weeks in Aug., and first week Nov.*

St-Michel. In a 16th-century building behind the ducal palace, warmly lit, intimate, and filled with antiques (but not stuffy), this is one of the finest restaurants in the region. It has recently been acquired by German chef Joerg Glauben, who is making new friends in Luxembourg with his lobster salad with green asparagus tips, pigeon stuffed with foie gras and accompanied by rhubarb compote, and sumptuous desserts. The wine list is exhaustive. *32 rue de l'Eau, tel. 223215. Reservations required. AE, DC, MC, V. Closed Sat.–Sun. and 3 weeks in Aug.*

Expensive **La Lorraine.** Strategically placed on the place d'Armes, with terrace tables under its awnings, this seafood restaurant caters to tourists passing by but also serves serious meals upstairs in a formal dining room. A retail shop around the corner shows off the coast-fresh quality of their wares: Heaps of briny oysters, glistening turbot and sole, wriggling crabs. Once prepared, they live up to their promise: Baked skate in hazelnut butter with capers, puff-pastry with sole, and morel are good bets. *7 pl. d'Armes, tel. 474620. Reservations advised. Jacket advised indoors. AE, DC, MC, V. Closed Sat. lunch, Sun. and 3 weeks in Aug./Sept.*

Speltz. In a chic, restored 17th-century home in the middle of the pedestrian shopping area, this stylish restaurant caters to a young business crowd, serving a reasonable prix-fixe lunch that may include Vosges quail in Armagnac gelée, or venison stew with herbed *spätzle* (small dumplings). *8 rue Chimay, tel. 474950. Reservations advised. Jacket and tie advised. AE, DC, MC, V. Closed Sat., Sun., Easter week, and 2 weeks in July/Aug.*

Moderate **Ancre d'Or.** This tidy, friendly brasserie, just off the place
★ Guillaume, serves a wide variety of old-time Luxembourgish specialties as well as good *cuisine bourgeoise.* Try their judd mat gardebounen, *kuddelfleck* (breaded tripe), or *treipen* (rich blood sausages served with red cabbage and apple sauce). The apple tart (Luxembourgish style, with custard base) is homemade. Portions are generous, service friendly, and the clientele local. *23 rue du Fossé, tel. 472973. Reservations advised at lunch. MC, V. Closed Sun.*

Kamakura. If heavy Western cuisine palls, take the elevator from the Citadelle du St-Esprit to the up-and-coming Grund and try this chic Japanese restaurant. A number of fixed-price menus offer a variety of delicate, nouvelle-accented dishes, artfully presented and graciously served. A la carte specialties, considerably more expensive, include impeccably fresh sashimi (raw fish) and light tempura vegetables. *2–4 rue Munster, tel. 470604. Reservations accepted. AE, DC, MC, V. Closed Sun.*

★ **La Trattoria dei Quattro.** Despite an undesirable location—on one of the sleazier back streets around the avenue de la Gare shopping area–this restaurant merits the trip off the beaten track. It's set in a 150-year-old town house with an impressive carved wooden ceiling and fireplace. Excellent homemade pastas include *maccheroni alla Sarda* (sauced with tomato, onion, tuna, and fennel seeds) and *bucatini alla melanzani e funghi* (with eggplant and mushrooms). *64 rue Fort-neipperg, tel. 490039. Reservations accepted. AE, DC, MC, V. Closed Sun.*

★ **Mousel's Cantine.** Directly adjoining the great Mousel brewery (there are beer taps that feed from tanks within), this fresh, comfortable café serves up heaping platters of local specialties—braised and grilled ham, sausage, gardebounen (fava beans), sauerkraut, and fried potatoes—to be washed down with crockery steins of creamy *Gezwickelte Béier* (unfiltered beer). The front café is brighter, with sanded tabletops, but the tiny fluorescent-lit dining room has windows into the brewery. *46 montée de Clausen, tel. 470198. Reservations advised. MV, V. Closed Sun.*

Inexpensive **Ems.** Directly across the street from the train station, this lively diner-equivalent (vinyl booths, posted specials) draws a loyal clientele for its vast portions of *moules* (mussels) in a rich wine-and-garlic broth, accompanied by *frites* (french fries) and a bottle of sharp, cold Auxerrois or Rivaner. For dessert, try one of the huge ice-cream specialties. Food is served until 1 AM. *30 pl. de la Gare, tel. 487799. Reservations not necessary. AE, DC, MC, V.*

Taverne Bit. With sanded tabletops and dark-wood banquettes, this is a cozy and very local pub, where you can drink a *clensch* (stein) of draft Bitburger beer (from just across the German border) and have a plate of sausage with good potato salad, a plate of cold ham, or *kachkeis*, the pungent local cheese spread, served with baked potatoes. It's just off the Parking Glacis. *43 allée Scheffer, tel. 460751. Reservations not necessary. No credit cards. Closed Sat. PM, Sun.*

Lodging

Hotels in Luxembourg City are located in three main areas: the town center, the station area, and the area close to the airport. By far the largest number are around the station. Most hotels are modern, but a warm welcome and high standards compensate for the relative lack of character.

Ratings Price categories are determined by the cost of a double room (Continental breakfast is sometimes included in the room price). Best bets are indicated by a star ★.

Category	Cost
Very Expensive	over Flux 8,000
Expensive	Flux 5,000–8,000
Moderate	Flux 2,500–5,000
Inexpensive	under Flux 2,500

Very Expensive ★ **Le Royal.** In the city center, on the Wall Street of Luxembourg and within steps of parks, shopping, and the old town, this is the best choice for luxury. It's solid, modern (opened 1984), and sleek, with a great deal of lacquer, marble, and glass. Opt for a back room toward the park if possible; those facing the boulevard Royal have traffic noise leaking through the double-glazed windows. The piano bar is popular, as is the brasserie Le Jardin, especially when the fountain terrace is open. *12 blvd. Royal, tel. 41616; fax 225948. 180 rooms with bath. Facilities: 2 restaurants, piano bar, exercise equipment, pool, hairdresser; sauna and tennis for a fee. AE, DC, MC, V.*

Expensive ★ **Cravat.** This charming Luxembourg relic—moderately grand, modestly glamorous—continues to hold forth at the best location in town, straddling the valley and the old town. Built in several phases since the turn of the century, it features a mix of solid old architectural details; and though corridors have a dated, institutional air, the rooms are fresh and welcoming in a variety of tastefully retro styles. The Deco coffee shop still draws fur-hatted ladies of a certain age to tea. *29 blvd. F. D. Roosevelt, tel. 221975; fax 226711. 60 rooms with bath. Facilities: restaurant, coffee shop, bar. AE, DC, MC, V.*

Parc. This modern hotel complex, with extensive conference facilities and an outdoor swimming pool, is just outside city limits and traffic-clogged streets. It is especially useful as a base for excursions to the Ardennes. Rooms are restful, and the restaurant quite acceptable. *120 route d'Echternach, Dommeldange, tel. 435643, fax 436903. 271 rooms. Facilities: restaurant, bar, conference rooms, parking. AE, DC, MC, V.*

Moderate **Arcotel.** Opened in 1985 on the busy shopping street between the old town and the train station, this airtight, modernized hotel provides a quiet getaway from the city outside. Decorated in warm shades of beige and rose, with polished wood and brass, it offers solid baths and extra comforts—hair dryers in the bathroom, drinks in the Bokhara-lined lounge—to make up for typically small rooms. *43 av. de la Gare, tel. 494001; fax 405624. 30 rooms with bath. Facilities: breakfast room (no restaurant). AE, DC, MC, V.*

★ **Auberge du Coin.** At the edge of a quiet, dignified residential area but within easy reach of the station and the old town, this pleasant hotel was completely renovated in 1989 in pure "new Luxembourg" style—stone and terra-cotta floors, wood-framed double windows, polished oak, Persian rugs, and tropical plants. Rooms are freshly furnished in bright knotty pine with new tile baths. There's a lovely French restaurant and a comfortable oak-and-stone bar as well. Prices are at the high end of this category; the nine-room matching annex down the street, which has no elevator, costs slightly less. *2 blvd. de la Petrusse, tel. 402101; fax 403666. 32 rooms with bath. Facilities: restaurant, bar. AE, DC, MC, V.*

Empire. Slick, freshly decorated, simple, and aimed at single businesspeople (there are only three double rooms), this station hotel offers all comforts and a few bargain no-bath rooms (though all have toilets). Both a pizzeria and a French restaurant adjoin. *34 pl. de la Gare, tel. 485252; fax 491937. 31 rooms with bath. Facilities: restaurant, pizzeria, bar. AE, DC, MC, V.*

★ **Italia.** This is a valuable and remarkably inexpensive find in the *gare* area: a former private apartment converted into hotel rooms, some with plaster details and cabinetry left behind. Rooms are solid and freshly furnished, all with private tiled bathrooms. The somewhat pricey restaurant downstairs is one of the city's better Italian eateries. *15–17 rue d'Anvers, tel. 486626; fax 480807. 20 rooms with bath. Facilities: restaurant, bar, garden. AE, DC, MC, V.*

Inexpensive **Bristol.** Though on a street near the train station that is lined with strip joints and flophouses (as well as legitimate shops and restaurants), this modest hotel offers comfortable, secure lodging and fresh decor. The lobby/bar is warm and familial, and baths are newly refurbished. A few bathless rooms on the first and fourth floors go for bargain rates. *11 rue de Strasbourg, tel. 485830; fax 486480. 30 rooms, 22 with shower/toilet. Facilities: bar for guests only. AE, DC, MC, V.*

★ **Carlton.** In this vast 1918 hotel, buffered from the rue de Strasbourg scene by a rank of stores and opening onto a quiet inner court, budget travelers will find roomy, quiet quarters. The beveled glass, oak parquet, and terrazzo floors are original—but so are the toilets, all down the hall. Each room has antique beds, floral-print comforters, and a sink; wood floors, despite creaks, are white-glove clean. *9 rue de Strasbourg, tel. 484802; fax 486480. 50 rooms without toilet. Facilities: breakfast room, bar. No credit cards.*

20 Malta

The Mediterranean island of Malta, and its two sister islands, Gozo and Comino, enjoy a mild, sunny climate and attractive bays and beaches—a felicitous setting for such a festive and hospitable people.

For those interested in history and archaeology, tiny Malta—with only 28 kilometers (17 miles) between its two farthest points—displays the remains of a long and eventful history. Among the most fascinating ruins are Neolithic temples and stone megaliths left by prehistoric inhabitants. In AD 60, St. Paul, shipwrecked here, converted the people to Christianity. Other, less welcome visitors, attracted by Malta's strategic position, conquered and ruled. These included the Phoenicians, Carthaginians, Romans, Arabs, Normans, and Aragonese.

The Knights of the Order of St. John of Jerusalem arrived here in 1530 after they had been driven from their stronghold on the island of Rhodes by the Ottoman emperor Suleiman the Magnificent. In 1565, with only a handful of men, the Knights held Malta against the Ottoman Turks in a dramatic and bloody siege. They ruled the islands until Napoleon arrived in 1798 and left massive fortifications, rich architecture, and the city of Valletta, Malta's capital.

The British drove the French out in 1800 and gave the island the distinctive British feel that it still retains. In 1942, during World War II, King George VI awarded the Maltese people the George Cross for their courage in withstanding repeated German and Italian attacks, especially from the air. Malta gained independence from Britain in 1964 and was declared a republic within the Commonwealth in 1974. On December 2–3, 1989, the island hosted the first Bush-Gorbachev summit, marking the beginning of improved relations between the two superpowers.

Essential Information

Before You Go

When to Go The archipelago is a year-round delight, but May through October is the time of the main tourist season. April and May are the months for spring freshness; the summer months can be very hot, though sometimes tempered by sea breezes. August is just too hot for touring. If you visit in the winter, you'll find the climate pleasant and mild, but you may encounter sudden rainstorms.

Climate The following are the average daily maximum and minimum temperatures for Valletta.

Jan.	58F	14C	May	71F	22C	Sept.	81F	27C
	50	10		61	16		71	22
Feb.	59F	15C	June	79F	26C	Oct.	75F	24C
	51	10		67	19		66	19
Mar.	61F	16C	July	84F	29C	Nov.	67F	20C
	52	11		72	22		60	16
Apr.	65F	18C	Aug.	85F	29C	Dec.	61F	16C
	56	13		73	23		54	12

Currency The unit of currency is the Maltese lira (Lm), also sometimes referred to as the pound. It's divided into 100 cents, and the cents are divided into 10 mils; but in recent years the mils have dropped out of circulation. There are Lm 20, Lm 10, Lm 5, and Lm 2 bills; coins—1¢, 2¢, 5¢, 10¢, 25¢, 50¢, and Lm 1—are bronze and silver. At

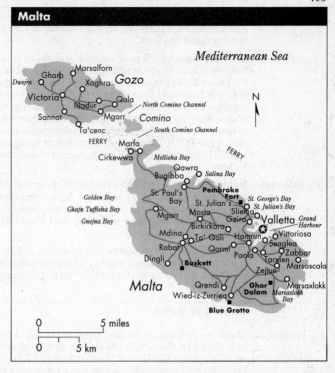

Malta

Mediterranean Sea

Gozo

Dwejra Gharb Marsalforn
Xaghra
Victoria Qala
Nadur North Comino Channel
Sannat Mgarr *Comino*
Ta'cenc South Comino Channel
FERRY Marfa
Cirkewwa Mellieha Bay
Qawra Salina Bay
Bugibba
FERRY
St. Paul's Pembroke Fort
Golden Bay Bay St. George's Bay
Ghajn Tuffieha Bay St. Julian's St. Julian's Bay
Mgarr Mosta Sliema
Gnejna Bay Gzira Valletta *Grand Harbour*
Birkirkara
Mdina Ta' Qali Hamrun Vittoriosa
Rabat Qormi Senglea
Dingli Paola Zabbar
Buskett Tarxien Marsascala
Zejtun
Malta Qrendi Ghar Marsaxlokk
Wied-iz-Zurrieq Dalam *Marsaxlokk Bay*
Blue Grotto

N

0 — 5 miles
0 — 5 km

press time (spring 1994), the exchange rate was Lm .35 to the dollar and Lm .56 to the pound sterling.

What It Will Cost — Malta is one of the cheapest holiday destinations in Europe, though with the rapid tourist development, prices are inevitably rising. Prices tend to be uniform across the island, except in Sliema and Valletta, the capital, where they are slightly higher.

Sample Prices — Cup of coffee, 25¢ (Maltese); bottle of beer, 25¢; Coca-Cola, 20¢.

Customs on Arrival — You may bring into Malta, duty-free, 200 cigarettes, one bottle of liquor, one bottle of wine, and one bottle of perfume. You may bring in up to Lm 50 in currency.

Language — The spelling of many Maltese words can be bewildering. Fortunately, both Maltese and English are the official languages on the island, so you shouldn't experience any problems. Italian is widely spoken, too.

Getting Around

By Car — The roads around Valletta are busy most mornings, but a new road network has made it easier to reach Sliema–St. Julian's from the airport. Road conditions are fairly good, but driving around the island can be a trial. Driving is on the left-hand side of the road. Speed limits are 40 kph (25 mph) in towns, 65 kph (40 mph) elsewhere. International and British driving licenses are acceptable. Be careful on roundabouts

By Bus — Most routes throughout the island are via Valletta, which facilitates travel out of the capital but makes cross-country trips a bit longer.

Public transportation is very inexpensive. Though some of the old green buses show their age, they are usually on time and plans are in hand to renew the fleet.

By Boat Daily car/passenger ferries operate year-round from Cirkewwa to Mġarr on Gozo. Telephone 243964 in Malta; 571884 in Cirkewwa; and 556114 or 556743 in Gozo for details. The crossing from Marfa to Mġarr in Gozo lasts 25 minutes, with shuttle service in summer and departures every hour in winter. The round-trip fare is Lm 1.50 adults, 50¢ children. There is also one service weekdays from Pietà to Gozo, leaving in the morning and taking an hour and 15 minutes each way. The round-trip fare from Mġarr (passenger plus car) is Lm 4.50. A ferry service links the tourist resort town of Sliema to Valletta.

By Helicopter **Malta Air Charter** (tel. 882916 or 882920) flies to and from Gozo several times daily and offers helicopter sightseeing tours. Flight time to Gozo is 10 minutes and costs Lm 17 round-trip (open return date) and Lm 15 (same-day return). Twenty- and 40-minute tours cost Lm 12 and Lm 20, respectively.

By Taxi There are plenty of metered taxis available, and fares are reasonable compared with those in other European countries. Be sure the meter is switched on when your trip starts, or bargain first. Tip the driver 10%.

Staying in Malta

Telephones There is direct dialing to most parts of the world from Malta. The best place to make calls is either from your hotel or from the Overseas Telephone Division of Telemalta at St. Julian's, Qawra, St. Paul's Bay, Sliema, Valletta, and Luqa International Airport. The international dialing access code is 00. Overseas telephone operator: tel. 194; time check: tel. 195; flight inquiries: tel. 249600.

Mail Airmail letters to the United States cost 20¢; postcards cost 20¢. Airmail letters to the United Kingdom cost 14¢; postcards 14¢.

Opening and Closing Times **Banks** are open weekdays 8:30–12:45, Tuesday and Friday 2:30–4, Saturday 8:30–noon (11:30 in summer). Banks in tourist areas are also open in the afternoon.

Museums run by the Museums Department are generally open mid-June through September, daily 8–2; October through mid-June, daily 8:30–5; closed holidays. Other museums' hours may vary slightly, so check locally.

Shops are open Monday–Saturday 9–1 and 4–7.

National Holidays January 1; February 10 (St. Paul's shipwreck); March 19 (St. Joseph's Day); March 31 (Freedom Day); April 14 (Good Friday); May 1 (Workers' Day); June 7 (Sette Giugno); June 29 (Sts. Peter and Paul); August 15 (Assumption, or Santa Marija); September 8 (Our Lady of Victories); September 21 (Independence Day); December 8 (Immaculate Conception); December 13 (Republic Day); December 25.

Dining There is a good choice of restaurants, ranging from expensive hotel restaurants to fast-food hamburger joints. Local specialties include *torta tal-lampuki* (dorado fish pie), *dentici* (sea bream), and tuna. *Minestra* is the local variant of minestrone soup, and the *timpana* (baked macaroni and meat) is filling. Rabbit, stewed or fried, is a national dish. Accompany your meal with the locally produced wine: *Marsovin* comes in red, white, or rosé; *Lachryma Vitis*, in red or white—try sampling the house wines, too. Maltese beers are excellent; highly popular are Cisk Lager and Hop Leaf. Lowenbrau recently began brewing in Malta, too. Try Kinnie, a refreshing local nonalcoholic citrus and herb drink.

Precautions The water in Malta is safe to drink, with the only drawback being its salty taste: Many prefer bottled mineral water.

Dress A jacket and tie are suggested for higher-priced restaurants. Otherwise, casual dress is acceptable.

Ratings Prices are for a three-course meal, not including wine, sales tax, and tip. Best bets are indicated by a star ★.

Category	Cost*
Expensive	over Lm 9
Moderate	Lm 6–Lm 9
Inexpensive	under Lm 6

*10% sales tax is charged on meals eaten in all restaurants

Lodging Malta has a variety of lodgings, from modern hotels to modest guest houses. There are also self-contained complexes geared mainly to package tours.

Ratings Prices are for two people sharing a double room and exclude the 5% room tax.

Category	Cost
Very Expensive	over Lm 35
Expensive	Lm 22–Lm 35
Moderate	Lm 12–Lm 22
Inexpensive	under Lm 12

Tipping A tip of 10% is expected when a service charge is not included.

Valletta

Arriving and Departing

By Plane There are no direct flights from the United States, but several airlines, including **Air Malta,** fly from London, Paris, Frankfurt, Athens, and Rome to Luqa Airport, 6 kilometers (4 miles) south of Valletta.

Between the Airport and Downtown There is a local bus service that passes through the town of Luqa on its way to Valletta, with a stop in front of the airport. It operates every 10 or 15 minutes from 6 AM to 11 PM; the trip takes about 30 minutes, and the fare is about 10¢.

Taxis are also available and prices are posted on a board at the taxi stand.

By Boat The **Gozo Channel Co.** (tel. 243964) operates weekly car and passenger ferries from Catania, Sicily, during the summer. **Sea Malta** (Flagstone Wharf, Marsa, tel. 232230) operates ferries year-round, three times a week (Tuesday, Friday, Sunday) from Syracuse, Catania, and Reggio Calabria, and a weekly (Thursday) ferry service from Naples.

Virtu (tel. 318854) runs an express ferry service from Catania (Tuesday, Thursday, Saturday, Sunday); Pozzallo (Monday, Thursday, Sunday); and Licata (Wednesday, Sunday).

Important Addresses and Numbers

Tourist Information
Gozo (Mġarr Harbor, tel. 553343; Victoria, tel. 558106).
St. Julian's Bay (Balluta Bay, tel. 342671 or 342672).
Sliema (Bisazza St., tel. 313409).
Valletta (1 City Gate Arcade, tel. 237747; Luqa Airport, tel. 249600; or 280 Republic St., tel. 224444 or 228282).

Embassies
U.S. Development House (St. Anne St., Floriana, tel. 243653). British High Commission (7 St. Anne St., Floriana, tel. 233134).

Emergencies
Hospital: St. Luke's (Gwardamangia, tel. 241251) or Craig Hospital (Gozo, tel. 556851). Police (tel. 191). Ambulance (tel. 196). Fire Brigade (tel. 199).

Travel Agencies
Thomas Cook (Il-Pjazzetta, Tower Road, Sliema, tel. 344225). American Express (representative) (Brockdorff, 14 Zachary St., Valletta, tel. 232141).

Guided Tours

Orientation
Sightseeing tours are arranged by local travel agents and the large hotels. There are half-day, full-day, and "Malta by Night" coach tours; rates vary according to the sights covered and whether or not meals are included. Contact the tourist offices above for details. Beware of cheap tours: A number of outlets offer "guided" tours at very low prices. These usually turn out to be rip-offs, the guide being the driver himself, who is far from qualified. Officially licensed guides should wear an identification tag.

One-hour boat tours of the harbor of Valletta leave regularly from Sliema jetty. Prices vary; buy tickets at most travel agencies.

Personal Guides
Licensed guides can be hired through the tourist information office at the City Gate Arcade in Valletta.

Exploring Valletta

The minicity of Valletta, with ornate palaces and museums, protected by massive honey-colored fortifications, was built by the Knights of the Order of St. John, who occupied the island from 1530 to 1798.

The main entrance to the city is through the arched **City Gate** (where all bus routes end), which leads onto Republic Street, the spine of the city and the main shopping street. From Republic Street, other streets are laid out on a grid pattern. Some streets are stepped. Houses along the narrow streets have overhanging wooden balconies, which visiting artists love to paint.

Valletta's small size makes it ideal to explore on foot. Before setting out along Republic Street, stop at the tourist information office for maps, brochures, and a copy of *What's On*. Two blocks farther, on your left, is the Auberge de Provence (the hostel of the knights from Provence), which now houses the **National Museum of Archaeology.** Its collection includes finds from Malta's many prehistoric sites— Tarxien, Hagar Qim, and the Hypogeum at Paola. You'll see pottery, statuettes, temple carvings, and, on the upper floor, finds from Punic and Roman tombs. *Republic St., tel. 225577. Admission: Lm 1; day tickets (good at 4 other museums on the same day) Lm 1.50. Open mid-June–Sept., daily 8–2; Oct.–mid-June, daily 8:30–5; closed holidays.*

From Republic Street, turn right at the Inter-Flora kiosk and head to St. John's Square. Dominating the square is **St. John's co-Cathedral.** This was the Order of St. John's own church, completed in 1578. It is by far Malta's most important treasure. A side chapel was given to each national group of knights, who decorated it in their own distinctive way. The cathedral **museum** includes the oratory in which hangs *The Beheading of St. John,* the masterpiece painted by Caravaggio when he was staying on Malta in 1608. In the museum, you'll find a rich collection of Flemish tapestries based on drawings by Poussin and Rubens, antique embroidered vestments, and illuminated manuscripts. *St. John's Sq. Museum admission: 60¢. Open weekdays 9:30–12:30 and 1:30–4:30, Sat. 9:30–12:30.*

While in St. John's Square, visit the **Government Craft Center,** which has a wide range of traditional, handmade goods. *Open weekdays 9–7, Sat. 9–1 and 4–7.*

Continue along Republic Street to the **Grand Master's Palace,** where Malta's parliament sits. You can walk through the shady courtyards. Inside, friezes in the sumptuously decorated state apartments depict scenes from the history of the Knights. There is also a gallery with Gobelin tapestries. At the back of the building is the **Armoury of the Knights,** with displays of arms and armor down through the ages. *Republic St. Admission: Lm 1. Open mid-June–Sept., daily 8–2; Oct.–mid-June, 8:30–5; closed holidays.*

Also on Republic Street, spend some time at **Casa Rocca Piccola,** a traditional 16th-century Maltese house. Continue to **Fort St. Elmo,** built by the Knights to defend the harbor. Though completely destroyed during the siege of 1565, it was rebuilt by succeeding military leaders. Today part of the fort houses the **War Museum,** with its collection of military objects largely related to Malta's role in World War II. Here you can see an Italian E-boat and the *Faith,* one of three Gloster Gladiator biplanes that defended the island. The other two, *Hope* and *Charity,* were shot down in the air battles of 1940–41. *St. Elmo. Admission: Lm 1. Open mid-June–Sept., daily 8–2; Oct.–mid-June, daily 8:30–5; closed holidays.*

Continue along the seawall to the **Hospital of the Order** at the end of Merchants Street. This gracious building has been converted into the Mediterranean Conference Center. For an excellent introduction to the island, see the "Malta Experience," a multimedia presentation on the history of Malta that is given here daily. *Admission: Lm 2.*

Continue along the seawall past the siege bell memorial and climb up to the **Upper Barrakka Gardens.** Once part of the city's defenses, they're now a pleasant area from which to watch the comings and goings in the Grand Harbour.

Then walk down to Merchants Street, which is dominated by an open-air market. Here, with some haggling, you may snap up a good bargain. Next, cut along South Street, across Republic Street, to the **National Museum of Fine Art.** The former 18th-century palace has paintings that date from the 15th century to the present, including works by Tintoretto, Preti, and Tiepolo, as well as local artists.

South St., tel. 225769. Admission: Lm 1. Open mid-June–Sept., daily 8–2; Oct.–mid-June, daily 8:30–5; closed holidays.

Valletta's neighboring towns of **Sliema** and **Ta' Xbiex** offer seaside resort facilities.

Dining

For details and price-category definitions, *see* Dining in Staying in Malta, *above.*

Moderate **Bologna.** This restaurant situated in the heart of the city specializes in Italian cuisine. *59 Republic St., tel. 246149. AE, DC, MC, V.*

★ **Giannini.** Atop Valletta's mighty bastions, this is one of the city's most elegant restaurants. Leading local politicians and the fashionable set dine here on Maltese-Italian cuisine, especially seafood, while enjoying the marvelous view. *23 Windmill St., tel. 237121 or 236575. Reservations required. AE, DC, MC, V.*

★ **Pappagall.** This restaurant in Valletta is popular with locals and visitors alike. Traditional Maltese food is featured, and the bustling atmosphere is warm and friendly. *Melita St., tel. 236195. Reservations advised. AE, DC, MC, V. Closed Sun.*

Scalini. An attractive cellar restaurant with walls of Malta's golden limestone, it features seafood and Italian-style pastas. The fixed-price menu is a good value. *32B South St., tel. 246221. Dress: casual. Reservations advised. AE, DC, MC, V.*

Inexpensive **The Lantern.** This friendly spot is run by two brothers. The 18th-century town-house location may not win any design awards, but the food is delicious and served in a traditional Maltese atmosphere. *20 Sapper St., tel. 237521. Reservations advised. Closed Sun.*

Pizzeria Bologna. A street-level pizza house beside the Grand Master's Palace serves delicious pizzas with an interesting choice of ingredients. *59B Republic St., tel. 238014. Open until 9 PM.*

Lodging

For details and price-category definitions, *see* Lodging in Staying in Malta, *above.*

Very Expensive **Holiday Inn Crowne Plaza.** This large resort hotel is in Sliema, close to the sea and the major shopping area. It offers a full range of resort activities from swimming and windsurfing to dining and dancing. *Tigne St., Sliema, tel. 341173, fax 311292. 182 rooms with bath. Facilities: restaurant, bar, pool, tennis, gym, sauna. AE, DC, MC, V.*

Expensive **Grand Hotel des Lapins.** A modern building on the banks of the Ta' Xbiex seafront, this hotel has contemporary decor, and it overlooks Malta's newest yacht marina. It's popular with businesspeople, but offers resort facilities, too. *Ta' Xbiex Seafront, tel. 342551, fax 343902. 191 rooms with bath. Facilities: restaurant, bar, pool, tennis. AE, DC, MC, V.*

Moderate **Castille.** For a touch of old Malta, stay at the Castille in what used to be a 16th-century palazzo. This is a gracious, comfortable, Old World hotel with a friendly, relaxed ambience. It has an ideal central location, close to the museums and the bus terminus. There's a good rooftop restaurant with an excellent fixed-price menu offering several choices. A pianist plays most evenings during dinner, and the views across the harbor are stunning. *St. Paul St., tel. 243677 or 243678, fax 243679. 38 rooms with bath. Facilities: coffee shop-bar, sun terrace. AE.*

Osborne. Centrally located in Valletta, it has spacious rooms and undistinguished decor. Spend a few minutes in the rooftop lounge and enjoy the view. *South St., tel. 243656, fax 232120. 60 rooms with bath. Facilities: restaurant. AE, DC, MC, V.*

Beyond Valletta

It is impractical to attempt a tour of Malta and Gozo in one day. Allow at least two days for the main island—three to include Valletta—and one full day for Gozo.

The rest of Malta has much to offer, ranging from strange prehistoric sites to richly decorated churches.

The Southeast Leaving Valletta, head first for the **Hypogeum** at **Paola,** 6 kilometers (3½ miles) south of the capital. This massive area of underground chambers was used for burials more than 4,000 years ago. Built on three levels, the chambers descend to 40 feet beneath the ground, and there are examples of fine carving to be seen. *Admission: Lm 1. Closed for restoration; scheduled to reopen in mid-1994.*

Nearby is **Tarxien,** an ordinary suburban town with extraordinary megalithic monuments. The **Tarxien Temples** are three interconnecting temples with curious carvings, oracular chambers, and altars, all dating from about 2800 BC. *Admission: Lm 1. Open mid-June–Sept., daily 8–2; Oct.–mid-June, daily 8:30–5; closed holidays.*

Northeast of Paola, across the Grand Harbour from Valletta, lie evidences of the reign of the Knights of St. John: the **Cottonera Lines**—massive coastal defensive walls—and the city of **Vittoriosa,** dominated by the looming Fort St. Angelo and site of a 17th-century church as well as an Inquisitor's Palace built by the Knights.

Turning southward, you can visit the fishing and resort towns of **Marsaskala** and **Marsaxlokk** on the southeast coast and then head west to **Ghar Dalam.** A cave here was found to contain the semifossilized remains of long-extinct species of dwarf elephants and hippopotamuses that roamed the island about 125,000 years ago. You can visit the cave and see the fossils on display in the small museum. *Admission: Lm 1. Open mid-June–Sept., daily 8–2; Oct.–mid-June, daily 8:30–5; closed holidays.*

Follow the coast first south through **Birzebbugia,** a beach town, and **Kalafrana,** where the U.S. and Russian leaders met in 1989, and then northwest to the **Blue Grotto,** near Wied iz-Zurrieq. This is part of a group of water-filled caves made vivid by the phosphorescent marine life that colors the water a distinctive and magical blue. You can reach the grotto only by sea. Boatmen will take you there for about Lm 2.

Nearby are the prehistoric temples of **Hagar Qim** and **Mnajdpa.** *Admission: Lm 1. Open mid-June–Sept., daily 8–2; Oct.–mid-June, daily 8:30–5; closed holidays.*

Central Malta Take the northwest route to Rabat and Mdina, visiting **Buskett,** a very old and colorful garden, along the way. This trip is best in the spring when the orange and lemon trees are in blossom. In **Rabat,** visit the beautiful **St. Paul's Church,** built next to a grotto where St. Paul is said to have taken refuge when he was shipwrecked on Malta in AD 60. Also of interest are the 4th-century **catacombs** of St. Paul and St. Agatha, unusual for their rock agate tables where mourners held celebratory meals for the dead. *Admission: Lm 1. Open mid-*

June–Sept., daily 8–2; Oct.–mid-June, daily 8:30–5; closed holidays.

The Crafts Village at Ta' Qali is geared mainly toward tourists. Browse through the shops, but be cautious when buying. Here, in this converted World War II aerodrome, you can see filigree silver, gold jewelry, and hand-blown Mdina glass being made by age-old methods. There are also leather workshops and pottery shops selling gaily colored items. Some of the seconds in the glass workshops are good buys; the faults are often noticeable only to those with a trained eye.

Adjoining Rabat is **Mdina,** Malta's ancient walled capital. The Maltese have a special love for what is often called the Silent City. It certainly lives up to its sobriquet: Traffic here is limited to residents' cars, and the noise of the busy world outside somehow doesn't penetrate the thick, golden walls. Wandering through the peaceful streets is like entering an earlier age. Visit the serene baroque cathedral of **St. Peter and St. Paul** for a look at Preti's 17th-century wall painting, *The Shipwreck of St. Paul,* and the Cathedral museum to see the Dürer woodcuts and illuminated manuscripts. *Admission: 60¢. Open Mon.–Sat. 9–1 and 2–5.*

On your way out of the city you can visit the **National Museum of Natural History** (Vilhena Palace, tel. 455–951) and the **Mdina Dungeons** (St. Publius Sq., tel. 450–267) for a feel of the old Malta.

Continue to **Mosta** to see the **Church of St. Mary.** The Rotunda, as it is also known, has the third-largest unsupported dome in Europe, after St. Sofia in Istanbul and St. Peter's in Rome. You can also see a replica of the bomb that crashed through the dome during a service in 1942 and fell to the ground without exploding—a miraculous escape for those in the crowded church.

Gozo Head for the northwest tip of the island through the beach and water-sports centers near **St. Paul's Bay** and along Mellieha Bay, and take a ferry from Cirkewwa to **Gozo,** Malta's lusher, quieter sister island. The capital, Victoria, is a charming old town with attractive cafés and bars around the main square. In it lies the hilltop citadel of **Gran Castello,** with an impressive Baroque cathedral. The museum here offers displays of ceremonial silver and manuscripts. *Admission: Lm 1. Open mid-June–Sept., daily 8–2; Oct.–mid-June, daily 8:30–5; closed holidays.*

The town also has a **Folklore Museum** (Milite Bernardo St.) and an impressive archaeological collection in the **Archaeological Museum** (Cathedral Square). *Admission to each: Lm 1. Open mid-June–Sept., daily 8–2; Oct.–mid-June, daily 8:30–5; closed holidays.*

On Xaghra plateau stands the extraordinary pair of **Ggantija Prehistoric Temples.** *Admission: Lm 1. Open mid-June–Sept., daily 8–2; Oct.–mid-June, daily 8:30–5; closed holidays.*

In the town of **Xaghra** itself, there are two underground alabaster caves with delicately colored stalagmites and stalactites. In the cliffs nearby is the cave where the sea nymph Calypso, mentioned in Homer's *Odyssey,* is said to have lived; with such stunning views and the sandy beach, it's easy to imagine that the myth might be true.

Dining and Lodging

For details and price-category definitions, *see* Dining and Lodging in Staying in Malta, *above.*

Gozo
Lodging

Ta' Ċenċ. Surprisingly, the little island of Gozo harbors one of the best hotels in this part of the Mediterranean. The Ta' Ċenċ is a luxurious paradise, and its location on the coast about 4 miles out of Victoria ensures guests' privacy and accommodates a full range of water sports. For this reason it's favored for top-level conventions, though it's small enough to be exclusive. *Ta' Ċenċ, near Sannat, tel. 561522 or 561525, fax 558199. 82 rooms with bath. Facilities: restaurant, bar, pools, tennis, disco. AE, DC, MC, V. Very Expensive.*

Calypso. This modern hotel has so many services and facilities that it's almost like a small town in itself. The choice of dining spots includes a Chinese restaurant. The rooms are comfortably furnished and have balconies, most with sea views. *Marsalforn, tel. 562000; fax 562012. 92 rooms with bath. Facilities: restaurants, nightclub, rooftop splash pool, boutique, bank. AE, DC, MC, V. Moderate.*

Cornucopia. For pleasant, personal service and a restful vacation, try this lovingly restored farmhouse near the village of Xaghra—it's an ideal base for exploring the island, and the sea is just a short drive away. There's a good restaurant and barbecues in the summer. *10 Gnien Imrik St., Xaghra, tel. 556486 or 553866; fax 552910. 52 rooms with bath. Facilities: restaurant, pool. AE, DC, MC, V. Moderate.*

Qawra
Lodging

Suncrest Hotel. At this modern, 9-story turquoise-and-white complex overlooking Salina Bay in the northern part of the island, the atmosphere is relaxed and informal. Rooms have fresh, white walls and marble-tile floors that are covered with rugs in winter. *Qawra Coast Rd., Qawra, tel. 577101, fax 575478. 427 rooms with bath. Facilities: cafe, 3 restaurants, bar, pool, tennis, gym, sauna, beach. AE, DC, MC, V. Very Expensive.*

Rabat
Lodging

Medina. This is a good value close to the island's old capital, Mdina. It is not luxurious but is quite comfortable nonetheless, with a full fitness center and an indoor heated swimming pool. *Labour Ave., Rabat, tel. 453230, fax 455738. 40 rooms with bath. MC, V. Moderate.*

St. Julian's
Dining

San Giuliano. St. Julian's and Sliema are Malta's smartest seaside resorts and main entertainment districts as well as the site of many restaurants and discos, especially in nearby Paceville. The San Giuliano is a fashionable restaurant in a rustic, fishermen's-wharf setting. San Giuliano offers terrace dining directly on St. Julian's small fishing harbor. The menu features Maltese-Italian dishes. *Spinola Bay, tel. 332000. Reservations required. AE, DC, MC, V. Expensive.*

Barracuda. This characterful old house perched precariously on columns—thus commanding a superb view of St. Julian's Bay—is now one of Malta's most delightful and efficiently run restaurants. Seafood, not surprisingly, is the drawing card here. *194/5 Main St., St. Julian's, tel. and fax 337370. AE, DC, MC, V. Moderate.*

21 Norway

Norway has some of the most remote and dramatic scenery in Europe. Along the west coast, deep fjords knife into steep mountain ranges. Inland, cross-country ski trails follow frozen trout streams and downhill trails career through forests whose floors teem with wildflowers and berries during the summer. In older villages, wooden houses spill down toward docks where Viking ships—and later, whaling vessels—once were moored. Today the maritime horizon is dominated by tankers and derricks, for oil is now Norway's economic lifeblood. Fishing and timber, however, still provide many Norwegians with a staple income.

Inhabited since 1700 BC, Norway is today considered a peaceful nation. This was hardly so during the Viking period (the 8th–10th centuries AD), when, apart from vicious infighting at home, the Vikings were marauding as far afield as Seville and the Isle of Man. This fierce fighting spirit remained, despite Norway's subsequent centuries of subjugation by the Danes and Swedes. Independence came early this century but was put to the test during World War II, when the Germans occupied the country. Norwegian Resistance fighters rose to the challenge, eventually squashing Nazi efforts to develop atomic weapons.

The foundations for modern Norwegian culture were laid in the 19th century, during the period of union with Sweden, which lasted until 1905. Oslo blossomed at this time, and Norway produced its three greatest men of arts and letters: composer Edvard Grieg (1843–1907), dramatist Henrik Ibsen (1828–1906), and painter Edvard Munch (1863–1944). The polar explorers Roald Amundsen and Fridtjof Nansen also lived during this period.

All other facts aside, Norway is most famous for its fjords, which were formed during an ice age a million years ago. The ice cap burrowed deep into existing mountain-bound riverbeds, creating enormous pressure. There was less pressure along the coast, so the entrances to most fjords are shallow, about 155 meters (508 feet), while inland depths reach 1,240 meters (4,067 feet). Although Norway's entire coastline is riddled with fjords, the most breathtaking sights are on the west coast between Stavanger and Trondheim.

Oil-prosperous or fisherman-poor, friendly or taciturn, Norwegians remain outdoor fanatics, firmly in the grip of their country's natural beauty. Norway's high prices and its vastness (it is over 3,200 difficult road-kilometers [2,000 miles] long) are the only reasons the country isn't overrun with tourists. Norway is not quite as expensive as it was a few years ago because low inflation and increased competition in the tourist industry have kept prices stable. There are discount schemes and travel strategies that can lower the cost of traveling here even more (see What It Will Cost in Before You Go, below).

Essential Information

Before You Go

When to Go Cross-country skiing was born in Norway, and the country remains an important winter sports center. While much of the terrain is dark and impassable through the winter, you can cross-country or downhill ski within Oslo's city limits. January, February, and early March are good skiing months, and hotel rooms are plentiful then. Avoid late March and April, when sleet, rain, and countless thaws

Norway

0   200 miles
0   300 km

ATLANTIC OCEAN

Norwegian Sea

North Cape

Vardø
Vadsø
Hammerfest
Kirkenes
Alta
Masi
Kantokeino
Tromsø

FINLAND

Bardu
Narvik
Svolvoer
Vestfjorden
Bodø
Fauske
Saltdal

Arctic Circle

Mo i Rana
Umbukta
Sandnessjøen
Mosjøen
Brønnøysund
E6

S W E D E N

Gulf of Bothnia

Vikna
Namsos
Steinkjer
Trondheim
Meråker
Støren
Kristiansund N.
70
Oppdal
Røros
Tynset
Ålesund
E69
Dombås
Otta
Nordfjord
Koppang
Jostedalsbreen
Florø
Rena
Lillehammer
Sognefjorden
Lake Mjøsa
Hamar
Voss
E68
Eidsvoll
Bergen
Hønefoss
Hardangerfjorden
40
Haugesund
Kongsberg
Drammen
Larvik
Skien
11
★ **Oslo**
Sarpsborg
Fredrikstad
Sandefjord
Oslofjord

Baltic Sea

Stavanger
Egersund
Evje
Arendal
30
Grimstad
Mandal
Kristiansand S.
Skagerrak
Kattegat

and refreezings may ruin the good skiing snow and leave roads—and spirits—in bad shape. Bear in mind that the country virtually closes down for the five-day Easter holidays, when Norwegians make their annual migration to the mountains. If you plan to visit at this time, reserve well in advance. Hotels are more crowded and expensive during this period, but some offer discounts during the two weeks before Easter—which is a good time for skiing.

Summers are generally mild. Then there's the famous midnight sun: Even in the "southern" city of Oslo, night seems more like twilight around midnight, and dawn comes by 2 AM. The weather can be fickle, however, and rain gear and sturdy waterproof shoes are recommended even during the summer. The best times to avoid crowds in museums and on ferries and trains are May and September; Norwegians themselves are on vacation in July and the first part of August.

Climate The following are the average daily maximum and minimum temperatures for Oslo.

Jan.	28F	– 2C	May	61F	16C	Sept.	60F	16C
	19	– 7		43	6		46	8
Feb.	30F	– 1C	June	68F	20C	Oct.	48F	9C
	19	– 7		50	10		38	3
Mar.	39F	4C	July	72F	22C	Nov.	38F	3C
	25	– 4		55	13		31	– 1
Apr.	50F	10C	Aug.	70F	21C	Dec.	32F	0C
	34	1		54	12		25	– 4

Currency The unit of currency in Norway is the krone, written as Kr. on price tags but officially written as NOK. It is divided into 100 øre. Bills of NOK 50, 100, 500, and 1,000 are in general use. Coins are 50 øre and 1, 5, and 10 kroner. Credit cards are accepted in most hotels, stores, restaurants, and many gas stations and garages, but generally not in smaller shops and inns in rural areas. The exchange rate at press time (spring 1994) was NOK 6.80 to the dollar and NOK 10.5 to the pound sterling.

What It Will Cost Norway has a high standard—and cost—of living, but there are ways of saving money by taking advantage of some special offers for accommodations and travel during the tourist season and on weekends throughout the year.

Hotels in larger towns have special weekend and summer rates from late June to early August, and some chains have their own discount schemes—see Norway's annual accommodation guide. Discounts in rural hotels are offered to guests staying several days; meals are then included in the rate. Meals are generally expensive, so take hotel breakfast when it's offered. Alcohol is very expensive and is sold only during strictly regulated hours.

Sample Prices Cup of coffee, NOK 12–NOK 25; a half-liter of beer, NOK 30–NOK 50; soft drink, NOK 15–NOK 25; ham sandwich, NOK 30–NOK 40; 1-mile taxi ride, NOK 40 (for night rates, add 15%).

Customs on Arrival Residents of non-European countries who are over 16 may import duty-free into Norway 200 cigarettes or 500 grams of other tobacco goods, souvenirs, and gifts to the value of NOK 3,500. Residents of European countries who are over 16 may import 200 cigarettes or 250 grams of tobacco or cigars, a small amount of perfume or eau de cologne, and goods to the value of NOK 1,200. Anyone over 20 may bring in 1 liter of wine and 1 liter of liquor or 2 liters of wine and beer.

Language In larger cities, on public transportation, and in most commercial establishments, people speak English. Younger Norwegians generally speak it well—English is the main foreign language taught in schools, and movies and cable TV reinforce its popularity.

There are two official forms of the Norwegian language plus many dialects, so don't be disappointed if you've studied it but find that you can't understand everyone. Typical of Scandinavian languages, Norwegian's additional vowels—æ, ø, and å—come at the end of the alphabet.

Getting Around

By Car
Road Conditions Away from the major routes, roads are narrow and winding, so don't expect to cover more than 240 kilometers (150 miles) in a day, especially in fjord country. The climate plays havoc with the roads: Even the best roads suffer from frost, and the mountain passes may be closed in winter. Snow tires (preferably studded) are compulsory in winter; if you're planning to rent a car, choose a smaller model with front-wheel drive.

Rules of the Road Driving is on the right. The speed limit is 90 kph (55 mph) on highways, 80 kph (50 mph) on main roads, 50 kph (30 mph) in towns, and 30–40 kph (18–25 mph) in residential areas. Throughout the year, low-beam headlights are mandatory. For assistance contact **Norges Automobil Forbund (NAF)**—the Norwegian Automobile Association (Storgt. 2, 0155 Oslo, tel. 22341400). It is important to remember to yield to the vehicle approaching from the right. Passing areas on narrow roads are marked with a white M (for *Møteplass)* on a blue background.

Parking Street parking in cities and towns is clearly marked. There are also municipal parking lots. You cannot park on main roads or on bends. Details can be found in the leaflet "Parking in Oslo," available free from tourist offices and gas stations.

Gasoline Gas costs about NOK 7.50 per liter.

Breakdowns The Norwegian Automobile Association (NAF) patrols main roads and has emergency telephones on mountain roads. For NAF 24-hour service, dial 22341600.

By Train Trains are punctual and comfortable, and most routes are scenic. They fan out from Oslo and leave the coasts (except in the south) to buses and ferries. Reservations are required on all express (*ekspresstog*) and night trains. The Oslo–Bergen route is superbly scenic, while the Oslo–Trondheim–Bodø route takes you within the Arctic Circle. Do not miss the side trips from Myrdal to Flåm from the Oslo–Bergen line, and Dombås to Åndalsnes from the Oslo–Trondheim line. The trains leave Oslo from Sentralstasjonen (Oslo S or Central Station) on Jernbanetorget (at the beginning of Karl Johans gate).

Fares In addition to the Europe-wide passes (**Eurail** and **Inter-Rail**), **ScanRail** passes, good in Norway, Sweden, Denmark, and Finland, are also available. ScanRail passes offer set numbers of travel days within a specified period or one month of unlimited travel. They are available in the United States through **Rail Europe** (tel. 914/682–2999) and **DER Travel Service** (tel. 310/479–4411), and in Great Britain through **NSB Travel**, the Norwegian State Railway (21–24 Cockspur St., London SW1Y 5DA, tel. 071/930–6666). A **Norway Rail Pass** is available for one or two weeks' unlimited rail travel within Norway. In the United States the ticket is available through

ScanAm (tel. 800/545–2204), and in London, at **NSB Travel.** Reduced fares during off-peak times ("green" routes) are also available.

By Plane The remoteness of so much of Norway means that air travel is a necessity for many inhabitants. The main Scandinavian airline, **SAS,** operates a network, along with **Braathens SAFE** and **Widerøe.** Fares are high, but the time saved makes it attractive if you are in a hurry. For longer distances, flying can be cheaper than driving a rented car and paying for gas and incidentals. Inquire about "Visit Norway" passes, which give you relatively cheap domestic-flight coupons (usually good only for summer travel). Norwegian airlines can be contacted at the following addresses: **SAS** (Oslo City, Stenersgt. 1A, 0184 Oslo, tel. 81003300); **Braathens SAFE AS** (Haakon VII's gt. 2, 0161 Oslo, tel. 67597000 or 22834470); **Norsk Air** (Torp Airport, Sandefjord, tel. 33469000); and **Widerøe** (Mustads vei 1, 0283 Oslo, tel. 22736600).

By Bus The Norwegian bus network makes up for some of the limitations of the country's train system, and several of the routes are particularly scenic. For example, the north Norway bus service, starting at Fauske (on the train line to Bodø), goes right up to Kirkenes on the Russian-Norwegian border, covering the 1,000 kilometers (625 miles) within four days. Long-distance bus routes also connect Norway with all its Scandinavian neighbors. Most buses leave from Bussterminalen (Galleri Oslo, Schweigaardsgt. 10, tel. 22170166), close to Oslo Central Station.

By Ferry Norway's long, fjord-indented coastline is served by an intricate and essential network of ferries and passenger ships. A wide choice of services is available, from simple hops across fjords (saving many miles of traveling) and excursions among the thousands of islands to luxury cruises and long journeys up the coast. Most ferries carry cars. Reservations are required on journeys of more than one day but are not needed for simple fjord crossings. Many ferries are small and have limited space, so book ahead if possible; this will allow you to drive onto the ferry ahead of the cars that are waiting in line. Fares and exact times of departures depend on the season and availability of ships. Contact the main Norwegian travel office, Nortra, or the Norway Information Center (*see* Important Addresses and Numbers, *below*) for details.

One of the world's great sea voyages is aboard the mail-and-passenger ship called Hurtigruten, which runs up the Norwegian coast from Bergen to Kirkenes, a town well above the Arctic Circle. Contact the Bergen Line, (405 Park Ave., New York, NY 10022, tel. 800/323–7436), or the Tromsø Main Office, (tel. 77686088).

Nortra (Norwegian Travel Association; Postboks 499, Sentrum, 0150 Oslo, tel. 22427044, fax 22423189) will answer your queries about long-distance travel.

Staying in Norway

Telephones Norway's phone system is one of the world's most expensive, so try to make calls when rates are reduced (5 PM–8 AM weekdays and all day on weekends). Also, avoid using room phones in hotels. In public booths, place coins in the phone before dialing. The largest coins accepted are NOK 10, with most older phones taking only NOK 1 or NOK 5 coins, so make sure you have enough small change. The minimum deposit is NOK 2.

Local Calls The cost of calls within Norway varies according to distance: Within Oslo, the cost goes up according to the amount of time used after the three-minute flat fee. Check the Oslo phone book for dialing information. In 1993, telephone numbers throughout Norway changed from six digits to eight digits; area codes were eliminated.

International Calls To call North America, dial 095–1, then the area code and number. For the United Kingdom, dial 095–44, then the area code (minus the first 0) and number. Beginning in January 1995, you will need to dial 00 for an international connection.

Operators and Information For local information, dial 0180. For international information, dial 0181.

Mail Postal Rates Letters and postcards to the United States cost NOK 5.50 for the first 20 grams. For the United Kingdom, the rate is NOK 4.50 for the first 20 grams.

Receiving Mail Have letters marked "poste restante" after the name of the town, with the last name underlined. The service is free, and letters are directed to the nearest main post office. American Express offices will also hold mail (nonmembers pay a small charge on collection).

Shopping VAT Refunds Much of the 22% Norwegian value-added tax (VAT) will be refunded to visitors who spend more than NOK 300 in any single store. Ask for a special tax-free check and show your passport to confirm that you are not a resident. All purchases must be sealed and presented together with the tax-free check at the tax-free counter at ports, on ferries destined for abroad, and at airports and border posts. The VAT will be refunded, minus a service charge. General information about the tax-free system is available by calling tel. 67149901.

Opening and Closing Times **Banks** are open weekdays 8–3:30; summer hours are 8:15–3. (All post offices change money.)

Museums are usually open Tuesday to Sunday 10–3 or 4. Many, but not all, are closed on Monday.

Shops are usually open weekdays 9 or 10–5 (Thursday until 7) and Saturday 9–1 or 2, though times vary. Shopping malls are often open until 8 on weeknights.

National Holidays January 1; April 14–17 (Easter); May 1 (Labor Day); May 17 (Constitution Day); May 25 (Ascension); June 4 and 5 (Pentecost); December 25–26.

Dining The Norwegian diet emphasizes protein and carbohydrates. Breakfast is usually a large buffet of smoked fish, cheeses, sausage, cold meats, and whole-grain breads accompanied by tea, good coffee, or milk. Lunch is often similar to breakfast, or the famous, but not very filling, *smørbrød* open sandwich. Restaurant and hotel dinners are usually three-course meals, often starting with soup and ending with fresh fruit and berries. The main course may be salmon, trout, or other fish; alternatives can include lamb or pork, reindeer, or even ptarmigan. Remember that the most expensive part of eating is drinking (*see* What It Will Cost in Before You Go, *above*) and that alcohol is not served on Sunday in most areas except Oslo and a handful of other regions. One consolation is the quality of the water, which is still among the purest in the world, despite the growing problem of acid rain.

Mealtimes Lunch is from noon to 3 at restaurants featuring a *koldtbord*. This is a Scandinavian buffet, though few natives ever partake of it, except when dining at mountain resorts. Dinner has traditionally been early, but in hotels and major restaurants it is now more often from 6 to 11. Some rural places still serve dinner from 4 to 7, however.

Dress Jacket and tie or high-fashion casual wear are recommended for restaurants in the Very Expensive and Expensive categories, although during the summer, neat casual dress is acceptable in most places.

Ratings Prices are per person and include a first course, main course, and dessert, without wine or tip. Outside the major cities, prices are considerably less. Service is always included (*see* Tipping, *below*). Best bets are indicated by a star ★.

Category	Oslo
Very Expensive	over NOK 450
Expensive	NOK 300–NOK 450
Moderate	NOK 150–NOK 300
Inexpensive	under NOK 150

Lodging
Hotels Accommodations in Norway are usually spotless, and smaller establishments are often family-run. Service is thoughtful and considerate, right down to blackout curtains to block out the midnight sun. Passes are available for discounts in hotels. The **Scandinavian Bonus Pass,** costing approximately $23 and also valid in Denmark, Sweden, and Finland, gives up to 50% discounts in 250 hotels during summer (May 15–Oct. 1). In addition, children under 15 stay in their parents' room at no extra charge. Contact **Inter Nor Hotels** (Dronningensgt. 40, 0154 Oslo, tel. 22334200). Or consult Norway's accommodations guide, free from any tourist office. **Fjord Pass** (Fjord Tours, Box 1752, 5024 Bergen, tel. 55326550), which costs about $8, is valid at 298 establishments.

Camping Camping is a popular way of keeping costs down. There are more than 900 authorized campsites in the country, many set in spectacular surroundings. Prices vary according to the facilities provided: A family with a car and tent can expect to pay about NOK 100 per night. Some campsites have log cabins available from about NOK 250 per night. *Camping Norway* is available from tourist offices and **NAF** (the Norwegian Automobile Association), Storgaten 2, 0155 Oslo, tel. 22341400.

Youth Hostels There are about 90 youth hostels in Norway; some are schools or farms doing extra summer duty. You must be a member of the Youth Hostel Association (YHA) to stay in the hostels, but there are no age restrictions. Contact **Norske Vandrerhjem (NoVa)** (Dronningensgt. 26, 0154 Oslo, tel. 22421410).

International YHA guides are available to members in the United Kingdom and North America. (There are no age restrictions for membership.) In the United States, contact **American Youth Hostels Inc.** (733 15th St. NW, Suite 840, Washington, DC 20005, tel. 202/783–6161, fax 202/783–6171). In Canada, contact **Canadian Hostelling Association** (1600 James Naismith Dr., Suite 608, Gloucester, Ont. K1B 5N4, tel. 613/748–5638).

Rentals Norwegians escape to mountain cabins whenever they have a chance. Stay in one for a week or two and you'll see why—magnificent scenery; pure air; edible wild berries; and the chance to hike, fish, or cross-country ski. For information on renting cabins, farms, or private homes, write to Den Norske Hytteformidling A.S, Box 3404, Bjølsen, 0406 Oslo, tel. 22356710. Or get the brochure *Norsk Hytteferie* from tourist offices. An unusual alternative is to rent a *rorbu* (fisherman's dwelling) in the northerly Lofoten Islands. Contact Destination Lofoten, Box 210, N–8301 Svolvær, tel. 76073000.

Ratings Prices are summer rates and are for two people in a double room with bath and include breakfast, service, and all taxes. Best bets are indicated by a star ★.

Category	Major Cities	Other Areas
Very Expensive	over NOK 1,300	over NOK 1,000
Expensive	NOK 1,000–NOK 1,300	NOK 850–NOK 1,000
Moderate	NOK 800–NOK 1,000	NOK 650–NOK 850
Inexpensive	under NOK 800	under NOK 650

Tipping A 10%–12% service charge is added to most bills at hotels and restaurants. If you have had exceptional service, then give an additional 5% tip. Round off a taxi fare to the next higher unit, or a little more if the driver has been particularly helpful with luggage. If a doorman hails a taxi for you, you can give NOK 5. On sightseeing tours, tip the guide NOK 10–NOK 15 if you are satisfied. Tip with local currency only.

Oslo

Arriving and Departing

By Plane Oslo Fornebu Airport, about 20 minutes west of Oslo, has international and domestic services. Charter flights go to Gardermoen Airport, about 50 minutes north.

Between the Airport and Downtown Buses from Bussterminalen (Galleri Oslo) to Fornebu leave every 10 minutes (starting at 6 AM) during the week and every half hour on weekends; the fare is NOK 30. Alternatively, take bus No. 31 from Jernbanetorget, marked "Snarøya." The fare is NOK 20; the bus makes a round-trip once hourly. Buses meet flights to Gardermoen and take passengers to the Central Station; the fare is NOK 60. Taxis between Fornebu and downtown cost NOK 130.

By Train Trains on international or domestic long-distance and express routes arrive at Oslo Central Station. Suburban trains depart from Oslo Central Station, Stortinget, and National Theater Station.

Getting Around

By Public Transportation The **Oslo Card**—valid for one, two, or three days—entitles you to free admission to museums and galleries and unlimited travel on the Oslo Transport system and the Norwegian Railways commuter trains within the city limits; free parking; free admission to the Tusenfryd amusement park, public swimming pools, and racetracks; and discounts at various stores, cinemas, and sports centers. You can get the card at Oslo's tourist information offices and hotels (*see* Important Addresses and Numbers in Oslo, *below*). A one-day card costs NOK 110 adults, NOK 55 children; two days NOK 190 adults, NOK 80 children; three days NOK 240 adults, NOK 110 children.

If using public transportation only occasionally, you can get tickets (adults NOK 15, children NOK 7.50) at bus and subway stops. For NOK 35, the **Tourist Ticket** gives 24 hours' unlimited travel on any means of public transportation, including the summer ferries to Bygdøy. The **Flexikort** gives you 10 subway, bus, or streetcar rides for NOK 130, including transfers.

By Taxi A taxi is available if the roof light is on. There are taxi stands at Oslo Central Station and usually alongside Narvesen newsstands, or call 22388090; during peak hours, though, you may have to wait.

Important Addresses and Numbers

Tourist Information The **Oslo Tourist Information Office** (tel. 22830050) is at the **Norway Information Center,** Vestbaneplassen 1. Open Oct.–Apr., Mon.–Sat. 9–4; May, Mon.–Sat. 9–6; June, Mon.–Sat. 9–6, Sun. 9–4; July and Aug., daily 9–8; Sept., Mon.–Sat. 9–6. **Oslo Central Station,** tel. 22171124. Open 8 AM–11 PM. **Trafikanten,** Oslo Central Station, tel. 22177030. Open weekdays 7 AM–11 PM, weekends 8 AM–11 PM.

Embassies U.S. (Drammensvn. 18, tel. 22448550). Canadian (Oscarsgt. 20, tel. 22466955). U.K. (Thos. Heftyesgt. 8, tel. 22552400).

Emergencies Police (Grønlandsleiret 44, tel. 112 or 22669050, 24-hour service). **Ambulance:** 24-hour service (tel. 113 or 22117070). Dentist (Oslo Kommunale Tannlegevakt, Tøyen Center, Kolstadsgt. 18, tel. 22673000). Emergencies, weekdays 8 PM–11 PM, weekends and holidays 11 AM–2 PM. **Pharmacy: Jernbanetorgets Apotek** (Jernbanetorget 4B, tel. 22412482. Open 24 hours).

Post Office The main post office, located at Dronningensgate 15, is open Monday–Friday 8–8, Saturday 9–3. The **Telegraph Office** is at Kongensgate 21.

Books in English Tanum Libris (Karl Johans gt. 37–41, tel. 22411100), **Erik Qvist** (Drammensvn. 16, tel. 22445269, beside the U.S. Embassy).

Travel Agencies Winge (agent for American Express): Karl Johans gate 33/35, tel. 22412030; **Bennett:** Pilestredet 35, tel. 22943600 **Berg-Hansen** (agent for Thomas Cook): 3 Arbiensgate, tel. 22551901. **NSB Travel Agency:** Stortingsgate 28, tel. 22838850.

Guided Tours

Orientation Tours H. M. K. provides three three-hour tours and one full-day tour departing from the Rådhuset (harbor side). Tickets are available on the bus or from Oslo Tourist Information Office (*see* Important Addresses and Numbers, *above*). The "Oslo Highlights" morning tour goes to the Vigeland Sculpture Park, Holmenkollen Ski Jump, the Viking Ship Museum, and the *Kon-Tiki*. The "Art and History tour" includes Akershus Castle and Church, Gamle Aker Church, National Gallery, Stave Church at Norwegian Folk Museum, and Holmenkollen Ski Jump. *Each tour costs NOK 160 adults, NOK 80 children. Tours start daily at 10.*

The "Afternoon Tour" goes to the Holmenkollen Ski Jump, Vigeland Sculpture Park, the Viking Ships, and the polar ship *Fram* at Bygdøy. *Each tour costs NOK 160 adults, NOK 80 children. Open Apr.–Sept., daily at 1:30.*

The "Full Day Sightseeing Tour" lasts from 10 to 4:30 and includes most of what Oslo has to offer. *Tel. 22208206. Tour: NOK 300 adults, NOK 150 children under 12.*

Båtservice Sightseeing has seven different boat and/or bus tours departing from Rådhusbrygge 3—from a 50-minute minicruise (NOK 55 adults, NOK 25 children) departing every hour all summer to an all-day grand tour of Oslo by boat and bus (NOK 275 adults, NOK 140 children). Book at 22200715.

Walking Tours The "Oslo Guide" brochure (free from the tourist office) has several walking tours on its map. Some go farther afield and link up with public transportation.

Personal Guides Taxis give sightseeing tours in English for NOK 250 per hour. Call 22388070 for reservations.

Exploring Oslo

Oslo is a small capital city, with a population of just less than half a million. The downtown area is compact, but the geographic limits of Oslo spread out to include forests, fjords, and mountains, which give the city a pristine airiness that complements its urban dignity. Oslo has an excellent public transportation network. Explore downtown on foot, enjoying its museums and jazz clubs, then venture beyond via bus, streetcar, or train.

Numbers in the margin correspond to points of interest on the Oslo map.

Oslo's main street, **Karl Johans gate,** runs right through the center of town, from Oslo Central Station uphill to the Royal Palace. Half its length is closed to traffic, and it is in this section that you will find many of the city's shops and outdoor cafés.

❶ Start at the **Slottet** (Royal Palace), the king's residence. The neoclassical palace was built during the early 19th-century and is as sober, sturdy, and unpretentious as the Norwegian character. The surrounding park is open to the public, though the palace is not. Time your visit to coincide with the changing of the guard (daily at 1:30). When the king is in residence—signaled by a red flag—the Royal Guard strikes up the band.

❷ Walk down Karl Johans gate to the old **Universitet** (University), which is made up of the three big buildings on your left. The main hall of the university is decorated with murals by Edvard Munch (1863–1944), Norway's most famous artist. The hall (*aula*) is open only during July. The Nobel Peace Prize is presented there each year on December 10. *Admission to hall free. Open July, weekdays noon–2.*

❸ Behind the University is the **Nasjonalgalleriet** (National Gallery), Norway's largest public gallery. It has a small but high-quality selection of paintings by European artists, but of particular interest is the collection of works by Norwegian artists. Edvard Munch is represented here, but most of his work is in the Munch Museum (*see below*), east of the center. *Universitetgt. 13. Admission free. Open Mon., Wed., Fri., and Sat. 10–4, Thurs. 10–8, Sun. 11–3.*

❹ The **Historisk Museum** (Historical Museum) is in back of the National Gallery. It features displays of daily life and art from the Viking period, including treasures recovered from Viking ships. The Ethnographic Section houses a collection related to the great polar explorer Roald Amundsen, the first man to reach the South Pole. *Frederiksgt. 2. Admission free. Open summer, Tues.–Sun. 11–3; winter, Tues.–Sun. noon–3.*

⑤ Return to Karl Johans gate and cross over for a closer look at the **Nationaltheatret,** watched over by the statues of Bjørnstjerne Bjørnson and Henrik Ibsen. Bjørnson was the nationalist poet who wrote Norway's anthem. Internationally lauded playwright Ibsen wrote *Peer Gynt* (he personally requested Edvard Grieg's musical accompaniment), *A Doll's House*, and *Hedda Gabler*, among others. He worried that his plays, packed with allegory, myth, and sociological and emotional angst, might not have appeal outside Norway. Instead, they were universally recognized and changed the face of modern theater.

Time Out Inside the Grand Hotel, in the informal **Palmen,** salads and light meals are served along with pastries and cakes.

⑥ At the far end of the pond is **Stortinget** (Parliament), a bow-fronted yellow-brick building stretched across the block. It is open to visitors by request when Parliament is not in session: A guided tour takes visitors around the frescoed interior and into the debating chamber. *Karl Johans gt. 22, tel. 22313050. Admission free.*

⑦ Karl Johans gate is closed to traffic near the staid **Oslo Domkirke** (Cathedral). The much-renovated cathedral, consecrated in 1697, is modest by the standards of some other European capital cities, but the interior is rich with treasures, such as the Baroque carved wooden altarpiece and pulpit. The ceiling frescoes by Hugo Lous Mohr were done after World War II. The bronze door to the cathedral is also noteworthy. Behind the cathedral is an area of arcades, small restaurants, and street musicians. *Stortorvet 1. Admission free. Open weekdays 10–3.*

Facing the cathedral, turn right at Kirkegata. Three blocks down, turn right onto Rådhusgate and then almost immediately left onto **⑧** Kongens gate. This takes you to **Akershus Slott** (castle) on the harbor. The castle was built during the Middle Ages but restored in 1527 by Christian IV of Denmark—Denmark then ruled Norway—after it was damaged by fire. He then laid out the present city of Oslo (naming it Christiania after himself) around his new residence; Oslo's street plan still follows his design. Some rooms are open for guided tours, and the grounds form a park around the castle. The grounds also house the **Forsvarsmuseet** and **Hjemmefrontmuseum** (Norwegian Defense and Resistance museums). Both give you a feel for the Norwegian fighting spirit throughout history and especially during the German occupation, when the Nazis set up headquarters on this site and had a number of patriots executed here. *Akershus Castle and Museums. Entrance from Festningspl., tel. 22/412521. Admission: NOK 15 adults, NOK 5 children. Guided tours of the castle, May–Sept., Mon.–Sat. 11, 1, and 3, Sun. 1 and 3. Museums open weekdays 10–4, Sun. 12:30–4.*

⑨ Just behind Akershus Castle, in the direction of Oslo Central Station, is the **Museet for Samtidskunst** (the Museum of Contemporary Art), housed in the former Bank of Norway building. *Bankpl. 4, tel. 22335820. Admission free. Open Tues.–Fri. 11–7, Sat.–Sun. 11–4.*

Continue along the waterfront toward the central **harbor**—the heart of Oslo and head of the fjord. Shops and cafés stay open late at **⑩** **Aker Brygge,** the new quayside shopping and cultural center, with a theater, cinemas, and galleries among the shops, restaurants, and cafés. You don't have to buy anything—just sit amid the fountains and statues and watch the activities.

Oslo

KEY

AE American Express Office

ⓘ Tourist Information

— Rail Lines

Vigelandsparken

Bogstadveien · Prof. Dahls gt. · Industrigt. · Eilert Sundts gt. · Holte · Gabelenborgveien · Camilla Colletts vei · Oscars · Riddervolds gt. · Parkveien · Kirkeveien · Glydenlovens gt. · Nordraaks gt. · Tidemands gt. · Eckersbergs gt. · Frognerveien · Løvenskiolds · Arno Bergs Plass · Gyldenloves gt. · Skoveien · Drammensveien · Halvdan Svartes gt. · Nobels gt. · Thomas Heftyes · Gimleveien · veien · Borders Gate · Lille Frogner Alle · Kruses gate · Bygdøy allé · Elisenberg · Thomas · Bygdøy allé · Gabels gt. · Lapsetorget · U.S. Embassy · Dr · Sjølystveien · Dronning Blancas vei · Frognerstranda · Drammensveien · Heftyes · Fred. Stangs gt. · Niels Juels gate · Drammensveien · Parkveien · Cort Adelers · Heftyes gt. · Munkedamsveien · D · Frognerkilen · E18 · Filipstadveien · BYGDØY · Oscarshallveien · Museumsveien · Dronninghavn veien · Filipstadkaia · Huk aveny · Langvikbukta · Bygdøynes-veien · Løkenveien

⑫ ⑬ ⑭ ⑮

0 — 1 mile
0 — 1 km

N

Aker Brygge and harbor, **10**
Akershus Slott, **8**
Fram-Museet, **15**
Historisk Museum, **4**
Kon-Tiki Museum, **14**
Munch-Museet, **16**
Museet for Samtidskunst, **9**
Nasjonalgalleriet, **3**
Nationaltheatret, **5**
Norsk Folkemuseum, **12**
Oslo Domkirke, **7**
Rådhuset, **11**
Slottet, **1**
Stortinget, **6**
Universitetet, **2**
Vikingskipshuset, **13**

⓫ The large redbrick **Rådhuset** (City Hall) is on the waterfront, too: Note the friezes in the courtyard, depicting scenes from Norwegian folklore, then go inside and see murals depicting daily life in Norway, historical events, and Resistance activities. You can set your watch by the astronomical clock in the inner courtyard. *Admission free. Open Mon.–Sat. 9–3:30, Sun. noon–3. Tours daily.*

The **Norway Information Center** is on the right side across the street when facing the harbor. From nearby Pipervika Bay, you can board a ferry in the summertime for the seven-minute crossing of the fjord to the **Bygdøy** peninsula, where there is a complex of seafaring museums. *Ferries run Apr.–Sept., at 15 past and 15 to each hour.*

The first ferry stop is Dronningen. From here, walk up a well-
⓬ marked road to the **Norsk Folkemuseum** (Norwegian Folk Museum), a large park where historic farmhouses, some of them centuries old, have been collected from all over the country and reassembled. A whole section of 19th-century Oslo was moved here, as was a 12th-century wooden stave church. There are displays of weaving and sheepshearing on Sunday, and throughout the park there are guides in period costume. *Museumsvn. 10, tel. 22437020. Admission: NOK 35. Open summer, daily 10–6; winter, daily noon–4.*

Signs lead you around the corner to a second museum. The
⓭ **Vikingskipshuset** (Viking Ship Museum) contains 9th-century ships recovered from the fjord, where they had been ritually sunk while carrying the mortal remains of Viking kings and queens to the next world. Also on display are the treasures and jewelry that accompanied the royal bodies on their last voyage. The ornate craftsmanship evident in the ships and jewelry dispels any notion that the Vikings were skilled only in looting and pillaging. *Huk aveny. Admission: NOK 20 adults, NOK 10 children. Open Nov.–Mar., daily 11–3; Apr. and Oct., daily 11–4; May–Aug., daily 9–6; Sept., daily 11–5.*

Reboard the ferry or follow signs for the 20-minute walk to the
⓮ **Kon-Tiki Museum,** where the *Kon-Tiki* raft and the reed boat *RA II* are on view. Thor Heyerdahl made no concessions to the modern world when he crossed the Pacific *(Kon-Tiki)* and the Atlantic *(RA II)* in these boats. *Admission: NOK 20 adults, NOK 10 children. Open Oct.–Mar., daily 10:30–4; Apr.–May 17 and Sept., daily 10:30–5; May 18–Aug. 31, daily 9–6.*

Directly across from the Kon-Tiki Museum is a large triangular
⓯ building, the **Fram-Museet.** This museum is devoted to the polar ship *Fram,* the sturdy wooden vessel that belonged to bipolar explorer Fridtjof Nansen. (It was also used by Amundsen.) In 1893 Nansen led an expedition that reached latitude 86°14′N, the most northerly latitude to have been reached at that time. The book *Farthest North* tells his story. Active in Russian famine-relief work, Nansen received a Nobel Peace Prize in 1922. You can board the ship and imagine yourself in one of the tiny berths, and that outside a force-nine gale is blowing and the temperature is dozens of degrees below freezing. *Admission: NOK 15 adults, NOK 8 children. Open May 16–Aug., daily 9–5:45; May 1–15 and Sept., daily 10–4:45; Apr. and Oct., weekdays 11–2:45; Apr., Oct. and Nov., weekends 11:45–3:45.*

Time Out Before catching the ferry back to the center of Oslo, consider a meal or snack at **Lanternen Kro.** In summer you can sit on the terrace, which commands a view of the entire harbor. Or you can stop at **Rodeløkken Kafé** for homemade waffles and coffee. It's just a short walk from the Folk Museum, right near the king's farm.

Back at City Hall, board bus No. 29 to **Tøyen,** the area northeast of Oslo, where you'll find the **Munch-museet** (Munch Museum). In 1940, four years before his death, Munch bequeathed much of his work to the city of Oslo; the museum opened in 1963, the centennial of his birth. Although only a fraction of its 22,000 items—books, paintings, drawings, prints, sculptures, and letters—are on display, you can still get a sense of the tortured expressionism that was to have such an effect on European painting. *Tøyengt. 53. Admission: NOK 40 adults, NOK 10 children. Open June–Sept. 15, Mon.– Sat. 10–6, Sun. noon–6; Sept. 16–May, Tues.–Sat. 10–4, Thurs. 10–6, Sun. noon–6.*

Off the Beaten Track

The jury is still out on the question of the artistic merit of Gustav Vigeland's *Wheel of Life and Monolith,* but few would deny the perseverance involved in its creation. Over 15 meters (50 feet) high and covered with more than 100 linked human forms, this sculpture is the focal point of **Vigelandsparken,** in northwest Oslo. Open-air restaurants, tennis courts, and swimming pools provide additional diversions. To get there, take streetcar No. 2 or T-bane train Nos. 13, 14, 15, or 16 and get off at Majorstuen. *Free. Park open 24 hours.*

Walk down Frognerveien to Krusesgate and turn left for a view of what Oslo looked like 100 years ago. The decorative gingerbread houses are on the historic preservation list.

The **Holmenkollen ski jump,** at 62 meters (203 feet) above ground level, is one of the world's highest and the site of an international contest each March. At the base is a ski museum carved into the rock. To get there, board any Frognerseter/Holmenkollen suburban train from Nationaltheatret; get off at Holmenkollen and walk uphill to the jump. The half-hour train ride sweeps from underground up to 403 meters (1,322 feet) above sea level.

The forests within Oslo's vast city limits include 11 sports chalets geared to exercise and the outdoor life. The areas around **Skullerudstua** and **Skistua** are recommended for their walking and skiing trails. Contact Oslo Kommune (Forestry Services, Skogvesenet, tel. 22381870). Or, for winter or summer "safaris" through the forest by Land-Rover, contact the main tourist office (*see* Important Addresses and Numbers, *above*).

Head east on streetcar No. 9 (from Nationaltheatret or Jernbanetorget) to the Sjømannsskolen stop to see 5,000-year-old carvings on the runic stones near **Ekebergsletta park.** They are across the road from the park on Karlsborgveien and marked by a sign reading *Fortidsminne.* Walk through the park and take Oslogate and then Bispegata to the **Oslo Ladegård,** which has scale models of old Oslo on the site of the 13th-century Bispegard (Bishop's Palace). *Admission: NOK 20 adults, NOK 10 children. Open May–Sept.; guided tours on Wed. at 6 and Sun. at 1.*

Beyond Oslo, trips include a visit to **Lillehammer,** site of the 1994 Winter Olympics and home of **Maihaugen,** one of the largest open-air museums in northern Europe (tel. 61250135). Lillehammer is at the top of the long finger of **Lake Mjøsa** and is reached by train from Oslo Central Station in about two hours. A paddle steamer, **D/S *Skibladner,*** travels the length of the lake (six hours each way) in summer, making several stops. At the southern tip of the lake is **Eidsvoll,** where the Norwegians announced their new constitution in 1814, marking the end to centuries of domination by Denmark.

There are limitless possibilities for outdoor activities in the region, all within reach of Oslo.

Shopping

Gift Ideas Since prices in Norway are government-controlled, Oslo is the obvious place to do your shopping. The selection is widest here: Pewter, silver, glass, crystal, sheepskin, leather, and knitwear are all appealing samples of Norwegian craftsmanship.

Shopping Districts Many of the larger stores are in the area between Stortinget and the cathedral; much of this area is for pedestrians only. The **Basarhallene**, at the back of the cathedral, is an art and handicrafts boutique center. Oslo's newest shopping area, **Aker Brygge**, was once a shipbuilding wharf. Located right on the waterfront, it is a complex of booths, offices, and garden cafés. Check out Bogstadveien/Hegdehaugsveien, which runs from Majorstua to Parkveien. This street offers a good selection of stores and has plenty of places to rest your tired feet and quench your thirst. Shops stay open until 5 PM (Thursday to 7 PM).

Department Stores and Malls Oslo's department stores, **Steen & Strøm** and **Christiania Glasmagasin**, are both in the shopping district near the cathedral. **Paléet** on Karl Johans gate is a recent, elegant addition to Oslo's main street, with 40 shops and 10 restaurants.

Food and Flea Markets Every Saturday during spring, summer, and fall, there is a flea market at Vestkanttorget, two blocks away from Frogner Park. Check the papers for local flea markets.

Dining

For details and price-category definitions, *see* Dining in Staying in Norway, *above*. Best bets are indicated by a star ★.

Very Expensive ★ **Bagatelle.** Bagatelle was the first restaurant with a Norwegian chef serving Norwegian food to merit a Michelin star. Choose the five- or seven-course menus for the full range of Chef Hellstrøm's talents. The wine list is extensive, chairs are comfortable, service is impeccable, and the best of Norwegian contemporary art adorns the walls. *Bygdøy allé 3, tel. 22446397. Reservations recommended. AE, DC, MC, V. Open Mon.–Sat. 6 PM–11 PM.*

★ **D'Artagnan.** Among gourmands, D'Artagnan is a favorite. Stellar food and excellent service make this a place to remember. Try chef Freddie Nielsen's Grand Menu with an appropriate wine from the well-stocked cellar. *Øvre Slottsgt. 16, tel. 22415062. Reservations required. AE, DC, MC, V.*

★ **De Fem Stuer.** Chef Bent Stiansen, gold medalist in the Bocuse d'Or World Championships for Chefs in 1993, prepares food that is even better than the view. Enjoy modern versions of Norwegian specialties, with the accent on fish and game. *Holmenkollen Park Hotel, Kongevn. 26, tel. 22146090, fax 22146192. Reservations recommended. AE, DC, MC, V.*

Feinschmecker. Located in a fashionable residential area only minutes from the center of town, this restaurant specializes in modern Scandinavian cuisine. The desserts are especially good. Lars Erik Underthun, the silver medal winner at the 1991 Bocuse d'Or World Championships for Chefs, is in charge here. *Balchensgt. 5, tel. 22441777. Reservations required for dinner. AE, DC, MC, V. Closed Sun.*

Expensive **Babette's Gjestehus.** This warm and intimate restaurant has an international menu with a French accent. *Rådhuspassasjen, tel. 22416464. Reservations required. AE, DC, MC, V. No weekday lunch. Closed Sun.*

★ **Theatercafeen.** This Oslo institution is the last Viennese-style café in northern Europe and is a favorite with the literary and entertainment crowd. The daily menu is a good value. Save room for dessert, which the pastry chef also makes for Norway's royal family. *Hotel Continental, Stortingsgt. 24/26, tel. 22333200. Reservations required. AE, DC, MC, V.*

Moderate **Det Gamle Raadhus.** The "old city hall," Oslo's oldest restaurant, is located in a building dating from 1641. Specialties include mussels and fresh shrimp. *Nedre Slottsgt. 1, tel. 22420107. Reservations advised. AE, DC, MC, V. Closed Sun.*

★ **Dinner.** Though its name is not the best for a restaurant specializing in Szechuan-style cuisine, this is the best place for Chinese food, both hot and not so pungent. The mango pudding for dessert is wonderful. Don't bother with the other Chinese restaurants. *Arbeidergt. 2, tel. 22/42-68-90. Reservations advised. Dress: casual. AE, DC, MC, V. No lunch.*

Frognerseteren. Located just above the Holmenkollen Ski Jump, this restaurant looks down on the entire city. Take the Holmenkollbanen to the end station and then walk downhill to the restaurant. Follow the signs. The newly renovated upstairs room has the same view as the more expensive panorama veranda. There is also an outdoor café. *Voksenkollen, tel. 22143736. Reservations accepted. AE, DC, MC, V.*

Kastanjen. The short menu at this neighborhood restaurant changes often and features all seasonal ingredients. The three-course fixed-price dinner is an excellent value. *Bygdøy allé 18, tel. 22434467. Reservations recommended. AE, DC, MC, V. Closed Sun.*

A Touch of France. The bouillabaisse at this intimate, French brasserie is out of this world. *Øvre Slottsgt. 16, tel. 22425697. Reservations advised weekends. AE, DC, MC, V.*

Inexpensive **Kaffistova.** This cafeteria serves Norwegian "country-style" cook-
★ ing at reasonable prices. *Rosenkrantz' gt. 8, tel. 22429530. No reservations. AE, DC, MC, V.*

Lofotstua. This rustic fish restaurant has a cozy atmosphere and personal service. Good, moderately priced food is served—typical specialties include fresh cod and seafood from Lofoten. *Kirkevn 40, tel. 22469396. Reservations advised. AE, DC, MC, V. Closed Sat.*

Vegeta. Next to the Nationaltheatret bus and streetcar station, this is a popular spot for hot and cold vegetarian meals and salads. It is a nonsmoking restaurant. The all-you-can-eat specials offer top value. *Munkedamsvn. 3B, tel. 22834020. No reservations. No credit cards.*

Lodging

The tourist office's accommodations bureaus (open daily 8 AM–11 PM) in Oslo Central Station can help you find rooms in hotels, pensions, and private homes. You must apply in person and pay a fee of NOK 20 (NOK 10 children) plus 10% of the room rate, which will be refunded when you check in. For details and price-category definitions, *see* Lodging in Staying in Norway, *above*. Best bets are indicated by a star ★.

Very **Grand.** It's hard to beat the Grand's location on Oslo's main street,
Expensive opposite the Parliament and Studenterlunden. The hotel has com-
★ forts and history to match its name: Ibsen had a permanent table in

Grand Café, a famous Oslo rendezvous. The Palmen, just off the lobby, is where Oslo matrons drink their afternoon tea. *Karl Johans gt. 31, tel. 22429390, fax 22421225. 215 rooms with bath and shower, 60 suites. Facilities: 3 restaurants, 2 bars, indoor pool, health club, parking facilities. AE, DC, MC, V.*

★ **Holmenkollen Park Rica.** Near the ski jump, this hotel is an imposing building in the old romantic folkloric style with a luxurious annex. The rooms are bright, and most have balconies with excellent views of the city and the fjord. The hotel runs a shuttle bus for its guests, since it's a 20-minute drive from downtown. It's probably the best place for anyone hoping to do some skiing. *Kongevn. 26, tel. 22922000, fax 22141692. 191 rooms with bath. Facilities: 2 restaurants, bar, nightclub, whirlpool, sauna, indoor pool, ski trails. AE, DC, MC, V.*

SAS Scandinavia Hotel. The SAS is a comfortable business hotel with impeccable service. The airport bus stops right outside. Summit 21 is the rooftop lunch bar, with commanding views of the entire city. Downstairs you'll find a shopping center and the city air terminal. *Holbergs gt. 30, tel. 22113000, fax 22113017. 491 rooms with bath, 15 suites. Facilities: 2 restaurants, 2 bars, nightclub, indoor pool, disco. AE, DC, MC, V.*

Expensive **Ambassadeur.** Located just behind the Royal Palace, this hotel has 42 individually designed rooms and personalized service. The Ambassadeur restaurant serves modern Scandinavian food. *Camilla Colletts vei 15, tel. 22441835, fax 22444791. 42 rooms with bath or shower, 8 suites. Facilities: restaurant, bar, sauna. AE, DC, MC, V.*

SAS Park Royal Hotel. Ten minutes from Oslo, this hotel is clean, efficient, and convenient to Fornebu Airport. The rooms are American motel-style, and the top-class facilities are well suited for business stays. *Fornebuparken, Lysaker, tel. 67120220, fax 67120011. 254 rooms and 14 suites with bath. Facilities: restaurant, health club, tennis courts, direct airport check-in, executive office space. AE, DC, MC, V.*

Stefan. The service is cheerful and accommodating in this hotel in the center of Oslo. One of its main attractions is the popular restaurant on the top floor, with Oslo's best buffet lunch, featuring traditional Norwegian dishes. *Rosenkrantz' gt. 1, tel. 22429250, fax 22337022. 130 rooms with bath or shower. Facilities: restaurant. AE, DC, MC, V.*

Moderate **Bondeheimen.** Oslo's most Norwegian hotel has modern, comfortable rooms and a staff that wears national costumes. *Rosenkrantz' gt. 8, tel. 22429530, fax 22419437. 76 rooms with shower. Facilities: café, conference room. AE, DC, MC, V.*

★ **Cecil Hotel.** Built in 1989, just off Stortingsgata right in the heart of town, this bed-and-breakfast—only hotel is a good value for the money. *Stortingsgt. 8, tel. 22427000, fax 22422670. 110 rooms with bath. AE, DC, MC, V.*

Europa. This centrally located modern bed-and-breakfast is a moderately priced alternative to its next-door neighbor, the SAS Scandinavia Hotel. The rooms are comfortable (all have color TV), and there are special reductions for children. *St. Olavs gt. 31, tel. 22209990, fax 22112727. 158 rooms with bath. AE, DC, MC, V.*

Gabelshus Hotel. Only five minutes from the center of town, the Gabelshus is a moderate-size hotel on an attractive side street. The rooms are spacious and airy, and the hotel has the feel of a large country house. *Gabels gt. 16, tel. 22552260, fax 22442730. 45 rooms with bath. Facilities: restaurant. AE, DC, MC, V.*

Inexpensive **Gyldenløve.** Centrally located at Bogstadveien, this bed-and-breakfast hotel—renovated in 1992—offers quality at a reasonable price and 160 well-equipped rooms with all conveniences. *Bogstadvn. 20, tel. 22601090, fax 22603390. 156 rooms with bath or shower. AE, DC, MC, V.*

Haraldsheim. Oslo's youth hostel is one of Europe's largest. Most of the rooms have four beds, and those in the new wing all have showers. It is 4 kilometers (2½ miles) from city center on tram 1 or 7 to Sinsen. Breakfast is included. *Haraldsheimvn. 4, tel. 22155043, fax 22347197. 270 beds. No credit cards.*

Munch. This bed-and-breakfast hotel, renovated in 1994, has large but rather basic rooms. It's a 10-minute walk from downtown. *Munchsgt. 5, tel. 22424275, fax 22206469. 180 rooms with shower. AE, DC, MC, V.*

The Arts

Considering the size of the city, Oslo has a surprisingly good artistic life. Consult the "Oslo Guide" or "Oslo This Week" for details. Winter is *the* cultural season, with the **Nationaltheatret** featuring modern plays (all in Norwegian), classics, and a good sampling of Ibsen. **Det Norske Teatret** (Kristian IVs gate 8), one of Europe's most modern theater complexes, has musicals and plays.

Oslo's modern **Konserthuset** (Concert Hall), at Munkedamsveien 14, is the home of the Oslo Philharmonic, famous for its recordings of Tchaikovsky's symphonies. A smaller hall in the same building is the setting for performances of chamber music and—in summer only—folk dancing, held Monday and Thursday at 9 in July and August. In addition to the **Museum of Contemporary Art**, there's a good modern collection at the **Henie-Onstad Kunstsenter** (tel. 67543050) at Høvikodden. This center specializes in 20th-century art and was a gift from the Norwegian Olympic skater Sonja Henie and her husband, shipowner Niels Onstad. Open Mon. 11–5, Tue.–Fri. 9–9, Sat.–Sun., 11–7.

Nightlife

Oslo used to be a place where the sidewalks rolled up at 8. Now Karl Johans gate is a lively place into the wee hours. There are loads of music cafés and clubs, as well as more conventional night spots. A few good ones are **Barock** (Universitetsgt. 26, tel. 22424420), **Cruise Café** (Aker Brygge 1, tel. 22836430), **Rockefeller** (Torggt. 16—entrance from Mariboes gt., tel. 22203232), **Smuget** (Rosenkrantz gt. 22, tel. 22425262), and **Lipp** (Roald Amundsens gt. 2, tel. 22414400). Why not go to a movie? All films are screened in the original language with Norwegian subtitles. Tickets cost NOK 45.

The Coast Road to Stavanger

This tour follows the Sørlandet coast south of Oslo toward the busy port Kristiansand and then west to Stavanger. It is an area where whaling has given way to canneries, lumber, paper production, and petrochemicals. Yet the beauty of this 608-kilometer (380-mile) route has not been greatly marred, and you'll find seaside towns, rocky headlands, and stretches of forest (fjord country does not begin until north of Stavanger). The route outlined here follows the

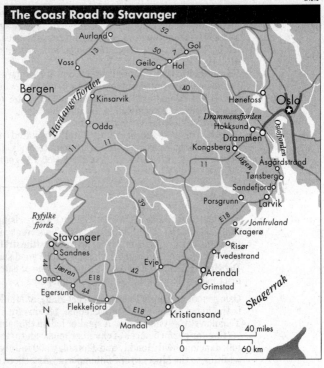

The Coast Road to Stavanger

coast, but it is also possible to reach Stavanger via an inland route through the Telemark region.

Getting Around

By Car Driving is recommended because it gives visitors the chance to stop at coastal villages that are either not served by trains or have only sporadic service. The route is simple: E18 as far as Flekkefjord, then Route 44 to Stavanger.

By Train The best train service is the Sørland line, which leaves Oslo Central Station and goes all the way to Stavanger. The Oslo–Drammen stretch is an engineering feat and features Norway's longest tunnel, an 11-kilometer (7-mile) construction through sheer rock.

By Bus Local buses cover the entire route, but they take much longer than the train. For details on fares and schedules, check with the tourist offices listed below or the main one in Oslo (*see* Important Addresses and Numbers in Oslo, *above*).

Guided Tours

During the summer there is a daily boat excursion from Oslo to the coastal resorts of Kragerø, Jomfruland, and Risør southwest of the capital in the direction of Stavanger. Sightseers return the same day, and refreshments are served on board. The excursion is organized by the Norway Information Center (*see* Important Addresses and Numbers, *above*).

Tourist Information

Arendal (Friholmsgt. 1, tel. 37022193).
Drammen (Rådhuset, tel. 32806210).
Flekkefjord (tel. 38324254).
Kristiansand (Dronningensgt. 2, tel. 38026065).
Larvik (Storgt. 48, tel. 33130100).
Stavanger (Stavanger Kulturhus, Sølvberget, tel. 51535100).
Tønsberg (Nedre Langgt. 36B, tel. 33310220).

Exploring the Coast Road to Stavanger

From Oslo, take E18 west for about 40 kilometers (25 miles) to the bustling port of **Drammen.** Located at the mouth of a large timber-floating river, Drammen operates as a processing and shipping center for lumber and paper products. Take a short detour west of town on Route 11, turn right on Kongsgate, and climb the mile-long series of spiraling tunnels leading to **Spiraltoppen** at **Bragernes Hill.** During the '50s, locals decided against any further quarrying of building stone and turned instead to tunneling for it. The result is this scenic and dramatic road with panoramic views of **Drammensfjord** and the larger **Oslofjord** beyond.

Return to E18 and continue to the coastal town of **Åsgårdstrand,** an unspoiled summer resort where Edvard Munch painted many of his best works. His small yellow frame house is open to visitors during the summer (admission: NOK 15). Farther along is **Tønsberg,** which inhabitants claim is Norway's oldest town, founded in AD 870. The steep hill, Slottsfjellet, beside the train station leads to the ruins of **Tønsberghus,** an extensive fortress and abbey. The outlook tower, built in 1870 to commemorate the town's millennium, has a good view of the coast. The rise of Oslo as Norway's capital led to the decline of Tønsberg, although it thrived as a whaling port in the 1700s.

Attractive **Sandefjord,** 15 kilometers (9 miles) down E18, is a port that served as the base for the Norwegian whaling fleet until after World War II, when large-scale competition from the Soviet Union and Japan made the operation uneconomical. The port remains busy as a depot for timber shipping.

Just beyond Sandefjord, E18 crosses the important lumbering river Lågen and then follows it to the port of **Larvik,** which is the terminus for ferries to Frederikshavn in Denmark. Like Tønsberg and Sandefjord, Larvik once looked to whaling for its livelihood, but it, too, has turned to lumber and ferrying for employment.

The **Maritime Museum** is located in the former customs house and chronicles Larvik's seafaring history. It emphasizes Thor Heyerdahl's voyages, with models of *Kon-Tiki* and *RA II. Admission charges and opening times vary; check with the tourist office.*

After Larvik, progress is faster, as E18 cuts across some of the narrower peninsulas on its way south. Side roads offer the chance to explore the smaller coastal village of **Kragerø,** where Edvard Munch spent many summers painting. Next is **Risør,** with picturesque, white-painted, patrician 19th-century harbor-front homes; and **Tvedestrand,** with charming old sections of town. They are all very popular summer resorts.

Arendal, 120 kilometers (75 miles) beyond Larvik, was once called the Venice of Scandinavia, but the canals have now been turned into wide streets. The atmosphere of bygone whaling prosperity in this and other Sørland ports is like that of Nantucket, with tidy cottages and grandiose captains' houses all within shouting distance of the docks. Explore Arendal's **Tyholmen quarter** for a glimpse into this 19th-century world.

Kristiansand is another 50 kilometers (31 miles) along the coast from Arendal. It is the largest town in Sørlandet and has important air, sea, road, and rail links. It was laid out during the 17th century in a grid pattern, with the imposing **Christiansholm Festning** guarding the eastern harbor approach. (Exhibitions are sometimes held inside the fort during the summer.) Just to the northeast of Kristiansand is the open-air **Vest-Agder Fylkesmuseum** (County Museum), with 30 old buildings and farms rebuilt in the local style of the 18th and 19th centuries. There are also displays of folklore and costumes. *Admission: NOK 20 adults, NOK 10 children. Open Mon.–Sat. 10–6, Sun. noon–6.*

A must for children is a visit to the nearby **Kardemomme By** (Cardamom Town) and the zoo and leisure park. *Tel. 38049700. Admission: NOK 150 adults, NOK 130 children. Open summer, daily 9–6; off-season, daily 10–3.*

Continue along E18 for another 30 kilometers (19 miles) to **Mandal,** Norway's most southerly town, famous for its beach, salmon, and 18th- and 19th-century houses. For the next 30 kilometers (19 miles), the road climbs and weaves its way through steep, wooded valleys and then descends to the fishing port of **Flekkefjord,** with its charming **Hollenderbyen,** or Dutch Quarter.

E18 heads inland here to Stavanger, but it is more rewarding to follow the coast road (Route 44) past the fishing port of **Egersund,** 40 kilometers (25 miles) ahead, and a little farther to **Ogna,** with its sandy beach. For the last hour or so before Stavanger, you will be in the region known as the **Jæren.** Flat and stony, it is the largest expanse of level terrain in this mountainous country. The mild climate and the absence of good harbors mean that the population here turned to agriculture, and the miles of stone walls are a testament to their labor.

Stavanger, at the end of the tour, is a former trading town that has become a champion (some environmentalists say victim) of the oil boom. It is now the fourth largest city in Norway. Drilling platforms and oil tankers take the place of fishing boats in the harbor. In sharp contrast to the new high-rise complexes, there is an old quarter with narrow cobbled lanes and clapboard houses at odd angles. The town is believed to date from the 8th century; its Anglo-Norman **Stavanger Domkirke** (cathedral), next to the central market, was established in 1125 by the bishop of Winchester in England. (Trading and ecclesiastical links between Norway and England were strong throughout the Middle Ages.)

Ledaal is a fine patrician mansion where the king resides when he's visiting Stavanger. It houses relics from the area and a special maritime display. Across the street is **Breidablikk** manor house, built by a Norwegian shipping magnate. An outstanding example of what Norwegians call "Swiss style" architecture, it has been perfectly preserved since the 1960s. Nearby **Ullandhaug** is a reconstructed Iron Age farm. The **Norsk Hermetikkmuseum** (Canning Museum) is a reconstructed sardine factory in use between 1890 and 1920; here you'll get a lesson in the production of sardines and fish conserves.

The **Norwegian Emigration Center** specializes in genealogy and family research, helping to bridge the gap between Norway and the families of Norwegians who emigrated to America. *Bergjelandsgt. 30, tel. 51501267. Open weekdays 9–3.*

The **Ryfylke fjords** north and east of Stavanger form the southern end of the fjord country. The city is a good base for exploring this region, with the "white fleet" of low-slung seabuses making daily excursions into even the most distant fjords of Ryfylke. The Lysefjord excursion is superb.

Dining and Lodging

For details and price-category definitions, *see* Dining and Lodging in Staying in Norway, *above*. Best bets are indicated by a star ★.

Arendal **Madam Reiersen.** This authentic restaurant on the waterfront
Dining serves good food in an informal atmosphere. *Nedre Tyholmsvn. 3, tel. 37021900. No reservations. AE, DC, MC, V. Moderate.*

Lodging **Inter Nor Tyholmen.** This new maritime hotel is located at Tyholmen, with the sea at close quarters and a splendid view of the fjord. It also boasts an open-air restaurant, Bryggekanten. *Teaterpl. 2, tel. 37026800, fax 37026801. 60 rooms with bath. Facilities: restaurant, bar. AE, DC, MC, V. Moderate.*

Drammen **Spiraltoppen Café.** Located at the top of Bragernes Hill, this café of-
Dining fers excellent views as well as good food. *Bragernesåsen, tel. 32837815. No reservations. AE, DC, MC, V. Moderate.*

Lodging **Rica Park.** This comfortable and centrally located hotel has well-equipped rooms and two good restaurants, a bar, and a nightclub. *Gamle Kirkepl. 3, tel. 32838280, fax 32895207. 103 rooms with bath or shower. Facilities: 2 restaurants, bar, nightclub. AE, DC, MC, V. Moderate.*

Kristiansand **Sjøhuset.** Seafood and fish are best bets in this rustic waterfront res-
Dining taurant. *Østre Strandgt. 12a, tel. 38026260. No reservations. AE, DC, MC, V. Moderate–Expensive.*

Lodging **Rica Fregatten.** You're right in the center of town in this medium-size hotel, a stone's throw from the Town Hall and Cathedral. The comfortable and well-appointed rooms were renovated in 1992, and there is a good restaurant, the Captain's Table. *Dronningens gt. 66, tel. 38021500, fax 38021019. 47 rooms with bath. Facilities: restaurant, bar. AE, DC, MC, V. Moderate.*

Larvik **Grand.** The rooms are spotless and service is attentive in this large
Dining and hotel overlooking the fjord. There is a choice of restaurants in which
Lodging to sample the local fish soup and smoked meat platters, particularly good at lunchtime. *Storgt. 38–40, tel. 33187800, fax 33187045. 97 rooms with bath. Facilities: restaurants. AE, DC, MC, V. Moderate.*

Sandefjord **Edgar Ludl's Gourmet.** Enjoy fish specialties prepared by Master
Dining Chef Ludl in the best restaurant outside Oslo. The seven-course
★ menu is an excellent choice. *Rådhusgt. 7, tel. 33462741, fax 33462741. Reservations advised. AE, DC, MC, V. Closed Sun. Moderate–Expensive.*

Lodging **Park.** Overlooking Sandefjord's attractive harbor, the imposing
★ Park is one of the best hotels in Norway. The rooms are large and comfortable, with excellent views over the water. The service is flawless. *Strandpromenaden 9, tel. 33465550, fax 33467900. 174 rooms with bath or shower. Facilities: restaurants, bar, pool, saunas. AE, DC, MC, V. Expensive.*

Stavanger **Sjøhuset Skagen.** This restored 17th-century wharf house specia-
Dining lizes in seafood plus lots of atmosphere. *Skagen 15, tel. 51895180,*
fax 51521472. Reservations advised. AE, DC, MC, V. Moderate.
Straen. This famous fish restaurant, located in the oldest part of
town, offers a wide selection of delicious fresh seafood. There is a
night club, a rock café, and a pub on the premises. *Nedre Strandgt.*
15, tel. 51526230, fax 51567798. AE, DC, MC, V. Closed Sun. Mod-
erate.

Lodging **Skagen Brygge.** This hotel incorporates three rehabilitated old sea
houses. Almost all rooms are different, from modern to old-fashioned maritime with exposed beams and brick-and-wood walls;
many have harbor views. The hotel has an arrangement with 15 restaurants in the area—it makes the reservations and the tab ends up
on your bill. *Skagenkaien 30, tel. 51894100, fax 51895883. 110 rooms*
with bath, 2 suites. Facilities: bar, pool, fitness center, conference
center. AE, DC, MC, V. Moderate–Expensive.
Grand Hotel. This hotel on the edge of the town center doesn't aim to
be fancy: Rooms are comfortable and bright, done in pastels and
white. In summer the rates drop significantly. *Klubbgt. 3, tel.*
51895800, fax 51895710. 92 rooms with bath. Facilities: breakfast
room, bar. AE, DC, MC, V. Inexpensive–Moderate.

Through Telemark to Bergen

Bergen is Norway's second-largest city. To get there, you pass
through the Telemark area, midway between Oslo and Bergen. This
region is characterized by steep valleys, pine forests, lakes, and
fast-flowing rivers that are full of trout. Morgedal, the cradle of skiing, is here. You'll go on to Hardangervidda, a wild mountain area
and national park that was the stronghold of Norway's Resistance
fighters during World War II, and then down to the beautiful
Hardangerfjord. Few places on earth match western Norway for
spectacular scenic beauty—this is the fabled land of the fjords.

Fjord transportation is good, since crossing fjords is a necessary as
well as a scenic way to travel in Norway. Hardangerfjorden,
Sognefjord, and Nordfjord are three of the deepest and most popular fjords. Local tourist offices will be able to recommend excursions
and travel routes.

Guided Tours

Bergen is the gateway to the fjords, and excursions cover most of the
last half of the tour below as well as the fjords farther north. Contact
the tourist information offices (*see below*) for details of these constantly changing tours.

Tourist Information

Bergen (Bryggen 7, tel. 55321480).
Drammen (Rådhuset, tel. 32806210).
Kinsarvik (tel. 53663112).
Kongsberg (Storgt. 35, tel. 32735000).
Røldal (tel. 53647259).

Exploring Through Telemark to Bergen

Take E18 west from Oslo to nearby **Drammen** (*see* Exploring the
Coast Road to Stavanger, *above*). Follow Route 11 through

Through Telemark to Bergen

Drammen and continue west for about 40 kilometers (25 miles) to **Kongsberg,** by the fast-flowing Lågen River. Kongsberg was founded in 1624 as a silver-mining town. Although there is no more mining, the old mines at Saggrenda are open for guided tours. **Norsk Bergverksmuseum** includes the Silver Mines Collection, the Ski Museum, and the Royal Mint Museum. In the center of town is an 18th-century Rococo church, which reflects the town's former source of wealth—silver.

Kongsberg is one of the gateways to Telemark, which is just beyond Meheia on the county border. Forests give way to rocky peaks and desolate spaces farther into the plateau. **Heddal** is the first stop in Telemark. Norway's largest stave church is here. Stave churches, built with wooden planks staked vertically into the ground or base, date from the medieval period and are found almost exclusively in southern Norway. The Heddal church is typical of stave churches in that it has richly carved ornamentation on the doors and around the aisle.

Route 11 climbs from Heddal and skirts the large Telemark plateau. You'll see the **Lifjell** area's highest peak, Røydalsnuten, 1,291 meters (4,234 feet), on the left before descending toward **Seljord,** on the lake of the same name. The countryside by the lake is richer than that on the plateau; meadows and pastureland run down to the lakefront. The attractive village of Seljord has ornamented wooden houses and a medieval church.

Continue south from Seljord, making sure to stay right (on Route 11) at the Brunkeberg crossroads, while the other road continues south to Kristiansand. You are now entering the steep valley of **Morgedal.** It was here in the last century that Sondre Nordheim developed the slalom method of skiing—*slalom* means "make turns." You can get the full story on the development of skiing at the **Olav Bjåland's Museum,** named for the south polar explorer and ski hero. *Admission NOK 15. Open June 20–Aug. 15, daily 10–5.*

Turn left at Høydalsmo for a scenic diversion to mountainbound **Dalen.** At Dalen is **Tokke I,** one of Europe's largest hydroelectric power stations. From here it's an 8-kilometer (5-mile) drive to **Eidsborg,** where there is a stave church and a dramatic view of the Dalen Valley.

Take Route 38 from Dalen along the Tokke Valley to **Åmot.** The 93-meter (305-foot) Hyllandfoss Falls were destroyed by the hydroelectric project, but the drive is still spectacular.

Rejoin Route 11 at Åmot. At the next crossroads **(Haukeligrend),** Route 11 really begins to climb, and you'll see why the Norwegians are so proud of keeping this route open all year. Before you leave Telemark, you'll pass through the 6-kilometer (4-mile) Haukeli Tunnel and then begin a long descent to **Røldal,** another lakefront village with a hydroelectric plant.

Turn north on Route 13 a few miles after Røldal, and drive to the **Sørfjord** at Odda. Continue along the fjord to the attractive village of **Kinsarvik.** For the best view of the junction of the Sørfjord and the mighty Hardangerfjord, take the ferry across the Sørfjord to Utne. On the dramatic 30-minute ferry crossing from Utne to Kvanndal, you will know why this area was such a rich source of inspiration for Romantic composer Edvard Grieg.

At Kvanndal, turn left on Route 7. The road follows the fjord west, then veers right to **Norheimsund.** After climbing another coastal mountain spur, it winds through the wild **Tokagjel Gorge** and across the mountains of **Kvamskogen,** then descends tortuously into Bergen, capital of the fjords.

Bergen, founded in 1070, is now Norway's second-largest city, with a population of 217,000. Before oil brought an influx of foreigners to Stavanger, it was the most international of the country's cities, having been an important trading and military center when Oslo was an obscure village. Bergen was a member of the medieval Hanseatic League and offered an ice-free harbor and convenient trading location on the west coast. Natives of Bergen still think of Oslo as a dour provincial town.

Despite numerous fires in its past, much of medieval Bergen has remained. Seven surrounding mountains set off the weathered wooden houses, cobbled streets, and Hanseatic-era warehouses of the **Bryggen** (harbor area).

The best way to get a feel for Bergen's medieval trading heyday is to visit the **Hanseatisk Museum** on the Bryggen. One of the oldest and st-preserved of Bergen's wooden buildings, it is furnished in 16th-century style. The guided tour is excellent. *Admission: NOK 30 adults, NOK 15 children. Open June–Aug., daily 9–5; May, Sept., daily 11–2; Oct.–Apr., Mon., Wed., Fri., Sun. 11–2.*

On the western end of the Vågen is the **Rosenkrantz tårnet** (tower), part of the **Bergenhus,** the 13th-century fortress guarding the harbor entrance. The tower and fortress were destroyed during World War II, but were meticulously restored during the '60s and are now rich with furnishings and household items from the 16th century. *Admission: NOK 15 adults, NOK 5 children. Open mid-May–mid-Sept., daily 10–4; mid-Sept.–mid-May, Sun. noon–3, or upon request.*

From Øvregaten, the back boundary of Bryggen, you can walk through the meandering back streets to the popular **Fløybanen,** the funicular (a cable car that runs on tracks on the ground). The funicular climbs a steep 326 meters (1,050 feet) to the top of Fløyen, one of the seven mountains guarding the city.

Troldhaugen manor on Nordås Lake, once home to Edvard Grieg, is now a museum and includes a new chamber music hall. Recitals are held each Wednesday and Sunday at 7:30 PM from late June through early August. *Troldhaugsvn, Hop, Bergen, tel. 55911791. Admission: NOK 30 adults, NOK 15 children. Open May–Sept., daily 9:30–5:30.*

Dining and Lodging

For details and price-category definitions, *see* Dining and Lodging in Staying in Norway, *above*. Best bets are indicated by a star ★.

Bergen
Dining
★ **Bellevue.** It's hard to imagine a more imposing or dramatic setting for a restaurant than the Bellevue's, high up on a hillside looking down on Bergen. The restaurant itself is a 17th-century manor house. Fine crystal and silverware accompany the excellent food. *Bellevuebakken 9, tel. 55310240. Reservations required. AE, DC, V. Very Expensive.*

★ **Lucullus.** This French-inspired seafood restaurant is, appropriately enough, in the Hotel Neptun. It has an excellent wine cellar, with special emphasis on white wines to go with the fish. *Walckendorffsgt. 8, tel. 55901000, fax 55233202. Reservations recommended. AE, DC, MC, V. Closed weekends. Very Expensive.*

Munkestuen Café. The locals regard this tiny mom-and-pop place as a hometown legend. Try the monkfish with hollandaise sauce or the fillet of roe deer with morels. *Klostergt. 12, tel. 55902149. Reservations required. AE, DC, MC, V. Closed Sat. and 3 weeks in July. No lunch. Moderate.*

Lodging **SAS Royal.** Located right at the harbor, the SAS Royal was opened in 1982 on the site of old warehouses. Ravaged by nine fires since 1170, the warehouses have been rebuilt each time in the same style, which SAS has incorporated into this well-equipped hotel. *Bryggen, tel. 55543000, fax 55324808. 267 rooms with bath. Facilities: 2 restaurants, pub, bar, discothèque, pool, sauna, conference center. AE, DC, MC, V. Moderate–Very Expensive.*

Augustin. This small but excellent hotel in the center of town has been recently restored to its original late–Art Nouveau character, complete with period furniture in the lobby. *C. Sundtsgt. 24, tel. 55230025, fax 55233130. 38 rooms with bath. AE, DC, MC, V. Inexpensive–Moderate.*

Bryggen Orion. Facing the harbor in the center of town, the hotel is surrounded by Bergen's most famous sights. *Bradbenken 3, tel. 55318080, fax 55329414. 229 rooms with bath. Facilities: restaurant, bar, nightclub. AE, DC, MC, V. Inexpensive–Moderate.*

Kinsarvik
Lodging
Kinsarvik Fjord Hotel. This handsome hotel near the busy ferry port offers good views of Hardangerfjord and the glacier. The rooms are bright and spacious. *Kinsarvik, tel. 53663100, fax 53663374. 62 rooms with bath or shower. AE, MC, V. Moderate.*

Kongsberg
Dining
Gamle Kongsberg Kro. Located by the waterfall at Nybrofossen, with a mini-golf course nearby, this newly restored café offers hearty Norwegian dishes at moderate prices. *Thornesvn. 4, tel. 32731633. No reservations. AE, DC, MC, V. Moderate.*

Utne
Dining and Lodging
Utne Hotel. The white frame house dates from 1722, and the hotel, the oldest in Norway, has been run by the same family since 1787. The Utne has all the cared-for atmosphere of an old home. The dining room is wood paneled and hand painted, decorated with copper pans, old china, and paintings. The rooms, many of which have good views of the ferry port and Hardangerfjord, are filled with period furniture. The Utne makes a good base for hiking or cycling. *Utne, tel. 53666983, fax 53666950. 24 rooms with bath or shower. AE, DC, MC, V. Moderate.*

Above Bergen: The Far North

The fjords continue northward from Bergen all the way to Kirkenes, at Norway's border with the Republic of Russia. Norway's north is for anyone eager to hike, climb, fish, bird-watch (seabirds), see Samiland—the land of the Sami ("Lapp")—or experience the unending days of the midnight sun in June and July. The Lofoten Islands present the grand face of the "Lofoten Wall"—a rocky, 96-kilometer-long (60-mile-long) massif surrounded by the sea and broken into six pieces. Svolvær, the most populated island, has a thriving summer artists' colony. It's also known for Lofotfisket, the winter cod fishing.

The major towns north of Bergen are Ålesund, Trondheim, Bodø, Narvik, Tromsø, Hammerfest, and Kirkenes. Cheaper accommodations are the rule in the north, whether you stay in a cabin, campsite, guest house, or *rorbu*—fishermen's huts in the islands that are available for rent outside the January to April fishing season. These days, many *rorbuer* are built to be motels.

Getting Around

By Ship One of the best ways to travel in northern Norway is the **Hurtigrute**, or coastal steamer, which begins in Bergen and turns around 2,000 nautical kilometers (1,250 miles) later at Kirkenes. Many steamers run this route, so you can stay at any of the ports for any length of time and pick up the next one coming through: Major tourist offices have schedules, and reservations are essential (*see* Important Addresses and Numbers in Oslo, *above*, and Getting Around by Ferry, *above*).

By Car E6 and its feeder roads are the only route available north of Trondheim, where the country narrows dramatically.

By Train Major train routes are Oslo–Bergen and Oslo–Trondheim–Bodø (the Trondheim–Bodø leg takes one day). From Bodø there are tours to the Lofoten and Vesterålen Islands and to the Væren Islands, two tiny, remote islands at the tail of the Lofoten chain. You can get to Svolvær, the Lofotens' main port, via ferry from Skutvik.

To get all the way to Nordkapp (the North Cape, the northernmost mainland point in Norway and Europe) and the Land of the Midnight Sun, you must continue your trip by bus from Fauske.

Tourist Information

Local tourist offices offer tour information, area maps, and tours.

Ålesund (Rådhuset [City Hall], tel. 70121202).
Bodø (Sjøgt. 21, tel. 75526000).
Hammerfest (tel. 78412185).
Harstad (Rikard Kaarbøsgt. 20, tel. 77063235).
Kirkenes (off the E6 in a wooden hut behind Rica Hotel [on Pasvikveien], tel. 78992544).
Narvik (Kongensgt. 66, tel. 76943309).
Svolvær (Torget 6, tel. 76073000).
Tromsø (Storgt. 61, tel. 77610000).
Trondheim (Munkegata 19, tel. 73929394).

Exploring the Far North

See the Norway country map for the location of towns on this tour.

The steamer is probably the best route from Ålesund to Trondheim because no main road connects them directly. **Ålesund,** a much-overlooked coastal city flanked by fjords, is perhaps the only example you'll find of true architectural eccentricity in Norway. After a fire here during the early 1900s, anyone who had any aspirations to architecture designed his or her own new home, and the result is a rich, playful mixture of styles ranging from austere to Art Nouveau. There are excellent tours of the Romsdal, Geiranger, and Hjørund fjords. Pick up the free "Ålesund Guide" and "On Foot in Ålesund" from the tourist office (*see* Tourist Information, *above*).

Trondheim sits at the southern end of Norway's widest fjord, Trondheimfjord. This waterbound city is the third largest in the country and is the traditional coronation place of Norwegian royalty. Construction of what is Scandinavia's largest medieval building, **Nidaros Domkirke** (Cathedral), started here in 1320 but was not completed until the early 1920s. For centuries it served as a goal for religious pilgrims. There is a historic fish market that is worth seeing. Scandinavia's two largest wooden buildings are in Trondheim. One is the rococo **Stiftsgården,** a royal palace built in 1774, and the other is a student dormitory.

After Trondheim, the country thins into a vertebral cord of land hugging the border with Sweden and hunching over the top of Finland. **Bodø,** the northern terminus of the Nordland railway, is the first major town above the Polar Circle. It is bathed in midnight sun from early June to mid-July. For those who want boat excursions to **coastal bird colonies** (the Væren Islands), Bodø is the best base. The city was bombed by the Germans in 1940. The stunning, contemporary **Bodø Cathedral,** its spire separated from the main building, was built after the war. Inside are rich, modern tapestries; outside is a war memorial. The **Nordland County Museum** depicts the life of the Sami, as well as regional history. *Prinsengt. 116, tel. 75526128. Admission: NOK 15 adults, children free. Open weekdays 9–3, weekends noon–3.*

If you want to see a real **maelstrom**—a furious natural whirlpool—inquire at the tourist office (*see* Tourist Information, *above*) about **Saltstraumen.**

Time Out Alongside the maelstrom is **Saltstraumen Hotel.** Try the poached halibut—delicious!

Bodø is considered a gateway to the Lofoten and Vesterålen islands; the tourist office will make the necessary arrangements.

The **Lofoten** islands are a 190-kilometer (118-mile) chain of mountaintops rising from the bottom of the sea like open jaws. During the summer, the farms, fjords, and fishing villages make it a major tourist attraction. Between January and March, thousands of fishermen from all over the country head for Lofoten to the annual Lofotfisket, the world's largest cod fishery.

Narvik is a rebuilt city, an "ice-free" seaport, and a major shipping center for iron ore. An excellent railway connects it to the mines across the Swedish border. The **Krigsminnemuseet** (War Memorial Museum) has gripping displays on wartime intrigues and suffering. *Kongensgt., near the main square. Admission: NOK 20. Open June*

15–Sept. 15, Mon.–Sat. 10–10, Sun. 11–5; Sept. 16–June 14, Mon.–Sat. 10–2.

Northeast of Lofoten on Hinnøya, Norway's largest island, is **Harstad,** where the population of 22,000 swells to 42,000 during the annual June cultural festival and its July deep-sea fishing festival.

Farther north on the mainland is **Tromsø,** self-dubbed "Paris of the North" for the nightlife inspired by the midnight sun. Looming over this remote arctic university town are 1,860-meter (6,100-foot) peaks with permanent snowcaps. Tromsø trails off into the islands: Half the town lives offshore. Its population is about 50,000. Be sure to see the spectacular **Ishavskatedralen** (cathedral), with its eastern wall made entirely of stained glass, across the long stretch of **Tromsø bridge.** Coated in aluminum, the bridge's triangular peaks make a bizarre mirror for the midnight sun.

Be sure to walk around old Tromsø (along the waterfront) and to visit the **Tromsø Museum,** which concentrates on science, the Sami, and northern churches. *Lars Thøringsvei 10, Folkeparken; take Bus 27 or 22. Admission: NOK 10 adults, NOK 5 children. Open June–Aug., daily 9–6; Sept.–May, weekdays 8:30–3:30, Sat. noon–3, Sun. 11–4.*

Hammerfest is the world's northernmost town. It is surrounded by Sami settlements and is home to the **Royal and Ancient Polar Bear Society.** Don't visit the society if you don't like real stuffed bears. *Town Hall basement. Admission free. Open in summer, weekdays 8–6, weekends 10–3.*

Hammerfest is an elegant, festive-looking port town despite having been razed twice in its history. During the late 19th century the town was leveled by fire. Years later, defeated German troops destroyed the town as they retreated to avoid leaving anything to the Russians.

Dining and Lodging

For details and price-category definitions, *see* Dining and Lodging in Staying in Norway, *above.*

Ålesund
Dining

Fjellstua. This mountaintop restaurant has tremendous views over the surrounding peaks, islands, and fjords. There are several different eating facilities here, but the main restaurant serves a variety of dishes and homemade desserts. *Fjellstua, tel. 70126582. Reservations not necessary. AE, DC, V. Closed Dec.–Easter. Moderate.*

Sjøbua. Located at Brunholmen on an old wharf, Sjøbua offers an excellent seafood selection. You can even pick your own dinner from a saltwater aquarium. *Brunholmgt. 1, tel. 70127100. Reservations recommended. AE, DC, MC, V. Moderate.*

Lodging

Bryggen. This dockside warehouse was converted into a hotel in 1990. There are splendid views over the water. *Apotekergt. 1–3, tel. 70126400, fax 70121180. 82 rooms with bath or shower. Facilities: sauna, solarium. AE, DC, MC, V. Moderate.*

Hotel Scandinavie. The impressive building with towers and arches dates from 1905, but the rooms are newly refurbished. *Løevenvoldgt. 8, tel. 70123131, fax 70129488. 70 rooms with bath. Facilities: 2 restaurants, bar, fitness room. AE, DC, MC, V. Moderate.*

Rica Parken. Renovated in 1990, this is the largest and best-equipped hotel in Ålesund. *Storgt. 16, tel. 70125050, fax 70122164.*

132 rooms with bath. Facilities: restaurants, bar, disco, sauna, gym. AE, DC, MC, V. Moderate.

Bodø **Marlene Restaurant.** Set within the SAS Royal hotel, the Marlene
Dining offers a superb seafood buffet throughout the summer. Be sure to try one of the salmon dishes. *Storgt. 2, tel. 75524100. Reservations advised. AE, DC, MC, V. Moderate–Expensive.*

Turisthytta. This mountaintop lodge (accessible by taxi) is a fine place to eat if you want to bask in the midnight sun. There is a good range of dishes, from snacks and open-faced sandwiches to fresh fish. *Turisthytta, tel. 75583300. Reservations advised. No credit cards. Closed in winter. Moderate.*

Lodging **SAS Royal.** This grandiose hotel is throbbing with life, with enough amenities to keep you entertained virtually around the clock. *Storgt. 2, tel. 75524100, fax 75527493. 190 rooms with bath. Facilities: restaurant, wine bar, nightclub, health club, sauna. AE, DC, MC, V. Expensive.*

Norrøna. This bed-and-breakfast–style establishment is comfortable, with a location just as grand as that of the SAS Royal next door. *Storgt. 4B, tel. 75525550, fax 75523388. 150 rooms with bath or shower. AE, DC, V. Moderate.*

Hammerfest **Hammerfest Hotel.** On the pleasant Rådhusplassen, this guest
Dining and house has handsome, harborview rooms for tolerable prices in a
Lodging town where hotels are expensive. *Strandgt. 2–4, tel. 78411622, fax 78412127. 54 rooms with bath or shower. Facilities: restaurant, cafeteria. AE, DC, MC, V. Expensive.*

Narvik **Inter-Nor Grand Royal Hotel.** This is a classy, handsome hotel, en-
Dining and hanced by a staff that is eager to please. The location, right by the
Lodging train station, is a plus, and there are many chances to try the skiing and fishing nearby. The Grand Royal was renovated in 1987 and the rooms are well equipped. *Kongensgt. 64, tel. 76941500, fax 76945531. 112 rooms with bath. Facilities: 2 restaurants, gym, sauna, nightclub. AE, DC, MC, V. Expensive.*

Svolvær **Nyvågar Rorbu.** Built in 1990, this hotel and recreation complex is a
Dining and 15-minute drive from the Svolvær Airport. Activities include fish-
Lodging ing trips, eagle safaris, and deep-sea rafting. *Kabelvåg, tel. 76078900, fax 76078950. 60 rooms with showers. Facilities: 2 restaurants, conference rooms. AE, DC, MC, V. Moderate–Expensive.*

Tromsø **SAS Royal.** Each room in this beautifully set hotel gives splendid
Dining and views over Tromsø's shoreline, although the location is in the heart
Lodging of town. *Sjøgt. 7, tel. 77600000, fax 77685474. 193 rooms with bath. Facilities: restaurant, bar, nightclub. AE, DC, MC, V. Expensive–Very Expensive.*

Saga. Situated on a pretty town square, the Saga combines its central location with the staff's expertise. Its restaurant has affordable, hearty meals, and the rooms—although somewhat basic—are quiet and comfortable. *Richard Withs Pl. 2, tel. 77681180, fax 77682380. 52 rooms with bath. Facilities: restaurant, cafeteria. AE, DC, MC, V. Moderate.*

Trondheim **Bryggen.** This popular restaurant, set near the Gamle Bybro (Old
Dining Town Bridge), serves a feast of Norwegian gourmet specialties with
★ a Gallic flourish. With a choice of creperie, wine and cheese room, and bistro serving French cuisine, you can't go wrong. *Ø Bakklandet 66, tel. 73520230. Reservations advised. AE, DC, MC, V. Expensive.*

Hos Magnus. The price:value ratio is excellent at this old-fashioned, cozy restaurant in the new part of Bryggen. The menu includes such modern dishes as cognac-marinated moose fillet with mustard dressing and grilled, marinated spiral pork chops. *Kjøpmannsgt. 63, tel. 73524110. Reservations advised. AE, DC, MC, V. Moderate.*

★ **Tavern på Sverresborg.** Outside the city, at the open-air Folk Museum, this restaurant serves Norwegian specialties. *Sverresborg, tel. 73520932. No reservations. No credit cards. Moderate.*

Lodging **Royal Garden.** Trondheim's finest hotel has excellent facilities for sports and fitness, as well as many features to help guests with disabilities. *Kjøpmannsgt. 73, tel. 73521100, fax 73531766. 297 rooms with bath. Facilities: 3 restaurants, bar, sauna, indoor pool, gymnasium. AE, DC, MC, V. Expensive.*

Ambassadeur. Take in the panoramic view from the roof terrace of this first-rate modern hotel, about 93 meters (101 yards) from the market square. The deep blue waters of the Trondheimsfjord reflect the dramatic and irregular coastline. Most rooms in the Ambassadeur have fireplaces, and some have balconies. *Elvegt. 18, tel. 73527050, fax 73527052. 34 rooms with bath. Facilities: restaurant, bar. AE, DC, MC, V. Moderate.*

★ **Bakeriet.** Built as a bakery in 1863, Trondheim's newest hotel opened in March 1991. Few rooms look alike, but all are large and stylish in their simplicity, with natural wood furniture and beige-and-red textiles. Although there's no restaurant, a hot evening meal is included in the room rate. *Brattørgt. 2, tel. 73525200, fax 73502330. 93 rooms with bath or shower. Facilities: sauna. AE, DC, MC, V. Inexpensive–Moderate.*

22 Poland

Poland is a land rich in natural beauty and contrasts. Its landscape varies from rolling plains with slow-moving rivers, broad fields, and scattered villages to lakes, forests, and marshes in the north and jagged mountains in the south. This makes possible a wide variety of outdoor activities, from hunting to hiking, sailing, and skiing.

Every one of the major cities, with the exception of Kraków and Łódź, had to be rebuilt after the destruction of World War II. Particularly fine restoration work has been done on Warsaw's Old Town and in Gdańsk on the Baltic coast.

Poland's geographic position between Germany and Russia has determined its history of almost continual war and struggle for independence since the late 18th century. After "liberation" by the Red Army in 1945, a Communist government was imposed. Although the country recovered economically and experienced rapid industrialization, more than 40 years of Communist rule left Poland in prolonged economic crisis. The hopes and aspirations of the postwar generations remained unfulfilled.

Social discontent erupted in 1980 with strikes and the formation of Solidarity, the first free trade union in the Communist bloc. After a year, martial law was imposed and Solidarity was banned. Though martial law was lifted in 1983, and Poland now has a democratically elected government, life for the average Pole remains hard, and no one has simple answers to the country's complicated political and economic problems. In spite of all this, the Polish people continue to be resilient, resourceful, and hopeful.

Poles openly welcome visitors; their uninhibited sense of hospitality makes them eager to please their guests. It is easy to make friends here and to exchange views with strangers on trains and buses. Poles have a passionate interest in all things Western, from current affairs to the arts, clothes, and music.

Essential Information

Before You Go

When to Go The official tourist season runs from May through September. The best times for sightseeing are late spring and early fall. Major cultural events usually take place in the cities during the fall. The early spring is often wet and windy.

Below are the average daily maximum and minimum temperatures for Warsaw.

Jan.	32F	0C	May	67F	20C	Sept.	66F	19C
	22	6		48	9		49	10
Feb.	32F	0C	June	73F	23C	Oct.	55F	13C
	21	- 6		54	12		41	5
Mar.	42F	6C	July	75F	24C	Nov.	42F	6C
	28	- 2		58	16		33	1
Apr.	53F	12C	Aug.	73F	23C	Dec.	35F	2C
	37	3		56	14		28	- 3

Currency The monetary unit in Poland is the złoty (zł). There are notes of 50, 100, 200, 500, 1,000, 2,000, 5,000, 10,000 20,000, 50,000, 100,000, 200,000, 500,000, 1,000,000, and 2,000,000 złotys; coins have gone out of circulation. At press time (spring 1994), the bank exchange rate was about zł 22,000 to the U.S. dollar and zł 32,500 to the pound

Poland

Bornholm (Denmark)

Baltic Sea

LITHUANIA

RUSSIA

GERMANY

CZECH REPUBLIC

SLOVAKIA

UKRAINE

HUNGARY

0 — 100 miles

0 — 150 km

N

sterling. Since spring 1989, the złoty has been legally exchangeable at a free market rate in banks (*Bank Narodowy* and *Pekao* are the largest) and private exchange bureaus (*Kantor wymiany walut*), which sometimes offer slightly better rates than do the banks. If you run out of złotys, you will find that Polish taxi drivers, waiters, and porters will usually accept dollars or any other Western currency.

Credit Cards American Express, Diners Club, MasterCard, and Visa are accepted in all major hotels, in the better restaurants and nightclubs, and for other tourist services. In small cafés and shops, credit cards may not be accepted.

What It Will Cost At press time (spring 1994), it was still illegal to import or export złotys. This may change if the new Polish government goes through with plans to make the złoty fully convertible on the international market. Still, don't buy more złotys than you need, or you will have to go to the trouble of changing them back at the end of your trip.

Poland is now one of the more expensive countries of Eastern Europe, and inflation is still high by Western standards, despite the reforms of 1990. Prices are highest in the big cities, especially in Warsaw. The more you stray off the tourist track, the cheaper your vacation will be.

Sample Prices A cup of coffee, zł 10,000–35,000; a bottle of beer, zł 10,000–30,000; a soft drink, zł 5,000–25,000; a ham sandwich, zł 15,000–40,000; 1-mile taxi ride, zł 20,000.

Museums Admission fees to museums and other attractions are also rising in line with inflation, and seem ever-changing. At press time (spring 1994), fees ranged from zł 10,000 to zł 80,000.

Visas U.S. and British citizens are no longer required to obtain visas for entry to Poland; Canadian citizens and citizens of other countries that have not yet abolished visas for Poles, must pay the equivalent of $35 (more for multiple-entry visas). Apply at any Orbis office (the official Polish tourist agency), an affiliated travel agent, or from the Polish Consulate General in any country. Each visitor must complete three visa application forms and provide two photographs. Allow about two weeks for processing. Visas are issued for 90 days but can be extended in Poland, if necessary, either through the local county police headquarters or through Orbis.

You can contact the **Polish Consulate General** at the following addresses: **In the United States:** 233 Madison Ave., New York, NY 10016 (tel. 212/391–0844); 1530 North Lake Shore Dr., Chicago, IL 60610 (tel. 312/337–8166); 2224 Wyoming Ave., Washington DC 20008 (tel. 202/234–2501). **In Canada:** 1500 Pine Ave., Montreal, Quebec H3G (tel. 514/937–9481); 2603 Lakeshore Blvd. W., Toronto, Ont. M8V 1G5 (tel. 416/252–5471). **In the United Kingdom:** 73 New Cavendish St., London W1 (tel. 071/636–4533).

Customs on Arrival Persons over 17 may bring in duty-free: personal belongings, including musical instruments, typewriter, radio, 2 cameras with 24 rolls of film; up to 250 cigarettes or 50 cigars and ½ liter each of wine and spirits; and goods to the value of $200. Any amount of foreign currency may be brought in but must be declared on arrival.

Language Polish is a Slavic language that uses the Roman alphabet but has several additional characters and diacritics. Because it has a much higher incidence of consonant clusters than English, most English speakers find it's a difficult language to decipher, much less pronounce. Most older Poles know German; the younger generation usually knows some English. In the big cities you will find people who speak English, especially in hotels, but you may have difficulty in the provinces and countryside.

Getting Around

By Car
Road Conditions Despite the extensive road network, driving conditions, even on main roads, have deteriorated in the past few years. Minor roads tend to be narrow and cluttered with horse-drawn carts and farm animals. Drivers in a hurry should stick to roads marked E or T.

Rules of the Road Driving is on the right, as in the United States. The speed limit on highways is 110 kph (68 mph) and on roads in built-up areas, 60 kph (37 mph). A built-up area is marked by a white rectangular sign with the name of the town on it.

Gasoline   The price of gas is between $5.50 and $6.50 for 10 liters of high octane. Filling stations are located every 30 kilometers (20 miles) or so and are usually open 6 AM–10 PM; there are some 24-hour stations.

Breakdowns   Poland's **Motoring Association** (PZMot) offers breakdown, repair, and towing services to members of various international insurance organizations. For names of affiliated organizations, check with Orbis before you leave home. Carry a spare-parts kit. For emergency road help, call 981.

Car Rentals   You can rent cars from Avis or Hertz at international airports or through Orbis offices. Rates vary according to season, car model, and mileage. Fly/drive vacations are also available through Orbis.

By Train   Poland's PKP railway network is extensive and inexpensive. Most trains have first- and second-class accommodations, but Western visitors usually prefer to travel first-class. You should arrive at the station well before departure time. The fastest trains are intercity and express trains, which require reservations. Some Orbis offices furnish information, reservations, and tickets. Overnight trains have first- and second-class sleeping cars and second-class couchettes. Most long-distance trains carry buffets, but the quality of the food is unpredictable and you may want to bring your own.

Fares   Polish trains run at three speeds—*ekspresowy* (express), *pośpieszny* (fast), and *osobowy* (slow)—and fares vary according to the speed of the train. You pay more for intercity and express; return tickets cost exactly twice the single fare.

By Plane   **LOT,** Poland's national airline, operates daily flights linking five main cities: **Warsaw, Kraków, Gdańsk, Wrocław,** and **Rzeszów.** Fares begin at about $60 round-trip and can be paid for in złotys. Tickets and information are available from LOT or Orbis offices. All flights booked through Orbis in the United Kingdom carry a discount, but it is cheaper to pay in local currency in Poland. Be sure to book well in advance, especially for the summer season.

By Bus   **PKS,** the national bus company, offers long-distance service to most cities. Express buses, on which you can reserve seats, are somewhat more expensive than trains but often—except in the case of a few major intercity routes—get to their destination more quickly. For really out-of-the-way destinations, the bus is often the only means of transportation. PKS bus stations are usually located near railway stations. Tickets and information are best obtained from Orbis. Warsaw's central bus terminal is at aleje Jerozolimskie 144.

Staying in Poland

Telephones   Public phone booths take tokens *(żetony)*: zł 1,000 for local calls and
Local Calls   zł 5,000, 10,000, or 20,000 for long-distance calls, which must be made from special booths, usually situated in post offices. Place a token in the groove on the side or top of the phone, lift the receiver, and dial the number. Many phones automatically absorb the token; in others you must push it into the machine when the call is answered. Card phones are gradually being introduced and can be used for both local and long-distance calls. Cards (zł 50,000 or 100,000) are available at post offices and some newspaper kiosks.

International   Post offices and first-class hotels have assigned booths, at which you
Calls   pay after the completion of your call. To place an international call, dial 901; for domestic long-distance calls, dial 900. There's a heavy surcharge on calls made from hotel rooms.

Information   For general information (including international codes), tel. 913.

Mail
Postal Rates Airmail letters to the United States cost zł 8,000; postcards, zł 5,000. Letters to the United Kingdom or Europe cost zł 6,000; postcards, zł 4,500. Post offices are open 8 AM–8 PM (except weekends). At least one post office is open 24 hours in every major city. In Warsaw the post office is located at ulica Świętokrzyska 31.

Opening and
Closing Times **Banks** are open weekdays 8 or 9 AM–3 PM or 6 PM.

Museum opening hours vary greatly, but they are generally open Tuesday–Sunday 9–5.

Shops. Food shops are open weekdays 7 AM–7 PM, Saturday 7 AM–1 PM; many are now open on Sunday, and there are a few all-night stores in most districts. Other stores are open weekdays 11 AM–7 PM and Saturday 9 AM–1 PM.

National
Holidays January 1; April 16 (Easter); May 1 (Labor Day); May 3 (Constitution Day); June 18 (Corpus Christi); August 15 (Assumption); November 1 (Remembrance); November 11 (rebirth of Polish state, 1918); December 25, 26.

Dining Polish food and drink are basically Slavic with Baltic overtones. There is a heavy emphasis on soups and meat (especially pork) as well as freshwater fish. Much use is made of cream, and pastries are rich and often delectable.

The most popular soup is *barszcz* (known to many Americans as borscht), a clear beet soup often served with such Polish favorites as sausage, cabbage, potatoes, sour cream, coarse rye bread, and beer. Other dishes include *pierogi* (a kind of ravioli), which may be stuffed with savory or sweet fillings; *gołąbki*, cabbage leaves stuffed with minced meat; *bigos*, sauerkraut with meat and mushrooms; and *flaki*, a select dish of tripe, served boiled or fried. Polish beer is good; vodka is a specialty and is often downed before, with, and after meals.

Zajazdy (roadside inns), which are less expensive than regular restaurants, serve more traditional food. As elsewhere in Central Europe, cafés are a way of life in Poland and are often stocked with delicious pastries and ice creams.

Mealtimes At home, Poles eat late lunches (their main meal) and late suppers. Many restaurants, however, close around 9 PM. Most hotel restaurants serve the evening meal until 10:30.

Precautions Tap water is unsafe, so ask for mineral water. Beware of meat dishes served in cheap snack bars. Avoid the food on trains.

Dress In Warsaw and Kraków, formal dress is customary at Very Expensive and Expensive restaurants. Casual dress is appropriate elsewhere.

Ratings Prices are for one person and include three courses and service but no drinks. Best bets are indicated by a star ★.

Category	Warsaw	Other Areas
Very Expensive	over zł 600,000	over zł 400,000
Expensive	zł 400,000–600,000	zł 200,000–400,000
Moderate	zł 150,000–400,000	zł 100,000–200,000
Inexpensive	under zł 150,000	under zł 100,000

Lodging
Hotels The government rates hotel accommodations on the basis of one to five stars. Orbis hotels, owned by the state tourist office and currently undergoing privatization, have almost all been accorded four or five stars and guarantee a reasonable standard of cleanliness and service. They range in price from Moderate to Very Expensive and include a number of foreign-built luxury hotels, such as the Inter-Continental. In recent years Orbis hotels have faced competition from a growing number of privately owned lodgings, often part of international chains and mostly at the top end of the price range.

Municipal Hotels and Dom Turysty hotels are run by local authorities or the Polish Tourist Association. They are often rather old and limited in bath and shower facilities. Prices are Inexpensive.

Roadside Inns A number of roadside inns, often very attractive, offer inexpensive food and a few guest rooms at moderate rates.

Private Rooms can be arranged either in advance through Orbis or on the
Accommodations spot at the local tourist information office. Villas, lodges, rooms, or houses are available, and the prices are often negotiable. Rates vary from about $6 for a room to more than $150 for a villa.

Ratings The following chart is based on a rate for two people in a double room, with bath or shower and breakfast. These prices are in U.S. dollars. Best bets are indicated by a star ★.

Category	Cost
Very Expensive	over $200
Expensive	$100–$200
Moderate	$50–$100
Inexpensive	under $50

Tipping Waiters get a standard 10% of the bill. Hotel porters and doormen should get about zł 20,000. In Warsaw and other big towns frequented by foreign tourists, waiters also often expect a tip to help find you a table. If you choose to tip in foreign currency (readily accepted), remember that $1 is about an hour's wage.

Warsaw

Arriving and Departing

By Plane All international flights arrive at Warsaw's Okęcie Airport (Port Lotniczy) just southwest of the city. Terminal 1 serves international flights; Terminal 2 serves domestic flights. For flight information, contact the airlines, or call the airport at tel. 02/650–42–20.

Between the LOT operates a regular bus service into Warsaw. Orbis cars and
Airport and minivans also transport visitors to their hotels. Warsaw city trans-
Downtown port bus 175, which runs past almost all major downtown hotels, leaves Okęcie every 10 minutes during peak hours, and every 14 minutes at other times. The trip takes about 15 minutes and the fare is zł 6,000.

By Train Trains to and from Western Europe arrive at Dworzec Centralny on aleje Jerozolimskie in the center of town. For tickets and information, contact Orbis.

By Car There are seven main access routes to Warsaw, all leading to the center of the city. Drivers heading to or from the West will use the E8 or E12 highways.

Getting Around

By Tram and Bus These are often crowded, but they are the cheapest way of getting around. Trams and buses (including express buses) cost zł 6,000. The bus fare goes up to zł 12,000 between 11 PM and 5:30 AM. Tickets must be bought in advance from **Ruch** newsstands or certain shops. You must cancel your own ticket in a machine on the tram or bus when you get on; watch others do it.

By Taxi Taxis are a relatively cheap ride—about zł 20,000 per mile (1.6 kilometers)—and are readily available at stands downtown; the Marriott and Victoria hotels have their own monogrammed fleets. There is an efficient radio taxi service, tel. 919, which is much cheaper than taxis at stands.

By Buggy Horse-drawn carriages can be rented at a negotiated price from the Old Town Market Square.

Important Addresses and Numbers

Tourist Information The **Center for Tourist Information** is open 9 to 6 weekdays, and 11 to 6 weekends; it is located at plac Zamkowy 1, tel. 02/635–1881. **Orbis** offices in Warsaw include: ulica Bracka 16, tel. 022/26–02–71; and ulica Marszałkowska 142, tel. 022/27–80–31 or 022/27–36–73.

Embassies U.S. (al. Ujazdowskie 29–31, tel. 02/628–30–41). **Canadian** (ul. Matejki 1/5, tel. 022/29–80–51). **U.K.** (al. Róż 1, tel. 02/628–10–01). **U.K. Consulate** (ul. Wawelska 14, tel. 022/25–30–31).

Emergencies Police (tel. 997). **Ambulance** (tel. 998). **Doctor** (tel. 998 or call your embassy).

Travel Agencies American Express (ul. Bagińskiego 1, tel. 02/635–20–02). **Thomas Cook** (ul. Nowy Świat 64, tel. 022/26–47–29). **Polish Motoring Association (PZMot,** al. Jerozolimskie 63, tel. 022/29–45–50).

Guided Tours

Bus tours of the city depart in the morning and afternoon from the major hotels. **Orbis** also has half-day excursions into the surrounding countryside. These usually include a meal and some form of traditional entertainment. Check for details with your hotel, the Orbis office, or tourist information office.

Exploring Warsaw

At the end of World War II, Warsaw lay in ruins, a victim of systematic Nazi destruction. Only one-third of its prewar population survived the horrors of German occupation. The experience has left its mark on the city and is visible everywhere in the memorial plaques describing mass executions of civilians and in the bullet holes on the facades of buildings. Against all the odds, Warsaw's survivors have rebuilt their historic city. The old districts have been painstakingly reconstructed according to old prints and paintings, including those of Belotto and Canaletto from the 18th century. The result, a city of warm pastel colors, is remarkable.

Surrounding the old districts, however, is the modern Warsaw, built since the war in utilitarian Socialist-Realist and later styles. Whether you like it or not is your business, but it is worth noting as a testimony to one approach to urban life. The sights of Warsaw are all relatively close to each other, making most attractions accessible by foot.

Numbers in the margin correspond to points of interest on the Warsaw map.

The Old Town

❶ A walking tour of the old historic district takes about two hours. Begin in the heart of the city at **plac Zamkowy** (Castle Square), where you will see a slender column supporting the **statue of Zygmunt (Sigismund) III Wasa,** the king who made Warsaw his capital in the early 17th century. It is the city's oldest monument and, symbolically, the first to be rebuilt after the wartime devastation. Dominating the
❷ square is the **Zamek Królewski** (Royal Castle). Restoring the interior or was a herculean task, requiring workers to relearn traditional skills, match ancient woods and fabrics, and even reopen abandoned quarries to find just the right kind of stone. *Plac Zamkowy 4, tel. 02/635-39-95. Admission: zł 60,000 adults, zł 30,000 children. Tours start hourly from the side entrance. Open Tues.–Sat. 10–2:30, Sun. 9–2:30.*

Enter the narrow streets of the **Stare Miasto** (Old Town), with its colorful medieval houses, cobblestone alleys, uneven roofs, and wrought-iron grillwork. On your right as you proceed along ulica
❸ Świętojańska is the **Bazylika świętego Jana** (Cathedral Church of St. John), the oldest church in Warsaw, dating back to the 14th century. Several Polish kings were crowned here. Soon you will reach the
❹ **Rynek Starego Miasta** (Old Market Square), the charming and intimate center of the old town. The old town hall, which once stood in the middle, was pulled down in the 19th century. It was not replaced, and today the square is full of open-air cafés, tubs of flowering plants, and the inevitable artists displaying their talents for the tourists. At night the brightly lighted Rynek (marketplace) is the place to go for good food and atmosphere.

Continue along ulica Nowomiejska until you get to the pinnacled
❺ red-brick **Barbakan,** a fine example of a 16th-century defensive fortification. From here you can see the partially restored town wall that was built to enclose the Old Town, and enjoy a splendid view of the Vistula River, with the district of Praga on its east bank.

Follow the street called ulica Freta to Warsaw's **Nowe Miasto** (New Town), which was founded at the turn of the 15th century. Rebuilt after the war in 18th-century style, this district has a more elegant
❻ and spacious feeling about it. Of interest here is the **Muzeum Marii Skłodowskiej-Curie,** where the woman who discovered radium and polonium was born. *Ul. Freta 16, tel. 022/31-80-92. Admission: zł 10,000 adults, zł 5,000 children. Open Tues.–Sat. 10–4:30, Sun. 10–2:30.*

Time Out The **U Pana Michała** tearooms (ul. Freta 4–6) offer a variety of teas—as well as coffee—for nonsmokers.

The Royal Route

All towns with kings had their Royal Routes; the one in Warsaw stretched south from Castle Square down Krakowskie Przedmieście, curving through Nowy Świat and on along aleje
❼ Ujazdowskie to the **Pałac Belweder** (Belvedere Palace) and Łazienki Park. Some of Warsaw's finest churches and palaces are found along this route, as well as the names of famous Poles. A few blocks south of plac Zamkowy on Krakowskie Przedmieście, you'll come to the
❽ **University of Warsaw** on your left. Farther down, on your right, the

Warsaw

Vistula

KEY

AE American Express Office
i Tourist Information

Park Łazienkowski

Major Attractions

Barbakan, **5**
Bazylika świętego
Jana, **3**
Kościół świętego
Krzyża, **9**
Muzeum Marii
Skłodowskiej–Curie, **6**

Pałac Belweder, **7**
Pałac
Łazienkowski, **10**
Plac Zamkowy, **1**
Rynek Starego
Miasta, **4**
University of
Warsaw, **8**

Wilanów, **11**
Zamek Królewski, **2**

Museum of
Literature, **13**
National Museum, **15**
Palace of Culture and
Science, **14**
Tomb of the Unkown
Soldier, **17**

Monument to the
Heroes of the
Ghetto, **16**
Monument to the
Heroes of Warsaw, **12**

Other Attractions

Church of the Blessed
Sacrament Sisters, **18**
Frederick Chopin
Society, **19**
Grand Theater of
Opera and Ballet, **20**

Central Station

1/2 mile

3/4 km

9 **Kościoł świętego Krzyża** (Holy Cross Church) contains a pillar in which the heart of the great Polish composer Frédéric Chopin is entombed. As you pass the statue of Nicolaus Copernicus, Poland's most famous astronomer, you enter the busy Nowy Świat thoroughfare. Crossing aleje Jerozolimskie, on your left is the **former headquarters of the Polish Communist party,** a large solid gray building typical of the Socialist-Realist architectural style, which now houses banks and Poland's new stock exchange.

Aleje Ujazdowskie is considered by many locals to be Warsaw's finest street. It is lined with magnificent buildings and has something of a French flavor to it. Down at its southern end, before the name inexplicably changes to Belwederska, the French-style landscaped **Park Łazienkowski** (Łazienki Park), with pavilions and a royal palace,
10 stands in refreshing contrast to the bustling streets. The **Pałac Łazienkowski** (Łazienki Palace), a gem of Polish neoclassicism, was the private residence of Stanisław August Poniatowski, last king of Poland. It overlooks a lake stocked with huge carp. At the impressionistic Chopin monument nearby, you can stop for a well-deserved rest and, on summer Sundays, listen to an open-air concert. *Tel. 02/ 621–62–41. Admission: zł 20,000 adults, zł 12,000 children. Open Tues.–Sat. 9:30–3.*

The Royal Route extends along ulica Belwederska, ulica Jana
11 Sobieskiego, and aleja Wilanowska to **Wilanów,** 10 kilometers (6 miles) from the town center. This charming Baroque palace was the summer residence of King Jan III Sobieski, who, in 1683, stopped the Ottoman advance on Europe at the Battle of Vienna. The palace interior is open and houses antique furniture and a fine poster museum. *Ul. Wiertnicza l, tel. 022/42–07–95. Admission: zł 30,000 adults, zł 15,000 children. Open Wed.–Mon. 10–2:30.*

Off the Beaten Track

Some 3 million Polish Jews were put to death by the Nazis during World War II ending the enormous Jewish contribution to Polish culture, tradition, and achievement. A simple monument to the **Heroes of the Warsaw Ghetto,** a slab of dark granite with a bronze bas relief, stands on ulica Zamenhofa in the Muranów district, the historic heart of the old prewar Warsaw Jewish district and ghetto under the Nazi regime. The Warsaw Ghetto uprising that broke out in April 1943 was put down with unbelievable ferocity, and the Muranów district was flattened. Today there are only bleak gray apartment blocks here.

With ironic humor, Warsaw locals tell you that the best vantage point from which to admire their city is atop the 37-story **Palace of Culture and Science.** Why? Because it is the only point from which you can't see the Palace of Culture and Science. This wedding-cake-style skyscraper was a personal gift from Stalin. Although it is disliked by Poles as a symbol of Soviet domination, it does afford a panoramic view and is the best example in Warsaw of 1950s "Socialist Gothic" architecture. *Plac Defilad, tel. 022/20–02–11 ext. 2777. Admission: zł 75,000 adults, zł 25,000 children. Open daily 9–5.*

Shopping

Nowy Świat, Krakowskie Przedmieście, and ulica Chmielna are lined with boutiques selling good-quality leather goods, clothing, and trinkets. Try the **Cepelia** stores (plac Konstytucji 5 and Rynek Starego Miasta 8–10) for a wide range of handicrafts, such as glass, enamelware, amber, and handwoven woolen rugs. **Orno** shops (Marszałkowska 83 and Nowy Świat 52) offer handmade jewelry and silverware. **Desa** stores (Marszałkowska 34) specialize in ornaments and objets d'art. Polish and imported wines and spirits can be found at most large delicatessens.

For the more adventurous there is a flea market, **Bazar Różyckiego,** on ulica Targowa 55, where you can find almost anything. An even bigger market, where visitors from all over Eastern Europe sell their wares, is open daily at the **Stadion Tysiąclecia** sports stadium, near Rondo Waszyngtona.

Dining

More and more interesting restaurants have been opening throughout the city, but some of the best and most atmospheric dining rooms are still to be found on and around the Rynek Starego Miasto (Old Market Square) in the Old Town. The area is brightly lighted at night and makes for a pleasant walk before or after dinner. Reservations for dinner can be made by telephone (by your hotel receptionist if you don't speak Polish), and, in the case of expensive and fashionable restaurants, this is usually necessary. For details and price-category definitions, *see* Dining in Staying in Poland, *above.*

Expensive   **Bazyliszek.** Dimly lighted and elegant, the Bazyliszek excels in such game as boar, venison, and duck. A good café and snack bar are located downstairs. *Rynek Starego Miasta 7/9, tel. 022/31–18–41. Reservations advised. AE, DC, MC, V.*

★ **Canaletto.** Located in the Victoria InterContinental hotel, this restaurant serves Polish specialties with a good selection of European wines. The two paintings of old Warsaw on the walls are by Canaletto himself. *Plac Piłsudskiego, tel. 022/27–92–91. Reservations advised. AE, DC, MC, V.*

★ **Flik.** A new restaurant in Mokotów, Flik is light and spacious and boasts a lantern-lit terrace overlooking the Morskie Oko park. The proprietors are interested in good food and tend toward nouvelle cuisine. Try the fresh salmon to start. *Ul. Puławska 43, tel. 022/49–43–34. Reservations advised. AE, DC, MC, V.*

Forum. Another good hotel restaurant, the Forum's menu offers traditional Polish mixed with conventional Central European meat dishes. Like Canaletto, it is frequented by Western businesspeople and tourists. *Ul. Nowogrodzka 24, tel. 02/621–01–19. Reservations advised. AE, DC, MC, V.*

Moderate   **Kamienne Schodki.** This intimate, candlelit restaurant is located in one of the Market Square's medieval houses. Its main specialty is duck; also try the pastries. *Rynek Starego Miasta 26, tel. 022/31–08–22. Reservations advised. AE, DC, MC, V.*

Pod Samsonem. This small restaurant, decorated in wood, has a smoke-filled Warsaw atmosphere and friendly waitresses. The fish and pierogi are good when available. *Ul. Freta 3/5, tel. 022/31–17–88. Reservations accepted. No credit cards.*

Lodging

Orbis hotels are recommended for convenience and high standards. The rooms are comfortable though standardized, with functional, nondescript carpeting and furniture. Some rooms are beginning to show signs of wear. Private accommodations are cheap and hospitable, and are available through Orbis or through the Center for Tourist Information. There is no off-season for tourism. For details and price-category definitions, *see* Lodging in Staying in Poland, *above*.

Very Expensive

Bristol. Warsaw's most famous hotel was reopened in December 1992 after more than a decade of renovation and modernization. Once owned by Ignacy Paderewski, the concert pianist who served as Poland's prime minister in 1919–1920, the Bristol was always at the center of Warsaw's social life. Distinguished guests have included Charles de Gaulle and Marlene Dietrich. *Krakowskie Przedmieście 42–44, tel. 02/625-25-25, fax 02/625-25-77. 163 rooms with bath, 43 suites. Facilities: 2 restaurants, 2 bars, café, satellite TV in suites, sauna, solarium, pool. AE, DC, MC, V.*

★ **Marriott.** The Warsaw Marriott was completed in late 1989, and at 40 stories (20 make up the hotel; the rest are set aside for office and retail shopping space), it is also the city's tallest building. Luxuries include 11 restaurants, 24-hour room service, and color TV in every room. *Al. Jerozolimskie 65, tel. 02/630-63-06, fax 022/30-52-39. 525 rooms with bath. Facilities: restaurants and bars, casino, health club, swimming pool, sauna, shopping arcade. AE, DC, MC, V.*

Expensive

Holiday Inn. This five-story hotel in the center of the city opened in 1989. All rooms are equipped with color TV offering four satellite programs. One floor is reserved for nonsmokers. *Ul. Złota 2, tel. 022/20-03-41, fax 022/30-05-69. 338 rooms with bath. Facilities: restaurants, bars, business center, health club, sauna. AE, DC, MC, V.*

Hotel Forum. The Swedes built this InterContinental chain hotel in the '70s. Frequented by businesspeople and the Arab community, it has a good restaurant. A room higher up will give you a view of the city. *Ul. Nowogrodzka 24, tel. 02/621-02-71, fax 022/25-81-57. 750 rooms, some with bath or shower. Facilities: restaurant, nightclub, hairdresser. AE, DC, MC, V.*

Victoria InterContinental. Frequented by Western businesspeople, this is a large 1970s hotel in an ideal location in the center of town. It has a variety of facilities, including a fine restaurant and nightclub. Try to get a room facing Victory Square. *Ul. Królewska 11, tel. 022/ 27-92-71, fax 022/27-98-56. 370 rooms, most with bath or shower. Facilities: restaurant, nightclub, casino, sauna, indoor pool. AE, DC, MC, V.*

Moderate

★ **Hotel Europejski.** This fine old Warsaw hotel is located in the heart of the city. It was built in the 19th century in neo-Renaissance style, and its decor is elegant and refined. The rooms are spacious and attractive; some have hosted kings, presidents, and diplomats. The hotel takes pride in its restaurant. *Krakowskie Przedmieście 13, tel. 022/26-50-51, fax 022/26-11-11. 279 rooms, most with bath or shower. Facilities: restaurant. AE, DC, MC, V.*

Hotel Solec. This comfortable, modest, '70s hotel is down by the river in a residential area of the central town. Food and service are good, but the hotel tends to be inundated with tour groups. *Ul. Zagórna 1, tel. 022/25-92-41, fax 022/21-64-42. 150 rooms with bath. AE, DC, MC, V.*

Novotel. This small member of the French Novotel chain is ideal for visitors with a car and is well situated near Warsaw's airport (fortunately, *not* under any flight paths). *Ul. 1 Sierpnia 1, tel. 022/46-40-51, fax 022/46-36-86. 150 rooms with bath. Facilities: restaurant, café, outdoor pool. AE, DC, MC, V.*

Orbis Grand. Conveniently located in the center of the city, this large hotel was built in the 1950s and is a prime example of the Socialist-Realist architecture of the period. It has a rooftop res-

taurant-café and offers live jazz, dancing, or cabaret in the evening.
*Ul. Krucza 28, tel. 022/29–40–51, fax 02/621–97–24. 415 rooms,
some with shower. Facilities: restaurant, nightclub, indoor pool,
hairdresser, Pewex shop. AE, DC, MC, V.*

★ **Zajazd Napoleoński.** This small, privately owned inn has an excellent restaurant and deluxe facilities. Napoleon reputedly stayed
here when his Grand Army passed through Warsaw on its way to
Russia. It is situated about 12.8 kilometers (8 miles) outside of town.
Book well in advance. *Ul. Płowiecka 83, tel. 022/15–30–68, fax 022/
15–22–16. 22 rooms with bath, 3 suites. Facilities: restaurant. AE,
DC, MC, V.*

The Arts

For information, buy the newspaper *Życie Warszawy* or *Gazeta
Wyborcza* at Ruch newsstands. Tickets can be ordered by your Orbis
hotel receptionist, through the tourist information center (pl.
Zamkowy 1, tel. 02/635–18–81), or at the ticket office on ulica
Marszałkowska 104.

Theaters There are 17 theaters in Warsaw, attesting to the popularity of this
art form, but none offers English performances. **Teatr Narodowy,**
opened in 1764 and the oldest in Poland, is on plac Teatralny; at press
time it was closed for repairs after a major fire, but it may be reopened during 1995. **Teatr Polski Kameralny** (Foksal 16) has a small
stage. **Współczesny** (Mokotowska 13) shows contemporary works.

Concerts **The National Philharmonic** puts on the best concerts. The hall is on
ulica Sienkiewicza 12. An excellent new concert hall, opened in 1992,
is the **Studio Concertowe Polskiego Radia** (Woronicza 17). In the
summer, free Chopin concerts take place both at the Chopin monument in **Łazienki Park** and each Sunday at **Żelazowa Wola,** the composer's birthplace, 58 kilometers (36 miles) outside Warsaw.

Opera **Teatr Wielki** (plac Teatralny) hosts the Grand Theater of Opera and
Ballet. It has a superb operatic stage—one of the largest in Europe.

Nightlife

Cabaret The Victoria, Forum, Grand, Europejski, and Marriott hotels all
have nightclubs that are popular with Westerners. The acts vary, so
check listings in the press. These clubs also present striptease and
jazz.

Bars **Gwiazdeczka** (Piwna 42) is a noisy, hip, upscale joint, popular with
chic young Warsovians. **The Irish Pub** (Koszykowa 1) is a fashionable
recent addition to Warsaw's night spots. **Harenda** (Krakowskie
Przedmieście 4–6), with an outdoor terrace in summer, is open all
night.

Jazz Clubs **Akwarium** (Emilii Platter) and **Wanda Warska's Modern Music Club**
(Stare Miasto) are popular jazz clubs. A new jazz club that is winning
a major following is **Jazz Club 77** (Marszałkowska 77–79).

Discos Apart from the hotels, the most popular discos are **Hybrydy** (Złota 7)
and **Stodoła** (Batorego 10), but these can be rough.

Cafés Warsaw is filled with cafés *(kawiarnie),* which move outdoors in the
summer. They are popular meeting places and usually serve delicious coffee and pastries in the best Central European style.

Ambassador is an elegant and brightly lit café with a tree-lined terrace for summer visitors. *Ul. Matejki 4.*
Bonbonierka was recently reopened as a vegetarian café-cum-res-

taurant, with cane furniture and a resident harpist. *Rynek Nowego Miasta 13–15.*

Le Petit Trianon is a tiny, intimate 18th-century French-style restaurant and café. It is difficult to find a seat, but worth it once you do. *Ul. Piwna 40.*

Telimena is a small corner café with an art gallery on the ground floor. *Krakowskie Przedmiéscie 27.*

Wilanowska has definitely seen better days, but its crumbling elegance has a certain appeal. *Plac Trzech Krzyży 3.*

Kraków and Environs

Kraków (Cracow), seat of Poland's oldest university and once the capital of the country (before losing the honor to Warsaw in 1611), is one of the few Polish cities that escaped devastation during World War II. Today Kraków's fine ramparts, towers, facades, and churches, illustrating seven centuries of Polish architecture, make it a major attraction for visitors. Its location—about 270 kilometers (160 miles) south of Warsaw—also makes it a good base for hiking and skiing trips in the mountains of southern Poland.

Also within exploring range from Kraków are the famous Polish shrine to the Virgin Mary at Częstochowa, and, at Auschwitz (Oświęcim), the grim reminder of man's capacity for inhumanity.

Getting Around

Kraków is reached by major highways—E7 direct from Warsaw and E82 from Częstochowa. Trains link Kraków with most major destinations in Poland; the station is in the city center near the Old Town, on ulica Pawia. The bus station is nearby.

Guided Tours

Bus or walking tours of Kraków and its environs are provided by **Orbis**. Horse-drawn carriages can be rented at the main market square for a negotiated price.

Tourist Information

Częstochowa (al. najświętszej Marii Panny 37/39, tel. 034/24–71–34).
Kraków (ul. Pawia 8, tel. 012/22–95–10).

Exploring Kraków

Numbers in the margin correspond to points of interest on the Kraków map.

Kraków's old city is ringed by a park called the **Planty**. The park replaced the old walls of the town, which were torn down in the mid-19th century. Begin your tour at **Brama Floriańska** (St. Florian's Gate), which leads to the old town. The gate is guarded by an imposing 15th-century fortress called the **Barbakan**. Enter the city, passing along ulica Floriańska, the beginning of the Royal Route through the town.

Time Out Don't pass up the chance to stop for refreshments at Kraków's most famous café, **Jama Michalikowa** (ul. Floriańska 45), which now has a nonsmoking area. It serves good coffee and excellent ice cream.

Kraków

0 ——— 440 yards
0 ——— 400 meters

KEY

AE American Express Office

Major Attractions
Brama Floriańska, **1**
Jagiellonian University, **5**
Kosciół Mariacki, **3**
Rynek Główny, **2**
Sukiennice, **4**
Wawel Castle and Cathedral, **6**

Other Attractions
Barbakan, **14**
Central Station, **8**
Czartoryski Museum, **15**
Ethnographic Museum, **13**
Helena Modrzejewska Stary Theater, **10**
Jagiellonian University Museum, **9**

K. Szymanowski State Philharmonic Hall, **11**
National Museum, **12**
St. Adalbert Romanesque Church, **7**

② Ulica Floriańska leads to the **Rynek Główny** (main market), one of the largest and finest Renaissance squares in Europe. The calm of this spacious square, with its pigeons and flower stalls, is interrupted every hour by four short bugle calls drifting down from the spire of the Church of the Virgin Mary. The plaintive notes recall a centuries-old tradition in memory of a trumpeter whose throat was pierced by a well-aimed enemy arrow as he was warning his fellow citizens of an impending Tartar attack. **③** The square Gothic **Kościół Mariacki** (Church of the Virgin Mary) contains a 15th-century wooden altarpiece—the largest in the world—carved by Wit Stwosz. The faces of the saints are reputedly those of Cracovian burghers. In the **④** center of the square stands a covered market called **Sukiennice** (Cloth Hall), built in the 14th century but remodeled during the Renaissance. The ground floor is still in business, selling trinkets and folk art souvenirs. *Open Mon.–Sat. 10–6, Sun. 10–5.*

From the Main Market, turn down ulica świętej Anny to No. 8, the **⑤** **Collegium Maius,** the oldest building of the famous **Jagiellonian University** (founded 1364). Its pride is the Italian-style arcaded courtyard. Inside is a museum where you can see the Copernicus globe, the first on which the American continents were shown, as well as astronomy instruments belonging to Kraków's most famous graduate. *Admission free. Courtyard open Mon.–Sat. 8–6. Museum shown by appointment only, 10–noon.*

⑥ Backtracking on ulica Grodzka will lead you to the **Wawel Castle and Cathedral.** This impressive complex of Gothic and Renaissance buildings stands on fortifications dating as far back as the 8th century. Inside the castle is a museum with an exotic collection of Oriental tents that were captured from the Turks at the battle of Vienna in 1683 and rare 16th-century Flemish tapestries. Wawel Cathedral is where, until the 18th century, Polish kings were crowned and buried. Until 1978, the cathedral was the principal church of the see of Archbishop Karol Wojtyła, now known as Pope John Paul II. *Ul. Grodzka, tel. 012/22–51–55. Castle. Admission: zł 30,000 adults, zł 15,000 children. Open Tues., Thurs., Sat., Sun. 10–3, Wed. and Fri. noon–6. Cathedral Museum. Admission: zł 20,000. Open Tues.– Sun. 10–3.*

About 50 kilometers (30 miles) west of Kraków is Oświęcim, better known by its German name, **Auschwitz.** Here 4 million victims, mostly Jews, were executed by the Nazis in the Auschwitz and Birkenau concentration camps. Auschwitz is now a museum, with restored crematoria and barracks housing dramatic displays of Nazi atrocities. The buildings at Birkenau, a 15-minute walk away, have been left just as they were found in 1945 by the Soviet Army. Oświęcim itself is an industrial town with good connections from Kraków; buses and trains leave Kraków approximately every hour, and signs in Oświęcim direct visitors to the camp. *Auschwitz: admission free. Open Mar. and Nov., Tues.–Sun. 8–4; Apr. and Oct., Tues.–Sun. 8–5; May and Sept., daily 8–6; June–Aug., daily 8–7; Dec.–Feb., Tues.–Sun. 8–3. Birkenau: open all times.*

Wieliczka, about 8 kilometers (5 miles) southeast of Kraków, is the oldest salt mine in Europe, in operation since the end of the 13th century. It is famous for its magnificent underground chapel hewn in crystal rock, the **Chapel of the Blessed Kinga.** *Admission: zł. 70,000 adults, zł 40,000 children. Open daily 9–4.*

Częstochowa, 120 kilometers (70 miles) from Kraków and reached by regular trains and buses, is the home of the holiest shrine in a country that is more than 90% Catholic. Inside the 14th-century **Pauline**

monastery on Jasna Góra (Light Hill) is the famous *Black Madonna*, a painting of Our Lady of Częstochowa attributed by legend to St. Luke. It was here that an invading Swedish army was halted in 1655 and finally driven out of the country. About 25 miles southwest of Kraków is the little town of **Wadowice**, birthplace of Pope John Paul II. *Wadowice Museum. Admission: zł 20,000 adults, zł 10,000 children. Open Tues.–Sat. 10–3, Sun. 10–5.*

Dining and Lodging

For details and price-category definitions, *see* Dining and Lodging in Staying in Poland, *above*.

Częstochowa
Lodging

Polonia. The Polonia makes a good base for exploring the Pauline monastery, and since most of the other guests are pilgrims, the atmosphere is an interesting mixture of piety and good fun. *Ul. Piłsudskiego 9, tel. 0–34/24–40–67, fax 0–34/65–11–05. 62 rooms, most with bath or shower. AE, DC, MC, V. Inexpensive.*

Kraków
Dining

Staropolska. Traditional Polish cuisine is served in a medieval setting. Try the pork, duck, or veal. *Ul. Sienna 4, tel. 012/22–58–21. Reservations advised. Expensive.*

★ **Wierzynek.** One of the best restaurants in the country, Wierzynek serves traditional Polish specialties and excels in soups and game. It was here, after a historic meeting in 1364, that the king of Poland wined and dined the Holy Roman Emperor Charles IV, five kings, and a score of princes. *Rynek Główny 15, tel. 012/22–14–04. Reservations advised. AE, DC, MC, V. Expensive.*

Dining and Lodging

Francuski. This small hotel is just inside the old town's walls, within walking distance of all the main sites. Built at the turn of the century, it offers an intimate atmosphere and friendly service. The rooms are elegant in a homey, East European way. The excellent restaurant is tranquil and plush and has a café with dancing. The hotel reopened in late 1991 after extensive renovations. *Ul. Pijarska 13, tel. 012/22–51–22, fax 012/22–52–70. 42 rooms, most with bath or shower. Facilities: restaurant, café. AE, DC, MC, V. Expensive.*

★ **Cracovia.** This large, Orbis-run, five-story hotel boasts one of the best restaurants in town. There is also a lively nightclub where Western tourists like to meet. *Al. marszałka F. Focha 1, tel. 012/22–86–66, fax 012/21–95–86. 427 rooms with bath. Facilities: restaurant, nightclub. AE, DC, MC, V. Moderate.*

Holiday Inn. This was the first Holiday Inn in Eastern Europe. Rather bland but comfortable with a fine restaurant, this high-rise establishment is pleasantly located near Cracow's Green Meadows. *Ul. Koniewa 7, tel. 012/37–50–44, fax 012/37–59–38. 310 rooms with bath. Facilities: restaurant, solarium, sauna, indoor pool. AE, DC, MC, V. Moderate.*

Lodging

Forum. Opened in 1988, this Orbis hotel stands on the south bank of the Vistula, commanding a fine view of the Wawel castle. *Ul. Marii Konopnickiej 28, tel. 012/66–95–00, fax 012/66–58–27. 280 rooms with bath. Facilities: restaurant, sauna, indoor pool, tennis courts, beauty salon. AE, DC, MC, V. Expensive.*

★ **Grand.** Reopened in 1990 after a 12-year renovation, this late-19th-century hotel in the heart of the Old Town is elegant and comfortable. It has reproduction period furniture but modern bathrooms and facilities. *Ul. Sławkowska 5–7, tel. 012/21–72–55, fax 012/21–83–60. 50 rooms with bath. Facilities: restaurant, café, exercise room. AE, DC, MC, V. Expensive.*

Europejski. This small, older hotel overlooking the Planty park has now been renovated, and most of the rooms have shower or bath. *Ul.*

Lubicz 5, tel. 012/22–09–11, fax 012/22–89–25. 55 rooms, some with bath. No credit cards. Inexpensive.

Gdańsk and the North

In contrast to Kraków and the south, Poland north of Warsaw is the land of medieval castles and châteaus, dense forests and lakes, and fishing villages and beaches. If you don't have a car, consider going straight to Gdańsk and making excursions from there.

Getting Around

Gdańsk is a major transportation hub, with an airport just outside town (and good bus connections to downtown) and major road and rail connections with the rest of the country.

Guided Tours

Orbis arranges an eight-day tour of Warsaw, Toruń, Gdańsk, and Poznań. It also handles group and individual tours of Toruń, Gdańsk, and the surrounding areas.

Tourist Information

Elbląg (ul. 3 Maja 1, tel. 050/247–76; Orbis, ul. Hetmańska 23, tel. 050/223–64).
Gdańsk (ul. Heweliusza 8, tel. 058/31–03–38; Orbis, pl. Górskiego 1, tel. 058/31–49–44).
Ostróda (Orbis, ul. Czarnieckiego 10, tel. 088/35–57).
Płock (ul. Tuńska 4, tel. 024/226–00; Orbis, al. Jachowa 47, tel. 024/229–89).
Toruń (ul. Kopernika 27, tel. 056/272–99; Orbis, ul. Żeglarska 31, tel. 056/261–30).

Exploring Gdańsk and the North

From Warsaw, follow routes E81 and 107 through **Płock**. Once you get through Płock's industrial area, you'll find a lovely medieval city that was, for a short time, capital of Poland. Worth seeing are the 12th-century cathedral, where two Polish kings are buried, and the dramatic 14th-century Teutonic castle. Continue through Włocławek to Toruń, where an overnight stay is recommended.

Toruń, birthplace of Nicolaus Copernicus, is an interesting medieval city that grew wealthy due to its location on the north-south trading route along the Vistula. Its old town district is a remarkably successful blend of Gothic buildings—churches, town hall, and burghers' homes—with Renaissance and Baroque patricians' houses. The Town Hall's Tower (1274) is the oldest town hall building in Poland. Don't leave without trying some of Toruń's famous gingerbread and honey cakes.

The route leading north from Toruń to Gdańsk passes through some of the oldest towns in Poland. Along the way are many medieval castles, châteaus, and churches that testify to the wealth and strategic importance of the area. Two short detours are a must: one is to **Kwidzyń** to see the original 14th-century castle and cathedral complex, which is free and open to the public. The other is to **Malbork.** This huge castle, 58 kilometers (36 miles) from Gdańsk, was one of the most powerful strongholds in medieval Europe. From 1308 to

Gdansk and the North

1457, it was the residence of the Grand Masters of the Teutonic Order. The Teutonic Knights were a thorn in Poland's side until their defeat at the battle of Grunwald in 1410. Inside Malbork castle is a museum with beautiful examples of amber—including lumps as large as melons and pieces containing perfect specimens of prehistoric insects. *tel. 055/3364. Open Tues.–Sat. 10–3, Sun. 10–5. Admission: zł 45,000 adults, zł 35,000 children.*

Gdańsk, once the free city of Danzig, is another of Poland's beautifully restored towns, displaying a rich heritage of Gothic, Renaissance, and Mannerist architecture. This is where the first shots of World War II were fired and where the free trade union Solidarity was born after strikes in 1980. The city's old town has a wonderful collection of historic town houses and narrow streets. The splendid Długa and Długi Targ streets (best for shopping) form the axis of the city and are good starting points for walks into other districts. The evocative **Solidarity Monument** stands outside the Lenin shipyards—erected in honor of workers killed by the regime during strikes in 1970. The nearby town of **Sopot** is Poland's most popular seaside resort.

For a different route back to Warsaw, follow highway E81 southeast through Poland's scenic forest and lake district. The area is rich in nature and wildlife attractions, as well as places of historical interest. Recommended is a diversion (or night stop) 42 kilometers (26 miles) east of Ostróda to the medieval town of **Olsztyn.** The old town was once administered and fortified by Copernicus.

About 30 kilometers (19 miles) farther south on E81 is **Olsztynek,** where the **Museum of Folk Buildings** has a collection of timber buildings from different parts of the country. They include a small Mazurian thatch-roofed church, an inn, a mill, a forge, old windmills, and thatched cottages, some of which have been furnished period-style. *Tel. 889/19–24–64. Admission: zł 25,000 adults, zł 10,000 children. Open May–Sept., Tues.–Sun. 9–4; closed Mon.*

Time Out Located on E81, 5 kilometers (3 miles) north of Olsztynek, the **Mazurski** is a good place to stop for a meal. The food varies, but is generally tasty. *Moderate.*

Another diversion, 17 kilometers (10½ miles) west of Olsztynek, is the **site of the battle of Grunwald,** possibly the greatest battle of the Middle Ages. Here on July 15, 1410, Władysław Jagiełło and his Polish Lithuanian army annihilated the Grand Master of the Teutonic Order, Ulrich von Jungingen, and thousands of his knights. A small museum on the site (open summer only, 10–10) graphically explains the course of the battle.

Dining and Lodging

For details and price-category definitions, *see* Dining and Lodging in Staying in Poland, *above.*

Elbląg **Karczma Słupska.** This is the best restaurant in town. It's usually
Dining crowded and specializes in fresh fish. *Ul. Krótka 1. No reservations. No credit cards. Moderate.*

Gdańsk **Pod Łososiem.** The name of this restaurant refers to salmon, which,
Dining if available on the day you visit, is highly recommended. *Ul. Szeroka 51, tel. 058/31–76–52. Reservations advised. AE, DC, MC, V. Expensive.*
Pod Wieżą. This restaurant has a reputation for good meat dishes and generous portions. If they're on the menu when you visit, try the *zupa rybna* (fish soup), veal steak with mushroom sauce, or roast duck with apples and brown rice. *Piwna 51, tel. 058/31–39–24. Reservations advised. AE, DC, MC, V. Expensive.*
★ **Kaszubska.** The specialties here come from Kashubia. Smoked fish dishes are highly recommended. *Ul. Kartuska 76, tel. 058/32–06–02. Reservations advised. AE, DC, MC, V. Moderate.*
★ **Tawerna.** This well-established restaurant overlooking the river serves traditional Polish and Germanic dishes such as pork cutlets and seafood. Yes, it's touristy, but the food is delicious. *Ul. Powroźnicza 19–20, off Długi Targ, tel. 058/31–92–48. Reservations advised. Dress: casual. AE, DC, MC, V. Moderate.*

Lodging **Hewelius.** This large, modern, high-rise hotel is within walking distance of the old town. The rooms are spacious, and blandly furnished, with all the modern conveniences. *Ul. Heweliusza 22, tel. 058/31–56–31, fax 31 058/31–19–22. 250 rooms, most with bath. Facilities: restaurant, nightclub. AE, DC, MC, V. Moderate.*
★ **Marina.** Built in 1982, this large high rise, popular with Western businesspeople, is one of the newer hotels in Poland and probably the best in town. Upper floors have splendid views. *Ul. Jelitkowska 20, tel. 058/53–20–79, fax 058/53–04–60. 193 rooms with bath or shower. Facilities: restaurant, nightclub, indoor pool, tennis courts, bowling alley. AE, DC, MC, V. Moderate.*

Olsztyn **Orbis Novotel.** This standard 1970s hotel is typical of the kind found
Lodging in Poland. It is, however, the most comfortable lodging in the area and is located in beautiful surroundings on the shores of lake Ukiel. *Ul. Sielska 4A, tel. 889/27–40–81, fax 889/27–54–03. 98 rooms with bath. Facilities: restaurant, pool. Moderate.*

Ostróda This town is not visited by many foreign tourists and is lacking in
Lodging good-quality facilities. The undistinguished **Panorama Hotel** is the
best, unless Orbis can locate private lodging for you. *Ul.
Krasickiego 23, tel. 089/82–22–27. Inexpensive.*

Toruń **Pod Kurantem.** Regional cuisine is featured in this attractive old
Dining wine cellar. Slow service is the penalty for popularity. *Rynek
★ Staromiejski 28. No telephone. No reservations. No credit cards.
Expensive.*
Wodnik. This large café along the banks of the Vistula is very popu-
lar with locals. *Blwd. Filadelfijski, tel. 056/287–55. AE, DC, MC,
V. Moderate.*
Zajazd Staropolski. This restaurant features excellent meat dishes
and soups in a restored 17th-century interior. *Ul. Żeglarska 10/14,
tel. 056/260–60. Reservations advised. AE, DC, MC, V. Moderate.*

Lodging **Helios.** This friendly, medium-size hotel is situated in the city center
and offers a good restaurant (albeit with slow service). *Ul.
Kraszewskiego 1, tel. 056/250–33, fax 856/235–65. 140 rooms, most
with bath or shower. Facilities: restaurant, sauna, nightclub, beauty parlor. AE, DC, MC, V. Moderate.*
Kosmos. A functional 1960s hotel, Kosmos is beginning to show
signs of wear and tear. It is situated near the river, in the city center. *Ul. Portowa 2, tel. 056/270–85. 180 rooms, most with bath or
shower. AE, DC, MC, V. Moderate.*

23 Portugal

Given its long Atlantic coastline, it isn't surprising that Portugal has been a maritime nation for most of its history. The valor of its seamen is well known; from the charting of the Azores archipelago in 1427 to the discovery of Japan in 1542, Portuguese explorers unlocked the major sea routes to southern Africa, India, the Far East, and the Americas. To commemorate the *descobrimentos*, this great era of exploration, a period that reached its height in the 15th century under the influence of Prince Henry the Navigator, the years 1988 to 2000 have been set aside for various celebrations throughout the country.

Despite its sailors' world-wide adventures, Portugal itself has remained relatively undiscovered. Although it shares the Iberian Peninsula with Spain, it attracts far fewer visitors—a strange fact, because Portugal has much to recommend it to tourists: fine beaches, beautiful castles, charming fishing villages, well-maintained hotels and *pousadas* (government-owned inns), excellent restaurants, and colorful folk traditions.

About the size of Indiana, Portugal is so small that its main attractions can be seen during a short visit; at the country's widest point the distance between the Atlantic and Spain is a mere 240 kilometers (150 miles). Short distances don't mean monotony, however, for this narrow coastal strip of land has more geographic and climatic variations than virtually any other nation in Western Europe.

Although Portugal has seen numerous divisions in modern times, the country has traditionally been divided into six historic provinces. Most visitors head for the low-lying plains of the southern Algarve or the region around the Lisbon/Estoril coast, but as traditional tourist destinations become more crowded, adventurous travelers are exploring in other directions. The northern and central provinces—Minho, Beiras, and Trás-os-Montes—are largely unspoiled, full of tiny villages and splendid scenery. The major drawbacks here are the comparative lack of first-class accommodations and poor secondary roads. With the recent infusion of substantial EC funds, however, this condition has been improving rapidly. The main highways from Lisbon to the North and the frontier are now in good shape. In the south the once fearsome EN125, which spans the Algarve from east to west, has been widened and largely tamed, and a high-speed trans-Algarve expressway is under construction.

Observant visitors are likely to notice differences between Portugal's northern and southern regions and people. The northern character is decidedly more Celtic, while in the south, Moorish ancestry is apparent. But throughout the country, the Portuguese people are welcoming wherever you meet them.

We have concentrated our Exploring sections on the southern part of the country—the section most frequented by foreign visitors—including Portugal's sophisticated capital of Lisbon, its coastal and wooded environs, and the Algarve.

Essential Information

Before You Go

When to Go The tourist season runs from spring through autumn, but some parts of the country—especially the Algarve, which boasts 3,000 hours of sunshine annually—are balmy even in winter. Hotel prices are greatly reduced between November and February, except in

Portugal

0   50 miles
0   50 km

N

Minho

Valença

Viana
do Castelo   *Lima*

Barcelos   Braga   Chaves   Bragança

Póvoa de Varzim   Guimarães   *Tâmega*

N15   Mirandela

Vila do Conde   Amarante   Vila Real   *Sabor*   Mogadouro

Oporto   Penafiel   *Douro*

Douro   Lamego   *Duoro*

Espinho   Oliveira   Moimenta
dos Azeméis   da Beira

S. Pedro
do Sul

ATLANTIC
OCEAN

Albergaria-a-Velha   *Vouga*   Viseu   Pinhel

Aveiro

Mealhada   Sta. Comba
Dão

Mira   Cantanhede   *Mondego*   Guarda

Coimbra   *Serra da Estrêla*

Figueira
da Foz   Arganil   Covilhã

E1/A1   *N110*   *Zêzere*   Fundão

Pombal   Penamacor

*Serra da
Gardunha*
N233

Leiria   Ourém   Proença-
a-Nova   Castelo
Branco

Nazaré   Batalha   Tomar

Alcobaça   Fátima   Abrantes   Nisa

Caldas
da Rainha   *Sra.
do Aire*   N118   *Tagus*

Óbidos   Torres
Novas

Aveiras de Cima   Portalegre

Torres Vedras   Santarém   Ponte
de Sor

Mafra   *Tejo*

Sintra   Vila Franca
de Xira   *Sorraia*   Avis

Cascais   Lisbon   Arraiolos   Estremoz   Elvas

Estoril   *N10*   Montemoro-Novo   *Sra. de Ossa*   Vila
Viçosa

Seixal   *A2*

Setúbal   *Sado*   Alcácer
do Sal   Évora   Reguengos   *Guadiana*

*Cabo
Espichel*   *N2*

Ferreira do
Alentejo   Moura

Sines   *E1*   Beja   Vilaverde de Ficalho

*Cabo de
Sines*   Santiago
do Cacem   Serpa

Castro
Verde   N122

Odemira   Ourique   *Chança*

N120   *Mira*   Mértola   *Guadiana*

Almodovar

Monchique

A L G A R V E

Vila do Bispo   Portimão   N125   Albufeira   S. Bráz de Alportel

Lagos   Tavira   Vila Real de
S. António

*Cabo de
S. Vicente*   Faro   Olhão

S P A I N

ATLANTIC OCEAN

Lisbon where business visitors keep prices uniformly high throughout the year.

Climate Since Portugal's entire coast is on the Atlantic Ocean, the country's climate is temperate year-round. Portugal rarely suffers the extremes of heat that Mediterranean countries do. Even in August, the hottest month, the Algarve and the Alentejo are the only regions where the midday heat may be uncomfortable, but most travelers go to the beaches there to swim and soak up the sun. What rain there is falls from November to March; December and January can be chilly outside the Algarve, and very wet to the north, but there is no snow except in the mountains of the Serra da Estrela in the northeast. The almond blossoms and vivid wildflowers that cover the countryside start to bloom early in February. The dry months, June–September, can turn much of the landscape the tawny color of a lion's hide, but there is always a breeze in the evening in Lisbon, as well as along the Estoril coast west of the capital.

The following are the average daily maximum and minimum temperatures for Lisbon.

Jan.	57F	14C	May	71F	21C	Sept.	79F	26C
	46	8		55	13		62	17
Feb.	59F	15C	June	77F	25C	Oct.	72F	22C
	47	8		60	15		58	14
Mar.	63F	17C	July	81F	27C	Nov.	63F	17C
	50	10		63	17		52	11
Apr.	67F	20C	Aug.	82F	28C	Dec.	58F	15C
	53	12		63	17		47	9

Currency The unit of currency in Portugal is the *escudo*, which can be divided into 100 centavos. Escudos come in bills of 500$00, 1,000$00, 2,000$00, 5,000$00, and 10,000$00. (In Portugal the dollar sign stands between the escudo and the centavo.) Coins come in 1$00, 2$50, 5$00, 10$00, 20$00, 50$00, 100$00, and 200$00. Newly minted 1$00, 5$00, and 10$00 yellow-colored coins can be confused for older coins still in circulation, so make sure you know exactly what you're spending.

At press time (spring 1994), the exchange rate was about 175$00 to the U.S. dollar and 250$00 to the pound sterling. Owing to the complications of dealing in millions of escudos, 1,000$00 is always called a *conto*, so 10,000$00 is referred to as 10 contos. You can change money in hotels and in larger shops and restaurants, but banks and *cambios* (exchange offices) usually give better rates.

What It Will Cost While the cost of hotels and restaurants in Portugal is still reasonable, inflation is pushing prices up. Some of Portugal's best food bargains are to be enjoyed in its many simple seaside restaurants. The most expensive areas are Lisbon, the Algarve, and the tourist resort areas along the Tagus estuary. The least expensive areas are country towns, which all have reasonably priced hotels and *pensões*, or pensions, as well as numerous café-type restaurants. A sales, or value-added, tax (called IVA) of 16% is imposed on hotel and restaurant bills, car rentals, and services like car repairs.

Sample Prices Cup of coffee, 100$00; bottle of beer, 125$00; soft drink, 175$00; bottle of house wine, 750$00; ham sandwich, 225$00; 1-mile taxi ride, 425$00; city bus ride, 140$00; museum entrance, 250$00.

Customs on Arrival Non–European-Union (EU) visitors over age 17 are allowed to bring the following items into Portugal duty-free: 200 cigarettes or 250 grams of tobacco, 1 liter of liquor (over 22% volume) or 2 liters (under 22% volume), 2 liters of wine, 100 ml of perfume, and a reasonable amount of personal effects (camera, binoculars, etc). There is no limit on money brought into the country. However, no more than 100,000$00 in Portuguese currency or the equivalent of 500,000$00 in foreign currency may be taken out without proof that an equal amount or more was brought into Portugal. Computerized customs services make random and often thorough checks on arrival.

Language Portuguese is easy to read by anyone with even slight knowledge of a Latin language, but it is difficult to pronounce and understand (most people speak quickly and elliptically). But in large cities and major resorts many people, especially the young, speak English and, occasionally, French.

Getting Around

By Car The few turnpikes (moderate tolls) and the major highways between
Road Lisbon and the coast, the Algarve, and Oporto are in good shape.
Conditions For the most part, road conditions in Portugal have greatly improved, but minor roads are often poor and winding with unpredictable surfaces.

New highways have made the once grueling drive between the Algarve and Lisbon a pleasure. EN 125, the principal east-west Algarve highway, has been widened and resurfaced, and the eastern section of the new Algarve highway from Albufeira to Vila Real de Santo António was due to open in mid-'94. New bridges have eliminated the formerly horrendous bottlenecks at Portimão and replaced the ferry across the Guadiana River from Vila Real de Santo António to Spain.

In the north, the IP5 makes the drive from Aveiro to the border with Spain near Guarda a pleasant one, and the IP4 connects Oporto through Vila Real to once-remote Bragança.

There's no superhighway from Lisbon leading east to the nearest frontier post at Badajoz, Spain, but the route over the Tagus bridge through Setúbal (turnpike from Lisbon), via Montemoro-Novo and Estremoz, is good and fast.

Rules of the Driving is on the right. At the junction of two roads of equal size,
Road traffic coming from the right has priority. Vehicles already in a traffic circle have priority over those entering it from any point. Traffic in the country is light, but local people are apt to walk in the road and occasional horse- or donkey-drawn carts may hold things up. After dark watch out for motorbikes and donkey carts without lights. Seat belts are obligatory. Horns should not be used in built-up areas, and a reflective red warning triangle, for use in a breakdown, must be carried. The speed limit on turnpikes is 120 kph (72 mph); on other roads it is 90 kph (54 mph), and in built-up areas, 50–60 kph (30–36 mph).

Parking Lisbon, Coimbra, and Oporto are experimenting with parking meters, although these are still rare. Parking lots and underground garages abound in major cities, but those in Lisbon and Oporto are no longer cheap. Parking on side streets is usually chaotic, and in Lisbon and Oporto it's often very difficult to find a parking space near city-center hotels.

Gasoline Gas prices are among the highest in Europe: 155$00 per liter for super and 145$00 for regular. Unleaded gas is now available for 140$00. Many gas stations around the country are self-service. Credit cards are widely accepted.

Breakdowns All large garages in and around towns have breakdown services. Special orange emergency (SOS) telephones are located at intervals on turnpikes and highways. Motorists in Portugal are very helpful; if your car breaks down, aid from a passing driver is usually forthcoming within a short time. The national automobile organization, **Automóvel Clube de Portugal** (Rua Rosa Araújo 24/26, 1200 Lisbon, tel. 01/356–3931) provides reciprocal membership with AAA and other European automobile associations, provided the membership is up-to-date.

By Train The Portuguese railway system is surprisingly extensive for such a small country. Trains are clean and leave on time, but there are few express runs except between Lisbon and Oporto, which takes just over three hours for the 210-mile journey. Several of the Oporto–Lisbon and Lisbon–Algarve trains take cars, as does one train a day between Lisbon, Castelo Branco, and Guarda. Cars must be at the station an hour before departure; prices are reasonable, and tickets can be bought then or in advance. Most trains have first- and second-class compartments; suburban lines around Lisbon have a single class. Tickets should be bought, and seats reserved if desired, at the stations or through travel agents, two or three days in advance. Advance reservations are essential on Lisbon–Oporto express trains. Timetables are mostly the same on Saturday and Sunday as on weekdays, except on suburban lines. **Wasteels–Expresso** (Av. António Augusto Aguiar 88, 1000 Lisbon, tel. 01/579655 or 01/579180) is reliable for all local and international train tickets and reservations.

Special **tourist passes** can be obtained through travel agents or at main train stations. These are valid for periods of 7, 14, or 21 days for first- and second-class travel on any domestic train service; mileage is unlimited. At press time (spring 1994), the cost was 15,200$00 for 7 days; 24,200$00 for 14 days; and 34,600$00 for 21 days. Child passes cost exactly half those amounts.

International trains to Madrid, Paris, and other parts of Europe depart from the Santa Apolonia Station in Lisbon and Campanhã in Oporto.

By Plane The internal air services of **TAP Air Portugal** are good. Lisbon is linked at least four times daily with Oporto and Faro; daily with Funchal (Madeira), more at peak periods; weekly with Porto Santo, an island some way off Madeira; and several times a week with the archipelago of the Azores. Flights to Viseu, Vila Real, and Bragança are all run by TAP (Praça Marques Pombal 3, 1200 Lisbon, tel. 01/386–1020). **LAR Transregional Airlines** (Rua C, Edifício 70, Aeroporto de Lisboa, tel. 01/8509) provides the most extensive domestic air service along with flights to Seville, Bordeaux, and Santiago de Compostela. **Portugália** (Av. Almirante Gago Coutinho 88, tel. 01/808999) has regular connections between Lisbon, Oporto, and Faro. **SATA-Air Açores** (Av. de Liberdade 261, tel. 01/535911) schedules regular flights between the various islands of the Azores.

By Bus The nationalized bus company, **Rodoviaria Nacional,** has passenger terminals in Lisbon (Av. Casal Ribeiro 18, tel. 01/545439), with regular bus services throughout Portugal. Several private companies offer luxury service between major cities. For information and reservations in Lisbon, contact the main tourist office (*see* Important Addresses and Numbers in Lisbon, *below*) or **Mundial Turismo** (Ave. António Augusto de Aguiar 90–A, tel. 01/356–3521). Most long-distance buses have toilet facilities, and the fares are often cheaper than for trains.

By Boat   Ferries across the river Tagus (Lisbon) leave from Praça do Comércio, Cais do Sodré, and Belém. From June to September, a two-hour boat excursion leaves the ferry station at Praça do Comércio in Lisbon daily at 2:30 PM. The price is 3,000$00. There are also cruises to Cascais; details from **Transtejo** (Terreiro do Paço, tel. 01/886–4100). In the United States, contact **Sea Air Holidays Ltd.** (733 Summer St., Stamford, CT 06901, tel. 800/732–6247) about cruises on the Douro river in an 80-cabin vessel, with weekly departures.

Boat trips on the river Douro (Oporto) are organized from May through October by **Porto Ferreira** (Rua da Cavalhosa, 19, Vila Nova de Gaia, Oporto, tel. 02/300866). They leave every day on the hour, except Saturday afternoon and Sunday. Overnight cruises are also available. Contact **Endouro** (Rua da Reboleira 49, 4000 Oporto, tel. 02/324236, fax 02/317260).

By Bicycle   **Tip Tours** (Ave. Costa Pinto 91-A, 2750 Cascais, tel. 01/483–5150 and 01/483–5159) rents out bicycles by the day or half day. **Cycling through the Centuries** (Box 10095, South Lake Tahoe, CA 96158, tel. 916/541–4713 or 800/246–4226 or, in Portugal, tel. 01/486–2044, fax 01/486–1409) offers bicycle tours throughout the country with accommodations in first-class hotels and romantic country inns. Each tour is accompanied by a guide, a mechanic, and a van for luggage.

Staying in Portugal

Telephones   The country code for Portugal is 351; for Lisbon, 1, Oporto, 2. Pay phones take 10$00, 20$00, and 50$00 coins; 10$00 is the minimum payment for short local calls (some pay phones may not accept the newly minted yellow-colored coins). Pay phones marked *credifone* will accept plastic phone cards, which can be purchased at post offices and most tobacconist shops. Long-distance calls cost less from 8 PM to 7 AM. All telephone calls are more expensive when made from a hotel, so it is wise to make international calls from a post office, where you will be assigned a private booth. Collect calls can also be made from post offices, and some telephone booths accept international calls. Access numbers to reach American long-distance operators are: for AT&T, 050–171288; for MCI, 0*010–480–0112; for Sprint, 050–171877.

Mail   Postal rates, both domestic and foreign, increase twice a year. Country post offices close for lunch and at 6 PM on weekdays; they are not open on weekends. Main post offices in towns are open weekdays 8:30 to 6. In Lisbon, the post office in the Praça dos Restauradores is open daily until 10 PM.

Receiving Mail   Mail can be sent in care of American Express Star (**Top Tours,** Av. Duque de Loulé 108, 1000 Lisbon, tel. 01/315–5877, fax 01/352–3227); there is no service charge. Main post offices also accept poste restante letters.

Shopping   Bargaining is not common in city stores or shops, but it is sometimes possible in flea markets, antiques shops, and outdoor markets that sell fruit, vegetables, and household goods. The **Centro de Turismo Artesanato** (Rua Castilho 61, 1200 Lisbon, tel. 01/353–4879) will ship goods abroad even if they were not bought in Portugal. By air to the United States, parcels take about three weeks; by sea, two months.

IVA Refunds   IVA tax on items over a certain value can be reclaimed, although the methods are time-consuming. For Americans and other non-EU residents, the tax paid on individual items costing more than 10,000$00 can be reclaimed in cash on presentation of receipts and a special *Tax-free Shopping Cheque* to special departments in airports (in Lisbon, near Gate 23). You can also have the check stamped at any border crossing and receive the refund by mail or credit card. Shops specializing in IVA-refund purchases are clearly marked throughout the country, and shop assistants can help with the forms. For details in Lisbon call 01/418–8703.

Opening and Closing Times **Banks** are open weekdays 8:30 to 3 PM; they do not close for lunch. There are automatic currency-exchange machines in Lisbon in the Praça dos Restauradores and in major cities.

Museums are usually open 10–12:30 and 2–5. Most close on Sunday afternoon, and they are all closed on Monday. Most palaces close on Tuesday.

Shops are open weekdays 9–1 and 3–7, Saturdays 9–1. Shopping malls and supermarkets in Lisbon and other cities remain open until 10 PM or midnight and are often open on Sunday.

National Holidays January 1; February 28 (Carnival begins); April 14 (Good Friday); April 25 (Anniversary of the Revolution); May 1 (Labor Day); June 2 (Corpus Christi); June 10 (National Day); August 15 (Assumption); October 5 (Day of the Republic); November 1 (All Saints Day); December 1 (Independence Day); December 8 (Immaculate Conception); December 25.

Dining Eating is taken quite seriously in Portugal, and, not surprisingly, seafood is a staple including *sardinhas assadas* (fresh-grilled sardines), a local favorite. Freshly caught lobster, crab, shrimp, tuna, sole, and squid are prepared in innumerable ways, and *caldeirada* is a piquant seafood stew made with a little bit of everything. In the Algarve, *cataplana* is a must: It's a mouth-watering mixture of clams, ham, tomatoes, onions, garlic, and herbs, named for the dish in which it is cooked. Meat lovers wax rhapsodic over northern-style *leitão da Bairrada* (roast suckling pig), *coelho á caçadora* (rabbit with potatoes, onions, garlic, and a splash of wine), and the tasty spiced sausages and smoked ham. There are some excellent local wines, and in modest restaurants even the *vinho da casa* (house wine) is usually very good. Desserts feature *doces de ovos* (egg and sugar confections), *pudim flan* (egg custard), egg and almond tarts, and always fruit. Water is generally safe, but visitors may want to drink bottled water—*sem gas* for still, *com gas* for fizzy—from one of the many excellent Portuguese spas.

Mealtimes Lunch usually begins around 1 PM; dinner is served at about 8 PM.

Dress and Reservations Jacket and tie are advised for most restaurants in the Expensive category, but otherwise casual dress is acceptable. Unless noted, reservations are not necessary.

Ratings Prices are per person, without alcohol. Taxes and service are usually included, but a tip of 5%–10% is always appreciated. Best bets are indicated by a star ★.

Category	All Areas
Very Expensive	over 6,000$00
Expensive	3,500$00–6,000$00

| Moderate | 2,000$00–3,500$00 |
| Inexpensive | under 2,000$00 |

*Per person, for a three-course meal, excluding drinks and service

Lodging Visitors have a wide choice of lodging in Portugal, which offers some of the lowest rates in Europe for accommodations. Hotels are graded from one up to five stars, as are the smaller inns called *estalagems*, which usually provide breakfast only. Pensões go up to four stars and often include meals. The state-subsidized *pousadas*, most of which are situated in castles, old monasteries, or have been built where there is a particularly fine view, are five-star luxury properties. *Residencials* (between a pensão and a hotel) are located in most towns and larger villages; most rooms have private baths or showers, and breakfast is usually included. They are extremely good value, around 4,000$00–6,000$00, but since they usually have only a few rooms, we don't review many residencials.

A recent innovation is *Turismo no Espaço Rural* (Tourism in the Country), in which private homeowners all over the country offer visitors a room and breakfast (and sometimes provide dinner on request). This is an excellent way to experience life on a country estate or in a small village. Details are available from several agencies, including **P.I.T.** (Alto da Pampilheira, Torre D2–8°A, 2750 Cascais, tel. 01/486–7958, fax 01/284–2901) and **Privetur** (Rua João Penha, 10, 1200 Lisbon, tel. 01/690549, fax 01/388–8115).

Tourist offices can help with reservations and will provide lists of the local hostelries without charge (except in Lisbon). Few international chains have hotels in Portugal.

Aparthotels, with double rooms, bath, and kitchenette, are to be found in the main resorts and are good value. Villas can be rented by the week or longer in the Algarve from various agents. Among the better-run complexes are the Luz Bay Club and Luz Ocean Club, at Luz near Lagos, whose well-designed villas have daily maid service.

Camping Camping has become increasingly popular in Portugal in recent years, and there are now more than 150 campsites throughout the country offering a wide range of facilities. The best equipped have markets, swimming pools, and tennis courts. For additional information, contact **Federação Portuguesa de Campismo** (Av. 5 Outubro 15-3, 1000 Lisbon, tel. 01/315–2715).

Ratings Highly recommended lodgings are indicated by a star ★.

Category	All Areas*
Very Expensive	over 40,000$00
Expensive	20,000$00–40,000$00
Moderate	14,000$00–20,000$00
Inexpensive	under 14,000$00

*Prices are for two people in a double room, based on high-season rates, including tax and service.

Tipping In Portugal, modest tips are usually the rule. Service is included in bills at hotels and most restaurants. In luxury hotels, give the porter who carries your luggage 200$00; in less expensive establishments, 100$00. If the maid brings your breakfast, give her 100$00 a day or 500$00 for a stay of a week. If you regularly dine in the hotel, give between 500$00 and 1,000$00 to your waiter at the end of your stay, somewhat less to the wine waiter if you order wine with every meal. Otherwise tip 5%–10% on restaurant bills, except at inexpensive establishments, where you may just leave any coins given in change. Taxi drivers get 10%; cinema and theater ushers who seat you, 20$00 to 50$00; train and airport porters, 100$00 per bag; service-station attendants, 10$00–20$00 for gas, 20$00–50$00 for checking tires and cleaning windshields; hairdressers, around 10%.

Lisbon

Arriving and Departing

By Plane Lisbon's Portela Airport is only about 20 minutes from the city by car or taxi. The airport is small, but has been recently modernized; for information, tel. 01/802060.

Between the There is a special bus service every 15 minutes, 7:30 AM–10 PM, from
Airport and outside the airport into the city center called the *Linha Verde* (Green
Downtown Line; 250$00). Taxis here are so cheap, however, that visitors would be wise to take one straight to their destination. The cost into Lisbon is about 1,500$00–2,000$00, and to Estoril or Sintra, 6,000$00. There are no trains or subways between the airport and the city, but there are car-rental desks.

By Train International trains from Paris and Madrid arrive at Santa Apolonia Station (tel. 01/888–4025), just east of the city center. There is a tourist office at the station and plenty of taxis and porters, but no car-rental firms. The Linha Verde bus also runs from here into the center.

Getting Around

Lisbon is a hilly city, and the sidewalks are paved with cobblestones, so walking can be tiring, even when you're wearing comfortable shoes. Fortunately, Lisbon's tram service is one of the best in Europe and buses go all over the city. A **Tourist Pass** for unlimited rides on the tram or bus costs 350$00 (420$00 June–Sept.) for 24 hours, 1,900$00 for a week, or 1,350$00 for four days; it can be purchased at the Cais do Sodré Station and other terminals.

By Tram and Buses and trams operate from 6 AM to midnight. Try tram routes 13,
Bus 24, 28, 29, and 30 for an inexpensive tour of the city; buses nos. 52 and 53 cross the Tagus bridge. There's a flat fare of 140$00.

By Subway The subway, called the Metropolitano, operates from 6:30 AM to 1 AM; it is modern and efficient but covers a limited route. If you use it, watch out for pickpockets during rush hour. Tickets cost 65$00.

By Taxi Taxis can be easily recognized by a lighted sign on green roofs. There are ranks in the main squares, and you can hail a cruising vehicle, though this can be difficult late at night. Taxis are metered and take up to four passengers at no extra charge. Rates start at 250$00, with an extra charge for luggage.

By Ferry Ferries cross the Tagus river from the Fluvial terminal, adjacent to Praça do Comércio, to the suburb of Cacilhas, famous for its fish restaurants; it's a 10-minute crossing and costs 85$00 (daily 7 AM–9:30 PM). Alternatively, ferries from the quay at Cais do Sodré to Cacilhas run all night.

Important Addresses and Numbers

Tourist The main Lisbon tourist office (tel. 01/346–3314 or 01/346–3643) is
Information located in the Palacio Foz, Praça dos Restauradores, at the Baixa
end of the Avenida da Liberdade, the main artery of the city; open
daily 9–8. The tourist office at Lisbon airport (tel. 01/849–4323 or
01/849–3689) is open daily 9–midnight.

Embassies **U.S.** (Av. Forças Armadas, tel. 01/726–6600); **Canadian** (Av. da
Liberdade 144-3, tel. 01/347–4892); **U.K.** (Rua S. Domingos à Lapa
37, tel. 01/396–1191).

Emergencies **SOS Emergencies** (tel. 115). **Police** (tel. 01/3466141). **Ambulance** (tel.
01/301–7777). **Fire Brigade** (tel. 01/606060). **Doctor:** British Hospital
(Rua Saraiva de Carvalho 49, tel. 01/395–5067). **Pharmacies:** open
weekdays 9–1, 3–7, Saturday 9–1; consult notice on door for nearest
one open on weekends or after hours, or call tel. 118 for additional
listings.

Travel **American Express Star** (c/o Top Tours, Av. Duque de Loule 108, tel.
Agencies and fax 01/315–5877). **Marcus & Harting** (Rossío 45–50, tel. 01/346–
9271). **Wagons-Lits** (Av. da Liberdade 103, tel. 01/342–6434 or 01/
346–3872). **Viagens Rawes** (Travessa do Corpo Santo 15, tel. 01/347–
4089).

Guided Tours

Orientation Various companies organize half-day tours of Lisbon and environs
Tours and also full-day trips to more distant places of interest. Those listed
and below are reliable and offer similar trips and prices. Reservations
Excursions can be made through any travel agent or hotel. A half-day tour of
Lisbon will cost about 4,500$00. A full- day trip north to Obidos,
Nazaré, and Fatima will run about 12,000$00, as will a full day east
on the "Roman Route" to Évora and Monsaraz. Companies are **RN
Gray Line Tours** (Av. Fontes Pereira de Melo 14–12°, tel. 01/
577523); **Capristanos** (Av. Duque de Loulé 47, tel. 01/543580);
Citirama (Av. Praia da Vitoria, 12–b, tel. 01/352–2594); and **Top
Tours** (Rua Luciano Cordeiro 116, tel. 01/352–0028).

Personal Contact the main Lisbon tourist office (*see* Important Addresses
Guides and Numbers, *above*). Beware of unauthorized guides who will approach you at popular attractions and try to "guide" you to a particular shop or restaurant. Another source is the Syndicate of Guide
Interpreters (Rua do Telhal 4, tel. 01/346–7170), or you can ask at
your hotel; the front desk may have a list of bilingual guides.

Exploring Lisbon

North of the river Tagus estuary, spread out over a string of hills,
Portugal's capital presents unending treats for the eye. Its wide
boulevards are bordered by black-and-white mosaic sidewalks made
up of tiny cobblestones called *calçada*. Modern, pastel-colored
apartment blocks vie for attention with Art Nouveau houses faced
with decorative tiles. Winding, hilly streets provide scores of
miradouros, natural vantage points that offer spectacular views of
the river and city.

Lisbon is not easily explored on foot. The steep inclines of many
streets present a tough challenge to the casual tourist, and places
that appear to be close to one another on a map are sometimes on
different levels. Yet the effort is worthwhile—judicious use of

trams, a funicular railway, and the majestic city-center elevator make walking tours enjoyable even on the hottest summer day.

With a population of around a million, Lisbon is a small capital by European standards. Its center stretches north from the spacious Praça do Comércio, one of the largest riverside squares in Europe, to the Rossío, a smaller square lined by shops and sidewalk cafés. This district is known as the Baixa (Lower Town), and it is one of the earliest examples of town planning on a large scale. The grid of parallel streets between the two squares was built after an earthquake and tidal wave destroyed much of the city in 1755. The Alfama, the old Moorish quarter that survived the earthquake, lies just east of the Baixa, while Belém, where many royal palaces and museums are, is about 5 kilometers (3 miles) west.

Numbers in the margin correspond to points of interest on the Lisbon map.

Castelo de São Jorge and the Alfama

The Moors, who imposed their rule on most of the southern Iberian Peninsula during the 8th century, left their mark on Lisbon in many ways. The most visible examples are undoubtedly the imposing castle, set on one of the city's highest hills; and the Alfama, a district of narrow, twisting streets that wind their way up toward the castle. The best way to tour this area of Lisbon is to take a taxi to the castle and walk down.

❶ Although the **Castelo de São Jorge** (St. George's Castle) is Moorish in construction, it stands on the site of a fortification used by the Visigoths in the 5th century. Today its idyllic atmosphere is disturbed only by the shrieks of the many peacocks that strut through the well-tended grounds, which are also home to swans, turkeys, ducks, ravens, and other birds. The castle walls enclose the ruins of a Muslim palace that was the residence of the kings of Portugal until the 16th century; there is also a small village with a surviving church, a few simple houses, and souvenir shops. Panoramic views of Lisbon can be seen from the walls, but visitors should take care, because the footing is uneven and slippery. *Admission free. Open Apr.–Sept., daily 9–9; Oct.–Mar., daily 9–7.*

❷ After leaving the castle by its impressive gate, wander down through the warren of streets that make up the **Alfama**. This jumble of whitewashed houses, with their flower-laden balconies and red-tile roofs, rests on foundations of dense bedrock. It's a notorious place for getting lost in, but it's relatively compact and you'll keep coming upon the same main squares and streets. Find your way to the Largo Rodrigues de Freitas, a street to the east of the castle, **❸** then take a look at the **Museu da Marioneta** (Puppet Museum) at No. 19A (Admission: 300$00. Open Tues.–Sun. 10–1 and 2–6). From there head south along the Rua de São Tomé to the Largo das Portas **❹** do Sol, where you'll find the **Museu de Artes Decorativas** (Museum of Decorative Arts) in the 17th-century mansion housing the Fundaçaõ Ricardo Espirito Santo. More than 20 workshops teach rare handicrafts—bookbinding, ormulu, carving, and cabinetmaking. The museum is closed for long-term restoration, but there are guided tours of the mansion and workshops; inquire at the tourist office.

❺ Head southwest past the Largo de Santa Luzia along the Rua do Limoeiro, which eventually becomes the Rua Augusto Rosa. This route takes you past the **Sé** (cathedral), founded in 1150, to commemorate the defeat of the Moors three years earlier. The Sé has an austere Romanesque interior enlivened by a splendid 13th-century cloister. *Largo da Sé. Admission to cathedral free, cloister 120$00. Open daily 8:30–noon and 2–6.*

Lisbon

Alfama, **2**
Castelo de São Jorge, **1**
Elevador da Glória, **9**
Elevador de Santa Justa, **14**
Fundaçao Calouste Gulbenkian , **8**

Igreja do Carmo, **13**
Igreja de São Roque, **11**
Largo do Chiado, **12**
Museu de Artes Decorativas, **4**
Museu da Marioneta, **3**

Parque Eduardo VII, **7**
Rossío, **6**
Sé, **5**
Solar do Vinho do Porto, **10**

Continue northwest from the cathedral along the Rua de Santo António da Sé, turn left along the Rua da Conceiçao, then right and north up the Rua Augusta. A 10-minute stroll along this street takes you through the **Baixa,** which is also one of Lisbon's main shopping and banking districts. Semipedestrianized, this old-fashioned area boasts a small crafts market, some of the best shoe shops in Europe, glittering jewelry stores, and a host of delicatessens selling anything from game birds to *queijo da serra*—a delicious mountain cheese from the Serra da Estrela range north of Lisbon.

Avenida da Liberdade
6 Rua Augusta leads into the **Rossío** (officially Praça Dom Pedro IV), Lisbon's principal square, which in turn opens on its northwestern end into the Praça dos Restauradores. This can be considered the beginning of modern Lisbon, for here the broad, tree-lined **Avenida da Liberdade** begins its northwesterly ascent, and ends just over 1.6 **7** kilometers (1 mile) away at the green expanses of the **Parque Eduardo VII.**

A leisurely stroll from the Praça dos Restauradores to the park takes about 45 minutes. As you make your way up the Avenida da Liberdade, you'll find several cafés at its southern end serving coffee and cool drinks. Most notable is the open-air *esplanada* (café), which faces the main post office on the right. You'll also pass through a pleasant mixture of ornate 19th-century architecture and Art Deco buildings from the '30s. In the park, rare flowers, trees, and shrubs thrive in the *estufa fria* (cold greenhouse) and the *estufa quente* (hot greenhouse). *Parque Eduardo VII. Admission: 75$00. Open winter, daily 9–5; summer, daily 9–6.*

Walk through the park to the northeast corner and then head north along the Avenida António Augusto de Aguiar. A 15-minute walk will bring you to the busy Praça de Espanha, to the right of which, in **8** the Parque de Palhava, is the renowned **Fundação Calouste Gulbenkian,** a cultural trust whose museum houses treasures collected by Armenian oil magnate Calouste Gulbenkian (1869–1955) and donated to the people of Portugal. There are superb examples of Greek and Roman coins, Persian carpets, Chinese porcelain, and paintings by such Old Masters as Rembrandt and Rubens, as well as impressionist and pre-Raphaelite works. *Ave. de Berna 45 tel. 01/795–0236. Admission: 200$00, free Sun. Open June–Sept., Tues., Thurs., Fri., and Sun. 10–5, Wed. and Sat. 2–7:30; Oct.–May, Tues.–Sun. 10–5; closed Mon. year-round.*

The complex also houses a good modern art museum (same times and price as the main museum) and two concert halls where music and ballet festivals are held during the winter and spring. Modestly priced tickets are available at the box office in the main building. Pick up an events brochure at the reception desk.

Bairro Alto
Lisbon's **Bairro Alto** (Upper Town) is largely made up of 18th- and 19th-century buildings that house an intriguing mixture of restaurants, theaters, nightclubs, churches, bars, and antiques shops. The **9** best way to start a tour of this area is via the **Elevador da Glória** (funicular railway), located on the western side of Avenida da Liberdade by the Praça dos Restauradores. The trip takes about a minute and drops passengers at the São Pedro de Alcăntara miradouro, a viewpoint that looks toward the castle and the Alfama (Cost: 140$00. Open 7 AM–midnight).

10 Across the street from the miradouro is the **Solar do Vinho do Porto** (Port Wine Institute), where, in its cozy, clublike lounge, visitors can sample more than 300 types and vintages of Portugal's most famous beverage—from the extra-dry white varieties to the older ruby-red vintages. *Rua S. Pedro de Alcãntara 45, tel. 01/342–3307. Admission free. Prices of tastings vary, starting at 160$00. Open Mon.–Sat. 10–10.*

From the institute, turn right and walk down Rua de São Pedro de Aleântara. On your left is the Largo Trindade Coelho, site of the highly decorative **Igreja de São Roque** (Church of São Roque). The church is best known for the flamboyant 18th-century **Capela de São João Baptista** (Chapel of St. John the Baptist), but it is nonetheless a showpiece in its own right. Adjoining the church is the **Museu de Arte Sacra** (Museum of Sacred Art). *Church open daily 8:30–6. Museum admission: 150$00. Open Tues.–Sun. 10–5.*

Continue south down Rua de São Pedro de Alcântara until you reach the **Largo do Chiado** on your left. The Chiado, once Lisbon's chic shopping district, was badly damaged by a fire in August 1988, but it still houses some of the city's most fashionable department stores.

Time Out The Chiado's wood-paneled coffee shops attract tourists and locals alike; the most popular of these is the **Brasileira**, which features a life-size statue of Fernando Pessoa, Portugal's national poet, at one of the sidewalk tables. *Rua Garrett 120, tel. 01/3469541. Closed Sun. Inexpensive.*

North of the Chiado, on the Largo do Carmo, lies the partially ruined **Igreja do Carmo** (Carmo Church), one of the few older structures in the area to have survived the 1755 earthquake. Today its sacristy houses an **archaeological museum.** *Museu Arqueologico. Largo do Carmo. Admission: 300$00. Open Oct.–Mar., Mon.–Sat. 10–1 and 2–5; Apr.–Sept., Mon.–Sat. 10–6.*

Return directly to the Praça dos Restauradores via the nearby **Elevador de Santa Justa** (the Santa Justa elevator), which is enclosed in a Gothic tower created by Raul Mesnier, the Portuguese protégé of Gustave Eiffel. *Cost: 140$00. Open 7 AM–midnight.*

Numbers in the margin correspond to points of interest on the Belém map.

Belém To see the best examples of that uniquely Portuguese, late-Gothic architecture known as Manueline, head for Belém, at the far southwestern edge of Lisbon. If you are traveling in a group of three or four, taxis are the cheapest means of transportation; otherwise take a No. 15, 16, or 17 tram from the Praça do Comércio for a more scenic, if bumpier, journey.

Trams Nos. 15 and 16 stop directly outside the **Mosteiro dos Jerónimos,** (Jerónimos Monastery), in the Praça do Império. This impressive structure was conceived and planned by King Manuel I at the beginning of the 16th century to honor the discoveries of Vasco da Gama. Construction began in 1502, and was largely financed by treasures brought back from the so-called *descobrimentos*—the "discoveries" made by the Portuguese in Africa, Asia, and South America. Don't miss the stunning double cloister with its arches and pillars heavily sculpted with marine motifs. *Admission to church free, cloisters: 400$00. Open June–Sept., Tues.–Sun. 10–6:30; Oct.–May, Tues.–Sun. 10–1 and 2:30–5.*

The **Museu de Marinha** (Maritime Museum) is at the west end of the monastery. Its huge collection reflects Portugal's long seafaring tradition, and exhibits range from early maps, model ships, and nav-

Monumento
dos Desco-
brimentos, **17**

Mosteiro dos
Jerónimos, **15**

Museu de
Marinha, **16**

Museu Nacional
do Coches, **19**

Palácio
da Ajuda, **20**

Torre de
Belém, **18**

Belém

N

R. Tristao Vaz

Av. da Ilha da Madeira

R. Gonçalves Zarco

Jardim
Botânico

Calçada do Galvão

Calçada da Ajuda

Av. do Restelo

Pr. de
Damão

Pr. de
Dio

R. Dom Fr. de Almeida

Pr. de
Malaca

Pr. Dr. A.
da Amha

R. dos Jerónimos

Jardim
Tropical

R. de Belém

R.Dom Fr. de Almeida

R. de São Fr. Xavier

Av. da Torre de Belém

R. Bartolomeu Dias

Rua de Belém

Pr. Afonso
de
Albuquerque

R. da
Junqueira

Pr. do
Império

Av. da India

Av. Marginal

Tagus River

0   1/4 mile
0   1/4 km

---

igational instruments to entire fishing boats and royal barges. *Admission: 300$00, free Sun. Open Tues.–Sun. 10–5.*

Time Out   There are a number of small restaurants and inexpensive cafés close to the monastery on Rua de Belém. Stop for coffee at the **Fabrica dos Pasteis de Belém** (the Belém Pastry Factory) to sample the delicious custard pastries served hot with cinammon and powdered sugar. *Rua de Belém 86–88.*

---

① Across from the monastery at the water's edge stands the **Monumento dos Descobrimentos**, a tall, white angular slab. Built in 1960, this modern tribute to the seafaring explorers stands on what was the departure point of many of their voyages. An interesting mosaic, surrounded by an intricate wave pattern of black-and-white stones, lies at the foot. Take the elevator to the top for river views. *Admission: 275$00. Open Tues.–Sun. 9:30–7.*

⑱ A 15-minute walk west of the monument brings you to the **Torre de Belém** (the Belém Tower), another fine example of Manueline architecture with openwork balconies, loggia, and domed turrets. Although it was built in the early 16th century on an island in the middle of the river Tagus, today the tower stands near the north bank—the river's course has changed over the centuries. *Av. de India. Admission: 400$00 June–Sept.; 250$00 Oct.–May. Open June–Sept., Tues.–Sun. 10–6:30; Oct.–May, Tues.–Sun. 10–1 and 2:30–5.*

⑲ Away from the Tagus and east of the monastery, on the Praça Afonso de Albuquerque, is the **Museu Nacional do Coches** (National Coach Museum), which houses one of the largest collections of coaches in the world. The oldest vehicle on display was made for Philip II of Spain in the late 16th century, but the most stunning exhibits are three golden Baroque coaches made in Rome for King John V in 1716. *Admission: June–Sept. 400$00, Oct.–May 250$00; free Sun. Open June–Sept., Tues.–Sun. 10–1 and 2:30–6:30; Oct.– May, Tues.–Sun. 10–1 and 2:30–5:30.*

㉐ Head north of the coach museum on Calçada da Ajuda to the **Palácio da Ajuda** (Ajuda Palace). Once a royal residence, this impressive building now contains a collection of 18th- and 19th-century paintings, furniture, and tapestries. *Largo da Ajuda. Admission: 250$00; free Sun. 10–2. Guided tours arranged on request. Open Thurs.–Tues. 10–5. Closed Wed.*

Off the Beaten Track

North of the city in the suburb of São Domingos de Benfica is one of the most beautiful private houses in the capital. The **Palácio da Fronteira,** built in the late 17th century, contains splendid reception rooms with 18th-century figurative tiles, contemporary furniture, and paintings, but it is the gardens that are unique. A long rectangular water tank is backed by 17th-century tiled panels of heroic-size knights on prancing horses. Stone steps at either side lead to a terraced walk above, between pyramid pavilions roofed with copper-colored tiles. This beautiful conceit is surrounded by a topiary garden, statuary, fountains, and terraces. *Largo de S. Domingos de Benfica 1. Admission to gardens: 300$00; to palace and gardens: 1,000$00. Open Mon.–Fri. for 1-hr. tour, but visitors must arrive between 10:45 and 11 AM. On Sat. a full guided tour costs 1,000$00 (gardens) or 1,500$00 (palace and gardens); arrive at 10:45 AM.*

In the wealthy district of Lapa, halfway between the Bairro Alto and Belém, stands the **Museu de Arte Antiga** (Ancient Art Museum) in a 17th-century palace, the only museum in Lisbon to rival the Gulbenkian. It has a beautifully displayed collection of Portuguese art, mainly 15th–19th century. The highlight is undoubtedly the *Saint Vincent Altarpiece* (1467–1470), masterpiece of Nuno Gonçalves. Its six panels show Vincent, the patron saint of Lisbon, receiving the homage of king, court, and citizens, and 60 different figures can be identified, including Henry the Navigator himself. *Rua das Janelas Verdes 95, Lapa. Admission 250$00, free Sun. 10–1. Open Tues.–Sun. 10–1 and 2–5. Tram No. 19 from Praça do Comércio.*

Shopping

Shopping Districts Since the fire that destroyed much of the Chiado in 1988, an extensive reconstruction project has made good progress. Another important shopping area is in the **Baixa** quarter (between the Rossío and the river Tagus). On Avenida Engeneiro Duarte Pacheco, west of Parque Eduardo VII, the blue-and-pink towers of the **Amoreiras,** a huge modern shopping center (open daily 9 AM–11 PM), dominate the Lisbon skyline.

Flea Markets The **Feira da Ladra** (flea market) is held on Tuesday morning and all day Saturday in the Largo de Santa Clara behind the Church of São Vicente, near the Alfama district.

Gift Ideas
Leather Goods Fine leather handbags and luggage are sold at **Galeão** (Rua Augusta 190) and at **Casa Canada** (Rua Augusta 232). Shoe stores abound in Lisbon, but they may have a limited selection of large sizes (the Portuguese have relatively small feet); the better shops can make shoes

to order, on short notice, however. Leather gloves can be purchased at a variety of specialty shops on Rua do Carmo and Rua Aurea.

Handicrafts **Viúva Lamego** (Largo do Intendente 25) has the largest selection of tiles and pottery, while **Fabrica Sant'Ana** (Rua do Alecrim 95), in the Bairro Alto, sells wonderful handpainted ceramics and tiles. For embroidered goods and baskets, try **Casa Regional da Ilha Verde** (Rua Paiva de Andrade 4) or **Tito Cunha** (Rua Aurea 286). **Casa Quintão** (Rua Ivens 30), probably has the largest selection of *arraiolos* rugs, the traditional, hand-embroidered Portuguese carpets, in town. For fine porcelain, visit **Vista Alegre** (Largo do Chiado 18), and for handcrafted pottery, try **Casa Ribeiro da Silva** (Trav. Fieus de Deus 69, Bairro Alto).

Jewelry and **Antonio da Silva** (Praça Luis de Camoes 40) at the top of the Chiado,
Antiques specializes in antique silver and jewelry, as does **Barreto e Goncalves** (Rua das Portas de Santo Antão 17). Most of the antiques shops are along the Rua Escola Politecnica, Rua Dom Pedro IV, Rua da Misericordia, and Rua do Alecrim. Look for characteristic Portuguese gold- and silver-filigree work at **Sarmento** (Rua do Ouro 251) in the Baixa.

Dining

For details and price-category definitions, *see* Dining in Staying in Portugal, *above*.

Very **António Clara.** Housed in an attractive Art Nouveau building in
Expensive north Lisbon, this restaurant serves French and international dishes with a flourish in an elegant room with a decorated ceiling, heavy draperies, and huge chandelier. The menu is seasonal and there's a fine wine list. *Av. República 38, tel. 01/796–6380. Reservations required. AE, DC, MC, V. Closed Sun.*

★ **Aviz.** One of the best and classiest restaurants in Lisbon, Aviz has a Belle Epoque decor—even the rest rooms are impressive—and an excellent French and international menu. The restaurant is hidden on a side street off the Baixa's Rua Garrett. *Rua Serpa Pinto 12, tel. 01/342–8391. Reservations required. AE, DC, MC, V. Closed Sat. lunch and Sun.*

Casa da Comida. Imaginative French and Portuguese fare is served in a former private house surrounding a flower-filled patio. *Travessa das Amoreiras 1, tel. 01/685376. Reservations advised. AE, DC, MC, V. Closed Sat. lunch and Sun.*

Gambrinus. One of Lisbon's older restaurants, Gambrinus is noted for its fish and shellfish. Enter through an inconspicuous door on a busy street to one of the restaurant's numerous small dining rooms. *Rua Portas de S. Antão 23–25, tel. 01/346–8974. Reservations advised. AE, DC, MC, V.*

Tagide. Delicious Portuguese food and wine are served in this fine old tile house that looks out over the Baixa and river. Try to secure a window table. *Largo Academia das Belas Artes 18–20, tel. 01/342–0720. Reservations advised. AE, DC, MC, V. Closed weekends.*

★ **Tavares Rico.** Superb food, an excellent wine list, and a handsome Edwardian dining room have made this one of Lisbon's most famous restaurants. *Rua Misericórdia 37, tel. 01/342–1112. Reservations required. AE, DC, MC, V. Closed Sat. and Sun. lunch.*

Expensive **Alcântara.** Ranked among the trendier, newer restaurants, this one
★ is smartly decorated with a glorious modernistic design. The menu features traditional Portuguese specialties and a good wine list. *Rua Maria Luisa Holstein 15, tel. 363–7176. Reservations advised. AE, DC, MC, V. Open until 2 AM for dinner only. Closed Tues.*

Michel. Innovative French cooking and an intimate atmosphere can be found in this attractive restaurant in the village within the walls of St. George's Castle. *Largo S. Cruz do Castelo 5, tel. 01/886–4338. Reservations advised. AE, DC, MC, V. Closed Sat. lunch and Sun.*

Solmar. This large restaurant near the Rossío, Lisbon's main square, is best known for its seafood and shellfish, but try the wild boar or venison in season. *Rua Portas de S. Antão 108, tel. 01/342–3371. AE, DC, MC, V.*

Sua Excêlencia. There's no written menu in this cozy little restaurant in the Lapa district. The English-speaking owner will personally talk you through the outstanding Portuguese dishes that are offered. *Rua do Conde 42, tel. 01/603614. Reservations advised. MC, V. Closed Wed., Sept., and weekend lunch.*

Moderate **Brasuca.** A comfortable Brazilian restaurant set in an old mansion on the edge of the Bairro Alto, the Brasuca serves a splendid *caipirinha* (rum cocktail), grills, and spicy meat stews. *Rua João Pereira da Rosa 7, tel. 01/342–8542. Reservations advised. AE, DC, MC, V. Closed Mon.*

★ **Cervejaria Trindade.** Prepare for hearty Portuguese cuisine served in a 19th-century Lisbon beer hall–restaurant adorned with colorful tiles. It specializes in seafood and is open until 2 AM. *Rua Nova da Trindade 20, tel. 01/346–3506. AE, DC, MC, V.*

Comida de Santo. The Brazilian-style food is excellent, and is served in an attractive, bohemian atmosphere. Lively Brazilian music ensures that this restaurant is packed during later hours. *Rua Engenheiro Miguel Pais 39, tel. 01/396–3339. AE, DC, MC, V.*

Inexpensive **Bonjardim.** Known as *Rei dos Frangos* (the King of Chickens), the Bonjardim specializes in the spit-roasted variety. Just off the Restauradores, it gets very crowded at peak hours; you may have to wait in line for a table, but it's worth it. *Travesssa S. Antão 11, tel. 01/342–7424. AE, DC, MC, V.*

Farah's Tandoori. A small simple place, Farah's is known as one of the best and friendliest Indian restaurants in Lisbon. All the curries, which are served with Indian bread, are sure bets for a good meal. *Rua de Sant'Ana a Lapa 73, tel. 01/609219. MC, V. Closed Tues.*

Lodging

Lisbon has a good array of accommodations in all price categories, ranging from major international chain hotels to charming little family-run establishments. During peak season reservations should be made well in advance. For details and price-category definitions, *see* Lodging in Staying in Portugal, *above.*

Very Expensive **Lisboa Sheraton and Towers.** This is a typical Sheraton hotel with a huge newly refurbished reception area and medium-size rooms. The 79 deluxe units in the Towers section, which has a separate reception desk in the lobby and a private lounge, are about the same size but are more luxuriously appointed. The hotel is centrally located and is just across the street from a large shopping center. Parking is difficult. *Rua Latino Coelho 1, tel. 01/575757, fax 01/547164. 384 rooms with bath. Facilities: restaurant, grill, bar, garage, pool, health club and sauna. AE, DC, MC, V.*

Meridien Lisboa. The rooms in this luxury hotel are a bit on the small side, but they are soundproofed and attractively decorated; the front ones overlook the Parque Eduardo VII, which means the hotel is ideally situated for downtown exploration. *Rua Castilho 149, tel.*

01/690400, fax 01/693231. 331 rooms with bath. Facilities: health club with sauna, shops, garage. AE, DC, MC, V.

★ **Ritz Lisboa.** One of the finest hotels in Europe, this Intercontinental is renowned for its excellent service. The large, handsomely decorated guest rooms all have terraces, and the elegantly appointed public rooms feature tapestries, antique reproductions, and fine paintings. The best rooms are in the front overlooking Parque Eduardo VII. There's convenient dining at the outstanding restaurant and grill. *Rua Rodrigo da Fonseca 88, tel. 01/692020, fax 01/691783. 304 rooms with bath. Facilities: 2 restaurants, bar, shops, garage. AE, DC, MC, V.*

Expensive **Lisboa Penta.** The city's largest hotel, the Penta is about midway be-
★ tween the airport and the city center, next to the U.S. Embassy and close to the Gulbenkian Foundation (shuttle-bus service to the center is available). The rooms are rather small, but each one has a terrace. *Av. dos Combatentes, tel. 01/726–5050, fax 01/726–4281. 592 rooms with bath. Facilities: restaurant, grill, 3 bars, outdoor pool, health club and solarium, squash courts, shops, garage. AE, DC, MC, V.*

Sofitel Lisboa. Tasteful modern architecture and a convenient location make this new hotel a favorite with the international business community. Moderately sized guest rooms are comfortably furnished in pleasing colors. The small elegant lobby is bordered by an intimate piano bar. *Av. da Liberdade 123–125, tel. 01/342–9202, fax 01/342–9222. 170 rooms with bath. Facilities: restaurant, bar, garage. AE, DC, MC, V.*

★ **Tivoli Lisboa.** Located on Lisbon's main avenue, this comfortable, well-run establishment has a large public area furnished with inviting armchairs and sofas. The guest rooms are all pleasant, but the ones in the rear are quieter. There's also a good restaurant, and the grill on the top floor has wonderful views of the city and the Tagus. *Av. da Liberdade 185, tel. 01/353–0182, fax 01/579461. 326 rooms with bath. Facilities: restaurant, grill, bar, outdoor pool, tennis courts, shops, garage. AE, DC, MC, V.*

Moderate **Albergaria Senhora do Monte.** The rooms in this unpretentious little
★ hotel, located in the oldest part of town near St. George's Castle, have terraces that offer some of the loveliest views of Lisbon, especially at night when the castle and Carmo ruins in the middle distance are softly illuminated. The top-floor grill has a picture window. *Calçada do Monte 39, tel. 01/886–6002, fax 01/877783. 28 rooms with bath. Facilities: restaurant, bar, grill. AE, DC, MC, V.*

Fenix. Located at the top of Avenida da Liberdade, this hotel with elegant interiors has largish guest rooms—many with fine views—and a pleasant first-floor lounge. Its restaurant serves good Portuguese food. *Praça Marquês de Pombal 8, tel. 01/386–2121, fax 01/386–0131. 119 rooms with bath. Facilities: restaurant, bar, parking. AE, DC, MC, V.*

Florida. This centrally located hotel has a pleasant atmosphere, guest rooms with marble-clad bathrooms, and is handily placed for downtown restaurants. *Rua Duque de Palmela 32, tel. 01/576145, fax 01/543584. 112 rooms with bath. Facilities: bar. AE, DC, MC, V.*

Novotel Lisboa. There's an attentive staff and a quiet, welcoming atmosphere at this pleasant, modern hotel near the U.S. Embassy. The public rooms are spacious and all benefit from recent renovation; guest rooms are spruce and comfortably equipped. *Av. Jose Malhoa, tel. 01/726–6022, fax 01/726–6496. 246 rooms with bath. Facilities: restaurant, bar, pool, garage. AE, MC, V.*

★ **York House.** A former 17th-century convent, this residencia is set in a shady garden, up a long flight of steps, near the Museu de Arte

Antiga (Museum of Ancient Art). It has a good restaurant, and full or half board is available. Book well in advance: This atmospheric place is small and has a loyal following. *Rua das Janelas Verdes 32, tel. 01/396–2435, fax 01/397–2793. 54 rooms with bath. Facilities: restaurant, bar, garden. AE, DC, MC, V.*

Inexpensive **Hotel Borges.** In the heart of the Chiado district, convenient for shopping, this dependable, old-fashioned hotel has good service and a charm that transcends its limited facilities. You're also only a step away from the famous Brasileira café, an excellent breakfast spot. *Rua Garrett 108–110, tel. 01/346–1951, fax 01/342–6617. Facilities: breakfast room, bar. MC, V.*

Flamingo. Another good-value choice near the top of the Avenida da Liberdade, this hotel has a friendly staff and pleasant guest rooms, though the ones in the front tend to be noisy. There's a pay parking lot right next door, which is a bonus in this busy area. *Rua Castilho 41, tel. 01/386–2191, fax 01/386–1216. 39 rooms with bath. Facilities: restaurant, bar, shops. AE, DC, MC, V.*

The Arts

Two local newspaper supplements provide listings of music, theater, ballet, film, and other entertainment in Lisbon: *Sete,* published on Wednesdays, and *Sabado,* published on Fridays.

Plays are performed in Portuguese at the **Teatro Nacional de D. Maria II** (Praça Dom Pedro IV, tel. 01/342–2210) year-round except in July. Classical music, opera, and ballet are presented in the beautiful **Teatro Nacional de Ópera de São Carlos** (Rua Serpa Pinto 9, tel. 01/346–5914). Classical music and ballet are also staged from autumn to summer by the **Fundação Calouste Gulbenkian** (Av. Berna 45, tel. 01/793–5131). Of particular interest is the annual Early Music and Baroque Festival held in churches and museums around Lisbon every spring; for details *see* the Gulbenkian Foundation in Exploring Lisbon, *above.* Otherwise, there are free recitals held regularly at the Bairro Alto churches of Carmo and São Roque, and at the Se (cathedral). The **Nova Filarmonica,** one of Portugal's national orchestras, performs concerts around the country throughout the year; consult local papers for details.

Nightlife

The most popular night spots in Lisbon are the *adegas tipicas* (wine cellars), where customers dine on Portuguese specialties, drink wine, and listen to the haunting melodies of *fado* (traditional Portuguese folk music). Most of these establishments are scattered throughout the Alfama and Bairro Alto districts. Try the **Senhor Vinho** (Rua do Meio a Lapa 18, tel. 01/397–7456. Closed Sun.), **Lisboa à Noite** (Rua das Gaveas 69, tel. 01/346–8557. Closed Sun.), or the **Machado** (Rua do Norte 91, tel. 01/346–0095. Closed Mon.). The singing starts at 10 PM, and reservations are advised. Lisbon's top spot for live jazz is **The Hot Clube** (Praça da Alegria 39, tel. 01/346–7369. Closed Sun.–Mon.), where sessions don't usually begin until 11 PM.

Bars and Discos The main areas for bars and discos are the Bairro Alto or along Avenida 24 de Julho, northwest of Cais do Sodre station. In the former, **Cena de Copas** (Rua da Barroca 103–105, tel. 01/347–3372) is still loud and fashionable, while **Pavilhão Chines** (Rua Dom Pedro V 89, tel. 01/342–4729) is decorated with extraordinary bric-a-brac from around the world. Along Avenida 24 de Julho, current favorites include **Café 24 de Julho** (no. 114) and **Café Central** (no. 110), while the nearby **Kremlin** disco (Rua Escadinhas da Praia 5, tel. 01/608768) continues to attract the trendiest Lisboetas. **Trumps** (Rua Imprensa Nacional 104b, tel. 01/397–1059) is the city's biggest gay disco; **Memorial** (Rua Gustavo Sequeira 42, tel. 01/396–8891) is popular with both lesbian and gay visitors.

The Portuguese Riviera, Sintra, and Queluz

Just 32 kilometers (20 miles) west of Lisbon lies a stretch of coastline known as the Portuguese Riviera. Over the years, the casino at Estoril and the beaches, both there and in Cascais, have provided playgrounds for the wealthy, as well as homes for expatriates and exiled European royalty.

Beaches here differ both in quality and cleanliness. Some display the blue Council of Europe flag, which signals a high standard of unpolluted water and sands, but others leave much to be desired. The waters off Cascais and Estoril are calm, though sullied as a result of their proximity to the meeting of the sea and Lisbon's Tagus estuary. To the north, around Guincho's rocky promontory and the Praia de Maças coast, the Atlantic Ocean is often windswept and rough but provides good surfing and windsurfing.

To the north of Cascais and Estoril lie the lush, green mountains of Sintra and to the northeast, the historic town of Queluz, dominated by its 18th-century rococo palace and formal gardens. The villas, châteaus, and luxury *quintas* (country properties) of Sintra contrast notably with Cascais and Estoril, where life revolves around the sea. The entire region offers comprehensive sports facilities: golf courses, horseback riding, fishing, tennis, squash, swimming, water sports, grand prix racing, mountain climbing, and country walks.

Getting Around

The area is served by three main roads—the often congested four-lane coastal road (the N6 Avenida Marginal), the N117/N249 to Sintra, and the A5 expressway, which links Lisbon with Cascais. A commuter train leaves every 15 to 30 minutes from Cais do Sodré Station in Lisbon for the trip to Estoril and then to Cascais, four stops farther. The 30-minute-total journey affords splendid sea views as it hugs the shore. A one-way ticket costs 160$00. Trains from Lisbon's Rossío station run every quarter of an hour to Queluz (145$00), taking 20 minutes, and on to Sintra (155$00), which takes 40 minutes.

Guided Tours

Catur (Largo da Academia Nacional de Belas Artes 12, tel. 01/346–7974) offers a nine-hour excursion that takes in principal sites; it costs 12,000$00 and includes lunch. **Citirama Viagens e Turismo SA** (Av. Praia de Vitória 12-B, tel. 01/355–8567) offers a similar tour at a lower price. Both tours have daily departures.

The Portuguese Riviera, Sintra, and Queluz

Tourist Information

Cascais (Viscount Luz 14–r/c, tel. 01/486–8204).
Estoril (Arcadas do Parque, tel. 01/468–0113).
Sintra (Praça da Republica 3, tel. 01/923–3919).

Exploring the Portuguese Riviera, Sintra, and Queluz

Leave Lisbon by car via the Estrada Marginal highway (following signs for Cascais/Estoril) and take the curving coastal route (the N6) to Estoril. Both Estoril and Cascais are favored residential areas; thanks to their special microclimate, they boast milder winters than does nearby Lisbon.

Estoril   **Estoril** is filled with grand homes and gardens, and many of its large mansions date from the last century when it was a favorite with the European aristocracy. Portugal's jet-set resort is expensive, with little in the way of sights. People-watching is always a satisfying pastime, and one of the best places for it is on the **Tamariz esplanade,** especially from an alfresco restaurant. A palm-studded coastline, plush accommodations, sports facilities, and restaurants are among Estoril's other attractions, but it is perhaps best known for its **casino,** an excellent gambling hall and night spot that includes a restaurant, bar, theater, and art gallery. A major open-air handicrafts and ceramics fair is held each summer (July–September), and many summer music concerts and ballets are staged here during the annual Estoril Festival in July and August (a schedule is available at the tourist office).

Time Out The luxurious **Hotel Palácio** (*see* Dining and Lodging, *below*), in Parque do Estoril, is worth a visit simply to take tea in one of its ample salons. During World War II, it was an espionage center where the Germans and Allies kept watch on each other in neutral Portugal, and where exiled European courts waited out the war.

Cascais Cascais lies less than 3.2 kilometers (2 miles) west of Estoril. A pretty but heavily developed tourist resort, it is packed with shopping centers, restaurants, cinemas, and hotels. The three beaches are small and crowded, and in summer, parking is a real headache. Even so, there are still some sights worth seeing, including the **Igreja de Nossa Senhora da Assunção** (Church of Our Lady of the Assumption), which contains paintings by Portuguese artist Josefa de Óbidos. *Largo da Assunção. Admission free. Open daily 9–1 and 5–8.*

Opposite the church is one of the entrances to the **Parque do Marachal Carmona** (open daily 9–6), in which there's a shallow lake, a café, and a small zoo. Walk through the park to its southern edge and you'll find the **Museu Conde de Castro Guimarães** (Museum of the Count of Castro Guimarães), a large stately home set in spacious grounds. It houses some good paintings, ceramics, furniture, and archaeological artifacts excavated locally. *Estrada da Boca do Inferno. Admission: 150$00, free Sun. Open Tues.–Sun. 11–12:30 and 2–5.*

Continue west from the museum along the coastal road (N247), and it's less than 2 kilometers (about 1¼ miles), in the direction of Guincho beach, to the notorious **Boca do Inferno**, or Hell's Mouth. This rugged section of coastline is made up of numerous grottoes; visitors are able to see the full impact of the sea as it pounds into the walkways and viewing platforms. A path leads down to secluded spots on the rocks below.

From the Boca do Inferno, it's a scenic 9-kilometer (5½-mile) drive along the coastal road to the superb rocky surfing beach at **Guincho.** From here, the road cuts inland and continues north to the turnoff for **Cabo da Roca,** whose windswept reaches and lighthouse mark continental Europe's westernmost landfall.

Back on the main road, turn into the hills at the end of Praia do Guincho (Guincho Beach). This is the beginning of the **Serra de Sintra** (Sintra Mountains), and here, at **Capuchos,** you can visit the tiny friary, built in 1560 by Franciscan monks. The 12 diminutive cells, hacked out of solid rock, are lined with cork for warmth and insulation—hence the nickname the "Cork Convent." *Admission 200$00. Open June–Sept., daily 10–6; Oct.–May, daily 10–5.*

Return to the main road and follow its winding course through the village of **Penedo,** which offers terrific views of the sea and the surrounding mountains, until you reach the world-renowned gardens of **Monserrate,** 5½ kilometers (3 miles) from the superb Palácio de Seteais hotel (*see below*). This botanical wonderland was laid out by Scottish gardeners in the mid-1800s and is the site of an exotic and architecturally extravagant domed Moorish-style palace (closed to visitors). In addition to a dazzling array of tree and plant species, the gardens house one of the largest collections of fern varieties in the world. *Admission: 200$00. Open June–Sept., daily 10–6; Oct.–May, daily 10–5.*

Time Out Follow signs to Seteais and stop for a meal at the **Palácio de Seteais** (Seteais Palace), built by a Dutchman in the 18th century. Now a luxury hotel (*see* Dining and Lodging, *below*), the Seteais has an excellent but expensive restaurant, and its stately rooms are decorated with delicate wall and ceiling frescoes. *Tel. 01/923–3200. AE, DC, MC, V.*

Sintra From here, the main road gently winds down toward **Sintra.** One of Portugal's oldest towns, Sintra is full of art, history, and architecture, and has ties to a host of famous and eccentric Englishmen, among them the poet Lord Byron, who stayed here in 1809 and started to write his epic, *Childe Harold.* At the center of the **Old Town** near the Hotel Tivoli Sintra stands the 14th-century **Palácio Nacional de Sintra** (Sintra Palace). This twin-chimneyed building, a combination of Moorish and Gothic architectural styles, was once the summer residence of the House of Avis, Portugal's royal line. Today it's a museum that houses some fine examples of mozarabic *azulejos* (handpainted tiles). *Admission: June–Sept. 400$00, Oct.– May 200$00, free Sun. morning. Open Thurs.–Tue. 10–1 and 2–5.*

If you stand on the steps of the palace and look up toward the Sintra Mountains, you can spot the 8th-century ruins of the **Castelo dos Mouros** (Moors' Castle), which defied hundreds of invaders until it was finally conquered by Dom Afonso Henriques in 1147. For a closer look, follow the steep, partially cobbled road that leads up to the ruins; or, if you're a romantic, rent one of the horse-drawn carriages outside the palace for the trip. From the castle's serrated walls, you can see why its Moorish architects chose the site: The panoramic views falling away on all sides are breathtaking. *Estrada da Pena. Admission free. Open June–Sept., daily 10–6; Oct.–May, daily 10–5.*

Farther up the same road you'll reach the **Palácio Nacional de Pena** (the Pena Palace), a Wagnerian-style extravaganza built by the King Consort Ferdinand Saxe-Coburg in 1840. It is a cauldron of clashing styles, from Arabian to Victorian, and was home to the final kings of Portugal, the last of whom went into exile in 1910 after a republican revolt. The nucleus of the palace is a convent commissioned by Dom Fernando, consort to Queen Dona Maria II. The palace is surrounded by a splendid park filled with a lush variety of trees and flowers brought from every corner of the Portuguese empire by Dom Fernando in the 1840s. *Admission for guided tour: June–Sept. 400$00, Oct.–May 200$00, free Sun. 10–2. Open Tues.– Sun. 10–5.*

Back in downtown Sintra, the **Museu do Brinquedo** (Toy Museum) houses an enjoyable collection of dolls and traditional toys from this region of Portugal. *Largo Latino Coelho 9. Admission: 200$00. Open Tues.–Sun. 10–12:30 and 2:30–5.*

If you're in the area on the second or fourth Sunday of each month, visit the **Feira de Sintra** (Sintra Fair) in the nearby village of **São Pedro de Sintra,** 2 kilometers (about 1¼ miles) to the south. This is one of the best-known fairs in the country.

Queluz From the fairgrounds, drive past a gas station to the traffic circle and take N249 back toward Lisbon, keeping an eye out for the left turnoff to **Queluz.** As soon as you swing off the main road, you'll be confronted by the magnificent **Palácio Nacional de Queluz** (Queluz Palace). Partially inspired by Versailles, this salmon-pink rococo palace was begun by Dom Pedro III in 1747 and took 40 years to complete. The formal landscaping and waterways that surround it are the work of the French designer Jean-Baptiste Robillon. Restored after a disastrous fire in 1934, the palace is used today for formal banquets, music festivals, and as accommodations for visiting heads of state. Visitors may walk through the elegant state rooms, including the Music Salon, the Hall of the Ambassadors, and the mirrored Throne Room with its crystal chandeliers and gilt trimmings. The 14-kilometer (8½-mile) drive back to Lisbon takes about 20 minutes. *Admission: June–Sept. 400$00, Oct.–May 200$00. Open Wed.–Mon. 10–1 and 2–5.*

Dining and Lodging

For details and price-category definitions, *see* Dining and Lodging in Staying in Portugal, *above*.

Cascais **João Padeiro.** This restaurant, located in the town center, serves the
Dining best sole in the region—and other seafood as well—amid cheerful surroundings. *Rua Visconde da Luz 12, tel. 01/483–0232. AE, DC, MC, V. Closed Tues. Expensive.*

Beira Mar. This well-established restaurant behind the fish market has a wide variety of fish and meat dishes. The atmosphere is comfortable and unpretentious. *Rua das Flores 6, tel. 01/483–0152. AE, DC, MC, V. Closed Tues. Moderate.*

Dining and **Hotel Albatroz.** Situated on a rocky outcrop, this attractive old
Lodging house, converted from an aristocrat's summer residence, is the most
★ luxurious of Cascais's hotels. Though it's been extended and modernized, most recently in 1993, it has retained its character, with charming bedrooms and a pleasant terrace bar. The restaurant boasts superior views of the sea and over the coast toward Lisbon; it specializes in fish dishes. *Rua Frederico Arouca 100, tel. 01/483–2821, fax 01/484–4827. 40 rooms with bath. Facilities: bar, restaurant, pool, garage. Restaurant reservations required. AE, DC, MC, V. Very Expensive (hotel), Expensive (restaurant).*

★ **Restaurante/Estalagem Muchaxo.** The sound of the sea accompanies your meal at this restaurant nestled on the rocks overlooking Guincho beach. It is one of the region's oldest and best-known eating places, and the Portuguese and fish specialties here are beautifully cooked and presented. There are also 24 rooms available for guests. *Praia do Guincho, tel. 01/487–0221, fax 01/487–0444. Restaurant reservations advised. AE, DC, MC, V. Moderate (inn), Expensive (restaurant).*

Estoril **A Choupana.** Just outside town, toward Lisbon, this restaurant
Dining overlooks the beach. You can sample high-quality fresh fish, seafood, and other local dishes and dance to a live band until 2 AM. *Estrada Marginal, São João de Estoril, tel. 01/468–3099. Reservations advised. AE, DC, MC, V. Expensive.*

The English Bar. This mock-Tudor-style establishment serves good international cuisine in friendly, comfortable surroundings. There are beautiful views over the beach to Cascais and an excellent wine list. *Av. Marginal, Monte Estoril, tel. 01/468–0413. Reservations advised. AE, DC, MC, V. Closed Sun. Moderate.*

★ **Restaurant Grill Four Seasons.** This elegant and famous establishment, in the Hotel Palácio (*see below*), serves buffets around the garden pool in summer and seeks perfection in the freshest food. *Parque do Estoril, tel. 01/468–0400. Reservations advised. AE, DC, MC, V. Expensive–Very Expensive.*

Restaurante Frolic. The Frolic is a friendly restaurant/bar next to Hotel Palácio. Try the delectable cakes. *Av. Clotilde, tel. 01/468–1219. AE, DC, MC, V. Closed Sun. Inexpensive.*

Dining and **Hotel Palácio.** During World War II, exiled European courts came to
Lodging this luxurious hotel to wait out the war. A complete renovation pro-
★ gram over the last few years has put a contemporary sparkle into its
elegant interior. The pastel rooms are decorated in Regency style
and the hotel contains one of Portugal's most famous restaurants
(*see above*). It's a two-minute walk to the beach, and golfers can use
the hotel's membership to tee off at the Estoril golf course. *Parque
do Estoril, tel. 01/468-0400, fax 01/468-4867. 162 rooms with bath.
Facilities: outdoor pool, restaurant, bar, gardens, sports facilities.
AE, DC, MC, V. Expensive-Very Expensive.*

Queluz **Restaurante de Cozinha Velha.** This restaurant was formerly the
Dining great kitchens of the adjoining Queluz Palace and is magnificently
★ decorated with an open fireplace that dominates the room. There
are some fine wines in the cellar to go with the traditional Portuguese cooking—a spicy *cataplana* (stew) of salmon, monkfish,
clams, and shrimp is just one superb main course. *Palácio Nacional
de Queluz, tel. 01/435-0232. Reservations advised. AE, DC, MC, V.
Expensive.*

Sintra **Restaurant Regional.** Excellent Portuguese regional cooking sets
Dining this restaurant apart from most of its competitors in Sintra—ask
about the local dishes. It's very central, close to the Camera Municipal (Town Hall). *Trav. do Municipio 1, tel. 01/923-4444. Reservations advised. AE, MC, V. Moderate.*
Solar de São Pedro. Highly recommended by its habitués, this restaurant specializes in Portuguese and French country cooking. Its
English-speaking host adds to the warm and friendly atmosphere.
*Largo da Feira 12, São Pedro de Sintra, tel. 01/923-1860. Reserva-
tions advised. AE, DC, MC, V. Closed Wed. Moderate.*

Lodging **Palácio de Seteais.** This luxurious former palace set in its own
grounds a kilometer from Sintra (*see* Exploring the Portuguese Riviera, *above*) houses a splendid restaurant. *Rua Barbosa do Bocage 8,
tel. 01/923-3200, fax 01/923-4277, 30 rooms with bath. Facilities:
restaurant, bar, pool, tennis courts, gardens, horseback riding,
parking. AE, DC, MC, V. Very Expensive.*
Tivoli Sintra. Right in the center of Sintra, the Tivoli has excellent
views over the valleys and its own welcoming restaurant, the
Monserrate. Prices are lower in the winter. *Praça da República, tel.
01/923-3505, fax 01/923-1572. 75 rooms with bath. Facilities: restaurant, bar, garage. AE, DC, MC, V. Expensive.*
Quinta das Sequóias. This lovely old antique-filled manor house (formerly known as the Casa da Tapada) is down a side road just 1 km (⅔
mile) beyond the Palácio de Seteais and makes an excellent touring
base. Its small size means advance booking is essential. *Apartado 4,
2710, tel. and fax 01/923-0342. 6 rooms with bath. Facilities: bar,
dinner on request, breakfast served, gardens, pool, sauna, parking.
AE, DC, MC, V. Moderate-Expensive.*

The Algarve

The Algarve, Portugal's southernmost holiday resort, encompasses
some 240 kilometers (150 miles) of sun-drenched coast below the
Serra de Monchique and the Serra do Caldeirão. It is the top destination for foreign visitors to Portugal. During the past three decades, this area, indelibly marked by centuries of Arab occupation,
has been heavily developed in an effort to create a playground for
international sun worshipers. Well known by Europeans as a holiday
center of clean, sandy beaches; championship golf courses; and local
color, this section of Portugal is only now being discovered by Amer-

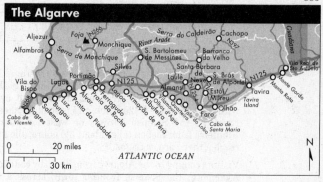

The Algarve

ATLANTIC OCEAN

0 — 20 miles
0 — 30 km

N

icans. Although some parts of the coastline have been seriously overbuilt, there are still a few picturesque fishing villages and secluded beaches to leaven the concentration of hotels, casinos, disco nightclubs, and sports facilities.

Getting Around

Faro, the capital of the Algarve, is only 45 minutes from Lisbon by air. **TAP Air Portugal** has daily service from Lisbon, and there are frequent international flights to Faro from London, Frankfurt, and Brussels. There is also daily bus and rail service between Lisbon and the major towns in the Algarve; trips take 4–6 hours, depending on your destination. The trip by car from Lisbon to Faro or Portimão takes about 3–3½ hours.

The main east-west highway in the Algarve is the two-lane N125, which extends 165 kilometers (100 miles) from Vila Real de Santo António, on the Spanish border, to Vila do Bispo, north of Cabo de São Vicente. This road does not run right along the coast, but turn-offs to beachside destinations mentioned here are posted along the route. A few kilometers inland a trans-Algarve expressway is under construction. Local rail and bus services link most of the villages and towns in the Algarve, and organized guided bus tours of some of the more noteworthy villages and towns depart from Faro, Quarteira, Vilamoura, Albufeira, Portimão, and Lagos.

Tourist Information

Local tourist offices can be found in the following towns:

Albufeira (Rua 5 de Outubro, tel. 089/512144).
Armação de Pêrá (Av. Marginal, tel. 082/312145).
Faro (Airport, tel. 089/818582; Rua da Misericorida 8/12, tel. 089/803604; Rua Ataide de Oliveira 100, tel. 089/803667).
Lagos (Largo Marquês de Pombal, tel. 082/763031).
Loulé (Edifico do Castelo, tel. 089/63900).
Monte Gordo (Av. Marginal, tel. 081/44495).
Olhão (Largo da Lagoa, tel. 089/713936).
Portimão (Largo 1° de Dezembro, tel. 082/23695).
Praia da Rocha (Av. Tomás Cabreira, tel. 082/22290).
Quarteira (Av. Infante de Sagres, tel. 082/312217).
Sagres (Promontório de Sagres, tel. 082/64125).
Silves (Rua 25 de Abril, tel. 082/442255).
Tavira (Praça da República, tel. 081/22511).

Vila Real de Santo António (Praça Marquês de Pombal, tel. 081/ 44495; Frontier Tourist Post, tel. 081/43272).

Exploring the Algarve

To reach the Algarve from Lisbon, cross the Tagus bridge and take the A2 toll road to Setúbal. Beyond here, the main IP1 (E1) highway runs via Alcácer-do-Sal, Grandola, and Ourique, eventually joining with the east–west N125. Albufeira is straight ahead; head east for Faro and the Spanish border, or west for Lagos. The trip to Albufeira from Lisbon takes about 3½ hours; allow another hour to reach either Faro or Lagos.

Visitors coming to the Algarve from Spain by car can now drive from Ayamonte, the Spanish frontier town, across a new suspension bridge over the River Guadiana to **Vila Real de Santo António**. This showcase of 18th-century Portuguese town planning is set out on a grid pattern, similar to the Baixa section of Lisbon, though there isn't really much to see here. A few miles west of this border town, pine woods and orchards break up the flat landscape around **Monte Gordo,** a town of brightly colored houses and extensive tourist facilities, including hotels, a casino, nightclubs, and discos. The long, flat stretch of beach here is steeply sloped, and swimmers quickly find themselves in deep water.

Tavira Continuing west past the excellent **Praia Verde** and **Manta Rota** beaches, you come to **Tavira,** which many people think the prettiest town in the Algarve. Situated at the mouth of the River Gilão, it is famous for its figs, cobbled old town streets, a seven-arched (and much-restored) Roman bridge, old Moorish defense walls, and interesting churches. There are good sand beaches on nearby **Tavira Island,** which is reached by ferry (May–mid-Oct., every 30–60 min; 130$00 round-trip) from the jetty at Quatro Águas, 2 km (1¼ mi) east of the town center, a 10-minute drive. Another 22 kilometers (14 miles) west lies the fishing port and market town of **Olhão.** Founded in the 18th century, Olhão is notable for its North African–style architecture—cube-shaped whitewashed buildings—and the best food markets in the Algarve, found down on the harborside. There are also ferries (July–Aug.; 9 a day, Sept.–June, 3–4 a day; 200$00 round-trip) from Olhão to the nearby sandy islands of **Armona** and **Culatra,** which both have excellent beaches.

Faro From Olhão it's just 9 kilometers (6 miles) to **Faro,** the provincial capital of the Algarve. When this city was finally taken by Afonso III in 1249, it ended the Arab domination of Portugal, and remnants of the medieval walls and gates that surrounded the city then can still be seen in the older district, the **Cidade Velha.** One of the gates, the **Arco da Vila,** with a white marble statue of St. Thomas Aquinas in a niche at the top, leads to the grand Largo de Sé. The Gothic **Sé** here has a stunning interior decorated with 17th-century tiles (Admission free. Open weekdays 10–noon, Sat. at 5 for service, Sun. 8–1). There are also several fascinating museums in Faro, notably the **Museu do Etnografia Regional** (Algarve Ethnographic Museum) on Rua do Pé da Cruz, with good historical and folkloric displays (Admission: 120$00. Open weekdays 9–noon and 2–6); and the **Museu Maritimo** (Maritime Museum) on Rua Comunidade Lusiada near the yacht basin, next to the Hotel Eva (Admission: 120$00. Open Mon.–Sat. 10–11 and 2:30–4:30). The **Museu Municipal** (Municipal Museum) on Largo Afonso III has a section dedicated to the Roman remains found at Milreu (Admission: 120$00. Open Mon.– Sat. 9:30–noon and 2–5). But best of the sights is really the **Capela**

dos Ossos (Chapel of Bones) in the Igreja do Carmo on Largo do Carmo, decorated with human bones taken from the monks' cemetery (Admission: 50$00. Open Mon.–Sat. 10–1 and 3–5). There's a large sand beach on Faro Island, the **Praia de Faro,** which is connected to land by road (bus No. 16 from the harbor gardens); or take the ferry from the jetty below the old town to the beach at Farol on Culatra island (*see* Olhão, *above*).

About 9 kilometers (6 miles) north of Faro, a road branches east from N2 to the village of **Estói,** where you'll find the 18th-century **Palácio do Visconde de Estói.** The palace itself is closed to the public, but visitors can stroll around the gardens (Admission free. Open Tues.–Sat. 9–12:30 and 2–5:30). Close by, a 10-minute walk down the main road, are the extensive 1st-century **Roman ruins** at **Milreu** (Admission free. Open Tues.–Sun. 10–12:30 and 2–5). Another worthwhile excursion from Faro is to **Loulé,** about 17 kilometers (10 miles) away; take N125–4 northwest from N125. This little market town in the hills was once a Moorish stronghold and is now best known for its crafts and the highly decorative white chimney stacks on its houses. You can usually see coppersmiths and leather craftsmen toiling in their workshops along the narrow streets.

You can also visit the restored ruins of a medieval Saracen **castle** (within which is the town's museum) and the recently restored 13th-century parish church nearby, which is decorated with handsome tiles and wood carvings and features an unusual wrought-iron pulpit. *Castle and museum at Largo D. Pedro I: Admission free. Open daily 9–12:30 and 2:30–5. Church at Largo Pr. C. da Silva: Admission free. Open Mon.–Sat. 9–12 and 2–5:30.*

Back on N125, in the town of **Almansil,** stop at the 18th-century Baroque chapel of **São Lourenço,** with its blue-and-white tile panels and intricate gilt work. The cottages next to the church have been transformed into a lovely art gallery. As you continue west, look for turnoffs to the south for the beach resort areas of Vale do Lobo, Quarteira, and Vilamoura. The tennis center at **Vale do Lobo,** one of the Algarve's earliest resort developments, is among the best in Europe. **Quarteira,** once a quiet fishing village, is now a bustling high-rise resort, with golf courses and tennis courts, as well as an excellent beach. **Vilamoura** is one of the most highly developed resort centers in the Algarve: There's a large yacht marina, several golf courses, a major tennis center, one of Europe's largest shooting centers, and other sports facilities, as well as modern luxury hotels and a casino.

Albufeira   If you continue on N125, you'll soon arrive at the **Albufeira** turnoff. At one time an attractive fishing village, the town has long since mushroomed into the Algarve's largest and busiest resort, too brash for many. Even the dried-up riverbed has been turned into a parking lot. But with its steep, narrow streets and hundreds of whitewashed houses snuggled on the slopes of nearby hills, Albufeira still has a distinctly Moorish flavor. Its attractions include the lively fish market (held daily); interesting rock formations, caves, and grottoes along the beach; and plenty of night life. Just about 14 kilometers (8 miles) west of the town is the erstwhile fishing village of **Armação de Pêra,** now a bustling resort that claims the largest beach in the Algarve. From here you can hop aboard one of the local boats that take sightseers on cruises to the caves and grottoes along the shore.

At **Lagoa,** a market town known for its wine, turn north to **Silves,** 8 kilometers (5 miles) up the N124-1. Once the Moorish capital of the Algarve, Silves lost its importance after it was almost completely destroyed by the 1755 earthquake. The 12th-century sandstone **fortress** (admission free, always open) together with its impressive parapets, was restored in 1835 and still dominates the town. Below the fortress stands the 12th–13th-century **Santa Maria da Sé** (Cathedral of Saint Mary), which was built upon the site of a Moorish mosque. (Admission free. Open daily 8:30–1 and 2:30–6.) The excellent **Museu Arqueologia** below the cathedral in Rua das Portas de Loulé features artifacts from prehistoric times through the 17th century. (Admission: 300$00. Open Mon.–Sat. 10–12:30 and 2–6). The **Cruz de Portugal,** a 16th-century limestone cross, stands on the road to Messines.

Portimão   Return to N125 and continue to **Portimão,** the most important fishing port in the Algarve. There was a settlement here at the mouth of the river Arade even before the Romans arrived. This is a cheerful, busy town and a good center for shopping. Although the colorful fishing boats now unload their catch at a modern terminal across the river, the open-air restaurants along the quay are a pleasant place to sample the local specialty: charcoal-grilled sardines with chewy fresh bread and red wine. Across the bridge, in **Ferragudo,** are the ruins of a 16th-century castle, and 3 kilometers (about 2 miles) south of Portimão is **Praia da Rocha.** Now dominated by high-rise apartments and hotels, this was the first resort in the Algarve to be developed; it can still boast of an excellent beach, made all the more interesting by a series of huge, colored rocks that have been worn by sea and wind into strange shapes.

For an entirely different aspect of the Algarve, you can drive north from Portimão on routes N124 and 266 about 24 kilometers (15 miles) into the hills of the Serra de Monchique to the highly attractive spa town of **Caldas de Monchique.** Besides its charming 19th-century buildings, in a shady wood, there's a theraputic spa that dates from Roman times, though the current spa building is resolutely modern.

Return to N125 to continue your route west through **Lagos,** a busy fishing port with an attractive harbor and some startling cove beaches in the vicinity that attract a bustling holiday crowd. Lagos has a venerable history—Henry the Navigator maintained a base here—most evident in its grand surviving **city walls** and the 17th-century harborside fort at **Ponta da Bandeira.** (Admission: 200$00. Open Tues.–Sat. 10–1 and 2–6, Sun. 10–1.) The 18th-century Baroque **Igreja de Santo António** (Church of Santo António), off Rua General Alberto Silveira, is renowned for its gilt, carved wood, and exuberant decoration. An amusing regional museum is alongside. (Admission 200$00. Open Tues–Sun. 9:30–12:30 and 2–5.) Lagos is the western terminus of the coastal railway that runs from Vila Real de Santo António.

Sagres   After Lagos, the terrain becomes more rugged as you approach the windy headland at **Sagres,** where some think Prince Henry established his famous school of navigation in the 15th century—the first of its kind. Take N268 south from N125 at Vila do Bispo to the promontory hundreds of feet above the sea. From here, a small road leads through the tunnel-like entrance to the **Forteleza de Sagres** (Sagres Fortress), which was rebuilt in the 17th century. The **Rosa dos Ventos** (compass rose), made of stone and earth, was uncovered in this century in the courtyard, but is believed by some to have been used by Prince Henry in his calculations. The **Graça Chapel** is also located inside the fortress (which is always open), as is a building believed to have been Henry's house.

There are spectacular views from here and from **Cabo de São Vicente** (Cape St. Vincent) 6 kilometers (4 miles) to the west, where most historians think Henry the Navigator founded his school. This point, the most southwesterly tip of the European continent, where the landmass juts into the rough waters of the Atlantic, is sometimes called *O Fim do Mundo,* "the end of the world." Admiral Nelson defeated the Spanish off this cape in 1797. The lighthouse at Cabo de São Vicente is said to have the strongest reflectors in Europe, casting a beam 96 kilometers (60 miles) out to sea; it is open to the public. From this breathtaking spot, where Pedro Álvares Cabral, Vasco da Gama, Ferdinand Magellan, and other great explorers learned their craft 500 years ago, you can return to the sybaritic diversions of the modern Algarve along N125.

Dining and Lodging

For details and price-category definitions, *see* Dining and Lodging in Staying in Portugal, *above.* In winter, particularly Jan.–Mar., hotel rates are discounted by as much as 40%.

Albufeira
Dining

A Ruina. A rustic restaurant on the beach, built on several levels, this is the place for good views and charcoal-grilled seafood. *Cais Herculano, Praia dos Pescadores, tel. 089/512094. No credit cards. Moderate.*

Cabaz da Praia. This long-established restaurant has a spectacular view of the main beach from its cliffside terrace. There's fine French-Portuguese cooking here—fish soup, imaginatively served fish, and chicken with seafood. *Praça Miguel Bombarda 7, tel. 089/512137. Reservations recommended. AE, MC, V. Closed Sat. lunch and Thur. Moderate.*

Dining and Lodging
★

Estalagem Vila Joya. One of the most luxurious restaurants and elegant inns in the Algarve has 14 Moorish-style rooms and three suites if you'd like to stay the night. The French-inspired food in the restaurant continues to impress. The inn is 4 km (2½ mi) west of town. *Praia da Galé, tel. 089/591839, fax 089/591201. Facilities: restaurant (reservations and jacket and tie required), bar, pool. AE, DC. Very Expensive.*

Lodging
★

Sheraton Algarve. This is a new luxury hotel in a spectacular cliff-top location 8 km (5 mi) east of town, overlooking the sea and with access to some of the Algarve's finest beaches. The architecture and decor blend traditional Moorish features with modern elements. *Praia da Falésia, tel. 089/501999, fax 089/501950. 215 rooms with bath. Facilities: restaurant, bar, 9-hole golf course, indoor and outdoor pools, gym, sauna, tennis. AE, DC, MC, V. Expensive–Very Expensive.*

Hotel Cerro Alagoa. On the hill above town, this hotel is the most comfortable of Albufeira's central lodgings. The smartly decorated guest rooms have private balconies; be sure to request a sea view. It's a 10-minute walk to the town center, but there's a courtesy bus service to both Albufeira and the local beaches. *Via Rápida, tel. 089/588261, fax 089/588262. 310 rooms with bath. Facilities: restaurant, bar, outdoor pool, fitness center, shop, garage. AE, DC, MC, V. Expensive.*

Alvor
Lodging
★

Golfe da Penina. This impressive golf hotel, on 360 well-maintained, secluded acres off the main road between Portimão and Lagos, has spacious, elegant public rooms, pleasant guest rooms, and offers attentive service. Most of the guest rooms have balconies; those in the back of the hotel face the Serra de Monchique and have the best views. The excellent golf courses were designed by Henry Cotton, and golf greens fees are waived for hotel guests. There's a special bus to the beach. *Montes de Alvor, tel. 082/415415, fax 082/415000. 192 rooms with bath. Facilities: 18-hole championship golf course plus two 9-hole courses, tennis, Olympic-sized pool, private beach, small private airport, sauna, billiards room, shops, water sports, horseback riding. AE, DC, MC, V. Very Expensive.*

Aparthotel Torralta. This large complex, offering good-size rooms, fully equipped kitchens, and daily maid service, is a very good value and has exceptionally low winter rates. *Praia de Alvor, tel. 082/459211, fax 082/459171. 655 units. Facilities: pools, horseback riding, restaurants, discos, tennis, shop. AE, DC, MC, V. Moderate.*

Armação de Pêra
Dining

A Santola. This well-established, delightful restaurant overlooking the beach is probably the best in town. There is a varied menu, but the seafood is especially good. Try the excellent cataplana. *Largo da Fortaleza, tel. 082/312332. Reservations advised. MC, V. Closed Sun. Moderate.*

Lodging

Hotel Garbe. The bar, lounge, and restaurant—all with terraces that provide unhindered views of the sea—maximize the superb location of this squat, white, central hotel. Rooms are modern and smartly furnished, and steps lead from the hotel to the beach below. *Av. Marginal, tel. 082/312194, fax 082/312087. 140 rooms with bath. Facilities: restaurant, bar, coffee shop, pool, garage. AE, DC, MC, V. Expensive.*

Caldas de Monchique
Dining and Lodging

Albergaria do Lageado. This hotel right in the center of the spa town, has rather small guest rooms, though they're attractively furnished and some overlook the lush gardens. The traditionally tiled dining room serves good home cooking, and there's a terrace for summer dining. *Caldas de Monchique, tel. 082/92616. 19 rooms with bath. Facilities: dining room, lounge, pool, gardens. No credit cards. Closed Nov.–Apr. Inexpensive.*

Faro
Dining

Cidade Velha. Located in an 18th-century house within the walls of the Old City, this small, intimate restaurant serves excellent international cuisine. *Rua Domingos Guieiro 19, tel. 089/27145. Reservations advised. Closed Sun., lunch Sat. and June–Sept. MC, V. Expensive.*

Adega Nova. Traditional Portuguese dishes are served at massive wooden tables at this restaurant that has plenty of atmosphere. *Rua Francisco Barreto 24, tel. 089/813433. No credit cards. Moderate.*

Lodging

Hotel Eva. This well-appointed modern hotel block is on the main square overlooking the yacht basin. The best rooms face the sea, and there's a courtesy bus to the beach. *Av. da República 1, tel. 089/803354, fax 089/802304. 150 rooms with bath. Facilities: pool, restaurant, disco. AE, DC, MC, V. Moderate.*

Casa de Lumena. This 150-year-old Faro mansion has been tastefully converted into a small hotel. Each room has its own individual ambience, and the courtyard Grapevine Bar is a pleasant place for a drink. *Praça Alexandre Herculano 27, tel. 089/801990, fax 089/804019. 12 rooms with bath. Facilities: restaurant, courtyard bar. AE, DC, MC, V. Inexpensive.*

Lagos
Dining

Alpendre. This is one of the oldest and best restaurants in the Algarve. The service is leisurely and the food excellent: French-influenced dishes complement the local fish and shellfish. *Rua António Barbosa Viana 17, tel. 082/762705. Reservations advised. AE, MC, V. Expensive.*

★ **Dom Sebastião.** Portuguese cooking and charcoal-grilled specials and fish are the main attractions at this cheerful restaurant. It has a wide range of Portuguese aged wines. *Rua 25 de Abril 20, tel. 082/*

762795. Reservations advised. AE, DC, MC, V. Closed Sun. in winter. Moderate–Expensive.

Lodging
★
Hotel de Lagos. This modern hotel is attractively laid out at the eastern edge of the old town and is within easy walking distance of all the sights and restaurants. The terraced rooms overlook the pool or across the river to the coast, and tiling is used effectively throughout, even on table lamps and table tops. There is a regular courtesy bus to the beach, where the hotel has outstanding club facilities. *Rua Nova da Aldeia, tel. 082/769967, fax 082/769920. 317 rooms with bath. Facilities: restaurant, bar, health club, pool, volleyball, windsurfing, tennis, billiards, garage. AE, DC, MC, V. Expensive.*

Monchique
Dining
★
Restaurant Teresinha. Simply decorated, this modest restaurant serves good country cooking: Try the local ham or one of the chicken recipes. Desserts are outstanding. The terrace overlooks a lovely valley and the coastline. *Estrada da Foia, tel. 082/92392. MC, V. Closed Mon. Inexpensive.*

Dining and
Lodging
Estalagem Abrigo da Montanha. This pleasant inn, noted for its garden of magnolias and camellias, serves excellent regional dishes. It also has 6 bedrooms, for which you'll need an advance reservation. *Estrada da Foia, tel. 082/92131, fax 082/93660. 6 rooms with bath. AE, DC, MC, V. Moderate (restaurant), Inexpensive (inn).*

Monte Gordo
Dining
Mota. The Mota is a lively, unpretentious restaurant with a covered terrace, right on the sand. Noted for its seafood and regional cuisine, it has live music in the evenings. *On the beach at Monte Gordo, tel. 081/42650. Reservations not necessary. No credit cards. Inexpensive.*

Lodging
Alcazar. This is one of the most attractive hotels in town, with unusual architecture and interior design—the sinuous arches and low molded ceilings recall a cave interior or that of an Arab tent. *Rua de Ceuta 9, tel. 081/512184, fax 081/512242. 95 rooms with bath. Facilities: restaurant, bar, shops, pool. AE, DC, MC, V. Moderate.*
Vasco da Gama. This long, relatively low-lying hotel occupies a choice position on the extensive, sandy beach—rooms with sea views cost more but are worth the extra expense. The staff is friendly and helpful. *Av. Infante Dom Henrique, tel. 081/511321, fax 081/511622. 200 rooms with bath. Facilities: restaurant, pool, tennis, bowling, disco, water sports. AE, DC, MC, V. Moderate.*

Olhos d' Agua
Dining
La Cigale. Located 9 km (5 ½ mi) east of Albufeira, this restaurant—one of the best known in the Algarve—combines French and native Portuguese cuisine. *On the beach, tel. 089/501637. Reservations advised. DC, MC, V. Closed Dec., Jan., Feb. Expensive.*

Portimão
Dining
A Lanterna. This well-run restaurant is located just over the bridge at Parchal, on the Ferragudo side. Its specialty is duck, but try the exceptional fish soup or smoked fish. *Parchal, tel. 082/23948. Reservations advised. MC, V. Closed Sun. Moderate.*
A Vela. A pleasant restaurant decorated in Moorish fashion, A Vela has a spacious open kitchen that produces a varied selection of tasty Portuguese and international specialties. *Rua Dr. Manuel de Almeida 97, tel. 082/414016. Reservations advised in summer. AE, DC, MC, V. Closed Sun. Moderate.*

Praia da
Rocha
Dining
Safari. This lively Portuguese seafront restaurant has a distinctly African flavor. Seafood and delicious Angolan recipes are the specialties. *Rua António Feu, tel. 082/415540. Reservations advised. AE, DC, MC, V. Moderate.*

Lodging **Algarve.** This modern, luxurious hotel is perched on a cliff top. Decorated in Moorish style, it has good-size rooms and a large, attentive staff. Leisure facilities are particularly good here, and the beach is just a step away from the hotel. *Av. Tomás Cabreira, tel. 082/ 415001, fax 082/415999. 220 rooms with bath. Facilities: restaurant, grill, 2 pools, disco, tennis courts, health center, bar. AE, DC, MC, V. Very Expensive.*

Hotel Bela Vista. A small, tastefully decorated beachfront hotel with magnificent traditional tiles, Hotel Bela Vista is one of the most delightful accommodations on the Algarve. *Av. Tomás Cabreira, tel. 082/24055, fax 082/415369. 14 rooms with bath. Facilities: bar, terrace, live music in summer. Early reservations essential. AE, DC, MC, V. Expensive.*

Sagres **Pousada do Infante.** Housed in a sprawling, traditional-style, red-
Dining and tile-roof building, this pousada affords spectacular views of the sea
Lodging and craggy rock cliffs. The moderate-size rooms are well appointed
★ and have small balconies. The restaurant has excellent fresh fish, good desserts, and more marvelous sea views. *8650 Sagres, tel. 082/ 64222, fax 082/64225. 39 rooms with bath. Facilities: restaurant, bar, tennis, pool. AE, DC, MC, V. Expensive.*

Santa Barbara **Hotel Apartamento La Reserve.** This intimate luxury hotel in the
de Nexe hills, 10 kilometers (6 miles) inland from Faro and set within a 6-acre
Dining and park, offers high-class guest accommodations, including small
Lodging apartments with verandas and sea views. However, don't fail to eat in the restaurant, which serves elegant cuisine with a French accent; local game is a specialty, and the wine list is very good. *Santa Barbara de Nexe, 8000 Faro, tel. 089/90234 or 089/90474, fax 089/ 90402. 12 rooms with bath, 8 apartments. Facilities: restaurant, bar, pool, tennis. No credit cards. Dinner only; reservations required. Closed Tues. Very Expensive (restaurant and hotel).*

Vale do Lobo **Dona Filipa.** One of the best hotels in the Algarve, the Dona Filipa
Dining and has a lavish and striking interior, pleasant rooms, and first-rate
Lodging service. Set in extensive, beautifully landscaped grounds near the beach, the hotel houses a chic restaurant that offers an excellent international menu. Greens fees for the nearby 18-hole golf course are included in room rates. *Vale do Lobo/Almansil, tel. 089/394141, fax 089/394288. 147 rooms with bath. Facilities: golf, pool, restaurant, tennis center. AE, DC, MC, V. Very Expensive.*

Vilamoura **Hotel Dom Pedro.** Situated in the heart of this highly successful va-
Lodging cation complex, the Dom Pedro is close to the casino and not far from the beach. Each room is attractively furnished and has its own balcony. *Tel. 089/389650, fax 089/315482. 263 rooms with bath. AE, DC, MC, V. Expensive.*

Vila Real de **Caves do Guadiana.** Located in a large, old-fashioned building facing
Santo António the fishing docks, this restaurant is well known for its seafood and
Dining Portuguese specialties. *Av. República 90, tel. 081/44498. No reservations. DC, MC. Closed Thurs. Inexpensive.*

24 Romania

Romania is not an easy place to visit as a tourist, but it is perhaps the most beautiful country in Eastern Europe. Its natural tourist attractions are varied, from the summer resorts on the Black Sea coast to the winter ski resorts in the rugged Carpathian Mountains; but perhaps even more surprising are the numerous medieval towns and traditional rural villages that are among the most unspoiled and unchanged in Europe.

The overthrow of the Ceauşescu regime in December 1989 started a continuing process of reform toward a Western-style democracy and market economy. Shortages are easing, and the range of available goods and services is increasing, although rising prices have hit many Romanians hard. But the many problems and inefficiencies remaining from Ceauşescu's time that tourists may encounter are often outweighed by the traditional hospitality that the Romanian people are free to express since the 1989 revolution.

Comparable in size to the state of Oregon, Romania is made up of the provinces of Walachia, Moldavia, and Transylvania and borders the Ukraine, Moldova, Bulgaria, Serbia, and Hungary. With a population of 23 million, Romania is a "Latin Island" in a sea of Slavs and Magyars. Its people are the descendants of the Dacian tribe and of the Roman soldiers who garrisoned this easternmost province of the Roman Empire. Barbaric invasions, struggles against the Turks, the Austro-Hungarian domination of Transylvania, and a strong French cultural influence have endowed them with a rich heritage to add to a folk culture that survives to this day.

Bucharest, with its wide, tree-lined avenues, Arcul de Triumf, and lively café life, was once known as the Paris of the East. Transylvania, a region wrapped in myth, is home to a sizable minority of Hungarians and a small minority of Germans with their own folk traditions and distinctive building styles. This area has long been a favorite with tourists because of the real and fictional sites associated with Dracula. Many enchanting Orthodox monasteries, including some of medieval origin that sport colorful frescoes on their outside walls, characterize the remote and mountainous region of Moldavia.

To the northeast of Bucharest lies the Danube Delta, a watery wilderness populated by fishermen (many of Ukrainian origin) and visited by hundreds of rare bird species. The Carpathian mountain ranges, which form a crown in the center of the country, offer the double pleasure of skiing during the winter and hiking during the summer. The unattractive effects of industrialization are generally confined to the cities, with life in the countryside remaining picturesquely simple. Horse and cart is a popular means of transportation, horse-drawn plows a common sight, and folk costume everyday wear in the northern regions of Maramures and Bukovina.

Romania is a bargain for package tourists. Prepaid package holidays to ski, spa, and seaside resorts offer the best available standards at a very reasonable cost. Independent travelers, however, often pay much more overall for their visit and find wide variations in quality. The country is now in the throes of privatization of its state monopolies, including its tourism industry. Much chaos has resulted from restructuring, and visitors may experience continual changes in prices, amenities, and quality of services. Nevertheless, conditions for visitors are improving all the time. More and better restaurants, refreshment facilities, and shops are opening in many of the larger towns.

Romania

If you are traveling independently, you may wish to take some food supplies with you. Vegetarians are warned that there is a limited range of produce available, especially in winter. However, most towns now have private markets where local farmers sell produce at very reasonable prices. Bread is usually available in Bucharest (shop early!), but it is often hard to find in the smaller towns. Dairy products remain in short supply, though cheese can usually be found at peasant markets.

Visitors should use water purification tablets or boil their tap water, since hepatitis is a danger in Romania. Alternatively, drinking-water fountains in most towns provide natural spring water, and bottled mineral water is available in many restaurants. All visitors should bring an emergency supply of toilet paper, a full first-aid kit, a flashlight for poorly lit streets and corridors, and, in summer, insect repellent. Since medical facilities do not meet Western standards, it is best to take along your own vitamins and medication (including needles and syringes for injections).

Romania enjoyed a period of comparative prosperity during the 1970s, but it is currently the poorest country in Europe after Albania. Petty theft is a widespread problem, although the streets are fairly safe at night. Romanians still have limited experience in dealing with foreigners and are sometimes envious of Westerners' wealth. Their efforts on your behalf may charm you, but they could also be cheating you. Tips, gifts, and even bribes are often expected, but use discretion or you may be regarded as patronizing.

Tourists nowadays may roam much as they wish, and many enjoy "discovering" old churches and buildings, museums, and craft workshops, or wandering through the beautiful countryside.

Romania is likely to remain underexplored until its serious economic difficulties are resolved, but, in the meantime, the package tourist is still assured a good price, while the intrepid independent traveler will experience a part of Europe rich in tradition, one that has largely avoided the pressures and complexities of modern times.

Essential Information

Before You Go

When to Go Bucharest, like Paris, is at its best during the spring. The Black Sea resorts open in mid- to late May and close at the end of September. Winter ski resorts in the Carpathians are now well developed and increasingly popular, while the best time for touring the interior is late spring to fall.

Climate The Romanian climate is temperate and generally free of extremes, but snow as late as April is not unknown, and the lowlands can be very hot in midsummer.

The following are the average daily maximum and minimum temperatures for Bucharest.

Jan.	34F	1C	May	74F	23C	Sept.	78F	25C
	19	- 7		51	10		52	11
Feb.	38F	4C	June	81F	27C	Oct.	65F	18C
	23	- 5		57	14		43	6
Mar.	50F	10C	July	86F	30C	Nov.	49F	10C
	30	- 1		60	16		35	2
Apr.	64F	18C	Aug.	85F	30C	Dec.	39F	4C
	41	5		59	15		26	- 3

Currency   The unit of currency is the *leu* (plural *lei*). There are coins of 1, 3, 5, 10, 20, 50, and 100 lei. Banknotes come in denominations of 200, 500, 1,000, and 5,000 lei. The Romanian currency is expected to continue to drop sharply in value, causing frequent price rises; costs are therefore best calculated in hard currency. At press time (spring 1994), the official exchange rate was approximately 1,420 lei to the dollar and 2,120 to the pound sterling. The price of a pack of Western cigarettes rose from 450 lei in 1993 to 2,000 lei in 1994, but because of exchange-rate inflation, the "real" cost only rose from 93¢ to $1.40. Prices of basic items, artificially low from Communism, are gradually being increased.

Because of high inflation, check on your arrival that low-denomination notes and coins are still in use. There is no longer an obligatory currency exchange, and an increasing number of licensed exchange offices (*casă de schimb*) have been competing to offer rates far higher than official rates, almost equal to those available on the illegal and risky black market. Retain your exchange receipts, as you may need to prove your money was changed legally. Except for air tickets, foreigners must pay in lei by law, though hard currency is widely accepted. The financial police (*garda financiară*) are useful if you experience difficulty. You may not import or export lei.

Credit Cards   Major credit cards are welcome in a number of major hotels and their restaurants, but are not accepted in most shops and independent restaurants.

What It Will Cost   Prices of hotels and restaurants can be as high as those in Western Europe as far as the independent traveler is concerned. Those with prepaid arrangements, however, may enjoy reductions of about 30% in some cases.

Sample Prices   Museum admission usually costs less than 50¢, a bottle of imported beer in a restaurant around $1.50; a bottle of good local wine in a top restaurant around $6. A one-mile taxi ride will cost around 60¢.

Visas   All visitors to Romania must have a visa, obtainable from Romanian embassies abroad or at border stations (for those with prepaid arrangements, the cost of the visa is often included). Send the visa fee ($31), a stamped, self-addressed envelope, and your passport to the relevant office: in the **United States,** Embassy of Romania, 1607 23rd Street, NW, Washington DC 20008, tel. 202/387–6902, fax 202/232–4748, or Romanian Consulate 573–577 Third Avenue, New York, NY 10016, tel. 212/682–9122, fax 212/972–8463; in **Canada,** Romanian Consulate, 111 Peter Street, Suite 530, Toronto, Ontario M5V 2H1, tel. 416/585–5802, fax 416/585–4798; Romanian Consulate, 1111 Street Urbain, Suite M-09, Montreal, Quebec H2Z 1Y6, tel. 514/876–1793, fax 514/876–1796; Embassy of Romania, 655 Rideau St., Ottawa, Ontario K1N 6A3, tel. 613/789–3709, fax 613/789–4365; in the **United Kingdom,** Consular Section of the Romanian Embassy, 4 Palace Green, London W8, tel. 071/937–9667, fax 071/937–8069.

Customs   You may bring in 2 cameras, 20 rolls of film, 1 small movie camera, 2 rolls of movie film, a typewriter, binoculars, a radio/tape recorder, a small television set, a bicycle, a stroller for a child, 200 cigarettes, 2 liters of liquor, and 4 of wine or beer. Gifts are permitted, though you may be charged duty for some electronic goods. Camping and sports equipment may be imported freely. Declare video cameras, personal computers, and expensive jewelry on arrival.

Souvenirs and gifts may be taken out of Romania, provided their value does not exceed 50% of the currency you have changed legally—so keep your receipts. In addition, you may export five paintings from the Plastic Artists' Union.

There is an increasing number of tempting antiques shops in Bucharest. Sales clerks may encourage you to make purchases, but exporting antiques is difficult and risky. It is possible to obtain export licenses for some items from the Patrimonium office (Calea Victoriei 118, 5th floor, tel. 01/6592070; open weekdays 12:30–3:30), but the process is very time-consuming, and there is no guarantee you'll succeed. If you are considering buying an antique, ask the shopowner to obtain a license for you before making a commitment.

Language Romanian sounds pleasantly familiar to anyone who speaks a smattering of French, Italian, or Spanish. French is widely spoken and understood in Romanian cities. Romanians involved with the tourist industry, in all hotels and major resorts, usually speak English.

Getting Around

By Car An adequate network of main roads covers the country, though the *Road* great majority are still a single lane wide in each direction. Some *Conditions* roads are badly potholed, and a few roads have not been paved. Progress may be impeded by convoys of farm machinery or slow-moving trucks, by horses and carts, or by herds of animals. Night driving can be dangerous: Roads and vehicles are lighted either poorly or not at all.

Rules of the Driving is on the right, as in the United States. Speed limits are 60 *Road* kph (37 mph) in built-up areas and 80 kph–90 kph (50 mph–55 mph) on all other roads. Driving after drinking any alcohol whatsoever is prohibited. Police are empowered to levy on-the-spot fines. Vehicle spot checks are frequent, but police are generally courteous to foreigners. Road signs are the same as in Western Europe.

Gasoline Gas stations are scarce and usually found on main roads at the edge of towns. They sell *regular* (90-octane), *premium* (98-octane), and *motorina* (diesel), but rarely unleaded gas. Prices remain well below those in Western Europe, but shortages sometimes cause waits of several hours. Gas coupons for foreigners—and the privilege of jumping to the front of the line—have been phased out. The Automobil Clubul Roman (*see below*) and tourist offices can provide visitors with a useful Tourist and Motor Car Map that pinpoints the location of each gas station.

Breakdowns **Automobil Clubul Roman** (ACR, Str. Take Ionescu 27, Bucharest, tel. 01/6502595, fax 01/3120434) offers mechanical assistance in case of breakdowns and medical and legal assistance at fixed rates in case of accidents. (It also arranges bus and driving tours and advance hotel bookings.) For breakdowns, dial tel. 927 in Bucharest and tel. 12345 elsewhere. Spare parts are scarce, so carry extras. Thefts of parts from vehicles under repair are frequent.

Car Rentals A number of international car rental companies have opened offices in Bucharest and other major towns. **Hertz** is in the former ACR building (Str. Cihoski 2, Bucharest, tel. 01/6114365, and also at

Bucharest's Otopeni Airport, tel. 01/6795284). **Europcar** is in the ONT Carpaţi building (B-dul. Magheru 7, tel. 01/6131540, fax 01/3120915).

By Train Romanian Railways (CFR) operates *expres, accelerat, rapide,* and *personal* trains; if possible, avoid the *personal* trains because they are very slow. Trains are inexpensive and often crowded, with carriages in poor repair. First class is worth the extra cost. A *vagon de dormit* (sleeper) or cheap *cuşeta*, with bunk beds, is available on longer journeys. It is always advisable to buy a seat reservation in advance, but you cannot buy the ticket itself at a train station more than one hour before departure. If your reserved seat is already occupied, it may have been sold twice. If you're in Bucharest and want to buy your ticket ahead of time, go to the Advance Booking Office, Strada Brezoianu 10, tel. 01/6132642/3/4 or, for international reservations, go to CFR International (B-dul I.C., Brătianu 44, tel. 01/6134008). You will be charged a small commission, but the process is less time-consuming than buying your ticket at the railway station.

By Plane **Tarom** operates daily flights to major Romanian cities from Bucharest's Baneasa Airport. During the summer, additional flights link Constanţa with major cities, including Cluj and Iaşi. Be prepared for delays and cancellations. Prices average $90 round-trip. External flights can be booked at the central reservations office, Strada Brezoianu 10, and at some major hotels. For domestic flights go to Piaţa Victoriei 1, tel. 01/6594185.

By Bus Bus stations, or *autogara*, are usually located near train stations. Buses are generally crowded and far from luxurious. Tickets are sold at the stations up to two hours before departure.

By Boat Regular passenger services operate on various sections of the Danube; tickets are available at the ports.

Staying in Romania

Telephones All large Romanian towns can be dialed directly, and international direct dialing is slowly being introduced in Bucharest. The system is stretched, and you may have to order and wait a long time for nonlocal calls. It is less expensive to telephone from the post office than from hotels. Post offices have a waiting system whereby you order your call and pay at the counter. When your call is ready, the name of the town or country you are phoning is announced, together with the number of the cabin you should proceed to for your call. Private business services are opening in large towns, offering phone, fax, and telex facilities. Coin-operated telephones at roadsides, airports, and train stations may work only for local calls.

Telephone numbers in Bucharest, and area codes throughout Romania, changed in late 1992 and again in 1994. The area code for Bucharest is now 01, and telephone numbers in the city now have 2, 3, 6, or 7 as a prefix, followed by a six-digit number. Long distance calls should now be prefixed with a 0 followed by the new area code for the county. For information dial the relevant area code, then 11515; in Bucharest it is 931 (A–L) and 932 (M–Z). Your hotel's front desk or a phone book will be much more helpful.

Mail The central post office in Bucharest is at Calea Victoriei 37 and is open Monday–Thursday 7:30 AM–7 PM, Friday–Saturday 8 AM–2 PM. The telephone section is open 24 hours a day.

Postal Rates Rates are increasing regularly in line with inflation, so check before you post.

Opening and Closing Times

Banks are open weekdays 9 to 12:30 or 1. Licensed exchange (schimb) bureaus are usually open weekdays and Saturday mornings, though private bureaus could have other hours.

Museums are usually open from 10 to 6, but it's best to check with local tourist offices. Most museums are closed on Monday, and some are also closed on Tuesday.

Shops are generally open Monday–Friday from 9 or 10 AM to 6 or 8 PM and close between 1 and 3, though some food shops open earlier. Many shops are closed on Saturday afternoons.

National Holidays

January 1; January 2; April 17 (Easter Monday); May 1; December 1; December 25; December 26.

Dining

Shortages have eased and poor standards have now improved sufficiently for the better hotels and restaurants to offer reasonable cuisine and menu choices. Elsewhere, expect poorly cooked dishes based around pork or beef. Vegetables and salads may be canned or pickled. Traditional Romanian main courses are not always offered, but you might try *gustare*, a platter of hot or cold mixed hors d'oeuvres, or *ciorbă*, a soup stock, slightly spicy and sour. Overcharging is a hazard outside the bigger restaurants with printed menus. You can insist on seeing the prices, but small establishments may genuinely not have a menu prepared for just one or two dishes.

Mealtimes

Outside Bucharest and the Black Sea and Carpathian resorts, many restaurants will have stopped serving by 9 PM, although an increasing number have begun staying open until 11 PM or later. Restaurants usually open at midday.

Precautions

The far less expensive *bufet expres, lacto vegetarian* snack bars, and *autoservire* cannot be recommended, but creamy cakes are available at the better *cofetarie* (coffee shops). Romanian coffee is served with grounds; instant coffee is called *nes*. You may want to bring your own coffee creamer, as milk is in short supply.

Dress

There are no dress rules as such, but Romanians themselves usually wear smart, informal clothes for an expensive evening out. Casual dress is appropriate elsewhere.

Ratings

Prices are per person and include first course, main course, and dessert, plus wine and tip. Because high inflation means local prices frequently change, ratings are given in dollars, which remain reasonably constant. Your bill will be in lei. Best bets are indicated by a star ★.

Category	Cost
Very Expensive	over $14
Expensive	$9–$14
Moderate	$5–$9
Inexpensive	under $5

Lodging

Prepaid arrangements through travel agencies abroad often benefit from discounted prices. Some schemes, such as fly-drive holidays, give bed-and-breakfast accommodation vouchers (these cannot be bought in Romania). Most places take vouchers; in deluxe hotels, you have to pay a little extra. Otherwise, book accommodations directly with hotels or through tourism agencies. Some agencies deal only with their local areas; those spawned from the formerly monolithic national tourism office (ONT)—the *agenţia de turism*—and from the former youth tourism bureau, now known as the *Biroul de Turism Și Tranzacții* (BTT), offer nationwide services. Avoid the cheap and often cheerless hotels used by many Romanians. Rooms in private homes can be booked through many of the ONT offices—this is a good alternative to hotels. Private citizens come to railway stations and offer spare rooms in their homes, but use discretion and be prepared to bargain. Inexpensive accommodations such as pensions or hostels are almost nonexistent, and student hostels are not available to foreigners.

Hotels The star system of hotel classification is only just being introduced in Romania. Instead, you will encounter Deluxe categories A and B, First-class categories A and B, and so on. Deluxe A is equivalent to five-star or Very Expensive, Deluxe B to four-star or Expensive, first-class A to three-star or Moderate, and first-class B to two-star or Inexpensive. Standards of facilities, including plumbing and hot water, may not be good even in the top hotels, and decline rapidly through the categories. Ask at the front desk when hot water will be available. In principle, at least, all hotels leave a certain quota of rooms unoccupied until 8 PM for unexpected foreign visitors.

Rentals A few delightfully rustic cottages may be rented at such ski resorts as Sinaia and Predeal. Details are available from Romanian tourist offices abroad (*see* Important Addresses and Numbers in Bucharest, *below*).

Camping There are more than 100 campgrounds in Romania; they provide an inexpensive way of exploring the country, but standards vary. The best ones are at Brașov, Cluj, Sibiu, and Suceava, which also offer reasonable bungalow accommodations. They all have showers with hot water at least some of the time. The worst ones have no running water apart from a natural spring and very unpleasant toilets. Rates vary. Usually campsites are clean and comfortable but are only for use during the summer. Details are available from Romanian tourist offices abroad.

Ratings The following hotel price categories are for two people in a double room. Guests staying in single rooms are charged a supplement. Prices are estimates for high season. Because of inflation, ratings are given according to hard-currency equivalents—but you must pay in lei. (Note that hotels may insist on your buying lei from them to pay your bill, unless you can produce an exchange receipt to prove you changed your money legally.) Rates in Bucharest are much higher than in the rest of the country due to a shortage of accommodations there and an increasing number of business travelers. Best bets are indicated by a star ★.

Category	Bucharest	Black Sea Coast/ Transylvania
Very Expensive	over $200	over $80
Expensive	$125–$200	$50–$80
Moderate	$70–$125	$30–$50
Inexpensive	under $70	under $30

Tipping A 12% service charge is added to meals at most restaurants. Elsewhere, a 10% tip is welcomed, and is expected by taxi drivers.

Bucharest

Arriving and Departing

By Plane All international flights to Romania land at Bucharest's Otopeni Airport (tel. 01/6333137), 16 kilometers (9 miles) north of the city.

Between the Airport and Downtown Bus no. 783 leaves the airport every 30 minutes between 7 AM and 10 AM, stopping in the main squares before terminating in Piata Unirii. The journey takes an hour and costs 20¢. Your hotel can arrange transport by car from the airport. Taxi drivers at the airport seek business aggressively and charge outrageously in dollars. Note that the "official" fare is in lei, the equivalent of about $12 with tip, so bargain.

By Train There are five main stations in Bucharest, though international lines operate from Gara de Nord (tel. 01/952). For tickets and information, go to the Advance Booking Office (Str. Brezoianu 10, tel. 01/6132642). For international trains, go to CFR International (B-dul I.C. Brătianu 44, tel. 01/6134008).

By Car There are three main access routes into the city—E70 west from the Hungarian border, E60 north via Braşov, and E70/E85 south to Bulgaria. Bucharest has poor signposting and many tortuous one-way systems: *Unde este centrul* (**oon**-day **yes**-tay **tchen**-trul)? or "Where is the town center?" is essential vocabulary.

Getting Around

Bucharest is spacious and sprawling. Though the old heart of the city and the two main arteries running the length of it are best explored on foot, long, wide avenues and vast squares make some form of transportation necessary. New tourist maps are being printed and can be found in bookstores; they may also be available at tourism agencies and hotels. It is generally safe on the streets at night, but watch out for vehicles and hidden potholes.

By Subway Four lines of the subway system are now in operation. Change is available from kiosks inside stations, and you may travel any distance. The system closes at 1 AM.

By Tram, Bus, and Trolley Bus These are uncomfortable, crowded, and infrequent, but service is extensive. A ticket valid for two trips of any length can be purchased from kiosks near bus stops or from tobacconists; validate your ticket when you board. There are also day and week passes *(abonaments)*, but more expensive *maxi taxis* (minibuses that stop on request) and express buses take fares on board. The system shuts down at midnight.

By Taxi Hail in the street, or phone 01/953—they speak English. The price should be around 40¢ a kilometer, charged in lei.

Important Addresses and Numbers

Tourist Information The main **Romanian National Tourist Office (ONT)** is located at 7 Boulevard General Magheru (tel. 01/6145160) and deals with all inquiries related to tourism (open weekdays 8–8 and weekends 8–2). There are ONT offices at Otopeni Airport, open 24 hours, and at the Gara de Nord, open 8–8 Monday–Saturday. ONT is currently being broken up and privatized, so its office signs in most Romanian towns now read *Agenţia de Turism*. The **Biroul de Turism şi Tranzacţii (BTT)** at Bulevardul Nicolae Bălcescu 21 (tel. 01/6133841) also has branches nationwide.

For information before your trip, write or call **in the United States** (573 Third Avenue, New York, NY 10016, tel. 212/697–6971); **in the United Kingdom** (17 Nottingham Street, London W1M 3RD, tel. 071/224–3692).

Guided Tours

A wide variety of tours is promised for 1995 from the growing number of competing tourism agencies, many of which maintain desks in the larger hotels. Tours range from sightseeing in the city—by car with your own driver, if you prefer—to weekend excursions to the Danube Delta or the monasteries of Bukovina.

Exploring Bucharest

The old story goes that a simple peasant named Bucur settled on the site upon which the city now stands. True or not, the name București was first officially used only in 1459, by none other than Vlad Țepeș, the real-life Dracula (sometimes known as Vlad the Impaler for his bloodthirsty habit of impaling unfortunate victims on wooden stakes). Two centuries later, this citadel on the Dimbovița (the river that flows through Bucharest) became the capital of Walachia, and after another 200 years, it was named the capital of Romania. The city gradually developed into a place of bustling trade and gracious living, with ornate and varied architecture, landscaped parks, busy, winding streets, and wide boulevards. It became known before the Second World War as the Paris of the Balkans, but its past glory is now only hinted at.

The high-rise Intercontinental Hotel now dominates the main crossroads at Piața Universității; northwards, up the main shopping streets of Bulevardul Nicolae Bălcescu, Bulevardul General Magheru, and Bulevardul Ana Ipătescu, only the occasional older building survives. However, along Calea Victoriei, a flavor of Bucharest's grander past can be savored, especially at the former royal palace opposite the Romanian senate (formerly Communist Party headquarters) in Piața Revoluției. Here, one also sees reminders of the December 1989 revolution, including the slow restoration of the domed National Library, gutted by fire, and bullet holes on walls nearby. Modest, touching monuments to the more than 1,000 people killed in the revolution can be found here, and Piața Universității has a wall still festooned with protest posters.

South along Calea Victoriei is the busy Lipscani trading district, a remnant of the old city that used to sprawl farther southward before it was bulldozed in Nicolae Ceaușescu's megalomaniacal drive to redevelop the capital. Piața Unirii is the hub of his enormously expensive and impractical vision, which involved the forced displacement of thousands of people and the demolition of many houses, churches, and synagogues. Cranes now stand eerily idle above unfinished tower blocks with colonnaded, white marble frontages. They flank a lengthy boulevard leading to the enormous, empty, and unfinished Palace of the People, second in size only to the Pentagon. With such a massive diversion of resources, it is not surprising that Bucharest is potholed and faded, and suffers shortages and erratic services. But happily, the city continues to offer many places of historic interest, as well as cinemas, theaters, concert halls, and an opera house.

Numbers in the margin correspond to points of interest on the Bucharest map.

Historic
Bucharest

A tour of this city should start at its core, the **Curtea Veche** (old Princely Court) and the Lipscani District. The Princely Court now ❶ houses **Muzeul Curtea Veche-Palatul Voievodal,** a museum exhibiting the remains of the palace built by Vlad Țepeș during the 15th century. One section of the cellar wall presents the palace's history from the 15th century onward. You can see the rounded river stones used in the early construction, later alternating with red brick, and later still in plain brick. Prisoners were once kept in these cellars, which extend far into the surrounding city; a pair of ancient skulls belonging to two young *boyars* (aristocrats), decapitated at the end of the 17th century, will interest some. *Str. Iuliu Maniu 31. Admission charged. Open Tues.–Sun. 10–6.*

❷ The **Biserica din Curtea Veche** (Curtea Veche Church), beside the Princely Court, was founded during the 16th century and remains ❸ an important center of worship in the city. Nearby, **Hanul lui Manuc** (Manuc's Inn), a renovated 19th-century inn arranged in the traditional Romanian fashion around a courtyard, now houses a hotel and restaurant. Manuc was a wealthy Armenian merchant who died in Russia by poisoning—at the hand of a famous French fortune-teller who, having forecast Manuc's death on a certain day, could not risk ruining her reputation. The 1812 Russian-Turkish Peace Treaty was signed here.

Nearby, **Lipscani** is a bustling area of narrow streets, open stalls, and small artisans' shops that combine to create the atmosphere of a bazaar. At Strada Selari 11–13, you'll find glassblowers hard at work; glassware is sold next door. In Hanul cu Tei, off Strada Lipscani, are many galleries, crafts, and gift shops. On Strada ❹ Stavreopolos, a small but exquisite **Biserica Ortodoxă** (Orthodox church) combines late-Renaissance and Byzantine styles with elements of the Romanian folk-art style. Go inside to look at the superb wood and stone carving and a richly ornate iconostasis, the painted screen that partitions off the altar. Boxes on either side of the entrance contain votive candles—for the living on the left, for the "sleeping" on the right.

Time Out

Down the road, at Strada Stavreopolos 3, is the **Carul cu Bere,** serving half-liter tankards of beer, appetizers, and Turkish coffee.

❺ At the end of the street is the **Muzeul Național de Istorie** (Romanian History Museum), which contains a vast collection of exhibits from neolithic to modern times. The Treasury, which can be visited and paid for separately, has a startling collection of objects in gold and precious stones—royal crowns, weapons, plates, and jewelry—dating from the 4th millennium BC through the 20th century. Opposite ❻ the Treasury is a full-size replica of **Columna Traiană** (Trajan's Column; the original is in Rome), commemorating a Roman victory over Dacia in AD 2. *Calea Victoriei 12. Admission charged. Treasury open Tues.–Sun. 10–5, last ticket at 4 PM. Museum open Wed.–Sun. 10–4.*

Turning north along the Calea Victoriei, you'll pass a military club ❼ and academy before reaching the pretty little **Crețulescu Church** on your left. Built in 1722, the church and some of its original frescoes were restored during the 1930s. Immediately north is a massive building, once the royal palace and now the Palace of the Republic. ❽ The **Muzeul de Artă al României** (National Art Museum) is housed here, with its fine collection of Romanian art, including works by the world-famous sculptor Brâncuși. The foreign section has a wonderful Brueghel collection and is well worth a visit. *Str. Stribei Voda 1. Museum admission charged. Open Wed.–Sun. 10–6.*

Opposite the palace, in Piaţa Revoluţiei, was the former headquarters of the Romanian Communist party. Before the revolution in December 1989, no one was allowed to walk in front of this building. During the uprising the square was a major site of the fighting that destroyed the National Library, parts of the Palace, and the Cina restaurant next to the **Ateneul Român** (Romanian Athenaeum Concert Hall). The Ateneul, dating from 1888, with its Baroque dome and Greek columns, survived the upheavals and still houses the George Enescu Philharmonic Orchestra.

Time Out The cafeteria of the **Hotel Bucureşti,** on Calea Victoriei, has excellent cakes.

Follow Calea Victoriei as far as the Piaţa Victoriei. Opposite is the **Muzeul de Ştiinţe Naturale "Grigore Antipa"** (Natural History Museum), with its exceptional butterfly collection and the skeleton of the dinosaur, *Dinotherium gigantissimum. Şoseaua Kiseleff 1. Admission charged. Open Tues.–Sun. 10–5.*

Next door, in an imposing redbrick building, is the impressive **Muzeul Iăranalui Român** (Museum of the Romanian Peasant). This museum, which reopened in 1990, has an excellent collection of costumes, icons, carpets, and other artifacts from rural life, including two 19th-century wooden churches. *Şoseaua Kiseleff 3. Admission charged. Open Tues.–Sun. 10–6.*

Şoseaua Kiseleff, a pleasant tree-lined avenue, brings you to the **Arcul de Triumf,** built in 1922 to commemorate the Allied victory in World War I. Originally constructed of wood and stucco, it was rebuilt during the 1930s and carved by some of Romania's most talented sculptors.

Still farther north lies Herăstrău Park, accommodating the fascinating **Muzeul Satului Romanesc** (Village Museum), as well as Herăstrău Lake. The museum is outstanding, with more than 300 authentic, fully furnished peasants' houses, with folk styles taken from all over Romania. *Şoseaua Kiseleff 28. Admission charged. Open winter, daily 8–4; summer, daily 10–7.*

Shopping

Gifts and Souvenirs New private shops are beginning to bring extra style and choice to Bucharest, but note the astonishing customs restrictions (*see* Customs in Before You Go, *above)* that prohibit exporting even bric-a-brac. Keep receipts of all purchases, regardless of their legal export status. The **Apollo** gallery, in the National Theater building next to the Intercontinental Hotel, and the galleries in the fascinating **Hanul cu Tei** off Strada Lipscani sell art that you may legally take home with you.

Market The main food market is in Piaţa Amzei, open seven days a week and best visited during the morning. It sells a limited variety of cheese, fruit, and flowers. If you decide to visit outlying flea markets such as Piaţa Obor, take a guide to avoid being hassled and ripped off.

Dining

The restaurants of the Continental, Bucureşti, and Intercontinental hotels are all recommended for a reasonable meal in pleasant sur-

Arcul de Triumf, **12**
Ateneul Român, **9**
Biserica din Curtea
Veche, **2**
Biserica Ortodoxă, **4**

Columna Traiană, **6**
Crețulescu Church, **7**
Curtea Veche, **1**
Hanul lui Manuc, **3**
Muzeul de Artă al
României, **8**

Muzeul de Știinţe
Naturale "Grigore
Antipa", **10**
Muzeul Național de
Istorie, **5**
Muzeul Satului
Romanesc, **13**

Muzeul Iăranalui
Român, **11**

KEY

[AE] American Express Office

7 Tourist Information

roundings. Some, like the **Balada,** at the top of the Intercontinental, offer a folklore show or live music. Although prices are not unreasonable, it is possible to rack up quite a total. Many restaurants have no menu, and waiters' recommendations can be expensive. Also note that most places will serve wine only by the bottle and not by the glass. For details and price-category definitions, *see* Dining in Staying in Romania, *above.*

Very Expensive **Casa Doina.** Recently refurbished, this historic restaurant, popular with the Bucharest elite between the wars, is once again one of the best in town. It serves Romanian and international cuisine in a relaxing atmosphere. In summer you can enjoy the terrace, which backs onto Kiseleff park. *B-dul. Kiseleff 4, tel. 01/6176715. Reservations advised. AE, DC, MC, V.*

Hotel Bucureşti. The restaurant in this modern hotel sometimes has a loud band playing in the evenings, but the air-conditioning makes it comfortable, and it is one of the few places where you can enjoy good, genuine Romanian cuisine. *Calea Victoriei 63–81, tel. 01/155850 or 154640. Reservations not necessary. AE, DC, MC, V.*

La Premiera. One of Bucharest's most popular restaurants is conveniently located at the back of the National Theatre. The good selection of Romanian and French cuisine includes excellent salads, even in winter. In summer, you can enjoy La Premiera's terrace. *Str. Arghezi 9, tel. 01/3124397. Reservations advised. AE, DC, V.*

Rapsodia. Located on the ground floor of the modern Hotel Intercontinental, this is a quiet, elegant restaurant with a pianist in the evenings. There is a wide choice of authentic Romanian and international dishes. *B-dul Nicolae Bălcescu 4–6. Reservations not necessary. AE, DC, MC, V.*

Expensive **Bistrot Pierrot.** A new German-run restaurant is in the basement of a turn-of-the-century building off Calea Victoriei. It serves mainly international cuisine, including a good-value Sunday brunch in intimate surroundings. *Str. Occidentului 44, tel. 01/6596155. Reservations advised. AE, DC, MC, V.*

Brâdet. This informal, privately run Lebanese restaurant is popular with expatriates and diplomats. It's east of the city center in the pleasant Cotroceni district. *Str. Carol Davilla 60, tel. 01/6386014. Reservations advised. No credit cards.*

Select Restaurant. Located in the pleasant primavera district, this restaurant offers good Romanian food at reasonable prices in a friendly atmosphere. Fish lovers will enjoy the locally caught sturgeon; the *mici* (small, spicy sausages) is also worthwhile. You can eat outside in summer. *Aleea Alexandru 18, tel. 01/6792177. Reservations advised. No credit cards.*

Moderate ★ **Dong Hai.** One of many recently opened Chinese restaurants in Bucharest, this large, well-decorated restaurant in the Lipscani district serves authentic Chinese cuisine. *Str. Blánari 14, tel. 01/6156494. Reservations not necessary. No credit cards.*

Lodging

Hotels in Bucharest are often heavily booked during the tourist season. If you don't have reservations, the ONT office will be of help in suggesting available alternatives. For details and price-category definitions, *see* Lodging in Staying in Romania, *above.*

Very Expensive **Helveţia.** Bucharest's first privately constructed hotel since World War II, the Helveţia has established itself as one of the capital's best hotels since opening in mid-1993. This is a small, quiet hotel with an emphasis on individual service and comfort. It is located a little north of the city center but is easily accessible by metro or taxi. *Str. Uruguay 29, tel. 01/3110566, fax 01/3110567. 30 rooms with bath. Facilities: restaurant, bar, café. AE, DC, MC, V.*

★ **Intercontinental.** Designed principally for business clients, the Intercontinental offers American-style accommodation in the city's tallest building. Every room is air-conditioned and has a balcony. *B-dul N. Bălcescu 4–6, tel. 01/6140400, fax 01/3120486. 423 rooms with bath. Facilities: fitness center, sun terrace, pool, nightclub, minicasino, 7 bars and restaurants. AE, DC, MC, V.*

Expensive **Bucureşti.** The city's largest hotel has an excellent central location and spacious, pleasantly furnished rooms. Its modern ambience is complemented by the vast range of facilities. *Calea Victoriei 63–81, tel. 01/6155850, fax 01/3120927. 402 rooms with bath. Facilities: 2 pools, health club, sauna, cafeteria, restaurant. AE, DC, MC, V.*

★ **Continental.** This small, turn-of-the-century hotel recalls Bucharest's more gracious past. Furnishings are traditional, but rooms have air-conditioning. It is excellently located in the city center, just north of the lively Lipscani district. *Calea Victoriei 56, tel. 01/6145348, fax 01/3120134. 53 rooms with bath. Facilities: restaurant, coffee shop, bar. AE, DC, MC, V.*

Flora. The modern Flora, situated on the outskirts of the city near Herăstrău Park, offers its cosmopolitan clientele top facilities for geriatric (antiaging) treatment. The sun terraces are havens of relaxation. Most guests stay in this quiet, restful hotel for at least two weeks. *B-dul Poligrafiei 1, tel. 01/6184640, fax 01/3128344. 155 rooms with bath. Facilities: pool, spa-care unit, health club, sauna, restaurant. AE, DC, MC, V.*

Moderate **Ambassador.** The 13-story Ambassador was built in 1937 and enjoys a fine central location. Although a little shabby, rooms are comfortably furnished. The restaurant is not recommended, but there is a good café. *B-dul General Magheru 6–8, tel. 01/6159080, fax 01/3121239. 233 rooms with bath. Facilities: restaurant, café. AE, DC, MC, V.*

Lebada. This pleasant hotel overlooks a lake on the southeast outskirts of Bucharest. *Str. Biruinţei 3, tel. 01/6243000, fax 01/3128041. Facilities: restaurant, outdoor terrace, bar, outdoor pool, sauna. AE, DC, MC, V.*

Lido. Conveniently located in the center of the city, this prewar hotel has been recently privatized and renovated to offer comfortable rooms and good facilities, including an outdoor swimming pool and terrace. *B-dul Magheru 5, tel. 01/6144930, fax 01/3126544. 92 rooms with bath. Facilities: restaurant, bar, nightclub, outdoor pool. AE, DC, MC, V.*

Parc. Located near Herăstrău Park and the Flora Hotel, the Parc is modern and within easy reach of the airport; many guests stay here before moving on to the Black Sea resorts. There's a good restaurant that provides music every evening. *B-dul Poligrafiei 3, tel. 01/6180950, fax 01/3128419. 314 rooms with bath. Facilities: restaurant, pool, sauna, tennis. AE, DC, MC, V.*

Inexpensive **Capitol.** The circa 1900 Capitol is situated in a lively part of town near the Cişmigiu Gardens. In days gone by, it was the stomping ground of Bucharest's mainstream artists and writers. Today the Capitol is modernized and offers comfortable rooms—though the literati have long since moved on. *Calea Victoriei 29, tel. 01/6139440. 70 rooms with bath. Facilities: restaurant. No credit cards.*

★ **Triumf.** This comfortable hotel is set on its own grounds slightly outside the city center near the Arcul de Triumf. Formerly the President, it used to serve only the Communist elite. This hotel is a good value. The more expensive rooms are miniapartments. *Şoseaua Kiseleff 12, tel. 01/6184110, fax 01/3128411. 98 rooms, 49 with bath. Facilities: restaurant, bar, tennis court. AE, DC, V.*

The Arts

You can enjoy Bucharest's lively theater and music life at prices well below those in the West. Tickets can be obtained directly from the theater or hall or from your hotel (for a commission fee). Performances usually begin at 7 PM (6 in winter). **Opera Română** (The Opera House, B-dul Mihail Kogălniceanu 70) has some good productions, but don't expect to find the same quality as you would in Prague or Budapest. The George Enescu Philharmonic Orchestra holds concerts at the **Ateneul Român** (Romanian Athenaeum in Piaţa Revoluţiei) or at the more modern **Studioul de Concerte al Radioteleviziunii** (Radio Concert Hall, Str. General Berthelot 62–64). The **Teatrul de Operetă** (Operetta House) is now located at the **Teatrul National** (National Theater, B-dul N. Bălcescu 2), which also offers serious drama. For lighter entertainment, try the **Teatrul de Comedie** (Comedy Theater, Str. Mandinesti); despite the language barrier, there is often enough spectacle to ensure a very good evening's entertainment. **Teatrul Tăndărică** (The Tandarica Puppet Theater, Calea Victoriei 50), has an international reputation, and the **Teatrul Evreesc de Stat** (State Jewish Theater, Str. Barasch 15), stages Yiddish-language performances. Don't miss the fine folkloric show at the **Rapsodia Română Artistic Ensemble** (Str. Lipscani 53). The **Cinematica Romana** (Str. Eforie 5) runs a daily program of old, undubbed American and English films.

Nightlife

Increasing numbers of bars and restaurants stay open late. Coffee shops, however, are usually closed after 8 PM.

Nightclubs   The **Lido, Ambassador,** and **Intercontinental** hotels have nightclubs with floor shows, and many others are popping up as well. **Vox Maris,** at the corner of Calea Victoriei and Bulevardul Mihail Kogălniceanu, and **Club A,** on Str. Blănari, are among several late-night discos. **Şarpele Roşu** (Str. Icoanei Piaţa Galaţi), or "Red Snake," has a pleasant, bohemian atmosphere, with Gypsy bands playing until 3 AM.

Cafés   Cafés with outdoor terraces remain a feature of the city. Try the **Lido** or, in winter, the excellent indoor **Ana Café** (Str. Aviator Radu Beller 6), just north of Piaţa Dorobanţi.

The Black Sea Coast and Danube Delta

The southeastern Dobrogea region, only 45 minutes by air from Bucharest, 210 kilometers (130 miles) by road, is one of the major focal points of Romania's rich history. Within a clearly defined area are the historic port of Constanţa; the Romanian Riviera pleasure coast; the renowned Murfatlar vineyards; Roman, Greek, and earlier ruins; and the Danube Delta, one of Europe's leading wildlife sanctuaries. The rapid development of the Black Sea resorts and increasing interest in the delta region mean that tourist amenities (such as hotels and restaurants) and train, bus, and plane connections are good.

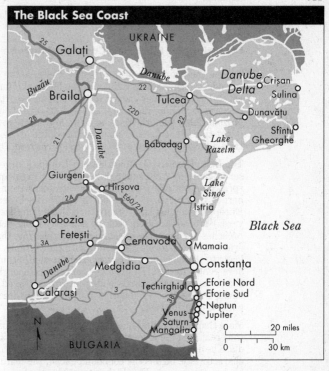

The Black Sea Coast

(Map showing: UKRAINE, Galaţi, Buzău, Brăila, Danube, Giurgeni, Hîrşova, Slobozia, Feteşti, Cernavodă, Medgidia, Călăraşi, Tulcea, Băbadag, Danube Delta, Crişan, Sulina, Dunavăţu, Sfîntu Gheorghe, Lake Razelm, Lake Sinoe, Istria, Mamaia, Constanţa, Techirghiol, Eforie Nord, Eforie Sud, Neptun, Jupiter, Venus, Saturn, Mangalia, Black Sea, BULGARIA, 20 miles, 30 km)

Getting Around

By Bus Bus trips from the Black Sea resorts and Constanta to the Danube Delta, the Murfatlar vineyards, Istria, and the sunken city of Adamclisi are arranged by tourism agencies.

By Car Rental cars, with or without drivers, are available through Societatea Comercială Litoral (formerly ONT) offices, hotels, and specialized agencies.

By Boat Regular passenger and sightseeing boats operate along the middle and southern arms of the Danube Delta. Motorboats are available for hire, or rent one of the more restful fishermen's boats.

Guided Tours

Tours always involve some hours on the road, so it is better to go for more than one day. The **Societatea Comercială Litoral** has the most tour experience. Try trips to the Bukovina monasteries, the Prahova Mountains, or, especially, the Danube Delta.

Tourist Information

Constanţa. Societatea Comercială Litoral (B-dul Tomis 69, tel. 041/617181, fax 041/611429). **BTT** (Hotel Tineretului, B-dul Tomis 20–26, tel. 041/515262, fax 041/516624).
Mamaia. Societatea Comercială Mamaia (Hotel Bucureşti, tel. 041/531025).
Tulcea. Societatea Comercială Deltarom (Hotel Delta, Str. Isaccei 2,

tel. 040/614720, fax 040/616260). **BTT** (Str. Babadag Bloc B1, tel. 040/612496, fax 040/616842).

Exploring the Black Sea Coast and Danube Delta

Tulcea, the main town of the Danube Delta, is the gateway to the splendors of the region. Built on seven hills and influenced by Turkish styles, this former market town is now an important sea and river port, as well as the center of the Romanian fish industry. The **Muzeul Deltei Dunării** (Danube Delta Museum) provides a good introduction to the flora, fauna, and way of life of the communities in the area. *Str. Progresului 32. Admission charged. Open daily 10–6.*

The **Delta Dunării** (Danube Delta) is Europe's largest wetlands reserve, covering 2,681 square kilometers (1,676 square miles), with a sprawling, watery wilderness that stretches from the Ukrainian border to a series of lakes north of the Black Sea resorts. It is Europe's youngest land—more than 43.7 square meters (47 square yards) are added each year by normal silting action. As it approaches the delta, the great Danube divides into three. The northernmost branch forms the border with the Ukraine, the middle arm leads to the busy port of Sulina, and the southernmost arm meanders gently toward the little port of Sfîntu Gheorghe. From these channels, countless canals widen into tree-fringed lakes, reed islands, and pools covered with water lilies; there are sand dunes and pockets of lush forest.

More than 80% of the delta area is water. Over 300 bird species visit the area; 70 of these species come from as far away as China and India. The delta is a natural stopover for migratory birds, but the most characteristic bird is the common pelican, the featured star of this bird-watchers' paradise. Fishing provides most of the area's inhabitants, many of whom are of Ukrainian origin, with a livelihood. Common sights are the long lines of fishing boats strung together to be towed by motorboats to remote fishing grounds. Smaller communities, such as Independența on the southern arm and Crišan on the middle arm, rent out the services of a fisherman and his boat to foreigners. The waters here are particularly rich in catfish, perch, carp, and caviar-bearing sturgeon.

There are good roads to the Black Sea resorts from Tulcea that take you to **Babadag** via the strange, eroded Măcin hills. It was here, according to local legend, that Jason and his Argonauts cast anchor in their search for the mythical golden fleece. Farther south is **Istria,** an impressive archaeological site, founded in 6 BC by Greek merchants from Miletus. There are traces of early Christian churches and baths and even residential, commercial, and industrial districts. A useful English-language booklet, available on the spot, will help make sense of the remains of several cultures.

Istria lies only 60 kilometers (37 miles) from **Mamaia,** the largest of the Black Sea resorts. Mamaia is situated on a strip of land bordered by the Black Sea and fine beaches on one side and the fresh waters of the Mamaia Lake on the other. All the resorts along this stretch of the coast have high-rise modern apartments, villas, restaurants, nightclubs, and discos. There are cruises down the coast to Mangalia and along the new channel linking the Danube with the Black Sea near Constanța. Sea-fishing expeditions can also be arranged for early risers, with all equipment provided. These resorts offer everything necessary for a complete vacation by the sea.

Constanţa is Romania's second-largest city and only a short ride by trolley bus from Mamaia. With a polyglot flavor characteristic of so many seaports, Constanţa is steeped in history. The famous Roman poet Ovid was exiled here from Rome in AD 8, probably for his part in court scandals and for the amorality of his poem *Ars amandi (The Art of Making Love)*. A city square has been named in his honor and provides a fine backdrop for a statue of him by the sculptor Ettore Ferrari. Behind the statue, in the former town hall, is one of the best museums in Europe, the **Muzuel Naţional de Istorie şi Arheologie** (National History and Archaeological Museum). Of special interest here are the statuettes of *The Thinker* and *The Seated Woman*, from the neolithic Hamangian culture (4000 to 3000 BC). Collections from the Greek, Roman, and Daco-Roman cultures are generally outstanding. *Piaţa Ovidiu 12. Admission charged. Open Tues.–Sun. 10–6.*

Near the museum is **Edificiu Roman cu Mozaic,** a Roman complex of warehouses and shops from the 4th century AD, including a magnificent mosaic floor measuring over 6,510 square meters (21,000 square feet) (Piaţa Ovidiu 1). Not far away are the remains of the Roman baths from the same period. The **Parcul Arheologic** (Archaeology Park) on Boulevard Republicii contains items dating from the 3rd and 4th centuries AD and from a 6th-century tower. Modern-day attractions include an **Acvariul,** or aquarium (Str. Februarie 16), and **Delfinariul,** the dolphinarium (B-dul Mamaia 265), which offers aquatic displays by trained dolphins.

A string of seaside resorts lies just south of Constanţa. **Eforie Nord** is an up-to-date thermal treatment center. A series of resorts built during the 1960s are named for the coast's GrecoRoman past— **Neptun, Jupiter, Venus,** and **Saturn.** Not in any way typically Romanian, these resorts offer good amenities for relaxed, seaside vacations. The old port of **Mangalia** is the southernmost resort.

Most of the old Greek city of **Callatis** lies underwater now, but a section of the walls and the remains of a Roman villa are still visible.

There are regular excursions from the seaside resorts to the **Columna Traiană** (replica of Trajan's Column), the **Podgoriile Murfatlar** (Murfatlar vineyards) for wine tastings, and the ruins of the Roman town at **Tropaeum Trajani.**

Dining and Lodging

For details and price-category definitions, *see* Dining and Lodging in Staying in Romania, *above.* Travelers are advised not to rely on credit cards in this region since many resorts are not yet equipped to accept them.

Constanţa **Cazinou.** A turn-of-the-century former casino situated close to the
Dining aquarium, the Cazinou is decorated in an ornate 20th-century style; there's an adjoining bar by the sea. Seafood dishes are the house specialties. *Str. Februarie 16, tel. 041/617416. Reservations advised. No credit cards. Very Expensive.*

Lodging **Continental.** Older, slightly less luxurious, but larger than the Palace, the Continental is conveniently situated near the open-air archaeological museum in the downtown area. *B-dul Republicii 20, tel. 041/15660. 140 rooms with bath. AE. Expensive.*
Palace. Located near the city's historic center, the large and gracious old Palace has recently been renovated. It has a good restaurant and a terrace overlooking the sea and the tourist port of Tomis.

Str. Remus Opreanu 5–7, tel. 041/14696. 132 rooms with bath. Facilities: restaurant. Expensive.

Crişan
Lodging
Lebăda. This is a comfortable hotel from which to make fishing trips into the more remote parts of the delta. *Sulina Canal, mile 14.5, tel. 040/14720. 74 rooms with bath. Facilities: restaurant, currency exchange. Moderate.*

Mamaia
Dining
Satul de Vacanţa. This holiday village is an attractive complex of traditional Romanian buildings, built in styles from all over Romania and featuring many small restaurants that serve local specialties. *Inexpensive–Expensive.*

Insula lui Ovidiu. This is a reed-thatched complex of rustic-style buildings with lively music every evening. A relaxed, informal atmosphere provides a good setting for delicious seafood dishes. *Lake Siurghiol. No phone. Reservations not necessary. Moderate.*

Lodging
Rex. One of King Carol's former residences, this is the largest and grandest of all the hotels in Mamaia. An outdoor swimming pool, an excellent restaurant, a bar, and a cafeteria are among its facilities. *Tel. 041/31595, fax 041/62292. 102 rooms with bath. AE, DC, MC, V. Very Expensive.*

Ambasador, Lido, and **Savoy.** Among the many modern hotels, these three are all newly built and moderately priced. They are grouped in a horseshoe around open-air pools near the beach at the north end of the resort. Contact them through the Societatea Comercială Mamaia (*see* Tourist Information, *above*). *Moderate.*

Tulcea
Lodging
Delta. A large, modern hotel on the banks of the Danube, the Delta currently has a mixed reputation. Amenities include a restaurant, bar, and cafeteria. *Str. Isaacei 2, tel. 040/14720, fax 040/16260. 117 rooms with bath. Moderate.*

Venus
Lodging
Dana. This is a new, privately run three-star hotel at the popular Venus resort. All rooms have balconies and showers. *Venus Resort, tel. 041/31503, fax 041/31465. 110 rooms with shower. Facilities: restaurant, terrace, shop, currency office. Expensive.*

25 Slovakia

Even if it had not developed separately for nearly a millennium under Hungarian and Habsburg rule, the newly independent Slovak Republic (Slovensko) would be different from its Bohemian neighbor (*see* Chapter 7) in a great many respects. The mountains are higher here; the veneer less sophisticated. The people seem more carefree, and the folk culture is particularly rich.

Although they speak a language closely related to Czech, the Slovaks have a strong sense of national identity, and indeed the two Slavic groups developed quite separately. Although united in the 9th century as part of the Great Moravian Empire, the Slovaks were conquered a century later by the Magyars and remained under Hungarian domination until 1918. After the Tartar invasions of the 13th century, many Saxons were invited to resettle the land, exploit the rich mineral resources, and thereby develop the economy. In the 15th and 16th centuries, Romanian shepherds migrated from Wallachia through the Carpathians into Slovakia, and the merging of these varied groups with the resident Slavs bequeathed to the region a rich folk culture and some unique forms of architecture, especially in the east.

Bratislava, the capital of Hungary for nearly 300 years until 1784, and now the capital of the new republic, is a disappointment to many visitors. The 40 years of Communist rule left a clear mark on the city, hiding its ancient beauty with hulking, and now dilapidated, futurist structures. Take time, however, to walk the picturesque streets of the Old Town, now undergoing frenzied revitalization. The city is filled with good concert halls, restaurants, and wine bars.

Most visitors head for the great peaks of the High Tatras. The smallest Alpine range in the world, the Tatras rise magnificently from the foothills of northern Slovakia. The tourist infrastructure here is very good, catering especially to hikers and skiers. Visitors who come to admire the peaks, however, often overlook the exquisite medieval towns of the Spiš in the plains and valleys below the Tatras and the beautiful 18th-century wood churches farther east.

Essential Information

Before You Go

When to Go Organized sightseeing tours run from April or May through October. Some monuments, especially castles, either close entirely or open for shorter hours during the winter. Hotel rates drop during the off-season except during festivals. The High Tatra mountains come into their own in winter (Dec.–Feb.), when skiers from all over Eastern Europe crowd the slopes and resorts. If you're not into skiing, try visiting the mountains in late spring (May or June) or fall, when the colors are dazzling and you'll have the hotels and restaurants pretty much to yourself.

Climate The following are the average daily maximum and minimum temperatures for Bratislava.

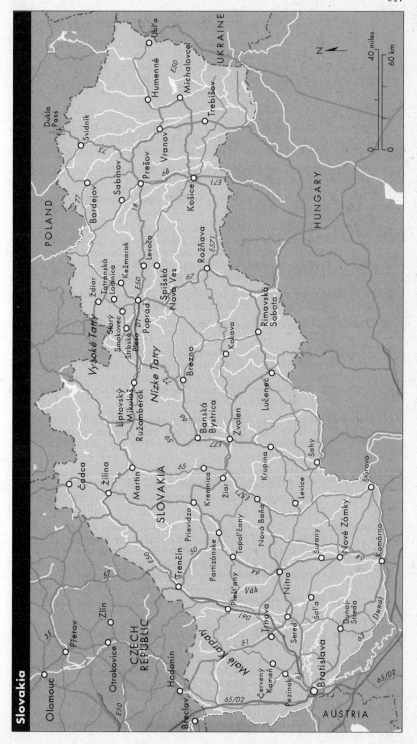

Slovakia

Jan.	36F	2C	May	70F	21C	Sept.	72F	22C
	27	- 3		52	11		54	12
Feb.	39F	4C	June	75F	24C	Oct.	59F	15C
	28	- 2		57	14		45	7
Mar.	48F	9C	July	79F	26C	Nov.	46F	8C
	34	1		61	16		37	3
Apr.	61F	16C	Aug.	79F	26C	Dec.	39F	4C
	43	6		61	16		32	0

Currency The unit of currency in Slovakia is the crown, or koruna, written as Sk, and divided into 100 haléř. There are bills of 20, 50, 100, 500, and 1,000 Sk and coins of 10, 20, and 50 haléř and 1, 2, 5, and 10 Sk.

At press time (spring 1994), the koruna was trading at around 32 Sk to the dollar and 45 Sk to the pound.

Credit cards are widely accepted in establishments used by foreign tourists.

What It Will Cost Costs are highest in Bratislava and only slightly less in the High Tatra resorts and main spas, although even in those places you can now find bargain private accommodations. The prices at tourist resorts in the outlying areas and off the beaten track are incredibly low. The least expensive areas are central and eastern Slovakia.

Sample Prices Cup of coffee, 10 Sk; beer (½ liter), 15 Sk; Coca-Cola, 10 Sk–15 Sk; ham sandwich, 30 Sk; 1-mile taxi ride, 100 Sk.

Museums Admission to museums, galleries, and castles ranges from 5 Sk to 50 Sk.

Visas U.S. and British citizens do not need visas to enter Slovakia. Visa requirements have been temporarily reintroduced for Canadian citizens; check whether this is still the case with the consulate. Apply to the Consulate of the Slovak Republic, 50 Rideau Terrace, Ottowa, Ontario K1M 2A1, tel. 316/749–4442.

Customs **On Arrival** Valuable items should be entered on your customs declaration. You can bring in 250 cigarettes (or their equivalent in tobacco), 2 liters of wine, 1 liter of spirits, ½ liter of eau de cologne, and gifts to the value of 1,000 Sk.

On Departure Crystal not purchased with hard currency may be subject to a tax of 100% of its retail price. To be on the safe side, hang on to all receipts. Only antiques bought at specially designated shops may be exported.

Language Slovak, a western-Slavic tongue closely related to both Czech and Polish, is the official language of Slovakia. Czech and Slovak are mutually comprehensible; if you speak Czech, you'll have little problem in Slovakia. Learning English is popular among young people, but German is still the most useful language for tourists.

Getting Around

By Car **Road Conditions** Main roads are usually good, if sometimes narrow, and traffic is light, especially away from main centers. **Bratislava** is not a good city for drivers, and finding a parking space can be a problem. Hence, for touring the capital, walking is the best option. It's very useful to have a car when exploring central and eastern Slovakia, however, where many of the interesting sights are outside the larger towns and are difficult to reach with mass transit.

Rules of the Road Drive on the right. Speed limits are 60 kph (37 mph) in built-up areas, 90 kph (55 mph) on open roads, and 110 kph (68 mph) on expressways. Seat belts are compulsory outside built-up areas; drinking and driving is strictly prohibited.

Gasoline Gasoline is expensive, averaging $3 a gallon. Service stations are usually located along main roads on the outskirts of towns and cities. Finding a station in Bratislava is difficult. Fill up on the freeway as you approach the city to avoid frustration. Lead-free gasoline, known as "Natural," is still available only at select stations, so tank up when you see it.

Breakdowns For accidents, call the emergency number (tel. 155). In case of an auto breakdown, in Bratislava contact the 24-hour service (tel. 07/ 249404). The *Auto Atlas ČSFR* (available at any bookstore) has a list of emergency road-repair numbers in various towns.

By Train Train service is erratic to all but the largest cities—**Poprad, Prešov, Košice,** and **Banská Bystrica.** Good, if slow, electric rail service, however, connects Poprad with the resorts of the **High Tatras.** If you're going just to the Tatras, you won't need any other kind of transportation.

By Bus Bus service in Bratislava is very cheap and reasonably frequent, and you can use it with confidence to reach any of the places in the tours below. You may have trouble reading the detailed information on the timetable, so try to ask if you're not sure where a particular bus is headed.

The bus network in Slovakia is dense, linking all of the towns on the tours given here. Leave a couple of extra days, however, to compensate for the infrequent service to the smaller towns.

Staying in Slovakia

Telephones These cost 1 Sk from a pay phone. Lift the receiver, place the coin in *Local Calls* the holder, dial, and insert the coin when your party picks up. Public phones are located in metro stations and on street corners; unfortunately, they're often out of order. Try asking in a hotel if you're stuck.

International You'll pay an enormous surcharge if you make calls from your hotel. *Calls* There's automatic dialing to many countries, including North America and the United Kingdom. For international inquiries, dial 0132 for the United States, Canada, or the United Kingdom. ATT's USADirect number for Slovakia is 004200010.

Mail Airmail letters to the United States and Canada cost 11 Sk up to 10 *Postal Rates* grams, postcards 6 Sk. Airmail letters to the United Kingdom cost 8 Sk up to 20 grams, postcards 5 Sk.

Receiving Mail Mail can be sent to Poste Restante at any main post office; there's no charge to claim it.

Opening and Banks are open weekdays 8–3. **Museums** are usually open Tues.– **Closing Times** Sun. 10–5. **Shops** are generally open weekdays 9–6 (Thurs. 9–8); some close between noon and 2. Many are also open Sat. 9–noon (department stores, 9–4).

National January 1; January 6 (Orthodox Easter); April 17 (Easter Monday); **Holidays** May 1 (Labor Day); July 5 (Sts. Cyril and Methodius); August 29 (anniversary of the Slovak National Uprising); September 1 (Constitution Day); December 25, 26.

Dining The options in Slovakia include restaurants, wine cellars, the more down-to-earth beer taverns, cafeterias, and a growing number of coffee shops and snack bars. Most restaurants are remarkably reasonable, but privatization is beginning to push up prices in a few places.

The most typical main dish is roast pork (or duck or goose) with sauerkraut. Dumplings in various forms or potatoes, generally with a rich gravy, accompany many dishes. Peppers are frequently used as well to spice up bland entrées. Look for *halušky*, a tasty Slovak noodle dish, usually served with sheep cheese. Fresh green vegetables and salads are still rare, but there are plenty of the pickled variety.

Mealtimes Lunch is usually from 11:30 to 2 or 3; dinner from 6 to 9:30 or 10. Some places are open all day, and in Bratislava you might find it easier to find a table during off hours.

Ratings Prices are reasonable by American standards, even in the more expensive restaurants. The following prices are for meals made up of a first course, main course, and dessert (excluding wine and tip). Best bets are indicated by a star ★.

Category	Cost
Very Expensive	over 600 Sk
Expensive	400 Sk–600 Sk
Moderate	200 Sk–400 Sk
Inexpensive	under 200 Sk

Lodging Travelers to Slovakia can choose from among hotels, motels, private accommodations, and campsites. Many older properties are gradually being renovated, and the best have great character and style. There is still an acute shortage of hotel rooms during the peak season, so make reservations well in advance. Many private room agencies are now in operation, and as long as you arrive before 9 PM, you should be able to get a room. The standards of facilities and services hardly match those in the West, so don't be surprised by faulty plumbing or indifferent reception clerks.

Hotels These are officially graded with from one to five stars. Many hotels used by foreign visitors—Interhotels—belong to Čedok and are mainly in the three- to five-star categories. These will have all or some rooms with bath or shower.

Private Accommodations Čedok can help you find a private room in Bratislava and other larger cities. These accommodations are invariably cheaper (around $20) and often more comfortable than hotels, though you may have to sacrifice something in privacy. You can also wander the main roads looking for signs declaring "Room Free," or more frequently, in German, "Zimmer Frei" or "Privatzimmer."

Rates Prices are for double rooms, generally not including breakfast. Prices at the lower end of the scale apply to low season. At certain periods, such as Easter or during festivals, there may be an increase of 15%–25%. Best bets are indicated by a star ★.

Category	Cost
Very Expensive	over $100
Expensive	$50–$100

Moderate	$15–$50
Inexpensive	under $15

Tipping Small sums of hard currency will certainly be most welcome. To reward good service in a restaurant, round up the bill to the nearest multiple of 10; 10% is considered appropriate on very large tabs. Tip porters who bring bags to your rooms 20 Sk. For room service, a 20 Sk tip is enough. In taxis, round up the bill by 10%. Give tour guides and helpful concierges between 20 Sk and 30 Sk for services rendered.

Bratislava

Arriving and Departing

By Plane The most convenient international airport for Bratislava is in Vienna, approximately 50 kilometers (30 miles) away. Four buses a day stop at Schwechat en route to Bratislava, or you could even take a taxi; the journey takes just over an hour, depending on the border crossing. From Prague's Ruzyně Airport you can take a ČSA domestic flight to Bratislava; the flight takes about an hour.

If time is a factor during your stay in Slovakia, flying may be an option to consider for reaching the relatively far-flung Tatras and eastern Slovakia. ČSA has reasonably priced daily flights from Prague and Bratislava to Poprad (the regional airport for the Tatras). For further information, contact the ČSA offices in Prague (tel. 02/2146) or Bratislava (tel. 07/311205).

By Train Reasonably efficient train service connects Prague and Bratislava. Trains leave from Prague's main station (Hlavní nádraží, and the journey takes five hours. There are four trains a day to and from Vienna, with the journey lasting just over an hour.

By Bus There are numerous buses from Prague to Bratislava; the journey costs less than 200 Sk and takes about five hours. From Vienna, there are four buses a day from Autobusbahnhof Wien Mitte. The journey takes between 1½ and two hours. The **Autobus Stanica** in Bratislava is just outside the center; you can take trolleybus No. 217 to Mierové námestie or bus No. 107 to the Castle (Hrad).

By Car There are good freeways from Prague to Bratislava via Brno (D1 and D2); the 315-kilometer (203-mile) journey takes about 3½ hours. From Vienna, take the A4 and then Route 8 to Bratislava. The 60-kilometer (37-mile) trip will take about 1½ hours.

Getting Around

By Car Bratislava is not a good city for drivers, and finding a parking space can be a problem; hence, for touring the republic's capital, walking is the best option. If you do need to rent a car, you can do so either at Čedok or at the Hotel Forum.

By Bus Bus service in Bratislava is very cheap and reasonably frequent, and you can use it with confidence to reach any of the main sights.

Important Addresses and Numbers

Tourist Information Bratislava has its own tourist information service, **Bratislava Tourist Information (BIS)** (Panská 18, tel. 07/33715 or 07/334370). The office is in the Old Town, a few steps down from Hlavné námestie. It's open weekdays 8–4:30 (8–6 in summer) and Saturday 8–1. The Čedok office (Jesenského 5, tel. 07/52002; open weekdays 9–6, Sat. 9–noon) can help with accommodations and provide information on Bratislava and surrounding areas.

Emergencies **Police:** tel. 158. **Ambulance:** tel. 155.

Late-night Pharmacies *(lekárna)* take turns staying open late or on Sunday.
Pharmacies Look for the list posted on the front door of each pharmacy. For af-ter-hours service, ring the bell; you will be served through a little hatch-door.

Guided Tours

The best tours of Bratislava are offered by **BIS** (*see* Tourist Informa-tion, *above*), although out of the summer season they are given only in German and only on weekends. These tours start at 2 PM at the National Theater; they last two hours and cost 270 Sk per person. Čedok offers tours from May through September on Wednesday and Saturday, starting at 1:45 from the Devin Hotel (Riečna ul. 4, tel. 07/330851). You can combine these with an afternoon tour of the Small Carpathians (departing at 4:45 PM, also from the Devin), which includes dinner at the Zochová Chata. Čedok can also arrange an indi-vidual guide at a cost of around 150 Sk.

Exploring Bratislava

Europe's newest capital city is on the move. Everywhere you look new shops are opening and older buildings are being renovated, as if the city's residents were trying to forget as quickly as possible the past 40 years when Bratislava played second fiddle to Prague. Avoid the newer, and shabbier, parts of the city and head instead for the peace and beauty of the Old Town.

Originally settled by a variety of Celts and Romans, the city became part of the Great Moravian Empire under Prince Břetislav. After a short period under the Bohemian Přemysl princes, Bratislava was brought into the Hungarian kingdom by Stephan I at the end of the 10th century. The Hungarians called it Pozsony; the German set-tlers, Pressburg; and the original Slovaks called it Bratislava after Prince Břetislav.

Numbers in the margin correspond to points of interest on the Brati-slava map.

❶ Begin your tour of the city at the modern square **Námestie SNP.** An abbreviation for *Slovenské Národné Povstanie* (Slovak National Up-rising), these three letters appear on streets, squares, bridges, and posters throughout Slovakia. This anti-Nazi resistance movement involved partisan fighting, organized partly but not exclusively by the Communists, in Slovakia's mountainous areas during the final years of the war. In 1992 this was the center for demonstrations in support of Slovak independence, and you will often see the Slovak flag (red, blue, and white with a double cross) flying from the parti-san's gun.

❷ From here walk up toward **Hurbanovo námestie.** Across the road, unobtrusively located between a large shoe store and a bookshop, is the enchanting entrance to the Old Town. A small bridge, decorated with wrought-iron railings and statues of St. John Nepomuk and St. Michael, takes you over the old mote, now blossoming with trees and fountains, into the intricate barbican, a set of gates and houses that

Dóm Sv.
Martina, **5**

Hrad, **7**

Hurbanovo
Námestie, **2**

Jezuitský
Kostol, **9**

Michalská
Brána, **3**

Most SNP, **6**

Námestie
SNP, **1**

Palác Uhorskej
Král'ovskej
Komory, **4**

Primaciálny
Palác, **11**

Stará
Radnica, **10**

Židovská
Ulica, **8**

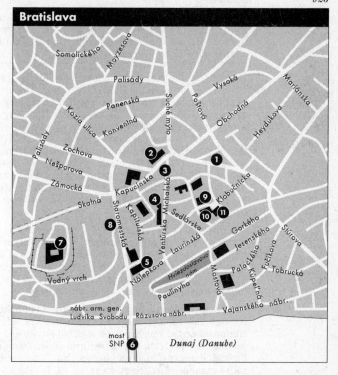

Bratislava

Dunaj (Danube)

❸ made up the medieval fortifications. After going through the first archway, you come to the narrow **Michalská ulica;** in front of you is the **Michalská brána** (Michael's Gate), the last remaining of the original three city gates.

❹ A little farther down Michalská ulica on the right is the **Palác Uhorskej král'ovskej komory** (Hungarian Royal Chamber), a Baroque palace that housed the Hungarian nobles' parliament from 1802 until 1848; it is now used as the University Library. Go through the arched passageway at the back of this building, and you'll emerge in a tiny square dominated by the **Church and Convent of the Poor Clares.**

❺ Follow Farská ulica up to the corner, and turn left on **Kapitulská ulica,** noticing the ground stone depicting two kissing lizards. At the bottom of the street is the side wall of the **Dóm svätého Martina** (St. Martin's Cathedral). Construction of this massive plain Gothic church, with its 280-foot steeple twinkling with gold trim, began in the 14th century. Between the 16th and 19th centuries, the Cathedral saw the coronation of 17 Hungarian royals. You can enter the church through a door on this side (Kapitulská ulica). The peace is disturbed by the noise of traffic zooming by on the elevated freeway built in the 1970s across the front entrance, reducing the church to an irrelevant religious relic.

❻ As you leave the church and walk around to the front, the freeway leading to the futuristic spaceship bridge, **Most SNP,** is the first thing you see. Follow the steps under the passageway and up the other side in the direction of the Castle.

Time Out At the top of the wood stairs, you come to the **Arkadia** restaurant and café, one of Bratislava's better private establishments, situated in a beautiful old house. Here you can get good coffee and desserts or a full meal before the ascent to the castle.

❼ Continue up the steps, through a Gothic arched gateway built in 1480, until you reach the **Hrad** (castle) area. The original fortifications date from the 9th century. The Hungarian kings expanded the castle into a large royal residence, and the Habsburgs turned it into a very successful defense against the Turks. Its current design, square with four corner towers, stems from the 17th century, although the existing castle had to be completely rebuilt after a disastrous fire in 1811. In the castle, you'll find the **Slovenské národné múzeum** (Slovak National Museum). The exhibits cover glassmaking, medieval warfare, and coinmaking. *Zámocká ul., tel. 07/ 311444. Admission: 40 Sk. adults, 10 Sk. children and students. Open Tues.–Sun., 10–5.*

❽ Leave the castle by the same route, but instead of climbing the last stairs by the Arkadia restaurant, continue down the old-world Beblaveho ulica. Continue along **Židovská ulica.** The name, Jews' Street, marks this area as the former Jewish ghetto. Walk up Židovská until you come to a thin concrete bridge that connects with the reconstructed city walls across the freeway.

Across the road you'll find steps leading down into the Old Town. Go through the Františkánske námestie into the adjoining square, **Hlavné námestie,** which is lined with old houses and palaces representing the spectrum of architectural styles from Gothic (No. 2), through Baroque (No. 4) and Rococo (No. 7), to a wonderfully decorative example of Art Nouveau at No. 10. To your immediate left as **❾** you come into the square is the richly decorated **Jezuitský kostol** (Jesuit Church). Next door is the colorful agglomeration of old bits **❿** and pieces that makes up the **Stará radnica** (Old Town Hall). The imaginative roofing stems from the end of the 15th century, and the wall paintings from the 16th century. Walk through the arched passageway, still with early Gothic ribbing, into a wonderfully cheery Renaissance courtyard with romantic arcades and gables. Toward the back of the courtyard, you'll find the entrance to the **Mestské múzeum** (City Museum), which documents Bratislava's varied past. *Primaciálne nám., tel. 07/334690. Admission: 4 Sk. adults, 1 Sk. children and students. Open Tues.–Sun. 10–5.*

⓫ Leaving the back entrance of the Old Town Hall, you come to the **Primaciálne námestie** (Primates' Square), with the glorious pale pink, classical elegance of the **Primaciálny palác** (Primates' Palace). If the building is open, go up to the dazzling hall of mirrors. In this room, Napoleon and Habsburg Emperor Franz I signed the Bratislava Peace of 1805, following Napoleon's victory at the Battle of Austerlitz.

Dining

For details and price-category definitions, *see* Dining in Staying in Slovakia, *above.*

★ **Klaštorná Vináreň.** Old Town dining can be a delight in the vaulted cellars of this old monastery. The spiciness of Slovak cooking comes alive in dishes like *Čikós tokáň,* a fiery mixture of pork, onions, and peppers. Wash it down with a glass of mellow red wine and a fire hose. *Bravcové ražníci* is milder, a tender pork shish kebab and fried potatoes. *Františkanská ul. 1, tel. 07/330430. Reservations advised. No credit cards. Closed Sun. Moderate–Expensive.*

Rybársky Cech. The name means "Fishermen's Guild," and this restaurant, which has Bratislava's smartest interior, is in the guild house on the river embankment below the castle. It's really two restaurants in one: freshwater fish is served upstairs; pricier saltwater varieties are offered on the ground floor. *Žižkova ul. 1, tel. 07/ 313049. Reservations advised. No credit cards. Closed Sat. Moderate–Expensive.*

Modrá Hviezda. The first of a new breed of small, privately owned wine cellars, the "Blue Star" eschews the international standards in favor of regional Slovak fare. Be sure to try the *bryndza* (baked sheep-cheese) pie and the tasty goulash. *Beblavého 14, tel. 07/ 332747. Reservations advised. No credit cards. Moderate.*

Michalská. This light, airy luncheon restaurant, with an adjacent stand-up buffet, is situated in a convenient spot in the heart of the old town. Soup, *halušky* (noodles with sheep cheese), and salad make a meal fit for a king. *Michalská ul. 1, tel. 07/332389. Reservations not necessary. No credit cards. Inexpensive.*

Stará Sladovňa. This mammoth beer hall in known lovingly, and fittingly, as "Mamut" to Bratislavans. Locals come here for the Bohemian beer on tap and for inexpensive, filling meals. The place seats almost 2,000, so don't worry about reservations. *Cintorínska ul. 32, tel. 07/51101. No credit cards. Inexpensive.*

Lodging

For details and price-category definitions, *see* Lodging in Staying in Slovakia, *above.*

★ **Danube.** Opened in 1992 to rival the Forum in atmosphere and services. The latter may retain an overall edge, but the Danube is the better value. The Danube also wins hands down on location—alongside the river, with a stunning view of the castle out the front door. *Rybné námestie 1, tel. 07/340833, fax 07/314311. 280 rooms with bath. Facilities: restaurants, nightclub, health club, pool, sauna, solarium. AE, DC, MC, V. Very Expensive.*

Forum Bratislava. The Forum opened in 1989 in downtown Bratislava, offering top facilities. It houses a French as well as a Slovak restaurant and several cafés and bars. *Hodžovo námestie 2, tel. 07/ 348111, fax 07/314645. 219 rooms with bath. Facilities: nightclub, saunas, pool, solarium, health club. AE, DC, MC, V. Very Expensive.*

Želing. This small, family-run pension is just outside the Old Town. Clean, cozy rooms and affordable prices compensate for the uninspiring, modern appearance. *Panenská 7, tel. 07/312982, fax 07/ 331207. 15 rooms without bath. Facilities: snack bar. No credit cards. Inexpensive.*

Highlights of Slovakia

Most visitors head for the great peaks of the High Tatras, with their excellent tourist facilities; and this is where most tours will take you. The mountains *are* spectacular, but also worth seeing are the exquisite medieval towns of **Spiš** in the plains and valleys below the High Tatras and the beautiful 18th-century country churches farther east. Away from main centers, these areas are short on tourist amenities, so if creature comforts are important to you, stick to the Tatras.

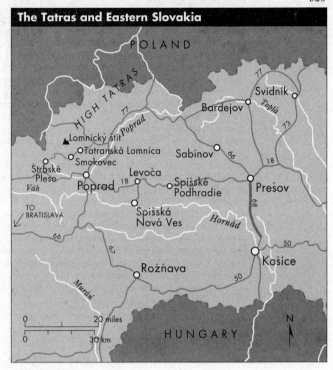

The Tatras and Eastern Slovakia

Getting Around

By Plane ČSA's 40-minute flights from Bratislava to Poprad connect with services from Prague once or twice daily and are reasonable.

By Train Train service is erratic to all but the largest cities—**Poprad, Prešov, Košice,** and **Banská Bystrica.** (Bratislava to Poprad by express train takes four hours.) Good, if slow, electric rail service, however, connects Poprad with the resorts of the **High Tatras.** If you're going just to the Tatras, you won't need any other kind of transportation.

By Bus The bus network is dense, linking all of the towns mentioned in Exploring Slovakia, *below.* Leave a couple of extra days, however, to compensate for infrequent service to smaller towns. Consult local timetables for specific information.

Guided Tours

Čedok's seven-day **Grand Tour of Slovakia,** which leaves from Bratislava every other Saturday from June through September, stops in the High Tatras, Kežmarok, Košice, and Banská Bystrica. The tour includes all meals and accommodations. For more information, contact the Čedok office in Bratislava (tel. 07/55280).

Slovair offers a novel biplane flight over the Tatras from Poprad airport. Contact the Čedok office in Poprad (tel. 092/23651). The Čedok office in Starý Smokovec (tel. 0969/2417) is also helpful in arranging tours of the Tatras and the surrounding area.

Tourist Information

Bardejov (Nám. Osloboditel'ov 46, tel. 0935/2134).
Bratislava (Štúrova 13, tel. 07/55280).
Prešov (Hlavná ul. 1, tel. 091/24040).
Smokovec (Starý Smokovec V/22, tel. 0969/2417).
Žilina (Hodžova ul. 9, tel. 089/23347).

Exploring Slovakia

Despite its charms, there's no denying that Bratislava is intensely industrial. If you're not going on to the mountains and fresh air of the High Tatras (*see below*), a good one- or two-day natural respite can be had less than an hour north of the city, in the **Malé Karpaty** (Small Carpathian) mountains. Drive or take the bus to the dusty wine-making town of **Modra**, and from there, follow the signs to **Zochová Chata**, some 8 kilometers (5 miles) away in the hills. The *chata* is really a cozy mountain chalet, with big rooms, plenty of period furniture, and a romantic *koliba* (tavern) that serves the best roast chicken in Slovakia. Trails fan out in all directions from the chata. For a full day's walk, follow the yellow-marked path about three hours to the Renaissance castle **Červený Kameň** ("red rock"). The blue-marked path will take you back to Zochová Chata.

Whether you travel by car, bus, or train, your route will follow the Vah Valley for most of the way to **Poprad**, a transit point for Slovakia's most magnificent natural treasure, the High Tatras. While Poprad itself is a dreary place, its suburb of **Spišská Sobota**, reached by bus Nos. 2, 3, or 4, is, however, a little gem. It was one of 24 small Gothic towns in a medieval region known as **Spiš**. Steep shingled roofs, high timberframed gables, and brick-arched doorways are the main features of the rich merchants' dwelling, usually grouped around a main square dominated by a Gothic church, often with a separate Renaissance bell tower. Keep in mind the name Pavol of Levoča, one of the great woodcarvers of the 16th century. The main altar in **Sv. Juraj** (the Church of St. George) is his work. The **museum** is worth a visit. *Admission: 4 Sk. Open Mon.–Sat. 9–4.*

Both an electric train network and a winding highway link Poprad with the resorts spread about on the lower slopes of the High Tatras. **Štrbské Pleso** is the highest of the towns and the best launching point for mountain excursions. A rewarding two-hour trek of moderate difficulty leads from here to **Popradské Pleso**, one of dozens of tiny, isolated Alpine lakes that dot the Tatras. **Smokovec** is really three resorts in one (Starý, Nový, and Horný) and has the most varied amenities. For the most effortless high-level trip, though, go to **Tatranská Lomnica**, from which a two-stage cable car will take you via Skalnaté Pleso to Lomnický štít, which at 8,635 feet high is the second-highest peak in the range. From Skalnaté Pleso, you can take the red-marked Magistrale trail down to **Hrebienok**, where you can board a funicular and ride down to Stary Smokovec. The **Museum of the Tatra National Park** at Tatranská Lomnica offers an excellent introduction to the area's natural and human history. *Admission: 6 Sk, 2 Sk for children. Open weekdays 8:30–noon and 1–5, weekends 8–noon.*

Leave Poprad on Highway 18 east. Restoration work on **Levoča**, the most famous of the Spiš towns, is well under way, and the overlays of Renaissance on Gothic are extremely satisfying to the eye (note especially Nos. 43, 45, 47, and 49 on the main square). Pavol of

Levoča's work on the main altar of **Sv. Jakub** (the Church of St. James) on the main square is both monumental in size and exquisite in its detail.

The surrounding countryside is dotted with more medieval towns. About 16 kilometers (10 miles) to the east, the massive, partly restored ruins of **Spiš Castle,** above Spišské Podhradie, dominate the surrounding pastures and orchards. Some of **Prešov's** fortifications survive, and its spindle-shaped main square is lined with buildings in the Gothic, Renaissance, and Baroque styles. You have now left Spiš and entered **Šariš,** a region whose proximity to the Orthodox east has left a unique legacy of both Orthodox and Greek Catholic (Uniate) churches. The Uniates are particularly interesting because, though they acknowledge the pope's supremacy, they have retained their own litergy and their clergy are permitted to marry.

Bardejov is a splendid walled town and makes the best center from which to set out on a journey of exploration, as long as you're prepared to get lost along some rough minor roads while seeking out the 17th- and 18th-century wooden churches of **Bodružal, Ladomirová, Mirola,** and **Šemetkovce**—and the right person to open them up for you. You'll find these churches east and northeast of **Svidník,** near the border with Poland (follow the road to the Dukla Pass). These churches jostle for attention with the dramatic collection of Nazi and Soviet tanks and planes dotted around this area to commemorate the fighting that took place in 1944. Easier to find is the 15th-century church of **Hvervartov** (Roman Catholic), 10 kilometers (6 miles) southwest of Bardejov—a fascinating example of timber Gothic with some famous 17th-century frescoes.

Dining and Lodging

For details and price-category definitions, *see* Dining and Lodging in Staying in Slovakia, *above.*

Bardejov
Lodging

Minerál. This rather sterile modern hotel lies in a quiet location in the spa town of Bardejovské kúpele, 3½ miles from Bardejov proper. *Bardejovské kúpele, tel. 0935/4122. 60 rooms with shower. Facilities: tennis courts. No credit cards. Moderate.*

Smokovec
Dining

Tatranská Kúria. The Tatranská's rustic decor and Slovak specialties will provide some insight into local life. Dishes include *rezeň kúria* (pork cutlets with a cheese and ham filling in a cheese pastry) and *bryndzové pirohy* (cheese-filled pastry served with cream and bacon). *Starý Smokovec, tel. 0969/2806. Reservations not necessary. No credit cards. Closes early. Moderate.*

Lodging

Bellevue. This modern high rise with well-appointed rooms lies about 200 yards from the resort center. Rates include breakfast and dinner. *Horný Smokovec, tel. 0969/2941. 103 rooms, 63 with bath. Facilities: saunas, pool. AE, DC, MC, V. Expensive.*

Grand Hotel. The town's oldest hotel has a wonderful air of faded fin-de-siècle elegance. It's right in the resort center, with a reasonable restaurant. Rooms without bath are Moderate. *Starý Smokovec, tel. 0969/2154. 83 rooms, some with bath. Facilities: restaurant, nightclub, pool, sauna. AE, DC, MC, V. Expensive.*

Villa Dr. Szontagh. Away from the action in Nový Smokovec, this steepled chalet, formerly known as the Tokájík, offers mostly peace and quiet. The darkly furnished rooms and public areas are well maintained, and the courtly staff goes out of its way to please. *Nový Smokovec, tel. 0969/2061. 11 rooms with bath. Facilities: restau-*

rant, wine cellar. Breakfast not included. No credit cards. Moderate.

Tatranská Lomnica

Dining

Zbojnícka Koliba. This tavern offers a small range of Slovak specialties prepared over an open fire, amid rustic decor and accompanied by folk music. *Near Grandhotel Praha, tel. 0969/967630. Reservations not necessary. No credit cards. Dinner only. Closed Sun. Moderate.*

Lodging

Grandhotel Praha. A renovated turn-of-the-century building, the Grandhotel has large, comfortable rooms decorated with a traditional touch. The restaurant has an air of elegance that is unusual in Slovakia. *Tel. 0969/967941. 92 rooms with bath. Facilities: restaurant, nightclub. AE, DC, MC, V. Expensive.*

26 Spain

Spain has long had a rather schizophrenic reputation as a vacation destination among English-speaking tourists. On the one hand, as Europe's premier package-vacation destination, the country is almost instinctively associated in many minds with the worst excesses of the cheap-holiday-in-the-sun, an image conjured up by the vast numbers of faceless hotels along the Mediterranean coasts. The other half of the equation is infinitely more appealing. For Spain is also the land of the fountain-singing courtyards of Moorish Granada and Córdoba, of dusty plains where Don Quixote fought imaginary enemies, and of timeless hilltop towns. Spain also acquired a new gloss on the international scene in 1992, when it played host to two major events of world stature: the Olympic Games in Barcelona, and the International Exposition in Seville. Both events brought with them major face-lifts to the cities and regions hosting them, as well as quite dramatic improvements to their infrastructures.

Still, if it's beaches you're after, there is the jet-set Costa del Sol in the south, or San Sebastián in the Basque country, formerly the summer capital of Spain. Farther west is the resort city of Santander and La Coruña, a long-standing favorite of British visitors. In the east is the Costa Brava, while to the south, around Alicante, is the Costa Blanca, with its most popular tourist center at Benidorm. When you tire of roasting in the sun, rent a car and head for one of the thousands of castles, ruins, or museums. Perhaps the number-one tourist attraction is the Alhambra, in Granada. Following close behind it come the Mosque of Córdoba, and the Alcázar and cathedral of Seville. Ávila is a historic walled town and Segovia boasts a Roman aqueduct and proud Alcázar. Madrid, the capital, contains some of the greatest art collections in the world, while Toledo, home of El Greco and boasting a cathedral, synagogues, and startling views, is one of Spain's greatest treasures. Finally, Barcelona, capital of Catalonia, has a sophistication built on its obsession with design, from Gaudí at the turn of the century right up to the present day.

Essential Information

Before You Go

When to Go The tourist season runs from Easter to mid-October. The best months for sightseeing are May, June, September, and early October, when the weather is usually pleasant and sunny without being unbearably hot. During July and August try to avoid Madrid or the inland cities of Andalusia, where the heat can be stifling and many places close down at 1 PM. If you visit Spain in high summer, the best bet is to head for the coastal resorts or to mountain regions such as the Pyrenees or Picos de Europa. The one exception to Spain's high summer temperatures is the north coast, where the climate is similar to that of northern Europe.

Visitors should be aware of the seasonal events that can clog parts of the country, reserving in advance if traveling during peak periods. Easter is always a busy time, especially in Madrid, Barcelona, and the main Andalusian cities of Seville, Córdoba, Granada, Málaga, and the Costa del Sol resorts. July and August, when most Spaniards and other Europeans take their annual vacations, see the heaviest crowds, particularly in coastal resorts. Holiday weekends are naturally busy, and major fiestas, such as Pamplona's running of the bulls, make advance booking essential and cause prices to soar. Off-season travel offers fewer crowds and lower rates in many hotels.

Spain

Bay of Biscay

El Ferrol
La Coruña
Villalba
Ribadeo
Luarca
Gijón
Ribadesella
Santander
S
Santiago de
Compostela
Lugo
Oviedo
Mieres
Cangas
de Onis
PICOS DE
EUROPA
Bilbao
Muros
C A N T A B R I A N
MTS.
Pontevedra
Vigo
Orense
Ponferrada
León
Burgos
Logro
Tui/Túy
Astorga
Benavente
Palencia
Valladolid
Duero
Zamora
Tordesillas
Salamanca
Adanero
Segovia
SIERRA DE GUADARRAMA
Guadalajara
Ciudad
Rodrigo
Avila
El Escorial
MADRID
PORTUGAL
Plasencia
SIERRA DE GREDOS
Toledo
Tara
Talavera
de la Reina
Aranjuez
Tajo
Guadalupe
Alcázar de
San Juan
Cáceres
Trujillo
Mérida
Guadiana
Ciudad
Real
Abenójar
Badajoz
Valdepeñas
Jerez de los
Caballeros
Zafra
Almadén
Fregenal
de la Sierra
SIERRA MORENA
Bailén
Linares
Ubeda
Córdoba
Baeza
Aroche
Jaén
Caz
Seville
Guadalquivir
Ecija
Baena
Carmona
Lucena
Guadix
Huelva
Granada
SIERRA
Gulf of
Cadiz
Antequera
Loja
COSTA DE LA LUZ
Sanlúcar de
Barrameda
Ronda
Nerja
Cádiz
Jerez de
la Frontera
Torremolinos
Málaga
Motril
ATLANTIC
OCEAN
Estepona
Fuengirola
Marbella
COSTA DEL SOL
Algeciras
Gibraltar
TO CANARY
ISLANDS
Strait of Gibraltar

Climate The following are the average daily maximum and minimum temperatures for Madrid.

Jan.	47F	9C	May	70F	21C	Sept.	77F	25C
	35	2		50	10		57	14
Feb.	52F	11C	June	80F	27C	Oct.	65F	18C
	36	2		58	15		49	10
Mar.	59F	15C	July	87F	31C	Nov.	55F	13C
	41	5		63	17		42	5
Apr.	65F	18C	Aug.	85F	30C	Dec.	48F	9C
	45	7		63	17		36	2

Currency The unit of currency in Spain is the peseta. There are bills of 1,000, 2,000, 5,000, and 10,000 ptas. Coins are 1 pta., 5, 25, 50, 100, 200, and 500 ptas. The 2- and 10-pta. coins and the old 100-pta. bills are rare but still legal tender. Note that pay phones in Spain won't accept the new, smaller 5- and 25-pta. coins first minted in 1991. Following the recent European currency shakeup, which resulted in several devaluations of the peseta, most foreigners find that their currency now goes farther in Spain than it had in recent years. At press time (spring 1994), the exchange rate was about 140 ptas. to the U.S. dollar and 205 ptas. to the pound sterling.

Credit Cards Most hotels, restaurants, and stores accept payment by credit card. Visa is the most widely accepted piece of plastic, followed by MasterCard (called EuroCard in Spain). More expensive establishments may also take American Express and Diners Club.

Changing Money The word to look for is "Cambio" (exchange). Most Spanish banks take a 1½% commission, though some less scrupulous places charge more; always check, as rates can vary greatly. To change money in a bank, you need your passport and a lot of patience, because filling out the forms takes time. Hotels offer rates lower than banks, but they rarely make a commission, so you may well break even. Restaurants and stores, with the exception of those catering to the tour bus trade, do not usually accept payment by dollars or traveler's checks. If you have a credit card with a Personal Identification Number (PIN), you'll be able to make withdrawals or get cash advances at most cash machines at Spanish banks.

Currency Regulations Visitors may take any amount of foreign currency in bills or traveler's checks into Spain as well as any amount of pesetas. When leaving Spain, you may take out only 100,000 ptas. per person in Spanish bank notes and foreign currency up to the equivalent of 500,000 ptas, unless you can prove you declared the excess at customs on entering the country.

What It Will Cost Prices rose fast during the first decade of Spain's democracy, and Spain's inflation rate was one of the highest in Europe. By the 1990s, however, inflation had been curbed; in 1994, it was just a little over 5%. Generally speaking, the cost of living in Spain is now on a par with that of most other European countries, and the days when Spain was the bargain basement of Europe are truly over, although the weakness of the peseta has somewhat improved the buying power of visitors from North America and the U.K. The 1992 completion of the country's integration into the European Community (EC) and the euphoria accompanying the Olympic games and Seville's Expo '92 were, unfortunately, accompanied by sometimes shocking price increases. These have been reversed to a certain extent, though Seville and Barcelona are still quite expensive. In general, the cost of lodging is roughly comparable to that in France and Great Britain. You can still eat fairly cheaply in Spain, but if you go to quality restaurants, it will cost you dearly; in general, the cost of lodging has risen to make up for the peseta devaluation, while restaurant prices remain stable. Snacks in cafés and bars are expensive by American or British standards, and alcohol is generally reasonable, except for cocktails in hotel bars. Trains and long-distance buses are relatively inexpensive, and car-rental rates are lower than in some European countries. City buses and subways are a good value, and cab fares are bargains compared with rates in the United States.

Taxes A value-added tax known as IVA was introduced in 1986 when Spain joined the European Community (EC). IVA is levied at 6% on most goods and services, but a luxury rate of 15% applies to five-star hotels and to car rental. IVA is always included in the purchase price of goods in stores, but for hotels and car rentals, the tax will be added to your bill. Many restaurants include IVA in their menu prices, but plenty—usually the more expensive ones—do not. Large stores, such as the Corte Inglés and Galerías Preciados, operate a tax refund plan for foreign visitors who are not EC nationals; but to qualify for this refund, you need to spend at least 48,000 ptas. in any one store and, in theory, on any one item. There is no airport tax in Spain.

Sample Prices A cup of coffee will cost around 125 ptas., a Coca-Cola 150 ptas., bottled beer 150 ptas., a small draught beer 100 ptas., a glass of wine in a bar 100 ptas., an American-style cocktail 400 ptas., a ham sandwich 300 ptas., an ice-cream cone about 150 ptas., a local bus or subway ride 125 ptas., and a one-mile taxi ride about 350 ptas.

Language In major cities and coastal resorts you should have no trouble finding people who speak English. In such places, reception staff in hotels of three or more stars are required to speak English. Don't expect the man in the street or the bus driver to speak English, although you may be pleasantly surprised.

Getting Around

By Car Roads marked A *(autopista)* are toll roads. N stands for national or
Road main roads, and C for country roads. A huge road improvement
Conditions scheme has been largely completed, but many N roads are still single-lane and the going can be slow. Tolls vary but are high; for example, Bilbao–Zaragoza 2,930 ptas., Salou–Valencia 2,065 ptas., Seville–Jerez 585 ptas.

Rules of the Driving is on the right, and horns and high-beam headlights may not
Road be used in cities. Front seat belts are compulsory. Children under age 10 may not ride in front seats. At traffic circles, give way to traffic coming from the right unless your road has priority. Your home driving license is essential and must be carried with you at all times, along with your car insurance and vehicle registration document. You will also need an International Driving License and a proof-of-insurance Green Card if you are bringing your own car into Spain. Speed limits are 120 kph (74 mph) on autopistas, 100 kph (62 mph) on N roads, 90 kph (56 mph) on C roads, and 60 kph (37 mph) in cities unless otherwise signed.

Parking Parking restrictions should be checked locally. In many cities, a blue line on the street indicates residents-only parking; other cars are towed promptly. In other places, curbside signs inform you of legal parking times. Never leave *anything* on view inside a parked car. Thefts are common, and it is safer to leave your car in one of the many paying parking lots; charges are reasonable.

Gasoline At press time, gas cost 106 ptas. a liter for super and 99 ptas. a liter for regular. Unleaded gas *(sin plomo)* is now available at a steadily increasing number of pumps. There is attendant service at most pumps, but there's no need to tip for just a fill-up. Most gas stations accept payment by credit card.

By Train The Spanish railroad system, known usually by its initials RENFE, has greatly improved in recent years. Air-conditioned trains are now widespread but by no means universal. Most overnight trains have first- and second-class sleeping cars and second-class *literas* (couchettes). Dining, buffet, and refreshment services are available on most long-distance trains. There are various types of trains—*talgo*, ELT (electric unit expresses), TER (diesel rail cars), and ordinary *expresos* and *rápidos*. Fares are determined by the kind of train you travel on and not just by the distance traveled. Talgos are by far the quickest, most comfortable, and the most expensive train; *expresos* and *rápidos* are the slowest and cheapest of the long-distance services. In spring 1992, a high-speed train known as the AVE (Alto Velocidad Español) began service between Madrid and Seville, reducing travel time between these cities from six to two and a half hours (fares vary, but the AVE can cost almost as much as flying). A few lines, such as the narrow-gauge FEVE routes along the north coast from San Sebastián to El Ferrol and on the Costa Blanca around Alicante, do not belong to the national RENFE network, and international rail passes are not valid on these lines.

Ticket Purchase and Seat Reservation Tickets can be bought from any station (whether or not it is your point of departure), and from downtown RENFE offices and travel agents displaying the blue and yellow RENFE sign. The latter are often best in the busy holiday season. At stations, buy your advance tickets from the window marked "Largo Recorrido, Venta Anticipada" (Long Distance, Advance Sales). Seat reservation can be made up to 60 days in advance and is obligatory on all the better long-distance services.

Fare Savers The **RENFE Tourist Card** is an unlimited-kilometers pass, valid for 8, 15, or 22 days' travel, and can be bought by anyone who lives outside Spain. It is available for first- or second-class travel and can be purchased from RENFE's General Representative in Europe (3 Ave. Marceau, 75116 Paris, France, tel. 14/723–52–00); from selected travel agencies and main railroad stations abroad; and within Spain, at RENFE travel offices and major long-distance stations such as those in Madrid, Barcelona, Port Bou, and Irún. At press time (spring 1994) the second-class pass cost 15,400 ptas. for 3 days, 24,200 ptas. for 5 days, and 37,400 ptas. for 10 days. RENFE has no representative in the United States.

Prices are determined according to when the train leaves. There are three price categories: *Valle* (low), *Llano* (regular), and *Punto* (high). On the most heavily used runs, Madrid–Barcelona or Madrid–Seville, for example, there is one *Valle* and one *Punto* train each day. The rest are in the *Llano* price category. The cheapest train generally departs early in the morning, while the most expensive leaves at midday.

By Plane **Iberia** and its subsidiary **Aviaco** operate a wide network of domestic flights, linking all the main cities and the Balearic Islands. Distances are great and internal airfares are high by U.S. standards, although deregulation is pushing prices lower. Flights from the mainland to the Balearics are heavily booked in summer, and the Madrid–Málaga route is frequently overbooked at Easter and in high season. A frequent shuttle service operates between Madrid and Barcelona. Iberia has its own offices in most major Spanish cities and acts as agent for Aviaco. In Madrid, Iberia headquarters are at Velázquez 130 (tel. 91/411–1011 for domestic reservations, and 91/329–4353 for international, or call Inforiberia for flight information, tel. 91/329–5767). Flights can also be booked at most travel agencies. Air Europa (91/305–5130) offers slightly cheaper scheduled service between Madrid and Barcelona as well as flights to the Canary Islands. For information on other airlines' flights to and within Spain, call the airline itself, or call the airport (tel. 91/305–8343/44/45/46) and ask for your airline.

By Bus   Spain has an excellent bus network, but there is no national or nationwide bus company. The network simply consists of numerous private regional bus companies *(empresas)* and there are therefore no comprehensive bus passes. Some of the buses on major routes are now quite luxurious, although this is not always the case in some of the more rural areas. Buses tend to be more frequent than trains, are sometimes cheaper, and often allow you to see more of the countryside. On major routes and at holiday times it is advisable to buy your ticket a day or two in advance. Some cities have central bus stations but in many, including Madrid and Barcelona, buses leave from various boarding points. Always check with the local tourist office. Bus stations, unlike train stations, usually provide luggage storage facilities.

Staying in Spain

Telephones   Pay phones are supposed to work with coins of 25 and either 50 or
Local Calls   100 ptas. (smaller 5- and 25-ptas. coins do not work in the machines). Twenty-five ptas. is the minimum for short local calls. In the older blue phones, place several coins in the slot, or in the groove on top of the phone, lift the receiver, and dial the number. Coins then fall into the machine as needed. In the newer green phones, place several coins in the slot, watch the display unit and feed as needed. These phones take 100-pta. coins. Area codes always begin with a 9 and are different for each province. In Madrid province, the code is 91; in Cantabria, it's 942. If you're dialing from outside the country, drop the 9.

International   Calling abroad can be done from any pay phone marked "Teléfono
Calls   Internacional." Though usable for short European calls, pay phones are feasible only for brief transatlantic calls. Use 50-pta. (or 100-pta. if the phone takes them) coins initially, then coins of any denomination to prolong your call. Dial 07 for international, wait for the tone to change, then 1 for the United States, or 44 for England, followed by the area code and number. For calls to England, omit the initial 0 from the area code. For lengthy international calls, go to the *telefónica*, a telephone office found in all sizable towns, where an operator assigns you a private booth and collects payment at the end of the call; this is the least expensive and by far the easiest way of phoning abroad. The cost of calls made from your hotel room includes a hefty service charge, even for collect calls.

Operators and   For the operator and information for the city you are in, dial 003; for
Information   information for the rest of Spain, just ask the 003 information operator. If you're in Madrid, dial 008 to make collect calls to countries in Europe; 005 for the rest of the world. Private long-distance companies now have special access numbers: ATT (tel. 900/99–00–11), MCI (tel. 900/99–00–14), Sprint (tel. 900/99–00–13), British Telcom (900–99–0044).

Mail	To the United States, airmail letters up to 15 grams and postcards

Mail
Postal Rates
To the United States, airmail letters up to 15 grams and postcards each cost 90 ptas. (These were the rates at press time [spring 1994]). To the United Kingdom and other EU countries, letters up to 20 grams and postcards each cost 45 ptas. To non–EU European countries, letters and postcards up to 20 grams cost 60 ptas. If you wish to expedite your overseas mail, send it *Urgente* for 160 ptas. over the regular airmail cost. Within Spain, letters and postcards each cost 27 ptas.; within a city in Spain, letters and postcards cost 17 ptas. Mailboxes are yellow with red stripes, and the slot marked "Extranjero" is the one for mail going abroad. Buy your stamps *(sellos)* at a post office *(correos)* or in a tobacco shop *(estanco)*.

Receiving Mail
If you're uncertain where you'll be staying, have mail sent to American Express or to the Poste Restante *(Lista de Correos)* of the local post office. To claim your mail, you'll need to show your passport. American Express has a $2 service charge per letter for non-cardholders. The Spanish mail is notoriously slow and not always very efficient.

Shopping
Sales Tax
Refunds
If you purchase goods up to a value of 48,000 ptas. or more in any one store (and in theory this should be on only *one* item), you are entitled to a refund of the IVA tax paid (usually 6% but more in the case of certain luxury goods), provided you leave Spain within three months. You will be given two copies of the sales invoice, which you must present at customs together with the goods as you leave Spain. Once the invoice has been stamped by customs, mail the blue copy back to the store, which will then mail your tax refund to you. If you are leaving via the airports of Madrid, Barcelona, Málaga or Palma de Mallorca, you can get your tax refund immediately from the Banco Exterior de España in the airport. The above does not apply to residents of EC countries, who must claim their IVA refund through customs in their own country. The Corte Inglés and Galerías Preciados department stores operate the above system, but don't be surprised if other stores are unfamiliar with the tax-refund procedure and do not have the necessary forms.

Bargaining
Prices in city stores and produce markets are fixed; bargaining is possible only in flea markets, some antiques stores, and with gypsy vendors, with whom it is *essential*, though you'd do best to turn them down flat as their goods are almost always fake and grossly overpriced.

Opening and Closing Times
Banks are open Monday through Saturday 9–2 from October through June; during the summer months they are closed on Saturdays.

Museums and churches. Opening times vary. Most are open in the morning, and most museums close one day a week, often Monday.

Post offices are usually open weekdays 9–2, but this can vary; check locally.

Stores are open weekdays from 9 or 10 until 1:30 or 2, then again in the afternoon from around 5 to 8. In some cities, especially in summer, stores close on Saturday afternoon. The Corte Inglés and Galerías Preciados department stores in major cities are open continuously from 10 to 8, and some stores in tourist resorts also stay open through the siesta.

National Holidays
January 1; January 6 (Epiphany); April 14 (Good Friday); May 1 (May Day); July 25 (St. James); August 15 (Assumption); October 12 (National Day); November 1 (All Saints' Day); December 6 (Constitution); December 8 (Immaculate Conception); December 25. Other holidays include May 2 (in the province of Madrid) and March 19 (St.

Joseph). These holidays are not celebrated in every region; always check locally.

Dining Visitors have a choice of restaurants, tapas bars, and cafés. Restaurants are strictly for lunch and dinner; they do not serve breakfast. Tapas bars are ideal for a glass of wine or beer accompanied by an array of savory tidbits *(tapas)*. Cafés, called *cafeterías*, are basically coffee shops serving snacks, light meals, tapas, pastries, and coffee, tea, and alcoholic drinks. They also serve breakfast and are perfect for afternoon tea.

Mealtimes Mealtimes in Spain are much later than in any other European country. Lunch begins between 1 and 2:30, with 2 being the usual time, and 3 more normal on Sunday. Dinner is usually available from 8:30 onward, but 10 PM is the usual time in the larger cities and resorts. An important point to remember is that lunch is the main meal, not dinner. Tapas bars are busiest between noon and 2 and from 8 PM on. Cafés are usually open from around 8 AM to midnight.

Precautions Tap water is said to be safe to drink in all but the remotest villages (in Madrid, tap water, from the surrounding Guadarrama Mountains, is excellent; in Barcelona, it's safe but tastes terrible). However, most Spaniards drink bottled mineral water; ask for either *agua sin gas* (without bubbles) or *agua con gas* (with). A good paella should be served only at lunchtime and should be prepared to order (usually 30 minutes); beware the all-too-cheap version.

Typical Dishes Paella—a mixture of saffron-flavored rice with seafood, chicken, and vegetables—is Spain's national dish. Gazpacho, a cold soup usually made of crushed garlic, tomatoes, and olive oil and garnished with diced vegetables, is a traditional Andalusian dish and is served mainly in summer. The Basque Country and Galicia are the gourmet regions of Spain, and both serve outstanding fish and seafood. Asturias is famous for its *fabadas* (bean stews), cider, and dairy products; Extremadura for its hams and sausages; and Castile for its roasts, especially *cochinillo* (suckling pig), *cordero asado* (roast lamb), and *perdiz* (partridge). The best wines are those from the Rioja and Penedés regions. Valdepeñas is a pleasant table wine, and most places serve a perfectly acceptable house wine; ask for *vino de la casa*. Sherries from Jerez de la Frontera make fine aperitifs; ask for a *fino* or a *manzanilla;* both are dry. In summer you can try *horchata*, a sweet white drink made from ground nuts, or *granizados de limón* or *de café*, lemon juice or coffee served over crushed ice. *Un café solo* is a small, black, espresso coffee, and *café con leche* is coffee with cream, cappuccino-style; weak black American-style coffee is hard to come by.

Dress In Very Expensive and Expensive restaurants, jacket and tie are the norm. Elsewhere, casual dress is appropriate.

Ratings Spanish restaurants are officially classified from five forks down to one fork, with most places falling into the two- or three-fork category. In our rating system, prices are per person and include a first course, main course, and dessert, but not wine or tip. Sales tax (IVA) is usually included in the menu price; check the menu for *IVA incluído* or *IVA no incluído*. When it's not included, an additional 6% (15% in the fancier restaurants) will be added to your bill. Most restaurants offer a fixed-price menu called a *menú del día;* however, this is often offered only at lunch, and at dinner tends to be merely a reheated midday offering. This is usually the cheapest way of eating; *à la carte* dining is more expensive. Service charges are never added to your bill; leave around 10%, less in inexpensive restaurants and bars. Major centers such as Madrid, Barcelona, Marbella, and

Seville tend to be a bit more expensive. Best bets are indicated by a star ★.

Category	All Areas
Very Expensive	over 9,000 ptas.
Expensive	6,000 ptas.–9,000 ptas.
Moderate	3,000 ptas.–6,000 ptas.
Inexpensive	under 3,000 ptas.

Lodging Spain has a wide range of accommodations, including luxury palaces, medieval monasteries, converted 19th-century houses, modern hotels, high rises on the coasts, and inexpensive hostels in family homes. All hotels and hostels are listed with their rates in the annual *Guía de Hoteles* available from bookstores and kiosks for around 1,000 ptas., or you can see a copy in local tourist offices. Rates are always quoted per room, and not per person. Single occupancy of a double room costs 80% of the normal price. Breakfast is rarely included in the quoted room rate; always check. The quality of rooms, particularly in older properties, can be uneven; always ask to see your room *before* you sign the acceptance slip. If you want a private bathroom in a less expensive hotel, state your preference for shower or bathtub; the latter usually costs more though many hotels have both.

Hotels and Hostels Hotels are officially classified from five stars (the highest) to one star, hostels from three stars to one star. Hostels—not the youth hostels associated with the English word—are usually a family home converted to provide accommodations that often occupy only part of a building. If an R appears on the blue hotel or hostel plaque, the hotel is classified as a *residencia*, and full dining services are not provided, though breakfast and cafeteria facilities may be available. A three-star hostel usually equates with a two-star hotel; two- and one-star hostels offer simple, basic accommodations. The main hotel chains are Husa, Iberotel Melia, Sol, and Tryp, and the state-run *paradores* (tourist hotels). Holiday Inn, InterContinental, and Forte also own some of the best hotels in Madrid, Barcelona, and Seville; only these and the paradores have any special character. The others mostly provide clean, comfortable accommodation in the two- to four-star range.

In many hotels rates vary fairly dramatically according to the time of year. The hotel year is divided into *temporada alta, media,* and *baja* (high, mid, and low season); high season usually covers the summer and Easter and Christmas periods, plus the major fiestas. IVA is rarely included in the quoted room rates, so be prepared for an additional 6%, or, in the case of luxury five-star hotels, 15%, to be added to your bill. Service charges are never included.

Paradors There are 85 state-owned-and-run paradors, many of which are located in magnificent medieval castles or convents or in places of great natural beauty. Most of these fall into the four-star category and are priced accordingly. Most have restaurants that specialize in local regional cuisine and serve a full breakfast. The most popular paradors (Granada's San Francisco parador, for example) are booked far in advance. For more information or to make reservations, contact **Paradores** (Requena 3, 28013 Madrid, tel. 91/559-0069, fax 91/559-3233), **Keytel International** (402 Edgware Rd.,

London, W2 1ED, UK, tel. 071/402–8182) or **Marketing Ahead Inc.,** 433 5th Ave., New York, NY 10016, USA, tel. 212/686–9213.

Villas   Villas are plentiful all along the Mediterranean coast, and cottages in Cantabria and Asturias on the north coast are available from a few agencies. Several agencies in both the United States and United Kingdom specialize in renting property; check with the Spanish National Tourist Office.

Camping   There are approximately 530 campsites in Spain, with the highest concentration along the Mediterranean coast. The season runs from April through October, though some sites are open year-round. Sites are listed in the annual publication *Guía de Campings* available from bookstores or local tourist offices, and further details are available from the Spanish National Tourist Office. Reservations for the most popular seaside sites can be made either directly with the site or through camping reservations at: Federación Española de Campings (Príncipe de Vergara 85, 2°-dcha, 28006 Madrid, tel. 91/ 562–9994).

Ratings   Prices are for two people in a double room and do not include breakfast. Best bets are indicated by a star ★.

Category	Major City	Other Areas
Very Expensive	over 20,000 ptas.	over 18,000 ptas.
Expensive	14,000–20,000 ptas.	12,000–18,000 ptas.
Moderate	9,000–14,000 ptas.	7,000–12,000 ptas.
Inexpensive	under 9,000 ptas.	under 7,000 ptas.

Tipping   Spaniards appreciate being tipped, though the practice is becoming less widespread. Restaurants and hotels are by law not allowed to add a service charge to your bill, though confusingly your bill for both will most likely say *servicios e impuestos incluídos* (service and tax included). Ignore this unhelpful piece of advice, and leave 10% in most restaurants where you have had a full meal; in humbler eating places, bars, and cafés, 5%–10% is enough, or you can round out the bill to the nearest 100 ptas. A cocktail waiter in a hotel will expect at least 30 ptas. a drink, maybe 50 ptas. in a luxury establishment. Tip taxi drivers about 5% to 10% when they use the meter, otherwise *nothing*—they'll have seen to it themselves. Gas-station attendants get no tip for pumping gas, but they get about 50 ptas. for checking tires and oil and cleaning windshields. Train and airport porters usually operate on a fixed rate of about 60 ptas.–100 ptas. a bag. Coat-check attendants get 25 ptas.–50 ptas., and restroom attendants get 10 ptas.–25 ptas. In top hotels doormen get 100 ptas.–150 ptas. for carrying bags to the check-in counter or for hailing taxis, and bellhops get 100 ptas. for room service or for each bag they carry to your room. In moderate hotels about 50 ptas. is adequate for the same services. Leave your chambermaid about 300 ptas. for a week's stay. There's no need to tip for just a couple of nights. The waiter in your hotel dining room will appreciate 500 ptas. a week.

Madrid

Arriving and Departing

By Plane   All international and domestic flights arrive at Madrid's Barajas Airport (tel. 91/305–8343), 16 kilometers (10 miles) northeast of town just off the N-II Barcelona highway. For information on arrival and departure times, call **Inforiberia** (tel. 91/329–5767) or the airline concerned.

Between the Airport and Downtown   Buses leave the national and international terminals every 15 minutes from 5:40 AM to 2 AM for the downtown terminal at Plaza de Colón just off the Paseo de la Castellana. The ride takes about 20 minutes and the fare at press time was 300 ptas. Most city hotels are then only a short taxi ride away. The fastest and most expensive route into town (usually about 1,500 ptas., but up to 2,000 ptas. plus tip in traffic) is by taxi. Pay what is on the meter plus 300 ptas. surcharge and 50 ptas. for each suitcase. By car, take the N-II, which becomes Avenida de América, into town, then head straight into Calle María de Molina and left on either Calle Serrano or the Castellana.

By Train   Madrid has three railroad stations. Chamartín, in the northern suburbs beyond the Plaza de Castilla, is the main station, with trains to France and the north (including Barcelona, Segovia, El Escorial, Santiago, and La Coruña). Most trains to Valencia, Alicante, and Andalusia now leave from here, too, but stop at Atocha station, at the southern end of Paseo del Prado on the Glorieta del Emperador Carlos V. Also departing from Atocha, where a new station was built in 1989, are trains to Toledo, Granada, Extremadura, and Lisbon. In 1992, a convenient new metro stop (Atocha RENFE) was opened in Atocha station, connecting it to the city subway system. The old Atocha station, designed by Eiffel, was refurbished and reopened in 1992 as the Madrid terminus for a new high-speed rail service to Seville. Norte (or Príncipe Pío), on Paseo de la Florida, in the west of town below the Plaza de España, is the departure point for local trains to the Madrid suburbs.

For all train information, call RENFE (tel. 91/563–0202, in Spanish only), or go to its offices at Alcalá 4, or on the second floor of Torre de Madrid in the Plaza de España, right above the main tourist office (open weekdays 9–3 and 5–7, Sat. 9–3). There's another RENFE office at Barajas Airport in the International Arrivals Hall, or you can purchase tickets at any of the three main stations, or from travel agents displaying the blue and yellow RENFE sign.

By Bus   Madrid has no central bus station. The two main bus stations are the Estación del Sur (Canarias 17, tel. 91/468–4200), nearest metro Palos de la Frontera, for buses to Toledo, La Mancha, Alicante, and Andalusia; and Auto-Rés (Plaza Conde de Casal 6, tel. 91/551–7200), nearest metro Conde de Casal, for buses to Extremadura, Cuenca, Salamanca, Valladolid, Valencia, and Zamora. Auto-Rés has a central ticket and information office at Salud 19 near the Hotel Arosa, just off Gran Vía. Buses to other destinations leave from various points, so check with the tourist office. The Basque country and most of north central Spain is served by Auto Continental (Alenza 20, nearest metro Ríos Rosas, tel. 91/533–0400). For Ávila, Segovia, and La Granja, Empresa La Sepulvedana (tel. 91/527–9537) leaves from Paseo de la Florida 11, next to the Norte station, a few steps from the Norte metro stop. Empresa Herranz (tel. 91/543–3645 or 91/543–8167), serving San Lorenzo de El Escorial and the Valley of the Fallen, departs from the base of Calle Fernandez de los Ríos, a few yards from the Moncloa metro stop. La Veloz (Avda. Mediterraneo 49, tel. 91/409–7602) serves Chinchón.

By Car The main roads are north–south, the Paseo de la Castellana and Paseo del Prado; and east–west, Calle de Alcalá, Gran Vía, and Calle de la Princesa. The M30 ring road circles Madrid and the M40 is an outer ring road scheduled for completion in 1995. For Burgos and France, drive north up the Castellana and follow the signs for the N-I. For Barcelona, head up the Castellana to Plaza Dr. Marañón, then right onto María de Molina and the N-II; for Andalusia and Toledo, head south down Paseo del Prado, then follow the signs to the N-IV and N401, respectively. For Segovia, Ávila, and El Escorial, head west along Princesa to Avenida Puerta de Hierro and onto the N-VI La Coruña road.

Getting Around

Madrid is a fairly compact city and most of the main sights can be visited on foot. But if you're staying in one of the modern hotels in the north of town off the Castellana, you may well need to use the bus or subway (metro). As a rough guide, the walk from the Prado to the Royal Palace at a comfortable sightseeing pace but without stopping takes around 30 minutes; from Plaza del Callao on Gran Vía to the Plaza Mayor, it takes about 15 minutes.

By Metro The subway offers the simplest and quickest means of transport and is open from 6 AM to 1:30 AM. Metro maps are available from ticket offices, hotels, and tourist offices. Fares at press time were 125 ptas. a ride. Savings can be made by buying a 10-ride ticket for 600 ptas. Keep some change (5, 25, 50, and 100 ptas.) handy for the ticket machines, especially after 10 PM; the machines give change and are handy for beating often long lines for tickets.

By Bus City buses are red and run from 6 AM to midnight (though check, as some stop earlier). Again there is a flat-fare system, with each ride costing 125 ptas. Route plans are displayed at bus stops *(paradas)*, and a map of the entire system is available from EMT (Empresa Municipal de Transportes) booths on Plaza de la Cibeles, Callao, or Puerta del Sol. Savings can be made by buying a **Bonobus** (600 ptas.), good for 10 rides, from EMT booths or any *estanco* or tobacco shop.

By Taxi Madrid has more than 18,000 taxis, and fares are low by New York or London standards. The meter starts at 150 ptas. and each additional kilometer costs 70 ptas. The average city ride costs about 500 ptas., and there is a surcharge of 150 ptas. between 11 PM and 6 AM and on holidays from 6 AM to 11 PM. A supplemental fare of 150 ptas. applies to trips to the bullring or soccer matches, and there is a charge of 50 ptas. per suitcase. The airport surcharge is 300 ptas. Cabs available for hire display a "Libre" sign during the day and a green light at night. They hold four passengers. Make sure the driver puts his meter on when you start your ride, and tip from 5% to 10% of the fare.

Important Addresses and Numbers

Tourist Information The main Madrid tourist office (tel. 91/541–2325) is on the ground floor of the Torre de Madrid in Plaza de España, near the beginning of Calle de la Princesa, and is open weekdays 9–7, Saturdays 9:30–1:30. Another Madrid Provincial Tourist Office (Duque de Medinacelli 2, tel. 91/429–4951) is conveniently located on a small street across from the Palace Hotel. The much less useful municipal tourist office is at Plaza Mayor 3 (tel. 91/366–4874) and is open weekdays

10–8, Saturdays 10–2. A third office is in the International Arrivals Hall of Barajas Airport (tel. 91/305–8656) and is open weekdays 8–8, Saturdays 9–1.

Embassies   **U.S.** (Serrano 75, tel. 91/577–4000), **Canadian** (Núñez de Balboa 35, tel. 91/431–4300), **U.K.** (Fernando el Santo 16, tel. 91/319–0200).

Emergencies   **Police:** (emergencies, tel. 091; Municipal Police, tel. 092 for towed cars or traffic accidents). To report lost passports, go to Los Madrazos 9 just off the top of Paseo del Prado (tel. 91/521–9350). **Ambulance:** tel. 91/522–2222 or 91/588–4400. **Doctor:** Your hotel reception will contact the nearest doctor for you. Emergency clinics: **Hospital 12 de Octubre** (Avda. Córdoba, tel. 91/390–8000) and **La Paz Ciudad Sanitaria** (Paseo de la Castellana 261, tel. 91/358–2600). English-speaking doctors are available at British-American Medical Unit (Conde de Aranda 7, tel. 91/435–1823). **Pharmacies:** A list of pharmacies open 24 hours *(farmacias de guardia)* is published daily in *El País*. Hotel receptions usually have a copy. **Company** (Puerta del Sol 14, tel. 91/521–3625) has English-speaking pharmacists. It does not stock American medicines but will recognize many American brand names.

Books in English   **Booksellers S.A.** (José Abascal 48, tel. 91/442–8104) and **Turner's English Bookshop** (Génova 3, tel. 91/310–4359).

Travel Agencies   **American Express** (Plaza de las Cortes 2, tel. 91/322–5500), **Marsans** (Gran Vía 59, tel. 91/547–7300), **Wagons-Lits** (Alcalá 23, tel. 91/522–4334).

Airlines   **Iberia** (Velázquez 130, tel. 91/411–1011 for domestic reservations or tel. 91/329–4353 for international flights; for flight information, call Inforiberia, tel. 91/329–5767), **British Airways** (Serrano 60, 5th floor, tel. 91/431–7575), and **TWA** (Plaza de Colón 2, tel. 91/310–1905 or 91/305–4290).

Guided Tours

Orientation Tours   City sightseeing tours are run by **Juliá Tours** (Gran Vía 68, tel. 91/571–2558), **Pullmantur** (Plaza de Oriente 8, tel. 91/541–1807), and **Trapsatur** (San Bernardo 23, tel. 91/542–6666). All three run the same tours, mostly in 48-seat buses and conducted in Spanish and English. Book tours directly with the offices above, through any travel agent, or through your hotel. Departure points are from the addresses above, though in many cases you can be picked up at your hotel. "Madrid Artístico" is a morning tour of the city with visits to the Royal Palace and Prado Museum, entrance fees included. The "Madrid Panorámico" tour includes the University City, Casa del Campo park, and the northern reaches of the Castellana. This is a half-day tour, usually in the afternoon, and makes an ideal orientation for the first-time visitor. Also offered are "Madrid de Noche," a night tour combining a drive round the illuminations, dinner in a restaurant, flamenco show, and cabaret at La Scala nightclub; and "Panorámico y Toros," on bullfight days only (usually Sunday), a panoramic drive and visit to a bullfight. Trapsatur also runs the *Madridvision* tourist bus, which makes a one-hour sightseeing tour of the city with recorded commentary in English. No advance reservation is necessary. Catch it in front of the Prado museum every 1½ hours beginning at 10:45 Monday through Saturday or 10:30 Sunday. A round-trip ticket costs 500 ptas. and a day pass, which allows you to get on or off at various attractions, is 1,000 ptas.

Walking and Special-Interest Tours Spanish-speaking people can take advantage of a hugely popular selection of tours recently launched by the **Ayuntamiento** (city hall) under the title "Discubre Madrid." Walking tours are held most mornings year-round and visit many of the capital's hidden corners, as well as the major sights. Special-interest tours include "Madrid's Railroads," "Medicine in Madrid," "Goya's Madrid," and "Commerce and Finance in Madrid." Some tours are by bus, others on foot. Schedules are listed in the "Discubre Madrid" leaflet available from the municipal tourist office and tickets can be purchased at the Patronato de Turismo (Calle Mayor 69, 91/588–2906).

Excursions **Juliá Tours, Pullmantur,** and **Trapsatur** run full- or half-day trips to El Escorial, Ávila, Segovia, Toledo, and Aranjuez, and in summer to Cuenca and Salamanca; for additional details, *see* Madrid Environs, *below*. The "Tren de la Fresa" (Strawberry Train) is a popular excursion on summer weekends; a 19th-century train carries passengers from the old Delicias Station to Aranjuez and back. Tickets can be obtained from RENFE offices, travel agents, and the Delicias Station (Paseo de las Delicias 61). Other one- or two-day excursions by train to such places as Ávila, Cuenca, or Salamanca are available on weekends in summer. Contact RENFE for details.

Exploring Madrid

Numbers in the margin correspond to points of interest on the Madrid map.

You can walk the following route in a day, or even half a day if you stop only to visit the Prado and Royal Palace. Two days should give you time for browsing. Begin in the Plaza Atocha, more properly known as the Glorieta del Emperador Carlos V, at the bottom of the Paseo del Prado, and check out what's showing in the **Centro de Arte Reina Sofía** (Reina Sofía Arts Center) opened by Queen Sofía in 1986. This converted hospital, home of art and sculpture exhibitions and symbol of Madrid's new cultural pride, is fast becoming one of Europe's most dynamic venues—a Madrileño rival to Paris's Pompidou Center. It also recently became home to Picasso's *Guernica*, the horrific painting depicting the April 1937 carpet bombing of the Basque Country's traditional capital by Nazi warplanes aiding Franco during the Spanish Civil War (1936–39). The main entrance is on Calle de Santa Isabel 52. *Tel. 91/467–5062. Admission: 400 ptas. Open Mon., Wed.–Sat. 10–9; Sun. 10–2:30.*

Walk up Paseo del Prado to Madrid's number-one sight, the famous **Museo del Prado** (Prado Museum), one of the world's most important art galleries. Plan on spending at least 1½ days here, though it will take at least two full days to view its treasures properly. Brace yourself for the crowds. The greatest treasures—the Velázquez, Murillo, Zurbarán, El Greco, and Goya galleries—are all on the upstairs floor. Two of the best works are Velázquez's *Surrender of Breda* and his most famous work, *Las Meninas*, which occupies a privileged position in a room of its own. The Goya galleries contain the artist's none-too-flattering royal portraits—Goya believed in painting the truth—his exquisitely beautiful *Marquesa de Santa Cruz*, and his famous *Naked Maja* and *Clothed Maja*, for which the 13th duchess of Alba was said to have posed. Goya's most moving works, the *Second of May* and the *Fusillade of Moncloa* or *Third of May*, vividly depict the sufferings of Madrid patriots at the hands of Napoleon's invading troops in 1808. Before you leave, feast your eyes on the fantastic flights of fancy of Hieronymus Bosch's *Garden of Earthly Delights* and his triptych *The Hay Wagon*, both downstairs on the

Major Attractions

Centro de Arte Reina Sofía, **1**
Cibeles Fountain, **7**
Convento de las Descalzas Reales, **10**
Museo del Prado, **2**
Museo Thyssen-Bornemisza, **4**
Palacio Real, **13**
Parque del Retiro, **5**
Plaza de la Villa, **12**
Plaza Mayor, **11**
Puerta de Alcalá, **6**
Puerta del Sol, **9**
Real Academia de San Fernando, **8**
Ritz, **3**
Royal Carriage Museum, **14**

Other Attractions

Biblioteca Nacional, **19**
Municipal Museum, **16**
Museo Arqueológico, **20**
Museo de Artes Decorativas, **21**
Museo de Cera (Wax Museum), **18**
Museo Romántico, **17**
Torre de Madrid, **15**

ground floor. *Paseo del Prado s/n, tel. 91/420–2836. Admission: 400 ptas., Open Tues.–Sat. 9–7, Sun. 9–2.*

❸ Across the street is the **Ritz,** the grand old lady of Madrid's hotels, built in 1910 by Alfonso XIII when he realized that his capital had no hotels elegant enough to accommodate the guests at his wedding in 1906. The Ritz garden is a delightfully aristocratic place to lunch in summer.

❹ The **Museo Thyssen-Bornemisza** across the plaza Neptuno was opened in 1992 in the Villahermosa Palace—elegantly renovated to include plenty of airy spaces and natural light. This ambitious collection of 800 paintings attempts to trace the history of Western art with examples from all the important movements beginning with 13th-century Italy. Among the museum's gems are the *Portrait of Henry VIII* by Hans Holbein, purchased from Princess Diana's grandfather, who used the money to buy a new Bugatti sports car. Two halls are devoted to the Impressionists and Post-Impressionists and contain many works by Pissarro and canvases by Renoir, Monet, Degas, Van Gogh, and Cézanne. Among the more recent movements represented are terror-filled examples of German Expressionism, but there are also soothing paintings by Georgia O'Keeffe and Andrew Wyeth. *Paseo del Prado 8, tel. 91/420–3944. Admission: 600 ptas., under 12 free. Open Tues.–Sun. 10–7.*

❺ The **Parque del Retiro** (Retiro Park) once a royal retreat, is today Madrid's prettiest park. Visit the beautiful rose garden, **La Rosaleda,** and enjoy the many statues and fountains. You can hire a carriage, row a boat on **El Estanque,** gaze up at the monumental **statue to Alfonso XII,** one of Spain's least notable kings though you wouldn't think so to judge by its size, or wonder at the **Monument to the Fallen Angel**—Madrid claims the dubious privilege of being the only capital to have a statue dedicated to the Devil. The **Palacio de Velázquez** and the beautiful steel-and-glass **Palacio de Cristal,** built as a tropical plant house in the 19th century, now host art exhibits.

❻ Leaving the Retiro via its northwest corner, you come to the Plaza de la Independencia, dominated by the **Puerta de Alcalá,** a grandiose gateway built in 1779 for Charles III. A customs post once stood beside the gate, as did the old bullring until it was moved to its present site at Ventas in the 1920s. At the turn of the century, the Puerta de Alcalá more or less marked the eastern limits of Madrid.

❼ Continue to the **Plaza de la Cibeles,** one of the great landmarks of the city, at the intersection of its two main arteries, the Castellana and Calle de Alcalá. If you can see it through the roar and fumes of the thundering traffic, the square's center is the **Cibeles Fountain,** the unofficial emblem of Madrid. Cybele, the Greek goddess of fertility, languidly rides her lion-drawn chariot, overlooked by the mighty **Palacio de Comunicaciónes,** a splendidly pompous cathedral-like building often jokingly dubbed Our Lady of Communications. In fact, it's the main post office, erected in 1918. The famous goddess looks her best at night when she's illuminated by floodlights.

Time Out   To rest your feet and sip a cup of coffee or a beer, head about one block up the center boulevard of the Paseo Recoletos and pull up a chair on the shady terrace or inside the air-conditioned, stained-glass bar of **El Espejo** (Paseo Recoletos 31).

Now head down the long and busy Calle de Alcalá toward the Puerta del Sol, resisting the temptation to turn right up the Gran Vía, which beckons temptingly with its mile of stores and cafés. Before

you reach the Puerta del Sol, art lovers may want to step inside the
❽ **Real Academia de San Fernando** at Alcalá 13. This recently refurbished fine arts gallery boasts an art collection second only to the
Prado's and features all the great Spanish masters: Velázquez, El
Greco, Murillo, Zurbarán, Ribera, and Goya. *Alcalá 13, tel. 91/532–
1546. Admission: 300 ptas. Open daily 9–2.*

❾ The **Puerta del Sol** is at the very heart of Madrid. Its name means
Gate of the Sun, though the old gate disappeared long ago. It's easy
to feel you're at the heart of things here—indeed, of all of Spain—
for the kilometer distances for the whole nation are measured from
the zero marker in front of the Police Headquarters. The square was
expertly revamped in 1986 and now accommodates both a copy of **La
Mariblanca** (a statue that 250 years ago adorned a fountain here)
and, at the bottom of Calle Carmen, the much-loved statue of the
bear and *madroño* (strawberry tree). The Puerta del Sol is inextri-
cably linked with the history of Madrid and of the nation. Here, half
a century ago, a generation of literati gathered in the long-gone
cafés to thrash out the burning issues of the day; and if you can cast
your thoughts back almost 200 years, you can conjure up the heroic
deeds of the patriots' uprising immortalized by Goya in the *Second
of May*.

This is a good place to break the tour if you've had enough sightseeing for one day. Head north up Preciados or Montera for some of the
busiest shopping streets in the city or southeast toward Plaza Santa
Ana for tavern-hopping in Old Madrid.

Time Out   If it's teatime (6–7 PM), don't miss **La Mallorquina** (Calle Mayor 2,
tel. 91/521–1201), an old pastry shop between Calle Mayor and
Arenal. Delicious pastries are sold at the downstairs counter; the
old-fashioned upstairs tea salon offers an age-old tea ritual and unbeatable views over the Puerta del Sol.

❿ Art lovers will want to make a detour to the **Convento de las
Descalzas Reales** on Plaza Descalzas Reales just above Arenal. It
was founded by Juana de Austria, daughter of Charles V, and is still
inhabited by nuns. Over the centuries the nuns, daughters of the
royal and noble, endowed the convent with an enormous wealth of
jewels, religious ornaments, superb Flemish tapestries, and the
works of such great masters as Titian and Rubens. A bit off the main
tourist track, it's one of Madrid's better-kept secrets. Your ticket
includes admission to the nearby, but less interesting, **Convento de
la Encarnación.** *Plaza de las Descalzas Reales, tel. 91/559–7404.
Admission: 350 ptas. Guided tours in Spanish only. Open Tues.–
Thurs., Sat. 10:30–12:30 and 4–5:30; Fri. 10:30–12:30, and Sun.
11–1:30.*

Walk up **Calle Mayor,** the Main Street of Old Madrid, past the shops
⓫ full of religious statues and satins for bishops' robes, to the **Plaza
Mayor,** the capital's greatest architectural showpiece. It was built in
1617–19 for Philip III—that's Philip on the horse in the middle. The
plaza has witnessed the canonization of saints, burning of heretics,
fireworks and bullfights, and is still one of the great gathering
places of Madrid.

Time Out   In summer you can relax over a drink in any of the delightful side-
walk cafés that adorn the square; in winter, head for the **Mesón del
Corregidor** (tel. 91/366–5056) at No. 8, near the Cuchilleros arch.
This colorful tavern restaurant has typical dishes and tapas.

If you're here in the morning, take a look inside the 19th-century steel-and-glass San Miguel market, a colorful provisions market, before continuing down Calle Mayor to the **Plaza de la Villa.** The square's notable cluster of buildings includes some of the oldest houses in Madrid. The **Casa de la Villa,** the Madrid city hall, was built in 1644 and has also served as the city prison and the mayor's home. Its sumptuous salons are occasionally open to the public; ask about guided tours, which are sometimes offered in English. An archway joins the Casa de la Villa to the **Casa Cisneros,** a palace built in 1537 for the nephew of Cardinal Cisneros, primate of Spain and infamous inquisitor general. Across the square, the **Torre de Lujanes** is one of the oldest buildings in Madrid. It once imprisoned Francis I of France, archenemy of the Emperor Charles V.

Time Out If it's lunchtime, close by is a moderately priced restaurant with turn-of-the-century decor: **Fuente Real** (Calle de las Fuentes 1, tel. 91/559–6613).

The last stop on the tour, but Madrid's second most important sight, is the **Palacio Real** (Royal Palace). This magnificent granite and limestone residence was begun by Philip V, the first Bourbon king of Spain, who was always homesick for his beloved Versailles, the opulence and splendor of which he did his best to emulate. His efforts were successful, to judge by the 2,800 rooms with their lavish Rococo decorations, precious carpets, porcelain, time pieces, mirrors, and chandeliers. From 1764, when Charles III first moved in, till the coming of the Second Republic and the abdication of Alfonso XIII in 1931, the Royal Palace proved a very stylish abode for Spanish monarchs. Today King Juan Carlos, who lives in the far less ostentatious Zarzuela Palace outside Madrid, uses it only for official state functions. The Palace can be visited only on guided tours, sometimes available in English. Allow 1½–2 hours for a visit. A *visita completa* (full visit), including the Royal Pharmacy, and other outbuildings, costs 500 ptas.; many visitors opt for the *Salones Oficiales* (State Rooms) ticket at 325 ptas. *Bailén s/n, tel. 91/559–7404. Admission: 500 ptas. for entire complex, 325 ptas. for palace only. Open Mon.–Sat. 9:30–5, Sun. 9–2. Closed during frequent official functions.*

The **Royal Carriage Museum,** which belongs to the palace, has a separate entrance on Paseo Vírgen del Puerto. One of its highlights is the wedding carriage of Alfonso XIII and his English bride, Victoria Eugenia, granddaughter of Queen Victoria, which was damaged by a bomb thrown at it in the Calle Mayor during their wedding procession in 1906; another is the chair that carried the gout-stricken old Emperor Charles V to his retirement at the remote monastery of Yuste. The museum has been closed for several years for restoration, so make sure to check at the Royal Palace to find out if it is open.

Off the Beaten Track

Stroll around the narrow streets of the **Chueca** between Hortaleza and Paseo de Recoletos. Look for the architectural features of the old houses; the dark, atmospheric bars and restaurants well known to discerning Madrileños; and the small stores with their wooden counters and brass fittings, many of which have been run by the same family for generations. Calle de las Infantas has some real gems: the **Bolsa de los Licores** at No. 13, selling wines and liqueurs from every corner of Europe; the splendid silver shop at No. 25; the

Old World grocery store **Casa Jerez** at No. 32. And don't miss the **Tienda de Vinos** restaurant in Augusto Figueroa, affectionately nicknamed "El Comunista" and long famed for its rock-bottom prices. The whole quarter seems to come straight from the pages of a 19th-century novel.

For a dramatic view of the northwest quadrant of the city and the adjoining Casa de Campo park, take the Metro to the Moncloa stop and climb the Faro de Moncloa, a recently opened 285-foot observatory. *Admission: 200 ptas. Open daily 10–1:45 and 4:30–7:15.*

The old **Lavapiés** quarter, between Calle Atocha and Embajadores, is another area with plenty of atmosphere. Traditionally one of the poorest parts of Old Madrid, it is now the home of artists and actors, writers and musicians. Health-food restaurants—a novelty in Spain generally—have flourished. You can get a good cheap lunch at **La Biotika,** Amor de Diós 3 (tel. 91/429–0780). Don't miss a restored old tenement building, **La Corrala,** Mesón de Paredes 32, where in summer you can watch a *zarzuela* performance in the ancient courtyard.

Casa Mingo (Paseo de la Florida 2, tel. 91/547–7918) is an Asturian tavern behind Norte Station. A real Madrid institution, it has long been famous for its Asturian cider, goat cheese, and succulent chicken at amazingly low prices.

Shopping

Gift Ideas   There are no special regional crafts associated with Madrid itself, but traditional Spanish goods are on sale in many stores. The **Corte Inglés** and **Galerías Preciados** department stores both stock good displays of Lladró porcelain, as do several specialist shops on the Gran Vía and behind the Plaza hotel on Plaza de España. Department stores stock good displays of fans, but for really superb examples, try the long-established **Casa Diego** in Puerta del Sol. Two stores opposite the Prado on Plaza Cánovas del Castillo, **Artesanía Toledana** and **El Escudo de Toledo,** have a wide selection of souvenirs, especially Toledo swords, inlaid marquetry ware, and pottery. Carefully selected handicrafts from all over Spain—ceramics, furniture, glassware, rugs, embroidery, and more—are sold at **Artespaña** (Hermosilla 14), a government-run crafts store.

Antiques   The main areas to see are the Plaza de las Cortes, the Carrera San Jerónimo, and the Rastro flea market, along the Ribera de Curtidores and the courtyards just off it.

Boutiques   Calle Serrano has the largest collection of smart boutiques and designer fashions. Another up-and-coming area is around Calle Argensola, just south of Calle Génova. **Loewe,** Spain's most prestigious leather store, has boutiques on Serrano 26 and Gran Vía 8. **Adolfo Domínguez,** one of Spain's top designers, has several boutiques in Salamanca, and another on Calle Orense in the north of town.

Shopping Districts   The main shopping area in the heart of Madrid is around the pedestrian streets of **Preciados** and **Montera,** between Puerta del Sol and Plaza Callao on Gran Vía. The smartest and most expensive district is the **Barrio de Salamanca** northeast of Cibeles, centered around Serrano, Velázquez, and Goya. **Calle Mayor** and the streets to the east of **Plaza Mayor** are lined with fascinating old-fashioned stores straight out of the 19th century.

Department Stores   **El Corte Inglés** is the biggest, brightest, and most successful Spanish chain store. Its main branch is on Preciados, just off the Puerta del Sol. **Galerías Preciados** is its main rival, with branches on Plaza Callao right off Gran Vía, Calle Arapiles, Goya corner of Conde de Peñalver, Serrano and Ortega y Gasset, and its newest branch at La Vaguada. Both stores are open Monday–Saturday 10–8, and neither closes for the siesta.

Food and Flea Markets   **The Rastro,** Madrid's most famous flea market, operates on Sundays from 9 to 2 around the Plaza del Cascorro and the Ribera de Curtidores. A **stamp and coin** market is held on Sunday mornings in the Plaza Mayor, and there's a **secondhand book** market most days on the Cuesta Claudio Moyano near Atocha Station.

Bullfighting

The Madrid bullfighting season runs from March to October. Fights are held on Sunday, and sometimes also on Thursday; starting times vary between 4:30 and 7 PM. The pinnacle of the spectacle may be seen during the three weeks of daily bullfights held during the San Isidro festivals in May. The bullring is at Las Ventas (formally known as the Plaza de Toros Monumental), Alcalá 237 (metro Ventas). You can buy your ticket there shortly before the fight, or, with a 20% surcharge, at the agencies that line Calle Victoria, just off Carrera San Jerónimo and Puerta del Sol.

Dining

For details and price-category definitions, *see* Dining in Staying in Spain, *above*.

Very Expensive ★   **Horcher.** Housed in a luxurious mansion at the edge of Retiro Park, this classic restaurant is renowned for its hearty but elegant fare, served with impeccable style. Specialties include the types of game dishes favored by Spanish aristocracy. Try the wild boar, venison, or roast wild duck with almond croquettes. The star appetizer is lobster salad with truffles. Other dishes such as stroganoff with mustard, pork chops with sauerkraut, and a chocolate-covered fruit and cake dessert called *baumkuchen* betray the Germanic roots of this restaurant, which originally opened in Berlin at the turn of the century. The dining room is intimate with rust brocade fabric on the walls and antique Austrian porcelains. A wide selection of French and German wines rounds out the menu. *Alfonso XII 6, tel. 91/532–3596. Reservations required. Jacket and tie advised. AE, DC, MC, V. Closed Sun.*

Viridiana. The trendiest of Madrid's gourmet restaurants, Viridiana has the relaxed atmosphere of a bistro and a black and white decor highlighted by photograms from Luis Buñuel's classic anti-clerical film of the same name. Iconoclast chef Abraham Garcia says "market-based" is too narrow a description of his creative menu, which changes every two weeks and includes such varied fare as red onions stuffed with *morcilla* (black pudding); soft flour tortillas wrapped around marinated fresh tuna; and filet mignon in white truffle sauce. If it's available, be sure to try the superb duck paté drizzled with sherry and served with tokay wine. The tangy grapefruit sherbet for dessert is a marvel. *Juan de Mena 14, tel. 91/531–5222. Reservations required. Dress: casual but neat. No credit cards. Closed Sun., Easter week, and Aug.*

Zalacaín. A deep apricot color scheme, set off by dark wood and gleaming silver give this restaurant the atmosphere of an exclusive villa. Zalacaín introduced *nouvelle cuisine* to Spain and continues to set the pace after 20 years at the top. Splurge on dishes such as prawn salad in avocado vinaigrette; scallops and leeks in Albariño wine; and roast pheasant with truffles. Service is correct, but somewhat stuffy. A fixed-price tasting menu allows you to sample the best of Zalacaín for about 6,500 ptas. *Alvarez de Baena, 4, tel. 91/ 561–5935. Reservations required. Jacket and tie recommended. AE, DC, V. Closed Sat. lunch, Sun., Easter week, and Aug.*

Expensive **El Cenador del Prado.** The Cenador's innovative menu features
★ French and Oriental touches, as well as exotic Spanish dishes not often found in restaurants. Dine in a baroque salmon and gold salon or a less formal plant-filled conservatory. The house specialty is *patatas a la importancia* (sliced potatoes fried in a sauce of garlic, parsley, and clams). Other possibilities include shellfish consommé with ginger raviolis, veal and eggplant in bechamel, or wild boar with prunes. For dessert try the cream-filled pastry called *cañas fritas*—a treat once served only at Spanish weddings. *Calle del Prado 4, tel. 91/429–1561.Reservations advised. Jacket and tie advised. AE, DC, MC, V. Closed Sat. lunch, Sun., Easter week, and 1st half of Aug.*

Gure-Etxea. Located in the heart of medieval Madrid on the trendy Plaza de Paja, this is one of the capital's most authentic Basque restaurants. The ground floor dining room is airy, high-ceilinged, and elegant; while brick walls line the downstairs eating area, giving it a rustic, farmhouse feel. As in the Basque country, you are waited on by women. Classic dishes here include *bacalao pil-pil* (spicy cod fried in garlic and oil, making the "pil-pil" sound), *rape, salsa verde* (monkfish in garlic and parsley sauce), and for dessert *leche frita* (fried custard). On weekdays a hearty and inexpensive plate of the day is added to the lunchtime menu. *Plaza de Paja 12, tel. 91/365– 6149. Reservations advised. AE, DC, V. Closed Sun., Easter week, and Aug.*

La Trainera. Fresh seafood—the best quality money can buy—is what La Trainera is all about. For decades this informal restaurant, with its nautical decor and maze of little dining rooms, has reigned as queen of Madrid's seafood houses. Crab, lobster, shrimp, mussels, and a dozen other types of shellfish are served by weight in *raciones.* While many Spanish diners share several plates of these delicacies as their entire meal, the grilled hake, sole, or turbot make an unbeatable second course, and it's a treat to watch the waiter expertly debone the fish at the table. Skip the listless house wine and go for a bottle of Albariño from the cellar. *Lagasca 60, tel. 91/576– 8035. Reservations advised. Dress: casual. MC, V. Closed Sun. and Aug.*

Moderate **Café Balear.** A sophisticated yet informal eatery that attracts a crowd of creative types from the fashion and advertising world, the Café Balear serves some of the best *paella* (rice dishes) in Madrid. Art prints and potted palms are the only nods to decoration in the stark white dining room. Specialties include *paella centolla* (rice with crab) and *arroz negro* (rice with squid in its ink), as well as a perfectly prepared *paella mixta* (rice, seafood, pork, and vegetables). *Sagunto 18, tel. 91/447–9115. Reservations advised. Dress: casual. AE, V. Closed Sun. and Mon. dinner.*

★ **Casa Botín.** Madrid's oldest and most famous restaurant, just off the Plaza Mayor, has been catering to diners since 1725. Its decor and food are traditionally Castilian, as are the wood-fired ovens used for cooking. *Cochinillo asado* (roast suckling pig) and *cordero asado* (roast lamb) are the specialties. It was a favorite with Hemingway and is somewhat touristy, but fun. Try to be seated in the basement *cueva* or the upstairs dining room. *Cuchilleros 17, tel. 91/366–4217. Reservations strongly advised. Jacket advised. AE, DC, MC. V.*

Casa Vallejo. With its homey dining room, friendly staff, creative menu, and reasonable prices, this restaurant is the well-kept secret of Madrid's budget gourmets. Try the tomato, zucchini, and cheese tart or artichokes and clams for starters, then follow up with duck breast in prune sauce or meatballs made with lamb, almonds, and pine nuts. Their fudge-and-raspberry pie is worth a trip in itself. *San Lorenzo 9, tel. 91/308–6158. Reservations required. Jacket advised. AE, MC, V. Closed Sat. lunch and Sun.*

La Cacharrería. The name of this restaurant in medieval Madrid means junkyard, and it's reflected in the decor, which is a funky mix of dusty calico, old lace, and gilt mirrors. The cooking, however, is surprisingly upscale with a market-based menu that changes daily and an excellent selection of wines. Venison stew and fresh tuna steaks with cava and leeks are among the specialties. Save room for the homemade lemon tart. *Moreria 9, tel. 91/365–3930. Reservations advised. Jacket advised. AE, DC, MC, V. Closed Sun.*

★ **La Gamella.** American-born chef Dick Stephens has created a new reasonably priced menu at this hugely popular dining spot. The sophisticated rust-red dining room, batik tablecloths, oversized plates, and attentive service remain the same. But much of the nouvelle cuisine has been replaced by more traditional fare, such as chicken in garlic, boeuf bourguignon, or steak tartar a la Jack Daniels. A few signature dishes such as sausage and red pepper quiche and the bittersweet chocolate paté for dessert remain and the lunchtime *menu del día* at 1,700 ptas. is a great value. *Alfonso XII 4, tel. 91/532–4509. Reservations advised. Dress: casual. AE, DC, MC, V. Closed Sun., Mon., and Aug. 15–Sept. 15.*

Inexpensive **Café La Plaza.** Strategically positioned between the Prado and Thyssen-Bornemisza art museums and open continuously from 10 AM to midnight, the Café La Plaza is an indispensable rest stop for tourists exploring Madrid. It's an upscale, self-service restaurant with a green-and-white garden party decor set among the exclusive boutiques of the Galería del Prado shopping center. Food is arranged on several circular tables. There's a do-it-yourself salad bar, a pasta bar, and an economical *menu del día*, which depending on the day might be Spanish-style chicken, breaded fish, or beef stew served with vegetables, bread, and wine. Breakfast, including bacon and eggs, is available until 12:30 and the café is also a good place to remember for afternoon coffee and pastries. *Plaza de las Cortes 7, tel. 91/429–6537. No reservations. Dress: casual. AE, V.*

★ **Casa Mingo.** Resembling an Asturian cider tavern, Casa Mingo is built into a stone wall beneath the Estación del Norte train station and across the street from the hermitage of San Antonio de la Florida. It's a bustling place and the only dishes offered are succulent roast chicken, salad, and sausages, all washed down with numerous bottles of sidra (hard cider). Inside, you'll share long plank tables with other diners, while in summer small tables are set up on the sidewalk. *Paseo de la Florida 2, tel. 91/547–7918. No reservations. Dress: casual. No credit cards.*

Lodging

Madrid hotel prices have come down greatly since the glory days of 1992, especially in the upper price brackets. The Ritz and Villamagna hotels, which once charged upwards of $600 a night, can now be enjoyed for $250 to $300, a room rate comparable to other world capitals. If that's still too steep, try bargaining. Surveys show that only 15% of hotel guests pay the posted room rate in Madrid; more savvy customers take advantage of a dizzying array of special offers. Be sure to ask for a business or professional discount, often up to 40% off. As most hotels in Madrid cater to business travelers, special weekend rates are widely available. You can generally save 50% on a Friday, Saturday, or Sunday night, and many hotels throw in extras, like meals or museum admissions. There are hotel reservation desks in the national and international terminals of the airport, and at Chamartín station (tel. 91/315–7894). Or you can contact **La Brújula** (tel. 91/559–9705) on the sixth floor of the Torre de Madrid in Plaza de España, which is open 9–9. It has English-speaking staff and can book hotels all over Spain for a fee of 200 ptas.

For details and price-category definitions, *see* Lodging in Staying in Spain, *above*.

Very Expensive

Palace. This dignified turn-of-the-century hotel opposite parliament and the Prado is a slightly less dazzling step-sister of the nearby Ritz but is full of charm and style. It has long been a favorite of politicians and journalists. Its Belle Epoque decor—especially the glass dome over the lounge—is superb. *Plaza de las Cortes 7, tel. 91/429–7551, fax 91/420–2547. 480 rooms, 20 suites. AE, DC, MC, V.*

★ **Ritz.** Spain's most exclusive hotel is elegant and aristocratic with beautiful rooms, spacious suites, and sumptuous public salons furnished with antiques and handwoven carpets. Its palatial restaurant is justly famous, and its garden terrace is the perfect setting for summer dining. Features are brunches with harp music on weekends and tea or supper chamber concerts from February through May. Close to the Retiro Park and overlooking the famous Prado Museum, it offers pure unadulterated luxury. *Plaza Lealtad 5, tel. 91/521–2857, fax 91/532–8776. 158 rooms. AE, DC, MC, V.*

Villamagna. Second in luxury only to the Ritz, the Villamagna's modern facade belies a palatial interior exquisitely furnished with 18th-century antiques. Set in a delightful garden, it offers all the facilities one would expect in a hotel of international repute. *Paseo de la Castellana 22, tel. 576–7500, fax 91/575–9504. 164 rooms. AE, DC, MC, V.*

Villa Real. Aubusson tapestries from the 19th century and English antiques set the tone in the lobby of this very personal hotel. The emphasis is on service and luxurious details, such as three telephones in every room and teletext service on TV. All rooms are split-level and have a slightly clubby masculine decor with leather sofas and dark red floral fabrics. The hotel looks over the Plaza de las Cortes and is convenient to almost everything. *Plaza de las Cortes 10, 28014, tel. 91/420–3767, fax 91/420–2547. 94 rooms, 20 suites. AE, DC, MC, V.*

Expensive

Alcalá. Close to the Retiro Park and Goya shopping area, this comfortable hotel has long been recognized for high standards. Bedrooms are well furnished, and the cafeteria serves a good lunch menu for around 1,200 ptas. The hotel restaurant, Le Basque (closed Sun. and Mon. lunch), is famed for its Basque culinary delights. *Alcalá 66, tel. 91/435–1060, fax 91/435–1105. 153 rooms. AE, DC, MC, V.*

El Prado. Wedged in among the classic buildings of Old Madrid, this skinny new hotel is within stumbling distance of the city's best bars and nightclubs. Rooms are soundproofed with double-paned glass and are surprisingly spacious. Decor includes pastel floral prints and gleaming marble baths. *Calle Prado 11, 28014, tel. 91/369–0234, fax 91/429–2829. 50 rooms with bath. AE, DC, MC, V.*

Lagasca. Opened in 1993 in the heart of the elegant Salamanca neighborhood, this hotel combines large brightly furnished rooms with an unbeatable location two blocks from Madrid's main shopping street, Calle Serrano. The marble lobbies border on the functional, but are fine to use as a meeting place. *Lagasca 64, 28001, tel. 91/575–4606, fax 91/575–1694. 100 rooms with bath. AE, DC, MC, V.*

★ **Reina Victoria.** One of Madrid's most historic and best loved hotels, the Reina Victoria faces two of the city's liveliest squares. Once a haven for bullfighters, the hotel now attracts a more upscale clientele, who are treated to large renovated rooms with a comfortable feel and magnificent views. *Plaza del Angel 7, 28014, tel. 91/531–4500, fax 91/522–0307. 110 rooms. AE, DC, MC, V.*

Tryp Ambassador. Located in the refurbished palace of the Dukes of Granada, this hotel sits on a quiet old street near the Royal Palace. A magnificent front door and three-story spiral staircase in the entryway greet visitors. Rooms are large and luxurious with separate sleeping and sitting areas. *Cuesta de Santo Domingo 5, 28013. tel. 91/541–6700, fax 91/559–1040. 182 rooms. AE, DC, MC, V.*

Moderate **Atlántico.** Hidden away on the third floor of a rather shabby building on Gran Via, this hotel will surprise you with its clean and modern rooms, each one decorated in a different color scheme and all with tile baths. Windows are soundproofed, and the hotel is always filled with an interesting assortment of international visitors. *Gran Via 38, 28013, tel. 91/522–6480, fax 91/531–0210. 60 rooms. AE, MC, V.*

Carlos V. If you like to be right in the center of things, this classic Madrid hotel on a quiet, pedestrian-only street is just a few steps away from the Puerta del Sol and Plaza Mayor. A suit of armor decorates the tiny lobby, while crystal chandeliers add elegance to a second-floor guest lounge. All rooms are bright and carpeted. *Maestro Victoria 5, 28013, tel. 91/531–4100, fax 91/531–3761. 67 rooms. AE, MC, V.*

★ **Inglés.** The exterior may seem shabby, but don't be deterred. The Inglés is a long-standing budget favorite. Its rooms are comfortable, with good facilities, and the location is a real bonus: You're a short walk from the Puerta del Sol one way, and from the Prado the other; inexpensive restaurants and atmospheric bars are right at hand. *Echegaray 10, tel. 91/429–6551, fax 91/420–2423. 58 rooms. AE, DC, MC, V.*

★ **Paris.** Overlooking the Puerta del Sol, the Paris is a stylish hotel full of old-fashioned appeal. It has an impressive turn-of-the-century lobby and a restaurant where you can dine for around 1,500 ptas. Recently refurbished, the hotel has managed to retain its character while adding modern amenities. *Alcalá 2, tel. 91/521–6496, fax 91/531–0188. 114 rooms. MC, V.*

Inexpensive **Lisboa.** Clean, small, and central, the Lisboa is a well-kept secret in the lively bar-and-restaurant neighborhood of Plaza Santa Ana. Rooms have tile floors and are sparsely furnished. They vary greatly in size and quality, so be sure to ask to see your room before taking it. *Ventura de la Vega 17, 28014, tel. 91/429–9894. 22 rooms. AE, DC, MC, V.*

Monaco. An eccentric and opulent delight, this hotel was once a haunt of the court of Alfonso XIII. All of the rooms are different, and many retain crumbling signs of grandeur such as murals on the ceiling, bas-relief figures, and gilt mirrors. Monaco is located in the lively, but drug-infested, neighborhood off Plaza Chueca. Once again, look before you buy. *Barbieri 5, 28004, tel. 91/522–4630, fax 91/521–1601. 33 rooms. AE, MC, V.*

Bars and Cafés

Bars **The Mesones.** The most traditional and colorful taverns are on Cuchilleros and Cava San Miguel just west of Plaza Mayor, where you'll find a whole array of mesones with such names as **Tortilla, Champiñón,** and **Boqueron.**

Old Madrid. Wander the narrow streets between Puerta del Sol and Plaza Santa Ana, which are packed with traditional tapas bars. Favorites here are the **Cervecería Alemana,** Plaza Santa Ana 6, a beer hall founded more than 100 years ago by Germans and patronized, inevitably, by Hemingway; **Los Gabrieles,** Echegaray 17, with magnificent ceramic decor; **La Trucha,** Manuel Fernández y González 3, with loads of atmosphere; and **Viva Madrid,** Fernández y González 7, a lovely old bar.

Calle Huertas. Fashionable bars with turn-of-the-century decor and chamber or guitar music, often live, line this street. **La Fídula** at No. 57 and **El Hecho** at No. 56 are two of the best.

Plaza Santa Barbara. This area just off Alonso Martínez is packed with fashionable bars and beer halls. Stroll along Santa Teresa, Orellana, Campoamor, or Fernando VI and take your pick. The **Cervecería Santa Barbara** in the plaza itself is one of the most colorful, a popular beer hall with a good range of tapas.

Cafés If you like cafés with an old-fashioned atmosphere, dark wooden counters, brass pumps, and marble-topped tables, try any of the following: **Café Comercial,** Glorieta de Bilbao 7; **Café Gijón,** Paseo de Recoletos 21, a former literary hangout and the most famous of the cafés of old, now one of the many café-terraces that line the Castellana; **Café León,** Alcalá 57, just up from Cibeles; and **El Espejo,** Paseo de Recoletos 31, with art-nouveau decor and an outdoor terrace in summer. And don't forget **La Mallorquina** tearooms on Puerta del Sol (*see* Exploring, *above*).

The Arts

Details of all cultural events are listed in the daily newspaper *El País* or in the weekly *Guía del Ocio.*

Concerts and The main concert hall is the new **Auditorio Nacional de Madrid** (tel.
Opera 91/337–0100), Príncipe de Vergara 146 (metro, Cruz del Royo), which opened at the end of 1988. The old **Teatro Real** on the Plaza de Oriente opposite the Royal Palace is being converted into Madrid's long-needed opera house and may reopen in 1995; inquire at the tourist office.

Zarzuela and Zarzuela, a combination of light opera and dance ideal for non-Span-
Dance ish speakers, is held at the **Teatro Nacional Lírico de la Zarzuela** (Jovellanos 4, tel. 91/429–8216). The season runs from October through July.

Theater If language is no problem, check out the fringe theaters in Lavapiés (*see* Off the Beaten Track, *above*) and the **Centro Cultural de la Villa** (tel. 91/575–6080) beneath the Plaza Colón, and the open-air events in the Retiro Park. Other leading theaters—you'll also need reasonable Spanish—include the **Círculo de Bellas Artes,** Marqués de Casa Riera 2, just off Alcalá 42 (tel. 91/531–7700); the **Teatro Español,** Príncipe 25 on Plaza Santa Ana (tel. 91/429–6297) for Spanish classics; and the **Teatro María Guerrero,** Tamayo y Baus 4 (tel. 91/319–4769), home of the Centro Dramático Nacional, for plays by García Lorca. Most theaters have two curtains, at 7 and 10:30 PM, and close on Mondays. Tickets are inexpensive and often easy to come by on the night of performance.

Films   Foreign films are mostly dubbed into Spanish, but movies in English are listed in *El País* or *Guía del Ocio* under "V.O.," meaning *versión original*. A dozen or so theaters now show films in English; some of the best bets are **Alphaville** and **Cines Renoir,** both in Martín de los Heros, just off Plaza España, and the **Filmoteca Español** (Santa Isabel 3), a city-run institution where classic V.O. films change daily.

Nightlife

Cabaret   **Florida Park** (tel. 91/573–7805), in the Retiro Park, offers dinner and a show that often features ballet, Spanish dance, or flamenco and is open Monday through Saturday from 9:30 PM, with shows at 10:45 PM. **Berlin** (Costanilla de San Pedro 11, tel. 91/366–2034) opens at 9:30 PM for a dinner that is good by most cabaret standards, followed by a show and dancing until 4 AM. **La Scala** (Rosario Pino 7, tel. 91/571–4411), in the Meliá Castilla hotel, is Madrid's top nightclub, with dinner, dancing, cabaret at 8:30, and a second, less expensive show around midnight. This is the one visited by most night tours.

Flamenco   Madrid offers the widest choice of flamenco shows in Spain; some are good, but many are aimed at the tourist trade. Dinner tends to be mediocre and overpriced, but it ensures the best seats; otherwise, opt for the show and a drink *(consumición)* only, usually starting around 11 PM and costing around 3,000 ptas.–3,500 ptas. **Arco de Cuchilleros** (Cuchilleros 7, tel. 91/266–5867), behind the Plaza Mayor, is one of the better, cheaper ones. **Café de Chinitas** (Torija 7, tel. 91/248–5135) and **Corral de la Morería** (Morería 17, tel. 91/265–8446 and 265–1137) are two of the more authentic places where well-known troupes perform. Another choice is **Corral de la Pacheca** (Juan Ramón Jiménez 26, tel. 91/359–2660). **Zambra** (Velázquez 8, tel. 91/435–4928), in the Hotel Wellington, is one of the smartest (jacket and tie essential), with a good show and dinner served into the small hours.

Jazz   The leading club of the moment is **Café Central** (Plaza de Angel 10), followed by **Clamores** (Albuquerque 14). Others include **Café Jazz Populart** (Huertas 22) and **El Despertar** (Torrecilla del Leal 18). Excellent jazz frequently comes to Madrid as part of city-hosted seasonal festivals; check the local press for listings and venues.

Casino   **Madrid's Casino** (tel. 91/856–1100) is 28 kilometers (17 miles) out at Torrelodones on the N-VI road to La Coruña. *Open 5 PM–4 AM. Free transportation service from Plaza de España 6.*

Madrid Environs

The beauty of the historic cities surrounding Madrid and the role they have played in their country's history rank them among Spain's most worthwhile sights. Ancient Toledo, the former capital, the great palace-monastery of El Escorial, the sturdy medieval walls of Avila, Segovia's Roman aqueduct and fairy-tale Alcázar, and the magnificent Plaza Mayor of the old university town of Salamanca all lie within an hour or so from the capital.

All the towns below, with the possible exception of Salamanca, can easily be visited on day-trips from Madrid. But if you've had your fill of the hustle and bustle of Spain's booming capital, you'll find it far more rewarding to tour from one place to another, spending a day or two in one or more of these fascinating locales. Then, long after the

Madrid Environs

day-trippers have gone home, you can enjoy the real charm of these small provincial towns and wander at leisure through their medieval streets.

Getting There from Madrid

Trains to Toledo leave from Madrid's Atocha Station; to Salamanca, Avila, Segovia and El Escorial from Chamartín station.

Getting Around

There's a direct train line between El Escorial, Ávila, and Salamanca; otherwise, train connections are poor and you'll do better to go by bus. All places are linked by bus services and the local tourist offices will advise on schedules. Toledo's bus station is on the Ronda de Castilla la Mancha (tel. 925/215850) just off the road from Madrid. Ávila's bus station is on Avenida de Madrid (tel. 918/220154); Segovia's is on Paseo Ezequiel González (tel. 911/427725); and Salamanca's is on Filiberto Villalobos 73 (tel. 923/236717). The N403 from Toledo to Ávila passes through spectacular scenery in the Sierra de Gredos mountains, as does the C505 Ávila–El Escorial route. From El Escorial to Segovia, both the Puerto de León and Puerto de Navacerrada mountain passes offer magnificent views. The N501 from Ávila to Salamanca will take you across the tawny plain of Castile.

Tourist Information

Ávila (Plaza de la Catedral 4, tel. 918/211387); open weekdays 8–3
and 4–6 (5–7 in summer), Saturday 9–1:30 only.
El Escorial (Floridablanca 10, tel. 91/8901554); open weekdays 10–2
and 3–4:45, Saturday 10–1:45.
Salamanca (Gran Vía 41, tel. 923/268571); open weekdays 9:30–2 and
4:30–8, Saturday 10–2. There's also an information booth on the Plaza Mayor (market side).
Segovia (Plaza Mayor 10, tel. 911/430328); open Monday–Saturday
9–2; also weekdays 4–6 in summer only.
Toledo (Puerta Nueva de Bisagra tel. 925/220843); open Monday–
Saturday 9–3 and 4–7, Sunday 9–3.

Exploring the Madrid Environs

The following tour goes from Toledo to El Escorial, the Valley of the
Fallen, La Granja, Segovia, Riofrio, Ávila, Alba de Tormes, and Salamanca.

Head south from Madrid on the road to Toledo. About 20 minutes
from the capital look left for a prominent rounded hill topped by a
statue of Christ. This is the **Hill of the Angels,** which marks the geographical center of the Iberian Peninsula. After 90 minutes of drab,
industrial scenery, the unforgettable silhouette of **Toledo** suddenly
rises before you, the imposing bulk of the Alcazar and the slender
spire of the cathedral dominating the skyline. This former capital,
where Moors, Jews, and Christians once lived in harmony, is now a
living national monument, depicting all the elements of Spanish civilization in hand-carved, sun-mellowed stone. For a stunning view
and to capture the beauty of Toledo as El Greco knew it, begin with a
panoramic drive around the Carretera de Circunvalación, crossing
over the Alcántara bridge and returning by way of the bridge of San
Martín. As you gaze at the city rising like an island in its own bend of
the Tagus, reflect how little the city skyline has changed in the four
centuries since El Greco painted *Storm Over Toledo.*

Toledo is a small city steeped in history and full of magnificent buildings. It was the capital of Spain under both Moors and Christians
until some whim caused Philip II to move his capital to Madrid in
1561. Begin your visit with a drink in one of the many terrace cafés
on the central **Plaza Zocodover,** study a map, and try to get your
bearings, for a veritable labyrinth confronts you as you try to find
your way to Toledo's great treasures. While here, search the
square's pastry shops for the typical marzipan candies *(mazapanes)*
of Toledo.

Begin your tour with a visit to the 13th-century **Cathedral,** seat of
the Cardinal Primate of Spain, and one of the great cathedrals of
Spain. Somber but elaborate, it blazes with jeweled chalices, gorgeous ecclesiastical vestments, historic tapestries, some 750
stained-glass windows, and paintings by Tintoretto, Titian, Murillo, El Greco, Velázquez, and Goya. The cathedral has two surprises:
a **Mozarabic chapel,** where Mass is still celebrated on Sundays according to an ancient Mozarabic rite handed down from the days of
the Visigoths (AD 419–711); and its unique **Transparente,** an
extravagent Baroque roof that gives a theatrical glimpse into heav-
en as the sunlight pours down through a mass of figures and clouds.
*Admission: 350 ptas. Open Tues.–Sat. 10:30–1:30 and 3:30–6 (7 in
summer), Sun. 10:30–1:30 and 4–6.*

En route to the real jewel of Toledo, the **Chapel of Santo Tomé,** you'll pass a host of souvenir shops on Calle Santo Tomé, bursting with damascene knives and swords, blue-and-yellow pottery from nearby Talavera, and El Greco reproductions. In the tiny chapel that houses El Greco's masterpiece, *The Burial of the Count of Orgaz,* you can capture the true spirit of the Greek painter who adopted Spain, and in particular Toledo, as his home. Do you recognize the sixth man from the left among the painting's earthly contingent? Or the young boy in the left-hand corner? The first is El Greco himself, the second his son Jorge Manuel—see 1578, the year of his birth, embroidered on his handkerchief. *Admission: 100 ptas. Open daily 10–1:45 and 3:30–5:45 (6:45 in summer).*

Not far away is **El Greco's House,** a replica containing copies of his works. *Tel. 925/224046. Closed for restoration until 1996.*

The splendid **Sinagoga del Tránsito** stands on the corner of Samuel Levi and Reyes Católicos. Commissioned in 1366 by Samuel Levi, chancellor to Pedro the Cruel, the synagogue shows Christian and Moorish as well as Jewish influences in its architecture and decoration—look at the stars of David interspersed with the arms of Castile and León. There's also a small **Sephardic Museum** chronicling the life of Toledo's former Jewish community. *Admission: 200 ptas. Open Tues.–Sat. 10–2 and 4–6, Sun. 10–2.*

Another synagogue, the incongruously named **Santa María la Blanca** (it was given as a church to the Knights of Calatrava in 1405), is just along the street. Its history may have been Jewish and Christian, but its architecture is definitely Moorish, for it resembles a mosque with five naves, horseshoe arches, and capitals decorated with texts from the Koran. *Admission: 100 ptas. Open daily 10–2 and 3:30–6 (until 7 in summer).*

Across the road is **San Juan de los Reyes,** a beautiful Gothic church begun by Ferdinand and Isabella in 1476. Wander around its fine cloisters and don't miss the iron manacles on the outer walls; they were placed there by Christians freed by the Moors. The Catholic Kings originally intended to be buried here, but then their great triumph at Granada in 1492 changed their plans. *Admission: 100 ptas. Open daily 10–1:30 and 3:30–5:45 (6:45 in summer).*

Walk down the hill through the ancient **Cambrón Gate** and your visit to Toledo is over. Should you have more time, however, head for the **Museum of Santa Cruz,** just off the Zocodover, with its splendid El Grecos. *Tel. 925/221036. Admission: 200 ptas. Open Mon. 10–2, 4:30–6:30, Tues.–Sat. 10–6:30, Sun. 10–2.*

Also consider a visit to the **Hospital de Tavera,** outside the walls, where you can see Ribera's amazing *Bearded Woman. Tel. 925/ 220451. Admission: 500 ptas. Open daily 10:30–1:30 and 3:30–6.*

In the foothills of the Guadarrama Mountains, 50 kilometers (31 miles) to the northwest of Madrid, and 120 kilometers (74 miles) from Toledo, lies **San Lorenzo del Escorial,** burial place of Spanish kings and queens. The **Monastery,** built by the religious fanatic Philip II as a memorial to his father, Charles V, is a vast rectangular edifice, conceived and executed with a monotonous magnificence worthy of the Spanish royal necropolis. It was designed by Juan de Herrera, Spain's greatest Renaissance architect. The **Royal Pantheon** contains the tombs of monarchs from Charles V to Alfonso XIII, grandfather of Juan Carlos, and those of their consorts. Only two kings are missing, Philip V, who chose to be buried in his beloved La Granja, and Ferdinand VI, buried in Madrid. In the **Pantheon of the**

Infantes rest the 60 royal children who died in infancy, and those queens who bore no heirs. The lavishly bejeweled tomb here belongs to Don Juan, bastard son of Charles V and half brother of Philip II, dashing hero and victor of the Battle of Lepanto. The monastery's other highlights are the magnificent **Library of Philip II**, with 40,000 rare volumes and 2,700 illuminated manuscripts, including the diary of Santa Teresa, and the **Royal Apartments.** Contrast the spartan private apartment of Philip II and the simple bedroom in which he died in 1598 with the beautiful carpets, porcelain, and tapestries with which his less austere successors embellished the rest of his somber monastery-palace. *Tel. 91/890–5905. Admission: 800 ptas. for the monastery and 500 ptas. for the Casita del Príncipe. Open Tues.–Sun. 10–6 (7 in summer). Last entry is 45 mins. before closing time.*

Eight kilometers (5 miles) along the road to Segovia, the mighty cross of the **Valley of the Fallen** looms up on your left. This vast basilica hewn out of sheer granite was built by General Franco between 1940 and 1959 as a monument to the dead of Spain's Civil War of 1936–39. Buried here are 43,000 war dead, José Antonio Primo de Rivera, founder of the Falangists and early martyr of the war, and Franco himself, who died in 1975. A funicular to the top of the monument costs 300 ptas. *Tel. 91/890–5611. Admission: 600 ptas. Open Tues.–Sat. 10–7 (6 in winter).*

A spectacular drive lies ahead for those who use the local road rather than the autoroute, from the resort of Navacerrada up through the Guadarrama Mountains by way of the **Navacerrada pass** at 1,860 meters (6,000 feet). The steep descent through fragrant pine forests via the hairpin bends of the Siete Revueltas (Seven Curves) brings you straight into La Granja.

The **Palace of La Granja,** with its splendid formal gardens and fountains, was built between 1719 and 1739 by the homesick Philip V, first Bourbon king of Spain and grandson of France's Louis XIV, to remind him of his beloved Versailles. The whole place is like an exquisite piece of France in a Spanish wood, and it's small wonder that Philip chose to be buried here in the splendor of his own creation rather than in the austerity of El Escorial. The splendid gardens are open until dusk and you can stroll around them for free except when the fountains are playing. *Tel. 911/470020. Palace admission: 500 ptas. Palace open Tues.–Sun. 10–6; winter, Tues.–Sat. 10–1:30 and 3–5, Sun. 10–2.*

From La Granja, a 10-minute drive will bring you to the golden-stone market town of **Segovia.** In front of you rises the majestic Roman aqueduct, its huge granite blocks held together without mortar. At its foot is a small bronze statue of Romulus and the wolf, presented by Rome in 1974 to commemorate the 2,000-year history of Spain's most complete Roman monument.

Drive around the base of the rock on which Segovia stands. The Ronda de Santa Lucía leads to the most romantic view of the Alcázar, perched high on its rock like the prow of a mighty ship. Return via the Carretera de los Hoyos for yet another magical view, this time of the venerable cathedral rising from the ramparts. Next, fend off the pestering gypsies around the aqueduct and make for the **Calle Real,** the main shopping street. As you climb, you'll pass the Romanesque church of **San Martín,** with its porticoed outer gallery. Continue to the picturesque **Plaza Mayor** with its colorful ceramic stalls (good bargains) and pleasant cafés set against the backdrop of ancient arcaded houses and one of the loveliest, externally, at least, Gothic cathedrals in Spain.

Segovia **cathedral** was the last Gothic cathedral to be built in Spain (the one in Ávila was the first). Begun in 1525 by order of Charles V, its interior is sadly disappointing, as many of its treasures were carried off by Napoleon's troops in the Peninsular War of the early 1800s. Its museum has the first book printed in Spain (1472). You should also seek out the tomb of Don Pedro, two-year-old son of Henry IV who slipped from his nurse's arms and tumbled to his death over the battlements of the Alcázar (his distraught nurse cast herself over after him). *Admission: 200 ptas. Open daily in summer, 10–7; in winter, Mon.–Sat. 10–1 and 3–6, Sun. 9:30–6.*

The turreted **Alcázar** with its *esgrafiado* facade—an architectural peculiarity of Segovia whereby houses were embellished with small pieces of coke—is largely a fanciful re-creation of the 1880s, the original 13th-century castle having been destroyed by fire in 1862. The view from its ramparts—and, even better, from its tower if you can manage the 156 steps—is breathtaking. The Alcázar served as a major residence of the Catholic Kings. Here Isabella met Ferdinand, and from here she set out to be crowned Queen of Castile. The interior successfully re-creates the era of this dual monarchy that established Spain's Golden Age. *Tel. 911/430176. Admission: 350 ptas. Open daily 10–6 in winter, 10–7 in summer.*

The **Palace of Riofrio,** 8 kilometers (5 miles) south of Segovia, off the road to San Rafael, was bought by Isabel Farnese, widow of Philip V, with the idea of turning it into a splendid dwelling along the lines of Madrid's Royal Palace. Her dream was never fulfilled, and the palace, which houses a small **Hunting Museum,** is now of minor importance. Far more attractive is its surrounding **parkland,** where deer will come right up to your car. *Admission: 400 ptas. Palace open Tues.–Sat. 10–1:30 and 3–5, Sun. 10–2.*

Ávila, almost 1,240 meters (4,000 feet) above sea level, is the highest provincial capital in Spain. Alfonso VI and his son-in-law, Count Raimundo de Borgoña, rebuilt the town and walls in 1090, bringing it permanently under Christian control. It is these walls, the most complete military installations of their kind in Spain, that give Ávila its special medieval quality. Thick and solid, with 88 towers tufted with numerous untidy storks' nests, they stretch for 2½ kilometers (1½ miles) around the entire city and make an ideal focus for the start of your visit. For a superb overall view and photo spot, drive out to the **Cuatro Postes,** three-quarters of a kilometer (half a mile) out on the road to Salamanca.

The personality of Santa Teresa the Mystic, to whom the city is dedicated, lives today as vividly as it did in the 16th century. Several religious institutions associated with the life of the saint are open to visitors, the most popular of which is the **Convent of Santa Teresa,** which stands on the site of her birthplace. There's an ornate Baroque chapel, a small gift shop, and a museum with some of her relics: her rosary, books, walking stick, a sole of her sandal, and her finger wearing her wedding ring. *Tel. 918/211030. Admission free. Located at Plaza de la Santa, just inside the southern gate. Open daily 9:30–1 and 3:30–7.*

Ávila's other ecclesiastical monuments are far older and more rewarding than those that commemorate the saint. The impregnable hulk of the **cathedral** is in many ways more akin to a fortress than a house of God. Though of Romanesque origin—the Romanesque sections are recognizable by their red and white brickwork—it is usual-

ly claimed as Spain's first Gothic cathedral. Inside, the ornate alabaster tomb of Cardinal Alonso de Madrigal, a 15th-century bishop
whose swarthy complexion earned him the nickname of "El Tostado"
(the toasted one) is thought to be the work of Domenico Fancelli,
who also sculpted the tomb of Prince Juan in Santo Tomás and the
sepulchers of the Catholic Kings in Granada's Royal Chapel. *Tel.
918/211641. Admission free. Cathedral open daily in summer 10–1
and 3:30–7, in winter 10–2. Museum admission: 200 ptas.*

The **Basilica of San Vicente,** just outside the walls, is one of Ávila's
finest Romanesque churches, standing on the spot where St. Vincent and his sisters Sabina and Cristeta were martyred in AD 306.
Here, too, Santa Teresa is said to have experienced the vision that
told her to reform the Carmelite order. *Admission: 50 ptas. Open
Tues.–Sun. 10–2 and 4–6 (7 in summer).*

Before continuing to the **Monastery of Santo Tomás,** you can relax in
the pleasant **Plaza de Santa Teresa** with its outdoor cafés and statue
of the saint erected for Pope John Paul's visit in 1982. Built between
1482 and 1493 by Ferdinand and Isabella, who used it as a summer
palace, it houses the tomb of their only son, Prince Juan—who died
at the age of 19 while a student at Salamanca—as well as the tomb of
that far less lovable character, the notorious Inquisitor General
Tomás de Torquemada. *Admission: monastery free, cloisters 50
ptas., Museum of Eastern Art 50 ptas. Open daily 10–1 and 4–7.*

From Ávila it's straight sailing all the way to Salamanca unless
you're a devotee of Santa Teresa and choose to take a small detour to
the old ducal town of **Alba de Tormes** to visit the **Carmelite Convent**
(open daily 9–2 and 4–8), where the saint is buried.

Salamanca is an ancient city, and your first glimpse of it is bound to
be unforgettable. Beside the road flows the Tormes River and beyond it rise the old houses of the city and the golden walls, turrets,
and domes of the Plateresque cathedrals. "Plateresque" comes from
plata (silver) and implies that the stone is chiseled and engraved as
intricately as that delicate metal. A superb example of this style is
the facade of the Dominican **Monastery of San Esteban** (150 ptas.;
open daily 9–1 and 4–7, 5–8 in summer), which you'll pass on your
way to the cathedrals. The **old cathedral** far outshines its younger
sister, the **new cathedral,** in beauty. (The new cathedral's funds ran
out during construction—1513–1733—leaving a rather bare interi-
or.) Inside the sturdy Romanesque walls of the old cathedral, built
between 1102 and 1160, your attention will be drawn to Nicolás Flor-
entino's stunning altarpiece with 53 brightly painted panels. Don't
miss the splendid **cloisters,** which now house a worthwhile collection
of religious art, and the **Degree Chapel,** where anxious students
sought inspiration on the night before their final exams. *New cathedral free; old cathedral and cloisters 200 ptas. Open daily 10–2 and
4–7.*

Founded by Alfonso IX in 1218, **Salamanca University** is to Spain
what Oxford University is to England. On its famous **doorway** in the
Patio de las Escuelas, a profusion of Plateresque carving surrounds
the medallions of Ferdinand and Isabella. See if you can find the famous frog and skull, said to bring good luck to students in their ex-
aminations. Inside, the **lecture room** of Fray Luis de León has
remained untouched since the days of the great scholar, and the
prestigious **Library** boasts some 50,000 parchment and leather-
bound volumes. *Tel. 923/294400, ext. 1150. Library admission: 200
ptas. Open Mon.–Sat. 10–2 and 4–8, Sun. 10–1.*

Now make for Salamanca's greatest jewel, the elegant 18th-century **Plaza Mayor.** Here you can browse in stores offering typical *charro* jewelry (silver and black flowerheads), head down the steps to the market in search of colorful tapas bars, or simply relax in an outdoor café. In this, the city's crowning glory, and the most exquisite square in Spain, you've found the perfect place to end your tour of Salamanca and Castile.

Dining and Lodging

For details and price-category definitions, *see* Dining and Lodging in Staying in Spain, *above.*

Ávila
Dining

El Fogón de Santa Teresa. Traditional Castilian roasts, lamb chops, and trout feature on the menu of this attractive restaurant in the vaults of the Palacio de Valderrábanos. *Alemania 3, tel. 918/211023. AE, DC, MC, V. Moderate.*

★ **El Molino de la Losa.** Situated on a spit of land jutting into the Adaja River, this restaurant occupies a restored 15th-century mill and has splendid views of Ávila's walls. Specialties include lamb roasted in a medieval-style wood oven and fresh river trout. *Bajada de la Losa 12, tel. 918/211101. AE, MC, V. Closed Mon. in winter. Moderate.*

★ **Mesón del Rastro.** This ancient inn tucked into the city walls is Ávila's most atmospheric place to dine. Local specialties include Ávila's famous veal *(ternera)* and *yemas de Santa Teresa*, a dessert made from candied egg yolks. *Plaza del Rastro 1, tel. 918/211218. AE, DC, MC, V. Moderate.*

Lodging
★

Palacio de Valderrábanos. Ávila's best hotel is located in a 15th-century mansion opposite the cathedral. It was once the residence of the first bishop of Ávila. *Plaza Catedral 9, tel. 918/211023, fax 918/256191. 73 rooms. AE, DC, MC, V. Expensive.*

Parador Raimundo de Borgoña. The location of this parador in a 15th-century palace just inside the northern walls of the city is superb. The rooms are decorated in traditional Castilian style and have spacious, well-equipped bathrooms. Some rooms also have four-poster beds and a view of the city walls. Its dining room is atmospheric and serves local Ávilan dishes, including the inevitable yemas, and the parador garden offers the only access to the walls. *Marqués de Canales y Chozas 16, tel. 918/211340, fax 918/226166. 62 rooms. AE, DC, MC, V. Expensive.*

Hostería de Bracamonte. Unpack your bags in any of the 19 rooms at this tiny, comfortable hotel and you'll feel as if you've moved into your own private medieval mansion. The entryway and lounge feature exposed stone walls and beam ceilings; guest rooms are decorated with canopy beds and fireplaces. *Bracamonte 6, tel. 918/251280, fax 918/213240. 19 rooms. MC, V. Moderate.*

El Escorial
Dining
★

Charolés. This elegant restaurant has a terrace above the street for summer dining. Its meat dishes are famous throughout the region. Try the *charolés a la pimienta* (pepper steak). Fresh fish is brought in daily from Spain's north coast. *Floridablanca 24, tel. 91/890-5975. Reservations required most weekends. AE, DC, MC, V. Expensive.*

Mesón de la Cueva. Founded in 1768, this atmospheric mesón has several small, rustic dining rooms. This inn is a must for ambience, and the food is good, too. *San Antón 4, tel. 91/890-1516. Reservations advised on weekends. AE, DC, MC, V. Moderate–Expensive.*

El Candil. One of the best of the many middle-range restaurants in El Escorial, El Candil is situated above a bar on the corner of Plaza San Lorenzo on the village's main street. In summer you can dine outdoors in the square, a delightful spot. *Reina Victoria 12, tel. 91/890–4103. AE, DC, MC, V. Moderate.*

Lodging **Victoria Palace.** The rooms at the back of this grand old-world hotel close to the monastery have balconies and a splendid view toward Madrid; there's a garden and pool, too. *Juan de Toledo 4, tel. 91/890–1511, fax 91/8901248. 89 rooms. AE, DC, MC, V. Expensive.*

Miranda Suizo. Rooms are comfortable in this charming old hotel on the main street, and the hotel café, with its dark wood fittings and marble tables, is right out of the 19th century. *Floridablanca 20, tel. 91/890–4711, fax 91/8904358. 47 rooms. AE, DC, MC, V. Moderate.*

Salamanca **Chapeau.** This chic spot carefully offers both meat and fish carefully
Dining roasted in its wood-fired ovens. Try their *pimientos rellenos*
★ (stuffed peppers) and orange mousse for dessert. *Gran Vía 20, tel. 923/271833. Reservations advised. AE, DC, MC, V. Closed Sun. in summer. Expensive.*

Chez Victor. Chez Victor attracts a regular clientele with its French-inspired cuisine. *Espoz y Mina 26, tel. 923/213123. Reservations advised. AE, DC, MC, V. Closed Sun. evening, Mon., and Aug. Expensive.*

El Mesón. There's plenty of colorful atmosphere and good traditional Castilian food in this typical mesón just off the Plaza Mayor, beside the Gran Hotel. *Plaza Poeta Iglesias 10, tel. 923/217222. AE, MC, V. Closed Jan. Moderate.*

Río de la Plata. This small, atmospheric restaurant close to El Mesón and the Gran Hotel, serves superb *farinato* sausage; it's a great find. *Plaza del Peso 1, tel. 923/219005. AE, MC, V. Closed Mon., July. Moderate.*

Lodging **Gran Hotel.** The *grande dame* of Salamanca's hotels got a face-lift in 1994 and now offers stylishly baroque lounges and refurbished yet old-fashioned, oversized rooms just steps from the Plaza Mayor. *Poeta Iglesias 3, 37001, tel. 923/213500, fax 923/213501. 109 rooms. AE, DC, MC, V. Expensive.*

Palacio del Castellanos. Opened in 1992 in an immaculately restored 15th-century palace, this hotel offers a much needed alternative to Salamanca's national parador (probably the ugliest in the chain). There is an exquisite interior patio and an equally beautiful restaurant. *San Pablo 58, tel. 923/261818, fax 923/261819. 69 rooms. AE, DC, MC, V. Expensive.*

Las Torres. Overlooking the Plaza Mayor, the down-at-the-heels look of this hotel is more than made up for by fabulous views of Spain's most beautiful square. The rooms are spartan but adequate; be sure to ask for one with balconies on the plaza. *Plaza Mayor 26, 37001, tel. 923/212100, fax 923/212101. 26 rooms. No credit cards. Moderate.*

Segovia **Casa Duque.** Located at the end of the main shopping street, this
Dining restaurant has several floors of beautifully decorated traditional dining rooms and is the main rival to the famous Cándido. There's plenty of local atmosphere, and the food is pure Castilian—try the *ponche segoviano* for dessert. *Cervantes 12, tel. 911/430537. Reservations advised on weekends. AE, DC, MC, V. Moderate–Expensive.*

★ **Mesón de Cándido.** Segovia's most prestigious restaurant has seven dining rooms pulsating with atmosphere and decorated with bullfighting memorabilia and photos of the dignitaries who have dined here over the years. Specialties are *cochinillo* (suckling pig) and *cordero asado* (roast lamb). *Plaza Azoguejo 5, tel. 911/425911. Res-*

ervations required for Sun. lunch. AE, DC, MC, V. Moderate–Expensive.

La Oficina. Traditional Castilian dishes are served in two delightful dining rooms that date back to 1893. It's just off Plaza Mayor. *Cronista Lecea 10, tel. 911/431643. AE, DC, MC, V. Moderate.*

Lodging **Los Linajes.** The advantages of this pleasant, modern hotel, built in Castilian style, are its central location and its superb views. *Dr. Velasco 9, tel. 911/431201, fax 911/431501. 53 rooms. AE, DC, MC, V. Expensive.*

★ **Parador.** To the north of town is this modern parador offering comfortable, spacious rooms and a pool. The views of the city, especially when illuminated, are magnificent. The restaurant offers superior parador cooking. *Off the N601 toward Valladolid, tel. 911/443737, fax 911/437362. 103 rooms. AE, DC, MC, V. Expensive.*

Infanta Isabel. A recently restored building with a Victorian feel houses this small, centrally located hotel—it's two steps off the Plaza Mayor and offers great views of Segovia's cathedral. Guest rooms are feminine and light, with white painted furnishings. *Plaza Mayor s/n, 40001, tel. 911/443105, fax 911/433240. 29 rooms. AE, MC, V. Moderate.*

Toledo **Asador Adolfo.** This restaurant is situated near the cathedral and is
Dining well known for its good food (try the superb roast meat and the *pimentos del piquillo rellenos de pescado*) and service. *Calle de la Granada 6, tel. 925/227321. AE, DC, MC, V. Closed Sun. evening. Expensive.*

★ **Hostal del Cardenal.** Toledo's best restaurant is set in the 17th-century palace of Cardinal Lorenzana, up against the city ramparts, and boasts five dining rooms and a delightful garden for summer dining. The first choice of every tourist, both food and service are excellent (try the roast suckling pig). *Paseo Recaredo 24, tel. 925/220862. Reservations required in high season. AE, MC, V. Expensive.*

Hierbabuena. Dine on a covered Moorish patio with crocheted tablecloths and plenty of natural light. The menu features gourmet dishes such as artichokes stuffed with seafood and steak in blue cheese sauce at surprisingly low prices. *Cristo de la Luz 9, tel. 925/223463. Reservations advised. MC, V. Moderate.*

La Abadia. Perfect for a light lunch, a sandwich, or a round of tapas, this stylish bar-restaurant features vaulted stone ceilings and a huge old wooden door. The dining room downstairs specializes in shish-kebabs, grilled meats, and salads. *Plaza San Nicolás 3. No phone. No reservations. No credit cards. Moderate.*

Venta de Aires. A century-old inn on the edge of town and not far from the Tajo River, this is where Toledanos go to eat partridge. Steaks and lamb are also expertly prepared. *Circo Romano 35, tel. 925/220545. Reservations advised on weekends. MC, V. Moderate.*

Lodging **Parador Conde de Orgaz.** This is one of Spain's most popular para-
★ dores, and the best and most expensive hotel in Toledo (a 15-minute drive from city center). It's a modern parador built in traditional Toledo style and stands on a hill across the river, commanding magnificent views of the city. Book far ahead. *Paseo de los Cigarrales, tel. 925/221850, fax 925/225166. 77 rooms. AE, DC, MC, V. Expensive.*

María Cristina. You'll pass this comfortable new hotel on your way from Madrid. Located beside the bullring, it opened in 1986 and provides excellent facilities. Its El Abside restaurant is fast gaining in prestige. *Marqués de Mendigorría 1, tel. 925/213202. 65 rooms. AE, V. Moderate.*

Pintor El Greco. Next door to the famous painter's house-museum, this friendly hotel occupies a building that was once a 17th-century bakery. Extensive renovation has resulted in a light and modern interior, with some antique touches such as exposed brick vaulting. *Alamillos del Transito 13, 45002, tel. 925/214250, fax 925/215819. 35 rooms. AE, DC, MC, V. Moderate.*

Maravilla. This simple but very central old-world hotel just off Plaza Zocodover has a good, old-fashioned restaurant. *Barrio Rey 7, tel. 925/223304. 18 rooms. AE, DC, MC, V. Inexpensive.*

Barcelona

Arriving and Departing

By Plane All international and domestic flights arrive at El Prat de Llobregat airport, 14 kilometers (8½ miles) south of Barcelona just off the main highway to Castelldefels and Sitges. For information on arrival and departure times, call the airport (tel. 93/478–5000 or 478–5032) or Iberia information (tel. 93/301–3993).

Between the Airport and Downtown The airport–city train leaves every 30 minutes between 6:30 AM and 11 PM and reaches the Barcelona Central (Sants) Station in 15 minutes; a new extension now carries you to the Plaça de Catalunya, at the head of the Rambla, in the heart of the old city. Taxis will then take you to your hotel. The Aerobus service connects the airport with Plaza Catalunya every 15 minutes between 6:25 AM and 11 PM; pay the driver the fare of 375 ptas. RENFE provides a bus service to the Central Station during the night hours. A cab from the airport to your hotel, including airport and luggage surcharges, will cost about 2,500 ptas.

By Train The old Terminal (or França) Station on Avenida Marquès de l'Argentera reopened in 1992 after major renovations and now serves as the main terminal for trains to France and some express trains to points in Spain. The Central (Sants) station, which had been the main station, serves suburban destinations as well as most cities in Spain. Inquire at the tourist office to find out which station you need. Many trains also stop at the Passeig de Gràcia underground station at the junction of Aragó. This station is closer to the Plaça de Catalunya and Rambla area than Central (Sants), but though tickets and information are available here, luggage carts and taxi ranks are not. Check with tourist offices for current travel information and phone numbers. For RENFE information, call 93/490–0202 (24 hours).

By Bus Barcelona has no central bus station, but many buses operate from the old Estació Vilanova (or Norte) at the end of Avenida Vilanova. **Juliá,** Ronda Universitat 5, runs buses to Zaragoza and Montserrat; and **Alsina Graëlls,** Ronda Universitat 4, to Lérída and Andorra.

Getting Around

Modern Barcelona above the Plaça de Catalunya is mostly built on a grid system, though there's no helpful numbering system as in the United States. The Gothic Quarter from the Plaça de Catalunya to the port is a warren of narrow streets, however, and you'll need a good street map to get around. Most sightseeing can be done on foot—you won't have any other choice in the Gothic Quarter—but you'll need to use the metro or buses to link sightseeing areas.

By Metro The subway is the fastest way of getting around, as well as the easiest to use. You pay a flat fare of 100 ptas. no matter how far you travel, or purchase a **targeta multiviatge,** good for 10 rides (600 ptas.).

Plans of the system are available from main metro stations or from branches of the Caixa savings bank.

By Bus City buses run from about 5:30 or 6 AM to 10:30 PM, though some stop earlier. Again, there's a flat-fare system (100 ptas.). Plans of the routes followed are displayed at bus stops. A reduced-rate *targeta multiviatge*, good for 10 rides, can be purchased at the transport kiosk on Plaça de Catalunya (600 ptas.).

By Taxi Taxis are black and yellow, and when available for hire show a "Libre" sign in the daytime and a green light at night. The meter starts at 350 ptas., and there are small supplements for luggage (100 ptas. per case), Sundays and fiestas, rides from a station or the port (varies according to zone), and for going to or from the bullring or a soccer match. The supplement to the airport is 300 ptas. over the meter total. There are cab stands all over town; cabs may also be flagged down on the street. Make sure the driver puts on his meter.

By Cable Car Montjuïc Funicular is a cog railroad that runs from the junction of
and Funicular Avenida Parallel and Nou de la Rambla to the Miramar Amusement Park on Montjuïc. It runs only when the amusement park is open (11–8:15 in winter, noon–2:45 and 4:30–9:25 in summer). A cable car (*teleferic*) then runs from the amusement park up to Montjuïc Castle (noon–8 daily in summer; winter, weekends only, 11–7:30).

A **Transbordador Aeri Harbor Cable Car** runs from Miramar on Montjuïc across the harbor to the Torre de Jaume I on Barcelona *moll* (jetty), and on to the Torre de Sant Sebastià at the end of Passeig Don Joan de Borbó in Barceloneta. You can board at either stage. The cable car runs from 11:30 AM to 6 PM in winter, 11 AM to 10 PM in summer.

To reach Tibidabo summit, take either bus No. 58 or the Ferrocarrils de la Generalitat train from Plaça de Catalunya to Avenida Tibidabo, then the *tramvía blau* (blue tram) to Peu del Funicular, and the Tibidabo Funicular from there to the Tibidabo Fairground. The funicular runs every half hour from 7:15 AM to 9:45 PM.

By Boat **Golondrinas** harbor boats operate short harbor trips from the Portal de la Pau near the Columbus Monument between 10 AM and 1:30 PM weekends only in winter, daily in summer between 10 AM and 8 PM.

Important Addresses and Numbers

Tourist The city's three main tourist offices are at the **Central** (Sants) train
Information station (tel. 93/491–4431; open daily 8–8), the **Francia** train station (tel. 93/319–5758; open daily 8–8), and at the **airport** (tel. 93/478–4704; open Mon.–Sat. 9:30–8).

Information on the province and city can be found at the useful office at Gran Vía 658 (tel. 93/301–7443; open weekdays 9–7, Sat. 9–2).

During special events and conferences, a tourist office is open at the **Palau de Congressos** (Avda. Maria Cristina, tel. 93/423–3101, ext. 8356); a small office with some pamphlets and maps is at the **Ajuntament** (Plaça Sant Jaume, tel. 93/402–7000, ext. 433; open summer, daily 9–8; and cultural information is available at the **Palau de la Virreina** (Rambla 99, tel. 93/301–7775; open daily 9:30–9).

American Visitors' Bureau (Gran Vía 591 between Rambla de Catalunya and Balmes, 3rd floor, tel. 93/301–0150 or 301–0032).

Consulates U.S. (Pg. Reina Elisenda 23, tel. 93/280–2227), **Canadian** (Vía Augusta 125, tel. 93/209–0634), **U.K.** (Diagonal 477, tel. 93/419–9044).

Emergencies **Police** (National Police, tel. 091; Municipal Police, tel. 092; Main Police [Policía Nacional] Station, Vía Laietana 43, tel. 93/301–6666). **Ambulance** (tel. 93/329–7766). **Doctor: Hospital Clínico** (Casanova 143, tel. 93/323–1414); **Hospital Evangélico** (Alegre de Dalt 87, tel. 93/219–7100).

English-Language Bookstores Several bookstalls on the Rambla sell English guidebooks and novels, but the bookstore at the Palau de la Virreina (Rambla 99) has the best selection. Also try **Librería Laie** (Pau Claris 85), **Librería Francesa** (Passeig de Gràcia 91), or *Come In* (Provença 203).

Travel Agencies **American Express** (Rosello 257, on the corner of Passeig de Gràcia, tel. 93/217–0070), **Wagons-Lits Cook** (Passeig de Gràcia 8, tel. 93/317–5500), **Viajes Iberia** (Rambla 130, tel. 93/317–9320), and **Bestours** (Diputación 241, tel. 93/487–8580).

Guided Tours

Orientation Tours City sightseeing tours are run by **Juliá Tours** (Ronda Universitat 5, tel. 93/317–6454) and **Pullmantur** (Gran Vía de les Corts Catalanes 635, tel. 93/318–5195). Tours leave from the above terminals, though it may be possible to be picked up at your hotel. The content and price of tours are the same with both agencies. A morning sightseeing tour visits the Gothic Quarter and Montjuïc; an afternoon tour concentrates on Gaudí and the Picasso Museum. Visits to Barcelona's Olympic sites are scheduled from May through October.

Excursions These are run by **Juliá Tours** and **Pullmantur** and are booked as above. Principal trips are a half-day tour to **Montserrat** to visit the monastery and shrine of the famous Black Virgin; a full-day trip to the **Costa Brava** resorts, including a boat cruise to Lloret de Mar; and a full-day trip to **Andorra** for tax-free shopping.

Exploring Barcelona

Numbers in the margin correspond to points of interest on the Barcelona map.

Barcelona, capital of Catalonia and Spain's second-largest city, thrives on its business acumen and industrial muscle. Its hardworking citizens are almost militant in their use of their own language—with street names, museum exhibits, newspapers, radio programs, and movies all in Catalan. Their latest cause for rejoicing was the realization of their long-cherished goal to host the Olympic Games, held in Barcelona in summer 1992 after a massive building program. The Games' legacy to the city includes a vastly improved ring road and several other highways; four new beaches and an entire new neighborhood in what used to be the rundown industrial district of Poble Nou; an adjoining marina; and a new sports stadium and pools on the hill of Montjuïc. This thriving metropolis also has a rich history and an abundance of sights. Few places can rival the narrow alleys of its Gothic Quarter for medieval atmosphere, the elegance and distinction of its Moderniste Eixample area, or the fantasies of Gaudí's whimsical imagination.

It should take you two full days of sightseeing to complete the following tour. The first part covers the Gothic Quarter, the Picasso Museum, and the Rambla. The second part takes you to Passeig de Gràcia, the Sagrada Família, and Montjuïc.

Start on Plaça de la Seu, where on Sunday morning the citizens of Barcelona gather to dance the *Sardana*, a symbol of Catalan pride.

❶ Step inside the magnificent Gothic **catedral** (cathedral) built between 1298 and 1450, though the spire and Gothic facade were not added until 1892. Highlights are the beautifully carved **choir stalls,** Santa Eulàlia's tomb in the crypt, the battle-scarred crucifix from Don Juan's galley in the **Lepanto Chapel,** and the cloisters. *Tel. 93/ 315–1554. Admission free. Open daily 7:45–1:30 and 4–7:45.*

❷ Around the corner is the **Museu Frederic Marès** (Frederic Marès Museum), where you can browse for hours among the miscellany of sculptor-collector Frederic Marès. Displayed here is everything from polychrome crucifixes to hat pins, pipes, and walking sticks. *Plaça Sant Iu 5, tel. 93/310–5800. Admission: 350 ptas. Open Tues.–Sat. 10–5, Sun. 10–2.*

❸ The neighboring **Plaça del Rei** embodies the very essence of the Gothic Quarter. Following Columbus's first voyage to America, the Catholic Kings received him in the **Saló de Tinell,** a magnificent banqueting hall built in 1362. Other ancient buildings around the square are the **Lieutenant's Palace;** the 14th-century **Chapel of St. Agatha,** built right into the Roman city wall; and the **Padellás Palace,** which houses the City History Museum.

❹ Cross Vía Laietana, walk down Princesa, and turn right into Montcada, where you come to one of Barcelona's most popular attractions, the **Museu Picasso** (Picasso Museum). Two 15th-century palaces provide a striking setting for the collections donated in 1963 and 1970, first by Picasso's secretary, then by the artist himself. The collection ranges from early childhood sketches done in Málaga to exhibition posters done in Paris shortly before his death. Of particular interest are his Blue Period pictures and his variations on Velázquez's *Las Meninas. Tel. 93/319–6310. Admission: 500 ptas. Open Tues.–Sat. 10–8, Sun. 10–3.*

Time Out At the bottom of Montcada, on the left, is **La Pizza Nostra** (Arc de Sant Vicens 2, tel. 93/319–9058), an ideal spot for a cup of coffee, a slice of cheesecake, or a pizza and a glass of wine. Or you may prefer the colorful *Xampanyet* across the street.

❺ **Santa Maria del Mar** is one of the loveliest Gothic churches in Barcelona. It was built between 1329 and 1383 in fulfillment of a vow made a century earlier by Jaume I to build a church for the Virgin of the Sailors. Its simple beauty is enhanced by a stunning rose window and magnificent soaring columns. *Open daily 8–1 and 4–7:30.*

❻ Continue up Carrer Argentería, cross Vía Laietana, and walk along Jaume I till you come to **Plaça Sant Jaume,** an impressive square built in the 1840s in the heart of the Gothic Quarter. The two imposing buildings facing each other across the square are very much older. The 15th-century **Ajuntament,** or City Hall, has an impressive black and gold mural (1928) by Josep María Sert (who also painted the murals for New York's Waldorf Astoria) and the famous **Saló de Cent,** from which the Council of One Hundred ruled the city from 1372 to 1714. The **Palau de la Generalitat,** seat of the Catalan Regional Government, is a 15th-century palace open to the public on Sunday mornings only.

Time Out Among the best lunch spots in this area are **Agut d'Avignon** and **La Cuineta** (*see* Dining, *below*), and **Tinell** (Frenería 8, tel. 93/315–4604).

❼ Continue along the Carrer Ferrán, with its attractive 19th-century shops and numerous Moderniste touches, to the **Plaça Reial.** Here in

Casa Milà, **16**

Catedral, **1**

Fundació Miró, **19**

Gran Teatre
del Liceu, **11**

Mançana de la
Discòrdia, **15**

Monument a Colon, **8**

Museu Nacional d'Art
de Catalunya, **18**

Museu Frederic
Marès, **2**

Museu Marítim, **9**

Museu Picasso, **4**

Palau de la
Virreina, **13**

Palau Güell, **10**

Plaça de Catalunya, **14**

Plaça del Rei, **3**

Plaça Reial, **7**

Plaça Sant Jaume, **6**

Rambla, **12**

Santa Maria del Mar, **5**

Temple Expiatori de la
Sagrada Família, **17**

Barcelona

this splendid 19th-century square, arcaded houses overlook the wrought-iron **Fountain of the Three Graces,** and lampposts designed by a young Gaudí in 1879. Watch out for drug pushers here; the safest and most colorful time to come is on a Sunday morning when crowds gather at the stamp and coin stalls and listen to soap-box orators.

Time Out   Nearby are two atmospheric restaurants, **Los Caracoles** (Esudellers 14) and **Can Culleretes** (Quintana 15).

---

8 Head to the bottom of Rambla and take an elevator to the top of the **Monument a Colon** (Columbus Monument) for a breathtaking view over the city. Columbus faces out to sea, overlooking a replica of his own boat, the *Santa María.* (Nearby you can board the cable car that crosses the harbor to Montjuïc.) *Admission: 350 ptas. adults, 150 ptas. children. Open Tues.–Sat. 10–2 and 3:30–6:30, Sun. 10–7.*

9 Our next stop is the **Museu Marítim** (Maritime Museum) housed in the 13th-century Atarazanas Reales, the old Royal Dockyards. The museum is packed with ships, figureheads, nautical paraphernalia, and several early navigation charts, including a map by Amerigo Vespucci, and the 1439 chart of Gabriel de Valseca from Mallorca, the oldest chart in Europe. *Plaça Portal de la Pau 1, tel. 93/318-3245. Admission: 300 ptas., Wed. 150 ptas. Open Tues.–Sat. 10–2 and 4–7, Sun. 10–2.*

10 Turn back up the Rambla to Nou de la Rambla. At No. 3 is Gaudí's **Palau Güell.** Gaudí built this mansion between 1885 and 1890 for his patron, Count Eusebi de Güell, and it's the only one of his houses that is readily open to the public. *Admission: 250 ptas. Open Tues.–Sat. 11–2 and 5–8.*

11 Back to the Rambla and our next landmark, the **Gran Teatre del Liceu,** on the corner of Sant Pau. Built between 1845 and 1847, the Liceu claims to be the world's oldest opera house and is the only one in Spain. A fairly mundane facade conceals an exquisite interior with ornamental gilt and plush red velvet fittings. Anna Pavlova danced here in 1930, and Maria Callas sang here in 1959. *Tel. 93/318-9122. Admission: free. Guided tours (some in English) weekdays 11:30 and 12:15; tel. reservations advised.*

12 This next stretch of the **Rambla** is the most fascinating. The colorful paving stones on the Plaça de la Boquería were designed by Joan Miró. Glance up at the swirling Moderniste dragon and the Art Nouveau street lamps. Then take a look inside the bustling **Boqueria Food Market** and the **Casa Antigua Figueras,** an old grocery store on the corner of Petxina, with a splendid mosaic facade.

13 The **Palau de la Virreina** was built by a viceroy from Peru in 1778. It's recently been converted into a major exhibition center, and you should check to see what's showing while you're in town. *Corner of Carme and Rambla de les Flors 99, tel. 93/301-7775. Admission: 500 ptas., Wed. 250 ptas. Open Tues.–Sat. 10–2 and 4:30–9, Sun. 10–2, Mon. 4:30–9. Last entrance 30 mins. before closing.*

On the next block is the 18th-century **Church of Betlem** (Bethlehem) and, opposite, the handsome ocher-hued **Palau Moja,** built in 1702.

14 The final stretch of the Rambla brings us past the cacaphonous bird market and out onto the busy **Plaça de Catalunya,** the frantic business center and transport hub of the modern city. The first stage of the tour ends here. You may want to head for the Corte Inglés department store across the square or for any of the stores on the nearby **Porta de l'Angel.** Alternatively, you can relax on the terrace of the ancient **Café Zurich** on the corner of Pelai, or stop at the colorful beer hall, the **Cervecería,** opposite the Hotel Continental.

Above the Plaça de Catalunya you come into modern Barcelona and an elegant area known as the **Eixample,** which was laid out in the late 19th century as part of the city's expansion scheme. Much of the building here was done at the height of the **Moderniste** movement, a Spanish and mainly Catalan offshoot of Art Nouveau, whose leading exponents were the architects Gaudí, Domènech i Montaner, and Puig i Cadafalch. The principal thoroughfares of the Eixample are the Rambla de Catalunya and the Passeig de Gràcia, where some of the city's most elegant shops and cafés are found. Moderniste houses are one of Barcelona's special drawing cards, so walk up **Passeig de** ⓯ **Gràcia** until you come to the **Mançana de la Discòrdia,** or Block of Discord, between Consell de Cent and Aragó. Its name is a pun on the word *mançana,* which means both "block" and "apple." The houses here are quite fantastic: The floral **Casa Lleó Morera** at No. 35 is by Domènech i Montaner. The pseudo-Gothic **Casa Amatller** at No. 41 is by Puig i Cadafalch. At No. 43 is Gaudí's **Casa Batlló.** Farther along the street on the right, on the corner of Provença, is ⓰ Gaudí's **Casa Milà** (Passeig de Gràcia 92), more often known as **La Pedrera** (which, along with Casa Batlló, was dramatically spruced up in conjunction with the 1992 Olympics). Its remarkable curving stone facade with ornamental balconies actually ripples its way around the corner of the block.

Time Out   You can ponder the vagaries of Gaudí's work over a drink in **Amarcord,** a terrace café in the Pedrera building. If you're feeling a bit homesick, sip a cocktail or munch a deep-pan pizza in the **Chicago Pizza Pie Factory** at Provença 300. For a more sedate, old-world tearoom, head for the **Salón de Té Mauri** on the corner of Rambla de Catalunya and Provença.

Now take the metro at Diagonal directly to Barcelona's most eccen- ⓱ tric landmark, Gaudí's **Temple Expiatori de la Sagrada Família** (Expiatory Church of the Holy Family). Far from finished at his untimely death in 1926—Gaudí was run over by a tram and died in a pauper's hospital—this striking creation will cause consternation or wonder, shrieks of protest or cries of rapture. In 1936 during the Spanish Civil War the citizens of Barcelona loved their crazy temple enough to spare it from the flames that engulfed all their other churches except the cathedral. An elevator takes visitors to the top of one of the towers for a magnificent view of the city. Gaudí is buried in the crypt. *Tel. 93/255–0247. Admission: 500 ptas. Open Sept.– June., daily 9–7; July–Aug., daily 9–9.*

Way across town to the south, the hill of **Montjuïc** was named for the Jewish cemetery once located on its slopes. Montjuïc is home to a castle, an amusement park, several delightful gardens, a model Spanish village, an illuminated fountain, the recently rebuilt Mies van der Rohe Pavilion, and a cluster of museums—all of which could keep you busy for a day or more. This was the principal venue for the 1992 Olympics.

⓲   One of the leading attractions here is the **Museu Nacional d'Art de Catalunya** (National Museum of Catalan Art) in the Palau Nacional atop a long flight of steps. The collection of Romanesque and Gothic art treasures—medieval frescoes and altarpieces, mostly from small churches and chapels in the Pyrenees—is simply staggering. Just three rooms were open at press time, but the entire museum

was expected to open by 1994 after extensive renovations; ask at the
tourist office for current information.

⑲ Nearby is the **Fundació Miró** (Miró Foundation), a gift from the artist Joan Miró to his native city. One of Barcelona's most exciting contemporary galleries, it has several exhibition areas, many of them
devoted to Miró's works. Miró himself now rests in the cemetery on
the southern slopes of Montjuïc. *Admission: 500 ptas. Open Tues.-
Sat. 11–7 (9:30 on Thurs.), Sun. 10:30–2:30.*

Off the Beaten Track

If you're hooked on **Moderniste** architecture, you can follow a walk-
ing trail around the **Dreta de l'Eixample,** the area to the right of
Rambla de Catalunya. Ask at a tourist office for a Gaudí or
Modernisme trail brochure for the Eixample. Attend a concert at
Domènech i Montaner's fantastic **Palau de la Música.** Make a trip to
the **Parc Güell,** Gaudí's magical but uncompleted attempt at creating
a garden city. *Open May–Aug., daily 10–9; Sept.–Apr., daily 10–7.
Metro: Lesseps. Bus: 24.*

Explore the **Gràcia** area, above the Diagonal. It's a small, once independent village within a large city, a warren of narrow streets,
changing name at every corner, and filled with tiny shops where
you'll find everything from old-fashioned tin lanterns to feather
dusters.

Take a stroll around **Barceloneta,** the old fishermen's quarter built
in 1755 below the Estació de França and the Ciutadella Park. Along
its narrow streets are atmospheric taverns. There are no-frills fish
restaurants on the Passeig D. Joan de Borbó and beach restaurants
along the Passeig Marítim that are well known to locals and worth
experiencing. Hike out to the end of the breakwater, the *rampeolas*
extending 2½ miles southeast into the Mediterranean, for a panoramic view of the city and a few breaths of fresh air.

Hunt out the tiny **Shoe Museum** in Plaça Sant Felip Neri, in a hidden
corner of the Gothic Quarter, between the cathedral and Bishop's
Palace. The collection includes clowns' shoes and a pair worn by
Pablo Casals. *Admission: 250 ptas. Open Tues.–Sun. 11–2.*

Shopping

Gift Ideas There are no special handicrafts associated with Barcelona, but
you'll have no trouble finding typical Spanish goods anywhere in
town. If you're into fashion and jewelry, then you've come to the
right place, as Barcelona makes all the headlines on Spain's booming
fashion front. **Xavier Roca i Coll,** Sant Pere mes Baix 24, just off
Laietana, specializes in silver models of Barcelona's buildings.

Antiques Carrer de la Palla and Banys Nous in the Gothic Quarter are lined
with antiques shops where you'll find old maps, books, paintings,
and furniture. An **antiques market** is held every Thursday morning
in Plaça Nova in front of the cathedral. The **Centre d'Antiquaris,**
Passeig de Gràcia 57, has some 75 antiques stores. **Gothsland,**
Consell de Cent 331, specializes in Moderniste designs.

Boutiques The most fashionable boutiques are in the **Galerías** on Passeig de
Gràcia and Rambla de Catalunya. Others are on Gran Vía between
Balmes and Pau Claris; and on the Diagonal between Ganduxer and
Passeig de Gràcia. **Adolfo Domínguez,** Spain's top designer, is at
Passeig de Gràcia 89 and Valencia 245; **Loewe,** Spain's top leather

store, is at Passeig de Gràcia 35 and Diagonal 570; **Joaquín Berao,** a top jewelry designer, is at Rosselló 277.

Shopping Districts Elegant shopping districts are the Passeig de Gràcia, Rambla de Catalunya, and the Diagonal. For more affordable, more old-fashioned, and typically Spanish-style shops, explore the area between Ramblas and Vía Laietana, especially around C. Ferran. The area around Plaça del Pi from Boquería to Portaferrisa and Canuda is recommended for young fashion stores and imaginative gift shops.

Department Stores El Corte Inglés is on the Plaça de Catalunya 14 (tel. 93/302–1212) and at Diagonal 617 (tel. 93/419–2828) near the María Cristina metro stop. **Galerías Preciados** is at Porta de l'Angel 19 just off the Plaça de Catalunya; Diagonal 471 on the Plaça Francesc Macià; and Avenida Meridiana 352. All are open Monday through Saturday 10–8.

Food and Flea Markets The **Boquería** or **Sant Josep Market** on the Ramblas between Carme and Hospital is a superb, colorful food market, held every day except Sunday. **Els Encants,** Barcelona's fascinating Flea Market, is held every Monday, Wednesday, Friday, and Saturday at the end of Dos de Maig on the Plaça Glòries Catalanes. **Sant Antoni Market,** at the end of Ronda Sant Antoni, is an old-fashioned food and clothes market, best on Sundays when there's a secondhand **book market** with old postcards, press cuttings, lithographs, and prints. There's a **stamp and coin market** in the Plaça Reial on Sunday mornings, and an **artists' market** in the Placeta del Pi just off the Rambla and Boquería on Saturday mornings.

Bullfighting

Barcelona has two bullrings, the **Monumental** on Gran Vía and Carles I, and the smaller **Les Arenes** on the Plaça d'Espanya, now mainly used for rock concerts. Bullfights are held on Sundays between March and October; check the newspaper for details. The official ticket office, where there is no markup on tickets, is at Muntaner 24 (tel. 93/453–3821) near Gran Vía. There's a **Bullfighting Museum** at the Monumental ring, open March–October, daily 10–1 and 5:30–7.

Bars and Cafés

Cafés and Tearooms Zurich (Plaça de Catalunya 35), on the corner of Pelai, is one of the oldest and most traditional cafés, perfect for watching the world go by. **The Croissant Show** (Santa Anna 10 just off the Rambla), is a small coffee and pastry shop, ideal for a quick mid-morning or afternoon break. **Salón de Té Mauri,** on the corner of Rambla de Catalunya and Provença, and **Salón de Té Libre i Serra** (Ronda Sant Pere 3), are both traditional tearooms with a good selection of pastries.

Tapas Bars You'll find these all over town, but two of the most colorful are **Alt Heidelberg** (Ronda Universitat 5), with German beer on tap and German sausages, and the **Cervecería** at the top of Ramblas, opposite the Hostal Continental. **Cal Pep** on Plaça de les Olles (near Santa Maria del Mar) is another popular spot.

Cocktail Bars These places are both popular and plentiful everywhere, but the two best areas are the **Passeig del Born,** which is near the Picasso Museum and very fashionable with the affluent young, and the **Eixample,** near Passeig de Gràcia. A bar called **Dry Martini** (Aribau 162), has more than 80 different gins; **Ideal Cocktail Bar,** at Aribau 89, has some good malt whiskeys. **El Paraigua,** on Plaça Sant Miquel, in the

Gothic Quarter behind the city hall, serves cocktails in a stylish setting with classical music. **Boadas** (Tallers 1), on the corner of Ramblas, has been going strong for over 50 years.

Champagne Bars *Xampanyerías*, serving sparkling Catalan *cava*, are popular all over town and are something of a Barcelona specialty. Try **Brut** (Trompetas 3), in the Picasso Museum area; **La Cava del Palau** (Verdaguer i Callis 10), near the Palau de la Música; **La Folie** (Bailén 169), one of the best; or **La Xampanyería** (Provença 236), on the corner of Enric Granados.

Special Cafés **Els Quatre Gats** (Montsiò 5, off Porta de l'Angel) is a reconstruction of the original café that opened in 1897, and a real Barcelona institution. Literary discussions, jazz, and classical music recitals take place in this café where Picasso held his first show, Albéniz and Granados played their piano compositions, and Ramón Casas painted two of its original murals. **Café de l'Opera** (Ramblas 74), right opposite the Liceu, is a long-standing Barcelona tradition, ideal for a coffee or drink at any time of day.

Dining

For details and price-category definitions, *see* Dining in Staying in Spain, *above*.

Very Expensive ★ **Eldorado Petit.** Luis Cruañas moved to Barcelona from the Costa Brava in 1984 and opened this restaurant, which rapidly became known as the best in Barcelona and one of the top restaurants in Spain. The setting—a private villa with a delightful garden for summer dining—is simply beautiful, and so is the cuisine. *Dolors Monserdá 51, tel. 93/204–5153. Reservations required. AE, MC, V. Closed Sun. and 2 weeks in Aug.*

Expensive **Agut d'Avignon.** This venerable Barcelona institution takes a bit of finding; it's near the junction of Ferran and Avinyó in the Gothic Quarter. The ambience is rustic and it's a favorite with businesspeople and politicians from over the road in the Generalitat. The cuisine is traditional Catalan and game specialties are recommended in season. *Trinidad 3, tel. 93/302–6034. Reservations required. AE, DC, MC, V. Closed Holy Week.*

La Cuineta. This small intimate restaurant in a 17th-century house just off Plaça Sant Jaume specializes in Catalan nouvelle cuisine. The decor is smart but charming, the service professional; and it's popular with businesspeople at lunchtime. *Paradis 4, tel. 93/315–0812. Reservations accepted. AE, DC, MC, V. Closed Mon.*

Quo Vadis. Located just off the Ramblas, near the Boquería Market and Betlem Church, is an unimpressive facade camouflaging one of Barcelona's most respected restaurants. Its much-praised cuisine includes delicacies like *pot pourri de setas* (wild mushrooms), *lubina al hinojo* (sea bass in fennel), and *hígado de ganso con ciruelas* (goose liver with plums). *Carmen 7, tel. 93/317–7447. Reservations advised. AE, DC, MC, V. Closed Sun.*

★ **Tram-Tram.** With prominent chef Isidro Soler at the helm in the kitchen and Reyes Lizán doing double-duty as hostess and pastry chef, Tram-Tram is one of Barcelona's fastest rising culinary stars. It's well worth the minor inconvenience of a ride out to the northwestern suburb of Sarrià (metro stop: Sarrià). Order the taster's menu and let Isidro have his way with your palate. You won't regret it. *Major de Sarrià 121, tel. 93/2048518. Reservations advised. AE, MC, V. Closed Sun. and Dec. 24–Jan. 6. Expensive.*

Moderate **Can Culleretes.** This picturesque old restaurant began life as a pastry shop in 1786, and it is one of the most atmospheric and reasonable finds in Barcelona. Located on an alleyway between Ferran and Boquería, its three dining rooms are decorated with photos of visiting celebrities. It serves real Catalan cooking and is very much a family concern; don't be put off by the prostitutes outside! *Quintana 5, tel. 93/317–3022. Reservations accepted. AE, MC, V. Closed Sun. evening and Mon.*

Los Caracoles. Just below the Plaça Reial is Barcelona's most famous restaurant, which caters to tourists but has real atmosphere. Its walls are hung thick with photos of bullfighters and visiting celebrities; its specialties are mussels, paella and, of course, snails (*caracoles*). Don't miss it; it's fun. *Escudellers 14, tel. 93/309–3185. Reservations accepted. AE, DC, MC, V.*

★ **Set Portes.** With plenty of old-world charm, this delightful restaurant near the waterfront has been going strong since 1836. The cooking is Catalan, the portions enormous, and specialties are *paella de pescado* and *zarzuela sete portes* (seafood casserole). *Passeig Isabel II 14, tel. 93/319–3033. Reservations advised on weekends. AE, DC, MC, V. Open 1 PM–1 AM.*

★ **Sopeta Una.** Dining in this delightful small restaurant with old-fashioned decor and intimate atmosphere is more like eating in a private home. The menu is in Catalan, all the dishes are Catalan, and the atmosphere is very genteel and middle class. For dessert, try the traditional Catalan *música*—a plate of raisins, almonds, and dried fruit served with a glass of muscatel. It's near the Palau de la Música; don't be put off by the narrow street. *Verdaguer i Callis 6, tel. 93/319–6131. Reservations accepted. V. Closed Sun., and Mon. AM.*

Inexpensive ★ **Agut.** Simple, hearty Catalan fare awaits you in this unpretentious restaurant in the lower reaches of the Gothic Quarter. Founded in 1924, its popularity has never waned. There's plenty of wine to wash down the traditional home cooking, but you won't find frills like coffee or liqueurs. *Gignàs 16, tel. 93/319–3315. Reservations not necessary. No credit cards. Closed Sun. evening, Mon., and July.*

★ **Egipte.** This small, friendly restaurant hidden away in a very convenient location behind the Boquería Market—though it's far better known to locals than to visitors—is a real find. Its traditional Catalan home cooking, huge desserts, and swift personable service all contribute to its popularity and good value. *Jerusalem 12, tel. 93/301–6208. No reservations. No credit cards.*

Lodging

For a city of its size and importance, Barcelona has long been underendowed with hotels. The 1992 Olympic Games, however, brought with them some new hotels—generally of the featureless modern variety—and also spurred the renovation and cleaning up of most of the older ones. Prices rose dramatically for the Games, but have fallen back to more reasonable levels now. Hotels around the Rambla and in the Gothic Quarter have plenty of old-world charm, but are less strong on creature comforts; those in the Eixample are mostly '50s or '60s buildings, often recently renovated; and the newest hotels are found out along the Diagonal or beyond, in the residential districts of Sarriá and Pedralbes. There are hotel reservation desks at the airport and Sants Central Station.

For details and price-category definitions, *see* Lodging in Staying in Spain, *above.*

Very Expensive

Avenida Palace. Right in the center of town, between the Rambla de Catalunya and Passeig de Gràcia, this hotel dates from 1952 but conveys a feeling of elegance and Old World style. Some rooms are rather plain, but most have been recently renovated and there's a superbly ornate lobby. *Gran Vía 605, tel. 93/301–9600, fax 93/318–1234. 211 rooms. AE, DC, MC, V.*

★ **Condes de Barcelona.** As this is one of Barcelona's most popular hotels, rooms need to be booked well in advance. The decor is stunning, with marble floors and columns, an impressive staircase, and an outstanding bar area, but no restaurant. Guest rooms are on the small side. *Passeig de Gràcia 75, tel. 93/487–3737; for reservations, 93/215–7931, fax 93/216–0835. 110 rooms. AE, DC, MC, V.*

Princesa Sofia. The Barcelona hotel most convenient to the airport, the Princesa Sofia is somewhat far from the hue and cry of downtown. For business, comfort, and convenience, though, it's one of the city's best guarantees. *Plaça Pius XII 4, tel. 93/330–7111, fax 93/411–2106. 505 rooms. Facilities: 3 restaurants, shops, fitness center, sauna, 2 pools. AE, DC, MC, V.*

★ **Ritz.** Founded in 1919 by Caesar Ritz, this is still the grand old lady of Barcelona hotels. Extensive refurbishment has now restored it to its former splendor. The entrance lobby is awe-inspiring, the rooms spacious, and the service impeccable. *Gran Vía 668, tel. 93/318–5200, fax 93/318–0148. 158 rooms. AE, DC, MC, V.*

Expensive

★ **Colón.** This cozy, older hotel has a unique charm and intimacy reminiscent of an English country hotel, though some refurbishing would be very welcome. It's in an ideal location right in the heart of the Gothic Quarter, and the rooms on the front overlook the cathedral and square. It was a great favorite of Joan Miró. *Avda. Catedral 7, tel. 93/301–1404, fax 93/317–2915. 148 rooms. AE, DC, MC, V.*

Regente. This smallish hotel on the corner of Valencia has a rooftop pool, plenty of style and charm, and a wonderful Modernista lobby. *Rambla de Catalunya 76, tel. 93/215–2570, fax 93/487–3227. 78 rooms. AE, DC, MC, V.*

Moderate

Gran Vía. Architectural features are the special charm of this 19th-century mansion, close to the main tourist office. The original chapel has been preserved, and you can have breakfast in a hall of mirrors, climb its Moderniste staircase, and call from elaborate Belle Epoque phone booths. *Gran Vía 642, tel. 93/318–1900, fax 93/318–9997. 53 rooms. AE, DC, MC, V.*

★ **Oriente.** Barcelona's oldest hotel opened in 1843. Its public rooms are a delight—the ballroom and dining rooms have lost none of their 19th-century magnificence—though the bedrooms have undergone rather featureless renovation. It's located just below the Liceu and its terrace café is the perfect place for a drink. *Rambla 45, tel. 93/302–2558. 142 rooms. AE, DC, MC, V.*

Rialto. In the heart of the Gothic Quarter, just two paces down from the Plaça Sant Jaume, this old 19th-century house has been renovated to high standards of comfort while preserving its charm. Here you're surrounded by sights, shops, and some of Barcelona's best restaurants. *Ferran 40, tel. 93/318–5212, fax 93/315–3819. 132 rooms. AE, DC, MC, V.*

Inexpensive

Continental. Something of a legend among cost-conscious travelers, this comfortable hostel with canopied balconies stands at the top of Ramblas, just below Plaça Catalunya. The rooms are homey and comfortable, the staff is friendly, and the location's ideal. Buffet breakfasts are a plus. *Rambla 136, tel. 93/301–2570, fax 93/302–7360. 32 rooms. V.*

España. The Domènech i Montaner–designed Modernista interior renders this hotel an amazing bargain for those who put architectural style before comfort. The high-ceilinged downstairs features a breakfast room decorated with mermaids, elaborate woodwork, and an Art Nouveau chimney in the cafeteria. The rooms themselves, however, are very basic, and the neighborhood can be a bit daunting for women walking alone. *Sant Pau 9–11, tel. 93/318–1758. 84 rooms. AE, DC, MC, V.*

The Arts

To find out what's on in town, look in the daily papers or in the weekly *Guía del Ocio*, available from newsstands all over town. *Actes a la Ciutat* is a weekly list of cultural events published by the Ajuntament and available from its information office on Plaça Sant Jaume.

Concerts Catalans are great music lovers, and their main concert hall is the **Palau de la Música** (Sant Francesc de Paula 2, tel. 93/268–1000). The ticket office is open weekdays 11–1 and 5–8 and Saturday 5–8 only. Its Sunday morning concerts are a popular tradition. Tickets are reasonable and can usually be purchased just before the concert.

Opera The **Gran Teatre del Liceu** is one of the world's finest opera houses, considered by some second only to Milan's La Scala. The box office for advance bookings is on Sant Pau 1 (tel. 93/318–9277), open weekdays 8–3, Saturday 9–1. Tickets for same-day performances are on sale in the Ramblas entrance 11–1:30 and 4 PM onward. Tickets are inexpensive by New York or London standards.

Dance **L'Espai de Dansa i Música de la Generalitat de Catalunya,** usually listed simply as *L'Espai* (the Space), (Travessera de Gràcia 63, tel. 93/201–2906), is now Barcelona's prime venue for ballet and contemporary dance. **El Mercat de les Flors** (Lleida 59, tel. 93/426–1875), not far from Plaça d'Espanya, continues to offer its traditionally rich program of modern dance and theater.

Theater Most theater performances are in Catalan, but Barcelona is also known for its experimental theater and for its mime troupes such as **ELS Joglars** and **La Claca** (language is not always an impediment). The best-known modern theaters are the **Teatre Lliure** (Montseny 47, in Gràcia, tel. 93/218–9251), **Mercat de les Flors** (*see* Dance, *above*), **Teatre Romea** (Hospital 51, tel. 93/317–7189), **Teatre Tívoli** (Casp 10, tel. 93/412–2063), and **Teatre Poliorama** (Rambla Estudios 115, tel. 93/317–7599).

Film Many theaters show foreign movies in their original languages. The **Filmoteca** (av. Sarrià 33, tel. 93/430–5007) often includes English films in its schedule.

Nightlife

Cabaret **Belle Epoque** (Muntaner 246, tel. 93/209–7385) is a beautifully decorated music hall with the most sophisticated shows. **El Mediévolo** (Gran Vía 459, tel. 93/243–1566) has medieval feasts and entertainment; it's all geared to tourists but fun.

Jazz Clubs Try **Abraxas Jazz Auditorium** (Gelabert 26); **La Cova del Drac** (Tuset 30, just off the Diagonal); and **Zeleste** (Almogávares 122).

Rock Check out **Zeleste** (Almogávares 122). Major concerts are usually held in sports stadiums; keep an eye out for posters.

Flamenco The best place is **El Patio Andaluz** (Aribau 242, tel. 93/209–3378). **El Cordobés** (Ramblas 35, tel. 93/317–6853) is aimed at tour groups but can be fun.

Casino The **Gran Casino de Barcelona** (tel. 93/893–3866), 42 kilometers (26 miles) south in Sant Pere de Ribes, near Sitges, also has a dance hall and some excellent international shows in a 19th-century atmosphere. Jacket and tie essential.

Moorish Spain

Stretching from the dark mountains of the Sierra Morena in the north, west to the plains of the Guadalquivir valley, and south to the mighty snowcapped Sierra Nevada, Andalucía rings with echoes of the Moors. In the kingdom they called Al-Andalus, these Muslim invaders from North Africa dwelt for almost 800 years, from their first conquest of Spanish soil (Gibraltar) in 711 to their expulsion from Granada in 1492. And to this day the cities and landscapes of Andalucía are rich in their legacy. The great Mosque of Córdoba, the magical Alhambra Palace in Granada, and the Giralda tower, landmark of Seville, were the inspired creations of Moorish architects and craftsmen working at the behest of Al-Andalus's Arab emirs. The brilliant white villages with narrow streets and sturdy-walled houses clustered round cool inner patios, the whitewashed facades with heavily grilled windows, and the deep wailing song of Andalucía's flamenco, so reminiscent of the muezzin's call to prayer, all stem from centuries of Moorish occupation.

Getting There from Madrid

Seville, Córdoba, and Granada all lie on direct train routes from Madrid. Service is frequent from both Chamartín and Atocha stations in Madrid, and includes overnight trains (to Seville and Granada), slower day trains, and express talgos. In addition, the high-speed AVE train connecting Seville and Atocha Station began service in 1992 on entirely new track; it's very expensive but has cut traveling time on that route from 5½–6 hours to about 2½ hours. Most bus service from Madrid to Moorish Spain operates out of the Estación del Sur (*see* Arriving and Departing in Madrid, *above*). If you drive, follow the N-IV, which takes you through the scorched orange plains of La Mancha to Córdoba, then along the Guadalquivir River to Seville. The N323 road, which splits from the N-IV at Bailén, takes you past lovely olive groves and rolling hills to Granada.

Getting Around

Seville and Córdoba are linked by direct train service. Buses are a better choice between Seville and Granada, and between Córdoba and Granada, as trains are relatively slow and infrequent and often involve a time-consuming change. **Seville**'s older bus station (tel. 95/441–7111) is between José María Osborne and Manuel Vazquez Sagastizabal; a new bus station is closer to downtown (Arjona, next to the Cachorro Bridge, tel. 95/490–8040). Check with the tourist office to determine which one you'll need. The city also has a spanking new train station, Santa Justa (at José Laquillo and Avda. Kansas City, tel. 95/454–0202), built in conjunction with the 1992 International Exposition. In **Granada**, the main bus station is Alsina Gräells (Camino de Ronda 97, tel. 958/251358). The train station is at the end of Avenida Andaluces; the RENFE office is located at Reyes Católicos 63, tel. 958/223119. **Córdoba** has no central bus depot, so

Moorish Spain

check at the tourist office for the appropriate company. The train station is on the Glorieta Conde de Guadalorce (RENFE office: Ronda de los Tejares 10, tel. 957/475884).

Driving in Moorish Spain, long an anathema to travelers, has been largely transformed by improvements made for the 1992 festivities. If you like winding roads and gorgeous landscapes, consider driving.

Guided Tours

Guided tours of Seville, Córdoba, Granada, and Ronda are run by **Juliá Tours, Pullmantur,** and **Trapsatur,** both from Madrid and resorts of the Costa del Sol; check with travel agents. Local excursions may be available from Seville to the sherry bodegas and equestrian museum of Jerez de la Frontera. From Granada, there's a weekly day trip to the villages of the Alpujarras; check details with tourist offices. In Córdoba, **Viajes Vincit** (Alonso de Burgos 1, tel. 957/472316) runs daily sightseeing tours of the city that include a visit to the Mosque.

Tourist Information

Córdoba (Plaza de Judá Leví, tel. 957/472000, and Palacio de Congresos y Exposiciones, Torrijos 10, tel. 957/471235).
Granada (Plaza Mariana Pineda 10, tel. 958/226688, and the less useful office at Corral del Carbón, Calle Mariana Pineda, tel. 958/225990).
Seville (Av. Constitución 21B, tel. 95/422–1404, not far from the ca-

thedral and Archives of the Indies, and the smaller office at Costurero de la Reina, Paseo de las Delícias 9, tel. 95/423–4465).

Exploring Moorish Spain

Our tour begins in Seville and continues to Carmona, Ecija, Córdoba, Baena, Granada, Sierra Nevada, Lanjarón, Orgiva, and Alpujarras.

The downside to a visit here, especially to Seville, is that petty crime, much of it directed against tourists, is rife. Purse snatching and thefts from cars, frequently when drivers are in them, are depressingly familiar. *Always* keep your car doors *and* trunk locked. *Never* leave any valuables in your car. Leave your passport, traveler's checks, and credit cards in your hotel's safe, *never* in your room. Don't carry expensive cameras or wear jewelry. Take only the minimum amount of cash with you. There comes a point, however—if your windshield is smashed or your bag is snatched, for example— when all the precautions in the world will prove inadequate. If you're unlucky, it's an equally depressing fact that the police, again especially in Seville, have adopted a distinctly casual attitude to such thefts, and often combine indifference to beleaguered tourists with rudeness in about equal measure. Frankly, there's little you can do except remain calm.

Numbers in the margin correspond to points of interest on the Seville map.

Seville Lying on the banks of the Guadalquivir, **Seville**—Spain's fourth-largest city and capital of Andalucía—is one of the most beautiful and romantic cities in Europe. Here in this city of the sensuous Carmen and the amorous Don Juan, famed for the spectacle of its Holy Week processions and April Fair, you'll come close to the spiritual heart of Moorish Andalucía. You'll also find some dramatic improvements, courtesy of the International Exposition hosted by the city in 1992. They include the development of La Cartuja Island, where the fairgrounds were built; seven new bridges and a refurbished riverfront esplanade; the new Maestranza opera house built on the river; improved roads in the city and throughout the region; and new railroad ❶ and bus stations. Begin your visit in the **catedral** (cathedral), begun in 1402, a century and a half after St. Ferdinand delivered Seville from the Moors. This great Gothic edifice, which took just over a century to build, is traditionally described in superlatives. It's the biggest and highest cathedral in Spain, the largest Gothic building in the world, and the world's third-largest church after St. Peter's in Rome and St. Paul's in London. And it boasts the world's largest carved wooden altarpiece. Despite such impressive statistics, the inside can be dark and gloomy with too many overly ornate Baroque trappings. But seek out the beautiful Virgins by Murillo and Zurbarán, and reflect on the history enshrined in these walls. In a silver urn before the high altar rest the precious relics of Seville's liberator, St. Ferdinand, said to have died from excessive fasting, and down in the crypt are the tombs of his descendants Pedro the Cruel, founder of the Alcázar, and his mistress María de Padilla. But above all, you'll want to pay your respects to Christopher Columbus, whose mortal vestiges are enshrined in a flamboyant mausoleum in the south aisle. Borne aloft by statues representing the four medieval kingdoms of Spain, it's to be hoped the great voyager has found peace at last after the transatlantic quarrels that carried his body from Valladolid to Santo Domingo and from Havana to Seville. *Ad-*

Seville

0 |_____| 440 yards
0 |_____| 400 meters

Major Attractions
Alcázar, **3**
Barrio de
Santa Cruz, **5**
Calle Betis, **9**
Catedral, **1**
Giralda, **2**
Maestranza
Bullring, **11**

Parque de
María Luisa, **6**
Patio de las
Banderas, **4**
Plaza de America, **8**
Plaza de España, **7**
Torre de Oro, **10**

Other Attractions
Museo Arte
Comtemporaneo, **12**
San Telmo Palace, **13**
Tobacco Factory
(University), **14**

*mission to cathedral and Giralda (see below): 500 ptas. Open Mon.-
Sat. 10–5, Sun. 10–4. Cathedral also open for Mass.*

Every day the bell that summons the faithful to prayer rings out
from a Moorish minaret, relic of the Arab mosque whose admirable
tower of Abu Yakoub the Sevillians could not bring themselves to de-
stroy. Topped in 1565–68 by a bell tower and weather vane and
❷ called the **Giralda,** this splendid example of Moorish art is one of the
marvels of Seville. In place of steps, a gently sloping ramp climbs to
the viewing platform 71 meters (230 feet) above Seville's rooftops.
St. Ferdinand is said to have ridden his horse to the top to admire the
view of the city he had conquered. Seven centuries later your view of
the Golden Tower and shimmering Guadalquivir will be equally
breathtaking. Try, too, to see the Giralda at night when the floodlights cast a new magic on this gem of Islamic art. *Open same hours
as Cathedral and visited on same ticket.*

❸ The high fortified walls of the **Alcázar** belie the exquisite delicacy of
the palace's interior. It was built by Pedro the Cruel—so known because he murdered his stepmother and four of his half-brothers—
who lived here with his mistress María de Padilla from 1350 to 1369.
Don't mistake this for a genuine Moorish palace as it was built more
than 100 years after the reconquest of Seville; rather, its style is Mudéjar—built by Moorish craftsmen working under orders of a Christian king. The Catholic Kings (Ferdinand and Isabella), whose only
son, Prince Juan, was born in the Alcázar in 1478, added a wing to
serve as administration center for their New World empire, and
Charles V enlarged it further for his marriage celebrations in 1526.
Pedro's Mudéjar palace centers around the beautiful **Patio de las
Doncellas** (Court of the Damsels) whose name pays tribute to the annual gift of 100 virgins to the Moorish sultans whose palace once
stood on the site. Resplendent with the most delicate of lacelike
stucco and gleaming azulejo decorations, it is immediately reminiscent of Granada's Alhambra, and is in fact the work of Granada
craftsmen. Opening off this are the apartments of María de Padilla,
whose hold over her lover, and seemingly her courtiers, too, was so
great that they apparently vied with one another to drink her bath
water!

The **Alcázar Gardens** are fragrant with jasmine and myrtle, an orange tree said to have been planted by Pedro the Cruel, and a lily
pond well stocked with fat, contented goldfish. The end of your visit
❹ brings you to the **Patio de las Banderas** for an unrivaled view of the
Giralda. *Palace and gardens admission: 600 ptas. Open Tues.–Sat.
10:30–5, Sun. 10–1.*

❺ The **Barrio de Santa Cruz,** with its twisting alleyways, cobbled
squares, and whitewashed houses, is a perfect setting for an operetta. Once the home of Seville's Jews, it was much favored by 17th-
century noblemen and today boasts some of the most expensive
properties in Seville. All the romantic images you've ever had of
Spain will come to life here: Every house gleams white or deep ocher
yellow; wrought-iron grilles adorn the windows, and every balcony
and patio is bedecked with geraniums and petunias. You'll find the
most beautiful patio at Callejón del Agua 12. Ancient bars nestle
side by side with antiques shops. Don't miss the famous **Casa Román**
bar in Plaza de los Venerables Sacerdotes with its ceilings hung
thick with some of the best hams in Seville, or the **Hostería del Laurel** next door, where in summer you can dine in one of the loveliest
squares in the city. Souvenir and excellent ceramic shops surround
the **Plaza Doña Elvira,** where the young of Seville gather to play guitars around the fountain and azulejo benches. And in the **Plaza**

Alianza, with its well-stocked antiques shops and **John Fulton gallery** (Fulton is the only American ever to qualify as a full-fledged bullfighter), stop a moment and admire the simplicity of the crucifix on the wall, framed in a profusion of bougainvillea.

⑥ Take a cab, or better still, hire a horse carriage from the Plaza Virgen de los Reyes, below the Giralda, and visit **Parque de María Luisa** (María Luisa Park), whose gardens are a delightful blend of formal design and wild vegetation, shady walkways and sequestered nooks. In the 1920s the park was redesigned to form the site of the 1929 Hispanic-American exhibition, and the impressive villas you see here today are the fair's remaining pavilions. Visit the mon-
⑦ umental **Plaza de España,** whose grandiose pavilion of Spain was the centerpiece of the exhibition. At the opposite end of the park you can feed the hundreds of white doves that gather round the fountains of
⑧ the lovely **Plaza de America;** it's a magical spot to while away the sleepy hours of the siesta.

⑨ An early evening stroll along the **Calle Betis** on the far side of the Guadalquivir is a delight few foreigners know about. Between the San Telmo and Isabel II bridges, the vista of the sparkling water,
⑩ the palm-lined banks, and the silhouette of the **Torre de Oro** (Tower of Gold) (built 1220; admission: 100 ptas., open Tues.–Fri. 10–2,
⑪ weekends 10–1) and the **Maestranza Bullring** (built 1760–63), one of Spain's oldest, is simply stunning. *Admission for plaza tours and bullfighting museum: 250 ptas. Open Mon.–Sat. 10–1:30).*

Thirty kilometers (19 miles) from Seville, the N-IV brings you to **Carmona.** This unspoiled Andalusian town of Roman and Moorish origin is worth a visit, either to stay at the parador or to enjoy its wealth of Mudéjar and Renaissance churches, and its streets of whitewashed houses of clear Moorish influence. Most worthwhile is the **Church of San Pedro** begun in 1466, whose extraordinary interior is an unbroken mass of sculptures and gilded surfaces, and whose tower, erected in 1704, is an unabashed imitation of Seville's famous Giralda. Carmona's most moving monument is its splendid **Roman Necropolis,** where in huge underground chambers some 900 family tombs dating from the 2nd to the 4th century AD have been chiseled out of the rock. *Admission: 250 ptas. Open Tues.–Fri. 10–2 and 4–6, weekends 10–2.*

A little farther along the N-IV brings you to **Ecija,** a dazzling white cluster reputed to be the hottest town in Spain–its nickname is *sarten de Andalucía,* "Andalusia's frying pan." With its history going back to Greek and Roman times, you'll find plenty of Renaissance and Baroque palaces here and a bewildering array of churches whose towers and turrets rise before you as you approach along the main road.

Numbers in the margin correspond to points of interest on the Córdoba map.

Córdoba   Ancient **Córdoba,** city of the caliphs, is one of Spain's oldest cities and the greatest embodiment of Moorish heritage in all Andalusia. From the 8th to the 11th centuries, the Moorish emirs and Caliphs of the West held court here and it became one of the Western world's greatest centers of art, culture, and learning. Moors, Christians, and Jews lived together in harmony within its walls. Two of Córdoba's most famous native sons were Averröes, the great Arab scientist, and Maimónides, the notable Jewish doctor and philoso-
❶ pher. But above all it is for its famous **Mezquita** (mosque), one of the finest built by the Moors, that Córdoba is known first and foremost. Its founder was Abd ar-Rahman I (756–788), and it was completed

Córdoba

Major Attractions
Judería, **3**
Maimónides Statue, **6**
Mezquita, **1**
Museo Taurino, **5**
Plaza Judá Levi, **4**

Synagogue, **7**
Virgen de los
Faroles, **2**

Other Attractions
Alcázar, **8**
Cristo de los
Faroles, **11**
Museo Arqueológico, **9**
Museo de
Bellas Artes, **10**

by Al Mansur (976–1002) around the year 987. As you step inside you'll come face to face with a forest of gleaming pillars of precious marble, jasper, and onyx, rising to a roof of red-and-white horseshoe arches, one of the most characteristic traits of Moorish architecture. Not even the heavy Baroque cathedral that Charles V so mistakenly built in its midst—and later regretted—can detract from the overpowering impact and mystery wrought by the art of these Moorish craftsmen. It was indeed a fitting setting for the original copy of the Koran and a bone from the arm of the Prophet Mohammed, holy relics once housed in the Mezquita that were responsible for bringing thousands of pilgrims to its doors in the great years before St. Ferdinand reconquered Córdoba for the Christians in 1236. The mosque opens onto the **Patio de los Naranjos** (Orange Tree Courtyard), perfumed in springtime by orange blossoms, and the bell tower, which served as the mosque's minaret. It's well worth climbing the uneven steps to the top for the view of the Guadalquivir river and the tiled rooftops of the old city. *Tel. 957–470512. Admission: 600 ptas. Open daily May–Sept., 10:30–1:30 and 4–7; Oct.–Apr., 10:30–1:30 and 3:30–5:30.*

Near the mosque, the streets of Torrijos, Cardenal Herrero, and Deanes are lined with tempting souvenir shops specializing in local handicrafts, especially the filigree silver and embossed leather for which Córdoba is famous. In her niche on Cardenal Herrero, the ❷ **Virgen de los Faroles** (Virgin of the Lanterns) stands demurely behind a lantern-hung grille, rather like a lovely lady awaiting a serenade. In a narrow alleyway off to your left is the **Callejón de las Flores**, its houses decked with hanging flower baskets. Now make ❸ your way westward to the old **Judería**, or Jewish quarter. On the ❹ **Plaza Judá Leví** you'll find the municipal tourist office. A few paces down, on Calle Manríquez, is another outstanding patio open to visitors.

❺ Overlooking the Plaza Maimónides (or Bulas) is the **Museo Taurino** (Museum of Bullfighting), housed in two delightful old mansions. You'll see a well-displayed collection of memorabilia, paintings, and posters by early 20th-century Córdoban artists, and rooms dedicated to great Córdoban *toreros*—even the hide of the bull that killed the legendary Manolete in 1947. *Tel. 957/472000, ext. 211. Admission: 200 ptas. Open Tues.–Sat. 9:30–1:30 and 5–8 (4–7 in winter).*

❻ A moving statue of the great Jewish philosopher **Maimónides** stands in the Plaza Tiberiades. A few paces along Judíos, you come to the ❼ only **synagogue** in Andalucía to have survived the expulsion of the Jews in 1492. It's one of only three remaining synagogues in Spain—the other two you saw in Toledo—built before 1492 and it boasts some fine Hebrew and Mudéjar stucco tracery and a women's gallery. *Tel. 957/298133. Admission: 75 ptas. Open Tues.–Sat. 10–2 and 3:30–5:30, Sun. 10–1:30.*

Across the way is the courtyard of El Zoco, a former Arab souk, with some pleasant shops and stalls, and sometimes a bar open in summer.

As you leave Córdoba and head for Granada, the N432 climbs from the Guadalquivir valley up into the mountains of central Andalucía. It is 63 kilometers (39 miles) to **Baena**, a picturesque Andalucían town of white houses clustered on the hillside, where you may want to stop for a drink and wander the narrow streets and squares as yet largely untouched by tourism. Mountain views line the route as the road twists toward its highest point, the 931-meter (3,000-foot)

Puerto del Castillo, before dropping down onto the *vega* (fertile plain) of Granada. At Pinos Puente, you can take a short detour to the village of **Fuente Vaqueros** where Federico García Lorca was born on June 5, 1898. In 1986, to commemorate the 50th anniversary of his assassination in Granada at the outbreak of the Civil War, his birthplace was restored as a museum. The nearby village of Valderrubio inspired his *Libro de Poemas* and *La Casa de Bernarda Alba. Museo de Lorca, open Jan., Feb., and July–Sept., Tues.–Sun. 10–1 and 6–8; Apr.–June, Tues.–Sun. 10–1 and 5–7; Oct.–Mar., Tues.–Sun. 10–1 and 4–6. Tours every hour on the hour.*

Numbers in the margin correspond to points of interest on the Granada map.

Granada   The city of **Granada** rises majestically on three hills dwarfed by the mighty snowcapped peaks of the Sierra Nevada, which boasts the highest roads in Europe. Atop one of these hills the pink-gold palace of the Alhambra, at once splendidly imposing yet infinitely delicate, gazes out across the rooftops and gypsy caves of the Sacromonte to the fertile *vega* rich in orchards, tobacco fields, and poplar groves. Granada, the last stronghold of the Moors and the most treasured of all their cities, fell finally to the Catholic Kings in January 1492. For Ferdinand and Isabella their conquest of Granada was the fulfillment of a long-cherished dream to rid Spain of the Infidel, and here ❶ they built the flamboyant **Capilla Real** (Royal Chapel) where they have lain side by side since 1521, later joined by their daughter Juana la Loca. Begin your tour in the nearby Plaza de Bib-Rambla, a pleasant square with flower stalls and outdoor cafés in summer, then ❷ pay a quick visit to the huge Renaissance **catedral** (cathedral) commissioned in 1521 by Charles V who thought the Royal Chapel "too small for so much glory" and determined to house his illustrious grandparents somewhere more worthy. But his ambitions came to little, for Granada Cathedral is a grandiose and gloomy monument, not completed until 1714, and is far surpassed in beauty and historic value by the neighboring Royal Chapel, which, despite the great emperor's plans, still houses the tombs of his grandparents and less fortunate mother. *Admission to Royal Chapel and cathedral: 200 ptas. each. Open Mar.–Sept., Mon.–Sat. 10:30–1 and 4–7; Oct.–Feb., Mon.–Sat. 11–1 and 3:30–6, Sun. 3:30–6.*

❸ The adjacent streets of the **Alcaicería,** the old Arab silk exchange, will prove a haven for souvenir hunters. Here you can find any number of local handicrafts inspired by Granada's Moorish heritage: brass and copperware, green and blue Fajalauza pottery, wooden boxes, tables and chess sets inlaid with mother of pearl, and woven goods from the villages of the Alpujarras in which the colors green, red, and black predominate. Across the Gran Vía de Colón, Granada's main shopping street, the narrow streets begin to wind ❹ up the slopes of the **Albaicín,** the old Moorish quarter, which is now a fascinating mixture of dilapidated white houses and beautiful *cármenes*, luxurious villas with fragrant gardens. Few visitors find ❺ their way to the balcony of **San Nicolás Church,** which affords an unforgettable view of the Alhambra, particularly when it is floodlit at night.

❻ The Cuesta de Gomérez climbs steeply to the **Alhambra precincts**, where the Duke of Wellington planted shady elms and Washington Irving tarried among the gypsies from whom he learned the Moorish legends so evocatively recounted in his *Tales of the Alhambra.* ❼ Above the **Puerta de la Justicia** the hand of Fatima, her fingers evoking the five laws of the Koran, beckons you inside the mystical Alhambra, the most imposing and infinitely beautiful of all Andalucía's

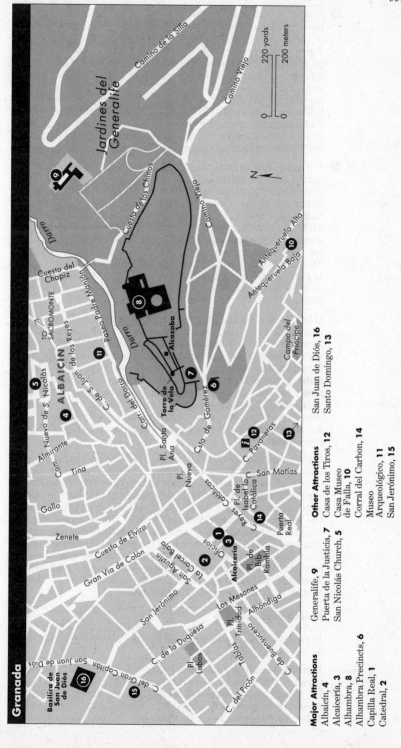

Granada

Major Attractions

Albaicín, **4**
Alcaicería, **3**
Alhambra, **8**
Alhambra Precincts, **6**
Capilla Real, **1**
Catedral, **2**

Generalife, **9**
Puerta de la Justicia, **7**
San Nicolás Church, **5**

Other Attractions

Casa de los Tiros, **12**
Casa Museo
de Falla, **10**
Corral del Carbon, **14**
Museo
Arqueológico, **11**
San Jerónimo, **15**

San Juan de Diós, **16**
Santo Domingo, **13**

8 Moorish monuments. The history of the **Alhambra** is woven through the centuries. Once inside its famous courts the legends of the Patio of the Lions, the Hall of the Two Sisters, and the murder of the Abencerrajes spring to life in a profusion of lacy walls, frothy stucco, gleaming tiles, and ornate domed ceilings. Here in this realm of myrtles and fountains, festooned arches and mysterious inscriptions, every corner holds its secret. Here the emirs installed their harems, accorded their favorites the most lavish of courts, and bathed in marble baths. In the midst of so much that is delicate the Baroque palace of Charles V seems an intrusion, heavy and incongruous, were it not for the splendid acoustics that make it a perfect setting for Granada's summer music festival.

9 Wisteria, jasmine, and roses line your route to the **Generalife,** the nearby summer palace of the caliphs, where crystal drops shower from slender fountains against a background of stately cypresses. The view of the white, clustered houses of the Albaicín, the Sacromonte riddled with gypsy caves, and the imposing bulk of the Alhambra towering above the tiled roofs of the city will etch on your memory an indelible image of this most beautiful setting and greatest Moorish legacy. *Admission to Alhambra and Generalife, 600 ptas. Free Sun. after 3. Open Nov.–Feb., daily 9–6, Mar.–Oct., daily 9–8. Floodlit visits Tues., Thurs., and Sat. 10 PM–midnight (Sat. 8–10 PM in winter). Ticket office closes 45 mins. before closing times above.*

If you have a day to spare, you can drive to the mountains of the nearby **Sierra Nevada.** The ski resort itself, where you can ski from December through May, is truly unmemorable, but the surrounding scenery viewed from the highest mountain route in Europe makes for a memorable day out. A bus leaves Granada daily at 9 AM and returns at around 5 PM; ask at the tourist office for details. Above the resort the road climbs to the Pico de Veleta, Spain's second-highest mountain at 3,100 meters (10,000 feet), and the view across the Alpujarra range to the sea at Motril is simply stunning. Away to the left rises the mighty Mulhacén, at 3,558 meters (11,477 feet), Spain's highest peak.

If you opt instead for a trip to the villages of the high **Alpujarras,** leave Granada on the N323 toward Motril, then branch east to **Lanjarón,** a delightful old spa town with an air of faded gentility. From **Orgiva,** the main town of the Alpujarras, the highest road in Europe ascends to picturesque villages like **Bubión, Capileira** beneath the summit of the Veleta, and **Trevélez,** Europe's highest village, on the slopes of Mulhacén. These ancient villages, only recently brushed by modern tourism, became the final refuge of the Moors as they fled the Conquest of Granada, and here they remained until their expulsion from Spain in 1609. With their squat, square houses and flat roofs so reminiscent of the land across the Straits of Gibraltar, they are the last vestige of Andalusia's great Moorish past.

Dining and Lodging

For details and price-category definitions, *see* Dining and Lodging in Staying in Spain, *above.*

Carmona **Parador Alcázar del Rey Don Pedro.** The beauty of this modern
Lodging parador is its splendid, peaceful setting in the ruins of the old Moor-
★ ish alcázar on top of the hill above Carmona, and its magnificent views across the vast fertile plain below. *Tel. 95/414–1010, fax 95/ 414–1010. 59 rooms. Facilities: pool. AE, DC, MC, V. Expensive.*

Córdoba **El Caballo Rojo.** The Red Horse, located close to the mosque, is
Dining Córdoba's most outstanding restaurant, famous throughout Anda-
★ lucía and all of Spain. The decor resembles a cool Andalusian patio,
and the menu features traditional specialties such as *rabo de toro*
(bull's tail); *salmorejo*, a local version of gazpacho with chunks of
ham and egg; and other exotic creations inspired by Córdoba's Moorish heritage. *Cardenal Herrero 28, tel. 957/475375. Reservations
advised. AE, DC, MC, V. Expensive.*

El Blasón. Under the same management as El Caballo Rojo, this
charming restaurant is fast gaining a name for fine food and unbeatable ambience. Located in an old inn with a pleasant tapas patio and
a whole array of restaurants upstairs, its specialties include *salmón
con naranjas* (salmon in oranges) and *ternera con salsa de
alcaparrones* (roast veal in caper sauce). *José Zorrilla 11, tel. 957/
480625. AE, DC, MC, V. Moderate.*

El Cardenal. Close to the mosque, beside the Marisa hotel, this restaurant in the heart of Córdoba's tourist center offers a stylish setting for lunch or dinner. A marble staircase with Oriental carpets
leads up to the second-floor dining room. Good food and professional
service complement the cool, agreeable atmosphere. *Cardenal
Herrero 14, tel. 957/480346. AE, DC, MC, V. Closed Sun. evening
and Mon. in winter. Moderate.*

★ **El Churrasco.** Ranking second only to El Caballo Rojo, this atmospheric restaurant with a patio is famous for its grilled meat dishes.
Specialties are, of course, *churrasco*, a pork dish in pepper sauce,
and an excellent salmorejo. *Romero 16, tel. 957/290817. AE, DC,
MC, V. Closed Aug. Moderate.*

La Almudaina. This attractive restaurant is located in a 15th-centu-
ry house and former school that overlooks the Alcázar at the entrance to the Judería. It has an Andalucían patio, and the decor and
cooking are both typical of Córdoba. *Campo Santo de los Mártires 1,
tel. 957/474342. AE, DC, MC, V. Closed Sun. evening. Moderate.*

Lodging **Conquistador.** This delightful contemporary hotel on the east side of
★ the mosque is built in Andalusian Moorish style with a charming patio and ceramic decor. The hotel itself has no restaurant, but guests
can dine in the attractive Mesón del Bandolero in Calle Torrijos on
the opposite side of the mosque. *Magistral González Francés 15, tel.
957/481102, fax 957/475079. 103 rooms. Facilities: pool, garage
parking. AE, DC, MC, V. Expensive–Very Expensive.*

El Califa. This is a small, modern hotel in a reasonably quiet, central
location in the heart of the old city. It accepts no tour groups, only
individual guests, and is a comfortable place to stay, with the sights
and shops close at hand. *Lope de Hoces 14, tel. 957/299400. 65 rooms.
MC, V. Moderate–Expensive.*

Marisa. A charming old Andalusian house whose location in the
heart of the old town overlooking the mosque's Patio de los Naranjos
is its prime virtue. You'll find the decor quaint and charming, and
the rates reasonable. *Cardenal Herrero 6, tel. 957/473142. 28
rooms. MC, V. Moderate.*

Granada **Baroca.** Located one block above the Camino de Ronda, the locals
Dining consider this Granada's best restaurant. The menu favors interna-
★ tional cuisine; desserts are especially good. Service is professional
and the ambience agreeable. *Pedro Antonio de Alarcón 34, tel. 958/
265061. Reservations advised. AE, DC, MC, V. Closed Sun. and
Aug. Expensive.*

Carmen de San Miguel. This is a restaurant to visit for its superb setting in a villa with an outdoor terrace and magnificent views over
Granada. Located on the Alhambra hill beside the Alhambra Palace
hotel, the setting is unbeatable, the food is average Continental-

style cuisine. *Paseo Torres Bermejas 3, tel. 958/226723. AE, DC, MC, V. Closed Sun. evening. Expensive.*

Cunini. Located in the center of town, close to the cathedral, Cunini has long been famous for the quality of its seafood. *Pescadería 9 or Capuchina 14, tel. 958/250777. Reservations advised. AE, DC, MC, V. Closed Mon. Expensive.*

Sevilla. This is a very atmospheric, colorful restaurant located in the Alcaicería beside the cathedral. There's a superb tapas bar at the entrance, and the dining room is picturesque but rather small and crowded. The menu can be rather tourist-oriented, but try their *sopa Sevillana* (fish soup). *Oficios 12, tel. 958/221223. AE, DC, MC, V. Closed Sun. Moderate.*

Los Manueles. This old inn is one of Granada's long-standing traditions. The walls are decorated with ceramic tiles, and the ceiling is hung with hams. There's lots of atmosphere, good old-fashioned service, and plenty of traditional Granada cooking. *Zaragoza 2, tel. 958/223413. AE, DC, MC, V. Inexpensive.*

Lodging **Parador de San Francisco.** Magnificently located in an old convent right within the Alhambra precincts, the parador was where Queen Isabella was entombed before the completion of the Royal Chapel. It's one of Spain's most popular hotels, and you need to book at least four months in advance. *Alhambra, tel. 958/221443, fax 958/222264. 38 rooms. AE, DC, MC, V. Very Expensive.*

★ **Alhambra Palace.** This flamboyant ocher-red Moorish-style palace was built about 1910 and sits halfway up the hill to the Alhambra. The mood is more harried than at the more isolated parador. Though recently renovated, it remains a conversation piece with rich carpets, tapestries, and Moorish tiles. Rooms overlooking the town are preferable. The terrace is the perfect place for an early evening drink as the sun sets over the Sierra Nevada. *Peña Partida 2, tel. 958/221468, fax 958/226404. 132 rooms. AE, DC, MC, V. Expensive–Very Expensive.*

América. A simple but charming hotel within the Alhambra precincts. It's very popular so you'll need to reserve a room months ahead. The location is magnificent, and guests can linger over breakfast on a delightful patio. *Real de la Alhambra 53, tel. 958/227471. 14 rooms. No credit cards. Open Mar.–Oct. only. Moderate.*

Juan Miguel. This comfortable, modern hotel right in the center of town opened in 1987. The rooms are well equipped, service is professional, and there's a good restaurant. *Acera del Darro 24, tel. 958/258912. 66 rooms. AE, DC, MC, V. Moderate.*

Inglaterra. Set in a period house just two blocks above the Gran Vía de Colón in the heart of town, this is a hotel that will appeal to those who prefer Old World charm to creature comforts, though accommodations are perfectly adequate for the reasonable rates. *Cetti Meriem 6, tel. 958/221559, fax 958/221586. 36 rooms. AE, DC, MC, V. Inexpensive.*

Seville **Egaña-Oriza.** This is currently one of Seville's most fashionable res-
Dining taurants. Basque specialties include *merluza con almejas en salsa*
★ *verde* (white fish in clam sauce) and *solomillo con foie en salsa de trufas* (steak with goose liver pâté in truffle sauce). It's opposite the old tobacco factory, now Seville University. *San Fernando 41, tel. 95/422–7271. Reservations required. AE, DC, MC, V. Closed Sat. lunch, Sun., and Aug. Expensive.*

La Albahaca. Set in an attractive old house in the heart of the Barrio Santa Cruz, the Albahaca offers plenty of style and atmosphere and original, imaginative cuisine. Specialties of the chef, who was formerly in the Hotel Alfonso XIII, are *ajo blanco con pasas de Corinto* (garlic with raisins) and *filetitos de ciervo con ciruelas* (venison and cherries). *Plaza Santa Cruz 12, tel. 95/422–0714. Reservations advised. AE, DC, MC, V. Closed Sun. Expensive.*

La Isla. Located in the center of town between the cathedral and the Convent of La Caridad, La Isla has long been famous for its superb seafood and paella. *Arfe 25, tel. 95/421–5376. AE, DC, MC, V. Closed Mon. and Aug. Expensive.*

San Marco. The brothers Ramacciotti serve Italian-influenced cuisine in an 18th-century mansion with a classic Andalusian patio—a wonderful spot for a summer meal. Try the *ravioli rellenos de lubina en salsa de almejas* (ravioli stuffed with sea bass in a clam sauce), *cordero relleno de espinacas y setas* (lamb stuffed with spinach and forest mushrooms), or any of a delectable array of desserts. *Cuna 6, tel. 95/421–2440. Reservations advised. AE, DC, MC, V. Closed Sun. and Aug. Expensive.*

El Bacalao. This popular fish restaurant, opposite the church of Santa Catalina, is in an Andalusian house decorated with ceramic tiles. As its name suggests, the house specialty is *bacalao* (cod); try the *bacalao con arroz* or the *bacalao al pilpil. Plaza Ponce de León 15, tel. 95/421–6670. Reservations advised. AE, DC, MC, V. Closed Sun. and Aug. Moderate.*

★ **La Judería.** This bright, modern restaurant near the Hotel Fernando III is fast gaining recognition for the quality of its Andalusian and international cuisine and reasonable prices. Fish dishes from the north of Spain and meat from Ávila are specialties. Try *cordero lechal* (roast baby lamb) or *urta a la roteña* (a fish dish unique to Rota). *Cano y Cueto 13, tel. 95/441–2052. Reservations required. AE, DC, MC, V. Closed Tues. and first 2 weeks in Aug. Moderate.*

★ **Mesón Don Raimundo.** Located in an old convent close to the cathedral, the atmosphere and decor are deliberately Sevillian. Its bar is the perfect place to sample a *fino* and some splendid tapas, and the restaurant, when not catering to tour groups, is one of Seville's most delightful. *Argote de Molina 26, tel. 95/422–3355. Reservations advised. AE, DC, MC, V. Closed Sun. evening. Moderate.*

Mesón Castellano. This recently refurbished old house opposite the church of San José is an ideal place for lunch after a morning's shopping on Calle Sierpes. Specialties are Castilian meat dishes. *Jovellanos 6, tel. 95/421–4028. Open for lunch only. AE, DC, MC, V. Closed Sun. Inexpensive.*

Lodging **Alfonso XIII.** This ornate Mudéjar-style palace was built for Alfonso XIII's visit to the 1929 exhibition. It is worth a visit for its splendid Moorish decor, despite the fact that parts of the hotel are faded and fall short of five-star expectations. Rooms are overpriced and desperately need to be redecorated. The restaurant is elegant but falls short of expectations also. *San Fernando 2, tel. 95/422–2850, fax 95/421–6033. 128 rooms and 21 suites. Facilities: restaurant, pool. AE, DC, MC, V. Very Expensive.*

Colón. This classic Seville hotel reopened at the end of 1988 after several years of renovation. The rooms and suites have been modernized to a high degree of comfort while retaining much of their style. It's located right in the heart of town, close to the main shopping center. You can dine in the elegant El Burladero restaurant or in the more typical La Tasca. *Canalejas 1, tel. 95/422–2900, fax 95/422–0938. 204 rooms and 14 suites. AE, DC, MC, V. Very Expensive.*

★ **Doña María.** Close to the cathedral, this is one of Seville's most charming hotels. Some rooms are small and plain; others are tastefully furnished with antiques. Room 310 has a four-poster double bed, and 305 two single four-posters; both have spacious bathrooms. There's no restaurant, but there's a rooftop pool with a good view of the Giralda. *Don Remondo 19, tel. 95/422–4990, fax 95/421–9546. 60 rooms. AE, DC, MC, V. Expensive.*

Bécquer. This functional, modern hotel with attentive service is convenient for the shopping center and offers comfortable if unexciting accommodations. It's one of the best moderate bets, with a parking garage but no restaurant. *Reyes Católicos 4, tel. 95/422–8900, fax 95/421–4400. Telex 72884. 120 rooms. AE, DC, MC, V. Moderate.*

Giralda. Recently modernized and extensively renovated, this is a comfortable, functional hotel with spacious, light rooms decorated in typical Castilian style. Located in a cul-de-sac off Avenida Menéndez Pelayo, it lies on the edge of the old city; rooms on the fifth floor are best. *Sierra Nevada 3, tel. 95/441–6661, fax 95/441–9352. 70 rooms, garage. AE, DC, MC, V. Moderate.*

Girarda. One of several very basic family-run hotels in the Barrio Santa Cruz, the Girarda is in an old, Moorish-style building with a colorful interior patio that also serves as a restaurant. Antonia Miranda runs the place in the absence of her bullfighter husband, Pedro Sanchez Martínez. *Justin de Neve 8, tel. 95/421–5113. 5 rooms. No credit cards. Inexpensive.*

Internacional. Well maintained and charming, this Old World hotel lies in the narrow streets of the old town near Casa Pilatos. *Aguilas 17, tel. 95/421–3207. 26 rooms. Inexpensive.*

Murillo. This picturesque hotel in the heart of the Barrio Santa Cruz was redecorated in 1987. The rooms are simple and small, but the setting is a virtue. You can't reach the hotel by car, but porters with trolleys will fetch your luggage from your taxi. *Lope de Rueda 7, tel. 95/421–6095, fax 95/421–9616. 61 rooms, 30 with bath, 31 with shower. AE, DC, MC, V. Inexpensive.*

The Arts and Nightlife

Granada
Flamenco There are several "impromptu" flamenco shows in the caves of the Sacromonte, but these can be dismally bad and little more than tourist rip-offs. Go only if accompanied by a Spanish friend who knows his way around or with a tour organized by a local agency. There are also two regular flamenco clubs that cater largely to tourists and tour groups: **Jardines Neptuno** (tel. 958/522533) and **Reina Mora** (tel. 958/278228). Both can be booked through your hotel.

Seville
Flamenco Regular flamenco clubs cater largely to tourists and cost about 3,500 ptas. per person, but their shows are colorful and offer a good introduction for the uninitiated. Try any of the following: **El Arenal** (Rodo 7, tel. 95/421–6492); **Los Gallos** (Plaza Santa Cruz 11, tel. 95/421–6981), a small intimate club in the heart of the Barrio Santa Cruz offering fairly pure flamenco; and **El Patio Sevillano** (Paseo de Colón, tel. 95/421–4120), which caters largely to tour groups.

Bullfights Corridas take place at the Maestranza bullring on Paseo de Colón, usually on Sunday from Easter through October. The best are during the April Fair. Tickets can be bought in advance from the windows at the ring (one of the oldest and most picturesque in Spain) or from the kiosks in Calle Sierpes (these charge a commission). The ring and a bullfighting museum may be visited year-round. Tel. 95/422–4576. Admission: 250 ptas. Open Mon.–Sat. 10–1:30.

Costa del Sol

What were impoverished fishing villages in the 1950s are now retirement villages and package-tour meccas for northern Europeans and
Americans. Despite the abuses of this naturally lovely area during
the boom years of the 1960s and '70s, and the continuing brashness of
the resorts that cater to the package-tour trade, the Costa del Sol
has managed to preserve at least some semblance of charm. Behind
the hideous concrete monsters—some of which are now being demolished—you'll come across old cottages and villas set in gardens
that blossom with jasmine and bougainvillea. The sun still sets over
miles of beaches and the lights of small fishing craft still twinkle in
the distance. Most of your time should be devoted to indolence—
sunbathing and swimming (though not in the polluted Mediterranean; all hotels have pools for this reason). When you need something
to do, you can head inland to the historic town of Ronda and the
perched white villages of Andalusia. You can also make a day trip to
Gibraltar or Tangier.

Getting There

Daily flights on Iberia and Aviaco connect Málaga with Madrid and
Barcelona. Iberia (tel. 95/213–6146, 47, or 48), British Airways, and
charter airlines such as Dan Air offer frequent service from London;
most other major European cities also have direct air links. You'll
have to make connections in Madrid for all flights from the United
States. Málaga Airport (tel. 95/224–0191) is 12 kilometers (7 miles)
west of the city. City buses run from the airport to the city every 20
minutes (fare: 100 ptas., 6:20 AM–10:40 PM); the Portillo bus company
(tel. 95/236–0191) has frequent service from the airport to
Torremolinos. A suburban train serving Málaga, Torremolinos, and
Fuegirola also stops at the airport every half hour. From Madrid, Málaga is easily reached by a half-dozen rapid trains a day.

Getting Around

Buses are the best means of transport on the Costa del Sol (as well as
from Seville or Granada). Málaga's long-distance station is on the
Paseo de los Tilos (tel. 95/235–0061); nearby, on Muelle de Heredía,
a smaller station serves suburban destinations. The main bus company serving the Costa del Sol is **Portillo** (offices at the bus station,
tel. 95/236–0191). **Alsina Gräells** (at the station, tel. 95/231–8295)
has service to Granada, Córdoba, Seville, and Nerja. The train station in Málaga (Explanada de la Estación, tel. 95/236–0202) is a 15-
minute walk from the city center, across the river. The **RENFE** office (Stracham 2, tel. 95/221–4127) is more convenient for tickets and
information.

Guided Tours

Organized one- and two-day excursions to places such as Seville,
Granada, Córdoba, Ronda, Gibraltar, and Tangier are run by **Juliá
Tours, Pullmantur,** and numerous smaller companies from all the
Costa del Sol resorts and can be booked through your hotel desk or
any travel agent.

Costa del Sol

Tourist Information

The most helpful tourist offices, by far, are in Málaga and Marbella. The Málaga office covers the entire province.

Estepona (Paseo Marítimo Pedro Manrique, tel. 95/280–0913).
Fuengirola (Av. Jesús Santos Rein 6, tel. 95/246–7457).
Gibraltar (On Cathedral Square, the Piazza, and John Mackintosh Square, tel. 9567/74950).
Málaga (Pasaje de Chinitas 4, tel. 95/221–3445, and at the airport in both national and international terminals).
Marbella (Glorieta de la Fontanilla, tel. 95/277–1442).
Nerja (Puerta del Mar 2, tel. 95/252–1531).
Ronda (Plaza de España 1, tel. 95/287–1272).
Torremolinos (Plaza Pablo Ruíz Picasso, tel. 95/237–1159).

Exploring the Costa del Sol

Our tour of the Costa del Sol begins in Nerja, some 50 kilometers (30 miles) to the east of Málaga, and takes us along the coast as far as Gibraltar, with a detour inland to the picturesque town of Ronda set high in the mountains.

Nerja is a small but expanding resort that so far has escaped the worst excesses of the property developers. Its growth to date has been largely confined to villages such as El Capistrano, one of the showpieces of the Costa del Sol. There's pleasant bathing here, though the sand is gray and gritty. The **Balcón de Europa** is a fantastic lookout, high above the sea. The famous **Cuevas de Nerja** (a series of stalactite caves) are off the road to Almuñecar and Almería. A kind of vast underground cathedral, they contain the world's largest known stalactite (62 meters [203 feet] long). *Tel. 95/252–0076. Admission: 300 ptas. Open daily summer 10:30–6, winter 10:30–2 and 3:30–6.*

Málaga is a busy port city with ancient streets and lovely villas set among exotic foliage, but it has little to recommend it to the overnight visitor. The central Plaza de la Marina, overlooking the port, is a pleasant place for a drink. The main shops are along the Calle Marqués de Larios.

The **Alcazaba** is a fortress begun in the 8th century when Málaga was the most important port of the Moorish kingdom. The ruins of the Roman amphitheater at its entrance were uncovered when the fort was restored. The inner palace dates from the 11th century when, for a short period after the breakup of the Caliphate of the West in Córdoba, it became the residence of the Moorish emirs. Today you'll find the **Archaeological Museum** here and a good collection of Moorish art. *Tel. 95/222–0043. Admission: 20 ptas. Open Mon.–Sat. 11–2 and 5–8, Sun. 10–2 (4–7 in winter).*

Energetic souls can climb through the Alcazaba gardens to the summit of **Gibralfaro.** Others can drive by way of Calle Victoria or take the parador minibus that leaves roughly every 1½ hours from near the cathedral on Molina Lario. The Gibralfaro fortifications were built for Yusuf I in the 14th century. The Moors called it Jebelfaro, which means "rock of the lighthouse," after the beacon that stood here to guide ships into the harbor and warn of invasions by pirates. Today the beacon has gone, but there's a small parador that makes a delightful place for a drink or a meal and has some stunning views.

As you approach **Torremolinos** through an ocean of concrete blocks, it's hard to grasp that as recently as the early 1960s this was an inconsequential fishing village. Today, this grossly overdeveloped resort is a prime example of 20th-century tourism run riot. The town center, with its brash Nogalera Plaza, is full of overpriced bars and restaurants. Much more attractive is the district of La Carihuela, farther west, below the Avenida Carlota Alexandra. You'll find some old fishermen's cottages here, a few excellent seafood restaurants, and a traffic-free esplanade for an enjoyable stroll on a summer evening.

Head west from Torremolinos, toward the similar but more staid resorts of **Benalmádena** and **Fuengirola,** both retirement havens for British and American senior citizens. A short drive from Fuengirola up into the mountains takes you to the picturesque—and over-photographed—village of **Mijas.** Though the vast tourist-oriented main square may seem like an extension of the Costa's tawdry bazaar, there are hillside streets of whitewashed houses where you'll discover an authentic village atmosphere that has changed little since the days before the tourist boom of the 1960s. Visit the bullring, the nearby church, and the chapel of Mijas's patroness, the Virgen de la Peña (to the side of the main square), and enjoy shopping for quality gifts and souvenirs.

Marbella is the most fashionable and sedate resort area along the coast. It does have a certain Florida land boom feel to it, but development has been controlled, and Marbella will, let's hope, never turn into another Torremolinos. The town's charming old Moorish quarter may be crowded with up-market boutiques and a modern, T-shirt-and-fudge section along the main drag; but when people speak of Marbella they refer both to the town and to the resorts—

some more exclusive than others—stretching 16 kilometers (10 miles) or so on either side of town, between the highway and the beach. If you're vacationing in southern Spain, this is the place to stay. There's championship golf and tennis, fashionable waterfront cafés, and trendy shopping arcades.

A short drive up into the hills behind Marbella brings you to the village of **Ojén.** Its typical streets are a far cry from the promenades of the coastal resorts. Look out for the traditional pottery sold here and for the picturesque cemetery, with its rows of burial-urn chambers.

Back on the coastal highway, Marbella's Golden Mile, with its mosque, Arab banks, and residence of King Fahd of Saudi Arabia, proclaims the ever-growing influence of wealthy Arabs in this playground of the rich. In **Puerto Banús,** Marbella's plush marina, with its flashy yachts, fashionable people, and expensive restaurants, the glittering parade outshines even St. Tropez in ritzy glamour.

Ronda is reached via a spectacular mountain road from San Pedro de Alcántara. One of the oldest towns in Spain, and last stronghold of the legendary Andalusian bandits, Ronda's most dramatic feature is its ravine, known as **El Tajo,** which is 279 meters (900 feet) across and divides the old Moorish town from the "new town" of El Mercadillo. Spanning the gorge is the **Puente Nuevo,** an amazing architectural feat built between 1755 and 1793, whose parapet offers dizzying views of the River Guadalevin way below. Countless people have plunged to their death from this bridge, including its own architect, who accidentally fell over while inspecting his work, and numerous victims of the Civil War of 1936–39 who were hurled into the ravine—an episode recounted in Hemingway's *For Whom the Bell Tolls.* Ronda is visited more for its setting, breathtaking views, and ancient houses than for any particular monument. Stroll the old streets of **La Ciudad;** drop in at the historic **Reina Victoria** hotel, built by the English from Gibraltar as a fashionable resting place on their Algeciras to Bobadilla railroad line; and visit the **bullring,** one of the earliest and most beautiful rings in Spain. Here Ronda's most famous native son, Pedro Romero (1754–1839), father of modern bullfighting, is said to have killed 5,600 bulls during his 30-year career; and in the **Bullfighting Museum** you can see posters dating back to the very first fights held in the ring in May 1785. The ring is privately owned now, but 3–4 fights a year are still held in the summer months. Tickets are exceedingly difficult to come by (tel. 95/287–6967, admission to ring and museum: 200 ptas., open daily 10–6:30). Above all, don't miss the cliff-top walk and the gardens of the **Alameda del Tajo,** where you can contemplate one of the most dramatic views in all of Andalucía.

Returning to the coast road, the next town is **Estepona,** which until recently marked the end of the urban sprawl of the Costa del Sol. Estepona lacks the hideous high rises of Torremolinos and Fuengirola, and set back from the main highway, it's not hard to make out the old fishing village this once was. Wander the streets of the Moorish village, around the central food market and the **Church of San Francisco,** and you'll find a pleasant contrast to the excesses higher up the coast.

Nineteen kilometers (11¾ miles) northwest of Estepona, the mountain village of **Casares** lies high in the Sierra Bermeja. Streets of ancient white houses perch on the slopes beneath a ruined Moorish castle. Admire the view of the Mediterranean and check out the village's thriving ceramics industry.

Between Estepona and Gibraltar, the highway is flanked by prosperous vacation developments known as *urbanizaciones*. These have mushroomed since the border between Spain and Gibraltar was reopened in 1985. The architecture here is much more in keeping with traditional Andalusian style than the concrete blocks of earlier developments. The new **Puerto de Sotogrande** near Manilva is one of the showpieces of the area.

Gibraltar

To enter **Gibraltar,** simply walk or drive across the border at La Línea and show your passport. In theory car drivers need an International Driver's License, insurance certificate, and registration book; in practice, these regulations are usually waived. It is also possible to fly into Gibraltar on daily flights from London but, as yet, there are no flights from Spanish airports. There are, however, plenty of bus tours from Spain. **Juliá Tours, Pullmantur,** and many smaller agencies, run daily tours (not Sunday) to Gibraltar from most Costa del Sol resorts. Alternatively, you can take the regular **Portillo** bus to La Línea and walk across the border. In summer, **Portillo** runs an inexpensive daily tour to Gibraltar from Torremolinos bus station. Once you reach Gibraltar the official language is English and the currency is the British pound sterling, though pesetas are also accepted.

The Rock of Gibraltar acquired its name in AD 711 when it was captured by the Moorish chieftain Tarik at the start of the Arab invasion of Spain. It became known as Jebel Tariq (Rock of Tariq), later corrupted to Gibraltar. After successive periods of Moorish and Spanish domination, Gibraltar was captured by an Anglo-Dutch fleet in 1704 and ceded to the British by the Treaty of Utrecht in 1713. This tiny British colony, whose impressive silhouette dominates the straits between Spain and Morocco, is a rock just 5⅘ kilometers (3⅗ miles) long, three-quarter kilometers (half a mile) wide, and 425 meters (1,369 feet) high.

On entering Gibraltar by road you have to cross the airport runway on the narrow strip of land that links the Rock with La Línea in Spain. Here you have a choice. You can either plunge straight into exploring Gibraltar town, or opt for a tour around the Rock. Several minibus tours are readily available at this point of entry.

Numbers in the margin correspond to points of interest on the Gibraltar map.

The tour around the Rock is best begun on the eastern side. As you enter Gibraltar, turn left down Devil's Tower Road, and drive as far
❶ as **Catalan Bay,** a small fishing village founded by Genoese settlers in the 18th century, and now one of the Rock's most picturesque resorts. The road continues on beneath water catchments that supply
❷ the colony's drinking water, to another resort, **Sandy Bay,** and then plunges through the Dudley Ward Tunnel to bring you out at the
❸ Rock's most southerly tip, **Punta Grande de Europa** (Europa Point). Stop here to admire the view across the Straits to the coast of Morocco, 22½ kilometers (14 miles) away. You are standing on what in ancient times was called one of the two Pillars of Hercules. Across the water in Morocco, a mountain between the cities of Ceuta and Tangier formed the second pillar. The Europa Point lighthouse has stood above the meeting point of the Atlantic and the Mediterranean since 1841. Plaques explain the history of the gun installations here,
❹ and, nearby on Europa Flats, you can see the **Nun's Well,** an ancient

Apes' Den, **10**

Casino, **7**

Catalan Bay, **1**

Cathedral of the Holy Trinity, **15**

Cathedral of St. Mary the Crowned, **16**

Gibraltar Museum, **17**

Governor's Residence, **13**

Great Siege Tunnel, **11**

Jews Gate, **8**

Koehler Gun, **19**

Law Courts, **14**

Nefusot Yehudada Synagogue, **18**

Nun's Well, **4**

Punta Grande de Europa, **3**

Rosia Bay, **6**

St. Michael's Cave, **9**

Sandy Bay, **2**

Shrine of Our Lady of Europe, **5**

Tower of Homage, **12**

Gibraltar

⑤ Moorish cistern, and the **Shrine of Our Lady of Europe,** venerated by sailors since 1462.

⑥ Europa Road winds its way high on the western slopes above **Rosia Bay,** to which Nelson's flagship, HMS *Victory*, was towed after the Battle of Trafalgar in 1805. Aboard were the dead of the battle, who are now buried in Trafalgar Cemetery on the southern edge of town, and the body of Admiral Nelson himself, preserved in a barrel of rum. He was then taken to London for burial.

⑦ Continue on Europa Road as far as the **casino** (Europa Rd., tel. 9567/76666, open daily 9 PM–4 AM) above the Alameda Gardens. Make a

⑧ sharp right here up Engineer Road to **Jews Gate,** an unbeatable lookout point over the docks and Bay of Gibraltar to Algeciras in Spain.

Here you can gain access to the **Upper Nature Preserve**, which includes St. Michael's Cave, the Ape's Den, the Great Siege Tunnel, **9** and the Moorish Castle (*see below*). Queens Road leads to **St. Michael's Cave**, a series of underground chambers adorned with stalactites and stalagmites, which provides an admirable setting for concerts, ballet, and drama. Sound-and-light shows are held here most days at 11 AM and 4 PM. A skull of Neanderthal Woman (now in the British Museum in London) was found in the caves some eight years *before* the world-famous discovery in Germany's Neander Valley in 1856. *Admission to the preserve, including all sites: £4.50 adults, £2.25 children 5 or under, plus £1.50 per vehicle. Open daily 10–6.*

10 Drive down Old Queen's Road to the **Apes' Den** near the **Wall of Charles V.** The famous Barbary apes are a breed of cinnamon-colored, tailless monkeys, natives of the Atlas Mountains in Morocco. Legend holds that as long as the apes remain, the British will continue to hold the Rock. Winston Churchill himself issued orders for the maintenance of the ape colony when its numbers began to dwindle during World War II. Today the apes are the responsibility of the British Army, and a special Officer in Charge of Apes is assigned to feed them twice daily at 8 AM and 4 PM.

Passing beneath the cable car that runs to the Rock's summit, drive up **11** to the **Great Siege Tunnel** at the northern end of the Rock. These huge galleries were carved out during the Great Siege of 1779–1783. Here, in 1878, the Governor, Lord Napier of Magdala, entertained ex-President Ulysses S. Grant at a banquet in **St. George's Hall.** From here, the **Holyland Tunnel** leads out to the east side of the Rock above Catalan Bay.

The last stop before the town is at the **Moorish Castle** on Willis Road. Built by the successors of the Moorish invader Tarik, the present **12** **Tower of Homage** was rebuilt by the Moors in 1333. Admiral Rooke hoisted the British flag from its top when he captured the Rock in 1704, and here it has flown ever since. The castle has been closed to the public and can be seen only from the outside.

Willis Road leads steeply down to the colorful, congested town of Gibraltar where the dignified Regency architecture of Britain blends with the shutters, balconies, and patios of southern Spain. Apart from the attraction of shops, restaurants, and pubs on Main Street, **13** you'll want to visit some of the following: the **Governor's Residence,** where the ceremonial Changing of the Guard once took place weekly **14** (it now occurs 4–5 times a year; ask at the tourist office); the **Law Courts,** where the famous case of the *Mary Celeste* sailing ship was **15** heard in 1872; the Anglican **Cathedral of the Holy Trinity;** the Catho- **16** lic **Cathedral of St. Mary the Crowned;** and the recently refurbished **17** **Gibraltar Museum,** whose exhibits recall the history of the Rock throughout the ages. *Gibraltar Museum, Bomb House La., tel. 9567–74289. Admission: £1.50 adults, £1 children. Open Mon.–Fri. 10–6, Sat. 10–2.*

18 Finally, the **Nefusot Yehudada Synagogue** on Line Wall Road is worth a look for its inspired architecture, and, if you're interested in **19** guns, the **Koehler Gun** in **Casemates Square** at the northern end of Main Street is an impressive example of the type of gun developed during the Great Siege.

Dining and Lodging

For details and price-category definitions, *see* Dining and Lodging in Staying in Spain, *above*.

Estepona
Dining

El Molino. Situated in an old windmill 12 km (8 mi) on the road to Malaga, this restaurant has offered classic French cuisine for some three decades. Try the *lubina al hinojo* (sea bass in fennel) or the delicious Chateaubriand steak. *Carretera N340 at Km 166, tel. 95/ 288–2135. Reservations advised. AE, DC, MC, V. No lunch. Closed Tues., Sun., and Jan. Expensive.*

Alcaría de Ramos. José Ramos, winner of the National Gastronomy Prize, opened this restaurant outside town in 1990, and it has quickly garnered a large and loyal following. Try the *ensalada de lentejas con salmón ahumado* (lentil salad with smoked salmon), followed by *cordero asado* (roast lamb) and the chef's justly famous fried ice cream. *Rte. N340, km. 167, tel. 95/288–6178. Reservations advised. V. Closed for lunch, Sun., and June 15–July 15. Moderate–Expensive.*

Lodging

Santa Marta. This is a small, quiet hotel with just 37 rooms in chalet bungalows set in a large, peaceful garden. Some rooms are a little faded after 30 years, but the tranquil setting is a plus. Good lunches are served by the pool. *Rte. N340, km. 173, tel. 95/288–8180. 37 rooms with bath. AE, MC, V. Open Apr.–Sept. only. Moderate.*

Gibraltar
Dining

La Bayuca. One of the Rock's longest-established restaurants, La Bayuca is renowned for its onion soup and Mediterranean dishes. Prince Charles and Prince Andrew have dined here while on naval service. *21 Turnbull's La., tel. 9567/75119. Reservations advised. AE, DC, MC, V. Closed Tues. and Sun. lunch. Expensive.*

Country Cottage. Opposite the Catholic cathedral, this is the place to go for a taste of Old England. Enjoy steak and kidney pie, Angus steak, and roast beef, by candlelight. *13 Giro's Passage, tel. 9567/ 70084. Reservations advised. AE, MC, V. Closed Sun. Moderate–Expensive.*

Lodging
★

Rock. The Rock has undergone a massive refurbishment program with the aim of bolstering its reputation as Gibraltar's supreme luxury hotel. You'll find a comfortable, old-fashioned English atmosphere, along with a pool, sun terrace, and gardens. Located on Gibraltar's western slopes, the hotel overlooks the town and harbor. *3 Europa Rd., tel. 9567/73000. 143 rooms with bath. AE, DC. Expensive.*

Bristol. This colonial-style hotel is just off Gibraltar's main street, right in the heart of town. Rooms are large and comfortable, and the tropical garden is a real haven for those guests who want to relax in peaceful isolation. *10 Cathedral Sq., tel. 9567/76800. 60 rooms with bath. AE, DC, MC, V. Moderate.*

Málaga
Dining

Café de Paris. The owner of this stylish restaurant in the Paseo Marítimo area is a former chef of Maxim's in Paris, and La Hacienda in Marbella. The *menú degustación* lets you try a little of everything. Specialties include *rodaballo con espinacas* (sea bass and spinach). *Vélez Málaga 8, tel. 95/222–5043. Reservations advised. AE, DC, MC, V. Closed Sun. Expensive.*

Antonio Martín. This is another old Málaga standby, with a splendid terrace overlooking the ocean, at the beginning of the Paseo Marítimo. It's long been famous for its fresh seafood and paella. Try the local *fritura malagueña. Paseo Marítimo 4, tel. 95/222–2113. Reservations advised. AE, DC, MC, V. Closed Sun. evening. Moderate.*

Casa Pedro. It's crowded and noisy, but Malgueños have been flosking to this no-frills fish restaurant for more than 50 years. Located in the seaside suburb of El Palo, the restaurant has a huge, bare dining room that overlooks the ocean. Try joining the hordes of local families who come here for lunch on Sundays. It's quieter at other times. *Quitapenas 121, El Paso beach (bus No. 11), tel. 95/229–0003. Reservations advised Sun. AE, DC, MC, V. Closed Mon. dinner and Nov. Moderate.*

La Cancela. This is a colorful restaurant in the center of town, just off Calle Granada. Dine indoors or alfresco. *Denís Belgrano 3, tel. 95/222–3125. Reservations not necessary. AE, DC, MC, V. Inexpensive.*

Lodging **Los Naranjos.** This small hotel owned by the Luz chain is situated on a pleasant avenue in a residential district a little to the east of the city center. There's a small garden in front, but rooms overlooking the street can be noisy. *Paseo de Sancha 35, tel. 95/222–4317. 41 rooms. AE, DC, V. Expensive.*

★ **Parador de Gibralfaro.** Located in a small wood on top of Gibralfaro mountain 3½ kilometers (2 miles) above the city, this tiny parador offers spectacular views over the city and bay. The Parador was closed for major renovations in 1993 and was not expected to reopen this year; check first with the tourist office. *Gibralfaro, tel. 95/222–1902. 12 rooms. AE, DC, MC, V. Expensive.*

Las Vegas. In a pleasant, though noisy, part of town, just east of the center, this recently renovated hotel has a dining room overlooking the Paseo Marítimo, an outdoor pool, and a large leafy garden. Rooms at the back enjoy a good view of the ocean. *Paseo de Sancha 22, tel. 95/221–7712. 100 rooms. AE, DC, MC, V. Moderate.*

Victoria. This small, recently renovated hostel in an old house just off Calle Larios offers excellent budget accommodations in a convenient central location. *Sancha de Lara 3, tel. 95/222–4223. 13 rooms. AE, V. Inexpensive.*

Marbella **La Hacienda.** This restaurant, owned by Belgian chef-proprietor
Dining Paul Schiff, belongs to the Relais Gourmand group and is one of the
★ highest rated in Spain. The menu reflects the influence of both Paul Schiff's native Belgium and his adopted Andalusia. The *menú degustación* at around 6,500 ptas. will enable you to sample the very best creations of this famous European chef. *Las Chapas, Rte. N340, km. 193, 12 km (7 mi) east on the road to Málaga; tel. 95/283–1116. Reservations required. AE, DC, MC, V. Closed Mon., Tues., and mid-Nov.–mid-Dec. Very Expensive.*

La Meridiana. Another of Marbella's most outstanding restaurants and a favorite with the local jet set, La Meridiana is located just west of town, toward Puerto Banús, and is famous for its original Bauhaus-type architecture and the superb quality and freshness of the ingredients. *Camino de la Cruz, tel. 95/277–6190. Reservations required. AE, DC, MC, V. Closed Mon., Tues. lunch, and lunch in summer. Very Expensive.*

La Dorada. Fresh fish and shellfish top the menu in this two-story building with an outdoor dining area on each floor. Specialties of the house include *fritura malagueña* (fried fish Malaga style) served sizzling and fresh from the pan, and excellent *mariscos* (shellfish), such as *coquinas* (small cockles), *cigalos* (small crayfish), and *bogavantes* (similar to crayfish). *Ctra. Cádiz-Málaga (N340), km. 176, tel. 95/282–1034. AE, DC, V. Closed Aug. Expensive.*

★ **La Fonda.** In a beautiful 18th-century house with antique furniture and located in one of the loveliest old squares in Marbella, La Fonda is owned by one of Madrid's leading restaurateurs. Its cuisine combines the best of Spanish, French, and Austrian influences, and it has been awarded the National Gastronomy Prize. A delightful patio filled with potted plants makes a perfect setting for summer dining. *Plaza del Santo Cristo 9, tel. 95/277–2512. Reservations advised. AE, DC, MC, V. Open for dinner only. Closed Sun. Expensive.*

Mesón del Pollo. This small, charming "house of chicken" illustrates how Marbella, despite tourism, remains truly Spanish. Porcelain lampshades, azulejo tiles, a dozen tables, and the scent of roasting chicken fill this popular lunch spot. Try the *pollo a la sevillana* dinner (roast chicken with squid, fried potatoes, salad, and cider) or *fritura malagueña,* or sample tapas of octopus or meatballs. *Antonio Martín, across from the El Fuerte Hotel, no tel. No reservations. No credit cards. Inexpensive.*

Lodging The only reason to stay in town is if you're on a tight budget and have no car. Students can stay in small, family-run hotels in the old quarter of Marbella for as little as $20 a night. There are a few reasonably priced, package-tour-type high-rise hotels only a block from the busy town beach. For most visitors, air-conditioning in summer is a must. The ocean is uninviting at times, thanks to improper pollution controls, so a hotel pool is a plus. Most visitors prefer to stay at one of the sparkling white resorts strung along the beach on either side of town. Finding the right one is critical.

★ **Los Monteros.** Situated 2½ kilometers (1½ miles) east of Marbella, on the road to Málaga, this deluxe hotel offers all the facilities of a top hotel, including an 18-hole golf course, seven tennis courts, three pools, horseback riding, and gourmet dining in its famous El Corzo Grill restaurant. This is the third most expensive hotel in Spain, after the Ritz and Villa Magna in Madrid. Eighty percent of the guests are British, which may explain the somewhat starched formality of the rooms. *Urb. Los Monteros, tel. 95/277–1700. 171 rooms. AE, DC, MC, V. Very Expensive.*

Marbella Club. The grande dame of Marbella tends to attract an older clientele. The bungalow-style rooms run from cramped to spacious, and the decor varies considerably; specify the type you prefer, but ask for a room that's been recently renovated. The grounds are exquisite. Breakfast is served on a patio where songbirds flit through the vegetation. *Rte. N340, km. 178, tel. 95/277–1300. 76 rooms. Facilities: restaurant, bar, gym, sauna, nightclub, hairdresser, tennis. AE, DC, MC, V. Very Expensive.*

Puente Romano. A spectacular, modern hotel and apartment complex of low, white-stucco buildings located 2 miles west of Marbella on the road to Puerto Banús. The "village" has a Roman bridge in its beautifully landscaped grounds as well as two pools, a tennis club, and a disco run by Régine. *Rte. N340, km. 184, tel. 95/277–0100. 220 rooms. AE, DC, V. Very Expensive.*

El Fuerte. This is the best of the few hotels in the center of Marbella, with simple, adequate rooms. It's located in a 1950s-type building in the midst of a large garden with an outdoor pool. *Avda. El Fuerte, tel. 95/286–1500. 146 rooms. AE, DC, V. Moderate.*

★ **Pilar.** This may be the best find in Marbella: a cheerful, relatively large, and charming hotel in a central location—and very fairly priced to boot. It was taken over in 1992 by Scotsman Michael Wright, a former butler and master of guest houses in Edinburgh. It's clean and intimate, and includes such delightful surprises as a log fire in winter. *Mesoncillo 4, tel. 95/282–9936. 17 rooms. Facilities: bar serving breakfast. No credit cards. Inexpensive.*

Mijas **Valparaíso.** *Pato a la naranja* (duck in an orange sauce) is one of the
Dining specialties served in a pleasant villa with garden and terrace on the

road from Fuengirola to Mijas. *Tel. 95/248–5996. AE, MC, V. Dinner only. Closed Sun. Nov.–May. Expensive.*

Mirlo Blanco. Here you can sample Basque specialties such as *txangurro* (crab) and *merluza a la vasca* (hake with asparagus, eggs, and clam sauce). *Plaza Constitución 13, tel. 95/248–5700. Reservations accepted. AE, MC, V. Moderate.*

Lodging **★ Byblos Andaluz.** In this new luxury hotel set in a huge garden of palms, cypresses, and fountains, you'll find every comfort. Facilities include pools, saunas, tennis, and an 18-hole golf course. Its Le Nailhac restaurant is famous for its French cuisine; special low-calorie meals are also available. *Urbano Mijas-Golf, tel. 95/247–3050, fax 95/247–6783. 144 rooms. AE, DC, MC, V. Very Expensive.*

★ Mijas. You'll find this hotel at the entrance to Mijas village. The hotel is modern and peaceful, with a delightful rose garden, terrace, and afternoon tea. *Urbano Tamisa, tel. 95/248–5800, fax 95/248–5825. 106 rooms. AE, DC, MC, V. Expensive.*

Nerja **Casa Luque.** This is one of the most authentically Spanish of Nerja's
Dining restaurants, located in a charming old Andalusian house behind the Balcón de Europa church. *Plaza Cavana 2, tel. 95/252–1004. Reservations accepted. AE, V. Closed Mon. and Feb. Moderate.*

Udo Heimer. A genial German is your host at this Art Deco villa. His menu is a combination of traditional German dishes and local produce. Try ham-stuffed pumpkin or prawns wrapped in bacon and served in a curried banana sauce. *Pueblo Andaluz 27, tel. 95/252–0032. AE, DC, MC, V. Reservations advised. No lunch. Closed Wed. and Jan.–Feb. Moderate.*

Lodging **Mónica.** Nerja's newest beach hotel opened in 1986. It's spacious and luxurious, with Moorish-style architecture. Facilities include tennis, pool, nightclub, and disco. *Playa Torrecilla, tel. 95/252–1100. 234 rooms. AE, DC, MC, V. Expensive.*

★ Parador. All the rooms in this small parador a little to the east of the center of Nerja have balconies overlooking the sea. There's a pleasant leafy garden and outdoor pool, and an elevator takes you down to the beach. *El Tablazo, tel. 95/252–0050, fax 95/252–1997. 73 rooms. AE, DC, MC, V. Expensive.*

Ronda **Don Miguel.** Located by the bridge over the Tajo gorge, the restau-
Dining rant's terrace offers spectacular views of the ravine. Lamb is a specialty; try *pierna de cordero lechal Don Miguel* (leg of baby lamb). *Villanueva 4, tel. 95/287–1090. Reservations advised. AE, DC, MC, V. Closed Sun. and Wed. in summer and mid-Jan.–mid-Feb. Expensive.*

Pedro Romero. Located opposite the bullring, this restaurant is, not surprisingly, packed with colorful taurine decor. Among the traditional regional recipes worth trying is the *sopa de mesón*—the soup of the house. *Virgen de la Paz 18, tel. 95/287–1110. AE, DC, MC, V. Moderate.*

Lodging **Reina Victoria.** A spectacularly situated Old-World hotel with a distinctly British air, the Reina Victoria sits atop the very rim of the gorge. Its views and style are tops, but its facilities are often overwhelmed by tour groups. *Jerez 25, tel. 95/287–1240, fax 95/287–1075. 89 rooms. AE, DC, MC, V. Moderate–Expensive.*

Polo. A cozy, old-fashioned hotel in the center of town, Polo sports a reasonably priced restaurant. The staff is friendly and the rooms simple but comfortable. *Mariano Soubiron 8, tel. 95/287–2447. 33 rooms. AE, DC, V. Moderate.*

Torremolinos **Casa Guaquin.** Casa Guaquin is widely known as the best seafood
Dining restaurant in the region. Changing daily catches are served on a seaside patio alongside such menu stalwarts as *coquillas al ajillo* (sea
cockles in garlic sauce). *Paseo Maritimo 63, tel. 95/238–4530. AE,
MC, V. Closed Thurs. and mid.-Dec.–mid-Jan. Moderate.*

El Atrio. This small, stylish restaurant is located in the Pueblo
Blanco. Its cuisine is predominantly French. In summer, you can
dine on the terrace. *Casablanca 9, tel. 95/238–8850. AE, MC, V.
Open 8 PM–midnight. Closed Sun. and Dec. Moderate.*

Juan. This is a good place to enjoy seafood in summer, with a sunny
outdoor patio facing the sea. The specialties include the great Costa
del Sol standbys: *sopa de mariscos* (shellfish soup), *dorada al horno*
(oven-roasted giltheads), and *fritura malagueña. Paseo Marítimo
29, La Carihuela, tel. 95/238–5656. AE, DC, MC, V. Moderate.*

Marrakech. The magic of Morocco is evoked in this splendid stucco-
and-tile palace. Couscous and tajine are served in big earthenware
dishes; lamb is stewed with prunes, raisins, or almonds; and delicious honey-coated pastries round off a sumptuous repast. *Av. Joan
Miro 7, tel. 95/238–2169. No reservations. No credit cards. Closed
Sun. and Mon. lunch. Moderate.*

Lodging **Cervantes.** This busy cosmopolitan hotel in the heart of town has
comfortable rooms, good service, and a well-known dining room on
its top floor. *Las Mercedes, tel. 95/238–4033, fax 95/238–4857. 393
rooms. Facilities: pool, sauna, nightclub. AE, DC, MC, V. Expensive.*

Tropicana. Located on the beach at the far end of the Carihuela is a
comfortable, relaxing resort hotel with several good restaurants
nearby. *Trópico 6, tel. 95/238–6600, fax 95/238–0568. 86 rooms. Facilities: pool. AE, DC, MC, V. Moderate.*

★ **Miami.** Set in an old Andalusian villa in a shady garden to the west of
the Carihuela, this is something of a find amid the ocean of concrete
blocks. *Aladino 14, tel. 95/238–5255. 26 rooms. No credit cards. Inexpensive.*

Canary Islands

Traditionally a popular spot for winter holidays, Spain's Canary Islands are becoming a year-round destination favored by sun-seekers
and nature lovers alike. The Canaries lie 70 miles off the coast of
southern Morocco in the Atlantic Ocean and enjoy mild, sunny
weather throughout the year. Each of the seven volcanic islands in
the archipelago is distinct. Some have lush tropical vegetation, poin-
settias as tall as trees, and banana plantations, while others are arid
and resemble an exotic moonscape of lava rock and sand dunes. Mt.
Teide (12,198 feet), Spain's highest peak and snowcapped for much
of the year, is located here. The islands are also home to six national
parks and dozens of other protected ecological zones in which visitors can hike through mist-shrouded forests of virgin laurel trees,
climb mountains, eat food cooked by nature over volcanic craters, or
scuba dive off long stretches of unspoiled coastline.

Tenerife Of all the Canary Islands **Tenerife** is the most popular and has the
greatest variety of scenery to offer visitors. Its beaches are small,
though, with volcanic black sand or sand imported from the Sahara
Desert.

The south coast resort of **Playa de las Americas,** built chock-a-block
with hotels, is where the majority of tourists stay. Located in the
most arid and barren zone of the island, it offers little apart from
sprawling hotel swimming pools and sizzling nightlife.

An hour northeast by super-highway is the pleasant provincial capital, **Santa Cruz,** known as the site of Spain's wildest fiesta, the pre-lenten Carnival, which takes place the weekends before and after Ash Wednesday. The **Museo Arqueológico Provincial** (Provincial Archeology Museum, Bravo Murillo 5) contains ceramics and mummies from the stone-age culture of the Guanches, the native people who inhabited the islands before they were conquered and colonized by the Spanish in the 15th century. The best thing to visit in Santa Cruz is the colorful weekday morning market, **Mercado de Nuestra Señora de Africa,** which sells everything from tropical fruits and flowers to canaries and parrots.

North of Santa Cruz are the university town of La Laguna and the island's first resort village, **Puerto de la Cruz.** Despite masses of high-rise hotels, the village has a small-town feel and a beautiful flower-filled central square.

Inland the road rises through banana plantations, almond groves, and pine forests to the entrance to **Mt. Teide National Park** (visitors center open daily 9–4). Before arriving at the foot of the mountain, you pass through a stark landscape called Las Cañadas del Teide, a violent jumble of rocks and minerals created by millions of years of volcanic activity. A cable car (admission 1,000 ptas; open daily 9–5, last trip up at 4) will take you within 534 feet of the top of Mt. Teide, where there are good views of the southern part of the island and neighboring Gran Canaria.

Also worth a visit are the north coast towns of **Icod de los Vinos,** which boasts a 3,000-year-old, 57-foot-tall dragon tree once worshipped by the ancient Guanches and a plaza surrounded by typical wood-balconied Canarian houses; and farther west, **Garachico,** the most peaceful and best-preserved village on this touristy isle.

Gran Canaria The "in" spot of the 60s and 70s, **Gran Canaria** has better beaches than Tenerife. Most visitors base themselves in the south coast resorts of **Playa del Inglés** and **Maspalomas,** where the white sand beach extends for 4 kilometers (2½ miles).

The central highlands of Gran Canaria provide a glimpse of rural island life. The road passes through numerous villages, and it is common to see farmers walking along the road laden with burlap sacks of potatoes. The **Parador Cruz de Tejada** specializes in traditional Canarian cuisine. Twenty-one kilometers (13 mi) beyond the parador is the **Mirador Los Pechos,** the highest viewpoint on the island.

Gran Canaria's capital, **Las Palmas,** is a vibrant Spanish city with an interesting old quarter called La Vegueta. Here you can wander cobblestone streets and visit the **Casa Museo Colón** (Columbus House and Museum, Colón 1; admission free), where the great navigator is said to have stayed when he stopped to repair the rudder on the *Pinta* before leaving to discover America. Lots of nautical paraphernalia is on display, as are ceramics and jewelry brought back by the Spanish from Mexico and Colombia. The real jewel of the capital, however, is **Las Canteras beach,** a sparkling-clean strand of white sand perfect for swimming or strolling.

Lanzarote Stark and dry, with landscapes of volcanic rock, **Lanzarote** enjoys good beaches and tasteful architecture—low-rise with a green-and-white color scheme—the latter due to the efforts of the late artist, César Manrique, a Lanzarote native who is all but worshipped for single-handedly saving the island from mass development. The **Jameos del Agua** (Water Cavern, Rte. GC710, 21 km (13 mi) north of

Arrecife) is a natural wonder created when molten lava streamed through an underground tunnel and hissed into the sea. Ponds in the caverns are home to a unique species of albino crab. The site also features an auditorium with fantastic acoustics for concerts and a restaurant/bar.

The **Parque National Timanfaya,** known as the fire mountains, takes up much of the southern part of the island. Here you can have a camel ride, take a guided coach tour of the volcanic zone, and eat lunch at one of the world's most unusual restaurants, **El Diablo,** where meat is cooked over the crater of a volcano using the earth's natural heat.

Fuerteventura The island of **Fuerteventura** was only recently discovered by tourists—mostly Germans—who come to windsurf and to enjoy the dunes of **Corralejo** and the endless white sand beaches of the **Sotovento** coast. Diving is good along the lengthy and lonely **Jandía Peninsula,** while the arid interior is largely the domain of goatherds.

La Palma Called the garden isle, **La Palma** has luxuriant foliage, tropical storms, rainbows, and black crescents of beach, the best known of which is **Los Cancajos.** Its capital, **Santa Cruz de la Palma,** was burned to the ground by pirates in 1533. It was rebuilt with assistance from the king of Spain and today remains one of the most beautiful and harmonious examples of Spanish colonial architecture.

La Gomera Tiny **La Gomera** is a paradise for the backpacking crowd. Ruggedly mountainous, it offers good hiking, and UNESCO protects its misty primeval laurel forests. La Gomera has a laid-back tropical feel with black sand beaches fringed by banana plantations. It is also the only island in the chain that has no airport and must be reached by ferry from Tenerife.

El Hierro The smallest and least-visited island in the Canaries, **El Hierro** is only for those who thrive on solitude. It is cool and windswept with a few black sand beaches, a highland pine forest for hiking, and good scuba diving around the volcanic southern tip of the island.

Dining and Lodging

For price-category definitions *see* Dining and Lodging in Essential Information, *above.*

Gran Canaria **Tenderete II.** Canarian cuisine is cherished at this unassuming little
Dining restaurant located in a shopping center. Typical soups and stews are always available for the first course, and it is one of the only restaurants in the islands that serves *gofio,* a traditional corn and barley pudding. The main course is always fish, grilled or baked in rock salt. *Av. de Tirajan, Edificio Aloe, Maspalomas, tel. 928/76–14–60. Reservations advised. Dress: casual. AE, DC, MC, V. Moderate.*

Lodging **Hotel Palm Beach.** One of the most sophisticated and luxurious hotels in the Canary Islands, the Palm Beach is located in the middle of a 1,000-year»old palm oasis at the edge of Maspalomas Beach. Spacious rooms have dark bamboo furniture, large marble baths, and terraces that overlook the sea or pool area. *Av. del Oasis s/n, 35106, Maspalomas, tel. 928/14–08–06, fax 928/14–51–08. 358 rooms with bath. Facilities: restaurant, bar, outdoor pool, tennis, shops, discotheque. AE, MC, V. Expensive.*

Lanzarote **La Era.** One of only three buildings that survived the eruption of the
Dining volcano that wiped out the town of Yaiza in 1730, this farmhouse restaurant offers simple dining rooms with blue-and-white checked tablecloths arranged around a center patio. This is a great place to try

regional dishes such as goat stew, *cherne* in cilantro sauce, or Canarian cheeses. *Barranco 3, Yaiza, tel. 928/83–00–16. Reservations not necessary. Dress: casual. AE, DC, MC, V. Inexpensive–Moderate.*

Dining and Lodging **Melia Salinas.** A stunning hotel built around an interior tropical garden, the Melia Salinas offers a chance to rub elbows with vacationing business and political leaders from all over Europe. Rooms have a tropical feel thanks to louvered closets and doors, and all include large, flower-filled terraces that face the sea. The hotel's restaurant, **La Graciosa,** Lanzarote's swankiest dining spot, overlooks the garden. A German chef prepares international cuisine with fresh island ingredients such as giant prawns, duck breast in plum sauce, and halibut wrapped in chard. *35509 Costa Teguise, tel. 928/59–00–40, fax 928/59–03–90. 310 rooms. Facilities: 2 restaurants, bar, outdoor pool, semi-private beach, tennis, squash, sauna, gym, shops. AE, DE, MC, V. Very Expensive.*

Tenerife Dining **Mesón El Drago.** In the village of El Socorro halfway between Santa Cruz and Puerto de la Cruz, this green-and-white 18th-century farmhouse with its brick floors and flower-filled patio has been converted into a showcase of typical Canarian cookery. Among the best dishes are *puchero canario,* a tangy stew of vegetables and meats, and fish casserole. *Urbanizacion San Gonzalo, El Socorro, tel. 922/54–30–01. Reservations advised weekends. Dress: casual. AE, MC, V. Open Tues.–Sun. for lunch, Fri. and Sat. for dinner. Expensive.*

Masia del Mar. There's no menu here; you simply point and choose among a vast array of fresh fish and shellfish in a big refrigerator case. Add a salad and a bottle of white wine to the order, and then find a seat on a wide terrace for a simple feast of the best food the Canary Islands has to offer, overlooking Las Caletas cove, about 5 kilometers (3 miles) west of Playa de las Americas. *Caleta de Adeje, tel. 922/71–02–41. Reservations not necessary. Dress: casual. MC, V. Moderate.*

Lodging **Gran Hotel Bahia del Duque.** This sprawling hotel is a jumble of pastel colored houses and palaces, with Renaissance windows, loggias, and quiet courtyards. Rooms feature oversized beds, summery wicker and pine furnishings, and rich architectural details such as scalloped plaster work and hand-painted ceramics. *38660 Adeje, tel. 922/75–00–00, fax 922/75–16–16. 362 rooms. Facilities: 5 restaurants, bars, 4 outdoor pools, gym, squash, sauna, beauty shop, tennis, sailing, diving. AE, MC, V. Expensive.*

Hotel Monopol. One of the town's first inns, this hotel has been lodging tourists for more than a century. Before that it was a private home built in 1742 in the Canarian patio style. Tropical plants fill the center courtyard. Rooms are simple but have good views of the sea or main plaza. *Quintana 15, 38400, Puerto de la Cruz, tel. 922/38–46–11, fax 922/37–03–10. 110 rooms with bath. Facilities: restaurant, 2 bars, outdoor pool, TV room. AE, MC, V. Moderate.*

27 Sweden

Sweden's 450,707 square kilometers (173,349 square miles) contain only 8.5 million people, so its population density ranks among Europe's lowest, and its vast open spaces and well-paved, uncrowded roads make it a country where you can easily escape the frantic pace of modern life. But the long, narrow shape of the country means that on a typical visit it is possible to explore only a relatively small area; it is unwise to be overly ambitious when planning your trip. The distances are considerable, especially by European standards—almost 1,600 kilometers (1,000 miles) as the crow flies, from north to south. The 2,128-kilometer (1,330-mile) train line from Trelleborg, in the far south, through endless birch forests to Riksgränsen, in the Arctic north, is the world's longest stretch of continuously electrified railroad.

The Swedish Travel and Tourism Council, which replaced the government-run Swedish Tourist Board in August 1992, has had an easier job marketing the country to overseas visitors in recent years due to the fall of the Swedish krona against other currencies. Visitors can expect to find Sweden up to 40% less expensive than in 1992. Those who visit Sweden usually return home raving about its high standards of lodging and dining. Even the most modest establishment is always spotless, and your hosts will welcome you warmly (almost certainly in excellent English, too).

Sweden's scenic attractions may not be as spectacular as the Norwegian fjords across the border, but the country offers a varied landscape, with forests, mountains, rushing rivers, more than 96,000 lakes, and a jagged coastline with countless archipelagoes. While Sweden is very much a modern country, it zealously guards its rural heritage. Most city dwellers have access to homes in the country to which they retreat as often as possible. Traditional arts and crafts are also highly prized.

The cities, too, make the most of their natural settings and are carefully planned, with an emphasis on light and open spaces. Stockholm, one of the most beautiful of European capitals, is the major metropolitan attraction, though Gothenburg, on the west coast, and Malmö, just across the sound from Denmark, are worthy of short visits as well.

Essential Information

Before You Go

When to Go In an attempt to encourage visitors from abroad, Sweden has extended the main tourist season to run from mid-May through mid-September. Bear in mind, however, that many attractions close in late August when the Swedes' own vacation season ends and children return to school. The weather can also be magnificent in the spring and fall, and there are plenty of tourists who prefer sightseeing when fewer people are around.

The concentrated nature of the Swedes' own vacation period—Sweden virtually shuts up shop for the entire month of July—can sometimes make it difficult to get hotel reservations during July and early August. On the other hand, the big city hotels, which cater mainly to business travelers, reduce their rates drastically in the summer, when their ordinary clients are on vacation. (If you're traveling fall through spring, the high season for business travel, be forewarned that prices are high.) Ask your travel agent about special discounts offered by the major hotel groups, or contact the tour-

Sweden

0   50 miles
0   75 km

Riksgränsen
Kiruna

Arctic Circle

*Norwegian
Sea*

Gällivare
Luleälven
Jokkmokk
400

Arjeplog
Tärnaby
Töre
Torneå
Arvidsjaur
Kalix
E79
Sorsele
95
Luleå
Storuman
Piteå
Lycksele
Skellefteå
342
Åsele
Umeälven
92
90
Umeå
Strömsund
Åre
Östersund
E75

Tännäs
Sundsvall
NORWAY
84
Ljungan
FINLAND
Idre
Hudiksvall
*Gulf
of
Bothnia*
70
Bollnäs
Mora
Söderhamn
62
Falun
Gävle
80
Klarälven
Borlänge
Avesta
Fagersta
E4
Karlstad
Uppsala
Västerås
Åland
E18
Mellerud
Mälaren
Stockholm
Strömstad
Vänern
Örebro
Gulf of Finland
Uddevalla
Trollhättan
Norrköping
Göteborg
(Gothenburg)
Vättern
*Gotska
Sandön*
ESTONIA
Linköping
Borås
40
Jönköping
*Baltic
Sea*
Nässjö
Visby
*Gulf of
Riga*
Falkenberg
E6
Värnamo
E06
Oskarshamn
Gotland
Halmstad
Växjö
Öland
LATVIA
23
Kalmar
Helsingborg
Karlskrona
Malmö
Kristianstad
DENMARK
LITHUANIA
Trelleborg
Ystad

ist information center, **Next Stop Sweden** (Box 10134, 121 28 Stockholm, tel. 08/725–5500, fax 08/649–8882). Once you're in Sweden, you might also pay a visit to **Upptäck Sverige Resor** (Discover Sweden Travel Agency, Hamngatan 27, tel. 08/791–8085, fax. 08/791–8889) for well-priced seasonal package tours throughout Sweden.

Climate Like the rest of northern Europe, Sweden has unpredictable summer weather, but, as a general rule, it is more likely to be rainy on the west coast than on the east. When the sun shines, the climate is usually agreeable; it is rarely hot. In Stockholm it never really gets dark in midsummer, while in the far north, above the Arctic Circle, the sun doesn't set between the end of May and the middle of July.

The following are the average daily maximum and minimum temperatures for Stockholm.

Jan.	30F	– 1C	May	58F	14C	Sept.	60F	15C
	23	– 5		43	6		49	9
Feb.	30F	– 1C	June	67F	19C	Oct.	49F	9C
	22	– 5		51	11		41	5
Mar.	37F	3C	July	71F	22C	Nov.	40F	5C
	26	– 4		57	14		34	1
Apr.	47F	8C	Aug.	68F	20C	Dec.	35F	3C
	34F	1C		55F	13C		28F	– 2C

Currency The unit of currency in Sweden is the krona (plural kronor), which is divided into 100 öre and is written as SEK or kr. Coins come in values of 50 öre and 1, 5, or 10 kronor, while bills come in denominations of 20, 50, 100, 500, and 1,000 SEK. Traveler's checks and foreign currency can be exchanged at banks all over Sweden and at post offices bearing the NB Exchange sign. At press time (spring 1994), the exchange rate was 7.35 kronor to the dollar and 10.75 kronor to the pound sterling.

What It Will Cost Sweden is seen as an expensive country but, in recent years, hotel prices have fallen in line with the European average. As in most countries, the most expensive hotels are found in major cities. Restaurant prices are generally high, but there are bargains to be had: Look for the *dagens rätt* (dish of the day) in many city restaurants. This costs about SEK 50–SEK 65 and can include a main dish, salad, soft drink, bread and butter, and coffee.

Many hotels have special low summer rates and cut prices during weekends in winter. But because of heavy taxes and excise duties, liquor prices remain among the highest in Europe. It pays to take in your maximum duty-free allowance. Value-added tax (known as *Moms* in Swedish) is imposed on most goods and services at a rate of 25%, with the exception of a 21% Moms on food, hotels, restaurants, and transportation. You can get a refund for most of the tax on goods if you take advantage of the tax-free shopping service offered at more than 13,000 stores throughout the country (*see* Shopping in Staying in Sweden, *below*).

Sample Prices Cup of coffee, SEK 10–SEK 15; bottle of beer, SEK 30–SEK 40; Coca-Cola, SEK 12–SEK 15; ham sandwich, SEK 25–SEK 35; 1-mile taxi ride, SEK 70 (depending on the taxi company).

Customs on Arrival You may bring duty-free into Sweden 400 cigarettes or 200 cigarillos or 100 cigars or 500 grams of tobacco. You may also import 1 liter of spirits and 1 liter of wine *or* 2 liters of beer, plus a reasonable amount of perfume and other goods to the value of SEK 600. Residents over the age of 15 of other European countries may bring duty-free into Sweden 200 cigarettes or 100 cigarillos, or 50 cigars or 250 grams of tobacco; visitors over 19 years old may import 1 liter of spirits, 1 liter of wine, and 2 liters of beer, plus a reasonable amount of perfume, and other goods to the value of SEK 600. There are no limits on the amount of foreign currency that can be imported or exported.

Language Virtually all Swedes you are likely to meet will speak English, for it is a mandatory subject in all schools and is the first foreign language that Swedish children learn. Some of the older people you encounter in the rural areas may not be so familiar with English, but you'll soon find someone who can help out.

Getting Around

By Car Sweden has an excellent highway network of more than 80,000 ki-
Road lometers (50,000 miles). The fastest routes are those with numbers
Conditions prefixed with an E (for "European"), some of which are the equivalent of American superhighways or British motorways—for part of the way, at least. Road E4, for instance, covers the entire distance from Malmö, in the south, to Stockholm, and on to Sundsvall and Umeå, in the north, finishing at Haparanda, on the border with Finland. All main and secondary roads are well surfaced, but some minor roads, particularly in the north, are graveled.

Rules of the You drive on the right and, no matter where you sit in a car, you must
Road wear a seat belt. You must also have low-beam headlights on at all times. Signs indicate five basic speed limits, ranging from 30 kph (19 mph) in school or playground areas to 110 kph (69 mph) on long stretches of E roads.

Parking Park on the right-hand side of the road, but if you want to park overnight, particularly in suburban areas, be sure not to do so on the night the street is being cleaned; signs should indicate when this occurs. Parking meters and, increasingly, timed ticket machines, are available for use in larger towns, usually between 8 AM and 6 PM. The fee varies from about SEK 4 to SEK 20 per hour. A circular sign with a red cross on a blue background with a red border means parking is prohibited. A yellow plate with a red border means restricted parking. The fees for parking tickets are extraordinarily high in Sweden.

Gasoline Sweden has some of the highest gasoline rates in Europe, about SEK 7.36 per liter, depending on the grade. Lead-free gasoline is readily available. Most gas stations are self-service places, indicated by the sign Tanka Själv. Many have automatic pumps, which accept SEK 50 or SEK 100 bills, where you can fill up at any time, night or day. Some take credit cards.

Breakdowns The **Larmtjänst** organization, run by a confederation of Swedish insurance companies, provides a 24-hour breakdown service. Its phone numbers are listed in all telephone books. A toll-free emergency number, tel. 020/910040, is also available.

By Train Sweden's rail network, mostly electrified, is highly efficient, and trains operate frequently, particularly on the main routes linking Stockholm with Gothenburg and Malmö. First- and second-class cars are provided on all main routes, and sleeping cars are available in both classes on overnight trains. On long-distance trains, there is usually a buffet or dining car. Seat reservations are advisable, and on some trains—indicated with R or IC on the timetable—they are compulsory. Reservations can be made right up to departure time at a cost of SEK 20 per seat (tel. 020/757575). In addition, the Swedish rail network operates several daily high-speed trains called the

X2000 between Stockholm and Gothenburg (the trip takes less than three hours).

Fares   On "Low price" or "Red" departures, fares are reduced by 50%, but careful planning is necessary to take advantage of the lower prices. Passengers paying low fares cannot make stopovers and the tickets are valid for only 36 hours.

By Plane   Sweden's domestic air network is highly developed. Most major cities are served by **SAS** (tel. 020/727555). From Stockholm, there are services to about 30 points around the country. SAS offers cut-rate round-trip "minifares" every day of the week on selected flights, and these fares are available on most services during the peak tourist season, from late June to mid-August. Some even more favorable offers on domestic flights are frequently available from the end of June through early August and during the Christmas and Easter seasons.

By Bus   Sweden has an excellent network of express bus services that provides an inexpensive and relatively speedy way of getting around the country. **Swebus** (tel. 08/237190 offers daily bus services from most major Swedish cities to various parts of Sweden. A number of other private companies operate weekend-only services on additional routes. In the far north of Sweden, post buses delivering mail to remote areas also carry passengers, providing an offbeat and inexpensive way to see the countryside.

By Boat   The classic boat trip in Sweden is the four-day journey along the Göta Canal between Gothenburg and Stockholm, operated by **Göta Kanal,** Gothenburg, tel. 031/806315.

By Bicycle   Cycling is popular in Sweden, and the country's uncongested roads make it ideal for extended bike tours. Bicycles can be rented throughout the country; inquire at the local tourist information office. Rental costs average around SEK 80 per day or SEK 400 per week. The **Swedish Touring Club** (STF) in Stockholm (tel. 08/790–3100) can give you information about cycling packages that include bike rental, overnight accommodations, and meals. **Cykelfrämjandet** (tel. 08/321680) has an English-language guide to cycling trips.

Staying in Sweden

Telephones   Sweden has plenty of pay phones, although they are not found (as in
Local Calls   many other European countries) in post offices. There are, however, special offices marked Tele or Telebutik from which you can make calls. To make calls from a pay phone, you should have SEK 1, SEK 5, or SEK 10 coins available. You can also purchase a *telefonkort* (telephone card) from a Telebutik, hospital, or *Pressbyrån* store for SEK 45 or SEK 80, which can be cheaper if you make numerous domestic calls. For a local call, you need two SEK 1 coins.

International   These can be made from any pay phone. For calls to the United
Calls   States and Canada, dial 009, then 1 (the country code), then wait for a second dial tone before dialing the area code and number. When dialing the United Kingdom, omit the initial zero on area codes (for Central London you would dial 009 followed by 44, wait for the second tone, then dial 71 and the local number). Making calls from your hotel room is convenient but can be expensive, so check with the front desk about rates first. You pay the normal rate at Telebutik offices.

Operators and   The international exchange number is 0018. Dial 07975 for directory
Information   assistance in Sweden, and 07977 for foreign inquiries.

Mail
Postal Rates Airmail letters and postcards to the United States and Canada weighing less than 20 grams cost SEK 6.00. Postcards and letters within Europe cost SEK 5.00.

Receiving Mail If you're uncertain where you will be staying, have your mail sent to Poste Restante, S-101 10 Stockholm. The address for collection is Vasagatan 28–32. A Poste Restante service is also offered by American Express (*see* Important Addresses and Numbers in Stockholm, *below*).

Shopping Swedish goods have earned an international reputation for elegance and quality, and any visitor to the country should spend some time exploring the many impressive shops and department stores. The midsummer tourist season is as good a time as any to go shopping, for that is when many stores have their annual sales. The best buys are glassware, stainless steel, pottery and ceramics, leather goods, and textiles. You will find a wide selection of goods available in such major stores as **NK, Åhléns, PUB,** and **Konsum,** which have branches all over the country.

High-quality furniture is a Swedish specialty, and it is worthwhile to visit one of the many branches of **IKEA,** a shop usually located on the outskirts of major towns. IKEA's prices are extremely competitive, and the company also operates an export service. For glassware at bargain prices, head for the "Kingdom of Glass" (*see* The West Coast and the Glass Country, *below*). All the major glassworks, including **Orrefors** and **Kosta Boda,** have large factory outlets where you can pick up "seconds" (normally indistinguishable from the perfect product) at only a fraction of the normal retail price. For clothing, the best center is Borås, not far from Gothenburg. Here you can find bargains from the leading mail-order companies. In country areas, look for the local **Hemslöjd** craft centers, featuring high-quality clothing and needlework items.

VAT Refunds About 13,000 Swedish shops—1,000 in Stockholm alone—participate in the tax-free shopping program for visitors, enabling you to claim a refund on most of the value-added tax that you have paid. Shops taking part in this service display a distinctive black, blue, and yellow sticker in the window. (Some stores offer the service only on purchases worth more than SEK 200.) Whenever you make a purchase in a participating store, the store wraps and seals your purchase and you are given a "Tax-Free shopping check" equivalent to the tax paid, less a handling charge. This check can be cashed when you leave Sweden and show your unopened packages, either at the airport or aboard ferries. You should have your passport with you when you make your purchase and when you claim your refund.

Opening and Closing Times **Banks** are open weekdays 9:30–3, but some stay open until 5:30 in larger cities. Banks at Stockholm's Arlanda Airport and Gothenburg's Landvetter Airport are open every day, with extended hours. **Forex** and **Valuta Specialisten** currency-exchange offices operate in downtown Stockholm, Gothenburg, and Malmö, also with extended hours.

Hours vary widely, but **museums** are typically open weekdays 10–4 or 10–5. Many are also open on weekends but may close on Monday.

Shops are generally open weekdays 9 or 9:30–6 and Saturday 9–1 or 9–4. Some department stores remain open until 8 or 10 on certain evenings, and some are also open Sunday noon–4 in major cities. Many supermarkets open on Sunday.

National Holidays January 1; January 6 (Epiphany); April 14 (Good Friday); April 17 (Easter Monday); May 1 (Labor Day); May 25 (Ascension); June 4, 5

(Pentecost); June 23 (Midsummer's Eve); June 24 (Midsummer's Day); November 4 (All Saints' Day); December 25, 26. Hotels and restaurants may close for some of these holidays.

Dining Swedish cuisine used to be considered somewhat uninteresting, but lately it has become much more cosmopolitan. The inevitable fast-food outlets, such as McDonald's and Burger King, have come on the scene, as well as Clock, the homegrown version. But there is also a good range of more conventional restaurants, from the usual top-class establishments to less expensive places where you can pick up a somewhat cheaper lunch or snack. Snacks can also be enjoyed in a *Konditori*, which offers inexpensive sandwiches, pastries, and pies with coffee, tea, or soft drinks. A cross between a café and a coffee shop, the Konditori can be found in every city and town.

Many restaurants all over the country specialize in *Husmanskost*—literally "home cooking"—which is based on traditional Swedish recipes.

Sweden is best known for its *smörgåsbord*, a word whose correct pronunciation defeats non-Swedes. It consists of a tempting buffet of hot and cold dishes, usually with a strong emphasis on seafood, notably herring, prepared in a wide variety of ways. Authentic smörgåsbord can be enjoyed all over the country, but the best is found in the many inns in Skåne, where you can eat as much as you want for about SEK 200. Many Swedish hotels serve a lavish smörgåsbord-style breakfast, often included in the room price. Do justice to your breakfast and you'll probably want to skip lunch!

Mealtimes Swedes eat early. Restaurants start serving lunch at about 11 AM, and outside the main cities you may find that they close quite early in the evening (often by 9) or may not open at all for dinner. Don't wait too long to look for someplace to have a meal.

Dress Except for the most formal restaurants, where a jacket and tie are preferable, casual—or casual chic—attire is perfectly acceptable for restaurants in all price categories.

Ratings Prices are per person and include a first course and main course, but no drinks. Service charges and Moms are included in the meal, so there is no need to tip. Best bets are indicated by a star ★.

Category	Cost
Very Expensive	over SEK 350
Expensive	SEK 250–SEK 350
Moderate	SEK 120–SEK 250
Inexpensive	under SEK 120

Lodging Sweden offers a wide range of accommodations, from simple village rooms and campsites to hotels of the highest international standard. Except at the major hotels in the larger cities that cater mainly to a business clientele, rates are fairly reasonable. Prices are normally on a per-room basis and include all taxes and service and usually breakfast. Apart from the more modest inns and the cheapest budget establishments, private baths and showers are now standard features, although it is just as well to double-check when making your reservation. Whatever their size, virtually all Swedish hotels provide scrupulously clean accommodations and courteous service. In Stockholm, there is a hotel reservation office—**Hotellcentralen**—at the central train station and at the Stockholm Tourist Center in the Sweden House. In other areas, local tourist offices will help you with hotel reservations.

Hotels You can get a good idea of the facilities and prices at a particular hotel by consulting the official annual guide, "Hotels in Sweden," obtainable free of charge from the Swedish Travel and Tourism Council. There is a good selection of hotels in all price categories in every town and city, though major international chains such as Sheraton have made only small inroads in Sweden thus far. The main homegrown chains are Scandic and RESO. The Sweden Hotels group has about 100 independently owned hotels and offers a central reservation office. The group also has its own classification scheme—A, B, or C—based on the facilities available at each establishment. CountrySide Sweden is a group of 35 handpicked resort hotels, some of them restored historic manor houses or centuries-old inns. Most have been family-run for generations.

House-Rental In Sweden, these are popular among other Europeans, particularly *Vacations* the British and Germans. There are about 250 chalet villages with amenities, such as grocery stores, restaurants, saunas, and tennis courts. You can often arrange such accommodations on the spot at local tourist information offices. An alternative is a package, such as the one offered by **Scandinavian Seaways,** that combines a ferry trip from Britain across the North Sea with a stay in a chalet village. Scandinavian Seaways is based in the United Kingdom at Parkeston Quay, Harwich, Essex (tel. 0255/240240). Their number in Gothenburg is 031/650600.

Camping Camping is also popular in Sweden. There are about 750 officially approved sites throughout the country, most located next to the sea or a lake and offering such activities as windsurfing, riding, and tennis. They are generally open between June 1 and September 1, though some are available year round. The National Swedish Camping Association publishes, in English, an abbreviated list of sites.

Ratings Prices are for two people in a double room, based on summer season rates, tax and breakfast are included. Best bets are indicated by a star ★.

Category	Cost
Very Expensive	over SEK 1,200
Expensive	SEK 970–SEK 1,200
Moderate	SEK 725–SEK 970
Inexpensive	under SEK 725

Tipping Swedes seldom expect tips. In hotels, tip the porter about SEK 5 per item). Taxi drivers do not expect a tip. A consistent but irritating feature of the Swedish restaurant scene is that you must always dispose of your coat or sports jacket, whether you want to or not; the fee for leaving a coat in the checkroom is between SEK 6 and SEK 15.

Stockholm

Arriving and Departing

By Plane All international flights arrive at Arlanda Airport, 40 kilometers (25 miles) north of the city. The airport is linked to Stockholm by a major freeway. For information on arrival and departure times, call the individual airlines.

Between the Buses leave both the international and domestic terminals every 10–
Airport and 15 minutes, from 7:10 AM to 10:30 PM, and run to the city terminal at
Downtown Klarabergsviadukten next to the central train station. The bus costs
SEK 50 per person. A bus-taxi package is available (tel. 08/670–1010)
for SEK 150 per person inside city limits and SEK 200 anywhere in the
Stockholm area. A taxi directly from the airport will cost at least SEK
250 (be sure to ask the driver if he offers the standard SEK 250 airport-
to-city rate before you get into the taxi), but a possible alternative if
you are not traveling alone is the SAS limousine service to any point in
greater Stockholm. It operates as a shared taxi at SEK 300 plus Moms.
If two or three people travel together in a limousine to the same address, only one pays the full rate; all others pay SEK 75 plus Moms.

By Train Major domestic and international trains arrive at Stockholm Central
Station on Vasagatan, in the heart of the city. This is also the terminus for local commuter services. For train information 7 AM–10 PM,
tel. 020/757575. At the station there is a ticket and information office,
where you can make seat or sleeping-car reservations. An automatic
ticket-issuing machine is also available. Seat reservations on the regular train cost SEK 20, couchettes SEK 75, and beds SEK 155. Seat reservations on the X2000, the high-speed train between Stockholm and
Gothenburg, costs SEK 245. Add SEK 689 for the first-class fare and
SEK 394 for the second-class fare.

By Bus Long-distance buses, from such places as Härnösand and Sundsvall,
arrive at Norra Bantorget, a few blocks north of the central train
station, and all others at Klarabergsviadukten, just beside the train
station. Bus tickets can also be bought at the railroad reservations
office.

By Car There are two main access routes from the west and south: the E20
main highway from Gothenburg and E4 from Malmö, which continues as the main route to Sundsvall, the far north, and Finland. All
routes to the city center are well marked.

Getting Around

The most cost-effective way of getting around Stockholm is to use a
Stockholmskortet (Key to Stockholm) card. Besides giving unlimited transportation on city subway, bus, and rail services, it offers
free admission to 60 museums and several sightseeing trips. The
card costs SEK 150 for 24 hours, SEK 300 for two days, and SEK 450
for three days. It is available from the tourist center at Sweden
House, at Kungsträdgården, and the Hotellcentralen accommodations bureau at the central train station.

Maps and timetables for all city transportation networks are available from the Stockholm Transit Authority (SL) information desks
at Norrmalmstorg or Sergels Torg. You can also obtain information
by phone (tel. 08/600–1000).

By Bus The Stockholm Transit Authority (SL) operates both the bus and
and Subway subway systems. Tickets for the two networks are interchangeable.

The subway system, known as T-banan (the *T* stands for tunnel), is
the easiest and fastest way of getting around the city. Some of the
stations offer permanent art exhibitions. Station entrances are
marked with a blue T on a white background. The T-banan has about
100 stations and covers more than 60 route-miles. Trains run frequently between 5 AM and 2 AM.

The subway and bus fare system is based on zones. The least you will pay is SEK 13, good for travel within one zone, such as downtown, for a short time period. You pay more if you travel in more than one zone.

Tickets are available at ticket counters, but it is cheaper to buy a special discount coupon that gives a significant savings compared with buying separate tickets each time you travel. The coupons are available at Pressbyrån newsstands. A one-day ticket for the city center alone, valid on both bus and subway, costs SEK 30. A ticket covering the entire Greater Stockholm area costs SEK 60 for 24 hours or SEK 115 for 72 hours. People under 18 or over 65 pay half price. Also available from the Pressbyrån newsstands are SEK 80 coupons, good for 10 subway rides in the central zone.

The Stockholm bus network is one of the world's largest. Services run not only within the central area but also to out-of-town points of interest, such as Waxholm, with its historic fortress, and Gustavsberg, with its well-known porcelain factory. Within greater Stockholm, buses run throughout the night.

By Train SL operates conventional train services from Stockholm Central Station to a number of nearby points, including Nynäshamn, a departure point for ferries to the island of Gotland. Trains also run from the Slussen station to the fashionable seaside resort of Saltsjöbaden.

By Taxi Thanks to a deregulation of the taxi market in December 1992, taxi prices have fallen considerably. Typically, a trip of 10 kilometers (6 miles) will cost SEK 82 between 6 AM and 7 PM on weekdays and SEK 92 on weekday nights; weekend prices are SEK 102, including Moms. Major taxi companies are Taxi Stockholm (tel. 08/150000), Taxi 1 (tel. 08/670–0000), and Taxikurir (tel. 08/300000).

Important Addresses and Numbers

Tourist Information The main tourist center is at **Sweden House** (Kungsträdgården, tel. 08/789–2490). During the peak tourist season (mid-May to mid-September), it is open weekdays 8:30–6; weekends 8–5. The current off-season hours are 9–5 and 9–2, respectively. Besides providing information, it is the main ticket center for sightseeing excursions. There are also information centers at the central train station, in the City Hall (summer only), and in the Kaknäs TV Tower. When planning to visit any of the tourist attractions in Stockholm, be sure to call ahead as opening times and prices are subject to change.

Embassies **U.S.** (Strandvägen 101, tel. 08/783–5300). **Canadian** (Tegelbacken 4, tel. 08/613–9900). **U.K.** (Skarpögatan 6–8, tel. 08/667–0140).

Emergencies **Police** (tel. 08/769–3000; emergencies only: 90000); **Ambulance** (tel. 90000); **Doctor** (Medical Care Information, tel. 08/644–9200)—tourists can get hospital attention in the district where they are staying or can contact the private clinic, **City Akuten** (tel. 08/117102); **Dentist** (tel. 08/654–1117); **Pharmacy: C. W. Scheele** (tel. 08/248280) (all are indicated by the sign Apotek).

English-Language Bookstores Most bookstores have a good selection of English books. **Akademibokhandeln** (Mäster Samuelsgatan 32, tel. 08/214890), which belongs to a chain of bookstores, has the widest selection of paperbacks, dictionaries, and maps in many languages.

Travel Agencies **American Express** (Birger Jarlsgatan 1, tel. 08/235330). **Thomas Cook** (Ulvsundavägen 178B, Bromma, tel. 88/764–5555).

Guided Tours

Orientation Tours Some 30 different tours—by foot, boat, bus, or a combination of these—are available during the summer. Some last only 30 minutes, others an entire day. A popular three-hour bus tour, costing SEK 200, runs daily at 9:45 AM and 1:45 PM. The tour includes City Hall, Storkyrkan in Gamla Stan, the Vasa Ship, and the Royal Palace, among other stops. Tickets can be purchased from the Excursion Shop at Sweden House. A convenient budget-price tour by boat and/or bus is SL's "Tourist Route" (Turistlinjen). The tour departs every 15 minutes during peak vacation periods and every half hour at other times; you can get on and off at any one of the 14 stops. This tour is free for holders of the Key to Stockholm card but is conducted in Swedish only.

Boat Tours You'll find a bewildering variety of tours available at Stockholm's quay. The **Waxholm Steamship Company** (tel. 08/679–5830) operates scheduled services to many islands in the archipelago on its famous white steamers. Trips range from one to three hours each way. Popular one-day excursions include Waxholm, Utö, Sandhamn, and Möja. Conventional sightseeing tours include a one-hour circular city tour run by the **Strömma Canal Company** (tel. 08/233375). It leaves from the Nybroplan quay every hour between 10 and 5 in summer.

Special-Interest Tours A range of special-interest tours is available in the Stockholm area, especially in summer. These include a weekend at a chalet in the archipelago, rental of a small fishing boat, or the chance to buy porcelain at the Gustavsberg porcelain factory, just outside Stockholm. Several outstanding 17th-century villas and estates within an hour or two of Stockholm have been converted into quaint, high-quality hotels, such as the stately Ulvhälls Herrgård in Strängnäs on Lake Mälaren. Contact the tourist center at the Sweden House for details.

Excursions Don't miss the boat trip to the 17th-century Palace of Drottningholm, the private residence of the Swedish Royal Family and a smaller version of Versailles. Departures are every half hour between 10 and 4:30 during the summer from the City Hall Bridge (Stadshusbron). Another popular trip goes from Stadshusbron to the ancient towns of Sigtuna and Skokloster. By changing boats you can continue to Uppsala to catch the train back to Stockholm. Information is available from the **Strömma Canal Company** (tel. 08/233375) or the Tourist Center at Sweden House.

Personal Guides Contact the **Guide Center** at **Stockholm Information Service** (tel. 08/789–2496).

Exploring Stockholm

Numbers in the margin correspond to points of interest on the Stockholm map.

Because Stockholm's main attractions are concentrated in a relatively small area, the city itself can be explored in a few days. But if you want to take advantage of some of the full-day excursions offered, it is worthwhile to devote a full week to your visit.

The city of Stockholm, built on 14 small islands among open bays and narrow channels, has been dubbed the "Venice of the North," but Stockholmers refer to their city simply as "Beauty on Water." It is a handsome, civilized city, full of parks, squares, and airy boulevards, yet it is also a bustling, modern metropolis. Glass-and-steel skyscrapers abound, but in the center you are never more than five minutes' walk from twisting, medieval streets and waterside walks.

The first written mention of Stockholm dates from 1252, when a powerful regent named Birger Jarl is said to have built a fortified castle here. And it must have been this strategic position, where the calm, fresh waters of Lake Mälaren meet the salty Baltic Sea, that prompted King Gustav Vasa to take over the city in 1523, and King Gustavus Adolphus to make it the heart of an empire a century later.

During the Thirty Years' War (1618–48), Sweden gained importance as a Baltic trading state, and Stockholm grew commensurately. But by the beginning of the 18th century, Swedish influence had begun to wane, and Stockholm's development slowed. It did not pick up until the Industrial Revolution, when the hub of the city moved north from the Old Town area.

City Hall and the Old Town Anyone in Stockholm with limited time should give priority to a tour of **Gamla Stan** (the Old Town), a labyrinth of narrow, medieval streets, alleys, and quiet squares on the island just south of the city center. Ideally, you should devote an entire day to this district. But before crossing the bridge from the city center, walk west across ❶ Stadshusbron to the modern-day **City Hall,** constructed in 1923 and now one of the symbols of Stockholm. Lavish mosaics adorn the walls of the **Golden Hall,** and the **Prince's Gallery** features a collection of large murals by Prince Eugene, brother of King Gustav V. Take the elevator halfway up, then climb the rest of the way to the top of the 106-meter (348-foot) tower for a magnificent view of the city. *Tel. 08/785–9074. Admission: SEK 25. Tours daily at 10 and noon; also at 11 and 2 in summer. Tower admission: SEK 15. Tower open May–Sept., daily 10–3.*

Retrace your steps over the bridge and head for Drottninggatan, the main walking street, and turn right onto Riksbron. Crossing into the Old Town, the first thing you'll see is the magnificent ❷ **Riddarholm Church,** where a host of Swedish kings are buried. *Tel. 08/789–8500. Admission: SEK 10. Open Mon.–Sat. 10–3, Sun. noon–3.*

❸ Proceed to the **Royal Palace,** preferably by noon, when you can see the colorful changing-of-the-guard ceremony. The smartly dressed guards seem superfluous, since tourists wander at will into the castle courtyard and around the grounds. Several separate attractions are open to the public. Be sure to visit the **Royal Armory,** with its outstanding collection of weaponry and royal regalia. The **Treasury** houses the Swedish crown jewels, including the regalia used for the coronation of King Erik XIV in 1561. You can also visit the **State Apartments,** where the king swears in each successive government. *Tel. 08/789–8500. Admission: SEK 40 for Armory and Treasury; SEK 30 for State Apartments. Call ahead for opening hours, as they are subject to change.*

From the palace, stroll down **Västerlånggatan,** one the main streets in the Old Town. This is a popular shopping area, brimming with boutiques and antiques shops. Walk down to the Skeppsbron waterfront, then head back toward the center over the Ström bridge, where anglers cast for salmon. If you feel like a rest, stop off at ❹ **Kungsträdgården** and watch the world go by. Originally built as a royal kitchen garden, the property was turned into a public park in 1562. During the summer, entertainment and activities abound, and you can watch people playing open-air chess with giant chess pieces. During the winter months, the park has a skating rink.

Djurgården Be sure to spend at least a day visiting the many attractions on the large island of **Djurgården.** Although it's only a short walk from the city center, the most pleasant way to approach it is by ferry from Skeppsbron, in the Old Town. The ferries drop you off near two of Stockholm's best-known attractions, the Vasa Museum and Gröna Lund Tivoli. Or you might want to take the reinstated streetcar, which runs along refurbished tracks from Norrmalmstorg, near the city center, to **Prince Eugene's Waldemarsudde,** (tel. 08/662–2800), an art museum in the former summer residence of a Swedish prince, on a peninsula in Djurgården. The *Vasa,* a restored 17th-century warship, is one of the oldest preserved war vessels in the world and has become Sweden's most popular tourist sight. It sank ignominiously in Stockholm Harbor on its maiden voyage in 1628, reportedly because it was not carrying sufficient ballast. Recovered in 1961, the ship has been restored to its original appearance and is housed in a ⑤ spectacular museum, the **Vasamuseet,** which opened in 1990. It features guided tours, films, and displays. *Gälarvarvet, tel. 08/666– 4800. Admission: SEK 40 adults, SEK 10 students. Open daily 9:30–7.*

⑥ **Gröna Lund Tivoli,** Stockholm's version of the famous Copenhagen amusement park, is a favorite family attraction, featuring hair-raising roller coasters as well as tamer delights. *Tel. 08/665–7000. Open late Apr.–early Sept. Call ahead for prices and hours, as they are subject to change.*

⑦ Just across the road is **Skansen,** a large, open-air folk museum showcasing 150 reconstructed traditional buildings from Sweden's different regions. Here you can see a variety of handicraft displays and demonstrations. There is also an attractive zoo—with many native Scandinavian species, such as lynxes, wolves, reindeer, and brown bears—as well as an excellent aquarium. *Tel. 08/663–0500. Call ahead for prices and times, as they are subject to change.*

Time Out For a mediocre snack and a great view, try the **Solliden Restaurant** at Skansen. Skansen also offers a selection of open-air snack bars and cafés; Gröna Lund has four different restaurants and many snack bars.

From the zoo, head back toward the city center. Just before the ⑧ Djurgårdsbron, you come to the **Nordic Museum,** which, like Skansen, provides insight into the way Swedish people have lived over the past 500 years. The collection includes displays of peasant costumes, folk art, and Sami culture. *Tel. 08/666–4600. Admission: SEK 30–SEK 50 adults. Call ahead for prices and hours.*

⑨ Once you're back on the "mainland," drop into the **Museum of National Antiquities.** Though its name is uninspiring, it houses some remarkable Viking gold and silver treasures. **The Royal Cabinet of Coin,** located in the same building, boasts the world's largest coin. *Tel. 08/783–9400. Narvavägen 13–17. Admission free.*

Stockholm Environs

The region surrounding Stockholm offers many attractions that can easily be seen on day trips from the capital.

One "must" is the trip to the majestic 16th-century **Gripsholm Castle,** at Mariefred, on the southern side of Lake Mälaren and about 64 kilometers (40 miles) from Stockholm. Gripsholm, with its drawbridge and four massive round towers, is one of Sweden's most romantic castles. There had been a castle on the site as early as the

Stockholm

Major Attractions
City Hall, **1**
Gröna Lund Tivoli, **6**
Kungsträdgården, **4**
Museum of National Antiquities, **9**
Nordic Museum, **8**
Riddarholm Church, **2**
Royal Palace, **3**
Skansen, **7**
Vasamuseet, **5**

Other Attractions
Cathedral, **22**
Concert Hall, **12**
House of Nobles, **20**
Kaknäs TV Tower, **15**
Kulturhuset, **23**
Museum of Far Eastern Antiquities, **18**
Museum of Modern Art, **14**
National Museum, **16**

NK, **24**
Parliament, **21**
Prince Eugene's Waldemarsudde, **25**
Royal Dramatic Theater, **11**
Royal Library, **13**
Royal Opera House, **17**
Stock Exchange, **10**
Supreme Court, **19**

ÖSTERMALM

Kommendörsgatan

Karlaplan

Sibyllegatan

Linnégatan

Narvavägen

Banérgatan

Karlavägen

LADUGÅRDSGÄRDET

Oxenstiernsgatan

Linnégatan

9

Artillerigatan

Skeppargatan

Grevgatan

Styrmangatan

Storgatan

Riddargatan

Gärdesgatan

Storgatan

15

Strandvägen

Strandvägen

Djurgårdsbron

Djurgårdsbrunnsviken

8

Rosendalsvägen

5

18

DJURGÅRDEN

14

SKEPPSHOLMEN

7

Svensksundsvägen

Sirishovsvägen

Alkärret

Djurgårdsvägen

Falkenbergsg.

Djurgårds
Slätten

Solfids backen

Singelbacken

Allmänna Gränd

KASTELL-
HOLMEN

6

25

Baltic →

BECKHOLMEN

Saltsjön

ömmen

KEY

N

AE American Express
Office

_i_ Tourist Information

——— Rail Lines

0   500 yards

0   500 meters

Stockholm Environs

N · Tärnsjö · Heby · 72 · Uppsala · Norrtälje · Sala · 55 · E4 · 76 · 276 · Skokloster Palace · Sigtuna · 70 · Enköping · E18 · Västerås · Mälaren · Vaxholm · Gustavsberg · Strängnäs · Södertälje · Stockholm · Eskilstuna · Gripsholm Castle · Mariefred · E3 · 225 · 67 · Ornö · 57 · Utö · 56 · Nynäshamn · Katrineholm · E4 · 53 · Baltic Sea · 55 · Nyköping · Öxelösund · 0 — 20 miles · 0 — 30 km · Bråviken · Norrköping

1380s, but it was destroyed, and King Gustav Vasa had the present building erected in 1577. Today the castle is best known for housing the Swedish state collection of portraits and is one of the largest portrait galleries in the world, with some 3,400 paintings.

The most pleasant way of traveling to Gripsholm from Stockholm is on the vintage steamer *Mariefred*, the last coal-fired ship on Lake Mälaren. Departures, between mid-June and late August, are from the city hall daily, except Monday, at 10 AM, leaving from Mariefred at 4:30. The journey takes 3½ hours each way, and there is a restaurant on board. *Tel. 08/669–8850. Round-trip fare: SEK 140. Castle tel. 0159/10194. Admission to castle: SEK 30.*

Another popular boat trip goes to **Skokloster Palace,** about 70 kilometers (44 miles) from Stockholm. Departures are from the city hall bridge (Stadshusbron) daily, except Monday and Friday, between early June and mid-August. The route follows the narrow inlets of Lake Mälaren along the "Royal Waterway" and stops at **Sigtuna,** an ancient trading center. You can get off the boat here; visit the town, which has medieval ruins and an 18th-century town hall; and catch the boat again on the return journey. Or stay on board and continue to Skokloster, an impressive palace dating from the 1650s. Built by the Swedish field marshal Carl Gustav Wrangel, it contains many of his trophies from the Thirty Years' War. Other attractions include what is reckoned to be the largest private collection of arms in the world, as well as some magnificent Gobelin tapestries. Next door to the palace is a motor museum that houses Sweden's largest collection of vintage cars and motorcycles. The round-trip boat fare is SEK 135, and there is a restaurant and cafeteria on board. *Palace* *tel. 018/386077. Admission to Skokloster Palace: SEK 50. Admission to motor museum: SEK 25. Open daily noon–4.*

Lovers of the sea could easily spend an entire week cruising among the 24,000 islands in the **Stockholm archipelago.** The **Båtluffarkortet** (Inter-Skerries Card), available from early June to mid-August, gives you 16 days' unlimited travel on the Waxholm Steamship Company boats, which operate scheduled services throughout the archipelago. The card is on sale in the Excursion Shop at the Sweden House Tourist Center and at the Waxholm Steamship Company terminal at Strömkajen. It costs SEK 230.

Off the Beaten Track

Just over 155 meters (508 feet) tall, the **Kaknäs TV Tower** at Gärdet is the highest structure in Scandinavia. From the top you can catch a magnificent view of the city and surrounding archipelago. Facilities include a cafeteria, restaurant, and gift shop. *Ladugårdsgärdet, tel. 08/667–8030. Admission: SEK 20.*

You can see the world's largest variety of water lilies at the **Bergianska Botanical Garden,** just north of the city center. The largest lily's leaves are more than 2.17 meters (7 feet) in diameter. *Frescati, tel. 08/153912.*

Fjäderholmarna (the Feather Islets), the collective name for a group of four secluded islands in the Stockholm archipelago, have been open to the public only since the early '80s, after 50 years as a military zone. There is a museum depicting life in the archipelago, as well as the largest aquarium in Scandinavia, housing many species of Baltic marine life. Boats leave from Slussen, Strömkajen, and Nybroplan in downtown Stockholm. *Fjäderholmarna, tel. 08/718–0100.*

Shopping

Gift Ideas Stockholm is an ideal place to find items that reflect the best in Swedish design and elegance, particularly glass, porcelain, furs, handicrafts, home furnishings, and leather goods. The quality is uniformly high, and you can take advantage of tax-free shopping in most stores (*see* Shopping in Staying in Sweden, *above*).

Department Stores The largest is **NK,** on Hamngatan, where you can find just about anything at the impressive collection of independently operated boutiques. Other major stores are **PUB,** on Hötorget, and **Åhléns City,** on Klarabergsgatan. All three are open Sundays. **Sturegallerian** is a covered shopping gallery built on the site of the former public baths at Stureplan. There are about 50 shops, plus a number of restaurants.

Shopping Districts The center of Stockholm's shopping activity has shifted from Kungsgatan to Hamngatan, a wide boulevard along which a huge, covered shopping complex called **Gallerian** has been built. The **Old Town** area is best for handicrafts, antiquarian bookshops, and art shops.

Food and Flea Markets One of the biggest flea markets in northern Europe is located in **Skärholmen** shopping center, a 20-minute subway ride from the downtown area. Market hours are weekdays 11–6, Saturday 9–3, Sunday 10–3. Superior food markets selling such Swedish specialties as marinated salmon and reindeer can be found on **Östermalmstorg** and **Hötorget.**

Glassware For the best buys, try **Nordisk Kristall,** on Kungsgatan, or **Rosenthal Studio-Haus,** on Birger Jarlsgatan. The latter operates its own shipping service. **Arioso,** on Västerlånggatan in the Old Town, is good for modern crystal and ceramics, and **Önskebutiken,** on the corner of Kungsgatan and Sveavägen, specializes in crystal as well as porcelain.

Handicrafts A good center for all kinds of Swedish handicrafts in wood and metal is **Svensk Hemslöjd,** on Sveavägen. It also sells embroidery kits and many types of weaving and knitting yarn. For elegant home furnishings and timeless fabrics, Stockholmers tend to favor **Svensk Tenn** on Strandvägen, best known for its selection of designer Josef Franck's furniture and fabrics. **Stockholms Läns Hemslöjdsförening,** on Drottninggatan, has a wide selection of Swedish folk costumes and handicraft souvenirs from different parts of Sweden.

Dining

Prices quoted here are per person and include a first course, main course, tax, and service, but not wine. For details and price-category descriptions, *see* Dining in Staying in Sweden, *above.* Best bets are indicated by a star ★.

Very **Operakällaren.** Located in part of the elegant Opera House building,
Expensive this is one of Stockholm's best-known traditional restaurants, featuring both Scandinavian and Continental cuisine. It is famed for its smörgåsbord, which is particularly good during the pre-Christmas period. The restaurant faces Kungsträdgården, the waterfront, and the Royal Palace. *Operahuset, tel. 08/111125. Reservations advised. AE, DC, MC, V.*

Paul and Norbert. A very cozy, 32-seat restaurant on Stockholm's most elegant avenue, Paul and Norbert is noted for its French-style cuisine, using indigenous wild game such as reindeer, elk, partridge, and grouse, as well as fish. The decor is rustic but refined. *Strandvägen 9, tel. 08/663–8183. Reservations required. AE, DC, MC, V. Closed weekends. Call for yearly closing dates.*

Ulriksdals Värdshus. This is a beautifully situated country inn, built in 1868 and set in a castle park on the outskirts of town. It offers both Swedish and international cuisines but is particularly noted for its lunchtime smörgåsbord. *Ulriksdals Slottspark, tel. 08/850815. Reservations advised. AE, DC, MC, V. Closed Sun. dinner.*

Expensive **Clas på Hörnet.** Located just outside the city center, Clas på Hörnet
★ is a small, intimate establishment occupying the ground floor of a restored 200-year-old town house, now a hotel (*see* Lodging, *below*). It offers a choice of international or Swedish cuisine. *Surbrunnsgatan 20, tel. 08/165136. Reservations advised. AE, DC, MC, V.*

★ **Den Gyldene Freden.** Once a favorite haunt of Stockholm's artists and composers, the 1722 Den Gyldene Freden has Old Town ambience. The cuisine is a tasteful combination of French and Swedish. Every Thursday, the Swedish Academy, whose members choose the winner of the Nobel Prize in literature, meets for lunch on the second floor. *Österlånggatan 51, tel. 08/249760. Reservations advised. AE, DC, MC, V. Closed Sun.*

Nils Emil. Frequented by members of the Swedish royal family, this unpretentious yet elegant restaurant is noted for its delicious Swedish cuisine and generous helpings. Walls are decorated with paintings of the Stockholm archipelago, birthplace of chef/owner Nils Emil. He likes to visit his patrons' tables to keep tabs on the quality of the meals and service. *Södermalm, Folkungagatan 122, tel. 08/407209. Reservations required. AE, DC, MC, V.*

★ **Stallmästaregården.** A historic old inn with an attractive courtyard and garden, Stallmästaregården is in the Haga Park, some distance from the city center. But the fine French and Swedish cuisine is well worth the journey. In the summer meals are served in the courtyard overlooking Brunnsviken Lake. A lower, fixed-price menu is available. *Norrtull, near Haga, tel. 08/610–1301. Reservations advised. AE, DC, MC, V.*

Wedholms Fisk. Serving only fresh fish and shellfish, this open and high-ceilinged restaurant is located across a small bay from the Royal Dramatic Theater. The tartar of salmon and grilled sole are noteworthy. Portions are generous. The artwork featuring Scandinavian artists is part of the owner's personal collection. *Nybrokajen 17, tel. 08/611–7874. Reservations advised. AE, DC, MC, V. Closed Sun. and July.*

Moderate **Bakfickan.** The name means "hip pocket" and is appropriate be-
★ cause this restaurant is tucked around the back of the Opera House complex. It's a budget-price alternative to the nearby Operakällaren and is particularly popular at lunchtime, offering Swedish home cooking and a range of daily dishes. Counter and table service are available. *Operahuset, tel. 08/207745. No reservations. AE, DC, MC, V. Closed Sun.*

Eriks Backficka. An extremely popular dining spot among locals, this eatery serves a wide variety of Swedish dishes. The bustling 120-seat restaurant is located a block from the elegant waterside street Strandvägen, a flight down from street level. The same owner operates Eriks Gamla Stan, one of Stockholm's most exclusive restaurants. *Frederikshovsgatan 4, tel. 08/660–1599. Reservations advised. AE, DC, MC, V. Closed weekends in July.*

Gondolen. Suspended under the gangway of the *Katarina* elevator at Slussen, Gondolen offers a magnificent view over the harbor, Lake Mälaren, and the Baltic Sea. The cuisine is international, and a range of fixed-price menus is available. *Slussen, tel. 08/640–2021. Reservations advised. AE, DC, MC, V.*

Martini. This popular, centrally located Italian restaurant is a great people-watching hangout. People line up to get a seat during the summer, when the terrace is open. The main restaurant is below street level, but the decor is light and the atmosphere bustling. *Norrmalmstorg 4, tel. 08/679–8220. Reservations advised. AE, DC, MC, V.*

Sturehof. Centrally located, with an unpretentious, nautical ambience, Sturehof's specialty is its seafood. It also boasts an English-style pub. *Stureplan 2, tel. 08/679–8750. Reservations advised. AE, DC, MC, V. Closed Sat. lunch, Sun.*

Inexpensive **Cassi.** This downtown restaurant specializes in French cuisine at reasonable prices. *Narvavägen 30, tel. 08/661–7461. Reservations not necessary. MC, V. Closed Sat.*

★ **Open Gate.** This popular, trendy Art Deco Italian-style trattoria is located near the Slussen locks, on the south side of Stockholm Harbor. Pasta dishes are the house specialty. *Högbergsgatan 40, tel. 08/643–9776. No reservations. AE, DC, MC, V.*

Örtagården. This vegetarian, non-smoking restaurant is one floor up from the Östermalmshallen market hall. It offers an attractive buffet of soups, salads, and hot dishes with turn-of-the-century atmosphere. *Nybrogatan 31, tel. 08/662–1728. MC, V.*

Lodging

Stockholm has plenty of hotels in higher price brackets, but relatively few in the Inexpensive category. Many hotels cut their rates by up to 50% in the summer season, however, so during this time even a hotel classified as Very Expensive can be affordable. The major chains also have a number of bargain plans available on weekends throughout the year and daily during the summer.

Almost 50 hotels offer the "Stockholm Package," providing accommodations for one night, costing between SEK 320 and SEK 635 per person, including breakfast and a Stockholmskortet (Key to Stockholm) card (*see* Getting Around, *above*). Get details of the package from the **Stockholm Information Service**, Excursion Shop, Box 7542, S-103 93 Stockholm (tel. 08/789–2490). Also, you can call **The Hotel Center** (tel. 08/240880) or reserve the package through travel agents.

If you arrive in Stockholm without a hotel reservation, **Hotellcentralen** in the central train station will arrange accommodations for you. The office is open November–March, weekdays 8–5 and weekends 8–2; April and October, daily 8–5; May and September, daily 8–7; and June–August, daily 7 AM–9 PM. There is a reservations office in the Sweden House (*see* Important Addresses and Numbers, *above*) as well. There's a small fee for each reservation, but advance telephone reservations are free of charge. Or phone one of the central reservations offices run by the major hotel groups: RESO (tel. 08/720–8100 or 08/720–8830), Scandic (tel. 08/610–5050), Sweden Hotels (tel. 08/204311), or Best Western (tel. 08/300420).

Prices quoted here are for two people in a double room. For details and price-category definitions, *see* Lodging in Staying in Sweden, *above*. Best bets are indicated by a star ★.

Very Expensive

Amaranten. Only five minutes' walk from the central train station, Amaranten is a large, modern hotel, that was built in 1969. The "executive tower" offers a roof garden and 52 rooms. Guests enjoy a gourmet restaurant and brasserie and a piano bar. *Kungsholmsgatan 31, tel. 08/654–1060, fax 08/652–6248. 410 rooms with bath. Facilities: sauna, pool, restaurants, piano bar, solarium. AE, DC, MC, V.*

★ **Continental.** Located in the city center across from the central train station, the Continental is popular with American guests. It was first opened in 1966 and was renovated in 1992. It offers three restaurants in different price brackets. *Klara Vattugränd 4, tel. 08/244020, fax 08/113695. 268 rooms with bath. Facilities: 3 restaurants. AE, DC, MC, V.*

★ **Diplomat.** This is an elegant hotel located within easy walking distance of Djurgården Park and Skansen and offering magnificent views over Stockholm Harbor. The building itself is a turn-of-the-century town house that was converted into a hotel in 1966. The teahouse is a popular spot for light meals. *Strandvägen 7C, tel. 08/663–5800, fax 08/783–6634. 133 rooms with bath. Facilities: teahouse. AE, DC, MC, V.*

Grand. Opposite the Royal Palace on the waterfront in the center of town, the Grand is a large, gracious, Old World–style hotel dating back to 1874. Guests are entitled to relax at the prestigious Sturebadet Health Spa. The two restaurants—French and Swedish—offer harbor views. The bar serves light snacks. *S. Blasieholmshamnen 8, tel. 08/679–3500, fax 08/611–8686. 321 rooms with bath, most with waterfront views. Facilities: sauna, 2 restaurants, beauty salon. AE, DC, MC, V.*

★ **Lady Hamilton.** Considered one of Stockholm's most desirable hotels, the Lady Hamilton, in the Old Town, was built as a private home in 1470 and has been a hotel only since 1980. It houses an extensive collection of antiques, including one of George Romney's portraits of Lady Hamilton. *Storkyrkobrinken 5, tel. 08/234680, fax 08/111148. 34 rooms with bath. Facilities: sauna, pool, cafeteria. AE, DC, MC, V.*

Reisen. The building which is in the Old Town on the waterfront, dates from 1819; it has a fine restaurant, a grill, and what is reputed to be the best piano bar in town. The swimming pool is built under medieval arches. *Skeppsbron 12–14, tel. 08/223260, fax 08/201559. 114 rooms with bath. Facilities: restaurants, piano bar, sauna, pool, library. AE, DC, MC, V.*

SAS Royal Viking. This is a large, modern hotel adjoining the central train station and the airport bus terminal. Some rooms are rather small. Check out the restaurant or the Sky bar on the top floor. There is an SAS check-in counter in the lobby. *Vasagatan 1, tel. 08/141000, fax 08/108180. 319 rooms with bath. Facilities: restaurant, bar, sauna, pool, rooms for people with disabilities. AE, DC, MC, V.*

SAS Strand. Acquired in 1986 by the SAS group, this is a gracious, Old World hotel. It was built in 1912 but was recently modernized. No two rooms are the same; many are furnished with antiques. The Piazza is an indoor restaurant with an outdoor feel to it; its specialty is Italian cuisine, and it has a superb wine list. An SAS check-in counter adjoins the main reception area. *Nybrokajen 9, tel. 08/678–7800, fax 08/611–2436. 138 rooms with bath. Facilities: restaurant, sauna, banquet rooms. AE, DC, MC, V.*

Scandic Crown. A modern hotel with a panoramic view of the Old Town and City Hall, the Scandic Crown is on Stockholm's increasingly trendy south side. Noteworthy is the Couronne d'Or, a French eatery, and a wine cellar with wines dating to 1650. *Guldgränd 8, tel. 08/702–2500, fax 08/642–8358. 264 rooms with bath. Facilities: 2 restaurants, bar, indoor pool, solarium, sauna. AE, DC, MC, V.*

Expensive ★ **Clas på Hörnet.** An 18th-century inn converted into a small hotel in 1982, Clas på Hörnet is just outside the city center. Its rooms, furnished with antiques of the period, go quickly. If you can't manage to reserve a night, at least have a meal in the gourmet restaurant (*see* Dining, *above*). *Surbrunnsgatan 20, tel. 08/165130, fax 08/612–5315. 10 rooms with bath. Facilities: restaurant. AE, DC, MC, V.*

Hotel Stockholm. You can't get much closer to the center of Stockholm than this modern hotel, which occupies the sixth and seventh floors of an office building on one of the city's main squares. Hotel Stockholm is a clean, efficient hotel intended for those who want to spend their waking hours shopping, sightseeing, or on business. Breakfast is included in the room rates. *Norrmalmstorg 1, tel. 08/678–1320, fax 08/611–2103. 93 rooms with shower or bath. Facilities: 30-seat conference room. AE, DC, MC, V. Closed Christmas–New Year's Day.*

Karelia. A turn-of-the-century building on one of the main shopping streets, Karelia has a Finnish atmosphere. There is a Finnish restaurant for dining and dancing plus a separate restaurant specializing in Russian cuisine—the only such one in Stockholm. *Birger Jarlsgatan 35, tel. 08/247660, fax 08/241511. 86 rooms with bath or shower. Facilities: 2 restaurants. AE, DC, MC, V.*

Lord Nelson. This companion hotel to the Lady Hamilton was built in much the same style. It's on a busy pedestrian street in the Old Town, so it's rather noisy at night. The atmosphere is distinctly nautical—even down to the cabin-size rooms. The café is open until 8 PM daily. *Västerlånggatan 22, tel. 08/232390, fax 08/101089. 31 rooms with bath. Facilities: café. AE, DC, MC, V. Closed Christmas and New Year's Day.*

Moderate   **Birger Jarl.** A short subway ride from the city center, Birger Jarl is a modern, characteristically Scandinavian hotel that opened in 1974. There is no full-service restaurant. *Tulegatan 8, tel. 08/151020, fax 08/673–7366. 241 rooms with bath. Facilities: sauna, pool, coffee shop. AE, DC, MC, V.*

City. A large, modern-style hotel built in the 1940s but modernized in 1982–83, City is located near the city center and the Hötorget market. It is owned by the Salvation Army, so alcohol is not served. Breakfast is served in the Winter Garden atrium. *Slöjdgatan 7, tel. 08/222240, fax 08/208224. 300 rooms with bath. Facilities: restaurant, café, sauna, rooms for people with disabilities. . AE, DC, MC, V.*

Gamla Stan. A quiet, cozy hotel in the Old Town, the Gamla Stan was recently renovated, and each room is uniquely decorated. Breakfast is included. *Lilla Nygatan 25, tel. 08/244450, fax 08/216483. 51 rooms with shower. AE, DC, MC, V. Closed Christmas–New Year's Day.*

Stockholm. This hotel has an unusual location—the upper floors of a downtown office building. The mainly modern decor is offset by traditional Swedish furnishings that help create a family atmosphere. Only breakfast is served. *Norrmalmstorg 1, tel. 08/678–1320, fax 08/611–2103. 92 rooms with bath. AE, DC, MC, V.*

Inexpensive   **Alexandra.** Located in the Södermalm area, to the south of the Old Town, the Alexandra is only five minutes by subway from the city center. It is a small, modern hotel that opened in the early 1970s. Only breakfast is served. *Magnus Ladulåsgatan 42, tel. 08/840320, fax 08/720–5353. 84 rooms with bath. Facilities: sauna, solarium. AE, DC, MC, V.*

Gustav af Klint. A "hotel ship" moored at Stadsgården quay, near Slussen subway station, the Gustav af Klint is divided into two sections—a hotel and a hostel. There is a cafeteria and restaurant, and you can dine on deck in summer. *Stadsgårdskajen 153, tel. 08/640–4077, fax 08/640–6416. 14 cabins with showers. 80 hostel beds. Facilities: restaurant, cafeteria. AE, MC, V.*

Långholmen. This former prison, built in 1724, was converted into a combined hotel and hostel in 1989. It is located on the island of Långholmen, which has popular beaches. The Inn, next door, serves Swedish home cooking, and the wine cellar offers light snacks. *Långholmen, tel. 08/668–0500, fax 08/841096. 101 rooms with shower. Facilities: mini-golf course and boule court. AE, DC, MC, V.*

The Arts

Stockholm's main theater and concert season runs from September through May or June, so there are not many major performances during the height of the tourist season. But for a list of events, pick up the free booklet "Stockholm This Week," available from hotels and tourist information offices. For tickets to theaters and shows try the **central reservation office** (tel. 08/108800).

Concerts   The city's main concert hall is **Konserthuset** (the Concert House) at Hötorget 8, home of the Stockholm Philharmonic Orchestra. The season runs from mid-September to mid-May. In addition to full-scale evening concerts, there are "coffee break" or lunchtime concerts some days (tel. 08/221800). During the summer, many city parks have free concerts. For information, phone 08/785–8182.

Opera   The season at the **Royal Opera House,** just across the bridge from the Royal Palace, runs from mid-August to early June and offers performances at top-class international standards (tel. 08/248240). And from early June to early September, there are performances of opera, ballet, and orchestral music at the exquisite **Drottningholm Court Theater,** which was the setting for Ingmar Bergman's film *The Magic Flute.* The original 18th-century stage machinery is still used in these productions. You can get to Drottningholm by subway and bus or by special theater-bus (leaving from the Grand hotel or Vasagatan, opposite the central train station). For tickets, call 08/660–8225.

Theater Stockholm has about 20 top-rank theaters, but dramatic productions are unlikely to interest those who don't understand Swedish. A better option is to go to a musical; several city theaters hold regular performances. Plays in English are featured at the **Regina Theater** (Drottninggatan 71A, tel. 08/207000).

Film English and American films predominate, and they are screened with the original soundtrack and Swedish subtitles. Programs are listed in the local evening newspapers, though titles are usually in Swedish. Movie buffs should visit **Filmstaden** (Film City), Mäster Samuelsgatan 25 (tel. 08/840500), where 15 cinemas under one roof show a variety of films from noon until midnight.

Nightlife

Cabaret Stockholm's biggest nightclub, **Börsen** (Jakobsgatan 6, tel. 08/787–8500), offers high-quality Swedish and international cabaret shows. Another popular spot is the **Cabaret Club** (Barnhusgatan 12, tel. 08/110608). Although it can accommodate 450 guests, reservations are advised.

Bars and Nightclubs **Café Opera** (tel. 08/110026) is a popular meeting place for young and old alike. It has the longest bar in town, plus dining and roulette, and dancing after midnight. **Riche** (tel. 08/611–8450) is another popular watering hole in the city center. Piano bars are also an important part of the Stockholm scene: Try the **Anglais Bar** at the Hotel Anglais (tel. 08/614–1600) or the **Clipper Club** at the Hotel Reisen, Skeppsbron (tel. 08/223260). Not to be forgotten is the recently renovated restaurant/bar **Berns Salon** (Berzelii Park 9, tel. 08/614–0500). Worth a visit is the Red Room, a private dining room on the second floor, where playwright August Strindberg once held court. Other popular clubs are **Sture Compagniet** (08/611–7800) at Stureplan and **Café Victoria** (tel. 08/101085) in Kungsträdgården.

Irish pubs have recently become very popular among the happy-hour crowds, with **Limerick** (Tegnérgatan 10, tel. 08/673–4398), **Dubliner** (Birger Jarlspassagen, tel. 08/697–7707), and **Bagpiper's Inn** (Rörstrandsgatan 21, tel. 08/311855) currently leading the pack.

Jazz Clubs **Fasching** (Kungsgatan 63, tel. 08/216267) is Stockholm's largest, but another popular spot is **Stampen** (Stora Nygatan 5, tel. 08/205793). Get here in good time if you want a seat, but phone first to be sure the establishment hasn't been reserved for a private party.

Discos **Galaxy** (Strömsborg, tel. 08/215400) is one of the most popular night spots, catering to a variety of musical tastes. There is an outdoor bar and dining area in summer. Others are **Downtown** (Norrlandsgatan 5A, tel. 08/119488) and **Karlsson** (Kungsgatan 65, tel. 08/119298).

Uppsala and the Folklore District

The area of Sweden referred to as the "Folklore District"—essentially the provinces of Dalarna (sometimes called Darlecarlia in English) and Värmland—is easily accessible from Stockholm and the best region in which to see some of the country's enduring folk traditions. This itinerary takes you to Dalarna through the ancient city of Uppsala and returns to Stockholm through the Bergslagen region, the heart of the centuries-old Swedish iron industry.

Getting Around

The route can be covered entirely by train. The ride from Stockholm to Uppsala takes only 45 minutes, and the service is fairly frequent. A car, however, will give you the flexibility to explore some of the attractions that are not easily accessible by public transportation.

Guided Tours

Uppsala is compact enough to explore on foot, and guided sightseeing tours are available; you can book a tour in advance by calling the Guide Service, tel. 018/274818.

Tourist Information

Falun (Stora Torget, tel. 023/83637).
Ludvika (Sporthallen, tel. 0240/86050).
Mora (Ångbåtskajen, tel. 0250/26550).
Örebro (Slottet, tel. 019/212121).
Rättvik (Torget, tel. 0248/70200).
Uppsala (Fyris Torg 8, tel. 018/117500 and 018/274800, and at Uppsala Castle in summer).

Exploring Uppsala and the Folklore District

Uppsala is really the cradle of Swedish civilization, so it is well worth spending a day or two exploring it. If you opt for a guided tour of the city, you should first stop by **Gamla Uppsala** (Old Uppsala), which is dominated by three huge burial mounds. During the 5th century AD, Aun, Egil, and Adils, the first Swedish kings, were buried here. Adjoining the burial mounds are a church, the seat of Sweden's first archbishop, built on the site of a former pagan temple, and the Odinsborg restaurant, where you can sample local mead, brewed from a 14th-century recipe. Check all prices and times listed below with the local tourist office, as they are subject to change.

Back in **Uppsala** itself, your first stop should be the enormous **cathedral,** with its twin towers dominating the city skyline. The cathedral has been the seat of the archbishop of the Swedish church for 700 years. Its present appearance owes much to major restoration work completed during the late 19th century. Make a point of visiting the **Cathedral Museum** in the north tower, which boasts one of Europe's finest collections of ecclesiastical textiles. *Admission charged. Open June–Aug., daily 8–8; Sept.–May, daily 8–6.*

Nearby, in a strategic position atop a hill, is **Uppsala Castle.** This prepossessing structure was built during the 1540s by King Gustav Vasa. Having broken his ties with the Vatican, the king was eager to

Uppsala and the Folklore District

show who was actually running the country. He arranged to have the cannons aimed directly at the archbishop's palace. *Admission: SEK 35. Open mid-Apr.–mid-June, daily 11–3; mid-June–mid Aug., daily 10–5.*

Uppsala is also the site of Scandinavia's oldest university, founded in 1477. Be sure to visit one of its most venerable buildings, the **Gustavianum,** located near the cathedral. Just below the cupola is the anatomical theater, where public dissections of executed convicts were a popular 17th-century tourist attraction.

One of Uppsala's most famous sons was Carl von Linné, known as Linnaeus. A professor of botany at the university during the 1740s, he developed a system of plant and animal classification that is still used today. You can visit the **gardens** he designed, as well as his former residence, now a **museum.** *Admission to garden: SEK 10. Admission to museum: SEK 10. Open May–Aug. daily 9–9; Sept., daily 9–7.*

From Uppsala, the route heads northwest through a pleasant agricultural landscape into the province of Dalarna, passing through **Säter,** one of the best-preserved wooden villages in Sweden. This is a pleasant spot in which to just wander around. For an overnight stop it is best to head for Falun, Dalarna's capital.

Falun is best known for a huge hole in the ground, referred to as the **"Great Pit."** The hole has been there since 1687, when an abandoned copper mine collapsed. Other mines on the site are still working today. You can take a guided tour down into some of the old shafts and hear the gruesome story of 17th-century miner Fat Mats, whose body was perfectly preserved in brine for 40 years following a cave-in. There is also a museum that tells the story of the local mining industry. *Admission to museum: SEK 5; Admission to mine shaft: SEK 55. Open May 1–Aug. 31, daily 10–4:30; Sept. 1–Nov. 15 and Mar. 1–Apr. 30, weekends only 12:30–4:30.*

Just outside Falun, at **Sundborn,** is the former home of Swedish artist Carl Larsson. Here, in an idyllic, lakeside setting, you can see a selection of his paintings, which owe much to local folk-art traditions. His grandchildren and great-grandchildren are on hand to show you around. *Admission: SEK 50. Open May–Sept., Mon.–Sat. 10–5, Sun. 1–5.*

The real center of Dalarna folklore is the area around **Lake Siljan,** by far the largest of the 6,000 lakes in the province. Begin your tour at the attractive lakeside village of **Tällberg,** or at **Mora,** toward the north end of the lake. In the neighboring village of **Rättvik,** hundreds of people wearing traditional costumes arrive in longboats to attend Midsummer church services. Mora itself is best known as the home of the artist Anders Zorn. His house and a museum featuring his paintings are open to the public. *Admission to museum: SEK 20. Admission to home: SEK 25. Open daily.*

Near Mora is the village of **Nusnäs,** where the famous, brightly colored **Dalarna wooden horses** are produced. You can visit either of the two workshops where they are made.

Heading south again you'll come to **Ludvika,** an important center of the old Bergslagen mining region. This region stretches from the forests of Värmland in the west to the coastal forges in the east. Ludvika has a notable open-air mining museum, **Gammelgården.** Check times and prices with the Ludvika Tourist Office. There is also a **Railway Engine Museum** that features three steam turbine-driven iron-ore engines, the only ones of their kind in the world. *Admission: SEK 20. Open June 1–Aug. 31, daily 10–6.*

Another local attraction is **Luosa Cottage.** The poet Dan Andersson lived here in the early part of the century so he could experience for himself the rigorous life of the local charcoal burners. An annual music and poetry festival is held at the cottage and in nearby towns in Andersson's memory in late July. *Admission to cottage: SEK 20. Open mid-May–Aug., Tues.–Sun. 11–5.*

Continuing south from Ludvika, you'll come to **Örebro,** a sizable town at the western edge of **Lake Hjälmaren,** which is connected to Lake Mälaren and the sea by the Hjälmare Canal. Örebro received its charter in the 13th century and developed as a trading center for the farmers and miners of the Bergslagen region. Rising from a small island in the Svartån River, right in the center of town, is an imposing **castle,** parts of which date to the 13th century. The castle is now the residence of the regional governor. Guided tours run from mid-June to the end of August. Check with the Örebro tourist office for further information. An added attraction is the excellent restaurant in the castle.

To get a feel for the Örebro of bygone days, wander around the **Wadköping** district, where a number of old houses and crafts workshops have been painstakingly preserved. At the north end of town is **Svampen** (The Mushroom), a water tower rising 59 meters (193 feet) into the air. If you take the elevator to the top, you'll get a magnificent view of the surrounding countryside. There is also a cafeteria and tourist office. *The tower is open Apr. 30–Sept. 5, daily 10–9.*

Direct train service from Örebro back to Stockholm operates at two-hour intervals, and the journey takes just under three hours. You can also take the hourly train to Hallsberg and change there to the frequent Gothenburg–Stockholm service.

Dining and Lodging

For details and price-category definitions, *see* Dining and Lodging in Staying in Sweden, *above*. Best bets are indicated by a star ★.

Falun **Bergmästaren.** In the town center, Bergmästaren is a small, cozy ho-
Lodging tel built in traditional Dalarna style and filled with antique furnishings. *Bergskolegränd 7, tel. 023/63600, fax 023/22524. 89 rooms,
most with bath. Facilities: sauna, solarium, restaurant. AE, DC,
MC, V. Expensive.*

Hotel Falun. Located in the center of the city, Hotel Falun is a medium-size hotel built in the 1950s. Breakfast is included. *Cen-
trumhuset, Trotzgatan 16, tel. 023/29180, fax 023/13006. 25 rooms,
most with showers. AE, DC, MC, V. Moderate.*

Ludvika **Grand.** A medium-size, modern-style hotel, the Grand is located in
Lodging the town center. *Eriksgatan 6, tel. 0240/18220, fax 0240/11018. 102
rooms with bath. Facilities: sauna, disco, 2 restaurants. AE, DC,
MC, V. Expensive.*

Rex. The Rex is a fairly basic but modern hotel conveniently located
near the city center. It was built in 1960. Its restaurant serves
breakfast only. *Engelbrektsgatan 9, tel. 0240/13690. 28 rooms, 15
with shower. AE, DC, MC, V. Closed 1 week in summer. Inexpensive.*

Mora **Siljan.** Taking its name from the nearby lake, the Siljan is a popular,
Lodging small but modern-style hotel. *Moragatan 6, tel. 0250/13000, fax
★ 0250/13098. 46 rooms, most with bath. Facilities: sauna, disco, restaurant. AE, DC, MC, V. Moderate.*

Örebro **RESO Grand.** Located in the heart of town, the Grand is the city's
Dining and largest hotel. It was built in 1985 and offers all the modern comforts.
Lodging *Fabriksgatan 23, tel. 019/150200, fax 019/185814. 221 rooms with
bath. Facilities: sauna, Jacuzzi, à la carte restaurant, VIP rooms.
AE, DC, MC, V. Expensive.*

Stora Hotellet. Across the street from the castle on the Svartån river, this hotel is one of the oldest in Sweden, dating back to 1858.
There is a cozy 13th-century cellar restaurant, Slottskällaren, and
an English pub, the Bishop's Arms. *Drottninggatan 1, tel. 019/
124360, fax 019/117890. 105 rooms with bath or shower. Facilities:
restaurant, pub, sauna. AE, DC, MC, V. Expensive.*

Tällberg **Åkerblads.** Located near the shores of Lake Siljan, Åkerblads is a
Lodging real rural Swedish experience. The hotel occupies a typical Dalarna
★ farmstead, parts of which date to the 16th century. It is run by the
14th and 15th generations of the Åkerblad family. A hotel since
1910, it was modernized in 1987. The restaurant serves table d'hôte
meals only. *793 03 Tällberg, tel. 0247/50800, fax 0247/50652. 64
rooms, some with bath. Facilities: sauna, Jacuzzi, restaurant, pub-
style bar. AE, DC, MC, V. Moderate.*

Uppsala **Domtrappkällaren.** One of the city's most popular restaurants,
Dining Domtrappkällaren is located in a 14th-century cellar near the cathe-
★ dral. The cuisine is a mixture of French and Swedish. *St.
Eriksgränd 5, tel. 018/130955, fax 018/153380. Reservations required. Facilities: restaurant. AE, DC, MC, V. Expensive.*

Lodging **Sara Gillet.** A centrally located, medium-size hotel, the Sara Gillet
was opened in 1971 and has been recently modernized. *Dragar-*

brunnsgatan 23, tel. 018/155360, fax 018/153380. 169 rooms with bath. AE, DC, MC, V. Expensive.

Grand Hotel Hörnan. An Old World, medium-size hotel opened in 1906, the Grand Hotel Hörnan is in the city center near the train station. *Bangårdsgatan 1, tel. 018/139380, fax 018/120311. 37 rooms with shower. AE, MC, V. Closed July. Moderate.*

The West Coast and the Glass Country

For many visitors traveling to Sweden by ferry, Gothenburg (or Göteborg) is the port of arrival. But those who arrive in Stockholm should not miss making a side trip to this great shipping city and Sweden's scenic western coast. This itinerary combines a western trip with a route through the Glass Country to the medieval fortress town of Kalmar, on the east coast.

Getting Around

As with the previous itinerary, the route can be followed by both train and car. Regular trains for Gothenburg depart from Stockholm's central train station about every hour, and normal travel time is about four hours. There are also four daily high-speed trains (the X2000), which take less than three hours between the two cities, but these require a supplementary fare of SEK 245. First-class seats include breakfast on morning trains and sandwich snacks the rest of the day. Seat reservations are compulsory on most trains to Gothenburg. There are also hourly flights to Gothenburg from Stockholm's Arlanda Airport between 7 AM and 10 PM on weekdays, slightly less frequently on weekends. The trip by air takes 55 minutes.

For getting around the city of Gothenburg itself, the best transportation option for the visitor is the **Göteborgskortet** (Key to Gothenburg) card, similar to the Key to Stockholm card. This entitles the user to free travel on all public transportation, free parking, and free admission to the Liseberg amusement park and all city museums. Prices for the card are SEK 120 for one day, SEK 200 for two days, and SEK 250 for three days. Cards for children under 18 are SEK 60 for one day, SEK 100 for two days, and SEK 140 for three days.

Guided Tours

In the summer, sightseeing tours of Gothenburg leave regularly from Kungsportsplatsen, just beside the city tourist office. They must be reserved at the office in advance. Tourboats run frequently in summer (*see* Exploring, *below*).

Tourist Information

Gothenburg (Kungsportsplatsen 2, tel. 031/100740).
Jönköping (Djurläkartorget, tel. 036/105050).
Kalmar (Larmgatan 6, tel. 0480/15350).
Malmö (Central Station, Skeppsbron, tel. 040/300150).
Växjö (Kronobergsgatan 8, tel. 0470/41410).

The West Coast and the Glass Country

Uddevalla · Trollhättan · Falköping · Lake Vättern · Norrköping · Linköping · Gothenburg (Göteborg) · Borås · Jönköping · Huskvarna · Nässjö · Västervik · Riddersberg · Varberg · Falkenberg · Värnamo · Oskarshamn · Alvesta · Halmstad · Växjö · Nybro · Kalmar · Laholm · Öland · Helsingborg · Hässleholm · Karlshamn · Karlskrona · Landskrona · Ronneby · DEN. · Malmö · Kristianstad · Baltic Sea · Kattegat · Trelleborg · Ystad

0   40 miles
0   60 km

N

Exploring the West Coast and the Glass Country

Visitors arriving in **Gothenburg** by car often drive straight through the city in their haste to reach their coastal vacation spots, but this attractive harbor city is a tourist destination in its own right. A quayside jungle of cranes and warehouses attests to the city's industrial might, yet within 10 minutes' walk of the waterfront is an elegant, modern city of broad avenues, green parks, and gardens. Most of the major attractions are within walking distance of each other, and there is an excellent streetcar network. In the summer, you can take a sightseeing trip on a vintage open-air streetcar.

Gothenburg's development was pioneered mainly by British merchants in the 19th century, when it acquired the nickname "Little London." But a more accurate name would have been "Little Amsterdam," for the city was designed during the 17th century by Dutch architects, who gave it its extensive network of straight streets divided by canals. There is only one major canal today, but you can explore it on one of the popular "Paddan" sightseeing boats. The boats got their name, Swedish for toad, because of their short, squat shape, necessary for negotiating the city's 20 low bridges. You embark at the **Paddan terminal** at Kungsportsplatsen. *Fare: SEK 55. Departures: early Apr.–early May, Sat. at 10:45; early May–mid-Sept., daily 10–5; late June–early Aug., daily 10–9. Check with Gothenburg tourist information for specific dates.*

The hub of Gothenburg is **Kungsportsavenyn**, better known as "The Avenue." It is a broad, tree-lined boulevard flanked with elegant shops, restaurants, and sidewalk cafés. In summer it has a distinctively Parisian air. The avenue ends at **Götaplatsen Square**, home of the municipal theater, concert hall, art museum, and library (where there's an excellent selection of English-language newspapers). Just off the avenue is **Trädgårdsföreningen,** an attractive park with a magnificent Palm House that was built in 1878 and recently restored, and a Butterfly House featuring 40 different species. *Admission to park: SEK 10. Admission to Palm House: SEK 25. Open May–Aug., daily 7 AM–9 PM; Sept.–Apr., daily 7–6. Admission to Butterfly House: SEK 25. Open June–Aug., Tues.–Sat. 10–5, Sun. 11–5; hours vary during rest of year; check with Butterfly House (tel. 031/611911) or tourist information.*

If you're interested in shopping, the best place to go is **Nordstan,** a covered complex of shops near the central train station. Many of its businesses participate in the tax-free shopping service.

In the harbor near the Nordstan shopping complex, you will find the new **Maritime Center.** The center houses a historic collection of ships, including a destroyer, a lightship, a trawler, and tugboats. *Admission: SEK 35. Open May–Aug., daily 11–5; late Feb.–late Nov., weekends 11–5.*

To reach **Jönköping,** the next stop on the journey, take the train from Gothenburg's central train station and change at Falköping.

Jönköping is an attractive town on the southern shores of **Lake Vättern,** Sweden's second-largest lake. Jönköping, which celebrated its 700th anniversary in 1984, is known as the "matchstick town." For it was here, during the 19th century, that the match-manufacturing industry got its start. The **Matchstick Museum,** built on the site of the first factory, has an exhibition on the development and manufacture of matches. *Open throughout the year. Check opening times with the Jönköping Tourist Office.*

A few miles from Jönköping is **Riddersberg,** former home of the famous wood sculptor Calle Örnemark, which can be reached by local bus from the Jönköping train station. The house has now been transformed into an arts center featuring exhibitions by various Swedish artists as well as some remarkable sculptures by Örnemark. Check opening times and prices with the Jönköping Tourist Office.

To the southeast of Jönköping lies **Växjö,** Kronoberg County's main town and the best center for exploring Sweden's Glass Country. It is also an important sightseeing destination for some 10,000 American visitors each year, for it was from this area that their Swedish ancestors set sail during the 19th century. The **Emigrants' House,** located in the town center, tells the story of the migration period, during which close to 1 million Swedes—one-quarter of the entire population—departed for the promised land. The museum exhibits provide a vivid sense of the rigorous journey, and an archive room and research center allow American visitors to trace their ancestry. On the second Sunday in August, Växjö celebrates "Minnesota Day." Swedes and Swedish-Americans come together to commemorate their common heritage with American-style square dancing and other festivities.

Many of Sweden's most famous glassworks are within easy reach of Växjö, and it is usually possible to take an organized sightseeing tour of the facilities. Inquire at the tourist office for information. The manufacture of Swedish glass dates to 1556, when Venetian glassblowers were first invited to the Swedish court. But it was another 200 years before glass manufacturing became a real Swedish industry. The area between Växjö and Kalmar was chosen for its dense forest, which offered limitless wood supplies for heating the furnaces. All the major Swedish glass companies, including **Orrefors** and **Kosta Boda,** still have their works in this area, and all of them are open to the public. They also have shops where you can pick up near-perfect seconds at bargain prices. *Open weekdays 9–6, Sat. 9–3, Sun. noon–4 (no glass manufacturing on Sat. and Sun. in winter).*

An attractive coastal town, **Kalmar** is dominated by its imposing seaside castle. The town was once known as the "lock and key" of Sweden, for it is situated on the southern frontier of the kingdom, and thus open to constant enemy invasion. The castle's history goes back 800 years, although the present building dates only from the 16th century, when it was rebuilt by King Gustav Vasa. *Admission: SEK 30. Open daily. Tel. 0480/56300 for hours. Closed major holidays.*

To return to Stockholm from Kalmar, catch the train to Alvesta (the service runs every two hours) and change there for the Stockholm service. Two trains—one day service and one night service—run direct to Stockholm each day. The journey takes about 6½ hours. **SAS** operates several flights a day to Stockholm from the Kalmar airport, located 5 kilometers (3 miles) from the town center. The trip takes about 45 minutes. For information, phone 0480/58800 or 0480/58811.

Dining and Lodging

For details and price-category definitions, *see* Dining and Lodging in Staying in Sweden, *above.* Best bets are indicated by a star ★.

Gothenburg
Dining
★ **Räkan.** An informal and popular restaurant, Räkan makes the most of an unusual gimmick. The tables are arranged around a long tank, and if you order shrimp, the house specialty, they arrive at your table in radio-controlled boats you navigate yourself. *Lorensbergsgatan 16, tel. 031/169839. Reservations required. AE, DC, MC, V. Closed lunchtime on weekends, Christmas, New Year's Day. Expensive (with moderate fixed-price menus also available).*

★ **Sjömagasinet.** Situated in a 200-year-old renovated shipping warehouse, this waterfront restaurant, with its view of the harbor and suspension bridge, specializes in fish. During the summer, an outdoor terrace is open. *Klippanskulturreservat, tel. 031/246510. Reservations required. AE, DC, MC, V. Expensive (with moderate fixed-price menu also available in the winter).*

Weise. A centrally located restaurant with a German-beercellar atmosphere, Weise was once a haunt of local painters and intellectuals and still retains something of that ambience. The tables and chairs date from 1892. It specializes in traditional Swedish home cooking, serving such dishes as pork and brown beans. *Linnégatan 54, tel. 031/131402. Reservations advised. AE, DC, MC, V. Moderate.*

Åtta Glas. A casual, lively restaurant in what was formerly a barge, Åtta Glas offers excellent views of the river and of Kungsportsbron, a bridge spanning the canal in the center of town. The two standard specials—ox fillet or grilled salmon—are the best deals at SEK 59, and a children's menu, which includes ice cream, is popular with families. The second floor boasts a bar, especially popular with the younger crowd on weekends. *Kungsportsbron, tel. 031/136015. Reservations advised. AE, DC, MC, V. Inexpensive.*

Lodging
★ **Sheraton Hotel and Towers.** Opened in 1986, the Sheraton Hotel and Towers is Gothenburg's most modern and spectacular international-style hotel. It features an atrium lobby and several restaurants with varying prices. *Södra Hamngatan 59–65, tel. 031/806000, fax 031/159888. 343 rooms with bath. Facilities: restaurants, health club. 16*

rooms especially equipped for people with disabilities. *AE, DC, MC, V. Very Expensive.*

★ **Eggers.** Dating to 1859, Eggers probably has more Old World character than any other hotel in the city. It is located near the train station and was most likely the last port of call in Sweden for many emigrants to the United States. The rooms feature antique furnishings. *Drottningtorget, tel. 031/806070, fax 031/154243. 77 rooms with bath. AE, DC, MC, V. Expensive.*

Liseberg Heden. Not far from the famous Liseberg amusement park, Liseberg Heden is a popular, modern, family hotel. It offers a sauna and gourmet restaurant. *Sten Sturegatan, tel. 031/200280, fax 031/165283. 160 rooms with bath. Facilities: restaurant, sauna. AE, DC, MC, V. Moderate.*

Hotel Klang. This family-run hotel is 10 minutes' walk from the central train station. The rooms are simple and clean. Only breakfast is served. *Stora Badhusetgatan 28, tel. 031/174050, fax 031/174058. 50 rooms with shower or bath. AE, DC, MC, V. Inexpensive.*

Jönköping **Mäster Gudmunds Källare.** Nestled in cozy, 16th-century cellar
Dining vaults and only two minutes from the train station is this particular-
★ ly inviting restaurant. The cuisine is international. *Kapellgatan 2, tel. 036/112633. Reservations advised. AE, DC, MC, V. Moderate.*

Lodging **Stora Hotellet.** Stora Hotellet is an old-fashioned establishment opened in 1861 but recently modernized. Its restaurant serves international cuisine. *Hotellplan, tel. 036/119300, fax 036/119320. 108 rooms with shower. Facilities: restaurant, bar, sauna. AE, DC, MC, V. Expensive.*

John Bauer Hotel (Best Western). Located in the center of town, this modern, family-run hotel overlooks Lake Munksjön. It was named after a local artist famous for his fairy-tale illustrations of trolls, forests, and mystical landscapes. *Södra Strandgatan 15, tel. 036/100500, fax 038/112788. 100 rooms with shower or bath. Facilities: bar, terrace, steam room, sauna, solarium, billiards. AE, DC, MC, V. Moderate.*

Kalmar **Slottshotellet.** Situated in a gracious old town house on a quiet
Lodging street, Slottshotellet does not look like a hotel from the outside. Inside, however, you'll find a host of modern facilities. Only breakfast is served. *Slottsvägen 7, tel. 0480/88260, fax 0480/11993. 36 rooms with shower. Facilities: sauna, solarium. AE, DC, MC, V. Expensive.*

Stadshotellet. Located in the city center, Stadshotellet is a large, Old World hotel. The main building dates from the 19th century. *Storgatan 14, tel. 0480/15180, fax 0480/15847. 138 rooms with bath or shower. Facilities: restaurant, Jacuzzi, disco. AE, DC, MC, V. Expensive.*

Continental. The Continental is a fairly basic but comfortable family hotel. Only breakfast is served. *Larmgatan 10, tel. 0480/15140, fax 0480/13755. 39 rooms, most with bath or shower. AE, DC, MC, V. Inexpensive.*

Växjö **Sara Statt.** A conveniently located, traditional hotel, Sara Statt is
Lodging popular with tour groups. The building dates from the early 19th century, but the rooms themselves are modern, and the hotel has a cozy bar and à la carte restaurant. *Kungsgatan 6, tel. 0470/13400, fax 0470/44837. 130 rooms with bath or shower. Facilities: restaurant, bar. AE, DC, MC, V. Expensive.*

Esplanad. Centrally located, Esplanad is a small, family hotel offering basic amenities; it has been recently renovated. Only breakfast is served. *Norra Esplanaden 21A, tel. 0470/22580, fax 0470/26226. 27 rooms, most with shower. MC, V. Inexpensive.*

28 Switzerland

In Switzerland they keep their coziness under strict control: An electric eye beams open a sliding glass door into a room lined with carved wood, copper, and old-fashioned rafters. That is the paradox of the Swiss, whose two primary aesthetics pitch high-tech urban efficiency against rustic Alpine comfort. Fiercely devout, rigorously clean, prompt as their world-renowned watches, the Swiss are a people who drink their eau de vie in firelit *stübli* (cozy little pubs)—but rarely on Sunday. Liquors here are measured with scientific precision into glasses marked for one or two centiliters, and the local wines come in sized carafes that are reminiscent of laboratory beakers. And as for passion—well, the "double" beds have separate mattresses and sheets that tuck firmly down the middle. (Foreigners with more lusty Latin tastes may request a French—that is, a standard double—bed.) Politically isolated, culturally self-contained, Switzerland remains economically aloof . . . even Europhobic. As their neighbors pull their wagons in a circle, breaking down internal borders to present a unified front to the world, the Swiss continue to choose their apples from bins marked *Inländer* (domestic), while the *Ausländer* varieties, from abroad, rot humbly beside them. Yet Switzerland itself is a country of contrasts: While cowbells tinkle on the slopes of Klewenalp, the hum of commerce in Zürich isn't far away. As befurred and bejeweled socialites shop in Geneva, across the country in Appenzell women stand beside their husbands on the Landsgemeinde-Platz to raise their hands in the local vote—a right they didn't win until 1990.

But the trains run on time. In fact, all Swiss public transportation is chillingly precise: Step up to a tram stop, check the posted arrival time, and watch your second hand sweep toward the 12 as the streetcar pulls into view. Sleek, swift national trains may be the best in the world, while the roads and autoroutes are direct, scenic, and pothole-free.

Switzerland comprises most of the attractions of its larger European neighbors—Alpine grandeur, urban sophistication, ancient villages, scintillating ski slopes, and all-around artistic excellence. It's the heart of the Reformation, the homeland of William Tell; its cities are full of historic landmarks, its countryside strewn with castles. The varied cuisine reflects an ethnic mix, with three distinct cultures dominating: French in the southwest, Italian in the southeast, and German—a 70% majority—in the north and east.

All these assets have combined to create a major center of tourism, and the Swiss are happy to pave the way. A welcoming if reserved people, many of them well versed in English, they have earned their age-old reputation as fine hosts. Their hotels and inns are famous for cleanliness and efficiency, and the notorious high prices are justified, for the most part, by standards unrivaled in the world.

Essential Information

Before You Go

When to Go Switzerland functions as a year-round tourist attraction. Winter sports begin around Christmas and usually last until mid-April, depending on the state of the snow. The countryside is a delight in spring when the wild flowers are in bloom, and the fall colors rival those in New England. In the Ticino (the Italian-speaking area) and around Lake Geneva (Lac Léman), summer stays late: There is often sparkling weather in September and October, and the popular

Switzerland

resorts are less crowded then. After that, though, beware: Throughout Switzerland, resorts may close up altogether in November and May. Always check with the local tourist office.

Climate Summer in Switzerland is generally warm and sunny, though the higher you go, of course, the cooler it gets, especially at night. Winter is cold everywhere: In low-lying areas the weather is frequently damp and overcast, while in the Alps there are often brilliantly clear days, but it is guaranteed to be cold and snowy—especially above 1,400 meters (4,600 feet).

Summer or winter, some areas of Switzerland are prone to an Alpine wind that blows from the south and is known as the *Föhn*. This gives rise to clear but rather oppressive weather, which the Swiss claim causes headaches. The only exception to the general weather patterns is the Ticino. Here, protected by the Alps, the weather is positively Mediterranean; even in winter, it is significantly warmer than elsewhere.

The following are the average daily maximum and minimum temperatures for Zürich.

Jan.	36F	2C	**May**	67F	19C	**Sept.**	69F	20C
	26	− 3		47	8		51	11
Feb.	41F	5C	**June**	73F	23C	**Oct.**	57F	14C
	28	− 2		53	12		43	6
Mar.	51F	11C	**July**	76F	25C	**Nov.**	45F	7C
	34	1		56	14		35	2
Apr.	59F	15C	**Aug.**	75F	24C	**Dec.**	37F	3C
	40	− 4		56	14		29	− 2

Currency The unit of currency is the Swiss franc (Fr.), divided into 100 rappen (known as centimes in French-speaking areas). There are coins of 5, 10, 20, and 50 rappen and of 1, 2, and 5 francs. The bills are of 10, 20, 50, 100, 500, and 1,000 francs.

At press time (spring 1994), the Swiss franc stood at 1.47 to the dollar and 2.21 to the pound sterling.

All banks will change your money, though many impose a minimum and a slight fee. Traveler's checks get a better exchange rate, as do cash advances on major credit cards. Main airports and train stations have exchange offices (bureaux de change) that are open longer hours than banks and often offer equally good rates of exchange. Most hotels and some restaurants will change money but usually at a far less favorable rate. Most major credit cards are generally, though not universally, accepted at hotels, restaurants, and shops.

What It Will Cost High standards of living mean that Switzerland is generally expensive: If it's luxury you're after, you'll pay more for it here than in almost any other European country. You'll find plenty of reasonably priced hotels and restaurants, however, if you look for them. Those who have visited Switzerland before will be surprised at how little prices have changed recently: Inflation has been less than 2% for years.

As in any other European country, the cities are more expensive than are the smaller towns. Zürich and Geneva are the priciest; Basel, Bern, and Lugano are also quite expensive. Holiday resorts—especially the better-known Alpine ski centers—rival cities for high prices. Elsewhere, prices drop appreciably, particularly off the beaten track and in the northeast.

Sample Prices Cup of coffee, 2.50 Fr.; bottle of beer, 2.50–3 Fr.; Coca-Cola, 2.50 Fr.; ham sandwich, 7 Fr.; a 1-mile taxi ride, 10 Fr. (more in Geneva, Lugano, or Zürich).

Customs on Arrival There are two levels of duty-free allowance for visitors to Switzerland. Residents of non-European countries may import 400 cigarettes or 100 cigars or 500 grams of tobacco, plus 2 liters of alcoholic beverage below 15% and 1 liter of alcoholic beverage in excess of 15%. Residents of European countries may import 200 cigarettes or 50 cigars or 250 grams of tobacco, plus 2 liters of alcoholic beverage below 15% and 1 liter of alcoholic beverage in excess of 15%. These allowances apply only to those age 17 and above.

There are no restrictions on the import or export of any currency.

Language French is spoken in the southwest, around Lake Geneva, and in the cantons of Fribourg, Neuchâtel, Jura, Vaud, and the western portion of Valais; Italian is spoken in the Ticino, and lilting dialects of German are spoken everywhere else—in more than 70% of the country, in fact. The Romance language called Romansh has regained a firm foothold throughout the Upper and Lower Engadine regions of the canton Graubünden, where it takes the form of five different dialects. English, however, is spoken widely. Many public signs are in English, as well as in the regional language, and all hotels, restaurants, tourist offices, train stations, banks, and shops will have someone who can speak English comfortably.

Getting Around

By Plane **Swissair** connects the cities of Zürich, Basel, and Geneva. The airline offers flexible packages (106 Calvert St., Hamson, NY 10528, tel. 800/688–7947) from April through October for the independent traveler who flies at least one way between North America and Europe on Swissair or Delta. "The Swiss Travel Invention" allows visitors to tailor-fit their Swiss holiday to include hotels, car rentals, rail vacations, and guided tours at great savings. Swissair also offers personalized ski packages consisting of round-trip flights, surface travel by rail or bus, and a choice of hotels at ski resorts. **Crossair** is Switzerland's domestic airline, flying between local airports and bringing in visitors from various Continental cities as well, including London, Rome, Barcelona, Berlin, and Amsterdam.

By Car
Road Conditions Swiss roads are usually well surfaced but wind about considerably—especially in the mountains. Don't plan on achieving high average speeds. When estimating likely travel times, look carefully at the map: There may be only 32.3 kilometers (20 miles) between one point and another, but there could also be a mountain pass along the way. There is a well-developed highway network, though some notable gaps still exist in the south along an east–west line, roughly between Lugano and Sion. Under some mountain passes, there are tunnels through which cars can be transported by train while passengers remain in the cars—an experience not unlike riding through the world's longest car wash.

A combination of steep or winding routes and hazardous weather conditions may close some roads during the winter. Dial 120 or 163 for bulletins and advance information on road conditions.

Rules of the Road Driving is on the right. In built-up areas, the speed limit is 50 kph (30 mph), and on main highways, it's 120 kph (75 mph). On other roads outside built-up areas, the limit is 80 kph (50 mph). Strongly contested efforts are being made to raise these limits.

Children under 12 are not permitted to sit in the front seat. Driving with parking lights is prohibited, and lights are mandatory in heavy rain and under other conditions of poor visibility; you *must* use headlights in road tunnels.

To use the main highways, you must display a disk or *vignette*, which you can buy from the Swiss National Tourist Office before you leave or at the border stations when you enter the country. As of January 1, 1995, it costs 40 Fr. and is valid until the end of the year. Cars rented within Switzerland already have these disks.

Traffic going up a mountain has priority except for postal buses coming down. A sign with a yellow posthorn on a blue background means that postal buses have priority.

During the winter, snow chains are advisable—sometimes mandatory. They can be rented in all areas, and snow-chain service stations have signs marked "Service de Chaînes à Neige," or "Schneekettendienst."

Parking Parking areas are clearly marked. Parking in public lots normally costs between .5 Fr. and 1 Fr. per hour.

Gasoline Lead-free (*sans plomb* or *bleifrei*) gas costs 1.46 Fr. per liter, and super costs 1.57 per liter. Leaded regular is no longer available.

Breakdowns Assistance is available through the telephone exchange: Ask for "Autohilfe." The Touring Club Suisse has a 24-hour breakdown service. Useful organizations are the **Automobile Club de Suisse** (ACS, Wasserwerkegasse 39, Bern) and the **Touring Club Suisse** (TCS, 9 rue Pierre Fatio, Geneva), both of which have branches throughout Switzerland.

By Train Switzerland's trains are among Europe's finest. Generally, they are swift (except through the mountains), immaculate, and unnervingly punctual. Don't linger between international connections: The Swiss don't wait for languorous travelers. If you plan to use the trains extensively, get a timetable (*Offizieles Kursbuch* or *Horaire*), which costs 14 Fr., or a portable, pocket version called "Fribo" for 10.80 Fr. A useful booklet called "Switzerland by Train," available from the Swiss National Tourist Office (SNTO), describes passes, itineraries, and discounts available to rail travelers.

Trains described as Inter-City or Express are the fastest, stopping only at principal towns. *Regionalzug* means a local train, often affording the most spectacular views. Meals, snacks, and drinks are provided on most main services; there are even McDonald's dining cars on some routes. Seat reservations are useful during rush hours and high season, especially on international trains.

Fares There are numerous concessions for visitors. The **Swiss Pass** is the best value, offering unlimited travel on Swiss Federal Railways, postal buses, lake steamers, and the local bus and tram service of 30 cities. It also gives reductions on many privately owned railways, cable cars, and mountain railways. It's available from the Swiss National Tourist Office and from travel agents outside Switzerland. The card is valid for eight days (186 Fr. 2nd-class, 266 Fr. 1st-class), 15 days (214 Fr. 2nd-class, 312 Fr. 1st-class), or one month (296 Fr. 2nd-class, 430 Fr. 1st-class). There is also a new 3-day **Flexi Pass** (148 Fr. 2nd-class, 222 Fr. 1st-class), which offers the same unlimited travel options of a regular Swiss Pass for any 3 days within a 15-day period. Prices are for second-class travel; first-class travel costs about 40% more.

Within some popular tourist areas, **Regional Holiday Season Tickets,** issued for 15 days, give 5 days of free travel by train, postal buses, steamers, and mountain railways, with half fare for the rest of the validity of the card. Central Switzerland offers a similar pass for 7 days, with 2 days of free travel. Prices vary widely, depending upon the region and period of validity, but if you like to cover a lot of ground, they do assure you of savings over full fare. Increasingly popular with tourists is a **Swiss Half-Fare Travel Card,** which allows half-fare travel for 30 days (85 Fr.) or one year (150 Fr.).

The new **Swiss Card,** which can be purchased in the United States through RailEurope (226–230 Westchester Ave., White Plains, NY 10604, tel. 800/438–7245) and at train stations at the Zürich and Geneva airports and in Basel, is valid for 30 days and grants full round-trip travel from your arrival point to any destination in the country, plus a half-price reduction on any further excursions during your stay (118 Fr. first class, 96 Fr. second class). For more information about train travel in Switzerland, get the free "Swiss Travel System" or "Discover Switzerland" brochures from the SNTO.

For 20 Fr. per bag round-trip, travelers holding tickets or passes on Swiss Federal Railways can forward their luggage to their final destination, allowing passengers to make stops on the way unencumbered.

By Bus Switzerland's famous yellow postal buses link main cities with villages off the beaten track. Both postal and city buses follow posted schedules to the minute: You can set your watch by them. Free timetables can be picked up at any post office.

The Swiss Pass (*see above*) gives unlimited travel on the postal buses, which venture well beyond rail routes. The postal buses pay special attention to hikers. You can get a free booklet, "The Best River and Lakeside Walks," from the SNTO. The booklet describes 28 walks you can enjoy by hopping on and off postal buses. Most walks take around three hours.

By Boat Drifting across a Swiss lake and stopping off here and there at picturesque villages nestling by the water makes a relaxing day's excursion, especially if you are lucky enough to catch one of the elegant old paddle steamers. Trips are scheduled on most of the lakes, with increased service in summer. Unlimited travel is free to holders of the **Swiss Pass** (*see above*). For those not traveling by train, there is also a **Swiss Boat Pass,** which allows half-fare travel on all lake steamers for the entire year (35 Fr., Jan. 1–Dec. 31).

By Bicycle Bikes can be rented at all train stations and returned to any station. Rates are 19 Fr. per day or 76 Fr. per week for a conventional bike, 31 Fr. per day and 124 Fr. per week for a mountain bike. Families can rent two adult bikes and bikes for the children for 48 Fr. per day, 208 Fr. per week. Groups get reductions according to the number of bikes involved. Reservations are necessary by 6 PM the day before use by individuals and a week ahead for groups. **Touring Club Suisse** (9 rue Pierre Fatio, CH-1211 Geneva 3, tel. 022/7851222) also rents bikes from its local offices at prices ranging from 14 Fr. to 24 Fr. per day.

Staying in Switzerland

Telephones There is direct dialing to every location in Switzerland. For local and
Local Calls international codes, consult the pink pages at the front of the telephone book.

| International Calls | You can dial most international numbers direct from Switzerland, adding a 00 before the country's code. If you want a number that cannot be reached directly, dial 114 for a connection. Dial 191 for international numbers and information. It's cheapest to use the booths in train stations and post offices; calls made from your hotel cost a great deal more. The PTT phone card, available in 10 Fr. and 20 Fr. units, allows you to call from any adapted public phone. You can buy cards at the post office or train station. Rates are lower between 5 PM and 7 PM, after 9 PM, and on weekends. Calls to the United States cost 1.80 Fr. per minute, to the United Kingdom 1 Fr. per minute. |

| Operators and Information | All telephone operators speak English, and instructions are printed in English in all telephone booths. |

| Mail Postal Rates | Mail rates are divided into first class (air mail) and second class (surface). Letters and postcards to the United States up to 20 grams cost 1.80 Fr. first class, .90 Fr. second class; to the United Kingdom, 1 Fr. first class, .80 Fr. second class. |

| Receiving Mail | If you're uncertain where you'll be staying, you can have your mail, marked Poste Restante or Postlagernd, sent to any post office in Switzerland. The sender's name and address must be on the back, and you'll need proof of identity to collect it. You can also have your mail sent to American Express for a small fee, payable when you collect it. |

| Shopping VAT Refunds | A 6.5% value-added tax (VAT) on all goods is included in the price. Nonresidents who have spent at least 500 Fr. at one time at a particular store may claim a VAT refund at the time of purchase, or the shop will send the refund to your home. In order to qualify for a refund, you *must* sign a form at the time of purchase and present it to Swiss customs on departure. |

| Bargaining | Don't try bargaining: Except at the humblest flea market, it just doesn't work. As with everything in Switzerland, prices are efficiently controlled. |

| Opening and Closing Times | **Banks** are open weekdays 8:30–4:30 or 5.

Museums times vary considerably, though many close on Monday. Check locally.

Shops are generally open 8–noon and 1:30–6:30. Some close at 4 on Saturday, and some are closed Monday morning. In cities, many large stores do not close for lunch. In train stations, some shops remain open until 9 PM, and in Geneva and Zürich airports, shops remain open on Sunday. |

| National Holidays | January 1, 2; April 14 (Good Friday); April 16, 17 (Easter); May 29 (Ascension); June 5 (Pentecost Sunday); December 25, 26. May 1 (Labor Day) and August 1 (National Day) are also celebrated, though not throughout the country. |

| Dining | Options range from luxury establishments to modest cafés, *stübli* (cozy little pubs), and restaurants specializing in local cuisine.

Because the Swiss are so good at preparing everyone else's cuisine, it is sometimes said that they have none of their own, but there definitely is a distinct and characteristic Swiss cuisine. Switzerland is the home of great cheeses—Gruyère, Emmentaler, Appenzeller, and Vacherin—which form the basis of many dishes. *Raclette* is cheese melted over a fire and served with potatoes and pickles, *Rösti* are hash brown potatoes, and *fondue* is a bubbling pot of melted cheeses flavored with garlic and kirsch, into which you dip chunks of bread. Other Swiss specialties to look for are *Geschnetzeltes* |

Kalbfleisch (veal bits in cream sauce), *polenta* (cornmeal mush) in the Italian region, and fine game in autumn. A wide variety of Swiss sausages make both filling and inexpensive meals, and in every region the breads are varied and superb.

Mealtimes At home, the main Swiss meal of the day is lunch, with a snack in the evening. Restaurants, however, are open at midday and during the evening; often limited menus are offered all day. Watch for *Tagesteller* or *menus* (fixed-price lunch platters or menus), which enable you to experience the best restaurants without paying high à la carte rates.

Dress Jacket and tie are suggested for restaurants in the Very Expensive and Expensive categories; casual dress is acceptable elsewhere.

Ratings Prices are per person, without wine or coffee, but including tip and taxes. Best bets are indicated by a star ★.

Category	Zürich/Geneva	Other Areas
Very Expensive	over 90 Fr.	over 70 Fr.
Expensive	50 Fr.–90 Fr.	40 Fr.–70 Fr.
Moderate	30 Fr.–50 Fr.	20 Fr.–40 Fr.
Inexpensive	under 30 Fr.	under 20 Fr.

Lodging Switzerland's accommodations cover a broad range, from the most luxurious hotels to the more economical rooms in private homes. Pick up the *Schweizer Hotelführer (Swiss Hotel Guide)* from the SNTO before you leave home. The guide is free and lists all the members of the Swiss Hotel Association (comprising nearly 90% of the nation's accommodations); it tells you everything you'll want to know. Some hotels choose not to pay dues to the SHA guide or to the local tourist office. Standards may be lower, but so may the prices.

Most hotel rooms today have private bath and shower; those that don't are usually considerably cheaper. Single rooms are generally about two-thirds the price of doubles, but this can vary considerably. Remember that the no-nonsense Swiss sleep in separate beds or, at best, a double with separate bedding. If you prefer more sociable arrangements, ask for the rare "matrimonial" or "French" bed. Service charges and taxes are included in the price quoted and the bill you pay. Breakfast is included unless there is a clear notice to the contrary. In resorts especially, half pension (choice of a noon or evening meal) may be included in the room price. If you choose to eat à la carte or elsewhere, the management will generally reduce your price. Give them plenty of notice, however.

All major towns and train stations have hotel-finding services, which sometimes charge a small fee. Local tourist offices will also help.

Hotels Hotels are graded from one star (the lowest) to five stars. Always confirm what you are paying before you register, and check the posted price when you get to your room. Major credit cards are generally accepted, but make sure beforehand.

Two important hotel chains are the Romantik Hotels and Restaurants and Relais et Châteaux, with premises that are generally either in historic houses or houses that have some special character. Another chain that has a good reputation is Best Western, affiliated with the familiar American chain. Relais du Silence hotels are usually isolated in a peaceful, natural setting—or urban oasis—with first-class comforts. The Check-In E and G ("Einfach und Gemütlich" or "Cheap and Cozy") Hotels are dependable small hotels, boardinghouses, and mountain lodges that offer accommodations at reasonable prices. Details are available from the SNTO, which also offers pamphlets recommending family hotels and a list of hotels and restaurants that cater specifically to Jewish travelers.

Rentals Switzerland has literally thousands of furnished chalets. Off-season, per-day prices are around 50 Fr. per person for four sharing a chalet. In peak season, prices would be at least twice that. Deluxe chalets cost much more. For more information, pick up an illustrated brochure from the **Swiss Touring Club** (9 rue Pierre Fatio, CH-1211 Geneva 3) or from **Uto-Ring AG** (Beethovenstr. 24, CH-8002 Zürich). In the United States, write to **Interhome** (36 Carlos Dr., Fairfield, NJ 07006). In Britain, contact **Interhome** (383 Richmond Rd., Twickenham, Middlesex TW1 2EF). You may save considerably if you write directly to the village or resort you wish to rent in, specifying your projected dates and number of beds needed: Prices start at around 20 Fr. per person without an agency's commission.

Ratings Prices are for two people in a double room with bath or shower, including taxes, service charges, and breakfast. Best bets are indicated by a star ★.

Category	Zürich/Geneva	Other Areas
Very Expensive	over 450 Fr.	over 250 Fr.
Expensive	250 Fr.–450 Fr.	180 Fr.–250 Fr.
Moderate	120 Fr.–250 Fr.	120 Fr.–180 Fr.
Inexpensive	under 120 Fr.	under 120 Fr.

Tipping Although restaurants include service charges of 15% with the taxes in your hotel and restaurant bill, you will be expected to leave a small additional tip: 1 Fr. or 2 Fr. per person for a modest meal, 5 Fr. for a first-class meal, and 10 Fr. at one of the exclusive gastronomic restaurants in the Very Expensive range. When possible, tip in cash. Elsewhere, give bathroom attendants 1 Fr. and hotel maids 2 Fr. Theater and opera-house ushers get 2 Fr. Hotel porters and doormen should get about 2 Fr. per bag in an upmarket hotel; 1 Fr. elsewhere.

Zürich

Arriving and Departing

By Plane Kloten (tel. 01/8127111) is Switzerland's most important airport and is among the most sophisticated in the world. Several airlines fly directly to Zürich from major cities in the United States, Canada, and the United Kingdom.

Swissair flies nonstop from New York, Chicago, Toronto, Montreal, Atlanta, Los Angeles, and Boston. "Fly Rail Baggage" allows Swissair passengers departing Switzerland to check their bags at any of 120 rail or postal bus stations throughout the country; luggage is automatically transferred to the airplane. At eight Swiss railway stations, passengers may complete all check-in procedures for Swissair flights, including boarding-pass issuance and baggage forwarding.

Between the Airport and Downtown Beneath the air terminals, there's a train station with an efficient, direct service into the Hauptbahnhof (main station) in the center of Zürich. Fast trains run every 10–15 minutes, and the trip takes about 10 minutes. The fare is 4.80 Fr., and the ticket office is in the airport. There are express trains to most Swiss cities at least every hour. Trains run from 6 AM to midnight.

Taxis are very expensive: about 40 Fr. into town. Some hotels provide their own bus service. Cars can be rented at the airport.

By Bus All bus services to Zürich will drop you at the Hauptbahnhof.

By Train Zürich is the northern crossroads of Switzerland, with swift and timely trains arriving from Basel, Geneva, Bern, and Lugano. All routes lead to the Hauptbahnhof in the city center.

By Car There are direct highways from the border crossings with France, Germany, and Italy. Germany is the nearest.

Getting Around

Although Zürich is Switzerland's largest city, it has a population of only 362,000 and is not large by European standards. That's one of its nicest features: You can explore it comfortably on foot.

By Bus and Streetcar The city's transportation network is excellent. **VBZ Züri-Line** (Zürich Public Transport) buses run from 5:30 AM to midnight, every six minutes on all routes at peak hours, and about every 12 minutes at other times. Before you board the bus, you must buy your ticket from the automatic vending machines found at every stop. A ticket for all travel for 24 hours is a good buy at 6.40 Fr. Free route plans are available from VBZ offices.

By Taxi Taxis are very expensive, with an 8 Fr. minimum, and should be avoided unless you have no other means of getting around.

Important Addresses and Numbers

Tourist Information The tourist office is located at Bahnhofplatz 15 (Main Station), tel. 01/2114000. Open Apr.–Oct., weekdays 8:30–9:30, weekends 8:30 AM–8:30 PM; Nov.–Mar., Mon.–Fri. 8:30–7:30, weekends 8:30–6:30.

Consulates U.S. (Zollikerstr. 141, tel. 01/4222566). U.K. (Dufourstr. 56, tel. 01/2611520).

Emergencies **Police** (tel. 117). **Ambulance** (tel. 144). **Doctor/Dentist Referral** (tel. 01/2616100). **Pharmacy: Bellevue** (Theaterstr. 14, tel. 01/2525600) offers an all-night service.

Books in English For books and magazines, try **Payot** (Bahnhofstr. 9). **Travel Book Shop** (Rindermarkt 20).

Travel Agencies **American Express** (Bahnhofstr. 20, tel. 01/2118370). **Kuoni** (Bahnhofplatz 7, tel. 01/2213411).

Guided Tours

Orientation Tours There are three bus tours available. The daily "Sights of Zürich" tour (22 Fr. adults, 11 Fr. children) gives a good general idea of the city in two hours. "In and Around Zürich" goes farther and includes an aerial cableway trip to Felsenegg. This is also a daily tour that takes 2½ hours; it costs 30 Fr. adults, 15 Fr. children. The May-to-

October tour, "Zürich by Night," takes in everything from folklore to striptease in 3½ hours (69 Fr.). All tours start from the main station. Contact the tourist office for reservations.

Walking Tours From May through October, daily guided walking tours (16 Fr. adults, 8 Fr. children 6–12) start from the tourist office and take roughly two hours.

Excursions There are many bus excursions to other areas, such as the Bernese Oberland, St. Gotthard, the Ticino, Lucerne, and Geneva. Since these depend on the season and weather, it's best to book them after you arrive and can check with the tourist office.

Exploring Zürich

Zürich is not at all what you'd expect. Stroll around on a fine spring day and you'll ask yourself if this can really be one of the great business centers of the world: The lake glistening and blue in the sun, the sidewalk cafés, the swans gliding in to land on the river, the hushed and haunted old squares of medieval guildhouses, the elegant shops. There's not a gnome (a mocking nickname for a Swiss banker) in sight. The point is that for all its economic importance, Zürich is a place where people enjoy life. Hardworking when need be, the Swiss love the good things in life and have the money to enjoy them.

Zürich started in 15 BC as a Roman customs post on the Lindenhof overlooking the river Limmat, but its growth really began around the 10th century AD. It became a free imperial city in 1336, a center of the Reformation in 1519, and then gradually assumed commercial importance during the 1800s. Today there is peace as well as prosperity here, and since Zürich is so compact, you can take it in in a morning's stroll.

Numbers in the margin correspond to points of interest on the Zürich map.

❶ Collect your map (it's essential) from the tourist office (Bahnhofplatz 15), then start your walk from the nearby **Bahnhofstrasse,** famous for its shops and cafés and as the center of the banking network, though you'd be unlikely to guess it. Take Rennweg on your left, and then turn left again into the Fortunagasse, a quaint medie-
❷ val street leading to the **Lindenhof,** a square where there are remains of Zürich's Roman origins. The fountain commemorates the ingenuity of the Zürich women who, when the city was besieged by the Habsburgs in 1292, donned armor and marched around the walls. The invaders thought they were reinforcements and beat a hasty retreat.

An alley on the right leads to a picturesque square dating from the
❸ Middle Ages, with the **Peterskirche,** Zürich's oldest parish church (13th century), which also happens to have the largest clockface in Europe. Walk down to the river and follow it to the 13th century
❹ **Fraumünster** (church), which has modern stained-glass windows by Chagall. There are two handsome guildhalls nearby: the **Zunfthaus zur Waag** hall of the linen weavers (Münsterhof 8), built in 1637, and the **Zunfthaus zur Meise** (Münsterhof 20), built during the 18th century for the wine merchants.

Time Out Head away from the river to the Bahnhofstrasse, then to Paradelplatz to visit **Sprüngli,** the famous café-sweets shop where glossy Zürichers gather to see and be seen. The chocolate truffles are sinfully rich.

Main Attractions
Altstadt
(Old Town), **9**
Bahnhof-
strasse, **1**
Fraumünster, **4**
Grossmünster, **7**
Kunsthaus, **5**
Limmatquai, **8**
Lindenhof, **2**
Niederdorf, **10**
Peterskirche, **3**
Schweizerisches
Landes-
museum, **11**
Wasserkirche, **6**

Other Attractions
Centre Le
Corbusier, **19**
Federal
Institute of
Technology, **12**
Opernhaus, **15**
Rathaus, **17**
Stadthaus, **18**
University of
Zürich, **13**
Wohn-
museum, **16**
Zoo, **14**

Zürich

Continue along Bahnhofstrasse to Bürkliplatz and cross the **Quai Bridge** to take in the impressive views of the lake and town. Art lovers might want to first continue up Rämistrasse to the **Kunsthaus** (Art Gallery), with its varied high-quality collection of medieval paintings, Dutch and Italian Baroque, and Impressionist works, as well as an excellent representation of Swiss artists, including nearly 100 works by Hodler. There also are representative works of the Dadaist movement, which was conceived in Zürich by French exile Hans Arp. *Heimpl. 1, tel. 01/2516755. Admission varies with exhibitions. Open Tues.–Thurs. 10–9, Fri.–Sun. 10–5.*

Now head left to the **Wasserkirche** (Water Church), dating from the 15th century and a lovely example of late-Gothic architecture. It is attached to the **Helmhaus**, originally an 18th-century cloth market.

❼ Now turn right toward the **Grossmünster** church, which dates from the 11th century. During the 3rd century AD, St. Felix and his sister Regula were martyred by the Romans. Legend maintains that having been beheaded, they then walked up the hill carrying their heads and collapsed on the spot where the Grossmünster now stands. On the south tower you can see a statue of Charlemagne (768–814), emperor of the West, who founded the church when his horse stumbled on the same site. During the 16th century, the Zürich reformer Huldrych Zwingli preached sermons here that were so threatening in their promise of fire and brimstone that Martin Luther himself was frightened.

❽ Back at the river on the **Limmatquai** are some of Zürich's most enchanting old buildings. Today most of them are restaurants. In the **Haus zum Ruden,** a 13th-century noblemen's hall, you will eat under a 300-year-old wooden ceiling. Other notable buildings here are the **Zunfthaus zur Saffran** (built in 1723 for haberdashers) and the **Zunfthaus zur Zimmerleuten** (built in 1708 for carpenters). The 17th-century Baroque **Rathaus** (Town Hall) is nearby.

❾ Turn right into the **Altstadt** (old town), and you will enter a maze of fascinating medieval streets where time seems to have stood still. The Rindermarkt, Napfplatz, and Kirchgasse all have their charming old houses.

❿ Head back to the river through **Niederdorf** (Zürich's nightlife district) and cross the bridge to the Hauptbahnhof. On the northern

⓫ edge of the Hauptbahnhof, go to the **Schweizerisches Landesmuseum,** housed in a curious 19th-century building, for a look at Swiss history. There are fascinating pre-Romanesque and Romanesque church art, glass paintings from the 15th to the 17th century, splendid ceramic stoves, gold and silver from Celtic times, and weapons from many ages. *Museumstr. 2, tel. 01/2186565. Admission free. Open Tues.–Sun. 10–5.*

Off the Beaten Track

Wealthy Zürich spends its money when the occasion calls for it, and as a result its citizens and visitors benefit from a surfeit of excellent museums and galleries—many of them rarely mentioned outside Zürich itself. One of the most outstanding is the **Stiftung Sammlung E.G. Bührle** (Collection of the E.G. Bührle Foundation), a once-private collection of European art housed in a suburban mansion. Especially noteworthy are its French Impressionist and early modern paintings. *Zollikerstr. 172, tel. 01/4220086. Admission: 6.60 Fr. adults, 3 Fr. children. Open Tues. and Fri. 2–5 and Wed. 5–8.*

The **Museum Rietberg** is a wonderful gathering of art from India, China, Africa, Japan, and Southeast Asia, contained in the neoclassical Villa Wesendonck, where Richard Wagner once lived (as in *Wesendonck Songs*). *Gablerstr. 15, tel. 01/2024528. Admission: 3 Fr. adults, children 1 Fr. Open Tues., Thurs.–Sun. 10–5, Wed. 10–9.*

The **Graphiksammlung** (Graphics Collection) of the Eidgenössische Technische Hochschule (Federal Institute of Technology) displays portions of its vast library of woodcuts, etchings, and engravings by European masters such as Dürer, Rembrandt, Goya, and Picasso. From time to time there are good thematic exhibitions drawn from the collection. *Rämistr. 101, tel. 01/6324046. Admission free. Open Mon., Tues., Thurs., Fri. 10–5; Wed. 10–8.*

Shopping

Gift Ideas Typical Swiss products, all of the highest quality, include watches in all price categories, clocks, jewelry, music boxes, embroidered goods, wood carvings, and the famous multiblade Swiss army pocket knife. You'll also find fine household linens, delicate cotton or woolen underthings, and Zürich-made Fogal hosiery.

Shopping Districts The **Bahnhofstrasse** is one of the most bountiful shopping streets in Switzerland. Here you'll find **Jelmoli** (Seidengasse 1), Switzerland's largest department store, carrying a wide range of tasteful Swiss goods. **Heimatwerk** (Bahnhofstr. 2) specializes in handmade Swiss crafts, all of excellent quality. For high fashion, go to **Trois Pommes** (Storchengasse 6/7) and **Grieder** (Bahnhofstrasse 30), and for the finest porcelain, glass, and silverware, visit **Sequin-Dormann** (Bahnhofstr. 69a). If you have a sweet tooth, stock up on truffles at **Sprüngli** (Paradeplatz).

In the **Old Town** and off the **Limmatquai,** you'll find boutiques, antiques shops, bookstores, and galleries in picturesque byways. The **Löwenstrasse** has a diversity of upscale shops; the **Langstrasse** is another good shopping area and often has slightly lower prices. Under the central train station, **Shopville** offers a variety of middle-class stores and snack bars.

Food and Flea Markets In many parts of town, there are lively markets where fruit, vegetables, and flowers are competitively priced. The best are at **Bürkliplatz, Helvetiaplatz,** and **Milkbuckstrasse** (open Tues. and Fri. 6 AM–11 AM).

At Bürkliplatz, at the lake end of the Bahnhofstrasse, there's a flea market that's open on Saturday 6 AM to 3:30 PM May through October, and a curio market is held at **Rosenhof** every Thursday and Saturday between April and Christmas.

Dining

You're likely to be served seconds in Zürich's generous restaurants, where the rest of your *Rösti* (hash brown potatoes) and *Geschnetzeltes Kalbfleisch nach Zürcher Art* (veal bits in cream sauce, "Zürich style") simmer in copper pans by your table while you relish the hefty first portion. This is a Germanic city, after all, though its status as a minor world capital means that most international cuisines are represented as well. But brace yourself: The cash register rings portentously when the waiter places your order. Watch for posted *Tagesteller* specials, a good source of savings. For details and price-category definitions, *see* Dining in Staying in Switzerland, *above*.

Very Expensive **Königstuhl.** This trendy, tongue-in-cheek take on Zürich's

★ *Zunfthäuser* (guildhalls) has caught on with a vengeance. Itself the Zunfthaus zur Schneidern (Cutters' Guildhall), with a relatively traditional meeting hall on the top floor, this complex consisting of bar, bistro, and first-class restaurant functions more as an antizunfthaus: It's been entirely redone in cool gray graphite and glass, with halogen lighting and broad, droll allusions to Zürich's heavy Teutonic taste. The cuisine is equally irreverent, with light, moderately priced suppers (appetizers, pastas) downstairs in the bistro and superb international experiments in the soigné restaurant upstairs. There's a lovely courtyard terrace for summer dining. *Stüssihofstatt 3, tel. 01/2617618. Bistro: reservations advised, jack-*

et advised. Restaurant: reservations required, jacket and tie advised. AE, DC, MC, V.

La Rotonde. Even when it's not illuminated by candlelight, the Dolder Grand Hotel's haute cuisine restaurant is one of the most romantic spots in Zürich. Housed in a great arc of a room, La Rotonde provides sweeping park views that attract the lunchtime business crowd. Main courses may include grilled salmon with finely diced lobster, scallops, and shrimp in a hazelnut oil sauce, and sweetbreads on a bed of *gnocchi* with asparagus and truffles. The 70 Fr. prix-fixe dinner is a particularly good value. For those who love hors d'oeuvres, there's a Sunday afternoon buffet of nothing but starters. *Dolder Grand Hotel, Kurhausstr. 65, tel. 01/2516231. Reservations advised. Jacket and tie required. AE, DC, MC, V.*

★ **Petermann's Kunststuben.** This is one of Switzerland's gastronomic meccas, and while it's south of the city center, in Küssnacht on the lake's eastern shore, it's more than worth the 8-kilometer (5-mile) pilgrimage. The ever-evolving, fish-based menu may include lobster with artichoke and almond oil; grilled turbot with lemon sauce and capers; or Tuscan dove with pine nuts and herbs. There are great wines available by the glass. *Seestr. 160, Küssnacht, tel. 01/9100715. Reservations required. Jacket and tie advised. AE, DC, MC, V. Closed Sun. and Mon.*

Tübli. Tucked on a back alley in the more venturesome Niederdorf neighborhood, this intimate little Züricher secret continues to draw insiders for some of the best—and most innovative—cuisine in the city center. Eschewing à la carte standbys for ever-changing weekly seven-course menus, chef Martin Surbeck experiments with almost indiscriminate pleasure with literally far-fetched ingredients: Portuguese *chocolat* for his fish carpaccio, Norwegian reindeer with mulberry-flower mousseline, or passion-fruit soufflé. *Schneggengasse 8, tel. 01/2512471. Reservations advised. Jacket advised. AE, DC, MC, V. Closed weekends.*

Expensive **Blaue Ente.** Part of a shopping gallery in a converted mill south of
★ the city center, this modern, upmarket restaurant and bar draw well-dressed crowds from advertising and the arts. In a setting of whitewashed brick and glass, with jazz filtering through from the adjoining bar, guests sample a pot-au-feu of clams, prawns, and saffron, or lamb with potato pancakes and eggplant. Take the No. 2 tram toward Tiefenbrunnen. *Mühle Tiefenbrunnen, tel. 01/4227706. Reservations required. Jacket advised. AE, DC, MC, V.*

★ **Kronenhalle.** From Stravinsky, Brecht, and Joyce to Nureyev, Deneuve, and St-Laurent, this beloved landmark has always drawn a stellar crowd for its genial atmosphere, hearty cooking, and astonishing collection of 20th-century art. Try the herring in double cream, tournedos with truffle sauce, or duck à l'orange with red cabbage and *Spätzli* (tiny dumplings). And be sure to have a cocktail in the adjoining bar: *Le tout* Zürich drinks here. *Rämistr. 4, tel. 01/2516669. Reservations advised. Jacket and tie advised. AE, DC, MC, V.*

Veltliner Keller. Though its rich, carved-wood decor borrows from Graubündner Alpine culture, this ancient and atmospheric dining spot is no tourist trap: The house, built in 1325 and functioning as a restaurant since 1551, has always stored Italian-Swiss Valtellina wines, which were carried over the Alps and imported to Zürich. The traditional kitchen favors heavy meat standards, but is flexible and reasonably deft with seafood as well. *Schlüsselgasse 8, tel. 01/2213228. Reservations advised. Jacket and tie advised. AE, DC, MC, V.*

Moderate **Oepfelchammer.** This was once the haunt of Zürich's beloved writer
★ Gottfried Keller, and, now restored, it still draws unpretentious literati. One room's dark and graffiti-scribbled bar, with sagging timbers and slanting floors; the other's a welcoming little dining room,
with carved oak paneling, a coffered ceiling, and pink damask
linens. The traditional meats—calf's liver, veal, tripe in white wine
sauce—come in generous portions; salads are fresh and seasonal.
It's always packed, and service can be slow, so stake out a table and
spend the evening. *Rindermarkt 12, tel. 01/2512336. Reservations
advised. Dress: casual. MC, V. Closed Sun.*

Zunfthaus zur Schmiden. The sense of history and the magnificent
mix of Gothic wood, leaded glass, and tile stoves justify a visit to this
popular landmark, the guildhouse of blacksmiths and barbers since
1412. All the classics are served in enormous portions, and there's a
considerable selection of alternatives, fish among them. The guild's
own house wine is fine. *Marktgasse 20, tel. 01/2515287. Reservations advised. Dress: casual but neat. AE, DC, MC, V.*

Inexpensive **Bierhalle Kropf.** Under the giant boar's head and century-old murals
★ that have been recently restored, businesspeople, workers, and
shoppers crowd shared tables to feast on generous hot dishes and a
great selection of sausages. The *Leberknödli* (liver dumplings) are
tasty, *Apfelköchli* (fried apple slices) tender and sweet, and the
bread chewy and delicious—though you pay for every chunk you eat.
*In Gassen 16, tel. 01/2211805. Reservations advised. Dress: casual.
AE, DC, MC, V.*

Rheinfelder Bierhaus. Dark and smoky, with every wooden table
squeezing in mixed parties of workers, bikers, shoppers, and tourists, this is a solid old institution in the Niederdorf area. There's rich
Rindpfeffer (preserved beef stew) with homemade *Spätzli*, tender
liver with *Rösti*, sausage dishes, and once a month, the chef's pride:
an incongruous but freshly homemade paella. *Marktgasse 19, tel.
01/2512991. Reservations not necessary. Dress: casual. No credit
cards.*

Zeughauskeller. Built as an arsenal in 1487, this enormous stone and
beam hall offers hearty meat platters and a variety of beers and
wines amid comfortable and friendly chaos. Waitresses are harried
and brisk, especially at lunchtime, when crowds are thick. They're
not unaccustomed to tourists, but locals consider this their home
away from home. *Bahnhofstr. 28 (at Paradeplatz), tel. 01/2112690.
Reservations advised at lunch. Dress: casual. No credit cards.*

Lodging

Zürich has an enormous range of hotels, from some of the most chic
and prestigious in the country to modest guest houses. Prices tend
to be higher than anywhere else in Europe, but you can be sure that
you will get what you pay for: Quality and good service are guaranteed. For details and price-category definitions, *see* Lodging in
Staying in Switzerland.

Very **Baur au Lac.** This is the hoary, highbrow patrician of Swiss hotels,
Expensive with luxury facilities but none of the glitz associated with the flashi-
★ er upstarts among prestige resorts. Its broad back is turned to the
commercial center, and its front rooms overlook the lake, canal, and
manicured lawns of the hotel's private park. Decor is posh, discreet,
and firmly fixed in the Age of Reason. In summer, meals are served
in the glassed park Pavilion along the canal; in winter, in the glowing Restaurant Français. The Grillroom is a business tradition.
Talstr. 1, CH–8022, tel. 01/2211650, fax 01/2118139. 156 rooms with

bath. Facilities: 3 restaurants, bar, disco, beauty shop, Rolls-Royce limousine service, parking. AE, DC, MC, V.

★ **Dolder Grand.** A cross between Camp David and Maria Theresa's summer palace, this sprawling Victorian fantasy-palace sits high on a wooded hill over Zürich, quickly reached from Römerhof by funicular railway (free for guests) and offering splendid views and complete self-sufficiency. It was opened in 1899 as a summer resort, a picturesque hodgepodge of turrets, cupolas, half-timbers, and mansards; the uncompromisingly modern wing was added in 1964, but from inside the connection is seamless. The garden and forest views behind nearly match those of the golf course, park, and city itself. Restaurant La Rotonde excels in traditional French cuisine (*see* Dining, *above*). *Kurhausstr. 65, CH-8032, tel. 01/2516231, fax 01/2518829. 207 rooms with bath. Facilities: French restaurant, terrace cafe, bar, hairdresser, underground parking, swimming pool with wave machine, 9-hole golf course, tennis courts, ice-skating rink. AE, DC, MC, V.*

★ **Savoy Baur en Ville.** The oldest hotel in Zürich, built in 1838, this luxurious downtown landmark was gutted in 1975 and reconstructed as an airtight urban gem. It's directly on the Paradeplatz and at the hub of the banking, shopping, and sightseeing districts. The rooms have a warm, postmodern decor, with pearwood cabinetry, brass, and chintz, and there are two fine restaurants—one French, the other Italian—as well as a city-slick café. *Paradeplatz, CH-8022, tel. 01/2115360, fax 01/2111467. 112 rooms with bath. Facilities: 2 restaurants, café. AE, DC, MC, V.*

Expensive
★ **Neues Schloss.** Headed by Bernard Seiler, an heir to the Zermatt hotel dynasty, this small, discreet hotel in the business district (southeast of Paradeplatz) shows its bloodlines, offering a cordial welcome, good service, and the warmth of a tastefully furnished private home. Its restaurant, Le Jardin, is airy and floral, and popular at lunch. *Stockerstr. 17, CH-8022, tel. 01/2016550, fax 01/2016418. 59 rooms with bath. Facilities: restaurant. AE, DC, MC, V.*

Splügenschloss. Constructed at the turn of the century as luxury apartments, this Relais et Châteaux property maintains an ornate and historic decor, with antiques in rooms as well as throughout public spaces. Some rooms have been paneled completely in Alpine-style pine, others in fussy florals. Its location southeast of the Neues Schloss may be a little out of the way for tourists, but atmosphere buffs will find it worth the effort. *Splügenstr. 2, CH-8002, tel. 01/2010800, fax 01/2014286. 55 rooms. Facilities: restaurant, bar. AE, DC, MC, V.*

★ **Zum Storchen.** In a stunning central location, tucked between Fraumünster and St. Peter on the gull-studded banks of the Limmat, this airy 600-year-old structure houses an impeccable modern hotel. It has warmly appointed rooms, some with French windows that open over the water, and a lovely terrace restaurant as well as a cozy, guildhouselike dining room. *Weinplatz 2, CH-8001, tel. 01/2115510, fax 01/2116451. 77 rooms with bath. Facilities: restaurant, terrace café, snack bar, bar. AE, DC, MC, V.*

Moderate
City. Near the Bahnhofstrasse, train station, and Löwenstrasse shopping district, this is a hotel in miniature, with small furnishings and baths and a high proportion of single rooms. It's recently been renewed to chic pastel polish, and some rooms fall in the Expensive category. *Löwenstr. 34, CH-8021, tel. 01/2112055, fax 01/2120036. 83 rooms. AE, DC, MC, V.*

★ **Rössli.** Young, trendy, and completely high-tech, this hip new spot in Oberdorf, near the Grossmünster, offers a refreshing antidote to Zürich's medievalism. Decor is white-on-white, with metallic-tiled baths, vivid lithographs, and splashy fabrics; hair dryers, robes, and fax connections keep services above average, especially for the price. The adjoining bar is very popular with young locals. *Rössligasse 7, CH-8001, tel. 01/2522121, fax 01/252213. 12 rooms with bath. Facilities: bar. AE, DC, MC, V.*

★ **Sonnenberg.** If you're traveling by car and want to avoid the urban rush, escape to this hillside refuge east of town. There are breathtaking views of the city, lake, and mountains, and landscaped grounds with a lovely terrace restaurant. The wood, stone, and beam decor reinforces the resort atmosphere. It's run by the friendly Wismer family. Take tram No. 3 or No. 8 to Klusplatz, then walk 10 minutes uphill. *Aurorastr. 98, CH-8030, tel. 01/2620062, fax 01/2620633. 35 rooms with bath. Facilities: restaurant, terrace cáfe. AE, DC, MC, V.*

Wellenberg. Another effort at high style but not as effective as the Rössli, this new, central hotel sports a postmodern retro look, with burled wood, black lacquer, Art Deco travel posters, and Hollywood photos. Rooms are relatively roomy, if occasionally garish, and the location—on Niederdorf's Hirschenplatz—is superb. Some rooms are expensive. *Niederdorfstr. 10, CH-8001, tel. 01/2624300, fax 01/2513130. 46 rooms with bath. AE, DC, MC, V.*

Inexpensive **St. Georges.** While this simple former pension has a fresh, bright lobby and breakfast room, guest rooms and corridors are considerably more spare, with toothpaste-green walls, red linoleum floors, and '60s pine furniture. Rooms are available with and without showers. Take tram No. 3 or No. 14 from the station to Stauffacher, west of the center; it's another five minutes on foot. *Weberstrasse 11, tel. 01/2411144. 44 rooms. Facilities: breakfast room. AE, DC, MC, V.*

Vorderer Sternen. On the edge of the Old Town and near the lake, this plain but adequate establishment takes in the bustle (and noise) of the city. It's steps from the opera house, theaters, art galleries, cinemas, and a shopping area; it's also close to the Bellevueplatz tram junction. There's a dependable and popular restaurant downstairs with moderate standards. *Theaterstr. 22, CH-8001 tel. 01/2514949, fax 01/2529063. 15 rooms without bath. AE, DC, MC, V.*

The Arts

Pick up *Zürich News,* published each week by the tourist office, to check what's on. Ticket reservations can be made through the **Billetzentrale** (Werdmühleplatz, tel. 01/2212283; open weekdays 10–6:30, Sat. 10–2). **Musik Hug** (Limmatquai 26, tel. 01/2212540) and **Jecklin** (Rämistr. 30, tel. 01/2617733) are good ticket sources as well.

The **Zürich Tonhalle Orchestra** (Claridenstr. 7, tel. 01/2063434) ranks among Europe's best. The **Opernhaus** (Falkenstr., tel. 01/2620909) is renowned for its adventurous opera, operetta, and ballet productions. The **Schauspielhaus** (Rämistr. 34, tel. 01/2655858) is one of the finest German-speaking theaters in the world. Zürich has 40 movie theaters, with English-language films appearing regularly.

Nightlife

Zürich has a lively nightlife scene, largely centered in the Niederdorf, parallel to the Limmat, across from the Hauptbahnhof. Many spots are short-lived, so check in advance. Informal dress is acceptable in most places, but again, check to make sure. The hotel porter is a good source of information.

Bars and Lounges The narrow bar at the **Kronenhalle** (Rämistr. 4, tel. 01/2511597) draws mobs of well-heeled locals and internationals for its prize-winning cocktails. The **Jules Verne Panorama Bar** (Uraniahaus, tel. 01/2111155) offers cocktails with a wraparound view of downtown Zürich. **Champagnertreff** in the Hotel Central (Central 1, tel. 01/2515555) is a popular Deco-look piano bar with several champagnes available by the glass. **Odeon** (Am Bellevue, tel. 01/2511650) serves a young, arty set until 4 AM. Some beer halls, including **Bierhalle Kropf** (In Gassen 16, tel. 01/2211805) and **Zeughauskeller** (Bahnhofstr. 28, tel. 01/2112690), serve a variety of draft beers in an old-Zürich atmosphere.

Cabaret/ Nightclubs There's a variety show (dancers, magicians) at **Polygon** (Marktgasse 17, tel. 01/2521110). There are strip shows all over town, as well as the traditional nightclub atmosphere at **Le Privé** (Stauffacherstr. 106, tel. 01/2416487), **Moulin Rouge** (Mühlegasse 14, tel. 01/2620730), and the slightly more sophisticated **Terrace** (Limmatquai 3, tel. 01/2511074).

Discos **Mascotte** (Theaterstr. 10, tel. 01/2524481) is, at the moment, popular with all ages on weeknights, but caters to young crowds on weekends. **Le Petit Prince** (Bleicherweg 21, tel. 01/2011739) attracts an upscale crowd. Even more exclusive is **Diagonal,** at the Hotel Baur au Lac (Talstr. 1, tel. 01/2117396), where you must be a hotel guest—or the guest of one. **Rasputine's** (Schützengasse 16, tel. 01/2115058) offers 40 different kinds of vodka.

Jazz Jazz clubs **Casa Bar** (Münstergasse 30, tel. 01/2612002) and **Moods** (Schlamtstrasse 5, tel. 01/2018130) offer jazz into the wee hours.

Excursion from Zürich: Liechtenstein

For an international day trip out of Zürich, dip a toe into tiny Liechtenstein: There isn't room for much more. Just 80 kilometers (50 miles) southeast on the Austrian border, this miniature principality covers a scant 158 square kilometers (61 square miles). An independent nation since 1719, Liechtenstein has a customs union with Switzerland, which means they share trains, currency, and diplomats—but not stamps, which is why collectors prize the local releases. It's easiest to get there by car, since Liechtenstein is so small that Swiss trains pass through without stopping. If you're using a train pass, ride to Sargans or Buchs and take a postbus across the border to Liechtenstein's capital, Vaduz.

Tourist Information The principal tourist office in Liechtenstein is at Städtle 37, Box 139, FL 9490, Vaduz, tel. 075/2321443. It's open weekdays 8–5:30, Sat. 9–4.

Exploring Liechtenstein Green and mountainous, its Rhineshores lined with vineyards, greater Liechtenstein is best seen by car. But if you're on foot, you won't be stuck: The postbuses are prompt and take you everywhere at a scenic snail's pace.

In fairy-tale **Vaduz,** Prince Johannes Adam Pius still lives in **Vaduz Castle,** a massive 16th-century fortress perched high on the cliff over the city. Only honored guests of the prince tour the interior, but its exterior and the views from the grounds are worth the climb. In the modern center of town, head for the tourist information office to have your passport stamped with the Liechtenstein crown. Upstairs, the **Prince's Art Gallery and the State Art Collection** showcase various sectors—say, 20th-century Spanish masters—of the vast royal collection. *Städtle 37, tel. 075/2322341. Admission: 3 Fr.*

adults, 1.5 Fr. children. Open Apr.–Oct., daily 10–noon and 1:30–5:30; Nov.–Mar., daily 10–noon and 1:30–5.

On the same floor, the **Postage Stamp Museum** attracts philatelists from all over the world to see the 300 frames of beautifully designed—and relatively rare—stamps. Place subscriptions here for future first-day covers. *Städtle 37, tel. 075/2366109. Admission free. Open Apr.–Oct., daily 10–noon and 1:30–5:30; Nov.–Mar., 10–noon and 1:30–5.*

Next, move on to the **Liechtenstein National Museum,** which houses historical artifacts, church carvings, ancient coins, and arms from the prince's collection. *Städtle 43, tel. 075/22310. Admission: 2 Fr. Open May–Sept., daily 10–noon and 1:30–5:30; Oct.–Apr., Tues.–Sun. 2–5:30; may be closed into 1995 for renovations.*

In **Schaan,** just north of Vaduz, visit the Roman excavations and the parish church built on the foundations of a Roman fort. Or drive up to the chalets of picturesque **Triesenberg** for spectacular views of the Rhine Valley. Higher still, **Malbun** is a sundrenched ski bowl with comfortable slopes and a low-key family ambience.

Dining   For details and price-category definitions, *see* Dining in Staying in Switzerland, *above.*

★ **Real.** Surrounded by slick, new decor, you'll find rich, old-style Austrian-French cuisine in all its buttery glory, prepared these days by Martin Real, son of the unpretentious former chef, Felix Real. The menu offers game, seafood, generous seasonal salads, soufflés, and an extraordinary wine list. Downstairs is a more casual stübli. There are 11 small but fresh decked rooms upstairs, with new tile baths. *Städtle 21, Vaduz, tel. 075/2322222. Reservations advised. Jacket and tie advised upstairs. AE, DC, MC, V. Very Expensive (restaurant), Expensive (hotel).*

★ **Wirtschaft zum Löwen.** Though there's plenty of French, Swiss, and Austrian influence, Liechtenstein has a cuisine of its own, and this is the place to try it. In a wood-shingled farmhouse on the Austrian border, the friendly Biedermann family serves tender homemade *Schwartenmagen* (the pressed porkmold known unfortunately as headcheese in English), pungent *Sauerkäse* (sour cheese), and *Käseknöpfli* (cheese dumplings), plus lovely meats and the local crusty, chewy bread. *Schellenberg, tel. 075/3731162. Reservations advised. V. Inexpensive.*

Lodging   For details and price-category definitions, *see* Lodging in Staying in Switzerland, *above.*

Park-Hotel Sonnenhof. A garden oasis commanding a superb view over the valley and mountains beyond, this hillside retreat offers discreet luxury minutes from downtown Vaduz. Some rooms open directly onto the lawns; others have balconies. It has an excellent restaurant exclusive to guests. *Mareestr. 29, tel. 075/2321192, fax 075/2320053. 29 rooms with bath. Facilities: indoor pool, sauna. AE, DC, MC, V. Very Expensive.*

Engel. Directly on the main tourist street, its café bulging with bus-tour crowds, this simple hotel/restaurant manages to maintain a local, comfortable ambience. The Huber family oversees the easygoing pub downstairs; the restaurant upstairs serves Chinese food. The rooms were renovated in winter 1991. *Städtle 13, tel. 075/2320313, fax 075/2331159. 17 rooms with bath. Facilities: restaurant, café, terrace. AE, DC, MC, V. Moderate.*

Alpenhotel. Well above the mists of the Rhine in sunny Malbun, this 82-year-old chalet has been remodeled and a modern wing added.

The old rooms are small and cozy; the higher-priced new rooms are modern and spare. The Vögeli family's welcoming smiles and good food have made it a local institution. *Tel. 075/2631181, fax 075/2639646. 25 rooms with bath. Facilities: restaurant, café, indoor pool. AE, DC, MC, V. Inexpensive.*

Geneva

Arriving and Departing

By Plane Cointrin (tel. 022/7993111), Geneva's airport, is served by several airlines that fly directly to the city from New York, Toronto, or London. Swissair also has flights from Chicago and Los Angeles. Check with individual airlines for their schedules.

Swissair ticketholders departing from Cointrin can check their luggage through to the airplane from 120 rail and postal bus stations, and also get their boarding passes at eight train stations.

Between the Airport and Downtown Cointrin has a direct rail link with Cornavin (tel. 022/7316450), the city's main train station, which is located in the center of town. Trains run about every 10 minutes from 5:30 AM to midnight. The trip takes about six minutes, and the fare is 5 Fr. for second class.

There is regular city bus service from the airport to the center of Geneva. The bus takes about 20 minutes, and the fare is 2 Fr. Some hotels have their own bus service.

Taxis, though plentiful, are very expensive, charging at least 25 Fr. to the city center. Tips are expected only for luggage.

By Train All services—domestic and international—use Cornavin Station in the center of the city. For information, dial 022/7316450.

By Bus Buses generally arrive at and depart from the bus station at place Dorcière, behind the English church in the city center.

By Car Since Geneva sits on France's doorstep, entry from France, just a few minutes away, is very convenient. Or enter from the north via Lausanne.

Getting Around

By Bus and Streetcar There are scheduled services by local buses and trains every few minutes on all routes. Before you board, you must buy your ticket from the machines at the stops (they have English instructions). For 2 Fr. you can use the system for one hour, changing as often as you like. Save money and buy a ticket covering unlimited travel all day within the city center for 5 Fr. If you have a **Swiss Pass,** you can travel free (*see* Getting Around Switzerland by Train, *above*).

By Taxi Taxis are extremely expensive; use them only if there's no alternative. There is a 5 Fr. minimum charge per passenger just to get into the cab plus a charge of 2 Fr. per kilometer.

Guided Tours

Orientation Tours Bus tours around Geneva are operated by **Key Tours** (tel. 022/7314140). They leave from the bus station in place Dorcière, behind the English church, at 2 (also at 10 AM in high season). These tours, which involve some walking in the Old Town, last about two hours and cost 26 Fr.

Special-Interest Tours	The United Nations organizes tours around the Palais des Nations. Take bus No. 8 or F past Nations to the Appia stop. Enter by the Pregny Gate in the avenue de la Paix. Tours, lasting about an hour, are given regularly from January through March and November to mid-December, weekdays 10–noon and 2–4; April through June, September, and October, daily 10–noon and 2–4; July and August, daily 9–noon and 2–6. They cost 8 Fr. for adults, 3.50 Fr. for children 6–18.

The tourist office will provide you with an audio-guided tour (in English) of the Old Town that covers 26 points of interest, complete with map, cassette, and player; rental is 10 Fr. A refundable deposit of 50 Fr. is required.

Excursions	There are bus excursions from Geneva to Lausanne, Montreux, the Mont Blanc area, the Jura, and the Bernese Oberland. They vary considerably according to the weather and time of year, so inquire locally.

Boat excursions vary for the same reasons. When the weather is good, take one of the delightful daylong trips that stop at some of the waterside villages on the vineyard-fringed lake; some trips also pass by or stop at the 13th-century Château de Chillon, the inspiration for Byron's *The Prisoner of Chillon*. Full details are available from **Mouettes Genevoises** (tel. 022/7322944), **Swissboat** (tel. 022/7367935), **Compagnie de Navigation** (tel. 022/3112521), or from the tourist office.

Tourist Information

The **Office du Tourisme de Genève** (Cornavin Station, tel. 022/7385200; open mid-Sept.–mid-June, Mon.–Sat. 9–6; late June–early Sept., weekdays 8–8, weekends 8–6). For information by mail, contact the administration at 1, rue de la Tour de l'Ile, Case Postale 5230, CH-1211 Genève. **Thomas Cook** (64 rue de Lausanne, tel. 022/7324555).

Exploring Geneva

Draped at the foot of the Juras and the Alps on the westernmost tip of Lake Geneva (or Lac Léman, as the natives know it), Geneva is the most cosmopolitan and graceful of Swiss cities and the stronghold of the French-speaking territory. Just a stone's throw from the French border and 160 kilometers (100 miles) or so from Lyon, its grand mansarded mansions stand guard beside the river Rhône, where yachts bob, gulls dive, and Rolls-Royces purr beside manicured promenades. The combination of Swiss efficiency and French savoir faire gives the city a chic polish, and the infusion of international blood from the United Nations adds a heterogeneity that is rare in cities with a population of only 160,000.

Headquarters of the World Health Organization and the International Red Cross, Geneva has always been a city of humanity and enlightenment, offering refuge to writers Voltaire, Hugo, Dumas, Balzac, and Stendhal, as well as to religious reformers Calvin and Knox. Byron, Shelley, Wagner, and Liszt all fled from scandals to Geneva's sheltering arms.

A Roman seat for 500 years (from 120 BC), then home to early Burgundians, Geneva flourished under bishop-princess into the 11th century, fending off the greedy dukes of Savoy in conflicts that lasted into the 17th century. Under the guiding fervor of Calvin, Geneva rejected Catholicism and became a stronghold of Protestant reforms. In 1798 it fell to the French, but joined the Swiss Confederation as a canton in 1815, shortly after Napoleon's defeat. The French accent remains nonetheless.

Numbers in the margin correspond to points of interest on the Geneva map.

❶ Start your walk from Gare de Cornavin (Cornavin Station) and head down the rue du Mont-Blanc to the **Pont du Mont-Blanc,** which spans the westernmost point of Lac Léman as it squeezes back into the Rhône. From the middle of the bridge (if it's clear) you can see the snowy peak of Mont Blanc itself, and from March through October you'll have a fine view of the **Jet d'Eau,** Europe's highest fountain, gushing 145 meters (475 feet) into the air.

❷ Back at the foot of the bridge, turn right onto quai du Mont-Blanc to reach the **Monument Brunswick,** the high-Victorian tomb of a duke of Brunswick who left his fortune to Geneva in 1873. Just north are the city's grandest hotels, overlooking a manicured garden walk and the embarkation points for excursion boats. If you continue north a considerable distance through elegant parks and turn inland on the ❸ avenue de la Paix, you'll reach the enormous **International Complex,** where the **Palais des Nations** houses the European seat of the United Nations. (You can also reach it by taking bus No. 8 or F from the train station. For guided tour information, *see* Special-Interest Tours, *above*.)

❹ Or turn left from the Pont du Mont-Blanc and walk down the elegant quai des Bergues. In the center of the Rhône is the **Ile Rousseau** (Rousseau Island), with a statue of the Swiss-born philosopher. ❺ Turn left onto the **Pont de l'Ile,** where the tall Tour de l'Ile, once a medieval prison, houses the tourist office. Turn left again and cross the place Bel-Air, the center of the business and banking district, ❻ and follow the rue de la Corraterie to the **place Neuve.** Here you'll see the **Grand Théâtre,** which hosts opera, ballet, and sometimes the Orchestre de la Suisse Romande (it also performs at nearby Victoria Hall), and the **Conservatoire de Musique.** Also at this address is the **Musée Rath,** with top-notch temporary exhibitions. *Tel. 022/ 3105270. Admission and hours vary with exhibition; check local listings.*

Above the ancient ramparts on your left are some of the wealthiest old homes in Geneva. Enter the gated park before you, the promenade des Bastions, site of the university, and keep left until you see ❼ the famous **Monument de la Réformation,** which pays homage to such Protestant pioneers as Bèze, Calvin, Farel, and Knox. Passing the uphill ramp and continuing to the farther rear gate, take the park exit just beyond the monument and turn left on the rue St-Leger, passing through the ivy-covered arch and winding into the **Vieille Ville,** or Old Town.

❽ When you reach the ancient place du Bourg-de-Four, once a Roman forum, turn right on rue des Chaudronniers and head for the **Musée d'Art et Histoire,** with its fine collection of paintings, sculpture, and archaeological relics. *2 rue Charles-Galland, tel. 022/3114340. Admission free. Open Tues.–Sun. 10–5.*

❾ Just beyond are the spiraling cupolas of the **Eglise Russe** (Russian ❿ Church) and the **Collection Baur** of Oriental arts. *8 rue Munier-Romilly, tel. 022/3461729. Admission: 5 Fr. Open Tues.–Sun. 2–6.*

Alternatively, from the place du Bourg-de-Four, head left up any ⓫ number of narrow streets and stairs toward the **Cathédrale St-**

Pierre, with its schizophrenic mix of Classical and Gothic styles. Under its nave (entrance outside) is concealed one of the biggest **archaeological digs** in Europe, a massive excavation of the cathedral's early Christian predecessors, now restored as a stunning maze of backlit walkways over mosaics, baptisteries, and ancient foundations. *Tel. 022/7385650. Admission to site: 5 Fr. Open Tues.–Sun. 10–1 and 2–6.*

⑫ Calvin worshiped in the cathedral; he made the **Temple de l'Auditoire,** a small Gothic church just south of the cathedral toward place du Bourg-de-Four, into his lecture hall, where he taught missionaries his doctrines of reform. *Place de la Taconnerie, tel. 022/ 738–5650. Open Oct.–May, weekdays 9–noon and 2–5, Sat. 9:30–12:30 and 2–5, Sun. 2–5; June–Sept., weekdays 9–noon and 2–6, Sat. 9:30–12:30 and 2–6, Sun. 2–6.*

Behind the Temple de l'Auditoire, on the rue de l'Hôtel de Ville, is
⑬ the 16th-century **Hôtel de Ville,** where in 1864, in the Alabama Hall, the Geneva Convention was signed by 16 countries, laying the foundations for the International Red Cross. *Individual visits by request. Guided group tours by advance arrangement, tel. 022/ 3272202.*

The winding, cobbled streets leading from the cathedral down to the modern city are lined with antiques shops, galleries, and unique but often expensive boutiques. The medieval Grand' Rue is the oldest in Geneva, the rue de l'Hôtel de Ville features lovely 17th-century homes, and the rue Calvin has noble mansions of the 18th century (No. 11 is on the site of Jean Calvin's house). No. 6 on the rue du
⑭ Puits-St-Pierre is the **Maison Tavel,** the oldest building in town and home of a vivid, intimate re-creation of daily life and urban history. *Tel. 022/3102900. Admission free. Open Tues.–Sun. 10–5.*

Down the hill, plunge back into the new city and one of the most luxurious shopping districts in Europe, which stretches temptingly between the quai Général-Guisan, rue du Rhône, rue de la Croix d'Or, and rue du Marché. It's tough enough to resist top name *prêt-à-porter* (ready-to-wear clothing), dazzling jewelry and watches, luscious chocolates, and luxurious furs and leathers, but the glittering bou-
⑮ tiques of the new three-story **Confédération-Centre**—where all the above are concentrated with a vengeance—could melt the strongest resolve. Escape across the quai, head back toward the lake, and
⑯ come to your senses in the **Jardin Anglais,** where the famous floral clock will tell you that it's time to stop.

Dining

Perch fresh from Lac Léman, cream-sauced *omble chevalier* (a kind of salmon trout), Lyonnaise *cardon* (a celerylike vegetable often served in casseroles), pigs' feet, and the famous cheese fondue are specialties of this most French of Swiss cities. Be warned: Many restaurants close on weekends. For details and price-category definitions, *see* Dining in Staying in Switzerland, *above.*

Very Expensive ★ **Le Béarn.** This elegant little restaurant in Empire style, dressed up with pretty porcelain and crystal, features modern, light, and creative cuisine: ravioli stuffed with Scotch salmon and oysters, preserved rabbit in green mustard sauce, and any number of truffle specialties, including a spectacular truffle soufflé. There are excellent Swiss and French wines. *4 quai de la Poste, tel. 022/3210028. Reservations required. Jacket and tie advised. AE, MC, V. Closed Sat. lunch and Sun.*

Cathédrale
St-Pierre, **11**

Collection Baur, **10**

Confédération-
Centre, **15**

Eglise Russe, **9**

Hôtel de Ville, **13**

Ile Rousseau, **4**

International
Complex, **3**

Jardin Anglais, **16**

Maison Tavel, **14**

Monument
Brunswick, **2**

Monument de la
Réformation, **7**

Musée d'Art et
Histoire, **8**

Place Neuve, **6**

Pont de l'Ile, **5**

Pont du Mont-Blanc, **1**

Temple de
l'Auditoire, **12**

Geneva

Rue de Berne

Rue Rossi

Rue des Pâquis

Rue Ph. Plantamour

③

Rue des Alpes

Pl. des
Alpes

Rue Adhémar-Fabri

②

Square du
Mont-Blanc

Quai du Mont-Blanc

Lac Léman

0 ____ 220 yards
0 ____ 200 meters

AE

Rue du
Mont-Blanc

Je Cendrier

Rue Kléberg

Pl. des
Bergues

①

Bergues

Pont des
Bergues

Pont de la
Rhône

Pont du Mont-Blanc

④

Ile
Rousseau

Promenade du Lac

Quai Gustav-Ador

Rue du lac

Rue Muzy

Pl. de la
Fusterie

Rue du Rhône

Pl.
Port

Jardin
Anglais ⑯

R. de la Scie

R. des Eaux-Vives

Place de
Molard

Quai Général - Guisan

Pl.
Longemalle

federation R. du Marché

⑮

Rue de la Croix d'Or Rue de Rive

Rue Versonnex

Rue d'Italie

Rue P.-Fatio

Blvd. Helvétique

Pl. des
Eaux
Vives

Ave. Pictet de
Rochemont

Rue de la Rôtisserie

Rue Jean-Calvin

Grand-Rue

des
Granges

la
Treille

Rue du Puits-
St-Pierre

⑭

⑪

⑫

⑬

Rue de l'Hôtel de Ville

Rue de la Fontaine

Rue Verdaine

Rond-Point
de Rive

Pl. du Pré
l'Évêque

Rue de la Terrassière

de la Croix-Rouge

⑦

Rue des
Chaudronniers

Pl. du Bourg-
de-Four

Rue Ferdinand-Hodler

R. d. Glacis-de-Rive

R. A.-Lachenal

Rue de Villereuse

⑧

Blvd. Jaques-Dalcroze

Rue Charles-Galland

Rue Toepffer

R. Sturm

⑨

Route de

St-Léger R. de l'Athénée

Blvd. Helvétique

R. Munier
Romilly

Place
Emile-Gayénot

Malagnou

Rue
Cours
des Bastions

R. le-Fort

R. le-Fort

⑩

Blvd. des
Tranchées

Les Continents. It's often a shock to find exceptional restaurants in modern business hotels, but this one—at the base of the Inter-Continental's 18 stories—serves contemporary French cuisine prepared by Irish super-chef Tommy Byrne. Try the warm salad of scallops with Oriental spices, pigeon pie, or grilled foie gras. All the international heads of state have met here during the peace conferences of the past 25 years. *7–9 ch. du Petit-Saconnex, tel. 022/ 7346091. Reservations required. Jacket and tie advised. AE, DC, MC, V. Closed Sat.; Sun. dinner.*

Expensive **La Cassolette.** Located in the heart of Carouge, the picturesque *cité*
★ *sarde* (Sardinian city) of old houses, tiny streets, and ancient courtyards, this modern and colorful upscale bistro features the imaginative cuisine of young chef Réné Fracheboud. Novel specialties— salmon and zucchini with dried tomatoes and curry oil, or veal sweetbreads and duck liver in bitter cocoa and Arabian coffee—are served on Miami-bright triangular platters, in high contrast to the very pink decor. There's an unusual list of lesser-known wines, available by the glass. *31 rue Jacques Dalphin, Carouge, tel. 022/ 3420318. Reservations advised. Dress: casual. No credit cards. Closed Sat. and Sun.*

La Mère Royaume. Only in Geneva could you find good, classic French cooking served in a pseudo-historic setting under the careful direction of a charming Italian couple. Even the name is Genevois: La Mère Royaume was a kind of Genevois Joan of Arc, who in 1602 repulsed the army of the duke of Savoy by dumping hot soup on the soldiers' heads. The main restaurant serves formal French standards—duck liver with raspberries, rack of lamb with garlic confit—but the rustic bistro offers inexpensive plats du jour. *9 rue des Corps-Saints, tel. 022/7327008. Reservations advised. Jacket and tie advised. AE, DC, MC, V. Closed Sat. lunch and Sun.*

Moderate **Boeuf Rouge.** Despite its kitschy decor this cozy and popular spot
★ delivers the real thing: rich, unadulterated Lyon cuisine, from the bacon, egg, and greens *salade Lyonnaise* to the homemade pistachio sausage with lentil salad; *boudin noir* (blood sausage) with apples; *andouillettes* (chitterling sausage) in mustard sauce; and authentic *tarte tatin. 17 rue Alfred-Vincent, tel. 022/7327537. Reservations advised. Dress: casual. V. Closed weekends.*

★ **La Favola.** Run by a young Ticinese couple from Locarno, this quirky little restaurant may be the most picturesque in town. The tiny dining room, at the top of a vertiginous spiral staircase, strikes a delicate balance between rustic and fussy, with its lace window panels, embroidered cloths, polished parquet, and rough-beamed ceiling sponge-painted in Roman shades of ochre and rust. The food finds the same delicate balance between country simple and city chic: carpaccio with olive paste or white truffles, rabbit in Gorgonzola. *15 rue Jean Calvin, tel. 022/3117437. Reservations advised. Dress: casual. MC, V. Closed weekends.*

Le Pied-de-Cochon. While visiting antiques shops and art galleries in the Vielle Ville, stop for lunch or supper in this old bistro, which retains its original beams and zinc-top bar. Crowded, noisy, smoky, lively, it faces the Palais de Justice and shelters famous lawyers who plead celebrated causes; there are artists and workers as well. The good, simple fare includes *pieds de cochon* (pigs' feet), of course, either grilled, with mushrooms, with lentils, or *dessossés* (boned), as well as simple Lyonnais dishes, including *petit salé* (pork belly), ham, grilled *andouillettes* (chitterling sausages), tripe, and salads. *4 place du Bourg-de-Four, tel. 022/3104797. Reservations advised. Dress: casual. AE, DC, MC, V. Closed weekends.*

Inexpensive ★ **Les Armures.** In the picturesque and historic hotel at the summit of the Old Town (*see* Lodging, *below*) and two steps from the Cathédrale St-Pierre, this atmospheric restaurant offers several dining halls, all decorated with authentic arms from the Middle Ages. The broad menu of Swiss specialties ranges from fondue to *choucroute* to *Rösti*, but some of the dishes are pure Genevois. There also are inexpensive pizzas and a good selection of salads and fruit tarts. Everyone comes here, from workers to politicians. *1 rue du Puits-St-Pierre, tel. 022/3103442. Reservations advised. Dress: casual. AE, DC, MC, V.*

★ **Taverne de la Madeleine.** Tucked into the commercial maze between the Rue de la Croix d'Or and the Old Town, by l'Eglise de la Madeleine, this casual, alcohol-free café claims to be the oldest eatery in Geneva. It's run by the city's temperance league, and thus loses the business clientele that insist on a pitcher of Fendant with their meals: All the more room for you to relax over homemade *choucroute*, perch, or fresh-baked fruit tarts in the charming Victorian upstairs dining room. There are big, fresh salads, vegetable plates, and a variety of loose-leaf teas. *20 rue Toutes-âmes, tel. 022/3106070. Reservations advised. Dress: casual. No credit cards.*

Lodging

For details and price-category definitions, *see* Lodging in Staying in Switzerland, *above.*

Very **Beau-Rivage.** Hushed and genteel, this grand old Victorian palace
Expensive has been largely restored to its 1865 splendor: It's all velvet, parquet, and frescoes, and there's a marble fountain in the lobby. Front rooms take in magnificent Right Bank views, as does the terrace restaurant on the first floor, over the prestigious French restaurant Le Chat Botté. In 1898, Empress Elizabeth of Austria died here after being shot only 100 meters away. *13 quai du Mont-Blanc, CH-1201, tel. 022/7310221, fax 022/7389847. 115 rooms with bath. Facilities: two restaurants, terrace café, bar, video. AE, DC, MC, V.*

★ **Le Richemond.** Under the management of the Armleder family since 1875, this Right Bank luxury landmark maintains its Victorian presence without looking like a museum. Nor does it feel like one: This is a lively, thriving, contemporary inn, proud of recent guests (Michael Jackson) as well as past ones (Colette, Miró, Chagall). Only the restaurant Le Gentilhomme indulges in museumlike conservatism: Amid pompous red velvet, crystal, and gilt, you can indulge in a meal Escoffier would have relished. There's classic but showy French cuisine, old wines, brandy, cigars, and your share of the 8 kilos of caviar they serve a day. *Jardin Brunswick, CH-1211, tel. 022/7311400, fax 022/7316709. 98 rooms with bath. Facilities: two restaurants, bar, terrace café, hairdresser. AE, DC, MC, V.*

Expensive **Les Armures.** In the heart of the Vielle Ville, this 17th-century archaeological treasure has been restored, and its charming original stonework, frescoes, and stenciled beams accompany impeccable modern comforts. Its few rooms are intimate, combining appropriate Old World furnishings with slick marble baths. Its casual restaurant is an Old Town must (*see* Dining, *above*). Approach by car can be difficult. *1 rue du Puits-St-Pierre, tel. 022/3109172, fax 022/3109846. 28 rooms with bath. Facilities: restaurant, bar, VCR. AE, DC, MC, V.*

★ **Metropole.** Built in 1855, lent to the city of Geneva to house Red Cross archives for prisoners of war and now lovingly restored by its management of 27 years, the Metropole has as much riverside splendor as its Right Bank sisters—at a lower price. There's a relaxed, unfussy ambience despite the grand scale, with leather and hunting prints mixed in with discreet pastels. Riverside rooms are noisier, over traffic, but the view compensates; ask for the quieter third or fourth floors. It's seconds from the best shopping and minutes from the Old Town. *34 quai Général-Guisan, tel. 022/3111344, fax 022/ 3111350. 140 rooms with bath. Facilities: two restaurants, terrace café, bar. AE, DC, MC, V.*

Moderate **Strasbourg-Univers.** A stylish oasis in the slightly sleazy train-station neighborhood, this just-renovated spot offers sleek decor, convenience, and four-star quality at a three-star price. The new look is marble and faux exotic wood; a few older, less flashy rooms, redone eight years ago, still don't show the wear. *10 rue Pradier, tel. 022/ 7322562, fax 022/7384208. 58 rooms with bath or shower. AE, DC, MC, V.*

★ **Touring-Balance.** The lower floors are tired but gracious, with French doors and a chic new paint job; ask to stay in the slick, solid high-tech rooms on the higher floors. There are gallery-quality lithos in every room. You can't beat the location for shopping and sightseeing. *13 pl. Longemalle, tel. 022/287122, fax 022/3104045. 64 rooms with bath. Facilities: restaurant, café. AE, DC, MC, V.*

Inexpensive **De la Cloche.** This once luxurious walk-up flat has tidy, tasteful new
★ decor that hasn't altered its period details, and the courtyard setting is so quiet you can hear birds in the garden. Good-size rooms with high ceilings share baths down the hall. The prices are still the lowest in town. *6 rue de la Cloche, tel. 022/7329481. 8 rooms without shower. Breakfast only. No credit cards.*

Des Tourelles. Once worthy of a czar, now host to the backpacking crowd, this fading Victorian offers enormous bay-windowed corner rooms, many with marble fireplaces, French doors, and views over the Rhône. The furnishings are sparse and strictly functional, but the staff is young and friendly. Bring earplugs: The location is extremely noisy, over roaring bridge traffic. *2 blvd. James-Fazy, tel. 022/7324423, fax 022/7327620. 25 rooms, some with shower. AE, DC, MC, V.*

Luzern

Arriving and Departing

By Plane The nearest international airport is **Kloten** in **Zürich,** approximately 54 kilometers (33 miles) from Luzern. **Swissair** flies in most often from the United States and the United Kingdom. Easy rail connections, departing hourly, whisk you on to Luzern within 50 minutes.

By Car It's easy to reach Luzern from Zürich by road, approaching from national expressway N3 south, connecting to N4 via the secondary E41, in the direction of Zug, and continuing on N4 to the city. Approaching from the southern, St. Gotthard Pass route, or after cutting through the Furka Pass by rail ferry, you descend below Andermatt to Altdorf, where a view-stifling tunnel sweeps you through to the shores of the lake and on to the city. Arriving from Basel in the northwest, it's a clean sweep by N2 into Luzern.

By Train Luzern functions as a rail crossroads, with express trains connecting hourly from Zürich and every two hours from Geneva, the latter with a change at Bern. For rail information, call the station (tel. 041/ 1573333).

Getting Around

Luzern's modest scale allows you to explore most of the city easily on foot, but you will want to resort to mass transit to visit far-flung attractions like the Verkehrshaus (Transit Museum) and nearby Alpine viewpoints.

By Bus The city bus system offers easy access throughout the urban area. If you're staying in a Luzern hotel, you will be eligible for a special **Guest-Ticket,** offering unlimited rides for two days for a minimal fee of 5 Fr.

By Taxi Given the small scale of the old town and the narrowness of most of its streets, taxis can prove a pricey encumbrance.

By Boat It's a crime to see this city and the surrounding mountainous region only from the shore; some of its most impressive landscapes can be seen from the decks of one of the cruise ships that ply the Vierwaldstättersee (Lake Lucerne). The boats of the Schiffahrtsgesellschaft des Vierwaldstättersee (tel. 041/404540) operate on a standardized, mass-transit-style schedule, criss-crossing the lake and stopping at scenic resorts and historic sites. Rides are included in a Swiss Pass or Swiss Boat Pass.

Important Addresses and Numbers

Tourist Information The city tourist office, near the Bahnhof (Frankenstrasse 1, tel. 041/517171), offers information April–October, weekdays 8:30–6, Saturday 9–5; May–October, Sunday 9–1 as well; and November–March, weekdays 8:30–noon and 2–6, Saturday 9–1. Another tourist information center has opened at Schweizerhofquai 2 (open May and October, weekdays 9–noon and 1–7, Saturday 9–noon and 1–4; June–September, weekdays 9–5, Saturday 9–4). There is also an accommodations service.

Emergencies **Police** (tel. 117). **Medical, dental, and pharmacy referral** (tel. 111). **Auto breakdown:** Tourist Club of Switzerland (tel. 140), **Swiss Automobile Club** (tel. 041/231000).

Guided Tours

Orientation Tours The Luzern tourist office offers a two-hour guided walking tour of Luzern, departing from the office daily at 10; from May through September, there are 4 PM tours as well. The 12 Fr. price includes a drink.

Excursions You may want to take a high-altitude day trip to **Mount Pilatus, Mount Rigi,** or—if you're bound for the highest—the **Titlis,** above Engelberg. All can be accomplished by combination train and cograil travel, though to mount the Titlis you must complete the journey by a series of cablecar rides. For information, check at the Central Switzerland regional tourist office (Vehkehrsverband Zentralschweiz, Alpenstr. 1, Luzern, tel. 041/511891) or at the city tourist office. Boat and bus trips to William Tell country—**Altdorf** and **Bürglen**—make the most of both scenery and local legend.

Exploring Luzern

Where the River Reuss flows out of the Vierwaldstättersee, Luzern's old town straddles the narrowed waters with the greater concentration of city life lying on the river's right bank. To get a feel for this riverfront center, start at the right-bank end of the prominent **Kapellbrücke,** with its flanking water tower. Stay on this side for the moment and head down the **Rathausquai,** lined with hotels and cafés on the right, a sloping reinforced bank on the left. Facing the end of a modern bridge (the Rathaus-Steg) stands the **Altes Rathaus** (Old Town Hall), built between 1599 and 1606 in the late-Renaissance style.

Numbers in the margin correspond to points of interest on the Luzern map.

① Just to the right of the Rathaus, the **Am Rhyn-Haus** (Am Rhyn House) contains an impressive collection of late paintings by Picasso. *Furrengasse, tel. 041/511773. Admission: 6 Fr. adults, 3 Fr. students. Open Jan.-Oct., daily 10-6; Nov.-Mar., daily 11-1 and 2-4.*

Turn right and climb the stairs past the ornately frescoed **Zunfthaus zu Pfistern,** a guild hall dating from the late 15th and early 16th century, to the Kornmarkt, former site of the local grain market. Cross the square and cut left into the **Weinmarkt,** the loveliest of Luzern's several squares. Its Gothic central fountain depicts St. Mauritius, patron saint of warriors, and its surrounding buildings are flamboyantly frescoed in 16th-century style.

② Leave the square from its west end, turn right on Kramgasse, and cross the Mühlenplatz to the **Spreuerbrücke,** a narrow, weathered all-wood covered bridge dating from 1408. Its interior gables frame a series of eerie, well-preserved paintings (by Kaspar Meglinger) of the Dance of Death; they date from the 17th century, though their style and inspiration—tracing to the plague that devastated Luzern and all of Europe in the 14th century—is medieval.

③ At the other end of the bridge, on the left bank, stands the stylish **Historisches Museum** (Historical Museum). Its exhibitions of city sculptures, Swiss arms and flags, and reconstructed rooms depict rural and urban life. The late-Gothic building was an armory, dating from 1567. *Pfistergasse 24, tel. 041/245424. Admission: 4 Fr. Open Tues.-Fri. 10-noon and 2-5, weekends 10-5.*

Time Out Follow Baselstrasse west to a funicular that carries you up (2 Fr.) to the **Château Gütsch,** where you can have a drink on the panoramic terrace and take in a bird's-eye view of the old town, the river, and the fortification walls.

④ From the end of the Spreuerbrücke, cut back upstream along Pfistergasse and turn left onto Bahnhofstrasse to reach the Baroque **Jesuitenkirche** (Jesuit Church), constructed 1667-78. Its symmetrical entrance is flanked by two onion-domed towers, added in 1893. Do not fail to go inside: Its vast interior, restored to mint condition, is a rococo explosion of gilt, marble, and epic frescoes.

⑤ Continue past the Rathaus-Steg bridge, but before you enter the **Kapellbrücke** (Chapel Bridge), take a look at its exterior from the right. It snakes diagonally across the water and, when it was built in the early 14th century, served as the division between the lake and the river. Its shingled roof and grand stone water tower (now housing a souvenir stand) are to Luzern what the Matterhorn is to Zermatt. Walk the length of this dark, creaky landmark; you'll see 112 gable panels, painted by Heinrich Wägmann in the 17th century, depicting Luzern and Swiss history, stories of St. Leodegar and St. Mauritius, Luzern's patron saints, and coats of arms from local patrician families.

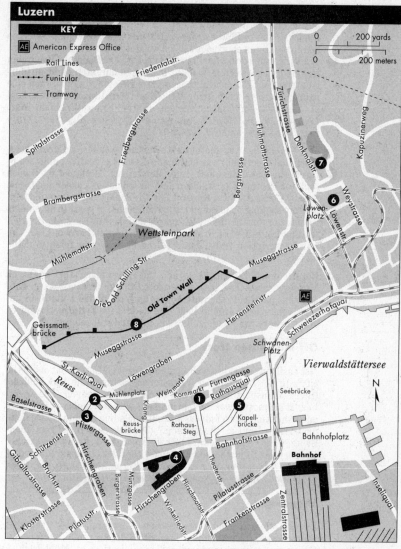

Luzern

KEY

AE American Express Office

—— Rail Lines

••••• Funicular

══ Tramway

0   200 yards

0   200 meters

Friedentalstr.

Spitalstrasse

Friedbergstrasse

Brambergstrasse

Zürichstrasse

Denkmalstr.

Kapuzinerweg

Fluhmattstrasse

Bergstrasse

7

Löwen-platz   **6**

Löwenstr.

Weystrasse

Mühlemattstr.

Wettsteinpark

Museggstrasse

Diebold Schilling-Str.

Old Town Wall

Hertensteinstr.

AE

Schweizerhofquai

Geissmatt-brücke

8

Museggstrasse

Löwengraben

Schwanen-Platz

Vierwaldstättersee

St.-Karli-Quai

Reuss

Mühlenplatz

Weinmarkt

Kornmarkt

Furrengasse

Rathausquai

Seebrücke

Baselstrasse

2

3

Pfistergasse

Reuss-brücke

Rathaus-Steg

Kramg.

1

5

Kapell-brücke

N

Schützenstr.

Gibraltarstrasse

Bruchstr.

Hirschengraben

Burgerstrasse

Mungasse

Hirschengraben

4

Theaterstr.

Hirschmattstr.

Winkelriedstr.

Bahnhofstrasse

Pilatusstrasse

Bahnhof

Bahnhofplatz

Zentralstrasse

Inseliquai

Klosterstrasse

Pilatusstr.

Frankenstrasse

Am Rhyn-Haus, **1**

Bourbaki-Panorama, **6**

Historisches
Museum, **3**

Jesuitenkirche, **4**

Kapellbrücke, **5**

Löwendenkmal, **7**

Spreuerbrücke, **2**

Zytturm, **8**

Now break away from the old town and work through thick pedestrian and bus traffic at Schwanenplatz to Haldenstrasse. Turn left on Zürichstrasse or Löwenstrasse and continue to **Löwenplatz,** which is dominated by an enormous conical wooden structure, like a remnant

6 of a Victorian world's fair. That's its spirit: The **Bourbaki-Panorama** was created between 1876 and 1878 as a genuine, step-right-up tourist attraction: The conical roof covers a sweeping, wraparound epic painting of the French Army of the East retreating into Switzerland at Verrières—a famous episode in the Franco-Prussian War. *Löwenpl., tel. 041/529942. Admission: 3 Fr. Open May–Sept., daily 9–6; Mar.–Apr. and Oct., daily 9–5.*

Just beyond lies yet another 19th-century wonder, a Luzern landmark that is certainly one of the world's most evocative public sculp-

7 tures: the **Löwendenkmal** (Lion Monument). Designed by Danish sculptor Berthel Thorwaldsen and carved out of a sheer sandstone face by Lucas Ahorn of Konstanz, it's a simple image of a dying lion, his chin sagging on his shield, a broken stump of spear in his side. It commemorates the 760 Swiss guards and their officers who died defending Louis XVI of France at the Tuileries in Paris in 1792. The Latin inscription translates: "To the bravery and fidelity of the Swiss."

Return down Löwenstrasse and, at Löwenplatz, turn right on Museggstrasse. This long street cuts through an original city gate and runs parallel to the **watchtowers** and **crenellated walls** of old Lu-

8 zern, constructed around 1400. The clock in the **Zytturm,** the fourth of the towers, was made in Basel in 1385 and still keeps time.

Off the Beaten Track

Not easily included in a walking tour of central Luzern but one of the city's (if not Switzerland's) greater attractions, the **Verkehrshaus** (Swiss Transport Museum) can be reached by steamer, car, or city bus. It's almost a world's fair in itself, with a complex of buildings and exhibitions both indoors and out, including dioramas, live demonstrations, and a "Swissorama" (360-degree screen) film about Switzerland. Every mode of transit is discussed, from stagecoaches and bicycles to jumbo jets and space capsules. *Lidostr. 5, tel. 041/ 314444. Admission: 15 Fr. adults, 8 Fr. children under 16. Open Mar.–Oct., daily 9–6; Nov.–Feb., weekdays 10–4, Sun. 10–5.*

Shopping

Luzern offers a good concentration of general Swiss goods: At **Sturzenegger** (Schwanenpl. 7, tel. 041/511958), you'll find fine St.-Gallen-made linens and embroidered niceties; at **Mühlebach & Birrer** (Kapellpl., tel. 041/516673) there's a selection of Alpen-style (although Austrian-made) Geiger clothing (boiled-wool jackets, edelweiss-embroidered sweaters) as well as Swiss-made handkerchiefs. **Schmid-Linder** (Denkmalstr. 9, tel. 041/514346) sells a comprehensive line of Swiss kitsch: cuckoo clocks, cowbells, embroidery, and a large stock of wood carvings from Brienz, in the Berner Oberland. **Innerschweizer Heimatwerk** (Franziskanerpl. 14, tel. 041/236944) sells nothing but goods—most of them contemporary rather than traditional—made in the region by independent craftspeople, from handweaving to ceramics and wooden toys. Watch dealers are unusually competitive, and the two enormous patriarchs of the business—**Gübelin** (Schweizerhofquai, tel. 041/ 515142) and **Bucherer** (Schwanenpl., tel. 041/437700) advertise heavily and offer inexpensive souvenirs to lure shoppers into their luxurious showrooms. Gübelin is the exclusive source for Audemars Piguet, Patek Philippe, and its own house brand; Bucherer represents Piaget and Rolex. An abundance of small shops carry Tissot, Rado, Corum, and others—but prices are controlled by the manufacturer, and discounts are rare. Watch for closeouts on out-of-date models.

Dining

Rooted in the German territory of Switzerland and the surrounding farmlands, Central Switzerland's native cuisine is down-home and hearty. Luzern takes pride in its *Kügelipaschtetli*, puffed pastry nests filled with tiny veal meatballs, mushrooms, cream sauce, occasionally raisins, and bits of chicken, pork, or sweetbreads. Watch for lake fish such as *Egli* (perch), *Hecht* (pike), *Forellen* (trout), and *Felchen* (whitefish). Though most often served baked or fried, a Luzern tradition offers them sautéed and sauced with tomatoes, mushrooms, and capers. After your meal here, have a steaming mug of coffee laced with *Träsch*, a harsh schnapps blended from the dregs of other eaux-de-vie; the locals leave their spoon in the cup as they drink. For details and price-category definitions, *see* Dining in Staying in Switzerland, *above*.

Moderate–Very Expensive ★ **La Vague (Hotel des Balances).** This chic combination upscale restaurant and casual bistro offers soigné decor, a shimmering riverside view, and adventurous, worldly, cuisine that features local fish. A standing fixed-price "menu de poissons du lac" may offer crayfish soup, grilled omble chevalier (a kind of salmon-trout) in vegetable vinaigrette, and steamed perch in chive butter. A house specialty is light, fresh fish fondue for two. *Weinmarkt, tel. 041/511851. Reservations advised. Dress: casual in bistro, jacket advised in restaurant. AE, DC, MC, V. Restaurant: Very Expensive. Bistro: Moderate.*

Expensive ★ **Wilden Mann.** You may choose the ancient original Burgerstube, all dark beams and family crests, its origins as a rest-stop for St. Gotthard travelers traced back to 1517; or you may opt for the more formal adjoining Liedertafel restaurant, with wainscoting, vaulting, and candlelight. On either side, the menu and prices are the same (with additional soup, salad, and sausage options in the Stube)—and the cooking is outstanding. *Bahnhofstr. 30, tel. 041/ 231666. Reservations advised. Dress: casual in Burgerstube, jacket advised in Liedertafel. AE, DC, MC, V.*

Moderate ★ **Galliker.** Step past the ancient façade into an all-wood room roaring with local action, where Luzerners drink, smoke, and bask in their culinary roots. Brisk, motherly waitresses serve the dishes Mutti used to make: Fresh *Kutteln* (tripe) in rich white wine sauce with cumin seeds; real *Kalbskopf* (chopped fresh veal head) served with heaps of green onions and warm vinaigrette; authentic Luzerner *Kügelipastetli;* and their famous simmered-beef pot-au-feu, served only on Tuesday, Wednesday, and Saturday. *Schützenstr. 1, tel. 041/221002. Reservations advised. Dress: casual. AE, MC, V. Closed Sun. and Mon., mid-July–mid-Aug.*

Rebstock/Hofstube. At the opposite end of the culinary spectrum from Galliker, this up-to-date kitchen offers modern, international fare, including rabbit, lamb, oriental, and organic vegetarian specialties. The lively bentwood brasserie hums with locals lunching by the bar, while the more formal, old-style restaurant glows with wood and brass under a low-beamed herringbone ceiling. *St.-*

Leodegarstr. 3, tel. 041/513581. Reservations advised. Dress: casual. AE, DC, MC, V.

Inexpensive **Zur Pfistern.** One of the architectural focal points of the old town waterfront, this floridly decorated old guildhouse—its origins trace back to 1341—offers a good selection of moderate meals in addition to higher-priced standards. Lake fish and *pastetli* (meat pies made with puffed pastry) are good local options. In summer the small first-floor balcony may provide the best seat in town for a postcard waterfront view. *Kornmarkt 4, tel. 041/513650. Reservations not necessary. Dress: casual. AE, DC, MC, V.*

Lodging

Luzern provides a convenient home base for excursions around the Vierwaldstättersee and all over the region. Unlike most Swiss cities, Luzern has high and low seasons, and drops prices considerably in winter. For details and price-category definitions, *see* Lodging in Staying in Switzerland, *above*.

Very **Chateau Gütsch.** Any antiquity in this "castle" built as a hotel in
Expensive 1888 is strictly contrived, but honeymooners, groups, and determined romantics seeking out storybook Europe enjoy the Disneyland-like experience: the turrets and towers worthy of Mad Ludwig of Bavaria, the cellars, crypts, and corridors lined with a hodgepodge of relics, not to mention the magnificent hilltop site above Luzern, once a lookout point. An extravagant renovation, reducing the number of fantasy-style rooms but enlarging them considerably, has bumped this lodging-attraction into the deluxe category. *Kanonenstr., tel. 041/220272, fax 041/220252. 49 rooms. Facilities: restaurant, terrace, outdoor pool, private forest. AE, DC, MC, V.*

Palace. Brilliantly refurbished and subtly modernized to take in broader lake views, the Palace sports a classic look with a touch of postmodern. Built in 1906 and regularly updated, the fifth-floor rooms were recently redone, and an entire sixth floor of new rooms was added. *Haldenstr. 10, tel. 041/502222, fax 041/516976. 185 rooms. Facilities: restaurant, bar, terrace, 2 saunas, steam bath, solarium, fitness center, parking. AE, DC, MC, V.*

Expensive **Des Balances.** Restored and renewed, outside and in, this riverfront
★ property built in the 19th century on the site of an ancient guildhouse gleams with style. State-of-the-art tile baths, up-to-date pastel decor, and one of the best sites in town make this the slickest in its price class. Nearly every window frames a period scene outdoors. *Metzgerrainle 7, tel. 041/511851, fax 041/516451. 57 rooms. Facilities: 2 restaurants, piano bar, riverfront balcony. AE, DC, MC, V.*

★ **Wilden Mann.** Living up to its reputation, the city's best-known hotel offers its guests a gracious and authentic experience of Old Luzern. Joining several old houses that once were part of the town wall, the structure has been renewed to maintain its Reformation ambience, with stone, beams, brass, hand-painted tiles, and burnished wood everywhere. Standard rooms have a prim 19th-century look. *Bahnhofstr. 30, tel. 041/231666, fax 041/231629. 43 rooms. Facilities: 2 restaurants. AE, DC, MC, V.*

Moderate **Des Alpes.** With a terrific riverfront location in the bustling heart of the old town, this historic hotel has been completely renovated inside to look like a laminate-and-vinyl chain motel. Rooms are generously proportioned, tidy, and sleek; front doubles, several with balconies, overlook the water and promenade. Cheaper back rooms face the old town. *Rathausquai 5, tel. 041/515825, fax 041/517451. 45 rooms. Facilities: restaurant, terrace café. AE, DC, MC, V.*

★ **Zum Weissen Kreuz.** Now renovated and upgraded, this former bargain hotel on the waterfront is slick, bright, and airtight, with tile, stucco, oak, and pine to soften the modern edges. Some rooms face the lake, others the old town. The restaurant Al Forno serves pasta and pizzas. *Furrengasse 19, tel. 041/514040, fax 041/514060. 22 rooms. Facilities: restaurant. AE, DC, MC, V.*

Inexpensive **Schlüssel.** On the Franziskanerplatz, with several rooms overlooking the Franciscan church and fountain, this spare, no-nonsense little lodging attracts young bargain hunters. It's a pleasant combination of tidy new touches (quarry tile, white paint) and antiquity: You can have dinner in a low, cross-vaulted "crypt" and admire the fine old lobby beams. *Franziskanerpl. 12, tel. 041/231061. 11 rooms. Facilities: restaurant. MC, V.*

★ **SSR Touristen.** Despite its friendly collegiate atmosphere, this cheery dormlike spot is anything but a backpackers' flophouse. It has a terrific setting on the Reuss, around the corner from the old town. Rooms are available with or without bath. *St. Karliquai, tel. 041/512474, fax 041/528414. 100 beds. AE, DC, MC, V.*

The Arts

Luzern hosts the **International Music Festival** for three weeks in August every year. Performances take place at the **Kunsthaus** (Frohburgstr. 6, tel. 041/233880). For more information, contact International Musikfestwochen (Postfach, CH-6002, Luzern, tel. 041/235272). The **Allgemeine Musikgesellschaft Luzern** (AML), the local orchestra in residence, offers a season of concerts from October through June, also in the Kunsthaus.

Nightlife

Bars and Lounges **Des Balances** hotel has a hip, upscale piano bar (Metzgerrainle 7, tel. 041/511851), and **Château Gütsch** *(Kanonenstrasse)* draws a sedate dinner-and-dancing crowd. **Mr. Pickwick** (Rathausquai 6, tel. 041/515927) is a Swiss version of an English pub.

Casinos The most sophisticated nightlife in Luzern is found in the **Casino** (Haldenstr. 6, tel. 041/512751), on the northern shore by the grand hotels. You can play boule in the Gambling Room (5 Fr. federally-imposed betting limit), dance in the **Babilonia** club, watch a strip show in the **Red Rose,** or have a Swiss meal in **Le Chalet** while watching a folklore display.

Discos **Flora Club** (Seidenhofstr. 5, tel. 041/244444) mixes dancing with folklore shows.

Folklore Besides the shows at the Casino and Flora Club, **Stadtkeller** (Sternenpl. 3, tel. 041/514733) transports you to the Valais Alps for cheese, yodeling, and dirndled dancers. **Nightboat** (Landungsbrücke 6, tel. 041/404540) sails every evening May through September at 8:45, offering drinks, meals, and a mid-cruise folklore show.

Lugano

Arriving and Departing

By Plane There are short connecting flights by **Crossair**—the Swiss domestic network—to Lugano Airport (tel. 091/505001) from Zürich, Geneva, Basel, and Bern, as well as from Paris, Nice, Rome, Florence, and Venice. The nearest intercontinental airport is at Milan, Italy, about 56 kilometers (35 miles) away.

Between the Airport and Downtown There is no longer a regular bus service between the local airport and central Lugano, 7 kilometers (4 miles) away; taxis, costing about 25 Fr. to the center, are the only option.

By Train There's a train from Zürich seven minutes past every hour, and the trip takes about three hours. If you're coming from Geneva, you can catch the Milan express at various times, changing at Domodossola and Bellinzona. Daytimes, there's a train 30 minutes past every hour from Milan's Centrale Station; the trip takes about 1½ hours. Always keep passports handy and confirm times with the SNTO. For train information in Lugano, tel. 091/226502.

By Car There are fast, direct highways from Milan and from Zürich. If you are planning to come from Geneva, check the weather conditions with the automobile associations beforehand.

Getting Around

By Bus Well-integrated services run regularly on all local routes. You must buy your ticket from the machine at the stop before you board.

By Train With or without a Swiss Pass, get a **Regional Holiday Season Ticket** for Lugano from the tourist office. One of these gives unlimited free travel for seven consecutive days on most rail and steamer routes and a 50% or 25% discount on longer trips. It costs 86 Fr. for adults (68 Fr. for holders of a Swiss Pass) and 39 Fr. for children 6–16. The newest version offers any three out of seven days free on most routes, with 50% or 25% reductions on the remaining four days. Its price is 66 Fr. for adults, 50 Fr. for Swiss Pass holders, and 30 Fr. for children.

By Taxi Though less expensive than in Zürich or Geneva, taxis are still not cheap, with a 10 Fr. minimum. In a pinch, call 091/512121 or 091/519191.

By Boat The **Navigation Company of Lake Lugano** (tel. 091/515223) offers cruise-boat excursions around the bay to the romantic fishing village of Gandria and toward the Villa Favorita. Use it like public transit, following a schedule and paying according to distance, or look into special tickets: Seven consecutive days' unlimited travel cost 50 Fr., 3 days within a week cost 44 Fr.; an all-day pass costs 30 Fr.

Guided Tours

The tourist office is the best source of information about hiking tours into the mountains surrounding Lugano; it offers several topographical maps and suggested itineraries. There are bus trips to Locarno, Ascona, Lake Como, Lake Maggiore, Milan, Venice, St. Moritz, Florence, the Alpine passes, and the Italian market in Como. A free guided walking tour of Lugano leaves the tourist office every Tuesday at 9:30 AM from April through October.

Tourist Information

Ente Turistico Lugano (riva Albertolli 5, CH-6901, tel. 091/214664; open October–June, weekdays 9–6; July–September, weekdays 9–6:30; April–October, Saturday 9–5).

Exploring Lugano

Its sparkling bay, with dark, conical mountains rising from the beautiful Lago di Lugano, has earned Lugano the nickname "Rio of the Old World." The largest city in the Ticino—the Italian-speaking corner of Switzerland—Lugano has not escaped some of the inevitable overdevelopment of a successful resort town. There's thick traffic, right up to the waterfront, much of it manic Italian-style, and it has more than its share of concrete waterfront high-rise hotels, with balconies skewed to claim rooms with a view no matter what the aesthetic cost.

But the view from the waterfront is unforgettable, the boulevards are fashionable, and the old quarter is still reminiscent of sleepy old towns in Italy. And the sacred *passeggiata*—the afternoon stroll to see and be seen that winds down every Italian day—asserts the city's true personality as a graceful, sophisticated Old World resort—not Swiss, not Italian . . . just Lugano.

Numbers in the margin correspond to points of interest on the Lugano map.

Start your walk under the broad porticoes of the tourist office and cross over to the tree-lined promenade, where you can stroll along the waterfront and take in stunning mountain views. Head left
➊ along the waterfront and into the **Parco Civico,** with its cacti, exotic shrubs, and more than 1,000 varieties of roses. There's an aviary, a tiny "deer zoo," and a fine view of the bay from its peninsula. The **Villa Ciani,** temporarily closed for renovations, contains paintings and sculpture from Tintoretto to Giacometti.

➋ There's also the canton's **Museo Cantonale di Storia Naturale** (Museum of Natural History), which contains exhibits on animals, plants, and mushrooms. *Viale Cattaneo 4, tel. 091/237827. Admission free. Open Tues.–Sat. 9–noon and 2–5.*

➌ If you continue left along the waterfront, you'll find the **Lido,** with a stretch of sandy beach, several swimming pools, and a restaurant. *Admission: 5 Fr. adults, 2 Fr. children 2–14.*

Or follow the promenade right until you reach the **Imbarcadero Centrale,** where steamers launch into the bay, and turn inland to the
➍ **Piazza della Riforma,** the scene of Lugano's vigorous Italian life, where the modish locals socialize in outdoor cafés. From here, enter the **Old Town** and follow the steep, narrow streets lined with chic Italian clothing shops and small markets offering pungent local cheeses and porcini mushrooms. Swiss culture asserts itself only at lunch stands, where *panini* (small sandwiches) are made not only of prosciutto, tuna, or mozzarella but of sauerkraut and sausage as well.

➎ On the street of the same name, you'll find the **Cathedral San Lorenzo,** with its graceful Renaissance facade and noteworthy frescoes inside. Then shop your way down the Via Nassa until you reach the
➏ **Church of Santa Maria degli Angioli** in Piazza Luini, started in 1455. Within, you'll find a splendid fresco of the *Passion and Crucifixion* by Bernardino Luini (1475–1532).

➐ Across the street, the waterfront **Giardino Belvedere** (Belvedere Gardens) frame 12 modern sculptures with palms, camelias, oleanders, and magnolias. At the far end, to your right, there's **public bathing** on the Riva Caccia. *Admission (bathing): 3 Fr., 2 Fr. children. Open mid-May–mid-Sept.*

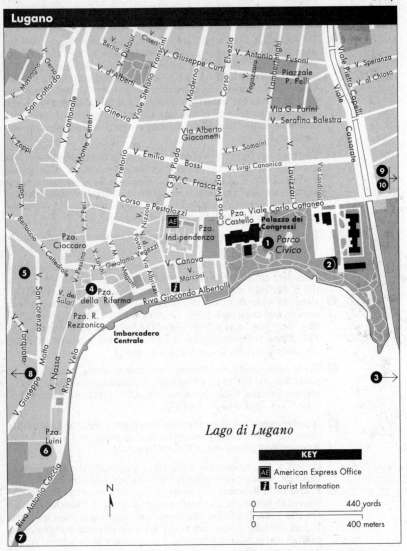

Lugano

Cathedral San Lorenzo, **5**

Church of Santa Maria degli Angioli, **6**

Giardino Belvedere, **7**

Lido, **3**

Museo Cantonale di Storia Naturale, **2**

Parco Civico, **1**

Parco Tassino, **8**

Parco degli Ulivi, **9**

Piazza della Riforma, **4**

Villa Favorita, **10**

If you want to see more of Lugano's luxurious parklands, take the funicular from the Old Town to the train station: Behind the station, **8** deer greet you as you enter the floral **Parco Tassino.** Or take bus No. **9** 2 east to the San Domenico stop in Castagnola to reach the **Parco degli Ulivi** (Olive Park), where you can climb the olive-lined slopes of Monte Brè for views of the surrounding mountains.

10 The dust has finally settled at the **Villa Favorita,** owned by art baron and *real* Baron Heinrich von Thyssen, and you'll find the villa not only completely renovated but also with a portion of its magnificent art collection back on the walls. In a controversial bidding war, much of the collection was transferred to Madrid—at least temporarily—but a significant display of 19th- and 20th-century paintings and watercolors from Europe and America remains, shown to better advantage than ever in the renewed space. Artists represented include Thomas Hart Benton, Giorgio de Chirico, Frederic Church, Lucien Freud, Edward Hopper, Franz Marc, Jackson Pollock, and Andrew Wyeth. *Strada Castagnola, tel. 091/516152. Admission: 12 Fr. Open Easter–Oct., Fri.–Sun. 10–5; during special exhibitions, Tues.–Sun. 10–5.*

Dining

The Ticinese were once poor mountain people, so their cuisine shares the earthy delights of the Piemontese: polenta, gnocchi, game, and mushrooms. But as in all prosperous resorts, the mink-and-Vuarnets set draws the best in upmarket international cooking. Fixed-price lunches are almost always cheaper, so dine as the Luganese do—before your siesta. That way you can sleep off the fruity local merlot wine before the requisite passeggiata. For details and price-category definitions, *see* Dining in Staying in Switzerland, *above*.

Very Expensive ★ **Al Portone.** The settings are formal, with silver and lace dressing up the stucco and stone, but the ambience is strictly easy. Chef Roberto Galizzi pursues *nuova cucina* (nouvelle cuisine, Italian-style) with ambition and flair, putting local spins on classics: roast veal kidneys with balsamic vinegar, pasta with white beans and lobster, seafood carpaccio, or the simple luxury of creamed potatoes with white truffle. *Viale Cassarate 3, tel. 091/235995. Reservations required. Jacket and tie advised. AE, DC, MC, V. Closed Sun. and Mon.*

★ **Santabbondio.** Ancient stone and terracotta blend with pristine pastels in this upgraded grotto, where superb and imaginative new Franco-Italian dishes are served in intimate little dining rooms and on a flower-filled terrace. Watch for lobster risotto, eggplant ravioli, or scallops in orange-basil sauce to confirm what locals assert—that Chef Martin Dalsass is the region's best. It's a cab ride from town, toward the airport, but worth the trip. *Via ai Grotti di Gentilino, Lugano/Sorengo, tel. 091/548535. Reservations advised. Jacket advised. AE, DC, MC, V. Closed Sat. lunch, Sun. night, and Mon.*

Expensive **Galleria.** Though the setting aspires to formal hauteur, with contemporary appointments and modern art, family warmth and vigor peek through the chinks in the facade, and in the end this is a comfortable source of good middle-class Italian cooking. *Via Vegezzi, tel. 091/236288. Reservations advised. Jacket advised. AE, DC, MC, V. Closed Sun.*

★ **Locanda del Boschetto.** The grill is the first thing you see in this nononsense restaurant, a specialist in simple but sensational seafood *alla griglia* (grilled). Crisp linens contrast with rustic wood touches, and the low-key service is helpful and down-to-earth. *Via Boschetto 8, tel. 091/542493. Reservations advised. AE, DC, MC, V. Closed Mon.*

Moderate **Al Barilotto.** Despite its generic pizzeria decor and American-style
★ salad bar, this restaurant draws local crowds for grilled meats, homemade pasta, and wood-oven pizza. Take bus No. 10 from the center. *Hôtel de la Paix, Via Calloni 18, tel. 091/542331. Reservations advised. AE, DC, MC, V.*

Inexpensive **La Tinera.** This tiny taverna crowds loyal locals, tourists, and fami-
★ lies onto wooden benches for authentic regional specialties, hearty meats, and pastas. Regional wine is served in traditional ceramic bowls. It's tucked down an alley off Via Pessina in the Old Town. *Via dei Gorini 2, tel. 091/235219. Reservations advised. AE, DC, MC, V.*

Sayonara. There's nothing Japanese about it: This is a modern urban pizzeria with several rooms that are crowded at lunchtime with a mix of tourists and shoppers. The old copper polenta pot stirs automatically year-round, with polenta offered in several combinations, one of them with mountain hare. *Via F. Soave 10, tel. 091/220170. Reservations not necessary. AE, DC, MC, V.*

Lodging

There are few Inexpensive hotels in the downtown area, but a brief drive into the surrounding countryside increases your options. Since this is a summer resort, many hotels close for the winter, so call ahead. For details and price-category definitions, *see* Lodging in Staying in Switzerland, *above.*

Very **Ticino.** In this warmly appointed, 16th-century house in the heart of
Expensive the Old Town, shuttered windows look out from every room onto a
★ glassed-in garden and courtyard, and there are vaulted halls lined with art and antiques. This member of the Romantik Hotels is steps away from the funicular to the station. *Piazza Cioccaro 1, tel. 091/227772, fax 091/236278. 23 rooms with bath. Facilities: restaurant, garden courtyard, parking. AE, DC, MC, V.*

★ **Villa Principe Leopoldo.** In a price range all its own, but with Old World service and splendor to match, this sumptuously appointed garden mansion sits on a hillside high over the lake. There is free transportation to the airport and town. *Via Montalbano 5, tel. 091/558855, fax 091/558825. 24 suites with bath. Facilities: restaurant, bar, pool, indoor golf, hydromassage, solarium, tennis courts, covered parking, sauna, whirlpool, fitness center. AE, DC, MC, V.*

Expensive **Du Lac.** This discreet and simple hotel offers you more lakefront luxury for your money than the glossier Grand Eden down the same beach. All rooms face the lake, but the sixth floor is the quietest. *Riva Paradiso 3, tel. 091/541921, fax 091/546173. 53 rooms with bath. Facilities: restaurant, terrace bar, pool, private swimming area on lake, sauna, solarium, massage room. AE, DC, MC, V.*

Moderate **Alba.** This solid little hotel, surrounded by landscaped grounds and
★ an interior that is lavish in the extreme, is ideal for lovers with a sense of camp or honeymooners looking for romantic privacy. Mirrors, gilt, plush, and crystal fill the public areas, and the beds are all ruffles and swags. *Via delle Scuole 11, tel. 091/543731, fax 091/544523. 25 rooms with bath. Facilities: restaurant, bar, garden. AE, DC, MC, V.*

International au Lac. This is a big, old-fashioned, friendly city hotel, half a block from the lake, with many lake-view rooms. It's next to

Santa Maria degli Angioli, on the edge of the shopping district and the Old Town. *Via Nassa 68, tel. 091/227541, fax 091/227544. 86 rooms with bath. Facilities: restaurant, garden. AE, DC, MC, V.*

★ **Park-Hotel Nizza.** This former villa (modernized in 1974) affords panoramic views from its spot on the lower slopes of San Salvatore, well above the lake, and thus is an uphill hike from town. The mostly small rooms are decorated with antique reproductions; there is no extra charge for lake views. An ultra-modern bar overlooks the lake, and a good restaurant serves vegetables (and even wine) from its own garden. There's a shuttle service to Paradiso. *Via Guidino 14, tel. 091/541771, fax 091/541773. 30 rooms with bath. Facilities: restaurant, bar, outdoor pool, garden. AE, DC, MC, V.*

San Carlo. The San Carlo offers one of the better deals in a high-priced town: It's small, clean, freshly furnished, and right on the main shopping street, a block from the waterfront. There are no frills, but the friendly atmosphere. *Via Nassa 28, tel. 091/227107, fax 091/228022. 22 rooms with bath. Facilities: breakfast only. AE, DC, MC, V.*

Inexpensive **Flora.** Though it's one of the cheapest hotels in town, this 70-year-
★ old lodging has been reasonably well maintained. The room decor is minimal, a holdover of the '60s (red-orange prints, wood-grain Formica), and the once-elegant dining hall has seen better days. But some rooms have balconies, and there's a sheltered garden terrace for balmy nights. *Via Geretta 16, tel. 091/541671, fax 091/542738. 33 rooms with bath. Facilities: restaurant, bar, terrace, small outdoor pool. AE, DC, MC, V.*

Zurigo. Ideally placed behind the tourist office and handy to parks, shopping, and promenades, this spartan hotel offers quiet comfort at rock-bottom rates, even in high season. Several rooms have full bathrooms. *Corso Pestalozzi 13, CH–6900, tel. and fax 091/234343. 25 rooms. Breakfast only. No credit cards.*

Bern

Arriving and Departing

By Plane **Belp** (tel. 031/9615516) is a small airport, 9 kilometers (6 miles) south of the city, with flights to and from most European capitals. A bus from the airport to the train station costs 12 Fr., a taxi about 35 Fr.

By Train Bern is a major link between Geneva, Zürich, and Basel, with fast connections running usually every hour from the enormous central station. The high-speed French TGV gets to Paris in 4½ hours.

By Car The Geneva-Zürich expressway runs by Bern, with crossroads leading to Basel and Lugano as well.

Getting Around

By Bus and Bern is a small, concentrated city, and it's easy to get around on foot.
Tram There are 6½ kilometers (4 miles) of covered shopping arcades in the center. Bus and tram service is excellent, however, if you don't feel like walking. Fares range from 1.40 Fr. to 2.20 Fr. Buy individual tickets from the dispenser at the tram or bus stop; the posted map will tell you the cost. Tourist cards for unlimited rides are available at 5 Fr. for one day, 7 Fr. for two, and 10 Fr. for three. Buy them at the bahnhof tourist office or from the public-transportation ticket office in the subway leading down to the main station (take the esca-

lator in front of Loeb's department store and turn right through the Christoffel Tower). A **Swiss Pass** will allow you to travel free.

By Taxi This cumbersome alternative to walking costs between 6 Fr. and 15 Fr. across town.

Important Addresses and Numbers

Tourist Information The tourist office is located at Bahnhofplatz (main station, tel. 031/3116611); it's open June–Sept., daily 9–8:30; Oct.–May, Mon.–Sat. 9–6:30 and Sun. 10–5.

Embassies U.S. (Jubiläumsstr. 93, tel. 031/3517011). **Canadian** (88 Kirchenfeldstr., tel. 031/3526381). **U.K.** (Thunstr. 50, tel. 031/3525021).

Emergencies **Police** (tel. 117). **Ambulance** (tel. 144). **Doctor/Dentist** (tel. 3119211). **All-night pharmacy** (tel. 3119211).

Guided Tours

Walking Tours A two-hour tour around the Old Town, covering all the principal sights, is offered by the tourist office from May–Oct., daily 10 and 2; Nov.–Mar., Sat. at 2; Apr., Mon.–Sat. at 2 for 19F.

Excursions Bern prides itself on its central location, and offers easy access to Zürich and Geneva as well as to the remote farmlands of the Bernese Mittelland, where you can visit the Emmental Valley. The most popular (though expensive) outing is up into the heights of the Jungfrau in the Alpine Bernese Oberland. The train passes through Interlaken, Lauterbrunne, Wengen, and Kleine Scheidegg to the Jungfraujoch, which, at 3,513 meters (11,333 feet), has the highest rail station in Europe. Contact the tourist office.

Exploring Bern

No cosmopolitan nonsense here: The local specialties are fatback and sauerkraut, the annual fair features the humble onion, and the president takes the tram to work. Walking down broad, medieval streets past squares teeming with farmers' markets and cafés full of shirt-sleeved politicos, you might forget that Bern is the federal capital—indeed, the geographic and political hub—of a sophisticated and prosperous nation.

It earned its pivotal position through a history of power and influence that dates to the 12th century, when Berchtold V of the Holy Roman Empire established a fortress on this gooseneck in the river Aare. By the 15th century the Bernese had overcome the Burgundians to expand their territories west to Geneva. Napoleon held them briefly—from 1798 until his defeat in 1815—but by 1848 Bern was back in charge, as the capital of the Swiss Confederation.

Today it's not the massive Bundeshaus (capitol building) that dominates the city, but the perfectly preserved arcades, the fountains, and the thick, sturdy towers of the Middle Ages. They're the reason UNESCO granted Bern World Landmark status, ranking it with the Pyramids and the Taj Mahal.

Numbers in the margin correspond to points of interest on the Bern map.

1 Start on the busy **Bahnhofplatz** in front of the grand old Schweizerhof hotel, facing the station. To your left is the **2** **Heiliggeistkirche** (Church of the Holy Spirit), finished in 1729 and at odds with both the modern and the medieval in Bern. Head right up

Bern

Anna Seiler
fountain, **6**
Bahnhofplatz, **1**
Bärengraben, **17**
Bernisches
Historisches
Museum, **19**

Bundeshaus, **23**
Gerechtigkeits-
brunnen, **15**
Heiliggeistkirche, **2**
Käfigturm, **5**
Kindlifresser-
brunnen, **9**

Kornhaus, **10**
Kunstmuseum
Bern, **3**
Läuferbrunnen, **16**
Marksman fountain, **7**
Münster, **18**

Naturhistorisches
Museum, **20**
Pfeiferbrunnen, **4**
Rathaus, **14**
Samson fountain, **12**
Schweizerisches
PTT-Museum, **22**

Schweizerisches
Schützenmuseum, **21**
Vennerbrunnen, **13**
Zähringer
fountain, **11**
Zytgloggeturm, **8**

Bollwerk and turn right into Kleeplatz and Hodlerstrasse, where
③ you'll come to the **Kunstmuseum Bern** on your left. Originally dedicated to collecting Swiss art, it houses an exceptional group of works
by Ferdinand Hodler, including some enormous, striking allegories;
there are landscapes and portraits as well. But the concentration is
no longer entirely Swiss, and early Bern masters mingle with Fra
Angelico, and Böcklin and Anker share space with artists of the caliber of Cézanne, Rouault, and Picasso. The museum's pride—and its
justified claim to fame—is its collection of more than 2,000 works by
Paul Klee, who lived in Bern. *Hodlerstrasse 8–12, tel. 031/3110944.
Admission: 4 Fr. Open Tues. 10–9; Wed.–Sun. 10–5.*

Walk down Spitalgasse outside the arcades to see some of the city's
stunning architecture; inside the sheltered walkways, you'll be seduced by modern shops and cafés.

④ Head for the **Pfeiferbrunnen** (Bagpiper Fountain), the first of the
city's many signature fountains erected between 1539 and 1546, and
⑤ the **Käfigturm** (Prison Tower), which dates from the 13th and 14th
centuries. There's a small museum of economic and cultural life inside. *Tel. 031/3112306. Admission free. Open Tues.–Fri. 9–1 and
2–6.*

⑥ ⑦ Continue down Marktgasse past the **Anna Seiler** and **Marksman**
⑧ **fountains** to the **Zytgloggeturm** (clock tower), built as a city gate in
1191 but transformed by the addition of an astronomical clock in
1530. To your right is the Theaterplatz, to your left the
⑨ **Kindlifresserbrunnen** (Ogre Fountain) and the Kornhausplatz,
⑩ where you will see the imposing 18th-century **Kornhaus** (granary),
its magnificent vaulted cellar a popular beer hall today. Now walk
past the clock tower and observe the clock from the east side. At four
minutes before every hour, you can see the famous mechanical puppet bears perform their ancient dance.

Continue down Kramgasse, past fine 18th-century houses and the
⑪ ⑫ **Zähringer** and **Samson fountains.** Turn left at the next small inter-
⑬ section and head for Rathausplatz, with its **Vennerbrunnen** (Ensign
⑭ Fountain), and the late-Gothic **Rathaus** (city hall), where the city
and cantonal government meet.

Head back to the main route, here named Gerechtigkeitsgasse, and
⑮ continue past the **Gerechtigkeitsbrunnen** (Justice Fountain) and
lovely patrician houses. Artisan shops, galleries, and antiquaries
line this leg of the endless arcades. Turn left at the bottom and head
down the steep Nydegg Stalden through one of the city's oldest sec-
⑯ tions, past the **Läuferbrunnen** (Messenger Fountain), to the river
Aare. Here the **Nydeggkirche** (Nydegg Church), on the right, was
built from 1341 to 1571 on the foundations of Berchtold V's ruined
fortress.

Cross the river by the **Untertorbrücke** (Bridge under the Gate), then
turn right and climb up to the **Nydeggbrücke.** Here you'll find the
⑰ **Bärengraben** (Bear Pits), where Bern keeps its famous live mascots.
According to legend, Berchtold named the town after the first animal he killed while hunting—a bear, since the woods were thick
with them.

Now cross the bridge and head back into town, turning left up
⑱ Junkerngasse to the magnificent Gothic **Münster** (cathedral), begun
in 1421. It features a fine portal (1490) depicting the *Last Judgment,*
recently restored and repainted in extravagant hues. There also are
stunning stained-glass windows, both originals and period reproductions.

Arty boutiques line the Münstergasse, leading to the **Casino,** which houses a concert hall and restaurants, but no casino. If you head even farther south (across the river yet again), you'll find Helvetiaplatz, a historic square surrounded by museums. The **⑲ Bernisches Historisches Museum** (Bern Historical Museum) has a prehistoric collection, 15th-century Flemish tapestries, and Bernese sculptures. Its fine Islamic holdings are imaginatively displayed. *Helvetiaplatz 5, tel. 031/3511811. Admission: 5 Fr. Open Tues.–Sun. 10–5.*

⑳ The **Naturhistorisches Museum** is one of Europe's major natural history museums. It features enormous wildlife dioramas and a splendid collection of Alpine minerals. *Bernastr. 15, tel. 031/3507111. Admission: 3 Fr. Open Mon. 2–5, Tues.–Sat. 9–5, and Sun. 10–5.*

㉑ The **Schweizerisches Schützenmuseum** (Swiss Shooting Museum) traces the development of firearms from 1817 and celebrates Swiss marksmanship beyond the apple-splitting accuracy of William Tell. It's in between the History and Natural History museums. *Bernastr. 5, tel. 031/3510127. Admission free. Open Tues.–Sat. 2–4, Sun. 10–noon and 2–4.*

㉒ The **Schweizerisches PTT-Museum** (Swiss Postal and Telecommunications Museum), now housed in its striking new building behind the Bernisches Historisches Museum, offers detailed documents, art, and artifacts of early technology to trace the history of the mail system in Switzerland, from Roman messengers to telegraph and radio. *Helvetiastr. 16, tel. 031/3387777. Admission: 2 Fr. adults. Open Tues.–Sun. 10–5.*

Alternatively, head back from the casino on Kochergasse past the **㉓** enormous domed **Bundeshaus** (Capitol). By night, be sure to stick to Kochergasse instead of the riverview promenade behind the capitol building; some visitors have been annoyed by obvious drug traffic.

Dining

While Bern teeters between two cultures politically, Teutonic conquers Gallic when it comes to cuisine. Dining in Bern is usually a down-to-earth affair, with Italian home cooking running a close second to the local standard fare of meat and potatoes. Specialties include the famous *Bernerplatte* (sauerkraut with boiled beef, fatty pork, sausages, ham, and tongue), *Buurehamme* (hot smoked ham), and *Ratsherrentopf* (rösti with roast veal, beef, liver, and sausage). Coffee and *Kuchen* (pastry) are the four-o'clock norm. For details and price-category definitions, *see* Dining in Staying in Switzerland, *above.*

Very Expensive **Bellevue-Grill.** When Parliament is in town, this haute-cuisine landmark is transformed from a local gourmet mecca to a political clubhouse where the movers-and-shakers put their heads together over healthy portions of updated classics—such as veal liver *Geschnetzeltes* with raspberries. *Kochergasse 3–5, tel. 031/3204545. Reservations advised. Jacket and tie advised. AE, DC, MC, V.*

★ **Schultheissenstube.** The intimate, rustic dining room, with a clublike bar in the center and an adjoining all-wood stübli, looks less like a gastronomic haven than a country pub, and the folksy music piped in furthers the delusion. Yet the cooking is sophisticated, international, and imaginative—duck breast in hazelnut vinaigrette, oyster-and-champagne risotto, seafood lasagne with saffron, Cornish hen with goose liver sauce. *Hotel Schweizerhof, Bahnhofplatz*

11, tel. 031/3114501. Reservations advised. Jacket and tie advised. AE, DC, MC, V. Closed Sun.

Expensive **Jack's Brasserie.** In the Hotel Schweizerhof, this street-level restaurant, with high ceilings, wainscoting, and roomy banquettes, is airy and bustling, frequented by shoppers, Parliament members, and businesspeople who enjoy its urbane atmosphere. You can enjoy a drink here by day or settle in at mealtime for a smartly served menu of French classics with a light touch. *Hotel Schweizerhof, Bahnhofplatz 11, tel. 031/3114501. Reservations advised. Jacket and tie advised. AE, DC, MC, V.*

★ **Zum Rathaus.** Across from the Rathaus in the Old Town, this atmospheric, all-wood landmark has been a restaurant since 1863, though the row house dates from the 17th century. Downstairs, the setting is casual and comfortable, while the upstairs "Marcuard-Stübli" is considerably more formal; during the summer, opt for the outdoor café on the Rathausplatz. The cooking ranges from local meat standards to game, salmon, and hearty pastries. *Rathausplatz 5, tel. 031/3116183. Reservations advised upstairs. Dress: casual downstairs, jacket suggested upstairs. AE, DC, MC, V. Closed Sun. and Mon.*

Moderate **Della Casa.** You can stay downstairs in the steamy, rowdy stübli,
★ where necktied businessmen roll up their sleeves and play cards, or you can head up to the restaurant, where they leave their jackets on. It's an unofficial parliament headquarters, with generous local and Italian specialties. *Schauplatzgasse 16, tel. 031/3112142. Reservations advised. Jacket advised. DC, MC, V. No credit cards downstairs. Closed Sat. eve. and Sun.*

★ **Lorenzini.** In a town where the cozy or stuffy holds sway, this hip, bright spot stands apart. Delicious homemade pasta and changing menus featuring the specialties of different Italian regions are served with authentic, contemporary flair. The clientele is a mix of voguish yuppies; the café-bar downstairs draws the young and even more seriously chic. *Marktgass-Passage 3, tel. 031/3117850. Reservations advised. Dress: casual but neat. DC, MC, V.*

Zunft zu Webern. Founded as a weavers' guildhouse and built in 1704, this classic building has been renovated on the ground floor in a slick but traditional style, with gleaming new wood and bright lighting. The cuisine reflects the sophisticated decor, with generous portions of such upgraded standards as lamb stew with saffron. *Gerechtigkeitsgasse 68, tel. 031/3114258. Reservations not necessary. Dress: casual. MC, V.*

Inexpensive **Brasserie zum Bärengraben.** Directly across from the bear pits, this
★ popular, easygoing little local institution, with the thinnest veneer of a French accent, serves inexpensive lunch specials to shoppers, tourists, businesspeople, and retirees, who settle in with a newspaper and a *dezi* (deciliter) of wine. The menu offers many old-style basics—*Kalbskopf am Vinaigrette* (chopped veal in vinaigrette), pig's feet, stuffed cabbage—and wonderful pastries. À la carte dining can be more expensive. *Muristalden 1, tel. 031/3314218. Reservations advised. Dress: casual. No credit cards.*

Harmonie. Run by the same family since 1900, this leaded-glass and old-wood café-restaurant serves inexpensive basics alongside pricier heavy-meat dinners: sausage-and-rösti, *Käseschnitte* (cheese toast), *bauern* omelets (farm-style, with bacon, potatoes, onions, and herbs), and fondue. It's lively and a little dingy, very friendly, and welcoming to foreigners. *Hotelgasse 3, tel. 031/3113840. Reservations not necessary. Dress: casual. No credit cards.*

★ **Klötzlikeller.** A cozy muraled wine cellar, this is much more intimate than the famous Kornhauskeller and just as lovely. There's a good, if limited, menu of meat specialties. *Gerechtigkeitsgasse 62, tel. 031/ 3117456. Reservations not necessary. Dress: casual. AE, MC, V.*

Kornhauskeller. This spectacular vaulted old wine cellar, under the Kornhaus granary, is now a popular beer hall with live music on weekends. Decent hot food is served as an after-thought. *Kornhausplatz 18, tel. 031/3111133. Reservations not necessary. Dress: casual. AE, DC, MC, V.*

Lodging

For details and price-category definitions, *see* Lodging in Staying in Switzerland, *above*.

Very Expensive ★ **Bellevue Palace.** This is a palace indeed, with a view that gives it an advantage over its friendly rival in luxury, the Schweizerhof. It is 75 years old, with Art Nouveau details that include a sweeping staircase and a spectacular stained-glass ceiling in the lobby. Decor in the rooms varies greatly, but each is deluxe. *Kochergasse 3–5, tel. 031/3204545, fax 031/3114743. 155 rooms with bath. Facilities: 2 restaurants, grill, bar, summer terrace café. AE, DC, MC, V.*

★ **Schweizerhof.** The quarters are roomy and luxuriously appointed (most double rooms are the size of junior suites and, at 320 Fr., a great value); halls are decorated with antiques from the collection of the Gauer family, the hotel's owners; and this grand, graceful landmark by the Bahnhof offers excellent service. *Bahnhofplatz 11, tel. 031/3114501, fax 031/3122179. 94 rooms with bath. Facilities: 3 restaurants, café, gourmet deli, bar, nightclub, conference rooms. AE, DC, MC, V.*

Expensive **Bären/Bristol.** These neighboring properties have been twinned as dependable business-class hotels, with modern interiors and first-class comforts. The Bärenbar, where bears figure heavily in the decor, serves drinks and snacks. *Schauplatzgasse 4–10, tel. 031/ 3113367, fax 031/3116983 (Bären); tel. 031/3110101, fax 031/3119479 (Bristol). 149 rooms, 91 with bath. Facilities: bar/café, video, sauna. AE, DC, MC, V.*

★ **Belle Epoque.** This relatively new hotel with period furnishings is more suggestive of fin de siècle Paris than you might expect in Germanic Bern: Every inch of the arcaded row house is filled with authentic Art Nouveau and Jugendstil antiques. Despite the historic look, amenities, including white-tile baths and electric blinds, are state-of-the-art. *Gerechtigkeitsgasse 18, tel. 031/3114336, fax 031/ 3113936. 17 rooms with bath. Facilities: piano bar, gallery. Breakfast only. AE, DC, MC, V.*

Bern. Behind a spare and imposing neoclassical facade, this former theater and formerly modest hotel has been transformed into a sleek, modern gem, with an airshaft garden "courtyard" lighting the better rooms. *Zeughausgasse 9, tel. 031/3121021, fax 031/ 3121147. 96 rooms with bath. Facilities: 2 restaurants, rooftop terrace café, piano bar. AE, DC, MC, V.*

Innere Enge. Opened in December 1992, this renovated early 18th-century inn has been transformed into a slick deluxe business hotel. Spacious, light, and airy thanks to generous windows that take in views toward the Bernese Alps, it's outside the city center. Marian's Jazzroom, in the Louis Armstrong Bar, features top jazz acts. Take Bus No. 21 ("Bremgarten") from the train station. *Engestr. 54, tel. 031/3096111, fax 031/3096112. 26 rooms with bath. Facilities: restaurant, café, jazz bar. AE, DC, MC, V. Expensive.*

Moderate **Goldener Adler.** The exterior of this 1764 building is a magnificent
★ patrician town house, but its interior is modern and modest, with
linoleum baths and severe Formica furniture. The ambience is comfortable and familial nonetheless: The same family has run it for
more than 100 years. *Gerechtigkeitsgasse 7, tel. 031/3111725, fax
031/3113761. 20 rooms with bath. Facilities: restaurant, terrace
café. AE, DC, MC, V.*

★ **Krebs.** A classic, small, Swiss hotel, Krebs is impeccable and solid,
managed with an eye on every detail. The spare decor is warmed
with wood and made comfortable by the personal, friendly service of
the Buri family. A handful of inexpensive rooms without bath offer
excellent value. *Genfergasse 8, tel. 031/3114942, fax 031/3111035. 44
rooms, 41 with shower. Facilities: restaurant. AE, DC, MC, V.*

Inexpensive **Glocke.** Though it's very plain and occasionally shabby, there's a
young, friendly management here and two lively restaurants, one a
"Swiss Chalet," with dancing and folklore shows, the other Italian.
The rooms have a fresh paint job, tile baths, and homey, unmatched
towels. A few rooms without baths cost less. *Rathausgasse 75, tel.
031/3113771, fax 031/3111008. 20 rooms, some with bath. Facilities:
2 restaurants, entertainment. AE, DC, MC, V.*

Goldener Schlüssel. This is a bright, tidy spot with wood, crisp
linens, and tiled baths. It's in the heart of the Old Town, so the rooms
are quieter in the back. There are two good restaurants serving
Swiss and international specialties. *Rathausgasse 72, tel. 031/
3110216, fax 031/3115688. 29 rooms, some with shower. Facilities: 2
restaurants. DC, MC, V.*

★ **Hospiz zur Heimat.** The elegant 18th-century exterior belies the
dormitory gloom inside, but the baths are new and the rooms are immaculate. It's in an excellent Old Town location. *Gerechtigkeitsgasse
50, tel. 031/3110436, fax 031/3123386. 40 rooms, some with bath.
Breakfast only. AE, DC, MC, V.*

Jardin. In a commercial neighborhood far above the Old Town, this is
a solid, roomy middle-class hotel, with fresh decor and baths in every room. It's easily reached by tram No. 9 to Breitenrainplatz.
*Militärstrasse 38, tel. 031/3330117, fax 031/3330943. 17 rooms with
bath. Facilities: restaurant. AE, DC, MC, V.*

Marthahaus. Take bus No. 20 over the Kornhaus Bridge to this
spare, old-style pension in a residential neighborhood north of the
Old Town, where rates are low and the service is friendly.
*Wyttenbachstrasse 22a, tel. 031/3324135. 20 rooms, 6 with bath.
Breakfast only. MC, V.*

Zermatt

Lying at an altitude of 1,616 meters (5,300 feet), Zermatt offers the
ultimate Swiss-Alpine experience: spectacular mountains, a roaring
stream, state-of-the-art transport facilities, and a broad range of
high-quality accommodations, some of them radiating rustic atmosphere, plus 230 kilometers (143 miles) of downhill runs and 7 kilometers (4 miles) of cross-country trails. But its greatest claim to fame
remains the **Matterhorn** (4,477 meters, 14,690 feet), which attracts
swarms of package-tour sightseers pushing shoulder to shoulder to
get yet another shot of this genuine wonder of the Western world.

Arriving and Departing

Zermatt is a car-free resort isolated at the end of the Mattertal, a
rugged valley at the eastern end of the Alpine canton of Valais. A
good mountain highway and the Brig-Visp-Zermatt Railway cut

south through the valley from Visp, the crossroads of the main Valais east–west routes. The airports of Zürich and Geneva are roughly equidistant from Brig, but by approaching from Geneva you can avoid crossing mountain passes.

By Train The Brig-Visp-Zermatt Railway, a private narrow-gauge rail system, runs from Brig to Visp, connecting on to Zermatt. All major rail routes connect through Brig, whether you approach from Geneva or Lausanne in the west, from the Lötschberg line that tunnels through from Kandersteg and the Bernese Oberland, or from the Simplon Pass that connects from Italy.

By Car You may drive up the Mattertal as far as Täsch, where you must abandon your car in a large parking lot and catch the train as it completes its climb into Zermatt.

Getting Around

Because Zermatt permits no private cars, your only means of transit are electric taxis that shuttle arriving guests to their hotels and back. The village is relatively small and easily covered on foot.

By Cable Car and Mountain Rail Hiking as well as skiing are Zermatt's raison d'être, but you may want to get a head start into the heights by riding part of the sophisticated network of cable cars, lifts, cogwheel rails, and even an underground metro that carry you above the village center into the wilderness. Excursions to the Klein, Matterhorn, and Gornergrat are particularly spectacular.

Important Addresses and Numbers

Tourist Information The main tourist office, the **Verkehrsbüro Zermatt,** is across from the train station (Bahnhofplatz, CH-3920 Zermatt, tel. 028/661181).

Emergencies **Police** (tel. 027/225656). **Ambulance** (tel. 028/672000).

Exploring Zermatt

Zermatt lies in a hollow of meadows and trees ringed by mountains—among them the broad **Monte Rosa** (4,554 meters/14,940 feet) and its tallest peak, the **Dufourspitze** (at 4,634 meters/15,200 feet, the highest point in Switzerland)—of which visitors hear relatively little, so all-consuming is the cult of the Matterhorn. But the Matterhorn deserves the idolatry: Though it has become an almost self-parodying icon, like the Eiffel Tower or the Statue of Liberty, this distinctive snaggle-toothed pyramid, isolated on all sides from surrounding peaks, is larger than life as it rears up over the village.

Despite its celebrity mountain, Zermatt remains a resort with its feet on the ground, protecting its regional quirks along with its wildlife and its tumbledown *mazots* (little grain-storage sheds raised on mushroomlike stone bases to keep the mice away), which crowd between glass-and-concrete chalets like old tenements between skyscrapers. Streets twist past weathered wood walls, flower boxes, and haphazard stone roofs until they break into open country that inevitably slopes uphill.

In 1891, the cog railway between Visp and Zermatt took its first summer run and began disgorging tourists with profitable regularity—though it didn't plow through in wintertime until 1927. But what really drew the first tourists and made Zermatt a household word was Edward Whymper's spectacular—and catastrophic—conquering of the Matterhorn in 1865. Whymper and his band of six made the successful trek to the mountain's summit before tragedy struck. During the treacherous descent, four of the men slid against one another and fell 4,000 feet to their death. The body of one was never recovered, but the others lie in the grim little cemetery behind the Zermatt church in the village center.

If you want to gain the broader perspective of high altitudes without risking life or limb, take the trip up the Gornergrat—the train is used for excursions as well as ski transport. Part of the rail system completed in 1898 and the highest open-air rail system in Europe (the tracks to the Jungfraujoch, though higher, bore through the face of the Eiger), it connects out of the main Zermatt train station and climbs slowly up the valley to the **Riffelberg,** which at 2,582 meters (8,469 feet) offers wide-open views of the Matterhorn. From **Rotenboden,** at 2,819 meters (9,246 feet), a short downhill walk leads to the **Riffelsee,** which obligingly provides photographers with a postcard-perfect reflection of the famous peak. At the end of the 9-kilometer (14½-mile) line, the train stops at the summit station of **Gornergrat** (3,130 meters/10,266 feet), and passengers pour onto the observation terraces to take in the majestic views of the Matterhorn, Monte Rosa, Gorner glacier, and scores of other peaks and glaciers. There's a departure every 24 minutes between 8 AM and 7 PM. The round-trip fare is 53 Fr. Bring warm clothes, sunglasses, and sturdy shoes.

Dining

Located at the German end of the mostly French canton of Valais, Zermatt offers a variety of French and German cooking, from veal and rösti to raclette and fondue. Specialties often feature pungent mountain cheese: *Käseschnitte,* for instance, are substantial little casseroles of bread, cheese, and often ham, baked until the whey saturates the crusty bread and the cheese browns to gold. Air-dried beef is another Valais treat: The meat is pressed into a dense brick and dried in mountain breezes. It is served in thin, translucent slices, with gherkins and crisp pickled onions. Alas, McDonald's has infiltrated this once-isolated retreat, and you now have to climb or ski to find memorable, cut-above dining. For price-category definitions, *see* Dining in Staying in Switzerland, *above.*

Moderate **Findlerhof.** Whether for long lunches between sessions on the slopes
★ or for the traditional wind-down après-ski, this mountain restaurant in tiny Findeln, between the Sunnegga and Blauherd ski areas, is still de rigueur, especially with the hip young English and Americans. The Matterhorn views are astonishing, the decor stylish, the staff chic—and the food surprisingly fine. Traditional hot dishes and nontraditional pastas share billing with good homemade desserts. *Findeln, tel. 028/672588. Dress: casual. No credit cards. Closed May–mid-June, Oct.–Nov.*

★ **Zum See.** Beyond Findeln in a tiny village by the same name, Zum See has become something of an institution, serving light meals of a quality and level of invention that would merit acclaim even if the restaurant weren't in the middle of nowhere at 1,766 meters (5,792 feet). During the summer its shaded picnic tables draw hikers who reward themselves with homemade pasta and fresh-cranked sorbet at the finish of a day's climb; during the winter its low, cozy log dining room gives skiers a glow with a fine assortment of brandies. *Tel. 028/672045. Reservations suggested in the evening. Dress: casual. No credit cards. Closed May–June, Oct.–mid-Nov.*

Inexpensive **Elsie Bar.** Directly across from the church, this popular, central après-ski haunt looks like a log cabin inside, and draws an international crowd into its barroom for cocktails, American-style. Light meals include cheese specialties and snails. *Tel. 028/672431. Dress: casual. AE, DC, MC, V.*

Lodging

At high season—Christmas and New Year's, Easter, and late summer—Zermatt's high prices rival those of Zürich and Geneva. But read the fine print carefully when you plan your visit: Most hotels include half-pension in their price, offering breakfast and your choice of a noon or evening meal. Hotels that call themselves "garni" do not offer pension dining plans. For price-category definitions, *see* Lodging in Staying in Switzerland.

Very **Mont Cervin.** One of the flagships of the Seiler dynasty, this is a
Expensive sleek, luxurious, and urbane mountain hotel. First built in 1852, it's
★ unusually low-slung for a grand hotel, with dark beams and classic decor; a few rooms are full of rustic stucco and carved blond wood. Jacket and tie are required in the guests' dining hall, and for the Friday gala buffet, it's black tie only. *Tel. 028/668888, fax 028/672878. 105 rooms with bath. Facilities: restaurant, grill, dancing, sports center, sauna, solarium, indoor pool. AE, DC, MC, V.*

Zermatterhof. The Cervin's rival for five-star luxury, this 19th-century hotel has recently undergone major renovations to better emphasize its rustic beginnings. Both restaurants, including the elegant newer one opened in 1993, are for guests only, with half-pension included in the price. *Tel. 028/661100, fax 028/674842. 93 rooms with bath. Facilities: 2 restaurants, sauna, fitness center, indoor pool. AE, DC, MC, V.*

Expensive **Monte Rosa.** Behind its graceful shuttered facade you will find flag-
★ stone floors, brass, stained and beveled glass, pine, fireplaces, and an elaborate Victorian dining hall, fully restored. The bar is an après-ski must. *Tel. 028/661131, fax 028/671160. 51 rooms. Facilities: restaurant, access to Mont Cervin pool, sauna, sun terrace. AE, DC, MC, V.*

Pollux. Constructed in 1978 and renovated in 1989, this simple but chic modern hotel is directly on the main pedestrian shopping street. A French restaurant serves seafood specialties, and an appealing old-fashioned stübli draws locals for its low-price lunches, snacks, and Valais cheese specialties; the terrace café sits directly on the busy street. *Tel. 028/671946, fax 028/675426. 32 rooms with bath. Facilities: restaurant, stübli, terrace, dancing, sauna, solarium, garden. AE, DC, MC, V.*

Moderate **Julen.** Its 1937 chalet-style construction, knotty-pine decor, and im-
★ peccable 1981 renovation qualify this lodge for membership in the Romantik chain, which assures guests of authentic regional comforts. The main restaurant offers French cooking, and the welcoming stübli serves lamb specialties from locally raised flocks. *Tel. 028/672481, fax 028/671481. 37 rooms with bath. Facilities: restaurant, café, terrace, sauna, solarium. AE, DC, MC, V.*

Romantica. Among the scores of anonymous modern hotels around Zermatt, this modest structure offers an exceptional location directly above the town center. Its tidy gardens and flower boxes, game trophies, and old-style stove soften the cookie-cutter look, and its plain rooms benefit from big windows and balconies. Views take in the mountains (though not the Matterhorn) over a graceful clutter of stone roofs. *Tel. 028/671505, fax 028/675815. 14 rooms with bath. Facilities: bar. AE, MC, V.*

Inexpensive **Alphubel.** Although it is surrounded by other hotels and is steps from the main street, this modest, comfortable pension feels off the beaten track—and it offers large sunny balconies in its south-side rooms. The interior reflects the 1954 construction—a little institutional—but there's a sauna in the basement guests can use for a slight surcharge. *Tel. 028/673003, fax 028/676684. 32 rooms, 16 with bath. Facilities: restaurant, sauna. AE, MC, V.*

★ **Mischabel.** This proud old budget pension—run by the same family for 40 years—provides comfort, atmosphere, and a central location few places can match at twice the price, with balconies on the south side framing a perfect Matterhorn view. Creaky, homey, and covered with knotty pine aged to the color of toffee, its rooms have sinks only, though you'll find linoleum-lined showers on every floor. *Tel. 028/671131, fax 028/676507. 28 rooms with bath. Facilities: restaurant. No credit cards.*

★ **Touring.** Its reassuringly traditional architecture and snug, sunny all-pine rooms, combined with an elevated location outside town and excellent Matterhorn views, make this an appealing choice for travelers who wish to avoid the chic "downtown" scene. Built in 1958 and tastefully updated in 1989, it's family-run, and rooms with Matterhorn views cost only 2 Fr. extra. *Tel. 028/671177, fax 028/674601. 24 rooms, 10 with bath. Facilities: restaurant, stübli. MC, V.*

29 Turkey

Turkey is one place to which the term "East meets West" really applies, both literally and figuratively. It is in Turkey's largest city, Istanbul, that the continents of Europe and Asia meet, separated only by the Bosporus, which flows 29 kilometers (18 miles) from the Black Sea to the Sea of Marmara.

Although most of Turkey's landmass is in Asia, Turkey has faced West politically since 1923, when Mustapha Kemal, better known as Atatürk, founded the modern republic. He transformed the remnants of the shattered Ottoman Empire into a secular state with a Western outlook. So thorough was this changeover—culturally, politically, and economically—that in 1987, 49 years after Atatürk's death, Turkey applied to the European Community (EC) for full membership. It has been a member of the North Atlantic Treaty Organization (NATO) since 1952.

For 16 centuries Istanbul, originally known as Byzantium, played a major part in world politics, first as the capital of the Eastern Roman Empire, when it was known as Constantinople, then as capital of the Ottoman Empire, the most powerful Islamic empire in the world, when it was renamed Istanbul. Atatürk moved the capital to Ankara at the inception of the Turkish Republic.

The legacy of the Greeks, Romans, Ottomans, and numerous other civilizations has made the country a vast outdoor museum. The most spectacular of the reconstructed classical sites are along the western Aegean coast and the southwest Mediterranean coast, which are lined with magnificent sandy beaches and sleepy little fishing villages, as well as busy holiday spots with sophisticated tourism facilities.

For those with more time, an extra five to seven days, an excursion inland to central Anatolia and the eroded lunar valleys of the Cappadocia area will show some of the enormous diversity of the landscapes and people of Turkey.

Essential Information

Before You Go

When to Go The height of the tourist season runs from April through October. July and August are the busiest and warmest months. April through June and September and October are the best months to visit archaeological sites or Istanbul and the Marmara area because the days are cooler and the crowds are smaller.

Climate The Mediterranean and Aegean coasts have mild winters and hot summers. You can swim in the sea from late April through October. The Black Sea coast is mild and damp, with a rainfall of 228 centimeters (90 inches) a year.

The following are the average daily maximum and minimum temperatures for Istanbul.

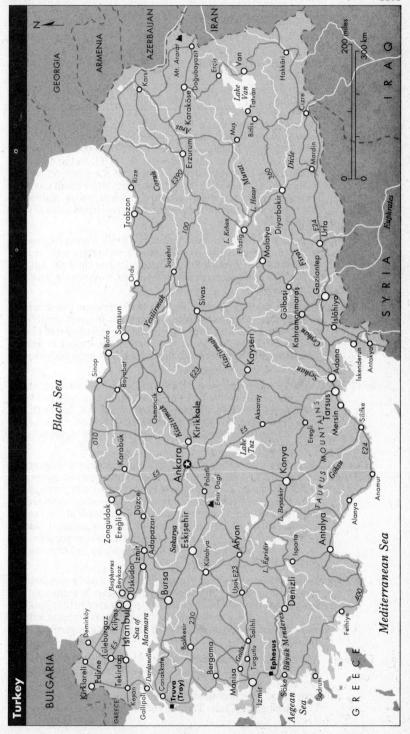

Turkey

Jan.	46F	8C	May	69F	21C	Sept.	76F	24C
	37	3		53	12		61	16
Feb.	47F	9C	June	77F	25C	Oct.	68F	20C
	36	2		60	16		55	13
Mar.	51F	11C	July	82F	28C	Nov.	59F	15C
	38	3		65	18		48	9
Apr.	60F	16C	Aug.	82F	28C	Dec.	51F	11C
	45	7		66	19		41	5

Currency The monetary unit is the Turkish lira (TL), which comes in bank notes of 10,000, 20,000, 50,000, 100,000, 250,000, and 500,000. Coins come in denominations of 500, 1,000, 2,500, and 5,000. At press time (spring 1994), the exchange rate was 35,714 TL to the dollar and 49,680 TL to the pound sterling. These rates are subject to wide fluctuation, so check close to your departure. Major credit cards and traveler's checks are widely accepted in hotels, shops, and expensive restaurants in cities and resorts, but rarely in villages and small shops and restaurants.

Be certain to retain your original exchange slips when you convert money into Turkish lira—you will need them to reconvert the money. Because the Turkish lira is worth a lot less than the dollar or most other foreign currencies, it's best to convert only what you plan to spend.

What It Will Cost Turkey is the least expensive of the Mediterranean countries. Although inflation hovers between 50% and 70%, frequent small devaluations of the lira keep prices fairly stable when measured against foreign currencies. Prices in this chapter are quoted in dollars, which indicate the real cost to the tourist more accurately than do the constantly increasing lira prices.

Sample Prices Coffee can range from about 30¢ to $2.50 a cup, depending on whether it's the less expensive Turkish coffee or American-style coffee and whether it's served in a luxury hotel or a café; tea, 20¢ to $2.50 a glass; local beer, $1–$3; soft drinks, $1–$4; lamb shish kebab, $1.50–$7; taxi, less than $1 for 1 mile; prices are 50% higher between midnight and 6 AM.

Customs On Arrival Turkish customs officials rarely look through tourists' luggage on arrival. You are allowed to take in 400 cigarettes, 50 cigars, 200 grams of tobacco, 1.5 kilograms of instant coffee, 500 grams of tea, and 2.5 liters of alcohol. An additional 600 cigarettes, 100 cigars, or 500 grams of tobacco may be imported if purchased at the Turkish duty-free shops on arrival. Register all valuable personal items in your passport on entry. Items at duty-free shops in airports are usually less expensive here than in duty-free shops in European airports or in in-flight offerings.

On Departure You must keep receipts of your purchases, especially such items as carpets, as proof that they were bought with legally exchanged currency. Also, it cannot be emphasized strongly enough that Turkey is extremely tough on anyone attempting to export antiques without authorization or anyone caught with illegal drugs, regardless of the amount.

Language Atatürk launched language reforms that replaced Arabic script with the Latin-based alphabet. English and German are widely spoken in cities and resorts. In the villages or in remote areas, you'll have a hard time finding anyone who speaks anything but Turkish. Try learning a few basic Turkish words; the Turks will love you for it.

Getting Around

By Car
Road
Conditions
Turkey has excellent roads—25,000 miles of well-maintained, paved highways—but signposts are few, lighting is scarce, and city traffic is chaotic. City streets and highways are jammed with vehicles operated by high-speed lunatics and drivers who constantly blast their horns. In Istanbul, it's safer and faster to drive on the modern highways. Avoid the many small one-way streets, since you never know when someone is going to barrel down one of them in the wrong direction. Better yet, leave your car in a garage and use public transportation or take taxis. Parking is a big problem in the cities and larger towns. Archaeological and historical sites are indicated by yellow signposts.

Rules of the Road
The best way to see Turkey is by car, but be warned that it has one of the highest accident rates in Europe. In general, Turkish driving conforms to Mediterranean customs, with driving on the right and passing on the left. But watch out for drivers passing on a curve or on the top of a hill. Other hazards are peasant carts, which are unlit at night, and motorcycles weaving in and out of traffic.

Gasoline
Throughout the country Mobil, Shell, and British Petroleum, as well as two Turkish oil companies, have gas stations that are open 24 hours on the main highways. Others are open from 6 AM to 10 PM.

Breakdowns
Before you start out, check with your hotel or a tourist information office about how, in case of an emergency, to contact one of the road rescue services available on some highways. Turkish mechanics in the villages will usually manage to get you going again, at least until you reach a city for full repairs. In the cities, entire streets are given over to car-repair shops. Prices are not high, but it's good to give a small tip to the person who does the actual repair work. If you're not in the shop during the repairs, take all the car documents with you. **The Touring and Automobile Club (TTOK)** (Sisli Halaskargazi Cad. 364, tel. 0/212/231–4631) gives information about driving in Turkey and offers a repair service.

By Train
Although there are express trains in Turkey, the term is usually a misnomer. These trains ply several long-distance routes, but they tend to be slow. The best trains are Fatih Expres, Anadolu, and Mavi. Dining cars on some trains have waiter service and serve surprisingly good and inexpensive food. Overnight expresses have sleeping cars and bunk beds.

Fares
Train fares tend to be less expensive than bus fares. Seats on the best trains, as well as those with sleeping berths, should be booked in advance. Round-trip fares are cheaper than two one-way fares. There are 10% student discounts (30% Dec.–May) and 30% discounts for groups of 24 or more. In railroad stations, buy tickets at windows marked "Bilgisayar Giseleri."

By Bus
Buses, which are run by private companies, are much faster than trains and provide excellent, inexpensive service. Buses are available, virtually around the clock, between all cities and towns. They are fairly comfortable and many are air-conditioned. Companies have their own fixed fares for different routes. Istanbul to Ankara, for instance, varies from $8 to $13; Istanbul to Izmir varies from $11 to $16. *Su* (bottled water) is included in the fare. You can purchase tickets at stands in a town's *otogar* (central bus terminal) or at branch offices in city centers. All seats are reserved. Fares vary among competing companies, but most buses between major cities are double-deckers and have toilets. Companies such as Varan, Ulusoy, and Pamukkale offer no-smoking seating. For very short

trips, or getting around within a city, take minibuses or a *dolmuş* (shared taxi). Both are inexpensive and comfortable.

By Plane **Turkish Airlines (THY)** operates an extensive domestic network. There are at least nine flights daily on weekdays between Istanbul and Ankara. During the summer, many flights between the cities and coastal resorts are added. Try to arrive at the airport at least 45 minutes before your flight because security checks, which are rigidly enforced without exception, can be time-consuming. Checked luggage is placed on trolleys on the tarmac and must be identified by boarding passengers before it is put on the plane. Unidentified luggage is left behind and checked for bombs or firearms.

THY offers several discounts on domestic flights: 10% for family members, including spouses; 50% for children under 13; 90% for children under two; and 50% for sports groups of seven or more. The THY sales office is at Taksim Square (tel. 212/252–1106; reservations by phone, tel. 212/574–8200).

By Boat **Turkish Maritime Lines** operates car ferry and cruise services from Istanbul. Cruises are in great demand, so make your reservations well in advance, either through the head office in Istanbul (Rihtim Cad. 1, Karaköy, tel. 212/244–0207) or through **Sunquest Holidays Ltd.** in London (Aldine House, Aldine St., London W128AW, tel. 081/800–5455).

The **Black Sea Ferry** sails from May through September from Istanbul to Samsun and Trabzon and back, from Karaköy Dock in Istanbul. One-way fares to Trabzon are about $30 for a reclining seat, $38 to $94 for cabins, and $50 for cars. The Istanbul to Izmir car ferry departs three days a week. The price of a one-way ticket with no meals included varies between $38 and $122, and $40 for a car.

Staying in Turkey

Telephones **Note:** All telephone numbers in Turkey now have seven local digits plus three-digit city codes. Intercity calls are preceded by 0.

Most pay phones are yellow, push-button models, although a few older, operator-controlled telephones are still in use. Multilingual directions are posted in phone booths.

Local Calls Public phones use *jetons* (tokens), which can be purchased for 1,000 TL at post offices and street booths. For a local call, deposit the token, wait until the light at the top of the phone goes off, then dial the number. If you need operator assistance for long-distance calls within Turkey, dial 131. For intercity automatic calls, dial 0, then dial the city code and the number. Jetons are available for 4,500 TL and 13,000 TL for long-distance calls. Far more practical than the jetons are telephone cards, available at post offices for 24,000 TL, 48,000 TL, and 80,000 TL.

International For all international calls dial 00, then dial the country code, area or
Calls city code, and the number. You can use the higher-price cards for this, or reach an international operator by dialing 132.

If you must make a call abroad, you're better off calling from a phone booth using a telephone credit card or asking the local post office if they have a *Kontörlü* telephone; hotels in Turkey, as elsewhere, have hefty service charges for international calls. The international country code for Turkey is 90.

Mail Post offices are painted bright yellow and have PTT (Post, Telegraph, and Telephone) signs on the front. The major ones are open

Monday–Saturday from 8 AM to 9 PM, Sundays from 9 to 7. Smaller branches open Monday–Saturday 8:30–5.

Receiving Mail If you're uncertain where you'll be staying, have mail sent to Post Restante, Merkez Postanesi (central post office) in the town of your choice.

Shopping The best part of shopping in Turkey is visiting the *bedestans*
Bargaining (bazaars), all brimming with copper and brassware items, hand-painted ceramics, alabaster and onyx goods, fabrics, and richly colored carpets. The key word for shopping in the bazaars is "bargain." You must be willing to bargain, and bargain hard. It's great fun once you get the hang of it. As a rule of thumb, offer 50% less after you're given the initial price and be prepared to go up by about 25% to 30% of the first asking price. It's both bad manners and bad business to underbid grossly or to start bargaining if you're not serious about buying. Outside the bazaars prices are usually fixed, although in resort areas some shopkeepers may be willing to bargain if you ask for a "better price." Part of the fun of roaming through the bazaars is having a free glass of *çay* (tea), which vendors will offer you whether you're a serious shopper or just browsing. Beware of antiques: Chances are you will end up with an expensive fake, but even if you do find the genuine article, it's illegal to export antiques of any type.

VAT Refunds Value-added tax (VAT) is nearly always included in the price. You can claim back the VAT if you buy articles from authorized shops. The net total value of articles subject to VAT on your invoice must be over a specified amount, depending on the nature of the goods, and these articles must be exported within three months of purchase. The invoice must be stamped by customs. Otherwise, mail the stamped invoice back to the dealer within one month of departure and the dealer will send back a check.

Opening and **Banks** are open weekdays, 8:30–noon and 1:30–5.
Closing Times
Mosques are usually open to the public, except during *namaz* (prayer hours), which are observed five times a day. These times are based on the position of the sun, so they vary throughout the seasons between the following hours: sunrise (5–7), lunchtime (noon–1, when the sun is directly overhead), afternoon (3–4), sunset (5–7), bedtime (9–10). Prayers last 30–40 minutes.

Museums are generally open Tuesday–Sunday, 9:30–4:30, and closed Monday. **Palaces,** open the same hours, are closed Thursday instead of Monday.

Shops are closed daily from 1 PM to 2 PM and all day Sunday. Generally they're open Monday–Saturday, 9:30–1 and 2–7. There are some exceptions in the resort areas, where shops stay open until 9 PM and are often open on Sunday.

National January 1; March 3 (sunset) to March 5 (sunset): *Seker Bayrami*
Holidays (sugar feast), three-day feast marking the end of Ramadan, a month-long Islamic observance that includes daytime fasting and is based on the Muhammadan lunar calendar, varying yearly; April 23 (National Independence and Children's Day); May 19 (Atatürk's Commemoration, Youth and Sports Day); May 11 (sunset) to May 14 (sunset): *Kurban Bayrami* (sacrificial feast), Turkey's most important religious holiday, celebrating Abraham's willingness to sacrifice his son to God, varying yearly according to the lunar calendar; August 30 (Victory Day); October 28 (half-day) and 29 (Republic Day).

Dining Turkish cuisine is among the best in the world. In Istanbul, even the tiniest little hole-in-the-wall serves delicious food. It's also extremely healthy, full of fresh vegetables, yogurt, legumes, and grains, not to mention fresh seafood, roast lamb, and kebabs made of lamb, beef, or chicken. Because Turkey is predominantly Muslim, pork is not readily available. But there's plenty of alcohol, including local beer and wine, which are excellent and inexpensive. Particularly good wines are Villa Doluca and Kavaklidere, available in *beyaz* (white) and *kirmizi* (red). The most popular local beer is Efes Pilsen. The national alcoholic drink, *raki*, is made from grapes and aniseed. Turks mix it with water or ice and sip it throughout their meal or serve it as an aperitif.

Hotel restaurants have English-language menus and usually serve a bland version of Continental cuisine. Far more adventurous and tasty are meals in *restorans* and in *lokantas* (Turkish restaurants). Most lokantas do not have menus because they serve only what's fresh and in season, which varies daily. At lokantas, you simply sit back and let the waiter bring food to your table, beginning with a tray of *mezes* (appetizers). You point to the dishes that look inviting and take as many as you want. Then you select your main course from fresh meat or fish—displayed in glass-covered refrigerated units—which is then cooked to order, or from a steam table laden with casseroles and stews. For lighter meals there are *kebabcis*, tiny restaurants specializing in kebabs served with salad and yogurt, and *pidecis*, selling *pides*, a pizzalike snack on flat bread, topped with butter, cheese, egg, or ground lamb, and baked in a wood-fired oven.

Mealtimes Lunch is generally served from noon to 3 and dinner from 7 to 10. In the cities you can find restaurants or cafés open virtually anytime of day or night, but in the villages, finding a restaurant open at odd hours can be a problem.

Dress Except for Very Expensive restaurants, where formal dress is appropriate, informal dress is acceptable at restaurants in all price categories.

Precautions Although tap water is heavily chlorinated, it is not safe to drink in cities and resorts. It's best to play it safe and drink *maden suyu* (bottled mineral water) or *şişe suyu* (bottled water), which is better tasting and inexpensive.

Ratings Prices are per person and include an appetizer, main course, and dessert. Wine and gratuities are not included. Best bets are indicated by a star ★.

Category	Major Cities	Other Areas
Very Expensive	over $40	over $30
Expensive	$25–$40	$20–$30
Moderate	$12–$25	$10–$20
Inexpensive	under $12	under $10

Lodging Hotels are officially classified in Turkey as HL (luxury), H1 to H5 (first- to fifth-class); motels, M1 to M2 (first- to second-class); and P, *pansiyons* (guest houses). The classification is misleading because the lack of a restaurant or a lounge automatically relegates the establishment to the bottom of the ratings. A lower-grade hotel may actually be far more charming and comfortable than one with a higher rating. There are also many local establishments that are licensed but not included in the official ratings list. You can obtain their names from local tourist offices.

Accommodations range from international luxury chains in Istanbul, Ankara, and Izmir to comfortable, family-run pansiyons. Plan ahead for the peak summer season, when resort hotels are often booked solid by tour companies. Turkey does not have central hotel reservations offices.

Rates vary from $10 to more than $200 a night for a double room. In the less expensive hotels, the plumbing and furnishings will probably leave much to be desired. You can find very acceptable, clean double rooms with bath for between $30 and $70, with breakfast included. Room rates are displayed in the reception area. It is accepted practice in Turkey to ask to see the room in advance.

Ratings Prices are for two people in a double room, including 20% VAT and a 10–15% service charge. Best bets are indicated by a star ★.

Category	Major Cities	Other Areas
Very Expensive	over $200	over $150
Expensive	$100–$200	$100–$150
Moderate	$60–$100	$50–$100
Inexpensive	under $60	under $50

Tipping Except at inexpensive restaurants, a 10% to 15% charge is added to the bill. Since the money does not necessarily find its way to the waiter, leave an additional 10% on the table or hand it to the waiter. In the top restaurants, waiters expect tips of between 10% and 15%. Hotel porters expect between $2 and $5, and the chambermaid, about $2 a day. Taxi drivers don't expect tips, although they are becoming accustomed to foreigners giving them something. Round off the fare to the nearest 500 TL. At Turkish baths, the staff that attends you expects to share a tip of 30% to 35% of the bill. Don't worry about missing them—they'll be lined up expectantly on your departure.

Istanbul

Arriving and Departing

By Plane All international and domestic flights arrive at Istanbul's Atatürk Airport. For arrival and departure information, call the individual airline or the airport's information desk (tel. 212/663–6433).

Between the Airport and Downtown Shuttle buses run between the airport's international and domestic terminals to the Turkish Airlines (THY) terminal in downtown Istanbul, at Meşrutiyet Caddesi, near the Galata Tower. Buses depart for the airport at the same address every hour from 6 AM to 11 PM. After that, departure time depends on the number of passengers. Allow at least 45 minutes for the bus ride. Plan to be at the airport two hours before your international flight because of the lengthy security and check-in procedures. The ride from the airport into town takes from 30 to 40 minutes, depending on traffic. Taxis charge about $15 to Taksim Square and $11 to Sultanahmet.

By Train Trains from the west arrive at Sirkeci station (tel. 212/527–0050 or 0051) in Old Istanbul. Eastbound trains to Anatolia depart from Haydarpasa station (tel. 212/348–8020) on the Asian side.

By Bus Buses arrive at Topkapi terminal (not to be confused with the area around the Topkapi Palace) just outside the city at the Cannon Gate. The smaller Trakya Otogari terminal is used for buses serving cities and villages on the European side of Turkey. The Anadolu Otogari serves Anatolian Turkey and European destinations. A few buses from Anatolia arrive at Harem terminal, on the eastern shore of the Bosporus. Some bus companies have *servis arabasi* (minibus services) to the hotel areas of Taksim Square and Aksaray. There are local buses (Nos. 83, 71, 72, 73, and 76 to Taksim and Nos. 84, 89, 92, 93, and 94 to Eminönü from Topkapi terminal), as well as *dolmuşlar* (shared taxis). If you arrive with baggage, it is much easier to take a taxi, which will cost about $8 to Taksim from the bus terminals and about $5 to Old Istanbul.

By Car If you drive in from the west, take the busy E5 highway, also called Londra Asfalti, which leads from Edirne to Atatürk Airport and on through the city walls at Cannon Gate (Topkapi). E5 heading out of Istanbul leads into central Anatolia and on to Iran and Syria. An alternative to E5, when leaving the city, is to take one of the numerous car ferries that ply the Sea of Marmara and the Dardanelles from Kabataş Dock, or try the overnight ferry to İzmir, which leaves from Sarayburnu.

Getting Around

The best way to get around all the magnificent monuments in Sultanahmet in Old Istanbul is to walk. They're all within easy distance of each other, along streets filled with peddlers, shoeshine boys, children playing, and craftsmen working. To get to other areas, you can take a bus or one of the many ferries that steam between the Asian and European continents; sea buses (*deniz otobüsü*) running between the continents, as well as to destinations such as the Princes' Islands, are fast and efficient. Dolmuş vehicles and taxis are plentiful, inexpensive, and more comfortable than city buses. A new tram system runs from Topkapi terminal, via Sultanahmet, to Sirkeci. Subway system construction is underway between Taksim and Levent, and there is the Tünel, a tiny underground train that's handy for getting up the steep hill from Karaköy to the bottom of Istiklal Caddesi. It runs every 10 minutes and costs about 25¢.

By Bus Buy a ticket before boarding a bus. You can buy tickets, individually or in books of 10, at ticket stands around the city. Shoeshine boys or men on the street will also sell them to you for a few cents more. Fares are about 25¢ per ride.

By Dolmuş These are shared taxis that stop at one of the blue and white dolmuş signs. The destination is shown either on a roof sign or a card in the front window. Many of them are classic American cars from the '50s.

By Taxi Taxis are inexpensive. Since most drivers do not speak English and may not know the street names, write down the street you want, the nearby main streets, and the name of the area. Taxis are metered. Although tipping is not expected, you should round off the fare to the nearest 500 TL.

By Boat For a fun and inexpensive ride, take the *Anadolu Kavaği* boat along the Bosporus to its mouth at the Black Sea. The boat leaves year-round from the Eminönü Docks, next to the Galata Bridge on the Old Istanbul side, at 10:30 AM and 1:30 PM, with two extra trips on weekdays and four extra trips on Sundays from April to September. The fare is $6 (round-trip). The trip takes one hour and 45 minutes one way. You can disembark at any of the stops and return by land if you wish. Regular ferries depart from Kabataş Dock, near Dolmabahçe Palace on the European side, to Üsküdar on the Asian side; and also from Eminönü Docks 1 and 2, near Sirkeci station.

Important Addresses and Numbers

Note: Telephone numbers in European and Asian Istanbul have been assigned different codes: the code for European Istanbul (for numbers beginning with 2, 5, or 6) is 0/212; for Asian Istanbul, dial 0/216 for local numbers beginning with 3 or 4.

Tourist Information Official tourist information offices are at **Atatürk Airport** (tel. 212/663–6363); the **Hilton Hotel** (tel. 212/233–0592); **Karaköy Yolcu Salonu,** International Maritime Passenger Terminal (tel. 212/249–5776); and in a pavilion in the **Sultanahmet** district of Old Istanbul (Divan Yolu Cad. 3, tel. 212/518–1802).

Consulates **U.S.** (Meşrutiyet Caddesi 147, Tepebaşi, Beyoğlu, tel. 212/251–3602). **Canada** (Büyükdere Caddesi 107/3, Bengün Han, tel. 212/272–5174). **U.K.** (Meşrutiyet Caddesi 34, Tepebaşi, Beyoğlu, tel. 212/293–7540).

Emergencies **Tourism Police** (tel. 212/528–5369 or 212/527–4503). **Ambulance** (tel. 177). **Doctors:** For an English-speaking doctor, call the American Hospital (Güzelbahçe Sok. 20, Nişantaşi, tel. 212/231–4050/69) or Beyoğlu Hospital (Kuledibi, Karaköy, tel. 212/251–5900). **Pharmacies:** There is one on duty 24 hours in every neighborhood; tel. 111 for details. Consult the notice in the window of any pharmacy for the name and address of the nearest all-night shop. One that's centrally located is **Taksim** in the Taksim district (Istiklal Cad. 17, tel. 212/249–2252).

English-Language Bookstores Dünya Aktuel Bookshop (Istiklal Cad. 469, tel. 212/249–1006) has several branches, including one each in the Hilton and the Sheraton hotels. **Net** (Yerebatan Cad. 15/3, Sultanahmet, tel. 212/520–8406), publishes tourism guides and **ABC Bookshop** (Istiklal Cad. 461, tel. 249–2414) sells English-language books and magazines.

Travel Agencies Most are concentrated along Cumhuriyet Caddesi, off Taksim Square, in the hotel area. They include **American Express** (Hilton Hotel, Cumhuriyet Cad., Harbiye, tel. 212/241–0248 or 212/241–0249); **Intra** (Halaskargazi Cad. 111/2, Harbiye, tel. 212/247–8174 or 212/240–3891); **Setur** (Cumhuriyet Cad. 107, Harbiye, tel. 212/230–0336); and **Vitur** (Cumhuriyet Cad. 269/4, Harbiye, tel. 212/230–0895).

Guided Tours

Tours are arranged through travel agencies (*see* Travel Agencies, above). Choices include the "Classical Tour," either half- or full-day. The half-day tour costs $25 and includes Sancta Sophia, the Museum of Turkish and Islamic Arts, the Hippodrome, Yerebatan Sarayi, and the Blue Mosque; the full-day tour costs $50, and, in addition to the above sights, includes Topkapi Palace, the Süleymaniye Mosque, the Covered or Egyptian Bazaar, and lunch. The "Bosporus Tour" costs $25 for a half day or $50 for a full day, and includes lunch at Sariyer and visits to the Dolmabahçe and Beylerbeyi palaces. The "Night Tour" costs $50 and includes dinner and drinks at Kervansaray or Galata, where there is a show. The full-day guided "Classical Tour" by private car costs between $60 and $90 per person.

Exploring Istanbul

Istanbul is a noisy, chaotic, and exciting city, where Asia meets Europe and spires and domes of mosques and medieval palaces dominate the skyline. At dawn, when the call to the muezzin's prayer rebounds from ancient minarets, many people are making their way home from the nightclubs and bars, while others are kneeling on their prayer rugs, facing Mecca.

Day and night, Istanbul has a schizophrenic air to it. Women in jeans, business suits, or elegant designer outfits pass women wearing the long skirts and head coverings that village women have worn for generations. Donkey-drawn carts vie with old Chevrolets and Pontiacs or shiny Toyotas and BMWs for dominance of the noisy, narrow streets, and the world's most fascinating Oriental bazaar competes with Western boutiques for the time and attention of both tourists and locals.

Ironically, Istanbul's Asian side is filled with Western-style sprawling suburbs, while its European side contains Old Istanbul—an Oriental wonderland of mosques, opulent palaces, and crowded bazaars. The Golden Horn, an inlet 6½ kilometers (4 miles) long, flows off the Bosporus on the European side, separating Old Istanbul from New Town. The center of New Town is Beyoğlu, a modern district filled with hotels, banks, and shops grouped around Taksim Square. There are three bridges spanning the Golden Horn: the Atatürk, the Galata, and the Haliç. The historic Galata Bridge, which has been replaced by a modern drawbridge, is a central landmark and a good place to get your bearings. From here, you can see the city's layout and its seven hills. The bridge will also give you a taste of Istanbul's frenetic street life. It's filled with peddlers selling everything from pistachio nuts and spices to curly-toed slippers fancy enough for a sultan; fishermen grill their catch on coal braziers and sell them to passersby. None of this sits well with motorists, who blast their horns constantly, usually to no avail. If you want to orient yourself in a quieter way, take a boat trip from the docks on the Eminönü side of the Galata Bridge up the Bosporus.

Numbers in the margin correspond to points of interest on the Istanbul map.

Old Istanbul (Sultanahmet) ❶ The number-one attraction in Istanbul is **Topkapı Palace** (Topkapı Saray), located on Seraglio Point in Old Istanbul, known as Sultanahmet. The palace, which dates from the 15th century, was the residence of a number of sultans and their harems until the mid-19th century. In order to avoid the crowds, try to get there by 9 AM, when the gates open. If you're arriving by taxi, tell the driver you want the Topkapı *Saray* (palace) in Sultanahmet, or you could end up at the Topkapı bus terminal on the outskirts of town.

Sultan Mehmet II built the first palace during the 1450s, shortly after the Ottoman conquest of Constantinople. Over the centuries, sultan after sultan added ever more elaborate architectural fantasies, until the palace eventually ended up with more than four courtyards and some 5,000 residents, many of them concubines and eunuchs. Topkapı was the residence and center of bloodshed and drama for the Ottoman rulers until the 1850s, when Sultan Abdül Mecit moved with his harem to the European-style Dolmabahçe Palace farther up the Bosphorus coast.

②
③ In Topkapı's outer courtyard are the **Church of St. Irene** (Aya Irini), open only during festival days for concerts, and the **Court of the Janissaries** (Merasim Avlusu), members of the sultan's elite guard.

Adjacent to the ticket office is the **Bab-i-Selam** (Gate of Salutation), built in 1524 by Süleyman the Magnificent, who was the only person allowed to pass through it. In the towers on either side, prisoners were kept until they were executed beside the fountain outside the gate in the first courtyard. In the second courtyard, amid the rose gardens, is the **Divan-i-Humayun,** the assembly room of the council of state, once presided over by the grand vizir (prime minister). The sultan would sit behind a latticed window, hidden by a curtain so no one would know when he was listening, although occasionally he would pull the curtain aside to comment.

One of the most popular tours in Topkapı is the **Harem,** a maze of nearly 400 halls, terraces, rooms, wings, and apartments grouped around the sultan's private quarters on the west side of the second courtyard. Forty rooms have been meticulously restored and are open to the public. Next to the entrance are the quarters of the eunuchs and about 200 of the lesser concubines, who were lodged in tiny cubicles, as cramped and uncomfortable as the main rooms of the Harem are large and opulent. Tours begin about every half hour. *Admission: $1.*

In the third courtyard is the **Treasury** (Hazine Dairesi), four rooms filled with jewels, including two uncut emeralds, each weighing 3½ kilograms (7.7 pounds), that once hung from the ceiling. Here, too, you will be dazzled by the emerald dagger used in the movie *Topkapi* and the 84-carat "Spoonmaker" diamond that, according to legend, was found by a pauper and traded for three wooden spoons.

Time Out Just past the Treasury, on the right side of the courtyard, are steps leading to a 19th-century Rococo Mecidiye pavilion, now the **Konyali Restaurant** (tel. 212/513–9696), which serves excellent Turkish food and has a magnificent view of the *seraglio* (sultan's household, including the harem) and the Golden Horn. On a terrace below is an outdoor café with an even better view. Go early or reserve a table to beat the tour-group crush. *Open Wed.–Mon. Lunch only.*

In the fourth and last courtyard of the Topkapı Palace are small, elegant summer houses, mosques, fountains, and reflecting pools scattered amid the gardens on different levels. Here you will find the **Erivan Kiosk,** also known as the Revan Kiosk, built by Murat IV in 1636 to commemorate his capture of Rivan in Caucasus. In another kiosk in the gardens, called the **Golden Cage** (Iftariye), the closest relatives of the reigning sultan lived in strict confinement under what amounted to house arrest. The custom began during the 1800s after the old custom of murdering all possible rivals to the throne had been abandoned. The confinement of the heirs apparently helped keep the peace, but it deprived them of any chance to prepare themselves for the formidable task of ruling a great empire. *Topkapi Palace. Admission: $4.25, harem $1. Open Wed.–Mon. 9:30–5:30.*

④ To the left as you enter the outer courtyard, a lane slopes downhill to three museums grouped together: the **Archaeological Museum** (Arkeoloji Müzesi), which houses a fine collection of Greek and Roman antiquities, including finds from Ephesus and Troy; the **Museum of the Ancient Orient** (Eski Şark Eserleri Müzesi), with Sumerian, Babylonian, and Hittite treasures; and the **Tiled Pavilion** (Çinili Köşkü), which houses ceramics from the early Seljuk and Os-

Archaeological
Museum, **4**

Blue Mosque, **6**

Church of St. Irene, **2**

Cistern Basilica, **9**

Court of the
Janissaries, **3**

Dolmabahçe
Mosque, **16**

Dolmabahçe Palace, **17**

Egyptian Bazaar, **13**

Flower Arcade, **15**

Galata Tower, **14**

Grand Bazaar, **10**

Hippodrome, **7**

Istanbul
University, **11**

Museum of Turkish
and Islamic Arts, **8**

Sancta Sophia, **5**

Süleymaniye
Mosque, **12**

Topkapı Palace, **1**

HARBIYE

TEŞVIKIYE

BEŞIKTAŞ

Yıldız
Parkı

Emlâk Cad.

Nüzhetiye Cad.

Kurtuluş Cad.

Bulvarı

Barbaros

Serencebey Yok.

Müvezzi Cad.

TO ORTAKÖY

Şair Nedim

Koçuk
Çiflik
Park

Spor Cad.

Barbaros

Beşiktaş
Cad.

Çırağan Cad.

Beşiktaş
Docks

Yenişehir dere Cad.

Cumhuriyet Cad.

Taşkışla Cad.

Kadirgalargeçit

Dolmabahçe Cad.

YENİŞEHIR

İnönü
Stadium

17

Askerocağı Cad.

Mete Cad.

Tarlabaşı Cad.

TAKSİM

Sıraselviler Cad.

Gümüssuyu Cad.

16

İstiklâl Cad.

Meydanı

KABATAŞ

Kabataş Ferry Dock

Saydam Cad.

15
ℹ

Yeni Çarşı

Kabataş
Seabus Terminal

Masruliyet Cad.

İstiklâl Cad.

BEYOĞLU

C.

Defterdar
Yokuşu

Bogaziçi (Bosporus)

Postacılar
S.

Tünel
Subway
Line

Meclisimebusan

14

Kemeralti Cad.

Necatibey Cad.

Kemankeş Cad.

Şemşi Paşa
Cad.

yvoda
Cad.

ℹ

ÜSKÜDAR

ad.

Karaköy Seabus Terminal

Karaköy
Ferry Dock

Doğancılar Cad.

Galata Bridge

Eminönü
Docks

Halk Cad.

EMİNÖNÜ

Kennedy Cad.

Seraglio
Point (Sarayburnu)

Sirkeci
Station

İhsaniye Sok.

İRKECİ

Gülhane
Park

Tıbbiye Cad.

OĞLU

4

1

Ankara Cad.

Hilaliahmer
Cad.

2

ULTANAHMET

9

3

Ayasofa
Sq.

Çeşme Kebir
Cad.

Divan Yolu

Alemdâr Cad.

5

ℹ

8

7

6

Baths of
Roxelana

Kabasakal Sok.

Çeşme Kebir
Cad.

Kavak İskelesi Cad.

ğler Sok.

Cad.

SELİMİYE

N

Sea of Marmara

TO PRINCES
ISLANDS

Haydarpaşa
Station

TO KADIKÖY

manli empires. The admission price covers all three museums. *Admission: $2. Open Tues.–Sun. 9:30–5.*

❺ Just outside the walls of Topkapi Palace is **Sancta Sophia** (Hagia Sofia in Greek, Ayasofya in Turkish), one of the world's greatest examples of Byzantine architecture. Built in AD 532 under the supervision of Emperor Justinian, it took 10,000 men and six years to complete. Sancta Sophia is made of ivory from Asia, marble from Egypt, and columns from the ruins of Ephesus. The dome, one of the most magnificent in the world, was also the world's largest until the dome at St. Peter's Basilica was built in Rome 1,000 years later. Sancta Sophia was the cathedral of Constantinople for 900 years, surviving earthquakes and looting Crusaders until 1453, when it was converted into a mosque by Mehmet the Conqueror. Minarets were added by succeeding sultans. Sancta Sophia originally had many mosaics depicting Christian scenes, which were plastered over by Süleyman I, who felt they were inappropriate for a mosque. In 1935, Atatürk converted Sancta Sophia into a museum. Shortly after that, American archaeologists discovered the mosaics, which were restored and are now on display.

According to legend, the **Sacred Column,** in the north aisle of the mosque, "weeps water" that can work miracles. It's so popular that, over the centuries, believers have worn a hole through the marble and brass column. You can stick your finger in it and make a wish. *Ayasofya Meydani. Admission: $4.25. Open Tues.–Sun. 9:30–5.*

❻ Across from Sancta Sophia is the **Blue Mosque** (Sultan Ahmet Camii), with its shimmering blue tiles, 260 stained-glass windows, and six minarets, as grand and beautiful a monument to Islam as Sancta Sophia was to Christianity. Mehmet Aga, also known as Sedefkar (Worker of Mother of Pearl) built the mosque during the reign of Sultan Ahmet I in eight years, beginning in 1609, nearly 1,100 years after the completion of Sancta Sophia. His goal was to surpass Justinian's masterpiece, and many in the world believe he succeeded.

Press through the throng of touts and enter the mosque at the side entrance that faces Sancta Sophia. You must remove your shoes and leave them at the entrance. Immodest clothing is not allowed, but an attendant at the door will lend you a robe if he feels you are not dressed appropriately. *Admission free. Open daily 9–5.*

The **Carpet and Kilim museums** (Hünkar Kasri) are in the mosque's stone-vaulted cellars and upstairs at the end of a stone ramp, where the sultans rested before and after their prayers. *Admission: $1.50 adults, 25¢ students. Open Tues.–Sat. 8:30–5.*

❼ The **Hippodrome** is a long park directly in front of the Blue Mosque. As a Roman stadium with 100,000 seats, it was once the focal point for public entertainment, including chariot races and circuses. It was also the site of many riots and public executions. What remain today are an **Egyptian Obelisk** (Dikilitas), the **Column of Constantinos** (Örme Sütun), and the **Serpentine Column** (Yilanli Sütun) taken from the Temple of Apollo at Delphi in Greece. You'll also encounter thousands of peddlers selling postcards, nuts, and trinkets.

On the western side of the Hippodrome is **Ibrahim Paşa Palace,** the grandiose residence of the son-in-law and grand vizir of Süleyman the Magnificent. Ibrahim Paşa was executed when he became too **❽** powerful for Süleyman's liking. The palace now houses the **Museum of Turkish and Islamic Arts,** which gives a superb insight into the lifestyles of Turks of every level of society, from the 8th century to the present. *Şifahane Sok, across from the Blue Mosque, in line with the Serpentine Column. Admission: $2.50. Open Tues.–Sun. 9:30–5.*

Walk back along the length of the Hippodrome and cross the busy main road, Divan Yolu. Turn left onto Hilaliahmer Caddesi. On your **9** left is the **Cistern Basilica** (Yerebatan Sarayı). This is an underground network of waterways first excavated by Emperor Constantine in the 3rd century and then by Emperor Justinian in the 6th century. It has 336 marble columns rising 8 meters (26 feet) to support Byzantine arches and domes. The cistern was always kept full as a precaution against long sieges. *Yerebatan Cad. Admission: $2. Open Wed.–Mon. 9–5.*

Time Out If you need some time out and want a real treat, spend an hour in a Turkish bath. One of the best is Cağaloğlu **Hamami**, near Sancta Sophia in a magnificent 18th-century building. *Ismail Gürkan Cad. 34, tel. 212/522–2424. Admission: $8 for self-service bath, $15 for full service, $24 for deluxe Ottoman massage. Open daily 8–8 for women; 7 AM–10 PM for men.*

10 The next grand attraction is the **Grand Bazaar** (Kapali Carsişi) about a quarter-mile northwest of the Hippodrome (a 15-minute walk or 5-minute taxi ride). The Grand Bazaar, also called the Covered Bazaar, is a maze of 65 winding, covered streets, with 4,000 shops, tiny cafés, and restaurants. Originally built by Mehmet the Conqueror in the 1450s, it was ravaged by two modern-day fires, one in 1954 that virtually destroyed it, and a smaller one in 1974. In both cases, the bazaar was quickly rebuilt. It's a shopper's paradise, filled with thousands of different items, including carpets, fabrics, clothing, brassware, furniture, and gold jewelry. *Yeniçeriler Cad. and Fuatpaşa Cad. Admission free. Open Apr.–Oct., Mon.–Sat. 8:30–7; Nov.–Mar., Mon.–Sat. 8:30–6:30.*

When you leave the bazaar, cross Fuatpaşa Caddesi and walk **11** around the grounds of **Istanbul University**, which has a magnificent gateway facing Beyazit Square. Follow Besim Ömer Paşa Caddesi, the western border of the university, to the right to the 16th-centu- **12** ry **Süleymaniye Mosque.** The mosque was designed by Sinan, the architectural genius who masterminded more than 350 buildings and monuments under the direction of Süleyman the Magnificent. This is Sinan's grandest and most famous monument, and the burial site of both himself and his patron, Süleyman. *Admission free. Open daily outside prayer hours.*

13 The Grand Bazaar isn't the only bazaar in Istanbul. Another one worth visiting is the **Egyptian Bazaar** (Misir Carsişi). You reach it by walking down Çarşi Caddesi to Çakmakçilar Yokuşu and Firincilar Sokak, and then into Sabunchani Sokak, where you will see the back of the bazaar. It was built in the 17th century as a means of rental income for the upkeep of the Yeni Mosque. The bazaar was once a vast pharmacy, filled with burlap bags overflowing with herbs and spices for folk remedies. Today, you're more likely to see bags full of fruit, nuts, Royal Jelly from the beehives of the Aegean coast, and white sacks spilling over with culinary spices. It's a lively, colorful scene. Nearby are the fruit and fish markets, which are equally colorful. *Next to Yeni Cami. Open Mon.–Sat. 8–7.*

Time Out **Pandeli.** Excellent food is served in this frenetic turn-of-the-century restaurant, with its domed alcoves. Try the *kağitta levrek* (paper-wrapped grilled sea bass). It can be reached up two flights of stairs over the arched gateway to the Egyptian Bazaar. *Misir Carsişi, Eminönü, tel. 212/527–3909. AE, DC, MC, V. Lunch only. Closed Sun. Moderate.*

New Town New Town is the area on the northern shore of the Golden Horn, the waterway that cuts through Istanbul and divides Europe from Asia.

⑭ The area's most prominent landmark is the **Galata Tower,** built by the Genoese in 1349 as part of their fortifications. In this century, it served as a fire lookout until 1960. Today it houses a restaurant and nightclub (*see* Nightlife, *below*), and a daytime viewing tower. *Büyük Hendek Cad. Admission: $1. Open daily 9–8.*

⑮ North of the tower is the **Flower Arcade** (Çiçek Pasaji), off Istiklâl Caddesi, a lively blend of tiny restaurants, bars, and street musicians.

Next head for Dolmabahçe Mosque and Dolmabahçe Palace, which are reached by following Istiklâl Caddesi to Taksim Square and then taking Inönü (Gümüssuyu) Caddesi around the square downhill to a

⑯ junction. You will see the **Dolmabahçe Mosque** on your right and the clock tower and gateway to Dolmabahçe Palace on your left. The mosque is a separate building from the palace. It was founded by Valide Sultan Bezmialem, mother of Abdül Mecit I, and was completed in 1853. *Admission free. Open daily outside prayer hours.*

⑰ The **Dolmabahçe Palace** was also built in 1853 and, until the declaration of the modern republic in 1923, was the residence of the last sultans of the Ottoman Empire. It was also the residence of Atatürk, who died here in 1938. The palace, floodlit at night, is an extraordinary mixture of Hindu, Turkish, and European styles of architecture and interior design. Queen Victoria's contribution to the lavishness was a chandelier weighing 4½ tons. Guided tours of the palace take about 80 minutes. *Gümüssuyu Cad. Admission: $4.80. Open Apr.–Oct. 9–4; Nov.–Mar. 9–3. Closed Mon. and Thurs.*

Shopping

Gift Ideas The **Grand Bazaar** (*see* Exploring Istanbul, *above*) is a treasure trove of all things Turkish—carpets, brass, copper, jewelry, textiles, and leather goods.

Stores Stores and boutiques are located in New Town on such streets as **Istiklâl Caddesi,** which runs off Taksim Square, and **Rumeli, Halaskargazi,** and **Valikonagi Caddeleri,** north of the Hilton Hotel. Two streets in the Kadiköy area that offer good shopping are **Bağdat** and **Bahariye Caddeleri.** In Altunizade on the Asian side, **Capitol,** a new and slick mall, offers shoppers movies and entertainment, too. **Ataköy Shopping and Tourism Center** is a large shopping and leisure mall near the airport, while **Akmerkez,** the newest of the malls in Etiler, draws those who like luxury and designer wear. Both malls are good places for children.

Markets **Balikpazari** (fish market) is in Beyoğlu Caddesi, off Istiklâl Caddesi. Despite its name, you will find anything connected with food at this market. A **flea market** is held in Beyazit Square, near the Grand Bazaar, every Sunday. A crafts market, with street entertainment, is open on Sundays along the Bosporus at Ortaköy. A weekend crafts market is also held on Bekar Sokak, off Istiklal Caddesi.

Dining

Istanbul has a wide range of eating establishments, with prices to match. Most of the major hotels have dining rooms serving rather bland international cuisine. It's far more rewarding to eat in Turkish restaurants. For details and price-category definitions, *see* Dining in Staying in Turkey, *above*.

Very Expensive

Club 29. This popular restaurant serves French and Turkish cuisines. After midnight a discotheque upstairs is open until 4 AM. *Nispetiye Cad. 29, Etiler, tel. 212/263–5411. Reservations required. AE, DC, MC, V. No lunch.*

Körfez. The specialty here is seafood dishes such as bass baked in salt. The restaurant boat ferries guests across the Bosporus from Rumeli Hisari. *Kanlica, tel. 216/413–4098. Reservations advised. AE, DC, MC, V. Closed Mon. and Nov.–Apr.*

Tugra. Located in the historic Çiragan Palace, this spacious and luxurious restaurant serves the most delectable of long-savored Ottoman recipes, including stuffed bluefish and Circassian chicken. The Bosporus view is framed by the palace's marble columns; high ceilings carry dazzlingly crafted glass chandeliers. *Cirağan Cad. 84, Beşiktaş, tel. 212/258–3377, ext. 7684. Reservations advised. AE, DC, MC, V.*

Expensive

Abdullah Efendi. Here you'll find a great selection of Istanbul fish and other dishes served in a garden overlooking the Bosporus. *Koru Caddesi 11, Emirgan, tel. 212/277–5721. Reservations advised. AE, DC, MC, V.*

Divan. You'll enjoy gourmet Turkish and international cuisine, elegant surroundings, and excellent service at this restaurant in the Divan hotel. *Cumhuriyet Cad. 2, Elmadağ, tel. 212/231–4100. Reservations advised. AE, DC, MC, V.*

Gelik. This restaurant in a two-story 19th-century villa is usually packed, often with people who want to savor its specialty: all types of meat cooked in deep wells. *Sahil Yolu, Ataköy, tel. 212/560–7284. Reservations advised. AE, DC, MC, V.*

Moderate

Borsa Lokantasi. This unpretentious restaurant serves some of the best food in Turkey. The baked lamb in eggplant purée and the stuffed artichokes are not to be missed. *Yaliköskü Cad. Yaliköskü Han 60–62, Eminönü, tel. 212/522–4173. Reservations not necessary. No credit cards. Lunch only. Closed Sun. Another branch at Halaskargazi Cad. 90/1, Osmanbey, tel. 212/232–4200. AE, DC, MC, V.*

Dört Mevsim. Located in a large Victorian building, Dört Mevsim is noted for its blend of Turkish and French cuisine and for its owners, Gay and Musa, an Anglo-Turkish couple who opened it in 1965. On any given day, you'll find them in the kitchen overseeing such delights as shrimp in cognac sauce and baked marinated lamb. *Istiklâl Cad. 509, Beyoğlu, tel. 212/245–8941. Reservations advised. AE, DC, MC, V. Closed Sun.*

Dunya. The frenetic traffic of the adjacent Ortaköy Square and waiters balancing appetizer trays is countered by the picturesque Bosporus view, which on summer nights includes many passing pleasure boats. The grilled cupra is a must, while mezes (appetizers) are always fresh and sumptuous. *Salhane sokak 10, Ortaköy, tel. 212/258–6385. Dress: casual. Reservations advised. No credit cards.*

Hanedan. The emphasis is on kebabs, all kinds, all excellent; there are better-than-average mezes as starters, too. The setting is lively, by the Besiktas ferry terminal. *Çiğdem Sok. 27, Besiktas, tel. 212/ 260-4854. Reservations advised. AE, MC, V.*

Inexpensive **Hacibaba.** This is a large, cheerful-looking place, with a terrace overlooking a churchyard. Fish, meat, and a wide variety of vegetable dishes are on display for your selection. Before you choose your main course, you'll be offered a tray of appetizers that can be a meal in themselves. *Istiklal Cad. 49, Taksim, tel. 212/244-1886. Reservations advised. AE, DC, MC, V.*

★ **Haci Salih.** A tiny, family-run restaurant, Haci Salih has only 10 tables, so you may have to line up and wait—but it's worth it. Traditional Turkish food is the fare here, with special emphasis on vegetable dishes and lamb. Alcohol is not served, but you can bring your own. *Anadolu Han 201, off Istiklâl Cad., Beyoğlu, tel. 212/ 243-4528. Reservations sometimes accepted. No credit cards. Lunch only. Closed Sun.*

Yakup. This cheery hole-in-the-wall is smoky and filled with locals rather than tourists, and it can get loud, especially if there is a soccer match on the television. From the stuffed peppers to the boreks and octopus salad, the mezes are several notches above average. *Asmali Mescit Sok. 35-37, Beyoğlu, tel. 212/249-2925. Reservations advised weekends. No credit cards.*

Lodging

The top hotels are located mainly around Taksim Square in New Town. Hotels generally include the 15% VAT and a service charge of 10–15% in the rate. Modern, middle-range hotels usually have a friendly staff, which compensates for the generally bland architecture and interiors. In Old Istanbul, the Aksaray, Laleli, Sultanahmet, and Beyazit areas have many conveniently located, inexpensive small hotels and family-run pansiyons. Istanbul has a chronic shortage of beds, so plan ahead. For details and price-category definitions, *see* Lodging in Staying in Turkey, *above*.

Very **Çirağan Palace.** This 19th-century Ottoman palace is the city's most
Expensive luxurious—and expensive—hotel. The setting is exceptional, right
★ on the Bosporus and adjacent to lush Yildiz Park. *Çirağan Cad. 84, Beşiktaş, tel. 212/258-3377, fax 212/259-6687. 340 rooms with bath. Facilities: Turkish bath, health spa, pool, bar, 4 restaurants, casino, shops. AE, DC, MC, V.*

Hilton. Lavishly decorated with Turkish rugs and large brass urns, this is one of the best Hiltons in the chain. Ask for a room with a view of the Bosporus. *Cumhuriyet Cad., Harbiye, tel. 212/231-4646, fax 212/240-4165. 510 rooms with bath. Facilities: Turkish baths, beauty and health spa, pool, rooftop bar and restaurant, tennis, squash, shopping arcade, casino, conference facilities. AE, DC, MC, V.*

★ **Pera Palace.** A grand hotel with a genuinely Turkish feel, the Pera Palace was built in 1892 to accommodate guests arriving on the *Orient Express*. Although it has been modernized, the hotel has lost none of its original Victorian opulence. Ask to see the room where Atatürk used to stay—it's been maintained with some of his personal belongings. *Meşrutiyet Cad. 98, Tepebaşi, tel. 212/251-4560, fax 212/251-4089. 145 rooms with bath. Facilities: bar. AE, DC, MC, V.*

Sheraton. Taksim Park provides a splendid setting for this hotel. All rooms have views of the Bosporus or the square. For a night's spree, try the rooftop restaurant and nightclub. *Taksim Park, Taksim, tel. 212/231-2121, fax 212/231-2180. 437 rooms with bath. Facilities: restaurant, bar, nightclub, pool, health and beauty spa. AE, DC, MC, V.*

Expensive **Ayasofia Pansiyons.** These guest houses are part of an imaginative project undertaken by the Touring and Automobile Club to restore a little street of historic wooden houses along the outer wall of Topkapı Palace. One of the houses has been converted into a library and two into pansiyons, furnished in late Ottoman style, with excellent dining rooms. During the summer, tea and refreshments are served in the gardens to guests and non-guests alike. *Soğukçeşme Sokak, Sultanahmet, tel. 212/513–3660, fax 212/512–3669. 63 rooms with bath. AE, MC, V.*

Divan. This is a quiet modern hotel with an excellent restaurant, located very close to Taksim Square. *Cumhuriyet Cad. 2, Şişli, tel. 212/231–4100, fax 212/248–8527. 180 rooms with bath. Facilities: restaurant, bar, tea shop, beauty salon. AE, DC, MC.*

★ **Yeşil Ev (Green House).** Practically next door to the Blue Mosque, this 19th-century building is decorated in old-fashioned Ottoman style with lace curtains and latticed shutters. Its high-walled garden restaurant is a verdant and peaceful oasis in the midst of frenetic Istanbul. *Kabasakal Sok. 5, Sultanahmet, tel. 212/517–6785, fax 212/517–6780. 20 rooms with bath. Facilities: restaurant and garden. AE, MC, V.*

Moderate **Barin.** Modern, clean, and comfortable, with good, friendly service, the Barin caters to business travelers as well as tourists. *Fevziye Cad. 7, Şehzadebaşi, tel. 212/513–9100, fax 212/526–4440. 65 rooms with bath. AE, DC, MC, V.*

★ **Barut's Guesthouse.** Quiet and secluded and in the heart of Old Istanbul, Barut's has a roof terrace overlooking the Sea of Marmara. A friendly, pleasant establishment, the hotel has a modern art gallery in its foyer. *Ishakpaşa Cad. 8, Sultanahmet, tel. 212/516–0357, fax 212/516–2944. 23 rooms with bath. MC, V.*

Büyük Londra. This is another Victorian hotel, similar to the Pera Palace, but not as grand, that has grown old gracefully. *Meşrutiyet Cad. 117, Tepebaşi, tel. 212/245–0670, fax 212/245–0671. 54 rooms with bath. AE, MC, V.*

Inexpensive **Berk Guest House.** Clean and exceptionally comfortable, this is run by an English-speaking couple, Güngör and Nevin Evrensel. Two rooms have balconies overlooking a garden. The guest house is expected to be expanded. *Kutlugün Sok. 27, Cankurtaran, Sultanahmet, tel. 212/516–9671, fax 212/517–7715. 7 rooms with bath. No credit cards.*

Oriental. Conveniently located near Taksim Square, it is minutes from sights such as Dolmabahçe Palace. The front rooms of this modest hotel have great views of the Bosporus. *Cihangir Cad. 60, Taksim, tel. 212/252–6870, fax 212/251–5321. 20 rooms with bath. Facilities: bar. AE, MC, V.*

The Arts

Entertainment in Istanbul ranges from the **Istanbul International Festival**—held late June through mid-July and attracting internationally renowned artists and performers—to local folklore and theatrical groups, some amateur, some professional. Because there is no central ticket agency, ask your hotel to help you. You can also pick up tickets at the box office or through a local tourist office.

For tickets to the Istanbul International Festival, apply to the **Istanbul Foundation for Culture and Arts** (Kültür ve Sanat Vakfı, Yildiz, Besiktaş, tel. 212/261–3294 and 212/260–9072). Performances, which include modern and classical music, ballet, opera, and theater, are given throughout the city in historic buildings, such as St.

Irene Church and Rumeli Castle. The highlight of the festival is the performance of Mozart's opera *Abduction from the Seraglio*, at Topkapi Palace, the site that inspired the opera. The season at the City of Istanbul's **Cemal Resit Rey Concert Hall** (tel. 212/248–9404 or 212/248–5392) runs from September through May and includes classical and jazz music, as well as ballet performed by visiting and local groups.

Concerts Tickets for performances at the main concert hall, **Atatürk Kültür Merkezi,** are available from the box office at Taksim Square (tel. 212/251–5600). From October through May, the **Istanbul State Symphony** gives performances here. It's also the location for ballet and dance companies. The Touring and Automobile Association organizes chamber music performances at **Beyaz Kösk** and **Hidiv Kasri,** two 19th-century minipalaces. For information, contact the **Touring and Automobile Association** (Halaskargazi Cad. 364, Şişli, tel. 212/231–4631).

Nightlife

Bars and Nightclubs Local young professionals patronize **Zihni** (Bronz Sok. 1A, Macka, tel. 212/246–9043) for lunch or evening cocktails. Open daily noon–3 and 6–10.

Kaktus (Istiklâl Cad., Imam Adnan Sokak 4, tel. 212/249–5979) is a French-style café and bar catering to local intellectuals, actors, and feminists. In warm weather, the chairs—and the customers—spill onto the sidewalk. Open daily 9 AM to 2 AM.

At the **Sherlock Holmes British Pub** (Calikusu Sokak 5, Levent, tel. 212/281–6372) an English and Turkish staff serve such pub delights as Guinness and steak and kidney pie. The music volume rises after 10 PM, as does the energy. Open noon until 3 AM.

Bebek Bar (Bebek Ambassadeurs Hotel, Cevdet Paşa Cad. 113, Bebek, tel. 212/263–3000) has views over the Bosporus. Open daily until 1 AM.

Orient Express Bar (Pera Palace Hotel, Meşrutiyet Cad. 98, Tepebaşi, tel. 212/251–4560) distills the atmosphere of old Istanbul with the lingering presence of the rich, powerful, and famous (from Atatürk to Italian king Victor Emmanuel to Josephine Baker) who once played here.

Tribunal (Istiklâl Cad. Muammer Karaca Cikmazi, 3, tel. 212/249–7179) once served as the French court and still retains the original brick inlay ceiling. Live bands perform authentic Gypsy, Greek, or Latin American music after 11 PM. Open 8 PM to 4 AM on weekends.

A well-established nightclub is **Kervansaray** (Cumhuriyet Cad. 30, Elmadağ, tel. 212/247–1630), where you can dine, dance, and watch belly-dancing shows. Open daily 8 PM–midnight. Two other good places for floor shows are **Balim** (Kemerhatun Mah. Hamalbaşi Cad. 8, Beyoğlu, tel. 212/249–5608) and **Olimpia** (Acar Sok. Tomtom Mah., off Istiklâl Cad., tel. 212/244–9456). **Galata Tower** (Kuledibi, tel. 212/245–1160) offers dinner between 8:30 and 10, with a Turkish show and dancing from 10 PM to 1 AM.

Jazz **Hayal Kahvesi** (Büyük Parmakkapi Sok. 19, Beyoğlu, tel. 212/244–2558) is a bohemian side-street bar with wood furniture and lace curtains. Local groups perform jazz, blues, and rock; Tuesday and Friday are jazz nights.

Discos A chic disco with space-age decor and hip atmosphere is **Juliana's,** which also offers live music (Swissotel The Bosporus, Macka, tel. 212/259–0940), open nightly 8 PM–4 AM. **Discorium** (Esentepe, tel. 212/274–8410) is highly recommended. Men are admitted only if accompanied by a woman. **Çubuklu 29** (Bahçeburun, Çubuklu, tel. 212/331–2829), situated by the Bosporus on the Asian side, is open from mid-June through September. **Şaziye** (Eytam Caddesi 21, Maçka tel. 212/232–4155 or 212/231–1401) turns into a popular disco after 11:30 PM; it has New Age decor.

The Aegean Coast

Some of the finest reconstructed Greek and Roman cities, including the fabled Pergamum, Ephesus, Aphrodisias, and Troy, are to be found in this region of Turkey. Bright yellow road signs pointing to historical sites or to those currently undergoing excavation are everywhere here. There are so many Greek and Roman ruins, in fact, that some haven't yet been excavated and others are going to seed.

Grand or small, all the sites are steeped in atmosphere and are best explored early in the morning or late in the afternoon, when there are fewer crowds. You can escape the heat of the day on one of the sandy beaches that line the coast.

Getting Around

The E24 from Çanakkale follows the coast until it turns inland at Kuşadasi to meet the Mediterranean again at Antalya. All the towns on the itinerary are served by direct bus routes, and there are connecting services to the ancient sites.

Guided Tours

The travel agencies in all the major towns offer tours of the historical sites. **Troy-Anzac Tours** (tel. 286/217–5849 or 286/217–5847), in central Çanakkale, has guided tours of the battlefields at Gallipoli. The tour takes about four hours and costs about $11 per person, including breakfast. Travel agencies along Teyyare Caddesi in Kuşadasi offer escorted tours to Ephesus; Priene, Miletus, and Didyma; and Aphrodisias and Pamukkale.

Tourist Information

Contact the tourist office in each town for names of travel agencies and licensed tour guides.

Ayvalik (Yat Limani Karşisi, tel. 266/312–2122).
Bergama (Zafer Mah. Izmir Cad. 54, tel. 232/633–1862).
Bursa (Ulu Cami Parki, Atatürk Cad. 1, tel. 224/221–2359).
Çanakkale (Iskele Meyd. 67, tel. 286/217–1187).
Çeşme (Iskele Meyd. 8, tel. 232/712–6653).
İzmir (Atatürk Cad. 418, Alsancak, tel. 232/422–0207; Gaziosmanpasa Bul. 1/C, tel. 232/484–2147).
Kuşadasi (Iskele Meyd. tel. 256/614–1103).

Exploring the Aegean Coast

Bursa **Bursa,** the first capital of the Ottoman Empire, is known as Yeşil (Green) Bursa, not only because of its many trees and parks but also

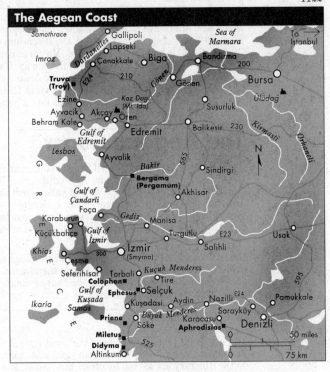

The Aegean Coast

Samothrace · Gallipoli · Lapseki · Imroz · Çanakkale · Biga · Bandirma · Sea of Marmara · To İstanbul · Dardanelles · E24 · 210 · Gönen · 200 · Bursa · Truva (Troy) · Ezine · Gönen · Susurluk · Ülüdağ · Kaz Dağı (Mt. Ida) · Ayvacik · Akçay · Oren · Behram Kale · Gulf of Edremit · Edremit · Balikesir · 230 · Kirmasti · Orhaneli · Lesbos · Ayvalik · Bakir · Sindirgi · N · Bergama (Pergamum) · Akhisar · Gulf of Çandarli · Foça · Gediz · Manisa · 565 · Karaburun · Küçükbahçe · Gulf of İzmir · Turgutlu · E23 · Usak · Khios · Çeşme · 300 · İzmir (Smyrna) · Salihli · 595 · Seferihisar · Torbali · Kuçuk Menderes · Tire · Colophon · Gulf of Kuşada · Ephesus · Selçuk · Samos · Kuşadasi · Aydin · Nazilli · E24 · Pamukkale · Ikaria · Priene · Büyük Menderes · Karacasu · Sarayköy · Denizli · Miletus · Söke · Aphrodisias · Didyma · 525 · Altinkum · 50 miles · 75 km

because of its **Yeşil Cami** (Green Mosque) and **Yeşil Türbe** (Green Mausoleum). Both the mosque and mausoleum derive their names from the green tiles that line the interior of the buildings. They are located opposite each other on Yeşil Caddesi (Green Avenue). *Admission free. Open daily outside prayer hours.*

Bursa is also the site of **Ülüdağ** (the Great Mountain), Turkey's most popular ski resort. To fully appreciate why the town is called Green Bursa, take a ride on the *teleferik* (cable car) from Namazgah Caddesi up the mountain for a panoramic view.

The town square is called **Heykel**, which means "statue," and is named for its statue of Atatürk. Off Heykel, along Atatürk Caddesi, is the **Ülü Cami** (Great Mosque) with its distinctive silhouette of 20 domes. *Admission free. Open daily outside prayer hours.*

Troy Long thought to be simply an imaginary city from Homer's *Iliad*, Troy was excavated in the 1870s by Heinrich Schliemann, a German amateur archaeologist who also found the remains of nine successive civilizations, one on top of the other, dating back 5,000 years. Considering Troy's fame, the site is surprisingly small. It's best to take a guided tour to appreciate fully the significance of this discovery and the unwavering passion of the man who proved that Troy was not just another ancient myth. *Admission: $2.50. Open daily 8–7.*

The E24 highway leads around the **Gulf of Edremit**, a glorious area of olive groves, pine forests, and small seaside resorts. **Ayvalik,** 5 kilometers (3 miles) off the main bus route, between Çanakkale and Izmir, is an ideal place to stay while visiting the ruins of ancient Pergamum, 40 kilometers (24 miles) away. From Ayvalik you can take boats to **Ali Bey Adasi,** a tiny island with pleasant waterfront restaurants, and to the Greek island of Lesbos.

Pergamum **Pergamum** is reached by driving southeast along E24 following the signs toward Bergama, the modern-day name of the ancient Greek-Roman site. If you're traveling by bus, be certain it is going all the way to Bergama, or you'll find yourself dropped off at the turn-in, 8 kilometers (5 miles) from the site.

Because the ruins of Pergamum are spread out over several miles, it's best to take a taxi from one site to the next. The most noteworthy places are the Asklepieion, the Ethnological Museum, the Red Hall, and the **Acropolis.** *Admission: $2.50. Open Apr.–Oct., daily 8:30–6:30; Nov.–Mar., daily 8:30–5:30*

Pergamum's glory peaked during the Greek Attalid dynasty (241–133 BC), when it was one of the world's most magnificent architectural and artistic centers—especially so under the rule of Eumenes II, who lavished his great wealth on the city. Greek rule continued until 133 BC, when the mad Attalus III died, bequeathing the entire kingdom to Rome.

The most famous building at the acropolis is the **library,** which once contained a collection of 200,000 books, all on papyrus. The library's collection was second only to the one in Alexandria, Egypt. When the troops of Julius Caesar burned down the library in Alexandria, Mark Antony consoled Cleopatra by shipping the entire collection of books from Pergamum to Alexandria. These, too, went up in flames 400 years later, in wars between Muslims and Christians.

İzmir The coastal area between Bergama and İzmir, 104 kilometers (64 miles), was once thick with ancient Greek settlements. Today only İzmir remains. Called Smyrna by the Greeks, it was a vital trading port that was often ravaged by wars and earthquakes. İzmir was completely destroyed by a fire in 1922 following Turkey's War of Independence against Greece. The war was a bloody battle to win back the Aegean coast, which had been given to the Greeks in the 1920 Treaty of Sèvres. Atatürk was in İzmir helping to celebrate the victory when celebrations soon turned to horror as the fire engulfed the city.

The city was quickly rebuilt, and it then became known by its Turkish name, İzmir. It's a lively, modern city filled with wide boulevards and apartment houses and office buildings. The center of the city is **Kültürpark,** a large green park that is the site of İzmir's industrial fair from late August to late September, a time when most hotels are full.

On top of İzmir's highest hill is the **Kadifekale** (Velvet Fortress), built in the 3rd century BC by Lysimachos. It is easily reached by dolmuş and is one of the few ancient ruins that was not destroyed in the fire. At the foot of the hill is the restored **Agora,** the market of ancient Smyrna. The modern-day marketplace is in **Konak Square,** a maze of tiny streets filled with shops and covered stalls. *Open 8–8. Closed Sun.*

Kuşadasi **Kuşadasi,** about 80 kilometers (50 miles) south of İzmir on Route 300, has grown since the late 1970s from a fishing village into a sprawling, hyperactive town geared to serving thousands of tourists who visit the nearby ruins and beaches. Although it's packed with curio shops, Kuşadasi has managed to retain a pleasant atmosphere.

Ephesus The major attraction near Kuşadasi is **Ephesus,** a city created by the Ionians in the 11th century BC and now one of the grandest reconstructed ancient sites in the world. It is the showpiece of Aegean archaeology. Ephesus was a powerful trading port and the sacred center for the cult of Artemis, Greek goddess of chastity, the moon, and hunting. The Ionians built a temple in her honor, one of the Seven Wonders of the Ancient World. During the Roman period, it became a shrine for the Roman goddess Diana. Today waterlogged foundations are all that remain of the temple.

Allow yourself one full day to tour Ephesus. The city is especially appealing out of season, when it can seem like a ghost town with its shimmering, long, white marble road grooved by chariot wheels.

Some of the splendors you can see here include the two-story **Library of Celsus;** houses of nobles, with their terraces and courtyards; a 25,000-seat **amphitheater,** still used today during the Selçuk Ephesus Festival of Culture and Art; remains of the municipal baths; and a brothel. *Admission: $5.50. Admission to the houses on the slopes: $1.20. Open daily 8:30–6 (summer), 8:30–5 (winter).*

Selçuk On Ayasoluk Hill in **Selçuk,** 4 kilometers (2½ miles) from Ephesus, is the restored **Basilica of St. John** (St. Jean Aniti), containing the tomb of the apostle. Near the entrance to the basilica is the **Ephesus Museum,** with two statues of Artemis. The museum also has marvelous frescoes and mosaics among its treasures. *Admission: $2.50. Basilica and museum open Tues.–Sun. 8:30–6.*

St. Paul and St. John preached in both Ephesus and Selçuk and changed the cult of Artemis into the cult of the Virgin Mary. **Meryemana,** 5 kilometers (3 miles) from Ephesus, has the **House of Mary,** thought to have been the place where St. John took the mother of Jesus after the crucifixion and where some believe she ascended to heaven. *Admission $1.20. Open daily 7:30–sunset.*

Priene, Miletus, and Didyma Priene and Miletus, 40 kilometers (25 miles) from Kuşadasi, are sister cities, also founded by the Ionians in 11 BC. Nearby is **Didyma,** a holy sanctuary dedicated to Apollo. **Priene,** on top of a steep hill, was an artistic and cultural center. Its main attraction is the **Temple of Athena,** a spectacular sight, with its five fluted columns and its backdrop of mountains and the fertile plains of the Meander River. You can also see the city's small amphitheater, gymnasium, council chambers, marketplace, and stadium. *Admission: $1.20. Open daily 8:30–6.*

Nearby, **Miletus,** once a prosperous port, was the first Greek city to use coins for money. It also became an Ionian intellectual center and home to such philosophers as Thales, Anaximander, and Anaximenes, all of whom made contributions to mathematics and the natural sciences. The city's most magnificent building is the **Great Theater,** a remarkably intact 25,000-seat amphitheater built by the Ionians and kept up by the Romans. Climb to the highest seats in the amphitheater for a view across the city to the bay. *Admission: ruins $1.20, museum $1.20. Open Tues.–Sun. 8:30–6.*

Didyma The temple of **Didyma** is reached by a 32-kilometer (20-mile) road called the **Sacred Way,** starting from Miletus at the bay. The temple's oracles were as revered as those of Delphi. Under the courtyard is a network of corridors whose walls would throw the oracle's voice into deep and ghostly echoes. The messages would then be interpreted by the priests. Fragments of bas-relief include a gigantic head of Medusa and a small statue of Poseidon and his wife, Amphitrite. *Admission: $1.20. Open daily 8:30–6.*

Pamukkale East of Kuşadasi, 215 kilometers (133 miles) away, is **Pamukkale,** which first appears as an enormous chalky white cliff rising some

102 meters (330 feet) from the plains. Mineral-rich volcanic spring water cascades over basins and natural terraces, crystallizing into white stalactites, curtains of solidified water seemingly suspended in air. The hot springs in the area were popular with the ancient Romans, who believed they had curative powers. You can see the remains of Roman baths among the ruins of nearby **Hierapolis.** The village of Pamukkale has many small hotels surrounding the hot springs, which are used today by people who still believe that they can cure a variety of problems, including rheumatism. Farther down in the village are inexpensive pansiyons, some also with hot springs. It's best to stay in Pamukkale overnight before heading on to the ruins of **Aphrodisias,** a city of 60,000 dedicated to Aphrodite, the Greek goddess of love and fertility. It thrived from 100 BC to AD 500. Aphrodisias is reached via **Karacasu,** a good place to stop for lunch; fresh trout is the local specialty. Aphrodisias is filled with marble baths, temples, and theaters, all overrun with wild blackberries and pomegranates. Across a field sprinkled with poppies and sunflowers is a well-preserved **stadium,** which was built for 30,000 spectators.

Dining and Lodging

For details and price-category definitions, *see* Dining and Lodging in Staying in Turkey, *above.*

Ayvalik
Lodging

Büyük Berk. This is a modern hotel on Ayvalik's best beach, about 3½ kilometers (2 miles) from the center of town. *Sarimsakli Mev., tel. 266/324–1045, fax 266/324–1194. 180 rooms with bath. Facilities: outdoor pool, restaurant, disco. AE, DC, MC, V. Moderate.*
Ankara Oteli. Located on Sarimsakli beach, just a few feet from the surf, the Ankara Oteli gives excellent value for the money. *Sarimsakli Mev., tel. 266/324–1195 or 266/324–1048, fax 266/324–0022. 57 rooms with bath. Facilities: café, bar, game room. No credit cards. Inexpensive.*

Bergama
Lodging

Tusan Bergama Moteli. On the main road leading into Bergama, the Tusan has a pool fed by hot springs. The rooms are simple and clean. *İzmir Yolu, Çati Mev., tel. 232/663–1173, fax 266/312–6284. 42 rooms with bath. No credit cards. Moderate.*

Bursa
Dining

Cumurcul. This old house converted into a restaurant is a local favorite. Grilled meats and fish are both attentively prepared. *Çekirge Cad. tel. 224/235–3707. Reservations advised. V. Moderate.*
Kebabcı Iskender. Bursa is famous for the dish served here, *Iskender Kebab* (Alexander's kebab), slivers of skewer-grilled meat served with tomato sauce and yogurt. *Ünü Cad. 7, Heykel, tel. 224/221–4615. Dress: casual. Reservations not necessary. No credit cards. Inexpensive.*

Lodging
★

Celik Palace. The main attraction of this luxurious hotel is a domed, Roman-style pool fed by hot springs. *Çekirge Cad. 79, tel. 224/235–3500, fax 224/236–1910. 173 rooms with bath. Facilities: restaurant, bar, pool, nightclub, disco. AE, DC, MC, V. Expensive.*
Ada Palas. Located near Kültür Park, this hotel has an inviting thermal pool. *Murat Cad. 21, tel. 224/236–1600, fax 224/236–4656. 39 rooms with bath. V. Moderate.*

Çanakkale and Troy
Lodging

Akol. This modern, new hotel is on the waterfront in Çanakkale; ask for a room with a terrace overlooking the Dardanelles. *Kordonboyu, tel. 286/217–9456, fax 286/217–2897. 138 rooms with bath. Facilities: bar, restaurant, outdoor pool, disco. AE, MC, V. Moderate.*
Büyük Truva. Near the center of Çanakkale, the Truva is an excel-

lent base for sightseeing. *Kordonboyu, tel. 286/217–1024, fax 286/ 217–0903. 66 rooms with bath. No credit cards. Moderate.*

Tusan. Surrounded by a pine forest on a beach at Güzelyali, north of Troy, the Tusan is one of the most popular hotels in the area. Be certain to reserve well in advance. *Güzelyali, tel. 286/232–8210 and 286/232–8204, fax 286/232–8226. 64 rooms with bath. MC, V. Closed Oct.–Feb. Inexpensive.*

Çeşme
Lodging

Kanuni Kervansaray. Built in 1528 during the reign of Süleyman the Magnificent, the Kervansaray is decorated in traditional Turkish style. It has an excellent restaurant, with outdoor dining in an ancient courtyard. Adjacent to the hotel is a medieval castle. *Çarşi Cad., tel. 232/712–7177 or 232/712–6492, fax 232/712–6496. 32 rooms with bath. AE, DC, MC, V. Expensive.*

İzmir
Lodging

Büyük Efes. Elegant but showing its age, this hotel is distinguished by a beautiful and relaxing enclosed garden. *Cumhuriyet Mey., tel. 232/484–4300, fax 232/441–5695. 446 rooms with bath. Facilities: restaurant, 2 outdoor pools, disco, auditorium, casino. AE, DC, MC, V. Very Expensive.*

Kismet. Tastefully decorated, the Kismet is a quiet, comfortable hotel with friendly service. *1377 Sok. 9, tel. 232/463–3853, fax 232/ 421–4856. 68 rooms with bath. Facilities: restaurant, bar, sauna. AE, MC, V. Moderate.*

Kuşadasi
Dining
★

Sultan Han. Full of atmosphere, with excellent food to boot, Sultan Han is an old house built around a courtyard, where the focal point is a gigantic tree. You can dine in the courtyard or upstairs in small rooms. One of the specialties is fresh seafood, which you select from platters piled high with fish and shellfish of every possible variety. Ask to have your after-dinner coffee served upstairs, where you can sit on cushions at low brass tables. *Bahar Sok. 8, tel. 256/614–3849. Reservations required. No credit cards. Expensive.*

★ **İbrahim Ustanin Yeri.** Hands down, this spot is the best restaurant in Kuşadasi. The barbecued shrimp and chicken are great, and the fish is always the day's catch. It's also one of the few restaurants around with no blaring TV. *Türkmen Mah. 50, Yıl Cad. 3, tel. 256/ 614–8063. Reservations suggested. AE, DC, MC, V. Moderate.*

Lodging

Club Kervansaray. A refurbished, 300-year-old caravansary, this hotel is decorated in the Ottoman style and loaded with charm and atmosphere. It's in the center of town and features a restaurant with a floor show. There's dancing after dinner in the courtyard, where the camels were once kept. *Atatürk Bul. 1, tel. 256/614–4115, fax 256/614–2423. 40 rooms with bath. Facilities: restaurant, café, nightclub, bar. AE, DC, MC, V. Expensive.*

★ **Kismet.** Although it's a small hotel, Kismet is run on a grand scale, surrounded by beautifully maintained gardens on a promontory overlooking the marina on one side and the Aegean on the other. Ask for rooms in the garden annex. Its popularity makes reservations a must. *Akyar Mev., tel. 256/614–2005, fax 256/614–4914. 98 rooms with bath. Facilities: private beach, restaurant. AE, MC, V. Closed Nov.–Mar. Expensive.*

Liman Hotel. Opened in 1993, this whitewashed building is dramatic, with black cast-iron balconies and black window frames. The front rooms overlook panoramic views of the town and the port. Friendly staff welcome you. *Kibris Cad., Buyral Sok. 4, tel. and fax 256/612–3149. 16 rooms with shower. Facilities: cafe, bar. No credit cards. Inexpensive.*

Pammukale
Lodging

Tusan. The best feature of the Tusan is its pool, one of the most inviting in the area. The rooms are basic and comfortable. The one-story building is at the top of a steep hill. *Tel. 258/272–2010, fax 258/272–2059. 47 rooms with bath. Facilities: restaurant, outdoor pool. AE, DC, MC, V. Moderate.*

Selçuk
Lodging

Hülya. This is a pleasant, family-run pansiyon, where one of the family members is a fisherman who brings in some of his daily catch. You can enjoy a delicious fish meal cooked to order. *Atatürk Cad., Özgür Sok. 15, tel. 232/892–2120. No credit cards. Inexpensive.*

Kale Han. Located in a refurbished stone inn, Kale Han is another pansiyon run by a warm, welcoming family. *Atatürk Cad. 49, tel. 232/892–6154, fax 232/892–2169. 50 rooms with shower. MC, V. Inexpensive.*

The Mediterranean Coast

Until the mid-1970s, Turkey's southwest coast was inaccessible to all but the most determined travelers—those intrepid souls in four-wheel-drive vehicles or on the backs of donkeys. Today well-maintained highways wind through the area and jets full of tourists arrive at the new Dalaman Airport.

Thanks to strict developmental control, the area has maintained its Turkish flavor, with low, whitewashed buildings and tiled roofs. The beaches are clean, and you can swim and snorkel in turquoise waters so clear that it is possible to see fish 6 meters (20 feet) below. There are excellent outdoor cafés and seafood restaurants in which to dine, and you won't find a shortage of bars, discos, and nightclubs.

Getting Around

By Car Although the highways between towns are well maintained, the smaller roads are usually unpaved and very rough.

By Boat There are lots of coves and picnic areas accessible only by boat. For a small fee, local fishermen will take you to and from the coves; also, you can take one of the many water taxis. Or charter a small yacht, with or without skipper, at the marinas of Bodrum and Marmaris. Many people charter boats and join small flotillas that leave the marinas daily for sightseeing in the summer. One of the most enjoyable ways to see the coast is to take a one- or two-week **Blue Voyage** cruise on a *gulet*, a wooden craft with a full crew. There are also three-night mini Blue Voyage trips for scuba divers and snorkelers. For information, contact the following Blue Voyage agencies: in the United States, **Club Voyages,** Box 7648, Shrewsbury, NJ 07702, tel. 908/291–8228; in the United Kingdom, **Explore,** 1 Frederick Street, Aldershot, Hants GU11 1LQ, tel. 02/523–19448; **Simply Turkey,** 8 Chiswick Terrace, Acton Lane, London W4, tel. 081/747–1011; **Falcon Sailing,** 13 Hillgate Street, London W8, tel. 071/727–0232.

Guided Tours and Tourist Information

Local tourist offices list all the guided tours for the area and will also arrange for local guides.

Bodrum (Iskele Meyd. 12, tel. 252/316–1091).
Dalaman (Dalaman Airport, tel. 252/692–1220).
Datça (Iskele Mah. Hükümet Binasi, tel. 252/712–3163 or 252/712–3546).
Kaş (Cumhuriyet Meyd. 5, tel. 242/836–1238).
Marmaris (Iskele Meyd. 39, tel. 252/412–1035).

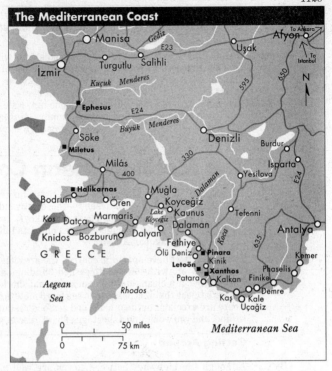

The Mediterranean Coast

(map showing locations including Manisa, Afyon, İzmir, Turgutlu, Salihli, Uşak, Ephesus, Söke, Miletus, Denizli, Burdur, Milás, Isparta, Halikarnas, Muğla, Yesilova, Bodrum, Ören, Koyceğiz, Marmaris, Kaunus, Tefenni, Datça, Dalaman, Antalya, Knidos, Bozburun, Dalyan, Fethiye, Kemer, GREECE, Ölü Deniz, Pinara, Kinik, Letoön, Xanthos, Phaselis, Patara, Kalkan, Finike, Kaş, Kale, Demre, Uçağiz, Rhodos, Aegean Sea, Mediterranean Sea)

0 — 50 miles
0 — 75 km

Exploring the Mediterranean Coast

Bodrum   **Bodrum,** which sits between two crescent-shaped bays, has for years been the favorite haunt of the Turkish upper classes. Today the elite are joined by thousands of foreign visitors, and the area is rapidly filling with hotels and guest houses, cafés, restaurants, and discos. Many compare it to St. Tropez on the French Riviera. Fortunately, it is still beautiful and unspoiled, with gleaming white-washed buildings covered with bougainvillea and magnificent unobstructed vistas of the bays. People flock to Bodrum not for its beach, which is a disappointment, but for its fine dining and nightlife. You'll find beautiful beaches in the outlying villages on the peninsula—**Torba, Türkbükü, Yalikavak, Turgutreis, Akyarlar, Ortakent, Bitez,** and **Gümbet.** Easy to reach by minibus or dolmuş, these villages are about an hour's drive away and have clean hotels and plenty of outdoor restaurants. One of the outstanding sights in Bodrum is **Bodrum Castle,** known as the **Castle of St. Peter.** Located between the two bays, the castle was built by crusaders in the 11th century. It has beautiful gardens and a **Museum of Underwater Archaeology.** *Castle and museum admission: $2.50. Open Tues.–Sun. 8:30–noon and 1–5.*

The peninsula is downright littered with ancient Greek and Roman ruins, although getting to some of them involves driving over rough dirt roads. Five kilometers (3 miles) from Bodrum is **Halikarnas,** a well-preserved 10,000-seat Greek amphitheater built in the 1st century BC and still used for town festivals. *Admission free. Open daily 8:30–sunset.*

Marmaris Another beach resort between two bays is **Marmaris,** which has some of the best sailing on the Mediterranean. It is 178 kilometers (111 miles) along Route 400 from Bodrum via Muğla. You'll climb steep, winding mountain passes, with cliffs that drop straight into the sea. The final 30 kilometers (19 miles) into Marmaris is a broad boulevard lined with eucalyptus trees. Marmaris, like Bodrum, is a sophisticated resort with boutiques, elegant restaurants, and plenty of nightlife. Nearby are quiet villages that are easy to reach by boat or taxi. One of these is **Knidos,** where you can see the ruins of Aphrodite's circular temple and an ancient theater. By road, Knidos is a very rough 108 kilometers (67 miles) from Marmaris. It's easier and quicker to take a boat. Another town is **Turunç,** worth a day's visit, especially for its beaches.

Freshwater **Lake Köyceğiz** can be reached by boat through the reed beds of the **Dalyan delta.** This entire area is a wildlife preserve, filled with such birds as kingfishers, kestrels, egrets, and cranes. Köyceğiz and **Dalyan** villages, both 20 minutes' drive from Dalaman Airport, are good stopping-off places for exploring the area. It costs about $20 to rent a boat with a boatsman to sail from Dalyan to the ruins and beach.

Ölü Deniz One of Turkey's greatest natural wonders is **Ölü Deniz,** an azure lagoon flanked by long, white beaches. The area is about 145 kilometers (90 miles) from Koyceğiz. There are a few wooden chalets in camping grounds and one beachfront hotel. Opposite the beach, you'll find small restaurants with rooftop bars, many with live music that goes on all night.

Southeast of Fethiye, near Route 400, are several ancient sites, including the ruins of **Pinara,** one of the most important cities of the former Roman province of Lycia. Near Pinara, up a steep and strenuous dirt road, you'll find nearly 200 Roman tombs cut honeycomb-fashion into the face of the cliffs. *Admission: $1.20. Open daily 8:30–sunset.*

Xanthos Return to Route 400 and head 18 kilometers (11 miles) south toward the village of Kinik. At Kinik leave the main highway and take a mile-long bumpy road to **Xanthos,** another major city of ancient Lycia. It was excavated in 1838; much of what was found here is now in the British Museum in London. What's left is still well worth the bumpy ride: the acropolis, the Tomb of Harpies, some plastercast reliefs, and ruins of some Byzantine buildings. *Admission: $1.20. Open daily 8:30–sunset.*

Patara and Kalkan Ten minutes from Xanthos is **Patara,** once the city's port. Here you'll find ruins scattered around the marshes and sand dunes. The area's long, wide beaches remain beautiful and unspoiled, despite the fact that they attract hundreds of Turkish families and tourists. The nearest place to stay is **Kalkan,** a fishing village 20 minutes away by minibus.

Kaş **Kaş,** 30 kilometers (18 miles) from Kalkan, is another fishing village that has become a popular resort and is also developing into a major yachting center. Although luxury hotels have replaced many of the tiny houses on the hills, there are still plenty of old-fashioned pansiyons for those on a budget. One of the attractions here is a day trip by boat to the underwater city of **Kekova,** where you can look overboard and see ancient Roman and Greek columns that were once part of a thriving city before the area was flooded. Kekova is especially popular with scuba divers and snorkelers, but to scuba-dive or fish in this area, a permit must be obtained from the directorate of the harbor and from the directorate of the ministry of tourism. Motorboats leave daily at 9:30 and cost about $15.

For romantic ruins, it would be hard to beat **Phaselis.** The Roman agora, theater, aqueduct, and a necropolis with fine sarcophagi are scattered throughout the pine woods that surround the Temple of Athena. Overgrown streets descend to the translucent water, which is ideal for swimming.

Kemer is the center of intensive touristic development, with hotels and restaurants, a well-equipped marina, and club-style holiday villages that make you forget you're in Turkey. The remaining 35 kilometers (26 miles) are increasingly occupied by villas and motels along the smooth pebbles of Konyalti Beach, which stretches to the outskirts of Antalya.

Antalya   The resort of **Antalya,** on the Mediterranean, is a good base for several worthwhile excursions. The city is on a beautifully restored harbor and is filled with narrow streets lined with small houses, restaurants, and pansiyons. On the hilltop are tea gardens where you can enjoy tea made in an old-fashioned samovar and look across the bay to the Taurus Mountains, which parallel the coast. To the right of the port is the 13th-century **Fluted Minaret** (Yivli Minare). The Hisar Café, Tophane tea garden, and Mermerli tea garden all overlook Antalya's harbor.

Dining and Lodging

For details and price-category definitions, *see* Dining and Lodging in Staying in Turkey, *above.*

Antalya   **Talya.** This is a luxurious resort hotel with its own beach that you
Lodging   reach by taking an elevator down the side of the cliff. From every
★   angle there's a view of the sea. It gets booked up quickly in high season. *Fevzi Çakmak Cad., tel. 242/248–6800, fax 242/241–5400. 204 rooms with bath. Facilities: disco, restaurant, pool, game room, fitness room, Turkish hamam, spa. AE, DC, MC, V. Very Expensive.*
Turban Adalya. Built in 1869 as a bank, the Turban Adalya has been imaginatively transformed into a luxurious hotel overlooking the colorful fishing port. *Kaleiçi Yat Limani, tel. 242/241–8066, fax 242/242–3679. 28 rooms with bath. Facilities: restaurant. AE, DC, MC, V. Expensive.*
Altun Pansiyon. The recently renovated pansiyon is located near the Fluted Minaret and minutes from the seaport. It has a well-stocked bar and a pleasant courtyard, and the staff is extremely helpful. *Kaleiçi Mev. 10, tel. 242/241–6624, fax 242/241–4010. 10 rooms with shower. No credit cards. Inexpensive.*

Bodrum   **Club Pirinç.** This restaurant has a pleasant bar, nine guest rooms, a
Dining   swimming pool, and offers Turkish-French cuisine. *Akçabuk Mev., Kumbahçe, tel. 252/316–2902. No credit cards. Expensive.*
Restaurant No. 7. Octopus casseroles are a specialty. *Eski Banka Sok. 7. Expensive.*
Balik Restaurant. Specialties include fish, meat, and chicken kebabs. *Yeniçarşi 28, tel. 252/316–1454. No credit cards. Moderate.*
Korfez Restaurant. This is a seaside fish restaurant. *Cumhuriyet Cad. 18, tel. 252/316–1169. No credit cards. Moderate.*

Lodging   **Manzara Aparhotel.** On a hill looking across the bay toward Bodrum Castle, the Manzara is a group of 20 small apartments, each with living room, kitchen, and terrace. At peak times, you may have to pay half-board. *Kumbahçe Mah. Meteoroloji Yani, tel. 252/316–1719,* *fax 252/316–1720. Facilities: restaurant, outdoor pool, bar. AE, V. Expensive.*

Merhaba Pansiyon. Here, on the waterfront, you'll find a beautiful roof terrace and simply furnished but clean rooms. *Akasya Sok. 5, tel. 252/316–2115. No credit cards. Inexpensive.*

Dalyan **Yali Restaurant.** This is a waterside eatery reached by a short
Dining boatride from Dalyan. It's also a good stopping-off point if you're planning a walk to the Kaunus ruins. *Tel. 252/284–1150. No credit cards. Inexpensive.*

Lodging **Hotel Turtle.** This is a quiet 10-room hotel tucked away in a bay of orchards on the lakeside. The hotel boat picks up guests from Dalyan. Vefa Ülkü, the owner, cooks excellent dishes served under a big plane tree. *Kücük Karaağac, Sultaniye Köyü, Köyceğiz, tel. 252/284–1487. No credit cards. Moderate.*

Kalkan **Kalkan Han.** A rambling old house in the back part of the village, the
Lodging Kalkan Han has a special treat for visitors: a roof terrace with sweeping views of the bay, a perfect place to enjoy breakfast. *Köyiçi Mev., tel. 242/844–1151. 16 rooms with bath. No credit cards. Closed Nov.–Apr. Moderate.*

Balikçi Han. This delightful pansiyon is in a converted 19th-century inn, directly on the waterfront. *Tel. 242/844–1075. 7 rooms with bath. No credit cards. Inexpensive.*

Kaş **Mercan.** On the eastern side of the harbor, the Mercan serves good,
Dining basic Turkish food in an attractive open-air setting. The water is so close you can actually hear fish jumping. *Hukumet Cad. No credit cards. Moderate.*

Lodging **Kaş Oteli.** This hotel has wonderful views of the Greek island of Kastellorizo. There's good swimming off the rocks in front of the hotel, or you can laze in the sun with drinks and snacks from the bar or restaurant. *Hastane Cad. 15, tel. 242/836–1271. Facilities: bar, restaurant. No credit cards. Closed Nov.–Apr. Moderate.*

Mimosa. Conveniently located on a hill near the bus station, this hotel has plain but perfectly adequate rooms, all with balconies and views. *Elmali Cad., tel. 242/836–1272. 22 rooms with bath. Facilities: swimming pool. No credit cards. Moderate.*

Çan Otel. Turkish carpets and antiques decorate this village house that's been lovingly restored and turned into a pansiyon. It's on a tiny side street near the harbor. *Off Hukumet Cad., tel. 242/836–1441. No credit cards. Inexpensive.*

Köyceğiz **Hotel Özay.** This lakeside hotel is quiet, modern, and efficiently run.
Lodging *Kordon Boyu 11, Köyceğiz, tel. 252/262–4300, fax 252/262–2000. 34 rooms with bath. Facilities: restaurant, bar, swimming pool. AE, DC, MC, V. Expensive.*

Hotel Deniz Feneri. The owner is an artist whose wood carvings hang in Golbasi Restaurant. The hotel is located in a picturesque square; the rooms are basic. *Atatürk Square, Köyceğiz, tel. 252/262–1777. No credit cards. Inexpensive.*

Ölü Deniz **Beyaz Yunus.** Wicker chairs and wooden floors fill this domed res-
Dining taurant, whose name means "white dolphin." The most elegant res-
★ taurant in the area, it's situated on a promontory near Padirali and serves Continental and Turkish cuisines imaginatively prepared and presented. *Tel. 252/616–6036. Reservations not necessary. No credit cards. Expensive.*

Kebabcı Salonu. You can grill meat at your table in this outdoor restaurant, where tables and chairs are clustered around trees in a field. Meals are served with meze, salad, and wine. *Behind Han*

Camp, no telephone. Reservations not necessary. No credit cards. Inexpensive.

Lodging **Meri Oteli.** Located on a steep incline above the lagoon, this is a series of bungalows, with rooms a bit down-at-the-heel but clean. These are the only accommodations at the lagoon. *Tel. 252/616–6060, fax 252/616–6456. 75 rooms with bath. Facilities: restaurant. AE, DC, MC, V. Moderate.*

Central Anatolia and Cappadocia

Cappadocia, an area filled with ruins of ancient civilizations, is in the eastern part of Anatolia and has changed little over the centuries. People travel between their farms and villages in horse-drawn carts, women drape their houses with strings of apricots and paprika for drying in the sun, and nomads pitch their black tents beside sunflower fields and cook on tiny fires that send smoke billowing through the tops of the tents. And in the distance, a minaret pierces the sky.

Getting Around

By Car There are good roads between Istanbul and the main cities of Anatolia—Ankara (the capital of Turkey), Konya, and Kayseri. The highways are generally well maintained and lead to all the major sites. Minor roads are full of potholes and are very rough. On narrow, winding roads, look out for oncoming trucks, whose drivers apparently don't believe in staying on their side of the road.

By Bus There is a good interlinking bus network between most towns and cities, and fares are reasonable.

By Train Though there are frequent trains between the main cities, they are almost nonexistent between small towns. It's much quicker to take a bus.

By Taxi Drivers are usually willing to take you to historical sites out of town for reasonable fares.

Guided Tours

As the Cappadocia area is so vast, you'll need at least two days to see the main sights. If you are driving, consider hiring a guide for about $15–$30 a day. Local tourist offices and hotels will be able to recommend guides and excursions.

Tourist Information

Check with local tourist offices for names of travel agencies and English-speaking guides.

Ankara (Gazi Mustafa Kemal Bul. 121, Demirtepe, tel. 312/229–2631).
Aksaray (Ankara Cad. Dinçer Apt. 2/2, tel. 382/213–2474).
Kayseri (Kagni Pazari 61, tel. 352/231–9295).
Konya (Mevlana Cad. 21, tel. 332/351–1074).
Nevşehir (Atatürk Cad. Hastane Yani, tel. 384/213–1137).
Ürgüp (Kayseri Cad. 37, tel. 384/341–4059).

Central Anatolia and Cappadocia

Mediterranean Sea

NORTHERN CYPRUS

Cyprus

0   50 miles
0   75 km

N

Exploring Central Anatolia and Cappadocia

An hour's drive, 30 kilometers (19 miles), to the northwest of Antalya is **Termessos,** which has an almost complete Roman amphitheater built on a mountainside, and the unexcavated remains of a Roman city on the other side of the mountain. There are organized tours to Termessos from Antalya. *Admission free. Open daily 9–5:30.*

Perge, 19 kilometers (11 miles) east of Antalya, has many Roman ruins to explore. You can climb up a 22,000-seat amphitheater, walk down a restored colonnaded street, visit well-preserved thermal baths and a Roman basilica, and see the spot where St. Paul preached his first sermon in AD 45. *Admission: $2.50. Open daily 9–5:30.*

Nearby is **Aspendos,** 44 kilometers (23 miles) to the east of Antalya, which contains Turkey's best-preserved amphitheater. The acoustics are so fine that modern-day performers don't need microphones or amplifiers. *Admission: $2.50. Open daily 9–5:30.*

Konya   **Konya,** home of the Whirling Dervishes, is reached by driving 427 kilometers (267 miles) northeast of Antalya past **Lake Beyşehir.** There is also a longer and more difficult road via **Lake Eğridir.** The Whirling Dervishes belong to a religious order founded in the 13th century by Celaleddin Rumi, or Melvana, a Muslim mystic, who said, "There are many ways of knowing God. I choose the dance and music." You can see the dervishes whirl to the sounds of a flute at the annual commemorative rites held in Konya in early December. Tickets are available from travel agencies or from the Konya tourist information office (*see above*).

Sultan Han, 95 kilometers (59 miles) northeast of Konya, is Anatolia's largest and best-preserved caravansary, once a place of rest and shelter for travelers and their camels plying the ancient trade routes.

Cappadocia **Cappadocia** roughly forms the triangular area between **Kayseri, Nevşehir,** and **Niğde.** Most of the main sights are within an even smaller triangular area linked by Ürgüp, Göreme, and Avanos. **Ürgüp** is the center from which to explore the villages and the best place to shop, as well as to arrange tours.

The softness of the rock in this area was ideal for hollowing out cave dwellings and forming defenses from invading armies. The Cappadocians carved out about 40 underground cities, with some structures as deep as 20 stories underground. The largest of these cities housed 20,000 people. Each had dormitories, dining halls, sewage disposal systems, ventilation chimneys, a cemetery, and a prison. Large millstones sealed off the entrances from enemies. Two of these cities are open to the public, one at **Derinkuyu,** 21 kilometers (13 miles) south of Nevşehir, and the other at **Kaymakli,** 30 kilometers (9 miles) south of Nevşehir. *Admission: $2.50. Open daily 8– sunset.*

The Christians also hid in these underground cities when the Islamic forces swept through Cappadocia in the 7th century. Some of the earliest relics of Christianity are to be found in the **Göreme Valley,** a few miles east of Nevşehir. There are dozens of old churches and monasteries covered by frescoes. For a history of the area, visit the **Göreme Open-Air Museum,** 1 kilometer (.62 miles) outside of Göreme village on the Ürgüp road. *Admission free. Open daily 8:30–5:30.*

Dining and Lodging

For details and price-category definitions, *see* Dining and Lodging in Staying in Turkey, *above.*

Avanos **Zelve.** This is a small modern hotel in the center of town. *Hükümet*
Lodging *Meydani, tel. 384/511–4524, fax 384/511–4687. 29 rooms with bath. AE, DC, MC, V. Moderate.*

Göreme **Ataman.** Run by tourist guide Abbas and his wife Şermin, this res-
Dining taurant is built into the face of a rock facing the lush Göreme valley and serves mostly French cuisine, as well as some Turkish. It is being expanded into a hotel. *Tel. 384/271–2310. Reservations not necessary. DC, MC, V. Inexpensive.*

Konya **Ali Baba Kebapçısı.** This restaurant serves good kebabs and is fa-
Dining mous for its Firin kebab, cooked over an open charcoal fire. *Eski Avukatlar Sokak 11/A, tel. 332/351–0307. Reservations not necessary. No credit cards. Inexpensive.*
Bolu Restaurant. You can eat dishes here for which Konya is renowned: *etli ekmek* (flat bread with ground lamb) and *tereyağli borek* (buttered pastries). *Pürküklü Mah. 31/c, tel. 332/352–4533. Reservations not necessary. Inexpensive.*

Lodging **Başak Palas.** An older but charming small hotel, Başak Palas is also comfortable. *Hukumet Alani 3, tel. 332/351–1338. 35 rooms, most with bath. No credit cards. Inexpensive.*

Ürgüp **Hanedan.** In the cellar of an old Greek house, the Hanedan is on a hill
Dining a short distance from town. You can sit on the terrace and watch the sunset across the plains toward the mountains. The food is very good and is presented with flair. *Nevşehir Yolu Üzeri, tel. 384/341–4266. Reservations required for groups. DC, MC, V. Moderate.*

Lodging **Büyük.** In the center of town, this is a friendly hotel that features folk dancing in the evenings—you're encouraged to join in but can just sit back and watch if you prefer. *Kayseri Cad., tel. 384/341–1060. 49 rooms with bath. No credit cards. Moderate.*

Hitit. The family-run Hitit is a comfortable, small hotel with a restaurant serving basic but enjoyable food. *Dumlupinar Cad. 54, tel. 384/341–1481. 15 rooms without bath. No credit cards. Inexpensive.*

Index

Adventure tours, 7
Air travel
from North America,
26–29
from United
Kingdom, 30–32
within Europe, 41–42
American Express,
11–13
Amsterdam, 566–583
air travel to, 41–42,
566
Ann Frankhuis, 572
autos in, 567
ballet in, 582
bars in, 572, 583
Begijnhof, 573
bicycling in, 567
boat in, 567
bookstores in, 568
buses in, 567
bus travel to, 36
casinos in, 583
Centraal Station, 568
Concertgebouw, 576
consulates in, 567
Dam, 568–572
Dam Palace, 572
dining in, 573, 575,
576, 578–580
Dokwerker, 574–575
emergencies in, 567
film in, 582
flower market, 573
gay and lesbian bars,
583
Golden Bend, 573
Heinekin Brewery,
577
Historisch Museum,
572
hotels in, 580–582
Jewish Amsterdam,
574
Joods Historisch
Museum, 575
Jordaan area of, 576
Koninklijk Paleis, 572
Leidseplein, 573
Maritime Quarter,
576
metro in, 567
Muntplein, 573
Museum
Amstelkring, 569

Museum Boat, 568,
575
Museum Het
Rembrandthuis, 574
music in, 574, 576,
582
Netherlands Theater
Institut, 573–574
Nieuwe Kerk, 569,
572
nightlife in, 582–583
Nooderkerk, 572
opera in, 582
Oude Kerk, 569
Portuguese
Synagogue, 574
Rijksmuseum, 575
Rijksmuseum Vincent
van Gogh, 575
St. Nicolasskerk, 569
Schreierstoren, 569
shopping in, 577–578
Singel, 576
Spui, 573
Stedelijk Museum,
575–576
taxis in, 567
theater in, 582
tourist information
in, 567
tours of, 568
train travel to, 566
travel agencies in,
568
Vondelpark, 576
Westerkerk, 572
Westermarkt, 572
Andorra, 46–54
air travel to, 50
Andorro La Vella, 51,
52–53
auto travel in, 48–49
business hours in, 49
bus travel in, 49
Can Pal, 52
Casa de la Vall, 51
churches in, 51–52
climate of, 47
consulates in, 51
La Cortinada, 52
currency of, 47–48
customs in, 48
dining in, 49–50,
52–54
emergencies in, 51

Encamp, 51
Les Escaldes, 51,
53–54
expenses in, 48
holidays in, 49
hotels in, 50, 52–54
language of, 48
mail in, 49
La Massana, 52
Ordino, 54
Pas de la Casa, 51, 54
Pont de St. Antoni,
52
Sanctuary of
Meritxell, 51–52
Santa Coloma, 52, 54
Santa Julia de Loria,
54
Sant Joan des
Caselles, 52
Sant Miguel
d'Engolasters, 51
Sant Romà de les
Bons, 51
shopping in, 52
telephones in, 49
tipping in, 50
tourist information
in, 51
tours of, 7, 51–52
train travel to, 50
travel agencies in, 51
Antwerp, 117–122
air travel to, 117
auto travel to, 117
boat excursion from,
120
bus travel to, 117
Centraalstation, 118
Diamond Quarter,
118
Diamondland, 118
dining in, 120–121
hotels in, 121–122
Koninklijk Museum
voor Schone
Kunsten, 120
Meir, 118
Museum Mayer
vanden Bergh, 118
Onze-Lieve
Vrouwkathedraal,
118
Plantin-Moretus
Museum, 120

Rubenshuis, 118
St. Annatunnel, 120
shopping in, 118
Steen, 118
streetcars in, 117
Torengebouw, 118
tourist information
in, 117
tours of, 117
train travel to, 117
vogelmarkt, 120
zoo, 118
Apartment rentals,
21–22
Architecture tours,
7–8
Art tours, 7–8
Athens, 522–539
Academy, 529
Acropolis, 528
Acropolis Museum,
529
Agora, 529
air travel to, 522
Areopagus, 529
auto travel to, 37, 523
bookstore in, 524
bouzoukias in, 539
bus travel in, 523
Byzantine Museum,
530
Cathedral of Athens,
529
Cathedral Square,
529
climate of, 515
concerts in, 538
dining in, 525, 529,
530, 531, 532–534
embassies in, 524
emergencies in, 524
Erechtheion temple,
528
Evzone guards, 525,
530
festivals in, 528,
537–538
film in, 538
guides in, 525
Hadrian's Arch, 528
Hephestaion, 529
hotels in, 534–537
Kaisariani
monastery, 530–531
Kolonaki, 530

'Little Cathedral,'
529
metro in, 523
Mikrolimano, 531
Mount Lycabettos,
530
Museum of the Agora
Excavations, 529
Museum of Cycladic
Art, 530
National
Archaeological
Museum, 529–530
National Gardens,
525
National Library, 529
nightlife in, 538–539
Odeon of Herodes
Atticus, 528
opera in, 538
Parliament Building,
525
Parthenon, 528–529
Plaka, 529
Presidential Palace,
530
Propylaea, 528
sea travel to, 523
Senate House of the
University, 529
shopping in, 531–532
Son-et-Lumière, 538
stadium, 528
Syntagma Square,
525
tavernas, 539
taxis in, 523–524
Temple of Olympian
Zeus, 525, 528
Temple of Wingless
Victory, 528
Theater of Dionysos,
528
theater in, 528
Tomb of the
Unknown Soldier,
525
tourist information
in, 524
tours of, 524–525
train travel to,
522–523
travel agencies in,
524
Austria, 55–93. See
also Innsbruck;
Salzburg; Vienna
airline of, 27
air travel in, 59–60
auto travel in, 59

bicycling in, 60
boat travel in, 60
Burg Kreuzenstein,
81
business hours in, 61
bus travel in, 60
churches in, 65, 69,
70, 71
climate in, 56, 58
currency in, 58
customs in, 58–59
Danube Valley of,
79–81
dining in, 61–62, 80
Dürnstein, 81
expenses in, 58
festivals in, 56
gardens in, 83
Göttweig, 79
holidays in, 61
hotels in, 62
Imperial Toll House,
81
Klosterneuburg, 80
Krems, 81
Langelebarn, 81
language in, 59
mail in, 60
Mautern, 81
Melk, 80
Minoritenkirche, 81
museums in, 61,
68–69, 72
opera in, 69, 77–78
shopping in, 61
Stein, 81
Stift Göttweig, 80
telephones in, 60
tipping in, 62
tourist information
in, 2, 64, 79
tours of, 5–10, 64, 79
train travel in, 59
Tulln, 80
zoos, 71
Auto leasing, 20
Auto rentals, 18–20

Baggage insurance,
17
Ballet. *See also*
Dance
in Amsterdam, 582
in Berlin, 420
in Copenhagen, 209
in Florence, 734
in Lisbon, 878
in London, 479–480
in Milan, 751–752
in Prague, 183

in Zürich, 1063
Ballooning, 8
Barcelona, 968–982
air travel to, 968
Barceloneta, 976
bars in, 977–978
bookstores in, 969
bullfighting in, 977
bus travel to, 968,
969
cabarets in, 981
cable cars in, 969
cafés in, 975, 977–978
casino in, 882
Cathedral, 971
Columbus Monument,
974
concerts in, 976, 981
consulates in, 969
dance in, 981
dining in, 971, 974,
978–979
Dreta de l'Eixample,
976
Eixample, 975
emergencies in, 969
film in, 981
Flamenco in, 982
Funicular in, 969
Gran Teatre del
Liceu, 974
harbor trips in, 969
hotels in, 979–981
Major de Gràcia, 976
Mançana de la
Discòrdia, 975
Maritime Museum,
974
metro in, 968–969
Miró Foundation, 976
Montjuïc, 975
Museum of Catalan
Art, 975–976
music in, 981
nightlife in, 981–982
opera in, 981
Palau de la Virreina,
974
Palau Güell, 974
Picasso Museum, 971
Plaça del Rei, 971
Plaça Reial, 971–974
Plaça Sant Jaume,
971
Porta de L'Angel, 975
Rambla, 974
Santa María del Mar,
971
Shoe Museum, 976
shopping in, 976–977

taxis in, 969
Temple Expiatori de
la Sagrada Família,
975
theater in, 981
tourist information
in, 969
tours of, 970
train travel to, 968
travel agencies in,
970
Bath, 489–491
Assembly Rooms, 489
dining in, 490–491
Holburne Museum,
489
hotels in, 491
Roman Baths
Museum, 489
Royal Crescent, 489
tourist information
in, 481
tours of, 481–482
travel to, 481
Baths, See also Spas
in Rome, 704
Belgium, 95–127. See
also Antwerp;
Bruges; Brussels
airline of, 27
auto leasing in, 20
auto travel in, 98
bicycling in, 44–45,
99
boat travel to, 34
business hours in, 99
bus travel in, 99
camping in, 101
churches in, 105, 108,
125
climate of, 97
currency in, 97
customs in, 97–98
dining in, 100
expenses in, 97
holidays in, 99–100
hotels in, 100–101
language in, 98
mail in, 99
museums in, 99, 104,
105, 109, 123, 125
sales-tax refunds in,
99
shopping in, 99
telephones in, 99
tipping in, 101
tourist offices of, 2
train travel in, 98–99
train travel to, 35–36
youth hostels in, 101

Berlin, *402–421*
Agyptisches
  Museum, *409*
air travel to, *402*
Altes Museum, *412*
auto travel to, *403*
Babylonian
  Processional Way,
  412
ballet in, *420*
Berlin cathedral, *412*
Berlin Philharmonic,
  405, 420
boat trips in, *404*
Bodemuseum, *412*
bookstores in, *404*
Brandenburger Tor,
  408, 410
buses in, *403, 404*
bus travel to, *403*
Checkpoint Charlie,
  408, 410
Checkpoint Charlie
  Museum, *408–409*
churches in, *405, 410,
  412, 413*
concerts in, *420*
consulates in, *404*
Deutsches
  Historisches
  Museum, *412*
Deutsche Staatsoper,
  410
dining in, *409, 410,
  413, 414–417*
East Berlin, *410–415,
  419–420*
emergencies in, *404*
Fischerinsel, *413*
Gemaldegalerie, *409*
Grunewald park, *409*
hotels in, *417–420*
Huguenot Museum,
  410
Humboldt University,
  410, 412
Kaiser Wilhelm
  Gedachtniskirche,
  405
Kreuzberg, *409*
Kunstgewerbe-
  museum, *405*
Märkisches Museum,
  413
Museumsinsel, *412*
Nationalgalerie, *412*
Neue
  Nationalgalerie, *405*
nightlife in, *421*
Nikolaikirche, *413*

opera in, *410, 420*
Palast der Republik,
  412
Pergamon Altar, *412*
Pergamon Museum,
  412
public transportation
  in, *403*
Rathaus, *412–413*
Rathaus Schöneberg,
  409
St. Hedwigs
  Kathedrale, *410*
Schauspielhaus, *410*
Schloss
  Charlottenburg, *409*
shopping in, *413*
Siegessaule, *408*
Soviet Victory
  monument, *408*
streetcars in, *403*
synagogue, *413*
taxis in, *403*
Tiergarten Park, *408*
tourist information
  in, *404*
tours of, *404*
train travel to,
  402–403
TV tower, *412*
U-Bahn and S-Bahn
  in, *403*
West Berlin,
  *405–410, 415–416,
  417–419*
Zoologischer Garten,
  405
Bern, *1087–1094*
air travel to, *1087*
auto travel to, *1087*
Bahnofplatz, *1088*
Bärengraben, *1090*
Bernisches
  Historisches
  Museum, *1091*
buses in, *1087–1088*
casino, *1091*
dining in, *1091–1093*
embassies in, *1088*
emergencies in, *1088*
fountains in, *1090*
Heilggeistkirche,
  1088
hotels in, *1093–1094*
Kornhaus, *1090*
Kunstmuseum Bern,
  1090
Münster, *1090*
Naturhistorisches
  Museum, *1091*

Pfeiferbrunnen, *1090*
Schweizerisches
  PTT-Museum, *1091*
Schweizerisches
  Schützenmuseum,
  1091
taxis in, *1088*
tourist information
  in, *1088*
tours of, *1088*
train travel to, *1087*
Bicycling, *8, 44–45*
in Amsterdam, *567*
in Austria, *60*
in Belgium, *99*
in Copenhagen, *195*
in Cork, *677*
in Denmark, *192*
in Finland, *226*
in Florence, *720*
in Germany, *345–346,
  381*
in Great Britain, *442*
in Holland, *563–564*
in Hungary, *604*
in Ireland, *652, 682*
in Luxembourg, *781*
in Portugal, *864*
in Rome, *699*
in Sweden, *1017*
in Switzerland, *1051*
Bratislava, *921–925*
air travel to, *921*
auto travel in, *921*
buses in, *921*
dining in, *924–925*
Dóm svätého
  Martina, *923*
emergencies in, *922*
hotels in, *925*
Hrad, *924*
Hurbanovo námestie,
  922
Jezuitský kostol, *924*
Most SNP, *923*
museums in, *923*
Námestie SNP, *922*
Palác Uhorskej
  král'oveskej komory,
  923
pharmacies, *922*
Primaciálny palác,
  924
Stará radnica, *924*
tourist information
  in, *921–922*
tours of, *922*
train travel to, *921*
Zidovská ulica, *924*
Bruges, *122–127*

auto travel to, *122*
Begijnhof, *125*
Belfort, *123*
boat trips, *123*
Burg, *123*
Dijver, *125*
dining in, *125, 126*
Groeninge Museum,
  125
Gruuthuse Museum,
  125
Heilig-Bloed Basiliek,
  123
Heilig-Bloed
  Museum, *123*
horse-drawn cabs in,
  122
hotels in, *126–127*
Landshuis, *123*
Markt, *123*
Memling Museum,
  125
Minnewater Park,
  125
Onze Lieve
  Vrouwekerk, *125*
Oude Griffie, *123*
Provinciaal Hof, *123*
Stadthius, *123*
tourist information
  in, *123*
tours of, *123*
train travel to, *122*
Brussels, *101–117*
air travel to, *101*
Atomium, *110*
auto travel to, *102*
Autoworld Museum,
  109
beer hall in, *108*
Biblotheque
  Nationale, *105*
Black Tower, *108*
boat travel to, *102*
bookstores in, *103*
Bourse, *108*
buses in, *102*
bus travel to, *102*
Butte de Lion, *109*
Cathédrale de St.
  Michel, *108*
Chunnel, *102*
Cinquantenaire, *109*
City Museum, *104*
dance in, *116*
dining in, *104, 109,
  111–113*
disco in, *117*
embassies in, *103*
emergencies in, *103*

European
Commission
Headquarters, *109*
film in, *116*
Galeries St-Hubert,
104, *111*
Grand' Place, *104*
Grand Sablon, *105*
Hôtel de Ville, *104*
hotels in, *113–115*
Maison d'Erasme, *110*
Maison du Roi, *104*
Manneken Pis, *104*
Marolles, *108*
métro in, *102*
Musée d'Art
Moderne, *105*
Musée de la Bande
Dessinée, *110*
Musée des Sciences
Naturelles, *109*
Musée Horta, *110*
Musée Instrumental,
105
Musée Royale d'Art
Ancien, *105*
music, *116*, *117*
nightlife in, *116–117*
Notre Dame de la
Chapelle, *108*
Notre Dame du
Sablon, *105*
opera in, *116*
Palais d'Egmont, *105*,
108
Palais de Justice, *108*
Palais de la Nation,
108
Palais Royale, *108*
Parc de Bruxelles,
108
Petit Sablon, *105*
place des Martyrs,
108
place du Jeu de Balle,
108
place Royale, *105*
Royal Museums of
Art and History, *109*
shopping in, *110–111*
taxis in, *102*
theater in, *116*
tourist information
in, *102–103*
tours of, *103*
train travel to, *102*
trams in, *102*
travel agencies in,
103
Waterloo, *109*

Wellington's
headquarters, *109*
Bucharest, *902–910*
air travel to, *902*
Arcul de Triumf, *905*
arts in, *910*
Ateneul Român, *905*
auto travel to, *902*
Biserica din Curtea
Veche, *904*
Biserica Ortodoxă,
904
buses in, *902*
cafés in, *904*, *910*
Crețulescu Church,
904
Curtea Veche, *904*
dining in, *904*, *905*,
908
Hanul lui Manuc, *904*
hotels in, *908–910*
Museul de Artă al
Romniei, *904–905*
music in, *910*
Muzeul Curtea
Veche-Palatul
Voievodal, *904*
Muzeul National de
Istorie, *904*
Muzeul Satului
Romanesc, *905*
nightlife in, *910*
shopping in, *905*
subway in, *902*
taxis in, *902*
tourist information
in, *902–903*
tours of, *903*
train travel to, *902*
trams in, *902*
Treasury, *904*
Budapest, *607–620*
air travel to, *607*
Állami Operaház, *614*
auto travel in, *607*
Belvárosi plébánia
templom, *613*
boat travel in, *608*
bookstores in, *608*
Budapest Történeti
Múzeum, *612*
bus travel to, *607*
coffeehouse in, *613*
concerts, *619*
dining in, *613*,
615–616
embassies in, *608*
emergencies in, *608*
folk dancing in, *619*
Gellèrt-hegy, *615*

Hadtörténeti
Múzeum, *612*
Halászbástya, *612*
hotels in, *617–619*
Jánoshegy, *615*
Királi Palota, *609*
Korzó, *613*
Legújabbkori
Történeti Múzeum,
609
Március 15 Tér, *613*
Mátyás templom, *612*
medieval synagogue,
612
Mezögazdasági
Múzeum, *614*
Millenneumi
Emlékmű, *614*
Műcsárnok, *614*
National Gallery,
609–612
Neprájzi Múzeum,
613
nightlife in, *619–620*
Olaf Palme sétány,
614
opera in, *614*
Parliament, *613*
public transportation
in, *607–608*
Roosevelt Tér, *613*
shopping in, *615*
Szépművészeti
Múzeum, *614*
Szt. István Bazilica,
614
taxis in, *607*
tourist information
in, *608*
tours of, *608–609*
train travel to, *607*
Várhegy (Castle
Hill), *609*
Zenetrtneti Mzeum,
612
Bulgaria, *129–153.*
See also Sofia
air travel in, *133*
Aladji Rock
Monastery, *146*
Albena, *146*, *147*
Archaeological
Museum, *145*
auto rentals in,
132–133, *149*
auto travel in, *37–39*,
132–133
Balčik, *146*
Baldwin's Tower, *151*
Black Sea Golden

Coast of, *144–148*
boat travel in, *133*,
144
Borovec, *152*
Botanical Gardens,
146
Burgas, *147*
business hours in, *133*
bus travel in, *133*,
144, *149*
churches in, *137*, *139*,
140
climate of, *129*, *131*
Copernicus
Astronomy Complex,
146
currency of, *131*
customs in, *132*
dining in, *133–134*,
147–148, *152–153*
Djuni, *147*
emergencies in, *136*
Etur, *151*
expenses in, *131*
Forty Martyrs
church, *151*
gardens in, *139*, *146*
Hadji Nikoli, *151*
history of, *129*
holidays in, *133*
hotels in, *134*, *146*,
147–148
hydrofoils in, *144*
Inland Bulgaria,
149–153
Kapana District, *151*
Kazanlak, *151*
Koprivštica, *149*, *152*
language in, *132*
Madara Horseman,
151
mail in, *133*
Marine Gardens, *146*
Maritime Park, *147*
mosques in, *137*
museums in, *131*,
139, *146*, *152*
National
Archaeological
Museum, *152*
National
Ethnographical
Museum, *151*
Naval Museum, *146*
Nesebâr, *146–147*
Pliska, *151*
Plovdiv, *151*, *152*
Rila Monastery, *152*
Roman ruins in,
145–146, *151*, *152*

Bulgaria *(continued)*
Saint Dimitrius,
  church of, *151*
Saints Peter and Paul
  Church, *151*
Shipka Pass, *151*
shopping in, *133*
Slånčev Brjag, *146*,
  147
Sozopol, *147*
Stoyan Bucharov
  National Theater,
  145
Strumna Street, *151*
Šumen, *151*
Sunny Beach, *144*
Sveti Konstantin and
  Golden Sands, *146*,
  147
telephones in, *133*
tipping in, *135*
tourist information
  in, *2*, *136*, *144*, *145*,
  149
tours of, *136*, *144*,
  149
train travel in, *133*,
  135, *149*
Trojan Monastery,
  150
Tszaravec, *150*
Valley of Roses, *149*,
  151
Varna, *144*–*146*, *148*
Veliki Preslav, *151*
Veliko Târnovo, *150*,
  153
visas for, *131*–*132*
Zlatni Pjasaci, *146*
Bullfighting
Museum of, *989*, *1000*
in Spain, *977*, *987*,
  996, *1000*
Buses
from United Kingdom
  to Europe, *36*–*37*
within Europe, *42*–*43*

Cambridge, *493*–*499*
auto travel to, *494*
bus travel to, *494*
Clare College, *494*
dining in, *496*–*497*
Downing College, *496*
Emmanuel College,
  496
Fitzwilliam Museum,
  496
hotels in, *498*–*499*
Kettle's Yard, *496*

King's College, *494*,
  496
Magdalene College,
  496
Mathematical Bridge,
  496
Pembroke College,
  496
Pepys Library, *496*
Peterhouse, *496*
Queen's College, *496*
St. John's College,
  496
tourist information
  in, *494*
tours of, *494*
train travel to, *494*
Trinity College, *494*
Camcorders, *15*–*16*
Cameras, *15*
Camping
in Belgium, *101*
in Czech Republic, *173*
in Denmark, *194*
in Finland, *228*
in France, *264*
in Germany, *342*
in Great Britain, *446*
in Hungary, *606*
in Ireland, *654*
in Italy, *696*–*697*
in Luxembourg, *780*
in Norway, *809*
in Portugal, *866*
in Romania, *901*
in Spain, *941*
in Sweden, *1020*
Canadian citizens
customs and duties
  for, *14*–*15*
passports and visas
  for, *13*
Cash machines, *12*
Casinos
in Barcelona, *982*
in France, *322*
in Gibraltar, *1002*
in London, *480*
in Luzern, *1081*
in Madrid, *958*
in Portugal, *880*
in Sofia, *143*
Castles. *See also*
  Palaces
in Austria, *71*, *72*
in Bohemia, *183*–*186*
in Bratislava, *924*
in Copenhagen, *200*,
  201, *203*, *204*
in Cork, *674*

in Cyprus, *162*, *166*
in Denmark, *200*,
  201, *203*, *204*
in Edinburgh, *507*
in Finland, *242*, *245*
in France, *282*,
  314–*315*
in Germany, *384*, *386*,
  387
in Gibraltar, *1003*
in Great Britain, *429*,
  482, *488*, *504*, *507*
in Hungary, *614*, *625*
in Innsbruck, *91*
in Ireland, *663*, *675*,
  679, *680*, *683*
in Italy, *737*
in Kraków, *852*
in Liechtenstein,
  1064
in Lisbon, *869*
in Luxembourg, *786*
in Milan, *746*
in Oslo, *813*
in Poland, *852*
in Portugal, *882*, *887*
in Prague, *177*
in Rome, *709*, *711*
in Slovakia, *927*, *928*
in Spain, *975*, *1003*
in Stockholm, *1025*,
  1028
in Sweden, *1036*
in Turkey, *1128*
in Warsaw, *843*
Channel Tunnel, *33*,
  36
**Children, traveling
  with,** *23*–*24*
**Churches and
  cathedrals**
in Andorra, *51*–*52*
in Austria, *69*, *70*, *89*
in Barcelona, *971*, *974*
in Belgium, *105*, *108*,
  118
in Berlin, *405*, *410*
in Bern, *1088*, *1090*
in Bratislava, *923*
in Brugge, *125*
in Brussels, *105*, *108*
in Bucharest, *904*
in Bulgaria, *137*, *139*,
  140, *145*, *146*, *150*,
  151
in Copenhagen, *200*,
  201, *202*, *204*
in Cork, *675*
in Cyprus, *159*, *166*
in Delft, *594*, *595*

in Denmark, *217*,
  218, *219*
in Dublin, *660*, *663*,
  664
in Edinburgh, *507*,
  509
in Finland, *231*, *234*,
  235, *243*, *244*
in Florence, *722*–*723*,
  727, *728*, *729*
in France, *295*, *300*,
  301, *303*, *307*, *308*,
  309, *314*, *315*, *325*
in Frankfurt, *363*,
  366
in Geneva, *1068*
in Germany, *347*, *352*,
  382, *384*, *385*, *386*,
  393, *394*, *395*
in Gibraltar, *1003*
in Great Britain, *460*,
  462, *464*, *465*, *482*,
  488, *497*, *500*, *502*,
  503, *507*, *509*
in Greece, *529*,
  530–*531*, *543*, *548*,
  549
in Hamburg, *376*
in Helsinki, *231*, *234*,
  235
in Holland, *569*, *572*,
  573, *585*, *586*, *595*
in Hungary, *612*, *614*,
  622, *625*
in Ireland, *675*, *685*
in Italy, *701*,
  704–*705*, *706*,
  707–*708*, *710*,
  722–*723*, *727*, *728*,
  729, *736*–*737*, *738*,
  739, *740*, *746*, *748*,
  758, *759*, *769*
in Kraków, *852*, *854*
in London, *454*, *460*,
  462, *464*, *465*
in Lugano, *1083*
in Luxembourg, *784*,
  785, *786*
in Luzern, *1076*
in Malta, *797*, *799*,
  800
in Milan, *746*, *748*
in Nicosia, *159*
in Norway, *813*, *824*,
  831, *832*
in Paris, *271*, *274*,
  275, *279*, *280*, *281*
in Poland, *843*, *846*,
  852, *854*
in Portugal, *872*, *881*,

886–887, 888
in Prague, 177
in Reykjavík, 634, 636
in Romania, 904
in Rome, 701, 704–705, 706, 707–708, 710
in Salzburg, 83, 85–86
in Slovakia, 927–928
in Sofia, 137, 139, 140
in Spain, 945, 948, 949, 950, 961, 963, 989, 990, 999
in Sweden, 1024
in Switzerland, 1076, 1083
in Toledo, 961
in Turkey, 1124, 1128
in Tuscany, 736–737, 738, 739, 740
in Uppsala, 1036
in Valletta, 797
in Venice, 758, 759
in Vienna, 69, 70
in Warsaw, 843
in York, 500
in Zürich, 1056, 1057, 1058
Climate, 10
Clothing, 10
Copenhagen, 195–210
air travel to, 41, 195
Amaliehavn Gardens, 201
Amalienborg Palace, 201
auto travel in, 195
ballet in, 209
bicycling in, 195
bookstores in, 196
Børsen, 200
Botansk Have, 203
buses in, 195
Christianborg-Slot, 200
concerts in, 209
Den Lille Havfrue, 202
Det Kongeliege Bibliotek, 200
dining in, 201, 203, 205–207
embassies in, 196
emergencies in, 196
Folketinget, 200
Frihedsmuseet, 202
Gammel and Nytorv square, 197

gardens in, 203
Helligånds Kirken, 201
Hirschprung Collection, 203
hotels in, 207–209
Kastellet, 202
Kongelige Teater, 201
Kongens Nytorv, 201
Kundindustrimuseet, 202
The Little Mermaid, 202
Lurblæserne, 197
Marmorikirken, 202
Minefield, 209
museums in, 197, 200, 202, 203
Nationalmuseet, 197
nightlife in, 209–210
Nikolaj Kirke, 201
Ny Carlsberg Glypotek, 203–204
Nyhavn Canal, 201
opera in, 209
Rådhus, 197–201
Rosenborg Slot, 203
Runde tårn, 202
Russiske Ortodoke Kirke, 202
sea travel to, 43
shopping in, 205
Slotsholmen, 197–201
Statens Museum for Kunst, 203
S-trains in, 195
Strøget, 197
synagogue in, 202
taxis in, 195
Teaterhistorisk Museum, 200
theater in, 209
Thorvaldsens Museum, 200
Tivoli, 203
Tøjhusetmuseet, 200
tourist information in, 195–196
tours of, 196
train travel to, 195
travel agencies in, 196
Tycho Brahe Planetarium, 204
university of, 202
Vor Frelser's Kirke, 200
Vor Frue Kirke, 202
Corfu, 44
Cork, 676–682

auto travel to, 677
bicycling in, 677
Blarney Castle, 675
Blarney Stone, 675
bus travel to, 677
Crawford Art Gallery, 675
dining in, 676–677
Fota Island, 675
hotels in, 676–677
Patrick Street, 674–675
Shandon Steeple, 675
shopping in, 675
tourist information in, 677
tours of, 677
train travel to, 677
Currency, 12
Customs and duties, 14–15
Cyprus, 155–166. See also Nicosia
Abbey of Bellapais, 166
airline of, 27
air travel to, 157, 165
amphitheater, 162
auto travel in, 37–38, 157, 165
Ayia Napa, 160, 163–164
Ayios Lazarus, 160
Bellapais, 166
boats to, 157
business hours in, 158
bus travel in, 157, 165
Castle of St. Hilarion, 166
churches in, 159, 160
climate in, 155–156
Curium, 162
currency in, 157, 165
customs in, 156
dining in, 162–163
embassies in, 158
emergencies in, 158
expenses in, 157, 165
Famagusta, 166
Gazimagusa, 166
Girne, 166
Green Line, 159
history of, 155
holidays in, 158
hotels in, 163–165
KEO Winery, 161
Kition, 160
Kolossi Castle, 162
Kykko Monastery,

161
Kyrenia, 165
Kyrenia Castle, 166
Lala Mustafa Pasha Mosque, 166
language in, 156
Larnaca, 160, 162–163, 164
Latchi, 162
Lefkosa, 166
Limassol, 161, 163, 164
mail in, 158
museums in, 159, 160, 161
Northern Cyprus, 165–166
Paphos, 161, 163, 164–165
Republic of, 157–165
Roman ruins in, 162
St. Hilarion, 166
Salamis, 166
Sanctuary of Appolo Hylates, 162
Selimiyre Mosque, 166
Shipwreck Museum, 166
shopping in, 158
Stavrovouni Monastery, 162
taxis in, 157–158
telephones in, 158
tipping in, 158
Tombs of the Kings, 161
tourist offices of, 2, 158
tours of, 158
Troodos Mountains, 161–162
Villa of Eustolios, 162
visas for, 156, 162
Czech Republic, 168–186. See also Prague
airline of, 27
air travel in, 171
auto travel in, 171
Bohemian spas and castles, 183–186
business hours in, 172
bus travel in, 171, 184
camping in, 173
České Budějovicae, 185–186
Česky Krumlov, 185, 186

Czech Republic
(continued)
Chod Museum, *185*
climate of, *170*
currency in, *170*
customs in, *170*
dining in, *172, 186*
Domažlice, *185*
expenses in, *170*
gardens in, *182*
history of, *168*
holidays in, *172*
hotels in, *172–173*
Hussite Museum, *186*
Karlovy Vary, *185, 186*
Kárlštejn, *184*
Krivoklát, *184*
Kvilda, *185*
language in, *170*
Lipno, *185*
mail in, *172*
Mariánské Lázné, *185, 186*
museums in, *170, 176, 177*
Přemysla Ottokara II Square, *185*
shopping in, *172, 180*
Šumava mountains, *185*
Tábor, *186*
telephones in, *171*
tipping in, *173*
tourist information in, *2, 174, 184*
tours of, *175, 184*
train travel in, *39, 171, 184*
visas for, *170*
Vltava River, *185*

Dance. *See also* Ballet
in Barcelona, *981*
in Berlin, *420*
in Brussels, *116*
in Madrid, *957*
in Munich, *360*
Delft, *590–598*
dining in, *597*
hotels in, *597*
Lambert van Meerten Museum, *595*
Nieuwe Kerk, *594*
Oude Kerk, *595*
Prinsehof, *595*
tourist information in, *592*
Denmark, *188–220.*

See also Copenhagen
Aalborg, *218, 219*
Ærøskøbing, *213*
air travel in, *195*
airline of, *27*
Arhus, *217, 219*
Auning, *218*
auto travel in, *191*
bicycling in, *192*
Billund, *219*
Brandt's Passage, *212*
Budolfi Kirke, *218*
business hours in, *192–193*
bus travel in, *191*
camping in, *194*
Carl-Henning Pederson and Else Afelt's Museum, *219*
Carl Nielsen Museum, *212*
churches in, *200, 201, 202, 204, 217, 218, 219*
climate of, *190*
currency of, *190*
customs in, *190*
Den Fynske Landsby, *212*
Den Gamla Gård, *212*
Den Gamle By, *217–218*
Den Georgafiske Have, *217*
dining in, *193, 213–215, 219–220*
Dollerup Bakker, *219*
Domkirke (Arhus), *219*
Domkirke (Roskilde), *204*
Domkirke (Viborg), *217*
Egeskov Slot, *213*
expenses in, *190*
Fåborg, *212, 214*
Fåborg Museum for Fynsk Malerkunst, *212*
farm vacations in, *194*
ferry travel in, *192*
Fyn Island, *210–215*
Gammel Estrup, *218*
gardens in, *201, 203, 217*
Graphic Museum, *212*
Haervejen, *218*
Hald Sø, *219*
Hans Christian Anderson Museum,

212
Helligandsklosteret, *218*
Helsingør-Kronburg Castle, *204*
Herning, *219*
holidays in, *193*
hotels in, *193–194, 213–215, 219–220*
inns in, *194*
Jelling, *217*
Jens Bangs Stenhus, *218*
Jylland, *215–220*
Kerteminde, *211*
Kolding, *215*
Koldinghus castle, *215*
Ladbyskibet, *211*
Langeland, *213*
language in, *190–191*
Legoland, *219*
Louisiana, *204*
mail in, *192*
Møesgard Prehistoric Museum, *218*
Montegården, *212*
Museum for Photographic Art, *212*
museums in, *192, 197, 200, 202, 203, 212, 218, 219*
Nyborg, *211, 214*
Nyborg Slot, *211*
Odense, *211, 214*
Randers, *218*
Ribe, *219, 220*
Roskilde, *204*
Rungstedlund, *205*
shopping in, *192, 205*
Silkeborg, *217*
Silkeborg Kulturhistoriske Museum, *217*
Skagen, *218, 220*
Skagens Museum, *218*
Svendborg, *213, 214*
Tåsinge, *213*
telephones in, *192*
tipping in, *194*
tourist information in, *210, 215*
tourist offices of, *2*
tours of, *210, 215*
train travel to, *35, 191–192, 195*
Troense, *213, 215*
Valdemars Slot, *213*

Vejle, *217, 220*
Viborg, *218*
Viking Ship Museum, *205*
Vor Frue Kirke, *217*
youth hostels in, *194*
Disabilities, travelers with, *24–25*
Doctors, *16*
Dublin, *655, 672*
Abbey Theatre, *660, 671*
air travel to, *655*
Archbishop Marsh's Library, *663*
auto travel to, *655*
Book of Kells, *661*
Brown Thomas, *662–663*
buses in, *655*
bus travel to, *655*
Charlemont House, *660*
Christ Church Cathedral, *663*
City Hall, *664*
Civic Museum, *663*
Custom House, *664*
dining in, *660, 661, 664, 666–668*
Dublin Castle, *663*
Dublin Crystal Glass Co., *665*
Dublin Writers Museum, *660*
embassies in, *656*
emergencies in, *656*
Four Courts, *664*
Gate Theater, *657*
Genealogical office, *662*
General Post Office, *657*
Grafton Street, *662*
Gresham Hotel, *672*
Guinness Brewery, *664*
Halfpenny Bridge, *665*
Heraldic Museum, *662*
hotels in, *669–671*
Howth, *665*
Hugh Lane Municipal Gallery of Modern Art, *660*
Irish Jewish Museum, *665*
Irish Museum of Modern Art, *665*

Irish Whiskey
Corner, *664*
Joyce Museum, *665*
Kilkenny Design
Workshops, *661*
Leinster House, *662*
Liffey (river), *656*,
664
Mansion House, *662*
Merrion Square, *661*
National Gallery,
661–662
National Library, *662*
National Museum,
662
nightlife in, *672*
O'Connell Bridge, *657*
O'Connell Street, *657*
Parliament House,
660
Parnell Square, *657*
Phoenix Park, *664*
Powerscourt Town
House, *663*
pubs in, *662*, *672*
Rotunda, *657*
Royal Hospital
Kilmainham, *665*
Royal Irish Academy,
662
St. Mary's Pro
Cathedral, *660*
St. Michan's, *664*
St. Patrick's
Cathedral, *663*
Sandycove, *665*
shopping in, *662–663*,
665–666
Stephen's Green,
660–661
taxis in, *655*
Temple Bar, *664*
theater in, *660*,
671–672
tourist information
in, *655–656*
tours of, *656*
train travel in,
655
travel agencies in,
656
Trinity College,
660–661

Edinburgh, *506–512*
air travel to, *506*
Arthur' Seat, *509*
auto travel to, *506*
bus travel to, *506*
Calton Hill, *510*

Canongate, *507*
Canongate Kirk, *509*
Castle Esplanade,
507
Charlotte Square, *510*
Crown Room, *507*
dining in, *509*,
510–512
Edinburgh Castle,
507
Edinburgh
International
Festival, *510*
Festival Fringe, *510*
Georgian House, *510*
Gladstone's Land, *509*
High Kirk of St.
Giles, *509*
Holyrood Park, *509*
hotels in, *510–512*
Huntly House, *509*
John Knox's House,
509
Lady Stair's House,
509
National Gallery of
Scotland, *510*
Netherbow Arts
Centre, *509*
Old Parliament Hall,
507
Palace of
Holyroodhouse, *509*
Queen Mary's
Apartments, *507*
Royal Mile, *507*
St. Andrew Square,
510
St. Margaret's
Chapel, *507*
Scott Monument, *510*
Scottish National
War Memorial, *507*
Tolbooth, *509*
tourist information
in, *507*
tours of, *507*
train travel to, *506*
Writers' Museum, *509*
Electricity, *11*
**Emergency assistance
companies,** *16*
England. *See* Great
Britain
EurailPasses, *20–21*

Ferries
from United Kingdom
to Europe, *32–37*
within Europe, *43–44*

Film, *15*
Finland, *222–253.* *See
also* Helsinki
airline of, *27*
air travel in, *225*, *241*
Amuri Museum of
Workers' Housing,
244
aquarium, *244*
Arctic Highway,
250–251
Arktikum, *250*
auto travel in, *225*,
241
bicycling in, *226*
boat travel in, *226*,
241
business hours in, *226*
bus travel in, *225–226*
camping in, *228*
churches in, *244*
climate of, *224*
currency of, *224*
customs in, *224–225*
dining in, *227*, *242*,
245–247, *251–253*
expenses in, *224*
farmhouses in, *228*
Finnish Glass
Museum, *245*
Gold Museum, *251*
Häme Castle, *245*
Hämeenlinna,
245–246
Hattula Church, *245*
history of, *222*
holidays in, *226–227*
hotels in, *227–228*,
242, *245–247*,
251–253
Iittala Glassworks,
245
Inari, *251–252*
Ivalo, *251*, *252*
Ivalo River, *251*
Kaleva Church, *244*
Kuopio, *243*, *246*
Lake Inari, *251*
Lakelands of,
240–247
language in, *225*
Lapland, Finnish,
247–253
Lappia Hall, *250*
Lenin Museum, *244*
Levitunturi, *252*
Lintula convent, *243*
Luostotuntiuri, *250*,
252
mail in, *226*

Menesjärvi, *251*
Monastery of Valamo,
243
Museum of the
Province of Lapland,
250
museums in, *243*,
245, *250*
Nasinnuela
Observation Tower,
244
Olavinlinna, *242*
opera in, *235*
Orthodox Church
Museum, *243*
planetarium, *244*
Poet's Way, *245*
Pöykköla Museum,
250
Puijo Tower, *243*
Punkaharju, *242*
Pyynikki, *244*
reindeer roundups in,
248–249
rental houses in, *228*
Retretti, *242*
Riihimäki, *245*
Rovaniemi, *250*,
252–253
Saariselkä, *251*, *253*
Salama, *242*
Sami Museum, *251*
Santa Claus's
Workshop, *250*
Sarah Hildén Art
Museum, *244*
Savonlinna, *242*,
246–247
shopping in, *226*
Sibelius birthplace,
245
Sodankylä, *250*
Tammerkoski Rapids,
244
Tampere, *243–245*,
247
Tankavaara, *251*, *253*
telephones in, *226*
tipping in, *228*
tourist information
in, *2*, *242*, *249–250*
tours of, *242*, *249*
train travel in, *225*
Urho Kekkonen
National Park, *251*
youth hostels in, *228*
Flight insurance, *17*
Florence, *719–735*
Accademia Gallery,
723

Florence *(continued)*
air travel to, *719*
auto travel in, *720*
ballet in, *734*
baptistry, *722*
Bargello, *727*
Barrett-Browning
  house, *728*
bell tower, *722*
bicycling in, *720*
Boboli Gardens, *728*
bookstores in, *721*
buses in, *720*
bus travel to, *720*
Casa Guadi, *728*
Church of San
  Lorenzo, *726*
concerts, *734*
consulates in, *720*
Davanzati Museum,
  729
dining in, *726, 728,*
  730–732
emergencies in,
  720–721
English Cemetery,
  729
Gallery of Modern
  Art, *728*
hotels in, *732–734*
Jewish Museum, *729*
Loggia del Mercato
  Nuovo, *723*
Medici Chapels, *726*
mopeds in, *720*
Museo Archeologico,
  726
Museo dell'Opera del
  Duomo, *722*
Museo di San Marco,
  726
Museo Nazionale, *727*
Museum of Santa
  Maria Novella, *727*
nightlife in, *734–735*
Orsanmichele, *722*
Ospedale degli
  Innocenti, *726*
Palatine Gallery, *728*
Palazzo Medici
  Riccardi, *726, 729*
Palazzo Pitti, *728*
Palazzo Vecchio, *723*
Piazza del Duomo,
  722
Piazza della Signoria,
  722, 723
Ponte Vecchio, *727*
San Lorenzo Market,
  726

San Miniato al
  Monte, *729*
Santa Croce, *727*
Santa Maria del
  Carmine, *728*
Santa Maria del
  Fiore, *722*
Santa Maria Novella,
  726–727
Santo Spirito, *728*
shopping in, *723,*
  729–730
Stibbert Museum,
  729
synagogue in, *729*
taxis in, *720*
tourist information
  in, *720*
tours of, *721*
train travel to,
  719–720
travel agencies in, *721*
Uffizi Gallery, *723*
France, *255–328. See*
  also Paris
Abbaye St-Ouen, *300*
airline of, *27*
air travel in, *42, 261*
Alabaster coast, *299*
Amboise, *315*
Ancienne Auberge du
  Père Ganne, *296*
Les Andelys, *300*
Angers, *317*
Antibes, *321, 326*
Arronmanches, *303*
auto travel in,
  259–260, 292–293,
  299, 306–307, 313,
  320
Autun, *309–310*
Auxerre, *308,*
  310–311
Avallon, *308, 311*
Azay-le-Rideau, *316*
Barbizon, *295–296,*
  297
Bayeux, *302, 303–304*
Beauce, *313*
Beaune, *309, 311*
bed-and-breakfasts
  in, *264*
Biarritz, *258*
bicycling in, *261*
Blois, *315, 317*
boat travel in, *261*
boat travel to, *34*
Burgundy, *306–313*
buses in, *261, 313*
business hours in, *262*

Caen, *302, 304*
Cagnes, *326*
camping in, *264*
Cannes, *321, 326*
Cathdrale
  Notre-Dame
  (Rouen), *300, 303*
Cathedral St-Etienne
  (Sens), *307, 308*
Cathedral of
  St-Gatien, *315–316*
Chablis, *308, 311*
Chambord, *315,*
  317–318
Channel Tunnel
  between Great
  Britain and, *36*
Chartres, *295,*
  297–298
Chartreuse de
  Champmol, *309*
château of Chaumont,
  315
château of
  Chenonceau, *315*
Château du Clos de
  Vougeot, *309*
Châteaudun, *314*
Château Gaillard,
  300
Château Grimaldi,
  321
château of Sully, *309*
Chinon, *316, 318*
churches in, *295, 300,*
  301, 303, 307, 308,
  309, 314, 315, 325
Clamecy, *308*
climate of, *258*
Clos-Lucé, *315*
Cluny, *310, 311–312*
currency of, *258–259*
customs in, *259*
D-Day, *303*
Deauville, *302, 304*
Dijon, *309, 312*
dining in, *262–263,*
  297–298, 303–306,
  310–313, 317–318,
  326–328
Etretat, *302, 304*
Euro Disney,
  296–297, 298
expenses in, *259*
Fécamp, *302, 305*
festivals in, *321*
film in, *290, 321*
Fontainebleau, *295,*
  298
Fontevraud, *316*

Fréjus, *321*
Gassin, *321*
George d'Apremont,
  295
Giverny, *300*
Grasse, *321, 326–327*
holidays in, *262*
Honfleur, *302, 305*
hotels in, *263–264,*
  303–306, 310–313,
  317–318, 326–328
Ile de France,
  292–298
Jumièges Abbey, *301*
Landing Museum,
  303
Langeais, *316*
language in, *252*
Loire Valley, *313–318*
Lyon, *306–313, 310,*
  312
Mâcon, *310*
Maeght Foundation,
  319
mail in, *262*
Menton, *325–326, 327*
Monaco, *322–325, 327*
Mont St-Michel, *303,*
  305
Morvan Regional
  Park, *308*
Mougins, *321,*
  327–328
Musée Chagall, *322*
Musée de la Bataille
  de Normandie, *303*
Musée de la
  Céramique, *301*
Musée de l'Ecole de
  Barbizon, *296*
Musée de
  l'Annonciade, *320*
Musée des Arts
  Décoratifs, *317*
Musée des
  Beaux-Arts (Lyon),
  310
Musée des
  Beaux-Arts (Rouen),
  301
Musée du Cheval, *317*
Musée du
  Gros-Horloge, *301*
Musée du Vin de
  Bourgogne, *309*
Musée Jean Cocteau,
  326
Musée Le Secq des
  Tournelles, *301*
Musée National des

Automates et Poupées d'Autrefois, *322, 325*

Musée Ochier, *310*

Musée Picasso, *321–322*

Musée Rolin, *310*

museums in, *262, 301, 302, 303, 308, 309, 310, 317, 321–322, 325*

Nice, *322*

Normandy, *299–306*

Notre-Dame de Chartres, *295*

Palais des Ducs, *309*

Palais de Justice, *300*

Palais Synodal, *308*

place Garibaldi, *322*

place Masséna, *322*

Port Grimaud, *321*

Puits de Moïse, *309*

Quarré-les-Tombes, *308*

Ramatuelle, *321*

Rambouillet, *294–295, 298*

Riviera, *318–328*

Rocher de la Pérouse, *308–309*

Rochers des Demoiselles, *295*

Roman ruins in, *310*

Rouen, *306*

St-Martin Church, *308*

St. Paul de Vence, *320*

St-Tropez, *320–321, 328*

St-Wandrille Abbey, *301*

Saône Valley, *306*

Saulieu, *309*

Saumur, *316–317, 318*

Sens, *307, 312*

shopping in, *262*

Siene Valley, *299*

telephones in, *261–262*

tipping in, *264–265*

tourist information in, *2, 294, 299, 307, 314, 320*

Tours, *315, 318*

tours of, *6–7, 293, 299, 307, 313, 320*

train travel in, *39, 260–261, 292, 299, 306–307, 313, 320*

train travel to, *35–36*

Les Trianons, *293*

Trouville, *302*

Vaux-le-Vicomte, *296*

Vendôme, *314*

Versailles, *294, 298*

Vézelay, *308, 312–313*

Villandry, *316*

villas in, *264*

visas for, *259*

William the Conqueror Cultural Center, *302*

youth hostels in, *264*

Frankfurt, *360–370*

air travel to, *31, 42, 360*

Alte Brücke, *367*

Alte Oper, *366*

auto travel to, *361*

bookstores in, *362*

Börse, *366*

bus travel to, *361*

Carmelite Monastery, *366*

consulates in, *361*

dining in, *367–369*

Eiserne Steg, *363*

emergencies in, *362*

Fountain of Justitia, *363*

Goethehaus und Goethemuseum, *366*

Hauptwache, *363*

hotels in, *369–370*

Jewish Museum, *367*

Kaiserdom, *363*

Kaisersaal, *363*

Karmeliterkirche, *366*

Katerinenkirche, *363*

Kuhhirtenturm, *367*

Leonhardskirche, *366*

Museum of Modern Art, *366–367*

Nikolaikirche, *363, 366*

Paulskirche, *363*

public transportation in, *361*

Rententurm, *363*

Römer, *363*

Römerberg, *363*

Römerberg Square, *363*

Sachsenhausen, *367*

Schaumainkai, *367*

Städelsches Kunstinstitut and Städische Galerie, *367*

taxis in, *361*

tourist information in, *2–3, 361*

tours of, *362*

train travel to, *361*

travel agencies in, *362*

Gardens

in Athens, *525*

in Austria, *83*

in Berlin, *409*

in Bulgaria, *139, 146*

in Czech Republic, *177*

in Denmark, *201, 203, 217*

in Florence, *728*

in Geneva, *1069*

in Germany, *385, 393*

in Great Britain, *462, 488–489*

in Hamburg, *373*

in Holland, *587–588*

in Iceland, *641*

in Ireland, *674*

in Italy, *709, 738*

in London, *462*

in Lugano, *1083*

in Malta, *797*

in Monaco, *325*

in Munich, *350*

in Paris, *274, 277*

in Spain, *986, 987*

in Stockholm, *1029, 1037*

Gay and Lesbian Travelers, *26*

Gdańsk, *854–857*

dining in, *856–857*

hotels in, *856–857*

Solidarity Monument, *855*

tourist information in, *854*

tours of, *854*

Geneva, *1066–1074*

air travel to, *1066*

auto travel to, *1066*

buses in, *1066*

Cathédral St-Pierre, *1068–1069*

Confédération Centre, *1069*

Conservatoire de Musique, *1068*

dining in, *1069, 1072–1073*

Grand Théâtre, *1068*

Hôtel de Ville, *1069*

hotels in, *1073–1074*

International Complex, *1068*

Jardin Anglais, *1069*

Jet D'Eau, *1068*

Maison Tavel, *1069*

Monument Brunswick, *1068*

Musée d'Art et Histoire, *1068*

Musée Rath, *1068*

opera in, *1068*

Pont de l'Ile, *1068*

Pont du Mont Blanc, *1068*

Reformation Monument, *1068*

Rousseau Island, *1068*

Russian church, *1068*

streetcars in, *1066*

taxis in, *1066*

Temple de l'Auditoire, *1069*

tourist information in, *1066*

tours of, *1066–1067*

train travel to, *1066*

Germany, *330–433.* *See also* Berlin; Frankfurt; Hamburg; Munich; Saxony and Thuringia

Achkarren, *395*

airline of, *27*

air travel in, *42, 337–338*

Alpirsback, *394*

auto travel in, *37–38, 335–336, 381*

Bacharach, *387, 388*

Baden-Baden, *396, 397*

Bad Godesberg, *384*

Bad Liebenzell, *393, 397–398*

Baiersbronn, *398*

bicycling in, *338, 381*

Black Forest, *391–402*

boat travel in, *338, 380*

boat travel to, *34*

Bonn, *388*

Boppard, *386, 389*

Burg Gutenfels, *387*

Burg Katz, *386*

Burg Maus, *386*

Germany *(continued)*
buses in, *337*
business hours in, *339*
Calw, *394*
camping in, *342*
castles in, *386*, *387*
churches in, *347*, *352*,
363, *366*, *376*, *382*,
384, *385*, *386*, *393*,
394, *395*
Claw, *398*
climate of, *334*
currency of, *334*
customs in, *335*
Deutsches Eck, *385*
dining in, *339–341*,
388–391, *394*, *395*,
396–402
Drachenfels, *384*
Ehrenbreitstein, *385*
expenses in, *334–335*
farm vacations in, *342*
Freiburg, *395*,
399–400
Freudenstadt, *394*,
400–401
Gutachtal Valley, *394*
Himmelreich, *395*
Hinterzarten, *401*
holidays in, *339*
hotels in, *341–342*,
388–391, *396–402*
Kaub, *386*, *389*
Koblenz, *384*,
389–390
Köln, *382*
Königswinter, *384*,
390
Landesmuseum, *385*
language in, *335*
Lorelei rock, *386*
Ludwig Museum, *385*
mail in, *339*
Mainz, *387*, *390–391*
Mittelrhein Museum,
385
Mummelsee Lake, *396*
Museum Ludwig, *385*
museums in, *339*,
383, *384*, *385*, *387*,
410, *412*
Nagold, *401*
Neubulach silver
mine, *394*
Oberwesel, *386*
Pfalzgrafenstein, *387*
Pforzheim, *393*, *401*
Remagen, *384*
rentals in, *342*
Reuchlinhaus, *393*

Rheinfels Castle, *386*
Rhine region of,
380–391
Roman ruins in, *384*,
386
Römisch-
Germanisches
Museum, *383*, *387*
Rüdesheim, *391*
St. Goar, *391*
St. Goarshausen, *386*,
391
Schiltach, *394*
Schluchsee, *395*
shopping in, *339*
Siebengebirge, *384*
Staufen, *395*
telephones in, *338–339*
tipping in, *343*
Titisee, *395*, *401*
tourist information
in, *3*, *381*, *393*
tours of, *382*, *393*
train travel in, *39*,
336–337, *380*
train travel to, *35*
Triberg, *401–402*
visas for, *335*
Wallraf-Richartz
Museum, *383*
Wine Road, *395*
Wolfach, *394*
youth hostels in, *342*
Gibraltar, *998*,
1001–1008
air travel to, *1001*
Apes' Den, *1003*
auto travel in, *37*
auto travel to, *1001*
bus travel in, *1001*
casino in, *1002*
Catalan Bay, *1001*
Cathedral of the Holy
Trinity, *1003*
Cathedral of St.
Mary the Crowned,
1003
dining in, *1004–1008*
Europa Point, *1001*
Gibraltar Museum,
1003
Governor's
Residence, *1003*
Holyland Tunnel,
1003
hotels in, *1004–1008*
Jews Gate, *1002*
Koehler Gun, *1003*
Law Courts, *1003*
Moorish Castle, *1003*

Nefusot Yehudada
Synagogue, *1003*
Nuns Well, *1001–1002*
Our Lady of Europe,
1002
Rosia Bay, *1002*
St. Michael's Cave,
1003
Sandy Bay, *1001*
tourist information
in, *3*,*998*
Tower of Homage,
1003
Upper Galleries, *1003*
Wall of Charles V,
1003
Great Britain,
435–512. *See also*
Bath; Cambridge;
Edinburgh; London;
Oxford; York
Abbeygate Street,
497
airline of, *27*
air travel to, *441*
air travel to Europe
from, *30–32*
Angel Hill, *497*
Anne Hathaway's
Cottage, *488*
auto travel in, *37–39*,
439–440, *451*, *481*
auto travel to Europe
from, *33–34*
Bath, *489–491*
bed-and-breakfasts
in, *445*
bicycling in, *45–46*,
442
Bladon, *486*
Blenheim Palace, *484*,
485
boat travel in, *442*
boat travel to Europe
from, *34–35*
Bolton Abbey, *502*
Bury St. Edmund's,
493, *497–498*
business hours in, *444*
bus travel in,
441–442, *481*
bus travel to Europe
from, *36–37*
camping in, *446*
Castle Howard, *504*
Channel Tunnel
between France and,
33
Chantry House, *483*
Chipping Campden,

488
Christ Church, *484*
churches in, *482*, *488*,
497, *500*, *502*, *503*,
507, *509*
climate of, *438*
Cotswolds, *486*
currency of, *438–439*
customs and duties
for citizens of, *15*
customs in, *439*
dining in, *444–445*,
454–455, *483*, *484*,
486, *488*, *490–493*,
498–499
Ely, *493*, *497*
Eton, *483*, *493*
expenses in, *439*
farmhouses in, *445*
Fountains Abbey and
Studley Royal, *503*
gardens in, *488–489*
Grantchester, *496*
Grassinton, *502*
Hall's Croft, *487*
Helmsley, *504*
Henley, *483*
Hidcote Manor
Garden, *488–489*
Historic Buildings,
445–446
holiday cottages in,
445
holidays in, *444*
Holy Trinity Church,
488
horse racing in, *497*
hotels in, *445–446*,
490–493, *498–499*
Magdalen College,
484
mail in, *443*
Marlow, *483*
Mary Arden's House,
486–487
Museum of Eton
Life, *483*
museums in, *444*,
454, *460*, *461*,
462–463, *467*, *483*,
484, *489*, *496*, *497*,
500, *502*, *507*, *509*,
510
National Horseracing
Museum, *497*
National Park
Centre, *503*
National Stud, *497*
Newby Hall, *503*
Newmarket, *497*

North York Moors, 503–504
Nunnington Hall, 504
Oxford, 484, 491–492
Queen Mary's Doll's House, 482–483
Rievaulx Abbey, 504
Roman ruins in, 489
Royal Shakespeare Theatre, 488
St. George's Chapel, 482
sea travel to, 29–30
Shakespeare Birthplace Trust, 486
shopping in, 443–444
Stained-Glass Museum, 497
Stratford, 481, 492–493
Stratford-upon-Avon, 486–488
Strid, 502
Swan, 488
telephones in, 442–443
theater in, 498
Theater Royal, 498
tipping in, 446
tourist offices of, 3, 481
tours of, 5–10, 481–482
train travel in, 440, 481
train travel to Europe from, 35–36
trip insurance for citizens of, 17–18
university housing in, 446
visas for residents of, 13
Warwick, 488
Warwick Castle, 488
Windsor, 481–483, 493
Woolstaplers Hall, 488
York, 499–506
Yorkshire Dales, 502
youth hostels in, 446
Greece, 514–557. *See also* Athens
Acrocorinth, 541
airline of, 27
air travel in, 27, 32, 519, 552
Akrotiri, 554

Ancient Thira, 554
Arahova, 548
Arch of the Emperor Galerius, 549
Archaeological Museum, 549
Argos, 542
arts in, 537–538, 545
auto rentals in, 18–20
auto travel in, 37–38, 518, 546, 552, 553
Avenue of the Lions, 554
boat travel in, 519, 552
buses in, 42–43
business hours in, 520
bus travel in, 519
Cathedral of St. Andrew's, 543
climate of, 515
Corinth, 541
Crete, 555–556
cruises in, 553
currency of, 515
customs in, 515
Daphni, 541
Delos, 554
Delphi, 548, 550
Delphi Museum, 548
dining in, 520–521, 543–545, 550–552, 556–557
Doric Temple of Apollo, 541
Eleusis, 541
Epidauros, 542
expenses in, 515
ferry service from, 44, 552, 553
Fort of Acrocorinth, 541
holidays in, 520
hotels in, 543–545, 550–552, 556–557, 521–522
islands of, 552–557
Kalambaka, 548, 550–551
Kamenes, 554
Knights' Hospital, 555
language in, 518
Lindos, 555
Lion Gate, 542
Livadia, 547
mail in, 520
mainland Greece, 546–552

Mallia, 555
Megalopolis, 542
Meteora, 548
monasteries in, 548–549
Monastery of Ossios Loukas, 548
Mount Olympus, 514, 546
Mount Parnassus, 514, 546
Museum of the Olympic Games, 544
museums in, 520, 529–530, 542, 543, 549, 555
Mycenae, 542
Mykonos, 553, 556
Nafplio, 542, 543–544
Olympia, 542, 544–545
Palace of the Grand Masters, 555
Palace of Knossos, 555
Patras, 543, 545
Peloponnese, 539–545
Rhodes, 554, 556–557
sanctuary of Dionysos, 554
Santorini, 554, 557
sea travel to, 44
shopping in, 520
telephones in, 519–520
Temple of Apollo, 548
theater in, 545
Thebes, 547
Thessaloniki, 549, 551–552
tipping in, 522
Tiryns, 542
tourist information in, 3, 541, 547, 553
tours of, 541, 546–547, 552
train travel in, 518–519
volcanoes, 552, 554
White Tower, 549

The Hague, 590–598
dining in, 597–598
Haags Gemeente-museum, 593
hotels in, 597–598
International Court of Justice, 593

Kloosterkerk, 593
Madurodam, 594
Mauritshuis, 592
Omniversum, 594
Rijksmuseum H.W. Mesdag, 593
Supreme Court, 593
tourist information in, 592
train travel to, 590
Vredespaleis, 593
Zorgvliet, 594
Hamburg, 370–379
air travel to, 370
Alter Botanischer Garten, 373
Aussenalster, 376
auto travel to, 371
Binnenalster, 376
Bismarck Memorial, 373
Blankenese, 373
bookstores in, 371
bus travel to, 370
consulates in, 371
dining in, 377–378
emergencies in, 371
Fischmarkt, 373
Grosse Wallanlagen, 373
Hauptbahnhof, 372
hotels in, 378–379
Jungfernstieg, 376
Kunsthalle, 377
Lundungsbrücken, 373
Museum für Hamburgische Geschichte, 373, 376
nightlife in, 379
Platen un Blomen, 373
public transportation in, 371
Rathaus, 376
Rathausmarkt, 376
Reeperbahn, 373, 379
St. Michael's Church, 376
taxis in, 371
tourist information in, 371
tours of, 371–372
train travel to, 370
travel agencies in, 371
Health and accident insurance, 17
Health precautions, 16

Helsinki, *228–240*
air travel to, *228*
Akseli Gallen
  Kallela's studio, *235*
boat travel in, *229*
bookstores, *230*
bus travel to, *229*
concerts in, *240*
dining in, *234, 235,*
  236–238
embassies in, *229*
emergencies in, *230*
festivals in, *240*
Finlandiatalo, *235*
Havis Amanda
  statue, *231*
hotels in, *238–240*
Kaivopuisto, *234*
Katajanokka, *231, 234*
Kauppatori, *231*
Lutheran Cathedral,
  234
Mannerheim statue,
  235
Market Hall, *234*
National Museum,
  235
National Theater, *235*
nightlife in, *240*
Nordic Arts Center,
  234
Olympia Terminal,
  234
Pohjoisesplanadi, *231*
Pohjoismainen
  Taidekeskus, *234*
Presidentinlinna, *231*
sea travel to, *229*
Senaatintori, *234*
shopping in, *234, 236*
Stockmann's, *234*
streetcars in, *229*
subways in, *229*
Suomen
  Kansallismuseo, *235*
Suomen
  Kansallisoppera, *235*
Suomenlinna, *234*
Swedish Theater, *234*
Tapiola, *235*
taxis in, *229*
Temppeliaukion
  Church, *235*
theater in, *240*
tourist information
  in, *229*
tours of, *230*
train travel to, *229*
travel agencies in,
  230

Tuomiokirkko, *234*
Uspenskin Kirkko,
  231
Valtion Taidemuseo
  Ateneum, *235*
Holland, *559–598. See
  also* Amsterdam;
  Delft; The Hague;
  Scheveningen
Aalsmeer, *587–588*
airline of, *27*
air travel to, *563*
Amersfoort, *584–585*
Apeldoorn, *585, 589*
Arnhem, *585*
auto travel in, *562,
  583*
bicycling in, *563–564*
Bloemenveiling, *588*
boat travel in, *591*
boat travel from
  United Kingdom to,
  34–35
buses in, *563, 583,
  591*
business hours in,
  564–565
Centraal Museum,
  586
churches in, *572, 573,
  585, 586, 595*
climate of, *561*
currency of, *561*
customs in, *562*
dining in, *565,
  588–590, 597–598*
Domkerk, *585*
expenses in, *561–562*
Frans Hals Museum,
  588
gardens in, *587–588*
Gouda, *586, 589*
Grote Kerk, *588*
Haarlem, *588, 587*
holidays in, *565*
Hortus Botanicus
  gardens, *587*
hotels in, *565–566,
  588–590, 597–598*
Keukenhof Gardens,
  587
Koopelport, *585*
Lakenhal, *587*
language in, *562*
Leiden, *587, 589–590*
Lisse, *587–588*
mail in, *564*
Molenmuseum De
  Valk, *587*
Museum Flehite, *585*

museums in, *562,
  569, 572–573, 574,
  575, 576, 585, 586,
  587, 588, 592, 593,
  596*
Pilgrim Fathers
  Documentatie
  Centrum, *587*
Rijksmuseum Het
  Catharijneconvent,
  586
Rijksmuseum Paleis
  Het Loo, *585*
Rijksmuseum van
  Speelklok tot
  Pierement, *586*
Rotterdam, *590–598*
Scheveningen, *594*
shopping in, *564*
Stedelijk Museum
  Het Catharina
  Gasthuis, *586–587*
telephones in, *564*
Teylers Museum, *588*
tipping in, *566*
tourist information
  in, *3, 584, 592*
tours of, *584, 591*
train travel in, *563,
  583, 590*
Utrecht, *585–586, 590*
Zandvoort, *584*
Home exchanges, *21*
Hostels, *22*
for older travelers,
  25–26
Hungary, *600–626.
  See also* Budapest
airline of, *27*
Aquincum, *621*
auto travel in, *603*
Balatonfüred, *623,
  625*
bicycling in, *604*
boat travel in, *604,
  620, 624*
business hours in, *605*
bus travel in, *604,
  624*
camping in, *606*
churches in, *612, 614,
  622, 625*
climate in, *602*
currency of, *602*
customs in, *603*
Danube Bend,
  620–623
dining in, *605,
  622–623, 625–626*
Esztergom, *622, 623*

expenses in, *602*
guest houses in, *606*
Herend, *625*
holidays in, *605*
hotels in, *605–606,
  623, 625–626*
Kereszteny Museum,
  622
Lake Balaton,
  623–626
language in, *603*
mail in, *604–605*
Margit Kovács
  Pottery Museum,
  622
museums in, *605,
  609, 611, 612, 614,
  622, 625*
Nagyvázsony castle,
  625
Nemesvámos, *625*
Nprajzi Mzeum, *613*
parks in, *614*
rentals in, *605–606*
Szabadtéri Néprajzi
  Mzeum, *622*
Szentendre, *621, 623*
telephones in, *604*
Tihany, *625, 626*
tipping in, *606*
tourist information
  in, *3, 608, 621, 624*
tours of, *608–609,
  621, 624*
train travel to,
  603–604, 624
Veszprém, *624, 626*
visas for, *602*
Visegrád, *622, 623*

Iceland, *628–644. See
  also* Reykjavík
airline of, *27*
air travel in, *630, 639*
Akureuyri, *641, 642*
auto travel in, *630,
  639*
bicycling in, *45–46*
Blönduós, *641, 642*
boat travel in, *639*
Borgarnes, *641, 642*
botanic gardens, *641*
Breiddalsvik, *640,
  642*
Búoir, *642*
business hours in, *631*
bus travel in, *630–631*
climate of, *628, 630*
countryside of,
  639–644

currency of, *630*
customs in, *630*
Dettifoss waterfall, *641*
dining in, *631–632*, *642–644*
Djúpivogur, *643*
Egilsstaðir, *640*, *643*
expenses in, *630*
Goðafoss waterfall, *641*
Hallormsstaður, *641*, *643*
Höfn, *640*, *643*
holidays in, *631*
hotels in, *632*, *642–644*
Húsavík, *641*, *643*
Hveragerði, *640*, *643*
Ísafjörður, *643*
Jökulsárlón, *640*
Kirkjubæjarklaustur, *640*, *643*
Lake Mývatn, *639*, *641*
language in, *630*
mail in, *631*
museums in, *636*
Mývatn, *639*, *643*
Ólafsvík, *641*, *643*
Sauðárkrókur, *641*, *643*
Seyðisfjörður, *641*, *644*
Skaftafell National Park, *640*, *644*
Skógar, *640*, *644*
Snæfelsnes, *641*
telephones in, *631*
tipping in, *632*
Tjörnes, *641*
tourist information in, *639*
tourist offices of, *3–4*
tours of, *639*, *641*
Vatnajökull, *640*
Vestfirðir, *642*
Innsbruck, *88–93*
air travel to, *88*
arts in, *93*
auto travel to, *88*
buses in, *88*
dining in, *91–92*
Ferdinandeum, *89*, *91*
Goldenes Dachl, *89*
Grassmayr Bell Foundry, *91*
Hofburg, *89*
Hofkirche, *89*
hotels in, *92–93*

Olympic Museum, *89*
Schgloss Ambras, *91*
taxis in, *88*
Tiroler Volksunstmuseum, *89*
tourist information in, *89*
tours of, *88*
train travel to, *88*
Triumphpforte, *91*
zoo, *91*

Insurance, *17–18*
for rental cars, *19–20*
Ireland, *646–686* See also Cork; Dublin
Ailwee Cave, *680*
airline of, *27*
air travel in, *651*
Aran Islands, *680*
auto travel in, *37–39*, *650–651*, *673*, *682*
Ballyporeen, *674*
bed-and-breakfasts in, *654*
Belleek, *685*
bicycling in, *652*, *673*, *682*
Blasket Islands, *679*
boat travel in, *652*
boat travel from United Kingdom to, *35*
Bundoran, *685*
Bunratty Castle, *679–680*
The Burren, *680*
business hours in, *652*
bus travel in, *651*, *673*, *682*
bus travel to, *36–37*
Cahir, *674*, *676*
camping in, *654*
Cashel, *674*, *676*
Cashel Bay, *685*
castles in, *663*, *675*, *679*, *680*, *683*
Cavan, *685*
churches in, *660*, *663*, *664*, *675*, *685*
Claddagh, *684*
Clare Heritage Center, *680*
Clarinbridge, *680*, *681*
Clifden, *684*, *685*
Cliffs of Moher, *680*
climate of, *647*
Cobh, *675*

Collooney, *685–686*
Cong, *686*
Connemara, *684*
Connemara National Park, *684*
Croagpatrick, *684*
Curragh, *674*
currency of, *647*
customs in, *650*
Derrynane House, *679*
Dingle Peninsula, *679*, *681*
dining in, *652–653*, *676–677*, *680*, *681–682*, *684*, *685–686*
Donegal, *685*
Doolin, *680*
Ennis, *680*, *681*
expenses in, *647*, *650*
Gaelteacht, *678*
Galway City, *683*, *686*
guest houses in, *654*
holidays in, *652*
horse racing in, *674*
hotels in, *653–654*, *676–677*, *681–682*, *685–686*
Inishmaan, *684*
Innishfree, *684*
Japanese Gardens, *674*
Kells, *685*
Kenmare, *679*, *681*
Kerry, *679*
Kildare, *674*
Killarney, *678*, *681*
Knappogue castle, *680*
Lahinch, *682*
language in, *650*
Limerick, *679*, *682*
Lisdoonvarna, *680*, *682*
Lissadell House, *684–685*
Lynch's Castle, *683*
mail in, *652*
Moycullen, *686*
Muckross, *678*
museums in, *652*, *660*, *661–662*, *664*, *665*, *684*
National Stud and Horse Museum, *674*
Northwest, *682–686*
Oughterand, *684*, *686*
The Pale, *674*
parks in, *664*, *678*

pubs in, *668*
Ring of Kerry, *679*
Rock of Cashel, *674*
Rossaveale, *684*
Salthill Promenade, *684*
Shannon region, *678–680*
shopping in, *652*
Skellig Rocks, *679*
Sligo Town, *684*, *686*
Sneem, *679*
Tara, hill of, *685*
Tarbet, *679*
telephones in, *652*
tipping in, *654*
tourist information in, *4*, *655*, *673*, *677*, *683*
tours of, *673*, *677*, *683*
train travel in, *673*, *677*, *682*
train travel to, *35–36*
Tralee, *678*, *679*
Waterville, *679*
Westport, *684*, *686*

Istanbul, *1107–1121*
air travel to, *1107*
Archaeological Museum, *1111*
auto travel to, *1108*
Bab-i-Salam, *1111*
bars in, *1120*
Blue Mosque, *1114*
boats in, *1108–1109*
bookstores in, *1109*
buses in, *1108*
bus travel to, *1108*
Carpet Museum, *1114*
Church of St. Irene, *1111*
Cistern Basilica, *1115*
Column of Constantinos, *1114*
concerts in, *1120*
consulates in, *1109*
dining in, *1111*, *1115–1116*, *1117–1118*
Divan-i-Huyayun, *1111*
Dolmabahçe Mosque, *1116*
Dolmabahçe Palace, *1116*
Dolmuş in, *1108*
Egyptian Bazaar, *1115*

Istanbul *(continued)*
Egyptian Obelisk, *1114*
emergencies, *1109*
festival in, *1119*
Flower Market, *1116*
Galata Tower, *1116*
Golden Cage, *1111*
Grand Bazaar, *1115*
Harem, *1111*
Hippodrome, *1114*
hotels in, *1118–1119*
Ibrahim Paşa Palace, *1114*
Istanbul University, *1115*
Kilim Museum, *1114*
Museum of the Ancient Orient, *1111*
Museum of Turkish and Islamic Arts, *1114*
New Town, *1116*
nightlife in, *1120–1121*
opera in, *1119–1120*
Sacred Column, *1114*
Sancta Sophia, *1114*
Serpentine Column, *1114*
shopping in, *1116*
Süleymaniye Mosque, *1115*
taxis in, *1108*
theater in, *1119*
Tiled Pavilion, *1111*, *1113*
Topkapi Palace, *1110*
tourist information in, *1109*
tours of, *1109–1110*
train travel to, *1108*
travel agencies in, *1109*
Treasury, *1111*
Turkish baths, *1115*
Italy, *688–775 See also* Florence; Milan; Rome; Venice
airline of, *27*
air travel in, *693, 767*
Amalfi, *770–771, 772*
Anacapri, *770*
Arezzo, *740, 741*
auto travel in, *692–693, 735, 767*
Baptistery (Pisa), *738*
bicycling in, *45–46*
boat travel in, *693–694, 767–768*
business hours in, *695*

bus travel in, *693, 699, 735, 767*
Campania region of, *766–775*
camping in, *696–697*
Capri, *770, 772*
Castel Nuovo, *768*
Certaldo, *738*
Certosa di San Martino, *769*
churches in, *701, 704–705, 706, 707–708, 710, 722–723, 727, 728, 729, 736–737, 738, 739, 740, 746, 748, 758, 759, 769*
climate of, *689*
Collegiata, Church of the, *739*
Cortona, *740, 741*
Crypt of St. Peter's, *708*
currency of, *689–692*
customs in, *692*
dining in, *695–696, 739, 741–744, 768–769*
Duomo (Pisa), *738*
Duomo (Pistoia), *737*
Duomo (Prato), *736*
expenses in, *692*
gardens in, *709, 738*
Gesù, *768*
Grotto Azzurra, *770*
Herculaneum, *769*
holidays in, *695*
hotels in, *696–697, 741–744*
language in, *692*
Leaning Tower (Pisa), *738*
Lucca, *737–738, 741–742*
mail in, *694*
Montepulciano, *742*
Museo Archeologico, *740*
Museo Archeologico Nazionale, *769*
Museo Correale, *770*
Museo dell'Accademia Etrusca, *740*
Museo dell'Opera del Duomo, *737*
Museo di Capodimonte, *769*
Museo Diocesano, *741*
museums in, *695, 701, 705, 706, 707,*

709, 712, 722, 723, 726, 727, 728, 729, 737, 740, 755, 759, 760, 761, 769
Naples, *768–769, 772–773*
Ostia Antica, *712*
Palazzo Reale, *768*
Petrarch's House, *740*
Piazza Grande, *740*
Pievescola, *742*
Pisa, *738, 742*
Pistoia, *737, 743*
Pompeii, *769–770*
Positano, *770–771, 773–774*
Prato, *736–737, 743*
Ravello, *771, 774*
rentals in, *696*
Roman ruins in, *740*
San Francesco, church of, *740*
San Gimignano, *739, 743*
San Giovanni Fuorcivitas, *737*
San Pietro, *761*
Santa Chiara, *768*
Santa Maria del Calcinaio, *740*
Santa Maria della Carceri, *737*
Santa Maria della Pieve, *740*
Sant'Andrea, *737*
shopping in, *694, 695*
Siena, *738–739, 743–744*
Sorrento, *770, 774–775*
telephones in, *694*
tipping in, *697*
tourist information in, *4, 699, 720, 735, 768*
tours of, *735, 768*
train travel in, *693, 735, 767*
Tuscany region of, *735–744*
Villa Reale, *738*
Villa Rufolo, *771*

Kraków, *850–854*
Auschwitz, *852*
Barbican, *850*
Church of the Virgin Mary, *852*
dining in, *850*
hotels in, *853–854*

Jagiellonian University, *852*
Main Market, *852*
Planty, *850*
St. Florian's Gate, *850*
Sukiennice, *852*
tourist information in, *850*
tours of, *850*
transportation to, *850*
Wieliczka, *852*
Laptop computers, *16*
Lefkosa. *See* Nicosia
Liechtenstein, *1064–1066*
dining in, *1065*
hotels in, *1065–1066*
Liechtenstein National Museum, *1065*
Malbun, *1065*
Postage Stamp Museum, *1065*
Prince's Art Gallery and the State Art Collection, *1064*
Schaan, *1065*
tourist information in, *1064*
Triesenberg, *1065*
Vaduz, *1064*
Vaduz Castle, *1064*
Lisbon, *867–879*
air travel to, *867*
Alfama, *869–871*
Bairro Alta, *871*
Baixa, *871*
ballet in, *878*
Belém, *872*
buses in, *867*
Castelo de São Jorge, *869*
dining in, *872, 873, 875–876*
embassies in, *868*
emergencies in, *868*
ferries in, *867*
Fundação Calouste Gulbenkian, *871*
funicular railway in, *871*
hotels in, *876–878*
Igreja de São Roque, *872*
Igreja do Carmo, *872*
Largo do Chiado, *872*
Monument to the Discoveries, *873*

Mosteiro dos Jerónimos, *872*
Museu da Artes Decorativas, *869*
Museu da Marioneta, *869*
Museu de Arte Sacra, *872*
Museu de Marinha, *872–873*
Museu Nacional do Coches, *873–874*
nightlife in, *878–879*
opera in, *878*
Palácio da Ajuda, *874*
Palácio da Fronteira, *874*
Parque Eduardo VII, *871*
Rossio, *871*
Sé, *869*
sea travel to, *29–30*
shopping in, *871, 874–875*
Solar do Vinho do Porto, *871–872*
subways in, *867*
taxis in, *867*
theater in, *878*
Torre de Belém, *873*
tourist information in, *868*
tours of, *868*
train travel to, *867*
trams in, *867*
travel agencies in, *868*
wine cellars in, *878*
London, *446–481*
Admiralty Arch, *455*
air travel to, *30–32, 446–447*
Albert Memorial, *461–462*
auto travel in, *451*
ballet in, *463*
Bank of England, *465, 479–480*
Banqueting House, *459–460*
The Barbican, *465*
Bayswater, *474–475*
Berkeley Square, *461*
Big Ben, *459*
Birdcage Walk, *458*
Bloomsbury, *463, 469–470, 475*
British Museum, *463*
Buckingham Palace, *455, 458*

Burlington Arcade, *460*
Burlington House, *460*
buses in, *448, 450*
Cabinet War Rooms, *458*
Camden Lock, *467*
Carlton House Terrace, *455*
Cenotaph, *459*
Changing of the Guard, *455*
Chapel Royal, *455*
Chapter House, *459*
Cheapside, *465*
Chelsea, *470, 475–476*
The City, *463–467, 470*
Clarence House, *455*
concerts, *479*
Cornhill, *465*
Covent Garden, *462–463, 470–471*
Crown Jewels, *466*
dining in, *460, 461, 462, 465, 466, 469–474*
Downing Street, *459*
drugstores in, *451*
embassies in, *451*
emergencies in, *451*
film in, *480*
Flower Walk, *462*
Greenwich, *467–468*
Guards Museum, *458*
Guildhall, *465*
Hampstead, *467*
Hampstead Heath, *467*
Henry VII's Chapel, *459*
Horse Guards Parade, *460*
hotels in, *474–478*
Hyde Park, *461–462*
Hyde Park Corner, *461*
Jermyn Street, *460*
Jewish Museum, *463*
Keats Grove, *467*
Kensington, *471–472, 475–476*
Kensington Gardens, *461*
Kensington Palace, *462*
Kenwood House, *467*
Knightsbridge, *472, 476–477*

Lancaster House, *455*
Leadenhall Market, *465*
Lloyd's of London, *465–466*
London International Financial Futures Exchange, *465*
London Transport Museum, *462*
London Wall, *464*
The Mall, *455*
Mansion House, *465*
Mayfair, *460–461, 472–473*
Museum of London, *464–465*
Museum of Mankind, *460*
National Gallery, *454*
National History Museum, *461*
National Maritime Museum, *467*
National Portrait Gallery, *454*
National Theatre, *478*
nightlife in, *480–481*
Notting Hill, *462, 473*
Old Royal Observatory, *468*
opera in, *462, 463, 479*
Palace of Westminster, *458*
Parliament Square, *458*
Piccadilly, *460*
Pyx Chamber, *459*
Queen's Gallery, *458*
Rotten Row, *461*
Royal Academy, *460*
Royal Exchange, *465*
Royal Mews, *458*
Royal Naval College, *468*
Royal Opera House, *462, 463*
St. James's, *460–461, 473–474*
St. James's Church, *460*
St. James's Palace, *455*
St. Martin-in-the-Fields Church, *454*
St. Mary-le-Bow, *465*
St. Paul's Cathedral, *464*

St. Paul's Church, *462*
St. Stephen's Tower, *459*
Science Museum, *461*
Serpentine, *461*
Shepherd Market, *461*
shopping in, *460, 462, 468–469*
Soho, *473–474*
taxis in, *450*
10 Downing Street, *459*
theater in, *478–479*
Theatre Museum, *463*
Theatre Royal Drury Lane, *462*
tourist information in, *451*
tours of, *452–453*
Tower of London, *466*
Trafalgar Square, *454*
train travel to, *447*
travel agencies in, *451*
Undercroft, *459*
Underground in, *448, 450*
Victoria, *476–477*
Victoria and Albert Museum, *461*
Victoria Tower, *459*
Wellington Barracks, *458*
West End, *477–478*
Westminster, *454–460*
Westminster Abbey, *459*
Whispering Gallery, *464*
Whitehall, *459*
York House, *455*
Lugano, *1081–1087*
air travel to, *1081–1082*
auto travel to, *1082*
Belvedere Gardens, *1083*
boat travel in, *1082*
buses in, *1082*
Cathedral of San Lorenzo, *1083*
Church of Santa Maria degli Angioli, *1083*
dining in, *1085–1086*
hotels in, *1086–1087*
Lido, *1083*
Museum of Natural History, *1083*

Lugano *(continued)*
Old Town, *1083*
Parco Civico, *1083*
Parco Tassino, *1085*
taxis in, *1082*
tourist information in, *1082*
tours of, *1082*
train travel to, *1082*
Villa Ciani, *1083*
Villa Favorita, *1085*
Luggage, *11*
Luxembourg, *777–790*
bicycling in, *781*
business hours in, *779*
camping in, *780*
castles in, *786*
churches in, *784, 785, 786*
climate of, *777–778*
currency of, *778*
customs in, *778*
Diekirch, *786*
dining in, *779, 786–788*
Echternach, *786*
expenses in, *778*
holidays in, *779*
hotels in, *779–780, 789–790*
language in, *779*
mail in, *779*
shopping in, *779*
telephones in, *779*
tipping in, *780*
tourist offices of, *4, 781*
train travel in, *780*
youth hostels in, *780*
Luxembourg City, *780–790*
air travel to, *780*
auto travel in, *781*
bicycling in, *781*
Bock promontory, *785*
bookstores in, *781*
buses in, *780*
Cathédrale Notre-Dame, *784*
chapel of St-Quiren, *785*
Citadelle du St-Ésprit, *782*
dining in, *784, 786–788*
embassies in, *781*
emergencies in, *781*
Grand Ducal Palace, *784*

hotels in, *789–780*
Maquette, *784*
Monument de la Solidarité Nationale, *782*
Musée National, *784*
Passerelle Viaduct, *782*
place de la Constitution, *782*
place Guillaume, *784*
shopping in, *786*
taxis in, *781*
tourist information in, *781*
tours of, *781–782*
train travel to, *780*
travel agencies in, *781*
Trois Tours, *785*
Luzern, *1074–1081*
air travel to, *1074*
Am Rhyn-Haus, *1076*
auto travel in, *1074*
boat travel in, *1075*
buses in, *1075*
casinos in, *1081*
dining in, *1079–1080*
emergencies, *1075*
Historisches Museum, *1076*
hotels in, *1080*
Jesuitenkirche, *1076*
Kapelbrücke, *1076*
Löwendenkmal, *1078*
Löwenplatz, *1078*
museums in, *1076*
music in, *1081*
nightlife in, *1081*
shopping in, *1078–1079*
Spreuerbrücke, *1076*
taxis in, *1075*
tourist information in, *1075*
tours of, *1075*
train travel to, *1074*
Verkehrshaus, *1078*

Madrid, *942–958*
airline office in, *944*
air travel to, *942*
auto travel in, *943*
bookstores in, *944*
bullfighting in, *952*
buses in, *942–943*
cafés in, *949, 957*
Calle Mayor, *949*
Casa Cisneros, *950*
Casa de la Villa, *959*

casino in, *958*
Chueca, *950*
Cibeles Fountain, *948*
Convento de las Descalzas Reales, *949*
dance in, *957*
dining in, *949, 950, 951, 952–954*
embassies in, *944*
emergencies in, *944*
environs of, *958–968*
Flamenco in, *958*
hotels in, *954–956*
Lavapiés Quarter, *951*
metro in, *943*
Monument to the Fallen Angel, *948*
Museo Thyssen-Bornemisza, *948*
nightlife in, *958*
opera in, *957*
Plaza de la Cibeles, *948*
Plaza de la Villa, *950*
Prado Museum, *945, 948*
Puerta de Alcalá, *948*
Puerta del Sol, *949*
Real Academia de San Fernando, *949*
Reina Sofia Arts Center, *945*
Retiro Park, *948*
Royal Carriage Museum, *950*
Royal Palace, *950*
shopping in, *951–952*
taxis in, *943*
theater in, *957–958*
tourist information in, *943–944*
tours of, *944–945*
train travel to, *942*
travel agencies in, *944*
Zarzuela in, *957*
Malta, *792–801. See also* Valletta
airline of, *27*
auto travel in, *793*
Blue Grotto, *799*
boat travel in, *794*
business hours in, *794*
Buskett, *799*
bus travel in, *793–794*
catacombs, *799*
churches in, *797, 799, 800*

climate of, *792*
currency of, *792–793*
customs in, *793*
dining in, *794–795, 800–801*
expenses in, *793*
Folklore Museum, *800*
Ggantija Prehistoric Temples, *800*
Ghar Dalam, *799*
Gozo, *800–801*
helicopter travel in, *794*
holidays in, *794*
hotels in, *795, 800–801*
Hypogeum, *799*
language in, *793*
mail in, *794*
Mdina, *800*
Mosta, *800*
museums in, *794, 796, 797, 800*
Qawra, *801*
Rabat, *799, 801*
St. Julians, *801*
Tarxien, *799*
taxis in, *794*
telephones in, *794*
tipping in, *795*
tourist offices of, *4*
Xaghra, *800*
Milan, *744–752*
air travel to, *744*
auto travel to, *745*
ballet in, *752*
buses in, *745*
cafés in, *746*
Castello Sforzesco, *746*
concerts in, *751*
dining in, *746, 748–750*
Duomo, *746*
Galleria, *746*
hotels in, *750–751*
opera in, *746, 751–752*
Piazza della Scala, *746*
Pinacoteca di Brera, *746*
San Lorenzo Maggiore, *748*
San Satiro, *748*
Santa Maria delle Grazie, *746*
Sant'Ambrogio, *746, 748*
shopping in, *748*

streetcars in, *745*
subways in, *745*
taxis in, *745*
Teatro alla Scala, *746*
tourist information
  in, *4, 745*
tours of, *745*
train travel to, *745*
Monaco, *322–325*
tourist information
  in, *4, 320*
Money, *11–12*
Munich, *344–360*
air travel to, *344*
Alte Peter, *352*
Alte Pinakothek, *351*
Altes Rathaus, *347*
Amalienburg, *352*
Asamkirche, *347, 350*
auto travel to, *344*
ballet in, *360*
bookstores in, *345*
Bürgersaal, *347*
bus travel to, *344*
concerts in, *359*
consulates in, *345*
dance in, *360*
dining in, *347, 350,*
  353–356
emergencies in, *345*
Englischer Garten,
  351
Feldherrnhalle, *350*
film, *360*
Frauenkirche, *347*
Hauptbahnhof, *346*
Haus der Kunst, *351*
Hertie, *346*
Hofgarten, *350*
hotels in, *356–359*
jazz clubs in, *360*
Justizpalast, *346*
Karlsplatz, *346*
Karlstor, *346*
Leopoldstrasse, *350*
Ludwigstrasse, *350*
Marienplatz, *347*
Marstallmuseum, *352*
Michaelskirche, *347*
Neue Pinakothek, *351*
Neues Rathaus, *347*
nightlife in, *360*
Olympic Park,
  351–352
opera in, *359*
public transportation
  in, *344–345*
Schloss
  Nymphenburg, *352*
Schwabing, *350*

shopping in, *352–353*
Siegestor, *350*
taxis in, *345*
theater in, *360*
Theatinerkirche, *350*
tourist information
  in, *345*
tours of, *345–346*
train travel to, *344*
travel agencies in,
  345
Viktualienmarkt, *350*
Museums
in Amsterdam, *569,*
  572–573, 574, 575,
  576
in Antwerp, *120*
in Athens, *529–530*
in Austria, *61, 68–69,*
  70, 71, 89
in Barcelona, *971,*
  974, 975–976
in Belgium, *105, 109,*
  120, 123, 125
in Berlin, *405, 409,*
  410, 412, 413
in Bern, *1091*
in Bratislava, *923*
in Bruges, *123, 125*
in Brussels, *105, 109*
in Bucharest, *904,*
  905
in Budapest, *609,*
  611, 612, 614
in Bulgaria, *137, 139,*
  145, 146, 151, 152
in Copenhagen, *197,*
  200, 202, 203
in Cork, *685*
in Cyprus, *159, 161,*
  166
in Czech Republic,
  176, 177, 185, 186
in Delft, *595*
in Denmark, *197,*
  200, 202, 203, 212,
  218, 219
in Dresden, *425, 426,*
  427
in Dublin, *660,*
  661–662, 664
in Edinburgh, *509,*
  510
in Finland, *243, 245,*
  250
in Florence, *722, 726,*
  727, 728, 729
in France, *301, 302,*
  303, 308, 309, 310,
  317, 321–322, 325

in Frankfurt, *366,*
  367
in Geneva, *1068*
in Germany, *351, 352,*
  383, 384, 385, 387
in Gibraltar, *1003*
in Great Britain, *483,*
  484, 489, 496, 497,
  500, 502, 507, 509,
  510
in Greece, *542, 543,*
  549, 555
in The Hague, *592,*
  593
in Hamburg, *373,*
  376, 377
in Helsinki, *235*
in Holland, *585, 586,*
  587, 588, 592, 593,
  596
in Hungary, *622, 625*
in Iceland, *637*
in Ireland, *675, 684*
in Istanbul, *1111*
in Italy, *701, 705,*
  706, 707, 709, 712,
  722, 723, 726, 727,
  728, 729, 737, 740,
  746, 755, 759, 760,
  761, 769
in Liechtenstein,
  1064, 1065
in Lisbon, *869, 871,*
  872, 873
in London, *454, 460,*
  461, 462–463, 467
in Lugano, *1083*
in Luxembourg, *782,*
  784
in Luzern, *1076*
in Madrid, *945, 948,*
  949, 950
in Malta, *796, 797,*
  800
in Nicosia, *159*
in Norway, *823, 824,*
  827, 828, 831, 832
in Oslo, *812, 813, 816,*
  817, 821
in Paris, *271, 275,*
  276, 278
in Poland, *853,*
  855–856
in Portugal, *874, 881,*
  882, 886,
in Prague, *176, 177*
in Reykjavík, *636*
in Romania, *912, 913*
in Rome, *701, 705,*
  706, 707, 712

in Salzburg, *83*
in Slovakia, *927, 928*
in Sofia, *137, 139*
in Spain, *961, 963,*
  989, 999
in Stockholm, *1025,*
  1028
in Sweden, *1036,*
  1037, 1038, 1042
in Toledo, *961, 963*
in Turkey, *1134*
in Tuscany, *737, 740*
in Uppsala, *1036,*
  1037, 1038
in Valletta, *796, 797*
in Venice, *755, 759,*
  760, 761
in Vienna, *68–69, 70,*
  71, 72, 73
in Warsaw, *843,*
  855–856
in York, *500, 502*
in Zürich, *1057,*
  1058
Music, *8–9, See also*
  Opera

Natural history tours,
  9
Netherlands. *See*
  Holland
Nicosia, *159–160*
Archbishop Makarios
  III Cultural
  Foundation, *159*
Byzantine Art
  Museum, *159*
Cyprus Folk Art
  Museum, *159*
Cyprus Museum,
  159–160
dining in, *163*
Greek War of
  Independence
  Gallery, *159*
hotels in, *164*
Laiki Yitonia, *159*
Leventis Museum,
  159
Municipal Gardens,
  160
Municipal Theatre,
  160
Museum of the
  National Struggle,
  159
St. John's Cathedral,
  159
Tripiotis Church,
  159

Norway, *803–834 See also* Oslo
airline of, *27*
air travel in, *42, 807*
Ålesund, *831, 832*
Åmot, *827*
Arendal, *823–824, 825*
Åsgårdstrand, *823*
auto travel in, *806, 822, 830*
Bergen, *826–829*
Bergenhus, *828*
bicycling in, *45–46*
Bodø, *831, 833*
Bragernes Hill, *823*
business hours in, *808*
bus travel in, *807, 822*
camping in, *809*
Christiansholm Fort, *824*
climate in, *805*
currency of, *805*
customs in, *805*
Dalen, *827*
dining in, *808–809, 829, 831, 832–833*
Drammen, *823, 825, 826*
Egersund, *824*
Eidsborg, *827*
expenses in, *805*
ferries in, *807*
Flekkefjord, *824*
Hammerfest, *832, 833*
Hanseatisk Museum, *828*
Heddal, *827*
holidays in, *808*
hotels in, *809–810, 829*
Jæren, *824*
Kardemomme By, *824*
Kinsarvik, *828, 829*
Kirkenes, *830*
Kongsberg, *829*
Kragerø, *823*
Kristiansand, *824, 825*
language in, *806*
Larvik, *823, 825*
Lillehammer, *817*
Lofoten islands, *831*
maelstrom in, *831*
mail in, *808*
Mandal, *824*
Maritime Museum (Larvik), *823*
Morgedal, *827*
museums in, *808, 812, 813, 816, 817,*

821, 823, 824, 827, 828, 831, 832
Narvik, *831, 833*
Nidaros Cathedral, *831*
Norheimsund, *828*
Olav Bjåland's Museum, *827*
rentals in, *809–810*
Risør, *823*
Røldal, *828*
Ryfylke fjords, *825*
Sandefjord, *823, 825*
sea travel in, *830*
Seljord, *827*
shopping in, *808*
Stavanger, *824–825, 826*
Stiftsgården, *831*
Svolvær, *833*
telephones in, *807–808*
tipping in, *810*
Tønsberg, *823*
Tønsberghus, *823*
tourist information in, *4, 811, 823, 830*
tours of, *811, 822*
train travel in, *39, 40, 806–807, 822, 830*
Troldhaugen, *828*
Tromsø, *833*
Trondheim, *831, 833–834*
Tvedestrand, *823*
Utne, *829*
youth hostels in, *809*
zoo, *824*

Older travelers, *25–26*
Opera
in Amsterdam, *582*
in Athens, *538–539*
in Barcelona, *981*
in Berlin, *420*
in Brussels, *116*
in Bucharest, *910*
in Budapest, *619*
in Copenhagen, *209*
in Dresden, *424–425*
in Frankfurt, *366*
in Geneva, *1068*
in Germany, *359*
in Helsinki, *235*
in Lisbon, *874*
in London, *462, 463, 479*
in Madrid, *957*
in Milan, *751–752*
in Munich, *359*

in Paris, *279–280, 281*
in Prague, *183*
in Rome, *718*
in Salzburg, *88*
in Stockholm, *1034–1035*
in Venice, *766*
in Vienna, *69, 77–78*
in Warsaw, *849*
Oslo, *810–821*
air travel to, *810*
Aker Brygge, *813*
Akershus Castle, *813*
bookstores in, *811*
buses to, *810*
concerts, *821*
Contemporary Art Museum, *813*
dining in, *813, 816, 818–819*
Domkirken, *813*
Ekebergseletta park, *817*
embassies in, *811*
emergencies in, *811*
forests in, *817*
Framhuset, *816*
Historisk Museum, *812*
Holmenkollen ski jump, *817*
hotels in, *819–821*
Karl Johans gate, *812*
Kon-Tiki Museum, *816*
Lillehammer, *817*
mail in, *811*
Munch-Museet, *817*
Nasjonalgalleriet, *812*
Nationalteatret, *813, 821*
nightlife in, *821*
Norsk Folkemuseum, *816*
Oslo Ladegård, *817*
post office in, *811*
public transportation in, *810*
Rådhuset, *816*
shopping in, *818*
Slottet, *812*
Storting, *813*
taxis in, *811*
tourist information in, *811*
tours of, *811–812*
Tøyen, *817*
train travel to, *810*
travel agencies in, *811*

Universitet, *812*
Vikingskiphuset, *816*
Oxford, *484–486*
Ashmolean Museum, *484*
Balliol College, *484*
Christ Church, *484*
dining in, *484, 491–492*
hotels in, *492*
Magdalen College, *484*
Oxford Story, *484*
St. Edmund Hall, *484*
Sheldonian Theatre, *484*
tourist information in, *481*

Palaces. *See also* Castles
in Amsterdam, *572*
in Bratislava, *923–924*
in Brussels, *104, 105, 108*
in Budapest, *627*
in Copenhagen, *200, 204*
in France, *294, 295, 309, 325*
in Great Britain, *484, 486, 507, 509*
in Holland, *585, 592, 593*
in Istanbul, *1110, 1114*
in Italy, *701, 706, 711, 712, 723, 758*
in London, *455, 458, 462*
in Luxembourg City, *784*
in Malta, *797, 799*
in Munich, *352*
in Oslo, *812, 831*
in Paris, *274, 280*
in Portugal, *874, 882, 887*
in Prague, *177*
in Spain, *950, 963, 971, 986*
in Stockholm, *1024, 1028*
in Venice, *758*
in Vienna, *68, 71, 72*
in Warsaw, *843, 846*
Paris, *265–292*
air travel to, *265*
Arc de Triomphe,

276–277
Arènes de Lutèce, 274
auto travel to, 265
Beaubourg, 280
boat tours of, 270
Bois de Boulogne, 276
Bois de Vincennes, 281–282
bookstores in, 267
Bourse du Commerce, 280
buses in, 266–267
bus travel to, 265
Canal St-Martin, 282
Centre Pompidou, 280
Champs-Elysées, 277, 278
Château de Vincennes, 282
Chinatown, 283
Conciergerie, 281
dance in, 290
dining in, 275, 279, 283–286
Eglise de la Madeleine, 279
Eglise St-Séverin, 271
Eiffel Tower, 276
embassies in, 267
emergencies in, 267
film in, 290
Galeries Lafayette, 280
gardens in, 274, 277
Grand Palais, 277
guillotine, 277
Les Halles, 280
Hôtel de Cluny, 271
Hôtel des Invalides, 275
Hôtel de Ville, 281
Hôtel Drouot, 282
hotels in, 286–290
Ile St-Louis, 271
Jardin des Plantes, 274
Jardin des Tuileries, 277
Jeu de Paume, 277
L'Etoile, 277
L'Etoile (Place Charles de Gaulle), 277
Louvre, 278
Louvre des Antiquaires, 280

Maison de Victor Hugo, 281
Marais quarter, 281
métro in, 266
Montmarte, 278–279
Moulin Rouge cabaret, 279
Musée de l'Armée, 275
Musée des Plans-Reliefs, 275
Musée d'Orsay, 275
Musée Marmottan, 276
Museum of Modern Art, 280
Musée Picasso, 280–281
Musée Rodin, 276
museums in, 271, 278
nightlife in, 291–292
Notre-Dame Cathedral, 271
Opéra, 279–280
opera in, 279–280, 290
Opéra Comique, 290
Opéra de la Bastille, 281
Orangerie, 277
Palais Bourbon, 275
Palais de Justice, 281
Palais de la Découverte, 277
Palais du Luxembourg, 274
Palais-Royal, 280
Panthéon, 271
Père Lachaise, 282
Petit Palais, 277
place de la Bastille, 281
place des Vosges, 281
place du tertre, 279
place Pigalle, 279
place Vendôme, 279
Pont Alexandre III, 275
Printemps, 280
rue de la Paix, 279
Sacré-Coeur, 278–279
Sainte-Chapelle, 281
St-Etienne du Mont, 274
St-Eustache, 280
St-Germain-des-Prés, 275
Saint-Paul-Saint-Louis, 281
St-Sulpice, 274

shopping in, 280, 283
Sorbonne, 271
square du Vert Galant, 281
taxis in, 267
theater in, 290
Tour de l'Horioge, 281
tourist information in, 267
tours of, 267, 270
train travel to, 265
travel agencies in, 267
Val de Grâce, 274
Passports and visas, 13–14
Poland, 836–857. *See also* Gdańsk; Kraków; Warsaw
airline of, 27
air travel in, 839, 854
Auschwitz, 852
auto travel in, 838–839
business hours in, 840
bus travel in, 839, 854
churches in, 271, 274, 275, 279, 280, 281
climate of, 836
currency of, 836–837
customs in, 838
Częstochowa, 852, 853
dining in, 840, 856–857
Elbgąg, 856
expenses in, 837–838
Grunwald, site of battle of, 856
holidays in, 840
hotels in, 841, 856–857
language in, 838
mail in, 840
Malbork, 854–855
museums in, 838, 840
Olsztyn, 855, 856
Olsztynek, 855
Ostróda, 857
Płock, 854
shopping in, 846–847
Sopot, 855
telephones in, 839
tipping in, 841
Toruń, 854
tourist information in, 4, 842, 850, 854
tours of, 842, 850,

854
train travel in, 839, 850, 854
visas for, 838
Wieliczka, 852
Portugal, 859–892. *See also* Lisbon
airline of, 27
air travel in, 863, 885
Albufeira, 887, 889
Algarve, 884–892
Almansil, 887
Alvor, 889–890
Armação de Pêrá, 887, 890
auto travel in, 37–38, 862–863, 885
beaches of, 188
bicycling in, 44–45, 864
boat travel in, 864
boat travel to, 34
Boca do Inferno, 881
buses in, 42–43, 863, 885
business hours, 865
Cabo da Roca, 881
Cabo São Vincente, 889
camping in, 866
Cascais, 881–882, 883
casino, 880
Castelo dos Mouros, 882
churches in, 872, 881, 886–887, 888
climate of, 861
currency of, 861
customs in, 861–862
dining in, 865–866, 881–882, 883–884, 889–892
Estói, 887
Estoril, 880–881, 883–884
expenses in, 861
fairs in, 882
Faro, 886–887, 890
Ferragudo, 888
festivals in, 882
holidays in, 865
hotels in, 866, 883–884, 889–892
Lagoa, 887
Lagos, 887, 890–891
language in, 862
Loulé, 887
mail in, 864
Monchique, 891
Monserrate, 881

Portugal *(continued)*
Monte Gordo, *886, 891*
Museu Arqueologia, *888*
Museu Conde de Castro Guimarães, *881*
Museu do Brinquedo, *882*
Museu do Etnografia Regional, *886*
Museu Martimo, *886*
museums in, *865, 869, 871, 872, 873, 874, 886*
Museu Municipal, *886*
Olhão, *886*
Olhos d'Agua, *891*
Palácio do Visconde de Estói, *887*
Palácio Nacional de Pena, *882*
Palácio Nacional de Queluz, *882–883*
Palácio Nacional de Sintra, *882*
parks in, *881*
Parque do Marachel Carmona, *881*
Penedo, *881*
Portimão, *888*
Praia de Rocha, *888, 891–892*
Quarteira, *887*
Queluz, *879, 882–883, 884*
Riviera, *879–884*
Roman ruins in, *887*
Sagres, *888, 892*
Santa Barbara de Nexe, *892*
sea travel to, *29–30*
Serra de Sintra, *881*
shopping in, *864–865*
Silves, *887–888*
Sintra, *879, 882, 884*
Tavira, *886–887*
telephones in, *864*
tipping in, *866–867*
tourist information in, *4, 880, 885*
tours of, *879*
train travel in, *40, 863, 879, 885–886*
Vale de Lobo, *892*
Vilamoura, *887, 892*
Vila Real de Santo António, *886, 892*
zoo, *881*
Prague, *173–183*
air travel to, *173*

ballet in, *183*
Bedřich Smetana museum, *176*
Betlémeska kaple, *176*
bookstores in, *174*
buses in, *174*
Charles Bridge, *176*
Chram svatého Mikuléše, *177*
Clock Tower, *176*
concerts in, *182*
dining in, *180–181*
embassies in, *174*
emergencies in, *174*
history of, *175*
hotels in, *181–182*
Hradčany (Prague Castle), *177*
Kafka, *176, 177, 180*
Královský palác (Royal Palace), *177*
Letenské Sady, *177*
Loreto, *177*
Národní Muzeum, *176*
nightlife in, *183*
Old Jewish Quarter, *176*
opera in, *183*
puppet shows in, *183*
shopping in, *180*
Staroměstske náměští, *176*
Státní židowské múzeum, *176*
subways in, *174*
taxis in, *174*
theater in, *183*
tourist information in, *174*
tours of, *175*
train travel to, *174*
Václavské náměští, *176*
Vyšehrad Castle, *177*

Rail passes, *20–21*
Rail tours, *9*
Rentals
of autos, *18–20*
of homes and villas, *21–22*
Reykjavík, *632–638*
air travel to, *632*
Arbjærsafn, *634*
Arnarhóll Hill, *634*
Ásgrímur Jónsson Museum, *636*
Asmundur Sveinsson Gallery, *634*

Austurvollŭr, *634*
Bernhöfstorfa, *634*
boat travel to, *632*
bookstores in, *633*
buses in, *633*
cathedral, *634*
coffee shops in, *634*
dining in, *636, 637–638*
Einar Jónsson Museum, *636*
embassies in, *633*
emergencies in, *633*
Hallgrímskirkja, *636*
hotels in, *638*
Kjarvalsstáir gallery, *636*
Museum of Natural History, *634*
National Museum, *636–637*
National Theatre, *636*
Nordic House, *636*
Opera, *636*
Perlan, *636*
shopping in, *637*
taxis in, *633*
tourist information in, *633*
tours of, *633*
travel agencies in, *633*
Romania, *894–914.*
See also Bucharest
airline of, *27*
air travel in, *899*
auto travel in, *898–899, 911*
Babadag, *912*
Black Sea Coast of, *910–914*
boat travel in, *899, 911*
business hours in, *900*
bus travel in, *899, 911*
Callatis, *913*
camping in, *901*
churches in, *904*
climate of, *896–897*
Constanţa, *913*
Crişan, *914*
currency of, *897*
customs in, *897–898*
Danube Delta, *912*
dining in, *900, 913–914*
expenses in, *897*
holidays in, *900*
hostels in, *901*

hotels in, *900–901, 913–914*
Istria, *912*
language in, *898*
mail in, *899*
Mamaia, *912*
Mangalia, *913*
museums in, *900, 904, 905, 912, 913*
rentals in, *901*
Roman ruins in, *913*
spas in, *913*
telephones in, *899*
tipping in, *901*
tourist information in, *4, 902, 911–912*
tours of, *903, 911*
train travel in, *899*
Tulcea, *912*
visas for, *897*
Roman ruins
in Austria, *71*
in Bulgaria, *145–146, 151, 152*
in Cyprus, *162*
in France, *310*
in Germany, *384, 386, 387*
in Great Britain, *489*
in Hungary, *621*
in Italy, *710, 711, 740*
in Portugal, *887*
in Romania, *913*
in Spain, *987*
in Turkey, *1123, 1125, 1129, 1131*
Rome, *697–719*
air travel to, *697*
Aracoeli, *701*
Arch of Constantine, *704*
Augusteo, *707*
auto travel to, *698*
Baths of Caracalla, *704*
bicycling in, *699*
bookstores in, *700*
buses in, *699*
bus travel to, *698*
cafés in, *706*
Campidoglio, *701*
Campo dei Fiori, *711*
Castel Sant'Angelo, *707*
Church of the Gesù, *710*
Church of Santa Maria dela Concezione, *706*
Circus Maximus, *704*

Colosseum, *704*
consulates in, *699*
dining in, *705, 710,*
  711, 713–716
emergencies in, *699*
Fabricio Bridge, *712*
Fontana di Trevi, *705*
Forum, *701, 704*
Fountain of the
  Barcaccia, *705*
Fountain of the Four
  Rivers, *711*
Fountain of the
  Tartarughe, *711*
Galleria Borghese,
  706
Galleria Doria
  Pamphii, *712*
Galleria Nazionale di
  Arte Antica, *706*
hotels in, *706,*
  716–718
Keats and Shelley
  Memorial House,
  705
metro in, *698–699*
mopeds in, *699*
Museo Capitolino,
  701
Museo Nazionale di
  Villa Giulia, *712*
nightlife in, *718–719*
opera in, *718*
Ostia Antica, *712*
Palatine Hill, *704*
Palazzo Barberini,
  706
Palazzo dei
  Conservatori, *701*
Palazzo Farnese, *711*
Palazzo Senatorio,
  701
Palazzo Spada, *711*
Pantheon, *710*
Pasetto, *707*
Piazza Barberini, *705*
Piazza del Popolo, *704*
Piazza di Spagna, *705*
Piazza Farnese, *711*
Piazza Navona, *711*
Piazza San Pietro,
  707
Piazza Venezia, *701*
Ponte Sant'Angelo,
  707
Porta Pinciana, *706*
Roman Forum, *701,*
  704
St. Peter's Basilica,
  707–708

St. Peter's Square,
  707
San Luigi dei
  Francesi, *710–711*
Sant'Agnese in
  Agone, *711*
Santa Maria del
  Popolo, *704–705*
Santa Maria Sopra
  Minerva, *710*
shopping in, *705,*
  712–713
Sistine Chapel, *709*
Spanish Steps, *705*
taxis in, *699*
Teatro di Marcello,
  711
Terrazza del Pincio,
  712
Tiberina Island, *712*
tourist information
  in, *699*
tours of, *700*
train travel to, *698*
travel agencies in,
  700
Trinità dei Monti, *705*
Triton, *705*
Vatican City, *707*
Vatican Gardens, *709*
Vatican Museums,
  707, 709–710
Vatican Palace, *707,*
  709
Villa Borghese, *706*

Salzburg, *81–88*
air travel to, *81*
Alter Markt, *85*
auto travel in, *82*
Baroque Museum, *83*
Bürgerspital, *83*
buses in, *82*
bus travel to, *81–82*
Carolino Augusteum
  Museum, *83*
dining in, *85, 86–87*
Dom, *83*
Festspielhaus, *83*
Festung
  Hohensalzburg, *85*
fiakers in, *82*
Franzikanerkirche,
  83
hotels in, *87–88*
Kollegialitätskirche,
  83
Landerstheater, *83*
Mirabell gardens, *83*
Mozarteum, *83*

Mozart's birthplace,
  85
opera in, *88*
Residenz, *85*
Residenzgalerie, *85*
St. George's Chapel,
  85
Schloss Hellblrunn,
  85
Schloss Mirabell, *83*
Stiftskirche St.
  Peter, *85*
taxis in, *82*
theater in, *88*
Tiegarten, *86*
tourist information
  in, *82*
tours of, *82*
train travel to, *81*
Wasserspiele, *86*
Saxony and
  Thuringia, *421–433*
Albertinum, *425*
Altes Rathaus, *427*
auto travel in, *423*
boat travel in, *423*
Buchenwald, *430*
bus travel in, *423*
Deutsche Hygiene
  Museum, *426*
dining in, *427, 428,*
  430–433
Dresden, *424–427,*
  431
Exhibition Pavilion,
  428
Goethehaus, *429*
Grassimuseum, *428*
Herderkirche, *430*
Historischer
  Friedhof, *430*
history of, *421–423*
hotels in, *430–433*
Katholische
  Hofkirche, *426*
Kirms-Krackow
  house, *430*
Leipzig, *427–428,*
  431–432
Museum der
  Bildenden Kunste,
  428
Nikolaikirche, *428*
opera in, *424, 428*
Schillerhaus, *429*
Schloss Belvedere,
  430
Schloss Pillnitz, *426*
Semper Opera house,
  424

Sempergalerie, *425*
Stadtschloss, *429*
streetcars in, *423*
taxis in, *423*
Thomaskirche, *427*
tourist information
  in, *424*
tours in, *424*
train travel in, *423*
Weimar, *428–431,*
  432–433
Wittumspalais, *429*
Zwinger, *425*
Scotland. *See* Great
  Britain
Sea travel
from North America,
  29–30
from United
  Kingdom, *34–35*
Ship travel
from United Kingdom
  to Europe, *34–35*
within Europe, *43–44*
Singles, tours for, *9*
Slovakia, *916–929.*
  See also Bratislava
airline of, *27*
air travel to, *926*
auto travel in,
  918–919
Bardejov, *928*
Bodružal, *928*
Bratislava, *921–925*
buses in, *919, 926*
business hours in, *919*
churches in, *923, 927,*
  928
climate of, *916, 918*
currency of, *918*
customs in, *918*
dining in, *919–920,*
  928–929
expenses in, *918*
history of, *916*
holidays in, *919*
hotels in, *920–921,*
  928–929
Hvervartov, *928*
language in, *918*
Levoča, *927*
mail in, *919*
museums in, *918,*
  924, 927
Museum of the Tatra
  National Park, *927*
Poprad, *927*
Prešov, *928*
shopping in, *919*
Smokovec, *927*

Slovakia *(continued)*
Spiš, *927*
Spiš Castle, *928*
Spišská Sobota, *927*
Štrbské Pleso, *927*
Sv. Jakub, *928*
Sv. Juraj, *927*
Svidník, *928*
Tatranská Lomnica, *927*
telephones in, *919*
tipping in, *921*
tourist information in, *2, 927*
tours of, *926*
train travel in, *39–40*
train travel to, *919, 926*
visas for, *918*
Zilina, *927*
Zochová Chata, *927*
Sofia, *135–143*
air travel to, *135*
art galleries in, *143*
auto rentals in, *136*
auto travel to, *136*
Banya Bashi Djamiya, *140*
Borisova Grodina, *139*
Boyana, *140*
buses in, *136*
casino in, *143*
Crypt Museum, *139*
dining in, *140–141*
Dragalevci Monastery, *140*
embassies in, *136*
emergencies in, *136*
hotels in, *141–143*
Hram-pametnik Alexander Nevski, *139*
Mavsolei Georgi Dimitrov, *137, 139*
Natzionalen Archeologicheski Musei, *137*
Natzionalen Dvoretz na Kulturata, *139*
Natzionalen Etnografski Musei, *139*
Natzionalen Istoricheski Musei, *137*
Natzionalna Hudozhestvena Galeria, *139*
nightlife in, *143*
Partiyniyat Dom, *137*

Plodshtad Sveta Nedelya, *137*
puppet theater in, *143*
Rotonda Sveti Georgi, *137*
shopping in, *140*
taxis in, *136*
tourist information in, *136*
tours of, *136–137*
train travel to, *135*
Tsentralen Universalen Magazin, *139*
Tsentralni Hali, *140*
Tzarkva Sveta Nedelya, *137*
Tzarkva Sveta Nikolai, *139*
Tzarkva Sveta Sovia, *139*
Spain, *931–1011. See also* Barcelona; Gibraltar; Madrid; Toledo
airline of, *27*
air travel in, *42, 936, 937, 997, 1001*
Alba de Tormes, *964*
Alcaicería, *990*
Alcazaba, *999*
Alcázar (Segovia), *963*
Alcázar (Seville), *986*
Alhambra, *990–992*
Alpujarras, *992*
Andalusia, *982–996*
auto rentals in, *18–20*
auto travel in, *935–936, 982, 1001*
Ávila, *963, 965*
Baena, *989*
Barrio Santa Cruz, *986*
Basilica of San Vicente, *964*
Benalmádena, *999*
bicycling in, *44–45*
boat travel from United Kingdom to, *34*
bullfighting in, *987, 996, 1000*
buses in, *42–43, 937, 959, 982–983, 997, 1001*
business hours in, *938*
camping in, *941*
Canary Islands,

1008–1011
Carmona, *987, 992*
Casares, *1000*
churches in, *960, 961, 962, 963–964, 971, 974, 975, 984, 987, 990, 1000, 1002, 1003*
climate of, *934*
Córdoba, *982–983, 987–990, 993*
Costa del Sol, *997–1008*
currency of, *934*
dining in, *939–940, 965–968, 992–996, 1010–1011*
Ecija, *987*
El Escorial, *965–966*
El Hierro, *1010*
Estepona, *998, 1000, 1004*
expenses in, *934–935*
Flamenco in, *996*
Fuengirola, *998, 999*
Fuerteventura, *1010*
Generalife, *992*
Gibraltar, *998, 1001–1008*
Giralda, *986*
Gran Canaria, *1009, 1010*
Granada, *982, 983, 990–992, 993–994, 996*
La Granja, *962*
holidays in, *938–939*
hostels in, *940*
hotels in, *940–941, 965–968, 992–996, 1010–1011*
Hunting Museum, *963*
language of, *935*
La Gomera, *1010*
La Palma, *1010*
Lanzarote, *1009–1010, 1011*
mail in, *938*
Málaga, *998, 999, 1004–1005*
Marbella, *998, 999–1000, 1005–1006*
María Luisa park, *987*
Mijas, *999, 1006–1007*
Moorish, *982–996*
mosques in, *982, 986*
Museum of Bullfighting, *989, 1000*
museums in, *938,

945, 948, 949, 950, 961, 963, 971, 974, 989, 990, 999, 1003*
Navacerrada pass, *962*
Nerja, *998–999, 1007*
nightlife in, *996*
Ojén, *1000*
Palace of Riofrio, *963*
paradors in, *940–941*
parks in, *948, 963, 987*
Puente Nuevo, *1000*
Puerto de Sotogrande, *1001*
Ronda, *998, 1000, 1007*
Salamanca, *964, 966*
Segovia, *962, 966–967*
Seville, *982, 983, 984–987, 994–996*
shopping in, *938*
Sierra Nevada, *992*
synagogues in, *961, 989*
telephones in, *937*
Tenerife, *1008*
tipping in, *941*
Toledo, *960, 967–968*
Torre de Oro, *987*
Torremolinos, *998, 999, 1008*
tourist information in, *5, 960, 983–984, 998*
tours of, *5, 983, 997*
train travel in, *39–40, 936, 959, 982–983, 997*
Trevélez, *992*
Valley of the Fallen, *962*
villas in, *941*
Spas
in Bohemia, *183–186*
in Germany, *396*
in Hungary, *623*
in Portugal, *888*
Sports tours, *9*
Stockholm, *1020–1036*
air travel to, *1020–1021*
auto travel to, *1021*
bars in, *1035*
Bergranska Botanical Garden, *1029*
bookstores in, *1022*
buses in, *1021–1022*
bus travel to, *1021*

City Hall, *1024*
concerts, *1034*
dining in, *1025*,
1030–1031
Djurgården, *1025*
embassies in, *1022*
emergencies in, *1022*
Fjäderholmarna, *1029*
Galma Stan, *1024*
Gripsholm Castle,
1025
Gröna Lund Tivoli,
1025
hotels in, *1031–1034*
Kaknas TV Tower,
1029
Kungsträgården,
1024
Museum of National
Antiquities, *1025*
nightlife in, *1035*
Nordic Museum, *1025*
opera in, *1034–1035*
Riddarholm Church,
1024
Royal Armory, *1024*
Royal Palace, *1024*
shopping in,
1029–1030
Skansen, *1025*
Skokloster Palace,
1028
Stockholm
archipelago, *1029*
subways in,
1021–1022
taxis in, *1022*
theater in, *1035*
tourist information
in, *1022*
tours of, *1023*
train travel in, *1022*
train travel to, *1021*
travel agencies in,
1022
Treasury, *1024*
Vasamuseet, *1025*
zoo, *1025*
Student travel, 22
Sweden, *1012–1044.*
See also Stockholm;
Uppsala
airline of, 27
air travel in, *41–42,*
1017, 1040
auto travel in, *1016,*
1040
bicycling in, *44–45,*
1017
boat travel in, *1017*

boat travel to, *34–35*
business hours in,
1018
bus travel in, *1017*
camping in, *1020*
churches in, *1024*
climate of, *1015*
currency of, *1015*
customs in,
1015–1016
Dalarna, *1038*
dining in, *1019,*
1043–1044
Emigrants' House,
1042
expenses in, *1015*
Falun, *1036,*
1037–1038
folklore district of,
1036–1040
Glass Country of,
1040–1044
Göteborgskortet,
1040
Gothenburg, *1041,*
1043–1044
holidays in,
1018–1019
hotels in, *1019–1020,*
1043–1044
Jönköping, *1042, 1044*
Kalmar, *1043, 1044*
Lake Hjälmaren,
1038
Lake Siljan, *1038*
Lake Vattern, *1042*
language in, *1016*
Ludvika, *1036, 1038,*
1039
mail in, *1018*
Matchstick Museum,
1042
Mora, *1036, 1038,*
1039
museums in, *1018,*
1025, 1028, 1036,
1037, 1038, 1042
Nusnäs, *1038*
Örebro, *1036, 1039*
Rättvik, *1036, 1038*
Riddersberg, *1042*
Säter, *1037*
shopping in, *1018,*
1042
Sundborn, *1038*
Tällberg, *1038, 1039*
telephones in, *1017*
tipping in, *1020*
tourist information
in, *5, 1022, 1040*

tours of, *1040*
Trädgärdsföreningen,
1042
train travel in, *39–40,*
1016–1017, 1040
Växjö, *1044*
Wadköping, *1038*
west coast of,
1040–1044
Switzerland,
1046–1098. See also
Bern; Geneva;
Lugano; Luzern;
Zürich
airline of, 27
air travel in, *1049,*
1094–1095
auto rentals in, *18–20*
auto travel in,
1049–1050, 1095
bicycling in, *44–45,*
1051
boat travel in, *1051*
business hours in,
1052
bus travel in, *1051*
climate of, *1048*
currency of, *1048*
customs in, *1049*
dining in, *1052–1053,*
1096–1097
emergencies in, *1095*
expenses in,
1048–1049
festivals in, *1081*
gardens in, *1083*
holidays in, *1052*
hotels in, *1053–1054,*
1097–1098
language in, *1049*
Luzern, *1074–1081*
mail in, *1052*
Matterhorn, *1094*
rental chalets in,
1054
shopping in, *1052*
telephones in,
1051–1052
tipping in, *1054*
tourist information
in, *5, 1055, 1095*
train travel in, *39–40,*
1050, 1051, 1095
Zermatt, *1094–1098*

Toledo, *958–961*
Cambrón Gate, *961*
cathedral in, *960*
Chapel of Santo
Tomé, *961*

El Greco's house, *961*
Hill of the Angels,
960
Hospital de Tavera,
961
Museum of Santa
Cruz, *961*
Plaza Zocodover, *960*
San Juan de los
Reyes, *961*
Santa María la
Blanca, *961*
Sephardic Museum,
961
Sinagoga del
Tránsito, *961*
Traveler's checks,
11–12
**Trip cancellation
insurance,** *17–18*
Trip insurance, *17–18*
Turkey, *1100–1135.*
See also Istanbul
Acropolis, *1123*
Aegean Coast,
1121–1127
airline of, 27
air travel in, *1104,*
1127
Aksaray, *1132*
Ankara, *1132*
Antalya, *1130*
Aphrodisias, *1125*
Aspendos, *1133*
auto travel in, *1103,*
1121, 1127, 1132
Avanos, *1134*
Ayvalik, *1122*
Bergama, *1121, 1125*
boat travel in, *1104,*
1127
Bodrum, *1128,*
1130–1131
Bursa, *1121*
buses in, *42–43,*
1103–1104, 1121,
1132
business hours in,
1105
Çankkale, *1122*
Cappadocia,
1132–1135
Castle of St. Peter,
1128
Central Anatolia,
1132–1135
Çesme, *1121, 1126*
churches in, *1124,*
1128
climate of, *1100, 1102*

Turkey (*continued*)
currency of, *1102*
customs in, *1102*
Dalaman, *1127*
Dalyan, *1129*, *1131*
Datça, *1127*
Derinkuyu, *1134*
Didyma, *1124*
dining in, *1106*,
   1125–1127,
   1130–1132,
   1134–1135
Ephesus, *1123–1124*
Ephesus Museum,
   1124
expenses in, *1102*
Göreme, *1134*
Göreme Open-Air
   Museum, *1134*
Greek ruins in, *1129*
Gulf of Edremit, *1122*
Halikarnas, *1128*
Hierapolis, *1125*
holidays in, *1105*
hotels in, *1106–1107*,
   1125–1127,
   1130–1132,
   1134–1135
House of Mary, *1124*
İzmir, *1122*, *1123*
Kadifekale, *1123*
Kalkan, *1129*, *1131*
Kaş, *1129*, *1131*
Kaymakli, *1134*
Kayseri, *1134*
Kekòva, *1129*
Kemer, *1130*
Knidos, *1129*
Konya, *1133*, *1134*
Köyceğiz, *1131*
Kuşadasi, *1123*, *1126*
language in, *1102*
mail in, *1104–1105*
Marmaris, *1129*
Mediterranean Coast,
   1127–1132
Miletus, *1124*
mosques in, *1116*, *1122*
museums in, *1105*,
   1114, *1124*, *1128*
Museum of
   Underwater
   Archaeology, *1128*
Nevşehir, *1134*
Olü Deniz, *1129*,
   1131–1132
Pammukale,
   1124–1125
Patara, *1129*
Pergamum, *1123*

Perge, *1133*
Phaselis, *1130*
Pinara, *1129*
Priene, *1124*
Roman ruins in, *1123*,
   1125, *1129*, *1133*
Selçuk, *1124*
shopping in, *1105*
Sultan Han, *1134*
taxis in, *1132*
telephones in, *1104*
Temple of Athena,
   1124
Termessos, *1133*
tipping in, *1107*
tourist information
   in, *5*, *1109*, *1121*,
   1127, *1132*
tours of, *1109*, *1121*,
   1127, *1132*
train travel in, *39–40*,
   1103, *1132*
Troy, *1122*
Turunç, *1129*
Ulu Cami, *1122*
Uludağ, *1122*
Ürgüp, *1134–1135*
Xanthos, *1129*

United Kingdom. *See*
   Great Britain
Uppsala, *1036–1040*
cathedral, *1036*
Cathedral Museum,
   1036
dining in, *1039–1040*
hotels in, *1039–1040*
Uppsala Castle, *1036*

Valleta, *795–799*
air travel to, *795*
Armoury of the
   Knights, *797*
boat travel to,
   795–796
buses to, *795*
City Gate, *796*
dining in, *798*
embassies in, *796*
emergencies in, *796*
Fort St. Elmo, *797*
Government Craft
   Center, *797*
Grand Master's
   Palace, *797*
Hospital of the
   Order, *797*
hotels in, *798–799*
National Museum of
   Archaeology, *796*

National Museum of
   Fine Art, *797–798*
St. John's
   Co-Cathedral, *797*
taxis in, *795*
tourist information
   in, *796*
tours of, *796*
travel agencies in,
   796
Upper Barracca
   Gardens, *797*
War Museum, *797*
Venice, *752–766*
Accademia Gallery,
   759, *760*
air travel to, *752*
auto travel to,
   752–753
Basilica di San
   Marco, *758*
boat travel in,
   753–754
bus travel to, *753*
Campanile di San
   Marco, *758*
concerts, *766*
consulates in, *754*
dining in, *758*,
   762–763
emergencies in, *754*
Frari, *759*
Ghetto, *761*
gondolas in, *754*
Grand Canal, *760*
hotels in, *763–765*
Madonna dell'Orto,
   761
Museo Correr, *755*
Museo Ebraico, *761*
museums in, *761*
nightlife in, *766*
opera in, *766*
Palazzo Ducale, *758*
Palazzo Venier dei
   Leoni, *761*
Peggy Guggenheim
   Museum, *760*
Piazza San Marco,
   755
Rialto Bridge, *760*
San Moisè, *758*
San Pietro, *761*
Santa Maria dei
   Miracoli, *760*
Santa Maria del
   Giglio, *758*
Santa Maria
   Formosa, *759*
San Zanipolo, *759*,

   760
Scuoli di San Rocco,
   759
shopping in, *759*, *761*
taxis in, *752*
tourist information
   in, *754*
tours of, *754–755*
Traghettos in,
   753–754
train travel to, *752*
travel agencies in,
   754
Vaporettos in, *753*
water taxis in, *753*
Video recorders,
   15–16
Videotape, *15–16*
Vienna, *62–79*
air travel to, *62–63*
Albertina, *65*
Am Hof, *71*
Anker-Uhr, *71*
Augustinerkirche, *65*
auto travel to, *63*
Bermuda Triangle,
   72–73
boat travel to, *63*
bookstores in, *64*
buses in, *63*
bus travel to, *63*
Café Central, *70*
dining in, *68*, *69*, *70*,
   71, *73–75*
Doll and Toy
   Museum, *73*
Donner Brunner, *70*
embassies in, *64*
emergencies in, *64*
Freud's apartment,
   72
Gloriette, *72*
Hofburg, *68*
Hofburgkapelle, *68*
Hoher Markt, *71*
hotels in, *75–77*
Hundertwasserhaus,
   72
Jewish Museum, *70*
Kaisergruft, *69–70*
Kapuzinerkirche, *69*
Karlskirche, *69*
Kirche am Hof, *71*
Kunst Haus Wien
   Museum, *73*
Kunsthistoriches
   Museum, *69*
Loos building, *68*
Maria am Gestade, *71*
Michaelertor, *68*

Mozart
  Erinnerungsräume,
  70
  Nationalbibliothek,
  65
  Naturhistoriches
  Museum, 69
  Neue Hofburg
  Museums, 68–69
  nightlife in, 78–79
  opera in, 69, 77–78
  Palais Ferstl, 70
  Pestsäule, 70
  Peterskirche, 70
  Ring, 65
  Ruprechtskirche, 71
  Sacher Hotel, 69
  Schatzkammer, 68
  Schloss Belvedere,
  72
  Schönbrunn Palace,
  71
  Schottenkirche, 71
  shopping in, 73
  Spanische Reitschule,
  65, 68
  Staatsoper, 77
  Stephansdom, 70
  streetcars in, 63
  subways in, 64
  Tabak Museum, 69
  taxis in, 64
  theater in, 77–78
  Theater Museum, 65
  Tiegarten, 71
  tourist information
  in, 64
  tours of, 64
  train travel to, 63
  travel agencies in, 64
  20th Century
  Museum, 72
  Uhrenmuseum, 71
  Vienna Woods, 72

Wagenburg, 72
  wine taverns in,
  78–79
Villa rentals, 21–22
Visas, 13–14

Warsaw, 841–850
  air travel to, 841
  auto travel in, 842
  Barbakan, 843
  Belvedere Palace,
  843
  buggies in, 842
  buses in, 842
  cafés in, 849
  concerts in, 849
  dining in, 843, 847
  embassies in, 842
  emergencies in, 842
  Heroes of the
  Warsaw Ghetto
  monument, 846
  Holy Cross Church,
  846
  hotels in, 847–849
  Łazienki Palace, 846
  Łazienki Park, 846
  Muzeum Marii-
  Skłodowskeij-Curie,
  843
  nightlife in, 849
  Nowe Miasto, 843
  Old Town, 843
  opera in, 849
  Palace of Culture and
  Science, 846
  Rynek Starego
  Miasta, 843
  shopping in, 846–847
  taxis in, 842
  tearooms in, 843
  theater in, 849
  tourist information
  in, 842

tours of, 842
  train travel to, 841
  trams in, 842
  travel agencies in, 842
  University of
  Warsaw, 843
  Wilanów, 846
  Zamek Królowski,
  843
Wine and food tours,
  9–10

York, 499–506
  auto travel to, 499
  bus travel to, 499
  Castle Museum, 500
  Chapter House, 500
  dining in, 502,
  504–506
  hotels in, 504–506
  Jorvik Viking
  Centre, 500
  Merchant
  Adventurers' Hall,
  502
  Minster, 500
  National Railway
  Museum, 502
  The Shambles, 502
  Stonegate, 502
  tourist information
  in, 500
  tours of, 500
  train travel to, 499
  Undercroft Museum
  and Treasury, 500
  walls of, 502
Youth hostels, 22
Youth travel, 22

Zoos
  in Antwerp, 118
  in Berlin, 405
  in Innsbruck, 91

in Ireland, 675
  in Norway, 824
  in Portugal, 881
  in Salzburg, 86
  in Stockholm, 1025
  in Vienna, 71
Zürich, 1054–1066
  air travel to,
  1054–1055
  Altstadt, 1058
  arts in, 1063
  auto travel to, 1055
  Bahnhofstrasse, 1056
  bookstores in, 1055
  buses in, 1055
  consulates in, 1055
  dining in, 1059–1061
  emergencies in, 1055
  Fraumünster, 1056
  Grossmünster, 1058
  Haus zum Ruden,
  1058
  hotels in, 1061–1063
  Limmatquai, 1058
  Lindenhof, 1056
  Niederdorf, 1058
  nightlife in,
  1063–1064
  Peterskirche, 1056
  Quai Bridge, 1057
  Rathaus, 1058
  Schweizerishes
  Landesmuseum,
  1058
  shopping in, 1059
  streetcars in, 1055
  taxis in, 1055
  tourist information
  in, 1055
  tours of, 1055–1056
  train travel to, 1055
  travel agencies in,
  1055
  Wasserkirche, 1057

Conversion Tables

Distance

Kilometers/ Miles
To change kilometers to miles, multiply kilometers by .621.
To change miles to kilometers, multiply miles by 1.61.

Km to Mi	Mi to Km
1 = .62	1 = 1.6
2 = 1.2	2 = 3.2
3 = 1.9	3 = 4.8
4 = 2.5	4 = 6.4
5 = 3.1	5 = 8.1
6 = 3.7	6 = 9.7
7 = 4.3	7 = 11.3
8 = 5.0	8 = 12.9
9 = 5.6	9 = 14.5

Meters/Feet
To change meters to feet, multiply meters by 3.28.
To change feet to meters, multiply feet by .305.

Meters to Feet	Feet to Meters
1 = 3.3	1 = .31
2 = 6.6	2 = .61
3 = 9.8	3 = .92
4 = 13.1	4 = 1.2
5 = 16.4	5 = 1.5
6 = 19.7	6 = 1.8
7 = 23.0	7 = 2.1
8 = 26.2	8 = 2.4
9 = 29.5	9 = 2.7

Weight

Kilograms/ Pounds
To change kilograms to pounds, multiply by 2.20.
To change pounds to kilograms, multiply by .453.

Kilo to Pound	Pound to Kilo
1 = 2.2	1 = .45
2 = 4.4	2 = .91
3 = 6.6	3 = 1.4
4 = 8.8	4 = 1.8
5 = 11.0	5 = 2.3

6 = 13.2		6 = 2.7
7 = 15.4		7 = 3.2
8 = 17.6		8 = 3.6
9 = 19.8		9 = 4.1

Grams/Ounces To change grams to ounces, multiply grams by .035.
To change ounces to grams, multiply ounces by 28.4.

Grams to Ounces	Ounces to Grams
1 = .04	1 = 28
2 = .07	2 = 57
3 = .11	3 = 85
4 = .14	4 = 114
5 = .18	5 = 142
6 = .21	6 = 170
7 = .25	7 = 199
8 = .28	8 = 227
9 = .32	9 = 256

Liquid Volume

Liters/U.S. Gallons To change liters to U.S. gallons, multiply liters by .264.
To change U.S. gallons to liters, multiply gallons by 3.79.

Liters to U.S. Gallons	U.S. Gallons to Liters
1 = .26	1 = 3.8
2 = .53	2 = 7.6
3 = .79	3 = 11.4
4 = 1.1	4 = 15.2
5 = 1.3	5 = 19.0
6 = 1.6	6 = 22.7
7 = 1.8	7 = 26.5
8 = 2.1	8 = 30.3
9 = 2.4	9 = 34.1

Personal Itinerary

Departure   *Date*

Time

Transportation

Arrival   *Date*   *Time*

Departure   *Date*   *Time*

Transportation

Accommodations

Arrival   *Date*   *Time*

Departure   *Date*   *Time*

Transportation

Accommodations

Arrival   *Date*   *Time*

Departure   *Date*   *Time*

Transportation

Accommodations

Personal Itinerary

Arrival *Date*   *Time*

Departure *Date*   *Time*

Transportation

Accommodations

Arrival *Date*   *Time*

Departure *Date*   *Time*

Transportation

Accommodations

Arrival *Date*   *Time*

Departure *Date*   *Time*

Transportation

Accommodations

Arrival *Date*   *Time*

Departure *Date*   *Time*

Transportation

Accommodations

Personal Itinerary

Arrival *Date*   *Time*

Departure *Date*   *Time*

Transportation

Accommodations

Arrival *Date*   *Time*

Departure *Date*   *Time*

Transportation

Accommodations

Arrival *Date*   *Time*

Departure *Date*   *Time*

Transportation

Accommodations

Arrival *Date*   *Time*

Departure *Date*   *Time*

Transportation

Accommodations

Addresses

Name

Address

Telephone

Name

Address

Telephone

Name

Address

Telephone

Name

Address

Telephone

Name

Address

Telephone

Name

Address

Telephone

Name

Address

Telephone

Name

Address

Telephone

Name

Address

Telephone

Name

Address

Telephone

Name

Address

Telephone

Name

Address

Telephone

Name

Address

Telephone

Name

Address

Telephone

Name

Address

Telephone

Name

Address

Telephone

Addresses

Name	*Name*
Address	*Address*
Telephone	*Telephone*
Name	*Name*
Address	*Address*
Telephone	*Telephone*
Name	*Name*
Address	*Address*
Telephone	*Telephone*
Name	*Name*
Address	*Address*
Telephone	*Telephone*
Name	*Name*
Address	*Address*
Telephone	*Telephone*
Name	*Name*
Address	*Address*
Telephone	*Telephone*
Name	*Name*
Address	*Address*
Telephone	*Telephone*
Name	*Name*
Address	*Address*
Telephone	*Telephone*

The only guide to explore a Disney World® you've never seen before:

The one for grown-ups.

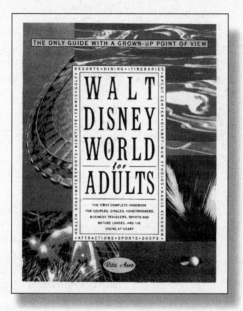

0-679-02490-5 $14.00 ($18.50 Can)

This is the only guide written specifically for the millions of adults who visit Walt Disney World® each year <u>without</u> kids. Upscale, sophisticated, packed full of facts and maps, *Walt Disney World® for Adults* provides up-to-date information on hotels, restaurants, sports facilities, and health clubs, as well as unique itineraries for adults. With *Walt Disney World® for Adults* in hand, you'll get the most out of one of the world's most fascinating, most complex playgrounds.

At bookstores everywhere, or call **1-800-533-6478.**

Fodor's Travel Guides

Available at bookstores everywhere, or call 1–800–533–6478, 24 hours a day.

U.S. Guides

Alaska

Arizona

Boston

California

Cape Cod, Martha's
Vineyard, Nantucket

The Carolinas & the
Georgia Coast

Chicago

Colorado

Florida

Hawaii

Las Vegas, Reno,
Tahoe

Los Angeles

Maine, Vermont,
New Hampshire

Maui

Miami & the Keys

New England

New Orleans

New York City

Pacific North Coast

Philadelphia & the
Pennsylvania Dutch
Country

The Rockies

San Diego

San Francisco

Santa Fe, Taos,
Albuquerque

Seattle & Vancouver

The South

The U.S. & British
Virgin Islands

USA

The Upper Great
Lakes Region

Virginia & Maryland

Waikiki

Walt Disney World and
the Orlando Area

Washington, D.C.

Foreign Guides

Acapulco, Ixtapa,
Zihuatanejo

Australia & New
Zealand

Austria

The Bahamas

Baja & Mexico's
Pacific Coast Resorts

Barbados

Berlin

Bermuda

Brittany & Normandy

Budapest

Canada

Cancún, Cozumel,
Yucatán Peninsula

Caribbean

China

Costa Rica, Belize,
Guatemala

The Czech Republic &
Slovakia

Eastern Europe

Egypt

Euro Disney

Europe

Florence, Tuscany &
Umbria

France

Germany

Great Britain

Greece

Hong Kong

India

Ireland

Israel

Italy

Japan

Kenya & Tanzania

Korea

London

Madrid & Barcelona

Mexico

Montréal &
Québec City

Morocco

Moscow &
St. Petersburg

The Netherlands,
Belgium &
Luxembourg

New Zealand

Norway

Nova Scotia, Prince
Edward Island &
New Brunswick

Paris

Portugal

Provence & the
Riviera

Rome

Russia & the Baltic
Countries

Scandinavia

Scotland

Singapore

South America

Southeast Asia

Spain

Sweden

Switzerland

Thailand

Tokyo

Toronto

Turkey

Vienna & the Danube
Valley

Special Series

Fodor's Affordables

Caribbean

Europe

Florida

France

Germany

Great Britain

Italy

London

Paris

**Fodor's Bed &
Breakfast and
Country Inns Guides**

America's Best B&Bs

California

Canada's Great
Country Inns

Cottages, B&Bs and
Country Inns of
England and Wales

Mid-Atlantic Region

New England

The Pacific
Northwest

The South

The Southwest

The Upper Great
Lakes Region

The Berkeley Guides

California

Central America

Eastern Europe

Europe

France

Germany & Austria

Great Britain &
Ireland

Italy

London

Mexico

Pacific Northwest &
Alaska

Paris

San Francisco

**Fodor's Exploring
Guides**

Australia

Boston &
New England

Britain

California

The Caribbean

Florence & Tuscany

Florida

France

Germany

Ireland

Italy

London

Mexico

New York City

Paris

Prague

Rome

Scotland

Singapore & Malaysia

Spain

Thailand

Turkey

Fodor's Flashmaps

Boston

New York

Washington, D.C.

Fodor's Pocket Guides

Acapulco

Bahamas

Barbados

Jamaica

London

New York City

Paris

Puerto Rico

San Francisco

Washington, D.C.

Fodor's Sports

Cycling

Golf Digest's Best
Places to Play

Hiking

The Insider's Guide
to the Best Canadian
Skiing

Running

Sailing

Skiing in the USA &
Canada

USA Today's Complete
Four Sports Stadium
Guide

**Fodor's Three-In-Ones
(guidebook, language
cassette, and phrase
book)**

France

Germany

Italy

Mexico

Spain

**Fodor's
Special-Interest
Guides**

Complete Guide to
America's National
Parks

Condé Nast Traveler
Caribbean Resort and
Cruise Ship Finder

Cruises and Ports
of Call

Euro Disney

France by Train

Halliday's New
England Food
Explorer

Healthy Escapes

Italy by Train

London Companion

Shadow Traffic's New
York Shortcuts and
Traffic Tips

Sunday in New York

Sunday in San
Francisco

Touring Europe

Touring USA:
Eastern Edition

Walt Disney World and
the Orlando Area

Walt Disney World
for Adults

**Fodor's Vacation
Planners**

Great American
Learning Vacations

Great American
Sports & Adventure
Vacations

Great American
Vacations

Great American
Vacations for Travelers
with Disabilities

National Parks and
Seashores of the East

National Parks
of the West

**The Wall Street
Journal Guides to
Business Travel**

AT LAST

YOUR OWN PERSONALIZED LIST
OF WHAT'S GOING ON IN THE
CITIES YOU'RE VISITING.

KEYED TO THE DAYS WHEN
YOU'LL BE THERE, CUSTOMIZED
FOR YOUR INTERESTS,
AND SENT TO YOU BEFORE YOU
LEAVE HOME.

GET THE INSIDER'S
PERSPECTIVE. . .

UP-TO-THE-MINUTE
ACCURATE
EASY TO ORDER
DELIVERED WHEN YOU NEED IT

Now there is a revolutionary way to get customized, time-sensitive travel information just before your trip.

Now you can obtain detailed information about what's going on in each city you'll be visiting <u>before</u> you leave home—up-to-the-minute, objective information about the events and activities that interest you most.

Travel Updates contain the kind of time-sensitive insider information you can get only from local contacts – or from city magazines and newspapers once you arrive. But now you can have the same information before you leave for your trip.

The choice is yours: current art exhibits, theater, music festivals and special concerts, sporting events, antiques and flower shows, shopping, fitness, and more.

The information comes from hundreds of correspondents and thousands of sources worldwide. Updated continuously, it's like having your own personal concierge or friend in the city.

You specify the cities and when you'll be there. We'll do the rest — personalizing the information for you the way no guidebook can.

It's the perfect extension to your Fodor's guide and the best way to make the most of your valuable travel time.

Your Itinerary:
Customized reports available for 160 destinations

**Use Order Form on back
or call 1-800-799-9609**

a...
air
tour
9902...
Regent's...
The annu...
in this an...
domain of R...
tion of R...
worthwhile. It'...
the perfomances...
Tickets are usually...
venue. Alternate t...
mances are cancelled...
given. For more inform...
Open-Air Theatre, Inner ...
NW1 4NP Open Air Thea...
Tel: 935-5756. Ends: 9-11-93.
International Air Tattoo
Held biennially, the world'...
military air display in...
demostra-...
tions, milit...
bands...

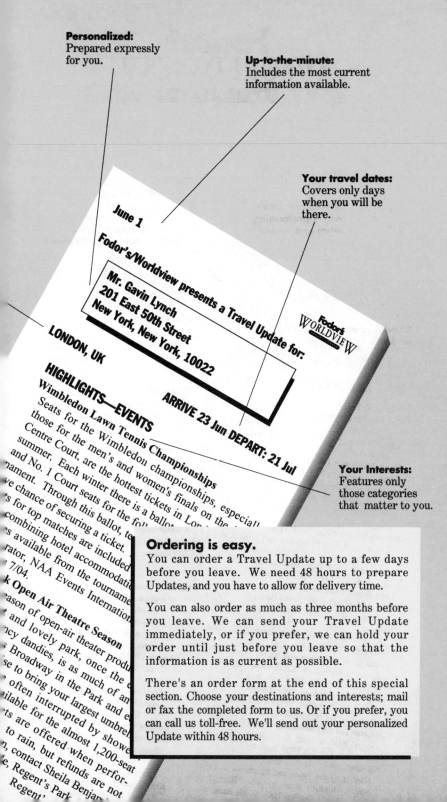

Personalized:
Prepared expressly for you.

Up-to-the-minute:
Includes the most current information available.

Your travel dates:
Covers only days when you will be there.

June 1

Fodor's/Worldview presents a Travel Update for:

Mr. Gavin Lynch
201 East 50th Street
New York, New York, 10022

Fodor's WORLDVIEW

LONDON, UK

ARRIVE 23 Jun DEPART: 21 Jul

Your Interests:
Features only those categories that matter to you.

HIGHLIGHTS—EVENTS

Wimbledon Lawn Tennis Championships

Seats for the Wimbledon championships, especiall those for the men's and women's finals on the Centre Court, are the hottest tickets in Lon summer. Each winter there is a ballo and No. 1 Court seats for the foll nament. Through this ballot, t e chance of securing a ticket. s for top matches are included combining hotel accommodati s available from the tourname rator, NAA Events Internation 7/04.

k Open Air Theatre Season

ason of open-air theater produ and lovely park, once the e ncy dandies, is as much of an Broadway in the Park and e se to bring your largest umbrel often interrupted by showe ilable for the almost 1,200-seat ts are offered when perfor- to rain, but refunds are not , Regent's Benja e, Regent's Park Regent'

Ordering is easy.

You can order a Travel Update up to a few days before you leave. We need 48 hours to prepare Updates, and you have to allow for delivery time.

You can also order as much as three months before you leave. We can send your Travel Update immediately, or if you prefer, we can hold your order until just before you leave so that the information is as current as possible.

There's an order form at the end of this special section. Choose your destinations and interests; mail or fax the completed form to us. Or if you prefer, you can call us toll-free. We'll send out your personalized Update within 48 hours.

Fodor's
WORLDVIEW
TRAVEL UPDATE

**Special concerts—
who's performing
what and where**

**One-of-a-kind,
one-time-only events**

**Special interest,
in-depth listings**

Children — Events
Angel Canal Festival
The festivities include a children's funfair, entertainers, a boat rally and displays on the water. Regent's Canal. Islington. N1. Tube: Angel. Tel: 267 9100. 11:30am-5:30pm. 7/04.
Blackheath Summer Kite Festival
Stunt kite displays with parachuting teddy bears and trade stands. Free admission. SE3. BR: Blackheath. 10am. 6/27.
Megabugs
Children will delight in this infestation of giant robotic insects, including a praying mantis 60 times life size. Mon-Sat 10am-6pm; Sun 11am-6pm. Admission 4.50 pounds. Natural History Museum, Cromwell Road. SW7. Tube: South Kensington. Tel: 938 9123. Ends 10/01.
Childminders
This establishment employs only women, providing nurses and qualified nannies to

Music — Jazz & Blues
Tito Puente's Golden Men of Latin Jazz
The father of mambo and Cuban rumba king comes to town. Royal Festival Hall. South Bank. SE1. Tube: Waterloo. Tel: 928 8800. 8pm. 7/15.
Georgie Fame and The New York Band
Riding a popular tide with his latest album, the smoky-voiced Fame and his keyboard are on a tour yet again. The Grand. Clapham Junction. SW11. BR: Clapham Junction. Tel: 738 9000. 7:30pm. 7/07.
Jacques Loussier Play Bach Trio
The French jazz classicist and colleagues. Kenwood Lakeside. Hampstead Lane. Kenwood. NW3. Tube: Golders Green, then bus 210. Tel: 413 1443. 7pm. 7/10.
Tony Bennett and Ronnie Scott
Royal Festival Hall. South Bank. SE1. Tube: Waterloo. Tel: 928 8800. 8pm. 7/11.
Santana
Royal Festival Hall. South Bank. SE1. Tube: Waterloo. Tel: 928 8800. 8pm. 7/12.
Count Basie Orchestra and Nancy Wilson Trio
Royal Festival Hall. South Bank. SE1. Tube: Waterloo. Tel: 928 8800. 8pm. 7/14.
King Pleasure and the Biscuit Boys
Royal Festival Hall. South Bank. SE1. Tube: Waterloo. Tel: 928 8800. 6:30 and 9pm. 7/16.
Al Green and the London Community Gospel Choir
Royal Festival Hall. South Bank. SE1. Tube: Waterloo. Tel: 928 8800. 8pm. 7/13.
BB King and Linda Hopkins
Mother of the blues and successor to Bessie Smith, Hopkins meets up with "Blues Boy" Royal Festival Hall. South Bank. SE

Music — Classical
Marylebone Sinfonia
Kenneth Gowen conducts music by Puccini and Rossini. Queen Elizabeth Hall. South Bank. SE1. Tube: Waterloo. Tel: 928 8800. 7:45pm. 7/16.
London Philharmonic
Franz Welser-Moest and George Benjamin conduct selections by Alexander Goehr, Messiaen, and some of Benjamin's own compositions. Queen Elizabeth Hall. South Bank. SE1. Tube: Waterloo. Tel: 928 8800. 8pm.
London Pro Arte Orchestra and Forest Choir
Murray Stewart conducts selections by Rossini, Haydn and Jonathan Willcocks. Queen Elizabeth Hall. South Bank. S Tube: Waterloo. Tel: 928 8800. 7:45pm. 7
Kensington Symphony Orchestra
Russell Keable conducts Dvorak's Dr

Here's what you get . . .

Detailed information about what's going on — precisely when you'll be there.

Show openings during your visit

Handy pocket-size booklet

Reviews by local critics

Exhibitions & Shows—Antique & Flower
Westminster Antiques Fair
Over 50 stands with pre-1830 furniture and other Victorian and earlier items. Thu-Fri 11am-8pm; Sat-Sun 11am-6pm. Admission 4 pounds, children free. Old Royal Horticultural Hall. Vincent Square. SW1. Tel: 0444/48 25 14. 6-24 thru 6/27.

Royal Horticultural Society Flower Show
The show includes displays of carnations, summer fruit and vegetables. Tue 11am-7pm; Wed 10am-5pm. Admission Tue 4 pounds, Wed 2 pounds. Royal Horticultural Halls. Greycoat Street and Vincent Square. SW1. Tube: Victoria. 7/20 thru 7/21.

Hampton Court Palace International Flower Show
Major international garden and flower show taking place in conjunction with

Theater — Musical
Sunset Boulevard
In June, the four Andrew Lloyd Webber musicals which dominated London's stages in the 1980s (Cats, Starlight Express, Phantom of the Opera and Aspects of Love) are joined by the composer's latest work, a show rumored to have his best music to date. The 1950 Billy Wilder film about a helpless young writer who is drawn into the world of a possessive, aging silent screen star offers rich opportunities for Webber's evolving style. Soaring, aching melodies, lush technical effects and psychological thrills are all expected. Patti Lupone stars. Mon-Sat at 8pm; matinee Thu-Sat at 3pm. In-person sales only at the box office; credit card bookings, Tel: 344 0055. Admission 15-32.50 pounds. Adelphi Theatre. The Strand. WC2. Tube: Charing Cross. Tel: 836 7611. Starts: 6/21.

Leonardo A Portrait of Love
A new musical about the great Renaissance artist and inventor comes in for a London pre-... tested by a brief run at Oxford's Old ... The work explores ...

Spectator Sports — Other Sports
Greyhound Racing: Wembley Stadium
This dog track offers good views of greyhound racing held on Mon, Wed and Fri. No credit cards. Stadium Way. Wembley. HA9. Tube: Wembley Park. Tel: 902 8833.

Benson & Hedges Cricket Cup Final
Lord's Cricket Ground. St. John's Wood Road. NW8. Tube: St. John's Wood. Tel: 289 1611. 11am. 7/10.

Business-Fax & Overnight Mail
Post Office, Trafalgar Square Branch
Offers a network of fax services, the Intelpost system, throughout the country and abroad. Mon-Sat 8am-8pm, Sun 9am-5pm. William IV Street. WC2. Tube: Charing Cross. Tel: 930 0500

Fodor's
WORLDVIEW
TRAVEL UPDATE

London, England
Arriving: June 23
Departing: July 21

Interest Categories

For <u>your</u> personalized Travel Update, choose the categories you're most interested in from this list. Every Travel Update automatically provides you with *Event Highlights* - the best of what's happening during the dates of your trip.

1.	**Business Services**	Fax & Overnight Mail, Computer Rentals, Photocopying, Protocol, Secretarial, Messenger, Translation Services

Dining

2.	**All Day Dining**	Breakfast & Brunch, Cafes & Tea Rooms, Late-Night Dining
3.	**Local Cuisine**	In Every Price Range—from Budget Restaurants to the Special Splurge
4.	**European Cuisine**	Continental, French, Italian
5.	**Asian Cuisine**	Chinese, Far Eastern, Japanese, Other
6.	**Americas Cuisine**	American, Mexican & Latin
7.	**Nightlife**	Bars, Dance Clubs, Casinos, Comedy Clubs, Ethnic, Pubs & Beer Halls
8.	**Entertainment**	Theater—Comedy, Drama, English Language, Musicals, Dance, Ticket Agencies
9.	**Music**	Country/Western/Folk, Classical, Traditional & Ethnic, Opera, Jazz & Blues, Pop, Rock
10.	**Children's Activities**	Events, Attractions
11.	**Tours**	Local Tours, Day Trips, Overnight Excursions, Cruises
12.	**Exhibitions, Festivals & Shows**	Antiques & Flower, History & Cultural, Art Exhibitions, Fairs & Craft Shows, Music & Art Festivals
13.	**Shopping**	Districts & Malls, Markets, Regional Specialities
14.	**Fitness**	Bicycling, Health Clubs, Hiking, Jogging
15.	**Recreational Sports**	Boating/Sailing, Fishing, Golf, Ice Skating, Skiing, Snorkeling/Scuba, Swimming, Tennis & Racquet
16.	**Spectator Sports**	Auto Racing, Baseball, Basketball, Boating & Sailing, Football, Golf, Horse Racing, Ice Hockey, Rugby, Soccer, Tennis, Track & Field, Other Sports

Please note that interest category content will vary by season, destination, and length of stay.

Destinations

The Fodor's/Worldview Travel Update covers more than 160 destinations world-wide. Choose the destinations that match your itinerary from this list. (Choose bulleted destinations only.)

Europe
- Amsterdam
- Athens
- Barcelona
- Berlin
- Brussels
- Budapest
- Copenhagen
- Dublin
- Edinburgh
- Florence
- Frankfurt
- French Riviera
- Geneva
- Glasgow
- Istanbul
- Lausanne
- Lisbon
- London
- Madrid
- Milan
- Moscow
- Munich
- Oslo
- Paris
- Prague
- Provence
- Rome
- Salzburg
* Seville
- St. Petersburg
- Stockholm
- Venice
- Vienna
- Zurich

United States (Mainland)
- Albuquerque
- Atlanta
- Atlantic City
- Baltimore
- Boston
* Branson, MO
* Charleston, SC
- Chicago
- Cincinnati
- Cleveland
- Dallas/Ft. Worth
- Denver
- Detroit
- Houston
* Indianapolis
- Kansas City
- Las Vegas
- Los Angeles
- Memphis

- Miami
- Milwaukee
- Minneapolis/ St. Paul
* Nashville
- New Orleans
- New York City
- Orlando
- Palm Springs
- Philadelphia
- Phoenix
- Pittsburgh
- Portland
* Reno/ Lake Tahoe
- St. Louis
- Salt Lake City
- San Antonio
- San Diego
- San Francisco
* Santa Fe
- Seattle
- Tampa
- Washington, DC

Alaska
- Alaskan Destinations

Hawaii
- Honolulu
- Island of Hawaii
- Kauai
- Maui

Canada
- Quebec City
- Montreal
- Ottawa
- Toronto
- Vancouver

Bahamas
- Abaco
- Eleuthera/ Harbour Island
- Exuma
- Freeport
- Nassau & Paradise Island

Bermuda
- Bermuda Countryside
- Hamilton

British Leeward Islands
- Anguilla

- Antigua & Barbuda
- St. Kitts & Nevis

British Virgin Islands
- Tortola & Virgin Gorda

British Windward Islands
- Barbados
- Dominica
- Grenada
- St. Lucia
- St. Vincent
- Trinidad & Tobago

Cayman Islands
- The Caymans

Dominican Republic
- Santo Domingo

Dutch Leeward Islands
- Aruba
- Bonaire
- Curacao

Dutch Windward Island
- St. Maarten/ St. Martin

French West Indies
- Guadeloupe
- Martinique
- St. Barthelemy

Jamaica
- Kingston
- Montego Bay
- Negril
- Ocho Rios

Puerto Rico
- Ponce
- San Juan

Turks & Caicos
- Grand Turk/ Providenciales

U.S. Virgin Islands
- St. Croix
- St. John
- St. Thomas

Mexico
- Acapulco
- Cancun & Isla Mujeres
- Cozumel
- Guadalajara
- Ixtapa & Zihuatanejo
- Los Cabos
- Mazatlan
- Mexico City
- Monterrey
- Oaxaca
- Puerto Vallarta

South/Central America
* Buenos Aires
* Caracas
* Rio de Janeiro
* San Jose, Costa Rica
* Sao Paulo

Middle East
* Jerusalem

Australia & New Zealand
- Auckland
- Melbourne
* South Island
- Sydney

China
- Beijing
- Guangzhou
- Shanghai

Japan
- Kyoto
- Nagoya
- Osaka
- Tokyo
- Yokohama

Pacific Rim/Other
* Bali
- Bangkok
- Hong Kong & Macau
- Manila
- Seoul
- Singapore
- Taipei

* Destinations available by 1/1/95

Fodor's WORLDVIEW TRAVEL UPDATE Order Form

THIS TRAVEL UPDATE IS FOR (Please print):

Name

Address

City   State   Country   ZIP

Tel # (   )   -   Fax # (   )   -

Title of this Fodor's guide:

Store and location where guide was purchased:

INDICATE YOUR DESTINATIONS/DATES: You can order up to three (3) destinations from the previous page. Fill in your arrival and departure dates for each destination. **Your Travel Update itinerary (all destinations selected) cannot exceed 30 days from beginning to end.**

		Month	Day		Month	Day
(Sample) *LONDON*	From:	6 /	21	To:	6 /	30
1	From:	/		To:	/	
2	From:	/		To:	/	
3	From:	/		To:	/	

CHOOSE YOUR INTERESTS: Select up to eight (8) categories from the list of interest categories shown on the previous page and circle the numbers below:

1   2   3   4   5   6   7   8   9   10   11   12   13   14   15   16

CHOOSE WHEN YOU WANT YOUR TRAVEL UPDATE DELIVERED (Check one):
❏ Please send my Travel Update immediately.
❏ Please hold my order until a few weeks before my trip to include the most up-to-date information.
Completed orders will be sent within 48 hours. Allow 7-10 days for U.S. mail delivery.

ADD UP YOUR ORDER HERE. *SPECIAL OFFER FOR FODOR'S PURCHASERS ONLY!*

	Suggested Retail Price	Your Price	This Order
First destination ordered	$ 9.95	$ 7.95	$ 7.95
Second destination (if applicable)	$ 6.95	$ 4.95	+
Third destination (if applicable)	$ 6.95	$ 4.95	+

DELIVERY CHARGE (Check one and enter amount below)

	Within U.S. & Canada	Outside U.S. & Canada
First Class Mail	❏ $2.50	❏ $5.00
FAX	❏ $5.00	❏ $10.00
Priority Delivery	❏ $15.00	❏ $27.00

ENTER DELIVERY CHARGE FROM ABOVE: +

TOTAL: $

METHOD OF PAYMENT IN U.S. FUNDS ONLY (Check one):
❏ AmEx ❏ MC ❏ Visa ❏ Discover ❏ Personal Check (U. S. & Canada only)
❏ Money Order/ International Money Order
Make check or money order payable to: Fodor's Worldview Travel Update

Credit Card —/—/—/—/—/—/—/—/—/—/—/—/—/—/—/—/— Expiration Date:___/___

Authorized Signature

SEND THIS COMPLETED FORM WITH PAYMENT TO:
Fodor's Worldview Travel Update, 114 Sansome Street, Suite 700, San Francisco, CA 94104

OR CALL OR FAX US 24-HOURS A DAY
Telephone **1-800-799-9609** • Fax **1-800-799-9619** (From within the U.S. & Canada)
(Outside the U.S. & Canada: Telephone 415-616-9988 • Fax 415-616-9989)

(Please have this guide in front of you when you call so we can verify purchase.)
Code: FTG   Offer valid until 12/31/95.